Business Statistics
of the United States
Patterns of Economic Change

10th Edition, 2005

Business Statistics
of the United States

Patterns of Economic Change

10th Edition, 2005

Editor
Cornelia J. Strawser

Associate Editor
Mark Siegal

BERNAN PRESS

© 2005 Bernan Press, an imprint of Bernan Associates, a division of the Kraus Organization Limited.

No part of this publication may be reproduced, stored in a retrieval system, or transmitted, in any form or by any means, electronic, mechanical, photocopying, recording, or otherwise, without the prior written permission of the copyright holder. Bernan Press does not claim copyright in U.S. government information.

ISBN: 1-886222-24-X

ISSN: 1086-8488

Printed by Automated Graphic Systems, Inc., White Plains, MD, on acid-free paper that meets the American National Standards Institute Z39-48 standard.

2006 2005   4 3 2 1

BERNAN PRESS
4611-F Assembly Drive
Lanham, MD 20706
800-274-4447
email: info@bernan.com
www.bernanpress.com

CONTENTS

ACKNOWLEDGEMENTS xiii
PREFACE xv
ARTICLE—"NEW PERSPECTIVES ON THE U.S. ECONOMY" xix
   I. COMPREHENSIVE REVISION OF THE NATIONAL INCOME AND PRODUCT ACCOUNTS xix
   II. NEW QUARTERLY REPORTS FROM THE CENSUS BUREAU xxiv
ARTICLE—"EXPANDED HISTORICAL STATISTICS GIVE PERSPECTIVE ON GROWTH, WAR, INFLATION,
      AND UNEMPLOYMENT" xxvii
SPECIAL NOTES—CURRENT STATISTICAL ISSUES AND PITFALLS xxxiv
ARTICLE—"EMPLOYMENT FROM THE BLS HOUSEHOLD AND PAYROLL SURVEYS: SUMMARY OF
      RECENT TRENDS" (REPRINTED FROM BUREAU OF LABOR STATISTICS INTERNET SITE) xxxvii
GENERAL NOTES l

PART A: THE U.S. ECONOMY 1

CHAPTER 1: NATIONAL INCOME AND PRODUCT AND CYCLICAL INDICATORS 3
Section 1a: Gross Domestic Product: Values, Quantities, and Prices 3
Figure 1-1: Output Per Capita 3
TABLES
      1-1: Gross Domestic Product 4
      1-2: Real Gross Domestic Product 5
      1-3: Contributions to Percent Change in Real Gross Domestic Product 6
Figure 1-2: Current-Dollar and Real Gross Domestic Product 7
Figure 1-3: Percent Changes in Current-Dollar and Real GDP 7
      1-4: Chain-Type Quantity Indexes for Gross Domestic Product and Domestic Purchases 8
      1-5: Chain-Type Price Indexes for Gross Domestic Product and Domestic Purchases 9
      1-6: Final Sales 10
      1-7: Per Capita Product and Income and U.S. Population 11
      1-8: Composite Indexes of Economic Activity and Selected Index Components 12
Section 1b: Income and Value Added 13
Figure 1-4: Factor Income by Type 13
TABLES
      1-9: Relation of Gross Domestic Product, Gross and Net National Product, National Income, and
          Personal Income 14
Figure 1-5: Difference Between GNP and GDP 16
      1-10: Gross Domestic Income by Type of Income 17
      1-11: National Income by Type of Income 19
      1-12: Gross Value Added of Domestic Corporate Business 21
      1-13: Gross Value Added of Nonfinancial Domestic Corporate Business in Current and Chained Dollars . . 22
Notes and Definitions 23

CHAPTER 2: INDUSTRIAL PRODUCTION AND CAPACITY UTILIZATION 35
Figure 2-1: Capacity Utilization: Total Manufacturing and High-Tech 35
TABLES
      2-1: Industrial Production Indexes by Market Groups 36
      2-2: Industrial Production Indexes by NAICS Industry Groups 40
      2-3: Capacity Utilization by NAICS Industry Groups 43
Notes and Definitions 46

CHAPTER 3: INCOME DISTRIBUTION AND POVERTY ... 49
Section 3a: Household and Family Income ... 49
Figure 3-1: Median and Mean Household Income ... 49
TABLES
- 3-1: Median Household Income ... 50
- 3-2: Median Family Income and Median Earnings by Sex ... 51
- 3-3: Shares of Aggregate Income Received by Each Fifth and Top 5 Percent of Households ... 52
- 3-4: Shares of Aggregate Income Received by Each Fifth and Top 5 Percent of Families ... 53

Section 3b: Poverty ... 54
Figure 3-2: Poverty Rates, Total, Children, and Seniors ... 54
TABLES
- 3-5: Average Poverty Thresholds by Family Size ... 55
- 3-6: Poverty Status by Type of Family, Race, and Hispanic Origin ... 56
- 3-7: Poverty Status of People by Sex and Age ... 60
- 3-8: Poverty Status of People Inside and Outside Metropolitan Areas, and People In and Near Poverty ... 61
- 3-9: Poor People 16 Years and Over by Work Experience ... 62

Section 3c: Alternative Measures and State Data ... 63
Figure 3-3: Median Household Income, Official and Alternative ... 63
TABLES
- 3-10: Median Household Income and Poverty Rates for People, Based on Alternative Definitions of Income ... 64

Figure 3-4: Poverty Rate, Official and Alternative Definitions of Income ... 65
- 3-11: Experimental Measures of Before-Tax and After-Tax Income ... 66
- 3-12: Median Income and Poverty Rates by State ... 67

Notes and Definitions ... 68

CHAPTER 4: CONSUMER INCOME AND SPENDING ... 73
Figure 4-1: Personal Saving Rate ... 73
TABLES
- 4-1: Personal Income and Its Disposition ... 74
- 4-2: Personal Consumption Expenditures: Current Dollars, Constant Dollars, and Price Indexes ... 76
- 4-3: Personal Consumption Expenditures by Major Type of Product ... 77
- 4-4: Chain-Type Quantity Indexes for Personal Consumption Expenditures by Major Type of Product ... 79
- 4-5: Personal Consumption Expenditures by Type of Expenditure ... 81

Figure 4-2: Personal Consumption Expenditures by Type of Expenditure ... 82
Notes and Definitions ... 83

CHAPTER 5: SAVING AND INVESTMENT; BUSINESS SALES AND INVENTORIES ... 87
Figure 5-1: National Saving, Investment, and Borrowing ... 87
TABLES
- 5-1: Saving and Investment ... 88
- 5-2: Gross Private Fixed Investment by Type ... 90

Figure 5-2: Private Fixed Investment by Type ... 92
- 5-3: Real Gross Private Fixed Investment by Type ... 93
- 5-4: Chain-Type Quantity Indexes for Private Fixed Investment by Type ... 95
- 5-5: Current-Cost Net Stock of Fixed Assets ... 97
- 5-6: Chain-Type Quantity Indexes for Net Stock of Fixed Assets ... 98
- 5-7: Inventories to Sales Ratios ... 99

Figure 5-3: Private Nonfarm Inventory/Sales Ratios ... 100
- 5-8: Manufacturing and Trade Sales and Inventories ... 101
- 5-9: Real Manufacturing and Trade Sales and Inventories ... 102
- 5-10: Capital Expenditures, 1996–2002 ... 103

5-11: Capital Expenditures for Structures and Equipment for Companies With Employees by Major NAICS Industry Sector, 1998–2002 104
Notes and Definitions 106

CHAPTER 6: GOVERNMENT 111
Section 6a: Federal Government in the National Income and Product Accounts 111
Figure 6-1: Federal Government Saving and Dis-Saving 111
TABLES
    6-1: Federal Government Current Receipts and Expenditures 112
    6-2: Federal Government Consumption Expenditures and Gross Investment 114
    6-3: Federal Government Defense and Nondefense Consumption Expenditures by Type 115
    6-4: National Defense Consumption Expenditures and Gross Investment: Selected Detail 116
    6-5: Federal Government Output, Lending and Borrowing, and Net Investment 117
    6-6: Chain-Type Quantity Indexes for Federal Government Defense and Nondefense Consumption Expenditures and Gross Investment 118
    6-7: Chain-Type Quantity Indexes for National Defense Consumption Expenditures and Gross Investment: Selected Detail 119
Section 6b: State and Local Government in the National Income and Product Accounts 120
Figure 6-2: State and Local Government Current Receipts and Expenditures 120
TABLES
    6-8: State and Local Government Current Receipts and Expenditures 121
    6-9: State and Local Government Consumption Expenditures and Gross Investment 123
    6-10: State and Local Government Output, Lending and Borrowing, and Net Investment 124
    6-11: Chain-Type Quantity Indexes for State and Local Government Consumption Expenditures and Gross Investment 125
    6-12: State Government Current Receipts and Expenditures 126
    6-13: Local Government Current Receipts and Expenditures 128
    6-14: State Government Consumption Expenditures and Gross Investment by Function 130
    6-15: Local Government Consumption Expenditures and Gross Investment by Function 131
Section 6c: Federal Government Budget Accounts 132
Figure 6-3: Defense Spending as a Percent of GDP 132
TABLES
    6-16: Federal Government Receipts and Outlays by Fiscal Year 133
    6-17: Federal Government Debt by Fiscal Year 136
Section 6d: Government Output and Employment 137
Figure 6-4: Government Employment 137
TABLES
    6-18: Chain-Type Quantity Indexes for Government Output 138
    6-19: Government Employment 139
Notes and Definitions 140

CHAPTER 7: U.S. FOREIGN TRADE AND FINANCE 147
Section 7a: Foreign Transactions in the National Income and Product Accounts 147
Figure 7-1: Receipts, Payments, and Balance on Current Account 147
TABLES
    7-1: Foreign Transactions in the National Income and Product Accounts 148
    7-2: Chain-Type Quantity Indexes for Exports and Imports of Goods and Services 149
    7-3: Chain-Type Price Indexes for Exports and Imports of Goods and Services 150
    7-4: Exports and Imports of Selected NIPA Types of Product 151
    7-5: Chain-Type Quantity Indexes for Exports and Imports of Selected NIPA Types of Product 152

Section 7b: U.S. International Transactions Accounts ... 153
Figure 7-2: Balance on Current Account and Financial Inflows and Outflows ... 153
TABLES
- 7-6: U.S. International Transactions ... 154
- 7-7: International Investment Position of the United States at Year-End ... 160

Section 7c: Exports and Imports ... 161
Figure 7-3: Foreign Trade Balances on Goods and Services ... 161
TABLES
- 7-8: U.S. Exports and Imports of Goods and Services ... 162
- 7-9: U.S. Exports of Goods by End-Use and Advanced Technology Categories ... 163
- 7-10: U.S. Imports of Goods by End-Use and Advanced Technology Categories ... 164
- 7-11: U.S. Exports and Imports of Goods by Principal End-Use Category in Constant Dollars ... 165
- 7-12: U.S. Exports of Goods by Selected Regions and Countries ... 166
- 7-13: U.S. Imports of Goods by Selected Regions and Countries ... 168
- 7-14: U.S. Exports of Services ... 170
- 7-15: U.S. Imports of Services ... 171
- 7-16: U.S. Export and Import Price Indexes ... 172

Notes and Definitions ... 173

CHAPTER 8: PRICES ... 183
Figure 8-1: Inflation Indicators ... 183
TABLES
- 8-1: Consumer Price Indexes ... 184

Figure 8-2: Consumer Prices: All Items, Medical Care, and Apparel ... 190
- 8-2: Producer Price Indexes and Purchasing Power of the Dollar ... 191
- 8-3: Producer Price Indexes by Major Commodity Groups ... 196
- 8-4: Producer Price Indexes for the Net Output of Selected NAICS Industry Groups ... 197
- 8-5: Prices Received and Paid by Farmers ... 198

Notes and Definitions ... 199

CHAPTER 9: EMPLOYMENT COSTS, PRODUCTIVITY, AND PROFITS ... 207
Figure 9-1: Change in Labor Productivity, Nonfarm Business ... 207
TABLES
- 9-1: Employment Cost Indexes—Total Compensation ... 208
- 9-2: Employment Cost Indexes—Wages and Salaries ... 209
- 9-3: Productivity and Related Data ... 210
- 9-4: Corporate Profits with Inventory Valuation Adjustment by Industry Group (SIC Basis) ... 212
- 9-5: Corporate Profits with Inventory Valuation Adjustment by Industry Group (NAICS Basis) ... 214

Notes and Definitions ... 215

CHAPTER 10: EMPLOYMENT, HOURS, AND EARNINGS ... 219
Section 10a: Labor Force, Employment, and Unemployment ... 219
Figure 10-1: Labor Force Participation Rate and Employment/Population Ratio ... 219
Figure 10-2: Unemployment Rate ... 219
TABLES
- 10-1: Civilian Population and Labor Force ... 220
- 10-2: Civilian Employment and Unemployment ... 221
- 10-3: Unemployment Rates ... 222
- 10-4: Insured Unemployment ... 224

Section 10b: Payroll Employment, Hours, and Earnings ... 225
Figure 10-3: Total Nonfarm Payroll Employment ... 225

TABLES
- 10-5: Nonfarm Payroll Employment by NAICS Supersector 226
- 10-6: Production or Nonsupervisory Workers on Private Nonfarm Payrolls by NAICS Supersector 228
- 10-7: Average Weekly Hours of Production or Nonsupervisory Workers on Private Nonfarm Payrolls by NAICS Supersector 229

Figure 10-4: Average Weekly Hours, Selected Industries 230
- 10-8: Indexes of Aggregate Weekly Hours of Production or Nonsupervisory Workers on Private Nonfarm Payrolls by NAICS Supersector 231
- 10-9: Average Hourly Earnings of Production or Nonsupervisory Workers on Private Nonfarm Payrolls by NAICS Supersector 232
- 10-10: Average Weekly Earnings of Production or Nonsupervisory Workers on Private Nonfarm Payrolls by NAICS Supersector 233

Notes and Definitions 234

CHAPTER 11: ENERGY 243
Figure 11-1: Energy Consumption and Prices 243
TABLES
- 11-1: Energy Supply and Consumption 244
- 11-2: Energy Consumption per Dollar of Real Gross Domestic Product 245

Notes and Definitions 246

CHAPTER 12: MONEY AND FINANCIAL MARKETS 247
Figure 12-1: Federal Funds Rate and 10-Year Treasury Securities Rate 247
TABLES
- 12-1: Money Stock Measures 248
- 12-2: Selected Components of the Money Stock 249
- 12-3: Aggregate Reserves of Depository Institutions and Monetary Base 250
- 12-4: Commercial Banks: Bank Credit and Selected Liabilities 251
- 12-5: Credit Market Debt Outstanding, By Borrower and Lender 253

Figure 12-2: Debt as a Percent of GDP 256
- 12-6: Household Assets, Liabilities, Net Worth, Financial Obligations, and Delinquency Rates 257

Figure 12-3: Ratios of Household Debt Service and Financial Obligations to Personal Income 259
- 12-7: Mortgage Debt Outstanding 260
- 12-8: Consumer Credit 261
- 12-9: Selected Interest Rates and Bond Yields 262
- 12-10: Common Stock Prices and Yields 264

Notes and Definitions 265

CHAPTER 13: INTERNATIONAL COMPARISONS 273
Figure 13-1: Real GDP Per Capita, United States and Japan 273
TABLES
- 13-1: International Comparisons: Growth Rates in Real Gross Domestic Product 274
- 13-2: International Comparisons: Real GDP Per Capita 275
- 13-3: International Comparisons: Real GDP per Employed Person 276
- 13-4: International Comparisons: Industrial Production Indexes 277
- 13-5: International Comparisons: Consumer Price Indexes 278
- 13-6: International Comparisons: Unemployment Rates and Civilian Labor Forces 279
- 13-7: Exchange Rates 280

Figure 13-2: International Value of the U.S. Dollar 281
Notes and Definitions 282

x BUSINESS STATISTICS OF THE UNITED STATES (BERNAN PRESS)

PART B: INDUSTRY PROFILES 285

CHAPTER 14: INDUSTRY DEFINITION AND STRUCTURE 287
Article — "The Structure of U.S. Industry: An Introduction to the North American Industry
  Classification System (NAICS)" 287
TABLE
  14-1: NAICS Industry Definitions: With Rough Derivation from SIC 289

CHAPTER 15: PRODUCT AND INCOME BY INDUSTRY 297
Figure 15-1: Output Change by NAICS Industry Group 297
TABLES
  15-1: Gross Domestic Product (Value Added) by SIC Industry Group, 1987–2000 .. 298
  15-2: Value Added (Gross Domestic Product) by NAICS Industry Group, 1998–2003, in Current Dollars ... 299
  15-3: Value Added (Gross Domestic Product) by NAICS Industry Group, 1998–2003, in Constant Dollars .. 300
Notes and Definitions 301

CHAPTER 16: EMPLOYMENT, HOURS, AND EARNINGS BY NAICS INDUSTRY 303
Figure 16-1: Net New Nonfarm Payroll Jobs by NAICS Industry Group 303
TABLES
  16-1: Nonfarm Employment by NAICS Sector and Industry 304
  16-2: Production or Nonsupervisory Workers on Private Nonfarm Payrolls by NAICS Industry 307
  16-3: Average Weekly Hours of Production or Nonsupervisory Workers on Private Nonfarm Payrolls
    by NAICS Industry 308
  16-4: Average Hourly Earnings of Production or Nonsupervisory Workers on Private Nonfarm Payrolls
    by NAICS Industry 309
  16-5: Average Weekly Earnings of Production or Nonsupervisory Workers on Private Nonfarm Payrolls
    by NAICS Industry 310
  16-6: Indexes of Aggregate Weekly Hours of Production or Nonsupervisory Workers on Private
    Nonfarm Payrolls by NAICS Industry 311
  16-7: Indexes of Aggregate Weekly Payrolls of Production or Nonsupervisory Workers on Private
    Nonfarm Payrolls by NAICS Industry 312
Notes and Definitions 313

CHAPTER 17: KEY SECTOR STATISTICS 315
Figure 17-1: New Orders for Durable Goods 315
TABLES
  17-1: Petroleum and Petroleum Products—Imports, Domestic Production, and Stocks 316
  17-2: New Construction Put in Place 317
  17-3: Housing Starts and Building Permits; Home Sales and Prices 319
  17-4: Manufacturers' Shipments 320
  17-5: Manufacturers' Inventories 325
  17-6: Manufacturers' New Orders 328
  17-7: Manufacturers' Unfilled Orders, Durable Goods Industries 330
  17-8: Motor Vehicle Sales and Inventories 332
  17-9: Retail and Food Services Sales 334
  17-10: Retail Inventories 337
  17-11: Merchant Wholesalers—Sales and Inventories 338
  17-12: Selected Service Industries—Receipts of Taxable Firms, 1986–1998, by SIC Industry 339
  17-13: Selected Service Industries—Revenue of Tax-Exempt Firms, 1986–1998, by SIC Industry 339
  17-14: Selected Service Industries—Revenue, 1998–2002, by NAICS Industry 340
  17-15: Selected Service Industries—Revenue—Total and E-Commerce, 1998–2002, by NAICS Industry .. 341
Notes and Definitions 342

PART C: HISTORICAL DATA ... 351

CHAPTER 18: SELECTED ANNUAL DATA, 1939–1947 ... 353
Figure 18-1: Real GDP, 1939–1947 ... 353
TABLE
    18-1: Selected Aggregate Economic Data, 1939–1947 ... 354
Notes and Definitions ... 356

CHAPTER 19: HISTORICAL DATA FOR SELECTED QUARTERLY SERIES ... 357
TABLES
    19-1: Gross Domestic Product ... 357
    19-2: Real Gross Domestic Product ... 361
    19-3: Contributions to Percent Change in Real Gross Domestic Product ... 362
    19-4: Chain-Type Quantity Indexes for Gross Domestic Product and Domestic Purchases ... 366
    19-5: Chain-Type Price Indexes for Gross Domestic Product and Domestic Purchases ... 370
    19-6: Personal Income and Its Disposition ... 374
    19-7: Inventories to Sales Ratios ... 378
    19-8: Federal Government Current Receipts and Expenditures ... 382
    19-9: State and Local Government Current Receipts and Expenditures ... 390
    19-10: U.S. International Transactions ... 398
    19-11: Productivity and Related Data ... 404
Notes and Definitions ... 412

CHAPTER 20: HISTORICAL DATA FOR SELECTED MONTHLY SERIES ... 413
TABLES
    20-1: Industrial Production and Capacity Utilization ... 413
    20-2: Summary Consumer and Producer Price Indexes ... 423
    20-3: Summary Labor Force, Employment, and Unemployment ... 433
    20-4: Nonfarm Payroll Employment, Hours, and Earnings ... 443
    20-5: Money Stock, Reserves, and Monetary Base ... 453
    20-6: Interest Rates, Bond Yields, and Stock Price Indexes ... 461
    20-7: Composite Indexes of Economic Activity and Selected Index Components ... 471
Notes and Definitions ... 479

PART D: REGIONAL AND STATE DATA ... 481

CHAPTER 21: REGIONAL AND STATE DATA ... 483
Figure 21-1: Per Capita Personal Income, United States and Selected States ... 483
TABLES
    21-1: Gross Domestic Product by Region and State ... 484
    21-2: Personal Income and Employment by Region and State ... 489
Notes and Definitions ... 519

INDEX ... 523

ACKNOWLEDGEMENTS

This volume would not have been possible without the knowledge, experience, judgment, and technical and organizational skills of Associate Editor Mark Siegal, who researched and compiled each data table and graph in this book with unfailing intelligence and efficiency.

Bernan's editorial and production departments, under the overall direction of Tamera Wells-Lee, did the copy editing, layout, and graphics preparation. Kara Prezocki prepared the layout and graphics, assisted by Rebecca Zayas. Jacalyn Houston served as the lead copy editor.

Jacalyn, Kara, and Rebecca capably handled all editorial and production aspects of this edition.

Also, thanks to Katherine DeBrandt, who worked on previous editions of *Business Statistics*, for her support and guidance as Bernan's Data Analyst Team Leader.

Finally, special thanks are due to the many federal agency personnel who, as always, responded generously to our frequent need for assistance in obtaining data and background information.

PREFACE

Business Statistics of the United States: Patterns of Economic Change, 10th Edition, 2005 is a basic desk reference for everyone requiring historical information about the U.S. economy since World War II, or needing background information for the interpretation of new economic data as they are reported. It contains some 3,000 economic time series, predominantly from federal government sources, presenting a rich selection of the data most needed for analysis of economic trends and patterns. Of equal importance with the data themselves are the extensive background notes that enable the user to understand the data, use them appropriately, and, if desired, seek additional information from the source agencies.

THE 2005 EDITION

Business Statistics: 2005, like the 2004 edition, provides a rich, deep, and comprehensive picture of the American economy. The subtitle introduced with last year's edition—*Patterns of Economic Change*—indicates the increased resources made available for analyzing the economic history of the past half-century, for observing past trends, and for providing the basis for projecting such trends into the future.

- Whereas editions prior to 2004 typically presented data for only the latest 30 years, *Business Statistics* now presents data for the entire half-century since the end of World War II, with summary data covering the war years 1939–1947 as well, enabling the user to refer to earlier periods of war, recession, recovery, and cycles of inflation and disinflation.
- New data using the new North American Industry Classification System give a much clearer picture of the most dynamic sectors of the "new economy."

As always, each table in the 2005 edition has been updated through the latest full year for which data were available (usually 2003) and all historical revisions to the data available as of November 2004 have been incorporated.

THE PLAN OF THE BOOK

The history of the U.S. economy in the period since World War II is told in the major U.S. government sets of statistical data: the National Income and Product Accounts compiled by the Bureau of Economic Analysis (BEA); the data on labor force, employment, hours, earnings, and productivity compiled by the Bureau of Labor Statistics (BLS); the price indexes also collected by BLS; and financial market data compiled mainly by the Board of Governors of the Federal Reserve System (FRB). All of these sets exist in both annual and either monthly or quarterly form dating from shortly after the end of World War II—beginning in 1946, 1947, or 1948.

In Part A, *Business Statistics* presents all annual values for major indicators and their significant components back to the earliest postwar year available, along with recent quarterly or monthly data. This enables easy calculation of growth rates for periods or subperiods and more flexible comparisons of recent values with historical data.

For many purposes, however, historical data at a higher frequency than annual are required: comparison of activity before and after business cycle turning points, for example, or observation of the effects of the outbreak or the end of war. For the main series presented in Part A, historical quarterly or monthly data are presented in Part C, all the way back to the beginning of the postwar period where available.

In both Part A and Part C, the presentation begins with the National Income and Product Accounts, or NIPAs. The NIPAs comprise a comprehensive, thorough, and internally consistent data set. They measure the value of the output of the U.S. economy (the Gross Domestic Product, or GDP); they factor that value into its quantity, or "real," and price components; and they show how the value of output is distributed between the labor and capital that produce it.

Production estimates for the "industrial" sectors of the economy—manufacturing, mining, and utilities—follow the presentation of the overall accounts.

Then, more detail is presented for the final demand components of production. GDP by definition consists of the sum of consumption expenditures, business investment, government purchases of goods and services, and exports minus imports—the elementary economics blackboard equation "GDP = C + I + G + X − M." Chapters on each of those demand components are presented in Part A.

Following those, there is a chapter on prices; two that are concerned with the amount and compensation of labor and capital inputs into production; one on energy inputs into production; and one on money and financial markets.

While we initially define and measure Gross Domestic Product by adding up its final demand categories, this output is produced in industries—some in the old-line heavy industries such as manufacturing, mining, and utilities, but an increasing share in the huge and heterogeneous group known as "service-producing" industries. Part A gives a number of summary measures of activity classified by industry or industrial sector—industrial production, profits, and employment-related data.

Industry data are presented in more detail in Part B. The user will not, however, find the same degree of historical continuity as in Part A. The pace of technological and organizational change that the American economy has experienced over the past half-century has been so rapid that the statistical industry definitions have had difficulty keeping up with it. It has proved impossible in many cases to produce historical data series that cover the entire postwar period and also reflect in a meaningful way the detailed industrial structure of the economy as it exists today.

The industries that were used to categorize data during most of the postwar period were originally defined in the 1930s and modified only modestly since then. They do not provide an adequate framework for analyzing economic activity in the twenty-first century. An up-to-date system called the North American Industry Classification System (NAICS) has been put into effect beginning in 1997, and has now been incorporated in nearly all of the government's statistical series. However, this system required breaks with the past at many disaggregated reporting levels, and data collected on the earlier Standard Industrial Classification system (SIC) are, in many areas, not easily convertible to the new system.

Different statistical agencies have dealt with this problem in different ways, and *Business Statistics* provides both detailed information for recent data and as much historical comparability as possible. For industrial production, the Federal Reserve Board has been able to carry estimates on the NAICS basis back to at least 1972 (1967 for some higher-level aggregates); these are shown in Chapters 2 and 20. The Bureau of Labor Statistics has calculated employment and related data back to 1939 for NAICS "supersectors," and these are shown in Chapters 10 and 18. On the other hand, the Census Bureau's capital expenditures survey gives data by NAICS industries beginning only in 1998 (Chapter 5).

In Part B, *Business Statistics* first presents a general description of NAICS and its differences from SIC, followed by a table summarizing the structure of the U.S. economy as specified in NAICS. This table indicates how the NAICS statistical system is organized and shows—very roughly in some cases—how each NAICS industry relates to the earlier SIC industries. In the chapters that follow, *Business Statistics* presents detailed industry data on the NAICS basis as far back as it is available. For the BLS employment and related data, this means data back to 1990. For the Census Bureau data on manufacturers' shipments, orders, and inventories, and wholesale and retail sales and stocks, this means data beginning in 1992. For these Census data, *Business Statistics* shows roughly comparable data for earlier years, with an overlap shown in the year 1992, so that comparisons at a broad level can be observed. For selected service industries, NAICS data are available only from 1998 forward. NIPA data by industry are presented on the NAICS basis as far back as available and on the SIC basis for earlier years.

Part C, Historical Data, begins with a table summarizing annual values for important economic aggregates for the years 1939–1947, giving some suggestion of the enormous changes the economy went through as it mobilized for World War II and subsequently demobilized. In the subsequent two chapters, quarterly or monthly data for NIPA data and other major indicators provide the opportunity to observe changes associated with all of the 10 business cycles that have been identified in the postwar period.

Part D, State and Regional Data, now includes not only data by state and region on personal income and employment back to 1969, but also values and quantity indexes for Gross Domestic Product by state and region for the years 1977–2001.

Notes and Definitions. Productive use of economic data requires accurate knowledge about the sources and meaning of the data. The Notes and Definitions for each chapter, shown immediately after that chapter's tables, contain definitions, descriptions of recent data revisions, and references to sources of additional technical information. They also include information about data availability and revision and release schedules, so that the user may readily access the latest current values if he or she needs to keep up with the data month by month or quarter by quarter.

THE HISTORY OF BUSINESS STATISTICS

The history of *Business Statistics* began with the publication, many years ago, by the U.S. Commerce Department's Bureau of Economic Analysis (BEA) of the first edition of a volume of the same name and general purpose. After 27 periodic editions, the last of which appeared in 1992, the BEA found it necessary, for budgetary and other reasons, to discontinue not only that publication but also maintenance of the database from which the publication was derived.

The individual statistical series gathered together here are publicly available. However, the task of gathering them from a number of sources within the government, plus a few private sources, and assembling them into one coherent database is impractical for most data users. Even when current data are more-or-less readily available, obtaining the full historical time series often is time-consuming and difficult. Definitions and other documentation can be inconvenient to find as well. Believing that a *Business Statistics* compilation was too valuable to be lost to the public, Bernan Press published the first edition of the present publication in 1995, edited by Dr. Courtenay M. Slater. The first edition received a warm welcome among users of economic data. Dr. Slater, formerly Chief Economist of the Department of Commerce, continued to edit and improve *Business Statistics* through four subsequent annual editions. The current editor worked with Dr. Slater on the fourth and fifth editions, and in subsequent editions has continued in the tradition established by Dr. Slater of ensuring high-quality data while revising and expanding the book's scope to include significant new aspects of the U.S. economy and longer historical background.

Most of the statistical data in this book are from federal government sources and are in the public domain. A few series are from private sources and further use may be subject to copyright restrictions. Sources and restrictions, if any, are given in the Notes and Definitions.

The data in this volume meet the publication standards of the federal statistical agencies from which they were obtained. Every effort has been made to select data that are accurate, meaningful, and useful. All statistical data are subject to error arising from sampling variability, reporting errors, incomplete coverage, imputation, and other causes. The responsibility of the editor and publisher of this volume is limited to reasonable care in the reproduction and presentation of data obtained from established sources.

The 2005 edition has been edited by Cornelia J. Strawser, in association with Mark Siegal.

Dr. Strawser is Senior Economic Consultant to Bernan Press. She edited the seventh, eighth, and ninth editions and was the co-editor on two previous editions of *Business Statistics*. She was co-editor of *Foreign Trade of the United States, 2001*, and also worked on the *Handbook of U.S. Labor Statistics*. She was formerly Senior Economist at the U.S. House of Representatives Budget Committee and has also served at the Senate Budget Committee, the Congressional Budget Office, and the Federal Reserve Board. Her fields of special concentration included analysis of current business conditions, including issues of economic measurement; monetary and fiscal policy; and income distribution and poverty.

Mark Siegal, a research editor with Bernan Press, served as the associate editor on this edition of *Business Statistics*. Mark previously worked as a staff assistant with the USDA Human Nutrition Research Center on Aging at Tufts University, and has a background in researching government data; statistics and data management; technical writing; and editing. Mark, also an assistant editor on *Business Statistics 2004* and *Vital Statistics of the United States*, has a B.S. in communication (with distinction in research) from Cornell University and a certificate in epidemiology from Tufts University.

The editor assumes full responsibility for the interpretations presented in this volume.

NEW PERSPECTIVES ON THE U.S. ECONOMY

I. COMPREHENSIVE REVISION OF THE NATIONAL INCOME AND PRODUCT ACCOUNTS

The 10th edition of *Business Statistics* incorporates the 2003 comprehensive revision of the National Income and Product Accounts (NIPAs)—the basic accounts for production, income, and demand in the U.S. economy—as further updated by the 2004 annual revision.

Over the half-century of history shown in this volume, the basic story of short-term fluctuations and long-term growth is the same as before these revisions. The basic concepts of production measurement and the categories in which the components of production are measured also remain the same. Growth rates over the postwar period are about the same as before. However, each of the two revisions in turn made both the 2001 recession and the subsequent recovery milder than had been previously portrayed.

For many students of the U.S. economy, the most significant consequences of the 2003 comprehensive revision may be the new clarity introduced into the accounts, the new distinctions made, and the new ways in which economic relationships are illuminated.

Major features of the 2003 comprehensive revision

The major definitional and classification changes are as follows, with the material in quotes taken directly from the Bureau of Economic Analysis:

- "A more complete and accurate measure of insurance services that results from estimating implicit services provided by property and casualty insurance companies." This smoothed the inappropriate movements that were caused by extraordinary disasters—such as hurricanes and the attack on September 11, 2001—under the previous treatment.
- "An improved measure of banking services that identifies services received by borrowers as well as by depositors." As a result of the overhaul of the banking measure, bank output growth in the United States was revised down, partly because services to business borrowers were redefined as intermediate rather than final output, and partly because more output was attributed to foreign offices.
- "A new treatment of government that recognizes that governments produce services and that goods and services purchased by governments are intermediate inputs." This treatment does not revise total gross domestic product (GDP), but makes offsetting changes in components.
- "An expanded definition of national income that includes all net incomes earned in production—a definition more consistent with international guidelines."

New and updated sources and methodologies were used to improve other sectors of the accounts. The base year for chained-dollar estimates of real output was updated from 1996 to 2000, as was the base year for all quantity and price indexes. While these base-year changes affect the *level* of every index and chained-dollar series, they do not of themselves have any effect on the statistics that convey the meanings of the series—the *growth rates* of real product and its components, and the *changes in price levels* that portray inflation.

Industry measures have been compiled and presented using the new North American Industry Classification System (NAICS); however, because NAICS represents such a sharp break from the old Standard Industrial Classification System (SIC), NAICS-based data are available only for a few recent years.

NIPA changes in Business Statistics

These new features have all been incorporated into the NIPA-based tables in *Business Statistics*. An overview of the major changes in each affected chapter follows. More detailed information is provided in the Notes and Definitions that follow each chapter.

Chapter 1. In the first section of Chapter 1, "Gross Domestic Product: Values, Quantities, and Prices," the structure and the underlying content of the tables are little changed from those presented in *Business Statistics* last year, although the shift in base years changes the levels of all quantity and price indexes and real-dollar measures.

The introduction of chain-weighted price and quantity indexes in recent years has made the measurement of real output more stable, because real GDP changes are no longer re-evaluated using price relationships from time periods far removed from those in which the changes actually take place. However, chain-weighting has complicated the analysis of real data. Specifically, it is now difficult for users of the data to break down the change in a total to changes in its component parts that add up to the total. *Business Statistics* therefore now includes Table 1-3, Contributions to Percent Change in Real Gross Domestic Product, as calculated by the Bureau of Economic Analysis.

The second section, entitled "Income and Value Added," incorporates many of the new and clarified definitions of income, in tables that make more clear the identity of the value of output and the value of the incomes generated by that output. Table 1-9 demonstrates the relationship of *domestic* income and product to *national* income and product, where "domestic" indicates income and product generated within the United States while "national" indicates income and product accruing to residents of the United States. "Domestic" and "national" income components are presented in Tables 1-10 and 1-11, where those differences can be identified in more detail.

Certain components of national and domestic income have been re-grouped. Certain fees for services that used to be included in "other labor income" have been reclassified as wages and salaries, and the bulk of the category formerly known as "other labor income" is now included in "supplements to wages and salaries," which comprises employer contributions to government and private social insurance and benefit funds. Business tax totals no longer include "nontaxes" which have been reclassified as transfer payments.

In Tables 1-12 and 1-13, *Business Statistics* provides an expanded presentation of "value added by"—formerly known as "GDP originating in"—domestic corporate business, financial and nonfinancial, and the income components of that value added. Real-dollar measures of the output of nonfinancial domestic corporate business are also now shown.

Chapter 4. The tables in this chapter have changed little in general outline, but are affected by the new base period for constant dollars and price and quantity indexes. In Table 4-1, Personal Income and Its Disposition, "nontaxes" are no longer lumped in with personal taxes but have been reclassified, mainly as transfer payments. "Supplements to wages and salaries" now include business payments to social insurance funds and pension and welfare funds. However, both the employer and the employee contributions to social insurance funds are subtracted in the calculation of "personal income," whose definition is therefore unchanged.

Chapter 5. Table 5-1, Saving and Investment, now includes a new measure of "net domestic investment," defined as the value of gross investment minus the value of the consumption of fixed capital. It also includes two new national saving rates—gross saving and net saving as a percent of gross national income. A new concept, "net lending or net borrowing," provides a measure similar to the "net foreign investment" concept formerly included in these tables. With an adjustment for "capital account transactions" (generally a small amount), it shows the amount by which national saving exceeds domestic investment and can be invested abroad. Where net lending or net borrowing has a negative sign, as has been the case in current years, domestic investment exceeds national saving and has been financed by capital inflows from abroad.

Chapter 6. This chapter reflects the new treatment of government in the NIPAs. It is a clarification of the role of government, not a quantitative re-evaluation. These definitional changes do not, of themselves, change total GDP in either current or constant dollars, or change the amount of government saving and investment, but they do provide new information on what the government produces and the flows between government and the rest of the economy.

Government performs two different functions that are specifically recognized in these accounts.

First, government produces output that adds to the overall output of goods and services. This output is broken down between "gross investment," which is production of fixed assets with lives longer than one year, and "consumption expenditures," which is all other government activity that uses productive resources, including payments to government employees for their services. Both government gross investment and government consumption expenditures are components of GDP, just as private gross investment and personal consumption are.

Second, government redistributes income by making payments of social benefits to persons, payments that are not in exchange for services performed in the period under measurement—for example, Social Security payments and payments for Medicare services. These payments are not components of the building-up of GDP, but affect the flow of incomes to individuals. Through these effects they may indirectly influence the level and composition of GDP—for example, by facilitating the use of medical care.

Governments finance all of their spending—investment, consumption, and social benefits and other transfer payments—with some combination of taxes, other receipts, and borrowing, as the new NIPA tables demonstrate.

Tables displaying "Current Receipts and Expenditures," such as Tables 6-1 and 6-8, include all current government spending, whether it generates GDP or redistributes income, and all current tax and other receipts. Investment spending is not included but spending does include a calculated value of the consumption of government fixed capital. In the receipts sections of these tables, personal current taxes exclude the "nontax" payments, which are now in transfer receipts. "Indirect business taxes" now exclude "nontaxes," again reclassified as transfer payments, and are renamed "Taxes on production and imports." Receipts of interest and other payments on assets are now shown separately in the receipts section instead of being netted against government interest and other payments, which now appear gross of such receipts in the expenditure section. This "grossing up" of course does not change net government saving.

Tables that follow complete the depiction of the role of governments in the production of GDP and in the balance of saving and investment. In Tables 6-2 and 6-9, government consumption spending is seen to be the total of employee compensation, consumption of fixed capital, and goods and services purchased from other sectors, adjusted to exclude own-account investment and sales to other sectors. This consumption spending plus government gross investment (which includes the own-account investment that was removed from the components of consumption spending) makes up the contribution of government to GDP. Tables 6-5 and 6-10 show the total "gross" output of government, which consists of the value added by the government labor force and capital stock and the value of the goods and services purchased. The same tables show net investment (gross investment minus capital consumption) and net lending, completing the accounting for the government contribution to national saving and investment as shown in Table 5-1.

Other tables in Chapter 6 present detail of government consumption expenditures and gross investment, including breakdowns of federal spending into defense and nondefense components, in current dollars and quantity indexes.

Chapter 7. Foreign transactions in the NIPAs are now closely aligned with the International Transactions Accounts (ITAs) in the definition of the current-account balance. (The actual measures will still differ because of slightly different definitions, including the fact that the NIPAs exclude U.S. territories overseas that are included in the ITAs.)

In Table 7-1, instead of "net foreign investment," the entry that used to be added to "payments to the rest of the world" to balance the accounts, the NIPAs now show "balance on current account," "capital transactions," and "net lending and net borrowing, national income and product accounts," the last being defined as the balance on current account less capital transfers to the rest of the world.

In Table 7-6, the ITAs also measure the balance on current account and the capital transactions (with the definitional differences mentioned above) and also measure directly (with an inevitable statistical discrepancy) the capital inflows and outflows that are associated with those transactions.

Chapter 15. Six years' worth of data by major industry using the new North American Industry Classification System (NAICS) became available in the 2003 and 2004 NIPA revisions. Accordingly, *Business Statistics* adds two new tables on product and income by NAICS industry. Because this is a relatively short span of time, available earlier data are shown on the old Standard Industrial Classification (SIC).

The concept formerly known as Gross Domestic Product Originating, or GDP by industry, has been renamed Value Added. This does not represent any significant change in the concept, which continues to be that portion of the GDP, priced at market prices (including taxes on production and imports, formerly included in "indirect business taxes and nontaxes"), that is produced in the industry, or—equivalently—the industry's gross output, valued at market prices, minus its purchases of intermediate goods and services. Because of the redefinition of income to include taxes on production and imports, the national income originating in an industry is now the same—except for statistical discrepancy—as the gross product or value added of that industry.

Measures of real industry output are shown in Table 15-1 as quantity indexes on the SIC basis for 1987–2000, and in Table 15-2 as chained-dollar measures on the NAICS basis for 1998–2000. Neither data set is available with a longer historical time span.

Value added statistics need to be used with some caution as measures of the relative importance of industries. The reason is the economically arbitrary assignment of "taxes on production and imports"—now included in both value added and income—to industries in the U.S. economy. They have been assigned to the industry with the legal liability to pay them.

If all of these taxes were property taxes, they would be related to the value of capital in the industry and could reasonably be considered part of the capital share of the value of production. If all these taxes were taxes on value added, as in many European countries, then they would be more or less proportional to value added and would not distort the share of that industry in the total income generated. However, in the United States, more than half of the taxes in this category are levied as excises, sales taxes, and customs duties. In the NIPA data, most sales taxes are allocated to retail trade, and most fuel taxes and all customs duties to wholesale trade. This allocation bears little relationship to the incidence of the tax—much of which is on the consumer, not the industry—or to the contribution of the legally liable industry, which simply passes them on.

The same considerations should lead to caution in calculating the shares of capital and labor in industry value added (data that are included in the industry accounts but not shown in this volume). Users interested in such calculations should refer to the detailed data in "Improved Annual Industry Accounts for 1998–2003," *Survey of Current Business*, June 2004, in which the tax data are presented for each industry; users may subtract these taxes for the purposes of calculating industry shares and capital and labor shares within industries.

Overall, the immense wealth of new data now provided in the NIPAs affords new opportunities for fruitful research and a deeper understanding of the U.S. economy.

Other NIPA innovations of special interest

Other new NIPA series have been introduced that are of great interest but, because of their relatively short histories, are not easily included in the main data tables in *Business Statistics*. Two of these are described and presented below.

Nonprofit institutions. In the NIPAs, the personal sector includes not only households but also "nonprofit institutions serving households" (NPISHs). This comprises all nonprofit institutions except for those that are considered to serve government and business, such as chambers of commerce and trade associations, which are included in the business sector instead.

For the years from 1992 through 2003, but only for annual (not quarterly) data, BEA now compiles and makes available tables showing personal income and its disposition for households and NPISHs separately. Each major type of income and expenditure is estimated separately for the two groups, and household receipts from NPISHs, purchases from NPISHs, and contributions to NPISHs are identified separately instead of being "netted out" as they are in the current quarterly accounts. These data provide answers to questions about how much of "personal saving" is in fact accounted for by NPISHs and whether these institutions are a factor in the observed changes in personal saving behavior. Saving estimates from these tables are shown in Table 1 below.

Table 1. Personal Saving: Households and Non-Profit Institutions Serving Households (NPISHs)

Year	Personal saving (billions of dollars)			NPISH saving as a percent of total personal saving	Saving as a percent of disposable income	
	Total personal	Household	NPISH		Total personal	Household
1992	366.0	352.6	13.5	3.7	7.7	7.5
1993	284.0	271.4	12.6	4.4	5.8	5.6
1994	249.5	238.8	10.6	4.2	4.8	4.7
1995	250.9	235.7	15.2	6.1	4.6	4.4
1996	228.4	206.9	21.6	9.5	4.0	3.7
1997	218.3	176.5	41.8	19.1	3.6	3.0
1998	276.8	240.3	36.5	13.2	4.3	3.8
1999	158.6	114.0	44.6	28.1	2.4	1.7
2000	168.5	116.6	51.9	30.8	2.3	1.6
2001	132.3	107.8	24.5	18.5	1.8	1.4
2002	159.2	137.7	21.5	13.5	2.0	1.8
2003	110.6	96.7	13.9	12.6	1.4	1.2

These results indicate that NPISHs have accounted for a surprisingly large proportion of personal saving in recent years, particularly in the stock-market boom years of 1999 and 2000. The significance of this and other important factors in personal saving is discussed in Marshall B. Reinsdorf, "Alternative Measures of Personal Saving," *Survey of Current Business*, September 2004.

These data and the data on income and outlays for the household and non-profit sectors on which they are based are available in Table 2-9 in the NIPA tables on the BEA Web site, <http://www.bea.gov>. The Reinsdorf article on saving measures and an article from the April 2003 *Survey*, "Income and Outlays of Households and of Nonprofit Institutions Serving Households," can be found on the same Internet site.

Market-based price indexes

Supplemental measures of the value and price of personal consumption expenditures are now available that exclude items not deflated by a detailed component of either the Consumer Price Index (CPI) or the Producer Price Index (PPI). In other words, the price observations that make up these new aggregate measures are all based on observed market transactions, and the new price measures are known as "market-based price indexes." Excluded are services furnished without payment by financial intermediaries, most insurance purchases, expenses of NPISHs, gambling, margins on used light motor vehicles, and expenditures by U.S. residents working and traveling abroad. The imputed rent for owner-occupied housing is included in the market-based index, since it is based on observed rentals of comparable homes. Household insurance premiums are also included in the market-based index, since they are deflated by the CPI for tenants' and household insurance; but excluded are medical and hospitalization and income loss insurance, expense of handling life insurance, motor vehicle insurance, and workers' compensation.

Market-based price indexes for total PCE and PCE excluding food and energy were published in the Technical Note to the GDP release beginning in June 2004. Beginning in November 2004, they will be shown in the GDP news release itself.

Index levels and changes for the market-based price indexes, as published in the Technical Note dated October 29, 2004, are shown in Table 2 below.

Table 2. Price Indexes for Personal Consumption Expenditures, Market-Based and Total

(Quarterly data are at seasonally adjusted annual rates.)

Year and quarter	Market-based PCE price index		Market-based PCE price index excluding food and energy		Percent change, total PCE price index	
	Index (2000 = 100)	Percent change	Index (2000 = 100)	Percent change	Total PCE	Total PCE excluding food and energy
2001	101.941	1.9	101.668	1.7	2.1	1.9
2002	103.113	1.1	103.185	1.5	1.4	1.8
2003	105.040	1.9	104.388	1.2	1.9	1.3
2001						
1st quarter	101.479	2.8	101.072	2.1	3.3	2.8
2nd quarter	102.003	2.1	101.408	1.3	2.6	2.1
3rd quarter	102.205	0.8	101.890	1.9	0.6	1.4
4th quarter	102.079	-0.5	102.304	1.6	0.6	2.6
2002						
1st quarter	102.242	0.6	102.560	1.0	0.9	1.2
2nd quarter	102.966	2.9	103.011	1.8	2.9	2.0
3rd quarter	103.424	1.8	103.449	1.7	2.0	2.0
4th quarter	103.820	1.5	103.722	1.1	1.4	0.9
2003						
1st quarter	104.601	3.0	103.952	0.9	3.2	1.5
2nd quarter	104.768	0.6	104.238	1.1	0.7	1.1
3rd quarter	105.294	2.0	104.572	1.3	1.6	0.9
4th quarter	105.496	0.8	104.790	0.8	1.2	1.3
2004						
1st quarter	106.334	3.2	105.261	1.8	3.3	2.1
2nd quarter	107.292	3.7	105.798	2.1	3.1	1.7
3rd quarter	107.670	1.4	106.057	1.0	1.1	0.7
Percent change, 2001:I to 2004:III	...	6.1	...	4.9	6.4	5.5

... = Not available.

Overall, for the period from the first quarter of 2001 to the third quarter of 2004 for which the market-based indexes are shown, they display somewhat less price increase than the PCE totals. There is a particularly sharp difference in the fourth quarter of 2001, when the total index rises while the market-based index falls. (This may be traceable in some way to the effects as measured of the September 11 attacks; the first places to look would be insurance and financial services, not included in the market-based measures.) In some later quarters, however, the market-based indexes show changes noticeably *higher* than the total PCE indexes. The editor is not aware of any studies as yet concerning the significance of the differences among these indexes and between them and the CPI; this should provide an interesting area for analysis.

II. NEW QUARTERLY REPORTS FROM THE CENSUS BUREAU

The Census Bureau has instituted new quarterly reports on growth areas of the U.S. economy, to provide additional business indicators and more current information for inclusion in the GDP.

Retail E-commerce sales

Beginning with the fourth quarter of 1999, the Census Bureau has collected data on e-commerce sales from the Monthly Retail Trade Survey sample (see Table 17-9 and its Notes and Definitions). E-commerce sales are sales of goods and services where an order is placed by the buyer or price and terms of sale are negotiated over an Internet, extranet, Electronic Data Interchange (EDI) network, electronic mail, or other online system. Payment may or may not be made online. Table 3 below shows the latest available data from this survey as of the *Business Statistics* press time—a release dated August 20, 2004, available on the Census Internet site <http://www.census.gov>.

E-commerce has grown from 0.7 percent of retail sales (not including food services) in the fourth quarter of 1999 to 1.9 percent in the fourth quarter of 2003—still a

Table 3. Quarterly U.S. Retail Sales: Total and E-Commerce

(Not seasonally adjusted.)

Year and quarter	Retail sales (millions of dollars)		E-commerce as a percent of total sales	Quarter-to-quarter percent change		Year-to-year percent change	
	Total	E-commerce		Total sales	E-commerce sales	Total sales	E-commerce sales
1999							
4th quarter	787 212	5 335	0.7	8.1	...	9.1	...
2000							
1st quarter	714 561	5 663	0.8	-9.2	6.1	11.2	...
2nd quarter	774 677	6 185	0.8	8.4	9.2	7.4	...
3rd quarter	768 139	7 009	0.9	-0.8	13.3	5.5	...
4th quarter	812 809	9 143	1.1	5.8	30.4	3.3	71.4
2001							
1st quarter	724 731	7 893	1.1	-10.8	-13.7	1.4	39.4
2nd quarter	802 662	7 794	1.0	10.8	-1.3	3.6	26.0
3rd quarter	779 096	7 821	1.0	-2.9	0.3	1.4	11.6
4th quarter	850 265	10 755	1.3	9.1	37.5	4.6	17.6
2002							
1st quarter	738 185	9 549	1.3	-13.2	-11.2	1.9	21.0
2nd quarter	814 626	10 005	1.2	10.4	4.8	1.5	28.4
3rd quarter	818 061	10 734	1.3	0.4	7.3	5.0	37.2
4th quarter	859 250	13 999	1.6	5.0	30.4	1.1	30.2
2003							
1st quarter	767 433	12 115	1.6	-10.7	-13.5	4.0	26.9
2nd quarter	852 760	12 718	1.5	11.1	5.0	4.7	27.1
3rd quarter	867 242	13 651	1.6	1.7	7.3	6.0	27.2
4th quarter	912 109	17 512	1.9	5.2	28.3	6.2	25.1
2004							
1st quarter	834 716	15 515	1.9	-8.5	-11.4	8.8	28.1
2nd quarter	919 041	15 654	1.7	10.1	0.9	7.8	23.1

... = Not available.

fairly small share of the total. E-commerce has been particularly strong, both in dollars and as a share of total retail, in the fourth quarter of each year, undoubtedly representing a significant holiday buying component. Beginning with the November 2004 release, seasonally adjusted estimates will be made available as well, which should leave the trend—already evident in year-ago comparisons—more clear in the quarter-to-quarter changes as well.

Quarterly revenue for selected services

The Census Bureau has just published the first data from the new Quarterly Services Survey, shown in Table 4 below. With only three quarters of not-seasonally-adjusted data, only very limited conclusions can be drawn. Presumably, post-holiday seasonal effects can be seen in the sharp first-quarter declines in many components, notably publishing and movies, while the tax-preparation season undoubtedly accounts for the strong first-quarter performance, followed by a second-quarter decline, in the accounting and related industry.

By the spring of 2005, when data for the fourth quarter of 2004 become available, it will be possible to do year-ago comparisons and better identify the trends for these important industries. The quarterly releases will be available on the Census Internet site.

These new quarterly Census data should eventually improve the quality of quarterly GDP data for these important and growing sectors and reduce the amount of revision necessary in annual benchmarking.

Table 4. Selected Services: Estimated Revenue for Employer Firms

(Not seasonally adjusted.)

NAICS code	Kind of business	Total revenue (millions of dollars)				Percent change	
		2004 year-to-date total	2Q 2004	1Q 2004	4Q 2003	2Q 2004 from 1Q 2004	1Q 2004 from 4Q 2003
51	**Information**	450 511	230 092	220 419	232 478	4.4	-5.2
511	Publishing industries	119 612	61 009	58 603	66 047	4.1	-11.3
51111	Newspaper publishers	24 963	12 851	12 112	13 018	6.1	-7.0
51112	Periodical publishers	17 593	9 336	8 257	9 150	13.1	-9.8
5111 pt	Book, database and directory, and other publishers	26 334	13 379	12 955	14 446	3.3	-10.3
5112	Software publishers	50 722	25 443	25 279	29 433	0.6	-14.1
512	Motion picture and sound recording industries	36 133	18 636	17 497	20 878	6.5	-16.2
513	Broadcasting and telecommunications	250 620	127 926	122 694	123 142	4.3	-0.4
5131	Radio and television broadcasting	29 016	15 714	13 302	14 176	18.1	-6.2
5132	Cable networks and program distribution	50 452	25 958	24 494	23 638	6.0	3.6
5133	Telecommunications	171 152	86 254	84 898	85 328	1.6	-0.5
51331	Wired telecommunications carriers	104 235	51 945	52 290	52 991	-0.7	-1.3
51332	Wireless telecommunications carriers (except satellite)	57 955	29 728	28 227	27 722	5.3	1.8
5133 pt	Other telecommunications	8 962	4 581	4 381	4 615	4.6	-5.1
514	Information services and data processing services	44 146	22 521	21 625	22 411	4.1	-3.5
5141	Information services	16 465	8 378	8 087	8 031	3.6	0.7
5142	Data processing services	27 681	14 143	13 538	14 380	4.5	-5.9
54	**Professional, scientific, and technical services**	477 709	246 140	231 569	232 157	6.3	-0.3
5412	Accounting, tax preparation, bookkeeping, and payroll services	50 750	23 455	27 295	21 522	-14.1	26.8
5413	Architectural, engineering, and related services	106 737	56 592	50 145	48 212	12.9	4.0
5415	Computer system design and related services	93 903	47 071	46 832	46 352	0.5	1.0
5416	Management, scientific, and technical consulting services	59 858	31 022	28 836	28 539	7.6	1.0
5418	Advertising and related services	33 820	17 510	16 310	17 124	7.4	-4.8
541 pt	Other professional, scientific, and technical services	132 641	70 490	62 151	70 408	13.4	-11.7
56	**Administrative and support and waste management and remediation services**	237 311	121 885	115 426	114 049	5.6	1.2
561	Administrative and support services	212 035	108 833	103 202	101 584	5.5	1.6
5613	Employment services	63 528	33 151	30 377	31 084	9.1	-2.3
5615	Travel arrangement and reservation services	13 347	7 237	6 110	5 872	18.4	4.1
561 pt	Other administrative and support services	135 160	68 445	66 715	64 628	2.6	3.2
562	Waste management and remediation services	25 276	13 052	12 224	12 465	6.8	-1.9

EXPANDED HISTORICAL STATISTICS GIVE PERSPECTIVE ON GROWTH, WAR, INFLATION, AND UNEMPLOYMENT

This edition of *Business Statistics of the United States* continues to provide a summary economic record of the Second World War and extensive detail describing the entire, remarkable half-century that has followed the end of that war. These data were introduced in last year's ninth edition, and have now been completely updated to include the results of the comprehensive 2003 revision of the National Income and Product Accounts.

Business Statistics enables its users to look at the postwar period as a whole; to compare the performance of the U.S. economy in different wars, large and small; to compare economic performance in each of the 10 postwar business cycles; and to examine the entire history of the cycle of inflation and disinflation that occurred from the 1960s through the 1990s.

Analytical techniques

In assessing the performance of an economy over longer periods of time, it is important to use analytical techniques that best allow underlying economic relationships to reveal themselves. In this article, and in the newly enhanced graphs and text included in nearly every *Business Statistics* data chapter, the editor will frequently make use of three such tools: the ratio-scale graph; the calculation of compound annual growth rates; and the use of cyclically comparable years to calculate longer-term trends.

Ratio-scale graphs. At the beginning of Chapter 1 (Figure 1-1) is a time series graph of output per capita from 1946 through 2003, drawn on a ratio scale. Output per capita is the constant-dollar value of each year's U.S. Gross Domestic Product (GDP) divided by the size of that year's U.S. population. The reader will quickly see that equal distances on the vertical scale of this graph do not represent equal 2000-dollar differences in values. However, equal vertical distances do represent equal *percent changes*. Any upward-sloping straight line plotted on this scale would represent a constant rate of growth over the period, and any downward-sloping straight line would represent a constant percentage rate of decline.

This ratio-scale graph was produced by the following three steps: (1) Convert the values to be graphed into natural (base e) logarithms. (2) Graph the natural logarithms. (3) For ease in interpretation, relabel the vertical scale on the graph of the logarithms, replacing the actual numerical value of the logarithm that was plotted with the numerical value of its antilog, that is, the original value.

This technique is only valid, of course, for data series that do not include zeroes or negative numbers, for which logs do not exist. Since percentage values such as the unemployment rate and percentage changes such as the inflation rate are already in percentage terms, and may include zero and/or negative values, they are not graphed in this fashion.

Compound annual growth rates. In the text of this article and in the highlights pages that precede and accompany most of the chapters, the editor has often used compound annual growth rates to summarize the long-term history of important economic processes such as economic and demographic growth and inflation.

The compound annual growth rate is the percentage rate which, compounded annually, would cause a quantity "X(t)" observed in a period "t" to grow (or decline) to a quantity "X(t+i)" over a period of "i" years. Using this procedure, growth percentages for different periods spanning different numbers of years can be reduced to a common scale for comparison. The formula for calculating such a growth rate, "r," is as follows:

$$r = \left(\sqrt[i]{X(t+i)/X(t)} - 1 \right) x 100.$$

When growth rates are functionally related to each other, such as the growth rates for output, hours worked, and output per hour worked (productivity), those rates will be arithmetically consistent as in the following formula, where "o" is the percentage growth rate for output, "h" the rate for hours worked, and "p" the growth rate for output per hour worked:

$$p = [(100 + o)/(100 + h) - 1]x100$$

When the percentage growth rates are not very far from zero, relationships of this kind can be approximated or verified by simple addition or subtraction of the relevant percentage rates. For example, the productivity growth rate of 2.4 percent is (approximately) the difference between the output growth rate of 3.6 percent and the hours growth rate of 1.2 percent.

Using cyclically comparable end points. For economic processes that have significant business-cycle components, such as output and employment, it is important to use comparable points in the business cycle for estimating underlying growth rates. One commonly used method is simply to calculate growth rates between years with similar, high rates of resource utilization. The broadest readily available measure of resource utilization is the unemployment rate, which was 3.8 percent in 1948 and 4.0 percent in 2000. Hence, in the analysis that follows, postwar long-term growth rates are typically calculated as the rates for the 52-year period from 1948 to 2000.

For comparisons using monthly or quarterly data, an alternative is to use the dates of business cycle peaks, which are shown in the Notes and Definitions to Table 1-8, as beginning and end points.

A half-century of economic growth and change

Real gross domestic product (GDP), the broadest measure of the output of the U.S. economy, grew an average 3.5 percent per year from 1948 to 2000. Year by year, the rate of change varied from +8.7 percent in 1950—when a cyclical recovery coincided with the outbreak of the Korean War—to –1.9 percent in the 1982 recession. (Table 1-3) Although there were 10 recessions in the postwar period—periods when output, employment, and other aggregate indicators all declined—they were outweighed by longer periods of expansion. (Table 1-8 and its Notes and Definitions)

GDP, by definition, is the sum of personal consumption spending, business investment, government consumption and investment, and exports, minus imports. In the standard blackboard equation, "GDP = C + I + G + X – M." This definition takes only final demands into account, eliminating any double-counting of intermediate stages of production. (See the Notes and Definitions to Chapters 1 and 15 for further explanation.) The measurement of GDP is based on summing these final demands, thereby not only providing the preferred measure of output but also illuminating the sources of demand.

The composition of GDP is best measured using current-dollar data, reflecting the actual relative prices in effect at the time. The shares of the major components have changed somewhat between 1948 and 2000. Personal consumption expenditures (PCE) rose from 65.0 percent to 68.7 percent of the total; private investment was almost unchanged at 17.9 percent to 17.7 percent; and government consumption and investment spending (federal, state, and local combined) rose from 15.1 percent to 17.6 percent. How could the consumption and government shares rise that much, with only a small slippage in investment? The answer lies in the other two terms of the equation. Imports increased from 3.8 percent to 15.0 percent, while exports only rose from 5.8 percent to 11.2 percent. Recall that imports are a subtraction from final demands in the calculation of GDP, because they represent demands that have been satisfied by foreign instead of domestic production. Thus, the United States is now consuming and investing more than it produces, reflected in an international balance on goods and services that is a negative 3.9 percent of GDP (11.2 minus 15.0, with a slight difference due to rounding) compared with a positive balance of 2.0 percent in 1948 (5.8 minus 3.8). (See Chapters 1 and 7.)

The increase in the volume of both export and import trade and the change in the net international balance from surplus to deficit are perhaps the most dramatic shifts that have taken place over the postwar period. At the end of World War II, the United States had what amounted to the world's only fully functioning economy among all the industrialized nations. War-devastated countries needed U.S. consumption and investment goods to survive and rebuild, and were not yet able to generate enough exports to pay for them; the U.S. positive export balance had to be financed by U.S. government grants and loans.

Today, industries all over the world can compete with ours, and many countries generate balance of payments surpluses. These surpluses represent saving within these countries, evidently in excess of their own investment needs or opportunities, which they can invest in the United States, thus financing the U.S. trade deficit. (See Chapter 7 for data on foreign trade and finance.) One of the principal debates about today's economy concerns the sustainability of the U.S. trade deficit and the associated capital inflow.

While the shares of total consumption and total investment in GDP changed relatively little, large and striking shifts can be seen within each category.

Consumers in the aggregate were able to devote a smaller share of their total consumption expenditures to food and tobacco, clothing and personal care, and household operation; a greater share to housing, transportation, and miscellaneous categories; and a much larger share to medical care. This includes medical care paid for by private and government insurance, including Medicare and Medicaid. (Table 4-5)

Within investment spending, the share of information processing equipment was up sharply over the half-century, while shares declined for the other three principal components—other equipment, nonresidential structures, and residential investment. (Table 5-2)

The federal government's consumption and investment spending as a share of GDP fell from 8.9 percent to 5.9

percent. This does not, however, give a complete picture of the role of federal spending in the economy. Total federal spending includes not only the categories classified as consumption and investment in the National Income and Product Accounts but also federal transfer payments, of which more than half are Social Security and Medicare; federal interest payments; and federal grants to state and local governments. (See Chapter 6.) The role of these latter three categories in final demand is represented by the consumption, investment, and state and local government spending that they support. Furthermore, the receipts side of the federal accounts also affects final demands through tax rates and flows.

Federal transfer payments grew from 4.7 percent of personal income in 1948 to 12.4 percent in 2000. One particularly significant factor was the growth in Medicare and Medicaid, neither of which existed in 1948. (Table 4-1)

Total personal interest income grew from 3.9 percent to 12.0 percent of total personal income. (Table 4-1) It is difficult to trace federal (and other) interest payments through the economy because of the duplicative payments and receipts generated by financial intermediation. Given that the federal share of total domestic nonfinancial debt plummeted from 59.2 percent in 1948 to 18.6 percent in 2000 (Table 12-5), it can be surmised that the growth in personal interest income did not arise principally from federal interest payments.

On the receipts side of the federal government accounts, current taxes and contributions for social insurance rose from 15.6 percent of GDP in 1948 to 20.4 percent in 2000. The latter percent is not representative of subsequent years, however, as it included unusually high receipts from the stock market boom and preceded the substantial tax cuts that began in 2001. By 2003, federal tax and social insurance receipts had fallen to 16.6 percent of GDP. (Tables 6-1 and 1-1)

Finishing the accounting for GDP by final demands, the state and local government spending share of GDP jumped from 6.1 percent in 1948 to 11.6 percent in 2000. Federal grants-in-aid rose from 10.1 percent to 18.7 percent of total state receipts. State and local taxes and social insurance contributions rose from 5.2 percent to 9.2 percent of GDP (Tables 6-8 and 1-1).

Labor force, employment, and productivity growth

The total U.S. population grew at a 1.3 percent annual rate from 1948 to 2000, while the growth in real GDP was more than double that rate, leading to a significant rate of increase in the average real standard of living as measured by per capita GDP. (Table 1-7 and Figure 1-1) This happened because more and more Americans went to work and because their productivity grew even faster than their work input.

Labor force and employment. The civilian labor force—the number of persons either working or seeking work—rose 1.7 percent per year, as the labor force participation rate rose from 58.8 percent to 67.1 percent of the working-age civilian noninstitutional population, reflecting increased participation by women in the paid work force. In addition, there was a shift of employment out of agriculture and into nonagricultural industries with significantly higher values of output per worker—a continuation of a trend that started at the dawn of the Industrial Revolution. Agricultural employment declined over the half-century and the total number of persons employed outside farms rose at a 1.9 percent rate. A separate count of nonfarm payroll jobs rose even faster, 2.1 percent. The payroll count is a count of jobs, so a person with two jobs is counted twice, whereas that person is counted only once as a "person employed." There are other important differences as well. (See Chapter 10, its Notes and Definitions, and the Special Notes.)

Unemployment, like economic growth, varied from year to year, with postwar unemployment rates ranging from a low of 2.9 percent in 1953, in the period of the Korean War, to 9.7 percent in 1982. At the height of World War II, even lower unemployment rates were achieved. (Tables 10-3 and 18-1)

Unemployment is, of course, directly related to economic growth over the business cycle—yet the relationship (known as "Okun's Law") is not always regular or predictable. Changes in productivity and the workweek affect the relationship of employment change to output change, and changes in labor force participation affect the relationship of the change in the unemployment rate to employment change.

Looking at the longer-term trend, output grew faster than employment during the past half-century because of increases in labor productivity, that is, output per hour worked. In Chapter 9, measures of productivity are presented for the total business sector, which was 78 percent of the value of GDP in 2000, and three important subsectors—nonfarm business, nonfinancial corporations, and manufacturing.

Hours worked and productivity. Business sector output per hour grew at a 2.4 percent annual rate from 1948 to 2000. This is the arithmetic result of business sector output growing 3.7 percent—slightly faster than total GDP—while aggregate hours worked (the number of jobs times the average workweek per job) rose only 1.3 percent on average.

Factoring the change in hours worked into its employment and average hours components reveals another salient fact about the last half-century—the decline in the average job's workweek. The number of jobs in the business sector increased from 1948 to 2000 at a 1.5 percent rate, while the average workweek—the number of hours worked *per job*—declined at a rate of 0.3 percent. (Table 9-3)

Does this mean that the average American worker is working shorter hours, or that the average American family can be supported by less paid work effort? No, because the precise meaning of "hours worked per job" must be understood. In the productivity accounts, as in the BLS payroll employment survey that provides much of the basic data for employment and hours worked, the employment concept is the number of jobs, not the number of persons. If more workers take second, part-time jobs, these measures show higher "employment," even though no more persons are employed, and a shorter average workweek. If a spouse or other previously nonworking family member takes a part-time job, employment increases and the "average workweek" declines, even while that family as a family unit is putting more time into paid employment.

Readers will note that Table 10-7 shows *increases* over the years in the average workweek in old-line, relatively well-paid sectors—natural resources and mining, manufacturing, and construction. In these sectors, employers often prefer paying overtime to taking on more workers. The extra cost of an additional worker in terms of additional health and other fringe benefit expenses is often a consideration. In the sectors where pay and benefits are lower, jobs, particularly part-time jobs without benefits, grow faster. Overall, the average workweek declines. (See Chapters 10 and 16.)

Interpretation and sources of labor productivity. As the Bureau of Labor Statistics points out, its measures of labor productivity "do not measure the specific contribution of labor, capital, or any other factor of production. Rather, they reflect the joint effects of many influences, including changes in technology; capital investment; level of output; utilization of capacity, energy, and materials; the organization of production; managerial skill; and the characteristics and effort of the work force." In measures of "total factor productivity," BLS undertakes further analysis of the sources of growth in output per hour. These can be found, along with extensive data on the composition and education of the work force, in *Handbook of U.S. Labor Statistics*, Bernan Press.

Data related to some of these sources of productivity are shown in *Business Statistics*. For the capital stock, Tables 5-5 and 1-1 indicate that the current-cost value of total fixed assets was 2.80 times the value of GDP in 1948 and 2.74 times GDP in 2000. The ratio of private fixed assets to GDP rose from 2.00 to 2.16, while the ratio of government assets declined from 0.80 to 0.58. The quantity indexes in Table 5-6 indicate that the quantity (that is, the constant-dollar value) of fixed assets rose somewhat more slowly than real GDP—from 1948 to 2000, private fixed assets grew at a 3.4 percent annual rate and government assets 2.4 percent. The growth in both kinds of capital stock was greater than the growth in labor input (aggregate hours), providing an explanation for some of the increase in labor productivity, but clearly the productivity of capital as well as that of labor was increasing.

In Chapter 11, *Business Statistics* provides measures of energy consumption, indicating a decline in overall energy use per real dollar of GDP—yet another instance of increased efficiency of a factor of production.

In Chapter 2 and Table 20-1, measures of capacity utilization are shown for the manufacturing sector for the entire postwar period, and for the mining and utility sectors from 1967 forward. Unfortunately, utilization rates are not available for other industries, which now make up a large share of GDP. Manufacturing utilization rates were about the same in the late 1990s and 2000 as they had been in 1948, suggesting that in that industry, long-term productivity increases probably cannot be explained by greater utilization of the capital stock.

Implications of productivity growth. Productivity growth interacts in important ways with labor compensation and inflation. In the business sector, the current-dollar value of compensation per hour worked (including wages, salaries, and employer-paid benefits) rose at a 5.7 percent annual rate from 1948 to 2000. However, the 2.4 percent increase in productivity meant that the labor cost of a unit of *output* only rose at a 3.2 percent annual rate. Since labor compensation now makes up about two-thirds of national income (Table 1-11), unit labor costs are often considered to be a major determinant of inflation. Indeed, inflation and unit labor costs track each other closely over longer periods: the 1948–2000 rate of increase in the average price (implicit deflator) of the business sector was also 3.2 percent.

Productivity growth is also considered to be a major determinant of the real wage, since it allows increases in compensation without increases in labor cost. The productivity accounts show that in the business sector, real hourly compensation rose at a 1.9 percent annual rate from 1948 to 2000, falling short of the 2.4 percent increase in productivity. However, the apparent difference between these two trends reflects not a decline in the share of the value of output going to employees as a group but a difference between the "market baskets" used to determine the real value of the two aggregates. The deflator for real compensation in this set of data is a variation of the consumer price index, while the gross product deflator that determines productivity is based on goods and services *produced* by the business sector rather than those *consumed* by U.S. consumers. Business sector output includes a substantial proportion of high-tech products, which have had dramatic price declines. Workers, on the other hand, buy proportionately fewer computers and other high-tech products and proportionately more commodity-based products, including imports. In other words, the average price of what workers buy went up more than the average price of what they produced. (Table 9-3)

A more complete accounting for the costs of production, taking capital as well as labor costs into account, can be observed in the productivity and cost data for nonfinancial corporations. These are only available back to 1958. To demonstrate some of the implications of these data, growth rates will be calculated here using 1960 as the earlier cyclical high. This is not entirely satisfactory, since the 1960 unemployment rate, at 5.5 percent, was markedly higher than the 4.0 percent registered in 2000.

In that 40-year span, compensation per hour at nonfinancial corporations rose 5.4 percent and productivity 1.9 percent, for a unit labor cost increase of 3.4 percent. Unit non-labor costs (capital consumption, interest, and indirect taxes) rose 3.9 percent and unit profits rose 2.0 percent. The total price of a unit of output—which is the sum of the unit cost and unit profits growth rates, weighted by their shares—rose at a 3.4 percent rate—once again, the same as the rise in unit labor cost. The relative decline in profits echoes the rise in interest and fall in profits indicated in the national income accounts, which in turn reflects the rise in corporate indebtedness shown in Table 12-5. (Tables 9-3, 1-8 through 1-11, and 12-5.)

Whose standard of living?

In everything written so far, this article has been concerned with averages—average GDP per capita, average output and real compensation per hour worked, and so forth. It is important to note that an average, known technically to statisticians as a "mean," is only one way of describing the central tendency of any set of statistical data, and not necessarily the one that produces the most representative number.

If we are interested in the economic well-being of a typical American family (or household), we would probably judge that the best single number to characterize that well-being would be the standard of living of a family (or household) situated at the middle of the income distribution. Half of all families would have higher income and half would have lower incomes. This is the measure known as the "median," and data on median incomes are presented in Chapter 3. Medians are not the same as averages or means, and in the case of income distributions they are invariably lower.

This difference is sometimes illustrated by the image of a millionaire walking into a working-class bar. The "average income" (mean income) of each person in the bar would jump, as a million dollars was added to the numerator of the average and just one unit to the denominator. However, the median would be little if at all changed, and this would accord with an accurate perception that the "typical" person in that bar had not experienced any increase in his income. Not only are income means higher than income medians; if the incomes of people at the upper end of the distribution increase faster than the incomes of those at the middle and bottom, then the means will also *increase* more than the medians.

In Chapter 3, it can be seen that real median family cash income increased 1.9 percent from 1948 to 2000 (again using years of comparable low unemployment). This is less than the 2.2 percent increase in real per capita GDP (a mean) during that period and also less than the 2.1 percent increase in real mean family income that can be derived from the census income data. Had the median income increased as fast as the census mean—implying no change in the income distribution—the median family would have had over $6,000 more income in 2000, in that year's dollars.

The increasing inequality in the income distribution can also be seen by comparing the 1948 and 2000 income shares shown in Chapter 3. The top 20 percent of families received 47.7 percent of all income in 2000, compared with 42.4 percent in 1948. The shares of each of the lower four quintiles declined. There is also a more comprehensive measure of income inequality known as the "Gini coefficient," which is discussed and shown in Chapter 3, including its Notes and Definitions.

It can be argued that the postwar growth in real income and productivity required increasing relative rewards for the successful, so that the hypothetical potential increase just calculated for the median family could never actually occur. This is not a question that can be definitively answered—certainly not based on the kind of data available here—but it can be noted that productivity increases were quite rapid during the earlier postwar years, before the trend toward a more unequal income distribution began. (See Chapters 3 and 9.)

Inflation and unemployment

A number of important price indicators are presented in *Business Statistics*, both in Chapter 8: Prices and also in Table 1-4, which shows chain-type price indexes for GDP and various subsectors. Users should note that price indexes measure the average level of prices, relative to some base year, while "inflation" is the annual percent *rate of change* in a price index.

Biases that emerge in the most popular indicator—the official Consumer Price Index for All Urban Consumers (CPI-U)—are not retroactively corrected. There are some alternative versions of the CPI that carry the improved methodologies currently in use back for some historical period. These are presented in *Business Statistics*; see Table 8-1 and the associated Notes and Definitions. One of these alternatives, the CPI-U-RS, is used by the Bureau of Labor Statistics to calculate historical values of real compensation (Chapter 9) and by the Census Bureau to calculate historical values of real median income (Chapter 3).

Because of this and other perceived shortcomings of the CPI, the monetary authorities at the Federal Reserve pay particular attention to the chain-type price indexes for personal consumption expenditures, total and excluding food and energy, derived from the National Income and Product Accounts, which use the same basic price data as the CPIs but process those data in a more consistent fashion and apply to a somewhat broader universe of prices. (See Table 1-4 and the Notes and Definitions to Chapter 1.) But all of these indexes tell a similar story about the inflation rate—that is, the rate of change in prices—for the broad sweep of the postwar period.

As the graph in Chapter 8 (Figure 8-1) shows, inflation was high in 1946 and 1947, as wartime price controls were dismantled and pent-up purchasing power from the war period was released. Prices declined in the 1949 recession but rose sharply in 1950 and 1951 with recovery and the outbreak of the Korean War. Inflation was negative again in 1955 in the aftermath of the war's end and the 1954 recession. It rose during two recoveries in 1956–1957 and 1960, but fell back to about 1 percent—generally judged to represent price stability because of remaining and irremediable biases in the price indexes—in the slack years of 1961 and 1962.

As the 1960s progressed, however, the federal government embarked on a stimulative fiscal policy, with the intent of attaining an unemployment rate lower than those observed in the 1950s and early 1960s. (See Table 10-3.) Then fiscal policy became even more stimulative as the buildup in military spending for the Vietnam War progressed, without any attempt to raise taxes or cut back on other spending until late in the decade. (See Chapter 6.) An attempt was made to hold wages and prices down using voluntary "guidelines" in the early 1960s, but it collapsed in 1966, and inflation continued to accelerate during the sustained period of high employment through 1969.

The 1970 recession failed to bring inflation down, and the 1971 recovery was weak. New expansionary moves to accelerate the recovery, including monetary stimulus and depreciation of the dollar, were undertaken in 1972, along with new price controls. But the 1972 decline in inflation was short-lived, followed by new highs as the controls collapsed and commodity prices soared. The 1975–1976 recession again gave only a temporary and incomplete respite, and inflation soared to double digits with recovery and new commodity price shocks.

Finally, under the impact of the most severe recession in the postwar period in 1981–1982, inflation began to unwind. A subsequent recession in 1990 ushered in even lower inflation rates throughout the rest of the 1990s, despite the achievement, late in that decade, of the lowest unemployment rates since 1969.

As the above narrative indicates, the 1950s and 1960s were characterized by an apparent inverse relationship, often interpreted as a "trade-off," between inflation and high employment, with inflation falling as an apparent consequence of unemployment rising. By the 1970s, however, inflation became more stubborn, and failed to respond proportionately and negatively to increases in unemployment—indeed, at times the two indicators rose together, a phenomenon known as "stagflation." This has often been ascribed to "supply shocks"—for example, bad harvests, oil embargoes, and OPEC price increases—which, unlike decreases in aggregate demand, tend to increase inflation even while depressing output. But in retrospect, many "supply shocks" should perhaps be considered as delayed reactions to demand shocks. To give an important example, oil prices tend to increase when the dollar has declined, and tend to fall during worldwide recession as in 1986. (See price data in Chapter 8 and data on the international value of the dollar in Table 13-7.)

In attempting to explain stagflation, economists now take account of the role of expectations in maintaining the momentum of a given inflation rate, which is believed to explain the worsening of the tradeoff in the 1970s. They were again surprised, however, by the combination of low unemployment and low inflation in the late 1990s. The surprise was greater among those economists who looked at the unemployment rate as the sole measure of resource utilization. In fact, the level of capacity utilization also plays a role in determining to what extent changes in aggregate demand affect prices and to what extent they lead to expanded volume of production instead. Federal Reserve Board measures (Table 2-3) indicate that average utilization of manufacturing capacity declined between the last three major business cycle peaks—from 1979 to 1989 and again from 1989 to 2000. This indicated less pressure on prices, helping to offset the effect of lower unemployment rates over the same intervals.

The issues involved in the relationships between inflation, economic growth, and unemployment are certainly not settled. Debate continues about the relative roles of monetary policy, tax rates and other aspects of fiscal policy, global competition, other supply considerations, labor market institutions, and expectations.

With respect to monetary policy, *Business Statistics* provides data on the monetary and reserve aggregates in Tables 12-1 through 12-3. Rates of change in money and reserves have provided increasingly inaccurate forecasts of inflation and are not widely considered to be valid indicators of the state of monetary policy anymore. The data on interest rates provided in Table 12-9, especially the federal funds rate which is directly controlled by the Federal Reserve, are currently the subject of more attention in assessing the monetary policy stance. However, they need to be converted to "real" interest rates—subtracting the inflation rate (actual or anticipated) from the nominal interest rate—to shed light on the size of the stimulative and inflationary effects of Federal Reserve policy.

War and the economy

Figure 6-3 makes clear how little impact federal spending on the wars against Afghanistan and Iraq could have had on the U.S. economy, at least as of Fiscal Year 2003. Relative to the value of GDP, defense spending had increased slightly but was not much higher than at the *low* point of the post–World War II demobilization. It was lower than Korean War levels (1950–1953), Vietnam War levels (1964–1975), and the 1980s defense buildup. (The 1990–1991 Gulf War was largely financed by U.S. allies, which actually led to a slight *decline* in the defense/GDP ratio.) However, analysts will continue to monitor defense spending, taking note of the tendency toward delayed recognition of war costs—for example, early Johnson-administration underestimates of Vietnam spending, and the failure of the Bush administration to submit any early estimates at all of Iraq War spending.

Business cycle comparisons

Business Statistics now also provides expanded data on earlier cyclical recoveries that users may compare with current data. The reference dates for all of the postwar business cycles are shown in the Notes and Definitions to Table 1-8. Monthly and quarterly data for major indicators such as output, employment, and unemployment for the entire postwar period are shown in Chapters 19 and 20. A few statistical pitfalls need to be avoided; see the Special Notes.

...and more

This article has provided examples of the kinds of data analysis newly possible with this expanded version of *Business Statistics*. Regional and industrial details are also available, along with information on business and consumer balance sheets. The editor anticipates that users will find this volume even more useful than previous editions, and welcomes input on ways to make it more helpful still. The editor can be contacted via email at cstrawser@bernan.com.

SPECIAL NOTES: CURRENT STATISTICAL ISSUES AND PITFALLS

Almost every day, some new set of information on the economy is released—a new estimate of the latest quarter's Gross Domestic Product, new figures on employment and unemployment, or a new month's inflation rate. Politicians, pundits, and stock market gurus give instant opinions on the significance of the new numbers. One of the purposes of *Business Statistics* is to provide background information to supplement and give perspective to this daily stream of new and updated economic data, and enable the users of this book to make their own informed judgments.

Sometimes the very richness of U.S. economic data makes comparisons and analysis more difficult for people who are not already immersed in the intricacies of the system. For example, one government agency issues two different estimates of what at first glance would seem to be the same thing, "employment." More generally, the constant labors of statistical agencies to incorporate new information and new understanding of the economy lead to frequent revisions of data.

To help users understand these difficulties, the Notes and Definitions at the end of each chapter in *Business Statistics* explain concepts, definitions, measurement methods, and revision procedures. In these Special Notes, the editor will discuss briefly the measurement of employment and the measurement of employee compensation per hour. The two measures of employment are discussed more fully and authoritatively in the article by the Bureau of Labor Statistics that follows, entitled "Employment from the BLS household and payroll surveys: summary of recent trends."

Measures of employment

Each month, the Bureau of Labor Statistics updates two distinct measures of aggregate employment in the U.S. economy.

One measure, total civilian employment, is a count of the number of civilians holding jobs. It is derived from a large sample survey of households (Current Population Survey, or CPS) and periodically benchmarked to population levels or "controls" established by the decennial Census and other more comprehensive data.

The other measure is nonfarm payroll employment. It is derived from a very large sample of employers (Current Employment Statistics, or CES) and is benchmarked each year to a comprehensive count of employment from the records of the unemployment insurance system.

Financial market participants, including Federal Reserve Chairman Greenspan and other analysts at the Federal Reserve Board, typically rely on the CES numbers for interpreting the recent course of the economy. Its large sample size and consequent relative stability make it easier to distinguish the "signal" from the "noise." (In the BLS article, it can be seen that the size of the over-the-month change in employment required to be statistically significant is 339,000 in the CPS series but only 108,000 in the CES series.)

In recent years some analysts have pointed out that the CPS has shown a stronger employment trend and suggested that it is a better measure. Analysts who give preference to CPS employment point out that it includes self-employment, which is omitted by definition from the CES. (Self-employment is covered and reported separately in the CPS; the series can be found on the BLS Internet site, <http://www.bls.gov>.) In addition, they hold that because the CPS is a survey of households it is not subject to the potential bias of the employer survey—a failure to pick up new businesses, at least until the annual benchmark.

However, there is also an important point to be made about potential bias and distortion in the CPS, which arises from the fact that it is anchored in projections of the total population. If these projections are in error—and they have been in the past, due to misestimates of international migration—then the errors will carry through to the estimates of the number employed. Furthermore, when the population "controls" are revised to reflect new information from the decennial Census or a new migration estimate, the adjustments are introduced in a "lump sum" in a single month, usually January. This makes for a discontinuity between the two adjoining months, and fails to spread the correction of the level over the months or years during which the misstatement gradually emerged. For examples, see the Notes and Definitions to Tables 10-1 through 10-3. For examples with orders of magnitude involved, see any issue of the BLS publication *Employment and Earnings*.

CES benchmark adjustments, on the other hand, are "wedged" back to the previous benchmark month, resulting in a smoother and more realistic pattern of revision. In addition, because the CES is a survey of employers, it will not be biased by errors in population estimates due to faulty estimates of migration. In the late 1990s, unlike the more recent period, the CES showed greater employment growth than the CPS—differences that were narrowed when new population numbers caused upward adjustment of CPS employment.

With respect to the new-firm problem, the benchmark adjustments to CES employment were downward for March 2001, 2002, and 2003, but an upward revision is now anticipated for 2004, based on preliminary tabulations of the benchmark data. BLS has incorporated increasingly sophisticated methods to make ongoing corrections for this problem and minimize the amount of revision.

In the article that follows this note, BLS details the characteristics of both series and calculates, for comparison with the CES payroll employment series, an "adjusted household survey" which makes all feasible adjustments for definitional differences and smooths the population control revisions. These adjustments "provide a partial explanation for the employment trend differences" but other differences remain that continue to be explored. BLS concludes that "both the payroll and household surveys are needed for a complete picture of the labor market. The payroll survey provides a highly reliable gauge of monthly change…[and] offers industry and geographic information at very detailed levels. The household survey provides a broader picture of employment including agriculture and the self-employed, as well as detailed information on the demographic composition of the employed and the unemployed."

Measures of employee compensation

Hourly earnings, wages, salaries, compensation—each of these terms is used to describe at least one data series in the U.S. statistical system, and each appears in at least one of three different data sets presented in *Business Statistics*. (Additional, more detailed data on labor compensation are presented in *Handbook of U.S. Labor Statistics*, Bernan Press.) It is important for the user to understand the characteristics of each of these series in order to select the one most suited for his or her purpose.

Wages typically mean gross amounts per hour paid to hourly workers. They are gross of withheld income and payroll taxes, dues, and other withholdings—in other words, they do not exclude those amounts—but they do exclude the employer share of payroll taxes and the cost of employer-provided benefits such as pensions and health insurance. Measures of wages and salaries together are presented in Chapter 9 and measures of hourly earnings are presented in Chapter 10, with precise definitions of each in the Notes and Definitions to those chapters.

Salaries represent gross amounts paid to those who are paid by the week, month, or year rather than by the hour. Measures of wages and salaries together are presented in Chapter 9, and salaried production or nonsupervisory workers are included in the hourly earnings measures in Chapter 10. As with wages, salaries do not exclude personal and payroll taxes on the individual or other withholdings, but do exclude the cost of employer-paid benefits and payroll taxes.

Compensation includes wages and salaries as defined above together with the employer-paid payroll taxes and benefit costs.

Compensation, then, represents the total cost of labor to the employer. Wages and salaries represent the gross taxable income to the employees. Only one measure in this book represents net spendable income after all income and payroll taxes—Personal Disposable Income, in Chapter 4. This includes not only labor income but also all forms of capital income. It is not broken down by industry or by income level, and like all other income averages it is a mean and, because of the skewed distribution of income, is biased as a measure of the income of a typical or median individual. (See "Whose Standard of Living?" in the article above on "Expanded Historical Statistics.") There are no currently reported measures of the concept of "worker take-home pay," but in the absence of any change in tax rates, the rate of change in worker paychecks can usually be inferred from the rate of change in a relevant measure of wages and salaries or hourly earnings.

Probably the principal use for *compensation* series, the use emphasized by the Federal Reserve System, is as an indicator of inflationary pressure. Labor costs represent about two-thirds of the cost of production on average. If labor costs rise faster than productivity, either because of the effects of a tight labor market or because of some autonomous source, there can be upward pressure on prices.

In evaluating trends in compensation, the differences between the two series presented in Chapter 9 are important. The Notes and Definitions for that chapter explain each one in a General Note and in the specific notes for each table. Briefly, the compensation component of the Productivity and Costs measures (Table 9-3) is simply an average of all compensation divided by all labor input, and will increase if there is a shift in the composition of output toward industries that pay their employees more, even if no individual worker experiences any increase in his or her hourly or weekly earnings. However, high-pay industries are typically high-productivity industries, and a shift toward those industries will also register as an increase in productivity even if productivity is unchanged in each individual industry. Thus, such a shift in the composition of output will not increase labor cost per unit of output or inflationary pressure.

The Employment Cost Index holds constant the composition of employment in order to isolate trends in hourly wages, salary rates, and compensation rates for individual occupations. One appropriate use of ECI measures would be to test the effect of changes in the unemployment rate or other measures of labor market tightness and other relevant variables on the rate of change in wages per unit of labor—the "Phillips Curve" relationship.

The Employment Cost Index includes sales commissions in its measures of wages and salaries. Since these are subject to temporary fluctuations that may not reflect underlying trends, ECIs excluding the sales occupations are also calculated and published.

Currently, the cost of stock options issued to employees is not included in the Employment Cost Index and is included in the compensation component of the productivity measures only with a lag. As illustrated in the Notes and Definitions, this led to large revisions in compensation per hour in some recent periods. Whether this is a significant failing in the Employment Cost Index depends on the extent to which employees accepted stock options as a substitute for demanding higher salaries and/or benefits. This substitution hypothesis has been suggested by anecdote and could be tested by comparing stock price data and relevant components of the Employment Cost Index.

Hourly earnings, as presented in Chapter 10, are a major source for the aggregate compensation measures in Productivity and Costs. They are reported monthly at the beginning of the following month, far more promptly than the quarterly measures, and represent the production or nonsupervisory workers that make up about four-fifths of the labor force, based on a very large sample survey of employers. Hourly earnings are described in the Notes and Definitions to Chapter 10; they exclude stock options and fluctuate as the composition of output and employment fluctuates between high- and low-pay industries. Weekly earnings, based on these hourly earnings data, are an important component of personal income and thus a major determinant of consumer income and purchasing power.

Hourly earnings give an early, if imperfect, indicator of inflationary wage pressures, subject to refinement and reinterpretation as the ECI data become available, while weekly earnings give an early look at recent income developments.

This article is reprinted from the Bureau of Labor Statistics Web site, <http://www.bls.gov/cps/ces_cps_trends.pdf>, published December 3, 2004.

Employment from the BLS household and payroll surveys: summary of recent trends

Overview

The Bureau of Labor Statistics (BLS) has two monthly surveys that measure employment levels and trends: the Current Population Survey (CPS), also known as the household survey, and the Current Employment Statistics (CES) survey, also known as the payroll or establishment survey.

Estimates from both surveys are published in the "Employment Situation" news release each month. The household and payroll surveys use different definitions of employment and distinct survey and estimation methods. To help data users better understand the differences in the surveys' employment measures and divergences that sometimes occur in their trends, the following information is provided.

- **Summary comparison of household and payroll survey concepts, definitions, and methodologies**

- **Employment trends as measured by the payroll and household surveys**

- **Possible causes of differences in employment trends**

- **Summary of recent changes made to each survey:**
  - **Population control adjustments to the household survey**
  - **Benchmark revisions to the payroll survey**

Summary comparison of household and payroll survey concepts, definitions, and methodologies

Major features and distinctions of the two surveys are compared below in Box 1.

Box 1. How the household and payroll surveys compare

Comparison by:	Household Survey (CPS)	Payroll Survey (CES)
Universe	Civilian noninstitutional population age 16 and over	Nonfarm wage and salary jobs
Type of survey	Monthly sample survey of approximately 60,000 households	Monthly sample survey of about 160,000 businesses and government agencies covering approximately 400,000 establishments
Major outputs	Labor force, employment, unemployment, and associated rates with significant demographic detail	Employment, hours, and earnings with significant industry and geographic detail
Reference period	Calendar week that includes the 12th of the month	Employer pay period that includes the 12th of the month (could be weekly, biweekly, monthly or other)
Employment concept	Estimate of employed persons (multiple jobholders are counted only once)	Estimate of jobs (multiple jobholders counted for each nonfarm payroll job)
Employment definition differences	Includes the unincorporated self employed, unpaid family workers, agriculture and related workers, private household workers, and workers absent without pay	Excludes all of the groups listed at left, except for the logging component of agriculture and related industries
Size of over-the-month change in employment required for a statistically significant movement	$\pm$339,000	$\pm$108,000
Benchmark adjustments to survey results	No direct benchmark for employment. Adjustments to underlying population base revised annually to intercensal estimates, and every 10 years to the decennial census	Employment benchmarked annually to employment counts derived primarily from Unemployment Insurance (UI) tax records

Employment trends as measured by the household and payroll surveys

Chart 1 shows employment from the household and payroll surveys from January 1994 through the most recent month. Two variations of household survey employment used in BLS research are presented (these variations differ from the official series that appears in the "Employment Situation" and in the public database available through the BLS website). The green household survey line represents a version of total household survey employment where the effects of sizeable population control revisions in January 2000, 2003, and 2004 have been smoothed. The red "adjusted" household survey line represents the smoothed household survey employment series that has been further modified to make it more similar in concept and definition to payroll survey employment. This adjustment to household survey employment subtracts from total employment agriculture and related employment, nonagricultural self employed, unpaid family and private household workers, and workers absent without pay from their jobs, and then adds nonagricultural wage and salary multiple jobholders.

Chart 1 shows that, because of its broader employment definition, the household survey employment level (green line) normally exceeds that of the payroll survey. When the household survey is adjusted to more closely match the payroll survey definition (red line), trend discrepancies between the two surveys are more discernible. In particular, there is an obvious multi-year period from the late 1990s until the onset of the recent recession when payroll employment was growing significantly faster than household survey employment. More recently, the two series converged.

Chart 1. Household and payroll survey employment, seasonally adjusted, 1994–2004

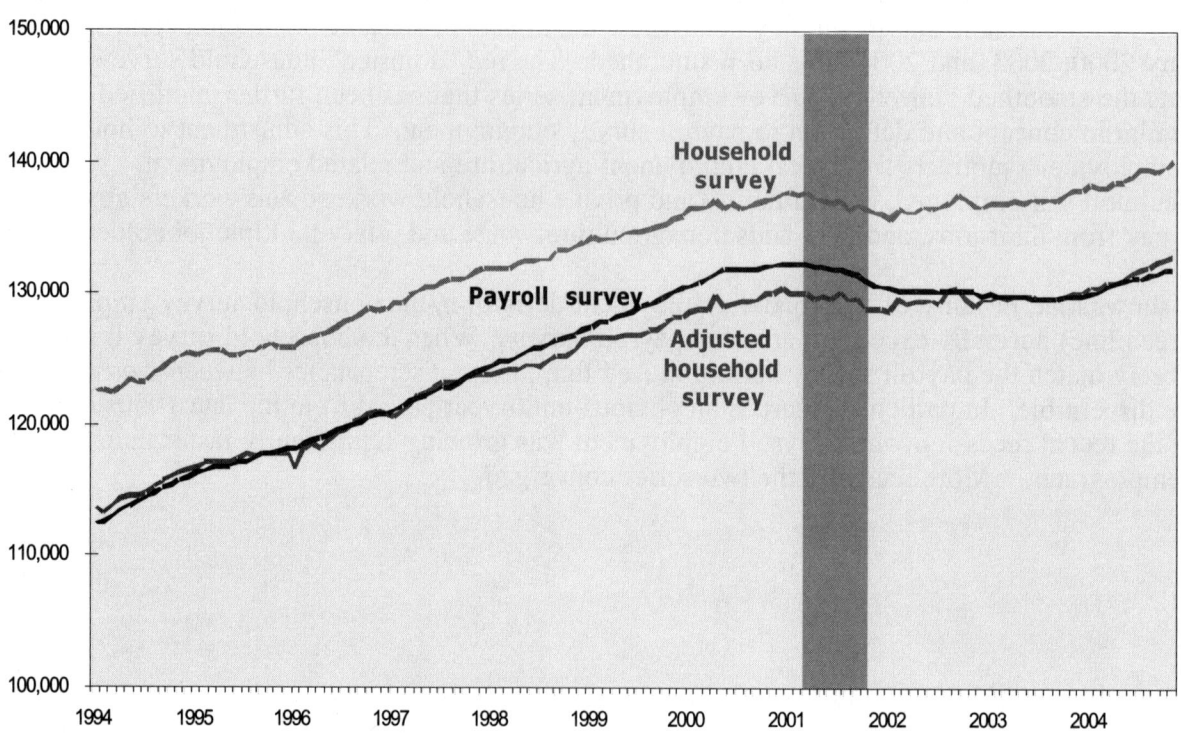

NOTE: The household series presented here has been smoothed for population control revisions. The "adjusted" household series has been smoothed for population control revisions and adjusted to an employment concept more similar to the payroll survey. Shaded area indicates recession.

SOURCE: Bureau of Labor Statistics, December 3, 2004.

Chart 2 shows the same payroll and household employment series as chart 1, but highlights only the recent recession and post-recessionary period from March 2001 through the most recent month. The Business Cycle Dating Committee of the National Bureau of Economic Research (NBER) designated March 2001 as the most recent business cycle peak and November 2001 as the most recent trough. (The NBER is a private, nonprofit, nonpartisan research organization that is the generally acknowledged arbiter of business cycle dating.)

From Chart 2, more recent trends in employment from the two surveys can be seen. Payroll employment declined for a number of months following the end of the recession, while household survey employment trended up. Since last fall, employment as measured by both surveys has increased.

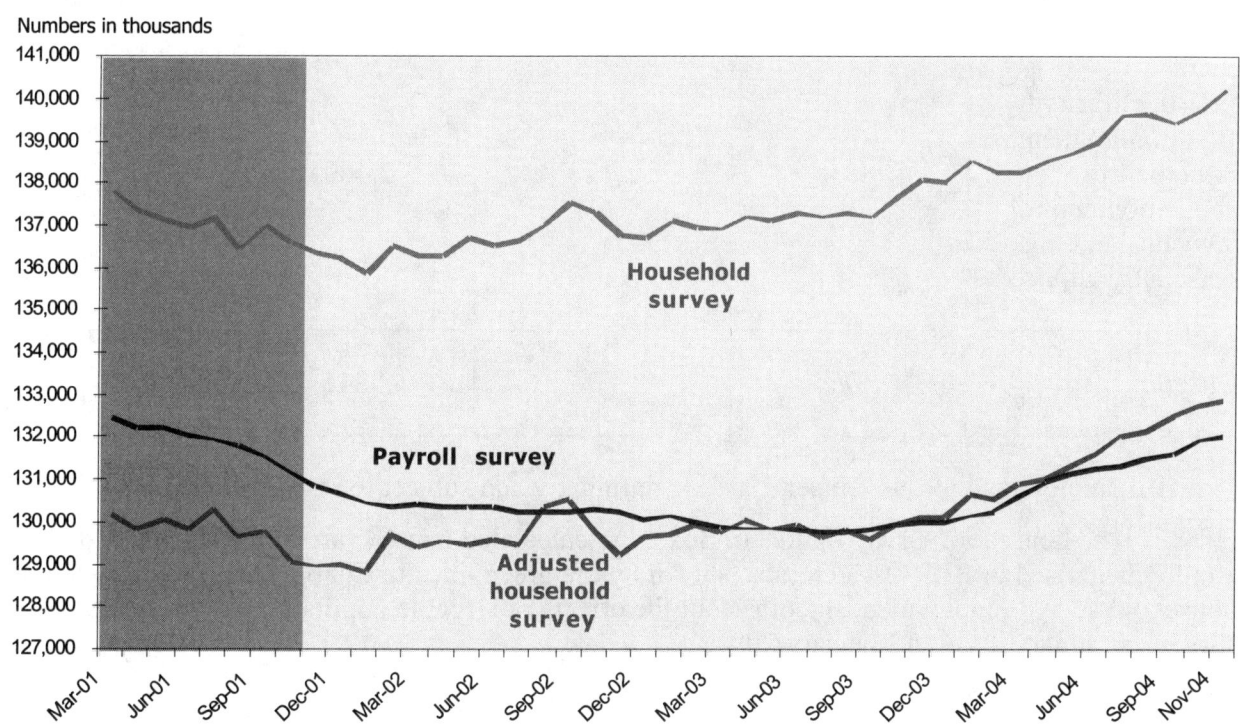

NOTE: The household series presented here has been smoothed for population control revisions. The "adjusted" household series has been smoothed for population control revisions and adjusted to an employment concept more similar to the payroll survey. Shaded area indicates recession.

SOURCE: Bureau of Labor Statistics, December 3, 2004.

Box 2 shows the change in employment levels from the payroll and household surveys as measured across the following time periods: 1) over the most recent month, 2) over the most recent year, 3) since March 2001, the most recent business cycle peak, and 4) since November 2001, the most recent business cycle trough. The peak and trough dates are determined by the National Bureau of Economic Research (NBER).

Box 2. Recent trends in payroll and household survey employment

Numbers in thousands

	Over-the-month change: October 2004– November 2004	Over-the-year change: November 2003– November 2004	From March 2001 (peak)– November 2004	From November 2001 (trough)– November 2004
Payroll survey: total nonfarm employment, seasonally adjusted[1]	112	2,048	-432	1,204
Household survey: total employment, smoothed for population control revisions and seasonally adjusted	483	2,128	2,409	3,855
Difference	371	80	2,841	2,651

[1] Payroll employment for November 2004 is preliminary and subject to revision.

NOTE: The household survey figures in Box 2 are calculated from a variation of household survey employment used in BLS research (also shown by the green lines in Charts 1 and 2). This version of household survey employment smoothes out the effects of sizeable population control revisions to the survey in January 2003 and January 2004.

Box 3 shows employment trends in the payroll and household surveys over the same periods as in Box 2, but this illustration uses adjusted household employment that is more comparable to the payroll survey (also shown in Charts 1 and 2). Even with this adjustment, the difference in employment change as measured by the two surveys since March or November of 2001 is substantial.

Box 3. Recent trends in payroll employment and household survey employment adjusted to an employment concept more similar to that of the payroll survey

Numbers in thousands

	Over-the-month change: October 2004–November 2004	Over-the-year change: November 2003–November 2004	From March 2001 (peak)–November 2004	From November 2001 (trough)–November 2004
Payroll survey: total nonfarm employment, seasonally adjusted[1]	112	2,048	-432	1,204
Household survey: total employment, smoothed for population control revisions, adjusted to be more like the payroll survey, and seasonally adjusted	107	2,772	2,706	3,923
Difference	5	724	3,138	2,719

[1] Payroll employment for November 2004 is preliminary and subject to revision.

NOTE: The household survey figures in Box 3 are calculated from a variation of household employment used in BLS research (also shown by the red lines in Charts 1 and 2). This version of household employment smoothes out the effects of sizeable population control revisions to the survey in January 2003 and January 2004. In addition, it adjusts household survey employment to make it more similar in concept and definition to payroll employment. This adjustment to household survey employment subtracts from total employment agriculture and related employment, nonagricultural self employed, unpaid family and private household workers, and workers on unpaid leave from their jobs, and then adds nonagricultural wage and salary multiple jobholders.

Possible causes of differences in employment trends

The following summarizes some issues with the surveys that are important when comparing changes in employment from the two sources.

Sampling error – The payroll survey has a much larger sample size than the household survey. The payroll survey's active sample covers approximately 400,000 business establishments *of all sizes* representing about one-third of total nonfarm employment. The household survey is much smaller at 60,000 households, covering a very small fraction of total employed persons. Household survey employment is therefore subject to larger sampling error, about 3 times that of the payroll survey on a monthly basis (see Box 1). When looking at short-term trends in either survey, especially over-the-month changes, it is essential to assess the statistical significance of the change. When comparing the two series over longer periods of time, however, other factors also need to be considered; some of these are discussed below.

Payroll survey benchmark – The payroll survey estimates are benchmarked once a year against a full universe count of employment derived from Unemployment Insurance (UI) tax records that nearly all employers are required to file. The payroll survey's last benchmark—to March 2003 employment records—resulted in a small downward revision of one-tenth of one percent. The preliminary estimate of the next benchmark revision—for March 2004—is for an upward revision of 236,000, or two-tenths of one percent. The historical average for benchmark revisions over the past decade has been plus or minus three-tenths of one percent. Hence, payroll employment continues to track closely with the universe of nonfarm payroll employment.

With regard to the benchmark source data, BLS has reviewed information from publicly available UI management reports concerning the timeliness of new business enrollments into the UI system. The findings are available in the report "Assessing the Timeliness of Business Births in BLS Establishment Statistics" on the BLS Internet site at <http://www.bls.gov/cew/eta581study.pdf>.

New business births in the payroll survey – The payroll survey sample does not include new firms immediately. They are incorporated with a lag. In the interim, a model-based estimate is used each month to account for employment resulting from new firm births. Based on the relatively small benchmark revision for March 2003, as well as comparisons to preliminary universe data for First Quarter 2004, the model appears to be performing well during the recent period. Additional information about the birth/death model used in the payroll survey estimates is on the BLS Internet site at <http://www.bls.gov/web/cesbd.htm>.

Job changing – Employment estimates from the payroll survey are a count of jobs, unlike the household survey which provides a count of employed persons. If a person changes jobs within a payroll survey reference period, which is defined as the pay period including the 12th of the month, both jobs will be counted by the payroll survey estimates. If the rate of job-to-job movement changes substantially over time, it could impact trends produced from the payroll survey. While there is no method to directly measure effects from job changing, BLS is researching this issue using job change rates from the household survey. The initial findings of this research are provided in the report "Effects of Job Changing on Payroll Survey Employment Trends" at <http://www.bls.gov/ces/cesjobch.pdf>.

Population controls in the household survey – Population controls determine the weights used in the household survey to adjust the sample results to the overall level of the U.S. population. The population controls are developed by the U.S. Census Bureau. They are derived from decennial census information and, between census years, from administrative and other data. There are limitations to the population control estimates due primarily to the difficulties associated with estimating the net international migration component. The population controls contributed significantly to the discrepancy between payroll and household survey employment in the 1980s and 1990s when the household survey showed less growth than the payroll survey.

The upward trend in household employment since the end of the 2001 recession has been largely a function of the estimated growth in population. That is to say, the proportion of the population that is employed remains below the 63.0 percent mark at the November 2001 trough. (See additional information on the recent household survey population control adjustments below.)

Worker classification in the household survey – As was illustrated in Box 3 above, adjusting for the measurable differences in the surveys' employment definitions resolves only a portion of the discrepancy. This adjustment process is imperfect, however, because precise data are not available in many cases to make the best possible adjustment. For example, some independent contractors are not reported as self employed in the household survey, but rather as wage and salary workers. This type of reporting issue limits BLS' ability to fully reconcile the two employment measures.

"Off-the-books" employment – Workers who are paid "off-the-books" are not reported in the payroll survey. The household survey could possibly include some of these workers, but BLS cannot determine the extent to which they might be reflected in household survey employment.

Summary
- BLS has estimated the measurable definitional differences between the household and payroll surveys and found they provide a partial explanation for the employment trend differences. There are a number of definitional differences between the surveys that cannot be readily measured or quantified. These differences may contribute to divergences in the surveys' trends, but their effects are either unknown or can only be conjectured. In addition, although BLS has devoted considerable attention to this issue, there may be other contributing factors that have not been identified.

- A summary of some of BLS' research was presented to the Federal Economic Statistics Advisory Committee (FESAC) in October 2003. The paper is available on the BLS Internet site at <http://www.bls.gov/bls/fesacp2101703.dpf>.

- BLS is continuing to investigate possible causes of recent divergences in employment growth between the payroll and household surveys. BLS also has implemented improvements that addressed past limitations. The redesign of the payroll survey, for example, led to the use of a probability sample, more frequent updating of the survey sample frame, and the development of a more effective means to estimate business births and deaths. With regard to the household survey population controls, the Census Bureau remains engaged in efforts to improve the intercensal population estimates. In particular, they have begun utilizing information from the large American Community Survey (ACS) to improve the estimates of net international migration.

- Both the payroll and household surveys are needed for a complete picture of the labor market. The payroll survey provides a highly reliable gauge of monthly change in nonfarm wage and salary employment. The survey has a large probability sample, and is benchmarked annually to a universe count of jobs derived from the unemployment insurance tax system. The payroll survey offers industry and geographic information at very detailed levels. The household survey provides a broader picture of employment including agriculture and the self employed, as well as detailed information on the demographic composition of the employed and the unemployed.

Population control adjustments to the household survey

January 2004 adjustment — As part of its annual review of intercensal population estimates, the U.S. Census Bureau determined that a *downward* adjustment should be made to the household survey population controls. This adjustment stemmed from revised estimates of net international migration for 2000 through 2003. In keeping with usual practice, the new controls were used in the survey starting with data for January 2004. Estimates for December 2003 and earlier months were *not* revised to reflect the new (lower) population controls.

A comparison of December 2003 data based on the old and new controls indicated that the population decrease caused declines in the labor force (-437,000), employment (-409,000), and unemployment (-27,000). The total unemployment rate, labor force participation rate, and employment-population ratio, however, were not affected. Additional details on the January 2004 population adjustments are provided in the table below.

January 2004 household survey population control adjustment effect

Employment status of the population, December 2003

(Numbers in thousands)

	December 2003 as published	December 2003 based on adjusted population controls	Difference[1]
Civilian noninstitutional population	222,509	221,949	-560
Civilian labor force	146,501	146,065	-437
Participation rate	65.8	65.8	0.0
Employed	138,556	138,147	-409
Employment-population ratio	62.3	62.2	0.0
Unemployed	7,945	7,918	-27
Unemployment rate	5.4	5.4	0.0
Not in labor force	76,007	75,884	-123

[1] Differences are calculated from unrounded estimates.

Previous population control adjustments — This latest population control adjustment follows two previous *increases* in the controls. With the release of January 2003 household data last year, BLS introduced two separate adjustments that increased the survey population controls.
1) Beginning in January 2000, household estimates reflect an increase in population resulting from the switch to the Census 2000 population controls.
2) In January 2003, household estimates reflect new, higher population controls. The upward adjustment resulted from higher estimates of net international migration in the population for 2000 through 2002.

Both of these adjustments in population controls resulted in an increase in the employment estimates from the household survey. The impact on employment of the January 2000 adjustment was about 1.6 million. The impact of the January 2003 adjustment was about 576,000.

Interpreting household data with the population control adjustments – The level shifts in household survey employment resulting from these population adjustments make it difficult for data users to compare changes in employment over time periods that include the "bumps." As a convenience to its data users, BLS created a research series that smoothes the level shifts in employment resulting from the January 2000, 2003, and 2004 population control adjustments. This household employment research series was used in Charts 1 and 2 and Box 2 above to provide a clearer picture for analysis. The full series, 1990–2003, is shown in the table below.

Household Survey Employment Smoothed for Population Controls, Seasonally Adjusted, January 1990–December 2003

(In thousands)

	January	February	March	April	May	June	July	August	September	October	November	December
1990	119,093	119,082	119,238	118,898	119,209	119,052	118,891	118,894	118,628	118,651	118,432	118,379
1991	118,089	117,915	117,823	118,293	117,634	117,845	117,785	117,712	118,169	118,052	118,033	117,740
1992	118,265	118,050	118,454	118,748	118,709	118,764	119,071	119,195	119,101	119,020	119,280	119,413
1993	119,503	119,715	119,995	119,938	120,594	120,781	120,970	121,373	121,081	121,363	121,722	122,031
1994	122,547	122,679	122,534	122,908	123,497	123,277	123,362	124,013	124,372	124,811	125,230	125,448
1995	125,402	125,681	125,720	125,722	125,207	125,321	125,629	125,677	125,972	126,241	126,052	125,963
1996	126,013	126,542	126,779	126,924	127,189	127,562	127,922	128,161	128,540	128,909	128,801	128,904
1997	129,358	129,370	129,981	130,247	130,584	130,544	130,970	131,172	131,194	131,368	131,859	131,898
1998	131,958	132,053	132,072	132,484	132,614	132,545	132,643	132,718	133,333	133,359	133,655	133,994
1999	134,436	134,276	134,381	134,402	134,775	134,855	134,905	135,097	135,227	135,529	135,862	136,092
2000	136,569	136,614	136,691	137,294	136,649	136,968	136,569	136,761	136,976	137,200	137,399	137,723
2001	137,889	137,687	137,852	137,396	137,191	136,978	137,234	136,464	137,027	136,612	136,406	136,258
2002	135,902	136,557	136,308	136,305	136,723	136,578	136,710	137,051	137,586	137,335	136,807	136,729
2003	137,134	136,997	136,971	137,240	137,158	137,317	137,240	137,320	137,263	137,704	138,133	138,070

NOTE: This series reflects seasonally adjusted household survey employment that has been revised from January 1990–December 2003 to smooth out the effects of population control revisions introduced in January 2000, 2003, and 2004.

Source: Bureau of Labor Statistics, Division of Labor Force Statistics, February 6, 2004

Box 3 used a variation of the smoothed household survey employment research series that was adjusted to be more similar in concept and definition to payroll employment. That series, which begins in January 1994, is provided below.

Household Survey Employment Smoothed for Population Controls and Adjusted to a Payroll Concept, Seasonally Adjusted
January 1994–November 2004

(In thousands)

	January	February	March	April	May	June	July	August	September	October	November	December
1994	113,747	113,312	113,901	114,425	114,649	114,664	114,832	115,277	115,836	116,114	116,456	116,716
1995	116,831	117,161	117,109	117,174	117,270	117,474	117,805	117,703	117,765	117,811	117,756	117,929
1996	116,807	118,281	118,655	118,258	118,933	119,395	119,637	120,199	120,498	120,823	121,231	120,807
1997	120,718	121,225	121,609	122,335	122,421	122,878	123,307	123,315	123,353	123,620	123,926	123,980
1998	123,991	124,131	124,335	124,191	124,586	124,564	124,500	124,948	125,349	125,368	125,908	126,473
1999	126,758	126,739	126,808	126,800	126,892	126,942	127,079	127,290	127,410	127,877	128,320	128,429
2000	128,843	128,941	128,958	130,061	129,216	129,378	129,511	129,525	129,630	130,147	130,119	130,509
2001	130,204	130,221	130,205	129,842	130,086	129,830	130,332	129,661	129,810	129,103	128,988	129,010
2002	128,816	129,735	129,434	129,600	129,512	129,634	129,479	130,372	130,549	129,826	129,229	129,649
2003	129,725	129,939	129,780	130,063	129,901	129,950	129,642	129,854	129,638	129,969	130,139	130,155
2004	130,667	130,543	130,940	131,037	131,327	131,642	132,109	132,214	132,527	132,804	132,911	

NOTE: This series represents not seasonally adjusted household survey employment that has been revised from January 1990–December 2003 to smooth out the effects of population control revisions introduced in January 2000, 2003, and 2004. The data from 1994 forward were then adjusted to an employment concept more similar to the payroll survey by subtracting from total employment agriculture and related employment, the self employed, unpaid family and private household workers, and workers on unpaid absences and then adding nonagricultural wage and salary multiple jobholders. The resulting employment series was then seasonally adjusted.

Source: Bureau of Labor Statistics, Division of Labor Force Statistics, December 3, 2004

GENERAL NOTES

These notes provide general information about the data in Tables 1-1 through 21-2. Specific Notes and Definitions providing information about data sources, definitions, methodology, revisions, and sources of additional information follow the tables in each chapter.

Main Divisions of the Book

The tables are divided into four main parts.

Part A (Tables 1-1 through 13-7) pertains to the U.S. economy as a whole. Generally, each table presents annual averages for the full period since World War II, or as far back as available, and quarterly or monthly values for the most recent year or years. (Full quarterly or monthly histories for major series are shown in Part C.) Some chapters present data for the United States only in aggregate, while others—such as industrial production, capital expenditures, and employment, hours and earnings—also have detail for major industry groups. Data by industry on industrial production (Chapter 2), capital expenditures (Table 5-11), profits (Table 9-5), and payroll employment, hours, and earnings (Tables 10-5 through 10-10) are classified using the new North American Industry Classification System (NAICS), as far back as such data are made available by the source agencies.

Part B focuses on the individual industries that together produce the Gross Domestic Product (GDP).

- Chapter 14 provides an overview of the NAICS, presenting the overall structure of the classification system, the definition of each major industry group, and the approximate relationships of each group to the industries in the old Standard Industrial Classification (SIC).
- Chapter 15 contains data on value added or GDP originating by industry, using NAICS for the years 1998–2003 and the SIC for 1987–2000.
- Chapter 16 provides further detail on payroll employment, hours, and earnings classified according to NAICS.
- Chapter 17 presents various data sets for key economic sectors. Some of the tables are based on definitions of products, rather than producing establishments, and are valid for either classification system. This is the case for Tables 17-1, Petroleum and Petroleum Products; 17-2, New Construction; 17-3, Housing Starts and Building Permits, Home Sales and Prices; and 17-8, Motor Vehicle Sales and Inventories. Tables 17-4 through 17-7 and 17-9 through 17-11, covering manufacturing and retail and wholesale trade, show overlapping data for the year 1992 using the old and new classification systems,

preserving the old-basis historical record for the years prior to 1992. Tables 17-14 and 17-15 for services firms also present data on the NAICS basis, while 17-12 and 17-13 show overlapping data for earlier years on SIC.

The 1987 SIC is published in *Standard Industrial Classification Manual, 1987*, Executive Office of the President, Office of Management and Budget (Washington, DC: U.S. Government Printing Office, 1988). The NAICS is fully described in U.S. Office of Management and Budget, *North American Industry Classification System: United States, 2002*, published by Bernan Press. Additional information is available on the Census Bureau Internet site <http://www.census.gov>.

Part C presents further historical detail. Chapter 18 shows selected data for the World War II years 1939–1947. These are shown on an annual basis only, as many of the series are not available quarterly or monthly. Chapters 19 and 20 present quarterly or monthly data back to the earliest postwar year available for major series; the corresponding annual values are shown in Part A.

Part D presents data by state and region, calculated by the Bureau of Economic Analysis, available on an annual basis only. Table 21-1 contains data on Gross Domestic Product originating by state, and Table 21-2 shows personal income, population, and employment.

Characteristics of the Tables and the Data

The table subtitles or column headings for the data tables normally indicate that the data are "seasonally adjusted" or "not seasonally adjusted" or "at a seasonally adjusted annual rate." These headings refer to the monthly or quarterly, rather than the annual, data. Annual data by definition require no seasonal adjustment. Annual values are normally calculated as totals or averages of unadjusted data, and such values are used in either adjusted or unadjusted data columns, or both.

Seasonal adjustment removes from the time series the average impact of variations that normally occur at about the same time each year due to, for example, weather, holidays, and tax payment dates.

A simplified example of the process of seasonal adjustment, or deseasonalizing, can indicate why it is so important for the interpretation of economic time series. Statisticians compare actual monthly data for a number of years with "moving average" trends of the monthly data for the 12 months centered on each month's data.

For example, they may find that in November, sales values are usually about 95 percent of the moving average, while in December, usual sales values are 110 percent of the average. Suppose that actual November sales in the current year are $100 and December sales are $105. The seasonally adjusted value for November will be $105 ($100/0.95) while the value for December will be $95 ($105/1.10). Thus, an apparent increase in the unadjusted data turns out to be a decrease when adjusted for the usual seasonal pattern.

The statistical method used to achieve the seasonal adjustment may vary from one data set to another. Many of the data are adjusted by a computer method known as X-12-ARIMA, developed by the Bureau of the Census. A description of the method is found in "New Capabilities and Methods of the X-12-ARIMA Seasonal Adjustment Program," David F. Findley, Brian C. Monsell, William R. Bell, Mark C. Otto and Bor-Chung Chen, *Journal of Business and Economic Statistics*, April 1998. A preprint version of this article can be downloaded from the Bureau of the Census Web site.

Data that are presented at *annual rates* show values at their annual equivalents—the values that would be registered if the rate of activity measured during a particular month or quarter were maintained for a full year. In other words, seasonally adjusted monthly values have been multiplied by 12 and quarterly values by 4 to yield annual rates.

Detail may not add to totals due to rounding. Annual data are typically calculated by source agencies as the annual totals or averages of not-seasonally-adjusted data, and therefore will not be precisely equal to the annual total or average of monthly seasonally-adjusted data. Seasonal adjustment procedures are typically multiplicative rather than additive, and as a result, seasonally adjusted data may not add or average to the annual figure.

Most of the data in this volume are from federal government sources and may be reproduced freely. A few series are from private sources and are used with permission; further use may be subject to copyright restrictions. A list of data sources is shown below.

The tables in this volume incorporate data revisions and corrections released by the source agencies through November 2004.

Data Sources

Most of the data in this volume are from the government agencies and private sources listed below. The specific source(s) for each individual data set is identified at the beginning of the Notes and Definitions for the relevant data pages.

Board of Governors of the Federal Reserve System
Washington, DC 20551

Data Inquiries and Publication Sales:
  Publications Services
  Mail Stop 127
  Board of Governors of the
  Federal Reserve System
  Washington, DC 20551
  Phone: (202) 452-3244 or 3245

Monthly Publication:
  Federal Reserve Bulletin

Internet Address:
  http://www.federalreserve.gov

Bureau of the Census
U.S. Department of Commerce
Washington, DC 20233

Internet Address:
  http://www.census.gov

Ordering data products:
  Call Center: 301-763-INFO (4636)
Email questions:
  webmaster@census.gov
E-sales: <ProductCatalog>

Bureau of Economic Analysis
U.S. Department of Commerce
Washington, DC 20230

Data Inquiries:
  Public Information Office:
  (202) 606-9900

Monthly Publication:
  Survey of Current Business
  Available by subscription. Call 202-512-1800 or go to <bookstore.gpo.gov>.

Internet Address:
  http://www.bea.gov

Bureau of Labor Statistics
U.S. Department of Labor
2 Massachusetts Ave., NE
Washington, DC 20212-0001
(202) 691-5200

Internet Address:
   http://www.bls.gov

Data Inquiries:
   Blsdata_staff@bls.gov

Monthly Publications:
   Monthly Labor Review
   Employment and Earnings
   Compensation and Working Conditions
   Producer Price Indexes
   CPI Detailed Report
   Available by subscription from the Superintendent of Documents (see address below)

Conference Board, The
845 Third Avenue, New York, NY 10022

Internet Address:
   http://www.tcb-indicators.org

Monthly Publication:
   Business Cycle Indicators Report

Employment and Training Administration
U.S. Department of Labor
200 Constitution Avenue, NW
Washington, DC 20210
1-877-US-2JOBS

Internet Address:
   http://www.doleta.gov
   http://www.itsc.state.md.us

Energy Information Administration
U.S. Department of Energy
1000 Independence Ave., SW
Washington, DC 20585

Data Inquiries and Publications:
   National Energy Information Center
   Phone: (202) 586-8800
   Email: infoctr@eia.doe.gov

Monthly Publication:
   Monthly Energy Review

Internet Address:
   http://www.eia.doe.gov

National Agricultural Statistics Service
U.S. Department of Agriculture
14th & Independence Ave., SW
Washington, DC 20250

Data Inquiries:
   Information Hotline: (800) 727-9540 or 202-720-3878

Publication Sales:
   Phone: (800) 999-6779
   Fax: (703) 834-0110

Internet Address:
   http://www.usda.gov/nass/

To order government publications:
   Superintendent of Documents
   Government Printing Office
   Washington, DC 20402
   (202) 512-1800

PART A

THE U.S. ECONOMY

CHAPTER 1: NATIONAL INCOME AND PRODUCT AND CYCLICAL INDICATORS

Section 1a: Gross Domestic Product: Values, Quantities, and Prices

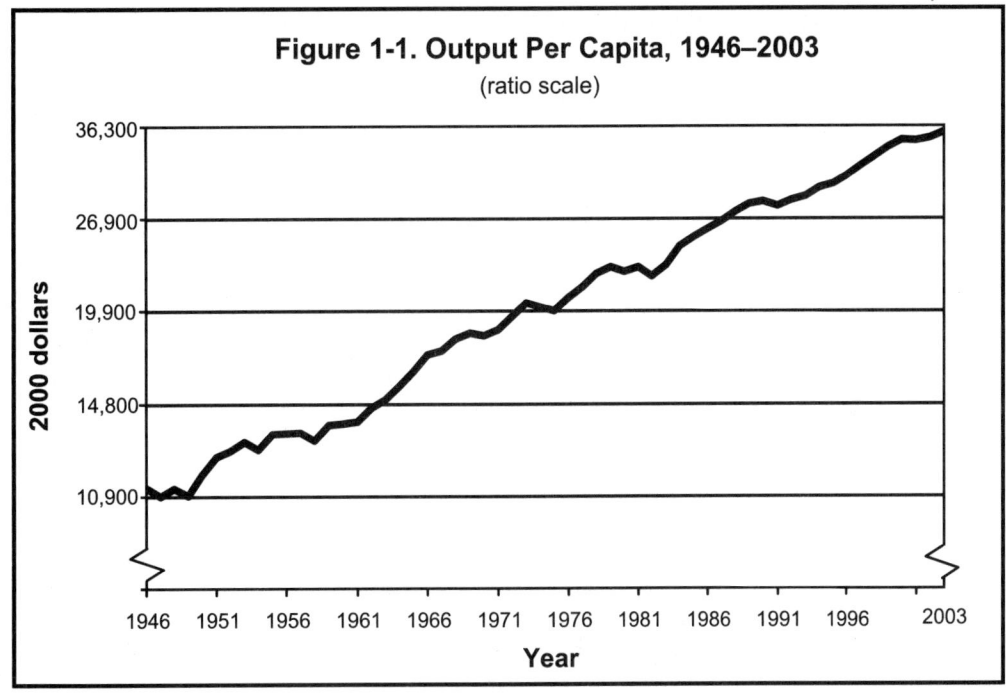

- Output of goods and services in the United States, expressed in constant 2000-value dollars to remove the effect of inflation (real Gross Domestic Product, or GDP), rose from $1.64 trillion in 1948 to $9.82 trillion in 2000—comparable high points in the business cycle. (Table 1-2) This was a nearly sixfold increase in real value over the 52-year period, with an average growth rate of 3.5 percent per year.
- Over the same period population nearly doubled, growing at a rate of 1.3 percent per year. As a result, real GDP per capita—the average value of production for each man, woman, and child in the population—rose at a rate of 2.2 percent per year, from $11,206 (2000 dollars) in 1948 to $34,760 in 2000. (Table 1-7) This value is charted in the graph above. It is graphed on a "ratio scale" so that equal vertical distances signify equal percent changes.
- As the graph indicates, growth is not always smooth or uninterrupted. There are periods of leveling off or decline, marking the periods identified as recessions in economic activity. (Table 1-8 and the associated Notes and Definitions)
- Measured in current dollars, the value of GDP rose even faster, reflecting increases in the average price level. Current-dollar GDP rose from $269 billion in 1948 to nearly $10 trillion in 2000. (Table 1-1) The price level in 2000 was more than six times that in 1948, reflecting an average inflation rate of 3.5 percent per year. (Table 1-5) Annual rates of increase in the chain-type price index for GDP ranged from 9 percent or more in 1947, 1974–1975, and 1980–1981 to changes of no more than 1.2 percent in 1949–1950, 1954, 1959, 1961, 1963, and 1998. Over the latest 10 years, inflation averaged only 1.8 percent.

Table 1-1. Gross Domestic Product

(Billions of dollars, quarterly data are at seasonally adjusted annual rates.)

NIPA Tables 1.1.5, 5.6.5A, 5.6.5B

Year and quarter	Gross domestic product	Personal consumption expenditures	Gross private domestic investment					Exports and imports of goods and services			Government consumption expenditures and gross investment		
			Total	Fixed investment		Change in private inventories		Net exports	Exports	Imports	Total	Federal	State and local
				Nonresidential	Residential	Nonfarm	Farm						
1946	222.3	144.3	31.1	17.3	7.8	6.2	-0.2	7.2	14.2	7.0	39.6	28.9	10.8
1947	244.2	162.0	35.0	23.5	12.1	1.2	-1.8	10.8	18.7	7.9	36.4	22.7	13.7
1948	269.2	175.0	48.1	26.8	15.6	3.0	2.7	5.5	15.5	10.1	40.6	24.2	16.3
1949	267.3	178.5	36.9	24.9	14.6	-2.1	-0.6	5.2	14.5	9.2	46.7	27.7	19.0
1950	293.8	192.2	54.1	27.8	20.5	5.9	-0.1	0.7	12.4	11.6	46.8	26.0	20.7
1951	339.3	208.5	60.2	31.8	18.4	8.9	1.0	2.5	17.1	14.6	68.1	45.1	23.0
1952	358.3	219.5	54.0	31.9	18.6	2.1	1.4	1.2	16.5	15.3	83.6	59.2	24.4
1953	379.4	233.1	56.4	35.1	19.4	1.2	0.7	-0.7	15.3	16.0	90.6	64.4	26.1
1954	380.4	240.0	53.8	34.7	21.1	-2.1	0.2	0.4	15.8	15.4	86.2	57.3	28.9
1955	414.8	258.8	69.0	39.0	25.0	5.6	-0.6	0.5	17.7	17.2	86.5	54.9	31.6
1956	437.5	271.7	72.0	44.5	23.6	4.9	-1.0	2.4	21.3	18.9	91.4	56.7	34.7
1957	461.1	286.9	70.5	47.5	22.2	0.7	0.1	4.1	24.0	19.9	99.7	61.3	38.3
1958	467.2	296.2	64.5	42.5	22.3	-2.3	2.0	0.5	20.6	20.0	106.0	63.8	42.2
1959	506.6	317.6	78.5	46.5	28.1	5.5	-1.6	0.4	22.7	22.3	110.0	65.4	44.7
1960	526.4	331.7	78.9	49.4	26.3	2.7	0.6	4.2	27.0	22.8	111.6	64.1	47.5
1961	544.7	342.1	78.2	48.8	26.4	2.1	0.9	4.9	27.6	22.7	119.5	67.9	51.6
1962	585.6	363.3	88.1	53.1	29.0	5.5	0.6	4.1	29.1	25.0	130.1	75.3	54.9
1963	617.7	382.7	93.8	56.0	32.1	5.1	0.5	4.9	31.1	26.1	136.4	76.9	59.5
1964	663.6	411.4	102.1	63.0	34.3	6.0	-1.2	6.9	35.0	28.1	143.2	78.5	64.8
1965	719.1	443.8	118.2	74.8	34.2	8.4	0.8	5.6	37.1	31.5	151.5	80.4	71.0
1966	787.8	480.9	131.3	85.4	32.3	14.1	-0.5	3.9	40.9	37.1	171.8	92.5	79.2
1967	832.6	507.8	128.6	86.4	32.4	9.0	0.9	3.6	43.5	39.9	192.7	104.8	87.9
1968	910.0	558.0	141.2	93.4	38.7	7.7	1.4	1.4	47.9	46.6	209.4	111.4	98.0
1969	984.6	605.2	156.4	104.7	42.6	9.2	0.0	1.4	51.9	50.5	221.5	113.4	108.2
1970	1 038.5	648.5	152.4	109.0	41.4	2.8	-0.8	4.0	59.7	55.8	233.8	113.5	120.3
1971	1 127.1	701.9	178.2	114.1	55.8	6.6	1.7	0.6	63.0	62.3	246.5	113.7	132.8
1972	1 238.3	770.6	207.6	128.8	69.7	8.8	0.3	-3.4	70.8	74.2	263.5	119.7	143.8
1973	1 382.7	852.4	244.5	153.3	75.3	14.4	1.5	4.1	95.3	91.2	281.7	122.5	159.2
1974	1 500.0	933.4	249.4	169.5	66.0	16.8	-2.8	-0.8	126.7	127.5	317.9	134.6	183.4
1975	1 638.3	1 034.4	230.2	173.7	62.7	-9.6	3.4	16.0	138.7	122.7	357.7	149.1	208.7
1976	1 825.3	1 151.9	292.0	192.4	82.5	18.0	-0.8	-1.6	149.5	151.1	383.0	159.7	223.3
1977	2 030.9	1 278.6	361.3	228.7	110.3	17.8	4.5	-23.1	159.4	182.4	414.1	175.4	238.7
1978	2 294.7	1 428.5	438.0	280.6	131.6	24.4	1.4	-25.4	186.9	212.3	453.6	190.9	262.6
1979	2 563.3	1 592.2	492.9	333.9	141.0	14.4	3.6	-22.5	230.1	252.7	500.8	210.6	290.2
1980	2 789.5	1 757.1	479.3	362.4	123.2	-0.2	-6.1	-13.1	280.8	293.8	566.2	243.8	322.4
1981	3 128.4	1 941.1	572.4	420.0	122.6	21.0	8.8	-12.5	305.2	317.8	627.5	280.2	347.3
1982	3 255.0	2 077.3	517.2	426.5	105.7	-20.7	5.8	-20.0	283.2	303.2	680.5	310.8	369.7
1983	3 536.7	2 290.6	564.3	417.2	152.9	9.6	-15.4	-51.7	277.0	328.6	733.5	342.9	390.5
1984	3 933.2	2 503.3	735.6	489.6	180.6	59.7	5.7	-102.7	302.4	405.1	797.0	374.4	422.6
1985	4 220.3	2 720.3	736.2	526.2	188.2	16.1	5.8	-115.2	302.0	417.2	879.0	412.8	466.2
1986	4 462.8	2 899.7	746.5	519.8	220.1	8.0	-1.5	-132.7	320.5	453.3	949.3	438.6	510.7
1987	4 739.5	3 100.2	785.0	524.1	233.7	33.6	-6.4	-145.2	363.9	509.1	999.5	460.1	539.4
1988	5 103.8	3 353.6	821.6	563.8	239.3	30.4	-11.9	-110.4	444.1	554.5	1 039.0	462.3	576.7
1989	5 484.4	3 598.5	874.9	607.7	239.5	27.7	0.0	-88.2	503.3	591.5	1 099.1	482.2	616.9
1990	5 803.1	3 839.9	861.0	622.4	224.0	12.2	2.4	-78.0	552.4	630.3	1 180.2	508.3	671.9
1991	5 995.9	3 986.1	802.9	598.2	205.1	0.9	-1.3	-27.5	596.8	624.3	1 234.4	527.7	706.7
1992	6 337.7	4 235.3	864.8	612.1	236.3	10.1	6.2	-33.2	635.3	668.6	1 271.0	533.9	737.0
1993	6 657.4	4 477.9	953.4	666.6	266.0	27.0	-6.2	-65.0	655.8	720.9	1 291.2	525.2	766.0
1994	7 072.2	4 743.3	1 097.1	731.4	301.9	51.8	12.1	-93.6	720.9	814.5	1 325.5	519.1	806.3
1995	7 397.7	4 975.8	1 144.0	810.0	302.8	42.2	-11.1	-91.4	812.2	903.6	1 369.2	519.2	850.0
1996	7 816.9	5 256.8	1 240.3	875.4	334.1	22.1	8.6	-96.2	868.6	964.8	1 416.0	527.4	888.6
1997	8 304.3	5 547.4	1 389.8	968.7	349.1	68.8	3.2	-101.6	955.3	1 056.9	1 468.7	530.9	937.8
1998	8 747.0	5 879.5	1 509.1	1 052.6	385.8	69.4	1.4	-159.9	955.9	1 115.9	1 518.3	530.4	987.9
1999	9 268.4	6 282.5	1 625.7	1 133.9	424.9	69.6	-2.7	-260.5	991.2	1 251.7	1 620.8	555.8	1 065.0
2000	9 817.0	6 739.4	1 735.5	1 232.1	446.9	57.8	-1.3	-379.5	1 096.3	1 475.8	1 721.6	578.8	1 142.8
2001	10 128.0	7 055.0	1 614.3	1 176.8	469.3	-31.7	0.0	-367.0	1 032.8	1 399.8	1 825.6	612.9	1 212.8
2002	10 487.0	7 376.1	1 579.2	1 063.9	504.1	12.7	-1.5	-424.9	1 005.0	1 429.9	1 956.6	680.8	1 275.8
2003	11 004.0	7 760.9	1 665.8	1 094.7	572.3	-1.5	0.3	-498.1	1 046.2	1 544.3	2 075.5	752.2	1 323.3
2001													
1st quarter	10 021.5	6 955.8	1 675.3	1 229.6	455.6	-12.9	3.0	-392.9	1 100.7	1 493.7	1 783.3	596.2	1 187.2
2nd quarter	10 128.9	7 017.5	1 647.7	1 187.1	467.6	-1.9	-5.1	-361.7	1 060.5	1 422.2	1 825.4	610.9	1 214.5
3rd quarter	10 135.1	7 058.5	1 613.0	1 167.2	477.6	-31.5	-0.3	-361.9	1 003.5	1 365.3	1 825.6	614.3	1 211.2
4th quarter	10 226.3	7 188.4	1 521.4	1 123.2	476.3	-80.5	2.3	-351.6	966.6	1 318.2	1 868.2	630.1	1 238.1
2002													
1st quarter	10 338.2	7 236.9	1 568.5	1 091.4	486.0	-11.9	3.0	-376.3	975.0	1 351.3	1 909.2	654.2	1 255.0
2nd quarter	10 445.7	7 339.3	1 577.0	1 061.2	501.8	14.9	-0.9	-415.4	1 008.1	1 423.5	1 944.9	676.6	1 268.3
3rd quarter	10 546.5	7 428.0	1 581.3	1 055.0	507.2	23.3	-4.2	-431.1	1 023.4	1 454.5	1 968.3	684.4	1 283.9
4th quarter	10 617.5	7 500.0	1 589.9	1 048.1	521.4	24.4	-4.0	-476.6	1 013.5	1 490.1	2 004.2	708.2	1 296.0
2003													
1st quarter	10 744.6	7 609.8	1 596.6	1 046.4	539.6	8.7	1.9	-503.3	1 019.8	1 523.0	2 041.4	723.4	1 318.0
2nd quarter	10 884.0	7 696.3	1 611.1	1 072.7	553.8	-16.2	0.9	-497.6	1 018.1	1 515.7	2 074.2	761.1	1 313.1
3rd quarter	11 116.7	7 822.5	1 696.6	1 113.3	586.9	-2.8	-0.9	-488.8	1 047.7	1 536.4	2 086.4	756.7	1 329.7
4th quarter	11 270.5	7 914.9	1 758.8	1 146.3	609.0	4.5	-0.9	-502.8	1 099.2	1 602.0	2 100.0	767.5	1 332.6

Table 1-2. Real Gross Domestic Product

(Billions of chained [2000] dollars, quarterly data are at seasonally adjusted annual rates.)

NIPA Tables 1.1.6, 5.6.6A, 5.6.6B

Year and quarter	Gross domestic product	Personal consumption expenditures	Gross private domestic investment					Exports and imports of goods and services			Government consumption expenditures and gross investment			Residual
			Total	Fixed investment		Change in private inventories		Net exports	Exports	Imports	Total	Federal	State and local	
				Nonresidential	Residential	Nonfarm	Farm							
1946	1 589.4	1 012.9	172.1	...	...	28.9	-0.9	...	64.6	47.0	396.8	...	...	-10.0
1947	1 574.5	1 031.6	165.3	...	...	4.0	-3.6	...	73.7	44.6	337.2	...	...	11.3
1948	1 643.2	1 054.4	211.2	...	...	11.3	4.9	...	58.0	52.0	361.7	...	...	9.9
1949	1 634.6	1 083.5	161.2	...	...	-7.8	-1.5	...	57.5	50.2	404.9	...	...	-22.3
1950	1 777.3	1 152.8	227.7	...	...	20.8	-0.3	...	50.3	59.3	405.3	...	...	0.5
1951	1 915.0	1 171.2	228.3	...	...	25.8	1.7	...	61.7	61.7	553.5	...	...	-38.0
1952	1 988.3	1 208.2	206.5	...	...	6.7	2.5	...	59.0	67.1	666.3	...	...	-84.6
1953	2 079.5	1 265.7	216.2	...	...	4.1	1.6	...	55.1	73.4	713.9	...	...	-98.0
1954	2 065.4	1 291.4	206.1	...	...	-6.8	0.4	...	57.7	69.8	665.1	...	...	-85.1
1955	2 212.8	1 385.5	256.2	...	...	17.0	-1.5	...	63.9	78.2	640.7	...	...	-55.3
1956	2 255.8	1 425.4	252.7	...	...	14.2	-2.6	...	74.4	84.5	641.0	...	...	-53.2
1957	2 301.1	1 460.7	241.7	...	...	2.2	0.4	...	80.9	88.1	669.5	...	...	-63.6
1958	2 279.2	1 472.3	221.7	...	...	-7.0	4.7	...	70.0	92.3	690.9	...	...	-83.4
1959	2 441.3	1 554.6	266.7	...	...	17.9	-3.8	...	77.2	101.9	714.3	...	...	-69.6
1960	2 501.8	1 597.4	266.6	...	...	8.8	1.4	...	90.6	103.3	715.4	...	...	-64.9
1961	2 560.0	1 630.3	264.9	...	...	7.0	2.1	...	91.1	102.6	751.3	...	...	-75.0
1962	2 715.2	1 711.1	298.4	...	...	18.3	1.4	...	95.7	114.3	797.6	...	...	-73.3
1963	2 834.0	1 781.6	318.5	...	...	17.0	1.2	...	102.5	117.3	818.1	...	...	-69.4
1964	2 998.6	1 888.4	344.7	...	...	19.7	-3.1	...	114.6	123.6	836.1	...	...	-61.6
1965	3 191.1	2 007.7	393.1	...	...	27.4	2.0	...	117.8	136.7	861.3	...	...	-52.1
1966	3 399.1	2 121.8	427.7	...	...	45.2	-1.1	...	126.0	157.1	937.1	...	...	-56.4
1967	3 484.6	2 185.0	408.1	...	...	28.4	2.1	...	128.9	168.5	1 008.9	...	...	-77.8
1968	3 652.7	2 310.5	431.9	...	...	23.7	3.3	...	139.0	193.6	1 040.5	...	...	-75.6
1969	3 765.4	2 396.4	457.1	...	...	27.8	0.0	...	145.7	204.6	1 038.0	...	...	-67.2
1970	3 771.9	2 451.9	427.1	...	...	7.8	-1.9	...	161.4	213.4	1 012.9	...	...	-68.0
1971	3 898.6	2 545.5	475.7	...	...	18.5	3.3	...	164.1	224.7	990.8	...	...	-52.8
1972	4 105.0	2 701.3	532.1	...	...	24.2	0.3	...	176.5	250.0	983.5	...	...	-38.4
1973	4 341.5	2 833.8	594.4	...	...	36.6	1.5	...	209.7	261.6	980.0	...	...	-14.8
1974	4 319.6	2 812.3	550.6	...	...	35.1	-3.6	...	226.3	255.7	1 004.7	...	...	-18.6
1975	4 311.2	2 876.9	453.1	...	...	-19.2	4.7	...	224.9	227.3	1 027.4	...	...	-43.8
1976	4 540.9	3 035.5	544.7	...	...	34.0	-1.3	...	234.7	271.7	1 031.9	...	...	-34.2
1977	4 750.5	3 164.1	627.0	...	...	32.1	5.9	...	240.3	301.4	1 043.3	...	...	-22.8
1978	5 015.0	3 303.1	702.6	...	...	40.9	1.7	...	265.7	327.6	1 074.0	...	...	-2.8
1979	5 173.4	3 383.4	725.0	...	...	21.5	3.5	...	292.0	333.0	1 094.1	...	...	11.9
1980	5 161.7	3 374.1	645.3	...	...	0.0	-5.8	...	323.5	310.9	1 115.4	...	...	14.3
1981	5 291.7	3 422.2	704.9	...	...	25.5	8.2	...	327.4	319.1	1 125.6	...	...	30.7
1982	5 189.3	3 470.3	606.0	...	...	-24.6	6.1	...	302.4	315.0	1 145.4	...	...	-19.8
1983	5 423.8	3 668.6	662.5	...	...	10.2	-14.2	...	294.6	354.8	1 187.3	...	...	-34.4
1984	5 813.6	3 863.3	857.7	...	...	66.5	5.1	...	318.7	441.1	1 227.0	...	...	-12.0
1985	6 053.7	4 064.0	849.7	...	...	17.5	5.7	...	328.3	469.8	1 312.5	...	...	-31.0
1986	6 263.6	4 228.9	843.9	...	...	10.1	-1.8	...	353.7	510.0	1 392.5	...	...	-45.4
1987	6 475.1	4 369.8	870.0	...	...	37.7	-7.4	...	391.8	540.2	1 426.7	...	...	-43.0
1988	6 742.7	4 546.9	890.5	...	...	32.7	-10.7	...	454.6	561.4	1 445.1	...	...	-33.0
1989	6 981.4	4 675.0	926.2	...	...	28.8	0.0	...	506.8	586.0	1 482.5	...	...	-23.1
1990	7 112.5	4 770.3	895.1	595.1	298.9	13.2	2.1	-54.7	552.5	607.1	1 530.0	659.1	868.4	-91.1
1991	7 100.5	4 778.4	822.2	563.2	270.2	1.0	-1.5	-14.6	589.1	603.7	1 547.2	658.0	886.8	-96.0
1992	7 336.6	4 934.8	889.0	581.3	307.6	10.3	5.8	-15.9	629.7	645.6	1 555.3	646.6	906.5	-89.1
1993	7 532.7	5 099.8	968.3	631.9	332.7	27.7	-6.1	-52.1	650.0	702.1	1 541.1	619.6	919.5	-78.6
1994	7 835.5	5 290.7	1 099.6	689.9	364.8	52.0	11.2	-79.4	706.5	785.9	1 541.3	596.4	943.3	-63.7
1995	8 031.7	5 433.5	1 134.0	762.5	353.1	41.3	-10.6	-71.0	778.2	849.1	1 549.7	580.3	968.3	-51.1
1996	8 328.9	5 619.4	1 234.3	833.6	381.3	21.7	6.8	-79.6	843.4	923.0	1 564.9	573.5	990.5	-38.5
1997	8 703.5	5 831.8	1 387.7	934.2	388.6	68.5	2.9	-104.6	943.7	1 048.3	1 594.0	567.6	1 025.9	-23.8
1998	9 066.9	6 125.8	1 524.1	1 037.8	418.3	71.2	1.4	-203.7	966.5	1 170.3	1 624.4	561.2	1 063.0	-14.6
1999	9 470.3	6 438.6	1 642.6	1 133.3	443.6	71.5	-3.0	-296.2	1 008.2	1 304.4	1 686.9	573.7	1 113.2	-5.8
2000	9 817.0	6 739.4	1 735.5	1 232.1	446.9	57.8	-1.3	-379.5	1 096.3	1 475.8	1 721.6	578.8	1 142.8	0.2
2001	9 890.7	6 910.4	1 598.4	1 180.5	448.5	-31.8	0.0	-399.1	1 036.7	1 435.8	1 780.3	601.4	1 179.0	1.6
2002	10 074.8	7 123.4	1 560.7	1 075.6	470.0	13.5	-1.6	-472.1	1 012.3	1 484.4	1 857.9	646.6	1 211.4	3.7
2003	10 381.3	7 355.6	1 628.8	1 110.8	511.2	-1.1	0.3	-518.5	1 031.8	1 550.3	1 909.4	689.6	1 219.8	0.8
2001														
1st quarter	9 875.6	6 853.1	1 670.3	1 234.4	444.0	-13.5	5.5	-398.2	1 097.2	1 495.4	1 749.6	588.5	1 161.1	0.7
2nd quarter	9 905.9	6 870.3	1 637.4	1 190.2	450.1	-1.1	-1.3	-385.2	1 060.6	1 445.8	1 783.0	601.4	1 181.6	0.9
3rd quarter	9 871.1	6 900.5	1 592.6	1 169.3	452.1	-31.1	1.0	-398.4	1 008.7	1 407.1	1 776.1	601.5	1 174.6	3.3
4th quarter	9 910.0	7 017.6	1 493.4	1 128.2	447.8	-81.7	-5.1	-414.5	980.3	1 394.9	1 812.7	614.2	1 198.5	1.9
2002														
1st quarter	9 993.5	7 049.7	1 552.5	1 099.8	457.8	-11.9	4.4	-444.9	991.6	1 436.5	1 833.5	626.4	1 207.2	2.1
2nd quarter	10 052.6	7 099.2	1 553.7	1 072.4	470.3	16.1	-7.9	-458.1	1 017.8	1 475.9	1 853.4	645.5	1 208.0	4.2
3rd quarter	10 117.3	7 149.9	1 569.2	1 069.5	473.6	24.6	-1.7	-469.8	1 025.5	1 495.3	1 863.1	650.1	1 213.1	2.0
4th quarter	10 135.9	7 194.6	1 567.3	1 060.9	478.5	25.3	-1.2	-515.4	1 014.5	1 529.8	1 881.6	664.5	1 217.3	6.1
2003														
1st quarter	10 184.4	7 242.2	1 564.0	1 060.5	487.3	9.6	0.1	-511.7	1 010.6	1 522.3	1 882.5	665.0	1 217.7	7.7
2nd quarter	10 287.4	7 311.4	1 577.6	1 090.6	497.9	-15.7	-1.8	-525.2	1 006.5	1 531.7	1 915.3	699.0	1 216.3	5.1
3rd quarter	10 472.8	7 401.7	1 659.4	1 131.1	523.8	-2.7	-0.7	-508.7	1 033.8	1 542.5	1 916.0	693.1	1 222.9	-4.9
4th quarter	10 580.7	7 466.8	1 714.1	1 161.0	535.9	4.6	3.5	-528.3	1 076.2	1 604.5	1 923.7	701.2	1 222.5	-4.7

Note: Chained (2000) dollar series are calculated as the product of the chain-type quantity index and the 2000 current-dollar value of the corresponding series, divided by 100. Because the formula for the chain-type quantity indexes uses weights of more than one period, the corresponding chained-dollar estimates are usually not additive. The residual line is the difference between the first line and the sum of the most detailed lines.

... = Not available.

Table 1-3. Contributions to Percent Change in Real Gross Domestic Product

NIPA Table 1.1.2

Year and quarter	Percent change at seasonally adjusted annual rate, GDP	Percentage points at seasonally adjusted annual rates										
		Personal consumption expenditures	Gross private domestic investment				Exports and imports of goods and services			Government consumption expenditures and gross investment		
			Total	Fixed investment		Change in private inventories	Net exports	Exports	Imports	Total	Federal	State and local
				Nonresidential	Residential							
1946	-11.0	6.36	7.46	2.24	2.39	2.84	3.82	3.25	0.57	-28.67	-29.06	0.39
1947	-0.9	1.20	-0.57	1.31	1.06	-2.93	1.08	0.91	0.17	-2.65	-3.32	0.68
1948	4.4	1.47	4.00	0.51	0.98	2.50	-2.18	-1.63	-0.55	1.08	0.71	0.37
1949	-0.5	1.79	-4.22	-0.93	-0.44	-2.85	0.08	-0.05	0.13	1.83	0.90	0.93
1950	8.7	4.28	5.74	0.86	2.03	2.84	-1.31	-0.66	-0.65	0.02	-0.56	0.58
1951	7.7	1.05	0.05	0.44	-1.14	0.75	0.81	0.98	-0.17	5.84	5.78	0.06
1952	3.8	1.95	-1.65	-0.18	-0.10	-1.37	-0.59	-0.22	-0.37	4.11	4.00	0.11
1953	4.6	2.91	0.70	0.80	0.18	-0.28	-0.70	-0.31	-0.39	1.67	1.33	0.34
1954	-0.7	1.25	-0.69	-0.20	0.42	-0.91	0.40	0.19	0.21	-1.64	-2.25	0.60
1955	7.1	4.57	3.45	1.01	0.90	1.54	-0.04	0.44	-0.48	-0.84	-1.39	0.55
1956	1.9	1.79	-0.23	0.55	-0.49	-0.29	0.37	0.70	-0.33	0.01	-0.24	0.25
1957	2.0	1.53	-0.71	0.16	-0.32	-0.54	0.25	0.43	-0.18	0.93	0.46	0.47
1958	-1.0	0.50	-1.25	-1.12	0.05	-0.18	-0.89	-0.69	-0.20	0.69	-0.01	0.70
1959	7.1	3.55	2.80	0.73	1.21	0.86	0.00	0.45	-0.45	0.76	0.42	0.34
1960	2.5	1.73	0.00	0.52	-0.39	-0.13	0.72	0.78	-0.06	0.03	-0.35	0.39
1961	2.3	1.30	-0.10	-0.06	0.01	-0.05	0.06	0.03	0.03	1.07	0.51	0.56
1962	6.1	3.11	1.81	0.78	0.46	0.57	-0.21	0.25	-0.47	1.36	1.07	0.29
1963	4.4	2.56	1.00	0.50	0.58	-0.08	0.24	0.35	-0.12	0.58	0.01	0.57
1964	5.8	3.71	1.25	1.07	0.30	-0.13	0.36	0.59	-0.23	0.49	-0.17	0.65
1965	6.4	3.91	2.16	1.65	-0.15	0.66	-0.30	0.15	-0.45	0.65	0.00	0.66
1966	6.5	3.50	1.44	1.29	-0.43	0.58	-0.29	0.36	-0.65	1.87	1.24	0.63
1967	2.5	1.81	-0.76	-0.15	-0.13	-0.49	-0.22	0.12	-0.34	1.68	1.17	0.51
1968	4.8	3.50	0.90	0.46	0.53	-0.10	-0.30	0.41	-0.70	0.73	0.10	0.63
1969	3.1	2.27	0.90	0.78	0.13	0.00	-0.04	0.25	-0.29	-0.06	-0.42	0.37
1970	0.2	1.42	-1.04	-0.06	-0.26	-0.73	0.34	0.56	-0.22	-0.55	-0.86	0.31
1971	3.4	2.38	1.67	0.00	1.10	0.58	-0.19	0.10	-0.29	-0.50	-0.85	0.36
1972	5.3	3.80	1.87	0.92	0.89	0.06	-0.21	0.42	-0.63	-0.16	-0.42	0.26
1973	5.8	3.05	1.96	1.50	-0.04	0.50	0.82	1.12	-0.29	-0.08	-0.41	0.33
1974	-0.5	-0.47	-1.30	0.09	-1.13	-0.27	0.75	0.58	0.18	0.52	0.08	0.44
1975	-0.2	1.42	-2.98	-1.14	-0.57	-1.27	0.89	-0.05	0.94	0.48	0.03	0.45
1976	5.3	3.48	2.84	0.52	0.90	1.41	-1.08	0.37	-1.45	0.10	0.00	0.09
1977	4.6	2.68	2.43	1.19	0.99	0.25	-0.72	0.20	-0.92	0.23	0.19	0.04
1978	5.6	2.76	2.16	1.69	0.35	0.12	0.05	0.82	-0.78	0.60	0.22	0.38
1979	3.2	1.52	0.61	1.23	-0.21	-0.41	0.66	0.82	-0.16	0.37	0.20	0.17
1980	-0.2	-0.17	-2.12	-0.04	-1.17	-0.91	1.68	0.97	0.71	0.38	0.39	-0.01
1981	2.5	0.90	1.59	0.74	-0.35	1.20	-0.15	0.12	-0.27	0.19	0.42	-0.23
1982	-1.9	0.87	-2.55	-0.51	-0.71	-1.34	-0.60	-0.73	0.12	0.35	0.35	0.01
1983	4.5	3.65	1.45	-0.16	1.33	0.29	-1.35	-0.22	-1.13	0.77	0.63	0.13
1984	7.2	3.44	4.63	2.05	0.64	1.95	-1.58	0.63	-2.21	0.70	0.30	0.40
1985	4.1	3.31	-0.17	0.82	0.07	-1.06	-0.42	0.23	-0.65	1.41	0.74	0.67
1986	3.5	2.62	-0.12	-0.36	0.55	-0.32	-0.30	0.54	-0.84	1.27	0.55	0.71
1987	3.4	2.17	0.51	-0.01	0.10	0.42	0.17	0.78	-0.61	0.52	0.36	0.17
1988	4.1	2.66	0.39	0.57	-0.05	-0.14	0.82	1.24	-0.42	0.27	-0.15	0.42
1989	3.5	1.86	0.64	0.61	-0.14	0.17	0.52	0.99	-0.47	0.52	0.14	0.39
1990	1.9	1.34	-0.53	0.05	-0.37	-0.21	0.43	0.81	-0.39	0.64	0.18	0.46
1991	-0.2	0.11	-1.20	-0.57	-0.37	-0.26	0.69	0.63	0.06	0.23	-0.02	0.24
1992	3.3	2.18	1.07	0.32	0.47	0.29	-0.04	0.68	-0.72	0.11	-0.15	0.26
1993	2.7	2.23	1.21	0.83	0.31	0.07	-0.59	0.32	-0.91	-0.18	-0.35	0.17
1994	4.0	2.52	1.93	0.91	0.39	0.63	-0.43	0.85	-1.29	0.00	-0.30	0.30
1995	2.5	1.81	0.48	1.08	-0.14	-0.46	0.11	1.04	-0.93	0.10	-0.20	0.30
1996	3.7	2.31	1.35	1.01	0.33	0.02	-0.14	0.91	-1.05	0.18	-0.08	0.26
1997	4.5	2.54	1.95	1.33	0.08	0.54	-0.34	1.30	-1.64	0.34	-0.07	0.41
1998	4.2	3.36	1.63	1.28	0.32	0.03	-1.16	0.27	-1.43	0.34	-0.07	0.41
1999	4.5	3.44	1.33	1.09	0.27	-0.03	-0.99	0.47	-1.46	0.67	0.14	0.54
2000	3.7	3.17	0.99	1.06	0.03	-0.10	-0.86	0.93	-1.79	0.36	0.05	0.31
2001	0.8	1.74	-1.39	-0.52	0.02	-0.88	-0.20	-0.60	0.40	0.60	0.23	0.37
2002	1.9	2.14	-0.37	-1.02	0.22	0.42	-0.70	-0.24	-0.46	0.79	0.46	0.33
2003	3.0	2.29	0.66	0.33	0.43	-0.10	-0.43	0.18	-0.61	0.52	0.43	0.09
2001												
1st quarter	-0.5	1.07	-2.44	-0.52	0.10	-2.01	-0.04	-0.59	0.56	0.92	0.46	0.46
2nd quarter	1.2	0.67	-1.28	-1.76	0.25	0.23	0.49	-1.45	1.94	1.35	0.52	0.83
3rd quarter	-1.4	1.20	-1.76	-0.83	0.08	-1.02	-0.56	-2.04	1.48	-0.28	0.00	-0.28
4th quarter	1.6	4.71	-3.95	-1.63	-0.18	-2.14	-0.66	-1.11	0.45	1.48	0.51	0.97
2002												
1st quarter	3.4	1.32	2.34	-1.13	0.42	3.05	-1.10	0.43	-1.53	0.85	0.49	0.36
2nd quarter	2.4	1.98	0.05	-1.06	0.51	0.60	-0.46	0.99	-1.45	0.81	0.78	0.03
3rd quarter	2.6	2.02	0.61	-0.12	0.13	0.59	-0.43	0.29	-0.72	0.40	0.19	0.21
4th quarter	0.7	1.74	-0.06	-0.33	0.20	0.07	-1.69	-0.42	-1.27	0.75	0.58	0.17
2003												
1st quarter	1.9	1.84	-0.10	-0.01	0.36	-0.45	0.14	-0.15	0.29	0.05	0.04	0.02
2nd quarter	4.1	2.72	0.54	1.10	0.44	-1.01	-0.50	-0.15	-0.34	1.35	1.40	-0.05
3rd quarter	7.4	3.58	3.16	1.50	1.09	0.57	0.64	1.02	-0.39	0.03	-0.23	0.26
4th quarter	4.2	2.50	2.04	1.07	0.50	0.47	-0.66	1.55	-2.22	0.31	0.33	-0.02

CHAPTER 1: NATIONAL INCOME AND PRODUCT AND CYCLICAL INDICATORS

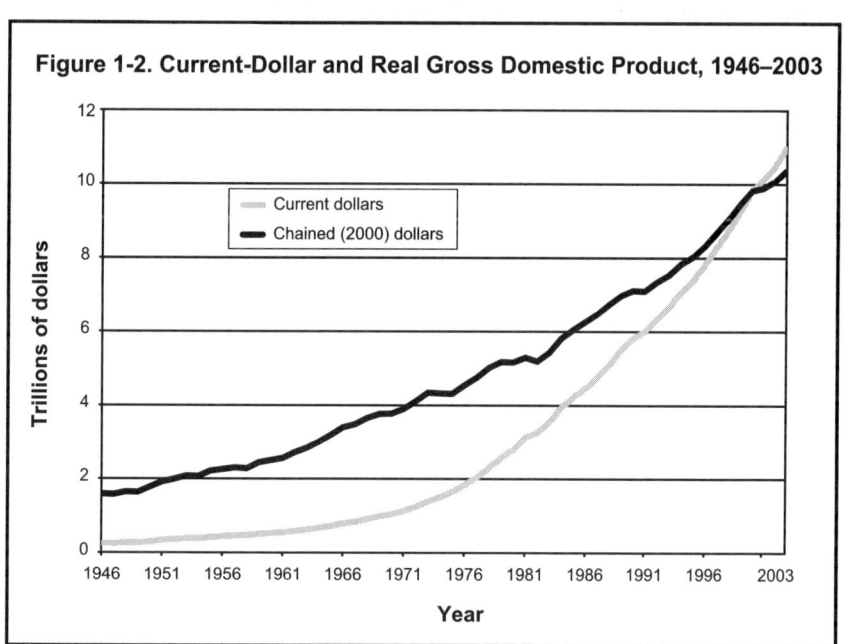

- Figure 1-2 graphs the value of GDP in current dollars and in real terms (chained 2000 dollars). Since real GDP is expressed in dollars of the year 2000, the two are the same in that year. Because prices increase in nearly every year, the current-dollar measure grows faster than the measure of real, or constant-dollar, GDP. (Tables 1-1 and 1-2)

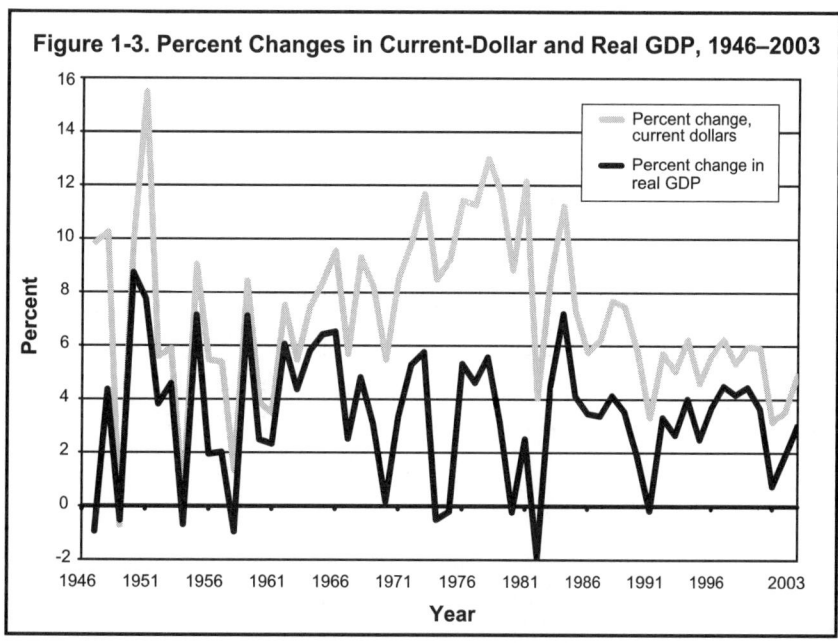

- The arithmetic scale used in Figure 1-2 seems to suggest ever-accelerating growth in GDP, but should not be interpreted that way. (See "Expanded Historical Statistics Give Perspective..." in the introductory material to this book.) Figure 1-3 depicts the same data in the form of year-to-year percent changes. The changes in real GDP, though quite variable, fluctuate around a value of about 3.5 percent, the average rate between the business cycle peak years of 1948 and 2000. The changes in nominal GDP, which are (roughly) the sum of the real change and the inflation rate, are more volatile. They are quite similar to the changes in real GDP, but somewhat higher, in years of low inflation. In years of high inflation, they are far above the changes in real GDP—and in 1974 and 1975, years of high nominal change, real GDP actually declined. (Tables 1-1 and 1-3)

Table 1-4. Chain-Type Quantity Indexes for Gross Domestic Product and Domestic Purchases

(Index numbers, 2000 = 100.)

NIPA Tables 1.1.3, 1.4.3, 2.3.3

Year and quarter	Gross domestic product, total	Personal consumption expenditures		Private fixed investment			Exports and imports of goods and services		Government consumption expenditures and gross investment			Gross domestic purchases
		Total	Excluding food and energy	Total	Nonresidential	Residential	Exports	Imports	Total	Federal	State and local	
1946	16.2	15.0	11.2	9.0	7.1	16.6	5.9	3.2	23.0	43.0	11.6	15.4
1947	16.0	15.3	11.7	10.8	8.2	21.3	6.7	3.0	19.6	31.8	13.2	15.1
1948	16.7	15.6	12.2	11.9	8.7	25.5	5.3	3.5	21.0	34.3	14.0	16.1
1949	16.7	16.1	12.6	10.9	7.9	23.6	5.2	3.4	23.5	37.6	16.2	16.0
1950	18.1	17.1	13.7	13.0	8.6	32.3	4.6	4.0	23.5	35.6	17.5	17.7
1951	19.5	17.4	13.8	12.4	9.0	27.0	5.6	4.2	32.2	59.0	17.6	18.9
1952	20.3	17.9	14.2	12.2	8.8	26.6	5.4	4.5	38.7	76.8	17.9	19.7
1953	21.2	18.8	14.9	13.0	9.6	27.5	5.0	5.0	41.5	82.9	18.8	20.8
1954	21.0	19.2	15.2	13.3	9.4	29.8	5.3	4.7	38.6	72.0	20.5	20.6
1955	22.5	20.6	16.5	15.0	10.4	34.6	5.8	5.3	37.2	65.5	21.9	22.0
1956	23.0	21.2	16.9	15.0	11.0	31.8	6.8	5.7	37.2	64.3	22.6	22.4
1957	23.4	21.7	17.3	14.9	11.2	29.8	7.4	6.0	38.9	66.6	24.0	22.8
1958	23.2	21.8	17.4	13.8	10.0	30.2	6.4	6.3	40.1	66.6	26.0	22.8
1959	24.9	23.1	18.6	15.7	10.8	37.8	7.0	6.9	41.5	68.7	27.0	24.4
1960	25.5	23.7	19.2	15.9	11.4	35.1	8.3	7.0	41.6	66.8	28.2	24.8
1961	26.1	24.2	19.7	15.8	11.3	35.2	8.3	7.0	43.6	69.6	29.9	25.4
1962	27.7	25.4	20.9	17.2	12.3	38.6	8.7	7.7	46.3	75.5	30.8	27.0
1963	28.9	26.4	22.0	18.6	13.0	43.2	9.4	8.0	47.5	75.5	32.7	28.1
1964	30.5	28.0	23.5	20.4	14.5	45.7	10.5	8.4	48.6	74.5	34.9	29.7
1965	32.5	29.8	25.1	22.5	17.0	44.3	10.7	9.3	50.0	74.5	37.3	31.7
1966	34.6	31.5	26.6	23.7	19.2	40.4	11.5	10.6	54.4	82.7	39.6	33.8
1967	35.5	32.4	27.6	23.3	18.9	39.1	11.8	11.4	58.6	91.0	41.6	34.8
1968	37.2	34.3	29.2	24.9	19.7	44.4	12.7	13.1	60.4	91.7	44.0	36.6
1969	38.4	35.6	30.4	26.5	21.2	45.7	13.3	13.9	60.3	88.5	45.5	37.7
1970	38.4	36.4	31.0	25.9	21.1	43.0	14.7	14.5	58.8	82.0	46.8	37.6
1971	39.7	37.8	32.5	27.9	21.1	54.8	15.0	15.2	57.6	75.7	48.2	39.0
1972	41.8	40.1	34.7	31.2	23.1	64.5	16.1	16.9	57.1	72.6	49.3	41.1
1973	44.2	42.0	36.9	34.1	26.4	64.1	19.1	17.7	56.9	69.5	50.7	43.1
1974	44.0	41.7	36.9	32.0	26.7	50.9	20.6	17.3	58.4	70.1	52.6	42.6
1975	43.9	42.7	37.7	28.5	24.0	44.3	20.5	15.4	59.7	70.4	54.5	42.1
1976	46.3	45.0	39.8	31.4	25.2	54.7	21.4	18.4	59.9	70.4	54.9	44.9
1977	48.4	47.0	41.8	35.9	28.0	66.4	21.9	20.4	60.6	71.9	55.1	47.3
1978	51.1	49.0	44.1	40.2	32.2	70.6	24.2	22.2	62.4	73.7	56.9	49.8
1979	52.7	50.2	45.5	42.5	35.5	68.0	26.6	22.6	63.5	75.5	57.8	51.1
1980	52.6	50.1	45.4	39.7	35.4	53.6	29.5	21.1	64.8	79.0	57.7	50.1
1981	53.9	50.8	46.4	40.6	37.4	49.3	29.9	21.6	65.4	82.8	56.6	51.4
1982	52.9	51.5	47.1	37.7	36.0	40.4	27.6	21.3	66.5	86.0	56.6	50.8
1983	55.2	54.4	50.3	40.5	35.5	57.1	26.9	24.0	69.0	91.7	57.3	53.7
1984	59.2	57.3	53.6	47.3	41.8	65.6	29.1	29.9	71.3	94.6	59.3	58.4
1985	61.7	60.3	56.9	49.8	44.6	66.6	30.0	31.8	76.2	102.0	63.0	61.0
1986	63.8	62.7	59.6	50.4	43.3	74.8	32.3	34.6	80.9	107.8	67.1	63.2
1987	66.0	64.8	61.8	50.7	43.3	76.3	35.7	36.6	82.9	111.7	68.0	65.2
1988	68.7	67.5	64.4	52.4	45.5	75.5	41.5	38.0	83.9	109.9	70.6	67.3
1989	71.1	69.4	66.4	53.9	48.1	73.2	46.2	39.7	86.1	111.6	73.0	69.2
1990	72.5	70.8	67.8	52.8	48.3	66.9	50.4	41.1	88.9	113.9	76.0	70.2
1991	72.3	70.9	67.9	49.4	45.7	60.5	53.7	40.9	89.9	113.7	77.6	69.6
1992	74.7	73.2	70.6	52.3	47.2	68.8	57.4	43.7	90.3	111.7	79.3	72.0
1993	76.7	75.7	73.2	56.8	51.3	74.4	59.3	47.6	89.5	107.1	80.5	74.3
1994	79.8	78.5	76.2	62.1	56.0	81.6	64.4	53.3	89.5	103.1	82.5	77.6
1995	81.8	80.6	78.6	66.1	61.9	79.0	71.0	57.5	90.0	100.3	84.7	79.4
1996	84.8	83.4	81.7	72.0	67.7	85.3	76.9	62.5	90.9	99.1	86.7	82.4
1997	88.7	86.5	85.3	78.7	75.8	86.9	86.1	71.0	92.6	98.1	89.8	86.4
1998	92.4	90.9	90.1	86.7	84.2	93.6	88.2	79.3	94.4	97.0	93.0	90.9
1999	96.5	95.5	95.2	93.9	92.0	99.3	92.0	88.4	98.0	99.1	97.4	95.8
2000	100.0	100.0	100.0	100.0	100.0	100.0	100.0	100.0	100.0	100.0	100.0	100.0
2001	100.8	102.5	102.9	97.0	95.8	100.4	94.6	97.3	103.4	103.9	103.2	100.9
2002	102.6	105.7	106.3	92.3	87.3	105.2	92.3	100.6	107.9	111.7	106.0	103.4
2003	105.7	109.1	109.8	96.9	90.2	114.4	94.1	105.0	110.9	119.1	106.7	106.9
2001												
1st quarter	100.6	101.7	101.7	100.0	100.2	99.3	100.1	101.3	101.6	101.7	101.6	100.8
2nd quarter	100.9	101.9	102.3	97.7	96.6	100.7	96.7	98.0	103.6	103.9	103.4	100.9
3rd quarter	100.6	102.4	102.8	96.6	94.9	101.2	92.0	95.3	103.2	103.9	102.8	100.7
4th quarter	100.9	104.1	104.7	93.9	91.6	100.2	89.4	94.5	105.3	106.1	104.9	101.3
2002												
1st quarter	101.8	104.6	105.2	92.9	89.3	102.4	90.4	97.3	106.5	108.2	105.6	102.4
2nd quarter	102.4	105.3	105.9	92.1	87.0	105.2	92.8	100.0	107.7	111.5	105.7	103.1
3rd quarter	103.1	106.1	106.8	92.1	86.8	106.0	93.5	101.3	108.2	112.3	106.2	103.8
4th quarter	103.2	106.8	107.3	91.9	86.1	107.1	92.5	103.7	109.3	114.8	106.5	104.4
2003												
1st quarter	103.7	107.5	107.9	92.5	86.1	109.0	92.2	103.2	109.3	114.9	106.6	104.9
2nd quarter	104.8	108.5	109.3	94.9	88.5	111.4	91.8	103.8	111.3	120.8	106.4	106.0
3rd quarter	106.7	109.8	110.6	98.9	91.8	117.2	94.3	104.5	111.3	119.8	107.0	107.7
4th quarter	107.8	110.8	111.4	101.4	94.2	119.9	98.2	108.7	111.7	121.2	107.0	108.9

Table 1-5. Chain-Type Price Indexes for Gross Domestic Product and Domestic Purchases

(Index numbers, 2000 = 100.)

NIPA Tables 1.1.4, 1.6.4, 2.3.4

Year and quarter	Gross domestic product											Gross domestic purchases
	Gross domestic product, total	Personal consumption expenditures		Private fixed investment			Exports and imports of goods and services		Government consumption expenditures and gross investment			
		Total	Excluding food and energy	Total	Nonresidential	Residential	Exports	Imports	Total	Federal	State and local	
1946	13.9	14.2	14.4	16.7	19.9	10.6	21.9	14.9	10.0	11.6	8.1	13.6
1947	15.5	15.7	15.6	19.6	23.2	12.6	25.4	17.8	10.8	12.3	9.1	15.1
1948	16.4	16.6	16.5	21.3	25.2	13.7	26.8	19.3	11.2	12.2	10.2	16.0
1949	16.4	16.5	16.6	21.7	25.8	13.9	25.2	18.4	11.5	12.7	10.3	16.0
1950	16.5	16.7	16.8	22.2	26.3	14.2	24.5	19.6	11.5	12.6	10.4	16.2
1951	17.6	17.8	17.8	24.1	28.8	15.2	27.7	23.7	12.3	13.2	11.4	17.4
1952	18.0	18.2	18.2	24.7	29.5	15.7	27.9	22.8	12.6	13.3	11.9	17.7
1953	18.2	18.4	18.6	24.9	29.7	15.8	27.8	21.8	12.7	13.4	12.2	17.9
1954	18.4	18.6	18.9	25.1	30.0	15.8	27.4	22.1	13.0	13.7	12.4	18.1
1955	18.7	18.7	19.1	25.5	30.4	16.2	27.7	22.0	13.5	14.5	12.6	18.4
1956	19.4	19.1	19.6	27.0	32.8	16.6	28.6	22.4	14.3	15.2	13.4	19.0
1957	20.0	19.6	20.2	27.9	34.5	16.6	29.7	22.6	14.9	15.9	14.0	19.7
1958	20.5	20.1	20.6	28.0	34.7	16.6	29.4	21.7	15.3	16.6	14.2	20.1
1959	20.8	20.4	21.0	28.3	35.1	16.6	29.4	21.9	15.4	16.4	14.5	20.4
1960	21.0	20.8	21.4	28.4	35.3	16.7	29.8	22.1	15.6	16.6	14.7	20.6
1961	21.3	21.0	21.6	28.3	35.1	16.8	30.3	22.1	15.9	16.9	15.1	20.9
1962	21.6	21.2	21.9	28.3	35.1	16.8	30.4	21.8	16.3	17.2	15.6	21.1
1963	21.8	21.5	22.2	28.3	35.1	16.7	30.3	22.3	16.7	17.6	15.9	21.4
1964	22.1	21.8	22.5	28.4	35.3	16.8	30.6	22.7	17.1	18.2	16.2	21.7
1965	22.5	22.1	22.8	28.9	35.7	17.3	31.5	23.1	17.6	18.7	16.7	22.1
1966	23.2	22.7	23.2	29.5	36.2	17.9	32.5	23.6	18.3	19.3	17.5	22.7
1967	23.9	23.2	23.9	30.4	37.1	18.5	33.7	23.7	19.1	19.9	18.5	23.4
1968	24.9	24.2	24.9	31.6	38.4	19.5	34.5	24.0	20.1	21.0	19.5	24.4
1969	26.2	25.3	26.1	33.1	40.0	20.9	35.6	24.7	21.3	22.1	20.8	25.6
1970	27.5	26.4	27.3	34.6	41.9	21.5	37.0	26.1	23.1	23.9	22.5	27.0
1971	28.9	27.6	28.5	36.3	43.9	22.8	38.4	27.7	24.9	26.0	24.1	28.4
1972	30.2	28.5	29.5	37.9	45.4	24.2	40.1	29.7	26.8	28.5	25.5	29.6
1973	31.9	30.1	30.5	40.0	47.1	26.3	45.4	34.8	28.7	30.4	27.5	31.3
1974	34.7	33.2	32.8	43.9	51.7	29.0	56.0	49.8	31.6	33.2	30.5	34.5
1975	38.0	36.0	35.5	49.4	58.8	31.7	61.7	54.0	34.8	36.6	33.5	37.8
1976	40.2	37.9	37.7	52.2	62.0	33.7	63.7	55.6	37.1	39.2	35.6	39.9
1977	42.8	40.4	40.1	56.3	66.3	37.1	66.3	60.5	39.7	42.2	37.9	42.6
1978	45.8	43.2	42.8	61.1	70.7	41.7	70.3	64.8	42.2	44.8	40.4	45.7
1979	49.6	47.1	45.7	66.6	76.4	46.4	78.8	75.9	45.8	48.2	43.9	49.7
1980	54.1	52.1	49.9	72.9	83.2	51.4	86.8	94.5	50.8	53.3	48.9	54.9
1981	59.1	56.7	54.2	79.7	91.2	55.6	93.2	99.6	55.8	58.5	53.7	59.9
1982	62.7	59.9	57.8	84.0	96.3	58.6	93.6	96.2	59.4	62.4	57.1	63.3
1983	65.2	62.4	60.8	83.9	95.4	59.9	94.0	92.6	61.8	64.6	59.7	65.5
1984	67.7	64.8	63.4	84.4	95.2	61.6	94.9	91.8	65.0	68.4	62.3	67.8
1985	69.7	66.9	65.8	85.5	95.9	63.2	92.0	88.8	67.0	70.0	64.7	69.8
1986	71.3	68.6	68.2	87.5	97.6	65.9	90.6	88.9	68.2	70.4	66.6	71.3
1987	73.2	70.9	70.8	89.1	98.4	68.6	92.9	94.3	70.1	71.2	69.4	73.5
1988	75.7	73.8	73.8	91.4	100.6	70.9	97.7	98.8	71.9	72.7	71.5	76.0
1989	78.6	77.0	76.9	93.6	102.7	73.2	99.3	100.9	74.1	74.7	73.9	78.9
1990	81.6	80.5	80.2	95.5	104.7	74.9	100.0	103.8	77.1	77.1	77.4	82.1
1991	84.5	83.4	83.3	97.0	106.3	75.9	101.3	103.4	79.8	80.2	79.7	84.8
1992	86.4	85.8	86.1	96.7	105.4	76.8	100.9	103.6	81.7	82.6	81.3	86.8
1993	88.4	87.8	88.3	97.8	105.5	79.9	100.9	102.7	83.8	84.8	83.3	88.7
1994	90.3	89.7	90.4	99.1	106.0	82.8	102.0	103.6	86.0	87.1	85.5	90.6
1995	92.1	91.6	92.4	100.3	106.2	85.8	104.4	106.4	88.4	89.5	87.8	92.5
1996	93.9	93.5	94.1	100.0	105.0	87.6	103.0	104.5	90.5	92.0	89.7	94.1
1997	95.4	95.1	95.6	99.8	103.7	89.8	101.2	100.8	92.1	93.5	91.4	95.4
1998	96.5	96.0	96.9	98.9	101.4	92.2	98.9	95.4	93.5	94.5	92.9	96.1
1999	97.9	97.6	98.3	98.9	100.1	95.8	98.3	96.0	96.1	96.9	95.7	97.6
2000	100.0	100.0	100.0	100.0	100.0	100.0	100.0	100.0	100.0	100.0	100.0	100.0
2001	102.4	102.1	101.9	101.0	99.7	104.6	99.6	97.5	102.5	101.9	102.9	102.0
2002	104.1	103.5	103.7	101.2	98.9	107.2	99.3	96.3	105.3	105.3	105.3	103.5
2003	106.0	105.5	105.1	102.4	98.5	112.0	101.4	99.6	108.7	109.1	108.5	105.6
2001												
1st quarter	101.5	101.5	101.2	100.4	99.6	102.6	100.3	99.9	101.9	101.3	102.2	101.4
2nd quarter	102.3	102.1	101.7	100.9	99.7	103.9	100.0	98.4	102.4	101.6	102.8	102.0
3rd quarter	102.7	102.3	102.1	101.4	99.8	105.6	99.5	97.1	102.8	102.1	103.1	102.2
4th quarter	103.1	102.4	102.7	101.4	99.6	106.4	98.6	94.6	103.1	102.6	103.3	102.4
2002												
1st quarter	103.5	102.7	103.0	101.1	99.2	106.2	98.3	94.1	104.1	104.4	104.0	102.7
2nd quarter	103.9	103.4	103.5	101.1	99.0	106.7	99.1	96.5	104.9	104.8	105.0	103.3
3rd quarter	104.3	103.9	104.0	101.0	98.6	107.1	99.8	97.3	105.7	105.3	105.8	103.7
4th quarter	104.8	104.3	104.3	101.7	98.8	109.0	99.9	97.4	106.5	106.6	106.5	104.2
2003												
1st quarter	105.5	105.1	104.6	102.2	98.7	110.8	100.9	100.1	108.4	108.8	108.2	105.2
2nd quarter	105.8	105.3	104.9	102.1	98.4	111.3	101.2	99.0	108.3	108.9	108.0	105.3
3rd quarter	106.2	105.7	105.2	102.4	98.4	112.1	101.4	99.6	108.9	109.2	108.7	105.7
4th quarter	106.6	106.0	105.5	103.1	98.7	113.7	102.1	99.8	109.2	109.4	109.0	106.1

Table 1-6. Final Sales

(Quarterly dollar data are at seasonally adjusted annual rates.)

NIPA Tables 1.4.4, 1.4.5, 1.4.6

Year and quarter	Final sales of domestic product			Final sales to domestic purchasers		
	Billions of dollars	Billions of chained (2000) dollars	Chain-type price index, 2000 = 100	Billions of dollars	Billions of chained (2000) dollars	Chain-type price index, 2000 = 100
1946	216.3	1 566.4	13.8	209.1	1 547.7	13.5
1947	244.7	1 598.5	15.3	233.9	1 562.8	15.0
1948	263.5	1 628.1	16.2	258.0	1 628.6	15.8
1949	270.0	1 666.7	16.2	264.7	1 666.6	15.9
1950	288.0	1 763.8	16.3	287.3	1 787.4	16.1
1951	329.4	1 889.4	17.4	326.9	1 900.0	17.2
1952	354.8	1 990.0	17.8	353.7	2 013.6	17.6
1953	377.4	2 087.7	18.1	378.1	2 127.1	17.8
1954	382.3	2 092.5	18.3	381.9	2 123.4	18.0
1955	409.8	2 209.2	18.6	409.3	2 242.8	18.3
1956	433.5	2 259.0	19.2	431.2	2 285.0	18.9
1957	460.3	2 316.9	19.9	456.2	2 338.3	19.5
1958	467.6	2 299.0	20.3	467.0	2 341.1	20.0
1959	502.7	2 442.7	20.6	502.3	2 487.4	20.2
1960	523.2	2 506.8	20.9	519.0	2 534.8	20.5
1961	541.7	2 566.8	21.1	536.8	2 594.6	20.7
1962	579.5	2 708.5	21.4	575.4	2 744.8	21.0
1963	612.1	2 830.3	21.6	607.2	2 862.4	21.2
1964	658.8	2 999.9	22.0	651.9	3 024.5	21.6
1965	709.9	3 173.8	22.4	704.3	3 211.2	21.9
1966	774.2	3 364.8	23.0	770.3	3 415.5	22.6
1967	822.7	3 467.6	23.7	819.2	3 528.1	23.2
1968	900.9	3 640.3	24.8	899.6	3 715.3	24.2
1969	975.4	3 753.7	26.0	974.0	3 832.6	25.4
1970	1 036.5	3 787.7	27.4	1 032.6	3 854.0	26.8
1971	1 118.9	3 893.4	28.7	1 118.2	3 969.3	28.2
1972	1 229.2	4 098.6	30.0	1 232.6	4 186.9	29.4
1973	1 366.8	4 315.9	31.7	1 362.7	4 373.4	31.2
1974	1 486.0	4 305.5	34.5	1 486.8	4 329.7	34.3
1975	1 644.6	4 352.5	37.8	1 628.6	4 338.2	37.5
1976	1 808.2	4 522.3	40.0	1 809.8	4 556.2	39.7
1977	2 008.6	4 721.6	42.5	2 031.7	4 789.5	42.4
1978	2 268.9	4 981.6	45.6	2 294.3	5 047.9	45.5
1979	2 545.3	5 161.2	49.3	2 567.9	5 194.2	49.4
1980	2 795.8	5 196.7	53.8	2 808.9	5 142.8	54.6
1981	3 098.6	5 265.1	58.9	3 111.2	5 217.9	59.6
1982	3 269.9	5 233.4	62.5	3 289.9	5 218.2	63.1
1983	3 542.4	5 454.0	65.0	3 594.1	5 507.3	65.3
1984	3 867.8	5 739.2	67.4	3 970.5	5 877.3	67.6
1985	4 198.4	6 042.1	69.5	4 313.6	6 204.2	69.5
1986	4 456.3	6 271.8	71.1	4 589.0	6 452.0	71.1
1987	4 712.3	6 457.2	73.0	4 857.5	6 626.5	73.3
1988	5 085.3	6 734.5	75.5	5 195.7	6 849.7	75.9
1989	5 456.7	6 962.2	78.4	5 544.8	7 041.6	78.8
1990	5 788.5	7 108.5	81.4	5 866.5	7 157.4	82.0
1991	5 996.3	7 115.0	84.3	6 023.8	7 115.2	84.7
1992	6 321.4	7 331.1	86.2	6 354.7	7 333.0	86.7
1993	6 636.6	7 522.3	88.2	6 701.6	7 566.4	88.6
1994	7 008.4	7 777.8	90.1	7 102.0	7 853.6	90.4
1995	7 366.5	8 010.2	92.0	7 457.9	8 076.8	92.3
1996	7 786.1	8 306.5	93.7	7 882.3	8 383.1	94.0
1997	8 232.3	8 636.6	95.3	8 333.9	8 740.4	95.3
1998	8 676.2	8 997.6	96.4	8 836.2	9 203.2	96.0
1999	9 201.5	9 404.0	97.8	9 462.0	9 701.3	97.5
2000	9 760.5	9 760.5	100.0	10 140.0	10 140.0	100.0
2001	10 159.7	9 920.9	102.4	10 526.7	10 320.5	102.0
2002	10 475.9	10 063.2	104.1	10 900.7	10 533.0	103.5
2003	11 005.3	10 379.9	106.0	11 503.4	10 894.2	105.6
2001						
1st quarter	10 031.4	9 883.2	101.5	10 424.4	10 280.8	101.4
2nd quarter	10 136.0	9 908.7	102.3	10 497.7	10 294.2	102.0
3rd quarter	10 166.9	9 899.9	102.7	10 528.8	10 299.1	102.2
4th quarter	10 304.5	9 992.3	103.1	10 656.1	10 408.4	102.4
2002						
1st quarter	10 347.2	10 000.4	103.5	10 723.5	10 444.7	102.7
2nd quarter	10 431.7	10 044.9	103.9	10 847.1	10 501.1	103.3
3rd quarter	10 527.4	10 095.2	104.3	10 958.5	10 562.7	103.8
4th quarter	10 597.1	10 112.5	104.8	11 073.7	10 623.3	104.2
2003						
1st quarter	10 734.0	10 173.3	105.5	11 237.3	10 680.8	105.2
2nd quarter	10 899.3	10 302.5	105.8	11 397.0	10 823.3	105.3
3rd quarter	11 120.4	10 473.9	106.2	11 609.2	10 979.4	105.7
4th quarter	11 267.4	10 569.6	106.6	11 770.1	11 093.2	106.1

Table 1-7. Per Capita Product and Income and U.S. Population

(Dollars, except as noted; quarterly data are at seasonally adjusted annual rates.)

NIPA Table 7.1

Year and quarter	Current dollars							Chained (2000) dollars						Population (mid-period, thousands)
	Gross domestic product	Personal income	Disposable personal income	Personal consumption expenditures				Gross domestic product	Disposable personal income	Personal consumption expenditures				
				Total	Durable goods	Nondurable goods	Services			Total	Durable goods	Nondurable goods	Services	
1946	1 572	1 263	1 141	1 021	111	585	324	11 241	8 011	7 164	325	3 489	3 320	141 389
1947	1 694	1 325	1 188	1 124	142	631	352	10 925	7 565	7 158	381	3 329	3 394	144 126
1948	1 836	1 431	1 300	1 194	156	659	379	11 206	7 832	7 191	399	3 284	3 464	146 631
1949	1 792	1 388	1 276	1 196	168	636	393	10 957	7 747	7 263	424	3 277	3 492	149 188
1950	1 937	1 510	1 385	1 267	203	648	417	11 717	8 306	7 600	509	3 324	3 607	151 684
1951	2 199	1 672	1 497	1 352	194	708	450	12 412	8 408	7 591	456	3 354	3 728	154 287
1952	2 283	1 754	1 550	1 399	187	731	481	12 668	8 534	7 698	436	3 427	3 826	156 954
1953	2 378	1 829	1 621	1 461	205	738	517	13 032	8 802	7 932	482	3 477	3 923	159 565
1954	2 342	1 813	1 627	1 478	196	737	545	12 719	8 757	7 952	472	3 460	4 011	162 391
1955	2 509	1 913	1 714	1 566	235	755	576	13 389	9 177	8 383	566	3 564	4 148	165 275
1956	2 601	2 019	1 801	1 615	227	777	611	13 410	9 450	8 474	534	3 621	4 279	168 221
1957	2 692	2 094	1 867	1 675	233	800	641	13 435	9 508	8 528	529	3 622	4 365	171 274
1958	2 683	2 119	1 898	1 701	215	814	672	13 088	9 433	8 455	479	3 597	4 456	174 141
1959	2 860	2 218	1 979	1 793	241	838	714	13 782	9 685	8 776	527	3 682	4 612	177 130
1960	2 912	2 277	2 022	1 835	240	846	750	13 840	9 735	8 837	527	3 662	4 721	180 760
1961	2 965	2 335	2 078	1 862	227	852	782	13 932	9 901	8 873	499	3 669	4 838	183 742
1962	3 139	2 448	2 171	1 947	251	872	823	14 552	10 227	9 170	549	3 727	5 000	186 590
1963	3 263	2 534	2 246	2 022	273	888	861	14 971	10 455	9 412	594	3 751	5 153	189 300
1964	3 458	2 681	2 410	2 144	295	931	918	15 624	11 061	9 839	640	3 880	5 393	191 927
1965	3 700	2 860	2 563	2 283	325	986	972	16 420	11 594	10 331	712	4 035	5 610	194 347
1966	4 007	3 072	2 734	2 446	347	1 062	1 037	17 290	12 065	10 793	763	4 208	5 821	196 599
1967	4 189	3 262	2 895	2 555	354	1 092	1 108	17 533	12 457	10 994	767	4 228	6 039	198 752
1968	4 533	3 547	3 114	2 780	402	1 174	1 203	18 196	12 892	11 510	843	4 377	6 292	200 745
1969	4 857	3 840	3 324	2 985	424	1 249	1 313	18 573	13 163	11 820	864	4 449	6 529	202 736
1970	5 064	4 090	3 587	3 162	414	1 326	1 421	18 391	13 563	11 955	826	4 504	6 712	205 089
1971	5 427	4 350	3 860	3 379	467	1 375	1 538	18 771	14 001	12 256	898	4 528	6 886	207 692
1972	5 899	4 729	4 140	3 671	526	1 467	1 678	19 555	14 512	12 868	1 001	4 677	7 200	209 924
1973	6 524	5 241	4 616	4 022	583	1 619	1 820	20 484	15 345	13 371	1 094	4 784	7 466	211 939
1974	7 013	5 716	5 010	4 364	572	1 798	1 994	20 195	15 094	13 148	1 009	4 645	7 570	213 898
1975	7 586	6 181	5 498	4 789	618	1 948	2 223	19 961	15 291	13 320	999	4 668	7 775	215 981
1976	8 369	6 762	5 972	5 282	728	2 102	2 452	20 822	15 738	13 919	1 116	4 848	8 012	218 086
1977	9 219	7 414	6 517	5 804	823	2 257	2 725	21 565	16 128	14 364	1 207	4 915	8 274	220 289
1978	10 307	8 255	7 224	6 417	906	2 472	3 039	22 526	16 704	14 837	1 258	5 046	8 569	222 629
1979	11 387	9 161	7 967	7 073	952	2 774	3 347	22 982	16 931	15 030	1 240	5 123	8 734	225 106
1980	12 249	10 134	8 822	7 716	940	3 057	3 719	22 666	16 940	14 816	1 129	5 057	8 785	227 726
1981	13 601	11 266	9 765	8 439	1 006	3 299	4 134	23 007	17 217	14 879	1 132	5 066	8 844	230 008
1982	14 017	11 951	10 426	8 945	1 034	3 392	4 519	22 346	17 418	14 944	1 120	5 065	8 944	232 218
1983	15 092	12 635	11 131	9 775	1 198	3 547	5 030	23 146	17 828	15 656	1 272	5 187	9 349	234 333
1984	16 638	13 915	12 319	10 589	1 381	3 742	5 466	24 593	19 011	16 343	1 445	5 346	9 644	236 394
1985	17 695	14 787	13 037	11 406	1 524	3 894	5 988	25 382	19 476	17 040	1 577	5 443	10 098	238 506
1986	18 542	15 466	13 649	12 048	1 674	3 982	6 391	26 024	19 906	17 750	1 714	5 587	10 302	240 683
1987	19 517	16 255	14 241	12 766	1 736	4 181	6 849	26 664	20 072	17 994	1 728	5 670	10 652	242 843
1988	20 827	17 358	15 297	13 685	1 851	4 421	7 413	27 514	20 740	18 554	1 816	5 802	10 983	245 061
1989	22 169	18 545	16 257	14 546	1 907	4 716	7 923	28 221	21 120	18 898	1 839	5 907	11 205	247 387
1990	23 195	19 500	17 131	15 349	1 895	4 996	8 457	28 429	21 281	19 067	1 813	5 932	11 398	250 181
1991	23 650	19 923	17 609	15 722	1 790	5 068	8 864	28 007	21 109	18 848	1 688	5 840	11 438	253 530
1992	24 668	20 870	18 494	16 485	1 882	5 179	9 424	28 556	21 548	19 208	1 763	5 878	11 680	256 922
1993	25 578	21 356	18 872	17 204	2 024	5 300	9 881	28 940	21 493	19 593	1 877	5 956	11 855	260 282
1994	26 844	22 176	19 555	18 004	2 210	5 455	10 339	29 741	21 812	20 082	2 009	6 088	12 058	263 455
1995	27 749	23 078	20 287	18 665	2 294	5 571	10 800	30 128	22 153	20 382	2 073	6 147	12 228	266 588
1996	28 982	24 176	21 091	19 490	2 419	5 767	11 304	30 881	22 546	20 835	2 209	6 230	12 443	269 714
1997	30 424	25 334	21 940	20 323	2 538	5 931	11 854	31 886	23 065	21 365	2 370	6 321	12 705	272 958
1998	31 674	26 880	23 161	21 291	2 717	6 096	12 478	32 833	24 131	22 183	2 608	6 498	13 090	276 154
1999	33 181	27 933	23 968	22 491	2 927	6 461	13 103	33 904	24 564	23 050	2 880	6 718	13 454	279 328
2000	34 760	29 848	25 472	23 863	3 057	6 895	13 911	34 760	25 472	23 863	3 057	6 895	13 911	282 425
2001	35 492	30 573	26 237	24 723	3 097	7 069	14 558	34 661	25 699	24 216	3 156	6 962	14 099	285 358
2002	36 383	30 804	27 157	25 590	3 178	7 217	15 195	34 953	26 227	24 713	3 329	7 068	14 324	288 240
2003	37 804	31 475	28 033	26 662	3 266	7 558	15 838	35 664	26 569	25 269	3 541	7 257	14 498	291 085
2001														
1st quarter	35 254	30 565	26 004	24 469	3 068	7 036	14 366	34 741	25 620	24 108	3 094	6 949	14 064	284 265
2nd quarter	35 546	30 601	25 996	24 627	3 035	7 077	14 515	34 763	25 450	24 110	3 084	6 930	14 094	284 952
3rd quarter	35 472	30 565	26 679	24 704	3 028	7 084	14 591	34 547	26 082	24 151	3 099	6 953	14 097	285 726
4th quarter	35 695	30 559	26 266	25 091	3 256	7 077	14 758	34 591	25 641	24 495	3 346	7 017	14 141	286 490
2002														
1st quarter	36 002	30,658	26 946	25 202	3 147	7 128	14 927	34 802	26 249	24 550	3 266	7 067	14 222	287 156
2nd quarter	36 290	30 910	27 255	25 498	3 153	7 218	15 126	34 924	26 363	24 664	3 293	7 064	14 313	287 840
3rd quarter	36 543	30 823	27 196	25 738	3 232	7 212	15 294	35 056	26 178	24 774	3 393	7 034	14 358	288 605
4th quarter	36 693	30 824	27 228	25 919	3 182	7 308	15 430	35 029	26 120	24 864	3 364	7 108	14 400	289 360
2003														
1st quarter	37 048	31 040	27 504	26 239	3 145	7 474	15 621	35 117	26 175	24 972	3 356	7 179	14 443	290 016
2nd quarter	37 442	31 324	27 779	26 476	3 257	7 443	15 776	35 390	26 389	25 152	3 509	7 190	14 475	290 689
3rd quarter	38 143	31 599	28 368	26 840	3 337	7 614	15 889	35 934	26 842	25 397	3 636	7 292	14 507	291 445
4th quarter	38 574	31 931	28 476	27 088	3 324	7 701	16 064	36 212	26 865	25 555	3 661	7 365	14 568	292 190

Table 1-8. Composite Indexes of Economic Activity and Selected Index Components

Year and month	Cyclical composite indexes, 1996 = 100				Selected components of leading index			Selected component of coincident index	Selected component of lagging index
	Leading	Coincident	Lagging	Ratio, coincident to lagging	Vendor performance (slower deliveries, diffusion index, percent)	Interest rate spread, 10-year Treasury bond less federal funds [1]	Index of consumer expectations [1,2]	Personal income less transfer payments (billions of 1996 dollars)	Consumer installment credit outstanding (percent of personal income)
1959	59.3	37.0	80.7	45.8	60.6	1.03	96.6	1 803.8	13.3
1960	58.4	37.7	83.1	45.4	35.7	0.90	98.3	1 857.5	14.2
1961	60.7	37.9	81.9	46.3	48.1	1.93	97.2	1 904.0	14.2
1962	62.8	39.7	82.6	48.1	48.8	1.24	98.0	2 007.7	14.3
1963	65.3	41.0	84.0	48.9	51.1	0.82	97.1	2 083.0	15.1
1964	68.2	42.9	85.5	50.1	62.8	0.69	99.2	2 208.1	15.9
1965	71.0	45.4	88.0	51.6	66.6	0.21	104.3	2 350.4	16.5
1966	72.2	48.1	91.1	52.8	73.0	-0.19	94.6	2 489.7	16.5
1967	72.6	49.6	92.5	53.6	44.0	0.85	94.2	2 583.1	16.1
1968	75.1	51.6	93.3	55.4	52.6	-0.01	91.4	2 715.4	15.7
1969	75.7	53.7	95.7	56.1	65.2	-1.53	88.5	2 835.3	15.8
1970	72.7	53.7	96.1	55.9	50.3	0.17	73.7	2 889.1	15.4
1971	76.5	54.5	93.2	58.5	48.0	1.50	77.1	2 956.8	15.5
1972	81.4	57.5	91.8	62.7	62.7	1.78	87.3	3 135.9	15.8
1973	82.4	60.7	95.1	63.9	88.0	-1.89	67.6	3 317.4	16.3
1974	77.0	61.1	99.0	61.8	65.8	-2.95	56.0	3 282.7	16.1
1975	75.5	59.1	95.4	61.9	30.2	2.16	65.5	3 239.7	14.9
1976	81.5	61.8	92.0	67.2	54.4	2.57	82.7	3 400.7	14.6
1977	84.2	64.9	92.5	70.2	55.7	1.88	81.3	3 559.8	14.9
1978	84.7	68.4	95.2	71.9	60.5	0.48	69.3	3 763.4	15.5
1979	82.9	70.7	99.1	71.3	57.9	-1.75	52.8	3 881.8	16.0
1980	80.5	70.4	100.1	70.3	40.6	-1.90	56.8	3 894.8	15.2
1981	81.0	71.4	99.1	72.0	46.3	-2.47	65.0	4 006.5	14.0
1982	80.6	70.0	97.0	72.1	43.5	0.74	62.7	4 043.8	13.8
1983	87.9	71.1	92.8	76.7	56.8	2.02	84.7	4 126.6	13.8
1984	90.6	75.8	96.1	78.8	57.3	2.21	92.7	4 458.4	14.6
1985	91.8	78.1	98.7	79.1	48.0	2.52	86.5	4 633.7	16.0
1986	93.7	79.8	99.3	80.4	50.6	0.88	85.8	4 770.8	17.0
1987	96.1	82.3	98.9	83.3	57.4	1.73	81.3	4 904.1	16.9
1988	96.6	85.4	99.8	85.6	57.7	1.28	85.2	5 093.4	16.8
1989	95.6	87.4	101.8	85.9	47.6	-0.72	85.3	5 254.2	16.8
1990	95.0	88.5	101.5	87.2	47.9	0.45	70.2	5 321.1	16.5
1991	94.8	87.5	99.0	88.4	47.3	2.17	70.3	5 256.0	15.9
1992	96.6	88.7	94.6	93.8	50.2	3.49	70.3	5 374.1	14.9
1993	97.5	90.7	94.2	96.3	51.6	2.85	72.8	5 430.4	15.0
1994	99.0	94.1	95.2	98.9	60.1	2.88	83.8	5 593.4	15.9
1995	98.2	97.1	99.1	98.0	52.8	0.74	83.2	5 759.9	17.5
1996	100.0	100.0	100.0	100.0	50.5	1.14	85.7	5 981.1	18.5
1997	103.0	103.6	100.5	103.1	53.9	0.89	97.7	6 269.4	18.6
1998	105.3	108.1	102.2	105.8	51.1	-0.09	98.3	6 714.1	18.4
1999	108.5	111.7	103.7	107.7	53.3	0.67	99.3	6 948.4	18.9
2000	109.4	115.4	106.5	108.4	53.3	-0.21	102.7	7 345.3	19.1
2001	108.5	114.8	105.0	109.3	48.0	1.13	82.3	7 376.4	20.2
2002	110.9	114.3	102.1	111.9	53.3	2.94	84.6	7 336.1	21.1
2003	112.3	114.7	99.8	114.9	53.0	2.89	81.4	7 417.4	21.3
2002									
January	110.8	114.1	103.3	110.5	50.8	3.31	91.3	7 337.3	20.9
February	111.0	114.1	103.0	110.8	51.1	3.17	87.2	7 350.3	20.9
March	111.1	114.0	103.0	110.7	52.6	3.55	92.7	7 358.6	21.0
April	110.8	114.2	102.5	111.4	53.6	3.46	89.1	7 353.1	21.0
May	111.4	114.3	102.2	111.8	53.9	3.41	92.7	7 363.8	21.0
June	111.1	114.5	102.0	112.3	54.9	3.18	87.9	7 374.6	21.1
July	111.0	114.4	101.9	112.3	54.8	2.92	81.0	7 339.2	21.2
August	110.8	114.4	101.9	112.3	53.7	2.52	80.6	7 319.4	21.3
September	110.3	114.3	101.6	112.5	56.5	2.12	79.9	7 306.1	21.3
October	110.3	114.3	101.5	112.6	53.1	2.19	73.1	7 317.5	21.3
November	111.0	114.4	101.2	113.0	51.8	2.71	78.5	7 312.9	21.3
December	111.1	114.2	101.1	113.0	52.4	2.79	80.8	7 300.7	21.3
2003									
January	111.0	114.4	101.1	113.2	52.0	2.81	72.8	7 313.9	21.5
February	110.6	114.2	101.2	112.8	52.4	2.64	69.9	7 318.8	21.4
March	110.4	114.2	101.0	113.1	53.4	2.56	69.6	7 324.1	21.3
April	110.5	114.1	100.7	113.3	50.1	2.70	79.3	7 345.1	21.4
May	111.6	114.3	100.5	113.7	51.4	2.31	91.4	7 392.9	21.4
June	112.0	114.4	99.8	114.6	50.6	2.11	86.4	7 412.5	21.3
July	112.8	114.7	99.6	115.2	51.4	2.97	83.7	7 430.0	21.3
August	113.2	114.7	99.6	115.2	53.3	3.42	82.5	7 437.9	21.3
September	113.3	114.9	99.0	116.1	53.1	3.26	80.8	7 451.6	21.4
October	113.9	115.2	99.0	116.4	54.1	3.28	83.0	7 488.2	21.4
November	114.2	115.6	98.4	117.5	56.0	3.30	88.1	7 542.8	21.2
December	114.5	115.8	98.0	118.2	58.6	3.29	89.8	7 550.6	21.2

[1] Not seasonally adjusted.
[2] Copyright, University of Michigan, Survey Research Center, first quarter 1966 = 100.

Section 1b: Income and Value Added

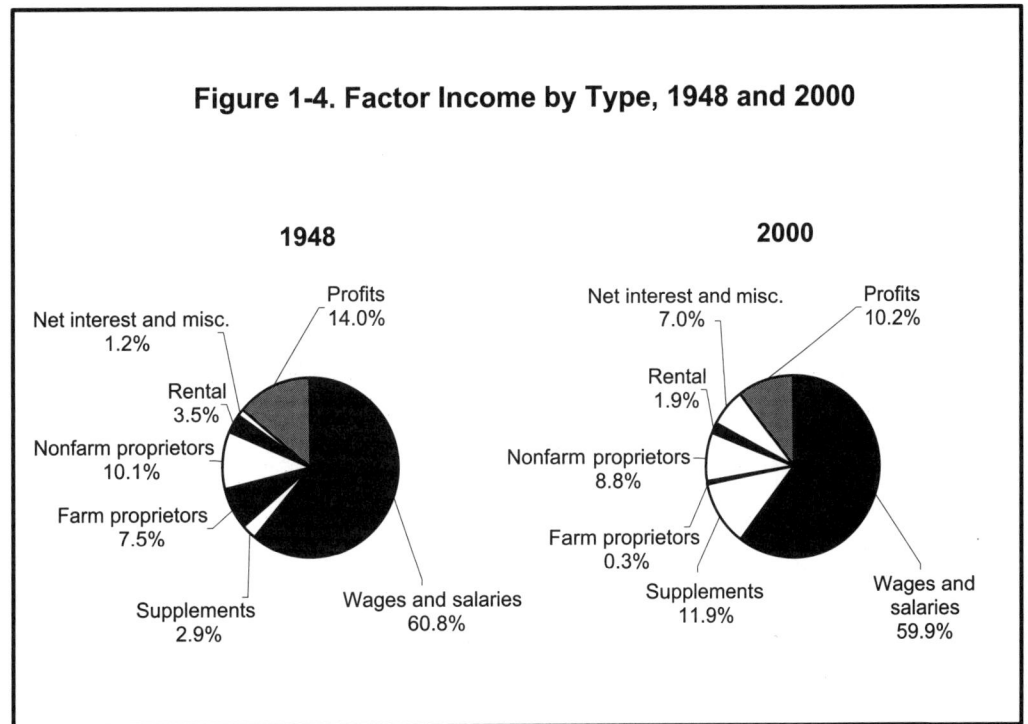

Figure 1-4. Factor Income by Type, 1948 and 2000

- The changing distribution of the national income over the postwar period is shown in the graph above, based on data in Table 1-11, and using years at comparable points in the business cycle. Labor compensation rose from 63.7 percent of "net national factor income" (formerly known simply as "national income") in 1948 to 71.8 percent in 2000. However, the wage and salary share was actually down slightly; the increase is accounted for by supplements to wages and salaries—the costs of fringe benefits, including health insurance, and of taxes to pay for Social Security and Medicare.
- Farm proprietors' share dropped from 7.5 percent in 1948—a year when American food was still providing relief for war-ravaged economies—to less than 1 percent in 2000. Shares going to nonfarm proprietors also declined over the period, though not as sharply. Proprietors' income includes the return to the labor input of the proprietors as well as to their land and other capital, so it cannot be attributed unequivocally to either capital or labor.
- The share of rental income of persons declined somewhat, despite the increase in rental income imputed to homeowners that is included in this income category.
- The share of capital incomes other than rental rose from 15.2 percent to 17.2 percent, with the interest portion rising sharply while the corporate profits portion declined, reflecting a shift in debt/equity relationships for U.S. corporations.

Table 1-9. Relation of Gross Domestic Product, Gross and Net National Product, National Income, and Personal Income

(Billions of dollars, quarterly data are at seasonally adjusted annual rates.)

NIPA Table 1.7.5

Year and quarter	Gross domestic product	Plus: Income receipts from the rest of the world	Less: Income payments to the rest of the world	Equals: Gross national product	Less: Consumption of fixed capital									Equals: Net national product
					Total	Private					Government			
						Total	Domestic business			House-holds and institutions	Total	General government	Government enterprises	
							Total	Capital consumption allowances	Less: Capital consumption adjustment					
1946	222.3	1.1	0.4	222.9	23.3	12.5	10.5	7.9	-2.6	1.9	10.8	10.5	0.3	199.6
1947	244.2	1.6	0.5	245.3	26.4	15.7	13.2	9.9	-3.4	2.5	10.7	10.3	0.4	218.9
1948	269.2	2.0	0.6	270.6	28.1	18.4	15.5	11.8	-3.8	2.9	9.7	9.2	0.5	242.5
1949	267.3	1.9	0.7	268.6	28.7	20.0	16.9	13.5	-3.4	3.1	8.7	8.2	0.5	239.9
1950	293.8	2.2	0.7	295.2	29.4	21.5	18.1	14.9	-3.2	3.3	8.0	7.5	0.5	265.8
1951	339.3	2.8	0.9	341.2	33.2	24.6	20.7	17.1	-3.6	3.8	8.7	8.1	0.6	308.0
1952	358.3	2.9	0.9	360.3	35.7	26.1	21.9	18.8	-3.1	4.2	9.6	8.9	0.6	324.6
1953	379.4	2.8	0.9	381.3	37.8	27.3	22.9	21.0	-1.9	4.4	10.5	9.8	0.7	343.5
1954	380.4	3.0	0.9	382.5	39.9	28.7	24.1	23.0	-1.1	4.7	11.2	10.4	0.7	342.6
1955	414.8	3.5	1.1	417.2	42.1	30.3	25.3	25.7	0.4	5.0	11.8	11.0	0.8	375.1
1956	437.5	3.9	1.1	440.3	46.4	33.6	28.1	27.9	-0.2	5.5	12.8	11.9	0.9	393.9
1957	461.1	4.3	1.2	464.1	49.9	36.3	30.4	30.3	-0.1	5.8	13.6	12.7	0.9	414.3
1958	467.2	3.9	1.2	469.8	52.0	38.1	32.1	31.6	-0.4	6.1	13.9	12.9	1.0	417.8
1959	506.6	4.3	1.5	509.3	53.0	38.6	32.2	33.5	1.4	6.4	14.5	13.5	1.0	456.3
1960	526.4	4.9	1.8	529.5	55.6	40.5	33.9	35.3	1.4	6.7	15.0	13.9	1.1	473.9
1961	544.7	5.3	1.8	548.2	57.2	41.6	34.7	36.7	2.0	6.9	15.6	14.4	1.2	491.0
1962	585.6	5.9	1.8	589.7	59.3	42.8	35.6	41.0	5.4	7.2	16.5	15.3	1.2	530.5
1963	617.7	6.5	2.1	622.2	62.4	44.9	37.5	43.5	6.0	7.5	17.5	16.2	1.3	559.8
1964	663.6	7.2	2.3	668.5	65.0	46.9	39.0	46.2	7.2	7.9	18.1	16.7	1.4	603.5
1965	719.1	7.9	2.6	724.4	69.4	50.5	41.9	49.5	7.6	8.5	18.9	17.4	1.5	655.0
1966	787.8	8.1	3.0	792.9	75.6	55.5	46.3	53.5	7.2	9.2	20.1	18.5	1.6	717.3
1967	832.6	8.7	3.3	838.0	81.5	59.9	50.0	57.9	7.8	9.9	21.6	19.8	1.8	756.5
1968	910.0	10.1	4.0	916.1	88.4	65.2	54.4	62.6	8.2	10.8	23.1	21.1	2.0	827.7
1969	984.6	11.8	5.7	990.7	97.9	73.1	61.2	68.9	7.7	12.0	24.8	22.6	2.2	892.8
1970	1 038.5	12.8	6.4	1 044.9	106.7	80.0	67.2	73.9	6.7	12.9	26.7	24.2	2.5	938.2
1971	1 127.1	14.0	6.4	1 134.7	115.0	86.7	72.5	79.5	6.9	14.2	28.3	25.5	2.8	1 019.7
1972	1 238.3	16.3	7.7	1 246.8	126.5	97.1	80.9	88.9	8.1	16.2	29.5	26.4	3.1	1 120.3
1973	1 382.7	23.5	10.9	1 395.3	139.3	107.9	89.9	97.0	7.1	18.0	31.4	27.8	3.5	1 256.0
1974	1 500.0	29.8	14.3	1 515.5	162.5	126.6	105.9	107.6	1.7	20.7	35.9	31.6	4.3	1 353.0
1975	1 638.3	28.0	15.0	1 651.3	187.7	147.8	124.4	118.5	-5.9	23.4	40.0	34.9	5.1	1 463.6
1976	1 825.3	32.4	15.5	1 842.1	205.2	162.5	136.9	128.6	-8.3	25.6	42.6	37.1	5.5	1 637.0
1977	2 030.9	37.2	16.9	2 051.2	230.0	184.3	155.3	146.2	-9.1	29.0	45.7	39.7	6.0	1 821.2
1978	2 294.7	46.3	24.7	2 316.3	262.3	212.8	179.3	165.5	-13.7	33.6	49.5	42.8	6.7	2 054.0
1979	2 563.3	68.3	36.4	2 595.3	300.1	245.7	206.9	190.0	-16.9	38.8	54.5	46.9	7.6	2 295.1
1980	2 789.5	79.1	44.9	2 823.7	343.0	281.1	236.8	217.1	-19.8	44.3	61.8	53.1	8.8	2 480.7
1981	3 128.4	92.0	59.1	3 161.4	388.1	317.9	268.9	269.3	0.4	49.0	70.1	60.2	10.0	2 773.3
1982	3 255.0	101.0	64.5	3 291.5	426.9	349.8	297.3	309.3	12.1	52.5	77.1	66.3	10.9	2 864.6
1983	3 536.7	101.9	64.8	3 573.8	443.8	362.1	307.4	347.8	40.4	54.7	81.7	70.2	11.5	3 130.0
1984	3 933.2	121.9	85.6	3 969.5	472.6	385.6	328.0	393.4	65.4	57.6	87.0	74.8	12.2	3 496.9
1985	4 220.3	112.4	85.9	4 246.8	506.7	414.0	353.0	445.4	92.4	61.0	92.7	79.8	12.9	3 740.1
1986	4 462.8	111.4	93.6	4 480.6	531.3	431.8	366.9	458.4	91.5	64.9	99.5	85.7	13.8	3 949.3
1987	4 739.5	123.2	105.3	4 757.4	561.9	455.3	385.7	475.1	89.4	69.5	106.7	92.1	14.6	4 195.4
1988	5 103.8	152.1	128.5	5 127.4	597.6	483.5	408.9	501.0	92.1	74.6	114.1	98.4	15.6	4 529.8
1989	5 484.4	177.7	151.5	5 510.6	644.3	522.1	440.6	523.1	82.5	81.5	122.2	105.3	16.9	4 866.3
1990	5 803.1	189.1	154.3	5 837.9	682.5	551.6	466.4	521.1	54.7	85.1	130.9	113.1	17.9	5 155.4
1991	5 995.9	168.9	138.5	6 026.3	725.9	586.9	497.4	530.1	32.7	89.5	139.1	120.2	18.8	5 300.4
1992	6 337.7	152.7	123.0	6 367.4	751.9	607.3	510.5	544.9	34.4	96.8	144.6	124.8	19.8	5 615.5
1993	6 657.4	156.2	124.3	6 689.3	776.4	624.7	524.6	569.3	44.7	100.1	151.8	130.6	21.1	5 912.9
1994	7 072.2	186.4	160.2	7 098.4	833.7	675.1	568.0	615.1	47.1	107.1	158.6	135.9	22.7	6 264.7
1995	7 397.7	233.9	198.1	7 433.4	878.4	713.4	600.2	651.8	51.6	113.2	165.0	141.4	23.6	6 555.1
1996	7 816.9	248.7	213.7	7 851.9	918.1	748.8	630.7	696.8	66.1	118.2	169.3	144.6	24.6	6 933.8
1997	8 304.3	286.7	253.7	8 337.3	974.4	800.3	675.2	756.5	81.3	125.1	174.1	148.2	25.9	7 362.8
1998	8 747.0	287.1	265.8	8 768.3	1 030.2	851.2	718.3	809.6	91.4	132.9	179.0	151.9	27.1	7 738.2
1999	9 268.4	320.8	287.0	9 302.2	1 101.3	914.3	769.8	883.6	113.7	144.5	187.0	158.4	28.6	8 200.9
2000	9 817.0	382.7	343.7	9 855.9	1 187.8	990.8	836.1	943.9	107.8	154.8	197.0	166.4	30.6	8 668.1
2001	10 128.0	322.4	278.8	10 171.6	1 281.5	1 075.5	903.7	1 028.7	124.9	171.7	206.0	172.7	33.3	8 890.2
2002	10 487.0	301.8	274.7	10 514.1	1 303.9	1 092.8	912.6	1 126.3	213.6	180.2	211.2	178.0	33.2	9 210.1
2003	11 004.0	329.0	273.9	11 059.2	1 353.9	1 135.9	942.6	1 225.6	283.0	193.3	218.1	183.6	34.5	9 705.2
2001														
1st quarter	10 021.5	361.8	323.0	10 060.2	1 240.5	1 038.4	873.6	967.3	93.7	164.8	202.0	170.6	31.4	8 819.8
2nd quarter	10 128.9	337.8	293.2	10 173.5	1 270.8	1 067.0	890.7	987.3	96.6	176.3	203.8	172.2	31.6	8 902.7
3rd quarter	10 135.1	306.0	289.3	10 151.8	1 332.7	1 121.3	949.8	1 052.8	103.0	171.5	211.4	173.4	37.9	8 819.1
4th quarter	10 226.3	284.2	209.6	10 300.9	1 281.8	1 075.2	900.8	1 107.2	206.4	174.4	206.6	174.5	32.1	9 019.1
2002														
1st quarter	10 338.2	288.5	265.0	10 361.7	1 287.1	1 078.5	902.6	1 123.0	220.4	175.8	208.6	176.0	32.7	9 074.7
2nd quarter	10 445.7	304.5	288.6	10 461.6	1 297.9	1 087.7	909.0	1 124.7	215.7	178.6	210.3	177.3	33.0	9 163.7
3rd quarter	10 546.5	312.9	287.8	10 571.7	1 309.3	1 097.4	915.8	1 127.1	211.3	181.6	211.9	178.5	33.4	9 262.4
4th quarter	10 617.5	301.2	257.5	10 661.2	1 321.5	1 107.6	923.0	1 130.2	207.2	184.7	213.8	180.2	33.6	9 339.7
2003														
1st quarter	10 744.6	304.8	268.0	10 781.3	1 334.0	1 118.4	930.5	1 148.7	218.3	187.9	215.6	181.6	34.0	9 447.3
2nd quarter	10 884.0	309.8	264.7	10 929.0	1 347.0	1 129.7	938.3	1 219.6	281.3	191.4	217.3	182.9	34.4	9 582.0
3rd quarter	11 116.7	329.8	278.2	11 168.3	1 360.6	1 141.5	946.5	1 255.5	309.0	195.0	219.1	184.4	34.7	9 807.7
4th quarter	11 270.9	371.8	284.6	11 358.1	1 374.2	1 153.8	955.0	1 278.4	323.3	198.8	220.4	185.4	35.0	9 983.9

Table 1-9. Relation of Gross Domestic Product, Gross and Net National Product, National Income, and Personal Income—Continued

(Billions of dollars, quarterly data are at seasonally adjusted annual rates.)

NIPA Table 1.7.5

Year and quarter	Net national product	Less: Statistical discrepancy	Equals: National income	Corporate profits with IVA and CCAdj	Taxes on production and imports less subsidies	Contributions for government social insurance	Less — Net interest and miscellaneous payments on assets	Business current transfer payments (net)	Current surplus of government enterprises	Wage accruals less disbursements	Plus — Personal income receipts on assets	Personal current transfer receipts	Equals: Personal income	Addenda: Gross national income
1946	199.6	1.2	198.5	17.8	15.7	6.6	1.9	0.7	...	0.0	12.3	10.6	178.6	221.8
1947	218.9	2.3	216.6	23.7	17.9	5.6	2.5	0.7	...	0.0	13.9	10.8	191.0	243.0
1948	242.5	-0.5	243.0	31.2	19.4	4.6	2.6	0.7	...	0.0	15.1	10.3	209.8	271.1
1949	239.9	1.8	238.0	29.1	20.6	4.9	2.9	0.7	...	0.0	16.0	11.2	207.1	266.7
1950	265.8	1.4	264.4	36.0	22.4	5.5	3.2	0.9	...	0.0	18.6	14.0	229.0	293.8
1951	308.0	3.6	304.3	41.2	24.0	6.6	3.7	1.2	...	0.1	19.1	11.4	258.0	337.6
1952	324.6	2.8	321.8	39.3	26.7	6.9	4.1	1.3	...	0.0	19.9	11.9	275.4	357.5
1953	343.5	4.0	339.5	39.7	29.0	7.1	4.7	1.2	...	-0.1	21.6	12.5	291.9	377.2
1954	342.6	3.2	339.4	38.8	29.0	8.1	5.6	1.0	...	0.0	23.2	14.3	294.5	379.3
1955	375.1	2.5	372.7	49.5	31.7	9.1	6.2	1.4	...	0.0	25.7	15.7	316.1	414.8
1956	393.9	-1.7	395.6	48.5	33.9	10.0	6.9	1.7	...	0.0	28.2	16.8	339.6	441.9
1957	414.3	0.0	414.3	48.4	36.0	11.4	8.0	1.9	...	0.0	30.6	19.5	358.7	464.1
1958	417.8	1.0	416.8	43.5	36.8	11.4	9.5	1.8	...	0.0	31.9	23.5	369.0	468.8
1959	456.3	0.5	455.8	55.7	40.0	13.8	9.6	1.8	1.0	0.0	34.6	24.2	392.8	508.9
1960	473.9	-0.9	474.9	53.8	43.4	16.4	10.6	1.9	0.9	0.0	37.9	25.7	411.5	530.4
1961	491.0	-0.6	491.6	54.9	45.0	17.0	12.5	2.0	0.8	0.0	40.1	29.5	429.0	548.8
1962	530.5	0.4	530.1	63.3	48.2	19.1	14.2	2.2	0.9	0.0	44.1	30.4	456.7	589.4
1963	559.8	-0.8	560.6	69.0	51.2	21.7	15.2	2.7	1.4	0.0	47.9	32.2	479.6	623.0
1964	603.5	0.8	602.7	76.5	54.6	22.4	17.4	3.1	1.3	0.0	53.8	33.5	514.6	667.7
1965	655.0	1.6	653.4	87.5	57.8	23.4	19.6	3.6	1.3	0.0	59.4	36.2	555.7	722.8
1966	717.3	6.3	711.0	93.2	59.3	31.3	22.4	3.5	1.0	0.0	64.1	39.6	603.9	786.6
1967	756.5	4.6	751.9	91.3	64.2	34.9	25.5	3.8	0.9	0.0	69.0	48.0	648.3	833.4
1968	827.7	4.6	823.2	98.8	72.3	38.7	27.1	4.3	1.2	0.0	75.2	56.1	712.0	911.5
1969	892.8	3.2	889.7	95.4	79.4	44.1	32.7	4.9	1.0	0.0	84.1	62.3	778.5	987.6
1970	938.2	7.3	930.9	83.6	86.7	46.4	39.1	4.5	0.0	0.0	93.5	74.7	838.8	1 037.6
1971	1 019.7	11.6	1 008.1	98.0	95.9	51.2	43.9	4.3	-0.2	0.6	101.0	88.1	903.5	1 123.1
1972	1 120.3	9.1	1 111.2	112.1	101.4	59.2	47.9	4.9	0.5	0.0	109.6	97.9	992.7	1 237.7
1973	1 256.0	8.6	1 247.4	125.5	112.1	75.5	55.2	6.0	-0.4	-0.1	124.7	112.6	1 110.7	1 386.7
1974	1 353.0	10.9	1 342.1	115.8	121.7	85.2	70.8	7.1	-0.9	-0.5	146.4	133.3	1 222.6	1 504.6
1975	1 463.6	17.7	1 445.9	134.8	131.0	89.3	81.6	9.4	-3.2	0.1	162.2	170.0	1 335.0	1 633.6
1976	1 637.0	25.1	1 611.8	163.3	141.5	101.3	85.5	9.5	-1.8	0.1	178.4	184.0	1 474.8	1 817.0
1977	1 821.2	22.3	1 798.9	192.4	152.8	113.1	101.1	8.4	-2.6	0.1	205.3	194.2	1 633.2	2 028.9
1978	2 054.0	26.6	2 027.4	216.6	162.2	131.3	115.0	10.6	-1.9	0.3	234.8	209.6	1 837.7	2 289.7
1979	2 295.1	46.0	2 249.1	223.2	171.9	152.7	138.9	13.0	-2.6	-0.2	274.7	235.3	2 062.2	2 549.2
1980	2 480.7	41.4	2 439.3	201.1	190.9	166.2	181.8	14.4	-4.8	0.0	338.7	279.5	2 307.9	2 782.3
1981	2 773.3	30.9	2 742.4	226.1	224.5	195.7	232.3	17.6	-4.9	0.1	421.9	318.4	2 591.3	3 130.4
1982	2 864.6	0.3	2 864.3	209.7	226.4	208.9	271.1	20.1	-4.0	0.0	488.4	354.8	2 775.3	3 291.2
1983	3 130.0	45.7	3 084.2	264.2	242.5	226.0	285.3	22.5	-3.1	-0.4	529.6	383.7	2 960.7	3 528.0
1984	3 496.9	14.6	3 482.3	318.6	269.3	257.5	327.1	30.1	-1.9	0.2	607.9	400.1	3 289.5	3 954.9
1985	3 740.1	16.7	3 723.4	330.3	287.3	281.4	341.3	34.8	0.8	-0.2	654.0	424.9	3 526.7	4 230.1
1986	3 949.3	47.0	3 902.3	319.5	298.9	303.4	366.8	36.6	1.3	0.0	695.5	451.0	3 722.4	4 433.6
1987	4 195.4	21.7	4 173.7	368.8	317.7	323.1	366.4	33.8	1.2	0.0	717.0	467.6	3 947.4	4 735.7
1988	4 529.8	-19.5	4 549.4	432.6	345.5	361.5	385.3	34.0	2.5	0.0	769.3	496.6	4 253.7	5 147.0
1989	4 866.3	39.7	4 826.6	426.6	372.1	385.2	432.1	39.2	4.9	0.0	878.0	543.4	4 587.8	5 470.9
1990	5 155.4	66.2	5 089.1	437.8	398.7	410.1	442.2	39.4	1.6	0.1	924.0	595.2	4 878.6	5 771.6
1991	5 300.4	72.5	5 227.9	451.2	430.2	430.2	418.2	39.9	5.7	-0.1	932.0	666.4	5 051.0	5 953.8
1992	5 615.5	102.7	5 512.8	479.3	453.9	455.0	388.5	42.4	7.6	-15.8	910.9	749.4	5 362.0	6 264.7
1993	5 912.9	139.5	5 773.4	541.9	467.0	477.7	365.7	40.7	7.2	6.4	901.8	790.1	5 558.5	6 549.8
1994	6 264.7	142.5	6 122.3	600.3	513.5	508.2	366.4	43.3	8.6	17.6	950.8	827.3	5 842.5	6 955.9
1995	6 555.1	101.2	6 453.9	696.7	524.2	532.8	367.1	46.9	11.4	16.4	1 016.4	877.4	6 152.3	7 332.3
1996	6 933.8	93.7	6 840.1	786.2	546.8	555.2	376.2	53.1	12.7	3.6	1 089.2	925.0	6 520.6	7 758.2
1997	7 362.8	70.7	7 292.2	868.5	579.1	587.2	415.6	49.9	12.6	-2.9	1 181.7	951.2	6 915.1	8 266.6
1998	7 738.2	-14.6	7 752.8	801.6	604.4	624.2	487.1	64.7	10.3	-0.7	1 283.2	978.6	7 423.0	8 783.0
1999	8 200.9	-35.7	8 236.7	851.3	629.8	661.4	495.4	67.4	10.1	5.2	1 264.2	1 022.1	7 802.4	9 337.9
2000	8 668.1	-127.2	8 795.2	817.9	664.6	702.7	559.0	87.1	5.3	0.0	1 387.0	1 084.0	8 429.7	9 983.1
2001	8 890.2	-89.6	8 979.8	767.3	673.3	731.1	566.3	92.8	-1.4	0.0	1 380.0	1 193.9	8 724.1	10 261.3
2002	9 210.1	-15.3	9 225.4	874.6	724.4	748.3	532.9	80.9	2.8	0.0	1 334.6	1 282.7	8 878.9	10 529.4
2003	9 705.2	25.6	9 679.6	1 021.1	751.3	773.2	543.0	77.7	9.5	0.0	1 322.7	1 335.4	9 161.8	11 033.6
2001														
1st quarter	8 819.8	-167.8	8 987.6	778.7	672.8	729.2	565.2	98.3	1.7	0.0	1 397.4	1 149.6	8 688.7	10 228.0
2nd quarter	8 902.7	-98.8	9 001.5	783.1	667.9	731.5	569.9	104.8	-1.1	0.0	1 388.7	1 185.7	8 719.9	10 272.3
3rd quarter	8 819.1	-71.1	8 890.3	714.5	658.2	731.9	565.5	65.7	-2.9	0.0	1 373.3	1 202.6	8 733.1	10 223.0
4th quarter	9 019.1	-20.9	9 039.9	793.0	694.5	731.9	564.8	102.5	-3.4	0.0	1 360.3	1 237.8	8 754.8	10 321.8
2002														
1st quarter	9 074.7	-61.8	9 136.5	838.2	708.4	745.7	549.2	89.6	-0.9	0.0	1 337.8	1 259.4	8 803.6	10 423.5
2nd quarter	9 163.7	-58.7	9 222.3	868.4	723.4	749.1	527.3	81.3	-0.1	0.0	1 340.2	1 284.0	8 897.1	10 520.3
3rd quarter	9 262.6	20.8	9 241.6	876.2	732.8	748.9	526.8	78.0	6.0	0.0	1 333.7	1 289.1	8 895.7	10 550.9
4th quarter	9 339.7	38.4	9 301.3	915.4	733.1	749.6	528.3	74.6	6.0	0.0	1 326.7	1 298.1	8 919.2	10 622.7
2003														
1st quarter	9 447.3	39.6	9 407.7	912.0	740.7	762.4	541.3	74.8	10.3	1.4	1 325.9	1 311.4	9 002.2	10 741.7
2nd quarter	9 582.0	13.2	9 568.8	986.2	737.7	768.9	542.8	76.9	9.8	-1.4	1 324.7	1 333.1	9 105.7	10 915.8
3rd quarter	9 807.7	36.6	9 771.1	1 057.1	757.4	776.7	542.8	78.9	9.3	0.0	1 314.4	1 346.2	9 209.3	11 131.7
4th quarter	9 983.9	12.8	9 971.1	1 129.1	769.4	785.0	545.3	80.1	8.7	0.0	1 325.8	1 350.7	9 330.0	11 345.2

... = Not available.

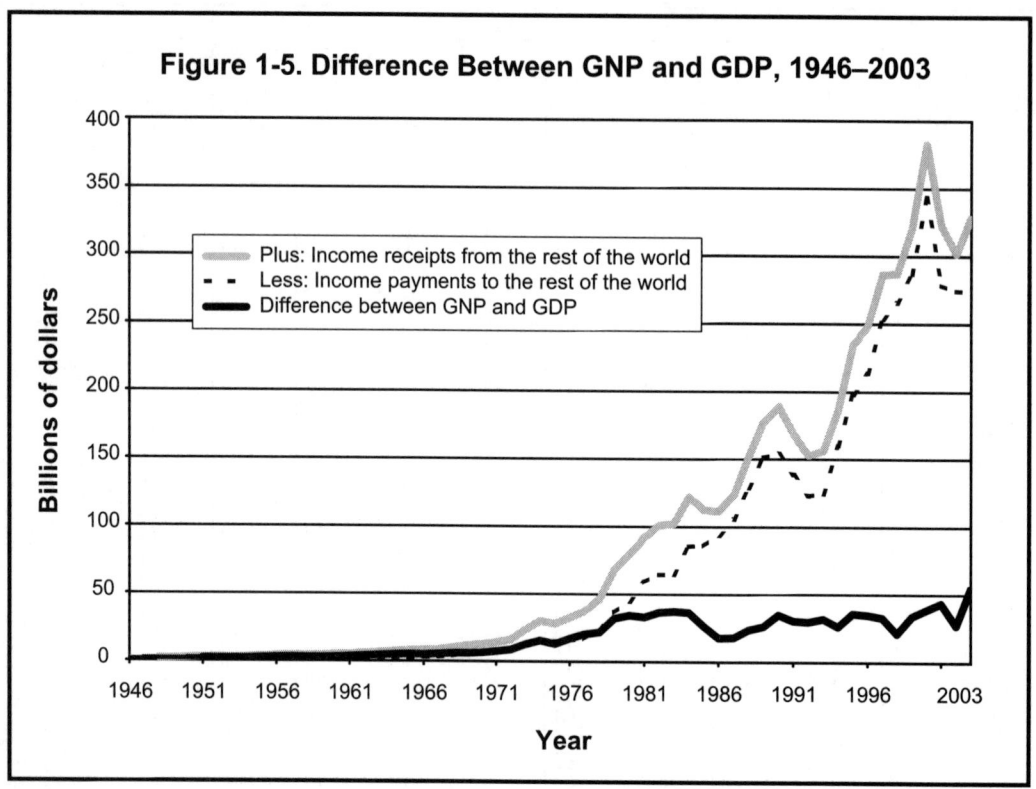

Figure 1-5. Difference Between GNP and GDP, 1946–2003

- Over the postwar period, income receipts by U.S. residents from the rest of the world have consistently exceeded income payments from U.S. industries to the rest of the world. In other words, U.S. residents have increasingly had more income to spend than was generated by production within the boundaries of the United States, and this was indicated by an excess of Gross National Product (GNP) over Gross Domestic Product (GDP). (Table 1-9)
- Most of the growth in this gap had occurred by the early 1980s. As a percentage of the value of GDP, the net excess of receipts over payments rose from 0.5 percent in 1948 to 1.2 percent in 1979 (comparing business cycle high years). Since then, the gap, while still rising in absolute value, dropped to 0.4 percent of GDP in 2000; in the latest year, it increased, but only to 0.5 percent of GDP. (Table 1-9)
- This relative decline in the gap reflects the deteriorating international investment position of the United States. The excess of U.S. assets abroad over foreign-owned assets in the United States peaked in 1980 and since then, as a result of balance of payments deficits and the associated inflows of foreign capital, has been reversed to a net indebtedness position of nearly $2.5 trillion in 2003. (Table 7-7)
- The gap between GNP and GDP reflects differences in three income components: compensation, net interest and miscellaneous payments, and corporate profits. Comparison between those elements as shown in the tables on national income (1-11) and domestic income (1-10) shows that profits earned by U.S. corporations still exceed those generated in the domestic economy, but net payments of interest by domestic industry are increasingly going to overseas lenders.

CHAPTER 1: NATIONAL INCOME AND PRODUCT AND CYCLICAL INDICATORS

Table 1-10. Gross Domestic Income by Type of Income
(Billions of dollars, quarterly data are at seasonally adjusted annual rates.)

NIPA Tables 1.1.5, 1.10

Year and quarter	Gross domestic income	Compensation of employees			Taxes on production and imports	Less: Subsidies	Net operating surplus					
								Private enterprises				
		Total	Wage and salary accruals	Supplements to wages and salaries			Total	Total	Net interest and miscellaneous payments, domestic industries	Business current transfer payments (net)	Proprietors' income with IVA and CCAdj	Rental income of persons with CCAdj
1946	221.1	119.7	112.0	7.6	16.8	1.2	...	62.5	1.9	0.7	35.6	7.1
1947	241.9	130.0	123.0	7.0	18.1	0.2	...	67.6	2.4	0.7	34.5	7.2
1948	269.7	141.9	135.5	6.4	19.7	0.3	...	80.3	2.5	0.7	39.3	7.9
1949	265.4	141.8	134.7	7.1	20.9	0.3	...	74.3	2.8	0.7	34.7	8.2
1950	292.4	155.2	147.2	8.0	23.0	0.6	...	85.4	3.1	0.9	37.6	9.2
1951	335.7	181.4	171.6	9.8	24.8	0.7	...	97.0	3.5	1.2	42.7	10.1
1952	355.6	196.2	185.6	10.5	27.1	0.4	...	97.0	4.0	1.3	43.1	11.2
1953	375.3	210.2	199.0	11.2	29.1	0.1	...	98.4	4.6	1.2	42.1	12.5
1954	377.2	209.2	197.3	11.9	28.9	-0.1	...	99.1	5.4	1.0	42.3	13.5
1955	412.3	225.8	212.2	13.5	31.5	-0.2	...	112.8	6.1	1.4	44.3	13.9
1956	439.2	244.6	229.1	15.5	34.3	0.4	...	114.3	6.8	1.7	45.8	14.2
1957	461.1	257.6	240.0	17.6	36.6	0.7	...	117.6	8.0	1.9	47.9	14.6
1958	466.2	259.6	241.4	18.2	37.7	0.9	...	117.7	9.4	1.8	50.1	15.4
1959	506.1	281.1	259.9	21.1	41.1	1.1	132.0	131.0	9.5	1.8	50.7	16.2
1960	527.3	296.6	273.0	23.6	44.6	1.1	131.8	130.8	10.4	1.9	50.8	17.1
1961	545.3	305.4	280.7	24.8	47.0	2.0	137.6	136.8	12.1	2.0	53.2	17.9
1962	585.3	327.2	299.5	27.8	50.4	2.3	150.6	149.7	13.8	2.2	55.4	18.8
1963	618.5	345.3	314.9	30.4	53.4	2.2	159.6	158.3	14.7	2.7	56.5	19.5
1964	662.8	370.7	337.8	32.9	57.3	2.7	172.4	171.1	16.9	3.1	59.4	19.6
1965	717.5	399.5	363.8	35.7	60.8	3.0	190.9	189.6	19.1	3.6	63.9	20.2
1966	781.5	442.6	400.3	42.3	63.3	3.9	204.0	203.0	21.9	3.5	68.2	20.8
1967	828.0	475.1	429.0	46.1	68.0	3.8	207.2	206.2	24.9	3.8	69.8	21.2
1968	905.4	524.3	472.0	52.3	76.5	4.2	220.5	219.3	26.7	4.3	74.3	20.9
1969	981.4	577.6	518.3	59.3	84.0	4.5	226.5	225.5	33.2	4.9	77.4	21.2
1970	1 031.2	617.2	551.5	65.7	91.5	4.8	220.6	220.6	39.9	4.5	78.4	21.4
1971	1 115.5	658.9	584.5	74.4	100.6	4.7	245.7	245.9	44.2	4.3	84.8	22.4
1972	1 229.2	725.1	638.8	86.4	108.1	6.6	276.1	275.6	48.9	4.9	95.9	23.4
1973	1 374.1	811.2	708.8	102.5	117.3	5.2	311.4	311.8	57.5	6.0	113.5	24.3
1974	1 489.1	890.3	772.3	118.0	125.0	3.3	314.6	315.6	72.7	7.1	113.1	24.3
1975	1 620.6	949.2	814.9	134.3	135.5	4.5	352.7	356.0	83.2	9.4	119.5	23.7
1976	1 800.1	1 059.4	899.8	159.6	146.6	5.1	394.1	396.0	85.2	9.5	132.2	22.3
1977	2 008.7	1 180.6	994.2	186.4	159.9	7.1	445.3	447.9	99.8	8.4	145.7	20.7
1978	2 268.1	1 336.2	1 121.3	214.9	171.2	8.9	507.4	509.3	116.2	10.6	166.6	22.1
1979	2 517.3	1 500.8	1 255.9	245.0	180.4	8.5	544.4	547.0	141.5	13.0	180.1	23.8
1980	2 748.1	1 651.9	1 377.7	274.2	200.7	9.8	562.3	567.2	183.0	14.4	174.1	30.0
1981	3 097.5	1 826.0	1 517.7	308.3	236.0	11.5	658.9	663.9	228.9	17.6	183.0	38.0
1982	3 254.7	1 926.0	1 593.9	332.1	241.3	15.0	675.4	679.4	267.0	20.1	176.3	38.8
1983	3 490.9	2 042.8	1 684.8	358.0	263.7	21.2	761.9	765.0	283.1	22.5	192.5	37.8
1984	3 918.6	2 255.8	1 855.3	400.5	290.2	21.0	920.9	922.8	327.1	30.1	243.3	40.2
1985	4 203.6	2 424.9	1 995.7	429.2	308.5	21.3	984.7	983.9	352.6	34.8	262.5	41.9
1986	4 415.8	2 571.9	2 116.6	455.3	323.7	24.8	1 013.7	1 012.4	386.6	36.6	275.7	33.5
1987	4 717.8	2 751.6	2 272.1	479.5	347.9	30.2	1 086.6	1 085.4	395.1	33.8	302.2	33.5
1988	5 123.3	2 968.1	2 453.8	514.2	374.9	29.4	1 212.1	1 209.6	417.8	34.0	341.6	40.6
1989	5 444.7	3 146.5	2 597.6	548.9	399.3	27.2	1 281.8	1 276.9	471.7	39.2	363.3	43.1
1990	5 736.8	3 340.5	2 756.3	584.2	425.5	26.8	1 315.1	1 313.5	481.1	39.4	380.6	50.7
1991	5 923.4	3 448.0	2 825.7	622.3	457.5	27.3	1 319.3	1 313.6	461.6	39.9	377.1	60.3
1992	6 235.0	3 638.4	2 967.5	670.9	483.8	29.9	1 390.8	1 383.2	428.9	42.4	427.6	78.0
1993	6 517.9	3 804.7	3 092.5	712.2	503.4	36.4	1 469.7	1 462.4	407.4	40.7	453.8	95.6
1994	6 929.7	4 001.2	3 253.8	747.5	545.6	32.2	1 581.3	1 572.8	413.3	43.3	473.3	119.7
1995	7 296.5	4 197.4	3 439.8	757.7	558.2	34.0	1 696.4	1 685.0	420.0	46.9	492.1	122.1
1996	7 723.2	4 394.7	3 627.3	767.3	581.1	34.3	1 863.6	1 850.9	438.9	53.1	543.2	131.5
1997	8 233.7	4 666.1	3 879.1	787.0	612.0	32.9	2 014.1	2 001.5	489.2	49.9	576.0	128.8
1998	8 761.6	5 023.9	4 187.3	836.7	639.8	35.4	2 103.1	2 092.8	564.1	64.7	627.8	137.5
1999	9 304.1	5 362.3	4 476.6	885.7	674.0	44.2	2 210.7	2 200.6	577.9	67.4	678.3	147.3
2000	9 944.1	5 787.3	4 833.8	953.4	708.9	44.3	2 304.5	2 299.1	661.2	87.1	728.4	150.3
2001	10 217.6	5 947.2	4 947.9	999.3	728.6	55.3	2 315.3	2 317.0	687.2	92.8	771.9	167.4
2002	10 502.3	6 074.9	4 981.7	1 093.2	762.6	38.2	2 399.1	2 396.3	658.2	80.9	769.6	170.9
2003	10 978.5	6 294.5	5 109.1	1 185.5	798.1	46.7	2 578.7	2 569.2	659.3	77.7	834.1	153.8
2001												
1st quarter	10 189.3	5 951.2	4 966.0	985.1	725.1	52.3	2 324.9	2 323.2	681.5	98.3	769.4	155.3
2nd quarter	10 227.7	5 949.8	4 956.5	993.2	726.3	58.4	2 339.3	2 340.4	691.2	104.8	770.6	161.7
3rd quarter	10 206.3	5 944.5	4 940.4	1 004.1	725.6	67.3	2 270.9	2 273.7	690.2	65.7	773.4	176.4
4th quarter	10 247.2	5 943.6	4 928.8	1 014.8	737.6	43.1	2 327.3	2 330.7	686.0	102.5	774.2	176.2
2002												
1st quarter	10 400.1	6 015.6	4 961.6	1 054.0	747.3	38.9	2 389.1	2 390.0	675.4	89.6	762.2	179.7
2nd quarter	10 504.4	6 073.9	4 985.9	1 088.0	760.1	36.8	2 409.2	2 409.2	657.1	81.3	769.0	184.7
3rd quarter	10 525.7	6 091.3	4 986.5	1 104.8	771.2	38.4	2 392.4	2 386.4	651.5	78.0	770.4	165.4
4th quarter	10 579.1	6 118.9	4 992.9	1 126.0	771.8	38.7	2 405.6	2 399.6	648.7	74.6	776.7	153.8
2003												
1st quarter	10 704.9	6 184.6	5 030.3	1 154.3	783.5	42.8	2 445.6	2 435.3	655.9	74.8	794.0	155.5
2nd quarter	10 870.8	6 251.2	5 077.5	1 173.7	792.9	55.2	2 534.9	2 525.1	653.5	76.9	825.7	144.1
3rd quarter	11 080.1	6 330.1	5 134.0	1 196.1	802.0	44.5	2 632.0	2 622.7	659.3	78.9	852.0	148.8
4th quarter	11 258.1	6 412.1	5 194.4	1 217.8	813.9	44.4	2 702.3	2 693.6	668.5	80.1	864.7	167.1

... = Not available.

Table 1-10. Gross Domestic Income by Type of Income—*Continued*

(Billions of dollars, quarterly data are at seasonally adjusted annual rates.)

NIPA Tables 1.1.5, 1.10

Year and quarter	Net operating surplus—*Continued*					Current surplus of government enterprises	Consumption of fixed capital			Statistical discrepancy	Gross domestic product
	Private enterprises—*Continued*										
	Corporate profits with IVA and CCAdj, domestic industries										
	Total	Taxes on corporate income	Profits after tax				Total	Private	Government		
			Total	Net dividends	Undistributed corporate profits						
1946	17.1	9.1	8.0	5.1	2.9	...	23.3	12.5	10.8	1.2	222.3
1947	22.7	11.3	11.4	5.6	5.8	...	26.4	15.7	10.7	2.3	244.2
1948	29.9	12.4	17.5	6.2	11.3	...	28.1	18.4	9.7	-0.5	269.2
1949	27.9	10.2	17.7	6.4	11.3	...	28.7	20.0	8.7	1.8	267.3
1950	34.7	17.9	16.8	7.9	9.0	...	29.4	21.5	8.0	1.4	293.8
1951	39.5	22.6	16.9	7.4	9.5	...	33.2	24.6	8.7	3.6	339.3
1952	37.4	19.4	18.0	7.5	10.5	...	35.7	26.1	9.6	2.8	358.3
1953	37.9	20.3	17.6	7.8	9.9	...	37.8	27.3	10.5	4.0	379.4
1954	36.9	17.6	19.3	7.9	11.4	...	39.9	28.7	11.2	3.2	380.4
1955	47.2	22.0	25.1	8.9	16.2	...	42.1	30.3	11.8	2.5	414.8
1956	45.7	22.0	23.7	9.5	14.2	...	46.4	33.6	12.8	-1.7	437.5
1957	45.3	21.4	23.8	9.9	14.0	...	49.9	36.3	13.6	0.0	461.1
1958	41.0	19.0	22.0	9.8	12.2	...	52.0	38.1	13.9	1.0	467.2
1959	53.0	23.7	29.2	10.7	18.5	1.0	53.0	38.6	14.5	0.5	506.6
1960	50.6	22.8	27.9	11.4	16.4	0.9	55.6	40.5	15.0	-0.9	526.4
1961	51.5	22.9	28.6	11.5	17.1	0.8	57.2	41.6	15.6	-0.6	544.7
1962	59.5	24.1	35.4	12.4	23.0	0.9	59.3	42.8	16.5	0.4	585.6
1963	64.9	26.4	38.5	13.6	25.0	1.4	62.4	44.9	17.5	-0.8	617.7
1964	72.0	28.2	43.8	15.0	28.9	1.3	65.0	46.9	18.1	0.8	663.6
1965	82.8	31.1	51.7	16.9	34.8	1.3	69.4	50.5	18.9	1.6	719.1
1966	88.7	33.9	54.8	17.8	37.0	1.0	75.6	55.5	20.1	6.3	787.8
1967	86.6	32.9	53.7	18.3	35.3	0.9	81.5	59.9	21.6	4.6	832.6
1968	93.2	39.6	53.5	20.2	33.4	1.2	88.4	65.2	23.1	4.6	910.0
1969	88.8	40.0	48.8	20.4	28.4	1.0	97.9	73.1	24.8	3.2	984.6
1970	76.5	34.8	41.8	20.4	21.4	0.0	106.7	80.0	26.7	7.3	1 038.5
1971	90.2	38.2	52.0	20.3	31.7	-0.2	115.0	86.7	28.3	11.6	1 127.1
1972	102.6	42.3	60.2	21.9	38.3	0.5	126.5	97.1	29.5	9.1	1 238.3
1973	110.6	50.0	60.6	23.1	37.5	-0.4	139.3	107.9	31.4	8.6	1 382.7
1974	98.3	52.8	45.5	23.5	22.1	-0.9	162.5	126.6	35.9	10.9	1 500.0
1975	120.2	51.6	68.6	26.4	42.2	-3.2	187.7	147.8	40.0	17.7	1 638.3
1976	146.8	65.3	81.5	30.1	51.4	-1.8	205.2	162.5	42.6	25.1	1 825.3
1977	173.3	74.4	98.9	33.7	65.2	-2.6	230.0	184.3	45.7	22.3	2 030.9
1978	193.8	84.9	108.9	39.6	69.3	-1.9	262.3	212.8	49.5	26.6	2 294.7
1979	188.6	90.0	98.6	41.5	57.1	-2.6	300.1	245.7	54.5	46.0	2 563.3
1980	165.7	87.2	78.5	47.3	31.1	-4.8	343.0	281.1	61.8	41.4	2 789.5
1981	196.4	84.3	112.1	58.3	53.8	-4.9	388.1	317.9	70.1	30.9	3 128.4
1982	177.1	66.5	110.6	61.3	49.2	-4.0	426.9	349.8	77.1	0.3	3 255.0
1983	229.2	80.6	148.5	71.3	77.2	-3.1	443.8	362.1	81.7	45.7	3 536.7
1984	282.0	97.5	184.5	78.5	106.0	-1.9	472.6	385.6	87.0	14.6	3 933.2
1985	292.2	99.4	192.8	85.7	107.1	0.8	506.7	414.0	92.7	16.7	4 220.3
1986	280.0	109.7	170.4	88.3	82.1	1.3	531.3	431.8	99.5	47.0	4 462.8
1987	320.8	130.4	190.4	95.6	94.8	1.2	561.9	455.3	106.7	21.7	4 739.5
1988	375.7	141.6	234.0	98.0	136.0	2.5	597.6	483.5	114.1	-19.5	5 103.8
1989	359.5	146.1	213.4	126.4	87.0	4.9	644.3	522.1	122.2	39.7	5 484.4
1990	361.7	145.4	216.3	144.1	72.2	1.6	682.5	551.6	130.9	66.2	5 803.1
1991	374.7	138.6	236.1	156.4	79.8	5.7	725.9	586.9	139.1	72.5	5 995.9
1992	406.2	148.7	257.5	159.9	97.7	7.6	751.9	607.3	144.6	102.7	6 337.7
1993	465.0	171.0	294.0	182.2	111.7	7.2	776.4	624.7	151.8	139.5	6 657.4
1994	523.2	193.7	329.5	197.4	132.0	8.6	833.7	675.1	158.6	142.5	7 072.2
1995	603.9	218.7	385.2	221.6	163.7	11.4	878.4	713.4	165.0	101.2	7 397.7
1996	684.3	231.7	452.6	257.3	195.3	12.7	918.1	748.8	169.3	93.7	7 816.9
1997	757.5	246.1	511.5	283.9	227.6	12.6	974.4	800.3	174.1	70.7	8 304.3
1998	698.7	248.3	450.4	309.2	141.2	10.3	1 030.2	851.2	179.0	-14.6	8 747.0
1999	729.8	258.6	471.1	295.7	175.5	10.1	1 101.3	914.3	187.0	-35.7	9 268.4
2000	672.2	265.2	407.0	348.4	58.6	5.3	1 187.8	990.8	197.0	-127.2	9 817.0
2001	597.6	204.1	393.5	330.1	63.4	-1.4	1 281.5	1 075.5	206.0	-89.6	10 128.0
2002	716.8	183.8	532.9	347.5	185.5	2.8	1 303.9	1 092.8	211.2	-15.3	10 487.0
2003	844.2	234.9	609.3	374.8	234.5	9.5	1 353.9	1 135.9	218.1	25.6	11 004.0
2001											
1st quarter	618.6	222.5	396.1	333.6	62.5	1.7	1 240.5	1 038.4	202.0	-167.8	10 021.5
2nd quarter	612.1	217.9	394.2	313.2	81.1	-1.1	1 270.8	1 067.0	203.8	-98.8	10 128.9
3rd quarter	567.9	197.6	370.3	339.1	31.2	-2.9	1 332.7	1 121.3	211.4	-71.1	10 135.1
4th quarter	591.8	178.6	413.3	334.3	79.0	-3.4	1 281.8	1 075.2	206.6	-20.9	10 226.3
2002											
1st quarter	683.2	168.9	514.2	339.3	174.9	-0.9	1 287.1	1 078.5	208.6	-61.8	10 338.2
2nd quarter	717.1	183.5	533.7	353.6	180.1	-0.1	1 297.9	1 087.7	210.3	-58.7	10 445.7
3rd quarter	721.1	188.3	532.8	332.9	199.9	6.0	1 309.3	1 097.4	211.9	20.8	10 546.5
4th quarter	745.7	194.7	551.0	364.0	187.0	6.0	1 321.5	1 107.6	213.8	38.4	10 617.5
2003											
1st quarter	755.1	224.0	531.0	348.7	182.4	10.3	1 334.0	1 118.4	215.6	39.6	10 744.6
2nd quarter	824.9	224.6	600.3	417.9	182.4	9.8	1 347.0	1 129.7	217.3	13.2	10 884.0
3rd quarter	883.7	238.7	644.9	361.0	284.0	9.3	1 360.6	1 141.5	219.1	36.6	11 116.7
4th quarter	913.3	252.3	660.9	371.5	289.5	8.7	1 374.2	1 153.8	220.4	12.8	11 270.9

... = Not available.

Table 1-11. National Income by Type of Income

(Billions of dollars, quarterly data are at seasonally adjusted annual rates.)

NIPA Tables 1.7.5, 1.12

Year and quarter	National income, total	Compensation of employees							Proprietors' income with IVA and CCAdj			Rental income of persons with CCAdj
		Total	Wage and salary accruals			Supplements to wages and salaries			Total	Farm	Nonfarm	
			Total	Government	Other	Total	Employer contributions for					
							Employee pension and insurance funds	Government social insurance				
1946	198.5	119.6	112.0	20.7	91.3	7.6	2.5	5.1	35.6	14.2	21.4	7.1
1947	216.6	130.1	123.1	17.5	105.6	7.0	3.0	3.9	34.5	14.4	20.2	7.2
1948	243.0	142.0	135.6	19.0	116.5	6.4	3.4	3.0	39.3	16.7	22.6	7.9
1949	238.0	141.9	134.7	20.8	113.9	7.1	3.8	3.3	34.7	12.0	22.7	8.2
1950	264.4	155.3	147.3	22.6	124.6	8.0	4.7	3.4	37.6	12.9	24.7	9.2
1951	304.3	181.4	171.6	29.2	142.4	9.8	5.7	4.1	42.7	15.3	27.4	10.1
1952	321.8	196.2	185.6	33.4	152.3	10.5	6.4	4.1	43.1	14.3	28.8	11.2
1953	339.5	210.2	199.0	34.3	164.7	11.2	7.0	4.2	42.1	12.1	30.0	12.5
1954	339.4	209.2	197.3	34.9	162.4	11.9	7.3	4.6	42.3	11.7	30.6	13.5
1955	372.7	225.7	212.2	36.6	175.6	13.5	8.4	5.2	44.3	10.6	33.7	13.9
1956	395.6	244.5	229.0	38.8	190.2	15.5	9.8	5.7	45.8	10.5	35.4	14.2
1957	414.3	257.5	240.0	41.0	198.9	17.6	11.2	6.4	47.9	10.4	37.4	14.6
1958	416.8	259.5	241.3	44.1	197.2	18.2	11.9	6.3	50.1	12.3	37.8	15.4
1959	455.8	281.0	259.8	46.1	213.8	21.1	13.3	7.9	50.7	10.0	40.6	16.2
1960	474.9	296.4	272.9	49.2	223.7	23.6	14.3	9.3	50.8	10.5	40.3	17.1
1961	491.6	305.3	280.5	52.5	228.0	24.8	15.2	9.6	53.2	11.0	42.2	17.9
1962	530.1	327.1	299.4	56.3	243.0	27.8	16.6	11.2	55.4	11.0	44.4	18.8
1963	560.6	345.2	314.9	60.0	254.8	30.4	18.0	12.4	56.5	10.8	45.7	19.5
1964	602.7	370.7	337.8	64.9	272.9	32.9	20.3	12.6	59.4	9.6	49.8	19.6
1965	653.4	399.5	363.8	69.9	293.8	35.7	22.7	13.1	63.9	11.8	52.1	20.2
1966	711.0	442.7	400.3	78.4	321.9	42.3	25.5	16.8	68.2	12.8	55.4	20.8
1967	751.9	475.1	429.0	86.5	342.5	46.1	28.1	18.0	69.8	11.5	58.4	21.2
1968	823.2	524.3	472.0	96.7	375.3	52.3	32.4	20.0	74.3	11.5	62.8	20.9
1969	889.7	577.6	518.3	105.6	412.7	59.3	36.5	22.8	77.4	12.6	64.7	21.2
1970	930.9	617.2	551.6	117.2	434.3	65.7	41.8	23.8	78.4	12.7	65.7	21.4
1971	1 008.1	658.9	584.5	126.8	457.8	74.4	47.9	26.4	84.8	13.2	71.6	22.4
1972	1 111.2	725.1	638.8	137.9	500.9	86.4	55.2	31.2	95.9	16.8	79.1	23.4
1973	1 247.4	811.2	708.8	148.8	560.0	102.5	62.7	39.8	113.5	28.9	84.6	24.3
1974	1 342.1	890.2	772.3	160.5	611.8	118.0	73.3	44.7	113.1	23.2	89.9	24.3
1975	1 445.9	949.1	814.8	176.2	638.6	134.3	87.6	46.7	119.5	21.7	97.8	23.7
1976	1 611.8	1 059.3	899.7	188.9	710.8	159.6	105.2	54.4	132.2	17.0	115.2	22.3
1977	1 798.9	1 180.5	994.2	202.6	791.6	186.4	125.3	61.1	145.7	15.7	130.0	20.7
1978	2 027.4	1 336.1	1 121.2	220.0	901.2	214.9	143.4	71.5	166.6	19.6	147.1	22.1
1979	2 249.1	1 500.8	1 255.8	237.1	1 018.7	245.0	162.4	82.6	180.1	21.8	158.3	23.8
1980	2 439.3	1 651.8	1 377.6	261.5	1 116.2	274.2	185.2	88.9	174.1	11.3	162.8	30.0
1981	2 742.4	1 825.8	1 517.5	285.8	1 231.7	308.3	204.7	103.6	183.0	18.7	164.3	38.0
1982	2 864.3	1 925.8	1 593.7	307.5	1 286.2	332.1	222.4	109.8	176.3	13.1	163.3	38.8
1983	3 084.2	2 042.6	1 684.6	324.8	1 359.8	358.0	238.1	119.9	192.5	6.0	186.5	37.8
1984	3 482.3	2 255.6	1 855.1	348.1	1 507.0	400.5	261.5	139.0	243.3	20.6	222.7	40.2
1985	3 723.4	2 424.7	1 995.5	373.9	1 621.6	429.2	281.5	147.7	262.3	20.8	241.5	41.9
1986	3 902.3	2 570.1	2 114.8	397.0	1 717.9	455.3	297.5	157.9	275.7	22.6	253.1	33.5
1987	4 173.7	2 750.2	2 270.7	422.6	1 848.1	479.5	313.2	166.3	302.2	28.7	273.5	33.5
1988	4 549.4	2 967.2	2 452.9	451.3	2 001.6	514.2	329.6	184.6	341.6	26.8	314.7	40.6
1989	4 826.6	3 145.2	2 596.3	480.2	2 116.2	548.9	355.2	193.7	363.3	33.0	330.3	43.1
1990	5 089.1	3 338.2	2 754.0	517.7	2 236.3	584.2	377.8	206.5	380.6	31.9	348.7	50.7
1991	5 227.9	3 445.2	2 823.0	546.8	2 276.2	622.3	407.1	215.1	377.1	26.7	350.4	60.3
1992	5 512.8	3 635.4	2 964.5	569.2	2 395.3	670.9	442.5	228.4	427.6	34.5	393.0	78.0
1993	5 773.4	3 801.4	3 089.2	586.8	2 502.4	712.2	472.4	239.8	453.8	31.2	422.6	95.6
1994	6 122.3	3 997.2	3 249.8	606.2	2 643.5	747.5	493.3	254.1	473.3	33.9	439.4	119.7
1995	6 453.9	4 193.3	3 435.7	625.5	2 810.2	757.7	493.6	264.0	492.1	22.7	469.5	122.1
1996	6 840.1	4 390.5	3 623.2	644.4	2 978.8	767.3	492.5	274.9	543.2	37.3	505.9	131.5
1997	7 292.2	4 661.7	3 874.7	668.1	3 206.6	787.0	497.5	289.5	576.0	34.2	541.8	128.8
1998	7 752.8	5 019.4	4 182.7	697.3	3 485.5	836.7	529.7	307.0	627.8	29.4	598.4	137.5
1999	8 236.7	5 357.1	4 471.4	729.3	3 742.1	885.7	562.4	323.3	678.3	28.6	649.7	147.3
2000	8 795.2	5 782.7	4 829.2	774.7	4 054.5	953.4	609.9	343.5	728.4	22.7	705.7	150.3
2001	8 979.8	5 942.1	4 942.8	815.9	4 126.9	999.3	642.7	356.6	771.9	19.7	752.2	167.4
2002	9 225.4	6 069.5	4 976.3	862.6	4 113.7	1 093.2	729.6	363.6	769.6	9.7	759.9	170.9
2003	9 679.6	6 289.0	5 103.6	897.9	4 205.6	1 185.5	808.9	376.6	834.1	21.8	812.3	153.8
2001												
1st quarter	8 987.6	5 946.2	4 961.1	798.0	4 163.0	985.1	629.3	355.8	769.4	21.9	747.5	155.3
2nd quarter	9 001.5	5 944.6	4 951.4	809.1	4 142.2	993.2	636.4	356.9	770.6	19.2	751.5	161.7
3rd quarter	8 890.3	5 939.3	4 935.2	822.2	4 113.0	1 004.1	647.2	356.9	773.4	17.7	755.7	176.4
4th quarter	9 039.9	5 938.3	4 923.4	834.1	4 089.4	1 014.8	657.9	356.9	774.2	20.0	754.1	176.2
2002												
1st quarter	9 136.5	6 010.2	4 956.2	850.7	4 105.6	1 054.0	691.5	362.5	762.2	10.8	751.4	179.7
2nd quarter	9 222.3	6 068.3	4 980.3	859.7	4 120.6	1 088.0	723.8	364.2	769.0	10.4	758.6	184.7
3rd quarter	9 241.6	6 086.0	4 981.2	866.8	4 114.4	1 104.8	740.9	363.9	770.4	8.7	761.7	165.4
4th quarter	9 301.3	6 113.4	4 987.3	873.2	4 114.1	1 126.0	762.0	364.0	776.7	8.8	767.9	153.8
2003												
1st quarter	9 407.7	6 179.1	5 024.7	889.2	4 135.6	1 154.3	782.7	371.6	794.0	13.8	780.2	155.5
2nd quarter	9 568.8	6 245.6	5 072.0	896.4	4 175.6	1 173.7	799.0	374.6	825.7	24.1	801.6	144.1
3rd quarter	9 771.1	6 324.7	5 128.6	901.1	4 227.5	1 196.1	817.9	378.2	852.0	24.8	827.2	148.8
4th quarter	9 971.1	6 406.7	5 188.9	905.0	4 283.9	1 217.8	835.9	381.9	864.7	24.7	840.0	167.1

Table 1-11. National Income by Type of Income—Continued

(Billions of dollars, quarterly data are at seasonally adjusted annual rates.)

NIPA Tables 1.7.5, 1.12

Year and quarter	Corporate profits with IVA and CCAdj					Net interest and miscellaneous payments	Taxes on production and imports	Less: Subsidies	Business current transfer payments (net)			Current surplus of government enterprises	Addendum: Net national factor income
	Total	Taxes on corporate income	Profits after tax						Total [1]	To persons	To government		
			Total	Net dividends	Undistributed corporate profits								
1946	17.8	9.1	8.7	5.6	3.2	1.9	16.8	1.2	0.7	0.4	0.3	...	182.1
1947	23.7	11.3	12.4	6.3	6.1	2.5	18.1	0.2	0.7	0.4	0.3	...	198.0
1948	31.2	12.4	18.7	7.0	11.7	2.6	19.7	0.3	0.7	0.4	0.4	...	222.9
1949	29.1	10.2	18.9	7.2	11.6	2.9	20.9	0.3	0.7	0.4	0.4	...	216.6
1950	36.0	17.9	18.1	8.8	9.3	3.2	23.0	0.6	0.9	0.6	0.3	...	241.2
1951	41.2	22.6	18.6	8.6	10.1	3.7	24.8	0.7	1.2	0.9	0.3	...	279.1
1952	39.3	19.4	19.9	8.6	11.3	4.1	27.1	0.4	1.3	0.9	0.4	...	293.9
1953	39.7	20.3	19.4	8.9	10.6	4.7	29.1	0.1	1.2	0.8	0.4	...	309.3
1954	38.8	17.6	21.2	9.3	11.9	5.6	28.9	-0.1	1.0	0.6	0.4	...	309.4
1955	49.5	22.0	27.5	10.5	17.0	6.2	31.5	-0.2	1.4	0.9	0.4	...	339.6
1956	48.5	22.0	26.5	11.3	15.3	6.9	34.3	0.4	1.7	1.2	0.5	...	359.9
1957	48.4	21.4	26.9	11.7	15.2	8.0	36.6	0.7	1.9	1.4	0.5	...	376.4
1958	43.5	19.0	24.5	11.6	13.0	9.5	37.7	0.9	1.8	1.2	0.6	...	378.1
1959	55.7	23.7	32.0	12.6	19.4	9.6	41.1	1.1	1.8	1.3	0.4	1.0	413.1
1960	53.8	22.8	31.0	13.4	17.6	10.6	44.6	1.1	1.9	1.3	0.5	0.9	428.7
1961	54.9	22.9	32.0	13.9	18.1	12.5	47.0	2.0	2.0	1.4	0.7	0.8	443.7
1962	63.3	24.1	39.2	15.0	24.1	14.2	50.4	2.3	2.2	1.5	0.7	0.9	478.8
1963	69.0	26.4	42.6	16.2	26.4	15.2	53.4	2.2	2.7	1.9	0.8	1.4	505.3
1964	76.5	28.2	48.3	18.2	30.1	17.4	57.3	2.7	3.1	2.2	0.9	1.3	543.6
1965	87.5	31.1	56.4	20.2	36.2	19.6	60.8	3.0	3.6	2.3	1.4	1.3	590.7
1966	93.2	33.9	59.3	20.7	38.7	22.4	63.3	3.9	3.5	2.1	1.4	1.0	647.2
1967	91.3	32.9	58.4	21.5	36.9	25.5	68.0	3.8	3.8	2.3	1.5	0.9	683.0
1968	98.8	39.6	59.2	23.5	35.6	27.1	76.5	4.2	4.3	2.8	1.5	1.2	745.4
1969	95.4	40.0	55.4	24.2	31.2	32.7	84.0	4.5	4.9	3.3	1.6	1.0	804.3
1970	83.6	34.8	48.9	24.3	24.6	39.1	91.5	4.8	4.5	2.9	1.6	0.0	839.7
1971	98.0	38.2	59.9	25.0	34.8	43.9	100.6	4.7	4.3	2.7	1.6	-0.2	908.1
1972	112.1	42.3	69.7	26.8	42.9	47.9	108.1	6.6	4.9	3.1	1.8	0.5	1 004.4
1973	125.5	50.0	75.5	29.9	45.6	55.2	117.3	5.2	6.0	3.9	2.0	-0.4	1 129.7
1974	115.8	52.8	63.0	33.2	29.8	70.8	125.0	3.3	7.1	4.7	2.4	-0.9	1 214.2
1975	134.8	51.6	83.2	33.0	50.2	81.6	135.5	4.5	9.4	6.8	2.6	-3.2	1 308.8
1976	163.3	65.3	98.1	39.0	59.0	85.5	146.6	5.1	9.5	6.7	2.8	-1.8	1 462.7
1977	192.4	74.4	118.0	44.8	73.2	101.1	159.9	7.1	8.4	5.1	3.3	-2.6	1 640.4
1978	216.6	84.9	131.8	50.8	81.0	115.0	171.2	8.9	10.6	6.5	4.1	-1.9	1 856.5
1979	223.2	90.0	133.2	57.5	75.7	138.9	180.4	8.5	13.0	8.2	4.8	-2.6	2 066.8
1980	201.1	87.2	113.9	64.1	49.9	181.8	200.7	9.8	14.4	8.6	5.7	-4.8	2 238.9
1981	226.1	84.3	141.8	73.8	68.0	232.3	236.0	11.5	17.6	11.2	6.4	-4.9	2 505.2
1982	209.7	66.5	143.2	77.7	65.4	271.1	241.3	15.0	20.1	12.4	7.8	-4.0	2 621.8
1983	264.2	80.6	183.6	83.5	100.1	285.3	263.7	21.2	22.5	13.8	8.7	-3.1	2 822.4
1984	318.6	97.5	221.1	90.8	130.3	327.1	290.2	21.0	30.1	19.7	10.4	-1.9	3 184.8
1985	330.3	99.4	230.9	97.6	133.4	341.3	308.5	21.3	34.8	22.3	12.6	0.8	3 400.5
1986	319.5	109.7	209.8	106.2	103.7	366.8	323.7	24.8	36.6	22.9	13.6	1.3	3 565.6
1987	368.8	130.4	238.4	112.3	126.1	366.4	347.9	30.2	33.8	20.2	13.6	1.2	3 821.1
1988	432.6	141.6	291.0	129.9	161.1	385.3	374.9	29.4	34.0	20.6	13.4	2.5	4 167.3
1989	426.6	146.1	280.5	158.0	122.6	432.1	399.3	27.2	39.2	23.5	15.7	4.9	4 410.3
1990	437.8	145.4	292.4	169.1	123.3	442.2	425.5	26.8	39.4	22.2	17.2	1.6	4 649.4
1991	451.2	138.6	312.6	180.7	131.9	418.2	457.5	27.3	39.9	17.9	22.0	5.7	4 752.1
1992	479.3	148.7	330.6	187.9	142.7	388.5	483.8	29.9	42.4	19.6	24.5	7.6	5 008.8
1993	541.9	171.0	370.9	202.8	168.1	365.7	503.4	36.4	40.7	14.4	26.6	7.2	5 258.4
1994	600.3	193.7	406.5	234.7	171.8	366.4	545.6	32.2	43.3	15.1	28.6	8.6	5 556.9
1995	696.7	218.7	478.0	254.2	223.8	367.1	558.2	34.0	46.9	19.0	26.5	11.4	5 871.4
1996	786.2	231.7	554.5	297.6	256.9	376.2	581.1	34.3	53.1	22.9	31.1	12.7	6 227.6
1997	868.5	246.1	622.4	334.5	287.9	415.6	612.0	32.9	49.9	19.4	29.7	12.6	6 650.6
1998	801.6	248.3	553.3	351.6	201.7	487.1	639.8	35.4	64.7	26.0	35.0	10.3	7 073.3
1999	851.3	258.6	592.6	337.4	255.3	495.4	674.0	44.2	67.4	34.1	35.9	10.1	7 529.4
2000	817.9	265.2	552.7	377.9	174.8	559.0	708.9	44.3	87.1	42.4	43.7	5.3	8 038.3
2001	767.3	204.1	563.2	370.9	192.3	566.3	728.6	55.3	92.8	50.0	47.5	-1.4	8 215.0
2002	874.6	183.8	690.7	390.0	300.7	532.9	762.6	38.2	80.9	33.7	46.7	2.8	8 417.4
2003	1 021.1	234.9	786.2	395.3	390.9	543.0	798.1	46.7	77.7	28.9	46.6	9.5	8 841.1
2001													
1st quarter	778.7	222.5	556.2	379.2	177.0	565.2	725.1	52.3	98.3	44.2	46.3	1.7	8 214.7
2nd quarter	783.1	217.9	565.2	370.1	195.1	569.9	726.3	58.4	104.8	48.9	46.9	-1.1	8 229.9
3rd quarter	714.5	197.6	516.9	366.0	150.9	565.5	725.6	67.3	65.7	60.0	49.6	-2.9	8 169.1
4th quarter	793.0	178.6	614.4	368.4	246.1	564.8	737.6	43.1	102.5	46.9	47.3	-3.4	8 246.4
2002													
1st quarter	838.2	168.9	669.3	378.7	290.6	549.2	747.3	38.9	89.6	39.6	46.8	-0.9	8 339.5
2nd quarter	868.4	183.5	685.0	389.2	295.8	527.3	760.1	36.8	81.3	34.2	46.6	-0.1	8 417.7
3rd quarter	876.2	188.3	687.9	395.3	292.6	526.8	771.2	38.4	78.0	32.3	46.7	6.0	8 424.7
4th quarter	915.4	194.7	720.6	396.9	323.7	528.3	771.8	38.7	74.6	28.9	46.8	6.0	8 487.5
2003													
1st quarter	912.0	224.0	688.0	396.0	292.0	541.3	783.5	42.8	74.8	29.2	45.3	10.3	8 581.9
2nd quarter	986.2	224.6	761.7	394.7	367.0	542.8	792.9	55.2	76.9	29.0	46.2	9.8	8 744.4
3rd quarter	1 057.1	238.7	818.4	394.1	424.2	542.8	802.0	44.5	78.9	28.9	47.2	9.3	8 925.4
4th quarter	1 129.1	252.3	876.8	396.4	480.4	545.3	813.9	44.4	80.1	28.8	47.5	8.7	9 112.8

[1] Includes net transfer payments to the rest of the world, not shown separately.
... = Not available.

Table 1-12. Gross Value Added of Domestic Corporate Business

(Billions of dollars, quarterly data are at seasonally adjusted annual rates.)

NIPA Table 1.14

Year and quarter	Gross value added of corporate business, total	Consumption of fixed capital	Net value added										Gross value added of financial corporate business
			Total	Compensation of employees	Taxes on production and imports less subsidies	Net operating surplus							
						Total	Net interest and miscellaneous payments	Business current transfer payments	Corporate profits with IVA and CCAdj				
									Total	Taxes on corporate income	Profits after tax		
											Total	Net dividends	Undistributed	
1946	104.4	7.0	97.4	69.9	9.8	17.8	0.1	0.6	17.1	9.1	8.0	5.1	2.9	5.1
1947	126.0	8.7	117.3	82.1	11.5	23.6	0.3	0.6	22.7	11.3	11.4	5.6	5.8	5.3
1948	144.5	10.1	134.4	91.1	12.7	30.5	0.0	0.6	29.9	12.4	17.5	6.2	11.3	6.1
1949	141.5	10.9	130.7	88.8	13.4	28.5	0.0	0.6	27.9	10.2	17.7	6.4	11.3	6.8
1950	160.4	11.6	148.8	98.7	14.8	35.3	-0.1	0.7	34.7	17.9	16.8	7.9	9.0	7.3
1951	183.9	13.2	170.7	114.6	15.9	40.3	-0.2	1.1	39.5	22.6	16.9	7.4	9.5	8.2
1952	192.6	14.0	178.6	123.0	17.3	38.2	-0.2	1.1	37.4	19.4	18.0	7.5	10.5	9.2
1953	206.2	14.8	191.4	134.0	18.5	38.9	0.0	1.0	37.9	20.3	17.6	7.8	9.9	10.2
1954	203.6	15.7	188.0	132.2	17.9	37.8	0.2	0.8	36.9	17.6	19.3	7.9	11.4	10.8
1955	229.5	16.6	212.9	144.6	19.8	48.5	0.2	1.2	47.2	22.0	25.1	8.9	16.2	11.8
1956	245.6	18.7	226.9	158.2	21.5	47.2	0.0	1.5	45.7	22.0	23.7	9.5	14.2	12.9
1957	256.9	20.5	236.4	166.5	22.8	47.1	0.2	1.7	45.3	21.4	23.8	9.9	14.0	13.8
1958	251.8	21.6	230.2	164.0	23.1	43.0	0.6	1.5	41.0	19.0	22.0	9.8	12.2	14.7
1959	281.9	21.8	260.1	180.3	25.6	54.2	-0.2	1.5	53.0	23.7	29.2	10.7	18.5	15.9
1960	293.9	23.3	270.6	190.7	27.8	52.0	-0.2	1.6	50.6	22.8	27.9	11.4	16.4	17.5
1961	302.1	23.9	278.2	195.6	28.9	53.7	0.4	1.8	51.5	22.9	28.6	11.5	17.1	18.4
1962	329.0	24.6	304.4	211.0	31.2	62.2	0.7	2.0	59.5	24.1	35.4	12.4	23.0	19.3
1963	349.5	26.0	323.5	222.7	33.2	67.7	0.4	2.4	64.9	26.4	38.5	13.6	25.0	19.7
1964	377.7	27.2	350.4	239.2	35.6	75.7	0.8	2.9	72.0	28.2	43.8	15.0	28.9	21.6
1965	414.4	29.4	385.0	259.9	37.8	87.3	1.2	3.3	82.8	31.1	51.7	16.9	34.8	23.2
1966	454.1	32.7	421.4	288.5	38.9	94.0	2.3	3.0	88.7	33.9	54.8	17.8	37.0	25.1
1967	479.3	35.6	443.6	308.4	41.4	93.8	4.0	3.3	86.6	32.9	53.7	18.3	35.3	28.1
1968	529.1	39.1	490.1	341.3	47.8	100.9	3.9	3.8	93.2	39.6	53.5	20.2	33.4	31.3
1969	576.7	44.2	532.5	378.6	52.9	101.0	7.8	4.4	88.8	40.0	48.8	20.4	28.4	36.2
1970	597.8	48.9	548.9	400.2	57.0	91.7	11.3	3.9	76.5	34.8	41.8	20.4	21.4	39.4
1971	646.1	52.9	593.2	425.3	62.8	105.2	11.5	3.5	90.2	38.2	52.0	20.3	31.7	43.1
1972	716.8	59.1	657.7	472.5	67.3	117.9	11.3	4.0	102.6	42.3	60.2	21.9	38.3	47.3
1973	802.6	65.9	736.6	533.9	74.1	128.6	13.0	5.0	110.6	50.0	60.6	23.1	37.5	51.8
1974	869.9	78.2	791.7	587.4	78.6	125.6	20.7	6.6	98.3	52.8	45.5	23.5	22.1	60.0
1975	944.4	92.9	851.6	614.9	84.5	152.2	23.4	8.6	120.2	51.6	68.6	26.4	42.2	67.8
1976	1 062.9	102.8	960.1	695.2	91.4	173.5	18.8	7.9	146.8	65.3	81.5	30.1	51.4	73.2
1977	1 205.2	117.4	1 087.8	784.8	100.0	203.0	23.3	6.4	173.3	74.4	98.9	33.7	65.2	85.8
1978	1 376.4	136.0	1 240.4	901.9	108.7	229.8	27.5	8.5	193.8	84.9	108.9	39.6	69.3	103.6
1979	1 530.7	157.2	1 373.4	1 023.4	115.0	235.0	34.9	11.5	188.6	90.0	98.6	41.5	57.1	114.7
1980	1 666.0	180.1	1 485.8	1 122.6	128.6	234.6	55.9	13.0	165.7	87.2	78.5	47.3	31.1	128.8
1981	1 893.3	205.3	1 688.0	1 243.9	154.4	289.7	77.7	15.6	196.4	84.3	112.1	58.3	53.8	147.3
1982	1 971.4	227.5	1 743.9	1 297.5	161.3	285.2	90.0	18.1	177.1	66.5	110.6	61.3	49.2	165.2
1983	2 121.0	236.0	1 885.0	1 371.2	177.4	336.3	86.6	20.6	229.2	80.6	148.5	71.3	77.2	188.0
1984	2 378.0	252.9	2 125.1	1 520.3	195.6	409.2	98.8	28.3	282.0	97.5	184.5	78.5	106.0	210.5
1985	2 535.3	274.0	2 261.3	1 630.9	209.0	421.4	96.9	32.3	292.2	99.4	192.8	85.7	107.1	233.3
1986	2 649.8	284.4	2 365.4	1 728.6	219.6	417.2	107.0	30.1	280.0	109.7	170.4	88.3	82.1	262.3
1987	2 837.9	300.0	2 537.9	1 849.8	233.4	454.8	108.3	25.6	320.8	130.4	190.4	95.6	94.8	280.8
1988	3 071.3	318.9	2 752.3	1 988.9	252.0	511.4	108.7	27.1	375.7	141.6	234.0	98.0	136.0	299.7
1989	3 235.0	344.6	2 890.4	2 097.6	267.5	525.3	129.4	36.5	359.5	146.1	213.4	126.4	87.0	322.7
1990	3 382.0	367.5	3 014.5	2 208.1	284.5	521.9	125.3	34.9	361.7	145.4	216.3	144.1	72.2	340.5
1991	3 468.9	395.7	3 073.2	2 253.0	307.9	512.3	101.7	35.8	374.7	138.6	236.1	156.4	79.8	369.2
1992	3 643.1	408.7	3 234.4	2 377.0	325.9	531.5	79.3	46.0	406.2	148.7	257.5	159.9	97.7	407.1
1993	3 824.8	421.3	3 403.5	2 489.2	343.5	570.8	72.1	33.7	465.0	171.0	294.0	182.2	111.7	427.0
1994	4 103.4	456.6	3 646.9	2 633.0	375.6	638.3	74.9	40.2	523.2	193.7	329.5	197.4	132.0	433.9
1995	4 354.5	486.9	3 867.6	2 774.1	384.1	709.3	66.4	39.1	603.9	218.7	385.2	221.6	163.7	475.0
1996	4 626.5	513.6	4 112.9	2 916.1	397.4	799.4	70.0	45.1	684.3	231.7	452.6	257.3	195.3	517.0
1997	4 983.6	553.6	4 430.0	3 125.0	415.7	889.3	95.4	36.3	757.5	246.1	511.5	283.9	227.6	581.8
1998	5 313.6	589.0	4 724.6	3 397.6	429.8	897.2	143.3	55.2	698.7	248.3	450.4	309.2	141.2	658.6
1999	5 655.0	632.0	5 023.0	3 645.2	449.4	928.4	142.3	56.3	729.8	258.6	471.1	295.7	175.5	704.1
2000	6 051.8	690.0	5 361.8	3 957.7	477.1	926.9	178.1	76.6	672.2	265.2	407.0	348.4	58.6	779.6
2001	6 099.4	752.5	5 346.9	4 016.7	473.6	856.6	171.3	87.7	597.6	204.1	393.5	330.1	63.4	805.9
2002	6 224.0	757.8	5 466.2	4 031.3	502.4	932.5	150.0	65.7	716.8	183.8	532.9	347.5	185.5	846.3
2003	6 518.0	782.5	5 735.5	4 147.6	523.2	1 064.7	155.5	65.0	844.2	234.9	609.3	374.8	234.5	911.2
2001														
1st quarter	6 137.8	724.9	5 412.9	4 039.9	478.8	894.2	184.8	90.8	618.6	222.5	396.1	333.6	62.5	822.0
2nd quarter	6 131.5	739.1	5 392.4	4 026.7	471.4	894.3	174.8	107.5	612.1	217.9	394.2	313.2	81.1	810.2
3rd quarter	6 055.5	797.0	5 258.5	4 007.3	457.7	793.5	165.9	59.6	567.9	197.6	370.3	339.1	31.2	776.3
4th quarter	6 072.9	749.2	5 323.7	3 992.7	486.7	844.3	159.7	92.8	591.8	178.6	413.3	334.3	79.0	815.2
2002														
1st quarter	6 152.8	749.7	5 403.1	3 997.7	492.3	913.1	154.0	75.9	683.2	168.9	514.2	339.3	174.9	843.1
2nd quarter	6 224.4	754.9	5 469.5	4 035.5	501.6	932.3	149.3	65.9	717.1	183.5	533.7	353.6	180.1	848.8
3rd quarter	6 240.7	760.5	5 480.2	4 041.4	507.5	931.3	148.1	62.1	721.1	188.3	532.8	332.9	199.9	847.9
4th quarter	6 278.2	766.3	5 511.9	4 050.7	507.9	953.3	148.4	59.1	745.7	194.7	551.0	364.0	187.0	845.4
2003														
1st quarter	6 325.9	772.5	5 553.4	4 070.5	515.9	967.0	151.7	60.2	755.1	224.0	531.0	348.7	182.4	882.9
2nd quarter	6 449.9	779.0	5 670.9	4 116.6	512.1	1 042.3	153.8	63.6	824.9	224.6	600.3	417.9	182.4	902.1
3rd quarter	6 594.1	785.8	5 808.3	4 171.9	529.0	1 107.5	156.8	67.0	883.7	238.7	644.9	361.0	284.0	925.1
4th quarter	6 702.1	792.9	5 909.3	4 231.5	535.7	1 142.1	159.7	69.1	913.3	252.3	660.9	371.5	289.5	934.6

Table 1-13. Gross Value Added of Nonfinancial Domestic Corporate Business in Current and Chained Dollars

(Billions of dollars, quarterly data are at seasonally adjusted annual rates.)

NIPA Table 1.14

Year and quarter	Current-dollar gross value added													Gross value added in billions of chained (2000) dollars
	Total	Consumption of fixed capital	Net value added											
			Total	Compensation of employees	Taxes on production and imports less subsidies	Net operating surplus								
						Total	Net interest and miscellaneous payments	Business current transfer payments	Corporate profits with IVA and CCAdj					
									Total	Taxes on corporate income	Profits after tax			
											Total	Net dividends	Undistributed	
1946	99.4	6.8	92.6	66.9	9.5	16.2	0.7	0.5	15.0	8.6	6.5	4.9	1.6	532.1
1947	120.6	8.4	112.2	78.8	11.2	22.2	0.8	0.6	20.9	10.8	10.1	5.4	4.8	569.2
1948	138.4	9.8	128.6	87.5	12.4	28.7	0.8	0.6	27.3	11.7	15.6	5.9	9.7	614.9
1949	134.7	10.6	124.2	84.9	13.0	26.3	1.0	0.6	24.8	9.3	15.5	6.0	9.5	610.3
1950	153.1	11.3	141.8	94.4	14.4	33.1	0.9	0.6	31.6	16.8	14.8	7.4	7.4	689.0
1951	175.7	12.9	162.9	109.8	15.4	37.7	1.0	0.8	35.9	21.1	14.8	7.0	7.7	728.8
1952	183.4	13.6	169.7	117.8	16.8	35.2	1.2	0.9	33.1	17.7	15.5	7.1	8.4	754.0
1953	195.9	14.4	181.6	128.2	17.9	35.5	1.3	1.0	33.2	18.4	14.9	7.2	7.6	808.6
1954	192.9	15.2	177.7	125.9	17.3	34.4	1.6	0.9	31.9	15.5	16.4	7.4	9.0	798.9
1955	217.7	16.1	201.7	137.9	19.2	44.6	1.6	1.0	41.9	20.1	21.8	8.4	13.4	896.0
1956	232.5	18.1	214.6	150.8	20.8	43.0	1.8	1.1	40.2	19.9	20.2	9.0	11.2	926.0
1957	243.1	19.9	223.2	158.4	22.0	42.7	2.2	1.2	39.4	19.0	20.4	9.2	11.2	937.9
1958	237.1	21.0	216.2	155.2	22.3	38.6	2.8	1.2	34.6	16.1	18.6	9.1	9.5	900.6
1959	266.0	21.1	244.9	170.8	24.4	49.7	2.9	1.3	45.5	20.7	24.8	9.8	15.0	1 000.7
1960	276.4	22.6	253.8	180.4	26.6	46.8	3.2	1.4	42.2	19.1	23.1	10.5	12.6	1 032.4
1961	283.7	23.2	260.5	184.5	27.6	48.4	3.7	1.5	43.2	19.4	23.8	10.6	13.2	1 054.8
1962	309.8	23.9	285.9	199.3	29.9	56.8	4.3	1.7	50.8	20.6	30.2	11.6	18.6	1 143.4
1963	329.9	25.2	304.7	210.1	31.7	62.9	4.7	1.7	56.5	22.8	33.8	12.4	21.3	1 211.1
1964	356.1	26.4	329.7	225.7	33.9	70.2	5.2	2.0	63.0	23.9	39.2	14.0	25.2	1 296.2
1965	391.2	28.4	362.8	245.4	36.0	81.4	5.8	2.2	73.3	27.1	46.2	16.2	30.0	1 403.3
1966	429.0	31.5	397.4	272.9	37.0	87.6	7.0	2.7	77.9	29.5	48.4	16.8	31.6	1 502.6
1967	451.2	34.3	416.8	291.1	39.3	86.4	8.4	2.8	75.2	27.8	47.3	17.3	30.1	1 539.8
1968	497.8	37.6	460.2	321.9	45.5	92.8	9.7	3.1	80.0	33.5	46.5	19.0	27.5	1 637.5
1969	540.5	42.4	498.1	357.1	50.2	90.8	12.7	3.2	74.9	33.3	41.6	19.0	22.5	1 701.2
1970	558.3	46.8	511.5	376.5	54.2	80.7	16.6	3.3	60.9	27.3	33.6	18.3	15.3	1 683.7
1971	603.0	50.7	552.4	399.4	59.5	93.4	17.6	3.7	72.1	30.0	42.1	18.1	24.0	1 751.5
1972	669.5	56.4	613.2	443.9	63.7	105.6	18.6	4.0	83.0	33.8	49.2	19.7	29.5	1 883.8
1973	750.8	62.7	688.1	502.2	70.1	115.8	21.8	4.7	89.4	40.4	49.0	20.8	28.2	1 997.8
1974	809.8	74.1	735.7	552.2	74.4	109.1	27.5	4.1	77.5	42.8	34.7	21.5	13.1	1 964.7
1975	876.7	87.9	788.7	575.5	80.2	133.1	28.4	5.0	99.6	41.9	57.7	24.6	33.2	1 937.8
1976	989.7	97.0	892.7	651.4	86.7	154.7	26.0	7.0	121.7	53.5	68.2	27.8	40.5	2 091.6
1977	1 119.4	110.5	1 008.8	735.3	94.6	178.9	28.5	9.0	141.4	60.6	80.9	30.9	50.0	2 245.0
1978	1 272.9	127.8	1 145.1	845.3	102.7	197.0	33.4	9.5	154.1	67.6	86.6	35.9	50.6	2 390.4
1979	1 415.9	147.3	1 268.6	959.9	108.8	200.0	41.8	9.5	148.8	70.6	78.1	37.6	40.5	2 462.1
1980	1 537.1	168.2	1 368.9	1 049.8	121.5	197.6	54.2	10.2	133.2	68.2	65.0	44.7	20.4	2 423.3
1981	1 746.0	191.5	1 554.5	1 161.5	146.7	246.4	67.2	11.4	167.7	66.0	101.7	52.5	49.2	2 500.0
1982	1 806.2	211.2	1 594.9	1 203.9	152.9	238.1	77.4	8.8	151.9	48.8	103.1	54.1	49.0	2 447.0
1983	1 933.0	217.6	1 715.4	1 266.9	168.0	280.5	77.0	10.5	192.9	61.7	131.2	63.2	68.0	2 572.8
1984	2 167.5	230.7	1 936.8	1 406.1	185.0	345.7	86.0	11.7	248.0	75.9	172.0	67.2	104.8	2 810.2
1985	2 302.0	247.4	2 054.6	1 504.2	196.6	353.8	91.5	16.1	246.3	71.1	175.2	72.0	103.2	2 940.0
1986	2 387.5	255.3	2 132.2	1 583.1	204.6	344.5	95.1	27.3	222.1	76.2	145.9	72.9	73.0	3 012.6
1987	2 557.1	266.5	2 290.6	1 687.8	216.8	386.0	96.4	29.9	259.7	94.2	165.5	76.3	89.2	3 172.2
1988	2 771.6	281.6	2 490.0	1 812.8	233.8	443.4	109.8	27.4	306.2	104.0	202.3	82.2	120.1	3 348.6
1989	2 912.3	301.6	2 610.7	1 914.7	248.2	447.9	142.0	23.0	282.9	101.2	181.7	105.4	76.4	3 401.5
1990	3 041.5	319.2	2 722.3	2 012.9	263.5	445.8	146.2	25.4	274.3	98.5	175.8	118.3	57.5	3 431.3
1991	3 099.7	341.4	2 758.3	2 048.4	285.7	424.2	135.9	26.7	261.5	88.6	172.9	125.5	47.4	3 408.1
1992	3 236.0	353.6	2 882.3	2 154.1	302.5	425.7	111.3	25.2	289.2	94.4	194.8	134.1	60.7	3 499.5
1993	3 397.8	363.4	3 034.4	2 244.8	318.8	470.8	102.0	29.6	339.2	108.0	231.2	149.1	82.1	3 604.4
1994	3 669.5	391.5	3 278.0	2 381.5	349.6	546.9	101.0	30.0	415.9	132.9	283.1	157.9	125.2	3 832.0
1995	3 879.5	415.0	3 464.5	2 509.8	356.9	597.8	115.2	30.2	452.5	141.0	311.4	178.0	133.5	3 999.1
1996	4 109.5	436.5	3 673.0	2 630.8	369.1	673.1	111.9	38.0	523.2	153.1	370.1	197.5	172.6	4 222.3
1997	4 401.8	467.1	3 934.7	2 812.9	385.5	736.3	124.0	39.0	573.4	161.9	411.5	215.9	195.6	4 493.0
1998	4 655.0	493.3	4 161.7	3 045.6	398.7	717.4	143.8	35.2	538.3	158.6	379.7	241.0	138.7	4 735.5
1999	4 950.8	523.8	4 427.0	3 267.7	416.6	742.7	160.2	45.0	537.6	171.2	366.3	224.6	141.7	5 009.9
2000	5 272.2	567.8	4 704.3	3 544.4	443.4	716.5	191.7	48.4	476.4	170.2	306.2	251.3	54.8	5 272.2
2001	5 293.5	646.8	4 646.7	3 595.9	439.1	611.8	204.0	50.6	357.2	111.7	245.5	245.4	0.1	5 229.7
2002	5 377.7	655.7	4 722.0	3 601.3	465.1	655.5	181.7	55.5	418.4	89.0	329.4	254.9	74.5	5 306.6
2003	5 606.8	676.4	4 930.5	3 696.2	483.4	750.8	170.8	63.5	516.4	130.0	386.4	275.4	111.0	5 520.2
2001														
1st quarter	5 315.8	616.6	4 699.1	3 616.6	444.4	638.2	202.0	51.9	384.2	127.6	256.6	248.4	8.2	5 295.0
2nd quarter	5 321.3	635.9	4 685.4	3 604.8	437.1	643.6	207.0	56.9	379.7	126.2	253.5	233.3	20.1	5 259.0
3rd quarter	5 279.1	683.6	4 595.5	3 587.6	423.3	584.7	205.8	37.8	341.1	110.9	230.2	252.2	-22.0	5 199.6
4th quarter	5 257.7	651.1	4 606.6	3 574.5	451.5	580.6	201.3	55.5	323.7	82.0	241.7	247.8	-6.0	5 165.2
2002														
1st quarter	5 309.6	648.1	4 661.5	3 571.2	456.4	633.9	193.3	54.8	385.8	73.2	312.7	250.2	62.5	5 237.8
2nd quarter	5 375.6	653.2	4 722.5	3 605.1	464.7	652.7	183.6	54.3	414.8	86.5	328.2	259.5	68.7	5 299.7
3rd quarter	5 392.8	658.2	4 734.6	3 610.3	469.7	654.5	177.4	55.3	421.8	93.6	328.2	243.7	84.5	5 330.5
4th quarter	5 432.9	663.3	4 769.5	3 618.7	469.8	681.0	172.5	57.4	451.1	102.6	348.5	266.3	82.3	5 358.4
2003														
1st quarter	5 443.0	668.5	4 774.5	3 627.4	477.1	669.9	171.4	58.4	440.1	120.5	319.5	255.5	64.0	5 366.5
2nd quarter	5 547.8	673.7	4 874.1	3 668.5	472.6	733.0	169.6	62.3	501.1	120.5	380.6	307.0	73.6	5 463.8
3rd quarter	5 669.0	679.0	4 990.0	3 717.9	489.3	783.2	170.2	65.7	547.3	132.2	415.1	265.6	149.5	5 579.6
4th quarter	5 767.5	684.3	5 083.3	3 771.0	495.0	817.2	172.1	67.8	577.3	146.8	430.5	273.6	156.9	5 670.7

CHAPTER 1: NATIONAL INCOME AND PRODUCT AND CYCLICAL INDICATORS

NOTES AND DEFINITIONS

TABLES 1-1 THROUGH 1-7, 1-9 THROUGH 1-13, AND 19-1 THROUGH 19-5
NATIONAL INCOME AND PRODUCT

SOURCE: U.S. DEPARTMENT OF COMMERCE, BUREAU OF ECONOMIC ANALYSIS (BEA)

All data on these pages are from the national income and product accounts (NIPAs). The data are as published in the 2003 comprehensive NIPA revisions and subsequently updated and revised as of August 2004.

Definitions and notes on the data:
Basic concepts of total output and income

The NIPAs depict the U.S. economy in several different dimensions. The bedrock concept is "Gross Domestic Product" (GDP), the market value of all goods and services produced by labor and property located in the United States.

In principle at least, GDP can be measured by summing the values created by each industry in the economy. But it can be more readily measured by summing up all the final demands for the economy's output. This final demand approach also has the advantage of depicting the origins of demand for economic production, whether by consumers, businesses, or government.

Because production for the market necessarily generates incomes equal to its value, there is an income total corresponding to the production value total that can also be measured, depicting the distribution of value among labor, capital, and other income recipients.

The structure and relationships of several of these major concepts are illustrated in Table 1-9, "Relation of Gross Domestic Product, Gross and Net National Product, National Income, and Personal Income," and Table 1-10, "Gross Domestic Income by Type of Income." The definitions of these concepts are as follows.

Gross domestic product (GDP), the featured measure of the value of U.S. output, is the market value of the goods and services produced by labor and property located in the United States. Market values represent output valued at the prices paid by the final customer, and therefore include taxes on production and imports, such as customs duties and taxes on sales and property. GDP is "gross" product in the sense that capital consumption allowances (economic depreciation) have not been deducted.

GDP is primarily measured by summing the values of personal consumption expenditures, gross private domestic investment (including change in private inventories and before deduction of charges for consumption of fixed capital), net exports of goods and services, and government consumption expenditures and gross investment. GDP so measured excludes duplication involving "intermediate" purchases of goods and services, that is, goods and services purchased by industries and used in production, because the value of such goods and services is already included in the value of the final products. Production of any intermediate goods not used in production in the current period is captured in the measurement of inventory change.

In concept, GDP is equal to the sum of the economic value added by (formerly also referred to as "gross product originating in") all industries in the United States. This, in turn, also makes it the conceptual equivalent of *"Gross Domestic Income" (GDI)*, a new concept introduced in the 2003 revision, which is the sum of the incomes earned in each domestic industry, plus the taxes on production and imports and less the subsidies that account for the difference between output value and factor input value. This derivation is shown in Table 1-10. Because the incomes and taxes can be measured directly, they can be summed to a total that is equivalent to GDP in concept, but differs because of imperfections in measurement. The difference between the two is known as the *statistical discrepancy*. It is expressed as GDP minus GDI.

Gross national product (GNP) refers to all goods and services produced by labor and property supplied by U.S. residents, whether located in the United States or abroad, expressed at market prices. It is equal to gross domestic product (GDP) plus income receipts from the rest of the world less income payments to the rest of the world. *Domestic* production and income refer to the *location* of the factors of production, with only factors located in the United States included; *national* production and income refer to the *ownership* of the factors of production, with only factors owned by United States residents included.

Before the comprehensive NIPA revisions made in 1991, GNP was the commonly used measure of U.S. production (the terminology survives in popular cultural references such as the name of a musical group and the "Gross National Parade"). In the earlier postwar years when international income flows were much smaller, the difference between GNP and GDP was inconsequential. But GDP is clearly preferable where it is to be compared with indicators such as employment, hours worked, and capital utilized—for example, in the calculation of labor and capital productivity—because it is confined to production taking place within the borders of the United States. It is also the measure used by almost all other countries and thus facilitates international comparisons.

The income-side aggregate corresponding to GNP is *gross national income*, shown as an addendum to Table 1-9. It consists of gross domestic income plus income receipts from the rest of the world less income payments to the rest of the world. It is used as the denominator for a national saving/income ratio, presented in Chapter 5. National income is the preferred measure for calculating and comparing saving, since it is the income aggregate from which that saving arises. As with GDP and gross domestic income, the statistical discrepancy indicates the difference between the product-side and income-side measurement of the same concept.

Net national product is the market value, net of depreciation, of goods and services attributable to the labor and property supplied by U.S. residents and is equal to GNP less the consumption of fixed capital. The measure of fixed capital consumption used relates only to fixed capital located in the United States. Investment in that capital is measured by private fixed investment and government gross investment.

National income has been redefined and now includes all net incomes (net of the consumption of fixed capital) earned in production. It now includes not only "factor incomes"—net incomes received by labor and capital as a result of their participation in the production process—but also "nonfactor charges"—taxes on production and imports, business transfer payments, and the current surplus of government enterprises, less subsidies. This change has been made to conform with the international guidelines for national accounts, *System of National Accounts 1993*. According to *SNA 1993*, these charges cannot be eliminated from the input and output prices.

Since national income now includes the nonfactor charges, it is conceptually equivalent to net national product and differs only by the amount of the statistical discrepancy.

The concept formerly known as "national income" is still included in the accounts, as an addendum item called "Net national factor income," which is shown in Table 1-11 and used as the denominator in the *Business Statistics* income shares graph. *Net national factor income* consists of compensation of employees; proprietors' income with inventory valuation and capital consumption adjustments; rental income of persons with capital consumption adjustment; corporate profits with inventory valuation and capital consumption adjustments; and net interest.

By definition, national income and its components exclude all income from capital gains, which has no counterpart on the production side of the accounts. This exclusion is accomplished (in part) by means of the inventory valuation and capital consumption adjustments, which will be described below in the definitions of the components of product and income.

Definitions and notes on the data: Imputation

The term *imputation* will appear from time to time in the definitions of product and income components below. Imputed values are values estimated by BEA statisticians for certain important product and income components that are not explicitly valued in the source data. Imputed values appear on both the product and income side of the accounts; they add equal amounts to income and spending, so that no imputed saving is created.

One important example is the imputed rent on owner-occupied housing. The building of such housing is counted as investment, yet in the monetary accounts of the household sector there is no income from that investment. In the NIPAs, the rent that each such house would earn if rented is estimated and added both to national and personal income, as part of rental payments, and to personal consumption expenditures, as part of expenditures on housing services.

Another important example is imputed interest. An individual keeps a monetary balance in a bank or other financial institution; he or she receives no interest, or below-market interest, but receives the institution's services, such as clearing checks and otherwise facilitating payments, with little or no charge. Where is the product generated by the institution's workers and capital? In the NIPAs, the depositor is imputed a market-rate-based interest return on his or her balance, which is then paid to the institution as an imputed service charge and therefore included in the value of the institution's output.

Definitions and notes on the data: Components of product

Personal consumption expenditures (PCE) is goods and services purchased by persons residing in the United States. PCE consists mainly of purchases of new goods and services by individuals from business. It includes purchases that are financed by insurance—for example, by medical insurance. In addition, PCE includes purchases of new goods and services by nonprofit institutions, net purchases of used goods ("net" here meaning purchases of used goods from business less sales of used goods to business) by individuals and nonprofit institutions, and purchases abroad of goods and services by U.S. residents traveling or working in foreign countries. PCE also includes purchases for certain goods and services provided by government agencies. (See Notes and Definitions for Tables 4-1 through 4-5 for additional information.) New annual accounts separate household and nonprofit institution expenditures and incomes; these are presented in the article at the beginning of this volume.

Gross private domestic investment consists of private fixed investment and change in private inventories.

Private fixed investment consists of both nonresidential and residential fixed investment. The term "residential" refers to the construction and equipping of living quarters for permanent occupancy; as will be seen below, hotels and motels are included in *nonresidential* fixed investment. Private fixed investment consists of purchases of fixed assets, which are commodities that will be used in a production process for more than one year, including replacements and additions to the capital stock, and it is measured "gross," before a deduction for consumption of existing fixed capital. It covers all investment by private businesses and nonprofit institutions in the United States, regardless of whether the investment is owned by U.S. residents. The residential component includes investment in owner-occupied housing; the homeowner is treated equivalently to a business in these investment accounts. (However, when GDP by sector is calculated, owner-occupied housing is no longer included in the business sector but is allocated to the households and institutions sector.) Private fixed investment does not include purchases of the same types of equipment and structures by government agencies, which are included in government gross investment, nor does it include investment by U.S. residents in other countries.

Nonresidential fixed investment is the total of nonresidential structures and nonresidential equipment and software.

Nonresidential structures consists of new construction, brokers' commissions on sales of structures, and net purchases of used structures by private business and by nonprofit institutions from government agencies (that is, purchases of used structures from government minus sales of used structures to government). New construction also includes hotels and motels, as well as mining exploration, shafts, and wells.

Nonresidential equipment and software consists of private business purchases, on capital account, of new machinery, equipment, and vehicles; purchases and in-house production of software; dealers' margins on sales of used equipment; and net purchases of used equipment from government agencies, persons, and the rest of the world, that is, purchases of such equipment minus sales of such equipment. It does not, however, include the estimated personal-use portion of equipment purchased for both business and personal use, which is included in PCE.

Residential private fixed investment consists of both residential structures and residential producers' durable equipment, that is, equipment such as appliances owned by landlords and rented to tenants. Investment in structures consists of new units, improvements to existing units, manufactured homes, brokers' commissions on the sale of residential property, and net purchases of used residential structures from government agencies—that is, purchases of such structures from government minus sales of such structures to government. As noted above, it includes investment in owner-occupied housing.

Change in private inventories is the change in the physical volume of inventories held by businesses, valued at the average price of the period. It differs from the change in the book value of inventories reported by most businesses; an *inventory valuation adjustment (IVA)* converts book value change using historical cost valuations to the change in physical volume, valued at average replacement cost.

Net exports of goods and services is *exports of goods and services* less *imports of goods and services*. It does not include income payments or receipts or transfer payments to and from the rest of the world.

Government consumption expenditures is the estimated value of the services produced by governments (federal, state, and local) for current consumption. Since these are generally not sold, there is no market valuation, and they are priced at the cost of inputs. The input costs consist of the compensation of general government employees; the estimated consumption of general government fixed capital including software (CFC, or economic depreciation); and the cost of goods and services purchased by government, less the value of sales to other sectors. The value of investment in equipment and structures produced by government workers and capital is also subtracted, and included in government investment instead. Government sales to other sectors consist primarily of tuition payments for higher education and charges for medical care.

This definition of government consumption expenditures differs in concept, but not in the amount contributed to GDP, from the treatment before the 2003 revision. In the new definition, goods and services purchased by government are considered to be intermediate output, whereas in the previous definition, they were considered as final sales. But since their value is added to the other components to yield total government consumption expenditures, the dollar total contributed to GDP is the same. The only practical difference is that the goods purchased disappear from the goods account and appear in the services account instead. In the industry sector accounts, the value added by government is also not changed: it continues to be measured as the sum of compensation and CFC, or equivalently as gross government output less the value of goods and services purchased. The new definition increases conformity with *SNA 1993*.

Gross government investment consists of general government and government enterprise expenditures for fixed assets (structures and equipment and software). Government inventory investment is included in government consumption expenditures.

Definitions and notes on the data: Real values, quantity and price indexes

Real, or chained (2000) dollar, estimates are estimates from which the effect of price change has been removed. Prior to the 1996 comprehensive revision, constant-dollar measures were obtained by combining real output measures for different goods and services using the relative prices of a single year as weights for the entire time span of the series. In the recent environment of rapid technological change, which has caused the prices of computers and electronic components to decline dramatically relative to other prices, this method distorted the measurement of economic growth and caused excessive revisions of growth rates at each benchmark revision. The current, chained-dollar measure changes the relative price weights each year as relative prices shift over time. As a result, historical growth rates are not revised to reflect recent changes in relative prices.

Chained-dollar estimates, although expressed for continuity's sake as if they had occurred according to the prices of a single year (currently 2000), are usually not additive; that is, because of the changes in price weights each year, the 2000-dollar components in any given table usually do not add to the 2000-dollar total. This difference for the major components of GDP is calculated by BEA and shown in Table 1-2. In time periods close to the base year, the difference between the sum of components and the total is usually quite small. Over longer periods, the differences become much larger. For this reason, the BEA no longer publishes chained-dollar estimates prior to 1990, except for selected aggregate series. For the more detailed components, historical trends and fluctuations in real volumes are represented by *chain-type quantity indexes*, which are presented in Tables 1-4, 4-4, 5-4, 5-6, and 19-2.

Chain-weighting leads to complexity in estimating the contribution of economic sectors to an overall change in output: for example, answering questions such as "How much is the rise in defense spending contributing to GDP growth?" The Bureau of Economic Analysis is now calculating and publishing such estimates, and *Business Statistics* reproduces these calculations in new Tables 1-3 and 19-3. To calculate contributions to growth for longer periods than those published by BEA, see Landefeld and Parker, "BEA's Chain Indexes, Time Series, and Measures of Long-Term Economic Growth," *Survey of Current Business*, May 1997, and "Preview of the Comprehensive Revision of the National Income and Product Accounts: BEA's New Featured Measures of Output and Prices," *Survey of Current Business*, July 1995.

GDP price indexes measure price changes between any two adjacent years (or quarters) for a fixed "market basket" of goods and services—the average quantities in those two years (or quarters). The annual measures are chained together to form an index with prices in 2000 set to equal 100. This avoids the substitution bias that arises when the quantity weights are held constant while the composition of output is changing; generally, this bias leads to an overstatement of price increase.

The use of the chain-type formula guarantees that a GDP price index change will differ only trivially from the change in the implicit deflator (ratio of current-dollar to real value). Therefore, *Business Statistics* is no longer publishing a separate table of implicit deflators.

Definitions and notes on the data: Aggregates of sales and purchases

Final sales of domestic product is GDP minus change in private inventories. Thus, it is the sum of personal consumption expenditures, gross private domestic fixed investment, government consumption expenditures and gross investment, and net exports of goods and services.

Gross domestic purchases is the market value of goods and services purchased by U.S. residents, regardless of where those goods and services were produced. It is GDP minus net exports (that is, minus exports plus imports) of goods and services; equivalently, it is the sum of personal consumption expenditures, gross private domestic investment, and government consumption expenditures and gross investment. The price index for gross domestic purchases is therefore a measure of price change for goods and services purchased by (rather than produced by) U.S. residents.

Final sales to domestic purchasers is gross domestic purchases minus change in private inventories.

Definitions and notes on the data: Components of income

There are now two different presentations of aggregate income for the United States: *Gross domestic income* (Table 1-10) and *National income* (Table 1-11). As noted above, "domestic income" refers to income generated from production within the United States, while "national income" refers to income received by residents of the United States. This means that some of the income components are different between the two tables. Domestic income payments include payments to the rest of the world from domestic industries, while national income payments exclude payments to the rest of the world but include payments received by U.S. residents from the rest of the world. These differences are seen in employee compensation, interest, and corporate profits. Taxes on production, imports, and corporate profits, business transfer payments, subsidies, proprietors' income, rental income, and the current surplus of government enterprises are the same in both accounts.

A third income aggregate is the well-known *personal income* account, whose derivation from national income is shown in Table 1-9. This will be discussed and defined in more detail in Chapter 4.

Compensation of employees is the income accruing to employees as remuneration for their work. It is the sum of wage and salary accruals and supplements to wages and salaries. In the domestic income account it is called "Compensation of employees, paid" and refers to all payments generated by domestic production including those to workers residing in the "rest of the world." In the national and personal income accounts it is a different amount called "Compensation of employees, received" (that is, received by U.S. residents) including from the rest of the world.

Wage and salary accruals consists of the monetary remuneration of employees, including the compensation of corporate officers; corporate directors' fees paid to directors who are also employees of the corporation; commissions, tips, and bonuses; voluntary employee contributions to certain deferred compensation plans, such as 401(k) plans; and receipts in kind that represent income. As of the 2003 revision, it now also includes judicial fees to jurors and witnesses, compensation of prison inmates, and marriage fees to justices of the peace, which were formerly included in "other labor income."

In concept, wage and salary accruals includes the value of the exercise by employees of "nonqualified stock options," in which an employee is allowed to buy stock for less than its current market price. (Actual measurement of these values involves a number of problems, particularly in the short run. Such stock options are not included in the Bureau of Labor Statistics wage data, which are the main source for current extrapolation of wages and salaries, and are not consistently reported in corporate financial statements. They are, however, generally included in the unemployment insurance wage data that are used to correct the preliminary wage and salary estimates.) Another form of stock option, the "incentive stock option," leads to a capital gain only and is not included in the definition of wages and salaries.

Wage and salary accruals include retroactive wage payments in the period for which earned, not when paid. In the NIPAs, wages accrued is the appropriate measure for both domestic and national income, and wages disbursed is the appropriate measure for personal income, since the latter concept focuses on what individuals receive. The difference, *wage accruals less disbursements*, is shown in Table 1-7. In practice, it is usually estimated as zero, and only appears in the case of a large and unusual payment.

Supplements to wages and salaries consists of *employer contributions for employee pension and insurance funds* and *employer contributions for government social insurance*.

Employer contributions for employee pension and insurance funds consists of employer payments (including payments in kind) to private pension and profit-sharing plans; private group health and life insurance plans; privately administered workers' compensation plans; government employee retirement plans; and supplemental unemployment benefit plans. This includes the major part of the former category "other labor income." The remainder of "other labor income" has been reclassified as wages and salaries, as noted above.

Employer contributions for government social insurance consists of employer payments under the following federal, state, and local government programs: Old-age, survivors, and disability insurance (Social Security); hospital insurance (Medicare); unemployment insurance; railroad retirement; pension benefit guaranty; veterans life insurance; publicly administered workers' compensation; military medical insurance; and temporary disability insurance.

Taxes on production and imports is included in the gross domestic income account to make it comparable in concept to Gross Domestic Product. It consists of federal excise taxes and customs duties and of state and local sales taxes, property taxes (including residential real estate taxes), motor vehicle licenses, severance taxes, other taxes, and special assessments. It is equal to the former "indirect business taxes and nontax liabilities" less most of the nontax liabilities, which have now been reclassified as business transfer payments.

Subsidies (payments by government to business other than purchases of goods and services) are now presented separately from the current surplus of government enterprises, which is presented as a component of net operating surplus. However, for the years prior to 1959, subsidies will continue to be presented net of the current surplus of government enterprises, because detailed data to separate the series for this period are not available.

Net operating surplus is a new aggregate—a grouping of the business income components of the gross domestic income account. It is a profits-like measure that shows business income after subtracting the costs of compensation of employees, taxes on production and imports (less subsidies), and consumption of fixed capital (CFC) from gross product, but before subtracting financing costs (such as net interest) and business transfer payments. Net operating surplus consists of the net operating surplus of private enterprises and the current surplus of government enterprises.

Net interest and miscellaneous payments, domestic industries consists of interest paid by domestic private enterprises and of rents and royalties paid by private enterprises to government, less interest received by domestic private enterprises. Interest received does not include that received by noninsured pension plans, which are recorded as being directly received by persons in personal income. Both interest categories include both monetary and imputed interest. In the *national* account, interest paid to the rest of the world is subtracted and interest received from the rest of the world is added. Interest payments on mortgage and home improvement loans and on home equity loans are included as net interest in the private enterprises account.

It should be noted that net interest does not include interest paid by federal, state, or local governments; in fact, government interest does not enter into the national and domestic income accounts, though it does appear as a component of personal income. The reason for this distinction is that interest paid by *business* is one of the income counterparts of the production side of the account: the value of business production (as measured by its output of goods and services) includes the value added by business capital, and interest is part of the total return to business capital.

There is no product flow, however, that is a counterpart to the payment of interest by *government*. The output of government does not have a market value. For purposes of GDP measurement, its contribution to GDP is estimated by BEA as the sum of compensation of employees, purchases of goods and services, and consumption of government fixed capital (see above, and also the Notes and Definitions to Chapter 6). This implies a conservative estimate that the net return to government capital is zero, which generates no income corresponding to the interest payment.

Of course, most federal government debt was not incurred to finance investment anyway, but rather to finance wars, avoid tax increases and spending cuts during recessions, or stimulate the economy.

Business current transfer payments, net consists of payments to persons, to government, and to the rest of the world by private business for which no current services are performed. Net insurance settlements—actual insured losses (or claims payable) less a normal level of losses—are treated as transfer payments. Payments to government consist of federal deposit insurance premiums, fines, regulatory and inspection fees, tobacco settlements, and other miscellaneous payments previously classified as "nontaxes." Taxes paid by domestic corporations to foreign governments, formerly classified in transfer payments, are now counted as taxes on corporate income.

In the NIPAs, capital income other than interest—corporate profits, proprietors' income, and rental income—is converted from the basis usually shown in the books of business and reported to the Internal Revenue Service to a basis that more closely represents income from current production. In the source data, depreciation of structures and equipment will probably reflect a historical cost basis and a possibly arbitrary service life allowed by law to be used for tax purposes. These values are adjusted by BEA to reflect the average actual life of the capital good and the cost of replacing it in the current period's prices. This conversion is done for all three forms of capital income. In addition, the measurement of income from current production is defined to exclude any element of capital gains, so corporate and proprietors' income also require an adjustment for inventory valuation to exclude any profits or losses that might appear in the books if the cost of inventory acquisition is not valued in the current period's prices. These two adjustments are called the *capital consumption adjustment (CCAdj)* and the *inventory valuation adjustment (IVA)*. They will be described in more detail below.

Proprietors' income with inventory valuation and capital consumption adjustments is the current-production income (including income in kind) of sole proprietorships and partnerships and of tax-exempt cooperatives. The imputed net rental income of owner-occupants of farm dwellings is included, but the imputed net rental income of owner-occupants of nonfarm dwellings is included in rental income of persons. Fees paid to outside directors of corporations are included. Proprietors' income excludes dividends and monetary interest received by nonfinancial business and rental incomes received by persons not primarily engaged in the real estate business; these incomes are included in dividends, net interest, and rental income of persons.

Rental income of persons with capital consumption adjustment is the net current-production income of persons from the rental of real property (except for the income of persons primarily engaged in the real estate business); the imputed net rental income of owner-occupants of nonfarm dwellings; and the royalties received by persons from patents, copyrights, and rights to natural resources. Consistent with the treatment of investment in owner-occupied housing as business investment, the homeowner is considered to receive as income the value of occupying the house and then to pay it to himself/herself as a component of consumer expenditures on services.

Corporate profits with inventory valuation and capital consumption adjustments (often referred to as "economic profits") is the current-production income, net of economic depreciation, of organizations treated as corporations in the NIPAs. These organizations consist of all entities required to file federal corporate tax returns, including mutual financial institutions and cooperatives subject to federal income tax; private noninsured pension funds; nonprofit institutions that primarily serve business; Federal Reserve Banks, which accrue the income stemming from the conduct of monetary policy; and federally sponsored credit agencies. With several differences, this income is measured as receipts less expenses as defined in federal tax law. Among these differences: receipts exclude capital gains and dividends received; expenses exclude depletion and capital losses and losses resulting from bad debts; inventory withdrawals are valued at replacement cost; and depreciation is on a consistent accounting basis and is valued at replacement cost. Because *national* income is defined as the income of U.S. residents, its profits component includes income earned abroad by U.S. corporations and excludes income earned in the United States by the rest of the world.

Taxes on corporate income consists of taxes on corporate income paid to government and to the rest of the world.

Taxes on corporate income paid to government (formerly "profits tax liability") is the sum of federal, state, and local income taxes on all income subject to taxes; this income includes capital gains and other income excluded from profits before tax. The taxes are measured on an accrual basis, net of applicable tax credits.

Taxes on corporate income paid to the rest of the world consists of nonresident taxes—that is, taxes paid by domestic corporations to foreign governments. These taxes were formerly classified as business transfer payments to the rest of the world.

Profits after tax is total corporate profits with IVA and CCAdj less taxes on corporate income. It consists of dividends and undistributed corporate profits.

Dividends is payments in cash or other assets, excluding the corporations' own stock, that are made by corporations to stockholders. In the domestic account, these are payments by domestic industries to stockholders in the United States and abroad; in the national account, these are all dividends received by U.S. residents. The payments are measured net of dividends received by U.S. corporations. Dividends paid to state and local government social insurance funds and general government are included.

Undistributed profits is corporate profits after tax with IVA and CCAdj less dividends.

Inventory valuation adjustment (IVA) for corporations is the difference between the cost of inventory withdrawals as valued in the source data used to determine profits before tax and the cost of withdrawals valued at replacement cost. In the NIPAs, inventory profits or losses are shown as adjustments to business income (corporate profits and nonfarm proprietors' income); they are shown as the IVA with the sign reversed. No adjustment is needed to farm proprietors' income because farm inventories are measured on a current-market-cost basis.

Consumption of fixed capital is a charge for the using up of private and government fixed capital located in the United States. It is based not on the depreciation schedules allowed in tax law but on studies of prices of used equipment and structures in resale markets. For general government and for nonprofit institutions that primarily serve individuals, it is recorded in government consumption expenditures and in personal consumption expenditures, respectively, and is also considered to be the value of the current services of the fixed capital assets owned and used by these entities.

Private capital consumption allowances consists of tax-return-based depreciation charges for corporations and nonfarm proprietorships and of historical-cost depreciation (calculated by BEA using a geometric pattern of price declines) for farm proprietorships, rental income of persons, and nonprofit institutions.

The private capital consumption adjustment (CCAdj) is the difference between private capital consumption allowances and private consumption of fixed capital, and therefore reflects the net effect of the two adjustments made to reported nonfarm business profits that convert historical to replacement costs and incorporate actual, rather than tax-based, service lives.

**Definitions and notes on the data:
Gross value added of Domestic Corporate Business**

Gross value added is the term now used for what was formerly called "Gross domestic product originating." It represents that share of the GDP produced in the specified sector or industry. Tables 1-12 and 1-13 show the current-dollar value of gross value added for all domestic corporate business and its financial and nonfinancial components. For the total and for nonfinancial corporations, consumption of fixed capital and net value added are shown as well, as is the allocation of net value added among employee compensation, taxes and transfer payments, and capital income. Constant-dollar values are also shown for nonfinancial corporations.

These data for nonfinancial corporations are often considered to be somewhat sturdier than data for the other sectors of the economy, since they exclude sectors whose outputs are difficult to evaluate—households, institutions, general government, and financial business—as well as excluding all noncorporate business.

**Definitions and notes on the data:
Per capita product and income estimates**

In Table 1-7, annual and quarterly measures of product, income, and consumption spending are expressed in per capita terms—the aggregate dollar amount divided by the U.S. population. Population data from 1991 forward reflect the results of Census 2000.

National per capita totals as shown in Table 1-17 are based on definitions of income and population that differ slightly from the sum of the states shown in Table 21-2. See the Notes and Definitions to Chapter 21 for explanation.

Revisions

NIPA data normally undergo revision at the end of July each year. Typically these annual revisions cover annual and quarterly data for the previous three years, but may also include more limited revisions to data for earlier years. Approximately once every five years the NIPA data undergo "benchmark" revision, at which times definitional or other comprehensive changes may affect data back to 1929—the earliest year for which official national accounts data are available. Shown here are the results of the latest comprehensive revision of the NIPAs, which was released in 2003.

In mid-2002, BEA inaugurated a new revision schedule for wages and salaries and related income-side components of the NIPAs. When "final" estimates of GDP are released each quarter, in June, September, December, and March following the end of that quarter, wages and salaries and related data will be revised for not only the "GDP" quarter but the previous quarter as well. Since these only affect income-side components, GDP itself will not be revised for that previous quarter. The purpose of this schedule change is to achieve a more timely incorporation of BLS quarterly tabulations of employees covered by state unemployment insurance. Previously, revisions based on these data were not incorporated until July of the following year. The same revision schedule will also be used in the monthly estimates of personal income.

Data availability

Annual data are available beginning with 1929; quarterly data begin with 1946 for current-dollar values and 1947 for quantity and price measures such as real GDP and the GDP price index. Not all data are available for all time periods.

New data normally are released toward the end of each month. The first estimates for each calendar quarter are released in the month after the quarter's end. Revisions for the most recent quarter are released in the second and third months after the quarter's end. As described above, wage and salary and related income-side components will be revised for previous quarters as well.

The most recent data are published each month in the *Survey of Current Business*; current and historical data may be obtained from the BEA Internet site at <http://www.bea.gov> and the STAT-USA subscription Internet site at <http://www.stat-usa.gov>.

References

Articles describing and presenting the NIPAs are found in the *Survey of Current Business*, available by mail subscription and on the BEA Web site.

The 2003 revision is presented and described in several articles in the *Survey*: "Improved Estimates of the National Income and Product Accounts for 1929–2002: Results of the Comprehensive Revision," February 2004; "Preview of the 2003 Comprehensive Revision of the National Income and Product Accounts: Statistical Changes," September 2003; "Preview of the 2003 Comprehensive Revision of the National Income and Product Accounts: New and Redesigned Tables," August 2003; "Preview of the 2003 Comprehensive Revision of the National Income and Product Accounts: Changes in Definitions and Classifications," June 2003; "Income and Outlays of Households and of Nonprofit Institutions Serving Households," April 2003; "Preview of Revised NIPA Estimates for 1997: Effects of Incorporating the 1997 Benchmark I-O Accounts and Proposed Definitional and Statistical Changes," January 2003; "Note on the Upcoming Comprehensive Revision of the National Income and Product Accounts," November 2002; and "Selected Issues in the Measurement of U.S. International Services," June 2002.

The previous comprehensive revision was presented in "Improved Estimates of the National Income and Product Accounts for 1929–99: Results of the Comprehensive Revision," April 2000.

General reference articles on NIPA concepts and methods in the *Survey of Current Business* are "Updated Summary NIPA Methodologies" (October 2002) and "A Guide to the NIPA's" (March 1998).

The treatment of employee stock options is discussed in Carol Moylan, "Treatment of Employee Stock Options in the U.S. National Economic Accounts," available on the BEA Web site.

TABLES 1-8 AND 20-7
COMPOSITE INDEXES OF ECONOMIC ACTIVITY

Source: The Conference Board

The composite indexes of leading, coincident, and lagging indicators are intended to help predict and identify peaks and troughs in the business cycle. They are calculated from sets of component series selected for their utility as indicators of stages of the business cycle. The component series originate from a variety of sources, as indicated below. Several component series that are not published elsewhere in this volume appear on the page with the composites. For the other components, references to the appropriate tables in *Business Statistics* are given below.

The classification of indicators into leading, coincident, and lagging series grows out of an approach to the study of economic fluctuations pioneered by Wesley C. Mitchell and Arthur F. Burns early in the twentieth century, and carried on by other researchers affiliated with the National Bureau of Economic Research (NBER). It was observed that indicators of business activity tended to move up and down over periods that were longer than a year and therefore were not accounted for by seasonal variation. Although these periods of expansion and contraction were not uniform in length, their recurrent nature has caused them to be called "business cycles."

Furthermore, researchers found that some indicators that described the general state of business activity, such as different measures of production and income, tended to move together, with their peaks occurring within a few months of each other and their low points, or troughs, also tending to occur at about the same time. These are the *coincident indicators*. Other indicators also moved cyclically, but their peaks and troughs came noticeably before the peaks and troughs in the coincident indicators; these are the *leading indicators*, which of course are of great interest to anyone with a stake in the future performance of the economy. Finally, still other indicators had peaks and troughs noticeably later than those in the coincident indicators; these are the *lagging indicators*. Lagging indicators can be valuable in observing whether cyclical imbalances have been corrected and preconditions exist for a new cycle phase.

The dates of business cycles are currently established by the Business Cycle Dating Committee of the NBER; this committee was formed in 1978. (The first NBER-established business cycle dates were published in 1929.) Business cycle dates are based on monthly data, and the identification of a recession does not always follow the common definition of recession as two consecutive quarters of decline in real GDP. In all, the NBER has identified 31 cycles since December 1854.

The monthly and quarterly dates of the cycles from the trough marking the end of the Great Depression to the latest announced trough are shown in the table below. Quarterly turning points are identified by Roman numerals. NBER considers that the trough month is both the end of the decline and the beginning of the recovery, based on the concept that the actual turning point was some particular day within that month; thus, the latest recession ended in November 2001 and the recovery also began in November 2001. Similarly, the peak month of March 2001 was both the last month of expansion and the first month of recession.

BUSINESS CYCLE REFERENCE DATES
1933–2001

TROUGH	PEAK
March 1933 (I)	May 1937 (II)
June 1938 (II)	February 1945 (I)
October 1945 (IV)	November 1948 (IV)
October 1949 (IV)	July 1953 (II)
May 1954 (II)	August 1957 (III)
April 1958 (II)	April 1960 (II)
February 1961 (I)	December 1969 (IV)
November 1970 (IV)	November 1973 (IV)
March 1975 (I)	January 1980 (I)
July 1980 (III)	July 1981 (III)
November 1982 (IV)	July 1990 (III)
March 1991 (I)	March 2001 (I)
November 2001 (IV)	

For additional information on NBER and its business cycle studies, see the NBER Internet site at <http://www.nber.org/cycles>.

The composite indexes were originally compiled and published by the Commerce Department, Bureau of Economic Analysis. In 1995, responsibility for compilation and publication was transferred to The Conference Board, a not-for-profit business research organization.

It is frequently said that the leading indicator index is designed to predict turning points in business activity six months in advance. However, the actual leads over the last six business cycles have varied between three and 15 months, and the index has sometimes turned down without a corresponding recession, so it is important not to rely mechanically on these composites.

Index components

The *index of leading economic indicators* consists of the following 10 components, with monthly data seasonally adjusted except as noted:

Average weekly hours are average hours worked per week by production workers in manufacturing. Source: Bureau of Labor Statistics. (Table 10-7)

Initial claims, unemployment insurance are average weekly claims for unemployment insurance under state programs. For inclusion in the leading index, the signs of the month-to-month changes are reversed, because claims increase when employment conditions worsen. Source: U.S. Department of Labor, Employment and Training Administration. (Table 10-4)

Manufacturers' new orders, consumer goods and materials are new orders, net of order cancellations, in billions of chained 1996 dollars. Source: Bureau of the Census, with inflation adjustment by The Conference Board. (See Table 17-6 for current-dollar data.)

Vendor performance, slower deliveries diffusion index tracks the relative speed with which goods-producing companies receive deliveries from their suppliers. An increase in this series indicates a slowdown in deliveries and is generally caused by increased demand for manufacturing materials. The survey asks purchasing managers if their suppliers' deliveries were obtained faster, slower, or the same as the previous month's deliveries. The index records the percentage reporting slower deliveries plus one-half of the percentage reporting no change in delivery speed. Source: National Association of Purchasing Management.

Manufacturers' new orders, nondefense capital goods are in billions of chained 1996 dollars. Source: Bureau of the Census, with inflation adjustment by The Conference Board. (See Table 17-6 for new orders for nondefense capital goods in current dollars.)

Building permits, new private housing units is the number of new private housing units authorized by local building permits. Source: Bureau of the Census. (Table 17-3)

Stock prices: 500 common stocks is an index based on 1941–1943 = 10. Source: Standard and Poor's Corporation. (Table 12-10)

Money supply (M2) is in billions of chained 1996 dollars. Source: Federal Reserve Board of Governors, with inflation adjustment by The Conference Board. (See Table 12-1 for the M2 money supply in current dollars.)

Interest rate spread is equal to the rate on 10-year treasury bonds less the rate on federal funds. The interest rate series are not seasonally adjusted. Source: Federal Reserve Board of Governors. (Table 12-9)

Index of consumer expectations is based on the first quarter of 1966 = 100. The monthly data are not seasonally adjusted. Source: University of Michigan, Survey Research Center. This is a copyrighted series used by permission; it may not be reproduced without written permission from the source.

The *index of coincident economic indicators* consists of the following four components, with monthly data seasonally adjusted:

Employees on nonagricultural payrolls are total wage and salary employees, in thousands. Source: Bureau of Labor Statistics. (Table 10-5)

Personal income less transfer payments is in billions of chained 1996 dollars (seasonally adjusted annual rate). Source: Bureau of Economic Analysis, with inflation adjustment by The Conference Board, using the implicit deflator for personal consumption expenditures (PCE). (See Table 4-1 for total personal income and transfer payments in current dollars, and Table 1-5 for the price index for PCE, which is usually the same as the implicit deflator.)

Index of industrial production is an index of the output of the mining, manufacturing, and utility sectors of the U.S. economy. The index is based on 1992 = 100. Source: Federal Reserve Board of Governors. (Table 2-1)

Manufacturing and trade sales are in millions of chained 1996 dollars. Source: Bureau of Economic Analysis. (Table 5-9)

The *index of lagging economic indicators* consists of the following seven components, with monthly data seasonally adjusted except as noted.

Average duration of unemployment is in weeks. As with initial claims, the signs of the month-to-month changes are reversed. Source: Bureau of Labor Statistics. (Table 10-2)

Ratio: manufacturing and trade inventories to sales is calculated from sales and inventories in chained 1996 dollars. Source: Bureau of Economic Analysis. (Table 5-9)

Manufacturing labor cost per unit of output is the percent change over a 6-month span in this monthly index, which is constructed by The Conference Board. (For the Bureau of Labor Statistics quarterly index of manufacturing unit labor cost, see Table 9-3.)

Average prime interest rate is an average percentage rate per annum used by banks to price short-term business loans; not seasonally adjusted. Source: Federal Reserve Board of Governors. (Table 12-9)

Commercial and industrial loans outstanding is in billions of chained 1996 dollars. Sources: Federal Reserve Board of Governors, with inflation adjustment by The Conference Board. (See Table 12-4 for current-dollar data.)

Consumer credit outstanding is expressed as a percent of personal income. Sources: Bureau of Economic Analysis (Table 4-1) and Federal Reserve Board of Governors. (Table 12-8)

Consumer price index for services is the annual rate of change in the services component of the Consumer Price Index. Source: Bureau of Labor Statistics. (Table 8-1)

Notes on the data

Each composite index is scaled so that its average monthly value equals 100 in a base year, currently 1996. Changes in the components are calculated and standardized, using the standard deviation of each component, to equalize the volatility of each component in an index. Beginning with the January 2001 release, indicators that are not available at publication time are estimated using statistical imputation (an autoregressive model); in subsequent months the imputations are replaced by the actual reported data. This imputation procedure allows earlier release each month of preliminary values for the composite indexes.

Annual revisions to the indexes are normally made each January; the latest was made in January 2003. The most recent comprehensive revisions, which included addition and deletion of components, were introduced in 1996.

Data availability

Data are published each month by The Conference Board. The monthly report *Business Cycle Indicators* is available by subscription from The Conference Board, 845 Third Avenue, New York, NY 10022. A monthly press release from The Conference Board, with information about the indexes and their components, is available at <http://www.tcb-indicators.org>. The full historical database (with monthly data back to 1959) is available by subscription from the same Internet site.

References

In addition to The Conference Board's *Business Cycle Indicators* (referenced above), see the *Survey of Current Business:* "Business Cycle Indicators: Upcoming Revision of the Composite Indexes" (October 1993).

CHAPTER 2: INDUSTRIAL PRODUCTION AND CAPACITY UTILIZATION

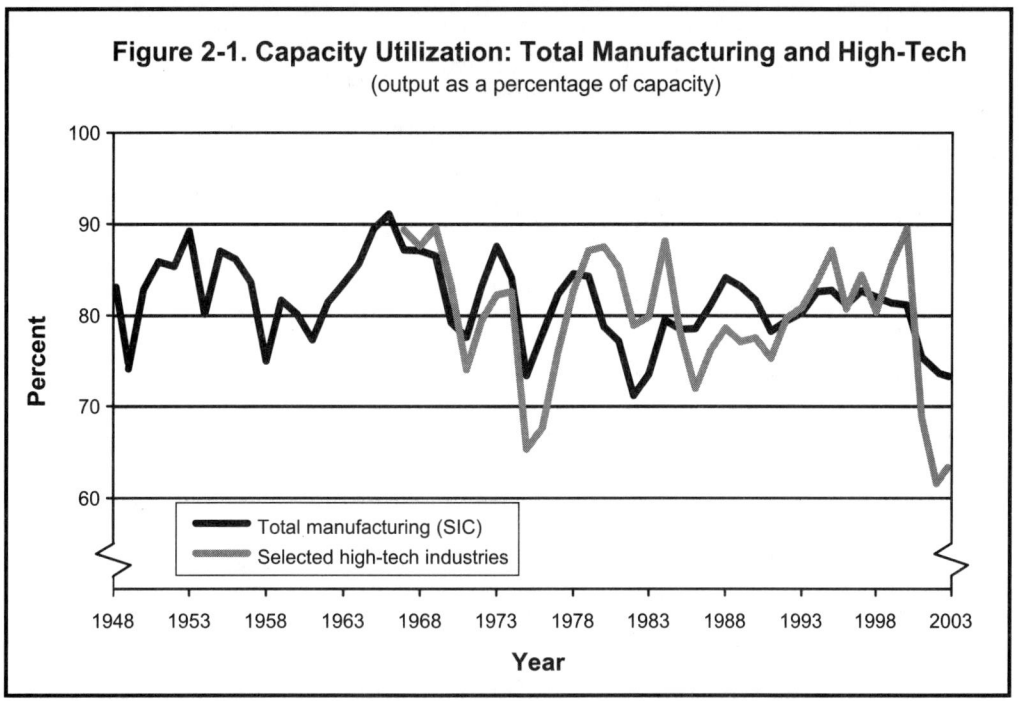

- Manufacturing capacity utilization is a key statistic for the U.S. economy, even though limited to a sector that by some measures is diminishing in importance. (The Federal Reserve also provides measures of capacity utilization for "total industry"—manufacturing, mining, and utilities. However, mining and utilities are less significant in the context of business cycle analysis, and much of the variation in capacity use by utilities is a result of transitory weather variations, not economic factors.) Manufacturing utilization is an important indicator of inflationary pressure—not adequately gauged by reliance on the labor force unemployment rate alone—and an element in the demand for new capital goods. (Table 2-3)
- The Federal Reserve continues to calculate and publish the utilization rate for manufacturing as defined in the old Standard Industrial Classification (SIC), which is therefore available for the entire postwar period, as shown in Figure 2-1. The SIC manufacturing definition is slightly broader than that in the new North American Industry Classification System (NAICS), including logging and publishing.
- The most recent cyclical highs in manufacturing utilization, in 1995 and 1997, fell short of peaks reached in some earlier years; this may have contributed to the low inflation rates of the late 1990s, which were surprising to analysts who looked only at the low and falling labor force unemployment rates of that period. (Figure 2-1; Tables 2-3, 20-1, and 10-3)
- Beginning with measures for 1967 the Federal Reserve provides measures of production and utilization for NAICS industries, making possible a clearer separation of high-tech and other industries. Capacity utilization in the high-tech industries (computers and office equipment, communications equipment, and semiconductors and related electronic components) was more volatile than in the rest of industry, as can be seen in Figure 2-1. At the height of the dot-com boom, high-tech utilization soared to 89.6 percent; at their lowest levels, high-tech industries used only 65.3 percent of capacity in 1975 and 61.5 percent in 2002. (Table 2-3)
- Industrial production increased 154 percent from 1967 to 2003, which translates into an annual average growth rate of 2.6 percent. The high-tech industries grew at an annual rate of 18.6 percent, while the rest of manufacturing, mining, and utilities grew at a 1.7 percent rate. Of the major market groups, consumer goods production grew at a 2.2 percent rate from 1967 to 2003; business equipment, 4.3 percent; defense and space equipment, 0.6 percent; construction supplies, 1.9 percent; energy materials, 1.1 percent; and non-energy materials, 3.3 percent. (Tables 2-1 and 2-2)

Table 2-1. Industrial Production Indexes by Market Groups

(Seasonally adjusted, 1997 = 100.)

Year and month	Total industrial production	Final products and nonindustrial supplies							
		Total	Consumer goods						
			Total	Durable consumer goods					Nondurable consumer goods
				Total	Automotive products	Home electronics	Appliances, furniture, and carpeting	Miscellaneous durable goods	Total
1967	43.7	42.6	48.7	36.3	37.0	2.0	48.6	48.4	54.4
1968	46.2	44.6	51.7	40.4	44.1	2.2	52.2	51.6	56.6
1969	48.3	46.3	53.6	42.1	44.3	2.3	55.0	55.8	58.5
1970	46.7	44.9	53.0	38.9	37.3	2.1	54.5	53.8	59.5
1971	47.4	45.5	56.0	44.0	47.5	2.3	57.5	56.8	61.2
1972	51.9	49.7	60.5	49.3	51.3	2.6	67.5	63.7	65.1
1973	56.1	53.4	63.3	52.9	55.5	3.0	72.9	66.6	67.1
1974	55.9	53.2	61.4	48.1	48.0	2.8	66.4	64.2	67.1
1975	50.9	49.4	59.0	43.7	46.1	2.4	56.8	57.1	66.0
1976	54.9	52.8	63.8	49.3	52.4	2.9	64.2	63.5	70.1
1977	59.1	57.2	67.7	55.3	59.1	3.4	72.1	70.3	72.6
1978	62.4	60.6	69.8	56.6	58.4	3.8	75.9	72.7	75.2
1979	64.2	62.6	68.8	54.5	52.6	3.8	76.1	73.2	74.8
1980	62.5	61.6	66.3	47.6	41.2	3.9	70.9	67.0	74.8
1981	63.4	62.9	66.8	48.3	42.5	4.0	69.9	68.0	75.2
1982	60.1	61.3	66.6	45.6	41.2	3.5	63.2	64.4	76.5
1983	61.7	62.9	69.0	50.5	47.3	5.2	69.8	66.2	77.3
1984	67.3	68.3	72.1	56.2	52.4	6.3	77.8	73.3	78.9
1985	68.1	70.0	72.7	56.2	52.2	6.5	77.2	73.3	79.9
1986	68.8	71.4	75.1	59.4	55.3	8.6	81.0	81.0	81.8
1987	72.3	74.8	78.1	62.7	58.5	8.4	85.3	85.3	84.7
1988	75.9	78.3	81.2	66.2	62.0	10.9	86.6	86.6	87.5
1989	76.6	79.0	81.4	67.5	64.1	11.4	87.6	87.6	87.2
1990	77.2	79.9	82.0	66.1	61.2	13.1	85.4	85.4	88.7
1991	76.1	78.6	82.0	63.6	57.9	15.6	79.5	79.5	90.0
1992	78.2	80.5	84.5	69.7	67.8	17.1	84.0	84.0	90.6
1993	80.8	83.1	87.4	76.6	75.3	26.9	88.8	88.8	91.9
1994	85.2	86.9	91.6	85.4	85.7	40.3	95.2	95.2	94.2
1995	89.3	90.4	94.5	89.7	89.1	61.0	94.7	94.7	96.5
1996	93.1	93.9	96.5	93.5	92.7	73.7	95.7	95.7	97.8
1997	100.0	100.0	100.0	100.0	100.0	100.0	100.0	100.0	100.0
1998	105.9	105.7	103.6	107.0	106.6	131.1	106.7	106.7	102.2
1999	110.6	108.7	105.3	113.5	116.5	145.5	109.9	109.9	102.1
2000	115.4	112.3	107.5	117.5	119.4	170.1	113.3	113.3	103.7
2001	111.5	109.3	105.9	110.4	113.9	132.7	109.1	109.1	104.0
2002	110.9	107.9	106.8	115.7	124.1	148.4	110.8	110.8	103.4
2003	111.0	108.0	106.0	118.0	129.0	181.0	111.0	98.0	102.0
2001									
January	114.2	111.9	106.6	109.2	107.2	141.8	110.4	105.6	105.3
February	113.6	111.2	106.4	109.3	109.2	129.9	111.2	103.9	105.0
March	113.2	110.8	106.1	111.3	114.3	129.7	109.8	103.5	103.9
April	112.8	110.5	106.5	110.7	113.7	127.6	108.7	103.4	104.6
May	112.3	110.1	106.6	111.3	116.1	131.6	107.8	102.0	104.5
June	111.6	109.6	106.3	110.5	114.8	123.3	107.6	102.2	104.4
July	111.1	109.2	106.0	111.8	118.0	108.1	109.2	102.2	103.6
August	110.9	108.6	105.9	110.0	114.8	115.6	109.2	100.6	104.0
September	110.2	107.8	105.4	109.4	113.2	124.3	109.9	99.7	103.6
October	109.9	107.5	105.5	108.3	110.8	141.3	108.5	98.9	104.0
November	109.4	106.9	104.9	110.5	115.1	158.4	108.1	98.0	102.6
December	109.1	107.0	105.4	112.8	119.2	161.3	108.6	98.4	102.5
2002									
January	109.7	107.3	106.3	112.7	118.1	172.4	109.1	98.5	103.6
February	109.9	107.3	106.3	113.7	119.6	165.8	110.7	99.0	103.4
March	110.3	107.7	106.8	113.9	119.9	151.9	111.5	100.1	104.0
April	110.8	107.9	107.0	114.4	122.3	132.9	111.1	100.5	104.1
May	111.0	107.8	106.5	114.9	122.7	129.0	112.8	100.9	103.2
June	111.7	108.6	107.6	116.1	125.2	123.9	113.2	101.3	104.4
July	111.5	108.3	107.5	116.8	127.4	133.0	111.2	100.4	103.9
August	111.5	108.2	107.1	116.8	128.0	140.3	108.8	100.1	103.5
September	111.3	108.2	107.3	117.0	127.1	150.6	109.7	100.6	103.6
October	111.0	108.0	106.7	115.9	124.9	151.2	109.0	100.7	103.2
November	111.2	107.8	106.6	118.8	129.5	163.9	110.8	100.8	102.1
December	110.6	107.3	105.6	116.8	124.9	166.2	111.1	100.9	101.5
2003									
January	111.2	108.1	106.6	119.4	129.5	184.7	111.0	100.3	101.9
February	111.6	108.6	107.0	117.2	127.1	167.2	110.4	99.2	103.2
March	110.8	107.9	106.3	116.4	125.7	170.8	109.8	98.6	102.6
April	110.1	106.9	105.3	115.5	124.4	172.7	110.0	97.5	101.4
May	110.0	107.1	105.5	115.3	123.5	168.8	111.7	97.5	101.8
June	110.0	106.8	105.0	116.2	125.7	169.4	110.8	97.7	100.9
July	110.8	107.5	105.8	118.2	129.1	170.7	112.2	97.8	101.3
August	110.9	107.6	105.7	117.4	127.3	179.2	112.0	97.4	101.4
September	111.5	108.0	106.1	120.8	135.0	183.2	110.6	97.1	100.9
October	111.8	108.2	106.0	119.8	131.8	196.2	110.6	97.6	101.1
November	112.9	109.3	107.1	121.3	133.0	202.8	112.3	98.9	102.1
December	113.1	109.5	107.3	121.2	133.1	202.7	111.4	99.0	102.3

Table 2-1. Industrial Production Indexes by Market Groups—Continued

(Seasonally adjusted, 1997 = 100.)

Year and month	Final products and nonindustrial supplies—Continued											
	Consumer goods—Continued						Business equipment				Defense and space equipment	Construction supplies	Business supplies
	Nondurable consumer goods—Continued												
	Nondurable nonenergy consumer goods					Consumer energy products	Total	Transit	Information processing	Industrial and other			
	Total	Foods and tobacco	Clothing	Chemical products	Paper products								
1967	55.4	57.8	96.9	30.7	54.4	48.2	24.4	70.7	2.8	50.7	90.9	52.6	37.0
1968	57.3	59.3	100.4	33.6	53.8	51.7	25.4	78.9	3.2	50.6	91.1	55.3	39.2
1969	59.0	60.9	101.9	35.2	55.8	55.3	27.1	77.8	3.5	53.9	86.7	57.7	41.7
1970	59.6	61.7	99.0	38.3	53.8	58.5	26.1	68.2	3.7	52.0	73.4	55.7	41.9
1971	61.1	63.6	98.4	40.5	54.9	61.2	24.8	66.0	3.4	49.7	66.0	57.5	43.2
1972	65.1	67.2	107.1	44.2	55.3	64.6	28.3	72.0	4.0	56.6	64.2	65.2	47.5
1973	67.3	69.0	109.2	47.6	57.2	65.7	32.7	86.7	4.6	64.4	69.9	70.7	50.4
1974	66.9	69.3	102.3	50.1	56.4	67.5	34.5	84.6	5.5	67.1	72.0	69.0	50.3
1975	65.2	68.2	99.4	48.3	53.2	68.9	30.5	74.0	5.0	58.9	73.2	58.5	46.4
1976	69.4	72.6	104.7	52.5	55.2	72.5	32.3	77.0	5.8	61.2	70.9	63.1	49.4
1977	71.9	74.1	109.9	54.7	60.4	75.3	37.4	92.1	7.6	66.8	63.4	68.7	53.5
1978	74.7	76.8	112.5	58.1	63.5	76.7	42.3	107.9	9.6	71.6	63.9	72.6	56.4
1979	73.7	76.3	106.3	58.2	64.1	78.6	47.6	124.9	12.1	75.9	68.7	74.4	58.4
1980	74.6	77.5	108.2	58.0	64.9	75.8	48.2	115.6	14.8	73.5	81.8	68.8	57.0
1981	75.1	77.9	108.1	58.8	66.4	75.3	49.5	108.0	17.4	73.3	88.7	67.6	58.4
1982	76.6	80.4	107.8	59.0	68.2	75.8	45.4	82.8	19.7	63.5	106.2	61.4	57.7
1983	77.6	80.5	110.8	59.6	71.1	76.3	45.3	82.3	22.1	58.8	107.0	65.7	60.4
1984	79.0	81.5	111.2	61.0	74.8	78.7	52.5	86.5	27.7	67.1	122.3	71.6	65.7
1985	80.2	83.9	106.3	61.6	78.6	78.7	54.6	89.6	30.0	68.0	136.9	73.4	67.4
1986	82.2	85.3	106.2	66.4	79.7	80.2	53.9	84.2	30.1	67.6	145.5	75.9	69.6
1987	85.0	87.3	107.0	71.5	84.2	83.1	57.3	87.0	33.7	70.0	148.3	80.5	73.8
1988	87.5	89.8	105.3	75.8	86.5	87.5	62.4	94.8	36.9	76.0	148.3	82.3	76.6
1989	87.0	89.1	100.4	77.3	86.9	88.0	64.4	99.3	37.7	78.5	148.3	81.9	77.7
1990	89.0	91.6	98.4	80.1	88.5	87.4	66.1	103.9	40.1	77.9	142.6	81.1	79.6
1991	89.9	92.1	98.0	83.0	89.1	90.1	64.6	106.4	39.9	73.9	131.6	76.6	78.5
1992	91.0	93.3	100.1	82.7	90.0	88.9	67.1	103.2	45.0	75.1	122.3	79.8	80.3
1993	91.7	92.6	102.0	85.0	92.1	92.8	69.7	95.3	48.1	80.2	115.6	83.4	82.9
1994	94.3	96.3	103.9	86.9	91.3	94.0	73.5	86.7	54.1	85.6	108.9	89.5	86.2
1995	96.4	98.8	103.3	90.4	92.0	96.5	79.4	81.8	64.4	90.9	106.0	91.4	89.9
1996	97.1	98.6	100.6	94.7	91.9	100.7	86.9	84.0	78.8	94.3	102.0	95.5	93.2
1997	100.0	100.0	100.0	100.0	100.0	100.0	100.0	100.0	100.0	100.0	100.0	100.0	100.0
1998	102.5	102.4	94.4	104.6	105.5	100.5	111.2	119.2	118.3	103.3	104.1	105.2	105.9
1999	101.8	100.4	90.6	106.2	107.9	104.1	117.1	118.1	141.9	101.0	101.4	107.9	110.7
2000	103.3	101.8	87.3	110.2	109.0	105.8	125.5	102.9	169.9	107.1	91.0	110.3	116.0
2001	103.5	101.8	78.2	115.8	106.7	106.5	117.6	97.7	165.3	97.1	102.6	105.2	111.6
2002	102.0	100.7	70.9	115.6	103.9	110.0	109.5	84.5	159.6	90.5	105.7	103.1	110.7
2003	100.0	97.0	63.0	116.0	109.0	111.0	110.0	76.0	174.0	90.0	112.0	102.0	112.0
2001													
January	103.7	101.7	84.8	112.8	108.7	112.8	126.0	97.2	181.0	104.9	97.8	108.4	115.6
February	103.9	101.7	84.4	114.8	106.7	110.3	124.3	97.6	176.2	104.0	97.4	107.6	114.1
March	103.1	100.9	83.8	114.1	106.0	108.2	123.4	100.3	173.4	102.8	100.3	107.2	113.3
April	104.1	102.4	82.9	114.2	107.9	107.2	122.0	100.5	172.2	100.8	102.0	106.6	112.0
May	104.5	101.7	80.7	119.4	107.1	104.9	119.8	100.6	168.7	98.5	102.1	106.3	111.6
June	104.3	103.2	78.9	115.6	107.0	105.3	118.1	99.6	165.7	97.2	103.8	105.9	111.2
July	103.3	101.1	78.0	116.0	108.0	105.5	117.1	99.6	164.0	96.2	105.1	105.3	110.8
August	103.4	101.4	75.6	117.0	107.2	107.4	114.7	98.3	158.4	94.9	104.6	104.2	111.0
September	103.3	102.7	73.3	114.9	106.3	105.2	112.8	97.2	156.4	92.9	105.4	103.7	110.0
October	103.6	102.1	72.9	117.6	105.6	106.5	111.5	95.2	155.5	91.7	105.0	102.1	110.2
November	102.5	101.2	71.7	116.3	104.6	102.9	110.8	94.0	154.9	91.2	104.1	102.2	109.5
December	102.6	101.2	71.4	116.6	105.5	102.1	110.1	91.8	156.9	90.0	104.1	102.4	109.4
2002													
January	103.3	101.8	70.9	118.6	104.9	105.3	110.0	90.8	155.9	90.5	103.7	101.9	109.2
February	102.9	102.3	70.2	116.1	104.5	105.8	109.8	90.4	157.1	89.8	103.3	102.7	109.3
March	103.3	102.7	70.4	116.3	104.9	107.8	109.5	88.7	157.7	89.8	103.9	103.9	109.8
April	102.6	102.6	69.8	114.2	103.0	111.4	109.4	87.3	156.7	90.4	104.3	103.5	110.7
May	101.8	101.0	70.8	114.3	103.2	110.1	109.7	85.2	156.8	91.6	104.5	103.9	111.3
June	102.9	102.3	72.2	115.7	102.5	111.6	110.1	84.8	159.2	91.5	105.3	104.0	111.1
July	102.4	101.1	72.3	116.4	102.6	111.5	109.0	83.3	158.1	90.6	105.0	102.6	111.6
August	102.3	101.2	71.3	115.5	103.4	109.5	109.7	83.1	160.0	91.2	106.1	103.3	111.2
September	102.6	101.2	72.1	116.3	104.7	108.6	109.3	82.1	160.7	90.6	107.2	103.4	111.1
October	101.6	99.8	70.3	115.5	105.5	110.8	108.8	80.4	161.5	90.2	107.9	103.2	111.7
November	99.7	96.9	71.1	114.7	104.6	113.5	109.6	80.1	164.3	90.5	107.1	102.8	111.0
December	98.8	96.0	69.4	113.9	102.8	114.3	109.2	77.9	167.0	89.7	109.7	102.1	110.9
2003													
January	100.1	97.6	68.0	114.6	106.3	110.7	109.8	78.1	169.0	89.8	110.3	102.7	111.8
February	100.2	97.1	66.6	115.3	108.5	117.6	110.6	76.7	172.1	90.6	111.0	101.9	112.6
March	100.6	97.6	65.7	115.7	109.6	112.1	110.0	76.2	172.3	89.8	111.0	101.2	111.9
April	100.1	96.9	64.0	116.3	108.6	108.5	108.7	75.0	170.0	88.9	110.3	100.6	111.1
May	100.0	97.1	64.1	115.6	109.0	110.4	108.6	74.4	170.8	88.8	111.8	100.8	111.0
June	99.8	97.1	62.2	114.4	110.2	107.1	109.0	74.0	170.9	89.4	111.8	100.8	110.6
July	99.6	97.3	61.6	114.4	108.4	109.8	109.3	73.9	172.5	89.5	112.1	101.5	111.5
August	99.3	96.2	59.7	116.5	108.8	111.1	110.0	74.5	174.7	89.6	113.0	101.9	111.2
September	99.1	96.0	59.7	116.3	108.2	109.4	111.2	77.1	175.4	90.3	113.7	102.3	111.3
October	99.5	95.7	60.7	117.4	109.7	109.0	110.8	75.9	178.5	89.2	113.7	103.1	112.1
November	100.5	96.4	61.2	120.0	110.6	109.9	112.7	76.7	178.4	92.0	113.3	104.4	112.8
December	100.1	96.1	61.2	118.7	109.7	113.0	113.2	77.8	177.6	92.5	112.4	104.1	113.4

Table 2-1. Industrial Production Indexes by Market Groups—Continued

(Seasonally adjusted, 1997 = 100.)

Year and month	Total	Materials									Energy materials
		Nonenergy materials									
		Total	Durable				Nondurable				
			Total	Consumer parts	Equipment parts	Other	Total	Textile	Paper	Chemical	
1967	44.2	37.6	32.9	50.3	13.8	57.1	46.8	66.0	46.9	34.0	68.9
1968	47.1	40.3	34.8	56.7	14.1	60.1	51.5	72.8	49.0	39.6	72.1
1969	49.9	42.8	36.6	57.1	15.0	64.0	55.7	74.8	53.2	43.9	75.7
1970	48.1	40.3	33.3	47.9	13.8	59.7	56.0	72.1	52.8	44.9	79.5
1971	48.9	41.0	33.4	53.0	13.8	57.5	58.4	75.5	55.1	47.6	80.2
1972	53.8	46.0	37.8	59.0	15.9	65.0	64.4	79.5	58.8	55.4	83.2
1973	58.7	50.9	43.1	68.5	18.7	72.0	67.6	77.3	63.4	61.1	85.2
1974	58.5	50.8	42.6	60.6	19.8	72.0	68.5	72.3	66.6	62.8	84.9
1975	52.1	43.7	35.7	48.9	17.0	60.2	61.4	70.8	57.9	52.6	84.0
1976	56.7	48.6	39.9	62.4	18.4	64.6	68.0	78.8	63.7	60.3	85.8
1977	60.7	52.7	43.6	68.4	20.9	68.5	72.9	84.0	66.6	67.0	88.5
1978	63.7	56.1	47.1	72.3	23.4	72.9	75.7	83.1	69.8	71.1	89.6
1979	65.4	57.7	48.6	68.3	25.8	74.7	77.1	82.4	72.6	74.0	92.0
1980	63.0	54.3	45.0	52.6	26.5	69.1	74.6	80.5	73.2	68.5	92.7
1981	63.3	54.5	45.1	50.1	27.2	69.3	75.2	78.7	74.6	69.1	93.6
1982	58.5	49.1	39.4	42.5	25.0	58.5	71.2	71.8	75.2	61.9	89.6
1983	60.0	52.4	42.0	51.7	25.5	61.2	76.3	80.6	80.0	68.5	86.8
1984	65.8	58.6	48.8	61.5	30.9	67.8	79.7	80.4	84.9	72.8	92.3
1985	65.7	58.6	49.2	63.9	31.0	67.3	79.0	76.1	84.4	71.4	91.7
1986	65.7	82.2	49.9	63.4	31.7	68.5	81.5	79.3	88.1	74.9	88.1
1987	69.2	85.0	53.4	65.1	34.7	73.3	86.3	89.0	92.4	81.3	90.2
1988	73.0	87.5	57.6	70.4	37.7	78.6	89.5	88.2	95.5	86.2	93.3
1989	73.5	87.0	57.8	66.8	38.9	78.9	90.4	90.1	95.4	87.4	94.2
1990	74.0	89.0	57.9	62.2	40.2	79.3	90.6	85.6	95.7	88.3	96.1
1991	72.9	89.9	56.3	58.9	40.3	75.9	89.6	85.5	93.7	87.1	96.2
1992	75.4	91.0	60.1	66.1	42.7	79.9	91.8	90.5	96.0	89.3	95.3
1993	77.9	91.7	64.1	75.1	45.4	83.0	92.8	94.2	96.0	89.7	95.5
1994	83.0	94.3	71.6	86.9	51.9	89.1	95.6	100.0	99.7	92.4	97.0
1995	87.9	96.4	79.4	90.5	64.1	92.4	96.5	98.3	102.2	93.1	98.5
1996	92.2	97.1	87.3	92.9	77.9	95.2	95.5	95.6	98.9	93.5	100.0
1997	100.0	100.0	100.0	100.0	100.0	100.0	100.0	100.0	100.0	100.0	100.0
1998	106.2	102.5	111.4	103.6	124.3	102.8	101.4	98.4	100.4	100.7	100.2
1999	113.1	101.8	124.6	113.3	154.4	104.4	103.0	96.4	102.2	103.9	100.2
2000	119.8	103.3	138.2	114.1	196.2	105.5	102.8	92.5	100.3	104.8	101.6
2001	114.6	103.5	131.2	101.1	196.6	98.1	96.7	81.8	94.5	98.2	100.4
2002	115.1	102.0	132.5	105.9	199.4	96.9	96.6	78.2	92.7	100.1	100.5
2003	115.8	119.9	135.2	106.9	214.5	95.1	95.3	70.2	90.3	99.9	100.6
2001											
January	117.4	121.8	135.2	99.4	205.0	101.8	99.6	86.7	97.5	101.2	101.2
February	116.9	121.1	134.1	101.4	203.5	99.8	99.4	84.0	98.6	101.0	101.5
March	116.4	120.1	133.7	101.9	203.4	98.8	97.9	85.9	96.1	99.1	101.8
April	115.9	119.7	133.3	102.3	200.3	99.5	97.4	85.8	95.9	97.4	101.3
May	115.2	118.9	132.4	102.6	198.0	98.9	96.8	83.8	94.8	97.7	100.7
June	114.2	117.7	131.0	101.3	195.2	98.3	95.9	81.6	93.6	96.9	100.4
July	113.7	117.5	130.8	102.0	192.5	98.9	95.7	80.4	93.2	97.0	99.2
August	114.0	117.5	130.3	101.5	192.9	97.9	96.2	80.6	94.2	97.8	100.3
September	113.4	116.8	129.1	99.4	192.0	97.1	96.2	80.5	94.1	97.7	99.9
October	113.3	116.4	128.6	98.8	192.6	96.3	96.1	79.0	93.0	98.8	100.4
November	112.7	116.0	128.3	99.9	192.0	95.6	95.4	76.9	92.3	97.9	99.6
December	112.0	115.3	128.1	102.3	191.4	94.4	94.2	76.4	90.7	96.0	98.7
2002											
January	113.0	116.6	129.1	103.1	192.6	95.2	95.7	77.8	92.0	98.4	99.3
February	113.4	116.8	129.7	104.7	192.6	95.6	95.5	77.5	91.3	98.4	100.1
March	113.9	117.4	130.3	104.6	193.5	96.2	96.0	78.8	90.5	99.9	100.4
April	114.8	118.4	131.6	105.8	195.7	96.9	96.6	79.1	92.2	100.4	100.7
May	115.3	119.2	132.4	105.0	199.0	97.3	97.3	79.4	93.3	101.5	100.6
June	116.0	120.0	133.6	105.9	201.2	98.1	97.5	79.7	92.5	101.6	101.2
July	116.2	120.0	133.5	107.1	201.2	97.2	97.8	79.7	93.7	102.1	101.6
August	116.1	120.3	134.5	106.8	203.9	98.0	97.2	78.2	93.2	101.1	100.5
September	115.7	120.0	134.1	106.7	203.8	97.5	96.9	77.8	93.3	100.5	99.7
October	115.3	119.5	134.0	106.3	203.2	97.7	96.0	77.0	93.1	98.9	99.8
November	115.9	119.8	134.3	108.8	203.5	96.9	96.3	77.4	93.8	99.2	100.9
December	115.3	119.0	133.0	106.1	203.0	96.1	96.2	75.7	93.1	99.6	101.0
2003											
January	115.5	119.4	134.0	108.8	203.9	96.3	95.7	74.4	91.5	99.5	100.6
February	115.8	119.3	133.7	107.1	205.2	96.0	96.0	74.3	91.3	100.1	101.7
March	114.7	118.7	132.7	106.0	205.1	94.9	95.9	73.2	91.8	99.6	99.8
April	114.5	118.3	132.2	104.8	206.0	94.1	95.5	71.8	90.6	100.2	100.2
May	114.1	117.9	132.1	103.9	207.9	93.8	94.8	70.4	90.5	98.1	99.6
June	114.4	118.3	133.1	105.0	210.5	94.0	94.5	69.9	90.7	97.0	99.6
July	115.4	119.2	134.6	105.9	214.2	94.6	94.8	67.8	90.9	98.5	100.9
August	115.5	119.2	134.9	104.8	218.2	94.1	94.4	67.0	89.3	99.1	101.0
September	116.4	120.8	137.0	109.2	221.6	94.4	95.1	67.5	89.6	100.8	100.4
October	116.9	121.3	138.2	108.4	224.2	95.7	95.0	68.3	88.7	100.4	100.9
November	117.9	122.7	139.8	109.2	227.7	96.8	96.0	69.3	89.1	102.5	100.9
December	118.2	123.0	140.2	109.9	228.8	96.7	96.2	68.8	89.7	102.8	101.4

. . . = Not available.

Table 2-1. Industrial Production Indexes by Market Groups—Continued
(Seasonally adjusted, 1997 = 100.)

Year and month	Special aggregates											
	Energy						Nonenergy					Total nonenergy excluding high-tech
	Total	Consumer energy products	Commercial energy products	Oil and gas well drilling	Converted fuels	Primary energy	Total	Selected high-tech				
								Total	Computers and office equipment	Communications equipment	Semiconductors and related components	
1967	60.2	48.2	35.3	...	59.6	77.7	40.4	0.8	...	...	...	53.2
1968	63.5	51.7	38.3	...	63.8	79.9	42.6	0.8	...	...	...	56.1
1969	66.9	55.3	40.2	...	68.2	82.7	44.6	0.9	...	...	...	58.4
1970	70.1	58.5	43.3	...	71.8	86.6	42.6	0.9	...	...	...	55.7
1971	71.4	61.2	45.5	...	73.8	86.0	43.2	0.9	...	...	...	56.7
1972	74.7	64.6	48.0	88.3	78.3	87.4	47.7	1.0	0.2	14.1	0.7	62.3
1973	76.6	65.7	50.6	83.1	81.3	88.4	52.0	1.3	0.2	15.2	1.0	67.7
1974	76.9	67.5	50.7	96.5	80.2	88.8	51.7	1.5	0.3	15.5	1.1	66.9
1975	77.2	68.9	52.5	108.9	77.3	89.5	46.2	1.3	0.3	13.4	0.9	59.7
1976	79.6	72.5	55.1	122.7	81.3	89.5	50.3	1.6	0.5	13.7	1.2	64.7
1977	82.7	75.3	57.0	155.8	84.3	92.1	54.6	2.2	0.7	16.8	1.6	69.6
1978	84.1	76.7	58.7	173.6	83.6	94.3	58.0	2.7	1.1	18.3	1.9	73.4
1979	86.6	78.6	61.4	185.1	86.7	96.4	59.8	3.6	1.5	21.9	2.5	74.8
1980	86.9	75.8	60.4	218.8	85.0	98.4	57.7	4.3	2.2	24.0	2.8	71.3
1981	88.2	75.3	62.0	262.9	83.8	100.4	58.4	5.1	3.0	24.9	3.2	71.4
1982	85.0	75.8	62.8	231.4	77.1	97.5	55.1	5.9	3.6	26.4	3.7	66.6
1983	82.5	76.3	64.0	179.3	76.9	93.3	57.7	7.0	5.1	25.6	4.4	69.0
1984	87.4	78.7	67.4	195.2	81.8	99.2	63.5	9.3	7.3	28.9	6.0	75.0
1985	87.1	78.7	69.9	178.8	81.4	98.6	64.7	9.9	8.5	29.0	6.2	76.1
1986	84.1	80.2	71.8	87.1	78.5	94.5	66.2	10.2	9.1	27.3	6.6	77.8
1987	86.5	83.1	75.6	84.0	82.5	95.1	69.9	12.3	11.7	27.9	8.4	81.4
1988	89.9	87.5	78.2	100.9	86.3	97.7	73.5	14.2	14.4	29.4	9.7	85.0
1989	90.9	88.0	81.1	87.8	89.6	97.1	74.1	15.0	15.0	29.5	10.7	85.4
1990	92.3	87.4	83.3	92.9	90.4	99.7	74.6	16.8	16.2	32.7	12.4	85.4
1991	92.8	90.1	84.6	72.4	90.4	99.7	73.1	18.0	16.8	32.5	14.2	83.2
1992	91.6	88.9	84.1	50.5	92.1	97.3	75.9	21.8	21.1	37.4	17.2	85.4
1993	93.2	92.8	86.5	70.4	93.8	96.5	78.6	25.6	26.1	42.8	20.0	87.6
1994	95.1	94.0	90.0	83.5	95.3	98.1	83.4	33.2	33.1	53.0	26.9	91.5
1995	97.0	96.5	93.2	81.3	96.7	99.6	87.9	47.3	46.9	62.6	41.8	93.8
1996	99.4	100.7	96.1	87.2	98.4	100.9	92.0	66.7	68.1	76.0	62.2	95.3
1997	100.0	100.0	100.0	100.0	100.0	100.0	100.0	100.0	100.0	100.0	100.0	100.0
1998	100.5	100.5	102.0	98.3	101.3	99.5	106.9	140.2	140.5	114.2	154.3	103.6
1999	101.5	104.1	105.9	82.0	102.9	98.4	112.2	201.3	176.3	140.9	255.5	104.9
2000	103.8	105.8	110.0	110.3	105.2	99.3	117.5	286.7	202.6	188.0	412.1	106.0
2001	103.7	106.5	111.6	125.0	101.4	99.5	112.8	291.1	193.8	172.9	454.4	101.1
2002	104.1	110.0	112.6	91.0	103.6	98.5	111.9	311.4	226.5	146.2	539.7	99.7
2003	104.5	110.7	113.4	93.7	102.9	98.9	112.2	369.3	265.7	154.6	684.6	98.7
2001												
January	105.9	112.8	112.5	132.7	102.9	100.0	115.6	311.1	204.0	203.8	457.2	103.2
February	105.4	110.3	112.4	131.6	103.8	99.9	114.9	306.4	200.6	194.5	460.1	102.7
March	105.2	108.2	112.1	135.6	103.8	100.4	114.4	304.1	199.2	188.2	464.3	102.3
April	104.6	107.2	111.2	139.8	103.9	99.5	114.1	297.4	198.2	182.9	451.5	102.3
May	103.7	104.9	111.8	136.5	102.6	99.4	113.7	292.3	195.1	178.3	445.6	101.9
June	103.7	105.3	112.9	133.3	100.1	100.1	112.8	286.6	188.4	173.3	442.5	101.3
July	102.7	105.5	111.4	129.8	99.3	98.7	112.5	281.0	181.1	170.2	437.2	101.1
August	103.8	107.4	112.6	122.6	102.0	99.0	111.9	277.0	177.4	162.3	443.5	100.7
September	102.9	105.2	111.4	118.4	99.5	99.7	111.3	277.0	180.3	158.3	448.0	100.1
October	103.4	106.5	111.5	117.7	100.9	99.7	110.9	282.9	188.7	156.8	461.9	99.5
November	101.8	102.9	109.6	109.0	99.5	99.3	110.5	286.7	200.2	153.5	468.3	99.1
December	100.9	102.1	110.0	99.9	99.1	98.2	110.4	291.3	212.1	152.4	472.4	98.8
2002												
January	101.8	105.3	108.6	98.5	100.0	98.5	111.0	291.3	221.3	145.3	476.2	99.3
February	102.6	105.8	110.4	94.1	101.9	98.7	111.0	294.1	224.2	147.2	479.1	99.3
March	103.3	107.8	111.4	92.0	103.7	98.2	111.4	295.8	219.7	147.8	489.1	99.6
April	104.7	111.4	113.9	87.0	103.8	98.8	111.7	298.9	211.9	148.8	507.7	99.8
May	104.2	110.1	113.3	86.1	103.5	98.8	112.0	302.3	207.0	147.5	528.4	100.0
June	104.9	111.6	113.1	89.2	104.2	99.3	112.7	308.3	209.3	150.0	541.9	100.5
July	105.3	111.5	114.2	90.2	106.4	98.7	112.4	311.2	217.2	144.0	554.6	100.2
August	103.8	109.5	111.8	90.6	103.8	98.4	112.7	318.9	227.0	144.4	569.4	100.2
September	103.2	108.6	112.5	91.6	105.6	96.2	112.6	323.2	235.6	142.6	578.4	100.0
October	104.2	110.8	115.8	92.1	104.0	97.2	112.0	325.8	242.6	140.8	582.6	99.4
November	105.2	113.5	113.3	89.0	103.3	99.2	112.0	332.5	248.7	146.7	587.0	99.2
December	105.6	114.3	113.5	92.1	103.2	99.5	111.2	334.7	253.8	149.8	582.0	98.5
2003												
January	104.7	110.7	115.4	89.4	105.0	98.0	112.1	335.7	257.5	148.6	583.5	99.3
February	107.0	117.6	115.4	92.1	106.8	98.7	112.1	344.0	258.6	157.4	593.4	99.1
March	104.2	112.1	113.3	90.9	101.2	98.5	111.7	345.9	257.0	158.6	599.4	98.7
April	103.5	108.5	112.0	93.3	100.3	99.5	111.1	348.3	254.5	156.5	615.8	98.0
May	103.6	110.4	112.3	96.0	98.7	99.3	111.0	352.9	253.8	156.0	634.7	97.8
June	102.5	107.1	108.9	94.6	99.5	99.1	111.2	359.6	256.4	155.4	657.8	97.9
July	104.3	109.8	112.5	94.0	103.4	99.1	111.8	369.1	261.9	152.6	693.0	98.3
August	104.7	111.1	112.0	95.4	104.4	98.8	111.7	382.6	266.7	154.6	732.7	98.0
September	103.8	109.4	111.5	94.5	101.8	99.2	112.7	388.1	272.2	152.6	751.6	98.9
October	104.4	109.0	114.2	95.0	103.3	99.2	113.0	397.4	277.9	156.0	771.1	98.9
November	104.7	109.9	115.3	94.6	104.9	98.5	114.2	402.8	283.8	154.6	787.3	100.0
December	106.1	113.0	118.0	94.6	105.3	99.1	114.2	404.7	288.7	152.0	794.6	99.9

. . . = Not available.

Table 2-2. Industrial Production Indexes by NAICS Industry Groups

(Seasonally adjusted, 1997 = 100.)

			Manufacturing (NAICS)										
	Total industrial production	Manu- facturing (SIC)	Total	Durable goods manufacturing									
Year and month				Total	Wood products	Nonmetallic mineral products	Primary metals	Fabricated metal products	Machinery	Computer and electronic products	Electrical equipment, appliances, and compo- nents	Motor vehicles and parts	Aerospace and misc. transport equipment
1967	43.7	40.6	...	...	...	...	...	...	...	...	...	...	...
1968	46.2	42.9	...	...	...	...	...	...	...	...	...	...	...
1969	48.3	44.8	...	...	...	...	...	...	...	...	...	...	...
1970	46.7	42.8	...	...	...	...	...	...	...	...	...	...	...
1971	47.4	43.5	...	...	...	...	...	...	...	...	...	...	...
1972	51.9	48.0	47.1	38.8	76.1	75.7	108.3	67.4	60.7	3.2	66.1	51.6	72.7
1973	56.1	52.3	51.5	43.6	73.6	81.2	126.0	74.4	70.2	3.8	74.3	59.0	82.8
1974	55.9	52.1	51.3	43.3	66.9	80.3	129.1	73.1	73.6	4.1	72.6	50.7	84.2
1975	50.9	46.6	45.8	37.5	62.0	71.9	100.2	63.2	64.2	3.7	58.2	44.2	79.9
1976	54.9	50.8	50.0	41.0	69.8	76.0	106.3	67.7	67.0	4.3	65.7	56.4	74.8
1977	59.1	55.2	54.3	45.1	75.4	80.9	107.3	73.5	73.2	5.5	72.5	64.2	75.4
1978	62.4	58.6	57.6	48.6	76.3	86.3	114.1	77.1	78.9	6.8	76.9	66.9	83.2
1979	64.2	60.4	59.4	51.0	73.8	86.2	116.7	80.5	83.2	8.4	80.1	61.2	96.8
1980	62.5	58.2	57.1	48.7	68.4	77.6	102.3	75.9	79.2	10.1	75.3	45.0	104.2
1981	63.4	58.8	57.7	49.2	66.9	74.3	102.6	75.4	78.5	11.6	74.4	43.9	99.1
1982	60.1	55.6	54.4	45.1	59.9	65.8	72.7	67.6	65.7	13.1	67.0	39.6	92.8
1983	61.7	58.2	57.0	47.2	69.5	70.8	74.2	68.2	59.3	15.0	69.3	50.5	88.7
1984	67.3	64.0	62.8	54.0	74.4	76.4	81.5	74.3	69.3	18.7	78.0	60.6	94.6
1985	68.1	65.1	63.8	55.3	75.3	77.7	75.2	75.2	69.5	20.0	76.8	62.9	101.1
1986	68.8	66.5	65.3	56.2	81.8	81.0	73.4	74.7	68.4	20.8	78.2	62.8	106.4
1987	72.3	70.2	68.9	59.4	89.2	85.4	79.2	76.1	69.7	23.5	79.3	65.1	110.3
1988	75.9	73.8	72.6	63.6	89.1	87.2	88.6	80.1	76.8	25.8	83.1	69.6	114.9
1989	76.6	74.4	73.2	64.2	87.8	86.4	86.7	79.4	79.6	26.5	81.8	68.8	121.2
1990	77.2	74.9	73.8	64.4	86.8	85.1	85.5	78.3	77.6	28.7	79.7	64.7	121.6
1991	76.1	73.4	72.4	62.4	81.3	78.4	80.3	74.8	72.9	29.8	75.6	61.8	117.0
1992	78.2	76.1	75.3	65.6	85.7	81.9	82.2	77.1	72.6	33.6	80.2	70.4	108.3
1993	80.8	78.8	78.1	69.3	86.7	83.6	86.2	80.0	78.1	37.1	85.2	77.8	101.0
1994	85.2	83.6	83.1	75.4	91.8	88.3	92.6	87.0	85.5	44.2	91.4	89.4	90.7
1995	89.3	88.0	87.8	81.9	94.0	90.9	93.7	92.3	91.5	57.5	93.5	92.0	86.4
1996	93.1	92.1	92.1	89.0	97.1	96.7	95.9	95.8	94.9	73.8	96.4	92.7	89.6
1997	100.0	100.0	100.0	100.0	100.0	100.0	100.0	100.0	100.0	100.0	100.0	100.0	100.0
1998	105.9	106.8	106.8	110.7	105.0	104.7	102.3	103.0	102.6	129.1	104.1	105.2	115.9
1999	110.6	112.1	112.3	119.9	108.8	106.1	101.7	103.8	100.4	169.0	105.9	116.4	111.8
2000	115.4	117.4	117.7	129.5	107.2	106.0	98.5	107.9	105.8	224.0	111.6	116.2	98.3
2001	111.5	112.7	113.1	123.5	100.6	101.4	89.0	100.1	93.8	226.1	100.9	105.6	106.3
2002	110.9	111.8	112.5	122.9	100.6	99.9	86.5	97.4	86.8	234.7	96.4	114.5	97.5
2003	111.2	112.2	112.6	125.4	99.1	100.8	84.7	94.6	86.8	266.9	93.9	117.0	94.6
2001													
January	114.2	115.4	115.8	127.4	98.9	104.2	93.3	104.9	102.5	238.4	109.0	99.4	103.9
February	113.6	114.8	115.3	126.5	98.5	104.1	90.6	103.0	102.0	234.9	105.7	102.4	103.9
March	113.2	114.3	114.9	126.6	100.0	103.4	88.8	102.3	99.9	233.9	104.1	106.8	106.1
April	112.8	114.1	114.5	125.8	100.0	102.6	91.1	101.8	98.3	230.8	102.5	106.3	107.4
May	112.3	113.5	114.0	124.8	101.2	102.1	90.8	101.0	95.1	227.4	101.6	108.3	107.6
June	111.6	112.7	113.1	123.6	102.0	101.8	90.8	100.0	93.9	224.4	100.2	106.8	107.5
July	111.1	112.4	112.7	123.4	100.8	101.1	91.5	100.0	92.2	221.3	98.9	109.3	107.2
August	110.9	111.8	112.1	122.1	102.0	100.2	89.7	99.2	91.4	218.3	99.7	106.6	107.6
September	110.2	111.2	111.5	120.9	102.7	100.3	89.0	97.6	89.6	217.9	98.4	104.0	108.5
October	109.9	110.8	111.2	120.1	100.0	98.2	86.2	97.7	87.5	220.1	97.6	101.9	107.6
November	109.4	110.5	110.9	120.3	100.2	100.3	85.9	96.5	87.2	221.5	96.3	105.7	105.6
December	109.1	110.4	110.7	120.4	101.3	98.6	80.1	96.8	85.9	224.1	96.4	109.8	102.7
2002													
January	109.7	111.0	111.4	120.8	102.3	97.9	84.8	96.5	86.8	224.3	97.4	108.8	102.4
February	109.9	111.0	111.5	121.1	101.2	99.0	85.2	96.8	86.9	225.1	98.0	110.8	100.7
March	110.3	111.4	111.9	121.4	102.5	99.2	86.7	96.8	87.0	226.1	96.9	110.7	100.3
April	110.8	111.6	112.3	122.0	101.5	99.4	85.7	97.4	87.0	226.9	97.1	113.4	99.0
May	111.0	111.9	112.6	122.7	101.1	100.0	86.6	98.2	87.6	229.2	98.6	113.5	97.5
June	111.7	112.6	113.3	123.5	101.9	99.3	87.3	98.3	87.8	233.0	98.7	115.8	96.9
July	111.5	112.4	113.1	123.3	100.4	98.8	85.7	98.1	86.4	233.9	97.6	117.8	95.3
August	111.5	112.6	113.4	124.1	100.5	100.3	88.6	98.0	87.5	238.3	94.8	117.9	96.3
September	111.3	112.5	113.1	123.8	99.5	101.4	86.7	97.4	86.8	241.2	93.8	117.0	96.4
October	111.0	111.9	112.4	123.5	100.1	101.1	87.9	97.7	86.1	242.4	94.1	115.1	95.7
November	111.2	111.9	112.6	124.5	98.4	100.9	88.8	96.5	86.5	246.5	94.8	118.9	94.6
December	110.6	111.3	111.9	123.6	97.5	101.2	84.3	96.6	85.6	248.9	94.8	114.6	94.8
2003													
January	111.2	112.0	112.6	124.8	98.5	101.4	88.3	96.2	85.2	251.1	93.5	118.7	94.7
February	111.6	112.1	112.4	124.5	98.4	99.8	88.0	95.7	86.5	253.6	94.6	116.0	94.1
March	110.8	111.8	112.0	123.6	97.0	100.3	83.5	95.0	86.3	254.6	93.0	114.4	94.3
April	110.1	111.1	111.3	122.8	97.1	99.9	83.8	94.0	85.4	254.6	92.8	113.0	93.7
May	110.0	111.0	111.2	122.8	97.0	99.3	82.2	93.2	86.2	258.0	92.4	112.0	94.2
June	110.0	111.2	111.4	123.6	97.7	100.0	82.7	93.3	86.3	260.5	93.6	113.8	94.0
July	110.8	111.8	112.2	124.8	99.6	100.8	82.9	94.2	85.9	266.7	92.9	116.6	93.8
August	110.9	111.8	112.1	124.9	98.7	100.9	82.5	93.2	86.7	273.7	93.0	114.9	94.9
September	111.5	112.7	113.2	127.1	98.7	100.4	83.0	94.4	87.3	277.1	93.9	122.7	95.0
October	111.8	112.9	113.3	127.2	101.2	101.5	84.7	94.6	86.3	282.9	94.4	119.9	95.0
November	112.9	114.2	114.6	128.8	103.8	102.5	86.8	95.3	89.7	285.3	95.9	120.5	95.6
December	113.1	114.2	114.7	129.3	102.0	102.6	88.0	95.6	89.6	285.3	96.7	121.3	96.2

. . . = Not available.

Table 2-2. Industrial Production Indexes by NAICS Industry Groups—Continued

(Seasonally adjusted, 1997 = 100.)

Year and month	Manufacturing (NAICS)—Continued											Other manufacturing (non-NAICS)
	Durable goods manufacturing—Continued		Nondurable goods manufacturing									
	Furniture and related products	Miscellaneous manufacturing	Total	Food, beverage, and tobacco products	Textile and product mills	Apparel and leather	Paper	Printing and support	Petroleum and coal products	Chemical	Plastics and rubber products	
1967	...	...	...	...	...	...	...	...	...	...	...	...
1968	...	...	...	...	...	...	...	...	...	...	...	...
1969	...	...	...	...	...	...	...	...	...	...	...	...
1970	...	...	...	...	...	...	...	...	...	...	...	...
1971	...	...	...	...	...	...	...	...	...	...	...	...
1972	60.6	49.7	61.3	66.8	74.4	109.0	62.6	46.8	77.7	53.1	37.5	66.9
1973	63.4	51.1	64.1	67.6	73.6	110.9	67.7	49.2	76.3	58.1	42.2	69.1
1974	58.4	49.9	64.4	68.5	67.7	104.2	70.6	47.7	82.4	60.3	41.0	69.6
1975	49.7	46.7	59.8	67.4	65.5	101.6	61.1	44.5	81.2	53.1	35.1	66.0
1976	55.5	50.8	65.2	72.0	72.9	106.8	67.5	47.8	90.0	59.4	38.8	68.1
1977	63.7	55.2	69.7	73.6	79.7	112.0	70.4	51.8	96.3	64.6	45.8	74.7
1978	68.7	56.3	72.1	76.2	79.5	114.5	73.6	54.8	97.3	67.9	47.3	77.4
1979	68.2	56.5	72.6	75.8	79.4	107.5	74.7	56.4	103.9	69.4	46.5	79.0
1980	65.8	53.4	70.3	77.0	76.1	109.6	74.5	56.8	92.1	65.6	41.4	81.8
1981	65.3	55.5	71.0	77.9	74.5	109.5	75.5	58.3	87.8	66.7	43.9	83.8
1982	61.5	56.2	69.9	80.1	69.0	108.9	74.2	62.7	83.9	62.4	43.1	84.7
1983	67.4	56.0	73.2	80.3	77.9	111.9	79.1	67.4	85.3	66.7	46.9	87.0
1984	75.6	60.7	76.6	81.4	79.9	111.8	83.1	73.4	87.2	70.6	54.2	91.1
1985	76.1	61.5	77.0	84.0	77.2	106.8	81.4	76.3	85.9	70.1	56.3	94.6
1986	79.6	63.0	79.2	85.1	80.4	106.3	84.8	80.2	85.4	73.2	58.6	96.7
1987	85.2	67.9	83.5	86.8	88.7	107.3	87.6	86.1	89.5	78.9	64.9	102.1
1988	84.1	74.4	86.3	89.2	87.9	105.4	91.1	88.8	92.3	83.4	67.9	101.7
1989	83.7	75.3	86.8	88.7	89.5	100.7	92.1	89.2	91.3	85.0	70.2	100.2
1990	82.0	79.1	88.2	91.2	85.9	98.4	92.0	92.5	91.4	87.0	72.0	99.0
1991	75.7	80.7	87.9	91.9	84.7	97.7	92.2	89.7	90.1	86.8	71.3	94.9
1992	81.7	84.1	90.1	93.1	89.3	100.3	94.5	94.6	89.7	88.0	76.7	92.8
1993	85.2	88.9	91.4	92.8	92.8	102.4	95.6	94.9	90.3	89.0	82.2	93.5
1994	88.1	89.5	94.6	96.0	97.9	103.6	99.7	95.9	92.8	91.3	89.0	92.8
1995	89.6	92.8	96.2	98.7	96.9	102.8	101.1	97.3	94.5	92.7	91.1	92.9
1996	90.3	97.5	96.5	98.0	94.7	100.4	98.0	98.0	96.7	94.6	94.3	92.1
1997	100.0	100.0	100.0	100.0	100.0	100.0	100.0	100.0	100.0	100.0	100.0	100.0
1998	107.1	106.0	101.5	102.8	98.8	94.6	101.1	101.0	99.9	101.8	103.4	106.5
1999	110.7	108.2	102.2	100.9	99.0	90.5	102.2	101.9	104.0	103.8	108.7	109.9
2000	113.0	114.8	102.8	102.2	97.2	87.3	99.9	102.3	101.9	105.5	110.5	112.2
2001	106.2	114.1	99.8	102.1	87.5	77.9	94.3	96.9	99.9	103.9	104.0	105.6
2002	103.4	116.0	99.2	101.3	83.9	70.8	93.5	93.7	100.6	105.3	104.3	102.0
2003	101.1	116.8	97.0	97.8	77.7	63.2	92.4	89.4	101.4	105.6	103.2	105.7
2001												
January	110.1	117.8	101.1	101.9	91.8	84.5	96.7	100.7	100.7	104.2	107.1	109.5
February	109.3	116.1	101.2	102.0	90.4	84.1	97.8	100.6	100.7	104.9	105.8	106.0
March	109.5	116.4	100.3	101.2	91.0	83.4	94.4	100.8	100.1	103.8	105.1	104.9
April	107.3	115.5	100.3	102.5	90.4	82.5	96.1	97.4	99.9	103.0	105.5	106.2
May	107.1	113.5	100.3	101.8	88.3	80.3	94.7	97.6	100.6	105.1	104.5	105.5
June	105.5	112.1	99.8	103.3	87.6	78.5	93.3	96.4	101.4	102.8	104.1	105.4
July	106.9	113.7	99.1	101.5	86.6	77.7	93.5	95.4	100.5	102.9	104.5	106.7
August	104.7	113.1	99.3	101.8	86.3	75.4	94.0	96.2	98.9	103.9	103.5	105.9
September	104.1	111.1	99.3	102.9	86.9	72.9	94.8	94.2	98.8	103.3	103.0	105.1
October	104.0	114.3	99.4	102.4	84.3	72.6	93.2	94.3	100.1	105.2	102.5	104.4
November	103.4	112.2	98.7	101.8	83.2	71.4	91.8	95.2	99.6	104.5	101.1	103.5
December	102.7	113.3	98.2	101.8	83.6	71.1	90.8	93.8	98.1	103.7	101.5	104.0
2002												
January	103.1	113.8	99.2	102.4	83.1	70.7	91.5	95.3	100.2	105.7	101.7	103.2
February	102.7	112.8	99.0	102.8	83.0	70.1	91.6	94.2	101.6	104.6	102.0	102.9
March	102.7	113.7	99.5	103.1	84.7	70.3	90.8	93.7	100.9	105.4	103.8	103.1
April	103.1	115.9	99.6	103.0	84.8	69.8	92.6	94.0	101.5	104.9	104.6	101.6
May	104.0	117.3	99.5	101.6	85.3	70.8	94.0	94.4	100.0	105.6	105.2	101.6
June	104.9	116.5	100.2	102.8	86.2	72.1	94.0	93.5	100.3	106.2	106.1	101.2
July	104.7	117.6	100.0	101.6	84.7	72.4	94.3	94.3	101.2	106.8	105.6	101.1
August	103.0	116.9	99.7	101.8	83.9	71.3	94.4	93.8	100.9	105.9	105.4	101.4
September	104.1	115.9	99.5	101.7	83.2	71.9	94.7	92.9	99.3	105.9	105.1	102.5
October	103.1	116.0	98.5	100.4	82.3	70.3	94.2	92.6	97.1	104.7	104.7	102.8
November	103.8	116.8	97.8	97.7	83.2	71.1	95.3	92.7	101.3	104.3	103.9	101.6
December	102.0	119.0	97.4	97.1	82.3	69.4	94.2	93.0	103.0	104.0	103.4	100.5
2003												
January	103.9	119.1	97.5	98.4	79.8	68.1	92.4	92.7	100.8	104.5	103.4	103.7
February	103.1	118.9	97.5	98.0	80.4	66.7	92.5	92.3	100.4	105.3	103.8	106.0
March	101.5	118.8	97.5	98.4	80.1	65.9	93.4	90.3	102.1	105.0	103.9	107.0
April	101.0	117.1	97.0	97.8	78.5	64.2	92.2	90.3	100.5	105.6	102.2	106.0
May	100.8	116.6	96.8	98.0	77.7	64.2	92.7	88.8	101.6	104.4	103.0	106.1
June	100.3	117.2	96.3	98.0	77.2	62.5	93.1	88.8	99.1	103.5	102.5	107.0
July	101.2	116.6	96.7	98.3	76.7	62.0	93.0	89.0	100.0	104.5	102.8	105.0
August	100.1	114.8	96.5	97.3	75.9	60.2	91.6	88.5	101.8	105.5	103.1	105.2
September	100.5	115.3	96.6	97.3	74.9	60.2	91.3	88.7	101.9	106.1	103.0	104.7
October	100.0	114.8	96.7	96.8	76.2	61.2	91.4	88.3	102.1	106.4	103.4	105.8
November	100.4	115.1	97.6	97.5	77.9	61.7	92.0	87.0	102.8	108.3	104.2	106.6
December	100.0	117.6	97.4	97.2	76.6	61.8	92.7	87.6	104.2	107.8	103.1	105.4

... = Not available.

Table 2-2. Industrial Production Indexes by NAICS Industry Groups—Continued

(Seasonally adjusted, 1997 = 100.)

Year and month	Mining	Utilities			Selected high-tech industries	Excluding selected high-tech industries	Stage-of-process groups		
		Total	Electric	Natural gas			Crude	Primary and semi-finished	Finished
1967	...	...	...	...	0.8	54.8	...	...	...
1968	...	...	...	...	0.8	57.8	...	...	...
1969	...	...	...	...	0.9	60.3	...	...	...
1970	...	...	...	...	0.9	58.2	...	...	...
1971	...	...	...	...	0.9	59.3	...	...	...
1972	98.7	56.5	46.4	110.4	1.0	64.7	...	...	...
1973	99.2	59.7	50.5	105.9	1.3	69.7	...	...	...
1974	97.8	59.4	50.8	102.4	1.5	69.0	...	...	...
1975	95.4	60.4	53.0	95.9	1.3	62.9	...	...	...
1976	96.1	63.1	56.4	95.0	1.6	67.6	...	...	...
1977	98.3	65.5	60.0	91.8	2.2	72.2	...	...	...
1978	101.4	67.3	61.9	92.5	2.7	75.6	...	...	...
1979	104.4	68.8	63.2	95.0	3.6	77.2	...	...	...
1980	106.4	69.3	64.3	93.0	4.3	74.4	...	...	...
1981	109.2	70.2	66.0	90.9	5.1	74.9	...	...	...
1982	103.8	68.0	64.4	85.4	5.9	70.4	...	...	...
1983	98.3	68.5	66.3	79.8	7.0	71.7	...	...	...
1984	104.6	72.5	70.1	84.9	9.3	77.4	...	...	...
1985	102.6	74.0	72.6	81.4	9.9	78.2	...	...	...
1986	95.2	74.6	74.2	77.4	10.2	78.9	92.0	64.3	69.3
1987	96.0	78.2	77.7	80.9	12.3	82.2	94.9	68.0	72.5
1988	98.4	82.6	82.0	85.9	14.2	85.8	98.2	71.6	76.2
1989	97.3	85.2	84.5	89.0	15.0	86.3	98.2	72.2	77.1
1990	98.8	86.8	86.9	86.0	16.8	86.6	99.7	72.3	78.4
1991	96.5	88.9	89.0	88.3	18.0	84.8	97.1	71.2	77.5
1992	94.4	88.9	88.5	90.8	21.8	86.4	96.3	74.1	79.3
1993	94.4	92.0	91.7	94.2	25.6	88.6	95.1	77.6	81.6
1994	96.6	93.9	93.7	94.9	33.2	92.1	97.1	83.0	85.1
1995	96.4	97.2	97.1	97.3	47.3	94.4	97.6	87.8	89.1
1996	98.1	100.0	99.7	102.0	66.7	96.0	97.3	92.6	92.7
1997	100.0	100.0	100.0	100.0	100.0	100.0	100.0	100.0	100.0
1998	98.2	102.5	104.1	93.4	140.2	103.1	98.2	106.8	106.7
1999	94.0	105.5	107.1	96.1	201.3	104.4	96.8	114.3	109.2
2000	96.3	108.6	110.2	99.1	286.7	105.7	96.7	121.0	113.1
2001	96.8	108.1	109.9	97.7	291.1	101.6	94.5	115.6	110.5
2002	93.0	111.3	113.3	99.9	311.4	100.5	92.6	116.3	108.6
2003	93.3	111.4	113.8	99.1	369.0	100.0	92.0	117.0	109.0
2001									
January	96.8	112.3	113.3	106.0	311.1	103.7	95.6	119.4	112.4
February	97.5	110.8	112.0	103.5	306.4	103.2	96.0	118.2	112.2
March	98.0	109.6	110.8	102.2	304.1	102.9	95.6	117.4	112.1
April	98.1	108.5	110.5	97.8	297.4	102.7	95.4	116.8	112.0
May	97.8	107.4	109.5	95.8	292.3	102.3	94.5	116.0	111.9
June	97.1	107.9	110.1	96.2	286.6	101.8	93.7	115.5	111.0
July	96.6	106.6	108.0	97.9	281.0	101.5	93.6	115.0	110.5
August	96.4	109.1	110.8	99.0	277.0	101.3	93.9	115.2	109.6
September	96.8	106.7	108.1	98.3	277.0	100.6	94.8	114.1	108.9
October	96.1	108.0	109.4	99.0	282.9	100.2	94.3	113.9	108.6
November	95.8	105.2	108.7	86.8	286.7	99.6	93.9	113.1	108.3
December	94.5	104.8	107.4	90.3	291.3	99.2	92.3	112.7	108.6
2002									
January	93.5	106.6	109.2	92.5	291.3	99.8	92.4	113.7	108.9
February	93.7	107.7	110.2	94.1	294.1	99.9	92.5	114.3	108.6
March	93.0	109.9	111.9	98.5	295.8	100.3	92.0	115.2	108.7
April	92.8	112.3	114.3	101.5	298.9	100.7	92.6	116.2	108.6
May	93.1	111.4	113.0	102.8	302.3	100.7	93.4	116.6	108.3
June	93.6	112.5	114.4	101.9	308.3	101.3	93.5	117.2	109.4
July	92.8	113.4	115.7	100.3	311.2	101.1	93.4	117.3	108.9
August	93.0	110.9	113.2	97.9	318.9	100.9	92.8	117.1	109.2
September	91.3	111.6	114.3	96.3	323.2	100.7	91.5	117.0	109.2
October	91.8	113.4	115.5	101.5	325.8	100.3	91.4	117.2	108.3
November	93.8	112.8	113.8	106.5	332.5	100.3	92.7	117.3	108.1
December	94.2	112.8	114.0	105.2	334.7	99.8	93.2	116.4	107.7
2003									
January	93.4	112.3	113.9	102.6	335.7	100.3	92.1	116.9	108.8
February	93.3	116.4	117.2	110.8	344.0	100.5	92.5	117.9	108.5
March	93.1	110.8	112.9	99.4	345.9	99.7	92.5	116.3	108.3
April	93.4	109.4	111.9	96.5	348.3	99.0	92.4	115.6	107.6
May	92.7	110.2	112.4	98.0	352.9	98.9	91.7	115.6	107.6
June	93.2	107.9	109.8	97.5	359.6	98.8	92.3	115.3	107.6
July	93.4	111.3	114.1	96.7	369.1	99.4	92.6	116.6	108.2
August	93.1	111.8	115.0	95.9	382.6	99.2	92.0	116.9	108.1
September	93.5	109.9	112.4	96.8	388.1	99.8	92.3	117.3	109.0
October	93.7	111.0	113.9	96.6	397.4	99.9	92.2	118.2	108.8
November	93.6	111.9	114.6	98.2	402.8	100.8	92.1	119.3	110.1
December	93.5	114.2	116.9	100.0	404.7	101.1	92.2	119.9	110.1

. . . = Not available.

Table 2-3. Capacity Utilization by NAICS Industry Groups
(Output as a percentage of capacity, seasonally adjusted.)

Year and month	Total industry	Total manufacturing (SIC)	Manufacturing (NAICS)										
			Total	Durable goods manufacturing									Aircraft and miscellaneous transportation equipment
				Total	Wood products	Nonmetallic mineral products	Primary metals	Fabricated metal products	Machinery	Computer and electronic products	Electrical equipment, appliances, and components	Motor vehicles and parts	
1967	87.0	87.2	...	87.5	...	75.7	85.0	86.4	90.4	...	...	78.9	94.1
1968	87.3	87.0	...	87.3	...	78.4	84.8	87.3	85.0	...	...	90.0	89.4
1969	87.3	86.5	...	86.9	...	79.7	88.1	86.2	86.4	...	...	86.5	84.2
1970	81.0	79.2	...	77.4	...	73.8	79.1	78.5	79.3	...	...	66.0	72.3
1971	79.3	77.6	...	75.0	...	75.5	72.6	78.4	73.3	...	...	78.6	63.2
1972	84.4	83.2	83.1	81.7	92.1	79.9	82.6	84.9	82.3	80.7	89.5	83.8	64.9
1973	88.3	87.5	87.7	88.4	87.8	84.4	94.0	90.8	92.0	85.4	97.7	91.7	73.1
1974	84.9	84.1	84.2	84.2	77.9	82.0	95.4	85.9	90.9	83.3	90.9	76.5	73.5
1975	75.5	73.4	73.3	71.4	71.1	73.1	74.3	72.0	77.0	68.9	71.0	65.5	69.3
1976	79.5	78.0	78.0	75.9	80.4	77.2	79.0	75.2	79.7	71.1	79.8	81.8	63.5
1977	83.2	82.3	82.2	81.0	86.5	82.0	80.3	79.6	85.1	77.5	86.3	92.1	63.6
1978	85.0	84.5	84.5	84.2	85.2	86.3	85.2	80.7	88.7	84.1	88.4	92.2	69.7
1979	85.0	84.2	84.2	84.6	80.7	84.6	86.7	81.8	90.7	87.4	89.4	81.5	79.0
1980	80.9	78.8	78.5	77.8	73.0	75.5	76.5	75.6	84.2	86.8	82.1	60.0	83.2
1981	79.9	77.2	76.9	75.6	70.9	71.9	77.6	73.4	82.3	84.2	79.0	57.7	76.9
1982	73.8	71.1	70.6	66.7	63.3	63.5	55.6	65.4	67.6	80.9	69.5	51.4	70.5
1983	74.8	73.5	73.1	68.7	73.6	69.5	59.3	66.5	61.7	80.8	72.4	67.1	67.1
1984	80.5	79.5	79.1	76.9	78.8	74.8	69.1	72.7	72.6	86.9	82.0	80.3	71.0
1985	79.4	78.4	77.9	75.9	79.2	74.8	67.3	74.0	72.2	79.6	79.7	81.8	74.4
1986	78.8	78.5	78.1	75.4	83.6	77.3	69.9	73.9	71.2	76.0	79.8	77.5	76.6
1987	81.3	81.2	80.7	77.8	88.2	81.2	78.9	75.2	72.4	78.8	81.0	77.0	78.9
1988	84.3	84.1	83.9	82.1	86.6	83.2	89.9	78.9	80.1	80.4	85.4	83.1	82.4
1989	83.6	83.2	83.0	81.3	83.7	82.2	86.9	78.4	82.9	78.1	84.4	79.6	86.9
1990	82.4	81.6	81.5	79.1	81.9	80.3	84.6	76.7	79.8	78.9	81.7	70.4	87.6
1991	79.6	78.3	78.2	74.8	76.5	73.5	79.6	72.9	75.0	76.8	77.2	63.8	84.6
1992	80.3	79.4	79.4	76.8	80.2	76.4	82.4	74.8	74.2	79.0	81.4	72.0	78.1
1993	81.3	80.3	80.2	78.5	80.1	77.9	86.6	75.7	78.6	78.7	85.5	77.8	72.8
1994	83.4	82.6	82.6	81.5	83.3	81.5	91.9	80.2	84.1	80.7	91.1	86.2	65.2
1995	83.6	82.7	82.8	82.0	83.0	82.8	89.6	82.2	86.2	84.2	90.1	82.8	61.8
1996	82.4	81.1	81.3	80.7	83.0	86.2	88.7	82.2	85.8	79.5	87.9	79.6	63.9
1997	83.6	82.6	82.8	82.6	82.1	86.7	89.3	81.7	87.0	82.0	86.7	82.7	70.7
1998	83.0	82.0	82.0	81.9	83.6	88.3	88.5	80.2	85.4	78.5	86.7	81.0	80.5
1999	82.4	81.4	81.3	81.5	84.5	86.5	86.1	77.3	80.6	81.2	84.8	86.4	76.3
2000	82.6	81.1	80.9	81.5	81.2	83.8	82.7	79.4	82.2	84.5	86.4	85.4	66.7
2001	77.4	75.4	75.1	73.2	74.6	78.5	76.7	73.0	71.8	69.1	77.6	76.1	71.5
2002	75.6	73.9	73.6	70.6	74.5	76.9	76.5	70.1	67.0	63.0	75.1	80.7	65.8
2003	74.8	73.4	72.8	70.2	74.1	77.7	75.0	67.8	67.7	64.5	73.9	80.3	64.0
2001													
January	80.1	78.0	77.8	77.1	73.9	81.3	79.1	77.3	78.6	78.3	83.6	72.5	70.1
February	79.5	77.4	77.2	76.1	73.5	81.1	77.0	75.8	78.1	75.9	81.1	74.5	70.0
March	79.0	76.9	76.8	75.8	74.4	80.4	75.8	75.1	76.5	74.4	79.9	77.5	71.5
April	78.6	76.6	76.3	75.0	74.3	79.6	77.9	74.7	75.2	72.3	78.7	77.0	72.3
May	78.1	76.1	75.9	74.2	75.1	79.1	77.9	73.9	72.7	70.4	78.0	78.2	72.4
June	77.5	75.4	75.1	73.2	75.5	78.8	78.2	73.0	71.8	68.6	77.0	77.0	72.3
July	77.0	75.1	74.7	72.8	74.6	78.1	79.1	72.9	70.5	66.9	76.1	78.6	72.0
August	76.7	74.6	74.3	71.9	75.3	77.4	77.8	72.1	69.9	65.3	76.7	76.5	72.3
September	76.1	74.1	73.8	71.0	75.8	77.4	77.4	70.8	68.5	64.5	75.8	74.5	72.9
October	75.8	73.8	73.4	70.3	73.8	75.7	75.7	75.2	70.8	67.0	64.5	75.3	72.8	72.4
November	75.3	73.5	73.2	70.3	73.9	77.3	75.1	69.8	66.7	64.3	74.4	75.4	71.0
December	75.1	73.4	73.0	70.2	74.7	76.0	70.2	69.9	65.8	64.3	74.6	78.2	69.1
2002													
January	75.4	73.7	73.4	70.3	75.4	75.4	74.5	69.6	66.5	63.8	75.5	77.3	69.0
February	75.4	73.7	73.4	70.3	74.6	76.2	75.0	69.7	66.7	63.3	76.0	78.6	67.8
March	75.6	73.8	73.5	70.3	75.7	76.4	76.4	69.7	66.8	62.9	75.3	78.4	67.6
April	75.8	73.9	73.7	70.5	75.0	76.5	75.7	70.1	66.9	62.5	75.5	80.2	66.8
May	75.8	74.1	73.8	70.8	74.7	77.0	76.5	70.7	67.5	62.5	76.8	80.2	65.8
June	76.2	74.4	74.2	71.1	75.4	76.5	77.3	70.7	67.7	62.9	76.9	81.7	65.4
July	76.0	74.3	74.0	70.8	74.4	76.1	75.9	70.6	66.7	62.5	76.1	83.0	64.4
August	75.9	74.3	74.1	71.1	74.5	77.3	78.5	70.5	67.6	63.0	74.0	82.9	65.1
September	75.7	74.2	73.9	70.8	73.9	78.2	76.9	70.1	67.2	63.1	73.3	82.1	65.2
October	75.4	73.7	73.3	70.5	74.5	77.9	77.9	70.3	66.7	62.8	73.7	80.6	64.7
November	75.4	73.6	73.3	70.9	73.2	77.8	78.7	69.4	67.1	63.2	74.2	83.2	64.0
December	74.9	73.1	72.8	70.2	72.6	78.0	74.8	69.5	66.4	63.2	74.3	80.0	64.1
2003													
January	75.2	73.6	73.1	70.7	73.5	78.2	78.3	69.2	66.2	63.2	73.3	82.7	64.1
February	75.4	73.5	73.0	70.4	73.4	77.0	78.0	68.8	67.2	63.3	74.2	80.6	63.7
March	74.8	73.3	72.6	69.7	72.4	77.4	74.0	68.3	67.1	63.1	73.0	79.3	63.8
April	74.2	72.7	72.1	69.1	72.5	77.1	74.2	67.5	66.5	62.6	73.0	78.2	63.4
May	74.1	72.6	72.0	69.0	72.5	76.6	72.8	67.0	67.2	63.0	72.7	77.2	63.8
June	74.0	72.7	72.0	69.3	73.0	77.1	73.3	67.0	67.3	63.1	73.7	78.3	63.6
July	74.5	73.0	72.5	69.8	74.5	77.7	73.4	67.6	67.0	64.2	73.2	80.0	63.4
August	74.5	73.0	72.4	69.8	73.7	77.8	73.0	66.8	67.7	65.5	73.3	78.6	64.2
September	74.9	73.6	73.0	70.8	73.8	77.5	73.4	67.6	68.2	65.9	74.1	83.7	64.3
October	75.0	73.6	73.1	70.8	75.7	78.3	74.9	67.7	67.5	66.9	74.6	81.6	64.3
November	75.7	74.4	73.8	71.6	77.7	79.0	76.7	68.2	70.2	67.0	75.8	81.7	64.8
December	75.8	74.4	73.9	71.7	76.3	79.1	77.8	68.4	70.2	66.6	76.5	82.0	65.1

... = Not available.

Table 2-3. Capacity Utilization by NAICS Industry Groups—Continued

(Output as a percentage of capacity, seasonally adjusted.)

Year and month	Manufacturing (NAICS)—Continued											Other manufacturing (non-NAICS)
	Durable goods manufacturing—Continued		Nondurable goods manufacturing									
	Furniture and related products	Miscellaneous manufacturing	Total	Food, beverage, and tobacco products	Textile and product mills	Apparel and leather	Paper	Printing and support	Petroleum and coal products	Chemical	Plastics and rubber products	
1967	91.9	...	86.3	85.0	...	...	89.7	...	94.9	78.9	88.3	...
1968	91.8	...	86.4	84.8	...	...	89.3	...	95.9	80.1	90.9	...
1969	93.7	...	86.0	85.0	...	...	90.9	...	96.6	78.9	89.8	...
1970	85.6	...	82.0	84.0	...	...	85.9	...	97.0	75.8	78.6	...
1971	87.1	...	81.6	83.9	...	...	86.5	...	96.1	75.0	78.9	...
1972	94.4	80.3	85.1	85.2	89.0	81.2	91.4	92.2	94.3	79.9	88.1	85.4
1973	94.0	79.3	86.6	84.7	86.1	81.9	95.2	93.8	90.6	83.8	92.4	84.6
1974	81.5	74.4	84.1	83.8	76.2	75.9	95.7	87.7	93.1	83.9	83.9	82.7
1975	67.5	67.9	76.0	80.3	72.6	74.5	81.0	79.2	83.9	71.5	69.9	77.2
1976	74.2	72.7	80.9	83.3	81.0	77.7	88.2	82.1	86.2	77.2	77.3	77.4
1977	82.6	78.1	84.0	82.8	88.8	81.3	90.6	85.9	87.9	80.5	88.0	83.3
1978	85.0	78.9	84.9	83.4	88.3	83.5	92.5	87.2	86.6	81.6	88.1	85.1
1979	80.8	77.8	83.6	81.4	87.9	78.6	91.3	85.8	90.2	81.4	83.1	85.5
1980	75.6	72.9	79.5	81.3	83.5	81.2	88.6	83.4	77.1	75.5	72.5	87.0
1981	72.9	75.5	78.8	80.9	80.4	80.8	87.2	81.0	74.0	75.2	75.6	87.3
1982	67.5	73.1	76.7	82.0	74.2	80.3	84.3	82.2	74.3	69.0	72.3	86.5
1983	73.4	70.8	79.8	81.6	82.8	83.0	88.3	84.6	78.8	73.0	79.5	86.9
1984	80.5	75.5	82.6	82.1	84.7	83.2	90.8	87.5	82.5	76.4	89.8	89.0
1985	78.8	73.1	81.1	83.1	81.2	79.7	87.2	85.8	82.3	74.4	86.3	90.8
1986	80.6	72.8	82.1	82.9	83.7	80.9	89.4	86.1	81.6	76.9	85.3	89.3
1987	84.5	76.3	85.1	83.4	91.1	82.8	90.9	89.3	84.1	81.6	90.3	90.1
1988	82.0	81.0	86.5	84.6	88.8	82.6	92.4	89.9	86.9	84.6	90.7	88.2
1989	80.3	79.3	85.3	83.2	88.7	80.5	91.1	88.2	86.8	84.5	87.1	86.1
1990	77.4	80.0	84.6	84.0	83.2	79.5	89.0	88.8	86.8	84.3	83.1	84.3
1991	71.6	78.6	82.6	83.2	81.2	80.6	86.9	83.9	84.3	81.9	79.0	80.0
1992	77.4	77.0	82.9	82.5	85.5	83.5	87.0	85.7	84.9	80.5	82.5	78.6
1993	80.1	79.2	82.5	80.8	87.3	85.5	86.3	84.7	86.9	79.4	86.2	80.8
1994	81.7	78.7	84.1	82.5	89.2	87.0	88.9	85.1	88.5	79.9	90.5	81.5
1995	81.3	79.4	83.9	83.2	86.1	85.9	90.0	84.7	89.3	79.5	88.4	80.8
1996	79.1	80.9	82.2	81.4	82.7	83.1	85.8	83.8	91.4	78.4	86.8	78.1
1997	82.0	80.5	83.0	81.5	85.6	82.3	86.6	82.9	93.5	80.3	87.5	79.9
1998	81.7	80.9	82.2	82.4	84.0	78.1	87.2	81.6	90.3	78.7	86.4	81.3
1999	81.2	77.8	80.9	79.5	84.2	76.0	88.1	80.3	92.4	77.3	85.9	83.1
2000	80.5	79.0	80.1	79.6	83.3	74.9	86.1	79.7	90.3	76.4	83.6	84.8
2001	74.0	75.7	77.8	79.5	76.7	68.9	82.1	76.9	88.1	74.0	78.6	80.4
2002	71.5	75.8	77.6	79.4	75.4	66.1	83.3	75.1	88.2	74.0	79.5	78.6
2003	69.9	76.4	76.4	77.2	71.8	63.6	83.6	72.1	88.2	73.2	79.9	82.8
2001												
January	77.3	79.6	78.7	79.3	79.5	73.5	83.6	79.1	89.0	74.7	80.5	83.0
February	76.6	78.1	78.8	79.4	78.4	73.3	84.6	79.2	89.0	75.1	79.6	80.4
March	76.6	78.1	78.0	78.8	79.1	73.0	81.8	79.5	88.5	74.2	79.1	79.7
April	75.0	77.2	78.1	79.8	78.8	72.4	83.4	77.0	88.2	73.5	79.5	80.7
May	74.7	75.6	78.1	79.3	77.1	70.7	82.3	77.3	88.7	74.9	78.8	80.2
June	73.5	74.4	77.8	80.4	76.7	69.3	81.2	76.6	89.4	73.2	78.6	80.2
July	74.4	75.2	77.3	79.1	75.9	68.8	81.5	75.8	88.5	73.2	79.0	81.2
August	72.8	74.6	77.4	79.3	75.9	67.1	82.1	76.7	87.0	73.8	78.3	80.7
September	72.4	73.1	77.5	80.3	76.6	65.1	83.0	75.2	86.9	73.4	78.1	80.2
October	72.2	75.1	77.6	79.9	74.5	65.1	81.7	75.3	88.0	74.7	77.7	79.7
November	71.8	73.6	77.1	79.5	73.6	64.3	80.7	76.1	87.5	74.0	76.8	79.1
December	71.2	74.2	76.7	79.5	74.1	64.3	79.9	75.1	86.2	73.4	77.2	79.5
2002												
January	71.5	74.4	77.5	80.0	73.8	64.2	80.7	76.3	88.0	74.8	77.3	79.0
February	71.1	73.7	77.4	80.3	73.9	64.0	80.9	75.4	89.1	73.9	77.6	78.8
March	71.1	74.2	77.8	80.6	75.6	64.4	80.4	75.1	88.5	74.3	79.0	79.1
April	71.4	75.6	77.9	80.6	75.8	64.3	82.2	75.3	89.1	73.9	79.7	78.0
May	71.9	76.6	77.9	79.5	76.4	65.5	83.5	75.6	87.7	74.3	80.2	78.1
June	72.6	76.0	78.4	80.6	77.3	67.0	83.7	74.9	88.0	74.6	80.9	77.9
July	72.4	76.8	78.3	79.7	76.2	67.6	84.1	75.5	88.7	75.0	80.5	77.9
August	71.2	76.3	78.1	79.8	75.6	67.0	84.3	75.1	88.5	74.2	80.4	78.3
September	72.0	75.7	77.9	79.8	75.1	67.9	84.7	74.4	87.0	74.2	80.2	79.3
October	71.3	75.8	77.2	78.9	74.5	66.9	84.5	74.2	85.1	73.3	80.0	79.7
November	71.7	76.3	76.7	76.8	75.5	67.9	85.6	74.3	88.8	72.8	79.4	78.9
December	70.4	77.8	76.4	76.3	74.8	66.8	84.6	74.6	90.2	72.6	79.1	78.1
2003												
January	71.8	77.9	76.5	77.5	72.7	65.9	83.1	74.4	88.2	72.8	79.3	80.7
February	71.2	77.8	76.5	77.2	73.4	65.0	83.3	74.1	87.8	73.3	79.6	82.7
March	70.1	77.7	76.6	77.5	73.4	64.7	84.2	72.6	89.2	73.1	79.9	83.5
April	69.8	76.6	76.2	77.2	72.1	63.5	83.2	72.6	87.8	73.4	78.7	82.8
May	69.7	76.3	76.1	77.3	71.6	63.9	83.8	71.5	88.6	72.5	79.4	83.0
June	69.3	76.7	75.8	77.4	71.3	62.7	84.3	71.6	86.3	71.8	79.2	83.8
July	69.9	76.3	76.2	77.7	71.1	62.7	84.3	71.9	87.0	72.4	79.6	82.3
August	69.2	75.1	76.1	76.9	70.5	61.3	83.1	71.5	88.4	73.1	80.0	82.5
September	69.5	75.4	76.2	77.0	69.8	61.8	82.8	71.9	88.4	73.4	80.1	82.3
October	69.2	75.1	76.3	76.7	71.2	63.3	82.9	71.6	88.4	73.5	80.6	83.2
November	69.5	75.3	77.0	77.2	73.0	64.2	83.6	70.7	88.9	74.8	81.4	84.0
December	69.2	77.0	76.9	77.1	72.0	64.8	84.3	71.2	90.0	74.4	80.7	83.1

... = Not available.

Table 2-3. Capacity Utilization by NAICS Industry Groups—*Continued*

(Output as a percentage of capacity, seasonally adjusted.)

Year and month	Mining	Utilities	Selected high-technology industries				Measures excluding selected high-technology industries		Stage-of-process groups		
			Total	Computers and office equipment	Communications equipment	Semiconductors and related electronic components	Total industry	Manufacturing	Crude	Primary and semi-finished	Finished
1967	81.2	94.5	89.4	...	...	...	86.9	86.8	81.1	85.0	88.2
1968	83.6	95.1	87.6	...	...	...	87.2	86.9	83.4	86.8	87.0
1969	86.8	96.6	89.6	...	...	...	87.0	86.2	85.6	87.9	85.4
1970	89.3	96.0	83.2	...	...	...	80.8	79.0	85.1	81.2	77.9
1971	87.9	94.4	74.0	...	...	...	79.7	77.9	84.3	81.3	75.4
1972	90.8	95.2	79.4	85.2	73.2	84.7	84.6	83.3	88.7	87.8	79.4
1973	91.9	94.1	82.2	82.5	76.0	92.1	88.5	87.8	90.8	92.0	83.1
1974	91.1	87.8	82.6	88.7	74.3	88.4	85.0	84.2	91.3	87.1	80.1
1975	89.2	84.3	65.3	69.8	62.5	64.2	75.9	73.8	84.1	74.8	73.5
1976	90.1	85.1	67.6	71.6	62.7	70.0	79.9	78.4	87.5	79.8	76.2
1977	90.4	84.8	76.0	73.6	74.6	80.5	83.5	82.6	89.7	84.4	79.3
1978	90.1	84.0	82.6	85.9	77.9	84.7	85.1	84.6	88.9	86.0	82.3
1979	91.1	85.5	87.0	83.5	87.8	91.0	85.0	84.1	89.5	85.9	82.0
1980	91.7	85.3	87.5	85.5	90.2	87.1	80.6	78.3	89.2	78.8	79.7
1981	91.6	84.1	85.2	86.7	87.5	81.8	79.6	76.8	89.5	77.1	78.3
1982	83.8	80.5	78.9	71.9	87.5	80.7	73.6	70.7	81.8	70.4	74.0
1983	78.4	79.5	79.8	77.2	80.8	82.0	74.5	73.2	78.5	74.2	73.7
1984	84.6	82.8	88.2	86.6	86.3	91.3	80.1	78.9	84.7	81.0	77.9
1985	83.4	82.4	78.1	77.5	82.9	75.4	79.5	78.5	83.3	79.9	77.3
1986	76.7	82.3	72.0	71.8	77.5	68.3	79.2	79.0	79.0	79.9	77.4
1987	79.5	84.0	76.2	73.9	78.0	77.5	81.6	81.5	83.0	82.8	79.0
1988	83.5	86.1	78.6	76.8	80.5	79.2	84.6	84.5	86.7	85.7	81.8
1989	84.3	86.7	77.1	74.9	78.8	78.1	84.0	83.7	87.5	84.5	81.3
1990	86.5	86.1	77.5	73.2	81.0	79.5	82.7	81.9	88.8	82.3	80.7
1991	84.8	86.8	75.3	68.1	74.7	81.3	79.8	78.5	86.0	79.4	77.9
1992	84.4	85.2	79.7	77.5	79.3	80.7	80.3	79.4	85.7	80.9	78.2
1993	85.7	87.7	80.8	80.8	79.1	81.4	81.3	80.2	85.5	83.0	78.2
1994	87.3	88.9	83.8	81.3	83.5	84.8	83.4	82.5	87.2	86.3	79.1
1995	87.1	90.0	87.1	83.2	84.3	89.9	83.4	82.3	87.9	86.4	79.2
1996	89.6	90.5	80.7	78.4	78.9	82.5	82.6	81.2	87.6	85.1	78.0
1997	90.8	89.1	84.4	81.8	79.3	88.7	83.5	82.4	89.0	85.7	79.8
1998	88.1	91.0	80.3	84.5	80.1	78.4	83.2	82.2	86.1	84.4	80.6
1999	85.7	92.5	85.4	85.2	84.5	86.0	82.1	80.9	85.9	84.8	78.8
2000	89.9	92.9	89.6	75.9	91.2	95.6	82.0	80.3	87.4	85.3	78.2
2001	89.0	89.8	68.8	65.9	70.6	69.2	78.1	76.1	85.1	78.6	74.3
2002	84.3	87.8	61.5	70.4	50.6	65.2	76.7	75.0	82.9	77.5	71.9
2003	84.9	83.7	63.9	70.9	50.6	70.1	75.9	74.5	83.5	76.8	71.0
2001											
January	90.1	94.8	81.0	68.8	89.6	81.9	80.1	77.8	86.6	82.2	76.2
February	90.6	93.3	78.0	67.4	84.3	79.5	79.7	77.4	86.9	81.2	75.9
March	90.8	92.1	75.8	67.0	80.3	77.4	79.3	77.1	86.4	80.4	75.7
April	90.7	90.9	72.7	66.9	77.0	72.9	79.1	77.0	86.2	79.8	75.5
May	90.2	89.7	70.2	66.1	74.0	69.7	78.8	76.7	85.3	79.0	75.3
June	89.3	89.9	67.7	64.1	70.9	67.3	78.3	76.2	84.5	78.5	74.7
July	88.6	88.5	65.3	61.9	68.7	64.8	78.0	76.1	84.2	78.1	74.2
August	88.2	90.3	63.4	60.9	64.6	64.1	77.8	75.7	84.4	78.0	73.5
September	88.4	88.0	62.5	62.0	62.1	63.3	77.2	75.2	85.1	77.1	73.0
October	87.6	88.7	63.0	64.9	60.6	63.8	76.9	74.8	84.6	76.9	72.8
November	87.1	86.0	62.9	68.6	58.4	63.4	76.3	74.5	84.1	76.2	72.5
December	85.9	85.3	63.0	72.4	57.2	62.8	76.0	74.3	82.6	75.8	72.6
2002											
January	84.8	86.4	62.1	74.9	53.8	62.2	76.4	74.7	82.6	76.4	72.7
February	84.9	86.9	61.8	75.1	53.7	61.6	76.4	74.7	82.7	76.7	72.4
March	84.2	88.2	61.3	72.7	53.2	61.9	76.7	74.9	82.2	77.2	72.4
April	84.0	89.8	61.1	69.0	52.8	63.4	76.9	75.1	82.8	77.7	72.2
May	84.2	88.6	61.0	66.3	51.6	65.1	76.9	75.2	83.5	77.9	71.9
June	84.7	89.0	61.3	65.9	51.9	65.9	77.3	75.6	83.6	78.2	72.5
July	84.0	89.2	61.1	67.1	49.2	66.6	77.1	75.4	83.6	78.2	72.1
August	84.2	86.8	61.7	68.9	48.9	67.5	76.9	75.4	83.1	77.9	72.1
September	82.7	86.9	61.8	70.2	47.8	67.7	76.7	75.3	82.0	77.7	72.1
October	83.2	87.9	61.5	71.1	46.9	67.4	76.5	74.8	82.1	77.8	71.3
November	85.1	87.1	62.0	71.7	48.5	67.0	76.4	74.7	83.3	77.7	71.1
December	85.4	86.7	61.7	72.1	49.3	65.6	76.0	74.2	83.8	77.0	70.8
2003											
January	84.8	85.9	61.2	72.1	48.7	64.9	76.4	74.8	82.9	77.2	71.4
February	84.7	88.7	62.1	71.6	51.4	65.1	76.5	74.7	83.4	77.8	71.1
March	84.6	84.1	61.8	70.4	51.8	64.8	75.9	74.5	83.5	76.6	71.0
April	84.9	82.8	61.6	69.1	51.1	65.7	75.4	73.9	83.5	76.0	70.5
May	84.3	83.1	61.9	68.3	50.9	66.7	75.3	73.8	83.0	75.9	70.4
June	84.8	81.1	62.5	68.5	50.7	68.2	75.2	73.9	83.6	75.6	70.4
July	85.0	83.4	63.6	69.5	49.9	70.8	75.6	74.2	83.9	76.3	70.8
August	84.8	83.5	65.4	70.3	50.7	73.7	75.5	74.0	83.4	76.4	70.6
September	85.2	81.8	65.8	71.3	50.1	74.5	75.9	74.6	83.8	76.6	71.2
October	85.4	82.4	66.8	72.4	51.3	75.3	76.0	74.6	83.8	77.0	71.1
November	85.3	82.8	67.2	73.4	50.9	75.8	76.7	75.4	83.7	77.7	71.9
December	85.3	84.2	66.9	74.2	50.1	75.4	76.8	75.5	83.9	78.0	71.8

... = Not available.

NOTES AND DEFINITIONS

TABLES 2-1 THROUGH 2-3 AND 20-1
INDUSTRIAL PRODUCTION AND CAPACITY UTILIZATION

Source: Board of Governors of the Federal Reserve System

The *industrial production index* measures changes in the physical volume or quantity of output of manufacturing, mining, and electric and gas utilities. *Capacity utilization* is calculated by dividing a seasonally adjusted industrial production index for an industry or group of industries by a related index of productive capacity.

Around the 15th day of each month, the Federal Reserve issues estimates of industrial production and capacity utilization for the previous month. The production estimates are in the form of index numbers (currently 1997 = 100) reflecting the monthly levels of total output of the nation's factories, mines, and gas and electric utilities expressed as a percent of the monthly average in the 1997 base year. Capacity estimates are expressed as index numbers, 1997 *output* = 100 (not 1997 *capacity*), and capacity utilization is measured by the production index as a percent of the capacity index. Since for each industry the bases of those two indexes are the same, this procedure yields production as a percent of capacity. Monthly estimates are subject to revision in each of the three subsequent months, as well as annual and comprehensive revisions in subsequent years. Monthly series are seasonally adjusted using the Census X-12 ARIMA program.

Definitions and notes on the data

The index of industrial production measures a large portion of the goods output of the national economy on a monthly basis. That portion, together with construction, has also accounted for the bulk of the variation in output over the course of many historical business cycles. The substantial industrial detail included in the index illuminates structural developments in the economy.

The total industrial production index and indexes for its major components are constructed from individual industry series (295 series for data from 1997 forward) based on the 2002 North American Industry Classification System (NAICS). See Chapter 14 of this volume for a description of NAICS and a table outlining its structure.

The Federal Reserve has been able to provide a much longer continuous historical series on the NAICS basis than other government agencies. In a major research effort, the Fed and the Center for Economic Studies of the Bureau of the Census re-coded data from seven Censuses of Manufactures, beginning in 1963, to establish benchmark NAICS data for output, value added, and capacity utilization. The resulting indexes are shown annually for the full 31 years (37 for aggregate levels) in Tables 2-1 through 2-3 and monthly in Table 20-1.

However, the Fed's featured indexes for total industry and total manufacturing do not observe the reclassifications under NAICS of the logging industry to agriculture and the publishing industry to the Information sector. (The reason cited by the Fed was to avoid "changing the scope or historical continuity of these statistics.") Totals without those industries are also published, however, for users who may prefer the new NAICS definitions.

The individual series are grouped in two ways: market groups and industry groups.

Market groups. For analyzing market trends and product flows, the individual series are grouped into final products, nonindustrial supplies, and industrial materials. Final products are those purchased by consumers, businesses, or government for final use. Nonindustrial supplies are expected to become inputs in nonindustrial sectors, such as construction, agriculture, and services. Materials comprise industrial output requiring further processing within the industrial sector.

Final products are divided into consumer goods and equipment, and equipment is divided into business equipment and defense and space equipment. Further subdivisions of each market group are based on type of product and the market destination for the product.

Industry groups typically are groupings by 3-digit NAICS industries and major aggregates of these industries—for example, durable and nondurable manufacturing, mining, and utilities. Indexes are also calculated for stage-of-processing industry groups—crude, primary and semifinished, and finished processing. The stage-of-processing grouping is a new feature in the 2002 revision, replacing the two narrower and less refined "primary processing manufacturing" and "advanced processing manufacturing" groups previously published. *Crude processing* consists of logging, much of mining, and certain basic manufacturing activities in the chemical, paper, and metals industries. *Primary and semifinished processing* represents industries producing materials and parts used as inputs by other industries. *Finished processing* includes industries producing goods in their finished form for use by consumers, business investment, and government.

The indexes of industrial production are constructed with data from a variety of sources. Current monthly estimates of production are based on measures of physical output where possible and appropriate. For a few high-tech industries, the estimated value of nominal output is deflated by a corresponding price index. For industries in which such direct measurement is not possible monthly, output is inferred from production-worker hours or the use of electric power, adjusted for trends in output relative to input derived from annual and benchmark revisions.

In annual and benchmark revisions, the individual indexes are revised using data from the quinquennial Censuses of Manufactures and Mineral Industries and the Annual Survey of Manufactures and Survey of Plant Capacity, prepared by the Bureau of the Census; deflators from the Producer Price Indexes and other sources; the Minerals Yearbook, prepared by the Department of the Interior; publications of the Department of Energy; and other sources.

The weights used in computing the indexes are based on Census value added—the difference between the value of production and the cost of materials and supplies consumed. (Census value added differs in some respects from the economic concept of industry value added used in the National Income and Product Accounts [NIPAs]. Industry value added is not available in sufficient detail for the industrial production indexes. See Chapter 15 for data and description of value added by industry.) Beginning with 1972, the index uses a version of the Fisher-ideal index formula, that is, a chain-weighting system similar to that in the NIPAs. See Notes and Definitions to Chapter 1. Chain-weighting keeps the index from being distorted by the use of obsolete relative prices.

For the purpose of these value-added weights, value added per unit of output is based on data from the Censuses of Manufacturing and Mineral Industries, the Census Bureau's Annual Survey of Manufactures, and revenue and expense data reported by the Department of Energy and the American Gas Association, projected into recent years using changes in relevant producer price indexes.

To separate seasonal movements from cyclical patterns and underlying trends, each component of the index is seasonally adjusted by the Census X-12 ARIMA method.

The index does not cover production on farms, in the construction industry, in transportation, or in various trade and service industries. A number of groups and subgroups include data for individual series not published separately.

Capacity utilization is calculated for the manufacturing, mining, and electric and gas utilities industries. Output is measured by seasonally adjusted indexes of industrial production. The capacity indexes attempt to capture the concept of sustainable maximum output, which is defined as the greatest level of output that a plant can maintain within the framework of a realistic work schedule, taking account of normal downtime, and assuming sufficient availability of inputs to operate the machinery and equipment in place. The 85 individual capacity indexes are based on a variety of data, including capacity data measured in physical units compiled by government agencies and trade associations, Census Bureau surveys of utilization rates and investment, and estimates of growth of the capital stock.

Revisions

Revisions to data for recent years normally occur annually, late in the year, taking into account additional source data that have become available. The 2004 revision was released in December 2004, too late for inclusion in this volume. Data for 2000 through 2002 were revised in November 2003 and are included in this volume. Late in 2002, a comprehensive historical revision was introduced, converting the index to the NAICS classification system, updating the base year from 1992 to 1997, and introducing newly available and more comprehensive data and improved methods for measuring the output of communications equipment, as well as the usual annual data updating.

A previous comprehensive revision in 1997 moved the reference year from 1987 to 1992 = 100 and introduced annual (instead of quinquennial) updating of the value-added weights for each industry. In the January 2001 revision, recalculation of the value-added weights each month was introduced.

Data availability

Data are available monthly in Federal Reserve release G.17. Selected data are subsequently published monthly in the *Federal Reserve Bulletin*. Historical data may be purchased on diskette from Publications Services, Board of Governors of the Federal Reserve System. Current and historical data and background information are available on the Federal Reserve Internet site at <http://www.federalreserve.gov>.

Chain-weighting makes it difficult for the user to analyze in detail the sources of aggregate output change. An Explanatory Note included in each month's index release provides some assistance for the user, including a reference to a Web site location representing the exact contribution of a monthly change in a component index to the monthly change in the total index.

References

The G.17 release each month contains extensive explanatory material, as well as references for further detail. The 2003 annual revision is described in "Industrial Production and Capacity Utilization: The 2003 Annual Revision" in the *Federal Reserve Bulletin*, Winter 2004.

The latest comprehensive revision is described in "Industrial Production and Capacity Utilization: The 2002 Historical and Annual Revision," *Federal Reserve Bulletin*, April 2003. The aggregation method is described in *Bulletin* articles in March 2001 and February 1997. *Bulletin* articles are also available on the FRB Internet site.

An earlier detailed description of the industrial production index, together with a history of the index, a glossary of terms, and a bibliography is presented in *Industrial Production—1986 Edition*, available from the Publication Services, Board of Governors of the Federal Reserve System.

CHAPTER 3: INCOME DISTRIBUTION AND POVERTY

Section 3a: Household and Family Income

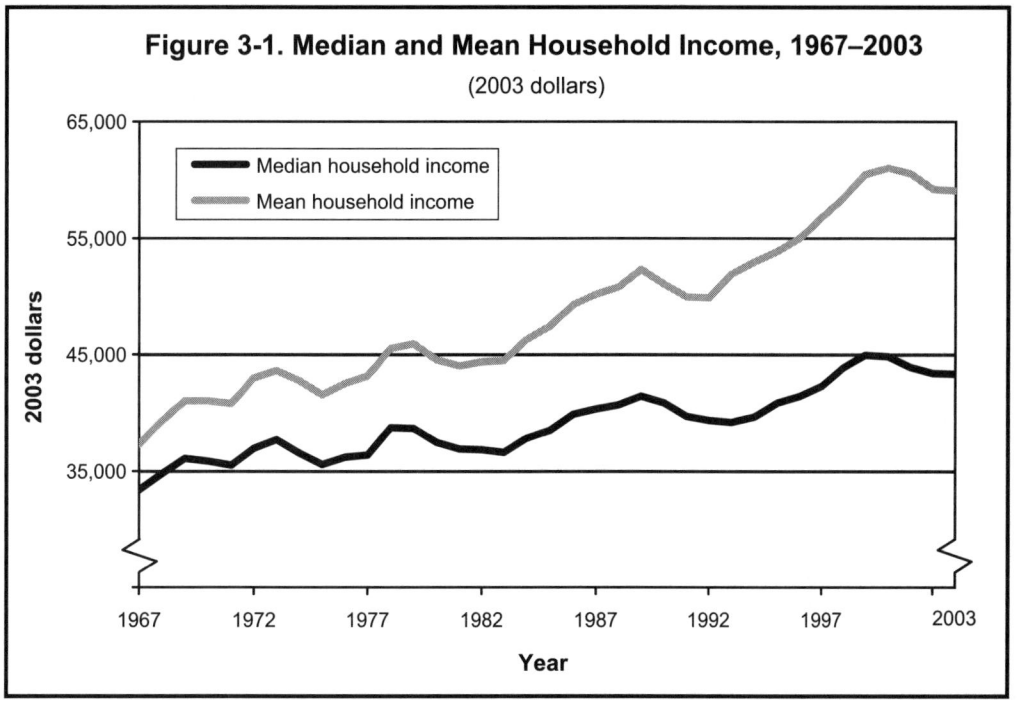

Figure 3-1. Median and Mean Household Income, 1967–2003

- Measured as cash income before taxes, median household income in 2003 was $43,318, down 3.6 percent in constant (2003) dollars from the 1999 all-time high. Between the 1969 business cycle peak and 1999, real median household income rose an average 0.7 percent per year. (Table 3-1)
- The Census Bureau also tabulates "mean income," which is the sum of all the reported household incomes divided by the number of households. The mean is higher than the median when the distribution of income is skewed upward, with very large incomes at the top of the distribution, and it rises faster than the median when the income distribution is becoming more unequal. (See "Whose Standard of Living?" in "Expanded Historical Statistics..." at the beginning of this book.) Mean household income peaked one year later, in 2000; rose at a 1.3 percent annual rate from 1969 to 2000; and declined 3.2 percent from 2000 to 2003. (Table 3-3)
- Measures of income distribution confirm an increase in income inequality. The "Gini coefficient" has risen from 0.388 in 1968 to a high of 0.466 in 2001, and was only slightly lower in 2003. (Table 3-3)
- In earlier postwar years, the Census Bureau did not tabulate household income but did measure median family income. ("Households" is the larger group, including not only families but also individuals living apart from any family member.) In constant dollars, median family income rose at a 3.3 percent annual rate between cycle peaks in 1948 and 1969 and slowed to 0.9 percent from 1969 to 2000. Thus, family income over the latest three decades rose faster than household income. The family income data also indicate a marked slowdown from the first two postwar decades in the rate of increase in the standard of living for the typical family. (Table 3-2)
- In another contrast to the more recent period, inequality in family incomes declined between 1947 and 1968. (Table 3-4)
- The ratio of women's to men's earnings for year-round, full-time workers has increased from 0.607 in 1960 to 0.766 in 2002, but fell back in 2003 as men's earnings increased while those of women declined. (Table 3-2)

Table 3-1. Median Household Income

(2003 dollars.)

Year	All races	White		Black	Asian, Native Hawaiian, and other Pacific Islander	Hispanic (of any race)
		Total	Not Hispanic			
1967	33 338	34 766	...	20 186	...	...
1968	34 746	36 178	...	21 333	...	...
1969	36 074	37 648	...	22 756	...	...
1970	35 832	37 321	...	22 716	...	...
1971	35 463	37 094	...	21 911	...	...
1972	36 953	38 767	39 320	22 629	...	29 256
1973	37 700	39 511	39 859	23 257	...	29 207
1974	36 537	38 211	38 537	22 724	...	29 061
1975	35 559	37 187	37 467	22 324	...	26 715
1976	36 155	37 874	38 646	22 521	...	27 272
1977	36 359	38 235	38 993	22 563	...	28 523
1978	38 693	40 224	40 981	24 173	...	30 317
1979	38 649	40 523	41 094	23 792	...	30 622
1980	37 447	39 506	40 206	22 760	...	28 864
1981	36 868	38 954	39 516	21 859	...	29 573
1982	36 811	38 537	39 183	21 841	...	27 699
1983	36 593	38 375	...	21 777	...	27 869
1984	37 767	39 843	40 670	22 697	...	28 630
1985	38 510	40 614	41 527	24 163	...	28 478
1986	39 868	41 914	42 867	24 148	...	29 387
1987	40 357	42 520	43 689	24 269	49 904	29 943
1988	40 678	43 003	44 188	24 514	48 212	30 419
1989	41 411	43 560	44 497	25 906	51 720	31 404
1990	40 865	42 622	43 597	25 488	52 475	30 475
1991	39 679	41 580	42 573	24 771	48 007	29 887
1992	39 364	41 385	42 774	24 098	48 570	29 035
1993	39 165	41 320	42 840	24 487	48 073	28 690
1994	39 613	41 779	43 127	25 816	49 703	28 756
1995	40 845	42 871	44 564	26 842	48 682	27 401
1996	41 431	43 379	45 277	27 411	50 517	29 073
1997	42 294	44 542	46 376	28 630	51 716	30 434
1998	43 825	46 110	47 831	28 572	52 562	31 929
1999	44 922	46 720	48 742	30 808	56 251	33 938
2000	44 853	46 910	48 734	31 690	59 559	35 429
2001	43 882	46 261	48 119	30 625	55 736	34 880
2002	43 381	...	...	...	...	33 861
2003	43 318	...	...	...	...	32 997
By race:						
Race alone:						
2002	...	46 119	47 974	29 691	53 832	...
2003	...	45 631	47 777	29 645	55 699	...
Race alone or in combination:						
2002	...	...	...	29 845	53 483	...
2003	...	...	...	29 689	55 262	...

... = Not available.

Table 3-2. Median Family Income and Median Earnings by Sex

(Constant dollars, as noted.)

Year	Median family income (2001 dollars, except as noted)						Median earnings of year-round, full-time workers (2003 dollars)	
	All families	Married couples			Male householder [1]	Female householder [1]	Male workers	Female workers
		Total	Wife in workforce	Wife not in workforce				
1947	20 402	20 927	...	...	19 762	14 620	...	...
1948	19 846	20 375	...	...	20 518	12 853	...	...
1949	19 584	20 139	24 311	19 275	17 781	13 256	...	...
1950	20 668	21 458	24 927	20 643	19 397	11 968	...	...
1951	21 391	22 129	26 709	20 959	19 909	12 803	...	...
1952	22 040	23 009	27 763	21 599	20 482	12 663	...	...
1953	23 825	24 550	30 357	23 123	23 101	13 789	...	...
1954	23 252	24 179	29 775	22 605	22 398	12 801	...	...
1955	24 706	25 718	31 439	24 192	23 431	13 818	...	...
1956	26 387	27 453	32 885	25 642	23 003	15 203	...	...
1957	26 506	27 525	32 777	25 796	24 451	14 747	...	...
1958	26 387	27 570	32 233	25 847	22 097	14 218	...	...
1959	27 930	29 193	34 571	27 414	23 785	14 251	...	...
1960	28 464	29 746	34 947	27 958	24 615	15 032	28 253	17 142
1961	28 764	30 279	36 052	28 047	25 424	15 012	29 161	17 278
1962	29 585	31 110	37 061	28 631	28 368	15 552	29 701	17 612
1963	30 627	32 313	38 175	29 598	27 986	15 738	30 457	17 953
1964	31 773	33 529	39 516	30 655	28 015	16 726	31 178	18 441
1965	33 152	34 620	40 967	31 413	29 297	16 831	31 575	18 921
1966	34 861	36 277	42 794	32 991	29 770	18 560	32 975	18 979
1967	35 629	37 911	44 715	34 183	30 604	19 286	33 520	19 369
1968	37 275	39 486	46 145	35 474	31 614	19 333	34 392	20 001
1969	39 034	41 385	48 121	36 742	34 511	19 954	36 358	21 402
1970	38 954	41 516	48 465	36 732	35 579	20 107	36 784	21 838
1971	38 878	41 543	48 585	36 833	32 970	19 331	36 921	21 970
1972	40 764	43 650	50 962	38 710	37 790	19 590	38 878	22 495
1973	41 590	44 961	52 585	39 405	37 072	20 006	40 117	22 719
1974	40 513	43 719	50 935	38 406	36 607	20 373	38 710	22 744
1975	39 784	43 113	49 985	36 979	37 684	19 847	38 446	22 613
1976	41 023	44 438	51 371	38 207	35 269	19 777	38 347	23 082
1977	41 271	45 414	52 251	38 832	37 427	20 018	39 183	23 088
1978	43 601	47 803	54 647	39 933	39 463	21 101	40 403	24 016
1979	44 255	48 417	56 171	40 005	37 976	22 323	39 948	23 834
1980	42 776	47 086	54 691	38 603	35 646	21 177	39 354	23 675
1981	41 642	46 622	54 400	37 805	36 994	20 386	39 161	23 197
1982	41 151	45 693	53 285	37 404	35 368	20 167	38 464	23 750
1983	41 444	46 006	54 135	36 908	36 832	19 877	38 338	24 381
1984	42 858	48 012	56 210	38 235	37 819	20 759	39 120	24 903
1985	43 518	48 798	57 163	38 530	35 496	21 434	39 451	25 476
1986	45 393	50 551	59 089	39 761	38 465	21 029	40 443	25 993
1987	46 151	51 976	60 726	39 698	37 564	21 880	40 179	26 188
1988	46 285	52 321	61 408	39 137	38 572	22 065	39 828	26 306
1989	47 166	53 141	62 404	39 631	38 390	22 667	39 155	26 889
1990	46 429	52 394	61 432	39 747	38 146	22 237	37 773	27 052
1991	45 551	51 959	61 052	38 119	35 934	21 156	38 751	27 071
1992	45 221	51 795	61 544	37 309	34 096	21 051	38 800	27 465
1993	44 586	51 880	61 771	36 454	31 929	21 043	38 119	27 263
1994	45 820	53 118	62 984	36 834	32 787	21 546	37 882	27 263
1995	46 843	54 284	64 390	37 344	35 017	22 713	37 753	26 966
1996	47 516	55 836	65 580	37 910	35 497	22 366	37 522	27 677
1997	49 017	56 741	66 726	39 624	36 250	23 122	38 487	28 542
1998	50 689	58 761	69 142	40 303	38 698	24 037	39 836	29 148
1999	51 996	60 202	70 668	41 029	39 723	25 209	40 170	29 048
2000	52 148	60 748	71 167	41 098	38 780	26 434	39 792	29 334
2001	51 407	60 335	70 834	40 782	36 590	25 745	39 775	30 360
2003 dollars:								
2002	[2]53 911	[2]62 657	...	...	42 667	29 665	40 332	30 895
2003	[2]53 991	[2]62 405	...	...	41 959	29 307	40 668	30 724

[1]No spouse present.
[2]Family households.
. . . = Not available.

Table 3-3. Shares of Aggregate Income Received by Each Fifth and Top 5 Percent of Households

Year	Number (thousands)	Upper limit of each fifth (2003 dollars)				Lower limit of top 5 percent (2003 dollars)	Share of aggregate income (percent)						Mean income (2003 dollars)	Gini coefficient
		Lowest fifth	Second fifth	Third fifth	Fourth fifth		Lowest fifth	Second fifth	Third fifth	Fourth fifth	Highest fifth	Top 5 percent		
1967	60 813	14 002	27 303	38 766	55 265	88 678	4.0	10.8	17.3	24.2	43.8	17.5	37 287	0.399
1968	62 214	14 912	28 271	40 522	56 937	89 076	4.2	11.1	17.5	24.4	42.8	16.6	39 310	0.388
1969	63 401	15 369	29 499	42 658	59 772	93 743	4.1	10.9	17.5	24.5	43.0	16.6	41 041	0.391
1970	64 778	15 126	28 981	42 158	60 148	95 090	4.1	10.8	17.4	24.5	43.3	16.6	41 030	0.394
1971	66 676	14 927	28 456	41 874	59 708	94 818	4.1	10.6	17.3	24.5	43.5	16.7	40 786	0.396
1972	68 251	15 434	29 724	43 939	62 878	101 215	4.1	10.5	17.1	24.5	43.9	17.0	43 009	0.401
1973	69 859	15 844	30 100	44 650	64 500	102 243	4.2	10.5	17.1	24.6	43.6	16.6	43 599	0.397
1974	71 163	16 064	29 675	43 725	63 477	101 433	4.4	10.6	17.1	24.7	43.1	15.9	42 727	0.395
1975	72 867	15 143	28 478	42 930	61 765	98 484	4.4	10.5	17.1	24.8	43.2	15.9	41 523	0.397
1976	74 142	15 615	28 879	43 956	63 247	100 839	4.4	10.4	17.1	24.8	43.3	16.0	42 528	0.398
1977	76 030	15 573	29 201	44 287	64 564	104 377	4.4	10.3	17.0	24.8	43.6	16.1	43 132	0.402
1978	77 330	16 398	30 823	46 609	67 874	109 348	4.3	10.3	16.9	24.8	43.7	16.2	45 540	0.402
1979	80 776	16 457	30 605	47 018	68 318	111 445	4.2	10.3	16.9	24.7	44.0	16.4	45 912	0.404
1980	82 368	15 977	29 814	45 693	67 028	108 894	4.3	10.3	16.9	24.9	43.7	15.8	44 537	0.403
1981	83 527	15 772	29 059	45 222	66 878	108 822	4.2	10.2	16.8	25.0	43.8	15.6	44 045	0.406
1982	83 918	15 548	29 217	44 820	66 920	111 516	4.1	10.1	16.6	24.7	44.5	16.2	44 362	0.412
1983	85 290	15 769	29 388	45 061	68 154	113 187	4.1	10.0	16.5	24.7	44.7	16.4	44 506	0.414
1984	86 789	16 175	30 167	46 345	70 092	117 253	4.1	9.9	16.4	24.7	44.9	16.5	46 274	0.415
1985	88 458	16 306	30 739	47 322	71 433	119 459	4.0	9.7	16.3	24.6	45.3	17.0	47 394	0.419
1986	89 479	16 586	31 679	48 928	73 853	125 264	3.9	9.7	16.2	24.5	45.7	17.5	49 255	0.425
1987	91 124	16 724	31 745	49 554	74 893	125 321	3.8	9.6	16.1	24.3	46.2	18.2	50 189	0.426
1988	92 830	17 006	32 124	50 063	75 593	127 958	3.8	9.6	16.0	24.3	46.3	18.3	50 826	0.427
1989	93 347	17 329	32 950	50 643	76 946	131 443	3.8	9.5	15.8	24.0	46.8	18.9	52 319	0.431
1990	94 312	17 059	32 293	49 404	75 341	129 307	3.9	9.6	15.9	24.0	46.6	18.6	51 046	0.428
1991	95 669	16 580	31 611	48 825	74 759	126 969	3.8	9.6	15.9	24.2	46.5	18.1	49 947	0.428
1992	96 426	16 190	31 017	48 697	74 533	127 230	3.8	9.4	15.8	24.2	46.9	18.6	49 905	0.434
1993	97 107	16 256	30 938	48 632	75 594	131 178	3.6	9.0	15.1	23.5	48.9	21.0	51 935	0.454
1994	98 990	16 484	30 940	49 234	77 154	134 835	3.6	8.9	15.0	23.4	49.1	21.2	52 958	0.456
1995	99 627	17 261	32 261	50 346	78 061	135 448	3.7	9.1	15.2	23.3	48.7	21.0	53 865	0.450
1996	101 018	17 239	32 405	51 369	79 395	139 541	3.7	9.0	15.1	23.3	49.0	21.4	55 008	0.455
1997	102 528	17 601	33 373	52 574	81 719	144 636	3.6	8.9	15.0	23.2	49.4	21.7	56 794	0.459
1998	103 874	18 164	34 271	54 478	84 529	148 995	3.6	9.0	15.0	23.2	49.2	21.4	58 443	0.456
1999	106 434	18 915	35 234	55 615	87 459	156 744	3.6	8.9	14.9	23.2	49.4	21.5	60 420	0.458
2000	108 209	19 142	35 250	55 731	87 341	155 121	3.6	8.9	14.8	23.0	49.8	22.1	61 031	0.462
2001	109 297	18 674	34 619	55 076	86 771	156 395	3.5	8.7	14.6	23.0	50.1	22.4	60 488	0.466
2002	111 278	18 326	34 142	54 380	85 941	153 438	3.5	8.8	14.8	23.3	49.7	21.7	59 177	0.462
2003	112 000	17 984	34 000	54 453	86 867	154 120	3.4	8.7	14.8	23.4	49.8	21.4	59 067	0.464

Table 3-4. Shares of Aggregate Income Received by Each Fifth and Top 5 Percent of Families

Year	Number of families (thousands)	Share of aggregate income (percent)						Mean family income (2001 dollars)						Gini coefficient
		Lowest fifth	Second fifth	Third fifth	Fourth fifth	Highest fifth	Top 5 percent	Lowest fifth	Second fifth	Third fifth	Fourth fifth	Highest fifth	Top 5 percent	
1947	37 237	5.0	11.9	17.0	23.1	43.0	17.5	...	...	...	...	...	...	0.376
1948	38 624	4.9	12.1	17.3	23.2	42.4	17.1	...	...	...	...	...	...	0.371
1949	39 303	4.5	11.9	17.3	23.5	42.7	16.9	...	...	...	...	...	...	0.378
1950	39 929	4.5	12.0	17.4	23.4	42.7	17.3	...	...	...	...	...	...	0.379
1951	40 578	5.0	12.4	17.6	23.4	41.6	16.8	...	...	...	...	...	...	0.363
1952	40 832	4.9	12.3	17.4	23.4	41.9	17.4	...	...	...	...	...	...	0.368
1953	41 202	4.7	12.5	18.0	23.9	40.9	15.7	...	...	...	...	...	...	0.359
1954	41 951	4.5	12.1	17.7	23.9	41.8	16.3	...	...	...	...	...	...	0.371
1955	42 889	4.8	12.3	17.8	23.7	41.3	16.4	...	...	...	...	...	...	0.363
1956	43 497	5.0	12.5	17.9	23.7	41.0	16.1	...	...	...	...	...	...	0.358
1957	43 696	5.1	12.7	18.1	23.8	40.4	15.6	...	...	...	...	...	...	0.351
1958	44 232	5.0	12.5	18.0	23.9	40.6	15.4	...	...	...	...	...	...	0.354
1959	45 111	4.9	12.3	17.9	23.8	41.1	15.9	...	...	...	...	...	...	0.361
1960	45 539	4.8	12.2	17.8	24.0	41.3	15.9	...	...	...	...	...	...	0.364
1961	46 418	4.7	11.9	17.5	23.8	42.2	16.6	...	...	...	...	...	...	0.374
1962	47 059	5.0	12.1	17.6	24.0	41.3	15.7	...	...	...	...	...	...	0.362
1963	47 540	5.0	12.1	17.7	24.0	41.2	15.8	...	...	...	...	...	...	0.362
1964	47 956	5.1	12.0	17.7	24.0	41.2	15.9	...	...	...	...	...	...	0.361
1965	48 509	5.2	12.2	17.8	23.9	40.9	15.5	...	...	...	...	...	...	0.356
1966	49 214	5.6	12.4	17.8	23.8	40.5	15.6	10 854	24 095	34 477	46 154	78 770	120 953	0.349
1967	50 111	5.4	12.2	17.5	23.5	41.4	16.4	11 031	24 666	35 454	47 549	83 960	132 839	0.358
1968	50 823	5.6	12.4	17.7	23.7	40.5	15.6	11 880	25 910	37 016	49 505	84 590	130 398	0.348
1969	51 586	5.6	12.4	17.7	23.7	40.6	15.6	12 269	27 096	38 773	51 941	88 955	136 630	0.349
1970	52 227	5.4	12.2	17.6	23.8	40.9	15.6	12 096	26 747	38 674	52 168	89 709	136 602	0.353
1971	53 296	5.5	12.0	17.6	23.8	41.1	15.7	12 100	26 339	38 538	52 191	89 894	137 065	0.355
1972	54 373	5.5	11.9	17.5	23.9	41.4	15.9	12 619	27 533	40 441	55 227	95 782	146 840	0.359
1973	55 053	5.5	11.9	17.5	24.0	41.1	15.5	12 949	28 047	41 210	56 319	96 628	145 828	0.356
1974	55 698	5.7	12.0	17.6	24.1	40.6	14.8	13 188	27 840	40 645	55 686	93 832	136 863	0.355
1975	56 245	5.6	11.9	17.7	24.2	40.7	14.9	12 664	26 772	39 807	54 503	91 848	134 735	0.357
1976	56 710	5.6	11.9	17.7	24.2	40.7	14.9	12 972	27 453	40 952	55 954	94 174	137 832	0.358
1977	57 215	5.5	11.7	17.6	24.3	40.9	14.9	12 908	27 592	41 498	57 244	96 438	140 591	0.363
1978	57 804	5.4	11.7	17.6	24.2	41.1	15.1	13 412	29 085	43 673	60 171	102 104	149 623	0.363
1979	59 550	5.4	11.6	17.5	24.1	41.4	15.3	13 552	29 300	44 188	60 835	104 345	154 454	0.365
1980	60 309	5.3	11.6	17.6	24.4	41.1	14.6	13 045	28 397	42 898	59 516	100 206	142 451	0.365
1981	61 019	5.3	11.4	17.5	24.6	41.2	14.4	12 654	27 517	42 087	59 089	99 145	138 539	0.369
1982	61 393	5.0	11.3	17.2	24.4	42.2	15.3	11 950	27 115	41 403	58 734	101 489	145 204	0.380
1983	62 015	4.9	11.2	17.2	24.5	42.4	15.3	11 781	27 105	41 703	59 436	103 056	148 587	0.382
1984	62 706	4.8	11.1	17.1	24.5	42.5	15.4	12 194	27 920	43 077	61 600	107 058	154 787	0.383
1985	63 558	4.8	11.0	16.9	24.3	43.1	16.1	12 347	28 333	43 744	62 704	111 435	166 528	0.389
1986	64 491	4.7	10.9	16.9	24.1	43.4	16.5	12 694	29 310	45 409	64 881	116 862	177 463	0.392
1987	65 204	4.6	10.7	16.8	24.0	43.8	17.2	12 677	29 671	46 073	65 940	120 507	188 647	0.393
1988	65 837	4.6	10.7	16.7	24.0	44.0	17.2	12 789	29 783	46 346	66 561	122 128	190 821	0.395
1989	66 090	4.6	10.6	16.5	23.7	44.6	17.9	13 047	30 354	47 157	67 846	127 746	204 638	0.401
1990	66 322	4.6	10.8	16.6	23.8	44.3	17.4	12 914	30 120	46 388	66 711	123 980	194 531	0.396
1991	67 173	4.5	10.7	16.6	24.1	44.2	17.1	12 337	29 285	45 439	65 904	121 080	187 351	0.397
1992	68 216	4.3	10.5	16.5	24.0	44.7	17.6	11 853	28 588	45 164	65 648	122 164	192 339	0.404
1993	68 506	4.1	9.9	15.7	23.3	47.0	20.3	11 749	28 217	44 715	66 285	133 927	231 154	0.429
1994	69 313	4.2	10.0	15.7	23.3	46.9	20.1	12 272	29 035	45 851	67 777	136 589	234 331	0.426
1995	69 597	4.4	10.1	15.8	23.2	46.5	20.0	12 994	29 938	46 873	68 582	137 785	236 303	0.421
1996	70 241	4.2	10.0	15.8	23.1	46.8	20.3	12 792	30 158	47 704	69 704	141 118	244 157	0.425
1997	70 884	4.2	9.9	15.7	23.0	47.2	20.7	13 261	31 072	49 025	71 888	147 691	258 483	0.429
1998	71 551	4.2	9.9	15.7	23.0	47.3	20.7	13 585	31 975	50 608	74 216	152 756	267 366	0.430
1999	72 031	4.3	9.9	15.6	23.0	47.2	20.3	14 149	32 924	51 977	76 642	156 973	270 695	0.428
2000	73 778	4.3	9.8	15.4	22.7	47.7	21.1	14 516	33 190	52 163	76 878	161 299	285 824	0.433
2001	74 340	4.2	9.7	15.4	22.9	47.7	21.0	14 021	32 466	51 538	76 646	159 644	280 312	0.435

... = Not available.

Section 3b: Poverty

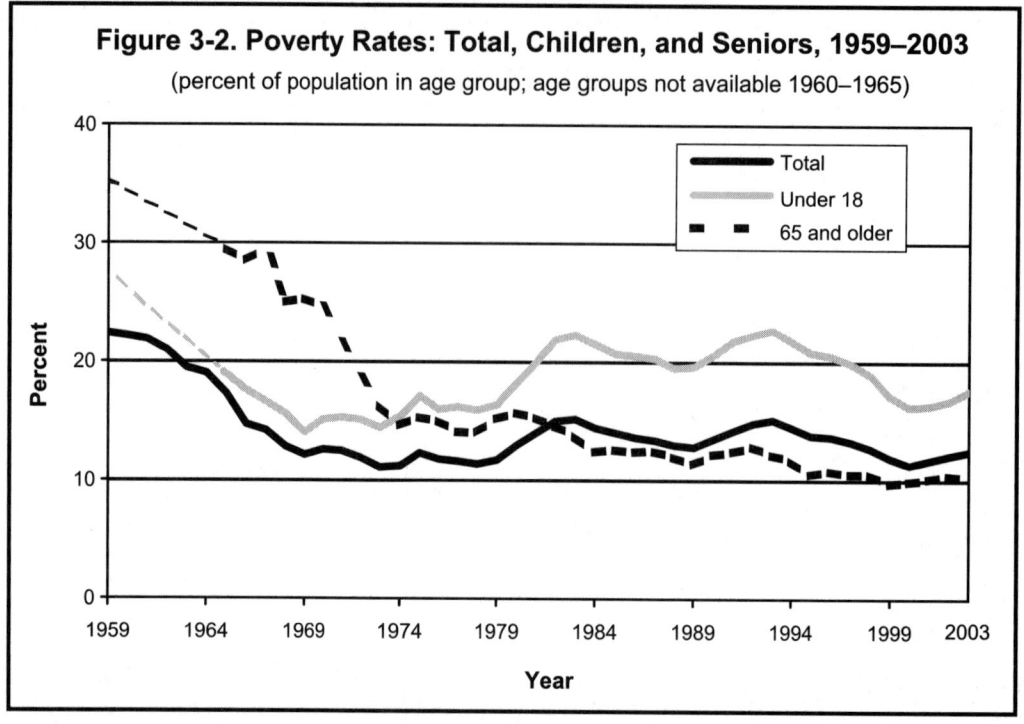

Figure 3-2. Poverty Rates: Total, Children, and Seniors, 1959–2003
(percent of population in age group; age groups not available 1960–1965)

- The percentage of Americans with family incomes below the poverty line has increased from 11.3 percent in 2000, which was near the all-time low reached in 1973, to 12.5 percent in 2003. (Table 3-6)
- The poverty rate for senior citizens (65 and older) was 10.2 percent in 2003, slightly lower than the rate for people 18 to 64. This has not always been the case. In 1959, the first poverty rate calculations showed more than one-third of all seniors in poverty, compared with 17 percent for working-age adults. But between 1959 and 1974, ad hoc legislative changes raised Social Security benefits by a cumulative 104 percent—exceeding the 69 percent increase in consumer prices—and since then, each year's payments have been indexed to the rate of change in the CPI-W (see Chapter 8). Because workers' earnings and incomes have not always kept up with inflation in the period since 1974, while Social Security cost-of-living adjustments have done so, the gap between senior poverty and working-age poverty has continued to narrow, and in some years been zero or negative. (Table 3-7)
- The poverty rate for children, on the other hand, has always been higher than the average. The gap between the poverty rates for children and for working-age adults has been as high as 10 percentage points (in 1959 and 1993, for example) and as low as 6.2 points (in 2001). (Table 3-7)
- Poverty among Hispanics was 22.5 percent in 2003 compared with 8.2 percent for non-Hispanic Whites. Poverty among Blacks was 24.4 percent, and 11.8 percent among Asians. For both those groups, poverty rates including persons who reported more than one race (permitted for the first time in the survey for 2002) were little different from those reporting one race only. (Table 3-6)

CHAPTER 3: INCOME DISTRIBUTION AND POVERTY

Table 3-5. Average Poverty Thresholds by Family Size

(Dollars.)

Year	Unrelated individuals			Families of 2 people			Families, all ages								CPI-U, all items (1982–1984 = 100)
	All ages	Under 65 years	65 years and older	All ages	Householder under 65 years	Householder 65 years and over	3 people	4 people	5 people	6 people	7 people or more (before 1980)	7 people	8 people	9 people	
1959	1 467	1 503	1 397	1 894	1 952	1 761	2 324	2 973	3 506	3 944	4 849	...	...	...	29.2
1960	1 490	1 526	1 418	1 924	1 982	1 788	2 359	3 022	3 560	4 002	4 921	...	...	...	29.6
1961	1 506	1 545	1 433	1 942	2 005	1 808	2 383	3 054	3 597	4 041	4 967	...	...	...	29.9
1962	1 519	1 562	1 451	1 962	2 027	1 828	2 412	3 089	3 639	4 088	5 032	...	...	...	30.3
1963	1 539	1 581	1 470	1 988	2 052	1 850	2 442	3 128	3 685	4 135	5 092	...	...	...	30.6
1964	1 558	1 601	1 488	2 015	2 079	1 875	2 473	3 169	3 732	4 193	5 156	...	...	...	31.0
1965	1 582	1 626	1 512	2 048	2 114	1 906	2 514	3 223	3 797	4 264	5 248	...	...	...	31.5
1966	1 628	1 674	1 556	2 107	2 175	1 961	2 588	3 317	3 908	4 388	5 395	...	...	...	32.5
1967	1 675	1 722	1 600	2 168	2 238	2 017	2 661	3 410	4 019	4 516	5 550	...	...	...	33.4
1968	1 748	1 797	1 667	2 262	2 333	2 102	2 774	3 553	4 188	4 706	5 789	...	...	...	34.8
1969	1 840	1 893	1 757	2 383	2 458	2 215	2 924	3 743	4 415	4 958	6 101	...	...	...	36.7
1970	1 954	2 010	1 861	2 525	2 604	2 348	3 099	3 968	4 680	5 260	6 468	...	...	...	38.8
1971	2 040	2 098	1 940	2 633	2 716	2 448	3 229	4 137	4 880	5 489	6 751	...	...	...	40.5
1972	2 109	2 168	2 005	2 724	2 808	2 530	3 339	4 275	5 044	5 673	6 983	...	...	...	41.8
1973	2 247	2 307	2 130	2 895	2 984	2 688	3 548	4 540	5 358	6 028	7 435	...	...	...	44.4
1974	2 495	2 562	2 364	3 211	3 312	2 982	3 936	5 038	5 950	6 699	8 253	...	...	...	49.3
1975	2 724	2 797	2 581	3 506	3 617	3 257	4 293	5 500	6 499	7 316	9 022	...	...	...	53.8
1976	2 884	2 959	2 730	3 711	3 826	3 445	4 540	5 815	6 876	7 760	9 588	...	...	...	56.9
1977	3 075	3 152	2 906	3 951	4 072	3 666	4 833	6 191	7 320	8 261	10 216	...	...	...	60.6
1978	3 311	3 392	3 127	4 249	4 383	3 944	5 201	6 662	7 880	8 891	11 002	...	...	...	65.2
1979	3 689	3 778	3 479	4 725	4 878	4 390	5 784	7 412	8 775	9 914	12 280	...	...	...	72.6
1980	4 190	4 290	3 949	5 363	5 537	4 983	6 565	8 414	9 966	11 269	13 955	12 761	14 199	16 896	82.4
1981	4 620	4 729	4 359	5 917	6 111	5 498	7 250	9 287	11 007	12 449	...	14 110	15 655	18 572	90.9
1982	4 901	5 019	4 626	6 281	6 487	5 836	7 693	9 862	11 684	13 207	...	15 036	16 719	19 698	96.5
1983	5 061	5 180	4 775	6 483	6 697	6 023	7 938	10 178	12 049	13 630	...	15 500	17 170	20 310	99.6
1984	5 278	5 400	4 979	6 762	6 983	6 282	8 277	10 609	12 566	14 207	...	16 096	17 961	21 247	103.9
1985	5 469	5 593	5 156	6 998	7 231	6 503	8 573	10 989	13 007	14 696	...	16 656	18 512	22 083	107.6
1986	5 572	5 701	5 255	7 138	7 372	6 630	8 737	11 203	13 259	14 986	...	17 049	18 791	22 497	109.6
1987	5 778	5 909	5 447	7 397	7 641	6 872	9 056	11 611	13 737	15 509	...	17 649	19 515	23 105	113.6
1988	6 022	6 155	5 674	7 704	7 958	7 157	9 435	12 092	14 304	16 146	...	18 232	20 253	24 129	118.3
1989	6 310	6 451	5 947	8 076	8 343	7 501	9 885	12 674	14 990	16 921	...	19 162	21 328	25 480	124.0
1990	6 652	6 800	6 268	8 509	8 794	7 905	10 419	13 359	15 792	17 839	...	20 241	22 582	26 848	130.7
1991	6 932	7 086	6 532	8 865	9 165	8 241	10 860	13 924	16 456	18 587	...	21 058	23 582	27 942	136.2
1992	7 143	7 299	6 729	9 137	9 443	8 487	11 186	14 335	16 952	19 137	...	21 594	24 053	28 745	140.3
1993	7 363	7 518	6 930	9 414	9 728	8 740	11 522	14 763	17 449	19 718	...	22 383	24 838	29 529	144.5
1994	7 547	7 710	7 108	9 661	9 976	8 967	11 821	15 141	17 900	20 235	...	22 923	25 427	30 300	148.2
1995	7 763	7 929	7 309	9 933	10 259	9 219	12 158	15 569	18 408	20 804	...	23 552	26 237	31 280	152.4
1996	7 995	8 163	7 525	10 233	10 564	9 491	12 516	16 036	18 952	21 389	...	24 268	27 091	31 971	156.9
1997	8 183	8 350	7 698	10 473	10 805	9 712	12 802	16 400	19 380	21 886	...	24 802	27 593	32 566	160.5
1998	8 316	8 480	7 818	10 634	10 972	9 862	13 003	16 660	19 680	22 228	...	25 257	28 166	33 339	163.0
1999	9 035	9 214	8 494	11 549	11 920	10 710	14 126	18 103	21 396	24 163	...	27 551	30 796	36 606	166.6
2000	8 791	8 959	8 259	11 235	11 589	10 418	13 740	17 604	20 815	23 533	...	26 750	29 701	35 150	172.2
2001	9 039	9 214	8 494	11 569	11 920	10 715	14 128	18 104	21 405	24 195	...	27 517	30 627	36 286	177.1
2002	9 183	9 359	8 628	11 756	12 110	10 885	14 348	18 392	21 744	24 576	...	28 001	30 907	37 062	179.9
2003	9 393	9 573	8 825	12 015	12 321	11 122	14 680	18 810	22 245	25 122	...	28 544	31 589	37 656	184.0

. . . = Not available.

Table 3-6. Poverty Status by Type of Family, Race, and Hispanic Origin

(Thousands of people or families, percent of population.)

Year, race, and Hispanic origin	All people			Married-couple families [1]			Female householder, no spouse present [1]			Unrelated individuals		
	Number of people	Below poverty level		Number of families	Below poverty level		Number of families	Below poverty level		Number of people	Below poverty level	
		Number	Percent		Number	Percent		Number	Percent		Number	Percent
All Races												
1959	176 557	39 490	22.4	39 335	...	...	4 493	1 916	42.6	10 699	4 928	46.1
1960	179 503	39 851	22.2	39 624	...	...	4 609	1 955	42.4	10 888	4 926	45.2
1961	181 277	39 628	21.9	40 405	...	...	4 643	1 954	42.1	11 146	5 119	45.9
1962	184 276	38 625	21.0	40 923	...	...	4 741	2 034	42.9	11 013	5 002	45.4
1963	187 258	36 436	19.5	41 311	...	...	4 882	1 972	40.4	11 182	4 938	44.2
1964	189 710	36 055	19.0	41 648	...	...	5 006	1 822	36.4	12 057	5 143	42.7
1965	191 413	33 185	17.3	42 107	...	...	4 992	1 916	38.4	12 132	4 827	39.8
1966	193 388	28 510	14.7	42 553	...	...	5 171	1 721	33.1	12 271	4 701	38.3
1967	195 672	27 769	14.2	43 292	...	...	5 333	1 774	33.3	13 114	4 998	38.1
1968	197 628	25 389	12.8	43 842	...	...	5 441	1 755	32.3	13 803	4 694	34.0
1969	199 517	24 147	12.1	44 436	...	...	5 591	1 827	32.7	14 626	4 972	34.0
1970	202 183	25 420	12.6	44 739	...	...	6 001	1 952	32.5	15 491	5 090	32.9
1971	204 554	25 559	12.5	45 752	...	...	6 191	2 100	33.9	16 311	5 154	31.6
1972	206 004	24 460	11.9	46 314	...	...	6 607	2 158	32.7	16 811	4 883	29.0
1973	207 621	22 973	11.1	46 812	2 482	5.3	6 804	2 193	32.2	18 260	4 674	25.6
1974	209 362	23 370	11.2	47 069	2 474	5.3	7 230	2 324	32.1	18 926	4 553	24.1
1975	210 864	25 877	12.3	47 318	2 904	6.1	7 482	2 430	32.5	20 234	5 088	25.1
1976	212 303	24 975	11.8	47 497	2 606	5.5	7 713	2 543	33.0	21 459	5 344	24.9
1977	213 867	24 720	11.6	47 385	2 524	5.3	8 236	2 610	31.7	23 110	5 216	22.6
1978	215 656	24 497	11.4	47 692	2 474	5.2	8 458	2 654	31.4	24 585	5 435	22.1
1979	222 903	26 072	11.7	49 112	2 640	5.4	8 705	2 645	30.4	26 170	5 743	21.9
1980	225 027	29 272	13.0	49 294	3 032	6.2	9 082	2 972	32.7	27 133	6 227	22.9
1981	227 157	31 822	14.0	49 630	3 394	6.8	9 403	3 252	34.6	27 714	6 490	23.4
1982	229 412	34 398	15.0	49 908	3 789	7.6	9 469	3 434	36.3	27 908	6 458	23.1
1983	231 700	35 303	15.2	50 081	3 815	7.6	9 896	3 564	36.0	29 158	6 740	23.1
1984	233 816	33 700	14.4	50 350	3 488	6.9	10 129	3 498	34.5	30 268	6 609	21.8
1985	236 594	33 064	14.0	50 933	3 438	6.7	10 211	3 474	34.0	31 351	6 725	21.5
1986	238 554	32 370	13.6	51 537	3 123	6.1	10 445	3 613	34.6	31 679	6 846	21.6
1987	240 982	32 221	13.4	51 675	3 011	5.8	10 696	3 654	34.2	32 992	6 857	20.8
1988	243 530	31 745	13.0	52 100	2 897	5.6	10 890	3 642	33.4	34 340	7 070	20.6
1989	245 992	31 528	12.8	52 317	2 931	5.6	10 890	3 504	32.2	35 185	6 760	19.2
1990	248 644	33 585	13.5	52 147	2 981	5.7	11 268	3 768	33.4	36 056	7 446	20.7
1991	251 192	35 708	14.2	52 457	3 158	6.0	11 693	4 161	35.6	36 845	7 773	21.1
1992	256 549	38 014	14.8	53 090	3 385	6.4	12 061	4 275	35.4	36 842	8 075	21.9
1993	259 278	39 265	15.1	53 181	3 481	6.5	12 411	4 424	35.6	38 038	8 388	22.1
1994	261 616	38 059	14.5	53 865	3 272	6.1	12 220	4 232	34.6	38 538	8 287	21.5
1995	263 733	36 425	13.8	53 570	2 982	5.6	12 514	4 057	32.4	39 484	8 247	20.9
1996	266 218	36 529	13.7	53 604	3 010	5.6	12 790	4 167	32.6	40 727	8 452	20.8
1997	268 480	35 574	13.3	54 321	2 821	5.2	12 652	3 995	31.6	41 672	8 687	20.8
1998	271 059	34 476	12.7	54 778	2 879	5.3	12 796	3 831	29.9	42 539	8 478	19.9
1999	276 208	32 791	11.9	56 290	2 748	4.9	12 818	3 559	27.8	43 977	8 400	19.1
2000	278 944	31 581	11.3	56 598	2 637	4.7	12 903	3 278	25.4	45 624	8 653	19.0
2001	281 475	32 907	11.7	56 755	2 760	4.9	13 146	3 470	26.4	46 392	9 226	19.9
2002	285 317	34 570	12.1	57 327	3 052	5.3	13 626	3 613	26.5	47 156	9 618	20.4
2003	287 699	35 861	12.5	57 725	3 115	5.4	13 791	3 856	28.0	47 594	9 713	20.4
White												
1959	156 956	28 484	18.1	36 217	...	...	3 547	1 233	34.8	9 154	4 041	44.1
1960	158 863	28 309	17.8	36 400	...	...	3 673	1 252	34.0	9 405	4 047	43.0
1961	160 306	27 890	17.4	37 185	...	...	3 608	1 208	33.5	9 589	4 143	43.2
1962	162 842	26 672	16.4	37 657	...	...	3 627	1 230	33.9	9 494	4 059	42.7
1963	165 309	25 238	15.3	37 799	...	...	3 797	1 191	31.4	9 725	4 089	42.0
1964	167 313	24 957	14.9	38 171	...	...	3 882	1 125	29.0	10 415	4 241	40.7
1965	168 732	22 496	13.3	38 632	...	...	3 860	1 196	31.0	10 477	3 988	38.1
1966	170 247	19 290	11.3	39 007	...	...	4 010	1 036	25.7	10 686	3 860	36.1
1967	172 038	18 983	11.0	39 821	...	...	4 008	1 037	25.9	11 318	4 132	36.5
1968	173 732	17 395	10.0	40 355	...	...	4 053	1 021	25.2	11 955	3 849	32.2
1969	175 349	16 659	9.5	40 802	...	...	4 165	1 069	25.7	12 570	4 036	32.1
1970	177 376	17 484	9.9	41 092	...	...	4 408	1 102	25.0	13 500	4 161	30.8
1971	179 398	17 780	9.9	42 039	...	...	4 489	1 191	26.5	14 214	4 214	29.6
1972	180 125	16 203	9.0	42 585	...	...	4 672	1 135	24.3	14 495	3 935	27.1
1973	181 185	15 142	8.4	43 805	2 306	5.3	4 853	1 190	24.5	15 761	3 730	23.7
1974	182 376	15 736	8.6	43 049	1 977	4.6	5 208	1 289	24.8	16 295	3 555	21.8
1975	183 164	17 770	9.7	43 311	2 363	5.5	5 380	1 394	25.9	17 503	3 972	22.7
1976	184 165	16 713	9.1	43 397	2 071	4.8	5 467	1 379	25.2	18 594	4 213	22.7
1977	185 254	16 416	8.9	43 423	2 028	4.7	5 828	1 400	24.0	19 869	4 051	20.4
1978	186 450	16 259	8.7	43 636	2 033	4.7	5 918	1 391	23.5	21 257	4 209	19.8
1979	191 742	17 214	9.0	44 751	2 099	4.7	6 052	1 350	22.3	22 587	4 452	19.7

[1] These numbers and rates refer to families rather than people.
. . . = Not available.

Table 3-6. Poverty Status by Type of Family, Race, and Hispanic Origin—Continued

(Thousands of people or families, percent of population.)

Year, race, and Hispanic origin	All people			Married-couple families [1]			Female householder, no spouse present [1]			Unrelated individuals		
	Number of people	Below poverty level		Number of families	Below poverty level		Number of families	Below poverty level		Number of people	Below poverty level	
		Number	Percent		Number	Percent		Number	Percent		Number	Percent
White—Continued												
1980	192 912	19 699	10.2	44 860	2 437	5.4	6 266	1 609	25.7	23 370	4 760	20.4
1981	194 504	21 553	11.1	45 007	2 712	6.0	6 620	1 814	27.4	23 913	5 061	21.2
1982	195 919	23 517	12.0	45 252	3 104	6.9	6 507	1 813	27.9	24 300	5 041	20.7
1983	197 496	23 984	12.1	45 470	3 125	6.9	6 796	1 926	28.3	25 206	5 189	20.6
1984	198 941	22 955	11.5	45 643	2 858	6.3	6 941	1 878	27.1	26 094	5 181	19.9
1985	200 918	22 860	11.4	45 924	2 815	6.1	7 111	1 950	27.4	27 067	5 299	19.6
1986	202 282	22 183	11.0	46 410	2 591	5.6	7 227	2 041	28.2	27 143	5 198	19.2
1987	203 605	21 195	10.4	46 510	2 382	5.1	7 297	1 961	26.9	28 290	5 174	18.3
1988	205 235	20 715	10.1	46 877	2 294	4.9	7 342	1 945	26.5	29 315	5 314	18.1
1989	206 853	20 785	10.0	46 981	2 329	5.0	7 306	1 858	25.4	29 993	5 063	16.9
1990	208 611	22 326	10.7	47 014	2 386	5.1	7 512	2 010	26.8	30 833	5 739	18.6
1991	210 133	23 747	11.3	47 124	2 573	5.5	7 727	2 192	28.4	31 207	5 872	18.8
1992	213 060	25 259	11.9	47 383	2 677	5.7	7 868	2 245	28.5	31 170	6 147	19.7
1993	214 899	26 226	12.2	47 452	2 757	5.8	8 131	2 376	29.2	32 112	6 443	20.1
1994	216 460	25 379	11.7	47 905	2 629	5.5	8 031	2 329	29.0	32 569	6 292	19.3
1995	218 028	24 423	11.2	47 877	2 443	5.1	8 284	2 200	26.6	33 399	6 336	19.0
1996	219 656	24 650	11.2	47 650	2 416	5.1	8 339	2 276	27.3	34 247	6 463	18.9
1997	221 200	24 396	11.0	48 070	2 312	4.8	8 308	2 305	27.7	34 858	6 593	18.9
1998	222 837	23 454	10.5	48 461	2 400	5.0	8 529	2 123	24.9	35 563	6 386	18.0
1999	225 361	22 169	9.8	49 493	2 207	4.5	8 462	1 901	22.5	36 441	6 411	17.6
2000	227 846	21 645	9.5	49 473	2 181	4.4	8 574	1 820	21.2	37 699	6 454	17.1
2001	229 675	22 739	9.9	49 612	2 242	4.5	8 641	1 939	22.4	38 294	6 996	18.3
White Alone												
2002	230 376	23 466	10.2	49 923	2 510	5.0	8 885	2 004	22.6	38 575	7 105	18.4
2003	231 866	24 272	10.5	50 025	2 504	5.0	9 058	2 171	24.0	38 913	7 225	18.6
White, Not Hispanic												
1973	170 488	12 864	7.5	...	...	...	...	...	...	15 158	3 602	23.8
1974	171 463	13 217	7.7	41 155	1 700	4.1	4 676	1 005	21.5	15 699	3 364	21.4
1975	172 417	14 883	8.6	41 447	2 036	4.9	4 786	1 079	22.5	16 879	3 746	22.2
1976	173 235	14 025	8.1	41 437	1 759	4.2	4 849	1 059	21.8	17 912	3 959	22.1
1977	173 563	13 802	8.0	41 338	1 750	4.2	5 156	1 039	20.2	19 114	3 825	20.0
1978	174 731	13 755	7.9	41 574	1 790	4.3	5 236	1 047	20.0	20 410	3 957	19.4
1979	178 814	14 419	8.1	42 527	1 810	4.3	5 473	1 062	19.4	21 638	4 179	19.3
1980	179 798	16 365	9.1	42 564	2 083	4.9	5 593	1 264	22.6	22 455	4 474	19.9
1981	180 909	17 987	9.9	42 653	2 353	5.5	5 910	1 436	24.3	22 950	4 769	20.8
1982	181 903	19 362	10.6	42 847	2 648	6.2	5 778	1 413	24.5	23 329	4 701	20.2
1983	181 393	19 538	10.8	42 768	2 649	6.2	5 982	1 501	25.1	23 894	4 746	19.9
1984	182 469	18 300	10.0	42 872	2 400	5.6	6 081	1 422	23.4	24 671	4 659	18.9
1985	183 455	17 839	9.7	43 036	2 316	5.4	6 180	1 460	23.6	25 544	4 789	18.7
1986	184 119	17 244	9.4	43 370	2 081	4.8	6 255	1 542	24.7	25 525	4 668	18.3
1987	184 936	16 029	8.7	43 422	1 847	4.3	6 287	1 443	23.0	26 439	4 613	17.4
1988	185 961	15 565	8.4	43 591	1 763	4.0	6 287	1 426	22.7	27 552	4 746	17.2
1989	186 979	15 599	8.3	43 710	1 798	4.1	6 255	1 355	21.7	28 055	4 466	15.9
1990	188 129	16 622	8.8	43 682	1 799	4.1	6 408	1 480	23.1	28 688	5 002	17.4
1991	189 116	17 741	9.4	43 724	1 918	4.4	6 553	1 610	24.6	29 215	5 261	18.0
1992	189 001	18 202	9.6	43 661	1 978	4.5	6 629	1 637	24.7	28 775	5 350	18.6
1993	190 843	18 882	9.9	43 745	2 042	4.7	6 798	1 699	25.0	29 681	5 570	18.8
1994	192 543	18 110	9.4	44 178	1 915	4.3	6 764	1 678	24.8	30 157	5 500	18.2
1995	190 951	16 267	8.5	43 771	1 664	3.8	6 792	1 463	21.5	30 586	5 303	17.3
1996	191 459	16 462	8.6	43 276	1 628	3.8	6 875	1 538	22.4	31 410	5 455	17.4
1997	191 859	16 491	8.6	43 427	1 501	3.5	6 826	1 598	23.4	32 049	5 632	17.6
1998	192 754	15 799	8.2	43 669	1 639	3.8	6 909	1 428	20.7	32 573	5 352	16.4
1999	192 565	14 735	7.7	44 443	1 474	3.3	6 770	1 248	18.4	33 189	5 412	16.3
2000	193 691	14 366	7.4	44 278	1 435	3.2	6 891	1 226	17.8	33 943	5 356	15.8
2001	194 538	15 271	7.8	44 124	1 477	3.3	6 886	1 305	19.0	34 603	5 882	17.0
White Alone, Not Hispanic												
2002	194 144	15 567	8.0	44 109	1 628	3.7	7 072	1 374	19.4	34 614	5 947	17.2
2003	194 595	15 902	8.2	44 200	1 575	3.6	7 121	1 455	20.4	34 683	6 015	17.3

[1] These numbers and rates refer to families rather than people.
... = Not available.

Table 3-6. Poverty Status by Type of Family, Race, and Hispanic Origin—Continued

(Thousands of people or families, percent of population.)

Year, race, and Hispanic origin	All people			Married-couple families [1]			Female householder, no spouse present [1]			Unrelated individuals		
	Number of people	Below poverty level		Number of families	Below poverty level		Number of families	Below poverty level		Number of people	Below poverty level	
		Number	Percent		Number	Percent		Number	Percent		Number	Percent
Black												
1959	18 013	9 927	55.1	...	...	...	...	...	...	1 430	815	57.0
1966	21 206	8 867	41.8	...	...	...	...	...	...	...	777	54.4
1967	21 590	8 486	39.3	3 118	...	...	1 272	716	56.3	...	809	49.3
1968	21 944	7 616	34.7	3 141	...	...	1 327	706	53.2	...	777	46.3
1969	22 011	7 095	32.2	3 323	...	...	1 384	737	53.3	1 819	850	46.7
1970	22 515	7 548	33.5	3 301	...	...	1 535	834	54.3	1 791	865	48.3
1971	22 784	7 396	32.5	3 289	...	...	1 642	879	53.5	1 884	866	46.0
1972	23 144	7 710	33.3	3 233	...	...	1 822	972	53.3	2 028	870	42.9
1973	23 512	7 388	31.4	3 360	...	...	1 849	974	52.7	2 183	828	37.9
1974	23 699	7 182	30.3	3 357	435	13.0	1 934	1 010	52.2	2 359	927	39.3
1975	24 089	7 545	31.3	3 352	479	14.3	2 004	1 004	50.1	2 402	1 011	42.1
1976	24 399	7 595	31.1	3 406	450	13.2	2 151	1 122	52.2	2 559	1 019	39.8
1977	24 710	7 726	31.3	3 260	429	13.1	2 277	1 162	51.0	2 860	1 059	37.0
1978	24 956	7 625	30.6	3 244	366	11.3	2 390	1 208	50.6	2 929	1 132	38.6
1979	25 944	8 050	31.0	3 433	453	13.2	2 495	1 234	49.4	3 127	1 168	37.3
1980	26 408	8 579	32.5	3 392	474	14.0	2 634	1 301	49.4	3 208	1 314	41.0
1981	26 834	9 173	34.2	3 535	543	15.4	2 605	1 377	52.9	3 277	1 296	39.6
1982	27 216	9 697	35.6	3 486	543	15.6	2 734	1 535	56.2	3 051	1 229	40.3
1983	27 678	9 882	35.7	3 454	535	15.5	2 871	1 541	53.7	3 287	1 338	40.7
1984	28 087	9 490	33.8	3 469	479	13.8	2 964	1 533	51.7	3 501	1 255	35.8
1985	28 485	8 926	31.3	3 680	447	12.2	2 874	1 452	50.5	3 641	1 264	34.7
1986	28 871	8 983	31.1	3 742	403	10.8	2 967	1 488	50.1	3 714	1 431	38.5
1987	29 362	9 520	32.4	3 681	439	11.9	3 089	1 577	51.1	3 977	1 471	37.0
1988	29 849	9 356	31.3	3 722	421	11.3	3 223	1 579	49.0	4 095	1 509	36.8
1989	30 332	9 302	30.7	3 750	443	11.8	3 275	1 524	46.5	4 180	1 471	35.2
1990	30 806	9 837	31.9	3 569	448	12.6	3 430	1 648	48.1	4 244	1 491	35.1
1991	31 313	10 242	32.7	3 631	399	11.0	3 582	1 834	51.2	4 505	1 590	35.3
1992	32 411	10 827	33.4	3 777	490	13.0	3 738	1 878	50.2	4 410	1 569	35.6
1993	32 910	10 877	33.1	3 715	458	12.3	3 828	1 908	49.9	4 608	1 541	33.4
1994	33 353	10 196	30.6	3 842	336	8.7	3 716	1 715	46.2	4 649	1 617	34.8
1995	33 740	9 872	29.3	3 713	314	8.5	3 769	1 701	45.1	4 756	1 551	32.6
1996	34 110	9 694	28.4	3 851	352	9.1	3 947	1 724	43.7	4 989	1 606	32.2
1997	34 458	9 116	26.5	3 921	312	8.0	3 926	1 563	39.8	5 316	1 645	31.0
1998	34 877	9 091	26.1	3 979	290	7.3	3 813	1 557	40.8	5 390	1 752	32.5
1999	35 756	8 441	23.6	4 150	295	7.1	3 797	1 487	39.2	5 668	1 562	27.5
2000	35 425	7 982	22.5	4 214	266	6.3	3 785	1 300	34.3	5 885	1 702	28.9
2001	35 871	8 136	22.7	4 234	328	7.8	3 838	1 351	35.2	5 873	1 692	28.8
Black Alone												
2002	35 678	8 602	24.1	4 165	331	7.9	4 003	1 433	35.8	5 858	1 800	30.7
2003	35 989	8 781	24.4	4 146	321	7.8	3 986	1 473	36.9	6 034	1 781	29.5
Black Alone or in Combination												
2002	37 207	8 884	23.9	4 268	340	8.0	4 072	1 454	35.7	6 034	1 851	30.7
2003	37 503	9 108	24.3	4 259	331	7.8	4 068	1 496	36.8	6 194	1 814	29.3
Asian and Pacific Islander												
1987	6 322	1 021	16.1	...	...	...	...	...	...	516	138	26.8
1988	6 447	1 117	17.3	...	...	...	...	...	...	651	160	24.5
1989	6 673	939	14.1	...	...	...	...	...	...	712	144	20.2
1990	7 014	858	12.2	...	...	...	...	...	...	668	124	18.5
1991	7 192	996	13.8	...	...	...	...	...	...	785	209	26.6
1992	7 779	985	12.7	...	...	...	...	...	...	828	193	23.3
1993	7 434	1 134	15.3	...	...	...	...	...	...	791	228	28.8
1994	6 654	974	14.6	...	...	...	...	...	...	696	179	25.7
1995	9 644	1 411	14.6	...	...	...	...	...	...	1 013	260	25.6
1996	10 054	1 454	14.5	...	...	...	...	...	...	1 120	255	22.8
1997	10 482	1 468	14.0	...	...	...	...	...	...	1 134	327	28.9
1998	10 873	1 360	12.5	...	...	...	...	...	...	1 266	257	20.3
1999	11 955	1 285	10.7	...	...	...	...	...	...	1 415	270	19.1
2000	12 672	1 258	9.9	...	...	...	...	...	...	1 588	350	22.0
2001	12 465	1 275	10.2	...	...	...	...	...	...	1 682	393	23.4
Asian Alone												
2002	11 541	1 161	10.1	2 286	135	5.9	337	48	14.2	1 613	390	24.2
2003	11 856	1 401	11.8	2 497	200	8.0	348	83	23.8	1 494	375	25.1
Asian Alone or in Combination												
2002	12 487	1 243	10.0	2 344	137	5.9	354	51	14.3	1 708	417	24.4
2003	12 891	1 527	11.8	2 576	203	7.9	378	89	23.5	1 590	402	25.3

[1] These numbers and rates refer to families rather than people.
... = Not available.

Table 3-6. Poverty Status by Type of Family, Race, and Hispanic Origin—Continued

(Thousands of people or families, percent of population.)

Year, race, and Hispanic origin	All people			Married-couple families [1]			Female householder, no spouse present [1]			Unrelated individuals		
	Number of people	Below poverty level		Number of families	Below poverty level		Number of families	Below poverty level		Number of people	Below poverty level	
		Number	Percent		Number	Percent		Number	Percent		Number	Percent
Hispanic (of Any Race)												
1972	10 588	2 414	22.8	...	...	...	...	...	...	488	162	33.2
1973	10 795	2 366	21.9	1 876	239	12.7	411	211	51.4	526	157	29.9
1974	11 201	2 575	23.0	1 926	278	14.4	462	229	49.6	617	201	32.6
1975	11 117	2 991	26.9	1 896	335	17.7	522	279	53.6	645	236	36.6
1976	11 269	2 783	24.7	1 978	312	15.8	517	275	53.1	716	266	37.2
1977	12 046	2 700	22.4	2 104	280	13.3	561	301	53.6	797	237	29.8
1978	12 079	2 607	21.6	2 089	248	11.9	542	288	53.1	886	264	29.8
1979	13 371	2 921	21.8	2 282	298	13.1	610	300	49.2	991	286	28.8
1980	13 600	3 491	25.7	2 365	363	15.3	706	362	51.3	970	312	32.2
1981	14 021	3 713	26.5	2 414	366	15.1	750	399	53.2	1 005	313	31.1
1982	14 385	4 301	29.9	2 448	465	19.0	767	425	55.4	1 018	358	35.1
1983	16 544	4 633	28.0	2 752	437	17.7	860	454	52.8	1 364	457	33.5
1984	16 916	4 806	28.4	2 824	469	16.6	905	483	53.4	1 481	545	36.8
1985	18 075	5 236	29.0	2 962	505	17.0	980	521	53.1	1 602	532	33.2
1986	18 758	5 117	27.3	3 118	518	16.6	1 032	528	51.2	1 685	553	32.8
1987	19 395	5 422	28.0	3 196	556	17.4	1 082	565	52.2	1 933	598	31.0
1988	20 064	5 357	26.7	3 398	547	16.1	1 112	546	49.1	1 864	597	32.0
1989	20 746	5 430	26.2	3 395	549	16.2	1 116	530	47.5	2 045	634	31.0
1990	21 405	6 006	28.1	3 454	605	17.5	1 186	573	48.3	2 254	774	34.3
1991	22 070	6 339	28.7	3 532	674	19.1	1 261	627	49.7	2 146	667	31.1
1992	25 646	7 592	29.6	3 940	743	18.8	1 348	664	49.3	2 577	881	34.2
1993	26 559	8 126	30.6	4 038	770	19.1	1 498	772	51.6	2 717	972	35.8
1994	27 442	8 416	30.7	4 236	827	19.5	1 485	773	52.1	2 798	926	33.1
1995	28 344	8 574	30.3	4 247	803	18.9	1 604	792	49.4	2 947	1 092	37.0
1996	29 614	8 697	29.4	4 520	815	18.0	1 617	823	50.9	2 985	1 066	35.7
1997	30 637	8 308	27.1	4 804	836	17.4	1 612	767	47.6	2 976	1 017	34.2
1998	31 515	8 070	25.6	4 945	775	15.7	1 728	756	43.7	3 218	1 097	34.1
1999	34 632	7 876	22.7	5 273	758	14.4	1 827	717	39.3	3 481	1 068	30.7
2000	35 955	7 747	21.5	5 426	772	14.2	1 826	664	36.4	3 978	1 163	29.2
2001	37 312	7 997	21.4	5 778	799	13.8	1 922	711	37.0	3 981	1 211	30.4
2002	39 216	8 555	21.8	6 189	927	15.0	2 033	717	35.3	4 364	1 255	28.8
2003	40 300	9 051	22.5	6 228	976	15.7	2 138	792	37.0	4 620	1 325	28.7

[1] These numbers and rates refer to families rather than people.
... = Not available.

Table 3-7. Poverty Status of People by Sex and Age

(Thousands of people, percent of population.)

Year	Poverty status of people by sex				Poverty status of people by age					
	Males below poverty level		Females below poverty level		Children under 18 below poverty level		People 18 to 64 years old below poverty level		People 65 years and older below poverty level	
	Number (thousands)	Poverty rate	Number (thousands)	Poverty rate	Number (thousands)	Poverty rate	Number (thousands)	Poverty rate	Number (thousands)	Poverty rate
1959	...	...	...	...	17 552	27.3	16 457	17.0	5 481	35.2
1966	12 225	13.0	16 265	16.3	12 389	17.6	11 007	10.5	5 114	28.5
1967	11 813	12.5	15 951	15.8	11 656	16.6	10 725	10.0	5 388	29.5
1968	10 793	11.3	14 578	14.3	10 954	15.6	9 803	9.0	4 632	25.0
1969	10 292	10.6	13 978	13.6	9 691	14.0	9 669	8.7	4 787	25.3
1970	10 879	11.1	14 632	14.0	10 440	15.1	10 187	9.0	4 793	24.6
1971	10 708	10.8	14 841	14.1	10 551	15.3	10 735	9.3	4 273	21.6
1972	10 190	10.2	14 258	13.4	10 284	15.1	10 438	8.8	3 738	18.6
1973	9 642	9.6	13 316	12.5	9 642	14.4	9 977	8.3	3 354	16.3
1974	10 313	10.2	13 881	12.9	10 156	15.4	10 132	8.3	3 085	14.6
1975	10 908	10.7	14 970	13.8	11 104	17.1	11 456	9.2	3 317	15.3
1976	10 373	10.1	14 603	13.4	10 273	16.0	11 389	9.0	3 313	15.0
1977	10 340	10.0	14 381	13.0	10 288	16.2	11 316	8.8	3 177	14.1
1978	10 017	9.6	14 480	13.0	9 931	15.9	11 332	8.7	3 233	14.0
1979	10 535	10.0	14 810	13.2	10 377	16.4	12 014	8.9	3 682	15.2
1980	12 207	11.2	17 065	14.7	11 543	18.3	13 858	10.1	3 871	15.7
1981	13 360	12.1	18 462	15.8	12 505	20.0	15 464	11.1	3 853	15.3
1982	14 842	13.4	19 556	16.5	13 647	21.9	17 000	12.0	3 751	14.6
1983	15 182	13.5	20 084	16.8	13 911	22.3	17 767	12.4	3 625	13.8
1984	14 537	12.8	19 163	15.9	13 420	21.5	16 952	11.7	3 330	12.4
1985	14 140	12.3	18 923	15.6	13 010	20.7	16 598	11.3	3 456	12.6
1986	13 721	11.8	18 649	15.2	12 876	20.5	16 017	10.8	3 477	12.4
1987	14 029	12.0	18 518	15.0	12 843	20.3	15 815	10.6	3 563	12.5
1988	13 599	11.5	18 146	14.5	12 455	19.5	15 809	10.5	3 481	12.0
1989	13 366	11.2	18 162	14.4	12 590	19.6	15 575	10.2	3 363	11.4
1990	14 211	11.7	19 373	15.2	13 431	20.6	16 496	10.7	3 658	12.2
1991	15 082	12.3	20 626	16.0	14 341	21.8	17 586	11.4	3 781	12.4
1992	16 222	12.9	21 792	16.6	15 294	22.3	18 793	11.9	3 928	12.9
1993	16 900	13.3	22 365	16.9	15 727	22.7	19 781	12.4	3 755	12.2
1994	16 316	12.8	21 744	16.3	15 289	21.8	19 107	11.9	3 663	11.7
1995	15 683	12.2	20 742	15.4	14 665	20.8	18 442	11.4	3 318	10.5
1996	15 611	12.0	20 918	15.4	14 463	20.5	18 638	11.4	3 428	10.8
1997	15 187	11.6	20 387	14.9	14 113	19.9	18 085	10.9	3 376	10.5
1998	14 712	11.1	19 764	14.3	13 467	18.9	17 623	10.5	3 386	10.5
1999	14 079	10.4	18 712	13.2	12 280	17.1	17 289	10.1	3 222	9.7
2000	13 536	9.9	18 045	12.6	11 587	16.2	16 671	9.6	3 323	9.9
2001	14 327	10.4	18 580	12.9	11 733	16.3	17 760	10.1	3 414	10.1
2002	15 162	10.9	19 408	13.3	12 133	16.7	18 861	10.6	3 576	10.4
2003	15 783	11.2	20 078	13.7	12 866	17.6	19 443	10.8	3 552	10.2

... = Not available.

Table 3-8. Poverty Status of People Inside and Outside Metropolitan Areas, and People In and Near Poverty

(Thousands of people, percent of population.)

Year	Inside metropolitan areas						Outside metropolitan areas		Total in and near poverty (income below 1.25 times the poverty level)		Near-poor (income between 1 and 1.25 times poverty level)	
	Number (thousands)	Poverty rate	Central city		Outside central city		Number (thousands)	Poverty rate	Number (thousands)	Percent	Number (thousands)	Percent
			Number (thousands)	Poverty rate	Number (thousands)	Poverty rate						
1959	17 019	15.3	10 437	18.3	6 582	12.2	21 747	33.2	54 942	31.1	15 452	8.7
1960	...	...	...	...	...	...	...	...	54 560	30.4	14 709	8.2
1961	...	...	...	...	...	...	...	...	54 280	30.0	14 652	8.1
1962	...	...	...	...	...	...	...	...	53 119	28.8	14 494	7.9
1963	...	...	...	...	...	...	...	...	50 778	27.1	14 342	7.7
1964	...	...	...	...	...	...	...	...	49 819	26.3	13 764	7.3
1965	...	...	...	...	...	...	...	...	46 163	24.1	12 978	6.8
1966	...	...	...	...	...	...	...	...	41 267	21.3	12 757	6.6
1967	13 832	10.9	8 649	15.0	5 183	7.5	13 936	20.2	39 206	20.0	11 437	5.8
1968	12 871	10.0	7 754	13.4	5 117	7.3	12 518	18.0	35 905	18.2	10 516	5.3
1969	13 084	9.5	7 993	12.7	5 091	6.8	11 063	17.9	34 665	17.4	10 518	5.3
1970	13 317	10.2	8 118	14.2	5 199	7.1	12 103	16.9	35 624	17.6	10 204	5.0
1971	14 561	10.4	8 912	14.2	5 649	7.2	10 999	17.2	36 501	17.8	10 942	5.3
1972	14 508	10.3	9 179	14.7	5 329	6.8	9 952	15.3	34 653	16.8	10 193	4.9
1973	13 759	9.7	8 594	14.0	5 165	6.4	9 214	14.0	32 828	15.8	9 855	4.7
1974	13 851	9.7	8 373	13.7	5 477	6.7	9 519	14.2	33 666	16.1	10 296	4.9
1975	15 348	10.8	9 090	15.0	6 259	7.6	10 529	15.4	37 182	17.6	11 305	5.4
1976	15 229	10.7	9 482	15.8	5 747	6.9	9 746	14.0	35 509	16.7	10 534	5.0
1977	14 859	10.4	9 203	15.4	5 657	6.8	9 861	13.9	35 659	16.7	10 939	5.1
1978	15 090	10.4	9 285	15.4	5 805	6.8	9 407	13.5	34 155	15.8	9 658	4.5
1979	16 135	10.7	9 720	15.7	6 415	7.2	9 937	13.8	36 616	16.4	10 544	4.7
1980	18 021	11.9	10 644	17.2	7 377	8.2	11 251	15.4	40 658	18.1	11 386	5.1
1981	19 347	12.6	11 231	18.0	8 116	8.9	12 475	17.0	43 748	19.3	11 926	5.3
1982	21 247	13.7	12 696	19.9	8 551	9.3	13 152	17.8	46 520	20.3	12 122	5.3
1983	21 750	13.8	12 872	19.8	8 878	9.6	13 516	18.3	47 150	20.3	11 847	5.1
1984	...	...	...	...	...	...	...	...	45 288	19.4	11 588	5.0
1985	23 275	12.7	14 177	19.0	9 097	8.4	9 789	18.3	44 166	18.7	11 102	4.7
1986	22 657	12.3	13 295	18.0	9 362	8.4	9 712	18.1	43 486	18.2	11 116	4.7
1987	23 054	12.3	13 697	18.3	9 357	8.3	9 167	17.0	43 032	17.9	10 811	4.5
1988	23 059	12.2	13 615	18.1	9 444	8.3	8 686	16.0	42 551	17.5	10 806	4.4
1989	22 917	12.0	13 592	18.1	9 326	8.0	8 611	15.7	42 653	17.3	11 125	4.5
1990	24 510	12.7	14 254	19.0	10 255	8.7	9 075	16.3	44 837	18.0	11 252	4.5
1991	26 827	13.7	15 314	20.2	11 513	9.6	8 881	16.1	47 527	18.9	11 819	4.7
1992	28 380	14.2	16 346	20.9	12 034	9.9	9 634	16.9	50 592	19.7	12 578	4.9
1993	29 615	14.6	16 805	21.5	12 810	10.3	9 650	17.2	51 801	20.0	12 536	4.8
1994	29 610	14.2	16 098	20.9	13 511	10.3	8 449	16.0	50 401	19.3	12 342	4.7
1995	28 342	13.4	16 269	20.6	12 072	9.1	8 083	15.6	48 761	18.5	12 336	4.7
1996	28 211	13.2	15 645	19.6	12 566	9.4	8 318	15.9	49 310	18.5	12 781	4.8
1997	27 273	12.6	15 018	18.8	12 255	9.0	8 301	15.9	47 853	17.8	12 280	4.6
1998	26 997	12.3	14 921	18.5	12 076	8.7	7 479	14.4	46 036	17.0	11 560	4.3
1999	25 278	11.3	13 404	16.5	11 874	8.3	7 513	14.3	45 030	16.3	12 239	4.4
2000	24 603	10.8	13 257	16.3	11 346	7.8	6 978	13.4	43 612	15.6	12 030	4.3
2001	25 446	11.1	13 394	16.5	12 052	8.2	7 460	14.2	45 320	16.1	12 413	4.4
2002	27 096	11.6	13 784	16.7	13 311	8.9	7 474	14.2	47 084	16.5	12 514	4.4
2003	28 367	12.1	14 551	17.5	13 816	9.1	7 495	14.2	48 687	16.9	12 826	4.5

... = Not available.

Table 3-9. Poor People 16 Years and Over by Work Experience

(Thousands of people, percent of total poor people.)

Year	Total number of poor people, 16 years and over	Worked						Did not work	
		Number	Percent of total poor	Worked year-round, full-time		Worked less than year-round or full-time		Number	Percent of total poor
				Number	Percent of total poor	Number	Percent of total poor		
1978	16 914	6 599	39.0	1 309	7.7	5 290	31.3	10 315	61.0
1979	16 803	6 601	39.3	1 394	8.3	5 207	31.0	10 202	60.7
1980	18 892	7 674	40.6	1 644	8.7	6 030	31.9	11 218	59.4
1981	20 571	8 524	41.4	1 881	9.1	6 643	32.3	12 047	58.6
1982	22 100	9 013	40.8	1 999	9.0	7 014	31.7	13 087	59.2
1983	22 741	9 329	41.0	2 064	9.1	7 265	31.9	13 412	59.0
1984	21 541	8 999	41.8	2 076	9.6	6 923	32.1	12 542	58.2
1985	21 243	9 008	42.4	1 972	9.3	7 036	33.1	12 235	57.6
1986	20 688	8 743	42.3	2 007	9.7	6 736	32.6	11 945	57.7
1987	20 546	8 258	40.2	1 821	8.9	6 437	31.3	12 288	59.8
1988	20 323	8 363	41.2	1 929	9.5	6 434	31.7	11 960	58.8
1989	19 952	8 376	42.0	1 908	9.6	6 468	32.4	11 576	58.0
1990	21 242	8 716	41.0	2 076	9.8	6 640	31.3	12 526	59.0
1991	22 530	9 208	40.9	2 103	9.3	7 105	31.5	13 322	59.1
1992	23 951	9 739	40.6	2 211	9.2	7 528	31.4	14 212	59.3
1993	24 832	10 144	40.8	2 408	9.7	7 736	31.2	14 688	59.1
1994	24 108	9 829	40.8	2 520	10.5	7 309	30.3	14 279	59.2
1995	23 077	9 484	41.1	2 418	10.5	7 066	30.6	13 593	58.9
1996	23 472	9 586	40.8	2 263	9.6	7 323	31.2	13 886	59.2
1997	22 753	9 444	41.5	2 345	10.3	7 099	31.2	13 309	58.5
1998	22 256	9 133	41.0	2 804	12.6	6 329	28.4	13 123	59.0
1999	21 762	9 251	42.5	2 559	11.8	6 692	30.8	12 511	57.5
2000	21 080	8 511	40.4	2 439	11.6	6 072	28.8	12 569	59.6
2001	22 245	8 530	38.3	2 567	11.5	5 963	26.8	13 715	61.7
2002	23 601	8 954	37.9	2 635	11.2	6 318	26.8	14 647	62.1
2003	24 266	8 820	36.3	2 636	10.9	6 183	25.5	15 446	63.7

Section 3c: Alternative Measures and State Data

Figure 3-3. Median Household Income: Official and Alternative, 1979–2002
(2002 dollars)

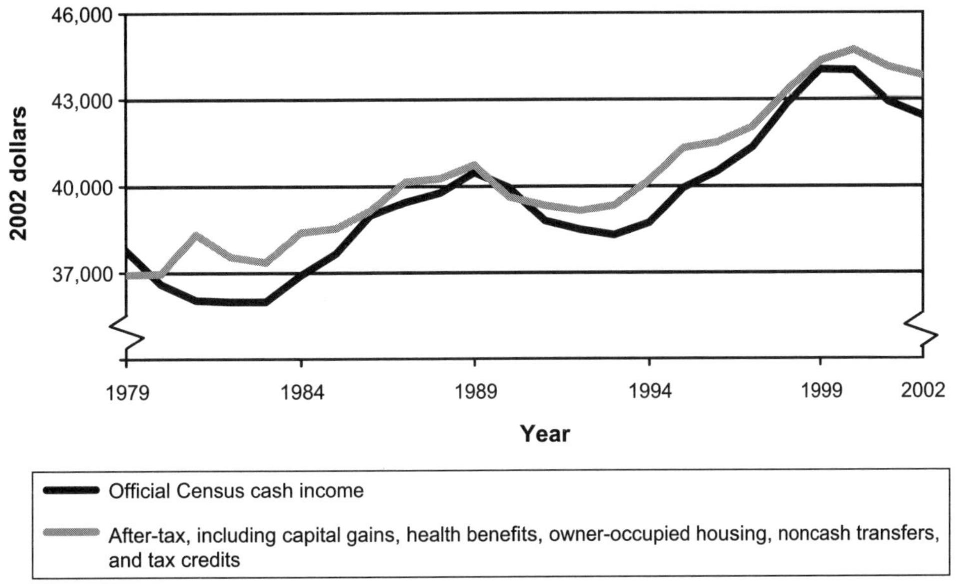

— Official Census cash income
— After-tax, including capital gains, health benefits, owner-occupied housing, noncash transfers, and tax credits

- The official income statistics just quoted are based on cash income before taxes. The Census Bureau has also developed a model to calculate alternative measures that define income more broadly and include the effects of taxes and of in-kind transfer payments such as food stamps. These estimates have not been updated since 2001, except for revised after-tax values for 2001 and 2002, nor extended to 2003. For Figure 3-3 above, the editor has converted historical 2001-dollar values for the years 1979 through 2000 to 2002 dollars, using the ratio of the CPIs for those two years, to provide a continuous historical comparison of the official income data and the most comprehensive, after-tax income series. As the graph indicates, other income sources, taxes, and transfers have mitigated some of the cyclical fluctuations in income in the period from 1979 to 2002 and improved the record of real median income growth, from 12.2 percent in the official numbers to 18.6 percent in the comprehensive numbers. (Table 3-10, with data conversion by the editor)
- In the more comprehensive measure, household income inequality as measured by the Gini coefficient is less than in the official definition but has increased more from 1979 to 2002. Indeed, the 2002 Gini coefficient for after-tax-and-transfer income was little different from the 1979 coefficient for the official measure, which is before-tax and includes only cash transfers such as Social Security. In other words, the redistributive effects of the tax and noncash transfer systems have been offset by the increasing inequality in before-tax income. (Table 3-10)

Table 3-10. Median Household Income and Poverty Rates for People, Based on Alternative Definitions of Income

Year	Definition 1: Money income excluding capital gains (current official measure)				Definition 4: Money income before taxes and transfers, plus health insurance supplements			
	Median income (2001 dollars)	Poverty rate (percent)		Gini coefficient	Median income (2001 dollars)	Poverty rate (percent)		Gini coefficient
		Official threshold	CPI-U-X1 threshold			Official threshold	CPI-U-X1 threshold	
1979	37 192	11.7	10.6	0.403	36 659	18.8	17.8	0.460
1980	36 035	13.0	11.5	0.401	34 826	20.1	19.0	0.462
1981	35 478	14.0	12.2	0.404	34 057	21.1	19.8	0.466
1982	35 423	15.0	13.2	0.409	33 649	22.0	20.6	0.475
1983	35 438	15.2	13.7	0.412	34 082	21.8	20.6	0.478
1984	36 343	14.4	12.8	0.413	35 202	20.8	19.5	0.477
1985	37 059	14.0	12.5	0.418	35 853	20.4	19.1	0.486
1986	38 365	13.6	12.2	0.423	37 308	19.9	18.7	0.505
1987	38 835	13.4	12.0	0.424	37 549	19.7	18.7	0.488
1988	39 144	13.0	11.7	0.425	38 065	19.7	18.6	0.489
1989	39 850	12.8	11.4	0.429	38 773	19.4	18.3	0.492
1990	39 324	13.5	12.1	0.426	37 702	19.9	18.8	0.487
1991	38 183	14.2	12.7	0.425	36 493	21.1	20.0	0.490
1992	37 880	14.8	13.4	0.430	36 103	22.1	20.9	0.497
1993	37 688	15.1	13.7	0.448	35 983	22.6	21.4	0.514
1994	38 119	14.5	13.2	0.450	36 830	22.0	20.8	0.515
1995	39 306	13.8	12.3	0.444	37 856	21.1	19.9	0.509
1996	39 869	13.7	12.2	0.447	38 614	20.8	19.5	0.511
1997	40 699	13.3	11.8	0.448	39 567	20.3	19.1	0.513
1998	42 173	12.7	11.3	0.446	40 859	19.3	18.1	0.509
1999	43 355	11.9	10.6	0.445	42 267	18.7	17.6	0.508
2000	43 327	11.3	10.3	0.447	42 348	18.0	17.0	0.506
2001	42 228	11.7	10.4	0.450	41 346	18.5	17.4	0.510
2002	...	12.1	10.8	0.448	...	19.3	18.1	...
2002 Dollars								
2001	42 900	...	...	...	42 004	...	...	...
2002	42 409	...	...	...	41 294	...	...	...

Year	Definition 14: Income after all taxes and transfers				Definition 15: Income after all taxes and transfers, plus net imputed return on equity in own home			
	Median income (2001 dollars)	Poverty rate (percent)		Gini coefficient	Median income (2001 dollars)	Poverty rate (percent)		Gini coefficient
		Official threshold	CPI-U-X1 threshold			Official threshold	CPI-U-X1 threshold	
1979	34 099	8.9	7.9	0.359	36 352	7.5	6.7	0.352
1980	32 997	10.1	8.6	0.354	36 379	8.2	7.0	0.347
1981	32 242	11.5	9.8	0.358	37 721	8.7	7.3	0.350
1982	32 555	12.3	10.6	0.366	36 951	9.9	8.5	0.359
1983	33 064	12.7	11.0	0.374	36 763	10.4	9.0	0.368
1984	33 728	12.0	10.4	0.378	37 781	9.9	8.6	0.372
1985	34 363	11.7	10.1	0.385	37 925	9.9	8.6	0.381
1986	35 795	11.3	9.8	0.409	38 517	10.1	8.6	0.404
1987	36 275	11.0	9.5	0.382	39 516	9.7	8.3	0.380
1988	36 371	10.8	9.5	0.385	39 642	9.4	8.2	0.384
1989	37 103	10.4	8.9	0.389	40 091	9.1	7.7	0.387
1990	36 529	10.9	9.5	0.382	38 998	9.8	8.5	0.381
1991	36 031	11.4	9.9	0.380	38 705	10.3	8.9	0.379
1992	36 318	11.9	10.5	0.385	38 517	10.7	9.5	0.381
1993	36 667	12.1	10.7	0.398	38 713	11.2	9.8	0.395
1994	37 279	11.1	9.8	0.400	39 563	10.0	8.8	0.395
1995	38 417	10.3	9.0	0.394	40 670	9.4	8.1	0.388
1996	38 776	10.2	8.9	0.398	40 844	9.3	8.1	0.392
1997	39 440	10.0	8.8	0.403	41 379	9.2	8.0	0.397
1998	40 859	9.5	8.2	0.405	42 632	8.8	7.6	0.399
1999	41 707	8.9	7.7	0.408	43 657	8.2	6.9	0.402
2000	41 709	8.8	7.6	0.410	44 009	8.0	6.9	0.402
2001	41 533	9.0	7.8	0.412	43 237	8.3	7.2	0.407
2002	...	9.4	8.2	0.405	...	8.6	7.5	0.400
2002 Dollars (revised)								
2001	42 398	...	...	...	44 116	...	...	...
2002	42 117	...	...	...	43 812	...	...	...

Note: See Notes and Definitions for explanation of alternative definitions and thresholds, and of the Gini coefficient.
... = Not available.

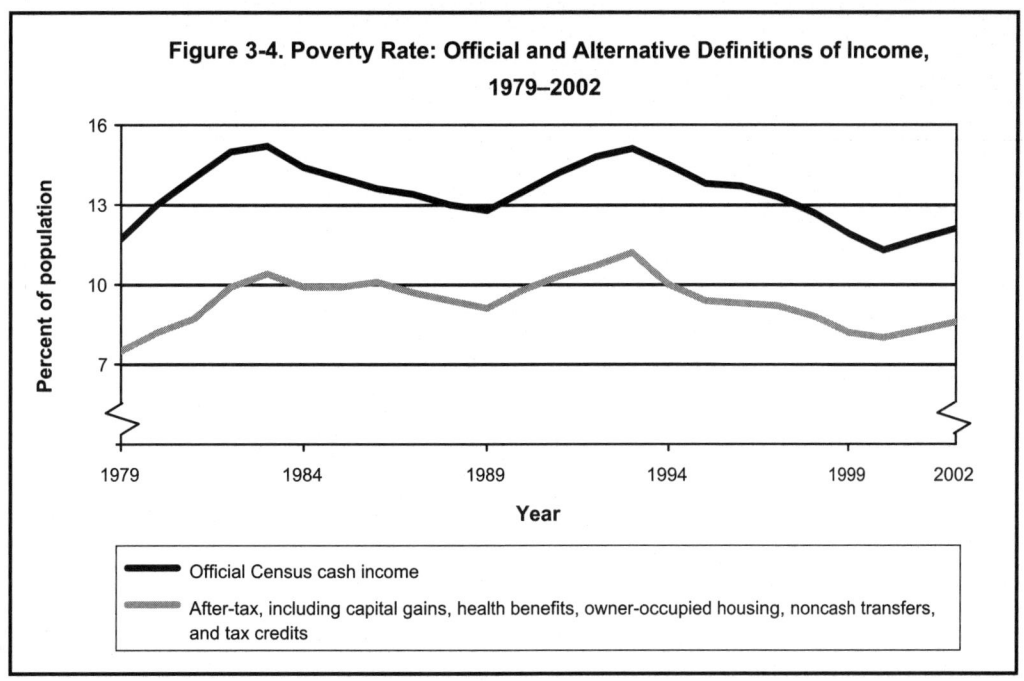

- Including the broader income definition and the effects of the earned income tax credit and noncash transfers, the poverty rate relative to the official poverty threshold is lower, as shown in the graph above. (Recent Census Bureau research, based on recommendations by the National Academy of Sciences, suggests that thresholds and income definitions should *both* be adjusted, resulting in poverty rates somewhat higher than the official rate. Rates following these recommendations were calculated only for 2001 and 2002 and are not shown in this volume, since *Business Statistics* focuses on longer time series. See references in Notes and Definitions.) The broader income definition mitigates, but does not eliminate, business-cycle fluctuations in the poverty rate. However, the broader income definition also indicates a 1.1 percentage point rise in the poverty rate from 1979 to 2002, *more* than the 0.4 point increase in the official measure. (Table 3-10)
- Cash transfers, which are dominated by Social Security, play a greater role in the reduction of poverty than the tax system, including the Earned Income Tax Credit, and noncash transfers, as can be seen by comparing the poverty rates using Definitions 1, 4, and 14. (Table 3-10)

Table 3-11. Experimental Measures of Before-Tax and After-Tax Income

Year	Number of households	2002 dollars		Share of aggregate income						Gini coefficient
		Mean income	Median income	Lowest fifth	Second fifth	Third fifth	Fourth fifth	Highest fifth	Top 5 percent	
BEFORE TAX										
1980	82 368	43 539	36 608	4.2	10.2	16.8	24.8	44.1	16.5	0.399
1981	83 527	43 059	36 042	4.1	10.1	16.7	24.8	44.4	16.5	0.402
1982	83 918	43 369	35 986	4.0	10.0	16.5	24.5	45.0	17.0	0.406
1983	85 290	43 865	36 001	4.0	9.9	16.4	24.6	45.1	17.1	0.407
1984	86 789	45 238	36 921	4.0	9.9	16.3	24.6	45.2	17.1	0.406
1985	88 458	46 332	37 648	3.9	9.8	16.2	24.4	45.6	17.6	0.406
1986	89 479	48 152	38 975	3.8	9.7	16.2	24.3	46.1	18.0	0.407
1987	91 124	49 065	39 453	3.8	9.6	16.1	24.3	46.2	18.2	0.424
1988	92 830	49 688	39 767	3.8	9.6	16.0	24.3	46.3	18.3	0.425
1989	93 347	51 148	40 484	3.8	9.5	15.8	24.0	46.8	18.9	0.429
1990	94 312	49 902	39 949	3.8	9.6	15.9	24.0	46.6	18.6	0.426
1991	95 669	48 829	38 791	3.8	9.6	15.9	24.2	46.5	18.1	0.425
1992	96 426	48 788	38 482	3.7	9.4	15.8	24.2	46.9	18.6	0.431
1993	97 107	50 772	38 287	3.6	9.0	15.1	23.5	48.9	21.0	0.448
1994	98 990	51 771	38 726	3.6	8.9	15.0	23.4	49.1	21.2	0.450
1995	99 627	52 659	39 931	3.7	9.1	15.2	23.4	48.6	21.0	0.444
1996	101 018	53 776	40 503	3.7	8.9	15.2	23.2	49.0	21.4	0.447
1997	102 528	55 522	41 346	3.6	8.9	15.0	23.2	49.4	21.7	0.448
1998	103 874	57 134	42 844	3.6	9.0	15.0	23.2	49.2	21.4	0.446
1999	106 434	59 067	43 915	3.6	8.9	14.9	23.2	49.4	21.5	0.445
2000	108 209	59 664	43 764	3.6	8.9	14.9	23.0	49.6	21.9	0.447
2001	109 297	59 134	42 900	3.5	8.7	14.6	23.0	50.1	22.4	0.450
2002	111 278	57 852	42 409	...	...	...	...	...	...	...
AFTER TAX										
1980	82 368	33 636	30 078	4.9	11.6	17.9	25.1	40.6	14.1	0.358
1981	83 527	33 059	29 331	4.9	11.5	17.8	25.0	40.9	14.2	0.362
1982	83 918	33 765	29 494	4.7	11.3	17.5	24.8	41.8	14.8	0.371
1983	85 290	34 509	29 850	4.7	11.1	17.4	24.8	42.1	15.0	0.375
1984	86 789	35 520	30 522	4.7	11.0	17.2	24.8	42.3	15.2	0.377
1985	88 458	36 099	30 926	4.6	11.0	17.2	24.7	42.6	15.4	0.379
1986	89 479	37 075	31 863	4.4	10.9	17.2	24.8	42.6	15.3	0.380
1987	91 124	38 013	32 609	4.5	10.9	17.2	24.8	42.5	15.4	0.382
1988	92 830	38 520	32 765	4.5	10.9	17.1	24.6	42.9	15.8	0.384
1989	93 347	39 433	33 296	4.6	10.8	16.9	24.4	43.3	16.2	0.388
1990	94 312	38 942	32 749	4.5	10.8	16.9	24.3	43.5	16.5	0.390
1991	95 669	38 165	32 132	4.5	10.8	16.9	24.6	43.2	16.0	0.388
1992	96 426	38 217	31 998	4.4	10.6	16.8	24.5	43.6	16.5	0.393
1993	97 107	39 330	32 002	4.3	10.4	16.3	24.0	45.0	18.1	0.407
1994	98 990	39 987	32 375	4.4	10.4	16.3	23.9	45.1	18.1	0.407
1995	99 627	40 535	33 103	4.5	10.5	16.4	23.9	44.6	17.9	0.401
1996	101 018	41 091	33 450	4.5	10.5	16.3	24.0	44.7	17.9	0.402
1997	102 528	42 074	34 244	4.4	10.5	16.3	24.0	44.8	18.0	0.403
1998	103 874	42 930	35 328	4.5	10.6	16.5	24.1	44.3	17.4	0.398
1999	106 434	43 920	36 251	4.6	10.6	16.6	24.2	44.0	17.1	0.395
2000	108 209	44 107	36 096	4.5	10.5	16.5	24.1	44.4	17.8	0.398
2001	109 297	43 865	35 563	4.4	10.4	16.3	24.0	44.9	18.2	0.403
2002	111 278	44 323	35 812	...	...	...	...	...	...	...

. . . = Not available.

Table 3-12. Median Income and Poverty Rates by State

State	Median household money income (2003 dollars)			Poverty rate (percent)		
	3-year-average median, 2001–2003	2-year average		3-year-average median, 2001–2003	2-year average	
		2001–2002	2002–2003		2001–2002	2002–2003
United States	43 527	43 631	43 349	12.1	11.9	12.3
Alabama	37 419	37 501	37 860	15.1	15.2	14.7
Alaska	55 143	56 797	52 910	9.0	8.7	9.2
Arizona	42 062	42 511	40 905	13.9	14.1	13.5
Arkansas	33 259	33 887	32 565	18.5	18.8	18.8
California	48 979	48 819	48 912	12.9	12.8	13.1
Colorado	50 224	50 366	49 670	9.4	9.2	9.7
Connecticut	55 004	55 024	54 788	7.9	7.8	8.2
Delaware	50 451	51 166	49 903	7.7	7.9	8.2
District of Columbia	42 597	41 373	42 505	17.3	17.6	16.9
Florida	38 572	38 372	38 934	12.7	12.6	12.6
Georgia	43 535	44 083	43 180	12.0	12.1	11.5
Hawaii	49 839	48 842	50 110	10.7	11.4	10.3
Idaho	40 230	39 159	40 476	11.0	11.4	10.8
Illinois	45 607	45 834	44 421	11.8	11.5	12.7
Indiana	42 124	41 974	42 206	9.2	8.8	9.5
Iowa	41 985	42 285	41 687	8.5	8.3	9.1
Kansas	43 622	43 316	43 914	10.3	10.1	10.4
Kentucky	38 161	38 774	37 270	13.7	13.4	14.3
Louisiana	34 307	34 707	34 147	16.9	16.9	17.2
Maine	37 619	37 872	37 405	11.8	11.9	12.5
Maryland	55 213	56 663	55 007	7.7	7.3	8.0
Massachusetts	52 084	52 649	50 976	9.7	9.5	10.1
Michigan	45 176	45 253	44 358	10.8	10.5	11.5
Minnesota	54 480	55 309	54 348	7.1	6.9	6.9
Mississippi	31 887	31 466	32 159	17.9	18.9	17.2
Missouri	43 492	43 357	43 759	10.1	9.8	10.3
Montana	34 375	34 509	34 871	14.0	13.4	14.3
Nebraska	44 357	44 548	43 875	9.9	10.0	10.2
Nevada	46 118	46 585	45 586	9.0	8.0	9.9
New Hampshire	55 166	54 965	56 078	6.0	6.1	5.8
New Jersey	55 221	54 809	55 932	8.2	8.0	8.3
New Mexico	35 265	35 346	35 687	18.0	17.9	18.0
New York	43 160	43 346	42 858	14.2	14.1	14.2
North Carolina	38 096	38 504	37 315	14.2	13.4	15.0
North Dakota	38 212	37 112	38 720	11.7	12.7	10.6
Ohio	43 535	43 542	43 591	10.4	10.1	10.3
Oklahoma	36 733	37 149	36 598	14.0	14.6	13.5
Oregon	42 429	42 825	42 199	11.7	11.3	11.7
Pennsylvania	43 869	44 337	43 202	9.9	9.5	10.0
Rhode Island	45 205	45 452	44 050	10.7	10.3	11.3
South Carolina	38 791	38 946	38 579	14.0	14.7	13.5
South Dakota	39 829	39 983	39 131	10.9	10.0	12.1
Tennessee	37 529	37 532	37 701	14.3	14.5	14.4
Texas	40 934	41 765	40 170	15.8	15.3	16.3
Utah	49 143	49 077	49 116	9.8	10.2	9.5
Vermont	43 212	43 188	43 623	9.4	9.8	9.2
Virginia	52 587	51 489	52 776	9.3	8.9	10.0
Washington	45 960	45 186	46 863	11.4	10.8	11.8
West Virginia	31 210	30 434	31 397	16.9	16.6	17.1
Wisconsin	46 782	47 039	46 612	8.8	8.2	9.2
Wyoming	41 501	40 975	41 614	9.1	8.8	9.4

NOTES AND DEFINITIONS

TABLES 3-1 THROUGH 3-12
INCOME DISTRIBUTION AND POVERTY

SOURCE: U.S. DEPARTMENT OF COMMERCE, BUREAU OF THE CENSUS

All data in this chapter are derived from the Current Population Survey (CPS), which is also the source of data on labor force, employment, and unemployment. (See the Notes and Definitions for Tables 10-1 through 10-3.) Early in each year, the 60,000 households in this monthly survey are asked additional questions concerning earnings and other income in the previous year. This survey, informally known as the "March supplement," is now formally known as the Current Population Survey Annual Social and Economic Supplement (ASEC). It was previously called the Annual Demographic Supplement.

The population represented by the survey is the civilian noninstitutional population of the United States and members of the Armed Forces in the United States living off post or with their families on post, but excluding all other members of the Armed Forces. Because it is a survey of households, homeless persons are not included.

Racial classification and Hispanic origin

In 2002 and all earlier years, the CPS allowed respondents to report identification with only one race group. Beginning in 2003, the CPS is now allowing respondents to choose more than one race. Since the income data for 2002 were collected in early 2003, the income data for the years 2002 and 2003 incorporate for the first time data in which one individual could be reported in more than one race group. In the 2000 Census, about 2.6 percent of people reported more than one race.

This means that the 2002–2003 data classified by race are not strictly comparable with race-classified data for 2001 and earlier years. As alternative approaches to dealing with this problem, the Census Bureau has, in a number of cases, tabulated two different race concepts for each racial category. In the case of Blacks, for example, this means there is one income measure for "Black alone," consisting of persons who report Black and no other race, and one for "Black alone or in combination," which includes all the "Black alone" reporters *plus* those who report Black in combination with any other race. The tables in this volume show both the "alone" and the "alone or in combination" values, where available.

The racial classifications used in the CPS are *White*; *Black*; *Asian, Native Hawaiian and Other Pacific Islander*; and *American Indian and Alaska Native*. The Census Bureau does not publish CPS data for the last group because it is too small to provide statistically reliable information.

Hispanic origin is a separate question in the survey, not a racial classification, and Hispanics may be of any race. According to the Census Bureau, "Being Hispanic was reported by 11.8 percent of White householders who reported only one race; 2.7 percent of Black householders who reported only one race; 26.5 percent of American Indian and Alaska Native householders who reported only one race; and 10.0 percent of Native Hawaiian and Other Pacific Islander householders who reported only one race.... Data users should exercise caution when interpreting aggregate results for the Hispanic population or for race groups because these populations consist of many distinct groups that differ in socioeconomic characteristics, culture, and recency of immigration." ("Income, Poverty, and Health Insurance Coverage in the United States: 2003," pp. 1–2.) A subgroup of *White Non-Hispanic* is shown in some tables.

Definitions

Households consist of all persons who occupy a housing unit. A household includes the related family members and all the unrelated persons, if any, such as lodgers, foster children, wards, or employees who share the housing unit. A person living alone in a housing unit or a group of unrelated persons sharing a housing unit as partners is also counted as a household. The count of households excludes group quarters.

A *family* is a group of two or more persons related by birth, marriage, or adoption who reside together.

Unrelated individuals are persons 15 years old and over who are not living with any relatives. The poverty status of unrelated individuals is determined independently of income of other persons with whom they may share a household.

Median income is the amount of household income that divides the ranked income distribution into two equal groups, half having incomes above the median, half having incomes below the median. The medians for persons are based on persons 15 years old and over with income.

Where available, historical income figures are shown in constant *2003 dollars*. Some data for earlier years are shown in *2001* or *2002 dollars* as calculated in a previous year's report, because the Census Bureau has not updated them. These data can be converted to dollars of another year using the ratio of the CPI-U in the desired year to the CPI-U for the year used in the series to be converted; for example, for Figure 8-3, the editor converted 2001-dollar incomes to 2002-dollar incomes by multiplying by the ratio of the CPI-U in 2002 (261.9) to the CPI-U in 2001 (257.8), which is 1.0159.

In either case, the constant-dollar figures are Census Bureau estimates, converted from current-dollar values using the *CPI-U-RS* (which shows the same changes as the CPI-U in the most recent years). This index measures changes in prices for past periods using the methodologies of the current CPI, and is similar in concept and behavior to the deflators used in the NIPAs for consumer income and spending. See the Notes and Definitions for Table 8-1 for further explanation of the CPI-U-RS.

Mean income is the amount obtained by dividing the total aggregate income of a group by the number of units in that group. Income means are higher than medians because of the skewed nature of the income distribution; see the section "Whose standard of living?" in the article at the beginning of this book.

Earnings include wages, salaries, armed forces pay, commissions, tips, piece-rate payments, and cash bonuses, before deductions such as taxes, bonds, pensions, and union dues; net income from nonfarm self-employment; and net income from farm self-employment.

Income, in the official definition used in the survey, is money income including earnings as defined above; unemployment compensation; workers' compensation; Social Security; Supplemental Security Income; cash public assistance (welfare payments); veterans' payments; survivor benefits; disability benefits; pension or retirement income; interest income; dividends (but not capital gains); rents, royalties, and payments from estates or trusts; educational assistance, such as scholarships or grants; child support; alimony; financial assistance from outside of the household; and other cash income regularly received, such as foster child payments, military family allotments, and foreign government pensions. Receipts not counted as income include capital gains or losses, withdrawals of bank deposits, money borrowed, tax refunds, gifts, and lump-sum inheritances or insurance payments.

The poverty population is the number of people with family or individual incomes below a specified level intended to measure the cost of a minimum standard of living. These minimum levels vary by size and composition of family and are known as *poverty thresholds*. The poverty thresholds are based on a definition developed by Mollie Orshansky of the Social Security Administration in 1964 and are adjusted each year for price increase, using the percent change in the Consumer Price Index for all urban consumers (CPI-U). For more information, see Gordon Fisher, "The Development of the Orshansky Thresholds and Their Subsequent History as the Official U.S. Poverty Measure," available on the Census Bureau Internet site at <http://www.census.gov/hhes/poverty/povmeas/papers/orshansky.html>. The *poverty rate* for a demographic group is the number of poor people or families in that group expressed as a percentage of the total number of people or families in the group.

Average poverty thresholds. The actual poverty thresholds used to calculate poverty rates vary not only with the size of the family but with the number of children in the family; for example, the threshold for a three-person family in 2003 was $14,393 if there were no children in the family but $14,824 if the family consisted of one adult and two children. To give a general sense of the "poverty line," the Census Bureau also publishes the *average* threshold for each size family, based on the actual mix of family types in that year. These are the values shown in Table 3-5 to represent the history of poverty thresholds. The average value for three-person families, as shown in Table 3-5, was $14,680, a weighted average of the values actually used for the three different possible family compositions.

A person with *work experience* is one who, during the preceding calendar year, did any work for pay or profit or worked without pay on a family-operated farm or business at any time during the year, on a part-time or full-time basis. A year-round worker is one who worked for 50 weeks or more during the preceding calendar year. A person is classified as having worked full time if he or she worked 35 hours or more per week during a majority of the weeks worked. A year-round, full-time worker is a person who worked 35 or more hours per week and 50 or more weeks during the previous calendar year.

Income distribution

Income distribution is portrayed by dividing the total ranked distribution of families or households into *fifths* or *quintiles*, and also tabulating separately the top 5 percent (which is also included in the highest fifth). The households or families are arrayed from those with the lowest income to those with the highest income, then divided into five groups each containing one-fifth of the total number of households. Within each quintile, incomes are summed and calculated as a share of total income for all quintiles, and averaged to show the average or mean income within that quintile.

A statistical measure that summarizes the dispersion of income across the entire income distribution is the *Gini coefficient* (also known as Gini ratio or index of income concentration), which can take values ranging from 0 to 1. A Gini value of 1 indicates "perfect" inequality: that is, one household having all the income and the rest having none. A value of 0 indicates "perfect" equality: that is, all households having equal shares of income. There are small differences between the Gini coefficients presented in the report's main tables and those presented in the tables comparing alternative definitions of income. In the latter, the coefficients were recalculated, for comparability with the other income definitions, using a slightly different method.

Alternative definitions of income

The Census Bureau calculates "alternative" income and poverty measures based on a number of different definitions of income, but the same concept of the poverty threshold, as the official measure. These measures in many cases require simulation—use of data from sources other than the CPS to estimate elements of family and individual income as reported in the CPS. *Business Statistics* shows median household income and poverty rates according to three of these alternative definitions, with the statistics according to the official definition also shown for comparison in the same table. This year these data were not updated through 2003 nor published in the basic income and poverty report. However, after-tax measures for 2001 and 2002 were revised to incorporate an improved tax model. The revised data and the earlier data for the years through 2002 are available on the Internet. (Table 3-10)

Definition 1 (labeled "MI" in the most recent reports) is the official Census definition of money income described above.

Definition 4 is Definition 1 income *minus* government cash transfers (Social Security, unemployment compensation, workers' compensation, veteran's payments, railroad retirement, black lung payments, government education assistance, Supplemental Security Income, and welfare payments), *plus* realized capital gains and employers' payments for health insurance coverage. Capital gains and health insurance are not collected in the CPS but are simulated using statistical data from the Internal Revenue Service and the National Medical Care Expenditure Survey. Definition 4 is, in effect, the income generated by the workings of the economy before government interventions in the form of taxes and transfer payments.

Definition 14 ("MI – Tx + NC" in recent reports) is income after all government income and earnings tax and transfer interventions. It consists of Definition 4 income *minus* payroll taxes and federal and state income taxes, *plus* the Earned Income Credit; all of the cash transfers listed above as being subtracted from money income to yield Definition 4; the "fungible" value of Medicare and Medicaid (see below for definition); the value of regular-price school lunches provided by government; and the value of noncash transfers, including food stamps, rent subsidies, and free and reduced-price school lunches. The tax information is not collected in the CPS but is simulated using statistical data from the Internal Revenue Service, Social Security payroll tax formulas, and a model of each state's income tax regulations.

The "fungible" value approach to medical benefits counts such benefits as income only to the extent that they free up resources that could have been spent on medical care. Therefore, if family income is not sufficient to cover the family's basic food and housing requirements, Medicare and Medicaid are treated as having no income value. Data on average Medicare and Medicaid outlays per enrollee are used in the valuation process.

Food stamp values are reported in the March CPS. Estimates of other government subsidy payments use data from the Department of Agriculture (for school lunches) and the 1985 American Housing Survey.

Definition 15 ("MI – Tx + NC + HE") is Definition 14 income *plus* the net imputed return on equity in owner-occupied housing—the calculated annual benefit of converting one's home equity into an annuity, net of property taxes. This concept can be thought of as measuring the extent to which equity in the home relieves the owner of the need for rental or mortgage payments. Information from the 1987 American Housing Survey is used to assign values of home equity and amounts of property taxes. Because disposable personal income in the NIPAs includes the imputed rent on owner-occupied housing plus most of the cash and in-kind transfers included in Definitions 14 and 15, Definition 15 is the Census income definition closest to the NIPA concept.

For each of these income definitions, poverty rates are also calculated and shown in this table for the years through 2002 using poverty thresholds that have been adjusted for price increase using the CPI-U-X1, instead of the CPI-U, which is used in the official thresholds. (See Notes and Definitions to Table 8-1.) The CPI-U-X1 is used with the intention of removing an upward bias that emerged in the CPI-U and CPI-W in the late 1970s and early 1980s due to a faulty method of measuring housing prices. Any upward bias in the price index used to inflate the poverty thresholds leads to an upward bias in the poverty rate as well *relative to the poverty rates estimated before the bias emerged*. (This is a bias in the behavior of the time series, not necessarily a bias in the level of poverty. As detailed below, there are other factors that can bias poverty thresholds and rates relative to some "real" definition of poverty.) After 1985, the rental equivalence method used in the CPI-U-X1 is also used to calculate the changes in the official CPI-U, and no further differences in *level* appear between the poverty rates using the CPI-U and using the CPI-U-X1.

A new table available on the Census Internet site this year shows the distribution by quintiles of before-tax and after-tax household income. This is shown in Table 3-11, along with the Gini ratios derived from both sets of data. *Before-tax income* is cash income as defined in the official income measures. *After-tax income* includes the earned income credit; excludes capital gains and capital losses; and reflects federal and state personal income taxes, federal retirement or FICA (Social Security and Medicare) payroll taxes, and property taxes on own home.

Experimental poverty measures

While the alternative poverty rates shown in Table 3-10, by using broader definitions of income and/or eliminating some price-index bias, seem to remedy *some* of the shortcomings of the official definition, they do not reflect improved data now available that can be used to measure need in a much more precise way than Mollie Orshansky could when she calculated the original poverty threshold. Experimental poverty measures which redefine both income and need are discussed in "Poverty in the United States: 2002" (see below for complete reference), including data on experimental measures for 2001 and 2002 using six different definitions. These two years of data were subsequently revised to incorporate the improved tax model and are available on the Census Internet site under the title "Alternative Poverty Estimates Based on National Academy of Sciences (NAS) Recommendations Using Revised Tax Model: 2001 and 2002." Each of these experimental measures yields a *higher* poverty rate than the official definition, due to the redefinition of the need thresholds (whereas the measures that redefine only income and/or the price index cited above yield *lower* rates). The experimental alternatives do not change significantly between 2001 and 2002, whereas the official measure indicates a statistically significant 0.4 percentage point increase. Because of the relatively short time span for which these measures are available and the lack of consensus on a preferred definition, they are not shown in this volume. For more information, see "Poverty in the United States: 2002," pp. 14–17; Kathleen Short, U.S. Census Bureau, Current Population Reports, P60-216, *Experimental Poverty Measures: 1999*; and additional studies on the Web site <http://www.census.gov/hhes/poverty/povmeas.html>.

Notes on the data

The following are the principal changes that may affect year-to-year comparability of income and poverty data from the CPS.

Beginning in 1952, the estimates are based on 1950 census population controls. Earlier figures were based on the 1940 census.

Beginning in 1962, 1960 census sample design and population controls are fully implemented.

With 1971 and 1972 data, 1970 census sample design and population controls were introduced.

With 1984 data, 1980 census sample design was introduced; 1980 population controls were introduced, and were extended back to 1979 data.

With 1993 data, there was a major redesign of the CPS, including computer-assisted interviewing. The limits used to "code" reported income amounts were changed, resulting in reporting of higher income values for the highest income families and, consequently, an exaggerated year-to-year increase in income inequality. (It is possible that this jump actually reflects in just one year an increase that had emerged more gradually, so that the distribution measures for 1993 and later years are properly comparable with data for decades earlier.) In addition, 1990 Census population controls were introduced, and were extended back to the 1992 data.

Data for 2001 implemented population controls based on Census 2000, which were also used to reestimate 2000 and for some data 1999 as well. Data from 2000 forward also incorporate results from a 28,000-household sample expansion.

For more information on these and other changes that could affect comparability, see "Current Population Survey Technical Paper 63RV: Design and Methodology" (March 2002) and footnotes to CPS historical income tables, both available at the Census Web site <http://www.census.gov/hhes/income>.

Data availability

Data are published annually in late summer or early fall by the Bureau of the Census, in a series with the general title *Current Population Reports: Consumer Income, P60*. Data in this report were derived from P60-226, "Income, Poverty, and Health Insurance Coverage in the United States, 2003," August 2004; P60-221, "Money Income in the United States: 2002," September 2003; and P60-222, "Poverty in the United States: 2002," September 2003. These reports also contain extensive explanations and references to other relevant sources.

All reports and data are available on the Census Internet site at <http://www.census.gov>, under the general headings of "Income" and "Poverty."

CHAPTER 4: CONSUMER INCOME AND SPENDING

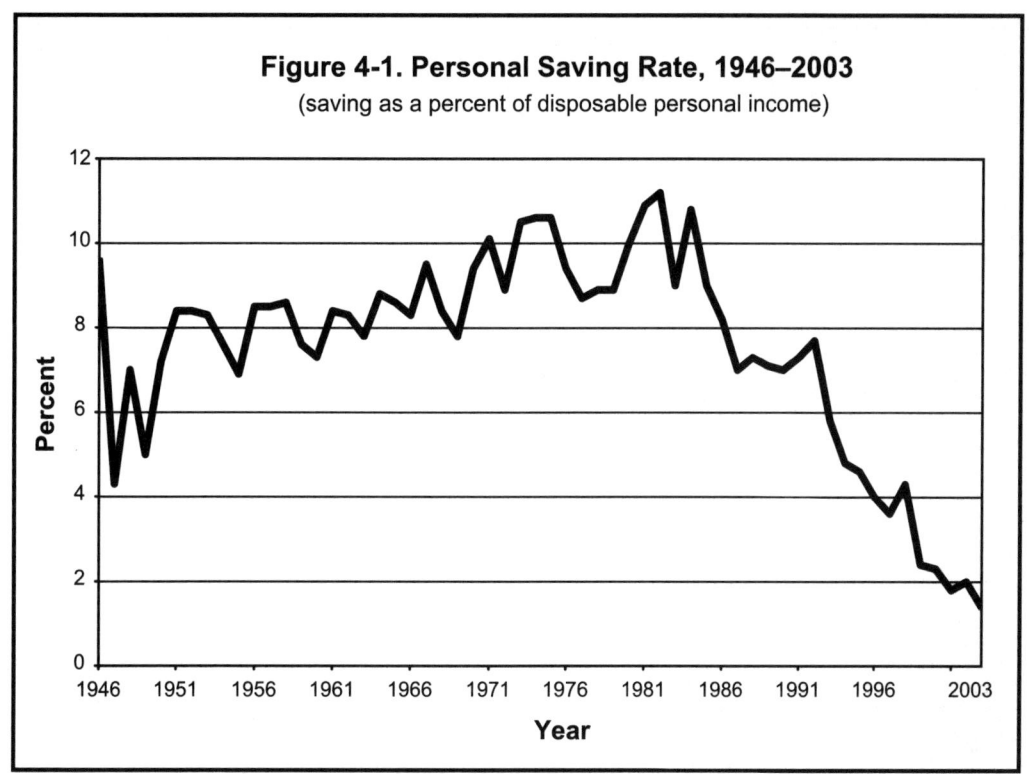

Figure 4-1. Personal Saving Rate, 1946–2003
(saving as a percent of disposable personal income)

- Personal saving is defined as aggregate disposable, that is, after-tax, personal income less aggregate personal outlays for consumption, interest, and transfers. The personal saving rate—saving as a percent of disposable income—averaged 8 percent to 10 percent for much of the postwar period, but commenced a marked downtrend around 1987, reaching 2.3 percent or less from 1999 through 2003. (Table 4-1) It should be noted that personal income by definition does not include any capital gains, while the taxes on realized capital gains are deducted to get after-tax income along with all other income taxes. Capital gains are a source of spending power in addition to current disposable income: they can be converted into cash by asset sales and by refinancing. These sources have been particularly strong in recent years, and the wealth of individuals may therefore be growing more rapidly than these saving data suggest. Nevertheless, the smaller saving flow out of personal income contributes to the need for foreign financing to fill the gap between investment and national saving. (Table 5-1)
- Labor compensation, excluding social insurance taxes, made up 60.3 percent of total personal income in 2000, down from 65.4 percent in 1948. ("Contributions for social insurance," such as Social Security taxes, are excluded from both the numerator and the denominator of this percentage.) Transfer payments accounted for a rising share of personal income. It should be noted that just as "consumption expenditures" in the National Income and Product Accounts includes all spending financed by government health insurance programs such as Medicare and Medicaid, the transfer payment component of income as defined here includes the equivalent payments on behalf of persons by these same programs. Proprietors' and rental income made up a declining share, while the shares of dividends and especially interest rose. (Table 4-1)

Table 4-1. Personal Income and Its Disposition

(Billions of current dollars, except as noted; quarterly data are at seasonally adjusted annual rates.) NIPA Table 2.1

Year and quarter	Personal income													
					Personal income receipts on assets			Personal current transfer receipts						
									Government social benefits to persons					
	Total	Compensation of employees, received	Proprietors' income with IVA and CCAdj	Rental income of persons with CCAdj	Total	Personal interest income	Personal dividend income	Total	Total	Social Security and Medicare	Government unemployment insurance	Veterans	Family assistance	Other
1946	178.6	119.6	35.6	7.1	12.3	6.7	5.6	10.6	10.1	0.4	1.1	7.0	1.1	0.6
1947	191.0	130.1	34.5	7.2	13.9	7.6	6.3	10.8	10.4	0.5	0.8	7.0	0.3	1.9
1948	209.8	141.9	39.3	7.9	15.1	8.1	7.0	10.3	9.9	0.6	0.9	5.9	0.4	2.2
1949	207.1	141.9	34.7	8.2	16.0	8.8	7.2	11.2	10.9	0.7	1.9	5.3	0.5	2.6
1950	229.0	155.3	37.6	9.2	18.6	9.7	8.8	14.0	13.4	1.0	1.5	7.7	0.6	2.7
1951	258.0	181.4	42.7	10.1	19.1	10.5	8.6	11.4	10.5	1.9	0.9	4.6	0.6	2.6
1952	275.4	196.2	43.1	11.2	19.9	11.3	8.6	11.9	11.0	2.2	1.1	4.3	0.5	2.9
1953	291.9	210.3	42.1	12.5	21.6	12.7	8.9	12.5	11.7	3.0	1.0	4.1	0.5	3.0
1954	294.5	209.2	42.3	13.5	23.2	14.0	9.3	14.3	13.7	3.6	2.2	4.2	0.6	3.2
1955	316.1	225.7	44.3	13.9	25.7	15.2	10.5	15.7	14.8	4.9	1.5	4.4	0.6	3.3
1956	339.6	244.5	45.8	14.2	28.2	16.9	11.3	16.8	15.6	5.7	1.5	4.4	0.6	3.4
1957	358.7	257.5	47.9	14.6	30.6	18.9	11.7	19.5	18.1	7.3	1.9	4.5	0.7	3.7
1958	369.0	259.5	50.1	15.4	31.9	20.3	11.6	23.5	22.2	8.5	4.1	4.7	0.8	4.1
1959	392.8	281.0	50.7	16.2	34.6	22.0	12.6	24.2	22.9	10.2	2.8	4.6	0.9	4.5
1960	411.5	296.4	50.8	17.1	37.9	24.5	13.4	25.7	24.4	11.1	3.0	4.6	1.0	4.7
1961	429.0	305.3	53.2	17.9	40.1	26.2	13.9	29.5	28.1	12.6	4.3	5.0	1.1	5.1
1962	456.7	327.1	55.4	18.8	44.1	29.1	15.0	30.4	28.8	14.3	3.1	4.7	1.3	5.5
1963	479.6	345.2	56.5	19.5	47.9	31.7	16.2	32.2	30.3	15.2	3.0	4.8	1.4	5.9
1964	514.6	370.7	59.4	19.6	53.8	35.6	18.2	33.5	31.3	16.0	2.7	4.7	1.5	6.4
1965	555.7	399.5	63.9	20.2	59.4	39.2	20.2	36.2	33.9	18.1	2.3	4.9	1.7	7.0
1966	603.9	442.7	68.2	20.8	64.1	43.4	20.7	39.6	37.5	20.8	1.9	4.9	1.9	8.1
1967	648.3	475.1	69.8	21.2	69.0	47.5	21.5	48.0	45.8	25.8	2.2	5.6	2.3	9.9
1968	712.0	524.3	74.3	20.9	75.2	51.6	23.5	56.1	53.3	30.5	2.1	5.9	2.8	11.9
1969	778.5	577.6	77.4	21.2	84.1	59.9	24.2	62.3	59.0	33.1	2.2	6.7	3.5	13.4
1970	838.8	617.2	78.4	21.4	93.5	69.2	24.3	74.7	71.7	38.6	4.0	7.7	4.8	16.6
1971	903.5	658.3	84.8	22.4	101.0	75.9	25.0	88.1	85.4	44.7	5.8	8.8	6.2	20.0
1972	992.7	725.1	95.9	23.4	109.6	82.8	26.8	97.9	94.8	49.8	5.7	9.7	6.9	22.7
1973	1 110.7	811.3	113.5	24.3	124.7	94.8	29.9	112.6	108.6	60.9	4.4	10.4	7.2	25.7
1974	1 222.6	890.7	113.1	24.3	146.4	113.2	33.2	133.3	128.6	70.3	6.8	11.8	8.0	31.7
1975	1 335.0	949.0	119.5	23.7	162.2	129.3	32.9	170.0	163.1	81.5	17.6	14.5	9.3	40.2
1976	1 474.8	1 059.2	132.2	22.3	178.4	139.5	39.0	184.0	177.3	93.3	15.8	14.4	10.1	43.7
1977	1 633.2	1 180.4	145.7	20.7	205.3	160.6	44.7	194.2	189.1	105.3	12.7	13.8	10.6	46.7
1978	1 837.7	1 335.8	166.6	22.1	234.8	184.0	50.7	209.6	203.2	116.9	9.1	13.9	10.8	52.5
1979	2 062.2	1 501.0	180.1	23.8	274.7	217.3	57.4	235.3	227.1	132.5	9.4	14.4	11.1	59.6
1980	2 307.9	1 651.8	174.1	30.0	338.7	274.7	64.0	279.5	270.8	154.8	15.7	15.0	12.5	72.8
1981	2 591.3	1 825.7	183.0	38.0	421.9	348.3	73.6	318.4	307.2	182.1	15.6	16.1	13.1	80.2
1982	2 775.3	1 925.9	176.3	38.8	488.4	410.8	77.6	354.8	342.4	204.6	25.1	16.4	12.9	83.4
1983	2 960.7	2 043.0	192.5	37.8	529.6	446.3	83.3	383.7	369.9	222.2	26.2	16.6	13.8	91.0
1984	3 289.5	2 255.4	243.3	40.2	607.9	517.2	90.6	400.1	380.4	237.8	15.9	16.4	14.5	95.9
1985	3 526.7	2 424.9	262.3	41.9	654.0	556.6	97.4	424.9	402.6	253.0	15.7	16.7	15.2	102.0
1986	3 722.4	2 570.1	275.7	33.5	695.5	589.5	106.0	451.0	428.0	268.9	16.3	16.7	16.1	109.9
1987	3 947.4	2 750.2	302.2	33.5	717.0	604.9	112.2	467.6	447.4	282.6	14.5	16.6	16.4	117.3
1988	4 253.7	2 967.2	341.6	40.6	769.3	639.5	129.7	496.6	476.0	300.2	13.2	16.9	16.9	128.8
1989	4 587.8	3 145.2	363.3	43.1	878.0	720.2	157.8	543.4	519.9	325.6	14.3	17.3	17.5	145.3
1990	4 878.6	3 338.2	380.6	50.7	924.0	755.2	168.8	595.2	573.1	351.8	18.0	17.8	19.2	166.2
1991	5 051.0	3 445.3	377.1	60.3	932.0	751.7	180.3	666.4	648.5	381.7	26.6	18.3	21.1	200.8
1992	5 362.0	3 651.2	427.6	78.0	910.9	723.4	187.4	749.4	729.8	414.4	38.9	19.3	22.2	234.9
1993	5 558.5	3 794.9	453.8	95.6	901.8	699.6	202.2	790.1	775.7	443.4	34.1	20.1	22.8	255.3
1994	5 842.5	3 979.6	473.3	119.7	950.8	716.8	234.0	827.3	812.2	475.4	23.5	20.1	23.2	270.0
1995	6 152.3	4 177.0	492.1	122.1	1 016.4	763.2	253.2	877.4	858.4	506.8	21.4	20.9	22.6	286.7
1996	6 520.6	4 386.9	543.2	131.5	1 089.2	793.0	296.2	925.0	902.1	537.7	22.0	21.7	20.3	300.4
1997	6 915.1	4 664.6	576.0	128.8	1 181.7	848.7	333.0	951.2	931.8	563.2	19.9	22.5	17.9	308.3
1998	7 423.0	5 020.1	627.8	137.5	1 283.2	933.2	349.9	978.6	952.6	575.1	19.5	23.4	17.4	317.3
1999	7 802.4	5 352.0	678.3	147.3	1 264.2	928.6	335.6	1 022.1	988.0	588.9	20.3	24.3	17.9	336.7
2000	8 429.7	5 782.7	728.4	150.3	1 387.0	1 011.0	376.1	1 084.0	1 041.6	620.8	20.3	25.1	18.4	357.0
2001	8 724.1	5 942.1	771.9	167.4	1 380.0	1 011.0	369.0	1 193.9	1 143.9	668.5	31.7	26.7	18.1	398.9
2002	8 878.9	6 069.5	769.6	170.9	1 334.6	946.7	387.9	1 282.7	1 248.9	708.3	53.2	29.9	17.7	440.0
2003	9 161.8	6 289.0	834.1	153.8	1 322.7	929.9	392.8	1 335.4	1 306.4	733.8	52.8	32.3	18.3	469.2
2001														
1st quarter	8 688.7	5 946.2	769.4	155.3	1 397.4	1 020.2	377.2	1 149.6	1 105.3	655.3	25.2	26.1	18.4	380.4
2nd quarter	8 719.9	5 944.6	770.6	161.7	1 388.7	1 020.6	368.2	1 185.7	1 136.8	663.5	28.3	26.4	18.2	400.5
3rd quarter	8 733.1	5 939.3	773.4	176.1	1 373.3	1 009.2	364.1	1 202.6	1 142.7	675.0	32.9	26.5	18.0	390.2
4th quarter	8 754.8	5 938.3	774.2	176.2	1 360.3	994.0	366.4	1 237.8	1 190.9	680.4	40.6	27.7	17.9	424.5
2002														
1st quarter	8 803.6	6 010.2	762.2	179.7	1 337.8	961.2	376.6	1 259.4	1 219.9	699.5	42.3	28.9	17.6	431.5
2nd quarter	8 897.1	6 068.3	769.0	184.7	1 340.2	953.1	387.1	1 284.0	1 249.7	705.9	60.3	29.6	17.6	436.4
3rd quarter	8 895.7	6 086.0	770.4	165.4	1 333.7	940.5	393.2	1 289.1	1 256.8	711.2	56.8	30.2	17.6	441.0
4th quarter	8 919.2	6 113.4	776.7	153.8	1 326.7	932.1	394.6	1 298.1	1 269.3	716.4	53.4	30.7	17.8	451.0
2003														
1st quarter	9 002.2	6 177.7	794.0	155.5	1 325.9	932.4	393.5	1 311.4	1 282.2	722.8	50.4	31.9	18.1	459.0
2nd quarter	9 105.7	6 247.0	825.7	144.1	1 324.7	932.4	392.3	1 333.1	1 304.1	731.1	54.8	32.3	18.3	467.7
3rd quarter	9 209.3	6 324.7	852.0	148.8	1 314.4	922.8	391.6	1 346.2	1 317.4	736.6	54.3	32.5	18.4	475.5
4th quarter	9 330.0	6 406.7	864.7	167.1	1 325.8	932.0	393.8	1 350.7	1 322.0	744.9	51.6	32.4	18.5	474.6

Table 4-1. Personal Income and Its Disposition—*Continued*

(Billions of current dollars, except as noted; quarterly data are at seasonally adjusted annual rates.)

NIPA Table 2.1

Year and quarter	Personal income—*Continued*		Less: Personal current taxes	Equals: Disposable personal income	Less: Personal outlays						Equals: Personal saving		Disposable personal income, billions of chained (2000) dollars
	Personal current transfer receipts—*Cont.* From business (net)	Less: Contributions for government social insurance			Total	Personal consumption expenditures	Personal interest payments	Personal current transfer payments			Billions of dollars	Percent of disposable personal income	
								Total	To government	To the rest of the world (net)			
1946	0.4	6.6	17.2	161.4	145.9	144.3	0.7	0.9	0.2	0.7	15.5	9.6	1 132.7
1947	0.4	5.6	19.8	171.2	163.8	162.0	0.9	0.9	0.2	0.7	7.4	4.3	1 090.3
1948	0.4	4.6	19.2	190.6	177.3	175.0	1.3	1.0	0.3	0.7	13.4	7.0	1 148.4
1949	0.4	4.9	16.7	190.4	180.9	178.5	1.6	0.8	0.3	0.5	9.5	5.0	1 155.8
1950	0.6	5.5	18.9	210.1	195.0	192.2	2.0	0.8	0.3	0.4	15.1	7.2	1 260.0
1951	0.9	6.6	27.1	231.0	211.5	208.5	2.2	0.7	0.3	0.4	19.5	8.4	1 297.3
1952	0.9	6.9	32.0	243.4	222.9	219.5	2.6	0.8	0.4	0.4	20.5	8.4	1 339.4
1953	0.8	7.1	33.2	258.6	237.1	233.1	3.2	0.9	0.4	0.5	21.5	8.3	1 404.5
1954	0.6	8.1	30.2	264.3	244.3	240.0	3.4	0.9	0.4	0.5	20.0	7.6	1 422.1
1955	0.9	9.1	32.9	283.3	263.6	258.8	4.0	0.8	0.4	0.4	19.7	6.9	1 516.7
1956	1.2	10.0	36.6	303.0	277.2	271.7	4.6	1.0	0.5	0.5	25.8	8.5	1 589.7
1957	1.4	11.4	38.9	319.8	292.8	286.9	4.9	1.1	0.6	0.5	27.0	8.5	1 628.5
1958	1.2	11.4	38.5	330.5	302.2	296.2	5.0	1.0	0.6	0.5	28.3	8.6	1 642.6
1959	1.3	13.8	42.3	350.5	323.9	317.6	5.5	0.8	0.3	0.5	26.7	7.6	1 715.5
1960	1.3	16.4	46.1	365.4	338.8	331.7	6.2	0.8	0.3	0.5	26.7	7.3	1 759.7
1961	1.4	17.0	47.3	381.8	349.6	342.1	6.5	1.0	0.5	0.5	32.2	8.4	1 819.2
1962	1.5	19.1	51.6	405.1	371.3	363.3	7.0	1.1	0.5	0.5	33.8	8.3	1 908.2
1963	1.9	21.7	54.6	425.1	391.8	382.7	7.9	1.2	0.5	0.7	33.3	7.8	1 979.1
1964	2.2	22.4	52.1	462.5	421.7	411.4	8.9	1.3	0.6	0.7	40.8	8.8	2 122.8
1965	2.3	23.4	57.7	498.1	455.1	443.8	9.9	1.4	0.6	0.8	43.0	8.6	2 253.3
1966	2.1	31.3	66.4	537.5	493.1	480.9	10.7	1.6	0.8	0.8	44.4	8.3	2 371.9
1967	2.3	34.9	73.0	575.3	520.9	507.8	11.1	2.0	1.0	1.0	54.4	9.5	2 475.9
1968	2.8	38.7	87.0	625.0	572.2	558.0	12.2	2.0	1.0	1.0	52.8	8.4	2 588.0
1969	3.3	44.1	104.5	674.0	621.4	605.2	14.0	2.2	1.1	1.1	52.5	7.8	2 668.7
1970	2.9	46.4	103.1	735.7	666.2	648.5	15.2	2.6	1.3	1.3	69.5	9.4	2 781.7
1971	2.7	51.2	101.7	801.8	721.2	701.9	16.6	2.8	1.5	1.3	80.6	10.1	2 907.9
1972	3.1	59.2	123.6	869.1	791.9	770.6	18.1	3.1	1.8	1.4	77.2	8.9	3 046.5
1973	3.9	75.5	132.4	978.3	875.6	852.4	19.8	3.4	1.8	1.5	102.7	10.5	3 252.3
1974	4.7	85.2	151.0	1 071.6	958.0	933.4	21.2	3.4	2.1	1.3	113.6	10.6	3 228.5
1975	6.8	89.3	147.6	1 187.4	1 061.9	1 034.4	23.7	3.8	2.5	1.3	125.6	10.6	3 302.6
1976	6.7	101.3	172.3	1 302.5	1 180.2	1 151.9	23.9	4.4	3.0	1.3	122.3	9.4	3 432.2
1977	5.1	113.1	197.5	1 435.7	1 310.4	1 278.6	27.0	4.8	3.5	1.3	125.3	8.7	3 552.9
1978	6.5	131.3	229.4	1 608.3	1 465.8	1 428.5	31.9	5.4	3.9	1.5	142.5	8.9	3 718.8
1979	8.2	152.7	268.7	1 793.5	1 634.4	1 592.2	36.2	5.9	4.3	1.6	159.1	8.9	3 811.2
1980	8.6	166.2	298.9	2 009.0	1 807.5	1 757.1	43.6	6.8	5.0	1.8	201.4	10.0	3 857.7
1981	11.2	195.7	345.2	2 246.1	2 001.8	1 941.1	49.3	11.4	6.0	5.5	244.3	10.9	3 960.0
1982	12.4	208.9	354.1	2 421.2	2 150.4	2 077.3	59.5	13.6	7.1	6.6	270.8	11.2	4 044.9
1983	13.8	226.0	352.3	2 608.4	2 374.8	2 290.6	69.2	15.0	8.1	6.9	233.6	9.0	4 177.7
1984	19.7	257.5	377.4	2 912.0	2 597.3	2 503.3	77.0	16.9	9.2	7.8	314.8	10.8	4 494.1
1985	22.3	281.4	417.4	3 109.3	2 829.3	2 720.3	90.4	18.6	10.4	8.2	280.0	9.0	4 645.2
1986	22.9	303.4	437.3	3 285.1	3 016.7	2 899.7	96.1	20.9	12.0	9.0	268.4	8.2	4 791.0
1987	20.2	323.1	489.1	3 458.3	3 216.9	3 100.2	93.6	23.1	13.2	9.9	241.4	7.0	4 874.5
1988	20.6	361.5	505.0	3 748.7	3 475.8	3 353.6	96.8	25.4	14.8	10.6	272.9	7.3	5 082.6
1989	23.5	385.2	566.1	4 021.7	3 734.5	3 598.5	108.2	27.8	16.5	11.4	287.1	7.1	5 224.8
1990	22.2	410.1	592.8	4 285.8	3 986.4	3 839.9	116.1	30.4	18.4	12.0	299.4	7.0	5 324.2
1991	17.9	430.2	586.7	4 464.3	4 140.1	3 986.1	118.5	35.6	22.6	13.0	324.2	7.3	5 351.4
1992	19.6	455.0	610.6	4 751.4	4 385.4	4 235.3	111.8	38.3	26.0	12.3	366.0	7.7	5 536.3
1993	14.4	477.7	646.6	4 911.9	4 627.9	4 477.9	107.3	42.7	28.5	14.2	284.0	5.8	5 594.2
1994	15.1	508.2	690.7	5 151.8	4 902.4	4 743.3	112.8	46.3	30.9	15.4	249.5	4.8	5 746.4
1995	19.0	532.8	744.1	5 408.2	5 157.3	4 975.8	132.7	48.9	32.6	16.2	250.9	4.6	5 905.7
1996	22.9	555.2	832.1	5 688.5	5 460.0	5 256.8	150.3	52.9	34.9	18.0	228.4	4.0	6 080.9
1997	19.4	587.2	926.3	5 988.8	5 770.5	5 547.4	163.9	59.2	38.2	21.0	218.3	3.6	6 295.8
1998	26.0	624.2	1 027.0	6 395.9	6 119.1	5 879.5	174.5	65.2	40.6	24.6	276.8	4.3	6 663.9
1999	34.1	661.4	1 107.5	6 695.0	6 536.4	6 282.5	181.0	73.0	44.7	28.3	158.6	2.4	6 861.3
2000	42.4	702.7	1 235.7	7 194.0	7 025.6	6 739.4	204.7	81.5	50.0	31.5	168.5	2.3	7 194.0
2001	50.0	731.1	1 237.3	7 486.8	7 354.5	7 055.0	212.2	87.2	54.2	33.0	132.3	1.8	7 333.3
2002	33.7	748.3	1 051.2	7 827.7	7 668.5	7 376.1	197.2	95.3	59.5	35.7	159.2	2.0	7 559.5
2003	28.9	773.2	1 001.9	8 159.9	8 049.3	7 760.9	185.3	103.1	64.9	38.2	110.6	1.4	7 733.8
2001													
1st quarter	44.2	729.2	1 296.6	7 392.1	7 253.5	6 955.8	212.4	85.3	52.6	32.6	138.6	1.9	7 283.0
2nd quarter	48.9	731.5	1 312.3	7 407.6	7 318.9	7 017.5	214.9	86.5	53.6	32.9	88.7	1.2	7 252.1
3rd quarter	60.0	731.9	1 110.3	7 622.8	7 361.2	7 058.5	214.5	88.3	54.7	33.6	261.6	3.4	7 452.2
4th quarter	46.9	731.9	1 230.0	7 524.8	7 484.4	7 188.4	207.2	88.8	56.0	32.9	40.5	0.5	7 346.0
2002													
1st quarter	39.6	745.7	1 065.8	7 737.8	7 528.5	7 236.9	199.3	92.3	57.5	34.8	209.3	2.7	7 537.6
2nd quarter	34.2	749.1	1 052.1	7 845.0	7 635.0	7 339.3	202.1	93.7	58.9	34.8	210.0	2.7	7 588.4
3rd quarter	32.3	748.9	1 046.7	7 849.0	7 722.9	7 428.0	198.6	96.3	60.2	36.1	126.1	1.6	7 555.1
4th quarter	28.9	749.6	1 040.3	7 878.8	7 787.6	7 500.0	188.8	98.7	61.5	37.2	91.2	1.2	7 558.0
2003													
1st quarter	29.2	762.4	1 025.7	7 976.5	7 897.0	7 609.8	187.1	100.0	62.8	37.2	79.5	1.0	7 591.2
2nd quarter	29.0	768.9	1 030.7	8 075.0	7 982.9	7 696.3	184.8	101.8	64.2	37.6	92.1	1.1	7 671.1
3rd quarter	28.9	776.7	941.7	8 267.6	8 107.8	7 822.5	183.3	102.1	65.6	36.5	159.8	1.9	7 822.9
4th quarter	28.8	785.0	1 009.4	8 320.5	8 209.4	7 914.9	185.9	108.6	67.0	41.6	111.1	1.3	7 849.6

Table 4-2. Personal Consumption Expenditures: Current Dollars, Constant Dollars, and Price Indexes

(Billions of dollars, except as noted; quarterly data are at seasonally adjusted annual rates.)

NIPA Tables 2.3.4, 2.3.5, 2.3.6

Year and quarter	Personal consumption expenditures											
	Current dollars				Chained (2000) dollars				Chain-type price indexes (2000 = 100)			
	Total	Durable goods	Nondurable goods	Services	Total	Durable goods	Nondurable goods	Services	Total	Durable goods	Nondurable goods	Services
1946	144.3	15.8	82.7	45.8	...	...	...	...	14.2	34.3	16.8	9.8
1947	162.0	20.4	90.9	50.7	...	...	...	...	15.7	37.2	18.9	10.4
1948	175.0	22.9	96.6	55.6	...	...	...	...	16.6	39.1	20.1	10.9
1949	178.5	25.1	94.9	58.6	...	...	...	...	16.5	39.6	19.4	11.2
1950	192.2	30.7	98.2	63.3	...	...	...	...	16.7	39.8	19.5	11.6
1951	208.5	29.9	109.2	69.5	...	...	...	...	17.8	42.5	21.1	12.1
1952	219.5	29.3	114.7	75.4	...	...	...	...	18.2	42.9	21.3	12.6
1953	233.1	32.7	117.8	82.5	...	...	...	...	18.4	42.5	21.2	13.2
1954	240.0	31.9	119.7	88.4	...	...	...	...	18.6	41.6	21.3	13.6
1955	258.8	38.8	124.7	95.2	...	...	...	...	18.7	41.4	21.2	13.9
1956	271.7	38.1	130.8	102.8	...	...	...	...	19.1	42.5	21.5	14.3
1957	286.9	40.0	137.1	109.8	...	...	...	...	19.6	44.1	22.1	14.7
1958	296.2	37.4	141.7	117.0	...	...	...	...	20.1	44.9	22.6	15.1
1959	317.6	42.7	148.5	126.5	...	...	...	...	20.4	45.7	22.8	15.5
1960	331.7	43.3	152.8	135.6	...	...	...	...	20.8	45.4	23.1	15.9
1961	342.1	41.8	156.6	143.8	...	...	...	...	21.0	45.6	23.2	16.2
1962	363.3	46.9	162.8	153.6	...	...	...	...	21.2	45.8	23.4	16.5
1963	382.7	51.6	168.2	162.9	...	...	...	...	21.5	45.9	23.7	16.7
1964	411.4	56.7	178.6	176.1	...	...	...	...	21.8	46.1	24.0	17.0
1965	443.8	63.3	191.5	189.0	...	...	...	...	22.1	45.7	24.4	17.3
1966	480.9	68.3	208.7	203.8	...	...	...	...	22.7	45.5	25.2	17.8
1967	507.8	70.4	217.1	220.3	...	...	...	...	23.2	46.2	25.8	18.3
1968	558.0	80.8	235.7	241.6	...	...	...	...	24.2	47.7	26.8	19.1
1969	605.2	85.9	253.1	266.1	...	...	...	...	25.3	49.1	28.1	20.1
1970	648.5	85.0	272.0	291.5	...	...	...	...	26.4	50.1	29.4	21.2
1971	701.9	96.9	285.5	319.5	...	...	...	...	27.6	52.0	30.4	22.3
1972	770.6	110.4	308.0	352.2	...	...	...	...	28.5	52.5	31.4	23.3
1973	852.4	123.5	343.1	385.8	...	...	...	...	30.1	53.3	33.8	24.4
1974	933.4	122.3	384.5	426.6	...	...	...	...	33.2	56.7	38.7	26.3
1975	1 034.4	133.5	420.7	480.2	...	...	...	...	36.0	61.8	41.7	28.6
1976	1 151.9	158.9	458.3	534.7	...	...	...	...	37.9	65.3	43.3	30.6
1977	1 278.6	181.2	497.1	600.2	...	...	...	...	40.4	68.1	45.9	32.9
1978	1 428.5	201.7	550.2	676.6	...	...	...	...	43.2	72.0	49.0	35.5
1979	1 592.2	214.4	624.5	753.3	...	...	...	...	47.1	76.8	54.1	38.3
1980	1 757.1	214.2	696.1	846.9	...	...	...	...	52.1	83.3	60.4	42.3
1981	1 941.1	231.3	758.9	950.8	...	...	...	...	56.7	88.9	65.1	46.7
1982	2 077.3	240.2	787.6	1 049.4	...	...	...	...	59.9	92.4	67.0	50.5
1983	2 290.6	280.8	831.2	1 178.6	...	...	...	...	62.4	94.2	68.4	53.8
1984	2 503.3	326.5	884.6	1 292.2	...	...	...	...	64.8	95.6	70.0	56.7
1985	2 720.3	363.5	928.7	1 428.1	...	...	...	...	66.9	96.6	71.5	59.3
1986	2 899.7	403.0	958.4	1 538.3	...	...	...	...	68.6	97.7	71.3	62.0
1987	3 100.2	421.7	1 015.3	1 663.3	...	...	...	...	70.9	100.5	73.7	64.3
1988	3 353.6	453.6	1 083.5	1 816.5	...	...	...	...	73.8	101.9	76.2	67.5
1989	3 598.5	471.8	1 166.7	1 960.0	...	...	...	...	77.0	103.7	79.8	70.7
1990	3 839.9	474.2	1 249.9	2 115.9	4 770.3	453.5	1 484.0	2 851.7	80.5	104.6	84.2	74.2
1991	3 986.1	453.9	1 284.8	2 247.4	4 778.4	427.9	1 480.5	2 900.0	83.4	106.1	86.8	77.5
1992	4 235.3	483.6	1 330.5	2 421.2	4 934.3	453.0	1 510.1	3 000.8	85.8	106.8	88.1	80.7
1993	4 477.9	526.7	1 379.4	2 571.8	5 099.8	488.4	1 550.4	3 085.7	87.8	107.8	89.0	83.3
1994	4 743.3	582.2	1 437.2	2 723.9	5 290.7	529.4	1 603.9	3 176.6	89.7	110.0	89.6	85.7
1995	4 975.8	611.6	1 485.1	2 879.1	5 433.5	552.6	1 638.6	3 259.9	91.6	110.7	90.6	88.3
1996	5 256.8	652.6	1 555.5	3 048.7	5 619.4	595.9	1 680.4	3 356.0	93.5	109.5	92.6	90.8
1997	5 547.4	692.7	1 619.0	3 235.8	5 831.8	646.9	1 725.3	3 468.0	95.1	107.1	93.8	93.3
1998	5 879.5	750.2	1 683.6	3 445.7	6 125.8	720.3	1 794.4	3 615.0	96.0	104.2	93.8	95.3
1999	6 282.5	817.6	1 804.8	3 660.0	6 438.6	804.6	1 876.6	3 758.0	97.6	101.6	96.2	97.4
2000	6 739.4	863.3	1 947.2	3 928.8	6 739.4	863.3	1 947.2	3 928.8	100.0	100.0	100.0	100.0
2001	7 055.0	883.7	2 017.1	4 154.3	6 910.4	900.7	1 986.7	4 023.2	102.1	98.1	101.5	103.3
2002	7 376.1	916.2	2 080.1	4 379.8	7 123.4	959.6	2 037.4	4 128.6	103.5	95.5	102.1	106.1
2003	7 760.9	950.7	2 200.1	4 610.1	7 355.6	1 030.6	2 112.4	4 220.3	105.5	92.2	104.2	109.2
2001												
1st quarter	6 955.8	872.1	2 000.0	4 083.7	6 853.1	879.5	1 975.2	3 997.9	101.5	99.1	101.3	102.1
2nd quarter	7 017.5	864.7	2 016.6	4 136.2	6 870.3	878.9	1 974.7	4 016.0	102.1	98.4	102.1	103.0
3rd quarter	7 058.5	865.1	2 024.2	4 169.1	6 900.5	885.6	1 986.5	4 027.8	102.3	97.7	101.9	103.5
4th quarter	7 188.4	932.8	2 027.5	4 228.0	7 017.6	958.7	2 010.3	4 051.2	102.4	97.3	100.9	104.4
2002												
1st quarter	7 236.9	903.5	2 046.8	4 286.5	7 049.7	937.8	2 029.3	4 084.1	102.7	96.3	100.9	105.0
2nd quarter	7 339.3	907.5	2 077.7	4 354.0	7 099.2	947.8	2 033.2	4 119.7	103.4	95.7	102.2	105.7
3rd quarter	7 428.0	932.8	2 081.3	4 413.9	7 149.9	979.3	2 030.2	4 143.8	103.9	95.2	102.5	106.5
4th quarter	7 500.0	920.8	2 114.6	4 464.7	7 194.6	973.4	2 056.8	4 166.9	104.3	94.6	102.8	107.2
2003												
1st quarter	7 609.8	912.1	2 167.5	4 530.2	7 242.2	973.2	2 082.0	4 188.7	105.1	93.7	104.1	108.2
2nd quarter	7 696.3	946.8	2 163.6	4 585.9	7 311.4	1 020.0	2 090.1	4 207.7	105.3	92.8	103.5	109.0
3rd quarter	7 822.5	972.7	2 219.2	4 630.6	7 401.7	1 059.6	2 125.3	4 227.9	105.7	91.8	104.4	109.5
4th quarter	7 914.9	971.1	2 250.1	4 693.6	7 466.8	1 069.7	2 152.0	4 256.7	106.0	90.7	104.6	110.3

. . . = Not available.

Table 4-3. Personal Consumption Expenditures by Major Type of Product

(Billions of dollars, quarterly data are at seasonally adjusted annual rates.)

NIPA Table 2.3.5

Year and quarter	Personal consumption expenditures, total	Durable goods				Nondurable goods					
		Total	Motor vehicles and parts	Furniture and household equipment	Other	Total	Food	Clothing and shoes	Gasoline and oil	Fuel oil and coal	Other
1946	144.3	15.8	4.1	8.4	3.2	82.7	47.4	18.2	3.4	2.5	11.3
1947	162.0	20.4	6.6	10.6	3.3	90.9	52.3	18.8	4.0	3.0	12.8
1948	175.0	22.9	8.0	11.5	3.4	96.6	54.2	20.1	4.8	3.4	14.1
1949	178.5	25.1	10.6	11.3	3.2	94.9	52.5	19.3	5.3	3.1	14.7
1950	192.2	30.7	13.7	13.7	3.3	98.2	53.9	19.6	5.5	3.4	15.8
1951	208.5	29.9	12.2	14.1	3.6	109.2	60.7	21.3	6.1	3.5	17.6
1952	219.5	29.3	11.4	14.0	3.9	114.7	64.1	22.0	6.8	3.5	18.4
1953	233.1	32.7	13.9	14.7	4.1	117.8	65.4	22.2	7.4	3.4	19.4
1954	240.0	31.9	12.8	14.8	4.3	119.7	66.8	22.3	7.8	3.5	19.3
1955	258.8	38.8	17.7	16.4	4.6	124.7	68.6	23.3	8.6	3.8	20.4
1956	271.7	38.1	15.8	17.3	5.0	130.8	71.4	24.4	9.4	3.9	21.7
1957	286.9	40.0	17.6	17.2	5.2	137.1	75.1	24.5	10.2	4.1	23.2
1958	296.2	37.4	15.1	16.9	5.4	141.7	77.9	24.9	10.6	4.2	24.2
1959	317.6	42.7	18.9	18.1	5.7	148.5	80.6	26.4	11.3	4.0	26.1
1960	331.7	43.3	19.7	18.0	5.7	152.8	82.3	27.0	12.0	3.8	27.7
1961	342.1	41.8	17.8	18.3	5.7	156.6	84.0	27.6	12.0	3.8	29.2
1962	363.3	46.9	21.5	19.3	6.1	162.8	86.1	29.0	12.6	3.8	31.4
1963	382.7	51.6	24.4	20.7	6.6	168.2	88.2	29.8	13.0	4.0	33.1
1964	411.4	56.7	26.0	23.2	7.5	178.6	93.5	32.4	13.6	4.1	35.0
1965	443.8	63.3	29.9	25.1	8.2	191.5	100.7	34.1	14.8	4.4	37.6
1966	480.9	68.3	30.3	28.2	9.8	208.7	109.3	37.4	16.0	4.7	41.4
1967	507.8	70.4	30.0	30.0	10.4	217.1	112.4	39.2	17.1	4.8	43.5
1968	558.0	80.8	36.1	32.9	11.8	235.7	122.2	43.2	18.6	4.7	47.0
1969	605.2	85.9	38.4	34.7	12.9	253.1	131.5	46.5	20.5	4.6	50.2
1970	648.5	85.0	35.5	35.7	13.7	272.0	143.8	47.8	21.9	4.4	54.1
1971	701.9	96.9	44.5	37.8	14.6	285.5	149.7	51.7	23.2	4.6	56.4
1972	770.6	110.4	51.1	42.4	16.9	308.0	161.4	56.4	24.4	5.1	60.8
1973	852.4	123.5	56.1	47.9	19.5	343.1	179.6	62.5	28.1	6.3	66.6
1974	933.4	122.3	49.5	51.5	21.3	384.5	201.8	66.0	36.1	7.8	72.7
1975	1 034.4	133.5	54.8	54.5	24.2	420.7	223.2	70.8	39.7	8.4	78.5
1976	1 151.9	158.9	71.3	60.2	27.4	458.3	242.5	76.6	43.0	10.1	86.0
1977	1 278.6	181.2	83.5	67.2	30.5	497.1	262.6	84.1	46.9	11.1	92.4
1978	1 428.5	201.7	93.1	74.3	34.3	550.2	289.6	94.3	50.1	11.5	104.7
1979	1 592.2	214.4	93.5	82.7	38.2	624.5	324.7	101.2	66.2	14.4	118.0
1980	1 757.1	214.2	87.0	86.7	40.5	696.1	356.0	107.3	86.7	15.4	130.6
1981	1 941.1	231.3	95.8	92.1	43.4	758.9	383.5	117.2	97.9	15.8	144.5
1982	2 077.3	240.2	102.9	93.4	43.9	787.6	403.4	120.5	94.1	14.5	155.2
1983	2 290.6	280.8	126.5	106.6	47.7	831.2	423.8	130.9	93.1	13.6	169.8
1984	2 503.3	326.5	152.1	119.0	55.4	884.6	447.4	142.5	94.6	13.9	186.3
1985	2 720.3	363.5	175.9	128.5	59.0	928.7	467.6	152.1	97.2	13.6	198.2
1986	2 899.7	403.0	194.1	143.0	66.0	958.4	492.0	163.1	80.1	11.3	211.9
1987	3 100.2	421.7	195.0	153.4	73.2	1 015.3	515.2	174.4	85.4	11.2	229.1
1988	3 353.6	453.6	209.4	163.7	80.5	1 083.5	553.5	185.5	88.3	11.7	244.5
1989	3 598.5	471.8	215.3	171.6	84.9	1 166.7	591.6	198.9	98.6	11.9	265.7
1990	3 839.9	474.2	212.8	171.6	89.8	1 249.9	636.8	204.1	111.2	12.9	285.0
1991	3 986.1	453.9	193.5	171.7	88.7	1 284.8	657.5	208.7	108.5	12.4	297.8
1992	4 235.3	483.6	213.0	178.7	91.9	1 330.5	669.3	221.9	112.4	12.2	314.7
1993	4 477.9	526.7	234.0	193.4	99.3	1 379.4	691.9	229.9	114.1	12.4	331.1
1994	4 743.3	582.2	260.5	213.4	108.3	1 437.2	720.6	238.1	116.2	12.8	349.5
1995	4 975.8	611.6	266.7	228.6	116.3	1 485.1	740.9	241.7	120.2	13.1	369.2
1996	5 256.8	652.6	284.9	242.9	124.8	1 555.5	768.7	250.2	130.4	14.3	391.9
1997	5 547.4	692.7	305.1	256.2	131.4	1 619.0	796.2	258.1	134.4	13.3	416.9
1998	5 879.5	750.2	336.1	273.1	141.0	1 683.6	829.8	270.9	122.4	11.5	449.0
1999	6 282.5	817.6	370.8	293.9	153.0	1 804.8	873.1	286.3	137.9	11.9	495.6
2000	6 739.4	863.3	386.5	312.9	163.9	1 947.2	925.2	297.7	175.7	15.8	532.9
2001	7 055.0	883.7	407.9	312.1	163.7	2 017.1	967.9	297.7	171.6	15.4	564.4
2002	7 376.1	916.2	426.1	319.9	170.1	2 080.1	1 005.8	302.1	163.4	14.1	594.7
2003	7 760.9	950.7	440.1	328.0	182.6	2 200.1	1 064.5	307.2	191.3	16.9	620.1
2001											
1st quarter	6 955.8	872.1	395.5	312.3	164.3	2 000.0	953.8	299.8	180.2	17.5	548.7
2nd quarter	7 017.5	864.7	390.8	310.7	163.2	2 016.6	961.9	297.1	183.6	15.2	558.8
3rd quarter	7 058.5	865.1	393.7	309.9	161.5	2 024.2	972.9	295.0	170.8	15.2	570.5
4th quarter	7 188.4	932.8	451.5	315.5	165.8	2 027.5	983.1	299.0	152.0	13.8	579.7
2002											
1st quarter	7 236.9	903.5	414.5	319.8	169.3	2 046.8	994.6	303.9	147.8	12.6	588.0
2nd quarter	7 339.3	907.5	415.8	321.9	169.8	2 077.7	1 004.1	303.2	163.0	13.7	593.7
3rd quarter	7 428.0	932.8	444.6	318.5	169.7	2 081.3	1 006.2	297.7	166.1	14.3	596.9
4th quarter	7 500.0	920.8	429.7	319.4	171.6	2 114.6	1 018.4	303.6	176.5	15.8	600.2
2003											
1st quarter	7 609.8	912.1	421.4	316.8	174.0	2 167.5	1 039.5	299.9	201.9	17.2	608.9
2nd quarter	7 696.3	946.8	442.4	323.9	180.5	2 163.6	1 052.2	303.6	180.1	15.5	612.3
3rd quarter	7 822.5	972.7	452.5	333.3	186.9	2 219.2	1 074.6	311.0	190.9	16.7	626.0
4th quarter	7 914.9	971.1	444.1	338.0	189.0	2 250.1	1 091.8	314.4	192.5	18.2	633.1

Table 4-3. Personal Consumption Expenditures by Major Type of Product—Continued

(Billions of dollars, quarterly data are at seasonally adjusted annual rates.)

NIPA Table 2.3.5

Year and quarter	Services					Transportation	Medical care	Recreation	Other
	Total	Housing	Household operation						
			Total	Electricity and gas	Other household operation				
1946	45.8	14.2	6.8	2.1	4.7	4.9	4.9	3.7	11.3
1947	50.7	16.0	7.5	2.3	5.1	5.2	5.7	3.8	12.5
1948	55.6	17.9	8.1	2.6	5.5	5.7	6.5	3.8	13.6
1949	58.6	19.6	8.6	2.9	5.6	5.8	6.7	3.8	14.0
1950	63.3	21.7	9.5	3.3	6.2	6.0	7.2	3.9	15.0
1951	69.5	24.3	10.4	3.7	6.7	7.0	7.7	4.0	16.0
1952	75.4	27.0	11.2	4.1	7.1	7.4	8.5	4.3	17.1
1953	82.5	29.9	12.1	4.5	7.6	8.0	9.5	4.5	18.5
1954	88.4	32.3	12.7	5.0	7.7	8.2	10.5	4.8	20.0
1955	95.2	34.4	14.2	5.5	8.7	8.6	11.2	5.2	21.7
1956	102.8	36.7	15.4	6.1	9.3	9.2	12.1	5.6	23.8
1957	109.8	39.3	16.4	6.5	9.9	9.7	13.4	5.6	25.4
1958	117.0	42.0	17.5	7.1	10.4	9.9	14.8	5.8	27.0
1959	126.5	45.0	18.7	7.6	11.1	10.6	16.4	6.4	29.4
1960	135.6	48.2	20.3	8.3	12.0	11.2	17.7	6.9	31.3
1961	143.8	51.2	21.2	8.8	12.4	11.6	19.0	7.4	33.3
1962	153.6	54.7	22.4	9.4	13.0	12.3	21.2	8.0	35.0
1963	162.9	58.0	23.6	9.9	13.8	12.9	23.0	8.5	36.9
1964	176.1	61.4	25.0	10.4	14.6	13.8	26.4	9.1	40.4
1965	189.0	65.4	26.5	10.9	15.6	14.7	28.6	9.6	44.2
1966	203.8	69.5	28.1	11.5	16.6	15.9	31.5	10.4	48.4
1967	220.3	74.1	30.0	12.2	17.8	17.4	34.7	11.1	53.0
1968	241.6	79.8	32.3	13.0	19.2	19.3	40.1	12.5	57.7
1969	266.1	86.9	35.0	14.1	21.0	21.6	45.8	13.8	62.9
1970	291.5	94.1	37.8	15.3	22.4	24.0	51.7	15.1	68.8
1971	319.5	102.8	41.1	16.9	24.2	26.8	58.4	16.3	74.0
1972	352.2	112.6	45.4	18.8	26.7	29.6	65.6	17.6	81.4
1973	385.8	123.3	49.9	20.4	29.5	31.6	73.3	19.7	88.0
1974	426.6	134.8	55.8	24.0	31.8	34.1	82.3	22.5	97.1
1975	480.2	147.7	64.0	29.2	34.8	37.9	95.6	25.4	109.7
1976	534.7	162.2	72.5	33.2	39.3	42.5	109.1	28.4	120.1
1977	600.2	180.2	81.8	38.5	43.3	48.7	125.3	31.4	132.8
1978	676.6	202.4	91.2	43.0	48.2	53.4	143.1	34.7	151.8
1979	753.3	227.3	100.3	47.8	52.5	59.9	161.0	38.8	166.2
1980	846.9	256.2	113.7	57.5	56.2	65.2	184.4	43.6	183.8
1981	950.8	289.7	126.8	64.8	62.0	70.3	216.7	50.6	196.7
1982	1 049.4	315.2	142.5	74.2	68.3	72.9	243.3	56.8	218.8
1983	1 178.6	341.0	157.0	82.4	74.6	81.1	274.3	63.6	261.6
1984	1 292.2	374.5	169.4	86.5	82.9	93.2	303.2	69.7	282.1
1985	1 428.1	412.7	181.8	90.8	91.1	104.5	331.5	77.7	319.8
1986	1 538.3	448.4	187.7	89.2	98.5	111.1	357.5	83.7	349.9
1987	1 663.3	483.7	195.4	90.9	104.5	120.9	392.2	90.0	381.2
1988	1 816.5	521.5	207.3	96.3	111.0	133.4	442.8	102.1	409.4
1989	1 960.0	557.4	221.1	101.0	120.0	142.0	492.5	114.3	432.8
1990	2 115.9	597.9	227.3	101.0	126.2	147.7	556.0	125.9	461.0
1991	2 247.4	631.1	238.6	107.4	131.2	145.3	608.9	132.9	490.6
1992	2 421.2	658.5	250.7	108.9	141.9	157.7	672.2	146.6	535.5
1993	2 571.8	683.9	269.9	118.2	151.7	172.7	715.1	160.4	569.8
1994	2 723.9	726.1	286.2	120.7	165.5	190.6	752.9	171.4	596.7
1995	2 879.1	764.4	298.7	122.2	176.5	207.7	797.9	187.9	622.5
1996	3 048.7	800.1	318.5	129.4	189.1	226.5	833.5	202.5	667.6
1997	3 235.8	842.6	337.0	131.3	205.6	245.7	873.0	215.1	722.4
1998	3 445.7	894.6	350.5	129.8	220.7	259.5	921.4	229.3	790.5
1999	3 660.0	948.4	364.8	130.6	234.1	276.4	961.1	248.6	860.7
2000	3 928.8	1 006.5	390.1	143.3	246.8	291.3	1 026.8	268.3	945.9
2001	4 154.3	1 073.7	409.0	156.7	252.3	292.8	1 113.8	284.1	980.7
2002	4 379.8	1 144.8	409.0	152.6	256.4	288.0	1 210.3	299.6	1 028.2
2003	4 610.1	1 188.4	431.3	167.3	264.0	294.0	1 301.1	317.2	1 078.1
2001									
1st quarter	4 083.7	1 047.0	418.3	168.9	249.4	297.4	1 079.5	280.5	960.9
2nd quarter	4 136.2	1 065.6	409.6	157.3	252.3	296.1	1 101.0	282.6	981.2
3rd quarter	4 169.1	1 082.3	408.8	154.3	254.5	290.7	1 125.4	284.9	977.0
4th quarter	4 228.0	1 099.9	399.3	146.2	253.2	287.1	1 149.4	288.6	1 003.7
2002									
1st quarter	4 286.5	1 121.8	400.6	146.5	254.1	287.6	1 173.7	293.6	1 009.3
2nd quarter	4 354.0	1 140.0	406.7	151.6	255.0	288.8	1 197.9	297.8	1 022.9
3rd quarter	4 413.9	1 153.2	410.9	153.0	258.0	287.2	1 222.5	300.9	1 039.2
4th quarter	4 464.7	1 164.2	417.7	159.2	258.5	288.3	1 247.0	306.0	1 041.5
2003									
1st quarter	4 530.2	1 174.5	426.6	164.9	261.6	291.5	1 267.6	310.8	1 059.3
2nd quarter	4 585.9	1 182.7	428.9	166.3	262.6	293.0	1 290.5	315.5	1 075.3
3rd quarter	4 630.6	1 193.4	431.8	166.7	265.0	295.1	1 312.1	319.0	1 079.1
4th quarter	4 693.6	1 202.8	438.1	171.2	266.8	296.5	1 334.0	323.4	1 098.8

Table 4-4. Chain-Type Quantity Indexes for Personal Consumption Expenditures by Major Type of Product

(Index numbers, 2000 = 100, seasonally adjusted.)

NIPA Table 2.3.3

Year and quarter	Personal consumption expenditures, total	Durable goods				Nondurable goods					
		Total	Motor vehicles and parts	Furniture and household equipment	Other	Total	Food	Clothing and shoes	Gasoline and oil	Fuel oil and coal	Other
1946	15.0	5.3	5.3	3.9	7.1	25.3	35.1	15.1	16.0	231.0	14.3
1947	15.3	6.4	7.7	4.5	6.7	24.6	33.8	14.4	17.1	243.3	14.2
1948	15.6	6.8	8.7	4.7	6.8	24.7	33.4	14.5	18.2	244.5	14.8
1949	16.1	7.3	11.2	4.6	6.4	25.1	33.6	14.6	19.7	215.7	15.8
1950	17.1	8.9	14.4	5.6	6.8	25.9	34.3	15.0	20.5	231.8	17.0
1951	17.4	8.1	12.2	5.3	6.9	26.6	35.2	14.9	22.3	231.2	17.7
1952	17.9	7.9	11.0	5.4	7.4	27.6	36.4	15.7	24.1	224.7	18.5
1953	18.8	8.9	13.6	5.6	7.7	28.5	37.7	15.9	25.4	217.2	19.2
1954	19.2	8.9	13.0	5.8	8.1	28.9	38.5	15.9	26.2	221.4	19.1
1955	20.6	10.8	17.8	6.5	8.9	30.3	40.1	16.7	28.5	235.3	20.1
1956	21.2	10.4	15.1	6.8	9.6	31.3	41.4	17.1	30.2	235.8	21.0
1957	21.7	10.5	15.8	6.6	9.7	31.9	42.2	17.0	31.4	233.8	21.7
1958	21.8	9.7	13.1	6.5	9.9	32.2	42.2	17.1	32.9	242.7	22.2
1959	23.1	10.8	15.6	7.0	10.5	33.5	43.7	18.0	34.6	231.8	23.5
1960	23.7	11.0	16.6	6.9	10.4	34.0	44.0	18.2	35.8	222.0	24.6
1961	24.2	10.6	14.9	7.0	10.3	34.6	44.5	18.5	36.1	211.4	25.9
1962	25.4	11.9	17.7	7.5	11.0	35.7	45.1	19.4	37.7	210.9	27.7
1963	26.4	13.0	20.0	8.0	11.7	36.5	45.6	19.7	38.8	221.3	29.0
1964	28.0	14.2	21.1	9.0	13.1	38.2	47.4	21.3	40.9	230.0	30.3
1965	29.8	16.0	24.5	9.9	14.5	40.3	50.0	22.1	42.9	240.8	32.1
1966	31.5	17.4	25.0	11.2	17.2	42.5	52.1	23.6	45.5	247.8	34.7
1967	32.4	17.6	24.4	11.7	18.0	43.2	52.8	23.8	47.0	247.9	35.6
1968	34.3	19.6	28.4	12.4	19.6	45.1	55.4	24.8	50.3	234.7	37.1
1969	35.6	20.3	29.6	12.8	20.5	46.3	56.8	25.2	53.7	222.4	38.2
1970	36.4	19.6	26.6	12.9	21.5	47.4	58.5	24.9	57.0	206.9	39.5
1971	37.8	21.6	31.7	13.4	21.8	48.3	59.1	26.1	59.8	199.9	39.7
1972	40.1	24.3	36.3	14.9	24.6	50.4	61.0	27.9	62.2	219.7	41.8
1973	42.0	26.8	39.6	16.5	27.7	52.1	61.2	29.8	65.4	238.6	44.6
1974	41.7	25.0	32.8	16.7	28.5	51.0	60.2	29.4	62.2	188.3	44.5
1975	42.7	25.0	33.0	16.3	29.6	51.8	61.7	30.4	64.1	184.8	43.0
1976	45.0	28.2	40.0	17.4	31.9	54.3	64.9	31.8	66.6	207.5	44.6
1977	47.0	30.8	44.2	18.9	34.2	55.6	66.1	33.6	68.7	200.9	45.3
1978	49.0	32.4	46.1	20.0	36.5	57.7	66.8	36.9	70.3	199.3	48.6
1979	50.2	32.3	43.1	21.1	37.9	59.2	68.1	38.8	69.3	185.2	51.4
1980	50.1	29.8	37.3	20.7	35.1	59.1	68.7	39.7	65.4	143.2	52.2
1981	50.8	30.1	38.1	20.7	35.6	59.8	68.8	42.2	66.3	120.1	53.3
1982	51.5	30.1	39.1	20.3	35.0	60.4	69.9	42.8	67.2	111.5	53.0
1983	54.4	34.5	46.7	23.1	37.0	62.4	71.9	46.0	68.7	111.6	54.3
1984	57.3	39.6	54.5	25.8	42.4	64.9	73.5	49.9	70.8	111.2	57.4
1985	60.3	43.6	61.6	28.1	44.4	66.7	75.2	52.2	72.2	112.5	58.8
1986	62.7	47.8	66.2	31.6	48.9	69.1	77.0	56.4	75.7	116.7	60.5
1987	64.8	48.6	63.8	33.9	52.0	70.7	78.0	58.4	77.8	115.1	62.9
1988	67.5	51.5	67.4	36.2	54.8	73.0	81.1	60.2	79.8	119.4	64.3
1989	69.4	52.7	67.3	38.1	56.0	75.0	82.5	63.6	81.5	116.5	66.4
1990	70.8	52.5	66.3	38.3	56.6	76.2	84.8	63.2	80.8	105.8	67.7
1991	70.9	49.6	58.6	38.7	54.1	76.0	84.7	63.4	79.9	104.8	67.4
1992	73.2	52.5	63.4	40.8	55.0	77.6	85.2	66.9	83.1	107.3	68.7
1993	75.7	56.6	67.1	45.1	59.2	79.6	86.7	69.7	85.2	109.6	71.1
1994	78.5	61.3	71.5	50.1	63.6	82.4	88.8	73.4	86.3	114.9	74.6
1995	80.6	64.0	70.4	55.4	67.8	84.2	89.4	76.4	87.9	118.2	77.7
1996	83.4	69.0	73.8	61.8	73.0	86.3	90.2	80.2	89.9	116.5	81.3
1997	86.5	74.9	78.8	69.1	77.7	88.6	91.4	82.6	92.7	107.0	85.7
1998	90.9	83.4	87.7	78.2	83.9	92.2	93.6	88.4	96.9	101.3	90.3
1999	95.5	93.2	96.4	89.7	92.6	96.4	96.6	95.0	100.4	103.7	95.4
2000	100.0	100.0	100.0	100.0	100.0	100.0	100.0	100.0	100.0	100.0	100.0
2001	102.5	104.3	105.0	106.0	99.6	102.0	101.6	102.0	101.5	95.8	103.1
2002	105.7	111.2	110.9	115.3	104.3	104.6	103.6	106.4	102.9	97.1	106.3
2003	109.1	119.4	117.0	125.8	113.8	108.5	107.6	110.9	103.6	97.4	110.6
2001											
1st quarter	101.7	101.9	101.6	103.5	99.6	101.4	101.3	100.9	102.7	101.3	101.5
2nd quarter	101.9	101.8	100.5	104.9	99.2	101.4	101.4	101.4	98.8	94.0	102.5
3rd quarter	102.4	102.6	101.6	106.2	98.3	102.0	101.7	101.7	100.2	94.9	103.5
4th quarter	104.1	111.1	116.3	109.6	101.1	103.2	102.1	104.1	104.2	92.8	104.8
2002											
1st quarter	104.6	108.6	107.4	113.3	103.3	104.2	102.8	106.3	104.4	92.1	105.9
2nd quarter	105.3	109.8	108.3	115.1	103.9	104.4	103.6	106.2	101.6	96.5	106.0
3rd quarter	106.1	113.4	115.7	115.4	104.3	104.3	103.5	105.1	101.3	97.1	106.1
4th quarter	106.8	112.8	112.3	117.4	105.6	105.6	104.4	107.9	104.2	102.8	107.1
2003											
1st quarter	107.5	112.7	110.7	118.0	108.0	106.9	106.1	107.7	105.0	95.0	108.8
2nd quarter	108.5	118.1	116.8	123.1	112.5	107.3	106.8	109.9	101.2	90.4	109.4
3rd quarter	109.8	122.7	120.5	129.4	116.3	109.1	108.3	112.5	102.0	97.7	111.4
4th quarter	110.8	123.9	119.9	132.5	118.3	110.5	109.0	113.6	106.1	106.5	113.0

Table 4-4. Chain-Type Quantity Indexes for Personal Consumption Expenditures by Major Type of Product
—*Continued*

(Index numbers, 2000 = 100, seasonally adjusted.) NIPA Table 2.3.3

Year and quarter	Services								
	Total	Housing	Household operation			Transportation	Medical care	Recreation	Other
			Total	Electricity and gas	Other household operation				
1946	11.9	11.5	11.2	9.2	11.8	19.8	7.7	11.1	14.3
1947	12.5	12.5	12.0	10.3	12.3	19.6	8.2	10.5	14.5
1948	12.9	13.2	12.6	11.4	12.6	19.6	9.0	10.2	14.8
1949	13.3	14.0	13.1	12.4	12.8	18.9	9.4	10.1	14.9
1950	13.9	15.0	14.2	14.1	13.6	18.7	10.0	10.0	15.4
1951	14.6	16.0	15.1	15.8	14.1	20.3	10.5	10.1	15.5
1952	15.3	17.1	15.6	17.2	14.0	20.6	11.0	10.3	16.1
1953	15.9	18.0	16.3	18.5	14.5	21.2	11.5	10.4	16.7
1954	16.6	18.9	17.0	20.3	14.5	20.9	12.3	10.6	17.4
1955	17.4	19.8	18.6	21.9	16.1	21.7	12.8	11.1	18.1
1956	18.3	20.8	19.9	23.8	17.1	22.6	13.6	11.7	18.8
1957	19.0	21.8	20.7	25.3	17.5	23.0	14.4	11.3	19.4
1958	19.8	22.9	21.4	26.7	17.9	22.6	15.3	11.3	20.2
1959	20.8	24.1	22.3	28.3	18.4	23.5	16.5	12.0	21.2
1960	21.7	25.4	23.4	29.9	19.2	24.3	17.1	12.7	21.9
1961	22.6	26.6	24.2	31.4	19.7	24.6	17.9	13.3	22.8
1962	23.7	28.1	25.4	33.6	20.4	25.5	19.4	14.0	23.3
1963	24.8	29.4	26.5	35.2	21.1	26.6	20.7	14.6	24.2
1964	26.3	30.8	27.8	37.1	22.1	28.0	23.0	15.2	25.8
1965	27.7	32.5	29.2	38.8	23.2	29.2	24.1	15.6	27.5
1966	29.1	34.0	30.6	41.0	24.3	30.8	25.4	16.3	28.9
1967	30.6	35.6	32.2	43.3	25.5	32.5	26.4	16.8	30.7
1968	32.1	37.4	33.6	45.8	26.3	34.5	28.4	17.8	31.8
1969	33.7	39.4	35.3	48.5	27.5	36.3	30.4	18.8	32.4
1970	35.0	40.8	36.6	50.8	28.3	37.3	32.1	19.6	33.7
1971	36.4	42.6	37.2	52.4	28.5	38.7	34.1	20.3	34.6
1972	38.5	45.1	39.2	55.5	29.9	41.1	36.5	21.3	36.2
1973	40.3	47.4	41.1	57.1	31.8	42.2	39.1	23.1	37.0
1974	41.2	49.8	41.6	57.8	32.1	42.5	40.5	24.7	36.1
1975	42.7	51.3	43.5	61.0	33.4	42.9	42.5	26.1	37.4
1976	44.5	52.8	45.3	63.2	34.9	44.2	44.5	27.9	39.1
1977	46.4	54.2	47.7	66.3	36.9	47.4	46.7	29.7	40.8
1978	48.6	56.8	50.2	69.2	39.1	49.0	48.9	31.1	42.6
1979	50.0	59.1	51.7	69.7	41.2	50.4	50.9	32.5	42.8
1980	50.9	60.9	53.1	71.6	42.2	47.9	52.7	34.1	42.5
1981	51.8	62.5	52.6	70.4	42.1	46.5	55.4	37.1	41.9
1982	52.9	62.8	53.0	71.3	42.3	45.9	56.2	39.7	44.5
1983	55.8	64.1	54.7	73.4	43.7	48.9	58.5	42.7	50.1
1984	58.0	66.8	56.1	73.8	45.8	53.6	60.2	44.8	52.0
1985	61.3	69.5	58.4	75.8	48.3	58.4	62.7	48.1	56.7
1986	63.1	71.3	59.4	75.0	50.5	60.7	65.2	49.9	58.0
1987	65.8	73.5	62.1	77.7	53.2	63.1	68.6	51.9	61.0
1988	68.5	75.8	65.0	81.6	55.4	66.3	72.0	56.7	62.5
1989	70.6	77.8	67.6	83.3	58.7	67.2	74.0	60.7	64.3
1990	72.6	79.7	68.3	81.9	60.5	67.2	77.7	63.6	65.7
1991	73.8	81.5	69.2	84.5	60.4	64.0	80.3	64.0	66.7
1992	76.4	82.7	71.1	84.0	63.8	66.7	84.1	68.6	69.1
1993	78.5	83.6	74.6	88.5	66.8	69.5	85.4	72.8	72.0
1994	80.9	86.4	77.8	89.9	70.9	75.0	86.4	76.3	73.6
1995	83.0	88.2	80.2	90.8	74.2	79.6	88.3	81.7	74.5
1996	85.4	89.5	83.9	94.0	78.2	85.0	89.8	85.2	77.2
1997	88.3	91.7	87.2	93.3	83.9	90.4	91.8	87.8	80.8
1998	92.0	94.3	91.5	95.4	89.4	93.4	94.5	91.3	86.9
1999	95.7	97.2	95.3	96.4	94.7	97.3	96.3	96.1	92.8
2000	100.0	100.0	100.0	100.0	100.0	100.0	100.0	100.0	100.0
2001	102.4	102.7	100.2	98.3	101.4	98.9	104.7	102.5	101.5
2002	105.1	105.5	101.0	101.0	101.0	96.1	111.0	104.9	102.7
2003	107.4	106.9	102.6	102.7	102.5	95.3	115.3	108.2	104.7
2001									
1st quarter	101.8	101.8	101.9	103.6	100.8	100.6	102.6	102.4	100.9
2nd quarter	102.2	102.5	99.8	96.9	101.7	100.1	103.8	102.2	101.9
3rd quarter	102.5	103.0	100.0	97.0	101.9	98.2	105.4	102.3	101.3
4th quarter	103.1	103.6	99.1	95.8	101.1	96.7	107.0	103.0	102.0
2002									
1st quarter	104.0	104.6	99.6	97.4	100.9	96.8	108.8	104.2	101.9
2nd quarter	104.9	105.4	101.1	100.7	101.4	96.4	110.3	104.6	102.5
3rd quarter	105.5	105.9	101.2	101.3	101.1	95.6	111.7	105.0	103.2
4th quarter	106.1	106.2	102.3	104.6	100.8	95.5	113.0	106.0	103.1
2003									
1st quarter	106.6	106.5	102.4	104.0	101.4	95.9	113.9	106.8	103.7
2nd quarter	107.1	106.7	101.7	100.8	102.2	95.3	114.9	107.9	104.5
3rd quarter	107.6	107.1	102.2	100.9	103.0	95.1	115.8	108.6	104.9
4th quarter	108.3	107.3	104.1	105.1	103.4	95.0	116.7	109.6	105.8

Table 4-5. Personal Consumption Expenditures by Type of Expenditure

(Billions of dollars.)

NIPA Table 2.5.5

Year	Personal consumption expenditures	Food and tobacco	Clothing, accessories, and jewelry	Personal care	Housing	Household operation	Medical care	Personal business	Transportation	Recreation	Education and research	Religious and welfare activities	Foreign travel and other, net
1939	67.2	20.9	8.4	1.0	9.4	9.6	3.1	3.0	6.5	3.5	0.7	1.0	0.2
1940	71.3	22.0	8.9	1.0	9.7	10.4	3.3	3.1	7.3	3.8	0.8	1.0	0.1
1941	81.1	25.4	10.5	1.2	10.4	11.8	3.6	3.2	8.6	4.3	0.8	1.1	0.1
1942	89.0	30.7	13.1	1.4	11.2	12.7	4.1	3.3	5.6	4.7	0.9	1.2	0.2
1943	99.9	35.8	16.0	1.6	11.8	13.1	4.5	3.7	5.6	5.0	1.1	1.5	0.3
1944	108.7	39.3	17.5	1.8	12.3	14.0	5.1	3.9	5.9	5.4	1.1	1.7	0.6
1945	120.0	43.5	19.6	2.0	12.8	15.5	5.4	4.1	6.8	6.2	1.1	1.8	1.2
1946	144.3	50.7	22.0	2.1	14.2	19.9	6.6	4.7	12.4	8.6	1.2	2.0	-0.1
1947	162.0	56.1	22.8	2.2	16.0	23.7	7.4	5.2	15.8	9.3	1.5	2.1	0.0
1948	175.0	58.2	24.2	2.3	17.9	26.1	8.4	5.6	18.4	9.7	1.7	2.3	0.3
1949	178.5	56.6	23.3	2.3	19.6	25.7	8.7	5.8	21.7	10.0	1.8	2.3	0.6
1950	192.2	58.1	23.7	2.4	21.7	29.1	9.4	6.4	25.2	11.2	1.9	2.4	0.7
1951	208.5	65.2	25.6	2.7	24.3	31.1	10.2	6.9	25.3	11.7	2.1	2.6	0.9
1952	219.5	69.0	26.6	2.9	27.0	31.5	11.2	7.2	25.6	12.3	2.2	3.0	1.1
1953	233.1	70.5	27.0	3.1	29.9	33.0	12.2	8.0	29.4	13.1	2.3	3.1	1.5
1954	240.0	71.7	27.2	3.4	32.3	33.7	13.3	8.8	28.8	13.6	2.5	3.3	1.5
1955	258.8	73.6	28.4	3.7	34.4	37.3	14.2	9.8	35.0	14.6	2.7	3.5	1.6
1956	271.7	76.7	29.7	4.1	36.7	39.8	15.5	10.7	34.4	15.5	3.0	3.9	1.7
1957	286.9	80.7	30.0	4.6	39.3	41.2	17.1	11.4	37.4	15.9	3.4	4.1	1.7
1958	296.2	83.9	30.3	4.9	42.0	42.4	18.7	12.2	35.5	16.3	3.7	4.4	1.9
1959	317.6	87.2	32.0	5.2	45.0	45.0	20.6	13.1	40.7	17.7	4.0	5.1	2.0
1960	331.7	89.2	32.7	5.6	48.2	46.7	22.2	14.1	42.8	18.5	4.4	5.2	2.1
1961	342.1	91.1	33.5	6.1	51.2	48.2	23.9	15.3	41.5	19.3	4.7	5.3	2.0
1962	363.3	93.3	35.0	6.7	54.7	51.0	26.5	15.9	46.4	20.8	5.1	5.5	2.3
1963	382.7	95.7	36.0	7.0	58.0	54.0	28.7	16.7	50.2	22.4	5.6	5.7	2.5
1964	411.4	101.1	39.1	7.5	61.4	58.4	32.3	18.4	53.3	24.6	6.2	6.6	2.6
1965	443.8	108.8	41.4	8.1	65.4	62.1	34.7	20.1	59.4	26.9	7.0	7.1	2.9
1966	480.9	117.8	45.5	9.0	69.5	67.2	38.0	22.0	62.2	30.9	8.0	7.7	3.1
1967	507.8	121.4	47.8	9.8	74.1	70.8	41.4	23.7	64.5	33.1	8.9	8.5	3.8
1968	558.0	131.6	52.5	10.5	79.8	76.3	47.7	26.0	73.9	36.7	10.1	9.3	3.7
1969	605.2	141.3	56.2	10.9	86.9	81.1	54.2	28.9	80.4	40.0	11.3	10.0	4.0
1970	648.5	154.6	57.6	11.5	94.1	84.8	61.3	31.8	81.5	43.1	12.7	11.0	4.5
1971	701.9	161.0	61.8	11.7	102.8	90.1	68.5	34.3	94.5	46.0	13.9	12.5	4.8
1972	770.6	173.6	67.1	12.3	112.6	99.5	76.7	37.7	105.1	51.5	15.3	14.0	5.2
1973	852.4	192.9	74.7	13.6	123.3	111.4	85.3	41.3	115.8	57.6	16.9	15.0	4.7
1974	933.4	215.9	79.3	14.8	134.8	123.6	95.5	46.6	119.7	63.4	18.5	16.7	4.7
1975	1 034.4	238.3	85.6	16.1	147.7	135.7	109.9	54.9	132.4	70.5	20.6	18.3	4.4
1976	1 151.9	259.3	93.7	17.5	162.2	152.0	124.7	60.5	156.8	78.2	22.5	20.8	3.8
1977	1 278.6	279.6	102.8	19.9	180.2	170.5	142.1	67.2	179.1	85.5	24.2	23.2	4.3
1978	1 428.5	307.8	115.1	21.9	202.4	189.6	162.3	78.9	196.7	96.1	26.8	26.6	4.3
1979	1 592.2	343.9	123.4	23.8	227.3	212.0	183.3	85.9	219.6	108.9	29.8	30.3	4.1
1980	1 757.1	376.8	132.3	25.5	256.2	233.3	209.6	95.2	238.9	117.5	33.5	34.8	3.5
1981	1 941.1	406.3	143.8	27.1	289.7	254.5	245.2	102.3	264.0	130.8	37.6	39.2	0.4
1982	2 077.3	427.7	147.0	28.0	315.2	271.9	274.8	115.1	270.0	140.9	41.3	43.0	2.5
1983	2 290.6	451.3	161.1	32.2	341.0	296.7	310.0	143.6	300.7	156.9	45.4	46.1	5.4
1984	2 503.3	476.6	175.8	35.5	374.5	322.8	343.7	151.8	339.9	174.8	49.4	51.8	6.6
1985	2 720.3	498.4	188.3	38.8	412.7	343.6	376.4	177.5	377.7	189.7	53.9	55.7	7.7
1986	2 899.7	524.2	204.1	42.3	448.4	359.6	407.4	198.3	385.2	206.9	58.1	61.9	3.3
1987	3 100.2	549.8	218.9	46.5	483.7	376.3	447.6	213.6	401.3	226.8	63.2	66.7	6.1
1988	3 353.6	588.2	235.7	50.1	521.5	398.6	505.0	224.2	431.1	251.7	70.2	74.4	2.8
1989	3 598.5	630.3	252.5	53.8	557.4	423.2	561.9	236.3	455.9	272.4	77.7	81.0	-3.7
1990	3 839.9	677.8	261.5	56.9	597.9	433.3	635.1	250.9	471.7	290.2	83.7	88.7	-7.7
1991	3 986.1	699.9	263.5	58.5	631.1	444.3	692.9	279.7	447.3	302.0	89.3	92.9	-15.2
1992	4 235.3	717.3	280.9	62.0	658.5	466.0	761.1	306.7	483.2	321.3	96.0	102.3	-20.0
1993	4 477.9	740.6	293.4	64.4	683.9	497.5	809.0	330.0	520.8	351.0	101.5	106.5	-20.6
1994	4 743.3	767.9	306.3	68.1	726.1	529.6	853.3	336.1	567.3	383.4	107.3	115.3	-17.4
1995	4 975.8	790.1	314.5	72.8	764.4	553.5	905.0	349.6	594.6	418.1	114.3	120.4	-21.4
1996	5 256.8	820.1	327.2	77.0	800.1	586.6	950.7	376.0	641.8	448.4	122.6	130.5	-24.2
1997	5 547.4	850.0	337.4	82.9	842.6	616.2	1 002.8	412.9	685.2	474.5	129.7	134.2	-21.1
1998	5 879.5	888.7	356.3	86.2	894.6	641.8	1 069.4	446.1	718.0	505.8	140.0	146.0	-13.3
1999	6 282.5	944.8	379.6	89.5	948.4	675.2	1 130.8	491.6	785.0	546.1	150.5	154.5	-13.5
2000	6 739.4	1 003.7	397.0	93.4	1 006.5	719.3	1 218.3	539.1	853.0	585.7	163.8	172.5	-13.0
2001	7 055.0	1 052.0	397.1	94.5	1 073.7	740.3	1 327.3	536.5	872.4	604.0	178.1	186.5	-7.4
2002	7 376.1	1 095.0	404.4	95.8	1 144.8	746.0	1 444.9	552.1	877.5	628.3	190.7	202.9	-6.4
2003	7 760.9	1 152.6	412.3	96.9	1 188.4	779.6	1 557.2	577.7	925.5	660.7	201.7	211.2	-2.7

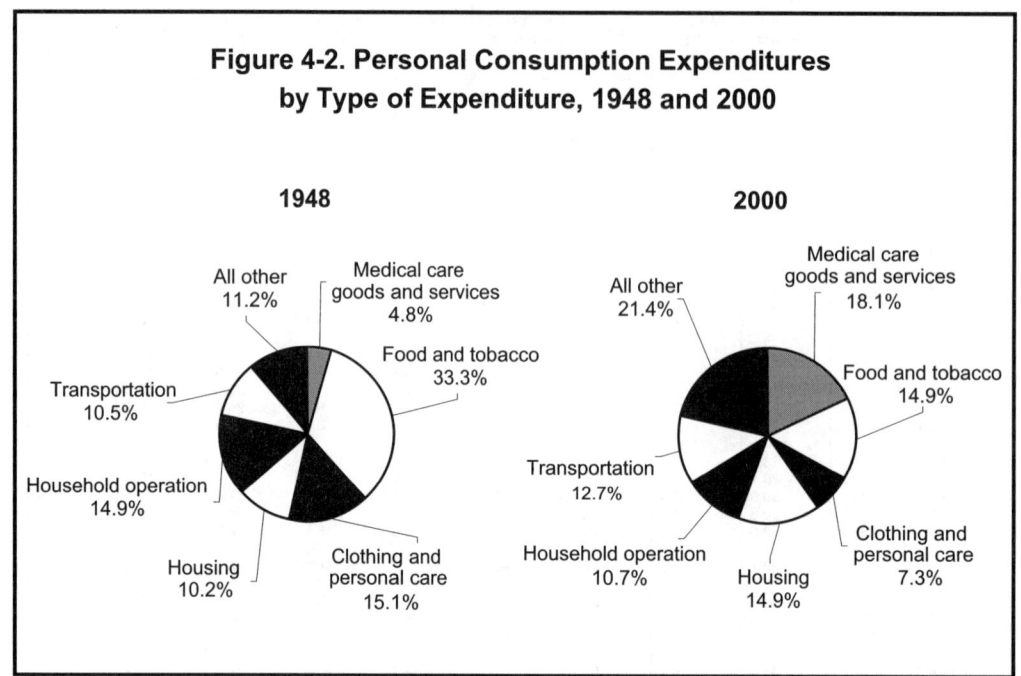

Figure 4-2. Personal Consumption Expenditures by Type of Expenditure, 1948 and 2000

- Spending for medical care goods and services in 2000 made up 18.1 percent of personal consumption spending—more than 3-1/2 times the 1948 percentage. This includes medical care payments made by government and private insurance on behalf of individuals as well as consumer payments out of pocket. (Table 4-5)
- In 2000, much smaller shares were required for food and tobacco and for clothing and personal care than in 1948, as can be seen on the graph. Household operation claimed a smaller share but housing itself a larger one. Transportation rose slightly and the "all other" share doubled. It should be noted that the nonprofit sector is included in this tabulation, and its spending on education, research, religious, and welfare activities is included in the "all other" category. (Table 4-5)

NOTES AND DEFINITIONS

SOURCE: U.S. DEPARTMENT OF COMMERCE, BUREAU OF ECONOMIC ANALYSIS

All personal income and personal consumption expenditure series are from the national income and product accounts (NIPAs). All quarterly series are shown at a seasonally adjusted annual rate. Current and constant dollar values are in billions of dollars. Indexes of price and quantity are based on the average for the year 2000 = 100.

In all these tables, the personal sector includes nonprofit institutions serving households. On an annual basis only, tables are also now available in which income, spending, and saving are estimated separately for households and nonprofit institutions. These data are available for the years 1992 through 2002 and are discussed in the article at the beginning of this book, "New Perspectives on the U.S. Economy." These tables are available on the BEA Web site as Table 2.9.

In several cases, the Notes and Definitions below will refer to *imputations* or *imputed values*. See the Notes and Definitions to Chapter 1 for an explanation of imputation and the role it plays in national and personal income measurement.

TABLES 4-1 THROUGH 4-4 AND 19-6
SOURCES AND DISPOSITION OF PERSONAL INCOME; PERSONAL CONSUMPTION EXPENDITURE BY MAJOR TYPE OF PRODUCT

Definitions

Personal income is the income received by persons residing in the United States from participation in production; from government and business transfer payments; and from government interest, which is treated like a transfer payment rather than income from participation in production. *Persons* refers to individuals, nonprofit institutions that primarily serve individuals, private noninsured welfare funds, and private trust funds. Proprietors' income is treated in its entirety as received by individuals. Life insurance carriers and private noninsured pension funds are not counted as persons, but their saving is credited to persons.

Personal income is the sum of compensation received by employees, proprietors' income with inventory valuation and capital consumption adjustments, rental income of persons with capital consumption adjustment, personal receipts on assets, and personal current transfer receipts, less contributions for social insurance.

Personal income differs from national income in that it includes current transfer payments and interest received by persons, regardless of source, while it excludes both employee and employer contributions for social insurance; business transfer payments, interest payments, and other payments on assets other than to persons; taxes on production and imports less subsidies; the current surplus of government enterprises; and undistributed corporate profits with IVA and CCAdj.

Compensation of employees, received is the sum of wage and salary accruals and supplements to wages and salaries, both as defined in the *national* income account (see Table 1-7 and the Notes and Definitions to Chapter 1), less an adjustment item *Wage accruals less disbursements*, the effect of which is to put retroactive wage payments into the quarter *in* which the wages were paid rather than the quarter *for* which they were paid. This adjustment item is zero in most quarters. It is shown in Table 1-7 but not in Tables 4-1 or 19-6. As in *national* income, this component refers to compensation received by residents of the United States, including compensation from the rest of the world, but excludes compensation from domestic industries to workers residing in the rest of the world.

Wage and salary disbursements consists of the monetary remuneration of employees, including the compensation of corporate officers; corporate directors' fees paid to directors who are also employees of the corporation; the value of the exercise by employees of "nonqualified stock options;" commissions, tips, and bonuses; voluntary employee contributions to certain deferred compensation plans such as 401(k) plans; receipts in kind that represent income; and judicial fees to jurors and witnesses, compensation of prison inmates, and marriage fees to justices of the peace, which were formerly included in "other labor income."

Supplements to wages and salaries consists of employer contributions for employee pension and insurance funds and for government social insurance.

Proprietors' income with inventory valuation and capital consumption adjustments is the current-production income (including income-in-kind) of sole proprietors and partnerships and of tax-exempt cooperatives. The imputed net rental income of owner-occupants of farm dwellings is included. Dividends and monetary interest received by proprietors of nonfinancial business and rental incomes received by persons not primarily engaged in the real estate business are excluded; these incomes are included in rental income of persons and personal income receipts on assets. Fees paid to outside directors of corporations are included. The two valuation adjustments are designed to obtain income measures that exclude any element of capital gains: inventory withdrawals are valued at replacement, rather than historical, cost, and charges for depreciation are on a consistent accounting basis and are valued at replacement cost.

Rental income of persons with capital consumption adjustment is the net current-production income of persons from the rental of real property (other than income of persons primarily engaged in the real estate business); the imputed net rental income of owner-occupants of nonfarm dwellings; and the royalties received by persons from patents, copyrights, and rights to natural resources. The capital consumption adjustment converts charges for depreciation to a consistent accounting basis valued at replacement cost.

Personal income receipts on assets consists of personal interest income and personal dividend income.

Personal interest income is the interest income (monetary and imputed) of persons from all sources, including interest paid by government to government employee retirement plans as well as government interest paid directly to persons.

Personal dividend income is the dividend income of persons from all sources, excluding capital gains distributions. It equals net dividends paid by corporations (dividends paid by corporations less dividends received by corporations) less a small amount of corporate dividends received by general government. Dividends received by government employee retirement systems are included in personal dividend income.

Personal current transfer receipts is income payments to persons for which no current services are performed. It consists of government social benefits to persons and net receipts from business.

Government social benefits to persons consists of benefits from the following social insurance funds:

Old-age, survivors, disability, and health insurance (*Social Security and Medicare*);

Unemployment insurance;

Veterans' benefits;

Family assistance, which consists of aid to families with dependent children and, beginning with 1996, assistance programs operating under the Personal Responsibility and Work Opportunity Reconciliation Act of 1996;

Other, which includes pension benefit guaranty; workers' compensation; military medical insurance; temporary disability insurance; food stamps; black lung; supplemental security income; public assistance (including Medicaid); and educational assistance. Government payments to nonprofit institutions, other than for work under research and development contracts, also are included. Payments from government employee retirement plans are not included.

Contributions for government social insurance, which is subtracted to arrive at personal income, includes payments by employers, employees, self-employed, and other individuals who participate in the following programs: Old-age, survivors, and disability insurance (Social Security); hospital insurance and supplementary medical insurance (Medicare); unemployment insurance; railroad retirement; veterans' life insurance; and temporary disability insurance. Contributions to government employee retirement plans are not included in this item.

In the 2003 revision there was a change in the tabular presentation of contributions for government social insurance, but not in the concept of personal income. Before the revision, the components of personal income included only wages and salaries and "other labor income," and *personal* contributions for social insurance were subtracted from that total. In the revision, the total compensation concept presented in the table includes wages and salaries and all supplements, including the *employer* social insurance payments, and both the *employer* and *employee* contributions are then subtracted to arrive at personal income. In either case, the effect is to end up with a personal income figure that is net of all social insurance taxes but not net of personal income taxes.

Personal current taxes is tax payments (net of refunds) by persons residing in the United States that are not chargeable to business expense, including taxes on income, on realized net capital gains, and on personal property. As of the 1999 revisions, estate and gift taxes are classified as capital transfers and are not included in personal current taxes.

Disposable personal income is personal income less personal current taxes. It is the income from current production that is available to persons for spending or saving. Disposable personal income in chained (2000) dollars represents the inflation-adjusted value of disposable personal income.

Personal outlays is the sum of *personal consumption expenditures* (defined below), *personal interest payments*, and *personal current transfer payments*.

Personal current transfer payments to government includes donations, fees, and fines paid to federal, state, and local governments. These were formerly classified as "personal nontax payments" and included in the old total "personal tax and nontax payments."

Personal current transfer payments to the rest of the world (net) is personal remittances in cash and in kind to the rest of the world less such remittances from the rest of the world.

Personal saving is derived by subtracting personal outlays from disposable personal income. It is the current saving of individuals (including proprietors), nonprofit institutions that primarily serve individuals, life insurance carriers, retirement funds (now including those of government employees), private noninsured welfare funds, and private trust funds. Conceptually, personal saving may also be viewed as the sum of the net acquisition of financial assets and the change in physical assets less the sum of net borrowing and consumption of fixed capital. In either case, it is defined to exclude capital gains, whether realized or unrealized.

Note that in the context of national income accounting the term just defined is "*saving*," not "savings." "Saving" refers to a *flow* of income during a particular time span (a year or a quarter, for example) that is not consumed and is therefore available to finance a commensurate *flow* of investment during that time span. "Savings" denotes an accumulated *stock* of monetary funds—possibly the cumulative effects of successive periods of *saving*—available to the owner in asset form, such as a bank savings account.

Personal consumption expenditures (PCE) is goods and services purchased by persons residing in the United States. Persons are defined as individuals and nonprofit institutions that primarily serve individuals. Most of PCE consists of purchases of new goods and services by individuals from business, including purchases financed by insurance (for example, by medical insurance). In addition, PCE includes purchases of new goods and services by nonprofit institutions, net purchases of used goods by individuals and nonprofit institutions, and purchases abroad of goods and services by U.S. residents traveling or working in foreign countries. PCE also includes purchases for certain goods and services provided by the government, primarily tuition payments for higher education, charges for medical care, and charges for water and sanitary services. Finally, PCE includes imputed purchases that keep PCE invariant to changes in the way that certain activities are carried out. For example, to take account of the value of the services provided by owner-occupied housing, PCE includes an imputation equal to the estimated rent homeowners would pay if they rented their houses from themselves. (Actual purchases of residential structures by individuals are classified as gross private domestic investment.)

Tables 4-3 and 4-4 present personal consumption expenditures classified by major type of product: *durable goods*, *nondurable goods*, and *services*. Each of these three major categories is then subdivided according to major type of expenditure. In general, *durable goods* are commodities that can be stored or inventoried and that have an average life of at least three years. *Nondurable goods* are all other commodities that can be stored or inventoried.

This classification system can be misleading with respect to the objective of spending. For example, the *medical care* component of services does not include drugs and medicines, which are included in nondurable goods. For a more precise classification of consumption spending by objective, available only on an annual basis, see Table 4-5 and its description below.

Revisions

Data in this book reflect the 2003 comprehensive revisions to the NIPAs and all further revisions available through August 2004.

See the Notes and Definitions to Chapter 1 for an explanation of a new revision schedule for wages and salaries and related components of the income side of the NIPAs. This will mean revisions once a quarter of as many as seven months of previous data, affecting incomes and saving but not PCE or other components of GDP.

An important conceptual change was made in the 1999 comprehensive revision of the NIPAs affecting the concepts of personal income and saving, in that the retirement plans of federal, state, and local employees are now treated like private pensions; formerly they were treated as government social insurance programs. The most significant differences are that employer contributions to, and the dividends and interest received by, these retirement funds are now treated as a component of personal income; but benefits paid by the plans are treated as transactions within the personal sector rather than transfer payments. In other words, this conceptual revision raised employer contributions for employee pension and insurance funds and dividends and interest, while reducing transfer payments received and personal contributions for social insurance. The effect was to move the accumulation of assets in these pension funds from the government surplus to the personal saving sector.

Data availability

Monthly data are released monthly in a BEA press release, normally the first business day following the monthly release of the latest national income and product account (NIPA) estimates. Monthly and quarterly data are subsequently published each month in the *Survey of Current Business*. Current and historical data are available on the BEA Internet site at <http://www.bea.gov>, and may also be obtained from the STAT-USA subscription Internet site at <http://www.stat-usa.gov>.

References

The latest revision is presented and described in an article on the National Income and Product Accounts in the August 2004 *Survey of Current Business*. A discussion of monthly estimates of personal income and its disposition appears in the November 1979 *Survey of Current Business*. A more detailed description of concepts, sources, and methods used in estimating personal consumption expenditures appears in *Personal Consumption Expenditures* (NIPA Methodology Paper No. 6, 1990), available on the BEA Internet site from the National Technical Information Service (NTIS Accession No. PB 90-254244). Additional and more recent information can be found in the articles listed in the Notes and Definitions for Tables 1-1 through 1-10.

TABLE 4-5
PERSONAL CONSUMPTION EXPENDITURES BY TYPE OF EXPENDITURE

SOURCE: BUREAU OF ECONOMIC ANALYSIS

In this table, also derived from the NIPA accounts, annual estimates of the current-dollar value of PCE are presented by "type of expenditure" instead of "by type of product," the latter of which is the classification scheme used in Tables 4-3 and 4-4. The "type of expenditure" tabulations provide a more precise delineation of consumer spending by its ultimate objective, and cut across the categories of durable goods, nondurable goods, and services that are used in the quarterly estimates. The definitions of the expenditure types given below explain the relationship of each to the categories used in the "type of product" tables.

Definitions

Food and tobacco includes food, beverages including alcoholic, and tobacco products whether purchased for home consumption or on the premises of eating and drinking places. All the components are included in nondurable goods in the "major type of product" classification system.

Clothing, accessories, and jewelry includes clothing and shoes from the nondurable goods category, jewelry and watches from durables, and cleaning, storage, and repair of clothing and shoes from services.

Personal care includes toilet articles and preparations from nondurable goods and barbershops, beauty parlors, and health clubs from services.

Housing includes rents paid for rental housing, imputed rent of owner-occupied dwellings, and rent of hotels, motels, clubs, schools, and other group housing, all from the services group.

Household operation includes furniture, appliances, and other durable household goods from durable goods; "semidurable" furnishings (such as textile goods), household supplies, and stationery from nondurable goods; and utilities, communications, domestic service, maintenance, insurance, and miscellaneous services.

Medical care includes drug preparations and sundries from nondurable goods, ophthalmic and orthopedic products from durable goods, and the services of medical professionals, hospitals, nursing homes, and health insurance.

Personal business includes financial, legal, funeral, and miscellaneous services.

Transportation includes purchase of motor vehicles and parts from the durable goods category; gasoline and oil from nondurables; and tolls, insurance, transit, taxis, rail, bus, airline, and other transportation services.

Recreation includes books, "wheel goods" (other than those classified in transportation), photo equipment, boats, pleasure aircraft, video, audio, musical instruments, computers, and software from durable goods; toys, sports supplies, flowers, seeds, and potted plants from nondurables; and a long list of recreational and cultural services, including gambling.

Education and research includes all education and research expenditures in the service category, including the research of nonprofit institutions.

Religious and welfare activities are all classified as services in the "major type of product" system. For nonprofits, this category equals current expenditures (including consumption of fixed capital) of religious, social welfare, foreign relief, and political organizations, museums, libraries, and foundations. The expenditures are net of receipts—such as those from meals, rooms, and entertainments—accounted for separately in consumer expenditures, and exclude relief payments within the United States and expenditures by foundations for education and research. For proprietary and government institutions, the value for this category equals receipts from users.

Foreign travel and other, net consists of foreign travel spending (services) and other expenditures abroad (nondurables) by U.S. residents *less* expenditures in the United States by nonresidents (services) and personal remittances in kind to nonresidents (nondurables). Negative figures indicate that the sum of the first two terms is less than the sum of the second two terms—in practice, that spending in the United States by foreigners exceeds spending on foreign travel by U.S. residents. Beginning with 1981, foreign travel spending by U.S. residents includes U.S. students' expenditures abroad, and expenditures in the United States by nonresidents includes nonresidents' student and medical care expenditures in the United States.

Data availability and revisions

Data are published once a year in supplemental NIPA tables in the *Survey of Current Business*, most recently in September 2003, reflecting the most recent NIPA revisions. They are also available on the BEA Web site referenced above.

CHAPTER 5: SAVING AND INVESTMENT; BUSINESS SALES AND INVENTORIES

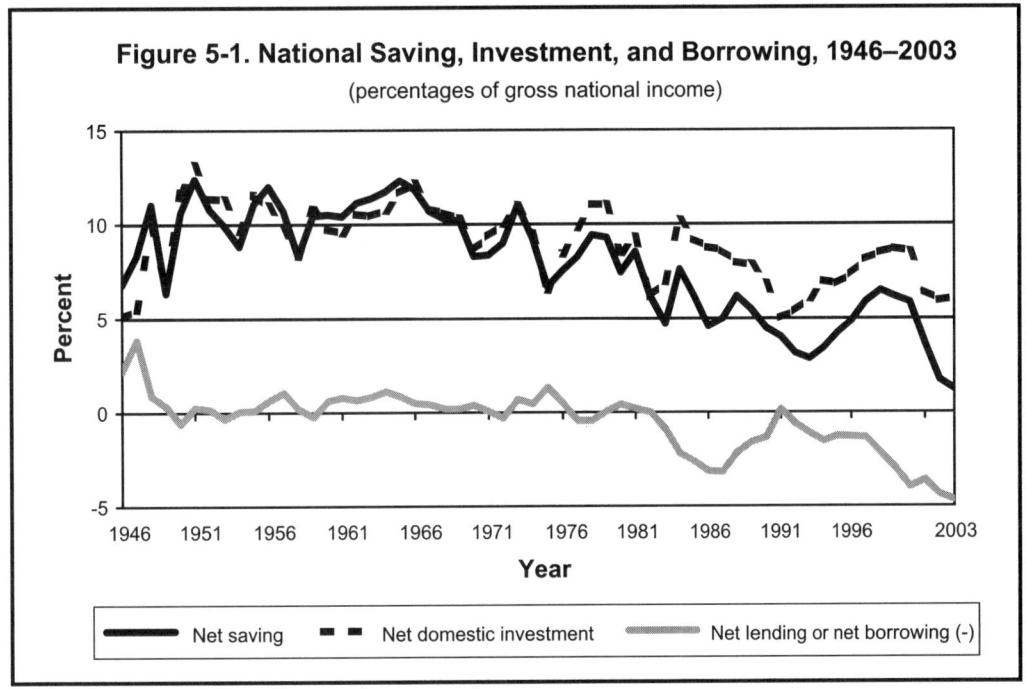

- The current-dollar amount of net saving in the U.S. economy (excluding allowances for capital consumption) fell to 1.2 percent of gross national income (GNI) in 2003—a postwar record low, and the lowest national saving rate since 1934. In 2000, the national net saving rate was 5.8 percent, which was already significantly lower than between the end of the war and the early 1970s. Since 2000, the federal budget position has swung from saving into borrowing by more than half a trillion dollars, and personal saving also declined, partly offset by an increase in retained corporate profits. (Tables 1-9 and 5-1)
- Net investment (gross investment minus depreciation) declined less than net saving between 2000 and 2003, financed by an increase in borrowing overseas (a larger negative entry on the graph above) from 4.0 percent to 4.7 percent of GNI. (Tables 1-9 and 5-1)
- In terms of physical quantities, total fixed investment rose 741 percent from 1948 to 2000, for an annual growth rate of 4.2 percent. Nonresidential investment rose 1,057 percent, with structures increasing 292 percent and total equipment and software up 1,780 percent. Residential investment rose 291 percent. (Table 5-4)
- The current-dollar value of the net stock of fixed assets was 2.76 times the value of GDP in 2000, little changed from 2.80 in 1948. A rise in the private stock/GDP ratio was more than offset by a decline in the ratio of government stock to GDP. (Table 5-5)

Table 5-1. Saving and Investment

(Billions of dollars, except as noted; quarterly data are at seasonally adjusted annual rates.)

NIPA Tables 1.7.5, 5.1

Year and quarter	Gross saving												
		Net saving						Consumption of fixed capital					
			Private			Government			Private			Government	
	Total	Total	Total	Personal saving	Undistributed corporate profits with IVA and CCAdj	Federal	State and local	Total	Total	Domestic business	Households and institutions	Federal	State and local
1946	38.4	15.1	18.6	15.5	3.2	-5.0	1.5	23.3	12.5	10.5	1.9	9.3	1.5
1947	46.6	20.2	13.5	7.4	6.1	5.3	1.4	26.4	15.7	13.2	2.5	8.8	1.8
1948	58.0	29.9	25.1	13.4	11.7	3.6	1.2	28.1	18.4	15.5	2.9	7.6	2.1
1949	45.6	16.9	21.1	9.5	11.6	-5.7	1.5	28.7	20.0	16.9	3.1	6.6	2.1
1950	60.6	31.2	24.4	15.1	9.3	5.5	1.3	29.4	21.5	18.1	3.3	5.8	2.1
1951	75.0	41.8	29.6	19.5	10.1	9.6	2.6	33.2	24.6	20.7	3.8	6.1	2.6
1952	74.2	38.5	31.8	20.5	11.3	3.7	3.0	35.7	26.1	21.9	4.2	6.8	2.7
1953	75.1	37.4	32.1	21.5	10.6	1.8	3.5	37.8	27.3	22.9	4.4	7.6	2.8
1954	73.4	33.5	31.9	20.0	11.9	-1.6	3.2	39.9	28.7	24.1	4.7	8.3	2.9
1955	88.0	45.9	36.7	19.7	17.0	5.7	3.5	42.1	30.3	25.3	5.0	8.7	3.1
1956	99.4	53.0	41.0	25.8	15.3	7.6	4.4	46.4	33.6	28.1	5.5	9.3	3.5
1957	99.6	49.7	42.2	27.0	15.2	3.3	4.2	49.9	36.3	30.4	5.8	9.8	3.9
1958	90.8	38.8	41.3	28.3	13.0	-5.4	2.9	52.0	38.1	32.1	6.1	9.9	4.0
1959	106.2	53.2	46.0	26.7	19.4	3.3	3.8	53.0	38.6	32.2	6.4	10.2	4.2
1960	111.3	55.8	44.3	26.7	17.6	7.2	4.3	55.6	40.5	33.9	6.7	10.6	4.4
1961	114.3	57.1	50.2	32.2	18.1	2.6	4.3	57.2	41.6	34.7	6.9	10.9	4.7
1962	124.9	65.7	57.9	33.8	24.1	2.5	5.2	59.3	42.8	35.6	7.2	11.5	5.0
1963	133.2	70.8	59.7	33.3	26.4	5.4	5.7	62.4	44.9	37.5	7.5	12.1	5.4
1964	143.4	78.4	71.0	40.8	30.1	1.0	6.4	65.0	46.9	39.0	7.9	12.3	5.7
1965	158.5	89.1	79.2	43.0	36.2	3.3	6.5	69.4	50.5	41.9	8.5	12.7	6.2
1966	168.7	93.1	83.1	44.4	38.7	2.3	7.8	75.6	55.5	46.3	9.2	13.2	6.9
1967	170.5	89.0	91.4	54.4	36.9	-9.4	7.0	81.5	59.9	50.0	9.9	14.0	7.5
1968	182.0	93.6	88.4	52.8	35.6	-2.3	7.5	88.4	65.2	54.4	10.8	14.8	8.3
1969	198.3	100.4	83.7	52.5	31.2	8.7	8.0	97.9	73.1	61.2	12.0	15.5	9.3
1970	192.7	86.0	94.0	69.5	24.6	-15.2	7.1	106.7	80.0	67.2	12.9	16.1	10.6
1971	208.9	93.9	115.8	80.6	34.8	-28.4	6.5	115.0	86.7	72.5	14.2	16.5	11.8
1972	237.5	111.0	119.8	77.2	42.9	-24.4	15.6	126.5	97.1	80.9	16.2	16.6	12.8
1973	292.0	152.7	148.3	102.7	45.6	-11.3	15.7	139.3	107.9	89.9	18.0	17.1	14.3
1974	301.5	139.0	143.4	113.6	29.8	-13.8	9.3	162.5	126.6	105.9	20.7	18.2	17.7
1975	297.0	109.2	175.8	125.6	50.2	-69.0	2.5	187.7	147.8	124.4	23.4	19.7	20.2
1976	342.1	137.0	181.3	122.3	59.0	-51.7	7.4	205.2	162.5	136.9	25.6	21.4	21.3
1977	397.5	167.5	198.5	125.3	73.2	-44.1	13.1	230.0	184.3	155.3	29.0	23.1	22.6
1978	478.0	215.7	223.5	142.5	81.0	-26.5	18.7	262.3	212.8	179.3	33.6	25.0	24.5
1979	536.7	236.6	234.9	159.1	75.7	-11.3	13.0	300.1	245.7	206.9	38.8	27.0	27.5
1980	549.4	206.5	251.3	201.4	49.9	-53.6	8.8	343.0	281.1	236.8	44.3	30.1	31.8
1981	654.7	266.6	312.3	244.3	68.0	-53.3	7.6	388.1	317.9	268.9	49.0	33.8	36.3
1982	629.1	202.2	336.2	270.8	65.4	-131.9	-2.2	426.9	349.8	297.3	52.5	37.6	39.5
1983	609.4	165.6	333.7	233.6	100.1	-173.0	4.9	443.8	362.1	307.4	54.7	40.8	40.9
1984	773.4	300.9	445.0	314.8	130.3	-168.1	23.9	472.6	385.6	328.0	57.6	44.6	42.3
1985	767.5	260.7	413.4	280.0	133.4	-175.0	22.3	506.7	414.0	353.0	61.0	48.1	44.6
1986	733.5	202.2	372.0	268.4	103.7	-190.8	21.0	531.3	431.8	366.9	64.9	51.6	47.9
1987	796.8	234.9	367.4	241.4	126.1	-145.0	12.4	561.9	455.3	385.7	69.5	55.2	51.4
1988	915.0	317.4	434.0	272.9	161.1	-134.5	17.9	597.6	483.5	408.9	74.6	59.3	54.8
1989	944.7	300.4	409.7	287.1	122.6	-130.1	20.8	644.3	522.1	440.6	81.5	63.5	58.7
1990	940.4	258.0	422.7	299.4	123.3	-172.0	7.2	682.5	551.6	466.4	85.1	67.9	63.0
1991	964.1	238.2	456.1	324.2	131.9	-213.7	-4.2	725.9	586.9	497.4	89.5	72.2	66.9
1992	948.2	196.3	493.0	366.0	142.7	-297.4	0.7	751.9	607.3	510.5	96.8	74.7	69.9
1993	962.4	186.0	458.6	284.0	168.1	-273.5	0.9	776.4	624.7	524.6	100.1	77.9	73.8
1994	1 070.7	237.1	438.9	249.5	171.8	-212.3	10.5	833.7	675.1	568.0	107.1	80.2	78.5
1995	1 184.5	306.2	491.1	250.9	223.8	-197.0	12.0	878.4	713.4	600.2	113.2	81.9	83.1
1996	1 291.1	373.0	489.0	228.4	256.9	-141.6	25.8	918.1	748.8	630.7	118.2	82.0	87.2
1997	1 461.1	486.6	503.3	218.3	287.9	-55.8	39.1	974.4	800.3	675.2	125.1	82.5	91.6
1998	1 598.7	568.6	477.8	276.8	201.7	38.8	52.0	1 030.2	851.2	718.3	132.9	82.8	96.2
1999	1 674.3	573.0	419.0	158.6	255.3	103.6	50.4	1 101.3	914.3	769.8	144.5	84.8	102.1
2000	1 770.5	582.7	343.3	168.5	174.8	189.5	50.0	1 187.8	990.8	836.1	154.8	87.2	109.8
2001	1 657.6	376.1	324.6	132.3	192.3	46.7	4.8	1 281.5	1 075.5	903.7	171.7	88.2	117.8
2002	1 484.3	180.3	459.8	159.2	300.7	-254.5	-25.0	1 303.9	1 092.8	912.6	180.2	89.0	122.1
2003	1 487.7	133.8	501.5	110.6	390.9	-364.5	-3.2	1 353.9	1 135.9	942.6	193.3	90.2	127.9
2001													
1st quarter	1 745.3	504.8	315.7	138.6	177.0	156.6	32.5	1 240.5	1 038.4	873.6	164.8	87.9	114.2
2nd quarter	1 704.0	433.2	283.8	88.7	195.1	123.6	25.8	1 270.8	1 067.0	890.7	176.3	88.3	115.6
3rd quarter	1 647.9	315.2	412.4	261.6	150.9	-88.6	-8.6	1 332.7	1 121.3	949.8	171.5	88.4	122.9
4th quarter	1 533.1	251.2	286.5	40.5	246.1	-4.7	-30.6	1 281.8	1 075.2	900.8	174.4	88.2	118.4
2002													
1st quarter	1 549.7	262.6	499.9	209.3	290.6	-208.5	-28.8	1 287.1	1 078.5	902.6	175.8	88.7	120.0
2nd quarter	1 528.5	230.6	505.8	210.0	295.8	-251.6	-23.6	1 297.9	1 087.7	909.0	178.6	88.8	121.5
3rd quarter	1 451.5	142.2	418.7	126.1	292.6	-255.1	-21.3	1 309.3	1 097.4	915.8	181.6	89.0	122.9
4th quarter	1 407.4	85.9	414.9	91.2	323.7	-302.7	-26.3	1 321.5	1 107.6	923.0	184.7	89.7	124.2
2003													
1st quarter	1 375.0	41.0	371.6	79.5	292.0	-281.6	-49.0	1 334.0	1 118.4	930.5	187.9	89.7	126.0
2nd quarter	1 436.0	89.0	459.1	92.1	367.0	-364.3	-5.7	1 347.0	1 129.7	938.3	191.4	90.0	127.3
3rd quarter	1 518.1	157.5	584.0	159.8	424.2	-433.0	6.5	1 360.6	1 141.5	946.5	195.0	90.5	128.5
4th quarter	1 621.7	247.6	591.5	111.1	480.4	-379.2	35.3	1 374.2	1 153.8	955.0	198.8	90.7	129.7

Table 5-1. Saving and Investment—Continued

(Billions of dollars, except as noted; quarterly data are at seasonally adjusted annual rates.)

NIPA Tables 1.7.5, 5.1

Year and quarter	Gross domestic investment, capital account transactions, and net lending, NIPAs							Net domestic investment	Gross national income	Gross saving as a percentage of gross national income	Net saving as a percentage of gross national income
	Total	Gross domestic investment			Capital account transactions (net)	Net lending or net borrowing (-), NIPAs	Statistical discrepancy				
		Total	Private	Government							
1946	39.6	34.6	31.1	3.5	...	4.9	1.2	11.3	221.8	17.3	6.8
1947	48.8	39.6	35.0	4.6	...	9.3	2.3	13.2	243.0	19.2	8.3
1948	57.5	55.1	48.1	7.0	...	2.4	-0.5	27.0	271.1	21.4	11.0
1949	47.4	46.6	36.9	9.7	...	0.9	1.8	17.9	266.7	17.1	6.3
1950	62.0	63.9	54.1	9.8	...	-1.8	1.4	34.4	293.8	20.6	10.6
1951	78.7	77.8	60.2	17.6	...	0.9	3.6	44.5	337.6	22.2	12.4
1952	77.0	76.3	54.0	22.3	...	0.6	2.8	40.6	357.5	20.7	10.8
1953	79.2	80.4	56.4	24.0	...	-1.3	4.0	42.7	377.2	19.9	9.9
1954	76.6	76.3	53.8	22.5	...	0.2	3.2	36.4	379.3	19.3	8.8
1955	90.5	90.0	69.0	21.0	...	0.4	2.5	47.9	414.8	21.2	11.1
1956	97.7	94.9	72.0	22.9	...	2.8	-1.7	48.5	441.9	22.5	12.0
1957	99.6	94.8	70.5	24.4	...	4.8	0.0	45.0	464.1	21.5	10.7
1958	91.9	91.0	64.5	26.5	...	0.9	1.0	38.9	468.8	19.4	8.3
1959	106.7	107.8	78.5	29.3	...	-1.2	0.5	54.8	508.9	20.9	10.4
1960	110.4	107.2	78.9	28.3	...	3.2	-0.9	51.6	530.4	21.0	10.5
1961	113.8	109.5	78.2	31.3	...	4.3	-0.6	52.3	548.8	20.8	10.4
1962	125.3	121.4	88.1	33.3	...	3.9	0.4	62.2	589.4	21.2	11.1
1963	132.4	127.4	93.8	33.6	...	5.0	-0.8	65.0	623.0	21.4	11.4
1964	144.2	136.7	102.1	34.6	...	7.5	0.8	71.7	667.7	21.5	11.7
1965	160.0	153.8	118.2	35.6	...	6.2	1.6	84.4	722.8	21.9	12.3
1966	175.0	171.1	131.3	39.8	...	3.9	6.3	95.5	786.6	21.4	11.8
1967	175.1	171.6	128.6	43.0	...	3.6	4.6	90.1	833.4	20.5	10.7
1968	186.6	184.8	141.2	43.6	...	1.7	4.6	96.5	911.5	20.0	10.3
1969	201.5	199.7	156.4	43.3	...	1.8	3.2	101.8	987.6	20.1	10.2
1970	200.0	196.0	152.4	43.6	...	4.0	7.3	89.3	1 037.6	18.6	8.3
1971	220.5	219.9	178.2	41.8	...	0.6	11.6	104.9	1 123.1	18.6	8.4
1972	246.6	250.2	207.6	42.6	...	-3.6	9.1	123.7	1 237.7	19.2	9.0
1973	300.7	291.3	244.5	46.8	...	9.3	8.6	152.1	1 386.7	21.1	11.0
1974	312.3	305.7	249.4	56.3	...	6.6	10.9	143.2	1 504.6	20.0	9.2
1975	314.7	293.3	230.2	63.1	...	21.4	17.7	105.6	1 633.6	18.2	6.7
1976	367.2	358.4	292.0	66.4	...	8.9	25.1	153.2	1 817.0	18.8	7.5
1977	419.8	428.8	361.3	67.5	...	-9.0	22.3	198.8	2 028.9	19.6	8.3
1978	504.6	515.0	438.0	77.1	...	-10.4	26.6	252.7	2 289.7	20.9	9.4
1979	582.8	581.4	492.9	88.5	...	1.4	46.0	281.2	2 549.2	21.1	9.3
1980	590.9	579.5	479.3	100.3	...	11.4	41.4	236.6	2 782.3	19.7	7.4
1981	685.6	679.3	572.4	106.9	...	6.3	30.9	291.2	3 130.4	20.9	8.5
1982	629.4	629.5	517.2	112.3	-0.2	0.0	0.3	202.6	3 291.2	19.1	6.1
1983	655.1	687.2	564.3	122.9	-0.2	-31.8	45.7	243.4	3 528.0	17.3	4.7
1984	788.0	875.0	735.6	139.4	-0.2	-86.7	14.6	402.4	3 954.9	19.6	7.6
1985	784.1	895.0	736.2	158.8	-0.3	-110.5	16.7	388.3	4 230.1	18.1	6.2
1986	780.5	919.7	746.5	173.2	-0.3	-138.9	47.0	388.4	4 433.6	16.5	4.6
1987	818.5	969.2	785.0	184.3	-0.4	-150.4	21.7	407.3	4 735.7	16.8	5.0
1988	895.5	1 007.7	821.6	186.1	-0.5	-111.7	-19.5	410.1	5 147.0	17.8	6.2
1989	984.3	1 072.6	874.9	197.7	-0.3	-88.0	39.7	428.4	5 470.9	17.3	5.5
1990	1 006.7	1 076.7	861.0	215.7	6.6	-76.6	66.2	394.2	5 771.6	16.3	4.5
1991	1 036.6	1 023.2	802.9	220.3	4.5	9.0	72.5	297.3	5 953.8	16.2	4.0
1992	1 051.0	1 087.9	864.8	223.1	0.6	-37.5	102.7	336.0	6 264.7	15.1	3.1
1993	1 102.0	1 172.4	953.4	219.0	1.3	-71.7	139.5	395.9	6 549.8	14.7	2.8
1994	1 213.2	1 318.4	1 097.1	221.4	1.7	-106.9	142.5	484.7	6 955.9	15.4	3.4
1995	1 285.7	1 376.7	1 144.0	232.7	0.9	-91.9	101.2	498.4	7 332.3	16.2	4.2
1996	1 384.8	1 485.2	1 240.3	244.9	0.7	-101.0	93.7	567.1	7 758.2	16.6	4.8
1997	1 531.7	1 641.9	1 389.8	252.2	1.0	-111.3	70.7	667.5	8 266.6	17.7	5.9
1998	1 584.1	1 771.5	1 509.1	262.4	0.7	-188.1	-14.6	741.3	8 783.0	18.2	6.5
1999	1 638.5	1 912.4	1 625.7	286.8	4.8	-278.7	-35.7	811.2	9 337.9	17.9	6.1
2000	1 643.3	2 040.0	1 735.5	304.5	0.8	-397.4	-127.2	852.1	9 983.1	17.7	5.8
2001	1 567.9	1 938.3	1 614.3	324.0	1.1	-371.5	-89.6	656.9	10 261.3	16.2	3.7
2002	1 468.9	1 926.6	1 579.2	347.4	1.3	-458.9	-15.3	622.7	10 529.4	14.1	1.7
2003	1 513.3	2 024.2	1 665.8	358.5	3.1	-514.0	25.6	670.3	11 033.6	13.5	1.2
2001											
1st quarter	1 577.5	1 988.5	1 675.3	313.2	1.1	-412.0	-167.8	748.0	10 228.0	17.1	4.9
2nd quarter	1 605.2	1 981.6	1 647.7	333.9	1.0	-377.4	-98.8	710.7	10 272.3	16.6	4.2
3rd quarter	1 576.8	1 929.3	1 613.0	316.3	1.2	-353.7	-71.1	596.6	10 223.0	16.1	3.1
4th quarter	1 512.2	1 854.0	1 521.4	332.7	1.0	-342.9	-20.9	572.2	10 321.8	14.9	2.4
2002											
1st quarter	1 487.9	1 910.8	1 568.5	342.3	1.1	-424.1	-61.8	623.7	10 423.5	14.9	2.5
2nd quarter	1 469.8	1 924.1	1 577.0	347.1	1.1	-455.3	-58.7	626.1	10 520.3	14.5	2.2
3rd quarter	1 472.3	1 932.4	1 581.3	351.1	1.4	-461.6	20.8	623.1	10 550.9	13.8	1.3
4th quarter	1 445.8	1 939.2	1 589.9	349.2	1.4	-494.7	38.4	617.7	10 622.7	13.2	0.8
2003											
1st quarter	1 414.7	1 948.9	1 596.6	352.3	1.6	-535.9	39.6	614.9	10 741.7	12.8	0.4
2nd quarter	1 449.3	1 967.4	1 611.1	356.7	6.2	-524.8	13.2	620.8	10 915.8	13.2	0.8
3rd quarter	1 554.7	2 059.0	1 696.6	362.4	3.3	-507.5	36.6	698.4	11 131.7	13.6	1.4
4th quarter	1 634.6	2 121.2	1 758.8	362.4	1.2	-487.8	12.8	747.0	11 345.2	14.3	2.2

. . . = Not available.

Table 5-2. Gross Private Fixed Investment by Type

(Billions of dollars, quarterly data are at seasonally adjusted annual rates.)

NIPA Table 5.3.5

Year and quarter	Total gross private fixed investment	Nonresidential									
		Total	Structures						Equipment and software		
			Total	Commercial and health care	Manufacturing	Power and communication	Mining exploration, shafts, and wells	Other nonresidential structures	Total	Information processing equipment and software	
										Total	Computers and peripheral equipment
1947	35.5	23.5	8.1	1.1	1.7	1.8	0.9	2.6	15.3	1.7	...
1948	42.4	26.8	9.5	1.5	1.4	2.4	1.2	2.9	17.3	1.8	...
1949	39.6	24.9	9.2	1.4	1.0	2.7	1.2	2.9	15.7	1.6	...
1950	48.3	27.8	10.0	1.8	1.1	2.8	1.4	2.9	17.8	1.8	...
1951	50.3	31.8	12.0	1.9	2.1	3.0	1.7	3.2	19.9	2.1	...
1952	50.5	31.9	12.2	1.6	2.3	3.1	2.0	3.3	19.7	2.4	...
1953	54.5	35.1	13.6	2.1	2.2	3.6	2.1	3.5	21.5	2.7	...
1954	55.8	34.7	13.9	2.6	2.0	3.3	2.3	3.6	20.8	2.4	...
1955	64.0	39.0	15.2	3.4	2.3	3.3	2.5	3.7	23.9	2.8	...
1956	68.1	44.5	18.2	4.2	3.2	4.1	2.7	4.0	26.3	3.4	...
1957	69.7	47.5	19.0	4.1	3.6	4.5	2.6	4.1	28.6	4.0	...
1958	64.9	42.5	17.6	4.2	2.4	4.4	2.4	4.2	24.9	3.6	...
1959	74.6	46.5	18.1	4.6	2.1	4.3	2.5	4.7	28.4	4.0	0.0
1960	75.7	49.4	19.6	4.8	2.9	4.4	2.3	5.2	29.8	4.9	0.2
1961	75.2	48.8	19.7	5.5	2.8	4.1	2.3	5.0	29.1	5.3	0.3
1962	82.0	53.1	20.8	6.2	2.8	4.1	2.5	5.2	32.3	5.7	0.3
1963	88.1	56.0	21.2	6.1	2.9	4.4	2.3	5.6	34.8	6.5	0.7
1964	97.2	63.0	23.7	6.8	3.6	4.8	2.4	6.2	39.2	7.4	0.9
1965	109.0	74.8	28.3	8.2	5.1	5.4	2.4	7.2	46.5	8.5	1.2
1966	117.7	85.4	31.3	8.3	6.6	6.3	2.5	7.8	54.0	10.7	1.7
1967	118.7	86.4	31.5	8.2	6.0	7.1	2.4	7.8	54.9	11.3	1.9
1968	132.1	93.4	33.6	9.4	6.0	8.3	2.6	7.3	59.9	11.9	1.9
1969	147.3	104.7	37.7	11.7	6.8	8.7	2.8	7.8	67.0	14.6	2.4
1970	150.4	109.0	40.3	12.5	7.0	10.2	2.8	7.8	68.7	16.6	2.7
1971	169.9	114.1	42.7	14.9	6.3	11.0	2.7	7.9	71.5	17.3	2.8
1972	198.5	128.8	47.2	17.6	5.9	12.1	3.1	8.6	81.7	19.5	3.5
1973	228.6	153.3	55.0	19.8	7.9	13.8	3.5	9.9	98.3	23.1	3.5
1974	235.4	169.5	61.2	20.6	10.0	15.1	5.2	10.3	108.2	27.0	3.9
1975	236.5	173.7	61.4	17.7	10.6	15.7	7.4	10.1	112.4	28.5	3.6
1976	274.8	192.4	65.9	18.1	10.1	18.2	8.6	11.0	126.4	32.7	4.4
1977	339.0	228.7	74.6	20.3	11.1	19.3	11.5	12.5	154.1	39.2	5.7
1978	412.2	280.6	93.6	25.3	16.2	21.4	15.4	15.2	187.0	48.7	7.6
1979	474.9	333.9	117.7	33.5	22.0	24.6	19.0	18.5	216.2	58.5	10.2
1980	485.6	362.4	136.2	41.0	20.5	27.3	27.4	20.0	226.2	68.8	12.5
1981	542.6	420.0	167.3	48.3	25.4	30.0	42.5	21.2	252.7	81.5	17.1
1982	532.1	426.5	177.6	55.8	26.1	29.6	44.8	21.3	248.9	88.3	18.9
1983	570.1	417.2	154.3	55.8	19.5	25.8	30.0	23.3	262.9	100.1	23.9
1984	670.2	489.6	177.4	70.6	20.9	26.5	31.3	28.1	312.2	121.5	31.6
1985	714.4	526.2	194.5	84.1	24.1	26.5	27.9	31.8	331.7	130.3	33.7
1986	739.9	519.8	176.5	80.9	21.0	28.3	15.7	30.7	343.3	136.8	33.4
1987	757.8	524.1	174.2	80.8	21.2	25.4	13.1	33.7	349.9	141.2	35.8
1988	803.1	563.8	182.8	86.3	23.2	25.0	15.7	32.5	381.0	154.9	38.0
1989	847.3	607.7	193.7	88.3	28.8	27.5	14.9	34.3	414.0	172.6	43.1
1990	846.4	622.4	202.9	87.5	33.6	26.3	17.9	37.6	419.5	177.2	38.6
1991	803.3	598.2	183.6	68.9	31.4	31.6	18.5	33.2	414.6	182.9	37.7
1992	848.5	612.1	172.6	64.5	29.0	33.9	14.2	31.0	439.6	199.9	44.0
1993	932.5	666.6	177.2	69.4	23.6	33.2	16.6	34.5	489.4	217.6	47.9
1994	1 033.3	731.4	186.8	75.4	28.9	31.2	16.4	34.9	544.6	235.2	52.4
1995	1 112.9	810.0	207.3	83.1	35.5	33.1	15.0	40.6	602.8	263.0	66.1
1996	1 209.5	875.4	224.6	91.5	38.2	29.2	16.8	49.0	650.8	290.1	72.8
1997	1 317.8	968.7	250.3	104.3	37.6	28.8	22.4	57.3	718.3	330.3	81.4
1998	1 438.4	1 052.6	275.2	115.4	40.5	33.6	23.4	62.3	777.3	363.4	87.2
1999	1 558.8	1 133.9	282.2	124.3	32.6	39.5	20.6	65.2	851.7	411.0	96.0
2000	1 679.0	1 232.1	313.2	137.6	31.8	46.8	27.2	69.9	918.9	467.6	101.4
2001	1 646.1	1 176.8	322.6	134.9	29.5	49.6	39.2	69.4	854.2	437.0	85.4
2002	1 568.0	1 063.9	271.6	116.7	16.4	49.1	29.3	60.0	792.4	400.5	81.4
2003	1 667.0	1 094.7	261.6	111.6	14.2	40.3	35.6	59.9	833.1	431.2	95.3
2001											
1st quarter	1 685.2	1 229.6	323.9	143.8	33.1	44.8	35.8	66.3	905.7	470.8	97.3
2nd quarter	1 654.7	1 187.1	325.7	139.4	31.1	48.7	39.8	66.7	861.4	442.8	88.3
3rd quarter	1 644.8	1 167.2	335.8	131.5	30.1	50.8	43.5	79.9	831.4	422.0	77.5
4th quarter	1 599.6	1 123.2	305.2	125.0	23.8	54.1	37.6	64.7	818.1	412.5	78.4
2002											
1st quarter	1 577.4	1 091.4	290.0	121.6	18.9	56.2	31.7	61.6	801.4	401.7	80.5
2nd quarter	1 563.0	1 061.2	273.4	118.0	16.9	49.5	27.5	61.5	787.8	398.2	79.5
3rd quarter	1 562.2	1 055.0	262.7	114.6	15.0	45.3	29.2	58.7	792.3	404.9	83.1
4th quarter	1 569.5	1 048.1	260.1	112.7	14.8	45.5	28.8	58.3	788.0	397.2	82.6
2003											
1st quarter	1 586.0	1 046.4	253.6	110.4	13.8	41.9	30.4	57.2	792.8	407.9	85.6
2nd quarter	1 626.4	1 072.7	262.3	112.0	14.5	38.9	35.5	61.3	810.4	419.3	91.5
3rd quarter	1 700.2	1 113.3	262.3	112.3	14.3	37.5	38.1	60.1	851.1	442.8	99.7
4th quarter	1 755.2	1 146.3	268.2	111.5	14.3	43.1	38.3	60.9	878.1	454.7	104.5

. . . = Not available.

Table 5-2. Gross Private Fixed Investment by Type—Continued

(Billions of dollars, quarterly data are at seasonally adjusted annual rates.)

NIPA Table 5.3.5

Year and quarter	Nonresidential—Continued					Residential						
	Equipment and software—Continued						Residential structures					
	Information processing equipment and software—Continued		Industrial equipment	Transportation equipment	Other nonresidential equipment	Total	Total	Permanent site			Other residential structures	Residential equipment
	Software[1]	Other information processing						Total	Single family	Multifamily		
1947	...	1.7	4.6	4.9	4.1	12.1	11.8	8.3	...	...	3.5	0.3
1948	...	1.8	4.6	5.5	5.4	15.6	15.3	11.2	...	...	4.2	0.3
1949	...	1.6	3.7	5.7	4.7	14.6	14.3	10.7	...	...	3.7	0.3
1950	...	1.8	4.5	6.4	5.1	20.5	20.2	16.1	...	...	4.0	0.4
1951	...	2.1	5.7	6.6	5.5	18.4	18.1	13.8	...	...	4.3	0.4
1952	...	2.4	5.9	5.7	5.6	18.6	18.2	13.4	...	...	4.9	0.4
1953	...	2.7	6.7	6.6	5.6	19.4	19.0	13.9	...	...	5.1	0.4
1954	...	2.4	7.1	6.0	5.3	21.1	20.7	15.4	...	...	5.3	0.4
1955	...	2.8	7.3	7.5	6.3	25.0	24.6	18.6	...	...	6.0	0.4
1956	...	3.4	8.8	7.4	6.7	23.6	23.1	16.5	...	...	6.6	0.5
1957	...	4.0	9.6	8.3	6.7	22.2	21.7	15.1	...	...	6.6	0.5
1958	...	3.6	8.2	6.1	6.9	22.3	21.9	15.4	13.1	2.3	6.4	0.5
1959	0.0	4.0	8.5	8.3	7.6	28.1	27.5	19.7	16.7	3.0	7.9	0.6
1960	0.1	4.6	9.4	8.5	7.1	26.3	25.8	17.5	14.9	2.6	8.3	0.5
1961	0.2	4.8	8.8	8.0	7.0	26.4	25.9	17.4	14.1	3.3	8.5	0.5
1962	0.2	5.1	9.3	9.8	7.5	29.0	28.4	19.9	15.1	4.8	8.5	0.5
1963	0.4	5.4	10.0	9.4	8.8	32.1	31.5	22.4	16.0	6.4	9.1	0.6
1964	0.5	5.9	11.4	10.6	9.9	34.3	33.6	24.1	17.6	6.4	9.5	0.6
1965	0.7	6.7	13.7	13.2	11.0	34.2	33.5	23.8	17.8	6.0	9.7	0.7
1966	1.0	8.0	16.2	14.5	12.7	32.3	31.6	21.8	16.6	5.2	9.8	0.7
1967	1.2	8.2	16.9	14.3	12.4	32.4	31.6	21.5	16.8	4.7	10.1	0.7
1968	1.3	8.7	17.3	17.6	13.0	38.7	37.9	26.7	19.5	7.2	11.1	0.9
1969	1.8	10.4	19.1	18.9	14.4	42.6	41.6	29.2	19.7	9.5	12.4	1.0
1970	2.3	11.6	20.3	16.2	15.6	41.4	40.2	27.1	17.5	9.5	13.2	1.1
1971	2.4	12.2	19.5	18.4	16.3	55.8	54.5	38.7	25.8	12.9	15.8	1.3
1972	2.8	13.2	21.4	21.8	19.0	69.7	68.1	50.1	32.8	17.2	18.0	1.5
1973	3.2	16.3	26.0	26.6	22.6	75.3	73.6	54.6	35.2	19.4	19.0	1.7
1974	3.9	19.2	30.7	26.3	24.3	66.0	64.1	43.4	29.7	13.7	20.7	1.9
1975	4.8	20.2	31.3	25.2	27.4	62.7	60.8	36.3	29.6	6.7	24.5	1.9
1976	5.2	23.1	34.1	30.0	29.6	82.5	80.4	50.8	43.9	6.9	29.6	2.1
1977	5.5	28.0	39.4	39.3	36.3	110.3	107.9	72.2	62.2	10.0	35.7	2.4
1978	6.3	34.8	47.7	47.3	43.2	131.6	128.9	85.6	72.8	12.8	43.3	2.7
1979	8.1	40.2	56.2	53.6	47.9	141.0	137.8	89.3	72.3	17.0	48.6	3.2
1980	9.8	46.4	60.7	48.4	48.3	123.2	119.8	69.6	52.9	16.7	50.2	3.4
1981	11.8	52.5	65.5	50.6	55.2	122.6	118.9	69.4	52.0	17.5	49.5	3.6
1982	14.0	55.3	62.7	46.8	51.2	105.7	102.0	57.0	41.5	15.5	45.0	3.7
1983	16.4	59.8	58.9	53.5	50.4	152.9	148.6	95.0	72.5	22.4	53.7	4.2
1984	20.4	69.6	68.1	64.4	58.1	180.6	175.9	114.6	86.4	28.2	61.3	4.7
1985	23.8	72.9	72.5	69.0	59.9	188.2	183.1	115.9	87.4	28.5	67.2	5.1
1986	25.6	77.7	75.4	70.5	60.7	220.1	214.6	135.2	104.1	31.0	79.4	5.5
1987	29.0	76.4	76.7	68.1	63.9	233.7	227.9	142.7	117.2	25.5	85.2	5.8
1988	34.2	82.8	84.2	72.9	69.0	239.3	233.2	142.4	120.1	22.3	90.9	6.1
1989	41.9	87.6	93.3	67.9	80.2	239.5	233.4	143.2	120.9	22.3	90.1	6.1
1990	47.6	90.9	92.1	70.0	80.2	224.0	218.0	132.1	112.9	19.3	85.8	6.0
1991	53.7	91.5	89.3	71.5	70.8	205.1	199.4	114.6	99.4	15.1	84.8	5.7
1992	57.9	98.1	93.0	74.7	72.0	236.3	230.4	135.1	122.0	13.1	95.3	5.9
1993	64.3	105.4	102.2	89.4	80.2	266.0	259.9	150.9	140.1	10.8	109.0	6.1
1994	68.3	114.6	113.6	107.7	88.1	301.9	295.6	176.4	162.3	14.1	119.2	6.2
1995	74.6	122.3	129.0	116.1	94.7	302.8	296.5	171.4	153.5	17.9	125.1	6.3
1996	85.5	131.9	136.5	123.2	101.0	334.1	327.8	191.1	170.8	20.3	136.7	6.3
1997	107.5	141.4	140.4	135.5	112.1	349.1	342.8	198.1	175.2	22.9	144.8	6.3
1998	124.0	152.2	146.4	144.0	123.5	385.8	379.3	224.0	199.4	24.6	155.3	6.6
1999	152.6	162.4	147.0	167.6	126.0	424.9	417.8	251.3	223.8	27.4	166.6	7.0
2000	176.2	190.0	159.2	160.8	131.2	446.9	439.5	265.0	236.8	28.3	174.5	7.4
2001	174.7	177.0	146.7	141.7	128.8	469.3	461.9	279.4	249.1	30.3	182.5	7.4
2002	161.7	157.3	138.6	126.0	127.3	504.1	496.6	298.8	265.9	33.0	197.7	7.5
2003	165.8	170.0	139.8	126.6	135.5	572.3	564.3	345.9	310.6	35.3	218.4	8.0
2001												
1st quarter	182.8	190.6	160.1	142.7	132.2	455.6	448.2	270.5	241.0	29.5	177.7	7.4
2nd quarter	176.1	178.4	148.4	142.3	127.9	467.6	460.2	278.3	248.5	29.8	181.9	7.3
3rd quarter	172.1	172.4	141.6	138.2	129.6	477.6	470.2	285.5	255.1	30.4	184.7	7.3
4th quarter	167.6	166.5	136.6	143.7	125.3	476.3	468.9	283.2	251.8	31.5	185.6	7.5
2002												
1st quarter	163.3	157.9	142.5	134.3	122.9	486.0	478.5	286.1	254.0	32.2	192.3	7.5
2nd quarter	160.6	158.2	136.9	125.1	127.6	501.8	494.2	297.4	264.0	33.3	196.8	7.6
3rd quarter	163.8	158.0	137.9	120.7	128.7	507.2	499.8	301.8	268.5	33.3	198.0	7.5
4th quarter	159.3	155.3	136.9	123.9	130.1	521.4	513.8	310.0	277.0	33.0	203.8	7.5
2003												
1st quarter	161.0	161.4	139.7	116.1	129.0	539.6	532.0	327.1	292.1	35.0	204.9	7.6
2nd quarter	162.8	165.0	139.3	121.4	130.3	553.8	545.9	331.7	297.1	34.6	214.2	7.8
3rd quarter	169.1	174.0	140.8	128.8	138.7	586.9	578.7	350.7	315.0	35.7	228.0	8.2
4th quarter	170.5	179.7	139.5	140.0	144.0	609.0	600.6	374.0	338.2	35.9	226.6	8.4

[1] Excludes software "embedded," or bundled, in computers and other equipment.
... = Not available.

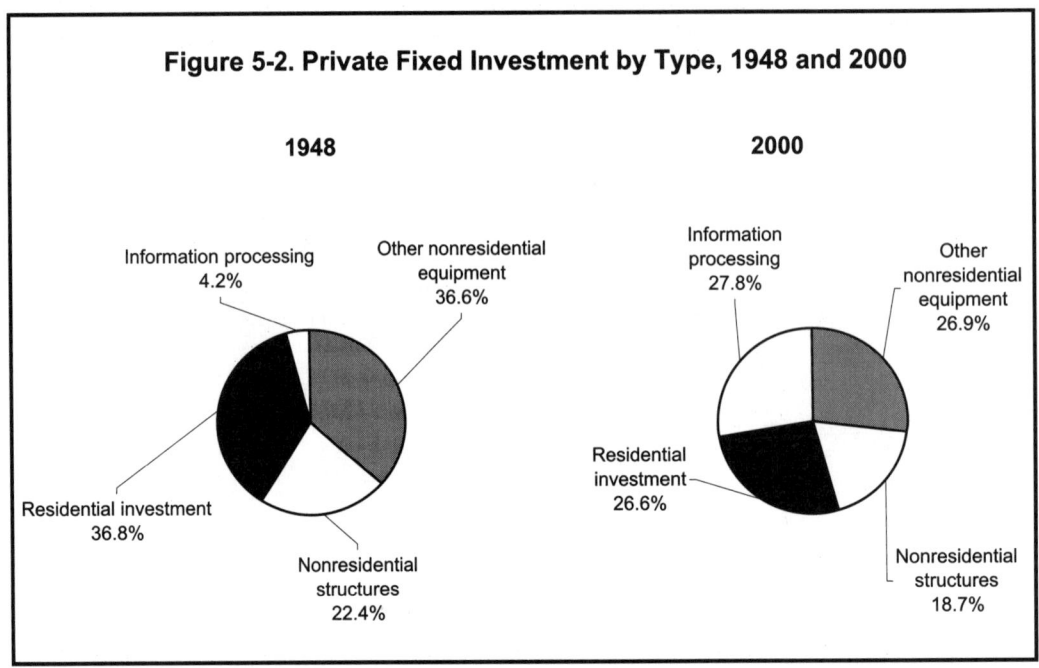

- Residential fixed investment accounted for a smaller percentage of the value of total private investment spending in 2000 than in 1948. As the graph shows, the share of nonresidential spending rose and its composition changed sharply, as investment in information processing equipment rose to over one-fourth of all private investment spending, while the shares of other kinds of equipment and of nonresidential structures declined. (Table 5-2)

Table 5-3. Real Gross Private Fixed Investment by Type

(Billions of chained [2000] dollars, quarterly data are at seasonally adjusted annual rates.)

NIPA Table 5.3.6

Year and quarter	Total gross private fixed investment	Nonresidential									
		Total	Structures						Equipment and software		
			Total	Commercial and health care	Manufac-turing	Power and communi-cation	Mining exploration, shafts, and wells	Other nonresiden-tial structures	Total	Information processing equipment and software	
										Total	Computers and peripheral equipment [1]
1990	886.6	595.1	275.2	119.6	45.4	33.4	26.6	50.4	355.0	100.7	...
1991	829.1	563.2	244.6	92.9	41.8	39.6	26.0	43.8	345.9	105.9	...
1992	878.3	581.3	229.9	86.4	38.4	42.0	21.5	40.6	371.1	122.2	...
1993	953.5	631.9	228.3	89.9	30.2	39.3	24.8	43.8	417.4	138.2	...
1994	1 042.3	689.9	232.3	94.1	35.7	35.6	23.9	42.8	467.2	155.7	...
1995	1 109.6	762.5	247.1	99.7	42.1	36.3	20.3	47.9	523.1	182.7	...
1996	1 209.2	833.6	261.1	107.4	44.2	31.3	21.5	56.4	578.7	218.9	...
1997	1 320.6	934.2	280.1	118.6	42.3	30.1	25.3	63.9	658.3	269.9	...
1998	1 455.0	1 037.8	294.5	125.4	43.7	34.7	23.3	67.4	745.6	328.9	...
1999	1 576.3	1 133.3	293.2	129.4	33.9	40.8	21.3	67.9	840.2	398.5	...
2000	1 679.0	1 232.1	313.2	137.6	31.8	46.8	27.2	69.9	918.9	467.6	...
2001	1 629.4	1 180.5	306.1	130.3	28.5	48.2	32.0	66.6	874.2	459.0	...
2002	1 548.9	1 075.6	251.6	109.8	15.4	46.7	23.6	56.4	826.5	439.6	...
2003	1 627.3	1 110.8	237.4	102.1	13.1	37.4	29.0	54.9	879.2	492.4	...
1992											
1st quarter	839.9	554.5	228.2	84.5	40.4	41.3	21.1	39.8	348.4	113.6	...
2nd quarter	873.0	576.5	228.2	85.2	38.4	41.9	20.3	41.2	367.9	119.9	...
3rd quarter	886.3	588.2	230.3	86.8	37.3	42.1	21.4	41.6	377.0	126.4	...
4th quarter	914.0	606.0	233.1	89.0	37.4	42.8	23.3	39.8	391.0	128.6	...
1993											
1st quarter	919.1	609.6	226.9	89.3	30.6	41.6	24.1	40.7	398.3	132.1	...
2nd quarter	939.7	625.9	226.6	89.8	28.9	39.4	23.6	44.4	413.1	134.8	...
3rd quarter	956.3	632.8	227.7	88.5	30.5	38.2	24.5	45.6	418.6	141.8	...
4th quarter	998.7	659.3	231.9	92.0	30.6	37.9	27.0	44.5	439.7	144.4	...
1994											
1st quarter	1 011.6	665.9	222.4	87.7	31.4	36.2	23.7	43.1	452.1	149.0	...
2nd quarter	1 036.0	679.3	235.0	96.9	35.6	35.2	23.3	43.8	455.7	152.7	...
3rd quarter	1 046.4	692.0	234.7	96.0	36.6	35.4	23.8	42.7	467.4	157.1	...
4th quarter	1 075.1	722.6	237.1	95.8	39.1	35.6	25.0	41.7	493.7	164.0	...
1995											
1st quarter	1 099.6	752.1	243.1	99.0	40.0	37.2	22.0	44.4	516.5	171.6	...
2nd quarter	1 095.5	757.4	247.9	100.3	43.3	37.3	20.0	46.1	517.8	180.2	...
3rd quarter	1 110.1	762.5	249.8	100.1	43.0	36.4	19.6	49.7	521.2	184.1	...
4th quarter	1 133.3	777.9	247.7	99.3	42.0	34.4	19.6	51.5	537.0	194.8	...
1996											
1st quarter	1 161.8	797.1	252.1	99.6	44.3	32.8	20.4	54.4	551.6	205.1	...
2nd quarter	1 199.7	820.0	257.6	106.0	43.4	31.2	21.9	54.9	568.7	214.1	...
3rd quarter	1 227.4	847.3	260.7	109.4	42.5	30.1	21.9	56.8	591.8	224.3	...
4th quarter	1 247.8	870.1	273.8	114.5	46.8	30.9	22.1	59.3	602.9	232.0	...
1997											
1st quarter	1 272.0	892.2	276.2	119.4	42.4	29.1	24.8	60.7	621.8	246.6	...
2nd quarter	1 299.4	914.3	273.7	114.6	40.9	29.5	25.6	63.2	644.7	260.7	...
3rd quarter	1 349.6	961.1	284.2	120.9	43.6	30.6	25.1	64.1	680.5	280.6	...
4th quarter	1 361.4	969.0	286.3	119.4	42.2	31.3	25.7	67.8	686.3	291.5	...
1998											
1st quarter	1 402.4	1 001.6	286.7	120.8	44.8	34.0	23.6	63.5	717.2	309.9	...
2nd quarter	1 444.5	1 032.5	298.0	126.7	44.6	34.9	24.0	67.9	737.3	322.7	...
3rd quarter	1 465.1	1 042.4	295.5	124.7	43.2	35.1	23.9	68.6	749.1	332.2	...
4th quarter	1 507.7	1 074.7	297.6	129.5	42.1	35.0	21.8	69.5	778.6	350.7	...
1999											
1st quarter	1 531.0	1 094.0	292.0	128.4	38.1	36.7	20.0	68.9	802.7	369.5	...
2nd quarter	1 568.6	1 127.3	294.1	129.5	34.3	39.2	21.7	69.6	833.5	395.8	...
3rd quarter	1 598.6	1 154.4	291.8	129.9	32.6	42.6	20.5	66.2	862.4	412.8	...
4th quarter	1 606.9	1 157.3	294.8	129.9	30.5	44.8	22.8	66.9	862.3	415.8	...
2000											
1st quarter	1 651.1	1 196.7	299.9	130.8	31.0	44.7	24.2	69.2	896.7	442.9	...
2nd quarter	1 689.1	1 238.6	312.5	136.7	33.0	45.7	26.9	70.2	926.0	465.7	...
3rd quarter	1 686.4	1 245.2	319.7	140.8	31.6	47.8	28.2	71.3	925.5	473.8	...
4th quarter	1 689.4	1 247.9	320.6	141.9	31.6	49.0	29.4	68.8	927.3	488.1	...
2001											
1st quarter	1 678.2	1 234.4	313.8	140.8	32.4	44.1	31.7	64.6	920.8	485.7	...
2nd quarter	1 640.5	1 190.2	310.6	135.4	30.2	47.6	32.6	64.4	879.2	461.4	...
3rd quarter	1 621.9	1 169.3	315.1	126.1	28.9	49.1	34.1	76.1	852.9	447.3	...
4th quarter	1 577.0	1 128.2	284.9	118.9	22.6	52.2	29.7	61.1	843.8	441.7	...
2002											
1st quarter	1 559.6	1 099.8	270.7	115.3	17.9	53.9	25.6	58.2	830.1	434.1	...
2nd quarter	1 545.9	1 072.4	253.9	111.3	15.9	47.2	22.0	57.9	820.6	435.5	...
3rd quarter	1 546.6	1 069.5	243.0	107.7	14.0	42.8	23.4	55.1	829.8	446.5	...
4th quarter	1 543.5	1 060.9	238.9	104.7	13.7	42.8	23.4	54.2	825.5	442.2	...
2003											
1st quarter	1 552.7	1 060.5	230.7	101.6	12.7	39.2	24.3	52.7	834.6	460.0	...
2nd quarter	1 593.4	1 090.6	238.7	102.9	13.4	36.1	28.9	56.4	856.7	475.7	...
3rd quarter	1 660.6	1 131.1	237.9	102.8	13.2	34.6	31.0	55.1	899.7	507.1	...
4th quarter	1 702.7	1 161.0	242.4	101.2	13.1	39.6	32.0	55.4	925.6	526.6	...

[1] See Notes and Definitions.
... = Not available.

Table 5-3. Real Gross Private Fixed Investment by Type—Continued

(Billions of chained [2000] dollars, quarterly data are at seasonally adjusted annual rates.)   NIPA Table 5.3.6

Year and quarter	Nonresidential—Continued					Residential						
	Equipment and software—Continued					Total	Residential structures					Residential equipment
	Information processing equipment and software—Continued		Industrial equipment	Transportation equipment	Other nonresidential equipment		Total	Permanent site			Other residential structures	
	Software 2	Other information processing						Total	Single family	Multifamily		
1990	39.9	80.1	109.2	81.0	96.0	298.9	292.6	181.3	154.2	26.7	111.6	6.0
1991	45.1	79.6	102.2	78.8	82.0	270.2	264.0	156.1	135.1	20.6	107.8	5.8
1992	53.0	84.4	104.0	80.2	81.6	307.6	301.4	182.0	164.1	17.5	119.5	6.0
1993	59.3	90.9	112.9	95.1	89.3	332.7	326.4	194.3	179.7	14.1	132.1	6.1
1994	65.1	99.4	122.9	111.4	96.5	364.8	358.6	217.6	198.9	18.2	141.2	6.1
1995	71.6	107.0	134.9	120.6	101.7	353.1	346.8	203.2	180.6	22.6	143.4	6.2
1996	84.1	117.2	139.9	125.4	105.6	381.3	375.1	222.3	197.3	25.0	152.8	6.2
1997	108.8	127.3	143.0	135.9	115.8	388.6	382.4	223.5	196.6	26.9	158.8	6.1
1998	129.4	143.2	148.1	145.4	125.7	418.3	411.9	244.7	218.1	26.6	167.1	6.4
1999	157.2	158.0	147.9	167.7	126.7	443.6	436.6	262.9	234.2	28.7	173.6	7.0
2000	176.2	190.0	159.2	160.8	131.2	446.9	439.5	265.0	236.8	28.3	174.5	7.4
2001	173.8	181.7	145.7	142.8	126.9	448.5	441.1	266.6	237.1	29.5	174.5	7.4
2002	163.6	164.3	137.4	125.6	124.5	470.0	462.5	277.3	246.3	31.0	185.1	7.6
2003	171.2	179.4	137.6	121.6	131.2	511.2	503.0	306.3	274.2	32.1	196.6	8.3
1992												
1st quarter	49.7	81.4	100.1	71.7	79.9	296.1	289.9	173.8	155.4	18.0	116.2	5.9
2nd quarter	52.0	82.7	102.2	83.6	79.6	307.4	301.3	184.7	164.1	20.2	116.9	5.9
3rd quarter	54.0	86.8	104.8	78.4	82.9	308.2	302.0	182.8	165.8	16.6	119.4	5.9
4th quarter	56.4	86.7	109.0	87.2	83.9	318.6	312.3	186.9	171.3	15.3	125.4	6.1
1993												
1st quarter	57.5	87.2	110.0	86.1	87.6	320.1	313.8	188.6	174.3	13.8	125.3	6.1
2nd quarter	58.6	88.7	110.6	98.5	88.5	323.8	317.5	188.8	174.8	13.5	128.8	6.1
3rd quarter	60.0	93.1	112.1	91.5	89.3	335.0	328.7	194.5	179.3	14.7	134.1	6.2
4th quarter	61.1	94.8	118.8	104.3	92.0	351.9	345.7	205.4	190.5	14.4	140.3	6.0
1994												
1st quarter	63.0	96.5	119.7	109.3	94.1	358.8	352.8	213.3	197.5	15.2	139.6	6.0
2nd quarter	64.4	98.0	120.6	105.2	95.7	370.9	364.8	222.5	204.6	17.4	142.5	6.1
3rd quarter	66.0	100.1	123.9	108.0	97.0	367.0	360.9	219.7	199.7	19.6	141.4	6.1
4th quarter	67.1	102.9	127.6	123.2	99.3	362.3	355.9	214.8	193.8	20.7	141.3	6.3
1995												
1st quarter	68.1	106.6	133.2	130.5	102.3	354.2	347.9	208.2	186.2	21.8	139.8	6.2
2nd quarter	70.2	107.6	135.3	117.7	101.5	342.9	336.6	196.4	174.7	21.6	140.1	6.1
3rd quarter	72.7	105.8	136.2	115.4	101.1	353.6	347.2	200.5	177.2	23.2	146.6	6.2
4th quarter	75.6	108.0	135.0	118.6	102.1	361.6	355.3	207.9	184.1	23.8	147.3	6.2
1996												
1st quarter	78.6	113.0	138.2	117.1	103.0	371.1	364.9	215.2	190.4	24.8	149.7	6.1
2nd quarter	81.9	116.2	140.8	120.8	104.3	386.8	380.5	227.0	200.2	26.9	153.5	6.3
3rd quarter	85.4	119.6	139.5	132.0	107.1	385.7	379.6	225.1	201.1	23.8	154.5	6.1
4th quarter	90.3	120.1	141.2	131.8	108.0	381.8	375.5	221.9	197.4	24.5	153.6	6.2
1997												
1st quarter	99.8	120.9	140.5	132.2	110.6	383.1	377.0	221.4	195.1	26.3	155.5	6.1
2nd quarter	105.1	124.1	143.2	135.2	112.4	387.9	381.8	224.2	197.0	27.3	157.5	6.1
3rd quarter	111.8	131.1	143.9	142.3	119.4	389.7	383.5	222.2	196.0	26.2	161.1	6.1
4th quarter	118.7	133.1	144.2	133.8	120.8	393.6	387.5	226.2	198.4	27.9	161.1	6.2
1998												
1st quarter	122.1	139.5	151.1	134.7	125.0	401.8	395.5	232.9	205.0	27.9	162.6	6.3
2nd quarter	126.2	142.2	149.4	140.3	127.8	412.9	406.5	239.5	213.5	26.1	166.9	6.4
3rd quarter	131.5	143.1	145.9	146.8	126.5	424.1	417.7	249.3	223.3	26.0	168.4	6.5
4th quarter	137.8	148.1	146.2	159.8	123.8	434.3	427.7	257.2	230.6	26.6	170.6	6.6
1999												
1st quarter	144.9	149.8	145.6	161.4	127.5	438.1	431.3	261.1	232.5	28.6	170.3	6.7
2nd quarter	154.5	157.0	147.4	165.7	125.1	441.8	434.9	260.3	231.8	28.4	174.6	7.0
3rd quarter	162.2	162.8	149.2	174.6	126.1	444.5	437.3	262.0	232.8	29.2	175.3	7.2
4th quarter	167.2	162.4	149.3	169.1	128.2	449.9	442.7	268.4	239.6	28.8	174.4	7.2
2000												
1st quarter	171.4	179.9	156.3	166.1	131.3	454.5	447.1	272.6	243.5	29.0	174.6	7.3
2nd quarter	175.8	187.7	159.7	167.0	133.6	450.4	443.1	268.8	239.7	29.1	174.3	7.3
3rd quarter	176.2	192.3	161.9	159.5	130.4	441.2	433.8	259.3	232.4	26.8	174.5	7.4
4th quarter	181.2	200.2	159.0	150.7	129.6	441.6	434.2	259.5	231.5	28.0	174.6	7.4
2001												
1st quarter	181.4	193.7	159.3	145.3	130.9	444.0	436.6	263.7	234.6	29.1	172.8	7.4
2nd quarter	174.1	182.9	147.3	144.5	126.3	450.1	442.7	268.4	239.1	29.3	174.3	7.4
3rd quarter	172.3	177.8	140.6	137.6	127.6	452.1	444.8	269.7	240.3	29.4	175.1	7.3
4th quarter	167.4	172.2	135.4	144.0	122.8	447.8	440.4	264.6	234.5	30.1	175.8	7.5
2002												
1st quarter	163.8	163.7	141.5	134.1	120.4	457.8	450.3	268.3	237.7	30.6	182.0	7.5
2nd quarter	162.9	164.9	136.0	124.3	125.1	470.3	462.7	277.6	246.0	31.6	185.1	7.6
3rd quarter	165.9	165.4	136.6	121.9	125.7	473.6	466.0	280.9	249.5	31.4	185.1	7.5
4th quarter	161.7	163.2	135.4	121.9	126.7	478.5	470.9	282.6	252.0	30.6	188.3	7.6
2003												
1st quarter	164.9	169.6	137.9	113.9	125.2	487.3	479.5	292.3	260.3	32.0	187.1	7.7
2nd quarter	166.8	173.7	137.3	120.5	126.1	497.9	489.8	295.8	264.1	31.7	194.1	8.1
3rd quarter	174.6	183.9	138.4	124.3	134.0	523.8	515.3	310.9	278.3	32.6	204.4	8.5
4th quarter	178.5	190.4	136.8	127.8	139.3	535.9	527.2	326.4	294.1	32.2	200.6	8.7

2Excludes software "embedded," or bundled, in computers and other equipment.

Table 5-4. Chain-Type Quantity Indexes for Private Fixed Investment by Type

(Index numbers, 2000 = 100.)

NIPA Table 5.3.3

Year and quarter	Total gross private fixed investment	Nonresidential									
		Total	Structures						Equipment and software		
			Total	Commercial and health care	Manufacturing	Power and communication	Mining exploration, shafts, and wells	Other nonresidential structures	Total	Information processing equipment and software	
										Total	Computers and peripheral equipment
1947	10.8	8.2	24.2	7.1	47.9	34.3	30.9	34.9	5.1	0.2	...
1948	11.9	8.7	25.5	9.1	35.3	41.0	37.9	34.9	5.3	0.2	...
1949	10.9	7.9	24.6	8.4	25.3	43.1	38.4	35.3	4.7	0.2	...
1950	13.0	8.6	26.4	10.8	27.8	42.9	45.6	34.9	5.1	0.2	...
1951	12.4	9.0	28.4	10.4	48.8	43.1	47.9	34.1	5.3	0.2	...
1952	12.2	8.8	28.3	8.1	52.2	43.5	53.3	34.3	5.1	0.2	...
1953	13.0	9.6	30.8	11.1	49.9	47.8	58.2	35.6	5.6	0.3	...
1954	13.3	9.4	31.9	13.8	46.7	43.7	64.4	37.5	5.3	0.2	...
1955	15.0	10.4	34.2	17.9	51.1	41.6	69.3	37.6	6.0	0.3	...
1956	15.0	11.0	37.8	20.3	67.1	48.6	67.0	37.2	6.2	0.3	...
1957	14.9	11.2	37.7	19.3	71.2	50.5	63.3	37.2	6.3	0.3	...
1958	13.8	10.0	35.7	20.3	49.1	48.5	59.2	38.9	5.4	0.3	...
1959	15.7	10.8	36.5	22.0	43.8	46.5	60.7	42.9	6.1	0.3	*
1960	15.9	11.4	39.4	23.4	59.3	47.0	57.0	47.7	6.3	0.4	*
1961	15.8	11.3	40.0	26.7	58.0	44.0	58.1	46.6	6.2	0.4	*
1962	17.2	12.3	41.8	29.7	58.6	44.3	60.9	47.6	6.9	0.5	*
1963	18.6	13.0	42.2	28.7	58.8	47.2	57.2	50.3	7.5	0.6	*
1964	20.4	14.5	46.6	31.2	70.7	51.4	61.2	55.2	8.5	0.7	*
1965	22.5	17.0	54.1	36.6	97.8	56.9	60.5	62.0	10.0	0.8	*
1966	23.7	19.2	57.8	35.7	121.5	64.9	57.3	64.4	11.6	1.1	*
1967	23.3	18.9	56.3	34.3	106.9	71.0	54.8	63.0	11.5	1.1	*
1968	24.9	19.7	57.1	37.5	102.9	78.9	55.1	55.8	12.3	1.2	*
1969	26.5	21.2	60.2	43.3	108.2	78.9	57.5	55.4	13.3	1.5	*
1970	25.9	21.1	60.4	43.9	104.5	86.3	54.1	52.1	13.2	1.7	*
1971	27.9	21.1	59.4	47.9	86.3	87.0	50.0	48.8	13.3	1.8	*
1972	31.2	23.1	61.2	52.3	75.4	90.7	53.7	49.3	15.1	2.0	*
1973	34.1	26.4	66.2	54.7	93.4	96.5	57.3	53.1	17.8	2.4	*
1974	32.0	26.7	64.8	51.3	106.4	90.4	68.1	48.7	18.3	2.7	*
1975	28.5	24.0	58.0	39.9	102.0	83.1	79.5	43.0	16.5	2.7	*
1976	31.4	25.2	59.4	39.4	94.2	90.6	85.8	45.2	17.6	3.1	0.1
1977	35.9	28.0	61.8	41.5	96.8	89.2	96.9	47.7	20.2	3.8	0.1
1978	40.2	32.2	70.8	47.3	129.1	93.5	110.5	54.1	23.3	4.9	0.2
1979	42.5	35.5	79.7	56.4	158.6	97.0	117.7	59.5	25.3	5.9	0.3
1980	39.7	35.4	84.4	61.9	132.7	97.9	165.4	57.7	24.4	6.9	0.5
1981	40.6	37.4	91.1	66.9	150.6	100.4	192.3	55.8	25.4	8.0	0.7
1982	37.7	36.0	89.5	72.8	145.4	94.8	177.7	52.7	24.1	8.5	0.9
1983	40.5	35.5	79.9	70.7	105.2	81.6	147.2	55.6	25.4	10.0	1.3
1984	47.3	41.8	91.0	86.0	108.8	83.3	167.3	65.1	30.5	12.6	2.2
1985	49.8	44.6	97.5	99.3	121.7	82.4	149.1	71.7	32.4	14.1	2.7
1986	50.4	43.3	86.8	92.3	102.3	87.9	87.3	67.4	33.0	15.2	3.1
1987	50.7	43.3	84.3	89.0	99.7	78.2	85.4	71.4	33.5	16.1	3.9
1988	52.4	45.5	84.9	91.6	105.2	73.8	93.7	66.5	36.0	18.0	4.5
1989	53.9	48.1	86.6	90.5	126.0	76.6	84.7	67.9	38.6	20.5	5.5
1990	52.8	48.3	87.9	86.9	142.8	71.3	97.9	72.1	38.6	21.5	5.4
1991	49.4	45.7	78.1	67.5	131.5	84.7	95.7	62.6	37.6	22.6	5.9
1992	52.3	47.2	73.4	62.8	120.7	89.8	79.2	58.1	40.4	26.1	8.0
1993	56.8	51.3	72.9	65.3	94.8	83.9	91.3	62.7	45.4	29.6	10.3
1994	62.1	56.0	74.2	68.4	112.2	76.0	88.1	61.3	50.8	33.3	12.8
1995	66.1	61.9	78.9	72.5	132.3	77.6	74.7	68.6	56.9	39.1	19.3
1996	72.0	67.7	83.4	78.1	139.1	66.8	79.3	80.7	63.0	46.8	27.8
1997	78.7	75.8	89.4	86.2	132.9	64.4	93.0	91.5	71.6	57.7	40.3
1998	86.7	84.2	94.0	91.2	137.4	74.2	85.8	96.4	81.1	70.3	58.2
1999	93.9	92.0	93.6	94.1	106.5	87.2	78.3	97.2	91.4	85.2	82.5
2000	100.0	100.0	100.0	100.0	100.0	100.0	100.0	100.0	100.0	100.0	100.0
2001	97.0	95.8	97.7	94.7	89.7	103.0	117.8	95.3	95.1	98.2	102.4
2002	92.3	87.3	80.3	79.8	48.4	99.7	86.8	80.7	89.9	94.0	113.8
2003	96.9	90.2	75.8	74.2	41.3	79.9	106.9	78.6	95.7	105.3	151.3
2001											
1st quarter	100.0	100.2	100.2	102.3	101.9	94.1	116.5	92.5	100.2	103.9	109.5
2nd quarter	97.7	96.6	99.2	98.4	95.1	101.6	119.9	92.2	95.7	98.7	103.3
3rd quarter	96.6	94.9	100.6	91.7	90.9	104.9	125.4	109.0	92.8	95.7	95.3
4th quarter	93.9	91.6	91.0	86.4	71.0	111.5	109.3	87.5	91.8	94.5	101.4
2002											
1st quarter	92.9	89.3	86.4	83.8	56.2	115.1	94.4	83.3	90.3	92.8	107.5
2nd quarter	92.1	87.0	81.1	80.9	50.0	100.9	80.9	83.0	89.3	93.1	108.7
3rd quarter	92.1	86.8	77.6	78.3	44.1	91.4	86.0	78.9	90.3	95.5	117.8
4th quarter	91.9	86.1	76.3	76.1	43.1	91.5	86.0	77.6	89.8	94.6	121.1
2003											
1st quarter	92.5	86.1	73.7	73.8	40.1	83.7	89.4	75.4	90.8	98.4	130.9
2nd quarter	94.9	88.5	76.2	74.8	42.2	77.2	106.4	80.7	93.2	101.7	143.4
3rd quarter	98.9	91.8	76.0	74.7	41.6	73.9	114.0	78.8	97.9	108.4	159.8
4th quarter	101.4	94.2	77.4	73.5	41.2	84.6	117.7	79.3	100.7	112.6	171.1

... = Not available.
* = Quantity more than zero but less than 0.05.

Table 5-4. Chain-Type Quantity Indexes for Private Fixed Investment by Type—Continued

(Index numbers, 2000 = 100.)

NIPA Table 5.3.3

Year and quarter	Nonresidential—Continued					Residential						
	Equipment and software—Continued						Residential structures					
	Information processing equipment and software—Continued		Industrial equipment	Transportation equipment	Other nonresidential equipment	Total	Total	Permanent site			Other residential structures	Residential equipment
	Software[1]	Other information processing						Total	Single family	Multifamily		
1947	...	2.3	26.8	16.1	22.7	21.3	21.9	26.3	...	...	15.4	7.3
1948	...	2.3	24.8	16.8	27.7	25.5	26.3	32.6	...	...	17.0	7.6
1949	...	2.1	19.1	16.7	23.3	23.6	24.3	30.8	...	...	14.8	7.1
1950	...	2.3	22.1	18.5	24.6	32.3	33.3	45.3	...	...	15.9	9.0
1951	...	2.5	24.8	17.8	24.8	27.0	27.8	36.2	...	...	15.7	8.3
1952	...	2.9	25.7	14.7	25.0	26.6	27.3	34.1	...	...	17.4	8.3
1953	...	3.2	28.3	17.4	24.4	27.5	28.2	35.2	...	...	18.1	8.7
1954	...	2.9	29.2	15.3	23.0	29.8	30.6	38.7	...	...	18.9	8.9
1955	...	3.3	29.0	19.4	27.0	34.6	35.6	45.7	...	...	20.9	10.2
1956	...	3.8	32.0	17.5	27.9	31.8	32.6	39.6	...	...	22.3	11.3
1957	...	4.3	32.4	18.7	26.3	29.8	30.5	36.0	...	...	22.5	11.3
1958	...	3.9	27.0	13.6	26.7	30.2	30.8	36.9	34.6	51.8	21.9	12.0
1959	*	4.2	27.4	18.0	28.7	37.8	38.7	47.0	44.0	66.6	26.6	13.8
1960	0.1	4.9	29.6	18.6	26.3	35.1	36.0	41.5	38.9	58.6	27.7	13.0
1961	0.1	5.2	28.0	17.6	26.0	35.2	36.1	41.3	36.8	73.9	28.3	13.0
1962	0.1	5.5	29.4	21.7	27.8	38.6	39.5	47.1	39.3	107.4	28.5	13.8
1963	0.2	5.7	31.8	21.0	32.3	43.2	44.2	53.4	41.9	144.2	30.7	15.4
1964	0.2	6.2	35.9	23.7	35.8	45.7	46.8	57.0	46.0	143.2	31.8	16.5
1965	0.3	7.1	42.4	29.7	39.7	44.3	45.3	54.5	45.0	128.7	31.7	18.4
1966	0.5	8.3	48.7	32.7	44.7	40.4	41.1	47.8	40.0	107.9	31.3	18.8
1967	0.6	8.3	48.9	31.6	42.2	39.1	39.8	45.6	39.2	93.7	31.2	19.3
1968	0.6	8.6	47.9	38.0	42.7	44.4	45.2	53.6	43.1	135.4	32.8	23.0
1969	0.8	9.9	51.1	39.5	45.6	45.7	46.4	55.1	41.0	168.5	33.5	26.2
1970	1.1	10.7	51.9	32.4	47.6	43.0	43.4	49.9	35.6	164.9	33.9	28.6
1971	1.1	10.8	47.6	35.0	47.5	54.8	55.5	67.2	49.4	209.9	38.5	32.0
1972	1.3	11.5	51.3	40.7	53.8	64.5	65.4	81.3	58.7	262.8	42.2	38.4
1973	1.5	13.9	60.7	48.9	62.8	64.1	64.8	80.9	57.4	270.2	41.3	43.2
1974	1.8	15.4	65.4	44.3	62.0	50.9	51.1	58.6	44.1	174.0	40.2	44.0
1975	2.1	14.8	55.4	38.2	57.4	44.3	44.3	44.8	40.2	77.6	43.6	41.0
1976	2.3	16.2	55.7	42.4	57.9	54.7	55.0	58.9	56.0	75.2	49.3	43.1
1977	2.4	19.5	59.0	51.6	65.2	66.4	67.0	76.0	72.0	99.6	53.9	47.2
1978	2.8	23.2	65.7	57.0	71.8	70.6	71.2	79.5	74.4	112.2	59.1	51.3
1979	3.5	26.0	70.4	59.5	73.2	68.0	68.4	74.4	65.9	137.1	59.7	56.2
1980	4.1	28.0	67.4	48.6	65.8	53.6	53.6	52.3	43.3	122.7	55.7	56.3
1981	4.8	29.6	66.3	47.2	67.6	49.3	49.2	48.2	39.4	118.0	50.8	56.2
1982	5.5	29.8	60.5	41.8	58.5	40.4	40.0	37.6	30.2	96.2	43.8	54.0
1983	6.5	31.3	55.7	47.1	56.3	57.1	57.0	61.4	52.5	131.8	50.8	60.3
1984	8.3	35.7	63.8	56.1	63.8	65.6	65.6	72.1	60.9	161.0	56.1	66.8
1985	9.8	36.8	66.7	58.3	64.4	66.6	66.5	71.2	60.4	156.9	59.8	72.1
1986	11.0	38.3	66.4	56.1	63.2	74.8	74.7	79.5	69.1	161.5	67.9	78.0
1987	12.5	36.8	64.8	53.3	65.0	76.3	76.2	80.6	74.7	127.4	69.9	81.2
1988	14.9	39.3	68.0	56.2	68.1	75.5	75.3	77.7	73.8	108.7	72.0	83.9
1989	19.2	41.1	72.8	50.6	76.1	73.2	73.0	75.7	71.7	108.5	69.1	84.4
1990	22.6	42.1	68.6	50.4	73.2	66.9	66.6	68.4	65.1	94.6	64.0	81.9
1991	25.6	41.9	64.2	49.0	62.5	60.5	60.1	58.9	57.1	72.9	61.8	78.7
1992	30.1	44.4	65.3	49.9	62.2	68.8	68.6	68.7	69.3	62.0	68.5	81.1
1993	33.7	47.9	70.9	59.1	68.1	74.4	74.3	73.3	75.9	50.0	75.7	82.7
1994	37.0	52.3	77.2	69.3	73.6	81.6	81.6	82.1	84.0	64.5	80.9	83.2
1995	40.7	56.3	84.7	75.0	77.5	79.0	78.9	76.7	76.3	80.0	82.2	84.3
1996	47.7	61.7	87.9	78.0	80.5	85.3	85.3	83.9	83.3	88.5	87.6	83.9
1997	61.8	67.0	89.8	84.5	88.3	86.9	87.0	84.3	83.0	95.3	91.0	83.2
1998	73.5	75.4	93.0	90.4	95.8	93.6	93.7	92.3	92.1	94.2	95.8	87.6
1999	89.2	83.1	92.9	104.3	96.6	99.3	99.3	99.2	98.9	101.7	99.5	95.3
2000	100.0	100.0	100.0	100.0	100.0	100.0	100.0	100.0	100.0	100.0	100.0	100.0
2001	98.7	95.6	91.5	88.8	96.7	100.4	100.4	100.6	100.1	104.3	100.0	100.4
2002	92.9	86.5	86.3	78.1	94.9	105.2	105.2	104.6	104.0	109.8	106.1	102.8
2003	97.2	94.4	86.4	75.6	100.0	114.4	114.4	115.6	115.8	113.7	112.6	112.2
2001												
1st quarter	103.0	101.9	100.0	90.3	99.8	99.3	99.3	99.5	99.1	103.1	99.0	100.5
2nd quarter	98.8	96.3	92.5	89.8	96.3	100.7	100.7	101.3	101.0	103.7	99.9	99.9
3rd quarter	97.8	93.6	88.3	85.5	97.3	101.2	101.2	101.7	101.5	104.1	100.3	99.8
4th quarter	95.1	90.6	85.1	89.5	93.6	100.2	100.2	99.8	99.1	106.5	100.7	101.4
2002												
1st quarter	93.0	86.1	88.9	83.3	91.8	102.4	102.5	101.2	100.4	108.4	104.3	102.3
2nd quarter	92.5	86.8	85.4	77.3	95.3	105.2	105.3	104.7	103.9	111.7	106.1	103.4
3rd quarter	94.2	87.0	85.8	75.8	95.8	106.0	106.0	106.0	105.4	111.1	106.1	102.3
4th quarter	91.8	85.9	85.0	75.8	96.6	107.1	107.1	106.6	106.4	108.2	107.9	103.3
2003												
1st quarter	93.6	89.3	86.6	70.8	95.4	109.0	109.1	110.3	109.9	113.3	107.3	105.2
2nd quarter	94.7	91.4	86.2	74.9	96.1	111.4	111.4	111.6	111.5	112.1	111.2	110.2
3rd quarter	99.1	96.8	86.9	77.3	102.2	117.2	117.2	117.3	117.5	115.2	117.1	115.0
4th quarter	101.3	100.2	85.9	79.5	106.1	119.9	119.9	123.2	124.2	113.9	115.0	118.5

[1]Excludes software "embedded," or bundled, in computers and other equipment.
. . . = Not available.
* = Quantity more than zero but less than 0.05.

Table 5-5. Current-Cost Net Stock of Fixed Assets

(Billions of dollars, year-end estimates.)

Year	Total	Private				Government				Private and government fixed assets				Government, by level	
		Total	Nonresidential		Residential	Total	Nonresidential		Residential	Total	Nonresidential		Residential	Federal	State and local
			Equipment and software	Structures			Equipment and software	Structures			Equipment and software	Structures			
1939	283.9	222.4	30.3	75.3	116.7	61.6	3.6	57.7	0.3	283.9	33.9	133.0	117.0	14.0	47.6
1940	308.9	241.3	32.7	80.5	128.1	67.6	4.0	63.1	0.5	308.9	36.7	143.5	128.7	15.7	51.9
1941	353.2	268.6	38.1	90.7	139.9	84.5	7.7	75.8	1.0	353.2	45.8	166.5	140.9	24.4	60.2
1942	403.7	286.7	38.6	97.5	150.6	117.0	20.9	94.4	1.7	403.7	59.5	191.9	152.3	49.7	67.4
1943	451.3	302.0	38.9	99.6	163.5	149.3	45.4	101.3	2.6	451.3	84.3	201.0	166.0	80.8	68.5
1944	484.7	314.8	39.1	101.0	174.7	169.9	65.5	101.6	2.8	484.7	104.6	202.6	177.6	103.0	66.9
1945	526.2	337.8	44.5	109.0	184.3	188.4	75.8	109.6	3.0	526.2	120.3	218.6	187.3	118.9	69.5
1946	616.8	416.5	53.6	135.8	227.1	200.3	70.7	125.7	4.0	616.8	124.2	261.5	231.1	122.4	77.9
1947	709.5	495.0	65.2	162.4	267.4	214.4	62.0	146.8	5.6	709.5	127.2	309.2	273.0	121.1	93.3
1948	753.6	539.0	79.1	171.9	288.0	214.6	52.2	157.4	5.0	753.6	131.3	329.3	293.0	113.0	101.6
1949	756.1	556.3	82.7	171.1	302.5	199.8	44.3	150.3	5.2	756.1	127.1	321.3	307.7	102.8	96.9
1950	841.2	629.6	97.0	193.0	339.6	211.5	40.5	164.6	6.4	841.2	137.5	357.7	346.0	102.3	109.3
1951	924.3	687.6	107.5	211.4	368.7	236.7	44.3	184.5	7.9	924.3	151.7	395.9	376.6	113.9	122.9
1952	976.9	722.8	112.2	223.1	387.4	254.1	50.7	195.9	7.4	976.9	163.0	419.1	394.8	123.9	130.2
1953	1 010.5	751.2	121.0	228.3	401.9	259.3	57.5	193.9	7.9	1 010.5	178.5	422.3	409.7	130.5	128.8
1954	1 057.9	782.6	125.6	233.6	423.4	275.2	64.1	200.6	10.6	1 057.9	189.7	434.2	434.0	140.7	134.5
1955	1 150.9	854.1	139.2	258.7	456.2	296.9	69.5	219.7	7.6	1 150.9	208.7	478.5	463.8	147.5	149.4
1956	1 249.5	920.4	156.6	285.5	478.2	329.1	74.1	246.1	8.9	1 249.5	230.7	531.6	487.2	159.8	169.3
1957	1 310.0	966.9	169.7	303.0	494.2	343.2	76.2	257.5	9.4	1 310.0	245.9	560.5	503.6	165.7	177.4
1958	1 351.8	990.6	174.6	306.8	509.2	361.3	77.9	273.2	10.2	1 351.8	252.5	580.0	519.4	171.7	189.5
1959	1 405.6	1 034.0	183.4	319.3	531.3	371.6	82.4	278.1	11.1	1 405.6	265.8	597.3	542.4	175.9	195.7
1960	1 452.4	1 067.3	189.8	325.4	552.2	385.1	85.2	288.1	11.8	1 452.4	275.0	613.5	564.0	180.0	205.1
1961	1 507.7	1 103.2	193.1	337.8	572.3	404.4	89.2	302.7	12.6	1 507.7	282.3	640.5	584.9	187.0	217.4
1962	1 575.9	1 145.2	200.7	351.1	593.4	430.7	96.5	320.8	13.5	1 575.9	297.2	671.9	606.9	197.9	232.8
1963	1 633.2	1 181.7	209.2	364.4	608.0	451.6	99.2	338.7	13.7	1 633.2	308.4	703.1	621.8	203.5	248.1
1964	1 740.2	1 266.6	222.1	387.5	657.0	473.7	102.0	357.1	14.6	1 740.2	324.1	744.6	671.6	209.0	264.7
1965	1 856.8	1 352.8	239.6	415.5	697.6	504.0	104.6	384.1	15.3	1 856.8	344.3	799.6	712.9	216.0	288.0
1966	2 015.0	1 470.0	266.5	449.1	754.4	544.9	109.8	418.7	16.4	2 015.0	376.3	867.8	770.8	226.7	318.2
1967	2 170.5	1 581.9	292.5	483.7	805.7	588.6	116.4	454.9	17.3	2 170.5	408.9	938.6	823.0	240.9	347.7
1968	2 385.4	1 746.5	323.5	532.8	890.2	638.9	120.9	498.6	19.4	2 385.4	444.4	1 031.4	909.6	253.0	385.9
1969	2 601.8	1 898.6	358.0	588.2	952.3	703.2	125.1	556.5	21.6	2 601.8	483.1	1 144.7	973.9	267.4	435.8
1970	2 835.2	2 052.8	393.9	650.8	1 008.2	782.4	131.1	628.2	23.1	2 835.2	525.0	1 279.0	1 031.2	285.3	497.1
1971	3 133.7	2 286.2	422.5	730.5	1 133.2	847.5	132.2	689.5	25.9	3 133.7	554.6	1 419.9	1 159.1	299.5	548.0
1972	3 449.4	2 526.0	455.6	803.0	1 267.4	923.4	134.0	760.4	29.0	3 449.4	589.6	1 563.4	1 296.4	322.5	600.9
1973	3 914.9	2 876.1	511.4	912.3	1 452.3	1 038.8	136.2	869.9	32.8	3 914.9	647.6	1 782.2	1 485.0	349.5	689.3
1974	4 665.8	3 389.2	634.9	1 101.5	1 652.7	1 276.6	149.7	1 090.3	36.6	4 665.8	784.6	2 191.8	1 689.4	403.3	873.3
1975	5 047.9	3 706.8	726.2	1 188.7	1 791.8	1 341.1	164.4	1 136.6	40.1	5 047.9	890.6	2 325.4	1 832.0	426.6	914.5
1976	5 504.7	4 086.6	804.3	1 293.5	1 988.9	1 418.1	178.7	1 194.6	44.8	5 504.7	983.1	2 488.1	2 033.6	462.8	955.3
1977	6 171.0	4 663.8	906.9	1 435.7	2 321.2	1 507.1	195.0	1 260.6	51.5	6 171.0	1 101.9	2 696.3	2 372.7	485.7	1 021.4
1978	6 988.9	5 340.9	1 034.8	1 629.1	2 677.0	1 648.0	207.8	1 380.7	59.6	6 988.9	1 242.6	3 009.7	2 736.5	524.0	1 124.0
1979	8 064.5	6 187.5	1 202.0	1 877.2	3 108.2	1 877.0	225.2	1 581.0	70.9	8 064.5	1 427.2	3 458.2	3 179.1	583.9	1 293.1
1980	9 198.0	7 049.0	1 395.9	2 148.5	3 504.6	2 148.9	251.5	1 819.7	77.8	9 198.0	1 647.4	3 968.2	3 582.3	648.0	1 501.0
1981	10 142.0	7 781.3	1 553.2	2 458.5	3 769.7	2 360.7	282.9	1 992.6	85.2	10 142.0	1 836.1	4 451.1	3 854.9	697.1	1 663.6
1982	10 697.0	8 205.7	1 644.0	2 621.1	3 940.6	2 491.3	307.5	2 093.4	90.3	10 697.0	1 951.5	4 714.6	4 030.9	735.5	1 755.8
1983	11 046.5	8 495.6	1 700.7	2 695.2	4 099.7	2 550.9	337.9	2 112.2	100.8	11 046.5	2 038.6	4 807.4	4 200.5	772.4	1 778.5
1984	11 646.7	8 996.4	1 797.3	2 868.0	4 331.1	2 650.3	360.9	2 184.7	104.6	11 646.7	2 158.2	5 052.8	4 435.7	810.6	1 839.7
1985	12 277.5	9 511.0	1 914.3	3 032.0	4 564.7	2 766.5	383.7	2 277.0	105.8	12 277.5	2 297.9	5 309.0	4 670.6	842.4	1 924.1
1986	13 077.6	10 141.4	2 042.3	3 169.2	4 929.9	2 936.2	411.5	2 414.9	109.7	13 077.6	2 453.8	5 584.1	5 039.6	885.2	2 051.0
1987	13 842.8	10 750.2	2 151.8	3 349.8	5 248.5	3 092.6	437.2	2 535.8	119.6	13 842.8	2 589.1	5 885.6	5 368.2	921.5	2 171.1
1988	14 706.1	11 454.8	2 300.5	3 579.9	5 574.3	3 251.3	471.1	2 645.0	135.2	14 706.1	2 771.6	6 224.9	5 709.5	977.3	2 274.0
1989	15 568.8	12 140.3	2 458.1	3 798.6	5 883.6	3 428.5	508.3	2 775.8	144.4	15 568.8	2 966.4	6 574.5	6 028.0	1 031.2	2 397.4
1990	16 317.5	12 716.9	2 606.1	3 999.7	6 111.0	3 600.7	551.1	2 900.4	149.2	16 317.5	3 157.2	6 900.1	6 260.2	1 078.9	2 521.8
1991	16 711.8	12 989.7	2 678.8	4 062.6	6 248.3	3 722.1	583.9	2 988.0	150.2	16 711.8	3 262.7	7 050.6	6 398.5	1 122.5	2 599.6
1992	17 421.3	13 536.2	2 735.4	4 201.2	6 599.9	3 885.1	613.3	3 112.8	159.0	17 421.3	3 348.6	7 314.0	6 758.9	1 169.4	2 715.7
1993	18 238.1	14 173.9	2 754.1	4 414.9	7 004.9	4 064.3	637.0	3 257.0	170.3	18 238.1	3 391.1	7 671.9	7 175.1	1 209.0	2 855.2
1994	19 358.9	15 063.7	2 906.1	4 652.2	7 505.4	4 295.2	665.8	3 447.7	181.7	19 358.9	3 571.9	8 099.9	7 687.1	1 260.7	3 034.5
1995	20 298.8	15 794.2	3 086.1	4 868.2	7 839.8	4 504.7	674.8	3 641.7	188.2	20 298.8	3 760.9	8 509.9	8 028.0	1 291.3	3 213.4
1996	21 297.2	16 615.4	3 249.6	5 095.2	8 270.6	4 681.8	674.8	3 810.5	196.5	21 297.2	3 924.5	8 905.7	8 467.1	1 315.5	3 366.3
1997	22 451.8	17 550.6	3 413.6	5 406.5	8 730.6	4 901.2	671.4	4 032.9	196.8	22 451.8	4 085.0	9 439.4	8 927.5	1 334.7	3 566.5
1998	23 732.3	18 631.2	3 611.2	5 720.0	9 300.1	5 101.1	677.1	4 217.1	206.9	23 732.3	4 288.3	9 937.1	9 507.0	1 355.8	3 745.3
1999	25 273.2	19 874.3	3 864.1	6 023.5	9 986.7	5 398.9	698.2	4 480.7	219.9	25 273.2	4 562.3	10 504.2	10 206.7	1 398.9	4 000.0
2000	26 941.0	21 228.3	4 130.3	6 422.3	10 675.7	5 712.7	703.0	4 778.0	231.7	26 941.0	4 833.3	11 200.3	10 907.4	1 424.6	4 288.1
2001	28 499.0	22 519.1	4 251.9	6 802.4	11 464.8	5 979.9	711.3	5 021.9	246.7	28 499.0	4 963.2	11 824.4	11 711.5	1 446.8	4 533.1
2002	29 829.8	23 581.9	4 350.8	7 035.1	12 195.9	6 247.9	725.2	5 263.8	259.0	29 829.8	5 076.0	12 298.9	12 454.9	1 468.8	4 779.1
2003	31 395.4	24 902.2	4 528.3	7 248.6	13 125.4	6 493.2	742.1	5 477.4	273.7	31 395.4	5 270.4	12 726.0	13 399.1	1 498.4	4 994.8

Table 5-6. Chain-Type Quantity Indexes for Net Stock of Fixed Assets

(Index numbers, 2000 = 100.)

Year	Total	Private				Government				Private and government fixed assets				Government, by level	
		Total	Nonresidential		Residential	Total	Nonresidential		Residential	Total	Nonresidential		Residential	Federal	State and local
			Equipment and software	Structures			Equipment and software	Structures			Equipment and software	Structures			
1939	15.25	15.57	5.96	20.79	18.04	15.21	3.43	19.85	2.04	15.25	5.21	20.30	17.97	11.83	16.58
1940	15.58	15.81	6.19	20.90	18.33	15.91	3.63	20.69	3.42	15.58	5.42	20.73	18.26	12.80	17.17
1941	16.23	16.12	6.52	21.07	18.66	17.81	6.71	22.10	6.20	16.23	6.17	21.44	18.61	18.70	17.50
1942	17.29	16.07	6.42	20.96	18.71	22.77	19.63	24.78	9.26	17.29	8.02	22.57	18.71	37.17	17.53
1943	18.48	15.94	6.28	20.71	18.65	28.75	44.68	25.85	13.16	18.48	11.42	22.92	18.74	60.75	17.37
1944	19.46	15.89	6.33	20.57	18.58	33.63	68.64	26.16	14.10	19.46	14.71	22.98	18.69	80.43	17.19
1945	19.87	15.98	6.71	20.60	18.52	35.31	76.94	26.31	14.32	19.87	16.15	23.06	18.64	87.48	17.04
1946	19.78	16.53	7.29	21.12	19.02	32.67	63.16	26.09	15.89	19.78	14.83	23.26	19.15	77.16	17.05
1947	19.90	17.23	8.18	21.57	19.72	30.41	50.31	26.11	16.38	19.90	13.89	23.52	19.85	67.76	17.25
1948	20.21	18.02	9.04	22.13	20.58	28.75	39.61	26.36	16.68	20.21	13.21	23.96	20.71	60.14	17.59
1949	20.63	18.67	9.57	22.65	21.35	28.20	34.02	26.89	17.69	20.63	12.93	24.48	21.47	56.26	18.16
1950	21.26	19.55	10.20	23.28	22.48	27.75	28.55	27.56	18.59	21.26	12.77	25.13	22.58	52.49	18.86
1951	22.09	20.32	10.80	23.98	23.35	28.84	30.49	28.42	19.98	22.09	13.55	25.89	23.45	54.62	19.57
1952	22.96	21.02	11.28	24.63	24.19	30.36	34.06	29.44	21.55	22.96	14.45	26.70	24.29	58.42	20.29
1953	23.90	21.80	11.89	25.38	25.06	31.96	37.84	30.52	22.96	23.90	15.48	27.60	25.15	62.30	21.10
1954	24.79	22.57	12.28	26.18	26.01	33.33	39.80	31.77	23.60	24.79	16.09	28.58	26.09	64.62	22.13
1955	25.77	23.50	12.85	27.07	27.15	34.48	40.62	33.03	24.11	25.77	16.69	29.62	27.22	65.80	23.26
1956	26.72	24.40	13.42	28.11	28.15	35.61	41.37	34.27	24.76	26.72	17.29	30.75	28.21	66.87	24.40
1957	27.64	25.26	14.00	29.11	29.04	36.76	41.86	35.56	25.94	27.64	17.87	31.88	29.11	67.73	25.63
1958	28.46	25.95	14.20	29.98	29.93	38.10	42.56	37.01	28.03	28.46	18.13	32.99	30.01	68.97	27.01
1959	29.49	26.84	14.58	30.85	31.14	39.66	44.36	38.45	30.38	29.49	18.71	34.10	31.24	71.02	28.40
1960	30.49	27.73	15.02	31.86	32.20	41.07	45.53	39.89	32.12	30.49	19.25	35.29	32.31	72.52	29.78
1961	31.50	28.58	15.37	32.88	33.25	42.74	47.39	41.47	34.22	31.50	19.80	36.55	33.37	74.65	31.28
1962	32.65	29.58	15.92	33.97	34.43	44.49	49.61	43.04	36.59	32.65	20.58	37.84	34.55	76.97	32.82
1963	33.86	30.68	16.57	35.04	35.78	46.15	50.98	44.78	37.81	33.86	21.33	39.19	35.90	78.53	34.52
1964	35.22	31.94	17.45	36.29	37.22	47.83	52.13	46.60	39.13	35.22	22.25	40.69	37.34	79.79	36.36
1965	36.69	33.37	18.71	37.86	38.58	49.50	52.65	48.54	40.54	36.69	23.42	42.42	38.69	80.58	38.33
1966	38.23	34.82	20.26	39.53	39.73	51.36	53.71	50.60	42.05	38.23	24.92	44.25	39.84	81.74	40.44
1967	39.69	36.15	21.61	41.10	40.82	53.30	55.11	52.66	43.76	39.69	26.28	46.03	40.92	82.85	42.67
1968	41.20	37.59	23.04	42.68	42.10	55.04	55.30	54.76	45.44	41.20	27.55	47.83	42.20	82.96	44.99
1969	42.72	39.12	24.62	44.36	43.42	56.52	54.95	56.63	47.56	42.72	28.88	49.60	43.51	82.58	47.12
1970	44.06	40.49	25.91	46.00	44.60	57.76	54.35	58.23	49.73	44.06	29.92	51.22	44.69	81.95	49.00
1971	45.44	42.00	27.04	47.55	46.25	58.66	52.16	59.76	51.83	45.44	30.58	52.76	46.34	80.39	50.74
1972	47.04	43.79	28.57	49.15	48.26	59.53	50.40	61.15	53.58	47.04	31.66	54.26	48.35	79.14	52.35
1973	48.80	45.78	30.76	50.90	50.23	60.46	49.06	62.50	55.25	48.80	33.34	55.84	50.32	78.21	53.93
1974	50.29	47.41	32.76	52.50	51.60	61.52	48.77	63.79	56.83	50.29	35.02	57.29	51.70	77.84	55.46
1975	51.43	48.58	33.96	53.77	52.68	62.58	48.76	65.02	58.72	51.43	36.05	58.54	52.78	77.68	56.93
1976	52.75	49.98	35.26	55.02	54.17	63.64	49.10	66.19	60.20	52.75	37.22	59.75	54.28	77.76	58.32
1977	54.35	51.76	37.12	56.34	56.14	64.56	49.37	67.21	61.60	54.35	38.87	60.95	56.25	77.87	59.53
1978	56.24	53.86	39.51	58.05	58.25	65.64	49.69	68.44	62.76	56.24	40.98	62.45	58.36	78.06	60.93
1979	58.22	56.03	42.10	60.11	60.22	66.86	50.70	69.70	63.89	58.22	43.35	64.18	60.32	78.50	62.43
1980	59.85	57.77	43.94	62.35	61.56	68.11	51.92	70.93	65.32	59.85	45.11	65.99	61.66	79.11	63.90
1981	61.44	59.47	45.76	64.85	62.67	69.21	53.32	71.95	67.01	61.44	46.88	67.86	62.77	80.01	65.07
1982	62.66	60.76	46.81	67.20	63.40	70.21	55.11	72.76	68.58	62.66	48.04	69.56	63.51	81.08	66.03
1983	64.07	62.24	47.98	68.99	64.83	71.34	57.86	73.53	70.46	64.07	49.43	70.92	64.94	82.69	66.99
1984	65.99	64.29	50.17	71.31	66.60	72.77	61.47	74.50	72.06	65.99	51.82	72.67	66.72	84.70	68.22
1985	68.07	66.45	52.34	74.00	68.40	74.54	66.21	75.66	74.03	68.07	54.35	74.71	68.51	87.32	69.67
1986	70.16	68.59	54.48	76.08	70.52	76.48	71.37	76.97	76.12	70.16	56.91	76.46	70.64	90.20	71.27
1987	72.19	70.64	56.28	78.11	72.69	78.45	76.59	78.34	78.31	72.19	59.16	78.20	72.82	93.23	72.87
1988	74.19	72.70	58.37	80.04	74.77	80.23	80.59	79.71	80.25	74.19	61.51	79.90	74.90	95.20	74.58
1989	76.16	74.72	60.61	81.95	76.71	82.03	84.95	81.05	81.96	76.16	64.03	81.56	76.85	97.00	76.36
1990	77.99	76.50	62.29	83.99	78.37	84.01	89.40	82.59	83.85	77.99	66.08	83.40	78.51	98.86	78.37
1991	79.39	77.79	63.28	85.41	79.72	85.87	92.68	84.20	85.48	79.39	67.37	84.89	79.86	100.21	80.38
1992	80.82	79.13	64.29	86.50	81.37	87.63	95.38	85.78	87.28	80.82	68.61	86.20	81.50	101.32	82.37
1993	82.62	81.01	66.05	88.10	83.32	89.10	96.57	87.29	90.28	82.62	70.36	87.75	83.47	101.67	84.22
1994	84.43	82.96	68.84	89.03	85.44	90.40	96.91	88.75	91.55	84.43	72.81	88.91	85.57	101.46	86.04
1995	86.45	85.13	72.31	90.37	87.47	91.82	97.11	90.38	93.08	86.45	75.83	90.37	87.60	101.32	88.01
1996	88.77	87.63	76.40	91.98	89.75	93.49	97.40	92.28	94.66	88.77	79.40	92.11	89.86	101.78	90.09
1997	91.27	90.38	81.34	93.82	92.04	95.08	97.23	94.17	95.82	91.27	83.61	93.97	92.12	101.35	92.36
1998	94.02	93.43	87.01	95.84	94.58	96.54	97.75	95.95	97.32	94.02	88.56	95.89	94.64	100.84	94.68
1999	96.97	96.67	93.42	97.78	97.29	98.23	98.94	97.92	98.81	96.97	94.22	97.84	97.32	100.54	97.26
2000	100.00	100.00	100.00	100.00	100.00	100.00	100.00	100.00	100.00	100.00	100.00	100.00	100.00	100.00	100.00
2001	102.55	102.69	103.91	101.92	102.68	101.90	101.17	102.18	101.43	102.55	103.51	102.03	102.66	99.46	102.88
2002	104.81	104.95	106.50	102.98	105.54	104.08	102.97	104.58	102.93	104.81	105.98	103.66	105.48	99.36	105.96
2003	107.20	107.35	109.30	103.79	108.74	106.31	105.09	106.98	104.34	107.20	108.68	105.14	108.64	99.54	108.98

CHAPTER 5: SAVING AND INVESTMENT; BUSINESS SALES AND INVENTORIES

Table 5-7. Inventories to Sales Ratios

(Seasonally adjusted, ratio of inventories at end of quarter to monthly rate of sales during the quarter, annual data are for fourth quarter.)

NIPA Tables 5.7.5A, 5.7.5B, 5.7.6A, 5.7.6B

Year and quarter	Total private inventories to final sales of domestic business		Nonfarm inventories to			
			Final sales of domestic business		Final sales of goods and structures	
	Current dollars	Chained (2000) dollars	Current dollars	Chained (2000) dollars	Current dollars	Chained (2000) dollars
1947	5.99	3.60	2.69	2.19	3.38	3.34
1948	5.37	3.77	2.83	2.30	3.63	3.51
1949	4.88	3.60	2.60	2.17	3.36	3.30
1950	5.45	3.53	2.87	2.24	3.68	3.39
1951	5.33	3.62	2.89	2.40	3.78	3.61
1952	4.70	3.61	2.76	2.39	3.69	3.59
1953	4.50	3.61	2.76	2.39	3.75	3.59
1954	4.33	3.40	2.64	2.23	3.54	3.35
1955	4.06	3.33	2.71	2.24	3.61	3.36
1956	4.11	3.33	2.79	2.30	3.74	3.48
1957	4.05	3.36	2.74	2.32	3.74	3.52
1958	4.09	3.33	2.65	2.25	3.62	3.42
1959	3.90	3.26	2.67	2.27	3.67	3.48
1960	3.89	3.27	2.67	2.29	3.67	3.51
1961	3.80	3.20	2.59	2.24	3.58	3.45
1962	3.79	3.21	2.59	2.29	3.60	3.51
1963	3.62	3.15	2.55	2.27	3.56	3.49
1964	3.50	3.07	2.54	2.26	3.54	3.49
1965	3.46	2.99	2.50	2.24	3.47	3.42
1966	3.59	3.16	2.67	2.44	3.74	3.75
1967	3.54	3.25	2.71	2.54	3.86	3.92
1968	3.43	3.23	2.62	2.53	3.76	3.91
1969	3.52	3.30	2.70	2.62	3.89	4.08
1970	3.47	3.29	2.70	2.63	3.92	4.13
1971	3.43	3.24	2.63	2.59	3.83	4.07
1972	3.44	3.09	2.54	2.50	3.66	3.90
1973	3.86	3.13	2.74	2.57	3.91	4.01
1974	4.11	3.37	3.22	2.82	4.73	4.50
1975	3.69	3.17	2.88	2.62	4.24	4.17
1976	3.62	3.14	2.91	2.63	4.32	4.21
1977	3.55	3.13	2.88	2.62	4.29	4.18
1978	3.63	3.06	2.87	2.58	4.20	4.06
1979	3.82	3.08	3.05	2.60	4.47	4.08
1980	3.86	3.05	3.13	2.60	4.69	4.13
1981	3.78	3.20	3.16	2.71	4.80	4.31
1982	3.58	3.15	2.97	2.64	4.67	4.26
1983	3.35	2.91	2.79	2.49	4.39	3.98
1984	3.36	2.98	2.85	2.56	4.50	4.07
1985	3.15	2.92	2.70	2.50	4.36	4.03
1986	2.91	2.84	2.52	2.44	4.12	3.92
1987	2.98	2.84	2.60	2.47	4.25	3.99
1988	2.96	2.75	2.58	2.43	4.22	3.92
1989	2.92	2.75	2.55	2.44	4.22	3.94
1990	2.90	2.77	2.54	2.46	4.27	4.02
1991	2.75	2.77	2.43	2.46	4.17	4.07
1992	2.63	2.67	2.30	2.36	3.99	3.90
1993	2.57	2.63	2.27	2.35	3.92	3.86
1994	2.60	2.67	2.31	2.38	3.99	3.88
1995	2.61	2.63	2.33	2.38	4.05	3.88
1996	2.49	2.56	2.23	2.30	3.87	3.74
1997	2.44	2.60	2.19	2.34	3.82	3.78
1998	2.33	2.59	2.12	2.35	3.67	3.75
1999	2.35	2.60	2.15	2.37	3.76	3.79
2000	2.39	2.62	2.18	2.40	3.85	3.86
2001	2.20	2.55	2.01	2.33	3.57	3.74
2002	2.22	2.56	2.02	2.35	3.73	3.83
2003	2.15	2.42	1.94	2.22	3.52	3.55
2001						
1st quarter	2.37	2.61	2.16	2.39	3.82	3.84
2nd quarter	2.33	2.61	2.12	2.39	3.76	3.84
3rd quarter	2.29	2.61	2.09	2.39	3.72	3.84
4th quarter	2.20	2.55	2.01	2.33	3.57	3.74
2002						
1st quarter	2.20	2.55	2.01	2.33	3.61	3.77
2nd quarter	2.20	2.55	2.01	2.34	3.65	3.79
3rd quarter	2.21	2.55	2.02	2.34	3.68	3.79
4th quarter	2.22	2.56	2.02	2.35	3.73	3.83
2003						
1st quarter	2.23	2.55	2.03	2.34	3.76	3.80
2nd quarter	2.17	2.51	1.98	2.30	3.66	3.72
3rd quarter	2.15	2.45	1.94	2.24	3.53	3.59
4th quarter	2.15	2.42	1.94	2.22	3.52	3.55

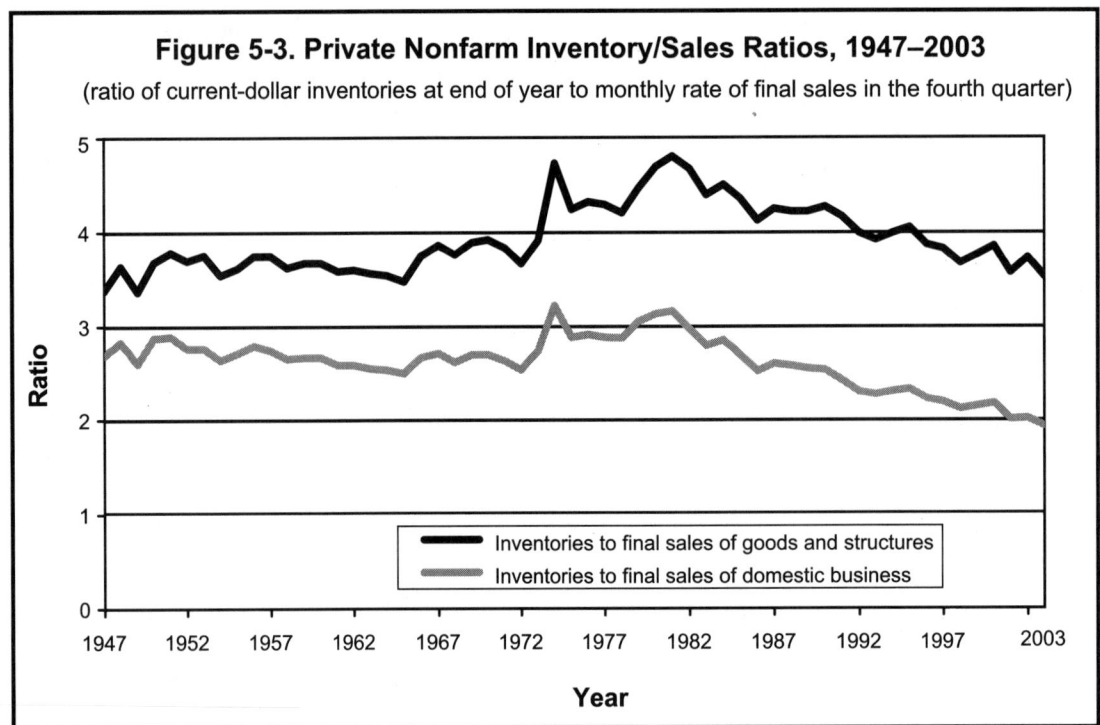

Figure 5-3. Private Nonfarm Inventory/Sales Ratios, 1947–2003

- Inventories play a key role in the business cycle, and ratios of inventories to sales are important cyclical indicators. During business expansions, if production and sales are rising at sustainable rates, inventory-building proceeds in line with sales increases, and ratios of inventories to sales are stable; they may even decline if sales run ahead of production and expectations. On the other hand, if production gets ahead of sales, or sales take an unexpected dip, there can be "involuntary" inventory accumulation. In that case, I/S ratios rise and production must be cut back. In the graph above, this can be most strikingly seen in the high ratios associated with the severe 1974–1975 and 1981–1982 recessions. (Table 5-7)
- In addition to these cyclical movements, the broadest ratios of inventories to monthly business sales rates for total GDP show a downtrend over the postwar period, as shown in the lower line on the graph. Abstracting from shorter-term movements, and confirming this trend, is the decline in the ratios between the earliest and latest pre-recession ratios, 1947 and 1999. However, this decline may simply reflect the shift in the composition of GDP toward *services*, which require relatively less inventory support. When nonfarm inventories are compared with final sales of *goods and structures* only, as in the higher line on the graph, 1999 ratios are actually higher than those of 1947, whether measured in current or 2000 dollars. This seems to suggest that inventory efficiencies achieved by individual firms may not have translated into inventory efficiency for the economy as a whole. (Table 5-7)
- Interrupting the trend in both ratios is a period of increase extending from about 1966 through the early 1980s. This coincides with a period of high and rising inflation, which may have given firms incentives to hold inventory in excess of production needs as a hedge against, or speculation on, price increase. (Table 5-7 and Chapter 8)

Table 5-8. Manufacturing and Trade Sales and Inventories

Classification basis, year and month	Sales, billions of dollars					Inventories, billions of dollars, end of period, seasonally adjusted				Ratios, inventories to monthly sales, seasonally adjusted			
	Not seasonally adjusted, total	Seasonally adjusted				Total	Manufac-turing	Retail trade	Merchant wholesalers	Total	Manufac-turing	Retail trade	Merchant wholesalers
		Total	Manufac-turing	Retail trade	Merchant wholesalers								
SIC Basis													
1973	1 844.1	1 844.1	875.2	511.6	457.4	...	...	...	...	...	...	...	...
1974	2 134.9	2 134.9	1 017.5	541.7	575.8	...	...	...	...	...	...	...	...
1975	2 186.4	2 186.4	1 039.1	587.7	559.6	...	...	...	...	...	...	...	...
1976	2 449.8	2 449.8	1 185.6	655.9	608.4	...	...	...	...	...	...	...	...
1977	2 754.2	2 754.2	1 358.4	722.1	673.6	...	...	...	...	...	...	...	...
1978	3 123.8	3 123.8	1 522.9	804.0	797.0	...	...	...	...	...	...	...	...
1979	3 572.4	3 572.4	1 727.2	896.6	948.6	...	...	...	...	...	...	...	...
1980	3 926.8	3 926.8	1 852.7	956.9	1 117.2	...	...	121.1	122.6	...	...	...	...
1981	4 269.9	4 269.9	2 017.5	1 038.2	1 214.2	...	...	132.7	129.7	...	...	1.48	1.25
1982	4 171.5	4 171.5	1 960.2	1 068.7	1 142.5	573.9	311.9	134.6	127.4	1.67	1.95	1.49	1.36
1983	4 431.4	4 431.4	2 070.6	1 170.2	1 190.7	590.3	312.4	147.8	130.1	1.56	1.78	1.44	1.28
1984	4 921.5	4 921.5	2 288.2	1 286.9	1 346.4	649.8	339.5	167.8	142.5	1.53	1.73	1.49	1.23
1985	5 071.0	5 071.0	2 334.5	1 375.0	1 361.5	664.0	334.7	181.9	147.4	1.55	1.73	1.52	1.28
1986	5 165.0	5 165.0	2 335.9	1 449.6	1 379.5	662.7	322.7	186.5	153.6	1.55	1.68	1.56	1.32
1987	5 492.8	5 492.8	2 475.9	1 541.3	1 475.6	709.8	338.1	207.8	163.9	1.50	1.59	1.55	1.29
1988	5 965.9	5 965.9	2 695.4	1 656.2	1 614.2	767.2	369.4	219.0	178.8	1.49	1.57	1.54	1.30
1989	6 324.5	6 324.5	2 840.4	1 759.0	1 725.1	815.5	391.2	237.2	187.0	1.52	1.63	1.58	1.28
1990	6 550.9	6 550.9	2 912.2	1 844.6	1 794.1	840.7	405.1	239.8	195.8	1.52	1.65	1.56	1.29
1991	6 513.8	6 513.8	2 878.2	1 855.9	1 779.7	834.7	391.0	243.4	200.4	1.53	1.65	1.54	1.33
1992	6 806.1	6 806.1	3 004.7	1 951.6	1 849.8	842.9	382.5	252.2	208.2	1.48	1.54	1.52	1.32
NAICS Basis													
1992	6 494.7	6 494.7	2 904.0	1 859.1	1 731.6	840.2	379.2	268.0	193.1	1.53	1.57	1.67	1.31
1993	6 816.9	6 816.9	3 020.5	1 986.4	1 810.0	867.4	380.1	286.1	201.2	1.50	1.51	1.68	1.31
1994	7 328.0	7 328.0	3 238.1	2 156.3	1 933.6	930.7	400.3	312.2	218.1	1.47	1.44	1.66	1.29
1995	7 862.7	7 862.7	3 479.7	2 268.3	2 114.7	989.1	425.2	329.6	234.3	1.48	1.44	1.72	1.30
1996	8 249.7	8 249.7	3 597.2	2 412.7	2 239.8	1 008.6	430.8	340.6	237.2	1.46	1.43	1.67	1.28
1997	8 689.5	8 689.5	3 834.7	2 520.3	2 334.5	1 049.5	443.8	351.0	254.8	1.42	1.37	1.64	1.27
1998	8 924.4	8 924.4	3 899.8	2 644.8	2 379.8	1 082.0	449.2	365.1	267.7	1.44	1.39	1.62	1.32
1999	9 450.4	9 450.4	4 031.9	2 878.9	2 539.6	1 142.3	463.6	394.2	284.4	1.41	1.35	1.59	1.30
2000	10 022.3	10 022.3	4 208.6	3 070.2	2 743.6	1 200.7	481.4	417.7	301.6	1.41	1.35	1.59	1.29
2001	9 828.7	9 828.7	3 970.5	3 156.8	2 701.5	1 146.2	452.2	406.0	287.9	1.44	1.42	1.58	1.32
2002	9 864.2	9 864.2	3 891.8	3 230.1	2 742.3	1 163.7	444.2	430.5	289.0	1.40	1.37	1.56	1.25
2003	10 284.0	10 284.0	3 999.1	3 399.5	2 885.3	1 185.5	438.6	451.5	295.4	1.37	1.33	1.56	1.21
2000													
January	737.8	827.9	352.9	250.7	224.3	1 144.9	463.7	394.1	287.1	1.38	1.31	1.57	1.28
February	789.7	821.5	343.7	254.2	223.6	1 150.7	466.6	395.5	288.5	1.40	1.36	1.56	1.29
March	878.6	834.0	350.4	257.4	226.2	1 155.5	467.3	397.4	290.7	1.39	1.33	1.54	1.29
April	807.6	834.6	353.5	253.6	227.5	1 162.1	470.2	398.9	293.1	1.39	1.33	1.57	1.29
May	859.6	832.6	351.0	254.0	227.7	1 168.7	470.2	403.6	294.9	1.40	1.34	1.59	1.30
June	887.3	840.6	355.3	254.6	230.7	1 178.9	474.0	407.9	297.0	1.40	1.33	1.60	1.29
July	787.2	835.8	351.2	255.0	229.5	1 180.6	476.0	406.8	297.8	1.41	1.36	1.60	1.30
August	860.7	832.2	348.2	254.9	229.1	1 188.7	477.2	412.6	298.9	1.43	1.37	1.62	1.30
September	858.6	843.9	353.3	259.2	231.4	1 188.4	477.4	411.9	299.1	1.41	1.35	1.59	1.29
October	851.2	838.8	348.5	258.1	232.2	1 194.5	479.5	414.4	300.6	1.42	1.38	1.61	1.29
November	833.6	834.4	346.7	257.4	230.4	1 201.2	481.8	417.1	302.3	1.44	1.39	1.62	1.31
December	870.4	838.7	347.7	257.7	233.3	1 200.7	481.4	417.7	301.6	1.43	1.38	1.62	1.29
2001													
January	762.9	829.7	337.9	260.0	231.9	1 203.8	484.3	418.2	301.3	1.45	1.43	1.61	1.30
February	775.0	838.0	346.7	260.3	231.1	1 200.2	483.4	415.7	301.0	1.43	1.39	1.60	1.30
March	862.1	827.9	341.6	258.3	228.0	1 196.7	479.9	415.8	301.0	1.45	1.40	1.61	1.32
April	804.3	820.9	332.0	262.4	226.5	1 197.6	479.6	416.3	301.8	1.46	1.44	1.59	1.33
May	860.2	830.7	339.3	263.8	227.6	1 197.5	477.2	417.3	303.0	1.44	1.41	1.58	1.33
June	851.6	817.7	332.0	262.5	223.1	1 190.4	473.2	416.5	300.7	1.46	1.43	1.59	1.35
July	780.0	816.4	330.8	261.1	224.6	1 185.8	470.3	417.4	298.1	1.45	1.42	1.60	1.33
August	850.5	817.0	330.1	262.1	224.8	1 186.0	466.6	421.6	297.7	1.45	1.41	1.61	1.32
September	797.1	802.9	320.4	258.0	224.6	1 179.5	462.9	420.3	296.4	1.47	1.44	1.63	1.32
October	842.7	818.0	321.9	276.3	219.8	1 162.6	460.3	408.4	293.9	1.42	1.43	1.48	1.34
November	807.8	807.4	320.1	267.2	220.1	1 151.9	456.4	405.1	290.4	1.43	1.43	1.52	1.32
December	834.5	806.0	321.9	264.6	219.5	1 146.2	452.2	406.0	287.9	1.42	1.40	1.53	1.31
2002													
January	745.0	808.9	323.8	263.9	221.2	1 144.4	448.9	408.5	287.0	1.41	1.39	1.55	1.30
February	745.7	808.9	320.1	265.8	223.0	1 141.1	446.4	410.3	284.4	1.41	1.39	1.54	1.28
March	827.5	807.4	318.5	265.6	223.3	1 139.6	445.4	409.7	284.5	1.41	1.40	1.54	1.27
April	817.0	822.3	325.9	269.7	226.7	1 137.4	444.6	410.2	282.6	1.38	1.36	1.52	1.25
May	851.4	819.7	326.0	266.2	227.5	1 141.0	442.9	415.1	283.0	1.39	1.36	1.56	1.24
June	836.6	820.7	322.8	269.0	228.8	1 143.5	442.4	416.6	284.5	1.39	1.37	1.55	1.24
July	808.4	829.3	328.4	271.6	229.3	1 150.1	442.6	420.7	286.8	1.39	1.35	1.55	1.25
August	858.3	831.4	326.2	272.8	232.4	1 151.2	442.8	420.6	287.7	1.38	1.36	1.54	1.24
September	828.3	826.9	326.2	269.0	231.8	1 156.8	443.6	424.9	288.4	1.40	1.36	1.58	1.24
October	858.0	831.4	329.3	270.8	231.3	1 156.8	443.5	426.6	286.6	1.39	1.35	1.58	1.24
November	822.9	832.3	326.5	272.0	233.8	1 158.5	442.5	429.2	286.8	1.39	1.36	1.58	1.23
December	865.3	829.9	323.4	274.5	232.0	1 163.7	444.2	430.5	289.0	1.40	1.37	1.57	1.25
2003													
January	780.7	841.1	329.7	276.2	235.2	1 165.8	444.2	433.0	288.6	1.39	1.35	1.57	1.23
February	771.4	834.0	325.6	272.9	235.6	1 172.1	446.1	436.8	289.3	1.41	1.37	1.60	1.23
March	864.6	846.8	330.8	278.3	237.7	1 175.1	445.2	439.5	290.5	1.39	1.35	1.58	1.22
April	834.0	835.2	322.6	279.1	233.5	1 176.6	445.2	440.8	290.5	1.41	1.38	1.58	1.24
May	859.2	834.8	323.9	277.9	233.0	1 172.9	444.0	439.6	289.2	1.41	1.37	1.58	1.24
June	871.8	847.9	328.6	282.6	236.6	1 172.5	442.7	441.0	288.9	1.38	1.35	1.56	1.22
July	845.4	861.2	337.2	285.2	238.8	1 172.3	440.8	442.5	289.0	1.36	1.31	1.55	1.21
August	871.4	860.7	331.7	289.0	240.0	1 169.0	439.6	439.4	290.0	1.36	1.33	1.52	1.21
September	882.7	866.8	337.6	287.6	241.5	1 173.4	438.3	443.9	291.2	1.35	1.30	1.54	1.21
October	906.3	873.5	339.8	287.3	246.4	1 177.5	438.7	446.3	292.5	1.35	1.29	1.55	1.19
November	852.4	879.9	341.5	290.7	247.7	1 181.7	438.1	450.1	293.5	1.34	1.28	1.55	1.18
December	944.1	891.3	348.5	291.3	251.5	1 185.5	438.6	451.5	295.4	1.33	1.26	1.55	1.17

... = Not available.

Table 5-9. Real Manufacturing and Trade Sales and Inventories

(Billions of chained [1996 or 2000] dollars, ratios; seasonally adjusted; annual figures are averages of seasonally adjusted monthly data.)

Classification basis, year and month	Sales, monthly average				Inventories, end of period				Ratios, end-of-period inventories to monthly average sales			
	Total	Manufacturing	Retail trade	Merchant wholesalers	Total	Manufacturing	Retail trade	Merchant wholesalers	Total	Manufacturing	Retail trade	Merchant wholesalers
SIC Basis (1996 dollars)												
1973	408.3	203.8	114.8	90.6	537.1	281.6	144.4	103.5	1.32	1.38	1.26	1.14
1974	405.8	199.0	109.4	97.3	567.5	302.8	142.3	113.7	1.40	1.52	1.30	1.17
1975	376.2	179.0	110.1	87.5	546.6	295.2	135.3	107.1	1.45	1.65	1.23	1.22
1976	403.5	195.4	117.4	91.4	578.9	309.3	145.7	115.0	1.43	1.58	1.24	1.26
1977	431.8	211.2	123.2	98.0	607.3	317.9	153.9	127.2	1.41	1.51	1.25	1.30
1978	458.5	221.3	129.1	108.4	645.7	332.5	164.1	141.3	1.41	1.50	1.27	1.30
1979	469.5	224.2	131.3	114.0	666.7	345.3	164.1	148.9	1.42	1.54	1.25	1.31
1980	454.9	211.5	126.5	116.4	669.2	345.7	159.5	155.7	1.47	1.63	1.26	1.34
1981	457.7	213.1	127.0	117.1	685.7	350.3	168.4	159.5	1.50	1.64	1.33	1.36
1982	439.1	202.9	125.8	110.3	663.4	334.6	164.5	157.8	1.51	1.65	1.31	1.43
1983	460.7	212.4	135.1	113.5	675.3	334.2	177.9	157.9	1.47	1.57	1.32	1.39
1984	499.3	229.3	144.8	125.4	740.6	363.2	199.7	172.6	1.48	1.58	1.38	1.38
1985	513.8	233.5	151.2	129.4	755.3	356.9	215.1	180.6	1.47	1.53	1.42	1.40
1986	533.6	237.6	159.6	136.6	762.4	353.1	218.5	189.2	1.43	1.49	1.37	1.38
1987	553.2	248.0	164.2	141.3	799.5	361.6	239.7	197.6	1.45	1.46	1.46	1.40
1988	579.1	259.4	171.3	148.6	832.7	378.5	247.4	205.9	1.44	1.46	1.44	1.39
1989	590.5	261.9	175.6	153.1	864.6	392.7	261.9	209.2	1.46	1.50	1.49	1.37
1990	593.9	261.4	177.3	155.3	880.1	401.6	260.2	217.1	1.48	1.54	1.47	1.40
1991	586.4	257.1	174.0	155.3	878.2	394.9	260.8	221.9	1.50	1.54	1.50	1.43
1992	607.7	266.4	179.9	161.5	886.6	390.1	265.4	230.9	1.46	1.46	1.48	1.43
1993	632.7	274.5	188.7	169.4	912.0	393.7	280.8	237.3	1.44	1.43	1.49	1.40
1994	670.3	290.1	201.0	179.2	959.2	405.8	301.4	252.0	1.43	1.40	1.50	1.41
1995	699.5	301.1	208.2	190.2	996.4	419.9	313.6	263.0	1.42	1.39	1.51	1.38
1996	726.0	309.5	218.5	198.0	1 016.4	430.0	321.0	265.4	1.40	1.39	1.47	1.34
NAICS Basis (2000 dollars)												
1997	737.1	324.1	219.8	190.2	1 025.1	430.7	340.6	254.1	1.39	1.33	1.55	1.34
1998	774.7	335.6	234.2	203.2	1 081.4	449.3	357.9	274.4	1.40	1.34	1.53	1.35
1999	819.4	346.2	253.6	218.9	1 143.8	466.3	385.5	292.0	1.40	1.35	1.52	1.33
2000	844.8	350.2	265.9	228.7	1 188.3	474.2	407.1	307.0	1.41	1.35	1.53	1.34
2001	834.8	331.2	274.0	228.7	1 147.9	452.8	396.3	298.6	1.38	1.37	1.45	1.31
2002	846.2	327.7	284.5	233.8	1 166.2	445.4	422.6	297.9	1.38	1.36	1.49	1.27
2003	866.9	328.3	300.7	238.0	1 165.7	430.2	435.6	299.7	1.35	1.31	1.45	1.26
2000												
January	847.1	357.5	263.4	227.2	1 143.9	465.1	384.6	294.1	1.35	1.30	1.46	1.30
February	835.0	345.8	265.8	223.5	1 147.0	466.4	385.4	295.2	1.37	1.35	1.45	1.32
March	843.3	350.6	267.4	225.3	1 149.7	465.6	387.6	296.5	1.36	1.33	1.45	1.32
April	846.8	355.1	263.6	227.9	1 156.0	467.8	389.7	298.4	1.37	1.32	1.48	1.31
May	843.9	352.6	264.2	227.1	1 161.1	467.5	393.7	299.9	1.38	1.33	1.49	1.32
June	848.5	354.6	263.9	229.8	1 169.3	470.6	396.7	302.0	1.38	1.33	1.50	1.31
July	845.1	350.3	265.2	229.5	1 173.5	471.6	398.9	302.9	1.39	1.35	1.50	1.32
August	844.8	348.3	266.1	230.3	1 178.2	472.0	401.9	304.2	1.40	1.36	1.51	1.32
September	850.8	351.8	268.8	230.5	1 178.8	471.5	402.4	304.8	1.39	1.34	1.50	1.32
October	846.2	347.0	267.7	231.3	1 184.5	473.1	405.3	306.2	1.40	1.36	1.51	1.32
November	840.9	344.2	266.7	229.6	1 189.4	474.8	406.8	307.7	1.41	1.38	1.53	1.34
December	845.1	344.8	267.4	232.7	1 188.3	474.2	407.1	307.0	1.41	1.38	1.52	1.32
2001												
January	836.5	335.1	269.4	231.4	1 189.9	476.6	406.5	306.8	1.42	1.42	1.51	1.33
February	845.6	344.1	269.6	231.5	1 186.0	475.5	403.5	306.9	1.40	1.38	1.50	1.33
March	837.9	339.8	268.2	229.2	1 182.1	472.0	402.9	307.2	1.41	1.39	1.50	1.34
April	830.3	329.4	272.0	227.9	1 184.2	471.7	404.2	308.3	1.43	1.43	1.49	1.35
May	838.1	336.1	272.4	228.7	1 184.5	469.5	405.0	309.9	1.41	1.40	1.49	1.36
June	827.5	329.7	271.2	225.3	1 178.5	466.1	404.3	308.0	1.42	1.41	1.49	1.37
July	832.2	331.0	271.4	228.8	1 174.4	464.0	404.4	305.9	1.41	1.40	1.49	1.34
August	834.0	330.6	273.6	228.8	1 173.6	461.7	406.0	305.8	1.41	1.40	1.48	1.34
September	817.9	319.5	268.4	228.1	1 169.6	458.9	405.7	304.9	1.43	1.44	1.51	1.34
October	842.9	325.4	289.5	227.2	1 157.5	457.8	396.5	303.2	1.37	1.41	1.37	1.33
November	836.3	325.0	281.7	228.6	1 147.9	455.5	391.9	300.6	1.37	1.40	1.39	1.32
December	838.7	328.2	280.6	228.7	1 147.9	452.8	396.3	298.6	1.37	1.38	1.41	1.31
2002												
January	841.7	330.7	279.9	230.3	1 150.5	451.1	401.1	298.1	1.37	1.36	1.43	1.29
February	841.4	326.5	282.5	231.7	1 146.5	449.6	401.1	295.5	1.36	1.38	1.42	1.28
March	834.7	322.9	281.0	229.8	1 146.1	449.1	401.3	295.6	1.37	1.39	1.43	1.29
April	846.1	329.3	283.6	233.2	1 145.1	448.4	402.7	293.8	1.35	1.36	1.42	1.26
May	846.0	330.5	280.8	234.3	1 147.9	446.9	406.4	294.4	1.36	1.35	1.45	1.26
June	846.3	326.5	284.0	235.7	1 151.6	446.1	409.3	295.8	1.36	1.37	1.44	1.26
July	852.2	331.2	286.6	234.5	1 155.0	446.2	410.6	297.8	1.36	1.35	1.43	1.27
August	852.6	328.9	287.5	236.5	1 154.3	446.3	409.9	297.9	1.35	1.36	1.43	1.26
September	845.1	326.5	283.6	234.9	1 158.4	446.5	413.9	297.6	1.37	1.37	1.46	1.27
October	847.7	328.8	285.8	232.9	1 157.7	445.9	416.1	295.3	1.37	1.36	1.46	1.27
November	851.5	326.7	287.6	236.9	1 161.5	444.4	421.2	295.6	1.36	1.36	1.47	1.25
December	849.2	323.4	291.0	234.6	1 166.2	445.4	422.6	297.9	1.37	1.38	1.45	1.27
2003												
January	854.6	327.2	292.0	235.0	1 166.3	444.3	424.5	297.2	1.37	1.36	1.45	1.27
February	838.8	319.4	286.7	231.5	1 170.3	444.7	428.0	297.3	1.40	1.39	1.49	1.28
March	847.6	322.7	291.5	232.7	1 170.7	442.3	429.6	298.5	1.38	1.37	1.47	1.28
April	848.4	319.6	294.4	233.6	1 169.3	441.6	429.2	298.2	1.38	1.38	1.46	1.28
May	853.0	322.9	295.7	234.3	1 165.9	440.1	427.9	297.5	1.37	1.36	1.45	1.27
June	864.6	326.2	300.6	237.9	1 166.2	438.6	429.9	297.5	1.35	1.35	1.43	1.25
July	877.1	333.9	304.0	239.7	1 166.6	436.7	431.6	298.0	1.33	1.31	1.42	1.24
August	873.0	327.5	306.6	239.2	1 161.5	435.4	428.2	297.7	1.33	1.33	1.40	1.24
September	879.0	333.2	305.5	240.8	1 165.6	433.5	433.3	298.6	1.33	1.30	1.42	1.24
October	883.0	333.5	306.6	243.6	1 167.7	432.9	435.4	299.2	1.32	1.30	1.42	1.23
November	888.5	334.4	311.9	243.4	1 167.9	431.0	437.7	299.0	1.32	1.29	1.40	1.23
December	895.2	339.7	312.8	244.4	1 165.7	430.2	435.6	299.7	1.30	1.27	1.39	1.23

Table 5-10. Capital Expenditures, 1996–2002

(Millions of dollars.)

Capital expenditures	All companies						
	1996	1997	1998	1999	2000	2001	2002
TOTAL	807 070	871 765	970 897	1 046 952	1 161 029	1 109 004	1 008 450
Structures	243 427	273 298	329 111	320 078	364 407	363 748	348 894
New	223 588	254 451	284 491	296 496	329 525	335 538	308 027
Used	19 839	18 849	44 620	23 583	34 882	28 210	40 867
Equipment	563 641	598 466	641 786	726 874	796 622	745 256	659 556
New	526 016	562 019	606 210	689 553	750 626	706 617	618 872
Used	37 625	36 447	35 577	37 321	45 996	38 639	40 684
Not distributed as structures or equipment	2	0	0	0	0	0	0
CAPITAL LEASE AND CAPITALIZED INTEREST EXPENSES [1]							
Capital leases	15 675	16 066	16 533	17 140	19 545	15 529	15 654
Capitalized interest	...	...	...	...	...	...	...

Capital expenditures	Companies with employees						
	1996	1997	1998	1999	2000	2001	2002
TOTAL	707 110	772 343	896 452	974 631	1 089 862	1 052 344	928 046
Structures	204 345	236 166	300 283	293 787	338 120	346 221	315 579
New	191 867	225 107	260 008	276 094	309 541	323 871	286 777
Used	12 478	11 060	40 275	17 693	28 579	22 349	28 801
Equipment	502 762	536 177	596 169	680 843	751 742	706 123	612 467
New	481 785	515 965	570 397	656 344	718 227	679 090	584 422
Used	20 977	20 212	25 773	24 499	33 515	27 033	28 045
Not distributed as structures or equipment	2	0	0	0	0	0	0
CAPITAL LEASE AND CAPITALIZED INTEREST EXPENSES [1]							
Capital leases	13 023	14 549	15 631	16 594	19 184	15 500	15 412
Capitalized interest	6 827	7 273	9 799	9 591	11 423	11 969	...

Capital expenditures	Companies without employees						
	1996	1997	1998	1999	2000	2001	2002
TOTAL	99 960	99 422	74 445	72 322	71 168	56 660	80 404
Structures	39 082	37 132	28 828	26 291	26 287	17 527	33 316
New	31 721	29 344	24 483	20 402	19 984	11 667	21 250
Used	7 361	7 789	4 345	5 889	6 303	5 860	12 066
Equipment	60 878	62 289	45 617	46 030	44 880	39 133	47 088
New	44 231	46 054	35 813	33 209	32 399	27 528	34 450
Used	16 648	16 235	9 804	12 821	12 481	11 605	12 638
Not distributed as structures or equipment	0	0	0	0	0	0	0
CAPITAL LEASE AND CAPITALIZED INTEREST EXPENSES [1]							
Capital leases	2 652	1 517	902	546	361	29	242
Capitalized interest	...	...	...	...	...	...	...

[1] Included in data shown above.
... = Not available.

Table 5-11. Capital Expenditures for Structures and Equipment for Companies With Employees by Major NAICS Industry Sector, 1998–2002

(Millions of dollars.)

Year and type of expenditure	Total	Forestry, fishing, and agricultural services (113–115)	Mining (21)	Utilities (22)	Construction (23)	Manufacturing (31–33)			Wholesale trade (42)	Retail trade (44–45)	Transportation and warehousing (48–49)	Information (51)
						Total	Durable goods industries (321, 327, 33)	Nondurable goods industries (31, 322–326)				
1998												
Total expenditures	896 452	854	40 424	36 010	26 867	203 587	117 901	85 685	29 169	57 276	51 287	96 487
Structures, total	300 283	206	26 503	18 574	7 062	39 028	19 406	19 622	7 480	25 105	13 036	24 721
New	260 008	158	24 714	17 771	4 749	37 122	18 449	18 673	6 738	23 104	12 365	24 218
Used	40 275	49	1 789	804	2 313	1 906	957	949	742	2 001	671	503
Equipment, total	596 169	648	13 921	17 436	19 805	164 559	98 496	66 063	21 690	32 171	38 251	71 766
New	570 397	603	12 625	17 266	15 346	159 363	95 571	63 792	20 470	30 359	33 409	70 827
Used	25 773	46	1 296	170	4 458	5 196	2 925	2 271	1 220	1 812	4 842	939
1999												
Total expenditures	974 631	1 716	30 586	42 802	23 110	196 399	117 005	79 394	32 442	64 063	57 299	122 827
Structures, total	293 787	344	17 626	21 241	1 753	33 985	17 320	16 665	7 264	29 494	14 122	34 924
New	276 094	331	17 039	20 784	1 505	32 814	16 581	16 233	6 508	28 670	13 859	33 733
Used	17 693	13	587	457	248	1 171	739	432	756	824	263	1 191
Equipment, total	680 843	1 371	12 960	21 561	21 356	162 414	99 685	62 729	25 179	34 569	43 178	87 903
New	656 344	1 190	12 167	20 545	18 600	157 715	96 434	61 281	23 714	33 567	40 425	85 310
Used	24 499	182	793	1 016	2 756	4 699	3 251	1 448	1 465	1 002	2 752	2 593
2000												
Total expenditures	1 089 862	1 488	42 522	61 302	25 049	214 827	133 786	81 041	33 579	69 791	59 851	160 177
Structures, total	338 120	139	28 620	29 472	2 803	39 434	21 228	18 207	8 923	32 037	13 457	41 502
New	309 541	134	25 500	29 258	2 583	36 643	19 748	16 895	8 364	30 413	13 190	40 062
Used	28 579	5	3 120	214	220	2 791	1 480	1 312	559	1 624	267	1 440
Equipment, total	751 742	1 350	13 902	31 830	22 245	175 393	112 558	62 835	24 656	37 754	46 394	118 675
New	718 227	1 086	12 854	27 937	17 788	169 454	108 703	60 751	23 610	36 428	43 455	117 835
Used	33 515	264	1 048	3 893	4 458	5 939	3 856	2 083	1 046	1 326	2 938	841
2001												
Total expenditures	1 052 344	1 532	51 278	82 823	24 802	192 835	118 875	73 959	29 981	66 917	57 756	144 793
Structures, total	346 221	226	32 678	38 093	3 859	39 815	22 032	17 784	6 932	30 010	16 594	41 742
New	323 871	149	31 825	36 504	3 389	38 001	20 701	17 301	5 357	29 118	14 479	41 384
Used	22 349	77	853	1 588	470	1 814	1 331	483	1 575	892	2 116	358
Equipment, total	706 123	1 306	18 600	44 731	20 943	153 019	96 844	56 176	23 049	36 906	41 161	103 051
New	679 090	1 091	17 567	42 939	17 432	148 397	94 251	54 145	20 757	35 074	38 521	102 410
Used	27 033	215	1 033	1 792	3 511	4 623	2 592	2 030	2 292	1 833	2 640	641
2002												
Total expenditures	928 046	1 902	42 309	67 137	25 372	163 291	90 059	73 233	27 859	59 368	47 774	88 924
Structures, total	315 579	184	24 354	32 558	2 317	32 519	15 859	16 660	6 014	25 937	12 181	26 361
New	286 777	118	23 444	31 064	1 616	30 884	15 073	15 811	5 573	24 702	10 255	26 226
Used	28 801	66	910	1 494	700	1 635	786	849	441	1 234	1 926	135
Equipment, total	612 467	1 718	17 955	34 579	23 055	130 772	74 199	56 573	21 846	33 432	35 593	62 562
New	584 422	1 311	16 419	34 382	19 249	124 754	71 373	53 381	19 490	31 559	31 880	62 260
Used	28 045	407	1 536	196	3 806	6 018	2 826	3 192	2 355	1 873	3 713	303

Note: Detail may not add up to total because of rounding.

Table 5-11. Capital Expenditures for Structures and Equipment for Companies With Employees by Major NAICS Industry Sector, 1998–2002—*Continued*

(Millions of dollars.)

Year and type of expenditure	Finance and insurance (52)	Real estate and rental and leasing (53)	Professional, scientific, and technical services (54)	Management of companies and enterprises (55)	Administrative and support and waste management (56)	Educational services (61)	Health care and social assistance (62)	Arts, entertainment, and recreation (71)	Accommodation and food services (72)	Other services, except public administration (81)	Structure and equipment expenditures serving multiple industries
1998											
Total expenditures	118 173	85 184	22 277	1 821	13 110	12 983	47 109	8 994	20 822	20 627	3 392
Structures, total	27 221	36 775	4 886	753	4 288	9 109	23 971	5 045	12 045	13 737	738
New	16 858	24 109	4 572	502	3 745	8 734	21 328	4 838	10 402	13 280	699
Used	10 362	12 666	314	251	543	374	2 643	206	1 643	457	39
Equipment, total	90 952	48 409	17 390	1 068	8 822	3 874	23 138	3 949	8 777	6 890	2 654
New	90 058	46 877	16 868	1 030	8 346	3 825	22 465	3 752	8 005	6 296	2 609
Used	894	1 532	522	38	476	49	672	197	772	594	46
1999											
Total expenditures	130 101	100 629	29 546	6 065	16 227	13 532	51 342	13 355	23 328	16 902	2 359
Structures, total	20 080	33 903	6 780	1 668	2 875	9 767	25 922	8 119	13 431	9 975	516
New	17 918	30 295	6 168	1 509	2 773	9 140	24 159	7 971	11 391	9 033	495
Used	2 162	3 608	613	159	102	627	1 763	148	2 040	941	21
Equipment, total	110 021	66 726	22 766	4 397	13 353	3 766	25 420	5 236	9 897	6 928	1 843
New	109 577	63 555	22 153	4 319	12 323	3 668	24 945	5 125	9 324	6 370	1 752
Used	444	3 171	613	78	1 029	97	475	111	573	558	91
2000											
Total expenditures	133 684	92 456	34 055	5 054	17 506	18 223	52 166	19 125	26 307	21 125	1 572
Structures, total	23 010	24 815	8 141	1 570	4 032	13 699	26 868	12 245	13 873	13 274	206
New	20 298	17 793	7 470	955	3 504	12 965	23 999	11 627	12 879	11 705	200
Used	2 712	7 022	671	615	528	735	2 869	618	993	1 569	6
Equipment, total	110 675	67 641	25 914	3 484	13 475	4 523	25 299	6 880	12 434	7 852	1 366
New	109 678	62 175	24 847	3 403	12 723	4 338	24 407	6 161	11 501	7 192	1 357
Used	997	5 466	1 067	81	752	186	892	719	933	659	10
2001											
Total expenditures	131 105	82 674	30 464	3 035	15 785	17 377	52 932	14 974	21 365	29 006	911
Structures, total	22 744	20 489	7 258	933	3 527	12 852	27 030	8 998	12 248	20 031	163
New	19 571	17 325	6 793	869	3 367	11 860	25 241	8 157	11 402	18 918	162
Used	3 173	3 164	465	64	160	991	1 789	841	846	1 112	0
Equipment, total	108 361	62 185	23 206	2 102	12 258	4 525	25 902	5 976	9 117	8 976	749
New	107 268	60 295	22 330	2 019	11 644	4 238	24 573	5 590	7 921	8 300	725
Used	1 093	1 891	876	83	613	287	1 329	386	1 196	676	24
2002											
Total expenditures	125 697	96 720	26 635	3 141	14 590	19 446	59 097	13 823	22 461	21 286	1 213
Structures, total	24 934	38 004	7 279	1 068	3 271	14 640	30 350	7 942	12 212	13 260	193
New	19 815	31 644	6 574	1 048	2 943	13 586	27 332	7 497	10 903	11 362	191
Used	5 119	6 360	706	20	328	1 055	3 018	445	1 309	1 899	3
Equipment, total	100 763	58 717	19 356	2 073	11 319	4 806	28 747	5 881	10 249	8 026	1 020
New	100 217	56 479	18 576	2 058	10 461	4 620	27 922	5 601	9 294	6 876	1 014
Used	546	2 238	780	16	857	186	825	280	955	1 149	6

Note: Detail may not add up to total because of rounding.

NOTES AND DEFINITIONS

TABLES 5-1 THROUGH 5-4 AND 5-7
GROSS SAVING AND INVESTMENT ACCOUNTS; INVENTORIES TO SALES RATIOS

SOURCE: U.S. DEPARTMENT OF COMMERCE, BUREAU OF ECONOMIC ANALYSIS

Revisions

Data in these tables reflect revisions to the national income and product accounts (NIPAs) available through August 2004.

Definitions: Table 5-1

Gross saving is saving before the deduction of allowances for the consumption, that is, the using up, of fixed capital. It represents the amount of saving available to finance gross investment. Net saving is gross saving less allowances for fixed capital consumption, and represents the amount of saving available for financing new capital spending.

Personal saving is derived by subtracting personal outlays from disposable personal income; see Chapter 4. It is the current net saving of individuals (including proprietors of unincorporated businesses), nonprofit institutions that primarily serve individuals, life insurance carriers, retirement funds, private noninsured welfare funds, and private trust funds. Conceptually, personal saving may also be viewed as the sum for all persons (including institutions as just defined) of the net acquisition of financial assets and the change in physical assets less the sum of net borrowing and consumption of fixed capital. In either case, it is defined to exclude capital gains, that is, it excludes profits on the sale of homes, securities, and other property—whether realized or unrealized—and includes the noncorporate inventory valuation and capital consumption adjustments (IVA and CCAdj). (See Notes and Definitions to Tables 1-1 through 1-12.)

Undistributed profits is corporate profits after tax less dividends, with the corporate IVA and corporate CCAdj. (See Notes and Definitions to Tables 1-1 through 1-12.)

Government net saving was formerly called "current surplus (deficit-) of general government." See Chapter 6 for further detail on the government accounts. Where current receipts of government exceed current expenditures, government has a current surplus, indicated by a positive value, and saving is made available to finance investment by government or other sectors—for example, by the repayment of debt, which can free up funds for private investment. Where current expenditures exceed current receipts, there is a government deficit, indicated by a negative value, and government must borrow, drawing on funds that would otherwise be available for private investment.

Consumption of fixed capital is a charge for the using up of private and government fixed capital, including software, located in the United States. It is based on studies of prices of used equipment and structures in resale markets. For general government and for nonprofit institutions that primarily serve individuals, it is recorded in government consumption expenditures and in personal consumption expenditures, respectively, as the value of the current services of the fixed capital assets owned and used by these entities. *Private consumption of fixed capital* consists of tax-return-based depreciation charges for corporations and nonfarm proprietorships and of historical-cost depreciation (calculated by the Bureau of Economic Analysis [BEA] using a geometric pattern of price declines) for farm proprietorships, rental income of persons, and nonprofit institutions, *minus* the capital consumption adjustments. (In other words, from the point of view of saving, the CCAdj is taken out of book depreciation and added to income and profits—it is a reallocation from one form of gross saving to another.)

Gross private domestic investment consists of gross private fixed investment and change in private inventories. See the Notes and Definitions for Chapter 1.

Gross government investment consists of federal, state, and local general government and government enterprise expenditures for fixed assets (structures, equipment, and software). Government inventory investment is included in government consumption expenditures. For more detail, see Chapter 6.

Capital account transactions, net is net cash or in-kind transfers between the United States and the rest of the world that are linked to the acquisition or disposition of an asset rather than the purchase or sale of currently produced goods and services. When positive it represents a net transfer from the United States to the rest of the world; when negative, a net transfer from the rest of the world. This represents a definitional category introduced in the 1999 revision. Estimates are available only from 1982 forward.

Net lending or net borrowing (-), NIPAs is equal to the international balance on current account as measured in the NIPAs (see Chapter 7) less capital account transactions, net. When positive, this represents net investment by the United States in the rest of the world; when negative, it represents net borrowing by the United States from the rest of the world. Before 1982, net lending or net borrowing equals the NIPA balance on current account, as estimates of capital account transactions are not available.

By definition, gross national saving must equal the sum of gross domestic investment, capital account transactions, and net international lending or borrowing. In practice, because of differences in measurement, they differ by the same *statistical discrepancy* calculated in the product and income accounts (see Chapter 1). Where the statistical discrepancy is negative, measured investment, capital transactions, and net international transactions have fallen short of measured saving.

Gross national income is national income plus the consumption of fixed capital (see Chapter 1). This is a new concept introduced in the 2003 revision. It is conceptually equal to gross national product, but differs by the statistical discrepancy. It is an appropriate denominator for the national saving ratios. Saving was previously measured as a percent of gross national product; in the revision, it is instead measured as a percent of the income-side equivalent of gross national product. Since saving is measured as a residual from income, it seems more appropriate to involve the same measurement imperfections in both the numerator and the denominator of the fraction.

Definitions: Tables 5-2 through 5-4

Gross private fixed investment comprises both nonresidential and residential fixed investment. It consists of purchases of fixed assets, which are commodities that will be used in a production process for more than one year, including replacements and additions to the capital stock. It is "gross" because it is measured before a deduction for consumption of fixed capital. It covers all investment by private businesses and nonprofit institutions in the United States, regardless of whether the investment is owned by U.S. residents. It does not include purchases of the same types of equipment and structures by government agencies, which are included in government gross investment, or investment by U.S. residents in other countries.

Gross nonresidential fixed investment consists of structures, equipment, and software not related to personal residences.

Nonresidential structures consists of new construction, brokers' commissions on sales of structures, and net purchases (purchases less sales) of used structures by private business and by nonprofit institutions from government agencies. New construction also includes hotels, motels, and mining exploration, shafts, and wells.

Nonresidential equipment and software consists of private business purchases, on capital account, of new machinery, equipment, and vehicles; purchases and in-house production of software; dealers' margins on sales of used equipment; and net purchases (purchases less sales) of used equipment from government agencies, persons, and the rest of the world. (It does not, however, include the personal-use portion of equipment purchased for both business and personal use, which is included in PCE.)

Residential private fixed investment consists of both structures and residential producers' durable equipment, that is, equipment owned by landlords and rented to tenants. Investment in *structures* consists of new units, improvements to existing units, manufactured homes, brokers' commissions on the sale of residential property, and net purchases (purchases less sales) of used structures from government agencies.

Real gross private investment (Table 5-3) and *Chain-type quantity indexes for private fixed investment* (Table 5-4). These are defined and explained in the Notes and Definitions to Chapter 1. The chained-dollar (2000) estimates in Table 5-3 are constructed by applying the changes in the chain-type quantity indexes, as shown in Table 5-4, to the 2000 current-dollar values; hence, they do not contain any information about time trends that is not already present in the quantity indexes.

Because the quantity indexes are chain-weighted at the basic level of aggregation, chained constant-dollar components generally do not add to the chained constant-dollar totals. For this reason, BEA only makes available 2000-dollar estimates back to 1990 (except for the very highest levels of aggregation of GDP), since the addition problem is less severe for years around the base year. However, the addition problem is so severe for computers that BEA does not publish even recent 2000-values for this component. BEA notes that "The quantity index for computers can be used to accurately measure the real growth rate of this component. However, because computers exhibit rapid changes in prices relative to other prices in the economy, the chained-dollar estimates should not be used to measure the component's relative importance or its contribution to the growth rate of more aggregate series...." Accurate estimates of these contributions are shown in BEA Table 5.3.2, which is published in the *Survey of Current Business* and can be found on the BEA Web site.

Definitions: Table 5-7

Inventories to sales ratios. The ratios shown in Table 5-7 are based on the inventory estimates underlying the measurement of inventory change in the NIPAs. They include data and estimates not only for the inventories held in manufacturing and trade (see the following Tables 5-8 and 5-9) but also for stocks held by all other businesses in the U.S. economy.

For the current-dollar ratios, inventories at the end of each quarter are valued in the prices that prevailed at the end of that quarter. For the constant-dollar ratios, they are valued in chained (2000) dollars. In both cases, the inventory/sales ratio is the value of the inventories at the end of the quarter divided by quarterly total sales at *monthly* rates (that is, quarterly totals divided by 3). In other words, they represent how many months' supply businesses had on hand at the end of the period. Annual data are those for the fourth quarter.

Data availability

Current data for some of these series are included in the monthly release of the latest NIPA estimates. All of the series are subsequently published each month in the *Survey of Current Business*. Current and historical data may be obtained from the BEA Internet site at <http://www.bea.gov> or the STAT-USA subscription Internet site at <http://www.stat-usa.gov>.

References

Sources of information about the NIPAs are listed in the Notes and Definitions for Tables 1-1 through 1-12.

**TABLE 5-5 AND 5-6
CURRENT-COST NET STOCK OF FIXED ASSETS; CHAIN-TYPE QUANTITY INDEXES FOR NET STOCK OF FIXED ASSETS**

Integrated with the NIPAs, BEA calculates measures of the level of the *stock* of fixed assets in the U.S. economy, or what is commonly called the "capital stock." (The fixed investment component of the GDP is a *flow*, the increment of new capital goods into the capital stock.) These two tables present two measures of the capital stock.

At the time *Business Statistics* went to press, new and revised data for the years 1993–2003 were available, but previous years' data had not been revised for comparability. However, the differences at the aggregate level for the overlap year 1993 were less than 0.2 percent, and the editor believes that the data are reasonably (if not strictly) comparable between 1992 and 1993.

Definitions and methods

The definitions of the capital stock categories are the same as used in the GDP investment categories (see Notes and Definitions to Tables 5-2 through 5-4, above).

The values of fixed capital and depreciation typically reported by businesses are inadequate for economic analysis and in general are not used in these measures. In business reports, capital is generally valued at historical costs—each year's capital acquisition in the prices of the year acquired—and therefore the totals represent a mixture of pricing bases. Reported depreciation is generally based on historical cost and on depreciation rates allowable by federal income tax law rather than a realistic rate of economic depreciation.

In these data, the *net stock of fixed assets* is measured by a perpetual inventory method. That is, net stock at any given time is the cumulative value of past gross investment less the cumulative value of past depreciation, including damages from disasters and war losses that exceed normal depreciation, such as the attack on September 11, 2001.

Gross investment is the gross fixed investment component of GDP. Depreciation for privately owned assets is the value of "consumption of fixed capital" in the NIPAs that is subtracted from gross domestic product in order to yield net domestic product. For government assets, the NIPA value of consumption of fixed capital does *not* include disaster and war loss damage, but the value of these damages is calculated by BEA and subtracted from the capital stock assets.

The initial calculations using this perpetual inventory method are performed in real terms for each type of asset. They are then aggregated to higher levels using an annual-weighted Fisher-type index; see the definition of *Real or chained-dollar estimates* in the Notes and Definitions to Chapter 1. This provides the *Chain-type quantity indexes* shown in Table 5-6. Growth rates in these indexes measure the real growth in the capital stock.

The real values are also converted to a *current-cost* basis to yield the values shown in Table 5-5. They are converted by multiplying the real values by the appropriate price index for the period under consideration. A major use of the current-cost net stock figures is comparison with the value of output in that year; for example, the current-cost net stock of fixed assets for the total economy divided by the current-dollar value of GDP yields a capital/output ratio for the entire economy. Growth rates in current-cost values will reflect both the real growth measured by the quantity indexes and the increase in the value at current prices of the existing stock.

Data availability

The fixed asset values are revised and updated periodically in articles in the *Survey of Current Business*. The 1993–2003 values shown here are from the September 2004 issue; earlier years are from May 2004. Revisions and updates are available on the BEA Web site.

References

The latest revision is presented and described in "Fixed Assets and Consumer Durable Goods for 1993–2003," *Survey of Current Business*, September 2004. Data for earlier years are presented and described in "Fixed Assets and Consumer Durable Goods: Preliminary Estimates for 2002 and Revised Estimates for 1925–2001," *Survey of Current Business*, May 2004. The fixed asset measures are described in *Fixed Assets and*

Consumer Durable Goods in the United States, 1925–97 (September 2003), available on the BEA Web site.

TABLES 5-8 AND 5-9
MANUFACTURING AND TRADE SALES AND INVENTORIES

SOURCES: U.S. DEPARTMENT OF COMMERCE, BUREAU OF THE CENSUS (CURRENT DOLLAR SERIES) AND U.S. DEPARTMENT OF COMMERCE, BUREAU OF ECONOMIC ANALYSIS (CONSTANT DOLLAR SERIES)

The current dollar data on these pages draw together summary data from the separate series on manufacturers' shipments, inventories, and orders; merchant wholesalers' sales and inventories; and retail sales and inventories, all of which are included in Part B of this book. Generally, current-dollar inventories are collected on a current cost (or pre-LIFO) basis. See the notes to Tables 17-4, 17-5, and 17-9 through 17-11 for further information about these data.

Data for recent years are compiled using the new North American Industry Classification System (NAICS), replacing the old Standard Industrial Classification (SIC).

- The Census Bureau has restated the current-dollar historical data on the NAICS basis back to January 1992. To allow the user to observe the difference between the two systems, and to "link" the new data to older data if a longer time series is required, *Business Statistics* is republishing the previous SIC-based annual data up through 1992, providing an overlap with the new data in that year.
- The Bureau of Economic Analysis has restated the constant-dollar data on the NAICS basis back to the beginning of 1997. *Business Statistics* is publishing the previous SIC-based annual data through 1996. BEA provides overlapping data on its Web site; see reference below.

In the NAICS, a few major industries have been taken out of manufacturing and trade entirely. Publishing and aerospace research activities have been reclassified from manufacturing to the new information industry, and food services and drinking places have been reclassified from retail trade to a new services category, Accommodation and Food Services, which also includes hotels and the like. A number of other activities have been moved within the broad category of manufacturing and trade. Food items made in retail establishments have been reclassified into manufacturing. A significant number of businesses previously classified as wholesale have been shifted to retail. Finally, the retail trade data, and therefore total manufacturing and trade, are no longer subdivided into durable and nondurable goods.

Based on these current-dollar values and relevant price data, estimates of real sales, inventories, and inventory-sales ratios are made by the Bureau of Economic Analysis (BEA). Note, however, that annual figures for sales are shown as annual *totals* in Table 5-8 but as *averages* of the monthly data in Table 5-9.

Inventory values are as of the end of the month or year. In Table 5-8, annual values for monthly current-dollar inventory-sales ratios are averages of seasonally adjusted monthly data. However, for the real ratios in Table 5-9, annual figures for inventory-sales ratios are calculated by BEA as year-end (that is, December) inventories divided by the monthly average of sales for the entire year. In all cases, the ratios in these two tables, like those in Table 5-7, represent the number of months' sales on hand as inventory at the end of the reporting period.

Data availability

Sales, inventories, and inventory-sales ratios for manufacturers, merchant wholesalers, and retailers are published monthly by the Census Bureau in a press release entitled "Manufacturing and Trade Inventories and Sales"; recent data are available on the Internet site at <http://www.census.gov/mtis/www/mtis.html>.

Sales and inventories in constant dollars are published regularly by the Bureau of Economic Analysis in the *Survey of Current Business*, most recently in the July 2004 issue. More recently updated data are available from the STAT-USA subscription Internet site at <http://www.stat-usa.gov> and on the BEA Internet site at <http://www.bea.gov>. On the latter, click on "Gross Domestic Product;" then, under "Supplemental Estimates," click "Underlying Detail Tables" and then "List of Underlying Detail Tables."

References

Further information comparing NAICS and SIC industries can be found on the Census Internet site, <http://www.census.gov>.

For information about the 1996 historical revisions to sales and inventories in constant dollars, see "Real Inventories, Sales, and Inventory-Sales Ratios for Manufacturing and Trade, 1977–95," *Survey of Current Business*, May 1996.

TABLES 5-10 AND 5-11
ANNUAL CAPITAL EXPENDITURES

SOURCE: U.S. DEPARTMENT OF COMMERCE, CENSUS BUREAU

These data are from the Census Bureau's Annual Capital Expenditures Survey (ACES). The survey provides detailed information on capital investment in new and used structures and equipment by nonfarm businesses for the years 1996 through 2002.

The survey is based on a sample of approximately 46,000 companies with employees and 15,000 non-employer businesses (businesses with an owner but no employees). For companies with employees, Census reports data for the years 1998 through 2002 for 132 separate industry categories from the North American Industry Classification System (NAICS); Table 5-11 shows these data for the major NAICS sectors. Total capital expenditures, with no industry detail, are reported for the non-employer businesses and shown in Table 5-10, where they can be compared with the totals for companies with employees, for the years 1996 through 2002.

Capital expenditures include all capitalized costs during the year for both new and used structures and equipment, including software, chargeable to fixed asset accounts for which depreciation or amortization accounts are ordinarily maintained. For projects lasting longer than one year, this definition includes gross additions to construction-in-progress accounts, even if the asset was not in use and not yet depreciated. For capital leases, the company using the asset (lessee) is asked to include the cost or present value of the leased assets in the year in which the lease was entered into. Also included in capital expenditures are capitalized leasehold improvements and capitalized interest charges on loans used to finance capital projects.

Data availability

The *Annual Capital Expenditure Survey: 2002* was published by the Census Bureau in February 2004 and, in addition to new data for 2002, contains data for 2000 and revised data for 2001. Previous surveys using NAICS, each containing the latest year's data and revisions for the preceding year, were issued in January 2003, April 2002, and May 2001. The 1998 and 1997 surveys show data by industry using the 1987 Standard Industrial Classification (SIC). Current and past surveys are available on the Census Internet site, <http://www.census.gov/csd/ace>.

CHAPTER 6: GOVERNMENT

Section 6a: Federal Government in the National Income and Product Accounts

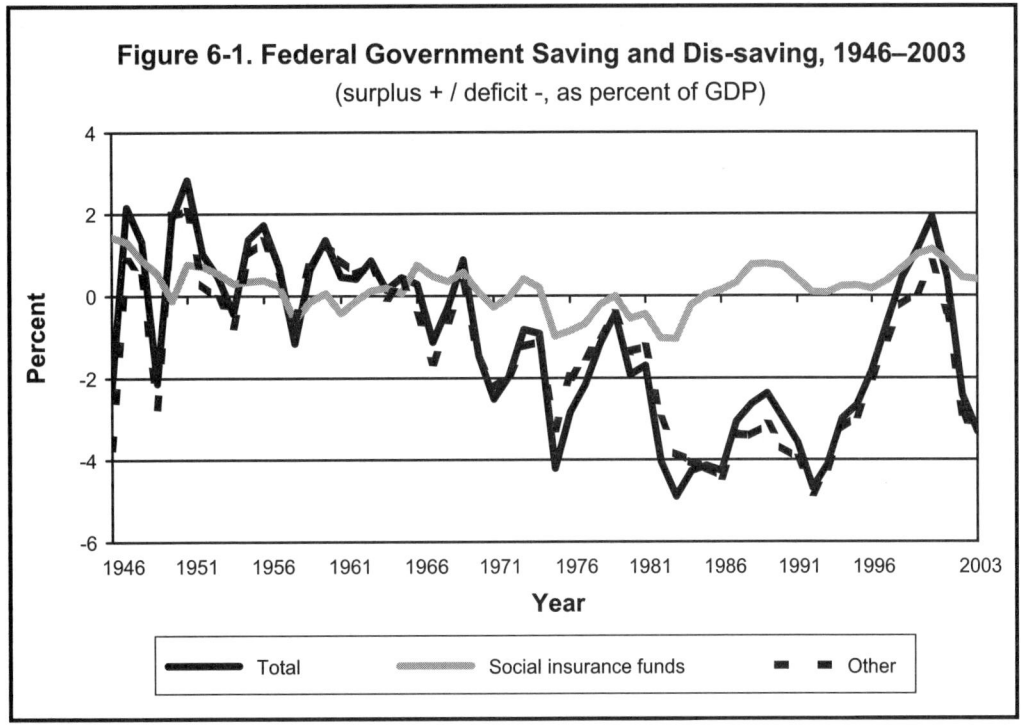

Figure 6-1. Federal Government Saving and Dis-saving, 1946–2003
(surplus + / deficit -, as percent of GDP)

- Net federal government saving is measured as current receipts minus current expenditures in the National Income and Product Accounts, and separated into two components—social insurance funds (such as Social Security and Medicare) and other. Investment spending is not counted as a current expenditure, but current expenditures do include an allowance for consumption of the government's capital stock. Since the changes in Social Security funding enacted in 1983, the federal government's social insurance funds have made a modest positive contribution to national saving. The remainder of the federal current budget has swung from large deficits to significant positive saving and back to deficit since the early 1980s. Periods of economic slack (recessions and early recoveries) produce deficits more or less automatically, as existing tax laws and spending programs produce different rates of receipts and spending in response to the changes in economic activity. Spending changes and changes in tax law also have significant effects. (Tables 6-1 and 1-1)
- Total federal government current expenditures have changed little as a percent of GDP: they were 20.0 percent in 1946 and 20.4 percent in 2003. The composition of those expenditures changed over that period, however. The interest share was little changed, but consumption expenditures fell from 60 percent to 29 percent of total federal spending, while social benefits (for example, Medicare and Social Security) rose from 20 percent to 43 percent, and grants to state and local governments from 2 percent to 15 percent. (Tables 6-1 and 1-1)
- Federal government nondefense consumption spending, in real terms (as measured by the quantity index), increased 551 percent from 1946 to 2003, for an annual rate of increase of 3.3 percent per year. Federal nondefense gross investment spending was up 1,689 percent, 5.2 percent per year. Defense consumption spending was up only 68 percent, or 0.9 percent per year, largely reflecting the fact that the armed forces were far larger in 1946 than they are now. Defense investment spending, however, rose 586 percent, or 3.4 percent per year, as defense spending shifted toward equipment. (Table 6-6)

Table 6-1. Federal Government Current Receipts and Expenditures

(National Income and Product Accounts, calendar years, billions of dollars, quarterly data are at seasonally adjusted annual rates.)

NIPA Table 3.2

Year and quarter	Current receipts													
	Total	Tax receipts							Contributions for government social insurance	Income receipts on assets			Current transfer receipts	Current surplus of government enterprises
		Total	Personal current taxes	Taxes on production and imports		Taxes on corporate income				Total	Interest receipts	Rents and royalties		
				Total	Excise taxes	Total	Federal Reserve banks	Other						
1946	39.5	32.7	16.4	7.7	7.2	8.6	0.0	8.6	6.5	...	...	...	0.3	...
1947	42.8	37.1	18.8	7.7	7.2	10.7	0.1	10.6	5.4	...	...	...	0.3	...
1948	42.4	37.6	18.1	7.8	7.4	11.8	0.2	11.6	4.4	...	...	...	0.3	...
1949	37.9	32.8	15.4	7.9	7.5	9.6	0.2	9.4	4.7	...	...	...	0.3	...
1950	48.8	43.3	17.4	8.7	8.2	17.2	0.2	17.0	5.3	...	...	...	0.2	...
1951	62.9	56.3	25.4	9.2	8.6	21.7	0.3	21.4	6.4	...	...	...	0.3	...
1952	65.8	58.9	30.2	10.1	9.6	18.6	0.3	18.3	6.6	...	...	...	0.3	...
1953	68.6	61.5	31.3	10.7	10.2	19.5	0.3	19.1	6.8	...	...	...	0.3	...
1954	62.5	54.4	28.1	9.5	9.0	16.9	0.3	16.6	7.8	...	...	...	0.3	...
1955	71.1	62.0	30.5	10.4	9.8	21.1	0.3	20.8	8.8	...	...	...	0.3	...
1956	75.8	65.9	33.9	11.0	10.3	20.9	0.4	20.5	9.6	...	...	...	0.4	...
1957	79.3	67.9	36.0	11.5	10.8	20.4	0.5	19.9	11.0	...	...	...	0.4	...
1958	76.0	64.7	35.5	11.2	10.4	18.0	0.5	17.4	11.0	...	...	...	0.4	...
1959	87.0	73.3	38.5	12.2	11.2	22.5	0.9	21.6	13.4	0.0	...	0.0	0.4	-0.1
1960	93.9	76.5	41.8	13.1	12.0	21.4	0.9	20.6	16.0	1.4	1.3	0.0	0.4	-0.3
1961	95.5	77.5	42.7	13.2	12.2	21.5	0.7	20.8	16.5	1.5	1.4	0.1	0.5	-0.5
1962	103.6	83.3	46.5	14.2	13.0	22.5	0.8	21.7	18.6	1.7	1.6	0.1	0.5	-0.5
1963	111.8	88.6	49.1	14.7	13.5	24.6	0.9	23.7	21.0	1.8	1.7	0.1	0.6	-0.3
1964	111.8	87.8	46.0	15.5	14.2	26.1	1.6	24.6	21.7	1.8	1.7	0.1	0.7	-0.3
1965	120.9	95.7	51.1	15.5	13.9	28.9	1.3	27.6	22.7	1.9	1.8	0.1	1.1	-0.3
1966	137.9	104.8	58.6	14.5	12.6	31.4	1.6	29.8	30.5	2.1	2.0	0.1	1.2	-0.6
1967	146.9	109.9	64.4	15.2	13.3	30.0	1.9	28.1	34.0	2.5	2.3	0.2	1.1	-0.6
1968	171.2	129.8	76.4	17.0	14.7	36.1	2.5	33.6	37.8	2.9	2.7	0.2	1.1	-0.3
1969	192.5	146.1	91.7	17.9	15.5	36.1	3.0	33.0	43.1	2.7	2.5	0.2	1.1	-0.5
1970	186.0	138.0	88.9	18.2	15.7	30.6	3.5	27.1	45.3	3.1	2.8	0.2	1.1	-1.5
1971	191.7	138.7	85.8	19.1	16.0	33.5	3.4	30.1	50.0	3.5	3.1	0.3	1.1	-1.6
1972	220.1	158.4	102.8	18.6	15.6	36.6	3.2	33.4	57.9	3.6	3.3	0.4	1.3	-1.1
1973	250.4	173.1	109.6	19.9	16.7	43.3	4.3	38.9	74.0	3.8	3.4	0.4	1.3	-1.8
1974	279.5	192.2	126.5	20.2	16.5	45.1	5.6	39.6	83.5	4.2	3.6	0.5	1.4	-1.8
1975	277.2	187.0	120.7	22.2	16.4	43.6	5.4	38.2	87.5	4.9	4.3	0.6	1.5	-3.6
1976	322.5	218.1	141.2	21.6	17.0	54.6	5.9	48.7	99.1	5.9	5.2	0.7	1.6	-2.2
1977	363.4	247.4	162.2	22.9	17.5	61.6	5.9	55.7	110.3	6.7	5.8	0.9	1.9	-2.9
1978	423.5	286.9	188.9	25.6	18.5	71.4	7.0	64.4	127.9	8.5	7.4	1.1	2.4	-2.1
1979	486.2	326.2	224.6	26.0	18.5	74.4	9.3	65.1	148.9	10.7	9.2	1.5	2.8	-2.3
1980	532.1	355.9	250.0	34.0	26.9	70.3	11.7	58.6	162.6	13.7	11.3	2.3	3.5	-3.6
1981	619.4	408.1	290.6	50.3	41.7	65.7	14.0	51.7	191.8	18.3	14.8	3.5	3.8	-2.5
1982	616.6	386.8	295.0	41.4	32.8	49.0	15.2	33.8	204.9	22.2	18.3	3.8	5.2	-2.4
1983	642.3	393.6	286.2	44.8	35.7	61.3	14.2	47.1	221.8	23.8	20.4	3.5	6.0	-2.9
1984	709.0	425.7	301.4	47.8	35.9	75.2	16.1	59.2	252.8	26.6	22.8	3.9	7.3	-3.4
1985	773.3	460.6	336.0	46.4	34.3	76.3	17.8	58.5	276.5	29.1	25.7	3.5	9.4	-2.4
1986	815.2	479.6	350.1	44.0	30.3	83.8	17.8	66.0	297.5	31.4	29.0	2.4	8.2	-1.5
1987	896.6	544.0	392.5	46.3	30.7	103.2	17.7	85.4	315.9	27.9	25.6	2.3	10.7	-2.0
1988	958.2	566.7	402.9	50.3	33.9	111.1	17.4	93.8	353.1	30.0	28.0	2.0	10.8	-2.3
1989	1 037.4	621.7	451.5	50.2	32.7	117.2	21.6	95.6	376.3	28.6	26.5	2.1	12.4	-1.6
1990	1 081.5	642.8	470.2	51.4	33.9	118.1	23.6	94.5	400.1	30.2	27.6	2.6	13.5	-5.1
1991	1 101.3	636.1	461.3	62.2	45.3	109.9	20.8	89.2	418.6	30.1	27.4	2.8	17.9	-1.4
1992	1 147.2	660.4	475.3	63.7	45.4	118.8	16.8	102.0	441.8	25.7	23.1	2.6	19.4	-0.1
1993	1 222.5	713.4	505.5	66.7	46.9	138.5	16.0	122.5	463.6	26.2	23.5	2.7	21.1	-1.8
1994	1 320.8	781.9	542.7	79.4	57.9	156.7	20.5	136.3	493.7	23.4	20.6	2.7	22.3	-0.4
1995	1 406.5	845.1	586.0	75.9	56.1	179.3	23.4	155.9	519.2	23.7	21.2	2.5	19.1	-0.6
1996	1 524.0	932.4	663.4	73.2	54.0	190.6	20.1	170.5	542.8	26.9	23.0	4.0	23.1	-1.2
1997	1 653.1	1 030.6	744.3	78.2	58.6	203.0	20.7	182.3	576.4	25.9	21.4	4.5	19.9	0.3
1998	1 773.8	1 116.8	825.8	81.1	61.5	204.2	26.6	177.7	613.8	21.5	17.7	3.8	21.5	0.1
1999	1 891.2	1 195.7	893.0	83.9	64.7	213.0	25.4	187.6	651.6	21.5	18.0	3.5	22.7	-0.3
2000	2 053.8	1 313.6	999.1	87.8	66.7	219.4	25.3	194.1	691.7	25.2	20.1	5.1	25.7	-2.3
2001	2 016.2	1 252.2	994.5	85.8	65.2	164.7	27.1	137.6	717.5	24.9	18.4	6.5	27.1	-5.5
2002	1 847.3	1 069.0	831.2	87.3	67.4	143.4	24.5	118.9	733.8	20.3	15.5	4.9	24.8	-0.6
2003	1 877.0	1 064.5	775.8	89.4	67.9	191.4	22.0	169.3	758.2	23.0	16.5	6.5	25.5	5.8
2001														
1st quarter	2 089.2	1 323.0	1 047.3	87.6	65.8	180.7	29.6	151.1	716.4	26.4	19.8	6.6	27.2	-3.8
2nd quarter	2 080.5	1 315.6	1 045.7	86.9	66.3	176.6	28.0	148.7	718.1	25.2	18.6	6.7	27.3	-5.7
3rd quarter	1 895.4	1 132.0	881.0	84.2	64.3	159.7	26.6	133.2	717.9	24.4	17.9	6.5	27.1	-6.1
4th quarter	1 999.6	1 238.1	1 004.1	84.6	64.4	141.6	24.3	117.4	717.6	23.5	17.3	6.2	26.6	-6.2
2002														
1st quarter	1 844.6	1 070.4	846.9	85.1	66.3	131.4	25.4	105.9	731.3	21.3	16.0	5.3	25.4	-3.7
2nd quarter	1 850.5	1 074.1	835.6	87.8	68.0	143.2	25.6	117.6	734.6	20.2	15.1	5.1	24.9	-3.3
3rd quarter	1 847.9	1 066.6	824.4	88.2	67.9	146.9	24.2	122.7	734.3	19.9	15.3	4.7	24.7	2.4
4th quarter	1 846.2	1 064.8	817.7	88.0	67.2	152.2	22.8	129.4	734.9	19.8	15.4	4.4	24.3	2.3
2003														
1st quarter	1 888.6	1 089.7	809.6	90.3	68.6	183.1	24.0	159.1	747.7	19.4	14.7	4.7	25.1	6.6
2nd quarter	1 902.5	1 094.2	811.6	89.6	68.2	183.1	22.8	160.4	754.0	22.8	16.4	6.4	25.4	6.0
3rd quarter	1 816.4	999.3	709.2	88.0	66.7	194.3	21.2	173.1	761.6	24.3	17.0	7.3	25.8	5.5
4th quarter	1 900.6	1 074.9	772.5	89.6	68.1	204.9	20.1	184.8	769.5	25.5	17.9	7.6	25.6	5.0

... = Not available.

Table 6-1. Federal Government Current Receipts and Expenditures—Continued

(National Income and Product Accounts, calendar years, billions of dollars, quarterly data are at seasonally adjusted annual rates.)

NIPA Table 3.2

Year and quarter	Current expenditures											Net federal government saving, NIPA (surplus + / deficit -)		
	Total	Consumption expenditures	Government social benefits		Other current transfer payments		Interest payments			Subsidies		Total	Social insurance funds	Other
			Total	To persons	Total	Grants-in-aid to state and local governments	Total	To persons and business	To the rest of the world					
1946	44.5	27.0	8.7	8.7	3.3	1.0	4.0	...	0.0	1.6		-5.0	3.2	-8.2
1947	37.6	20.9	8.4	8.4	3.6	1.6	4.1	...	0.0	0.6		5.3	3.2	2.1
1948	38.8	21.2	7.2	7.2	5.6	1.7	4.2	...	0.0	0.6		3.6	2.4	1.2
1949	43.5	23.3	8.2	8.2	7.0	1.9	4.3	...	0.0	0.7		-5.7	1.5	-7.2
1950	43.3	22.1	10.2	10.2	5.5	1.9	4.5	...	0.0	1.0		5.5	-0.3	5.8
1951	53.3	34.4	7.9	7.9	5.2	2.0	4.6	...	0.0	1.2		9.6	2.6	7.0
1952	62.1	44.2	8.1	8.1	4.3	2.2	4.6	...	0.1	0.9		3.7	2.6	1.1
1953	66.8	48.3	8.7	8.7	4.3	2.3	4.7	...	0.1	0.7		1.8	2.1	-0.3
1954	64.2	43.9	10.7	10.7	4.1	2.3	4.8	...	0.1	0.6		-1.6	1.2	-2.8
1955	65.3	43.9	11.5	11.5	4.5	2.4	4.8	...	0.1	0.6		5.7	1.5	4.2
1956	68.3	45.1	12.3	12.3	4.4	2.5	5.2	...	0.2	1.2		7.6	1.7	5.9
1957	76.0	49.5	14.5	14.5	4.7	2.9	5.7	...	0.2	1.6		3.3	1.1	2.2
1958	81.4	50.9	18.2	18.2	5.2	3.3	5.4	...	0.1	1.8		-5.4	-2.7	-2.7
1959	83.6	50.0	18.6	18.6	7.6	3.8	6.3	...	0.3	1.1		3.3	-0.7	4.0
1960	86.7	49.8	20.1	19.9	7.4	4.0	8.4	8.0	0.3	1.1		7.2	0.4	6.8
1961	92.8	51.6	23.3	23.1	8.0	4.5	7.9	7.6	0.3	2.0		2.6	-2.3	5.0
1962	101.1	57.8	23.7	23.5	8.6	5.0	8.6	8.3	0.3	2.3		2.5	-0.6	3.1
1963	106.4	60.8	24.9	24.6	9.2	5.6	9.3	8.9	0.4	2.2		5.4	0.8	4.5
1964	110.8	62.8	25.4	25.2	9.8	6.5	10.0	9.6	0.5	2.7		1.0	1.3	-0.2
1965	117.6	65.7	27.6	27.3	10.7	7.2	10.6	10.1	0.5	3.0		3.3	0.5	2.9
1966	135.7	75.9	30.2	29.9	14.0	10.1	11.6	11.1	0.5	3.9		2.3	6.0	-3.7
1967	156.2	87.1	36.9	36.5	15.7	11.7	12.7	12.1	0.6	3.8		-9.4	4.1	-13.5
1968	173.5	95.4	42.2	41.9	17.1	12.7	14.6	13.9	0.7	4.1		-2.3	3.2	-5.5
1969	183.8	98.4	46.1	45.8	19.0	14.6	15.8	15.0	0.8	4.5		8.7	5.7	3.0
1970	201.1	98.6	56.1	55.6	23.9	19.3	17.7	16.7	1.0	4.8		-15.2	1.0	-16.2
1971	220.0	102.0	66.6	66.1	29.0	23.2	17.9	16.1	1.8	4.6		-28.4	-3.0	-25.3
1972	244.4	107.7	73.3	72.9	38.6	31.7	18.8	16.1	2.7	6.6		-24.4	-0.6	-23.8
1973	261.7	108.9	85.2	84.5	39.7	34.8	22.8	19.0	3.8	5.1		-11.3	5.8	-17.1
1974	293.3	118.0	103.9	103.3	41.8	36.3	26.0	21.7	4.3	3.2		-13.8	3.2	-17.0
1975	346.2	129.6	133.0	132.3	50.5	45.1	28.9	24.4	4.5	4.3		-69.0	-16.2	-52.9
1976	374.3	137.2	143.9	143.1	54.6	50.7	33.8	29.3	4.5	4.9		-51.7	-15.6	-36.1
1977	407.5	150.7	152.9	152.1	60.0	56.6	37.1	31.6	5.5	6.9		-44.1	-13.8	-30.2
1978	450.0	163.3	163.3	162.4	69.4	65.5	45.3	36.7	8.7	8.7		-26.5	-4.6	-21.9
1979	497.5	179.0	183.7	182.8	70.8	66.3	55.7	44.6	11.1	8.2		-11.3	0.2	-11.4
1980	585.7	207.5	220.7	219.6	78.4	72.3	69.7	57.0	12.7	9.4		-53.6	-15.5	-38.1
1981	672.7	238.3	251.4	250.1	78.2	72.5	93.9	76.6	17.3	11.1		-53.3	-13.8	-39.5
1982	748.5	263.3	282.4	281.2	76.4	69.5	111.8	92.5	19.3	14.5		-131.9	-33.8	-98.1
1983	815.4	286.5	304.3	303.0	78.7	71.6	124.6	105.6	19.0	20.8		-173.0	-37.3	-135.7
1984	877.1	310.0	310.5	309.2	86.0	76.7	150.3	129.1	21.2	20.6		-168.1	-8.7	-159.4
1985	948.2	338.4	326.6	325.4	92.7	80.9	169.4	146.3	23.1	20.9		-175.0	1.7	-176.7
1986	1 006.0	358.2	345.3	343.7	99.9	87.6	178.2	153.5	24.6	24.5		-190.8	6.4	-197.2
1987	1 041.6	374.3	358.2	356.7	94.7	83.9	184.6	158.4	26.2	29.9		-145.0	15.2	-160.2
1988	1 092.7	382.5	379.1	377.5	102.8	91.6	199.3	167.6	31.7	29.0		-134.5	39.7	-174.1
1989	1 167.5	399.2	412.2	410.6	109.8	98.3	219.3	181.0	38.4	26.8		-130.1	43.1	-173.2
1990	1 253.5	419.8	447.2	445.4	122.7	111.4	237.5	196.7	40.8	26.4		-172.0	43.0	-215.0
1991	1 315.0	439.5	494.2	492.0	103.5	131.6	250.9	210.1	40.9	26.9		-213.7	25.7	-239.4
1992	1 444.6	445.2	551.7	549.8	167.0	149.1	251.3	212.2	39.1	29.5		-297.4	6.5	-303.9
1993	1 496.0	441.9	582.4	580.5	182.3	163.7	253.4	214.0	39.4	36.0		-273.5	5.6	-279.1
1994	1 533.1	440.8	607.6	605.5	191.6	174.7	261.3	217.1	44.2	31.8		-212.3	17.9	-230.3
1995	1 603.5	440.5	642.7	640.8	196.3	184.1	290.4	236.6	53.8	33.7		-197.0	19.0	-216.0
1996	1 665.8	446.3	680.0	677.9	208.2	191.2	297.3	232.0	65.3	34.0		-141.8	13.9	-155.7
1997	1 708.9	457.7	706.3	704.2	212.5	198.6	300.0	221.3	78.6	32.4		-55.8	30.6	-86.4
1998	1 734.9	454.6	719.2	716.9	227.4	212.8	298.6	219.6	79.3	35.0		38.8	59.0	-20.2
1999	1 787.6	475.1	738.0	735.7	248.0	232.9	282.7	208.1	74.5	43.8		103.6	94.1	9.6
2000	1 864.4	499.3	772.5	770.0	265.6	247.3	283.3	200.3	83.0	43.8		189.5	112.3	77.1
2001	1 969.5	531.9	841.4	838.7	290.0	276.1	258.6	176.2	82.4	47.6		46.7	87.0	-40.3
2002	2 101.8	592.7	919.7	917.0	323.2	304.4	229.0	152.9	76.1	37.2		-254.5	47.7	-302.1
2003	2 241.6	658.6	958.9	956.1	363.6	339.9	214.1	142.1	72.0	46.4		-364.5	45.5	-410.0
2001														
1st quarter	1 932.6	518.4	817.3	814.6	278.1	266.2	274.5	188.6	85.9	44.3		156.6	102.6	54.0
2nd quarter	1 956.9	528.0	831.2	828.5	290.1	278.3	263.7	178.7	85.0	44.0		123.6	95.2	28.4
3rd quarter	1 984.0	532.7	849.4	846.7	286.1	272.8	253.3	173.4	80.0	62.5		-88.6	80.9	-169.5
4th quarter	2 004.3	548.4	867.6	865.0	305.8	286.6	242.8	164.0	78.8	39.7		-4.7	69.3	-74.1
2002														
1st quarter	2 053.1	570.7	897.7	895.1	319.2	291.9	228.5	150.0	78.4	37.0		-208.5	63.9	-272.4
2nd quarter	2 102.1	586.3	924.2	921.5	319.0	304.2	236.5	159.4	77.1	36.1		-251.6	43.6	-295.2
3rd quarter	2 103.1	593.4	927.6	924.8	319.4	305.4	226.2	150.7	75.5	36.6		-255.1	42.2	-297.3
4th quarter	2 148.8	620.3	929.4	926.6	335.4	316.3	224.7	151.3	73.4	39.0		-302.7	40.9	-343.6
2003														
1st quarter	2 170.2	634.3	941.4	938.6	339.4	314.3	213.9	141.9	72.0	42.5		-281.6	48.4	-330.1
2nd quarter	2 266.9	665.7	957.2	954.4	370.3	345.1	217.7	146.7	71.0	54.6		-364.4	41.8	-406.2
3rd quarter	2 249.4	663.0	964.5	961.7	366.6	343.0	210.1	138.2	71.9	45.3		-433.0	44.4	-477.4
4th quarter	2 279.8	671.3	972.5	969.6	378.0	357.2	214.7	141.4	73.3	43.2		-379.2	47.2	-426.4

... = Not available.

Table 6-2. Federal Government Consumption Expenditures and Gross Investment

(National Income and Product Accounts, calendar years, billions of dollars, quarterly data are at seasonally adjusted annual rates.)

NIPA Tables 3.9.5, 3.10.5

Year and quarter	Federal government consumption expenditures and gross investment												
	Total	Consumption expenditures					Gross investment						
		Total	Compensation of general government employees	Consumption of general government fixed capital	Intermediate goods and services purchased [1]	Less: own-account investment and sales to other sectors	Total	National defense			Nondefense		
								Total	Structures	Equipment and software	Total	Structures	Equipment and software
1946	28.9	27.0	16.2	9.3	5.3	3.7	1.9	1.5	0.3	1.2	0.4	0.0	0.4
1947	22.7	20.9	10.3	8.8	2.5	0.6	1.8	0.9	0.2	0.8	0.8	0.3	0.5
1948	24.2	21.2	9.6	7.6	4.6	0.5	3.0	2.0	0.4	1.6	1.0	0.7	0.4
1949	27.7	23.3	10.7	6.6	6.4	0.3	4.4	2.9	0.4	2.6	1.4	1.1	0.3
1950	26.0	22.1	11.1	5.8	5.7	0.4	3.9	2.4	0.5	1.9	1.6	1.2	0.4
1951	45.1	34.4	16.6	6.1	12.6	0.9	10.7	9.1	2.0	7.1	1.5	1.1	0.4
1952	59.2	44.2	19.3	6.8	18.7	0.6	15.0	13.4	3.3	10.1	1.6	1.1	0.5
1953	64.4	48.3	19.1	7.6	22.3	0.6	16.1	14.7	3.3	11.4	1.4	1.1	0.3
1954	57.3	43.9	18.3	8.2	18.1	0.7	13.3	12.1	2.7	9.4	1.2	0.9	0.3
1955	54.9	43.9	19.0	8.6	17.7	1.3	10.9	10.1	2.1	8.0	0.9	0.6	0.2
1956	56.7	45.1	19.6	9.2	17.1	0.8	11.6	10.5	2.1	8.4	1.2	0.9	0.3
1957	61.3	49.5	20.2	9.7	20.8	1.3	11.9	10.5	2.3	8.2	1.4	1.1	0.2
1958	63.8	50.9	21.3	9.8	21.1	1.3	12.9	11.3	2.6	8.7	1.6	1.4	0.2
1959	65.4	50.0	21.7	10.1	19.3	1.2	15.4	13.7	2.5	11.2	1.7	1.5	0.2
1960	64.1	49.8	22.6	10.5	17.8	1.1	14.3	12.3	2.2	10.1	2.0	1.7	0.3
1961	67.9	51.6	23.7	10.7	18.2	1.0	16.3	13.9	2.4	11.5	2.4	1.9	0.6
1962	75.3	57.8	25.2	11.3	22.4	1.1	17.4	14.5	2.0	12.5	2.9	2.1	0.8
1963	76.9	60.8	26.5	11.9	23.5	1.2	16.1	12.6	1.6	11.0	3.5	2.3	1.2
1964	78.5	62.8	28.5	12.2	23.3	1.2	15.6	11.5	1.3	10.2	4.2	2.5	1.6
1965	80.4	65.7	30.0	12.5	24.6	1.3	14.7	10.0	1.1	8.9	4.7	2.8	1.9
1966	92.5	75.9	34.3	13.0	30.3	1.7	16.7	11.8	1.3	10.5	4.9	2.8	2.1
1967	104.8	87.1	37.9	13.8	36.8	1.3	17.7	13.5	1.2	12.3	4.2	2.2	1.9
1968	111.4	95.4	41.9	14.5	40.3	1.3	16.0	12.2	1.2	10.9	3.8	2.1	1.7
1969	113.4	98.4	44.9	15.2	39.8	1.4	15.0	11.3	1.5	9.9	3.6	1.9	1.7
1970	113.5	98.6	48.3	15.8	35.9	1.4	14.8	11.1	1.3	9.8	3.8	2.1	1.7
1971	113.7	102.0	51.7	16.1	35.7	1.5	11.7	7.5	1.8	5.7	4.2	2.5	1.7
1972	119.7	107.7	55.4	16.2	38.4	2.3	12.0	7.5	1.8	5.7	4.5	2.7	1.8
1973	122.5	108.9	57.4	16.5	37.7	2.8	13.6	8.7	2.1	6.6	4.9	3.1	1.8
1974	134.6	118.0	62.0	17.6	41.7	3.4	16.6	11.1	2.2	8.9	5.6	3.4	2.2
1975	149.1	129.6	68.4	19.0	45.2	3.0	19.5	13.0	2.3	10.7	6.5	4.1	2.4
1976	159.7	137.2	73.3	20.5	46.2	2.8	22.6	15.3	2.1	13.2	7.3	4.6	2.7
1977	175.4	150.7	79.9	22.1	52.4	3.8	24.7	16.7	2.4	14.4	8.0	5.0	3.0
1978	190.9	163.3	85.8	24.0	58.2	4.5	27.6	17.8	2.5	15.3	9.8	6.1	3.7
1979	210.6	179.0	91.8	25.8	66.9	5.6	31.6	21.4	2.5	18.9	10.2	6.3	4.0
1980	243.8	207.5	102.5	28.7	82.3	6.2	36.3	24.3	3.2	21.1	12.0	7.1	4.9
1981	280.2	238.3	115.1	32.3	97.0	6.2	41.9	28.9	3.2	25.7	13.0	7.7	5.3
1982	310.8	263.3	125.3	36.0	108.2	6.1	47.5	34.7	4.0	30.8	12.7	6.8	6.0
1983	342.9	286.5	132.3	39.0	121.3	6.1	56.4	41.9	4.8	37.1	14.5	6.7	7.8
1984	374.4	310.0	149.4	42.8	124.5	6.7	64.4	48.7	4.9	43.8	15.7	7.0	8.7
1985	412.8	338.4	159.0	46.1	140.2	6.9	74.4	57.5	6.2	51.3	16.9	7.3	9.6
1986	438.6	358.2	163.1	49.6	152.4	6.9	80.4	62.9	6.8	56.1	17.5	8.0	9.5
1987	460.1	374.3	170.3	53.1	158.7	7.9	85.8	66.4	7.7	58.8	19.4	9.0	10.4
1988	462.3	382.5	178.0	56.9	156.4	8.7	79.8	61.3	7.4	53.9	18.6	6.8	11.7
1989	482.2	399.2	185.7	60.9	162.1	9.4	83.0	62.7	6.4	56.3	20.3	6.9	13.4
1990	508.3	419.8	193.9	65.1	171.2	10.3	88.5	65.9	6.1	59.8	22.6	8.0	14.6
1991	527.7	439.5	205.9	69.1	175.9	11.3	88.2	63.4	4.6	58.8	24.8	9.2	15.7
1992	533.9	445.2	210.7	71.4	174.3	11.3	88.8	61.6	5.2	56.3	27.2	10.3	16.9
1993	525.2	441.9	211.9	74.4	166.6	11.0	83.3	55.2	5.1	50.1	28.1	11.2	16.9
1994	519.1	440.8	209.8	76.4	167.6	13.0	78.3	52.9	5.7	47.2	25.4	10.5	14.9
1995	519.2	440.5	206.8	77.9	166.4	10.6	78.8	51.4	6.3	45.1	27.3	10.8	16.5
1996	527.4	446.3	210.7	78.0	168.8	11.1	81.1	52.1	6.7	45.4	29.1	11.2	17.9
1997	530.9	457.7	212.9	78.0	175.9	9.1	73.2	44.9	5.7	39.2	28.3	9.8	18.5
1998	530.4	454.6	215.1	78.0	171.5	9.9	75.8	45.0	5.1	39.9	30.8	10.6	20.2
1999	555.8	475.1	221.3	79.6	182.7	8.5	80.7	47.7	5.0	42.8	33.0	10.6	22.4
2000	578.8	499.3	233.8	81.6	193.8	9.8	79.5	48.8	5.0	43.8	30.7	8.3	22.3
2001	612.9	531.9	242.9	82.8	215.3	9.1	81.0	50.2	4.6	45.6	30.8	8.3	22.5
2002	680.8	592.7	266.8	83.6	251.3	9.1	88.1	55.4	4.4	51.0	32.7	9.9	22.9
2003	752.2	658.6	293.5	84.9	289.0	8.8	93.6	60.4	5.3	55.1	33.2	10.2	23.0
2001													
1st quarter	596.2	518.4	238.8	82.3	207.0	9.7	77.8	47.6	4.8	42.9	30.1	8.0	22.1
2nd quarter	610.9	528.0	240.9	82.8	212.6	8.4	83.0	50.3	4.7	45.6	32.7	8.0	24.7
3rd quarter	614.3	532.7	244.3	83.0	213.9	8.6	81.6	51.6	4.3	47.3	30.1	8.4	21.6
4th quarter	630.1	548.4	247.6	82.9	227.8	9.9	81.6	51.2	4.6	46.6	30.4	8.8	21.6
2002													
1st quarter	654.2	570.7	261.8	83.3	235.3	9.7	83.5	51.4	4.2	47.2	32.1	9.7	22.4
2nd quarter	676.6	586.3	264.8	83.4	246.2	8.1	90.2	55.7	4.4	51.2	34.6	9.7	24.9
3rd quarter	684.4	593.4	266.6	83.6	253.9	10.8	91.0	58.4	4.5	53.9	32.5	9.9	22.7
4th quarter	708.2	620.3	273.9	84.3	269.9	7.8	87.9	56.2	4.6	51.6	31.7	10.3	21.4
2003													
1st quarter	723.4	634.3	290.3	84.3	267.7	8.0	89.1	57.3	4.8	52.5	31.8	10.0	21.8
2nd quarter	761.2	665.7	294.1	84.7	296.9	10.1	95.4	59.9	4.9	55.0	35.4	10.6	24.8
3rd quarter	756.7	663.0	294.7	85.2	292.3	9.3	93.7	61.0	5.7	55.3	32.8	10.5	22.2
4th quarter	767.5	671.3	294.9	85.3	299.2	8.1	96.2	63.4	5.7	57.7	32.8	9.7	23.1

[1] Includes general government intermediate inputs for goods and services sold to other sectors and for own-account investment.

Table 6-3. Federal Government Defense and Nondefense Consumption Expenditures by Type

(National Income and Product Accounts, calendar years, billions of dollars, quarterly data are at seasonally adjusted annual rates.)

NIPA Table 3.10.5

Year and quarter	Defense consumption expenditures [1]						Nondefense consumption expenditures [1]					
	Total	Compensation of general government employees	Consumption of general government fixed capital	Intermediate goods and services purchased [2]			Total	Compensation of general government employees	Consumption of general government fixed capital	Intermediate goods and services purchased [2]		
				Durable goods	Nondurable goods	Services				Durable goods	Nondurable goods	Services
1946	23.7	14.1	8.8	0.5	0.7	2.2	3.3	2.1	0.5	0.1	0.4	1.2
1947	17.3	7.8	8.2	0.3	0.3	0.7	3.6	2.5	0.6	0.1	0.4	0.7
1948	16.3	6.9	7.0	0.8	0.7	1.1	4.9	2.6	0.6	0.1	0.8	1.1
1949	16.9	7.8	6.0	1.0	0.8	1.5	6.4	2.9	0.6	0.1	2.1	1.0
1950	17.2	8.0	5.2	1.7	0.9	1.5	4.9	3.1	0.6	0.1	0.5	0.9
1951	30.1	13.5	5.4	4.4	2.3	5.0	4.3	3.1	0.6	0.1	0.1	0.7
1952	38.9	16.1	6.2	8.0	2.8	6.1	5.3	3.2	0.6	0.1	0.5	1.3
1953	41.2	16.0	6.9	9.1	4.2	5.1	7.1	3.1	0.6	0.1	2.4	1.3
1954	37.1	15.4	7.6	6.8	3.2	4.2	6.9	2.9	0.6	0.1	2.2	1.4
1955	36.9	15.8	8.0	6.0	1.7	5.9	7.1	3.2	0.6	0.1	2.5	1.6
1956	38.8	16.1	8.5	6.1	1.7	6.7	6.3	3.5	0.6	0.1	0.8	1.7
1957	43.2	16.5	9.0	6.7	2.2	9.3	6.3	3.7	0.6	0.1	0.8	1.8
1958	44.1	17.0	9.1	7.1	2.1	9.5	6.8	4.3	0.7	0.0	0.7	1.7
1959	40.1	17.3	9.5	5.1	1.8	6.9	9.8	4.4	0.7	0.0	3.3	2.1
1960	41.0	17.7	9.8	4.4	1.9	7.7	8.7	5.0	0.7	0.1	1.1	2.5
1961	42.7	18.3	10.0	3.6	2.3	8.8	9.0	5.4	0.7	0.1	0.4	3.0
1962	46.6	19.4	10.6	4.6	2.9	9.6	11.3	5.8	0.8	0.2	1.5	3.6
1963	48.3	20.1	11.1	4.7	2.7	10.2	12.4	6.4	0.9	0.3	1.2	4.5
1964	48.8	21.6	11.2	4.0	2.9	9.7	14.0	7.0	1.0	0.4	1.1	5.3
1965	50.6	22.6	11.3	4.2	3.2	9.9	15.1	7.4	1.2	0.5	1.1	5.7
1966	60.0	26.3	11.6	6.2	4.7	12.2	15.9	8.0	1.5	0.5	0.4	6.4
1967	70.0	29.3	12.1	6.2	7.3	15.5	17.1	8.6	1.7	0.4	1.2	6.2
1968	77.2	32.4	12.7	7.5	8.4	16.4	18.3	9.5	1.8	0.4	1.9	5.7
1969	78.2	34.7	13.2	6.5	7.6	16.5	20.2	10.1	2.0	0.3	3.0	5.9
1970	76.6	36.6	13.6	6.1	5.4	15.2	22.1	11.7	2.1	0.3	2.0	7.1
1971	77.1	38.2	13.8	4.6	4.4	16.3	24.9	13.4	2.3	0.3	2.1	8.1
1972	79.5	40.5	13.8	5.7	4.7	15.5	28.2	14.8	2.4	0.3	2.4	9.9
1973	79.4	41.4	14.0	5.5	4.3	15.3	29.4	16.0	2.5	0.2	1.9	10.4
1974	84.5	44.1	14.7	5.2	5.2	16.9	33.4	18.0	2.8	0.2	2.6	11.7
1975	90.9	47.9	15.7	6.0	5.1	17.4	38.7	20.5	3.2	0.2	2.8	13.7
1976	95.8	50.3	17.1	5.8	4.5	18.8	41.4	23.1	3.4	0.3	3.5	13.3
1977	104.2	53.6	18.4	8.0	4.5	20.4	46.5	26.3	3.7	0.3	4.4	14.7
1978	112.7	57.5	20.0	9.6	4.9	21.7	50.6	28.3	4.0	0.4	4.9	16.7
1979	123.8	61.7	21.3	11.3	6.2	24.2	55.1	30.1	4.5	0.5	5.2	19.4
1980	143.7	68.6	23.5	12.8	10.0	30.2	63.8	34.0	5.2	0.7	7.4	21.3
1981	167.3	78.8	26.3	16.2	11.8	35.8	71.0	36.3	6.0	0.6	11.2	21.4
1982	191.2	87.4	29.2	19.6	11.5	45.4	72.1	37.9	6.7	0.6	9.1	22.1
1983	208.8	92.4	31.7	25.1	11.3	49.5	77.7	39.9	7.3	0.9	10.6	23.9
1984	232.9	107.5	34.8	27.1	10.4	54.7	77.1	41.8	7.9	0.9	6.4	24.9
1985	253.7	115.3	37.5	29.3	10.0	63.4	84.7	43.6	8.7	1.0	9.5	27.1
1986	268.0	118.8	40.2	31.9	10.2	68.7	90.3	44.3	9.3	1.0	12.4	28.2
1987	283.6	123.5	43.0	33.8	10.3	75.1	90.6	46.8	10.1	1.1	6.9	31.6
1988	293.6	126.9	46.0	33.5	10.6	79.0	88.9	51.1	10.9	1.2	-0.1	32.2
1989	299.5	131.7	49.1	32.0	10.8	78.3	99.7	54.0	11.8	1.3	5.7	33.9
1990	308.1	134.5	52.4	31.6	11.0	81.8	111.7	59.3	12.7	1.5	5.7	39.6
1991	319.8	141.8	55.5	31.0	10.7	84.3	119.7	64.0	13.6	1.6	6.3	42.1
1992	315.3	143.0	57.3	28.4	9.4	81.3	129.8	67.7	14.2	1.7	6.9	46.7
1993	307.6	138.7	59.5	26.4	8.5	78.8	134.2	73.3	14.8	1.6	7.4	43.9
1994	300.7	134.7	61.0	22.9	7.6	80.5	140.1	75.1	15.3	1.6	7.0	48.1
1995	297.3	130.8	61.8	20.9	6.3	81.1	143.2	76.0	16.1	1.7	7.3	49.1
1996	302.5	133.3	61.2	20.8	7.6	83.6	143.8	77.3	16.7	1.8	7.2	47.8
1997	304.7	132.8	60.4	20.9	7.6	86.5	153.0	80.1	17.6	1.8	8.2	51.0
1998	300.7	131.6	59.6	21.0	7.0	84.7	153.9	83.5	18.4	1.7	8.2	49.0
1999	312.9	133.5	59.8	22.3	8.2	92.2	162.2	87.8	19.8	1.7	6.7	51.6
2000	321.5	138.9	60.2	22.3	10.4	92.7	177.8	94.8	21.4	1.8	8.5	58.1
2001	342.4	145.7	60.4	22.5	10.3	107.2	189.5	97.2	22.4	1.9	9.9	63.6
2002	382.0	161.6	60.7	23.5	11.5	128.8	210.7	105.2	23.0	2.2	11.4	74.0
2003	436.1	181.2	61.5	25.6	13.1	158.4	222.5	112.3	23.4	2.2	11.3	78.6
2001												
1st quarter	335.8	143.4	60.2	21.0	9.9	105.9	182.6	95.4	22.1	1.9	9.2	59.2
2nd quarter	338.0	144.0	60.4	22.9	10.7	102.8	189.9	97.0	22.4	1.9	11.4	62.9
3rd quarter	341.4	146.3	60.6	24.4	10.1	103.3	191.3	98.1	22.5	2.0	9.3	64.9
4th quarter	354.3	149.1	60.2	21.6	10.3	116.8	194.1	98.5	22.7	2.0	9.8	67.4
2002												
1st quarter	367.1	158.1	60.5	22.1	10.4	119.7	203.7	103.7	22.8	2.2	10.6	70.4
2nd quarter	376.0	160.3	60.5	23.4	11.6	123.6	210.3	104.5	22.9	2.2	12.2	73.2
3rd quarter	380.0	161.2	60.6	24.9	11.3	128.1	213.4	105.5	23.0	2.3	11.6	75.8
4th quarter	404.8	166.8	61.1	23.5	12.8	143.6	215.5	107.1	23.2	2.2	11.1	76.7
2003												
1st quarter	410.1	178.7	61.0	23.0	15.3	135.3	224.2	111.6	23.3	2.1	9.7	82.3
2nd quarter	446.7	181.3	61.3	26.7	14.1	167.4	219.0	112.8	23.4	2.1	11.4	75.3
3rd quarter	437.1	182.1	61.7	26.0	11.2	160.1	225.9	112.6	23.5	2.2	12.0	80.8
4th quarter	450.2	182.7	61.8	26.5	11.6	170.6	221.1	112.2	23.5	2.3	12.2	76.0

[1] Excludes government sales to other sectors and government own-account investment (construction and software).
[2] Includes general government intermediate inputs for goods and services sold to other sectors and for own-account investment.

Table 6-4. National Defense Consumption Expenditures and Gross Investment: Selected Detail
(National Income and Product Accounts, calendar years, billions of dollars, quarterly data are at seasonally adjusted annual rates.)

NIPA Table 3.11.5

Year and quarter	Consumption expenditures									Gross investment			
	Compensation of general government employees		Intermediate goods and services purchased [1]							Equipment and software			
			Durable goods	Nondurable goods		Services							
	Military	Civilian	Aircraft	Petroleum products	Ammunition	Research and development	Installation support	Weapons support	Personnel support	Aircraft	Missiles	Ships	Electronics and software
1972	27.0	13.5	2.7	1.8	2.0	5.1	4.4	1.6	1.7	2.6	1.5	1.8	0.8
1973	27.6	13.8	2.4	1.7	1.7	5.3	4.3	1.6	1.5	2.3	1.5	1.6	0.9
1974	29.1	15.0	2.0	2.8	1.4	5.7	4.7	1.8	1.8	2.3	1.7	2.2	1.0
1975	31.1	16.8	2.1	2.9	1.1	5.9	4.9	1.7	2.1	3.6	1.3	2.2	1.2
1976	32.4	17.8	2.0	2.5	0.6	6.4	5.4	1.9	2.3	3.4	1.4	2.4	1.3
1977	34.0	19.7	3.3	2.4	0.8	6.8	6.2	2.1	2.2	3.7	1.2	3.1	1.5
1978	36.2	21.3	3.5	2.5	1.0	7.1	6.3	2.4	2.6	3.7	1.1	3.9	1.8
1979	38.7	22.9	4.8	3.6	1.2	7.7	7.3	2.9	2.7	4.8	1.8	4.3	2.1
1980	43.5	25.1	5.6	6.8	1.4	10.2	8.5	4.4	3.0	6.1	2.3	4.1	2.6
1981	50.5	28.3	7.8	7.7	1.6	12.4	9.3	5.2	4.0	7.5	2.8	5.1	3.2
1982	56.6	30.8	10.2	6.8	2.1	14.1	13.7	6.0	5.8	8.4	3.4	6.2	3.8
1983	59.8	32.7	13.6	6.4	2.5	14.5	15.5	7.3	6.4	10.1	4.6	7.1	4.6
1984	72.8	34.8	14.0	5.9	2.2	16.2	17.0	8.6	6.7	10.9	5.7	8.0	5.6
1985	78.2	37.2	15.4	5.8	1.3	21.7	17.2	9.8	8.4	13.4	6.6	9.0	7.0
1986	80.6	38.1	17.2	3.6	3.6	23.8	18.5	10.4	9.4	17.9	7.9	8.9	7.8
1987	83.7	39.8	18.2	3.9	2.8	27.0	19.1	11.0	10.9	17.6	8.7	8.8	8.7
1988	85.2	41.7	17.9	3.5	3.5	31.5	19.0	9.8	11.4	13.5	7.8	8.6	9.2
1989	87.4	44.3	16.4	4.2	3.1	28.6	19.0	10.3	12.4	12.2	8.8	10.0	9.6
1990	89.1	45.4	14.8	5.3	2.8	26.1	22.1	11.7	13.0	12.0	11.2	10.8	9.9
1991	93.8	48.0	13.6	4.7	2.7	21.9	23.8	10.2	12.7	9.2	10.8	10.2	9.7
1992	93.2	49.8	12.2	3.5	2.6	23.7	23.2	8.5	14.4	8.3	10.6	10.1	9.8
1993	88.0	50.7	10.7	3.2	2.5	22.9	25.4	7.5	13.7	9.3	7.9	8.7	9.9
1994	84.3	50.4	9.2	3.0	1.8	22.5	26.3	8.6	14.7	10.5	5.7	8.1	9.3
1995	81.3	49.5	8.9	2.8	1.2	21.7	25.8	9.1	16.1	9.0	4.7	8.0	8.8
1996	84.0	49.4	8.8	3.4	1.4	24.8	26.0	7.2	17.0	9.2	4.1	6.8	9.0
1997	83.8	49.0	9.4	2.9	1.7	26.3	25.3	8.4	18.5	5.8	2.9	6.1	9.0
1998	83.4	48.2	9.9	2.1	1.9	23.6	24.7	8.7	19.3	5.8	3.3	6.4	9.1
1999	85.2	48.3	10.5	2.6	1.9	26.6	25.0	9.3	22.4	7.0	2.8	6.8	9.8
2000	89.4	49.5	9.8	4.1	1.8	26.3	24.9	9.6	22.9	7.8	2.7	6.6	10.1
2001	95.4	50.3	9.8	4.2	2.1	30.6	27.3	12.0	27.5	8.5	3.3	7.2	9.8
2002	107.7	53.9	9.8	4.6	2.5	39.0	30.5	14.1	34.6	9.4	3.2	8.7	9.8
2003	125.1	56.1	10.5	4.9	2.6	47.6	34.8	16.9	42.7	9.3	3.4	9.5	10.3
1996													
1st quarter	83.5	49.9	8.6	3.4	1.4	23.5	25.5	6.8	16.6	13.7	4.3	7.0	8.6
2nd quarter	83.9	49.6	8.8	3.3	1.5	24.3	26.8	6.8	16.6	9.9	4.2	7.2	9.2
3rd quarter	84.3	49.3	9.1	3.7	1.1	24.0	26.0	6.3	16.0	7.6	4.2	6.6	9.3
4th quarter	84.1	48.7	8.7	3.2	1.5	27.4	25.6	8.8	18.8	5.4	3.6	6.3	8.9
1997													
1st quarter	84.6	49.6	9.2	3.3	1.9	22.8	25.6	7.7	18.0	4.4	2.7	5.6	9.1
2nd quarter	83.9	49.2	10.2	3.0	1.5	28.9	25.5	8.5	19.1	3.6	2.7	6.7	9.1
3rd quarter	83.8	48.9	8.5	2.7	1.7	26.0	25.5	8.5	18.5	6.9	3.0	6.4	9.1
4th quarter	82.8	48.5	9.5	2.7	1.7	27.4	24.5	8.8	18.4	8.4	3.0	5.8	8.8
1998													
1st quarter	83.9	49.0	9.1	2.3	1.6	20.1	24.4	7.5	17.0	4.2	2.9	6.3	9.0
2nd quarter	83.4	48.1	9.6	2.1	1.4	24.8	24.7	8.5	19.7	5.0	2.6	6.0	9.3
3rd quarter	83.5	48.3	10.0	2.0	2.5	22.6	25.4	8.6	20.2	6.7	4.6	6.5	9.2
4th quarter	82.9	47.4	10.8	1.8	2.0	26.8	24.3	10.0	20.1	7.2	2.9	6.9	9.0
1999													
1st quarter	85.0	48.2	9.5	1.7	1.7	27.4	24.4	8.2	20.9	5.9	2.8	6.8	8.6
2nd quarter	84.7	48.5	10.9	2.4	1.8	21.0	24.7	8.4	20.8	6.7	2.7	6.6	10.2
3rd quarter	85.1	48.7	11.5	3.5	2.3	25.6	25.0	9.0	22.4	8.7	2.8	6.5	10.4
4th quarter	85.9	48.0	10.0	2.6	1.8	32.1	26.0	11.4	25.5	6.6	3.1	7.1	9.9
2000													
1st quarter	88.6	49.4	10.5	4.1	1.6	23.7	23.9	6.8	20.5	9.3	2.3	6.1	9.9
2nd quarter	88.7	49.5	9.6	3.6	1.6	27.8	25.2	10.2	24.9	6.9	2.4	6.8	10.2
3rd quarter	90.5	49.7	10.2	4.1	2.1	24.1	25.5	10.3	23.8	8.1	2.2	6.7	9.9
4th quarter	90.0	49.5	9.1	4.4	1.9	29.4	25.1	11.0	22.6	6.8	3.9	6.8	10.3
2001													
1st quarter	94.2	49.3	8.8	4.4	1.9	30.2	27.3	12.3	27.2	6.8	3.6	7.2	9.8
2nd quarter	94.3	49.7	9.6	4.2	2.1	30.2	26.3	11.6	25.5	7.0	3.5	7.4	9.8
3rd quarter	95.3	50.9	11.2	4.2	2.2	28.9	26.8	10.9	26.8	10.7	3.0	6.9	9.7
4th quarter	97.9	51.2	9.4	4.0	2.1	33.2	28.6	13.3	30.6	9.5	3.1	7.3	9.8
2002													
1st quarter	105.1	53.0	9.2	3.7	2.4	34.7	29.6	13.0	31.6	7.3	3.4	8.1	9.7
2nd quarter	106.3	54.0	9.9	4.6	2.6	37.5	29.8	12.8	32.8	9.4	3.2	8.5	9.9
3rd quarter	106.8	54.3	10.2	4.3	2.7	36.6	30.5	14.6	35.9	10.3	2.9	8.9	10.2
4th quarter	112.6	54.3	10.1	5.8	2.4	47.2	31.9	16.0	38.2	10.5	3.1	9.0	9.4
2003													
1st quarter	122.6	56.1	9.5	8.1	2.1	37.3	31.6	13.5	37.2	9.4	2.8	8.8	9.8
2nd quarter	126.0	55.3	11.3	5.6	2.7	54.6	35.4	17.9	43.3	9.2	2.8	10.0	9.8
3rd quarter	125.9	56.2	10.3	2.9	2.8	45.0	35.9	17.7	43.9	8.5	3.3	10.0	10.7
4th quarter	125.7	56.9	11.1	2.9	2.9	53.4	36.4	18.6	46.4	10.2	4.4	9.3	11.1

[1] Includes general government intermediate inputs for goods and services sold to other sectors and for own-account investment.

CHAPTER 6: GOVERNMENT

Table 6-5. Federal Government Output, Lending and Borrowing, and Net Investment

(National Income and Product Accounts, calendar years, billions of dollars, quarterly data are at seasonally adjusted annual rates.)

NIPA Tables 3.2, 3.10.5

Year and quarter	Output						Net lending (net borrowing -)							Net investment
	Gross		Value added		Intermediate goods and services purchased [1]		Net saving, current (surplus +, deficit -)	Plus: capital transfer receipts	Minus			Plus: consumption of fixed capital	Equals: Net lending (borrowing -)	
	Defense	Non-defense	Defense	Non-defense	Defense	Non-defense			Gross investment	Capital transfer payments	Net purchases of non-produced assets			
1946	26.4	4.4	22.9	2.6	3.5	1.8	-5.0	0.7	1.9	0.1	...	9.3	...	-7.4
1947	17.3	4.3	16.0	3.1	1.3	1.2	5.3	0.8	1.8	0.1	...	8.8	...	-7.0
1948	16.4	5.2	13.9	3.2	2.6	2.0	3.6	0.9	3.0	0.3	...	7.6	...	-4.6
1949	17.0	6.6	13.8	3.5	3.2	3.2	-5.7	0.7	4.4	0.4	...	6.6	...	-2.2
1950	17.3	5.3	13.2	3.7	4.1	1.6	5.5	0.6	3.9	0.4	...	5.8	...	-1.9
1951	30.6	4.6	18.9	3.7	11.7	0.9	9.6	0.7	10.7	0.4	...	6.1	...	4.6
1952	39.1	5.7	22.3	3.8	16.9	1.9	3.7	0.8	15.0	0.5	...	6.8	...	8.2
1953	41.5	7.5	23.0	3.7	18.5	3.8	1.8	0.9	16.1	0.6	...	7.6	...	8.5
1954	37.3	7.3	23.0	3.5	14.3	3.8	-1.6	0.9	13.3	0.6	...	8.3	...	5.0
1955	37.3	7.9	23.7	3.8	13.6	4.1	5.7	1.0	10.9	0.7	...	8.7	...	2.2
1956	39.1	6.7	24.7	4.1	14.5	2.6	7.6	1.3	11.6	0.8	...	9.3	...	2.3
1957	43.7	7.1	25.5	4.4	18.1	2.7	3.3	1.4	11.9	1.3	...	9.8	...	2.1
1958	44.7	7.4	26.1	5.0	18.6	2.4	-5.4	1.3	12.9	2.3	...	9.9	...	3.0
1959	40.5	10.6	26.7	5.1	13.8	5.5	3.3	1.4	15.4	3.1	...	10.2	...	5.2
1960	41.5	9.4	27.4	5.6	14.0	3.7	7.2	1.8	14.3	2.6	0.5	10.6	2.1	3.7
1961	43.1	9.6	28.3	6.1	14.7	3.5	2.6	2.0	16.3	2.9	0.5	10.9	-4.2	5.4
1962	47.0	11.9	30.0	6.6	17.0	5.3	2.5	2.1	17.4	3.1	0.6	11.5	-5.0	5.9
1963	48.7	13.2	31.1	7.3	17.6	5.9	5.4	2.2	16.1	3.6	0.5	12.1	-0.5	4.0
1964	49.3	14.8	32.7	8.0	16.5	6.8	1.0	2.6	15.6	4.1	0.6	12.3	-4.4	3.3
1965	51.2	15.9	33.9	8.6	17.3	7.3	3.3	2.8	14.7	4.0	0.5	12.7	-0.4	2.0
1966	60.9	16.7	37.9	9.5	23.0	7.2	2.3	3.0	16.7	4.4	0.6	13.2	-3.2	3.5
1967	70.4	18.0	41.4	10.2	29.0	7.8	-9.4	3.1	17.7	4.3	-0.2	14.0	-14.0	3.7
1968	77.4	19.3	45.1	11.3	32.3	8.0	-2.3	3.1	16.0	6.0	-0.9	14.8	-5.4	1.2
1969	78.4	21.3	47.9	12.1	30.5	9.2	8.7	3.6	15.0	5.9	0.1	15.5	6.8	-0.5
1970	76.8	23.2	50.3	13.8	26.6	9.3	-15.2	3.7	14.8	5.3	-0.3	16.1	-15.2	-1.3
1971	77.3	26.1	52.0	15.7	25.3	10.4	-28.4	4.6	11.7	5.9	-0.4	16.5	-24.5	-4.8
1972	80.2	29.8	54.3	17.2	25.8	12.6	-24.4	5.4	12.0	6.0	-0.7	16.6	-19.7	-4.6
1973	80.5	31.2	55.4	18.6	25.1	12.6	-11.3	5.1	13.6	6.0	-3.2	17.1	-5.5	-3.5
1974	86.1	35.2	58.8	20.8	27.3	14.4	-13.8	4.8	16.6	7.9	-5.7	18.2	-9.6	-1.6
1975	92.1	40.4	63.7	23.7	28.5	16.8	-69.0	4.9	19.5	9.7	-0.4	19.7	-73.1	-0.2
1976	96.4	43.6	67.3	26.5	29.1	17.1	-51.7	5.6	22.6	10.6	-2.4	21.4	-55.5	1.2
1977	105.0	49.5	72.1	30.0	32.9	19.5	-44.1	7.2	24.7	11.1	-1.4	23.1	-48.3	1.6
1978	113.6	54.3	77.5	32.3	36.2	22.0	-26.5	5.2	27.6	11.9	-0.6	25.0	-35.1	2.6
1979	124.8	59.7	83.0	34.7	41.8	25.1	-11.3	5.5	31.6	14.4	-2.8	27.0	-22.0	4.6
1980	145.0	68.6	92.1	39.2	52.9	29.4	-53.6	6.5	36.3	16.6	-4.0	30.1	-65.9	6.2
1981	168.9	75.5	105.1	42.3	63.8	33.2	-53.3	6.9	41.9	15.6	-5.5	33.8	-64.6	8.1
1982	193.1	76.4	116.7	44.6	76.4	31.8	-131.9	7.5	47.5	14.6	-3.6	37.6	-145.1	9.9
1983	210.1	82.5	124.2	47.1	85.9	35.4	-173.0	5.8	56.4	15.5	-4.9	40.8	-193.5	15.6
1984	234.6	82.0	142.4	49.8	92.2	32.2	-168.1	6.0	64.4	17.7	-3.9	44.6	-195.6	19.8
1985	255.5	89.8	152.8	52.3	102.7	37.5	-175.0	6.4	74.4	19.4	-1.1	48.1	-213.2	26.3
1986	269.8	95.3	159.0	53.7	110.8	41.6	-190.8	7.0	80.4	20.0	-3.0	51.6	-229.6	28.8
1987	285.8	96.4	166.6	56.8	119.2	39.6	-145.0	7.2	85.8	19.0	-0.4	55.2	-186.9	30.6
1988	296.0	95.3	172.9	62.0	123.1	33.3	-134.5	7.6	79.8	19.6	-0.1	59.3	-166.9	20.5
1989	302.0	106.7	180.8	65.8	121.1	40.9	-130.1	8.9	83.0	20.1	-0.7	63.5	-160.1	19.5
1990	311.4	118.7	186.9	72.0	124.5	46.7	-172.0	11.6	88.5	28.1	-0.7	67.9	-208.3	20.6
1991	323.2	127.7	197.3	77.7	125.9	50.0	-213.7	11.0	88.2	26.3	0.2	72.2	-245.3	16.0
1992	319.4	137.1	200.3	81.8	119.1	55.3	-297.4	11.3	88.8	22.4	0.2	74.7	-322.9	14.1
1993	311.9	141.0	198.2	88.1	113.7	52.9	-273.5	12.9	83.3	24.5	0.2	77.9	-290.7	5.4
1994	306.7	147.1	195.7	90.5	111.0	56.7	-212.3	15.1	78.3	25.9	0.2	80.2	-221.4	-1.9
1995	301.0	150.2	192.6	92.1	108.3	58.1	-197.0	14.9	78.8	27.7	-7.4	81.9	-199.2	-3.1
1996	306.6	150.9	194.6	94.1	112.0	56.8	-141.8	17.5	81.1	28.2	-3.8	82.0	-147.8	-0.9
1997	308.1	158.6	193.2	97.7	115.0	60.9	-55.8	20.6	73.2	29.1	-7.6	82.5	-47.4	-9.3
1998	303.9	160.7	191.3	101.8	112.6	58.9	38.8	25.2	75.8	28.8	-5.6	82.8	47.8	-7.0
1999	315.9	167.6	193.3	107.6	122.7	60.0	103.6	28.8	80.7	36.1	-0.9	84.8	101.3	-4.1
2000	324.6	184.6	199.2	116.2	125.4	68.4	189.5	28.1	79.5	36.2	-0.3	87.2	189.4	-7.7
2001	345.9	195.1	206.0	119.6	139.9	75.4	46.7	28.0	81.0	40.8	-0.7	88.2	41.8	-7.2
2002	386.0	215.7	222.3	128.1	163.8	87.6	-254.5	25.3	88.1	48.3	0.2	89.0	-276.8	-0.9
2003	439.6	227.8	242.7	135.7	197.0	92.1	-364.5	22.0	93.6	61.9	-0.2	90.2	-407.6	3.4
2001														
1st quarter	340.4	187.7	203.6	117.4	136.8	70.3	156.6	28.5	77.8	38.8	-3.9	87.9	160.3	-10.1
2nd quarter	340.8	195.6	204.4	119.4	136.4	76.2	123.6	30.6	83.0	41.2	-1.3	88.3	119.6	-5.3
3rd quarter	344.6	196.7	206.8	120.5	137.8	76.1	-88.6	26.5	81.6	41.2	2.3	88.4	-98.9	-6.8
4th quarter	358.0	200.3	209.3	121.2	148.7	79.2	-4.7	26.3	81.6	42.0	0.1	88.2	-14.0	-6.6
2002														
1st quarter	370.7	209.7	218.6	126.5	152.1	83.2	-208.5	27.0	83.5	46.4	0.2	88.7	-222.9	-5.2
2nd quarter	379.4	215.0	220.8	127.4	158.6	87.6	-251.6	24.8	90.2	43.8	-0.1	88.8	-272.0	1.4
3rd quarter	386.0	218.1	221.8	128.5	164.3	89.6	-255.1	27.2	91.0	43.9	0.6	89.0	-274.4	2.0
4th quarter	407.9	220.2	227.9	130.3	179.9	90.0	-302.7	22.2	87.9	59.0	0.1	89.7	-337.8	-1.8
2003														
1st quarter	413.4	229.0	239.7	134.9	173.6	94.1	-281.6	23.0	89.1	54.8	-2.7	89.7	-310.2	-0.6
2nd quarter	450.8	225.0	242.6	136.2	208.2	88.8	-364.4	20.0	95.4	65.1	-1.0	90.0	-413.9	5.4
3rd quarter	441.1	231.1	243.8	136.1	197.3	95.0	-433.0	22.0	93.7	66.3	3.4	90.5	-483.9	3.2
4th quarter	453.2	226.2	244.5	135.7	208.7	90.4	-379.2	22.9	96.2	61.5	-0.7	90.7	-422.6	5.5

[1] Includes general government intermediate inputs for goods and services sold to other sectors and for own-account investment.
... = Not available.

Table 6-6. Chain-Type Quantity Indexes for Federal Government Defense and Nondefense Consumption Expenditures and Gross Investment

(Index numbers, 2000 = 100.)

NIPA Table 3.9.3, 3.10.3

Year and quarter	Defense consumption expenditures [1]						Defense gross investment	Nondefense consumption expenditures [1]						Non-defense gross investment
	Total	Compensation of general government employees	Consumption of general government fixed capital	Intermediate goods and services purchased [2]				Total	Compensation of general government employees	Consumption of general government fixed capital	Intermediate goods and services purchased [2]			
				Durable goods	Nondurable goods	Services					Durable goods	Nondurable goods excluding CCC inventory change	Services	
1946	72.4	159.6	92.7	16.0	64.9	16.8	18.4	17.6	41.9	11.4	17.7	77.5	19.5	6.1
1947	49.4	86.9	75.8	8.0	24.1	4.5	9.9	19.0	51.2	11.6	19.5	18.1	8.5	12.2
1948	47.2	84.5	61.7	18.5	46.3	6.8	19.3	26.7	57.9	11.8	14.3	34.6	12.0	14.8
1949	47.3	89.4	52.3	22.8	55.1	8.9	28.2	32.6	55.1	12.0	12.2	39.7	11.1	19.9
1950	48.3	94.4	45.7	39.0	58.3	8.6	22.2	25.3	61.3	12.2	12.4	17.8	10.5	22.6
1951	82.1	163.5	44.7	93.4	153.0	24.7	78.8	21.1	56.3	12.4	12.3	31.3	7.7	20.3
1952	106.1	188.2	49.7	165.6	200.0	33.3	114.0	24.8	55.0	12.4	11.3	19.5	13.1	19.7
1953	110.8	184.3	55.5	185.4	321.2	26.8	127.7	32.3	50.4	12.4	10.4	19.5	13.1	17.3
1954	96.5	172.8	59.4	134.9	211.2	22.5	104.1	31.1	47.8	12.4	11.7	18.9	14.2	15.6
1955	90.2	164.0	60.6	114.4	97.0	29.4	84.1	30.5	48.4	12.3	9.7	21.8	14.7	11.1
1956	90.4	159.7	60.9	108.2	95.7	33.0	80.5	26.8	49.5	12.1	9.9	33.9	16.1	14.2
1957	96.5	157.5	61.2	113.3	115.7	44.3	76.3	25.9	50.9	12.0	9.1	46.9	15.8	15.9
1958	94.3	148.3	61.2	117.4	117.8	43.6	81.3	25.9	52.5	12.1	7.1	20.9	14.6	18.8
1959	87.2	144.3	62.5	83.9	98.5	39.2	97.0	37.5	52.6	12.0	5.4	57.5	19.1	18.9
1960	88.2	144.2	64.2	71.3	105.6	44.5	87.4	32.9	56.9	11.9	6.5	45.5	22.4	22.2
1961	90.4	147.1	65.4	58.5	130.3	48.7	96.9	32.5	58.3	12.1	11.7	53.1	26.5	26.9
1962	96.6	153.4	67.4	72.4	165.1	51.0	100.3	39.6	61.4	12.8	19.0	52.8	30.8	31.4
1963	97.6	150.7	69.1	73.0	153.6	54.8	86.6	43.2	65.0	14.1	26.4	58.8	38.7	36.9
1964	95.1	150.6	69.9	61.7	169.6	50.1	78.6	46.2	66.5	15.7	34.2	63.2	44.4	42.4
1965	95.4	150.8	69.8	63.9	183.2	49.7	68.6	48.3	67.7	18.0	43.7	63.5	45.8	48.4
1966	108.9	166.1	70.0	93.1	261.3	59.2	79.3	48.6	70.4	20.5	45.4	74.4	49.8	49.8
1967	123.1	180.7	71.3	91.9	401.9	70.4	89.5	50.8	73.9	22.5	39.8	80.4	45.9	40.4
1968	128.4	183.1	72.4	106.4	460.2	71.6	78.5	50.9	75.6	23.8	31.8	64.5	40.6	35.4
1969	123.3	183.3	72.1	88.8	408.4	67.7	69.5	53.5	76.3	24.7	27.7	81.1	39.6	32.1
1970	112.1	170.0	71.0	79.5	284.3	61.8	63.3	53.3	77.3	25.3	22.1	83.1	45.0	30.4
1971	103.4	157.1	68.0	57.2	232.4	61.8	40.3	55.8	79.9	25.5	21.2	79.1	49.1	31.9
1972	97.1	145.1	64.3	73.1	236.8	54.9	30.1	60.1	82.2	25.6	22.8	88.9	58.1	33.0
1973	90.0	137.6	61.3	67.6	176.0	51.4	33.9	59.4	82.4	25.9	18.0	76.8	58.3	34.0
1974	87.1	135.5	59.3	58.4	152.1	52.1	41.4	62.7	86.5	26.3	15.6	84.5	59.0	35.0
1975	85.0	133.6	58.5	60.7	126.0	48.9	46.0	64.8	88.0	26.8	16.7	63.9	62.1	36.3
1976	83.5	130.9	58.5	54.5	102.8	49.7	50.1	64.7	92.4	27.5	18.0	80.9	55.7	39.0
1977	84.4	129.8	58.8	69.0	96.0	50.4	51.2	67.4	94.5	28.3	20.7	92.5	59.0	41.0
1978	85.3	130.6	59.1	77.1	96.8	49.7	50.9	70.2	96.9	29.6	26.1	108.1	63.4	48.5
1979	86.4	129.5	59.7	83.3	99.7	51.5	58.1	71.4	96.8	31.2	31.5	108.2	67.9	47.3
1980	89.7	130.3	60.8	87.3	109.0	58.0	62.2	75.1	99.4	33.1	36.8	106.8	67.5	51.0
1981	94.8	134.3	62.3	101.8	115.3	63.8	68.6	76.3	96.5	35.2	32.7	177.1	61.4	50.8
1982	101.2	137.4	64.4	111.7	114.8	76.5	77.1	73.0	94.7	37.2	28.1	126.2	59.1	47.2
1983	106.6	139.5	67.5	132.0	120.2	81.0	90.5	75.7	96.0	39.8	42.8	132.1	62.0	53.6
1984	109.8	141.5	71.8	133.4	113.8	87.2	103.3	73.0	96.1	43.2	46.4	138.1	62.6	57.6
1985	116.4	144.1	77.5	143.2	111.8	99.1	124.4	77.1	96.3	46.6	47.4	121.1	65.5	61.5
1986	121.8	144.8	84.1	153.0	141.1	104.7	142.5	80.0	94.9	50.0	47.8	107.0	65.5	63.0
1987	126.3	146.1	90.6	162.5	138.2	111.1	155.6	78.8	96.6	53.2	53.5	121.9	72.2	69.1
1988	127.7	144.3	95.9	167.1	133.2	114.0	144.0	75.0	99.0	56.5	55.9	120.0	71.8	64.7
1989	126.8	144.3	100.1	160.4	129.0	110.3	144.9	81.4	99.6	59.8	61.5	106.5	72.8	69.0
1990	125.9	143.4	104.0	154.6	115.2	110.3	149.3	88.0	104.5	63.3	70.0	113.6	82.4	75.3
1991	125.8	142.9	107.0	147.6	117.3	110.0	140.7	89.1	104.2	66.9	72.1	96.8	84.8	81.5
1992	119.3	134.5	108.8	132.8	108.5	103.7	135.3	94.6	106.1	69.7	78.1	118.6	92.7	90.0
1993	114.2	128.7	109.2	120.8	99.5	98.4	118.3	93.4	106.0	72.2	76.0	118.5	85.6	92.1
1994	109.0	122.1	108.3	103.7	90.6	98.2	110.2	94.1	103.0	74.1	76.2	115.0	92.0	82.2
1995	105.2	115.4	106.7	94.2	74.3	96.6	104.3	92.6	98.9	76.3	78.4	112.7	92.0	87.1
1996	103.3	110.5	105.1	93.5	82.1	97.9	105.1	90.6	96.3	79.7	87.3	108.4	88.6	93.3
1997	102.1	106.5	103.5	93.9	82.7	99.2	92.4	93.7	95.7	83.6	92.4	116.8	92.3	92.0
1998	99.5	103.2	101.8	94.9	85.6	95.3	93.4	92.7	96.8	88.1	92.5	114.9	87.8	101.8
1999	101.0	100.7	100.8	100.8	95.3	102.2	97.6	94.5	97.0	94.3	92.3	91.8	91.0	108.9
2000	100.0	100.0	100.0	100.0	100.0	100.0	100.0	100.0	100.0	100.0	100.0	100.0	100.0	100.0
2001	103.9	100.7	99.8	100.9	104.7	112.2	104.1	104.5	99.9	103.9	112.5	118.6	107.3	100.3
2002	111.4	103.4	99.7	105.1	125.7	131.5	115.9	111.9	101.8	107.0	132.5	146.0	121.9	107.5
2003	121.4	107.1	100.4	113.7	135.7	156.8	126.2	114.7	104.2	108.9	132.8	141.6	126.8	109.4
2001														
1st quarter	102.6	100.5	99.8	94.3	95.4	111.7	98.3	101.5	99.4	102.7	107.3	109.1	100.3	98.1
2nd quarter	103.0	100.7	99.8	102.5	105.5	108.0	103.7	105.2	100.5	103.5	111.2	112.6	106.5	105.9
3rd quarter	103.3	100.8	99.9	109.7	100.4	107.7	106.7	105.3	100.6	104.4	114.3	121.5	109.5	98.0
4th quarter	106.7	100.9	99.8	96.9	117.5	121.2	107.6	105.8	99.3	105.2	117.3	131.1	113.0	99.1
2002														
1st quarter	108.4	102.6	99.6	99.1	122.4	123.7	107.7	108.6	100.3	106.0	128.2	143.4	116.7	104.9
2nd quarter	110.6	103.5	99.6	104.6	137.6	126.9	116.4	111.6	101.0	106.8	131.4	149.7	120.8	113.5
3rd quarter	110.9	104.0	99.7	111.5	115.4	130.3	122.1	113.3	102.2	107.4	137.0	145.3	124.6	107.1
4th quarter	115.7	103.5	99.8	105.1	127.3	145.1	117.2	114.3	103.6	107.9	133.5	145.6	125.6	104.4
2003														
1st quarter	114.4	105.9	100.0	102.4	143.8	135.5	119.8	116.2	104.1	108.4	129.3	123.7	133.8	104.7
2nd quarter	124.7	107.4	100.3	118.5	150.6	166.3	125.3	113.0	104.6	108.8	127.1	139.7	121.8	116.6
3rd quarter	121.7	107.6	100.5	115.8	122.9	158.0	127.3	116.2	104.3	109.1	135.3	150.8	130.1	108.0
4th quarter	124.8	107.5	100.8	117.9	125.5	167.5	132.3	113.6	103.9	109.5	139.6	152.3	121.5	108.4

[1] Excludes government sales to other sectors and government own-account investment (construction [b]and software).
[2] Includes general government intermediate inputs for goods and services sold to other sectors and for own-account investment.

Table 6-7. Chain-Type Quantity Indexes for National Defense Consumption Expenditures and Gross Investment: Selected Detail

(Index numbers, 2000 = 100.)

NIPA Table 3.11.3

Year and quarter	Consumption expenditures									Gross investment			
	Compensation of general government employees		Intermediate goods and services purchased [1]							Equipment and software			
			Durable goods	Nondurable goods		Services							
	Military	Civilian	Aircraft	Petroleum products	Ammunition	Research and development	Installation support	Weapons support	Personnel support	Aircraft	Missiles	Ships	Electronics and software
1972	147.9	139.5	82.6	414.8	336.9	45.7	60.6	61.7	43.1	50.4	51.5	99.5	7.6
1973	139.5	133.7	69.0	262.5	262.8	45.7	55.2	58.0	34.8	44.3	53.8	84.0	8.3
1974	134.5	137.2	53.6	238.6	179.7	45.4	55.5	62.1	39.5	44.4	59.6	103.6	8.3
1975	131.6	137.2	49.4	200.8	125.1	43.5	52.9	54.1	39.4	67.2	43.5	92.7	9.6
1976	128.4	135.5	41.4	166.4	62.8	45.1	54.3	57.0	38.8	62.9	37.0	95.0	10.1
1977	127.3	134.2	63.2	141.5	85.8	46.6	57.1	56.7	34.2	65.7	29.0	110.9	11.2
1978	126.1	139.0	64.6	140.8	99.2	46.0	53.3	61.7	35.8	62.0	23.9	124.8	13.8
1979	124.1	139.6	80.4	143.2	110.2	47.6	56.9	67.8	34.2	77.7	48.1	128.4	15.1
1980	125.4	139.4	87.3	158.5	110.5	58.7	60.5	91.3	33.7	93.0	69.4	112.9	18.5
1981	129.4	143.4	112.5	155.7	124.8	68.0	62.1	97.6	41.3	107.6	80.5	128.7	22.0
1982	131.7	148.0	131.6	146.5	153.8	73.2	85.0	106.0	56.7	108.2	103.9	150.0	25.4
1983	134.0	149.8	160.2	156.9	180.4	72.3	93.1	123.2	60.6	122.9	131.5	166.7	31.0
1984	135.6	152.3	151.4	156.5	152.7	78.1	99.1	140.5	62.0	132.1	158.1	176.6	39.0
1985	137.6	156.4	162.7	159.2	91.1	103.1	97.3	155.5	75.7	180.4	180.3	194.1	49.9
1986	138.9	155.6	179.9	159.1	245.1	110.7	100.1	162.9	80.3	275.1	228.6	187.4	57.0
1987	140.6	156.0	192.7	163.4	186.0	124.6	99.9	168.4	87.5	315.6	260.0	182.3	65.2
1988	139.6	152.6	199.5	137.6	214.7	146.7	95.6	146.9	81.8	259.3	236.7	172.7	68.9
1989	138.9	154.1	188.1	151.1	179.6	130.9	94.8	148.4	83.6	237.2	271.1	191.7	72.1
1990	139.2	150.5	165.3	149.8	162.0	117.1	104.5	162.7	81.3	218.8	352.0	202.3	74.8
1991	140.7	145.8	147.9	148.0	152.8	96.6	110.6	135.6	74.6	157.4	354.0	181.5	73.6
1992	128.7	145.0	129.0	123.8	145.1	101.8	106.5	108.3	80.3	137.7	350.1	175.4	77.7
1993	122.1	141.0	111.8	119.0	144.0	96.8	114.9	91.4	74.4	148.8	254.0	147.9	78.3
1994	116.2	132.9	94.9	122.5	99.2	93.6	116.1	102.3	76.8	148.6	186.9	133.1	74.8
1995	110.2	125.0	90.4	111.2	63.5	90.0	109.8	106.1	81.0	120.1	158.1	125.3	71.6
1996	106.1	118.6	89.7	112.3	74.3	102.4	109.0	81.6	83.0	117.3	140.9	105.8	77.0
1997	103.5	112.4	95.8	100.9	91.3	105.9	105.2	92.9	88.5	81.6	104.2	93.8	80.9
1998	100.9	107.2	101.7	99.2	103.4	93.3	101.6	94.7	89.9	82.1	117.7	99.1	86.5
1999	99.1	103.4	107.4	108.5	105.2	103.4	101.9	99.3	101.5	85.4	105.7	105.0	95.7
2000	100.0	100.0	100.0	100.0	100.0	100.0	100.0	100.0	100.0	100.0	100.0	100.0	100.0
2001	102.0	98.3	98.6	122.0	114.3	114.5	106.4	122.2	115.3	116.8	126.9	109.6	99.0
2002	105.8	99.0	99.4	157.7	140.9	143.5	116.3	140.5	140.3	133.5	122.1	131.0	102.2
2003	111.5	98.8	104.6	150.8	143.8	171.4	128.2	164.8	167.7	132.8	126.8	142.1	111.1
1996													
1st quarter	107.3	119.0	87.5	119.9	75.9	97.2	108.2	78.1	81.9	153.4	146.3	109.4	71.6
2nd quarter	106.3	120.5	89.8	114.0	80.4	101.0	112.6	77.1	81.4	136.2	143.7	113.0	78.4
3rd quarter	106.0	119.1	93.1	123.9	61.0	99.2	108.8	71.3	78.0	105.5	144.2	102.5	80.2
4th quarter	105.0	115.6	88.3	91.4	80.0	112.3	106.6	99.7	90.9	74.0	129.6	98.5	77.5
1997													
1st quarter	104.1	114.7	93.5	101.6	103.5	93.2	106.8	86.0	87.0	59.2	100.1	86.2	80.4
2nd quarter	103.1	113.4	104.6	104.9	81.0	116.8	106.6	94.2	91.5	49.6	98.4	102.3	80.9
3rd quarter	103.4	112.1	87.2	100.1	89.7	104.0	105.9	94.5	88.4	97.6	108.5	98.2	81.9
4th quarter	102.5	109.6	98.0	96.9	91.0	109.5	101.6	97.0	87.1	119.8	109.6	88.5	80.5
1998													
1st quarter	101.9	108.8	93.8	102.7	86.1	80.1	101.7	82.5	80.6	61.9	106.4	96.9	83.9
2nd quarter	100.9	107.7	99.0	101.0	78.5	98.4	102.3	93.5	92.7	70.8	94.7	92.7	87.8
3rd quarter	101.0	107.2	102.7	99.9	137.4	89.4	103.8	94.0	93.9	97.1	163.2	100.3	87.4
4th quarter	100.0	105.1	111.5	93.1	111.6	105.5	98.8	108.6	92.5	98.4	106.6	106.6	87.0
1999													
1st quarter	99.1	104.3	97.7	99.2	92.8	107.8	99.8	88.8	95.8	72.3	101.6	106.4	83.9
2nd quarter	98.6	103.6	111.6	112.4	99.6	82.2	101.0	90.1	94.8	81.6	102.2	103.4	99.3
3rd quarter	99.6	102.9	118.2	136.6	127.8	99.6	101.4	96.9	101.5	106.7	104.3	100.8	102.1
4th quarter	99.3	102.9	102.2	85.7	100.6	124.0	105.2	121.5	113.8	81.1	114.5	109.5	97.6
2000													
1st quarter	99.2	100.5	106.9	110.5	90.1	91.2	96.9	72.3	90.4	116.6	83.4	92.6	98.5
2nd quarter	99.2	102.0	97.3	99.6	86.9	106.0	101.7	106.4	108.9	88.8	89.0	102.8	101.6
3rd quarter	100.6	99.6	103.4	97.6	116.1	91.6	101.6	107.1	103.4	105.8	80.6	101.0	97.7
4th quarter	101.1	98.0	92.4	92.3	107.0	111.2	99.8	114.1	97.2	88.8	147.0	103.6	102.3
2001													
1st quarter	101.8	98.0	89.0	111.3	103.5	113.6	107.4	125.5	115.4	91.4	136.6	109.0	98.4
2nd quarter	102.1	98.0	97.2	111.2	116.8	112.9	103.3	118.8	107.5	93.1	135.3	112.9	98.7
3rd quarter	101.7	99.3	113.5	116.0	119.4	107.9	104.0	110.4	111.9	144.7	115.4	104.4	99.0
4th quarter	102.5	98.0	94.9	149.3	117.4	123.5	111.0	134.2	126.3	137.9	120.2	112.0	100.1
2002													
1st quarter	105.3	97.5	93.0	153.6	133.8	128.8	114.8	130.3	129.4	104.9	131.5	124.2	100.4
2nd quarter	105.9	99.2	99.6	189.6	145.7	138.3	114.7	127.5	133.5	135.0	122.0	129.5	102.6
3rd quarter	106.1	100.0	102.8	126.8	148.9	134.5	115.5	145.5	144.9	146.7	113.2	134.5	106.4
4th quarter	105.8	99.3	102.2	160.9	135.1	172.5	120.3	158.6	153.2	147.3	121.7	135.9	99.5
2003													
1st quarter	109.6	99.1	94.4	204.0	116.4	135.3	117.9	132.3	147.7	134.3	106.8	131.7	104.1
2nd quarter	112.7	97.3	112.6	188.2	149.9	197.2	130.5	175.1	170.8	131.4	108.1	149.3	104.4
3rd quarter	112.3	98.8	102.0	108.0	153.6	161.9	131.8	172.1	172.0	119.8	125.5	148.9	114.8
4th quarter	111.6	100.0	109.4	102.9	155.1	191.1	132.6	179.4	180.3	145.7	166.8	138.5	121.3

[1] Includes general government intermediate inputs for goods and services sold to other sectors and for own-account investment.

Section 6b: State and Local Government in the National Income and Product Accounts

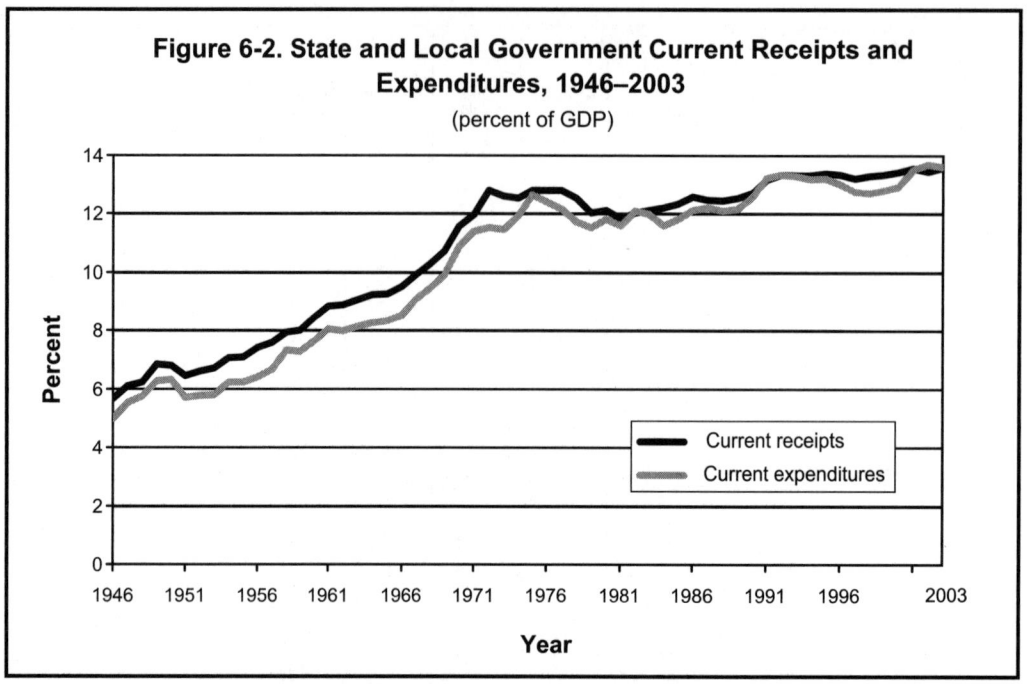

Figure 6-2. State and Local Government Current Receipts and Expenditures, 1946–2003 (percent of GDP)

- Both the current receipts and the current spending of state and local governments have increased as a share of GDP over the postwar period. However, the trend of the increase slowed over the decade of the 1970s, reflecting the weaker economy and the "tax revolt" associated with California's Proposition 13 in 1978. Because state governments, unlike the federal government, are bound by constraints on deficit spending, they have generally run modest surpluses ("net saving") in their current accounts, particularly in their social insurance funds. (Table 6-8)
- State and local governments, responsible for much of the infrastructure of the national transportation, education, and justice systems, do nearly three times as much gross investment spending as the federal government. Their gross investment rose 1,820 percent in real terms from 1946 to 2003, for an annual rate of increase of 5.3 percent. (Tables 6-2, 6-9, and 6-11)
- Though they are constrained against deficits in their annual budgets, state and local governments can and do borrow for investment by issuing bonds. Their gross investment generally exceeds their current surpluses, so that they are usually net borrowers with respect to the rest of the economy. (Table 6-10)
- Looking at the accounts for state and local governments separately, both levels have been net borrowers of funds in most postwar years, financing new investment in excess of the using up of old capital. (Tables 6-12 and 6-13)
- For both state and local governments, transportation spending dominates the economic affairs function. For states, transportation and higher education together made up 43 percent of all their spending in 2001. For local governments, transportation and elementary and secondary education accounted for 59 percent of their total spending. (Tables 6-14 and 6-15)

Table 6-8. State and Local Government Current Receipts and Expenditures

(National Income and Product Accounts, calendar years, billions of dollars, quarterly data are at seasonally adjusted annual rates.)

NIPA Table 3.3

Year and quarter	Current receipts												
	Total	Current tax receipts							Taxes on corporate income	Contributions for government social insurance	Income receipts on assets		
		Total	Personal current taxes		Taxes on production and imports						Total	Interest receipts	Rents and royalties
			Total	Income taxes	Total	Sales taxes	Property taxes	Other					
1946	12.6	10.5	0.9	0.4	9.1	2.9	4.8	1.4	0.5	0.2	0.4	0.3	0.1
1947	14.9	12.0	1.0	0.5	10.4	3.5	5.3	1.6	0.6	0.2	0.4	0.3	0.1
1948	16.8	13.7	1.1	0.6	11.9	4.1	5.9	1.8	0.7	0.2	0.5	0.3	0.2
1949	18.3	15.0	1.4	0.7	13.0	4.3	6.6	2.1	0.6	0.2	0.5	0.3	0.2
1950	20.0	16.5	1.5	0.8	14.2	4.8	7.1	2.3	0.8	0.2	0.5	0.3	0.2
1951	21.9	18.1	1.7	0.9	15.6	5.4	7.7	2.5	0.9	0.2	0.6	0.4	0.2
1952	23.7	19.7	1.8	1.0	17.0	5.8	8.4	2.8	0.8	0.3	0.7	0.4	0.2
1953	25.5	21.1	1.9	1.0	18.4	6.3	9.1	3.0	0.8	0.3	0.7	0.5	0.3
1954	26.9	22.2	2.1	1.1	19.4	6.5	9.7	3.2	0.8	0.3	0.8	0.5	0.3
1955	29.4	24.4	2.4	1.3	21.0	7.1	10.4	3.5	1.0	0.3	0.9	0.6	0.3
1956	32.4	27.0	2.7	1.6	23.3	8.0	11.5	3.8	1.0	0.4	1.0	0.7	0.3
1957	35.0	29.0	2.9	1.7	25.1	8.6	12.6	3.9	1.0	0.4	1.1	0.7	0.3
1958	37.1	30.6	3.1	1.8	26.5	10.0	13.8	2.8	1.0	0.4	1.1	0.8	0.4
1959	40.6	33.8	3.8	2.2	28.8	11.1	14.8	2.9	1.2	0.4	1.1	0.9	0.3
1960	44.5	37.0	4.2	2.5	31.5	12.2	16.2	3.1	1.2	0.5	1.3	1.0	0.3
1961	48.1	39.7	4.6	2.8	33.8	13.0	17.6	3.2	1.3	0.5	1.4	1.1	0.4
1962	52.0	42.8	5.0	3.2	36.3	14.0	19.0	3.3	1.5	0.5	1.5	1.1	0.4
1963	56.0	45.8	5.4	3.4	38.7	15.0	20.2	3.5	1.7	0.6	1.6	1.2	0.4
1964	61.3	49.8	6.1	4.0	41.8	16.5	21.7	3.7	1.8	0.7	1.9	1.5	0.4
1965	66.5	53.9	6.6	4.4	45.3	18.2	23.2	3.9	2.0	0.8	2.2	1.8	0.4
1966	74.9	58.8	7.8	5.4	48.8	20.0	24.5	4.3	2.2	0.8	2.6	2.1	0.5
1967	82.5	64.0	8.6	6.1	52.8	21.4	27.0	4.4	2.6	0.9	3.0	2.4	0.6
1968	93.5	73.4	10.6	7.8	59.5	25.1	29.9	4.6	3.3	0.9	3.5	2.8	0.7
1969	105.5	82.5	12.8	9.8	66.0	28.6	32.8	4.7	3.6	1.0	4.3	3.6	0.8
1970	120.1	91.3	14.2	10.9	73.3	31.6	36.7	5.0	3.7	1.1	5.2	4.3	0.8
1971	134.9	101.7	15.9	12.4	81.5	35.4	40.4	5.7	4.3	1.2	5.5	4.6	0.9
1972	158.4	115.6	20.9	17.2	89.4	39.8	43.2	6.4	5.3	1.3	5.9	4.9	1.0
1973	174.3	126.3	22.8	18.9	97.4	44.1	46.4	7.0	6.0	1.5	7.8	6.6	1.1
1974	188.1	136.0	24.5	20.4	104.8	48.2	49.0	7.7	6.7	1.7	10.2	8.9	1.3
1975	209.6	147.4	26.9	22.5	113.2	51.7	53.4	8.1	7.3	1.8	11.2	9.8	1.3
1976	233.7	165.7	31.1	26.3	125.0	57.8	58.2	9.0	9.6	2.2	10.4	9.0	1.3
1977	259.9	183.7	35.4	30.4	136.9	64.0	63.2	9.7	11.4	2.8	11.7	10.4	1.3
1978	287.6	198.2	40.5	35.0	145.6	71.0	63.7	10.9	12.1	3.4	14.7	13.3	1.3
1979	308.4	212.0	44.0	38.2	154.4	77.3	64.4	12.7	13.6	3.9	20.1	18.1	1.9
1980	338.2	230.0	48.9	42.6	166.7	82.9	68.8	15.0	14.5	3.6	26.3	23.1	3.1
1981	370.2	255.8	54.6	47.9	185.7	90.7	77.1	17.9	15.4	3.9	32.0	28.5	3.3
1982	391.4	273.2	59.1	51.9	200.0	96.2	85.3	18.5	14.0	4.0	36.7	33.1	3.5
1983	428.6	300.9	66.1	58.3	218.9	107.7	91.9	19.4	15.9	4.1	41.4	37.0	4.3
1984	480.2	337.3	76.0	67.5	242.5	121.0	99.7	21.8	18.8	4.7	47.7	42.6	4.9
1985	521.1	363.7	81.4	72.1	262.1	131.1	107.5	23.5	20.2	4.9	54.9	49.4	5.4
1986	561.6	389.5	87.2	77.4	279.7	139.9	116.2	23.7	22.7	6.0	58.4	52.0	6.2
1987	590.6	422.1	96.6	86.0	301.6	150.3	126.4	24.9	23.9	7.2	58.1	52.6	5.3
1988	635.6	452.8	102.1	90.6	324.6	162.4	136.5	25.7	26.0	8.4	60.5	55.9	4.4
1989	687.3	488.0	114.6	102.3	349.1	172.3	149.9	26.9	24.2	9.0	65.7	61.4	4.1
1990	737.8	519.1	122.6	109.6	374.1	184.3	161.5	28.3	22.5	10.0	68.4	64.1	4.2
1991	789.2	544.3	125.3	111.7	395.3	190.7	176.1	28.6	23.6	11.6	68.0	63.1	4.5
1992	845.7	579.8	135.3	120.4	420.1	204.3	184.7	31.1	24.4	13.1	64.8	59.6	4.8
1993	886.9	604.7	141.1	126.2	436.8	216.4	187.3	33.1	26.9	14.1	61.4	56.2	4.5
1994	942.9	644.2	148.0	132.2	466.3	231.4	199.4	35.5	30.0	14.5	63.2	57.9	4.5
1995	990.2	672.1	158.1	141.7	482.4	242.7	202.6	37.0	31.7	13.6	68.4	62.9	4.5
1996	1 043.3	709.6	168.7	152.3	507.9	256.2	212.4	39.4	33.0	12.5	73.3	67.3	4.6
1997	1 097.4	749.9	182.0	164.7	533.8	268.7	223.5	41.6	34.1	10.8	77.8	71.5	4.8
1998	1 163.2	794.9	201.2	183.0	558.8	283.9	231.0	43.9	34.9	10.4	80.9	74.6	4.6
1999	1 236.7	840.4	214.5	195.5	590.2	301.6	242.8	45.8	35.8	9.8	85.3	78.4	5.1
2000	1 319.5	893.2	236.6	217.3	621.1	316.6	254.6	49.9	35.5	11.0	92.2	84.0	6.3
2001	1 373.0	915.8	242.7	223.1	642.8	321.1	269.3	52.4	30.2	13.6	88.8	80.3	6.5
2002	1 411.9	926.5	220.1	199.6	675.3	329.1	291.5	54.7	31.2	14.5	81.6	73.2	6.2
2003	1 494.9	969.2	226.1	204.6	708.7	343.9	305.0	59.7	34.4	15.0	81.0	71.3	7.1
2001													
1st quarter	1 367.2	919.1	249.2	230.1	637.5	322.8	262.6	52.1	32.4	12.7	91.6	83.1	6.6
2nd quarter	1 397.4	937.9	266.6	246.9	639.4	320.5	266.5	52.4	31.9	13.5	89.9	81.4	6.6
3rd quarter	1 354.8	899.9	229.3	209.5	641.4	317.7	271.3	52.4	29.2	14.0	87.7	79.3	6.5
4th quarter	1 372.5	906.2	225.8	205.9	652.9	323.5	276.7	52.7	27.4	14.4	85.9	77.5	6.4
2002													
1st quarter	1 380.9	909.4	218.8	199.0	662.1	324.8	284.1	53.3	28.5	14.4	83.5	75.2	6.2
2nd quarter	1 404.1	919.7	216.5	195.9	672.3	328.6	289.5	54.2	30.9	14.5	81.9	73.7	6.1
3rd quarter	1 423.9	937.3	222.3	201.7	683.0	332.6	294.2	56.1	31.9	14.6	80.9	72.6	6.2
4th quarter	1 438.5	939.7	222.6	201.8	683.8	330.4	298.2	55.3	33.3	14.7	80.1	71.5	6.4
2003													
1st quarter	1 437.7	941.1	216.1	195.0	693.2	335.8	300.5	57.0	31.9	14.7	80.9	71.7	6.7
2nd quarter	1 484.6	955.2	219.0	198.0	703.3	340.8	303.5	59.0	32.9	14.9	80.6	71.2	7.0
3rd quarter	1 511.4	981.9	232.5	210.6	714.0	346.8	306.6	60.7	35.4	15.1	80.6	70.8	7.3
4th quarter	1 545.8	998.8	236.9	214.6	724.3	352.3	309.6	62.4	37.6	15.5	81.7	71.5	7.6

Table 6-8. State and Local Government Current Receipts and Expenditures—Continued

(National Income and Product Accounts, calendar years, billions of dollars, quarterly data are at seasonally adjusted annual rates.)

NIPA Table 3.3

Year and quarter	Current receipts—Continued					Current expenditures					Net state and local government saving, NIPA (surplus + / deficit -)		
	Current transfer receipts				Current surplus of government enterprises	Total	Consumption expenditures	Government social benefits to persons	Interest payments	Subsidies	Total	Social insurance funds	Other
	Total	Federal grants-in-aid	From business (net)	From persons									
1946	1.2	1.0	0.1	0.2	0.4	11.1	9.2	1.5	0.5	...	1.5	0.1	1.4
1947	1.8	1.6	0.1	0.2	0.4	13.5	10.9	2.0	0.5	...	1.4	0.1	1.4
1948	2.0	1.7	0.1	0.2	0.3	15.5	12.3	2.7	0.5	...	1.2	0.1	1.1
1949	2.2	1.9	0.1	0.3	0.4	16.8	13.7	2.7	0.5	...	1.5	0.1	1.4
1950	2.3	1.9	0.1	0.3	0.4	18.6	14.9	3.2	0.6	...	1.3	0.1	1.2
1951	2.5	2.0	0.1	0.3	0.5	19.4	16.1	2.6	0.6	...	2.6	0.1	2.5
1952	2.6	2.2	0.1	0.3	0.5	20.7	17.1	2.9	0.7	...	3.0	0.1	2.9
1953	2.8	2.3	0.1	0.3	0.6	22.0	18.2	3.0	0.8	...	3.5	0.1	3.4
1954	2.9	2.3	0.2	0.4	0.7	23.7	19.7	3.1	0.9	...	3.2	0.1	3.1
1955	3.0	2.4	0.2	0.4	0.8	25.9	21.6	3.3	1.1	...	3.5	0.1	3.4
1956	3.2	2.5	0.2	0.4	0.9	28.0	23.4	3.3	1.2	...	4.4	0.1	4.3
1957	3.6	2.9	0.2	0.5	0.9	30.8	25.8	3.6	1.4	...	4.2	0.1	4.1
1958	4.1	3.3	0.2	0.5	0.9	34.2	28.6	4.0	1.5	...	2.9	0.0	2.8
1959	4.2	3.8	0.1	0.3	1.1	36.9	30.7	4.3	1.8	0.0	3.8	0.0	3.8
1960	4.5	4.0	0.2	0.3	1.2	40.2	33.5	4.6	2.1	0.0	4.3	0.0	4.3
1961	5.2	4.5	0.2	0.4	1.3	43.8	36.6	5.0	2.2	0.0	4.3	0.0	4.3
1962	5.8	5.0	0.2	0.5	1.4	46.8	39.0	5.3	2.4	0.0	5.2	0.0	5.2
1963	6.4	5.6	0.3	0.5	1.6	50.3	41.9	5.7	2.7	0.0	5.7	0.0	5.7
1964	7.3	6.5	0.3	0.5	1.6	54.9	45.8	6.2	2.9	0.0	6.4	0.0	6.3
1965	8.0	7.2	0.3	0.5	1.7	60.0	50.2	6.7	3.1	0.0	6.5	0.1	6.4
1966	11.1	10.1	0.3	0.7	1.6	67.2	56.1	7.6	3.4	0.0	7.8	0.1	7.6
1967	13.1	11.7	0.5	0.9	1.5	75.5	62.6	9.2	3.7	0.0	7.0	0.1	6.9
1968	14.2	12.7	0.5	1.0	1.5	86.0	70.4	11.4	4.2	0.0	7.5	0.1	7.3
1969	16.2	14.6	0.5	1.1	1.5	97.5	79.9	13.2	4.4	0.0	8.0	0.2	7.8
1970	21.1	19.3	0.6	1.2	1.5	113.0	91.5	16.1	5.3	0.0	7.1	0.2	6.9
1971	25.2	23.2	0.6	1.4	1.4	128.5	102.7	19.3	6.5	0.0	6.5	0.2	6.2
1972	34.0	31.7	0.7	1.7	1.6	142.8	113.2	22.0	7.5	0.1	15.6	0.3	15.4
1973	37.3	34.8	0.9	1.7	1.5	158.6	126.0	24.1	8.5	0.1	15.7	0.3	15.4
1974	39.3	36.3	1.1	2.0	0.9	178.7	143.7	25.3	9.6	0.1	9.3	0.4	9.0
1975	48.7	45.1	1.2	2.4	0.4	207.1	165.1	30.8	11.1	0.2	2.5	0.5	2.0
1976	55.0	50.7	1.4	2.9	0.4	226.3	179.5	34.1	12.5	0.2	7.4	0.6	6.8
1977	61.4	56.6	1.6	3.3	0.3	246.6	195.9	37.0	13.7	0.2	13.1	1.0	12.2
1978	71.1	65.5	1.9	3.7	0.3	268.9	213.2	40.8	14.9	0.2	18.7	1.5	17.2
1979	72.7	66.3	2.2	4.1	-0.3	295.4	233.3	44.3	17.2	0.3	13.0	1.8	11.2
1980	79.5	72.3	2.5	4.7	-1.2	329.4	258.4	51.2	19.4	0.4	8.8	1.3	7.5
1981	81.0	72.5	2.9	5.7	-2.4	362.7	282.3	57.1	22.8	0.4	7.6	1.3	6.3
1982	79.1	69.5	3.2	6.4	-1.6	393.6	304.9	61.2	27.1	0.5	-2.2	1.2	-3.4
1983	82.4	71.6	3.6	7.2	-0.2	423.7	324.1	66.9	32.3	0.4	4.9	1.2	3.7
1984	89.0	76.7	4.2	8.1	1.5	456.2	347.7	71.2	37.0	0.4	23.9	1.4	22.5
1985	94.5	80.9	4.4	9.2	3.2	498.7	381.8	77.3	39.4	0.3	22.3	1.3	21.0
1986	105.0	87.6	6.7	10.6	2.8	540.7	417.9	84.3	38.2	0.3	21.0	1.9	19.1
1987	100.0	83.9	4.9	11.2	3.1	578.1	440.9	90.7	46.2	0.3	12.4	2.2	10.2
1988	109.0	91.6	5.4	12.0	4.8	617.6	470.4	98.5	48.4	0.4	17.9	2.5	15.4
1989	118.1	98.3	6.4	13.4	6.5	666.5	502.1	109.3	54.6	0.4	20.8	2.3	18.5
1990	133.5	111.4	7.1	14.9	6.7	730.5	544.6	127.7	57.9	0.4	7.2	2.0	5.3
1991	158.2	131.6	7.9	18.7	7.1	793.3	574.6	156.5	61.7	0.4	-4.2	2.4	-6.5
1992	180.3	149.1	9.2	21.9	7.7	845.0	602.7	180.0	61.9	0.4	0.7	3.1	-2.4
1993	197.7	163.7	10.5	23.5	9.0	886.0	630.3	195.2	60.2	0.4	0.9	4.2	-3.3
1994	211.9	174.7	12.0	25.2	9.0	932.4	663.3	206.7	62.0	0.3	10.5	4.6	5.8
1995	224.1	184.1	13.5	26.5	12.0	978.2	696.1	217.6	64.2	0.3	12.0	4.0	8.0
1996	234.1	191.2	15.2	27.8	13.9	1 017.5	724.8	224.3	68.1	0.3	25.8	2.8	23.0
1997	246.6	198.6	17.7	30.3	12.3	1 058.3	758.9	227.6	71.4	0.4	39.1	1.2	38.0
1998	266.8	212.8	22.1	31.9	10.2	1 111.2	801.4	235.8	73.6	0.4	52.0	1.7	50.3
1999	290.8	232.9	23.0	34.9	10.4	1 186.3	858.9	252.4	74.6	0.4	50.4	1.7	48.7
2000	315.4	247.3	28.8	39.2	7.7	1 269.5	917.8	271.7	79.5	0.5	50.0	2.0	47.9
2001	350.8	276.1	31.4	43.3	4.0	1 368.2	969.8	305.2	85.5	7.7	4.8	2.6	2.2
2002	385.9	304.4	32.8	48.7	3.3	1 436.9	1 016.5	331.9	87.4	1.0	-25.0	1.6	-26.6
2003	425.9	339.9	32.2	53.8	3.7	1 498.1	1 058.5	350.3	88.9	0.3	-3.2	1.1	-4.3
2001													
1st quarter	338.2	266.5	30.1	41.6	5.5	1 334.7	951.7	290.7	84.2	8.0	32.5	2.6	29.9
2nd quarter	351.6	278.3	30.5	42.7	4.6	1 371.6	963.6	308.3	85.3	14.4	25.8	2.7	23.1
3rd quarter	350.0	272.8	33.3	43.9	3.2	1 363.4	976.6	295.9	86.0	4.8	-8.6	2.6	-11.2
4th quarter	363.3	286.6	31.5	45.2	2.8	1 403.1	987.1	326.0	86.6	3.4	-30.6	2.4	-33.0
2002													
1st quarter	370.8	291.9	32.3	46.7	2.8	1 409.8	996.2	324.8	86.9	1.9	-28.8	2.0	-30.8
2nd quarter	384.8	304.2	32.5	48.1	3.2	1 427.7	1 011.5	328.3	87.3	0.7	-23.6	1.7	-25.3
3rd quarter	387.6	305.4	32.9	49.4	3.6	1 445.3	1 023.8	332.0	87.7	1.8	-21.3	1.4	-22.8
4th quarter	400.3	316.3	33.4	50.7	3.7	1 464.8	1 034.6	342.6	87.9	-0.3	-26.3	1.3	-27.6
2003													
1st quarter	397.4	314.3	31.3	51.8	3.6	1 486.6	1 054.8	343.6	87.9	0.3	-49.0	1.1	-50.1
2nd quarter	430.1	345.1	31.9	53.1	3.8	1 490.2	1 051.8	349.7	88.1	0.6	-5.7	1.1	-6.7
3rd quarter	429.9	343.0	32.5	54.4	3.8	1 504.9	1 061.0	355.7	88.9	-0.7	6.5	1.1	5.4
4th quarter	446.1	357.2	33.1	55.8	3.7	1 510.5	1 066.3	352.3	90.7	1.2	35.3	1.2	34.1

. . . = Not available.

Table 6-9. State and Local Government Consumption Expenditures and Gross Investment

(National Income and Product Accounts, calendar years, billions of dollars, quarterly data are at seasonally adjusted annual rates.)

NIPA Tables 3.9.5, 3.10.5

Year and quarter	Total	State and local government consumption expenditures and gross investment									Gross investment		
		Consumption expenditures [1]											
		Total	Compensation of general government employees	Consumption of general government fixed capital	Intermediate goods and services purchased [2]	Own-account investment	Less			Total	Structures	Equipment and software
							Sales to other sectors					
							Total	Tuition and related educational charges	Health and hospital charges			
1946	10.8	9.2	6.2	1.2	2.8	0.1	0.9	0.1	0.2	1.6	1.4	0.2
1947	13.7	10.9	7.3	1.5	3.4	0.1	1.1	0.1	0.2	2.8	2.5	0.3
1948	16.3	12.3	8.5	1.7	3.6	0.2	1.3	0.1	0.3	4.0	3.6	0.4
1949	19.0	13.7	9.4	1.7	4.2	0.2	1.4	0.1	0.3	5.3	4.9	0.5
1950	20.7	14.9	10.1	1.7	4.9	0.3	1.6	0.1	0.3	5.9	5.4	0.5
1951	23.0	16.1	11.2	2.0	4.9	0.3	1.7	0.1	0.3	7.0	6.4	0.5
1952	24.4	17.1	12.3	2.2	4.9	0.4	1.8	0.2	0.3	7.3	6.7	0.6
1953	26.1	18.2	13.3	2.2	4.9	0.4	1.9	0.2	0.4	7.9	7.3	0.6
1954	28.9	19.7	14.7	2.2	5.2	0.4	2.0	0.2	0.4	9.2	8.5	0.7
1955	31.6	21.6	15.8	2.4	6.0	0.4	2.2	0.2	0.5	10.0	9.3	0.8
1956	34.7	23.4	17.6	2.8	5.9	0.5	2.4	0.2	0.6	11.3	10.4	0.9
1957	38.3	25.8	19.6	3.0	6.4	0.5	2.6	0.3	0.7	12.5	11.5	1.1
1958	42.2	28.6	21.6	3.1	7.5	0.6	3.0	0.3	0.9	13.5	12.5	1.1
1959	44.7	30.7	23.1	3.3	8.3	0.8	3.2	0.4	1.0	13.9	12.8	1.1
1960	47.5	33.5	25.5	3.5	8.9	0.8	3.5	0.4	1.0	13.9	12.7	1.2
1961	51.6	36.6	27.9	3.7	9.7	0.8	3.9	0.5	1.0	15.0	13.8	1.3
1962	54.9	39.0	30.2	3.9	10.1	0.9	4.4	0.6	1.3	15.9	14.5	1.3
1963	59.5	41.9	32.9	4.2	10.8	1.0	4.9	0.7	1.3	17.5	16.0	1.5
1964	64.8	45.8	35.9	4.5	11.9	1.0	5.5	0.8	1.5	19.0	17.2	1.8
1965	71.0	50.2	39.3	4.9	13.4	1.1	6.3	1.0	1.8	20.8	19.0	1.9
1966	79.2	56.1	44.1	5.5	14.9	1.2	7.2	1.2	2.1	23.1	21.0	2.1
1967	87.9	62.6	49.5	6.0	16.5	1.2	8.2	1.4	2.5	25.3	23.0	2.3
1968	98.0	70.4	55.9	6.6	18.7	1.3	9.5	1.6	3.2	27.7	25.2	2.4
1969	108.2	79.9	62.6	7.4	21.8	1.4	10.6	1.9	3.5	28.3	25.6	2.7
1970	120.3	91.5	71.1	8.4	25.4	1.5	11.8	2.4	3.8	28.7	25.8	3.0
1971	132.8	102.7	79.2	9.4	29.2	1.6	13.5	2.9	4.6	30.1	27.0	3.1
1972	143.8	113.2	87.7	10.2	32.2	1.7	15.2	3.2	5.6	30.6	27.1	3.5
1973	159.2	126.0	98.0	11.3	35.4	1.7	17.0	3.7	6.6	33.2	29.1	4.1
1974	183.4	143.7	107.7	14.1	42.7	2.1	18.7	4.0	7.4	39.6	34.7	4.9
1975	208.7	165.1	121.2	15.9	50.7	2.1	20.6	4.3	8.5	43.6	38.1	5.5
1976	223.3	179.5	133.0	16.6	55.2	2.0	23.3	4.7	9.9	43.8	38.1	5.7
1977	238.7	195.9	145.1	17.5	61.1	2.0	25.8	5.2	10.9	42.8	36.9	5.9
1978	262.6	213.2	158.9	18.9	66.9	2.3	29.2	5.8	12.7	49.5	42.8	6.6
1979	290.2	233.3	174.3	21.1	74.3	2.9	33.4	6.4	15.2	56.8	49.0	7.8
1980	322.4	258.4	193.0	24.3	82.0	3.3	37.6	7.2	17.3	64.0	55.1	8.9
1981	347.3	282.3	210.1	27.8	91.6	3.5	43.7	8.3	21.0	65.0	55.4	9.5
1982	369.7	304.9	227.4	30.3	100.6	3.7	49.7	9.4	24.5	64.8	54.2	10.6
1983	390.5	324.1	243.0	31.2	109.6	4.0	55.7	10.7	27.8	66.4	54.2	12.2
1984	422.6	347.7	261.1	32.0	119.0	4.6	59.8	11.7	29.4	75.0	60.5	14.4
1985	466.2	381.8	284.7	33.7	134.0	5.2	65.4	12.8	32.0	84.4	67.6	16.8
1986	510.7	417.9	307.3	36.2	151.6	5.7	71.5	13.9	34.8	92.8	74.2	18.6
1987	539.4	440.9	328.8	39.0	156.2	6.1	76.9	15.0	37.0	98.4	78.8	19.6
1988	576.7	470.4	353.7	41.5	166.0	6.7	84.1	16.6	40.3	106.3	84.8	21.5
1989	616.9	502.1	380.5	44.4	178.8	7.8	93.8	18.4	45.0	114.7	88.7	26.0
1990	671.9	544.6	414.6	48.0	194.0	8.6	103.5	20.3	50.0	127.2	98.5	28.7
1991	706.7	574.6	439.8	51.1	208.4	9.3	115.4	22.7	57.0	132.1	103.2	28.9
1992	737.0	602.7	463.9	53.4	224.0	9.5	129.1	25.5	65.3	134.3	104.2	30.1
1993	766.0	630.3	486.7	56.3	239.7	9.7	142.7	27.5	73.1	135.7	104.5	31.2
1994	806.3	663.3	511.2	59.5	256.0	10.1	153.3	29.4	78.8	143.0	108.7	34.3
1995	850.0	696.1	533.5	63.4	274.8	10.6	165.0	31.2	85.0	154.0	117.3	36.7
1996	888.6	724.8	552.7	66.7	289.6	11.0	173.2	33.0	86.6	163.8	126.8	36.9
1997	937.8	758.9	575.5	70.2	308.5	12.2	183.2	35.5	89.9	178.9	139.5	39.4
1998	987.9	801.4	603.3	73.9	331.4	12.6	194.6	38.1	95.9	186.5	143.6	43.0
1999	1 065.0	858.9	633.1	78.7	364.6	13.5	203.9	40.9	98.4	206.0	159.7	46.4
2000	1 142.8	917.8	669.4	84.8	399.0	14.9	220.6	44.3	105.5	225.0	176.0	49.0
2001	1 212.8	969.8	710.8	89.9	428.3	16.7	242.7	49.7	118.5	243.0	192.4	50.6
2002	1 275.8	1 016.5	750.0	94.3	457.5	17.6	267.7	56.3	132.6	259.3	208.2	51.0
2003	1 323.3	1 058.5	778.2	98.7	494.3	18.0	294.7	63.8	147.2	264.9	213.4	51.5
2001												
1st quarter	1 187.2	951.7	692.0	88.3	421.1	16.0	233.6	47.2	112.8	235.4	185.7	49.7
2nd quarter	1 214.5	963.6	704.0	89.4	427.0	17.0	239.7	48.9	116.8	250.9	200.4	50.6
3rd quarter	1 211.2	976.6	717.4	90.4	431.3	16.7	245.7	50.5	120.4	234.6	183.7	51.0
4th quarter	1 238.1	987.1	730.0	91.6	434.0	16.8	251.6	52.0	123.9	251.0	199.9	51.1
2002												
1st quarter	1 255.0	996.2	736.9	92.7	442.2	17.4	258.2	53.7	127.3	258.8	207.7	51.1
2nd quarter	1 268.3	1 011.5	745.8	93.9	453.5	17.4	264.3	55.4	130.7	256.9	205.8	51.0
3rd quarter	1 283.9	1 023.8	754.7	94.9	462.6	17.7	270.8	57.1	134.3	260.1	208.9	51.3
4th quarter	1 296.0	1 034.6	762.5	95.9	471.5	17.8	277.6	59.0	138.0	261.4	210.6	50.8
2003												
1st quarter	1 318.0	1 054.8	768.0	97.3	491.5	17.8	284.2	60.8	141.6	263.2	212.2	51.0
2nd quarter	1 313.1	1 051.8	773.1	98.2	489.4	17.7	291.1	62.7	145.3	261.4	210.3	51.1
3rd quarter	1 329.7	1 061.0	782.2	99.2	495.9	18.3	298.1	64.7	148.9	268.7	217.0	51.7
4th quarter	1 332.6	1 066.3	789.4	100.0	500.5	18.2	305.4	66.9	152.8	266.2	214.2	52.0

[1] Excludes government sales to other sectors and government own-account investment (construction and software).
[2] Includes general government intermediate inputs for goods and services sold to other sectors and for own-account investment.

Table 6-10. State and Local Government Output, Lending and Borrowing, and Net Investment

(National Income and Product Accounts, calendar years, billions of dollars, quarterly data are at seasonally adjusted annual rates.)

NIPA Tables 3.3, 3.10.5

Year and quarter	Output			Net lending (net borrowing -)							Net investment
	Gross	Value added	Intermediate goods and services purchased [1]	Net saving, current (surplus +, deficit -)	Plus: capital transfer receipts	Minus			Plus: consumption of fixed capital	Equals: Net lending (borrowing -)	
						Gross investment	Capital transfer payments	Net purchases of nonproduced assets			
1946	10.2	7.4	2.8	1.5	0.2	1.6	...	0.1	1.5	1.6	0.1
1947	12.2	8.8	3.4	1.4	0.3	2.8	...	0.1	1.8	0.6	1.0
1948	13.8	10.2	3.6	1.2	0.4	4.0	...	0.1	2.1	-0.4	1.9
1949	15.3	11.1	4.2	1.5	0.5	5.3	...	0.2	2.1	-1.4	3.2
1950	16.7	11.8	4.9	1.3	0.6	5.9	...	0.3	2.1	-2.1	3.8
1951	18.1	13.2	4.9	2.6	0.7	7.0	...	0.3	2.6	-1.5	4.4
1952	19.3	14.4	4.9	3.0	0.7	7.3	...	0.3	2.7	-1.1	4.6
1953	20.5	15.5	4.9	3.5	0.8	7.9	...	0.3	2.8	-1.1	5.1
1954	22.1	16.9	5.2	3.2	0.8	9.2	...	0.4	2.9	-2.6	6.3
1955	24.2	18.2	6.0	3.5	1.0	10.0	...	0.6	3.1	-3.1	6.9
1956	26.3	20.4	5.9	4.4	1.1	11.3	...	0.7	3.5	-2.9	7.8
1957	29.0	22.6	6.4	4.2	1.6	12.5	...	0.7	3.9	-3.5	8.6
1958	32.2	24.7	7.5	2.9	2.7	13.5	...	0.8	4.0	-4.7	9.5
1959	34.8	26.5	8.3	3.8	3.5	13.9	...	0.8	4.2	-3.2	9.7
1960	37.9	28.9	8.9	4.3	3.0	13.9	...	0.9	4.4	-3.1	9.5
1961	41.3	31.6	9.7	4.3	3.3	15.0	...	1.0	4.7	-3.8	10.3
1962	44.3	34.2	10.1	5.2	3.5	15.9	...	1.1	5.0	-3.2	10.9
1963	47.9	37.1	10.8	5.7	4.1	17.5	...	1.2	5.4	-3.5	12.1
1964	52.3	40.4	11.9	6.4	4.7	19.0	...	1.3	5.7	-3.4	13.3
1965	57.6	44.2	13.4	6.5	4.7	20.8	...	1.3	6.2	-4.6	14.6
1966	64.5	49.6	14.9	7.8	5.1	23.1	...	1.4	6.9	-4.7	16.2
1967	72.0	55.5	16.5	7.0	5.1	25.3	...	1.4	7.5	-7.1	17.8
1968	81.2	62.5	18.7	7.5	6.8	27.7	...	1.4	8.3	-6.4	19.4
1969	91.9	70.0	21.8	8.0	6.8	28.3	...	1.0	9.3	-5.1	19.0
1970	104.9	79.5	25.4	7.1	6.2	28.7	...	1.1	10.6	-6.0	18.1
1971	117.9	88.6	29.2	6.5	7.0	30.1	...	1.6	11.8	-6.4	18.3
1972	130.0	97.9	32.2	15.6	7.3	30.6	...	1.7	12.8	3.4	17.8
1973	144.7	109.3	35.4	15.7	7.3	33.2	...	1.7	14.3	2.4	18.9
1974	164.5	121.8	42.7	9.3	9.2	39.6	...	1.9	17.7	-5.3	21.9
1975	187.9	137.1	50.7	2.5	11.0	43.6	...	1.9	20.2	-11.9	23.4
1976	204.8	149.7	55.2	7.4	12.0	43.8	...	1.7	21.3	-4.9	22.5
1977	223.7	162.6	61.1	13.1	13.1	42.8	...	1.6	22.6	4.5	20.2
1978	244.7	177.8	66.9	18.7	13.7	49.5	...	1.6	24.5	5.8	25.0
1979	269.6	195.4	74.3	13.0	16.2	56.8	...	1.7	27.5	-1.8	29.3
1980	299.3	217.3	82.0	8.8	18.6	64.0	...	1.8	31.8	-6.6	32.2
1981	329.5	237.9	91.6	7.6	17.8	65.0	...	2.0	36.3	-5.3	28.7
1982	358.3	257.7	100.6	-2.2	16.9	64.8	...	2.0	39.5	-12.6	25.3
1983	383.7	274.1	109.6	4.9	18.0	66.4	...	2.2	40.9	-4.9	25.5
1984	412.1	293.1	119.0	23.9	20.1	75.0	...	2.6	42.3	8.8	32.7
1985	452.4	318.4	134.0	22.3	22.0	84.4	...	3.1	44.6	1.5	39.8
1986	495.1	343.5	151.6	21.0	23.0	92.8	...	3.7	47.9	-4.6	44.9
1987	524.0	367.8	156.2	12.4	22.3	98.4	...	4.2	51.4	-16.4	47.0
1988	561.1	395.2	166.0	17.9	23.1	106.3	...	4.3	54.8	-14.8	51.5
1989	603.7	424.9	178.8	20.8	23.4	114.7	...	4.9	58.7	-16.6	56.0
1990	656.7	462.6	194.0	7.2	25.0	127.2	...	5.7	63.0	-37.7	64.2
1991	699.4	490.9	208.4	-4.2	25.8	132.1	...	5.8	66.9	-49.4	65.2
1992	741.3	517.3	224.0	0.7	26.9	134.3	...	5.9	69.9	-42.8	64.4
1993	782.7	543.0	239.7	0.9	28.6	135.7	...	5.8	73.8	-38.2	61.9
1994	826.7	570.7	256.0	10.5	29.9	143.0	...	6.2	78.5	-30.4	64.5
1995	871.7	596.9	274.8	12.0	32.4	154.0	...	6.6	83.1	-33.0	70.9
1996	908.9	619.3	289.6	25.8	33.9	163.8	...	6.1	87.2	-22.9	76.6
1997	954.3	645.8	308.5	39.1	35.3	178.9	...	5.8	91.6	-18.7	87.3
1998	1 008.6	677.2	331.4	52.0	36.0	186.5	...	7.5	96.2	-9.9	90.3
1999	1 076.4	711.8	364.6	50.4	39.9	206.0	...	8.6	102.1	-22.3	103.9
2000	1 153.2	754.2	399.0	50.0	43.7	225.0	...	8.8	109.8	-30.4	115.2
2001	1 229.1	800.8	428.3	4.8	48.6	243.0	...	9.2	117.8	-81.1	125.2
2002	1 301.8	844.3	457.5	-25.0	51.8	259.3	...	9.8	122.1	-120.2	137.2
2003	1 371.2	876.9	494.3	-3.2	51.5	264.9	...	10.0	127.9	-98.7	137.0
2001											
1st quarter	1 201.4	780.3	421.1	32.5	46.5	235.4	...	9.0	114.2	-51.2	121.2
2nd quarter	1 220.4	793.4	427.0	25.8	49.0	250.9	...	9.2	115.6	-69.8	135.3
3rd quarter	1 239.0	807.8	431.3	-8.6	49.0	234.6	...	9.4	122.9	-80.6	111.7
4th quarter	1 255.6	821.6	434.0	-30.6	49.9	251.0	...	9.5	118.4	-122.9	132.6
2002											
1st quarter	1 271.8	829.6	442.2	-28.8	54.1	258.8	...	9.7	120.0	-123.2	138.8
2nd quarter	1 293.1	839.7	453.5	-23.6	51.0	256.9	...	9.8	121.5	-117.7	135.4
3rd quarter	1 312.2	849.6	462.6	-21.3	50.9	260.1	...	9.9	122.9	-117.6	137.2
4th quarter	1 330.0	858.4	471.5	-26.3	51.3	261.4	...	9.9	124.2	-122.2	137.2
2003											
1st quarter	1 356.8	865.3	491.5	-49.0	46.8	263.2	...	9.9	126.0	-149.3	137.2
2nd quarter	1 360.7	871.3	489.4	-5.7	52.2	261.4	...	9.9	127.3	-97.5	134.1
3rd quarter	1 377.4	881.4	495.9	6.5	56.2	268.7	...	10.0	128.5	-87.5	140.2
4th quarter	1 390.0	889.4	500.5	35.3	50.9	266.2	...	10.0	129.7	-60.4	136.5

[1]Includes general government intermediate inputs for goods and services sold to other sectors and for own-account investment.
... = Not available.

Table 6-11. Chain-Type Quantity Indexes for State and Local Government Consumption Expenditures and Gross Investment

(Index numbers, 2000 = 100.)

NIPA Tables 3.9.3, 3.10.3

Year and quarter	State and local government consumption expenditures and gross investment											
	Total	Consumption expenditures [1]								Gross investment		
		Total	Compensation of general government employees	Consumption of general government fixed capital	Intermediate goods and services purchased [2]	Own-account investment	Less Sales to other sectors			Total	Structures	Equipment and software
							Total	Tuition and related educational charges	Health and hospital charges			
1946	11.6	14.2	18.4	10.7	5.8	6.1	6.6	3.8	4.8	5.8	7.8	1.4
1947	13.2	15.2	19.8	10.8	6.5	10.3	7.5	4.2	4.6	8.9	12.0	2.0
1948	14.0	15.3	20.3	11.0	6.4	12.9	7.7	5.0	5.4	11.3	15.2	2.6
1949	16.2	16.7	21.8	11.4	7.6	17.2	8.8	5.7	6.1	15.3	21.1	2.7
1950	17.5	17.7	22.5	11.9	8.7	18.1	9.6	5.6	5.8	17.3	24.2	2.7
1951	17.6	17.7	23.0	12.4	8.1	20.2	9.4	5.6	5.9	17.9	25.0	2.9
1952	17.9	17.9	23.8	12.9	7.9	23.8	9.6	5.9	6.0	18.3	25.5	3.1
1953	18.8	18.5	24.8	13.4	7.9	22.6	10.0	6.3	6.3	19.9	27.8	3.3
1954	20.5	19.3	25.9	14.1	8.2	23.6	10.6	6.9	6.9	23.8	33.4	3.6
1955	21.9	20.6	27.0	14.9	9.3	23.3	11.7	7.7	7.7	25.9	36.6	3.5
1956	22.6	21.3	28.8	15.7	9.0	26.1	12.2	8.8	8.8	26.5	37.2	4.0
1957	24.0	22.4	30.3	16.7	9.4	26.4	12.9	10.1	10.0	28.4	39.3	4.9
1958	26.0	24.2	32.2	17.7	10.8	28.3	14.4	11.5	12.6	31.2	43.6	4.9
1959	27.0	25.2	33.4	18.7	11.6	38.3	15.2	12.3	13.2	32.1	44.8	5.2
1960	28.2	26.6	35.2	19.8	12.2	35.9	15.7	13.6	12.2	32.5	44.9	5.9
1961	29.9	28.1	37.0	20.9	13.1	37.6	16.8	14.9	12.5	35.1	48.6	6.0
1962	30.8	28.9	38.2	22.0	13.6	40.0	18.7	16.9	14.6	36.4	50.2	6.5
1963	32.7	30.3	40.2	23.3	14.5	44.9	20.5	19.3	15.2	39.6	54.4	7.4
1964	34.9	32.3	42.6	24.7	15.8	44.4	22.5	22.6	16.4	42.4	58.0	8.4
1965	37.3	34.4	45.2	26.3	17.4	45.6	25.0	26.2	18.7	45.4	62.1	9.0
1966	39.6	36.5	47.9	28.0	18.8	48.1	27.3	29.7	21.3	48.4	66.0	9.9
1967	41.6	38.2	49.7	29.8	20.3	46.7	30.1	33.1	24.2	51.4	70.2	10.3
1968	44.0	40.7	52.7	31.6	22.3	49.2	33.0	37.2	28.3	53.7	73.4	10.8
1969	45.5	43.3	55.1	33.3	24.7	49.5	34.5	41.0	29.3	51.5	69.5	11.6
1970	46.8	45.9	57.5	34.9	27.2	50.1	36.2	47.7	29.8	48.3	64.4	12.1
1971	48.2	48.1	59.8	36.3	29.7	50.1	39.5	53.7	34.7	46.9	62.2	12.3
1972	49.3	49.9	61.9	37.6	31.5	48.8	42.3	57.0	39.8	45.4	59.2	13.7
1973	50.7	51.7	64.1	38.9	32.6	47.4	44.2	61.5	44.1	45.6	58.7	15.3
1974	52.6	54.0	66.4	40.3	34.4	50.5	44.2	61.3	45.5	46.0	58.5	16.7
1975	54.5	56.7	68.4	41.6	37.1	47.6	44.6	61.4	46.7	45.6	58.1	16.4
1976	54.9	57.5	69.2	42.8	38.2	42.0	47.1	63.4	49.7	44.8	57.0	16.1
1977	55.1	58.6	70.2	43.8	39.3	38.3	48.6	66.0	50.6	42.1	53.2	15.8
1978	56.9	59.7	71.8	44.7	40.3	41.3	50.9	69.6	54.1	45.9	58.3	16.7
1979	57.8	60.1	73.0	45.8	40.3	47.7	53.2	71.5	58.7	48.2	60.8	18.3
1980	57.7	60.0	73.9	47.0	39.0	49.7	54.1	73.9	59.2	48.4	60.5	19.5
1981	56.6	59.8	73.7	48.0	39.3	47.5	56.4	75.5	62.9	44.3	54.6	19.4
1982	56.6	60.7	74.0	48.9	41.0	47.9	58.1	75.4	64.8	41.6	50.1	20.6
1983	57.3	61.4	73.5	49.8	43.6	47.5	60.2	77.8	66.4	42.1	49.6	23.5
1984	59.3	62.5	73.8	51.1	45.4	52.8	60.0	77.7	64.9	47.3	55.0	27.5
1985	63.0	65.8	75.8	52.9	50.1	57.0	62.0	77.7	66.4	52.4	60.3	31.9
1986	67.1	69.9	77.9	55.0	56.7	61.0	64.1	78.3	68.1	56.0	64.1	34.9
1987	68.0	70.8	79.2	57.1	56.6	62.3	65.1	78.8	68.1	57.4	65.5	36.4
1988	70.6	73.2	81.9	59.5	58.1	65.2	66.4	81.3	68.2	60.4	68.4	39.4
1989	73.0	75.4	84.2	62.4	59.9	72.8	68.2	83.8	68.7	63.7	69.8	46.8
1990	76.0	77.8	86.5	65.7	61.8	76.3	69.5	85.6	69.4	68.7	75.0	51.1
1991	77.6	79.4	87.3	68.9	64.7	79.7	71.8	87.0	72.4	70.3	77.5	50.5
1992	79.3	81.3	88.5	71.9	68.1	78.9	75.0	88.7	76.6	71.2	77.8	52.9
1993	80.5	83.0	89.5	74.7	71.4	78.5	78.6	87.6	81.1	70.5	76.0	54.7
1994	82.5	85.1	90.8	77.4	74.9	79.3	81.4	87.7	84.3	72.5	76.6	60.2
1995	84.7	87.0	92.4	80.3	77.7	80.4	84.4	88.0	88.1	75.7	79.2	64.7
1996	86.7	88.6	93.6	83.3	79.5	81.4	86.0	88.2	87.7	79.1	83.1	66.7
1997	89.8	91.0	95.3	86.8	83.4	89.0	88.9	90.3	89.8	84.9	88.5	73.7
1998	93.0	94.4	96.9	90.9	90.0	90.7	92.9	92.9	94.9	87.4	88.4	84.1
1999	97.4	98.1	98.3	95.4	96.6	94.6	95.2	96.1	95.6	94.6	94.9	93.7
2000	100.0	100.0	100.0	100.0	100.0	100.0	100.0	100.0	100.0	100.0	100.0	100.0
2001	103.2	102.6	102.1	104.5	105.5	109.1	106.8	106.6	108.9	105.7	105.7	105.5
2002	106.0	104.8	103.4	108.7	111.8	112.5	113.8	113.1	117.8	110.7	111.2	109.1
2003	106.7	105.6	103.5	112.8	115.6	111.9	119.1	118.2	124.3	111.5	111.4	111.9
2001												
1st quarter	101.6	101.3	101.0	102.8	103.2	105.8	104.0	103.8	104.9	102.9	102.9	102.9
2nd quarter	103.4	101.9	101.8	103.9	104.4	111.8	106.0	105.9	107.7	109.4	110.5	105.0
3rd quarter	102.8	103.0	102.6	105.0	106.1	109.3	107.7	107.6	110.3	101.9	100.8	106.4
4th quarter	104.9	104.0	103.2	106.1	108.3	109.7	109.6	109.1	112.8	108.4	108.6	107.9
2002												
1st quarter	105.6	104.3	103.2	107.1	109.7	112.8	111.4	110.9	115.1	111.2	111.9	108.4
2nd quarter	105.7	104.7	103.4	108.1	111.2	111.8	113.0	112.2	117.1	109.8	110.1	108.8
3rd quarter	106.2	105.0	103.4	109.2	112.6	112.7	114.6	113.7	118.8	110.9	111.1	109.9
4th quarter	106.5	105.4	103.6	110.2	113.8	112.5	116.0	115.5	120.2	111.1	111.6	109.2
2003												
1st quarter	106.6	105.4	103.5	111.3	114.4	111.3	117.1	116.9	121.6	111.1	111.4	110.1
2nd quarter	106.4	105.5	103.4	112.3	115.3	110.7	118.5	118.2	123.2	110.1	109.9	111.0
3rd quarter	107.0	105.6	103.4	113.3	116.0	113.2	119.8	118.4	125.2	113.0	113.0	112.8
4th quarter	107.0	105.8	103.7	114.4	116.6	112.3	121.1	119.4	127.1	111.8	111.4	113.7

[1] Excludes government sales to other sectors and government own-account investment (construction and software).
[2] Includes general government intermediate inputs for goods and services sold to other sectors and for own-account investment.

Table 6-12. State Government Current Receipts and Expenditures

(National Income and Product Accounts, calendar years, billions of dollars.)

Year	Current receipts										Current expenditures	
	Total	Personal tax and nontax receipts		Corporate profits tax accruals	Indirect business tax and nontax accruals			Contributions for social insurance	Grants-in-aid		Total [1]	Consumption expenditures
		Total [1]	Income taxes		Total [1]	Sales taxes	Property taxes		Federal	Local		
1959	21.1	3.2	2.0	1.1	12.7	10.0	0.5	0.4	3.4	0.3	19.9	8.8
1960	22.8	3.6	2.3	1.2	13.7	10.8	0.5	0.5	3.5	0.3	21.5	9.5
1961	24.6	3.9	2.5	1.3	14.6	11.6	0.5	0.5	4.0	0.3	23.4	10.2
1962	26.7	4.3	2.8	1.5	15.7	12.6	0.6	0.5	4.4	0.3	25.4	10.9
1963	28.7	4.6	3.1	1.6	16.7	13.4	0.6	0.6	4.9	0.3	27.6	11.8
1964	31.4	5.2	3.6	1.8	18.0	14.5	0.6	0.7	5.4	0.3	30.1	12.8
1965	34.7	5.7	3.9	1.9	19.9	16.1	0.7	0.8	6.1	0.3	33.6	14.2
1966	41.0	6.7	4.8	2.2	22.0	18.0	0.7	0.8	8.9	0.4	38.6	15.9
1967	45.2	7.4	5.3	2.5	23.6	19.4	0.7	0.9	10.3	0.5	44.7	18.2
1968	52.6	9.2	6.9	3.1	27.2	22.8	0.8	0.9	11.6	0.6	51.0	20.5
1969	60.0	11.2	8.6	3.4	30.4	25.7	0.9	1.0	13.3	0.7	58.2	23.3
1970	67.2	12.4	9.6	3.5	33.2	28.2	0.9	1.1	16.2	0.8	67.8	26.9
1971	76.3	14.0	11.0	4.0	36.8	31.4	1.0	1.2	19.4	0.9	77.4	30.1
1972	93.0	18.5	15.2	5.0	41.3	35.2	1.1	1.3	25.8	1.1	86.3	32.8
1973	100.1	20.5	16.8	5.7	45.4	38.8	1.2	1.5	25.8	1.2	96.0	36.9
1974	108.1	22.0	18.0	6.3	49.2	42.0	1.1	1.7	27.6	1.3	108.0	44.0
1975	121.3	24.2	19.9	6.9	52.7	44.7	1.4	1.8	33.9	1.8	125.4	51.1
1976	137.5	28.2	23.4	9.1	58.6	49.9	1.5	2.2	37.1	2.3	138.7	55.9
1977	153.2	32.3	27.2	10.8	64.3	55.0	1.5	2.8	40.6	2.4	150.2	60.8
1978	171.0	37.1	31.6	11.5	71.3	60.8	1.9	3.4	45.2	2.5	164.7	67.3
1979	186.4	40.6	34.6	12.9	78.5	65.7	2.3	3.9	48.3	2.2	182.5	75.3
1980	205.9	45.6	39.1	13.7	85.9	70.0	2.6	3.6	54.7	2.4	205.9	85.2
1981	224.7	50.6	43.6	14.5	95.4	76.5	2.7	3.9	57.7	2.6	226.4	94.1
1982	230.5	54.7	47.0	13.1	99.6	80.3	2.8	4.0	56.0	3.1	241.4	101.4
1983	252.9	61.6	53.2	14.9	109.6	90.0	3.0	4.1	58.6	4.1	257.0	107.4
1984	284.7	71.4	61.9	17.4	122.9	100.9	3.4	4.7	63.3	5.0	277.5	115.7
1985	305.5	76.9	66.1	18.7	132.5	109.0	3.5	4.9	67.3	5.2	302.7	126.3
1986	329.9	82.7	70.7	20.8	140.6	115.8	3.6	6.0	74.5	5.3	327.0	135.5
1987	349.6	92.2	79.1	21.8	148.0	124.6	3.7	7.2	74.9	5.5	350.9	144.1
1988	373.4	95.5	81.2	23.8	158.0	134.2	4.0	8.4	82.1	5.6	376.5	153.5
1989	404.8	108.9	93.3	22.2	167.5	142.8	4.3	9.0	91.5	5.7	406.7	164.4
1990	434.2	114.9	97.9	20.4	178.0	151.5	4.6	10.0	104.7	6.2	447.2	178.2
1991	473.2	122.9	102.3	21.5	185.0	157.1	4.9	11.6	124.6	7.6	495.5	186.1
1992	515.9	132.1	108.7	22.1	197.8	167.6	5.2	13.1	141.8	9.0	537.8	193.1
1993	553.6	138.6	114.6	24.3	211.5	179.1	6.1	14.1	155.0	10.1	572.8	203.0
1994	590.7	146.5	121.4	27.3	226.2	191.4	6.9	14.5	165.2	11.0	606.1	213.7
1995	622.7	155.9	129.6	29.1	238.8	201.5	7.5	13.6	174.2	11.1	636.2	223.3
1996	649.7	166.4	139.1	30.0	250.8	210.9	7.8	12.5	178.0	12.0	661.6	230.5
1997	685.0	181.2	152.7	30.9	265.2	222.0	8.0	10.8	183.5	13.4	686.8	239.7
1998	726.0	196.5	166.6	31.3	280.9	233.5	8.6	10.1	193.8	13.4	723.1	249.5
1999	775.8	213.8	182.3	31.6	295.3	246.2	8.7	9.7	212.5	12.9	782.8	270.0
2000	828.9	232.6	199.5	32.3	311.7	255.7	8.2	9.2	229.5	13.6	846.6	296.1
2001	859.5	234.5	199.9	26.3	317.6	259.9	7.9	9.2	257.7	14.2	923.5	319.1

[1] Includes components not shown separately.

Table 6-12. State Government Current Receipts and Expenditures—Continued

(National Income and Product Accounts, calendar years, billions of dollars.)

Year	Current expenditures—Continued				Current surplus or deficit (-), national income and product accounts			Addenda			
	Transfer payments to persons	Grants-in-aid to local governments	Net interest paid	Subsidies less current surplus of enterprises	Total	Social insurance funds	Other	Consumption of fixed capital	Capital transfers received, net	Gross investment	Net lending or net borrowing (-) [1]
1959	3.6	7.7	0.1	-0.3	1.2	0.0	1.2	1.8	2.3	6.4	-1.5
1960	3.8	8.5	0.1	-0.4	1.3	0.0	1.3	1.9	1.7	5.7	-1.3
1961	4.1	9.4	0.1	-0.4	1.2	0.0	1.2	2.0	2.0	6.6	-1.9
1962	4.4	10.3	0.2	-0.4	1.3	0.0	1.3	2.1	2.1	7.0	-2.0
1963	4.7	11.3	0.2	-0.4	1.1	0.0	1.1	2.3	2.6	8.0	-2.6
1964	5.1	12.4	0.2	-0.4	1.3	0.0	1.3	2.5	3.1	8.5	-2.2
1965	5.5	14.2	0.2	-0.5	1.1	0.1	1.0	2.7	3.1	9.1	-2.8
1966	6.4	16.7	0.1	-0.5	2.4	0.1	2.3	3.0	3.4	10.4	-2.3
1967	7.7	19.2	0.1	-0.5	0.5	0.1	0.4	3.3	3.1	11.1	-4.8
1968	9.5	22.0	-0.4	-0.6	1.6	0.1	1.5	3.6	4.0	11.6	-3.0
1969	10.8	25.3	-0.6	-0.6	1.8	0.2	1.6	4.1	3.7	12.4	-3.0
1970	12.9	29.2	-0.7	-0.5	-0.6	0.2	-0.8	4.7	3.3	13.4	-6.2
1971	15.3	33.0	-0.5	-0.5	-1.1	0.2	-1.3	5.2	3.6	14.1	-7.1
1972	17.5	36.8	-0.4	-0.4	6.7	0.3	6.4	5.6	3.6	14.6	0.6
1973	19.4	41.1	-1.0	-0.4	4.1	0.3	3.8	6.3	3.1	15.2	-2.4
1974	19.9	45.9	-1.6	-0.2	0.1	0.4	-0.3	8.1	3.5	16.6	-5.8
1975	24.2	51.4	-1.2	-0.1	-4.1	0.5	-4.6	9.0	4.5	17.0	-8.5
1976	26.9	56.2	-0.2	-0.1	-1.2	0.6	-1.8	9.2	4.7	16.8	-4.9
1977	29.1	60.7	-0.3	-0.1	3.0	1.0	2.0	9.5	4.8	16.0	0.7
1978	32.0	67.2	-1.6	-0.1	6.3	1.5	4.8	10.1	4.9	17.7	2.9
1979	35.4	75.3	-3.5	0.1	3.9	1.8	2.1	11.2	6.1	21.2	-0.8
1980	41.3	83.7	-4.6	0.4	0.0	1.3	-1.3	13.1	7.6	23.5	-3.6
1981	46.7	90.4	-5.4	0.7	-1.7	1.3	-3.0	15.2	6.7	23.8	-4.4
1982	51.0	94.4	-5.6	0.4	-10.9	1.2	-12.1	16.6	6.1	23.0	-12.0
1983	55.9	98.9	-5.0	0.0	-4.1	1.2	-5.3	17.0	7.2	24.0	-4.9
1984	59.8	108.7	-6.0	-0.5	7.2	1.4	5.8	17.2	8.7	28.6	3.5
1985	65.2	120.0	-7.3	-1.3	2.8	1.3	1.5	18.1	10.6	32.8	-2.4
1986	71.5	128.9	-7.2	-1.5	2.9	1.9	1.0	19.5	11.1	35.7	-3.5
1987	77.5	137.8	-7.0	-1.3	-1.3	2.2	-3.5	21.2	10.5	38.0	-9.2
1988	84.5	148.4	-8.0	-1.7	-3.1	2.5	-5.6	22.4	11.6	41.4	-12.1
1989	94.5	159.5	-9.3	-2.2	-1.9	2.3	-4.2	23.7	11.5	43.2	-11.5
1990	111.2	169.4	-9.3	-2.1	-13.0	2.0	-15.0	25.3	12.2	47.3	-24.6
1991	137.7	181.9	-7.8	-2.2	-22.3	2.4	-24.7	26.6	12.5	48.6	-33.7
1992	159.6	194.8	-6.7	-2.8	-21.9	3.1	-25.0	27.5	13.5	49.9	-32.7
1993	173.7	205.9	-6.2	-3.4	-19.2	4.2	-23.4	28.8	14.4	52.0	-29.8
1994	184.6	218.8	-7.1	-3.7	-15.4	4.6	-20.0	30.5	15.5	56.3	-27.4
1995	195.0	231.5	-9.3	-4.0	-13.5	4.0	-17.5	32.7	16.3	59.1	-25.3
1996	202.6	242.3	-9.6	-3.9	-11.9	2.7	-14.6	34.6	17.0	60.8	-23.1
1997	206.9	255.4	-11.3	-3.6	-1.8	1.1	-2.9	36.6	18.1	65.6	-14.8
1998	214.4	274.1	-11.3	-3.2	2.9	0.6	2.3	38.4	18.4	69.8	-12.5
1999	230.8	297.6	-12.5	-2.7	-7.0	0.9	-7.9	40.9	21.1	76.4	-24.2
2000	248.3	319.3	-14.3	-2.4	-17.7	0.1	-17.8	44.1	23.0	80.5	-34.0
2001	279.7	334.5	-14.3	4.9	-64.0	-0.1	-63.9	46.6	25.6	86.9	-81.8

[1] Includes components not shown separately.

Table 6-13. Local Government Current Receipts and Expenditures

(National Income and Product Accounts, calendar years, billions of dollars.)

Year	Current receipts										Current expenditures	
	Total	Personal tax and nontax receipts		Corporate profits tax accruals	Indirect business tax and nontax accruals			Contributions for social insurance	Grants-in-aid		Total [1]	Consumption expenditures
		Total [1]	Income taxes		Total [1]	Sales taxes	Property taxes		Federal	State		
1959	25.7	1.0	0.2	0.0	16.6	1.2	14.3	0.0	0.4	7.7	23.2	22.3
1960	28.3	1.1	0.3	0.0	18.2	1.3	15.7	0.0	0.5	8.5	25.3	24.4
1961	31.0	1.2	0.3	0.0	19.8	1.4	17.0	0.0	0.6	9.4	27.9	26.8
1962	33.5	1.4	0.3	0.0	21.2	1.5	18.4	0.0	0.6	10.3	29.6	28.5
1963	36.3	1.5	0.4	0.0	22.7	1.6	19.7	0.0	0.8	11.3	31.6	30.6
1964	39.6	1.6	0.5	0.0	24.5	1.9	21.1	0.0	1.1	12.4	34.5	33.5
1965	43.1	1.6	0.5	0.0	26.2	2.1	22.5	0.0	1.1	14.2	37.7	36.6
1966	47.6	2.0	0.6	0.0	27.7	2.0	23.8	0.0	1.2	16.7	42.4	40.9
1967	53.6	2.4	0.8	0.2	30.3	1.9	26.2	0.0	1.5	19.2	47.1	45.1
1968	59.6	2.5	0.9	0.3	33.7	2.3	29.1	0.0	1.1	22.0	53.7	50.6
1969	66.7	2.9	1.1	0.2	37.0	2.9	31.9	0.0	1.3	25.3	60.6	56.9
1970	77.4	3.2	1.3	0.2	41.6	3.5	35.7	0.0	3.2	29.2	69.8	65.1
1971	87.0	3.6	1.5	0.3	46.3	4.0	39.5	0.0	3.8	33.0	79.5	73.3
1972	97.3	4.3	2.0	0.3	50.0	4.6	42.2	0.0	5.9	36.8	88.3	81.0
1973	108.7	4.2	2.0	0.3	54.1	5.2	45.2	0.0	9.0	41.1	97.1	89.9
1974	117.6	4.7	2.3	0.3	58.0	6.1	47.9	0.0	8.7	45.9	108.4	100.5
1975	131.4	5.3	2.6	0.4	63.1	7.0	52.0	0.0	11.2	51.4	125.0	114.3
1976	145.4	5.9	2.8	0.5	69.2	7.9	56.7	0.0	13.6	56.2	137.0	124.2
1977	159.4	6.5	3.2	0.6	75.6	9.0	61.7	0.0	16.0	60.7	149.4	135.7
1978	173.0	7.2	3.4	0.6	77.6	10.2	61.8	0.0	20.4	67.2	160.6	147.0
1979	182.0	7.9	3.6	0.6	80.1	11.5	62.1	0.0	18.1	75.3	172.9	159.8
1980	196.7	8.3	3.5	0.7	86.4	12.8	66.2	0.0	17.6	83.7	187.9	175.2
1981	212.7	10.0	4.3	0.9	96.6	14.2	74.4	0.0	14.8	90.4	203.5	190.5
1982	227.3	11.3	4.9	0.9	107.2	15.9	82.5	0.0	13.5	94.4	218.7	205.4
1983	242.2	12.1	5.1	1.0	117.2	17.7	88.9	0.0	13.0	98.9	233.2	217.6
1984	265.3	13.3	5.6	1.4	128.6	20.1	96.3	0.0	13.3	108.7	248.7	233.7
1985	288.9	14.3	6.0	1.5	139.5	22.1	104.0	0.0	13.6	120.0	269.4	254.2
1986	312.2	15.9	6.8	1.8	152.5	24.1	112.6	0.0	13.1	128.9	294.3	275.4
1987	329.7	16.4	6.9	2.1	164.4	25.7	122.7	0.0	9.0	137.8	316.2	295.0
1988	354.3	18.5	8.6	2.2	175.7	27.3	132.8	0.0	9.5	148.4	335.6	314.4
1989	379.4	20.0	9.3	2.1	191.0	29.9	144.4	0.0	6.8	159.5	358.1	338.6
1990	404.7	21.1	9.8	2.1	205.4	31.7	156.5	0.0	6.7	169.4	389.1	367.5
1991	432.3	22.4	10.4	2.2	218.8	33.0	167.9	0.0	7.0	181.9	417.7	390.0
1992	460.2	24.3	10.9	2.3	231.4	34.6	177.6	0.0	7.4	194.8	443.1	408.5
1993	485.5	26.1	11.4	2.6	243.3	36.9	185.0	0.0	7.6	205.9	464.8	426.5
1994	513.0	28.2	12.0	2.7	253.9	39.6	190.7	0.0	9.4	218.8	488.9	448.9
1995	537.7	30.6	12.9	2.6	262.8	42.1	196.1	0.0	10.2	231.5	508.9	471.4
1996	565.1	33.3	13.8	3.0	274.1	44.6	203.6	0.0	12.4	242.3	531.7	496.1
1997	595.2	35.8	14.9	3.3	287.4	47.3	212.3	0.0	13.3	255.4	562.5	526.8
1998	635.9	39.0	16.0	3.3	303.0	50.7	221.7	0.0	16.5	274.1	598.0	558.8
1999	678.8	42.0	17.4	3.2	317.4	54.4	230.6	0.0	18.6	297.6	633.5	594.6
2000	718.1	44.8	18.6	3.3	332.7	58.6	239.8	0.0	18.0	319.3	682.4	641.8
2001	750.4	46.7	18.7	2.7	346.8	61.4	249.5	0.0	19.7	334.5	717.8	674.6

[1] Includes components not shown separately.

Table 6-13. Local Government Current Receipts and Expenditures—Continued

(National Income and Product Accounts, calendar years, billions of dollars.)

Year	Current expenditures—Continued				Current surplus or deficit (-), national income and product accounts			Addenda			
	Transfer payments to persons	Grants-in-aid to state governments	Net interest paid	Subsidies less current surplus of enterprises	Total	Social insurance funds	Other	Consumption of fixed capital	Capital transfers received, net	Gross investment	Net lending or net borrowing (-) [1]
1959	0.7	0.3	0.7	-0.8	2.5	...	2.5	2.4	1.2	7.5	-1.8
1960	0.8	0.3	0.7	-0.9	3.0	...	3.0	2.6	1.3	8.2	-1.7
1961	0.9	0.3	0.9	-1.0	3.1	...	3.1	2.7	1.3	8.4	-1.8
1962	0.9	0.3	0.9	-1.0	3.9	...	3.9	2.9	1.4	8.8	-1.1
1963	1.0	0.3	0.9	-1.2	4.7	...	4.7	3.1	1.5	9.5	-0.8
1964	1.0	0.3	0.9	-1.2	5.1	...	5.1	3.3	1.6	10.5	-1.1
1965	1.1	0.3	0.9	-1.2	5.4	...	5.4	3.6	1.6	11.8	-1.9
1966	1.3	0.4	0.9	-1.1	5.2	...	5.2	3.9	1.8	12.7	-2.5
1967	1.6	0.5	0.9	-1.0	6.5	...	6.5	4.3	2.0	14.2	-2.2
1968	2.0	0.6	1.4	-0.9	5.9	...	5.9	4.7	2.9	16.1	-3.4
1969	2.4	0.7	1.5	-0.9	6.1	...	6.1	5.3	3.2	15.9	-2.1
1970	3.2	0.8	1.6	-0.9	7.6	...	7.6	5.9	2.9	15.4	0.1
1971	4.0	0.9	2.2	-0.8	7.5	...	7.5	6.6	3.4	16.0	0.6
1972	4.5	1.1	2.7	-1.1	9.0	...	9.0	7.2	3.7	16.0	2.9
1973	4.7	1.2	2.3	-1.0	11.6	...	11.6	8.0	4.2	18.0	4.8
1974	5.4	1.3	1.8	-0.6	9.2	...	9.2	9.6	5.7	23.1	0.4
1975	6.6	1.8	2.5	-0.2	6.4	...	6.4	11.2	6.5	26.6	-3.5
1976	7.3	2.3	3.3	-0.1	8.4	...	8.4	12.1	7.3	27.1	-0.2
1977	8.0	2.4	3.3	0.0	10.0	...	10.0	13.1	8.3	26.7	3.8
1978	8.8	2.5	2.4	0.1	12.4	...	12.4	14.3	8.8	31.7	2.8
1979	8.9	2.2	1.3	0.6	9.1	...	9.1	16.3	10.1	35.7	-1.4
1980	9.9	2.4	-0.8	1.2	8.8	...	8.8	18.7	11.0	40.5	-3.4
1981	10.4	2.6	-2.1	2.1	9.2	...	9.2	21.1	11.1	41.2	-1.3
1982	10.2	3.1	-1.7	1.7	8.6	...	8.6	22.9	10.9	41.8	-0.8
1983	11.0	4.1	-0.2	0.7	9.0	...	9.0	23.9	10.8	42.4	-0.1
1984	11.4	5.0	-0.8	-0.6	16.6	...	16.6	25.1	11.4	46.3	5.1
1985	12.1	5.2	-0.5	-1.6	19.5	...	19.5	26.6	11.4	51.6	3.9
1986	12.9	5.3	1.7	-1.0	17.9	...	17.9	28.4	11.9	57.2	-1.4
1987	13.3	5.5	3.9	-1.5	13.5	...	13.5	30.3	11.9	60.4	-7.3
1988	14.1	5.6	4.2	-2.7	18.7	...	18.7	32.5	11.6	64.9	-4.9
1989	15.0	5.7	2.7	-3.9	21.3	...	21.3	35.1	12.0	71.5	-6.4
1990	16.6	6.2	3.0	-4.2	15.6	...	15.6	37.8	12.8	79.9	-17.7
1991	18.9	7.6	5.7	-4.5	14.6	...	14.6	40.4	13.1	83.5	-19.4
1992	20.5	9.0	9.5	-4.4	17.1	...	17.1	42.4	13.5	84.5	-15.5
1993	21.7	10.1	11.7	-5.2	20.7	...	20.7	45.1	14.3	84.2	-8.3
1994	22.3	11.0	11.5	-4.8	24.1	...	24.1	48.4	14.2	88.0	-6.0
1995	22.8	11.1	9.8	-6.2	28.8	...	28.8	51.4	16.0	96.7	-5.6
1996	21.7	12.0	10.5	-8.6	33.4	...	33.4	54.3	16.8	103.0	-3.8
1997	20.7	13.4	10.4	-8.8	32.7	...	32.7	57.6	17.2	117.6	-15.2
1998	20.9	13.4	11.6	-6.7	37.9	...	37.9	61.0	17.6	121.2	-10.9
1999	21.9	12.9	11.8	-7.7	45.3	...	45.3	65.5	18.6	134.9	-12.4
2000	23.0	13.6	11.4	-7.4	35.7	...	35.7	70.9	20.8	143.4	-23.0
2001	24.8	14.2	12.2	-8.0	32.6	...	32.6	77.1	22.7	149.3	-24.1

[1] Includes components not shown separately.
... = Not available.

Table 6-14. State Government Consumption Expenditures and Gross Investment by Function

(National Income and Product Accounts, calendar years, billions of dollars.)

Year	Consumption expenditures and gross investment												
	Total [1]	General public service	Public order and safety		Economic affairs		Housing and community services	Health	Education			Income security	
			Total [1]	Prisons	Total [1]	Transportation			Total [1]	Elementary and secondary	Higher	Total [1]	Welfare and social services
1959	15.4	1.2	0.8	0.5	8.7	7.2	0.0	1.8	2.6	0.2	2.1	0.4	0.3
1960	15.5	1.3	0.9	0.5	8.3	6.7	0.0	1.8	2.8	0.2	2.3	0.4	0.3
1961	17.0	1.4	0.9	0.5	9.2	7.4	0.0	2.0	3.2	0.2	2.6	0.3	0.3
1962	18.2	1.4	1.0	0.5	9.8	8.0	0.0	2.0	3.6	0.2	3.0	0.4	0.3
1963	20.1	1.5	1.1	0.6	10.7	8.9	0.0	2.2	4.2	0.2	3.6	0.4	0.3
1964	21.6	1.8	1.2	0.6	11.2	9.1	0.0	2.4	4.7	0.2	4.0	0.4	0.4
1965	23.6	2.0	1.3	0.7	11.9	9.7	0.0	2.5	5.3	0.2	4.4	0.5	0.4
1966	26.6	2.4	1.4	0.7	13.2	10.8	0.0	2.7	6.4	0.3	5.2	0.6	0.5
1967	29.7	2.6	1.6	0.8	14.1	11.3	0.0	3.0	7.6	0.4	6.2	0.7	0.6
1968	32.6	3.1	1.8	0.9	15.1	12.2	0.0	3.3	8.4	0.4	6.7	0.8	0.8
1969	36.2	3.9	2.1	1.0	16.0	12.8	0.0	3.8	9.4	0.4	7.5	1.0	0.9
1970	40.8	4.0	2.4	1.2	17.9	14.4	0.0	4.4	10.8	0.5	8.5	1.2	1.1
1971	44.9	4.4	2.7	1.3	19.3	15.4	0.0	5.0	11.9	0.5	9.3	1.5	1.4
1972	48.1	4.8	3.1	1.5	19.8	15.7	0.0	5.3	13.1	0.5	10.2	1.8	1.7
1973	52.8	5.8	3.5	1.7	20.7	16.3	0.0	5.5	14.7	0.5	11.7	2.4	2.2
1974	61.3	6.9	4.1	2.0	24.2	19.2	0.0	6.5	16.4	0.5	13.0	2.9	2.7
1975	68.9	7.9	4.7	2.3	26.4	20.8	0.3	7.4	18.2	0.7	14.1	3.5	3.3
1976	73.4	8.3	5.2	2.7	26.6	20.3	0.2	8.1	20.2	0.7	15.8	4.1	3.9
1977	77.8	9.0	5.8	3.1	27.1	20.5	0.2	9.0	21.3	0.7	16.7	4.7	4.4
1978	86.1	9.9	6.9	3.6	29.9	22.6	0.3	9.9	22.9	0.9	18.1	5.4	5.1
1979	97.6	11.6	8.2	4.2	34.4	26.3	0.3	11.0	25.3	1.0	20.1	6.0	5.7
1980	110.0	13.6	9.5	4.8	38.6	29.3	0.4	12.7	28.1	1.1	22.4	6.3	6.0
1981	119.1	14.4	10.6	5.5	41.3	31.1	0.3	13.6	31.0	1.2	25.1	7.0	6.6
1982	125.9	15.2	12.1	6.5	42.8	31.9	0.3	14.2	33.1	1.2	27.0	7.4	7.0
1983	133.1	16.9	13.5	7.4	44.7	33.6	0.2	13.9	34.5	1.1	28.4	8.5	8.1
1984	146.3	19.3	15.2	8.4	49.3	37.5	0.2	14.7	37.2	1.2	30.9	9.3	8.8
1985	161.5	21.4	17.5	10.0	53.8	41.2	0.2	16.0	41.2	1.3	34.3	10.1	9.6
1986	174.1	24.0	19.3	11.3	57.6	43.9	0.3	17.0	43.9	1.4	36.6	10.7	10.1
1987	185.4	25.8	21.5	12.7	60.7	46.2	0.5	18.3	45.7	1.5	37.7	11.4	10.7
1988	198.0	26.6	23.9	14.2	64.1	48.7	0.8	19.7	48.8	1.6	40.4	12.5	11.7
1989	210.8	28.6	26.6	16.1	65.4	48.9	1.1	20.7	52.7	1.8	43.4	13.7	12.8
1990	228.8	30.5	30.3	18.6	70.7	52.9	1.4	22.3	56.2	2.0	46.3	15.3	14.2
1991	238.4	31.8	32.5	20.1	72.9	54.4	1.7	22.4	57.9	2.2	47.9	16.9	15.6
1992	246.9	33.0	34.0	21.0	75.6	56.0	1.9	21.7	60.1	2.4	49.6	18.5	17.0
1993	258.9	34.2	36.2	22.6	78.9	58.4	2.0	21.8	63.5	2.4	52.6	20.2	18.5
1994	274.2	36.5	39.4	25.0	82.9	61.9	2.2	21.6	66.7	2.3	55.4	22.6	20.8
1995	287.1	37.4	42.8	27.2	85.9	64.1	2.5	22.0	69.6	2.7	57.3	24.4	22.2
1996	295.8	37.7	45.5	28.8	89.1	67.1	2.3	21.8	71.2	3.0	58.2	25.3	22.9
1997	310.3	40.9	48.5	30.4	93.6	71.1	2.2	20.5	74.5	3.2	61.1	27.1	24.4
1998	323.9	43.4	50.5	31.1	98.0	75.4	2.3	18.9	78.5	3.4	64.3	29.3	26.3
1999	351.4	47.4	55.1	33.7	106.6	82.3	2.6	21.2	83.6	3.6	68.5	31.7	28.8
2000	382.4	52.4	60.3	36.5	113.6	87.2	2.9	24.8	90.8	3.8	74.4	34.3	31.4
2001	410.4	57.0	64.5	38.8	121.5	94.5	2.8	27.0	97.5	4.0	80.1	36.3	33.3

[1] Includes components not shown separately.

Table 6-15. Local Government Consumption Expenditures and Gross Investment by Function

(National Income and Product Accounts, calendar years, billions of dollars.)

Year	Consumption expenditures and gross investment												
	Total [1]	General public service	Public order and safety		Economic affairs		Housing and community services	Health	Education			Income security	
			Total [1]	Prisons	Total [1]	Transpor-tation			Total [1]	Elementary and secondary	Higher	Total	Welfare and social services
1959	29.7	2.3	3.3	0.2	4.6	3.9	2.7	1.3	14.5	14.0	0.3	0.3	0.3
1960	32.4	2.5	3.6	0.3	5.1	4.3	2.7	1.4	16.1	15.5	0.3	0.4	0.4
1961	35.0	2.8	3.8	0.3	5.2	4.4	2.9	1.5	17.6	17.0	0.3	0.4	0.4
1962	37.1	2.9	4.0	0.3	5.4	4.5	3.3	1.5	18.7	18.1	0.3	0.5	0.5
1963	39.8	3.1	4.2	0.3	6.0	4.9	3.0	1.6	20.5	19.7	0.4	0.5	0.5
1964	43.7	3.4	4.5	0.3	6.3	5.0	3.6	1.7	22.7	21.8	0.5	0.6	0.6
1965	48.1	3.8	4.8	0.4	7.1	5.4	3.8	1.8	25.1	24.0	0.6	0.7	0.7
1966	53.3	4.1	5.3	0.4	7.4	6.0	3.9	1.9	28.7	27.3	0.9	0.9	0.9
1967	58.8	4.6	5.8	0.4	8.2	6.5	4.1	2.1	31.7	30.1	1.1	1.0	1.0
1968	66.2	5.5	6.8	0.5	9.0	7.3	5.0	2.4	34.9	33.1	1.2	1.2	1.2
1969	72.2	6.0	7.5	0.5	9.4	7.6	4.9	2.7	38.6	36.5	1.4	1.5	1.5
1970	79.9	6.7	8.5	0.6	9.6	7.7	5.1	3.1	43.2	40.7	1.8	1.8	1.8
1971	88.6	7.6	9.7	0.8	10.0	8.0	5.5	3.7	47.9	45.0	2.1	2.1	2.1
1972	96.3	8.8	10.7	0.9	10.8	8.6	5.6	3.7	52.3	49.0	2.5	2.5	2.5
1973	107.3	10.3	11.9	1.0	11.9	9.5	6.3	4.2	57.6	53.9	2.8	2.7	2.7
1974	122.8	12.2	13.5	1.2	14.3	11.3	7.7	5.0	64.3	60.0	3.3	3.0	3.0
1975	140.1	14.7	15.5	1.4	15.8	12.7	8.6	5.3	73.6	68.6	3.8	3.3	3.3
1976	150.5	16.2	17.0	1.6	16.6	13.0	9.2	5.0	79.7	74.5	4.0	3.5	3.5
1977	161.5	18.1	18.5	1.8	17.7	13.7	9.0	5.5	85.4	79.7	4.4	3.9	3.9
1978	177.7	19.5	20.7	1.9	20.8	15.4	11.0	5.8	91.9	85.9	4.6	4.0	4.0
1979	194.3	20.5	22.6	2.1	23.4	17.3	12.3	5.7	101.1	94.7	4.9	4.4	4.4
1980	214.5	22.1	25.1	2.5	26.1	19.5	14.7	6.4	110.4	103.2	5.5	5.0	5.0
1981	230.5	23.9	28.3	2.8	28.8	21.1	14.5	6.5	117.9	110.1	6.0	5.5	5.5
1982	245.7	25.4	31.5	3.3	30.3	22.6	14.3	6.7	126.0	117.7	6.4	5.9	5.9
1983	258.4	26.9	33.9	3.8	31.3	23.6	13.8	6.4	133.5	125.2	6.1	6.7	6.7
1984	278.1	28.4	36.3	4.3	32.5	24.9	15.4	6.9	145.2	136.6	6.2	7.1	7.1
1985	303.3	31.0	40.1	4.9	35.5	26.4	16.7	7.4	157.7	148.4	6.6	7.8	7.8
1986	329.5	33.8	43.8	5.7	37.7	28.6	18.7	7.4	171.8	161.7	7.3	8.5	8.5
1987	352.1	35.3	47.4	6.6	38.1	30.1	20.7	8.4	184.8	173.9	7.8	9.0	9.0
1988	376.2	37.6	51.0	7.3	39.4	31.5	21.5	9.1	199.1	187.1	8.7	9.6	9.6
1989	406.9	41.0	56.3	8.5	41.6	33.7	22.2	9.9	215.6	202.4	9.5	10.7	10.7
1990	444.2	44.7	61.7	9.6	45.4	37.2	24.1	11.3	234.0	219.7	10.3	12.0	12.0
1991	469.8	47.7	66.3	10.4	47.1	38.8	24.9	11.6	247.8	232.7	10.8	12.9	12.9
1992	489.1	50.2	71.3	11.0	48.2	39.7	25.0	11.8	256.8	242.6	9.8	13.9	13.9
1993	506.8	52.8	74.6	11.4	50.8	42.3	23.6	10.8	267.5	252.4	10.5	14.7	14.7
1994	532.7	56.2	79.4	12.2	53.4	44.8	23.0	10.9	281.8	265.7	11.3	15.3	15.3
1995	563.4	59.3	84.2	12.9	54.8	45.7	24.0	9.7	302.2	285.5	11.6	15.6	15.6
1996	594.6	62.0	90.2	13.8	57.0	48.2	25.5	10.6	318.9	301.7	11.8	16.0	16.0
1997	639.4	70.6	95.7	14.3	63.6	52.5	27.0	10.1	340.5	321.8	12.6	16.5	16.5
1998	675.4	75.4	103.2	15.9	65.7	54.6	25.8	12.0	359.4	339.7	13.3	17.8	17.8
1999	724.6	82.3	109.5	17.0	70.8	58.4	25.4	14.4	385.6	364.8	14.0	19.1	19.1
2000	779.3	89.9	118.5	18.4	76.2	61.3	23.9	16.4	415.1	392.8	15.0	21.1	21.1
2001	819.5	90.5	127.9	19.6	77.4	64.9	25.4	16.9	439.8	416.5	15.6	22.5	22.5

[1] Includes components not shown separately.

Section 6c: Federal Government Budget Accounts

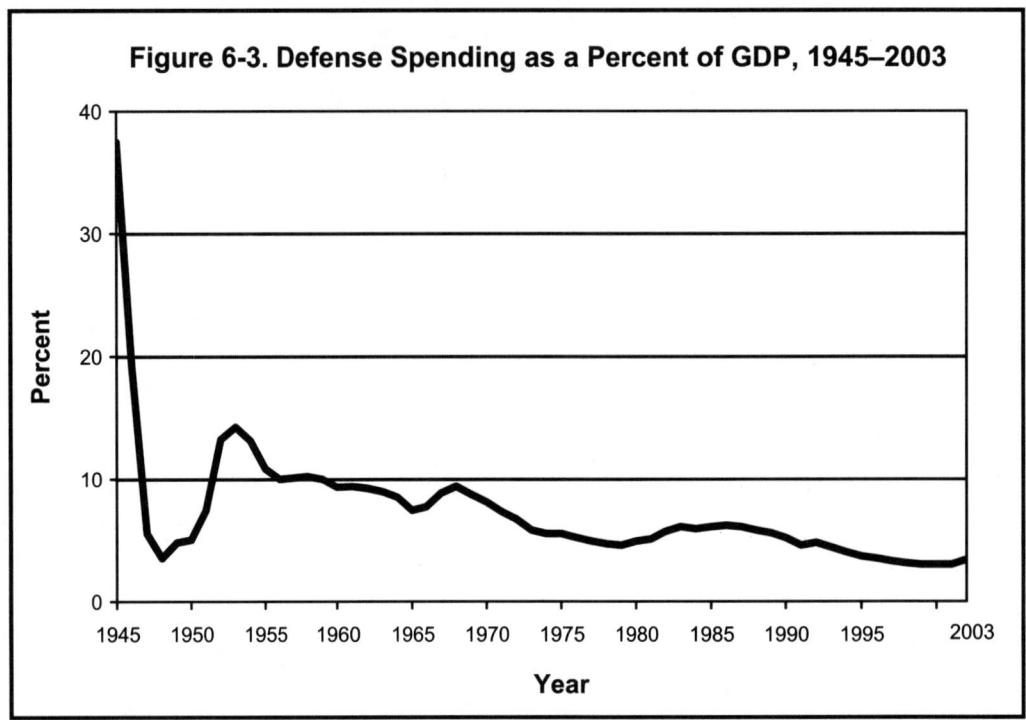

Figure 6-3. Defense Spending as a Percent of GDP, 1945–2003

- From fiscal year 2001 to fiscal year 2003, defense spending increased from 3.0 percent to 3.7 percent of GDP. This was similar to the increase at the beginning of the defense buildup of the 1980s, and less than the increases associated with the Korean and Vietnam wars. The ratio remained low compared with the postwar "cold war" decades. Defense outlays as defined in the budget data used in this table include both consumption and investment spending, but do not include an allowance for the consumption of fixed capital. (Table 6-16)
- After declining between 1993 and 2001, federal debt held by the public as a percent of GDP increased in 2002 and 2003. While the level of this ratio appears low by postwar standards, its direction of change may be more significant. Notably, the ratio was over 100 percent in 1945 and 1946, but its rapid decline in subsequent years meant that stability in the level of federal debt left room for the rapid expansion of private debt that financed the postwar boom. (Table 6-17)
- Over two-thirds (69 percent) of federal borrowing from the public during fiscal year 2003 was from foreign and international investors, who at the end of 2003 held over one-third (37 percent) of the total debt held by the public. (Table 6-17).

Table 6-16. Federal Government Receipts and Outlays by Fiscal Year [1]

(Budget Accounts, millions of dollars.)

Year	Fiscal year GDP	Receipts, outlays, deficit, and financing							Receipts by source				
		Total receipts (net)	Total outlays (net)	Budget surplus or deficit (-)			Sources of financing, total		Individual income taxes	Corporate income taxes	Social insurance taxes and contributions		
				Total	On-budget	Off-budget	Borrowing from the public	Other financing			Employment taxes and contributions	Unemployment insurance	Other retirement contributions
1939	89 100	6 295	9 141	-2 846	-3 362	516	...	...	1 029	1 127	1 593		
1940	96 800	6 548	9 468	-2 920	-3 484	564	...	...	892	1 197	725	1 015	45
1941	114 100	8 712	13 653	-4 941	-5 594	653	5 451	-510	1 314	2 124	827	1 056	57
1942	144 300	14 634	35 137	-20 503	-21 333	830	19 530	973	3 263	4 719	1 064	1 299	89
1943	180 300	24 001	78 555	-54 554	-55 595	1 041	60 013	-5 459	6 505	9 557	1 338	1 477	229
1944	209 200	43 747	91 304	-47 557	-48 735	1 178	57 030	-9 473	19 705	14 838	1 557	1 644	272
1945	221 400	45 159	92 712	-47 553	-48 720	1 167	50 386	-2 833	18 372	15 988	1 592	1 568	291
1946	222 700	39 296	55 232	-15 936	-16 964	1 028	6 679	9 257	16 098	11 883	1 517	1 316	282
1947	233 200	38 514	34 496	4 018	2 861	1 157	-17 522	13 504	17 935	8 615	1 835	1 329	259
1948	256 700	41 560	29 764	11 796	10 548	1 248	-8 069	-3 727	19 315	9 678	2 168	1 343	239
1949	271 300	39 415	38 835	580	-684	1 263	-1 948	1 368	15 552	11 192	2 246	1 205	330
1950	273 200	39 443	42 562	-3 119	-4 702	1 583	4 701	-1 582	15 755	10 449	2 648	1 332	358
1951	320 300	51 616	45 514	6 102	4 259	1 843	-4 697	-1 405	21 616	14 101	3 688	1 609	377
1952	348 700	66 167	67 686	-1 519	-3 383	1 864	432	1 087	27 934	21 226	4 315	1 712	418
1953	372 600	69 608	76 101	-6 493	-8 259	1 766	3 625	2 868	29 816	21 238	4 722	1 675	423
1954	377 100	69 701	70 855	-1 154	-2 831	1 677	6 116	-4 962	29 542	21 101	5 192	1 561	455
1955	395 900	65 451	68 444	-2 993	-4 091	1 098	2 117	876	28 747	17 861	5 981	1 449	431
1956	427 000	74 587	70 640	3 947	2 494	1 452	-4 460	513	32 188	20 880	7 059	1 690	571
1957	450 900	79 990	76 578	3 412	2 639	773	-2 836	-576	35 620	21 167	7 405	1 950	642
1958	460 000	79 636	82 405	-2 769	-3 315	546	7 016	-4 247	34 724	20 074	8 624	1 933	682
1959	490 200	79 249	92 098	-12 849	-12 149	-700	8 365	4 484	36 719	17 309	8 821	2 131	770
1960	518 900	92 492	92 191	301	510	-209	2 139	-2 440	40 715	21 494	11 248	2 667	768
1961	529 900	94 388	97 723	-3 335	-3 766	431	1 517	1 818	41 338	20 954	12 679	2 903	857
1962	567 800	99 676	106 821	-7 146	-5 881	-1 265	9 653	-2 507	45 571	20 523	12 835	3 337	875
1963	599 200	106 560	111 316	-4 756	-3 966	-789	5 968	-1 212	47 588	21 579	14 746	4 112	946
1964	641 400	112 613	118 528	-5 915	-6 546	632	2 871	3 044	48 697	23 493	16 959	3 997	1 007
1965	687 500	116 817	118 228	-1 411	-1 605	194	3 929	-2 518	48 792	25 461	17 358	3 803	1 081
1966	755 800	130 835	134 532	-3 698	-3 068	-630	2 936	762	55 446	30 073	20 662	3 755	1 129
1967	810 200	148 822	157 464	-8 643	-12 620	3 978	2 912	5 731	61 526	33 971	27 823	3 575	1 221
1968	868 500	152 973	178 134	-25 161	-27 742	2 581	22 919	2 242	68 726	28 665	29 224	3 346	1 354
1969	948 300	186 882	183 640	3 242	-507	3 749	-11 437	8 195	87 249	36 678	34 236	3 328	1 451
1970	1 012 900	192 807	195 649	-2 842	-8 694	5 852	5 090	-2 248	90 412	32 829	39 133	3 464	1 765
1971	1 080 300	187 139	210 172	-23 033	-26 052	3 019	19 839	3 194	86 230	26 785	41 699	3 674	1 952
1972	1 176 900	207 309	230 681	-23 373	-26 423	3 050	19 340	4 033	94 737	32 166	46 120	4 357	2 097
1973	1 311 000	230 799	245 707	-14 908	-15 403	495	18 533	-3 625	103 246	36 153	54 876	6 051	2 187
1974	1 438 900	263 224	269 359	-6 135	-7 971	1 836	2 789	3 346	118 952	38 620	65 888	6 837	2 347
1975	1 560 800	279 090	332 332	-53 242	-55 260	2 018	51 001	2 241	122 386	40 621	75 199	6 771	2 565
1976	1 738 800	298 060	371 792	-73 732	-70 512	-3 220	82 704	-8 972	131 603	41 409	79 901	8 054	2 814
TQ [1]	459 600	81 232	95 975	-14 744	-13 339	-1 405	18 105	-3 361	38 801	8 460	21 801	2 698	720
1977	1 974 400	355 559	409 218	-53 659	-49 760	-3 899	53 595	64	157 626	54 892	92 199	11 312	2 974
1978	2 218 300	399 561	458 746	-59 185	-54 919	-4 266	58 022	1 163	180 988	59 952	103 881	13 850	3 237
1979	2 502 400	463 302	504 028	-40 726	-38 742	-1 984	33 180	7 546	217 841	65 677	120 058	15 387	3 494
1980	2 725 400	517 112	590 941	-73 830	-72 710	-1 120	71 617	2 213	244 069	64 600	138 748	15 336	3 719
1981	3 058 600	599 272	678 241	-78 968	-73 948	-5 020	77 487	1 481	285 917	61 137	162 973	15 763	3 984
1982	3 225 500	617 766	745 743	-127 977	-120 040	-7 937	135 165	-7 188	297 744	49 207	180 686	16 600	4 212
1983	3 442 700	600 562	808 364	-207 802	-208 014	212	212 693	-4 891	288 938	37 022	185 766	18 799	4 429
1984	3 846 700	666 486	851 853	-185 367	-185 629	262	169 707	15 660	298 415	56 893	209 658	25 138	4 580
1985	4 148 900	734 088	946 396	-212 308	-221 671	9 363	200 285	12 023	334 531	61 331	234 646	25 758	4 759
1986	4 406 700	769 215	990 430	-221 215	-237 946	16 731	233 363	-12 148	348 959	63 143	255 062	24 098	4 742
1987	4 654 000	854 353	1 004 082	-149 728	-169 298	19 570	149 130	598	392 557	83 926	273 028	25 575	4 715
1988	5 011 900	909 303	1 064 455	-155 152	-193 951	38 800	161 863	-6 711	401 181	94 508	305 093	24 584	4 658
1989	5 401 700	991 190	1 143 646	-152 456	-205 210	52 754	139 100	13 356	445 690	103 291	332 859	22 011	4 546
1990	5 737 000	1 031 969	1 253 165	-221 195	-277 786	56 590	220 842	353	466 884	93 507	353 891	21 635	4 522
1991	5 934 200	1 055 041	1 324 369	-269 328	-321 525	52 198	277 441	-8 113	467 827	98 086	370 526	20 922	4 568
1992	6 240 600	1 091 279	1 381 655	-290 376	-340 463	50 087	310 738	-20 362	475 964	100 270	385 491	23 410	4 788
1993	6 578 400	1 154 401	1 409 489	-255 087	-300 434	45 347	248 659	6 428	509 680	117 520	396 939	26 556	4 805
1994	6 964 200	1 258 627	1 461 877	-203 250	-258 904	55 654	184 669	18 581	543 055	140 385	428 810	28 004	4 661
1995	7 325 100	1 351 830	1 515 802	-163 972	-226 387	62 415	171 313	-7 341	590 244	157 004	451 045	28 878	4 550
1996	7 697 400	1 453 062	1 560 535	-107 473	-174 061	66 588	129 695	-22 222	656 417	171 824	476 361	28 584	4 469
1997	8 186 600	1 579 292	1 601 250	-21 958	-103 322	81 364	38 271	-16 313	737 466	182 293	506 751	28 202	4 418
1998	8 626 300	1 721 798	1 652 585	69 213	-29 982	99 195	-51 245	-17 968	828 586	188 677	540 014	27 484	4 333
1999	9 127 000	1 827 454	1 701 891	125 563	1 873	123 690	-88 736	-36 827	879 480	184 680	580 880	26 480	4 473
2000	9 708 400	2 025 218	1 788 773	236 445	86 626	149 819	-222 559	-13 886	1 004 462	207 289	620 451	27 640	4 761
2001	10 040 700	1 991 194	1 863 770	127 424	-33 257	160 681	-90 189	-37 235	994 339	151 075	661 442	27 812	4 713
2002	10 373 400	1 853 173	2 010 970	-157 797	-317 456	159 659	220 780	-62 983	858 345	148 044	668 547	27 619	4 594
2003	10 828 300	1 782 342	2 157 637	-375 295	-536 128	160 833	373 212	2 083	793 699	131 778	674 981	33 366	4 631

[1] Fiscal years through 1976 are from July 1 through June 30. Beginning with October 1976 (fiscal year 1977), fiscal years are from October 1 through September 30. The period from July 1 through September 30, 1976 is a separate fiscal period known as the transition quarter (TQ) and not included in any fiscal year.
... = Not available.

Table 6-16. Federal Government Receipts and Outlays by Fiscal Year [1]—Continued

(Budget Accounts, millions of dollars.)

Year	Receipts by source—Continued				Outlays by function						
	Excise taxes	Estate and gift taxes	Customs deposits	Miscellaneous receipts	National defense	International affairs	General science, space, and technology	Energy	Natural resources and environment	Agriculture	Commerce and housing credit
1939	1 871	675			...	...	...	...	...	...	...
1940	1 977	353	331	14	1 660	51	...	88	997	369	550
1941	2 552	403	365	14	6 435	145	...	91	817	339	398
1942	3 399	420	369	11	25 658	968	4	156	819	344	1 521
1943	4 096	441	308	50	66 699	1 286	1	116	726	343	2 151
1944	4 759	507	417	48	79 143	1 449	48	65	642	1 275	624
1945	6 265	637	341	105	82 965	1 913	111	25	455	1 635	-2 630
1946	6 998	668	424	109	42 681	1 935	34	41	482	610	-1 857
1947	7 211	771	477	84	12 808	5 791	5	18	700	814	-923
1948	7 356	890	403	168	9 105	4 566	1	292	780	69	306
1949	7 502	780	367	241	13 150	6 052	48	341	1 080	1 924	800
1950	7 550	698	407	247	13 724	4 673	55	327	1 308	2 049	1 035
1951	8 648	708	609	261	23 566	3 647	51	383	1 310	-323	1 228
1952	8 852	818	533	359	46 089	2 691	49	474	1 233	176	1 278
1953	9 877	881	596	379	52 802	2 119	49	425	1 289	2 253	910
1954	9 945	934	542	429	49 266	1 596	46	432	1 007	1 817	-184
1955	9 131	924	585	341	42 729	2 223	74	325	940	3 514	92
1956	9 929	1 161	682	427	42 523	2 414	79	174	870	3 486	506
1957	10 534	1 365	735	573	45 430	3 147	122	240	1 098	2 288	1 424
1958	10 638	1 393	782	787	46 815	3 364	141	348	1 407	2 411	930
1959	10 578	1 333	925	662	49 015	3 144	294	382	1 632	4 509	1 933
1960	11 676	1 606	1 105	1 212	48 130	2 988	599	464	1 559	2 623	1 618
1961	11 860	1 896	982	918	49 601	3 184	1 042	510	1 779	2 641	1 203
1962	12 534	2 016	1 142	843	52 345	5 639	1 723	604	2 044	3 562	1 424
1963	13 194	2 167	1 205	1 022	53 400	5 308	3 051	530	2 251	4 384	62
1964	13 731	2 394	1 252	1 086	54 757	4 945	4 897	572	2 364	4 609	418
1965	14 570	2 716	1 442	1 594	50 620	5 273	5 823	699	2 531	3 955	1 157
1966	13 062	3 066	1 767	1 876	58 111	5 580	6 717	612	2 719	2 447	3 245
1967	13 719	2 978	1 901	2 107	71 417	5 566	6 233	782	2 869	2 990	3 979
1968	14 079	3 051	2 038	2 491	81 926	5 301	5 524	1 037	2 988	4 545	4 280
1969	15 222	3 491	2 319	2 909	82 497	4 600	5 020	1 010	2 900	5 826	-119
1970	15 705	3 644	2 430	3 424	81 692	4 330	4 511	997	3 065	5 166	2 112
1971	16 614	3 735	2 591	3 858	78 872	4 159	4 182	1 035	3 915	4 290	2 366
1972	15 477	5 436	3 287	3 632	79 174	4 781	4 175	1 296	4 241	5 259	2 222
1973	16 260	4 917	3 188	3 920	76 681	4 149	4 032	1 237	4 775	4 854	931
1974	16 844	5 035	3 334	5 368	79 347	5 710	3 980	1 303	5 697	2 230	4 705
1975	16 551	4 611	3 676	6 712	86 509	7 097	3 991	2 916	7 346	3 036	9 947
1976	16 963	5 216	4 074	8 027	89 619	6 433	4 373	4 204	8 184	3 170	7 619
TQ [1]	4 473	1 455	1 212	1 611	22 269	2 458	1 162	1 129	2 524	983	931
1977	17 548	7 327	5 150	6 531	97 241	6 353	4 736	5 770	10 032	6 787	3 093
1978	18 376	5 285	6 573	7 419	104 495	7 482	4 926	7 992	10 983	11 357	6 254
1979	18 745	5 411	7 439	9 252	116 342	7 459	5 235	9 180	12 135	11 236	4 686
1980	24 329	6 389	7 174	12 748	133 995	12 714	5 832	10 156	13 858	8 839	9 390
1981	40 839	6 787	8 083	13 790	157 513	13 104	6 469	15 166	13 568	11 323	8 206
1982	36 311	7 991	8 854	16 161	185 309	12 300	7 200	13 527	12 998	15 944	6 256
1983	35 300	6 053	8 655	15 600	209 903	11 848	7 935	9 353	12 672	22 901	6 681
1984	37 361	6 010	11 370	17 060	227 413	15 876	8 317	7 073	12 593	13 613	6 959
1985	35 992	6 422	12 079	18 571	252 748	16 176	8 627	5 609	13 357	25 565	4 337
1986	32 919	6 958	13 327	20 008	273 375	14 152	8 976	4 690	13 639	31 449	5 059
1987	32 457	7 493	15 085	19 518	281 999	11 649	9 216	4 072	13 363	26 606	6 435
1988	35 227	7 594	16 198	20 259	290 361	10 471	10 841	2 297	14 606	17 210	19 164
1989	34 386	8 745	16 334	23 328	303 559	9 585	12 838	2 706	16 182	16 919	29 710
1990	35 345	11 500	16 707	27 978	299 331	13 764	14 444	3 341	17 080	11 958	67 600
1991	42 402	11 138	15 949	23 623	273 292	15 851	16 111	2 436	18 559	15 183	76 271
1992	45 569	11 143	17 359	27 284	298 350	16 107	16 409	4 500	20 025	15 205	10 919
1993	48 057	12 577	18 802	19 465	291 086	17 248	17 030	4 319	20 239	20 363	-21 853
1994	55 225	15 225	20 099	23 164	281 642	17 083	16 227	5 219	21 026	15 046	-4 228
1995	57 484	14 763	19 301	28 561	272 066	16 434	16 724	4 936	21 915	9 778	-17 808
1996	54 014	17 189	18 670	25 534	265 753	13 496	16 709	2 839	21 524	9 159	-10 472
1997	56 924	19 845	17 928	25 465	270 505	15 228	17 174	1 475	21 227	9 032	-14 624
1998	57 673	24 076	18 297	32 658	268 456	13 109	18 219	1 270	22 300	12 206	1 014
1999	70 414	27 782	18 336	34 929	274 873	15 243	18 125	912	23 968	23 011	2 647
2000	68 865	29 010	19 914	42 826	294 495	17 216	18 633	-1 061	25 031	36 465	3 207
2001	66 232	28 400	19 369	37 812	305 500	16 493	19 784	38	25 623	26 204	5 878
2002	66 989	26 507	18 602	33 926	348 555	22 351	20 767	482	29 454	21 957	-391
2003	67 524	21 959	19 862	34 542	404 920	21 208	20 873	-775	29 703	22 600	-1 607

[1]Fiscal years through 1976 are from July 1 through June 30. Beginning with October 1976 (fiscal year 1977), fiscal years are from October 1 through September 30. The period from July 1 through September 30, 1976 is a separate fiscal period known as the transition quarter (TQ) and not included in any fiscal year.
... = Not available.

Table 6-16. Federal Government Receipts and Outlays by Fiscal Year [1]—Continued

(Budget Accounts, millions of dollars.)

Year	Outlays by function—Continued										
	Transportation	Community and regional development	Education, employment, and social services	Health	Medicare	Income security	Social Security	Veterans benefits and services	Administration of justice	General government	Net interest
1939	...	...	...	...	...	...	...	...	...	...	...
1940	392	285	1 972	55	...	1 514	28	570	81	274	899
1941	353	123	1 592	60	...	1 855	91	560	92	306	943
1942	1 283	113	1 062	71	...	1 828	137	501	117	397	1 052
1943	3 220	219	375	92	...	1 739	177	276	154	673	1 529
1944	3 901	238	160	174	...	1 503	217	-126	192	900	2 219
1945	3 654	243	134	211	...	1 137	267	110	178	581	3 112
1946	1 970	200	85	201	...	2 384	358	2 465	176	825	4 111
1947	1 130	302	102	177	...	2 820	466	6 344	176	1 114	4 204
1948	787	78	191	162	...	2 499	558	6 457	170	1 045	4 341
1949	916	-33	178	197	...	3 174	657	6 599	184	824	4 523
1950	967	30	241	268	...	4 097	781	8 834	193	986	4 812
1951	956	47	235	323	...	3 352	1 565	5 526	218	1 097	4 665
1952	1 124	73	339	347	...	3 655	2 063	5 341	267	1 163	4 701
1953	1 264	117	441	336	...	3 823	2 717	4 519	243	1 209	5 156
1954	1 229	100	370	307	...	4 434	3 352	4 613	257	799	4 811
1955	1 246	129	445	291	...	5 071	4 427	4 675	256	651	4 850
1956	1 450	92	591	359	...	4 734	5 478	4 891	302	1 201	5 079
1957	1 662	135	590	479	...	5 427	6 661	5 005	303	1 360	5 354
1958	2 334	169	643	541	...	7 535	8 219	5 350	325	655	5 604
1959	3 655	211	789	685	...	8 239	9 737	5 443	356	926	5 762
1960	4 126	224	968	795	...	7 378	11 602	5 441	366	1 184	6 947
1961	3 987	275	1 063	913	...	9 683	12 474	5 705	400	1 354	6 716
1962	4 290	469	1 241	1 198	...	9 207	14 365	5 619	429	1 049	6 889
1963	4 596	574	1 458	1 451	...	9 311	15 788	5 514	465	1 230	7 740
1964	5 242	933	1 555	1 788	...	9 657	16 620	5 675	489	1 518	8 199
1965	5 763	1 114	2 140	1 791	...	9 469	17 460	5 716	535	1 499	8 591
1966	5 730	1 105	4 363	2 543	64	9 678	20 694	5 916	563	1 603	9 386
1967	5 936	1 108	6 453	3 351	2 748	10 261	21 725	6 735	618	1 719	10 268
1968	6 316	1 382	7 634	4 390	4 649	11 816	23 854	7 032	659	1 757	11 090
1969	6 526	1 552	7 548	5 162	5 695	13 076	27 298	7 631	766	1 939	12 699
1970	7 008	2 392	8 634	5 907	6 213	15 655	30 270	8 669	959	2 320	14 380
1971	8 052	2 917	9 849	6 843	6 622	22 946	35 872	9 768	1 306	2 442	14 841
1972	8 392	3 423	12 529	8 674	7 479	27 650	40 157	10 720	1 653	2 960	15 478
1973	9 066	4 605	12 745	9 356	8 052	28 276	49 090	12 003	2 141	9 774	17 349
1974	9 172	4 229	12 457	10 733	9 639	33 713	55 867	13 374	2 470	10 032	21 449
1975	10 918	4 322	16 022	12 930	12 875	50 176	64 658	16 584	2 955	10 408	23 244
1976	13 739	5 442	18 910	15 734	15 834	60 799	73 899	18 419	3 328	9 747	26 727
TQ [1]	3 358	1 569	5 169	3 924	4 264	14 985	19 763	3 960	891	3 895	6 949
1977	14 829	7 021	21 104	17 302	19 345	61 060	85 061	18 022	3 605	12 833	29 901
1978	15 521	11 841	26 710	18 524	22 768	61 505	93 861	18 961	3 813	12 015	35 458
1979	18 079	10 480	30 223	20 494	26 495	66 376	104 073	19 914	4 173	12 293	42 633
1980	21 329	11 252	31 843	23 169	32 090	86 557	118 547	21 169	4 584	13 028	52 533
1981	23 379	10 568	33 151	26 866	39 149	100 299	139 584	22 973	4 769	11 429	68 766
1982	20 625	8 347	26 611	27 445	46 567	108 155	155 964	23 938	4 712	10 914	85 032
1983	21 334	7 564	26 196	28 641	52 588	123 031	170 724	24 824	5 105	11 235	89 808
1984	23 669	7 673	26 921	30 417	57 540	113 352	178 223	25 588	5 663	11 817	111 102
1985	25 838	7 680	28 593	33 542	65 822	128 979	188 623	26 262	6 270	11 588	129 478
1986	28 117	7 233	29 777	35 936	70 164	120 633	198 757	26 327	6 572	12 564	136 017
1987	26 222	5 051	28 922	39 967	75 120	124 088	207 353	26 750	7 553	7 560	138 611
1988	27 272	5 294	30 933	44 487	78 878	130 377	219 341	29 386	9 236	9 465	151 803
1989	27 608	5 362	35 330	48 390	84 964	137 426	232 542	30 031	9 474	9 249	168 981
1990	29 485	8 532	37 176	57 716	98 102	148 655	248 623	29 058	9 993	10 575	184 347
1991	31 099	6 813	41 234	71 183	104 489	172 441	269 015	31 305	12 276	11 719	194 448
1992	33 332	6 841	42 743	89 497	119 024	199 527	287 585	34 064	14 426	13 039	199 344
1993	35 004	9 149	47 376	99 415	130 552	209 934	304 585	35 671	14 955	13 086	198 713
1994	38 066	10 625	43 277	107 122	144 747	217 114	319 565	37 584	15 268	11 333	202 932
1995	39 350	10 749	51 020	115 418	159 855	223 736	335 846	37 890	16 247	13 967	232 134
1996	39 565	10 745	48 310	119 378	174 225	229 663	349 671	36 985	17 596	11 956	241 053
1997	40 767	11 055	48 961	123 843	190 016	234 952	365 251	39 313	20 243	12 821	243 984
1998	40 343	9 776	50 503	131 442	192 822	237 663	379 215	41 781	22 938	15 603	241 119
1999	42 533	11 870	50 591	141 074	190 447	242 356	390 037	43 212	26 082	15 599	229 756
2000	46 853	10 623	53 754	154 533	197 113	253 575	409 423	47 083	28 501	12 959	222 951
2001	54 447	11 773	57 143	172 270	217 384	269 615	432 958	45 039	30 205	14 259	206 168
2002	61 833	12 981	70 544	196 544	230 855	312 530	455 980	50 984	35 171	16 814	170 951
2003	67 069	18 850	82 568	219 576	249 433	334 432	474 680	57 018	35 408	22 987	153 076

[1] Fiscal years through 1976 are from July 1 through June 30. Beginning with October 1976 (fiscal year 1977), fiscal years are from October 1 through September 30. The period from July 1 through September 30, 1976 is a separate fiscal period known as the transition quarter (TQ) and not included in any fiscal year.
... = Not available.

Table 6-17. Federal Government Debt by Fiscal Year [1]

(Billions of dollars, except as noted.)

Year	Federal government debt held by the public at end of fiscal year		Gross public debt at end of fiscal year held by:						
	Debt held by the public (billions of dollars)	Debt/GDP ratio (percent)	Total	Social Security funds	Other U.S. government accounts	Federal Reserve System	Private investors		
							Total	Foreign and international investors	Domestic investors
1945	235	106.3	260	7	18	22	213	...	...
1946	242	108.6	271	8	21	24	218	...	...
1947	224	95.6	257	9	24	22	202	...	...
1948	216	84.3	252	10	26	21	195	...	...
1949	214	78.9	253	11	27	19	195	...	...
1950	219	80.1	257	13	25	18	201	...	...
1951	214	66.8	255	15	26	23	191	...	...
1952	215	61.6	259	17	28	23	192	...	...
1953	218	58.5	266	18	29	25	194	...	...
1954	224	59.4	271	20	26	25	199	...	...
1955	227	57.3	274	21	27	24	203	...	...
1956	222	51.9	273	23	28	24	198	...	...
1957	219	48.7	272	23	30	23	196	...	...
1958	226	49.1	280	24	29	25	201	...	...
1959	235	47.7	287	23	30	26	209	...	...
1960	237	45.6	291	23	31	27	210	...	...
1961	238	44.8	293	23	31	27	211	...	...
1962	248	43.6	303	22	33	30	218	...	...
1963	254	42.4	310	21	35	32	222	...	...
1964	257	40.1	316	22	37	35	222	...	...
1965	261	37.9	322	22	39	39	222	12	209
1966	264	35.0	328	22	43	42	222	12	210
1967	267	32.8	340	26	48	47	220	11	209
1968	290	33.3	369	28	51	52	237	11	227
1969	278	29.3	366	32	56	54	224	10	214
1970	283	28.0	381	38	60	58	225	14	211
1971	303	28.0	408	41	64	66	238	32	206
1972	322	27.3	436	44	70	71	251	49	202
1973	341	26.1	466	44	81	75	266	59	206
1974	344	23.8	484	46	94	81	263	57	206
1975	395	25.3	542	48	99	85	310	66	244
1976	477	27.5	629	45	107	95	383	70	313
TQ [1]	496	27.2	644	44	105	97	399	75	324
1977	549	27.9	706	40	118	105	444	96	349
1978	607	27.4	777	35	134	115	492	121	371
1979	640	25.6	829	33	156	116	525	120	404
1980	712	26.1	909	32	165	121	591	122	469
1981	789	25.8	995	27	178	124	665	131	534
1982	925	28.6	1 137	19	193	134	790	141	649
1983	1 137	33.1	1 372	32	202	156	982	160	822
1984	1 307	34.0	1 565	32	225	155	1 152	176	976
1985	1 507	36.4	1 817	40	270	170	1 337	223	1 115
1986	1 741	39.5	2 121	46	334	191	1 550	266	1 284
1987	1 890	40.7	2 346	65	391	212	1 678	280	1 398
1988	2 052	40.9	2 601	104	445	229	1 822	346	1 476
1989	2 191	40.5	2 868	157	520	220	1 971	395	1 576
1990	2 412	42.0	3 206	215	580	234	2 177	440	1 737
1991	2 689	45.3	3 598	268	641	259	2 430	477	1 953
1992	3 000	48.2	4 002	319	683	296	2 703	535	2 168
1993	3 248	49.5	4 351	366	737	326	2 923	591	2 331
1994	3 433	49.4	4 643	423	788	355	3 078	656	2 422
1995	3 604	49.2	4 921	483	833	374	3 230	800	2 430
1996	3 734	48.5	5 181	550	898	391	3 343	978	2 365
1997	3 772	46.1	5 369	631	966	425	3 348	1 218	2 130
1998	3 721	42.9	5 478	730	1 027	458	3 263	1 217	2 046
1999	3 632	39.8	5 606	855	1 118	497	3 136	1 281	1 854
2000	3 410	35.1	5 629	1 007	1 212	511	2 898	1 058	1 840
2001	3 320	33.1	5 770	1 170	1 280	534	2 785	1 006	1 780
2002	3 540	34.1	6 198	1 329	1 329	604	2 936	1 200	1 736
2003	3 914	36.1	6 760	1 485	1 362	656	3 257	1 459	1 798

[1]Fiscal years through 1976 are from July 1 through June 30. Beginning with October 1976 (fiscal year 1977), fiscal years are from October 1 through September 30. The period from July 1 through September 30, 1976 is a separate fiscal period known as the transition quarter (TQ) and not included in any fiscal year.
... = Not available.

Section 6d: Government Output and Employment

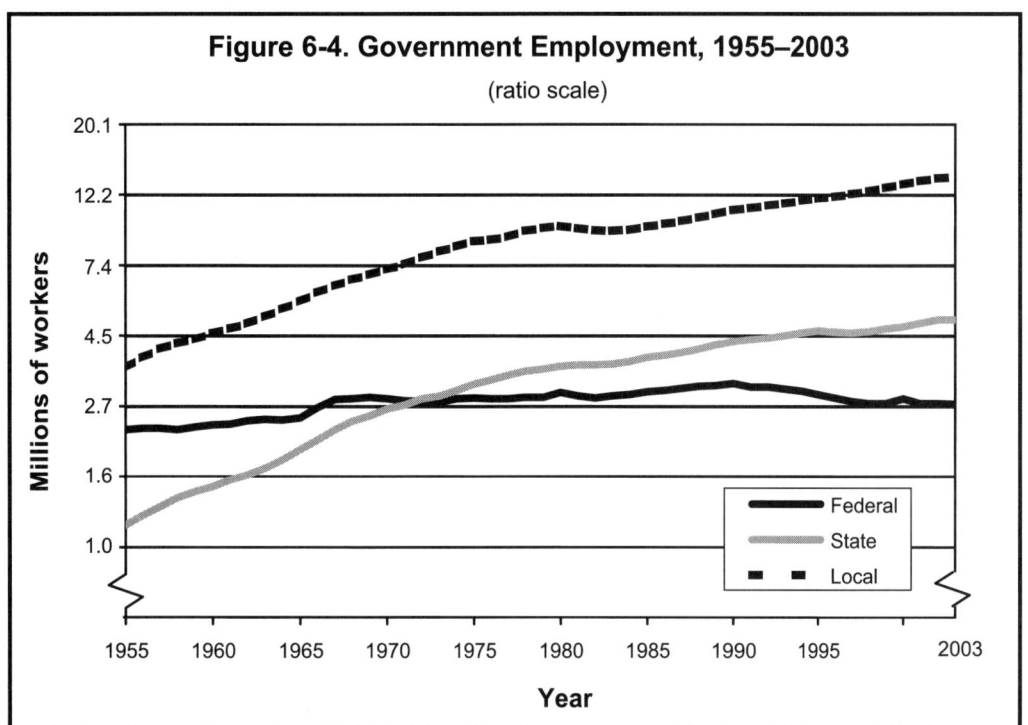

Figure 6-4. Government Employment, 1955–2003

- Since 1955, total employment of civilians by all levels of government has increased 207 percent and risen from 13.8 percent to 16.6 percent of total payroll employment. Federal employment rose 20 percent; state government rose 330 percent, with half of the increase due to education; and local government rose 288 percent, with 58 percent of the rise due to education. (Tables 6-19 and 8-4)
- Reported Defense Department civilian employment continued to decline in 2002 and 2003, even as defense spending was rising absolutely and as a percent of GDP. It should be noted that the figures shown here are for civilian employees only, as compiled by the Bureau of Labor Statistics, and exclude the active-duty armed forces, defense contractors, and employees of the Central Intelligence Agency and the National Security Agency. (Table 6-19 and Notes and Definitions)
- A more comprehensive picture of government activity in the context of GDP can be found in the new definition and presentation of the gross output and value added of government in the National Income and Product Accounts. Current-dollar data are found in Tables 6-5 and 6-10, and quantity indexes in Table 6-18. Looking at the quantity indexes, from 1947 (the first year of relatively normal defense spending following World War II) to 2003, the real gross output of the federal government has increased 205 percent, with nondefense activity rising faster than defense spending. For both defense and nondefense, the volume of intermediate goods and services purchased rose far faster than value added by government itself (where value added comprises the input of government employees and government-owned capital). The changes for defense were particularly striking, as gross output increased 147 percent, value added only 11 percent, and intermediate goods and services 1,990 percent. (Table 6-18)
- Real gross output of state and local governments rose 678 percent over the same period, with value added rising 464 percent and goods and services purchased rising 1,672 percent. (Table 6-18)

Table 6-18. Chain-Type Quantity Indexes for Government Output

(Index numbers, 2000 = 100.)

NIPA Table 3.10.3

Year and quarter	Federal government									State and local government		
	Gross output of general government			Value added			Intermediate goods and services purchased [1]			Gross output of general government	Value added	Intermediate goods and services purchased [1]
	Total	Defense	Nondefense	Total	Defense	Nondefense	Total	Defense	Nondefense			
1946	59.0	80.4	23.2	106.8	145.4	34.2	17.5	21.7	12.7	12.9	17.4	5.8
1947	38.8	49.0	21.6	75.4	95.0	40.3	7.6	7.1	7.9	13.9	18.5	6.5
1948	39.6	47.1	27.4	69.7	84.4	44.8	13.2	12.8	13.1	14.1	19.0	6.4
1949	41.3	47.1	32.4	66.6	80.5	43.1	18.2	16.0	20.3	15.5	20.3	7.6
1950	39.7	48.1	26.2	66.6	78.6	47.2	15.7	19.4	10.2	16.5	21.0	8.7
1951	60.0	82.6	21.9	87.6	112.1	44.1	32.7	50.9	6.1	16.4	21.5	8.1
1952	75.7	105.4	25.6	97.6	127.8	43.3	50.2	76.6	11.7	16.7	22.2	7.9
1953	81.4	110.2	32.8	98.0	130.0	40.2	58.9	82.8	23.6	17.3	23.2	7.9
1954	72.1	96.0	31.8	95.5	127.1	38.5	46.0	61.4	23.1	18.0	24.2	8.2
1955	69.0	90.3	32.9	93.3	123.5	38.8	42.6	54.7	24.5	19.3	25.3	9.3
1956	67.0	90.3	27.5	92.3	121.6	39.5	40.2	56.2	16.1	20.0	26.9	9.0
1957	71.1	96.6	27.8	92.0	120.7	40.4	47.1	67.5	16.1	21.0	28.4	9.4
1958	69.7	94.8	27.3	89.4	116.1	41.5	46.8	68.1	14.4	22.7	30.1	10.8
1959	69.2	87.1	38.9	88.6	114.9	41.5	46.6	55.3	33.1	23.8	31.4	11.6
1960	68.1	88.2	33.9	90.3	115.9	44.4	43.1	56.4	22.6	25.1	33.0	12.2
1961	69.3	90.2	33.6	92.1	118.2	45.5	43.6	58.0	21.3	26.5	34.8	13.1
1962	75.8	96.5	40.5	95.9	122.8	47.9	52.0	65.5	31.2	27.5	36.0	13.6
1963	77.8	97.4	44.2	96.8	122.4	51.0	54.8	67.5	35.3	29.0	37.9	14.5
1964	77.3	95.0	46.9	97.7	122.9	52.7	53.0	62.4	38.5	31.0	40.2	15.8
1965	78.4	95.6	48.8	98.4	122.9	54.5	54.4	63.5	40.4	33.1	42.6	17.4
1966	87.2	109.5	49.1	104.9	131.4	57.5	65.1	82.5	38.4	35.3	45.2	18.8
1967	96.4	122.6	51.6	111.7	140.2	60.7	76.0	99.5	40.1	37.0	47.1	20.3
1968	99.5	127.6	51.9	113.5	142.1	62.5	80.2	107.3	39.0	39.6	49.9	22.3
1969	97.4	122.6	54.4	113.8	142.1	63.3	75.7	97.2	42.8	42.0	52.2	24.7
1970	90.4	111.5	54.2	109.0	133.9	64.2	66.8	83.1	41.6	44.4	54.5	27.2
1971	85.9	102.8	56.7	103.9	125.0	66.1	63.1	74.9	44.5	46.8	56.7	29.7
1972	84.2	97.1	61.5	98.9	116.1	67.8	65.4	73.3	52.3	48.7	58.6	31.5
1973	79.7	90.6	60.5	95.2	110.3	68.1	59.9	65.7	50.1	50.4	60.7	32.6
1974	79.2	88.0	63.6	94.9	108.1	71.2	59.2	62.6	53.2	52.4	62.9	34.4
1975	78.2	85.4	65.5	94.3	106.6	72.4	57.6	58.6	55.6	54.7	64.8	37.1
1976	77.0	83.3	65.8	94.5	105.0	75.8	54.9	56.0	52.7	55.6	65.7	38.2
1977	78.8	84.3	69.0	94.7	104.4	77.6	58.5	58.9	57.4	56.7	66.7	39.3
1978	80.5	85.2	72.2	95.9	105.1	79.8	60.9	60.1	61.5	58.0	68.2	40.3
1979	81.9	86.3	74.0	95.8	104.7	80.2	63.9	62.9	64.9	58.8	69.4	40.3
1980	85.2	89.8	77.0	97.4	105.7	82.7	69.1	69.3	68.2	58.8	70.4	39.0
1981	88.7	94.9	77.6	98.9	108.8	81.3	74.9	76.7	71.0	58.9	70.3	39.3
1982	91.6	101.3	74.1	100.5	111.6	80.6	79.2	87.2	64.4	59.9	70.8	41.0
1983	95.9	106.4	77.1	102.8	114.2	82.5	85.8	95.0	68.7	60.8	70.5	43.6
1984	97.2	109.7	74.6	105.1	117.2	83.6	85.9	98.8	62.2	61.8	70.9	45.4
1985	103.0	116.3	78.8	108.1	121.1	84.8	95.0	108.8	69.7	64.8	73.0	50.1
1986	107.4	121.6	81.8	110.0	124.0	84.7	102.8	117.2	76.0	68.7	75.1	56.7
1987	110.1	126.1	80.9	112.9	127.2	86.9	105.2	123.6	71.6	69.6	76.5	56.6
1988	110.0	127.7	77.6	114.3	128.0	89.7	102.9	126.1	60.9	71.8	79.1	58.1
1989	111.6	126.7	83.9	115.7	129.4	91.0	104.8	121.8	73.7	74.0	81.6	59.9
1990	113.3	126.2	90.1	117.8	130.2	95.7	106.1	119.4	81.8	76.2	84.0	61.8
1991	113.8	126.0	91.8	118.5	130.9	96.4	106.2	118.0	84.7	78.0	85.1	64.7
1992	111.3	119.7	96.4	116.0	126.0	98.5	103.8	109.8	92.7	80.1	86.5	68.1
1993	107.4	114.7	94.5	113.8	122.3	99.0	97.4	103.0	87.3	82.1	87.7	71.4
1994	104.8	110.2	95.2	110.1	117.5	97.1	96.4	98.8	92.0	84.3	89.2	74.9
1995	101.2	105.5	93.7	106.0	112.6	94.4	93.7	94.5	92.3	86.4	91.0	77.7
1996	99.4	103.8	91.6	103.0	108.8	93.0	93.5	95.9	89.2	88.0	92.4	79.5
1997	99.1	102.3	93.5	101.1	105.6	93.4	95.8	97.0	93.7	90.6	94.3	83.4
1998	97.3	99.6	93.2	100.0	102.7	95.1	92.9	94.6	90.0	94.1	96.2	90.0
1999	98.5	101.0	94.1	99.1	100.7	96.5	97.4	101.4	90.2	97.5	97.9	96.6
2000	100.0	100.0	100.0	100.0	100.0	100.0	100.0	100.0	100.0	100.0	100.0	100.0
2001	103.8	104.0	103.6	100.5	100.5	100.7	109.3	109.6	108.7	103.5	102.4	105.5
2002	111.1	111.5	110.4	102.5	102.3	102.7	125.5	126.4	123.7	106.7	104.0	111.8
2003	118.3	121.2	113.2	105.2	105.2	105.1	140.5	147.7	127.1	108.3	104.5	115.6
2001												
1st quarter	102.1	103.0	100.5	100.2	100.3	100.0	105.2	107.3	101.4	101.9	101.2	103.2
2nd quarter	103.4	102.9	104.3	100.7	100.4	101.1	107.9	106.9	109.9	102.8	102.0	104.4
3rd quarter	103.6	103.2	104.3	100.8	100.6	101.2	108.2	107.5	109.6	104.0	102.8	106.1
4th quarter	106.2	106.8	105.3	100.5	100.6	100.3	115.6	116.7	113.7	105.1	103.5	108.3
2002												
1st quarter	108.2	108.5	107.7	101.6	101.7	101.4	119.1	119.3	118.6	105.7	103.7	109.7
2nd quarter	110.3	110.5	110.0	102.3	102.4	102.0	123.7	123.7	123.7	106.4	103.9	111.2
3rd quarter	111.6	111.6	111.6	102.9	102.7	103.2	125.9	125.9	126.1	106.9	104.1	112.6
4th quarter	114.4	115.5	112.5	103.1	102.4	104.4	133.1	136.8	126.4	107.5	104.3	113.8
2003												
1st quarter	114.2	114.2	114.3	104.5	104.2	104.9	130.5	130.4	130.7	107.7	104.3	114.4
2nd quarter	120.1	124.6	111.9	105.4	105.4	105.4	144.8	156.7	123.0	108.1	104.4	115.3
3rd quarter	119.1	121.6	114.6	105.5	105.6	105.2	142.0	148.0	130.8	108.4	104.5	116.0
4th quarter	120.0	124.5	111.9	105.4	105.6	104.9	144.6	155.8	124.0	108.8	104.9	116.6

[1] Includes general government intermediate inputs for goods and services sold to other sectors and for own-account investment.

Table 6-19. Government Employment

(Calendar years; payroll employment, thousands, seasonally adjusted, except as noted.)

Year and month	Total government employment	Federal			State			Local		
		Total	Department of Defense (not seasonally adjusted)	Postal Service (not seasonally adjusted)	Total	Education	State government hospitals (not seasonally adjusted)	Total	Education	Local government hospitals (not seasonally adjusted)
1946	5 705	2 365	746	473	...	...	...	...	...	...
1947	5 567	1 985	499	471	...	...	...	...	...	...
1948	5 742	1 954	511	498	...	...	...	...	...	...
1949	5 950	2 001	531	527	...	...	...	...	...	...
1950	6 120	2 023	533	516	...	...	...	...	...	...
1951	6 502	2 415	797	521	...	...	...	...	...	...
1952	6 727	2 539	868	542	...	...	...	...	...	...
1953	6 758	2 418	818	530	...	...	...	...	...	...
1954	6 858	2 295	744	533	...	...	...	...	...	...
1955	7 021	2 295	744	534	1 168	308	...	3 558	1 751	...
1956	7 386	2 318	749	539	1 249	334	...	3 819	1 884	...
1957	7 724	2 326	729	555	1 328	363	...	4 071	2 026	...
1958	7 946	2 298	695	567	1 415	389	...	4 232	2 115	...
1959	8 192	2 342	699	578	1 484	420	...	4 366	2 198	...
1960	8 464	2 381	681	591	1 536	448	...	4 547	2 314	...
1961	8 706	2 391	683	601	1 607	474	...	4 708	2 411	...
1962	9 004	2 455	697	601	1 669	511	...	4 881	2 522	...
1963	9 341	2 473	687	603	1 747	557	...	5 121	2 674	...
1964	9 711	2 463	676	604	1 856	609	...	5 392	2 839	...
1965	10 191	2 495	679	619	1 996	679	...	5 700	3 031	...
1966	10 910	2 690	741	686	2 141	775	...	6 080	3 297	...
1967	11 525	2 852	802	719	2 302	873	...	6 371	3 490	...
1968	11 972	2 871	801	729	2 442	958	...	6 660	3 649	...
1969	12 330	2 893	815	737	2 533	1 042	...	6 904	3 785	...
1970	12 687	2 865	756	741	2 664	1 104	...	7 158	3 912	...
1971	13 012	2 828	731	731	2 747	1 149	...	7 437	4 091	...
1972	13 465	2 815	720	703	2 859	1 188	459	7 790	4 262	467
1973	13 862	2 794	696	698	2 923	1 205	472	8 146	4 433	477
1974	14 303	2 858	698	710	3 039	1 267	483	8 407	4 584	483
1975	14 820	2 882	704	699	3 179	1 323	503	8 758	4 722	489
1976	15 001	2 863	693	676	3 273	1 371	518	8 865	4 786	492
1977	15 258	2 859	676	657	3 377	1 385	538	9 023	4 859	494
1978	15 812	2 893	661	660	3 474	1 367	541	9 446	4 958	535
1979	16 068	2 894	649	673	3 541	1 378	538	9 633	4 989	571
1980	16 375	3 000	645	673	3 610	1 398	530	9 765	5 090	604
1981	16 180	2 922	655	675	3 640	1 420	515	9 619	5 095	622
1982	15 982	2 884	690	684	3 640	1 433	494	9 458	5 049	635
1983	16 011	2 915	699	685	3 662	1 450	471	9 434	5 020	644
1984	16 159	2 943	716	706	3 734	1 488	459	9 482	5 076	623
1985	16 533	3 014	738	750	3 832	1 540	449	9 687	5 221	608
1986	16 838	3 044	736	792	3 893	1 561	438	9 901	5 358	601
1987	17 156	3 089	736	815	3 967	1 586	439	10 100	5 469	606
1988	17 540	3 124	719	835	4 076	1 621	446	10 339	5 590	619
1989	17 927	3 136	735	838	4 182	1 668	442	10 609	5 740	632
1990	18 415	3 196	722	825	4 305	1 730	426	10 914	5 902	646
1991	18 545	3 110	702	813	4 355	1 768	417	11 081	5 994	653
1992	18 787	3 111	702	800	4 408	1 799	419	11 267	6 076	665
1993	18 989	3 063	670	793	4 488	1 834	414	11 438	6 206	673
1994	19 275	3 018	657	821	4 576	1 882	407	11 682	6 329	673
1995	19 432	2 949	627	850	4 635	1 919	395	11 849	6 453	669
1996	19 539	2 877	597	867	4 606	1 911	376	12 056	6 592	648
1997	19 664	2 806	588	866	4 582	1 904	360	12 276	6 759	632
1998	19 909	2 772	550	881	4 612	1 922	346	12 525	6 921	630
1999	20 307	2 769	525	890	4 709	1 983	344	12 829	7 120	626
2000	20 790	2 865	510	880	4 786	2 031	343	13 139	7 294	622
2001	21 118	2 764	504	873	4 905	2 113	345	13 449	7 479	628
2002	21 513	2 766	499	842	5 029	2 243	349	13 718	7 654	642
2003	21 575	2 756	496	809	5 017	2 266	349	13 802	7 698	652
2003										
January	21 618	2 785	500	820	5 021	2 249	349	13 812	7 702	645
February	21 625	2 787	499	816	5 028	2 260	349	13 810	7 702	647
March	21 616	2 789	494	813	5 024	2 259	348	13 803	7 697	648
April	21 597	2 768	489	813	5 020	2 260	348	13 809	7 701	648
May	21 541	2 769	489	811	5 013	2 257	348	13 759	7 657	649
June	21 567	2 763	493	809	4 996	2 248	351	13 808	7 707	653
July	21 561	2 758	497	806	4 990	2 249	350	13 813	7 721	655
August	21 580	2 750	500	804	4 997	2 259	351	13 833	7 742	654
September	21 539	2 747	497	801	5 019	2 279	350	13 773	7 674	654
October	21 560	2 736	496	801	5 031	2 290	350	13 793	7 687	654
November	21 544	2 723	497	798	5 023	2 283	351	13 798	7 685	657
December	21 544	2 720	499	817	5 027	2 286	349	13 797	7 687	657

... = Not available.

NOTES AND DEFINITIONS

TABLES 6-1 THROUGH 6-11, 6-18, 19-8, AND 19-9 FEDERAL, STATE, AND LOCAL GOVERNMENT IN THE NATIONAL INCOME AND PRODUCT ACCOUNTS

SOURCE: U.S. DEPARTMENT OF COMMERCE, BUREAU OF ECONOMIC ANALYSIS

These data are from the national income and product accounts (NIPAs), as published in the 2003 comprehensive NIPA revisions and as subsequently revised and updated through August 2004. For general information on the NIPAs and the 2003 revision, see the Notes and Definitions for Tables 1-1 through 1-7.

A new framework for the government accounts

In the 2003 revision, a new framework is used for government consumption expenditures—federal, state, and local—that explicitly recognizes the services produced by general government. Governments serve several functions in the economy. The functions recognized in the NIPAs are the production of nonmarket services; the consumption of these services, in that the value of the services provided to the general public is treated as government consumption expenditures; and the provision of transfer payments. These functions are financed through taxation and through contributions to social insurance funds, and in the world's capital markets.

In the new framework, the value of the government services, most of which are not sold in the market, is measured as the sum of the costs of the three major inputs: compensation, consumption of fixed capital (CFC), and intermediate goods and services purchased. The purchase from the private sector of goods and services by government, classified as final sales to government before the 2003 revision, is reclassified as intermediate purchases.

The value of government final purchases of consumption expenditures and gross investment, which constitutes the contribution of government demand to the GDP, is not changed by this reclassification, since it was previously defined as the sum of compensation, CFC, and goods and services purchased. However, the distribution of GDP by type of product is changed—final sales of goods are reduced, and services increased by the same amount.

In addition to this change in the conceptual framework, a number of the categories of government receipts and expenditures have been redefined to draw distinctions more precisely. For example, items that used to be called "nontax payments" and included with taxes are now classified as transfer or fee payments and not included in taxes.

Finally, the concept previously known as "Current surplus or deficit(-), national income and product accounts" has been renamed "Net government saving." This recognizes, in part, the role of government in the capital markets. When government runs a current surplus, "net government saving" is positive, and funds are made available (for example, by repayment of outstanding debt) to finance investment—both private-sector capital spending and government investment. When government runs a current deficit, or "dis-saves," it must borrow funds that would otherwise be available to finance investment.

However, "net government saving" does not give a complete picture of governments' role in capital markets, because it is based on current receipts and expenditures alone and does not include government investment activity.

The federal *budget* accounts (see Tables 6-16 and 6-17) do not draw a distinction between current and capital spending. The accounts of individual state and local governments typically do separate capital from current spending, and allow capital spending to be financed by borrowing even when deficit financing of current spending is constitutionally forbidden. However, neither federal nor state and local governments typically show depreciation as a current expense in the way that is standard to private-sector accounting.

In the NIPAs, the capital spending of all levels of government is treated the same way the NIPAs treat private investment spending. A depreciation entry for existing capital (CFC) is calculated, using estimated replacement costs and realistic depreciation rates, and entered as one element of government current expenditures and output. Capital spending is excluded from current expenditures but appears in the account for "net lending or borrowing(-)."

"Net lending or borrowing(-)" is a concept introduced in a previous comprehensive revision, now shown along with its derivation in *Business Statistics* in Tables 6-5 and 6-10. It consists of current net saving as defined above, plus the consumption of fixed capital (CFC, from the current expenditure account), minus gross investment, plus capital transfer receipts, and minus capital transfer payments and net purchases of non-produced assets. The logic is that when CFC exceeds actual investment expenditures, governments have positive saving and can lend (or repay debt); if gross investment exceeds CFC, government must borrow to finance the difference, indicating negative saving and requiring borrowing.

Notes on the data

Government receipts and expenditures data are derived from the accounts of the U.S. government and from a Census Bureau survey of *Government Finances* covering state and local governments. However, BEA makes a number of adjustments to the data to convert them from fiscal year to calendar year and quarter bases and to agree with the concepts of national income accounting. Data are converted from the cash basis usually found in financial statements to the timing bases required for the NIPAs. In the NIPAs, receipts from businesses generally are on an accrual basis, purchases of goods and services are recorded when delivered, and receipts from and transfer payments to persons are on a cash basis. The federal receipts and expenditure data from the NIPAs in Tables 6-1 through 6-7 therefore differ from the federal receipts and outlay data in Table 6-16 in that, among other differences, the latter are by fiscal year and are on a modified cash basis.

The NIPA data on government receipts and expenditures record transactions of governments (federal, state, and local) with other U.S. residents and foreigners. Each entry in the government receipts and expenditures account has a corresponding entry elsewhere in the NIPAs. Thus, for example, the sum of personal current taxes received by federal and state and local governments (Tables 6-1 and 6-8) is equal to personal current taxes paid, as shown in the personal income table (4-1).

Definitions: general

In the 2003 revision, several items appear separately that were previously treated as "negative expenditures" and netted against other items on the expenditures side. This "grossing up" of the accounts raises both receipts and outlays and has no effect on net saving. "Grossing up" has been applied to taxes from the rest of the world, interest receipts (back to 1960 for the federal government and back to 1946 for state and local governments), dividends, and the current surplus of government enterprises (back to 1959).

Definitions: current receipts

Current tax receipts includes personal current taxes, taxes on production and imports, taxes on corporate income and (for the federal government only) taxes from the rest of the world. The taxes from the rest of the world are mostly income taxes and are not shown in the tables here.

Personal current taxes is personal tax payments from residents of the United States that are not chargeable to business expense. Personal taxes includes taxes on income, including on realized net capital gains, and on personal property. Personal contributions for social insurance are not included in this category. As of the 1999 revisions, estate and gift taxes are classified as capital transfers and are no longer included in personal current taxes. However, estate and gift taxes continue to be included in federal government receipts in Table 6-16.

Taxes on production and imports consists of federal excise taxes and customs duties and of state and local sales taxes, property taxes (including residential real estate taxes), motor vehicle licenses, severance taxes, other taxes, and special assessments. Before the 2003 revision, these taxes were a component of "indirect business tax and nontax liabilities."

Taxes on corporate income covers federal, state, and local government income taxes on all corporate income subject to taxes. This income includes capital gains and other income excluded from NIPA profits. The taxes are measured on an accrual basis, net of applicable tax credits.

Contributions for social insurance includes employer and personal contributions for Social Security, Medicare, unemployment insurance, and other government social insurance programs. As of the 1999 revisions, contributions to government employee retirement plans are no longer included in this category; these plans are now treated the same as private pension plans.

Income receipts on assets consists of *interest*, dividends (not shown separately here), and *rents and royalties*.

Interest receipts (1960 to date for federal; 1946 to date for state and local) consists of monetary and imputed interest received on loans and investments. In the NIPAs this no longer includes interest received by government employee retirement plans, which is now credited to personal income instead. However, such interest received is still deducted from interest paid in the budget accounts shown in Table 6-16. In the NIPAs, before the indicated years, receipts are deducted from aggregate interest payments, hence not shown as receipts, and net interest is presented on the expenditure side. In the federal budget accounts in Table 6-16, net interest is the interest expenditure concept used throughout the period covered.

Current transfer receipts includes receipts in categories other than those specified above from persons and business. In the case of the state and local government accounts (Table 6-8) it also includes *federal grants-in-aid*, a component of federal transfer payments on the expenditure side. Receipts from business and persons were previously included with income taxes in "tax and nontax payments." They consist of federal deposit insurance premiums and other nontaxes (largely fines and regulatory and inspection fees), state and local fines and other nontaxes (largely donations and tobacco settlements), and net insurance settlements paid to governments as policyholders.

The *current surplus of government enterprises* is their current operating revenue and subsidies received from other levels of government less their current expenses. No deduction is made for depreciation charges and net interest paid.

Definitions: consumption expenditures, saving, and gross investment

Government consumption expenditures is expenditures by governments (federal or state and local) on services for current consumption. It includes *compensation of general government employees* (including employer contributions to retirement plans, as of the 1999 revision), an allowance for *consumption of general government fixed capital* including purchases of goods and services software (depreciation), and *Intermediate goods and services purchased*. (See general discussion above for explanation.) The estimated value of *own-account investment*—investment goods, including software, produced by government resources and purchased inputs—is subtracted here, and added to *government gross investment*. *Sales to other sectors*—primarily tuition payments for higher education and charges for medical care—are also deducted.

Government social benefits are payments to individuals for which the individuals do not render current services. Examples are Social Security benefits, Medicare, Medicaid, unemployment benefits, and public assistance. Retirement payments to retired government employees from their pension plans are no longer included in this category.

Government social benefits to persons are payments to persons resident in the United States (with a corresponding entry of an equal amount in the personal income accounts). Government social benefits to the rest of the world—not shown separately here—appear only in the federal government account, and are transfers, mainly retirement benefits, to former residents of the United States.

Other current transfer payments (federal account only) include *Grants-in-aid to state and local governments* and military and nonmilitary grants to foreign governments, not shown separately.

Federal grants-in-aid are net payments from federal to state and local governments to help finance programs such as health (Medicaid), public assistance (for example, the old Aid to Families with Dependent Children and the new Temporary Assistance for Needy Families), and education. Investment grants to state and local governments for highways, transit, air transportation, and water treatment plants are now classified as capital transfers and no longer included in this category. However, such investment grants continue to be included as federal government outlays in Table 6-16.

Interest payments is monetary interest paid to U.S. and foreign persons and businesses and to foreign governments on public debt and other financial obligations. As noted above, from 1960 forward for the federal government and 1946 forward for state and local governments, this represents gross total, not net, interest payments. Before those dates in the NIPAs, and throughout the federal budget accounts presented in Table 6-16, net instead of aggregate interest is shown, that is, gross total interest paid less interest received.

Subsidies are monetary grants paid by government to business, including to government enterprises at another level of government. Subsidies no longer include federal maritime construction subsidies, which are now classified as a capital transfer. For years prior to 1959, subsidies will continue to be presented net of the current surplus of government enterprises, because detailed data to separate the series for this period are not available.

Net saving, NIPA (Surplus+/deficit-), is the sum of current receipts less the sum of current expenditures. This is shown separately for *Social insurance funds* (mainly Social Security) and *Other* (all other government). As of the 1999 revisions, net saving—particularly that of state and local governments—is measured as being significantly smaller than before that revision, because the net accumulations of government employee retirement plans are now classified as personal saving rather than in the government sector.

Gross government investment consists of general government and government enterprise expenditures for fixed assets—structures, equipment, and software. The expenditures include the compensation of government employees and the purchase of goods and services as intermediate inputs associated with government production of fixed assets. Government inventory investment is included in government consumption expenditures.

Capital consumption. Consumption of fixed capital (CFC; economic depreciation) is included in government consumption expenditures as a partial measure of the value of the services of general government fixed assets, including structures, equipment, and software.

Definitions: output and net investment

In Tables 6-5 and 6-10, the gross output and value added of government are presented, as described in the general discussion above. *Gross output* of government is the sum of the *intermediate goods and services purchased* by government and the value added by government as a producing industry. *Value added* consists of compensation of general government employees and consumption of general government fixed capital. Because this depreciation allowance is the only entry on the product side of the accounts measuring the output associated with such capital, a zero *net* return on these assets is implicitly assumed.

Gross output minus own-account investment and sales to other sectors (see above) yields *government consumption expenditures*, which represents the contribution of government consumption spending to final demands in the GDP.

The values of *net investment* shown in these tables are calculated by the editor, as gross investment minus the consumption of fixed capital.

Definitions: chain-type quantity indexes

Chain-type quantity indexes represent changes over time in real values, removing the effects of inflation. Indexes for key categories in the government expenditure accounts, as well as for government gross output, value added, and intermediate goods and services purchased, use the chain formula described in the Notes and Definitions to Chapter 1, and are expressed as index numbers with the average for the year 2000 equal to 100.

Data availability

The most recent data are published each month in the *Survey of Current Business*. Current and historical data may be obtained from the BEA Internet site at <http://www.bea.gov> and the STAT-USA subscription Internet site at <http://www.stat-usa.gov>.

References

See the references regarding the 2003 comprehensive revision of the NIPAs in the Notes and Definitions to Chapter 1.

For information on the classification of government expenditures into current consumption and gross investment, first undertaken in the 1996 comprehensive revisions, see the *Survey of Current Business* article "Preview of the Comprehensive Revision of the National Income and Product Accounts: Recognition of Government Investment and Incorporation of a New Methodology for Calculating Depreciation," September 1995. Other sources of information about the NIPAs are listed in the Notes and Definitions for Tables 1-1 through 1-10.

**TABLES 6-12 THROUGH 6-15
STATE GOVERNMENT CURRENT RECEIPTS AND EXPENDITURES; LOCAL GOVERNMENT CURRENT RECEIPTS AND EXPENDITURES; STATE GOVERNMENT CONSUMPTION EXPENDITURES AND GROSS INVESTMENT BY FUNCTION; LOCAL GOVERNMENT CONSUMPTION EXPENDITURES AND GROSS INVESTMENT BY FUNCTION**

SOURCE: BUREAU OF ECONOMIC ANALYSIS

In the standard presentation of the NIPAs, for example, Tables 6-8 through 6-11 above, state and local governments are combined. Annual measures for aggregate state governments and aggregate local governments were published in the June 2003 *Survey of Current Business*. As *Business Statistics* went to press, they had not been revised to reflect the 2003 comprehensive revision of the NIPAs as described in the Notes and Definitions to Chapter 1 and to Tables 6-1 through 6-11 above.

Definitions

The functions as defined in Tables 6-14 and 6-15, which include consumption expenditures and gross investment combined, are roughly similar to the federal government spending concept and functions displayed in Table 6-16. Specifically:

General public service includes executive and legislative functions, tax collection and financial management, and other.

Public order and safety includes police, fire, law courts, and *prisons*.

Economic affairs includes general economic and labor affairs, agriculture, energy, natural resources, *transportation*, and other. *Transportation* includes highways, air transportation, water transportation, transit, and railroads.

Housing and community services includes water, sewerage, sanitation, and other.

Education includes *elementary and secondary* and *higher* education, libraries, and other.

Income security includes disability, *welfare and social services*, and other transfer payments to individuals.

Total consumption expenditures and gross investment includes the groups listed above, *health*, and recreation and culture.

Data availability and references

These data are described and published in "Receipts and Expenditures of State Government and of Local Governments, 1959–2001," *Survey of Current Business*, June 2003.

**TABLE 6-16
FEDERAL GOVERNMENT RECEIPTS AND OUTLAYS BY FISCAL YEAR**

SOURCE: U.S. OFFICE OF MANAGEMENT AND BUDGET

These data on federal government receipts and outlays are on a modified cash basis and are from the *Budget of the United States Government: Historical Tables*. The data are by federal fiscal years: July 1–June 30 through 1976 and October 1–September 30 for 1977 and subsequent years. The period July 1–September 30, 1976, is a separate fiscal period known as the transition quarter (TQ) and is not included in any fiscal year.

There are numerous differences in both timing and definition between these estimates and the NIPA estimates in Tables 6-1 through 6-7. See the Notes and Definitions for those tables, above, for definitional differences that were introduced with the 1999 comprehensive revision.

Definitions

The definitions in these tables are not affected by the 2003 or 1999 changes in the government sectors of the National Income and Product Accounts.

Receipts are composed of taxes or other compulsory payments to the government and gifts. Other types of payments to government are netted against outlays.

Outlays occur when the federal government liquidates an obligation through a cash payment or when interest accrues on public debt issues. Beginning with the data for 1992, outlays include the subsidy cost of direct and guaranteed loans made. Before 1992, the costs and repayments associated with such loans are recorded on a cash basis. As noted above, various types of nontax receipts are netted against cash outlays. These accounts do not distinguish between investment outlays and current consumption, and do not include allowances for depreciation.

The *total surplus (deficit-)* is receipts minus outlays.

On-budget and off-budget. By law, two government programs that are included in the federal receipts and outlays totals are "off-budget"—old age, survivors, and disability insurance (Social Security) and the Postal Service. The former accounts for nearly all of the off-budget activity. The surplus (deficit-) not accounted for by these two programs is the on-budget surplus or deficit.

Sources of financing are the means by which the total deficit is financed or the surplus is distributed. By definition, sources of financing sum to the total deficit or surplus with the sign reversed. The principal source is *borrowing from the public*, shown as a positive number, that is, the increase in the debt held by the public. When there is a budget surplus, as in Fiscal Years 1998 to 2000, debt can be reduced, indicated by a minus sign in this column. *Other financing* includes drawdown (or buildup, shown here with a minus sign) in Treasury cash balances, seigniorage on coins, direct and guaranteed loan account cash transactions, and miscellaneous other transactions.

Outlays by function present outlays according to the major purpose of the spending. Functional classifications cut across departmental and agency lines. Most categories of offsetting receipts are netted against cash outlays in the appropriate function, but there is also a category of *undistributed offsetting receipts* (not shown) that includes proceeds from the sale or lease of assets and payments from federal agencies to federal retirement funds and the Social Security and Medicare trust funds.

In order to provide authoritative comparisons of these budget values with the overall size of the economy, a special calculation of gross domestic product by fiscal year (supplied to the Office of Management and Budget by the Bureau of Economic Analysis) is included in this table.

References

Definitions and budget concepts are discussed in *Budget of the United States: Historical Tables*, available from the Government Printing Office and on the Internet site listed below.

Data availability

The annual data are from the *Budget of the United States Government: Historical Tables* and are available on the Internet site at <http://www.gpo.gov/usbudget>.

Similarly classified data for the latest month, the year-ago month, and the current and year-ago fiscal year to date are published in the *Monthly Treasury Statement* prepared by the Financial Management Service, U.S. Department of the Treasury. For those who need up-to-date budget information, this publication is available on the Financial Management Service Internet site at <http://www.fms.treas.gov>. Because these monthly figures are never revised to agree with the final annual data, they are not published in this volume.

TABLE 6-17
FEDERAL GOVERNMENT DEBT BY FISCAL YEAR

Debt outstanding at the end of each fiscal year is from the *Budget of the United States Government*. Most securities are recorded at sales price plus amortized discount or less amortized premium.

Definitions

Federal government debt held by the public consists of all federal debt held outside the federal government accounts—by individuals, financial institutions including the Federal Reserve Banks, and foreign individuals, businesses, and central banks. It does not include federal debt held by federal government trust funds such as the Social Security trust fund. The level and change of the ratio of this debt to the value of GDP provide proportional measures of the impact of federal borrowing on credit markets.

Gross public debt—total. This is the total debt owed by the U.S. Treasury. It includes a small amount of matured debt. It consists of *debt held by Social Security funds, debt held by other U.S. government accounts, debt held by Federal Reserve Banks,* and *debt held by private investors.*

The "debt subject to statutory limitation," not shown here, corresponds closely to the gross debt in concept and size, but there are some relatively minor definitional differences specified by law. The debt limit can only be changed by an Act of Congress. For information on the debt subject to limit and other debt subjects, see the latest *Budget of the United States Government: Historical Statistics and Analytical Perspectives.*

Debt held by Social Security funds shows the trust fund balances of the Old-Age, Survivors and Disability Insurance funds (OASDI).

Debt held by other U.S. government accounts shows the holdings of all other trust fund accounts including the Medicare trust funds.

Debt held by Federal Reserve System shows the investments of the Federal Reserve System, largely acquired in Federal Reserve System open market operations undertaken to implement monetary policy.

Debt held by private investors is all Treasury debt not held by U.S. government funds or the Federal Reserve System, with a breakdown between *domestic* holdings and *foreign and international* holdings, which include holdings of international institutions.

Notes on the data

Gross federal debt, total debt held by federal government accounts, debt held by the public, and debt held by the Federal Reserve System are found in the budget *Historical Statistics* volume, Table 7.1. "Social Security funds" is calculated by the editor as the sum of the OASI and DI trust fund balances in Table 13.1 of the same volume. "Foreign and international investors" is shown in the budget *Analytical Perspectives* volume in the chapter on "Federal borrowing and debt," and is only available from 1965 to date. In the foreign investors series, some year-to-year comparisons are affected by benchmark and conceptual revisions, which have been made at the end of the years 1979, 1985, 1990, 1995, 1999, 2000, and 2002.

The other column entries have been derived by the editor by subtraction. "Private investors" is debt held by the public minus the holdings of the Federal Reserve. "Other U.S. government accounts" is total holdings by federal government accounts minus Social Security holdings. "Domestic investors" is total private investors minus foreign and international investors.

Data availability

For the end-of-fiscal-year data see *Historical Tables* and *Analytical Perspectives in the Budget of the United States Government,* available on the Internet site at <http://www.gpo.gov/usbudget>.

Recent quarterly data, but measured on a somewhat different basis, are found in the *Treasury Bulletin* in the chapter on "Ownership of Federal Securities (OFS)," tables OFS-1 and OFS-2. The *Bulletin* can be accessed on the Internet at <http://www.fms.treas.gov/bulletin>. Holdings by Social Security funds are also available in the *Bulletin* in the chapter on "Federal Debt," Table FD-3. The Disability Fund is listed separately from the Old-Age and Survivors Fund.

**TABLE 6-19
GOVERNMENT EMPLOYMENT**

SOURCE: U.S. DEPARTMENT OF LABOR, BUREAU OF LABOR STATISTICS (SEE NOTES AND DEFINITIONS TO TABLE 10-5)

Government payroll employment includes federal, state, and local activities such as legislative, executive, and judicial functions, as well as all government-owned and government-operated business enterprises, establishments, and institutions (arsenals, navy yards, hospitals, etc.), and government force account construction. The figures relate to civilian employment only. BLS considers regular full-time teachers (private and governmental) to be employed during the summer vacation period whether or not they are specifically paid in those months.

Employment in federal government establishments reflects employee counts as of the pay period including the 12th of the month. Federal government employment excludes employees of the Central Intelligence Agency and the National Security Agency.

CHAPTER 7: U.S. FOREIGN TRADE AND FINANCE

Section 7a: Foreign Transactions in the National Income and Product Accounts

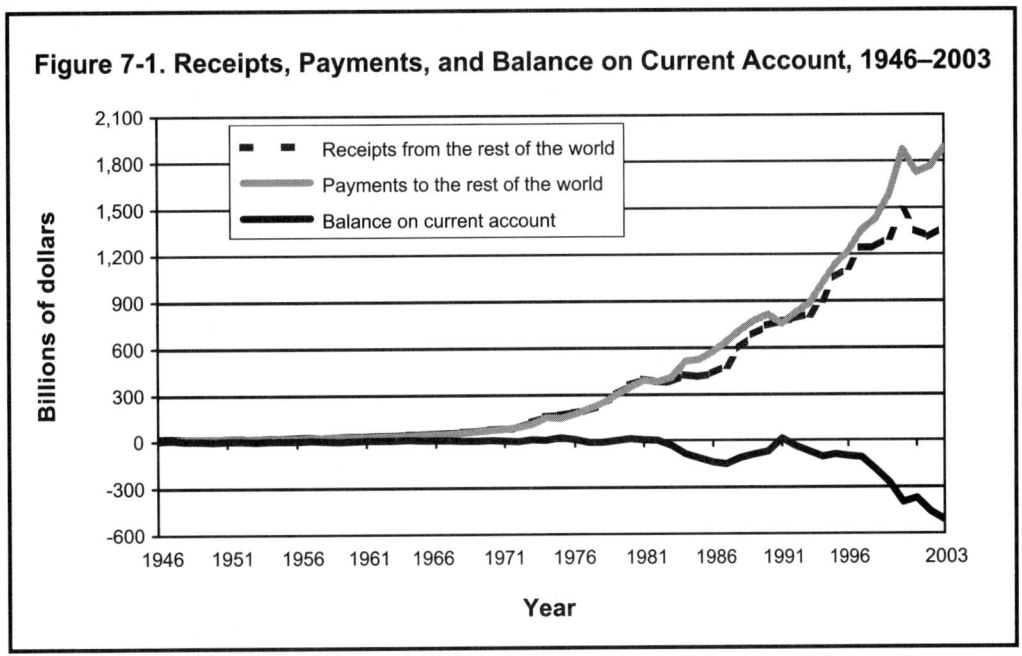

Figure 7-1. Receipts, Payments, and Balance on Current Account, 1946–2003

- For much of the earlier postwar period, U.S. current receipts from the rest of the world (exports and income receipts) and current payments to the rest of the world (imports, income payments, and net tax and transfer payments) were in rough balance. Indeed, in most of those years there was a surplus of receipts over payments—a positive balance on current account—that enabled the United States to invest in the economies of the rest of the world. (Table 7-1)
- Beginning in 1983, however, large current-account deficits emerged, requiring capital inflows from abroad to finance in most years. The only current-account surplus since then occurred in 1991 when payments from other countries financed most of the cost of the Gulf War. (Table 7-1)
- The current-account deficit of $511 billion in 2003 comprised a deficit of $556 billion on goods; a surplus of $58 billion on services; a surplus of $55 billion on income payments; and net payments of $68 billion in taxes and transfer payments. (Table 7-1)
- All the major categories of goods and services in Table 7-5 show long-term growth in quantity of both exports and imports. Between 1967 and 2003, the slowest-growing category—imports of foods and feeds—tripled, and the fastest-growing—imports of capital goods, except automotive—was 120 times greater in real terms. The greatest growth has been in capital goods and in "other private services" (financial, professional, and computer-related). In both of those categories, the quantity of imports has grown even faster than the quantity of exports. (Table 7-5)

Table 7-1. Foreign Transactions in the National Income and Product Accounts

(Billions of dollars, quarterly data are at seasonally adjusted annual rates.)

NIPA Table 4.1

Year and quarter	Current receipts from the rest of the world					Current payments to the rest of the world						Balance on current account, NIPAs	Net lending or net borrowing (-), NIPAs
	Total	Exports of goods and services			Income receipts	Total	Imports of goods and services			Income payments	Current taxes and transfer payments (net)		
		Goods [1]		Services [1]			Goods [1]		Services [1]				
		Durable	Non-durable				Durable	Non-durable					
1946	15.2	5.0	6.7	2.4	1.1	10.3	1.5	3.6	1.9	0.4	2.9	4.9	4.9
1947	20.3	8.5	7.6	2.6	1.6	11.1	1.8	4.2	2.0	0.5	2.6	9.3	9.3
1948	17.6	6.6	6.6	2.3	2.0	15.2	2.4	5.2	2.5	0.6	4.5	2.4	2.4
1949	16.4	6.1	6.1	2.3	1.9	15.6	2.1	4.8	2.4	0.7	5.6	0.9	0.9
1950	14.5	5.1	5.1	2.1	2.2	16.4	3.0	6.1	2.5	0.7	4.0	-1.8	-1.8
1951	19.9	6.6	7.6	2.9	2.8	19.0	3.8	7.4	3.4	0.9	3.5	0.9	0.9
1952	19.3	6.9	6.5	3.0	2.9	18.7	4.1	6.7	4.5	0.9	2.5	0.6	0.6
1953	18.2	6.9	5.5	2.9	2.8	19.4	4.1	6.9	5.0	0.9	2.5	-1.3	-1.3
1954	18.9	7.1	5.8	2.9	3.0	18.6	3.6	6.7	5.1	0.9	2.3	0.2	0.2
1955	21.2	8.2	6.2	3.3	3.5	20.7	4.5	7.1	5.7	1.1	2.5	0.4	0.4
1956	25.2	9.8	7.8	3.7	3.9	22.5	5.2	7.6	6.1	1.1	2.4	2.8	2.8
1957	28.3	10.9	8.6	4.5	4.3	23.5	5.3	8.0	6.7	1.2	2.3	4.8	4.8
1958	24.4	9.0	7.4	4.1	3.9	23.5	5.0	8.0	7.1	1.2	2.3	0.9	0.9
1959	27.0	8.9	7.5	6.3	4.3	28.2	6.6	8.7	7.0	1.5	4.3	-1.2	-1.2
1960	31.9	11.3	9.2	6.6	4.9	28.7	6.4	8.9	7.6	1.8	4.1	3.2	3.2
1961	32.9	11.5	9.4	6.7	5.3	28.6	6.0	9.0	7.6	1.8	4.2	4.3	4.3
1962	35.0	12.0	9.7	7.4	5.9	31.1	6.9	9.9	8.1	1.8	4.3	3.9	3.9
1963	37.6	12.7	10.7	7.7	6.5	32.6	7.4	10.3	8.4	2.1	4.4	5.0	5.0
1964	42.3	14.7	12.0	8.3	7.2	34.7	8.4	11.0	8.7	2.3	4.3	7.5	7.5
1965	45.0	15.8	12.0	9.4	7.9	38.8	10.4	11.8	9.3	2.6	4.7	6.2	6.2
1966	49.0	17.5	13.2	10.2	8.1	45.1	13.3	13.1	10.7	3.0	5.0	3.9	3.9
1967	52.1	18.4	13.7	11.3	8.7	48.6	14.5	13.2	12.2	3.3	5.4	3.6	3.6
1968	58.0	21.0	14.3	12.6	10.1	56.3	18.8	15.1	12.6	4.0	5.7	1.7	1.7
1969	63.7	23.7	14.6	13.7	11.8	61.9	20.8	16.1	13.7	5.7	5.8	1.8	1.8
1970	72.5	27.1	17.4	15.2	12.8	68.5	22.8	18.1	14.9	6.4	6.3	4.0	4.0
1971	77.0	27.5	18.0	17.4	14.0	76.4	26.6	19.9	15.8	6.4	7.6	0.6	0.6
1972	87.1	31.0	20.8	19.0	16.3	90.7	33.3	23.6	17.3	7.7	8.8	-3.6	-3.6
1973	118.8	41.4	32.6	21.3	23.5	109.5	40.8	31.0	19.3	10.9	7.4	9.3	9.3
1974	156.5	56.5	44.5	25.7	29.8	149.8	50.3	54.2	22.9	14.3	8.1	6.6	6.6
1975	166.7	63.8	45.8	29.1	28.0	145.4	45.6	53.4	23.7	15.0	7.6	21.4	21.4
1976	181.9	69.0	48.7	31.7	32.4	173.0	56.8	67.8	26.5	15.5	6.3	8.9	8.9
1977	196.6	72.0	51.6	35.7	37.2	205.6	69.2	83.4	29.8	16.9	6.2	-9.0	-9.0
1978	233.1	85.3	60.1	41.5	46.3	243.6	89.0	88.4	34.8	24.7	6.7	-10.4	-10.4
1979	298.5	108.0	76.0	46.1	68.3	297.0	100.4	112.3	39.9	36.4	8.0	1.4	1.4
1980	359.9	133.3	92.5	55.0	79.1	348.5	111.9	136.6	45.3	44.9	9.8	11.4	11.4
1981	397.3	140.1	99.0	66.1	92.0	390.9	126.0	141.8	49.9	59.1	14.1	6.3	6.3
1982	384.2	124.7	90.3	68.2	101.0	384.4	125.1	125.4	52.6	64.5	16.7	-0.2	0.0
1983	378.9	120.4	86.9	69.7	101.9	410.9	147.3	125.4	56.0	64.8	17.5	-32.1	-31.8
1984	424.2	132.4	93.2	76.7	121.9	511.2	192.4	143.9	68.8	85.6	20.5	-86.9	-86.7
1985	414.5	137.2	85.0	79.8	112.4	525.3	204.2	139.1	73.9	85.9	22.2	-110.8	-110.5
1986	431.9	142.6	83.4	94.5	111.4	571.2	238.8	131.2	83.3	93.6	24.3	-139.2	-138.9
1987	487.1	162.9	94.6	106.4	123.2	637.9	264.2	150.6	94.3	105.3	23.5	-150.8	-150.4
1988	596.2	208.8	117.0	118.3	152.1	708.4	294.8	157.3	102.4	128.5	25.5	-112.2	-111.7
1989	681.0	239.8	129.5	134.0	177.7	769.3	310.4	174.4	106.7	151.5	26.4	-88.3	-88.0
1990	741.5	262.0	134.6	155.7	189.1	811.5	314.7	193.4	122.3	154.3	26.9	-70.1	-76.6
1991	765.7	282.3	141.3	173.3	168.9	752.3	315.7	185.0	123.6	138.5	-10.6	13.5	9.0
1992	788.0	300.6	147.4	187.4	152.7	824.9	346.9	198.1	123.6	123.0	33.4	-36.9	-37.5
1993	812.1	314.0	145.9	195.9	156.2	882.5	386.6	206.2	128.1	124.3	37.3	-70.4	-71.7
1994	907.3	349.7	160.4	210.8	186.4	1 012.5	454.2	222.6	137.7	160.2	37.8	-105.2	-106.9
1995	1 046.1	394.1	189.2	228.9	233.9	1 137.1	511.0	246.5	146.1	198.1	35.4	-91.0	-91.9
1996	1 117.3	421.8	196.6	250.2	248.7	1 217.6	533.6	273.8	157.4	213.7	39.1	-100.3	-101.0
1997	1 242.0	483.0	204.7	267.6	286.7	1 352.2	588.3	297.1	171.5	253.7	41.6	-110.2	-111.3
1998	1 243.1	487.1	193.8	275.1	287.1	1 430.5	636.5	292.5	186.9	265.8	48.8	-187.4	-188.1
1999	1 312.1	503.3	193.9	294.0	320.8	1 585.9	714.7	330.8	206.3	287.0	47.2	-273.9	-278.7
2000	1 478.9	569.2	215.1	311.9	382.7	1 875.6	820.7	422.8	232.3	343.7	56.1	-396.6	-397.4
2001	1 355.2	521.1	210.1	301.6	322.4	1 725.6	754.7	413.2	231.9	278.8	47.0	-370.4	-371.5
2002	1 306.8	486.9	210.1	308.0	301.8	1 764.4	770.1	419.5	240.2	274.7	59.8	-457.7	-458.9
2003	1 375.2	497.1	229.3	319.8	329.0	1 886.1	800.2	481.8	262.3	273.9	67.9	-510.9	-514.0
2001													
1st quarter	1 462.5	570.3	218.7	311.8	361.8	1 873.4	807.0	451.5	235.2	323.0	56.8	-411.0	-412.0
2nd quarter	1 398.3	535.9	213.9	310.7	337.8	1 774.6	758.4	422.8	241.0	293.2	59.2	-376.3	-377.4
3rd quarter	1 309.5	498.6	205.8	299.0	306.0	1 661.9	734.7	400.8	229.8	289.3	7.3	-352.5	-353.7
4th quarter	1 250.8	479.7	202.1	284.8	284.2	1 592.6	718.7	377.7	221.7	209.6	64.8	-341.8	-342.9
2002													
1st quarter	1 263.4	474.9	201.4	298.7	288.5	1 686.4	740.8	376.9	233.6	265.0	70.1	-422.9	-424.1
2nd quarter	1 312.6	493.0	209.7	305.5	304.5	1 766.8	774.1	414.4	235.1	288.6	54.7	-454.2	-455.3
3rd quarter	1 336.4	499.0	214.5	310.0	312.9	1 796.5	783.1	430.3	241.1	287.8	54.2	-460.2	-461.6
4th quarter	1 314.6	480.7	214.8	318.0	301.2	1 808.0	782.4	456.5	251.1	257.5	60.4	-493.4	-494.7
2003													
1st quarter	1 324.6	482.0	226.3	311.4	304.8	1 858.8	777.2	491.5	254.3	268.0	67.7	-534.2	-535.9
2nd quarter	1 327.9	486.2	223.6	308.3	309.8	1 846.4	791.2	471.4	253.1	264.7	66.0	-518.6	-524.8
3rd quarter	1 377.5	496.4	229.6	321.7	329.8	1 881.7	792.3	478.0	266.1	278.2	67.1	-504.3	-507.5
4th quarter	1 471.0	523.7	237.6	337.9	371.8	1 957.6	840.0	486.4	275.6	284.6	71.0	-486.6	-487.8

[1]Exports and imports of certain goods, primarily military equipment purchased and sold by the federal government, are included in services. Beginning with 1986, repairs and alterations of equipment are reclassified from goods to services.

Table 7-2. Chain-Type Quantity Indexes for Exports and Imports of Goods and Services

(Index numbers, 2000 = 100.)

NIPA Table 4.2.3

Year and quarter	Exports of goods and services					Imports of goods and services				
	Total	Goods [1]			Services [1]	Total	Goods [1]			Services [1]
		Total	Durable	Nondurable			Total	Durable	Nondurable	
1967	11.76	10.64	7.47	20.84	14.91	11.42	9.40	5.12	20.74	22.89
1968	12.68	11.48	8.17	22.05	16.05	13.12	11.34	6.52	23.50	23.30
1969	13.29	12.08	8.83	22.26	16.65	13.87	11.96	6.97	24.37	24.77
1970	14.72	13.46	9.66	25.53	18.13	14.46	12.43	7.16	25.70	26.06
1971	14.97	13.41	9.59	25.56	19.53	15.23	13.47	7.89	27.29	25.32
1972	16.10	14.85	10.60	28.42	19.40	16.94	15.31	9.07	30.48	26.39
1973	19.13	18.26	13.20	34.31	20.78	17.73	16.39	9.66	32.87	25.50
1974	20.64	19.71	15.24	33.99	22.40	17.33	15.93	9.70	30.82	25.47
1975	20.51	19.25	14.92	33.09	23.77	15.40	13.92	7.92	28.60	24.37
1976	21.41	20.17	15.13	36.27	24.48	18.41	17.07	9.71	35.09	26.05
1977	21.92	20.43	15.10	37.54	26.06	20.43	19.15	10.98	39.08	27.35
1978	24.23	22.71	16.83	41.57	28.23	22.20	20.87	12.70	40.35	29.30
1979	26.64	25.40	19.16	45.32	29.10	22.57	21.23	12.99	40.82	29.70
1980	29.51	28.42	21.37	50.97	30.92	21.07	19.65	13.09	35.15	29.04
1981	29.87	28.11	20.60	52.30	34.21	21.62	20.06	14.18	34.09	30.71
1982	27.59	25.57	17.91	50.72	33.26	21.35	19.55	14.34	32.10	32.35
1983	26.88	24.84	17.54	48.69	32.71	24.04	22.21	17.28	34.19	34.96
1984	29.07	26.80	19.43	50.61	35.63	29.89	27.58	23.00	38.94	43.72
1985	29.95	27.79	21.00	49.29	36.05	31.83	29.31	25.30	39.41	47.05
1986	32.26	29.22	22.22	51.26	41.33	34.56	32.31	27.64	44.06	47.64
1987	35.74	32.46	25.37	54.32	45.50	36.60	33.81	28.87	46.28	53.21
1988	41.47	38.57	31.48	59.87	49.62	38.04	35.18	30.07	48.05	55.01
1989	46.23	43.17	35.91	64.72	54.72	39.71	36.69	31.42	49.93	57.68
1990	50.39	46.81	39.75	67.46	60.48	41.14	37.77	32.25	51.65	61.43
1991	53.74	50.04	42.70	71.44	64.08	40.91	37.74	32.43	51.07	59.85
1992	57.44	53.79	46.11	76.06	67.59	43.75	41.26	35.82	54.85	58.32
1993	59.29	55.53	48.51	75.51	69.73	47.58	45.42	40.07	58.66	60.03
1994	64.45	60.94	54.38	79.09	74.10	53.26	51.47	46.69	62.93	63.42
1995	70.98	68.07	62.13	84.20	78.79	57.54	56.10	52.04	65.52	65.49
1996	76.93	74.09	69.37	86.81	84.48	62.54	61.34	57.61	69.82	69.09
1997	86.08	84.72	81.90	92.35	89.51	71.04	70.17	67.05	77.20	75.60
1998	88.16	86.61	84.53	92.28	92.08	79.30	78.36	75.77	84.14	84.22
1999	91.97	89.91	88.48	93.77	97.21	88.39	88.08	86.73	90.90	90.04
2000	100.00	100.00	100.00	100.00	100.00	100.00	100.00	100.00	100.00	100.00
2001	94.57	93.87	91.73	99.59	96.30	97.29	96.83	93.76	102.90	99.71
2002	92.34	90.07	86.24	100.32	97.99	100.59	100.41	97.62	105.89	101.57
2003	94.12	92.02	87.97	102.84	99.33	105.05	105.13	101.66	111.93	104.75
1998										
1st quarter	88.24	87.20	85.10	92.90	90.80	76.64	75.71	73.14	81.43	81.56
2nd quarter	87.30	85.14	82.78	91.58	92.80	78.75	77.87	74.97	84.38	83.34
3rd quarter	86.93	85.34	83.29	90.89	90.95	79.75	78.65	75.54	85.66	85.53
4th quarter	90.19	88.78	86.94	93.75	93.76	82.06	81.22	79.41	85.07	86.47
1999										
1st quarter	89.41	86.96	85.44	91.07	95.63	84.17	83.49	81.40	88.01	87.76
2nd quarter	90.42	87.95	86.18	92.72	96.71	87.17	86.79	85.17	90.18	89.16
3rd quarter	92.81	90.85	89.51	94.43	97.79	90.21	90.04	88.70	92.80	91.09
4th quarter	95.24	93.87	92.77	96.84	98.70	92.01	91.99	91.65	92.61	92.14
2000										
1st quarter	96.77	95.86	95.51	96.81	99.06	95.64	95.47	95.68	94.97	96.60
2nd quarter	99.61	99.02	99.58	97.52	101.09	99.37	99.43	99.15	99.94	99.08
3rd quarter	102.16	103.27	103.06	103.81	99.38	102.70	102.76	102.60	103.08	102.40
4th quarter	101.46	101.85	101.85	101.86	100.47	102.29	102.35	102.57	102.01	101.92
2001										
1st quarter	100.08	100.44	100.03	101.52	99.19	101.33	101.46	99.05	106.14	100.62
2nd quarter	96.75	95.84	94.11	100.43	99.02	97.97	96.88	93.79	102.92	103.69
3rd quarter	92.01	90.64	87.91	97.90	95.44	95.35	94.73	91.67	100.77	98.59
4th quarter	89.42	88.57	84.87	98.49	91.56	94.52	94.26	90.51	101.78	95.92
2002										
1st quarter	90.45	88.15	84.05	99.17	96.16	97.34	96.56	93.81	101.99	101.36
2nd quarter	92.84	91.08	87.34	101.12	97.22	100.01	100.06	97.98	104.14	99.86
3rd quarter	93.55	91.73	88.35	100.79	98.05	101.33	101.50	99.18	106.08	100.56
4th quarter	92.54	89.31	85.23	100.21	100.52	103.67	103.52	99.51	111.35	104.50
2003										
1st quarter	92.18	90.18	85.32	103.10	97.15	103.15	103.04	98.94	111.00	103.83
2nd quarter	91.81	90.01	85.95	100.83	96.31	103.79	104.33	100.74	111.36	101.28
3rd quarter	94.30	92.19	87.94	103.52	99.54	104.52	104.33	100.57	111.65	105.54
4th quarter	98.17	95.69	92.69	103.93	104.31	108.73	108.82	106.38	113.72	108.36

[1] Exports and imports of certain goods, primarily military equipment purchased and sold by the federal government, are included in services. Beginning with 1986, repairs and alterations of equipment are reclassified from goods to services.

Table 7-3. Chain-Type Price Indexes for Exports and Imports of Goods and Services

(Index numbers, 2000 = 100.)

NIPA Table 4.2.4

Year and quarter	Exports of goods and services					Imports of goods and services				
	Total	Goods [1]			Services [1]	Total	Goods [1]			Services [1]
		Total	Durable	Nondurable			Total	Durable	Nondurable	
1967	33.73	38.56	43.39	30.65	24.29	23.69	23.75	34.60	15.07	22.86
1968	34.46	39.16	45.14	30.08	25.26	24.05	24.07	35.16	15.22	23.30
1969	35.63	40.37	47.11	30.44	26.31	24.68	24.75	36.28	15.58	23.78
1970	36.99	42.19	49.31	31.74	26.81	26.14	26.43	38.74	16.64	24.62
1971	38.36	43.32	50.45	32.76	28.58	27.74	27.78	41.10	17.29	26.85
1972	40.15	44.47	51.47	33.95	31.47	29.68	29.91	44.72	18.35	28.19
1973	45.43	51.62	55.04	44.13	32.94	34.84	35.26	51.48	22.33	32.61
1974	55.97	65.32	65.09	60.89	36.74	49.85	52.76	63.24	41.59	38.78
1975	61.68	72.60	75.12	64.38	39.21	54.00	57.18	70.19	44.14	41.92
1976	63.71	74.46	80.15	62.46	41.58	55.62	58.71	71.32	45.72	43.82
1977	66.30	77.17	83.82	63.92	43.92	60.52	64.08	76.76	50.50	46.93
1978	70.34	81.62	88.98	67.25	47.10	64.80	68.36	85.45	51.80	51.20
1979	78.81	92.40	99.03	77.99	50.77	75.88	80.61	94.25	65.09	57.82
1980	86.80	101.28	109.60	84.33	57.02	94.51	101.71	104.21	91.95	67.10
1981	93.22	108.43	119.47	87.98	61.97	99.59	107.38	108.33	98.36	70.01
1982	93.65	107.19	122.31	82.79	65.73	96.24	103.04	106.34	92.40	70.06
1983	94.02	106.41	120.58	82.98	68.31	92.63	98.73	103.87	86.72	68.91
1984	94.89	107.33	119.66	85.66	69.06	91.83	98.05	101.97	87.39	67.73
1985	91.98	101.96	114.83	80.17	70.94	88.81	94.19	98.34	83.51	67.65
1986	90.64	98.62	112.74	75.62	73.34	88.87	92.08	105.26	70.44	75.25
1987	92.87	101.17	112.81	80.98	74.94	94.25	98.65	111.52	76.97	76.32
1988	97.69	107.69	116.52	90.85	76.45	98.77	103.35	119.45	77.46	80.11
1989	99.31	109.08	117.32	93.04	78.50	100.94	106.27	120.39	82.61	79.66
1990	99.98	108.03	115.79	92.77	82.54	103.83	108.18	118.90	88.56	85.68
1991	101.31	107.91	116.12	91.94	86.69	103.42	106.70	118.63	85.70	88.88
1992	100.89	106.19	114.51	90.08	88.86	103.55	106.20	117.99	85.41	91.26
1993	100.90	105.59	113.73	89.83	90.07	102.67	104.95	117.56	83.14	91.87
1994	102.03	106.72	112.96	94.28	91.21	103.63	105.76	118.56	83.66	93.46
1995	104.38	109.25	111.44	104.46	93.14	106.41	108.57	119.65	88.98	96.06
1996	102.99	106.41	106.81	105.27	94.95	104.53	105.87	112.87	92.77	98.05
1997	101.23	103.50	103.60	103.05	95.86	100.82	101.47	106.90	91.01	97.69
1998	98.91	100.22	101.24	97.61	95.77	95.35	95.33	102.36	82.22	95.55
1999	98.31	98.87	99.94	96.11	96.97	95.96	95.46	100.41	86.07	98.63
2000	100.00	100.00	100.00	100.00	100.00	100.00	100.00	100.00	100.00	100.00
2001	99.62	99.32	99.80	98.08	100.39	97.50	97.00	98.09	94.98	100.13
2002	99.28	98.66	99.18	97.36	100.77	96.33	95.28	96.12	93.71	101.82
2003	101.40	100.64	99.26	103.63	103.22	99.62	98.07	95.91	101.82	107.78
1998										
1st quarter	99.77	101.49	102.14	99.76	95.68	96.72	97.19	103.95	84.54	94.46
2nd quarter	99.23	100.71	101.59	98.44	95.69	95.66	95.75	102.76	82.66	95.35
3rd quarter	98.46	99.63	100.76	96.73	95.68	94.52	94.34	101.54	80.92	95.50
4th quarter	98.17	99.05	100.45	95.52	96.04	94.51	94.06	101.18	80.77	96.90
1999										
1st quarter	97.96	98.71	100.18	94.96	96.15	94.02	93.48	101.13	79.18	96.88
2nd quarter	98.15	98.63	99.97	95.21	96.97	95.27	94.67	100.42	83.78	98.45
3rd quarter	98.35	98.80	99.68	96.53	97.23	96.63	96.10	100.07	88.49	99.46
4th quarter	98.81	99.33	99.94	97.73	97.53	97.91	97.57	100.02	92.83	99.74
2000										
1st quarter	99.46	99.64	99.85	99.10	99.01	99.32	99.18	100.30	97.05	100.05
2nd quarter	99.99	100.03	99.93	100.32	99.88	99.49	99.47	100.24	98.02	99.55
3rd quarter	100.22	100.12	100.17	99.98	100.49	100.51	100.57	100.03	101.62	100.16
4th quarter	100.33	100.21	100.06	100.59	100.63	100.69	100.77	99.43	103.31	100.23
2001										
1st quarter	100.35	100.17	100.17	100.15	100.78	99.93	99.80	99.30	100.68	100.61
2nd quarter	100.02	99.78	100.06	99.02	100.61	98.42	98.11	98.56	97.23	100.05
3rd quarter	99.51	99.13	99.66	97.76	100.45	97.09	96.47	97.70	94.16	100.34
4th quarter	98.62	98.17	99.31	95.39	99.74	94.56	93.61	96.79	87.86	99.51
2002										
1st quarter	98.34	97.83	99.26	94.44	99.57	94.11	93.13	96.22	87.52	99.22
2nd quarter	99.06	98.36	99.16	96.40	100.75	96.48	95.56	96.26	94.22	101.34
3rd quarter	99.80	99.16	99.21	98.94	101.35	97.30	96.17	96.21	96.05	103.24
4th quarter	99.91	99.29	99.09	99.65	101.41	97.42	96.27	95.80	97.06	103.47
2003										
1st quarter	100.92	100.15	99.25	102.07	102.77	100.06	99.03	95.72	104.76	105.46
2nd quarter	101.16	100.56	99.38	103.10	102.62	98.96	97.33	95.71	100.13	107.60
3rd quarter	101.36	100.41	99.16	103.10	103.63	99.61	97.91	96.01	101.24	108.57
4th quarter	102.15	101.44	99.26	106.27	103.87	99.84	98.01	96.22	101.14	109.50

[1]Exports and imports of certain goods, primarily military equipment purchased and sold by the federal government, are included in services. Beginning with 1986, repairs and alterations of equipment are reclassified from goods to services.

Table 7-4. Exports and Imports of Selected NIPA Types of Product

(Billions of dollars; quarterly data are at seasonally adjusted annual rates.)

NIPA Table 4.2.5

Year and quarter	Exports							Imports						
	Goods					Services		Goods					Services	
	Foods, feeds, and beverages	Industrial supplies and materials	Capital goods, except automotive	Automotive vehicles, engines, and parts	Consumer goods, except automotive	Travel	Other private services (financial, professional, etc.)	Foods, feeds, and beverages	Industrial supplies and materials, except petroleum and products	Petroleum and products	Capital goods, except automotive	Automotive vehicles, engines, and parts	Consumer goods, except automotive	Travel	Other private services (financial, professional, etc.)
1967	5.0	10.0	9.9	2.8	2.1	1.6	0.7	4.6	9.9	2.1	2.5	2.4	4.2	3.2	0.4
1968	4.8	11.0	11.1	3.5	2.3	1.8	0.8	5.3	12.0	2.4	2.8	4.0	5.4	3.0	0.5
1969	4.7	11.7	12.4	3.9	2.6	2.0	0.9	5.2	11.7	2.6	3.4	5.1	6.5	3.4	0.6
1970	5.9	13.8	14.7	3.9	2.8	2.3	1.0	6.1	12.2	2.9	4.0	5.7	7.4	4.0	0.6
1971	6.1	12.6	15.4	4.7	2.9	2.5	1.3	6.4	13.6	3.7	4.3	7.6	8.4	4.4	0.7
1972	7.5	13.9	16.9	5.5	3.6	2.8	1.5	7.3	16.0	4.7	5.9	9.0	11.1	5.0	0.8
1973	15.2	19.7	22.0	7.0	4.8	3.4	1.7	9.1	19.2	8.4	8.3	10.7	12.9	5.5	0.9
1974	18.6	29.9	30.9	8.8	6.4	4.0	3.0	10.6	27.0	26.6	9.8	12.4	14.4	6.0	1.9
1975	19.2	29.3	36.6	10.8	6.6	4.7	3.7	9.6	23.6	27.0	10.2	12.1	13.2	6.4	2.3
1976	19.8	31.6	39.1	12.2	8.0	5.7	4.5	11.5	28.5	34.6	12.3	16.8	17.2	6.9	2.9
1977	19.7	33.2	39.8	13.5	8.9	6.2	4.9	14.0	33.4	45.0	14.0	19.4	21.8	7.5	3.2
1978	25.7	38.4	47.5	15.2	11.4	7.2	6.2	15.8	39.3	42.6	19.3	25.0	29.4	8.5	3.9
1979	30.5	53.3	60.2	17.9	14.0	8.4	7.3	18.0	45.0	60.4	24.6	26.6	31.3	9.4	4.6
1980	36.3	68.0	76.3	17.4	17.8	10.6	8.6	18.6	47.3	79.5	31.6	28.3	34.3	10.4	5.1
1981	38.8	65.7	84.2	19.7	17.7	12.9	13.2	18.6	52.0	78.4	37.1	31.0	38.4	11.5	6.3
1982	32.2	61.8	76.5	17.2	16.1	12.4	16.9	17.5	45.4	62.0	38.4	34.3	39.7	12.4	7.4
1983	32.1	57.1	71.7	18.5	14.9	10.9	17.6	18.8	51.1	55.1	43.7	43.0	47.3	13.2	7.3
1984	32.2	61.9	77.0	22.4	15.1	17.2	18.6	21.9	62.6	58.1	60.4	56.5	61.1	22.9	8.2
1985	24.6	59.4	79.3	24.9	14.6	17.8	19.4	21.8	59.2	51.4	61.3	64.9	66.3	24.6	9.4
1986	23.5	59.0	82.8	25.1	16.7	20.4	28.5	24.4	62.5	34.3	72.0	78.1	79.4	25.9	14.2
1987	25.2	67.4	92.7	27.6	20.3	23.6	29.8	24.8	66.1	42.9	85.1	85.2	88.8	29.3	17.7
1988	33.8	84.2	119.1	33.4	27.0	29.4	31.6	24.9	76.6	39.6	102.2	87.9	96.4	32.1	18.9
1989	36.3	95.3	136.9	35.0	36.0	36.2	37.2	24.9	78.8	50.9	112.4	87.2	103.6	33.4	20.4
1990	35.2	101.8	153.1	36.1	43.6	43.0	40.8	26.4	78.2	62.3	116.3	88.4	104.9	37.4	23.9
1991	35.8	106.1	166.6	39.7	46.7	48.4	48.3	26.2	75.6	51.7	121.0	85.7	107.6	35.3	27.6
1992	40.3	105.0	176.5	46.7	51.3	54.7	50.6	27.6	82.4	51.6	134.6	91.7	122.4	38.6	26.1
1993	40.6	102.8	182.9	51.3	54.6	57.9	53.8	27.9	88.7	51.5	152.9	102.4	133.7	40.7	28.7
1994	42.0	115.7	205.8	57.3	59.9	58.4	61.3	31.0	105.0	51.3	185.0	118.1	145.9	43.8	32.6
1995	50.5	141.3	234.5	61.3	64.3	63.4	65.5	33.2	119.9	56.0	222.2	123.6	159.4	44.9	36.2
1996	55.5	141.0	254.0	64.2	70.1	69.8	73.7	35.7	125.2	72.7	228.5	128.7	171.9	48.1	40.5
1997	51.5	152.6	295.9	73.3	78.0	73.4	84.5	39.7	135.3	71.7	253.4	139.5	194.1	52.1	44.6
1998	46.4	142.8	299.9	72.4	80.3	71.3	92.6	41.2	142.5	50.6	269.4	148.7	217.1	56.5	49.6
1999	46.0	142.4	311.2	75.3	80.9	74.8	105.2	43.6	147.9	67.8	295.7	179.0	242.0	59.0	58.1
2000	47.9	166.6	357.0	80.4	89.4	82.4	109.3	46.0	172.8	120.2	347.0	195.9	282.0	64.7	64.0
2001	49.4	155.3	321.7	75.4	88.3	71.9	116.3	46.6	164.8	103.6	298.0	189.8	284.5	60.2	70.9
2002	49.6	153.5	290.4	78.9	84.4	66.7	124.7	49.7	158.4	103.5	283.3	203.7	308.0	58.0	77.2
2003	55.0	168.3	293.6	80.7	89.9	64.5	134.0	55.8	174.3	133.1	295.8	210.2	334.0	56.6	86.3
1998															
1st quarter	49.9	149.6	302.2	76.7	78.9	71.7	89.0	41.2	141.9	54.0	268.3	144.4	211.0	54.7	46.5
2nd quarter	46.1	143.7	293.0	71.6	80.7	72.7	92.7	41.3	144.7	53.2	269.0	145.7	217.3	56.5	49.3
3rd quarter	42.9	139.1	296.7	67.0	81.2	69.2	93.5	41.0	142.3	49.4	267.0	142.8	219.4	56.8	50.7
4th quarter	46.8	139.0	307.6	74.3	80.4	71.7	95.3	41.4	141.2	45.8	273.5	161.9	220.9	57.9	51.9
1999															
1st quarter	43.8	134.0	302.0	73.2	78.8	72.5	102.4	42.3	138.5	42.1	278.9	170.3	230.1	57.2	56.2
2nd quarter	45.8	138.0	301.2	74.7	79.4	73.4	104.3	43.9	143.2	63.7	291.6	175.2	234.6	58.3	58.5
3rd quarter	47.9	143.3	315.4	75.9	81.0	75.3	106.1	43.7	150.6	79.6	300.8	183.5	246.6	59.2	58.9
4th quarter	46.4	154.3	326.5	77.2	84.4	78.1	107.9	44.5	159.2	85.7	311.5	186.9	257.0	61.1	58.7
2000															
1st quarter	46.4	160.2	329.5	83.5	87.6	81.9	106.3	44.9	164.9	107.8	320.4	197.3	266.7	65.1	61.5
2nd quarter	47.9	163.3	356.4	80.2	88.8	84.1	108.0	45.9	169.9	117.9	346.2	195.4	280.0	64.6	62.6
3rd quarter	49.7	171.6	374.2	79.2	91.6	81.4	110.2	46.8	176.7	127.9	362.2	197.4	287.0	64.3	65.1
4th quarter	47.4	171.5	367.9	78.5	89.5	82.2	112.8	46.4	179.6	127.1	359.3	193.5	294.4	64.8	66.9
2001															
1st quarter	49.7	165.2	364.2	73.5	92.7	82.9	114.1	45.7	186.2	125.3	339.4	189.1	291.7	63.5	68.2
2nd quarter	49.7	157.9	331.8	76.8	91.5	78.5	114.9	45.7	167.6	108.6	299.9	190.4	286.6	66.9	71.4
3rd quarter	49.3	151.5	302.1	76.5	85.1	69.5	116.4	48.0	157.0	97.1	280.0	191.6	282.4	58.4	72.0
4th quarter	49.0	146.6	288.8	74.9	84.0	56.7	119.8	47.1	148.4	83.4	272.8	188.0	277.3	51.9	72.0
2002															
1st quarter	49.1	145.2	285.8	75.0	82.6	64.8	122.4	47.3	148.0	82.3	277.4	193.9	288.2	57.8	75.8
2nd quarter	49.3	154.7	294.1	80.4	84.6	64.7	125.0	49.1	157.4	103.0	285.9	203.5	306.7	57.0	74.8
3rd quarter	50.5	156.7	297.2	81.8	85.3	65.3	124.3	50.4	161.5	106.4	285.1	209.9	315.7	57.3	77.4
4th quarter	49.6	157.3	284.7	78.6	85.0	72.2	127.2	52.0	166.7	122.2	284.9	207.7	321.4	60.1	80.9
2003															
1st quarter	52.7	167.0	283.2	79.8	86.8	63.4	130.4	54.2	171.9	144.2	284.8	206.1	328.7	57.2	84.0
2nd quarter	53.3	165.7	284.1	81.0	88.4	57.4	132.9	55.1	170.8	123.2	292.9	210.7	329.2	51.2	85.0
3rd quarter	55.3	167.4	293.8	79.5	90.8	64.9	134.7	55.6	176.1	130.6	294.8	206.1	330.6	57.6	86.5
4th quarter	58.8	172.9	313.3	82.4	93.7	72.3	137.9	58.5	178.3	134.4	310.8	217.8	347.5	60.4	89.6

Table 7-5. Chain-Type Quantity Indexes for Exports and Imports of Selected NIPA Types of Product

(Index numbers, 2000 = 100.)

NIPA Table 4.2.3

Year and quarter	Exports							Imports							
	Goods					Services		Goods						Services	
	Foods, feeds, and beverages	Industrial supplies and materials	Capital goods, except automotive	Automotive vehicles, engines, and parts	Consumer goods, except automotive	Travel	Other private services (financial, professional, etc.)	Foods, feeds, and beverages	Industrial supplies and materials, except petroleum and products	Petroleum and products	Capital goods, except automotive	Automotive vehicles, engines, and parts	Consumer goods, except automotive	Travel	Other private services (financial, professional, etc.)
1967	26.36	23.08	4.04	17.27	7.81	9.91	2.54	35.29	24.28	20.44	0.77	8.39	5.92	17.14	1.75
1968	25.94	26.26	4.16	21.28	8.49	10.24	2.63	40.04	28.90	23.54	0.88	13.06	7.48	15.53	1.98
1969	25.40	27.46	4.41	23.00	9.09	11.18	2.89	37.94	27.35	26.27	1.03	15.95	8.82	16.85	2.20
1970	30.65	30.75	4.93	22.47	9.64	12.06	3.09	40.53	27.64	28.37	1.07	16.31	9.49	19.44	2.30
1971	29.84	27.80	5.15	25.47	9.67	12.59	3.59	41.84	30.12	32.45	1.06	19.89	9.98	19.42	2.54
1972	35.22	29.61	5.64	28.59	11.30	13.52	4.00	44.54	33.05	39.63	1.36	21.55	12.17	21.01	2.62
1973	45.60	36.43	7.16	33.56	13.78	15.53	4.36	45.67	33.27	56.30	1.68	22.24	12.49	19.82	2.93
1974	40.86	37.49	8.94	37.44	17.14	16.90	7.12	42.25	32.41	54.20	1.79	23.62	11.24	17.79	5.90
1975	43.23	32.79	9.08	39.42	15.80	18.27	8.26	37.37	27.30	53.30	1.70	18.75	8.71	17.16	6.67
1976	49.05	35.42	8.96	41.21	17.82	20.82	9.56	42.54	33.25	64.27	2.06	24.84	11.24	18.25	8.01
1977	49.01	35.71	8.81	41.51	19.27	20.86	9.85	42.11	35.77	77.32	2.20	26.31	13.58	18.81	8.39
1978	60.55	39.47	10.06	42.62	22.25	22.41	11.67	47.28	39.17	73.10	2.84	28.47	16.68	19.43	9.80
1979	64.23	45.20	12.08	42.89	23.39	24.03	13.00	48.53	37.63	73.94	3.47	27.53	16.81	18.95	11.10
1980	72.41	51.30	14.10	36.12	28.35	26.84	13.89	42.24	32.84	59.72	4.09	27.28	16.93	18.93	11.33
1981	73.93	47.84	14.15	35.71	27.18	29.62	19.87	43.95	35.65	52.33	4.82	26.40	18.54	20.02	13.35
1982	69.46	46.40	12.51	29.26	24.46	26.41	23.96	44.80	32.32	45.06	5.24	28.25	19.38	23.74	15.14
1983	66.39	44.14	12.07	30.27	22.37	22.30	23.67	48.62	38.38	44.54	6.34	34.58	23.32	26.89	14.18
1984	64.60	46.40	13.37	35.72	22.26	33.26	24.00	55.08	47.60	47.05	9.48	44.44	29.44	49.15	15.89
1985	55.91	46.67	14.69	38.87	21.60	32.93	23.96	57.46	47.87	44.18	10.68	49.79	32.14	54.25	17.71
1986	57.68	48.75	16.03	38.23	23.89	36.74	34.02	58.82	50.41	54.62	12.12	53.90	35.61	50.43	25.44
1987	61.73	49.97	18.51	41.21	28.11	40.54	34.06	60.29	49.92	57.05	13.84	55.31	36.76	59.80	28.93
1988	67.84	56.33	23.53	48.91	35.91	48.91	35.63	57.90	50.46	63.10	15.96	53.92	37.30	61.45	30.85
1989	70.75	62.58	27.29	50.14	46.21	58.46	41.11	59.22	49.33	68.06	18.07	52.45	39.03	63.32	35.90
1990	73.20	66.23	31.59	50.17	54.13	65.94	43.21	61.49	50.07	68.97	19.48	52.72	38.34	67.65	38.87
1991	74.65	70.80	34.55	53.75	56.05	69.86	49.12	58.71	49.15	65.55	20.94	49.18	38.99	61.26	43.16
1992	84.50	72.10	37.86	62.03	60.35	77.51	50.06	61.98	54.04	67.94	24.26	51.72	43.05	63.07	40.76
1993	83.96	70.20	40.34	67.60	63.43	81.30	52.14	62.70	58.63	74.98	28.29	56.86	46.63	66.16	43.70
1994	83.99	74.12	46.54	74.75	69.35	81.70	58.50	64.13	67.37	79.61	34.76	63.56	50.52	68.51	49.82
1995	93.15	79.87	55.43	78.89	73.51	87.60	61.25	65.71	70.74	78.21	42.80	64.62	54.40	69.05	55.29
1996	91.66	83.60	64.24	81.83	79.08	94.21	67.64	72.26	74.90	84.38	50.29	66.84	58.49	71.76	61.10
1997	91.84	90.83	78.76	92.64	87.29	96.90	76.58	79.60	81.05	88.20	63.05	72.30	66.85	77.95	67.28
1998	90.93	89.84	82.12	91.39	89.90	93.09	83.98	85.42	89.81	93.94	72.46	76.96	75.79	88.11	76.53
1999	94.44	90.89	86.65	94.43	90.91	95.14	96.91	93.39	93.67	94.46	83.19	92.01	85.08	89.82	89.56
2000	100.00	100.00	100.00	100.00	100.00	100.00	100.00	100.00	100.00	100.00	100.00	100.00	100.00	100.00	100.00
2001	102.86	96.10	90.18	93.56	99.19	86.93	106.32	104.61	96.37	103.71	88.60	96.96	101.71	95.27	110.85
2002	100.81	96.39	82.36	97.41	95.21	81.35	114.06	110.15	99.13	101.15	87.16	103.78	111.25	89.20	118.37
2003	102.51	98.86	84.19	98.86	100.90	77.13	121.01	118.67	100.74	107.57	92.36	106.48	120.90	81.07	131.49
1998															
1st quarter	95.42	91.70	81.86	96.87	88.06	94.13	80.48	84.65	87.43	89.02	70.41	74.53	73.21	86.49	71.93
2nd quarter	89.64	89.34	79.88	90.47	90.30	95.21	83.89	84.92	90.27	97.32	71.99	75.34	75.81	88.09	76.19
3rd quarter	84.83	88.45	81.71	84.68	91.00	90.17	84.82	85.78	90.51	97.60	72.62	74.16	76.87	89.17	78.18
4th quarter	93.81	89.86	85.01	93.54	90.22	92.84	86.72	86.34	91.02	91.84	74.83	83.81	77.27	88.70	79.80
1999															
1st quarter	88.63	87.40	83.63	92.13	88.58	93.90	93.61	89.85	89.53	92.72	76.70	87.82	80.49	87.23	86.02
2nd quarter	93.59	89.52	83.67	93.87	89.32	93.57	95.47	92.11	98.95	81.71	90.09	82.53	89.17	88.91
3rd quarter	98.94	90.81	88.15	95.30	91.08	95.23	98.01	94.46	94.56	97.49	85.54	94.24	86.85	90.43	90.97
4th quarter	96.60	95.82	91.13	96.43	94.67	97.87	100.55	95.76	98.47	88.69	88.79	95.87	90.43	92.44	92.32
2000															
1st quarter	96.68	97.48	92.37	104.20	98.02	101.00	97.77	96.52	99.64	94.45	91.58	101.03	94.15	98.43	96.30
2nd quarter	98.49	97.94	100.02	99.87	99.26	102.02	99.11	99.21	99.73	102.82	99.39	99.74	99.26	99.42	98.20
3rd quarter	106.04	102.32	104.66	98.41	102.36	98.24	100.17	102.15	100.99	102.22	104.45	100.62	101.85	99.57	100.91
4th quarter	98.79	102.27	102.96	97.52	100.36	98.75	102.96	102.11	99.64	100.51	104.58	98.62	104.74	102.57	104.60
2001															
1st quarter	103.27	99.28	101.67	91.34	104.03	99.64	103.68	100.47	100.04	113.68	99.31	96.46	103.82	100.35	106.37
2nd quarter	104.27	96.18	92.69	95.16	103.01	94.07	105.18	102.51	95.13	102.52	88.75	97.36	102.37	106.38	111.91
3rd quarter	101.21	94.61	84.91	94.81	95.58	84.26	106.40	108.91	95.50	94.39	83.82	98.11	101.03	92.24	112.62
4th quarter	102.71	94.34	81.44	92.92	94.13	69.76	110.00	106.54	94.82	104.26	82.52	95.91	99.61	82.09	112.52
2002															
1st quarter	103.35	94.26	80.66	92.71	93.22	79.65	112.62	107.11	95.54	102.77	84.77	99.02	103.87	91.99	117.90
2nd quarter	102.73	97.63	83.29	99.41	95.69	78.72	113.96	109.75	98.27	97.92	87.65	103.81	110.86	88.28	113.94
3rd quarter	99.98	96.93	84.38	100.96	96.19	79.55	113.42	111.26	100.48	95.20	87.66	106.87	114.02	86.21	117.94
4th quarter	97.16	96.75	81.10	96.57	95.75	87.49	116.26	112.48	102.23	108.70	88.56	105.43	116.24	90.30	123.71
2003															
1st quarter	102.68	99.16	80.83	97.90	97.67	76.26	118.46	115.41	98.82	106.99	88.70	104.71	119.05	84.66	128.04
2nd quarter	101.27	97.51	81.16	99.35	99.31	69.26	120.29	117.36	99.79	106.27	91.34	106.89	119.16	73.17	129.60
3rd quarter	103.84	98.74	84.44	97.39	101.93	77.39	121.00	118.33	102.28	106.44	91.97	104.52	119.65	82.44	131.31
4th quarter	102.25	100.01	90.33	100.81	104.70	85.60	124.28	123.57	102.47	110.59	97.43	109.79	125.72	83.99	136.99

Section 7b: U.S. International Transactions Accounts

Figure 7-2. Balance on Current Account and Financial Inflows and Outflows, 1960–2003

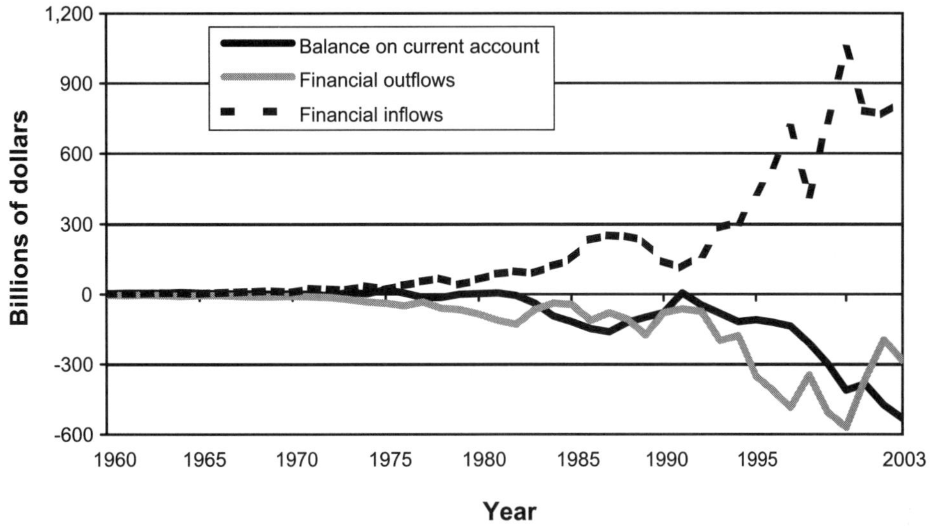

- The U.S. current-account international balance is also recorded in the International Transactions Accounts (ITAs). The definitional differences between this and the balance in the NIPAs are minor (see Notes and Definitions) and the trends in the two measures are similar. The ITAs not only measure the current account surplus or deficit (commonly known as the "balance of payments") but also measure directly the financial flows that are required to finance it. (Table 7-6)
- In Figure 7-2 above, the current-account balance since 1960 is shown, culminating in a $531 billion deficit in 2003. U.S. investment in assets abroad contributes a further outflow, amounting to $283 billion in 2003. Financing the sum of these is a financial inflow, or increase in foreign-owned assets in the United States, of $829 billion. The net of the financial flows does not exactly equal the current-account balance because of a capital transactions item (usually small) and the ITA statistical discrepancy. (Table 7-6)
- Private foreign investment here ("Other foreign assets in the United States") has been declining since 2000. Foreign governments, however, have stepped up their acquisition of U.S. assets ("Foreign official assets in the United States") to prevent a greater decline in the international value of the dollar. (Tables 7-6 and 13-7)
- Before the 1980s, the United States was a net creditor with respect to the rest of the world. That is, the value of U.S.-owned assets abroad exceeded the value of foreign-owned assets in the United States. Since then, the persistent net financial inflows associated with the current-account deficits have cumulated, resulting in a growing net debtor status, with the value of foreign-owned assets in the United States exceeding the value of U.S.-owned assets abroad by about $2 1/2 trillion as of the end of 2003. (Table 7-7)

Table 7-6. U.S. International Transactions

(Millions of dollars, seasonally adjusted.)

Year and quarter	Current account									
	Exports of goods and services and income receipts									
						Income receipts				
							Income receipts on U.S. assets abroad			
	Total	Exports of goods and services	Exports of goods	Exports of services	Total	Total	Direct investment receipts	Other private receipts	U.S. government receipts	Compensation of employees
1960	30 556	25 940	19 650	6 290	4 616	4 616	3 621	646	349	...
1961	31 402	26 403	20 108	6 295	4 999	4 999	3 823	793	383	...
1962	33 340	27 722	20 781	6 941	5 618	5 618	4 241	904	473	...
1963	35 776	29 620	22 272	7 348	6 157	6 157	4 636	1 022	499	...
1964	40 165	33 341	25 501	7 840	6 824	6 824	5 106	1 256	462	...
1965	42 722	35 285	26 461	8 824	7 437	7 437	5 506	1 421	510	...
1966	46 454	38 926	29 310	9 616	7 528	7 528	5 260	1 669	599	...
1967	49 353	41 333	30 666	10 667	8 021	8 021	5 603	1 781	636	...
1968	54 911	45 543	33 626	11 917	9 367	9 367	6 591	2 021	756	...
1969	60 132	49 220	36 414	12 806	10 913	10 913	7 649	2 338	925	...
1970	68 387	56 640	42 469	14 171	11 748	11 748	8 169	2 671	907	...
1971	72 384	59 677	43 319	16 358	12 707	12 707	9 160	2 641	906	...
1972	81 986	67 222	49 381	17 841	14 765	14 765	10 949	2 949	866	...
1973	113 050	91 242	71 410	19 832	21 808	21 808	16 542	4 330	936	...
1974	148 484	120 897	98 306	22 591	27 587	27 587	19 157	7 356	1 074	...
1975	157 936	132 585	107 088	25 497	25 351	25 351	16 595	7 644	1 112	...
1976	172 090	142 716	114 745	27 971	29 375	29 375	18 999	9 043	1 332	...
1977	184 655	152 301	120 816	31 485	32 354	32 354	19 673	11 057	1 625	...
1978	220 516	178 428	142 075	36 353	42 088	42 088	25 458	14 788	1 843	...
1979	287 965	224 131	184 439	39 692	63 834	63 834	38 183	23 356	2 295	...
1980	344 440	271 834	224 250	47 584	72 606	72 606	37 146	32 898	2 562	...
1981	380 928	294 398	237 044	57 354	86 529	86 529	32 549	50 300	3 680	...
1982	366 983	275 236	211 157	64 079	91 747	91 747	29 469	58 160	4 118	...
1983	356 106	266 106	201 799	64 307	90 000	90 000	31 750	53 418	4 832	...
1984	399 913	291 094	219 926	71 168	108 819	108 819	35 325	68 267	5 227	...
1985	387 612	289 070	215 915	73 155	98 542	98 542	35 410	57 633	5 499	...
1986	407 098	310 033	223 344	86 689	97 064	96 156	36 938	52 806	6 413	908
1987	457 053	348 869	250 208	98 661	108 184	107 190	46 288	55 592	5 311	994
1988	567 862	431 149	320 230	110 919	136 713	135 718	58 445	70 571	6 703	995
1989	648 290	487 003	359 916	127 087	161 287	160 270	61 981	92 638	5 651	1 017
1990	706 975	535 233	387 401	147 832	171 742	170 570	65 973	94 072	10 525	1 172
1991	727 557	578 344	414 083	164 261	149 214	147 924	58 718	81 186	8 019	1 290
1992	750 648	616 883	439 631	177 252	133 766	131 970	57 538	67 316	7 115	1 796
1993	778 920	642 863	456 943	185 920	136 057	134 237	67 246	61 865	5 126	1 820
1994	869 775	703 254	502 859	200 395	166 521	164 578	77 344	83 106	4 128	1 943
1995	1 004 631	794 387	575 204	219 183	210 244	208 065	95 260	108 092	4 713	2 179
1996	1 077 731	851 602	612 113	239 489	226 129	223 948	102 505	116 852	4 591	2 181
1997	1 191 441	934 637	678 366	256 271	256 804	254 534	115 323	135 652	3 559	2 270
1998	1 194 803	933 495	670 416	263 079	261 308	258 871	103 963	151 307	3 601	2 437
1999	1 259 665	966 443	683 965	282 478	293 222	290 474	131 626	155 651	3 197	2 748
2000	1 421 429	1 070 980	771 994	298 986	350 449	347 614	151 839	191 929	3 846	2 835
2001	1 293 345	1 006 653	718 712	287 941	286 692	283 761	128 665	151 535	3 561	2 931
2002	1 242 739	975 940	681 833	294 107	266 799	263 861	147 291	113 267	3 303	2 938
2003	1 314 888	1 020 503	713 122	307 381	294 385	291 354	187 522	99 135	4 697	3 031
1998										
1st quarter	302 200	235 788	171 060	64 728	66 412	65 822	27 423	37 545	854	590
2nd quarter	298 801	231 787	165 559	66 228	67 014	66 414	27 396	38 097	921	600
3rd quarter	293 039	228 924	164 054	64 870	64 115	63 499	23 361	39 250	888	616
4th quarter	300 761	236 994	169 743	67 251	63 767	63 136	25 784	36 415	937	631
1999										
1st quarter	300 137	233 131	164 302	68 829	67 006	66 311	29 201	36 199	911	695
2nd quarter	307 252	236 420	166 144	70 276	70 832	70 135	31 630	37 694	811	697
3rd quarter	319 816	244 254	172 989	71 265	75 562	74 888	33 981	40 161	746	674
4th quarter	332 465	252 639	180 530	72 109	79 826	79 144	36 816	41 597	731	682
2000										
1st quarter	341 606	258 481	185 253	73 228	83 125	82 403	37 085	44 252	1 066	722
2nd quarter	355 236	266 611	191 227	75 384	88 625	87 936	38 140	48 657	1 139	689
3rd quarter	360 310	273 591	198 811	74 780	86 719	86 001	36 306	48 850	845	718
4th quarter	364 277	272 296	196 703	75 593	91 981	91 275	40 309	50 170	796	706
2001										
1st quarter	350 473	268 713	193 976	74 737	81 760	80 998	34 109	45 996	893	762
2nd quarter	334 755	259 295	185 030	74 265	75 460	74 742	33 106	40 859	777	718
3rd quarter	311 400	243 935	172 648	71 287	67 465	66 731	30 833	35 048	850	734
4th quarter	296 718	234 710	167 058	67 652	62 008	61 291	30 617	29 632	1 042	717
2002										
1st quarter	299 663	236 208	165 123	71 085	63 455	62 697	33 462	28 422	813	758
2nd quarter	312 230	244 924	172 034	72 890	67 306	66 584	36 561	29 317	706	722
3rd quarter	317 911	248 369	174 371	73 998	69 542	68 812	38 823	29 139	850	730
4th quarter	312 935	246 439	170 305	76 134	66 496	65 768	38 445	26 389	934	728
2003										
1st quarter	315 676	247 999	173 459	74 540	67 677	66 936	40 748	25 345	843	741
2nd quarter	317 367	248 474	174 554	73 920	68 893	68 163	42 704	24 218	1 241	730
3rd quarter	329 508	255 723	178 251	77 472	73 785	73 016	47 229	24 498	1 289	769
4th quarter	352 336	268 306	186 858	81 448	84 030	83 239	56 843	25 074	1 322	791

... = Not available.

Table 7-6. U.S. International Transactions—*Continued*

(Millions of dollars, seasonally adjusted.)

Year and quarter	Current account—*Continued*									
	Imports of goods and services and income payments [1]									
						Income payments				
							Income payments on foreign-owned assets in the U.S.			
	Total	Imports of goods and services	Imports of goods	Imports of services	Total	Total	Direct investment payments	Other private payments	U.S. government payments	Compensation of employees
1960	-23 670	-22 432	-14 758	-7 674	-1 238	-1 238	-394	-511	-332	...
1961	-23 453	-22 208	-14 537	-7 671	-1 245	-1 245	-432	-535	-278	...
1962	-25 676	-24 352	-16 260	-8 092	-1 324	-1 324	-399	-586	-339	...
1963	-26 970	-25 410	-17 048	-8 362	-1 560	-1 560	-459	-701	-401	...
1964	-29 102	-27 319	-18 700	-8 619	-1 783	-1 783	-529	-802	-453	...
1965	-32 708	-30 621	-21 510	-9 111	-2 088	-2 088	-657	-942	-489	...
1966	-38 468	-35 987	-25 493	-10 494	-2 481	-2 481	-711	-1 221	-549	...
1967	-41 476	-38 729	-26 866	-11 863	-2 747	-2 747	-821	-1 328	-598	...
1968	-48 671	-45 293	-32 991	-12 302	-3 378	-3 378	-876	-1 800	-702	...
1969	-53 998	-49 129	-35 807	-13 322	-4 869	-4 869	-848	-3 244	-777	...
1970	-59 901	-54 386	-39 866	-14 520	-5 515	-5 515	-875	-3 617	-1 024	...
1971	-66 414	-60 979	-45 579	-15 400	-5 435	-5 435	-1 164	-2 428	-1 844	...
1972	-79 237	-72 665	-55 797	-16 868	-6 572	-6 572	-1 284	-2 604	-2 684	...
1973	-98 997	-89 342	-70 499	-18 843	-9 655	-9 655	-1 610	-4 209	-3 836	...
1974	-137 274	-125 190	-103 811	-21 379	-12 084	-12 084	-1 331	-6 491	-4 262	...
1975	-132 745	-120 181	-98 185	-21 996	-12 564	-12 564	-2 234	-5 788	-4 542	...
1976	-162 109	-148 798	-124 228	-24 570	-13 311	-13 311	-3 110	-5 681	-4 520	...
1977	-193 764	-179 547	-151 907	-27 640	-14 217	-14 217	-2 834	-5 841	-5 542	...
1978	-229 870	-208 191	-176 002	-32 189	-21 680	-21 680	-4 211	-8 795	-8 674	...
1979	-281 657	-248 696	-212 007	-36 689	-32 961	-32 961	-6 357	-15 481	-11 122	...
1980	-333 774	-291 241	-249 750	-41 491	-42 532	-42 532	-8 635	-21 214	-12 684	...
1981	-364 196	-310 570	-265 067	-45 503	-53 626	-53 626	-6 898	-29 415	-17 313	...
1982	-355 975	-299 391	-247 642	-51 749	-56 583	-56 583	-2 114	-35 187	-19 282	...
1983	-377 488	-323 874	-268 901	-54 973	-53 614	-53 614	-4 120	-30 501	-18 993	...
1984	-473 923	-400 166	-332 418	-67 748	-73 756	-73 756	-8 443	-44 158	-21 155	...
1985	-483 769	-410 950	-338 088	-72 862	-72 819	-72 819	-6 945	-42 745	-23 129	...
1986	-530 142	-448 572	-368 425	-80 147	-81 571	-78 893	-6 856	-47 412	-24 625	-2 678
1987	-594 443	-500 552	-409 765	-90 787	-93 891	-91 553	-7 676	-57 659	-26 218	-2 338
1988	-663 741	-545 715	-447 189	-98 526	-118 026	-116 179	-12 150	-72 314	-31 715	-1 847
1989	-721 607	-580 144	-477 665	-102 479	-141 463	-139 177	-7 045	-93 768	-38 364	-2 286
1990	-759 290	-616 097	-498 438	-117 659	-143 192	-139 728	-3 450	-95 508	-40 770	-3 464
1991	-734 563	-609 479	-491 020	-118 459	-125 084	-121 058	2 266	-82 452	-40 872	-4 026
1992	-765 507	-655 975	-536 528	-119 447	-109 531	-104 779	-2 189	-63 509	-39 081	-4 752
1993	-823 799	-713 058	-589 394	-123 664	-110 741	-105 609	-7 943	-58 290	-39 376	-5 132
1994	-951 008	-801 633	-668 690	-132 943	-149 375	-143 423	-22 150	-77 081	-44 192	-5 952
1995	-1 080 005	-890 652	-749 374	-141 278	-189 353	-183 090	-30 318	-97 149	-55 623	-6 263
1996	-1 159 355	-955 544	-803 113	-152 431	-203 811	-197 511	-33 093	-97 800	-66 618	-6 300
1997	-1 287 010	-1 042 815	-876 470	-166 345	-244 195	-237 529	-42 950	-112 878	-81 701	-6 666
1998	-1 355 917	-1 098 363	-917 103	-181 260	-257 554	-250 560	-38 418	-127 988	-84 154	-6 994
1999	-1 509 732	-1 229 695	-1 029 980	-199 715	-280 037	-272 082	-53 437	-138 120	-80 525	-7 955
2000	-1 779 188	-1 449 324	-1 224 408	-224 916	-329 864	-322 345	-56 910	-180 918	-84 517	-7 519
2001	-1 632 465	-1 369 345	-1 145 900	-223 445	-263 120	-255 034	-12 783	-159 825	-82 426	-8 086
2002	-1 657 301	-1 397 675	-1 164 728	-232 947	-259 626	-251 246	-46 460	-128 672	-76 114	-8 380
2003	-1 778 117	-1 517 011	-1 260 674	-256 337	-261 106	-252 573	-68 657	-111 874	-72 042	-8 533
1998										
1st quarter	-333 905	-270 730	-227 353	-43 377	-63 175	-61 488	-9 117	-31 187	-21 184	-1 687
2nd quarter	-337 651	-272 941	-228 197	-44 744	-64 710	-63 002	-10 189	-31 410	-21 403	-1 708
3rd quarter	-338 641	-273 415	-227 430	-45 985	-65 226	-63 460	-9 088	-33 426	-20 946	-1 766
4th quarter	-345 722	-281 280	-234 123	-47 157	-64 442	-62 609	-10 023	-31 965	-20 621	-1 833
1999										
1st quarter	-351 303	-286 522	-238 715	-47 807	-64 781	-62 827	-10 667	-31 769	-20 391	-1 954
2nd quarter	-366 856	-299 442	-250 093	-49 349	-67 414	-65 430	-13 174	-32 086	-20 170	-1 984
3rd quarter	-388 302	-315 293	-264 363	-50 930	-73 009	-71 005	-15 508	-35 535	-19 962	-2 004
4th quarter	-403 270	-328 438	-276 809	-51 629	-74 832	-72 819	-14 087	-38 730	-20 002	-2 013
2000										
1st quarter	-427 348	-348 079	-293 664	-54 415	-79 269	-77 390	-15 972	-41 012	-20 406	-1 879
2nd quarter	-441 169	-357 057	-301 569	-55 488	-84 112	-82 234	-15 912	-45 059	-21 263	-1 878
3rd quarter	-454 026	-370 466	-312 780	-57 686	-83 560	-81 720	-13 333	-47 045	-21 342	-1 840
4th quarter	-456 650	-373 727	-316 395	-57 332	-82 923	-81 001	-11 693	-47 802	-21 506	-1 922
2001										
1st quarter	-443 079	-366 044	-309 396	-56 648	-77 035	-75 029	-7 556	-46 000	-21 473	-2 006
2nd quarter	-417 608	-348 311	-290 214	-58 097	-69 297	-67 291	-4 089	-41 944	-21 258	-2 006
3rd quarter	-401 578	-333 211	-277 881	-55 330	-68 367	-66 346	-7 084	-39 266	-19 996	-2 021
4th quarter	-370 205	-321 780	-268 409	-53 371	-48 425	-46 370	5 944	-32 615	-19 699	-2 055
2002										
1st quarter	-392 457	-329 967	-273 520	-56 447	-62 490	-60 396	-8 320	-32 467	-19 609	-2 094
2nd quarter	-416 557	-348 297	-291 395	-56 902	-68 260	-66 130	-12 796	-34 047	-19 287	-2 130
3rd quarter	-423 484	-355 285	-296 778	-58 507	-68 199	-66 155	-15 096	-32 190	-18 869	-2 044
4th quarter	-424 804	-364 127	-303 035	-61 092	-60 677	-58 567	-10 250	-29 968	-18 349	-2 110
2003										
1st quarter	-437 067	-373 385	-311 402	-61 983	-63 682	-61 557	-15 415	-28 146	-17 996	-2 125
2nd quarter	-434 873	-371 854	-310 087	-61 767	-63 019	-60 899	-16 362	-26 785	-17 752	-2 120
3rd quarter	-444 497	-377 973	-312 886	-65 087	-66 524	-64 402	-18 589	-27 844	-17 969	-2 122
4th quarter	-461 679	-393 800	-326 299	-67 501	-67 879	-65 713	-18 289	-29 099	-18 325	-2 166

[1] A minus sign indicates imports of goods and services, or payments of incomes.
... = Not available.

Table 7-6. U.S. International Transactions—Continued

(Millions of dollars, seasonally adjusted.)

Year and quarter	Current account—Continued				Capital account transactions, net [2]	Financial account						
	Unilateral current transfers, net [2]					U.S.-owned assets abroad, net [2]					
	Total	U.S. government		Private remittances and other transfers		Total	U.S. official reserve assets, net				
		Grants	Pensions and other transfers				Total	Gold	Special drawing rights	Reserve position in the IMF	Foreign currencies
1960	-4 062	-3 367	-273	-423	...	-4 099	2 145	1 703	0	442	0
1961	-4 127	-3 320	-373	-434	...	-5 538	607	857	0	-135	-115
1962	-4 277	-3 453	-347	-477	...	-4 174	1 535	890	0	626	19
1963	-4 392	-3 479	-339	-575	...	-7 270	378	461	0	29	-112
1964	-4 240	-3 227	-399	-614	...	-9 560	171	125	0	266	-220
1965	-4 583	-3 444	-463	-677	...	-5 716	1 225	1 665	0	-94	-346
1966	-4 955	-3 802	-499	-655	...	-7 321	570	571	0	537	-538
1967	-5 294	-3 844	-571	-879	...	-9 757	53	1 170	0	-94	-1 023
1968	-5 629	-4 256	-537	-836	...	-10 977	-870	1 173	0	-870	-1 173
1969	-5 735	-4 259	-537	-939	...	-11 585	-1 179	-967	0	-1 034	822
1970	-6 156	-4 449	-611	-1 096	...	-8 470	3 348	787	16	389	2 156
1971	-7 402	-5 589	-696	-1 117	...	-11 758	3 066	866	468	1 350	382
1972	-8 544	-6 665	-770	-1 109	...	-13 787	706	547	7	153	-1
1973	-6 913	-4 748	-915	-1 250	...	-22 874	158	0	9	-33	182
1974	-9 249	-7 293	-939	-1 017	...	-34 745	-1 467	0	-172	-1 265	-30
1975	-7 075	-5 101	-1 068	-906	...	-39 703	-849	0	-66	-466	-317
1976	-5 686	-3 519	-1 250	-917	...	-51 269	-2 558	0	-78	-2 212	-268
1977	-5 226	-2 990	-1 378	-859	...	-34 785	-375	-118	-121	-294	158
1978	-5 788	-3 412	-1 532	-844	...	-61 130	732	-65	1 249	4 231	-4 683
1979	-6 593	-4 015	-1 658	-920	...	-64 915	6	-65	3	-189	257
1980	-8 349	-5 486	-1 818	-1 044	...	-85 815	-7 003	0	1 136	-1 667	-6 472
1981	-11 702	-5 145	-2 041	-4 516	...	-113 054	-4 082	*	-730	-2 491	-861
1982	-16 544	-6 087	-2 251	-8 207	199	-127 882	-4 965	0	-1 371	-2 552	-1 041
1983	-17 310	-6 469	-2 207	-8 635	209	-66 373	-1 196	0	-66	-4 434	3 304
1984	-20 335	-8 696	-2 159	-9 479	235	-40 376	-3 131	0	-979	-995	-1 156
1985	-21 998	-11 268	-2 138	-8 593	315	-44 752	-3 858	0	-897	908	-3 869
1986	-24 132	-11 883	-2 372	-9 877	301	-111 723	312	0	-246	1 501	-942
1987	-23 265	-10 309	-2 409	-10 548	365	-79 296	9 149	0	-509	2 070	7 588
1988	-25 274	-10 537	-2 709	-12 028	493	-106 573	-3 912	0	127	1 025	-5 064
1989	-26 169	-10 860	-2 775	-12 534	336	-175 383	-25 293	0	-535	471	-25 229
1990	-26 654	-10 359	-3 224	-13 070	-6 579	-81 234	-2 158	0	-192	731	-2 697
1991	10 752	29 193	-3 775	-14 665	-4 479	-64 388	5 763	0	-177	-367	6 307
1992	-33 133	-16 320	-4 043	-12 770	-557	-74 410	3 901	0	2 316	-2 692	4 277
1993	-37 108	-17 036	-4 104	-15 968	-1 299	-200 552	-1 379	0	-537	-44	-797
1994	-36 799	-14 978	-4 556	-17 265	-1 723	-178 937	5 346	0	-441	494	5 293
1995	-34 104	-11 190	-3 451	-19 463	-927	-352 264	-9 742	0	-808	-2 466	-6 468
1996	-38 583	-15 401	-4 466	-18 716	-654	-413 409	6 668	0	370	-1 280	7 578
1997	-40 410	-12 472	-4 191	-23 747	-1 044	-485 475	-1 010	0	-350	-3 575	2 915
1998	-48 443	-13 270	-4 305	-30 868	-740	-347 829	-6 783	0	-147	-5 119	-1 517
1999	-46 755	-13 774	-4 406	-28 575	-4 843	-503 640	8 747	0	10	5 484	3 253
2000	-55 684	-16 714	-4 705	-34 265	-809	-569 798	-290	0	-722	2 308	-1 876
2001	-46 581	-11 517	-5 798	-29 266	-1 083	-366 768	-4 911	0	-630	-3 600	-681
2002	-59 382	-17 097	-5 125	-37 160	-1 260	-198 014	-3 681	0	-475	-2 632	-574
2003	-67 439	-21 865	-5 341	-40 233	-3 079	-283 414	1 523	0	601	1 494	-572
1998											
1st quarter	-10 869	-2 365	-1 080	-7 424	-191	-72 938	-444	0	-182	-85	-177
2nd quarter	-11 174	-2 209	-1 094	-7 871	-180	-137 128	-1 945	0	73	-1 032	-986
3rd quarter	-11 956	-2 882	-1 055	-8 019	-203	-57 020	-2 025	0	189	-2 078	-136
4th quarter	-14 443	-5 814	-1 075	-7 554	-166	-80 745	-2 369	0	-227	-1 924	-218
1999											
1st quarter	-10 899	-2 574	-1 066	-7 259	-188	-84 290	4 068	0	562	3	3 503
2nd quarter	-11 316	-3 097	-1 074	-7 145	-169	-180 642	1 159	0	-190	1 413	-64
3rd quarter	-11 092	-2 847	-1 085	-7 160	-175	-125 226	1 951	0	-184	2 268	-133
4th quarter	-13 448	-5 256	-1 181	-7 011	-4 311	-113 483	1 569	0	-178	1 800	-53
2000											
1st quarter	-12 129	-2 884	-1 168	-8 077	-194	-214 667	-554	0	-180	-237	-137
2nd quarter	-12 645	-3 173	-1 179	-8 293	-189	-108 046	2 020	0	-180	2 328	-128
3rd quarter	-13 481	-3 637	-1 183	-8 661	-228	-86 485	-346	0	-182	1 300	-1 464
4th quarter	-17 435	-7 020	-1 177	-9 238	-198	-160 602	-1 410	0	-180	-1 083	-147
2001											
1st quarter	-14 083	-2 426	-1 316	-10 341	-269	-211 382	190	0	-189	574	-195
2nd quarter	-14 690	-2 479	-1 291	-10 920	-260	-84 086	-1 343	0	-156	-1 015	-172
3rd quarter	-1 719	-2 867	-1 305	2 453	-297	37 302	-3 559	0	-145	-3 242	-172
4th quarter	-16 087	-3 745	-1 886	-10 456	-257	-108 601	-199	0	-140	83	-142
2002											
1st quarter	-17 411	-6 397	-1 271	-9 743	-281	-34 144	390	0	-109	652	-153
2nd quarter	-13 562	-3 287	-1 279	-8 996	-271	-133 373	-1 843	0	-107	-1 607	-129
3rd quarter	-13 427	-3 075	-1 282	-9 070	-361	21 574	-1 416	0	-132	-1 136	-148
4th quarter	-14 980	-4 338	-1 292	-9 350	-347	-52 069	-812	0	-127	-541	-144
2003											
1st quarter	-16 815	-5 833	-1 320	-9 662	-406	-102 665	83	0	897	-644	-170
2nd quarter	-16 369	-5 832	-1 335	-9 202	-1 552	-110 962	-170	0	-102	86	-154
3rd quarter	-16 639	-5 447	-1 334	-9 858	-821	-8 138	-611	0	-97	-383	-131
4th quarter	-17 617	-4 753	-1 352	-11 512	-300	-61 647	2 221	0	-97	2 435	-117

[2] A minus sign indicates net unilateral transfers to foreigners, net capital or financial outflows, or increases in U.S. official assets.
... = Not available.
* = Less than $500,000 (+/-).

Table 7-6. U.S. International Transactions—Continued

(Millions of dollars, seasonally adjusted.)

Year and quarter	Financial account—Continued								
	U.S.-owned assets abroad, net [3]—Continued								
	U.S. government assets other than official reserve assets, net				U.S. private assets, net				
								U.S. claims	
	Total	U.S. credits and other long-term assets	Repayments on U.S. credits and other long-term assets	U.S. foreign currency holdings and short-term assets	Total	Direct investment	Foreign securities	On unaffiliated foreigners reported by U.S. nonbanking concerns	Reported by U.S. banks, not included elsewhere
1960	-1 100	-1 214	642	-528	-5 144	-2 940	-663	-394	-1 148
1961	-910	-1 928	1 279	-261	-5 235	-2 653	-762	-558	-1 261
1962	-1 085	-2 128	1 288	-245	-4 623	-2 851	-969	-354	-450
1963	-1 662	-2 204	988	-447	-5 986	-3 483	-1 105	157	-1 556
1964	-1 680	-2 382	720	-19	-8 050	-3 760	-677	-1 108	-2 505
1965	-1 605	-2 463	874	-16	-5 336	-5 011	-759	341	93
1966	-1 543	-2 513	1 235	-265	-6 347	-5 418	-720	-442	233
1967	-2 423	-3 638	1 005	209	-7 386	-4 805	-1 308	-779	-495
1968	-2 274	-3 722	1 386	62	-7 833	-5 295	-1 569	-1 203	233
1969	-2 200	-3 489	1 200	89	-8 206	-5 960	-1 549	-126	-570
1970	-1 589	-3 293	1 721	-16	-10 229	-7 590	-1 076	-596	-967
1971	-1 884	-4 181	2 115	182	-12 940	-7 618	-1 113	-1 229	-2 980
1972	-1 568	-3 819	2 086	165	-12 925	-7 747	-618	-1 054	-3 506
1973	-2 644	-4 638	2 596	-602	-20 388	-11 353	-671	-2 383	-5 980
1974	366	-5 001	4 826	541	-33 643	-9 052	-1 854	-3 221	-19 516
1975	-3 474	-5 941	2 475	-9	-35 380	-14 244	-6 247	-1 357	-13 532
1976	-4 214	-6 943	2 596	133	-44 498	-11 949	-8 885	-2 296	-21 368
1977	-3 693	-6 445	2 719	33	-30 717	-11 890	-5 460	-1 940	-11 427
1978	-4 660	-7 470	2 941	-131	-57 202	-16 056	-3 626	-3 853	-33 667
1979	-3 746	-7 697	3 926	25	-61 176	-25 222	-4 726	-5 014	-26 213
1980	-5 162	-9 860	4 456	242	-73 651	-19 222	-3 568	-4 023	-46 838
1981	-5 097	-9 674	4 413	164	-103 875	-9 624	-5 699	-4 377	-84 175
1982	-6 131	-10 063	4 292	-360	-116 786	-4 556	-7 983	6 823	-111 070
1983	-5 006	-9 967	5 012	-51	-60 172	-12 528	-6 762	-10 954	-29 928
1984	-5 489	-9 599	4 490	-379	-31 757	-16 407	-4 756	533	-11 127
1985	-2 821	-7 657	4 719	117	-38 074	-18 927	-7 481	-10 342	-1 323
1986	-2 022	-9 084	6 089	973	-110 014	-23 995	-4 271	-21 773	-59 975
1987	1 006	-6 506	7 625	-113	-89 450	-35 034	-5 251	-7 046	-42 119
1988	2 967	-7 680	10 370	277	-105 628	-22 528	-7 980	-21 193	-53 927
1989	1 233	-5 608	6 725	115	-151 323	-43 447	-22 070	-27 646	-58 160
1990	2 317	-8 410	10 856	-130	-81 393	-37 183	-28 765	-27 824	12 379
1991	2 924	-12 879	16 776	-974	-73 075	-37 889	-45 673	11 097	-610
1992	-1 667	-7 408	5 807	-66	-76 644	-48 266	-49 166	-387	21 175
1993	-351	-6 311	6 270	-310	-198 822	-83 950	-146 253	766	30 615
1994	-390	-5 383	5 088	-95	-183 893	-80 167	-63 190	-36 336	-4 200
1995	-984	-4 859	4 125	-250	-341 538	-98 750	-122 394	-45 286	-75 108
1996	-989	-5 025	3 930	106	-419 088	-91 885	-149 315	-86 333	-91 555
1997	68	-5 417	5 438	47	-484 533	-104 803	-116 852	-121 760	-141 118
1998	-422	-4 678	4 111	145	-340 624	-142 644	-124 204	-38 204	-35 572
1999	2 750	-6 175	9 559	-634	-515 137	-224 934	-116 236	-97 704	-76 263
2000	-941	-5 182	4 265	-24	-568 567	-159 212	-121 908	-138 790	-148 657
2001	-486	-4 431	3 873	72	-361 371	-142 349	-84 644	-8 520	-125 858
2002	345	-5 251	5 701	-105	-194 678	-134 835	15 889	-45 425	-30 307
2003	537	-7 279	7 981	-165	-285 474	-173 799	-72 337	-28 932	-10 406
1998									
1st quarter	-80	-1 192	1 134	-22	-72 414	-41 844	-17 951	-7 822	-4 797
2nd quarter	-483	-1 156	699	-26	-134 700	-44 689	-41 461	-20 363	-28 187
3rd quarter	188	-1 286	1 336	138	-55 183	-20 479	9 283	-15 658	-28 329
4th quarter	-47	-1 044	942	55	-78 329	-35 634	-74 075	5 639	25 741
1999									
1st quarter	118	-1 314	1 554	-122	-88 476	-68 498	4 196	-47 211	23 037
2nd quarter	-392	-2 167	1 887	-112	-181 409	-50 190	-68 182	-27 021	-36 016
3rd quarter	-686	-1 595	1 026	-117	-126 491	-64 062	-38 290	-13 663	-10 476
4th quarter	3 710	-1 099	5 092	-283	-118 762	-42 185	-13 960	-9 809	-52 808
2000									
1st quarter	-127	-1 750	1 329	294	-213 986	-34 934	-31 042	-79 800	-68 210
2nd quarter	-570	-1 371	860	-59	-109 496	-52 029	-36 671	-25 287	4 491
3rd quarter	114	-1 051	1 266	-101	-86 253	-39 618	-30 863	-14 121	-1 651
4th quarter	-358	-1 010	810	-158	-158 834	-32 633	-23 332	-19 582	-83 287
2001									
1st quarter	77	-1 094	1 071	100	-211 649	-35 381	-23 855	-46 769	-105 644
2nd quarter	-783	-1 330	573	-26	-81 960	-26 783	-48 700	-7 507	1 030
3rd quarter	77	-1 011	1 118	-30	40 784	-44 327	13 139	1 824	70 148
4th quarter	143	-996	1 111	28	-108 545	-35 857	-25 228	43 932	-91 392
2002									
1st quarter	133	-853	994	-8	-34 667	-30 668	5 325	-11 863	2 539
2nd quarter	42	-565	566	41	-131 572	-34 244	-5 886	-23 262	-68 180
3rd quarter	-27	-1 375	1 452	-104	23 017	-35 834	21 624	-4 119	41 346
4th quarter	197	-2 458	2 689	-34	-51 454	-34 087	-5 174	-6 181	-6 012
2003									
1st quarter	53	-2 428	2 445	36	-102 801	-40 837	-26 619	-11 207	-24 138
2nd quarter	310	-1 591	1 975	-74	-111 102	-34 049	8 429	-22 480	-63 002
3rd quarter	483	-1 532	2 035	-20	-8 010	-45 206	-28 312	35 845	29 663
4th quarter	-309	-1 728	1 526	-107	-63 559	-53 705	-25 835	-31 090	47 071

[3] A minus sign indicates financial outflows.

Table 7-6. U.S. International Transactions—Continued
(Millions of dollars, seasonally adjusted.)

Year and quarter	Financial account—Continued											
	Foreign-owned assets in the United States, net [4]											
	Foreign official assets in the United States, net								Other foreign assets in the United States, net			
	Total	Total			Other U.S. government liabilities	U.S. liabilities reported by U.S. banks, not included elsewhere	Other foreign official assets	Total	Direct investment	U.S. Treasury securities	U.S. securities other than Treasury securities	U.S. currency
			U.S. government securities										
			Total	U.S. Treasury securities	Other								
1960	2 294	1 473	655	655	...	215	603	...	821	315	-364	282	...
1961	2 705	765	233	233	...	25	508	...	1 939	311	151	324	...
1962	1 911	1 270	1 409	1 410	-1	152	-291	...	641	346	-66	134	...
1963	3 217	1 986	816	803	12	429	742	...	1 231	231	-149	287	...
1964	3 643	1 660	432	434	-2	298	930	...	1 983	322	-146	-85	...
1965	742	134	-141	-134	-7	65	210	...	607	415	-131	-358	...
1966	3 661	-672	-1 527	-1 548	21	113	742	...	4 333	425	-356	906	...
1967	7 379	3 451	2 261	2 222	39	83	1 106	...	3 928	698	-135	1 016	...
1968	9 928	-774	-769	-798	29	-15	10	...	10 703	807	136	4 414	...
1969	12 702	-1 301	-2 343	-2 269	-74	251	792	...	14 002	1 263	-68	3 130	...
1970	6 359	6 908	9 439	9 411	28	-456	-2 075	...	-550	1 464	81	2 189	...
1971	22 970	26 879	26 570	26 578	-8	-510	819	...	-3 909	367	-24	2 289	...
1972	21 461	10 475	8 470	8 213	257	182	1 638	185	10 986	949	-39	4 507	...
1973	18 388	6 026	641	59	582	936	4 126	323	12 362	2 800	-216	4 041	...
1974	35 341	10 546	4 172	3 270	902	301	5 818	254	24 796	4 760	697	378	1 100
1975	17 170	7 027	5 563	4 658	905	1 517	-2 158	2 104	10 143	2 603	2 590	2 503	1 500
1976	38 018	17 693	9 892	9 319	573	4 627	969	2 205	20 326	4 347	2 783	1 284	1 500
1977	53 219	36 816	32 538	30 230	2 308	1 400	773	2 105	16 403	3 728	534	2 437	1 900
1978	67 036	33 678	24 221	23 555	666	2 476	5 551	1 430	33 358	7 897	2 178	2 254	3 000
1979	40 852	-13 665	-21 972	-22 435	463	-40	7 213	1 135	54 516	11 877	4 060	1 351	3 000
1980	62 612	15 497	11 895	9 708	2 187	615	-159	3 145	47 115	16 918	2 645	5 457	4 500
1981	86 232	4 960	6 322	5 019	1 303	-338	-3 670	2 646	81 272	25 195	2 927	6 905	3 200
1982	96 589	3 593	5 085	5 779	-694	605	-1 747	-350	92 997	12 635	7 027	6 085	4 000
1983	88 694	5 845	6 496	6 972	-476	602	545	-1 798	82 849	10 372	8 689	8 164	5 400
1984	117 752	3 140	4 703	4 690	13	739	555	-2 857	114 612	24 468	23 001	12 568	4 100
1985	146 115	-1 119	-1 139	-838	-301	844	645	-1 469	147 233	19 742	20 433	50 962	5 200
1986	230 009	35 648	33 150	34 364	-1 214	2 195	1 187	-884	194 360	35 420	3 809	70 969	4 100
1987	248 634	45 387	44 802	43 238	1 564	-2 326	3 918	-1 007	203 247	58 470	-7 643	42 120	5 400
1988	246 522	39 758	43 050	41 741	1 309	-467	-319	-2 506	206 764	57 735	20 239	26 353	5 800
1989	224 928	8 503	1 532	149	1 383	160	4 976	1 835	216 425	68 274	29 618	38 767	5 900
1990	141 571	33 910	30 243	29 576	667	1 868	3 385	-1 586	107 661	48 494	-2 534	1 592	18 800
1991	110 808	17 389	16 147	14 846	1 301	1 367	-1 484	1 359	93 420	23 171	18 826	35 144	15 400
1992	170 663	40 477	22 403	18 454	3 949	2 191	16 571	-688	130 186	19 823	37 131	30 043	13 400
1993	282 040	71 753	53 014	48 952	4 062	1 313	14 841	2 585	210 287	51 362	24 381	80 092	18 900
1994	305 989	39 583	36 827	30 750	6 077	1 564	3 665	-2 473	266 406	46 121	34 274	56 971	23 400
1995	438 562	109 880	72 712	68 977	3 735	-105	34 008	3 265	328 682	57 776	91 544	77 249	12 300
1996	551 096	126 724	120 679	115 671	5 008	-982	5 704	1 323	424 372	86 502	147 022	103 272	17 362
1997	706 809	19 036	-2 161	-6 690	4 529	-881	22 286	-208	687 773	105 603	130 435	161 409	24 782
1998	423 569	-19 903	-3 589	-9 921	6 332	-3 326	-9 501	-3 487	443 472	179 045	28 581	156 315	16 622
1999	740 210	43 543	32 527	12 177	20 350	-2 863	12 964	915	696 667	289 444	-44 497	298 834	22 407
2000	1 046 896	42 758	35 710	-5 199	40 909	-1 825	5 746	3 127	1 004 138	321 274	-69 983	459 889	5 315
2001	782 859	28 059	54 620	33 700	20 920	-2 309	-29 978	5 726	754 800	167 021	-14 378	393 885	23 783
2002	768 246	113 990	89 016	60 466	28 550	137	21 221	3 616	654 256	72 411	100 432	285 500	21 513
2003	829 173	248 573	194 568	169 685	24 883	-564	49 420	5 149	580 600	39 890	113 432	250 981	16 640
1998													
1st quarter	79 170	11 072	13 946	11 336	2 610	-954	-964	-956	68 098	19 759	-6 535	63 237	746
2nd quarter	155 055	-10 235	-20 051	-20 305	254	-760	9 744	832	165 290	20 391	21 814	56 146	2 349
3rd quarter	75 963	-46 640	-30 917	-32 823	1 906	-281	-12 948	-2 494	122 603	23 490	-5 082	6 628	7 277
4th quarter	113 381	25 900	33 433	31 871	1 562	-1 331	-5 333	-869	87 481	115 405	18 384	30 304	6 250
1999													
1st quarter	109 283	4 381	6 793	800	5 993	-1 244	-1 273	105	104 902	28 759	-13 327	49 157	2 440
2nd quarter	247 860	-757	-916	-6 708	5 792	-1 085	1 761	-517	248 617	140 759	-11 412	70 205	3 057
3rd quarter	156 858	12 625	14 798	12 963	1 835	-767	-1 617	211	144 233	50 758	3 685	86 202	4 697
4th quarter	226 210	27 294	11 852	5 122	6 730	233	14 093	1 116	198 916	69 169	-23 443	93 270	12 213
2000													
1st quarter	248 698	22 542	24 311	16 204	8 107	-430	-2 270	931	226 156	52 094	-15 199	129 306	-2 661
2nd quarter	247 559	6 952	6 738	-3 596	10 334	-899	209	904	240 607	91 669	-22 883	88 189	989
3rd quarter	246 185	11 354	3 673	-10 599	14 272	-185	7 554	312	234 831	79 979	-13 413	122 138	757
4th quarter	304 456	1 910	988	-7 208	8 196	-311	253	980	302 546	97 534	-18 488	120 256	6 230
2001													
1st quarter	332 155	21 333	19 590	16 016	3 574	-601	1 341	1 003	310 822	59 145	-17 659	129 474	2 311
2nd quarter	207 866	-19 965	-9 634	-19 566	9 932	-1 154	-10 205	1 028	227 831	59 338	-11 916	108 537	2 772
3rd quarter	22 936	15 653	14 545	14 761	-216	-205	-675	1 988	7 283	13 783	-7 998	60 748	8 203
4th quarter	219 902	11 038	30 119	22 489	7 630	-349	-20 439	1 707	208 864	34 755	23 195	95 126	10 497
2002													
1st quarter	165 989	12 801	10 337	4 420	5 917	-597	2 335	726	153 188	28 407	10 333	73 782	4 525
2nd quarter	229 135	53 312	25 942	19 374	6 568	365	26 099	906	175 823	2 195	18 837	99 718	7 183
3rd quarter	150 075	17 720	20 001	9 124	10 877	464	-3 590	845	132 355	9 927	54 068	43 931	2 556
4th quarter	223 047	30 157	32 736	27 548	5 188	-95	-3 623	1 139	192 890	31 882	17 194	68 069	7 249
2003													
1st quarter	246 105	48 986	39 845	30 277	9 568	-437	8 325	1 253	197 119	32 523	8 974	56 723	4 927
2nd quarter	218 553	65 245	45 958	42 668	3 290	-16	18 552	751	153 308	-544	53 254	92 407	1 458
3rd quarter	134 202	50 663	27 293	23 953	3 340	-41	22 019	1 392	83 539	-2 810	46 490	18 090	2 768
4th quarter	230 311	83 679	81 472	72 787	8 685	-70	524	1 753	146 632	10 719	4 714	83 761	7 487

[4] A minus sign indicates financial outflows or decrease in foreign official assets in the United States.
... = Not available.

Table 7-6. U.S. International Transactions—Continued

(Millions of dollars, seasonally adjusted.)

Year and quarter	Financial account—Continued		Statistical discrepancy [5]		Balance on						
	Foreign-owned assets in the United States, net [4]—Cont.										
	Other foreign assets in the United States, net—Cont.										
	U.S. liabilities		Total	Seasonal adjustment discrepancy	Goods	Services	Goods and services	Income	Goods, services, and income	Unilateral current transfers	Current account
	To unaffiliated foreigners reported by U.S. nonbanking concerns	Reported by U.S. banks not included elsewhere									
1960	-90	678	-1 019	0	4 892	-1 385	3 508	3 379	6 887	-4 062	2 824
1961	226	928	-989	0	5 571	-1 376	4 195	3 755	7 950	-4 127	3 822
1962	-110	336	-1 124	0	4 521	-1 151	3 370	4 294	7 664	-4 277	3 387
1963	-37	898	-360	0	5 224	-1 014	4 210	4 596	8 806	-4 392	4 414
1964	75	1 818	-907	0	6 801	-779	6 022	5 041	11 063	-4 240	6 823
1965	178	503	-457	0	4 951	-287	4 664	5 350	10 014	-4 583	5 431
1966	476	2 882	629	0	3 817	-877	2 940	5 047	7 987	-4 955	3 031
1967	584	1 765	-205	0	3 800	-1 196	2 604	5 274	7 878	-5 294	2 583
1968	1 475	3 871	438	0	635	-385	250	5 990	6 240	-5 629	611
1969	792	8 886	-1 516	0	607	-516	91	6 044	6 135	-5 735	399
1970	2 014	-6 298	-219	0	2 603	-349	2 254	6 233	8 487	-6 156	2 331
1971	369	-6 911	-9 779	0	-2 260	957	-1 303	7 272	5 969	-7 402	-1 433
1972	815	4 754	-1 879	0	-6 416	973	-5 443	8 192	2 749	-8 544	-5 795
1973	1 035	4 702	-2 654	0	911	989	1 900	12 153	14 053	-6 913	7 140
1974	1 844	16 017	-2 558	0	-5 505	1 213	-4 292	15 503	11 211	-9 249	1 962
1975	319	628	4 417	0	8 903	3 501	12 404	12 787	25 191	-7 075	18 116
1976	-578	10 990	8 955	0	-9 483	3 401	-6 082	16 063	9 981	-5 686	4 295
1977	1 086	6 719	-4 099	0	-31 091	3 845	-27 246	18 137	-9 109	-5 226	-14 335
1978	1 889	16 141	9 236	0	-33 927	4 164	-29 763	20 408	-9 355	-5 788	-15 143
1979	1 621	32 607	24 349	0	-27 568	3 003	-24 565	30 873	6 308	-6 593	-285
1980	6 852	10 743	20 886	0	-25 500	6 093	-19 407	30 073	10 666	-8 349	2 317
1981	917	42 128	21 792	0	-28 023	11 852	-16 172	32 903	16 731	-11 702	5 030
1982	-2 383	65 633	36 630	0	-36 485	12 329	-24 156	35 164	11 008	-16 544	-5 536
1983	-118	50 342	16 162	0	-67 102	9 335	-57 767	36 386	-21 381	-17 310	-38 691
1984	16 626	33 849	16 733	0	-112 492	3 419	-109 073	35 063	-74 010	-20 335	-94 344
1985	9 851	41 045	16 478	0	-122 173	294	-121 880	25 723	-96 157	-21 998	-118 155
1986	3 325	76 737	28 590	0	-145 081	6 543	-138 538	15 494	-123 044	-24 132	-147 177
1987	18 363	86 537	-9 048	0	-159 557	7 874	-151 684	14 293	-137 391	-23 265	-160 655
1988	32 893	63 744	-19 289	0	-126 959	12 393	-114 566	18 687	-95 879	-25 274	-121 153
1989	22 086	51 780	49 605	0	-117 749	24 607	-93 142	19 824	-73 318	-26 169	-99 486
1990	45 133	-3 824	25 211	0	-111 037	30 173	-80 864	28 550	-52 314	-26 654	-78 968
1991	-3 115	3 994	-45 688	0	-76 937	45 802	-31 135	24 130	-7 005	10 752	3 747
1992	13 573	16 216	-47 705	0	-96 897	57 804	-39 093	24 234	-14 859	-33 133	-47 991
1993	10 489	25 063	1 797	0	-132 451	62 256	-70 195	25 316	-44 879	-37 108	-81 987
1994	1 302	104 338	-7 297	0	-165 831	67 452	-98 379	17 146	-81 233	-36 799	-118 032
1995	59 637	30 176	24 107	0	-174 170	77 905	-96 265	20 891	-75 374	-34 104	-109 478
1996	53 736	16 478	-16 826	0	-191 000	87 058	-103 942	22 318	-81 624	-38 583	-120 207
1997	116 518	149 026	-84 311	0	-198 104	89 926	-108 178	12 609	-95 569	-40 410	-135 979
1998	23 140	39 769	134 557	0	-246 687	81 819	-164 868	3 754	-161 114	-48 443	-209 557
1999	76 247	54 232	65 095	0	-346 015	82 763	-263 252	13 185	-250 067	-46 755	-296 822
2000	170 672	116 971	-62 846	0	-452 414	74 070	-378 344	20 585	-357 759	-55 684	-413 443
2001	66 110	118 379	-29 307	0	-427 188	64 496	-362 692	23 572	-339 120	-46 581	-385 701
2002	77 990	96 410	-95 028	0	-482 895	61 160	-421 735	7 173	-414 562	-59 382	-473 944
2003	84 014	75 643	-12 012	0	-547 552	51 044	-496 508	33 279	-463 229	-67 439	-530 668
1998											
1st quarter	39 833	-48 942	36 533	7 013	-56 293	21 351	-34 942	3 237	-31 705	-10 869	-42 574
2nd quarter	30 722	33 868	32 277	-1 949	-62 638	21 484	-41 154	2 304	-38 850	-11 174	-50 024
3rd quarter	14 976	75 314	38 818	-11 754	-63 376	18 885	-44 491	-1 111	-45 602	-11 956	-57 558
4th quarter	-62 391	-20 471	26 934	6 695	-64 380	20 094	-44 286	-675	-44 961	-14 443	-59 404
1999											
1st quarter	51 307	-13 434	37 260	4 723	-74 413	21 022	-53 391	2 225	-51 166	-10 899	-62 065
2nd quarter	16 928	29 080	3 871	696	-83 949	20 927	-63 022	3 418	-59 604	-11 316	-70 920
3rd quarter	-8 777	7 668	48 121	-11 542	-91 374	20 335	-71 039	2 553	-68 486	-11 092	-79 578
4th quarter	16 789	30 918	-24 163	6 117	-96 279	20 480	-75 799	4 994	-70 805	-13 448	-84 253
2000											
1st quarter	72 433	-9 817	64 034	7 226	-108 411	18 813	-89 598	3 856	-85 742	-12 129	-97 871
2nd quarter	28 796	53 847	-40 746	-1 200	-110 342	19 896	-90 446	4 513	-85 933	-12 645	-98 578
3rd quarter	16 914	28 456	-52 275	-10 250	-113 969	17 094	-96 875	3 159	-93 716	-13 481	-107 197
4th quarter	52 529	44 485	-33 848	4 235	-119 692	18 261	-101 431	9 058	-92 373	-17 435	-109 808
2001											
1st quarter	112 097	25 454	-13 815	6 712	-115 420	18 089	-97 331	4 725	-92 606	-14 083	-106 689
2nd quarter	-173	69 273	-25 977	-2 634	-105 184	16 168	-89 016	6 163	-82 853	-14 690	-97 543
3rd quarter	-23 171	-44 282	31 956	-9 618	-105 233	15 957	-89 276	-902	-90 178	-1 719	-91 897
4th quarter	-22 643	67 934	-21 470	5 541	-101 351	14 281	-87 070	13 583	-73 487	-16 087	-89 574
2002											
1st quarter	45 704	-9 563	-21 359	10 292	-108 397	14 638	-93 759	965	-92 794	-17 411	-110 205
2nd quarter	20 607	27 283	22 398	-1 206	-119 361	15 988	-103 373	-954	-104 327	-13 562	-117 889
3rd quarter	-242	22 115	-52 288	-14 052	-122 407	15 491	-106 916	1 343	-105 573	-13 427	-119 000
4th quarter	11 921	56 575	-43 782	4 963	-132 730	15 042	-117 688	5 819	-111 869	-14 980	-126 849
2003											
1st quarter	69 410	24 562	-4 828	11 091	-137 943	12 557	-125 386	3 995	-121 391	-16 815	-138 206
2nd quarter	-2 257	8 990	27 836	-3 121	-135 533	12 153	-123 380	5 874	-117 506	-16 369	-133 875
3rd quarter	12 721	6 280	6 385	-13 418	-134 635	12 385	-122 250	7 261	-114 989	-16 639	-131 628
4th quarter	4 140	35 811	-41 404	5 449	-139 441	13 947	-125 494	16 151	-109 343	-17 617	-126 960

[4] A minus sign indicates financial outflows or decrease in foreign official assets in the United States.
[5] Sum of credits and debits with the sign reversed.

Table 7-7. International Investment Position of the United States at Year-End

(Millions of dollars.)

Year	U.S. net international investment position		U.S.-owned assets abroad									
	Direct investment at current cost	Direct investment at market value	Total, direct investment at current cost	Total, direct investment at market value	Official reserve assets	Other U.S. government assets	Direct investment		Foreign bonds	Foreign corporate stocks	U.S. nonbank claims	U.S. bank claims
							Current cost	Market value				
1976	164 832	...	456 964	...	44 094	44 978	222 283	...	34 704	9 453	20 317	81 135
1977	171 440	...	512 278	...	53 376	48 567	246 078	...	39 329	10 110	22 256	92 562
1978	206 423	...	621 227	...	69 450	53 187	285 005	...	42 148	11 236	29 385	130 816
1979	316 926	...	786 701	...	143 260	58 851	336 301	...	41 966	14 803	34 491	157 029
1980	360 838	...	929 806	...	171 412	65 573	388 072	...	43 524	18 930	38 429	203 866
1981	339 767	...	1 001 667	...	124 568	70 893	407 804	...	45 675	16 467	42 752	293 508
1982	328 954	235 947	1 108 436	961 015	143 445	76 903	374 059	226 638	56 604	17 442	35 405	404 578
1983	298 304	257 393	1 210 974	1 129 673	123 110	81 664	355 643	274 342	58 569	26 154	131 329	434 505
1984	160 695	134 088	1 204 900	1 127 132	105 040	86 945	348 342	270 574	62 810	25 994	130 138	445 631
1985	54 343	96 886	1 287 396	1 302 712	117 930	89 792	371 036	386 352	75 020	44 383	141 872	447 363
1986	-36 209	100 782	1 469 396	1 594 652	139 875	91 850	404 818	530 074	85 724	72 399	167 392	507 338
1987	-80 007	50 529	1 646 527	1 758 711	162 370	90 681	478 062	590 246	93 889	94 700	177 368	549 457
1988	-178 470	10 466	1 829 665	2 008 365	144 179	87 892	513 761	692 461	104 187	128 662	197 757	653 227
1989	-259 506	-46 987	2 070 868	2 350 235	168 714	86 643	553 093	832 460	116 949	197 345	234 307	713 817
1990	-245 347	-164 495	2 178 978	2 294 085	174 664	84 344	616 655	731 762	144 717	197 596	265 315	695 687
1991	-309 259	-260 819	2 286 456	2 470 629	159 223	81 422	643 364	827 537	176 774	278 976	256 295	690 402
1992	-431 198	-452 305	2 331 696	2 466 496	147 435	83 022	663 830	798 630	200 817	314 266	254 303	668 023
1993	-306 956	-144 268	2 753 648	3 091 421	164 945	83 382	723 526	1 061 299	309 666	543 862	242 022	686 245
1994	-323 397	-135 251	2 987 118	3 315 135	163 394	83 908	786 565	1 114 582	310 391	626 762	322 980	693 118
1995	-458 462	-305 836	3 486 272	3 964 558	176 061	85 064	885 506	1 363 792	413 310	790 615	367 567	768 149
1996	-495 055	-360 024	4 032 307	4 650 837	160 739	86 123	989 810	1 608 340	481 411	1 006 135	450 578	857 511
1997	-820 682	-822 732	4 567 906	5 379 128	134 836	86 198	1 068 063	1 879 285	543 396	1 207 787	545 524	982 102
1998	-899 966	-1 075 377	5 090 938	6 174 518	146 006	86 768	1 196 021	2 279 601	578 012	1 474 983	588 322	1 020 826
1999	-775 488	-1 046 688	5 965 143	7 390 427	136 418	84 227	1 414 355	2 839 639	521 625	2 003 716	704 517	1 100 285
2000	-1 388 745	-1 588 556	6 231 236	7 393 643	128 400	85 168	1 531 607	2 694 014	532 511	1 852 842	836 559	1 264 149
2001	-1 889 680	-2 308 161	6 270 408	6 898 707	129 961	85 654	1 686 635	2 314 934	502 061	1 612 673	839 303	1 414 121
2002	-2 233 018	-2 553 407	6 413 535	6 613 320	158 602	85 309	1 839 995	2 039 780	501 762	1 345 117	908 024	1 574 726
2003	-2 430 682	-2 650 990	7 202 692	7 863 968	183 577	84 772	2 069 013	2 730 289	502 130	1 972 244	614 672	1 776 284

Year	Foreign-owned assets in the United States										
	Total, direct investment at current cost	Total, direct investment at market value	Foreign official assets	Direct investment in the United States		U.S. Treasury securities	U.S. currency	Corporate and other bonds	Corporate stocks	U.S. nonbank liabilities	U.S. bank liabilities
				Current cost	Market value						
1976	292 132	...	104 445	47 528	...	7 028	11 792	11 964	42 949	12 961	53 465
1977	340 838	...	140 867	55 413	...	7 562	13 656	11 456	39 779	11 921	60 184
1978	414 804	...	173 057	68 976	...	8 910	16 569	11 457	42 097	16 019	77 719
1979	469 775	...	159 852	88 579	...	14 210	19 552	10 269	48 318	18 669	110 326
1980	568 968	...	176 062	127 105	...	16 113	24 079	9 545	64 569	30 426	121 069
1981	661 900	...	180 425	164 623	...	18 505	27 295	10 694	64 391	30 606	165 361
1982	779 482	725 068	189 109	184 842	130 428	25 758	31 265	16 709	76 279	27 532	227 988
1983	912 670	872 280	194 468	193 708	153 318	33 846	36 776	17 454	96 357	61 731	278 330
1984	1 044 205	993 044	199 678	223 538	172 377	62 121	40 797	32 421	96 056	77 415	312 179
1985	1 233 053	1 205 826	202 482	247 223	219 996	87 954	46 036	82 290	125 578	86 993	354 497
1986	1 505 605	1 493 870	241 226	284 701	272 966	96 078	50 122	140 863	168 940	90 703	432 972
1987	1 726 534	1 708 182	283 058	334 552	316 200	82 588	55 584	166 089	175 643	110 187	518 833
1988	2 008 135	1 997 899	322 036	401 766	391 530	100 877	61 261	191 314	200 978	144 548	585 355
1989	2 330 374	2 397 222	341 746	467 886	534 734	166 541	67 118	231 673	251 191	167 093	637 126
1990	2 424 325	2 458 580	373 293	505 346	539 601	152 452	85 933	238 903	221 741	213 406	633 251
1991	2 595 715	2 731 448	398 538	533 404	669 137	170 295	101 317	274 136	271 872	208 908	637 245
1992	2 762 894	2 918 801	437 263	540 270	696 177	197 739	114 804	299 287	300 160	220 666	652 705
1993	3 060 604	3 235 689	509 422	593 313	768 398	221 501	133 734	355 822	340 627	229 038	677 147
1994	3 310 515	3 450 386	535 227	617 982	757 853	235 684	157 185	368 077	371 618	239 817	784 925
1995	3 944 734	4 270 394	682 873	680 066	1 005 726	326 995	169 484	459 080	510 769	300 424	815 043
1996	4 527 362	5 010 861	820 823	745 619	1 229 118	433 903	186 846	539 308	625 805	346 810	828 248
1997	5 388 588	6 201 860	873 716	824 136	1 637 408	538 137	211 628	618 837	893 888	459 407	968 839
1998	5 990 904	7 249 895	896 174	920 044	2 179 035	543 323	228 250	724 619	1 178 824	485 675	1 013 995
1999	6 740 631	8 437 115	951 088	1 101 709	2 798 193	440 685	250 657	825 175	1 526 116	578 046	1 067 155
2000	7 619 981	8 982 199	1 030 708	1 421 017	2 783 235	381 630	255 972	1 068 566	1 554 448	738 904	1 168 736
2001	8 160 088	9 206 868	1 082 296	1 513 514	2 560 294	358 483	279 755	1 343 071	1 478 301	798 314	1 306 354
2002	8 646 553	9 166 727	1 212 723	1 505 171	2 025 345	457 670	301 268	1 600 414	1 186 233	864 632	1 518 442
2003	9 633 374	10 514 958	1 474 161	1 553 955	2 435 539	542 542	317 908	1 852 971	1 538 079	466 543	1 887 215

... = Not available.

Section 7c: Exports and Imports

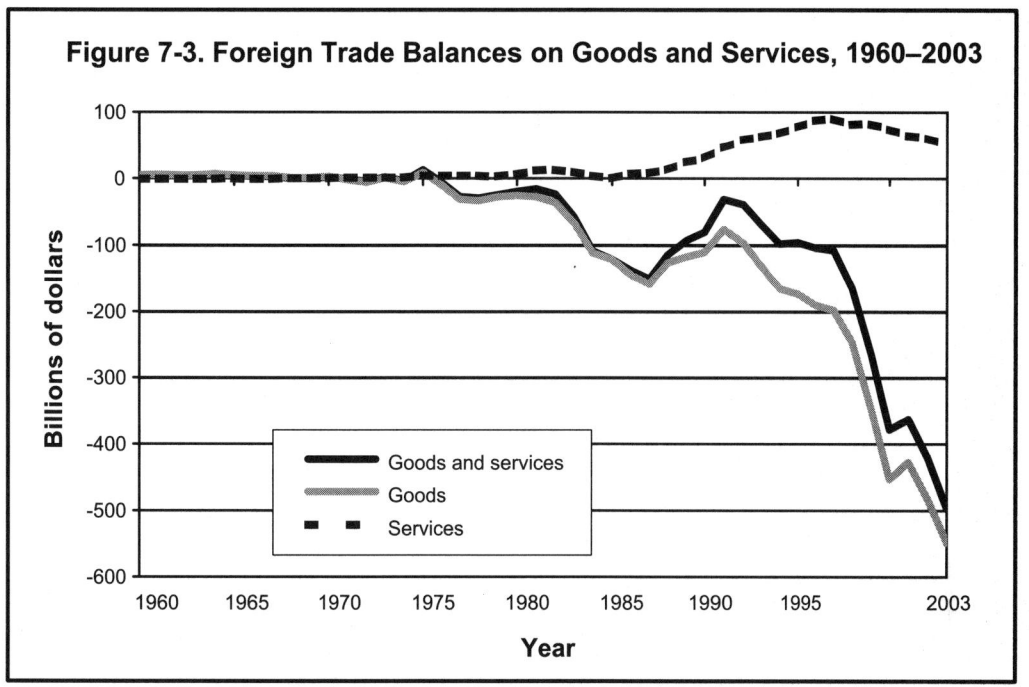

Figure 7-3. Foreign Trade Balances on Goods and Services, 1960–2003

- U.S. imports of goods and services exceeded exports by nearly $500 billion in 2003 for yet another new record. Both exports and imports increased, but exports by more than imports—not only absolutely (in dollars) but also in terms of percentage rise. (Table 7-8)
- The trade deficit in goods likewise set a new record. Less than a 10th of it was offset by the surplus in services trade, which has shrunk from $90 billion in 1997 to $51 billion in 2003. (Table 7-8)
- Canada and Mexico are principal trading partners of the United States, with relations governed by the North American Free Trade Agreement (NAFTA). Goods exports to and imports from these two countries in 2003 were double those figures for the Euro area. U.S. goods imports from those two countries about equaled the sum of imports from Japan, China, and the newly industrialized countries (NICS) of Asia, while exports to the NAFTA countries were about double the total to Japan, China, and the Asian NICS. (Tables 7-12 and 7-13)
- For U.S. services trade, "other private services" is the largest single category. This includes such activities as education, financial services, and many types of business and professional services. The United States had a surplus of $48 billion on "other private services" in 2003, about the same as in 2001 and 2002. This category accounted for 94 percent of the total surplus in services in 2003. (Tables 7-14, 7-15, and 7-8)

Table 7-8. U.S. Exports and Imports of Goods and Services

(Balance of payments basis; millions of dollars, seasonally adjusted.)

Year and month	Goods and services			Goods			Services		
	Exports	Imports	Balance	Exports	Imports	Balance	Exports	Imports	Balance
1960	25 940	22 432	3 508	19 650	14 758	4 892	6 290	7 674	-1 384
1961	26 403	22 208	4 195	20 108	14 537	5 571	6 295	7 671	-1 376
1962	27 722	24 352	3 370	20 781	16 260	4 521	6 941	8 092	-1 151
1963	29 620	25 410	4 210	22 272	17 048	5 224	7 348	8 362	-1 014
1964	33 341	27 319	6 022	25 501	18 700	6 801	7 840	8 619	-779
1965	35 285	30 621	4 664	26 461	21 510	4 951	8 824	9 111	-287
1966	38 926	35 987	2 939	29 310	25 493	3 817	9 616	10 494	-878
1967	41 333	38 729	2 604	30 666	26 866	3 800	10 667	11 863	-1 196
1968	45 543	45 293	250	33 626	32 991	635	11 917	12 302	-385
1969	49 220	49 129	91	36 414	35 807	607	12 806	13 322	-516
1970	56 640	54 386	2 254	42 469	39 866	2 603	14 171	14 520	-349
1971	59 677	60 979	-1 302	43 319	45 579	-2 260	16 358	15 400	958
1972	67 222	72 665	-5 443	49 381	55 797	-6 416	17 841	16 868	973
1973	91 242	89 342	1 900	71 410	70 499	911	19 832	18 843	989
1974	120 897	125 190	-4 293	98 306	103 811	-5 505	22 591	21 379	1 212
1975	132 585	120 181	12 404	107 088	98 185	8 903	25 497	21 996	3 501
1976	142 716	148 798	-6 082	114 745	124 228	-9 483	27 971	24 570	3 401
1977	152 301	179 547	-27 246	120 816	151 907	-31 091	31 485	27 640	3 845
1978	178 428	208 191	-29 763	142 075	176 002	-33 927	36 353	32 189	4 164
1979	224 131	248 696	-24 565	184 439	212 007	-27 568	39 692	36 689	3 003
1980	271 834	291 241	-19 407	224 250	249 750	-25 500	47 584	41 491	6 093
1981	294 398	310 570	-16 172	237 044	265 067	-28 023	57 354	45 503	11 851
1982	275 236	299 391	-24 156	211 157	247 642	-36 485	64 079	51 749	12 329
1983	266 106	323 874	-57 767	201 799	268 901	-67 102	64 307	54 973	9 335
1984	291 094	400 166	-109 072	219 926	332 418	-112 492	71 168	67 748	3 420
1985	289 070	410 950	-121 880	215 915	338 088	-122 173	73 155	72 862	294
1986	310 033	448 572	-138 538	223 344	368 425	-145 081	86 689	80 147	6 543
1987	348 869	500 552	-151 684	250 208	409 765	-159 557	98 661	90 787	7 874
1988	431 149	545 715	-114 566	320 230	447 189	-126 959	110 919	98 526	12 393
1989	487 003	580 144	-93 141	359 916	477 665	-117 749	127 087	102 479	24 607
1990	535 233	616 097	-80 864	387 401	498 438	-111 037	147 832	117 659	30 173
1991	578 344	609 479	-31 135	414 083	491 020	-76 937	164 261	118 459	45 802
1992	616 883	655 975	-39 093	439 631	536 528	-96 897	177 252	119 447	57 804
1993	642 863	713 058	-70 195	456 943	589 394	-132 451	185 920	123 664	62 256
1994	703 254	801 633	-98 379	502 859	668 690	-165 831	200 395	132 943	67 452
1995	794 387	890 652	-96 265	575 204	749 374	-174 170	219 183	141 278	77 905
1996	851 602	955 544	-103 942	612 113	803 113	-191 000	239 489	152 431	87 058
1997	934 637	1 042 815	-108 178	678 366	876 470	-198 104	256 271	166 345	89 926
1998	933 495	1 098 363	-164 868	670 416	917 103	-246 687	263 079	181 260	81 819
1999	966 443	1 229 695	-263 252	683 965	1 029 980	-346 015	282 478	199 715	82 763
2000	1 070 980	1 449 324	-378 344	771 994	1 224 408	-452 414	298 986	224 916	74 070
2001	1 006 653	1 369 345	-362 692	718 712	1 145 900	-427 188	287 941	223 445	64 496
2002	975 940	1 397 675	-421 735	681 833	1 164 728	-482 895	294 107	232 947	61 160
2003	1 020 503	1 517 011	-496 508	713 122	1 260 674	-547 552	307 381	256 337	51 044
2001									
January	90 057	125 300	-35 243	65 024	106 052	-41 028	25 033	19 248	5 785
February	90 101	119 516	-29 415	65 369	100 910	-35 541	24 732	18 606	6 126
March	88 554	121 228	-32 674	63 583	102 434	-38 851	24 971	18 794	6 177
April	86 826	118 332	-31 506	62 113	98 756	-36 643	24 713	19 576	5 137
May	87 290	115 286	-27 996	62 722	95 906	-33 184	24 568	19 380	5 188
June	85 179	114 695	-29 517	60 196	95 552	-35 357	24 983	19 143	5 840
July	82 889	113 027	-30 137	58 265	93 891	-35 625	24 624	19 136	5 488
August	83 708	112 074	-28 366	58 881	92 810	-33 929	24 827	19 264	5 563
September	77 337	108 111	-30 774	55 501	91 180	-35 679	21 836	16 931	4 905
October	78 008	108 823	-30 815	56 047	91 532	-35 485	21 961	17 291	4 670
November	78 393	108 042	-29 650	55 827	90 183	-34 357	22 566	17 859	4 707
December	78 310	104 917	-26 607	55 185	86 694	-31 509	23 125	18 223	4 902
2002									
January	78 429	108 070	-29 642	55 114	89 495	-34 382	23 315	18 575	4 740
February	78 494	111 087	-32 593	54 928	91 879	-36 951	23 566	19 208	4 358
March	79 284	110 811	-31 527	55 080	92 146	-37 066	24 204	18 665	5 539
April	81 047	115 002	-33 955	57 052	96 400	-39 348	23 995	18 602	5 393
May	81 624	115 643	-34 019	57 216	96 839	-39 623	24 408	18 804	5 604
June	82 253	117 651	-35 398	57 766	98 156	-40 390	24 487	19 495	4 992
July	82 741	116 864	-34 123	58 274	97 389	-39 115	24 467	19 475	4 992
August	83 096	119 294	-36 198	58 252	99 982	-41 730	24 844	19 312	5 532
September	82 532	119 127	-36 595	57 845	99 408	-41 563	24 687	19 719	4 968
October	82 225	117 157	-34 932	57 071	97 183	-40 112	25 154	19 974	5 180
November	82 942	122 545	-39 602	57 532	102 277	-44 744	25 410	20 268	5 142
December	81 274	124 424	-43 151	55 703	103 575	-47 873	25 571	20 849	4 722
2003									
January	82 037	123 391	-41 354	57 078	102 688	-45 610	24 959	20 703	4 256
February	82 828	123 203	-40 375	57 887	102 681	-44 794	24 941	20 522	4 419
March	83 134	126 792	-43 659	58 495	106 033	-47 539	24 639	20 759	3 880
April	81 310	123 829	-42 519	57 317	103 496	-46 179	23 993	20 333	3 660
May	82 581	123 408	-40 827	57 816	102 915	-45 099	24 765	20 493	4 272
June	84 581	124 617	-40 035	59 420	103 676	-44 255	25 161	20 941	4 220
July	85 611	126 425	-40 814	60 092	104 769	-44 677	25 519	21 656	3 863
August	84 105	124 290	-40 185	58 234	102 627	-44 393	25 871	21 663	4 208
September	86 009	127 259	-41 251	59 926	105 490	-45 565	26 083	21 769	4 314
October	88 107	129 596	-41 490	61 170	107 345	-46 176	26 937	22 251	4 686
November	90 133	130 128	-39 994	63 075	107 818	-44 742	27 058	22 310	4 748
December	90 067	134 077	-44 011	62 613	111 135	-48 523	27 454	22 942	4 512

Table 7-9. U.S. Exports of Goods by End-Use and Advanced Technology Categories

(Census basis, except as noted; billions of dollars; seasonally adjusted, except as noted.)

Year and month	Total exports of goods			Principal end-use category						Advanced technology products [1]
	Total: Balance of payments basis	Net adjustments	Total: Census basis	Foods, feeds, and beverages	Industrial supplies and materials		Capital goods, except automotive	Automotive vehicles, engines, and parts	Consumer goods (nonfood) except automotive	Other goods	
					Total	Petroleum and products					
1978	142.08	-1.59	143.66	25.68	39.59	1.95	47.50	15.16	11.38	...	...
1979	184.44	2.64	181.80	30.50	58.50	2.44	60.18	17.90	13.98	...	...
1980	224.25	3.55	220.70	36.28	72.09	3.57	76.28	17.44	17.75	...	...
1981	237.04	3.31	233.74	38.84	70.19	4.56	84.17	19.69	17.70	...	...
1982	211.16	-1.12	212.28	32.20	64.05	6.87	76.50	17.23	16.13	...	...
1983	201.80	0.09	201.71	32.09	58.94	5.59	71.66	18.46	14.93	...	...
1984	219.93	1.18	218.74	32.20	64.12	5.43	77.01	22.42	15.09	...	...
1985	215.92	3.29	212.62	24.57	61.16	5.71	79.32	24.95	14.59	...	...
1986	223.34	-3.13	226.47	23.52	64.72	4.43	82.82	25.10	16.73	...	...
1987	250.21	-3.70	253.90	25.23	70.05	4.63	92.71	27.58	20.31	...	...
1988	320.23	-3.11	323.34	33.77	90.02	4.48	119.10	33.40	26.98	...	...
1989	359.92	-3.08	363.00	36.34	98.36	6.46	136.94	35.05	36.01	...	...
1990	387.40	-5.57	392.97	35.18	105.55	8.36	153.07	36.07	43.60	20.73	...
1991	414.08	-7.77	421.85	35.79	109.69	8.40	166.72	39.72	46.65	23.66	...
1992	439.63	-8.54	448.17	40.34	109.59	7.62	176.50	46.71	51.31	24.39	...
1993	456.94	-7.92	464.86	40.59	111.89	7.49	182.85	51.35	54.56	23.89	...
1994	502.86	-9.77	512.63	41.96	121.55	6.97	205.82	57.31	59.86	26.50	...
1995	575.20	-9.54	584.74	50.47	146.37	8.10	234.46	61.26	64.31	28.72	...
1996	612.11	-12.96	625.08	55.53	147.98	9.63	253.99	64.24	70.11	33.85	...
1997	678.37	-10.82	689.18	51.51	158.32	10.42	295.87	73.30	77.96	33.51	...
1998	670.42	-11.72	682.14	46.40	148.31	8.08	299.87	72.39	80.29	35.44	...
1999	683.97	-11.83	695.80	45.98	147.52	8.62	310.79	75.26	80.92	35.32	...
2000	771.99	-9.92	781.92	47.87	172.62	12.01	356.93	80.36	89.38	34.77	227.39
2001	718.71	-10.39	729.10	49.41	160.10	10.64	321.71	75.44	88.33	34.11	199.63
2002	681.83	-11.27	693.10	49.62	156.81	10.34	290.44	78.94	84.36	32.94	178.57
2003	713.12	-11.65	724.77	55.03	173.04	12.69	293.62	80.69	89.91	32.49	180.21
2000											
January	61.41	-1.13	62.54	3.88	13.71	0.95	27.86	6.99	7.16	2.95	16.66
February	61.32	-1.10	62.41	3.77	14.02	0.78	27.11	6.93	7.37	3.21	16.44
March	62.44	-0.69	63.14	3.96	14.70	1.02	27.40	6.97	7.38	2.73	18.55
April	63.13	-0.69	63.81	3.93	13.87	0.96	29.40	6.60	7.33	2.68	18.12
May	62.85	-0.79	63.63	3.99	13.72	0.87	29.34	6.64	7.18	2.77	18.62
June	65.20	-0.80	66.00	4.06	14.15	0.81	30.31	6.81	7.69	2.98	20.18
July	64.99	-0.72	65.71	4.12	14.09	0.87	30.82	6.44	7.49	2.76	18.26
August	66.99	-0.78	67.76	4.23	14.68	1.07	31.53	6.77	7.68	2.87	19.76
September	66.85	-0.72	67.56	4.09	15.19	1.12	31.20	6.59	7.72	2.78	20.12
October	66.01	-0.84	66.85	4.01	14.96	1.42	30.82	6.66	7.36	3.03	20.26
November	65.80	-0.89	66.69	3.94	15.09	1.10	30.71	6.48	7.49	2.99	19.54
December	65.03	-0.79	65.82	3.90	14.45	1.06	30.44	6.48	7.53	3.02	20.91
2001											
January	65.02	-0.85	65.87	3.96	14.27	0.94	30.94	6.14	7.64	2.91	18.29
February	65.37	-0.75	66.11	4.12	14.46	0.89	30.99	6.04	7.81	2.71	18.06
March	63.58	-0.77	64.35	4.34	14.22	0.88	29.12	6.20	7.72	2.74	20.63
April	62.11	-0.69	62.81	4.27	13.95	0.93	27.92	6.26	7.70	2.71	16.54
May	62.72	-1.05	63.77	4.11	13.93	0.95	28.39	6.35	7.96	3.04	17.25
June	60.20	-0.91	61.10	4.04	13.45	0.92	26.64	6.59	7.23	3.16	17.72
July	58.27	-1.03	59.30	4.04	12.93	0.85	25.89	6.20	7.28	2.96	14.87
August	58.88	-0.77	59.65	4.23	13.20	0.98	25.56	6.54	7.11	3.00	15.75
September	55.50	-0.87	56.38	4.06	12.32	0.79	24.07	6.38	6.89	2.66	14.80
October	56.05	-0.94	56.99	4.11	12.60	0.78	24.17	6.29	7.00	2.82	15.68
November	55.83	-0.88	56.71	4.11	12.39	0.78	24.16	6.42	6.88	2.75	14.92
December	55.19	-0.88	56.07	4.02	12.38	0.95	23.87	6.02	7.13	2.66	15.11
2002											
January	55.11	-0.74	55.85	4.17	12.32	0.75	23.87	6.14	6.86	2.49	13.61
February	54.93	-0.88	55.81	4.17	12.30	0.79	23.52	6.27	6.98	2.58	12.96
March	55.08	-1.07	56.15	3.94	12.33	0.73	24.06	6.33	6.81	2.69	17.10
April	57.05	-0.82	57.87	3.99	12.94	0.80	24.35	6.70	7.12	2.77	14.40
May	57.22	-1.26	58.47	4.03	13.28	0.81	24.45	6.70	7.01	3.00	14.76
June	57.77	-0.88	58.65	4.30	13.31	0.80	24.71	6.71	7.02	2.60	16.41
July	58.27	-0.93	59.20	4.33	13.23	0.85	24.80	6.83	7.21	2.80	14.86
August	58.25	-1.01	59.26	4.18	13.46	0.95	24.73	6.95	7.08	2.87	15.13
September	57.85	-0.86	58.71	4.10	13.38	0.87	24.77	6.68	7.03	2.74	14.84
October	57.07	-0.99	58.06	3.86	13.19	0.91	24.32	6.66	7.18	2.87	15.73
November	57.53	-0.93	58.46	4.24	13.55	0.98	24.25	6.53	7.11	2.78	14.62
December	55.70	-0.91	56.61	4.31	13.53	1.11	22.60	6.46	6.95	2.76	14.15
2003											
January	57.08	-0.75	57.83	4.38	14.04	1.12	23.05	6.59	7.30	2.47	13.06
February	57.89	-0.91	58.79	4.34	14.11	1.20	24.10	6.61	7.07	2.57	13.53
March	58.50	-0.98	59.47	4.45	14.54	1.21	23.65	6.75	7.34	2.75	15.98
April	57.32	-1.19	58.50	4.39	14.10	1.05	23.17	6.72	7.21	2.92	13.95
May	57.82	-0.96	58.77	4.38	14.11	1.05	23.58	6.86	7.26	2.58	13.97
June	59.42	-1.02	60.44	4.56	14.56	1.09	24.29	6.67	7.62	2.75	15.42
July	60.09	-1.04	61.13	4.67	14.89	1.01	24.51	6.75	7.54	2.77	14.75
August	58.23	-1.05	59.29	4.47	14.13	0.97	24.10	6.36	7.47	2.77	14.47
September	59.93	-1.09	61.02	4.69	14.18	1.00	24.85	6.78	7.70	2.82	15.23
October	61.17	-0.77	61.94	4.79	14.63	0.95	25.48	6.94	7.59	2.51	16.29
November	63.08	-1.10	64.18	5.02	14.64	0.99	26.84	6.76	7.98	2.93	16.93
December	62.61	-0.80	63.41	4.88	15.12	1.05	26.00	6.91	7.85	2.65	16.63

[1] Not seasonally adjusted.
... = Not available.

Table 7-10. U.S. Imports of Goods by End-Use and Advanced Technology Categories

(Census basis, except as noted; billions of dollars; seasonally adjusted, except as noted.)

Year and month	Total imports of goods			Principal end-use category							Advanced technology products [1]
	Total: Balance of payments basis	Net adjustments	Total: Census basis	Foods, feeds, and beverages	Industrial supplies and materials		Capital goods, except automotive	Automotive vehicles, engines, and parts	Consumer goods (nonfood) except automotive	Other goods	
					Total	Petroleum and products					
1978	176.00	1.31	174.69	15.84	79.26	...	19.29	25.11	29.40	...	...
1979	212.01	2.60	209.41	18.01	102.67	...	24.49	26.51	31.22	...	...
1980	249.75	4.23	245.52	18.55	124.96	...	30.72	28.13	34.22	...	...
1981	265.07	3.76	261.31	18.53	131.10	...	36.86	30.80	38.30	...	...
1982	247.64	3.70	243.94	17.47	107.82	...	38.22	34.26	39.66	...	...
1983	268.90	7.18	261.72	18.56	105.63	...	42.61	42.04	46.59	...	...
1984	332.42	1.91	330.51	21.92	122.72	...	60.15	56.77	61.19	...	...
1985	338.09	1.71	336.38	21.89	112.48	...	60.81	65.21	66.43	...	...
1986	368.43	2.75	365.67	24.40	101.37	...	71.86	78.25	79.43	...	...
1987	409.77	3.48	406.28	24.81	110.67	...	84.77	85.17	88.82	...	...
1988	447.19	5.26	441.93	24.93	118.06	...	101.79	87.95	96.42	...	...
1989	477.37	3.72	473.65	25.08	132.40	...	112.45	87.38	102.26	...	...
1990	498.34	2.36	495.98	26.65	143.41	62.16	116.04	87.69	105.29	16.09	...
1991	490.98	2.53	488.45	26.21	131.38	51.78	120.80	84.94	107.78	15.94	...
1992	536.46	3.80	532.66	27.61	138.64	51.60	134.25	91.79	122.66	17.71	...
1993	589.44	8.78	580.66	27.87	145.61	51.50	152.37	102.42	134.02	18.39	...
1994	668.59	5.33	663.26	27.87	145.61	51.28	152.37	102.42	134.02	18.39	...
1995	749.57	6.03	743.54	33.18	181.85	56.16	221.43	123.80	159.91	23.39	...
1996	803.33	8.04	796.77	35.74	204.43	72.75	228.07	128.95	172.00	26.11	...
1997	876.37	6.66	869.70	39.69	213.77	71.77	253.28	139.81	193.81	29.34	...
1998	917.18	5.28	911.90	41.24	200.14	50.90	269.56	149.05	216.52	35.39	...
1999	1 029.99	5.37	1 024.62	43.60	221.39	67.81	295.72	178.96	241.91	43.04	...
2000	1 224.42	6.40	1 218.02	45.98	298.98	120.28	347.03	195.88	281.83	48.33	222.08
2001	1 145.90	4.90	1 141.00	46.64	273.87	103.59	297.99	189.78	284.29	48.42	195.18
2002	1 164.73	3.36	1 161.37	49.69	267.69	103.51	283.32	203.74	307.84	49.08	195.15
2003	1 260.67	3.55	1 257.12	55.83	313.82	133.10	295.83	210.17	333.88	47.59	207.03
2000											
January	94.62	0.72	93.90	3.67	21.70	7.95	26.24	16.73	21.72	3.84	14.67
February	96.84	0.94	95.90	3.69	23.53	9.28	26.54	16.09	22.03	4.02	15.44
March	99.90	0.72	99.18	3.87	24.71	9.74	27.33	16.49	22.88	3.90	17.63
April	99.52	0.28	99.24	3.83	23.46	9.17	28.47	16.41	23.20	3.88	16.51
May	99.94	0.29	99.65	3.82	24.19	9.56	28.67	15.95	23.27	3.75	17.82
June	103.45	0.43	103.02	3.82	25.68	10.75	29.41	16.50	23.47	4.13	19.11
July	103.57	0.22	103.35	3.89	25.85	10.65	29.36	16.54	23.65	4.06	18.51
August	104.03	0.36	103.67	3.92	25.27	10.46	30.02	16.35	23.85	4.26	20.04
September	107.03	0.63	106.40	3.89	26.47	10.90	31.17	16.44	24.22	4.21	21.12
October	106.67	0.61	106.06	3.86	26.42	11.13	30.28	16.65	24.77	4.08	21.40
November	104.65	0.65	103.99	3.94	25.43	10.41	29.60	16.21	24.64	4.18	20.38
December	104.22	0.55	103.67	3.80	26.28	10.29	29.94	15.50	24.13	4.03	19.46
2001											
January	106.05	0.58	105.47	3.90	27.99	11.32	28.83	16.00	24.62	4.14	17.67
February	100.91	0.56	100.35	3.80	25.89	10.46	27.82	15.61	23.16	4.08	16.12
March	102.43	0.58	101.85	3.74	25.32	9.53	28.20	15.68	25.10	3.82	18.61
April	98.76	0.59	98.16	3.75	24.15	9.41	25.86	15.93	24.31	4.17	16.13
May	95.91	0.76	95.15	3.77	23.37	8.87	24.59	15.70	23.53	4.19	15.26
June	95.55	0.57	94.98	3.92	22.79	8.87	24.52	15.96	23.76	4.02	16.65
July	93.89	0.21	93.68	4.01	21.92	8.06	23.87	15.99	23.85	4.04	16.49
August	92.81	0.24	92.57	3.94	21.64	8.10	23.54	16.25	23.26	3.93	15.42
September	91.18	0.22	90.96	4.05	21.36	8.13	22.58	15.67	23.43	3.88	14.77
October	91.53	0.21	91.32	4.03	20.67	7.47	22.98	15.72	23.89	4.04	17.02
November	90.18	0.21	89.98	3.97	19.95	6.92	22.76	15.90	23.33	4.07	16.16
December	86.69	0.17	86.53	3.77	18.84	6.45	22.45	15.38	22.05	4.04	14.89
2002											
January	89.50	0.23	89.26	3.86	19.42	6.89	22.78	15.64	23.53	4.04	14.78
February	91.88	0.22	91.66	3.99	19.60	6.54	23.10	16.54	24.42	4.02	14.50
March	92.15	0.27	91.87	3.96	19.90	7.15	23.46	16.29	24.07	4.19	16.20
April	96.40	0.31	96.09	4.03	22.38	8.91	23.74	16.96	24.94	4.04	15.53
May	96.84	0.30	96.54	4.10	22.26	8.57	23.71	16.94	25.44	4.09	15.63
June	98.16	0.30	97.86	4.15	22.05	8.28	24.03	16.98	26.26	4.40	16.37
July	97.39	0.29	97.10	4.20	22.17	8.54	23.89	16.98	25.87	4.01	16.96
August	99.98	0.30	99.68	4.23	23.13	9.11	23.78	17.79	26.70	4.06	16.55
September	99.41	0.31	99.10	4.16	23.17	8.96	23.61	17.72	26.33	4.11	16.83
October	97.18	0.32	96.86	4.08	24.08	10.11	22.32	17.02	25.31	4.05	17.39
November	102.28	0.29	101.99	4.41	24.37	10.04	24.38	17.50	27.42	3.92	17.60
December	103.58	0.23	103.35	4.51	25.19	10.41	24.52	17.40	27.57	4.16	16.80
2003											
January	102.69	0.23	102.45	4.51	25.54	11.05	24.26	17.13	27.07	3.95	15.41
February	102.68	0.22	102.47	4.43	26.53	12.10	23.41	17.05	27.09	3.97	14.32
March	106.03	0.25	105.78	4.60	28.40	12.89	23.54	17.35	28.01	3.90	16.82
April	103.50	0.26	103.24	4.67	25.62	10.90	24.35	17.05	27.57	3.98	16.35
May	102.92	0.35	102.56	4.63	24.28	9.45	24.38	17.68	27.68	3.90	15.85
June	103.68	0.48	103.20	4.47	25.17	10.46	24.51	17.95	27.01	4.09	17.28
July	104.77	0.21	104.56	4.56	26.31	11.05	24.46	17.75	27.44	4.05	17.49
August	102.63	0.47	102.15	4.56	25.95	10.88	24.19	16.25	27.39	3.81	16.24
September	105.49	0.31	105.18	4.79	26.14	10.72	25.06	17.51	27.78	3.91	18.80
October	107.35	0.28	107.07	4.79	25.99	10.46	25.37	18.01	28.93	3.99	19.96
November	107.82	0.26	107.55	4.88	25.83	10.83	25.64	18.10	29.08	4.02	18.63
December	111.14	0.23	110.91	4.95	28.06	12.31	26.69	18.34	28.85	4.03	19.87

[1] Not seasonally adjusted.
... = Not available.

Table 7-11. U.S. Exports and Imports of Goods by Principal End-Use Category in Constant Dollars

(Census basis; billions of 2000 chain-weighted dollars, except as noted; seasonally adjusted.)

Year and month	Exports							Imports						
	Total	Foods, feeds, and beverages	Industrial supplies and materials	Capital goods, except automotive	Automotive vehicles, engines, and parts	Consumer goods (nonfood) except automotive	Other goods	Total	Foods, feeds, and beverages	Industrial supplies and materials	Capital goods, except automotive	Automotive vehicles, engines, and parts	Consumer goods (nonfood) except automotive	Other goods
1986 [1]	227.20	22.30	57.30	75.80	21.70	...	...	365.40	24.40	101.30	71.80	78.20	79.40	...
1987 [1]	254.10	24.30	66.70	86.20	24.60	...	...	406.20	24.80	111.00	84.50	85.00	88.70	...
1988 [1]	322.40	32.30	85.10	109.20	29.30	...	...	441.00	24.80	118.30	101.40	87.70	95.90	...
1989 [1]	363.80	37.20	99.30	138.80	34.80	...	...	473.20	25.10	132.30	113.30	86.10	102.90	...
1990 [1]	393.60	35.10	104.40	152.70	37.40	39.22	18.70	495.30	26.60	146.20	116.40	87.30	105.70	14.46
1991 [1]	421.70	35.70	109.70	166.70	40.00	40.42	21.11	488.50	26.50	131.60	120.70	85.70	108.00	14.15
1992 [1]	448.20	40.30	109.10	175.90	47.00	43.60	21.71	532.70	27.60	138.60	134.30	91.80	122.70	15.46
1993 [1]	471.17	40.19	111.08	190.02	51.93	54.03	23.91	591.45	28.03	151.26	160.16	100.73	132.92	18.35
1994 [1]	522.29	40.43	114.17	225.76	56.54	58.97	26.41	675.05	29.52	168.80	199.56	112.13	144.22	20.82
1994	482.34	41.41	127.50	165.92	60.49	62.41	28.03	628.41	29.53	216.50	120.69	124.86	143.41	21.80
1995	531.74	45.70	136.13	192.70	64.02	66.02	28.79	682.73	30.28	222.84	145.53	126.99	154.37	23.01
1996	588.10	44.24	144.48	228.74	66.63	70.86	33.61	753.96	33.53	236.42	175.55	131.33	165.33	25.69
1997	666.61	44.12	156.35	280.22	75.18	77.82	33.38	858.67	36.75	252.73	219.82	141.98	188.23	29.06
1998	682.35	43.84	155.76	292.61	73.38	80.86	36.15	959.84	39.54	277.01	252.14	150.86	213.38	35.81
1999	704.29	45.35	156.88	308.44	75.99	81.42	36.12	1 075.39	43.18	281.43	289.21	180.17	239.60	43.70
2000	781.92	47.87	172.62	356.93	80.36	89.38	34.77	1 218.02	45.98	298.98	347.03	195.88	281.83	48.33
2001	733.58	49.14	164.85	321.92	75.13	88.38	34.15	1 177.64	47.76	297.51	306.31	189.86	286.48	48.79
2002	699.04	48.07	162.20	293.00	78.30	84.67	32.85	1 220.74	50.94	300.07	300.09	203.24	313.01	50.30
2003	714.07	48.86	166.69	298.60	79.62	89.31	31.35	1 284.25	55.65	311.69	317.07	208.52	339.94	47.87
2000														
January	62.89	3.89	14.05	27.80	7.01	7.17	2.98	95.61	3.61	23.77	25.96	16.78	21.58	3.88
February	62.60	3.75	14.19	27.13	6.95	7.36	3.22	96.67	3.64	24.63	26.30	16.14	21.92	4.05
March	63.18	3.93	14.74	27.43	6.97	7.38	2.73	99.39	3.84	25.09	27.17	16.54	22.83	3.91
April	63.86	3.87	13.90	29.48	6.61	7.33	2.68	100.10	3.77	24.54	28.27	16.45	23.15	3.89
May	63.53	3.90	13.66	29.40	6.64	7.17	2.77	100.59	3.82	25.29	28.56	15.93	23.24	3.76
June	65.87	4.02	14.07	30.30	6.82	7.69	2.98	102.94	3.86	25.56	29.38	16.47	23.54	4.13
July	65.65	4.17	14.04	30.78	6.44	7.47	2.75	102.81	3.92	25.33	29.35	16.51	23.64	4.05
August	67.84	4.42	14.62	31.51	6.76	7.67	2.87	103.34	3.93	24.97	30.02	16.33	23.85	4.24
September	67.41	4.12	15.04	31.17	6.57	7.72	2.78	105.41	3.91	25.34	31.26	16.44	24.27	4.21
October	66.72	4.04	14.84	30.82	6.65	7.36	3.02	105.26	3.88	25.25	30.59	16.63	24.85	4.07
November	66.60	3.93	15.02	30.70	6.47	7.50	2.98	103.15	4.03	24.21	29.87	16.19	24.73	4.17
December	65.77	3.86	14.45	30.42	6.47	7.56	3.01	102.77	3.79	25.01	30.28	15.48	24.24	3.98
2001														
January	65.78	3.89	14.32	30.88	6.13	7.65	2.90	104.91	3.89	27.06	29.12	15.97	24.72	4.06
February	66.05	4.12	14.46	30.91	6.03	7.82	2.70	100.39	3.84	25.40	28.20	15.59	23.27	4.03
March	64.35	4.31	14.32	29.06	6.19	7.74	2.73	103.28	3.72	26.27	28.57	15.67	25.18	3.81
April	62.83	4.28	14.07	27.82	6.23	7.72	2.70	100.13	3.81	25.25	26.41	15.94	24.44	4.17
May	63.92	4.15	14.11	28.33	6.31	7.99	3.03	96.87	3.85	24.12	25.18	15.74	23.68	4.19
June	61.38	4.05	13.78	26.60	6.56	7.25	3.16	97.31	4.06	23.98	25.13	15.99	23.97	4.04
July	59.71	3.98	13.42	25.89	6.17	7.28	2.96	97.24	4.17	24.18	24.61	16.04	24.03	4.10
August	60.22	4.13	13.77	25.68	6.51	7.11	3.01	96.32	4.11	23.97	24.36	16.30	23.46	4.00
September	56.85	3.97	12.83	24.16	6.35	6.87	2.66	94.41	4.18	23.36	23.47	15.68	23.64	3.94
October	57.72	4.09	13.27	24.29	6.26	6.98	2.83	96.65	4.16	24.47	23.97	15.70	24.16	4.13
November	57.65	4.15	13.19	24.27	6.40	6.87	2.77	96.44	4.05	24.95	23.78	15.89	23.61	4.17
December	57.13	4.03	13.30	24.03	6.00	7.10	2.69	93.70	3.91	24.51	23.51	15.36	22.33	4.15
2002														
January	56.84	4.12	13.20	24.03	6.10	6.88	2.51	96.34	3.94	24.83	23.95	15.65	23.81	4.15
February	56.94	4.25	13.18	23.66	6.23	7.02	2.61	99.19	4.21	25.06	24.35	16.51	24.78	4.15
March	57.09	3.98	13.15	24.12	6.29	6.85	2.71	98.14	4.11	23.89	24.77	16.29	24.49	4.33
April	58.65	4.00	13.54	24.50	6.66	7.17	2.78	100.88	4.15	25.00	25.04	16.94	25.38	4.14
May	59.21	4.04	13.82	24.65	6.65	7.06	3.01	101.02	4.19	24.45	25.06	16.95	25.89	4.20
June	59.28	4.25	13.73	24.98	6.66	7.06	2.60	102.57	4.30	24.39	25.39	16.94	26.73	4.51
July	59.50	4.16	13.48	25.04	6.79	7.24	2.78	101.55	4.33	24.31	25.30	16.93	26.28	4.10
August	59.47	3.96	13.73	24.96	6.90	7.09	2.85	103.91	4.37	25.04	25.16	17.74	27.11	4.16
September	58.74	3.77	13.59	25.03	6.62	7.05	2.70	102.86	4.22	24.61	25.03	17.66	26.79	4.20
October	58.09	3.62	13.31	24.58	6.59	7.19	2.83	100.19	4.13	25.14	23.84	16.91	25.74	4.13
November	58.48	3.91	13.74	24.52	6.46	7.13	2.74	106.39	4.46	26.24	26.02	17.42	27.95	4.00
December	56.77	4.00	13.75	22.93	6.39	6.96	2.73	107.69	4.53	27.12	26.18	17.31	28.05	4.24
2003														
January	57.59	4.06	13.95	23.34	6.51	7.30	2.42	104.82	4.49	25.56	25.90	17.06	27.54	4.00
February	58.15	4.04	13.69	24.38	6.52	7.04	2.50	103.28	4.41	24.97	25.03	16.95	27.63	4.00
March	58.67	4.13	13.92	23.97	6.67	7.31	2.67	105.75	4.55	25.98	25.20	17.25	28.55	3.89
April	57.81	4.06	13.61	23.47	6.64	7.19	2.84	105.95	4.63	25.92	26.06	16.94	28.09	4.02
May	58.00	3.93	13.69	23.88	6.78	7.23	2.51	106.32	4.64	25.50	26.14	17.57	28.22	3.94
June	59.59	4.11	14.05	24.64	6.59	7.56	2.66	106.02	4.50	25.62	26.20	17.82	27.46	4.11
July	60.32	4.21	14.45	24.84	6.65	7.48	2.68	107.07	4.56	26.43	26.17	17.63	27.89	4.07
August	58.65	4.10	13.63	24.59	6.27	7.42	2.68	104.49	4.59	25.86	25.90	16.14	27.89	3.84
September	60.11	4.08	13.61	25.43	6.69	7.64	2.71	107.74	4.79	26.18	26.87	17.40	28.29	3.93
October	60.79	4.08	13.97	26.07	6.83	7.51	2.40	109.93	4.78	26.25	27.33	17.80	29.49	4.01
November	62.62	4.11	13.88	27.41	6.67	7.88	2.79	110.00	4.85	25.85	27.54	17.88	29.57	4.03
December	61.77	3.97	14.23	26.60	6.81	7.76	2.51	112.89	4.87	27.59	28.74	18.08	29.32	4.03

[1] Data on the 2000 chain-weighted dollar basis are only available for 1994 to date. To provide more historical data, values in 1992 dollars are shown for the years 1986–1994.
... = Not available.

Table 7-12. U.S. Exports of Goods by Selected Regions and Countries

(Census f.a.s. basis; millions of dollars, not seasonally adjusted.)

Year and month	Total, all countries	Selected regions				Selected countries					
		European Union	Euro area	Asian NICS	OPEC	Brazil	Canada	China	France	Germany	Hong Kong
1972	...	...	...	...	...	1 243	13 070	...	1 609	2 808	...
1973	...	...	...	...	...	1 916	16 146	...	2 263	3 756	...
1974	...	28 268	...	...	6 723	3 088	21 281	807	2 942	4 985	882
1975	...	22 862	...	...	10 767	3 056	22 948	304	3 031	5 194	808
1976	...	25 406	...	...	12 566	2 809	25 677	135	3 446	5 731	1 115
1977	...	26 476	...	...	14 019	2 490	27 738	171	3 503	5 989	1 292
1978	...	32 051	...	...	16 655	2 981	30 540	824	4 166	6 957	1 625
1979	...	42 582	...	...	15 051	3 442	37 599	1 724	5 587	8 478	2 083
1980	...	53 679	...	...	17 759	4 344	40 331	3 755	7 485	10 960	2 686
1981	...	52 363	...	...	21 533	3 798	44 602	3 603	7 341	10 277	2 635
1982	...	47 932	...	...	22 863	3 423	37 887	2 912	7 110	9 291	2 453
1983	201 708	44 311	...	...	16 905	2 557	43 345	2 173	5 961	8 737	2 564
1984	218 743	46 976	...	...	14 387	2 640	51 777	3 004	6 037	9 084	3 062
1985	212 621	48 994	...	16 918	12 480	3 140	53 287	3 856	6 096	9 050	2 786
1986	226 471	53 154	...	18 289	10 844	3 885	55 512	3 106	7 216	10 561	3 030
1987	253 904	60 575	...	23 548	11 058	4 040	59 814	3 497	7 943	11 748	3 983
1988	323 335	75 755	...	34 816	13 994	4 267	71 622	5 021	9 970	14 348	5 687
1989	363 836	86 331	...	38 404	13 196	4 804	78 809	5 755	11 579	16 862	6 246
1990	392 924	98 027	...	40 741	13 679	5 062	83 866	4 807	13 652	18 693	6 841
1991	421 764	103 123	...	45 628	19 054	6 148	85 150	6 278	15 346	21 302	8 137
1992	448 161	102 958	...	48 592	21 960	5 751	90 594	7 418	14 593	21 249	9 077
1993	465 090	96 973	...	52 502	19 500	6 058	100 444	8 763	13 267	18 932	9 874
1994	512 626	102 818	...	59 595	17 868	8 102	114 439	9 282	13 619	19 229	11 441
1995	584 742	123 671	...	74 234	19 533	11 439	127 226	11 754	14 245	22 394	14 232
1996	625 075	127 710	...	75 768	22 275	12 718	134 210	11 993	14 455	23 495	13 966
1997	689 182	140 773	...	78 225	25 526	15 915	151 767	12 862	15 965	24 458	15 117
1998	682 138	149 035	...	63 269	25 154	15 142	156 603	14 241	17 729	26 657	12 925
1999	695 797	151 814	...	70 989	20 166	13 203	166 600	13 111	18 877	26 800	12 652
2000	781 918	165 065	116 212	84 624	19 078	15 321	178 941	16 185	20 362	29 448	14 582
2001	729 100	158 768	112 903	71 982	20 053	15 880	163 424	19 182	19 865	29 995	14 028
2002	693 103	143 691	105 863	69 770	18 812	12 376	160 923	22 128	19 016	26 630	12 594
2003	724 771	151 731	113 132	71 601	17 279	11 211	169 924	28 368	17 053	28 832	13 521
2000											
January	57 679	12 031	8 352	5 981	1 484	1 008	13 605	863	1 571	2 103	915
February	61 179	13 254	8 965	5 853	1 705	1 058	14 969	973	1 553	2 235	1 011
March	68 948	14 496	10 335	7 301	1 418	1 141	17 086	1 331	1 830	2 832	1 246
April	63 302	13 591	9 777	6 845	1 438	1 055	14 794	1 228	1 702	2 784	1 170
May	64 673	14 010	9 821	6 773	1 366	1 184	15 834	1 526	1 639	2 498	1 135
June	68 002	13 982	9 797	7 687	1 373	1 435	16 054	1 336	1 677	2 314	1 262
July	60 029	12 005	8 633	7 557	1 375	1 361	12 153	1 643	1 485	2 182	1 181
August	68 255	13 588	9 652	7 699	1 732	1 442	15 325	1 429	1 669	2 470	1 333
September	67 391	14 214	10 085	7 501	1 901	1 443	14 847	1 333	1 633	2 471	1 311
October	69 635	14 282	10 007	7 584	2 071	1 453	15 725	1 487	1 706	2 464	1 288
November	67 614	14 313	10 120	6 811	1 630	1 332	15 159	1 450	1 787	2 451	1 305
December	65 211	15 302	10 669	7 032	1 585	1 410	13 390	1 587	2 110	2 645	1 426
2001											
January	62 162	13 645	9 827	6 443	1 705	1 265	13 667	1 188	1 642	2 546	1 046
February	62 743	14 531	10 463	6 508	1 483	1 169	13 357	1 290	1 972	2 928	1 170
March	70 358	15 346	11 032	6 988	2 287	1 412	15 524	1 856	2 042	2 892	1 379
April	62 015	13 632	9 476	5 841	1 688	1 295	14 403	1 399	1 610	2 508	1 317
May	64 931	14 163	9 676	5 786	1 670	1 486	15 108	1 596	1 687	2 605	1 112
June	63 334	13 715	9 487	5 895	1 653	1 514	15 051	1 786	1 749	2 432	1 295
July	54 611	11 325	7 896	5 866	1 653	1 434	11 700	1 487	1 233	2 443	1 145
August	60 111	12 627	8 974	5 641	1 530	1 476	13 764	1 930	1 404	2 389	1 162
September	55 232	12 035	8 506	6 120	1 577	1 249	12 423	1 428	1 613	2 255	1 217
October	60 701	13 056	9 489	5 727	1 624	1 134	13 895	1 648	1 700	2 371	1 064
November	57 900	12 143	8 850	5 771	1 597	1 344	13 214	1 675	1 644	2 173	1 024
December	55 003	12 551	9 227	5 395	1 586	1 100	11 319	1 901	1 570	2 453	1 098
2002											
January	52 667	11 408	8 249	5 216	1 238	1 016	12 062	1 569	1 543	2 022	900
February	53 061	12 153	8 983	4 619	1 348	1 004	12 368	1 530	1 872	2 183	911
March	60 728	13 298	9 842	6 289	1 431	1 076	13 954	1 621	1 801	2 530	1 134
April	58 146	12 079	8 758	5 819	1 591	1 059	14 114	1 545	1 578	2 133	1 043
May	59 884	11 948	8 829	5 817	2 043	969	14 586	1 774	1 570	2 084	1 054
June	59 920	11 908	8 578	6 408	1 431	1 017	14 214	2 206	1 532	2 197	1 135
July	55 032	10 537	7 722	6 313	1 569	970	11 607	1 848	1 249	1 990	1 035
August	59 491	11 752	8 460	6 246	1 492	1 134	13 913	1 840	1 287	2 147	1 113
September	57 277	11 571	8 521	5 813	1 924	1 053	13 334	2 024	1 503	2 328	1 117
October	61 975	13 015	9 748	6 078	1 646	1 159	14 702	1 963	1 993	2 402	1 009
November	59 671	12 470	9 470	5 614	1 641	1 037	13 908	2 161	1 704	2 419	1 089
December	55 249	11 553	8 679	5 539	1 459	882	12 161	2 049	1 384	2 194	1 055
2003											
January	54 854	11 823	8 809	5 064	1 126	809	12 890	2 070	1 369	2 160	947
February	55 917	12 091	8 936	5 704	1 358	812	13 293	2 049	1 314	2 426	954
March	63 524	13 884	10 084	6 265	1 562	937	15 360	2 423	1 717	2 803	1 183
April	59 162	12 929	9 823	5 366	1 279	847	14 646	2 122	1 568	2 477	1 061
May	59 984	12 709	9 377	5 399	1 242	882	15 208	1 984	1 458	2 490	1 063
June	61 570	12 678	9 359	6 092	1 624	942	15 003	2 120	1 521	2 262	1 078
July	57 070	11 553	8 564	6 226	1 387	951	12 030	2 067	1 193	2 210	1 075
August	58 611	11 962	8 757	6 391	1 449	1 031	12 990	2 034	1 265	2 315	1 147
September	60 239	12 159	9 190	5 753	1 640	924	14 518	2 091	1 331	2 191	1 218
October	66 389	13 575	10 329	6 481	1 514	1 034	15 555	2 778	1 439	2 659	1 288
November	64 492	13 627	10 379	6 155	1 514	1 001	14 598	3 320	1 418	2 470	1 189
December	62 959	12 742	9 525	6 705	1 584	1 040	13 834	3 310	1 460	2 370	1 318

Note: See Notes and Definitions for definitions of regional groupings.
... = Not available.

Table 7-12. U.S. Exports of Goods by Selected Regions and Countries—Continued

(Census f.a.s. basis; millions of dollars, not seasonally adjusted.)

Year and month	Selected countries—Continued										
	Indonesia	Italy	Japan	Malaysia	Mexico	Netherlands	Singapore	South Korea	Taiwan	United Kingdom	Venezuela
1972	...	1 434	4 963	...	1 982	...	...	...	...	2 658	924
1973	...	2 119	8 313	...	2 937	...	...	...	...	3 564	1 033
1974	...	2 752	10 679	...	4 855	3 979	988	...	1 427	4 574	1 768
1975	...	2 867	9 563	...	5 141	4 183	994	...	1 660	4 527	2 243
1976	...	3 071	10 145	...	4 990	4 645	965	...	1 635	4 801	2 628
1977	...	2 790	10 529	...	4 806	4 796	1 172	...	1 798	5 951	3 171
1978	...	3 361	12 885	...	6 680	5 683	1 462	...	2 340	7 116	3 728
1979	...	4 362	17 581	...	9 847	6 907	2 331	...	3 271	10 635	3 934
1980	1 545	5 511	20 790	...	15 145	8 669	3 033	...	4 337	12 694	4 573
1981	1 302	5 360	21 823	...	17 789	8 595	3 003	...	4 305	12 439	5 445
1982	2 025	4 616	20 966	...	11 817	8 604	3 214	...	4 367	10 645	5 206
1983	1 466	3 908	21 894	...	9 082	7 767	3 759	...	4 667	10 621	2 811
1984	1 216	4 375	23 575	...	11 992	7 554	3 675	...	5 003	12 210	3 377
1985	795	4 625	22 631	...	13 635	7 269	3 476	5 956	4 700	11 273	3 399
1986	946	4 838	26 882	...	12 392	7 848	3 380	6 355	5 524	11 418	3 141
1987	767	5 530	28 249	...	14 582	8 217	4 053	8 099	7 413	14 114	3 586
1988	1 059	6 775	37 725	...	20 628	10 117	5 768	11 232	12 129	18 364	4 612
1989	1 247	7 215	44 494	...	24 982	11 364	7 345	13 478	11 335	20 837	3 025
1990	1 897	7 987	48 585	...	28 375	13 016	8 019	14 399	11 482	23 484	3 107
1991	1 891	8 570	48 125	3 900	33 277	13 511	8 804	15 505	13 182	22 046	4 656
1992	2 779	8 721	47 813	4 363	40 592	13 752	9 626	14 639	15 250	22 800	5 444
1993	2 770	6 464	47 892	6 064	41 581	12 839	11 678	14 782	16 168	26 438	4 590
1994	2 809	7 183	53 488	6 969	50 844	13 582	13 020	18 025	17 109	26 900	4 039
1995	3 360	8 862	64 343	8 816	46 292	16 558	15 333	25 380	19 290	28 857	4 640
1996	3 977	8 797	67 607	8 546	56 792	16 662	16 720	26 621	18 460	30 962	4 750
1997	4 522	8 995	65 549	10 780	71 388	19 827	17 696	25 046	20 366	36 425	6 602
1998	2 299	8 991	57 831	8 957	78 773	18 978	15 694	16 486	18 165	39 058	6 516
1999	2 038	10 091	57 466	9 060	86 909	19 437	16 247	22 958	19 131	38 407	5 354
2000	2 402	11 060	64 924	10 938	111 349	21 836	17 806	27 830	24 406	41 570	5 550
2001	2 521	9 916	57 452	9 358	101 297	19 485	17 652	22 181	18 122	40 714	5 642
2002	2 556	10 057	51 449	10 344	97 470	18 311	16 218	22 576	18 382	33 205	4 430
2003	2 516	10 561	52 004	10 914	97 412	20 695	16 560	24 073	17 448	33 828	2 831
2000											
January	169	827	4 772	697	7 965	1 558	1 239	1 986	1 841	3 045	363
February	201	820	4 992	742	8 464	1 795	1 195	2 053	1 595	3 689	420
March	237	930	5 899	826	9 641	1 897	1 621	2 433	2 001	3 516	492
April	201	883	4 968	854	9 044	1 675	1 325	2 425	1 925	3 193	531
May	177	822	5 109	830	9 144	1 786	1 274	2 384	1 981	3 533	437
June	177	907	5 758	1 113	9 408	1 833	1 499	2 576	2 349	3 561	453
July	229	861	5 094	1 011	9 084	1 627	1 504	2 288	2 584	2 903	407
August	206	876	5 677	1 040	10 449	1 858	1 669	2 442	2 255	3 325	499
September	211	1 369	5 526	1 043	9 756	1 831	1 754	2 378	2 058	3 494	479
October	227	946	5 546	985	10 332	2 057	1 662	2 476	2 158	3 636	451
November	177	849	5 760	933	9 927	1 959	1 516	2 243	1 748	3 683	426
December	190	969	5 824	863	8 137	1 960	1 548	2 147	1 911	3 994	593
2001											
January	234	918	5 253	899	8 648	1 809	1 434	2 150	1 813	3 374	461
February	203	889	5 222	778	8 768	1 821	1 541	2 025	1 772	3 486	411
March	218	968	5 897	1 011	9 272	1 912	1 689	2 217	1 703	3 700	517
April	217	792	5 033	887	8 198	1 756	1 233	1 627	1 664	3 719	451
May	239	841	4 878	679	8 649	1 594	1 550	1 692	1 433	4 036	494
June	201	808	4 986	682	8 405	1 627	1 453	1 783	1 365	3 824	524
July	185	720	4 308	689	7 675	1 290	1 434	1 774	1 513	3 087	477
August	198	735	4 604	700	9 023	1 530	1 370	1 747	1 362	3 252	511
September	173	724	4 336	678	7 700	1 363	1 523	2 000	1 380	3 157	416
October	212	961	4 352	715	9 273	1 501	1 766	1 532	1 365	3 190	499
November	198	770	4 287	720	8 346	1 614	1 475	1 858	1 414	2 936	481
December	243	790	4 296	920	7 337	1 668	1 183	1 776	1 339	2 952	400
2002											
January	136	714	3 945	726	7 734	1 460	1 386	1 706	1 224	2 764	374
February	198	797	3 862	688	7 250	1 480	1 069	1 487	1 152	2 771	379
March	201	885	4 744	1 253	7 624	1 710	1 705	1 877	1 573	2 985	365
April	195	824	3 901	960	8 258	1 714	1 329	1 931	1 516	2 957	320
May	222	933	4 262	856	8 530	1 593	1 235	1 991	1 538	2 702	677
June	195	775	4 670	1 003	8 088	1 531	1 538	1 975	1 760	2 966	272
July	198	836	4 493	828	7 963	1 353	1 323	1 890	2 066	2 456	304
August	282	823	4 791	907	8 559	1 514	1 600	1 919	1 614	2 914	329
September	187	679	4 138	798	8 283	1 505	1 133	1 974	1 588	2 643	400
October	212	977	4 151	874	9 221	1 476	1 583	1 982	1 504	2 904	374
November	268	914	4 412	723	8 606	1 490	1 302	1 800	1 423	2 619	470
December	262	901	4 082	728	7 354	1 484	1 015	2 044	1 425	2 524	165
2003											
January	238	956	3 919	719	7 780	1 529	1 069	1 726	1 322	2 670	121
February	207	752	4 136	689	7 093	1 550	1 425	2 162	1 163	2 781	188
March	233	849	4 470	848	7 805	1 861	1 566	2 182	1 335	3 300	183
April	194	787	4 475	917	7 816	1 816	1 146	1 919	1 240	2 729	179
May	192	1 071	4 562	983	8 082	1 590	1 312	1 825	1 199	2 939	182
June	200	866	4 403	896	8 012	1 667	1 341	2 115	1 559	2 949	218
July	184	746	4 238	976	7 904	1 524	1 599	1 949	1 604	2 655	279
August	195	736	4 298	913	7 941	1 610	1 847	1 860	1 538	2 818	288
September	173	748	4 163	970	8 534	1 586	1 258	1 885	1 391	2 577	241
October	193	1 110	4 384	998	9 520	2 031	1 450	2 111	1 633	2 821	308
November	248	961	4 481	946	8 621	2 081	1 262	2 199	1 504	2 806	348
December	260	979	4 475	1 058	8 304	1 850	1 286	2 139	1 962	2 782	296

... = Not available.

Table 7-13. U.S. Imports of Goods by Selected Regions and Countries

(Census Customs basis; millions of dollars, not seasonally adjusted.)

Year and month	Total, all countries	Selected regions				Selected countries					
		European Union	Euro area	Asian NICS	OPEC	Brazil	Canada	China	France	Germany	Hong Kong
1972	...	...	...	...	...	942	14 927	...	1 369	4 250	...
1973	...	...	...	...	...	1 189	17 715	...	1 732	5 345	...
1974	...	19 035	...	...	...	1 700	21 924	...	2 257	6 324	...
1975	...	16 610	...	...	...	1 464	21 747	...	2 137	5 382	...
1976	...	17 848	...	...	...	1 737	26 237	...	2 509	5 592	...
1977	...	22 087	...	...	...	2 241	29 599	...	3 032	7 238	...
1978	...	29 009	...	...	...	2 826	33 525	...	4 051	9 962	...
1979	...	33 295	...	...	...	3 118	38 046	...	4 768	10 955	...
1980	...	35 958	...	...	...	3 715	41 455	...	5 247	11 681	...
1981	...	41 624	...	...	...	4 475	46 414	...	5 851	11 379	...
1982	...	42 509	...	...	...	4 285	46 477	...	5 545	11 975	...
1983	261 723	43 892	...	...	...	4 946	52 130	...	6 025	12 695	...
1984	330 510	57 360	...	...	...	7 621	66 478	...	8 113	16 996	...
1985	336 383	67 822	...	...	22 800	7 526	69 006	3 862	9 482	20 239	8 396
1986	365 672	75 736	...	...	19 750	6 813	68 253	4 771	10 129	25 124	8 891
1987	406 283	81 188	...	...	23 953	7 865	71 085	6 294	10 730	27 069	9 854
1988	441 926	84 939	...	...	22 962	9 294	81 398	8 511	12 509	26 362	10 238
1989	473 647	85 153	...	...	30 601	8 410	87 953	11 989	13 013	24 832	9 739
1990	495 980	91 868	...	...	38 017	7 976	91 372	15 224	13 124	28 109	9 488
1991	488 452	86 481	...	59 277	32 644	6 717	91 064	18 969	13 333	26 137	9 279
1992	532 663	93 993	...	62 384	33 200	7 609	98 630	25 728	14 797	28 820	9 793
1993	580 658	97 941	...	64 572	31 739	7 479	111 216	31 540	15 279	28 562	9 554
1994	663 256	110 875	...	71 388	31 685	8 683	128 406	38 787	16 699	31 744	9 696
1995	743 543	131 871	...	82 008	35 197	8 830	145 349	45 543	17 209	36 844	10 291
1996	795 289	142 947	...	82 760	44 285	8 773	155 893	51 513	18 646	38 945	9 865
1997	869 704	157 528	...	86 164	44 025	9 626	168 201	62 558	20 636	43 122	10 288
1998	911 896	176 380	...	85 961	33 925	10 102	173 256	71 169	24 016	49 842	10 538
1999	1 024 618	195 227	...	95 102	41 978	11 314	198 711	81 788	25 709	55 228	10 528
2000	1 218 022	220 019	163 520	111 438	67 090	13 853	230 838	100 018	29 800	58 513	11 449
2001	1 140 999	220 057	166 373	93 202	59 754	14 466	216 268	102 278	30 408	59 077	9 646
2002	1 161 366	225 771	172 573	91 850	53 245	15 781	209 088	125 193	28 240	62 506	9 328
2003	1 257 121	244 826	187 204	92 818	68 344	17 910	221 595	152 436	29 219	68 113	8 851
2000											
January	87 188	15 345	11 530	8 375	4 382	1 099	17 579	6 902	2 329	4 207	961
February	91 688	16 772	12 192	7 971	4 826	1 091	18 092	6 585	2 092	4 474	842
March	103 244	19 988	14 651	8 555	5 414	1 053	20 762	6 424	2 636	5 410	796
April	95 141	17 801	13 324	8 223	5 000	1 024	18 638	7 071	2 442	5 018	731
May	101 067	18 762	13 839	8 992	5 452	1 101	19 836	7 850	2 625	4 829	916
June	104 527	17 992	13 307	9 665	6 085	1 421	20 391	8 542	2 362	4 644	1 016
July	101 986	18 415	13 728	9 772	5 884	1 224	16 889	9 246	2 368	4 940	1 063
August	108 166	18 362	13 845	10 303	6 193	1 414	19 815	10 054	2 248	5 295	1 151
September	106 355	17 834	13 514	10 340	6 158	1 178	19 379	10 062	2 317	4 710	1 231
October	113 812	20 399	15 133	10 417	6 520	1 070	20 500	10 612	2 821	5 162	1 043
November	106 395	19 939	14 767	9 846	5 653	1 043	19 969	9 067	2 775	4 961	898
December	98 453	18 410	13 690	8 979	5 524	1 135	18 990	7 605	2 785	4 866	802
2001											
January	101 869	18 896	14 082	9 064	5 793	1 360	20 442	8 428	2 525	4 875	982
February	91 639	17 861	13 275	7 286	4 781	1 050	18 263	6 376	2 344	4 846	617
March	103 536	20 172	15 379	8 416	5 642	1 202	19 976	7 590	3 309	5 345	751
April	96 265	19 218	14 508	7 669	5 439	1 077	18 733	7 687	2 734	5 378	662
May	96 605	19 039	14 431	7 578	5 790	1 261	19 603	7 758	2 612	5 219	759
June	95 663	17 843	13 484	7 733	5 224	1 188	18 915	8 398	2 303	4 783	868
July	94 625	19 522	14 876	7 784	5 300	1 211	15 793	8 975	2 629	5 423	930
August	96 728	17 466	13 495	7 694	4 933	1 428	18 001	10 043	2 364	5 055	910
September	89 484	15 292	11 553	7 323	4 872	1 209	16 698	9 928	1 873	4 147	915
October	101 177	20 147	15 071	8 261	4 717	1 175	17 542	10 808	2 714	5 037	922
November	91 705	18 015	13 524	7 595	3 778	1 183	17 170	8 879	2 469	4 582	712
December	81 703	16 587	12 694	6 800	3 487	1 123	15 132	7 409	2 533	4 387	619
2002											
January	85 111	16 057	12 180	7 275	3 733	1 093	16 335	8 415	2 284	4 195	836
February	83 473	16 651	12 876	6 478	3 298	1 024	16 180	8 021	2 184	4 636	603
March	91 415	18 829	14 445	7 185	3 898	1 104	17 481	7 259	2 465	5 255	589
April	96 891	18 997	14 189	7 635	4 512	1 250	18 186	9 098	2 576	5 185	674
May	97 649	18 932	14 229	7 753	4 586	1 261	18 794	9 847	2 043	4 900	738
June	96 415	18 236	13 848	7 437	4 153	1 384	17 436	10 727	2 311	4 620	787
July	100 472	20 953	16 084	7 988	4 714	1 400	15 911	11 213	2 687	5 796	934
August	102 277	18 168	14 043	8 027	5 139	1 581	17 943	12 671	2 201	5 108	867
September	99 429	17 705	13 475	7 935	4 880	1 350	17 862	12 292	2 166	4 914	861
October	106 251	20 897	16 032	7 862	5 130	1 649	19 044	11 455	2 526	5 993	896
November	102 564	19 711	15 057	8 349	4 591	1 296	17 685	12 570	2 275	5 750	818
December	99 418	20 635	16 116	7 927	4 611	1 390	16 232	11 625	2 523	6 156	725
2003											
January	97 491	18 192	14 291	7 821	4 827	1 434	17 735	11 404	2 354	4 877	822
February	93 154	18 057	13 585	6 517	4 745	1 305	17 184	9 630	2 215	4 860	564
March	105 842	21 275	16 203	7 185	6 565	1 535	19 823	10 110	2 329	6 271	563
April	103 869	20 531	15 757	7 874	6 296	1 427	18 454	11 522	2 424	5 943	625
May	102 068	20 234	15 277	7 233	5 653	1 398	18 668	11 885	2 237	5 883	626
June	103 958	20 512	15 691	7 749	5 608	1 479	18 574	12 127	2 461	5 736	692
July	107 631	21 665	16 682	8 071	5 821	1 647	17 079	13 439	2 524	5 785	871
August	102 307	18 619	14 523	7 390	5 568	1 634	17 584	13 765	2 278	5 135	839
September	108 322	19 746	14 728	8 102	5 738	1 465	19 361	14 748	2 347	5 016	920
October	117 158	22 255	16 720	8 732	5 956	1 635	20 138	16 458	2 617	6 060	958
November	106 066	20 868	16 208	7 819	5 414	1 348	18 641	14 157	2 551	6 046	696
December	109 255	22 873	17 537	8 325	6 152	1 603	18 354	13 193	2 881	6 501	678

Note: See Notes and Definitions for definitions of regional groupings.
. . . = Not available.

Table 7-13. U.S. Imports of Goods by Selected Regions and Countries—Continued

(Census Customs basis; millions of dollars, not seasonally adjusted.)

Year and month	Selected countries—Continued										
	Indonesia	Italy	Japan	Malaysia	Mexico	Netherlands	Singapore	South Korea	Taiwan	United Kingdom	Venezuela
1972	...	1 757	9 064	...	1 632	...	...	...	...	2 987	1 298
1973	...	2 002	9 676	...	2 306	...	...	...	...	3 657	1 787
1974	...	2 585	12 338	...	3 390	1 433	...	...	...	4 061	4 671
1975	...	2 397	11 268	...	3 059	1 083	...	...	...	3 784	3 624
1976	...	2 530	15 504	...	3 598	1 080	...	...	...	4 254	3 574
1977	...	3 037	18 550	...	4 694	1 477	...	...	...	5 141	4 084
1978	...	4 102	24 458	...	6 094	1 603	...	...	...	6 514	3 545
1979	...	4 918	26 248	...	8 800	1 852	...	...	...	8 028	5 166
1980	5 183	4 313	30 701	...	12 520	1 910	...	...	...	9 755	5 297
1981	6 022	5 189	37 612	...	13 765	2 366	...	...	...	12 835	5 566
1982	4 224	5 301	37 744	...	15 566	2 494	...	...	...	13 095	4 768
1983	5 285	5 455	41 183	...	16 776	2 970	...	...	...	12 470	4 938
1984	5 461	7 935	57 135	...	18 020	4 069	...	...	...	14 492	6 543
1985	4 569	9 674	68 783	...	19 132	4 081	4 260	10 031	16 396	14 937	6 537
1986	3 312	10 607	81 911	...	17 302	4 066	4 725	12 729	19 791	15 396	5 097
1987	3 394	11 040	84 575	...	20 271	3 964	6 201	16 987	24 622	17 341	5 579
1988	3 150	11 576	89 519	...	23 260	4 559	7 973	20 105	24 714	17 976	5 157
1989	3 529	11 933	93 586	...	27 162	4 810	8 950	19 742	24 326	18 319	6 771
1990	3 341	12 723	89 655	...	30 172	4 972	9 839	18 493	22 667	20 288	9 446
1991	3 241	11 764	91 511	6 102	31 130	4 811	9 957	17 019	23 023	18 413	8 179
1992	4 529	12 314	97 414	8 294	35 211	5 300	11 313	16 682	24 596	20 093	8 181
1993	5 435	13 216	107 246	10 563	39 917	5 443	12 798	17 118	25 102	21 730	8 140
1994	6 547	14 802	119 156	13 982	49 494	6 007	15 358	19 629	26 706	25 058	8 371
1995	7 435	16 348	123 479	17 455	61 684	6 405	18 560	24 184	28 972	26 930	9 721
1996	8 250	18 325	115 187	17 829	74 297	6 583	20 343	22 655	29 907	28 979	13 173
1997	9 188	19 408	121 663	18 027	85 938	7 293	20 075	23 173	32 629	32 659	13 477
1998	9 341	20 959	121 845	19 000	94 629	7 599	18 356	23 942	33 125	34 838	9 181
1999	9 525	22 357	130 864	21 424	109 721	8 475	18 191	31 179	35 204	39 237	11 335
2000	10 367	25 043	146 479	25 568	135 926	9 671	19 178	40 308	40 503	43 345	18 623
2001	10 104	23 790	126 473	22 340	131 338	9 515	15 000	35 181	33 375	41 369	15 251
2002	9 643	24 220	121 429	24 009	134 616	9 849	14 802	35 572	32 148	40 745	15 094
2003	9 515	25 414	118 037	25 440	138 060	10 953	15 138	37 229	31 599	42 795	17 136
2000											
January	790	1 792	10 204	1 702	9 583	718	1 401	2 954	3 060	2 949	1 283
February	703	1 956	11 721	1 776	10 365	728	1 423	2 833	2 873	3 465	1 497
March	832	2 154	12 810	2 029	11 653	898	1 473	3 134	3 152	4 119	1 516
April	738	1 986	12 452	1 881	10 555	795	1 386	2 956	3 150	3 422	1 390
May	830	2 063	11 946	2 023	11 367	859	1 517	3 121	3 438	3 796	1 541
June	919	2 092	12 174	2 209	11 944	771	1 625	3 497	3 526	3 586	1 623
July	877	2 244	12 557	2 228	10 947	824	1 647	3 494	3 568	3 594	1 560
August	1 010	2 158	12 535	2 401	12 306	784	1 837	3 622	3 693	3 693	1 562
September	962	2 306	11 484	2 412	12 344	777	1 785	3 627	3 696	3 283	1 542
October	978	2 103	14 065	2 527	12 814	903	1 705	3 890	3 779	3 956	1 807
November	883	2 151	12 461	2 265	11 940	854	1 788	3 741	3 420	3 947	1 727
December	847	2 037	12 070	2 117	10 109	760	1 592	3 439	3 147	3 538	1 575
2001											
January	957	2 084	11 143	1 869	10 706	835	1 499	3 514	3 069	3 857	1 678
February	763	1 946	11 380	1 746	10 297	725	1 306	2 811	2 553	3 547	1 324
March	918	2 173	12 076	1 932	12 045	860	1 373	3 125	3 167	3 634	1 475
April	764	1 928	11 562	1 736	10 481	831	1 290	2 824	2 893	3 685	1 410
May	859	2 044	9 606	1 704	11 431	880	1 280	2 758	2 782	3 567	1 339
June	856	1 981	9 969	2 066	11 438	777	1 187	2 861	2 817	3 327	1 401
July	939	2 253	10 318	1 849	10 578	734	1 205	2 844	2 805	3 550	1 329
August	926	2 105	10 219	1 895	11 565	745	1 203	2 754	2 827	3 172	1 300
September	771	1 448	9 457	1 771	10 687	690	1 066	2 782	2 561	2 747	992
October	899	2 133	11 187	2 118	11 909	889	1 289	3 159	2 890	3 919	1 160
November	771	1 857	10 288	1 941	10 873	775	1 288	3 010	2 586	3 476	965
December	682	1 837	9 269	1 714	9 329	774	1 015	2 740	2 426	2 889	878
2002											
January	746	1 730	8 674	1 775	9 982	679	1 199	2 756	2 486	3 046	916
February	672	1 714	9 426	1 748	10 023	715	1 050	2 539	2 285	2 860	753
March	765	1 939	10 466	1 942	11 055	765	1 179	2 940	2 477	3 253	1 035
April	764	1 975	10 699	1 901	11 471	889	1 209	3 021	2 731	3 702	1 057
May	849	2 052	9 167	2 036	11 929	888	1 300	3 075	2 639	3 588	1 257
June	827	2 007	10 090	2 098	11 311	800	1 022	2 748	2 880	3 327	1 197
July	942	2 421	10 230	2 182	11 293	875	1 245	2 931	2 879	3 767	1 497
August	968	2 154	10 081	2 307	11 854	766	1 375	2 882	2 902	3 372	1 582
September	851	1 737	10 074	2 032	11 409	789	1 232	3 068	2 774	3 257	1 722
October	773	2 163	10 561	2 067	12 658	952	1 334	3 047	2 585	3 723	1 654
November	781	2 033	10 815	2 009	11 484	823	1 356	3 410	2 766	3 507	1 459
December	707	2 295	11 143	1 912	10 148	907	1 301	3 155	2 745	3 344	965
2003											
January	728	2 003	9 110	1 891	10 831	883	1 421	2 861	2 717	3 003	400
February	715	1 808	9 441	1 651	10 958	849	1 106	2 643	2 204	3 493	690
March	810	2 291	10 435	1 936	11 783	959	1 231	2 897	2 494	3 729	1 458
April	855	2 118	10 333	2 041	11 155	951	1 333	3 342	2 574	3 515	1 648
May	793	2 054	9 106	1 990	11 495	825	1 285	2 751	2 571	3 559	1 581
June	761	2 109	9 739	2 169	11 420	935	1 365	3 070	2 622	3 525	1 533
July	868	2 487	10 129	2 331	11 125	955	1 239	3 241	2 720	3 711	1 539
August	797	2 169	9 089	2 223	11 403	878	1 065	2 776	2 709	3 171	1 706
September	799	1 779	9 442	2 297	11 817	917	1 346	3 023	2 815	3 647	1 620
October	949	2 105	10 787	2 435	12 966	1 011	1 342	3 674	2 758	4 136	1 648
November	767	2 157	10 187	2 228	11 693	941	1 124	3 397	2 602	3 430	1 539
December	673	2 334	10 241	2 249	11 417	849	1 281	3 555	2 812	3 876	1 773

... = Not available.

Table 7-14. U.S. Exports of Services

(Balance of payments basis, millions of dollars, seasonally adjusted.)

Year and month	Total	Travel	Passenger fares	Other transportation	Royalties and license fees	Other private services (financial, professional, etc.)	Transfers under U.S. military sales contracts [1]	U.S. government miscellaneous services
1960	6 290	919	175	1 607	837	570	2 030	153
1961	6 295	947	183	1 620	906	607	1 867	164
1962	6 941	957	191	1 764	1 056	585	2 193	195
1963	7 348	1 015	205	1 898	1 162	613	2 219	236
1964	7 840	1 207	241	2 076	1 314	651	2 086	265
1965	8 824	1 380	271	2 175	1 534	714	2 465	285
1966	9 616	1 590	317	2 333	1 516	814	2 721	326
1967	10 667	1 646	371	2 426	1 747	951	3 191	336
1968	11 917	1 775	411	2 548	1 867	1 024	3 939	353
1969	12 806	2 043	450	2 652	2 019	1 160	4 138	343
1970	14 171	2 331	544	3 125	2 331	1 294	4 214	332
1971	16 358	2 534	615	3 299	2 545	1 546	5 472	347
1972	17 841	2 817	699	3 579	2 770	1 764	5 856	357
1973	19 832	3 412	975	4 465	3 225	1 985	5 369	401
1974	22 591	4 032	1 104	5 697	3 821	2 321	5 197	419
1975	25 497	4 697	1 039	5 840	4 300	2 920	6 256	446
1976	27 971	5 742	1 229	6 747	4 353	3 584	5 826	489
1977	31 485	6 150	1 366	7 090	4 920	3 848	7 554	557
1978	36 353	7 183	1 603	8 136	5 885	4 717	8 209	620
1979	39 692	8 441	2 156	9 971	6 184	5 439	6 981	520
1980	47 584	10 588	2 591	11 618	7 085	6 276	9 029	398
1981	57 354	12 913	3 111	12 560	7 284	10 250	10 720	517
1982	64 079	12 393	3 174	12 317	5 603	17 444	12 572	576
1983	64 307	10 947	3 610	12 590	5 778	18 192	12 524	666
1984	71 168	17 177	4 067	13 809	6 177	19 255	9 969	714
1985	73 155	17 762	4 411	14 674	6 678	20 035	8 718	878
1986	86 689	20 385	5 582	15 438	8 113	28 027	8 549	595
1987	98 661	23 563	7 003	17 027	10 174	29 263	11 106	526
1988	110 919	29 434	8 976	19 311	12 139	31 111	9 284	664
1989	127 087	36 205	10 657	20 526	13 818	36 729	8 564	587
1990	147 832	43 007	15 298	22 042	16 634	40 251	9 932	668
1991	164 261	48 385	15 854	22 631	17 819	47 748	11 135	690
1992	177 252	54 742	16 618	21 531	20 841	50 292	12 387	841
1993	185 920	57 875	16 528	21 958	21 695	53 510	13 471	883
1994	200 395	58 417	16 997	23 754	26 712	60 841	12 787	887
1995	219 183	63 395	18 909	26 081	30 289	65 048	14 643	818
1996	239 489	69 809	20 422	26 074	32 470	73 340	16 446	928
1997	256 271	73 426	20 868	27 006	33 228	84 113	16 675	955
1998	263 079	71 325	20 098	25 604	35 626	92 095	17 405	926
1999	282 478	74 801	19 785	26 916	39 670	104 493	15 928	885
2000	298 986	82 400	20 687	29 803	43 233	108 287	13 790	786
2001	287 941	71 893	17 926	28 442	40 696	115 614	12 539	831
2002	294 107	66 728	17 046	29 195	44 219	124 181	11 943	795
2003	307 381	64 509	15 693	31 833	48 227	133 818	12 491	810
2001								
January	25 033	6 885	1 795	2 540	3 407	9 416	915	75
February	24 732	6 831	1 656	2 438	3 363	9 472	898	74
March	24 971	7 019	1 649	2 499	3 348	9 455	928	73
April	24 713	6 629	1 594	2 444	3 424	9 428	1 127	67
May	24 568	6 434	1 626	2 372	3 419	9 503	1 147	67
June	24 983	6 556	1 645	2 418	3 398	9 625	1 274	67
July	24 624	6 502	1 667	2 388	3 290	9 567	1 139	71
August	24 827	6 491	1 756	2 470	3 284	9 651	1 103	72
September	21 836	4 381	1 084	2 192	3 314	9 702	1 092	71
October	21 961	4 239	1 100	2 294	3 456	9 875	931	66
November	22 566	4 787	1 137	2 200	3 492	9 971	915	64
December	23 125	5 139	1 217	2 187	3 500	9 948	1 070	64
2002								
January	23 315	5 217	1 391	2 282	3 390	10 025	945	65
February	23 566	5 406	1 412	2 280	3 414	10 055	934	65
March	24 204	5 569	1 421	2 402	3 478	10 363	906	65
April	23 995	5 322	1 349	2 389	3 680	10 309	880	66
May	24 408	5 406	1 476	2 382	3 759	10 412	907	66
June	24 487	5 439	1 454	2 383	3 808	10 372	964	67
July	24 467	5 365	1 387	2 430	3 810	10 323	1 085	67
August	24 844	5 495	1 527	2 509	3 817	10 299	1 130	67
September	24 687	5 461	1 374	2 445	3 810	10 328	1 203	66
October	25 154	5 867	1 421	2 486	3 744	10 526	1 042	68
November	25 410	6 073	1 420	2 576	3 744	10 589	941	67
December	25 571	6 108	1 414	2 631	3 765	10 581	1 006	66
2003								
January	24 959	5 467	1 302	2 544	3 837	10 761	980	68
February	24 941	5 390	1 303	2 538	3 877	10 837	929	67
March	24 639	5 005	1 220	2 601	3 914	10 914	918	67
April	23 993	4 404	1 092	2 584	3 951	10 911	984	67
May	24 765	4 909	1 185	2 539	3 982	11 087	996	67
June	25 161	5 047	1 245	2 586	4 010	11 171	1 034	68
July	25 519	5 269	1 320	2 629	4 029	11 171	1 034	67
August	25 871	5 401	1 357	2 613	4 057	11 232	1 143	68
September	26 083	5 546	1 359	2 651	4 089	11 255	1 115	68
October	26 937	5 899	1 389	2 863	4 141	11 432	1 146	67
November	27 058	6 041	1 445	2 805	4 164	11 431	1 104	68
December	27 454	6 131	1 476	2 880	4 176	11 615	1 108	68

[1] Contains goods that cannot be separately identified.

Table 7-15. U.S. Imports of Services

(Balance of payments basis, millions of dollars, seasonally adjusted.)

Year and month	Total	Travel	Passenger fares	Other transportation	Royalties and license fees	Other private services (financial, professional, etc.)	Direct defense expenditures [1]	U.S. government miscellaneous services
1960	7 674	1 750	513	1 402	74	593	3 087	254
1961	7 671	1 785	506	1 437	89	588	2 998	268
1962	8 092	1 939	567	1 558	100	528	3 105	296
1963	8 362	2 114	612	1 701	112	493	2 961	370
1964	8 619	2 211	642	1 817	127	527	2 880	415
1965	9 111	2 438	717	1 951	135	461	2 952	457
1966	10 494	2 657	753	2 161	140	506	3 764	513
1967	11 863	3 207	829	2 157	166	565	4 378	561
1968	12 302	3 030	885	2 367	186	668	4 535	631
1969	13 322	3 373	1 080	2 455	221	751	4 856	586
1970	14 520	3 980	1 215	2 843	224	827	4 855	576
1971	15 400	4 373	1 290	3 130	241	956	4 819	592
1972	16 868	5 042	1 596	3 520	294	1 043	4 784	589
1973	18 843	5 526	1 790	4 694	385	1 180	4 629	640
1974	21 379	5 980	2 095	5 942	346	1 262	5 032	722
1975	21 996	6 417	2 263	5 708	472	1 551	4 795	789
1976	24 570	6 856	2 568	6 852	482	2 006	4 895	911
1977	27 640	7 451	2 748	7 972	504	2 190	5 823	951
1978	32 189	8 475	2 896	9 124	671	2 573	7 352	1 099
1979	36 689	9 413	3 184	10 906	831	2 822	8 294	1 239
1980	41 491	10 397	3 607	11 790	724	2 909	10 851	1 214
1981	45 503	11 479	4 487	12 474	650	3 562	11 564	1 287
1982	51 749	12 394	4 772	11 710	795	8 159	12 460	1 460
1983	54 973	13 149	6 003	12 222	943	8 001	13 087	1 568
1984	67 748	22 913	5 735	14 843	1 168	9 040	12 516	1 534
1985	72 862	24 558	6 444	15 643	1 170	10 203	13 108	1 735
1986	80 147	25 913	6 505	17 766	1 401	13 146	13 730	1 686
1987	90 787	29 310	7 283	19 010	1 857	16 485	14 950	1 893
1988	98 526	32 114	7 729	20 891	2 601	17 667	15 604	1 921
1989	102 479	33 416	8 249	22 172	2 528	18 930	15 313	1 871
1990	117 659	37 349	10 531	24 966	3 135	22 229	17 531	1 919
1991	118 459	35 322	10 012	24 975	4 035	25 590	16 409	2 116
1992	119 447	38 552	10 603	23 767	5 161	25 267	13 835	2 263
1993	123 664	40 713	11 410	24 524	5 032	27 645	12 086	2 255
1994	132 943	43 782	13 062	26 019	5 852	31 451	10 217	2 560
1995	141 278	44 916	14 663	27 034	6 919	35 080	10 043	2 623
1996	152 431	48 078	15 809	27 403	7 837	39 556	11 061	2 687
1997	166 345	52 051	18 138	28 959	9 161	43 567	11 707	2 762
1998	181 260	56 483	19 971	30 363	11 235	48 174	12 185	2 849
1999	199 715	58 963	21 315	34 139	13 107	56 035	13 335	2 821
2000	224 916	64 705	24 274	41 425	16 468	61 688	13 473	2 883
2001	223 445	60 200	22 633	38 682	16 538	67 675	14 835	2 882
2002	232 947	58 044	19 969	38 407	19 235	75 271	19 101	2 920
2003	256 337	56 613	20 957	44 768	20 049	85 829	25 117	3 004
2001								
January	19 248	5 340	1 971	3 845	1 383	5 317	1 152	240
February	18 606	5 248	1 907	3 296	1 370	5 382	1 162	241
March	18 794	5 297	1 920	3 306	1 362	5 503	1 164	242
April	19 576	5 784	2 031	3 444	1 357	5 588	1 130	242
May	19 380	5 601	2 006	3 363	1 354	5 679	1 135	242
June	19 143	5 340	2 099	3 207	1 354	5 749	1 152	242
July	19 136	5 314	2 197	3 128	1 351	5 723	1 180	243
August	19 264	5 363	2 235	3 111	1 358	5 734	1 221	242
September	16 931	3 934	1 463	2 905	1 374	5 740	1 274	241
October	17 291	3 965	1 588	3 001	1 413	5 709	1 380	235
November	17 859	4 398	1 581	3 030	1 426	5 761	1 428	235
December	18 223	4 616	1 635	3 049	1 435	5 794	1 457	237
2002								
January	18 575	4 780	1 652	2 977	1 423	6 065	1 433	245
February	19 208	4 848	1 635	2 953	1 974	6 099	1 451	248
March	18 665	4 825	1 587	2 926	1 442	6 162	1 475	248
April	18 602	4 599	1 574	3 194	1 450	6 031	1 511	243
May	18 804	4 694	1 595	3 192	1 481	6 057	1 544	241
June	19 495	4 959	1 705	3 162	1 774	6 076	1 578	241
July	19 475	4 806	1 652	3 282	1 655	6 216	1 622	242
August	19 312	4 567	1 597	3 269	1 685	6 299	1 653	242
September	19 719	4 941	1 580	3 201	1 680	6 396	1 680	241
October	19 974	4 823	1 889	3 246	1 581	6 514	1 677	244
November	20 268	4 979	1 698	3 444	1 553	6 638	1 713	243
December	20 849	5 223	1 805	3 565	1 537	6 713	1 764	242
2003								
January	20 703	4 945	1 715	3 567	1 531	6 847	1 850	248
February	20 522	4 769	1 672	3 458	1 539	6 923	1 912	249
March	20 759	4 598	1 620	3 771	1 559	6 993	1 970	248
April	20 333	4 083	1 583	3 792	1 606	6 979	2 040	250
May	20 493	4 265	1 603	3 611	1 637	7 047	2 081	249
June	20 941	4 442	1 689	3 706	1 669	7 077	2 108	250
July	21 656	4 738	1 846	3 884	1 711	7 143	2 083	251
August	21 663	4 902	1 875	3 639	1 736	7 152	2 108	251
September	21 769	4 769	1 791	3 790	1 757	7 263	2 148	251
October	22 251	4 938	1 853	3 783	1 753	7 429	2 243	252
November	22 310	4 953	1 894	3 697	1 766	7 470	2 278	252
December	22 942	5 211	1 816	4 072	1 785	7 509	2 296	253

[1] Contains goods that cannot be separately identified.

Table 7-16. U.S. Export and Import Price Indexes

(2000 = 100, not seasonally adjusted.)

Year and month	Exports			Imports		
	All commodities	Agricultural	Nonagricultural	All commodities	Petroleum [1]	Nonpetroleum
1989	94.7	110.5	92.7	91.1	61.2	96.0
1990	95.5	105.1	94.4	94.0	75.5	97.1
1991	96.3	103.4	95.4	94.2	67.3	98.7
1992	96.3	102.5	95.7	94.9	62.9	100.0
1993	96.9	104.4	96.2	94.6	57.7	100.6
1994	98.9	109.4	98.0	96.2	54.3	103.2
1995	103.9	119.0	102.5	100.6	59.8	107.2
1996	104.5	132.6	101.6	101.6	71.1	106.4
1997	103.1	120.6	101.3	99.1	66.0	104.1
1998	99.7	108.8	98.8	93.1	44.8	100.4
1999	98.4	101.1	98.2	93.9	60.1	99.0
2000	100.0	100.0	100.0	100.0	100.0	100.0
2001	99.2	101.2	99.0	96.5	82.8	98.5
2002	98.2	103.2	97.8	94.1	85.3	96.2
2003	99.7	112.3	98.8	96.9	103.2	97.3
1999						
January	98.5	106.2	97.8	91.3	37.1	99.5
February	98.3	103.7	97.8	91.2	36.9	99.4
March	97.9	100.6	97.7	91.5	42.0	99.0
April	98.1	101.0	97.9	92.4	50.6	98.8
May	98.2	101.4	97.9	93.1	54.3	99.0
June	98.2	101.1	97.9	92.9	54.5	98.8
July	98.1	98.9	98.0	93.8	61.9	98.6
August	98.4	100.8	98.2	94.8	69.1	98.7
September	98.5	100.7	98.3	95.8	74.9	98.9
October	98.8	100.6	98.7	96.0	76.1	99.0
November	99.0	99.6	99.0	96.7	79.2	99.4
December	99.0	98.9	99.0	97.4	84.2	99.4
2000						
January	99.2	99.0	99.2	97.8	87.2	99.4
February	99.6	100.0	99.6	99.7	100.2	99.7
March	100.0	100.4	100.0	99.9	99.4	100.0
April	100.0	101.3	99.9	98.5	88.1	100.1
May	100.2	101.9	100.1	98.8	92.1	99.9
June	100.1	100.5	100.0	100.2	101.9	99.9
July	100.0	98.3	100.2	100.2	100.4	100.2
August	99.8	96.3	100.1	100.4	101.3	100.3
September	100.4	99.4	100.5	101.6	111.8	100.0
October	100.3	99.9	100.3	101.2	108.7	100.0
November	100.3	100.9	100.2	101.2	109.8	99.9
December	100.1	102.0	99.9	100.5	99.0	100.7
2001						
January	100.3	102.5	100.1	100.5	93.1	101.6
February	100.2	101.0	100.1	99.9	93.3	100.8
March	100.0	101.3	99.9	98.3	87.2	100.0
April	99.9	100.8	99.8	97.8	86.2	99.5
May	99.6	100.8	99.5	98.0	90.3	99.2
June	99.4	100.9	99.3	97.6	89.4	98.9
July	99.0	101.8	98.8	96.1	84.6	97.8
August	98.8	102.8	98.5	96.0	86.1	97.5
September	99.0	102.5	98.6	95.9	86.7	97.3
October	98.3	100.7	98.1	93.7	73.4	96.8
November	97.8	99.2	97.7	92.3	63.8	96.6
December	97.6	100.2	97.4	91.4	59.9	96.2
2002						
January	97.5	100.9	97.2	91.6	63.0	96.1
February	97.3	98.3	97.2	91.6	65.7	95.7
March	97.6	98.9	97.5	92.8	76.9	95.8
April	98.0	99.6	97.8	94.3	86.7	96.3
May	98.0	99.5	97.8	94.4	88.4	96.2
June	98.0	100.7	97.8	94.1	85.3	96.2
July	98.3	103.4	97.9	94.5	88.5	96.2
August	98.5	105.2	97.9	94.8	91.8	96.3
September	98.8	108.6	98.0	95.5	97.1	96.4
October	98.7	106.6	98.1	95.5	97.0	96.4
November	98.8	108.7	98.0	94.6	89.0	96.3
December	98.6	108.2	97.8	95.2	94.0	96.5
2003						
January	99.0	108.0	98.0	97.0	108.0	97.0
February	99.5	107.9	98.8	98.5	119.9	97.1
March	99.7	107.5	99.1	99.1	118.6	98.1
April	99.6	107.9	99.0	96.0	96.3	97.1
May	99.7	110.6	98.8	95.3	91.5	96.9
June	99.5	110.0	98.7	96.2	96.4	97.3
July	99.4	109.9	98.6	96.7	101.4	97.3
August	99.4	108.8	98.7	96.7	103.2	97.0
September	99.8	114.7	98.6	96.2	97.2	97.3
October	100.0	117.5	98.7	96.3	98.8	97.2
November	100.5	122.2	98.8	96.8	100.9	97.4
December	100.8	122.7	99.1	97.5	106.0	97.7

[1] Petroleum and petroleum products.

NOTES AND DEFINITIONS

This chapter presents data from two different data systems on international flows of goods, services, income payments, and financial transactions as they impact the U.S. economy. Tables 7-1 through 7-5 present data on the value, quantities, and prices of foreign transactions in the National Income and Product Accounts (NIPAs). Table 7-6 shows foreign transactions in the U.S. International Transactions Accounts (ITAs). Both sets of accounts are prepared by the Bureau of Economic Analysis, and draw on the same source data. The source data are presented in greater detail in Tables 7-8 through 7-15 and the Notes and Definitions thereto. Table 7-16 presents selected summary values for export and import price indexes compiled by the Bureau of Labor Statistics, which are used in converting current-dollar values to constant-dollar values.

Because of certain differences in concept, scope, and definitions, the aggregate values of international transactions in the NIPAs (as shown in Tables 7-1 and 7-4) are not exactly equal to similar concepts in the ITAs, which are the source for the data in Tables 7-6 through 7-15. The principal sources of difference are as follows:
- The NIPAs cover only the 50 states and the District of Columbia. The international transactions accounts also include U.S. territories and Puerto Rico;
- Differences in the treatment of gold; and
- Differences in the treatment of services without payment by financial intermediaries except life insurance carriers (imputed interest).

A reconciliation of the two sets of international accounts is published regularly as part of the NIPAs, most recently in the June 2004 *Survey of Current Business*, p. D-84, Table 2.

TABLES 7-1 AND 7-4
FOREIGN TRANSACTIONS IN THE NATIONAL INCOME AND PRODUCT ACCOUNTS

SOURCE: U.S. DEPARTMENT OF COMMERCE, BUREAU OF ECONOMIC ANALYSIS

See the Notes and Definitions to Chapter 1 for an overview of the National Income and Product Accounts.

In the 2003 comprehensive revision, the NIPA foreign transactions account is split into two accounts—the current account and the capital account. (This change had already been made in the ITAs.) Most international transactions fall into the current account, but occasionally there are substantial flows in the capital account when major assets are transferred, such as the U.S. government's transfer of the Panama Canal to the Republic of Panama in 1999.

Definitions

In accordance with the split between current and capital account, there are now two NIPA measures of the balance of international transactions.

The *balance on current account, national income and product accounts* is *current receipts from the rest of the world* minus *current payments to the rest of the world*. A negative value indicates that current payments exceed current receipts.

Net lending or net borrowing(-), national income and product accounts is equal to the balance on current account less capital transfers to the rest of the world (net). Capital transfer payments to the rest of the world (net)—not shown separately in Table 7-1, but a similar measure is shown in the ITAs in Table 7-6—are cash or in-kind transfers that are linked to the acquisition or disposition of an existing asset. (In contrast, the current account is limited to flows associated with current production of goods and services.) Net lending or net borrowing provides an indirect measure of the net acquisition of foreign assets by U.S. residents less the net acquisition of U.S. assets by foreign residents. (These asset flows are measured directly in the ITAs. See Table 7-6 and its Notes and Definitions for a more extensive discussion of the relationship between the balances on current and capital account and international asset flows.)

Current receipts from the rest of the world is *exports of goods and services* plus *income receipts*.

Current payments to the rest of the world is *imports of goods and services* plus *income payments* plus *Current taxes and transfer payments (net)*.

Exports and imports of goods and services. Goods are products that can be stored or inventoried. Services are products that cannot be stored and are consumed at the place and time of their purchase. Goods include expenditures abroad by U.S. residents except for travel. Services include foreign travel by U.S. residents, expenditures in the United States by foreign travelers, and exports and imports of certain goods, primarily military equipment purchased and sold by the federal government. See the following paragraph for the definition of "travel."

Table 7-4 shows values for selected components of total goods and services; the components shown will not add to the total because of omitted items. In the case of *goods*, a miscellaneous "other" category is not shown. In the case of *services*, only two components are shown: *travel*, which does not include passenger fares but does include, as imports, all other spending abroad by tourists from the United States, and as exports, spending by foreign tourists in the United States; and a category called "Other private services," which includes the professional and financial services (for example, computer services) which have accounted for a large part of the long-term growth in the service category. (The remaining components of total services are: transfers under U.S. military agency sales contracts; passenger fares; other transportation; royalties and license fees; and a miscellaneous, smaller "other" category.)

Income receipts and payments. Income receipts—receipts from abroad of factor (labor or capital) income by U.S. residents—are analogous to exports, and are combined with them to yield total *Current receipts from the rest of the world. Income payments* by U.S. entities of factor income to entities abroad are analogous to imports.

Current taxes and transfer payments (net) consist of net payments between the U.S. and abroad that do not involve payment for the services of the labor or capital factors of production, purchase of currently produced goods and services, or transfer of an existing asset. It includes net flows from persons, from government, and from business. The types of payments included are personal remittances from U.S. residents to the rest of the world, net of remittances from foreigners to U.S. residents; government grants; and transfer payments from businesses. Only the net payment to the rest of the world is shown. It is usually positive, with transfers from the United States to abroad exceeding the reverse flow. There was an exception in 1991 when U.S. allies in the Gulf War reimbursed the United States for the cost of the war. This resulted in net payments to the United States from the rest of the world and therefore appears as a negative entry in the net transfer payments column.

TABLES 7-2, 7-3 AND 7-5
CHAIN-TYPE QUANTITY AND PRICE INDEXES FOR NIPA FOREIGN TRANSACTIONS

These indexes represent the separation of the current-dollar values in Tables 7-1 and 7-4 into their real quantity and price trends components. See the Notes and Definitions to Chapter 1 for a general explanation of chained-dollar estimates of real output and prices. As explained there, quantity indexes are shown instead of constant-dollar estimates because BEA no longer publishes its real output estimates before 1990 in any detail in the constant-dollar form. Therefore, quantity indexes are the only comprehensive source of information about longer-term trends in real volumes.

TABLES 7-6 AND 19-9
U.S. INTERNATIONAL TRANSACTIONS

SOURCE: U.S. DEPARTMENT OF COMMERCE, BUREAU OF ECONOMIC ANALYSIS

The U.S. international transactions accounts, or "balance of payments," provide a comprehensive view of economic and financial transactions between the United States and foreign countries, measured in current dollars only (unlike the NIPAs in which price and quantity trends are also estimated). Direct measurement of the values of asset flows further distinguishes this set of accounts from the NIPAs.

The International Transactions Account (ITA) is subdivided into three sets of accounts, each comprising credit and debit items. In concept, all of these items together provide a complete accounting for U.S. international transactions and should therefore sum to zero. In practice, there are substantial discrepancies due to measurement problems. See the Definitions below for an explanation of the "statistical discrepancy" in these accounts, which is different from the measure of the same name in the NIPAs.

The balance on the "current account" is the most frequently quoted statistic from these accounts, and is frequently, but imprecisely, called the "trade balance." (See the Definitions below for the correct definitions of "trade balance" and "merchandise trade balance", both of which differ from the current account balance.) The current account includes exports and imports of goods and of travel, transportation, and other services; receipts and payments of income between U.S. and foreign residents; and foreign aid and other current transfers. The "financial account" covers most international flows of capital, private and official, including direct investment. A "capital account," which is small relative to the other two accounts, includes certain transactions in existing assets.

More detailed data on exports and imports of goods and services as they are measured in these accounts are shown in Tables 7-8 through 7-15.

Definitions

Unlike the practice in the NIPA accounts, each category of transaction in the ITAs is presented either as a "*credit*," with an implicit plus sign, or as a "*debit*," with a minus sign. The signs indicate the direction of ultimate impact on the overall balance.

Credits (+): The following items are treated as credits in the international transactions accounts: Exports of goods and services and income receipts; unilateral current transfers to the United States; capital account transactions receipts; financial inflows, that is, increases in foreign-owned assets (U.S. liabilities) and decreases in U.S.-owned assets (U.S. claims).

Debits (-): The following items are treated as debits in the international transactions accounts, indicated by minus signs in the data cells: Imports of goods and services and income payments; unilateral current transfers to foreigners; capital accounts transactions payments; financial outflows, that is, decreases in foreign-owned assets (U.S. liabilities) and increases in U.S.-owned assets (U.S. claims).

This convention of credits and debits is used only in the ITAs in Table 7-6. In this table, import values all have a negative sign. Import values are shown without negative signs both in the NIPA tables (7-1 and 7-4) and in the detailed tables from the Census on exports and imports of goods and services (7-8 through 7-15).

The *balance on goods* is the excess of exports of goods over imports of goods. (A minus sign indicates an excess of imports over exports.) A very similar concept that appears in monthly trade reports is called the "merchandise trade balance."

The *balance on services* is the excess of service exports over service imports. (A minus sign indicates an excess of imports over exports.)

The *balance on goods and services* is the sum of the balance on goods and the balance on services. This is the concept that is accurately described as the "balance of trade."

The *balance on income* is the excess of income receipts from abroad over income payments to foreigners. (A minus sign indicates an excess of payments over receipts.)

The *balance on goods, services, and income* is the excess of exports of goods, services, and income over imports of goods, services, and income. It is equal to the sum of the balance on goods and services and the balance on income. (A minus sign indicates an excess of imports over exports.)

The *balance on unilateral transfers* is equal to unilateral transfers, net, that is, transfers to the United States minus transfers from the United States. This category includes U.S. government grants, pensions, and other transfers, and private remittances and other transfers. It includes an adjustment for the difference between actual and normal insured losses; see the entry below, in the Notes for Tables 7-8 through 7-15, concerning the measurement of insurance services.

The *balance on current account* is equal to the sum of the balance on goods, services, and income and the balance on unilateral transfers.

The *capital account* covers net capital transfers and the acquisition and disposal of nonproduced nonfinancial assets. The major types of *capital transfers* are debt forgiveness and assets that accompany immigrants.

Nonproduced nonfinancial assets include rights to natural resources, patents, copyrights, trademarks, franchises, and leases.

The *financial account* includes all other inflows and outflows of capital, that is, changes in U.S.-owned assets abroad and foreign-owned assets in the United States, including official reserve assets, direct investment, securities, currency, and bank deposits.

In concept, the balance on current account is necessarily offset exactly by the net financial and capital inflow or outflow; for example, a U.S. current account deficit results in more dollars held by foreigners, which *must* be reflected in additional claims on the United States held by foreigners, whether in the form of U.S. currency, securities, loans, or other forms of ownership or obligation. But because of different and incomplete data sources, the financial and capital accounts do not exactly offset the current account. The statistical discrepancy in the U.S. international accounts—the sum of all credits and debits, with the sign reversed—measures the amount by which the measured net financial and capital flow would have to be augmented (or diminished, in the case of a negative discrepancy) to offset the current account balance exactly. (In the quarterly accounts, a part of this discrepancy, the seasonal adjustment discrepancy, results from separate seasonal adjustments.) The statistical discrepancy in the international accounts is not the same as the statistical discrepancy in the national income and product accounts, which arises from measurement differences between domestic output and domestic income.

Notes on the data

Exports and imports of goods in the international transactions account exclude exports of goods under U.S. military agency sales contracts identified in Census Bureau export documents and imports of goods under direct defense expenditures identified in import documents. They also reflect various other adjustments (for valuation, coverage, and timing) of Census Bureau statistics to a balance-of-payments basis. See Tables 7-9 and 7-10 and the associated Notes and Definitions for further information.

Services include some goods, mainly military equipment (included in transfers under military agency sales contracts); major equipment, other materials, supplies, and petroleum products purchased abroad by U.S. military agencies (included in direct defense expenditures abroad); and fuels purchased by airline and steamship operators (included in other transportation).

U.S. government grants include transfers of goods and services under U.S. military grant programs. The data for 1974 include extraordinary U.S. government transactions with India.

Beginning in 1982, *private remittances and other transfers* includes taxes paid by U.S. private residents to foreign governments and taxes paid by private nonresidents to the U.S. government.

At the present time, all U.S. Treasury-owned *gold* is held in the United States.

Beginning with the data for 1982, *direct investment income* and the reinvested earnings component of direct investment financial flows are measured on a current-cost (replacement-cost) basis after adjustment to reported depreciation, depletion, and expensed exploration and development costs. For prior years, depreciation is valued in terms of the historical cost of assets and reflects a mix of prices for the various years in which capital investments were made. See *Survey of Current Business*, July 1999, pages 65–67, and *Survey of Current Business*, June 1992, pages 72ff.

Repayments on U.S. credits and other long-term assets includes sales of foreign obligations to foreigners. The data for 1974 include extraordinary U.S. government transactions with India, described in "Special U.S. Government Transactions," *Survey of Current Business*, June 1974, page 27.

Foreign official assets in the United States. U.S. Treasury securities consists of bills, certificates, marketable bonds and notes, and nonmarketable convertible and nonconvertible bonds and notes; *other U.S. government securities* consists of U.S. Treasury and Export-Import Bank obligations, not included elsewhere, and of debt securities of U.S. government corporations and agencies; *other U.S. government liabilities* includes, primarily, U.S. government liabilities to foreign official authorities associated with military agency sales contracts and other transactions arranged with or through foreign official agencies; *other foreign official assets* consists of official investments in U.S. corporate stocks and in debt securities of private corporations and state and local governments.

Estimates of *U.S. currency flows abroad* were introduced for the first time as part of the July 1997 revisions. Data for 1974 and subsequent years were affected (see *Survey of Current Business*, July 1997). Beginning with the 1998 revisions, currency flows are published separately from U.S. Treasury securities.

For 1978–1983, *U.S. Treasury securities* includes foreign-currency-denominated notes sold to private residents abroad.

Revisions

The international transactions accounts are revised annually in July. Changes in definitions and methodology, as well as the incorporation of newly available source data, may be introduced in these revisions.

Data availability

Quarterly and annual data are available. Data first are reported in a press release and subsequently published in an article in the *Survey of Current Business*, which can also be found on the BEA Internet site. Revisions to historical data are published annually. The most recent historical revisions also appear in the July 2004 issue of the *Survey*. Complete historical data may be purchased on diskette from BEA. Historical data also are available on the BEA Internet site at <http://www.bea.doc.gov>.

References

Discussions of the impact of changes in methodology and incorporation of new data sources are found in the July (June for 1995 and earlier) issues of the *Survey of Current Business* each year, the most recent being "Annual Revision of the U.S. International Accounts, 1989–2003" (July 2004).

The Balance of Payments of the United States: Concepts, Data Sources, and Estimating Procedures (May 1990), available on the BEA Internet site or from NTIS (Accession No. PB 90-268715) describes the methodology in detail and provides a list of data sources.

TABLE 7-7
INTERNATIONAL INVESTMENT POSITION OF THE UNITED STATES

SOURCE: U.S. DEPARTMENT OF COMMERCE, BUREAU OF ECONOMIC ANALYSIS

The data presented in Tables 7-1 through 7-6 all represent *flows* of goods, services, and money over the designated time periods. Table 7-7, in contrast, is a measure of *stocks*, that is, total holdings, of money and other claims. The data on the international investment position of the United States measure the extent to which the United States and its residents hold claims of ownership on foreigners, or are creditors of foreigners; the extent to which foreigners, including foreign governments, hold claims of ownership on assets located in the United States or are creditors of U.S. residents and entities; and the net difference between the two amounts. This difference measures the amount by which the United States is a net creditor of the rest of the world or a net debtor to the rest of the world. A position of net U.S. indebtedness is represented by a minus sign in the net international investment position.

Changes in the net investment position can arise in two principal ways. The first way is through inflows or outflows of capital. A net inflow of capital increases U.S. indebtedness to foreigners, while a net outflow increases foreigners' indebtedness to the United States. A deficit in the U.S. international current account requires an equivalent inflow of foreign capital, while a surplus would require an equivalent outflow of U.S. capital; see notes on Table 7-6. The second way is through valuation adjustments, which are of several kinds: market prices of assets can change; changes in exchange rates can cause revaluation of foreign-currency-denominated assets; and there can be miscellaneous other adjustments due to changes in coverage, statistical discrepancies, and the like.

CHAPTER 7: U.S. FOREIGN TRADE AND FINANCE

Definitions

Direct investment occurs when an individual or business in one country (the parent) obtains a lasting interest in, and a degree of influence over the management of, a business enterprise in another country (the affiliate). The U.S. data define this degree of interest to be ownership of at least 10 percent of the voting securities of an incorporated business enterprise or the equivalent interest in an unincorporated business enterprise.

When direct investment positions are valued at the historical costs carried on the books of the affiliated companies, much of the investment will reflect the price levels of earlier time periods. Therefore, before calculating the overall U.S. position, BEA estimates the *aggregate* direct investment totals using two alternative valuation bases. *Detailed* direct investment data by country and industry are available only on a historical cost basis.

At *current cost*, the portion of the direct investment position representing parents' shares of their affiliates' tangible assets (property, plant, equipment, and inventories) is revalued to replacement cost in today's money, using a perpetual inventory model, appropriate price indexes, and appropriate depreciation allowances. (The same methodology is used for the U.S. stock of fixed assets; see the Notes and Definitions to Table 5-5.) This is an adjustment made to the asset side of the balance sheet and reflects prices of tangible assets only.

The *market value* method revalues the owners' equity portion of the direct investment positions using general country indexes of stock market prices. This adjustment is made on the liability and owner's equity side of the balance sheet. Stock price changes reflect changes not only in the value of tangible assets but also in the value of intangible assets and in the outlook for a country or industry.

Market values are more volatile than current cost, reflecting the volatility of stock markets. Note, for example, that in some years the total market value of direct investment is significantly greater than the current replacement cost, while in other years, such as 1982 through 1984, it is less.

U.S. official reserve assets include gold, valued at the current market price; special drawing rights; the U.S. reserve position in the International Monetary Fund; and official holdings of foreign currencies.

Other U.S. government assets include other U.S. government claims on foreigners and holdings of foreign currency and short-term assets.

U.S. nonbank claims are U.S. claims on affiliated foreigners reported by U.S. nonbanking concerns.

U.S. bank claims are claims on foreigners, such as loans and commercial paper, held by U.S. banks and not reported elsewhere in the accounts.

Foreign official assets include foreign government holdings of claims on the United States, including U.S. government securities and other liabilities and deposits held by such governments in U.S. banks.

Foreign-owned assets in the United States, other than official assets, also include *U.S. Treasury securities, U.S. currency, corporate and other bonds, corporate stocks, U.S. liabilities (to foreigners) reported by U.S. nonbanking concerns*, and *U.S. bank liabilities* (such as deposits) *to foreigners*.

Data availability

The annual (year-end) data are presented each year, along with revisions for earlier years and a descriptive article, in the July issue of the *Survey of Current Business*. The articles and the data are available on the BEA Internet site at <http://www.bea.doc.gov>.

References

Relevant articles in the July 2004 *Survey of Current Business* are: "The International Investment Position of the United States at Yearend 2003" and "Direct Investment Position for 2003: Country and Industry Detail." For background on the valuation of direct investment and other components, see "Valuation of the U.S. Net International Investment Position," *Survey of Current Business*, May 1991. Also see the references for Table 7-6.

TABLES 7-8 THROUGH 7-15
EXPORTS AND IMPORTS OF GOODS AND SERVICES

SOURCES: U.S. DEPARTMENT OF COMMERCE, BUREAU OF THE CENSUS AND BUREAU OF ECONOMIC ANALYSIS (BEA)

These tables present the source data that are used to build up the aggregate measures of goods and services flows shown in Tables 7-1 through 7-6. These data are compiled and published monthly, making trends evident before the publication of the quarterly aggregate estimates. They also provide more detail than the quarterly aggregates.

Monthly and annual data on exports and imports of goods are compiled by the Bureau of the Census from documents collected by the U.S. Customs Service. BEA makes certain adjustments to these data (described below) to place the estimates on a "balance of payments" basis—a basis consistent with the national and international accounts. Data on exports and imports of services are prepared by BEA from a variety of sources. Monthly data on services are available from the beginning of 1992.

Annual and quarterly data for earlier years are available as part of the international transactions accounts. Current data on goods and services are available each month in a joint Census-BEA press release.

In the case of some of the detailed breakdowns of exports and imports, for example, by end-use categories, monthly data may not sum exactly to annual totals. This is because of later revisions, made only to annual data and not allocated to monthly data. Also, the constant-dollar figures expressed in 2000 dollars are now calculated using chain weights, so that in general the 2000-dollar detail will not add to the 2000-dollar totals.

In addition, monthly and annual data on exports and imports of goods for individual countries and various country groupings do not reflect subsequent revisions of annual total data. These country data are compiled by the Census Bureau for all countries, of which only a selection of the most significant ones is shown here. The full set of data can be accessed on the Census Internet site at <http://www.census.gov>.

Definitions: Goods

Goods: Census Basis. The Census basis goods data are compiled from documents collected by the U.S. Customs Service and reflect the movement of goods between foreign countries and the 50 states, the District of Columbia, Puerto Rico, the U.S. Virgin Islands, and U.S. Foreign Trade Zones. They include government and nongovernment shipments of goods. They exclude shipments between the United States and its territories and possessions, transactions with U.S. military, diplomatic and consular installations abroad, U.S. goods returned to the United States by its Armed Forces, personal and household effects of travelers, and in-transit shipments. The general import values reflect the total arrival of merchandise from foreign countries that immediately enters consumption channels, warehouses, or Foreign Trade Zones.

For *imports*, the value reported is the U.S. Customs Service appraised value of merchandise (generally, the price paid for merchandise for export to the United States). Import duties, freight, insurance, and other charges incurred in bringing merchandise to the United States are excluded.

Exports are valued at the f.a.s. (free alongside ship) value of merchandise at the U.S. port of export, based on the transaction price including inland freight, insurance, and other charges incurred in placing the merchandise alongside the carrier at the U.S. port of exportation.

Goods: Balance of payments (BOP) basis. Goods on a Census basis are adjusted by the BEA to goods on a BOP basis to bring the data in line with the concepts and definitions used to prepare the international and national accounts. Broadly, the adjustments include changes in ownership that occur without goods passing into or out of the customs territory of the United States. These adjustments are necessary to supplement coverage of the Census basis data, to eliminate duplication of transactions recorded elsewhere in the international accounts, and to value transactions according to a standard definition.

The *export* adjustments include: (1) Deduction of *U.S. military sales contracts*, because the Census Bureau has included these contracts in the goods data, but BEA includes them in the service category "Transfers Under U.S. Military Sales Contracts." BEA's source material for these contracts is more comprehensive, but does not distinguish between goods and services. (2) Addition of *private gift parcels* mailed to foreigners by individuals through the U.S. Postal Service. (Only commercial shipments are covered in Census goods exports.) (3) Addition to *nonmonetary gold exports* of gold purchased by foreign official agencies from private dealers in the United States and held at the Federal Reserve Bank of New York. The Census data include only gold that leaves the customs territory. (4) *Smaller adjustments* include deductions for repairs of goods, exposed motion picture film, and military grant aid, and additions for sales of fish in U.S. territorial waters, exports of electricity to Mexico, and vessels and oil rigs that change ownership without export documents being filed.

The *import* adjustments include: (1) On *inland freight in Canada*, the customs value for imports for certain Canadian goods is the point of origin in Canada. The BEA makes an addition for the inland freight charges of transporting these Canadian goods to the U.S. border. (2) An addition is made to *nonmonetary gold imports* for gold sold by foreign official agencies to private purchasers out of stock held at the Federal Reserve Bank of New York. The Census Bureau data include only gold that enters the customs territory. (3) A deduction is made for *imports by U.S. military agencies* because the Census Bureau has included these contracts in the goods data, but BEA includes them in the service category "Direct Defense Expenditures." BEA's source material is more comprehensive, but does not distinguish between goods and services. (4) *Smaller adjustments* include deductions for repairs of goods and for exposed motion picture film, and additions for imported electricity from Mexico, conversion of vessels for commercial use, and repairs to U.S. vessels abroad.

Definitions: Services

The statistics are estimates of service transactions between foreign countries and the 50 states, the District of Columbia, Puerto Rico, the U.S. Virgin Islands, and other U.S. territories and possessions. Transactions with U.S. military, diplomatic, and consular installations abroad are excluded because they are considered to be part of the U.S. economy. Services are shown in the broad categories described below. For six of these, the categories are the same for imports and exports. For the seventh, exports is "Transfers under U.S. Military Sales Contracts" while for imports the category is "Direct Defense Expenditures."

Travel—Purchases of services and goods by U.S. travelers abroad and by foreign visitors to the United States. A traveler is defined as a person who stays for a period of less than one year in a country of which the person is not a resident. Included are expenditures for food, lodging, recreation, gifts, and other items incidental to a foreign visit. Not included are the international costs of the travel itself, which are covered in *passenger fares* (see below).

Passenger fares—Fares paid by residents of one country to residents in other countries. Receipts consist of fares received by U.S. carriers from foreign residents for travel between the United States and foreign countries and between two foreign points. Payments consist of fares paid by U.S. residents to foreign carriers for travel between the United States and foreign countries.

Break in series: Travel and passenger fares—Beginning with data for 1984, these items incorporate results from a survey administered by the U.S. Travel and Tourism Administration. See *Survey of Current Business*, June 1989, pages 57ff.

Other transportation—Charges for the transportation of goods by ocean, air, waterway, pipeline, and rail carriers to and from the United States. Includes freight charges, operating expenses that transportation companies incur in foreign ports, and payments for vessel charter and aircraft and freight car rentals. (*Break in series.* Estimates of freight charges for the transportation of goods by truck between the United States and Canada are included in the data beginning with 1986. Reliable estimates for earlier years are not available. See *Survey of Current Business*, June 1994, pages 70ff.)

Royalties and license fees—Transactions with foreign residents involving intangible assets and proprietary rights, such as the use of patents, techniques, processes, formulas, designs, know-how, trademarks, copyrights, franchises, and manufacturing rights. The term "royalties" generally refers to payments for the utilization of copyrights or trademarks, and "license fees" generally refers to payments for the use of patents or industrial processes.

Other private services—Includes transactions with "affiliated" foreigners for which no identification by type is available and transactions with unaffiliated foreigners.

The term "affiliated" refers to a direct investment relationship, which exists when a U.S. person has ownership or control, directly or indirectly, of 10 percent or more of a foreign business enterprise, or when a foreign person has a similar interest in a U.S. enterprise.

Transactions with "unaffiliated" foreigners in this "other private services" category consist of education services; financial services; insurance services; telecommunications services; and business, professional, and technical services. Included in the last group are advertising services; computer and data processing services; database and other information services; research, development, and testing services; management, consulting, and public relations services; legal services; construction, engineering, architectural, and mining services; industrial engineering services; installation, maintenance and repair of equipment; and other services, including medical services and film and tape rental.

The "insurance" component of "other private services" was previously measured as premiums less actual losses paid or recovered. Furthermore, catastrophic losses were entered immediately when the loss occurred rather than when the insurance claim was actually paid out. This led to sharp swings in any month where catastrophic losses occurred, such as a large hurricane or September 2001. In the accounts as revised in July 2003 and presented here, insurance services are now measured as premiums less "normal" losses. Normal losses consist of a measure of expected regularly occurring losses based on six years of past experience *plus* an additional allowance for catastrophic loss. Catastrophic losses when they occur are added in equal increments to the estimate of regularly occurring losses over the 20 years following their occurrence. Because adoption of this methodology introduces a difference between actual and normal losses, an amount equal to the difference is entered in the international accounts as a current unilateral transfer.

BEA conducts surveys of international transactions in financial services and "selected services" (largely business, professional, and technical services). Beginning with data for 1986, *other private services* includes estimates of business, professional, and technical services from the BEA surveys of selected services. (See *Survey of Current Business*, June 1989, pages 57ff.)

Breaks in series: Royalties and license fees and other private services—These items are presented on a gross basis beginning in 1982. The definition of exports is revised to exclude U.S. parents' payments to foreign affiliates and to include U.S. affiliates' receipts from foreign parents. The definition of imports is revised to include U.S. parents' payments to foreign affiliates and to exclude U.S. affiliates' receipts from foreign parents.

Transfers under U.S. military sales contracts (exports only)—Exports of goods and services in which U.S. government military agencies participate. Includes both goods, such as equipment, and services, such as repair services and training, that cannot be separately identified. Transfers of goods and services under U.S. military grant programs are included.

Direct defense expenditures (imports only)—Expenditures incurred by U.S. military agencies abroad, including expenditures by U.S. personnel, payments of wages to foreign residents, construction expenditures, payments for foreign contractual services, and procurement of foreign goods. Included are both goods and services that cannot be separately identified.

U.S. government miscellaneous services—Transactions of U.S. Government nonmilitary agencies with foreign residents. Most of these transactions involve the provision of services to, or purchases of services from, foreigners; transfers of some goods are also included.

Services estimates are based on quarterly, annual, and benchmark surveys and partial information generated from monthly reports. Service transactions are estimated at market prices. Estimates are seasonally adjusted when statistically significant seasonal patterns are present.

Definitions: Area groupings

European Union—Austria, Belgium, Denmark, Finland, France, Germany, Greece, Ireland, Italy, Luxembourg, Netherlands, Portugal, Spain, Sweden, and United Kingdom.

Euro Area—Austria, Belgium, Finland, France, Germany, Greece, Ireland, Italy, Luxembourg, Netherlands, Portugal, and Spain. Greece entered the euro area beginning in January 2001, and is included in the data for 2001 and later years but not in the data for 2000.

Asian Newly Industrialized Countries (NICS)—Hong Kong, South Korea, Singapore, and Taiwan.

Organization of Petroleum Exporting Countries (OPEC)—Algeria, Gabon, Indonesia, Iran, Iraq, Kuwait, Libya, Nigeria, Qatar, Saudi Arabia, United Arab Emirates, and Venezuela.

Notes on the data

U.S./Canada data exchange and substitution. The data for U.S. exports to Canada are derived from import data compiled by Canada. The use of Canada's import data to produce U.S. export data requires several alignments in order to compare the two series. *Coverage*: Canadian imports are based on country of origin. U.S. goods shipped from a third country are included. U.S. exports exclude these foreign shipments. U.S. export coverage also excludes certain Canadian postal shipments. *Valuation*: Canadian imports are valued at point of origin in the United States. However, U.S. exports are valued at the port of exit in the United States and include inland freight charges, making the U.S. export value slightly larger. Canada requires inland freight to be reported. *Reexports*: U.S. exports include reexports of foreign goods. Again, the aggregate U.S. export figure is slightly larger. *Exchange Rate*: Average monthly exchange rates are applied to convert the published data to U.S. currency.

End-use categories and seasonal adjustment of trade in goods. Goods are initially classified under the Harmonized System, which describes and measures the characteristics of goods traded. Combining trade into approximately 140 export and 140 import end-use categories makes it possible to examine goods according to their principal uses. These categories are used as the basis for computing the seasonal and working-day adjusted data. These adjusted data are then summed to the six end-use aggregates for publication.

The seasonal adjustment procedure is based on a model that estimates the monthly movements as percentages above or below the general level of each end-use commodity series (unlike other methods that redistribute the actual series values over the calendar year). Imports of petroleum and petroleum products are adjusted for the length of the month.

Data availability

Data are released in a monthly joint Census-BEA press release (FT-900) about six weeks after the end of the month to which the data pertain. The data on trade in goods by end-use category (BOP basis) and trade in services are subsequently published each month in the *Survey of Current Business*. Additional data and information on goods is obtainable from the Foreign Trade Division, Bureau of the Census, Washington, DC 20233. Additional data and information on services is obtainable from the Balance of Payments Division, Bureau of Economic Analysis, Washington, DC 20230. Current releases and some historical data are available on the Bureau of the Census Internet site at <http://www.census.gov/foreign-trade/www/>.

Revisions

Data for recent years normally are revised annually. In some cases, revisions to annual totals are not distributed to monthly data, which therefore may not sum to the revised total shown. Data on trade in services may be subject to extensive revision as part of BEA's annual revision of the international transactions accounts, usually released in July.

References

Discussion of the impact of changes in methodology and incorporation of new data sources are found in discussions of annual revisions of the international transactions accounts in the July issue of the BEA publication, *Survey of Current Business*, the most recent being "Annual Revision of the U.S. International Accounts, 1989–2003" (July 2004).

TABLE 7-16
EXPORT AND IMPORT PRICE INDEXES

SOURCE: U.S. DEPARTMENT OF LABOR, BUREAU OF LABOR STATISTICS (BLS)

The BLS International Price Program produces monthly and quarterly export and import price indexes for non-military goods traded between the United States and the rest of the world.

Definitions

The *export* price index provides a measure of price change for all products sold by U.S. residents (businesses and individuals located within the geographic boundaries of the United States, whether or not owned by U.S. citizens) to foreign buyers.

The *import* price index provides a measure of price change for goods purchased from other countries by U.S. residents.

Notes on the data

Published index series use a base year of 2000 = 100 where possible.

The product universe for both the import and export indexes includes raw materials, agricultural products, and manufactures. Price data are collected primarily by mail questionnaire, in all but a few cases directly from the exporter or importer.

To the extent possible, the data refer to prices at the U.S. border for exports and at either the foreign border or the U.S. border for imports. For nearly all products, the prices refer to transactions completed during the first week of the month and represent the actual price for which the product was bought or sold, including discounts, allowances, and rebates.

For the export price indexes, the preferred pricing basis is f.a.s. (free alongside ship) U.S. port of exportation. Where necessary, adjustments are made to reported prices to place them on this basis. An attempt is made to collect two prices for imports: f.o.b. (free on board) at the port of exportation and c.i.f. (cost, insurance, and freight) at the U.S. port of importation. Adjustments are made to account for changes in product characteristics in order to obtain a "pure" measure of price change.

The indexes are weighted indexes of the Laspeyres type. The values assigned to each weight category are based on trade value figures compiled by the Bureau of the Census. They are reweighted annually, with a two-year lag (because concurrent value data are not available).

Data availability

Indexes are published monthly in a press release and a more detailed report. Selected data subsequently are published in the *Monthly Labor Review*. Indexes are published for detailed product categories, as well as for all commodities. Aggregate import indexes by country or region of origin also are available, as are indexes for selected categories of internationally traded services. Additional information is available from the Division of International Prices, Bureau of Labor Statistics. Complete historical data are available on the BLS Internet site at <http://www.bls.gov>.

References

"BLS to Produce Monthly Indexes of Export and Import Prices," *Monthly Labor Review* (December 1988) and Chapter 15, "International Price Indexes," *BLS Handbook of Methods* Bulletin 2490 (April 1997).

CHAPTER 8: PRICES

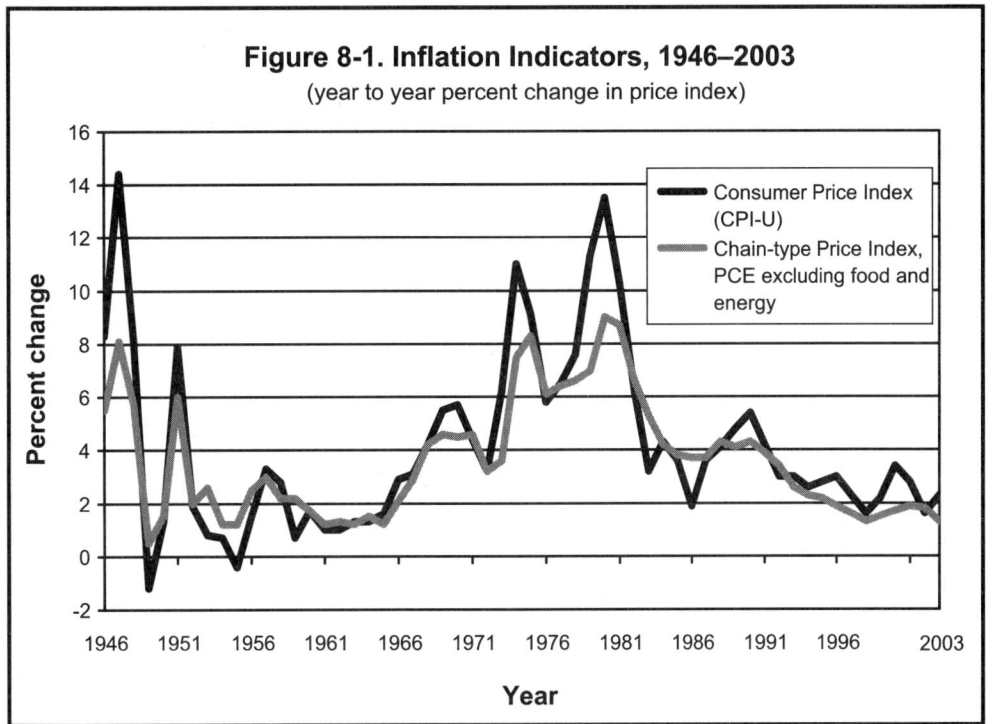

Figure 8-1. Inflation Indicators, 1946–2003
(year to year percent change in price index)

- The Consumer Price Index for all urban consumers (CPI-U) is the most widely used measure of the general price level, and percent changes in the CPI-U are the most widely used measures of inflation. Economists also are interested in an "underlying rate of inflation," free of the volatile, short-term, and often supply-determined fluctuations of food and energy prices. In the graph, overall inflation as measured by the official CPI-U is shown along with one measure of the underlying rate, the chain-type price index for personal consumption expenditures excluding food and energy. (Tables 8-1 and 1-5)
- Some past values of the official CPI-U are biased by the use of methodology that turned out to be faulty. Because the CPI is so widely used in law and contracts, it is not retroactively corrected. However, the chain-type price indexes, such as the one graphed above, and some alternative versions of the CPI shown in Table 8-1 apply the current improved methodologies to historical data to provide more consistent series.
- All the price indexes, however, tell the same basic story. Prices rose sharply as World War II controls were lifted and when the Korean War broke out. In the following periods of economic slack—1949, 1955, and 1959–1961—prices reverted to near-stability. But this was not true following the more sustained rises in inflation in the 1960s and 1970s; in each of those cases, the subsequent recession left inflation significantly higher than before. Only after the inflation of the late 1970s and early 1980s and the subsequent severe recession, with its high rates of unemployment and low rates of capacity utilization (see Tables 10-3 and 2-3), has inflation subsided to levels comparable with the early postwar period. (Table 8-1)
- From 1946 to 2003, commodity prices in the CPI-U rose an average 3.4 percent per year, but service prices increased at a 4.9 percent annual rate. (Table 8-1)
- The Producer Price Index (PPI) measures prices at the point of production, rather than the consumer level, and only covers commodities, whereas the CPI covers both commodities and services. For these reasons, the PPI for finished goods—the most widely used component of the PPI—fluctuates more (both up and down) than the aggregate CPI-U, but has a less inflationary trend. (Table 8-2)
- The PPI data set also includes prices for intermediate materials, supplies, and components and crude materials for further processing. Intermediate materials prices fluctuate more than those of finished goods, and crude materials prices most of all. (Table 8-2)

Table 8-1. Consumer Price Indexes

(All urban consumers; 1982–1984 = 100; seasonally adjusted, except as noted.)

Year and month	All items			Food and beverages										
	Not seasonally adjusted	Seasonally adjusted		Total	Total food	Food at home							Food away from home	Alcoholic beverages
		Index	Percent change			Total	Cereals and bakery products	Meats, poultry, fish, and eggs	Dairy and related products	Fruits and vege-tables	Non-alcoholic beverages	Other food at home		
1946	19.5	19.5	8.3	...	19.8	...	16.4	...	26.0	20.4	...	...	...	...
1947	22.3	22.3	14.4	...	24.1	25.8	20.4	...	29.3	22.4	12.0	...	...	...
1948	24.1	24.1	8.1	...	26.1	28.0	22.4	...	32.2	23.0	13.1	...	...	...
1949	23.8	23.8	-1.2	...	25.0	26.9	22.3	...	29.4	23.3	14.2	...	...	...
1950	24.1	24.1	1.3	...	25.4	27.3	22.6	...	29.0	22.4	20.0	...	...	...
1951	26.0	26.0	7.9	...	28.2	30.3	24.7	...	32.4	24.4	22.1	...	...	...
1952	26.5	26.5	1.9	...	28.7	30.8	25.3	...	33.8	26.9	22.2	...	...	...
1953	26.7	26.7	0.8	...	28.3	30.3	25.8	...	33.2	26.0	22.8	...	21.5	39.6
1954	26.9	26.9	0.7	...	28.2	30.1	26.4	...	32.1	25.6	27.1	...	21.9	40.6
1955	26.8	26.8	-0.4	...	27.8	29.5	26.8	...	32.1	26.0	24.3	...	22.1	40.5
1956	27.2	27.2	1.5	...	28.0	29.6	27.2	...	32.9	27.3	25.4	...	22.6	41.0
1957	28.1	28.1	3.3	...	28.9	30.6	28.3	...	33.9	27.2	25.2	...	23.4	42.1
1958	28.9	28.9	2.8	...	30.2	32.0	28.8	...	34.4	29.1	23.4	...	24.1	42.0
1959	29.1	29.1	0.7	...	29.7	31.2	29.1	...	34.6	28.7	21.3	...	24.8	42.4
1960	29.6	29.6	1.7	...	30.0	31.5	29.7	...	35.4	29.4	21.1	...	25.4	43.1
1961	29.9	29.9	1.0	...	30.4	31.8	30.3	...	35.9	29.5	21.1	...	26.0	43.3
1962	30.2	30.2	1.0	...	30.6	32.0	30.9	...	35.7	29.8	20.8	...	26.7	43.4
1963	30.6	30.6	1.3	...	31.1	32.4	31.4	...	35.6	31.5	21.1	...	27.3	43.8
1964	31.0	31.0	1.3	...	31.5	32.7	31.5	...	35.9	32.7	23.6	...	27.8	44.2
1965	31.5	31.5	1.6	...	32.2	33.5	31.9	...	36.0	32.6	23.4	...	28.4	44.6
1966	32.4	32.4	2.9	...	33.8	35.2	33.3	...	38.3	33.3	23.3	...	29.7	45.4
1967	33.4	33.4	3.1	35.0	34.1	35.1	34.0	38.0	40.0	33.3	23.1	29.3	31.3	46.4
1968	34.8	34.8	4.2	36.2	35.3	36.3	34.2	39.1	41.3	35.9	23.5	29.8	32.9	48.0
1969	36.7	36.7	5.5	38.1	37.1	38.0	35.2	42.6	42.7	36.4	24.2	30.7	34.9	49.7
1970	38.8	38.8	5.7	40.1	39.2	39.9	37.1	44.6	44.7	37.8	27.1	32.9	37.5	52.1
1971	40.5	40.5	4.4	41.4	40.4	40.9	38.8	44.1	46.1	39.7	28.1	34.3	39.4	54.2
1972	41.8	41.8	3.2	43.1	42.1	42.7	39.0	48.0	46.8	41.6	28.0	34.6	41.0	55.4
1973	44.4	44.4	6.2	48.8	48.2	49.7	43.5	60.9	51.2	47.4	30.1	36.7	44.2	56.8
1974	49.3	49.3	11.0	55.5	55.1	57.1	56.5	62.2	60.7	55.2	35.9	47.8	49.8	61.1
1975	53.8	53.8	9.1	60.2	59.8	61.8	62.9	67.0	62.6	56.9	41.3	55.4	54.5	65.9
1976	56.9	56.9	5.8	62.1	61.6	63.1	61.5	68.0	67.7	58.4	49.4	56.4	58.2	68.1
1977	60.6	60.6	6.5	65.8	65.5	66.8	62.5	67.4	69.5	63.8	74.4	68.4	62.6	70.0
1978	65.2	65.2	7.6	72.2	72.0	73.8	68.1	77.6	74.2	70.9	78.7	73.6	68.3	74.1
1979	72.6	72.6	11.3	79.9	79.9	81.8	74.9	89.0	82.8	76.6	82.6	79.0	75.9	79.9
1980	82.4	82.4	13.5	86.7	86.8	88.4	83.9	92.0	90.9	82.1	91.4	88.4	83.4	86.4
1981	90.9	90.9	10.3	93.5	93.6	94.8	92.3	96.0	97.4	92.0	95.3	94.9	90.9	92.5
1982	96.5	96.5	6.2	97.3	97.4	98.1	96.5	99.6	98.8	97.0	97.9	97.3	95.8	96.7
1983	99.6	99.6	3.2	99.5	99.4	99.1	99.6	99.2	100.0	97.3	99.8	99.5	100.0	100.4
1984	103.9	103.9	4.3	103.2	103.2	102.8	103.9	101.3	101.3	105.7	102.3	103.1	104.2	103.0
1985	107.6	107.6	3.6	105.6	105.6	104.3	107.9	100.1	103.2	108.4	104.3	105.7	108.3	106.4
1986	109.6	109.6	1.9	109.1	109.0	107.3	110.9	104.5	103.3	109.4	110.4	109.4	112.5	111.1
1987	113.6	113.6	3.6	113.5	113.5	111.9	114.8	110.5	105.9	119.1	107.5	110.5	117.0	114.1
1988	118.3	118.3	4.1	118.2	118.2	116.6	122.1	114.3	108.4	128.1	107.5	113.1	121.8	118.6
1989	124.0	124.0	4.8	124.9	125.1	124.2	132.4	121.3	115.6	138.0	111.3	119.1	127.4	123.5
1990	130.7	130.7	5.4	132.1	132.4	132.3	140.0	130.0	126.5	149.0	113.5	123.4	133.4	129.3
1991	136.2	136.2	4.2	136.8	136.3	135.8	145.8	132.6	125.1	155.8	114.1	127.3	137.9	142.8
1992	140.3	140.3	3.0	138.7	137.9	136.8	151.5	130.9	128.5	155.4	114.3	128.8	140.7	147.3
1993	144.5	144.5	3.0	141.6	140.9	140.1	156.6	135.5	129.4	159.0	114.6	130.5	143.2	149.6
1994	148.2	148.2	2.6	144.9	144.3	144.1	163.0	137.2	131.7	165.0	123.2	135.6	145.7	151.5
1995	152.4	152.4	2.8	148.9	148.4	148.8	167.5	138.8	132.8	177.7	131.7	140.8	149.0	153.9
1996	156.9	156.9	3.0	153.7	153.3	154.3	174.0	144.8	142.1	183.9	128.6	142.9	152.7	158.5
1997	160.5	160.5	2.3	157.7	157.3	158.1	177.6	148.5	145.5	187.5	133.4	147.3	157.0	162.8
1998	163.0	163.0	1.6	161.1	160.7	161.1	181.1	147.3	150.8	198.2	133.0	150.8	161.1	165.7
1999	166.6	166.6	2.2	164.6	164.1	164.2	185.0	147.9	159.6	203.1	134.3	153.5	165.1	169.7
2000	172.2	172.2	3.4	168.4	167.8	167.9	188.3	154.5	160.7	204.6	137.8	155.6	169.0	174.7
2001	177.1	177.1	2.8	173.6	173.1	173.4	193.8	161.3	167.1	212.2	139.2	159.6	173.9	179.3
2002	179.9	179.9	1.6	176.8	176.2	175.6	198.0	162.1	168.1	220.9	139.2	160.8	178.3	183.6
2003	184.0	184.0	2.3	180.5	180.0	179.4	202.8	169.3	167.9	225.9	139.8	162.6	182.1	187.2
2003														
January	181.7	182.2	0.3	177.8	177.1	176.0	200.1	162.2	165.6	221.1	140.3	161.7	179.9	185.8
February	183.1	183.2	0.5	178.7	178.1	177.2	201.6	164.5	166.4	222.0	140.0	162.4	180.7	185.9
March	184.2	184.0	0.4	179.0	178.4	177.4	202.4	164.2	167.4	222.4	139.8	162.5	181.0	186.6
April	183.8	183.4	-0.3	179.0	178.4	177.3	201.7	165.2	166.7	220.7	140.2	162.2	181.1	186.4
May	183.5	183.3	-0.1	179.4	178.8	177.9	202.5	165.6	166.2	224.0	140.3	162.4	181.5	186.7
June	183.7	183.5	0.1	180.2	179.6	179.0	202.9	167.4	164.8	228.1	140.4	163.0	181.9	187.1
July	183.9	183.8	0.2	180.4	179.8	179.0	203.5	168.3	165.5	229.1	138.1	162.4	182.3	187.2
August	184.6	184.5	0.4	181.0	180.5	180.0	203.6	169.9	167.9	228.2	139.8	162.9	182.6	187.1
September	185.2	185.1	0.3	181.5	180.9	180.6	203.7	171.2	170.3	227.4	139.6	163.0	182.8	187.9
October	185.0	184.9	-0.1	182.3	181.8	181.7	203.5	174.0	171.0	228.9	140.2	163.1	183.3	188.1
November	184.5	184.6	-0.2	183.1	182.6	182.8	203.8	178.7	170.3	229.5	139.0	162.3	183.8	188.6
December	184.3	184.9	0.2	184.0	183.5	184.0	204.1	180.5	172.2	230.3	140.0	163.2	184.3	188.7

... = Not available.

Table 8-1. Consumer Price Indexes—Continued

(All urban consumers; 1982–1984 = 100, except as noted; seasonally adjusted, except as noted.)

Year and month	Housing												
	Total	Shelter						Fuels and utilities				Household furnishings and operations	
		Total	Rent of shelter [1]	Rent of primary residence	Lodging away from home [2]	Owners' equivalent rent of primary residence [1]	Tenants' and household insurance [2,3]	Total	Fuels		Water and sewer and trash collection services [2]	Total	Household operations [2,3]
									Fuel oils and other fuels	Gas (piped) and electricity			
1946	...	...	...	...	...	...	...	...	7.9	18.3	...	...	...
1947	...	...	...	...	...	...	...	...	9.0	18.2	...	...	...
1948	...	...	...	...	...	...	...	...	10.6	18.7	...	...	...
1949	...	...	...	...	...	...	...	...	10.9	19.2	...	...	...
1950	...	...	...	...	...	...	...	...	11.3	19.2	...	...	...
1951	...	...	...	...	...	...	...	...	11.8	19.3	...	...	...
1952	...	...	...	...	...	...	...	...	12.1	19.5	...	...	...
1953	...	22.0	...	33.9	...	...	...	22.5	12.6	19.9	...	...	...
1954	...	22.5	...	35.1	...	...	...	22.6	12.6	20.2	...	...	...
1955	...	22.7	...	35.6	...	...	...	23.0	12.7	20.7	...	...	...
1956	...	23.1	...	36.3	...	...	...	23.6	13.3	20.9	...	...	...
1957	...	24.0	...	37.0	...	...	...	24.3	14.0	21.1	...	...	...
1958	...	24.5	...	37.6	...	...	...	24.8	13.7	21.9	...	...	...
1959	...	24.7	...	38.2	...	...	...	25.4	13.9	22.4	...	...	...
1960	...	25.2	...	38.7	...	...	...	26.0	13.8	23.3	...	...	...
1961	...	25.4	...	39.2	...	...	...	26.3	14.1	23.5	...	...	...
1962	...	25.8	...	39.7	...	...	...	26.3	14.2	23.5	...	...	...
1963	...	26.1	...	40.1	...	...	...	26.6	14.4	23.5	...	...	...
1964	...	26.5	...	40.5	...	...	...	26.6	14.4	23.5	...	...	...
1965	...	27.0	...	40.9	...	...	...	26.6	14.6	23.5	...	...	...
1966	...	27.8	...	41.5	...	...	...	26.7	15.0	23.6	...	...	...
1967	30.8	28.8	...	42.2	...	...	...	27.1	15.5	23.7	...	42.0	...
1968	32.0	30.1	...	43.3	...	...	...	27.4	16.0	23.9	...	43.6	...
1969	34.0	32.6	...	44.7	...	...	...	28.0	16.3	24.3	...	45.2	...
1970	36.4	35.5	...	46.5	...	...	...	29.1	17.0	25.4	...	46.8	...
1971	38.0	37.0	...	48.7	...	...	...	31.1	18.2	27.1	...	48.6	...
1972	39.4	38.7	...	50.4	...	...	...	32.5	18.3	28.5	...	49.7	...
1973	41.2	40.5	...	52.5	...	...	...	34.3	21.1	29.9	...	51.1	...
1974	45.8	44.4	...	55.2	...	...	...	40.7	33.2	34.5	...	56.8	...
1975	50.7	48.8	...	58.0	...	...	...	45.4	36.4	40.1	...	63.4	...
1976	53.8	51.5	...	61.1	...	...	...	49.4	38.8	44.7	...	67.3	...
1977	57.4	54.9	...	64.8	...	...	...	54.7	43.9	50.5	...	70.4	...
1978	62.4	60.5	...	69.3	...	...	...	58.5	46.2	55.0	...	74.7	...
1979	70.1	68.9	...	74.3	...	...	...	64.8	62.4	61.0	...	79.9	...
1980	81.1	81.0	...	80.9	...	...	...	75.4	86.1	71.4	...	86.3	...
1981	90.4	90.5	...	87.9	...	...	...	86.4	104.6	81.9	...	93.0	...
1982	96.9	96.9	...	94.6	...	...	...	94.9	103.4	93.2	...	98.0	...
1983	99.5	99.1	102.7	100.1	...	102.5	...	100.2	97.2	101.5	...	100.2	...
1984	103.6	104.0	107.7	105.3	...	107.3	...	104.8	99.4	105.4	...	101.9	...
1985	107.7	109.8	113.9	111.8	...	113.2	...	106.5	95.9	107.1	...	103.8	...
1986	110.9	115.8	120.2	118.3	...	119.4	...	104.1	77.6	105.7	...	105.2	...
1987	114.2	121.3	125.9	123.1	...	124.8	...	103.0	77.9	103.8	...	107.1	...
1988	118.5	127.1	132.0	127.8	...	131.1	...	104.4	78.1	104.6	...	109.4	...
1989	123.0	132.8	138.0	132.8	...	137.4	...	107.8	81.7	107.5	...	111.2	...
1990	128.5	140.0	145.5	138.4	...	144.8	...	111.6	99.3	109.3	...	113.3	...
1991	133.6	146.3	152.1	143.3	...	150.4	...	115.3	94.6	112.6	...	116.0	...
1992	137.5	151.2	157.3	146.9	...	155.5	...	117.8	90.7	114.8	...	118.0	...
1993	141.2	155.7	162.0	150.3	...	160.5	...	121.3	90.3	118.5	...	119.3	...
1994	144.8	160.5	167.0	154.0	...	165.8	...	122.8	88.8	119.2	...	121.0	...
1995	148.5	165.7	172.4	157.8	...	171.3	...	123.7	88.1	119.2	...	123.0	...
1996	152.8	171.0	178.0	162.0	...	176.8	...	127.5	99.2	122.1	...	124.7	...
1997	156.8	176.3	183.4	166.7	...	181.9	...	130.8	99.8	125.1	...	125.4	...
1998	160.4	182.1	189.6	172.1	109.0	187.8	99.8	128.5	90.0	121.2	101.6	126.6	101.5
1999	163.9	187.3	195.0	177.5	112.3	192.9	101.3	128.8	91.4	120.9	104.0	126.7	104.5
2000	169.6	193.4	201.3	183.9	117.5	198.7	103.7	137.9	129.7	128.0	106.5	128.2	110.5
2001	176.4	200.6	208.9	192.1	118.6	206.3	106.2	150.2	129.3	142.4	109.6	129.1	115.6
2002	180.3	208.1	216.7	199.7	118.3	214.7	108.7	143.6	115.5	134.4	113.0	128.3	119.0
2003	184.8	213.1	221.9	205.5	119.3	219.9	114.8	154.5	139.5	145.0	117.2	126.1	121.8
2003													
January	182.8	211.3	219.8	203.1	118.6	218.2	113.9	147.4	132.6	137.6	114.7	127.5	120.8
February	183.3	211.4	220.0	203.5	117.4	218.5	114.1	150.3	148.0	139.9	115.1	127.7	122.0
March	184.1	211.5	220.3	203.9	116.3	218.8	114.0	156.5	159.8	146.5	115.7	127.0	121.6
April	184.1	211.8	220.4	204.5	116.3	219.0	114.2	155.3	142.5	146.2	116.0	126.8	121.2
May	184.7	212.8	221.5	205.1	120.1	219.4	114.3	155.4	135.2	146.6	116.4	126.3	121.3
June	184.8	212.7	221.5	205.3	119.2	219.4	115.2	156.3	134.5	147.7	116.7	126.1	121.8
July	185.1	213.3	222.1	205.8	120.1	219.9	115.6	156.0	136.4	147.1	117.2	125.9	121.7
August	185.3	213.7	222.4	206.3	119.8	220.4	115.8	156.0	138.0	146.8	117.8	125.6	121.8
September	185.5	214.0	222.8	206.7	119.7	220.8	115.9	156.5	136.6	147.3	118.3	125.1	122.3
October	185.8	214.7	223.6	207.0	121.5	221.3	116.0	155.4	135.6	145.9	118.8	125.2	122.6
November	185.7	214.9	223.7	207.4	120.7	221.6	114.3	154.3	136.9	144.2	119.5	125.0	122.4
December	186.1	215.3	224.1	207.8	122.0	221.9	114.3	155.0	136.2	145.0	119.9	124.9	122.6

[1] December 1982 = 100.
[2] December 1997 = 100.
[3] Not seasonally adjusted.
... = Not available.

Table 8-1. Consumer Price Indexes—Continued

(All urban consumers; 1982–1984 = 100, except as noted; seasonally adjusted.)

Year and month	Apparel					Transportation							Motor vehicle parts and equipment	Motor vehicle maintenance and repair
	Total	Men's and boys' apparel	Women's and girls' apparel	Infants' and toddlers' apparel	Footwear	Total	Private transportation							
							Total	New and used motor vehicles			Motor fuel			
								Total 2	New vehicles	Used cars and trucks	Total	Gasoline (all types)		
1946	34.4	35.1	48.0	...	22.2	16.7	18.3	...	34.1	...	14.5	14.5	...	15.8
1947	39.9	41.6	55.6	43.8	27.7	18.5	20.8	...	34.1	...	16.4	16.4	...	17.1
1948	42.5	43.9	58.9	41.2	30.3	20.6	23.0	...	37.3	...	18.6	18.6	...	18.1
1949	40.8	42.7	55.7	38.4	30.1	22.1	24.4	...	40.9	...	19.1	19.1	...	18.6
1950	40.3	42.5	53.8	37.8	30.5	22.7	24.5	...	41.2	...	19.0	19.0	...	18.9
1951	43.9	46.0	57.9	41.5	34.5	24.1	25.6	...	43.1	...	19.5	19.5	...	20.4
1952	43.5	46.2	57.2	39.3	33.8	25.7	27.3	...	46.8	...	20.0	20.0	...	20.8
1953	43.1	45.9	56.6	39.2	33.8	26.5	27.8	...	47.3	26.7	21.2	21.2	...	22.0
1954	43.1	45.6	56.1	37.0	34.2	26.1	27.1	...	46.5	22.7	21.8	21.8	...	22.7
1955	42.9	45.1	55.6	37.6	34.5	25.8	26.7	...	44.9	21.5	22.1	22.1	...	23.2
1956	43.7	45.9	56.0	37.6	36.4	26.2	27.1	...	46.1	20.7	22.8	22.8	...	24.2
1957	44.5	46.6	56.3	37.7	37.5	27.7	28.6	...	48.6	23.2	23.8	23.8	...	25.0
1958	44.6	46.4	56.2	37.3	38.1	28.6	29.5	...	50.1	24.0	23.4	23.5	...	25.4
1959	45.0	46.3	56.5	36.9	39.7	29.8	30.8	...	52.3	26.8	23.7	23.7	...	26.0
1960	45.7	47.2	56.7	36.8	41.1	29.8	30.6	...	51.6	25.0	24.4	24.4	...	26.5
1961	46.1	47.7	56.9	35.5	41.4	30.1	30.8	...	51.6	26.0	24.1	24.1	...	27.1
1962	46.3	48.0	56.8	34.8	42.0	30.8	31.4	...	51.4	28.4	24.3	24.3	...	27.5
1963	46.9	48.6	57.3	34.8	42.5	30.9	31.6	...	51.1	28.7	24.2	24.2	...	27.8
1964	47.3	49.3	57.6	34.9	42.6	31.4	32.0	...	50.9	30.0	24.1	24.1	...	28.2
1965	47.8	49.9	58.1	35.1	43.4	31.9	32.5	...	49.8	29.8	25.1	25.1	...	28.7
1966	49.0	51.2	59.2	35.4	46.0	32.3	32.9	...	48.9	29.0	25.6	25.6	...	29.2
1967	51.0	53.1	61.9	35.8	48.2	33.3	33.8	...	49.3	29.9	26.4	26.4	...	30.4
1968	53.7	56.1	65.6	37.3	50.8	34.3	34.8	...	50.7	...	26.8	26.8	...	32.1
1969	56.8	59.7	69.2	38.4	53.9	35.7	36.0	...	51.5	30.9	27.6	27.7	...	34.1
1970	59.2	62.2	71.8	39.2	56.8	37.5	37.5	...	53.1	31.2	27.9	27.9	...	36.6
1971	61.1	63.9	74.4	40.0	58.6	39.5	39.4	...	55.3	33.0	28.1	28.1	...	39.3
1972	62.3	64.7	76.2	41.1	60.3	39.9	39.7	...	54.8	33.1	28.4	28.4	...	41.1
1973	64.6	67.1	78.8	42.5	62.8	41.2	41.0	...	54.8	35.2	31.2	31.2	...	43.2
1974	69.4	72.4	83.5	54.2	66.6	45.8	46.2	...	58.0	36.7	42.2	42.2	...	47.6
1975	72.5	75.5	85.5	64.5	69.6	50.1	50.6	...	63.0	43.8	45.1	45.1	...	53.7
1976	75.2	78.1	87.9	68.0	72.3	55.1	55.6	...	67.0	50.3	47.0	47.0	...	57.6
1977	78.6	81.7	90.6	74.6	75.7	59.0	59.7	...	70.5	54.7	49.7	49.7	...	61.9
1978	81.4	83.5	92.4	77.4	79.0	61.7	62.5	...	75.9	55.8	51.8	51.8	77.6	67.0
1979	84.9	85.4	94.0	79.0	85.3	70.5	71.7	...	81.9	60.2	70.1	70.2	85.1	73.7
1980	90.9	89.4	96.0	85.5	91.8	83.1	84.2	...	88.5	62.3	97.4	97.5	95.3	81.5
1981	95.3	94.2	97.5	92.9	96.7	93.2	93.8	...	93.9	76.9	108.5	108.5	101.0	89.2
1982	97.8	97.6	98.5	96.3	99.1	97.0	97.1	...	97.5	88.8	102.8	102.8	103.6	96.0
1983	100.2	100.3	100.2	101.1	99.8	99.3	99.3	...	99.9	98.7	99.4	99.4	100.7	100.3
1984	102.1	102.1	101.3	102.6	101.1	103.7	103.6	...	102.6	112.5	97.9	97.8	95.6	103.8
1985	105.0	105.0	104.9	107.2	102.3	106.4	106.2	...	106.1	113.7	98.7	98.6	95.9	106.8
1986	105.9	106.2	104.0	111.8	101.9	102.3	101.2	...	110.6	108.8	77.1	77.0	95.4	110.3
1987	110.6	109.1	110.4	112.1	105.1	105.4	104.2	...	114.4	113.1	80.2	80.1	96.1	114.8
1988	115.4	113.4	114.9	116.4	109.9	108.7	107.6	...	116.5	118.0	80.9	80.8	97.9	119.7
1989	118.6	117.0	116.4	119.1	114.4	114.1	112.9	...	119.2	120.4	88.5	88.5	100.2	124.9
1990	124.1	120.4	122.6	125.8	117.4	120.5	118.8	...	121.4	117.6	101.2	101.0	100.9	130.1
1991	128.7	124.2	127.6	128.9	120.9	123.8	121.9	...	126.0	118.1	99.4	99.2	102.2	136.0
1992	131.9	126.5	130.4	129.3	125.0	126.5	124.6	...	129.2	123.2	99.0	99.0	103.1	141.3
1993	133.7	127.5	132.6	127.1	125.9	130.4	127.5	91.8	132.7	133.9	98.0	97.7	101.6	145.9
1994	133.4	126.4	130.9	128.1	126.0	134.3	131.4	95.5	137.6	141.7	98.5	98.2	101.4	150.2
1995	132.0	126.2	126.9	127.2	125.4	139.1	136.3	99.4	141.0	156.5	100.0	99.8	102.1	154.0
1996	131.7	127.7	124.7	129.7	126.6	143.0	140.0	101.0	143.7	157.0	106.3	105.9	102.2	158.4
1997	132.9	130.1	126.1	129.0	127.6	144.3	141.0	100.5	144.3	151.1	106.2	105.8	101.9	162.7
1998	133.0	131.8	126.1	126.1	128.0	141.6	137.9	100.1	143.4	150.6	92.2	91.6	101.1	167.1
1999	131.3	131.1	123.3	129.0	125.7	144.4	140.5	100.1	142.9	152.0	100.7	100.1	100.5	171.9
2000	129.6	129.7	121.5	130.6	123.8	153.3	149.1	100.8	142.8	155.8	129.3	128.6	101.5	177.3
2001	127.3	125.7	119.3	129.2	123.0	154.3	150.0	101.3	142.1	158.7	124.7	124.0	104.8	183.5
2002	124.0	121.7	115.8	126.4	121.4	152.9	148.8	99.2	140.0	152.0	116.6	116.0	106.9	190.2
2003	120.9	118.0	113.1	122.1	119.6	157.6	153.6	96.5	137.9	142.9	135.8	135.1	107.8	195.6
2003														
January	122.0	118.6	113.7	123.0	121.9	156.4	152.5	97.8	138.6	148.3	130.8	130.2	107.8	193.6
February	121.6	118.4	113.5	122.8	121.2	159.1	155.4	97.7	138.4	148.4	142.3	141.7	108.2	194.1
March	121.0	119.4	112.8	122.5	119.2	161.4	157.7	97.8	138.8	148.5	150.7	150.0	107.9	194.2
April	120.5	118.5	112.6	122.2	118.2	158.4	154.6	97.6	138.3	148.4	137.7	136.9	107.7	194.6
May	120.4	117.5	112.6	122.9	118.4	156.1	152.0	97.4	138.0	147.9	127.0	126.3	107.8	194.9
June	120.8	117.2	113.2	122.3	119.5	156.3	152.1	97.2	137.7	147.4	127.6	126.9	107.7	195.3
July	120.6	117.1	112.9	121.7	119.3	156.5	152.3	96.8	137.5	145.7	128.9	128.2	107.6	196.3
August	120.7	116.7	113.1	122.5	119.3	158.4	154.4	96.5	138.1	143.3	137.9	137.2	107.9	196.1
September	120.9	117.8	112.9	123.4	119.8	159.9	156.0	95.5	137.5	139.0	146.9	146.3	107.7	196.3
October	121.2	118.0	113.8	122.3	119.7	157.7	153.6	94.9	137.2	135.1	137.9	137.3	107.9	196.7
November	120.6	118.1	112.9	120.3	119.3	155.6	151.4	94.5	137.1	132.0	130.9	130.3	107.9	197.0
December	120.2	118.1	112.5	119.3	119.0	155.3	151.1	94.0	137.0	131.0	130.9	130.4	107.7	197.9

2December 1997 = 100.
... = Not available.

Table 8-1. Consumer Price Indexes—Continued

(All urban consumers; 1982–1984 = 100, except as noted; seasonally adjusted.)

Year and month	Transportation—Continued		Medical care					Recreation		Education and communication			
					Medical care services						Education		
	Public transportation	Transportation services	Medical care, total	Medical care commodities	Total	Professional services	Hospital and related services	Total [2]	Video and audio [2]	Total [2]	Total [2]	Educational books and supplies	Tuition, other school fees, and childcare
1946	9.4	12.7	12.5	34.2	10.4	...	...	...	...	...	...	...	...
1947	9.9	13.2	13.5	36.7	11.3	...	...	...	...	...	...	...	...
1948	11.2	14.7	14.4	38.6	12.1	...	...	...	...	...	...	...	...
1949	12.4	16.3	14.8	39.2	12.5	...	...	...	...	...	...	...	...
1950	13.4	17.4	15.1	39.7	12.8	...	...	...	...	...	...	...	...
1951	14.8	19.0	15.9	40.8	13.4	...	...	...	...	...	...	...	...
1952	15.8	20.4	16.7	41.2	14.3	...	...	...	...	...	...	...	...
1953	16.8	21.7	17.3	41.5	14.8	...	...	...	...	...	...	...	...
1954	18.0	22.6	17.8	42.0	15.3	...	...	...	...	...	...	...	...
1955	18.5	22.7	18.2	42.5	15.7	...	...	...	...	...	...	...	...
1956	19.2	23.0	18.9	43.4	16.3	...	...	...	...	...	...	...	...
1957	19.9	24.1	19.7	44.6	17.0	...	...	...	...	...	...	...	...
1958	20.9	25.6	20.6	46.1	17.9	...	...	...	...	...	...	...	...
1959	21.5	26.5	21.5	46.8	18.7	...	...	...	...	...	...	...	...
1960	22.2	27.2	22.3	46.9	19.5	...	...	...	...	...	...	...	...
1961	23.2	27.8	22.9	46.3	20.2	...	...	...	...	...	...	...	...
1962	24.0	28.3	23.5	45.6	20.9	...	...	...	...	...	...	...	...
1963	24.3	28.6	24.1	45.2	21.5	...	...	...	...	...	...	...	...
1964	24.7	29.2	24.6	45.1	22.0	...	...	...	...	...	...	...	...
1965	25.2	30.3	25.2	45.0	22.7	...	...	...	...	...	...	...	...
1966	26.1	31.6	26.3	45.1	23.9	...	...	...	...	...	...	...	...
1967	27.4	32.6	28.2	44.9	26.0	30.9	...	...	...	...	...	33.7	...
1968	28.7	33.9	29.9	45.0	27.9	32.5	...	...	...	...	...	35.4	...
1969	30.9	36.3	31.9	45.4	30.2	34.7	...	...	...	...	...	37.4	...
1970	35.2	40.2	34.0	46.5	32.3	37.0	...	...	...	...	...	38.8	...
1971	37.8	43.4	36.1	47.3	34.7	39.4	...	...	...	...	...	41.4	...
1972	39.3	44.4	37.3	47.4	35.9	40.8	...	...	...	...	...	44.2	...
1973	39.7	44.7	38.8	47.5	37.5	42.2	...	...	...	...	...	45.6	...
1974	40.6	46.3	42.4	49.2	41.4	45.8	...	...	...	...	...	47.2	...
1975	43.5	49.8	47.5	53.3	46.6	50.8	...	...	...	...	...	50.3	...
1976	47.8	56.9	52.0	56.5	51.3	55.5	...	...	...	...	...	53.7	...
1977	50.0	61.5	57.0	60.2	56.4	60.0	...	...	...	...	...	56.9	...
1978	51.5	64.4	61.8	64.4	61.2	64.5	55.1	...	...	...	...	61.6	59.8
1979	54.9	69.5	67.5	69.0	67.2	70.1	61.0	...	...	...	...	65.7	64.7
1980	69.0	79.2	74.9	75.4	74.8	77.9	69.2	...	...	...	...	71.4	71.2
1981	85.6	88.6	82.9	83.7	82.8	85.9	79.1	...	...	...	...	80.3	79.9
1982	94.9	96.1	92.5	92.3	92.6	93.2	90.3	...	...	...	...	91.0	90.5
1983	99.5	99.1	100.6	100.2	100.7	99.8	100.5	...	...	...	...	100.3	99.7
1984	105.7	104.8	106.8	107.5	106.7	107.0	109.2	...	...	...	...	108.7	109.8
1985	110.5	110.0	113.5	115.2	113.2	113.5	116.1	...	...	...	...	118.2	119.7
1986	117.0	116.3	122.0	122.8	121.9	120.8	123.1	...	...	...	...	128.1	129.6
1987	121.1	121.9	130.1	131.0	130.0	128.8	131.6	...	...	...	...	138.1	140.0
1988	123.3	128.0	138.6	139.9	138.3	137.5	143.9	...	...	...	...	148.1	151.0
1989	129.5	135.6	149.3	150.8	148.9	146.4	160.5	...	...	...	...	158.0	162.7
1990	142.6	144.2	162.8	163.4	162.7	156.1	178.0	...	...	...	...	171.3	175.7
1991	148.9	151.2	177.0	176.8	177.1	165.7	196.1	...	...	...	...	180.3	191.4
1992	151.4	155.7	190.1	188.1	190.5	175.8	214.0	...	...	...	...	190.3	208.5
1993	167.0	162.9	201.4	195.0	202.9	184.7	231.9	90.7	96.5	85.5	78.4	197.6	225.3
1994	172.0	168.6	211.0	200.7	213.4	192.5	245.6	92.7	95.4	88.8	83.3	205.5	239.8
1995	175.9	175.9	220.5	204.5	224.2	201.0	257.8	94.5	95.1	92.2	88.0	214.4	253.8
1996	181.9	180.5	228.2	210.4	232.4	208.3	269.5	97.4	96.6	95.3	92.7	226.9	267.1
1997	186.7	185.0	234.6	215.3	239.1	215.4	278.4	99.6	99.4	98.4	97.3	238.4	280.4
1998	190.3	187.9	242.1	221.8	246.8	222.2	287.5	101.1	101.1	100.3	102.1	250.8	294.2
1999	197.7	190.7	250.6	230.7	255.1	229.2	299.5	102.0	100.7	101.2	107.0	261.7	308.4
2000	209.6	196.1	260.8	238.1	266.0	237.7	317.3	103.3	101.0	102.5	112.5	279.9	324.0
2001	210.6	201.9	272.8	247.6	278.8	246.5	338.3	104.9	101.5	105.2	118.5	295.9	341.1
2002	207.4	209.1	285.6	256.4	292.9	253.9	367.8	106.2	102.8	107.9	126.0	317.6	362.1
2003	209.3	216.3	297.1	262.8	306.0	261.2	394.8	107.5	103.6	109.8	134.4	335.4	386.7
2003													
January	205.9	212.9	292.4	260.5	300.6	257.8	384.7	106.9	103.4	109.2	130.1	328.0	374.0
February	205.5	213.3	293.1	260.5	301.5	258.3	386.5	107.1	103.4	109.5	130.8	329.9	376.1
March	206.7	213.9	293.7	261.3	302.0	258.7	387.5	107.2	103.3	109.4	131.5	331.7	378.1
April	207.2	214.9	294.3	261.5	302.7	259.4	388.6	107.2	103.5	109.5	132.3	332.6	380.4
May	209.7	215.9	295.4	261.8	304.1	260.8	389.8	107.4	103.5	109.4	133.0	333.8	382.5
June	210.7	216.6	296.3	261.7	305.3	261.0	393.1	107.6	103.6	109.3	133.7	335.1	384.6
July	211.8	217.4	297.4	263.0	306.4	261.7	395.9	107.7	103.7	109.6	134.3	336.4	386.3
August	210.6	217.2	298.3	263.7	307.3	261.7	398.0	107.7	103.7	110.0	136.1	339.4	391.5
September	210.2	217.5	299.6	264.9	308.6	262.6	400.3	107.8	103.9	110.2	136.6	336.6	393.5
October	212.0	219.2	300.3	264.9	309.6	263.3	401.2	107.7	103.9	110.2	137.2	338.2	395.2
November	211.3	218.8	301.3	264.7	311.0	263.7	405.1	107.9	104.0	110.4	137.8	337.7	397.2
December	209.7	218.2	302.7	265.4	312.6	264.9	407.0	108.0	103.9	110.6	138.8	345.8	399.5

[2] December 1997 = 100.
... = Not available.

Table 8-1. Consumer Price Indexes—Continued

(All urban consumers; 1982–1984 = 100, except as noted; seasonally adjusted, except as noted.)

Year and month	Education and communication—Continued					Other goods and services				
	Communication					Total	Tobacco and smoking products	Personal care		
		Information and information processing								
				Information and information processing other than telephone services						
	Total [2]	Total [2,3]	Telephone services [2,3]	Total [3,4]	Personal computers and peripheral equipment [2,3]			Total	Personal care products [3]	Personal care services [3]
1946	...	...	...	...	...	...	18.2	22.7	27.6	...
1947	...	...	...	...	...	...	19.8	25.4	33.2	...
1948	...	...	...	...	...	...	20.7	26.3	34.2	...
1949	...	...	...	...	...	...	21.3	26.2	33.0	...
1950	...	...	...	...	...	...	21.7	26.2	32.2	...
1951	...	...	...	...	...	...	22.4	28.7	35.7	...
1952	...	...	...	...	...	...	23.5	29.0	35.0	...
1953	...	...	...	...	...	...	24.5	29.3	34.8	24.1
1954	...	...	...	...	...	...	24.9	29.4	34.6	24.4
1955	...	...	...	...	...	...	25.0	29.9	34.6	25.6
1956	...	...	...	...	...	...	25.5	31.2	35.4	27.2
1957	...	...	...	...	...	...	26.3	32.3	36.6	28.3
1958	...	...	...	...	...	...	27.1	33.4	37.9	29.0
1959	...	...	...	...	...	...	28.1	34.1	38.2	30.0
1960	...	...	...	...	...	...	29.1	34.6	38.2	31.0
1961	...	...	...	...	...	...	29.3	34.8	38.1	31.5
1962	...	...	...	...	...	...	29.5	35.4	38.5	32.2
1963	...	...	...	...	...	...	30.4	35.9	38.6	33.0
1964	...	...	...	...	...	...	31.2	36.3	38.6	33.9
1965	...	...	...	...	...	...	32.6	36.6	38.4	34.8
1966	...	...	...	...	...	...	34.2	37.3	38.0	36.4
1967	...	...	...	...	...	35.1	35.5	38.4	38.6	38.1
1968	...	...	...	...	...	36.9	37.8	40.0	39.8	40.1
1969	...	...	...	...	...	38.7	39.8	42.0	41.6	42.2
1970	...	...	...	...	...	40.9	43.1	43.5	42.7	44.2
1971	...	...	...	...	...	42.9	44.9	44.9	44.0	45.7
1972	...	...	...	...	...	44.7	47.4	46.0	45.2	46.8
1973	...	...	...	...	...	46.4	48.7	48.1	46.4	49.7
1974	...	...	...	...	...	49.8	51.1	52.8	51.5	53.9
1975	...	...	...	...	...	53.9	54.7	57.9	58.0	57.7
1976	...	...	...	...	...	57.0	57.0	61.7	61.3	61.9
1977	...	...	...	...	...	60.4	59.8	65.7	64.7	66.4
1978	...	...	...	...	...	64.3	63.0	69.9	68.2	71.3
1979	...	...	...	...	...	68.9	66.8	75.2	72.9	77.2
1980	...	...	...	...	...	75.2	72.0	81.9	79.6	83.7
1981	...	...	...	...	...	82.6	77.8	89.1	87.8	90.2
1982	...	...	...	...	...	91.1	86.5	95.4	95.1	95.7
1983	...	...	...	...	...	101.1	103.4	100.3	100.7	100.0
1984	...	...	...	...	...	107.9	110.1	104.3	104.2	104.4
1985	...	...	...	...	...	114.5	116.7	108.3	107.6	108.9
1986	...	...	...	...	...	121.4	124.7	111.9	111.3	112.5
1987	...	...	...	...	...	128.5	133.6	115.1	113.9	116.2
1988	...	...	...	...	...	137.0	145.8	119.4	118.1	120.7
1989	...	...	...	96.3	...	147.7	164.4	125.0	123.2	126.8
1990	...	...	...	93.5	...	159.0	181.5	130.4	128.2	132.8
1991	...	...	...	88.6	...	171.6	202.7	134.9	132.8	137.0
1992	...	...	...	83.7	...	183.3	219.8	138.3	136.5	140.0
1993	96.7	97.7	...	78.8	...	192.9	228.4	141.5	139.0	144.0
1994	97.6	98.6	...	72.0	...	198.5	220.0	144.6	141.5	147.9
1995	98.8	98.7	...	63.8	...	206.9	225.7	147.1	143.1	151.5
1996	99.6	99.5	...	57.2	...	215.4	232.8	150.1	144.3	156.6
1997	100.3	100.4	...	50.1	...	224.8	243.7	152.7	144.2	162.4
1998	98.7	98.5	100.7	39.9	78.2	237.7	274.8	156.7	148.3	166.0
1999	96.0	95.5	100.1	30.5	53.5	258.3	355.8	161.1	151.8	171.4
2000	93.6	92.8	98.5	25.9	41.1	271.1	394.9	165.6	153.7	178.1
2001	93.3	92.3	99.3	21.3	29.5	282.6	425.2	170.5	155.1	184.3
2002	92.3	90.8	99.7	18.3	22.2	293.2	461.5	174.7	154.7	188.4
2003	89.7	87.8	98.3	16.1	17.6	298.7	469.0	178.0	153.5	193.2
2003										
January	91.6	90.3	100.4	17.1	19.5	296.7	472.4	176.1	153.0	190.6
February	91.6	90.1	100.5	16.9	19.1	297.5	472.7	176.7	153.3	190.9
March	91.1	89.5	99.7	16.8	19.0	297.1	467.2	177.0	153.3	191.7
April	90.6	88.6	98.7	16.7	18.7	297.9	467.9	177.5	154.1	192.5
May	90.0	87.9	98.1	16.4	18.0	297.8	465.6	177.7	153.6	193.0
June	89.4	87.2	97.5	16.2	17.5	297.9	463.5	178.0	153.8	192.8
July	89.4	87.5	98.1	16.0	17.2	299.1	469.1	178.3	154.2	193.2
August	89.0	87.0	97.8	15.7	16.7	299.7	471.8	178.5	153.5	193.9
September	88.9	86.7	97.4	15.6	16.3	299.9	468.7	179.0	153.4	195.4
October	88.5	86.4	97.1	15.6	16.5	300.2	469.5	179.1	153.6	195.6
November	88.4	86.2	97.2	15.4	16.3	300.1	469.1	179.1	153.2	194.2
December	88.1	86.2	97.2	15.3	16.2	300.8	470.4	179.5	153.4	194.3

[2] December 1997 = 100.
[3] Not seasonally adjusted.
[4] December 1988 = 100.

Table 8-1. Consumer Price Indexes—Continued

(All urban consumers, except as noted; 1982–1984 = 100, except as noted; seasonally adjusted, except as noted.)

Year and month	Commodity and service groups of CPI-U		Special indexes in CPI-U					Supplemental all items indexes based on CPI-U			Consumer Price Index, Urban wage earners and clerical workers (CPI-W) [5]
				All items less							
	Commodities	Services	Energy	Food	Energy	Food and energy		CPI-U-X1 [5]	CPI-U-RS [6]	C-CPI-U [7]	
						Index	Percent change				
1946	22.9	14.1	...	19.8	...	...	...	...	...	...	19.6
1947	27.6	14.7	...	21.7	...	...	...	24.2	...	...	22.5
1948	29.6	15.6	...	23.3	...	...	...	26.2	...	...	24.2
1949	28.8	16.4	...	23.5	...	...	...	25.9	...	...	24.0
1950	29.0	16.9	...	23.8	...	...	...	26.2	...	...	24.2
1951	31.6	17.8	...	25.3	...	...	...	28.3	...	...	26.1
1952	32.0	18.6	...	25.9	...	...	...	28.8	...	...	26.7
1953	31.9	19.4	...	26.4	...	...	...	29.0	...	...	26.9
1954	31.6	20.0	...	26.6	...	...	...	29.2	...	...	27.0
1955	31.3	20.4	...	26.6	...	...	...	29.1	...	...	26.9
1956	31.6	20.9	...	27.1	...	...	...	29.6	...	...	27.3
1957	32.6	21.8	21.5	28.0	28.9	28.9	...	30.5	...	...	28.3
1958	33.3	22.6	21.5	28.6	29.7	29.6	2.4	31.4	...	...	29.1
1959	33.3	23.3	21.9	29.2	29.9	30.2	2.0	31.6	...	...	29.3
1960	33.6	24.1	22.4	29.7	30.4	30.6	1.3	32.2	...	...	29.8
1961	33.8	24.5	22.5	30.0	30.7	31.0	1.3	32.5	...	...	30.1
1962	34.1	25.0	22.6	30.3	31.1	31.4	1.3	32.8	...	...	30.4
1963	34.4	25.5	22.6	30.7	31.5	31.8	1.3	33.3	...	...	30.8
1964	34.8	26.0	22.5	31.1	32.0	32.3	1.6	33.7	...	...	31.2
1965	35.2	26.6	22.9	31.6	32.5	32.7	1.2	34.2	...	...	31.7
1966	36.1	27.6	23.3	32.3	33.5	33.5	2.4	35.2	...	...	32.6
1967	36.8	28.8	23.8	33.4	34.4	34.7	3.6	36.3	...	...	33.6
1968	38.1	30.3	24.2	34.9	35.9	36.3	4.6	37.7	...	...	35.0
1969	39.9	32.4	24.8	36.8	38.0	38.4	5.9	39.4	...	...	36.9
1970	41.7	35.0	25.5	39.0	40.3	40.8	6.3	41.3	...	...	39.0
1971	43.2	37.0	26.5	40.8	42.0	42.7	4.7	43.1	...	...	40.7
1972	44.5	38.4	27.2	42.0	43.4	44.0	3.0	44.4	...	...	42.1
1973	47.8	40.1	29.4	43.7	46.1	45.6	3.6	47.2	...	...	44.7
1974	53.5	43.8	38.1	48.0	50.6	49.4	8.3	51.9	...	...	49.6
1975	58.2	48.0	42.1	52.5	55.1	53.9	9.1	56.2	...	...	54.1
1976	60.7	52.0	45.1	56.0	58.2	57.4	6.5	59.4	...	...	57.2
1977	62.4	56.0	49.4	59.6	61.9	61.0	6.3	63.2	...	...	60.9
1978	66.8	60.8	52.5	63.9	66.7	65.5	7.4	67.5	104.3	...	65.6
1979	76.6	67.5	65.7	71.2	73.4	71.9	9.8	74.0	114.1	...	73.1
1980	86.0	77.9	86.0	81.5	81.9	80.8	12.4	82.3	126.7	...	82.9
1981	93.2	88.1	97.7	90.4	90.1	89.2	10.4	90.1	138.6	...	91.4
1982	97.0	96.0	99.2	96.3	96.1	95.8	7.4	95.6	146.8	...	96.9
1983	99.8	99.4	99.9	99.7	99.6	99.6	4.0	99.6	152.9	...	99.8
1984	103.2	104.6	100.9	104.0	104.3	104.6	5.0	103.9	159.0	...	103.3
1985	105.4	109.9	101.6	108.0	108.4	109.1	4.3	107.6	164.3	...	106.9
1986	104.4	115.4	88.2	109.8	112.6	113.5	4.0	109.6	167.3	...	108.6
1987	107.7	120.2	88.6	113.6	117.2	118.2	4.1	113.6	173.0	...	112.5
1988	111.5	125.7	89.3	118.3	122.3	123.4	4.4	118.3	179.3	...	117.0
1989	116.7	131.9	94.3	123.7	128.1	129.0	4.5	124.0	187.0	...	122.6
1990	122.8	139.2	102.1	130.3	134.7	135.5	5.0	130.7	196.3	...	129.0
1991	126.6	146.3	102.5	136.1	140.9	142.1	4.9	136.2	203.4	...	134.3
1992	129.1	152.0	103.0	140.8	145.4	147.3	3.7	140.3	208.5	...	138.2
1993	131.5	157.9	104.2	145.1	150.0	152.2	3.3	144.5	213.7	...	142.1
1994	133.8	163.1	104.6	149.0	154.1	156.5	2.8	148.2	218.2	...	145.6
1995	136.4	168.7	105.2	153.1	158.7	161.2	3.0	152.4	223.5	...	149.8
1996	139.9	174.1	110.1	157.5	163.1	165.6	2.7	156.9	229.5	...	154.1
1997	141.8	179.4	111.5	161.1	167.1	169.5	2.4	160.5	234.4	...	157.6
1998	141.9	184.2	102.9	163.4	170.9	173.4	2.3	163.0	237.7	...	159.7
1999	144.4	188.8	106.6	167.0	174.4	177.0	2.1	166.6	242.7	...	163.2
2000	149.2	195.3	124.6	173.0	178.6	181.3	2.4	172.2	250.8	102.0	168.9
2001	150.7	203.4	129.3	177.8	183.5	186.1	2.6	177.1	257.8	104.3	173.5
2002	149.7	209.8	121.7	180.5	187.7	190.5	2.4	179.9	261.9	105.6	175.9
2003	151.2	216.5	136.5	184.7	190.6	193.2	1.4	184.0	267.9	[8]107.7	179.8
2003											
January	150.6	213.5	130.4	183.1	189.3	192.2	0.1	181.7	264.5	[8]106.4	178.2
February	152.0	214.1	137.5	184.1	189.6	192.4	0.1	183.1	266.6	[8]107.2	179.3
March	152.9	214.9	144.9	185.0	189.7	192.5	0.1	184.2	268.2	[8]107.9	180.2
April	151.4	215.2	138.1	184.3	189.8	192.6	0.1	183.8	267.6	[8]107.7	179.4
May	150.2	216.1	132.9	184.1	190.2	193.0	0.2	183.5	267.2	[8]107.5	179.1
June	150.4	216.4	133.7	184.2	190.4	193.1	0.1	183.7	267.5	[8]107.6	179.4
July	150.5	216.9	134.1	184.5	190.7	193.4	0.2	183.9	267.8	[8]107.7	179.6
August	151.5	217.3	138.3	185.2	191.0	193.6	0.1	184.6	268.8	[8]108.0	180.4
September	152.1	217.8	142.8	185.8	191.1	193.7	0.1	185.2	269.6	[8]108.3	180.9
October	151.2	218.4	137.8	185.5	191.5	194.0	0.2	185.0	269.4	[8]108.2	180.6
November	150.5	218.4	133.7	185.0	191.6	194.0	0.0	184.5	268.7	[8]107.8	180.1
December	150.7	218.9	134.1	185.2	191.9	194.1	0.1	184.3	268.4	[8]107.6	180.4

[5]Not seasonally adjusted; see Notes and Definitions for more information.
[6]December 1977 = 100; not seasonally adjusted; see Notes and Definitions for more information.
[7]December 1999 = 100; not seasonally adjusted; see Notes and Definitions for more information.
[8]Interim values.
. . . = Not available.

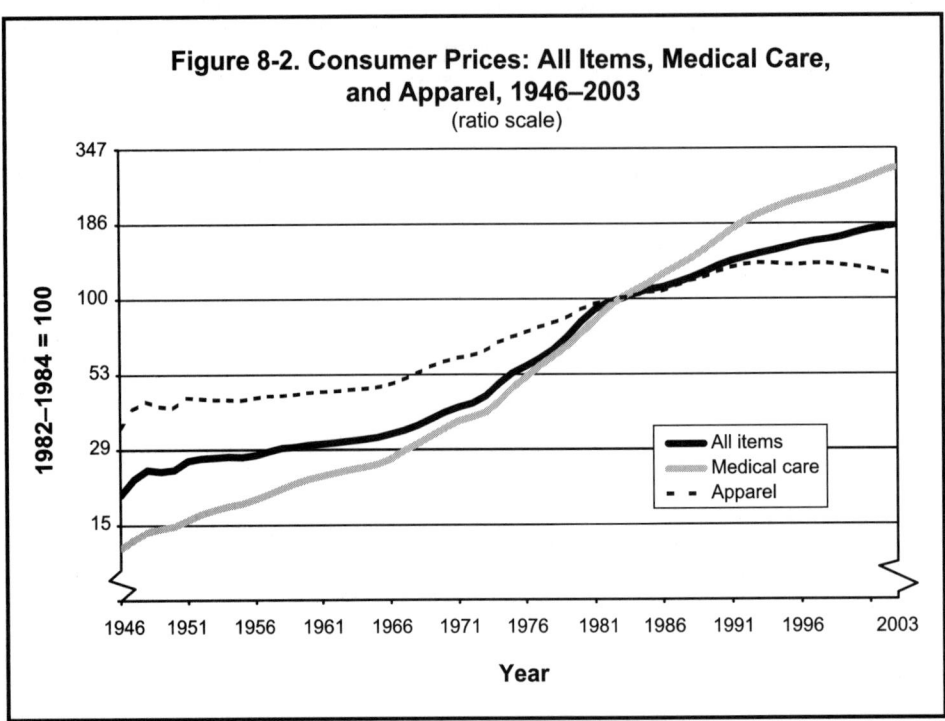

Figure 8-2. Consumer Prices: All Items, Medical Care, and Apparel, 1946–2003

- Figure 8-2 charts two components of the Consumer Price Index (CPI-U) along with the all-items total. Since all three indexes have the base years 1982–1984, they converge in those years. But over the years the trends of the two components are very different. Apparel has been one of the areas most subject to international competition, and the apparel index shows far less growth than the overall average of prices. Medical care, on the other hand, has little or no price competition from producers in other countries; is often paid for not directly by consumers but by third-party insurers, both government and private; is characterized by trend growth in demand, reflecting rising income and expectations and technological innovations; and arguably has been overstated in the CPI due to the difficulties of making quality adjustments. (Quality adjustments have been much improved in recent years, but such improvements are not retroactively introduced into the CPI.) (Table 8-1)

Table 8-2. Producer Price Indexes and Purchasing Power of the Dollar

(1982 = 100, seasonally adjusted.)

Year and month	Finished goods		Finished consumer goods				Finished consumer goods, except foods			Capital equipment		
		Percent change from previous period		Finished consumer foods					Nondurable goods less foods		Manufacturing industries	Nonmanufacturing industries
	Total		Total	Total	Crude	Processed	Total	Durable goods		Total		
1947	26.4	...	28.6	31.9	39.3	31.1	27.4	32.9	24.2	19.8	17.5	21.9
1948	28.5	8.0	30.8	34.9	42.4	34.0	29.2	35.2	25.7	21.6	19.1	23.8
1949	27.7	-2.8	29.4	32.1	40.1	31.1	28.6	36.1	24.7	22.7	20.0	25.0
1950	28.2	1.8	29.9	32.7	36.5	32.4	29.0	36.5	25.1	23.2	20.6	25.5
1951	30.8	9.2	32.7	36.7	41.9	36.2	31.1	38.9	27.0	25.5	22.7	27.9
1952	30.6	-0.6	32.3	36.4	44.6	35.4	30.7	39.2	26.3	25.9	23.2	28.3
1953	30.3	-1.0	31.7	34.5	41.6	33.6	31.0	39.5	26.6	26.3	23.5	28.7
1954	30.4	0.3	31.7	34.2	37.5	34.0	31.1	39.8	26.7	26.7	23.9	29.0
1955	30.5	0.3	31.5	33.4	39.1	32.7	31.3	40.2	26.8	27.4	24.7	29.8
1956	31.3	2.6	32.0	33.3	39.1	32.7	32.1	41.6	27.3	29.5	26.8	31.8
1957	32.5	3.8	32.9	34.4	38.5	34.1	32.9	42.8	27.9	31.3	28.5	33.6
1958	33.2	2.2	33.6	36.5	41.0	36.1	32.9	43.4	27.8	32.1	29.3	34.5
1959	33.1	-0.3	33.3	34.8	37.3	34.7	33.3	43.9	28.2	32.7	29.8	35.1
1960	33.4	0.9	33.6	35.5	39.8	35.2	33.5	43.8	28.4	32.8	30.2	34.8
1961	33.4	0.0	33.6	35.4	38.0	35.3	33.4	43.6	28.4	32.9	30.3	34.8
1962	33.5	0.3	33.7	35.7	38.4	35.6	33.4	43.4	28.4	33.0	30.5	34.9
1963	33.4	-0.3	33.5	35.3	37.8	35.2	33.4	43.1	28.5	33.1	30.6	34.8
1964	33.5	0.3	33.6	35.4	38.9	35.2	33.3	43.3	28.4	33.4	31.0	35.1
1965	34.1	1.8	34.2	36.8	39.0	36.8	33.6	43.2	28.8	33.8	31.5	35.4
1966	35.2	3.2	35.4	39.2	41.5	39.2	34.1	43.4	29.3	34.6	32.5	36.0
1967	35.6	1.1	35.6	38.5	39.6	38.8	34.7	44.1	30.0	35.8	33.8	37.0
1968	36.6	2.8	36.5	40.0	42.5	40.0	35.5	45.1	30.6	37.0	35.0	38.2
1969	38.0	3.8	37.9	42.4	45.9	42.3	36.3	45.9	31.5	38.3	36.2	39.5
1970	39.3	3.4	39.1	43.8	46.0	43.9	37.4	47.2	32.5	40.1	38.1	41.3
1971	40.5	3.1	40.2	44.5	45.8	44.7	38.7	48.9	33.5	41.7	39.6	43.0
1972	41.8	3.2	41.5	46.9	48.0	47.2	39.4	50.0	34.1	42.8	40.5	44.2
1973	45.6	9.1	46.0	56.5	63.6	55.8	41.2	50.9	36.1	44.2	42.2	45.3
1974	52.6	15.4	53.1	64.4	71.6	63.9	48.2	55.5	44.0	50.5	48.8	51.2
1975	58.2	10.6	58.2	69.8	71.7	70.3	53.2	61.0	48.9	58.2	56.5	58.9
1976	60.8	4.5	60.4	69.6	76.7	69.0	56.5	63.7	52.4	62.1	60.3	62.9
1977	64.7	6.4	64.3	73.3	79.5	72.7	60.6	67.4	56.8	66.1	64.5	66.8
1978	69.8	7.9	69.4	79.9	85.8	79.4	64.9	73.6	60.0	71.3	70.1	71.8
1979	77.6	11.2	77.5	87.3	92.3	86.8	73.5	80.8	69.3	77.5	77.1	77.7
1980	88.0	13.4	88.6	92.4	93.9	92.3	87.1	91.0	85.1	85.8	86.0	85.7
1981	96.1	9.2	96.6	97.8	104.4	97.2	96.1	96.4	95.8	94.6	94.9	94.4
1982	100.0	4.1	100.0	100.0	100.0	100.0	100.0	100.0	100.0	100.0	100.0	100.0
1983	101.6	1.6	101.3	101.0	102.4	100.9	101.2	102.8	100.5	102.8	102.3	103.0
1984	103.7	2.1	103.3	105.4	111.4	104.9	102.2	104.5	101.1	105.2	104.9	105.4
1985	104.7	1.0	103.8	104.6	102.9	104.8	103.3	106.5	101.7	107.5	107.4	107.6
1986	103.2	-1.4	101.4	107.3	105.6	107.4	98.5	108.9	93.3	109.7	109.7	109.7
1987	105.4	2.1	103.6	109.5	107.1	109.6	100.7	111.5	94.9	111.7	111.8	111.6
1988	108.0	2.5	106.2	112.6	109.8	112.7	103.1	113.8	97.3	114.3	115.5	113.9
1989	113.6	5.2	112.1	118.7	119.6	118.6	108.9	117.6	103.8	118.8	120.3	118.2
1990	119.2	4.9	118.2	124.4	123.0	124.4	115.3	120.4	111.5	122.9	124.5	122.2
1991	121.7	2.1	120.5	124.1	119.3	124.4	118.7	123.9	115.0	126.7	127.8	126.3
1992	123.2	1.2	121.7	123.3	107.6	124.4	120.8	125.7	117.3	129.1	129.3	129.0
1993	124.7	1.2	123.0	125.7	114.4	126.5	121.7	128.0	117.6	131.4	131.2	131.4
1994	125.5	0.6	123.3	126.8	111.3	127.9	121.6	130.9	116.2	134.1	133.2	134.3
1995	127.9	1.9	125.6	129.0	118.8	129.8	124.0	132.7	118.8	136.7	135.8	137.0
1996	131.3	2.7	129.5	133.6	129.2	133.8	127.6	134.2	123.3	138.3	137.2	138.6
1997	131.8	0.4	130.2	134.5	126.6	135.1	128.2	133.7	124.3	138.2	137.7	138.4
1998	130.7	-0.8	128.9	134.3	127.2	134.8	126.4	132.9	122.2	137.6	137.9	137.4
1999	133.0	1.8	132.0	135.1	125.5	135.9	130.5	133.0	127.9	137.6	138.5	137.3
2000	138.0	3.8	138.2	137.2	123.5	138.3	138.4	133.9	138.7	138.8	139.5	138.6
2001	140.7	2.0	141.5	141.3	127.7	142.4	141.4	134.0	142.8	139.7	140.4	139.4
2002	138.9	-1.3	139.4	140.1	128.5	141.0	138.8	133.0	139.8	139.1	140.0	138.7
2003	143.3	3.2	145.3	145.9	130.0	147.2	144.7	133.1	148.4	139.5	139.9	139.3
2003												
January	141.1	1.3	142.5	142.3	121.0	144.1	142.2	132.6	144.9	139.1	139.9	138.7
February	142.8	1.2	144.8	142.8	117.8	144.8	145.2	132.6	149.4	139.0	139.7	138.6
March	144.6	1.3	147.0	143.2	124.6	144.8	148.1	134.1	152.8	139.8	139.8	139.7
April	142.5	-1.5	144.3	144.3	135.5	145.0	144.0	132.4	147.7	139.1	139.6	138.8
May	141.9	-0.4	143.5	144.5	133.7	145.4	142.8	132.7	145.8	139.2	139.5	139.0
June	142.7	0.6	144.5	145.1	122.6	146.9	144.0	132.5	147.6	139.2	139.8	138.9
July	142.8	0.1	144.6	144.7	124.2	146.3	144.3	132.7	148.0	139.4	139.9	139.1
August	143.5	0.5	145.5	145.8	129.5	147.1	145.0	132.9	148.9	139.7	140.0	139.5
September	143.8	0.2	146.0	147.5	135.4	148.5	145.0	132.8	149.0	139.6	140.0	139.4
October	144.7	0.6	147.1	150.5	134.1	151.9	145.4	133.9	149.0	140.0	140.1	140.0
November	144.5	-0.1	146.7	150.1	134.5	151.4	145.0	134.0	148.5	140.1	140.2	140.0
December	144.8	0.2	147.2	150.4	147.5	150.6	145.6	133.5	149.5	139.9	140.2	139.7

... = Not available.

Table 8-2. Producer Price Indexes and Purchasing Power of the Dollar—Continued

(1982 = 100, seasonally adjusted.)

Year and month	Intermediate materials, supplies, and components												
		Materials and components for manufacturing					Materials and components for construction	Processed fuels and lubricants			Containers, nonreturnable	Supplies	
	Total	Total	Materials for food manufacturing	Materials for nondurable manufacturing	Materials for durable manufacturing	Components for manufacturing		Total	Manufacturing industries	Nonmanufacturing industries		Total	Manufacturing industries
1947	23.3	24.9	36.9	33.5	17.5	21.3	22.5	14.4	17.3	12.5	23.4	28.5	23.4
1948	25.2	26.8	38.0	35.4	19.8	23.0	24.9	16.4	19.3	14.5	24.4	29.8	24.7
1949	24.2	25.7	32.7	32.3	20.4	23.4	24.9	14.9	17.6	13.2	24.5	28.0	24.6
1950	25.3	26.9	34.0	33.9	21.5	24.3	26.2	15.2	17.9	13.6	25.2	29.0	26.3
1951	28.4	30.5	37.9	39.3	23.9	27.6	28.7	15.9	18.7	14.1	29.6	32.6	29.3
1952	27.5	29.3	36.4	35.4	24.0	27.6	28.5	15.7	18.5	13.9	28.0	32.6	28.5
1953	27.7	29.7	36.5	35.1	25.0	28.1	29.0	15.8	18.5	14.2	28.0	31.0	28.7
1954	27.9	29.8	36.1	34.5	25.6	28.3	29.1	15.8	18.5	14.1	28.5	31.7	29.1
1955	28.4	30.5	35.0	34.7	26.9	29.5	30.3	15.8	18.5	14.2	28.9	31.2	30.8
1956	29.6	32.0	35.2	35.2	28.5	32.2	31.8	16.3	19.1	14.6	31.0	32.0	32.2
1957	30.3	32.7	35.8	35.7	29.5	33.5	32.0	17.2	20.1	15.6	32.4	32.3	33.4
1958	30.4	32.8	36.6	35.3	29.7	33.8	32.0	16.2	19.1	14.5	33.2	33.1	33.9
1959	30.8	33.3	35.3	35.9	30.4	34.2	32.9	16.2	19.1	14.3	33.0	33.5	34.8
1960	30.8	33.3	35.7	35.9	30.4	34.0	32.7	16.6	19.7	14.6	33.4	33.3	36.2
1961	30.6	32.9	36.9	35.1	30.0	33.7	32.2	16.8	19.9	14.8	33.2	33.7	35.8
1962	30.6	32.7	36.1	34.9	30.0	33.4	32.1	16.7	19.9	14.7	33.6	34.5	36.0
1963	30.7	32.7	37.9	34.6	30.0	33.4	32.2	16.6	19.8	14.5	33.2	35.0	35.8
1964	30.8	33.1	37.3	34.8	30.6	33.7	32.5	16.2	19.4	14.1	32.9	34.7	35.9
1965	31.2	33.6	38.3	35.2	31.2	34.2	32.8	16.5	19.6	14.4	33.5	35.0	36.1
1966	32.0	34.3	40.0	35.4	31.8	35.4	33.6	16.8	19.9	14.7	34.5	36.5	37.1
1967	32.2	34.5	39.2	35.2	32.3	36.5	34.0	16.9	20.1	14.8	35.0	36.8	37.6
1968	33.0	35.3	39.8	35.6	33.4	37.3	35.7	16.5	19.8	14.2	35.9	37.1	38.7
1969	34.1	36.5	42.0	36.0	35.2	38.5	37.7	16.6	20.0	14.4	37.2	37.8	39.8
1970	35.4	38.0	44.3	36.5	37.0	40.6	38.3	17.7	21.5	15.2	39.0	39.7	41.4
1971	36.8	38.9	45.7	37.0	38.1	41.9	40.8	19.5	23.6	16.6	40.8	40.8	42.5
1972	38.2	40.4	47.0	38.5	39.9	42.9	43.0	20.1	24.5	16.9	42.7	42.5	43.3
1973	42.4	44.1	57.2	42.6	43.1	44.3	46.5	22.2	26.4	19.4	45.2	51.7	45.6
1974	52.5	56.0	82.0	54.6	55.4	51.1	55.0	33.6	35.5	32.7	53.3	56.8	53.3
1975	58.0	61.7	82.1	61.4	60.8	57.8	60.1	39.4	41.9	38.0	60.0	61.8	59.4
1976	60.9	64.0	70.6	64.8	64.8	60.8	64.1	42.3	44.8	41.1	63.1	65.8	62.6
1977	64.9	67.4	71.9	66.8	70.2	64.5	69.3	47.7	51.0	46.2	65.9	69.3	66.6
1978	69.5	72.0	81.0	69.2	76.2	69.2	76.5	49.9	53.7	48.1	71.0	72.9	71.2
1979	78.4	80.9	89.9	78.3	87.3	75.8	84.2	61.6	64.3	60.4	79.4	80.2	78.1
1980	90.3	91.7	103.7	91.2	97.1	84.6	91.3	85.0	85.5	84.7	89.1	89.9	87.2
1981	98.6	98.7	102.1	100.5	100.7	94.7	97.9	100.6	100.2	101.0	96.7	96.9	95.2
1982	100.0	100.0	100.0	100.0	100.0	100.0	100.0	100.0	100.0	100.0	100.0	100.0	100.0
1983	100.6	101.2	101.3	98.5	103.0	102.4	102.8	95.4	96.2	94.9	100.4	101.8	101.5
1984	103.1	104.1	106.3	102.1	104.9	105.0	105.6	95.7	97.1	94.6	105.9	104.1	105.0
1985	102.7	103.3	101.5	100.5	103.3	106.4	107.3	92.8	93.8	92.0	109.0	104.4	107.3
1986	99.1	102.2	98.4	98.1	101.2	107.5	108.1	72.7	75.1	71.2	110.3	105.6	108.3
1987	101.5	105.3	100.8	102.2	106.2	108.8	109.8	73.3	75.9	71.7	114.5	107.7	110.0
1988	107.1	113.2	106.0	112.9	118.7	112.3	116.1	71.2	73.3	69.9	120.1	113.7	114.8
1989	112.0	118.1	112.7	118.5	123.6	116.4	121.3	76.4	78.3	75.3	125.4	118.1	119.8
1990	114.5	118.7	117.9	118.0	120.7	119.0	122.9	85.9	87.3	85.0	127.7	119.4	122.1
1991	114.4	118.1	115.3	116.7	117.2	121.0	124.5	85.3	88.4	83.4	128.1	121.4	124.4
1992	114.7	117.9	113.9	115.4	117.2	122.0	126.5	84.5	87.5	82.6	127.7	122.7	125.9
1993	116.2	118.9	115.6	115.5	119.1	123.0	132.0	84.7	88.1	82.6	126.4	125.0	128.5
1994	118.5	122.1	118.5	119.2	125.2	124.3	136.6	83.1	86.1	81.1	129.7	127.0	130.7
1995	124.9	130.4	119.5	135.1	135.6	126.5	142.1	84.2	87.1	82.3	148.8	132.1	137.0
1996	125.7	128.6	125.3	130.5	131.3	126.9	143.6	90.0	92.4	88.4	141.1	135.9	138.7
1997	125.6	128.3	123.2	129.6	132.8	126.4	146.5	89.3	92.0	87.6	136.0	135.9	139.4
1998	123.0	126.1	123.2	126.7	128.0	125.9	146.8	81.1	85.8	78.1	140.8	134.8	140.6
1999	123.2	124.6	120.8	124.9	125.1	125.7	148.9	84.6	87.9	82.5	142.5	134.2	140.7
2000	129.2	128.1	119.2	132.6	129.0	126.2	150.7	102.0	100.9	102.3	151.6	136.9	143.5
2001	129.7	127.4	124.3	131.8	125.1	126.4	150.6	104.5	105.7	103.5	153.1	138.7	145.4
2002	127.8	126.1	123.2	129.2	124.7	126.1	151.3	96.3	98.7	94.8	152.1	138.9	144.7
2003	133.7	129.7	134.4	137.2	127.9	125.9	153.6	112.6	116.0	110.5	153.7	141.5	146.5
2003													
January	131.1	127.9	129.4	133.5	126.3	125.8	151.8	106.5	107.0	106.3	153.4	140.1	145.1
February	133.6	129.5	130.3	138.1	127.0	125.8	152.2	114.1	113.2	114.7	153.7	140.7	145.6
March	136.4	130.1	129.6	140.0	126.9	125.9	152.3	125.7	124.2	126.6	153.8	141.2	146.4
April	133.2	129.3	130.0	137.4	126.6	126.0	152.8	112.0	115.9	109.6	154.0	141.2	146.7
May	132.3	129.2	130.9	136.8	126.7	126.1	152.6	107.7	112.5	104.7	153.9	141.5	146.7
June	133.1	129.5	134.1	137.3	126.7	126.0	152.7	110.8	116.0	107.5	154.1	141.4	146.6
July	133.3	129.1	132.7	136.3	127.0	125.8	153.3	112.4	117.7	109.0	153.8	141.4	146.7
August	134.1	129.8	134.7	137.6	127.4	125.9	153.5	114.6	119.7	111.4	153.6	141.2	146.7
September	134.0	129.8	136.6	136.5	128.5	125.9	154.9	113.0	118.4	109.6	153.5	141.6	146.7
October	134.4	130.5	141.1	137.3	129.6	125.8	155.4	112.7	117.5	109.7	153.2	141.9	146.7
November	134.4	130.8	141.6	137.4	130.6	125.9	155.9	111.3	115.9	108.4	153.4	142.7	146.8
December	134.9	131.0	141.1	138.1	131.4	125.8	156.0	112.8	115.8	110.9	153.5	142.8	146.9

Table 8-2. Producer Price Indexes and Purchasing Power of the Dollar—Continued

(1982 = 100, seasonally adjusted.)

Year and month	Intermediate materials, supplies, and components—Continued			Total	Foodstuffs and feedstuffs	Crude materials for further processing						
	Supplies—Continued						Nonfood materials					
	Nonmanufacturing industries					Total	Nonfood materials except fuel			Crude fuel		
	Total	Feeds	Other supplies				Total	Manu-facturing	Construc-tion	Total	Manu-facturing industries	Nonmanu-facturing industries
1947	31.8	60.8	26.5	31.7	45.1	...	24.0	24.0	23.5	7.5	6.5	8.5
1948	33.1	61.8	27.9	34.7	48.8	...	26.7	26.7	25.7	8.9	7.7	10.0
1949	30.4	52.5	26.7	30.1	40.5	...	24.3	24.1	26.6	8.8	7.6	9.9
1950	31.0	52.5	27.5	32.7	43.4	...	27.8	27.7	26.9	8.8	7.6	9.9
1951	35.1	58.5	31.3	37.6	50.2	...	32.0	32.1	28.5	9.0	7.7	10.1
1952	35.5	63.5	30.7	34.5	47.3	...	27.8	27.6	28.5	9.0	7.7	10.2
1953	32.8	51.9	30.1	31.9	42.3	...	26.6	26.3	29.6	9.3	8.0	10.6
1954	33.7	56.2	30.1	31.6	42.3	...	26.1	25.8	30.5	8.9	7.6	10.1
1955	31.8	44.7	30.7	30.4	38.4	...	27.5	27.3	31.5	8.9	7.6	10.1
1956	32.3	42.5	31.9	30.6	37.6	...	28.6	28.3	32.9	9.5	8.2	10.7
1957	32.1	39.4	32.6	31.2	39.2	...	28.2	27.8	34.3	10.1	8.7	11.4
1958	32.8	42.7	32.8	31.9	41.6	...	27.1	26.6	35.1	10.2	8.8	11.5
1959	33.1	43.6	32.8	31.1	38.8	...	28.1	27.6	35.4	10.4	8.9	11.7
1960	32.1	37.2	33.2	30.4	38.4	...	26.9	26.3	35.9	10.5	9.0	11.8
1961	32.9	40.9	32.9	30.2	37.9	...	27.2	26.6	35.9	10.5	9.0	11.8
1962	33.8	43.6	33.2	30.5	38.6	...	27.1	26.5	36.1	10.4	8.9	11.8
1963	34.6	45.9	33.2	29.9	37.5	...	26.7	26.1	36.0	10.5	9.0	11.9
1964	34.1	45.0	32.9	29.6	36.6	...	27.2	26.6	35.9	10.5	9.0	11.9
1965	34.5	45.9	33.0	31.1	39.2	...	27.7	27.2	36.1	10.6	9.0	11.9
1966	36.2	50.0	33.8	33.1	42.7	...	28.3	27.8	36.3	10.9	9.3	12.3
1967	36.3	48.3	34.5	31.3	40.3	21.1	26.5	25.8	37.0	11.3	9.7	12.8
1968	36.4	46.5	35.4	31.8	40.9	21.6	27.1	26.3	38.4	11.5	9.9	13.1
1969	36.9	46.4	36.0	33.9	44.1	22.5	28.4	27.6	39.8	12.0	10.2	13.8
1970	38.9	49.9	37.6	35.2	45.2	23.8	29.1	28.3	42.1	13.8	11.3	16.6
1971	39.9	50.4	38.9	36.0	46.1	24.7	29.4	28.4	44.1	15.7	12.6	19.3
1972	42.0	56.1	39.8	39.9	51.5	27.0	32.3	31.5	45.0	16.8	13.5	20.6
1973	54.7	97.3	42.7	54.5	72.6	34.3	42.9	42.7	46.2	18.6	14.8	22.9
1974	58.4	90.2	50.5	61.4	76.4	44.1	54.5	55.0	50.0	24.8	19.1	31.8
1975	62.9	84.0	58.9	61.6	77.4	43.7	50.0	49.7	55.9	30.6	24.4	38.0
1976	67.3	95.1	62.0	63.4	76.8	48.2	54.9	54.7	59.6	34.5	29.0	40.5
1977	70.7	99.3	65.2	65.5	77.5	51.7	56.3	56.0	63.1	42.0	37.2	47.4
1978	73.8	95.5	69.7	73.4	87.3	57.5	61.9	61.5	68.7	48.2	43.1	53.8
1979	81.2	106.9	76.3	85.9	100.0	69.6	75.5	75.6	76.6	57.3	53.1	62.0
1980	91.1	110.6	87.5	95.3	104.6	84.6	91.8	92.3	87.9	69.4	66.7	72.5
1981	97.8	111.3	95.4	103.0	103.9	101.8	109.8	110.9	96.8	84.8	83.6	86.2
1982	100.0	100.0	100.0	100.0	100.0	100.0	100.0	100.0	100.0	100.0	100.0	100.0
1983	102.0	109.1	101.0	101.3	101.8	100.7	98.8	98.6	100.1	105.1	105.8	104.4
1984	103.7	104.2	103.7	103.5	104.7	102.2	101.0	100.8	103.1	105.1	105.6	104.6
1985	103.0	86.6	105.3	95.8	94.8	96.9	94.3	93.1	105.7	102.7	102.7	102.5
1986	104.2	90.5	106.2	87.7	93.2	81.6	76.0	72.6	106.5	92.2	91.1	93.6
1987	106.6	94.6	108.3	93.7	96.2	87.9	88.5	84.7	114.8	84.1	82.1	86.3
1988	113.2	115.0	112.7	96.0	106.1	85.5	85.9	81.5	126.5	82.1	80.1	84.5
1989	117.2	114.4	117.5	103.1	111.2	93.4	95.8	91.0	136.9	85.3	83.9	87.0
1990	118.0	102.8	120.2	108.9	113.1	101.5	107.3	102.5	145.2	84.8	82.9	87.0
1991	119.9	101.3	122.5	101.2	105.5	94.6	97.5	92.2	147.5	82.9	82.3	84.1
1992	121.1	103.0	123.7	100.4	105.1	93.5	94.2	87.9	162.1	84.0	83.1	85.2
1993	123.2	105.4	125.8	102.4	108.4	94.7	94.1	85.6	193.6	87.1	85.9	88.6
1994	125.1	105.8	127.9	101.8	106.5	94.8	97.0	88.3	199.1	82.4	81.7	83.6
1995	129.5	103.4	133.2	102.7	105.8	96.8	105.8	97.3	201.7	72.1	72.5	72.9
1996	134.4	133.1	134.6	113.8	121.5	104.5	105.7	97.6	195.7	92.6	90.7	94.3
1997	134.1	129.1	134.8	111.1	112.2	106.4	103.5	95.0	201.4	101.3	98.4	103.3
1998	132.2	100.2	136.2	96.8	103.9	88.4	84.5	76.7	196.0	86.7	84.8	88.5
1999	131.4	89.2	136.5	98.2	98.7	94.3	91.1	83.0	195.7	91.2	90.0	92.9
2000	134.1	94.6	138.8	120.6	100.2	130.4	118.0	108.7	193.4	136.9	136.9	139.3
2001	135.8	96.8	140.5	121.0	106.1	126.8	101.5	93.2	181.7	151.4	150.2	154.2
2002	136.3	98.1	140.9	108.1	99.5	111.4	101.0	92.5	181.4	117.3	113.4	119.8
2003	139.0	106.6	143.1	135.3	113.5	148.2	116.9	107.5	180.8	185.7	176.4	189.9
2003												
January	137.7	100.9	142.2	127.9	107.0	140.3	114.3	105.1	179.8	169.9	161.8	173.7
February	138.3	102.2	142.8	134.5	107.6	151.6	121.7	112.0	180.9	186.6	177.1	190.8
March	138.7	102.8	143.1	152.3	106.2	184.2	121.6	111.9	180.5	271.5	255.4	277.9
April	138.7	102.6	143.1	128.2	107.7	140.3	110.2	101.2	179.6	176.9	168.4	180.9
May	138.9	105.0	143.2	130.1	109.7	142.1	108.8	99.9	179.9	183.7	174.7	187.9
June	139.0	105.0	143.2	135.7	108.8	152.7	113.7	104.5	179.1	203.0	192.4	207.6
July	138.9	104.5	143.2	131.9	106.1	148.2	114.9	105.6	178.6	189.1	179.5	193.5
August	138.6	101.5	143.2	130.6	110.0	142.6	117.0	107.6	180.2	171.2	163.0	175.1
September	139.2	107.8	143.2	134.1	117.7	142.8	113.9	104.6	181.2	176.9	168.4	180.9
October	139.5	109.2	143.4	137.9	127.7	141.4	119.7	110.1	182.0	163.3	155.8	167.0
November	140.4	118.6	143.5	137.9	126.9	142.1	122.1	112.3	182.7	161.2	153.9	164.8
December	140.6	118.4	143.6	142.6	127.3	150.1	125.9	116.0	184.9	175.3	166.9	179.3

. . . = Not available.

Table 8-2. Producer Price Indexes and Purchasing Power of the Dollar—Continued

(1982 = 100, seasonally adjusted.)

Year and month	Finished energy goods	Finished goods excluding			Finished consumer goods excluding		Intermediate materials		Intermediate materials less			Crude materials		
		Foods	Energy	Foods and energy	Energy	Foods and energy	Foods and feeds	Energy goods	Foods and feeds	Energy	Foods and energy	Energy materials	Less energy	Nonfood materials less energy
1947	...	...	...	...	...	...	...	...	22.2	...	...	...	...	...
1948	...	...	...	...	...	...	...	...	24.1	...	...	...	...	...
1949	...	...	...	...	...	...	...	...	23.5	...	...	...	...	...
1950	...	...	...	...	...	...	...	...	24.6	...	...	...	...	...
1951	...	...	...	...	...	...	...	...	27.6	...	...	...	...	...
1952	...	...	...	...	...	...	...	...	26.7	...	...	...	...	...
1953	...	...	...	...	...	...	...	...	27.0	...	...	...	...	...
1954	...	...	...	...	...	...	...	...	27.2	...	...	...	...	...
1955	...	...	...	...	...	...	...	...	28.0	...	...	...	...	...
1956	...	...	...	...	...	...	...	...	29.3	...	...	...	...	...
1957	...	...	...	...	...	...	...	...	30.1	...	...	...	...	...
1958	...	...	...	...	...	...	...	...	30.1	...	...	...	...	...
1959	...	...	...	...	...	...	...	...	30.5	...	...	...	...	...
1960	...	...	...	...	...	...	...	...	30.7	...	...	...	...	...
1961	...	...	...	...	...	...	...	...	30.3	...	...	...	...	...
1962	...	...	...	...	...	...	...	...	30.2	...	...	...	...	...
1963	...	...	...	...	...	...	...	...	30.1	...	...	...	...	...
1964	...	...	...	...	...	...	...	...	30.3	...	...	...	...	...
1965	...	...	...	...	...	...	...	...	30.7	...	...	...	...	...
1966	...	...	...	...	...	...	...	...	31.3	...	...	...	...	...
1967	...	35.0	...	...	...	...	41.8	...	31.7	...	...	...	...	...
1968	...	35.9	...	...	...	...	41.5	...	32.5	...	...	...	...	...
1969	...	36.9	...	...	...	...	42.9	...	33.6	...	...	...	...	...
1970	...	38.2	...	...	...	...	45.6	...	34.8	...	...	...	...	...
1971	...	39.6	...	...	...	...	46.7	...	36.2	...	...	...	...	...
1972	...	40.4	...	...	...	...	49.5	...	37.7	...	...	...	...	...
1973	...	42.0	...	48.1	...	50.4	70.3	...	40.6	...	44.3	...	...	70.8
1974	26.2	48.8	...	53.6	58.7	55.5	83.6	33.1	50.5	56.2	54.0	27.8	78.4	83.3
1975	30.7	54.7	62.4	59.7	63.9	60.6	81.6	38.7	56.6	61.7	60.2	33.3	75.9	69.3
1976	34.3	58.1	64.8	63.1	65.7	63.7	77.4	41.5	60.0	64.7	63.8	35.3	77.6	80.2
1977	39.7	62.2	68.6	66.9	69.4	67.3	79.6	46.8	64.1	68.5	67.6	40.4	78.1	79.8
1978	42.3	66.7	74.0	71.9	74.9	72.2	84.8	49.1	68.6	73.4	72.5	45.2	87.5	87.8
1979	57.1	74.6	80.7	78.3	81.7	78.8	94.5	61.1	77.4	81.7	80.7	54.9	101.5	106.2
1980	85.2	86.7	88.4	87.1	89.3	87.8	105.5	84.9	89.4	91.4	90.3	73.1	106.5	113.1
1981	101.5	95.6	95.4	94.6	95.7	94.6	104.6	100.5	98.2	98.2	97.7	97.7	105.7	111.7
1982	100.0	100.0	100.0	100.0	100.0	100.0	100.0	100.0	100.0	100.0	100.0	100.0	100.0	100.0
1983	95.2	101.8	102.5	103.0	102.4	103.1	103.6	95.3	100.5	101.7	101.6	98.7	102.6	105.3
1984	91.2	103.2	105.5	105.5	105.6	105.7	105.7	95.5	103.0	104.6	104.7	98.0	106.3	111.7
1985	87.6	104.6	107.2	108.1	107.0	108.4	97.3	92.6	103.0	104.7	105.2	93.3	97.0	104.9
1986	63.0	101.9	109.7	110.6	109.7	111.1	96.2	72.6	99.3	104.5	104.9	71.8	95.4	103.1
1987	61.8	104.0	112.3	113.3	112.5	114.2	99.2	73.0	101.7	107.3	107.8	75.0	100.9	115.7
1988	59.8	106.5	115.8	117.0	116.3	118.5	109.5	70.9	106.9	114.6	115.2	67.7	112.6	133.0
1989	65.7	111.8	121.2	122.1	122.1	124.0	113.8	76.1	111.9	119.5	120.2	75.9	117.7	137.9
1990	75.0	117.4	126.0	126.6	127.2	128.8	113.3	85.5	114.5	120.4	120.9	85.9	118.6	136.3
1991	78.1	120.9	129.1	131.1	130.0	133.7	111.1	85.1	114.6	120.8	121.4	80.4	110.9	128.2
1992	77.8	123.1	131.1	134.2	131.8	137.3	110.7	84.3	114.9	121.3	122.0	78.8	110.7	128.4
1993	78.0	124.4	132.9	135.8	133.5	138.5	112.7	84.6	116.4	123.2	123.8	76.7	116.3	140.2
1994	77.0	125.1	134.2	137.1	134.2	139.0	114.8	83.0	118.7	126.3	127.1	72.1	119.3	156.2
1995	78.1	127.5	136.9	140.0	136.9	141.9	114.8	84.1	125.5	134.0	135.2	69.4	123.5	173.6
1996	83.2	130.5	139.6	142.0	140.1	144.3	128.1	89.8	125.6	133.6	134.0	85.0	130.0	155.8
1997	83.4	130.9	140.2	142.4	141.0	145.1	125.4	89.0	125.7	133.7	134.2	87.3	123.5	156.5
1998	75.1	129.5	141.1	143.7	142.5	147.7	116.2	80.8	123.4	132.4	133.5	68.6	113.6	142.1
1999	78.8	132.3	143.0	146.1	145.2	151.7	111.1	84.3	123.9	131.7	133.1	78.5	107.9	135.2
2000	94.1	138.1	144.9	148.0	147.4	154.0	111.7	101.7	130.1	135.0	136.6	122.1	111.7	145.2
2001	96.7	140.4	147.6	150.0	150.8	156.9	115.9	104.1	130.5	135.1	136.4	122.3	112.2	130.7
2002	88.8	138.3	147.3	150.2	150.8	157.6	115.5	95.9	128.5	134.5	135.8	102.0	108.7	135.7
2003	102.0	142.4	149.0	150.5	153.1	157.9	125.9	111.9	134.2	137.7	138.5	147.2	123.4	152.5
2003														
January	97.0	140.6	147.8	150.0	151.4	157.4	120.7	105.5	131.7	136.2	137.2	140.1	116.0	142.7
February	104.2	142.6	147.8	149.9	151.6	157.3	121.7	113.6	134.3	137.1	138.2	153.9	117.8	147.9
March	109.2	144.7	148.6	150.8	152.4	158.3	121.4	125.0	137.2	137.5	138.6	200.2	116.7	147.6
April	101.3	141.8	148.2	150.0	152.1	157.3	121.6	111.4	133.9	137.3	138.3	138.8	117.3	145.8
May	98.2	141.0	148.4	150.1	152.4	157.5	123.0	106.7	132.9	137.4	138.4	141.4	118.7	145.6
June	101.0	141.8	148.6	150.1	152.6	157.5	125.2	110.0	133.6	137.5	138.4	156.2	118.1	145.9
July	101.5	142.1	148.6	150.3	152.5	157.7	124.1	111.7	133.9	137.3	138.2	148.7	116.9	148.6
August	102.9	142.6	149.0	150.5	153.0	157.8	124.4	114.4	134.6	137.5	138.4	139.7	120.5	151.5
September	102.8	142.6	149.5	150.5	153.7	157.8	127.8	112.1	134.4	138.0	138.7	138.2	127.2	155.6
October	102.4	143.0	150.7	151.2	155.4	158.7	131.3	111.9	134.6	138.5	139.1	134.3	135.8	160.3
November	101.7	142.8	150.6	151.2	155.2	158.7	134.7	110.4	134.5	138.9	139.3	132.5	137.0	167.2
December	103.1	143.1	150.6	151.0	155.3	158.6	134.3	111.9	135.0	139.2	139.6	141.8	138.7	172.2

... = Not available.

Table 8-2. Producer Price Indexes and Purchasing Power of the Dollar—*Continued*

(1982 = 100, except as noted; not seasonally adjusted.)

Year and month	Finished goods						Capital equipment	Intermediate materials, supplies, and components	Crude materials for further processing	Purchasing power of the dollar	
	Total	Finished consumer goods								Producer prices for finished goods (1982–1984 = $1.00)	Consumer prices (CPI-U, 1982–1984 = $1.00)
		Total	Foods	Consumer goods except foods							
				Total	Durable goods	Nondurable goods less foods					
1947	26.4	28.6	31.9	27.4	32.9	24.2	19.8	23.3	31.7	3.855	4.474
1948	28.5	30.8	34.9	29.2	35.2	25.7	21.6	25.2	34.7	3.571	4.151
1949	27.7	29.4	32.1	28.6	36.1	24.7	22.7	24.2	30.1	3.674	4.193
1950	28.2	29.9	32.7	29.0	36.5	25.1	23.2	25.3	32.7	3.609	4.151
1951	30.8	32.7	36.7	31.1	38.9	27.0	25.5	28.4	37.6	3.304	3.846
1952	30.6	32.3	36.4	30.7	39.2	26.3	25.9	27.5	34.5	3.326	3.765
1953	30.3	31.7	34.5	31.0	39.5	26.6	26.3	27.7	31.9	3.359	3.735
1954	30.4	31.7	34.2	31.1	39.8	26.7	26.7	27.9	31.6	3.348	3.717
1955	30.5	31.5	33.4	31.3	40.2	26.8	27.4	28.4	30.4	3.337	3.732
1956	31.3	32.0	33.3	32.1	41.6	27.3	29.5	29.6	30.6	3.251	3.678
1957	32.5	32.9	34.4	32.9	42.8	27.9	31.3	30.3	31.2	3.131	3.549
1958	33.2	33.6	36.5	32.9	43.4	27.8	32.1	30.4	31.9	3.065	3.457
1959	33.1	33.3	34.8	33.3	43.9	28.2	32.7	30.8	31.1	3.075	3.427
1960	33.4	33.6	35.5	33.5	43.8	28.4	32.8	30.8	30.4	3.047	3.373
1961	33.4	33.6	35.4	33.4	43.6	28.4	32.9	30.6	30.2	3.047	3.340
1962	33.5	33.7	35.7	33.4	43.4	28.4	33.0	30.6	30.5	3.038	3.304
1963	33.4	33.5	35.3	33.4	43.1	28.5	33.1	30.7	29.9	3.047	3.265
1964	33.5	33.6	35.4	33.3	43.3	28.4	33.4	30.8	29.6	3.038	3.220
1965	34.1	34.2	36.8	33.6	43.2	28.8	33.8	31.2	31.1	2.984	3.166
1966	35.2	35.4	39.2	34.1	43.4	29.3	34.6	32.0	33.1	2.891	3.080
1967	35.6	35.6	38.5	34.7	44.1	30.0	35.8	32.2	31.3	2.859	2.993
1968	36.6	36.5	40.0	35.5	45.1	30.6	37.0	33.0	31.8	2.781	2.873
1969	38.0	37.9	42.4	36.3	45.9	31.5	38.3	34.1	33.9	2.678	2.726
1970	39.3	39.1	43.8	37.4	47.2	32.5	40.1	35.4	35.2	2.589	2.574
1971	40.5	40.2	44.5	38.7	48.9	33.5	41.7	36.8	36.0	2.513	2.466
1972	41.8	41.5	46.9	39.4	50.0	34.1	42.8	38.2	39.9	2.435	2.391
1973	45.6	46.0	56.5	41.2	50.9	36.1	44.2	42.4	54.5	2.232	2.251
1974	52.6	53.1	64.4	48.2	55.5	44.0	50.5	52.5	61.4	1.935	2.029
1975	58.2	58.2	69.8	53.2	61.0	48.9	58.2	58.0	61.6	1.749	1.859
1976	60.8	60.4	69.6	56.5	63.7	52.4	62.1	60.9	63.4	1.674	1.757
1977	64.7	64.3	73.3	60.6	67.4	56.8	66.1	64.9	65.5	1.573	1.649
1978	69.8	69.4	79.9	64.9	73.6	60.0	71.3	69.5	73.4	1.458	1.532
1979	77.6	77.5	87.3	73.5	80.8	69.3	77.5	78.4	85.9	1.311	1.380
1980	88.0	88.6	92.4	87.1	91.0	85.1	85.8	90.3	95.3	1.156	1.215
1981	96.1	96.6	97.8	96.1	96.4	95.8	94.6	98.6	103.0	1.059	1.098
1982	100.0	100.0	100.0	100.0	100.0	100.0	100.0	100.0	100.0	1.018	1.035
1983	101.6	101.3	101.0	101.2	102.8	100.5	102.8	100.6	101.3	1.002	1.003
1984	103.7	103.3	105.4	102.2	104.5	101.1	105.2	103.1	103.5	0.981	0.961
1985	104.7	103.8	104.6	103.3	106.5	101.7	107.5	102.7	95.8	0.972	0.928
1986	103.2	101.4	107.3	98.5	108.9	93.3	109.7	99.1	87.7	0.986	0.913
1987	105.4	103.6	109.5	100.7	111.5	94.9	111.7	101.5	93.7	0.966	0.880
1988	108.0	106.2	112.6	103.1	113.8	97.3	114.3	107.1	96.0	0.942	0.846
1989	113.6	112.1	118.7	108.9	117.6	103.8	118.8	112.0	103.1	0.896	0.807
1990	119.2	118.2	124.4	115.3	120.4	111.5	122.9	114.5	108.9	0.854	0.766
1991	121.7	120.5	124.1	118.7	123.9	115.0	126.7	114.4	101.2	0.836	0.734
1992	123.2	121.7	123.3	120.8	125.7	117.3	129.1	114.7	100.4	0.826	0.713
1993	124.7	123.0	125.7	121.7	128.0	117.6	131.4	116.2	102.4	0.816	0.692
1994	125.5	123.3	126.8	121.6	130.9	116.2	134.1	118.5	101.8	0.811	0.675
1995	127.9	125.6	129.0	124.0	132.7	118.8	136.7	124.9	102.7	0.796	0.656
1996	131.3	129.5	133.6	127.6	134.2	123.3	138.3	125.7	113.8	0.775	0.638
1997	131.8	130.2	134.5	128.2	133.7	124.3	138.2	125.6	111.1	0.772	0.623
1998	130.7	128.9	134.3	126.4	132.9	122.2	137.6	123.0	96.8	0.779	0.614
1999	133.0	132.0	135.1	130.5	133.0	127.9	137.6	123.2	98.2	0.765	0.600
2000	138.0	138.2	137.2	138.4	133.9	138.7	138.8	129.2	120.6	0.737	0.581
2001	140.7	141.5	141.3	141.4	134.0	142.8	139.7	129.7	121.0	0.723	0.565
2002	138.9	139.4	140.1	138.8	133.0	139.8	139.1	127.8	108.1	0.733	0.556
2003	143.3	145.3	145.9	144.7	133.1	148.4	139.5	133.7	135.3	0.710	0.544
2003											
January	140.8	141.9	142.0	141.6	133.2	143.8	139.3	131.1	127.3	0.723	0.550
February	142.3	144.0	142.3	144.4	133.1	147.9	139.2	133.5	134.0	0.715	0.546
March	144.2	146.3	142.8	147.4	134.4	151.7	139.9	136.2	152.2	0.706	0.543
April	142.1	143.8	144.0	143.5	132.5	146.9	139.1	133.0	128.0	0.716	0.544
May	142.0	143.7	144.6	143.0	132.4	146.3	139.0	132.5	130.9	0.717	0.545
June	143.0	145.0	145.2	144.6	131.8	148.9	138.9	133.5	136.5	0.712	0.544
July	143.0	145.1	144.9	144.8	131.7	149.2	138.9	133.7	132.6	0.712	0.544
August	143.7	145.9	146.3	145.4	131.8	150.0	139.2	134.1	131.3	0.708	0.542
September	144.0	146.4	148.0	145.5	131.1	150.4	138.9	134.1	134.7	0.707	0.540
October	145.5	147.8	151.0	146.2	135.6	149.4	140.8	134.1	138.0	0.699	0.540
November	144.5	146.5	150.1	144.8	135.0	147.6	140.5	134.1	137.0	0.704	0.542
December	144.5	146.7	150.3	145.0	134.3	148.2	140.2	134.5	141.1	0.704	0.543

Table 8-3. Producer Price Indexes by Major Commodity Groups

(1982 = 100, not seasonally adjusted.)

Year and month	All commodities	Farm products	Processed foods and feeds	Industrial commodities												
				Total	Textile products and apparel	Hides, leather, and related products	Fuels and related products and power	Chemicals and related products	Rubber and plastics products	Lumber and wood products	Pulp, paper, and allied products	Metals and metal products	Machinery and metal equipment	Furniture and household durables	Nonmetallic mineral products	Transportation equipment	Miscellaneous products
1947	25.6	45.1	33.0	22.7	50.6	31.7	11.1	32.1	29.2	25.8	25.1	18.2	19.3	37.2	20.7	...	26.6
1948	27.7	48.5	35.3	24.6	52.8	32.1	13.1	32.8	30.2	29.5	26.2	20.7	20.9	39.4	22.4	...	27.7
1949	26.3	41.9	32.1	24.1	48.3	30.4	12.4	30.0	29.2	27.3	25.1	20.9	21.9	40.1	23.0	...	28.2
1950	27.3	44.0	33.2	25.0	50.2	32.9	12.6	30.4	35.6	31.4	25.7	22.0	22.6	40.9	23.5	...	28.6
1951	30.4	51.2	36.9	27.6	56.0	37.7	13.0	34.8	43.7	34.1	30.5	24.5	25.3	44.4	25.0	...	30.3
1952	29.6	48.4	36.4	26.9	50.5	30.5	13.0	33.0	39.6	33.2	29.7	24.5	25.3	43.5	25.0	...	30.2
1953	29.2	43.8	34.8	27.2	49.3	31.0	13.4	33.4	36.9	33.1	29.6	25.3	25.9	44.4	26.0	...	31.0
1954	29.3	43.2	35.4	27.2	48.2	29.5	13.2	33.8	37.5	32.5	29.6	25.5	26.3	44.9	26.6	...	31.3
1955	29.3	40.5	33.8	27.8	48.2	29.4	13.2	33.7	42.4	34.1	30.4	27.2	27.2	45.1	27.3	...	31.3
1956	30.3	40.0	33.8	29.1	48.2	31.2	13.6	33.9	43.0	34.6	32.4	29.6	29.3	46.3	28.5	...	31.7
1957	31.2	41.1	34.8	29.9	48.3	31.2	14.3	34.6	42.8	32.8	33.0	30.2	31.4	47.5	29.6	...	32.6
1958	31.6	42.9	36.5	30.0	47.4	31.6	13.7	34.9	42.8	32.5	33.4	30.0	32.1	47.9	29.9	...	33.3
1959	31.7	40.2	35.6	30.5	48.1	35.9	13.7	34.8	42.6	34.7	33.7	30.6	32.8	48.0	30.3	...	33.4
1960	31.7	40.1	35.6	30.5	48.6	34.6	13.9	34.8	42.7	33.5	34.0	30.6	33.0	47.8	30.4	...	33.6
1961	31.6	39.7	36.2	30.4	47.8	34.9	14.0	34.5	41.1	32.0	33.0	30.5	33.0	47.5	30.5	...	33.7
1962	31.7	40.4	36.5	30.4	48.2	35.3	14.0	33.9	39.9	32.2	33.4	30.2	33.0	47.2	30.5	...	33.9
1963	31.6	39.6	36.8	30.3	48.2	34.3	13.9	33.5	40.1	32.8	33.1	30.3	33.1	46.9	30.3	...	34.2
1964	31.6	39.0	36.7	30.5	48.5	34.4	13.5	33.6	39.6	33.5	33.0	31.1	33.3	47.1	30.4	...	34.4
1965	32.3	40.7	38.0	30.9	48.8	35.9	13.8	33.9	39.7	33.7	33.3	32.0	33.7	46.8	30.4	...	34.7
1966	33.3	43.7	40.2	31.5	48.9	39.4	14.1	34.0	40.5	35.2	34.2	32.8	34.7	47.4	30.7	...	35.3
1967	33.4	41.3	39.8	32.0	48.9	38.1	14.4	34.2	41.4	35.1	34.6	33.2	35.9	48.3	31.2	...	36.2
1968	34.2	42.3	40.6	32.8	50.7	39.3	14.3	34.1	42.8	39.8	35.0	34.0	37.0	49.7	32.4	...	37.0
1969	35.6	45.0	42.7	33.9	51.8	41.5	14.6	34.2	43.6	44.0	36.0	36.0	38.2	50.7	33.6	40.4	38.1
1970	36.9	45.8	44.6	35.2	52.4	42.0	15.3	35.0	44.9	39.9	37.5	38.7	40.0	51.9	35.3	41.9	39.8
1971	38.1	46.6	45.5	36.5	53.3	43.4	16.6	35.6	45.2	44.7	38.1	39.4	41.4	53.1	38.2	44.2	40.8
1972	39.8	51.6	48.0	37.8	55.5	50.0	17.1	35.6	45.3	50.7	39.3	40.9	42.3	53.8	39.4	45.5	41.5
1973	45.0	72.7	58.9	40.3	60.5	54.5	19.4	37.6	46.6	62.2	42.3	44.0	43.7	55.7	40.7	46.1	43.3
1974	53.5	77.4	68.0	49.2	68.0	55.2	30.1	50.2	56.4	64.5	52.5	57.0	50.0	61.8	47.8	50.3	48.1
1975	58.4	77.0	72.6	54.9	67.4	56.5	35.4	62.0	62.2	62.1	59.0	61.5	57.9	67.5	54.4	56.7	53.4
1976	61.1	78.8	70.8	58.4	72.4	63.9	38.3	64.0	66.0	72.2	62.1	65.0	61.3	70.3	58.2	60.5	55.6
1977	64.9	79.4	74.0	62.5	75.3	68.3	43.6	65.9	69.4	83.0	64.6	69.3	65.2	73.2	62.6	64.6	59.4
1978	69.9	87.7	80.6	67.0	78.1	76.1	46.5	68.0	72.4	96.9	67.7	75.3	70.3	77.5	69.6	69.5	66.7
1979	78.7	99.6	88.5	75.7	82.5	96.1	58.9	76.0	80.5	105.5	75.9	86.0	76.7	82.8	77.6	75.3	75.5
1980	89.8	102.9	95.9	88.0	89.7	94.7	82.8	89.0	90.1	101.5	86.3	95.0	86.0	90.7	88.4	82.9	93.6
1981	98.0	105.2	98.9	97.4	97.6	99.3	100.2	98.4	96.4	102.8	94.8	99.6	94.4	95.9	96.7	94.3	96.1
1982	100.0	100.0	100.0	100.0	100.0	100.0	100.0	100.0	100.0	100.0	100.0	100.0	100.0	100.0	100.0	100.0	100.0
1983	101.3	102.4	101.8	101.1	100.3	103.2	95.9	100.3	100.8	107.9	103.3	101.8	102.7	103.4	101.6	102.8	104.8
1984	103.7	105.5	105.4	103.3	102.7	109.0	94.8	102.9	102.3	108.0	110.3	104.8	105.1	105.7	105.4	105.2	107.0
1985	103.2	95.1	103.5	103.7	102.9	108.9	91.4	103.7	101.9	106.6	113.3	104.4	107.2	107.1	108.6	107.9	109.4
1986	100.2	92.9	105.4	100.0	103.2	113.0	69.8	102.6	101.9	107.2	116.1	103.2	108.8	108.2	110.0	110.5	111.6
1987	102.8	95.5	107.9	102.6	105.1	120.4	70.2	106.4	103.0	112.8	121.8	107.1	110.4	109.9	110.0	112.5	114.9
1988	106.9	104.9	112.7	106.3	109.2	131.4	66.7	116.3	109.3	118.9	130.4	118.7	113.2	113.1	111.2	114.3	120.2
1989	112.2	110.9	117.8	111.6	112.3	136.3	72.9	123.0	112.6	126.7	137.8	124.1	117.4	116.9	112.6	117.7	126.5
1990	116.3	112.2	121.9	115.8	115.0	141.7	82.3	123.6	113.6	129.7	141.2	122.9	120.7	119.2	114.7	121.5	134.2
1991	116.5	105.7	121.9	116.5	116.3	138.9	81.2	125.6	115.1	132.1	142.9	120.2	123.0	121.2	117.2	126.4	140.8
1992	117.2	103.6	122.1	117.4	117.8	140.4	80.4	125.9	115.1	146.6	145.2	119.2	123.4	122.2	117.3	130.4	145.3
1993	118.9	107.1	124.0	119.0	118.0	143.7	80.0	128.2	116.0	174.0	147.3	119.2	124.0	123.7	120.0	133.7	145.4
1994	120.4	106.3	125.5	120.7	118.3	148.5	77.8	132.1	117.6	180.0	152.5	124.8	125.1	126.1	124.2	137.2	141.9
1995	124.7	107.4	127.0	125.5	120.8	153.7	78.0	142.5	123.8	178.1	172.2	134.5	126.6	128.2	129.0	139.7	145.4
1996	127.7	122.4	133.3	127.3	122.4	150.5	85.8	142.1	123.8	176.1	168.7	131.0	126.5	130.4	131.0	141.7	147.7
1997	127.6	112.9	134.0	127.7	122.6	154.2	86.1	143.6	123.2	183.8	167.9	131.8	125.9	130.8	133.2	141.6	150.9
1998	124.4	104.6	131.6	124.8	122.9	148.0	75.3	143.9	122.6	179.1	171.7	127.8	124.9	131.3	135.4	141.2	156.0
1999	125.5	98.4	131.1	126.5	121.1	146.0	80.5	144.2	122.5	183.6	174.1	124.6	123.4	131.7	138.9	141.8	166.6
2000	132.7	99.5	133.1	134.8	121.4	151.5	103.5	151.0	125.5	178.2	183.7	128.1	124.0	132.6	142.5	143.8	170.8
2001	134.2	103.8	137.3	135.7	121.3	158.4	105.3	151.8	127.2	174.4	184.8	125.4	123.7	133.2	144.3	145.2	181.3
2002	131.1	99.0	136.2	132.4	119.9	157.6	93.2	151.9	126.8	173.3	185.9	125.9	122.9	133.5	146.2	144.6	182.4
2003	138.1	111.5	143.4	139.1	119.8	162.3	112.9	161.8	130.1	177.4	190.0	129.2	121.9	133.9	148.2	145.7	179.6
2003																	
January	135.3	104.1	139.2	136.7	119.7	160.8	106.5	158.0	127.8	171.7	188.5	127.6	122.3	133.7	146.8	145.3	179.5
February	137.6	104.6	139.9	139.3	119.6	162.2	114.9	162.2	128.7	173.2	188.8	128.3	122.1	133.6	147.5	145.5	179.5
March	141.2	104.0	140.1	143.6	119.7	162.3	129.6	164.5	129.9	172.6	189.1	128.5	122.1	133.6	147.8	146.9	179.9
April	136.8	105.6	140.7	138.2	119.7	162.8	110.0	162.2	130.9	172.9	189.6	128.2	122.1	133.8	148.5	144.9	179.1
May	136.7	109.2	141.4	137.8	119.9	161.0	108.5	162.1	131.0	173.1	189.9	128.3	122.1	133.9	148.4	144.8	179.1
June	138.0	107.3	143.2	139.2	119.7	160.8	114.3	162.2	130.5	173.8	190.2	128.3	122.0	134.0	148.2	144.3	179.3
July	137.7	105.5	142.7	139.1	119.6	160.8	114.0	160.9	130.4	176.9	190.3	128.4	121.9	134.1	148.2	144.3	179.0
August	138.0	109.0	143.6	139.1	119.9	161.9	113.7	161.2	130.5	177.8	190.4	129.0	121.8	133.9	148.3	144.6	179.3
September	138.5	116.1	145.2	139.1	120.0	162.9	113.0	161.4	130.4	184.0	190.6	129.5	121.7	133.6	148.5	144.1	179.6
October	139.3	124.4	148.5	139.2	119.9	163.7	110.7	162.1	130.5	184.1	190.8	130.2	121.6	133.9	148.5	148.7	180.0
November	138.9	123.7	148.2	138.8	120.0	163.6	108.6	162.1	130.4	184.4	191.1	131.4	121.6	134.3	148.9	147.9	180.4
December	139.5	124.3	147.5	139.5	120.1	164.2	111.0	163.1	130.7	183.9	190.9	133.1	121.5	133.9	148.8	147.4	180.5

... = Not available.

Table 8-4. Producer Price Indexes for the Net Output of Selected NAICS Industry Groups

(Various index bases, not seasonally adjusted.)

Year and month	Mining		Manufacturing (Dec. 1984 = 100)									
	Total (Dec. 1984 = 100)	Oil and gas extraction (Dec. 1985 = 100)	Total	Food manufacturing	Leather and products	Petroleum and coal products	Chemicals	Plastics and rubber products	Nonmetallic mineral products	Primary metals	Fabricated metal products	Furniture and related products
1985	...	...	...	99.0	101.3	...	100.7	100.0	102.1	99.4	100.6	101.9
1986	77.0	76.9	98.4	100.3	103.0	66.6	100.5	100.3	103.8	97.0	101.0	103.9
1987	75.0	74.3	100.9	102.6	106.6	70.5	103.6	100.9	104.5	101.0	102.1	106.4
1988	70.6	68.5	104.4	107.1	113.4	67.7	113.0	106.7	105.8	113.0	107.4	111.4
1989	76.4	75.7	109.6	112.2	118.0	75.7	119.6	110.2	107.9	118.8	112.6	115.6
1990	81.8	82.7	114.5	116.2	122.6	91.4	121.0	111.3	110.0	116.5	115.1	119.1
1991	78.4	77.9	115.9	116.5	124.8	83.1	124.4	113.7	112.3	113.1	116.6	121.6
1992	76.9	76.5	117.4	116.9	127.0	80.3	125.8	114.2	112.8	111.7	117.2	122.9
1993	76.4	76.2	119.1	118.7	129.0	77.6	127.2	115.4	115.4	111.4	118.2	125.4
1994	73.3	71.1	120.7	120.1	130.6	74.8	130.0	117.1	119.6	117.0	120.3	129.7
1995	71.0	66.6	124.2	121.7	134.1	77.2	143.4	123.3	124.3	128.2	124.8	133.3
1996	84.4	84.8	127.1	127.1	134.7	87.4	145.8	123.1	125.8	123.7	126.2	136.2
1997	86.1	87.5	127.5	127.9	137.1	85.6	147.1	122.8	127.4	124.7	127.6	138.2
1998	70.8	68.3	126.2	126.3	137.1	66.3	148.7	122.1	129.3	120.9	128.7	139.7
1999	78.0	78.5	128.3	126.3	136.5	76.8	149.7	122.2	132.6	115.8	129.1	141.3
2000	113.5	126.8	133.5	128.5	137.9	112.8	156.7	124.6	134.7	119.8	130.3	143.3
2001	114.3	127.5	134.6	132.8	141.3	105.3	158.4	125.9	136.0	116.1	131.0	145.1
2002	96.6	107.0	133.7	132.0	141.1	98.8	157.3	125.5	137.1	116.2	131.7	146.3
2003	131.3	160.1	137.1	137.4	142.8	122.0	164.6	128.4	138.0	118.4	132.9	147.4
2003												
January	126.0	152.5	135.7	133.9	142.4	116.5	160.9	126.3	137.6	117.9	132.4	147.0
February	137.4	170.2	137.6	134.5	142.4	138.0	162.3	127.2	137.8	118.0	132.5	147.1
March	169.1	220.0	138.7	134.8	142.4	145.9	165.2	128.1	137.7	118.0	132.7	147.2
April	124.5	150.2	136.3	135.1	142.7	118.7	166.7	129.1	138.1	117.8	132.7	147.3
May	126.3	152.7	135.8	135.7	142.2	111.0	165.8	129.2	138.0	117.8	132.7	147.4
June	137.1	169.3	136.3	137.1	142.7	116.0	165.0	128.8	137.7	117.8	132.7	147.5
July	131.6	160.7	136.4	137.0	142.9	118.3	164.5	128.6	137.8	117.7	132.9	147.6
August	125.5	151.1	137.0	137.8	142.8	124.0	164.2	128.7	138.0	117.8	132.9	147.5
September	124.7	149.4	137.1	139.0	143.2	122.1	164.8	128.6	138.2	118.1	133.1	147.2
October	122.7	146.1	138.2	141.8	143.2	120.9	165.2	128.6	138.2	119.0	133.1	147.6
November	121.5	143.7	137.7	141.5	143.4	115.5	165.0	128.5	138.7	120.0	133.3	147.5
December	129.0	155.1	137.7	141.1	143.4	117.5	165.3	128.8	138.6	121.4	133.7	147.6

Year and month	Transportation and warehousing					Health care and social assistance			Other services industries (Dec. 1996 = 100)			
	Air transportation (Dec. 1992 = 100)	Rail transportation (Dec. 1996 = 100)	Pipeline transportation (June 1986 = 100)		Postal service (June 1989 = 100)	Offices of physicians (Dec. 1996 = 100)	Home health care (Dec. 1996 = 100)	Hospitals (Dec. 1992 = 100)	Legal services	Architectural, engineering, and related services	Employment services	Accommodation
			Crude oil	Refined petroleum products								
1985	...	...	...	...	85.3	...	...	...	...	...	...	...
1986	...	...	...	...	86.5	...	...	...	...	...	...	...
1987	...	...	96.9	101.0	86.5	...	...	...	...	...	...	...
1988	...	...	92.7	100.9	96.6	...	...	...	...	...	...	...
1989	...	...	92.3	100.5	100.0	...	...	...	...	...	...	...
1990	...	...	94.2	100.8	100.0	...	...	...	...	...	...	...
1991	...	...	94.4	101.1	117.9	...	...	...	...	...	...	...
1992	...	...	94.8	101.2	119.8	...	...	...	...	...	...	...
1993	105.6	...	95.0	101.3	119.8	...	...	102.5	...	...	...	...
1994	108.5	...	102.5	103.4	119.8	...	...	106.2	...	...	...	...
1995	113.7	...	113.4	104.6	132.2	...	...	110.0	...	...	...	...
1996	121.1	...	104.7	104.3	132.3	...	...	112.6	...	...	...	...
1997	125.3	100.5	96.0	105.3	132.3	101.0	103.3	113.6	102.5	102.2	101.0	104.2
1998	124.5	101.7	96.8	104.8	132.3	103.2	106.2	114.6	106.1	105.1	103.2	108.1
1999	130.8	101.3	95.5	104.9	135.3	105.5	107.1	116.4	108.7	108.5	105.2	112.7
2000	147.7	102.6	101.0	105.3	135.2	107.3	111.1	119.4	112.5	111.8	107.3	116.2
2001	157.2	104.5	111.1	108.5	143.4	110.4	114.0	123.0	117.9	115.9	108.2	121.3
2002	157.8	106.6	112.3	111.0	150.2	110.3	116.6	127.5	121.7	121.1	108.9	121.3
2003	162.1	108.8	111.1	112.7	155.0	112.1	117.0	134.9	125.6	124.3	111.4	122.0
2003												
January	161.4	107.3	110.4	110.9	155.0	110.5	116.4	132.4	125.0	124.6	110.6	121.6
February	160.2	107.5	110.4	110.9	155.0	110.4	117.0	132.8	125.1	123.7	111.1	122.2
March	161.8	108.3	111.0	110.9	155.0	111.4	117.0	132.9	125.1	123.7	111.0	122.6
April	162.2	109.1	111.4	112.0	155.0	111.8	116.4	133.4	125.2	123.9	111.3	122.2
May	162.0	108.7	111.4	112.4	155.0	112.2	116.1	134.4	125.2	123.9	111.1	122.3
June	162.3	109.2	111.4	112.9	155.0	112.2	116.2	134.4	125.3	124.1	111.2	122.5
July	162.6	109.2	111.5	112.8	155.0	112.5	116.1	135.3	125.4	124.2	111.3	123.3
August	163.1	109.1	111.5	112.9	155.0	112.7	116.2	135.4	125.4	124.2	111.7	122.7
September	162.0	109.3	111.3	114.1	155.0	112.7	116.5	135.3	126.0	124.7	111.9	120.4
October	162.2	109.4	110.9	114.2	155.0	112.7	118.5	137.5	126.3	124.7	112.1	122.6
November	162.3	109.4	110.9	114.4	155.0	112.9	119.0	137.6	126.4	124.8	111.8	121.2
December	162.7	109.6	110.9	114.4	155.0	112.8	119.0	137.6	126.5	125.3	112.1	120.5

... = Not available.

Table 8-5. Prices Received and Paid by Farmers

(1990–1992 = 100, not seasonally adjusted.)

Year and month	Prices received by farmers															Prices paid by farmers [1]		Ratio of prices received to prices paid
	All farm products	Crops									Livestock and products				Food commodities	All items	Production items	
		Total	Food grains	Feed grains and hay	Cotton	Tobacco	Oil-bearing crops	Fruit and nuts	Commercial vegetables	Potatoes and dry beans	Total	Meat animals	Dairy products	Poultry and eggs				
1975	73	88	128	112	68	56	93	46	66	78	62	56	67	83	69	47	55	158
1976	75	87	105	105	99	63	97	45	67	75	64	57	74	83	71	50	59	150
1977	73	83	83	87	100	66	119	54	70	71	64	56	74	81	71	53	61	138
1978	83	89	102	88	91	72	110	72	74	73	78	75	81	87	83	58	67	144
1979	94	98	121	100	96	75	121	77	79	65	90	90	92	90	95	66	76	144
1980	98	107	136	115	114	80	118	73	80	93	89	84	100	91	96	75	85	131
1981	100	111	138	122	111	94	122	76	99	126	89	82	105	94	97	82	92	121
1982	94	98	119	103	92	99	103	78	92	88	90	86	104	89	93	86	94	109
1983	98	108	120	125	104	96	118	71	96	89	88	81	104	95	95	86	92	113
1984	101	111	117	127	108	98	125	85	97	111	91	83	103	109	98	89	94	114
1985	91	98	108	105	93	92	96	84	95	87	86	78	97	97	89	86	91	106
1986	87	87	89	84	91	82	89	83	92	81	88	80	96	105	87	85	86	103
1987	89	86	83	72	98	83	90	93	105	89	91	90	96	87	91	87	87	102
1988	99	104	113	102	95	86	126	96	104	88	93	91	93	98	99	91	90	108
1989	104	109	127	109	98	96	118	99	103	131	100	94	104	111	104	96	95	108
1990	104	103	100	105	107	97	105	97	102	133	105	105	105	105	104	99	99	105
1991	100	101	94	101	108	102	99	112	100	99	99	101	94	99	99	100	100	99
1992	98	101	113	98	88	101	100	99	111	88	97	96	100	97	99	101	101	97
1993	101	102	105	99	89	101	108	93	117	107	100	100	98	105	102	104	104	97
1994	100	105	119	106	109	102	110	90	109	110	95	90	99	106	98	106	106	94
1995	102	112	134	112	127	103	104	97	121	107	92	85	98	107	99	109	108	93
1996	112	127	157	146	122	105	128	118	111	114	99	87	114	120	108	115	115	98
1997	107	115	128	117	112	104	131	110	118	90	98	92	102	113	105	118	119	90
1998	102	107	103	100	107	104	107	112	123	99	97	79	119	117	101	115	113	89
1999	96	97	91	86	85	102	83	115	110	100	95	83	110	110	96	115	111	83
2000	96	96	85	86	82	107	85	98	121	93	97	94	94	106	97	120	116	80
2001	102	99	91	91	64	107	80	109	133	98	106	97	115	115	105	123	120	83
2002	98	105	104	99	56	108	88	105	137	129	90	87	93	94	97	124	119	79
2003	107	111	108	104	85	107	107	106	138	103	103	103	96	110	107	128	124	83
2001																		
January	97	94	93	89	86	115	84	86	121	81	100	97	100	105	97	124	121	78
February	100	98	91	91	80	116	80	84	147	89	102	98	100	111	101	124	121	81
March	103	99	92	91	68	99	78	97	138	86	107	103	106	116	105	124	120	83
April	106	103	92	90	70	82	75	105	137	92	109	103	112	116	108	124	121	85
May	108	105	95	90	67	...	77	96	144	90	110	103	119	115	110	124	120	87
June	107	102	91	91	65	...	80	122	121	96	113	104	124	117	110	124	120	86
July	108	104	88	95	64	107	86	127	125	105	112	102	124	119	110	123	120	88
August	110	109	90	96	62	104	86	129	145	125	111	100	126	120	113	123	120	89
September	106	102	92	93	60	108	81	128	134	102	111	96	131	121	109	123	120	86
October	94	88	90	86	51	109	74	126	103	91	104	91	119	120	96	123	119	76
November	94	90	89	86	46	114	77	114	110	106	99	86	110	117	97	122	118	77
December	95	97	91	92	51	113	78	96	171	114	93	85	103	99	98	122	117	78
2002																		
January	95	94	89	90	45	116	76	84	158	123	96	90	104	101	96	122	117	78
February	98	102	85	91	46	113	77	83	191	127	96	93	100	96	100	122	117	80
March	105	118	85	91	47	98	79	96	270	141	94	92	96	96	108	123	118	85
April	94	100	84	92	45	...	80	91	121	138	89	87	96	87	93	123	118	76
May	96	104	86	94	44	...	83	105	115	148	89	85	93	92	94	123	118	78
June	97	104	95	97	56	...	88	114	110	159	90	85	88	100	95	123	118	79
July	99	109	105	102	58	106	96	119	116	175	88	87	85	94	97	123	119	80
August	100	113	115	110	57	103	98	122	121	129	87	84	87	93	97	124	120	81
September	98	109	129	111	59	104	88	124	119	103	85	81	89	92	95	124	121	79
October	95	101	129	105	65	106	90	123	106	92	87	84	93	86	93	125	121	76
November	97	103	124	104	71	115	97	110	110	104	89	86	91	96	96	125	120	78
December	98	103	125	106	73	115	98	93	104	108	91	88	91	96	95	125	121	78
2003																		
January	99	103	117	105	75	120	99	80	113	105	96	93	90	108	97	127	122	78
February	99	103	106	106	77	119	100	82	114	107	95	95	87	104	96	128	123	77
March	99	106	102	106	80	104	101	87	123	113	93	93	84	103	97	128	124	77
April	101	110	99	107	75	70	104	96	132	116	93	96	84	99	99	128	124	79
May	105	116	102	110	76	...	109	107	140	117	96	100	84	103	104	127	123	83
June	107	118	102	109	75	...	109	116	157	111	99	101	84	109	107	127	123	84
July	105	109	98	102	76	103	104	121	121	105	101	101	93	109	105	127	123	83
August	109	113	109	102	76	104	101	124	140	98	105	104	102	112	110	127	123	86
September	111	111	110	101	92	108	97	124	146	92	110	108	111	115	113	128	125	87
October	113	111	111	96	112	109	111	123	144	86	116	115	115	118	116	129	126	88
November	116	115	116	99	105	114	122	116	159	95	117	116	110	124	120	129	126	90
December	114	116	121	104	106	115	126	92	170	96	112	110	106	121	116	129	126	88

[1] Includes commodities, services, interest, taxes, and wage rates.
... = Not available.

NOTES AND DEFINITIONS

TABLES 8-1 AND 20-2
CONSUMER PRICE INDEXES

SOURCE: U.S. DEPARTMENT OF LABOR, BUREAU OF LABOR STATISTICS (BLS)

The Consumer Price Index (CPI) is a statistical measure of the average change in the cost to consumers of a market basket of goods and services purchased by urban consumers. The reference base for the total index and most of its components currently is 1982–1984 = 100; however, new products that have been introduced into the index since January 1982 are necessarily shown on later reference bases.

Except as noted, all of the consumer price indexes in this volume are components of the *CPI-U*, the index using the average market basket for all urban consumers, who comprised about 87 percent of the noninstitutional population in 1993–1995. Beginning with January 2002, the market basket represents expenditures in 1999–2000. Between January 1998 and December 2001, weights from 1993 to 1995 were used. Beginning with January 2004, the expenditure weights will represent expenditures in 2001–2002. From now forward, the weights will be updated at 2-year intervals. Previously, new weights were introduced only at the time of a major revision, translating into a lag of a decade or more.

A slightly different index that is widely used for adjusting wages and government benefits is the *CPI-W*, which represents the buying habits only of urban wage earners and clerical workers—about 32 percent of the noninstitutional population in 1993–1995. The total CPI-W is displayed in the last column of the last page of Table 8-1.

The CPI was overhauled and updated in the latest major revision effective January 1998. In addition, new products and improved methods are regularly introduced into the index, usually in January.

The latest change in methods was the introduction of a geometric mean formula for calculating many of the basic components of the index. Beginning with the index for January 1999, this formula is used for categories comprising approximately 61 percent of total consumer spending. The new formula allows for the possibility that some consumers may react to changing relative prices within a category by substituting items whose relative prices have declined for products whose relative prices have risen, while maintaining their overall level of satisfaction. The geometric mean formula is not being used for categories where demand elasticities are low and possibilities for substitution are limited, such as housing, utilities, and many health care services. The list of categories where the geometric mean is used is re-evaluated from time to time, and the geometric mean formula was introduced for two more categories in January 2004—cable and satellite television and radio services, and eyeglasses and eye care.

The CPI-U was introduced in 1978. Before that time, only CPI-W data were available. The movements of the CPI-U before 1978 are based on the changes in the CPI-W. The index levels are different, however, because the two indexes differed in the 1982–1984 base period.

There are several important differences between the CPI and measures of consumption spending and prices such as those in the National Income and Product Accounts. One of these has to do with the possibility of revision. Because the official CPI-U and CPI-W are so widely used in "escalation," that is, the calculation of cost-of-living adjustments for wages and for government payments and tax variables, these indexes are not retrospectively revised to incorporate new information and methods. (An exception is occasionally made for outright error, as happened in September 2000 with respect to the data for January through August of that year.) Instead, the new information and methods of calculation are introduced in the current index and affect future index changes only. See *Supplemental Indexes*, below, for information on certain special CPI indexes, published in this volume, that can be used to provide more consistent historical information.

Notes on the data

The CPI is based on prices of food, clothing, shelter, fuel, utilities, transportation, medical care, and other goods and services that people buy for day-to-day living. The quantity and quality of these items are kept essentially constant between revisions so that only price changes will be measured. All taxes directly associated with the purchase and use of items, such as sales and property taxes, are included in the index; the effects of income and payroll tax changes are not.

As of 2003, data collected from about 23,000 retail establishments and about 37,000 housing units in 87 urban areas across the country are used to develop the U.S. city average.

Periodic major revisions of the indexes, in addition to updating the content and weights of the market basket of goods and services, update the statistical sample of urban areas, outlets, and unique items used in calculating the CPI and improve the statistical methods used. In addition, retail outlets and items are resampled on a rotating 5-year basis; adjustments for changing quality are made at times of major product changes, such as the annual auto model changeover; and other methodological changes are introduced from time to time.

CPI weights for 1964–1977 were derived from reported expenditures of a sample of wage-earner and clerical-worker families and individuals in 1960–1961 and adjusted for price changes between the survey dates and 1963. Weights for 1978–1986 were derived from a consumer expenditure survey (CES) undertaken over the 1972–1974 period and adjusted for price change between the survey dates and December 1977. For 1987 to 1997, the spending patterns reflected in the CPI were derived from a CES undertaken over the 1982–1984 period, and the reported expenditures were adjusted for price change between the survey dates and December 1986.

The CES is composed of two separate surveys: an interview survey and a diary survey, both conducted by the Bureau of the Census for BLS. Each expenditure reported in the two surveys is coded to detailed categories, which are then combined in expenditure classes and ultimately into major expenditure groups. Data as of 1998 are grouped into eight such groups: (1) food and beverages, (2) housing, (3) apparel, (4) transportation, (5) medical care, (6) recreation, (7) education and communication, and (8) other goods and services. Education and communication and recreation are new groups, and several subcategories have been rearranged as well.

The expenditure base of the CPI that is established by the CES encompasses only out-of-pocket consumer spending. Consumers also benefit from goods and services that are financed by government and private insurance, particularly in the medical care area. In the NIPAs, personal consumption expenditures (PCE) includes all spending whether purchased out of pocket or financed by government or employer-financed insurance, whereas the CES includes only out-of-pocket spending and payment of insurance premiums by individuals. For this reason, there is a large difference between the relatively small weight of medical care spending in the CPI and the markedly greater percentage of PCE accounted for by total medical care spending.

Seasonally adjusted national CPI indexes are published for selected series for which there is a significant seasonal pattern of price change. The factors currently in use were derived by the X-12-ARIMA seasonal adjustment method. Some series with extreme or sharp movements are seasonally adjusted using X-12-ARIMA Intervention Analysis Seasonal Adjustment. Seasonally adjusted indexes and seasonal factors for the preceding 5 years are updated annually based on data through the previous December. Because of these revisions, BLS advises against use of seasonally adjusted data for escalation. Detailed descriptions of BLS seasonal adjustment procedures are available upon request from the Bureau of Labor Statistics.

Definitions

Definitions of the major CPI groupings were modified beginning with the data for January 1998 and carried back to 1993. The definitions below are these current definitions.

The *food and beverage index* includes both food at home and food away from home (restaurant meals and other food bought and eaten away from home).

The *housing index* measures changes in rental costs and in expenses connected with the acquisition and operation of a home. The CPI-U, beginning with data for January 1983, and the CPI-W, beginning with data for January 1985, reflect a change in the methodology used to compute the homeownership component. A rental equivalence measure replaced an asset-price approach. The central purpose of the change was to separate shelter costs from the investment component of homeownership so that the index would reflect only the cost of shelter services provided by owner-occupied homes. In addition to these measures of the cost of shelter, the housing category includes insurance, fuel, utilities, and household furnishings and operations.

The *apparel index* includes the purchase of apparel and footwear.

The *private transportation index* includes prices paid by urban consumers on such items as new and used automobiles and other vehicles, gasoline, motor oil, tires, repairs and maintenance, insurance, registration fees, driver's licenses, parking fees, etc. Auto finance charges, like mortgage interest payments, are considered to be a cost of asset acquisition, not of current consumption, and therefore are no longer included in the CPI. City bus, streetcar, subway, taxicab, intercity bus, airplane, and railroad coach fares are some of the components of the *public transportation index*.

The *medical care index* includes prices for professional medical services; hospital and related services; prescription and nonprescription drugs; and other medical care commodities. The portion of health insurance premiums used to cover the costs of these medical goods and services is distributed among the items; the portion of health insurance costs attributable to administrative expenses and profits of insurance providers constitutes a separate health insurance item. Effective with the January 1997 data, the method of calculating the hospital cost component was changed from the pricing of individual commodities and services to a more comprehensive cost-of-treatment approach.

Recreation includes components formerly in housing, apparel, entertainment, and "other."

Education and communication is a new group including components formerly in housing and "other," such as telephone services and computers.

Other goods and services now includes tobacco, personal care, and miscellaneous.

Supplemental indexes

The *CPI-U-X1* is a special version of the CPI that has been used by many researchers to provide a more historically consistent series. As explained above, the official CPI-U treated homeownership on an asset price basis until January 1983 and then changed to a rental equivalence method. The CPI-U-X1 incorporates a rental equivalence approach to homeowners' costs for the years 1967–1982 as well. It is rebased to the December 1982 value of the CPI-U (1982–1984 = 100); thus it is identical to the CPI-U in December 1982 and all subsequent periods, and for this reason is not updated or published in the CPI news release.

The *CPI-U-RS* is a "research series" CPI that retroactively incorporates estimates of the effects of most of the methodological changes that have been implemented since 1978, including the rental equivalence method, new or improved quality adjustments, and improvement of formulas to eliminate bias and allow for some consumer substitution within categories. This index is calculated from 1977 forward. Unlike the other CPI measures, its reference base is December 1977 = 100. Thus, although it generally shows less increase than the official index, its current *levels* are considerably higher. Unlike the official CPIs and the CPI-U-X1, its historical values will be revised each time that a significant change is made in the calculation of the current index. This index is not seasonally adjusted, and not included in the CPI news release; it is available on the BLS Internet site.

The *C-CPI-U* (Chained Consumer Price Index for All Urban Consumers) is a new, supplemental index that is published in the monthly CPI news release beginning in August 2002. It is available only from December 1999 to date and is calculated with the base December 1999 = 100; it is not seasonally adjusted. It is designed to be a closer approximation to a true cost-of-living index than the CPI-U and the CPI-W, which are based on a fixed market basket rather than the economic concept of a fixed basket of "consumer satisfaction."

The C-CPI-U is a "superlative" index, using a method known as the "Tornqvist" formula to incorporate the composition of consumer spending in the current period as well as in the earlier base period. Because it requires consumer expenditure data for the current as well as the earlier period, its final version can only be calculated after the expenditure data became available—about 2 years before the current period—and is approximated in more recent periods, making more extensive use of the "geometric mean" formula (see above). Of the data shown in this volume, the values for 2002 and earlier are "final" and the values for 2003 are "interim." At this writing, values announced each month for 2004 are "initial."

Data availability

The indexes are initially issued in a press release about 2 weeks following the month to which the data pertain. The *CPI Detailed Report* is issued about a month after the press release. Seasonally adjusted values for the preceding 5 years are revised with each year's release of the January index.

Selected CPI data are published monthly in the *Monthly Labor Review*, which also contains periodic articles analyzing price developments. Complete historical data are available on the BLS Internet site at <http://www.bls.gov>.

References

Two special issues of the *Monthly Labor Review* cover the CPI in detail. The December 1996 issue describes the subsequently implemented 1997 and 1998 revisions in a series of articles, and the December 1993 issue on "The Anatomy of Price Change" includes: "The Consumer Price Index: Underlying Concepts and Caveats"; "Basic Components of the CPI: Estimation of Price Changes"; "The Commodity Substitution Effect in CPI Data, 1982–1991"; and "Quality Adjustment of Price Indexes." The new formula for calculating basic components is described in "Incorporating a geometric mean formula into the CPI," *Monthly Labor Review*, October 1998. The CPI-U-RS is described in "Consumer Price Index research series using current methods, 1978–1998," *Monthly Labor Review*, June 1999. The C-CPI-U is discussed in the news release on the July 2002 CPI, available on the BLS Internet site.

For a detailed discussion of the treatment of homeownership, see "Changing the Homeownership Component of the Consumer Price Index to Rental Equivalence," *CPI Detailed Report* (January 1983).

BLS Handbook of Methods Bulletin 2490 (April 1997), Chapter 17, "Consumer Price Indexes," described the methodology used in computing the CPI.

For a comprehensive, up-to-date professional review of CPI concepts and methodology, see Charles Schultze and Christopher Mackie, ed., *At What Price? Conceptualizing and Measuring Cost-of-Living and Price Indexes*, Washington, DC: National Academy Press, 2001. Earlier discussions include: "Using Survey Data to Assess Bias in the Consumer Price Index," *Monthly Labor Review* (April 1998); Joel Popkin, "Improving the CPI: The Record and Suggested Next Steps," *Business Economics*, Vol. XXXII, No. 3 (July 1997), pages 42–47; *Measurement Issues in the Consumer Price Index*, Bureau of Labor Statistics, U.S. Department of Labor, June 1997; *Toward a More Accurate Measure of the Cost of Living*, Final Report to the Senate Finance Committee from the Advisory Commission to Study the Consumer Price

Index, December 4, 1996 (the "Boskin Commission" report); and *Government Price Statistics*, U.S. Congress Joint Economic Committee, 87th Congress, 1st Session, January 24, 1961 (the "Stigler Committee" report).

TABLES 8-2 THROUGH 8-4 AND 20-2
PRODUCER PRICE INDEXES

SOURCE: U.S. DEPARTMENT OF LABOR, BUREAU OF LABOR STATISTICS

Producer Price Indexes (PPI) measure average changes in prices received by domestic producers. They are organized in three systems: by stage of processing, by commodity group, and by industry. Most of the indexes currently are published on a base of 1982 = 100, but there are a number of exceptions for products introduced since 1982, identified in this book in the column headings for the individual series.

Table 8-2 presents price indexes for commodities by stage of processing. Table 8-3 presents data by major commodity groups; this is the grouping that has the longest continuous history. In recent years, the major commodity groups—particularly the totals for all commodities and industrial commodities—have been de-emphasized because they aggregate successive stages of processing and thus often exaggerate price trends. This effect was particularly acute in the energy price crisis of the early 1970s. To avoid this problem, the stage-of-processing groups were introduced in 1978. However, the individual commodity groups (for example, textile products and apparel) provide a much longer perspective on individual industrial sectors than is available in industry groupings, and are presented here for that reason.

Table 8-4—new to this edition of *Business Statistics*—presents PPIs for the net output of selected industry groups. As the coverage of the PPI is expanded, indexes for additional industries are frequently introduced, but new industries may only go back to the most recent December. This volume includes only those industry groupings with at least 7 years of historical data.

Definitions

The *stage-of-processing* PPI indexes organize commodities by class of buyer and degree of fabrication. These have been the featured measures since 1978. The three major indexes are (1) *finished goods*, commodities that will not undergo further processing and are ready for sale to the ultimate user (such as automobiles, meats, apparel, and machine tools); (2) *intermediate materials, supplies, and components*, commodities that have been processed but require further processing before they become finished goods (such as steel mill products, cotton yarns, lumber, and flour), as well as physically complete goods that are purchased by business firms as inputs for their operations (such as diesel fuel and paper boxes); and (3) *crude materials* for further processing, products entering the market for the first time which have not been manufactured or fabricated but which will be processed before becoming finished goods (such as ores, scrap metals, crude petroleum, raw cotton, and livestock).

PPIs for the *net output* of industries and their products are grouped according to the North American Industry Classification System (NAICS). For each industry they include not only measures of price change for the products "primary" to that industry (products made primarily but not necessarily exclusively by that industry) but also measures of changes in prices received by establishments classified in the industry for products or services chiefly made in some other industry. Thus, they are designed to be compatible with other economic time series organized by industry, such as data on shipments, employment, wages, and productivity.

Notes on the data

The probability sample used for calculating the PPI provides more than 100,000 price quotations per month, selected to represent the movement of prices of all commodities produced in the manufacturing; agriculture, forestry, and fishing; mining; and gas and electricity and public utility sectors. In addition, new PPIs are gradually being introduced for the products of industries in the transportation, trade, finance, and services sectors.

To the extent possible, prices used in calculating the PPI represent prices received by domestic producers in the first important commercial transaction for each commodity. These indexes attempt to measure only price changes; that is, changes in receipts per unit of measurement not influenced by changes in quality, quantity sold, terms of sale, or level of distribution. Most quotations are the selling prices of selected manufacturers or other producers, although a few prices are those quoted on organized exchanges or markets. Transaction prices are sought instead of list or book prices.

Price data are generally collected monthly, primarily by mail questionnaire. Most prices are obtained directly from producing companies on a voluntary and confidential basis. Prices generally are reported for the Tuesday of the week containing the 13th day of the month.

The name "Producer Price Index" became effective with the release of March 1978 data, replacing the term "Wholesale Price Index." The change was made to reflect the coverage of the data more accurately. At the same time, there was a shift in analytical emphasis from the All Commodities Index and other traditional commodity grouping indexes to the Finished Goods Index and other stage-of-processing indexes.

The BLS revises the Producer Price Index weighting structure periodically when data from economic censuses become available. Beginning with data for January 2002, the weights used to construct the PPI reflect 1997 shipments values as measured by the 1997 Economic Censuses and other sources. Data for 1996 through 2001 reflect 1992 shipments values; 1992 through 1995 reflect 1987 shipment values; 1987 through 1991 reflect 1982 values; 1976 through 1986 reflect 1972 values; and 1967 through 1975 reflect 1963 values.

BLS has been working for a number of years on a comprehensive overhaul of the theory, methods, and procedures used to construct the PPI. One aspect of this overhaul was the already mentioned shift in emphasis beginning in 1978 to the stage-of-processing measures. Other changes that have been phased in since 1978 include the replacement of judgment sampling with probability sampling techniques; expansion to systematic coverage of the net output of virtually all industries in the mining and manufacturing sectors; introduction of measures for selected services industries, including retail trade; a shift from a commodity to an industry orientation; the exclusion of imports from, and the inclusion of exports in, the survey universe.

Seasonal factors for the PPI are revised annually to take into account the most recent 12 months of data. Seasonally adjusted data for the previous 5 years are subject to these annual revisions.

Data availability

The indexes are initially issued in a press release about 2 weeks following the end of the month to which the data pertain and subsequently are published in greater detail in the monthly BLS publication, *PPI Detailed Report.* Each month, data for the fourth previous month are revised to reflect late reports and corrections.

Selected PPI data also are published monthly in the *Monthly Labor Review*, which also contains periodic articles analyzing price developments. Historical data tables providing annual and monthly data for all available periods for all published series are available on request from BLS. Complete historical data are available on the BLS Internet site at <http://www.bls.gov>.

References

The following *Monthly Labor Review* articles and technical notes contain background information: "Comparing PPI Energy Indexes to Alternative Data Sources" (December 1998); "Are Producer Prices Good Proxies for Export Prices?" (October 1997); "Effect of 1992 Weights on Producer Price Indexes" (July 1996); "Hospital Price Inflation: What Does the PPI Tell Us?" (July 1996); "Seasonal Adjustment of Producer Price Index for Passenger Cars" (June 1996); "Effect of Updated Weights on Producer Price Indexes" (March 1993); "Milestones in the Producer Price Index Methodology and Presentation" (August 1989); "New Stage of Process Price System Developed for the Producer Price Index" (April 1988); "Improving the Measurement of Producer Price Changes" (April 1977).

BLS Handbook of Methods Bulletin 2490 (April 1997), Chapter 14, "Producer Prices," describes the methodology used in computing the PPI.

**TABLE 8-2
PURCHASING POWER OF THE DOLLAR**

SOURCE: U.S. DEPARTMENT OF LABOR, BUREAU OF LABOR STATISTICS; CALCULATIONS BY EDITORS

The purchasing power of the dollar measures changes in the quantity of goods and services a dollar will buy at a particular date compared with a selected base date. It must be defined in terms of: (1) the specific commodities and services that are to be purchased with the dollar; (2) the market level (producer, retail, etc.) at which they are purchased; and (3) the dates for which the comparison is to be made. Thus, the purchasing power of the dollar for a selected period, compared with another period, may be measured in terms of a single commodity or a large group of commodities; for example, all goods and services purchased by consumers at retail, or all finished commodities sold in primary markets.

Broad prices indexes calculated by BLS that have been used to calculate the purchasing power of the dollar in the United States include: (1) the Producer Price Index (PPI) for Finished Goods, which relates to prices received by the producers of finished commodities at the primary market level, and (2) two versions of the Consumer Price Index, which measures average changes in retail prices of goods and services—the CPI-U and the CPI-W. These indexes are described above in the sections of the Notes and Definitions pertaining to the Producer Price Index and the Consumer Price Index, respectively.

The purchasing power of the dollar is computed by dividing the price index number for the base period by the price index number for the date to be compared, and expressing the result in dollars and cents. The base period is the period in which the price index equals 100, and the purchasing power is therefore $1.00. In this book, 1982 through 1984 is used as the base period for the two indexes shown so that they can be readily compared.

Purchasing power estimates in terms of both the CPI-U and the CPI-W are calculated by BLS and published in the CPI press release. The CPI-U version is used here. The comparable purchasing power in terms of the PPI is calculated by the editors of *Business Statistics*, after rebasing the index from its published 1982 base to 1982–1984 = 100. In all cases, the purchasing power measure is based on indexes not adjusted for seasonal variation.

TABLE 8-5
PRICES RECEIVED AND PAID BY FARMERS

SOURCE: U.S. DEPARTMENT OF AGRICULTURE, NATIONAL AGRICULTURAL STATISTICS SERVICE (NASS)

The data on prices received and paid by farmers represent prices farmers received for commodities sold and prices paid for production input goods and services. Prices are weighted and aggregated into price indexes. These indexes provide measures of relative price changes for agricultural outputs and inputs. These price measures are based on voluntary reports from agribusiness firms, merchants, dealers, and farmers. Data are collected at regular intervals using mailed inquiries, telephone, and personal enumeration. In January 1995, these data were converted to a reference base of 1990–1992 = 100. Prices-paid indexes were available only quarterly for several years but have been published monthly beginning with January 1996, with monthly indexes for 1995 constructed for historical comparison.

Definitions

Prices received by farmers represent sales from producers to first buyers. They include all grades and qualities. The average commodity price from the survey multiplied by the total quantity marketed theoretically should give the total cash receipts for the commodity.

Prices paid by farmers represent the average costs of inputs purchased by farmers and ranchers to produce agricultural commodities. Conceptually, the average price when multiplied by quantity purchased should equal total producer expenditures for the item.

Ratio of prices received to prices paid is the ratio of the index of prices received for all farm products to the index of prices paid for all commodities and services. (For some years, prices paid are available only for the first month of each quarter. Each month's ratio of prices received to prices paid is based on the latest data available.)

Notes on the data

In 1995, NASS reweighted and reconstructed the prices paid and received indexes. The indexes are now based on 5-year moving average weights compared with fixed weights previously. The changes in the construction of the indexes simplified updating component items and reference periods while maintaining appropriate weights. The overall changes to the weighting and construction of the indexes did not have a significant effect on the index levels and therefore had little effect on the level of parity prices. Indexes are now published on a 1990–1992 = 100 base. As required by law, the parity ratio (ratio of prices received to prices paid) also continues to be published on a base of 1910–1914 = 100.

Prices paid. Since 1995, the Prices Paid Survey of items purchased by farm establishments has been conducted annually in April. Surveys are conducted for feed, seed, fertilizer, agricultural chemicals, fuel, and farm machinery. About 135 selected items are priced to represent groups of similar items purchased which make up the major production expenditure categories. The number of input items consumed on farms is so extensive that it is not feasible to collect price data for all of the inputs. Items on the questionnaire are described in the simplest way consistent with definite identification. Firms are requested to report the prices for the most commonly sold item that meets the general specification on the questionnaire.

Reported data are summarized to regional estimates and then weighted to U.S. prices. Weights are based on available consumption or expenditure information. Average prices, including state and local taxes, are used in computing the indexes and are published in *Agricultural Prices* for the same month as the survey. Regional prices are published for feed, fuel, and fertilizer. U.S. prices are published for the remaining items surveyed.

Bureau of Labor Statistics (BLS) indexes are used to measure price change for the months when no survey data are collected. The BLS indexes measure price changes for farm supplies and repairs, autos and trucks, building materials, and marketing containers. Before 1995, quarterly prices-paid surveys were conducted by NASS. Quarterly feeder livestock surveys still are conducted.

Revisions: prices paid. Any revisions are published in the monthly and in annual issues of *Agricultural Prices*. The basis for revision must be supported by additional data that directly affect the level of the estimate. More revisions are likely in April when separate prices paid surveys are conducted.

Survey procedures: prices received. Primary sales data used to determine grain prices are obtained from probability samples of mills and elevators. These procedures ensure that virtually all grain moving into commercial channels has a chance of being included in the survey. Livestock prices are obtained from packers, stockyards, auctions, dealers, and market check data. Inter-farm sales of grain and livestock are not included since they represent very small percentages of total marketings. Grain marketed for seed is also excluded. Fruit and vegetable prices are obtained from sample surveys and market check data.

Summary and estimation procedures: prices received. Survey quantities sold are expanded by strata to state levels and used to weight average strata prices to a state average. State prices are then weighted to a U.S. price.

Revisions: prices received. For most items, the current month's price represents a 3–5 day period around the mid-month. Previous month's prices represent actual dollars received for quantities sold during the entire month. Revisions are published in monthly issues of *Agricultural Prices* and in the annual summary published in July. A schedule of monthly revisions is published in the December issue of *Agricultural Prices* and in the July annual summary.

Reliability: prices received. U.S. price estimates generally have a sampling error of less than one-half percent for the major commodities such as corn, wheat, soybeans, cotton, and rice.

Data availability

Prices paid and received by farmers are available each month in a press release issued around the end of the month. Data are subsequently published monthly in *Agricultural Prices*. Data also are available on the NASS Internet site at <http://www.usda.gov/nass/>.

Reference

"Revised Prices Received and Paid Indexes, United States, 1975–1993 for Base Periods 1910–1914 = 100 and 1990–1992 = 100," *Statistical Bulletin* number 917 (National Agricultural Statistics Service, February 1995).

CHAPTER 9: EMPLOYMENT COSTS, PRODUCTIVITY AND PROFITS

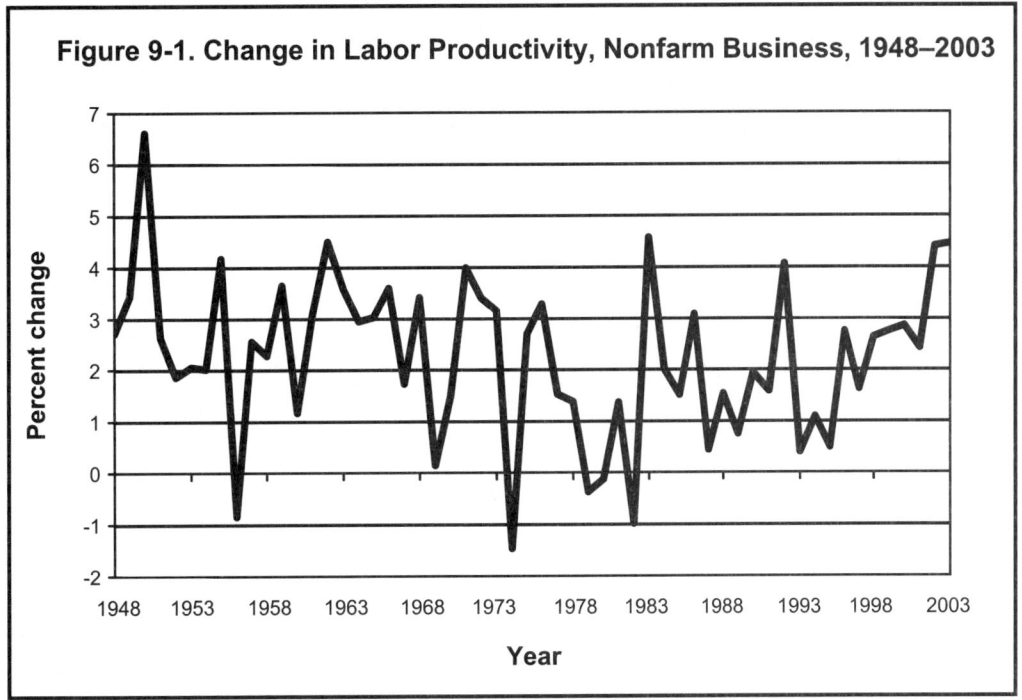

Figure 9-1. Change in Labor Productivity, Nonfarm Business, 1948–2003

- Typically, for most of the postwar period, output per hour in nonfarm business declined in recession years. In 2001, however, productivity growth barely slowed, and it rose to 4.4 percent in both 2002 and 2003—the best back-to-back years on record. (Table 9-3)
- Unit labor costs declined in 2002 and 2003, signaling an absence of any inflationary pressures on the cost front. Increases in compensation per hour averaging 3.7 percent were more than offset by the productivity increases. (Table 9-3)
- For nonfinancial businesses, unit profits and "unit nonlabor costs" (for example, depreciation and interest) can be calculated separately. Unit nonlabor costs rose rapidly in 2001—which is typical of recession, since such costs cannot be reduced as fast as output declines—but declined in 2002 and 2003. Unit profits, which had been declining since 1997, rose sharply in 2002 and 2003. (Table 9-3)
- Between 2000 and 2003, average hourly wages and salaries for all private industry workers as measured in the Employment Cost Index, measured in current dollars and holding constant the mix of industries and occupations, rose at a 3.2 percent annual rate. (Table 9-2) Total compensation per hour rose at a 3.8 percent rate, driven by rising costs of medical benefits. (Table 9-1) Both increases exceeded the 2.2 percent rate of CPI inflation (Table 8-1), implying increases in real wages and compensation. But the increase in real worker compensation fell short of the 3.8 percent rate of increase in worker productivity, even allowing for the difference between the productivity deflator and the CPI. (Table 9-3)
- Total corporate profits with IVA surged 14 percent in 2003 and surpassed the previous high reached in 1997. (Tables 9-4 and 9-5) Comparing 2003 with 1999—the highest pre-recession year for which data on the new NAICS classification are available—indicates that the increase over those four years was entirely accounted for by domestic financial industries and by the "rest of the world" (profits of U.S. corporations earned elsewhere). Of the domestic nonfinancial businesses, only the oil, retail trade, and "other nonfinancial" (mainly services) industries regained their pre-recession profits levels. (Table 9-5)

Table 9-1. Employment Cost Indexes—Total Compensation

(June 1989 [not seasonally adjusted] = 100; annual values are for December, not seasonally adjusted; quarterly values, seasonally adjusted, except as noted.)

Year and quarter	All civilian workers [1]	State and local government workers	Private industry workers													
			All private industry workers	Private industry workers excluding sales occupations [2]	By occupational group				By industry division							
									Goods-producing industries			Service-producing industries				
					Production and nonsupervisory occupations [2]	White-collar occupations	Blue-collar occupations	Service occupations	Total	Construction	Manufacturing	Total	Transportation and utilities	Wholesale trade	Retail trade	Finance, insurance, and real estate [2]	Services
1979	...	...	59.1	58.7	...	57.4	61.3	58.8	60.7	...	60.1	57.7	...	...	...	...	...
1980	...	...	64.8	64.8	...	62.9	67.5	64.4	66.7	...	66.0	63.3	...	...	...	...	...
1981	70.2	66.1	71.2	71.2	71.4	69.2	74.0	70.4	73.3	...	72.5	69.5	...	...	...	...	...
1982	74.8	70.8	75.8	75.9	76.1	73.7	78.4	76.3	77.8	...	76.9	74.1	...	...	...	...	...
1983	79.1	75.1	80.1	80.2	80.4	78.4	82.3	80.5	81.6	...	80.8	78.9	...	...	...	...	...
1984	83.2	80.1	84.0	84.3	84.2	82.4	85.8	85.8	85.4	...	85.0	82.9	...	...	...	...	...
1985	86.8	84.6	87.3	87.3	87.3	86.4	88.5	88.4	88.2	88.2	87.8	86.6	90.0	...	88.8	85.9	84.1
1986	89.9	89.0	90.1	90.2	89.8	89.4	90.9	91.1	91.0	90.7	90.7	89.3	92.0	88.7	90.8	88.6	87.7
1987	93.1	93.0	93.1	93.4	92.8	92.7	93.7	93.3	93.8	94.0	93.4	92.6	94.8	92.2	93.0	90.4	92.2
1988	97.7	98.2	97.6	97.7	97.5	97.3	97.9	98.2	97.9	98.0	97.6	97.3	97.5	96.1	98.4	96.2	97.5
1989	102.6	104.3	102.3	102.1	102.4	102.4	101.9	102.5	102.1	102.4	102.0	102.3	101.2	104.5	101.6	101.4	102.9
1990	107.6	110.4	107.0	107.1	106.9	107.4	106.4	107.3	107.0	105.6	107.2	107.0	105.1	106.5	106.0	105.5	109.3
1991	112.2	114.4	111.7	112.0	111.5	112.2	111.0	112.4	111.9	109.9	112.2	111.6	109.7	111.1	110.5	110.0	114.0
1992	116.1	118.6	115.6	115.9	115.5	115.9	115.0	115.9	116.1	113.8	116.5	115.2	113.5	114.4	113.4	111.3	118.9
1993	120.2	121.9	119.8	120.2	119.7	120.2	119.3	119.5	120.6	116.5	121.3	119.3	117.5	117.8	116.8	116.4	123.1
1994	123.8	125.6	123.5	123.9	123.1	124.1	122.6	122.9	124.3	120.8	125.1	122.8	122.1	121.5	120.1	118.9	126.6
1995	127.2	129.3	126.7	127.1	126.3	127.6	125.6	125.2	127.3	123.4	128.3	126.2	126.6	127.0	122.7	123.1	129.4
1996	130.9	132.7	130.6	130.8	130.0	131.7	129.0	128.9	130.9	126.4	132.1	130.2	130.4	130.9	127.4	126.0	133.4
1997	135.2	135.7	135.1	135.2	134.2	136.7	132.3	134.1	134.1	129.7	135.3	135.3	134.2	135.1	131.7	134.5	138.5
1998	139.8	139.8	139.8	139.4	139.0	142.0	135.9	138.0	137.8	134.3	138.9	140.5	139.3	142.8	135.6	142.5	142.7
1999	144.6	144.6	144.6	144.5	143.1	146.9	140.5	142.6	142.5	138.7	143.6	145.3	142.3	148.5	140.7	148.3	147.6
2000	150.6	148.9	150.9	150.9	149.5	153.6	146.4	148.1	148.8	146.7	149.3	151.7	148.3	154.4	146.6	155.7	154.1
2001	156.8	155.2	157.2	157.2	155.5	160.1	151.9	154.8	154.4	153.0	154.6	158.2	155.5	159.5	153.2	161.3	161.0
2002	162.2	161.5	162.3	162.4	160.5	165.2	157.3	159.8	160.1	157.9	160.5	163.1	161.7	166.7	155.8	168.5	165.4
2003	168.4	166.8	168.8	169.0	166.6	172.0	163.6	164.9	166.5	163.3	167.1	169.7	167.0	172.0	161.0	180.9	171.4
1995																	
1st quarter	124.9	126.4	124.5	125.0	124.1	125.2	123.5	123.3	125.5	121.3	126.0	124.0	123.8	123.3	121.0	120.2	127.4
2nd quarter	125.8	127.4	125.4	125.7	125.0	126.2	124.3	123.9	126.2	121.8	126.8	125.0	124.8	124.6	121.7	121.8	128.3
3rd quarter	126.5	128.3	126.2	126.5	125.8	126.9	125.0	124.5	126.9	122.8	127.3	125.8	125.9	126.1	122.3	122.7	128.8
4th quarter	127.3	129.1	126.9	127.1	126.3	127.8	125.8	125.0	127.8	123.7	128.4	126.5	126.8	127.2	123.0	123.1	129.5
1996																	
1st quarter	128.3	129.9	127.9	128.3	127.5	128.9	126.6	125.6	128.5	124.5	129.1	127.6	127.7	127.6	124.6	124.5	130.7
2nd quarter	129.2	130.8	128.9	129.2	128.6	129.9	127.5	126.3	129.6	125.1	130.3	128.6	128.5	129.1	124.7	126.3	131.8
3rd quarter	130.1	131.5	129.8	130.2	129.2	131.0	128.0	127.1	130.4	125.6	131.2	129.5	129.2	129.9	125.9	126.7	132.6
4th quarter	131.0	132.5	130.7	130.8	130.0	132.0	129.2	128.6	131.3	126.7	132.1	130.4	130.6	131.1	127.8	126.0	133.5
1997																	
1st quarter	131.9	133.2	131.6	131.9	131.1	133.0	129.7	129.5	131.6	127.4	132.5	131.5	131.1	133.0	128.6	128.6	134.6
2nd quarter	132.9	133.9	132.6	133.0	132.1	134.0	130.7	130.6	132.9	128.4	133.8	132.5	131.8	133.6	129.6	129.4	135.7
3rd quarter	133.9	134.6	133.7	134.1	133.2	135.1	131.6	132.7	133.8	129.4	134.5	133.6	132.8	134.6	130.8	130.5	136.9
4th quarter	135.2	135.4	135.2	135.2	134.2	137.0	132.5	133.8	134.4	130.0	135.4	135.6	134.3	135.2	132.1	134.5	138.6
1998																	
1st quarter	136.2	136.5	136.1	136.4	135.3	138.0	133.2	134.9	135.2	130.8	136.2	136.6	135.7	137.9	133.1	136.7	139.3
2nd quarter	137.3	137.5	137.3	137.5	136.6	139.3	134.1	135.7	136.3	132.4	137.0	137.7	137.1	138.3	134.3	138.4	140.3
3rd quarter	138.7	138.6	138.7	138.8	138.0	141.0	135.1	137.0	137.2	133.2	138.2	139.5	138.4	140.8	135.6	141.0	141.7
4th quarter	139.7	139.5	139.8	139.4	139.0	142.3	136.1	137.7	138.0	134.6	139.0	140.7	139.4	143.0	136.1	142.5	142.8
1999																	
1st quarter	140.2	140.4	140.2	140.5	139.3	142.3	137.0	139.1	138.9	135.8	139.7	140.8	139.7	142.9	136.7	141.5	143.5
2nd quarter	141.7	141.6	141.7	141.9	140.8	144.0	138.0	140.2	139.9	136.7	140.6	142.6	140.9	144.3	139.0	145.8	144.6
3rd quarter	143.0	142.6	143.1	143.2	141.9	145.5	139.3	140.6	141.1	137.7	142.0	144.0	141.7	146.3	139.7	147.6	145.9
4th quarter	144.6	144.2	144.7	144.5	143.1	147.2	140.7	142.2	142.7	138.9	143.8	145.6	142.5	148.7	141.2	148.3	147.7
2000																	
1st quarter	146.4	145.5	146.6	146.5	145.3	149.2	142.6	143.4	144.9	141.0	145.7	147.4	143.9	150.2	143.1	152.0	149.4
2nd quarter	147.9	146.6	148.2	148.2	146.9	150.9	143.9	145.0	146.7	143.0	147.3	149.0	145.6	151.3	144.6	153.1	151.2
3rd quarter	149.3	147.2	149.8	149.8	148.4	152.5	145.4	146.2	148.2	145.0	148.7	150.5	147.2	152.1	146.0	155.2	152.7
4th quarter	150.7	148.6	151.1	150.9	149.5	154.0	146.7	147.8	149.2	146.9	149.6	152.1	148.5	154.7	147.1	155.7	154.3
2001																	
1st quarter	152.3	150.2	152.7	153.0	151.4	155.6	148.2	149.6	150.7	148.4	151.1	153.7	150.6	155.3	148.6	157.9	156.5
2nd quarter	153.8	152.0	154.2	154.4	152.7	157.2	149.1	150.9	152.2	150.1	152.3	155.2	152.3	157.2	149.5	159.5	157.8
3rd quarter	155.3	153.7	155.7	156.0	154.3	158.6	150.9	152.3	153.4	151.6	153.3	156.9	153.3	158.6	150.7	160.9	159.8
4th quarter	156.9	154.8	157.4	157.2	155.5	160.5	152.3	154.5	154.9	153.1	155.0	158.6	155.8	160.0	153.6	161.3	161.2
2002																	
1st quarter	158.3	156.1	158.8	159.0	157.1	161.8	153.5	156.1	156.2	154.3	156.3	160.0	157.4	162.1	153.4	165.2	162.6
2nd quarter	159.9	157.6	160.5	160.5	158.7	163.6	154.9	157.2	157.7	155.0	157.7	161.8	158.7	165.6	155.5	167.3	163.7
3rd quarter	161.1	159.4	161.5	161.6	159.7	164.5	156.2	158.8	159.0	156.2	159.1	162.8	160.5	165.9	155.8	168.0	164.6
4th quarter	162.5	161.1	162.8	162.4	160.5	165.7	157.7	159.7	160.8	158.0	161.0	163.7	162.0	167.4	156.2	168.5	165.7
2003																	
1st quarter	164.5	162.7	165.0	165.1	162.6	168.0	159.6	161.5	163.3	159.3	163.6	165.8	163.3	169.6	156.5	176.7	167.1
2nd quarter	166.0	164.3	166.4	166.6	164.1	169.1	161.2	162.6	164.9	160.9	164.9	167.1	165.2	170.5	157.3	178.3	168.4
3rd quarter	167.6	165.2	168.2	168.1	165.7	171.1	162.7	163.9	166.5	162.2	166.5	169.0	166.2	172.0	159.7	180.2	170.1
4th quarter	168.9	166.5	169.5	169.0	166.6	172.5	164.1	165.0	167.6	163.4	167.6	170.4	167.4	172.8	161.3	180.9	171.7

[1] Includes private industry and state and local government workers. Federal government workers are not included.
[2] Not seasonally adjusted.
... = Not available.

Table 9-2. Employment Cost Indexes—Wages and Salaries

(June 1989 [not seasonally adjusted] = 100; annual values are for December, not seasonally adjusted; quarterly values, seasonally adjusted, except as noted.)

Year and quarter	All civilian workers [1]	State and local government workers	Private industry workers														
			All private industry workers	Private industry workers excluding sales occupations [2]	By occupational group				Goods-producing industries			Service-producing industries					
					Production and nonsupervisory occupations [2]	White-collar occupations	Blue-collar occupations	Service occupations	Total	Construction	Manufacturing	Total	Transportation and utilities	Wholesale trade	Retail trade	Finance, insurance, and real estate [2]	Services
1975	...	...	45.9	45.8	45.7	44.9	47.0	46.6	46.9	...	46.3	45.1	45.5	...	...	...	43.5
1976	...	...	49.2	49.0	49.1	47.9	50.8	50.2	50.4	54.4	49.7	48.2	49.4	...	52.5	...	45.8
1977	...	...	52.6	52.4	52.5	51.1	54.7	53.4	54.3	58.0	53.6	51.4	54.0	50.4	55.5	...	48.2
1978	...	...	56.6	56.4	56.6	54.7	59.2	58.1	58.8	62.5	58.1	55.1	58.1	54.2	60.3	52.8	51.5
1979	...	...	61.5	61.4	61.7	59.5	64.5	62.2	63.7	67.0	63.0	60.0	63.6	58.5	65.0	59.7	55.8
1980	...	...	67.1	67.0	67.5	64.6	70.7	67.3	69.7	72.9	68.9	65.3	70.7	64.4	69.6	64.1	60.6
1981	72.2	68.3	73.0	73.0	73.6	70.5	76.7	72.9	75.7	79.3	74.9	71.1	76.6	69.4	74.8	70.5	67.0
1982	76.7	72.8	77.6	77.7	78.2	75.1	81.0	79.1	80.0	83.4	79.1	75.9	82.1	73.7	77.8	75.1	72.4
1983	80.6	76.6	81.4	81.5	82.0	79.6	84.1	82.7	83.2	85.8	82.5	80.2	86.3	78.2	81.1	80.5	77.2
1984	84.2	81.2	84.8	85.3	85.2	83.0	87.1	87.8	86.4	86.9	86.1	83.7	89.2	82.5	85.3	79.8	82.1
1985	87.8	85.7	88.3	88.4	88.6	87.1	90.1	89.9	89.4	89.6	89.2	87.7	92.5	86.1	89.4	87.1	85.0
1986	90.9	90.3	91.1	91.2	91.0	90.1	92.4	92.3	92.3	91.8	92.1	90.3	94.2	89.3	91.3	89.5	88.4
1987	94.1	94.1	94.1	94.5	93.9	93.4	95.2	94.5	95.2	94.8	95.2	93.4	96.2	93.0	93.7	90.6	93.2
1988	98.1	98.7	98.0	98.0	97.9	97.8	98.2	98.7	98.2	98.3	98.1	97.8	98.6	96.4	98.5	96.3	97.8
1989	102.4	103.9	102.0	101.9	102.2	102.4	101.6	102.3	102.0	101.7	101.9	102.2	101.2	105.2	101.6	101.3	102.5
1990	106.8	109.4	106.1	106.2	105.9	106.6	105.2	106.4	105.8	103.7	106.2	106.3	104.6	106.2	105.3	104.8	108.3
1991	110.6	113.2	110.0	110.2	109.6	110.7	108.8	110.6	109.7	106.8	110.3	110.2	108.4	110.3	109.2	108.4	112.2
1992	113.6	116.6	112.9	113.2	112.6	113.7	111.6	112.9	112.8	108.9	113.7	113.0	111.8	113.5	111.8	108.3	116.1
1993	117.1	119.7	116.4	116.6	115.9	117.5	114.8	115.3	116.1	111.1	117.3	116.6	115.4	116.4	115.0	112.9	119.6
1994	120.4	123.4	119.7	120.0	119.1	120.8	118.0	118.8	119.6	114.7	120.8	119.7	119.6	119.9	117.8	114.2	123.0
1995	123.9	127.3	123.1	123.4	122.4	124.3	121.4	121.4	122.9	117.4	124.3	123.2	123.7	125.5	120.6	118.4	126.0
1996	128.0	130.9	127.3	127.5	126.5	128.7	125.1	125.7	126.8	120.8	128.4	127.5	127.0	129.6	125.8	122.2	130.5
1997	132.8	134.4	132.3	132.4	131.2	134.2	129.1	131.1	130.6	124.9	132.2	133.1	131.3	133.6	130.6	130.6	136.2
1998	137.7	138.5	137.4	136.9	136.4	139.9	133.2	135.3	135.2	129.3	136.8	138.4	135.1	141.3	134.8	139.8	140.8
1999	142.5	143.5	142.2	142.0	140.4	144.8	137.7	139.6	139.7	133.6	141.5	143.3	137.9	146.5	139.6	145.2	146.0
2000	147.9	148.3	147.7	147.6	146.0	150.6	142.8	144.9	145.2	140.7	146.5	148.9	142.3	151.6	145.2	151.7	151.8
2001	153.4	153.7	153.3	153.3	151.5	156.1	148.3	150.6	150.5	146.3	151.7	154.5	149.2	154.8	150.7	156.0	158.2
2002	157.8	158.6	157.5	157.5	155.2	160.4	152.4	154.5	155.0	150.2	156.5	158.6	154.1	161.0	152.7	162.6	161.7
2003	162.3	161.9	162.3	162.4	159.4	165.9	156.1	157.8	158.7	154.0	160.1	163.9	156.5	165.3	156.5	174.5	166.7
1995																	
1st quarter	121.3	124.3	120.6	121.0	119.9	121.7	119.0	119.4	120.4	115.0	121.9	120.7	121.1	121.1	118.9	115.0	123.8
2nd quarter	122.2	125.3	121.5	121.8	121.0	122.7	120.1	120.0	121.4	115.5	122.9	121.6	122.1	122.4	119.4	117.0	124.5
3rd quarter	123.1	126.1	122.4	122.6	121.8	123.5	120.8	120.8	122.1	116.5	123.5	122.5	122.9	124.0	120.2	118.0	125.3
4th quarter	123.9	127.0	123.2	123.4	122.4	124.4	121.4	121.4	122.9	117.6	124.3	123.3	123.7	125.5	120.9	118.4	126.0
1996																	
1st quarter	125.1	127.8	124.4	124.7	123.7	125.8	122.5	122.2	123.9	118.5	125.4	124.7	124.5	126.3	122.9	119.8	127.5
2nd quarter	126.2	128.8	125.6	125.7	124.9	126.9	123.7	123.0	125.1	119.4	126.5	125.8	125.1	127.8	123.0	121.9	128.8
3rd quarter	127.0	129.7	126.4	126.8	125.6	127.9	124.3	124.1	126.1	120.1	127.7	126.6	125.9	128.5	124.1	122.2	129.6
4th quarter	128.0	130.6	127.4	127.5	126.5	128.8	125.1	125.7	126.8	121.1	128.4	127.7	127.0	129.6	126.2	122.2	130.6
1997																	
1st quarter	129.1	131.4	128.5	128.6	127.7	130.2	126.0	126.6	127.5	122.2	129.1	129.0	128.2	131.6	127.1	124.5	131.7
2nd quarter	130.2	132.2	129.7	129.9	128.8	131.2	127.3	127.6	128.9	123.4	130.3	130.1	128.9	132.1	128.3	125.3	133.1
3rd quarter	131.3	133.1	130.9	131.2	130.1	132.6	128.3	129.9	129.9	124.5	131.3	131.4	130.0	133.0	129.7	126.4	134.6
4th quarter	132.8	134.1	132.5	132.4	131.2	134.4	129.1	131.1	130.6	125.2	132.2	133.3	131.3	133.5	131.0	130.6	136.3
1998																	
1st quarter	133.9	135.2	133.7	133.7	132.3	135.7	130.2	132.1	132.0	126.1	133.7	134.4	132.1	136.4	131.9	132.6	137.2
2nd quarter	135.1	136.1	134.8	134.8	133.6	136.9	131.3	133.0	133.2	127.8	134.6	135.5	132.8	136.9	133.1	134.8	138.4
3rd quarter	136.6	137.1	136.5	136.3	135.2	138.9	132.4	134.4	134.3	128.3	136.0	137.5	134.3	139.3	135.0	138.1	139.9
4th quarter	137.7	138.2	137.6	136.9	136.4	140.1	133.2	135.3	135.2	129.6	136.8	138.6	135.1	141.2	135.2	139.8	140.9
1999																	
1st quarter	138.3	139.1	138.1	138.2	136.8	140.3	134.3	136.7	136.3	130.8	137.9	138.9	135.4	141.0	136.2	137.2	142.2
2nd quarter	139.8	140.4	139.7	139.6	138.2	142.0	135.6	137.8	137.3	131.6	139.0	140.7	136.8	142.0	138.1	142.4	143.3
3rd quarter	141.1	141.7	140.9	140.8	139.3	143.4	136.8	138.0	138.5	132.9	140.2	142.0	137.5	144.3	138.7	144.5	144.4
4th quarter	142.5	143.2	142.3	142.0	140.4	145.0	137.7	139.6	139.7	133.8	141.5	143.5	137.9	146.5	140.0	145.2	146.1
2000																	
1st quarter	144.0	144.4	143.9	143.5	142.1	146.6	139.1	141.0	141.3	136.1	142.9	145.0	138.5	147.8	142.1	148.7	147.4
2nd quarter	145.4	145.5	145.4	145.1	143.7	148.2	140.5	142.5	143.0	137.8	144.4	146.4	140.0	148.8	143.4	149.5	149.2
3rd quarter	146.7	146.6	146.7	146.5	145.0	149.6	141.9	143.5	144.3	139.3	145.7	147.8	141.3	149.7	144.6	151.7	150.4
4th quarter	147.9	148.0	147.9	147.6	146.0	150.9	142.8	144.9	145.2	140.8	146.5	149.1	142.3	151.8	145.6	151.7	151.9
2001																	
1st quarter	149.4	149.4	149.4	149.5	147.7	152.3	144.6	146.4	147.0	142.3	148.5	150.5	143.7	152.0	146.9	153.9	153.8
2nd quarter	150.8	150.9	150.8	150.8	149.0	153.6	145.9	147.5	148.6	143.7	150.0	151.8	145.7	153.7	147.6	154.6	155.1
3rd quarter	152.1	152.4	152.0	152.2	150.3	154.7	147.5	148.7	149.5	145.0	150.7	153.1	146.7	154.3	148.6	155.8	156.9
4th quarter	153.4	153.4	153.5	153.3	151.5	156.4	148.3	150.6	150.5	146.3	151.7	154.7	149.2	155.2	151.1	156.0	158.3
2002																	
1st quarter	154.7	154.5	154.8	154.9	152.7	157.7	149.6	152.0	151.7	147.3	153.1	156.1	150.5	157.5	150.9	160.3	159.5
2nd quarter	156.1	155.7	156.2	156.1	154.0	159.2	150.9	152.8	153.1	148.0	154.5	157.6	152.1	160.3	152.5	162.0	160.4
3rd quarter	157.0	157.1	156.9	157.0	154.7	159.9	151.7	153.9	153.9	148.9	155.4	158.3	153.4	160.6	152.7	162.4	161.2
4th quarter	157.8	158.3	157.7	157.5	155.2	160.8	152.4	154.5	155.0	150.2	156.5	158.9	154.1	161.6	153.1	162.6	161.8
2003																	
1st quarter	159.3	159.3	159.3	159.4	156.4	162.6	153.6	155.5	156.3	151.0	158.0	160.6	154.8	163.7	153.1	171.1	162.8
2nd quarter	160.3	160.5	160.3	160.5	157.4	163.6	154.6	156.1	157.4	152.2	159.0	161.5	155.6	163.5	153.7	172.4	164.1
3rd quarter	161.5	160.6	161.7	161.7	158.8	165.1	155.6	157.1	158.3	153.4	159.7	163.2	156.0	165.0	156.1	174.1	165.6
4th quarter	162.3	161.6	162.5	162.4	159.4	166.3	156.1	157.8	158.7	154.0	160.1	164.2	156.5	166.1	156.8	174.5	166.9

[1]Includes private industry and state and local government workers. Federal government workers are not included.
[2]Not seasonally adjusted.
... = Not available.

Table 9-3. Productivity and Related Data

(1992 = 100, seasonally adjusted.)

Year and quarter	Business sector								Nonfarm business sector							
	Output per hour of all persons	Output	Hours of all persons	Compensation per hour	Real compensation per hour	Unit labor costs	Unit nonlabor payments	Implicit price deflator	Output per hour of all persons	Output	Hours of all persons	Compensation per hour	Real compensation per hour	Unit labor costs	Unit nonlabor payments	Implicit price deflator
1947	32.4	20.4	63.0	7.0	40.9	21.7	18.7	20.6	37.0	20.1	54.2	7.5	43.3	20.2	17.8	19.3
1948	33.9	21.5	63.5	7.6	41.0	22.5	20.7	21.8	38.0	20.9	55.1	8.1	43.6	21.3	19.4	20.6
1949	34.7	21.3	61.4	7.7	42.1	22.3	20.5	21.6	39.3	20.8	53.0	8.3	45.4	21.2	20.0	20.8
1950	37.5	23.4	62.3	8.3	44.5	22.1	21.6	21.9	41.9	22.9	54.7	8.8	47.5	21.1	20.8	21.0
1951	38.7	24.9	64.4	9.1	45.2	23.5	23.7	23.6	43.0	24.6	57.3	9.6	47.8	22.3	22.4	22.4
1952	39.7	25.7	64.6	9.6	47.0	24.2	23.2	23.8	43.8	25.3	57.9	10.1	49.5	23.2	22.3	22.8
1953	41.1	26.9	65.4	10.2	49.6	24.9	22.6	24.0	44.7	26.6	59.4	10.7	51.9	23.9	22.2	23.3
1954	42.0	26.6	63.2	10.6	50.8	25.1	22.6	24.2	45.6	26.1	57.3	11.0	53.1	24.2	22.3	23.5
1955	43.8	28.7	65.6	10.8	52.3	24.8	24.0	24.5	47.5	28.3	59.7	11.4	55.3	24.1	23.6	23.9
1956	43.8	29.1	66.6	11.5	55.0	26.4	23.5	25.3	47.1	28.8	61.1	12.1	57.8	25.8	23.1	24.8
1957	45.1	29.6	65.7	12.3	56.7	27.2	24.2	26.1	48.3	29.4	60.8	12.8	59.2	26.6	23.8	25.6
1958	46.4	29.1	62.7	12.8	57.5	27.7	24.8	26.6	49.4	28.7	58.2	13.4	59.8	27.1	24.1	26.0
1959	48.1	31.4	65.4	13.4	59.5	27.8	25.2	26.8	51.2	31.2	60.9	13.9	61.8	27.1	24.9	26.3
1960	48.9	32.0	65.5	13.9	60.9	28.4	24.9	27.1	51.8	31.8	61.3	14.5	63.3	27.9	24.3	26.6
1961	50.6	32.7	64.5	14.5	62.6	28.5	25.3	27.3	53.4	32.4	60.6	15.0	64.8	28.0	24.8	26.8
1962	52.9	34.8	65.7	15.1	64.7	28.5	26.1	27.6	55.8	34.6	62.0	15.6	66.7	27.9	25.8	27.1
1963	55.0	36.4	66.2	15.6	66.1	28.4	26.6	27.7	57.8	36.2	62.7	16.1	68.1	27.8	26.3	27.3
1964	56.8	38.7	68.1	16.2	67.7	28.5	27.3	28.1	59.5	38.7	65.0	16.6	69.3	27.9	27.1	27.6
1965	58.8	41.4	70.4	16.8	69.1	28.6	28.4	28.5	61.3	41.4	67.5	17.1	70.5	27.9	28.0	28.0
1966	61.2	44.2	72.3	17.9	71.7	29.3	29.0	29.2	63.5	44.4	69.8	18.2	72.6	28.6	28.7	28.6
1967	62.5	45.1	72.1	19.0	73.5	30.3	29.5	30.0	64.6	45.1	69.8	19.2	74.5	29.7	29.2	29.5
1968	64.6	47.3	73.2	20.5	76.3	31.7	30.4	31.2	66.8	47.5	71.1	20.7	77.1	31.0	30.2	30.7
1969	64.9	48.8	75.1	21.9	77.4	33.8	30.8	32.6	66.9	48.9	73.1	22.1	78.1	33.1	30.4	32.1
1970	66.2	48.7	73.6	23.6	78.8	35.6	31.4	34.1	67.9	48.9	72.0	23.7	79.1	34.9	31.1	33.5
1971	69.0	50.6	73.3	25.1	80.2	36.3	34.1	35.5	70.6	50.7	71.8	25.2	80.7	35.7	33.7	35.0
1972	71.2	53.9	75.6	26.7	82.6	37.4	35.7	36.8	73.0	54.1	74.1	26.9	83.2	36.8	34.9	36.1
1973	73.5	57.6	78.5	28.9	84.4	39.4	37.5	38.7	75.3	58.0	77.1	29.1	84.8	38.6	35.3	37.4
1974	72.3	56.8	78.6	31.7	83.3	43.9	40.0	42.4	74.2	57.3	77.2	31.9	83.8	43.0	38.1	41.2
1975	74.8	56.3	75.3	35.0	84.1	46.7	46.3	46.6	76.2	56.3	73.9	35.1	84.5	46.1	44.8	45.6
1976	77.2	60.0	77.7	38.0	86.4	49.2	48.7	49.0	78.7	60.2	76.5	38.1	86.6	48.4	47.8	48.1
1977	78.5	63.3	80.7	41.0	87.6	52.2	51.5	52.0	79.9	63.6	79.6	41.2	88.0	51.5	50.7	51.2
1978	79.3	67.3	84.8	44.6	89.1	56.2	54.8	55.6	81.0	67.8	83.7	44.8	89.6	55.3	53.4	54.6
1979	79.4	69.6	87.7	48.9	89.4	61.6	58.2	60.4	80.7	70.0	86.6	49.1	89.7	60.8	56.5	59.2
1980	79.2	68.8	86.9	54.2	89.2	68.4	61.3	65.8	80.6	69.2	85.9	54.4	89.5	67.5	60.4	64.9
1981	80.8	70.7	87.5	59.4	89.3	73.5	69.1	71.8	81.7	70.7	86.5	59.7	89.9	73.1	67.8	71.1
1982	80.2	68.6	85.5	63.6	90.4	79.3	70.2	75.9	80.9	68.4	84.6	64.0	90.8	79.1	69.5	75.5
1983	83.1	72.3	87.0	66.8	90.4	79.7	76.5	78.5	84.6	72.9	86.2	66.6	90.9	78.8	76.2	77.9
1984	85.3	78.6	92.1	69.1	90.7	81.0	80.4	80.8	86.3	78.9	91.4	69.5	91.1	80.5	79.4	80.1
1985	87.2	82.2	94.2	72.4	91.9	83.0	82.2	82.7	87.6	82.2	93.8	72.6	92.2	82.9	81.7	82.5
1986	89.9	85.3	94.9	76.2	94.9	84.8	82.8	84.1	90.3	85.4	94.6	76.4	95.2	84.6	82.6	83.9
1987	90.4	88.3	97.7	79.0	95.3	87.5	83.3	85.9	90.7	88.4	97.5	79.2	95.4	87.3	83.0	85.7
1988	91.7	92.1	100.3	83.1	96.6	90.6	85.4	88.6	92.1	92.4	100.3	83.1	96.6	90.2	85.1	88.3
1989	92.6	95.4	103.0	85.3	95.1	92.1	91.5	91.9	92.8	95.7	103.1	85.2	95.0	91.9	90.9	91.5
1990	94.5	96.9	102.5	90.6	96.2	95.9	93.9	95.1	94.6	97.1	102.7	90.4	96.0	95.6	93.6	94.9
1991	96.0	96.1	100.2	95.0	97.4	99.0	96.8	98.2	96.1	96.3	100.2	95.0	97.4	98.8	97.0	98.1
1992	100.0	100.0	100.0	100.0	100.0	100.0	100.0	100.0	100.0	100.0	100.0	100.0	100.0	100.0	100.0	100.0
1993	100.3	103.1	102.8	102.2	99.7	101.9	102.5	102.1	100.4	103.4	103.0	102.0	99.5	101.6	102.9	102.1
1994	101.5	108.2	106.7	103.8	99.2	102.3	106.6	103.9	101.5	108.3	106.6	103.8	99.1	102.2	107.1	104.0
1995	101.6	111.4	109.6	106.0	98.9	104.3	108.2	105.7	102.0	111.8	109.5	105.9	98.8	103.8	109.2	105.8
1996	104.6	116.5	111.4	109.6	99.6	104.8	111.8	107.4	104.8	116.8	111.5	109.5	99.5	104.5	112.0	107.3
1997	106.5	122.7	115.1	113.1	100.6	106.1	113.8	109.0	106.5	122.8	115.4	112.9	100.4	106.0	114.5	109.1
1998	109.4	128.6	117.6	119.9	105.1	109.6	109.8	109.7	109.3	128.9	117.9	119.6	104.9	109.4	110.8	109.9
1999	112.6	135.2	120.1	125.6	107.9	111.6	109.2	110.7	112.3	135.6	120.7	125.1	107.5	111.4	110.7	111.1
2000	115.9	140.5	121.3	134.5	111.8	116.1	107.2	112.7	115.5	140.8	121.9	134.0	111.4	116.0	108.7	113.3
2001	118.8	141.0	118.7	140.1	113.3	118.0	109.9	114.9	118.3	141.3	119.4	139.3	112.7	117.7	111.5	115.4
2002	123.9	143.5	115.8	144.5	115.0	116.6	114.9	116.0	123.5	143.9	116.5	143.8	114.5	116.5	116.8	116.6
2003	129.5	149.0	115.1	150.5	117.1	116.2	119.6	117.4	129.0	149.4	115.8	149.7	116.5	116.1	121.1	117.9
2001																
1st quarter	117.0	141.1	120.7	138.8	113.0	118.7	106.4	114.1	116.5	141.4	121.4	138.1	112.5	118.6	107.9	114.6
2nd quarter	118.4	141.4	119.4	139.7	112.8	117.9	109.9	114.9	118.1	141.9	120.2	138.9	112.2	117.6	111.6	115.4
3rd quarter	118.8	140.3	118.1	140.4	113.2	118.2	110.2	115.2	118.5	140.8	118.9	139.6	112.5	117.8	111.9	115.6
4th quarter	120.9	141.0	116.6	141.5	114.2	117.0	113.1	115.6	120.4	141.2	117.3	140.7	113.5	116.8	114.7	116.0
2002																
1st quarter	122.7	142.2	115.9	143.2	115.2	116.7	113.4	115.5	122.4	142.6	116.5	142.6	114.7	116.4	115.1	116.0
2nd quarter	123.2	142.9	116.0	144.4	115.2	117.2	113.6	115.9	122.8	143.2	116.7	143.8	114.7	117.1	115.4	116.5
3rd quarter	124.7	144.3	115.7	145.0	115.0	116.3	115.7	116.1	124.1	144.5	116.4	144.3	114.4	116.2	117.7	116.8
4th quarter	125.0	144.7	115.7	145.5	114.8	116.3	116.8	116.5	124.6	145.0	116.4	144.7	114.3	116.1	118.9	117.2
2003																
1st quarter	126.2	145.5	115.3	147.4	115.3	116.8	117.7	117.1	125.8	145.9	116.0	146.6	114.7	116.6	119.6	117.7
2nd quarter	128.6	147.5	114.7	149.6	116.8	116.4	119.0	117.3	127.8	147.8	115.6	148.7	116.1	116.3	120.4	117.8
3rd quarter	131.2	150.8	114.9	151.7	117.7	115.6	120.8	117.5	130.6	151.1	115.7	150.9	117.1	115.5	122.3	118.0
4th quarter	132.0	152.3	115.4	153.2	118.7	116.0	120.7	117.7	131.7	152.8	116.1	152.5	118.2	115.9	121.9	118.1

Table 9-3. Productivity and Related Data—Continued

(1992 = 100, seasonally adjusted.)

Year and quarter	Nonfinancial corporations										Manufacturing					
	Output per hour of all employees	Output	Employee hours	Compensation per hour	Real compensation per hour	Unit costs			Unit profits	Implicit price deflator	Output per hour of all persons	Output	Hours of all persons	Compensation per hour	Real compensation per hour	Unit labor costs
						Total	Labor costs	Nonlabor costs								
1947	...	...	...	...	...	...	...	...	...	...	...	...	...	...	...	...
1948	...	...	...	...	...	...	...	...	...	...	...	...	...	...	...	...
1949	...	...	...	...	...	...	...	...	...	...	...	...	...	...	...	...
1950	...	...	...	...	...	...	...	...	...	...	...	...	...	...	...	...
1951	...	...	...	...	...	...	...	...	...	...	...	...	...	...	...	...
1952	...	...	...	...	...	...	...	...	...	...	...	...	...	...	...	...
1953	...	...	...	...	...	...	...	...	...	...	...	...	...	...	...	...
1954	...	...	...	...	...	...	...	...	...	...	...	...	...	...	...	...
1955	...	...	...	...	...	...	...	...	...	...	...	...	...	...	...	...
1956	...	...	...	...	...	...	...	...	...	...	...	...	...	...	...	...
1957	...	...	...	...	...	...	...	...	...	...	...	...	...	...	...	...
1958	53.6	25.7	48.0	15.0	67.2	26.7	28.0	23.2	46.5	28.5	...	...	...	...	...	...
1959	56.1	28.6	50.9	15.6	69.3	26.2	27.7	21.9	55.0	28.7	...	...	...	...	...	...
1960	57.0	29.5	51.8	16.2	70.8	26.9	28.4	23.0	49.5	28.9	...	...	...	...	...	...
1961	58.8	30.1	51.3	16.7	72.4	27.1	28.4	23.5	49.5	29.1	...	...	...	...	...	...
1962	61.3	32.7	53.3	17.4	74.4	26.9	28.3	23.1	53.7	29.3	...	...	...	...	...	...
1963	63.5	34.6	54.5	17.9	75.7	26.8	28.2	23.1	56.5	29.5	...	...	...	...	...	...
1964	64.5	37.0	57.5	18.2	76.2	26.8	28.3	22.9	58.8	29.7	...	...	...	...	...	...
1965	66.0	40.1	60.7	18.8	77.1	26.9	28.4	22.8	63.2	30.2	...	...	...	...	...	...
1966	67.1	42.9	63.9	19.8	79.2	27.8	29.5	23.0	62.7	30.9	...	...	...	...	...	...
1967	68.1	44.0	64.6	20.9	81.1	29.0	30.7	24.3	59.1	31.7	...	...	...	...	...	...
1968	70.5	46.8	66.4	22.5	83.7	30.3	31.9	25.9	59.1	32.9	...	...	...	...	...	...
1969	70.5	48.6	69.0	24.0	84.8	32.5	34.1	28.1	53.3	34.4	...	...	...	...	...	...
1970	70.8	48.1	67.9	25.7	85.9	35.1	36.3	31.7	43.7	35.9	...	...	...	...	...	...
1971	73.8	50.1	67.9	27.3	87.4	36.0	37.0	33.1	49.8	37.2	...	...	...	...	...	...
1972	75.2	53.8	71.6	28.8	89.2	37.0	38.3	33.4	53.3	38.4	...	...	...	...	...	...
1973	75.9	57.1	75.2	31.0	90.4	39.3	40.8	35.2	54.1	40.6	...	...	...	...	...	...
1974	74.3	56.1	75.5	33.9	89.2	44.3	45.7	40.5	47.7	44.6	...	...	...	...	...	...
1975	77.3	55.4	71.7	37.3	89.7	47.6	48.2	45.9	62.2	48.9	...	...	...	...	...	...
1976	79.7	59.8	75.0	40.3	91.8	49.3	50.6	45.5	70.4	51.2	...	...	...	...	...	...
1977	81.8	64.2	78.4	43.5	93.0	51.7	53.2	47.7	76.2	53.9	...	...	...	...	...	...
1978	82.8	68.3	82.5	47.6	95.1	55.6	57.5	50.5	78.0	57.6	...	...	...	...	...	...
1979	82.0	70.4	85.8	51.9	94.9	61.1	63.3	55.1	73.1	62.2	...	...	...	...	...	...
1980	81.3	69.2	85.2	57.2	94.1	68.8	70.4	64.5	66.5	68.6	...	...	...	...	...	...
1981	82.7	71.4	86.4	62.4	93.9	75.0	75.5	73.6	81.2	75.5	...	...	...	...	...	...
1982	83.1	69.9	84.1	66.5	94.4	80.3	79.9	81.3	75.1	79.8	...	...	...	...	...	...
1983	86.2	73.5	85.3	68.9	94.0	80.3	80.0	81.2	90.7	81.2	...	...	...	...	...	...
1984	88.4	80.3	90.8	71.9	94.3	81.1	81.3	80.7	106.7	83.4	...	...	...	...	...	...
1985	90.5	84.0	92.9	75.2	95.4	83.0	83.1	82.8	101.3	84.7	...	...	...	...	...	...
1986	92.4	86.1	93.2	78.9	98.3	85.4	85.4	85.3	89.2	85.7	...	...	...	...	...	...
1987	94.4	90.7	96.1	81.6	98.3	86.0	86.4	84.9	99.0	87.2	88.4	91.7	103.8	80.7	97.3	91.4
1988	96.5	95.7	99.1	84.9	98.7	87.4	87.9	86.1	110.6	89.5	90.0	96.3	107.0	83.6	97.2	92.8
1989	95.1	97.2	102.2	87.0	97.0	91.8	91.4	92.8	100.6	92.6	90.3	97.2	107.6	86.1	96.0	95.3
1990	95.6	98.1	102.5	91.1	96.8	95.8	95.3	97.1	96.7	95.9	92.9	97.6	105.0	90.1	95.7	97.0
1991	97.8	97.4	99.6	95.5	97.9	98.9	97.6	102.3	92.8	98.4	95.4	96.0	100.5	95.4	97.8	100.0
1992	100.0	100.0	100.0	100.0	100.0	100.0	100.0	100.0	100.0	100.0	100.0	100.0	100.0	100.0	100.0	100.0
1993	100.6	103.0	102.4	101.8	99.3	100.8	101.2	99.7	113.9	101.9	102.7	104.1	101.4	102.3	99.8	99.6
1994	102.6	109.5	106.8	103.6	98.9	100.8	101.0	100.5	131.3	103.6	106.1	110.0	103.8	105.6	100.9	99.6
1995	103.3	114.3	110.6	105.3	98.3	101.8	102.0	101.3	136.9	104.9	109.9	115.0	104.6	107.5	100.3	97.8
1996	107.2	120.7	112.6	108.5	98.6	100.9	101.2	99.9	149.9	105.3	113.9	118.6	104.2	109.9	99.8	96.5
1997	109.9	128.4	116.9	111.7	99.4	101.2	101.7	99.8	154.4	105.9	118.0	125.1	106.0	112.1	99.7	95.0
1998	113.0	135.3	119.7	118.1	103.6	103.2	104.5	99.9	137.5	106.3	123.6	130.7	105.7	119.0	104.4	96.2
1999	116.6	143.2	122.8	123.5	106.1	104.6	106.0	101.0	129.8	106.9	128.1	134.6	105.1	123.7	106.2	96.6
2000	120.8	150.7	124.7	132.0	109.7	108.0	109.2	104.8	109.3	108.1	134.1	138.6	103.4	135.0	112.2	100.7
2001	123.0	149.4	121.5	137.3	111.1	112.1	111.7	113.2	82.6	109.5	136.9	132.3	96.6	138.1	111.7	100.9
2002	128.4	151.6	118.1	141.5	112.7	111.0	110.2	113.0	95.4	109.6	146.5	131.5	89.7	147.4	117.3	100.6
2003	135.4	157.7	116.5	147.3	114.6	109.5	108.8	111.5	113.2	109.8	154.1	131.6	85.4	159.9	124.5	103.8
2001																
1st quarter	122.2	151.3	123.9	135.5	110.4	110.6	111.0	109.6	87.8	108.6	134.9	135.2	100.2	138.4	112.7	102.6
2nd quarter	122.8	150.3	122.4	136.7	110.4	111.6	111.4	112.2	87.3	109.4	135.8	133.3	98.2	137.4	111.0	101.2
3rd quarter	123.0	148.6	120.8	137.9	111.1	112.8	112.1	114.7	79.4	109.8	136.9	131.1	95.8	137.3	110.6	100.3
4th quarter	123.9	147.6	119.1	139.3	112.5	113.4	112.4	116.2	75.8	110.1	140.4	129.7	92.4	139.4	112.5	99.3
2002																
1st quarter	126.3	149.7	118.5	139.9	112.6	111.6	110.8	114.0	89.1	109.6	143.8	130.5	90.7	144.1	115.9	100.2
2nd quarter	127.9	151.4	118.4	141.3	112.7	111.2	110.5	112.9	94.7	109.7	145.7	131.8	90.4	147.0	117.2	100.8
3rd quarter	129.2	152.3	117.9	142.1	112.7	110.7	110.0	112.7	95.7	109.4	147.8	132.4	89.5	148.6	117.8	100.5
4th quarter	130.2	153.1	117.6	142.9	112.8	110.4	109.7	112.3	101.8	109.6	148.8	131.3	88.2	149.9	118.3	100.7
2003																
1st quarter	131.3	153.4	116.8	144.1	112.7	110.7	109.8	113.2	99.2	109.7	151.0	131.3	87.0	155.7	121.8	103.1
2nd quarter	134.1	156.1	116.4	146.3	114.2	109.7	109.1	111.4	111.0	109.8	152.1	130.1	85.6	158.5	123.8	104.2
3rd quarter	137.2	159.4	116.2	148.5	115.3	109.0	108.2	111.1	118.7	109.9	156.0	131.5	84.3	161.6	125.5	103.6
4th quarter	138.9	162.0	116.7	150.0	116.2	108.7	108.0	110.5	123.2	110.0	157.2	133.5	84.9	163.9	127.0	104.2

. . . = Not available.

Table 9-4. Corporate Profits with Inventory Valuation Adjustment by Industry Group (SIC Basis)

(Billions of dollars.)

NIPA Tables 6.16B, 6.16C

Classification basis, year and quarter	Total	Domestic industries										
		Financial			Nonfinancial							
		Total	Federal Reserve Banks	Other	Total	Manufacturing						
						Total	Durable goods					
							Primary metal industries	Fabricated metal products	Industrial machinery and equipment	Electronic and other electric equipment	Motor vehicles and equipment	Other
1972 SIC BASIS												
1948	33.7	32.5	0.2	2.5	29.7	17.5	1.6	0.8	1.3	0.6	1.4	1.8
1949	31.5	30.3	0.2	3.1	27.0	16.2	1.5	0.7	1.3	0.8	2.1	1.7
1950	38.3	37.0	0.2	3.1	33.7	21.0	2.3	1.1	1.6	1.2	3.1	2.6
1951	43.6	41.8	0.3	3.4	38.1	24.7	3.1	1.3	2.3	1.3	2.4	2.8
1952	41.2	39.3	0.3	4.1	34.9	21.7	1.9	1.0	2.3	1.5	2.4	2.6
1953	40.7	38.9	0.4	4.4	34.0	22.0	2.5	1.0	1.9	1.4	2.6	2.6
1954	39.0	37.1	0.3	4.8	32.0	19.9	1.7	0.9	1.7	1.2	2.1	2.9
1955	48.1	45.8	0.3	5.0	40.5	26.1	2.9	1.1	1.7	1.1	4.1	3.5
1956	47.8	44.9	0.5	5.2	39.3	24.8	3.0	1.1	2.1	1.2	2.2	3.1
1957	47.5	44.4	0.6	5.4	38.5	24.1	3.1	1.1	2.0	1.5	2.6	3.1
1958	42.7	40.2	0.6	5.9	33.7	19.5	1.9	0.9	1.5	1.3	0.9	2.9
1959	53.5	50.8	0.7	6.9	43.2	26.5	2.3	1.1	2.2	1.7	3.0	3.5
1960	51.5	48.3	0.9	7.5	39.9	23.8	2.0	0.8	1.8	1.3	3.0	2.7
1961	51.8	48.5	0.8	7.6	40.2	23.4	1.6	1.0	1.9	1.3	2.5	2.9
1962	57.0	53.3	0.9	7.7	44.7	26.3	1.6	1.2	2.4	1.5	4.0	3.4
1963	62.1	58.1	1.0	7.3	49.8	29.7	2.0	1.3	2.6	1.6	4.9	4.0
1964	68.6	64.1	1.1	7.6	55.4	32.6	2.5	1.5	3.3	1.7	4.6	4.4
1965	78.9	74.2	1.3	8.0	64.9	39.8	3.1	2.1	4.0	2.7	6.2	5.2
1966	84.6	80.1	1.7	9.1	69.3	42.6	3.6	2.4	4.6	3.0	5.2	5.2
1967	82.0	77.2	2.0	9.2	66.0	39.2	2.7	2.5	4.2	3.0	4.0	4.9
1968	88.8	83.2	2.5	10.3	70.4	41.9	1.9	2.3	4.2	2.9	5.5	5.6
1969	85.5	78.9	3.1	10.5	65.3	37.3	1.4	2.0	3.8	2.3	4.8	4.9
1970	74.4	67.3	3.5	11.9	52.0	27.5	0.8	1.1	3.1	1.3	1.3	2.9
1971	88.3	80.4	3.3	14.3	62.8	35.1	0.8	1.5	3.1	2.0	5.2	4.1
1972	101.2	91.7	3.3	15.8	72.6	41.9	1.7	2.2	4.5	2.9	6.0	5.6
1973	115.3	100.4	4.5	16.0	79.9	47.2	2.3	2.7	4.9	3.2	5.9	6.2
1974	109.5	92.1	5.7	14.5	71.9	41.4	5.0	1.8	3.3	0.6	0.7	4.0
1975	135.0	120.4	5.6	14.6	100.2	55.2	2.8	3.3	5.1	2.6	2.3	4.7
1976	165.6	149.0	5.9	19.1	124.1	71.3	2.1	3.9	6.9	3.8	7.4	7.3
1977	194.7	175.6	6.1	25.8	143.7	79.3	1.0	4.5	8.6	5.9	9.4	8.5
1978	222.4	199.6	7.6	31.9	160.0	90.5	3.6	5.0	10.7	6.7	9.0	10.5
1979	231.8	197.2	9.4	30.9	156.8	89.6	3.5	5.3	9.5	5.6	4.7	8.5
1980	211.4	175.9	11.8	22.2	141.9	78.3	2.7	4.4	8.0	5.2	-4.3	2.7
1981	219.1	189.4	14.4	14.7	160.3	91.1	3.1	4.5	9.0	5.2	0.3	-2.6
1982	191.0	158.5	15.2	10.8	132.4	67.1	-4.7	2.7	3.1	1.7	0.0	2.1
1983	226.5	191.4	14.6	20.9	155.9	76.2	-4.9	3.1	4.0	3.5	5.3	8.4
1984	264.6	228.1	16.4	18.0	193.7	91.8	-0.4	4.7	6.0	5.1	9.2	14.6
1985	257.5	219.4	16.3	29.5	173.5	84.3	-0.9	4.9	5.7	2.6	7.4	10.1
1986	253.0	213.5	15.5	41.2	156.8	57.9	0.9	5.2	0.8	2.7	4.6	12.1
1987	301.4	253.4	15.7	44.1	193.5	86.3	2.6	5.5	5.4	5.9	3.7	17.6
1987 SIC BASIS												
1987	301.4	253.4	15.7	44.1	193.5	86.3	2.6	5.5	5.4	5.9	3.7	17.6
1988	363.9	306.9	17.6	51.1	238.2	121.2	6.0	6.5	11.1	7.7	6.2	16.5
1989	367.4	300.3	20.2	57.8	222.3	110.9	6.4	6.4	12.2	9.3	2.7	14.2
1990	396.6	320.5	21.4	73.0	226.1	113.1	3.5	6.0	11.8	8.5	-1.9	15.9
1991	427.9	351.4	20.3	103.9	227.3	98.0	1.5	5.3	5.7	10.0	-5.4	17.3
1992	458.3	385.2	17.8	111.9	255.4	99.5	0.0	6.2	7.5	10.4	-1.0	17.4
1993	513.1	436.1	16.2	120.6	299.3	115.6	0.4	7.4	7.5	15.2	6.0	19.4
1994	564.6	487.6	18.1	101.8	367.7	147.0	2.3	11.1	9.1	22.8	7.8	21.3
1995	656.0	563.2	22.5	139.7	401.0	173.7	7.1	11.8	14.8	21.5	0.0	25.8
1996	736.1	634.2	22.1	150.5	461.6	188.8	5.6	14.5	16.9	20.1	4.2	29.2
1997	812.3	701.4	23.8	169.2	508.4	209.0	6.3	17.0	16.7	25.3	4.8	33.0
1998	738.5	635.5	25.2	140.7	469.6	173.5	6.5	16.4	19.5	8.9	5.9	30.1
1999	776.8	655.3	26.3	170.1	458.9	175.2	2.4	16.2	12.4	5.3	7.3	35.3
2000	759.3	613.6	30.8	173.0	409.8	166.3	1.2	15.4	16.3	4.7	-1.5	28.8
1998												
1st quarter	752.0	643.1	25.0	147.9	470.2	178.5	6.9	14.9	14.4	12.2	6.4	28.8
2nd quarter	732.5	626.3	25.2	136.4	464.7	170.1	6.2	16.7	19.5	8.3	3.5	27.4
3rd quarter	743.5	647.3	25.4	136.9	485.0	176.6	6.1	18.5	20.4	6.6	4.5	31.3
4th quarter	725.9	625.3	25.1	141.8	458.4	168.8	6.8	15.7	23.7	8.3	9.3	32.9
1999												
1st quarter	771.3	657.3	24.9	163.0	469.5	175.0	3.8	15.9	9.8	4.3	8.9	33.9
2nd quarter	773.2	656.5	25.5	157.8	473.2	182.5	3.1	15.7	12.8	4.9	6.1	37.8
3rd quarter	766.8	648.3	26.2	175.3	446.8	174.2	1.5	16.2	12.3	6.9	7.3	34.3
4th quarter	796.1	659.1	28.6	184.5	446.0	169.1	1.2	17.1	14.7	4.9	6.7	35.3
2000												
1st quarter	766.8	635.7	30.0	179.5	426.2	172.6	2.1	18.8	12.6	2.5	1.2	33.3
2nd quarter	773.5	634.9	30.5	164.5	440.0	186.1	2.0	16.2	16.1	8.7	0.3	33.7
3rd quarter	756.3	611.7	31.1	171.1	409.6	164.9	0.5	15.2	18.1	3.4	-2.4	27.3
4th quarter	740.7	572.1	31.7	176.8	363.6	141.6	0.3	11.3	18.1	4.1	-5.2	21.0

Table 9-4. Corporate Profits with Inventory Valuation Adjustment by Industry Group (SIC Basis)—*Continued*

(Billions of dollars.)

NIPA Tables 6.16B, 6.16C

Classification basis, year and quarter	Domestic industries—*Continued*												Rest of the world
	Nonfinancial—*Continued*												
	Manufacturing—*Continued*					Transportation and public utilities				Wholesale trade	Retail trade	Other	
	Nondurable goods												
	Total	Food and kindred products	Chemicals and allied products	Petroleum and coal products	Other	Total	Transportation	Communications	Electric, gas, and sanitary services				
1972 SIC BASIS													
1948	10.0	1.9	1.7	2.8	3.7	3.0	1.5	0.4	1.1	2.4	3.2	3.5	1.3
1949	8.1	1.6	1.8	1.9	2.8	3.0	1.2	0.5	1.4	1.9	2.8	3.1	1.1
1950	9.0	1.6	2.3	2.3	2.7	4.1	1.9	0.7	1.5	2.1	3.0	3.5	1.3
1951	11.4	1.4	2.8	2.8	4.4	4.7	1.9	1.0	1.8	2.6	2.6	3.6	1.7
1952	10.0	1.8	2.3	2.3	3.6	5.0	1.9	1.1	2.0	2.3	2.7	3.3	1.9
1953	10.0	1.8	2.2	2.7	3.3	5.0	1.6	1.2	2.2	1.8	2.3	3.0	1.8
1954	9.5	1.6	2.2	2.8	2.9	4.7	1.0	1.3	2.4	1.7	2.3	3.3	2.0
1955	11.8	2.2	3.0	3.0	3.6	5.7	1.5	1.7	2.5	2.4	2.9	3.5	2.4
1956	12.0	1.8	2.8	3.3	4.1	5.9	1.4	1.8	2.7	2.2	2.6	3.9	2.8
1957	10.8	1.8	2.8	2.6	3.6	5.9	1.1	2.0	2.7	2.2	2.6	3.8	3.1
1958	10.2	2.1	2.5	2.1	3.4	5.9	0.9	2.3	2.7	2.2	2.6	3.5	2.5
1959	12.9	2.5	3.5	2.6	4.3	7.1	1.1	2.8	3.1	2.9	3.3	3.4	2.7
1960	12.2	2.2	3.1	2.6	4.2	7.5	0.9	3.0	3.6	2.5	2.8	3.3	3.1
1961	12.1	2.4	3.3	2.3	4.2	7.9	1.0	3.2	3.7	2.5	3.0	3.4	3.3
1962	12.3	2.4	3.2	2.2	4.4	8.5	1.0	3.6	3.9	2.8	3.4	3.6	3.8
1963	13.3	2.7	3.7	2.2	4.7	9.5	1.4	3.9	4.2	2.8	3.6	4.1	4.1
1964	14.5	2.7	4.1	2.4	5.3	10.2	1.6	4.0	4.6	3.4	4.5	4.7	4.5
1965	16.5	2.9	4.6	2.9	6.1	11.0	2.1	4.3	4.6	3.8	4.9	5.4	4.7
1966	18.6	3.3	4.9	3.4	6.9	12.0	2.3	4.8	4.9	4.0	4.9	5.9	4.5
1967	18.0	3.3	4.3	4.0	6.4	10.9	1.3	4.8	4.8	4.1	5.7	6.1	4.8
1968	19.4	3.2	5.3	3.8	7.1	11.0	1.0	5.1	4.9	4.6	6.4	6.6	5.6
1969	18.1	3.1	4.6	3.4	7.0	10.7	0.7	5.4	4.6	4.9	6.4	6.1	6.6
1970	17.0	3.2	3.9	3.7	6.1	8.3	-0.1	4.8	3.6	4.4	6.0	5.8	7.1
1971	18.5	3.6	4.5	3.8	6.6	8.9	0.7	4.1	4.1	5.2	7.2	6.4	7.9
1972	19.2	3.0	5.3	3.3	7.6	9.5	1.5	3.9	4.0	6.9	7.4	7.0	9.5
1973	22.0	2.5	6.2	5.4	7.9	9.1	1.3	4.3	3.4	8.2	6.6	8.7	14.9
1974	26.1	2.6	5.3	10.9	7.3	7.6	2.0	4.1	1.5	11.5	2.3	9.1	17.5
1975	34.5	8.6	6.4	10.1	9.5	11.0	1.0	4.3	5.7	13.8	8.2	12.0	14.6
1976	39.9	7.1	8.2	13.5	11.1	15.3	3.0	5.7	6.5	12.9	10.5	14.0	16.5
1977	41.4	6.9	7.8	13.1	13.6	18.6	3.7	6.6	8.3	15.6	12.4	17.8	19.1
1978	45.1	6.2	8.3	15.8	14.8	21.8	4.1	8.6	9.1	15.6	12.3	19.8	22.9
1979	52.5	5.8	7.2	24.8	14.7	17.0	3.5	7.5	6.0	18.8	9.8	21.6	34.6
1980	59.5	6.1	5.7	34.7	13.1	18.4	2.7	7.7	8.0	17.2	6.2	21.8	35.5
1981	71.6	9.2	8.0	40.0	14.5	20.3	1.7	8.6	10.0	22.4	9.9	16.7	29.7
1982	62.1	7.3	5.1	34.7	15.0	23.1	-0.1	8.6	14.6	19.6	13.4	9.2	32.6
1983	56.7	6.3	7.4	23.9	19.1	29.5	3.2	9.9	16.4	21.0	18.7	10.4	35.1
1984	52.6	6.8	8.2	17.6	20.1	40.1	6.1	12.8	21.3	29.5	21.1	11.1	36.6
1985	54.6	8.8	6.6	18.7	20.5	33.8	1.8	14.2	17.8	23.9	22.2	9.2	38.1
1986	31.7	7.5	7.5	-4.7	21.3	35.8	3.4	17.6	14.7	24.1	23.5	15.5	39.5
1987	45.6	11.4	14.4	-1.5	21.3	41.9	3.4	19.4	19.1	18.6	23.4	23.4	48.0
1987 SIC BASIS													
1987	45.6	11.4	14.4	-1.5	21.3	41.9	3.4	19.4	19.1	18.6	23.4	23.4	48.0
1988	67.1	12.0	18.6	12.7	23.7	48.4	7.9	19.5	21.1	20.1	20.3	28.3	57.0
1989	59.7	11.1	18.2	6.5	23.9	43.3	1.3	18.2	23.9	21.8	20.8	25.5	67.1
1990	69.2	14.3	16.8	16.4	21.7	44.2	-0.4	20.1	24.5	19.2	20.7	29.0	76.1
1991	63.6	18.1	16.2	7.3	22.0	53.3	2.3	23.5	27.5	21.7	26.7	27.5	76.5
1992	59.0	18.2	16.0	-0.9	25.6	58.4	2.3	27.7	28.4	25.1	32.6	39.7	73.1
1993	59.7	16.4	15.9	2.7	24.7	69.5	7.0	32.9	29.6	26.3	39.1	48.9	76.9
1994	72.6	19.9	23.2	1.2	28.3	83.2	10.5	36.7	36.1	30.9	46.2	60.4	77.1
1995	92.8	27.1	27.9	7.1	30.6	85.8	11.5	33.6	40.8	27.3	43.1	71.2	92.8
1996	98.2	22.1	26.4	15.0	34.7	91.3	15.7	35.0	40.7	39.8	51.9	89.7	101.9
1997	105.9	24.6	32.3	17.3	31.7	84.2	19.0	25.5	39.7	47.6	64.2	103.4	110.9
1998	86.2	21.9	26.5	6.7	31.1	78.9	21.6	21.4	35.8	52.3	73.4	91.5	103.0
1999	96.4	28.1	25.2	4.3	38.9	56.8	15.8	4.6	36.3	52.6	74.6	99.7	121.5
2000	101.5	25.7	16.0	29.1	30.7	43.8	15.2	1.3	27.3	56.9	70.1	72.8	145.7
1998													
1st quarter	94.9	23.6	30.5	9.4	31.3	76.8	20.6	22.1	34.1	50.2	71.3	93.4	108.8
2nd quarter	88.5	24.6	22.9	8.9	32.1	81.0	21.5	24.0	35.5	52.6	72.5	88.6	106.2
3rd quarter	89.2	25.8	24.9	7.3	31.3	86.7	24.2	25.1	37.4	57.5	73.8	90.4	96.2
4th quarter	72.0	13.6	27.6	1.3	29.6	71.0	20.3	14.5	36.3	48.8	76.0	93.8	100.5
1999													
1st quarter	98.5	28.5	31.8	0.6	37.6	62.6	16.8	9.2	36.6	54.8	79.4	97.7	113.9
2nd quarter	102.1	28.6	31.8	4.0	37.7	52.1	16.0	3.4	32.8	53.1	79.0	106.6	116.6
3rd quarter	95.8	27.0	22.1	8.2	38.5	52.5	13.5	1.3	37.6	49.3	69.6	101.2	118.5
4th quarter	89.1	28.2	14.9	4.4	41.6	59.9	17.0	4.5	38.4	53.3	70.5	93.2	137.0
2000													
1st quarter	102.1	28.3	20.0	15.3	38.6	47.5	14.7	-0.3	33.0	52.4	75.5	78.3	131.1
2nd quarter	109.2	25.4	17.4	33.8	32.7	42.4	19.4	-3.4	26.4	63.2	70.8	77.4	138.5
3rd quarter	102.8	28.2	13.3	33.9	27.4	43.2	15.7	0.4	27.1	62.9	70.3	68.3	144.6
4th quarter	91.9	21.0	13.2	33.4	24.3	42.2	11.2	8.4	22.6	48.9	63.9	67.0	168.6

Table 9-5. Corporate Profits with Inventory Valuation Adjustment by Industry Group (NAICS Basis)

(Billions of dollars.)

NIPA Table 6.16D

Year and quarter	Total	Domestic industries											
		Financial			Nonfinancial								
		Total	Federal Reserve Banks	Other financial	Total	Utilities	Manufacturing						
							Total	Durable goods					
								Fabricated metal products	Machinery	Computer and electronic products	Electrical equipment, appliances, and components	Motor vehicles, bodies and trailers, and parts	Other durable goods
1998	738.5	635.5	25.2	140.2	470.1	32.7	157.0	16.7	15.6	3.9	6.1	6.4	34.6
1999	776.8	655.3	26.3	168.0	461.1	33.1	150.6	16.5	12.4	-6.5	6.3	7.3	36.4
2000	759.3	613.6	30.8	169.4	413.4	24.4	144.3	15.5	8.2	4.0	5.6	-1.0	27.7
2001	719.2	549.5	28.3	199.3	322.0	24.7	52.6	9.9	2.7	-48.5	1.9	-9.2	17.8
2002	756.8	599.0	22.9	253.3	322.8	11.4	50.7	9.3	1.6	-32.9	-0.2	-6.0	19.8
2003	860.4	683.4	19.2	280.6	383.6	18.8	67.3	10.1	-0.5	-15.4	-3.2	-6.2	11.8
2001													
1st quarter	750.5	590.4	31.1	199.7	359.6	27.2	87.8	12.1	12.1	-18.7	4.3	-7.7	15.0
2nd quarter	756.0	585.0	29.1	194.9	361.0	29.3	79.8	10.7	4.2	-37.2	2.1	-9.9	25.0
3rd quarter	689.1	542.5	27.6	184.2	330.8	26.1	49.1	9.6	-6.7	-59.3	1.1	-6.1	23.1
4th quarter	681.3	480.2	25.5	218.2	236.5	16.2	-6.3	7.1	1.1	-78.6	0.0	-13.2	8.3
2002													
1st quarter	711.7	556.6	23.8	250.9	281.9	8.2	33.0	8.8	2.5	-47.1	1.5	-11.0	19.3
2nd quarter	747.5	596.2	23.7	256.2	316.2	10.8	46.4	9.3	1.7	-37.0	-0.4	-2.5	18.8
3rd quarter	761.2	606.1	22.6	254.5	329.0	12.9	57.5	9.0	1.8	-25.7	-0.2	-4.2	19.9
4th quarter	806.8	637.1	21.4	251.6	364.2	13.5	65.6	10.3	0.4	-21.6	-1.5	-6.3	21.4
2003													
1st quarter	798.7	641.8	20.9	271.6	349.2	17.1	54.8	6.4	-3.4	-17.5	-1.5	0.6	8.1
2nd quarter	823.5	662.2	19.9	275.5	366.8	15.3	54.1	10.6	-0.9	-14.8	-2.7	-9.0	8.4
3rd quarter	877.2	703.8	18.5	287.6	397.6	18.6	66.8	10.1	1.1	-15.2	-4.3	-11.4	12.2
4th quarter	941.9	726.1	17.6	287.8	420.7	24.3	93.4	13.2	1.1	-14.0	-4.4	-5.0	18.4

Year and quarter	Domestic industries—Continued											Rest of the world, net
	Nonfinancial—Continued											
	Manufacturing—Continued					Wholesale trade	Retail trade	Transportation and warehousing	Information	Other nonfinancial		
	Nondurable goods											
	Total	Food and beverage and tobacco products	Petroleum and coal products	Chemical products	Other nondurable goods							
1998	73.6	21.8	4.9	25.1	21.8	53.2	66.4	21.0	20.1	119.8		103.0
1999	78.3	30.7	1.8	23.0	22.7	55.5	65.2	16.1	10.5	130.1		121.5
2000	84.3	25.4	26.9	14.2	17.8	59.7	59.6	14.9	-17.6	128.2		145.7
2001	78.0	28.0	29.6	12.6	7.8	52.1	71.0	1.3	-25.6	145.9		169.7
2002	58.9	24.1	4.0	17.1	13.6	51.0	78.1	-1.3	-11.2	144.2		157.8
2003	70.7	27.7	14.8	21.2	7.1	47.9	77.7	10.5	-0.7	162.1		176.9
2001												
1st quarter	70.7	22.3	34.4	5.6	8.3	46.7	66.7	2.9	-21.5	149.8		160.1
2nd quarter	84.9	30.4	33.3	14.0	7.2	47.8	66.3	4.1	-21.1	154.9		171.0
3rd quarter	87.4	28.8	32.3	16.2	10.1	53.8	72.3	3.3	-25.4	151.5		146.6
4th quarter	69.2	30.3	18.6	14.6	5.7	60.2	78.6	-5.2	-34.4	127.4		201.2
2002												
1st quarter	59.1	27.4	3.8	16.2	11.7	51.3	76.3	-1.0	-17.5	131.6		155.1
2nd quarter	56.4	24.7	2.8	15.4	13.5	57.0	79.8	-4.1	-13.7	140.0		151.3
3rd quarter	57.1	24.5	4.0	16.5	12.1	46.5	78.7	-2.7	-11.7	147.8		155.1
4th quarter	63.0	20.0	5.5	20.5	17.1	49.3	77.7	2.4	-1.8	157.4		169.6
2003												
1st quarter	62.0	22.5	15.2	20.0	4.3	43.1	74.7	5.2	-6.5	160.8		157.0
2nd quarter	62.6	25.4	12.5	18.9	5.8	45.1	82.6	12.4	-1.8	159.1		161.4
3rd quarter	74.2	28.6	12.6	24.5	8.5	53.1	78.9	11.9	6.7	161.7		173.4
4th quarter	84.1	34.2	18.7	21.3	9.8	50.1	74.7	12.4	-1.0	166.8		215.8

CHAPTER 9: EMPLOYMENT COSTS, PRODUCTIVITY, AND PROFITS

NOTES AND DEFINITIONS

General note on data on compensation per hour

Included in this chapter are two different data series with similar names but markedly different behavior. Both are compiled and published by the Bureau of Labor Statistics, but the sources and methods of compilation are different. Users should be aware of these differences and consequent differences in the uses and interpretations of the two series.

The *Employment Cost Index* measures changes in *hourly compensation* for all civilian workers (except federal government) and a number of industry and occupational subgroups including all nonfarm private industry. It is constructed by analogy with the Consumer Price Index, holding constant the composition of employment in order to isolate trends in hourly compensation that take place for individual occupations. It is based on a sample survey and is not subject to benchmark revision, although the seasonal adjustments for quarterly movements are subject to recalculation and revision. It is frequently, and appropriately, used as the best available measure of the general trend of wages and the extent of inflationary pressure exerted on prices by labor costs. By design, it excludes any representation of employee stock options. Being based on a sample survey, it is measured "from the bottom up," starting with reports from individual employers and aggregating to higher levels.

The *Compensation per hour* component of the report on productivity and costs is calculated and published for total business, nonfarm business, nonfinancial corporations, and manufacturing. This is a "top-down" measure, starting with aggregate estimates of compensation and hours, then dividing the former by the latter. It is affected by changes in the composition of employment: if the composition of employment shifted toward higher-paid employees and/or industries, compensation per hour would rise even if there was no increase in hourly compensation for any individual worker.

In addition, *Compensation per hour* includes the value of exercised stock options as expensed by companies. Since these values are not reported currently but are incorporated at revisions to more comprehensive benchmark levels, this can lead to dramatic revisions. For example, the rise from a year earlier for compensation per hour in nonfarm business for the third quarter of 2000 was initially reported at 5.1 percent; last year, it was revised to 7.9 percent; but the latest estimate is 6.4 percent. The rise from a year earlier in the third quarter of 2001 was originally reported at 6.0 percent and is now shown at only 3.3 percent.

For both of these reasons, *Compensation per hour* should not be considered as an indicator of wage trends, especially for the great majority of workers. It is useful in conjunction with the productivity series, since aggregate productivity is subject to the same composition shifts, since higher-productivity industries also have higher-paid employees on average. Hence, the measure of *unit labor costs* is not distorted when the composition of output shifts toward higher-productivity industries, since the shift affects similarly the numerator and denominator of the ratio.

TABLES 9-1 AND 9-2
EMPLOYMENT COST INDEXES

SOURCE: U.S. DEPARTMENT OF LABOR, BUREAU OF LABOR STATISTICS (BLS)

The Employment Cost Index (ECI) is a quarterly measure of the change in the cost of labor, free from the influence of employment shifts among occupations and industries. It uses a fixed market basket of labor, similar in concept to the Consumer Price Index's fixed market basket of goods and services, to measure changes over time in employer costs of employing labor. Data are quarterly in all cases; in most cases, index levels have a base period of June 1989 (not seasonally adjusted) = 100.

Definitions

Total compensation includes wages, salaries, and the employer's costs for employee benefits. Excluded from wages and salaries and employee benefits are the value of stock option exercises and also such items as payment-in-kind, free room and board, and tips.

Wages and salaries consist of straight-time earnings per hour before payroll deductions, including production bonuses, incentive earnings, commissions, and cost-of-living adjustments. These wage rates exclude premium pay for overtime and for work on weekends and holidays, shift differentials, and nonproduction bonuses such as lump-sum payments provided in lieu of wage increases.

Benefits include the cost to employers for paid leave—vacations, holidays, sick leave, and other leave; supplemental pay—premium pay for work in addition to the regular work schedule (such as overtime, weekends, and holidays), shift differentials, and nonproduction bonuses (such as referral bonuses and lump-sum payments provided in lieu of wage increases); insurance benefits—life, health, short-term disability, and long-term disability; retirement and savings benefits—defined benefit and defined contribution plans; legally required benefits—Social Security, Medicare, federal and state unemployment insurance, and workers' compensation; and other benefits—severance pay and supplemental unemployment plans.

Private industry workers are workers in private nonfarm industry, not including proprietors, the self-employed, or private household workers.

Civilian workers includes private nonfarm industry workers and workers in state and local government. Federal workers are not included.

Notes on the data

Employee benefit costs are calculated as cents per hour worked for benefits ranging from employer payments for Social Security to paid time off for holidays.

The data are collected from probability samples of around 37,300 occupational observations in around 8,500 sample establishments in private industry, and around 3,650 occupations within around 800 establishments in state and local governments. Samples are rotated over approximately 5 years.

The sample establishments were classified in industry categories based on the 1987 Standard Industrial Classification (SIC). (Beginning with the indexes for 2004, the North American Industry Classification System [NAICS] is used for industry classification and the 2000 Standard Occupational Classification for occupations.) Within an establishment, specific job categories were selected and classified into about 500 occupational classifications according to the 1990 Census of Population. Data are collected each quarter for the pay period including the 12th day of March, June, September, and December.

Aggregate indexes are calculated using fixed employment weights. Beginning with March 1995, ECI weights are based on 1990 fixed employment counts, primarily from the BLS Occupational Employment Survey. From June 1986 through December 1994, ECI measures were based on 1980 census employment counts, while prior to June 1986, they were based on 1970 census employment counts. Use of fixed weights ensures that changes in the indexes reflect only changes in hourly compensation, not employment shifts among industries or occupations with different levels of wages and compensation. This feature distinguishes the ECI from other compensation series such as average hourly earnings (see Table 10-9 and its Notes and Definitions) and the compensation per hour component of the productivity series (see Table 9-3 and its Notes and Definitions, also the General Note above), each of which is affected by such employment shifts.

Data availability

Data for wages and salaries for the private nonfarm economy are available beginning with data for 1975; data for compensation begin with 1980. The series for state and local government and the civilian nonfarm economy begin with 1981. All are available on the BLS Internet site at <http://www.bls.gov>.

Wage and salary change and compensation cost change data also are available from BLS by major occupational and industry groups, as well as by region and bargaining status. Wage and salary change information is available from 1975 to the present for most of these series. Compensation cost change data are available from 1980 to the present for most series. For 10 occupational and industry series, benefit cost change data are available from the early 1980s to the present. For state and local governments and the civilian economy (state and local governments plus private industry), wage and salary change and compensation cost change data are available for major occupational and industry series. BLS provides data for all these series from June 1981 to the present.

Updates are available about four weeks following the end of the reference quarter. Reference quarters end in March, June, September, and December.

References

Explanatory notes including references are included in each quarter's ECI news release, available on the BLS Internet site. References include: Chapter 8, "National Compensation Measures," *BLS Handbook of Methods* Bulletin 2490 (April 1997); *Employment Cost Indexes, 1975–1999*, BLS Bulletin 2532 (includes details on the sample design and seasonal adjustment methodology); and the following *Monthly Labor Review* articles: "Is the ECI Sensitive to the Method of Aggregation" (June 1997); "Employment Cost Index Rebased to June 1989" (April 1990); "Measuring the Precision of the Employment Cost Index" (March 1989); "Employment Cost Index to Replace Hourly Earnings Index" (July 1988); and "Estimation Procedures for the Employment Cost Index" (May 1982).

TABLES 9-3 AND 19-10
PRODUCTIVITY AND RELATED DATA

SOURCE: U.S. DEPARTMENT OF LABOR, BUREAU OF LABOR STATISTICS (BLS)

Productivity measures relate real physical output to real input. As such, they encompass a family of measures that includes single-factor input measures, such as output per unit of labor input or output per unit of capital input, as well as measures of multifactor productivity (output per unit of combined labor and capital inputs). The indexes published in this book are indexes of labor productivity expressed in terms of output per hour. Data are provided for four sectors of the economy: business, nonfarm business, the nonfinancial corporate sector, and manufacturing. All data are presented as indexes, 1992 = 100.

Definitions

Output per hour of all persons (labor productivity) is the value of goods and services in constant prices produced per hour of labor input. Because nonfinancial corporations by definition include no self-employed persons, productivity in this sector is expressed as *output per hour of all employees.*

Compensation per hour is the wages and salaries of employees plus employers' contributions for social insurance and private benefit plans, and the wages, salaries, and supplementary payments for the self-employed—the sum of these divided by hours at work. Included in compensation is the value of exercised stock options that companies report as a charge against earnings. These are not reported quarterly, so that recent values are estimated based on extrapolation. They are revised to actual values when the data become available.

Real compensation per hour is compensation per hour deflated by the CPI-U-RS for the period 1978 through 2003. (For explanation of the CPI-U-RS, see Notes and Definitions for Table 8-1.) Changes in the CPI-W are used for data before 1978.

Unit labor costs are the labor costs expended in the production of a unit of output and are derived by dividing compensation by output.

Unit nonlabor payments include profits, depreciation, interest, rental income of persons, and indirect taxes per unit of output. They are computed by subtracting compensation of all persons from current-dollar value of output and dividing by output.

Unit nonlabor costs is available for nonfinancial corporations only. It contains all the components of unit nonlabor payments except unit profits (and rental income of persons, which for nonfinancial corporations is zero by definition).

Hours of all persons are the total hours at work of payroll workers, self-employed persons, and unpaid family workers. In the case of the data for nonfinancial corporations, there are no self-employed persons and the data represent *employee hours.*

Notes on the data

The output for the business sector is equal to constant-dollar gross domestic product less the following: the rental value of owner-occupied dwellings; the output of nonprofit institutions; the output of paid employees of private households; and general government output. The measures are derived from NIPA data supplied by the U.S. Department of Commerce, Bureau of Economic Analysis (BEA). For manufacturing, annual estimates of sectoral output are produced by the BLS. Quarterly manufacturing output indexes derived from the Federal Reserve Board of Governors' monthly indexes of industrial production are adjusted to these annual measures by the BLS, and used to project the quarterly values in the current period.

Nonfinancial corporate output excludes unincorporated businesses and financial corporations from business sector output. It accounted for about 54 percent of the value of GDP in 1996. For this sector, it is possible to calculate unit profits and unit nonlabor costs separately.

Compensation and hours data are developed from BLS and BEA data. The primary source for hours and employment is the BLS Current Employment Statistics (CES) program (see Notes and Definitions for Tables 10-5 through 10-10). The CES provides data on hours paid for production or nonsupervisory workers. Paid hours of nonproduction and supervisory workers are estimated by the BLS Office of Productivity and Technology. Weekly paid hours are adjusted to hours at work using the annual BLS Hours at Work survey, conducted for this purpose. For paid employees, hours at work differs from hours paid in that it excludes paid vacation and holidays, paid sick leave, and other paid personal or administrative leave.

Although the labor productivity measures relate output to labor input, they do not measure the contribution of labor or any other specific factor of production. Rather, they reflect the joint effect of many influences, including changes in technology; capital investment; level of output; utilization of capacity, energy, and materials; the organization of production; managerial skill; and the characteristics and efforts of the work force.

Revisions

Data for recent years are revised frequently to take account of revisions in the output and labor input measures that underlie the estimates. Customarily, all revisions to source data are reflected in the release following the source data revision. Data in this volume reflect the December 2003 and midyear 2004 revisions of the National Income and Product Accounts.

Data availability

Most of the series begin in 1959. Series are available quarterly and annually. Quarterly measures are based entirely on seasonally adjusted data. For some detailed manufacturing series (not shown here), only annual averages are available. Productivity indexes are published early in the second and third months of each quarter, reflecting new data for preceding quarters. Complete historical data are available on the BLS Internet site at <http://www.bls.gov>.

BLS also publishes productivity estimates for a number of individual industries. A listing is given in *Productivity Measures for Selected Industries and Government Services*, BLS Bulletin 2440.

References

Chapter 10, "Productivity Measures: Business Sector and Major Subsectors," *BLS Handbook of Methods* Bulletin 2490 (April 1997), and the following *Monthly Labor Review* articles: "Alternative Measures of Supervisory Employee Hours and Productivity Growth" (April 2004); "Possible Measurement Bias in Aggregate Productivity Growth" (February 1999); "Improvements to the Quarterly Productivity Measures" (October 1995); "Hours of Work: A New Base for BLS Productivity Statistics" (February 1990); and "New Sector Definitions for Productivity Series" (October 1976).

TABLE 9-4 AND 9-5
CORPORATE PROFITS WITH INVENTORY VALUATION ADJUSTMENT BY INDUSTRY GROUP

SOURCE: U.S. DEPARTMENT OF COMMERCE, BUREAU OF ECONOMIC ANALYSIS

These profits measures are derived from the National Income and Product Accounts (NIPAs). See the Notes and Definitions to Chapter 1 for definitions. Note that this industry breakdown of profits incorporates the inventory valuation adjustment (IVA), which eliminates any capital gain element in profits arising from changes in the prices at which stocks are valued, but does not incorporate the capital consumption adjustment (CCAdj), which adjusts historical costs to replacement costs and uses actual rather than tax-based service lives. (The reason is that the CCAdj is calculated at an aggregate level, whereas the IVA is calculated at an industry level.)

Beginning in 1998, data are compiled on the NAICS basis, as shown in Table 9-5. Data for earlier years based on the December 2003 revision—including an overlap for the years 1998 through 2000—are still based on the older Standard Industrial Classification system (SIC) and are shown back to 1948 on that basis; these have not been revised and are as shown in previous years' *Business Statistics*. See Chapter 14 for an outline and discussion of NAICS and its relation to SIC.

CHAPTER 10: EMPLOYMENT, HOURS, AND EARNINGS

Section 10a: Labor Force, Employment, and Unemployment

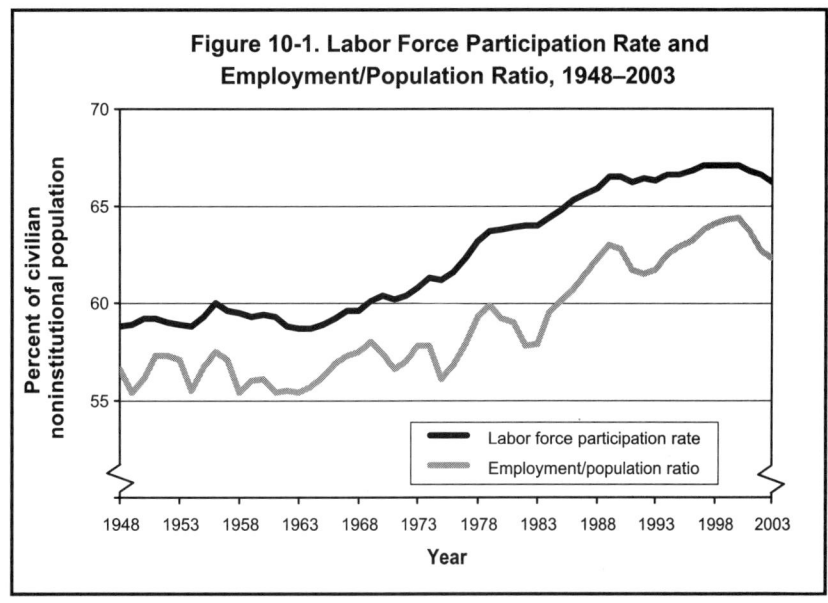

- The civilian noninstitutional population of working age only grew 1.4 percent from 1948 to 2000. Employment growth has been considerably more rapid than population growth, however. This was made possible by the rise in the labor force participation rate that began in the late 1960s and continued, interrupted only by recessions, through the late 1990s. The entire increase in the labor force participation rate was due to women, who increased their share of labor force and employment as the participation rate of men declined. (Table 10-1)
- After peaking in 2000, both labor force and employment declined relative to population in each following year. (Table 10-1)

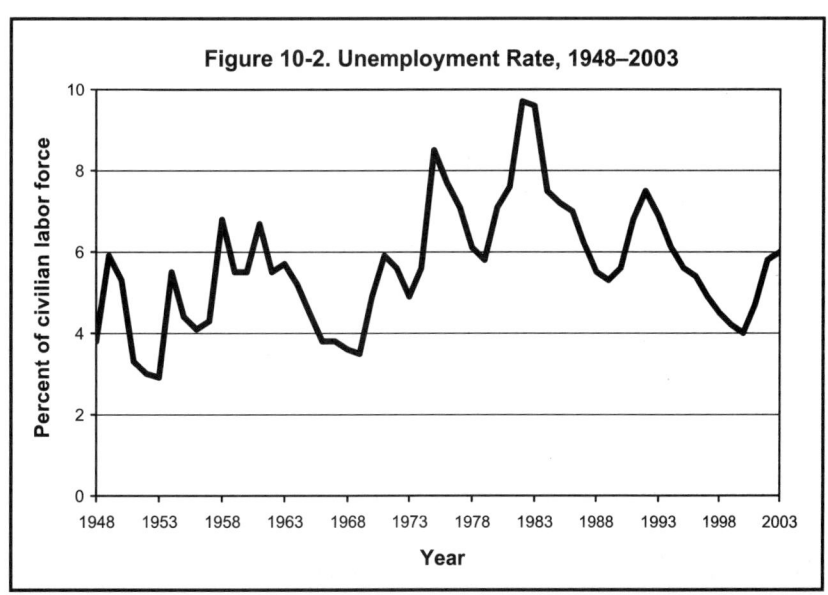

- The unemployment rate was almost the same in 1948 and 2000 — 3.8 percent and 4.0 percent, respectively. In the intervening years, annual average unemployment fluctuated between 2.9 percent (at its low point associated with the Korean War) and 9.7 percent (at its high point in the 1982 recession). (Table 10-3)
- The unemployment rate increased each year following its recent low point in 2000. (Table 10-3)

Table 10-1. Civilian Population and Labor Force [1]

(Thousands of persons, 16 years of age and over.)

| Year and month | Civilian noninstitutional population | Not seasonally adjusted | | | Civilian labor force (seasonally adjusted) | | | | Both sexes, 16 to 19 years | Not in labor force, want a job, seasonally adjusted |
| | | Civilian labor force | | | Total | | Persons 20 years and over | | | |
		Total	Employed	Unemployed	Thousands of persons	Participation rate [2]	Men	Women		
1948	103 068	60 621	58 343	2 276	60 621	58.8	40 687	15 500	4 435	...
1949	103 994	61 286	57 651	3 637	61 286	58.9	41 022	15 978	4 288	...
1950	104 995	62 208	58 918	3 288	62 208	59.2	41 316	16 678	4 216	...
1951	104 621	62 017	59 961	2 055	62 017	59.2	40 655	17 259	4 103	...
1952	105 231	62 138	60 250	1 883	62 138	59.0	40 558	17 517	4 064	...
1953	107 056	63 015	61 179	1 834	63 015	58.9	41 315	17 674	4 027	...
1954	108 321	63 643	60 109	3 532	63 643	58.8	41 669	17 997	3 976	...
1955	109 683	65 023	62 170	2 852	65 023	59.3	42 106	18 825	4 092	...
1956	110 954	66 552	63 799	2 750	66 552	60.0	42 658	19 599	4 296	...
1957	112 265	66 929	64 071	2 859	66 929	59.6	42 780	19 873	4 275	...
1958	113 727	67 639	63 036	4 602	67 639	59.5	43 092	20 285	4 260	...
1959	115 329	68 369	64 630	3 740	68 369	59.3	43 289	20 587	4 492	...
1960	117 245	69 628	65 778	3 852	69 628	59.4	43 603	21 185	4 841	...
1961	118 771	70 459	65 746	4 714	70 459	59.3	43 860	21 664	4 936	...
1962	120 153	70 614	66 702	3 911	70 614	58.8	43 831	21 868	4 916	...
1963	122 416	71 833	67 762	4 070	71 833	58.7	44 222	22 473	5 139	...
1964	124 485	73 091	69 305	3 786	73 091	58.7	44 604	23 098	5 388	...
1965	126 513	74 455	71 088	3 366	74 455	58.9	44 857	23 686	5 910	...
1966	128 058	75 770	72 895	2 875	75 770	59.2	44 788	24 431	6 558	...
1967	129 874	77 347	74 372	2 975	77 347	59.6	45 354	25 475	6 521	...
1968	132 028	78 737	75 920	2 817	78 737	59.6	45 852	26 266	6 619	...
1969	134 335	80 734	77 902	2 832	80 734	60.1	46 351	27 413	6 970	...
1970	137 085	82 771	78 678	4 093	82 771	60.4	47 220	28 301	7 249	3 907
1971	140 216	84 382	79 367	5 016	84 382	60.2	48 009	28 904	7 470	4 441
1972	144 126	87 034	82 153	4 882	87 034	60.4	49 079	29 901	8 054	4 476
1973	147 096	89 429	85 064	4 365	89 429	60.8	49 932	30 991	8 507	4 474
1974	150 120	91 949	86 794	5 156	91 949	61.3	50 879	32 201	8 871	4 541
1975	153 153	93 775	85 846	7 929	93 775	61.2	51 494	33 410	8 870	5 292
1976	156 150	96 158	88 752	7 406	96 158	61.6	52 288	34 814	9 056	5 217
1977	159 033	99 009	92 017	6 991	99 009	62.3	53 348	36 310	9 351	5 777
1978	161 910	102 251	96 048	6 202	102 251	63.2	54 471	38 128	9 652	5 459
1979	164 863	104 962	98 824	6 137	104 962	63.7	55 615	39 708	9 638	5 439
1980	167 745	106 940	99 303	7 637	106 940	63.8	56 455	41 106	9 378	5 682
1981	170 130	108 670	100 397	8 273	108 670	63.9	57 197	42 485	8 988	5 819
1982	172 271	110 204	99 526	10 678	110 204	64.0	57 980	43 699	8 526	6 563
1983	174 215	111 550	100 834	10 717	111 550	64.0	58 744	44 636	8 171	6 484
1984	176 383	113 544	105 005	8 539	113 544	64.4	59 701	45 900	7 943	6 054
1985	178 206	115 461	107 150	8 312	115 461	64.8	60 277	47 283	7 901	5 908
1986	180 587	117 834	109 597	8 237	117 834	65.3	61 320	48 589	7 926	5 848
1987	182 753	119 865	112 440	7 425	119 865	65.6	62 095	49 783	7 988	5 721
1988	184 613	121 669	114 968	6 701	121 669	65.9	62 768	50 870	8 031	5 370
1989	186 393	123 869	117 342	6 528	123 869	66.5	63 704	52 212	7 954	5 312
1990	189 164	125 840	118 793	7 047	125 840	66.5	64 916	53 131	7 792	5 481
1991	190 925	126 346	117 718	8 628	126 346	66.2	65 374	53 708	7 265	5 745
1992	192 805	128 105	118 492	9 613	128 105	66.4	66 213	54 796	7 096	6 172
1993	194 838	129 200	120 259	8 940	129 200	66.3	66 642	55 388	7 170	6 346
1994	196 814	131 056	123 060	7 996	131 056	66.6	66 921	56 655	7 481	6 218
1995	198 584	132 304	124 900	7 404	132 304	66.6	67 324	57 215	7 765	5 670
1996	200 591	133 943	126 708	7 236	133 943	66.8	68 044	58 094	7 806	5 451
1997	203 133	136 297	129 558	6 739	136 297	67.1	69 166	59 198	7 932	4 941
1998	205 220	137 673	131 463	6 210	137 673	67.1	69 715	59 702	8 256	4 812
1999	207 753	139 368	133 488	5 880	139 368	67.1	70 194	60 840	8 333	4 568
2000	212 577	142 583	136 891	5 692	142 583	67.1	72 010	62 301	8 271	4 413
2001	215 092	143 734	136 933	6 801	143 734	66.8	72 816	63 016	7 902	4 590
2002	217 570	144 863	136 485	8 378	144 863	66.6	73 630	63 648	7 585	4 677
2003	221 168	146 510	137 736	8 774	146 510	66.2	74 623	64 716	7 170	4 726
2002										
January	216 506	143 228	134 177	9 051	143 842	66.4	73 113	63 103	7 626	4 812
February	216 663	144 266	135 443	8 823	144 546	66.7	73 274	63 631	7 641	4 547
March	216 823	144 334	135 558	8 776	144 384	66.6	73 275	63 322	7 787	4 628
April	217 006	144 158	135 903	8 255	144 675	66.7	73 459	63 582	7 633	4 612
May	217 198	144 527	136 559	7 969	144 902	66.7	73 787	63 520	7 595	4 785
June	217 407	145 940	137 181	8 758	144 738	66.6	73 683	63 450	7 605	4 724
July	217 630	146 189	137 495	8 693	144 879	66.6	73 715	63 566	7 598	4 817
August	217 866	145 565	137 295	8 271	145 146	66.6	73 871	63 743	7 532	4 617
September	218 107	145 167	137 377	7 790	145 606	66.8	74 074	63 878	7 654	4 682
October	218 340	145 320	137 551	7 769	145 442	66.6	73 921	63 985	7 536	4 496
November	218 548	144 854	136 684	8 170	145 109	66.4	73 678	63 980	7 451	4 791
December	218 741	144 807	136 599	8 209	145 157	66.4	73 725	64 056	7 376	4 566
2003										
January	219 897	145 301	135 907	9 395	145 875	66.3	74 014	64 490	7 371	4 644
February	220 114	145 693	136 433	9 260	145 898	66.3	74 241	64 359	7 298	4 580
March	220 317	145 801	136 783	9 018	145 818	66.2	74 209	64 490	7 120	4 974
April	220 540	145 925	137 424	8 501	146 377	66.4	74 510	64 632	7 235	4 462
May	220 768	146 067	137 567	8 500	146 462	66.3	74 523	64 699	7 240	4 727
June	221 014	148 117	138 468	9 649	146 917	66.5	74 675	64 989	7 254	4 687
July	221 252	147 822	138 503	9 319	146 652	66.3	74 660	64 835	7 157	4 829
August	221 507	146 967	138 137	8 830	146 622	66.2	74 682	64 836	7 104	4 826
September	221 779	146 166	137 731	8 436	146 610	66.1	74 905	64 608	7 097	4 816
October	222 039	146 787	138 619	8 169	146 892	66.2	74 942	64 899	7 051	4 885
November	222 279	146 969	138 700	8 269	147 187	66.2	75 188	64 917	7 082	4 572
December	222 509	146 501	138 556	7 945	146 878	66.0	75 044	64 846	6 987	4 714

[1]Changes in survey design, population estimates, and methodology in 1994 and several other years affect year-to-year comparisons. See Notes and Definitions for more information.
[2]Labor force as a percent of civilian noninstitutional population.
... = Not available.

Table 10-2. Civilian Employment and Unemployment [1]

(Thousands of persons, 16 years and over, except as noted; seasonally adjusted.)

Year and month	Employment							Unemployment						
	Total		By age and sex			By industry		Total	Long-term [3]	Persons 20 years and over		Both sexes, 16 to 19 years	Average (mean) weeks unemployed	Median weeks unemployed
	Thousands of persons	Ratio: employment to population [2]	Persons 20 years and over		Both sexes, 16 to 19 years	Agricultural	Nonagricultural			Men	Women			
			Men	Women										
1948	58 343	56.6	39 382	14 936	4 026	7 629	50 714	2 276	309	1 305	564	409	8.6	...
1949	57 651	55.4	38 803	15 137	3 712	7 658	49 993	3 637	684	2 219	841	576	10.0	...
1950	58 918	56.1	39 394	15 824	3 703	7 160	51 758	3 288	782	1 922	854	513	12.1	...
1951	59 961	57.3	39 626	16 570	3 767	6 726	53 235	2 055	303	1 029	689	336	9.7	...
1952	60 250	57.3	39 578	16 958	3 719	6 500	53 749	1 883	232	980	559	345	8.4	...
1953	61 179	57.1	40 296	17 164	3 720	6 260	54 919	1 834	210	1 019	510	307	8.0	...
1954	60 109	55.5	39 634	17 000	3 475	6 205	53 904	3 532	812	2 035	997	501	11.8	...
1955	62 170	56.7	40 526	18 002	3 642	6 450	55 722	2 852	702	1 580	823	450	13.0	...
1956	63 799	57.5	41 216	18 767	3 818	6 283	57 514	2 750	533	1 442	832	478	11.3	...
1957	64 071	57.1	41 239	19 052	3 778	5 947	58 123	2 859	560	1 541	821	497	10.5	...
1958	63 036	55.4	40 411	19 043	3 582	5 586	57 450	4 602	1 452	2 681	1 242	678	13.9	...
1959	64 630	56.0	41 267	19 524	3 838	5 565	59 065	3 740	1 040	2 022	1 063	654	14.4	...
1960	65 778	56.1	41 543	20 105	4 129	5 458	60 318	3 852	957	2 060	1 080	712	12.8	...
1961	65 746	55.4	41 342	20 296	4 108	5 200	60 546	4 714	1 532	2 518	1 368	828	15.6	...
1962	66 702	55.5	41 815	20 693	4 195	4 944	61 759	3 911	1 119	2 016	1 175	721	14.7	...
1963	67 762	55.4	42 251	21 257	4 255	4 687	63 076	4 070	1 088	1 971	1 216	884	14.0	...
1964	69 305	55.7	42 886	21 903	4 516	4 523	64 782	3 786	973	1 718	1 195	872	13.3	...
1965	71 088	56.2	43 422	22 630	5 036	4 361	66 726	3 366	755	1 435	1 056	874	11.8	...
1966	72 895	56.9	43 668	23 510	5 721	3 979	68 915	2 875	526	1 120	921	837	10.4	...
1967	74 372	57.3	44 294	24 397	5 682	3 844	70 527	2 975	448	1 060	1 078	839	8.7	2.3
1968	75 920	57.5	44 859	25 281	5 781	3 817	72 103	2 817	412	993	985	838	8.4	4.5
1969	77 902	58.0	45 388	26 397	6 117	3 606	74 296	2 832	375	963	1 015	853	7.8	4.4
1970	78 678	57.4	45 581	26 952	6 144	3 463	75 215	4 093	663	1 638	1 349	1 106	8.6	4.9
1971	79 367	56.6	45 912	27 246	6 208	3 394	75 972	5 016	1 187	2 097	1 658	1 262	11.3	6.3
1972	82 153	57.0	47 130	28 276	6 746	3 484	78 669	4 882	1 167	1 948	1 625	1 308	12.0	6.2
1973	85 064	57.8	48 310	29 484	7 271	3 470	81 594	4 365	826	1 624	1 507	1 235	10.0	5.2
1974	86 794	57.8	48 922	30 424	7 448	3 515	83 279	5 156	955	1 957	1 777	1 422	9.8	5.2
1975	85 846	56.1	48 018	30 726	7 104	3 408	82 438	7 929	2 505	3 476	2 684	1 767	14.2	8.4
1976	88 752	56.8	49 190	32 226	7 336	3 331	85 421	7 406	2 366	3 098	2 588	1 719	15.8	8.2
1977	92 017	57.9	50 555	33 775	7 688	3 283	88 734	6 991	1 942	2 794	2 535	1 663	14.3	7.0
1978	96 048	59.3	52 143	35 836	8 070	3 387	92 661	6 202	1 414	2 328	2 292	1 583	11.9	5.9
1979	98 824	59.9	53 308	37 434	8 083	3 347	95 477	6 137	1 241	2 308	2 276	1 555	10.8	5.4
1980	99 303	59.2	53 101	38 492	7 710	3 364	95 938	7 637	1 871	3 353	2 615	1 669	11.9	6.5
1981	100 397	59.0	53 582	39 590	7 225	3 368	97 030	8 273	2 285	3 615	2 895	1 763	13.7	6.9
1982	99 526	57.8	52 891	40 086	6 549	3 401	96 125	10 678	3 485	5 089	3 613	1 977	15.6	8.7
1983	100 834	57.9	53 487	41 004	6 342	3 383	97 450	10 717	4 210	5 257	3 632	1 829	20.0	10.1
1984	105 005	59.5	55 769	42 793	6 444	3 321	101 685	8 539	2 737	3 932	3 107	1 499	18.2	7.9
1985	107 150	60.1	56 562	44 154	6 434	3 179	103 971	8 312	2 305	3 715	3 129	1 468	15.6	6.8
1986	109 597	60.7	57 569	45 556	6 472	3 163	106 434	8 237	2 232	3 751	3 032	1 454	15.0	6.9
1987	112 440	61.5	58 726	47 074	6 640	3 208	109 232	7 425	1 983	3 369	2 709	1 347	14.5	6.5
1988	114 968	62.3	59 781	48 383	6 805	3 169	111 800	6 701	1 610	2 987	2 487	1 226	13.5	5.9
1989	117 342	63.0	60 837	49 745	6 759	3 199	114 142	6 528	1 375	2 867	2 467	1 194	11.9	4.8
1990	118 793	62.8	61 678	50 535	6 581	3 223	115 570	7 047	1 525	3 239	2 596	1 212	12.0	5.3
1991	117 718	61.7	61 178	50 634	5 906	3 269	114 449	8 628	2 357	4 195	3 074	1 359	13.7	6.8
1992	118 492	61.5	61 496	51 328	5 669	3 247	115 245	9 613	3 408	4 717	3 469	1 427	17.7	8.7
1993	120 259	61.7	62 355	52 099	5 805	3 115	117 144	8 940	3 094	4 287	3 288	1 365	18.0	8.3
1994	123 060	62.5	63 294	53 606	6 161	3 409	119 651	7 996	2 860	3 627	3 049	1 320	18.8	9.2
1995	124 900	62.9	64 085	54 396	6 419	3 440	121 460	7 404	2 363	3 239	2 819	1 346	16.6	8.3
1996	126 708	63.2	64 897	55 311	6 500	3 443	123 264	7 236	2 316	3 146	2 783	1 306	16.7	8.3
1997	129 558	63.8	66 284	56 613	6 661	3 399	126 159	6 739	2 062	2 882	2 585	1 271	15.8	8.0
1998	131 463	64.1	67 135	57 278	7 051	3 378	128 085	6 210	1 637	2 580	2 424	1 205	14.5	6.7
1999	133 488	64.3	67 761	58 555	7 172	3 281	130 207	5 880	1 480	2 433	2 285	1 162	13.4	6.4
2000	136 891	64.4	69 634	60 067	7 189	2 464	134 427	5 692	1 318	2 376	2 235	1 081	12.6	5.9
2001	136 933	63.7	69 776	60 417	6 740	2 299	134 635	6 801	1 752	3 040	2 599	1 162	13.1	6.8
2002	136 485	62.7	69 734	60 420	6 332	2 311	134 174	8 378	2 904	3 896	3 228	1 253	16.6	9.1
2003	137 736	62.3	70 415	61 402	5 919	2 275	135 461	8 774	3 378	4 209	3 314	1 251	19.2	10.1
2002														
January	135 715	62.7	69 323	60 019	6 374	2 360	133 359	8 126	2 587	3 790	3 084	1 252	14.6	8.5
February	136 362	62.9	69 490	60 456	6 417	2 373	134 046	8 184	2 623	3 785	3 175	1 224	15.1	8.3
March	136 106	62.8	69 451	60 151	6 503	2 348	133 710	8 278	2 728	3 824	3 170	1 284	15.5	8.4
April	136 096	62.7	69 555	60 189	6 353	2 375	133 782	8 578	2 832	3 905	3 393	1 281	16.2	8.8
May	136 505	62.8	69 955	60 224	6 325	2 270	134 236	8 397	2 948	3 832	3 295	1 270	16.9	9.6
June	136 353	62.7	69 789	60 225	6 339	2 191	134 087	8 384	2 998	3 893	3 224	1 267	16.9	11.1
July	136 478	62.7	69 854	60 299	6 325	2 341	134 094	8 400	2 923	3 861	3 267	1 273	16.7	8.9
August	136 811	62.8	70 004	60 572	6 235	2 146	134 639	8 335	2 872	3 867	3 171	1 297	16.4	8.9
September	137 337	63.0	70 206	60 717	6 414	2 288	135 127	8 269	2 976	3 869	3 160	1 240	17.7	9.5
October	137 079	62.8	69 978	60 704	6 397	2 421	134 666	8 363	3 071	3 943	3 281	1 139	17.8	9.6
November	136 545	62.5	69 612	60 754	6 179	2 296	134 269	8 565	3 105	4 066	3 226	1 272	17.7	9.4
December	136 459	62.4	69 569	60 750	6 141	2 345	134 098	8 698	3 312	4 157	3 306	1 235	18.5	9.6
2003														
January	137 447	62.5	69 940	61 391	6 117	2 301	135 176	8 428	3 175	4 075	3 100	1 254	18.5	9.7
February	137 318	62.4	70 174	61 106	6 039	2 205	135 166	8 581	3 176	4 068	3 253	1 260	18.7	9.5
March	137 300	62.3	70 213	61 219	5 868	2 235	135 054	8 519	3 168	3 995	3 271	1 252	18.1	9.7
April	137 578	62.4	70 290	61 343	5 945	2 162	135 486	8 799	3 318	4 220	3 289	1 290	19.4	10.1
May	137 505	62.3	70 182	61 397	5 926	2 194	135 311	8 957	3 294	4 341	3 302	1 314	19.2	10.1
June	137 673	62.3	70 190	61 610	5 873	2 229	135 348	9 245	3 510	4 485	3 379	1 381	19.6	11.7
July	137 604	62.2	70 269	61 479	5 856	2 217	135 240	9 048	3 559	4 391	3 356	1 301	19.3	10.1
August	137 693	62.2	70 324	61 467	5 902	2 327	135 282	8 929	3 561	4 358	3 369	1 202	19.2	10.0
September	137 644	62.1	70 596	61 191	5 857	2 341	135 401	8 966	3 511	4 309	3 417	1 240	19.6	10.1
October	138 095	62.2	70 726	61 524	5 846	2 410	135 722	8 797	3 478	4 216	3 375	1 205	19.4	10.3
November	138 533	62.3	70 964	61 597	5 972	2 418	136 172	8 653	3 484	4 224	3 320	1 109	20.0	10.4
December	138 479	62.2	71 099	61 521	5 859	2 245	136 180	8 398	3 403	3 945	3 326	1 128	19.6	10.4

[1]Changes in survey design, population estimates, and methodology in 1994 and several other years affect year-to-year comparisons. See Notes and Definitions for more information.
[2]Civilian employment as a percent of the civilian noninstitutional population.
[3]Fifteen weeks and over.
... = Not available.

Table 10-3. Unemployment Rates [1]

(Unemployment as a percent of the civilian labor force in group; seasonally adjusted, except as noted.)

Year and month	All civilian workers	By age and sex			By race		Persons of Hispanic origin	By marital status			By industry of last job [2,3]				
		20 years and over		Both sexes, 16 to 19 years	White	Black		Married men, spouse present	Married women, spouse present	Women who maintain families [2]	Private nonagricultural wage and salary workers				
		Men	Women								Total	Construction	Manufacturing		
													Total	Durable goods	Nondurable goods
1948	3.8	3.2	3.6	9.2	...	...	...	...	...	...	4.5	...	...	...	...
1949	5.9	5.4	5.3	13.4	...	...	...	...	...	...	7.3	...	...	...	...
1950	5.3	4.7	5.1	12.2	...	...	...	...	...	...	6.3	...	...	...	...
1951	3.3	2.5	4.0	8.2	...	...	...	...	...	...	3.9	...	...	...	...
1952	3.0	2.4	3.2	8.5	...	...	...	...	...	...	3.6	...	...	...	...
1953	2.9	2.5	2.9	7.6	...	...	...	...	...	...	3.4	...	...	...	...
1954	5.5	4.9	5.5	12.6	5.0	...	...	...	...	...	6.7	...	...	...	...
1955	4.4	3.8	4.4	11.0	3.9	...	...	2.6	3.7	...	5.1	...	...	...	...
1956	4.1	3.4	4.2	11.1	3.6	...	...	2.3	3.6	...	4.7	...	...	...	...
1957	4.3	3.6	4.1	11.6	3.8	...	...	2.8	4.3	...	4.9	...	...	...	...
1958	6.8	6.2	6.1	15.9	6.1	...	...	5.1	6.5	...	7.9	...	...	...	...
1959	5.5	4.7	5.2	14.6	4.8	...	...	3.6	5.2	...	6.1	...	...	...	...
1960	5.5	4.7	5.1	14.7	5.0	...	...	3.7	5.2	...	6.2	...	...	...	...
1961	6.7	5.7	6.3	16.8	6.0	...	...	4.6	6.4	...	7.5	...	...	...	...
1962	5.5	4.6	5.4	14.7	4.9	...	...	3.6	5.4	...	6.1	...	...	...	...
1963	5.7	4.5	5.4	17.2	5.0	...	...	3.4	5.4	...	6.1	...	...	...	...
1964	5.2	3.9	5.2	16.2	4.6	...	...	2.8	5.1	...	5.4	...	...	...	...
1965	4.5	3.2	4.5	14.8	4.1	...	...	2.4	4.5	...	4.6	...	...	...	...
1966	3.8	2.5	3.8	12.8	3.4	...	...	1.9	3.7	...	3.8	...	...	...	...
1967	3.8	2.3	4.2	12.9	3.4	...	...	1.8	4.5	4.9	3.9	...	...	...	...
1968	3.6	2.2	3.8	12.7	3.2	...	...	1.6	3.9	4.4	3.6	...	...	...	...
1969	3.5	2.1	3.7	12.2	3.1	...	...	1.5	3.9	4.4	3.5	...	...	...	...
1970	4.9	3.5	4.8	15.3	4.5	...	...	2.6	4.9	5.4	5.2	...	...	...	...
1971	5.9	4.4	5.7	16.9	5.4	...	...	3.2	5.7	7.3	6.2	...	...	...	...
1972	5.6	4.0	5.4	16.2	5.1	10.4	...	2.8	5.4	7.2	5.7	...	...	...	...
1973	4.9	3.3	4.9	14.5	4.3	9.4	7.5	2.3	4.7	7.1	4.9	...	...	...	...
1974	5.6	3.8	5.5	16.0	5.0	10.5	8.1	2.7	5.3	7.0	5.7	...	...	...	...
1975	8.5	6.8	8.0	19.9	7.8	14.8	12.2	5.1	7.9	10.0	9.1	...	...	...	...
1976	7.7	5.9	7.4	19.0	7.0	14.0	11.5	4.2	7.1	10.1	7.9	...	...	...	...
1977	7.1	5.2	7.0	17.8	6.2	14.0	10.1	3.6	6.5	9.4	7.1	...	...	...	...
1978	6.1	4.3	6.0	16.4	5.2	12.8	9.1	2.8	5.5	8.5	5.9	...	...	...	...
1979	5.8	4.2	5.7	16.1	5.1	12.3	8.3	2.8	5.1	8.3	5.8	...	...	...	...
1980	7.1	5.9	6.4	17.8	6.3	14.3	10.1	4.2	5.8	9.2	7.4	...	...	...	...
1981	7.6	6.3	6.8	19.6	6.7	15.6	10.4	4.3	6.0	10.4	7.7	...	...	...	...
1982	9.7	8.8	8.3	23.2	8.6	18.9	13.8	6.5	7.4	11.7	10.1	...	...	...	...
1983	9.6	8.9	8.1	22.4	8.4	19.5	13.7	6.5	7.0	12.2	9.9	...	...	...	...
1984	7.5	6.6	6.8	18.9	6.5	15.9	10.7	4.6	5.7	10.3	7.4	...	...	...	...
1985	7.2	6.2	6.6	18.6	6.2	15.1	10.5	4.3	5.6	10.4	7.2	...	...	...	...
1986	7.0	6.1	6.2	18.3	6.0	14.5	10.6	4.4	5.2	9.8	7.0	...	...	...	...
1987	6.2	5.4	5.4	16.9	5.3	13.0	8.8	3.9	4.3	9.2	6.2	...	...	...	...
1988	5.5	4.8	4.9	15.3	4.7	11.7	8.2	3.3	3.9	8.1	5.5	...	...	...	...
1989	5.3	4.5	4.7	15.0	4.5	11.4	8.0	3.0	3.7	8.1	5.3	...	...	...	...
1990	5.6	5.0	4.9	15.5	4.8	11.4	8.2	3.4	3.8	8.3	5.8	...	...	...	...
1991	6.8	6.4	5.7	18.7	6.1	12.5	10.0	4.4	4.5	9.3	7.1	...	...	...	...
1992	7.5	7.1	6.3	20.1	6.6	14.2	11.6	5.1	5.0	10.0	7.8	...	...	...	...
1993	6.9	6.4	5.9	19.0	6.1	13.0	10.8	4.4	4.6	9.7	7.1	...	...	...	...
1994	6.1	5.4	5.4	17.6	5.3	11.5	9.9	3.7	4.1	8.9	6.3	...	...	...	...
1995	5.6	4.8	4.9	17.3	4.9	10.4	9.3	3.3	3.9	8.0	5.8	...	...	...	...
1996	5.4	4.6	4.8	16.7	4.7	10.5	8.9	3.0	3.6	8.2	5.5	...	...	...	...
1997	4.9	4.2	4.4	16.0	4.2	10.0	7.7	2.7	3.1	8.1	5.0	...	...	...	...
1998	4.5	3.7	4.1	14.6	3.9	8.9	7.2	2.4	2.9	7.2	4.6	...	...	...	...
1999	4.2	3.5	3.8	13.9	3.7	8.0	6.4	2.2	2.7	6.4	4.3	...	...	...	...
2000	4.0	3.3	3.6	13.1	3.5	7.6	5.7	2.0	2.7	5.9	4.1	6.2	3.5	3.2	4.0
2001	4.7	4.2	4.1	14.7	4.2	8.6	6.6	2.7	3.1	6.6	5.0	7.1	5.2	5.2	5.2
2002	5.8	5.3	5.1	16.5	5.1	10.2	7.5	3.6	3.7	8.0	6.2	9.2	6.7	6.9	6.2
2003	6.0	5.6	5.1	17.5	5.2	10.8	7.7	3.8	3.7	8.5	6.3	9.3	6.6	6.9	6.1
2003															
January	5.8	5.5	4.8	17.0	5.1	10.5	7.9	3.6	3.3	8.0	7.0	14.0	7.2	7.8	6.1
February	5.9	5.5	5.1	17.3	5.1	10.7	7.7	3.7	3.6	9.0	6.9	14.0	6.7	6.9	6.5
March	5.8	5.4	5.1	17.6	5.1	10.3	7.7	3.8	3.7	8.4	6.6	11.8	6.8	6.7	7.0
April	6.0	5.7	5.1	17.8	5.2	10.8	7.6	3.8	3.7	8.5	6.2	9.3	6.7	7.3	5.8
May	6.1	5.8	5.1	18.1	5.4	10.7	8.1	3.9	3.7	8.3	6.2	8.4	6.5	6.9	5.9
June	6.3	6.0	5.2	19.0	5.5	11.6	8.2	4.3	3.9	8.7	6.6	7.9	7.0	7.3	6.6
July	6.2	5.9	5.2	18.2	5.4	11.1	8.1	3.9	3.9	9.0	6.3	7.5	6.9	7.4	6.0
August	6.1	5.8	5.2	16.9	5.4	10.9	7.8	3.9	3.9	8.4	6.1	7.1	6.7	6.9	6.4
September	6.1	5.8	5.3	17.5	5.3	11.1	7.5	3.8	3.9	8.5	6.1	7.6	6.8	7.3	5.9
October	6.0	5.6	5.2	17.1	5.1	11.4	7.3	3.8	3.8	8.4	5.9	7.4	6.0	6.3	5.4
November	5.9	5.6	5.1	15.7	5.2	10.4	7.4	3.7	3.8	8.3	5.9	7.8	5.9	6.2	5.3
December	5.7	5.3	5.1	16.1	5.0	10.3	6.6	3.3	3.9	8.4	5.7	9.3	5.9	5.9	5.8

[1]Changes in survey design, population estimates, and methodology in 1994 and several other years affect year-to-year comparisons. See Notes and Definitions for more information.
[2]Not seasonally adjusted.
[3]Includes industries not shown separately.
... = Not available.

Table 10-3. Unemployment Rates [1]—Continued

(Unemployment as a percent of the civilian labor force in group; not seasonally adjusted, except as noted.)

Year and month	By industry of last job [3]—Continued						Agriculture and related	Government workers	By occupation					Augmented unemployment rate [4], seasonally adjusted
	Private nonagricultural wage and salary workers—Continued								Management, professional, and related occupations	Sales and office occupations	Natural resources, construction, and maintenance occupations	Production, transportation, and material moving occupations	Service occupations	
	Transportation and utilities	Wholesale and retail trade	Financial activities	Professional and business services	Education and health services	Leisure and hospitality								
1948	...	...	...	...	...	...	...	...	...	...	...	...	...	...
1949	...	...	...	...	...	...	...	...	...	...	...	...	...	...
1950	...	...	...	...	...	...	...	...	...	...	...	...	...	...
1951	...	...	...	...	...	...	...	...	...	...	...	...	...	...
1952	...	...	...	...	...	...	...	...	...	...	...	...	...	...
1953	...	...	...	...	...	...	...	...	...	...	...	...	...	...
1954	...	...	...	...	...	...	...	...	...	...	...	...	...	...
1955	...	...	...	...	...	...	...	...	...	...	...	...	...	...
1956	...	...	...	...	...	...	...	...	...	...	...	...	...	...
1957	...	...	...	...	...	...	...	...	...	...	...	...	...	...
1958	...	...	...	...	...	...	...	...	...	...	...	...	...	...
1959	...	...	...	...	...	...	...	...	...	...	...	...	...	...
1960	...	...	...	...	...	...	...	...	...	...	...	...	...	...
1961	...	...	...	...	...	...	...	...	...	...	...	...	...	...
1962	...	...	...	...	...	...	...	...	...	...	...	...	...	...
1963	...	...	...	...	...	...	...	...	...	...	...	...	...	...
1964	...	...	...	...	...	...	...	...	...	...	...	...	...	...
1965	...	...	...	...	...	...	...	...	...	...	...	...	...	...
1966	...	...	...	...	...	...	...	...	...	...	...	...	...	...
1967	...	...	...	...	...	...	...	...	...	...	...	...	...	...
1968	...	...	...	...	...	...	...	...	...	...	...	...	...	...
1969	...	...	...	...	...	...	...	...	...	...	...	...	...	...
1970	...	...	...	...	...	...	...	...	...	...	...	...	...	...
1971	...	...	...	...	...	...	...	...	...	...	...	...	...	...
1972	...	...	...	...	...	...	...	...	...	...	...	...	...	10.2
1973	...	...	...	...	...	...	...	...	...	...	...	...	...	9.4
1974	...	...	...	...	...	...	...	...	...	...	...	...	...	10.0
1975	...	...	...	...	...	...	...	...	...	...	...	...	...	13.3
1976	...	...	...	...	...	...	...	4.4	...	...	...	...	...	12.5
1977	...	...	...	...	...	...	...	4.2	...	...	...	...	...	12.2
1978	...	...	...	...	...	...	...	4.0	...	...	...	...	...	10.8
1979	...	...	...	...	...	...	...	3.8	...	...	...	...	...	10.5
1980	...	...	...	...	...	...	...	4.1	...	...	...	...	...	11.8
1981	...	...	...	...	...	...	...	4.7	...	...	...	...	...	12.3
1982	...	...	...	...	...	...	...	4.9	...	...	...	...	...	14.8
1983	...	...	...	...	...	...	...	5.3	...	...	...	...	...	14.6
1984	...	...	...	...	...	...	...	4.5	...	...	...	...	...	12.2
1985	...	...	...	...	...	...	...	3.9	...	...	...	...	...	11.7
1986	...	...	...	...	...	...	...	3.6	...	...	...	...	...	11.4
1987	...	...	...	...	...	...	...	3.5	...	...	...	...	...	10.5
1988	...	...	...	...	...	...	...	2.8	...	...	...	...	...	9.5
1989	...	...	...	...	...	...	...	2.8	...	...	...	...	...	9.2
1990	...	...	...	...	...	...	...	2.7	...	...	...	...	...	9.5
1991	...	...	...	...	...	...	...	3.3	...	...	...	...	...	10.9
1992	...	...	...	...	...	...	...	3.6	...	...	...	...	...	11.8
1993	...	...	...	...	...	...	...	3.3	...	...	...	...	...	11.3
1994	...	...	...	...	...	...	...	3.4	...	...	...	...	...	10.4
1995	...	...	...	...	...	...	...	2.9	...	...	...	...	...	9.5
1996	...	...	...	...	...	...	...	2.9	...	...	...	...	...	9.1
1997	...	...	...	...	...	...	...	2.6	...	...	...	...	...	8.3
1998	...	...	...	...	...	...	...	2.3	...	...	...	...	...	7.7
1999	...	...	...	...	...	...	...	2.2	...	...	...	...	...	7.3
2000	3.4	4.3	2.4	4.8	2.5	6.6	9.0	2.1	1.8	3.8	5.3	5.1	5.2	6.9
2001	4.3	4.9	2.9	6.1	2.8	7.5	11.2	2.2	2.3	4.4	6.4	6.4	5.8	7.7
2002	4.9	6.1	3.5	7.9	3.4	8.4	10.1	2.5	3.0	5.6	7.8	7.6	6.6	8.7
2003	5.3	6.0	3.5	8.2	3.6	8.7	10.2	2.8	3.1	5.5	8.1	7.9	7.1	8.9
2003														
January	6.3	6.7	3.6	8.9	3.2	9.3	13.2	2.8	3.2	5.5	11.1	9.0	7.4	8.7
February	5.8	6.1	3.4	8.9	3.2	10.0	14.7	2.4	3.1	5.5	11.0	8.5	7.8	8.7
March	5.9	5.9	4.0	9.1	2.9	8.9	12.9	2.6	2.9	5.3	9.7	8.6	7.9	8.9
April	5.0	6.0	3.6	8.3	3.4	8.5	12.0	2.2	2.9	5.3	8.3	8.0	7.1	8.8
May	4.9	6.2	3.6	8.4	3.5	7.9	10.2	2.4	3.0	5.7	7.5	8.1	6.5	9.1
June	5.5	6.9	4.0	8.5	4.4	8.6	6.9	3.5	3.5	6.3	7.4	8.7	6.9	9.2
July	5.4	6.6	3.1	8.2	4.0	8.4	8.2	3.8	3.7	5.7	7.0	8.5	6.6	9.2
August	4.8	5.6	3.7	7.2	4.3	9.0	10.7	3.7	3.6	5.6	6.8	7.5	6.9	9.1
September	4.7	5.9	3.3	8.0	3.7	8.8	6.2	2.7	3.2	5.9	6.6	6.9	6.7	9.1
October	4.8	5.7	3.3	8.1	3.6	8.3	8.5	2.4	2.9	5.4	6.7	6.8	7.2	9.0
November	5.1	5.4	3.3	7.7	3.8	9.0	10.3	2.7	2.9	5.0	7.2	7.7	7.2	8.7
December	5.0	5.0	3.0	7.6	3.5	8.2	10.9	2.5	2.8	4.9	7.8	7.0	6.7	8.6

[1]Changes in survey design, population estimates, and methodology in 1994 and several other years affect year-to-year comparisons. See Notes and Definitions for more information.
[3]Includes industries not shown separately.
[4]See Notes and Definitions.
. . . = Not available.

Table 10-4. Insured Unemployment

(Averages of weekly data; thousands of persons, except as noted.)

Year and month	State programs (seasonally adjusted)			Federal programs (not seasonally adjusted)					
				Initial claims		Persons claiming benefits			
	Initial claims	Insured unemployment	Insured unemployment rate (percent) [1]	Federal employees	Newly discharged veterans	Federal employees	Newly discharged veterans	Railroad retirement	Extended benefits
1967	226	1 204	...	...	...	...	...	...	...
1968	198	1 096	...	...	...	...	...	...	...
1969	197	1 093	...	...	...	...	...	...	...
1970	292	1 797	...	...	...	...	...	...	...
1971	294	2 145	4.0	...	...	...	...	...	...
1972	263	1 851	3.5	...	...	...	...	...	...
1973	245	1 625	2.8	...	...	...	...	...	...
1974	356	2 258	3.5	...	...	...	...	...	...
1975	474	3 963	6.0	...	...	...	...	...	...
1976	381	2 969	4.5	...	...	...	...	...	...
1977	376	2 657	3.9	...	...	...	...	...	...
1978	343	2 353	3.3	...	...	...	...	...	...
1979	384	2 428	3.0	...	...	...	...	...	...
1980	480	3 317	3.9	...	...	...	...	...	...
1981	451	3 030	3.5	...	...	...	...	...	...
1982	579	4 042	4.6	...	...	...	...	...	...
1983	442	3 384	3.9	...	...	...	...	...	...
1984	372	2 455	2.8	...	...	...	...	...	...
1985	390	2 584	2.9	...	...	...	...	...	...
1986	376	2 627	2.8	2.13	2.52	20.24	17.11	...	...
1987	326	2 293	2.4	2.19	2.57	21.29	17.71	...	9.51
1988	313	2 089	2.1	2.32	2.74	22.91	18.13	13.28	1.17
1989	329	2 172	2.1	2.14	2.31	22.17	15.09	10.37	0.61
1990	387	2 526	2.4	2.45	2.54	23.89	18.43	10.56	2.36
1991	448	3 336	3.1	2.55	2.93	30.50	22.12	10.73	32.16
1992	407	3 215	3.1	2.75	4.95	32.10	60.25	8.77	4.61
1993	342	2 759	2.6	2.55	3.94	32.06	54.90	7.40	7.59
1994	343	2 680	2.5	2.54	3.02	32.21	37.65	6.21	31.09
1995	357	2 583	2.4	4.57	2.51	31.68	29.78	5.48	14.27
1996	351	2 558	2.3	7.33	2.13	29.84	24.30	5.40	5.53
1997	322	2 307	2.0	2.01	1.75	23.58	19.66	4.00	5.35
1998	317	2 216	1.9	1.64	1.41	19.60	15.68	3.19	6.43
1999	299	2 191	1.8	1.48	1.18	16.85	14.25	3.24	3.05
2000	304	2 124	1.7	1.73	1.05	18.60	12.54	3.92	0.58
2001	403	2 974	2.3	1.47	1.15	18.57	13.98	...	0.57
2002	403	3 564	2.8	1.46	1.22	17.54	16.07	...	10.79
2003	399	3 516	2.8	1.56	1.46	18.22	19.68	...	22.30
2001									
January	340	2 395	1.9	2.36	1.21	27.69	13.60	...	0.00
February	368	2 490	2.0	1.38	1.11	25.87	13.77	...	0.00
March	384	2 579	2.0	1.07	1.07	22.32	13.45	...	1.07
April	394	2 686	2.1	1.23	1.02	18.07	12.96	...	2.61
May	393	2 809	2.2	1.10	0.99	15.32	12.75	...	2.39
June	396	2 938	2.3	1.45	1.04	14.53	12.56	...	0.85
July	396	3 022	2.4	1.84	1.25	15.70	12.95	...	0.00
August	397	3 116	2.4	1.23	1.34	16.43	13.92	...	0.00
September	438	3 269	2.6	1.22	1.29	15.28	14.30	...	0.00
October	486	3 549	2.8	1.74	1.33	16.18	15.20	...	0.00
November	450	3 673	2.9	1.52	1.11	17.00	15.51	...	0.00
December	421	3 603	2.8	1.58	1.09	19.16	16.55	...	0.01
2002									
January	408	3 555	2.8	1.81	1.24	20.30	16.81	...	12.96
February	394	3 565	2.8	1.11	1.10	18.77	16.56	...	32.84
March	411	3 598	2.8	0.99	1.03	16.56	15.76	...	26.14
April	426	3 662	2.8	1.26	1.04	15.30	14.66	...	4.02
May	409	3 688	2.9	1.24	0.99	13.49	14.06	...	3.00
June	385	3 614	2.8	1.57	1.05	13.93	13.56	...	1.36
July	385	3 492	2.7	1.78	1.23	16.16	13.84	...	0.52
August	394	3 516	2.7	1.33	1.40	18.75	15.00	...	1.82
September	414	3 570	2.8	1.44	1.44	17.77	16.19	...	7.06
October	413	3 583	2.8	1.69	1.59	18.94	17.70	...	12.03
November	397	3 505	2.7	1.69	1.26	19.23	18.87	...	12.47
December	417	3 510	2.8	1.71	1.29	21.76	20.13	...	15.55
2003									
January	394	3 425	2.7	1.93	1.49	22.74	20.74	...	24.93
February	406	3 460	2.8	1.25	1.27	20.63	20.68	...	17.30
March	422	3 530	2.8	1.06	1.27	18.03	19.70	...	17.63
April	433	3 600	2.9	1.10	1.16	15.32	18.04	...	16.94
May	424	3 677	2.9	1.18	1.08	13.34	16.99	...	16.06
June	419	3 678	2.9	1.68	1.20	13.88	16.58	...	15.38
July	407	3 600	2.9	2.02	1.35	16.61	16.74	...	13.87
August	400	3 594	2.8	1.32	1.66	18.30	17.84	...	20.02
September	400	3 582	2.8	1.66	1.77	18.14	19.50	...	32.18
October	388	3 506	2.8	1.74	1.89	19.51	21.51	...	33.33
November	368	3 397	2.7	1.87	1.56	19.82	23.16	...	30.46
December	362	3 305	2.6	1.94	1.84	22.34	24.70	...	29.52

[1] Insured unemployed as a percent of employment covered by state programs.
... = Not available.

Section 10b: Payroll Employment, Hours, and Earnings

Figure 10-3. Total Nonfarm Payroll Employment, 1946–2003
(ratio scale)

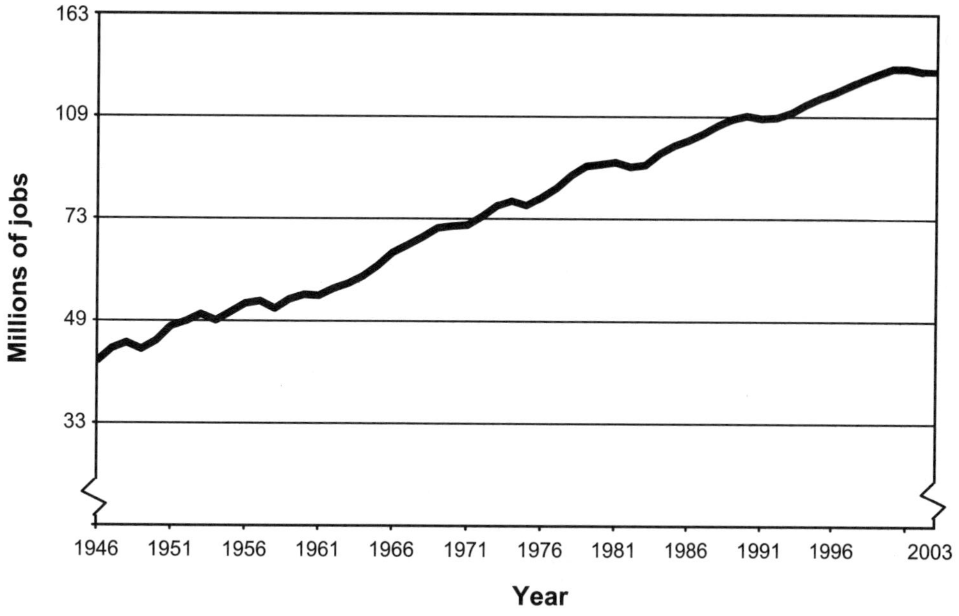

- Over the postwar period, the number of jobs on nonfarm payrolls in the United States increased at an average 2.1 percent annual rate between the 1948 and 2000 cycle peaks. As the graph shows, job growth has been temporarily interrupted by a number of recessions in which employment leveled off or declined. The latest recession is the first in the postwar period to have employment declines for two successive calendar years. (Table 10-5)
- A further indication of the pervasiveness of the recent recession in jobs is the diffusion index, which shows the percent of industries in which employment is stagnant or falling. Diffusion indexes below 50 percent are indicative of recession. In the short recession of 1980 and even in the severe recession of 1982, this index was below 50 percent only for a year or so. In 1990–1991, it remained there for two years, and in the latest recession, the index shows pervasive job declines for three years running, 2001 through 2003. (Table 10-5)

Table 10-5. Nonfarm Payroll Employment by NAICS Supersector

(Thousands; seasonally adjusted, except as noted.)

Year and month	Total	Private							Service-providing				
		Total	Goods-producing						Total	Private			
			Total	Natural resources and mining	Construction	Manufacturing				Total	Trade, transportation, and utilities		
						Total	Durable	Nondurable			Total	Wholesale trade	Retail trade
1946	41 759	36 054	16 122	885	1 724	13 513	7 535	5 978	25 637	19 932	8 945	1 962	4 118
1947	43 945	38 379	17 314	976	2 051	14 287	8 079	6 208	26 631	21 064	9 452	2 116	4 393
1948	44 954	39 213	17 579	1 014	2 241	14 324	8 028	6 296	27 376	21 634	9 716	2 230	4 524
1949	43 843	37 893	16 464	948	2 236	13 281	7 240	6 041	27 379	21 430	9 579	2 227	4 520
1950	45 287	39 167	17 343	924	2 405	14 013	7 809	6 204	27 945	21 824	9 694	2 255	4 580
1951	47 930	41 427	18 703	956	2 678	15 070	8 738	6 332	29 227	22 725	10 089	2 335	4 758
1952	48 909	42 182	18 928	928	2 709	15 291	8 979	6 312	29 981	23 254	10 302	2 408	4 880
1953	50 310	43 552	19 733	902	2 700	16 131	9 690	6 441	30 577	23 820	10 504	2 444	5 012
1954	49 093	42 235	18 515	825	2 688	15 002	8 773	6 229	30 578	23 720	10 357	2 454	4 999
1955	50 744	43 722	19 234	828	2 881	15 524	9 161	6 363	31 510	24 489	10 612	2 505	5 158
1956	52 473	45 087	19 799	859	3 082	15 858	9 435	6 424	32 674	25 288	10 921	2 583	5 315
1957	52 959	45 235	19 669	864	3 007	15 798	9 452	6 346	33 290	25 566	10 942	2 593	5 328
1958	51 426	43 480	18 319	801	2 862	14 656	8 480	6 176	33 107	25 161	10 656	2 551	5 267
1959	53 374	45 182	19 163	789	3 050	15 325	8 988	6 337	34 211	26 018	10 960	2 638	5 453
1960	54 296	45 832	19 182	771	2 973	15 438	9 071	6 367	35 114	26 650	11 147	2 690	5 589
1961	54 105	45 399	18 647	728	2 908	15 011	8 711	6 300	35 458	26 752	11 040	2 681	5 560
1962	55 659	46 655	19 203	709	2 997	15 498	9 099	6 399	36 455	27 451	11 215	2 737	5 672
1963	56 764	47 423	19 385	694	3 060	15 631	9 226	6 405	37 379	28 038	11 367	2 780	5 781
1964	58 391	48 680	19 733	697	3 148	15 888	9 414	6 474	38 658	28 947	11 677	2 856	5 977
1965	60 874	50 683	20 595	694	3 284	16 617	9 973	6 644	40 279	30 089	12 139	2 967	6 262
1966	64 020	53 110	21 740	690	3 371	17 680	10 803	6 878	42 280	31 370	12 611	3 080	6 530
1967	65 931	54 406	21 882	679	3 305	17 897	10 952	6 945	44 049	32 524	12 950	3 158	6 711
1968	68 023	56 050	22 292	671	3 410	18 211	11 137	7 074	45 731	33 759	13 334	3 236	6 977
1969	70 512	58 181	22 893	683	3 637	18 573	11 396	7 177	47 619	35 288	13 853	3 344	7 295
1970	71 006	58 318	22 179	677	3 654	17 848	10 762	7 086	48 827	36 139	14 144	3 418	7 463
1971	71 335	58 323	21 602	658	3 770	17 174	10 229	6 944	49 734	36 721	14 318	3 424	7 657
1972	73 798	60 333	22 299	672	3 957	17 669	10 630	7 039	51 499	38 034	14 788	3 547	8 038
1973	76 912	63 050	23 450	693	4 167	18 589	11 414	7 176	53 462	39 600	15 349	3 688	8 371
1974	78 389	64 086	23 364	755	4 095	18 514	11 432	7 082	55 025	40 721	15 693	3 823	8 536
1975	77 069	62 250	21 318	802	3 608	16 909	10 266	6 643	55 751	40 932	15 606	3 810	8 600
1976	79 502	64 501	22 025	832	3 662	17 531	10 640	6 891	57 477	42 476	16 128	3 920	8 966
1977	82 593	67 334	22 972	865	3 940	18 167	11 132	7 035	59 620	44 362	16 765	4 055	9 359
1978	86 826	71 014	24 156	902	4 322	18 932	11 770	7 162	62 670	46 858	17 658	4 280	9 879
1979	89 932	73 864	24 997	1 008	4 562	19 426	12 220	7 206	64 935	48 868	18 303	4 485	10 180
1980	90 528	74 154	24 263	1 077	4 454	18 733	11 679	7 054	66 265	49 891	18 413	4 557	10 244
1981	91 289	75 109	24 118	1 180	4 304	18 634	11 611	7 023	67 172	50 991	18 604	4 634	10 364
1982	89 677	73 695	22 550	1 163	4 024	17 363	10 610	6 753	67 127	51 145	18 457	4 575	10 372
1983	90 280	74 269	22 110	997	4 065	17 048	10 326	6 722	68 171	52 160	18 668	4 559	10 635
1984	94 530	78 371	23 435	1 014	4 501	17 920	11 050	6 870	71 095	54 936	19 653	4 788	11 223
1985	97 511	80 978	23 585	974	4 793	17 819	11 034	6 784	73 926	57 393	20 379	4 915	11 733
1986	99 474	82 636	23 318	829	4 937	17 552	10 795	6 757	76 156	59 318	20 795	4 935	12 078
1987	102 088	84 932	23 470	771	5 090	17 609	10 767	6 842	78 618	61 462	21 302	5 003	12 419
1988	105 345	87 806	23 909	770	5 233	17 906	10 969	6 938	81 436	63 897	21 974	5 153	12 808
1989	108 014	90 087	24 045	750	5 309	17 985	11 004	6 981	83 969	66 042	22 510	5 284	13 108
1990	109 487	91 072	23 723	765	5 263	17 695	10 736	6 959	85 764	67 349	22 666	5 268	13 182
1991	108 374	89 829	22 588	739	4 780	17 068	10 219	6 849	85 787	67 241	22 281	5 185	12 896
1992	108 726	89 940	22 095	689	4 608	16 799	9 945	6 854	86 631	67 845	22 125	5 110	12 828
1993	110 844	91 855	22 219	666	4 779	16 774	9 900	6 873	88 625	69 636	22 378	5 093	13 021
1994	114 291	95 016	22 774	659	5 095	17 021	10 131	6 890	91 517	72 242	23 128	5 247	13 491
1995	117 298	97 866	23 156	641	5 274	17 241	10 372	6 869	94 142	74 710	23 834	5 433	13 897
1996	119 708	100 169	23 410	637	5 536	17 237	10 485	6 752	96 299	76 759	24 239	5 522	14 143
1997	122 776	103 113	23 886	654	5 813	17 419	10 704	6 716	98 890	79 227	24 700	5 664	14 389
1998	125 930	106 021	24 354	645	6 149	17 560	10 910	6 650	101 576	81 667	25 186	5 795	14 609
1999	128 993	108 686	24 465	598	6 545	17 322	10 830	6 492	104 528	84 221	25 771	5 893	14 970
2000	131 785	110 996	24 649	599	6 787	17 263	10 876	6 388	107 136	86 346	26 225	5 933	15 280
2001	131 826	110 707	23 873	606	6 826	16 441	10 335	6 107	107 952	86 834	25 983	5 773	15 239
2002	130 341	108 828	22 557	583	6 716	15 259	9 483	5 775	107 784	86 271	25 497	5 652	15 025
2003	129 931	108 356	21 817	571	6 722	14 525	8 970	5 555	108 114	86 538	25 275	5 606	14 912
2003													
January	130 190	108 572	22 122	572	6 712	14 838	9 180	5 658	108 068	86 450	25 375	5 627	14 946
February	130 031	108 406	22 005	574	6 661	14 770	9 129	5 641	108 026	86 401	25 352	5 629	14 925
March	129 921	108 305	21 949	571	6 661	14 717	9 092	5 625	107 972	86 356	25 328	5 628	14 912
April	129 901	108 304	21 880	568	6 689	14 623	9 025	5 598	108 021	86 424	25 326	5 626	14 929
May	129 873	108 332	21 859	570	6 715	14 574	8 993	5 581	108 014	86 473	25 302	5 618	14 917
June	129 859	108 292	21 805	573	6 718	14 514	8 958	5 556	108 054	86 487	25 266	5 609	14 908
July	129 814	108 253	21 744	571	6 721	14 452	8 908	5 544	108 070	86 509	25 225	5 597	14 897
August	129 789	108 209	21 712	569	6 739	14 404	8 886	5 518	108 077	86 497	25 225	5 586	14 912
September	129 856	108 317	21 697	568	6 754	14 375	8 867	5 508	108 159	86 620	25 252	5 585	14 927
October	129 944	108 384	21 674	569	6 754	14 351	8 854	5 497	108 270	86 710	25 272	5 582	14 948
November	130 027	108 483	21 686	571	6 771	14 344	8 874	5 470	108 341	86 797	25 261	5 593	14 922
December	130 035	108 491	21 668	570	6 774	14 324	8 868	5 456	108 367	86 823	25 211	5 598	14 876

Table 10-5. Nonfarm Payroll Employment by NAICS Supersector—Continued

(Thousands; seasonally adjusted, except as noted.)

Year and month	Service-providing—Continued						Government							Diffusion index, 6-month span, private industry [2]
	Private—Continued						Total	Federal		State		Local		
	Information	Financial activities	Professional and business services	Education and health services	Leisure and hospitality	Other services		Total	Department of Defense [1]	Total	Education	Total	Education	
1946	1 594	1 619	2 666	1 885	2 485	737	5 705	2 365	746	...	...	...	...	...
1947	1 658	1 674	2 828	2 015	2 650	788	5 567	1 985	499	...	...	...	...	...
1948	1 669	1 742	2 893	2 077	2 726	812	5 742	1 954	511	...	...	...	...	...
1949	1 583	1 768	2 853	2 097	2 729	820	5 950	2 001	531	...	...	...	...	...
1950	1 625	1 825	2 928	2 144	2 769	839	6 120	2 023	533	...	...	...	...	...
1951	1 718	1 890	3 061	2 221	2 877	870	6 502	2 415	797	...	...	...	...	...
1952	1 736	1 964	3 128	2 281	2 950	894	6 727	2 539	868	...	...	...	...	...
1953	1 785	2 036	3 215	2 335	3 030	916	6 758	2 418	818	...	...	...	...	...
1954	1 693	2 118	3 197	2 385	3 034	936	6 858	2 295	744	...	...	...	...	...
1955	1 735	2 212	3 320	2 491	3 140	978	7 021	2 295	744	1 168	308	3 558	1 751	...
1956	1 778	2 299	3 437	2 593	3 242	1 018	7 386	2 318	749	1 249	334	3 819	1 884	...
1957	1 780	2 348	3 504	2 676	3 267	1 050	7 724	2 326	729	1 328	363	4 071	2 026	...
1958	1 674	2 386	3 449	2 695	3 243	1 058	7 946	2 298	695	1 415	389	4 232	2 115	...
1959	1 718	2 454	3 591	2 822	3 365	1 107	8 192	2 342	699	1 484	420	4 366	2 198	...
1960	1 728	2 532	3 694	2 937	3 460	1 152	8 464	2 381	681	1 536	448	4 547	2 314	...
1961	1 693	2 590	3 744	3 030	3 468	1 188	8 706	2 391	683	1 607	474	4 708	2 411	...
1962	1 723	2 656	3 885	3 172	3 557	1 243	9 004	2 455	697	1 669	511	4 881	2 522	...
1963	1 735	2 731	3 990	3 288	3 639	1 288	9 341	2 473	687	1 747	557	5 121	2 674	...
1964	1 766	2 811	4 137	3 438	3 772	1 346	9 711	2 463	676	1 856	609	5 392	2 839	...
1965	1 824	2 878	4 306	3 587	3 951	1 404	10 191	2 495	679	1 996	679	5 700	3 031	...
1966	1 908	2 961	4 517	3 770	4 127	1 475	10 910	2 690	741	2 141	775	6 080	3 297	...
1967	1 955	3 087	4 720	3 986	4 269	1 558	11 525	2 852	802	2 302	873	6 371	3 490	...
1968	1 991	3 234	4 918	4 191	4 453	1 638	11 972	2 871	801	2 442	958	6 660	3 649	...
1969	2 048	3 404	5 156	4 428	4 670	1 731	12 330	2 893	815	2 533	1 042	6 904	3 785	...
1970	2 041	3 532	5 267	4 577	4 789	1 789	12 687	2 865	756	2 664	1 104	7 158	3 912	...
1971	2 009	3 651	5 328	4 675	4 914	1 827	13 012	2 828	731	2 747	1 149	7 437	4 091	...
1972	2 056	3 784	5 523	4 863	5 121	1 900	13 465	2 815	720	2 859	1 188	7 790	4 262	...
1973	2 135	3 920	5 774	5 092	5 341	1 990	13 862	2 794	696	2 923	1 205	8 146	4 433	...
1974	2 160	4 023	5 974	5 322	5 471	2 078	14 303	2 858	698	3 039	1 267	8 407	4 584	...
1975	2 061	4 047	6 034	5 497	5 544	2 144	14 820	2 882	704	3 179	1 323	8 758	4 722	...
1976	2 111	4 155	6 287	5 756	5 794	2 244	15 001	2 863	693	3 273	1 371	8 865	4 786	...
1977	2 185	4 348	6 587	6 052	6 065	2 359	15 258	2 859	676	3 377	1 385	9 023	4 859	79.7
1978	2 287	4 599	6 972	6 427	6 411	2 505	15 812	2 893	661	3 474	1 367	9 446	4 958	76.2
1979	2 375	4 843	7 312	6 767	6 631	2 637	16 068	2 894	649	3 541	1 378	9 633	4 989	57.9
1980	2 361	5 025	7 544	7 072	6 721	2 755	16 375	3 000	645	3 610	1 398	9 765	5 090	37.5
1981	2 382	5 163	7 782	7 357	6 840	2 865	16 180	2 922	655	3 640	1 420	9 619	5 095	58.0
1982	2 317	5 209	7 848	7 515	6 874	2 924	15 982	2 884	690	3 640	1 433	9 458	5 049	36.8
1983	2 253	5 334	8 039	7 766	7 078	3 021	16 011	2 915	699	3 662	1 450	9 434	5 020	78.2
1984	2 398	5 553	8 464	8 193	7 489	3 186	16 159	2 943	716	3 734	1 488	9 482	5 076	72.6
1985	2 437	5 815	8 871	8 657	7 869	3 366	16 533	3 014	738	3 832	1 540	9 687	5 221	57.6
1986	2 445	6 128	9 211	9 061	8 156	3 523	16 838	3 044	736	3 893	1 561	9 901	5 358	57.6
1987	2 507	6 385	9 608	9 515	8 446	3 699	17 156	3 089	736	3 967	1 586	10 100	5 469	69.5
1988	2 585	6 500	10 090	10 063	8 778	3 907	17 540	3 124	719	4 076	1 621	10 339	5 590	66.3
1989	2 622	6 562	10 555	10 616	9 062	4 116	17 927	3 136	735	4 182	1 668	10 609	5 740	53.7
1990	2 688	6 614	10 848	10 984	9 288	4 261	18 415	3 196	722	4 305	1 730	10 914	5 902	43.4
1991	2 677	6 558	10 714	11 506	9 256	4 249	18 545	3 110	702	4 355	1 768	11 081	5 994	45.0
1992	2 641	6 540	10 970	11 891	9 437	4 240	18 787	3 111	702	4 408	1 799	11 267	6 076	62.8
1993	2 668	6 709	11 495	12 303	9 732	4 350	18 989	3 063	670	4 488	1 834	11 438	6 206	70.7
1994	2 738	6 867	12 174	12 807	10 100	4 428	19 275	3 018	657	4 576	1 882	11 682	6 329	80.4
1995	2 843	6 827	12 844	13 289	10 501	4 572	19 432	2 949	627	4 635	1 919	11 849	6 453	68.5
1996	2 940	6 969	13 462	13 683	10 777	4 690	19 539	2 877	597	4 606	1 911	12 056	6 592	77.5
1997	3 084	7 178	14 335	14 087	11 018	4 825	19 664	2 806	588	4 582	1 904	12 276	6 759	79.9
1998	3 218	7 462	15 147	14 446	11 232	4 976	19 909	2 772	550	4 612	1 922	12 525	6 921	69.4
1999	3 419	7 648	15 957	14 798	11 543	5 087	20 307	2 769	525	4 709	1 983	12 829	7 120	68.9
2000	3 631	7 687	16 666	15 109	11 862	5 168	20 790	2 865	510	4 786	2 031	13 139	7 294	59.0
2001	3 629	7 807	16 476	15 645	12 036	5 258	21 118	2 764	504	4 905	2 113	13 449	7 479	32.2
2002	3 395	7 847	15 976	16 199	11 986	5 372	21 513	2 766	499	5 029	2 243	13 718	7 654	34.7
2003	3 198	7 974	15 997	16 577	12 125	5 393	21 575	2 756	496	5 017	2 266	13 802	7 698	40.5
2003														
January	3 258	7 915	15 902	16 432	12 171	5 397	21 618	2 785	500	5 021	2 249	13 812	7 702	33.6
February	3 233	7 933	15 906	16 465	12 116	5 396	21 625	2 787	499	5 028	2 260	13 810	7 702	31.1
March	3 221	7 945	15 871	16 488	12 107	5 396	21 616	2 789	494	5 024	2 259	13 803	7 697	31.7
April	3 214	7 968	15 897	16 538	12 084	5 397	21 597	2 768	489	5 020	2 260	13 809	7 701	31.7
May	3 203	7 987	15 943	16 564	12 078	5 396	21 541	2 769	489	5 013	2 257	13 759	7 657	33.5
June	3 194	7 988	15 967	16 576	12 097	5 399	21 567	2 763	493	4 996	2 248	13 808	7 707	37.8
July	3 188	7 995	16 021	16 568	12 118	5 394	21 561	2 758	497	4 990	2 249	13 813	7 721	36.2
August	3 174	7 996	15 998	16 591	12 117	5 396	21 580	2 750	500	4 997	2 259	13 833	7 742	36.5
September	3 175	8 004	16 051	16 622	12 126	5 390	21 539	2 747	497	5 019	2 279	13 773	7 674	40.5
October	3 166	7 990	16 070	16 678	12 147	5 387	21 560	2 736	496	5 031	2 290	13 793	7 687	39.4
November	3 172	7 985	16 114	16 705	12 178	5 382	21 544	2 723	497	5 023	2 283	13 798	7 685	42.6
December	3 175	7 981	16 159	16 731	12 192	5 374	21 544	2 720	499	5 027	2 286	13 797	7 687	41.7

[1] Not seasonally adjusted.
[2] See Notes and Definitions for explanation. September value used to represent year.
... = Not available.

Table 10-6. Production or Nonsupervisory Workers on Private Nonfarm Payrolls by NAICS Supersector

(Thousands, seasonally adjusted.)

Year and month	Total private	Natural resources and mining	Construction	Manufacturing	Trade, transportation, and utilities			Information	Financial activities	Professional and business services	Education and health services	Leisure and hospitality	Other services
					Total	Wholesale trade	Retail trade						
1947	...	866	1 938	12 453	...	...	...	...	...	...	...	...	...
1948	...	898	2 106	12 383	...	...	...	...	...	...	...	...	...
1949	...	829	2 100	11 355	...	...	...	...	...	...	...	...	...
1950	...	811	2 251	12 032	...	...	...	...	...	...	...	...	...
1951	...	838	2 493	12 808	...	...	...	...	...	...	...	...	...
1952	...	801	2 510	12 797	...	...	...	...	...	...	...	...	...
1953	...	772	2 491	13 437	...	...	...	...	...	...	...	...	...
1954	...	691	2 467	12 300	...	...	...	...	...	...	...	...	...
1955	...	688	2 628	12 735	...	...	...	...	...	...	...	...	...
1956	...	709	2 804	12 869	...	...	...	...	...	...	...	...	...
1957	...	702	2 730	12 640	...	...	...	...	...	...	...	...	...
1958	...	630	2 573	11 532	...	...	...	...	...	...	...	...	...
1959	...	615	2 730	12 089	...	...	...	...	...	...	...	...	...
1960	...	596	2 651	12 074	...	...	...	...	...	...	...	...	...
1961	...	556	2 582	11 612	...	...	...	...	...	...	...	...	...
1962	...	538	2 656	11 986	...	...	...	...	...	...	...	...	...
1963	...	525	2 719	12 051	...	...	...	...	...	...	...	...	...
1964	40 575	526	2 794	12 298	10 303	...	...	1 217	2 390	3 360	3 303	3 278	1 107
1965	42 302	523	2 906	12 905	10 702	...	...	1 268	2 434	3 515	3 443	3 443	1 161
1966	44 292	517	2 977	13 703	11 095	...	...	1 334	2 492	3 715	3 623	3 607	1 230
1967	45 185	501	2 903	13 714	11 369	...	...	1 365	2 585	3 890	3 818	3 734	1 306
1968	46 519	491	2 986	13 908	11 688	...	...	1 394	2 700	4 067	4 008	3 898	1 379
1969	48 246	501	3 177	14 147	12 152	...	...	1 438	2 841	4 252	4 196	4 089	1 452
1970	48 180	496	3 158	13 490	12 388	...	...	1 422	2 922	4 321	4 305	4 185	1 494
1971	48 151	474	3 238	13 034	12 502	...	...	1 392	2 978	4 354	4 372	4 286	1 521
1972	49 971	494	3 425	13 497	12 954	2 920	7 257	1 437	3 066	4 518	4 531	4 467	1 583
1973	52 235	502	3 576	14 227	13 437	3 041	7 551	1 504	3 164	4 748	4 747	4 664	1 666
1974	52 846	550	3 469	14 040	13 700	3 148	7 673	1 516	3 217	4 907	4 941	4 766	1 740
1975	51 010	581	2 990	12 576	13 578	3 121	7 714	1 416	3 227	4 939	5 088	4 821	1 795
1976	52 916	606	2 999	13 127	14 038	3 212	8 048	1 459	3 300	5 153	5 309	5 046	1 880
1977	55 207	636	3 209	13 591	14 579	3 323	8 396	1 514	3 452	5 404	5 561	5 284	1 978
1978	58 188	658	3 544	14 150	15 329	3 509	8 861	1 586	3 645	5 717	5 874	5 588	2 099
1979	60 403	737	3 760	14 458	15 843	3 667	9 113	1 650	3 825	5 993	6 157	5 772	2 209
1980	60 372	785	3 623	13 667	15 907	3 708	9 158	1 626	3 957	6 197	6 442	5 850	2 318
1981	60 960	861	3 469	13 492	16 004	3 753	9 238	1 633	4 052	6 396	6 694	5 944	2 414
1982	59 465	834	3 208	12 315	15 821	3 662	9 254	1 564	4 055	6 421	6 812	5 976	2 458
1983	60 005	698	3 240	12 121	15 999	3 639	9 494	1 502	4 128	6 581	7 032	6 161	2 542
1984	63 316	714	3 614	12 821	16 797	3 821	9 964	1 631	4 289	6 918	7 368	6 491	2 672
1985	65 436	686	3 868	12 648	17 427	3 935	10 399	1 660	4 476	7 258	7 770	6 817	2 827
1986	66 802	577	3 984	12 449	17 769	3 941	10 704	1 663	4 698	7 532	8 107	7 066	2 957
1987	68 700	541	4 088	12 537	18 196	3 989	10 986	1 717	4 861	7 859	8 488	7 310	3 104
1988	71 029	545	4 199	12 765	18 771	4 132	11 306	1 775	4 894	8 256	8 956	7 587	3 280
1989	72 927	526	4 257	12 805	19 230	4 235	11 565	1 807	4 931	8 648	9 432	7 833	3 459
1990	73 684	538	4 115	12 669	19 032	4 198	11 308	1 866	4 973	8 889	9 748	8 299	3 555
1991	72 520	515	3 674	12 164	18 640	4 122	11 008	1 871	4 911	8 748	10 212	8 247	3 539
1992	72 786	478	3 546	12 020	18 506	4 071	10 931	1 871	4 908	8 971	10 555	8 406	3 526
1993	74 591	462	3 704	12 070	18 752	4 072	11 104	1 896	5 057	9 451	10 908	8 667	3 623
1994	77 382	461	3 973	12 361	19 392	4 196	11 502	1 928	5 183	10 078	11 338	8 979	3 689
1995	79 845	458	4 113	12 566	19 984	4 361	11 841	2 007	5 165	10 645	11 765	9 330	3 812
1996	81 773	461	4 325	12 532	20 325	4 423	12 057	2 096	5 279	11 161	12 123	9 565	3 907
1997	84 158	479	4 546	12 673	20 698	4 523	12 274	2 181	5 415	11 896	12 478	9 780	4 013
1998	86 316	473	4 807	12 729	21 059	4 605	12 440	2 217	5 605	12 566	12 791	9 947	4 124
1999	88 430	438	5 105	12 524	21 576	4 673	12 772	2 351	5 728	13 184	13 089	10 216	4 219
2000	90 336	446	5 295	12 428	21 965	4 686	13 040	2 502	5 737	13 790	13 362	10 516	4 296
2001	89 983	457	5 332	11 677	21 709	4 555	12 952	2 530	5 810	13 588	13 846	10 662	4 373
2002	88 393	436	5 196	10 768	21 337	4 474	12 774	2 398	5 872	13 049	14 311	10 576	4 449
2003	87 606	419	5 112	10 200	21 066	4 395	12 649	2 354	5 965	12 923	14 523	10 626	4 419
2003													
January	87 948	422	5 136	10 465	21 161	4 426	12 675	2 364	5 931	12 902	14 468	10 654	4 445
February	87 780	423	5 087	10 406	21 138	4 420	12 659	2 357	5 939	12 898	14 478	10 611	4 443
March	87 546	419	5 083	10 346	21 114	4 419	12 653	2 352	5 947	12 822	14 438	10 597	4 428
April	87 560	417	5 100	10 263	21 113	4 418	12 663	2 350	5 962	12 845	14 498	10 589	4 423
May	87 541	419	5 109	10 233	21 084	4 408	12 654	2 349	5 971	12 869	14 512	10 579	4 416
June	87 533	420	5 110	10 181	21 047	4 393	12 644	2 351	5 975	12 895	14 521	10 609	4 424
July	87 510	419	5 105	10 136	21 019	4 384	12 640	2 353	5 982	12 925	14 524	10 626	4 421
August	87 513	417	5 116	10 104	21 032	4 376	12 658	2 348	5 983	12 921	14 540	10 636	4 416
September	87 581	415	5 129	10 077	21 066	4 378	12 669	2 350	5 991	12 962	14 546	10 634	4 411
October	87 628	419	5 120	10 058	21 073	4 368	12 691	2 350	5 978	12 988	14 584	10 653	4 405
November	87 625	419	5 137	10 048	21 040	4 374	12 652	2 359	5 961	13 002	14 589	10 671	4 399
December	87 617	419	5 146	10 044	20 985	4 377	12 612	2 360	5 959	13 032	14 601	10 682	4 389

... = Not available.

Table 10-7. Average Weekly Hours of Production or Nonsupervisory Workers on Private Nonfarm Payrolls by NAICS Supersector

(Hours per week, seasonally adjusted.)

Year and month	Total private	Natural resources and mining	Construction	Manufacturing		Trade, transportation, and utilities			Information	Financial activities	Professional and business services	Education and health services	Leisure and hospitality	Other services
				Average weekly hours	Overtime hours	Total	Wholesale trade	Retail trade						
1947	...	42.3	38.7	40.5	...	...	...	...	...	...	...	...	...	...
1948	...	41.1	38.6	40.1	...	...	...	...	...	...	...	...	...	...
1949	...	38.2	38.2	39.2	...	...	...	...	...	...	...	...	...	...
1950	...	39.8	37.9	40.6	...	...	...	...	...	...	...	...	...	...
1951	...	40.2	38.6	40.7	...	...	...	...	...	...	...	...	...	...
1952	...	40.5	39.4	40.8	...	...	...	...	...	...	...	...	...	...
1953	...	40.7	38.4	40.6	...	...	...	...	...	...	...	...	...	...
1954	...	40.3	37.7	39.7	...	...	...	...	...	...	...	...	...	...
1955	...	42.3	37.6	40.8	...	...	...	...	...	...	...	...	...	...
1956	...	42.3	38.0	40.5	2.8	...	...	...	...	...	...	...	...	...
1957	...	41.7	37.5	39.9	2.3	...	...	...	...	...	...	...	...	...
1958	...	40.6	37.3	39.2	2.0	...	...	...	...	...	...	...	...	...
1959	...	42.1	37.5	40.3	2.7	...	...	...	...	...	...	...	...	...
1960	...	41.9	37.2	39.8	2.5	...	...	...	...	...	...	...	...	...
1961	...	42.1	37.4	39.9	2.4	...	...	...	...	...	...	...	...	...
1962	...	42.5	37.5	40.5	2.8	...	...	...	...	...	...	...	...	...
1963	...	43.0	37.8	40.6	2.8	...	...	...	...	...	...	...	...	...
1964	38.5	43.4	37.7	40.8	3.1	39.7	...	...	38.2	37.2	37.4	35.5	32.8	36.3
1965	38.6	43.7	37.9	41.2	3.6	39.6	...	...	38.3	37.1	37.3	35.2	32.5	36.1
1966	38.5	44.1	38.1	41.4	3.9	39.1	...	...	38.3	37.2	37.0	34.9	31.9	35.8
1967	37.9	43.9	38.1	40.6	3.3	38.5	...	...	37.6	36.9	36.6	34.5	31.3	35.4
1968	37.7	44.0	37.8	40.7	3.5	38.2	...	...	37.6	36.8	36.3	34.1	30.8	35.0
1969	37.5	44.3	38.4	40.6	3.6	37.9	...	...	37.6	36.9	36.3	34.1	30.4	35.0
1970	37.0	43.9	37.8	39.8	2.9	37.6	...	...	37.2	36.6	35.9	33.8	30.0	34.7
1971	36.8	43.7	37.6	39.9	2.9	37.4	...	...	37.0	36.4	35.5	33.3	29.9	34.2
1972	36.9	44.0	37.0	40.6	3.4	37.4	39.8	35.1	37.3	36.4	35.5	33.3	29.7	34.2
1973	36.9	43.8	37.2	40.7	3.8	37.2	39.6	34.8	37.3	36.4	35.5	33.3	29.4	34.1
1974	36.4	43.7	37.1	40.0	3.2	36.8	39.2	34.3	37.0	36.3	35.3	33.1	29.1	33.9
1975	36.0	43.7	36.9	39.5	2.6	36.4	39.1	34.0	36.6	36.2	35.1	33.0	28.8	33.8
1976	36.1	44.2	37.3	40.1	3.1	36.3	39.1	33.8	36.7	36.2	34.9	32.7	28.5	33.6
1977	35.9	44.7	37.0	40.3	3.4	36.0	39.2	33.3	36.8	36.2	34.7	32.5	28.1	33.4
1978	35.8	44.9	37.3	40.4	3.6	35.6	39.2	32.7	36.8	36.1	34.6	32.3	27.7	33.2
1979	35.6	44.7	37.5	40.2	3.3	35.4	39.2	32.4	36.6	35.9	34.4	32.2	27.4	33.0
1980	35.2	44.9	37.5	39.7	2.8	35.0	38.8	31.9	36.3	36.0	34.3	32.1	27.0	33.0
1981	35.2	45.1	37.4	39.8	2.8	34.9	38.9	31.9	36.3	36.0	34.3	32.1	26.9	33.0
1982	34.7	44.1	37.2	38.9	2.3	34.6	38.7	31.7	35.8	36.0	34.2	32.1	26.8	33.0
1983	34.9	43.9	37.6	40.1	2.9	34.6	38.8	31.6	36.2	35.9	34.4	32.1	26.8	33.0
1984	35.1	44.6	38.2	40.7	3.4	34.7	38.9	31.6	36.6	36.2	34.3	32.0	26.7	32.9
1985	34.9	44.6	38.2	40.5	3.3	34.4	38.8	31.2	36.5	36.1	34.2	31.9	26.4	32.8
1986	34.7	43.6	37.9	40.7	3.4	34.1	38.7	31.0	36.4	36.1	34.3	32.0	26.2	32.9
1987	34.7	43.5	38.2	40.9	3.7	34.1	38.5	31.0	36.5	36.0	34.3	32.0	26.3	32.8
1988	34.6	43.3	38.2	41.0	3.8	33.8	38.5	30.9	36.1	35.6	34.2	32.0	26.3	32.9
1989	34.5	44.1	38.3	40.9	3.8	33.8	38.4	30.7	36.1	35.6	34.2	32.0	26.1	32.9
1990	34.3	45.0	38.3	40.5	3.8	33.7	38.4	30.6	35.8	35.5	34.2	31.9	26.0	32.8
1991	34.1	45.3	38.1	40.4	3.8	33.7	38.4	30.4	35.6	35.5	34.0	31.9	25.6	32.7
1992	34.2	44.6	38.0	40.7	4.0	33.8	38.6	30.7	35.8	35.6	34.0	32.0	25.7	32.6
1993	34.3	44.9	38.4	41.1	4.4	34.1	38.5	30.7	36.0	35.5	34.0	32.0	25.9	32.6
1994	34.5	45.3	38.8	41.7	5.0	34.3	38.8	30.9	36.0	35.5	34.1	32.0	26.0	32.7
1995	34.3	45.3	38.8	41.3	4.7	34.1	38.6	30.8	36.0	35.5	34.0	32.0	25.9	32.6
1996	34.3	46.0	38.9	41.3	4.8	34.1	38.6	30.7	36.4	35.5	34.1	31.9	25.9	32.5
1997	34.5	46.2	38.9	41.7	5.1	34.3	38.8	30.9	36.3	35.7	34.3	32.2	26.0	32.7
1998	34.5	44.9	38.8	41.4	4.8	34.2	38.6	30.9	36.6	36.0	34.3	32.2	26.2	32.6
1999	34.3	44.2	39.0	41.4	4.8	33.9	38.6	30.8	36.7	35.8	34.4	32.1	26.1	32.5
2000	34.3	44.4	39.2	41.3	4.7	33.8	38.8	30.7	36.8	35.9	34.5	32.2	26.1	32.5
2001	34.0	44.6	38.7	40.3	4.0	33.5	38.4	30.7	36.9	35.8	34.2	32.3	25.8	32.3
2002	33.9	43.2	38.4	40.5	4.2	33.6	38.0	30.9	36.5	35.6	34.2	32.4	25.8	32.0
2003	33.7	43.6	38.4	40.4	4.2	33.6	37.8	30.9	36.2	35.5	34.1	32.3	25.6	31.4
2003														
January	33.8	43.4	38.7	40.3	4.3	33.5	37.6	30.9	35.9	35.6	34.3	32.5	25.9	31.8
February	33.7	43.5	37.7	40.4	4.3	33.5	37.7	30.9	36.2	35.6	34.2	32.4	25.6	31.7
March	33.8	44.2	38.7	40.4	4.1	33.6	37.8	30.9	36.3	35.6	34.3	32.3	25.6	31.6
April	33.6	43.3	37.8	40.1	4.0	33.5	37.7	30.9	36.2	35.5	34.0	32.3	25.6	31.4
May	33.7	43.8	38.5	40.2	4.1	33.5	37.9	30.8	36.3	35.6	34.2	32.3	25.7	31.4
June	33.7	43.6	38.4	40.3	4.1	33.5	37.8	30.8	36.3	35.5	34.1	32.3	25.5	31.4
July	33.6	43.3	38.3	40.1	4.1	33.4	37.8	30.7	36.3	35.5	34.1	32.3	25.4	31.3
August	33.6	43.6	38.5	40.2	4.1	33.5	37.9	30.9	36.2	35.5	33.9	32.4	25.5	31.3
September	33.6	43.6	38.4	40.4	4.2	33.5	37.8	30.9	36.1	35.4	33.9	32.3	25.5	31.2
October	33.7	43.7	38.4	40.5	4.3	33.6	38.0	30.9	36.1	35.5	34.0	32.3	25.6	31.3
November	33.8	43.9	38.5	40.8	4.5	33.6	38.0	30.9	36.3	35.5	34.1	32.4	25.7	31.2
December	33.6	43.6	38.1	40.6	4.5	33.5	37.8	30.8	36.2	35.3	33.8	32.4	25.6	31.0

... = Not available.

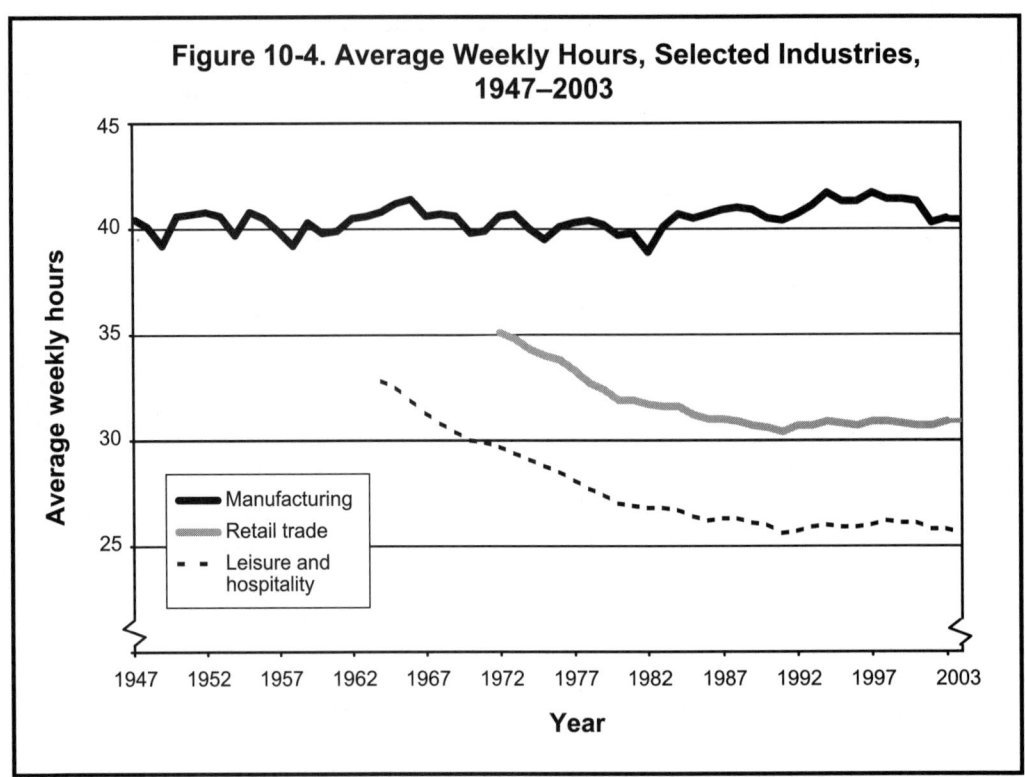

Figure 10-4. Average Weekly Hours, Selected Industries, 1947–2003

- The hours per week worked on the average private nonfarm production or nonsupervisory job have fallen from 38.5 in 1964 to 33.7 in 2003. It should be noted that these are hours per job, not per person. A worker with two half-time jobs enters this average as two workers with 20 hours per week each, not one worker with 40 hours. (Table 10-7)
- The downtrend in the all-industry average reflects increases in the number of part-time jobs and the increasing role of retail trade, leisure and hospitality (restaurants, hotels, and motels), and other service-producing industries where such jobs are frequently found. As the graph above shows, manufacturing—which accounts for a steadily declining share of employment—displays no long-term downtrend in the workweek; if anything, factory workers have on average worked longer hours since the early 1980s. There is also no downtrend for construction or natural resources and mining. But there has been a downtrend in recent decades for retail trade and leisure and hospitality, which already had shorter workweeks and which are accounting for an increasing share of total employment. (Tables 10-5 and 10-7)

Table 10-8. Indexes of Aggregate Weekly Hours of Production or Nonsupervisory Workers on Private Nonfarm Payrolls by NAICS Supersector

(2002 = 100, seasonally adjusted.)

Year and month	Total private	Natural resources and mining	Construction	Manu-facturing	Trade, transportation, and utilities			Information	Financial activities	Profes-sional and business services	Education and health services	Leisure and hospitality	Other services
					Total	Wholesale trade	Retail trade						
1947	...	194.7	37.6	115.7	...	...	...	...	...	...	...	...	...
1948	...	196.0	40.7	114.0	...	...	...	...	...	...	...	...	...
1949	...	168.3	40.2	102.2	...	...	...	...	...	...	...	...	...
1950	...	171.6	42.7	112.0	...	...	...	...	...	...	...	...	...
1951	...	179.1	48.2	119.8	...	...	...	...	...	...	...	...	...
1952	...	172.2	49.5	119.8	...	...	...	...	...	...	...	...	...
1953	...	166.7	47.9	125.3	...	...	...	...	...	...	...	...	...
1954	...	148.1	46.6	112.1	...	...	...	...	...	...	...	...	...
1955	...	154.7	49.5	119.3	...	...	...	...	...	...	...	...	...
1956	...	159.4	53.3	119.7	...	...	...	...	...	...	...	...	...
1957	...	155.5	51.3	115.8	...	...	...	...	...	...	...	...	...
1958	...	135.8	48.0	103.8	...	...	...	...	...	...	...	...	...
1959	...	137.4	51.3	111.9	...	...	...	...	...	...	...	...	...
1960	...	132.8	49.4	110.2	...	...	...	...	...	...	...	...	...
1961	...	124.2	48.4	106.3	...	...	...	...	...	...	...	...	...
1962	...	121.5	49.8	111.3	...	...	...	...	...	...	...	...	...
1963	...	120.0	51.4	112.2	...	...	...	...	...	...	...	...	...
1964	52.2	121.3	52.8	115.1	57.0	...	...	53.0	42.5	28.2	25.3	39.4	28.2
1965	54.6	121.6	55.2	122.0	59.0	...	...	55.5	43.3	29.4	26.2	41.0	29.4
1966	56.9	121.1	56.8	130.1	60.5	...	...	58.3	44.3	30.8	27.3	42.2	30.9
1967	57.2	117.0	55.4	127.8	61.1	...	...	58.6	45.7	31.9	28.4	42.9	32.4
1968	58.5	114.9	56.5	130.1	62.2	...	...	59.9	47.6	33.1	29.5	44.1	33.9
1969	60.5	118.1	61.0	131.9	64.3	...	...	61.7	50.2	34.6	30.9	45.6	35.6
1970	59.5	115.7	59.8	123.3	64.9	...	...	60.4	51.1	34.7	31.3	46.1	36.3
1971	59.1	109.9	61.0	119.2	65.1	...	...	58.7	51.9	34.7	31.4	46.9	36.5
1972	61.6	115.6	63.4	125.7	67.5	68.4	64.4	61.1	53.4	36.0	32.6	48.6	37.9
1973	64.3	117.0	66.7	132.9	69.6	71.0	66.4	64.1	55.1	37.8	34.1	50.3	39.9
1974	64.3	127.7	64.5	128.9	70.2	72.7	66.7	64.0	55.8	38.8	35.3	50.8	41.4
1975	61.3	134.9	55.2	113.9	68.9	71.8	66.4	59.1	55.9	38.9	36.2	50.9	42.6
1976	63.8	142.4	56.0	120.8	70.9	73.9	68.8	61.1	57.1	40.3	37.5	52.8	44.3
1977	66.3	151.1	59.4	125.8	73.1	76.7	70.7	63.5	59.7	42.1	39.0	54.4	46.3
1978	69.5	156.9	66.2	131.2	76.1	81.0	73.4	66.6	63.0	44.3	40.9	56.6	48.8
1979	71.8	175.2	70.6	133.3	78.3	84.6	74.7	69.0	65.8	46.3	42.7	57.9	51.2
1980	71.0	187.2	68.0	124.4	77.6	84.8	74.0	67.4	68.1	47.7	44.6	57.9	53.6
1981	71.6	206.2	64.9	123.1	78.0	86.0	74.5	67.6	69.8	49.2	46.3	58.7	55.8
1982	69.0	195.5	59.7	109.9	76.4	83.4	74.2	64.0	69.8	49.2	47.1	58.7	56.8
1983	70.0	162.8	61.0	111.6	77.2	83.3	76.0	62.1	70.9	50.7	48.8	60.5	58.9
1984	74.3	169.3	69.1	119.6	81.2	87.5	79.8	68.0	74.2	53.2	50.9	63.6	61.7
1985	76.2	162.7	73.9	117.5	83.5	89.9	82.2	69.1	77.3	55.6	53.5	66.1	65.1
1986	77.5	133.5	75.5	116.3	84.5	89.8	83.9	69.1	81.2	57.8	55.9	68.0	68.2
1987	79.7	125.2	78.1	117.8	86.5	90.5	86.3	71.4	83.7	60.3	58.5	70.5	71.5
1988	82.1	125.6	80.4	120.2	88.6	93.6	88.5	73.1	83.4	63.3	61.8	73.0	75.7
1989	84.1	123.2	81.7	120.3	90.5	95.9	90.0	74.4	83.9	66.3	65.2	74.9	79.8
1990	84.4	128.6	78.8	117.7	89.5	94.9	87.5	76.2	84.5	68.1	67.2	78.9	81.8
1991	82.6	123.8	70.1	112.8	87.4	93.3	84.8	76.1	83.3	66.7	70.2	77.3	81.2
1992	83.1	113.3	67.5	112.4	87.3	92.4	85.1	76.5	83.5	68.4	72.9	79.3	80.6
1993	85.5	110.3	71.3	113.9	89.0	92.4	86.3	78.0	85.9	71.9	75.4	82.2	82.8
1994	89.2	111.0	77.3	118.3	92.7	95.8	89.8	79.2	88.0	77.0	78.3	85.6	84.5
1995	91.6	110.2	79.9	119.0	95.1	99.2	92.3	82.5	87.8	81.2	81.2	88.5	87.1
1996	93.8	112.7	84.3	118.8	96.6	100.7	93.7	86.9	89.8	85.2	83.4	90.8	89.1
1997	97.1	117.6	88.6	121.4	98.8	103.4	95.9	90.4	92.6	91.5	86.7	93.4	91.9
1998	99.4	112.8	93.4	121.0	100.3	104.8	97.2	92.6	96.5	96.7	88.9	95.5	94.3
1999	101.5	102.9	99.7	118.9	101.9	106.2	99.5	98.5	98.0	101.7	90.6	97.9	96.3
2000	103.6	105.1	104.0	117.7	103.5	107.1	101.3	104.9	98.5	106.6	92.8	100.6	97.8
2001	102.1	108.3	103.2	108.1	101.5	102.9	100.5	106.6	99.5	104.0	96.6	100.7	99.1
2002	100.0	100.0	100.0	100.0	100.0	100.0	100.0	100.0	100.0	100.0	100.0	100.0	100.0
2003	98.6	97.0	98.2	94.6	98.5	98.0	98.8	97.3	101.4	98.8	101.3	99.7	97.3
2003													
January	99.3	97.3	99.5	96.8	98.8	98.0	99.1	96.8	101.0	99.2	101.4	101.1	99.2
February	98.8	97.8	96.0	96.5	98.7	98.1	98.7	97.4	101.2	98.9	101.2	99.6	98.8
March	98.9	98.4	98.5	95.9	98.9	98.4	99.0	97.4	101.3	98.6	100.6	99.4	98.2
April	98.3	96.0	96.5	94.5	98.6	98.1	99.0	97.1	101.3	97.9	101.0	99.4	97.4
May	98.6	97.5	98.5	94.4	98.5	98.4	98.7	97.3	101.7	98.6	101.1	99.7	97.3
June	98.6	97.3	98.2	94.2	98.3	97.8	98.6	97.4	101.5	98.5	101.2	99.2	97.4
July	98.2	96.4	97.9	93.3	97.9	97.6	98.2	97.5	101.6	98.8	101.2	98.9	97.1
August	98.2	96.6	98.6	93.2	98.2	97.7	99.0	97.0	101.6	98.2	101.6	99.4	97.0
September	98.3	96.2	98.6	93.4	98.4	97.5	99.1	96.8	101.5	98.5	101.4	99.4	96.5
October	98.7	97.3	98.4	93.5	98.7	97.7	99.3	96.8	101.6	99.0	101.6	100.0	96.7
November	99.0	97.7	99.0	94.1	98.6	97.9	99.0	97.7	101.3	99.4	102.0	100.5	96.3
December	98.4	97.1	98.2	93.6	98.0	97.4	98.3	97.5	100.7	98.7	102.1	100.2	95.4

... = Not available.

Table 10-9. Average Hourly Earnings of Production or Nonsupervisory Workers on Private Nonfarm Payrolls by NAICS Supersector

(Dollars, seasonally adjusted.)

Year and month	Total private	Natural resources and mining	Construction	Manufacturing	Trade, transportation, and utilities			Information	Financial activities	Professional and business services	Education and health services	Leisure and hospitality	Other services
					Total	Wholesale trade	Retail trade						
1947	...	1.43	1.12	1.10	...	...	...	...	...	...	...	...	...
1948	...	1.61	1.29	1.20	...	...	...	...	...	...	...	...	...
1949	...	1.67	1.37	1.25	...	...	...	...	...	...	...	...	...
1950	...	1.72	1.44	1.32	...	...	...	...	...	...	...	...	...
1951	...	1.88	1.60	1.45	...	...	...	...	...	...	...	...	...
1952	...	1.95	1.71	1.53	...	...	...	...	...	...	...	...	...
1953	...	2.08	1.86	1.63	...	...	...	...	...	...	...	...	...
1954	...	2.09	1.96	1.66	...	...	...	...	...	...	...	...	...
1955	...	2.15	2.03	1.74	...	...	...	...	...	...	...	...	...
1956	...	2.27	2.15	1.84	...	...	...	...	...	...	...	...	...
1957	...	2.39	2.29	1.93	...	...	...	...	...	...	...	...	...
1958	...	2.42	2.40	1.99	...	...	...	...	...	...	...	...	...
1959	...	2.50	2.51	2.08	...	...	...	...	...	...	...	...	...
1960	...	2.55	2.65	2.15	...	...	...	...	...	...	...	...	...
1961	...	2.59	2.78	2.20	...	...	...	...	...	...	...	...	...
1962	...	2.65	2.89	2.27	...	...	...	...	...	...	...	...	...
1963	...	2.70	2.99	2.34	...	...	...	...	...	...	...	...	...
1964	2.53	2.76	3.08	2.41	2.85	...	...	4.35	2.29	3.17	2.01	1.06	1.14
1965	2.63	2.87	3.23	2.49	2.94	...	...	4.47	2.38	3.28	2.12	1.14	1.25
1966	2.73	3.00	3.41	2.60	3.04	...	...	4.56	2.47	3.39	2.23	1.23	1.37
1967	2.85	3.14	3.63	2.71	3.15	...	...	4.68	2.58	3.51	2.36	1.34	1.49
1968	3.02	3.30	3.92	2.89	3.32	...	...	4.85	2.75	3.65	2.49	1.49	1.62
1969	3.22	3.54	4.30	3.07	3.48	...	...	5.05	2.92	3.84	2.68	1.64	1.81
1970	3.40	3.77	4.74	3.23	3.65	...	...	5.25	3.07	4.04	2.88	1.78	2.01
1971	3.63	3.99	5.17	3.45	3.86	...	...	5.53	3.23	4.26	3.11	1.90	2.24
1972	3.90	4.28	5.55	3.70	4.23	4.58	3.52	5.87	3.37	4.50	3.33	2.03	2.46
1973	4.14	4.59	5.89	3.97	4.45	4.80	3.69	6.17	3.55	4.72	3.54	2.15	2.67
1974	4.43	5.09	6.29	4.31	4.74	5.11	3.92	6.52	3.80	5.01	3.82	2.34	2.95
1975	4.73	5.68	6.78	4.71	5.02	5.45	4.14	6.92	4.08	5.29	4.09	2.52	3.21
1976	5.06	6.19	7.17	5.09	5.31	5.75	4.36	7.37	4.30	5.60	4.39	2.71	3.51
1977	5.44	6.70	7.56	5.55	5.67	6.12	4.65	7.84	4.58	5.95	4.72	2.96	3.84
1978	5.87	7.44	8.11	6.05	6.10	6.61	5.00	8.34	4.93	6.32	5.07	3.25	4.19
1979	6.33	8.20	8.71	6.57	6.55	7.12	5.34	8.86	5.31	6.71	5.44	3.54	4.56
1980	6.84	8.97	9.37	7.15	7.04	7.68	5.71	9.47	5.82	7.22	5.93	3.89	5.05
1981	7.43	9.89	10.24	7.86	7.55	8.28	6.09	10.21	6.34	7.80	6.49	4.26	5.61
1982	7.86	10.64	11.04	8.36	7.91	8.81	6.34	10.76	6.82	8.30	7.00	4.52	6.11
1983	8.19	11.14	11.36	8.70	8.23	9.27	6.60	11.18	7.32	8.70	7.39	4.76	6.51
1984	8.48	11.54	11.56	9.05	8.45	9.61	6.73	11.50	7.65	8.98	7.67	4.87	6.79
1985	8.73	11.87	11.75	9.40	8.60	9.88	6.83	11.81	7.97	9.28	7.98	4.98	7.10
1986	8.92	12.14	11.92	9.59	8.74	10.07	6.93	12.08	8.37	9.55	8.25	5.07	7.38
1987	9.13	12.17	12.15	9.77	8.92	10.32	7.02	12.36	8.73	9.85	8.57	5.17	7.69
1988	9.43	12.45	12.52	10.05	9.15	10.71	7.23	12.63	9.07	10.22	8.96	5.37	8.08
1989	9.80	12.91	12.98	10.35	9.46	11.12	7.46	12.99	9.54	10.69	9.46	5.62	8.58
1990	10.19	13.40	13.42	10.78	9.83	11.58	7.71	13.40	9.99	11.14	10.00	5.88	9.08
1991	10.50	13.82	13.65	11.13	10.08	11.95	7.89	13.90	10.42	11.50	10.49	6.06	9.39
1992	10.76	14.09	13.81	11.40	10.30	12.21	8.12	14.29	10.86	11.78	10.87	6.20	9.66
1993	11.03	14.12	14.04	11.70	10.55	12.57	8.36	14.86	11.36	11.96	11.21	6.32	9.90
1994	11.32	14.41	14.38	12.04	10.80	12.93	8.61	15.32	11.82	12.15	11.50	6.46	10.18
1995	11.64	14.78	14.73	12.34	11.10	13.34	8.85	15.68	12.28	12.53	11.80	6.62	10.51
1996	12.03	15.10	15.11	12.75	11.46	13.80	9.21	16.30	12.71	13.00	12.17	6.82	10.85
1997	12.49	15.57	15.67	13.14	11.90	14.41	9.59	17.14	13.22	13.57	12.56	7.13	11.29
1998	13.00	16.20	16.23	13.45	12.39	15.07	10.05	17.67	13.93	14.27	13.00	7.48	11.79
1999	13.47	16.33	16.80	13.85	12.82	15.62	10.45	18.40	14.47	14.85	13.44	7.76	12.26
2000	14.00	16.55	17.48	14.32	13.31	16.28	10.86	19.07	14.98	15.52	13.95	8.11	12.73
2001	14.53	17.00	18.00	14.76	13.70	16.77	11.29	19.80	15.59	16.33	14.64	8.35	13.27
2002	14.95	17.19	18.52	15.29	14.02	16.98	11.67	20.20	16.17	16.81	15.21	8.58	13.72
2003	15.35	17.58	18.95	15.74	14.34	17.36	11.90	21.01	17.13	17.20	15.64	8.76	13.84
2003													
January	15.18	17.36	18.78	15.58	14.20	17.19	11.83	20.64	16.71	16.98	15.53	8.72	13.94
February	15.27	17.34	18.81	15.62	14.28	17.28	11.86	20.74	16.79	17.17	15.56	8.78	13.98
March	15.27	17.45	18.83	15.63	14.28	17.26	11.85	20.82	16.82	17.17	15.56	8.74	13.89
April	15.25	17.60	18.90	15.64	14.24	17.29	11.81	20.89	16.95	17.20	15.45	8.73	13.78
May	15.31	17.47	18.95	15.68	14.30	17.32	11.87	21.01	17.02	17.21	15.56	8.75	13.82
June	15.34	17.52	18.97	15.72	14.35	17.37	11.91	20.98	17.16	17.16	15.61	8.76	13.82
July	15.40	17.57	18.97	15.73	14.39	17.40	11.94	21.18	17.41	17.20	15.64	8.78	13.82
August	15.41	17.62	19.01	15.79	14.40	17.43	11.95	21.22	17.39	17.20	15.69	8.77	13.82
September	15.41	17.66	19.05	15.84	14.38	17.44	11.94	21.21	17.27	17.19	15.70	8.78	13.81
October	15.43	17.72	19.06	15.83	14.41	17.47	11.95	21.21	17.29	17.25	15.73	8.78	13.80
November	15.46	17.79	19.06	15.89	14.44	17.47	11.97	21.10	17.30	17.29	15.77	8.82	13.81
December	15.45	17.91	19.04	15.93	14.41	17.46	11.95	20.99	17.30	17.25	15.81	8.84	13.80

... = Not available.

Table 10-10. Average Weekly Earnings of Production or Nonsupervisory Workers on Private Nonfarm Payrolls by NAICS Supersector

(Dollars, seasonally adjusted.)

Year and month	Total private	Natural resources and mining	Construction	Manufacturing	Trade, transportation, and utilities			Information	Financial activities	Professional and business services	Education and health services	Leisure and hospitality	Other services
					Total	Wholesale trade	Retail trade						
1947	...	60.49	43.34	44.55	...	...	...	...	...	...	...	...	...
1948	...	66.17	49.79	48.12	...	...	...	...	...	...	...	...	...
1949	...	63.79	52.33	49.00	...	...	...	...	...	...	...	...	...
1950	...	68.46	54.58	53.59	...	...	...	...	...	...	...	...	...
1951	...	75.58	61.76	59.02	...	...	...	...	...	...	...	...	...
1952	...	78.98	67.37	62.42	...	...	...	...	...	...	...	...	...
1953	...	84.66	71.42	66.18	...	...	...	...	...	...	...	...	...
1954	...	84.23	73.89	65.90	...	...	...	...	...	...	...	...	...
1955	...	90.95	76.33	70.99	...	...	...	...	...	...	...	...	...
1956	...	96.02	81.70	74.52	...	...	...	...	...	...	...	...	...
1957	...	99.66	85.88	77.01	...	...	...	...	...	...	...	...	...
1958	...	98.25	89.52	78.01	...	...	...	...	...	...	...	...	...
1959	...	105.25	94.13	83.82	...	...	...	...	...	...	...	...	...
1960	...	106.85	98.58	85.57	...	...	...	...	...	...	...	...	...
1961	...	109.04	103.97	87.78	...	...	...	...	...	...	...	...	...
1962	...	112.63	108.38	91.94	...	...	...	...	...	...	...	...	...
1963	...	116.10	113.02	95.00	...	...	...	...	...	...	...	...	...
1964	97.41	119.78	116.12	98.33	113.15	...	...	166.17	85.19	118.56	71.36	34.77	41.38
1965	101.52	125.42	122.42	102.59	116.42	...	...	171.20	88.30	122.34	74.62	37.05	45.13
1966	105.11	132.30	129.92	107.64	118.86	...	...	174.65	91.88	125.43	77.83	39.24	49.05
1967	108.02	137.85	138.30	110.03	121.28	...	...	175.97	95.20	128.47	81.42	41.94	52.75
1968	113.85	145.20	148.18	117.62	126.82	...	...	182.36	101.20	132.50	84.91	45.89	56.70
1969	120.75	156.82	165.12	124.64	131.89	...	...	189.88	107.75	139.39	91.39	49.86	63.35
1970	125.80	165.50	179.17	128.55	137.24	...	...	195.30	112.36	145.04	97.34	53.40	69.75
1971	133.58	174.36	194.39	137.66	144.36	...	...	204.61	117.57	151.23	103.56	56.81	76.61
1972	143.91	188.32	205.35	150.22	158.20	182.28	123.55	218.95	122.67	159.75	110.89	60.29	84.13
1973	152.77	201.04	219.11	161.58	165.54	190.08	128.41	230.14	129.22	167.56	117.88	63.21	91.05
1974	161.25	222.43	233.36	172.40	174.43	200.31	134.46	241.24	137.94	176.85	126.44	68.09	100.01
1975	170.28	248.22	250.18	186.05	182.73	213.10	140.76	253.27	147.70	185.68	134.97	72.58	108.50
1976	182.67	273.60	267.44	204.11	192.75	224.83	147.37	270.48	155.66	195.44	143.55	77.24	117.94
1977	195.30	299.49	279.72	223.67	204.12	239.90	154.85	288.51	165.80	206.47	153.40	83.18	128.26
1978	210.15	334.06	302.50	244.42	217.16	259.11	163.50	306.91	177.97	218.67	163.76	90.03	139.11
1979	225.35	366.54	326.63	264.11	231.87	279.10	173.02	324.28	190.63	230.82	175.17	97.00	150.48
1980	240.77	402.75	351.38	283.86	246.40	297.98	182.15	343.76	209.52	247.65	190.35	105.03	166.65
1981	261.54	446.04	382.98	312.83	263.50	322.09	194.27	370.62	228.24	267.54	208.33	114.59	185.13
1982	272.74	469.22	410.69	325.20	273.69	340.95	200.98	385.21	245.52	283.86	224.70	121.14	201.63
1983	285.83	489.05	427.14	348.87	284.76	359.68	208.56	404.72	262.79	299.28	237.22	127.57	214.83
1984	297.65	514.68	441.59	368.34	293.22	373.83	212.67	420.90	276.93	308.01	245.44	130.03	223.39
1985	304.68	529.40	448.85	380.70	295.84	383.34	213.10	431.07	287.72	317.38	254.56	131.47	232.88
1986	309.52	529.30	451.77	390.31	298.03	389.71	214.83	439.71	302.16	327.57	264.00	132.83	242.80
1987	316.81	529.40	464.13	399.59	304.17	397.32	217.62	451.14	314.28	337.86	274.24	135.97	252.23
1988	326.28	539.09	478.26	412.05	309.27	412.34	223.41	455.94	322.89	349.52	286.72	141.23	265.83
1989	338.10	569.33	497.13	423.32	319.75	427.01	229.02	468.94	339.62	365.60	302.72	146.68	282.28
1990	349.29	602.54	513.43	436.16	331.55	444.48	235.62	479.50	354.65	380.61	319.27	152.47	297.91
1991	358.06	625.42	520.41	449.73	339.19	459.27	240.15	495.20	369.57	391.09	334.55	155.16	306.91
1992	367.83	629.02	525.13	464.43	348.68	470.51	249.63	512.01	386.01	400.64	348.29	159.54	315.08
1993	378.40	634.77	539.81	480.80	359.33	484.46	256.89	535.25	403.02	406.20	359.08	163.45	322.69
1994	390.73	653.14	558.53	502.12	370.38	501.17	265.77	551.28	419.20	414.16	368.14	168.00	332.44
1995	399.53	670.32	571.57	509.26	378.79	515.14	272.56	564.98	436.12	426.44	377.73	171.43	342.36
1996	412.74	695.07	588.48	526.55	390.64	533.29	282.76	592.68	451.49	442.81	388.27	176.48	352.62
1997	431.25	720.11	609.48	548.22	407.57	559.39	295.97	622.40	472.37	465.51	404.65	185.81	368.63
1998	448.04	727.28	629.75	557.12	423.30	582.21	310.34	646.52	500.95	490.00	418.82	195.82	384.25
1999	462.49	721.74	655.11	573.17	434.31	602.77	321.63	675.32	517.57	510.99	431.35	202.87	398.77
2000	480.41	734.92	685.78	590.65	449.88	631.40	333.38	700.89	537.37	535.07	449.29	211.79	413.41
2001	493.20	757.92	695.89	595.19	459.53	643.45	346.16	731.11	558.02	557.84	473.39	215.19	428.64
2002	506.07	741.97	711.82	618.75	471.27	644.38	360.81	738,17	575.51	574.66	492.74	221.26	439.76
2003	517.36	766.83	727.11	636.07	481.10	657.12	367.28	761.13	608.87	586.68	505.76	224.35	434.49
2003													
January	513.08	753.42	726.79	627.87	475.70	646.34	365.55	740.98	594.88	582.41	504.73	225.85	443.29
February	514.60	754.29	709.14	631.05	478.38	651.46	365.29	750.79	597.72	587.21	504.14	224.77	443.17
March	516.13	771.29	728.72	631.45	479.81	652.43	366.17	755.77	598.79	588.93	502.59	223.74	438.92
April	512.40	762.08	714.42	627.16	477.04	651.83	364.93	756.22	601.73	584.80	499.04	223.49	432.69
May	515.95	765.19	729.58	630.34	479.05	656.43	365.60	762.66	605.91	588.58	502.59	224.88	433.95
June	516.96	763.87	728.45	633.52	480.73	656.59	366.83	761.57	609.18	585.16	504.20	223.38	433.95
July	517.44	760.78	726.55	630.77	480.63	657.72	366.56	768.83	618.06	586.52	505.17	223.01	432.57
August	517.78	768.23	731.89	634.76	482.40	660.60	369.26	768.16	617.35	583.08	508.36	223.64	432.57
September	517.78	769.98	731.52	639.94	481.73	659.23	368.95	765.68	611.36	582.74	507.11	223.89	430.87
October	519.99	774.36	731.90	641.12	484.18	663.86	369.26	765.68	613.80	586.50	508.08	224.77	431.94
November	522.55	780.98	733.81	648.31	485.18	663.86	369.87	765.93	614.15	589.59	510.95	226.67	430.87
December	519.12	780.88	725.42	646.76	482.74	659.99	368.06	759.84	610.69	583.05	512.24	226.30	427.80

... = Not available.

NOTES AND DEFINITIONS

General note on employment data

This chapter includes two different data sets measuring employment. Both are compiled and published by the Bureau of Labor Statistics (BLS), but the two sets differ in their sources and other characteristics. Users should be aware of these differences and consequent differences in the uses and interpretations of data from the two systems. These differences are discussed below and also in the "Special Notes" and the article by BLS entitled "Employment From the BLS Household and Payroll Surveys: Summary of Recent Trends," at the front of the book.

One set of employment estimates comes from a large sample survey of U.S. households, the Current Population Survey. The numbers in the sample are blown up to match the latest estimates of the total U.S. population. In their scope (that is, the universe that they are planned to measure), these are the most comprehensive estimates. Their total is of all civilian workers, including farm, household, self-employed, and unpaid family workers that are excluded from the other set of estimates.

However, CPS data are characterized by periodic discontinuities when new benchmarks for Census measures of the total population are introduced. These updates are made in one month, usually January, and the official data for previous months are *not* modified to provide a smooth transition. Therefore, shorter-term comparisons, for a year or two or for a business cycle phase, will be misleading if such a discontinuity is included in the period. Currently, this will be the case for data for January 2003 and following months, which should not be directly compared with the data for 2002 and earlier years presented in this volume; for data for January 2004 and following months, not comparable with the 2003 data in this volume; and also for a break between 1999 and 2000.

It should also be noted that the CPS is a count of persons employed, not of jobs. A person appears in these data only once no matter how many jobs he or she may hold.

The CPS employment estimates provide the best information on the breakdown of employment by demographic characteristics (age, race, and Hispanic origin, for example) and by occupation. Few of these breakdowns are shown in *Business Statistics*, but many of them can be found in Bernan's *Handbook of U.S. Labor Statistics*.

The second set of employment estimates—the payroll survey—comes from a large survey of employers. It is benchmarked annually to a survey of all employers. Benchmark data are introduced with a smooth adjustment back to the previous benchmark, thus preserving the continuity of the series and making it more appropriate for measurement of employment change over the business cycle or other short periods. The scope of the survey is wage and salary workers on nonfarm payrolls, and it is a count of jobs: a person with more than one job is counted as employed in each job.

The payroll survey provides the most reliable and detailed information on the breakdown of employment by industry—for example, the data shown in Table 16-1.

These and other conceptual and technical differences between the two sets of estimates are described in more detail in the Notes and Definitions below.

TABLES 10-1 THROUGH 10-3 AND 20-3 LABOR FORCE, EMPLOYMENT, AND UNEMPLOYMENT

SOURCE: U.S. DEPARTMENT OF LABOR, BUREAU OF LABOR STATISTICS (BLS)

The labor force, employment, and unemployment data are derived from the Current Population Survey (CPS), a sample survey of households conducted each month by the Bureau of the Census for the Bureau of Labor Statistics. The data pertain to the U.S. civilian noninstitutional population 16 years of age and over.

Due to changes in questionnaire design and survey methodology, data for 1994 and subsequent years are not fully comparable with data for 1993 and earlier years. In addition, discontinuities in the reported numbers of persons in the population, employment, unemployment, and labor force are introduced whenever periodic updates are made to U.S. population estimates. Population controls based on Census 2000 have been introduced beginning with the data for January 2000, which therefore are not comparable with data for December 1999 and earlier. Data for 1990 through 1999 incorporate 1990 census-based population controls and are not comparable with the years preceding. An additional large population adjustment was introduced in January 2003, and yet another in January 2004, making the data from that time forward not comparable with the 2003 data shown in this volume. Other discontinuities have been introduced in various earlier years, usually with January data. See "Notes on the Data" below for additional information.

For the most part, these population adjustments distort comparisons involving the *numbers of persons* in the population, labor force, and employment. They generally have negligible effects on the *percentages* that comprise the most important features of the CPS, that is, the unemployment rates, the labor force participation rates, and the employment/population ratios.

Beginning with the data for January 2000, data classified by industry and occupation use the 2002 NAICS (see Chapter 14) and the 2000 Standard Occupational Classification System. This creates breaks in the time series between December 1999 and January 2000 for occupational and industry data at all levels of aggregation. For this reason, nearly all of the unemployment rates by industry and occupation shown in Table 10-3 are shown only from 2000 forward, and are not seasonally adjusted (since not enough years of data have passed to provide reliable seasonal factors).

In January 2003 changes were introduced that affected classification by race and Hispanic origin. (It is very important to note that Hispanic origin is not a racial category and Hispanics may be of any race.) These changes caused discontinuities in the data between December 2002 and January 2003.

- Individuals in the sample are now asked whether they are of Hispanic ethnicity *before* being asked about their race. Prior to 2003, individuals were asked their ethnic origin *after* they were asked about their race. Furthermore, they are now asked directly if they are Spanish, Hispanic, or Latino. Previously, they were identified based on their or their ancestors' country of origin.

- Individuals in the sample are now allowed to choose more than one race category. Before 2003, they were required to select a single primary race. This change had no impact on the overall civilian noninstitutional population and labor force but did reduce the population and labor force levels of whites and of blacks beginning in January 2003, since individuals who reported more than one race are now excluded from those groups.

BLS estimates, based on a special survey, that these changes reduced the population and labor force levels for whites by about 950,000 and 730,000, respectively, and for blacks by about 320,000 and 240,000, respectively, while having little or no impact on their unemployment rates. The changes did not affect the size of the Hispanic population or labor force, but did cause an increase of about half a percentage point in their unemployment rate.

Definitions

The *civilian noninstitutional population* comprises all civilians 16 years of age and older who are not inmates of penal or mental institutions, sanitariums, or homes for the aged, infirm, or needy.

Civilian employment includes those civilians who (1) worked for pay or profit at any time during the week that includes the 12th day of the month (the survey week) or who worked unpaid for 15 hours or more in a family-operated enterprise or (2) were temporarily absent from regular jobs because of vacation, illness, industrial dispute, bad weather, or similar reasons. Each employed person is counted only once; those who hold more than one job are counted in the job at which they worked the greatest number of hours during the survey week. *Unemployed persons* are all civilians who were not employed (according to the above definition) during the survey week, but were available for work, except for temporary illness, and had made specific efforts to find employment sometime during the prior four weeks. Persons who did not look for work because they were on layoff are also counted as unemployed.

The *civilian labor force* comprises all civilians classified as employed or unemployed.

Civilians in the noninstitutional population, 16 years of age and over, who are not classified as employed or unemployed are defined as "not in the labor force." This group includes those engaged in own-home housework, in school, unable to work because of long-term illness, retired, too old, seasonal workers for whom the survey week fell in an "off" season (not reported as unemployed), persons who became discouraged and gave up the search for work, and the voluntarily idle. Also included are those doing only incidental work (less than 15 hours) in a family business during the survey week.

Not in the labor force, want a job consists of persons who are not employed; are not counted as unemployed under the criteria given above; but who did want a job at the time of the survey.

The civilian *labor force participation rate* represents the percent of the civilian noninstitutional population (age 16 and over) that is in the civilian labor force.

The *employment to population ratio* represents the percent of the civilian noninstitutional population (age 16 and over) that is employed.

The *long-term unemployed* are persons currently unemployed (searching or on layoff) who have been unemployed for 15 consecutive weeks or longer. If a person ceases to look for work for two weeks or more, or is temporarily employed, the continuity of long-term unemployment is broken. If he or she starts searching for work or is laid off again, the monthly CPS will record the length of his or her unemployment as the time since the search was recommenced or since the latest layoff.

Median and average weeks unemployed are summary measures of the length of time that persons classified as unemployed have been looking for work. For persons on layoff, the duration represents the number of full weeks they have been on layoff. Mean number of weeks is the arithmetic average computed by aggregating all the weeks of unemployment experienced by all unemployed persons (during their current spell of unemployment) and dividing by the number of unemployed. Median number of weeks unemployed is the number of weeks of unemployment experienced by the person at the midpoint of the distribution of all unemployed persons, ranked by duration of unemployment.

The civilian *unemployment rate* is the number of unemployed as a percent of the civilian labor force. The unemployment rates for groups within the civilian population (such as, for example, males 20 years and over) are the number of unemployed in a group as a percent of the labor force in that group. The unemployment rates by industry and occupation refer to experienced wage and salary workers and are based on industry or occupation of the last job held, according to the NAICS or the 2000 Standard Occupational System.

The *augmented unemployment rate* is a broader measure of potential labor availability used by the Federal Reserve Board, based on BLS data. The numbers shown here, as percentages, are calculated by the editors of *Business Statistics* using the Federal Reserve definition: the numerator, augmented unemployment, is the number of unemployed plus those who are not in the labor force and want a job; the denominator, the augmented labor force, is the number in the civilian labor force plus the number of those who are not in the labor force and want a job.

Notes on the data

The CPS data are collected monthly by trained interviewers from sample households selected to represent the U.S. population 16 years of age and older. Sample size was about 60,000 households from mid-1989 to mid-1995 but was reduced in two stages to about 50,000 households beginning in January 1996, establishing the level maintained from 1996 through 2000. Beginning with the data for July 2001, the sample size has been increased back to 60,000 households, as part of a plan to meet the requirements of the State Children's Health Insurance Program legislation. The data collected are based on the activity or status reported for the calendar week, Sunday through Saturday, that includes the 12th day of the month. Households are interviewed on a rotating basis so that three-fourths of the sample is the same for any two consecutive months and one-half is common with the same month a year earlier.

Data relating to 1994 and subsequent years are not strictly comparable with data for 1993 and earlier years because of the introduction of a major redesign of the survey questionnaire and collection methodology. The redesign includes new and revised questions for the classification of individuals as employed or unemployed, the collection of new data on multiple job holding, a change in the definition of discouraged workers, and the implementation of more completely automated data collection.

The 1994 redesign of the CPS was the most extensive in many years. However, there are other significant periods of year-to-year noncomparability in the labor force data, which typically result from the introduction of new decennial census data into the CPS estimation procedures, expansions of the sample, and other improvements made to increase the reliability of the estimates. Each change introduces a discontinuity, usually between December of the previous year and January of the newly altered year. The discontinuities are usually minor or negligible with respect to figures expressed as percents (for example, unemployment rate or labor force participation rate), but can be significant with respect to levels (for example, labor force and employment in thousands of persons). A list of the major discontinuities follows. They occur in January unless otherwise indicated.

- 1953: 1950 census data introduced.
- 1960: Alaska and Hawaii included.
- 1962: 1960 census data introduced.
- 1972: 1970 census data introduced.
- March 1973: further 1970 census data introduced, affecting racial groups.
- July 1975: adjustment for refugee inflow.
- 1978: sample expansion and revised estimation procedures.
- 1982: change in estimation procedures.
- 1986, with revisions carried back to 1980: adjustment for better estimates of immigration.
- 1994: 1990 census data introduced and carried back to 1990.
- 1997: new estimates of immigration and emigration.
- 1998: new population estimates and estimation procedures.
- 1999: new information on immigration.
- 2000: Census 2000 data introduced, using the 2002 NAICS and the 2000 Standard Occupational Classification System.
- 2003: Further population estimates introduced (based on an annual population update and therefore not carried back to 2000).
- 2004: Population controls updated to reflect revised migration estimates.

For further information on any of these changes, including the magnitude of the discontinuity introduced, see the BLS publication *Employment and Earnings*, February 2004.

Nonagricultural employment estimates from the CPS differ in level and trend from estimates compiled from establishment payrolls and shown in Table 10-5. The differences are attributable in part to differences in definitions and coverage and in part to differences in sample design, collection methodology, and the sampling variability inherent in the surveys.

- The CPS data cover the total farm and nonfarm economy and include domestics and other private household workers, self-employed persons, and unpaid family workers who worked 15 hours or more

in the survey week in family-operated enterprises. The payroll or establishment survey, on the other hand, covers only employees on payrolls of nonfarm establishments.
- Persons holding more than one job during the survey week are counted once in the household survey, but multiple jobholders are counted each time (that is, on each payroll) in the establishment survey.
- Persons with a job but not at work (that is, absent because of bad weather, work stoppages, personal reasons, and so forth) are included in the household survey but are excluded from the payroll survey if on leave without pay for the entire payroll period.

The monthly labor force, employment, and unemployment data are seasonally adjusted by the X-12-ARIMA method. All seasonally adjusted civilian labor force and unemployment rate statistics, as well as the major employment and unemployment estimates, are computed by aggregating independently adjusted series. For example, the seasonally adjusted level of total unemployment is the sum of the seasonally adjusted levels of unemployment for the four sex-age groups (men and women 16 to 19, and men and women 20 years and over). Seasonally adjusted employment is the sum of the seasonally adjusted levels of employment for the same four groups. The seasonally adjusted civilian labor force is the sum of all eight components. Finally, the seasonally adjusted civilian worker unemployment rate is calculated by taking total seasonally adjusted unemployment as a percent of the total seasonally adjusted civilian labor force. Seasonal adjustment factors are revised at the end of each year to reflect recent experience, and the revisions affect the preceding four years as well. See *Employment and Earnings*, February 2004, for further information.

Data availability

Data for each month usually are released on the first Friday of the following month in a press release that also contains data from the establishment survey (Tables 10-5 through 10-10). The press release and data are available on the BLS Internet site, <http://www.bls.gov>. Data are subsequently published in the BLS monthly periodical *Employment and Earnings*, which also contains detailed explanatory notes. Selected data are published each month in the *Monthly Labor Review*, which also contains frequent articles analyzing labor force, employment, and unemployment developments.

Monthly and annual data beginning with 1948 are available. Historical unadjusted data are published in *Labor Force Statistics Derived from the Current Population Survey*, BLS Bulletin 2307. Historical seasonally adjusted data are available from BLS upon request. Complete historical data are available on the BLS Internet site at <http://www.bls.gov>.

Seasonal adjustment factors are revised for the five latest years each year, with the release of December data in early January. New population controls are introduced with the release of January data in early February.

References

Historical background on the CPS, as well as a description of the 1994 redesign, are found in three articles in the September 1993 *Monthly Labor Review*: "Why Is It Necessary to Change"; "Redesigning the Questionnaire"; and "Evaluating Changes in the Estimates." The redesign also is described in the February 1994 issue of *Employment and Earnings*. See also Chapter 1, "Labor Force Data Derived from the Current Population Survey," *BLS Handbook of Methods*, Bulletin 2490 (April 1997).

**TABLE 10-4
INSURED UNEMPLOYMENT**

SOURCE: U.S. DEPARTMENT OF LABOR, EMPLOYMENT AND TRAINING ADMINISTRATION

State programs of unemployment insurance cover operations of regular programs under state unemployment insurance laws. In 1976, the law was amended to extend coverage (effective January 1, 1978) to include virtually all state and local government employees plus many agricultural and domestic workers.

The federal civilian employees unemployment insurance program (UCFE) provides unemployment insurance protection to civilian employees of the federal government or of wholly or partially owned instrumentalities, with the following exceptions: elective officers in the executive and legislative branches of government, certain foreign service personnel, temporary emergency workers, and other small groups.

Unemployment compensation for ex-service members (UCX) provides unemployment insurance protection to veterans under the law of the state in which the claim for compensation is filed.

An *initial claim* is the first claim in a benefit year filed by a worker after losing his job, or the first claim filed at the beginning of a subsequent period of unemployment in the same benefit year. The initial claim establishes the starting date for any insured unemployment that may result if the claimant is unemployed for one week or longer. Transitional claims (filed by persons as they start a new benefit year in a continuing spell of unemployment) are excluded; therefore, the data more closely represent instances of new unemployment.

Monthly averages in this book are averages, calculated by the editors, of the weekly data published by the

Employment and Training Administration. Annual data are averages of the monthly data.

Data availability

Data are published in weekly press releases from the Employment and Training Administration. These releases are available on their Internet site at <http://www.doleta.gov>. Also, historical data on weekly claims are available at the Department of Labor's Information Technology Support Center at <http://www.itsc.state.md.us>.

TABLES 10-5, 10-6, 16-1, 16-2, AND 20-4 NONFARM PAYROLL EMPLOYMENT

SOURCE: U.S. DEPARTMENT OF LABOR, BUREAU OF LABOR STATISTICS (BLS)

These nonfarm employment data, as well as the hours and earnings data in Tables 10-7 through 10-10, 16-3 through 16-7, and 20-4, are compiled from payroll records. Information is reported monthly on a voluntary basis to the BLS and its cooperating state agencies by a large sample of establishments representing all industries except farming.

The survey, originally based on a stratified quota sample, has been replaced on a phased-in basis by a stratified probability sample. The new sampling procedure went into effect for wholesale trade in June 2000; for mining, construction, and manufacturing in June 2001; and for retail trade, transportation and public utilities, finance, insurance, and real estate in June 2002. The phase-in was completed in June 2003 when it was extended to the service industries. The phase-in schedule was slightly different for the state and area series.

The sample has always been very large. Currently, it includes about 160,000 businesses and government agencies covering approximately 400,000 individual worksites, accounting for about one-third of total benchmark employment of payroll workers.

These data, formally known as the Current Employment Statistics (CES) survey, often are referred to as the "establishment data" or the "payroll data" and are also known as the BLS-790 survey. The data by industry conform to the definitions in the new North American Industry Classification System (NAICS) beginning in 2003. BLS has reconstructed historical time series to conform with NAICS, and all published series have a NAICS-based history extending back to at least January 1990. For total nonfarm and other high-level aggregates, NAICS history extends back to January 1939. For more detailed series, the starting date for NAICS data varies depending on the scope of the definitional changes between the old Standard Industrial Classification (SIC) and NAICS.

Definitions

An *establishment* is an economic unit that produces goods or services (such as a factory or store) at a single location and is engaged in one type of economic activity. *Employment* comprises all persons who received pay (including holiday and sick pay) for any part of the payroll period including the 12th day of the month. Included are all full-time and part-time workers in nonfarm establishments. Persons holding more than one job are counted in each establishment that reports them. Not covered are proprietors, the self-employed, unpaid volunteer or family workers, farm workers, domestic workers in households, and military personnel; salaried officers of corporations are included.

Persons on an establishment payroll who are on paid sick leave (when pay is received directly from the employer), on paid holiday or vacation, or who work during a portion of the pay period even though they are unemployed or on strike during the rest of the period are counted as employed. Not counted as employed are persons who are laid off, on leave without pay, or on strike for the entire period, or who are hired but have not been paid during the period.

Intermittent workers are counted if they performed any service during the month. BLS considers regular full-time teachers (private and governmental) to be employed during the summer vacation period whether or not they are specifically paid in those months.

The *government* division includes federal, state, and local activities such as legislative, executive, and judicial functions, as well as the Postal Service and all government-owned and government-operated business enterprises, establishments, and institutions (arsenals, navy yards, hospitals, state-owned utilities, and so forth), and government force account construction. The definition and measurement of federal government employment has been changed somewhat. The previous national series was an end-of-month federal employee count produced by the Office of Personnel Management that excluded some workers, mostly employees who work in Department of Defense-owned establishments such as military base commissaries. The national series now includes these workers. Also, employment is now estimated from a sample of federal establishments, is benchmarked annually to counts from unemployment insurance tax records, and reflects employee counts as of the pay period including the 12th of the month, consistent with other CES industry series. As before, however, the CES excludes the military and employees of the Central Intelligence Agency, the National Security Agency, and the Defense Intelligence Agency.

Nonfarm employment in these series differs from the measures in the household survey (Tables 10-1 and 10-2) in that, among other factors, it excludes domestics and other private household workers, self-employed persons, and unpaid family workers. Persons holding more than one job during the survey week are counted once in the household survey, but multiple jobholders are counted each time (that is, on each payroll) in the establishment survey. Persons with a job but not at work (that is, absent because of bad weather, work stoppages, personal reasons, and so on) are included in the household survey but are excluded from the payroll survey if on leave without pay for the entire payroll period. Finally, there is no age limit in the establishment survey, whereas the household survey is limited to persons 16 years and older.

The monthly *diffusion index of employment change*, currently based on 278 private nonfarm industries, represents the percent of those industries in which the seasonally adjusted level of employment in that month was higher than six months earlier, plus one-half of the percent of industries with unchanged employment. For example, the diffusion index reported for September represents the change from March to September. *Business Statistics* uses the September value to represent the year, since it spans the year's midpoint. Diffusion indexes measure the dispersion of economic gains and losses, with values below 50 percent associated with recessions.

Production or nonsupervisory workers. These data are collected for the private nonfarm sector and cover all production and related workers in mining and manufacturing; construction workers in construction; and nonsupervisory workers in transportation, communication, electric, gas, and sanitary services; wholesale and retail trade; finance, insurance, and real estate; and services. These groups account for about four-fifths of the total employment on private nonagricultural payrolls.

Production and related workers include working supervisors and all nonsupervisory workers (including group leaders and trainees) engaged in fabricating, processing, assembling, inspecting, receiving, storing, handling, packing, warehousing, shipping, trucking, hauling, maintenance, repair, janitorial, guard services, product development, auxiliary production for plant's own use (for example, power plant), record keeping, and other services closely associated with these production operations.

Construction workers include the following employees in the construction division of the NAICS: working supervisors, qualified craft workers, mechanics, apprentices, laborers, and the like, engaged in new work, alterations, demolition, repair, maintenance, and so on, whether working at the site of construction or working in shops or yards at jobs (such as precutting and preassembling) ordinarily performed by members of the construction trades.

Nonsupervisory employees include employees (not above the working supervisory level) such as office and clerical workers, repairers, salespersons, operators, drivers, physicians, lawyers, accountants, nurses, social workers, research aides, teachers, drafters, photographers, beauticians, musicians, restaurant workers, custodial workers, attendants, line installers and repairers, laborers, janitors, guards, and other employees at similar occupational levels whose services are closely associated with those of the employees listed.

Notes on the data

Benchmark adjustments. The establishment survey data are adjusted annually to comprehensive counts of employment, called "benchmarks." Benchmark information on employment, by industry, is compiled by state agencies from reports of establishments covered under state unemployment insurance laws, in an annual compilation of administrative data known as the ES-202. These tabulations cover about 98 percent of all employees on nonfarm payrolls. Benchmark data for the residual are obtained from the records of the Social Security Administration and a number of other agencies in private industry or government. The latest benchmark adjustment, which is incorporated in the data in this volume, lowered the employment level in March 2003 by 122,000 jobs below the previous estimate.

The estimates for the benchmark month are compared with new benchmark levels, industry by industry. If revisions are necessary, the monthly series of estimates between benchmark periods are adjusted by graduated amounts between the new benchmark and the preceding one, and the new benchmark level for each industry is then carried forward to the current month by use of the sample changes.

The probability sampling frame and sample are updated twice a year with new quarters of UI-based data which help keep the sample up to date by adding new firm births and deleting business deaths. Additional model-based procedures are used to estimate business births and deaths that occur after the latest quarterly report. A principal purpose of these procedures is to better capture cyclical turning points.

Not-seasonally-adjusted data for all months since the last benchmark to which the series has been adjusted are subject to revision.

Seasonal adjustment. The seasonal movements that recur periodically—such as warm and cold weather, holidays, vacations, and so on—are generally the largest single component of month-to-month changes in employment. After adjusting the data to remove such seasonal variation, the basic trends are more evident. BLS uses X-12 ARIMA software to produce the seasonal factors and performs concurrent seasonal adjustment, developing new factors each month using the most current data. For many series a special procedure called REGARIMA is also used to adjust for regular, predictable events not always associated with the same calendar month, such as the occurrence of certain holidays ("movable feasts") and the length of the interval (four or five weeks) between the survey weeks.

Seasonal adjustment factors are directly applied to the component levels. Seasonally adjusted totals for employment series are then obtained by aggregating seasonally adjusted components directly, while hours and earnings series represent weighted averages of the seasonally adjusted component series. Seasonally adjusted data are not published for a small number of series characterized by small seasonal components relative to their trend and/or irregular components. These series, however, are used in aggregating to broader seasonally adjusted levels.

Seasonal adjustment factors for federal government employment are derived from unadjusted data that include Christmas temporary workers employed by the Postal Service. The number of temporary census workers for the decennial census was removed, however, from the calculation of seasonal adjustment factors.

Revisions of the seasonally adjusted data, usually for the most recent five-year period, are made once a year coincident with the benchmark revisions.

Data availability

Employment data by industry division are available beginning with 1919. Data for each month usually are released on the first Friday of the following month in a press release that also contains data from the household survey (Tables 10-1 through 10-3). Data are subsequently published in the BLS monthly periodical *Employment and Earnings*, which also contains detailed explanatory notes. Selected data are published each month in the *Monthly Labor Review*, which also contains frequent articles analyzing labor force, employment, and unemployment developments. Press releases and complete historical data are available on the BLS Internet site at <http://www.bls.gov>.

Benchmark revisions and revised seasonally adjusted data for recent years are made each year with the release of January data in early February. Before 2004, the benchmark revisions were not made until June; the acceleration is due to earlier availability of the benchmark UI (ES-202) data.

References

The extensive changes incorporated in June 2003 are described in "Recent Changes in the National Current Employment Statistics Survey," *Monthly Labor Review*, June 2003, and in the "Explanatory Notes" in any subsequent issue of *Employment and Earnings*. The revisions made with the January 2004 data are described in "BLS National Establishment Estimates Revised to Incorporate March 2003 Benchmarks," *Employment and Earnings*, February 2004. Descriptive material is also available on the BLS Internet site. Also see Chapter 2, "Employment, Hours, and Earnings from the Establishment Survey," *BLS Handbook of Methods*, Bulletin 2490 (April 1997).

TABLES 10-7, 10-8, 16-3, 16-6, AND 20-4 AVERAGE HOURS PER WEEK; AGGREGATE EMPLOYEE HOURS

SOURCE: U.S. DEPARTMENT OF LABOR, BUREAU OF LABOR STATISTICS (BLS)

See the Notes and Definitions to Tables 10-5 and 10-6, just preceding, for an overall description of the "establishment" or "payroll" survey that is the source of hours data.

Definitions

Hours represent the average weekly hours for which production or nonsupervisory workers received pay. Average weekly hours are different from standard or scheduled hours. Such factors as unpaid absenteeism, labor turnover, part-time work, and work stoppages cause average weekly hours to be lower than scheduled hours of work for an establishment. These hours pertain to jobs, not to persons; thus, a person with two half-time jobs is represented as two jobs each with a 20-hour workweek in this series, not as one person with a 40-hour week.

Overtime hours represent the portion of average weekly hours which was in excess of regular hours and for which overtime premiums were paid. Weekend and holiday hours are included only if overtime premiums were paid. Hours for which only shift differential, hazard, incentive, or other similar types of premiums were paid are excluded.

Production or nonsupervisory workers. See the Notes and Definitions to Tables 10-5 and 10-6.

Aggregate hours. These provide a partial measure of labor input to the industry. Data pertain to production and nonsupervisory workers in nonfarm establishments. The indexes are obtained by multiplying seasonally adjusted production or nonsupervisory worker employment by seasonally adjusted average weekly hours and dividing by the monthly average for the 2002 period. For total private, goods-producing, service-producing, and major industry divisions, the indexes are obtained by summing the seasonally adjusted aggregate weekly employee hours for the component industries and dividing by the monthly average for the 2002 period.

Notes on the data

Benchmark adjustments. Independent benchmarks are not available for the hours and earnings series. At the time of the annual adjustment of the employment series to new benchmarks, the levels of hours and earnings may be affected by the revised employment weights (which are used in computing the industry averages for hours and earnings), as well as by the changes in seasonal adjustment factors also introduced with the benchmark revision.

Method of computing industry series. "Average weekly hours" for individual industries are computed by dividing production or nonsupervisory worker hours (reported by establishments classified in each industry) by the number of production or nonsupervisory workers reported for the same establishments. Estimates for divisions and major industry groups are averages (weighted by employment) of the figures for component industries.

Seasonal adjustment. Hours and earnings series are seasonally adjusted by applying factors directly to the corresponding unadjusted series. Data for some industries are not seasonally adjusted because the seasonal component is small relative to the trend-cycle and/or irregular components and consequently cannot be separated with sufficient precision.

Data availability

See "Data availability" for Tables 10-5 and 10-6, above.

References

See references for Tables 10-5 and 10-6, above.

TABLES 10-9, 10-10, 16-4, 16-5, AND 20-4
HOURLY AND WEEKLY EARNINGS

SOURCE: U.S. DEPARTMENT OF LABOR, BUREAU OF LABOR STATISTICS (BLS)

See the Notes and Definitions to Tables 10-5 and 10-6 for an overall description of the "establishment" or "payroll" survey that is the source of these earnings data.

Definitions

Earnings are the payments that production or nonsupervisory workers receive during the survey period (before deductions for taxes and other items), including premium pay for overtime or late-shift work but excluding irregular bonuses, tips, and other special payments.

Production or nonsupervisory workers. See the Notes and Definitions to Tables 10-5 and 10-6.

Notes on the data

The hours and earnings series are based on reports of gross payroll and corresponding paid hours for full- and part-time production and related workers, construction workers, or nonsupervisory workers who received pay for any part of the pay period that included the 12th of the month.

Total payrolls are before deductions, such as for the employee share of old-age and unemployment insurance, group insurance, withholding taxes, bonds, and union dues. The payroll figures also include pay for overtime, holidays, vacations, and sick leave (paid directly by the employer for the period reported). Excluded from the payroll figures are fringe benefits (health and other types of insurance, contributions to retirement, paid by the employer, and the employer share of payroll taxes); bonuses (unless earned and paid regularly each pay period); other pay not earned in the pay period reported (retroactive pay); tips; and the value of free rent, fuel, meals, or other payment in kind. The exclusion of tips is particularly significant for hotels, motels, and eating and drinking places.

Average hourly earnings data are on a "gross" basis; that is, they reflect not only changes in basic hourly and incentive wage rates but also such variable factors as premium pay for overtime and late-shift work, and changes in output of workers paid on an incentive basis. Also, shifts in the volume of employment between relatively high-paid and low-paid work affect the general average of hourly earnings.

Averages of hourly earnings should not be confused with *wage rates*, which represent the rates stipulated for a given unit of work or time, while earnings refer to the actual return to the worker for a stated period of time. The earnings series do not represent total labor cost to the employer because of the exclusion of irregular bonuses, retroactive items, the cost of employer-provided benefits, payroll taxes paid by employers, and earnings for those employees not covered under the production-worker or nonsupervisory-worker definition. Additionally, average weekly earnings are not the amounts available to workers for spending, since they do not reflect such deductions as those for income and Social Security taxes.

Method of computing industry series. Average hourly earnings are obtained by dividing the reported total production or nonsupervisory worker payroll by the total production or nonsupervisory worker hours. Estimates for both hours and hourly earnings for nonfarm divisions and major industry groups are employment-weighted averages of the figures for component industries.

Average weekly earnings are computed by multiplying average hourly earnings by average weekly hours. In addition to the factors mentioned above, which exert varying influences upon average hourly earnings, average weekly earnings are affected by changes in the length of the workweek, part-time work, work stoppages, labor turnover, and absenteeism. Persistent long-term increases in the proportion of part-time workers in retail trade and many of the service industries have reduced average workweeks and have similarly affected the average weekly earnings series.

Average weekly earnings are per job, not per person; a person with two half-time jobs will be reflected as two jobs with low weekly earnings rather than one person with the total earnings from his or her two jobs.

Benchmark adjustments. Independent benchmarks are not available for the hours and earnings series. At the time of the annual adjustment of the employment series to new benchmarks, the levels of hours and earnings may be affected by the revised employment weights (which are used in computing the industry averages for hours and earnings), as well as by the changes in seasonal adjustment factors also introduced with the benchmark revision.

Seasonal adjustment. Hours and earnings series are seasonally adjusted by applying factors directly to the corresponding unadjusted series; seasonally adjusted average weekly earnings are the product of seasonally adjusted hourly earnings and weekly hours.

Data availability

See "Data availability" for Tables 10-5 and 10-6 above.

References

See references for Tables 10-5 and 10-6 above.

CHAPTER 11: ENERGY

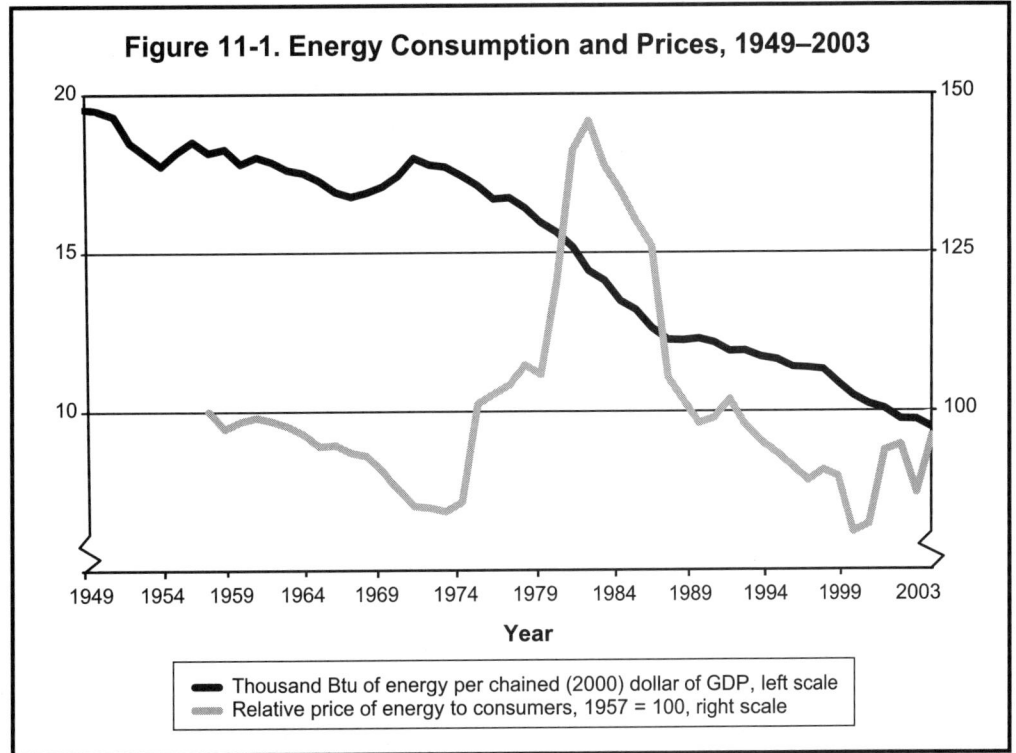

Figure 11-1. Energy Consumption and Prices, 1949–2003

- Thousand Btu of energy per chained (2000) dollar of GDP, left scale
- Relative price of energy to consumers, 1957 = 100, right scale

- Throughout the postwar period, there has been a long-term downtrend in the relationship of energy use to real gross domestic product (GDP). This may be because the relative share of services and high-tech goods in the composition of output is rising, with a correspondingly falling relative importance of energy-intensive production processes such as primary metals and chemicals manufacturing. Still, this trend is striking in light of the continued rise in motor vehicle use, air conditioning, air travel, and other consumer uses of energy. (Table 11-2)
- Changes in energy prices relative to other prices provide only a partial explanation, as the graph suggests. The decline in energy use—which can also be viewed as an increase in energy efficiency—accelerated as energy prices rose from 1973 through 1981. From 1981 through 1998, the increase in energy efficiency continued (though more slowly) while the relative price of energy declined. In 2002, energy prices fell and efficiency leveled off; in 2003, energy prices rose and relative energy use resumed its decline. (Tables 11-2 and 8-1)
- Comparing business cycle peak years 1973 and 2000, the greatest savings in energy relative to GDP were achieved in industrial use, which rose only 6 percent between those years while real GDP increased by 126 percent and industrial production rose 106 percent. But relative economies were also achieved in aggregate use of energy for residential and commercial purposes, which rose 54 percent, and for transportation, which rose 43 percent. (Table 11-1)
- Most of the decline in energy relative to GDP in recent years has been in the use of petroleum and natural gas. Before 1973, on the other hand, oil and gas use was rising relative to GDP while the use of other energy sources was declining. (Table 11-2)
- Imports supplied 32 percent of total U.S. energy consumption in 2003, compared with 19 percent in 1973 and only 5 percent in 1949. Domestic production of both crude oil and natural gas increased up until the early 1970s. Both have declined since then, with the greater decline in crude oil. Domestic coal production and nuclear energy generation have increased. Geothermal generation has increased but remains very small. (Table 11-1)

Table 11-1. Energy Supply and Consumption

(Quadrillion Btu.)

Year and month	Imports	Exports	Production, by source								Consumption, by end-use sector			
			Total [1]	Coal	Natural gas	Crude oil	Natural gas plant liquids	Nuclear electric power	Hydro-electric power	Geo-thermal energy	Total	Residential and commercial	Industrial	Transpor-tation
1949	1.448	1.592	31.722	11.974	5.377	10.683	0.714	0.000	1.425	...	31.982	9.275	14.717	7.990
1950	1.913	1.465	35.540	14.060	6.233	11.447	0.823	0.000	1.415	...	34.616	9.890	16.233	8.493
1951	1.892	2.622	38.751	14.419	7.416	13.037	0.920	0.000	1.424	...	36.974	10.263	17.669	9.042
1952	2.146	2.365	37.917	12.734	7.964	13.281	0.998	0.000	1.466	...	36.748	10.443	17.302	9.003
1953	2.313	1.866	38.181	12.278	8.339	13.671	1.062	0.000	1.413	...	37.664	10.340	18.201	9.123
1954	2.348	1.696	36.518	10.542	8.682	13.427	1.113	0.000	1.360	...	36.639	10.590	17.146	8.903
1955	2.790	2.286	40.148	12.370	9.345	14.410	1.240	0.000	1.360	...	40.208	11.185	19.472	9.551
1956	3.207	2.945	42.622	13.306	10.002	15.180	1.283	0.000	1.435	...	41.754	11.698	20.196	9.860
1957	3.529	3.439	42.983	13.061	10.605	15.178	1.289	0.000	1.516	...	41.787	11.686	20.205	9.897
1958	3.884	2.050	40.133	10.783	10.942	14.204	1.287	0.002	1.592	...	41.645	12.333	19.307	10.005
1959	4.076	1.534	41.949	10.778	11.952	14.933	1.383	0.002	1.548	...	43.466	12.800	20.316	10.349
1960	4.188	1.477	42.804	10.817	12.656	14.935	1.461	0.006	1.608	0.001	45.087	13.667	20.823	10.597
1961	4.437	1.377	43.280	10.447	13.105	15.206	1.549	0.020	1.656	0.002	45.739	14.032	20.937	10.770
1962	4.994	1.473	44.877	10.901	13.717	15.522	1.593	0.026	1.816	0.002	47.828	14.839	21.768	11.221
1963	5.087	1.835	47.174	11.849	14.513	15.966	1.709	0.038	1.771	0.004	49.646	15.261	22.730	11.655
1964	5.447	1.815	49.056	12.524	15.298	16.164	1.803	0.040	1.886	0.005	51.817	15.730	24.090	11.998
1965	5.892	1.829	50.676	13.055	15.775	16.521	1.883	0.043	2.059	0.004	54.017	16.509	25.075	12.434
1966	6.146	1.829	53.534	13.468	17.011	17.561	1.996	0.064	2.062	0.004	57.017	17.517	26.397	13.102
1967	6.159	2.115	56.379	13.825	17.943	18.651	2.177	0.088	2.347	0.007	58.908	18.541	26.616	13.752
1968	6.905	1.998	58.225	13.609	19.068	19.308	2.321	0.142	2.349	0.009	62.419	19.665	27.888	14.866
1969	7.676	2.126	60.541	13.863	20.446	19.556	2.420	0.154	2.648	0.013	65.621	21.000	29.114	15.506
1970	8.342	2.632	63.501	14.607	21.666	20.401	2.512	0.239	2.634	0.011	67.844	22.105	29.641	16.098
1971	9.535	2.151	62.723	13.186	22.280	20.033	2.544	0.413	2.824	0.012	69.289	22.959	29.601	16.729
1972	11.387	2.118	63.920	14.092	22.208	20.041	2.598	0.584	2.864	0.031	72.704	24.036	30.953	17.716
1973	14.613	2.033	63.585	13.992	22.187	19.493	2.569	0.910	2.861	0.043	75.708	24.437	32.653	18.612
1974	14.304	2.203	62.372	14.074	21.210	18.575	2.471	1.272	3.177	0.053	73.991	24.046	31.819	18.119
1975	14.032	2.323	61.357	14.989	19.640	17.729	2.374	1.900	3.155	0.070	71.999	24.308	29.447	18.244
1976	16.760	2.172	61.602	15.654	19.480	17.262	2.327	2.111	2.976	0.078	76.012	25.476	31.429	19.099
1977	19.948	2.052	62.052	15.755	19.565	17.454	2.327	2.702	2.333	0.077	78.000	25.866	32.307	19.820
1978	19.106	1.920	63.137	14.910	19.485	18.434	2.245	3.024	2.937	0.064	79.986	26.637	32.733	20.615
1979	19.460	2.855	65.948	17.540	20.076	18.104	2.286	2.776	2.931	0.084	80.903	26.469	33.962	20.471
1980	15.796	3.695	67.241	18.598	19.908	18.249	2.254	2.739	2.900	0.110	78.289	26.442	32.152	19.696
1981	13.719	4.307	67.007	18.377	19.699	18.146	2.307	3.008	2.758	0.123	76.342	25.990	30.836	19.513
1982	11.861	4.608	66.574	18.639	18.319	18.309	2.191	3.131	3.266	0.105	73.253	26.457	27.704	19.088
1983	11.752	3.693	64.106	17.247	16.593	18.392	2.184	3.203	3.527	0.129	73.101	26.411	27.511	19.176
1984	12.471	3.786	68.832	19.719	18.008	18.848	2.274	3.553	3.386	0.165	76.736	27.239	29.643	19.851
1985	11.781	4.196	67.647	19.325	16.980	18.992	2.241	4.076	2.970	0.198	76.469	27.393	28.958	20.122
1986	14.151	4.021	67.087	19.509	16.541	18.376	2.149	4.380	3.071	0.219	76.782	27.527	28.375	20.877
1987	15.398	3.812	67.608	20.141	17.136	17.675	2.215	4.754	2.635	0.229	79.225	28.184	29.519	21.524
1988	17.296	4.366	68.951	20.738	17.599	17.279	2.260	5.587	2.334	0.217	82.844	29.640	30.818	22.382
1989	18.766	4.661	69.364	21.346	17.847	16.117	2.158	5.602	2.837	0.317	84.957	30.930	31.396	22.622
1990	18.817	4.752	70.729	22.456	18.326	15.571	2.175	6.104	3.046	0.336	84.668	30.181	31.918	22.589
1991	18.335	5.141	70.362	21.594	18.229	15.701	2.306	6.422	3.016	0.346	84.595	30.873	31.527	22.195
1992	19.372	4.937	69.933	21.629	18.375	15.223	2.363	6.479	2.617	0.349	85.949	30.734	32.673	22.542
1993	21.273	4.258	68.260	20.249	18.584	14.494	2.408	6.410	2.892	0.364	87.578	32.037	32.668	22.883
1994	22.390	4.061	70.676	22.111	19.348	14.103	2.391	6.694	2.683	0.338	89.248	32.194	33.557	23.503
1995	22.260	4.511	71.156	22.029	19.082	13.887	2.442	7.075	3.205	0.294	91.211	33.317	33.941	23.960
1996	23.702	4.633	72.472	22.684	19.344	13.723	2.530	7.087	3.590	0.316	94.224	34.803	34.905	24.511
1997	25.215	4.514	72.389	23.211	19.394	13.658	2.495	6.597	3.640	0.325	94.727	34.746	35.167	24.808
1998	26.581	4.299	72.787	23.935	19.613	13.235	2.420	7.068	3.297	0.328	95.146	35.016	34.777	25.357
1999	27.252	3.715	71.652	23.186	19.341	12.451	2.528	7.610	3.268	0.331	96.774	35.981	34.679	26.108
2000	28.973	4.006	71.218	22.623	19.662	12.358	2.611	7.862	2.811	0.317	98.905	37.582	34.616	26.705
2001	30.157	3.770	71.792	23.529	20.205	12.282	2.547	8.033	2.201	0.311	96.378	37.570	32.527	26.276
2002	29.406	3.661	70.933	22.698	19.495	12.163	2.559	8.143	2.675	0.328	98.026	38.502	32.830	26.683
2003	31.036	4.065	70.320	22.311	19.602	12.026	2.346	7.973	2.779	0.314	98.188	38.803	32.525	26.863
2002														
January	2.414	0.292	6.278	2.117	1.669	1.051	0.211	0.740	0.221	0.029	8.849	3.926	2.799	2.124
February	2.148	0.290	5.607	1.873	1.496	0.954	0.198	0.644	0.204	0.026	7.928	3.379	2.611	1.942
March	2.427	0.266	5.947	1.871	1.669	1.058	0.220	0.658	0.213	0.028	8.421	3.425	2.799	2.200
April	2.434	0.292	5.826	1.864	1.617	1.019	0.215	0.610	0.245	0.025	7.782	2.909	2.682	2.193
May	2.510	0.294	6.063	1.897	1.677	1.065	0.224	0.658	0.270	0.028	7.830	2.774	2.772	2.284
June	2.442	0.308	5.858	1.770	1.613	1.029	0.209	0.693	0.285	0.026	7.910	2.956	2.687	2.263
July	2.528	0.270	5.997	1.791	1.684	1.037	0.213	0.735	0.258	0.029	8.452	3.306	2.791	2.346
August	2.588	0.344	6.052	1.912	1.652	1.045	0.224	0.739	0.213	0.028	8.374	3.223	2.795	2.347
September	2.349	0.301	5.739	1.916	1.554	0.942	0.212	0.673	0.173	0.027	7.691	2.853	2.651	2.183
October	2.566	0.333	5.833	1.962	1.601	0.964	0.217	0.631	0.174	0.028	7.843	2.820	2.786	2.238
November	2.550	0.313	5.737	1.833	1.607	0.974	0.212	0.642	0.200	0.027	8.057	3.090	2.755	2.214
December	2.450	0.359	5.995	1.891	1.657	1.025	0.203	0.719	0.219	0.028	8.888	3.839	2.701	2.349
2003														
January	2.422	0.377	6.040	1.935	1.684	1.040	0.204	0.722	0.199	0.027	9.285	4.322	2.817	2.144
February	2.174	0.300	5.444	1.715	1.525	0.940	0.190	0.636	0.198	0.025	8.469	3.826	2.650	1.995
March	2.579	0.316	5.957	1.858	1.706	1.046	0.200	0.626	0.246	0.027	8.428	3.493	2.729	2.208
April	2.603	0.333	5.792	1.863	1.618	1.005	0.191	0.593	0.253	0.025	7.686	2.852	2.651	2.188
May	2.738	0.357	5.983	1.889	1.665	1.031	0.181	0.649	0.302	0.025	7.680	2.747	2.679	2.255
June	2.656	0.351	5.843	1.845	1.602	0.992	0.177	0.670	0.288	0.026	7.622	2.781	2.591	2.248
July	2.746	0.339	5.936	1.844	1.651	0.994	0.191	0.727	0.249	0.026	8.285	3.215	2.724	2.341
August	2.725	0.334	5.943	1.866	1.648	1.006	0.197	0.721	0.231	0.026	8.391	3.234	2.754	2.397
September	2.660	0.325	5.789	1.884	1.612	0.989	0.198	0.664	0.184	0.026	7.590	2.754	2.606	2.229
October	2.662	0.349	5.927	1.951	1.650	1.013	0.211	0.627	0.185	0.026	7.821	2.728	2.798	2.297
November	2.452	0.338	5.635	1.748	1.588	0.968	0.206	0.622	0.199	0.026	7.915	2.970	2.741	2.205
December	2.618	0.345	6.030	1.912	1.654	1.003	0.200	0.716	0.244	0.029	9.017	3.874	2.790	2.354

[1] Includes categories not shown separately.
... = Not available.

Table 11-2. Energy Consumption per Dollar of Real Gross Domestic Product

Year	Energy consumption (quadrillion Btu)			Gross domestic product (billions of chained [2000] dollars)	Energy consumption per dollar of GDP (thousand Btu per chained [2000] dollar)		
	Total	Petroleum and natural gas	Other energy		Total	Petroleum and natural gas	Other energy
1949	31.982	17.028	14.954	1 634.6	19.57	10.42	9.15
1950	34.616	19.284	15.332	1 777.3	19.48	10.85	8.63
1951	36.974	21.477	15.497	1 915.0	19.31	11.21	8.09
1952	36.748	22.505	14.243	1 988.3	18.48	11.32	7.16
1953	37.664	23.462	14.202	2 079.5	18.11	11.28	6.83
1954	36.639	24.169	12.470	2 065.4	17.74	11.70	6.04
1955	40.208	26.253	13.955	2 212.8	18.17	11.86	6.31
1956	41.754	27.551	14.203	2 255.8	18.51	12.21	6.30
1957	41.787	28.122	13.665	2 301.1	18.16	12.22	5.94
1958	41.645	29.190	12.455	2 279.2	18.27	12.81	5.46
1959	43.466	31.040	12.426	2 441.3	17.80	12.71	5.09
1960	45.087	32.305	12.782	2 501.8	18.02	12.91	5.11
1961	45.739	33.143	12.596	2 560.0	17.87	12.95	4.92
1962	47.828	34.780	13.048	2 715.2	17.61	12.81	4.81
1963	49.646	36.104	13.542	2 834.0	17.52	12.74	4.78
1964	51.817	37.589	14.228	2 998.6	17.28	12.54	4.74
1965	54.017	39.014	15.003	3 191.1	16.93	12.23	4.70
1966	57.017	41.396	15.621	3 399.1	16.77	12.18	4.60
1967	58.908	43.228	15.680	3 484.6	16.91	12.41	4.50
1968	62.419	46.189	16.230	3 652.7	17.09	12.65	4.44
1969	65.621	49.016	16.605	3 765.4	17.43	13.02	4.41
1970	67.844	51.315	16.529	3 771.9	17.99	13.60	4.38
1971	69.289	53.030	16.259	3 898.6	17.77	13.60	4.17
1972	72.704	55.645	17.059	4 105.0	17.71	13.56	4.16
1973	75.708	57.352	18.356	4 341.5	17.44	13.21	4.23
1974	73.991	55.187	18.804	4 319.6	17.13	12.78	4.35
1975	71.999	52.678	19.321	4 311.2	16.70	12.22	4.48
1976	76.012	55.520	20.492	4 540.9	16.74	12.23	4.51
1977	78.000	57.053	20.947	4 750.5	16.42	12.01	4.41
1978	79.986	57.966	22.021	5 015.0	15.95	11.56	4.39
1979	80.903	57.789	23.114	5 173.4	15.64	11.17	4.47
1980	78.289	54.596	23.693	5 161.7	15.17	10.58	4.59
1981	76.342	51.859	24.483	5 291.7	14.43	9.80	4.63
1982	73.253	48.736	24.516	5 189.3	14.12	9.39	4.72
1983	73.101	47.411	25.690	5 423.8	13.48	8.74	4.74
1984	76.736	49.558	27.178	5 813.6	13.20	8.52	4.67
1985	76.469	48.756	27.713	6 053.7	12.63	8.05	4.58
1986	76.782	48.904	27.878	6 263.6	12.26	7.81	4.45
1987	79.225	50.609	28.616	6 475.1	12.24	7.82	4.42
1988	82.844	52.774	30.070	6 742.7	12.29	7.83	4.46
1989	84.957	53.923	31.034	6 981.4	12.17	7.72	4.45
1990	84.668	53.282	31.386	7 112.5	11.90	7.49	4.41
1991	84.595	52.994	31.601	7 100.5	11.91	7.46	4.45
1992	85.949	54.362	31.587	7 336.6	11.72	7.41	4.31
1993	87.578	55.193	32.385	7 532.7	11.63	7.33	4.31
1994	89.248	56.512	32.736	7 835.5	11.39	7.21	4.19
1995	91.221	57.338	33.884	8 031.7	11.36	7.14	4.23
1996	94.224	58.954	35.270	8 328.9	11.31	7.08	4.24
1997	94.727	59.594	35.133	8 703.5	10.88	6.85	4.05
1998	95.146	59.869	35.277	9 066.9	10.49	6.60	3.90
1999	96.774	60.970	35.804	9 470.3	10.22	6.44	3.79
2000	98.905	62.320	36.585	9 817.0	10.07	6.35	3.74
2001	96.378	61.239	35.139	9 890.7	9.74	6.19	3.55
2002	98.026	62.064	35.962	10 074.8	9.73	6.16	3.57
2003	98.188	61.612	36.576	10 381.3	9.46	5.93	3.52

NOTES AND DEFINITIONS

TABLES 11-1 AND 11-2
ENERGY SUPPLY AND CONSUMPTION

SOURCES: U.S. DEPARTMENT OF ENERGY, ENERGY INFORMATION ADMINISTRATION; U.S. DEPARTMENT OF COMMERCE, BUREAU OF ECONOMIC ANALYSIS

Definitions

The *British thermal unit (Btu)* is a measure used to combine data for different energy sources into a consistent aggregate. It is the amount of energy required to raise the temperature of 1 pound of water 1 degree Fahrenheit when the water is near 39.2 degrees Fahrenheit. To illustrate one of the factors used to convert volumes to Btu, conventional motor gasoline has a heat content of 5.253 million Btu per barrel. For further information, see *Monthly Energy Review*, Appendix A.

Notes on the data

These data are published in the *Monthly Energy Review*, Tables 1.1, 1.2, 1.8, and 2.1. Consumption by end-use sector is based on total, not net, consumption. The gross domestic product (GDP) data used to calculate energy consumption per dollar of GDP are from the Bureau of Economic Analysis (see *Business Statistics*, Table 1-2, and its Notes and Definitions).

Energy Production. Crude oil includes lease condensates. Hydroelectric power includes electrical utility and industrial generation. Energy production components not shown here (the difference between total production and the sum of the categories shown) include energy generated for distribution from wood, waste, alcohol, solar, and wind sources and an allowance for net hydroelectric energy losses related to pumped storage.

The sum of domestic energy production and net imports of energy does not equal domestic energy consumption. The difference is attributed to inventory changes; losses and gains in conversion, transportation, and distribution; the addition of blending compounds; shipments of anthracite to U.S. Armed Forces in Europe; and adjustments to account for discrepancies between reporting systems.

References

Energy Information Administration, *Monthly Energy Review*. Current and historical data are available on the EIA Internet site at <http://www.eia.doe.gov>.

CHAPTER 12: MONEY AND FINANCIAL MARKETS

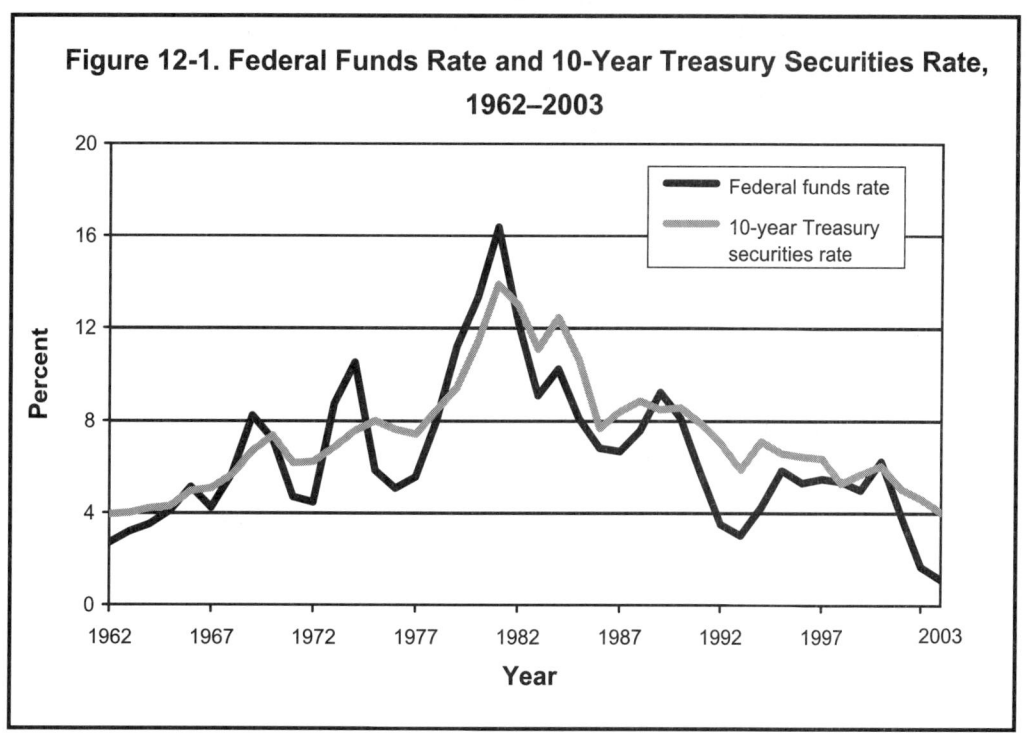

Figure 12-1. Federal Funds Rate and 10-Year Treasury Securities Rate, 1962–2003

- Inflation has fallen back to the levels of the early postwar period (see Chapter 8), and as the graph shows, the same has happened with interest rates. (Table 12-9)
- Comparisons of interest rates and other financial data over the half-century span are not always straightforward, because financial institutions and instruments have changed. In particular, interest rates were held low until 1952 because the Federal Reserve was pegging Treasury bill and bond rates. Rates before 1953 are therefore not shown in Table 12-9, and for many series are not available. Since then, rates have been free to reflect changing degrees of monetary tightness as well as changing inflation expectations and fluctuating views of the productivity of capital.
- In the short-term markets, where Federal Reserve policy governs the price of overnight money, the effective Federal Funds rate was 0.98 percent at the end of 2003, even lower than in years such as 1958 when the economy was slack and inflation expectations were nonexistent. This rate had averaged 16 percent in 1981 because of high inflation and tight monetary policy. Similar comparisons can be made looking at the rate on the three-month Treasury bill. (Table 12-9)
- In the longer-term market, the 10-year Treasury rate in 2003 fell to a level last seen in 1963. (Table 12-9)
- Treasury bonds are risk-free, and market rates on these bonds are usually taken as a pure representation of the sum of inflation expectations and the "real" (after-inflation) interest rate. Corporate bond rates, on the other hand, include a risk premium, and even the top-rated bonds (Aaa) commanded higher rates in 2003 than in the early postwar period, although far lower than the double-digit rates reached in the early 1980s. (Table 12-9)
- Even after the post-2000 decline in the stock market, stock valuations have remained high relative to earnings and dividends. The recent dividend-price and earnings-price ratios shown in Table 12-10 (the inverse of valuation, since stock prices are the denominator rather than the numerator) remain well below rates registered in the years before 1997.

Table 12-1. Money Stock Measures

(Billions of dollars, monthly data are averages of daily figures, annual data are for December.)

Year and month	Seasonally adjusted			Not seasonally adjusted		
	M1	M2	M3	M1	M2	M3
1959	140.0	297.8	299.7	143.6	300.6	302.4
1960	140.7	312.4	315.2	144.5	315.3	318.0
1961	145.2	335.5	340.8	149.2	338.5	343.7
1962	147.8	362.7	371.3	151.9	365.8	374.0
1963	153.3	393.2	405.9	157.5	396.4	408.7
1964	160.3	424.7	442.4	164.9	428.3	445.5
1965	167.8	459.2	482.1	172.6	463.1	485.5
1966	172.0	480.2	505.4	176.9	483.7	508.6
1967	183.3	524.8	557.9	188.4	528.0	560.9
1968	197.4	566.8	607.2	202.8	569.7	610.0
1969	203.9	587.9	615.9	209.4	590.1	618.2
1970	214.4	626.5	677.1	220.1	627.8	678.2
1971	228.3	710.3	776.0	234.5	711.2	776.6
1972	249.2	802.3	885.9	256.1	803.1	886.2
1973	262.9	855.5	985.0	270.2	856.5	985.2
1974	274.2	902.1	1 069.9	281.8	903.5	1 070.8
1975	287.1	1 016.2	1 170.2	295.3	1 017.8	1 173.3
1976	306.2	1 152.0	1 310.0	314.5	1 153.5	1 313.6
1977	330.9	1 270.3	1 470.4	340.0	1 273.0	1 476.2
1978	357.3	1 366.0	1 644.6	367.9	1 370.8	1 652.6
1979	381.8	1 473.7	1 808.7	393.2	1 479.0	1 815.2
1980	408.5	1 599.8	1 995.5	419.5	1 604.8	2 000.8
1981	436.7	1 755.4	2 254.6	447.0	1 760.3	2 259.0
1982	474.8	1 910.3	2 460.7	485.8	1 918.2	2 469.1
1983	521.4	2 126.5	2 697.6	533.3	2 137.0	2 708.5
1984	551.6	2 309.9	2 990.9	564.6	2 322.0	3 004.6
1985	619.8	2 495.7	3 208.3	633.3	2 507.7	3 221.6
1986	724.6	2 732.3	3 499.4	739.8	2 745.0	3 513.3
1987	750.2	2 831.4	3 686.8	765.4	2 843.4	3 698.7
1988	786.6	2 994.4	3 928.9	803.1	3 006.8	3 941.1
1989	792.8	3 158.4	4 076.9	810.6	3 171.5	4 089.4
1990	824.8	3 279.2	4 154.1	842.7	3 292.0	4 165.1
1991	896.9	3 379.1	4 207.7	915.6	3 393.4	4 220.9
1992	1 025.0	3 432.8	4 219.7	1 045.6	3 449.2	4 234.9
1993	1 129.9	3 484.7	4 281.8	1 153.3	3 504.9	4 300.8
1994	1 150.5	3 497.7	4 364.8	1 174.2	3 519.2	4 384.4
1995	1 127.0	3 641.4	4 630.9	1 152.1	3 664.8	4 653.4
1996	1 079.3	3 817.0	4 978.8	1 104.5	3 837.8	5 001.5
1997	1 072.5	4 031.9	5 453.5	1 096.9	4 053.8	5 481.6
1998	1 096.1	4 384.1	6 044.6	1 120.2	4 407.5	6 079.4
1999	1 124.0	4 649.0	6 544.7	1 147.9	4 677.0	6 587.9
2000	1 087.9	4 932.7	7 112.9	1 112.0	4 967.2	7 166.0
2001	1 179.3	5 448.6	8 025.0	1 205.1	5 486.6	8 091.6
2002	1 217.2	5 794.5	8 552.4	1 242.6	5 833.1	8 616.8
2003	1 293.4	6 062.5	8 845.6	1 319.1	6 102.7	8 904.1
2001						
January	1 095.3	4 988.4	7 223.4	1 099.4	4 993.1	7 249.8
February	1 099.4	5 027.4	7 290.0	1 087.1	5 021.5	7 320.7
March	1 107.7	5 086.9	7 363.1	1 106.8	5 112.7	7 414.4
April	1 110.6	5 151.1	7 498.2	1 122.1	5 186.8	7 531.3
May	1 115.5	5 152.4	7 554.8	1 110.5	5 124.1	7 536.9
June	1 123.6	5 190.3	7 629.6	1 122.6	5 175.9	7 617.0
July	1 135.6	5 221.2	7 669.0	1 136.3	5 205.1	7 628.3
August	1 147.3	5 253.4	7 677.6	1 141.3	5 241.5	7 640.1
September	1 199.1	5 363.2	7 833.4	1 190.6	5 354.8	7 782.5
October	1 162.8	5 355.0	7 875.3	1 156.1	5 341.0	7 826.5
November	1 166.5	5 398.1	7 955.9	1 165.8	5 404.7	7 964.7
December	1 179.3	5 448.6	8 025.0	1 205.1	5 486.6	8 091.6
2002						
January	1 184.6	5 476.0	8 046.1	1 187.1	5 474.6	8 073.3
February	1 186.1	5 505.7	8 090.1	1 172.7	5 492.3	8 115.2
March	1 190.0	5 517.4	8 110.0	1 190.3	5 541.5	8 161.6
April	1 179.9	5 522.7	8 133.6	1 190.3	5 554.5	8 158.4
May	1 184.0	5 552.2	8 169.4	1 179.6	5 522.0	8 145.1
June	1 188.3	5 573.9	8 180.8	1 188.4	5 559.8	8 169.2
July	1 194.2	5 615.8	8 221.6	1 195.0	5 602.0	8 187.5
August	1 182.9	5 651.5	8 284.8	1 178.3	5 646.8	8 256.1
September	1 190.5	5 677.9	8 321.3	1 183.2	5 672.3	8 274.5
October	1 201.8	5 722.7	8 348.3	1 194.1	5 710.5	8 303.5
November	1 204.5	5 767.2	8 479.4	1 202.7	5 784.0	8 499.0
December	1 217.2	5 794.5	8 552.4	1 242.6	5 833.1	8 616.8
2003						
January	1 220.4	5 825.5	8 564.8	1 222.0	5 819.9	8 582.9
February	1 235.1	5 867.3	8 601.9	1 221.5	5 845.1	8 615.2
March	1 240.6	5 891.1	8 633.4	1 240.6	5 905.8	8 673.5
April	1 246.1	5 933.8	8 670.4	1 255.8	5 962.8	8 692.0
May	1 257.7	5 985.1	8 725.2	1 253.7	5 953.1	8 700.6
June	1 271.0	6 026.1	8 774.6	1 271.6	6 009.5	8 764.8
July	1 273.4	6 066.1	8 849.0	1 274.3	6 053.4	8 819.6
August	1 281.5	6 106.6	8 888.6	1 279.0	6 111.8	8 871.4
September	1 281.4	6 083.9	8 879.6	1 274.0	6 083.3	8 841.8
October	1 284.1	6 069.1	8 856.8	1 275.9	6 063.6	8 823.0
November	1 283.4	6 065.8	8 844.4	1 280.8	6 087.1	8 868.1
December	1 293.4	6 062.5	8 845.6	1 319.1	6 102.7	8 904.1

Table 12-2. Selected Components of the Money Stock

(Billions of dollars, monthly data are averages of daily figures, seasonally adjusted, annual data are for December.)

Year and month	Currency	Demand deposits	Other checkable deposits	Repurchase agreements	Eurodollars	Money market funds		Savings deposits		Small time deposits		Large time deposits	
						Retail	Institutional	At banks	At thrifts	At banks	At thrifts	At banks	At thrifts
1959	28.8	110.8	0.0	0.0	0.7	0.0	0.0	54.8	91.7	8.9	2.5	1.2	0.0
1960	28.7	111.6	0.0	0.0	0.8	0.0	0.0	58.3	100.8	9.7	2.8	2.0	0.0
1961	29.3	115.5	0.0	0.0	1.5	0.0	0.0	64.2	111.3	11.1	3.7	3.9	0.0
1962	30.3	117.1	0.0	0.0	1.6	0.0	0.0	71.3	123.4	15.5	4.6	7.0	0.0
1963	32.2	120.6	0.1	0.0	1.9	0.0	0.0	76.8	137.6	19.9	5.7	10.8	0.0
1964	33.9	125.8	0.1	0.0	2.4	0.0	0.0	82.9	152.4	22.4	6.8	15.2	0.0
1965	36.0	131.3	0.1	0.0	1.8	0.0	0.0	92.4	164.5	26.7	7.8	21.2	0.0
1966	38.0	133.4	0.1	0.0	2.2	0.0	0.0	89.9	163.3	38.7	16.3	23.1	0.0
1967	40.0	142.5	0.1	0.0	2.2	0.0	0.0	94.1	169.6	50.7	27.1	30.9	0.0
1968	43.0	153.6	0.1	0.0	2.9	0.0	0.0	96.1	172.8	63.5	37.1	37.4	0.0
1969	45.7	157.3	0.2	4.9	2.7	0.0	0.0	93.8	169.8	71.6	48.8	20.4	0.0
1970	48.6	164.7	0.1	3.0	2.4	0.0	0.0	98.6	162.3	79.3	71.9	44.4	0.7
1971	52.0	175.1	0.2	5.2	2.9	0.0	0.0	112.8	179.4	94.7	95.1	56.1	1.5
1972	56.2	191.6	0.2	6.6	3.8	0.0	0.0	124.8	196.6	108.2	123.5	70.8	2.5
1973	60.8	200.3	0.3	12.8	5.8	0.1	0.0	128.0	198.7	116.8	149.0	107.4	3.6
1974	67.0	205.1	0.4	14.5	8.5	1.4	0.2	136.8	201.8	123.1	164.8	139.3	5.4
1975	72.8	211.3	0.9	13.8	10.0	2.4	0.5	161.2	227.6	142.3	195.5	123.3	6.4
1976	79.5	221.5	2.7	24.0	15.2	1.8	0.6	201.8	251.4	155.5	235.2	110.3	7.8
1977	87.4	236.4	4.2	32.2	21.7	1.8	1.0	218.8	273.4	167.5	278.0	135.0	10.2
1978	96.0	249.5	8.5	44.4	35.1	5.8	3.5	216.5	265.4	185.1	335.8	179.1	16.5
1979	104.8	256.6	16.8	48.8	52.7	33.9	10.4	195.0	228.8	235.5	398.7	190.9	32.2
1980	115.3	261.2	28.1	58.1	61.4	62.5	16.0	185.7	214.5	286.2	442.3	215.2	45.0
1981	122.5	231.4	78.7	67.8	88.8	151.7	38.2	159.0	184.9	347.7	475.4	250.5	53.8
1982	132.5	234.1	104.1	71.8	104.2	184.5	48.8	190.1	210.0	379.9	471.0	261.9	63.7
1983	146.2	238.5	132.1	97.5	116.6	136.1	40.9	363.2	321.7	350.9	433.1	219.4	96.7
1984	156.1	243.4	147.1	107.6	108.9	164.9	62.3	389.3	315.4	387.9	500.9	255.1	147.1
1985	167.7	267.0	179.5	121.5	104.2	174.9	65.3	456.6	358.6	386.4	499.3	269.9	151.8
1986	180.4	302.8	235.2	146.2	115.7	208.4	86.2	533.5	407.4	369.4	489.0	268.6	150.4
1987	196.7	287.7	259.2	178.3	121.5	222.8	93.7	534.8	402.6	391.7	529.3	299.1	162.7
1988	212.0	287.0	280.6	196.7	131.7	244.3	93.8	542.4	383.9	451.2	585.9	337.8	174.5
1989	222.2	278.5	285.1	169.0	109.4	320.6	112.0	541.1	352.6	533.8	617.6	366.5	161.5
1990	246.5	276.9	293.7	151.5	103.3	357.7	139.5	581.5	341.7	610.7	562.7	359.5	121.1
1991	267.1	289.7	332.4	131.2	92.3	372.3	188.4	664.7	379.6	602.3	463.3	333.3	83.5
1992	292.2	340.1	384.5	141.6	79.5	352.6	212.8	754.1	433.0	508.1	360.0	285.6	67.3
1993	321.6	385.6	414.6	172.6	72.8	353.6	216.2	785.2	434.0	467.9	314.1	273.9	61.6
1994	354.0	383.9	403.9	196.4	86.3	381.4	210.1	752.3	397.1	502.5	313.8	309.6	64.8
1995	372.1	389.3	356.6	198.6	94.0	449.1	263.3	774.5	359.4	574.8	356.5	359.4	74.2
1996	394.1	401.0	275.5	210.6	114.6	517.7	321.7	905.8	367.3	593.3	353.5	437.1	77.9
1997	424.6	394.2	245.3	254.2	147.4	592.4	395.1	1 022.0	377.1	625.2	342.7	539.8	85.0
1998	459.9	378.4	249.3	294.0	150.0	732.9	539.0	1 186.9	416.7	625.9	325.6	589.2	88.3
1999	517.7	354.9	242.8	337.0	170.4	832.7	635.6	1 286.9	451.3	634.5	319.5	660.8	91.9
2000	531.6	310.3	237.8	366.0	194.5	924.5	789.4	1 422.1	454.1	699.4	344.8	727.4	102.9
2001	582.0	332.5	256.8	378.9	210.0	987.6	1 193.6	1 736.0	572.9	633.6	339.1	679.2	114.8
2002	627.4	303.4	278.6	480.9	228.6	915.9	1 245.3	2 053.2	716.3	589.9	302.1	685.5	117.5
2003	663.9	312.6	309.2	513.4	288.7	801.5	1 113.2	2 328.0	830.4	536.4	272.8	747.7	120.2
2001													
January	534.6	312.7	239.7	364.7	198.9	941.8	826.7	1 443.8	456.1	702.8	348.5	739.2	105.6
February	536.9	312.7	241.5	353.6	205.0	945.6	889.5	1 466.6	464.3	701.2	350.3	707.6	106.9
March	539.5	314.6	245.4	349.7	217.9	961.9	918.1	1 494.6	475.0	697.6	350.2	682.9	107.5
April	542.5	310.9	249.0	372.4	212.1	981.7	950.3	1 532.4	483.3	691.9	351.2	703.0	109.4
May	545.6	312.7	249.2	375.0	211.8	961.5	995.2	1 544.3	493.0	684.7	353.4	709.6	110.8
June	548.1	312.7	254.9	375.5	212.2	968.3	1 026.6	1 566.2	502.4	677.7	352.0	715.1	109.8
July	554.3	314.4	258.9	374.2	216.2	968.1	1 041.5	1 583.4	512.4	671.3	350.4	704.4	111.6
August	563.1	318.8	257.2	371.7	213.4	962.9	1 033.2	1 608.2	520.1	667.4	347.5	690.9	114.9
September	568.6	364.7	257.7	363.0	215.2	974.3	1 086.0	1 650.9	529.5	663.0	346.4	690.4	115.6
October	572.5	330.5	251.7	360.0	210.3	982.4	1 152.7	1 665.1	543.8	657.6	343.2	681.3	116.0
November	576.6	329.0	252.8	378.2	214.1	984.4	1 171.5	1 704.3	555.8	648.1	339.1	679.1	114.8
December	582.0	332.5	256.8	378.9	210.0	987.6	1 193.6	1 736.0	572.9	633.6	339.1	679.2	114.8
2002													
January	587.4	330.2	259.0	376.8	209.5	978.9	1 183.9	1 767.8	584.8	626.3	333.7	684.4	115.5
February	591.6	327.3	259.2	375.0	215.5	971.4	1 192.5	1 797.1	602.1	619.5	329.5	686.2	115.2
March	595.0	326.8	260.3	373.2	217.4	957.3	1 198.0	1 812.2	618.6	613.4	326.1	689.2	114.8
April	599.1	310.9	261.9	371.1	216.4	946.4	1 206.2	1 833.3	631.9	608.3	322.8	701.9	115.3
May	604.0	307.6	264.5	367.5	211.9	942.0	1 206.9	1 863.5	637.2	611.4	314.1	718.6	112.4
June	609.4	305.8	265.2	369.8	210.6	937.6	1 202.3	1 881.5	645.0	610.6	310.9	713.1	111.2
July	615.1	304.3	267.0	373.6	209.9	944.4	1 198.1	1 903.5	655.7	608.4	309.6	713.0	111.2
August	617.7	290.2	267.2	400.9	210.8	941.3	1 196.0	1 947.0	666.7	605.4	308.2	713.0	112.7
September	619.2	293.3	270.2	423.5	214.4	927.5	1 181.7	1 974.8	678.3	600.4	306.3	710.7	113.1
October	621.1	298.9	274.0	422.3	221.6	922.4	1 148.9	2 003.8	692.9	597.0	304.7	718.2	114.6
November	623.8	296.6	276.3	445.0	226.3	922.7	1 214.6	2 041.3	701.4	594.2	303.2	709.7	116.5
December	627.4	303.4	278.6	480.9	228.6	915.9	1 245.3	2 053.2	716.3	589.9	302.1	685.5	117.5
2003													
January	630.9	301.9	279.8	472.6	236.6	904.6	1 219.8	2 085.5	728.8	586.0	300.2	691.2	118.9
February	635.4	308.3	283.6	485.4	238.1	897.9	1 205.4	2 110.3	744.1	582.4	297.7	687.0	118.7
March	639.0	307.7	286.1	497.4	241.6	889.5	1 193.8	2 126.9	759.3	578.8	296.1	691.7	117.7
April	642.0	310.5	286.0	501.6	249.3	883.8	1 176.6	2 162.0	773.0	574.8	294.2	691.0	118.0
May	644.6	314.7	290.8	511.3	261.3	882.4	1 153.9	2 189.9	794.0	570.1	291.1	696.4	117.3
June	646.4	321.8	295.2	517.2	262.5	879.7	1 155.0	2 221.7	800.0	565.9	287.9	695.3	118.5
July	648.0	319.1	298.8	498.2	269.8	867.8	1 193.8	2 269.6	812.6	557.6	285.0	699.6	121.5
August	650.8	320.9	302.2	497.6	279.1	864.0	1 174.7	2 302.5	826.2	550.7	281.7	707.6	123.0
September	654.1	313.4	306.3	502.1	280.1	852.1	1 175.6	2 291.3	834.3	545.5	279.4	715.4	122.5
October	658.3	312.2	305.9	511.4	286.8	824.9	1 154.1	2 301.2	840.0	541.8	277.0	713.3	122.1
November	661.3	308.6	305.8	513.3	286.4	813.3	1 131.7	2 321.5	834.4	538.2	274.7	726.0	121.2
December	663.9	312.6	309.2	513.4	288.7	801.5	1 113.2	2 328.0	830.4	536.4	272.8	747.7	120.2

Table 12-3. Aggregate Reserves of Depository Institutions and Monetary Base

(Millions of dollars, monthly data are averages of daily figures, adjusted for seasonality and changes in reserve requirements, annual data are for December.)

Year and month	Reserves				Monetary base
	Total	Nonborrowed	Nonborrowed plus extended credit	Required	
1959	11 109	10 168	10 168	10 603	40 880
1960	11 247	11 172	11 172	10 503	40 977
1961	11 499	11 366	11 366	10 915	41 853
1962	11 604	11 344	11 344	11 033	42 957
1963	11 730	11 397	11 397	11 239	45 003
1964	12 011	11 747	11 747	11 605	47 161
1965	12 316	11 872	11 872	11 892	49 620
1966	12 223	11 690	11 690	11 884	51 565
1967	13 180	12 952	12 952	12 805	54 579
1968	13 767	13 021	13 021	13 341	58 357
1969	14 168	13 049	13 049	13 882	61 569
1970	14 558	14 225	14 225	14 309	65 013
1971	15 230	15 104	15 104	15 049	69 108
1972	16 645	15 595	15 595	16 361	75 167
1973	17 021	15 723	15 723	16 717	81 073
1974	17 550	16 823	16 970	17 292	87 535
1975	17 822	17 692	17 704	17 556	93 887
1976	18 388	18 335	18 335	18 115	101 515
1977	18 990	18 420	18 420	18 800	110 324
1978	19 753	18 885	18 885	19 521	120 445
1979	20 720	19 248	19 248	20 279	131 143
1980	22 015	20 325	20 328	21 501	142 004
1981	22 443	21 807	21 956	22 124	149 021
1982	23 600	22 966	23 152	23 100	160 127
1983	25 367	24 593	24 595	24 806	175 467
1984	26 896	23 710	26 314	26 061	187 237
1985	31 541	30 223	30 722	30 478	203 540
1986	38 841	38 015	38 317	37 668	223 432
1987	38 918	38 141	38 624	37 899	239 847
1988	40 428	38 712	39 956	39 366	256 869
1989	40 430	40 164	40 184	39 489	267 668
1990	41 699	41 374	41 397	40 035	293 262
1991	45 451	45 258	45 259	44 461	317 509
1992	54 332	54 208	54 209	53 178	350 758
1993	60 460	60 378	60 378	59 390	386 465
1994	59 369	59 160	59 160	58 209	418 196
1995	56 430	56 173	56 173	55 140	434 388
1996	50 149	49 994	49 994	48 733	451 904
1997	46 848	46 523	46 523	45 163	479 826
1998	45 254	45 138	45 138	43 741	513 894
1999	41 928	41 607	41 607	40 631	593 709
2000	38 677	38 467	38 467	37 249	585 104
2001	41 411	41 344	41 344	39 760	635 936
2002	40 442	40 362	40 362	38 433	682 151
2003	42 843	42 797	42 797	41 804	720 978
2001					
January	37 847	37 774	37 774	36 463	588 053
February	38 427	38 376	38 376	36 920	589 841
March	38 278	38 220	38 220	36 879	591 977
April	38 354	38 303	38 303	37 077	594 869
May	38 483	38 270	38 270	37 464	598 094
June	39 027	38 798	38 798	37 665	601 500
July	39 568	39 285	39 285	38 160	607 771
August	39 809	39 626	39 626	38 601	615 828
September	58 085	54 700	54 700	39 069	640 082
October	45 476	45 349	45 349	44 150	630 645
November	40 999	40 915	40 915	39 558	630 420
December	41 411	41 344	41 344	39 760	635 936
2002					
January	41 640	41 590	41 590	40 245	641 534
February	41 571	41 541	41 541	40 201	646 160
March	40 883	40 804	40 804	39 462	649 124
April	40 595	40 524	40 524	39 383	652 862
May	39 429	39 317	39 317	38 168	656 818
June	39 288	39 146	39 146	38 049	662 257
July	39 435	39 243	39 243	38 057	668 273
August	39 703	39 370	39 370	38 095	670 801
September	39 036	38 807	38 807	37 550	672 264
October	39 132	38 989	38 989	37 597	674 482
November	39 880	39 609	39 609	38 242	677 713
December	40 442	40 362	40 362	38 433	682 151
2003					
January	40 840	40 813	40 813	39 132	685 645
February	41 095	41 070	41 070	39 129	690 639
March	41 087	41 065	41 065	39 453	693 925
April	40 696	40 666	40 666	39 153	696 642
May	40 884	40 829	40 829	39 263	700 151
June	42 348	42 186	42 186	40 485	702 786
July	43 314	43 183	43 183	41 379	705 363
August	45 581	45 252	45 252	41 814	710 239
September	44 289	44 109	44 109	42 779	712 123
October	43 394	43 287	43 287	41 921	715 834
November	43 034	42 966	42 966	41 545	718 968
December	42 843	42 797	42 797	41 804	720 978

Table 12-4. Commercial Banks: Bank Credit and Selected Liabilities

(All commercial banks in the United States, billions of dollars, seasonally adjusted, annual data are for December.)

Year and month	Bank credit								
	Total	Securities in bank credit			Loans and leases in bank credit				
		Total	U.S. government securities	Other securities	Total	Commercial and industrial	Real estate		
							Total	Revolving home equity	Other
1947	111.0	77.0	72.1	4.8	34.0	14.4	8.9	...	...
1948	109.1	70.8	65.7	5.1	38.3	15.3	10.3	...	...
1949	115.7	76.3	70.5	5.9	39.4	13.8	11.0	...	...
1950	120.4	72.2	65.1	7.1	48.2	17.6	12.9	...	...
1951	126.5	72.4	64.5	8.0	54.1	21.3	14.1	...	...
1952	134.1	74.3	66.3	7.9	59.8	23.6	15.0	...	...
1953	139.7	77.0	67.7	9.4	62.7	23.6	16.1	...	...
1954	150.8	85.8	74.9	10.8	65.0	22.9	17.6	...	...
1955	152.2	76.5	65.6	10.9	75.7	27.2	19.9	...	...
1956	158.0	73.2	62.1	11.1	84.9	33.0	21.7	...	...
1957	162.7	73.5	61.0	12.4	89.2	34.7	22.3	...	...
1958	184.1	85.9	70.5	15.4	98.2	35.4	25.1	...	...
1959	189.5	77.4	61.9	15.5	112.1	39.5	28.1	...	...
1960	197.6	79.5	63.9	15.6	118.1	42.4	28.7	...	...
1961	213.1	88.2	70.4	17.9	124.8	44.1	30.2	...	...
1962	231.0	92.2	70.7	21.5	138.8	47.7	34.0	...	...
1963	250.7	92.6	67.4	25.2	158.1	52.5	38.9	...	...
1964	270.4	94.7	66.7	28.1	175.6	58.7	43.5	...	...
1965	297.1	96.1	64.3	31.9	201.0	69.5	48.9	...	...
1966	318.6	97.2	61.0	36.2	221.4	79.3	53.8	...	...
1967	350.5	111.4	70.7	40.6	239.2	86.5	58.2	...	...
1968	390.5	121.9	73.8	48.1	268.6	96.5	64.8	...	...
1969	401.6	112.4	64.2	48.2	289.2	106.9	69.9	...	...
1970	434.4	129.7	73.4	56.3	304.6	111.6	72.9	...	...
1971	485.2	147.5	79.8	67.7	337.6	118.0	81.7	...	...
1972	555.3	160.6	85.4	75.2	394.7	133.6	98.8	...	...
1973	638.6	168.4	89.7	78.7	470.1	162.8	119.4	0.0	119.4
1974	701.7	173.8	87.9	85.9	527.9	193.0	132.5	0.0	132.5
1975	732.9	206.7	117.9	88.9	526.2	184.3	137.2	0.0	137.2
1976	790.7	228.6	137.3	91.3	562.1	186.3	151.3	0.0	151.3
1977	876.0	236.3	137.4	98.9	639.7	205.8	178.0	0.0	178.0
1978	989.4	242.2	138.4	103.8	747.2	239.0	213.5	0.0	213.5
1979	1 111.4	260.7	147.2	113.4	850.7	282.2	245.0	0.0	245.0
1980	1 207.1	296.8	173.2	123.6	910.3	314.5	265.7	0.0	265.7
1981	1 302.7	311.1	181.8	129.3	991.6	353.3	287.5	0.0	287.5
1982	1 412.3	338.6	204.7	133.9	1 073.7	396.4	303.8	0.0	303.8
1983	1 566.7	403.8	263.4	140.4	1 163.0	419.1	334.8	0.0	334.8
1984	1 733.4	406.6	262.9	143.7	1 326.9	479.4	380.8	0.0	380.8
1985	1 922.2	455.9	273.8	182.2	1 466.3	506.5	431.0	0.0	431.0
1986	2 106.6	510.0	312.8	197.2	1 596.5	544.0	499.9	0.0	499.9
1987	2 255.3	535.0	338.9	196.1	1 720.2	575.0	595.7	32.2	563.5
1988	2 432.7	561.7	366.0	195.7	1 871.0	611.7	676.4	42.6	633.8
1989	2 602.2	584.7	399.5	185.2	2 017.5	642.7	769.2	53.5	715.6
1990	2 749.7	634.9	456.0	178.9	2 114.9	645.6	856.6	66.4	790.2
1991	2 856.4	747.2	566.9	180.3	2 109.2	623.4	882.8	74.3	808.5
1992	2 954.1	841.8	664.9	176.9	2 112.3	599.4	906.0	78.5	827.5
1993	3 112.4	915.6	730.8	184.8	2 196.7	590.3	947.0	78.1	868.9
1994	3 318.2	939.9	721.6	218.3	2 378.3	650.3	1 010.7	80.5	930.2
1995	3 601.0	984.0	701.1	282.9	2 617.0	723.8	1 089.5	84.5	1 004.9
1996	3 756.9	984.4	702.6	281.8	2 772.6	784.7	1 140.1	90.9	1 049.2
1997	4 099.4	1 098.9	755.6	343.1	3 000.7	854.1	1 242.7	105.0	1 137.7
1998	4 532.9	1 237.0	797.6	439.5	3 295.9	947.4	1 332.9	103.9	1 229.0
1999	4 763.1	1 282.8	815.6	467.2	3 480.3	998.6	1 471.1	101.5	1 369.6
2000	5 216.4	1 348.2	792.4	555.8	3 868.2	1 086.8	1 650.5	130.0	1 520.5
2001	5 427.6	1 493.5	853.0	640.5	3 934.1	1 027.0	1 779.7	155.8	1 623.9
2002	5 885.5	1 721.1	1 029.1	692.0	4 164.4	962.9	2 021.2	213.5	1 807.7
2003	6 249.5	1 850.9	1 104.5	746.4	4 398.6	891.5	2 215.6	280.8	1 934.9
2002									
January	5 409.4	1 487.4	838.5	648.9	3 921.9	1 015.9	1 780.1	158.7	1 621.4
February	5 424.9	1 489.5	835.3	654.2	3 935.5	1 019.1	1 788.4	161.8	1 626.6
March	5 425.1	1 489.4	851.3	638.1	3 935.7	1 013.7	1 797.8	166.8	1 631.0
April	5 450.8	1 502.7	866.4	636.3	3 948.0	1 003.7	1 807.7	171.5	1 636.2
May	5 494.5	1 530.1	885.3	644.8	3 964.4	997.6	1 828.2	179.0	1 649.2
June	5 542.7	1 558.7	904.6	654.1	3 984.0	991.2	1 854.6	185.2	1 669.4
July	5 584.4	1 589.7	914.4	675.3	3 994.7	980.5	1 880.8	191.9	1 688.9
August	5 660.8	1 628.3	942.9	685.4	4 032.4	979.5	1 905.7	196.7	1 709.0
September	5 720.6	1 647.0	966.5	680.5	4 073.6	974.9	1 933.4	200.4	1 733.0
October	5 747.0	1 646.0	979.9	666.1	4 101.0	969.4	1 964.0	204.6	1 759.4
November	5 818.7	1 686.6	1 007.6	679.1	4 132.1	966.4	1 990.3	208.5	1 781.8
December	5 885.5	1 721.1	1 029.1	692.0	4 164.4	962.9	2 021.2	213.5	1 807.7
2003									
January	5 888.5	1 721.6	1 037.7	683.9	4 167.0	958.2	2 046.4	218.0	1 828.3
February	5 970.0	1 766.9	1 067.6	699.3	4 203.2	949.7	2 078.4	223.1	1 855.3
March	6 008.4	1 777.7	1 076.8	700.8	4 230.7	943.2	2 102.0	230.1	1 871.9
April	6 048.7	1 779.5	1 098.4	681.1	4 269.2	942.9	2 126.2	235.2	1 891.1
May	6 152.8	1 832.7	1 125.1	707.6	4 320.1	934.6	2 146.9	239.1	1 907.9
June	6 206.2	1 855.6	1 143.4	712.2	4 350.6	925.0	2 171.9	244.7	1 927.2
July	6 194.6	1 814.7	1 110.5	704.2	4 379.9	926.6	2 197.9	248.5	1 949.4
August	6 179.8	1 777.3	1 080.0	697.3	4 402.5	918.4	2 234.0	252.7	1 981.3
September	6 185.0	1 788.9	1 071.1	717.8	4 396.1	907.9	2 245.3	258.5	1 986.8
October	6 161.5	1 804.8	1 081.2	723.6	4 356.7	893.6	2 227.6	265.5	1 962.1
November	6 198.0	1 832.0	1 097.1	734.9	4 366.0	888.4	2 206.8	273.2	1 933.6
December	6 249.5	1 850.9	1 104.5	746.4	4 398.6	891.5	2 215.6	280.8	1 934.9

... = Not available.

Table 12-4. Commercial Banks: Bank Credit and Selected Liabilities—Continued

(All commercial banks in the United States, billions of dollars, seasonally adjusted, annual data are for December.)

| Year and month | Bank credit—Continued ||| Deposits | Selected liabilities ||||
| | Loans and leases in bank credit—Continued ||| | Borrowings |||
	Consumer	Security	Other		Total	From banks in the U.S.	From nonbanks in the U.S.
1947	5.7	2.3	2.8	...	...	...	...
1948	6.9	2.5	3.2	...	...	...	...
1949	8.1	2.9	3.5	...	...	...	...
1950	10.2	3.1	4.3	...	...	...	...
1951	10.7	2.7	5.2	...	...	...	...
1952	12.7	3.2	5.3	...	...	...	...
1953	14.7	3.6	4.8	...	...	...	...
1954	14.9	4.4	5.1	...	...	...	...
1955	17.3	5.1	6.1	...	...	...	...
1956	19.1	4.8	6.2	...	...	...	...
1957	20.0	4.6	7.6	...	...	...	...
1958	20.4	4.7	12.7	...	...	...	...
1959	24.1	5.0	15.4	...	...	...	...
1960	26.3	5.2	15.6	...	...	...	...
1961	27.6	6.1	16.8	...	...	...	...
1962	30.3	6.6	20.2	...	...	...	...
1963	34.2	7.9	24.6	...	...	...	...
1964	39.5	8.3	25.7	...	...	...	...
1965	45.0	8.0	29.7	...	...	...	...
1966	47.7	8.3	32.4	...	...	...	...
1967	51.2	9.6	33.8	...	...	...	...
1968	57.7	10.5	39.2	...	...	...	...
1969	62.6	10.0	39.8	...	...	...	...
1970	65.3	10.4	44.5	...	...	...	...
1971	73.3	10.9	53.9	...	...	...	...
1972	85.4	14.4	62.5	...	...	...	...
1973	98.3	11.2	78.4	651.6	70.5	44.1	26.4
1974	102.1	10.6	89.6	718.9	76.3	47.8	28.6
1975	104.6	12.7	87.5	759.3	72.1	45.1	27.0
1976	115.9	17.7	91.0	815.3	95.5	56.3	39.2
1977	138.1	20.7	97.2	899.4	111.7	61.8	49.9
1978	164.6	19.1	110.9	996.7	138.4	72.6	65.8
1979	184.5	17.4	121.6	1 069.3	176.6	97.4	79.2
1980	179.2	17.2	133.6	1 181.6	212.3	118.1	94.2
1981	182.7	20.2	148.0	1 247.4	256.0	142.3	113.7
1982	188.2	23.6	161.7	1 365.5	282.2	153.9	128.3
1983	213.2	26.5	169.4	1 478.8	282.8	149.1	133.7
1984	253.6	34.1	179.0	1 607.0	316.9	165.8	151.1
1985	294.5	42.9	191.4	1 752.1	372.6	192.4	180.1
1986	314.5	38.6	199.5	1 911.2	410.2	213.3	196.9
1987	327.7	34.8	187.0	1 971.7	427.2	222.2	204.9
1988	354.8	40.3	187.9	2 111.0	491.2	252.1	239.1
1989	375.3	40.9	189.3	2 237.3	552.5	282.9	269.6
1990	380.8	44.4	187.4	2 339.5	575.8	296.6	279.2
1991	363.9	53.9	185.2	2 468.0	496.8	222.6	274.2
1992	356.3	63.4	187.2	2 501.1	498.8	213.4	285.4
1993	387.6	86.4	185.5	2 535.3	535.8	214.4	321.4
1994	448.2	75.8	193.3	2 536.2	622.1	257.1	365.0
1995	491.4	83.2	229.1	2 668.9	697.1	288.4	408.7
1996	512.9	75.3	259.6	2 868.1	729.9	299.5	430.3
1997	502.6	94.4	306.9	3 118.8	854.7	307.0	547.7
1998	496.9	145.3	373.3	3 331.4	1 021.6	320.3	701.4
1999	490.6	149.8	370.2	3 533.6	1 125.8	346.4	779.4
2000	539.1	177.3	414.4	3 851.5	1 243.4	379.9	863.5
2001	555.8	146.0	425.6	4 240.0	1 253.9	406.6	847.4
2002	586.4	190.2	403.6	4 504.1	1 415.0	422.7	992.3
2003	629.5	215.2	446.8	4 765.0	1 476.4	386.1	1 090.3
2002							
January	556.1	153.7	416.1	4 252.9	1 244.3	407.4	836.9
February	560.8	156.7	410.5	4 262.0	1 239.7	403.2	836.5
March	563.4	160.1	400.7	4 301.3	1 215.6	389.1	826.4
April	568.3	167.3	401.0	4 316.3	1 221.8	386.8	834.9
May	571.1	169.3	398.2	4 349.5	1 236.2	388.9	847.3
June	570.2	169.3	398.7	4 364.1	1 229.1	381.9	847.2
July	564.9	176.1	392.5	4 399.7	1 226.3	385.6	840.7
August	574.1	177.7	395.4	4 437.9	1 282.5	401.9	880.6
September	581.2	182.6	401.5	4 451.4	1 324.2	413.7	910.5
October	583.2	183.4	401.0	4 475.0	1 345.0	416.2	928.8
November	584.4	186.8	404.2	4 510.9	1 381.7	424.6	957.0
December	586.4	190.2	403.6	4 504.1	1 415.0	422.7	992.3
2003							
January	585.6	176.4	400.4	4 522.6	1 356.1	390.2	965.9
February	589.3	184.2	401.6	4 548.5	1 381.7	395.9	985.9
March	590.2	191.9	403.5	4 591.7	1 406.1	401.8	1 004.3
April	589.1	191.7	419.2	4 613.1	1 406.3	396.8	1 009.5
May	597.5	215.0	426.1	4 641.3	1 443.7	393.7	1 050.0
June	600.8	216.8	436.1	4 687.7	1 484.6	410.3	1 074.3
July	601.3	217.7	436.4	4 729.8	1 524.2	411.9	1 112.4
August	600.7	214.6	434.8	4 769.5	1 523.6	414.9	1 108.8
September	601.6	212.2	429.2	4 749.0	1 498.1	400.0	1 098.1
October	596.9	220.1	418.6	4 707.0	1 454.6	386.2	1 068.4
November	625.9	228.7	416.3	4 747.4	1 452.4	383.8	1 068.6
December	629.5	215.2	446.8	4 765.0	1 476.4	386.1	1 090.3

. . . = Not available.

Table 12-5. Credit Market Debt Outstanding, By Borrower and Lender

(Billions of dollars, except as noted; end of period; not seasonally adjusted.)

Year and quarter	Credit market debt outstanding													
		Owed by:												
		Domestic financial sectors			Domestic nonfinancial sectors									
					Total		Federal government			Households		Nonfinancial business		
	Total	Total	Federal government-related	Private	Billions of dollars	Percent of GDP	Total	Treasury securities	Budget agency securities and mortgages	Billions of dollars	Percent of DPI	Total	Corporate	
													Total	Percent of sector value added
1945	355.0	1.9	0.9	1.0	348.1	156.0	251.5	251.2	0.3	28.0	18.4	56.0	44.6	46.7
1946	350.8	3.0	1.2	1.8	339.8	152.9	228.0	227.9	0.1	35.2	21.8	63.9	49.8	50.1
1947	367.7	3.8	1.3	2.5	351.6	144.0	220.8	220.7	0.1	43.9	25.6	72.6	56.6	46.9
1948	382.2	5.3	1.6	3.7	363.2	134.9	215.1	214.2	0.9	52.4	27.5	80.0	62.7	45.3
1949	397.5	6.1	1.4	4.7	377.5	141.2	217.7	216.7	1.0	60.2	31.6	83.0	64.2	47.7
1950	425.3	8.5	1.8	6.7	402.8	137.1	216.5	216.1	0.4	72.9	34.7	92.1	70.3	45.9
1951	449.2	9.6	2.1	7.5	425.0	125.3	216.1	215.8	0.2	81.5	35.3	103.9	78.7	44.8
1952	484.6	11.1	2.2	8.9	458.4	127.9	221.4	220.8	0.6	93.6	38.5	112.6	84.9	46.3
1953	516.7	12.7	2.2	10.5	487.7	128.6	228.4	226.2	2.3	105.8	40.9	117.7	89.1	45.5
1954	541.8	12.3	2.1	10.1	512.9	134.8	230.8	228.5	2.3	117.1	44.3	123.9	92.6	48.0
1955	582.0	15.3	3.2	12.1	550.1	132.6	230.0	228.4	1.6	137.6	48.6	136.4	101.2	46.5
1956	611.4	17.9	4.0	13.9	576.1	131.7	224.1	222.8	1.4	152.5	50.3	149.1	110.8	47.6
1957	642.7	20.8	5.1	15.7	603.2	130.8	221.9	220.1	1.8	165.0	51.6	161.3	120.5	49.5
1958	681.6	21.0	5.2	15.8	639.9	137.0	231.1	229.0	2.1	175.8	53.2	172.3	127.6	53.8
1959	738.6	27.7	7.5	20.2	689.5	136.1	238.0	236.2	1.8	197.7	56.4	187.1	136.3	51.2
1960	780.0	32.5	8.1	24.4	724.3	137.6	236.0	234.0	1.9	215.1	58.9	201.0	145.2	52.5
1961	828.1	34.9	8.9	26.0	767.8	141.0	243.2	240.7	2.5	231.6	60.7	215.2	152.7	53.8
1962	887.6	39.4	10.5	28.9	820.6	140.1	250.0	246.8	3.3	253.5	62.6	233.3	163.1	52.6
1963	953.5	46.6	12.0	34.6	876.0	141.8	253.8	250.7	3.2	280.2	65.9	252.8	173.7	52.7
1964	1 027.9	53.0	12.7	40.3	940.0	141.6	259.9	255.9	4.0	309.4	66.9	275.0	187.5	52.7
1965	1 106.5	61.9	15.1	46.8	1 007.2	140.1	261.5	257.0	4.5	337.9	67.8	304.6	207.6	53.1
1966	1 187.0	72.9	20.3	52.5	1 074.7	136.4	265.1	259.3	5.8	360.4	67.1	339.1	232.1	54.1
1967	1 267.7	71.6	20.4	51.2	1 152.7	138.5	278.1	268.2	9.9	380.7	66.2	376.6	259.1	57.4
1968	1 372.8	84.0	24.4	59.6	1 242.8	136.6	290.6	277.6	13.0	412.3	66.0	413.8	285.1	57.3
1969	1 493.1	111.5	33.8	77.7	1 332.3	135.3	287.4	276.8	10.6	444.6	66.0	462.0	317.8	58.8
1970	1 602.3	127.8	43.6	84.1	1 422.5	137.0	299.5	289.9	9.6	460.2	62.6	512.5	361.3	64.7
1971	1 753.2	138.9	49.5	89.3	1 557.7	138.2	324.4	315.9	8.5	503.0	62.7	563.6	389.5	64.6
1972	1 937.6	162.8	57.9	104.8	1 713.7	138.4	339.4	330.1	9.3	559.9	64.4	633.7	427.9	63.9
1973	2 175.4	209.8	77.9	131.9	1 898.2	137.3	346.3	336.7	9.6	630.6	64.5	726.5	492.7	65.6
1974	2 412.6	258.3	98.6	159.7	2 073.1	138.2	358.2	348.8	9.4	686.1	64.0	820.5	548.9	67.8
1975	2 620.7	260.4	108.9	151.6	2 264.7	138.2	443.9	434.9	8.9	739.2	62.3	862.2	569.4	64.9
1976	2 908.3	283.9	123.1	160.8	2 508.3	137.4	513.1	503.7	9.3	823.6	63.2	933.8	610.4	61.7
1977	3 296.8	337.8	145.5	192.3	2 829.6	139.3	569.4	560.9	8.4	951.4	66.3	1 052.7	685.5	61.2
1978	3 784.6	412.5	182.6	229.9	3 214.5	140.1	621.9	614.9	7.0	1 110.5	69.0	1 186.5	759.5	59.7
1979	4 285.8	504.9	231.8	273.1	3 606.5	140.7	657.7	652.1	5.6	1 280.6	71.4	1 346.1	842.9	59.5
1980	4 734.9	578.1	276.6	301.5	3 957.9	141.9	735.0	730.0	5.0	1 401.5	69.8	1 477.0	909.1	59.1
1981	5 271.5	682.4	324.0	358.3	4 366.4	139.6	820.5	815.9	4.5	1 512.7	67.3	1 661.2	1 026.5	58.8
1982	5 779.0	778.1	388.9	389.2	4 788.3	147.1	981.8	978.1	3.7	1 582.1	65.3	1 810.6	1 116.6	61.8
1983	6 477.2	882.7	456.6	426.1	5 364.8	151.7	1 167.0	1 163.4	3.6	1 738.9	66.7	1 997.8	1 229.1	63.6
1984	7 441.7	1 052.4	531.2	521.2	6 151.2	156.4	1 364.2	1 360.8	3.4	1 949.5	66.9	2 323.9	1 437.1	66.3
1985	8 628.9	1 257.3	631.7	625.6	7 132.3	169.0	1 589.9	1 586.6	3.3	2 277.5	73.2	2 587.0	1 615.5	70.2
1986	9 809.7	1 593.6	810.3	783.3	7 975.1	178.7	1 805.9	1 802.2	3.6	2 535.6	77.2	2 881.5	1 839.5	77.0
1987	10 820.5	1 895.5	977.6	917.9	8 677.6	183.1	1 949.8	1 944.6	5.2	2 752.2	79.6	3 134.6	2 033.9	79.5
1988	11 862.2	2 145.8	1 098.4	1 047.4	9 461.7	185.4	2 104.9	2 082.3	22.6	3 039.6	81.1	3 422.2	2 234.2	80.6
1989	12 830.4	2 399.3	1 247.8	1 151.4	10 166.2	185.4	2 251.2	2 227.0	24.2	3 333.8	82.9	3 636.0	2 401.1	82.4
1990	13 768.7	2 630.3	1 418.4	1 211.9	10 849.6	187.0	2 498.1	2 465.8	32.4	3 597.2	83.9	3 761.9	2 533.1	83.3
1991	14 428.7	2 812.9	1 564.2	1 248.6	11 311.9	188.7	2 776.4	2 757.8	18.6	3 787.3	84.8	3 670.6	2 477.3	79.9
1992	15 260.5	3 111.6	1 720.4	1 391.2	11 830.2	186.7	3 080.3	3 061.6	18.8	3 988.6	83.9	3 666.7	2 502.9	77.3
1993	16 211.3	3 411.2	1 885.7	1 525.5	12 411.6	186.4	3 336.5	3 309.9	26.6	4 227.6	86.1	3 695.3	2 549.8	75.0
1994	17 251.6	3 884.2	2 173.4	1 710.8	12 989.9	183.7	3 492.3	3 465.6	26.7	4 550.4	88.3	3 841.2	2 682.9	73.1
1995	18 463.7	4 333.6	2 377.7	1 955.8	13 674.2	184.8	3 636.7	3 608.5	28.2	4 875.6	90.2	4 116.8	2 909.6	75.0
1996	19 801.0	4 866.2	2 609.2	2 257.1	14 390.7	184.1	3 781.7	3 755.1	26.6	5 208.1	91.6	4 371.8	3 092.3	75.2
1997	21 214.4	5 449.4	2 822.8	2 626.6	15 156.9	182.5	3 804.8	3 778.3	26.5	5 518.7	92.1	4 762.7	3 382.3	76.8
1998	23 350.8	6 513.2	3 294.4	3 218.8	16 198.2	185.2	3 752.2	3 723.7	28.5	5 956.7	93.1	5 350.9	3 780.4	81.2
1999	25 473.2	7 567.4	3 887.7	3 679.7	17 253.2	186.2	3 681.0	3 652.7	28.3	6 440.8	96.2	5 954.5	4 188.5	84.6
2000	27 188.1	8 372.7	4 319.7	4 053.0	18 105.9	184.4	3 385.1	3 357.8	27.3	7 012.9	97.5	6 515.5	4 545.7	86.2
2001	29 161.8	9 272.3	4 962.3	4 310.0	19 229.7	189.9	3 379.5	3 352.7	26.8	7 640.9	102.1	6 911.2	4 774.4	90.2
2002	31 320.7	10 102.3	5 509.0	4 593.3	20 552.9	196.0	3 637.0	3 609.8	27.3	8 372.4	107.0	7 101.4	4 808.6	89.4
2003	34 007.4	11 085.3	6 083.1	5 002.2	22 272.2	202.4	4 033.1	4 008.2	24.9	9 252.3	113.4	7 427.1	4 987.1	88.9
2000														
1st quarter	25 857.1	7 704.7	3 944.0	3 760.7	17 471.4	181.4	3 653.5	3 625.7	27.8	6 507.0	92.2	6 131.1	4 319.4	83.1
2nd quarter	26 226.4	7 918.2	4 039.4	3 878.8	17 635.9	179.5	3 463.9	3 435.7	28.2	6 670.2	93.4	6 315.5	4 437.1	84.5
3rd quarter	26 640.8	8 114.7	4 168.5	3 946.2	17 829.0	180.8	3 410.1	3 382.5	27.6	6 838.9	94.1	6 400.2	4 482.1	84.3
4th quarter	27 188.1	8 372.7	4 319.7	4 053.0	18 105.9	181.9	3 385.1	3 357.8	27.3	7 012.9	95.9	6 515.5	4 545.7	85.4
2001														
1st quarter	27 614.3	8 560.1	4 428.7	4 131.4	18 349.7	183.1	3 408.8	3 382.0	26.8	7 087.0	95.9	6 634.2	4 626.8	87.0
2nd quarter	27 982.4	8 762.2	4 602.0	4 160.2	18 533.0	183.0	3 251.3	3 224.3	27.0	7 268.0	98.1	6 759.7	4 703.3	88.4
3rd quarter	28 525.9	9 015.4	4 806.7	4 208.7	18 850.8	186.0	3 319.9	3 293.0	27.0	7 435.7	97.5	6 835.0	4 741.0	89.8
4th quarter	29 161.8	9 272.3	4 962.3	4 310.0	19 229.7	188.0	3 379.5	3 352.7	26.8	7 640.9	101.5	6 911.2	4 774.4	90.8
2002														
1st quarter	29 590.8	9 448.6	5 132.0	4 316.6	19 466.1	188.3	3 430.2	3 403.9	26.3	7 749.1	100.1	6 966.8	4 800.0	90.4
2nd quarter	30 088.3	9 646.1	5 253.0	4 393.1	19 768.0	189.2	3 451.3	3 424.5	26.8	7 930.2	101.1	7 016.3	4 805.1	89.4
3rd quarter	30 581.4	9 828.9	5 368.0	4 461.0	20 086.6	190.5	3 540.8	3 513.6	27.2	8 118.8	103.4	7 034.0	4 786.7	88.8
4th quarter	31 320.7	10 102.3	5 509.0	4 593.3	20 552.9	193.6	3 637.0	3 609.8	27.3	8 372.4	106.3	7 101.4	4 808.6	88.5
2003														
1st quarter	31 845.3	10 321.3	5 632.8	4 688.5	20 854.6	194.1	3 700.6	3 673.7	26.9	8 523.4	106.9	7 164.6	4 847.0	89.0
2nd quarter	32 564.1	10 518.4	5 743.1	4 775.3	21 392.5	196.5	3 806.9	3 779.9	27.0	8 789.9	108.9	7 274.8	4 918.7	88.7
3rd quarter	33 225.0	10 785.0	5 940.5	4 844.5	21 801.3	196.1	3 914.5	3 887.5	27.0	9 027.3	109.2	7 329.8	4 934.8	87.0
4th quarter	34 007.4	11 085.3	6 083.1	5 002.2	22 272.2	197.6	4 033.1	4 008.2	24.9	9 252.3	111.2	7 427.1	4 987.1	86.5

. . . = Not available.

Table 12-5. Credit Market Debt Outstanding, By Borrower and Lender—Continued

(Billions of dollars, except as noted; end of period; not seasonally adjusted.)

Year and quarter	Credit market debt outstanding owed by: —Continued				Credit market assets held by:								
	Domestic nonfinancial sectors —Continued			Foreign credit market debt held in United States	Total	Government-related sectors						Selected domestic financial sectors	
	Nonfinancial business—Continued		State and local governments			Total	Federal government	Government-sponsored enterprises	Federally related mortgage pools	State and local governments	State and local retirement funds	Total, selected sectors	Monetary authority
	Nonfarm noncorporate	Farm											
1945	4.8	6.6	12.6	5.0	355.0	17.2	5.2	2.0	0.0	7.5	2.5	218.5	24.3
1946	7.2	7.0	12.7	8.0	350.8	20.0	8.3	2.1	0.0	6.8	2.8	219.0	23.5
1947	8.5	7.4	14.3	12.3	367.7	25.5	12.6	2.3	0.0	7.5	3.1	228.5	22.6
1948	9.2	8.1	15.7	13.7	382.2	28.3	13.9	2.7	0.0	8.2	3.5	235.7	23.5
1949	10.2	8.5	16.6	13.9	397.5	30.6	15.3	2.6	0.0	8.6	4.1	245.0	19.0
1950	12.3	9.5	21.2	14.0	425.3	33.2	16.0	3.1	0.0	9.4	4.7	262.3	20.7
1951	14.3	10.8	23.6	14.7	449.2	36.2	17.2	3.5	0.0	10.1	5.4	280.9	23.6
1952	16.1	11.6	30.8	15.1	484.6	40.6	18.8	3.6	0.1	11.7	6.4	303.2	24.1
1953	17.1	11.5	35.8	16.3	516.7	44.9	20.8	3.7	0.1	12.6	7.7	322.9	25.3
1954	18.9	12.3	41.1	16.6	541.8	47.3	20.5	4.0	0.1	13.5	9.2	346.1	25.0
1955	21.5	13.7	46.1	16.6	582.0	51.4	21.1	5.0	0.1	14.7	10.5	368.4	24.4
1956	23.7	14.6	50.4	17.4	611.4	55.6	21.8	6.0	0.1	15.9	11.7	390.0	24.7
1957	25.2	15.6	55.0	18.8	642.7	59.1	22.4	7.3	0.2	15.9	13.3	410.7	23.8
1958	27.7	17.0	60.7	20.8	681.6	62.8	23.9	7.7	0.2	16.1	15.0	444.0	26.3
1959	31.9	18.9	66.7	21.4	738.6	70.1	25.7	9.9	0.2	17.5	16.8	470.9	26.7
1960	35.8	20.0	72.2	23.2	780.0	76.0	26.7	11.1	0.2	19.1	18.9	502.5	27.0
1961	41.0	21.6	77.8	25.5	828.1	82.0	28.4	12.1	0.3	20.1	21.1	540.7	28.8
1962	46.4	23.9	83.8	27.5	887.6	89.4	30.4	13.7	0.4	21.7	23.2	586.5	30.5
1963	52.6	26.4	89.2	30.8	953.5	96.6	31.9	15.3	0.5	23.3	25.6	637.1	33.7
1964	58.5	29.0	95.6	35.0	1 027.9	104.7	34.7	16.0	0.6	25.0	28.3	694.2	36.6
1965	64.7	32.3	103.2	37.5	1 106.5	115.5	37.6	18.3	0.9	27.5	31.3	757.0	40.6
1966	71.5	35.5	110.0	39.5	1 187.0	129.8	42.7	23.3	1.3	27.5	34.9	803.9	43.7
1967	78.7	38.8	117.4	43.3	1 267.7	138.5	47.3	23.3	2.0	27.6	38.3	869.1	49.1
1968	87.1	41.6	126.1	46.1	1 372.8	154.4	52.3	26.5	2.5	31.4	41.6	942.1	53.0
1969	99.6	44.6	138.3	49.2	1 493.1	175.6	55.4	35.1	3.2	36.4	45.5	998.7	57.2
1970	103.6	47.6	150.3	52.1	1 602.3	191.5	58.2	43.9	4.8	35.1	49.6	1 071.9	62.2
1971	122.6	51.6	166.7	56.6	1 753.2	201.1	60.3	45.0	9.5	33.4	52.9	1 181.6	69.6
1972	149.0	56.8	180.7	61.1	1 937.6	223.0	62.2	49.0	14.4	40.1	57.4	1 325.8	71.2
1973	168.5	65.4	194.8	67.4	2 175.4	260.2	64.9	64.4	18.0	49.8	63.1	1 491.4	80.5
1974	198.4	73.3	208.2	81.2	2 412.6	304.7	72.2	85.3	21.5	56.4	69.4	1 631.1	85.3
1975	210.7	82.1	219.4	95.6	2 620.7	346.1	85.8	89.8	28.5	63.8	78.3	1 764.0	93.5
1976	231.2	92.2	237.8	116.0	2 908.3	398.6	93.7	94.5	40.7	82.0	87.7	1 959.8	100.3
1977	261.3	105.9	256.2	129.4	3 296.8	471.6	103.6	101.4	56.8	110.6	99.2	2 217.6	108.9
1978	304.8	122.2	295.6	157.6	3 784.6	582.6	120.6	128.1	70.4	147.5	116.0	2 512.9	117.4
1979	357.5	145.7	322.2	174.3	4 285.8	696.0	141.4	158.1	94.8	175.2	126.6	2 824.5	124.5
1980	406.4	161.5	344.4	198.9	4 734.9	804.5	165.5	184.5	114.0	193.4	147.2	3 092.4	128.0
1981	456.8	177.8	372.1	222.8	5 271.5	931.1	189.9	217.7	129.0	225.6	169.0	3 399.1	136.9
1982	509.5	184.5	413.8	212.6	5 779.0	1 058.9	205.8	233.7	178.5	250.1	190.7	3 640.2	144.5
1983	580.3	188.4	461.1	229.8	6 477.2	1 177.7	215.3	236.4	244.8	282.4	198.8	4 046.3	159.2
1984	698.8	187.9	513.6	238.0	7 441.7	1 339.7	232.6	265.9	289.0	319.0	233.2	4 602.8	167.6
1985	798.0	173.4	677.9	239.3	8 628.9	1 618.0	251.2	291.0	367.9	455.6	252.4	5 177.6	186.0
1986	886.0	156.0	752.1	241.0	9 809.7	1 920.0	258.0	307.6	531.6	525.8	297.1	5 880.5	205.5
1987	956.3	144.4	841.0	247.4	10 820.5	2 155.5	242.8	330.9	669.4	583.6	328.8	6 439.3	230.1
1988	1 054.2	133.7	895.0	254.8	11 862.2	2 295.9	217.4	364.2	745.3	618.6	350.5	6 971.2	240.6
1989	1 100.5	134.4	945.2	265.0	12 830.4	2 484.3	209.4	359.9	869.5	664.1	381.5	7 390.4	233.3
1990	1 093.3	135.4	992.3	288.8	13 768.7	2 742.1	243.0	373.9	1 019.9	703.4	402.0	7 769.3	241.4
1991	1 058.5	134.8	1 077.7	304.0	14 428.7	2 951.5	250.9	388.9	1 156.5	750.6	404.6	8 043.4	272.5
1992	1 028.4	135.3	1 094.5	318.7	15 260.5	3 163.1	238.9	458.1	1 272.0	752.3	441.8	8 466.6	300.4
1993	1 007.9	137.6	1 152.2	388.5	16 211.3	3 386.4	229.5	546.7	1 356.8	784.9	468.6	9 061.0	336.7
1994	1 015.9	142.4	1 105.9	377.5	17 251.6	3 563.4	214.5	667.9	1 472.4	729.9	478.7	9 563.5	368.2
1995	1 062.0	145.2	1 045.0	456.0	18 463.7	3 689.6	207.7	762.8	1 570.7	638.6	509.8	10 291.6	380.8
1996	1 130.7	148.8	1 029.1	544.1	19 801.0	3 895.1	206.4	833.8	1 711.7	604.8	538.4	10 882.1	393.1
1997	1 225.4	155.0	1 070.7	608.1	21 214.4	4 173.4	209.7	934.2	1 826.3	605.0	598.3	11 729.2	431.4
1998	1 405.3	165.3	1 138.3	639.4	23 350.8	4 864.8	221.4	1 251.5	2 019.0	709.7	663.2	12 874.9	452.5
1999	1 595.5	170.6	1 176.9	652.6	25 473.2	5 606.4	260.9	1 538.8	2 293.5	810.4	702.8	13 962.5	478.1
2000	1 788.4	181.5	1 192.3	709.6	27 188.1	6 134.9	272.6	1 794.4	2 493.2	822.6	752.0	14 921.0	511.8
2001	1 944.7	192.0	1 298.1	659.9	29 161.8	6 855.1	278.6	2 099.1	2 831.8	930.5	715.2	15 970.5	551.7
2002	2 093.0	199.9	1 442.0	665.5	31 320.7	7 431.2	288.2	2 323.2	3 158.6	953.3	708.0	17 133.7	629.4
2003	2 232.5	207.6	1 559.7	649.8	34 007.4	8 078.6	285.6	2 565.0	3 489.0	1 010.1	728.9	18 234.4	666.7
2000													
1st quarter	1 642.4	169.4	1 179.8	681.1	25 857.1	5 695.2	263.6	1 577.4	2 323.5	813.9	716.8	14 199.4	501.9
2nd quarter	1 701.9	176.5	1 186.3	672.3	26 226.4	5 804.4	263.4	1 642.7	2 356.6	818.9	722.9	14 376.1	505.1
3rd quarter	1 738.9	179.1	1 179.9	697.1	26 640.8	5 941.0	271.2	1 702.8	2 415.9	818.8	732.3	14 640.3	511.5
4th quarter	1 788.4	181.5	1 192.3	709.6	27 188.1	6 134.9	272.6	1 794.4	2 493.2	822.6	752.0	14 921.0	511.8
2001													
1st quarter	1 826.7	180.7	1 219.7	704.6	27 614.3	6 257.7	274.7	1 868.3	2 535.8	846.3	732.5	15 151.7	523.9
2nd quarter	1 868.1	188.3	1 254.0	687.2	27 982.4	6 486.1	275.2	1 946.2	2 637.4	880.1	747.2	15 371.1	535.1
3rd quarter	1 904.2	189.8	1 260.1	659.8	28 525.9	6 684.5	279.0	2 030.2	2 760.5	893.3	721.6	15 653.0	534.1
4th quarter	1 944.7	192.0	1 298.1	659.9	29 161.8	6 855.1	278.6	2 099.1	2 831.8	930.5	715.2	15 970.5	551.7
2002													
1st quarter	1 976.2	190.5	1 320.0	676.1	29 590.8	7 064.4	280.9	2 163.1	2 956.4	936.9	727.0	16 153.1	575.4
2nd quarter	2 014.4	196.9	1 370.1	674.2	30 088.3	7 174.8	280.0	2 203.3	3 042.6	938.5	710.4	16 336.6	590.7
3rd quarter	2 047.9	199.5	1 393.0	665.9	30 581.4	7 272.1	287.7	2 259.2	3 085.2	937.0	703.0	16 678.0	604.2
4th quarter	2 093.0	199.9	1 442.0	665.5	31 320.7	7 431.2	288.2	2 323.2	3 158.6	953.3	708.0	17 133.7	629.4
2003													
1st quarter	2 119.3	198.3	1 466.1	669.4	31 845.3	7 544.7	283.7	2 376.9	3 226.6	954.5	703.0	17 411.4	641.5
2nd quarter	2 153.2	202.8	1 521.0	653.2	32 564.1	7 658.4	281.7	2 401.3	3 289.1	969.2	717.1	17 840.9	652.1
3rd quarter	2 189.3	205.7	1 529.8	638.7	33 225.0	7 909.4	286.7	2 550.2	3 371.3	989.5	711.7	17 967.8	656.1
4th quarter	2 232.5	207.6	1 559.7	649.8	34 007.4	8 078.6	285.6	2 565.0	3 489.0	1 010.1	728.9	18 234.4	666.7

. . . = Not available.

Table 12-5. Credit Market Debt Outstanding, By Borrower and Lender—*Continued*

(Billions of dollars, except as noted; end of period; not seasonally adjusted.)

Year and quarter	Credit market assets held by:—*Continued*											
	Selected domestic financial sectors—*Continued*										Households	Foreign holdings in United States	All other financial and non-financial sectors
	Commercial banks	Savings institutions	Credit unions	Life insurance companies	Other insurance companies	Private pension funds	Money market mutual funds	Mutual funds	Asset-backed security issuers	Finance companies			
1945	117.7	23.9	0.2	41.2	3.5	3.9	0.0	0.2	0.0	3.6	91.0	3.1	25.2
1946	111.6	26.7	0.2	44.4	4.1	4.1	0.0	0.3	0.0	4.1	90.3	2.4	19.1
1947	114.9	29.1	0.3	47.4	4.8	4.4	0.0	0.3	0.0	4.7	91.5	3.0	19.2
1948	113.2	31.2	0.5	50.9	5.7	4.7	0.0	0.3	0.0	5.7	93.7	3.1	21.4
1949	119.0	33.6	0.6	54.4	6.4	5.0	0.0	0.4	0.0	6.6	94.6	3.4	23.9
1950	125.6	36.7	0.7	57.9	7.2	5.3	0.0	0.4	0.0	7.8	96.2	4.8	28.8
1951	132.8	39.5	0.8	61.6	7.8	6.0	0.0	0.5	0.0	8.3	96.9	4.9	30.3
1952	141.4	44.1	1.1	65.9	8.7	7.2	0.0	0.5	0.0	10.2	104.6	5.1	31.1
1953	145.2	49.5	1.4	70.6	9.9	8.5	0.0	0.5	0.0	11.9	109.6	5.8	33.5
1954	154.9	55.5	1.6	75.4	10.8	9.8	0.0	0.7	0.0	12.3	109.5	6.4	32.4
1955	159.2	63.2	2.0	80.5	11.5	11.2	0.0	0.8	0.0	15.6	117.6	6.7	37.9
1956	164.8	70.2	2.4	85.6	11.9	12.7	0.0	1.1	0.0	16.7	124.9	7.3	33.6
1957	170.1	77.0	2.9	90.5	12.6	14.5	0.0	1.2	0.0	18.3	131.9	7.5	33.4
1958	185.0	85.5	3.1	95.5	13.4	16.2	0.0	1.5	0.0	17.6	132.7	7.5	34.6
1959	189.7	95.1	3.8	100.5	14.6	17.9	0.0	1.8	0.0	20.8	142.8	11.7	43.1
1960	199.7	104.2	4.5	105.6	15.5	19.7	0.0	2.0	0.0	24.3	150.9	12.6	38.0
1961	215.9	115.3	4.9	110.9	16.5	21.2	0.0	2.4	0.0	24.7	154.9	13.1	37.5
1962	235.2	128.3	5.6	116.9	18.0	22.9	0.0	2.6	0.0	26.5	158.2	14.8	38.7
1963	252.8	144.5	6.3	123.3	18.7	24.8	0.0	2.8	0.0	30.1	159.8	15.9	44.0
1964	276.1	160.2	7.2	130.3	19.5	27.2	0.0	3.2	0.0	34.0	166.2	16.9	45.9
1965	305.1	173.5	8.2	137.8	20.6	29.1	0.0	3.9	0.0	38.2	170.2	17.2	46.6
1966	323.1	181.7	9.4	145.9	22.0	31.9	0.0	5.1	0.0	41.0	190.8	16.5	46.0
1967	359.8	195.0	10.2	153.3	23.5	32.8	0.0	4.3	0.0	41.2	196.3	18.9	44.8
1968	398.7	208.9	11.7	160.7	25.4	33.8	0.0	4.1	0.0	45.7	206.7	19.3	50.2
1969	418.3	221.5	13.8	167.6	27.0	34.6	0.0	5.1	0.0	53.4	217.0	18.8	83.0
1970	455.3	236.8	15.2	174.6	30.9	36.6	0.0	5.7	0.0	54.6	216.3	29.8	92.8
1971	506.5	271.7	17.2	182.8	34.6	35.0	0.0	5.5	0.0	58.7	204.0	56.5	109.9
1972	575.7	314.5	20.1	192.5	38.3	40.5	0.0	6.0	0.0	66.9	199.5	65.1	124.2
1973	662.4	348.0	23.7	204.8	41.8	46.8	0.0	6.6	0.0	77.0	220.6	66.0	137.2
1974	737.5	369.7	26.4	217.7	46.4	55.6	0.8	7.4	0.0	84.2	262.3	71.9	142.7
1975	768.8	415.2	31.7	234.6	53.7	71.2	1.5	8.0	0.0	85.7	278.0	80.7	151.8
1976	833.2	477.5	38.4	258.3	66.2	77.8	2.1	8.4	0.0	97.6	283.4	91.2	175.3
1977	924.6	548.1	45.6	285.8	83.7	88.2	1.9	12.3	0.0	118.4	290.2	142.1	175.3
1978	1 052.6	614.4	52.0	318.9	100.2	98.7	5.1	12.5	0.0	141.0	330.1	170.5	188.6
1979	1 181.8	671.9	53.8	352.0	113.7	120.8	24.9	14.5	0.0	166.6	400.6	161.0	203.7
1980	1 289.9	722.7	53.0	385.1	123.5	151.4	42.0	17.1	0.0	179.7	425.4	186.5	226.1
1981	1 398.2	748.7	55.0	419.8	132.0	178.7	107.5	20.2	0.0	202.2	443.7	216.7	280.9
1982	1 482.9	756.7	57.3	463.2	137.0	225.4	137.6	25.4	0.0	210.2	506.7	255.1	318.2
1983	1 626.1	879.5	69.4	513.8	138.6	267.4	119.7	34.9	3.0	234.5	589.7	281.2	382.3
1984	1 800.1	1 018.6	85.0	570.1	150.3	305.8	164.1	53.9	19.8	267.4	694.5	357.9	446.7
1985	1 989.5	1 097.6	98.4	646.6	176.5	328.9	178.2	129.9	34.8	311.2	849.5	431.9	552.0
1986	2 187.6	1 191.0	113.9	734.5	219.2	333.5	213.1	259.9	71.4	351.0	866.2	543.7	599.3
1987	2 323.0	1 310.3	131.3	823.1	258.6	347.1	215.0	291.1	113.2	396.4	1 027.6	595.5	602.6
1988	2 479.5	1 409.3	148.8	927.2	287.9	369.1	225.5	304.5	147.6	431.3	1 228.5	698.3	668.3
1989	2 647.4	1 316.0	156.0	1 028.3	317.5	420.7	293.7	327.2	201.1	449.2	1 316.1	816.1	823.4
1990	2 772.5	1 176.5	166.6	1 134.5	344.0	464.2	371.3	360.1	266.9	471.2	1 555.3	888.7	813.4
1991	2 853.3	1 013.2	179.4	1 218.9	376.6	489.6	403.9	440.2	342.7	453.0	1 633.7	904.8	895.3
1992	2 948.6	937.4	197.1	1 304.4	389.4	515.6	408.6	566.4	445.4	453.3	1 675.0	989.3	966.4
1993	3 090.8	914.1	218.7	1 415.5	422.7	551.8	429.0	725.9	528.0	427.9	1 650.8	1 108.7	1 004.4
1994	3 254.3	920.8	246.8	1 487.5	446.4	591.4	459.0	718.8	594.1	476.2	1 946.1	1 216.0	962.6
1995	3 520.1	913.3	263.0	1 587.5	468.7	607.9	545.5	771.3	707.3	526.2	1 956.1	1 490.2	1 036.3
1996	3 707.7	933.2	288.5	1 657.0	491.2	601.4	634.3	820.2	810.3	545.1	2 154.1	1 832.6	1 037.1
1997	4 031.9	928.5	305.3	1 751.1	515.3	647.1	721.9	901.1	927.4	568.2	2 140.0	2 085.2	1 086.6
1998	4 336.1	965.5	324.2	1 828.0	521.1	621.1	965.1	1 028.4	1 186.7	645.5	2 264.3	2 231.2	1 115.6
1999	4 648.3	1 032.6	351.7	1 886.0	518.2	720.4	1 147.8	1 076.8	1 360.0	742.6	2 392.1	2 316.0	1 196.1
2000	5 006.3	1 088.8	379.7	1 943.9	509.4	724.2	1 290.9	1 097.7	1 517.2	851.2	2 235.2	2 590.8	1 306.1
2001	5 210.5	1 133.4	421.2	2 074.8	518.4	708.3	1 536.9	1 223.8	1 745.1	846.6	2 104.8	2 916.9	1 314.5
2002	5 614.9	1 167.0	463.9	2 307.8	558.3	729.5	1 511.6	1 368.0	1 915.8	867.6	2 010.1	3 394.8	1 350.9
2003	5 960.8	1 293.3	514.5	2 488.3	625.2	733.6	1 398.5	1 505.7	2 096.0	951.8	2 154.4	3 933.1	1 606.8
2000													
1st quarter	4 727.1	1 043.7	359.0	1 902.2	515.4	712.2	1 217.1	1 058.3	1 385.9	776.8	2 352.4	2 395.1	1 215.0
2nd quarter	4 849.5	1 060.4	370.1	1 914.1	510.8	713.4	1 159.4	1 072.4	1 408.2	812.6	2 336.0	2 443.1	1 266.7
3rd quarter	4 930.5	1 080.0	374.8	1 935.1	512.4	722.7	1 212.5	1 087.1	1 443.2	830.5	2 269.0	2 494.8	1 295.7
4th quarter	5 006.3	1 088.8	379.7	1 943.9	509.4	724.2	1 290.9	1 097.7	1 517.2	851.2	2 235.2	2 590.8	1 306.1
2001													
1st quarter	5 013.8	1 100.1	387.0	1 969.6	510.0	716.7	1 404.2	1 114.0	1 563.6	849.0	2 173.4	2 688.0	1 343.5
2nd quarter	5 041.5	1 115.8	392.4	2 004.8	510.0	715.0	1 414.3	1 160.4	1 602.3	879.6	2 123.1	2 737.4	1 264.7
3rd quarter	5 100.6	1 118.4	408.4	2 054.8	511.3	713.5	1 494.9	1 187.6	1 668.5	860.8	2 095.5	2 806.8	1 286.1
4th quarter	5 210.5	1 133.4	421.2	2 074.8	518.4	708.3	1 536.9	1 223.8	1 745.1	846.4	2 104.8	2 916.9	1 314.5
2002													
1st quarter	5 231.3	1 137.4	434.3	2 141.2	527.6	717.6	1 496.9	1 280.2	1 776.8	834.4	2 115.9	2 978.8	1 278.7
2nd quarter	5 328.3	1 131.1	452.9	2 192.3	536.4	720.6	1 419.6	1 295.1	1 821.0	848.2	2 137.1	3 124.3	1 315.5
3rd quarter	5 476.2	1 154.0	455.1	2 265.7	541.9	728.2	1 411.2	1 335.8	1 845.0	860.8	2 028.9	3 239.9	1 362.5
4th quarter	5 614.9	1 167.0	463.9	2 307.8	558.3	729.5	1 511.6	1 368.0	1 915.8	867.6	2 010.1	3 394.8	1 350.9
2003													
1st quarter	5 673.6	1 214.6	473.7	2 377.0	572.3	731.3	1 485.5	1 415.6	1 965.3	861.1	1 949.5	3 489.7	1 450.0
2nd quarter	5 831.3	1 239.0	495.3	2 436.5	584.7	737.4	1 479.6	1 480.9	2 020.6	883.5	1 944.7	3 683.8	1 436.2
3rd quarter	5 831.8	1 261.5	517.7	2 471.6	601.9	734.4	1 438.1	1 478.5	2 051.7	924.2	2 047.8	3 772.2	1 527.8
4th quarter	5 960.8	1 293.3	514.5	2 488.3	625.2	733.6	1 398.5	1 505.7	2 096.0	951.8	2 154.4	3 933.1	1 606.8

. . . = Not available.

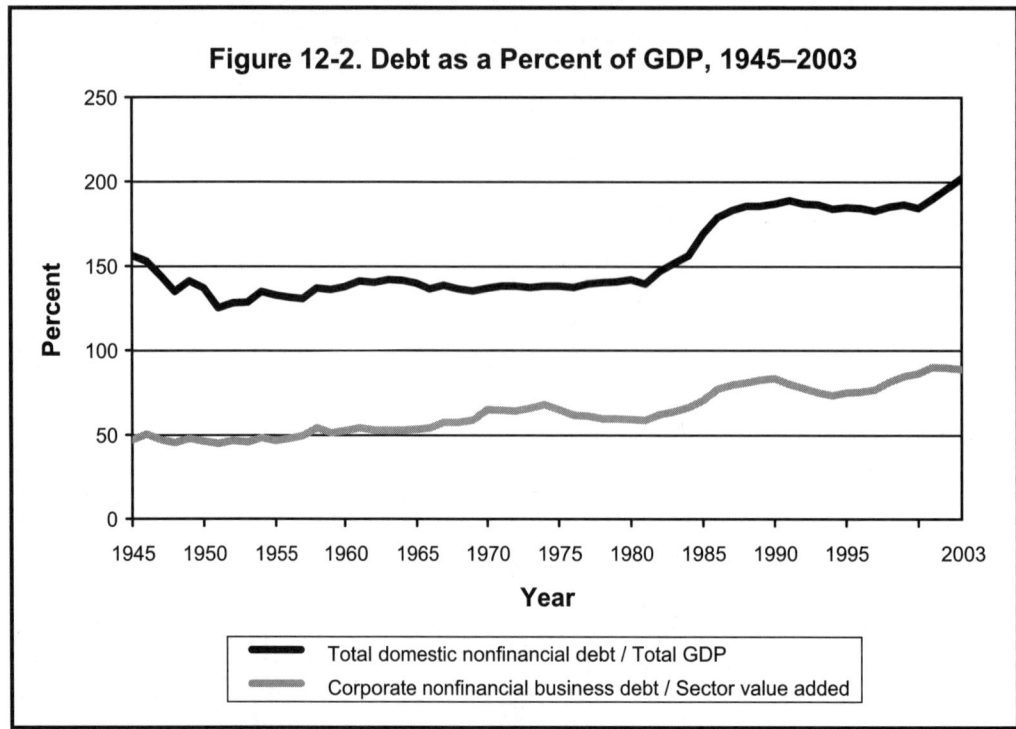

- After a pause during the 1990s, the ratio of the total debt owed by all domestic nonfinancial sectors at the end of the year to the year's GDP rose to another post–World War II record between 2000 and 2003. Over those three years, the fastest rate of debt growth occurred in the household sector. (Tables 12-5 and 1-1)
- Household debt can also be assessed relative to aggregate personal disposable income. Household debt reached a level higher than a year's aggregate personal disposable income in 2001 and continued to climb in the subsequent two years. (Tables 12-5 and 4-1)
- The debt of nonfinancial corporate business can be compared with its own contribution to GDP (value added), as graphed in Figure 12-2. This ratio reached a postwar high in 2001 but has declined slightly since then. (Tables 12-5 and 1-13)
- In the other sectors—federal, state, and local government, noncorporate farm and nonfarm business—debt increases were rapid compared to aggregate GDP between 2000 and 2003. (Tables 12-5 and 1-1)

Table 12-6. Household Assets, Liabilities, Net Worth, Financial Obligations, and Delinquency Rates

(Billions of dollars, except as noted; end of period; not seasonally adjusted, except as noted.)

Year and quarter	Financial assets of the household sector [1]													
	Total [2]	Checkable deposits and currency	Time and savings deposits	Money market fund shares	U.S. savings bonds	Other Treasury securities	Agency securities	Municipal securities	Corporate and foreign bonds	Mortgages	Corporate equities	Mutual fund shares	Security credit	Life insurance reserves
1945	560.6	54.0	50.3	0.0	42.9	23.6	0.1	3.9	8.4	12.2	109.5	1.2	0.7	39.6
1946	601.6	58.9	56.6	0.0	44.2	21.0	0.1	3.8	7.5	13.7	101.3	1.3	0.7	43.4
1947	640.7	58.7	60.1	0.0	46.2	18.8	0.1	4.5	6.6	15.0	98.8	1.4	0.7	46.5
1948	662.6	56.3	62.3	0.0	47.8	18.0	0.1	4.6	6.7	16.2	97.5	1.5	0.7	49.4
1949	681.5	54.4	65.0	0.0	49.3	18.0	0.0	3.7	6.3	17.0	105.0	3.1	0.7	52.1
1950	735.2	56.9	67.4	0.0	49.6	16.9	0.1	5.5	6.0	17.6	128.7	3.3	1.0	55.0
1951	800.3	61.0	72.2	0.0	49.1	16.3	0.1	5.7	6.3	18.6	151.1	3.5	0.9	57.8
1952	829.0	63.1	79.6	0.0	49.2	18.2	0.0	11.0	6.0	19.2	151.0	3.9	0.7	60.7
1953	846.5	64.3	87.8	0.0	49.4	18.7	0.2	13.9	6.0	20.2	145.8	4.2	0.7	63.7
1954	925.2	66.0	96.9	0.0	50.0	16.1	0.2	16.0	4.9	21.4	198.8	6.1	1.0	66.4
1955	1 014.8	67.0	105.4	0.0	50.2	18.6	0.6	19.2	5.0	22.7	248.3	7.8	0.9	69.3
1956	1 083.6	68.8	114.7	0.0	50.1	20.1	1.0	21.9	6.1	24.3	271.0	9.1	0.9	72.7
1957	1 096.0	67.8	126.5	0.0	48.2	23.3	1.5	23.9	7.2	26.2	244.5	8.7	0.9	75.5
1958	1 224.0	70.1	140.3	0.0	47.7	20.9	0.8	24.6	7.9	28.8	322.3	13.2	1.2	78.5
1959	1 300.0	72.4	151.5	0.0	45.9	25.7	2.3	28.4	8.2	30.8	357.3	15.8	1.0	82.0
1960	1 348.6	74.1	163.4	0.0	45.6	26.6	1.0	31.0	10.6	33.5	359.8	17.0	1.1	85.2
1961	1 493.1	72.9	181.6	0.0	46.5	25.5	0.6	32.5	10.8	36.8	443.2	22.9	1.2	88.6
1962	1 535.3	72.5	207.4	0.0	47.0	26.8	0.2	32.1	10.2	39.0	431.2	20.9	1.2	92.4
1963	1 633.9	77.3	233.4	0.0	48.2	24.7	0.0	32.1	10.1	40.5	469.9	24.8	1.2	96.6
1964	1 788.6	79.9	259.3	0.0	49.1	24.5	0.3	34.9	10.3	42.1	544.1	28.5	1.7	101.1
1965	1 955.5	86.5	286.8	0.0	49.7	25.1	1.1	36.5	9.2	42.6	616.1	34.4	2.5	105.9
1966	1 979.0	88.9	305.5	0.0	50.3	28.8	5.9	41.2	11.9	44.6	548.3	33.9	2.7	110.6
1967	2 229.8	99.3	340.4	0.0	51.2	27.7	6.3	38.2	16.3	46.5	682.1	43.0	4.9	115.5
1968	2 496.7	108.7	370.8	0.0	51.9	29.8	6.1	36.5	21.4	49.0	815.3	49.5	7.0	120.3
1969	2 453.0	105.3	378.3	0.0	51.8	36.4	7.2	36.4	21.3	49.1	578.1	41.5	5.2	125.4
1970	2 547.3	112.5	419.4	0.0	52.1	25.4	11.5	35.4	29.5	50.0	562.3	40.4	4.4	130.7
1971	2 836.4	125.8	483.3	0.0	54.4	14.8	10.6	31.9	36.5	47.3	638.2	48.1	4.9	137.1
1972	3 246.8	137.2	554.1	0.0	57.7	14.5	4.9	32.4	38.4	48.2	797.4	50.6	5.0	143.9
1973	3 259.7	145.2	615.5	0.0	60.4	21.5	3.7	39.0	41.3	47.2	587.1	38.7	4.9	151.3
1974	3 237.2	149.9	670.0	2.4	63.3	24.5	8.3	47.1	52.9	50.5	369.1	28.2	3.9	158.4
1975	3 699.6	150.6	747.9	3.7	67.4	34.1	1.1	50.0	62.9	50.4	492.7	34.4	4.5	168.6
1976	4 195.2	160.6	848.0	3.4	72.0	22.2	4.6	52.5	71.1	52.8	630.1	36.2	5.7	177.8
1977	4 459.2	174.7	950.1	3.0	76.8	18.2	0.3	56.3	60.8	55.3	536.4	35.6	5.7	187.8
1978	4 993.7	188.1	1 050.8	8.5	80.7	19.4	0.6	80.1	50.5	62.4	542.4	36.2	8.5	199.4
1979	5 727.5	205.5	1 120.7	38.3	79.9	64.7	0.3	96.2	44.6	71.6	662.0	39.4	10.4	210.3
1980	6 601.9	219.3	1 239.0	62.2	72.5	87.5	5.3	104.5	30.0	87.2	875.4	45.6	16.2	220.6
1981	6 998.7	261.4	1 307.3	148.1	68.2	84.5	1.2	131.3	30.5	101.4	780.1	46.6	14.7	230.1
1982	7 589.7	276.2	1 414.1	180.3	68.4	101.0	1.2	170.6	24.4	110.9	832.5	57.3	17.8	238.0
1983	8 357.1	283.6	1 614.0	149.1	71.5	143.3	0.3	211.8	26.7	111.2	936.2	87.7	20.6	246.7
1984	8 878.2	295.1	1 840.2	191.0	74.5	183.8	12.7	251.6	27.5	102.6	863.1	104.6	21.6	252.8
1985	10 013.2	312.6	1 970.3	193.3	79.8	182.7	6.9	348.0	77.4	119.7	1 058.1	197.9	35.1	264.3
1986	11 138.5	425.1	2 058.4	228.8	93.3	157.2	7.0	355.4	107.2	115.5	1 330.3	333.2	44.0	282.6
1987	11 823.6	427.4	2 177.4	250.0	101.1	180.0	11.9	453.6	123.9	124.2	1 306.2	381.7	39.1	309.5
1988	13 003.7	424.5	2 354.5	265.3	109.6	256.5	28.4	524.2	116.6	125.9	1 585.0	400.1	40.9	335.7
1989	14 406.3	424.1	2 434.0	341.7	117.7	247.0	49.3	547.7	162.9	134.5	1 939.8	462.9	53.2	365.3
1990	14 816.0	412.1	2 465.0	368.6	126.2	345.0	68.9	575.0	233.5	143.5	1 770.1	456.6	62.4	391.7
1991	16 343.3	461.3	2 394.1	383.1	138.1	364.6	38.7	614.4	299.0	145.7	2 517.3	570.3	87.0	418.6
1992	17 151.2	569.8	2 291.9	342.2	157.3	441.0	-7.8	578.9	335.9	139.9	2 857.1	706.7	76.2	447.7
1993	18 358.3	615.0	2 183.3	341.8	171.9	473.7	-66.1	534.8	358.3	132.5	3 223.5	969.2	102.3	484.8
1994	19 002.9	584.3	2 153.7	352.5	179.9	665.7	51.0	483.1	396.1	123.7	3 081.6	981.9	109.0	520.4
1995	21 608.2	543.5	2 280.8	450.2	185.0	621.5	73.8	429.2	482.3	116.3	4 122.6	1 153.1	127.6	566.2
1996	24 058.6	470.2	2 434.1	500.7	187.0	681.9	171.6	394.0	556.2	108.7	4 847.1	1 501.2	162.9	610.7
1997	27 521.0	436.4	2 559.6	582.3	186.5	596.3	223.6	413.0	563.5	101.1	6 272.9	1 957.7	215.5	665.0
1998	30 474.5	421.9	2 680.5	712.9	186.6	560.9	288.9	416.0	650.0	98.3	7 120.1	2 397.1	276.7	718.3
1999	34 894.0	364.3	2 799.1	825.0	186.5	646.5	362.4	435.6	587.0	106.5	9 168.1	2 987.4	323.9	783.9
2000	33 853.7	232.3	3 091.0	970.8	184.8	436.9	405.8	438.0	569.8	117.4	7 762.6	2 905.3	412.4	819.1
2001	32 326.3	335.3	3 298.8	1 129.2	190.3	320.5	328.9	489.3	564.7	125.4	6 466.3	2 750.8	454.3	880.0
2002	30 027.8	358.7	3 582.3	1 088.7	194.9	178.4	219.1	585.3	597.6	136.0	4 853.7	2 443.8	412.7	920.9
2003	34 265.6	316.3	3 907.3	989.0	203.8	251.8	485.5	618.7	352.4	147.4	6 146.7	3 182.4	475.4	1 013.2
2000														
1st quarter	35 751.6	311.0	2 892.2	907.5	185.3	592.3	370.7	433.1	587.2	109.8	9 318.3	3 183.8	371.2	801.0
2nd quarter	35 098.1	267.0	2 957.8	874.1	184.6	478.0	403.8	454.0	628.2	112.3	8 790.0	3 105.6	359.5	806.5
3rd quarter	35 126.7	220.7	3 026.5	906.7	184.3	414.9	426.5	447.8	604.2	114.9	8 558.7	3 139.0	373.0	818.7
4th quarter	33 853.7	232.3	3 091.0	970.8	184.8	436.9	405.8	438.0	569.8	117.4	7 762.6	2 905.3	412.4	819.1
2001														
1st quarter	31 990.8	268.4	3 199.4	1 053.0	184.8	403.2	305.4	457.9	619.7	119.2	6 584.2	2 612.1	412.0	823.0
2nd quarter	32 883.3	266.6	3 226.8	1 020.9	185.5	312.9	305.8	489.9	623.7	121.3	6 963.3	2 809.6	412.9	840.3
3rd quarter	30 886.1	278.3	3 278.2	1 077.0	186.4	317.0	326.0	480.2	577.8	123.2	5 785.3	2 478.3	494.8	844.0
4th quarter	32 326.3	335.3	3 298.8	1 129.2	190.3	320.5	328.9	489.3	564.7	125.4	6 466.3	2 750.8	454.3	880.0
2002														
1st quarter	32 567.0	362.7	3 444.0	1 109.4	191.9	306.1	324.3	515.9	565.1	127.9	6 346.1	2 809.1	427.5	894.2
2nd quarter	30 979.2	335.8	3 472.8	1 047.3	192.7	257.4	305.5	558.6	604.4	130.7	5 474.1	2 633.2	400.5	901.2
3rd quarter	29 095.3	310.5	3 578.8	1 061.7	193.3	261.6	248.8	554.2	544.9	133.5	4 475.0	2 338.9	401.3	902.9
4th quarter	30 027.8	358.7	3 582.3	1 088.7	194.9	178.4	219.1	585.3	597.6	136.0	4 853.7	2 443.8	412.7	920.9
2003														
1st quarter	29 917.7	356.3	3 728.4	1 077.8	196.9	218.2	200.5	586.6	503.6	138.8	4 680.3	2 431.4	429.6	936.3
2nd quarter	31 725.2	345.7	3 789.1	1 030.3	199.1	287.8	156.5	613.3	449.0	141.6	5 364.4	2 762.2	515.1	959.7
3rd quarter	32 414.3	299.3	3 859.0	986.7	201.5	258.8	345.9	602.7	395.5	144.5	5 499.3	2 905.5	503.4	973.0
4th quarter	34 265.6	316.3	3 907.3	989.0	203.8	251.8	485.5	618.7	352.4	147.4	6 146.7	3 182.4	475.4	1 013.2

[1] Includes nonprofit organizations.
[2] Includes components not shown separately.

Table 12-6. Household Assets, Liabilities, Net Worth, Financial Obligations, and Delinquency Rates —Continued

(Billions of dollars, except as noted; end of period; not seasonally adjusted, except as noted.)

Year and quarter	Financial assets of the household sector [1]—Continued			Tangible assets of the household sector		Debt as a percent of total assets [1]	Total liabilities [1]	Net worth [1]	Ratios to disposable personal income (percent, seasonally adjusted)				Consumer credit card accounts held at banks, percents	
	Pension fund reserves	Bank personal trusts	Equity in non-corporate business	Total [1]	Household real estate [3]				Household debt service	Household financial obligations			Delinquency rate (seas. adjusted)	Charge-off rate
										Total	Home-owners	Renters		
1945	12.3	0.0	195.9	181.3	116.0	3.8	30.3	711.6	...	...	...	...	...	...
1946	13.5	0.0	228.6	212.9	133.4	4.3	37.1	777.3	...	...	...	...	...	...
1947	15.8	0.0	259.7	253.6	158.9	4.9	46.1	848.3	...	...	...	...	...	...
1948	18.3	0.0	275.0	284.9	180.0	5.5	54.7	892.8	...	...	...	...	...	...
1949	21.1	0.0	277.3	310.2	196.9	6.1	63.0	928.7	...	...	...	...	...	...
1950	24.3	0.0	293.6	357.7	222.4	6.7	76.3	1 016.5	...	...	...	...	...	...
1951	27.9	0.0	319.8	398.2	249.1	6.8	85.0	1 113.6	...	...	...	...	...	...
1952	33.5	0.0	321.2	431.0	272.7	7.4	97.4	1 162.6	...	...	...	...	...	...
1953	38.5	0.0	320.8	460.0	293.1	8.1	110.1	1 196.4	...	...	...	...	...	...
1954	43.9	0.0	325.0	486.7	315.4	8.3	122.4	1 289.6	...	...	...	...	...	...
1955	52.0	0.0	334.4	530.6	344.7	8.9	143.5	1 401.9	...	...	...	...	...	...
1956	58.2	0.0	350.8	573.0	371.4	9.2	158.8	1 497.8	...	...	...	...	...	...
1957	64.6	0.0	362.7	608.0	394.4	9.7	171.2	1 532.8	...	...	...	...	...	...
1958	75.0	0.0	377.6	634.3	415.9	9.5	183.3	1 675.0	...	...	...	...	...	...
1959	85.0	0.0	378.5	669.4	441.1	10.0	205.7	1 763.6	...	...	...	...	...	...
1960	93.9	0.0	388.8	700.4	464.4	10.5	223.4	1 825.7	...	...	...	...	...	...
1961	107.2	0.0	405.6	732.0	488.6	10.4	241.2	1 983.8	...	...	...	...	...	...
1962	113.7	0.0	422.1	765.3	510.8	11.0	263.3	2 037.3	...	...	...	...	...	...
1963	128.0	0.0	426.8	800.8	531.3	11.5	292.0	2 142.7	...	...	...	...	...	...
1964	144.8	0.0	446.0	843.9	557.0	11.8	321.2	2 311.3	...	...	...	...	...	...
1965	162.0	0.0	472.5	888.6	582.2	11.9	350.7	2 493.4	...	...	...	...	...	...
1966	172.5	0.0	506.0	960.2	624.5	12.3	373.9	2 565.3	...	...	...	...	...	...
1967	195.6	0.0	530.9	1 026.4	660.2	11.7	398.1	2 858.2	...	...	...	...	...	...
1968	218.7	0.0	576.0	1 148.6	740.8	11.3	433.2	3 212.0	...	...	...	...	...	...
1969	230.9	135.2	610.3	1 252.9	804.3	12.0	463.3	3 242.6	...	...	...	...	...	...
1970	253.8	137.9	641.1	1 331.8	845.6	11.9	478.7	3 400.4	...	...	...	...	...	...
1971	293.5	163.0	707.4	1 453.4	925.8	11.7	525.2	3 764.5	...	...	...	...	...	...
1972	349.3	187.1	788.6	1 644.3	1 064.7	11.4	587.2	4 304.0	...	...	...	...	...	...
1973	358.5	175.0	926.0	1 864.2	1 213.9	12.3	654.8	4 469.2	...	...	...	...	...	...
1974	367.5	147.3	1 038.2	1 971.6	1 219.3	13.2	710.6	4 498.2	...	...	...	...	...	...
1975	467.0	169.3	1 139.0	2 186.8	1 369.1	12.6	765.8	5 120.6	...	...	...	...	...	...
1976	534.5	195.9	1 269.7	2 431.7	1 541.6	12.4	855.2	5 771.6	...	...	...	...	...	...
1977	589.9	194.0	1 434.5	2 823.2	1 831.9	13.1	986.3	6 296.1	...	...	...	...	...	...
1978	691.4	206.7	1 667.3	3 269.4	2 149.4	13.4	1 149.9	7 113.3	...	...	...	...	...	...
1979	801.1	230.7	1 936.2	3 802.5	2 534.1	13.4	1 322.3	8 207.7	...	...	...	...	...	...
1980	970.4	265.3	2 183.1	4 271.7	2 867.2	12.9	1 453.0	9 420.6	10.6	15.4	13.3	23.7	...	...
1981	1 065.0	271.6	2 342.6	4 729.3	3 213.9	12.9	1 565.2	10 162.8	10.7	15.6	13.5	24.1	...	...
1982	1 291.8	288.5	2 387.9	4 953.2	3 367.2	12.6	1 639.0	10 903.8	10.6	15.7	13.8	22.5	...	...
1983	1 541.0	318.1	2 450.9	5 196.0	3 522.1	12.8	1 807.2	11 745.9	10.6	15.6	13.7	22.8	...	...
1984	1 710.8	331.1	2 451.1	5 822.0	4 027.4	13.3	2 017.7	12 682.5	11.0	16.0	14.0	23.8	...	...
1985	2 085.0	384.3	2 510.8	6 500.3	4 574.0	13.8	2 367.7	14 145.7	11.9	17.1	14.9	25.7	...	3.0
1986	2 325.1	429.1	2 644.4	7 096.4	5 001.1	13.9	2 633.5	15 601.4	12.3	17.7	15.5	26.4	...	3.5
1987	2 497.3	442.1	2 766.4	7 655.6	5 410.5	14.1	2 840.4	16 638.8	12.0	17.4	15.3	26.3	...	3.3
1988	2 748.1	470.3	2 932.1	8 307.7	5 883.7	14.3	3 139.9	18 171.5	11.8	17.1	15.1	25.3	...	3.3
1989	3 221.1	541.4	3 071.3	8 963.1	6 376.3	14.3	3 450.1	19 919.3	12.1	17.4	15.5	24.7	...	3.3
1990	3 376.3	551.7	3 150.3	9 163.3	6 475.5	15.0	3 719.3	20 260.0	12.0	17.4	15.5	24.7	...	3.9
1991	3 854.3	639.3	3 116.2	9 431.6	6 708.8	14.7	3 934.3	21 840.6	11.5	17.0	15.2	23.6	5.3	4.7
1992	4 153.9	660.6	3 083.0	9 780.2	7 018.5	14.8	4 139.2	22 791.5	10.8	16.2	14.3	23.4	4.7	4.6
1993	4 616.1	691.3	3 179.2	10 095.9	7 248.0	14.9	4 408.0	24 046.2	10.8	16.2	14.2	23.9	3.9	3.4
1994	4 883.8	699.4	3 371.9	10 416.1	7 405.4	15.5	4 735.4	24 683.6	11.2	16.7	14.5	25.2	3.3	3.1
1995	5 676.2	803.0	3 589.5	11 020.3	7 870.3	14.9	5 072.8	27 555.7	11.9	17.5	15.2	27.0	3.9	4.0
1996	6 316.2	871.7	3 827.5	11 482.7	8 194.6	14.7	5 429.9	30 111.5	12.1	17.7	15.4	27.2	4.6	4.7
1997	7 255.8	942.5	4 116.9	12 146.2	8 652.2	13.9	5 786.5	33 880.7	12.1	17.7	15.5	27.3	4.8	5.6
1998	8 123.2	1 001.0	4 368.7	13 150.4	9 408.2	13.7	6 253.5	37 371.4	12.1	17.5	15.2	28.2	4.7	5.3
1999	9 111.4	1 130.4	4 600.5	14 217.0	10 253.7	13.1	6 819.1	42 291.9	12.4	17.9	15.5	29.2	4.5	4.6
2000	8 901.3	1 095.8	4 993.7	15 524.3	11 267.0	14.2	7 402.3	41 975.7	12.8	18.2	15.7	30.5	4.6	4.7
2001	8 444.1	960.7	5 054.1	16 774.6	12 358.2	15.6	7 989.2	41 111.6	13.3	18.8	16.2	31.4	4.7	6.3
2002	7 754.1	840.9	5 267.8	18 204.3	13 559.6	17.4	8 680.5	39 551.7	13.3	18.8	16.2	32.1	4.9	5.4
2003	8 960.6	932.5	5 660.8	19 853.8	14 988.5	17.1	9 603.4	44 516.0	13.1	18.3	15.8	30.8	4.5	5.9
2000														
1st quarter	9 343.7	1 178.2	4 678.0	14 531.9	10 506.1	12.9	6 942.8	43 340.7	12.3	17.7	15.3	29.1	4.4	4.6
2nd quarter	9 211.2	1 155.5	4 812.5	14 882.8	10 752.3	13.3	7 091.4	42 889.6	12.5	17.8	15.5	29.5	4.5	4.2
3rd quarter	9 301.6	1 169.2	4 913.4	15 224.6	11 029.8	13.6	7 264.8	43 086.5	12.6	17.9	15.5	29.8	4.5	4.3
4th quarter	8 901.3	1 095.8	4 993.7	15 524.3	11 267.0	14.2	7 402.3	41 975.7	12.8	18.2	15.7	30.5	4.6	4.7
2001														
1st quarter	8 374.7	1 000.5	5 059.0	15 898.2	11 588.0	14.8	7 435.8	40 453.2	12.9	18.3	15.8	30.5	4.8	5.1
2nd quarter	8 659.8	1 024.7	5 097.1	16 208.9	11 864.5	14.8	7 616.2	41 475.9	13.1	18.5	16.0	30.8	5.0	5.2
3rd quarter	8 046.6	916.5	5 142.0	16 519.1	12 139.1	15.5	7 846.4	39 558.9	12.9	18.2	15.7	30.8	5.0	5.2
4th quarter	8 444.1	960.7	5 054.1	16 774.6	12 358.2	15.6	7 989.2	41 111.6	13.3	18.8	16.2	31.4	4.7	6.3
2002														
1st quarter	8 553.8	963.2	5 088.6	17 061.7	12 608.7	15.6	8 095.1	41 533.6	13.1	18.6	16.0	31.5	4.9	7.7
2nd quarter	8 069.6	893.5	5 146.9	17 441.4	12 920.9	16.4	8 256.3	40 164.3	13.1	18.6	16.0	31.7	4.8	6.1
3rd quarter	7 485.6	811.6	5 217.5	17 867.9	13 275.7	17.3	8 426.4	38 536.8	13.3	18.7	16.1	32.0	4.8	5.7
4th quarter	7 754.1	840.9	5 267.8	18 204.3	13 559.6	17.4	8 680.5	39 551.7	13.3	18.8	16.2	32.1	4.9	5.4
2003														
1st quarter	7 664.6	819.6	5 332.0	18 487.2	13 796.6	17.6	8 845.3	39 559.6	13.3	18.7	16.2	31.8	4.6	5.6
2nd quarter	8 239.7	877.0	5 381.6	18 792.3	14 050.8	17.4	9 203.0	41 314.6	13.2	18.6	16.1	31.4	4.5	5.8
3rd quarter	8 424.2	885.0	5 503.3	19 182.7	14 381.0	17.5	9 421.6	42 175.5	13.1	18.3	15.9	30.9	4.2	5.2
4th quarter	8 960.6	932.5	5 660.8	19 853.8	14 988.5	17.1	9 603.4	44 516.0	13.1	18.3	15.8	30.8	4.5	5.9

[1] Includes nonprofit organizations.
[3] Excludes nonprofit organizations.
. . . = Not available.

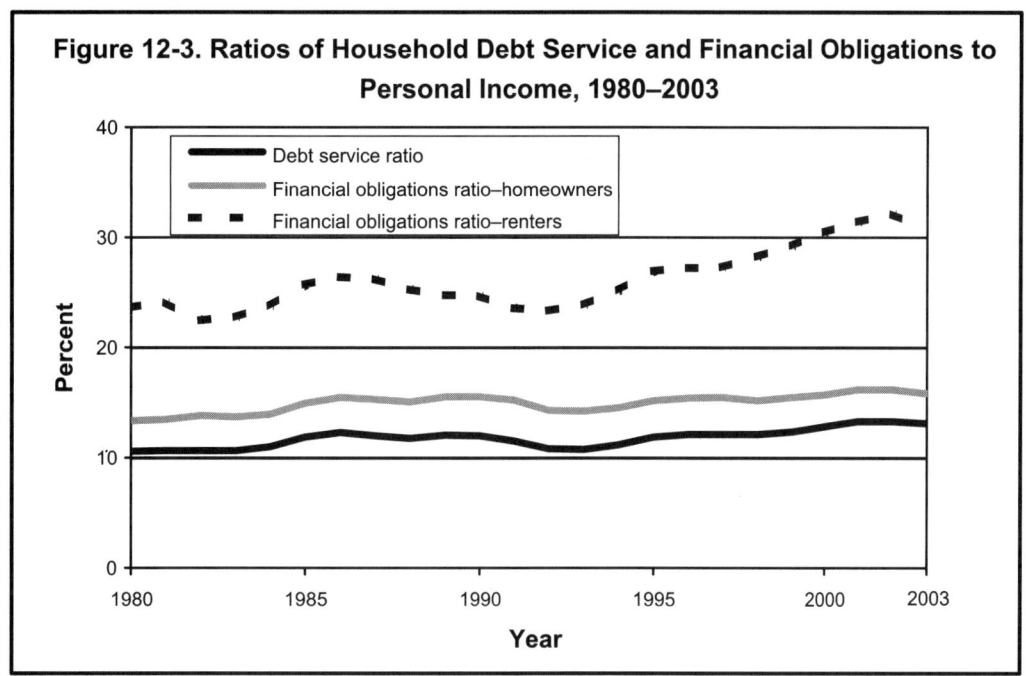

Figure 12-3. Ratios of Household Debt Service and Financial Obligations to Personal Income, 1980–2003

- The Federal Reserve calculates aggregate household debt service (payments of principal and interest) and total financial obligations as a percent of aggregate personal disposable income for the period 1980 to date. These measures provide meaningful supplements to the ratio of the total level of household debt to income (as shown in Table 12-5), because lengthening maturities and lower interest rates can mitigate much of the burden of a high level of debt. Like the debt-income ratio, the debt service ratio reached a new high at the end of 2002. Unlike the debt-income ratio, it has declined slightly since then, reflecting the decline in interest rates. (Tables 12-5, 12-6, and 12-9)
- With increasing homeownership, a trend increase in the debt service ratio might be expected and no cause for concern. Other long-term trends have also come into play—increasing credit card use, the increasing use of second mortgage (home equity) credit to finance purchases that used to be financed with consumer credit, and the increased use of auto leasing in place of auto purchase with consumer credit finance. To assess the financial condition of the personal sector while accounting for all of these trends as well, the Federal Reserve last year introduced financial obligations ratios, which include all debt service, rental payments on primary residences, property taxes, homeowners' insurance, and automobile lease payments. Furthermore, the Federal Reserve estimates the breakdown between homeowners and renters so that a ratio can be calculated for each group. (Table 12-6)
- Financial obligations ratios for both groups are, of course, higher than the ratio for debt service alone. Reflecting the lower average incomes of the renters' group, the ratio for renters is about double the ratio for homeowners. For each ratio, the same time pattern as that of the debt service ratio holds: a 22-year high at the end of 2002, followed by a relatively small decline in 2003. Both seem to show a long-term upward trend, more pronounced in the case of renters. (Table 12-6)
- Additional evidence of the long-term trend toward more debt is seen in the ratio of aggregate household debt to aggregate household financial and tangible assets. (Table 12-6)

Table 12-7. Mortgage Debt Outstanding

(Billions of dollars, except as noted; end of period; not seasonally adjusted.)

Year and quarter	Total	By type of property					By type of holder							
		Home		Multi-family residences	Commercial	Farm	Commercial banks	Savings institutions	Life insurance companies	Federal and related agencies	Mortgage pools or trusts			Other
		Billions of dollars	Percent of value of real estate								Total [1]	Federally related agencies	ABS issuers	
1945	36	19	14	5	8	5	5	10	7	2	0	0	0	10
1946	42	23	15	5	9	5	7	12	7	2	0	0	0	12
1947	49	28	16	6	10	5	9	14	9	2	0	0	0	15
1948	56	33	17	7	11	5	11	16	11	2	0	0	0	17
1949	63	37	17	8	12	6	12	18	13	2	0	0	0	18
1950	73	45	18	9	13	6	14	22	16	3	0	0	0	20
1951	82	51	19	11	14	7	15	25	19	3	0	0	0	21
1952	91	58	21	11	14	7	16	29	21	4	0	0	0	21
1953	101	66	22	12	16	8	17	34	23	5	0	0	0	22
1954	113	75	24	13	17	8	19	40	26	5	0	0	0	24
1955	129	88	25	13	19	9	21	48	29	5	0	0	0	26
1956	144	98	26	14	22	10	23	55	33	6	0	0	0	28
1957	156	107	27	15	24	10	23	60	35	7	0	0	0	30
1958	172	117	28	17	27	11	26	68	37	8	0	0	0	33
1959	191	130	29	19	30	12	28	77	39	10	0	0	0	36
1960	208	141	30	21	33	13	29	86	42	11	0	0	0	40
1961	228	153	31	24	37	14	30	96	44	12	0	0	0	45
1962	252	167	33	27	42	15	34	109	47	12	0	0	0	49
1963	278	184	35	30	47	17	39	125	51	11	1	1	0	52
1964	306	201	36	35	51	19	44	140	55	12	1	1	0	55
1965	334	219	38	38	56	21	50	153	60	13	1	1	0	58
1966	358	232	37	41	61	23	54	160	65	16	1	1	0	61
1967	381	245	37	45	66	25	59	170	68	19	2	2	0	64
1968	411	262	35	48	73	27	65	182	70	23	3	3	0	68
1969	442	280	35	53	79	29	71	194	72	28	3	3	0	74
1970	472	294	35	60	87	30	73	205	74	34	5	5	0	80
1971	520	321	35	70	97	32	83	231	75	37	10	10	0	85
1972	592	360	34	83	114	35	99	268	77	40	14	14	0	94
1973	669	402	33	93	134	40	119	300	81	47	18	18	0	104
1974	731	438	36	100	148	45	132	321	86	61	21	21	0	110
1975	788	477	35	101	161	50	136	351	89	73	29	29	0	111
1976	873	538	35	106	174	55	151	398	92	76	41	41	0	116
1977	1 002	631	34	114	193	64	179	459	97	84	57	57	0	126
1978	1 154	741	34	125	215	73	214	517	106	100	70	70	0	146
1979	1 321	859	34	135	239	87	245	565	118	121	95	95	0	176
1980	1 462	962	34	143	260	97	263	594	131	143	114	114	0	217
1981	1 584	1 035	32	142	300	107	284	612	138	160	129	129	0	261
1982	1 666	1 075	32	146	334	111	301	576	142	177	179	179	0	291
1983	1 856	1 192	34	161	389	114	331	627	151	188	245	245	0	314
1984	2 097	1 326	33	186	472	112	381	710	157	202	300	289	11	347
1985	2 377	1 524	33	206	542	106	431	766	172	213	393	368	25	403
1986	2 664	1 726	35	239	603	95	505	785	194	202	550	532	19	428
1987	2 965	1 924	36	259	694	88	595	824	212	189	702	669	32	443
1988	3 282	2 158	37	275	766	83	677	888	233	192	787	745	41	505
1989	3 553	2 383	37	288	801	80	771	873	254	198	923	870	53	534
1990	3 807	2 619	40	288	821	79	849	802	268	239	1 088	1 020	68	561
1991	3 959	2 787	42	285	807	79	881	705	260	266	1 273	1 156	117	573
1992	4 071	2 956	42	272	763	80	901	628	242	286	1 447	1 272	175	568
1993	4 207	3 117	43	269	740	81	948	598	224	326	1 572	1 357	216	538
1994	4 378	3 298	45	270	727	83	1 013	596	216	316	1 714	1 472	242	523
1995	4 568	3 469	44	276	739	85	1 090	597	213	308	1 833	1 571	263	526
1996	4 842	3 698	45	288	769	87	1 145	628	208	294	2 017	1 712	305	549
1997	5 163	3 940	46	300	833	91	1 245	632	207	285	2 203	1 826	376	591
1998	5 656	4 301	46	334	923	97	1 337	644	214	292	2 537	2 019	518	633
1999	6 258	4 722	46	373	1 060	104	1 495	668	231	320	2 892	2 294	599	652
2000	6 821	5 134	46	404	1 172	110	1 660	723	236	341	3 161	2 493	667	700
2001	7 502	5 651	46	448	1 285	118	1 790	758	243	373	3 616	2 832	784	722
2002	8 336	6 332	47	487	1 390	126	2 058	781	250	434	4 033	3 159	874	779
2003	9 352	7 150	48	545	1 523	134	2 256	871	261	537	4 548	3 489	1 059	880
2000														
1st quarter	6 370	4 798	46	380	1 088	105	1 547	680	229	320	2 934	2 323	610	659
2nd quarter	6 533	4 919	46	389	1 118	107	1 614	701	233	330	2 981	2 357	625	674
3rd quarter	6 684	5 036	46	395	1 143	109	1 649	721	235	334	3 058	2 416	642	689
4th quarter	6 821	5 134	46	404	1 172	110	1 660	723	236	341	3 161	2 493	667	700
2001														
1st quarter	6 944	5 225	45	413	1 194	111	1 688	740	235	344	3 228	2 536	692	708
2nd quarter	7 141	5 383	45	424	1 220	114	1 722	752	237	353	3 353	2 637	715	724
3rd quarter	7 327	5 524	46	435	1 253	116	1 737	758	239	359	3 494	2 760	734	739
4th quarter	7 502	5 651	46	448	1 285	118	1 790	758	243	373	3 616	2 832	784	722
2002														
1st quarter	7 662	5 786	46	454	1 302	119	1 800	746	243	381	3 764	2 956	808	727
2nd quarter	7 871	5 953	46	464	1 333	122	1 873	743	245	392	3 875	3 043	833	743
3rd quarter	8 084	6 131	46	471	1 357	125	1 962	774	246	408	3 937	3 085	851	758
4th quarter	8 336	6 332	47	487	1 390	126	2 058	781	250	434	4 033	3 159	874	779
2003														
1st quarter	8 560	6 524	47	495	1 413	128	2 099	816	251	456	4 149	3 227	922	789
2nd quarter	8 854	6 767	48	510	1 448	130	2 193	834	254	490	4 263	3 289	974	820
3rd quarter	9 123	6 983	49	524	1 485	132	2 264	852	257	525	4 371	3 371	1 000	854
4th quarter	9 352	7 150	48	545	1 523	134	2 256	871	261	537	4 548	3 489	1 059	880

[1] Outstanding principal balances of mortgage-backed securities issued or guaranteed by the holder indicated.

Table 12-8. Consumer Credit

(Outstanding at end of period, billions of dollars.)

Year and month	Seasonally adjusted			Not seasonally adjusted							
		By major credit type			By major holder						
	Total	Revolving	Non-revolving	Total	Commercial banks	Finance companies	Credit unions	Federal government and Sallie Mae	Savings institutions	Nonfinancial businesses	Securitized pools [1]
1945	6.6	0.0	6.6	6.8	2.2	0.9	0.0	0.0	0.3	3.4	0.0
1946	9.4	0.0	9.4	9.8	3.8	1.5	0.0	0.0	0.4	4.0	0.0
1947	12.9	0.0	12.9	13.3	5.4	2.4	0.1	0.0	0.6	4.9	0.0
1948	15.8	0.0	15.8	16.3	6.6	3.2	0.1	0.0	0.7	5.8	0.0
1949	18.8	0.0	18.8	19.4	7.7	4.3	0.2	0.0	0.7	6.4	0.0
1950	23.2	0.0	23.2	23.9	9.7	5.3	0.3	0.0	0.9	7.7	0.0
1951	24.6	0.0	24.6	25.4	10.0	5.6	0.3	0.0	0.9	8.5	0.0
1952	29.7	0.0	29.7	30.5	12.3	7.1	0.6	0.0	0.9	9.7	0.0
1953	33.7	0.0	33.7	34.6	14.0	8.6	0.9	0.0	1.0	10.1	0.0
1954	35.0	0.0	35.0	36.0	14.3	9.1	1.1	0.0	1.1	10.5	0.0
1955	41.9	0.0	41.9	42.9	17.2	11.8	1.3	0.0	1.4	11.2	0.0
1956	45.4	0.0	45.4	46.6	18.9	12.7	1.7	0.0	1.5	11.8	0.0
1957	48.1	0.0	48.1	49.2	20.2	13.2	2.1	0.0	1.6	12.1	0.0
1958	48.4	0.0	48.4	49.5	20.7	12.3	2.3	0.0	1.8	12.3	0.0
1959	56.0	0.0	56.0	57.2	24.2	14.1	2.9	0.0	2.1	14.0	0.0
1960	60.0	0.0	60.0	61.2	26.4	15.4	3.4	0.0	2.4	13.5	0.0
1961	62.2	0.0	62.2	63.4	27.9	15.5	3.6	0.0	2.9	13.6	0.0
1962	68.1	0.0	68.1	69.3	30.6	17.3	4.1	0.0	3.0	14.3	0.0
1963	76.6	0.0	76.6	77.9	34.7	19.6	4.5	0.0	3.6	15.5	0.0
1964	86.0	0.0	86.0	87.4	39.8	21.6	5.4	0.0	3.7	16.8	0.0
1965	96.0	0.0	96.0	97.5	45.2	23.9	6.5	0.0	3.9	18.1	0.0
1966	101.8	0.0	101.8	103.4	48.2	24.8	7.5	0.0	4.0	19.0	0.0
1967	106.8	0.0	106.8	108.6	51.7	24.6	8.3	0.0	4.1	19.9	0.0
1968	117.4	2.0	115.4	119.3	58.5	26.1	9.7	0.0	4.3	20.8	0.0
1969	127.2	3.6	123.6	129.2	63.4	27.8	11.7	0.0	4.4	21.9	0.0
1970	131.6	5.0	126.6	133.7	65.6	27.6	13.0	0.0	4.4	23.0	0.0
1971	146.9	8.2	138.7	149.2	74.3	29.2	14.8	0.0	4.7	26.2	0.0
1972	166.2	9.4	156.8	168.8	87.0	31.9	17.0	0.0	5.1	27.8	0.0
1973	190.1	11.3	178.7	193.0	99.6	35.4	19.6	0.0	8.5	29.8	0.0
1974	198.9	13.2	185.7	201.9	103.0	36.1	21.9	0.0	9.1	31.8	0.0
1975	204.0	14.5	189.5	207.0	106.1	32.6	25.7	0.0	10.1	32.6	0.0
1976	225.7	16.5	209.2	229.0	118.0	33.7	31.2	0.0	10.8	35.2	0.0
1977	260.6	37.4	223.1	264.9	140.3	37.3	37.6	0.5	11.8	37.4	0.0
1978	306.1	45.7	260.4	311.3	166.5	44.4	45.2	0.9	13.1	41.2	0.0
1979	348.6	53.6	295.0	354.6	185.7	55.4	47.4	1.5	20.0	44.6	0.0
1980	351.9	55.0	297.0	358.0	180.2	62.2	44.1	2.6	22.7	46.2	0.0
1981	371.3	60.9	310.4	377.9	184.2	70.1	46.7	4.8	24.0	48.1	0.0
1982	389.8	66.3	323.5	396.7	190.9	75.3	48.8	6.4	26.6	48.7	0.0
1983	437.1	79.0	358.0	444.4	213.7	83.3	56.1	4.6	31.5	55.7	0.0
1984	517.3	100.4	416.9	526.6	258.8	89.9	67.9	5.6	44.2	60.2	0.0
1985	599.7	124.5	475.2	610.6	297.2	111.7	74.0	6.8	57.6	63.3	0.0
1986	654.8	141.1	513.7	666.4	320.2	134.0	77.1	8.2	62.9	64.0	0.0
1987	686.3	160.9	525.5	698.6	334.1	140.0	81.0	10.0	65.3	68.1	0.0
1988	731.9	184.6	547.3	745.2	360.8	144.7	88.3	13.2	66.8	71.4	0.0
1989	794.6	211.2	583.4	809.3	383.3	138.9	91.7	16.0	62.5	69.6	47.3
1990	808.2	238.6	569.6	824.4	382.0	133.4	91.6	19.2	49.6	71.9	76.7
1991	798.0	263.8	534.3	815.6	370.2	121.6	90.3	21.1	42.2	67.3	103.0
1992	806.1	278.4	527.7	824.8	362.9	118.1	91.7	24.2	37.4	70.3	120.3
1993	865.7	309.9	555.7	886.2	395.7	116.1	101.6	27.2	37.9	77.2	130.5
1994	997.1	365.6	631.6	1 021.0	458.8	134.4	119.6	37.1	38.5	86.6	146.1
1995	1 140.6	443.1	697.5	1 168.0	502.0	152.1	131.9	44.2	40.1	85.1	212.6
1996	1 242.2	498.9	743.2	1 271.7	526.8	154.9	144.1	51.3	44.7	77.7	272.1
1997	1 310.6	527.3	783.4	1 339.6	512.6	167.5	152.4	57.8	47.2	84.8	317.4
1998	1 412.2	574.3	837.8	1 442.9	508.9	183.3	155.4	65.7	52.4	87.8	389.4
1999	1 519.9	597.1	922.8	1 550.2	499.8	201.6	167.9	84.7	61.7	86.0	448.4
2000	1 692.6	665.2	1 027.4	1 726.5	541.5	220.5	184.4	104.0	64.8	90.0	521.3
2001	1 828.8	708.9	1 119.9	1 865.2	558.4	238.1	189.6	119.5	71.1	88.8	599.7
2002	1 905.0	719.1	1 185.9	1 942.6	587.2	237.8	195.7	129.6	68.7	86.5	637.1
2003	1 986.7	734.1	1 252.6	2 025.5	636.4	295.4	205.9	114.6	77.9	70.3	625.0
2002											
January	1 835.3	709.1	1 126.1	1 841.4	557.1	231.8	188.5	122.4	71.2	71.8	598.6
February	1 843.2	708.3	1 134.9	1 834.9	551.9	235.0	187.4	123.1	71.2	69.7	596.5
March	1 855.9	710.8	1 145.1	1 844.4	550.7	234.3	187.7	124.1	71.3	76.7	599.5
April	1 862.5	713.3	1 149.2	1 849.9	556.0	233.2	188.9	124.3	70.4	75.5	601.5
May	1 869.7	714.6	1 155.2	1 861.4	557.5	234.5	190.7	124.9	69.5	78.9	605.4
June	1 877.7	717.0	1 160.8	1 868.4	554.9	238.3	191.6	125.1	68.7	76.4	613.5
July	1 886.8	719.1	1 167.7	1 875.2	557.3	245.0	194.0	125.7	67.6	75.7	609.9
August	1 892.4	722.5	1 169.9	1 893.6	572.4	243.1	195.5	128.2	66.5	78.3	609.6
September	1 895.9	721.0	1 174.9	1 897.6	575.7	249.7	195.9	134.3	65.5	72.7	603.8
October	1 900.6	720.9	1 179.7	1 905.0	577.4	242.8	197.1	132.9	66.6	74.2	614.0
November	1 901.5	721.1	1 180.4	1 912.1	580.3	233.1	196.8	131.2	67.6	75.0	628.1
December	1 905.0	719.1	1 185.9	1 942.6	587.2	237.8	195.7	129.6	68.7	86.5	637.1
2003											
January	1 924.2	722.9	1 201.3	1 931.3	582.1	238.5	195.5	131.7	68.7	73.1	641.7
February	1 926.3	724.3	1 201.9	1 918.3	581.5	240.1	195.0	131.0	68.6	69.5	632.6
March	1 924.7	724.9	1 199.9	1 912.7	575.3	233.2	194.0	125.9	68.6	75.6	640.2
April	1 937.7	726.5	1 211.2	1 925.0	576.9	240.8	195.8	124.1	70.3	74.4	642.6
May	1 950.9	730.7	1 220.2	1 942.4	582.4	239.8	197.1	122.0	72.1	79.9	649.1
June	1 949.9	726.1	1 223.8	1 940.0	584.2	244.3	198.9	120.4	73.8	75.1	643.3
July	1 955.0	725.0	1 230.0	1 942.8	583.4	264.3	201.1	118.5	73.4	75.0	627.1
August	1 965.6	727.6	1 237.9	1 966.2	590.3	276.4	202.9	118.1	73.0	78.1	627.4
September	1 975.7	730.7	1 245.0	1 977.5	593.7	284.0	203.4	122.5	72.7	74.7	626.6
October	1 982.7	733.1	1 249.7	1 987.2	589.0	290.0	204.1	120.3	74.4	72.3	637.1
November	1 982.1	735.8	1 246.3	1 993.3	620.2	292.4	204.4	117.4	76.1	63.6	619.1
December	1 986.7	734.1	1 252.6	2 025.5	636.4	295.4	205.9	114.6	77.9	70.3	625.0

[1] Outstanding balances of pools upon which securities have been issued; these balances are no longer carried on the balance sheets of the loan originators.
. . . = Not available.

Table 12-9. Selected Interest Rates and Bond Yields

(Percent per annum.)

Year and month	Short-term rates							
	Federal funds	Federal Reserve discount rate [1]	Eurodollar deposits, 1-month	U.S. Treasury bills, secondary market, 3-month	U.S. Treasury bills, secondary market, 6-month	Commercial paper, 3-month [2]	CDs (secondary market), 3-month	Bank prime rate
1954	...	...	...	0.94	...	...	...	...
1955	1.79	...	...	1.72	...	...	...	...
1956	2.73	2.77	...	2.62	...	...	...	3.77
1957	3.11	3.12	...	3.22	...	...	...	4.20
1958	1.57	2.15	...	1.77	3.01	...	...	3.83
1959	3.31	3.36	...	3.39	3.81	...	...	4.48
1960	3.21	3.53	...	2.87	3.20	...	...	4.82
1961	1.95	3.00	...	2.35	2.59	...	...	4.50
1962	2.71	3.00	...	2.77	2.90	...	...	4.50
1963	3.18	3.23	...	3.16	3.26	...	...	4.50
1964	3.50	3.55	...	3.55	3.68	...	3.92	4.50
1965	4.07	4.04	...	3.95	4.05	...	4.36	4.54
1966	5.11	4.50	...	4.86	5.06	...	5.45	5.63
1967	4.22	4.19	...	4.29	4.61	...	4.99	5.63
1968	5.66	5.17	...	5.34	5.47	...	5.82	6.31
1969	8.21	5.87	...	6.67	6.86	...	7.23	7.96
1970	7.17	5.95	...	6.39	6.51	...	7.55	7.91
1971	4.67	4.88	6.40	4.33	4.52	5.25	5.00	5.73
1972	4.44	4.50	5.00	4.06	4.47	4.66	4.66	5.25
1973	8.74	6.45	9.19	7.04	7.20	8.21	9.30	8.03
1974	10.51	7.83	10.79	7.85	7.95	10.05	10.29	10.81
1975	5.82	6.25	6.35	5.79	6.10	6.26	6.44	7.86
1976	5.05	5.50	5.26	4.98	5.26	5.24	5.27	6.84
1977	5.54	5.46	5.75	5.26	5.52	5.54	5.63	6.83
1978	7.94	7.46	8.33	7.18	7.58	7.93	8.21	9.06
1979	11.20	10.29	11.66	10.05	10.04	10.95	11.20	12.67
1980	13.35	11.77	13.77	11.39	11.32	12.61	13.02	15.26
1981	16.39	13.42	16.72	14.04	13.81	15.34	15.93	18.87
1982	12.24	11.01	12.74	10.60	11.06	11.90	12.27	14.85
1983	9.09	8.50	9.38	8.62	8.74	8.88	9.07	10.79
1984	10.23	8.80	10.45	9.54	9.78	10.12	10.39	12.04
1985	8.10	7.69	8.12	7.47	7.65	7.95	8.04	9.93
1986	6.80	6.32	6.78	5.97	6.02	6.49	6.51	8.33
1987	6.66	5.66	6.88	5.78	6.03	6.82	6.87	8.21
1988	7.57	6.20	7.69	6.67	6.91	7.66	7.73	9.32
1989	9.21	6.93	9.16	8.11	8.03	8.99	9.09	10.87
1990	8.10	6.98	8.15	7.50	7.46	8.06	8.15	10.01
1991	5.69	5.45	5.81	5.38	5.44	5.87	5.83	8.46
1992	3.52	3.25	3.62	3.43	3.54	3.75	3.68	6.25
1993	3.02	3.00	3.07	3.00	3.12	3.22	3.17	6.00
1994	4.21	3.60	4.34	4.25	4.64	4.66	4.63	7.15
1995	5.83	5.21	5.86	5.49	5.56	5.93	5.92	8.83
1996	5.30	5.02	5.32	5.01	5.08	5.41	5.39	8.27
1997	5.46	5.00	5.52	5.06	5.18	5.60	5.62	8.44
1998	5.35	4.92	5.45	4.78	4.83	[2]5.37	5.47	8.35
1999	4.97	4.62	5.15	4.64	4.75	5.22	5.33	8.00
2000	6.24	5.73	6.33	5.82	5.90	6.33	6.46	9.23
2001	3.88	3.40	3.81	3.40	3.34	3.65	3.71	6.91
2002	1.67	1.17	1.71	1.61	1.68	1.70	1.73	4.67
2003	1.13	...	1.14	1.01	1.05	1.13	1.15	4.12
2002								
January	1.73	1.25	1.74	1.65	1.73	1.72	1.74	4.75
February	1.74	1.25	1.78	1.73	1.82	1.80	1.82	4.75
March	1.73	1.25	1.83	1.79	2.01	1.87	1.91	4.75
April	1.75	1.25	1.79	1.72	1.93	1.83	1.87	4.75
May	1.75	1.25	1.78	1.73	1.86	1.80	1.82	4.75
June	1.75	1.25	1.78	1.70	1.79	1.78	1.81	4.75
July	1.73	1.25	1.77	1.68	1.70	1.76	1.79	4.75
August	1.74	1.25	1.74	1.62	1.60	1.71	1.73	4.75
September	1.75	1.25	1.77	1.63	1.60	1.74	1.76	4.75
October	1.75	1.25	1.75	1.58	1.56	1.71	1.73	4.75
November	1.34	0.83	1.37	1.23	1.27	1.37	1.39	4.35
December	1.24	0.75	1.35	1.19	1.24	1.32	1.34	4.25
2003								
January	1.24	...	1.28	1.17	1.20	1.27	1.29	4.25
February	1.26	[1]2.25	1.26	1.17	1.18	1.25	1.27	4.25
March	1.25	[1]2.25	1.24	1.13	1.13	1.21	1.23	4.25
April	1.26	[1]2.25	1.26	1.13	1.14	1.23	1.24	4.25
May	1.26	[1]2.25	1.25	1.07	1.08	1.20	1.22	4.25
June	1.22	[1]2.20	1.08	0.92	0.92	1.02	1.04	4.22
July	1.01	[1]2.00	1.04	0.90	0.95	1.03	1.05	4.00
August	1.03	[1]2.00	1.05	0.95	1.03	1.06	1.08	4.00
September	1.01	[1]2.00	1.06	0.94	1.01	1.06	1.08	4.00
October	1.01	[1]2.00	1.05	0.92	1.00	1.06	1.10	4.00
November	1.00	[1]2.00	1.04	0.93	1.02	1.08	1.11	4.00
December	0.98	[1]2.00	1.08	0.90	0.99	1.07	1.10	4.00

[1]Federal Reserve Bank of New York. Through 2002, represents the rate for adjustment credit. Beginning in 2003, represents the rate for primary credit. See Notes and Definitions.
[2]Prior to September 1997 this series represents both nonfinancial and financial commercial paper rates. Beginning September 1997, rates for financial companies only are shown. See Notes and Definitions.
. . . = Not available.

Table 12-9. Selected Interest Rates and Bond Yields—Continued

(Percent per annum.)

Year and month	U.S. Treasury securities, constant maturities					Bond yields			Fixed-rate first mortgages
	1-year	3-year	10-year	20-year	30-year	Domestic corporate (Moody's)		State and local bonds (Bond Buyer)	
						Aaa	Baa		
1954	...	...	...	...	...	2.90	3.51	2.39	...
1955	...	...	...	...	...	3.05	3.53	2.48	...
1956	...	...	...	...	...	3.36	3.88	2.76	...
1957	...	...	...	...	...	3.89	4.71	3.28	...
1958	...	...	...	...	...	3.79	4.73	2.73	...
1959	...	...	...	...	...	4.38	5.05	2.73	...
1960	...	...	...	...	...	4.41	5.19	2.73	...
1961	...	...	...	...	...	4.35	5.08	3.45	...
1962	3.10	3.47	3.95	...	...	4.33	5.02	3.15	...
1963	3.36	3.67	4.00	...	...	4.26	4.86	3.17	...
1964	3.85	4.03	4.19	...	...	4.41	4.83	3.21	...
1965	4.15	4.22	4.28	...	...	4.49	4.87	2.92	...
1966	5.20	5.23	4.93	...	...	5.13	5.67	2.92	...
1967	4.88	5.03	5.07	...	...	5.51	6.23	3.94	...
1968	5.69	5.68	5.64	...	...	6.18	6.94	4.45	...
1969	7.12	7.02	6.67	...	...	7.03	7.81	5.72	...
1970	6.90	7.29	7.35	...	...	8.04	9.11	6.33	...
1971	4.89	5.66	6.16	...	...	7.39	8.56	3.72	...
1972	4.95	5.72	6.21	...	...	7.21	8.16	3.81	7.38
1973	7.32	6.96	6.85	...	...	7.44	8.24	3.90	8.04
1974	8.20	7.84	7.56	...	...	8.57	9.50	3.93	9.19
1975	6.78	7.50	7.99	...	...	8.83	10.61	4.00	9.04
1976	5.88	6.77	7.61	...	...	8.43	9.75	6.64	8.86
1977	6.08	6.68	7.42	...	7.75	8.02	8.97	5.68	8.84
1978	8.34	8.29	8.41	...	8.49	8.73	9.49	6.02	9.63
1979	10.65	9.70	9.43	...	9.28	9.63	10.69	6.52	11.19
1980	12.00	11.51	11.43	...	11.27	11.94	13.67	8.59	13.77
1981	14.80	14.46	13.92	...	13.45	14.17	16.04	11.33	16.63
1982	12.27	12.93	13.01	...	12.76	13.79	16.11	11.66	16.08
1983	9.58	10.45	11.10	...	11.18	12.04	13.55	9.51	13.23
1984	10.91	11.92	12.46	...	12.41	12.71	14.19	10.10	13.87
1985	8.42	9.64	10.62	...	10.79	11.37	12.72	9.10	12.42
1986	6.45	7.06	7.67	...	7.78	9.02	10.39	7.32	10.18
1987	6.77	7.68	8.39	...	8.59	9.38	10.58	7.64	10.20
1988	7.65	8.26	8.85	...	8.96	9.71	10.83	7.68	10.34
1989	8.53	8.55	8.49	...	8.45	9.26	10.18	7.23	10.32
1990	7.89	8.26	8.55	...	8.61	9.32	10.36	7.27	10.13
1991	5.86	6.82	7.86	...	8.14	8.77	9.80	6.92	9.25
1992	3.89	5.30	7.01	...	7.67	8.14	8.98	6.44	8.40
1993	3.43	4.44	5.87	6.29	6.59	7.22	7.93	5.60	7.33
1994	5.32	6.27	7.09	7.49	7.37	7.97	8.63	6.18	8.35
1995	5.94	6.25	6.57	6.95	6.88	7.59	8.20	5.95	7.95
1996	5.52	5.99	6.44	6.83	6.71	7.37	8.05	5.76	7.80
1997	5.63	6.10	6.35	6.69	6.61	7.27	7.87	5.52	7.60
1998	5.05	5.14	5.26	5.72	5.58	6.53	7.22	5.09	6.94
1999	5.08	5.49	5.65	6.20	5.87	7.05	7.88	5.43	7.43
2000	6.11	6.22	6.03	6.23	5.94	7.62	8.37	5.71	8.06
2001	3.49	4.09	5.02	5.63	5.49	7.08	7.95	5.15	6.97
2002	2.00	3.10	4.61	5.43	...	6.49	7.80	5.04	6.54
2003	1.24	2.10	4.01	4.96	...	5.66	6.76	4.75	5.82
2002									
January	2.16	3.56	5.04	5.69	5.45	6.55	7.87	5.16	7.00
February	2.23	3.55	4.91	5.61	5.40	6.51	7.89	5.11	6.89
March	2.57	4.14	5.28	5.93	...	6.81	8.11	5.29	7.01
April	2.48	4.01	5.21	5.85	...	6.76	8.03	5.22	6.99
May	2.35	3.80	5.16	5.81	...	6.75	8.09	5.19	6.81
June	2.20	3.49	4.93	5.65	...	6.63	7.95	5.09	6.65
July	1.96	3.01	4.65	5.51	...	6.53	7.90	5.02	6.49
August	1.76	2.52	4.26	5.19	...	6.37	7.58	4.95	6.29
September	1.72	2.32	3.87	4.87	...	6.15	7.40	4.74	6.09
October	1.65	2.25	3.94	5.00	...	6.32	7.73	4.88	6.11
November	1.49	2.32	4.05	5.04	...	6.31	7.62	4.95	6.07
December	1.45	2.23	4.03	5.01	...	6.21	7.45	4.85	6.05
2003									
January	1.36	2.18	4.05	5.02	...	6.17	7.35	4.90	5.92
February	1.30	2.05	3.90	4.87	...	5.95	7.06	4.81	5.84
March	1.24	1.98	3.81	4.82	...	5.89	6.95	4.76	5.75
April	1.27	2.06	3.96	4.91	...	5.74	6.85	4.74	5.81
May	1.18	1.75	3.57	4.52	...	5.22	6.38	4.41	5.48
June	1.01	1.51	3.33	4.34	...	4.97	6.19	4.33	5.23
July	1.12	1.93	3.98	4.92	...	5.49	6.62	4.74	5.63
August	1.31	2.44	4.45	5.39	...	5.88	7.01	5.10	6.26
September	1.24	2.23	4.27	5.21	...	5.72	6.79	4.92	6.15
October	1.25	2.26	4.29	5.21	...	5.70	6.73	4.89	5.95
November	1.34	2.45	4.30	5.17	...	5.65	6.66	4.73	5.93
December	1.31	2.44	4.27	5.11	...	5.62	6.60	4.65	5.88

... = Not available.

Table 12-10. Common Stock Prices and Yields

Year and month	Stock price indexes			Yields based on Standard and Poor's composite (percent)	
	Dow Jones industrials (30 stocks)	Standard and Poor's composite (500 stocks) (1941–1943 = 10)	Nasdaq composite (Feb. 5, 1971 = 100)	Dividend-price ratio	Earnings-price ratio
1955	442.72	40.49	...	4.08	7.95
1956	493.01	46.62	...	4.09	7.55
1957	475.71	44.38	...	4.35	7.89
1958	491.66	46.24	...	3.97	6.23
1959	632.12	57.38	...	3.23	5.78
1960	618.04	55.85	...	3.47	5.90
1961	691.55	66.27	...	2.98	4.62
1962	639.76	62.38	...	3.37	5.82
1963	714.81	69.87	...	3.17	5.50
1964	834.05	81.37	...	3.01	5.32
1965	910.88	88.17	...	3.00	5.59
1966	873.60	85.26	...	3.40	6.63
1967	879.12	91.93	...	3.20	5.73
1968	906.00	98.70	...	3.07	5.67
1969	876.72	97.84	...	3.24	6.08
1970	753.19	83.22	...	3.83	6.45
1971	884.76	98.29	107.44	3.14	5.41
1972	950.71	109.20	128.52	2.84	5.50
1973	923.88	107.43	109.90	3.06	7.12
1974	759.37	82.85	76.29	4.47	11.59
1975	802.49	86.16	77.20	4.31	9.15
1976	974.92	102.01	89.90	3.77	8.90
1977	894.63	98.20	98.71	4.62	10.79
1978	820.23	96.02	117.53	5.28	12.03
1979	844.40	103.01	136.57	5.47	13.46
1980	891.41	118.78	168.61	5.26	12.66
1981	932.92	128.05	203.18	5.20	11.96
1982	884.36	119.71	188.97	5.81	11.60
1983	1 190.34	160.41	285.43	4.40	8.03
1984	1 178.48	160.46	248.88	4.64	10.02
1985	1 328.23	186.84	290.19	4.25	8.12
1986	1 792.76	236.34	366.96	3.49	6.09
1987	2 275.99	286.83	402.57	3.08	5.48
1988	2 060.82	265.79	374.43	3.64	8.01
1989	2 508.91	322.84	437.81	3.45	7.42
1990	2 678.94	334.59	409.17	3.61	6.47
1991	2 929.33	376.18	491.69	3.24	4.79
1992	3 284.29	415.74	599.26	2.99	4.22
1993	3 522.06	451.41	715.16	2.78	4.46
1994	3 793.77	460.42	751.65	2.82	5.83
1995	4 493.76	541.72	925.19	2.56	6.09
1996	5 742.89	670.50	1 164.96	2.19	5.24
1997	7 441.15	873.43	1 469.49	1.77	4.57
1998	8 625.52	1 085.50	1 794.91	1.49	3.46
1999	10 464.88	1 327.33	2 728.15	1.25	3.17
2000	10 734.90	1 427.22	3 783.67	1.15	3.63
2001	10 189.13	1 194.18	2 035.00	1.32	2.95
2002	9 226.43	993.94	1 539.73	1.61	2.92
2003	8 993.59	965.23	1 647.17	1.77	3.84
2002					
January	9 923.80	1 140.21	1 976.77	1.38	...
February	9 891.05	1 100.67	1 799.72	1.43	...
March	10 500.95	1 153.79	1 863.05	1.37	2.15
April	10 165.18	1 112.03	1 758.80	1.42	...
May	10 080.48	1 079.27	1 660.31	1.47	...
June	9 492.44	1 014.05	1 505.49	1.58	2.70
July	8 616.52	903.59	1 346.09	1.76	...
August	8 685.48	912.55	1 327.36	1.72	...
September	8 160.78	867.81	1 251.07	1.80	3.68
October	8 048.12	854.63	1 241.91	1.86	...
November	8 625.72	909.93	1 409.15	1.73	...
December	8 526.66	899.18	1 387.15	1.77	3.14
2003					
January	8 474.59	895.84	1 389.56	1.80	...
February	7 916.18	837.62	1 313.26	1.95	...
March	7 977.73	846.62	1 348.50	1.93	3.57
April	8 332.09	890.03	1 409.83	1.83	...
May	8 623.41	935.96	1 524.18	1.75	...
June	9 098.07	988.00	1 631.75	1.66	3.55
July	9 154.39	992.54	1 716.85	1.71	...
August	9 284.78	989.53	1 724.82	1.78	...
September	9 492.54	1 019.44	1 856.22	1.73	3.87
October	9 682.46	1 038.73	1 907.89	1.71	...
November	9 762.20	1 049.90	1 939.25	1.69	...
December	10 124.66	1 080.64	1 956.98	1.67	4.38

... = Not available.

NOTES AND DEFINITIONS

TABLES 12-1, 12-2, AND 20-5
MONEY STOCK MEASURES; SELECTED COMPONENTS OF THE MONEY STOCK

SOURCE: BOARD OF GOVERNORS OF THE FEDERAL RESERVE SYSTEM

Estimates of three monetary aggregates (M1, M2, and M3) and the components of these measures are published weekly. The monthly data are averages of daily figures.

Definitions

M1 consists of (1) currency outside the U.S. Treasury, Federal Reserve Banks, and the vaults of depository institutions; (2) travelers checks of nonbank issuers; (3) demand deposits at all commercial banks other than those due to depository institutions, the U.S. government, and foreign banks and official institutions, less cash items in the process of collection and Federal Reserve float; and (4) other checkable deposits, consisting of negotiable order of withdrawal (NOW) and automatic transfer service (ATS) accounts at depository institutions, credit union share draft accounts, and demand deposits at thrift institutions.

M2 consists of M1 plus savings deposits (including money market deposit accounts), small-denomination time deposits (time deposits—including retail repurchase agreements [RPs]—in amounts of less than $100,000), and balances in retail money market mutual funds. It excludes individual retirement account (IRA) and Keogh balances at depository institutions and money market funds.

M3 consists of M2 plus large-denomination time deposits (in amounts of $100,000 or more), balances in institutional money funds, RP liabilities (overnight and term) issued by all depository institutions, and Eurodollars (overnight and term) held by U.S. residents at foreign branches of U.S. banks worldwide and at all banking offices in the United Kingdom and Canada. It excludes amounts held by depository institutions, the U.S. government, money funds, and foreign banks and official institutions.

Currency consists of currency outside the U.S. Treasury, the Federal Reserve Banks, and the vaults of depository institutions.

Demand deposits consists of demand deposits at commercial banks and foreign-related institutions other than those due to depository institutions, the U.S. government, and foreign banks and official institutions, less cash items in the process of collection and Federal Reserve float.

Other checkable deposits consists of NOW and ATS balances at all depository institutions; credit union share draft balances; and demand deposits at thrift institutions.

Repurchase agreements (RPs) are commitments by depository institutions to repurchase securities (often government securities) that a client has purchased from the institution. A repurchase agreement constitutes a ready source of liquidity for the client, similar in nature to other components of M2 and M3. Both overnight and longer-term repurchase agreements are included in the data.

Eurodollars are dollar-denominated deposits—both overnight and term—held by U.S. residents at foreign branches of U.S. banks worldwide and at all banking offices in the United Kingdom and Canada.

Savings deposits includes money market deposit accounts and other savings deposits at both commercial banks and thrift institutions.

Small time deposits are those issued at commercial banks and thrift institutions in amounts of less than $100,000. Retail RPs are included. All IRA and Keogh account balances at commercial banks and thrift institutions are subtracted from small time deposits.

Large time deposits are those issued in amounts of $100,000 or more at commercial banks and thrift institutions, excluding those booked at international banking facilities. Deposits held at commercial banks by money market mutual funds, depository institutions, the U.S. government, and foreign banks and official institutions also are excluded.

Notes on the data

Seasonal adjustment. Seasonally adjusted M1 is calculated by summing currency, travelers checks, demand deposits, and other checkable deposits, each seasonally adjusted separately. Seasonally adjusted M2 is computed by adjusting each of its non-M1 components and then adding this result to seasonally adjusted M1. Similarly, seasonally adjusted M3 is obtained by adjusting each of its non-M2 components and then adding this result to seasonally adjusted M2.

Revisions. Money stock measures are revised annually, usually in February, based on a benchmark and seasonal factor review. These revisions typically extend back a number of years. The monetary aggregates were redefined in major revisions in 1980.

Data availability

Estimates are released weekly in Federal Reserve Statistical Release H.6, "Money Stock, Liquid Assets, and

Debt Measures" and are subsequently published each month in the *Federal Reserve Bulletin*. Historical data beginning with 1959 are available from Publications Services, Board of Governors of the Federal Reserve System. Current and historical data are available on the Federal Reserve Internet site at <http://www.federalreserve.gov/releases/>.

References

An explanation of the 1980 redefinition of the monetary aggregates is found in the *Federal Reserve Bulletin* for February 1980.

TABLES 12-3 AND 20-5
AGGREGATE RESERVES OF DEPOSITORY INSTITUTIONS AND MONETARY BASE

SOURCE: BOARD OF GOVERNORS OF THE FEDERAL RESERVE SYSTEM

The data presented here are in millions of dollars, seasonally adjusted and adjusted for changes in reserve requirements ("break-adjusted") so as to provide a consistent gauge of the effect of Federal Reserve open-market operations. To illustrate, an observed increase in reserves will not represent an easing in monetary conditions if it is simply equal to an increase in reserves required by the Federal Reserve. Therefore, the mandated increases and decreases are deducted to provide the "break-adjusted" series. Monthly data are averages of daily figures. Annual data are for December.

Definitions

Total reserves consists of reserve balances with Federal Reserve Banks plus vault cash used to satisfy reserve requirements. Seasonally adjusted, break-adjusted total reserves equal seasonally adjusted, break-adjusted required reserves plus unadjusted excess reserves.

Seasonally adjusted, break-adjusted *nonborrowed reserves* equal seasonally adjusted, break-adjusted total reserves less unadjusted total borrowings of depository institutions from the Federal Reserve.

Extended credit consists of borrowing at the discount window under the terms and conditions established for the extended credit program to help depository institutions deal with sustained liquidity pressures. Because there is not the same need to repay such borrowing promptly as there is with traditional short-term adjustment credit, the money market impact of extended credit is similar to that of nonborrowed reserves. The extended credit program has not been used in recent years but was significant in the 1980s.

To adjust *required reserves* for discontinuities due to regulatory changes in reserve requirements, a multiplicative procedure is used to estimate what required reserves would have been in past periods had current reserve requirements been in effect. Break-adjusted required reserves include required reserves against transactions deposits and personal time and savings deposits (but not reservable nondeposit liabilities).

The seasonally adjusted, break-adjusted *monetary* base consists of (1) seasonally adjusted, break-adjusted total reserves plus (2) the seasonally adjusted currency component of the money stock plus (3) for all quarterly reporters on the "Report of Transaction Accounts, Other Deposits and Vault Cash" and for all those weekly reporters whose vault cash exceeds their required reserves, the seasonally adjusted, break-adjusted difference between current vault cash and the amount applied to satisfy current reserve requirements.

Data availability

Data are released weekly in Federal Reserve Release H.3 and subsequently published in the *Federal Reserve Bulletin*. Historical data are available from the Money and Reserves Projections Section, Division of Monetary Affairs, Board of Governors of the Federal Reserve System, Washington, DC 20551. Current and historical data also are available on the Federal Reserve Internet site at <http://www.federalreserve.gov/releases/>.

TABLE 12-4
COMMERCIAL BANKS: BANK CREDIT AND SELECTED LIABILITIES

SOURCE: BOARD OF GOVERNORS OF THE FEDERAL RESERVE SYSTEM

These data on the assets and liabilities of commercial banks are published in the Federal Reserve's H.8 Release.

Definitions and notes on the data

The data are for all commercial banks in the United States. This category covers the following types of institutions in the 50 states and the District of Columbia: domestically chartered commercial banks that report weekly (large domestic); other domestically chartered commercial banks (small domestic); branches and agencies of foreign banks, and Edge Act and Agreement corporations (foreign related institutions). International Banking Facilities are excluded.

Data are collected weekly for Wednesday values; monthly data are pro rata averages of Wednesday values; annual data represent December figures.

Data are complete for large domestic banks. Data for others are estimated on the basis of weekly samples and end of quarter condition reports. Data are adjusted for breaks caused by reclassifications of assets and liabilities.

Data before 1988 are based on a previous version of the H.8, the G.7 release on Loans and Securities at Commercial Banks, and the G.10 on Major Nondeposit Funds of Commercial Banks.

Security loans—a component of *loans and leases in bank credit*—consist of loans to purchase and carry securities, and reverse repurchase agreements with brokers and dealers and others. In a reverse RP a bank has provided liquidity to a borrower by buying a security from him, which the borrower promises to repurchase at a certain date.

Interbank loans, cash assets, and other assets are not components of bank credit and are omitted from Table 12-4. Interbank loans include loans made to commercial banks, reverse repurchase agreements with commercial banks, and federal funds sold to commercial banks.

Selected liabilities show *deposits and borrowings*. Two components of total liabilities, "net due to foreign offices" and "other liabilities," are omitted.

Revisions

Data are revised annually to reflect new benchmark information and revised seasonal factors.

Data availability

Assets and Liabilities of Commercial Banks, Federal Reserve Release H.8, is issued each Friday around 4:30 p.m. eastern time. Selected data are subsequently published in the *Federal Reserve Bulletin*. Historical data may be purchased on diskette from Publications Services, Board of Governors of the Federal Reserve System. Current and historical data are available on the Federal Reserve Internet site at <http://www.federalreserve.gov/releases/>.

TABLE 12-5
CREDIT MARKET DEBT OUTSTANDING, BY BORROWER AND LENDER

SOURCE: BOARD OF GOVERNORS OF THE FEDERAL RESERVE SYSTEM

The flow of funds accounts, compiled quarterly by the Federal Reserve Board, supplement the national income and product accounts by providing a comprehensive and detailed accounting of financial transactions, with a balance sheet for each financial and nonfinancial sector of the economy. Table 12-5 shows the credit market debt that is owed by the major sectors in the economy, and it also shows the major lending sectors in the credit markets. One purpose of these statistics is to show the comparative growth of the various sectors.

Aggregates of these data can include multiple layers of financial intermediation, such as banks making advances to finance companies that are lending to households. In macroeconomic analysis, the most widely used flow of funds measure is the total debt of domestic nonfinancial sectors. By eliminating the financial sectors, this measure has little duplication due to financial intermediation. It is used by the Federal Reserve along with the monetary aggregates as an indicator of monetary conditions.

Definitions and notes on the data

Quarterly data on debt outstanding are shown on an end-of-period basis, not adjusted for seasonal variation or for "breaks" or discontinuities in the series. Because of these discontinuities, caution should be used in interpreting *changes* in debt levels. Break-adjusted values of the changes or "flows" can be found in the quarterly Flow-of-Funds report, along with a suggested method for calculating percent changes.

The data on credit market debt exclude corporate equities and mutual fund shares.

Data for the current and preceding years are revised each year to reflect revisions in source data.

Sectors owing debt:

Domestic financial sectors:

Federal government-related sectors include government sponsored enterprises (GSEs) such as "Fannie Mae" (originally the Federal National Mortgage Association) and "Freddie Mac" (originally the Federal Home Loan Mortgage Corporation); agency and GSE-backed mortgage pools; and the monetary authority (Federal Reserve). However, the Federal Reserve usually has no credit market debt.

The *private* sector includes commercial banks and bank holding companies, savings institutions, credit unions, life insurance companies, asset-backed securities (ABS) issuers, brokers and dealers, finance and mortgage companies, REITs (real estate investment trusts), and funding corporations.

Domestic nonfinancial sectors:

Federal government consists of all federal government agencies and funds that are in the unified budget. The District of Columbia government, however, is included in the state and local sector.

Treasury securities as shown here exclude securities issued by the Treasury but held by agencies within the U.S. government (e.g., in the Social Security trust funds). In this respect it corresponds to "Federal debt," shown in Table 6-17, except that the latter table uses a fiscal year rather than a calendar year basis. Federal government debt as shown here is smaller than the official total public debt and the "debt subject to limit," both of which also include the securities held by U.S. government agencies. The value shown here is considered a more accurate measure than those larger aggregates of the effect of government borrowing in relation to the economy and credit markets.

Budget agency securities and mortgages are those issued by government-owned corporations and agencies, such as the Export-Import Bank, that issue securities individually.

Households also include personal trusts and nonprofit organizations.

State and local governments represent operating funds only. Retirement funds are included in the financial sector.

Foreign credit market debt held in the United States shows foreign credit market debt owed to U.S. residents. This debt is included along with the debt of domestic financial and nonfinancial sectors in total credit market debt outstanding.

Percentage measures:

Table 12-5 includes three measures of relative debt burdens, calculated by the editor.

Domestic nonfinancial debt as a percent of GDP is the total debt owed by domestic nonfinancial sectors as a percent of the current-dollar value of total Gross Domestic Product (Table 1-1).

Household debt as a percent of DPI is the value of debt owed by households as a percent of the current-dollar value of disposable personal income (Table 4-1).

Corporate nonfinancial business debt as a percent of sector value added is the total debt owed by domestic corporate nonfinancial business as a percent of the current-dollar gross value added of domestic corporate nonfinancial business (Table 1-13).

Credit market assets held by sector

Government related sectors:

This grouping includes two nonfinancial and three financial sectors. The nonfinancial sectors are the *Federal government*, as reflected in the U.S. Budget accounts, and the operations of *state and local governments*, including the District of Columbia. *State and local employee retirement funds* are shown separately as a financial sector. Other government related financial sectors are the following:

Government-sponsored enterprises are financial institutions that provide credit to housing, agriculture, and other specific areas of the economy, such as Federal Home Loan Banks, Fannie Mae, Freddie Mac, and others.

Federally related mortgage pools are entities established for bookkeeping purposes that record the issuance of pooled securities representing an interest in mortgages originally held by federally related agencies such as Fannie Mae. Rather than being composed of a group of institutions, the sector is made up of a set of contractual arrangements in regard to pooled mortgages.

Selected domestic financial sectors:

This grouping includes major financial sectors, such as *commercial banks*, *savings institutions*, and *credit unions*. The *monetary authority* (the Federal Reserve) has also been put in this grouping because it is sometimes included in banking sector totals. Other financial sectors are *life insurance companies*, *other insurance companies*, and *private pension funds*. Additional sectors are *money market mutual funds*, which issue shares and invest in short-term liquid assets; *mutual funds*, whose investments are not restricted to the short-term area; *asset backed security (ABS) issuers*, which issue debt obligations that are backed by pooled assets, a financial procedure similar to that of federally related mortgage pools; and *finance companies*, which provide credit to businesses and individuals.

Private domestic nonfinancial sectors:

Households are the dominant private nonfinancial lenders.

A number of small lending sectors, nonfinancial and financial, are included in the category "*Other*." One of those is nonfinancial business, a sector that is important on the borrowing side, but not on the lending side.

Data availability

Debt estimates are released quarterly, about nine weeks following the end of a quarter, in Federal Reserve Statistical Release Z.1, "Flow of Funds of the United States," and are subsequently published in the *Federal Reserve Bulletin*. Releases and data on diskettes are available from Publications Services, Board of Governors of the Federal Reserve System. Current and historical data also are available on the Federal Reserve Internet site at<http://www.federalreserve.gov/releases>.

References

A *Guide to the Flow of Funds Accounts* can be purchased from Publications Services, Board of Governors of the Federal Reserve System. The *Federal Reserve Bulletin* for July 2001 includes an article on "The U.S. Flow of Funds Accounts and Their Uses."

TABLE 12-6
HOUSEHOLD ASSETS, LIABILITIES, NET WORTH, FINANCIAL OBLIGATIONS, AND DELINQUENCY RATES

SOURCE: BOARD OF GOVERNORS OF THE FEDERAL RESERVE SYSTEM

The quarterly data on household sector assets, liabilities, and net worth are obtained from the Federal Reserve Board's flow of funds accounts. These also are the source of the credit market data in Table 12-5. A general description of the flow of funds accounts is provided in the Notes and Definitions to Table 12-5, above.

The household debt service ratio relates required debt service (interest and principal) payments to disposable personal income. The financial obligations ratios include not only required debt payments but also rental payments, automobile lease payments, homeowners' insurance, and property taxes and are also expressed as a percent of disposable personal income. Unlike the debt service ratio, the financial obligations ratios are not distorted by the trends toward debt-financed homeownership in preference to rental, and toward auto leasing in preference to loan financing.

The delinquency and charge-off rates relate delinquent (past due 30 days or more) and charged-off consumer credit card credit at commercial banks to total bank holdings of that type of credit.

Definitions and notes on the data

Quarterly data on holdings of *financial assets* are shown on an end-of-period basis, not adjusted for seasonal variations. Data for the current and preceding years are revised each year to reflect revisions in source data. For most categories, the values for the household sector are calculated as residuals. That is, starting with known totals, such as total Treasury securities, amounts held by other sectors are subtracted, and the remainders are assigned to the household sector.

Financial assets of the household sector include nonprofit organizations, which are difficult to estimate separately, but exclude holdings by unincorporated businesses.

The table shows total household ownership of *checkable deposits and currency, time and savings deposits, money market fund shares, U.S. savings bonds, other Treasury securities, agency securities, municipal securities, corporate and foreign bonds, mortgages, corporate equities, mutual fund shares, security credit, life insurance reserves, pension fund reserves, bank personal trusts,* and *equity in noncorporate business*. Pension fund reserves include insurance and pension fund reserves of federal, state, and local government employee funds—but not the Social Security system—as well as private industry funds. Included in total *financial assets,* but not shown separately, are foreign deposits, open market paper, and claims on insurance companies, such as unearned premium reserves of other insurance companies and health insurance reserves of life insurance companies.

Tangible assets complete the asset side of the household balance sheet. Tangible assets comprise real estate, equipment and software owned by nonprofit organizations, and consumer durable goods. *Household real estate* is valued at market value, while equipment, software, and consumer durables are valued at replacement (current) cost.

Debt as a percent of total assets is calculated by the editor as household credit market debt outstanding, from Table 12-5, as a percent of the total of tangible and financial assets in this table. It covers both households and nonprofit organizations.

Total liabilities consists of household credit market debt, as shown in Table 12-5, plus security credit, trade payables of nonprofit organizations, and deferred and unpaid life insurance premiums.

Net worth is the sum of the value of financial and tangible assets minus total liabilities.

The *household debt-service and financial obligations ratios* are estimated on a quarterly basis by the Federal Reserve based on aggregate and consumer survey data and are seasonally adjusted, unlike almost all of the other data in Table 12-6. Fourth-quarter values are shown to represent the calendar year. The denominator for the aggregate ratio is personal disposable income from the National Income and Product Accounts (NIPAs) (see Chapter 4). The allocation of the NIPA data between *renters* and *homeowners* is estimated by the Federal Reserve based on data from the Federal Reserve's triennial Survey of Consumer Finances and the Current Population Survey (see Chapter 3).

Debt service payments are the minimum required monthly payments of principal and interest on mortgage debt (including home equity loans), revolving credit (credit-card debt), and auto, student, mobile-home, recreational vehicle, marine, and personal loans.

The *financial obligations ratios* include, in addition to debt service, rental payments on primary residences, property taxes, homeowners' insurance, and automobile lease payments.

Delinquency and charge-off rates of credit card accounts held at banks are compiled from the quarterly FFIEC (Federal Financial Institutions Examination Council) Consolidated Reports of Condition and Income (FFIEC 031 through 034) and pertain to all insured U.S.-chartered commercial banks. The *delinquency rate* is loans past due 30 days or more and still accruing interest as well as those in nonaccrual status, measured as a percentage of end-of-period loans. The *charge-off rate* is the value of loans removed from the books and charged against loss reserves, measured net of recoveries as a percentage of average loans and annualized.

Data availability

Household asset estimates are released quarterly, about nine weeks following the end of a quarter, in the Federal Reserve Statistical Release Z.1, "Flow of Funds Accounts of the United States." Further information on data availability is given in the Notes to Table 12-5, a table that is also based on the flow of funds accounts.

The revised debt service ratio and the new financial obligations ratios are described in "Recent Changes to a Measure of U.S. Household Debt Service," *Federal Reserve Bulletin*, October 2003. The data are estimated by the Federal Reserve about three months after the end of each quarter. Current and historical data are available on the Internet site at <http://www.federalreserve.gov/releases>.

Delinquency and charge-off rates of credit card accounts held at banks are also available on the Federal Reserve Internet site, listed under Charge-off and Delinquency Rates on Loans at Commercial Banks, approximately 60 days after the end of the quarter.

TABLE 12-7
MORTGAGE DEBT OUTSTANDING

SOURCE: BOARD OF GOVERNORS OF THE FEDERAL RESERVE SYSTEM

These data are published in the Federal Reserve's "Flow of Funds Accounts." They are based on reports from various government and private organizations.

Definitions and notes on the data

Home mortgages include home equity loans; these are also shown separately in the Flow of Funds Accounts.

Multifamily residential refers to mortgages on structures of five or more units.

Mortgage pools or trusts show mortgages that were refinanced by their holders through the issuance of mortgage-backed securities. They are shown in two columns: refinancings by *Federally related agencies*—mainly the Federal National Mortgage Association (Fannie Mae), the Federal Home Loan Mortgage Corporation (Freddie Mac), and the Government National Mortgage Association (Ginnie Mae)—and refinancings by private conduits (these are referred to as ABS issuers in the Flow of Funds Accounts, which stands for issuers of asset-backed securities).

Other holders include a variety of groups including finance companies, individuals, state and local governments, credit unions, and others.

Home mortgage debt as a percentage of the value of real estate is calculated by the editor, using total home mortgage debt as a percentage of the value of household real estate shown in Table 12-6.

Data availability

Mortgage debt data are compiled quarterly, about 9 weeks following the end of the quarter, in Federal Reserve Statistical Release Z.1, "Flow of Funds Accounts of the United States." Similar data are also provided in Table 1.54 on Mortgage Debt Outstanding in the *Federal Reserve Bulletin*. Releases and data on diskettes are available from Publications Services, Board of Governors of the Federal Reserve System. Current and historical data are available on the Federal Reserve Internet site at <http://www.federalreserve.gov/releases>.

TABLE 12-8
CONSUMER CREDIT

SOURCE: BOARD OF GOVERNORS OF THE FEDERAL RESERVE SYSTEM

The consumer credit series cover most short- and intermediate-term credit extended to individuals through regular business channels, excluding loans secured by real estate (e.g., first and second mortgages and home equity credit). In October 2003 the scope of the statistics was extended to incorporate student loans extended by the federal government and by SLM Holding Corporation (SLM), the parent company of Sallie Mae. The historical data have been revised back to 1977 to reflect this inclusion. The household debt series presented in Table 12-5 is more comprehensive, comprising both mortgage and consumer debt. Consumer credit is categorized by major types of credit and by major holders.

Definitions and notes on the data

The major types of consumer credit are *revolving* and *nonrevolving*. *Revolving credit* includes credit arising from purchases on credit card plans of retail stores and banks, cash advances and check credit plans of banks, and some overdraft credit arrangements. *Non-revolving credit* includes automobile loans (new and passenger automobiles), mobile home loans, and all other loans not included in revolving credit, such as loans for education, boats, trailers, or vacations. These loans may be secured or unsecured.

Debt secured by real estate (including first liens, junior liens, and home equity loans) is excluded. Credit extended to governmental agencies and nonprofit or charitable organizations, as well as credit extended to business or to individuals exclusively for business purposes, is excluded.

Categories of *holders* include *commercial banks, finance companies, credit unions, federal government and Sallie Mae, savings institutions, nonfinancial businesses, and pools of securitized assets*. Retailers and gasoline companies are included in the nonfinancial businesses category. *Pools of securitized assets* comprises the outstanding balances of pools upon which securities have been issued; these balances are no longer carried on the balance sheets of the loan originators.

The consumer credit series are based on comprehensive benchmark data that become available periodically. Current monthly estimates are brought forward from the latest benchmarks in accordance with weighted changes indicated by sample data. Classifications are made on a "holder" basis. Thus, installment paper sold by retail outlets is included in figures for the banks and finance companies that purchased the paper.

The amount of outstanding credit represents the sum of the balances in the installment receivable accounts of financial institutions and retail outlets at the end of each month.

The estimates of the amount of credit outstanding include any finance and insurance charges included as part of the installment contract. Unearned income on loans is included in some cases where lenders cannot separate the components.

The seasonally adjusted data are adjusted for differences in the number of trading days and for seasonal influences. The seasonal factors used are derived by the X-11-ARIMA process.

Data availability

Current data are available monthly in the Federal Reserve Statistical Release G.19, Consumer Credit, and in the *Federal Reserve Bulletin*. The data for earlier years may be purchased on diskette from Publication Services, Board of Governors of the Federal Reserve System. Current and historical data are available on the Federal Reserve Internet site at <http://www.federalreserve.gov/releases/>.

**TABLES 12-9, 12-10 AND 20-6
INTEREST RATES, BOND YIELDS, STOCK PRICES AND YIELDS**

SOURCES: BOARD OF GOVERNORS OF THE FEDERAL RESERVE SYSTEM; MOODY'S INVESTORS SERVICE; THE BOND BUYER; DOW JONES, INC.; STANDARD AND POOR'S CORPORATION; NEW YORK STOCK EXCHANGE

Definitions and notes on the data

Interest rates and bond yields are percents per year and are averages of business day figures, except as noted.

The daily effective *federal funds rate* is a weighted average of rates on trades through New York brokers. Monthly figures include each calendar day in the month. Annualized figures use a 360-day year.

The *Federal Reserve discount rate* is the rate for discount window borrowing at the Federal Reserve Bank of New York. Monthly figures include each calendar day in the month. Annualized figures use a 360-day year.

Beginning in January 2003 the rules governing the discount window programs were revised. "Adjustment credit," which was extended at a below-market rate, was replaced with a new type called "primary credit," available for very short terms as a backup source of liquidity to depository institutions in generally sound financial condition in the judgment of the lending Federal Reserve Bank. Primary credit is to be extended at a rate above the federal funds rate, eliminating the incentive for institutions to exploit the spread of money market rates over the discount rate.

Through December 2002, Table 12-9 displays the "adjustment credit" rate. Beginning in February 2003, the new "Primary credit" rate is shown. The rule change, and the change in discount rates shown, did not entail a change in the stance of monetary policy, which continues to be measured by the level of the federal funds rate.

The *Eurodollar rate* shown is the bid rate for Eurodollar deposits at about 9:30 a.m. Eastern time for 1-month deposits. Annualized figures use a 360-day year.

The *U.S. Treasury bills, 3-month rate* and the *U.S. Treasury bills, 6-month rate* shown are the yields on these securities based on their prices as traded in the secondary market. The rates are quoted on a discount basis, and annualized figures use a 360-day year.

Commercial paper, 3-month rates are interpolated from data on certain commercial paper trades settled by the Depository Trust Company. This company is a clearing house and custodian for nearly all domestic commercial paper activity. The trades, which are on a discount basis, represent sales of commercial paper by dealers or direct issuers. Annualized figures use a 360-day year. Prior to September 1997 the series represents both nonfinancial and financial commercial paper; beginning September 1997 only rates for financial companies are shown, introducing a slight discontinuity into the series.

CDs (secondary market), 3-month rates are averages of dealer offering rates on nationally traded certificates of deposit. Annualized figures use a 360-day year.

The *bank prime rate* is one of several base rates used by banks to price short-term business loans. It is the rate posted by a majority of the top 25 (by assets in domestic offices) insured U.S.-chartered commercial banks. Monthly figures include each calendar day in the month. Annualized figures use a 360-day year.

U.S. Treasury securities. The rates shown for 1-year, 3-year, 10-year, 20-year, and 30-year securities are yields on actively traded issues adjusted to constant maturities. Yields on Treasury securities at "constant maturity" are interpolated by the U.S. Treasury from the daily yield curve. This curve, which relates the yield on a security to its time to maturity, is based on the closing market bid yields on actively traded Treasury securities in the over-the-counter market. These market yields are calculated from composites of quotations reported by U.S. government securities dealers to the Federal Reserve Bank of New York. The constant maturity yield values are read from the yield curve at fixed maturities. This method provides a yield for a 10-year maturity, for example, even if no outstanding security has exactly 10 years remaining to maturity. The 30-year series was discontinued as of February 2002, because the Treasury is no longer issuing such bonds. The current 20-year series begins in 1993 and is not comparable with an earlier 20-year series. For further information, see Table 1.35 in the *Federal Reserve Bulletin* and the historical data series on the Federal Reserve Internet site.

Domestic corporate bond yields. The rates shown are for general obligation bonds based on Thursday figures and are provided by Moody's Investors Service and republished by the Federal Reserve. The Aaa rates through December 6, 2001 are averages of Aaa utility and Aaa industrial bond rates. As of December 7, 2001, these rates are averages of Aaa industrial bonds only.

The *state and local bond yields* are the Bond Buyer index as republished by the Federal Reserve. The index is based on 20 state and local government general obligation bonds of mixed quality maturing in 20 years or less. Quotes are as of Thursday.

The *fixed rate mortgage rates* are primary market contract interest rates on commitments for fixed-rate conventional 30-year first mortgages. The rates are obtained by the Federal Reserve from the Federal Home Loan Mortgage Corporation (FHLMC).

Stock price indexes. The *Dow Jones industrial* average is an average of 30 stocks compiled by Dow Jones, Inc. The *Standard and Poor's composite* is an index of 500 stocks based on 1941–1943 = 10 compiled by Standard and Poor's Corporation. The *dividend-price ratio* is compiled by Standard and Poor's, covering the 500 stocks in the S&P index, and represents aggregate cash dividends (based on the latest known annual rate) divided by aggregate market value based on Wednesday closing prices. The *earnings-price ratio* measures earnings (after taxes) for four quarters ending with the indicated quarter as a ratio to the price index for the last day of that quarter. Monthly data are averages of weekly figures; annual data are averages of monthly or quarterly figures. The *Nasdaq composite index* is an average of over 4,000 stocks traded on the Nasdaq exchange.

Data availability

Interest rates and bond yields are published weekly in the Federal Reserve's H.15 release. Most are subsequently published in the *Federal Reserve Bulletin*. The starting dates for individual interest rate series vary; some date back to 1911, and many begin in the 1950s and 1960s. Historical data may be purchased on diskette from Publications Services, Board of Governors of the Federal Reserve System. Current and historical data are available on the Federal Reserve Internet site at <http://www.federalreserve.gov/releases/>. Stock market data are published monthly in *Economic Indicators*, available by subscription from the Superintendent of Documents, Government Printing Office, Washington, DC 20402-9328; and annually in *Economic Report of the President*, available from the same source. Some historical interest rate data not available on the Federal Reserve Internet site were taken from the *Economic Report of the President*.

CHAPTER 13: INTERNATIONAL COMPARISONS

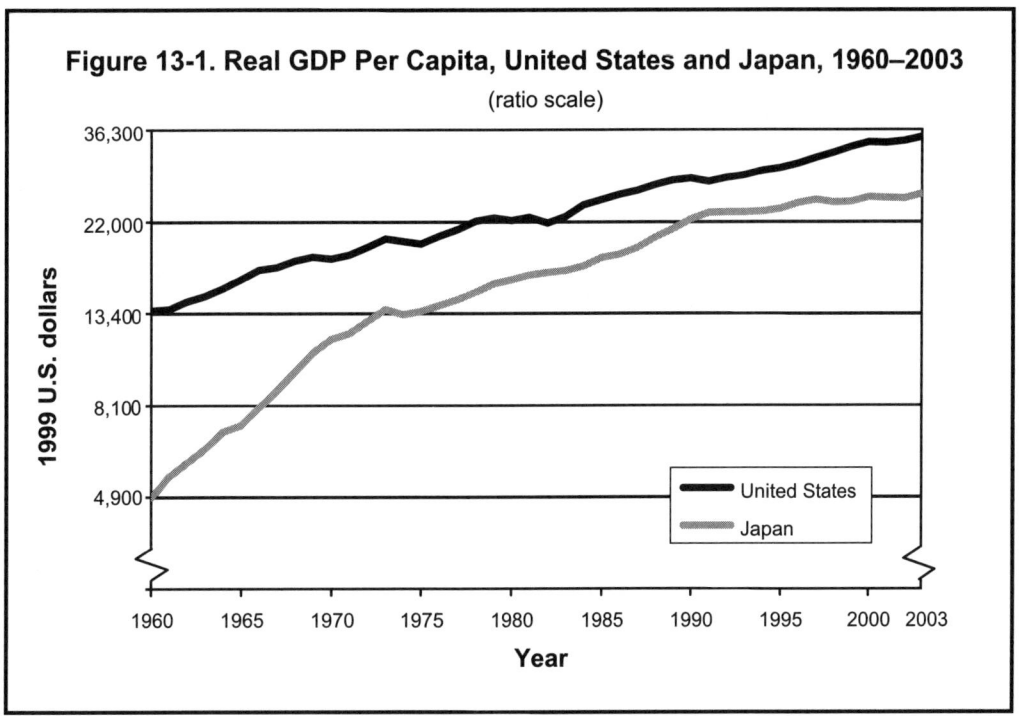

Figure 13-1. Real GDP Per Capita, United States and Japan, 1960–2003

- In the United States, gross domestic product per capita grew at a 2.2 percent annual rate between 1960 and 2000. The major industrial nations that had the next-highest average levels of living in 1960—Germany, the United Kingdom, and Canada—grew at similar rates of 2.0 percent, 2.2 percent, and 2.3 percent respectively. (German growth would have been higher, perhaps 2.2 percent, but for the effect of unification of West Germany with the poorer East in 1991.) Industrial nations that were further behind in 1960—Japan, France, and Italy—grew faster: 3.9 percent, 2.5 percent, and 2.7 percent respectively. The growth paths of the United States and Japan are compared in Figure 13-1 above. (Table 13-2)
- In Japan and in the three European countries that are compared in the per capita Tables 13-2 and 13-3, the growth in GDP per employed person—a measure of labor productivity—was almost identical to the growth in GDP per capita. In other words, growth in productivity and in potential living standards was the same. In the United States and Canada, on the other hand, growth in GDP per employee was only around 1.6 percent per year. In these two North American countries, productivity growth was *less* than per capita output growth, meaning that a significant fraction of the growth in GDP per capita was obtained not from greater efficiency but by putting a larger proportion of the population to work. (Tables 13-2 and 13-3)
- Inflation in 2003, as measured by the consumer price index, was low in six of the seven industrial countries shown, while Japan suffered its fifth successive year of deflation. (Table 13-5)
- Changes in unemployment between 2000 and 2003 were diverse. The United States had the largest increase, while unemployment declined in Italy and the United Kingdom. (Table 13-6)

Table 13-1. International Comparisons: Growth Rates in Real Gross Domestic Product
(Percent change at annual rate.)

Year	Total, world	Advanced economies					
		Total	Major advanced economies				
			Total	United States [1]	Japan	Germany	France
1985–1994	3.3	3.0	2.8	2.9	3.4	2.7	2.1
1995	3.7	2.8	2.4	2.7	1.8	1.7	1.8
1996	4.0	3.0	2.7	3.6	3.5	0.8	1.1
1997	4.2	3.5	3.2	4.4	1.9	1.4	1.9
1998	2.8	2.7	2.8	4.3	-1.1	2.0	3.6
1999	3.6	3.4	3.0	4.1	0.2	2.0	3.2
2000	4.8	3.9	3.5	3.8	2.8	2.9	4.2
2001	2.4	1.0	0.8	0.3	0.4	0.8	2.1
2002	3.0	1.8	1.6	2.4	0.2	0.2	1.2
2003 [2]	3.2	1.8	1.8	2.6	2.0	*	0.5

Year	Advanced economies—Continued				Special groupings, advanced economies		
	Major advanced economies—Continued			Other advanced economies	European Union	Euro area	Newly industrialized Asian economies
	Italy	United Kingdom	Canada				
1985–1994	2.1	2.6	2.5	3.8	2.4	...	7.8
1995	2.9	2.9	2.8	4.3	2.5	2.2	7.5
1996	1.1	2.6	1.6	3.6	1.7	1.4	6.3
1997	2.0	3.4	4.2	4.2	2.6	2.3	5.8
1998	1.8	2.9	4.1	1.9	3.0	2.9	-2.4
1999	1.7	2.4	5.5	4.8	2.8	2.8	8.0
2000	3.1	3.1	5.3	5.1	3.6	3.5	8.4
2001	1.8	2.1	1.9	1.6	1.7	1.5	0.8
2002	0.4	1.9	3.3	3.0	1.1	0.9	4.8
2003 [2]	0.4	1.7	1.9	1.9	0.8	0.5	2.3

Year	Developing countries					Countries in transition			
	Total	Africa	Developing Asia	Middle East, Malta, and Turkey	Western Hemisphere	Total	Central and eastern Europe	Commonwealth of Independent States and Mongolia	Russia
1985–1994	5.2	1.9	7.7	3.0	3.1	-2.1	...	...	...
1995	6.1	3.0	9.0	4.0	1.8	-1.5	5.5	-5.5	-4.1
1996	6.6	5.6	8.3	5.3	3.6	-0.6	4.0	-3.5	-3.6
1997	5.9	3.0	6.6	6.1	5.2	1.9	2.5	1.4	1.4
1998	3.5	3.2	4.0	3.7	2.3	-0.9	2.5	-3.2	-5.3
1999	3.9	2.7	6.2	0.9	0.2	4.1	2.3	5.2	6.3
2000	5.7	3.0	6.8	6.0	4.0	7.1	3.9	9.1	10.0
2001	4.1	3.7	5.8	2.0	0.7	5.1	3.1	6.4	5.0
2002	4.6	3.1	6.4	4.8	-0.1	4.2	3.0	4.9	4.3
2003 [2]	5.0	3.7	6.4	5.1	1.1	4.9	3.4	5.8	6.0

[1]These data were compiled before the December 2003 comprehensive revision.
[2]IMF estimates, January 2004.
. . . = Not available.
* = Figure is zero or negligible.

Table 13-2. International Comparisons: Real GDP Per Capita

(1999 U.S. dollars.)

Year	United States	Japan	Germany [1]	France	United Kingdom	Italy	Canada
1960	13 545	4 912	10 648	8 876	10 411	7 764	11 104
1961	13 636	5 495	10 993	9 268	10 579	8 369	11 225
1962	14 241	5 911	11 372	9 711	10 606	8 816	11 771
1963	14 652	6 365	11 579	10 047	11 080	9 241	12 144
1964	15 291	7 003	12 227	10 593	11 617	9 404	12 697
1965	16 070	7 249	12 739	11 005	11 809	9 635	13 275
1966	16 921	8 006	12 977	11 484	11 975	10 135	13 884
1967	17 159	8 790	12 907	11 929	12 201	10 770	14 044
1968	17 808	9 727	13 562	12 345	12 658	11 392	14 569
1969	18 177	10 761	14 437	13 103	12 868	12 009	15 127
1970	17 999	11 626	15 018	13 730	13 119	12 552	15 307
1971	18 371	11 973	15 317	14 252	13 316	12 736	15 638
1972	19 138	12 800	15 868	14 754	13 754	13 063	16 285
1973	20 048	13 636	16 542	15 432	14 703	13 824	17 244
1974	19 764	13 290	16 554	15 808	14 500	14 459	17 709
1975	19 535	13 534	16 406	15 693	14 424	14 078	17 840
1976	20 378	13 928	17 363	16 294	14 814	14 923	18 573
1977	21 105	14 403	17 895	16 743	15 183	15 210	18 992
1978	22 046	15 028	18 454	17 229	15 687	15 709	19 571
1979	22 492	15 720	19 223	17 723	16 093	16 530	20 193
1980	22 183	16 038	19 346	17 916	15 736	17 070	20 210
1981	22 516	16 438	19 329	18 032	15 502	17 180	20 575
1982	21 870	16 679	19 161	18 400	15 817	17 278	19 750
1983	22 652	16 886	19 566	18 577	16 370	17 486	20 087
1984	24 069	17 303	20 198	18 792	16 763	17 964	21 055
1985	24 841	18 101	20 659	18 972	17 316	18 493	21 861
1986	25 469	18 446	21 129	19 334	17 959	18 959	22 169
1987	26 095	19 076	21 438	19 716	18 737	19 523	22 808
1988	26 928	20 196	22 101	20 501	19 628	20 284	23 633
1989	27 619	21 139	22 676	21 230	19 998	20 851	23 819
1990	27 823	22 332	23 518	21 669	20 093	21 245	23 507
1991	27 409	23 111	22 034	21 775	19 749	21 528	22 741
1992	27 947	23 206	22 357	21 991	19 745	21 650	22 669
1993	28 324	23 178	21 954	21 705	20 167	21 387	22 944
1994	29 107	23 270	22 403	22 075	21 013	21 801	23 784
1995	29 485	23 598	22 723	22 365	21 561	22 400	24 198
1996	30 222	24 345	22 831	22 534	22 097	22 607	24 334
1997	31 206	24 767	23 106	22 884	22 776	23 019	25 111
1998	32 133	24 486	23 564	23 577	23 430	23 401	25 923
1999	33 181	24 552	24 029	24 234	24 014	23 766	27 135
2000	34 019	25 140	24 686	25 029	24 852	24 437	28 290
2001	33 839	25 050	24 849	25 419	25 215	24 797	28 490
2002	34 235	24 999	24 850	25 585	25 552	24 831	29 151
2003	34 960	25 587	24 813	25 578	26 039	24 894	29 489

[1] Data prior to 1991 are for West Germany only. In 1991, real GDP per capita in West Germany alone was $24,389 (1999 U.S. dollars).

Table 13-3. International Comparisons: Real GDP per Employed Person

(1999 U.S. dollars.)

Year	United States	Japan	Germany [1]	France	United Kingdom	Italy	Canada
1960	35 853	9 837	22 646	20 865	22 606	18 531	31 514
1961	36 673	10 858	23 369	22 017	22 924	19 925	32 004
1962	38 219	11 657	24 374	23 491	23 079	21 224	33 280
1963	39 342	12 574	25 000	24 550	24 203	22 792	34 187
1964	40 735	13 776	26 643	25 865	25 220	23 511	35 194
1965	42 312	14 335	27 911	27 018	25 550	24 887	36 147
1966	43 762	15 471	28 778	28 216	25 988	26 814	36 986
1967	43 824	16 838	29 655	29 463	26 942	28 386	37 037
1968	44 992	18 491	31 246	30 810	28 215	30 259	38 328
1969	45 267	20 502	33 062	32 469	28 811	32 336	39 168
1970	45 092	22 354	34 294	33 870	29 548	33 896	39 782
1971	46 427	23 172	35 199	35 331	30 597	34 541	41 054
1972	47 487	24 992	36 550	36 679	31 506	35 722	42 039
1973	48 620	26 403	37 879	38 146	33 105	37 530	42 948
1974	47 488	26 189	38 418	38 994	32 578	38 906	42 964
1975	47 932	27 066	38 984	39 226	32 571	38 080	43 174
1976	48 892	27 913	41 278	40 572	33 716	40 159	44 653
1977	49 381	28 793	42 392	41 532	34 498	40 981	45 536
1978	49 998	30 018	43 310	42 713	35 350	42 336	46 022
1979	50 173	31 342	44 392	43 904	35 844	44 187	46 000
1980	49 817	32 006	44 147	44 495	35 471	45 072	45 330
1981	50 506	32 788	44 238	45 210	36 206	45 461	45 361
1982	49 935	33 230	44 350	46 344	37 285	45 654	45 407
1983	51 519	33 366	45 782	47 182	38 751	46 071	46 255
1984	53 063	34 293	46 995	48 068	38 889	47 345	47 782
1985	54 164	35 895	47 594	49 143	39 698	48 296	48 731
1986	54 811	36 585	48 045	50 137	41 050	49 177	48 451
1987	55 250	37 863	48 405	51 019	42 324	50 530	49 093
1988	56 309	39 791	49 819	52 892	42 883	51 968	49 983
1989	57 152	41 197	50 883	54 189	42 520	53 097	50 198
1990	57 547	42 951	52 233	55 163	42 490	53 295	49 929
1991	57 989	43 736	45 830	55 653	42 790	53 044	49 704
1992	59 607	43 589	47 569	56 813	43 943	53 710	50 442
1993	60 389	43 500	47 698	57 044	45 586	54 598	51 235
1994	61 458	43 739	48 897	58 138	47 294	56 642	52 648
1995	62 128	44 403	49 638	58 589	48 134	58 363	53 150
1996	63 552	45 726	50 169	59 013	48 980	58 633	53 598
1997	64 988	46 152	50 953	59 874	49 724	59 594	54 552
1998	66 743	46 047	51 386	60 984	50 774	60 033	55 336
1999	68 682	46 639	51 811	61 707	51 522	60 362	56 836
2000	69 459	47 905	52 360	62 392	52 885	61 029	58 329
2001	69 784	48 150	52 583	62 639	53 593	60 912	58 722
2002	71 534	48 731	53 003	62 954	54 085	60 044	59 443
2003	73 097	50 060	53 538	63 131	54 802	59 512	59 353

[1] Data prior to 1991 are for West Germany only. In 1991, real GDP per capita in West Germany alone was $53,537 (1999 U.S. dollars).
. . . = Not available.

Table 13-4. International Comparisons: Industrial Production Indexes

(1990 = 100, seasonally adjusted.)

Year and month	United States	Japan	Germany (Federal Republic)	France	United Kingdom	Italy	Canada
1945	23.5	...	...	...	...	...	...
1946	20.3	...	...	...	...	...	...
1947	22.9	...	...	...	...	...	...
1948	23.8	1.8	8.6	...	36.0	11.8	...
1949	22.5	2.3	12.7	...	38.6	12.7	...
1950	26.0	2.9	15.4	...	41.5	14.1	...
1951	28.2	3.9	18.4	22.8	43.1	15.8	...
1952	29.3	4.2	19.6	22.8	41.7	16.2	...
1953	31.8	5.0	21.3	23.1	43.6	17.5	...
1954	30.0	5.4	24.2	25.3	47.3	19.1	...
1955	33.8	5.9	29.9	27.6	50.0	20.6	...
1956	35.3	7.3	32.5	31.3	50.5	22.2	...
1957	35.8	8.6	34.5	34.2	51.6	23.9	...
1958	33.5	8.5	34.4	35.5	51.4	24.7	...
1959	37.5	10.1	36.7	35.9	53.9	27.4	...
1960	38.3	12.7	40.7	39.1	57.8	31.6	...
1961	38.6	15.1	43.7	41.5	58.0	35.1	33.4
1962	41.8	16.3	45.6	43.9	58.6	38.5	36.8
1963	44.3	18.2	47.0	46.1	60.9	41.8	39.2
1964	47.3	21.1	50.9	49.0	65.2	42.3	43.1
1965	52.1	21.9	53.7	49.8	67.2	44.3	47.0
1966	56.7	24.8	54.1	52.8	68.0	49.4	50.0
1967	57.9	29.6	52.8	54.0	67.6	53.2	51.6
1968	61.1	34.2	57.9	56.1	70.7	56.4	55.2
1969	63.9	39.6	65.1	62.6	73.1	58.4	58.9
1970	61.8	45.0	69.1	66.0	73.5	62.2	58.0
1971	62.7	46.2	69.9	69.1	73.1	62.2	61.3
1972	68.6	49.6	72.2	74.2	74.4	64.9	66.7
1973	74.1	57.0	76.6	79.7	81.0	71.2	74.6
1974	73.7	54.8	75.3	81.8	79.4	74.4	76.0
1975	67.0	48.7	70.6	74.5	75.1	67.5	70.5
1976	72.1	54.1	75.9	81.5	77.6	75.9	75.2
1977	77.5	56.4	77.7	82.9	81.6	76.8	77.7
1978	81.8	59.9	78.9	84.8	83.9	78.2	80.4
1979	84.2	64.3	82.8	88.6	87.2	83.4	84.3
1980	81.8	67.3	83.0	87.6	81.5	88.1	81.5
1981	82.9	68.0	81.4	86.7	78.9	86.7	83.1
1982	78.6	68.3	78.9	86.0	80.4	84.0	75.0
1983	80.6	70.4	79.3	86.0	83.3	81.3	79.8
1984	87.8	77.0	81.6	87.5	83.4	84.1	89.5
1985	88.8	79.8	85.6	88.1	88.0	85.0	94.5
1986	89.6	79.7	87.3	89.1	90.1	88.0	93.8
1987	93.9	82.4	87.6	90.9	93.7	91.5	98.4
1988	98.4	90.7	90.7	94.6	98.2	97.0	103.6
1989	99.2	96.0	95.0	98.0	100.3	100.0	103.5
1990	100.0	100.0	100.0	100.0	100.0	100.0	100.0
1991	98.4	101.9	102.9	98.8	96.1	99.3	95.8
1992	101.0	96.1	100.4	97.6	95.6	99.1	96.9
1993	104.3	92.0	92.4	93.9	97.9	96.7	101.2
1994	109.8	92.5	95.3	97.4	103.1	101.6	108.3
1995	115.1	95.4	96.2	99.1	105.9	107.7	112.0
1996	120.1	98.5	96.8	99.0	106.3	102.9	113.3
1997	128.9	102.5	100.4	102.7	107.5	106.7	119.7
1998	136.2	95.6	104.6	108.1	108.5	108.2	123.9
1999	142.6	96.1	105.3	108.7	109.9	107.0	131.1
2000	148.8	101.0	111.2	113.1	112.0	111.5	141.9
2001	143.8	94.8	111.4	114.4	110.2	110.3	137.7
2002	143.0	93.7	110.3	113.0	107.5	108.7	140.4
2003	143.4	96.7	110.7	112.7	107.3	108.3	140.9
2002							
January	143.1	93.2	111.6	113.2	107.8	109.1	134.9
February	143.4	94.4	111.2	113.1	107.6	110.0	136.8
March	143.9	94.8	112.1	113.2	107.8	109.9	137.0
April	144.5	94.6	112.2	114.5	108.3	109.4	139.2
May	144.6	98.4	111.4	113.6	109.7	111.2	138.1
June	145.7	97.4	113.7	113.5	104.4	110.6	138.7
July	145.4	98.1	112.4	113.4	106.9	111.2	140.1
August	145.4	98.5	114.2	114.3	107.5	109.9	139.9
September	145.2	99.3	113.5	113.2	107.6	110.5	139.9
October	144.8	99.4	112.4	112.3	106.5	109.9	140.2
November	145.0	99.2	113.6	112.8	106.9	110.2	139.7
December	144.3	98.9	111.5	112.3	107.5	109.8	139.9
2003							
January	145.0	100.4	113.2	113.4	106.7	109.6	140.8
February	145.5	98.8	113.2	113.6	107.6	109.8	140.1
March	144.5	99.2	113.4	113.4	107.0	109.5	139.3
April	143.6	98.2	112.9	113.3	106.7	109.2	138.5
May	143.5	99.4	112.3	111.1	106.9	107.9	138.1
June	143.5	98.7	111.3	111.9	107.3	108.9	137.1
July	144.5	98.5	113.9	112.7	107.8	110.5	137.9
August	144.6	98.1	111.2	112.4	106.9	110.5	137.0
September	145.4	101.9	111.0	113.4	107.1	109.8	139.5
October	145.8	102.8	114.0	114.2	108.0	109.9	140.2
November	147.2	103.9	114.6	113.4	107.1	110.2	140.4
December	147.5	103.4	114.5	113.4	107.3	110.2	141.6

. . . = Not available.

Table 13-5. International Comparisons: Consumer Price Indexes

(1982–1984 = 100, except as noted; not seasonally adjusted; percent changes are from previous year's average for annual data, from the same quarter of the previous year for quarterly data.)

Year and month	United States		Japan		Germany [1]		France		United Kingdom		Italy		Canada	
	Index	Percent change	Index	Percent change	Index	Percent change	Index	Percent change	Index	Percent change	Index	Percent change	Index	Percent change
1950	24.1	...	14.8	...	34.5	...	11.1	...	9.8	...	...	...	21.6	...
1951	26.0	7.9	17.2	16.2	37.2	7.8	13.0	17.1	10.7	9.2	...	...	23.9	10.6
1952	26.5	1.9	18.0	4.7	38.0	2.2	14.6	12.3	11.7	9.3	...	...	24.5	2.5
1953	26.7	0.8	19.2	6.7	37.3	-1.8	14.4	-1.4	12.1	3.4	10.3	...	24.2	-1.2
1954	26.9	0.7	20.5	6.8	37.3	0.0	14.3	-0.7	12.3	1.7	10.6	2.9	24.4	0.8
1955	26.8	-0.4	20.2	-1.5	38.0	1.9	14.5	1.4	12.9	4.9	10.9	2.8	24.4	0.0
1956	27.2	1.5	20.3	0.5	39.0	2.6	14.8	2.1	13.5	4.7	11.2	2.8	24.8	1.6
1957	28.1	3.3	20.9	3.0	39.8	2.1	15.3	3.4	14.0	3.7	11.4	1.8	25.6	3.2
1958	28.9	2.8	20.8	-0.5	40.6	2.0	17.6	15.0	14.4	2.9	11.7	2.6	26.3	2.7
1959	29.1	0.7	21.1	1.4	41.0	1.0	18.7	6.2	14.5	0.7	11.7	0.0	26.6	1.1
1960	29.6	1.7	21.8	3.3	41.6	1.5	19.4	3.7	14.6	0.7	11.9	1.7	26.9	1.1
1961	29.9	1.0	23.0	5.5	42.6	2.4	20.0	3.1	15.1	3.4	12.2	2.5	27.1	0.7
1962	30.2	1.0	24.6	7.0	43.8	2.8	21.0	5.0	15.8	4.6	12.7	4.1	27.4	1.1
1963	30.6	1.3	26.4	7.3	45.1	3.0	22.0	4.8	16.1	1.9	13.7	7.9	27.9	1.8
1964	31.0	1.3	27.4	3.8	46.2	2.4	22.7	3.2	16.6	3.1	14.5	5.8	28.4	1.8
1965	31.5	1.6	29.5	7.7	47.8	3.5	23.3	2.6	17.4	4.8	15.2	4.8	29.1	2.5
1966	32.4	2.9	31.0	5.1	49.4	3.3	23.9	2.6	18.1	4.0	15.5	2.0	30.2	3.8
1967	33.4	3.1	32.3	4.2	50.1	1.4	24.6	2.9	18.5	2.2	16.1	3.9	31.3	3.6
1968	34.8	4.2	34.0	5.3	50.8	1.4	25.7	4.5	19.4	4.9	16.3	1.2	32.5	3.8
1969	36.7	5.5	35.8	5.3	51.8	2.0	27.3	6.2	20.5	5.7	16.7	2.5	34.0	4.6
1970	38.8	5.7	38.5	7.5	53.5	3.3	28.8	5.5	21.8	6.3	17.5	4.8	35.1	3.2
1971	40.5	4.4	40.9	6.2	56.2	5.0	30.3	5.2	23.8	9.2	18.4	5.1	36.2	3.1
1972	41.8	3.2	42.9	4.9	59.2	5.3	32.2	6.3	25.5	7.1	19.4	5.4	37.9	4.7
1973	44.4	6.2	47.9	11.7	63.2	6.8	34.6	7.5	27.9	9.4	21.6	11.3	40.7	7.4
1974	49.3	11.0	59.1	23.4	67.6	7.0	39.3	13.6	32.3	15.8	25.7	19.0	45.2	11.1
1975	53.8	9.1	66.0	11.7	71.7	6.1	43.9	11.7	40.1	24.1	30.0	16.7	50.1	10.8
1976	56.9	5.8	72.2	9.4	74.8	4.3	48.2	9.8	46.8	16.7	35.1	17.0	53.8	7.4
1977	60.6	6.5	78.1	8.2	77.4	3.5	52.7	9.3	54.2	15.8	41.0	16.8	58.1	8.0
1978	65.2	7.6	81.4	4.2	79.4	2.6	57.5	9.1	58.7	8.3	46.0	12.2	63.3	9.0
1979	72.6	11.3	84.4	3.7	82.4	3.8	63.6	10.6	66.6	13.5	52.8	14.8	69.1	9.2
1980	82.4	13.5	90.9	7.7	86.7	5.2	72.3	13.7	78.5	17.9	64.0	21.2	76.1	10.1
1981	90.9	10.3	95.4	5.0	92.2	6.3	82.0	13.4	87.9	12.0	75.4	17.8	85.6	12.5
1982	96.5	6.2	98.0	2.7	97.1	5.3	91.6	11.7	95.4	8.5	87.8	16.4	94.9	10.9
1983	99.6	3.2	99.8	1.8	100.2	3.2	100.5	9.7	99.8	4.6	100.7	14.7	100.4	5.8
1984	103.9	4.3	102.1	2.3	102.7	2.5	107.9	7.4	104.8	5.0	111.5	10.7	104.7	4.3
1985	107.6	3.6	104.2	2.1	104.7	1.9	114.2	5.8	111.1	6.0	121.8	9.2	108.9	4.0
1986	109.6	1.9	104.8	0.6	104.5	-0.2	117.2	2.6	114.9	3.4	129.0	5.9	113.4	4.1
1987	113.6	3.6	104.9	0.1	104.6	0.1	120.9	3.2	119.7	4.2	135.1	4.7	118.4	4.4
1988	118.3	4.1	105.7	0.8	105.7	1.1	124.2	2.7	125.6	4.9	141.9	5.0	123.2	4.1
1989	124.0	4.8	108.1	2.3	108.8	2.9	128.6	3.5	135.4	7.8	150.8	6.3	129.3	5.0
1990	130.7	5.4	111.4	3.1	111.7	2.7	133.0	3.4	148.2	9.5	160.5	6.5	135.5	4.8
1991	136.2	4.2	115.1	3.3	115.9	3.8	137.2	3.2	156.9	5.9	170.6	6.3	143.1	5.6
1992	140.3	3.0	117.0	1.7	86.1	5.1	140.6	2.5	162.7	3.7	179.4	5.2	145.3	1.5
1993	144.5	3.0	118.5	1.3	89.9	4.4	143.5	2.1	165.3	1.6	187.5	4.5	147.9	1.8
1994	148.2	2.6	119.3	0.7	92.3	2.7	145.9	1.7	169.3	2.4	195.0	4.0	148.2	0.2
1995	152.4	2.8	119.2	-0.1	93.9	1.7	148.4	1.7	175.2	3.5	205.1	5.2	151.4	2.1
1996	156.9	3.0	119.3	0.1	95.3	1.5	151.3	2.0	179.4	2.4	213.4	4.0	153.8	1.6
1997	160.5	2.3	121.5	1.8	97.1	1.9	153.2	1.3	185.1	3.2	217.7	2.0	156.2	1.6
1998	163.0	1.6	122.2	0.6	98.0	0.9	154.3	0.7	191.4	3.4	222.0	2.0	157.7	0.9
1999	166.6	2.2	121.8	-0.3	98.6	0.6	155.0	0.5	194.3	1.5	225.7	1.7	160.5	1.7
2000	172.2	3.4	121.0	-0.7	100.0	1.4	157.7	1.7	200.1	3.0	231.4	2.5	164.8	2.7
2001	177.1	2.8	120.1	-0.7	102.0	2.0	160.3	1.6	203.6	1.7	237.8	2.7	169.0	2.6
2002	179.9	1.6	119.1	-0.8	103.4	1.4	163.4	1.9	207.0	1.7	243.7	2.5	172.8	2.2
2003	184.0	2.3	118.7	-0.3	104.5	1.1	166.8	2.1	213.0	2.9	250.3	2.7	177.6	2.8
2001														
1st quarter	...	3.4	...	-0.4	...	1.7	...	1.3	...	2.5	...	2.9	...	2.8
2nd quarter	...	3.4	...	-0.7	...	2.5	...	2.0	...	1.9	...	3.1	...	3.6
3rd quarter	...	2.7	...	-0.8	...	2.1	...	1.8	...	1.8	...	2.8	...	2.7
4th quarter	...	1.9	...	-1.0	...	1.6	...	1.4	...	1.0	...	2.4	...	1.1
2002														
1st quarter	...	1.3	...	-1.4	...	1.9	...	2.1	...	1.2	...	2.4	...	1.5
2nd quarter	...	1.3	...	-0.9	...	1.2	...	1.6	...	1.2	...	2.3	...	1.3
3rd quarter	...	1.6	...	-0.8	...	1.1	...	1.8	...	1.5	...	2.4	...	2.3
4th quarter	...	2.2	...	-0.5	...	1.2	...	2.1	...	2.6	...	2.8	...	3.8
2003														
1st quarter	...	2.9	...	-0.2	...	1.2	...	2.4	...	3.1	...	2.7	...	4.5
2nd quarter	...	2.1	...	-0.2	...	0.9	...	1.9	...	3.0	...	2.7	...	2.8
3rd quarter	...	2.2	...	-0.2	...	1.0	...	1.9	...	2.9	...	2.7	...	2.1
4th quarter	...	1.9	...	-0.3	...	1.2	...	2.2	...	2.7	...	2.5	...	1.7

[1]Former West Germany only, 1950–1991. From 1992 forward, unified Germany, 2000 = 100. In 1991, the index for unified Germany, 2000 = 100, was 81.9.
... = Not available.

Table 13-6. International Comparisons: Unemployment Rates and Civilian Labor Forces [1]

(Quarterly data are seasonally adjusted.)

Year and quarter	United States		Japan		Germany [2]		France		United Kingdom		Italy		Canada	
	Unemployment rate	Labor force (thousands)	Unemployment rate	Labor force (thousands)	Unemployment rate	Labor force (thousands)	Unemployment rate	Labor force (thousands)	Unemployment rate	Labor force (thousands)	Unemployment rate	Labor force (thousands)	Unemployment rate	Labor force (thousands)
1959	5.5	68 369	2.3	43 320	2.0	25 850	1.6	18 480	2.8	23 880	4.8	21 020	5.6	6 286
1960	5.5	69 628	1.7	44 120	1.1	25 990	1.5	18 520	2.2	24 130	3.7	20 820	6.5	6 462
1961	6.7	70 459	1.5	44 610	0.6	26 160	1.2	18 530	2.0	24 380	3.2	20 830	6.7	6 575
1962	5.5	70 614	1.3	45 040	0.6	26 210	1.4	18 720	2.7	24 720	2.8	20 680	5.5	6 670
1963	5.7	71 833	1.3	45 430	0.5	26 290	1.6	19 100	3.3	24 940	2.4	20 240	5.2	6 805
1964	5.2	73 091	1.2	46 040	0.4	26 270	1.2	19 430	2.5	25 070	2.7	20 220	4.4	6 994
1965	4.5	74 455	1.2	46 780	0.3	26 360	1.6	19 650	2.1	25 240	3.5	19 900	3.6	7 207
1966	3.8	75 770	1.4	47 850	0.3	26 290	1.6	19 850	2.3	25 320	3.7	19 620	3.4	7 493
1967	3.8	77 347	1.3	48 810	1.3	25 730	2.1	20 070	3.3	25 290	3.4	19 800	3.8	7 747
1968	3.6	78 737	1.2	49 690	1.1	25 690	2.7	20 190	3.2	25 180	3.5	19 780	4.5	7 951
1969	3.5	80 734	1.1	50 140	0.6	25 960	2.3	20 470	3.1	25 160	3.5	19 620	4.4	8 194
1970	4.9	82 771	1.2	50 730	0.5	26 240	2.5	20 800	3.1	25 110	3.2	19 720	5.7	8 395
1971	5.9	84 382	1.3	51 120	0.6	26 380	2.8	21 000	3.9	24 950	3.3	19 660	6.2	8 639
1972	5.6	87 034	1.4	51 320	0.7	26 470	2.9	21 150	4.2	25 190	3.8	19 450	6.2	8 897
1973	4.9	89 429	1.3	52 590	0.7	26 780	2.8	21 430	3.2	25 440	3.7	19 590	5.5	9 276
1974	5.6	91 949	1.4	52 440	1.6	26 660	2.9	21 660	3.1	25 470	3.1	19 900	5.3	9 639
1975	8.5	93 775	1.9	52 530	3.4	26 430	4.2	21 770	4.6	25 730	3.4	20 090	6.9	9 974
1976	7.7	96 158	2.0	53 100	3.4	26 290	4.6	22 050	5.9	25 900	3.9	20 290	6.8	10 391
1977	7.1	99 009	2.0	53 820	3.4	26 330	5.2	22 380	6.4	26 050	4.1	20 510	7.8	10 650
1978	6.1	102 251	2.3	54 610	3.3	26 520	5.4	22 540	6.3	26 260	4.1	20 570	8.1	11 006
1979	5.8	104 962	2.1	55 210	2.9	26 860	6.1	22 780	5.4	26 350	4.4	20 850	7.3	11 377
1980	7.1	106 940	2.0	55 740	2.8	27 260	6.5	22 930	7.0	26 520	4.4	21 120	7.3	11 707
1981	7.6	108 670	2.2	56 320	4.0	27 540	7.6	23 090	10.5	26 590	4.9	21 320	7.3	12 067
1982	9.7	110 204	2.4	56 980	5.6	27 710	8.3	23 320	11.3	26 560	5.4	21 410	10.6	12 139
1983	9.6	111 550	2.7	58 110	6.9	27 670	8.6	23 400	11.8	26 610	5.9	21 590	11.5	12 368
1984	7.5	113 544	2.8	58 480	7.1	27 800	10.0	23 560	11.8	27 200	5.9	21 670	10.9	12 579
1985	7.2	115 461	2.6	58 820	7.2	28 020	10.5	23 620	11.2	27 433	6.0	21 800	10.2	12 825
1986	7.0	117 834	2.8	59 410	6.6	28 240	10.6	23 760	11.2	27 568	7.5	22 290	9.2	13 075
1987	6.2	119 865	2.9	60 050	6.3	28 390	10.8	23 890	10.7	27 827	7.9	22 350	8.4	13 331
1988	5.5	121 669	2.5	60 860	6.3	28 610	10.3	23 980	8.8	28 204	7.9	22 660	7.3	13 589
1989	5.3	123 869	2.3	61 920	5.7	28 840	9.6	24 170	7.2	28 594	7.8	22 530	7.1	13 848
1990	5.6	125 840	2.1	63 050	5.0	29 410	9.1	24 290	6.8	28 719	7.0	22 670	7.7	14 044
1991	6.8	126 346	2.1	64 280	5.6	39 075	9.5	24 440	8.4	28 602	6.9	22 940	9.8	14 135
1992	7.5	128 105	2.2	65 040	6.7	39 005	9.9	24 440	9.7	28 339	7.3	22 910	10.6	14 177
1993	6.9	129 200	2.5	65 470	8.0	39 102	11.3	24 480	10.4	28 165	10.2	22 570	10.8	14 308
1994	6.1	131 056	2.9	65 780	8.5	39 074	11.8	24 670	9.6	28 149	11.2	22 450	9.5	14 400
1995	5.6	132 304	3.2	65 990	8.2	38 980	11.3	24 760	8.7	28 157	11.8	22 460	8.6	14 517
1996	5.4	133 943	3.4	66 450	9.0	39 142	11.9	25 010	8.1	28 260	11.7	22 570	8.8	14 669
1997	4.9	136 297	3.4	67 200	9.9	39 415	11.8	25 130	7.0	28 417	11.9	22 680	8.4	14 958
1998	4.5	137 673	4.1	67 240	9.3	39 754	11.3	25 460	6.3	28 479	12.0	22 960	7.7	15 237
1999	4.2	139 368	4.7	67 090	8.5	39 375	10.6	25 790	6.0	28 769	11.5	23 130	7.0	15 536
2000	4.0	142 583	4.8	66 990	7.8	39 302	9.1	26 070	5.5	28 930	10.7	23 340	6.1	15 789
2001	4.7	143 734	5.1	66 870	7.9	39 459	8.4	26 350	5.1	29 053	9.6	23 540	6.4	16 027
2002	5.8	144 863	5.4	66 240	8.6	39 413	8.7	26 590	5.2	29 288	9.1	23 750	7.0	16 475
2003	6.0	146 510	5.3	66 010	9.3	39 276	9.3	26 730	5.0	29 490	8.8	23 880	6.9	16 819
1998														
1st quarter	4.6	...	3.7	...	9.8	...	11.5	...	6.4	...	11.9	...	8.0	...
2nd quarter	4.4	...	4.2	...	9.4	...	11.3	...	6.3	...	12.0	...	7.7	...
3rd quarter	4.5	...	4.3	...	9.1	...	11.2	...	6.3	...	12.0	...	7.6	...
4th quarter	4.4	...	4.5	...	8.9	...	11.1	...	6.2	...	12.0	...	7.4	...
1999														
1st quarter	4.3	...	4.7	...	8.8	...	11.0	...	6.2	...	11.8	...	7.3	...
2nd quarter	4.3	...	4.8	...	8.7	...	10.8	...	6.1	...	11.7	...	7.3	...
3rd quarter	4.3	...	4.8	...	8.6	...	10.5	...	5.9	...	11.5	...	6.9	...
4th quarter	4.1	...	4.7	...	8.5	...	10.1	...	5.9	...	11.3	...	6.3	...
2000														
1st quarter	4.0	...	4.8	...	8.3	...	9.6	...	5.8	...	11.2	...	6.1	...
2nd quarter	4.0	...	4.7	...	8.1	...	9.3	...	5.5	...	10.9	...	6.1	...
3rd quarter	4.0	...	4.7	...	8.0	...	9.0	...	5.4	...	10.5	...	6.1	...
4th quarter	3.9	...	4.8	...	7.8	...	8.7	...	5.2	...	10.1	...	6.1	...
2001														
1st quarter	4.2	...	4.8	...	7.9	...	8.5	...	5.1	...	10.0	...	6.2	...
2nd quarter	4.4	...	4.9	...	8.0	...	8.4	...	5.0	...	9.7	...	6.3	...
3rd quarter	4.8	...	5.2	...	8.0	...	8.5	...	5.1	...	9.5	...	6.5	...
4th quarter	5.6	...	5.5	...	8.1	...	8.6	...	5.2	...	9.4	...	6.8	...
2002														
1st quarter	5.7	...	5.4	...	8.3	...	8.5	...	5.1	...	9.2	...	7.1	...
2nd quarter	5.8	...	5.4	...	8.5	...	8.6	...	5.2	...	9.2	...	6.9	...
3rd quarter	5.7	...	5.5	...	8.7	...	8.7	...	5.2	...	9.1	...	7.0	...
4th quarter	5.9	...	5.4	...	8.9	...	8.9	...	5.1	...	9.0	...	6.9	...
2003														
1st quarter	5.8	...	5.4	...	9.2	...	9.0	...	5.1	...	9.0	...	6.7	...
2nd quarter	6.1	...	5.4	...	9.4	...	9.2	...	5.0	...	8.8	...	6.9	...
3rd quarter	6.1	...	5.2	...	9.4	...	9.4	...	5.0	...	8.7	...	7.2	...
4th quarter	5.9	...	5.1	...	9.3	...	9.4	...	4.9	...	8.6	...	6.8	...

[1]Data for other countries adjusted to approximate U.S. concepts.
[2]Data prior to 1991 are for West Germany only. In 1991, the unemployment rate for West Germany alone was 4.3 percent.
... = Not available.

Table 13-7. Exchange Rates

(Not seasonally adjusted.)

Year and month	Foreign currency per U.S. dollar						Trade-weighted exchange indexes of value of U.S. dollar					
							Nominal				Price-adjusted	
	European currency unit	Japanese yen	German mark	French franc	British pound	Canadian dollar	G-10 countries (March 1973 = 100)	Broad (January 1997 = 100)	Major currencies (March 1973 = 100)	Other important trading partners (January 1997 = 100)	Broad (March 1973 = 100)	Other important trading partners (March 1973 = 100)
1971	...	346.62	3.4673	5.4889	0.4092	1.0099	117.81	...	...	...	...	...
1972	...	303.11	3.1889	5.0448	0.4005	0.9908	109.07	...	...	...	...	...
1973	...	271.40	2.6719	4.4549	0.4084	1.0002	99.14	29.72	100.28	1.95	98.40	94.80
1974	...	291.94	2.5873	4.8104	0.4277	0.9781	101.41	30.55	102.06	2.06	95.96	88.32
1975	...	296.77	2.4614	4.2885	0.4521	1.0173	98.50	31.64	102.35	2.30	94.28	88.70
1976	...	296.48	2.5184	4.7805	0.5567	0.9861	105.63	33.58	105.95	2.60	94.17	87.43
1977	...	268.38	2.3225	4.9149	0.5733	1.0635	103.35	34.60	105.48	2.91	92.41	87.77
1978	...	210.46	2.0089	4.5101	0.5214	1.1408	92.39	32.95	96.33	3.05	86.73	86.54
1979	...	219.21	1.8331	4.2545	0.4720	1.1716	88.07	33.34	94.94	3.27	87.83	86.93
1980	...	226.58	1.8183	4.2269	0.4304	1.1694	87.39	34.41	94.85	3.61	89.36	86.31
1981	...	220.45	2.2606	5.4348	0.4978	1.1989	103.26	38.08	103.55	4.11	96.53	88.76
1982	...	249.05	2.4281	6.5761	0.5727	1.2339	116.50	44.22	114.21	5.28	105.86	99.22
1983	...	237.45	2.5545	7.6220	0.6601	1.2326	125.32	49.91	118.12	7.14	110.35	108.59
1984	...	237.59	2.8483	8.7439	0.7521	1.2952	138.34	57.02	125.85	9.44	117.54	115.08
1985	...	238.47	2.9443	8.9870	0.7792	1.3659	143.24	64.15	130.58	12.76	122.40	122.91
1986	...	168.50	2.1711	6.9258	0.6821	1.3898	112.27	59.89	107.26	16.00	106.78	126.41
1987	...	144.63	1.7976	6.0111	0.6117	1.3261	96.95	58.29	94.86	19.31	98.06	123.85
1988	...	128.14	1.7561	5.9565	0.5621	1.2309	92.75	59.00	88.17	23.37	91.50	113.25
1989	...	138.00	1.8792	6.3753	0.6111	1.1841	98.52	65.08	91.81	28.96	93.15	107.84
1990	...	144.82	1.6159	5.4449	0.5630	1.1670	89.05	70.22	87.82	39.47	91.49	110.77
1991	...	134.51	1.6585	5.6388	0.5667	1.1460	89.73	73.30	86.37	46.07	90.08	110.26
1992	...	126.75	1.5624	5.2956	0.5699	1.2088	86.64	76.10	84.89	52.60	88.19	106.62
1993	...	111.23	1.6537	5.6644	0.6662	1.2902	93.17	82.89	87.15	63.11	89.56	104.00
1994	...	102.19	1.6219	5.5467	0.6531	1.3659	91.32	90.40	85.63	80.61	89.40	104.11
1995	...	94.11	1.4331	4.9889	0.6337	1.3727	84.30	92.50	80.80	92.59	86.94	104.14
1996	...	108.81	1.5049	5.1158	0.6410	1.3637	87.34	97.40	84.60	98.26	88.97	101.06
1997	...	121.06	1.7339	5.8361	0.6106	1.3849	96.35	104.44	91.23	104.67	93.73	102.12
1998	...	130.99	1.7593	5.8979	0.6034	1.4836	98.82	116.48	95.75	126.03	101.69	115.49
1999	0.9387	113.73	1.8359	6.1575	0.6184	1.4858	...	116.87	94.02	129.94	101.06	114.16
2000	1.0832	107.80	2.1185	7.1053	0.6598	1.4855	...	119.44	101.57	129.80	105.00	114.34
2001	1.1171	121.57	2.1848	7.3275	0.6946	1.5487	...	125.91	107.66	135.86	111.08	118.95
2002	1.0578	125.22	2.0688	6.9384	0.6656	1.5704	...	126.75	105.98	140.55	111.30	121.57
2003	0.8838	115.97	1.7285	5.7972	0.6120	1.4013	...	119.28	93.08	144.02	104.60	123.34
2001												
January	1.0666	116.67	2.0860	6.9963	0.6768	1.5032	...	122.72	103.49	134.77	108.11	117.80
February	1.0863	116.23	2.1247	7.1259	0.6885	1.5216	...	123.41	104.80	134.31	108.94	117.59
March	1.1010	121.51	2.1533	7.2219	0.6923	1.5587	...	125.42	107.30	135.21	110.71	118.46
April	1.1204	123.77	2.1914	7.3495	0.6970	1.5578	...	126.39	108.45	135.71	111.54	119.04
May	1.1424	121.77	2.2344	7.4940	0.7010	1.5411	...	126.24	108.51	135.26	111.61	119.22
June	1.1724	122.35	2.2930	7.6904	0.7133	1.5245	...	127.08	109.53	135.67	112.55	119.81
July	1.1608	124.50	2.2703	7.6143	0.7068	1.5308	...	127.50	109.59	136.61	112.72	120.20
August	1.1094	121.37	2.1699	7.2774	0.6958	1.5399	...	125.41	107.15	135.42	110.75	118.92
September	1.0972	118.61	2.1459	7.1969	0.6831	1.5679	...	125.77	106.70	137.05	111.22	120.29
October	1.1050	121.45	2.1611	7.2481	0.6896	1.5717	...	126.61	107.64	137.60	111.47	119.81
November	1.1258	122.41	2.2019	7.3847	0.6966	1.5922	...	127.13	108.99	136.66	111.84	118.46
December	1.1221	127.59	2.1947	7.3606	0.6938	1.5788	...	127.20	109.50	136.02	111.52	117.84
2002												
January	1.1323	132.68	2.2146	7.4274	0.6982	1.5997	...	128.79	111.20	137.20	112.89	118.65
February	1.1211	128.20	2.1928	7.3542	0.6927	1.5802	...	129.54	111.97	137.79	113.45	118.60
March	1.1407	131.06	2.2311	7.4826	0.7027	1.5877	...	128.79	110.95	137.57	113.18	119.19
April	1.1287	130.77	2.2075	7.4036	0.6930	1.5815	...	128.42	110.14	137.93	113.13	119.93
May	1.0906	126.38	2.1330	7.1536	0.6850	1.5502	...	126.90	107.14	138.97	111.65	120.76
June	1.0459	123.29	2.0456	6.8605	0.6740	1.5318	...	125.51	104.32	140.11	110.39	121.70
July	1.0065	117.90	1.9686	6.6023	0.6425	1.5456	...	123.76	101.76	140.01	108.84	121.55
August	1.0224	118.99	1.9997	6.7067	0.6507	1.5694	...	125.20	103.21	141.18	110.24	122.71
September	1.0198	121.08	1.9945	6.6891	0.6425	1.5761	...	126.14	103.43	143.19	110.95	124.03
October	1.0192	123.91	1.9934	6.6856	0.6421	1.5780	...	127.06	103.90	144.73	111.56	124.97
November	0.9987	121.61	1.9533	6.5511	0.6365	1.5715	...	125.78	102.44	143.96	110.08	123.51
December	0.9810	121.89	1.9186	6.4347	0.6304	1.5592	...	125.13	101.47	144.00	109.20	123.18
2003												
January	0.9414	118.81	1.8412	6.1752	0.6182	1.5414	...	123.64	98.78	144.92	107.97	123.78
February	0.9272	119.34	1.8135	6.0824	0.6219	1.5121	...	123.53	97.73	146.53	108.16	125.23
March	0.9261	118.69	1.8114	6.0751	0.6319	1.4761	...	123.04	97.03	146.53	108.05	125.78
April	0.9206	119.90	1.8006	6.0388	0.6354	1.4582	...	122.01	96.71	144.42	107.01	123.70
May	0.8654	117.37	1.6925	5.6765	0.6164	1.3840	...	117.97	92.23	142.02	103.44	121.83
June	0.8566	118.33	1.6753	5.6188	0.6021	1.3525	...	117.36	91.15	142.41	103.15	122.68
July	0.8799	118.70	1.7209	5.7717	0.6165	1.3821	...	118.57	93.00	142.17	104.36	122.59
August	0.8964	118.66	1.7533	5.8803	0.6274	1.3963	...	119.93	94.13	143.67	105.72	124.04
September	0.8875	114.80	1.7359	5.8219	0.6190	1.3634	...	118.57	92.31	143.46	104.47	123.58
October	0.8537	109.50	1.6697	5.5999	0.5955	1.3221	...	116.21	88.82	143.83	102.01	123.01
November	0.8540	109.18	1.6702	5.6016	0.5918	1.3130	...	116.07	88.51	144.10	101.27	122.01
December	0.8131	107.74	1.5903	5.3338	0.5709	1.3128	...	114.51	86.27	144.27	99.64	121.87

. . . = Not available.

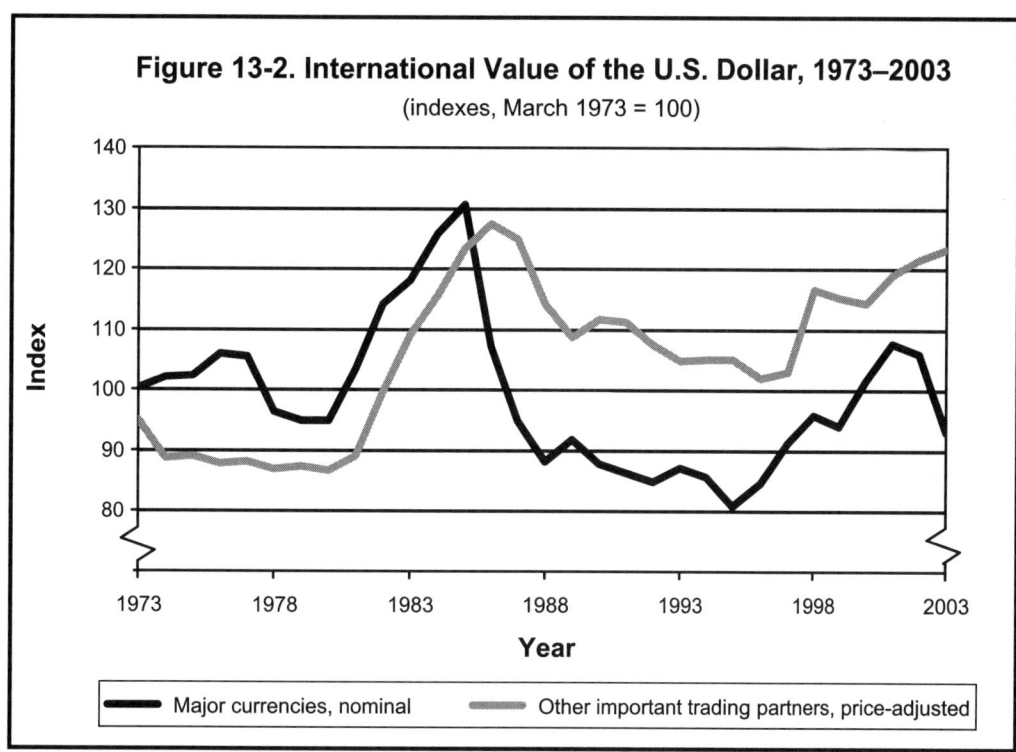

- The value of the U.S. dollar against the new European currency, the euro, rose 36 percent between January 1999, when the euro was introduced, and June 2001. In that month the dollar bought 1.1724 euros, up from only 0.8627 euros in January 1999. (This exchange rate is frequently quoted as dollars to one euro rather than euros to a dollar; in those terms the euro was worth $1.159 in January 1999 but only $0.853 in June 2001. The dollars-per-euro rate is high when the *euro* is strong. In the method used in *Business Statistics*, the rate is high when the *dollar* is strong, for consistency with the other measures shown in the table.) Between the June 2001 high and December 2003, the dollar fell back to a value of 0.8131 euros, lower than at the time of the euro's introduction. (Table 13-7)
- Indexes of the dollar's international value give a broader picture than the exchange rate against the euro or any other single currency. Figure 13-2 above displays two such indexes. One shows the dollar against seven major currencies—the euro, the British pound, the Canadian dollar, the Japanese yen, and the currencies of Switzerland, Australia, and Sweden. These are all major industrial countries whose currencies are freely traded on world markets. Measured against these major currencies in terms of annual averages, the dollar depreciated 13.5 percent from a high in 2001 to 2003—a big change but only half the size of the two-year drop from 1985 to 1987. Dollar depreciation seems unsurprising in the light of the large current-account deficits detailed in Chapter 7. (Table 13-7 and Chapter 7)
- However, the dollar has *not* depreciated against the emerging-market currencies ("Other important trading partners") that account for much of our trade deficit, and therefore is not functioning to bring trade closer to balance in the way anticipated in basic economic theory. The reason is that many such countries, especially China, are able to control the international values of their currencies (via direct capital controls, for example) and keep their currencies from appreciating relative to the dollar to maintain their competitiveness in the U.S. market. The result is that the dollar has actually appreciated further relative to "other important trading partners" (OITP), whether measured in nominal or in price-adjusted terms. The price-adjusted OITP index is shown in Figure 13-2 because it is the preferred measure of competitiveness over the longer term, for reasons described in the Notes and Definitions. (Table 13-7)

NOTES AND DEFINITIONS

TABLE 13-1
INTERNATIONAL COMPARISONS: GROWTH RATES IN REAL GROSS DOMESTIC PRODUCT

SOURCE: ECONOMIC REPORT OF THE PRESIDENT, ANNUAL REPORT OF THE COUNCIL OF ECONOMIC ADVISERS, FEBRUARY 2004

This table is reprinted from the 2004 *Annual Report* of the U.S. Council of Economic Advisers. It is based on data from the U.S. Department of Commerce, Bureau of Economic Analysis, and the International Monetary Fund. Because these data were compiled in 2003, the data for recent years may differ somewhat from the latest available data, such as the U.S. GDP data shown in Chapter 1 of this volume.

TABLES 13-2 AND 13-3
INTERNATIONAL COMPARISONS: REAL GDP PER CAPITA, REAL GDP PER EMPLOYED PERSON

SOURCE: BUREAU OF LABOR STATISTICS

Real GDP per capita can be taken as a rough measure of *potential economic welfare*, that is, the potential standard of living available to a country's residents. Because income distributions are typically "skewed," GDP per capita, which is an average or "mean," should not be taken as a representation of the standard of living actually enjoyed by a typical ("median") individual. (See the subsection "Whose standard of living?" in the article "Expanded Historical Statistics..." at the beginning of this volume.)

Real GDP per employee, on the other hand, is a rough measure of *productivity* (ignoring any differences in hours worked by employees).

The GDP, population, and employment measures for each country come from its own national accounts and population sources. Not all countries use annual chain-weighted methods such as those incorporated in U.S. GDP (see Notes and Definitions to Chapter 1). Some of the employment and population figures have been recalculated for greater comparability by BLS. GDP figures are converted from national currency values to U.S. dollar equivalents using Purchasing Power Parities (PPPs) published by the OECD in the OECD-Eurostat PPP Program.

PPPs are currency conversion rates that allow output in different currency units to be expressed in a common unit of value (U.S. dollars in this case). They are preferred to international market exchange rates for this purpose because, according to BLS, "At best, market exchange rates represent only the relative prices of goods and services that are traded internationally, not the relative value of total domestic output, which also consists of goods, and particularly services, that are not traded internationally, or which are isolated from the effects of foreign trade. Market exchange rates also are affected by...currency traders' views of the stability of governments in various countries, relative interest rates among countries, and other incentives for holding financial assets in one currency rather than another."

Measuring PPPs is difficult and subject to error, and BLS points out that statistics using PPPs should be used with caution. "The per capita GDPs of most OECD countries fall within a relatively narrow range, and changes in rankings can occur as a result of relatively minor adjustments to PPP estimates."

References

U.S. Department of Labor, Bureau of Labor Statistics, Office of Productivity and Technology, "Comparative Real Gross Domestic Product Per Capita and Per Employed Person, Fourteen Countries, 1960–2003," July 26, 2004, available at <http://www.bls.gov/fls>.

TABLE 13-4
INTERNATIONAL COMPARISONS: INDUSTRIAL PRODUCTION INDEXES

SOURCE: THE CONFERENCE BOARD

These data have been collected by The Conference Board from national sources, such as the Federal Reserve Board which is the source for U.S. data (see Chapter 2), and placed on a common comparison base, 1990 = 100.

TABLE 13-5
INTERNATIONAL COMPARISONS: CONSUMER PRICE INDEXES

SOURCE: U.S. DEPARTMENT OF LABOR, BUREAU OF LABOR STATISTICS

These data are prepared by the BLS Office of Productivity and Technology, based on national consumer price indexes as published by each country. The most recent updating was made on June 3, 2004. The data have not been adjusted for comparability across countries. National differences exist with respect to population coverage, frequency of market basket weight changes, and treatment of homeowner costs. BLS links published indexes together to form historical series and rebases the foreign indexes to the U.S. base 1982–1984. The data for Germany are for West Germany only through 1991, then for unified Germany from 1992 forward. A footnote on the table provides a unified Germany index for 1991 that is used to calculate the change from 1991 to 1992 and could be used to "link" the newer with the older series. For a description of the U.S. index, see the Notes and Definitions for Table 8-1.

TABLE 13-6
INTERNATIONAL COMPARISONS: UNEMPLOYMENT RATES AND CIVILIAN LABOR FORCES

SOURCE: U.S. BUREAU OF LABOR STATISTICS

These data have been adjusted by BLS to approximate U.S. concepts and definitions. (See Notes and Definitions for Tables 10-1 through 10-3.) The German data are for West Germany only through 1990, and for unified Germany from 1991 to the present. Adding former East Germany raised the 1991 unemployment rate from 4.3 percent, for West Germany alone, to 5.6 percent for unified Germany.

No adjustment is made to unemployment rates from Canada. Slight adjustments are made to those from Japan. Substantial adjustments were made to the Italian data prior to a 1992 definitional change. For France, Germany, and the United Kingdom before 1992, unemployment adjustment factors were based on annual household labor force surveys.

The concept of "layoff" differs from country to country. In the United States and Canada, persons who are laid off are classified as unemployed. The employees do not remain on the payroll, receive no payments from their firms, and are frequently not rehired. However, in Europe and Japan, these people are classified as employed. In general, employers reduce hours or days worked, rather than letting people go for weeks without work: The workers continue to receive pay, which is supplemented by a subsidy for time not worked. Because of these differences, the strict U.S. definition of unemployment is not applied on this point.

The adjusted statistics use the age at which compulsory schooling ends in each country instead of the U.S. standard of 16 years and older. This is 16 years in France and in the United Kingdom since 1973; 15 years in Canada, Japan, Germany, and Italy since 1993, and the United Kingdom before 1973; and 14 years in Italy before 1993. Data pertain to the noninstitutional population except in Japan and Germany, where the institutionalized population of working age is included.

There are several breaks in the series due to changes in methods or definitions. Among the more important of these are ones for the United States (1994), France (1992), Germany (1983 and 1991), and Italy (1986, 1991, and 1993).

The most recent updating was made on June 23, 2004. These data and more in-depth information on measurement procedures and standards are available from the Bureau of Labor Statistics Internet site at <http://www.bls.gov>.

TABLE 13-7
EXCHANGE RATES

SOURCE: BOARD OF GOVERNORS OF THE FEDERAL RESERVE SYSTEM

Definitions and notes on the data

This table shows measures of the U.S. dollar relative to foreign currencies—both to the currencies of some important individual countries and to average values for major groups of countries. All measures are defined as the foreign currency price of the U.S. dollar, so that where the value is relatively high, the dollar is relatively "strong"—but less competitive—and the other currencies in question are relatively "weak" and more competitive.

For consistency, this is done in *Business Statistics* even in the case of currencies that are commonly quoted, in the financial press and elsewhere, as dollars per foreign currency unit instead of foreign currency units per dollar. Notably, this is the case for the new euro and for the British pound. Where *Business Statistics* shows the 2000 value of the dollar as 1.0832 euros, the more usual statement would be that during 2000 the euro on average was worth $0.9232 (one divided by 1.0832). Where *Business Statistics* shows the 2000 value of the dollar as 0.6598 British pounds, the more usual statement would be that the pound averaged $1.5156. The Canadian dollar is also sometimes quoted relative to the U.S. dollar, rather than as shown here.

Foreign exchange rates shown are averages of the daily noon buying rates in New York City for cable transfers payable in foreign currencies; annual figures are averages of monthly data.

The introduction in January 1999 of the euro as the common currency for 11 European countries—Austria, Belgium, Finland, France, Germany, Ireland, Italy, Luxembourg, Netherlands, Portugal, and Spain—marked a major change in the international currency system. A 12th country, Greece, entered the European Monetary Union in January 2001. The values of the currencies of these countries no longer fluctuate relative to each other, but the value of the euro still fluctuates relative to the dollar and to currencies for countries outside the European Monetary Union. The currency and coins of the individual countries continued to circulate from 1999 through the end of 2001; in January 2002, new euro currency and coins were introduced, replacing the currency and coins of the individual countries. Once a country has entered the monetary union, its value relative to the dollar continues to fluctuate—but due only to fluctuations in the value of the euro relative to the dollar.

To provide continuous series after 1998 for Germany and France, *Business Statistics* converts the euro to its equivalent in the former currencies for those countries, using the following fixed values for 1 euro: 1.95583 German marks and 6.55957 French francs.

There is no fully satisfactory historical equivalent to the euro. For comparisons over time, the Federal Reserve Board uses a "restated German mark," derived simply by dividing each historical value of the mark by the euro conversion factor, 1.95583. The same trends can be derived using the values for the mark shown in this table.

Trade-weighted indexes of the value of the dollar against groups of foreign currencies also appear in this table. In each case, weighted averages of the individual currency values of the dollar are set at 100 in a base period. The weights are based on goods trade only, excluding trade in services. Base periods differ for different indexes.

The first four columns show the more familiar type of foreign exchange indexes, which use nominal values of each currency. The last two columns are price-adjusted (they are indexes of "real" exchange rates), aggregating values of the dollar in terms of each currency that have been adjusted for inflation, using each country's consumer price index. Where any currency has had an episode of hyperinflation with the consequent huge depreciation in terms of the dollar, the nominal index will not reflect the actual competitiveness of the dollar in terms of that currency over the longer term. Because there have been hyperinflations in some of the countries making up the Broad Index and its Other Important Trading Partners component (see below), price-adjusted indexes are also shown for those two groupings in the final two columns.

G-10 Index (March 1973 = 100): This measure is an index of the exchange value of the U.S. dollar in terms of the weighted average currencies of the G-10 (other industrialized) countries, which are Belgium, Canada, France, Germany, Italy, Japan, the Netherlands, Sweden, Switzerland, and the United Kingdom. Unlike the three indexes that follow, the weights in this index, which represented "multilateral" (world market) trade shares, were fixed. The Federal Reserve stopped calculating this index as of December 1998.

The three newer indexes use weights that focus more directly on U.S. competitiveness and that change as trade flows shift. Each country's weight is based on an average of the country's share of U.S. imports, the country's share of U.S. exports, and the country's share of exports that go to other countries that are large importers of U.S. goods.

The Broad Index (January 1997 = 100): The new overall index includes currencies of all countries that have a share of U.S. nonoil goods imports or nonagricultural goods exports of at least 0.5 percent. The list of currencies and the weights are updated each year. These countries are then classified as either Major Currencies or Other Important Trading Partners as outlined below.

Major Currency Index (March 1973 = 100): This index serves purposes similar to those of the discontinued G-10 index, and its level and movements are similar. It is a measure of the competitiveness of U.S. goods in the major industrial countries and a gauge of financial pressure on the dollar. The index includes countries whose currencies are traded in deep and relatively liquid financial markets and circulate widely outside the country of issue, and for which information on short and long-term interest rates is readily available. As of December 2003, this index includes the currencies of the following countries: Canada, the euro countries, Japan, United Kingdom, Switzerland, Australia, and Sweden.

Other Important Trading Partners (OITP) Index (January 1997 = 100): This index captures the competitiveness of U.S. goods in key emerging markets in Latin America, Asia, the Middle East, and Eastern Europe, whose currencies do not circulate widely outside the country of issue. Hyperinflations and large depreciations for some of these countries have led to a persistent upward trend in the nominal version of this index. Hence, the nominal OITP index is mainly useful for analysis of short-term developments, and the price-adjusted index is shown to give a more appropriate measure of longer-term competitiveness. The countries that make up this index were, as of December 2003, Mexico, China, Taiwan, South Korea, Singapore, Hong Kong, Malaysia, Brazil, Thailand, Indonesia, Philippines, Russia, India, Saudi Arabia, Israel, Argentina, Venezuela, Chile, and Colombia.

References and data availability

More information on the dollar value indexes can be found in the article "New Summary Measures of the Foreign Exchange Value of the Dollar," *Federal Reserve Bulletin*, vol. 84 (October 1998). This is available on the Federal Reserve Web site at <www.federalreserve.gov>, as are the exchange rate indexes, weighting and descriptions for the indexes, and the H.10 and G.5 releases containing daily, weekly, and monthly data for bilateral exchange rates.

Additional information can be found on the Federal Reserve Bank of St. Louis Web site at <http://www.stls.frb.org/fred/data/exchange.html>.

PART B

INDUSTRY PROFILES

CHAPTER 14: INDUSTRY DEFINITION AND STRUCTURE

THE STRUCTURE OF U.S. INDUSTRY: AN INTRODUCTION TO THE NORTH AMERICAN INDUSTRY CLASSIFICATION SYSTEM (NAICS)

This volume of *Business Statistics* incorporates data based on the new North American Industry Classification System (NAICS) for all of the major government statistical series that use classification by industry. New in this volume are NAICS series on industry value added and producer price indexes for the net output of NAICS industries.

Industry data collection is important because demands for goods and services are channeled into demands for labor and capital through the industries in which the goods and services are produced. NAICS delineates industries that are better defined in relation to today's demands, and groups together industries that are more closely related to each other by technology. Notable examples of these new features of NAICS are the more detailed data available on service industries; the more rational grouping of the computer and electronic product manufacturing subsector; and the new "Information" sector.

As a guide to the contents of the new NAICS categories, the editor has prepared a table of "NAICS Industry Definitions," showing the NAICS two-digit industry sectors and their component three-digit subsectors. The table follows this introduction and precedes the chapters of statistical tables. Where the short NAICS sector titles are not sufficiently self-explanatory, parenthetical listings are shown of the component activities.

For the user who needs information on the ways that the new classifications do—and do not—relate to the old Standard Industrial Classification System (SIC), a column has been added showing a rough match between the 2002 NAICS and the 1987 SIC. It must be emphasized that this match is approximate, not exact, and does not reflect every aspect of the change in classification systems. But even without providing exact equivalents, this column indicates just how thoroughly the SIC industries have been mixed and matched to comprise the new industries, and therefore explains why it has been so difficult for the statistical agencies to produce longer spans of historical data on the new basis.

As a further illustration, in this table the reader will note frequent references to parts of SIC industries that have been parceled out among different NAICS industries. In some cases the editor has included in parentheses the part of the old SIC industry that has been included in the new NAICS industry. For an example, see the entry for the new NAICS subsector 711, "Performing arts and spectator sports," demonstrating that this subsector includes dinner theaters, which used to be included in "Eating places" (which in turn were a subdivision of retail trade).

(For an idea of the orders of magnitude of noncomparability among roughly matched industries, the reader may refer to Table 17-4, Manufacturers' Shipments. In this table—and in the three tables that follow, derived from the same survey—the editor has shown values for 1992 on both classification bases for roughly matching industries such as Nonmetallic mineral products, Primary metals, Fabricated metal products, and Transportation equipment. Despite the basic similarities in general definition between these industries in the old and new systems, the tabulated values can be quite different, and it is evident that roughly matched industries cannot be viewed as continuous series.)

NAICS industries are groupings of producing units—not of products as such—and are grouped according to similarity of production processes. This is done in order to collect consistent data on inputs and outputs, and thus measure important concepts such as productivity and input-output parameters. This emphasis on production process helps to explain a number of the ways in which NAICS differs from SIC.

- Manufacturing activities at retail locations, such as bakeries, have been classified separately from the retail activity and put in the food manufacturing industry.
- Central administrative offices of companies have a new sector of their own; for example, the headquarters office of a food-producing corporation is no longer considered part of the food manufacturing industry but is part of sector 55, Management of companies and enterprises.
- Reproduction of packaged software, classified as a "business service" in the SIC, is now classified as a manufacturing process, in sector 334, Computer and electronic product manufacturing.
- "Electronic markets and agents and brokers," once undifferentiated components of wholesale trade industries, now have their own sector, 425.
- Retail trade in NAICS (sectors 44 and 45) now includes establishments such as office supply stores, computer and software stores, building materials dealers, plumbing supply stores, and electrical supply stores, that display merchandise and use mass-media advertising to sell to individuals as well as to businesses, and were formerly classified in wholesale trade.

References

The reader needing more precise information on NAICS definitions and differences from the SIC should refer to Executive Office of the President, Office of Management and Budget, *North American Industry Classification System: United States, 1997*, which contains matches between the 1997 NAICS and the 1987 SIC, and *North American Industry Classification System: United States, 2002*, which contains matches showing the relatively few changes from the 1997 NAICS to the 2002 NAICS. Both volumes are available from Bernan. These volumes describe fully the development and application of the new classification system, and are the sources for the material presented here. Information is also available on the NAICS Web site, <http://www.census.gov/naics>. Additional background information can also be found in Bernan, *Business Statistics of the United States: 2002*, pp. xxiv–xxviii.

Table 14-1. NAICS Industry Definitions: With Rough Derivation from SIC

NAICS Code	NAICS 2-digit industry sector and 3-digit industry subsector	Roughly corresponding major component SIC industry group or industry
11	AGRICULTURE, FORESTRY, FISHING AND HUNTING	Division A, Agriculture, forestry, and fishing; 241, Logging
111	Crop production	
112	Animal production	
113	Forestry and logging	
114	Fishing, hunting and trapping	
115	Agriculture and forestry support activities	
21	MINING	Division B, Mining
211	Oil and gas extraction	
212	Mining, except oil and gas (includes coal mining, mining for ores, and mining and quarrying of nonmetallic minerals)	
213	Support activities for mining (includes oil and gas well drilling and other support activities)	
22	UTILITIES	49, Electric, gas, and sanitary services (with some exclusions)
221	Utilities (includes electric power generation, transmission and distribution; natural gas distribution; water, sewage, irrigation, steam, and air-conditioning systems)	
23	CONSTRUCTION	Division C, Construction
236	Construction of buildings	
237	Heavy and civil engineering construction	
238	Specialty trade contractors	
31-33	MANUFACTURING	Division D, Manufacturing (excluding 241, Logging; 271, 272, 273, and 274, Publishing; and with other exclusions and inclusions)
311	Food manufacturing	20, Food and kindred products, excluding 208, Beverages
312	Beverage and tobacco product manufacturing	208, Beverages; 21, Tobacco products
313	Textile mills	221-4, 226, 228, Yarns, fabrics, and finishing

n.e.c. = Not elsewhere classified.

Table 14-1. NAICS Industry Definitions: With Rough Derivation from SIC—Continued

NAICS Code	NAICS 2-digit industry sector and 3-digit industry subsector	Roughly corresponding major component SIC industry group or industry
314	Textile product mills (including household and miscellaneous products)	227, Carpets and rugs; 229, Miscellaneous textile products
315	Apparel manufacturing	23, Apparel; 225, Knitting mills
316	Leather and allied product manufacturing	31, Leather and leather products
321	Wood product manufacturing	24, Lumber and wood products, excluding 241, Logging
322	Paper manufacturing	26, Paper and allied products
323	Printing and related support activities, including quick and instant	275-9, Commercial printing and miscellaneous printing and trade services
324	Petroleum and coal products manufacturing (includes refineries, asphalt, oil and grease, and coke manufacturing)	29, Petroleum and coal products
325	Chemical manufacturing (includes basic organic and inorganic chemicals; plastics materials; synthetic fibers and rubber; agricultural chemicals; pharmaceuticals and medicine; paint, adhesives, cleaning and toilet preparations, ink, explosives, and misc.)	28, Chemicals and allied products
326	Plastics and rubber products	30, Rubber and misc. plastics products
327	Nonmetallic mineral product manufacturing (includes pottery, plumbing fixtures, bricks and structural clay products, glass and products, cement and concrete, lime, gypsum, and stone products)	32, Stone, clay and glass products
331	Primary metal manufacturing (primary and secondary ferrous and nonferrous metals, rolling, drawing, and extruding, and foundries)	33, Primary metal industries
332	Fabricated metal product manufacturing (includes forging and stamping, cutlery, hardware, structural metal work, boilers, containers, machine shops, valves, fixtures, bearings, metal testing, small arms, ordnance, ammunition)	34, Fabricated metal products
333	Machinery manufacturing (includes machinery for agriculture, construction, mining, manufacturing, commercial, and service industries, metalworking machinery, turbine and power transmission, pumps and compressors, elevators and material handling, cranes and misc. general purpose machinery)	Parts of 35, Industrial machinery and equipment; 36, Electronic and other electric equipment; and 38, Instruments and related products
334	Computer and electronic product manufacturing (includes electronic computers and equipment, communications equipment, audio and video equipment, semiconductors and other electronic components, electromedical equipment, navigation, measuring, and controlling instruments, reproducing software and media)	Parts of 357, Computer and office equipment; 36, Electronic and other electric equipment; 38, Instruments and related products; 73, Business services; and 78, Motion picture services
335	Electrical equipment and appliance manufacturing (includes electrical lighting, household appliances, electrical equipment, batteries, wire and cable manufacturing)	Parts of 36, Electronic and other electric equipment and 335, Nonferrous wire drawing
336	Transportation equipment manufacturing (includes motor vehicles and parts, truck trailers, aerospace products and parts, railroad rolling stock, ship and boat building and repairing, motorcycles, bicycles, military armored vehicles, and parts)	37, Transportation equipment
337	Furniture and related product manufacturing	25, Furniture and fixtures; parts of other industries
339	Miscellaneous manufacturing (includes medical equipment and supplies, jewelry, silverware, sporting goods, toys, games, office supplies, art supplies, burial caskets, and other goods)	Parts of 38, Instruments; 39, Miscellaneous; 25, Furniture; and other industries

n.e.c. = Not elsewhere classified.

Table 14-1. NAICS Industry Definitions: With Rough Derivation from SIC—Continued

NAICS Code	NAICS 2-digit industry sector and 3-digit industry subsector	Roughly corresponding major component SIC industry group or industry
42	WHOLESALE TRADE	
423	Merchant wholesalers, durable goods	Parts of 50, Wholesale trade-durable goods, and other industries
424	Merchant wholesalers, nondurable goods	Parts of 51, Wholesale trade-nondurable goods, and other industries
425	Electronic markets and agents and brokers	Parts of 50 and 51, Wholesale trade
44-45	RETAIL TRADE	
441	Motor vehicle and parts dealers	Parts of 55, Automotive dealers and service stations, Wholesale trade, and other industries
442	Furniture and home furnishings stores	Parts of 57, Furniture and homefurnishing stores, Wholesale trade, and other industries
443	Electronics and appliance stores	5722, Household appliance stores; 5734, Computer and software stores; 5946, Camera and photo supply stores; and parts of wholesale trade and other industries
444	Building material and garden supply stores	52, Retail building materials and garden supplies, and parts of Wholesale trade
445	Food and beverage stores	54, Food stores, and 5921, Liquor stores
446	Health and personal care stores	5912, Drug stores and proprietary stores, and parts of Wholesale trade, Food stores and Miscellaneous stores
447	Gasoline stations (including stations with convenience stores)	Parts of 55, Automotive dealers and service stations, and 54, Food stores
448	Clothing and clothing accessories stores	56, Apparel and accessory stores; 5944, Jewelry stores; and 5948, Luggage and leather goods stores
451	Sporting goods, hobby, book and music stores	Parts of 59, Miscellaneous retail; 57, Furniture and homefurnishing stores; and other industries
452	General merchandise stores (includes department stores, warehouse clubs, superstores, and other general merchandise)	53, General merchandise, and parts of other retail
453	Miscellaneous store retailers (includes florists, office supply & stationery, gift, used merchandise, pet, manufactured and mobile home, tobacco, and misc. other store retailers)	Parts of 59, Misc. retail, and other industries
454	Nonstore retailers (includes electronic shopping and auctions, mail order, vending machines, and fuel and other direct selling)	Parts of 59, Misc. retail, and 517, Wholesale petroleum
48-49	TRANSPORTATION AND WAREHOUSING	
481	Air transportation	Parts of 45, Transportation by air
482	Rail transportation	Parts of 40, Railroad transportation
483	Water transportation	Parts of 44, Water transportation
484	Truck transportation	Parts of 42, Trucking and warehousing
485	Transit and ground passenger transportation	Parts of 41, Local and suburban transportation

n.e.c. = Not elsewhere classified.

Table 14-1. NAICS Industry Definitions: With Rough Derivation from SIC—Continued

NAICS Code	NAICS 2-digit industry sector and 3-digit industry subsector	Roughly corresponding major component SIC industry group or industry
486	Pipeline transportation	46, Pipelines except natural gas, and parts of 492, Gas production and distribution
487	Scenic and sightseeing transportation	Parts of 41, Local and suburban, 44, Water, 45, Air, 47, Transportation services, and 7999, Amusement and recreation n.e.c.
488	Support activities for transportation	Parts of 11 industries in transportation, communications, manufacturing, and services
491	Postal service	4311, U.S. Postal Service, and part of 7389, Business services n.e.c.
492	Couriers and messengers	4513, Air couriers, and 4215, Courier services except air
493	Warehousing and storage	Parts of 422, Public warehousing and storage
51	INFORMATION	
511	Publishing industries, except Internet	
5111	Newspaper, book, and directory publishers	Parts of 271, Newspapers, 272, Periodicals, 273, Books, 274, Misc. publishing, 277, Greeting cards, and 733, Mailing, reproduction, and stenographic services
5112	Software publishers	Part of 7372, Prepackaged software
512	Motion picture and sound recording industries (includes music books and sheet music)	781, Motion picture production and services; 783, Motion picture theaters; and parts of 782, Motion picture distribution and services, and other manufacturing and service industries
515	Broadcasting, except Internet	483, Radio and television broadcasting; part of 484, Cable and other pay TV services
516	Internet publishing and broadcasting	Parts of publishing and service industries
517	Telecommunications	Parts of 481, Telephone communications, 482, Telegraph and other communications, and 484, Cable and other pay TV services
518	ISPs, search portals, and data processing	7374, Data processing and preparation; 7375, Information retrieval services; and parts of other service industries
519	Other information services (includes news syndicates, libraries, archives, and other information services)	8231, Libraries, and parts of other service industries
52	FINANCE AND INSURANCE	
521	Monetary authorities-central bank	6011, Federal Reserve Banks
522	Credit intermediation and related activities (includes commercial banking, savings institutions, credit unions, credit card issuing, sales financing, consumer lending, real estate credit, trade financing, loan brokers, and processing and clearing)	Parts of 60, Depository institutions, and 61, Nondepository institutions
523	Securities, commodity contracts, investments	62, Security and commodity brokers, and parts of 60, Depository institutions, 61, Nondepository institutions, 63, Insurance carriers, and 67, Holding and other investment offices
524	Insurance carriers and related activities	64, Insurance agents, brokers, and service, and parts of 63, Insurance carriers
525	Funds, trusts, and other financial vehicles	672, Investment offices; 6798, Real estate investment trusts; parts of 63, Insurance carriers, and 673, Trusts

n.e.c. = Not elsewhere classified.

Table 14-1. NAICS Industry Definitions: With Rough Derivation from SIC—Continued

NAICS Code	NAICS 2-digit industry sector and 3-digit industry subsector	Roughly corresponding major component SIC industry group or industry
53	REAL ESTATE AND RENTAL AND LEASING	
531	Real estate	Parts of 65, Real estate, and 4225, General warehousing and storage (mini-warehouses and self-storage units)
532	Rental and leasing services	7352, Medical equipment rental; 7377, Computer rental and leasing; 751, Automotive rentals, no drivers; 7841, Video tape rental; and parts of 4499, Water transportation n.e.c., 4741, Rental of railroad cars, 7299, Misc. personal services n.e.c., 735, Misc. equipment rental, 7922, Theatrical producers and services, and 7999, Amusement and recreation n.e.c.
533	Lessors of nonfinancial intangible assets (except copyrighted)	6794, Patent owners and lessors, and part of 6792, Oil royalty traders
54	PROFESSIONAL AND TECHNICAL SERVICES (includes legal, accounting, bookkeeping, architectural, engineering, design, computer design and programming, management and other consulting, scientific research and development, advertising and public relations, market research, polling, and other services)	0741, Veterinary services; 6541, Title abstract offices; 731, Advertising; 7221, Photographic studios, portrait; 7921, Tax return preparation; 7336, Commercial art and graphic design; 7361, Employment agencies; 7371, Computer programming; 7373, Computer systems design; 7376, Computer facilities management; 8111, Legal services; 871, Engineering and architectural services; 873, Research and testing; and parts of mining, 37 (aircraft and guided missiles), 73, Business services, 87, Engineering and management services, and other industries
55	MANAGEMENT OF COMPANIES AND ENTERPRISES	671, Holding companies, and establishments classified as auxilaries in producing industries
56	ADMINISTRATIVE AND WASTE SERVICES	
561	Administrative and support services (Includes office administrative, employment placement, temporary help, telephone call centers, collection agencies, credit bureaus, court reporting, travel arrangement, investigation and security, services to buildings, and other support services)	0782, Lawn and garden services, 0783 Ornamental shrub and tree services, 4724, Travel agencies, 4725, Tour operators, 7217, Carpet and upholstery cleaning, 732, credit reporting and collection, 7338, Secretarial and court reporting, 734, Services to buildings, 7363, Help supply services, 7381,Detective and armored car services, 7382, Security systems, 8744 Facilities support, and parts of 458, Airfields, 472, Passenger transportation arrangement, 495, Sanitary services, 729, Misc. personal services, 73, Business services, 769, Misc. repair shops, 7819, Services allied to motion pictures, 79, Amusement and recreation services, 86, Membership organizations, and 8741, Management services
562	Waste management and remediation services	4953, Refuse systems, and parts of 1799, Special trade contractors, 4212, Local trucking, 4959, Sanitary services, 735, Misc. equipment rental and leasing (portable toilet rental) and 769, Misc. repair shops
61	EDUCATIONAL SERVICES	82, Educational services, except 823, Libraries; and parts of 7231, Beauty shops, 7241, Barber shops, 7911, Dance studios, 7999, Amusement and recreation n.e.c. and 8748, Business consulting n.e.c. (educational testing services)
62	HEALTH CARE AND SOCIAL ASSISTANCE	
621	Ambulatory health care services	Offices and clinics for 801, Doctors, 802, Dentists, 803, Osteopaths, and 804, Other health practitioners; 8071, Medical laboratories; 8082, Home health care services; 4119, Ambulances; 4522, Air ambulances; and parts of 809, Health and allied services n.e.c.
622	Hospitals	806, Hospitals
623	Nursing and residential care facilities	805, Nursing and personal care facilities, and 836, Residential care
624	Social assistance	8322, Individual and family services, except parole and probation offices; 8331, Job training, and 8351, Child day care services

n.e.c. = Not elsewhere classified.

Table 14-1. NAICS Industry Definitions: With Rough Derivation from SIC—*Continued*

NAICS Code	NAICS 2-digit industry sector and 3-digit industry subsector	Roughly corresponding major component SIC industry group or industry
71	ARTS, ENTERTAINMENT, AND RECREATION	
711	Performing arts and spectator sports	7929, Bands and other entertainment groups; 7941, Professional sports clubs and promoters; 7948, Racing; parts of 5812, Eating places (dinner theaters) and 6512, Building operators (stadium and arena owners); and agents, artists, writers, performers, correspondents, taxidermists, and antique restorers, previously classified as part of 738, Misc. business services; 76, Misc. repair services; 7819, Motion picture services; 7999, Amusement and recreation n.e.c.; and 8999, Membership organizations, n.e.c.
712	Museums, historical sites, zoos, and parks	84, Museums, botanical, and zoological gardens, and part of 7999, Amusement and recreation n.e.c. (caverns and misc. commercial parks)
713	Amusements, gambling, and recreation	4493, Marinas; 793, Bowling centers; 7991, Physical fitness facilities; 7992, Public golf courses, 7995, Coin operated amusments; 7996, Amusement parks; 7997, Membership sports and recreation clubs; and parts of 7911, Dance studios, and 7999, Amusement and recreation n.e.c.
72	ACCOMMODATION AND FOOD SERVICES	
721	Accommodation (includes hotels, motels, bed-and-breakfast inns, RV parks, camps, and rooming and boarding houses)	70, Hotels and other lodging places
722	Food services and drinking places	5812, Eating places (other than dinner theaters), 5813, Drinking places, and parts of 4789, Transportation services n.e.c. (contract dining car operations), 5641, Retail bakeries, and 5963 Direct selling (mobile food wagons)
81	OTHER SERVICES, EXCEPT PUBLIC ADMINISTRATION	
811	Repair and maintenance	753, Automotive repair shops (other than tire retreading); 7542, carwashes; 7631, Watch, clock and jewelery repair; 7692, Welding repair; and parts of 3732 (boat repair), 7219 (clothing alteration and repair), 7251(shoe repair), 7378 (computer repair), 7549 (auto window tinting), 7622 (radio and tv repair), 7623 (refrigeration repair), 7629, Electrical repair n.e.c., 7641, Reupholstery and furniture repair, 7694, Armature, rewinding, and 7699, Repair services n.e.c.
812	Personal and laundry services	6553, Cemetery subdividers and developers; 7211, power laundries; 7212, Garment pressing and cleaners' agents; 7213, Linen supply; 7215, Coin operated laundries and cleaning; 7216, Drycleaning except rugs; 7218, Industrial launderers; 7261, Funeral service and crematories; 7384, photofinishing laboratories; 7521, Auto parking; and parts of 0752 (pet care), 6531, Real estate agents and managers (cemetery management), 7219 (diaper and misc. services), 7231 (beauty shops), 7241 (barber shops), 7251 (shoe shine parlors), and 7389 (apparel pressing for the trade, bail bonding)
813	Membership associations and organizations	6732, Educational, religious and charitable trusts; 8399, Social services n.e.c. (voluntary health organizations, human rights organizations, environment, conservation, and wildlife, and other grant making, giving, and social advocacy organizations); 8611, Business associations; 8621, Professional organizations; 8631, Labor organizations; 8651, Political organizations; 8661, Religious organizations; and parts of 6531, Real estate agents and managers (condominium associations), 8641, Civic and social organizations (all except tribal governments), and 8699, Membership organizations n.e.c. (all except motor travel clubs)
814	Private households	8811, Private households

n.e.c. = Not elsewhere classified.

Table 14-1. NAICS Industry Definitions: With Rough Derivation from SIC—*Continued*

NAICS Code	NAICS 2-digit industry sector and 3-digit industry subsector	Roughly corresponding major component SIC industry group or industry
92	PUBLIC ADMINISTRATION	
921	Executive, legislative, and general government	91, Executive, legislative, and general; 9311, Finance, taxation, and monetary policy; and part of 8641, Civic and social associations (tribal governments)
922	Justice, public order, and safety activities	92, Justice, public order, and safety, and part of 8322, Individual and family services (parole and probation)
923	Administration of human resource programs	94, Administration of human resources
924	Administration of environmental programs	951, Environmental quality
925	Community and housing program administration	953, Housing and urban development
926	Administration of economic programs	9611, Administration of general economic programs; 9631, Regulation and administration of utilities; 9641, Regulation of agricultural marketing; 9651, Misc. commercial regulation; and parts of 9621, Regulation and administration of transportation (all except air traffic control)
927	Space research and technology	9661, Space research and technology
928	National security and international affairs	97, National security and international affairs

n.e.c.= Not elsewhere classified.

CHAPTER 15: PRODUCT AND INCOME BY INDUSTRY

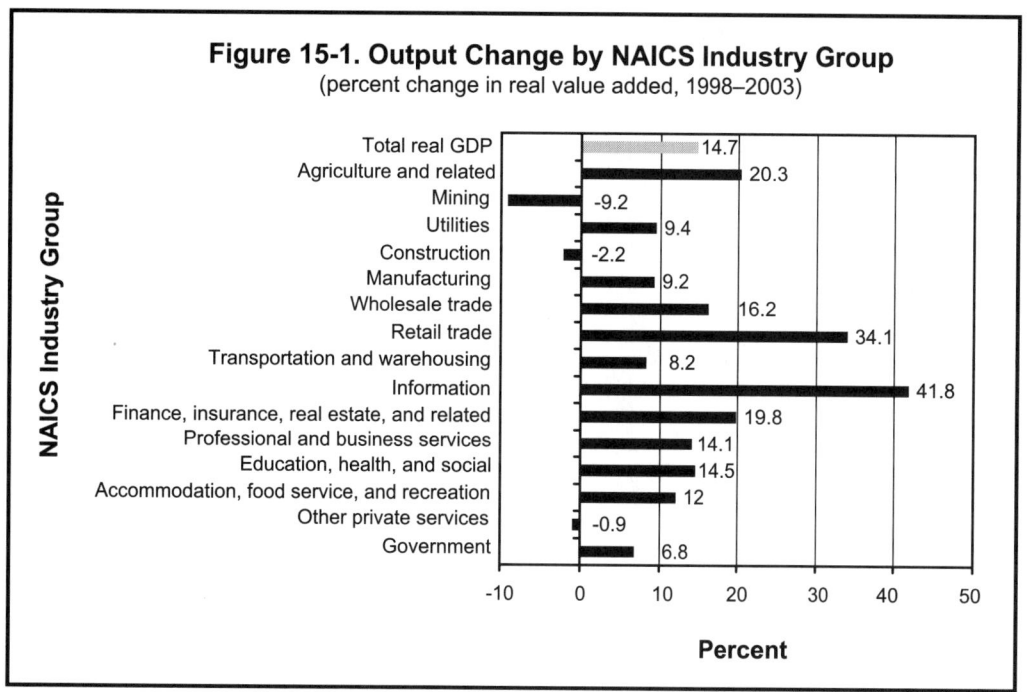

- Calculations of real output (value added in chained 2000 dollars) are available on a NAICS industry basis for the latest six years only. Between the first and the last of those years, 1998 and 2003, total real GDP rose 14.7 percent, for an annual rate of 2.8 percent. This figure presents a basis for comparison with component industry groups over the same years. It is lower than the potential national long-term growth rate, because 1998 was a year of fairly high activity with a 4.5 percent unemployment rate, and 2003 was a year of only partial recovery from recession with 6.0 percent unemployment. (Tables 15-3 and 10-3)
- Of the 15 industry groups represented in Table 15-3 and in Figure 15-1 above, there were four that expanded significantly faster than the average. The fastest-growing was information, whose output was up 42 percent. Next was retail trade, with a 34 percent increase. Agriculture and related industries and the finance, insurance, and real estate group each grew about 20 percent. (Table 15-3)
- Retail trade activity rose far more than U.S. output of agriculture and of manufactured products. Presumably, retail activity was increased relative to the domestic production of goods by the merchandising of imported products. (Table 15-3)
- The same industry groups can be assessed in terms of their relative importance using the statistics on current-dollar value added, although it should be remembered that "value added" includes taxes on production and imports, some of which are allocated to industries that may bear little of their ultimate incidence. Many sales taxes are allocated to the retail sector. Some excise taxes and all import duties are allocated to wholesale trade. Residential property taxes, including those on owner-occupied housing, are included in the real estate industry. Finance, insurance, real estate, and related industries accounted for 20 percent of GDP in 2003. Professional and business services accounted for 12 percent, and manufacturing 13 percent. The fastest-growing industry groups were smaller: information accounted for 5 percent and retail trade for 7 percent. (Table 15-2)

Table 15-1. Gross Domestic Product (Value Added) by SIC Industry Group, 1987–2000

(Billions of dollars; index numbers, 1996 = 100.)

Year and series definition	Gross domestic product	Private industries										
		Total	Agriculture, forestry, and fishing	Mining	Construction	Manufacturing		Transportation	Communications	Electric, gas, and sanitary services	Wholesale trade	Retail trade
						Durable goods	Nondurable goods					
VALUE												
1987	4 742.5	4 081.4	88.9	92.2	219.3	516.8	371.8	158.8	125.5	141.9	308.9	434.5
1988	5 108.3	4 401.8	89.1	99.2	237.2	566.3	413.6	169.2	132.8	147.0	346.6	461.5
1989	5 489.1	4 735.5	102.0	97.1	245.8	582.7	434.9	172.2	137.4	159.0	364.7	492.7
1990	5 803.2	4 996.7	108.3	111.9	248.7	586.6	454.0	177.4	148.1	165.4	376.1	507.8
1991	5 986.2	5 129.1	102.9	96.7	232.7	575.5	468.0	186.1	155.7	176.5	395.6	523.7
1992	6 318.9	5 424.5	111.7	87.6	234.4	594.0	488.0	193.4	163.9	181.2	414.6	551.7
1993	6 642.3	5 717.5	108.3	88.4	248.9	632.8	498.6	206.0	178.6	188.7	432.5	578.0
1994	7 054.3	6 096.7	118.5	90.2	275.3	694.1	529.1	223.2	190.7	197.4	479.2	620.6
1995	7 400.5	6 411.1	109.8	95.7	290.3	729.8	559.2	233.4	202.3	206.9	500.6	646.8
1996	7 813.2	6 792.8	130.4	113.0	316.4	748.4	567.6	243.4	214.7	208.3	529.6	687.1
1997	8 318.4	7 253.6	130.0	118.9	338.2	791.2	588.4	261.8	220.8	205.9	566.8	740.5
1998	8 781.5	7 678.2	128.0	100.2	380.8	830.7	600.8	288.7	238.5	204.8	607.9	790.4
1999	9 274.3	8 123.0	127.7	104.1	425.4	853.8	627.5	301.9	257.2	211.0	645.3	831.7
2000	9 824.6	8 606.9	134.3	133.1	461.3	886.4	633.9	313.7	279.1	216.5	696.8	887.3
QUANTITY INDEX												
1987	78.2	76.7	84.6	87.2	88.0	72.3	90.2	66.7	61.8	79.6	66.8	74.5
1988	81.5	80.2	77.6	101.3	93.0	79.1	93.6	68.8	65.6	82.2	71.6	79.3
1989	84.4	83.2	85.4	91.0	93.6	78.8	92.5	70.9	68.1	87.7	75.4	81.9
1990	85.9	84.5	90.9	93.6	91.9	78.2	91.7	74.2	72.3	91.2	74.6	81.4
1991	85.5	84.0	93.0	89.5	84.9	74.7	90.0	76.4	75.5	94.1	78.7	80.7
1992	88.1	86.6	100.2	84.7	85.9	76.0	91.6	79.5	78.9	92.8	84.0	82.9
1993	90.4	89.0	94.0	89.4	88.2	80.2	92.6	82.7	84.8	92.8	85.4	84.7
1994	94.0	93.0	104.1	95.6	93.9	87.7	97.1	89.8	88.9	94.5	90.9	89.8
1995	96.6	95.8	94.4	99.9	94.7	95.5	100.5	92.5	94.3	99.5	91.2	93.4
1996	100.0	100.0	100.0	100.0	100.0	100.0	100.0	100.0	100.0	100.0	100.0	100.0
1997	104.4	105.3	110.1	103.5	102.6	108.6	101.3	102.3	101.4	97.0	110.3	108.5
1998	108.9	110.3	111.5	105.9	110.3	119.3	97.9	106.0	107.7	93.0	125.3	116.4
1999	113.4	115.6	118.5	101.5	116.2	126.8	100.6	110.4	118.9	100.3	133.8	123.2
2000	117.6	120.1	127.8	90.1	119.5	139.5	98.3	116.1	133.6	102.7	141.7	132.3

Year and series definition	Private industries—Continued									Government		
	Finance, insurance, and real estate [1]				Services [1]				Statistical discrepancy	Total	Federal	State and local
	Total	Depository institutions	Real estate		Total	Business services	Health services	Other services				
			Nonfarm housing services	Other real estate								
VALUE												
1987	829.7	143.9	391.9	139.5	789.9	145.0	230.6	103.3	3.3	661.0	258.9	402.1
1988	893.7	147.6	424.3	162.0	887.9	166.9	253.6	119.8	-42.2	706.5	273.3	433.2
1989	954.5	157.2	456.7	174.0	976.0	183.7	280.7	135.8	16.3	753.6	287.1	466.5
1990	1 010.3	171.3	488.3	177.3	1 071.5	203.9	314.4	149.2	30.6	806.6	300.2	506.4
1991	1 072.2	193.9	515.5	173.6	1 123.8	205.3	345.3	150.0	19.6	857.1	322.4	534.7
1992	1 140.9	205.2	543.4	181.8	1 219.4	229.4	377.8	161.1	43.7	894.4	333.9	560.5
1993	1 205.3	200.9	558.1	193.5	1 287.7	247.6	394.5	170.6	63.8	924.8	336.2	588.6
1994	1 254.8	200.7	593.9	197.5	1 365.0	273.2	413.9	178.6	58.5	957.6	339.6	618.0
1995	1 347.2	227.4	628.9	203.7	1 462.4	302.0	433.1	194.4	26.5	989.5	342.3	647.2
1996	1 436.8	241.0	654.6	217.0	1 564.2	342.3	459.1	208.9	32.8	1 020.4	346.9	673.5
1997	1 569.9	273.9	679.1	241.0	1 691.5	395.5	472.2	229.7	29.7	1 064.8	354.7	710.1
1998	1 708.5	300.0	718.7	262.9	1 829.9	439.8	491.1	254.5	-31.0	1 103.3	359.9	743.4
1999	1 798.8	330.3	766.9	283.5	1 977.2	501.0	515.4	276.0	-38.8	1 151.3	369.8	781.5
2000	1 976.7	361.1	811.4	312.3	2 116.4	534.4	548.5	300.3	-128.5	1 217.7	389.5	828.2
QUANTITY INDEX												
1987	81.4	91.5	81.4	71.2	75.5	54.7	85.5	73.2	...	91.9	106.5	84.5
1988	84.2	90.3	84.2	83.5	80.2	61.0	86.9	79.9	...	94.2	107.4	87.5
1989	85.9	95.8	87.0	84.8	84.0	66.0	88.9	87.9	...	96.5	108.8	90.2
1990	87.0	101.2	88.6	84.3	87.1	70.5	92.2	91.6	...	98.8	110.9	92.7
1991	88.4	102.3	90.9	80.2	86.5	68.9	94.3	87.4	...	99.2	111.0	93.2
1992	90.3	97.4	93.0	87.9	89.0	74.4	96.4	86.8	...	99.5	110.2	94.1
1993	92.5	97.1	93.1	90.2	90.7	78.8	95.3	90.5	...	99.3	107.7	95.1
1994	93.8	94.6	96.5	90.5	93.2	86.2	95.5	92.0	...	99.6	105.8	96.4
1995	97.0	100.6	99.0	94.4	96.6	91.7	96.8	95.7	...	99.7	102.1	98.4
1996	100.0	100.0	100.0	100.0	100.0	100.0	100.0	100.0	...	100.0	100.0	100.0
1997	105.9	102.1	101.0	111.9	104.4	112.2	100.1	105.9	...	101.5	100.1	102.2
1998	112.9	106.4	103.5	123.9	108.6	120.0	100.4	114.2	...	102.6	100.2	103.9
1999	117.5	114.1	107.6	128.7	113.1	131.3	102.5	119.7	...	104.0	99.9	106.1
2000	124.8	119.2	110.4	136.2	116.7	134.4	106.3	126.3	...	106.7	102.3	108.9

Note: These data are reprinted without change from *Business Statistics 2004* in order to provide data for years prior to those shown in Tables 15-2 and 15-3.

[1] Includes industries not shown separately.
 . . . = Not available.

Table 15-2. Value Added (Gross Domestic Product) by NAICS Industry Group, 1998–2003, in Current Dollars

(Billions of current dollars.)

NAICS industry	1998	1999	2000	2001	2002	2003
Gross domestic product	8 747.0	9 268.4	9 817.0	10 100.8	10 480.8	10 987.9
Private industries	7 652.5	8 127.2	8 614.3	8 841.1	9 154.1	9 597.9
Agriculture, forestry, fishing, and hunting	102.4	93.8	98.0	103.0	98.6	112.0
Farms	78.9	68.8	71.5	75.5	70.7	...
Forestry, fishing, and related activities	23.5	25.0	26.5	27.4	27.9	...
Mining [1]	74.8	85.4	121.3	118.7	105.6	124.9
Oil and gas extraction	35.2	47.2	81.0	73.9	64.1	...
Mining, except oil and gas	27.0	27.5	27.0	27.0	26.1	...
Utilities	180.8	185.4	189.3	195.1	201.6	212.7
Construction	374.4	406.6	435.9	459.5	464.9	481.8
Manufacturing	1 343.9	1 373.1	1 426.2	1 346.0	1 351.6	1 392.8
Durable goods [1]	806.9	820.4	865.3	788.0	786.1	810.1
Computer and electronic products	165.7	162.8	185.6	141.6	139.9	...
Motor vehicles, bodies and trailers, and parts	108.8	115.4	118.1	108.0	119.3	...
Nondurable goods [1]	537.0	552.7	560.9	558.0	565.5	582.7
Food and beverage and tobacco products	137.5	153.6	154.8	161.6	168.8	...
Chemical products	153.4	157.1	157.1	157.2	167.9	...
Wholesale trade	542.9	577.7	591.7	603.0	622.9	642.9
Retail trade	598.6	635.5	662.4	687.7	765.8	792.2
Transportation and warehousing [1]	273.7	287.4	301.6	295.1	294.9	310.6
Air transportation	52.5	54.9	57.7	50.6	47.9	...
Rail transportation	24.5	24.7	25.5	25.3	24.3	...
Truck transportation	86.2	89.8	92.8	92.5	94.1	...
Transit and ground passenger transportation	13.8	14.4	14.5	15.7	16.3	...
Other transportation and support activities	59.9	64.8	70.2	69.3	70.7	...
Warehousing and storage	21.1	23.2	25.0	25.2	25.3	...
Information	381.6	439.3	458.3	474.8	484.0	536.1
Publishing industries (includes software)	96.7	118.7	116.7	118.6	120.1	...
Motion picture and sound recording industries	25.3	30.1	32.5	33.7	34.6	...
Broadcasting and telecommunications	229.8	253.8	271.3	281.3	283.9	...
Information and data processing services	29.8	36.7	37.7	41.2	45.4	...
Finance, insurance, real estate, rental, and leasing	1 684.6	1 798.4	1 931.0	2 028.0	2 125.7	2 228.4
Finance and insurance	641.1	679.8	740.5	770.1	804.0	863.6
Federal Reserve banks, credit intermediation, and related activities	277.7	308.0	319.0	352.3	374.8	...
Securities, commodity contracts, and investments	134.1	139.9	167.7	164.6	162.6	...
Insurance carriers and related activities	217.4	216.9	238.3	235.3	248.7	...
Funds, trusts, and other financial vehicles	11.9	15.0	15.5	17.9	17.9	...
Real estate and rental and leasing	1 043.5	1 118.6	1 190.5	1 257.8	1 321.7	1 364.9
Real estate	950.3	1 017.9	1 082.1	1 150.0	1 210.3	...
Rental and leasing services and lessors of intangible assets	93.2	100.6	108.3	107.8	111.5	...
Professional and business services	976.2	1 064.5	1 140.8	1 187.9	1 220.2	1 273.5
Professional, scientific, and technical services	565.3	613.9	675.1	710.9	723.5	753.3
Legal services	120.9	127.3	136.1	143.3	149.7	...
Computer systems design and related services	92.9	107.8	125.7	137.1	129.4	...
Miscellaneous professional, scientific, and technical services	351.6	378.8	413.3	430.6	444.3	...
Management of companies and enterprises	156.8	170.5	183.4	187.7	202.0	216.2
Administrative and waste management services	254.0	280.1	282.4	289.2	294.7	303.9
Administrative and support services	231.9	255.4	257.2	262.6	267.0	...
Waste management and remediation services	22.2	24.7	25.2	26.6	27.7	...
Educational services, health care, and social assistance	601.5	634.5	678.4	732.7	793.1	842.7
Educational services	67.6	72.8	79.2	85.8	91.5	96.8
Health care and social assistance	533.9	561.7	599.2	646.9	701.6	745.9
Ambulatory health care services	276.1	288.6	307.6	333.4	364.0	...
Hospitals and nursing and residential care facilities	214.5	225.6	238.6	256.0	276.0	...
Social assistance	43.3	47.6	53.0	57.5	61.7	...
Arts, entertainment, recreation, accommodation, and food services	306.0	327.8	350.1	358.9	371.5	385.2
Arts, entertainment, and recreation	76.8	83.8	88.7	94.8	99.6	104.9
Accommodation and food services	229.1	244.0	261.4	264.2	272.0	280.3
Accommodation	78.1	84.3	90.7	88.3	89.8	...
Food services and drinking places	151.1	159.7	170.8	175.9	182.1	...
Other services, except government	211.1	217.8	229.1	250.8	253.7	262.0
Government	1 094.5	1 141.2	1 202.7	1 259.6	1 326.7	1 390.0
Federal	352.9	361.9	378.7	386.9	408.9	...
General government	293.1	300.9	315.4	325.2	345.3	...
Government enterprises	59.9	61.0	63.4	61.7	63.6	...
State and local	741.6	779.4	823.9	872.7	917.8	...
General government	677.2	711.8	754.2	799.9	843.5	...
Government enterprises	64.4	67.6	69.7	72.8	74.3	...
Addenda						
Private goods-producing industries [2]	1 895.4	1 958.9	2 081.5	2 027.1	2 020.7	2 111.5
Private services-producing industries [3]	5 757.1	6 168.3	6 532.8	6 814.0	7 133.4	7 486.4

[1] Includes industries not shown separately.
[2] Consists of agriculture, forestry, fishing, and hunting; mining; construction; and manufacturing.
[3] Consists of utilities; wholesale trade; retail trade; transportation and warehousing; information; finance, insurance, real estate, rental, and leasing; professional and business services; educational services, health care, and social assistance; arts, entertainment, recreation, accommodation, and food services; and other services, except government.
... = Not available.

Table 15-3. Value Added (Gross Domestic Product) by NAICS Industry Group, 1998–2003, in Constant Dollars

(Billions of chained [2000] dollars.)

NAICS industry	1998	1999	2000	2001	2002	2003
Gross domestic product	9 066.9	9 470.3	9 817.0	9 866.6	10 083.0	10 398.0
Private industries	7 896.0	8 285.5	8 614.3	8 664.2	8 859.1	9 129.3
Agriculture, forestry, fishing, and hunting	84.6	87.4	98.0	97.8	100.0	101.8
Farms	61.6	62.9	71.5	68.5	69.8	...
Forestry, fishing, and related activities	22.9	24.5	26.5	29.6	30.5	...
Mining [1]	123.4	126.6	121.3	114.9	114.6	112.1
Oil and gas extraction	90.6	91.5	81.0	79.1	80.3	...
Mining, except oil and gas	24.5	26.7	27.0	25.6	24.1	...
Utilities	171.3	179.2	189.3	173.3	182.3	187.4
Construction	423.2	433.3	435.9	426.6	413.3	413.9
Manufacturing	1 286.2	1 342.1	1 426.2	1 349.1	1 380.9	1 404.9
Durable goods [1]	729.9	775.5	865.3	820.7	836.9	865.7
Computer and electronic products	96.3	125.4	185.6	186.4	207.8	...
Motor vehicles, bodies and trailers, and parts	111.8	114.6	118.1	108.2	125.0	...
Nondurable goods [1]	559.6	568.2	561.0	528.5	543.9	540.6
Food and beverage and tobacco products	153.1	155.1	154.8	151.0	150.4	...
Chemical products	149.8	157.1	157.1	152.9	163.8	...
Wholesale trade	564.7	594.1	591.7	626.6	640.5	656.3
Retail trade	598.8	633.9	662.4	708.3	764.4	803.0
Transportation and warehousing [1]	275.8	287.4	301.6	291.4	289.8	298.4
Air transportation	48.7	52.9	57.7	57.3	58.7	...
Rail transportation	24.4	24.8	25.5	24.5	22.8	...
Truck transportation	91.0	91.9	92.8	87.0	86.5	...
Transit and ground passenger transportation	14.3	14.7	14.5	15.1	15.3	...
Other transportation and support activities	62.6	66.2	70.2	67.2	67.8	...
Warehousing and storage	22.0	23.4	25.0	24.5	24.2	...
Information	377.0	437.5	458.3	474.5	489.3	534.7
Publishing industries (includes software)	100.8	121.2	116.7	115.3	117.1	...
Motion picture and sound recording industries	29.4	32.3	32.5	32.0	31.6	...
Broadcasting and telecommunications	217.3	248.3	271.3	287.5	297.7	...
Information and data processing services	29.8	36.2	37.7	39.8	43.0	...
Finance, insurance, real estate, rental, and leasing	1 741.7	1 834.3	1 931.0	1 976.8	2 009.7	2 086.4
Finance and insurance	634.6	678.1	740.5	762.0	773.9	829.7
Federal Reserve banks, credit intermediation, and related activities	305.8	328.4	319.0	337.8	337.1	...
Securities, commodity contracts, and investments	92.1	113.6	167.7	180.8	187.6	...
Insurance carriers and related activities	228.0	224.1	238.3	228.3	234.1	...
Funds, trusts, and other financial vehicles	25.7	20.4	15.5	15.3	15.7	...
Real estate and rental and leasing	1 108.6	1 157.0	1 190.5	1 214.7	1 235.7	1 257.5
Real estate	1 010.1	1 051.4	1 082.1	1 106.0	1 119.8	...
Rental and leasing services and lessors of intangible assets	98.6	105.6	108.3	108.6	115.9	...
Professional and business services	1 049.3	1 105.5	1 140.8	1 146.9	1 174.4	1 197.0
Professional, scientific, and technical services	585.9	623.9	675.1	682.5	685.9	699.3
Legal services	129.7	132.6	136.1	135.5	136.2	...
Computer systems design and related services	99.7	112.4	125.7	134.3	127.4	...
Miscellaneous professional, scientific, and technical services	356.6	379.0	413.3	412.8	422.1	...
Management of companies and enterprises	184.0	185.6	183.4	191.1	206.3	215.5
Administrative and waste management services	281.0	296.9	282.4	273.6	283.2	283.7
Administrative and support services	258.8	272.3	257.2	247.2	256.8	...
Waste management and remediation services	22.3	24.6	25.2	26.4	26.4	...
Educational services, health care, and social assistance	648.6	660.1	678.4	693.2	720.5	742.6
Educational services	75.6	77.1	79.2	80.2	80.6	80.9
Health care and social assistance	573.0	583.0	599.2	613.0	640.0	661.9
Ambulatory health care services	289.4	295.2	307.6	320.8	344.7	...
Hospitals and nursing and residential care facilities	236.0	237.6	238.6	237.9	240.8	...
Social assistance	47.7	50.2	53.0	54.4	55.1	...
Arts, entertainment, recreation, accommodation, and food services	327.2	339.0	350.1	352.7	359.5	366.5
Arts, entertainment, and recreation	84.7	87.9	88.7	90.7	92.1	94.2
Accommodation and food services	242.5	251.2	261.4	262.0	267.4	272.3
Accommodation	83.8	87.1	90.7	86.6	88.4	...
Food services and drinking places	158.7	164.1	170.8	175.5	179.1	...
Other services, except government	233.4	229.7	229.1	234.3	224.9	231.3
Government	1 165.7	1 178.7	1 202.7	1 213.6	1 228.5	1 245.0
Federal	375.5	373.0	378.7	373.3	377.5	...
General government	315.2	312.7	315.4	316.1	321.4	...
Government enterprises	60.4	60.4	63.4	57.4	56.3	...
State and local	790.1	805.7	823.9	840.3	851.0	...
General government	725.8	738.7	754.2	771.9	783.9	...
Government enterprises	64.4	67.0	69.7	68.5	67.2	...
Not allocated by industry [2]	-54.9	-22.9	0.0	-14.6	-19.5	...
Addenda						
Private goods-producing industries [3]	1 912.4	1 985.8	2 081.5	1 989.0	2 007.8	2 030.8
Private services-producing industries [4]	5 983.5	6 299.8	6 532.8	6 675.3	6 850.8	7 097.2

[1] Includes industries not shown separately.
[2] The value of not allocated by industry reflects the difference between the first line and the sum of the most detailed lines, as well as the differences in source data used to estimate GDP by industry and the expenditures measure of real GDP.
[3] Consists of agriculture, forestry, fishing, and hunting; mining; construction; and manufacturing.
[4] Consists of utilities; wholesale trade; retail trade; transportation and warehousing; information; finance, insurance, real estate, rental, and leasing; professional and business services; educational services, health care, and social assistance; arts, entertainment, recreation, accommodation, and food services; and other services, except government.
... = Not available.

NOTES AND DEFINITIONS

TABLES 15-1 THROUGH 15-3
VALUE ADDED (GROSS DOMESTIC PRODUCT) BY INDUSTRY

In the introduction to the Notes and Definitions to Chapter 1, it was observed that GDP, while primarily measured as the sum of final demands for goods and services, is also the sum of the values created by each industry in the economy. The NIPA industry accounts are designed to measure the contribution of each major industry to GDP. In June 2004, the BEA released a comprehensive revision and updating of these industry accounts for the years 1998–2003, using improved methods for integrating the industry accounts with the annual input-output accounts and the final-demand GDP calculations, and incorporating the new North American Industry Classification System (NAICS). Two important measures from these accounts—value added in current dollars and in chained (2000) dollars—are shown in Tables 15-2 and 15-3.

The 2004 revision also incorporates a change in terminology. An industry's contribution to total GDP, formerly referred to as "gross product originating" ("GPO") or "gross product by industry," is now called "value added." This is consistent with the use of the term "value added" in most economic writing. However, it should not be confused with a concept known as "Census value added" that is used in U.S. censuses and surveys of manufactures. Census value added is calculated at the individual establishment level and does not exclude purchased business services, which means it is not a true measure of economic value added.

Value added/gross product originating is calculated on an annual basis only. Current-dollar GDP and quantity indexes for real value added by industry using the older SIC (Standard Industrial Classification) system, which were calculated using the pre-revision methods for the years 1987 through 2000, are reprinted from last year's *Business Statistics* as Table 15-1 in order to provide a longer perspective. See Chapter 14 for the relationship of NAICS to SIC.

Definitions and notes on the data

An industry's value added or GPO is equal to the market value of its gross output (which consists of the value, including taxes, of sales or receipts and other operating income plus the value of inventory change) minus the value of its intermediate inputs (energy, raw materials, semifinished goods, and services that are purchased from domestic industries or from foreign sources).

In concept, this is also equal to the sum of compensation of employees, taxes on production and imports less subsidies, and gross operating surplus. (See Chapter 1 and its Notes and Definitions.)

Compensation of employees consists of wage and salary accruals and supplements to wages and salaries. This approximates the labor share of production, subject to the note below about proprietors' income.

Taxes on production and imports less subsidies. The taxes that fall into this classification include property taxes, sales and excise taxes, and Customs duties. They are allocated to the industry level at which they are assessed by law. Most sales taxes are allocated to retail trade; some sales taxes, most fuel taxes, and all customs duties to wholesale trade; and residential real property taxes, including those on owner-occupied dwellings, to the real estate industry.

For private sector businesses, *gross operating surplus* consists of business income (corporate profits before tax, proprietors' income, and rental income of persons); net interest and miscellaneous payments; business current transfer payments (net); and capital consumption allowances. For government, households, and institutions, it consists of consumption of fixed capital and (for government) government enterprises' current surplus. This approximates the capital share of production, though BEA notes that "an unknown portion [of proprietors' income"] reflects the labor contribution of proprietors."

The *quantity indexes of gross product by industry* represent estimates of the real output of each industry, net of intermediate inputs, based on chained constant-dollar estimates, and expressed as index numbers, 1996 = 100.

The preferred method for measuring real gross product by industry is known as "double deflation." This means constructing constant-dollar measures of the gross output of the industry and subtracting from those values constant-dollar measures of the intermediate inputs to the industry. In the new methodology this is used for all industries and the results are shown in Table 15-3 in chained (2000) dollars. See the Notes and Definitions to Chapter 1 for an explanation of chained-dollar methodology. In the older methodology, used for the years 1987 through 2000 in Table 15-1, the double-deflation method is used to calculate real output for most industry groups, and the real output series are expressed as quantity indexes, 1996 = 100.

Data for the most recent year are extrapolated using incomplete data.

Data availability and references

The estimates for 1998–2003 are published and described in "Improved Annual Industry Accounts for 1998–2003," *Survey of Current Business*, June 2004. Further background is given in "Preview of the Comprehensive Revision of the Annual Industry Accounts," *Survey of Current Business*, March 2004.

For the earlier estimates, concepts and methodology were described in "Improved Estimates of Gross Product by Industry for 1947–1998," *Survey of Current Business*, June 2000.

All *Survey* articles are available on the BEA Web site, <http://www.bea.gov>.

CHAPTER 16: EMPLOYMENT, HOURS, AND EARNINGS BY NAICS INDUSTRY

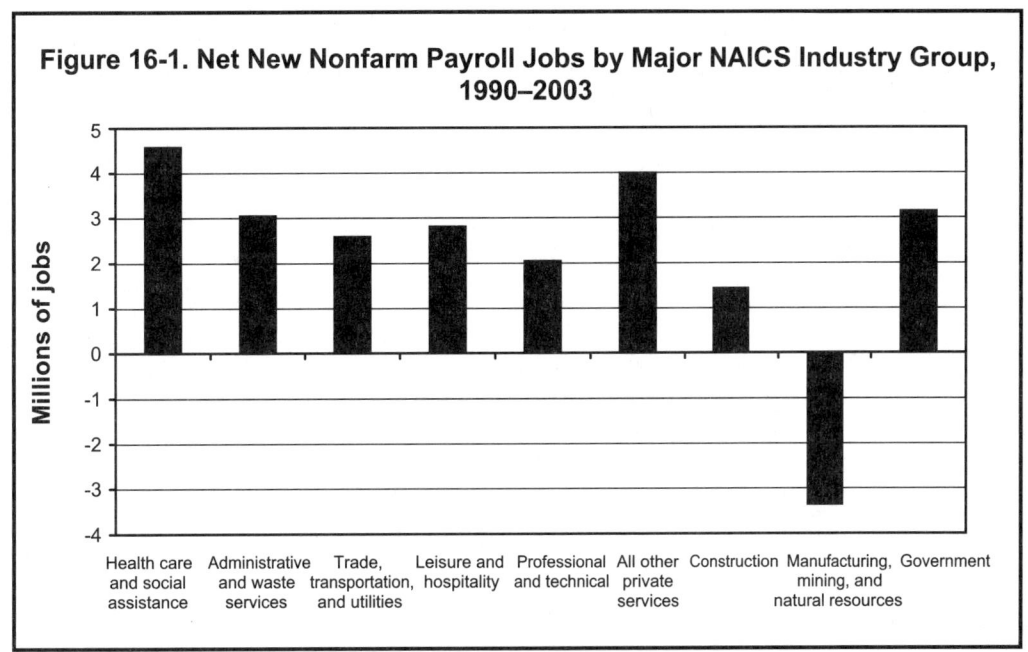

- Statistics on employment, hours, and earnings based on the new North American Industry Classification System (NAICS) have been tabulated back to 1990. Between 1990 and 2003, U.S. industries added 20.4 million jobs. Both were years of some economic slack, with the unemployment rate 5.6 percent in the earlier year and 6.0 percent in the latest year. But looking at the industry composition of job growth can give some idea of underlying trends. (Figure 16-1 and Table 16-1)
- Of the major sectors shown in the graph, health care and social assistance was the single biggest source of net new jobs, providing 4.6 million jobs of which 1.0 million were in social assistance and the rest in health care.
- Administrative and waste services provided 3.1 million net new jobs, of which 1.1 million were in the temporary help sector.
- Leisure and hospitality provided 2.8 million net new jobs, 2.0 million at food services and drinking places.
- Government provided 3.2 million net new jobs—2.9 million at local government and 0.7 million at state governments, partly offset by a loss at the federal level.
- Trade, transportation, and utilities added 2.6 million net new jobs, mostly at retail trade.
- Goods production at manufacturing and natural resource establishments lost 3.4 million jobs. Even the manufacturers of computer and electronic products lost jobs— 540,000 of them. There were, however, gains in net new jobs at computer *service* industries and in the new information sector, both of which are included in the "all other private services" category on the graph.
- Workweeks of around 40 hours characterized most of the goods-producing industries, while retail trade and some service industries, noticeably leisure and hospitality, had short average workweeks indicating many part-time jobs. (Table 16-3)
- Showing a somewhat similar pattern, average hourly earnings were high in most goods-producing industries (with the conspicuous exception of apparel) and low in leisure and hospitality and retail trade. (Table 16-4)

Table 16-1. Nonfarm Employment by NAICS Sector and Industry

(Wage and salary workers on nonfarm payrolls, thousands.)

Industry	1990	1991	1992	1993	1994	1995	1996	1997	1998	1999	2000	2001	2002	2003
Total nonfarm	109 487	108 374	108 726	110 844	114 291	117 298	119 708	122 776	125 930	128 993	131 785	131 826	130 341	129 931
Total private	91 072	89 829	89 940	91 855	95 016	97 866	100 169	103 113	106 021	108 686	110 996	110 707	108 828	108 356
Goods-producing	23 723	22 588	22 095	22 219	22 774	23 156	23 410	23 886	24 354	24 465	24 649	23 873	22 557	21 817
Natural resources and mining	765	739	689	666	659	641	637	654	645	598	599	606	583	571
Logging	84.6	78.7	78.7	81.0	82.0	82.5	80.7	82.1	80.0	80.8	79.0	73.5	70.4	68.5
Mining	680.1	660.5	609.8	584.9	576.5	558.1	556.4	571.3	564.7	517.4	520.2	532.5	512.2	502.3
Oil and gas extraction	190.2	191.0	182.2	170.9	162.4	151.7	146.9	144.1	140.8	131.2	124.9	123.7	121.9	122.9
Mining, except oil and gas [1]	302.2	285.1	271.8	250.9	255.2	252.4	249.4	249.5	243.1	234.5	224.8	218.7	210.6	202.7
Coal mining	136.0	125.6	117.5	100.2	103.5	96.7	90.5	89.4	85.3	78.6	72.2	74.3	74.4	70.4
Support activities for mining	188	184	156	163	159	154	160	178	181	152	171	190	180	177
Construction	5 263	4 780	4 608	4 779	5 095	5 274	5 536	5 813	6 149	6 545	6 787	6 826	6 716	6 722
Construction of buildings	1 413.0	1 252.9	1 187.3	1 227.4	1 300.8	1 325.4	1 380.2	1 435.4	1 508.8	1 586.3	1 632.5	1 588.9	1 574.8	1 575.9
Heavy and civil engineering	813.0	759.1	734.2	738.4	761.7	774.7	800.1	824.9	865.3	908.7	937.0	953.0	930.6	910.7
Specialty trade contractors	3 037.3	2 768.4	2 686.0	2 813.6	3 032.5	3 174.1	3 355.1	3 552.6	3 775.1	4 049.6	4 217.0	4 283.9	4 210.4	4 235.5
Manufacturing	17 695	17 068	16 799	16 774	17 021	17 241	17 237	17 419	17 560	17 322	17 263	16 441	15 259	14 525
Durable goods	10 736	10 219	9 945	9 900	10 131	10 372	10 485	10 704	10 910	10 830	10 876	10 335	9 483	8 970
Wood products	540.6	498.5	501.9	524.1	560.6	573.7	582.8	595.4	609.2	620.3	613.0	574.1	554.9	536.1
Nonmetallic mineral products	528.4	494.7	487.3	491.1	505.3	513.1	517.3	525.7	535.3	540.8	554.2	544.5	516.0	492.6
Primary metals	688.6	656.1	630.3	618.4	630.4	641.7	639.3	638.8	641.5	625.0	621.8	570.9	509.4	476.7
Fabricated metal products	1 610.0	1 541.3	1 497.2	1 509.5	1 565.3	1 623.4	1 647.5	1 695.8	1 739.5	1 728.4	1 752.6	1 676.4	1 548.5	1 478.4
Machinery	1 407.8	1 345.8	1 309.1	1 328.8	1 379.2	1 440.2	1 466.8	1 493.7	1 511.9	1 466.1	1 454.7	1 368.3	1 229.5	1 153.5
Computer and electronic products [1]	1 902.5	1 809.3	1 707.3	1 656.0	1 651.1	1 688.4	1 746.6	1 803.3	1 830.9	1 780.5	1 820.0	1 748.8	1 507.2	1 360.9
Computer and peripheral equipment	367.4	348.6	328.5	305.7	297.7	295.6	304.6	316.7	322.1	310.1	301.9	286.2	250.0	225.7
Communications equipment	231.5	220.6	209.7	210.3	218.0	232.8	237.6	243.9	246.4	237.4	247.7	233.9	185.8	157.0
Semiconductors and electronic components	574.0	546.6	519.4	519.4	535.4	571.0	606.6	639.8	649.8	630.5	676.3	645.4	524.5	461.8
Electronic instruments	626.3	590.0	548.5	517.6	493.4	482.0	489.1	493.9	500.2	489.6	478.6	475.1	450.0	429.3
Electrical equipment and appliances	633.1	597.7	579.4	575.8	588.5	592.8	591.0	586.3	591.6	588.0	590.9	556.9	496.5	459.9
Transportation equipment	2 133.3	2 028.2	1 976.9	1 913.7	1 936.1	1 977.2	1 973.7	2 026.2	2 077.0	2 087.3	2 055.8	1 937.9	1 828.9	1 775.4
Furniture and related products	601.4	561.0	562.8	575.4	600.2	606.7	603.8	615.1	641.2	664.8	679.7	642.4	604.1	573.5
Miscellaneous manufacturing	690.4	686.6	692.5	707.4	713.8	714.5	715.6	723.1	731.7	729.0	733.0	714.5	688.3	662.8
Nondurable goods	6 959	6 849	6 854	6 873	6 890	6 869	6 752	6 716	6 650	6 492	6 388	6 107	5 775	5 555
Food manufacturing	1 507.3	1 515.2	1 518.3	1 534.6	1 539.2	1 540.0	1 560.0	1 562.0	1 557.9	1 554.9	1 549.8	1 553.1	1 551.2	1 525.7	1 518.7
Beverages and tobacco products	217.7	214.7	208.5	207.1	204.6	202.6	204.4	206.3	208.9	208.3	207.0	209.0	207.4	200.6
Textile mills	491.8	479.9	479.0	478.7	477.6	468.5	443.2	436.2	424.5	397.1	378.2	332.9	290.9	260.3
Textile product mills	209.3	199.4	202.0	207.3	218.6	219.0	216.3	217.0	217.1	217.3	216.1	205.7	194.6	179.8
Apparel	929.1	902.6	905.2	882.5	856.3	814.1	743.1	700.2	639.0	555.6	496.8	426.5	359.7	312.7
Leather and allied products	133.2	124.4	120.8	118.1	113.9	104.9	94.2	89.5	82.9	74.9	68.8	58.0	50.2	45.2
Paper and paper products	647.2	638.5	639.6	639.7	639.4	639.5	631.4	630.6	624.9	615.6	604.7	577.6	546.6	519.0
Printing and related support activities	808.6	792.3	780.2	785.2	802.2	817.3	815.8	821.1	827.9	814.6	806.8	768.4	706.6	680.0
Petroleum and coal products	152.8	154.8	152.3	146.2	144.0	140.4	137.3	136.0	134.5	127.8	123.2	121.1	118.1	114.6
Chemicals	1 035.7	1 024.1	1 028.9	1 024.9	1 004.7	987.9	984.5	986.8	992.6	982.5	980.4	959.0	927.5	907.9
Plastics and rubber products	825.9	803.2	819.0	849.0	889.4	915.1	920.1	934.1	942.8	948.3	952.2	897.4	848.0	815.9
Service-providing	85 764	85 787	86 631	88 625	91 517	94 142	96 299	98 890	101 576	104 528	107 136	107 952	107 784	108 114
Private service-providing	67 349	67 241	67 845	69 636	72 242	74 710	76 759	79 227	81 667	84 221	86 346	86 834	86 271	86 538
Trade, transportation, and utilities	22 666	22 281	22 125	22 378	23 128	23 834	24 239	24 700	25 186	25 771	26 225	25 983	25 497	25 275
Wholesale trade	5 268.4	5 185.3	5 109.7	5 093.2	5 247.3	5 433.1	5 522.0	5 663.9	5 795.2	5 892.5	5 933.2	5 772.7	5 652.3	5 605.6
Durable goods	2 833.7	2 766.6	2 698.8	2 687.0	2 786.0	2 908.8	2 977.8	3 071.9	3 162.4	3 219.6	3 250.7	3 130.4	3 007.9	2 949.2
Nondurable goods	1 900.2	1 891.3	1 891.5	1 888.3	1 927.0	1 969.3	1 977.5	2 007.9	2 032.7	2 061.2	2 064.8	2 031.3	2 015.0	2 002.1
Electronic markets, agents, and brokers	534.5	527.4	519.4	517.9	534.4	555.0	566.7	584.1	600.1	611.8	617.7	611.1	629.4	654.3

[1] Includes other industries, not shown separately.

Table 16-1. Nonfarm Employment by NAICS Sector and Industry—Continued

(Wage and salary workers on nonfarm payrolls, thousands.)

Industry	1990	1991	1992	1993	1994	1995	1996	1997	1998	1999	2000	2001	2002	2003
Retail trade	13 182.3	12 896.4	12 827.9	13 020.5	13 490.8	13 896.7	14 142.5	14 388.9	14 609.3	14 970.1	15 279.8	15 238.6	15 025.1	14 911.5
Motor vehicle and parts dealers [1]	1 494.4	1 435.1	1 428.1	1 475.3	1 564.7	1 627.1	1 685.6	1 723.4	1 740.9	1 796.6	1 846.9	1 854.6	1 879.4	1 883.5
Automobile dealers	983.3	938.3	934.8	970.4	1 031.8	1 071.6	1 113.0	1 134.5	1 142.0	1 179.7	1 216.5	1 225.1	1 252.8	1 255.1
Furniture and home furnishings stores	431.5	412.8	410.3	418.6	441.6	461.2	474.2	484.7	499.1	524.4	543.5	541.2	538.7	542.9
Electronics and appliance stores	382.3	381.1	378.1	386.9	417.0	448.7	470.2	494.0	510.2	542.2	564.4	554.5	525.3	511.9
Building material and garden supply stores	891	863	872	892	946	982	1 007	1 043	1 062	1 101	1 142	1 152	1 176	1 191
Food and beverage stores	2 778.8	2 767.9	2 743.9	2 774.8	2 825.0	2 879.8	2 927.8	2 956.9	2 965.7	2 984.5	2 993.0	2 950.5	2 881.6	2 840.9
Health and personal care stores	792.0	788.5	780.2	778.6	797.0	811.9	826.4	853.3	876.0	898.2	927.6	951.5	938.8	943.0
Gasoline stations	910.2	889.3	876.4	881.2	902.3	922.3	946.4	956.2	961.3	943.5	935.7	925.3	895.9	879.9
Clothing and clothing accessories stores	1 313.0	1 275.8	1 249.1	1 259.9	1 261.7	1 246.3	1 220.6	1 235.9	1 268.6	1 306.6	1 321.6	1 321.1	1 312.5	1 296.7
Sporting goods, hobby, book, and music stores	532.0	527.7	534.4	545.2	577.6	605.8	614.0	626.2	635.4	664.3	685.7	679.2	661.3	645.0
General merchandise stores [1]	2 499.8	2 416.7	2 414.2	2 450.2	2 541.0	2 635.4	2 657.3	2 657.6	2 686.5	2 751.8	2 819.8	2 842.2	2 812.0	2 815.2
Department stores	1 493.9	1 440.8	1 445.2	1 486.8	1 560.4	1 629.8	1 645.0	1 653.5	1 679.2	1 709.2	1 755.0	1 768.3	1 684.0	1 618.8
Miscellaneous store retailers	738.2	734.7	736.8	752.9	795.7	841.1	874.3	913.2	950.3	985.5	1 007.1	993.3	959.5	934.1
Nonstore retailers	419.2	403.7	404.5	404.9	421.2	435.4	438.5	444.5	453.0	471.6	492.4	473.5	443.7	427.5
Transportation and warehousing	3 475.6	3 462.8	3 461.8	3 553.8	3 701.0	3 837.8	3 935.3	4 026.5	4 168.0	4 300.3	4 410.3	4 372.0	4 223.6	4 176.7
Air transportation	529.2	525.4	519.6	516.6	511.2	510.9	525.7	542.0	562.7	586.3	614.4	615.3	563.5	527.3
Rail transportation	271.8	255.6	248.1	242.2	234.6	232.5	225.2	221.0	225.0	228.8	231.7	226.7	217.8	215.4
Water transportation	56.8	57.4	56.7	52.8	52.3	50.8	51.0	50.7	50.5	51.7	56.0	54.0	52.6	52.5
Truck transportation	1 122.4	1 104.6	1 107.4	1 154.8	1 206.2	1 249.1	1 282.4	1 308.2	1 354.4	1 391.5	1 405.8	1 386.8	1 339.3	1 328.0
Transit and ground passenger transportation	274.2	283.9	287.9	299.9	316.6	327.9	339.1	349.6	362.7	371.0	372.1	374.8	380.8	380.3
Pipeline transportation	59.8	60.7	60.1	58.7	57.0	53.6	51.4	49.7	48.1	46.9	46.0	45.4	41.7	40.0
Scenic and sightseeing transportation	15.7	16.5	17.7	19.3	21.3	22.0	23.2	24.5	25.4	26.1	27.5	29.1	25.6	28.0
Support activities for transportation	364.1	376.6	369.9	381.8	404.7	430.4	445.8	473.4	496.8	518.1	537.4	539.2	524.7	516.3
Couriers and messengers	375.0	378.9	388.8	414.3	466.2	516.8	539.9	546.0	568.2	585.9	605.0	587.0	560.9	566.6
Warehousing and storage	406.6	403.2	405.6	413.4	431.0	443.8	451.8	461.5	474.2	494.1	514.4	513.8	516.7	522.3
Utilities	740.0	736.1	726.0	710.7	689.3	666.2	639.6	620.9	613.4	608.5	601.3	599.4	596.2	580.8
Information	2 688	2 677	2 641	2 668	2 738	2 843	2 940	3 084	3 218	3 419	3 631	3 629	3 395	3 198
Publishing industries, except Internet	870.6	863.4	854.2	873.1	891.0	910.7	927.2	955.5	982.3	1 004.8	1 035.0	1 020.7	964.1	926.4
Motion picture and sound recording industries	254.6	258.9	254.3	259.6	278.4	311.1	334.7	353.0	369.5	384.4	382.6	376.8	387.9	376.1
Broadcasting, except Internet	283.8	281.2	279.7	284.0	290.1	298.1	309.1	313.0	321.2	329.4	343.5	344.6	334.1	327.0
Internet publishing and broadcasting	16.7	16.2	16.1	16.4	16.9	18.6	21.0	23.5	27.1	37.1	50.5	45.5	33.7	30.0
Telecommunications	980.3	973.1	946.0	942.2	961.1	975.7	997.0	1 059.5	1 107.8	1 179.7	1 262.6	1 302.1	1 186.5	1 082.6
ISPs, search portals, and data processing	252.2	251.7	258.5	263.1	268.0	291.2	311.6	338.8	369.1	439.3	510.1	493.6	441.0	407.5
Other information services	29.9	32.9	32.3	29.4	32.8	38.2	39.4	40.1	41.4	43.8	46.2	46.1	47.3	48.1
Financial activities	6 614	6 558	6 540	6 709	6 867	6 827	6 969	7 178	7 462	7 648	7 687	7 807	7 847	7 974
Finance and insurance	4 978.6	4 937.3	4 914.7	5 035.5	5 135.2	5 071.7	5 154.2	5 305.1	5 532.0	5 668.4	5 680.4	5 773.1	5 817.3	5 920.5
Monetary authorities-central bank	24.0	24.2	23.7	23.4	23.4	23.0	22.8	22.1	21.7	22.6	22.8	23.0	23.4	22.7
Credit intermediation and related activities [1]	2 424.8	2 352.4	2 317.3	2 360.7	2 375.7	2 314.4	2 368.2	2 433.6	2 531.9	2 591.0	2 547.8	2 597.7	2 686.0	2 785.6
Depository credit intermediation [1]	1 908.5	1 830.7	1 769.0	1 760.5	1 736.7	1 700.2	1 691.4	1 696.6	1 708.9	1 709.7	1 681.2	1 701.2	1 733.0	1 752.1
Commercial banking	1 361.8	1 333.7	1 302.8	1 308.7	1 297.4	1 281.7	1 275.1	1 277.9	1 286.0	1 281.2	1 250.5	1 258.4	1 278.1	1 281.1
Securities, commodity contracts, investments	457.9	455.0	475.7	507.9	553.4	562.2	589.6	636.1	692.2	737.3	804.5	830.5	789.4	764.4
Insurance carriers and related activities	2 016.1	2 048.2	2 039.5	2 082.5	2 118.8	2 108.2	2 108.0	2 143.6	2 209.4	2 236.1	2 220.6	2 233.7	2 233.2	2 266.1
Funds, trusts, and other financial vehicles	55.7	57.5	58.5	61.0	63.9	63.9	65.6	69.8	76.9	81.5	84.8	88.3	85.4	81.7
Real estate and rental and leasing	1 634.9	1 620.8	1 625.5	1 673.8	1 731.5	1 755.4	1 814.3	1 872.8	1 930.3	1 979.0	2 006.8	2 034.5	2 029.6	2 053.6
Real estate	1 106.8	1 107.6	1 114.5	1 146.1	1 183.2	1 178.9	1 205.8	1 240.7	1 274.2	1 299.0	1 312.2	1 339.5	1 352.9	1 384.4
Rental and leasing services	514.2	499.4	496.4	511.0	529.9	557.4	587.7	609.5	630.8	653.1	666.8	666.3	649.1	640.8
Lessors of nonfinancial intangible assets	13.9	13.9	14.6	16.7	18.4	19.0	20.8	22.6	25.3	26.8	27.8	28.7	27.6	28.4

[1] Includes other industries, not shown separately.

Table 16-1. Nonfarm Employment by NAICS Sector and Industry—Continued

(Wage and salary workers on nonfarm payrolls, thousands.)

Industry	1990	1991	1992	1993	1994	1995	1996	1997	1998	1999	2000	2001	2002	2003
Professional and business services	10 848	10 714	10 970	11 495	12 174	12 844	13 462	14 335	15 147	15 957	16 666	16 476	15 976	15 997
Professional and technical services [1]	4 556.7	4 526.5	4 593.5	4 708.2	4 843.6	5 101.3	5 337.1	5 655.5	6 021.0	6 375.4	6 733.9	6 902.2	6 675.6	6 623.5
Legal services	943.6	946.0	949.8	963.9	965.6	959.2	968.4	987.5	1 021.1	1 051.4	1 065.7	1 091.3	1 115.3	1 136.8
Accounting and bookkeeping services	664.1	655.4	657.8	654.2	670.1	706.3	729.8	761.2	802.0	837.6	866.4	872.2	837.3	815.6
Architectural and engineering services	941.5	906.2	901.8	922.7	952.0	997.1	1 024.5	1 063.4	1 114.8	1 168.1	1 237.9	1 274.7	1 246.1	1 228.0
Computer systems design and related services	409.7	419.9	444.9	484.8	531.4	611.2	701.4	826.7	974.9	1 132.9	1 254.3	1 297.8	1 152.8	1 108.9
Management and technical consulting services	323.6	331.6	358.1	385.4	416.8	474.8	517.1	568.4	619.2	649.0	704.9	746.2	734.4	747.3
Management of companies and enterprises	1 667.4	1 638.1	1 623.4	1 640.1	1 665.9	1 685.8	1 702.7	1 729.7	1 756.1	1 773.8	1 796.0	1 779.0	1 705.4	1 675.5
Administrative and waste services	4 624.3	4 549.3	4 752.6	5 146.5	5 664.1	6 056.8	6 422.1	6 949.9	7 369.3	7 807.4	8 136.0	7 794.9	7 595.2	7 698.3
Administrative and support services [1]	4 394.9	4 317.0	4 515.9	4 897.8	5 403.4	5 783.4	6 140.0	6 659.4	7 069.9	7 496.9	7 823.1	7 477.6	7 276.8	7 376.4
Employment services [1]	1 493.7	1 448.7	1 592.5	1 865.1	2 226.5	2 425.2	2 600.8	2 927.2	3 217.0	3 551.5	3 817.0	3 437.1	3 246.5	3 336.2
Temporary help services	1 155.8	1 123.1	1 212.5	1 388.8	1 632.4	1 743.8	1 849.0	2 059.7	2 245.2	2 469.6	2 635.6	2 337.7	2 193.7	2 243.2
Business support services	504.6	503.3	524.5	549.0	574.4	629.8	678.3	733.9	772.2	780.5	786.7	779.7	756.6	747.4
Services to buildings and dwellings	1 174.6	1 150.9	1 159.7	1 197.9	1 267.4	1 302.4	1 361.5	1 424.1	1 460.0	1 534.7	1 570.5	1 606.2	1 606.1	1 631.7
Waste management and remediation services	229.4	232.4	236.7	248.6	260.7	273.3	282.0	290.5	299.3	310.5	312.9	317.3	318.3	321.9
Education and health services	10 984	11 506	11 891	12 303	12 807	13 289	13 683	14 087	14 446	14 798	15 109	15 645	16 199	16 577
Educational services	1 688.0	1 736.6	1 713.1	1 755.4	1 894.9	2 010.2	2 077.6	2 155.0	2 232.9	2 320.4	2 390.4	2 510.6	2 642.8	2 688.5
Health care and social assistance	9 295.8	9 769.8	10 178.0	10 548.1	10 911.7	11 278.4	11 604.9	11 932.2	12 213.5	12 477.1	12 718.0	13 134.0	13 555.7	13 888.0
Ambulatory health care services [1]	2 842	3 028	3 200	3 386	3 579	3 768	3 940	4 093	4 161	4 227	4 320	4 462	4 633.2	4 776
Offices of physicians	1 278.0	1 345.2	1 401.1	1 442.0	1 480.9	1 540.4	1 603.8	1 660.5	1 723.6	1 786.6	1 839.9	1 911.2	1 967.8	2 003.8
Outpatient care centers	260.5	271.4	286.5	303.1	314.5	328.8	340.2	352.1	363.3	375.4	386.4	399.7	413.0	423.2
Home health care services	287.5	340.7	393.4	463.8	553.2	621.8	667.2	702.8	659.5	629.6	633.3	638.6	679.8	727.1
Hospitals	3 512.6	3 617.3	3 711.4	3 740.0	3 724.0	3 733.7	3 772.8	3 821.6	3 892.4	3 935.5	3 954.3	4 050.9	4 159.6	4 252.5
Nursing and residential care facilities [1]	1 856.4	1 972.0	2 043.5	2 128.1	2 227.0	2 307.7	2 379.9	2 443.4	2 487.3	2 528.8	2 583.2	2 675.8	2 743.3	2 784.3
Nursing care facilities	1 169.8	1 240.2	1 273.4	1 319.3	1 377.1	1 413.0	1 448.4	1 474.6	1 489.3	1 501.0	1 513.6	1 546.8	1 573.2	1 582.8
Social assistance [1]	1 085.1	1 152.2	1 223.3	1 294.4	1 381.9	1 469.5	1 512.3	1 574.2	1 672.6	1 786.2	1 860.2	1 945.9	2 019.7	2 075.2
Child day care services	387.8	413.2	446.5	468.9	510.0	557.1	559.2	570.4	615.1	673.7	695.8	714.6	744.1	760.5
Leisure and hospitality	9 288	9 256	9 437	9 732	10 100	10 501	10 777	11 018	11 232	11 543	11 862	12 036	11 986	12 125
Arts, entertainment, and recreation	1 132	1 177	1 236	1 302	1 376	1 459	1 522	1 600	1 645	1 709	1 788	1 824	1 783	1 801
Performing arts and spectator sports	272.7	282.7	289.5	286.8	296.1	307.7	328.6	349.6	350.0	361.1	381.8	382.3	363.7	370.2
Museums, historical sites, zoos, and parks	68.0	71.0	75.0	78.3	81.8	83.9	88.9	93.8	97.4	103.1	110.4	115.0	114.0	114.1
Amusements, gambling, and recreation	791.3	823.4	871.8	936.8	997.7	1 067.8	1 104.5	1 156.5	1 197.9	1 244.9	1 295.7	1 327.1	1 305.0	1 316.6
Accommodations and food service	8 155.6	8 078.9	8 200.5	8 430.4	8 724.1	9 041.6	9 254.3	9 417.9	9 586.2	9 833.7	10 073.5	10 211.3	10 203.2	10 324.4
Accommodations	1 616.0	1 574.3	1 561.5	1 580.5	1 615.3	1 652.5	1 698.9	1 729.5	1 773.5	1 831.7	1 884.4	1 852.2	1 778.6	1 765.2
Food services and drinking places	6 539.6	6 504.6	6 639.0	6 849.9	7 108.7	7 389.1	7 555.4	7 688.5	7 812.7	8 002.0	8 189.1	8 359.1	8 424.6	8 559.2
Other services	4 261	4 249	4 240	4 350	4 428	4 572	4 690	4 825	4 976	5 087	5 168	5 258	5 372	5 393
Repair and maintenance	1 009.0	960.0	964.0	998.0	1 023.5	1 078.9	1 135.5	1 169.3	1 189.2	1 222.0	1 241.5	1 256.5	1 246.9	1 236.2
Personal and laundry service	1 119.9	1 109.2	1 098.9	1 116.0	1 120.3	1 143.9	1 165.7	1 180.4	1 205.6	1 220.3	1 242.9	1 255.0	1 257.2	1 258.2
Membership associations and organizations	2 132.2	2 179.5	2 177.1	2 236.4	2 284.5	2 348.9	2 389.1	2 474.9	2 581.3	2 644.4	2 683.3	2 746.4	2 867.8	2 898.0
Government	18 415	18 545	18 787	18 989	19 275	19 432	19 539	19 664	19 909	20 307	20 790	21 118	21 513	21 575
Federal	3 196	3 110	3 111	3 063	3 018	2 949	2 877	2 806	2 772	2 769	2 865	2 764	2 766	2 756
Federal, except U.S. Postal Service	2 370.5	2 296.2	2 310.7	2 269.4	2 197.2	2 098.8	2 009.8	1 940.2	1 891.3	1 879.5	1 984.8	1 891.0	1 923.8	1 947.0
U.S. Postal Service	825.1	813.2	800.0	793.2	820.6	849.9	867.2	866.0	880.5	889.7	879.7	873.0	842.4	809.1
State government	4 305	4 355	4 408	4 488	4 576	4 635	4 606	4 582	4 612	4 709	4 786	4 905	5 029	5 017
State government education	1 729.9	1 767.6	1 798.6	1 834.1	1 881.9	1 919.0	1 910.7	1 904.0	1 922.2	1 983.2	2 030.6	2 112.9	2 242.8	2 266.4
State government, excluding education	2 574.6	2 587.3	2 609.7	2 653.8	2 693.6	2 715.5	2 695.1	2 677.9	2 690.2	2 725.6	2 755.9	2 791.8	2 786.3	2 750.7
Local government	10 914	11 081	11 267	11 438	11 682	11 849	12 056	12 276	12 525	12 829	13 139	13 449	13 718	13 802
Local government education	5 902.1	5 994.1	6 075.9	6 206.3	6 329.4	6 453.1	6 592.3	6 758.5	6 920.9	7 120.4	7 293.9	7 479.3	7 654.4	7 698.1
Local government, excluding education	5 012.4	5 086.9	5 191.6	5 231.9	5 352.2	5 396.0	5 464.1	5 516.9	5 603.9	5 708.6	5 844.6	5 970.0	6 063.2	6 104.0

[1] Includes other industries, not shown separately.

Table 16-2. Production or Nonsupervisory Workers on Private Nonfarm Payrolls by NAICS Industry

(Wage and salary workers on nonfarm payrolls, thousands.)

Industry	1990	1991	1992	1993	1994	1995	1996	1997	1998	1999	2000	2001	2002	2003
Total private	73 684	72 520	72 786	74 591	77 382	79 845	81 773	84 158	86 316	88 430	90 336	89 983	88 393	87 606
Goods-producing	17 322	16 352	16 043	16 236	16 795	17 137	17 318	17 698	18 008	18 067	18 169	17 466	16 400	15 731
Natural resources and mining	538	515	478	462	461	458	461	479	473	438	446	457	436	419
Construction	4 115	3 674	3 546	3 704	3 973	4 113	4 325	4 546	4 807	5 105	5 295	5 332	5 196	5 112
Manufacturing	12 669	12 164	12 020	12 070	12 361	12 566	12 532	12 673	12 729	12 524	12 428	11 677	10 768	10 200
Durable goods	7 396	7 000	6 852	6 879	7 132	7 351	7 425	7 597	7 720	7 650	7 658	7 163	6 529	6 157
Wood products	449.9	412.8	417.0	436.8	468.7	477.5	484.9	496.6	507.9	514.4	505.6	468.3	448.7	431.9
Nonmetallic mineral products	413.2	384.1	378.4	380.7	392.3	399.7	404.8	412.5	420.6	426.0	439.5	427.1	398.8	373.6
Primary metals	525.1	496.9	478.7	473.3	487.4	500.3	500.3	501.6	505.3	491.9	490.0	446.9	396.2	369.7
Fabricated metal products	1 190.1	1 131.6	1 101.0	1 116.9	1 172.0	1 223.0	1 241.6	1 285.3	1 319.6	1 304.9	1 325.8	1 253.5	1 147.0	1 092.0
Machinery	937.6	883.6	856.3	874.1	921.1	968.5	983.2	1 005.5	1 014.7	977.0	959.9	889.1	785.4	733.7
Computer and electronic products	980.2	925.6	876.3	856.4	863.9	890.3	915.2	951.1	964.7	932.9	949.3	875.8	744.1	675.8
Electrical equipment and appliances	465.2	435.6	425.0	421.8	434.7	438.4	433.9	427.7	431.8	433.2	433.1	402.2	351.9	319.8
Transportation equipment	1 472.5	1 405.5	1 387.7	1 366.1	1 414.6	1 471.1	1 480.0	1 520.8	1 529.2	1 525.4	1 496.7	1 397.7	1 309.3	1 270.8
Furniture and related products	475.2	440.0	442.8	454.2	475.7	480.0	477.9	489.7	512.1	532.4	544.3	509.0	474.8	444.7
Miscellaneous manufacturing	487.2	484.2	489.1	498.2	502.1	502.2	503.3	506.6	514.3	512.2	513.2	493.1	472.5	444.9
Nondurable goods	5 273	5 164	5 168	5 192	5 229	5 215	5 107	5 076	5 009	4 873	4 770	4 514	4 239	4 043
Food manufacturing	1 165.0	1 174.2	1 182.0	1 195.3	1 200.4	1 221.0	1 227.7	1 227.7	1 227.6	1 228.7	1 227.9	1 221.3	1 202.3	1 193.5
Beverages and tobacco products	117.2	116.9	116.2	117.6	118.2	117.3	120.1	121.4	122.5	120.1	116.9	115.6	119.5	106.9
Textile mills	417.9	407.2	406.0	403.9	403.3	393.2	371.7	367.1	357.4	333.7	315.2	275.8	242.2	216.0
Textile products mills	170.1	160.9	163.0	167.2	176.0	176.3	173.4	174.7	173.9	173.4	171.8	163.9	153.7	141.7
Apparel	830.0	805.1	809.8	788.0	763.1	719.3	650.2	611.5	549.9	471.8	415.4	351.2	294.3	249.0
Leather and allied products	116.6	107.5	104.4	101.4	97.2	88.5	78.5	73.6	67.0	59.9	55.4	46.8	40.0	35.4
Paper and paper products	493.2	488.4	489.9	490.9	492.8	493.8	487.5	488.7	484.1	474.0	467.5	446.3	421.4	394.9
Printing and related support activities	597.6	581.7	573.6	579.7	591.4	599.1	594.0	597.0	598.4	585.1	575.7	544.4	492.6	470.9
Petroleum and coal products	97.5	97.4	96.8	93.0	90.9	88.8	87.2	87.8	87.1	84.6	83.1	80.9	78.0	74.6
Chemicals	620.3	599.7	586.2	590.1	595.6	598.4	595.1	593.3	600.6	595.2	587.7	562.2	531.9	525.4
Plastics and rubber products	647.7	624.8	639.8	664.7	699.6	719.8	721.3	732.7	740.4	747.0	753.6	705.3	662.7	634.7
Private service-providing	56 362	56 168	56 743	58 355	60 587	62 708	64 455	66 460	68 308	70 363	72 167	72 517	71 993	71 875
Trade, transportation, and utilities	19 032	18 640	18 506	18 752	19 392	19 984	20 325	20 698	21 059	21 576	21 965	21 709	21 337	21 066
Wholesale trade	4 198.3	4 122.2	4 070.7	4 072.2	4 196.4	4 360.8	4 423.2	4 523.2	4 605.0	4 673.1	4 686.4	4 555.1	4 473.5	4 394.5
Retail trade	11 308.4	11 007.9	10 931.4	11 104.0	11 502.1	11 841.0	12 056.7	12 273.6	12 439.8	12 771.5	13 039.8	12 952.3	12 774.0	12 648.7
Transportation and warehousing	2 940.8	2 928.4	2 934.3	3 019.4	3 152.8	3 260.2	3 339.3	3 406.8	3 521.6	3 641.9	3 753.2	3 718.2	3 611.3	3 555.5
Utilities	584.9	581.5	569.5	556.5	540.9	521.8	505.5	493.8	492.2	489.2	485.1	482.8	478.4	466.7
Information	1 866	1 871	1 871	1 896	1 928	2 007	2 096	2 181	2 217	2 351	2 502	2 530	2 398	2 354
Financial activities	4 973	4 911	4 908	5 057	5 183	5 165	5 279	5 415	5 605	5 728	5 737	5 810	5 872	5 965
Professional and business services	8 889	8 748	8 971	9 451	10 078	10 645	11 161	11 896	12 566	13 184	13 790	13 588	13 049	12 923
Education and health services	9 748	10 212	10 555	10 908	11 338	11 765	12 123	12 478	12 791	13 089	13 362	13 846	14 311	14 523
Leisure and hospitality	8 299	8 247	8 406	8 667	8 979	9 330	9 565	9 780	9 947	10 216	10 516	10 662	10 576	10 626
Other services	3 555	3 539	3 526	3 623	3 689	3 812	3 907	4 013	4 124	4 219	4 296	4 373	4 449	4 419

Table 16-3. Average Weekly Hours of Production or Nonsupervisory Workers on Private Nonfarm Payrolls by NAICS Industry

Industry	1990	1991	1992	1993	1994	1995	1996	1997	1998	1999	2000	2001	2002	2003
Total private	34.3	34.1	34.2	34.3	34.5	34.3	34.3	34.5	34.5	34.3	34.3	34.0	33.9	33.7
Goods–producing	40.1	40.1	40.2	40.6	41.1	40.8	40.8	41.1	40.8	40.8	40.7	39.9	39.9	39.8
Natural resources and mining	45.0	45.3	44.6	44.9	45.3	45.3	46.0	46.2	44.9	44.2	44.4	44.6	43.2	43.6
Construction	38.3	38.1	38.0	38.4	38.8	38.8	38.9	38.9	38.8	39.0	39.2	38.7	38.4	38.4
Manufacturing	40.5	40.4	40.7	41.1	41.7	41.3	41.3	41.7	41.4	41.4	41.3	40.3	40.5	40.4
Durable goods	41.1	40.9	41.3	41.9	42.6	42.1	42.1	42.6	42.1	41.9	41.8	40.6	40.8	40.8
Wood products	40.4	40.2	40.9	41.2	41.7	41.0	41.2	41.4	41.4	41.3	41.0	40.2	39.9	40.4
Nonmetallic mineral products	40.9	40.5	41.0	41.5	42.2	41.8	42.0	41.9	42.2	42.1	41.6	41.6	42.0	42.2
Primary metals	42.0	41.5	42.4	43.1	44.1	43.4	43.6	44.3	43.5	43.8	44.2	42.4	42.4	42.3
Fabricated metal products	41.0	40.8	41.2	41.6	42.3	41.9	41.9	42.3	41.9	41.7	41.9	40.6	40.6	40.7
Machinery	42.1	41.9	42.4	43.2	43.9	43.5	43.3	44.0	43.3	42.3	42.3	40.9	40.5	40.8
Computer and electronic products	41.3	40.9	41.4	41.8	42.2	42.2	41.9	42.5	41.8	41.5	41.4	39.8	39.7	40.4
Electrical equipment and appliances	41.2	41.5	41.8	42.4	43.0	41.9	42.1	42.1	41.8	41.8	41.6	39.8	40.1	40.6
Transportation equipment	42.0	41.9	41.9	43.0	44.3	43.7	43.8	44.2	43.6	43.3	43.3	41.9	42.5	41.9
Furniture and related products	38.0	37.8	38.7	39.0	39.3	38.5	38.3	39.1	39.4	39.3	39.2	38.3	39.2	38.9
Miscellaneous manufacturing	39.0	39.1	39.3	39.2	39.4	39.2	39.1	39.7	39.2	39.3	39.0	38.8	38.6	38.4
Nondurable goods	39.6	39.7	40.0	40.1	40.5	40.1	40.1	40.5	40.5	40.4	40.3	39.9	40.1	39.8
Food manufacturing	39.3	39.2	39.2	39.3	39.8	39.6	39.5	39.8	40.1	40.2	40.1	39.6	39.6	39.3
Beverages and tobacco products	38.9	38.8	38.7	38.3	39.3	39.3	39.7	40.0	40.3	41.0	42.0	40.9	39.4	39.1
Textile mills	40.2	40.7	41.3	41.6	41.9	40.9	40.8	41.6	41.0	41.0	41.4	40.0	40.6	39.1
Textile products mills	39.0	39.1	39.2	39.8	39.9	39.1	39.2	39.6	39.5	39.4	39.0	38.6	39.2	39.6
Apparel	34.8	35.4	35.6	35.5	35.7	35.3	35.2	35.5	35.5	35.4	35.7	36.0	36.7	35.6
Leather and allied products	37.4	37.6	37.9	38.4	38.2	37.7	37.8	38.2	37.4	37.2	37.5	36.4	37.5	39.3
Paper and paper products	43.6	43.6	43.8	43.8	44.2	43.4	43.5	43.9	43.6	43.6	42.8	42.1	41.9	41.5
Printing and related support activities	38.7	38.6	39.0	39.2	39.6	39.1	39.1	39.5	39.3	39.1	39.2	38.7	38.4	38.2
Petroleum and coal products	44.4	43.9	43.6	44.0	44.3	43.7	43.7	43.1	43.6	42.6	42.7	43.8	43.0	44.5
Chemicals	42.8	43.1	43.3	43.2	43.4	43.3	43.3	43.4	43.2	42.7	42.2	41.9	42.3	42.4
Plastics and rubber products	40.6	40.5	41.2	41.4	41.8	41.1	41.0	41.4	41.3	41.3	40.8	40.0	40.6	40.4
Private service–providing	32.5	32.4	32.5	32.5	32.7	32.6	32.6	32.8	32.8	32.7	32.7	32.5	32.5	32.4
Trade, transportation, and utilities	33.7	33.7	33.8	34.1	34.3	34.1	34.1	34.3	34.2	33.9	33.8	33.5	33.6	33.6
Wholesale trade	38.4	38.4	38.6	38.5	38.8	38.6	38.6	38.8	38.6	38.6	38.8	38.4	38.0	37.8
Retail trade	30.6	30.4	30.7	30.7	30.9	30.8	30.7	30.9	30.9	30.8	30.7	30.7	30.9	30.9
Transportation and warehousing	37.7	37.4	37.4	38.9	39.5	38.9	39.1	39.4	38.7	37.6	37.4	36.7	36.8	36.8
Utilities	41.5	41.5	41.7	42.1	42.3	42.3	42.0	42.0	42.0	42.0	42.0	41.4	40.9	41.1
Information	35.8	35.6	35.8	36.0	36.0	36.0	36.4	36.3	36.6	36.7	36.8	36.9	36.5	36.2
Financial activities	35.5	35.5	35.6	35.5	35.5	35.5	35.5	35.7	36.0	35.8	35.9	35.8	35.6	35.5
Professional and business services	34.2	34.0	34.0	34.0	34.1	34.0	34.1	34.3	34.3	34.4	34.5	34.2	34.2	34.1
Education and health services	31.9	31.9	32.0	32.0	32.0	32.0	31.9	32.2	32.2	32.1	32.2	32.3	32.4	32.3
Leisure and hospitality	26.0	25.6	25.7	25.9	26.0	25.9	25.9	26.0	26.2	26.1	26.1	25.8	25.8	25.6
Other services	32.8	32.7	32.6	32.6	32.7	32.6	32.5	32.7	32.6	32.5	32.5	32.3	32.0	31.4

Table 16-4. Average Hourly Earnings of Production or Nonsupervisory Workers on Private Nonfarm Payrolls by NAICS Industry

(Dollars.)

Industry	1990	1991	1992	1993	1994	1995	1996	1997	1998	1999	2000	2001	2002	2003
Total private	10.19	10.50	10.76	11.03	11.32	11.64	12.03	12.49	13.00	13.47	14.00	14.53	14.95	15.35
Goods–producing	11.46	11.76	11.99	12.28	12.63	12.96	13.38	13.82	14.23	14.71	15.27	15.78	16.33	16.80
Natural resources and mining	13.40	13.82	14.09	14.12	14.41	14.78	15.10	15.57	16.20	16.33	16.55	17.00	17.19	17.58
Construction	13.42	13.65	13.81	14.04	14.38	14.73	15.11	15.67	16.23	16.80	17.48	18.00	18.52	18.95
Manufacturing	10.78	11.13	11.40	11.70	12.04	12.34	12.75	13.14	13.45	13.85	14.32	14.76	15.29	15.74
Durable goods	11.40	11.81	12.09	12.41	12.78	13.05	13.45	13.83	14.07	14.46	14.93	15.38	16.02	16.46
Wood products	8.82	9.03	9.24	9.41	9.66	9.92	10.24	10.53	10.85	11.18	11.63	11.99	12.33	12.71
Nonmetallic mineral products	11.11	11.34	11.57	11.83	12.11	12.39	12.80	13.17	13.59	13.97	14.53	14.86	15.40	15.77
Primary metals	12.97	13.37	13.72	14.08	14.47	14.75	15.12	15.40	15.66	16.00	16.64	17.06	17.68	18.13
Fabricated metal products	10.64	10.97	11.16	11.40	11.64	11.91	12.26	12.64	12.97	13.34	13.77	14.19	14.68	15.01
Machinery	11.73	12.12	12.40	12.73	12.94	13.14	13.49	13.94	14.24	14.77	15.22	15.49	15.92	16.30
Computer and electronic products	10.89	11.35	11.64	11.95	12.19	12.29	12.75	13.24	13.85	14.37	14.73	15.42	16.20	16.68
Electrical equipment and appliances	10.00	10.30	10.50	10.70	10.90	11.30	11.80	12.20	12.50	12.90	13.20	13.78	13.98	14.35
Transportation equipment	14.44	15.12	15.59	16.22	16.94	17.21	17.67	18.00	17.92	18.24	18.89	19.48	20.64	21.25
Furniture and related products	8.52	8.74	9.00	9.24	9.51	9.75	10.08	10.50	10.88	11.27	11.72	12.14	12.61	12.98
Miscellaneous manufacturing	8.87	9.16	9.44	9.65	9.90	10.23	10.60	10.89	11.18	11.56	11.93	12.46	12.91	13.30
Nondurable goods	9.87	10.18	10.45	10.70	10.96	11.30	11.68	12.04	12.45	12.85	13.31	13.75	14.15	14.63
Food manufacturing	9.04	9.32	9.59	9.82	10.00	10.27	10.50	10.77	11.09	11.40	11.77	12.18	12.55	12.80
Beverages and tobacco products	13.24	13.65	14.07	14.30	14.97	15.40	15.73	16.00	16.03	16.54	17.40	17.67	17.73	17.96
Textile mills	8.17	8.49	8.82	9.12	9.35	9.63	9.88	10.22	10.58	10.90	11.23	11.40	11.73	12.00
Textile products mills	7.53	7.77	8.03	8.27	8.45	8.76	9.12	9.45	9.75	10.18	10.43	10.60	10.96	11.24
Apparel	6.22	6.43	6.60	6.74	6.95	7.22	7.45	7.76	8.05	8.35	8.60	8.82	9.10	9.56
Leather and allied products	7.18	7.43	7.68	7.88	8.23	8.50	8.94	9.31	9.68	9.93	10.35	10.69	11.00	11.67
Paper and paper products	12.06	12.45	12.78	13.13	13.49	13.94	14.38	14.76	15.20	15.58	15.91	16.38	16.85	17.32
Printing and related support activities	11.11	11.32	11.53	11.67	11.89	12.08	12.41	12.78	13.20	13.67	14.09	14.48	14.93	15.37
Petroleum and coal products	17.00	17.90	18.83	19.43	19.96	20.24	20.18	21.10	21.75	22.22	22.80	22.90	23.04	23.64
Chemicals	12.85	13.30	13.70	13.97	14.33	14.86	15.37	15.78	16.23	16.40	17.09	17.57	17.97	18.52
Plastics and rubber products	9.76	10.07	10.35	10.55	10.66	10.86	11.17	11.48	11.79	12.25	12.69	13.21	13.55	14.18
Private service–providing	9.71	10.05	10.33	10.60	10.87	11.19	11.57	12.05	12.59	13.07	13.60	14.16	14.56	14.96
Trade, transportation, and utilities	9.83	10.08	10.30	10.55	10.80	11.10	11.46	11.90	12.39	12.82	13.31	13.70	14.02	14.34
Wholesale trade	11.58	11.95	12.21	12.57	12.93	13.34	13.80	14.41	15.07	15.62	16.28	16.77	16.98	17.36
Retail trade	7.71	7.89	8.12	8.36	8.61	8.85	9.21	9.59	10.05	10.45	10.86	11.29	11.67	11.90
Transportation and warehousing	12.50	12.61	12.77	12.71	12.84	13.18	13.45	13.78	14.12	14.55	15.05	15.33	15.76	16.25
Utilities	16.14	16.70	17.17	17.95	18.66	19.19	19.78	20.59	21.48	22.03	22.75	23.58	23.96	24.76
Information	13.40	13.90	14.29	14.86	15.32	15.68	16.30	17.14	17.67	18.40	19.07	19.80	20.20	21.01
Financial activities	9.99	10.42	10.86	11.36	11.82	12.28	12.71	13.22	13.93	14.47	14.98	15.59	16.17	17.13
Professional and business services	11.14	11.50	11.78	11.96	12.15	12.53	13.00	13.57	14.27	14.85	15.52	16.33	16.81	17.20
Education and health services	10.00	10.49	10.87	11.21	11.50	11.80	12.17	12.56	13.00	13.44	13.95	14.64	15.21	15.64
Leisure and hospitality	5.88	6.06	6.20	6.32	6.46	6.62	6.82	7.13	7.48	7.76	8.11	8.35	8.58	8.76
Other services	9.08	9.39	9.66	9.90	10.18	10.51	10.85	11.29	11.79	12.26	12.73	13.27	13.72	13.84

Table 16-5. Average Weekly Earnings of Production or Nonsupervisory Workers on Private Nonfarm Payrolls by NAICS Industry

(Dollars.)

Industry	1990	1991	1992	1993	1994	1995	1996	1997	1998	1999	2000	2001	2002	2003
Total private	349.29	358.06	367.83	378.40	390.73	399.53	412.74	431.25	448.04	462.49	480.41	493.20	506.07	517.36
Goods–producing	459.55	471.32	482.58	498.82	519.58	528.62	546.48	568.43	580.99	599.99	621.86	630.04	651.61	669.23
Natural resources and mining	602.54	625.42	629.02	634.77	653.14	670.32	695.07	720.11	727.28	721.74	734.92	757.92	741.97	766.83
Construction	513.43	520.41	525.13	539.81	558.53	571.57	588.48	609.48	629.75	655.11	685.78	695.89	711.82	727.11
Manufacturing	436.16	449.73	464.43	480.80	502.12	509.26	526.55	548.22	557.12	573.17	590.65	595.19	618.75	636.07
Durable goods	468.43	483.28	499.59	519.92	544.66	549.49	566.53	589.10	591.68	606.67	624.38	624.54	652.97	671.53
Wood products	356.38	362.69	377.76	387.38	402.86	406.51	422.32	435.78	449.78	461.61	477.23	481.36	492.00	513.92
Nonmetallic mineral products	453.98	459.20	474.55	490.54	510.92	517.68	537.81	552.02	572.96	587.53	604.88	618.79	646.91	665.11
Primary metals	545.22	555.37	581.34	606.37	637.69	639.70	658.68	681.47	681.64	700.76	734.62	723.95	749.32	767.63
Fabricated metal products	436.12	447.98	459.64	474.21	492.07	498.48	513.57	534.48	543.20	555.86	576.68	576.60	596.38	610.33
Machinery	493.39	507.96	525.53	549.98	568.12	571.25	584.69	613.49	613.87	625.40	643.92	632.77	645.55	664.79
Computer and electronic products	450.09	464.25	482.09	499.15	514.92	518.25	534.42	562.69	579.70	596.25	609.70	613.07	642.87	674.68
Electrical equipment and appliances	412.42	426.96	439.04	451.28	470.21	471.63	496.69	515.73	522.51	538.98	550.56	548.00	560.24	582.68
Transportation equipment	606.87	633.87	652.95	697.16	750.67	751.74	773.95	795.82	774.82	796.25	817.98	817.08	877.87	890.32
Furniture and related products	324.08	330.49	348.03	360.63	373.87	375.06	385.68	410.38	428.50	443.38	459.69	464.57	494.01	505.23
Miscellaneous manufacturing	346.02	358.56	370.75	378.28	389.79	400.85	414.13	431.89	437.99	454.56	465.02	483.44	499.13	510.69
Nondurable goods	390.65	404.17	417.95	429.15	443.82	452.83	467.88	487.04	503.99	519.91	536.82	548.41	566.84	582.65
Food manufacturing	355.61	364.90	375.69	386.04	398.54	406.66	414.74	428.58	444.81	458.63	472.09	481.67	496.91	502.65
Beverages and tobacco products	515.73	530.09	544.25	547.60	588.39	605.00	624.82	639.69	646.26	679.06	730.35	721.68	698.39	702.75
Textile mills	328.11	345.48	364.45	379.74	391.64	394.17	403.08	425.53	434.15	447.38	464.51	456.64	476.52	469.47
Textile products mills	293.77	303.81	314.47	329.26	336.96	342.17	356.90	373.95	385.13	401.01	406.24	408.56	429.01	445.08
Apparel	216.10	227.76	235.20	239.45	248.33	254.85	261.90	275.61	286.07	295.20	307.00	317.15	333.66	340.22
Leather and allied products	268.32	279.41	291.11	302.85	314.18	319.98	337.86	355.63	361.87	369.80	388.46	388.83	412.99	458.26
Paper and paper products	525.71	542.26	560.27	575.49	596.19	604.74	625.38	647.55	662.20	679.24	681.34	690.06	705.62	719.21
Printing and related support activities	429.93	437.00	450.02	457.91	470.74	472.37	484.99	504.46	518.32	534.15	552.15	560.89	573.05	587.42
Petroleum and coal products	754.13	786.05	821.72	855.36	883.81	883.68	881.24	908.50	949.28	947.60	973.53	1 003.34	990.88	1 052.97
Chemicals	550.25	573.27	593.17	603.71	622.46	644.30	666.00	685.26	700.53	700.45	721.90	735.54	759.53	784.56
Plastics and rubber products	396.07	408.22	426.56	436.96	445.87	445.91	458.15	474.87	487.00	505.31	517.74	528.69	549.85	572.23
Private service–providing	315.49	325.31	335.46	345.03	354.97	364.14	376.72	394.77	412.78	427.30	445.00	460.32	472.88	484.00
Trade, transportation, and utilities	331.55	339.19	348.68	359.33	370.38	378.79	390.64	407.57	423.30	434.31	449.88	459.53	471.27	481.10
Wholesale trade	444.48	459.27	470.51	484.46	501.17	515.14	533.29	559.39	582.21	602.77	631.40	643.45	644.38	657.12
Retail trade	235.62	240.15	249.63	256.89	265.77	272.56	282.76	295.97	310.34	321.63	333.38	346.16	360.81	367.28
Transportation and warehousing	471.72	471.12	478.02	494.36	507.27	513.37	525.60	542.55	546.86	547.97	562.31	562.70	579.75	597.79
Utilities	670.40	693.40	716.36	756.35	789.98	811.52	830.74	865.26	902.94	924.59	955.66	977.18	979.09	1 016.94
Information	479.50	495.20	512.01	535.25	551.28	564.98	592.68	622.40	646.52	675.32	700.89	731.11	738.17	761.13
Financial activities	354.65	369.57	386.01	403.02	419.20	436.12	451.49	472.37	500.95	517.57	537.37	558.02	575.51	608.87
Professional and business services	380.61	391.09	400.64	406.20	414.16	426.44	442.81	465.51	490.00	510.99	535.07	557.84	574.66	586.68
Education and health services	319.27	334.55	348.29	359.08	368.14	377.73	388.27	404.65	418.82	431.35	449.29	473.39	492.74	505.76
Leisure and hospitality	152.47	155.16	159.54	163.45	168.00	171.43	176.48	185.81	195.82	202.87	211.79	215.19	221.26	224.35
Other services	297.91	306.91	315.08	322.69	332.44	342.36	352.62	368.63	384.25	398.77	413.41	428.64	439.76	434.49

Table 16-6. Indexes of Aggregate Weekly Hours of Production or Nonsupervisory Workers on Private Nonfarm Payrolls by NAICS Industry

(2002 = 100.)

Industry	1990	1991	1992	1993	1994	1995	1996	1997	1998	1999	2000	2001	2002	2003
Total private	84.4	82.6	83.1	85.5	89.2	91.6	93.8	97.1	99.4	101.5	103.6	102.1	100.0	98.6
Goods–producing	106.1	100.1	98.7	100.8	105.6	106.8	108.1	111.2	112.3	112.6	113.1	106.6	100.0	95.7
Natural resources and mining	128.6	123.8	113.3	110.3	111.0	110.2	112.7	117.6	112.8	102.9	105.1	108.3	100.0	97.0
Construction	78.8	70.1	67.5	71.3	77.3	79.9	84.3	88.6	93.4	99.7	104.0	103.2	100.0	98.2
Manufacturing	117.7	112.8	112.4	113.9	118.3	119.0	118.8	121.4	121.0	118.9	117.7	108.1	100.0	94.6
Durable goods	114.2	107.6	106.4	108.2	114.2	116.3	117.5	121.6	122.0	120.6	120.4	109.3	100.0	94.4
Wood products	101.5	92.6	95.2	100.5	109.1	109.3	111.6	114.8	117.5	118.6	115.8	105.0	100.0	97.6
Nonmetallic mineral products	100.8	92.8	92.6	94.2	98.8	99.7	101.5	103.2	105.8	106.9	109.1	106.1	100.0	94.0
Primary metals	131.5	122.9	120.8	121.4	128.0	129.3	129.9	132.3	131.1	128.4	128.9	113.0	100.0	93.2
Fabricated metal products	104.7	99.1	97.3	99.7	106.3	109.9	111.6	116.6	118.6	116.7	119.1	109.3	100.0	95.3
Machinery	123.9	116.3	113.9	118.6	127.0	132.3	133.8	139.0	137.4	129.9	127.6	114.1	100.0	94.0
Computer and electronic products	137.2	128.1	122.9	121.1	123.5	127.1	129.9	136.8	136.7	131.1	133.0	117.9	100.0	92.5
Electrical equipment and appliances	136.0	128.0	125.9	126.8	132.5	130.3	129.4	127.7	127.8	128.3	127.8	113.4	100.0	92.1
Transportation equipment	111.1	105.8	104.4	105.5	112.6	115.4	116.4	120.7	118.7	119.5	116.4	105.3	100.0	95.6
Furniture and related products	97.2	89.5	92.1	95.3	100.5	99.3	98.3	102.9	108.5	112.6	114.8	104.8	100.0	93.1
Miscellaneous manufacturing	104.0	103.8	105.2	106.9	108.2	107.7	107.7	110.0	110.3	110.3	109.5	104.8	100.0	93.6
Nondurable goods	123.0	120.8	121.7	122.6	124.7	123.1	120.5	120.9	119.4	116.1	113.3	106.0	100.0	94.8
Food manufacturing	96.2	96.6	97.3	98.7	100.5	101.6	101.8	102.6	103.4	103.8	103.5	101.5	100.0	98.5
Beverages and tobacco products	96.9	96.4	95.4	95.6	98.7	97.9	101.4	103.1	104.9	104.7	104.2	100.3	100.0	88.8
Textile mills	170.4	168.4	170.3	170.8	171.6	163.5	154.1	155.2	148.9	139.1	132.4	112.2	100.0	85.9
Textile products mills	110.3	104.5	106.0	110.6	116.6	114.4	112.8	114.8	114.1	113.5	111.1	105.0	100.0	93.2
Apparel	267.4	264.2	267.5	259.4	252.6	235.4	211.9	201.4	181.2	154.7	137.4	117.1	100.0	82.1
Leather and allied products	290.0	268.9	263.5	259.1	246.9	221.8	197.5	187.1	166.6	148.3	138.4	113.3	100.0	92.6
Paper and paper products	121.8	120.6	121.7	121.9	123.5	121.4	120.1	121.5	119.5	117.1	113.4	106.6	100.0	92.9
Printing and related support activities	122.3	118.7	118.4	120.3	123.8	123.9	122.8	124.6	124.3	120.9	119.4	111.5	100.0	95.2
Petroleum and coal products	128.9	127.5	126.0	122.0	120.0	115.5	113.5	112.7	113.4	107.6	105.8	105.6	100.0	99.1
Chemicals	118.2	115.0	112.9	113.4	115.1	115.4	114.7	114.6	115.4	113.1	110.4	104.7	100.0	99.0
Plastics and rubber products	97.7	94.2	98.1	102.4	108.8	109.9	110.1	112.7	113.8	114.6	114.3	105.0	100.0	95.3
Private service–providing	78.3	77.8	78.8	81.2	84.6	87.3	89.7	93.1	95.8	98.4	101.0	100.8	100.0	99.4
Trade, transportation, and utilities	89.5	87.4	87.3	89.0	92.7	95.1	96.6	98.8	100.3	101.9	103.5	101.5	100.0	98.5
Wholesale trade	94.9	93.3	92.4	92.4	95.8	99.2	100.7	103.4	104.8	106.2	107.1	102.9	100.0	98.0
Retail trade	87.5	84.8	85.1	86.3	89.8	92.3	93.7	95.9	97.2	99.5	101.3	100.5	100.0	98.8
Transportation and warehousing	83.5	82.4	82.7	88.4	93.8	95.6	98.3	101.0	102.7	103.2	105.6	102.8	100.0	98.5
Utilities	124.3	123.5	121.6	119.9	117.1	112.9	108.6	106.1	105.8	105.0	104.2	102.4	100.0	98.1
Information	76.2	76.1	76.5	78.0	79.2	82.5	86.9	90.4	92.6	98.5	104.9	106.6	100.0	97.3
Financial activities	84.5	83.3	83.5	85.9	88.0	87.8	89.8	92.6	96.5	98.0	98.5	99.5	100.0	101.4
Professional and business services	68.1	66.7	68.4	71.9	77.0	81.2	85.2	91.5	96.7	101.7	106.6	104.0	100.0	98.8
Education and health services	67.2	70.2	72.9	75.4	78.3	81.2	83.4	86.7	88.9	90.6	92.8	96.6	100.0	101.3
Leisure and hospitality	78.9	77.3	79.3	82.2	85.6	88.5	90.8	93.4	95.5	97.9	100.6	100.7	100.0	99.7
Other services	81.8	81.2	80.6	82.8	84.5	87.1	89.1	91.9	94.3	96.3	97.8	99.1	100.0	97.3

Table 16-7. Indexes of Aggregate Weekly Payrolls of Production or Nonsupervisory Workers on Private Nonfarm Payrolls by NAICS Industry

(2002 = 100.)

Industry	1990	1991	1992	1993	1994	1995	1996	1997	1998	1999	2000	2001	2002	2003
Total private	57.5	58.0	59.8	63.1	67.6	71.3	75.4	81.1	86.5	91.4	97.0	99.2	100.0	101.3
Goods-producing	74.5	72.1	72.4	75.8	81.7	84.8	88.6	94.1	97.9	101.4	105.7	103.0	100.0	98.5
Natural resources and mining	100.2	99.5	92.8	90.6	93.0	94.8	99.0	106.5	106.3	97.8	101.2	107.1	100.0	99.2
Construction	57.1	51.7	50.3	54.1	60.0	63.6	68.8	74.9	81.8	90.4	98.2	100.3	100.0	100.5
Manufacturing	82.9	82.1	83.8	87.1	93.2	96.1	99.0	104.3	106.4	107.7	110.2	104.3	100.0	97.4
Durable goods	81.3	79.3	80.3	83.9	91.1	94.7	98.7	105.0	107.1	108.9	112.2	104.9	100.0	97.0
Nondurable goods	85.7	86.9	89.9	92.7	96.6	98.3	99.4	102.9	105.1	105.5	106.6	103.0	100.0	98.0
Private service-providing	52.2	53.7	55.9	59.1	63.2	67.1	71.3	77.1	82.8	88.3	94.3	98.1	100.0	102.2
Trade, transportation, and utilities	62.8	62.9	64.2	67.0	71.4	75.3	79.0	83.9	88.6	93.2	98.3	99.2	100.0	100.8
Wholesale trade	64.7	65.7	66.4	68.4	73.0	77.9	81.8	87.8	93.0	97.7	102.7	101.7	100.0	100.2
Retail trade	57.8	57.4	59.2	61.9	66.3	70.0	74.0	78.8	83.8	89.1	94.3	97.3	100.0	100.8
Transportation and warehousing	66.3	65.9	67.0	71.3	76.4	79.9	83.8	88.3	92.0	95.3	100.8	99.9	100.0	101.5
Utilities	83.7	86.1	87.1	89.9	91.2	90.4	89.7	91.2	94.9	96.6	99.0	100.7	100.0	101.3
Information	50.5	52.3	54.1	57.3	60.0	64.1	70.2	76.7	81.0	89.7	99.1	104.5	100.0	101.2
Financial activities	52.2	53.7	56.1	60.3	64.3	66.7	70.5	75.7	83.1	87.7	91.2	95.9	100.0	107.5
Professional and business services	45.1	45.6	47.9	51.2	55.7	60.5	65.9	73.8	82.1	89.8	98.4	101.1	100.0	101.1
Education and health services	44.1	48.4	52.1	55.5	59.2	63.0	66.8	71.6	76.0	80.1	85.1	92.9	100.0	104.2
Leisure and hospitality	54.1	54.7	57.3	60.5	64.5	68.4	72.1	77.7	83.2	88.6	95.2	98.1	100.0	101.9
Other services	54.1	55.5	56.8	59.8	62.7	66.7	70.4	75.6	81.0	86.0	90.8	95.8	100.0	98.1

CHAPTER 16: EMPLOYMENT, HOURS, AND EARNINGS BY NAICS INDUSTRY

NOTES AND DEFINITIONS

TABLES 16-1 THROUGH 16-7
EMPLOYMENT, HOURS, AND EARNINGS BY NAICS INDUSTRY

See the Notes and Definitions to Tables 10-5 through 10-10 for definitions of employment, production or nonsupervisory workers, average weekly hours, average hourly earnings, average weekly earnings, and the indexes of aggregate weekly hours.

Indexes of aggregate weekly payrolls for private nonfarm production or nonsupervisory workers are calculated at the basic industry level as the product of average hourly earnings and aggregate weekly hours. At higher levels, payroll aggregates are the sum of the component aggregates. Index levels are calculated by dividing the current month's aggregate by the average of the 12 monthly figures for 2002.

See Chapter 14 for information on the NAICS.

CHAPTER 17: KEY SECTOR STATISTICS

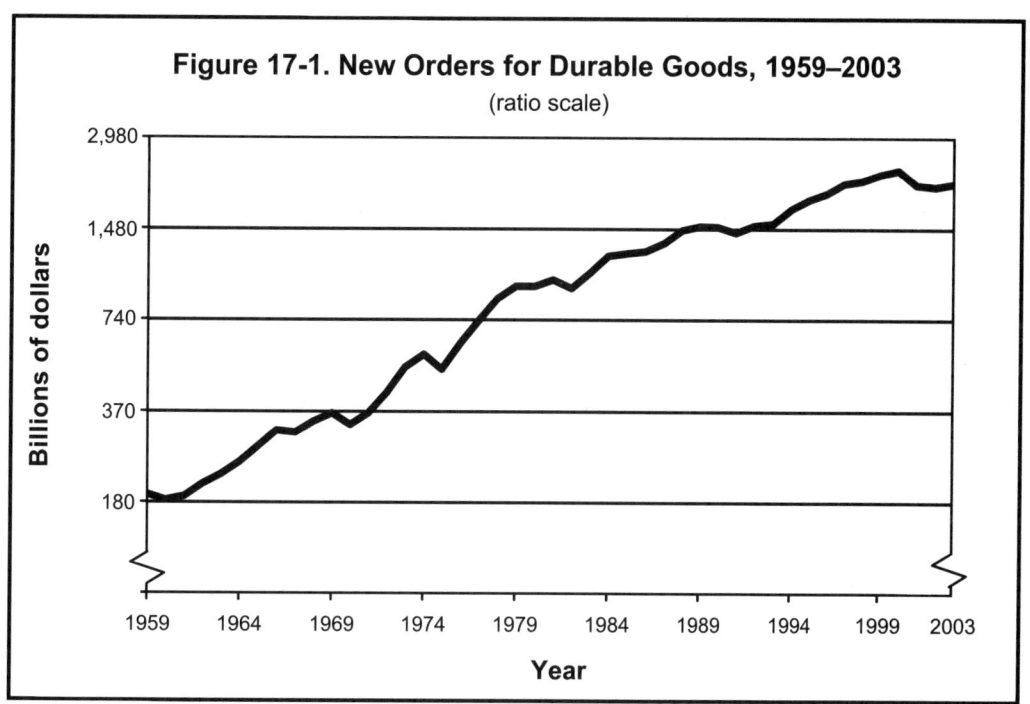

Figure 17-1. New Orders for Durable Goods, 1959–2003
(ratio scale)

- The value of new orders for durable goods at U.S. manufacturing firms is a sensitive indicator of the business cycle, shown in the graph above. From 2000 to 2002, the annual average of new orders dropped 12.3 percent, exceeding the severe decline from 1974 to 1975. In 2003, these orders saw a partial (3 percent) recovery. (Table 17-6)
- The value of manufacturers' inventories dropped 8.9 percent from the end of 2000 to the end of 2003. (Table 17-5)
- Between the end of 2000 and the end of 2003, order backlogs for nondefense capital goods declined 17.8 percent, but defense order backlogs rose 18.4 percent. (Table 17-7)
- As a percentage of the total supply of petroleum and products (domestic crude oil and natural gas liquids production plus net imports), net imports rose from 5.5 percent in 1949 to 60.3 percent in 2003. (Table 17-1)
- From 2000 to 2003, the value of construction put in place declined in a few sectors related to capital spending—office, commercial, communications, and manufacturing—but the construction sector as a whole continued to rise because of increases in residential and government spending. (Tables 17-2 and 17-3)
- The three years from 2000 to 2003 saw a very modest (less than 2 percent) decline in unit sales of cars and light trucks. Previous recessions in vehicle sales were far more severe: 31 percent from 1978 to 1982, and 20 percent from 1988 to 1991. (Table 17-8)
- The total value of retail and food service sales continued to grow during the most recent recession and recovery, and in 2003 was 11.3 percent above 2000. Sales by electronic shopping and mail-order grew from 1.9 percent of total retail sales in 1992 to 3.6 percent in 2000, with the sharpest jump in 2000, and have leveled off at that share in 2001 through 2003. (Table 17-9)
- E-commerce is still a small fraction of total revenues for surveyed service industries as a whole. The exceptions are the travel and reservation business and online information services. Growth in services revenues slowed in 2001 and 2002 and so did the growth of the e-commerce share. (Tables 17-14 and 17-15)

Table 17-1. Petroleum and Petroleum Products—Imports, Domestic Production, and Stocks

(Not seasonally adjusted.)

Year and month	Imports						Supply (thousands of barrels per day)					Stocks (end of period, millions of barrels)		
	Total energy-related petroleum products		Crude petroleum				Petroleum and products			Domestic production		Crude oil and petroleum products	Crude petroleum	
	Quantity (thousands of barrels)	Value (millions of dollars)	Quantity (thousands of barrels)		Value (millions of dollars)	Unit price (dollars per barrel)	Exports	Imports	Net imports	Crude oil	Natural gas plant liquids		Total	Strategic petroleum reserve
			Total	Average per day										
1949	...	...	...	...	...	...	327	645	318	5 046	430	603	253	0
1950	...	...	...	...	...	...	305	850	545	5 407	499	583	248	0
1951	...	...	...	...	...	...	422	844	422	6 158	561	634	256	0
1952	...	...	...	...	...	...	432	952	520	6 256	611	674	272	0
1953	...	...	...	...	...	...	402	1 034	633	6 458	654	726	274	0
1954	...	...	...	...	...	...	355	1 052	696	6 342	691	715	258	0
1955	...	...	...	...	...	...	368	1 248	880	6 807	771	715	266	0
1956	...	...	...	...	...	...	430	1 436	1 006	7 151	800	780	266	0
1957	...	...	...	...	...	...	568	1 574	1 007	7 170	808	841	282	0
1958	...	...	...	...	...	...	276	1 700	1 425	6 710	808	789	263	0
1959	...	...	...	...	...	...	211	1 780	1 569	7 054	879	809	257	0
1960	...	...	...	...	...	...	202	1 815	1 613	7 035	929	785	240	0
1961	...	...	...	...	...	...	174	1 917	1 743	7 183	991	825	245	0
1962	...	...	...	...	...	...	168	2 082	1 913	7 332	1 021	834	252	0
1963	...	...	...	...	...	...	208	2 123	1 915	7 542	1 098	836	237	0
1964	...	...	...	...	...	...	202	2 259	2 057	7 614	1 154	839	230	0
1965	...	...	...	...	...	...	187	2 468	2 281	7 804	1 210	836	220	0
1966	...	...	...	...	...	...	198	2 573	2 375	8 295	1 284	874	238	0
1967	...	...	...	...	...	...	307	2 537	2 230	8 810	1 409	944	249	0
1968	...	...	...	...	...	...	231	2 840	2 609	9 096	1 504	1 000	272	0
1969	...	...	...	...	...	...	233	3 166	2 933	9 238	1 590	980	265	0
1970	...	...	...	...	...	...	259	3 419	3 161	9 637	1 660	1 018	276	0
1971	...	...	...	...	...	...	224	3 926	3 701	9 463	1 693	1 044	260	0
1972	...	...	...	...	...	...	222	4 741	4 519	9 441	1 744	959	246	0
1973	...	...	1 392 970	3 816	4 593	3.30	231	6 256	6 025	9 208	1 738	1 008	242	0
1974	...	...	1 367 081	3 745	15 269	11.17	221	6 112	5 892	8 774	1 688	1 074	265	0
1975	...	...	1 584 730	4 342	18 374	11.59	209	6 056	5 846	8 375	1 633	1 133	271	0
1976	...	...	2 050 424	5 618	25 480	12.43	223	7 313	7 090	8 132	1 604	1 112	285	0
1977	...	...	2 519 806	6 904	33 583	13.33	243	8 807	8 565	8 245	1 618	1 312	348	7
1978	...	...	2 392 350	6 554	32 140	13.43	362	8 363	8 002	8 707	1 567	1 278	376	67
1979	...	...	2 467 315	6 760	46 100	18.68	471	8 456	7 985	8 552	1 584	1 341	430	91
1980	...	...	1 977 247	5 417	62 014	31.36	544	6 909	6 365	8 597	1 573	1 392	466	108
1981	...	...	1 763 072	4 830	61 940	35.13	595	5 996	5 401	8 572	1 609	1 484	594	230
1982	...	...	1 420 753	3 892	47 445	33.39	815	5 113	4 298	8 649	1 550	1 430	644	294
1983	...	...	1 293 819	3 545	38 184	29.51	739	5 051	4 312	8 688	1 559	1 454	723	379
1984	...	...	1 319 683	3 616	36 529	27.68	722	5 437	4 715	8 879	1 630	1 556	796	451
1985	...	...	1 260 856	3 454	33 034	26.20	781	5 067	4 286	8 971	1 609	1 519	814	493
1986	...	...	1 634 567	4 478	22 720	13.90	785	6 224	5 439	8 680	1 551	1 593	843	512
1987	...	...	1 744 957	4 781	29 321	16.80	764	6 678	5 914	8 349	1 595	1 607	890	541
1988	...	...	1 887 860	5 172	25 844	13.69	815	7 402	6 587	8 140	1 625	1 597	890	560
1989	...	...	2 146 552	5 881	35 400	16.49	859	8 061	7 202	7 613	1 546	1 581	921	580
1990	...	...	2 216 604	6 073	43 785	19.75	857	8 018	7 161	7 355	1 559	1 621	908	586
1991	2 828 953	50 646	2 146 064	5 880	37 463	17.46	1 001	7 627	6 626	7 417	1 659	1 617	893	569
1992	2 947 582	50 537	2 294 570	6 269	38 553	16.80	950	7 888	6 938	7 171	1 697	1 592	893	575
1993	3 257 008	50 210	2 543 374	6 968	38 469	15.13	1 003	8 620	7 618	6 847	1 736	1 647	922	587
1994	3 416 045	49 533	2 704 196	7 409	38 479	14.23	942	8 996	8 054	6 662	1 727	1 653	929	592
1995	3 361 882	53 835	2 767 312	7 582	43 750	15.81	949	8 835	7 886	6 560	1 762	1 563	895	592
1996	3 622 385	70 199	2 893 647	7 906	54 931	18.98	981	9 478	8 498	6 465	1 830	1 507	850	566
1997	3 802 574	69 288	3 069 430	8 409	54 226	17.67	1 003	10 162	9 158	6 452	1 817	1 560	868	563
1998	4 088 027	49 132	3 242 711	8 884	37 252	11.49	945	10 708	9 764	6 252	1 759	1 647	895	571
1999	4 081 181	65 931	3 228 092	8 844	50 890	15.76	940	10 852	9 912	5 881	1 850	1 493	852	567
2000	4 314 825	117 057	3 399 239	9 288	89 876	26.44	1 040	11 459	10 419	5 822	1 911	1 468	826	541
2001	4 475 026	100 792	3 471 067	9 510	74 293	21.40	971	11 871	10 900	5 801	1 868	1 586	862	550
2002	4 337 075	100 526	3 418 021	9 364	77 283	22.61	984	11 530	10 546	5 746	1 880	1 548	877	599
2003	4 654 638	129 485	3 676 006	10 071	99 167	26.98	1 027	12 264	11 238	5 681	1 719	1 568	907	638
2002														
January	369 816	6 220	295 494	9 532	4 813	16.29	861	11 088	10 228	5 848	1 827	1 591	875	555
February	310 404	5 321	246 411	8 800	4 086	16.58	1 175	10 904	9 729	5 871	1 900	1 576	887	560
March	335 337	6 755	267 037	8 614	5 145	19.27	853	11 198	10 345	5 883	1 901	1 573	895	561
April	377 653	8 748	296 134	9 871	6 671	22.53	890	11 765	10 876	5 859	1 925	1 588	891	567
May	379 179	9 181	296 505	9 565	7 041	23.75	910	11 769	10 859	5 924	1 936	1 611	898	571
June	347 732	8 267	270 677	9 023	6 321	23.35	880	11 753	10 873	5 915	1 870	1 616	894	576
July	366 643	8 880	290 855	9 382	6 903	23.73	839	11 624	10 785	5 770	1 846	1 611	883	579
August	375 036	9 380	296 068	9 551	7 276	24.58	1 138	11 890	10 752	5 811	1 937	1 596	878	582
September	343 765	8 932	272 653	9 088	6 951	25.49	1 015	11 075	10 059	5 411	1 898	1 574	858	587
October	289 617	10 472	315 720	10 185	8 288	26.25	962	11 893	10 931	5 363	1 875	1 573	881	590
November	370 416	9 171	286 298	9 543	6 927	24.19	1 026	12 268	11 242	5 597	1 891	1 578	884	596
December	371 477	9 198	284 170	9 167	6 862	24.15	1 272	11 100	9 828	5 699	1 760	1 548	877	599
2003														
January	362 626	10 220	273 338	8 817	7 587	27.76	1 212	11 104	9 892	5 785	1 758	1 504	873	599
February	320 153	10 084	250 262	8 938	7 601	30.37	1 067	10 921	9 854	5 791	1 812	1 460	870	599
March	390 535	12 366	294 768	9 509	8 958	30.39	1 051	12 044	10 993	5 817	1 729	1 474	881	599
April	399 601	10 813	318 088	10 603	8 273	26.01	1 053	12 599	11 546	5 774	1 701	1 496	891	600
May	406 979	10 126	319 111	10 294	7 673	24.05	1 097	12 918	11 822	5 733	1 564	1 533	889	603
June	402 804	10 535	312 982	10 433	7 980	25.50	1 065	13 001	11 936	5 701	1 582	1 560	893	609
July	422 313	11 598	335 511	10 823	8 975	26.75	976	12 736	11 760	5 526	1 649	1 570	897	612
August	398 306	11 307	319 674	10 312	8 809	27.56	947	12 769	11 822	5 595	1 703	1 572	898	618
September	393 522	10 686	316 796	10 560	8 372	26.43	960	12 868	11 908	5 683	1 761	1 598	911	624
October	404 183	10 902	329 992	10 645	8 672	26.28	970	12 373	11 402	5 635	1 818	1 602	926	631
November	364 670	9 975	291 352	9 712	7 733	26.54	933	11 712	10 780	5 560	1 839	1 598	915	634
December	388 945	10 872	314 131	10 133	8 535	27.17	990	12 033	11 043	5 579	1 723	1 568	907	638

. . . = Not available.

Table 17-2. New Construction Put in Place

(Billions of dollars, monthly data are at seasonally adjusted annual rates.)

Year and month	Total	Private											
		Total [1]	Residential	Office	Commercial		Health care	Educational	Amusement and recreation	Transportation	Communication	Power	Manufacturing
					Total [1]	Multi-retail							
1964	75.1	54.9	30.5	...	...	...	...	...	...	...	...	...	...
1965	81.9	60.0	30.2	...	...	...	...	...	...	...	...	...	...
1966	85.8	61.9	28.6	...	...	...	...	...	...	...	...	...	...
1967	87.2	61.8	28.7	...	...	...	...	...	...	...	...	...	...
1968	96.8	69.4	34.2	...	...	...	...	...	...	...	...	...	...
1969	104.9	77.2	37.2	...	...	...	...	...	...	...	...	...	...
1970	105.9	78.0	35.9	...	...	...	...	...	...	...	...	...	...
1971	122.4	92.7	48.5	...	...	...	...	...	...	...	...	...	...
1972	139.1	109.1	60.7	...	...	...	...	...	...	...	...	...	...
1973	153.8	121.4	65.1	...	...	...	...	...	...	...	...	...	...
1974	155.2	117.0	56.0	...	...	...	...	...	...	...	...	...	...
1975	152.6	109.3	51.6	...	...	...	...	...	...	...	...	...	...
1976	172.1	128.2	68.3	...	...	...	...	...	...	...	...	...	...
1977	200.5	157.4	92.0	...	...	...	...	...	...	...	...	...	...
1978	239.9	189.7	109.8	...	...	...	...	...	...	...	...	...	...
1979	272.9	216.2	116.4	...	...	...	...	...	...	...	...	...	...
1980	273.9	210.3	100.4	...	...	...	...	...	...	...	...	...	...
1981	289.1	224.4	99.2	...	...	...	...	...	...	...	...	...	...
1982	279.3	216.3	84.7	...	...	...	...	...	...	...	...	...	...
1983	311.9	248.4	125.8	...	...	...	...	...	...	...	...	...	...
1984	370.2	300.0	155.0	...	...	...	...	...	...	...	...	...	...
1985	403.4	325.6	160.5	...	...	...	...	...	...	...	...	...	...
1986	433.5	348.9	190.7	...	...	...	...	...	...	...	...	...	...
1987	446.6	356.0	199.7	...	...	...	...	...	...	...	...	...	...
1988	462.0	367.3	204.5	...	...	...	...	...	...	...	...	...	...
1989	477.5	379.3	204.3	...	...	...	...	...	...	...	...	...	...
1990	476.8	369.3	191.1	...	...	...	...	...	...	...	...	...	...
1991	432.6	322.5	166.3	...	...	...	...	...	...	...	...	...	...
1992	463.7	347.8	199.4	...	...	...	...	...	...	...	...	...	...
1993	491.0	375.1	225.1	20.0	34.4	11.5	14.9	4.8	4.6	4.7	9.8	23.6	23.4
1994	539.2	419.0	258.6	20.4	39.6	12.2	15.4	5.0	5.1	4.7	10.1	21.0	28.8
1995	557.8	427.9	247.4	23.0	44.1	12.0	15.3	5.7	5.9	4.8	11.1	22.0	35.4
1996	615.9	476.6	281.1	26.5	49.4	13.3	15.4	7.0	7.0	5.8	11.8	17.4	38.1
1997	653.4	502.7	289.0	32.8	53.1	12.2	17.4	8.8	8.5	6.2	12.5	16.4	37.6
1998	705.7	551.4	314.6	40.4	55.7	13.3	17.7	9.8	8.6	7.3	12.5	21.1	40.5
1999	766.1	596.3	350.6	45.1	59.4	15.2	18.4	9.8	9.6	6.5	18.4	21.1	32.6
2000	828.2	642.6	374.5	52.4	64.1	14.9	19.5	11.7	8.8	6.9	18.8	28.0	31.8
2001	858.3	652.5	388.3	49.7	63.6	16.4	19.5	12.8	7.8	7.1	19.6	30.0	29.5
2002	871.3	651.7	421.9	35.3	59.2	15.6	22.4	13.1	7.5	6.9	18.1	31.1	16.4
2003	915.7	690.0	476.1	30.4	57.7	15.5	23.6	13.4	7.9	6.5	12.4	27.9	14.2
2001													
January	831.6	640.1	371.7	57.6	63.3	16.3	20.4	12.3	7.3	7.3	20.2	21.2	34.4
February	832.3	638.3	376.9	55.7	64.5	17.2	19.6	12.0	7.4	7.2	19.3	19.4	31.4
March	850.5	646.9	376.2	56.8	64.3	16.3	20.8	12.2	7.8	7.5	18.6	24.3	33.7
April	856.7	649.3	380.4	54.0	65.6	17.3	19.4	12.2	7.7	7.5	20.6	25.5	32.0
May	865.1	654.3	383.5	51.8	64.4	16.7	19.8	12.0	7.8	7.4	22.6	29.7	30.3
June	874.4	663.8	389.8	53.5	63.9	16.4	19.0	12.6	8.4	7.3	19.4	32.9	31.4
July	878.8	669.1	400.1	50.5	65.3	16.6	19.1	12.5	8.0	7.1	18.9	30.9	30.9
August	865.3	660.0	395.6	47.0	63.3	15.8	18.9	12.9	7.8	7.0	20.2	32.2	29.8
September	858.2	655.6	395.1	44.4	62.8	16.5	19.2	13.6	7.8	6.5	19.8	31.7	30.1
October	855.9	647.6	388.9	44.5	62.6	15.8	19.6	13.9	8.0	6.6	19.0	34.4	26.3
November	858.7	648.8	397.8	42.1	62.6	15.7	18.8	14.0	8.2	6.6	18.7	34.2	22.4
December	863.9	652.1	397.5	40.0	62.2	16.1	19.7	14.0	7.7	7.0	18.4	40.8	22.9
2002													
January	857.2	635.8	382.8	39.7	64.0	17.6	20.6	13.6	7.9	6.7	18.3	40.2	20.6
February	863.7	639.2	392.7	38.5	61.9	16.6	20.5	13.6	8.0	6.7	19.5	38.4	18.9
March	860.7	647.4	404.2	36.9	63.4	16.2	20.9	13.8	7.6	7.1	18.6	36.4	18.2
April	865.8	652.5	410.8	37.6	61.7	17.0	21.3	14.1	7.6	7.1	18.2	34.8	17.6
May	868.9	649.8	416.4	36.4	59.3	15.3	22.2	13.7	7.5	6.9	18.3	31.1	17.1
June	865.7	648.0	420.7	34.7	58.6	15.1	23.1	12.6	7.8	7.0	18.9	28.4	16.4
July	869.7	649.2	427.6	35.1	56.3	14.3	22.8	12.4	7.4	6.6	18.5	28.4	15.7
August	868.8	649.0	428.8	34.0	58.0	15.1	22.9	12.4	7.5	7.1	17.7	26.7	14.8
September	873.8	653.4	433.5	33.8	59.2	15.8	23.2	12.5	7.2	6.8	16.9	26.7	14.4
October	878.0	659.2	437.3	33.0	57.9	15.0	24.0	13.1	7.6	6.7	17.9	27.7	14.8
November	884.9	662.7	441.6	32.8	57.1	15.4	24.1	13.4	7.0	6.8	17.0	29.2	14.8
December	889.9	662.6	448.1	31.7	54.3	14.2	23.3	12.8	6.9	6.7	17.3	28.4	14.3
2003													
January	898.6	671.5	456.6	30.6	56.8	14.8	23.1	12.9	6.5	7.1	12.9	32.1	13.6
February	891.7	667.9	455.6	29.2	54.5	14.3	23.8	12.9	7.0	7.3	11.8	33.4	13.6
March	890.0	671.2	457.2	29.2	56.8	15.1	23.9	13.2	7.5	6.8	12.3	30.7	14.2
April	892.9	672.3	458.9	29.3	57.4	15.0	23.6	13.3	7.7	6.7	12.3	29.8	14.0
May	901.0	678.3	461.5	28.8	58.4	15.1	23.8	13.9	7.8	6.4	12.3	26.9	14.9
June	906.8	677.8	465.1	30.5	59.0	16.1	24.0	13.8	8.0	6.4	12.6	24.0	14.7
July	909.4	681.1	472.5	30.1	59.0	15.8	23.6	13.7	7.8	6.3	13.0	21.7	13.9
August	922.0	691.7	481.0	30.2	60.4	16.1	22.9	13.7	7.9	6.3	12.1	23.5	14.3
September	930.8	701.2	487.6	30.5	57.9	15.4	23.1	13.8	8.2	6.5	12.5	26.3	14.8
October	942.2	714.1	495.6	32.5	58.1	15.9	23.9	13.2	8.9	6.3	12.6	27.9	14.9
November	947.7	721.1	504.2	32.1	57.0	16.3	23.9	12.7	8.7	6.1	13.1	29.6	14.4
December	948.9	727.0	511.3	31.5	56.7	16.0	24.0	13.4	8.4	6.3	11.8	31.2	13.6

[1] Includes categories not shown separately.
... = Not available.

Table 17-2. New Construction Put in Place—Continued

(Billions of dollars, monthly data are at seasonally adjusted annual rates.)

Year and month	Total	Public												Federal
		State and local												
		Total [1]	Residential	Office	Health care	Educational	Public safety	Amusement and recreation	Transportation	Power	Highway and street	Sewage and waste disposal	Water supply	
1964	20.2	16.5	...	...	...	...	...	...	...	...	...	...	...	3.7
1965	21.9	18.0	...	...	...	...	...	...	...	...	...	...	...	3.9
1966	23.8	20.0	...	...	...	...	...	...	...	...	...	...	...	3.8
1967	25.4	22.1	...	...	...	...	...	...	...	...	...	...	...	3.3
1968	27.4	24.2	...	...	...	...	...	...	...	...	...	...	...	3.2
1969	27.8	24.6	...	...	...	...	...	...	...	...	...	...	...	3.2
1970	27.9	24.8	...	...	...	...	...	...	...	...	...	...	...	3.1
1971	29.7	25.9	...	...	...	...	...	...	...	...	...	...	...	3.8
1972	30.0	25.8	...	...	...	...	...	...	...	...	...	...	...	4.2
1973	32.3	27.6	...	...	...	...	...	...	...	...	...	...	...	4.7
1974	38.1	33.0	...	...	...	...	...	...	...	...	...	...	...	5.1
1975	43.3	37.2	...	...	...	...	...	...	...	...	...	...	...	6.1
1976	44.0	37.2	...	...	...	...	...	...	...	...	...	...	...	6.8
1977	43.1	36.0	...	...	...	...	...	...	...	...	...	...	...	7.1
1978	50.1	42.0	...	...	...	...	...	...	...	...	...	...	...	8.1
1979	56.6	48.1	...	...	...	...	...	...	...	...	...	...	...	8.6
1980	63.6	54.0	...	...	...	...	...	...	...	...	...	...	...	9.6
1981	64.7	54.3	...	...	...	...	...	...	...	...	...	...	...	10.4
1982	63.1	53.1	...	...	...	...	...	...	...	...	...	...	...	10.0
1983	63.5	52.9	...	...	...	...	...	...	...	...	...	...	...	10.6
1984	70.2	59.0	...	...	...	...	...	...	...	...	...	...	...	11.2
1985	77.8	65.8	...	...	...	...	...	...	...	...	...	...	...	12.0
1986	84.6	72.2	...	...	...	...	...	...	...	...	...	...	...	12.4
1987	90.6	76.6	...	...	...	...	...	...	...	...	...	...	...	14.1
1988	94.7	82.5	...	...	...	...	...	...	...	...	...	...	...	12.3
1989	98.2	86.0	...	...	...	...	...	...	...	...	...	...	...	12.2
1990	107.5	95.4	...	...	...	...	...	...	...	...	...	...	...	12.1
1991	110.1	97.3	...	...	...	...	...	...	...	...	...	...	...	12.8
1992	115.8	101.5	...	...	...	...	...	...	...	...	...	...	...	14.4
1993	116.0	101.5	3.7	3.2	2.7	19.2	5.2	4.9	8.8	3.2	34.4	8.9	5.1	14.4
1994	120.2	105.8	3.4	3.6	2.9	20.5	5.4	5.6	8.6	2.8	37.3	8.7	4.7	14.4
1995	129.9	114.2	4.0	3.9	3.2	25.7	5.9	6.1	9.0	2.9	37.6	8.4	4.7	15.8
1996	139.3	123.9	4.2	4.4	3.4	28.6	6.7	6.1	10.0	2.5	39.5	9.8	5.6	15.3
1997	150.7	136.6	4.3	4.6	3.5	33.8	6.7	6.9	9.7	3.1	43.0	10.5	6.5	14.1
1998	154.3	140.0	4.3	4.6	2.9	35.0	7.6	7.7	10.2	2.5	44.8	9.9	6.7	14.3
1999	169.7	155.7	4.6	4.5	3.2	41.1	7.9	9.2	11.3	3.2	49.2	10.5	7.0	14.0
2000	185.5	171.4	4.2	6.3	3.9	45.6	8.1	10.6	14.2	3.9	53.1	10.2	7.0	14.2
2001	205.8	190.7	5.0	7.2	3.8	51.0	7.9	11.9	16.1	4.1	58.9	11.1	9.0	15.1
2002	219.6	203.1	5.2	8.0	4.4	57.5	7.6	11.7	17.3	3.2	60.6	12.7	9.7	16.6
2003	225.7	208.2	5.3	8.3	5.2	59.3	7.8	11.3	17.3	3.9	62.0	12.8	9.6	17.6
2001														
January	191.5	175.9	4.7	6.7	3.7	46.3	7.9	11.5	15.7	5.0	52.5	10.2	7.1	15.6
February	194.0	178.8	4.8	6.8	3.8	46.1	7.7	12.0	15.7	4.1	54.4	10.8	7.5	15.3
March	203.6	188.6	4.6	7.4	3.6	47.9	7.7	11.9	16.3	4.1	61.3	10.4	8.2	15.0
April	207.4	192.3	5.0	7.5	3.7	49.6	8.7	11.9	16.4	3.1	61.0	11.3	8.9	15.1
May	210.8	195.5	5.1	7.7	3.7	49.4	8.2	12.3	17.3	3.6	63.6	10.8	8.7	15.2
June	210.6	195.4	5.1	7.7	3.8	49.0	7.7	12.3	16.4	3.6	64.2	11.1	9.5	15.2
July	209.6	195.1	4.8	7.3	3.6	52.8	7.7	11.4	15.6	4.6	62.1	10.7	9.7	14.5
August	205.4	190.2	4.9	6.8	4.0	53.5	7.6	11.2	15.5	4.9	56.8	11.2	9.3	15.1
September	202.6	187.2	4.9	7.2	3.7	53.5	7.8	11.1	15.8	4.6	53.4	11.2	9.7	15.4
October	208.3	192.6	5.1	7.1	4.0	54.4	7.9	12.2	15.7	3.8	57.6	11.3	9.2	15.7
November	209.9	195.8	5.5	7.1	4.0	53.7	8.1	12.1	16.6	3.7	58.9	12.2	9.7	14.1
December	211.8	196.8	5.8	7.3	4.2	53.6	7.7	12.2	17.1	4.2	58.0	11.9	9.7	15.0
2002														
January	221.3	205.5	5.6	7.6	4.3	55.6	8.2	12.2	16.7	3.3	64.5	12.7	9.3	15.8
February	224.5	207.1	5.7	7.6	4.0	57.0	7.9	12.1	17.0	3.3	64.5	13.5	9.5	17.4
March	213.3	196.6	5.3	7.6	4.2	55.7	7.3	12.4	17.5	2.4	57.2	12.7	9.3	16.7
April	213.3	197.4	5.4	7.8	4.3	57.9	7.5	11.2	16.7	3.7	55.4	12.7	9.5	16.0
May	219.1	202.6	5.2	8.1	4.2	58.7	7.4	11.0	17.4	3.5	59.0	12.9	10.3	16.6
June	217.7	201.5	5.3	8.2	4.3	57.2	7.9	11.4	17.6	3.2	59.4	12.7	9.9	16.2
July	219.8	202.9	5.5	8.2	4.5	57.5	7.3	11.0	17.7	3.1	61.1	12.6	9.4	17.0
August	219.8	203.7	5.1	8.2	4.5	57.8	7.7	11.8	17.7	2.7	60.5	12.9	9.6	16.1
September	220.4	204.5	5.1	7.9	4.8	58.1	7.6	12.7	17.3	2.3	60.9	12.7	10.0	16.0
October	218.8	202.5	4.7	8.1	4.6	58.4	7.2	11.8	17.0	3.1	59.9	12.3	10.1	16.3
November	222.2	204.9	4.8	8.0	4.7	58.6	7.4	11.5	17.9	4.4	60.1	12.3	9.7	17.3
December	227.2	209.3	4.7	8.4	4.9	57.3	7.4	11.9	17.1	3.9	67.2	12.4	9.6	17.9
2003														
January	227.1	209.7	5.4	8.2	4.8	59.0	7.3	12.2	16.6	3.8	65.1	12.5	9.9	17.4
February	223.8	206.4	5.3	8.4	5.1	56.8	7.3	11.5	17.7	3.1	63.5	12.9	10.2	17.4
March	218.7	202.4	5.0	8.2	5.1	58.5	7.4	11.6	16.9	3.3	60.2	11.9	9.7	16.4
April	220.6	202.6	5.1	8.0	5.0	58.2	7.4	11.4	17.7	3.6	59.0	12.6	9.4	18.0
May	222.7	204.5	5.3	7.6	5.1	59.7	7.5	12.5	17.5	3.4	58.7	12.4	9.3	18.2
June	229.0	211.1	5.4	7.8	5.3	61.6	7.8	11.4	17.8	4.3	60.9	12.5	9.7	17.9
July	228.4	210.8	5.4	8.9	5.1	61.4	8.4	11.4	17.4	3.7	60.6	12.7	9.4	17.6
August	230.2	212.0	5.6	8.7	5.3	60.4	8.1	10.6	17.5	4.3	62.4	12.9	10.1	18.2
September	229.5	211.5	5.5	8.6	5.4	58.3	8.0	10.5	17.5	4.9	64.0	12.9	9.5	18.1
October	228.0	210.4	5.3	8.2	5.5	59.3	8.3	10.7	17.4	4.4	62.9	13.4	9.3	17.6
November	226.6	209.8	5.1	8.4	5.4	58.4	7.9	10.8	17.3	4.0	64.6	13.1	9.6	16.8
December	222.0	205.7	5.1	8.2	5.4	59.4	7.7	10.4	16.7	3.7	61.8	13.5	9.2	16.3

[1] Includes categories not shown separately.
... = Not available.

Table 17-3. Housing Starts and Building Permits; Home Sales and Prices

Year and month	Housing starts and building permits									Manufacturers' shipments of manufactured homes (thousands)		New home sales and prices		
	New private housing units (thousands)											Seasonally adjusted		Median sales price (dollars)
	Started (not seasonally adjusted)			Seasonally adjusted annual rate								Sold (thousands, annual rate)	For sale, end-of-period (thousands)	
				Started			Authorized by building permits [2]			Not seasonally adjusted	Seasonally adjusted annual rate			
	Total [1]	One-family structures	5 units or more	Total [1]	One-family structures	5 units or more	Total [1]	One-family structures	5 units or more					
1959	1 517	1 234	...	1 517	1 234	...	1 208	938	193	121	121	...	...	...
1960	1 252	995	...	1 252	995	...	998	746	187	104	104	...	...	...
1961	1 313	974	...	1 313	974	...	1 064	723	274	90	90	...	...	...
1962	1 463	991	...	1 463	991	...	1 187	716	383	118	118	...	...	...
1963	1 603	1 012	...	1 603	1 012	...	1 335	750	466	151	151	560	264	18 000
1964	1 529	970	450	1 529	970	450	1 286	720	465	191	191	565	250	18 900
1965	1 473	964	422	1 473	964	422	1 241	710	446	217	217	575	226	20 000
1966	1 165	779	325	1 165	779	325	972	563	348	217	217	461	194	21 400
1967	1 292	844	376	1 292	844	376	1 141	651	418	240	240	487	187	22 700
1968	1 508	899	527	1 508	899	527	1 353	695	574	318	318	490	213	24 700
1969	1 467	811	571	1 467	811	571	1 322	625	612	413	413	448	222	25 600
1970	1 434	813	536	1 434	813	536	1 352	647	617	401	401	485	220	23 400
1971	2 052	1 151	781	2 052	1 151	781	1 925	906	886	492	492	656	287	25 200
1972	2 357	1 309	906	2 357	1 309	906	2 219	1 033	1 037	576	576	718	409	27 600
1973	2 045	1 132	795	2 045	1 132	795	1 820	882	820	567	567	634	418	32 500
1974	1 338	888	382	1 338	888	382	1 074	644	366	329	329	519	346	35 900
1975	1 160	892	204	1 160	892	204	939	676	200	213	213	549	313	39 300
1976	1 538	1 162	289	1 538	1 162	289	1 296	894	310	246	246	646	353	44 200
1977	1 987	1 451	414	1 987	1 451	414	1 690	1 126	443	277	277	819	402	48 800
1978	2 020	1 433	462	2 020	1 433	462	1 800	1 183	487	276	276	817	414	55 700
1979	1 745	1 194	429	1 745	1 194	429	1 552	982	445	277	277	709	397	62 900
1980	1 292	852	330	1 292	852	330	1 191	710	366	222	222	545	337	64 600
1981	1 084	705	288	1 084	705	288	986	564	319	241	241	436	275	68 900
1982	1 062	663	320	1 062	663	320	1 000	546	366	240	240	412	253	69 300
1983	1 703	1 068	522	1 703	1 068	522	1 605	902	570	296	296	623	301	75 300
1984	1 750	1 084	544	1 750	1 084	544	1 682	922	617	296	296	639	353	79 900
1985	1 742	1 072	576	1 742	1 072	576	1 733	957	657	284	284	688	346	84 300
1986	1 805	1 179	542	1 805	1 179	542	1 769	1 078	584	244	244	750	357	92 000
1987	1 620	1 146	409	1 620	1 146	409	1 535	1 024	421	233	233	671	366	104 500
1988	1 488	1 081	348	1 488	1 081	348	1 456	994	386	218	218	676	368	112 500
1989	1 376	1 003	318	1 376	1 003	318	1 338	932	340	198	198	650	365	120 000
1990	1 193	895	260	1 193	895	260	1 111	794	263	188	188	534	321	122 900
1991	1 014	840	138	1 014	840	138	949	754	152	171	171	509	284	120 000
1992	1 200	1 030	139	1 200	1 030	139	1 095	911	138	210	210	610	265	121 500
1993	1 288	1 126	133	1 288	1 126	133	1 199	986	160	254	254	666	293	126 500
1994	1 457	1 198	224	1 457	1 198	224	1 372	1 068	241	304	304	670	336	130 000
1995	1 354	1 076	244	1 354	1 076	244	1 332	997	272	340	340	667	370	133 900
1996	1 477	1 161	271	1 477	1 161	271	1 426	1 070	290	363	362	757	322	140 000
1997	1 474	1 134	296	1 474	1 134	296	1 441	1 062	310	354	354	804	281	146 000
1998	1 617	1 271	303	1 617	1 271	303	1 612	1 188	356	373	373	886	294	152 500
1999	1 641	1 302	307	1 641	1 302	307	1 664	1 247	351	348	348	880	308	161 000
2000	1 569	1 231	299	1 569	1 231	299	1 592	1 198	329	250	250	877	298	169 000
2001	1 603	1 273	293	1 603	1 273	293	1 637	1 236	335	193	193	908	308	175 200
2002	1 705	1 359	308	1 705	1 359	308	1 748	1 333	341	168	168	973	339	187 600
2003	1 848	1 499	315	1 848	1 499	315	1 889	1 461	346	131	131	1 086	370	195 000
2002														
January	110	85	21	1 698	1 318	311	1 665	1 285	311	14	194	880	310	187 100
February	120	99	18	1 829	1 501	284	1 787	1 401	320	13	186	948	313	191 100
March	138	110	25	1 642	1 292	305	1 691	1 289	330	14	171	923	316	183 400
April	149	122	24	1 592	1 277	287	1 669	1 285	316	15	176	936	324	187 100
May	166	134	28	1 764	1 402	325	1 716	1 289	356	16	173	978	327	181 000
June	160	130	26	1 717	1 368	302	1 758	1 314	362	15	171	957	328	190 600
July	156	125	28	1 655	1 323	301	1 738	1 307	362	14	169	956	333	175 600
August	147	111	33	1 633	1 247	355	1 695	1 317	306	16	166	1 014	334	178 900
September	156	124	28	1 804	1 446	321	1 803	1 366	345	14	162	1 044	333	177 500
October	147	119	25	1 648	1 352	262	1 799	1 382	346	16	156	1 006	335	189 200
November	133	103	28	1 753	1 394	325	1 771	1 382	319	12	150	1 024	338	181 200
December	123	97	23	1 788	1 439	314	1 896	1 409	409	9	144	1 048	339	197 600
2003														
January	118	96	19	1 856	1 534	280	1 816	1 421	307	10	141	1 001	342	181 700
February	110	88	20	1 657	1 325	301	1 866	1 369	418	10	137	932	342	187 000
March	147	120	24	1 728	1 396	298	1 754	1 361	320	10	130	1 006	340	185 100
April	151	128	20	1 637	1 363	242	1 798	1 387	326	11	132	1 027	341	189 500
May	165	134	29	1 748	1 393	328	1 846	1 394	367	12	130	1 093	343	195 500
June	174	144	28	1 850	1 505	317	1 871	1 465	330	12	131	1 194	343	187 900
July	176	143	30	1 893	1 536	321	1 892	1 483	329	11	136	1 156	341	190 200
August	164	132	29	1 835	1 494	309	1 964	1 518	363	12	129	1 189	344	190 500
September	171	137	30	1 922	1 537	340	1 943	1 526	327	12	129	1 127	350	192 000
October	174	142	29	1 983	1 644	310	2 015	1 558	375	13	126	1 141	360	194 100
November	154	121	30	2 054	1 670	347	1 920	1 504	322	9	126	1 086	365	207 100
December	144	114	28	2 067	1 657	381	1 979	1 546	356	8	125	1 120	370	196 000

[1] Includes structures with 2 to 4 units, not shown separately.
[2] Data beginning with 1994 cover 19,000 permit issuing places; 1984–1993: 17,000 places; 1978–1983: 16,000 places; 1972–1977: 14,000 places; 1971: 13,000 places.
. . . = Not available.

Table 17-4. Manufacturers' Shipments

(Millions of dollars, adjusted for trading-day and calendar-month variation, but without seasonal adjustment.)

Classification basis, year and month	Total	NAICS durable goods industries									
		Total [1]	Nonmetallic mineral products	Primary metals		Fabricated metal products	Machinery	Computers and electronic products	Electrical equipment, appliances and components	Transportation equipment	
				Total	Iron and steel mills					Total	Motor vehicles and parts
SIC Basis [2]											
1958	326 971	162 632	9 543	26 541	15 533	21 359		41 129		39 223	20 411
1959	363 437	187 168	11 052	31 381	18 251	23 723		47 386		45 502	26 239
1960	370 535	190 440	10 879	31 307	18 140	23 947		48 426		47 631	29 263
1961	371 067	187 217	10 782	30 610	17 196	23 701		49 376		44 221	25 222
1962	400 294	206 958	11 298	32 543	18 073	26 162		53 993		52 146	31 979
1963	420 690	219 058	12 000	34 398	18 954	26 847		56 450		56 379	35 328
1964	447 968	235 327	12 652	38 876	21 625	28 866		62 425		58 151	36 557
1965	491 938	266 318	13 652	43 975	23 965	32 378		71 268		68 213	45 162
1966	538 436	295 405	14 301	47 943	24 551	36 775		83 483		72 500	45 058
1967	557 836	302 795	14 116	45 139	23 123	40 054		86 946		72 535	40 337
1968	602 744	331 490	15 465	48 717	24 908	43 638		90 742		83 527	49 465
1969	642 013	352 836	16 499	53 534	26 412	46 104		98 144		85 175	50 943
1970	633 663	337 876	16 454	51 995	25 189	44 210		98 301		74 539	42 538
1971	670 877	359 089	18 220	51 585	25 791	45 478		98 822		88 857	58 247
1972	756 321	407 844	20 875	58 490	28 712	51 487		113 658		94 706	63 923
1973	875 173	475 621	23 141	72 791	36 301	58 804		132 776		110 587	74 799
1974	1 017 477	530 074	25 503	95 686	49 718	67 212		151 725		108 244	68 631
1975	1 039 065	523 178	26 233	80 890	42 281	68 411		152 422		113 503	70 033
1976	1 185 563	607 475	29 618	93 082	46 764	77 560		170 998		141 028	95 380
1977	1 358 416	710 017	34 209	103 267	50 670	89 938		200 594		166 954	117 747
1978	1 522 858	812 776	40 238	118 175	59 228	101 245		232 598		188 773	131 999
1979	1 727 234	911 124	44 287	137 488	67 414	113 494		269 375		201 623	131 378
1980	1 852 689	929 027	44 473	134 057	61 612	116 071		293 428		186 516	104 560
1981	2 017 544	1 004 725	46 220	142 072	70 254	123 535		323 186		205 223	116 981
1982	1 960 214	950 541	43 515	104 874	46 928	119 236		312 501		201 347	112 270
1983	2 070 564	1 025 770	47 697	109 240	46 398	123 083		314 584		245 392	148 296
1984	2 288 184	1 175 276	53 101	120 315	51 978	138 107		373 437		284 593	181 993
1985	2 334 456	1 215 352	55 821	112 265	48 904	143 268		382 359		307 380	193 445
1986	2 335 881	1 238 859	59 254	107 865	45 718	143 063		378 385		322 688	198 811
1987	2 475 906	1 297 532	61 477	120 248	51 815	147 367		388 958		332 936	205 923
1988	2 695 432	1 421 501	63 145	149 837	64 294	159 505		431 666		354 849	222 353
1989	2 840 375	1 477 900	63 729	155 718	64 783	164 073		450 810		369 675	233 232
1990	2 912 228	1 485 313	63 728	148 787	62 826	165 064		455 265		370 328	217 295
1991	2 878 167	1 451 998	59 957	136 378	57 267	159 760		446 786		367 235	209 210
1992	3 004 727	1 541 866	62 521	138 287	58 449	166 532		475 426		399 270	238 384
NAICS Basis											
1992	2 904 024	1 518 862	61 902	123 789	55 947	170 403	186 589	273 728	81 813	433 611	279 197
1993	3 020 497	1 604 544	64 957	126 988	59 632	177 967	201 076	286 457	87 646	453 437	310 178
1994	3 238 112	1 764 061	70 598	142 976	67 087	194 113	224 920	320 769	95 531	494 745	364 840
1995	3 479 677	1 902 815	74 865	160 774	72 019	212 444	246 277	370 679	101 051	508 271	379 551
1996	3 597 188	1 978 597	81 308	157 638	71 814	222 995	257 459	399 516	105 283	516 030	387 394
1997	3 834 699	2 147 384	86 465	168 118	76 900	242 812	270 687	439 380	112 116	575 307	421 573
1998	3 899 813	2 231 588	92 501	166 109	75 871	253 720	280 651	443 768	116 024	612 882	439 590
1999	4 031 887	2 326 736	96 153	156 648	70 087	257 071	276 904	467 059	118 313	676 328	498 716
2000	4 208 584	2 373 688	97 329	156 598	70 470	268 213	291 548	510 639	125 443	639 861	471 180
2001	3 970 499	2 174 406	94 861	138 246	60 559	253 113	266 554	429 471	114 068	602 495	427 175
2002	3 891 753	2 131 404	88 222	135 930	61 999	252 232	255 651	392 026	103 673	624 129	450 136
2003	3 999 124	2 150 638	87 500	131 307	59 400	245 469	253 516	418 651	101 415	618 670	442 840
2002											
January	293 487	157 567	7 112	10 711	4 771	19 212	18 194	27 436	7 317	46 965	35 484
February	306 553	169 535	7 132	10 769	4 732	19 971	20 534	29 959	8 174	51 072	36 889
March	336 551	189 501	6 973	11 597	5 139	21 053	23 459	37 547	9 363	56 011	38 421
April	321 818	177 397	7 538	11 877	5 300	21 317	21 810	29 148	8 602	53 887	40 794
May	335 139	185 469	7 796	12 232	5 486	21 977	23 019	30 566	8 960	57 073	42 900
June	341 904	191 627	7 634	11 759	5 401	21 890	23 961	36 830	9 407	55 655	39 317
July	298 864	155 915	7 433	10 793	5 018	20 308	19 715	28 463	7 854	38 539	26 652
August	333 948	182 062	8 066	11 949	5 532	22 421	20 843	30 803	8 573	55 230	41 611
September	343 319	190 546	7 649	11 640	5 457	21 987	22 454	38 158	9 467	55 279	38 900
October	341 009	185 688	7 871	12 137	5 638	22 500	21 121	31 812	8 556	57 338	43 837
November	322 601	174 969	6 888	10 744	4 927	20 457	19 926	33 356	8 623	51 395	36 164
December	316 560	171 128	6 130	9 722	4 598	19 139	20 615	37 948	8 777	45 685	29 167
2003											
January	301 776	159 049	6 652	11 231	5 155	19 199	18 230	27 810	7 438	47 373	36 776
February	312 516	167 845	6 353	10 829	4 945	19 871	19 773	29 846	7 835	51 310	37 150
March	347 472	189 651	6 924	11 532	5 389	20 911	23 220	37 467	8 978	56 388	39 648
April	319 294	170 450	7 245	11 215	5 246	20 168	21 404	29 941	8 076	49 252	36 320
May	330 134	177 433	7 546	11 326	5 197	20 803	21 730	31 305	8 361	52 666	38 468
June	348 612	192 530	7 705	10 934	4 936	21 088	23 110	39 941	9 059	55 203	38 294
July	310 025	158 160	7 666	10 157	4 584	19 867	19 807	30 233	7 767	38 739	26 258
August	335 985	177 143	7 927	10 758	4 771	20 848	20 304	33 241	8 188	50 382	36 471
September	357 911	197 413	8 049	11 041	4 899	21 388	22 088	41 682	9 528	57 002	40 367
October	356 009	192 632	8 475	11 636	5 084	22 013	21 515	35 956	8 583	57 541	43 550
November	333 414	179 050	6 664	10 370	4 534	19 744	19 826	36 224	8 545	52 019	35 528
December	345 976	189 282	6 294	10 278	4 660	19 569	22 509	45 005	9 057	50 795	34 010

[1] Includes categories not shown separately.
[2] Data are for roughly similar categories in SIC classification system.
[3] SIC tobacco only, 1958–1992.
. . . = Not available.

Table 17-4. Manufacturers' Shipments—Continued

(Millions of dollars, adjusted for trading-day and calendar-month variation, but without seasonal adjustment.)

Classification basis, year and month	NAICS nondurable goods industries									
	Total [1]	Food products	Beverage and tobacco products [3]	Textiles	Textile products	Apparel	Paper products	Basic chemicals	Petroleum and coal products	Plastics and rubber products
SIC Basis [2]										
1958	164 339	59 738	3 868	12 417		...	12 707	23 093	15 188	7 310
1959	176 269	60 781	4 049	14 067		...	14 077	26 358	15 806	8 395
1960	180 095	62 468	4 367	13 791		...	14 308	26 509	16 349	8 483
1961	183 850	64 542	4 487	14 016		...	14 524	27 175	16 359	8 511
1962	193 336	66 935	4 531	15 185		...	15 382	29 266	16 716	9 335
1963	201 632	68 469	4 521	15 744		...	16 192	31 682	17 506	10 076
1964	212 641	71 594	4 653	17 000		...	17 019	34 148	17 855	10 749
1965	225 620	74 250	4 649	18 299		...	18 394	37 289	18 588	11 966
1966	243 031	79 665	4 772	19 600		...	20 211	40 569	19 857	13 181
1967	255 041	83 961	4 903	19 816		...	20 777	42 037	21 435	13 908
1968	271 254	87 328	4 937	21 970		...	22 093	45 491	22 548	15 585
1969	289 177	93 385	4 992	22 978		...	24 188	48 096	23 721	16 935
1970	295 787	98 535	5 350	22 614		...	24 573	49 195	24 200	16 754
1971	311 788	103 637	5 528	24 034		...	25 182	51 681	26 198	18 409
1972	348 477	115 054	5 919	28 065		...	28 004	58 130	27 918	21 662
1973	399 552	135 585	6 341	31 073		...	32 495	66 003	33 903	25 191
1974	487 403	161 884	7 139	32 790		...	41 514	85 387	57 229	28 828
1975	515 887	172 054	8 058	31 065		...	41 497	91 710	67 496	28 128
1976	578 088	180 830	8 786	36 387		...	47 939	106 467	80 022	32 880
1977	648 399	192 913	9 051	40 550		...	51 881	120 905	94 702	40 944
1978	710 082	215 989	9 951	42 281		...	56 777	132 262	100 967	44 823
1979	816 110	235 976	10 602	45 137		...	64 957	151 887	144 156	48 694
1980	923 662	256 191	12 194	47 256		...	72 553	168 220	192 969	49 157
1981	1 012 819	272 140	13 130	50 260		...	79 970	186 909	217 681	55 178
1982	1 009 673	280 529	16 061	47 516		...	79 698	176 254	203 404	57 307
1983	1 044 794	289 314	16 268	53 733		...	84 817	189 552	187 788	62 870
1984	1 112 908	304 584	17 473	56 336		...	95 525	205 963	184 488	72 938
1985	1 119 104	308 606	18 559	54 605		...	94 679	204 790	176 574	75 590
1986	1 097 022	318 203	19 146	57 188		...	99 865	205 711	122 605	78 379
1987	1 178 374	329 725	20 757	62 787		...	108 989	229 546	130 414	86 634
1988	1 273 931	354 084	23 809	64 627		...	122 882	261 238	131 682	95 485
1989	1 362 475	380 160	25 875	67 265		...	131 896	283 196	146 487	101 236
1990	1 426 915	391 728	29 856	65 533		...	132 424	292 802	173 389	105 250
1991	1 426 169	397 893	31 943	65 440		...	130 131	298 545	159 144	105 804
1992	1 462 861	406 964	35 198	70 753		...	133 201	305 420	150 227	113 593
NAICS Basis										
1992	1 385 162	358 494	85 687	52 923	24 763	61 535	127 122	319 501	150 095	113 827
1993	1 415 953	373 612	79 227	55 375	25 623	63 210	126 982	330 760	144 731	122 807
1994	1 474 051	379 786	83 434	58 607	27 233	64 894	136 922	350 098	143 339	134 288
1995	1 576 862	393 204	88 945	59 885	27 976	65 214	166 051	376 995	151 431	145 084
1996	1 618 591	404 173	94 033	59 796	28 515	64 237	152 860	385 919	174 181	149 773
1997	1 687 315	421 737	96 971	58 707	31 052	68 018	150 296	415 617	177 394	159 161
1998	1 668 225	428 479	102 359	57 416	31 137	64 932	154 984	416 742	137 957	163 736
1999	1 705 151	426 001	106 920	54 306	32 689	62 305	156 915	420 321	162 620	171 885
2000	1 834 896	435 229	111 692	52 112	33 654	60 339	165 298	449 159	235 134	178 236
2001	1 796 093	451 385	118 786	45 681	31 971	54 598	155 845	438 410	219 074	170 717
2002	1 760 349	450 183	109 832	43 170	34 232	53 621	151 530	424 143	206 879	178 383
2003	1 848 486	461 064	105 310	39 775	35 247	52 970	159 611	459 110	244 097	185 363
2002										
January	135 920	35 962	8 840	3 065	2 255	3 941	12 108	33 366	14 753	13 404
February	137 018	36 727	8 507	3 493	2 739	4 596	11 655	32 811	14 276	13 856
March	147 050	38 627	9 596	3 832	2 915	4 412	12 135	35 930	15 604	14 923
April	144 421	35 993	9 033	3 726	2 970	4 309	12 184	35 580	16 440	15 561
May	149 670	37 379	10 083	3 751	2 949	4 126	12 630	36 496	17 655	15 992
June	150 277	36 902	9 760	3 898	3 147	4 345	12 446	37 908	17 698	15 407
July	142 949	35 194	9 424	3 440	2 840	4 734	12 593	33 238	18 290	14 662
August	151 886	38 096	9 654	3 788	3 091	5 038	13 733	34 560	18 872	15 549
September	152 773	38 286	9 103	3 857	2 987	4 830	13 257	37 149	18 589	15 122
October	155 321	39 765	8 978	3 691	2 928	4 918	13 539	36 471	19 114	15 916
November	147 632	38 935	8 601	3 538	2 833	4 645	12 486	34 931	17 586	14 366
December	145 432	38 317	8 253	3 091	2 578	3 727	12 764	35 703	18 002	13 625
2003										
January	142 727	35 956	7 870	3 157	2 390	4 098	12 811	35 336	18 473	14 349
February	144 671	36 264	7 948	3 383	2 726	4 485	12 616	35 524	18 557	14 579
March	157 821	38 205	9 127	3 613	2 985	4 462	13 526	40 119	20 613	15 977
April	148 844	36 887	8 826	3 194	2 904	3 946	13 065	37 541	18 087	15 588
May	152 701	37 515	9 427	3 208	2 887	3 871	13 353	37 822	19 984	16 004
June	156 082	38 384	9 383	3 493	3 074	4 255	13 811	38 828	20 228	16 025
July	151 865	36 762	9 154	2 940	2 952	4 477	13 264	38 284	20 650	15 254
August	158 842	39 689	9 123	3 401	3 156	4 772	13 390	38 241	22 357	15 663
September	160 498	40 620	8 815	3 561	3 087	4 796	13 561	40 464	20 552	15 897
October	163 377	41 352	8 840	3 562	3 113	5 176	13 861	40 554	20 941	16 713
November	154 364	39 922	8 343	3 252	3 005	4 635	12 905	37 419	21 132	14 584
December	156 694	39 508	8 454	3 011	2 968	3 997	13 448	38 978	22 523	14 730

[1] Includes categories not shown separately.
[2] Data are for roughly similar categories in SIC classification system.
[3] SIC tobacco only, 1958–1992.
... = Not available.

Table 17-4. Manufacturers' Shipments—Continued

(Millions of dollars, seasonally adjusted.)

Classification basis, year and month	Total	NAICS durable goods industries									
		Total [1]	Nonmetallic mineral products	Primary metals		Fabricated metal products	Machinery	Computers and electronic products	Electrical equipment, appliances and components	Transportation equipment	
				Total	Iron and steel mills					Total	Motor vehicles and parts
SIC Basis [2]											
1958	326 971	162 632	9 543	26 541	15 533	21 359		41 129		39 223	20 411
1959	363 437	187 168	11 052	31 381	18 251	23 723		47 386		45 502	26 239
1960	370 535	190 440	10 879	31 307	18 140	23 947		48 426		47 631	29 263
1961	371 067	187 217	10 782	30 610	17 196	23 701		49 376		44 221	25 222
1962	400 294	206 958	11 298	32 543	18 073	26 162		53 993		52 146	31 979
1963	420 690	219 058	12 000	34 398	18 954	26 847		56 450		56 379	35 328
1964	447 968	235 327	12 652	38 876	21 625	28 866		62 425		58 151	36 557
1965	491 938	266 318	13 652	43 975	23 965	32 378		71 268		68 213	45 162
1966	538 436	295 405	14 301	47 943	24 551	36 775		83 483		72 500	45 058
1967	557 836	302 795	14 116	45 139	23 123	40 054		86 946		72 535	40 337
1968	602 744	331 490	15 465	48 717	24 908	43 638		90 742		83 527	49 465
1969	642 013	352 836	16 499	53 534	26 412	46 104		98 144		85 175	50 943
1970	633 663	337 876	16 454	51 995	25 189	44 210		98 301		74 539	42 538
1971	670 877	359 089	18 220	51 585	25 791	45 478		98 822		88 857	58 247
1972	756 321	407 844	20 875	58 490	28 712	51 487		113 658		94 706	63 923
1973	875 173	475 621	23 141	72 791	36 301	58 804		132 776		110 587	74 799
1974	1 017 477	530 074	25 503	95 686	49 718	67 212		151 725		108 244	68 631
1975	1 039 065	523 178	26 233	80 890	42 281	68 411		152 422		113 503	70 033
1976	1 185 563	607 475	29 618	93 082	46 764	77 560		170 998		141 028	95 380
1977	1 358 416	710 017	34 209	103 267	50 670	89 938		200 594		166 954	117 747
1978	1 522 858	812 776	40 238	118 175	59 228	101 245		232 598		188 773	131 999
1979	1 727 234	911 124	44 287	137 488	67 414	113 494		269 375		201 623	131 378
1980	1 852 689	929 027	44 473	134 057	61 612	116 071		293 428		186 516	104 560
1981	2 017 544	1 004 725	46 220	142 072	70 254	123 535		323 186		205 223	116 981
1982	1 960 214	950 541	43 515	104 874	46 928	119 236		312 501		201 347	112 270
1983	2 070 564	1 025 770	47 697	109 240	46 398	123 083		314 584		245 392	148 296
1984	2 288 184	1 175 276	53 101	120 315	51 978	138 107		373 437		284 593	181 993
1985	2 334 456	1 215 352	55 821	112 265	48 904	143 268		382 359		307 380	193 445
1986	2 335 881	1 238 859	59 254	107 865	45 718	143 063		378 385		322 688	198 811
1987	2 475 906	1 297 532	61 477	120 248	51 815	147 367		388 958		332 936	205 923
1988	2 695 432	1 421 501	63 145	149 837	64 294	159 505		431 666		354 849	222 353
1989	2 840 375	1 477 900	63 729	155 718	64 783	164 073		450 810		369 675	233 232
1990	2 912 228	1 485 313	63 728	148 787	62 826	165 064		455 265		370 328	217 295
1991	2 878 167	1 451 998	59 957	136 378	57 267	159 760		446 786		367 235	209 210
1992	3 004 727	1 541 866	62 521	138 287	58 449	166 532		475 426		399 270	238 384
NAICS Basis											
1992	2 904 024	1 518 862	61 902	123 789	55 947	170 403	186 589	273 728	81 813	433 611	279 197
1993	3 020 497	1 604 544	64 957	126 988	59 632	177 967	201 076	286 457	87 646	453 437	310 178
1994	3 238 112	1 764 061	70 598	142 976	67 087	194 113	224 920	320 769	95 531	494 745	364 840
1995	3 479 677	1 902 815	74 865	160 774	72 019	212 444	246 277	370 679	101 051	508 271	379 551
1996	3 597 188	1 978 597	81 308	157 638	71 814	222 995	257 459	399 516	105 283	516 030	387 394
1997	3 834 699	2 147 384	86 465	168 118	76 900	242 812	270 687	439 380	112 116	575 307	421 573
1998	3 899 813	2 231 588	92 501	166 109	75 871	253 720	280 651	443 768	116 024	612 882	439 590
1999	4 031 887	2 326 736	96 153	156 648	70 087	257 071	276 904	467 059	118 313	676 328	498 716
2000	4 208 584	2 373 688	97 329	156 598	70 470	268 213	291 548	510 639	125 443	639 861	471 180
2001	3 970 499	2 174 406	94 861	138 246	60 559	253 113	266 554	429 471	114 068	602 495	427 175
2002	3 891 753	2 131 404	88 222	135 930	61 999	252 232	255 651	392 026	103 673	624 129	450 136
2003	3 999 124	2 150 638	87 500	131 307	59 400	245 469	253 516	418 651	101 415	618 670	442 840
2002											
January	323 837	178 520	7 908	11 017	4 890	20 912	21 844	33 355	8 537	51 996	36 906
February	320 087	177 021	7 792	10 772	4 699	20 520	22 394	32 819	8 518	51 398	36 562
March	318 481	174 615	7 209	11 114	4 938	20 504	21 093	32 725	8 641	50 428	35 349
April	325 938	180 692	7 393	11 509	5 123	21 298	21 261	32 937	8 878	54 022	39 484
May	325 999	179 898	7 322	11 533	5 190	21 094	22 169	32 639	8 894	52 665	38 493
June	322 827	176 479	7 235	11 404	5 217	21 025	21 329	32 222	8 554	51 672	37 417
July	328 367	181 527	7 236	11 563	5 303	21 359	21 658	32 855	8 688	54 583	39 715
August	326 168	178 881	7 345	11 584	5 369	21 273	21 553	32 653	8 550	52 525	38 783
September	326 165	178 199	7 283	11 452	5 377	21 242	21 285	32 928	8 514	52 541	37 964
October	329 349	179 936	7 202	11 578	5 384	21 285	21 324	33 002	8 645	53 530	39 131
November	326 527	177 483	7 185	11 279	5 271	20 928	21 188	33 064	8 737	51 373	36 716
December	323 362	172 894	7 234	11 162	5 286	20 899	20 857	31 916	8 554	48 395	34 385
2003											
January	329 665	177 331	7 348	11 480	5 268	20 768	21 099	33 241	8 633	51 242	37 630
February	325 591	173 992	6 991	10 849	4 915	20 483	20 624	32 496	8 205	51 354	36 571
March	330 764	175 475	7 201	11 105	5 169	20 451	20 767	32 771	8 317	51 230	36 695
April	322 608	173 512	7 101	10 838	5 068	20 105	20 632	33 875	8 304	49 349	35 169
May	323 920	173 783	7 162	10 825	5 008	20 222	20 861	33 261	8 311	49 491	35 153
June	328 643	176 782	7 238	10 488	4 661	20 179	20 854	34 884	8 286	50 984	36 102
July	337 248	181 761	7 350	10 826	4 880	20 883	21 264	35 125	8 546	53 194	38 149
August	331 676	177 187	7 312	10 577	4 731	19 977	21 057	35 343	8 300	49 847	35 653
September	337 598	182 379	7 503	10 782	4 788	20 424	21 375	35 614	8 463	53 066	38 059
October	339 825	183 740	7 631	10 968	4 841	20 532	21 492	36 529	8 562	52 392	37 835
November	341 454	184 074	7 145	11 069	4 928	20 423	21 260	36 348	8 627	53 245	37 591
December	348 485	187 978	7 316	11 564	5 202	21 049	22 776	37 463	8 627	53 043	38 433

[1]Includes categories not shown separately.
[2]Data are for roughly similar categories in SIC classification system.
[3]SIC tobacco only, 1958–1992.
. . . = Not available.

Table 17-4. Manufacturers' Shipments—Continued
(Millions of dollars, seasonally adjusted.)

Classification basis, year and month	NAICS nondurable goods industries									
	Total [1]	Food products	Beverage and tobacco products [3]	Textiles	Textile products	Apparel	Paper products	Basic chemicals	Petroleum and coal products	Plastics and rubber products
SIC Basis [2]										
1958	164 339	59 738	3 868	12 417		...	12 707	23 093	15 188	7 310
1959	176 269	60 781	4 049	14 067		...	14 077	26 358	15 806	8 395
1960	180 095	62 468	4 367	13 791		...	14 308	26 509	16 349	8 483
1961	183 850	64 542	4 487	14 016		...	14 524	27 175	16 359	8 511
1962	193 336	66 935	4 531	15 185		...	15 382	29 266	16 716	9 335
1963	201 632	68 469	4 521	15 744		...	16 192	31 682	17 506	10 076
1964	212 641	71 594	4 653	17 000		...	17 019	34 148	17 855	10 749
1965	225 620	74 250	4 649	18 299		...	18 394	37 289	18 588	11 966
1966	243 031	79 665	4 772	19 600		...	20 211	40 569	19 857	13 181
1967	255 041	83 961	4 903	19 816		...	20 777	42 037	21 435	13 908
1968	271 254	87 328	4 937	21 970		...	22 093	45 491	22 548	15 585
1969	289 177	93 385	4 992	22 978		...	24 188	48 096	23 721	16 935
1970	295 787	98 535	5 350	22 614		...	24 573	49 195	24 200	16 754
1971	311 788	103 637	5 528	24 034		...	25 182	51 681	26 198	18 409
1972	348 477	115 054	5 919	28 065		...	28 004	58 130	27 918	21 662
1973	399 552	135 585	6 341	31 073		...	32 495	66 003	33 903	25 191
1974	487 403	161 884	7 139	32 790		...	41 514	85 387	57 229	28 828
1975	515 887	172 054	8 058	31 065		...	41 497	91 710	67 496	28 128
1976	578 088	180 830	8 786	36 387		...	47 939	106 467	80 022	32 880
1977	648 399	192 913	9 051	40 550		...	51 881	120 905	94 702	40 944
1978	710 082	215 989	9 951	42 281		...	56 777	132 262	100 967	44 823
1979	816 110	235 976	10 602	45 137		...	64 957	151 887	144 156	48 694
1980	923 662	256 191	12 194	47 256		...	72 553	168 220	192 969	49 157
1981	1 012 819	272 140	13 130	50 260		...	79 970	186 909	217 681	55 178
1982	1 009 673	280 529	16 061	47 516		...	79 698	176 254	203 404	57 307
1983	1 044 794	289 314	16 268	53 733		...	84 817	189 552	187 788	62 870
1984	1 112 908	304 584	17 473	56 336		...	95 525	205 963	184 488	72 938
1985	1 119 104	308 606	18 559	54 605		...	94 679	204 790	176 574	75 590
1986	1 097 022	318 203	19 146	57 188		...	99 865	205 711	122 605	78 379
1987	1 178 374	329 725	20 757	62 787		...	108 989	229 546	130 414	86 634
1988	1 273 931	354 084	23 809	64 627		...	122 882	261 238	131 682	95 485
1989	1 362 475	380 160	25 875	67 265		...	131 896	283 196	146 487	101 236
1990	1 426 915	391 728	29 856	65 533		...	132 424	292 802	173 389	105 250
1991	1 426 169	397 893	31 943	65 440		...	130 131	298 545	159 144	105 804
1992	1 462 861	406 964	35 198	70 753		...	133 201	305 420	150 227	113 593
NAICS Basis										
1992	1 385 162	358 494	85 687	52 923	24 763	61 535	127 122	319 501	150 095	113 827
1993	1 415 953	373 612	79 227	55 375	25 623	63 210	126 982	330 760	144 731	122 807
1994	1 474 051	379 786	83 434	58 607	27 233	64 894	136 922	350 098	143 339	134 288
1995	1 576 862	393 204	88 945	59 885	27 976	65 214	166 051	376 995	151 431	145 084
1996	1 618 591	404 173	94 033	59 796	28 515	64 237	152 860	385 919	174 181	149 773
1997	1 687 315	421 737	96 971	58 707	31 052	68 018	150 296	415 617	177 394	159 161
1998	1 668 225	428 479	102 359	57 416	31 137	64 932	154 984	416 742	137 957	163 736
1999	1 705 151	426 001	106 920	54 306	32 689	62 305	156 915	420 321	162 620	171 885
2000	1 834 896	435 229	111 692	52 112	33 654	60 339	165 298	449 159	235 134	178 236
2001	1 796 093	451 385	118 786	45 681	31 971	54 598	155 845	438 410	219 074	170 717
2002	1 760 349	450 183	109 832	43 170	34 232	53 621	151 530	424 143	206 879	178 383
2003	1 848 486	461 064	105 310	39 775	35 247	52 970	159 611	459 110	244 097	185 363
2002										
January	145 317	37 889	9 625	3 522	2 667	4 401	12 516	34 975	16 443	14 328
February	143 066	37 803	9 038	3 588	2 818	4 417	11 914	34 345	16 101	14 309
March	143 866	37 706	9 615	3 582	2 781	4 314	12 147	33 949	16 595	14 268
April	145 246	37 341	9 012	3 786	2 888	4 555	12 391	34 853	16 471	15 023
May	146 101	37 523	9 511	3 666	2 906	4 544	12 539	35 094	16 338	14 977
June	146 348	36 887	9 314	3 599	2 877	4 444	12 325	36 231	16 833	14 808
July	146 840	37 320	9 145	3 766	2 856	4 583	12 674	34 729	17 560	15 161
August	147 287	37 524	9 163	3 578	2 855	4 457	13 241	34 784	17 523	15 012
September	147 966	37 155	9 054	3 522	2 871	4 480	12 927	36 340	17 529	14 924
October	149 413	37 664	8 972	3 597	2 883	4 393	13 040	36 171	18 287	15 205
November	149 044	37 652	8 761	3 590	2 915	4 568	12 724	36 356	18 185	15 173
December	150 468	37 850	8 592	3 406	2 896	4 468	13 137	36 412	19 286	15 305
2003										
January	152 334	37 866	8 715	3 573	2 859	4 534	13 154	37 029	20 294	15 294
February	151 599	37 417	8 505	3 476	2 808	4 346	12 930	37 141	20 853	15 136
March	155 289	37 539	9 159	3 440	2 849	4 370	13 493	38 085	21 965	15 364
April	149 096	37 910	8 799	3 223	2 833	4 214	13 345	36 936	17 787	14 973
May	150 137	37 816	8 871	3 145	2 807	4 261	13 403	36 867	18 810	15 150
June	151 861	38 697	8 970	3 207	2 836	4 346	13 459	36 918	19 218	15 342
July	155 487	38 776	8 896	3 221	2 910	4 286	13 421	39 868	19 922	15 489
August	154 489	38 946	8 770	3 202	2 913	4 264	13 113	38 508	20 767	15 261
September	155 219	39 241	8 692	3 270	2 964	4 421	13 137	39 160	20 035	15 576
October	156 085	39 147	8 816	3 364	3 028	4 492	13 266	39 731	19 901	15 768
November	157 380	38 759	8 601	3 324	3 089	4 526	13 355	39 239	22 154	15 640
December	160 507	38 565	8 730	3 314	3 290	4 632	13 644	39 573	23 778	16 199

[1] Includes categories not shown separately.
[2] Data are for roughly similar categories in SIC classification system.
[3] SIC tobacco only, 1958–1992.
... = Not available.

Table 17-4. Manufacturers' Shipments—Continued

(Millions of dollars, seasonally adjusted.)

Classification basis, year and month	Construction supplies	Information technology industries	By topical categories				Consumer goods		
			Capital goods				Consumer goods		
			Total	Nondefense		Defense	Total	Durable	Nondurable
				Total	Excluding aircraft and parts				
SIC Basis [2]									
1958	23 286	...	46 552	...	...	...	...	...	...
1959	26 278	...	51 234	...	...	...	...	...	...
1960	25 886	...	52 171	...	...	...	...	...	...
1961	25 498	...	53 762	...	...	...	...	...	...
1962	27 019	...	58 711	...	...	...	...	...	...
1963	28 545	...	61 186	...	...	...	...	...	...
1964	30 692	...	64 837	...	...	...	...	...	...
1965	33 287	...	71 621	...	...	...	...	...	...
1966	35 643	...	84 792	...	...	...	...	...	...
1967	36 210	...	94 101	...	...	...	...	...	...
1968	39 621	...	99 702	72 405	...	27 297	...	...	...
1969	42 493	...	105 773	79 568	...	26 205	...	...	...
1970	41 945	...	102 285	78 907	...	23 378	...	...	...
1971	45 559	...	98 643	79 148	...	19 495	...	...	...
1972	54 119	...	107 198	87 762	...	19 436	...	...	...
1973	62 228	...	124 912	103 997	...	20 915	...	...	...
1974	69 146	...	143 828	122 674	...	21 154	...	...	...
1975	66 984	...	149 687	126 363	...	23 324	...	...	...
1976	77 948	...	162 172	135 540	...	26 632	...	...	...
1977	91 883	...	185 541	155 956	...	29 585	...	...	...
1978	106 017	...	217 165	186 427	...	30 738	...	...	...
1979	118 024	...	254 754	222 069	...	32 685	...	...	...
1980	118 429	...	287 132	246 797	...	40 335	...	...	...
1981	122 844	...	317 628	269 774	...	47 854	...	...	...
1982	115 777	...	312 298	252 098	...	60 200	...	...	...
1983	127 781	...	316 125	242 297	...	73 828	...	...	...
1984	141 230	...	361 205	278 900	...	82 305	...	...	...
1985	147 103	...	388 763	293 420	...	95 343	...	...	...
1986	154 113	...	396 158	289 969	...	106 189	...	...	...
1987	164 865	...	404 738	295 334	...	109 404	...	...	...
1988	175 594	...	438 089	333 402	...	104 687	...	...	...
1989	180 083	...	450 863	350 870	...	99 993	...	...	...
1990	180 604	...	473 175	370 804	...	102 371	...	...	...
1991	171 876	...	467 419	369 796	...	97 623	...	...	...
1992	184 498	...	481 257	389 448	...	91 809	...	...	...
NAICS Basis									
1992	281 232	236 015	566 268	471 485	435 696	94 783	1 108 692	263 323	845 369
1993	303 391	241 680	580 859	493 875	463 753	86 984	1 138 467	285 651	852 816
1994	332 734	264 092	616 435	538 203	512 327	78 232	1 203 162	325 995	877 167
1995	353 198	291 885	666 167	590 578	565 729	75 589	1 267 611	335 036	932 575
1996	371 401	311 028	704 635	630 932	605 295	73 703	1 304 283	339 730	964 553
1997	399 880	349 846	779 232	702 971	665 074	76 261	1 369 992	371 669	998 323
1998	418 756	362 564	821 736	747 046	695 717	74 690	1 364 326	385 918	978 408
1999	434 138	374 384	839 754	768 799	713 042	70 955	1 438 519	426 337	1 012 182
2000	444 812	399 751	875 396	808 345	757 617	67 051	1 514 377	405 308	1 109 069
2001	424 517	353 237	801 999	727 980	677 991	74 019	1 493 707	380 734	1 112 973
2002	419 040	319 391	753 048	673 223	634 549	79 825	1 472 647	396 590	1 076 057
2003	421 903	337 316	775 078	683 195	652 339	91 883	1 529 699	400 023	1 129 676
2002									
January	35 136	27 212	64 136	57 369	53 610	6 767	122 938	33 058	89 880
February	34 719	26 966	63 811	57 547	53 929	6 264	120 766	32 671	88 095
March	34 266	26 728	63 154	56 453	52 527	6 701	119 830	30 958	88 872
April	35 129	27 027	62 990	56 596	53 047	6 394	122 494	34 111	88 383
May	35 081	26 803	63 580	57 091	53 894	6 489	122 631	33 634	88 997
June	34 838	26 558	62 626	55 880	52 955	6 746	121 871	32 551	89 320
July	35 207	26 857	63 854	57 116	53 652	6 738	124 265	34 822	89 443
August	35 121	26 644	62 552	56 092	53 487	6 460	123 038	33 571	89 467
September	35 001	26 630	62 853	55 985	52 787	6 868	123 264	32 997	90 267
October	34 946	26 617	63 163	56 443	53 328	6 720	124 914	33 784	91 130
November	34 871	26 649	62 837	55 680	52 844	7 157	123 487	32 832	90 655
December	34 933	25 697	60 981	54 373	51 662	6 608	124 339	32 472	91 867
2003									
January	34 815	26 993	62 362	55 065	53 265	7 297	126 585	33 342	93 243
February	33 997	25 867	61 770	54 449	51 695	7 321	125 385	32 520	92 865
March	34 505	26 246	62 122	54 813	52 135	7 309	128 459	32 759	95 700
April	34 127	27 167	62 468	54 980	52 907	7 488	122 199	31 513	90 686
May	34 124	26 395	62 217	54 779	52 436	7 438	123 702	32 080	91 622
June	34 432	27 884	64 324	56 869	53 903	7 455	125 404	32 472	92 932
July	35 524	29 055	66 381	58 133	55 277	8 248	130 412	34 350	96 062
August	34 922	28 142	64 267	56 487	54 085	7 780	127 433	32 669	94 764
September	35 924	29 123	66 430	58 438	55 774	7 992	128 739	34 253	94 486
October	36 450	29 413	66 523	58 607	56 200	7 916	128 943	34 216	94 727
November	35 837	29 161	66 183	58 684	55 823	7 499	130 514	34 370	96 144
December	36 625	30 380	68 334	60 421	57 952	7 913	132 778	35 159	97 619

[2]Data are for roughly similar categories in SIC classification system.
... = Not available.

Table 17-5. Manufacturers' Inventories

(Current cost basis, end of period; seasonally adjusted, except as noted; millions of dollars.)

Classification basis, year and month	Total, not seasonally adjusted[1]	Total	NAICS durable goods industries										Durables total by stage of fabrication		
			Total[1]	Non-metallic mineral products	Primary metals		Fab-ricated metal products	Machinery	Com-puters and electronic products	Electrical equipment, appliances and components	Transportation equipment		Materials and supplies	Work in progress	Finished goods
					Total	Iron and steel mills					Total	Motor vehicles and parts			
SIC Basis[2]															
1958	49 995	50 203	30 194	1 217	5 153	3 287	4 186		8 630		6 650	1 815	9 970	12 408	7 816
1959	52 671	52 913	32 012	1 351	5 109	3 109	4 244		9 682		6 943	2 211	10 709	13 086	8 217
1960	53 580	53 786	32 337	1 429	5 488	3 385	4 292		9 804		6 415	2 080	10 306	12 809	9 222
1961	54 730	54 871	32 496	1 439	5 792	3 684	4 269		9 890		6 207	2 082	10 246	13 211	9 039
1962	58 060	58 172	34 565	1 460	5 702	3 494	4 387		11 212		6 628	2 334	10 794	14 124	9 647
1963	59 922	60 029	35 776	1 498	5 749	3 459	4 534		11 352		7 111	2 463	11 053	14 835	9 888
1964	63 293	63 410	38 421	1 590	5 953	3 560	5 011		12 573		7 707	2 899	11 946	16 158	10 317
1965	68 028	68 207	42 189	1 669	6 199	3 617	5 696		14 340		8 430	3 289	13 298	18 055	10 836
1966	77 745	77 986	49 852	1 784	7 031	4 075	6 347		17 242		10 454	3 470	15 464	21 908	12 480
1967	84 388	84 646	54 896	1 827	7 553	4 417	6 729		18 279		12 852	3 516	16 423	24 933	13 540
1968	90 235	90 560	58 732	1 918	7 547	4 207	7 506		18 925		14 413	3 879	17 344	27 213	14 175
1969	97 749	98 145	64 598	2 051	8 066	4 451	7 666		21 480		15 942	4 067	18 636	30 282	15 680
1970	101 246	101 599	66 651	2 239	8 995	4 990	7 907		22 910		14 648	4 178	19 149	29 745	17 757
1971	102 267	102 567	66 136	2 302	9 084	4 926	8 098		22 402		13 799	4 173	19 679	28 550	17 907
1972	107 900	108 121	70 067	2 430	9 617	5 387	8 408		23 670		14 775	4 670	20 807	30 713	18 547
1973	124 327	124 499	81 192	2 712	10 034	5 302	9 864		28 943		16 458	5 708	25 944	35 490	19 758
1974	157 595	157 625	101 493	3 403	13 447	6 820	13 387		36 420		19 197	6 688	35 070	42 530	23 893
1975	159 844	159 708	102 590	3 594	15 742	8 597	13 091		35 266		19 620	6 101	33 903	43 227	25 460
1976	174 867	174 636	111 988	3 841	17 699	10 035	14 304		37 839		20 886	7 814	37 457	46 074	28 457
1977	188 435	188 378	120 877	4 095	18 261	10 004	15 527		41 204		22 423	9 078	40 186	50 226	30 465
1978	209 113	211 691	138 181	4 710	19 420	10 719	17 296		48 249		26 170	10 357	45 198	58 848	34 135
1979	239 101	242 157	160 734	5 183	22 446	12 012	19 145		57 030		31 638	10 978	52 670	69 325	38 739
1980	261 700	265 215	174 788	5 674	23 055	12 153	19 532		62 796		35 900	9 864	55 173	76 945	42 670
1981	279 453	283 413	186 443	6 106	25 794	13 359	20 209		67 260		37 527	9 047	57 998	80 998	47 447
1982	307 212	311 852	200 444	6 506	24 174	12 556	21 440		73 008		43 005	8 534	59 136	86 707	54 601
1983	307 675	312 379	199 854	6 628	22 308	11 065	21 752		71 508		43 791	10 433	60 325	86 899	52 630
1984	334 236	339 516	221 330	7 042	22 444	11 087	23 330		80 396		50 770	11 680	66 031	98 251	57 048
1985	329 555	334 749	218 193	7 040	19 974	9 709	22 880		77 075		52 634	11 809	63 904	98 162	56 127
1986	317 567	322 654	211 997	7 093	18 436	8 567	22 094		71 041		53 363	11 445	61 331	97 000	53 666
1987	332 619	338 109	220 799	7 154	19 076	8 620	22 920		73 000		56 461	11 937	63 562	102 393	54 844
1988	363 300	369 374	242 468	7 496	22 422	10 495	24 950		79 352		63 202	12 310	69 611	112 958	59 899
1989	384 539	391 212	257 513	7 792	22 838	10 942	25 427		83 965		70 968	12 503	72 435	122 251	62 827
1990	397 850	405 073	263 209	8 205	22 560	11 045	25 044		82 586		77 640	13 504	73 559	124 130	65 520
1991	383 509	390 950	250 019	7 928	20 703	10 236	23 922		78 861		73 019	13 163	70 834	114 960	64 225
1992	374 906	382 510	238 105	8 006	19 981	9 809	23 815		77 797		63 290	13 081	69 459	104 424	64 222
NAICS Basis															
1992	369 673	379 183	238 416	8 001	17 945	9 676	26 114	36 282	44 545	12 215	66 743	17 008	69 823	104 341	64 252
1993	370 775	380 102	239 040	7 577	17 951	9 648	26 302	37 124	43 960	12 451	64 662	18 143	72 752	102 114	64 174
1994	390 540	400 335	253 444	7 828	20 078	10 474	28 209	40 901	47 092	13 748	65 241	20 155	78 680	106 676	68 088
1995	414 969	425 217	267 696	8 432	21 407	11 308	30 315	44 662	53 639	14 160	63 491	20 764	85 612	106 777	75 307
1996	420 680	430 816	272 787	8 733	21 716	11 686	31 308	45 384	50 947	13 928	68 427	21 177	86 365	110 651	75 771
1997	433 451	443 804	281 249	8 996	22 461	12 253	32 446	45 918	55 302	14 075	69 085	20 774	92 364	109 991	78 894
1998	438 845	449 231	290 874	9 015	22 023	12 358	32 866	47 115	52 164	14 005	80 153	21 233	93 614	115 328	81 932
1999	452 803	463 646	296 645	9 412	22 034	12 065	33 453	47 411	55 134	13 989	79 758	22 596	97 835	114 230	84 580
2000	470 084	481 396	306 682	9 939	21 922	12 334	34 745	50 535	65 775	15 006	71 717	22 789	106 018	111 270	89 394
2001	441 527	452 236	283 722	9 583	19 270	10 776	32 762	45 836	56 967	13 959	69 560	20 107	96 251	102 304	85 167
2002	433 756	444 188	271 789	9 459	18 899	10 774	31 788	43 479	51 384	12 690	68 030	20 764	89 408	97 383	84 998
2003	428 176	438 584	262 947	9 234	17 301	9 066	31 021	41 583	47 777	12 383	67 458	20 230	83 759	96 874	82 314
2002															
January	447 325	448 919	281 384	9 458	18 991	10 236	32 583	45 375	56 757	13 788	68 726	19 795	95 378	101 949	84 057
February	449 335	446 363	279 546	9 363	18 798	10 088	32 349	45 070	55 999	13 686	68 672	19 607	94 427	101 379	83 740
March	442 965	444 088	276 976	9 336	18 530	10 056	32 213	44 950	55 419	13 556	67 227	19 783	94 673	98 423	83 880
April	445 869	444 605	275 800	9 294	18 480	9 994	32 146	44 496	55 084	13 530	67 046	20 112	94 461	97 285	84 054
May	445 716	442 917	274 439	9 241	18 364	9 952	31 850	44 227	54 440	13 439	66 947	20 193	93 277	97 207	83 955
June	439 083	442 415	273 396	9 325	18 487	10 063	31 755	43 786	53 342	13 372	67 288	20 384	92 365	97 240	83 791
July	444 107	442 605	272 636	9 297	18 501	10 148	31 778	43 696	53 342	13 306	66 671	20 595	91 752	96 624	84 260
August	446 323	442 827	271 941	9 372	18 633	10 342	31 870	43 498	52 812	13 191	66 551	20 395	91 445	96 186	84 310
September	443 808	443 595	271 364	9 348	18 610	10 480	31 921	43 337	52 607	13 078	66 344	20 756	90 965	95 875	84 524
October	447 245	443 545	270 836	9 403	18 667	10 564	31 858	43 182	52 303	12 934	66 541	20 737	90 730	95 397	84 709
November	444 506	442 499	269 774	9 406	18 822	10 724	31 872	43 091	52 116	12 894	65 602	20 612	89 740	95 051	84 983
December	433 756	444 188	271 789	9 459	18 899	10 774	31 788	43 479	51 384	12 690	68 030	20 764	89 408	97 383	84 998
2003															
January	442 409	444 220	270 964	9 488	19 054	10 825	31 736	43 046	50 627	12 746	68 141	21 017	88 916	97 287	84 761
February	448 757	446 088	270 765	9 579	19 191	10 924	31 769	42 879	50 077	12 682	68 396	21 114	88 703	97 432	84 630
March	442 829	445 180	269 454	9 725	19 160	10 964	31 704	42 482	49 270	12 664	68 130	20 616	87 948	97 009	84 497
April	446 470	445 207	269 285	9 754	19 051	10 890	31 605	42 627	48 661	12 652	68 587	20 676	87 443	97 851	83 991
May	446 790	444 049	268 449	9 882	18 931	10 832	31 678	42 465	48 074	12 635	68 650	20 557	87 129	97 810	83 510
June	439 285	442 666	266 154	9 888	18 222	10 046	31 479	42 032	47 791	12 526	68 161	20 378	86 243	96 243	83 668
July	442 188	440 767	264 638	9 905	17 989	9 796	31 115	41 897	47 496	12 400	67 717	20 290	85 203	96 383	83 052
August	443 020	439 632	262 949	9 783	17 803	9 701	31 058	41 485	46 949	12 364	67 453	20 366	84 068	96 258	82 623
September	438 210	438 294	261 678	9 729	17 382	9 339	30 900	41 381	46 937	12 284	67 223	20 002	83 637	95 533	82 508
October	441 907	438 680	262 351	9 613	17 162	9 191	31 038	41 465	47 174	12 290	67 555	20 024	84 013	96 225	82 113
November	439 491	438 126	261 414	9 244	17 276	9 151	30 995	41 220	47 130	12 372	67 018	20 054	83 523	95 973	81 918
December	428 176	438 584	262 947	9 234	17 301	9 066	31 021	41 583	47 777	12 383	67 458	20 230	83 759	96 874	82 314

[1]Includes categories not shown separately.
[2]Data are for roughly similar categories in SIC classification system. Data prior to 1982 are not comparable to subsequent periods due to change in inventory valuation methods; see Notes and Definitions.

Table 17-5. Manufacturers' Inventories—*Continued*

(Current cost basis, end of period; seasonally adjusted, except as noted; millions of dollars.)

Classification basis, year and month	NAICS nondurable goods industries										Nondurables total by stage of fabrication		
	Total [1]	Food products	Beverage and tobacco products [4]	Textiles	Textile products	Apparel	Paper products	Basic chemicals	Petroleum and coal products	Plastics and rubber products	Materials and supplies	Work in process	Finished goods
SIC Basis [2]													
1958	20 009	5 302	1 982	2 148		...	1 430	2 995	1 634	1 033	8 676	2 827	8 506
1959	20 901	5 338	2 082	2 238		...	1 506	3 189	1 700	1 130	9 094	2 942	8 865
1960	21 449	5 492	2 193	2 301		...	1 543	3 298	1 667	1 163	9 097	2 947	9 405
1961	22 375	5 877	2 410	2 418		...	1 576	3 401	1 715	1 172	9 505	3 108	9 762
1962	23 607	6 198	2 404	2 585		...	1 702	3 659	1 786	1 277	9 836	3 304	10 467
1963	24 253	6 449	2 314	2 621		...	1 761	3 775	1 776	1 336	10 009	3 420	10 824
1964	24 989	6 629	2 306	2 682		...	1 783	3 959	1 760	1 430	10 167	3 531	11 291
1965	26 018	6 485	2 279	2 868		...	1 938	4 392	1 761	1 549	10 487	3 825	11 706
1966	28 134	6 973	2 206	3 045		...	2 170	4 951	1 808	1 771	11 197	4 226	12 711
1967	29 750	7 484	2 275	3 181		...	2 236	5 306	1 961	1 840	11 760	4 431	13 559
1968	31 828	8 009	2 218	3 610		...	2 309	5 542	2 035	2 018	12 328	4 852	14 648
1969	33 547	8 329	2 188	3 670		...	2 399	6 173	2 085	2 215	12 753	5 120	15 674
1970	34 948	8 738	2 052	3 676		...	2 735	6 749	2 161	2 386	13 168	5 271	16 509
1971	36 431	9 258	2 099	3 866		...	2 828	6 923	2 260	2 453	13 686	5 678	17 067
1972	38 054	9 673	2 355	4 056		...	2 896	7 079	2 142	2 695	14 677	5 998	17 379
1973	43 307	11 627	2 426	4 592		...	3 317	7 553	2 476	3 103	18 147	6 729	18 431
1974	56 132	14 625	3 024	5 044		...	4 816	11 579	3 945	4 023	23 744	8 189	24 199
1975	57 118	14 467	3 290	4 794		...	4 849	12 073	4 426	4 085	23 565	8 834	24 719
1976	62 648	15 695	3 416	5 232		...	5 299	13 319	4 711	4 581	25 847	9 929	26 872
1977	67 501	16 329	3 511	5 649		...	5 667	14 633	5 439	5 116	27 387	10 961	29 153
1978	73 510	18 073	3 669	5 935		...	6 114	16 018	5 330	5 801	29 619	12 085	31 806
1979	81 423	19 879	3 517	6 148		...	6 926	17 690	7 458	6 399	32 814	13 910	34 699
1980	90 427	21 710	3 721	6 648		...	7 802	20 066	9 693	6 435	36 606	15 884	37 937
1981	96 970	21 483	4 436	6 896		...	8 593	22 438	10 420	6 968	38 165	16 194	42 611
1982	111 408	23 016	6 873	6 723		...	9 022	24 448	17 009	7 748	44 039	18 612	48 757
1983	112 525	23 609	6 746	7 514		...	9 192	24 698	14 843	8 070	44 816	18 691	49 018
1984	118 186	24 182	6 533	7 827		...	10 299	26 420	14 260	8 904	45 692	19 328	53 166
1985	116 556	24 015	5 943	7 439		...	10 140	26 119	13 975	9 213	44 106	19 442	53 008
1986	110 657	23 884	5 449	7 191		...	10 254	25 743	8 791	9 285	42 335	18 124	50 198
1987	117 310	24 860	5 331	7 939		...	11 163	26 585	9 973	10 065	45 319	19 270	52 721
1988	126 906	27 122	5 286	8 384		...	12 495	29 792	9 196	11 367	49 396	20 559	56 951
1989	133 699	28 459	5 570	8 721		...	13 404	31 725	10 743	11 533	50 674	21 653	61 372
1990	141 864	29 714	5 974	8 732		...	13 640	34 001	13 432	12 292	52 645	22 817	66 402
1991	140 931	30 099	6 342	8 484		...	13 796	34 529	11 671	12 121	53 011	22 815	65 105
1992	144 405	30 996	6 668	8 710		...	14 010	35 720	11 350	12 541	54 007	23 532	66 866
NAICS Basis													
1992	140 767	26 445	11 667	6 468	3 516	8 919	13 451	37 544	11 664	12 660	53 126	23 438	64 203
1993	141 062	26 621	11 315	6 840	3 643	10 093	13 463	37 823	10 476	12 845	54 231	23 426	63 405
1994	146 891	27 560	10 979	7 192	3 932	10 491	13 736	38 863	11 308	14 297	57 114	24 491	65 286
1995	157 521	29 268	11 442	7 624	4 112	10 487	16 585	42 021	11 490	15 310	60 699	25 842	70 980
1996	158 029	29 585	12 383	7 238	4 093	8 787	15 260	43 329	12 780	15 801	59 066	26 500	72 463
1997	162 555	29 948	13 801	6 889	4 546	9 669	15 166	45 246	12 189	16 175	60 121	28 527	73 907
1998	158 357	29 211	13 909	6 934	4 222	9 481	14 793	45 502	9 703	16 193	58 139	27 075	73 143
1999	167 001	30 478	13 812	6 897	4 426	9 814	15 136	48 391	12 198	17 238	60 951	28 786	77 264
2000	174 714	31 750	14 023	6 479	4 928	9 513	15 306	52 236	13 824	18 035	61 268	30 065	83 381
2001	168 514	31 801	14 579	5 620	4 876	7 639	15 051	50 645	13 479	16 793	59 499	28 503	80 512
2002	172 399	32 497	14 481	4 947	4 920	7 042	14 714	50 974	15 449	19 313	59 071	30 418	82 910
2003	175 637	32 997	14 519	4 998	5 171	7 165	14 455	52 682	15 200	20 553	58 395	31 048	86 194
2002													
January	167 535	31 901	14 641	5 412	4 811	7 447	14 934	50 594	13 056	16 658	58 873	28 831	79 831
February	166 817	31 865	14 560	5 364	4 771	7 289	14 889	50 455	13 277	16 560	58 996	28 834	78 987
March	168 468	31 702	14 716	5 276	4 740	7 141	14 801	50 215	14 062	18 199	59 355	29 123	79 990
April	168 805	32 069	14 524	5 121	4 794	7 049	14 646	50 294	14 480	18 125	59 557	29 170	80 078
May	168 478	32 077	14 605	5 097	4 835	6 932	14 550	50 134	14 378	18 189	59 308	29 426	79 744
June	169 019	32 280	14 713	5 049	4 863	6 942	14 638	49 977	14 502	18 216	59 234	29 761	80 024
July	169 969	32 344	14 501	5 026	4 923	6 954	14 487	50 570	14 902	18 328	59 509	30 216	80 244
August	170 886	32 478	14 566	5 054	4 930	6 952	14 451	51 220	14 871	18 465	59 390	30 996	80 500
September	172 231	32 570	14 757	5 002	4 947	7 007	14 566	51 317	15 168	19 116	59 560	31 158	81 513
October	172 709	32 654	14 607	4 979	4 931	7 017	14 624	51 422	15 195	19 228	59 597	31 037	82 075
November	172 725	32 774	14 443	4 891	4 898	6 999	14 715	51 824	14 813	19 294	60 036	30 831	81 858
December	172 399	32 497	14 481	4 947	4 920	7 042	14 714	50 974	15 449	19 313	59 071	30 418	82 910
2003													
January	173 256	32 633	14 445	4 960	4 983	7 109	14 750	50 934	15 869	19 529	60 248	30 606	82 402
February	175 323	32 923	14 486	4 994	5 022	7 139	14 747	52 097	16 085	19 798	60 758	30 994	83 571
March	175 726	33 295	14 443	5 047	5 021	7 186	14 882	51 921	15 946	19 997	60 258	31 422	84 046
April	175 922	32 920	14 659	5 075	5 019	7 232	14 938	51 885	15 997	20 290	60 741	30 859	84 322
May	175 600	33 160	14 583	5 097	5 012	7 263	14 977	52 087	15 018	20 449	60 539	30 596	84 465
June	176 512	33 149	14 561	5 123	4 994	7 329	14 989	52 518	15 422	20 593	59 786	31 166	85 560
July	176 129	33 042	14 610	5 055	4 984	7 407	14 905	52 777	15 262	20 233	58 920	31 502	85 707
August	176 683	33 157	14 692	5 028	5 011	7 331	14 871	52 859	15 728	20 157	59 117	31 452	86 114
September	176 616	33 364	14 850	5 112	5 024	7 282	14 863	52 478	15 601	20 160	59 396	31 293	85 927
October	176 329	33 478	14 805	5 028	5 043	7 234	14 765	52 489	15 558	20 091	59 121	31 655	85 553
November	176 712	33 584	14 808	5 025	5 106	7 206	14 660	53 121	15 113	20 179	59 096	31 952	85 664
December	175 637	32 997	14 519	4 998	5 171	7 165	14 455	52 682	15 200	20 553	58 395	31 048	86 194

[1] Includes categories not shown separately.
[2] Data are for roughly similar categories in SIC classification system. Data prior to 1982 are not comparable to subsequent periods due to change in inventory valuation methods; see Notes and Definitions.
[4] SIC tobacco only, 1958ñ1992.
. . . = Not available.

Table 17-5. Manufacturers' Inventories—Continued

(Current cost basis, end of period; seasonally adjusted, except as noted; millions of dollars.)

Classification basis, year and month	Construction supplies	Information technology industries	Capital goods				Consumer goods		
			Total	Nondefense		Defense	Total	Durable	Nondurable
				Total	Excluding aircraft and parts				
SIC Basis [2]									
1958	3 762	...	11 381	...	...	...	...	...	...
1959	3 978	...	11 959	...	...	...	...	...	...
1960	4 079	...	11 737	...	...	...	...	...	...
1961	4 092	...	11 651	...	...	...	...	...	...
1962	4 223	...	12 960	...	...	...	...	...	...
1963	4 295	...	13 180	...	...	...	...	...	...
1964	4 551	...	14 267	...	...	...	...	...	...
1965	4 868	...	15 843	...	...	...	...	...	...
1966	5 325	...	19 791	...	...	...	...	...	...
1967	5 431	...	23 499	...	...	...	...	...	...
1968	5 805	...	25 709	18 158	...	7 551	...	...	...
1969	6 378	...	28 652	20 883	...	7 769	...	...	...
1970	6 867	...	27 859	22 810	...	5 049	...	...	...
1971	7 145	...	26 587	22 455	...	4 132	...	...	...
1972	7 603	...	27 667	23 337	...	4 330	...	...	...
1973	8 696	...	32 032	27 460	...	4 572	...	...	...
1974	11 076	...	39 605	34 583	...	5 022	...	...	...
1975	11 267	...	40 181	34 289	...	5 892	...	...	...
1976	12 540	...	41 046	34 449	...	6 597	...	...	...
1977	13 509	...	44 014	37 781	...	6 233	...	...	...
1978	15 100	...	52 237	45 660	...	6 577	...	...	...
1979	16 908	...	63 816	55 393	...	8 423	...	...	...
1980	17 513	...	74 531	63 692	...	10 839	...	...	...
1981	18 328	...	81 112	67 616	...	13 496	...	...	...
1982	18 580	...	92 601	73 748	...	18 853	...	...	...
1983	19 309	...	89 562	68 420	...	21 142	...	...	...
1984	20 552	...	102 615	75 466	...	27 149	...	...	...
1985	20 555	...	102 843	71 763	...	31 080	...	...	...
1986	20 348	...	99 104	67 631	...	31 473	...	...	...
1987	21 158	...	103 167	68 734	...	34 433	...	...	...
1988	22 925	...	114 207	77 448	...	36 759	...	...	...
1989	23 326	...	124 850	86 897	...	37 953	...	...	...
1990	23 714	...	128 997	90 894	...	38 103	...	...	...
1991	22 509	...	121 629	88 958	...	32 671	...	...	...
1992	22 779	...	110 261	84 351	...	25 910	...	...	...
NAICS Basis									
1992	36 752	40 240	121 038	97 454	79 005	23 584	104 422	21 924	82 498
1993	38 287	39 189	118 923	97 182	79 641	21 741	105 963	22 940	83 023
1994	40 873	41 588	123 825	103 433	85 827	20 392	110 851	25 198	85 653
1995	43 390	46 924	130 064	111 623	94 733	18 441	117 983	26 765	91 218
1996	44 073	43 617	133 152	115 321	93 556	17 831	117 946	26 261	91 685
1997	45 651	48 222	137 904	122 676	98 958	15 228	121 143	26 314	94 829
1998	46 410	45 522	145 575	127 230	97 520	18 345	118 752	26 204	92 548
1999	48 395	46 389	146 819	126 400	99 794	20 419	125 620	27 438	98 182
2000	50 384	53 085	149 608	131 918	110 481	17 690	132 234	28 657	103 577
2001	47 347	48 688	141 812	123 620	101 960	18 192	129 602	26 881	102 721
2002	47 267	43 592	131 053	112 905	93 598	18 148	132 444	27 524	104 920
2003	46 262	39 921	125 112	105 554	88 558	19 558	134 734	27 131	107 603
2002									
January	47 324	48 640	140 865	122 732	100 968	18 133	128 941	26 837	102 104
February	46 959	48 012	140 137	121 945	100 052	18 192	128 854	26 682	102 172
March	46 955	47 215	137 754	119 668	99 055	18 086	129 569	26 906	102 663
April	46 717	47 106	136 573	118 574	98 520	17 999	130 375	27 113	103 262
May	46 604	46 408	135 261	117 534	97 557	17 727	130 218	27 208	103 010
June	46 630	45 567	134 477	116 530	96 417	17 947	130 668	27 364	103 304
July	46 619	45 488	132 994	115 825	96 187	17 169	131 613	27 641	103 972
August	46 811	45 160	132 524	114 915	95 401	17 609	132 048	27 425	104 623
September	46 829	44 291	131 126	113 560	94 478	17 566	132 986	27 661	105 325
October	47 021	44 082	130 322	112 792	93 865	17 530	132 873	27 663	105 210
November	47 184	44 101	129 725	112 243	93 767	17 482	132 896	27 582	105 314
December	47 267	43 592	131 053	112 905	93 598	18 148	132 444	27 524	104 920
2003									
January	47 236	42 905	130 014	112 170	92 605	17 844	133 315	27 723	105 592
February	47 508	42 347	129 041	110 984	91 901	18 057	135 113	27 696	107 417
March	47 585	41 863	128 453	110 222	91 180	18 231	134 529	27 140	107 389
April	47 596	41 288	127 583	109 142	90 116	18 441	134 813	27 613	107 200
May	47 553	40 782	127 327	109 069	89 933	18 258	133 988	27 377	106 611
June	47 241	40 436	126 711	107 844	89 379	18 867	134 710	27 264	107 446
July	46 928	39 939	125 278	106 594	88 853	18 684	134 971	27 340	107 631
August	46 654	39 752	124 707	106 178	88 445	18 529	135 588	27 219	108 369
September	46 410	39 898	124 497	105 935	88 152	18 562	135 632	26 978	108 654
October	46 351	39 815	124 708	105 724	88 141	18 984	135 945	27 151	108 794
November	46 120	39 818	124 473	105 252	88 210	19 221	135 515	26 983	108 532
December	46 262	39 921	125 112	105 554	88 558	19 558	134 734	27 131	107 603

[2]Data are for roughly similar categories in SIC classification system. Data prior to 1982 are not comparable to subsequent periods due to change in inventory valuation methods; see Notes and Definitions.
... = Not available.

Table 17-6. Manufacturers' New Orders

(Net, millions of dollars, seasonally adjusted.)

Classification basis, year and month	Total [1]	NAICS durable goods industries											
		Total [1]	Primary metals			Fabricated metal products	Machinery	Computers and electronic products	Electrical equipment, appliances and components	Transportation equipment			
			Total [1]	Iron and steel mills	Aluminum and nonferrous metal products					Total [1]	Motor vehicles and parts	Non-defense aircraft and parts	Defense aircraft and parts
SIC Basis [2]													
1959	368 255	191 744	34 503	21 009	...	24 102		49 044		44 712	...	...	
1960	362 759	183 455	26 354	13 603	...	23 410		47 245		47 481	...	...	
1961	373 400	189 032	32 069	18 647	...	24 225		49 867		43 138	...	...	
1962	401 255	208 351	31 179	16 635	...	26 364		54 722		53 728	...	...	
1963	426 084	224 048	34 780	19 122	...	27 903		58 745		57 625	...	...	
1964	459 210	246 088	41 521	23 758	...	30 360		66 005		61 607	...	...	
1965	505 792	279 432	43 380	22 590	...	33 998		76 429		73 803	...	...	
1966	556 494	313 954	49 111	25 134	...	38 501		89 417		80 607	...	...	
1967	564 616	309 632	45 100	23 435	...	41 618		87 944		75 979	...	...	
1968	607 127	336 614	48 089	24 416	...	45 158		91 468		85 893	...	...	
1969	648 289	358 509	54 880	27 247	...	47 446		102 664		83 945	...	...	
1970	624 541	328 079	51 793	25 521	...	43 990		96 439		67 380	...		17 417
1971	671 134	358 856	51 284	25 571	...	44 305		98 525		89 900	...		22 459
1972	770 056	420 455	61 447	30 996	...	52 879		119 643		96 501	...		20 963
1973	912 279	511 525	78 395	39 413	...	64 733		147 437		118 194	...		26 669
1974	1 047 811	562 339	98 831	51 047	...	74 281		164 985		114 081	...		29 934
1975	1 022 133	503 485	75 034	38 611	...	64 349		147 473		109 050	...		26 869
1976	1 194 759	615 680	94 491	47 212	...	76 372		174 459		143 502	...		31 851
1977	1 382 309	732 422	105 689	52 103	...	92 028		206 245		175 446	...		40 625
1978	1 579 715	867 335	124 741	62 648	...	105 182		246 832		213 539	...		54 600
1979	1 771 603	953 796	139 783	66 968	...	117 428		281 974		223 226	...		67 818
1980	1 877 053	952 701	134 416	62 473	...	116 195		295 085		202 584	...		72 514
1981	2 015 982	1 003 845	137 286	67 457	...	123 245		324 629		203 482	...		63 530
1982	1 944 671	936 764	98 445	43 013	...	113 399		296 904		209 325	...		73 365
1983	2 106 726	1 057 677	113 884	49 123	...	122 760		321 010		261 359	...		86 952
1984	2 314 256	1 201 964	118 354	50 719	...	141 650		377 650		295 202	...		91 620
1985	2 346 410	1 228 268	112 276	49 079	...	142 300		381 747		311 482	...		100 889
1986	2 340 899	1 243 761	108 218	46 408	...	143 541		372 849		327 541	...		107 993
1987	2 510 890	1 329 712	125 989	54 763	...	150 716		394 381		348 224	...		114 835
1988	2 737 716	1 464 916	152 578	64 002	...	158 170		439 266		389 635	...		137 443
1989	2 872 514	1 512 664	152 814	62 752	...	160 037		449 533		411 434	...		153 430
1990	2 931 275	1 507 001	149 338	63 369	...	163 285		454 642		395 737	...		150 329
1991	2 866 841	1 438 187	134 657	56 366	...	158 401		441 109		363 366	...		132 645
1992	2 977 116	1 515 694	136 849	58 002	...	165 793		476 574		377 147	...		110 830
NAICS Basis [3]													
1992	...	...					...	...	...	...		...	...
1993	2 960 015	1 544 062	128 895	62 580	53 733	175 990	202 848	248 104	88 263	427 966	311 928	38 427	32 569
1994	3 199 686	1 725 635	146 503	67 619	64 594	196 567	232 226	274 776	96 919	487 253	367 306	39 309	31 524
1995	3 426 503	1 849 641	159 957	72 600	72 264	214 488	251 307	311 275	101 409	508 133	378 886	57 454	27 736
1996	3 567 384	1 948 793	158 066	71 301	70 657	227 447	258 405	327 288	104 837	552 024	385 712	72 094	32 520
1997	3 779 835	2 092 520	171 407	78 577	74 974	247 329	272 998	363 635	113 411	581 780	422 427	85 797	23 280
1998	3 808 143	2 139 918	160 743	72 378	71 274	253 847	278 100	372 433	115 711	600 205	440 934	84 150	23 854
1999	3 957 242	2 252 091	156 968	70 924	68 469	258 116	278 277	402 216	120 774	660 215	499 527	81 619	25 717
2000	4 161 472	2 326 576	153 625	68 181	67 122	270 021	294 608	436 415	126 196	663 326	468 470	99 249	31 326
2001	3 875 329	2 079 236	136 291	59 573	60 025	248 872	260 392	363 049	110 628	591 756	425 580	74 121	37 311
2002	3 800 930	2 040 581	134 089	61 884	56 545	249 408	244 559	325 378	103 013	617 098	450 183	65 295	40 087
2003	3 949 998	2 101 512	132 850	60 867	56 440	246 590	253 978	358 127	101 038	625 535	444 327	60 882	44 662
2002													
January	311 730	166 413	10 716	4 829	4 524	20 307	20 879	27 281	8 139	47 981	36 816	4 570	2 722
February	317 675	174 609	10 721	4 794	4 656	20 180	21 013	27 783	8 623	55 776	36 589	6 957	4 233
March	313 271	169 405	10 869	5 026	4 570	20 621	19 675	27 155	8 300	52 927	35 541	6 293	5 299
April	317 606	172 360	11 542	5 380	4 787	21 159	20 718	27 801	9 077	51 484	39 629	5 028	1 694
May	318 297	172 196	11 611	5 450	4 861	21 357	21 147	27 978	9 042	50 282	38 679	5 414	2 027
June	310 680	164 332	11 278	5 221	4 746	20 539	19 390	27 355	8 766	47 071	37 508	2 483	2 595
July	324 427	177 587	11 295	5 205	4 789	21 380	21 357	27 314	8 222	57 496	39 953	6 893	6 313
August	323 955	176 668	11 536	5 447	4 775	20 638	20 554	26 792	8 528	58 218	38 357	9 378	3 125
September	313 949	165 983	11 336	5 319	4 689	20 947	20 423	26 577	8 677	47 549	37 777	2 810	3 135
October	320 000	170 587	11 549	5 357	4 856	21 294	20 931	26 509	8 619	50 737	38 790	4 932	2 705
November	317 869	168 825	10 769	4 911	4 575	20 643	20 340	26 895	8 532	50 663	36 863	5 288	3 129
December	316 944	166 476	10 853	4 998	4 660	20 346	20 454	26 978	8 519	48 260	34 467	5 513	3 444
2003													
January	322 157	169 823	11 325	5 003	5 004	20 510	20 872	28 570	8 448	49 120	37 555	4 842	2 119
February	320 664	169 065	10 730	4 895	4 510	20 098	20 321	27 319	8 147	51 791	36 711	4 242	2 994
March	325 614	170 325	10 591	4 732	4 594	20 216	20 968	27 936	8 564	51 524	36 578	3 144	4 236
April	317 095	167 999	10 727	4 955	4 506	19 690	20 092	27 807	8 280	50 934	35 159	5 524	4 374
May	318 144	168 007	10 649	5 003	4 420	20 186	19 971	28 291	8 226	49 782	34 946	4 536	4 624
June	324 098	172 237	10 598	4 672	4 667	19 873	20 502	29 328	8 389	52 305	36 095	6 242	3 920
July	330 551	175 064	10 885	5 019	4 573	20 695	21 191	30 085	8 342	52 200	38 303	5 555	3 196
August	329 401	174 912	11 000	5 168	4 619	20 531	21 102	30 663	8 429	51 248	35 631	4 912	3 537
September	333 957	178 738	10 885	4 834	4 701	20 755	21 411	32 878	8 598	51 334	38 539	4 663	3 668
October	341 856	185 771	11 948	5 734	4 871	21 191	21 705	33 685	8 665	54 624	38 336	5 625	3 931
November	338 726	181 346	11 811	5 553	4 937	21 089	22 269	29 471	8 464	54 515	37 868	4 930	3 733
December	344 868	184 361	11 655	5 204	5 128	21 864	24 020	29 948	8 251	55 257	38 615	6 097	3 778

[1] Includes categories not shown separately.
[2] Data are for roughly similar categories in SIC classification system.
[3] Data excludes semiconductors. See Notes and Definitions.
... = Not available.

Table 17-6. Manufacturers' New Orders—Continued

(Net, millions of dollars, seasonally adjusted.)

Classification basis, year and month	Construction supplies	Information technology industries	By topical categories					Consumer goods		
			Capital goods							
				Nondefense ||				
			Total	Total	Excluding aircraft and parts	Defense	Total	Durable	Nondurable
SIC Basis [2]									
1959	...	...	...	...	...	...	...	...	...
1960	...	...	...	...	...	...	...	...	...
1961	...	...	...	...	...	...	...	...	...
1962	...	...	...	...	...	...	...	...	...
1963	...	...	...	...	...	...	...	...	...
1964	...	...	...	...	...	...	...	...	...
1965	...	...	...	...	...	...	...	...	...
1966	...	...	...	...	...	...	...	...	...
1967	...	...	...	...	...	...	...	...	...
1968	...	...	...	...	...	...	...	...	...
1969	...	...	...	84 549	...	23 790	...	...	...
1970	...	...	...	72 866	...	21 311	...	...	...
1971	...	...	...	80 185	...	18 787	...	...	...
1972	...	...	...	92 943	...	20 467	...	...	...
1973	...	...	...	119 108	...	23 409	...	...	...
1974	...	...	...	139 131	...	26 033	...	...	...
1975	...	...	...	118 635	...	24 765	...	...	...
1976	...	...	...	137 875	...	30 616	...	...	...
1977	...	...	...	164 168	...	34 624	...	...	...
1978	...	...	...	211 056	...	41 511	...	...	...
1979	...	...	...	253 844	...	33 795	...	...	...
1980	...	...	...	253 619	...	58 256	...	...	...
1981	...	...	...	261 666	...	58 881	...	...	...
1982	...	...	...	230 555	...	81 415	...	...	...
1983	...	...	...	235 489	...	96 105	...	...	...
1984	...	...	...	284 022	...	103 504	...	...	...
1985	...	...	...	294 544	...	109 505	...	...	...
1986	...	...	...	287 786	...	111 879	...	...	...
1987	...	...	...	313 127	...	111 639	...	...	...
1988	...	...	...	373 294	...	102 728	...	...	...
1989	...	...	...	395 855	...	93 398	...	...	...
1990	...	...	...	399 966	...	96 638	...	...	...
1991	...	...	...	365 655	...	87 213	...	...	...
1992	...	...	...	378 293	...	76 155	...	...	...
NAICS Basis [3]									
1992	...	...	...	...	...	...	...	...	...
1993	304 264	239 387	561 097	488 166	466 433	72 931	1 139 096	286 280	852 816
1994	335 962	265 010	616 252	542 094	523 461	74 158	1 203 225	326 058	877 167
1995	355 161	297 605	680 857	612 132	576 769	68 725	1 268 660	336 085	932 575
1996	373 536	310 074	737 268	648 797	607 174	88 471	1 305 517	340 964	964 553
1997	403 860	352 700	792 859	728 362	676 119	64 497	1 372 919	374 596	998 323
1998	419 330	365 723	809 727	745 600	698 279	64 127	1 364 268	385 860	978 408
1999	435 034	389 160	840 603	772 703	728 089	67 900	1 440 903	428 721	1 012 182
2000	446 792	409 500	910 933	831 335	767 754	79 598	1 515 799	406 730	1 109 069
2001	420 300	350 726	783 060	700 027	665 899	83 033	1 491 143	378 170	1 112 973
2002	418 315	314 473	727 158	647 894	617 878	79 264	1 471 270	395 213	1 076 057
2003	422 639	349 234	794 164	689 340	663 352	104 824	1 530 443	400 767	1 129 676
2002									
January	35 096	26 147	57 097	52 933	51 818	4 164	122 911	33 031	89 880
February	34 903	26 818	64 721	56 194	53 592	8 527	120 462	32 367	88 095
March	34 131	25 517	61 370	51 840	49 419	9 530	119 698	30 826	88 872
April	35 239	26 528	59 612	54 128	52 243	5 484	122 460	34 077	88 383
May	35 324	27 149	60 934	55 528	53 010	5 406	122 468	33 471	88 997
June	34 269	26 259	57 222	50 855	50 534	6 367	121 557	32 237	89 320
July	35 237	26 376	61 817	56 065	52 435	5 752	124 140	34 697	89 443
August	34 821	26 239	66 351	58 967	52 620	7 384	122 575	33 108	89 467
September	35 013	26 599	59 558	51 702	50 357	7 856	123 545	33 278	90 267
October	35 125	25 462	59 764	54 829	52 422	4 935	125 076	33 946	91 130
November	34 734	26 281	60 703	54 439	51 784	6 264	123 240	32 585	90 655
December	34 587	26 037	61 582	53 807	50 752	7 775	124 248	32 381	91 867
2003									
January	34 445	28 139	61 756	55 261	53 733	6 495	126 583	33 340	93 243
February	33 792	26 598	63 054	53 417	51 959	9 637	125 890	33 025	92 865
March	34 326	27 734	64 289	54 838	54 620	9 451	128 014	32 314	95 700
April	33 704	27 852	64 854	55 845	53 159	9 009	122 510	31 824	90 686
May	34 062	27 348	63 388	55 367	53 705	8 021	123 606	31 984	91 622
June	34 074	28 705	65 768	57 351	54 728	8 417	125 334	32 402	92 932
July	35 447	29 509	65 656	58 188	55 017	7 468	130 210	34 148	96 062
August	35 715	29 742	67 386	57 229	54 907	10 157	127 176	32 412	94 764
September	36 338	31 898	67 803	60 225	58 188	7 578	128 789	34 303	94 486
October	36 817	32 631	71 007	61 672	59 002	9 335	129 622	34 895	94 727
November	36 203	28 307	67 084	57 862	55 553	9 222	130 993	34 849	96 144
December	37 103	28 919	69 845	60 219	57 673	9 626	132 630	35 011	97 619

[2]Data are for roughly similar categories in SIC classification system.
[3]Data excludes semiconductors. See Notes and Definitions.
... = Not available.

Table 17-7. Manufacturers' Unfilled Orders, Durable Goods Industries

(End of period, millions of dollars, seasonally adjusted.)

Classification basis, year and month	Not seasonally adjusted, total	Seasonally adjusted, NAICS industries							
		Total [1]	Primary metals			Fabricated metal products	Machinery	Computers and electronic products	Electrical equipment, appliances and components
			Total [1]	Iron and steel mills	Aluminum and nonferrous metal products				
SIC Basis [2]									
1958	44 090	43 807	5 019	3 521	1 151	4 222		10 539	
1959	48 666	48 369	8 018	6 143	1 382	4 615		12 228	
1960	41 681	41 650	3 334	1 877	1 156	4 079		11 028	
1961	43 496	43 582	4 791	3 314	1 131	4 634		11 540	
1962	44 889	45 170	3 518	1 957	1 169	4 858		12 282	
1963	49 879	50 346	3 952	2 170	1 319	5 955		14 602	
1964	60 640	61 315	6 686	4 386	1 696	7 484		18 203	
1965	73 754	74 459	6 086	3 003	2 238	9 111		23 395	
1966	92 303	93 002	7 267	3 601	2 753	10 814		29 339	
1967	99 140	99 735	7 228	3 921	2 572	12 346		30 296	
1968	104 263	104 393	6 591	3 416	2 472	13 813		30 969	
1969	109 936	110 161	7 991	4 283	2 876	15 128		35 490	
1970	100 139	100 412	7 796	4 617	2 663	14 877		33 618	
1971	99 906	100 225	7 478	4 380	2 552	13 688		33 318	
1972	112 517	113 034	10 470	6 681	3 116	15 077		39 344	
1973	148 421	149 204	16 129	9 794	4 962	21 019		54 070	
1974	180 686	181 519	19 225	11 054	5 952	28 100		67 403	
1975	160 993	161 664	13 266	7 345	4 015	24 008		62 437	
1976	169 198	169 857	14 684	7 776	4 891	22 810		65 905	
1977	191 603	193 323	17 298	9 435	5 483	25 152		72 025	
1978	246 162	248 281	23 969	12 932	7 393	29 137		86 452	
1979	288 834	291 321	26 320	12 485	9 457	33 131		99 105	
1980	312 508	315 202	26 815	13 418	10 096	33 296		100 730	
1981	311 628	314 707	22 024	10 589	8 784	33 036		102 123	
1982	297 851	300 798	15 500	6 574	7 418	27 117		86 503	
1983	329 758	333 114	20 400	9 431	9 594	26 752		93 145	
1984	356 446	359 651	18 362	8 103	8 694	30 254		97 433	
1985	369 362	372 097	18 331	8 248	8 361	29 197		96 882	
1986	374 264	376 699	18 590	8 897	7 783	29 633		91 209	
1987	406 444	408 688	24 340	11 828	10 300	32 973		96 609	
1988	449 859	452 150	27 079	11 508	12 974	31 661		104 285	
1989	484 623	487 098	24 120	9 479	11 824	27 629		102 985	
1990	506 311	509 124	24 768	10 120	11 258	25 859		102 373	
1991	492 500	495 802	23 075	9 290	10 609	24 516		96 800	
1992	466 328	469 381	21 636	8 897	9 925	23 725		97 999	
NAICS Basis [3]									
1992	447 770	450 965	18 794	9 300	7 248	29 714	40 867	84 591	12 123
1993	422 314	425 665	20 862	12 434	6 398	27 756	42 638	81 251	12 769
1994	430 982	434 594	24 378	12 908	9 327	30 259	49 963	82 526	14 232
1995	443 497	447 338	23 456	13 423	7 976	32 338	55 209	89 001	14 593
1996	484 865	488 815	23 774	12 781	8 706	36 898	56 213	88 150	14 096
1997	508 480	513 166	27 158	14 495	9 942	42 091	58 748	91 119	15 432
1998	491 858	496 471	21 611	10 821	8 282	42 220	56 168	95 000	15 078
1999	500 749	505 941	22 004	11 711	8 211	43 301	57 749	113 968	17 551
2000	544 517	550 005	18 940	9 336	7 163	45 068	61 040	130 738	18 242
2001	512 520	517 590	16 934	8 323	6 145	40 680	54 598	127 441	14 665
2002	480 679	485 816	15 042	8 213	4 622	37 752	43 544	119 674	13 999
2003	502 416	506 298	16 475	9 526	4 604	38 954	43 907	129 533	13 621
2002									
January	513 565	510 293	16 633	8 262	5 899	40 075	53 633	126 177	14 267
February	517 782	512 426	16 582	8 357	5 808	39 735	52 252	125 686	14 372
March	519 462	512 007	16 337	8 445	5 517	39 852	50 834	124 907	14 031
April	516 015	508 336	16 370	8 702	5 314	39 713	50 291	124 432	14 230
May	511 206	505 261	16 448	8 962	5 195	39 976	49 269	124 398	14 378
June	499 512	497 705	16 322	8 966	5 099	39 490	47 330	124 122	14 590
July	499 609	498 562	16 054	8 868	4 954	39 511	47 029	123 378	14 124
August	498 174	501 299	16 006	8 946	4 847	38 876	46 050	122 467	14 102
September	488 171	494 297	15 890	8 888	4 773	38 581	45 188	121 330	14 265
October	481 835	490 267	15 861	8 861	4 749	38 590	44 795	120 156	14 239
November	477 626	487 009	15 351	8 501	4 593	38 305	43 947	119 387	14 034
December	480 679	485 816	15 042	8 213	4 622	37 752	43 544	119 674	13 999
2003									
January	486 552	483 871	14 887	7 948	4 721	37 494	43 317	120 566	13 814
February	489 568	484 649	14 768	7 928	4 595	37 109	43 014	121 094	13 756
March	492 408	485 178	14 254	7 491	4 547	36 874	43 215	121 938	14 003
April	493 389	485 534	14 143	7 378	4 542	36 459	42 675	121 739	13 979
May	492 209	485 829	13 967	7 373	4 393	36 423	41 785	122 840	13 894
June	489 445	487 360	14 077	7 384	4 485	36 117	41 433	123 360	13 997
July	486 595	485 959	14 136	7 523	4 383	35 929	41 360	123 616	13 793
August	486 358	490 036	14 559	7 960	4 378	36 483	41 405	125 288	13 922
September	484 496	492 006	14 662	8 006	4 364	36 814	41 441	128 163	14 057
October	491 677	500 307	15 642	8 899	4 396	37 473	41 654	131 589	14 160
November	495 329	503 869	16 384	9 524	4 495	38 139	42 663	131 002	13 997
December	502 416	506 298	16 475	9 526	4 604	38 954	43 907	129 533	13 621

[1] Includes categories not shown separately.
[2] Data are for roughly similar categories in SIC classification system.
[3] Data excludes semiconductors. See Notes and Definitions.

Table 17-7. Manufacturers' Unfilled Orders, Durable Goods Industries—Continued

(End of period, millions of dollars, seasonally adjusted.)

Classification basis, year and month	Transportation equipment				Construction materials and supplies	Information technology industries	By topical categories				Consumer durable goods
							Capital goods				
	Total [1]	Motor vehicles and parts	Non-defense aircraft and parts	Defense aircraft and parts			Total	Nondefense		Defense	
								Total	Excl. aircraft and parts		
SIC Basis [2]											
1958	19 094	...	...	...	3 149	...	...	...	...	...	967
1959	18 342	...	...	...	3 642	...	...	...	...	...	1 162
1960	18 217	...	...	...	3 094	...	...	...	...	...	1 067
1961	17 202	...	...	...	3 449	...	...	...	...	...	1 245
1962	18 844	...	...	...	3 480	...	...	...	...	...	1 153
1963	20 151	...	...	...	4 127	...	...	...	...	...	1 478
1964	23 664	...	...	...	5 182	...	...	...	...	...	1 620
1965	29 262	...	...	...	5 823	...	...	...	...	...	1 940
1966	37 376	...	...	...	6 728	...	...	...	...	...	2 109
1967	40 807	...	...	...	7 521	...	...	...	...	...	1 849
1968	43 023	...	...	...	8 205	...	...	47 608	...	23 152	2 129
1969	41 812	...	...	...	8 873	...	...	52 591	...	20 809	1 967
1970	34 720	...	26 198	...	8 880	...	...	46 544	...	18 804	2 078
1971	35 793	...	26 259	...	8 073	...	...	47 576	...	18 158	2 292
1972	37 627	...	26 151	...	8 810	...	...	52 781	...	19 261	2 914
1973	45 248	...	27 842	...	12 311	...	...	67 947	...	21 756	3 471
1974	51 118	...	30 506	...	15 125	...	...	84 495	...	26 558	2 582
1975	46 633	...	28 244	...	12 694	...	...	76 773	...	27 936	2 740
1976	49 078	...	29 421	...	11 592	...	...	79 121	...	31 826	2 862
1977	57 101	...	37 325	...	12 821	...	...	87 552	...	36 692	4 135
1978	81 782	...	54 417	...	14 408	...	...	112 277	...	47 425	4 864
1979	103 555	...	74 034	...	15 360	...	...	144 114	...	48 656	4 754
1980	119 700	...	88 051	...	15 410	...	...	150 973	...	66 636	4 388
1981	118 008	...	86 794	...	15 213	...	...	142 802	...	77 793	4 729
1982	125 879	...	93 703	...	11 981	...	...	121 082	...	99 052	4 860
1983	141 637	...	105 504	...	12 673	...	...	114 280	...	121 177	5 810
1984	152 189	...	117 923	...	13 102	...	...	119 424	...	142 324	5 603
1985	156 155	...	127 282	...	13 124	...	...	120 687	...	156 188	5 253
1986	161 145	...	133 565	...	13 677	...	...	118 429	...	161 705	5 815
1987	176 588	...	144 987	...	14 140	...	...	136 171	...	163 786	5 842
1988	211 575	...	174 721	...	14 557	...	...	176 069	...	161 878	5 703
1989	253 517	...	217 557	...	13 992	...	...	221 152	...	155 314	5 854
1990	279 082	...	242 208	...	14 021	...	...	250 314	...	149 844	5 215
1991	275 260	...	242 798	...	14 828	...	...	246 093	...	139 666	5 498
1992	253 076	...	222 194	...	14 706	...	...	234 817	...	124 047	5 047
NAICS Basis [3]											
1992	259 233	11 577	127 426	49 634	20 900	80 330	318 887	179 454	92 301	139 433	6 437
1993	233 703	13 337	110 787	46 684	21 774	78 044	299 110	173 715	95 048	125 395	7 133
1994	226 158	15 835	100 940	44 758	25 096	79 122	299 000	177 625	106 301	121 375	7 215
1995	225 909	15 133	109 271	42 482	27 158	85 022	314 009	199 417	117 634	114 592	8 211
1996	261 772	13 433	130 353	45 428	29 439	84 288	346 760	217 350	119 704	129 410	9 401
1997	268 127	14 310	143 399	41 115	33 596	87 414	360 764	243 059	131 164	117 705	12 383
1998	255 446	15 620	137 611	38 044	34 228	90 748	348 802	241 553	133 730	107 249	12 288
1999	239 244	16 396	126 662	35 973	35 155	105 777	350 161	245 884	149 249	104 277	14 694
2000	262 846	13 708	138 665	42 994	37 187	115 551	385 821	268 922	159 582	116 899	16 007
2001	252 387	12 126	122 521	52 552	32 804	112 975	366 787	240 676	147 164	126 111	13 419
2002	245 703	12 190	111 273	57 759	32 035	107 999	340 981	215 338	130 428	125 643	11 962
2003	251 900	13 486	104 675	62 132	32 779	119 555	359 490	221 087	141 220	138 403	12 766
2002											
January	248 372	12 036	120 095	52 518	32 764	111 910	359 748	236 240	145 372	123 508	13 392
February	252 750	12 063	119 826	54 023	32 948	111 762	360 658	234 887	145 035	125 771	13 088
March	255 249	12 255	119 134	56 431	32 813	110 551	358 874	230 274	141 927	128 600	12 956
April	252 711	12 400	117 419	55 305	32 923	110 052	355 496	227 806	141 123	127 690	12 922
May	250 328	12 586	116 543	54 386	33 166	110 398	352 850	226 243	140 239	126 607	12 759
June	245 727	12 677	113 011	54 008	32 597	110 099	347 446	221 218	137 818	126 228	12 445
July	248 640	12 915	113 347	57 096	32 627	109 618	345 409	220 167	136 601	125 242	12 320
August	254 333	12 489	117 074	57 366	32 327	109 213	349 208	223 042	135 734	126 166	11 857
September	249 341	12 302	113 640	57 331	32 339	109 182	345 913	218 759	133 304	127 154	12 138
October	246 548	11 961	112 317	57 096	32 518	108 027	342 514	217 145	132 398	125 369	12 300
November	245 838	12 108	111 604	57 050	32 381	107 659	340 380	215 904	131 338	124 476	12 053
December	245 703	12 190	111 273	57 759	32 035	107 999	340 981	215 338	130 428	125 643	11 962
2003											
January	243 581	12 115	111 304	56 652	31 665	109 145	340 375	215 534	130 896	124 841	11 960
February	244 018	12 255	109 618	56 489	31 460	109 876	341 659	214 502	131 160	127 157	12 465
March	244 312	12 138	106 829	57 493	31 281	111 364	343 826	214 527	133 645	129 299	12 020
April	245 897	12 128	107 110	58 533	30 858	112 049	346 212	215 392	133 897	130 820	12 331
May	246 188	11 921	106 224	59 943	30 796	113 002	347 383	215 980	135 166	131 403	12 235
June	247 509	11 914	106 433	60 547	30 438	113 823	348 827	216 462	135 991	132 365	12 165
July	246 515	12 068	106 086	60 295	30 361	114 277	348 102	216 517	135 731	131 585	11 963
August	247 916	12 046	105 666	60 419	31 154	115 877	351 221	217 259	136 553	133 962	11 706
September	246 184	12 526	104 692	60 572	31 568	118 652	352 594	219 046	138 967	133 548	11 756
October	248 416	13 027	104 831	61 123	31 935	121 870	357 078	222 111	141 769	134 967	12 435
November	249 686	13 304	103 900	61 840	32 301	121 016	357 979	221 289	141 499	136 690	12 914
December	251 900	13 486	104 675	62 132	32 779	119 555	359 490	221 087	141 220	138 403	12 766

[1] Includes categories not shown separately.
[2] Data are for roughly similar categories in SIC classification system.
[3] Data excludes semiconductors. See Notes and Definitions.
. . . = Not available.

Table 17-8. Motor Vehicle Sales and Inventories

Year and month	Retail sales of new passenger cars						Retail inventories of new domestic passenger cars (thousands of units, end of period)		
	Thousands of units, not seasonally adjusted			Millions of units, seasonally adjusted annual rate			Not seasonally adjusted	Seasonally adjusted	Inventory to sales ratio
	Total	Domestic	Imports	Total	Domestic	Imports			
1967	8 347.0	7 567.8	779.2	8.347	7.568	0.779	...	...	...
1968	9 654.6	8 624.8	1 029.8	9.654	8.625	1.030	...	...	...
1969	9 581.7	8 464.3	1 117.4	9.582	8.464	1.117	...	...	...
1970	8 402.6	7 119.4	1 283.2	8.403	7.119	1.283	...	...	...
1971	10 227.8	8 661.8	1 566.0	10.228	8.662	1.566	...	...	...
1972	10 873.3	9 252.6	1 620.7	10.873	9.253	1.621	1 311.0	1 379.0	1.700
1973	11 350.1	9 588.6	1 761.5	11.350	9.589	1.762	1 600.0	1 654.0	2.500
1974	8 773.7	7 361.8	1 411.9	8.774	7.362	1.412	1 672.0	1 730.0	3.400
1975	8 537.8	6 950.9	1 586.9	8.538	6.951	1.587	1 419.0	1 468.0	2.200
1976	9 994.0	8 492.0	1 502.0	9.994	8.492	1.502	1 465.0	1 494.0	1.900
1977	11 046.0	8 971.2	2 074.8	11.046	8.971	2.075	1 731.0	1 743.0	2.300
1978	11 164.0	9 163.9	2 000.1	11.164	9.164	2.000	1 729.0	1 731.0	2.300
1979	10 558.8	8 230.1	2 328.7	10.559	8.230	2.329	1 691.0	1 667.0	2.400
1980	8 981.8	6 581.4	2 400.4	8.982	6.581	2.401	1 448.0	1 440.0	2.600
1981	8 534.3	6 208.8	2 325.5	8.534	6.209	2.326	1 471.0	1 495.0	3.600
1982	7 979.4	5 758.2	2 221.2	7.980	5.758	2.221	1 126.0	1 127.0	2.200
1983	9 178.6	6 793.0	2 385.6	9.179	6.793	2.386	1 352.0	1 350.0	2.000
1984	10 390.2	7 951.7	2 438.5	10.390	7.952	2.439	1 415.0	1 411.0	2.100
1985	10 978.4	8 204.7	2 773.7	10.978	8.205	2.774	1 630.0	1 619.0	2.500
1986	11 405.7	8 215.0	3 190.7	11.406	8.215	3.191	1 499.0	1 515.0	2.000
1987	10 170.9	7 080.9	3 090.0	10.171	7.081	3.090	1 680.0	1 716.0	2.800
1988	10 545.6	7 539.4	3 006.2	10.546	7.539	3.006	1 601.0	1 601.0	2.300
1989	9 776.8	7 078.1	2 698.7	9.777	7.078	2.699	1 669.0	1 687.0	3.100
1990	9 300.2	6 896.9	2 403.3	9.300	6.897	2.403	1 408.0	1 418.0	2.600
1991	8 175.0	6 136.9	2 038.1	8.175	6.137	2.038	1 283.0	1 296.0	2.600
1992	8 214.4	6 276.6	1 937.8	8.214	6.277	1.938	1 276.0	1 288.0	2.300
1993	8 517.7	6 734.0	1 783.7	8.518	6.734	1.784	1 345.5	1 392.3	2.489
1994	8 990.4	7 255.2	1 735.2	8.990	7.255	1.735	1 378.6	1 409.6	2.335
1995	8 636.2	7 128.8	1 507.4	8.687	7.178	1.510	1 639.2	1 665.9	2.810
1996	8 526.8	7 253.7	1 273.1	8.527	7.254	1.273	1 441.4	1 485.4	2.463
1997	8 272.5	6 906.2	1 366.3	8.273	6.906	1.366	1 316.8	1 356.4	2.360
1998	8 142.1	6 763.9	1 378.2	8.142	6.764	1.378	1 270.5	1 336.0	2.381
1999	8 696.5	6 981.7	1 714.8	8.697	6.982	1.715	1 318.1	1 392.3	2.394
2000	8 852.1	6 832.8	2 019.3	8.852	6.833	2.019	1 330.5	1 360.8	2.400
2001	8 422.1	6 322.7	2 099.4	8.510	6.410	2.100	1 108.2	1 147.3	2.198
2002	8 102.4	5 871.3	2 231.1	8.082	5.854	2.228	1 105.6	1 162.3	2.381
2003	7 614.5	5 527.1	2 087.4	7.615	5.527	2.088	1 143.6	1 252.9	2.724
2001									
January	591.7	449.4	142.3	8.783	6.747	2.036	1 417.1	1 332.8	2.371
February	701.3	550.9	150.4	8.955	6.954	2.001	1 335.6	1 247.1	2.152
March	789.3	602.5	186.8	8.317	6.342	1.975	1 321.9	1 226.0	2.320
April	689.7	519.7	170.0	8.371	6.253	2.118	1 247.2	1 214.9	2.331
May	814.6	623.3	191.3	8.362	6.330	2.032	1 188.9	1 196.6	2.268
June	811.1	620.9	190.2	8.394	6.330	2.064	1 147.4	1 181.0	2.239
July	666.8	492.0	174.8	7.934	5.911	2.023	957.5	1 177.9	2.391
August	726.6	525.5	201.1	7.806	5.735	2.071	986.2	1 179.9	2.469
September	640.2	481.3	158.9	7.801	5.854	1.947	963.4	1 156.2	2.370
October	813.4	627.0	186.4	10.460	7.987	2.473	858.0	953.3	1.432
November	603.0	437.0	166.0	8.421	6.210	2.211	919.3	917.2	1.772
December	574.4	393.2	181.2	7.458	5.219	2.239	955.7	984.4	2.264
2002									
January	526.0	365.3	160.7	7.719	5.458	2.261	1 064.7	1 016.9	2.235
February	624.8	456.2	168.6	8.029	5.778	2.251	1 139.4	1 060.4	2.202
March	741.6	539.2	202.4	8.153	5.905	2.248	1 146.9	1 089.5	2.214
April	717.6	531.0	186.6	8.564	6.313	2.251	1 162.8	1 093.0	2.078
May	758.4	559.5	198.9	7.917	5.774	2.143	1 169.2	1 127.2	2.342
June	761.3	559.7	201.6	8.017	5.773	2.244	1 169.6	1 173.5	2.440
July	740.7	539.8	200.9	8.641	6.361	2.280	999.6	1 202.9	2.270
August	829.7	605.7	224.0	8.542	6.345	2.197	949.4	1 208.4	2.286
September	602.1	431.5	170.6	7.911	5.633	2.278	1 003.8	1 213.8	2.586
October	604.7	442.1	162.6	7.581	5.498	2.083	1 108.0	1 240.4	2.707
November	570.6	399.0	171.6	7.886	5.624	2.262	1 205.1	1 277.5	2.726
December	624.9	442.3	182.6	8.274	5.995	2.279	1 148.4	1 244.4	2.491
2003									
January	543.2	385.5	157.7	8.142	5.878	2.264	1 220.5	1 231.1	2.513
February	581.1	418.4	162.7	7.430	5.263	2.167	1 250.3	1 257.2	2.866
March	695.7	503.3	192.4	7.696	5.522	2.174	1 242.8	1 259.7	2.738
April	653.0	475.8	177.2	7.578	5.504	2.074	1 228.9	1 245.6	2.716
May	726.9	534.9	192.0	7.361	5.355	2.006	1 201.0	1 255.9	2.815
June	688.6	514.4	174.2	7.548	5.517	2.031	1 185.8	1 255.3	2.731
July	680.1	494.1	186.0	7.608	5.589	2.019	1 026.1	1 259.0	2.703
August	738.1	535.2	202.9	7.826	5.749	2.077	965.7	1 230.5	2.568
September	596.0	433.8	162.2	7.618	5.528	2.090	1 014.0	1 274.9	2.767
October	573.8	417.4	156.4	7.259	5.234	2.025	1 111.2	1 297.5	2.975
November	557.7	398.3	159.4	7.737	5.614	2.123	1 145.5	1 249.0	2.670
December	580.3	416.0	164.3	7.576	5.575	2.001	1 131.0	1 218.7	2.624

... = Not available.

Table 17-8. Motor Vehicle Sales and Inventories—Continued

Year and month	Retail sales of new trucks and buses								Unit sales of cars and light trucks (millions of units, seasonally adjusted annual rate)		
	Thousands of units, not seasonally adjusted				Millions of units, seasonally adjusted annual rate						
	Total	0–10,000 pounds		10,001 pounds and over	Total	0–10,000 pounds		10,001 pounds and over	Total	Domestic	Imports
		Domestic	Imports			Domestic	Imports				
1967	...	1 193.8	...	329.7	...	1.201	...	0.329	...	8.769	...
1968	...	1 464.2	...	343.3	...	1.463	...	0.343	...	10.087	...
1969	...	1 551.1	...	384.5	...	1.552	...	0.384	...	10.016	...
1970	...	1 408.5	...	337.3	...	1.408	...	0.335	...	8.528	...
1971	...	1 693.0	...	338.9	...	1.700	...	0.339	...	10.362	...
1972	...	2 122.5	...	437.4	...	2.116	...	0.437	...	11.369	...
1973	...	2 509.4	...	495.7	...	2.513	...	0.495	...	12.102	...
1974	...	2 180.1	...	423.9	...	2.176	...	0.424	...	9.538	...
1975	...	2 052.6	...	298.3	...	2.055	...	0.298	...	9.006	...
1976	3 300.5	2 738.3	237.5	324.7	3.296	2.733	0.239	0.324	12.966	11.225	1.741
1977	3 813.0	3 112.8	323.1	377.1	3.818	3.116	0.324	0.378	14.486	12.088	2.398
1978	4 256.8	3 481.1	335.9	439.8	4.249	3.469	0.340	0.440	14.973	12.633	2.340
1979	3 589.7	2 730.2	469.4	390.1	3.599	2.740	0.469	0.390	13.768	10.970	2.798
1980	2 487.4	1 731.1	484.6	271.7	2.482	1.731	0.480	0.271	11.192	8.312	2.881
1981	2 255.6	1 581.7	447.6	226.3	2.255	1.585	0.444	0.226	10.564	7.794	2.770
1982	2 562.8	1 967.5	410.4	184.9	2.569	1.971	0.413	0.185	10.363	7.729	2.634
1983	3 117.3	2 465.2	463.3	188.8	3.130	2.480	0.461	0.189	12.120	9.273	2.846
1984	4 093.1	3 207.2	607.7	278.2	4.085	3.199	0.609	0.278	14.197	11.150	3.047
1985	4 741.7	3 618.4	828.3	295.0	4.759	3.634	0.831	0.295	15.443	11.838	3.604
1986	4 912.1	3 671.4	967.2	273.5	4.918	3.676	0.969	0.273	16.051	11.891	4.160
1987	4 991.5	3 792.0	912.2	287.3	4.977	3.783	0.907	0.288	14.861	10.864	3.997
1988	5 231.9	4 199.7	697.9	334.3	5.225	4.194	0.697	0.334	15.436	11.733	3.703
1989	5 055.9	4 113.6	630.3	312.0	5.065	4.123	0.629	0.313	14.529	11.201	3.328
1990	4 837.0	3 956.8	602.7	277.5	4.841	3.960	0.602	0.278	13.863	10.857	3.006
1991	4 355.4	3 605.6	528.8	221.0	4.360	3.612	0.528	0.221	12.314	9.748	2.566
1992	4 892.2	4 247.0	395.9	249.3	4.894	4.247	0.398	0.248	12.860	10.524	2.336
1993	5 667.8	5 000.5	364.5	302.8	5.659	4.991	0.365	0.302	13.874	11.725	2.149
1994	6 407.3	5 658.2	396.3	352.8	6.408	5.659	0.396	0.354	15.045	12.914	2.131
1995	6 469.8	5 690.9	390.5	388.4	6.486	5.703	0.392	0.390	14.783	12.881	1.902
1996	6 921.8	6 131.8	430.9	359.1	6.915	6.127	0.430	0.357	15.084	13.381	1.703
1997	7 217.8	6 270.4	571.2	376.2	7.228	6.283	0.569	0.376	15.125	13.190	1.935
1998	7 815.8	6 745.3	646.2	424.3	7.788	6.720	0.644	0.425	15.506	13.484	2.022
1999	8 704.1	7 420.0	762.8	521.3	8.712	7.429	0.762	0.521	16.888	14.411	2.477
2000	8 953.5	7 650.8	840.8	461.9	8.951	7.649	0.841	0.461	17.342	14.481	2.861
2001	9 046.3	7 718.4	977.8	350.1	9.042	7.715	0.977	0.350	17.201	14.125	3.076
2002	9 030.2	7 646.9	1 060.9	322.4	8.998	7.619	1.058	0.322	16.759	13.474	3.286
2003	9 353.7	7 801.4	1 223.9	328.4	9.336	7.790	1.218	0.329	16.623	13.317	3.305
2001											
January	603.9	511.2	64.3	28.4	8.858	7.554	0.903	0.401	17.240	14.301	2.939
February	679.9	584.3	67.2	28.4	8.863	7.549	0.920	0.394	17.424	14.503	2.921
March	838.3	723.1	81.0	34.2	8.923	7.655	0.889	0.379	16.861	13.997	2.864
April	687.3	582.4	74.2	30.7	8.496	7.182	0.973	0.341	16.526	13.435	3.091
May	820.3	698.7	86.2	35.4	8.508	7.211	0.924	0.373	16.497	13.541	2.956
June	840.8	723.1	85.1	32.6	9.059	7.728	0.971	0.360	17.093	14.058	3.035
July	707.6	599.4	80.5	27.7	8.524	7.225	0.959	0.340	16.118	13.136	2.982
August	751.1	626.3	95.1	29.7	8.530	7.238	0.960	0.332	16.004	12.973	3.031
September	672.0	573.3	75.3	23.4	8.554	7.305	0.941	0.308	16.047	13.159	2.888
October	939.3	813.6	94.9	30.8	11.588	10.030	1.212	0.346	21.702	18.017	3.685
November	744.6	637.3	83.9	23.4	9.610	8.259	1.045	0.306	17.725	14.469	3.256
December	761.2	645.7	90.1	25.4	9.005	7.644	1.043	0.318	16.145	12.863	3.282
2002											
January	603.7	503.3	78.9	21.5	8.727	7.341	1.082	0.304	16.142	12.799	3.343
February	703.7	606.1	75.8	21.8	9.156	7.819	1.034	0.303	16.882	13.597	3.285
March	798.3	679.4	92.4	26.5	8.920	7.555	1.058	0.307	16.766	13.460	3.306
April	753.8	639.9	83.9	30.0	9.096	7.721	1.057	0.318	17.342	14.034	3.308
May	779.6	657.8	90.1	31.7	8.239	6.940	0.966	0.333	15.823	12.714	3.109
June	802.2	684.9	89.9	27.4	8.723	7.345	1.063	0.315	16.425	13.118	3.307
July	810.9	685.5	97.8	27.6	9.457	7.998	1.134	0.325	17.773	14.359	3.414
August	904.7	766.6	108.7	29.4	9.878	8.505	1.034	0.339	18.081	14.850	3.231
September	648.5	545.9	75.5	27.1	8.776	7.401	1.029	0.346	16.341	13.034	3.307
October	725.9	613.8	82.1	30.0	8.598	7.251	1.010	0.337	15.842	12.749	3.093
November	656.7	544.5	87.7	24.5	8.527	7.110	1.086	0.331	16.082	12.734	3.348
December	842.2	719.2	98.1	24.9	9.886	8.443	1.142	0.301	17.859	14.438	3.421
2003											
January	564.5	463.9	80.5	20.1	8.474	7.078	1.111	0.285	16.331	12.956	3.375
February	657.7	553.5	82.6	21.6	8.568	7.137	1.129	0.302	15.696	12.400	3.296
March	782.2	648.3	108.8	25.1	8.837	7.254	1.289	0.294	16.239	12.776	3.463
April	783.4	652.9	101.9	28.6	9.206	7.651	1.252	0.303	16.481	13.155	3.326
May	873.8	730.7	115.5	27.6	9.137	7.630	1.208	0.299	16.199	12.985	3.214
June	813.5	683.0	102.1	28.4	9.220	7.641	1.262	0.317	16.451	13.158	3.293
July	858.2	714.5	114.4	29.3	9.557	7.946	1.266	0.345	16.820	13.535	3.285
August	917.6	760.7	129.6	27.3	10.414	8.798	1.290	0.326	17.914	14.547	3.367
September	733.0	609.7	95.1	28.2	9.659	8.063	1.251	0.345	16.932	13.591	3.341
October	759.6	633.4	95.5	30.9	9.183	7.654	1.181	0.348	16.094	12.888	3.206
November	727.7	607.5	93.5	26.7	9.549	7.972	1.200	0.377	16.909	13.586	3.323
December	882.3	743.3	104.4	34.6	10.231	8.657	1.173	0.401	17.406	14.232	3.174

... = Not available.

Table 17-9. Retail and Food Services Sales

(All retail establishments and food services; millions of dollars; not seasonally adjusted.)

Classification basis, year and month	Retail and food services, total [1]	GAFO (department store type goods), total [2]	Motor vehicles and parts	Furniture and home furnishings	Electronics and appliances	Building materials and garden	Food and beverages	Health and personal care	Gasoline	Clothing and accessories	General merchandise	Nonstore retailers	Food services and drinking places
SIC Basis [3]													
1967	297 084	...	56 094	13 605	...	13 435	70 456	11 359	22 362	17 900	40 124	...	22 518
1968	329 336	...	64 314	15 257	...	15 602	75 899	12 378	24 750	19 707	44 019	...	25 279
1969	352 457	...	67 745	16 152	...	17 175	81 258	13 200	26 301	21 384	46 559	...	27 173
1970	374 989	...	65 241	17 043	...	18 080	89 990	14 567	28 903	22 095	49 163	...	30 476
1971	413 969	...	80 718	18 183	...	20 924	94 002	15 143	30 620	24 178	54 365	...	32 321
1972	458 267	...	92 335	21 199	...	24 123	100 589	16 139	33 072	26 367	59 656	...	35 738
1973	511 570	...	104 893	24 244	...	27 466	111 817	17 190	36 942	29 109	65 825	...	40 290
1974	541 686	...	97 551	25 982	...	27 347	126 312	18 595	43 054	30 077	69 540	...	44 606
1975	587 704	...	107 348	27 046	...	27 299	138 665	19 995	47 603	32 398	73 759	...	51 067
1976	655 859	...	130 169	30 300	...	33 259	148 218	21 710	52 037	34 706	79 500	...	57 331
1977	722 109	...	150 129	33 308	...	38 913	158 444	23 381	56 638	37 165	87 824	...	63 370
1978	804 019	...	168 065	36 832	...	45 170	175 425	25 607	59 889	42 649	97 215	...	71 828
1979	896 561	...	178 641	42 417	...	51 016	197 985	28 455	73 521	46 070	103 817	...	82 110
1980	956 921	...	164 149	44 238	...	50 794	220 224	30 951	94 093	49 296	108 955	...	90 058
1981	1 038 163	...	181 903	46 900	...	52 230	236 188	33 999	103 072	53 998	120 534	...	98 118
1982	1 068 747	...	192 440	46 761	...	50 994	246 122	36 440	97 440	55 570	124 624	...	104 593
1983	1 170 163	...	229 979	54 691	...	58 739	256 018	40 591	102 927	60 192	135 959	...	113 281
1984	1 286 914	...	273 320	61 432	...	67 077	271 909	44 011	107 565	64 341	150 283	...	121 321
1985	1 375 027	...	303 199	68 287	...	71 196	285 062	46 994	113 341	70 195	158 636	...	127 949
1986	1 449 636	...	326 138	75 714	...	77 104	297 019	50 546	102 093	75 626	169 397	...	139 415
1987	1 541 299	...	342 896	78 072	...	83 454	309 461	54 142	104 769	79 322	181 970	...	153 461
1988	1 656 202	...	372 570	85 390	...	91 056	325 493	57 842	110 341	85 307	192 521	...	167 993
1989	1 758 971	...	386 011	91 301	...	92 379	347 045	63 343	122 882	92 341	206 306	...	177 829
1990	1 844 611	...	387 605	91 545	...	94 640	368 333	70 558	138 504	95 819	215 514	...	190 149
1991	1 855 937	...	372 647	91 676	...	91 496	374 523	75 540	137 295	97 441	226 730	...	194 424
1992	1 951 589	...	406 935	96 947	...	100 838	377 099	77 788	136 950	104 212	246 420	...	200 164
NAICS Basis													
1992	2 062 495	536 894	427 609	54 994	42 763	160 171	371 451	90 794	156 556	120 346	247 968	81 299	203 415
1993	2 202 443	574 126	481 949	57 935	48 760	171 733	375 440	93 623	162 587	124 989	266 088	88 319	216 051
1994	2 381 946	619 580	550 095	62 766	57 413	190 817	385 265	97 299	171 416	129 327	285 278	98 518	225 629
1995	2 501 956	653 010	588 013	65 528	64 919	199 068	391 312	102 469	181 294	131 605	300 589	105 435	233 625
1996	2 655 590	685 254	635 251	69 415	68 515	212 759	402 020	110 199	194 601	136 860	315 398	119 512	242 896
1997	2 778 359	715 682	660 682	74 092	70 211	229 489	410 288	119 055	199 856	140 565	331 454	127 385	258 040
1998	2 917 431	762 480	699 457	78 574	75 981	243 490	421 579	130 228	191 749	149 442	351 706	133 320	272 646
1999	3 164 792	822 989	779 763	85 218	81 921	263 205	443 159	143 610	211 271	160 050	381 403	149 487	285 878
2000	3 376 616	872 390	816 631	91 662	86 362	275 996	459 211	156 861	247 160	167 864	406 204	175 702	306 430
2001	3 475 999	894 024	841 141	91 442	85 174	287 233	481 388	168 050	246 993	167 313	430 095	173 010	319 245
2002	3 563 579	926 751	846 248	93 689	89 930	299 893	489 445	181 111	244 796	171 759	451 365	177 264	333 457
2003	3 756 688	961 070	895 703	97 977	94 561	321 134	505 933	192 191	268 519	178 435	471 078	189 701	357 144
2001													
January	257 561	61 734	61 174	7 068	6 763	19 271	37 411	13 441	19 541	10 093	28 744	16 203	24 174
February	254 560	61 723	63 467	6 825	6 314	18 977	35 712	12 981	18 486	11 487	28 643	14 161	24 013
March	288 109	69 199	73 601	7 610	6 718	22 754	39 653	14 123	20 354	13 081	32 425	15 635	27 252
April	282 807	68 357	69 338	6 980	5 915	26 863	38 511	13 594	21 257	13 362	33 546	13 675	26 084
May	304 808	71 991	76 598	7 582	6 317	29 736	41 370	14 361	23 435	13 802	35 183	13 560	27 576
June	296 502	70 503	74 978	7 516	6 531	27 353	40 620	13 786	22 882	12 938	34 386	12 767	27 795
July	287 631	68 815	71 212	7 472	6 536	25 484	40 867	13 645	21 754	12 575	33 378	12 476	27 829
August	303 742	76 744	75 661	7 970	7 082	25 505	41 446	14 175	22 338	14 786	36 190	13 823	28 524
September	269 974	67 223	62 958	7 092	6 333	22 578	39 547	13 070	21 084	12 093	32 574	12 587	25 898
October	300 636	71 267	81 983	7 601	6 533	25 345	40 165	14 436	20 144	13 220	34 819	15 084	26 601
November	295 614	85 461	67 264	8 475	8 139	22 820	41 000	14 122	18 166	15 329	42 316	15 678	25 736
December	334 115	121 007	62 907	9 251	11 993	20 547	45 086	16 316	17 552	24 547	57 891	17 361	27 763
2002													
January	263 286	64 400	62 461	7 104	7 092	20 002	39 496	14 591	17 198	10 351	30 345	15 152	25 242
February	260 480	65 121	64 768	7 046	6 728	19 394	36 953	14 125	16 385	11 738	31 197	13 621	25 193
March	293 207	74 321	71 700	7 721	7 149	22 896	41 454	15 178	19 423	13 951	36 327	14 803	28 353
April	293 053	70 193	72 715	7 330	6 421	28 889	38 486	14 996	20 622	13 180	34 648	14 198	27 619
May	309 272	75 910	74 106	7 928	6 963	30 422	42 461	15 526	21 702	14 136	37 751	14 156	28 972
June	297 618	73 157	73 121	7 449	7 018	27 866	40 729	14 538	21 131	13 168	36 692	12 722	28 726
July	304 643	71 444	78 770	7 611	6 965	27 327	41 867	14 995	22 410	12 792	35 146	13 360	28 935
August	316 966	79 287	82 215	8 145	7 524	26 352	42 056	15 153	22 556	15 006	37 908	13 878	29 836
September	282 280	69 484	67 645	7 428	6 812	24 701	39 098	14 503	20 864	12 402	33 494	13 738	27 057
October	297 184	74 778	69 085	7 832	6 994	26 612	40 608	15 350	21 709	13 925	36 712	15 717	27 824
November	299 576	86 832	63 289	8 758	8 237	23 696	41 753	14 959	20 375	15 813	42 936	16 307	27 211
December	346 014	121 824	66 373	9 337	12 027	21 736	44 484	17 197	20 421	25 297	58 209	19 612	28 489
2003													
January	277 504	66 382	65 251	7 213	7 098	21 019	40 897	15 499	20 698	10 800	31 729	16 490	26 379
February	267 895	65 593	64 377	6 769	6 585	19 042	37 734	14 719	20 349	11 672	32 426	15 310	25 899
March	303 875	73 170	75 803	7 702	6 993	24 272	41 130	15 781	23 297	13 399	36 432	15 797	29 563
April	305 435	72 364	76 586	7 467	6 448	29 129	40 915	15 674	22 294	13 650	36 201	14 542	28 702
May	324 452	78 005	81 264	8 188	7 127	30 960	43 692	16 088	22 749	14 701	39 009	14 203	31 439
June	313 353	74 884	79 331	7 879	7 249	30 313	41 561	15 446	22 245	13 448	37 437	13 677	30 339
July	323 056	75 707	83 596	8 225	7 437	29 820	43 847	15 955	23 408	13 766	37 350	13 951	31 264
August	330 313	83 421	82 885	8 527	8 095	27 820	43 468	15 981	24 338	15 466	40 347	14 432	32 570
September	306 836	74 079	75 126	8 186	7 498	28 039	41 093	15 721	22 879	13 544	35 454	15 424	29 129
October	317 990	78 786	73 201	8 534	7 634	29 717	42 657	16 549	23 071	14 577	38 876	17 199	31 077
November	314 234	90 264	66 418	9 105	8 994	25 578	42 592	15 776	21 405	16 522	45 000	17 030	29 790
December	371 745	128 415	71 865	10 182	13 403	25 425	46 347	19 002	21 786	26 890	60 817	21 646	30 993

[1] Includes store categories not shown separately.
[2] Furniture, home furnishings, electronics, appliances, clothing, sporting goods, hobby, book, music, general merchandise, office supplies, stationery, and gifts.
[3] Data are for roughly similar categories in SIC classification system.
... = Not available.

Table 17-9. Retail and Food Services Sales—Continued

(All retail establishments and food services; millions of dollars; seasonally adjusted.)

Classification basis, year and month	Total	Retail and food services										
		Retail (NAICS industry categories)										
		Total	GAFO (department store type goods) [2]	Motor vehicles and parts	Furniture and home furnishings	Electronics and appliances	Building materials and garden	Food and beverages			Health and personal care	Gasoline
								Total	Groceries	Beer, wine, and liquor		
SIC Basis [3]												
1967	297 084	...	...	56 094	13 605	...	13 435	70 456	65 036	6 652	11 359	22 362
1968	329 336	...	...	64 314	15 257	...	15 602	75 899	69 873	7 258	12 378	24 750
1969	352 457	...	...	67 745	16 152	...	17 175	81 258	74 836	7 739	13 200	26 301
1970	374 989	...	...	65 241	17 043	...	18 080	89 990	82 556	8 412	14 567	28 903
1971	413 969	...	...	80 718	18 183	...	20 924	94 002	86 419	9 294	15 143	30 620
1972	458 267	...	...	92 335	21 199	...	24 123	100 589	92 856	9 814	16 139	33 072
1973	511 570	...	...	104 893	24 244	...	27 466	111 817	103 555	10 288	17 190	36 942
1974	541 686	...	...	97 551	25 982	...	27 347	126 312	117 182	11 087	18 595	43 054
1975	587 704	...	...	107 348	27 046	...	27 299	138 665	129 087	11 896	19 995	47 603
1976	655 859	...	...	130 169	30 300	...	33 259	148 218	137 992	12 442	21 710	52 037
1977	722 109	...	...	150 129	33 308	...	38 913	158 444	148 116	13 031	23 381	56 638
1978	804 019	...	...	168 065	36 832	...	45 170	175 425	164 234	13 630	25 607	59 889
1979	896 561	...	...	178 641	42 417	...	51 016	197 985	185 318	15 194	28 455	73 521
1980	956 921	...	...	164 149	44 238	...	50 794	220 224	205 630	16 882	30 951	94 093
1981	1 038 163	...	...	181 903	46 900	...	52 230	236 188	220 580	17 702	33 999	103 072
1982	1 068 747	...	...	192 440	46 761	...	50 994	246 122	230 696	18 146	36 440	97 440
1983	1 170 163	...	...	229 979	54 691	...	58 739	256 018	240 402	19 121	40 591	102 927
1984	1 286 914	...	...	273 320	61 432	...	67 077	271 909	258 465	18 273	44 011	107 565
1985	1 375 027	...	...	303 199	68 287	...	71 196	285 062	269 546	19 532	46 994	113 341
1986	1 449 636	...	...	326 138	75 714	...	77 104	297 019	280 833	19 929	50 546	102 093
1987	1 541 299	...	...	342 896	78 072	...	83 454	309 461	290 979	19 826	54 142	104 769
1988	1 656 202	...	...	372 570	85 390	...	91 056	325 493	307 173	19 638	57 842	110 341
1989	1 758 971	...	...	386 011	91 301	...	92 379	347 045	328 072	20 099	63 343	122 882
1990	1 844 611	...	...	387 605	91 545	...	94 640	368 333	348 243	21 722	70 558	138 504
1991	1 855 937	...	...	372 647	91 676	...	91 496	374 523	354 331	22 454	75 540	137 295
1992	1 951 589	...	...	406 935	96 947	...	100 838	377 099	358 148	21 698	77 788	136 950
NAICS Basis												
1992	2 062 495	1 859 080	536 894	427 609	54 994	42 763	160 171	371 451	337 925	21 825	90 794	156 556
1993	2 202 443	1 986 392	574 126	481 949	57 935	48 760	171 733	375 440	341 855	21 675	93 623	162 587
1994	2 381 946	2 156 317	619 580	550 095	62 766	57 413	190 817	385 265	351 056	22 240	97 299	171 416
1995	2 501 956	2 268 331	653 010	588 013	65 528	64 919	199 068	391 312	356 932	22 145	102 469	181 294
1996	2 655 590	2 412 694	685 254	635 251	69 415	68 515	212 759	402 020	366 075	23 300	110 199	194 601
1997	2 778 359	2 520 319	715 682	660 682	74 092	70 211	229 489	410 288	373 072	24 222	119 055	199 856
1998	2 917 431	2 644 785	762 480	699 457	78 574	75 981	243 490	421 579	382 426	25 697	130 228	191 749
1999	3 164 792	2 878 914	822 989	779 763	85 218	81 921	263 205	443 159	402 472	26 983	143 610	211 271
2000	3 376 616	3 070 186	872 390	816 631	91 662	86 362	275 996	459 211	415 250	29 217	156 861	247 160
2001	3 475 999	3 156 754	894 024	841 141	91 442	85 174	287 233	481 388	434 935	30 461	168 050	246 993
2002	3 563 579	3 230 122	926 751	846 248	93 689	89 930	299 893	489 445	441 682	31 056	181 111	244 796
2003	3 756 688	3 399 544	961 070	895 703	97 977	94 561	321 134	505 933	455 470	32 125	192 191	268 519
2001												
January	286 504	259 968	74 310	67 869	7 776	7 035	23 293	39 217	35 364	2 556	13 549	21 356
February	286 650	260 262	73 852	68 158	7 617	6 994	23 775	39 497	35 681	2 517	13 737	21 103
March	284 660	258 330	73 039	67 837	7 587	6 954	23 631	39 493	35 665	2 508	13 792	20 133
April	288 721	262 400	73 930	68 799	7 570	6 880	24 638	39 792	35 995	2 510	13 801	21 472
May	290 273	263 783	73 792	69 378	7 574	6 862	24 402	40 041	36 182	2 533	13 997	22 298
June	289 060	262 487	73 838	69 160	7 638	6 961	24 144	40 053	36 170	2 543	13 953	21 465
July	287 827	261 068	74 567	67 886	7 648	7 060	23 974	40 252	36 339	2 530	14 053	20 523
August	289 101	262 090	74 973	68 219	7 641	7 024	23 887	40 418	36 549	2 517	14 119	20 531
September	284 272	257 980	73 349	66 512	7 418	6 899	23 400	40 648	36 780	2 531	13 964	21 021
October	302 912	276 311	74 973	82 631	7 496	7 048	23 811	40 795	36 943	2 539	14 378	19 846
November	293 813	267 171	76 050	73 826	7 698	7 424	23 774	40 793	36 859	2 583	14 366	18 943
December	292 105	264 590	77 130	70 816	7 800	7 567	23 590	40 962	37 022	2 580	14 375	18 515
2002												
January	291 400	263 873	76 245	69 478	7 789	7 415	24 272	40 806	36 903	2 576	14 709	18 714
February	293 505	265 790	77 461	69 822	7 864	7 492	24 444	40 842	36 875	2 614	14 947	18 619
March	293 206	265 625	77 315	68 939	7 871	7 536	24 700	40 739	36 789	2 598	14 837	19 404
April	297 472	269 686	77 811	69 586	7 823	7 471	25 648	40 656	36 685	2 604	15 224	20 560
May	293 797	266 178	77 133	67 467	7 865	7 554	25 145	40 730	36 744	2 601	15 074	20 358
June	296 808	269 000	77 509	69 960	7 759	7 569	25 188	40 707	36 688	2 618	15 081	20 318
July	299 428	271 579	76 856	72 422	7 649	7 470	24 904	40 815	36 794	2 602	15 131	20 964
August	300 572	272 818	76 920	73 907	7 787	7 411	25 083	40 705	36 717	2 577	15 138	20 694
September	296 786	268 978	76 414	70 395	7 778	7 442	25 090	40 790	36 819	2 567	15 331	20 802
October	298 500	270 759	78 105	69 840	7 739	7 499	24 981	40 933	36 981	2 547	15 289	21 367
November	299 976	271 981	78 027	70 516	7 919	7 453	25 204	41 257	37 263	2 560	15 280	21 335
December	302 970	274 481	78 044	73 307	7 859	7 521	24 604	41 075	37 007	2 626	15 178	21 678
2003												
January	304 711	276 224	77 469	73 168	7 866	7 448	25 712	41 641	37 619	2 576	15 499	22 113
February	301 347	272 887	77 445	69 815	7 563	7 357	24 307	41 706	37 718	2 582	15 609	23 177
March	307 262	278 335	78 309	72 543	7 891	7 470	25 983	41 802	37 731	2 615	15 609	23 204
April	308 132	279 140	78 288	74 547	7 961	7 531	25 822	41 948	37 825	2 654	15 737	22 272
May	307 397	277 905	79 133	73 894	8 123	7 740	25 971	41 474	37 348	2 624	15 726	21 123
June	312 329	282 585	80 010	75 611	8 224	7 819	26 655	42 089	37 955	2 628	15 907	21 410
July	315 123	285 205	80 642	75 907	8 233	7 955	27 300	42 358	38 150	2 680	16 165	21 836
August	320 843	290 318	81 881	78 415	8 303	8 080	27 405	42 535	38 230	2 730	16 291	22 577
September	316 937	287 092	81 543	74 880	8 413	8 133	27 527	42 615	38 262	2 760	16 325	22 675
October	318 064	287 264	81 537	74 477	8 408	8 144	27 947	42 636	38 245	2 760	16 369	22 421
November	321 798	290 734	82 066	76 560	8 415	8 223	28 043	42 666	38 312	2 735	16 485	22 942
December	322 342	291 318	82 388	76 832	8 415	8 265	28 006	42 523	38 215	2 730	16 509	22 909

[2] Furniture, home furnishings, electronics, appliances, clothing, sporting goods, hobby, book, music, general merchandise, office supplies, stationery, and gifts.
[3] Data are for roughly similar categories in SIC classification system.
... = Not available.

Table 17-9. Retail and Food Services Sales—Continued

(All retail establishments and food services; millions of dollars; seasonally adjusted, except as noted.)

Classification basis, year and month	Retail and food services—Continued													Food services and drinking places
	Retail (NAICS industry categories)—Continued													
	Clothing and accessories				Shoes	Sporting goods, hobby, book, and music	General merchandise			Miscel-laneous store retailers	Nonstore retailers		
	Total [1]	Men's clothing	Women's clothing	Family clothing [4]			Total	Department stores [5]	Other general merchandise		Total [1]	Electronic shopping and mail-order	
SIC Basis [3]													
1967	17 900	3 519	6 812	3 569	3 606	...	40 124	29 183	...	...	...	...	22 518
1968	19 707	3 916	7 435	3 897	4 062	...	44 019	32 431	...	...	...	...	25 279
1969	21 384	4 382	7 842	4 204	4 577	...	46 559	34 754	...	...	...	...	27 173
1970	22 095	4 544	8 239	4 363	4 458	...	49 163	36 167	...	...	...	...	30 476
1971	24 178	4 903	9 222	5 046	4 524	...	54 365	40 472	...	...	...	...	32 321
1972	26 367	5 684	9 739	5 525	4 884	...	59 656	44 451	...	...	...	...	35 738
1973	29 109	6 193	10 732	5 959	5 600	...	65 825	49 342	...	...	...	...	40 290
1974	30 077	6 190	11 338	6 360	5 405	...	69 540	52 059	...	...	...	...	44 606
1975	32 398	6 619	12 438	6 725	5 751	...	73 759	55 702	...	...	...	...	51 067
1976	34 706	6 815	13 426	7 201	8 249	...	79 500	61 500	...	...	...	...	57 331
1977	37 165	7 042	12 537	7 972	7 058	...	87 824	68 856	...	...	...	...	63 370
1978	42 649	7 537	15 995	8 559	8 305	...	97 215	76 137	...	...	...	...	71 828
1979	46 070	7 763	17 030	9 397	9 693	...	103 817	81 161	...	...	...	...	82 110
1980	49 296	7 664	17 592	10 843	10 530	...	108 955	85 464	...	...	...	...	90 058
1981	53 998	7 910	19 060	12 251	11 821	...	120 534	95 638	...	...	...	...	98 118
1982	55 570	7 803	20 017	13 660	11 419	...	124 624	99 841	...	...	...	...	104 593
1983	60 192	7 958	21 847	15 384	11 949	...	135 959	108 637	...	...	...	...	113 281
1984	64 341	8 206	23 764	16 443	12 306	...	150 283	120 487	...	...	...	...	121 321
1985	70 195	8 458	26 149	17 827	13 054	...	158 636	126 412	...	...	...	...	127 949
1986	75 626	8 646	28 600	19 336	13 947	...	169 397	134 486	...	...	...	...	139 415
1987	79 322	9 017	29 208	21 472	14 594	...	181 970	144 017	...	...	...	...	153 461
1988	85 307	9 826	30 567	23 902	15 444	...	192 521	151 523	...	...	...	...	167 993
1989	92 341	10 507	32 231	26 375	17 290	...	206 306	160 524	...	...	...	...	177 829
1990	95 819	10 450	32 812	28 398	18 043	...	215 514	165 808	...	...	...	...	190 149
1991	97 441	10 435	32 865	30 521	17 504	...	226 730	172 922	...	...	...	...	194 424
1992	104 212	10 197	35 750	33 222	18 122	...	246 420	186 423	...	...	...	...	200 164
NAICS Basis													
1992	120 346	10 185	31 840	33 159	18 148	49 296	247 968	177 089	70 879	55 833	81 299	35 252	203 415
1993	124 989	9 968	32 377	35 311	18 528	52 368	266 088	187 685	78 403	62 601	88 319	40 725	216 051
1994	129 327	10 039	30 611	38 118	19 361	57 538	285 278	198 945	86 333	70 585	98 518	47 093	225 629
1995	131 605	9 322	28 723	40 014	19 759	60 922	300 589	205 920	94 669	77 177	105 435	52 741	233 625
1996	136 860	9 554	28 266	42 275	20 604	64 055	315 398	212 203	103 195	84 109	119 512	61 174	242 896
1997	140 565	10 077	27 851	45 259	20 788	65 573	331 454	220 108	111 346	91 669	127 385	70 136	258 040
1998	149 442	10 621	28 690	49 472	21 539	69 456	351 706	223 653	128 053	99 803	133 320	79 489	272 646
1999	160 050	10 540	30 251	53 800	21 967	74 045	381 403	231 048	150 355	105 782	149 487	92 440	285 878
2000	167 864	10 818	32 532	56 435	22 132	78 056	406 204	233 624	172 580	108 477	175 702	110 073	306 430
2001	167 313	10 318	32 925	56 750	22 130	79 818	430 095	229 906	200 189	105 097	173 010	109 158	319 245
2002	171 759	10 160	33 034	59 872	22 327	80 222	451 365	222 645	228 720	104 400	177 264	114 480	333 457
2003	178 435	10 463	33 812	62 689	22 610	79 447	471 078	214 129	256 949	104 865	189 701	121 177	357 144
2001													
January	14 183	913	2 749	3 268	1 847	6 367	35 586	20 108	15 478	8 637	15 100	9 213	26 536
February	14 260	903	2 805	3 554	1 807	6 722	34 861	19 304	15 557	8 766	14 772	9 020	26 388
March	13 968	890	2 737	4 335	1 809	6 670	34 408	18 692	15 716	9 026	14 831	9 228	26 330
April	14 101	846	2 776	4 495	1 878	6 597	35 428	19 137	16 291	8 709	14 613	9 140	26 321
May	13 932	871	2 717	4 508	1 872	6 615	35 380	19 087	16 293	8 972	14 332	9 179	26 490
June	13 888	861	2 717	4 392	1 838	6 561	35 424	19 020	16 404	8 883	14 357	9 237	26 573
July	13 963	855	2 733	4 399	1 895	6 630	35 896	19 178	16 718	8 892	14 291	9 177	26 759
August	14 102	867	2 802	5 076	1 885	6 715	36 070	19 248	16 822	8 801	14 563	9 318	27 011
September	13 230	798	2 672	4 201	1 768	6 577	35 990	18 938	17 052	8 573	13 748	8 522	26 292
October	14 017	863	2 792	4 626	1 814	6 704	36 530	19 118	17 412	8 726	14 329	9 173	26 601
November	13 819	847	2 725	5 586	1 849	6 930	36 935	19 258	17 677	8 637	14 026	9 079	26 642
December	14 124	846	2 739	8 310	1 850	6 733	37 460	19 195	18 265	8 593	14 055	9 167	27 515
2002													
January	14 223	836	2 780	3 359	1 889	6 768	36 758	19 111	17 647	8 594	14 347	9 413	27 527
February	14 487	860	2 837	3 595	1 924	6 733	37 506	19 147	18 359	8 690	14 344	9 470	27 715
March	14 413	882	2 795	4 719	1 878	6 778	37 432	19 033	18 399	8 530	14 446	9 357	27 581
April	14 542	859	2 831	4 409	1 916	6 620	38 096	19 249	18 847	8 727	14 733	9 533	27 786
May	14 148	839	2 737	4 644	1 864	6 716	37 569	18 696	18 873	8 667	14 885	9 571	27 619
June	14 381	844	2 789	4 613	1 881	6 599	37 913	18 724	19 189	8 783	14 742	9 453	27 808
July	14 148	851	2 694	4 686	1 837	6 635	37 645	18 452	19 193	8 735	15 061	9 640	27 849
August	14 225	838	2 712	5 437	1 831	6 639	37 500	18 378	19 122	8 862	14 867	9 604	27 754
September	13 754	837	2 661	4 370	1 779	6 712	37 338	18 118	19 220	8 868	14 678	9 480	27 808
October	14 569	850	2 699	5 242	1 851	6 719	38 169	18 633	19 536	8 763	14 891	9 555	27 741
November	14 372	846	2 726	6 069	1 843	6 774	38 251	18 173	20 078	8 529	15 091	9 677	27 995
December	14 567	846	2 808	8 729	1 865	6 638	38 127	18 060	20 067	8 682	15 245	9 686	28 489
2003													
January	14 596	833	2 764	3 637	1 819	6 652	37 639	17 929	19 710	8 710	15 180	9 661	28 487
February	14 243	811	2 695	3 656	1 864	6 449	38 584	18 027	20 557	8 520	15 557	9 819	28 460
March	14 508	834	2 733	4 695	1 875	6 460	38 731	17 750	20 981	8 560	15 574	9 805	28 927
April	14 443	844	2 719	4 714	1 813	6 581	38 484	17 704	20 780	8 593	15 221	9 877	28 992
May	14 685	866	2 748	5 046	1 844	6 507	38 682	17 809	20 873	8 726	15 254	9 840	29 492
June	14 863	878	2 773	4 787	1 854	6 673	39 071	17 864	21 207	8 742	15 521	10 041	29 744
July	15 054	868	2 843	5 097	1 893	6 589	39 471	17 972	21 499	8 725	15 612	10 124	29 918
August	15 092	889	2 833	5 557	1 940	6 874	40 153	18 125	22 028	8 846	15 747	10 094	30 525
September	15 081	898	2 881	4 846	1 917	6 659	39 958	17 948	22 010	8 766	16 060	10 328	29 845
October	15 117	888	2 877	5 340	1 935	6 616	39 977	17 830	22 147	8 870	16 282	10 382	30 800
November	15 284	896	2 937	6 262	1 943	6 628	40 239	17 750	22 489	8 951	16 298	10 384	31 064
December	15 348	922	2 955	9 052	1 938	6 659	40 413	17 797	22 616	8 882	16 557	10 585	31 024

[1] Includes store categories not shown separately.
[3] Data are for roughly similar categories in SIC classification system.
[4] Not seasonally adjusted
[5] Excluding leased departments.
. . . = Not available.

Table 17-10. Retail Inventories

(All retail stores; end of period, millions of dollars.)

Year and month	Not seasonally adjusted			Seasonally adjusted (NAICS industry categories)								
	Total	Excluding motor vehicles and parts	Motor vehicles and parts	Total	Excluding motor vehicles and parts	Motor vehicles and parts	Furniture, home furnishings, electronics, and appliances	Building materials and garden	Food and beverages	Clothing and accessories	General merchandise	
											Total	Department stores [1]
SIC Basis [2]												
1967	...	...	...	...	...	...	...	...	...	...	...	...
1968	...	...	...	...	...	...	...	...	...	...	...	...
1969	...	...	...	...	...	...	...	...	...	...	...	...
1970	...	...	...	...	...	...	...	...	...	...	...	...
1971	...	...	...	...	...	...	...	...	...	...	...	...
1972	53 791	42 126	11 665	55 079	43 224	11 855	4 414	4 268	5 981	5 200	11 743	8 214
1973	61 835	47 565	14 270	63 237	48 881	14 356	4 800	4 844	6 946	5 791	13 137	9 016
1974	69 644	52 874	16 770	71 067	54 330	16 737	5 439	5 131	8 043	6 071	13 647	9 632
1975	70 273	53 795	16 478	71 744	55 397	16 347	5 717	5 474	8 069	6 029	13 521	9 848
1976	77 617	58 994	18 623	79 273	60 853	18 420	6 115	6 481	8 709	6 516	14 886	11 037
1977	87 411	65 269	22 142	89 444	67 565	21 879	6 610	7 502	9 362	7 646	17 307	13 145
1978	100 242	74 752	25 490	102 694	77 506	25 188	7 876	8 397	10 193	8 914	19 853	14 829
1979	108 408	81 152	27 256	111 098	84 165	26 933	8 681	8 981	11 343	9 514	21 033	15 686
1980	117 857	92 190	25 667	121 078	95 525	25 553	9 207	9 685	13 390	10 929	23 171	16 814
1981	129 073	100 936	28 137	132 719	104 693	28 026	9 795	10 180	14 649	12 234	25 951	19 279
1982	130 797	102 360	28 437	134 628	106 276	28 352	9 714	10 203	15 248	12 392	26 548	19 645
1983	143 513	110 483	33 030	147 833	114 914	32 919	11 217	11 716	16 282	13 466	28 651	21 196
1984	162 773	123 493	39 280	167 812	128 808	39 004	12 433	12 890	17 624	14 641	34 392	25 750
1985	176 941	130 542	46 399	181 881	136 083	45 798	13 762	13 683	19 283	15 689	34 683	25 525
1986	181 651	135 461	46 190	186 510	141 264	45 246	14 340	14 033	19 612	16 067	35 743	26 412
1987	203 210	145 410	57 800	207 836	151 675	56 161	15 050	14 868	19 898	17 280	38 285	28 450
1988	214 824	153 909	60 915	219 047	160 140	58 907	16 311	16 157	21 601	18 079	39 179	29 987
1989	233 143	166 707	66 436	237 234	173 162	64 072	17 280	17 122	23 543	19 422	43 107	33 678
1990	236 152	170 635	65 517	239 815	176 708	63 107	17 442	17 015	25 038	19 690	42 377	33 387
1991	239 478	176 344	63 134	243 389	182 508	60 881	17 649	16 718	25 580	20 263	45 764	36 110
1992	248 198	181 697	66 501	252 185	188 051	64 134	17 934	17 234	25 738	22 249	48 630	38 033
NAICS Basis												
1992	263 276	189 752	73 524	268 003	196 748	71 255	16 483	25 300	27 467	27 448	49 783	38 333
1993	281 148	201 568	79 580	286 092	208 994	77 098	18 399	26 944	27 558	28 165	53 700	40 854
1994	307 117	216 661	90 456	312 227	224 550	87 677	20 661	29 506	28 171	29 573	56 830	42 136
1995	324 508	226 438	98 070	329 582	234 488	95 094	22 032	31 138	28 776	29 354	59 550	43 455
1996	335 347	233 464	101 883	340 621	241 742	98 879	22 434	32 359	29 744	29 830	60 611	44 124
1997	345 737	239 804	105 933	350 960	248 210	102 750	22 260	33 856	29 975	31 133	60 735	44 309
1998	359 646	251 840	107 806	365 068	260 483	104 585	22 817	36 355	31 178	32 360	61 675	43 525
1999	388 823	267 006	121 817	394 235	275 842	118 393	24 134	38 912	33 261	33 585	64 546	44 031
2000	412 148	276 897	135 251	417 652	285 855	131 797	25 522	40 642	32 986	36 460	65 302	42 974
2001	400 403	274 269	126 134	406 002	282 794	123 208	24 137	40 644	34 331	35 150	65 263	40 876
2002	425 250	281 767	143 483	430 512	290 288	140 224	25 217	43 429	34 455	36 624	66 952	39 346
2003	446 637	290 684	155 953	451 458	299 067	152 391	27 248	47 519	34 669	37 201	67 728	37 401
2001												
January	410 245	275 039	135 206	418 191	286 379	131 812	25 477	40 813	33 244	36 276	65 724	43 109
February	411 302	277 389	133 913	415 717	286 254	129 463	24 978	40 688	33 511	36 411	65 832	42 939
March	418 086	283 163	134 923	415 806	286 678	129 128	25 198	40 667	33 631	36 245	66 904	43 360
April	419 242	283 546	135 696	416 261	286 809	129 452	25 152	40 766	33 846	36 068	66 541	43 136
May	415 715	281 011	134 704	417 318	286 825	130 493	24 844	40 999	33 855	35 927	66 967	43 184
June	410 614	278 020	132 594	416 450	286 060	130 390	24 433	40 818	34 014	36 062	67 047	43 030
July	402 740	278 180	124 560	417 409	284 583	132 826	24 190	40 452	34 021	35 850	66 253	42 222
August	407 710	283 609	124 101	421 586	286 337	135 249	24 150	40 846	34 076	35 840	67 146	42 829
September	418 148	292 714	125 434	420 252	285 376	134 876	23 906	40 781	33 997	36 044	66 599	42 672
October	429 475	309 690	119 785	408 370	285 802	122 568	23 999	40 877	34 330	36 313	66 515	42 059
November	433 002	310 471	122 531	405 114	283 559	121 555	24 090	40 678	34 441	35 459	65 850	41 437
December	400 403	274 269	126 134	406 002	282 794	123 208	24 137	40 644	34 331	35 150	65 263	40 876
2002												
January	400 693	272 306	128 387	408 500	283 243	125 257	24 684	40 989	34 143	35 258	64 815	40 128
February	406 548	274 473	132 075	410 327	282 829	127 498	24 793	41 099	34 115	34 806	64 860	40 005
March	412 060	279 350	132 710	409 651	282 609	127 042	24 866	41 656	34 001	34 544	64 501	39 641
April	413 154	279 893	133 261	410 184	283 035	127 149	24 848	41 957	34 009	34 886	64 356	39 279
May	413 563	278 676	134 887	415 068	284 617	130 451	25 262	41 984	34 005	34 939	64 894	39 190
June	410 660	277 083	133 577	416 585	285 264	131 321	25 071	42 031	33 971	35 307	64 723	39 142
July	406 092	280 319	125 773	420 706	286 822	133 884	25 368	42 147	33 852	35 677	65 479	39 376
August	406 536	283 985	122 551	420 618	286 962	133 656	25 232	42 175	34 066	35 723	65 662	39 339
September	422 405	296 034	126 371	424 882	288 769	136 113	25 540	42 533	34 301	36 062	65 693	39 164
October	447 012	311 273	135 739	426 583	287 662	138 921	25 406	43 266	33 764	35 984	65 631	38 826
November	457 626	315 948	141 678	429 202	288 650	140 552	25 314	43 052	34 055	36 143	66 711	39 450
December	425 250	281 767	143 483	430 512	290 288	140 224	25 217	43 429	34 455	36 624	66 952	39 346
2003												
January	425 275	279 316	145 959	433 009	290 527	142 482	25 260	43 094	34 309	37 218	66 586	39 013
February	433 864	283 218	150 646	436 786	291 808	144 978	25 313	43 973	34 483	37 337	66 189	38 502
March	443 872	289 856	154 016	439 466	292 671	146 795	25 147	44 165	34 654	37 531	66 607	38 693
April	445 972	289 792	156 180	440 812	292 642	148 170	25 257	43 983	34 604	37 345	67 437	39 233
May	439 357	285 712	153 645	439 592	291 549	148 043	25 421	44 178	34 620	37 308	66 610	38 443
June	436 202	284 245	151 957	440 960	292 193	148 767	25 977	44 605	34 545	37 294	66 528	38 226
July	427 909	287 224	140 685	442 512	293 560	148 952	26 067	44 798	34 784	37 265	66 662	37 971
August	423 602	290 177	133 425	438 402	293 217	145 185	26 171	45 353	34 799	37 326	66 041	37 487
September	440 297	303 070	137 227	443 902	295 727	148 175	26 390	46 563	34 937	37 163	66 868	37 863
October	466 745	320 491	146 254	446 267	296 430	149 837	26 885	46 563	34 711	36 886	67 341	38 038
November	479 124	325 899	153 225	450 075	298 094	151 981	27 094	46 937	34 758	37 222	67 176	37 546
December	446 637	290 684	155 953	451 458	299 067	152 391	27 248	47 519	34 669	37 201	67 728	37 401

[1] Excluding leased departments.
[2] Data are for roughly similar categories in SIC classification system.
... = Not available.

Table 17-11. Merchant Wholesalers—Sales and Inventories

(Millions of dollars.)

Classification basis, year, and month	Not seasonally adjusted						Seasonally adjusted					
	Sales			Inventories (current cost, end of period)			Sales			Inventories (current cost, end of period)		
	Total	Durable goods establishments	Nondurable goods establishments	Total	Durable goods establishments	Nondurable goods establishments	Total	Durable goods establishments	Nondurable goods establishments	Total	Durable goods establishments	Nondurable goods establishments
SIC Basis[1]												
1972	358 388	168 879	189 509	...	...	...	358 388	168 879	189 509	...	...	...
1973	457 378	208 554	248 824	...	...	...	457 378	208 554	248 824	...	...	...
1974	575 786	255 863	319 923	...	...	...	575 786	255 863	319 923	...	...	...
1975	559 606	235 723	323 883	...	...	...	559 606	235 723	323 883	...	...	...
1976	608 381	263 605	344 776	...	...	...	608 381	263 605	344 776	...	...	...
1977	673 633	304 721	368 912	...	...	...	673 633	304 721	368 912	...	...	...
1978	796 961	372 176	424 785	...	...	...	796 961	372 176	424 785	...	...	...
1979	948 614	436 254	512 360	...	...	...	948 614	436 254	512 360	...	...	...
1980	1 117 187	486 509	630 678	124 015	78 849	45 166	1 117 187	486 509	630 678	122 631	79 372	43 259
1981	1 214 156	525 607	688 549	130 709	85 371	45 338	1 214 156	525 607	688 549	129 654	85 856	43 798
1982	1 142 535	480 318	662 217	128 514	84 806	43 708	1 142 535	480 318	662 217	127 428	85 222	42 206
1983	1 190 705	523 080	667 625	131 306	84 709	46 597	1 190 705	523 080	667 625	130 075	85 180	44 895
1984	1 346 392	622 361	724 031	143 458	94 895	48 563	1 346 392	622 361	724 031	142 452	95 474	46 978
1985	1 361 507	651 864	709 643	148 403	96 659	51 744	1 361 507	651 864	709 643	147 409	97 371	50 038
1986	1 379 514	681 691	697 823	154 081	101 369	52 712	1 379 514	681 691	697 823	153 574	102 349	51 225
1987	1 475 613	730 592	745 021	164 310	106 820	57 490	1 475 613	730 592	745 021	163 903	108 112	55 791
1988	1 614 249	801 751	812 498	179 828	115 613	64 215	1 614 249	801 751	812 498	178 801	117 045	61 756
1989	1 725 123	851 550	873 573	187 897	120 701	67 196	1 725 123	851 550	873 573	187 009	122 237	64 772
1990	1 794 072	880 767	913 305	196 881	124 839	72 042	1 794 072	880 767	913 305	195 833	126 461	69 372
1991	1 779 673	860 138	919 535	201 777	125 921	75 856	1 779 673	860 138	919 535	200 448	127 399	73 049
1992	1 849 798	908 917	940 881	209 675	130 044	79 631	1 849 798	908 917	940 881	208 302	131 509	76 793
NAICS Basis												
1992	1 731 623	832 807	898 816	194 199	117 827	76 372	1 731 623	832 807	898 816	193 056	119 334	73 722
1993	1 809 990	909 079	900 911	202 428	123 264	79 164	1 809 990	909 079	900 911	201 184	124 892	76 292
1994	1 933 598	1 004 153	929 445	219 265	135 929	83 336	1 933 598	1 004 153	929 445	218 119	137 800	80 319
1995	2 114 720	1 106 797	1 007 923	235 536	147 446	88 090	2 114 720	1 106 797	1 007 923	234 268	149 642	84 626
1996	2 239 784	1 156 617	1 083 167	237 871	150 360	87 511	2 239 784	1 156 617	1 083 167	237 186	152 637	84 549
1997	2 334 495	1 223 777	1 110 718	255 572	161 736	93 836	2 334 495	1 223 777	1 110 718	254 763	164 148	90 615
1998	2 379 824	1 265 755	1 114 069	268 462	171 480	96 982	2 379 824	1 265 755	1 114 069	267 689	174 107	93 582
1999	2 539 566	1 353 049	1 186 517	285 215	181 802	103 413	2 539 566	1 353 049	1 186 517	284 396	184 639	99 757
2000	2 743 557	1 421 462	1 322 095	302 922	190 874	112 048	2 743 557	1 421 462	1 322 095	301 618	193 835	107 783
2001	2 701 474	1 345 892	1 355 582	289 933	173 333	116 600	2 701 474	1 345 892	1 355 582	287 913	176 014	111 899
2002	2 742 285	1 334 066	1 408 219	291 358	171 335	120 023	2 742 285	1 334 066	1 408 219	288 990	173 906	115 084
2003	2 885 034	1 369 285	1 515 749	298 234	173 806	124 428	2 885 034	1 369 285	1 515 749	294 980	176 286	118 694
2001												
January	223 799	109 047	114 752	304 912	193 034	111 878	231 919	116 387	115 532	301 262	194 225	107 037
February	211 304	104 961	106 343	303 003	193 285	109 718	231 106	116 372	114 734	301 029	193 161	107 868
March	238 094	121 426	116 668	301 927	192 196	109 731	227 998	115 216	112 782	300 988	192 230	108 758
April	222 414	111 024	111 390	302 685	193 321	109 364	226 514	113 586	112 928	301 755	191 391	110 364
May	237 128	117 927	119 201	300 230	191 925	108 305	227 599	113 789	113 810	303 033	190 872	112 161
June	227 133	115 198	111 935	297 891	188 494	109 397	223 126	111 587	111 539	300 740	187 488	113 252
July	221 827	111 116	110 711	296 477	188 217	108 260	224 580	112 006	112 574	298 082	185 748	112 334
August	235 302	118 410	116 892	293 114	184 382	108 732	224 778	112 300	112 478	297 651	184 241	113 410
September	216 665	108 216	108 449	292 961	181 916	111 045	224 550	110 072	114 478	296 387	182 676	113 711
October	235 697	116 833	118 864	296 316	181 396	114 920	219 797	108 047	111 750	293 852	182 082	111 770
November	219 934	108 550	111 384	292 745	176 952	115 793	220 125	108 726	111 399	290 403	178 351	112 052
December	212 177	103 184	108 993	289 933	173 333	116 600	219 506	108 190	111 316	287 913	176 014	111 899
2002												
January	213 472	102 406	111 066	291 040	173 737	117 303	221 219	109 142	112 077	286 992	174 876	112 116
February	203 864	99 727	104 137	286 144	172 903	113 241	223 009	110 754	112 255	284 403	172 755	111 648
March	226 091	111 618	114 473	285 704	172 276	113 428	223 315	109 419	113 896	284 480	172 065	112 415
April	229 700	112 672	117 028	283 416	173 106	110 310	226 696	111 397	115 299	282 634	171 129	111 505
May	235 918	115 587	120 331	279 877	171 695	108 182	227 493	112 015	115 478	283 003	170 763	112 240
June	225 812	112 838	112 974	281 585	172 107	109 478	228 840	112 555	116 285	284 474	171 157	113 317
July	233 778	114 594	119 184	284 770	174 581	110 189	229 345	112 164	117 181	286 818	172 362	114 456
August	237 194	115 959	121 235	282 987	173 514	109 473	232 391	113 081	119 310	287 743	173 518	114 225
September	229 709	113 256	116 453	284 989	172 842	112 147	231 790	111 974	119 816	288 358	173 641	114 717
October	247 599	119 636	127 963	289 025	172 305	116 720	231 287	110 555	120 732	286 628	172 992	113 636
November	227 911	107 934	119 977	289 121	172 025	117 096	233 819	111 036	122 783	286 810	173 437	113 373
December	231 237	107 839	123 398	291 358	171 335	120 023	232 033	109 456	122 577	288 990	173 906	115 084
2003												
January	227 770	104 147	123 623	292 511	172 248	120 263	235 662	111 331	124 331	288 367	173 234	115 133
February	216 868	98 777	118 091	291 297	175 034	116 263	236 716	109 787	126 929	289 611	174 700	114 911
March	242 813	114 461	128 352	292 191	175 404	116 787	239 542	112 095	127 447	290 876	175 088	115 788
April	237 965	113 014	124 951	291 448	177 221	114 227	234 998	111 922	123 076	290 655	175 090	115 565
May	236 074	112 123	123 951	286 462	175 222	111 240	234 073	111 706	122 367	289 756	174 278	115 478
June	240 136	116 810	123 326	286 825	174 867	111 958	237 209	113 230	123 979	289 727	174 040	115 687
July	243 623	116 760	126 863	288 497	175 467	113 030	239 113	113 964	125 149	290 210	173 386	116 824
August	237 647	112 729	124 918	285 243	172 796	112 447	240 029	113 581	126 448	289 961	172 905	117 056
September	247 100	120 840	126 260	288 043	172 355	115 688	241 527	115 505	126 022	291 248	173 153	118 095
October	263 351	126 553	136 798	295 215	173 437	121 778	246 430	117 342	129 088	292 549	174 216	118 333
November	234 591	111 670	122 921	296 364	173 114	123 250	247 737	118 235	129 502	293 534	174 682	118 852
December	257 096	121 401	135 695	298 234	173 806	124 428	250 236	119 902	130 334	294 980	176 286	118 694

[1]Data are for roughly similar categories in SIC classification system.
... = Not available.

Table 17-12. Selected Service Industries—Receipts of Taxable Firms, 1986–1998, by SIC Industry

(By kind of business and SIC code, millions of dollars.)

Year	Arrangement of passenger transportation (472)	Real estate agents and managers (653)	Hotels, rooming houses, camps and other lodging places, except on membership basis (70, ex. 704)	Personal services (72)	Business services (73)	Automotive repair, services, and parking (75)	Miscellaneous repair services (76)	Motion pictures (78)
1986	7 465	48 360	47 634	39 587	170 250	53 867	22 478	23 740
1987	8 196	52 919	53 630	43 247	188 856	58 278	24 599	27 754
1988	9 521	58 980	58 637	48 329	223 369	66 053	27 659	31 746
1989	11 041	62 325	61 229	51 832	251 648	70 961	30 064	36 173
1990	12 276	63 023	64 225	54 736	280 699	73 722	32 848	39 982
1991	11 438	63 180	65 284	54 620	287 214	71 542	32 401	42 838
1992	11 926	73 115	71 038	59 597	309 439	78 511	35 238	45 662
1993	12 396	79 206	74 149	62 597	337 403	84 324	36 772	49 799
1994	13 125	80 947	79 555	66 105	375 067	91 865	40 683	53 504
1995	14 192	82 667	84 093	70 607	425 075	99 227	44 870	57 184
1996	15 354	90 186	88 961	73 905	484 242	106 638	46 101	60 279
1997	16 461	99 854	94 139	77 712	548 434	111 444	47 895	62 865
1998	17 038	108 639	100 650	82 798	638 500	119 978	52 365	66 229

Year	Amusement and recreation services (79)	Health services (80)	Legal services (81)	Vocational schools (824)	Social services (83)	Museums, art galleries, and botanical and zoological gardens (84)	Engineering, accounting, research, management and related services (87)
1986	33 984	173 885	63 390	3 327	...	...	127 885
1987	36 646	196 212	72 115	3 400	...	...	139 897
1988	41 272	221 741	81 636	4 263	...	...	160 446
1989	44 539	241 558	89 144	4 577	...	...	183 528
1990	50 126	271 212	97 640	4 519	15 509	144	198 395
1991	51 654	293 907	100 027	4 183	16 365	154	202 696
1992	57 699	321 653	108 443	4 429	18 201	192	215 624
1993	63 651	335 108	112 145	4 507	20 146	222	222 853
1994	68 453	351 419	114 603	4 710	22 498	231	235 447
1995	77 452	376 279	116 000	5 285	24 858	247	263 835
1996	85 733	398 353	124 659	6 190	27 694	273	292 260
1997	92 837	420 361	133 015	7 031	30 150	322	321 679
1998	97 512	444 727	141 827	8 268	31 970	388	360 823

... = Not available.

Table 17-13. Selected Service Industries—Revenue of Tax-Exempt Firms, 1986–1998, by SIC Industry

(By kind of business and SIC code, millions of dollars.)

Year	Camps and membership lodging (703, 704)	Selected amusement and recreation services (792, 7991, 7997, 7999)	Health services (80)	Legal aid societies and similar legal services (81)	Libraries (823)	Vocational schools (824)	Social services (83)	Museums, art galleries, and botanical and zoological gardens (84)	Selected membership organizations (86 [pt])	Research, development, and testing services (873)	Commercial, physical, and biological research (8731)	Non-commercial research organizations (8733)	Management and public relations services (874, ex. 8744)
1986	...	5 070	...	563	...	...	...	...	...	7 125	...	...	791
1987	...	5 858	...	665	...	...	...	...	...	8 304	...	...	902
1988	...	6 506	...	775	...	...	...	...	...	9 014	...	...	1 201
1989	...	7 163	...	944	...	...	...	...	...	9 975	...	...	1 494
1990	798	7 922	267 858	1 088	476	507	45 255	2 871	31 458	11 035	...	...	1 933
1991	782	8 160	298 168	1 162	481	486	49 055	3 048	33 288	11 463	...	...	2 150
1992	808	8 993	324 416	1 161	527	549	53 673	3 199	36 256	12 534	...	...	2 246
1993	817	10 279	345 081	1 190	606	569	59 052	3 615	39 426	13 180	...	...	2 588
1994	836	11 560	363 112	1 241	655	612	63 493	3 972	41 907	13 919	...	...	3 119
1995	846	12 778	385 210	1 278	730	696	70 303	4 295	45 873	14 493	5 951	7 688	3 732
1996	877	13 299	401 047	1 259	754	772	75 240	4 729	48 897	14 906	5 703	8 293	4 821
1997	929	14 600	414 990	1 446	850	871	83 235	6 231	51 098	16 839	5 950	9 953	6 583
1998	993	15 360	436 078	1 599	934	943	90 458	6 566	55 955	18 732	6 770	10 753	7 761

... = Not available.

Table 17-14. Selected Service Industries—Revenue, 1998–2002, by NAICS Industry

(Millions of dollars.)

NAICS code	Kind of business	1998	1999	2000	2001	2002
	Total for selected service industries	3 701 443	4 016 836	4 360 717	4 484 832	4 596 465
484	Truck transportation	173 458	187 191	199 360	196 584	198 201
492	Couriers and messengers	46 947	49 665	55 230	55 946	55 733
493	Warehousing and storage	12 073	12 565	13 101	13 615	15 304
51	Information	694 204	774 297	852 886	878 387	885 081
511	Publishing industries	202 142	219 876	233 935	233 625	232 869
512	Motion picture and sound recording industries	61 237	65 866	69 378	70 525	75 672
513	Broadcasting and telecommunications	382 429	426 598	470 920	489 328	486 204
514	Information services and data processing services	48 396	61 958	78 653	84 908	90 336
5231	Securities and commodity contracts intermediation and brokerage	165 288	200 161	234 237	195 746	167 367
532	Rental and leasing services	90 073	98 620	106 628	104 794	106 081
54	Professional, scientific, and technical services (except notaries and landscape architectural services)	745 427	813 217	894 781	932 172	940 970
56	Administrative and support and waste management and remediation services (except landscaping services)	352 223	390 195	427 993	430 516	442 558
561	Administrative and support services	310 374	344 758	381 029	383 386	395 877
562	Waste management and remediation services	41 849	45 437	46 964	47 130	46 682
62	Health care and social assistance	963 848	1 006 045	1 064 421	1 149 621	1 246 352
621	Ambulatory health care services	399 518	417 221	443 510	480 135	519 145
622	Hospitals	397 373	413 035	430 329	462 215	507 206
623	Nursing and residential care facilities	100 138	102 633	108 885	116 415	122 881
624	Social assistance	66 820	73 155	81 697	90 856	97 120
71	Arts, entertainment, and recreation	123 968	131 519	139 831	147 243	156 968
711	Performing arts, spectator sports, and related industries	50 337	53 319	56 800	59 867	64 820
712	Museums, historical sites, and similar institutions	7 222	7 671	8 291	8 237	7 803
713	Amusement, gambling, and recreation industries	66 409	70 529	74 740	79 139	84 345
81	Other services (except public administration, religious, labor, and political organizations, and private households)	333 934	353 361	374 249	380 208	381 850
811	Repair and maintenance	133 797	139 732	146 151	152 326	153 307
812	Personal and laundry services	88 436	94 003	99 631	103 426	107 162
813	Religious, grantmaking, civic, professional, and similar organizations (except religious, labor, and political organizations)	111 702	119 627	128 467	124 457	121 381

Table 17-15. Selected Service Industries—Revenue [1]—Total and E-Commerce, 1998–2002, by NAICS Industry

(Millions of dollars, percent.)

NAICS code	Description	Value of revenue, 2001		Value of revenue, 2002	
		Total	E-commerce revenue	Total	E-commerce revenue
	Total for selected service industries [1]	4 756 317	36 045	4 862 961	41 463
	Selected transportation and warehousing	235 659	2 810	237 485	3 429
484	Truck transportation	169 069	1 526	169 443	2 422
492	Couriers and messengers	53 317	1 192	53 101	913
493	Warehousing and storage	13 273	B	14 941	B
51	Information	870 684	10 438	876 984	11 059
511	Publishing industries	231 714	4 941	230 916	5 362
513	Broadcasting and telecommunications	487 799	2 516	484 652	2 549
51419	Online information services	32 347	1 850	31 842	1 823
	Selected finance	288 417	3 754	256 879	4 191
5231	Securities and commodity contracts intermediation and brokerage	191 007	3 570	163 080	4 071
532	Rental and leasing services	99 126	B	100 507	B
	Selected professional, scientific, and technical services	842 261	5 237	848 109	6 490
5415	Computer systems design and related services	174 367	3 526	162 175	4 267
	Selected administrative and support and waste management and remediation services	409 984	9 612	421 107	10 463
5615	Travel arrangement and reservation services	26 487	6 269	26 545	6 385
62	Health care and social assistance services	1 110 231	B	1 203 447	B
71	Arts, entertainment, and recreation services	128 904	B	137 236	B
72	Accommodation and food services	445 236	B	456 232	B
	Selected other services	325 815	656	324 975	1 097
811	Repair and maintenance	130 482	214	131 205	254
813	Religious, grantmaking, civic, professional, and similar organizations	124 457	383	121 381	639

NAICS code	Description	E-commerce as percent of total revenue				
		1998	1999	2000	2001	2002
	Total for selected service industries [1]	0.4	0.6	0.8	0.8	0.9
	Selected transportation and warehousing	0.8	0.9	1.1	1.2	1.4
484	Truck transportation	0.4	0.5	0.7	0.9	1.4
492	Couriers and messengers	2.2	2.3	2.3	2.2	1.7
493	Warehousing and storage	B	B	B	B	B
51	Information	0.4	0.7	1.1	1.2	1.3
511	Publishing industries	0.8	1.4	2.0	2.1	2.3
513	Broadcasting and telecommunications	0.1	0.2	0.4	0.5	0.5
51419	Online information services	3.6	5.1	6.4	5.7	5.7
	Selected finance	0.9	1.4	1.8	1.3	1.6
5231	Securities and commodity contracts intermediation and brokerage	1.3	2.0	2.5	1.9	2.5
532	Rental and leasing services	B	B	B	B	B
	Selected professional, scientific, and technical services	0.4	0.6	0.7	0.6	0.8
5415	Computer systems design and related services	1.3	1.9	2.0	2.0	2.6
	Selected administrative and support and waste management and remediation services	1.4	1.9	2.4	2.3	2.5
5615	Travel arrangement and reservation services	18.2	21.0	23.2	23.7	24.1
62	Health care and social assistance services	B	B	B	B	B
71	Arts, entertainment, and recreation services	B	B	B	B	B
72	Accommodation and food services	B	B	B	B	B
	Selected other services	0.1	0.1	0.2	0.2	0.3
811	Repair and maintenance	0.1	0.1	0.2	0.2	0.2
813	Religious, grantmaking, civic, professional, and similar organizations	0.1	0.1	0.2	0.3	0.5

[1] Includes data only for businesses with paid employees, except for accommodation and food services, which also includes businesses with and without paid employees. Note that accommodation and food services were not included in Table 17-14.

B = Data do not meet publication standards because of high sampling variability or poor response quality. Unpublished estimates derived from this table by subtraction should be used with caution and not be attributed to the U.S. Census Bureau.

NOTES AND DEFINITIONS

TABLE 17-1
PETROLEUM AND PETROLEUM PRODUCTS—IMPORTS, DOMESTIC PRODUCTION, AND STOCKS

SOURCES: IMPORTS: U.S. DEPARTMENT OF COMMERCE, BUREAU OF THE CENSUS (SEE NOTES AND DEFINITIONS TO TABLES 7-8 THROUGH 7-11); SUPPLY (NET IMPORTS AND DOMESTIC PRODUCTION) AND STOCKS: U.S. DEPARTMENT OF ENERGY, ENERGY INFORMATION ADMINISTRATION

Notes on the data

The import data in columns 1 through 6 of this table are those published as Exhibit 16: "Imports of Energy-related Petroleum Products, including Crude Petroleum" of the monthly Census-BEA foreign trade press release. *Total energy-related petroleum products* includes the following Standard International Trade Classification (SITC) commodity groupings: crude oil, petroleum preparations, and liquefied propane and butane gas.

The data in columns 7 through 11, on exports, imports, and net imports (imports minus exports) of petroleum and products and domestic production of crude oil and natural gas plant liquids, all expressed as thousands of barrels per day, and in columns 12 through 14 depicting stocks of crude oil in millions of barrels, are derived from the Department of Energy's weekly petroleum supply reporting system and are published in the Energy Information Administration publications *Petroleum Supply Monthly* and *Monthly Energy Review*. Stock totals are as of the end of the period. Geographic coverage includes the 50 states and the District of Columbia.

Data availability

Data on supply and stocks are available from the Energy Information Administration Internet site at <http://www.eia.doe.gov>. See the Notes and Definitions to Tables 7-8 through 7-11 for availability of import data.

TABLE 17-2
CONSTRUCTION PUT IN PLACE

SOURCE: U.S. DEPARTMENT OF COMMERCE, BUREAU OF THE CENSUS

The Census Bureau's estimates of the value of new construction put in place are intended to provide monthly estimates of the total dollar value of construction work done in the United States.

Definitions and notes on the data

The estimates cover all construction work done each month on new residential and nonresidential buildings and structures, public construction, and improvements to existing buildings and structures. Included are the cost of labor, materials, and equipment rental; cost of architectural and engineering work; overhead costs assigned to the project; interest and taxes paid during construction; and contractors' profits.

The total value put in place for a given period is the sum of the value of work done on all projects underway during this period, regardless of when work on each individual project was started or when payment was made to the contractors. For some categories, estimates are derived by distributing the total construction cost of the project by means of historic construction progress patterns. For some categories, published estimates do represent payments made during a period.

The statistics on the value of construction put in place result from direct measurement and indirect estimation. A series results from direct measurement when it is based on reports of the actual value of construction progress or construction expenditures obtained from a complete census or a sample survey. All other series are developed by indirect estimation using related construction statistics. On an annual basis, the estimates for series directly measured monthly, quarterly, or annually accounted for about 71 percent of total construction in 1998 (private multifamily residential, private residential improvements, private nonresidential buildings, farm nonresidential construction, public utility construction, all other private construction, and virtually all of public construction). On a monthly basis, directly measured data are available for about 55 percent of the value-in-place estimates.

Beginning in 1993, the Construction Expenditures Branch of the Manufacturing and Construction Division began collecting these data using a new classification system, basing project types on their end usage instead of building/nonbuilding types. Data collection on this system for federal construction began in January 2002.

With the changes in project classifications, data presented in these tables for 1993 to date are not directly comparable with data for previous years, except at aggregate levels. For that reason, *Business Statistics* shows earlier historical data only at those aggregate levels. Although some categories, such as lodging, office, education, or religion, have the same name as a category in previously published data, there have been changes within the classifications that make these values incomparable. For example, private medical office buildings were classified as "office" buildings previously, but under the new classification these buildings are in "health care."

The seasonally adjusted data are obtained by removing normal seasonal movement from the unadjusted data to bring out underlying trends and business cycles, using the Census X-12-ARIMA method. Seasonal adjustment accounts for month-to-month variations resulting from normal or average changes in any phenomena affecting the data such as weather conditions, the differing lengths of months, and the varying number of holidays, weekdays, and weekends within each month. It does not adjust for abnormal conditions within each month or for year-to-year variations in weather. The seasonally adjusted annual rate is the seasonally adjusted monthly rate multiplied by 12.

Residential includes new houses, town houses, apartments, and condominiums for sale or rent, built by the owner or for the owner on contract. It includes improvements inside and outside residential structures, such as remodeling, additions, major replacements, and addition of swimming pools and garages. Manufactured housing, houseboats, and maintenance and repair work are not included.

Office includes general office buildings, administration buildings, professional buildings, and financial institution buildings. Office buildings at manufacturing sites are classified as *manufacturing*, but office buildings owned by manufacturing companies but not at such a site are included in the *office* category. In the state and local government category, *office* includes capitols, city halls, courthouses, and similar buildings.

Commercial includes buildings and structures used by the retail, wholesale, farm, and selected service industries. One of the subgroups of this category is *multi-retail*, which includes department and variety stores, shopping centers and malls, and warehouse-type retail stores.

Health care includes hospitals, medical buildings, nursing homes, adult day-care centers, and similar institutions.

Educational includes schools at all levels, higher education, trade schools, libraries, museums, and similar institutions.

Amusement and recreation includes theme and amusement parks, sports structures not located at an educational institution, fitness centers and health clubs, neighborhood centers, camps, movie theaters, etc.

Transportation includes airport facilities, rail facilities, track, and bridges, bus, rail, maritime, and air terminals, docks, marinas, etc.

Communication includes telephone, television, and radio distribution and maintenance structures.

Power includes electricity production and distribution and gas and crude oil transmission, storage, and distribution.

Manufacturing includes all buildings and structures at manufacturing sites, but not the installation of production machinery or special-purpose equipment.

Included in *total private construction*, but not shown separately in these pages, are lodging facilities (hotels and motels), religious structures, and private public safety, sewage and waste disposal, water supply, highway and street, and conservation and development spending.

Included in *total state and local construction*, but not shown separately in these pages, are state and local construction of commercial buildings, conservation and development (dam, levee, jetty, and dredging), lodging, religious, and communication.

Public safety includes correctional facilities, police and sheriffs' stations, fire stations, etc.

Highway and street includes pavement, lighting, retaining walls, bridges, tunnels, toll facilities, and maintenance and rest facilities.

Sewage and waste disposal includes sewage systems, solid waste disposal, and recycling.

Water supply includes water supply, transmission, and storage facilities.

Among the data sources for construction expenditures are the Census Bureau's Survey of Construction, Building Permits Survey, Consumer Expenditure Survey (conducted for the Bureau of Labor Statistics), Annual Capital Expenditures Survey, and Construction Progress Reporting Survey; also, data from the F.W. Dodge Division of the McGraw-Hill Information Systems Company, the U.S. Department of Agriculture, and utility regulatory agencies.

Data availability

Data are released monthly in a press release. The release, more detailed data, and a discussion of methodologies can be found on the Census Web site, <http://www.census.gov/constructionspending>.

TABLE 17-3
HOUSING STARTS AND BUILDING PERMITS; HOME SALES AND PRICES

SOURCES: U.S. DEPARTMENT OF COMMERCE, BUREAU OF THE CENSUS

These data are mainly found in two major Bureau of the Census reports, "New Residential Construction" and "New Residential Sales." They cover new housing units intended for occupancy and maintained by the occupants, excluding hotels, motels, and group residential structures. Manufactured home units are reported in a separate survey.

Definitions

A *housing unit* is a house, an apartment, a group of rooms or a single room intended for occupancy as separate living quarters, that is, the occupants live separately from any other individuals in the building and the unit has a direct access from the outside of the building or through a common hall. Each apartment unit in an apartment building is counted as one housing unit. As of January 2000, a previous requirement that the residents must have the capability to eat separately has been eliminated. (Based on the old definition, some senior housing projects were excluded from the multifamily housing statistics because individual units did not have their own eating facilities.) Housing starts exclude group quarters such as dormitories or rooming houses, transient accommodations such as motels, and manufactured homes. Publicly owned housing units are excluded, but units in structures built by private developers with subsidies or for sale to local public housing authorities are both classified as private housing.

The *start* of construction of a privately owned housing unit is when excavation begins for the footings or foundation of a building intended primarily as a housekeeping residential structure and designed for nontransient occupancy. All housing units in a multifamily building are defined as being started when excavation for the building has begun.

One-family structures include fully detached, semi-detached, row houses, and town houses. In the case of attached units, each must be separated from the adjacent unit by a ground-to-roof wall to be classified as a one-unit structure and must not share facilities such as heating or water supply. Units built one on top of another and those built side-by-side which do not have a ground-to-roof wall and/or have common facilities are classified by the number of units in the structure.

Apartment buildings are defined as buildings containing *five units or more*. The type of ownership is not the criterion—a condominium apartment building is classified not as one-family but as a multifamily structure.

A *manufactured* home is a moveable dwelling, 8 feet or more wide and 40 feet or more long, designed to be towed on its own chassis, with transportation gear integral to the unit when it leaves the factory, and without need of a permanent foundation. Multiwides and expandable manufactured homes are included. Excluded are travel trailers, motor homes, and modular housing. The shipments figures are based on reports submitted by manufacturers on the number of homes actually shipped during the survey month. Shipments to dealers may not necessarily be placed for residential use in the same month as they are shipped. The number of manufactured "homes" used for nonresidential purposes (for example, offices) is not known.

Units authorized by building permits represent the approximately 97 percent of housing in permit-requiring areas.

The *start* occurs when excavation begins for the footing or foundation. Starts are estimated for all areas, regardless of whether permits are required.

New home *sales* are reported only for new single-family residential structures. The sales transaction must intend to include both the house and the land. Excluded are houses built for rent, houses built by the owner, and houses built by a contractor on the owner's land. A sale is reported when a deposit is taken or a sales agreement signed, which can occur prior to a permit being issued.

A house is *for sale* when a permit to build has been issued (or work begun in nonpermit areas) and a sales contract has not been signed nor a deposit accepted.

The *sales price* used in this survey is the price agreed upon between the purchaser and the seller at the time the first sales contract is signed or deposit made. It includes the price of the improved lot. The *median sales price* is the sales price of the house that falls on the middle point of a distribution by price of the total number of houses sold. Half of the houses sold have a sales price less than the median; half have a greater price. Changes in the *sales price* data reflect changes in the distribution of houses by region, size, etc., as well as changes in the prices of houses with identical characteristics.

Notes on the data

Monthly permit authorizations are based on data collected by a mail survey from a sample of 8,500 permit-issuing places, selected from a universe of 19,000 such places in the United States. Data for 1984 through 1993 represented 17,000 places; data for 1978 through 1983 are for 16,000 places; data for 1972 through 1977 are for 14,000 places; data for 1971 are for 13,000 places.

Housing starts and sales data are obtained from the Survey of Construction, in which Census field representatives sample both permit-issuing and non-permit-issuing places.

Effective with the data for April 2001 the Census Bureau made changes to the methodology used for new home sales, including discontinuing an adjustment for construction in areas where building permits are required without a permit being issued. It was believed that such unauthorized construction has virtually ceased. The upward adjustment was not phased out but dropped completely in revised estimates as of January 1999. The total effect of these changes was to lower the number of sales by about 2.9 percent relative to those published for earlier years.

Data availability and references

Housing start and building permit data have been collected by the Bureau of the Census monthly since 1959.

The monthly report for New Residential Construction (permits, starts, and completions) is issued around the middle of the following month. The monthly report and associated descriptions and historical data can be found at <http://www.census.gov/newresconst>.

The monthly report for New Residential Sales (sales, houses for sale, and prices) is issued toward the end of the following month. The monthly report and associated descriptions and historical data can be found at <http://www.census.gov/newhomesales>.

The manufactured housing data and background information can be accessed through <http://www.manufacturedhousing.org/statistics>.

**TABLES 17-4 THROUGH 17-7
MANUFACTURERS' SHIPMENTS, INVENTORIES, AND ORDERS**

SOURCE: U.S. DEPARTMENT OF COMMERCE, BUREAU OF THE CENSUS

These data are from the Bureau of the Census monthly M3 survey, a sample-based survey intended to provide measures of changes in the value of domestic manufacturing activity and indications of future production commitments. The sample includes most companies with $500 million or more in annual shipments and a selection of smaller ones. Currently, reported monthly data represent approximately 60 percent of shipments at the total manufacturing level.

One important technology industry, semiconductors, is represented in the shipments and inventories data in this report but not in new or unfilled orders. This affects the new and unfilled orders totals for computers and electronic products, durable goods industries, and total manufacturing. Based on recent shipments data, semiconductors account for about 15 percent of computers and electronic products, 3 percent of durable goods industries, and 1.5 percent of total manufacturing. Because semiconductors are intermediate materials and components rather than finished final products, the absence of these data does not distort new and unfilled orders data for important final demand categories such as capital goods and information technology.

The Census Bureau now compiles this survey on the NAICS classification system, and has restated historical data on the NAICS basis back to January 1992. To allow the user to observe the difference between levels of activity implied by the two systems, and to "link" the new data to older data if a longer time series is required, *Business Statistics* is republishing, on the same page with the new data, the previous SIC-based annual data up through 1992, providing an overlap with the new data in that year. Link factors can be calculated as the ratio of the 1992 NAICS value to the value of the most closely related SIC category. The SIC values multiplied by these link factors will yield a roughly comparable series without discontinuity. Where overlapping 1992 values are not available, as in the case of new orders, the link factor calculated on shipments can be used for an approximation.

Classification changes in NAICS

There were three major changes from SIC to NAICS affecting the level and trend of manufacturing as a whole: publishing was moved out of manufacturing to the new information industry; some research and development activities were moved out of aerospace manufacturing; and logging was moved out of manufacturing to the agriculture, forestry, fishing, and hunting group. A few relatively small activities, of which the largest are dental labs and retail bakeries, have been shifted into manufacturing based on similarity of production process.

In addition, there was a major rearrangement of industries within manufacturing, yielding groupings that are more relevant in today's economy. Three new industry groups—NAICS 333, Machinery; 334, Computers and Electronic Products; and 335, Electrical Equipment, Appliances, and Components—have been constituted, mainly from individual industries that were previously represented in SIC 35, Industrial Machinery (which included computers); SIC 36, Electronic and Electric Equipment; and SIC 38, Instruments. Other notable features in NAICS are moving beverages out of the food group into a new Beverages and Tobacco group and replacement of the old textile mill products group with two new groups, textile mills and textile products.

In many cases, the changes are so pervasive that it is not possible to match major SIC and NAICS industries. In Tables 17-4 through 17-7, SIC industries for 1992 and earlier years have been roughly aligned with the new NAICS categories, but a comparison of the old with the new data for 1992 indicates that in many cases, even after this alignment, the old and new industry groupings are still substantially different.

Definitions and notes on the data

Shipments. The value of shipments data represent net selling values, f.o.b. (free on board) plant, after discounts and allowances and excluding freight charges and excise taxes. For multi-establishment companies, the M3 reports typically are company- or division-level reports that encompass groups of plants or products. The data reported are usually net sales and receipts from customers and do not include the value of interplant transfers. The reported sales are used to calculate month-to-month changes that bring forward the estimates for the entire industry (that is, estimates of the statistical "universe") that have been developed from the Annual Survey of Manufactures (ASM). The value of products made elsewhere under contract from materials owned by the plant is also included in shipments, as well as receipts for contract work performed for others, resales, miscellaneous activities such as the sale of scrap and refuse, and installation and repair work performed by employees of the plant.

Inventories. Inventories in the M3 survey are collected on a current cost or pre-LIFO basis. Because different inventory valuation methods are reflected in the reported data, the estimates differ slightly from replacement cost estimates. Companies using the LIFO (last in, first out) method for valuing inventories report their pre-LIFO value; that is, the adjustment to their base-period prices is excluded. In the ASM, inventories are collected according to this same definition. However, there are discontinuities in the historical data in both surveys. Inventory data prior to 1982 are not comparable to later years because of changes in valuation methods. Until 1982, respondents were asked in the ASM to report their inventories at book values—that is, according to whatever method they used for tax purposes (LIFO, FIFO [first in, first out], and so forth). Because of this, the value of aggregate inventories for an industry was not precise. The change in instructions for reporting current cost inventories was carried to the monthly survey beginning in January 1987. The data for 1982 to 1987 were redefined (but not re-collected by survey) on a pre-LIFO or current cost basis.

Inventory data are requested from respondents by three stages of fabrication: finished goods, work in process, and raw materials and supplies. There are several limitations to the quality of these data for two reasons. First, response to the stage of fabrication inquiries is lower than for total inventories because not all companies keep their data monthly at this level of detail. Second, a product considered to be a finished good in one industry, such as steel mill shapes, may be reported as a raw material in another industry, such as stamping plants.

For some purposes, this difference in definitions is an advantage rather than a problem. When a factory accumulates inventory that it considers to be raw materials, it can be expected that that accumulation is intentional. But when a factory—whether a materials-making or a final-product producer—has a buildup of finished goods inventories, it may indicate involuntary accumulation as a result of sales falling short of expectations. Hence, the two types of accumulation can have different economic interpretations—even if they represent identical types of goods.

Like total inventories, stage of fabrication inventories are also benchmarked to the ASM data, but the stage of fabrication data are benchmarked at the major group level, as opposed to the level of total inventories, which is benchmarked at the individual industry level.

New orders, as reported in the monthly survey, are net of order cancellations and include orders received and filled during the month as well as orders received for future delivery. They also include the value of contract changes that increase or decrease the value of the unfilled orders to which they relate. Orders are defined to include those supported by binding legal documents such as signed contracts, letters of award, or letters of intent, although in some industries this definition may not be strictly applicable.

Unfilled orders include new orders (as defined above) that have not been reflected as shipments. Generally, unfilled orders at the end of the reporting period are equal to unfilled orders at the beginning of the period plus net new orders received less net shipments.

Series are adjusted for seasonal variation and variation in the number of trading days in the month using the X-12-ARIMA version of the Census Bureau's seasonal adjustment program.

Benchmarking and revisions

The M3 series are periodically benchmarked and seasonal adjustment factors are recalculated. In the latest benchmark, published in August 2003, and available on the Census Internet site, the data were benchmarked to the 2000 and 2001 Annual Surveys of Manufactures (ASM), new orders were adjusted to be consistent with the benchmarked shipments and inventory data, and other corrections were made; also, the seasonal adjustment factors were updated for all series.

Data availability and references

Data have been collected monthly since 1958.

An Advance Report on Durable Goods Manufacturers' Shipments, Inventories and Orders is available as a press release about 17 working days after the end of each month. It includes seasonally and not seasonally adjusted estimates of shipments, new orders, unfilled orders, and inventories for durable goods industries.

The Manufacturers' Shipments, Inventories, and Orders reports are released early in the following month. Content includes revisions to the advance durable goods data, estimates for nondurable goods industries, tabulations by market category, and ratios of shipments to inventories and to unfilled orders. Revisions may affect selected data for the two previous months.

Press releases, historical data, descriptions of the survey, and extensive documentation of the new NAICS including comparisons with the SIC are available on the Census Bureau Internet site at <http://www.census.gov>.

TABLE 17-8
MOTOR VEHICLE SALES AND INVENTORIES

Retail sales and inventories of cars, trucks, and buses. These estimates are prepared by the Bureau of Economic Analysis based on data from the American Automobile Manufacturers Association, Ward's Automotive Reports, and other sources. Seasonal adjustments are recalculated annually. Data are available on the BEA Internet site <http://www.bea.gov> as a part of the National Income and Product Accounts data set. They are also available on the STAT-USA subscription Internet site at <http://www.stat-usa.gov>.

TABLES 17-9 AND 17-10
RETAIL SALES AND INVENTORIES

SOURCE: U.S. DEPARTMENT OF COMMERCE, BUREAU OF THE CENSUS

Each month the Bureau of the Census prepares estimates of retail sales and inventories by kind of business based on a mail-out/mail-back survey of a sample of companies with one or more establishments that sell merchandise and related services to final consumers.

Retail sales and inventories are now compiled using the new NAICS classification system, replacing the old SIC. Historical data have been restated on the NAICS basis back to January 1992. To allow the user to observe the difference between levels of activity implied by the two systems, and to "link" the new data to older data if a longer time series is required, *Business Statistics* is republishing, on the same page with the new data, the previous SIC-based annual data up through 1992, providing an overlap with the new data in that year.

Classification changes in NAICS

- In NAICS, Eating and Drinking Places and Mobile Food Services have been reclassified out of retail into Sector 72, Accommodation and Food Services, which also includes hotels. The retail sales survey still collects and publishes sales data for food services and drinking places. It no longer includes them in the *retail* total, but they are included in a new *retail and food services* total.

- Some activities such as retail bakeries are shifted to manufacturing, based on use of the same production processes.
- Partly offsetting these losses, a significant number of businesses are shifted from wholesale to retail trade, including a number of sellers of lumber; construction and lawn equipment; electrical, plumbing, and farm supplies; computers; and office supplies. Establishments which are designed to attract walk-in customers and which use mass-media advertising are now classified as retail, even if they also serve business and institutional clients.

Data are published under the new NAICS system for a new group consisting of sporting goods, hobby, book, and music stores. In addition, total sales of *nonstore retailers* and a subgroup of nonstores—*electronic shopping and mail order houses*—are now published. *Store retailers* operate fixed point-of-sale locations designed to attract walk-in customers, display merchandise, use mass-media advertising, and may provide after-sales services. *Nonstore retailers*, on the other hand, sell by "infomercials," paper and electronic catalogs, door-to-door and in-home selling, portable stalls, or vending machines.

Subtotals of durable and nondurable goods are no longer published. They were always quite imprecise for retail sales, since general merchandise (including department) stores were included in nondurables and yet obviously sold substantial quantities of durable goods.

For further information see Chapter 14.

Special note on retail e-commerce

Beginning with the fourth quarter of 1999, the Census Bureau has conducted a quarterly survey of retail e-commerce sales. (The monthly survey does not report electronic shopping separately but combines it with mail-order.) This survey has not yet supplied a long enough history for a data page in *Business Statistics*, but the data available so far is presented and discussed in "New Perspectives on the U.S. Economy" at the beginning of this volume. The quarterly release is issued around the 20th of February, May, August, and November, and is available on the Census Bureau Internet site.

Definitions

Sales is the value of merchandise sold for cash or credit at retail or wholesale. Services that are incidental to the sale of merchandise, and excise taxes that are paid by the manufacturer or wholesaler and passed along to the retailer, are also included. Sales are net, after deductions for refunds and merchandise returns. Sales exclude sales taxes collected directly from customers and paid directly to a local, state, or federal tax agency. The sales estimates include only sales by establishments primarily engaged in retail trade, and are not intended to measure the total sales for a given commodity or merchandise line.

Inventories is the value of stocks of goods held for sale through retail stores, valued at cost, as of the last day of the report period. Stocks may be held either at the store or at warehouses that maintain supplies primarily intended for distribution to retail stores within the organization.

Inventory data prior to 1980 are not comparable to later years due to changes in valuation methods. Prior to 1980, inventories are book values of merchandise on hand at the end of the period and are valued according to the valuation method used by each respondent. Thus the aggregates are a mixture of LIFO (last in, first out) and non-LIFO values. Beginning with 1980, inventories are valued using methods other than LIFO in order to better reflect the current costs of goods held as inventory.

Leased departments are operations of one company conducted within the establishment or another company, such as jewelry counters or optical centers within department stores. The values for sales and inventories at department stores in Tables 17-9 and 17-10 exclude sales of leased departments.

GAFO (department store type goods) represents sales at general merchandise stores and at other stores that sell merchandise normally sold in department stores—clothing and accessories, furniture and home furnishings, electronics, appliances, sporting goods, hobby, book, music, office supplies, stationery, and gifts.

Notes on the data

The new NAICS-based data have been benchmarked to the 1997 Economic Census and the 1999, 2000, 2001, and 2002 Annual Retail Trade Surveys. Each year, the monthly series are benchmarked to the latest annual survey and new factors to adjust for seasonal, trading-day, and holiday variations are incorporated, using the Census X-12-ARIMA program.

The survey sample is stratified by kind of business and estimated sales. All firms with sales above applicable size cutoffs are included. Firms are selected randomly from the remaining strata. The sample used for the end-of-month inventory estimates is a subsample of the monthly sales sample, about one-third of the size of the sales sample.

New samples, designed to produce NAICS estimates, were introduced with the 1999 Annual Retail Trade Survey and the March 2001 monthly survey.

Data availability and references

An *Advance Monthly Retail Sales* report is released about nine working days after the close of the reference month, based on responses from a sub-sample of the complete retail sample.

Revised and more complete monthly *Retail Trade, Sales, and Inventories* reports are released six weeks after the close of the reference month. They contain preliminary figures for the current month and final figures for the prior 12 months. Statistics include retail sales, inventories, and ratios of inventories to sales. Data are both seasonally adjusted and unadjusted.

The *Annual Benchmark Report for Retail Trade* is released each spring. It includes updated seasonal adjustment factors; revised and benchmarked monthly estimates of sales and inventories; monthly data for the most recent 10 years; detailed annual estimates and ratios for the United States by kind of business; and comparable prior-year statistics and year-to-year changes.
Data and documentation are available on the Bureau of the Census Internet site at <http://www.census.gov>.

**TABLE 17-11
MERCHANT WHOLESALERS: SALES AND INVENTORIES**

SOURCE: U.S. DEPARTMENT OF COMMERCE, BUREAU OF THE CENSUS

These data are based on a monthly mail-out/mail-back sample survey conducted by the Bureau of the Census.

These data are now based on the new NAICS classification system, replacing the old SIC. Historical data have been restated on the NAICS basis back to January 1992. To allow the user to observe the difference between levels of activity implied by the two systems, and to "link" the new data to older data if a longer time series is required, *Business Statistics* is republishing, on the same page with the new data, the previous SIC-based annual data up through 1992, providing an overlap with the new data in that year.

Classification changes in NAICS

NAICS shifts a significant number of businesses from wholesale to retail, an important new criterion being whether or not the establishment is intended to solicit walk-in traffic. If it is, and if it uses mass-media advertising, it is now classified as retail, even if it also serves business and institutional clients. (See notes on retail trade, above, for the major categories involved in this shift.)

Definitions

Merchant wholesalers include merchant wholesalers that take title of the goods they sell, and jobbers, industrial distributors, exporters, and importers. Excluded are nonmerchant wholesalers such as manufacturer sales branches and offices; agents, merchandise or commodity brokers; and commission merchants.

Notes on the data

Inventory data prior to 1980 are not comparable to later years because of changes in valuation methods and are not included in this book. Prior to 1980, inventories are book values of stocks on hand at the end of the period and are valued according to the valuation method used by each respondent. Thus the aggregates are a mixture of LIFO (last in, first out) and non-LIFO values. Beginning with 1980 inventories are valued using methods other than LIFO in order to better reflect the current costs of goods held as inventory.

A survey has been conducted monthly since 1946. New samples are drawn every 5 years, most recently in 2001. The samples are updated every quarter to add new businesses and drop companies that are no longer active.

Data availability and references

Monthly Wholesale Trade, Sales and Inventories reports are released six weeks after the close of the reference month. They contain preliminary current-month figures and final figures for the previous month. Statistics include sales, inventories, and stock/sale ratios, along with standard errors. Data are both seasonally adjusted and unadjusted.

The *Annual Benchmark Report for Wholesale Trade* is released each spring. It contains estimated annual sales, monthly and year-end inventories, inventory-sales ratios, purchases, gross margins, and gross margin-sales ratios by kind of business. Annual estimates are benchmarked to the most recent census of wholesale trade. This report also presents the results of a benchmarking operation that revises monthly sales and inventories estimates. Seasonal adjustment factors are revised at the same time, and revised data for both seasonally adjusted and unadjusted values are published.

Data and documentation are available on the Bureau of the Census Internet site at <http://www.census.gov>.

TABLES 17-12 THROUGH 17-15
SELECTED SERVICE INDUSTRIES—
RECEIPTS AND REVENUE

SOURCE: U.S. DEPARTMENT OF COMMERCE, BUREAU OF THE CENSUS

The Census Service Annual Survey provides, for selected service industries, annual estimates of operating receipts of taxable firms, and revenues of private, nonprofit firms that are exempt from federal income taxation. The survey is based on a sample of establishments.

For the years 1986 through 1998, the data were collected using the old Standard Industrial Classification System (SIC), and were tabulated separately for taxable and nontaxable firms. Data from 1999 through 2001 were collected using the North American Industry Classification System (NAICS), and the data for each industry include both taxable and nontaxable firms.

See Chapter 14 for information on comparability of industries in the new and old classification systems.

The first quarterly estimates of revenue for selected service industries were published in September 2004, presenting data for the fourth quarter of 2003 and the first two quarters of 2004. They are presented and discussed in "New Perspectives on the U.S. Economy" at the beginning of this volume.

Notes on the data

In the SIC estimates for 1986–1998, separate estimates were developed for taxable and nontaxable firms in camps and membership lodging; selected amusement and recreation services; selected health services; legal services; libraries; vocational schools; social services; museums, art galleries, botanical gardens, and zoos; research, development, and testing services; and selected management and public relations services. Firms considered tax-exempt include membership lodging, membership organizations, and noncommercial research organizations. Firms in all remaining SICs were defined to be taxable. For tax-exempt firms, employer firms only were sampled; for all other kinds of business, data represent combined estimates for employer and nonemployer firms. Government-operated hospitals were included, while all other government establishments were excluded.

In Table 17-15, total and e-commerce revenues are reported for the service industries represented in Table 17-14 and also for NAICS industry 72, Accommodation and Food Services, which is not represented in Table 17-14.

Data availability

Data are published annually as *Current Business Reports, Service Annual Survey*. They are available on the Bureau of the Census Internet site at <http://www.census.gov>.

PART C

HISTORICAL DATA

CHAPTER 18: SELECTED ANNUAL DATA, 1939–1947

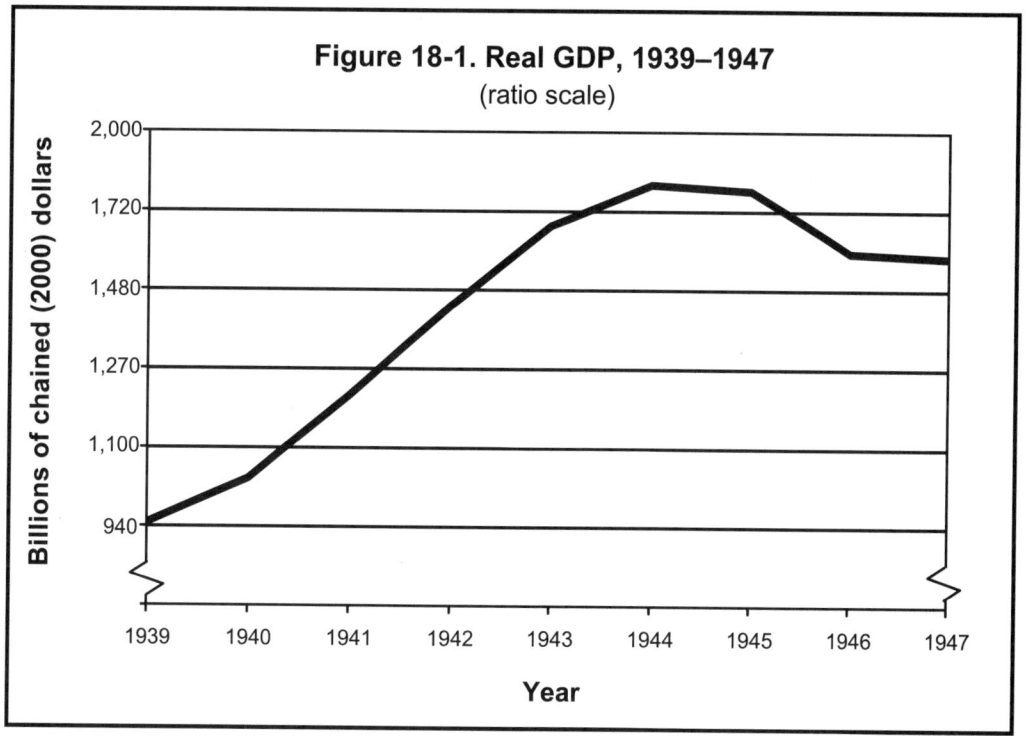

Figure 18-1. Real GDP, 1939–1947 (ratio scale)

- Real GDP grew 90 percent from 1939 to its wartime peak in 1944, an annual rate of 13.7 percent. It fell back during the subsequent demobilization, but in 1947 was still 65.6 percent above the 1939 level, representing growth from 1939 at an annual rate of 6.5 percent. Government military spending drove the wartime expansion but declined sharply after 1945.
- Real private investment spending rose from 1939 to 1941, declined during the war, but recovered at the war's end to more than double the 1939 level. Consumption spending in real terms rose in almost every year of the prewar, war, and postwar periods.
- Civilian employment rose by 8.7 million from 1939 to 1943, despite the withdrawal of members of the armed forces from the civilian population base. The rise in payroll jobs was even greater, at 11.9 million jobs. Workers left agriculture, household service, and other less-productive activities—included in civilian employment but not in the payroll series—for factory jobs making armaments, government positions, and other payroll employment.
- Unemployment fell to 1.2 percent of the labor force in 1944. When the demobilization ended, unemployment increased only to 3.9 percent, compared with 17.2 percent (excluding work relief) in 1939.
- Prices rose at an accelerating rate early in the war. Under price controls and rationing, inflation subsided to about 2-1/2 percent per year in 1944 and 1945, then rose again when the controls were lifted.
- Worker incomes increased during the wartime boom as employment, average hours, and hourly wages all rose. Consumption spending opportunities were limited by rationing and production controls. (For example, passenger cars were simply not produced, as the assembly lines were converted to build military vehicles.) This, along with "war bond" savings drives, contributed to a huge increase in personal saving, which peaked at 26.1 percent of disposable income in 1944. By 1947, the personal saving rate had returned to 4.3 percent, almost the same as its 1939 level.

Table 18-1. Selected Aggregate Economic Data, 1939–1947

Classification	1939	1940	1941	1942	1943	1944	1945	1946	1947
BILLIONS OF CURRENT DOLLARS (except as noted)									
Gross domestic product, total	92.2	101.4	126.7	161.9	198.6	219.8	223.1	222.3	244.2
Personal consumption expenditures, total	67.2	71.3	81.1	89.0	99.9	108.7	120.0	144.3	162.0
Durable goods	6.7	7.8	9.7	6.9	6.5	6.7	8.0	15.8	20.4
Nondurable goods	35.1	37.0	42.9	50.8	58.6	64.3	71.9	82.7	90.9
Services	25.4	26.5	28.5	31.4	34.8	37.6	40.1	45.8	50.7
Gross private domestic fixed investment, total	9.1	11.2	13.8	8.5	6.9	8.7	12.3	25.1	35.5
Nonresidential, total	6.1	7.7	9.7	6.3	5.4	7.4	10.6	17.3	23.5
Structures	2.2	2.6	3.3	2.2	1.8	2.4	3.3	7.4	8.1
Equipment and software	3.9	5.2	6.4	4.1	3.7	5.0	7.3	9.9	15.3
Residential	3.0	3.5	4.1	2.2	1.4	1.4	1.7	7.8	12.1
Change in private inventories	0.2	2.4	4.3	1.9	-0.7	-0.9	-1.5	6.0	-0.6
Net exports of goods and services	0.8	1.5	1.0	-0.3	-2.2	-2.0	-0.8	7.2	10.8
Exports	4.0	4.9	5.5	4.4	4.0	4.9	6.8	14.2	18.7
Imports	3.1	3.4	4.4	4.6	6.3	6.9	7.5	7.0	7.9
Government consumption expenditures and gross investment, total	14.8	15.0	26.5	62.7	94.8	105.3	93.0	39.6	36.4
Federal	6.0	6.5	18.0	54.1	86.5	97.0	84.1	28.9	22.7
National defense	1.5	2.5	14.3	51.1	84.2	94.5	82.0	25.2	18.2
State and local	8.8	8.6	8.6	8.6	8.4	8.4	9.0	10.8	13.7
Gross national product	92.5	101.7	127.2	162.3	198.9	220.1	223.4	222.9	245.3
National income, total	82.2	91.2	116.0	149.8	184.5	198.2	198.4	198.5	216.6
Compensation of employees	48.1	52.2	64.8	85.3	109.6	121.3	123.3	119.6	130.1
Proprietors' income with IVA and CCAdj	11.2	12.3	16.7	23.4	28.3	29.4	30.8	35.6	34.5
Farm	4.1	4.1	6.1	9.7	11.6	11.5	11.8	14.2	14.4
Nonfarm	7.1	8.2	10.6	13.7	16.7	18.0	19.0	21.4	20.2
Rental income of persons with CCAdj	3.8	3.9	4.5	5.5	6.1	6.5	6.7	7.1	7.2
Corporate profits with IVA and CCAdj	6.6	9.8	15.5	20.6	24.9	24.9	20.3	17.8	23.7
Net interest and miscellaneous payments	3.6	3.3	3.3	3.2	2.9	2.4	2.3	1.9	2.5
Taxes on production and imports	9.1	9.8	11.1	11.5	12.4	13.7	15.1	16.8	18.1
Less: Subsidies less current surplus of government enterprises	0.7	0.6	0.3	0.4	0.4	0.9	1.0	1.2	0.2
Business current transfer payments (net)	0.4	0.5	0.5	0.5	0.6	0.8	0.9	0.7	0.7
Personal income, total	72.9	78.5	96.1	123.5	152.2	166.0	171.7	178.6	191.0
Less: Personal current taxes	1.5	1.7	2.3	4.9	16.7	17.7	19.4	17.2	19.8
Equals: Disposable personal income (DPI)	71.4	76.8	93.8	118.6	135.4	148.3	152.2	161.4	171.2
Less: Personal outlays	68.2	72.4	82.3	90.0	100.8	109.7	121.2	145.9	163.8
Equals: Personal saving	3.2	4.4	11.5	28.6	34.6	38.7	31.1	15.5	7.4
As a percentage of DPI	4.5	5.7	12.2	24.1	25.6	26.1	20.4	9.6	4.3
Gross saving	13.6	18.5	29.8	39.8	44.9	39.9	29.8	38.4	46.6
Net saving	4.6	9.0	19.0	26.4	28.6	20.5	8.7	15.1	20.2
Net private saving	4.6	7.4	14.9	33.6	41.2	45.8	36.1	18.6	13.5
Net government saving, federal	-2.1	-0.3	2.2	-8.7	-14.1	-26.9	-29.0	-5.0	5.3
Net government saving, state and local	2.0	2.0	1.9	1.5	1.5	1.6	1.6	1.5	1.4
Consumption of fixed capital, private	7.6	7.9	8.8	9.9	10.0	10.5	10.9	12.5	15.7
Consumption of fixed capital, government	1.4	1.5	2.0	3.5	6.2	8.9	10.1	10.8	10.7
Gross domestic investment, total	13.8	18.0	28.9	39.0	45.2	44.4	35.0	34.6	39.6
Private	9.3	13.6	18.1	10.4	6.1	7.8	10.8	31.1	35.0
Government	4.5	4.4	10.8	28.5	39.1	36.6	24.1	3.5	4.6
Net lending or net borrowing (-), NIPAs	1.0	1.5	1.3	-0.1	-2.1	-2.0	-1.3	4.9	9.3
Net domestic investment	4.8	8.6	18.1	25.6	28.9	25.1	13.9	11.3	13.2
Gross saving as a percentage of gross national income	14.9	18.4	23.5	24.4	22.4	18.3	13.6	17.3	19.2
Net saving as a percentage of gross national income	5.0	9.0	15.0	16.2	14.3	9.4	4.0	6.8	8.3
BILLIONS OF CHAINED (2000) DOLLARS (except as noted)									
Real gross domestic product, total	950.7	1 034.1	1 211.1	1 435.4	1 670.9	1 806.5	1 786.3	1 589.4	1 574.5
Personal consumption expenditures	729.1	767.1	821.9	803.1	826.1	850.2	902.7	1 012.9	1 031.6
Gross private domestic investment	77.4	107.9	131.7	69.6	41.1	50.8	67.0	172.1	165.3
Exports	30.6	34.8	35.7	23.6	19.9	21.4	29.9	64.6	73.7
Imports	35.3	36.2	44.5	40.4	50.9	53.3	56.7	47.0	44.6
Government	196.0	201.5	335.1	788.6	1 173.3	1 320.5	1 152.9	396.6	337.2
Disposable personal income	774.9	826.5	950.7	1 069.9	1 119.9	1 160.7	1 145.3	1 132.7	1 090.3
Per capita (2000 dollars)	5 914	6 255	7 127	7 934	8 190	8 387	8 185	8 011	7 565
CHAIN-TYPE PRICE INDEXES, 2000 = 100									
Gross domestic product	9.69	9.77	10.41	11.26	11.89	12.17	12.48	13.93	15.49
Personal consumption expenditures	9.22	9.29	9.86	11.08	12.09	12.78	13.29	14.25	15.70

Table 18-1. Selected Aggregate Economic Data, 1939–1947—Continued

Classification	1939	1940	1941	1942	1943	1944	1945	1946	1947
CONSUMER AND PRODUCER PRICE INDEXES									
Consumer prices, all items; 1982–1984 = 100:									
All urban consumers (CPI-U)	13.9	14.0	14.7	16.3	17.3	17.6	18.0	19.5	22.3
Urban wage earners and clerical workers (CPI-W)	14.0	14.1	14.8	16.4	17.4	17.7	18.1	19.6	22.5
Producer prices, 1982 = 100:									
All commodities	13.3	13.5	15.1	17.0	17.8	17.9	18.2	20.8	25.6
Farm products	16.5	17.1	20.8	26.7	30.9	31.2	32.4	37.5	45.1
Industrial commodities	13.9	14.1	15.1	16.2	16.5	16.7	17.0	18.6	22.7
EMPLOYMENT STATUS OF THE CIVILIAN NONINSTITUTIONAL POPULATION, 14 AND OVER (Thousands of persons, except as noted)									
Civilian noninstitutional population	...	99 840	99 900	98 640	94 640	93 220	94 090	103 070	106 018
Civilian labor force	55 230	55 640	55 910	56 410	55 540	54 630	53 860	57 520	60 168
Participation rate, percent	...	55.7	56.0	57.2	58.7	58.6	57.2	55.8	56.8
Employment, total	45 750	47 520	50 350	53 750	54 470	53 960	52 820	55 250	57 812
Ratio, employment to population, percent	...	47.6	50.4	54.5	57.6	57.9	56.1	53.6	54.5
Agricultural	9 610	9 540	9 100	9 250	9 080	8 950	8 580	8 320	8 256
Nonagricultural	36 140	37 980	41 250	44 500	45 390	45 010	44 240	46 930	49 557
Unemployment	9 480	8 120	5 560	2 660	1 070	670	1 040	2 270	2 356
Percent of civilian labor force	17.2	14.6	9.9	4.7	1.9	1.2	1.9	3.9	3.9
NONFARM PAYROLL EMPLOYMENT (NAICS) (Thousands of persons, except as noted)									
Total	30 645	32 407	36 600	40 213	42 574	42 006	40 510	41 759	43 945
Private, total	26 606	28 156	31 874	34 621	36 353	35 819	34 428	36 054	38 379
Goods-producing, total	11 511	12 378	14 940	17 275	18 738	17 981	16 308	16 122	17 314
Natural resources and mining	856	927	967	1 010	958	926	864	885	976
Construction	1 205	1 352	1 852	2 234	1 627	1 152	1 190	1 724	2 051
Manufacturing, total	9 450	10 099	12 121	14 030	16 153	15 903	14 255	13 513	14 287
Durable goods	4 654	5 261	6 778	8 502	10 583	10 372	8 732	7 535	8 079
Nondurable goods, total	4 796	4 839	5 343	5 528	5 570	5 531	5 523	5 978	6 208
Private service-providing, total	15 094	15 778	16 934	17 347	17 615	17 839	18 121	19 932	21 064
Trade, transportation, and utilities, total	6 739	7 043	7 550	7 607	7 628	7 805	8 048	8 945	9 452
Wholesale trade	1 508	1 571	1 679	1 635	1 566	1 585	1 672	1 962	2 116
Retail trade	3 158	3 324	3 552	3 522	3 479	3 516	3 624	4 118	4 393
Information	1 141	1 196	1 342	1 470	1 605	1 635	1 581	1 594	1 658
Financial activities	1 386	1 424	1 466	1 455	1 431	1 414	1 435	1 619	1 674
Professional and business services	1 976	2 073	2 265	2 410	2 518	2 523	2 495	2 666	2 828
Education and health services	1 405	1 470	1 566	1 632	1 660	1 667	1 698	1 885	2 015
Leisure and hospitality	1 896	1 995	2 130	2 133	2 122	2 142	2 200	2 485	2 650
Other services	553	578	616	641	652	654	664	737	788
Government, total	4 040	4 251	4 726	5 592	6 222	6 187	6 082	5 705	5 567
Federal, total	950	1 045	1 406	2 322	3 047	3 071	2 945	2 365	1 985
Department of Defense, total	132	182	375	920	1 361	1 352	1 234	746	499
Service-providing	19 134	20 029	21 660	22 938	23 837	24 026	24 203	25 637	26 631
Manufacturing, production workers:									
Total (thousands)	8 163	8 737	10 641	12 447	14 407	14 031	12 445	11 781	12 453
Average weekly hours (number of hours per week)	37.7	38.2	40.7	43.2	45.1	45.4	43.6	40.4	40.5
Index of aggregate weekly hours (2002 = 100)	70.5	76.4	99.2	123.1	148.8	145.6	124.3	108.9	115.3
Average hourly earnings (dollars)	0.49	0.53	0.61	0.74	0.86	0.91	0.90	0.95	1.10
Average weekly earnings (dollars)	18.47	20.25	24.83	31.97	38.79	41.31	39.24	38.38	44.55
INDEXES OF INDUSTRIAL PRODUCTION (1997 = 100)									
Total	9.5	11.0	13.8	15.9	19.3	20.7	17.8	15.3	17.2
Products	9.3	10.4	13.2	15.0	18.6	20.3	17.2	15.0	16.7
Consumer goods	12.6	13.4	16.0	14.8	15.1	15.8	16.3	19.5	20.7
Materials	9.6	11.6	14.5	16.7	19.7	20.7	18.2	15.5	17.5
Manufacturing (SIC)	8.8	10.3	13.2	15.4	19.2	20.7	17.3	14.4	16.1

... = Not available.

NOTES AND DEFINITIONS

TABLE 18-1
SELECTED AGGREGATE ECONOMIC DATA, 1939–1947

For all these data, the sources, definitions, and availability are generally the same as for the identically titled series in Part A. Specific references to the appropriate chapter's Notes and Definitions are given below for each set of data, and differences in definitions where they exist (in the data on labor force, employment, and unemployment) are noted.

Gross domestic product and its components in current and constant dollars, gross national product, national income and its components, and chain-type price indexes: Chapter 1.

Personal income and its disposition and disposable personal income: Chapter 4.

Saving and investment: Chapter 5.

Consumer and producer price indexes: Chapter 8.

Civilian noninstitutional population, labor force, employment, and unemployment are as defined in the Notes and Definitions to Chapter 10 except that all the data for 1939 through 1947 in Chapter 18 pertain to persons 14 years of age and over. The data in Chapter 10 from 1947 to date are for persons 16 and over. The differences made by this difference in definitions can be observed in the two different sets of data for the overlap year 1947. Note that in that year the unemployment rates are the same—3.9 percent—but the labor force participation rate and the employment-population ratio are higher when the 14- and 15-year-olds are excluded. Data are from the Bureau of Labor Statistics, as published on their Web site and in the Appendix to the *Economic Report of the President*, February 2003.

Nonfarm employment and its components, and number, hours, and earnings for manufacturing production workers: Chapter 10. Note that because age is not specified in the Current Employment Survey, these data include any workers under 16 and always have done so.

Business cycle status and the duration of World War II

See the Notes and Definitions to Table 1-8 for the business cycle peaks and troughs occurring in this period. Note that the entire prewar and wartime period from June 1938 to February 1945 is construed as a business cycle expansion. (Also note that the June 1938 trough is not the one marking the end of the Great Depression—which terminated in March 1933—but the one marking the end of a 13-month recession in 1937–1938.)

World War II broke out in Europe in September 1939. The United States entered the war when attacked by Japan in December 1941. The end of the "wartime" expansion precedes the end of the war, as the European war ended in May 1945 and the Pacific war in August 1945. A brief "demobilization" recession occurred from February to October 1945, followed by the first postwar expansion, which lasted from October 1945 to November 1948.

CHAPTER 19: HISTORICAL DATA FOR SELECTED QUARTERLY SERIES

Table 19-1. Gross Domestic Product

(Billions of dollars, quarterly data are at seasonally adjusted annual rates.)

NIPA Tables 1.1.5, 1.4.5

Year and quarter	Gross domestic product	Personal consumption expenditures	Gross private domestic investment				Exports and imports of goods and services			Government consumption expenditures and gross investment			Addendum: Final sales of domestic product
			Total	Fixed investment		Change in private inventories	Net exports	Exports	Imports	Total	Federal	State and local	
				Nonresidential	Residential								
1947													
1st quarter	237.2	156.3	33.7	22.8	10.4	0.5	10.9	18.4	7.5	36.3	23.4	13.0	236.7
2nd quarter	240.5	160.2	32.4	23.2	10.4	-1.2	11.3	19.5	8.2	36.6	23.3	13.4	241.7
3rd quarter	244.6	163.7	32.7	23.3	12.3	-2.9	11.8	19.4	7.7	36.4	22.4	14.0	247.5
4th quarter	254.4	167.8	41.0	24.5	15.1	1.5	9.3	17.6	8.3	36.3	21.6	14.7	252.9
1948													
1st quarter	260.4	170.5	45.0	26.2	15.2	3.6	7.3	16.9	9.6	37.6	22.4	15.2	256.7
2nd quarter	267.3	174.3	48.1	26.0	16.3	5.9	5.2	15.2	10.0	39.7	23.8	15.9	261.5
3rd quarter	273.9	177.2	50.2	27.0	16.1	7.2	4.9	15.4	10.5	41.4	24.6	16.8	266.7
4th quarter	275.2	178.1	49.1	28.1	15.0	6.0	4.5	14.6	10.1	43.5	26.0	17.5	269.2
1949													
1st quarter	270.0	177.0	40.9	26.6	14.0	0.4	6.5	16.1	9.6	45.6	27.6	18.0	269.6
2nd quarter	266.2	178.6	34.0	25.5	13.7	-5.1	6.3	15.6	9.4	47.3	28.6	18.7	271.4
3rd quarter	267.7	178.0	37.3	24.1	14.5	-1.3	5.2	14.1	8.9	47.2	27.7	19.5	269.0
4th quarter	265.2	180.4	35.2	23.5	16.3	-4.7	3.0	12.1	9.1	46.6	26.9	19.7	269.9
1950													
1st quarter	275.2	183.1	44.4	24.2	18.1	2.0	2.2	11.7	9.5	45.6	25.5	20.0	273.2
2nd quarter	284.6	187.0	49.9	26.6	20.4	2.8	1.6	11.9	10.2	46.1	25.7	20.4	281.7
3rd quarter	302.0	200.7	56.1	29.6	22.3	4.2	-0.7	12.3	13.0	45.9	24.9	21.0	297.8
4th quarter	313.4	198.1	65.9	30.6	21.3	14.0	-0.2	13.5	13.7	49.5	27.9	21.6	299.3
1951													
1st quarter	329.0	209.4	62.1	30.9	20.8	10.4	0.2	15.0	14.9	57.4	35.2	22.1	318.6
2nd quarter	336.7	205.1	64.8	31.8	18.2	14.8	1.9	17.1	15.2	64.7	41.8	22.9	321.9
3rd quarter	343.6	207.8	59.4	32.5	17.2	9.7	3.7	18.1	14.3	72.6	49.2	23.4	333.8
4th quarter	348.0	211.8	54.4	32.2	17.5	4.7	4.2	18.2	14.0	77.6	53.9	23.7	343.3
1952													
1st quarter	351.3	213.1	55.2	32.4	18.0	4.7	3.7	18.7	15.0	79.2	55.4	23.8	346.5
2nd quarter	352.2	217.3	49.9	32.9	18.5	-1.5	2.0	16.6	14.6	83.1	58.5	24.6	353.7
3rd quarter	358.5	219.8	53.9	29.8	18.5	5.6	0.0	15.2	15.3	84.9	60.5	24.4	353.0
4th quarter	371.4	227.9	57.1	32.5	19.4	5.3	-1.0	15.3	16.3	87.4	62.4	25.0	366.1
1953													
1st quarter	378.4	231.5	57.9	34.3	19.7	3.9	-0.7	15.1	15.8	89.7	63.9	25.8	374.5
2nd quarter	382.0	233.3	58.1	34.8	19.8	3.6	-1.3	15.2	16.4	91.8	66.2	25.6	378.4
3rd quarter	381.1	234.0	57.4	35.9	19.2	2.3	-0.6	15.8	16.3	90.3	64.0	26.3	378.8
4th quarter	375.9	233.5	52.3	35.4	18.9	-2.0	-0.3	15.2	15.5	90.5	63.6	26.9	377.9
1954													
1st quarter	375.3	235.5	51.5	34.5	19.0	-2.0	-0.4	14.4	14.8	88.6	60.8	27.8	377.3
2nd quarter	376.0	238.3	51.2	34.3	20.3	-3.4	0.3	16.4	16.2	86.2	57.7	28.5	379.4
3rd quarter	380.8	240.7	54.7	35.0	21.8	-2.1	0.6	15.9	15.3	84.8	55.4	29.5	382.9
4th quarter	389.5	245.5	57.8	34.9	23.2	-0.3	1.1	16.6	15.5	85.0	55.2	29.8	389.8
1955													
1st quarter	402.6	251.8	64.2	35.4	25.0	3.8	1.1	17.3	16.2	85.4	54.6	30.8	398.8
2nd quarter	410.9	256.9	68.1	37.9	25.6	4.6	-0.2	16.9	17.1	86.0	54.7	31.3	406.3
3rd quarter	419.5	261.1	70.0	40.4	25.2	4.3	0.7	18.1	17.4	87.7	55.8	31.8	415.2
4th quarter	426.0	265.1	73.9	42.5	24.2	7.2	0.2	18.3	18.1	86.8	54.4	32.4	418.8
1956													
1st quarter	428.3	266.7	73.0	42.9	23.7	6.4	0.4	19.4	18.9	88.2	54.7	33.5	421.9
2nd quarter	434.2	269.4	71.4	43.9	23.9	3.6	1.9	20.9	19.0	91.5	57.1	34.4	430.6
3rd quarter	439.3	272.6	72.5	45.4	23.5	3.6	2.6	21.8	19.3	91.6	56.4	35.1	435.7
4th quarter	448.1	278.0	71.2	45.9	23.0	2.2	4.5	23.1	18.5	94.4	58.5	35.8	445.9
1957													
1st quarter	457.2	282.4	71.8	47.0	22.6	2.2	4.8	24.9	20.1	98.2	61.1	37.1	455.1
2nd quarter	459.2	284.7	71.9	47.1	22.2	2.7	4.1	24.4	20.3	98.4	60.5	38.0	456.5
3rd quarter	466.4	289.3	73.2	48.4	22.0	2.8	4.0	23.8	19.8	99.9	61.2	38.7	463.6
4th quarter	461.5	291.0	64.9	47.5	21.9	-4.5	3.4	23.0	19.6	102.3	62.7	39.6	466.1
1958													
1st quarter	454.0	290.5	60.5	43.6	20.9	-4.0	1.1	20.5	19.5	101.8	61.2	40.6	458.0
2nd quarter	458.1	293.4	58.7	42.0	21.0	-4.2	0.5	20.5	20.1	105.4	63.9	41.6	462.3
3rd quarter	471.7	298.5	65.5	41.4	22.5	1.5	0.9	20.6	19.7	106.9	64.2	42.7	470.2
4th quarter	485.0	302.3	73.2	43.1	24.9	5.2	-0.3	20.6	20.8	109.7	66.0	43.7	479.8
1959													
1st quarter	495.4	310.0	76.2	44.5	27.8	3.9	0.4	21.8	21.4	108.9	64.3	44.5	491.5
2nd quarter	508.4	316.0	82.2	46.1	28.8	7.3	0.0	22.6	22.5	110.2	65.5	44.7	501.2
3rd quarter	509.3	321.2	76.4	47.8	28.3	0.4	0.6	23.5	22.9	111.0	66.2	44.8	508.9
4th quarter	513.2	323.3	79.3	47.7	27.5	4.1	0.6	23.1	22.5	110.0	65.4	44.6	509.1
1960													
1st quarter	526.9	326.9	89.1	49.5	28.4	11.2	2.7	26.0	23.3	108.3	62.4	45.8	515.7
2nd quarter	526.1	332.7	79.7	50.3	26.1	3.2	4.2	27.6	23.5	109.5	62.4	47.2	522.9
3rd quarter	528.9	332.7	78.7	49.0	25.3	4.3	4.2	27.0	22.9	113.4	65.3	48.1	524.6
4th quarter	523.6	334.6	68.1	48.6	25.3	-5.8	5.8	27.5	21.7	115.1	66.3	48.8	529.4

Table 19-1. Gross Domestic Product—*Continued*

(Billions of dollars, quarterly data are at seasonally adjusted annual rates.)

NIPA Tables 1.1.5, 1.4.5

Year and quarter	Gross domestic product	Personal consumption expenditures	Gross private domestic investment				Exports and imports of goods and services			Government consumption expenditures and gross investment			Addendum: Final sales of domestic product
			Total	Fixed investment		Change in private inventories	Net exports	Exports	Imports	Total	Federal	State and local	
				Nonresidential	Residential								
1961													
1st quarter	527.9	335.1	70.3	47.5	25.3	-2.5	5.8	27.5	21.7	116.7	66.0	50.7	530.5
2nd quarter	539.0	340.1	75.8	48.4	25.5	1.8	5.5	27.4	21.9	117.6	66.8	50.8	537.2
3rd quarter	549.4	343.0	82.4	48.8	26.9	6.7	3.9	27.2	23.3	120.2	68.6	51.6	542.8
4th quarter	562.5	350.3	84.2	50.4	27.8	6.0	4.4	28.3	23.9	123.6	70.2	53.4	556.6
1962													
1st quarter	576.0	355.6	89.4	51.6	28.4	9.4	4.0	28.3	24.3	127.2	73.4	53.8	566.6
2nd quarter	583.2	361.2	87.9	53.2	29.2	5.4	5.8	30.7	24.9	128.3	73.9	54.4	577.8
3rd quarter	590.0	365.1	89.3	53.9	29.2	6.2	3.8	29.0	25.1	131.8	76.6	55.2	583.8
4th quarter	593.3	371.3	86.0	53.5	29.1	3.4	2.8	28.4	25.6	133.2	77.1	56.1	589.9
1963													
1st quarter	602.4	374.9	90.5	53.4	30.2	6.9	3.9	29.1	25.2	133.2	75.5	57.6	595.6
2nd quarter	611.2	379.0	92.2	55.1	32.2	4.8	6.5	32.4	25.9	133.4	74.9	58.5	606.3
3rd quarter	623.9	386.0	95.0	56.8	32.5	5.7	3.9	30.6	26.7	139.0	78.8	60.2	618.2
4th quarter	633.5	390.7	97.4	58.7	33.7	5.1	5.4	32.2	26.8	139.9	78.4	61.5	628.4
1964													
1st quarter	649.6	400.3	100.7	60.1	35.4	5.1	7.3	34.2	27.0	141.3	78.6	62.7	644.5
2nd quarter	658.8	408.3	100.6	61.9	34.2	4.5	7.1	34.8	27.7	142.9	78.4	64.5	654.4
3rd quarter	670.5	417.2	102.5	64.1	33.7	4.7	6.4	34.8	28.4	144.4	78.9	65.5	665.8
4th quarter	675.6	419.8	104.6	65.7	33.8	5.0	6.9	36.2	29.3	144.3	77.8	66.5	670.6
1965													
1st quarter	695.7	430.5	115.7	70.3	33.9	11.5	4.6	33.1	28.5	144.9	77.1	67.8	684.1
2nd quarter	708.1	437.4	115.8	73.1	34.2	8.6	7.5	39.1	31.7	147.4	77.5	69.9	699.6
3rd quarter	725.2	446.6	119.7	76.1	34.3	9.3	4.9	36.9	32.0	154.0	81.6	72.5	715.9
4th quarter	747.5	460.6	121.8	79.7	34.5	7.6	5.5	39.5	33.9	159.6	85.5	74.1	739.9
1966													
1st quarter	770.8	471.0	131.7	83.0	34.8	13.9	4.4	39.4	35.0	163.6	87.6	76.0	756.9
2nd quarter	779.9	476.1	130.7	85.2	33.2	12.3	5.2	41.5	36.2	167.9	90.0	77.9	767.6
3rd quarter	793.4	485.3	130.2	86.4	31.9	11.9	2.2	40.4	38.2	175.7	95.8	79.9	781.5
4th quarter	807.1	491.1	132.7	87.0	29.2	16.5	3.6	42.4	38.8	179.8	96.8	83.0	790.6
1967													
1st quarter	817.9	495.4	129.3	85.6	28.3	15.4	4.6	44.0	39.4	188.7	103.2	85.4	802.5
2nd quarter	822.5	504.5	123.7	85.7	31.6	6.3	4.5	43.5	39.0	189.7	102.9	86.8	816.1
3rd quarter	837.1	511.8	128.5	85.8	33.4	9.3	2.9	42.4	39.5	194.0	105.6	88.3	827.9
4th quarter	852.8	519.3	132.9	88.4	36.0	8.4	2.2	43.9	41.7	198.4	107.4	90.9	844.4
1968													
1st quarter	879.9	537.3	137.2	91.9	36.9	8.4	1.1	45.5	44.4	204.3	110.3	94.0	871.5
2nd quarter	904.2	551.2	143.4	91.2	38.2	14.1	1.9	47.4	45.4	207.7	110.7	97.0	890.2
3rd quarter	919.4	567.4	139.7	93.2	38.9	7.7	1.3	49.5	48.2	211.1	111.8	99.2	911.7
4th quarter	936.3	576.3	144.4	97.4	40.9	6.0	1.1	49.2	48.2	214.6	112.7	102.0	930.3
1969													
1st quarter	961.0	588.5	155.7	101.0	43.2	11.5	0.2	44.0	43.8	216.6	112.2	104.4	949.5
2nd quarter	976.3	599.9	155.7	103.0	43.4	9.2	1.2	53.9	52.7	219.5	112.1	107.4	967.0
3rd quarter	996.5	610.2	160.3	106.9	43.2	10.2	1.0	53.3	52.4	224.9	115.4	109.5	986.3
4th quarter	1 004.6	622.2	154.1	107.6	40.7	5.8	3.3	56.5	53.1	225.0	113.7	111.3	998.9
1970													
1st quarter	1 017.3	633.3	150.7	108.1	40.7	1.8	3.4	56.9	53.5	229.9	115.0	114.9	1 015.5
2nd quarter	1 033.2	643.3	153.9	109.4	39.4	5.1	5.4	60.6	55.2	230.7	112.7	118.0	1 028.2
3rd quarter	1 050.7	655.3	156.1	110.6	40.4	5.1	3.8	60.3	56.4	235.6	112.8	122.7	1 045.6
4th quarter	1 052.9	662.0	148.9	107.9	45.0	-4.0	3.2	61.1	57.9	238.9	113.3	125.6	1 056.9
1971													
1st quarter	1 098.3	681.0	171.3	110.4	48.6	12.3	4.4	63.1	58.7	241.6	112.9	128.7	1 086.1
2nd quarter	1 119.1	695.1	178.8	113.4	54.6	10.9	-0.2	63.1	63.3	245.3	113.5	131.8	1 108.2
3rd quarter	1 139.3	707.5	183.4	114.8	58.3	10.2	-0.1	65.4	65.5	248.5	114.7	133.8	1 129.1
4th quarter	1 151.7	723.8	179.2	118.0	61.5	-0.3	-1.7	60.3	61.9	250.3	113.6	136.8	1 152.0
1972													
1st quarter	1 190.6	741.2	193.2	123.3	66.6	3.2	-3.5	68.6	72.2	259.7	119.8	139.9	1 187.3
2nd quarter	1 225.9	759.8	206.5	126.3	68.2	12.0	-4.3	67.2	71.4	263.9	122.6	141.3	1 213.9
3rd quarter	1 249.7	778.3	212.4	129.1	69.6	13.7	-2.6	71.5	74.1	261.6	116.9	144.8	1 236.0
4th quarter	1 287.0	803.1	218.4	136.6	74.3	7.5	-3.1	76.1	79.2	268.6	119.4	149.2	1 279.5
1973													
1st quarter	1 335.5	827.7	232.5	144.1	77.9	10.6	-1.4	84.0	85.4	276.7	123.4	153.3	1 325.0
2nd quarter	1 371.9	843.3	246.0	152.1	75.8	18.2	2.5	91.9	89.5	280.1	123.3	156.8	1 353.7
3rd quarter	1 391.2	861.8	241.8	157.0	75.0	9.8	6.4	97.6	91.1	281.2	120.4	160.8	1 381.4
4th quarter	1 432.3	876.9	257.6	159.9	72.7	25.0	9.0	107.6	98.7	288.8	122.9	165.9	1 407.3
1974													
1st quarter	1 447.0	895.1	244.1	162.6	69.0	12.5	6.4	116.7	110.3	301.4	128.6	172.8	1 434.5
2nd quarter	1 485.3	923.7	252.3	167.4	67.5	17.4	-2.7	126.7	129.4	312.1	131.1	180.9	1 467.9
3rd quarter	1 514.2	952.5	245.4	172.5	67.4	5.6	-7.0	126.6	133.6	323.2	136.1	187.1	1 508.6
4th quarter	1 553.4	962.4	255.8	175.4	60.0	20.4	0.0	136.6	136.6	335.1	142.5	192.6	1 532.9

Table 19-1. Gross Domestic Product—*Continued*

(Billions of dollars, quarterly data are at seasonally adjusted annual rates.)

NIPA Tables 1.1.5, 1.4.5

Year and quarter	Gross domestic product	Personal consumption expenditures	Gross private domestic investment				Exports and imports of goods and services			Government consumption expenditures and gross investment			Addendum: Final sales of domestic product
			Total	Fixed investment			Net exports	Exports	Imports	Total	Federal	State and local	
				Nonresidential	Residential	Change in private inventories							
1975													
1st quarter	1 570.0	988.6	218.7	171.0	57.7	-10.0	16.5	141.4	124.9	346.3	144.0	202.2	1 580.0
2nd quarter	1 605.6	1 017.4	216.8	170.8	59.9	-14.0	21.6	136.8	115.2	349.8	144.9	204.9	1 619.6
3rd quarter	1 663.1	1 051.3	237.8	174.6	64.6	-1.4	12.0	134.1	122.1	362.0	151.4	210.6	1 664.5
4th quarter	1 714.6	1 080.2	247.6	178.6	68.7	0.3	13.8	142.5	128.7	372.9	156.0	216.9	1 714.2
1976													
1st quarter	1 772.6	1 114.0	274.8	183.9	76.2	14.7	4.7	143.6	138.9	379.1	156.3	222.8	1 757.9
2nd quarter	1 804.9	1 133.7	291.6	188.5	80.7	22.4	-0.5	146.6	147.1	380.1	157.8	222.3	1 782.4
3rd quarter	1 838.3	1 163.1	296.5	195.1	80.6	20.8	-4.1	151.8	155.8	382.8	159.9	223.0	1 817.5
4th quarter	1 885.3	1 196.9	304.9	201.9	92.5	10.5	-6.6	156.1	162.7	390.0	164.9	225.2	1 874.8
1977													
1st quarter	1 939.3	1 232.5	326.6	214.2	97.6	14.8	-21.1	155.4	176.4	401.4	169.8	231.5	1 924.5
2nd quarter	2 006.0	1 260.4	354.9	223.8	111.7	19.5	-21.1	161.9	183.0	411.8	174.8	237.0	1 986.6
3rd quarter	2 066.8	1 291.7	378.4	232.5	115.0	30.9	-20.6	162.3	182.9	417.3	176.5	240.8	2 035.9
4th quarter	2 111.6	1 329.8	385.5	244.5	116.9	24.1	-29.6	157.8	187.4	425.8	180.6	245.3	2 087.5
1978													
1st quarter	2 150.0	1 359.9	396.8	250.4	121.0	25.5	-38.7	164.6	203.3	431.9	183.0	249.0	2 124.5
2nd quarter	2 275.6	1 417.6	430.9	276.0	130.6	24.3	-22.6	186.2	208.8	449.8	189.2	260.6	2 251.4
3rd quarter	2 336.2	1 448.7	451.4	290.6	135.8	25.0	-23.8	191.3	215.1	459.9	192.4	267.4	2 311.2
4th quarter	2 417.0	1 487.9	472.8	305.3	139.0	28.5	-16.4	205.4	221.8	472.7	199.1	273.6	2 388.5
1979													
1st quarter	2 464.4	1 523.6	481.1	318.8	138.5	23.9	-18.2	211.7	229.8	477.8	202.3	275.5	2 440.5
2nd quarter	2 527.6	1 564.3	493.0	324.9	140.6	27.4	-22.2	220.9	243.1	492.5	207.9	284.6	2 500.2
3rd quarter	2 600.7	1 618.6	497.9	342.3	143.5	12.1	-23.0	234.3	257.3	507.3	211.8	295.5	2 588.6
4th quarter	2 660.5	1 662.2	499.5	349.6	141.4	8.6	-26.8	253.7	280.5	525.5	220.5	305.0	2 651.9
1980													
1st quarter	2 725.3	1 709.1	505.2	361.3	134.0	9.9	-35.8	268.5	304.3	546.8	231.7	315.1	2 715.4
2nd quarter	2 729.3	1 711.2	470.4	350.9	111.7	7.8	-15.2	277.4	292.6	562.8	243.0	319.8	2 721.5
3rd quarter	2 786.6	1 770.1	443.5	361.1	116.3	-33.9	5.5	284.7	279.2	567.6	243.6	324.0	2 820.5
4th quarter	2 916.9	1 838.1	497.9	376.2	130.8	-9.1	-6.7	292.5	299.2	587.5	256.8	330.8	2 926.0
1981													
1st quarter	3 052.7	1 893.7	563.1	393.1	131.3	38.8	-14.3	305.5	319.7	610.1	266.5	343.6	3 014.0
2nd quarter	3 085.9	1 925.5	551.4	410.8	128.9	11.7	-13.5	308.4	322.0	622.5	278.7	343.8	3 074.2
3rd quarter	3 178.7	1 965.1	592.8	428.4	120.4	44.0	-7.6	302.3	309.9	628.4	281.4	347.0	3 134.8
4th quarter	3 196.4	1 979.9	582.2	447.8	109.6	24.8	-14.8	304.7	319.4	649.0	294.2	354.8	3 171.6
1982													
1st quarter	3 186.8	2 018.0	526.4	443.1	104.8	-21.5	-16.3	293.2	309.5	658.6	298.7	359.9	3 208.2
2nd quarter	3 242.7	2 044.4	530.8	432.0	102.9	-4.2	-4.4	294.7	299.1	671.9	305.1	366.8	3 246.9
3rd quarter	3 276.2	2 092.4	528.7	419.5	103.5	5.8	-29.7	279.6	309.3	684.7	312.3	372.4	3 270.4
4th quarter	3 314.4	2 154.2	483.0	411.3	111.5	-39.8	-29.6	265.3	294.9	706.8	327.1	379.7	3 354.2
1983													
1st quarter	3 382.9	2 194.1	496.6	400.5	131.2	-35.1	-24.6	270.7	295.3	716.7	332.9	383.8	3 417.9
2nd quarter	3 484.1	2 258.2	542.2	402.9	147.0	-7.7	-45.4	272.5	318.0	729.1	342.1	387.0	3 491.8
3rd quarter	3 589.3	2 328.6	577.7	419.5	162.4	-4.2	-65.2	278.2	343.4	748.2	354.2	394.0	3 593.5
4th quarter	3 690.4	2 381.3	640.7	446.0	170.8	23.9	-71.4	286.6	358.0	739.8	342.5	397.3	3 666.5
1984													
1st quarter	3 809.6	2 427.6	709.7	460.1	176.6	73.0	-95.0	293.0	388.0	767.4	359.3	408.0	3 736.6
2nd quarter	3 908.6	2 486.3	735.1	484.4	181.4	69.3	-104.3	302.2	406.5	791.5	374.0	417.4	3 839.3
3rd quarter	3 978.2	2 524.9	753.5	500.7	181.4	71.3	-103.9	305.7	409.6	803.6	375.3	428.4	3 906.8
4th quarter	4 036.3	2 574.3	744.3	513.3	183.0	48.0	-107.8	308.6	416.4	825.5	388.8	436.7	3 988.3
1985													
1st quarter	4 119.5	2 645.7	720.0	520.5	183.3	16.2	-91.9	305.4	397.3	845.7	398.1	447.6	4 103.3
2nd quarter	4 178.4	2 690.1	735.3	528.5	185.1	21.6	-115.4	303.1	418.6	868.5	407.7	460.8	4 156.8
3rd quarter	4 261.3	2 758.7	727.2	522.2	188.8	16.3	-118.6	295.6	414.2	894.0	420.8	473.2	4 245.0
4th quarter	4 321.8	2 786.7	762.2	533.6	195.5	33.1	-134.9	304.0	438.9	907.8	424.7	483.1	4 288.7
1986													
1st quarter	4 385.6	2 830.3	763.8	527.2	206.3	30.3	-127.6	312.2	439.8	919.2	421.5	497.7	4 355.3
2nd quarter	4 425.7	2 862.0	753.0	517.5	219.8	15.7	-130.0	314.4	444.4	940.7	434.8	505.9	4 410.0
3rd quarter	4 493.9	2 933.5	732.5	513.5	226.1	-7.0	-139.5	320.4	459.8	967.4	452.1	515.3	4 500.9
4th quarter	4 546.1	2 973.2	736.7	521.2	228.3	-12.7	-133.8	335.2	469.0	970.0	446.2	523.9	4 558.8
1987													
1st quarter	4 613.8	3 008.0	765.0	506.8	230.1	28.0	-141.3	336.8	478.1	982.1	451.9	530.2	4 585.8
2nd quarter	4 690.0	3 075.3	767.6	518.2	232.9	16.5	-147.6	355.1	502.7	994.6	459.1	535.5	4 673.5
3rd quarter	4 767.8	3 141.6	769.5	534.2	234.2	1.0	-146.0	371.7	517.7	1 002.7	461.0	541.7	4 766.8
4th quarter	4 886.3	3 176.0	837.8	537.2	237.5	63.1	-145.9	392.0	537.9	1 018.4	468.2	550.2	4 823.2
1988													
1st quarter	4 951.9	3 256.8	797.6	546.2	234.4	17.0	-124.7	418.5	543.2	1 022.2	460.9	561.3	4 934.9
2nd quarter	5 062.8	3 316.4	820.4	562.3	238.4	19.7	-107.4	439.1	546.6	1 033.5	459.7	573.8	5 043.2
3rd quarter	5 146.6	3 384.0	825.7	567.5	240.0	18.2	-100.5	452.9	553.3	1 037.4	456.8	580.5	5 128.5
4th quarter	5 253.7	3 457.2	842.6	579.1	244.4	19.1	-109.0	465.8	574.8	1 062.9	471.8	591.1	5 234.7

Table 19-1. Gross Domestic Product—Continued

(Billions of dollars, quarterly data are at seasonally adjusted annual rates.)

NIPA Tables 1.1.5, 1.4.5

Year and quarter	Gross domestic product	Personal consumption expenditures	Gross private domestic investment				Exports and imports of goods and services			Government consumption expenditures and gross investment			Addendum: Final sales of domestic product
			Total	Fixed investment		Change in private inventories	Net exports	Exports	Imports	Total	Federal	State and local	
				Nonresidential	Residential								
1989													
1st quarter	5 367.1	3 511.3	884.1	591.3	244.6	48.2	-98.2	484.0	582.3	1 070.0	470.1	599.9	5 318.9
2nd quarter	5 454.1	3 573.9	878.2	601.9	240.2	36.0	-91.6	505.7	597.3	1 093.6	482.2	611.5	5 418.1
3rd quarter	5 531.9	3 630.9	870.3	621.9	238.4	10.0	-79.3	508.4	587.7	1 109.9	489.7	620.2	5 521.9
4th quarter	5 584.3	3 677.8	867.3	615.8	234.8	16.6	-83.5	515.2	598.7	1 122.7	486.9	635.8	5 567.7
1990													
1st quarter	5 716.4	3 762.6	880.0	626.9	239.2	13.9	-83.6	537.6	621.1	1 157.4	501.4	655.9	5 702.4
2nd quarter	5 797.7	3 815.9	882.5	617.9	230.9	33.7	-70.9	546.3	617.2	1 170.2	506.7	663.5	5 764.0
3rd quarter	5 849.4	3 879.6	866.8	626.1	218.8	21.9	-78.5	555.9	634.3	1 181.5	505.8	675.7	5 827.6
4th quarter	5 848.8	3 901.7	814.6	618.9	207.0	-11.3	-79.0	569.7	648.7	1 211.5	519.2	692.3	5 860.1
1991													
1st quarter	5 888.0	3 914.2	787.9	608.2	195.2	-15.6	-41.5	574.6	616.1	1 227.4	530.4	697.0	5 903.5
2nd quarter	5 964.3	3 970.3	784.0	601.4	200.7	-18.1	-24.3	592.3	616.6	1 234.3	532.9	701.4	5 982.4
3rd quarter	6 035.6	4 015.7	805.2	594.1	210.3	0.8	-22.7	602.6	625.3	1 237.5	527.3	710.2	6 034.8
4th quarter	6 095.8	4 044.1	834.4	589.0	214.2	31.2	-21.4	617.8	639.2	1 238.6	520.5	718.1	6 064.5
1992													
1st quarter	6 196.1	4 142.5	810.2	585.6	224.4	0.2	-14.2	627.4	641.6	1 257.6	526.8	730.7	6 195.9
2nd quarter	6 290.1	4 193.1	865.4	607.1	235.1	23.2	-33.7	628.0	661.7	1 265.3	530.0	735.3	6 266.9
3rd quarter	6 380.5	4 264.3	876.8	619.0	237.3	20.5	-39.6	641.8	681.4	1 278.9	539.6	739.3	6 360.0
4th quarter	6 484.3	4 341.1	906.6	636.7	248.6	21.3	-45.5	644.1	689.6	1 282.1	539.3	742.8	6 463.0
1993													
1st quarter	6 542.7	4 379.3	931.3	642.8	252.6	35.9	-50.0	645.1	695.1	1 282.1	528.9	753.2	6 506.8
2nd quarter	6 612.1	4 446.7	942.3	660.3	257.9	24.1	-65.2	654.3	719.6	1 288.3	524.7	763.6	6 588.0
3rd quarter	6 674.6	4 510.7	943.4	667.5	269.3	6.6	-70.9	651.6	722.5	1 291.5	521.7	769.8	6 668.0
4th quarter	6 800.2	4 574.9	996.5	695.7	284.1	16.7	-74.0	672.3	746.3	1 302.8	525.7	777.2	6 783.5
1994													
1st quarter	6 911.0	4 643.9	1 043.2	704.8	293.1	45.3	-77.6	681.2	758.8	1 301.5	513.3	788.2	6 865.7
2nd quarter	7 030.6	4 702.8	1 106.7	720.5	304.7	81.5	-94.6	706.3	801.0	1 315.7	516.2	799.5	6 949.1
3rd quarter	7 115.1	4 778.6	1 092.9	734.7	304.8	53.4	-99.7	737.2	836.9	1 343.4	528.6	814.8	7 061.7
4th quarter	7 232.2	4 847.9	1 145.5	765.6	304.8	75.1	-102.4	758.8	861.2	1 341.3	518.5	822.8	7 157.1
1995													
1st quarter	7 298.3	4 879.0	1 160.6	797.7	301.7	61.2	-102.7	780.7	883.4	1 361.4	523.5	837.9	7 237.1
2nd quarter	7 337.7	4 946.7	1 132.6	805.5	293.4	33.7	-114.3	797.7	912.0	1 372.7	523.3	849.3	7 304.0
3rd quarter	7 432.1	5 011.0	1 126.2	811.2	303.8	11.2	-78.2	830.9	909.1	1 373.0	520.3	852.7	7 420.8
4th quarter	7 522.5	5 066.4	1 156.6	825.8	312.4	18.3	-70.3	839.6	909.8	1 369.8	509.7	860.1	7 504.2
1996													
1st quarter	7 624.1	5 142.8	1 170.0	841.4	321.8	6.8	-84.2	848.2	932.4	1 395.6	527.8	867.8	7 617.3
2nd quarter	7 776.6	5 232.0	1 227.9	860.5	336.9	30.5	-97.0	859.6	956.6	1 413.7	533.6	880.0	7 746.2
3rd quarter	7 866.2	5 286.4	1 279.9	889.0	339.7	51.1	-116.7	860.8	977.5	1 416.6	522.8	893.8	7 815.1
4th quarter	8 000.4	5 366.1	1 283.3	910.7	337.9	34.7	-87.1	905.6	992.7	1 438.1	525.3	912.8	7 965.8
1997													
1st quarter	8 113.8	5 448.8	1 315.4	930.1	340.8	44.4	-103.0	919.7	1 022.7	1 452.7	523.5	929.2	8 069.4
2nd quarter	8 250.4	5 484.6	1 385.2	950.0	346.8	88.5	-88.3	955.5	1 043.8	1 468.9	535.6	933.3	8 162.0
3rd quarter	8 381.9	5 589.8	1 419.5	995.7	351.3	72.5	-99.6	975.6	1 075.2	1 472.2	532.8	939.4	8 309.4
4th quarter	8 471.2	5 666.4	1 439.1	998.9	357.5	82.7	-115.3	970.6	1 085.9	1 481.1	531.7	949.4	8 388.6
1998													
1st quarter	8 586.7	5 733.4	1 505.5	1 024.0	365.9	115.5	-129.2	965.2	1 094.4	1 477.0	520.3	956.7	8 471.2
2nd quarter	8 657.9	5 834.2	1 474.6	1 049.1	378.6	46.9	-162.4	949.6	1 112.0	1 511.5	534.4	977.1	8 611.0
3rd quarter	8 789.5	5 924.2	1 507.8	1 054.3	392.8	60.7	-174.2	938.3	1 112.5	1 531.7	530.5	1 001.2	8 728.8
4th quarter	8 953.8	6 026.2	1 548.6	1 082.7	406.0	59.9	-174.0	970.6	1 144.6	1 553.1	536.6	1 016.4	8 893.9
1999													
1st quarter	9 066.6	6 101.7	1 596.7	1 101.0	413.5	82.2	-207.5	960.1	1 167.6	1 575.6	540.6	1 035.0	8 984.4
2nd quarter	9 174.1	6 237.2	1 589.9	1 130.1	421.7	38.1	-252.1	972.8	1 224.9	1 599.1	545.9	1 053.2	9 136.0
3rd quarter	9 313.5	6 337.2	1 628.3	1 151.5	427.8	49.1	-285.2	1 000.5	1 285.7	1 633.2	560.0	1 073.2	9 264.4
4th quarter	9 519.5	6 453.7	1 687.7	1 153.0	436.5	98.2	-297.2	1 031.6	1 328.8	1 675.3	576.8	1 098.5	9 421.3
2000													
1st quarter	9 629.4	6 613.9	1 672.3	1 193.9	448.5	29.9	-346.4	1 055.1	1 401.5	1 689.6	565.3	1 124.3	9 599.6
2nd quarter	9 822.8	6 688.1	1 781.7	1 236.5	448.8	96.3	-366.9	1 091.8	1 458.7	1 720.0	586.6	1 133.4	9 726.5
3rd quarter	9 862.1	6 783.9	1 749.0	1 247.5	443.1	58.4	-400.7	1 122.4	1 523.1	1 729.9	581.2	1 148.6	9 803.7
4th quarter	9 953.6	6 871.6	1 738.9	1 250.3	447.2	41.4	-403.9	1 115.8	1 519.7	1 746.9	582.0	1 164.9	9 912.2
2001													
1st quarter	10 021.5	6 955.8	1 675.3	1 229.6	455.6	-9.9	-392.9	1 100.7	1 493.7	1 783.3	596.2	1 187.2	10 031.4
2nd quarter	10 128.9	7 017.5	1 647.7	1 187.1	467.6	-7.0	-361.7	1 060.5	1 422.2	1 825.4	610.9	1 214.5	10 136.0
3rd quarter	10 135.1	7 058.5	1 613.0	1 167.2	477.6	-31.8	-361.9	1 003.5	1 365.3	1 825.6	614.3	1 211.2	10 166.9
4th quarter	10 226.3	7 188.4	1 521.4	1 123.2	476.3	-78.2	-351.6	966.6	1 318.2	1 868.2	630.1	1 238.1	10 304.5
2002													
1st quarter	10 338.2	7 236.9	1 568.5	1 091.4	486.0	-8.9	-376.3	975.0	1 351.3	1 909.2	654.2	1 255.0	10 347.2
2nd quarter	10 445.7	7 339.3	1 577.0	1 061.2	501.8	14.0	-415.4	1 008.1	1 423.5	1 944.9	676.6	1 268.3	10 431.7
3rd quarter	10 546.5	7 428.0	1 581.3	1 055.0	507.2	19.1	-431.1	1 023.4	1 454.5	1 968.3	684.4	1 283.9	10 527.4
4th quarter	10 617.5	7 500.0	1 589.9	1 048.1	521.4	20.4	-476.6	1 013.5	1 490.1	2 004.2	708.2	1 296.0	10 597.1
2003													
1st quarter	10 744.6	7 609.8	1 596.6	1 046.4	539.6	10.6	-503.3	1 019.8	1 523.0	2 041.4	723.4	1 318.0	10 734.0
2nd quarter	10 884.0	7 696.3	1 611.1	1 072.7	553.8	-15.3	-497.6	1 018.1	1 515.7	2 074.2	761.1	1 313.1	10 899.3
3rd quarter	11 116.7	7 822.5	1 696.6	1 113.3	586.9	-3.7	-488.8	1 047.7	1 536.4	2 086.4	756.7	1 329.7	11 120.4
4th quarter	11 270.9	7 914.9	1 758.8	1 146.3	609.0	3.5	-502.8	1 099.2	1 602.0	2 100.0	767.5	1 332.6	11 267.4

Table 19-2. Real Gross Domestic Product

(Billions of chained [2000] dollars, quarterly data are at seasonally adjusted annual rates.)

NIPA Tables 1.1.6, 1.4.6

Year and quarter	Gross domestic product	Personal consumption expenditures	Gross private domestic investment				Exports and imports of goods and services			Government consumption expenditures and gross investment			Addendum: Final sales of domestic product
			Total	Fixed investment		Change in private inventories	Net exports	Exports	Imports	Total	Federal	State and local	
				Nonresidential	Residential								
1990													
1st quarter	7 112.1	4 757.1	920.0	603.9	321.0	14.1	-63.8	543.6	607.3	1 524.2	659.9	861.9	7 110.6
2nd quarter	7 130.3	4 773.0	920.1	593.5	308.6	33.9	-63.6	550.5	614.1	1 526.8	660.7	863.6	7 103.8
3rd quarter	7 130.8	4 792.6	898.4	597.2	291.1	22.8	-58.1	555.1	613.2	1 526.7	654.9	869.4	7 118.3
4th quarter	7 076.9	4 758.3	841.8	585.8	275.0	-9.3	-33.2	560.7	593.8	1 542.2	660.7	878.9	7 101.3
1991													
1st quarter	7 040.8	4 738.1	807.3	570.7	258.6	-14.4	-18.3	563.2	581.5	1 548.4	665.8	880.0	7 071.5
2nd quarter	7 086.5	4 779.4	803.5	565.3	264.7	-18.1	-14.3	583.8	598.1	1 553.7	667.7	883.5	7 120.2
3rd quarter	7 120.7	4 800.1	823.5	559.9	275.7	-0.1	-16.0	597.8	613.9	1 546.6	655.5	888.6	7 134.6
4th quarter	7 154.1	4 795.9	854.7	556.9	281.7	30.7	-9.6	611.6	621.2	1 540.4	642.8	895.2	7 133.8
1992													
1st quarter	7 228.2	4 875.0	835.8	554.5	296.1	1.8	-4.7	621.9	626.6	1 552.3	643.1	906.9	7 239.3
2nd quarter	7 297.9	4 903.0	890.7	576.5	307.4	22.9	-20.2	622.2	642.4	1 550.7	642.6	905.8	7 284.3
3rd quarter	7 369.5	4 951.8	900.2	588.2	308.2	19.6	-15.9	635.6	651.4	1 559.0	650.1	906.6	7 360.5
4th quarter	7 450.7	5 009.4	929.1	606.0	318.6	21.5	-23.0	639.1	662.1	1 559.3	650.4	906.6	7 440.3
1993													
1st quarter	7 459.7	5 027.3	950.3	609.6	320.1	36.7	-37.4	639.9	677.2	1 543.0	630.5	910.4	7 431.2
2nd quarter	7 497.5	5 071.9	957.8	625.9	323.8	24.3	-48.6	647.4	696.0	1 541.4	621.4	918.0	7 483.7
3rd quarter	7 536.0	5 127.3	957.8	632.8	335.0	7.0	-59.4	645.7	705.1	1 537.0	612.5	922.7	7 540.6
4th quarter	7 637.4	5 172.9	1 007.3	659.3	351.9	14.5	-63.0	667.0	730.1	1 542.7	614.1	926.9	7 633.7
1994													
1st quarter	7 715.1	5 230.3	1 050.6	665.9	358.8	46.3	-73.8	672.8	746.5	1 527.1	595.8	929.6	7 677.5
2nd quarter	7 815.7	5 268.0	1 112.0	679.3	370.9	83.0	-83.0	695.0	778.1	1 533.7	592.6	939.6	7 737.2
3rd quarter	7 859.5	5 305.7	1 092.4	692.0	367.0	51.7	-79.0	721.0	800.0	1 558.8	606.8	950.4	7 814.3
4th quarter	7 951.6	5 358.7	1 143.2	722.6	362.3	73.4	-81.9	737.3	819.2	1 545.5	590.5	953.7	7 882.3
1995													
1st quarter	7 973.7	5 367.2	1 154.6	752.1	354.2	60.8	-86.0	750.5	836.5	1 551.9	589.4	961.2	7 918.7
2nd quarter	7 988.0	5 411.7	1 123.8	757.4	342.9	34.6	-87.7	761.0	848.7	1 558.2	588.3	968.7	7 962.3
3rd quarter	8 053.1	5 458.8	1 113.1	762.5	353.6	7.9	-57.1	794.5	851.7	1 553.2	582.7	969.2	8 055.0
4th quarter	8 112.0	5 496.1	1 144.4	777.9	361.6	16.2	-53.1	806.6	859.7	1 535.5	560.6	974.1	8 104.8
1996													
1st quarter	8 169.2	5 544.6	1 160.2	797.1	371.1	3.0	-68.2	816.4	884.6	1 544.9	572.3	971.6	8 175.4
2nd quarter	8 303.1	5 604.9	1 220.0	820.0	386.8	24.5	-81.2	830.3	911.4	1 570.3	583.6	985.6	8 285.8
3rd quarter	8 372.7	5 640.7	1 280.8	847.3	385.7	57.5	-104.3	837.3	941.6	1 565.1	569.6	994.7	8 319.9
4th quarter	8 470.6	5 687.6	1 276.1	870.1	381.8	29.9	-64.9	889.5	954.4	1 579.2	568.5	1 010.0	8 444.7
1997													
1st quarter	8 536.1	5 749.1	1 302.9	892.2	383.1	34.7	-89.0	905.7	994.7	1 581.6	561.2	1 019.8	8 507.3
2nd quarter	8 665.8	5 775.8	1 389.6	914.3	387.9	94.2	-93.1	941.8	1 034.8	1 598.1	573.6	1 024.0	8 574.6
3rd quarter	8 773.7	5 870.7	1 417.5	961.1	389.7	72.3	-108.8	964.2	1 073.0	1 598.5	569.9	1 028.0	8 705.7
4th quarter	8 838.4	5 931.4	1 440.7	969.0	393.6	83.4	-127.6	963.2	1 090.9	1 597.9	565.7	1 031.8	8 758.6
1998													
1st quarter	8 936.2	5 996.8	1 515.8	1 001.6	401.8	116.9	-163.7	967.4	1 131.1	1 589.1	551.9	1 037.0	8 821.1
2nd quarter	8 995.3	6 092.1	1 491.7	1 032.5	412.9	50.4	-205.1	957.0	1 162.1	1 621.4	565.9	1 055.2	8 948.7
3rd quarter	9 098.9	6 165.7	1 525.8	1 042.4	424.1	64.2	-223.9	952.9	1 176.9	1 636.0	561.1	1 074.9	9 038.4
4th quarter	9 237.1	6 248.8	1 563.0	1 074.7	434.3	58.9	-222.3	988.7	1 211.0	1 651.1	566.1	1 084.9	9 182.2
1999													
1st quarter	9 315.5	6 311.3	1 606.6	1 094.0	438.1	79.5	-262.1	980.1	1 242.2	1 662.2	562.9	1 099.3	9 239.7
2nd quarter	9 392.6	6 409.7	1 607.8	1 127.3	441.8	41.7	-295.2	991.2	1 286.4	1 672.3	565.3	1 107.0	9 353.7
3rd quarter	9 502.2	6 476.7	1 647.4	1 154.4	444.5	50.8	-313.9	1 017.4	1 331.3	1 693.1	576.7	1 116.3	9 453.5
4th quarter	9 671.1	6 556.8	1 708.4	1 157.3	449.9	103.5	-313.7	1 044.1	1 357.9	1 720.2	589.9	1 130.2	9 569.3
2000													
1st quarter	9 695.6	6 661.3	1 678.0	1 196.7	454.5	26.9	-350.6	1 060.9	1 411.5	1 707.3	568.2	1 139.2	9 668.8
2nd quarter	9 847.9	6 703.3	1 788.6	1 238.6	450.4	99.3	-374.5	1 092.0	1 466.5	1 730.5	591.2	1 139.3	9 748.4
3rd quarter	9 836.6	6 768.9	1 742.6	1 245.2	441.2	56.2	-395.6	1 120.0	1 515.6	1 721.5	578.6	1 142.9	9 780.4
4th quarter	9 887.7	6 825.0	1 732.7	1 247.9	441.6	43.5	-397.2	1 112.3	1 509.5	1 727.1	577.2	1 149.9	9 844.3
2001													
1st quarter	9 875.6	6 853.1	1 670.3	1 234.4	444.0	-7.8	-398.2	1 097.2	1 495.4	1 749.6	588.5	1 161.1	9 883.2
2nd quarter	9 905.9	6 870.3	1 637.4	1 190.2	450.1	-2.5	-385.2	1 060.6	1 445.8	1 783.0	601.4	1 181.6	9 908.7
3rd quarter	9 871.1	6 900.5	1 592.6	1 169.3	452.1	-29.9	-398.4	1 008.7	1 407.1	1 776.1	601.5	1 174.6	9 899.9
4th quarter	9 910.0	7 017.6	1 493.4	1 128.2	447.8	-86.7	-414.5	980.3	1 394.9	1 812.7	614.2	1 198.5	9 992.3
2002													
1st quarter	9 993.5	7 049.7	1 552.5	1 099.8	457.8	-7.4	-444.9	991.6	1 436.5	1 833.5	626.4	1 207.2	10 000.4
2nd quarter	10 052.6	7 099.2	1 553.7	1 072.4	470.3	7.9	-458.1	1 017.8	1 475.9	1 853.4	645.5	1 208.0	10 044.9
3rd quarter	10 117.3	7 149.9	1 569.2	1 069.5	473.6	22.7	-469.8	1 025.5	1 495.3	1 863.1	650.1	1 213.1	10 095.2
4th quarter	10 135.9	7 194.6	1 567.3	1 060.9	478.5	23.8	-515.4	1 014.5	1 529.8	1 881.6	664.5	1 217.3	10 112.5
2003													
1st quarter	10 184.4	7 242.2	1 564.0	1 060.5	487.3	9.6	-511.7	1 010.6	1 522.3	1 882.5	665.0	1 217.7	10 173.3
2nd quarter	10 287.4	7 311.4	1 577.6	1 090.6	497.9	-17.6	-525.2	1 006.5	1 531.7	1 915.3	699.0	1 216.3	10 302.5
3rd quarter	10 472.8	7 401.7	1 659.4	1 131.1	523.8	-3.5	-508.7	1 033.8	1 542.5	1 916.0	693.1	1 222.9	10 473.9
4th quarter	10 580.7	7 466.8	1 714.1	1 161.0	535.9	8.6	-528.3	1 076.2	1 604.5	1 923.7	701.2	1 222.5	10 569.6

Table 19-3. Contributions to Percent Change in Real Gross Domestic Product

NIPA Table 1.1.2

Year and quarter	Percent change at seasonally adjusted annual rate, GDP	Personal consumption expenditures	Gross private domestic investment				Exports and imports of goods and services			Government consumption expenditures and gross investment		
			Total	Fixed investment		Change in private inventories	Net exports	Exports	Imports	Total	Federal	State and local
				Nonresidential	Residential							
1947												
1st quarter	...	...	...	...	...	...	...	...	...	...	...	...
2nd quarter	-0.5	4.55	-4.65	-0.58	-0.84	-3.24	-0.68	-0.43	-0.25	0.36	0.04	0.31
3rd quarter	-0.2	1.07	-1.65	-0.73	2.78	-3.70	-0.19	-1.75	1.56	0.66	0.00	0.66
4th quarter	6.0	-0.06	11.09	1.32	4.20	5.57	-4.15	-3.48	-0.67	-0.86	-1.24	0.39
1948												
1st quarter	6.5	1.32	6.71	2.72	-0.27	4.26	-2.74	-1.24	-1.50	1.25	1.28	-0.03
2nd quarter	7.3	3.04	4.21	-1.40	1.36	4.26	-2.94	-2.35	-0.59	2.97	2.24	0.73
3rd quarter	2.3	0.36	0.96	0.14	-0.74	1.56	-0.30	0.48	-0.78	1.31	0.83	0.49
4th quarter	1.0	1.94	-2.95	1.08	-1.74	-2.30	-0.58	-0.82	0.24	2.54	1.95	0.59
1949												
1st quarter	-5.8	0.28	-10.72	-2.04	-1.78	-6.90	2.75	2.33	0.41	1.70	0.74	0.96
2nd quarter	-1.2	3.69	-7.96	-1.54	-0.34	-6.08	0.05	-0.17	0.22	3.02	1.54	1.48
3rd quarter	4.6	0.18	4.97	-1.86	1.75	5.08	-1.33	-1.91	0.59	0.75	-0.42	1.17
4th quarter	-4.0	3.32	-2.95	-0.60	2.67	-5.02	-2.88	-2.70	-0.18	-1.50	-2.05	0.56
1950												
1st quarter	17.4	4.16	14.93	1.12	3.10	10.72	-0.55	-0.22	-0.33	-1.08	-1.86	0.78
2nd quarter	12.5	4.18	7.64	3.40	2.76	1.47	-0.50	0.23	-0.73	1.18	0.91	0.27
3rd quarter	16.6	14.05	6.52	3.53	1.66	1.32	-2.80	0.44	-3.25	-1.13	-1.15	0.02
4th quarter	7.5	-7.70	9.90	-0.06	-1.36	11.32	1.26	1.31	-0.05	4.04	4.02	0.01
1951												
1st quarter	4.9	6.42	-9.05	-1.04	-1.46	-6.55	0.76	0.81	-0.05	6.78	7.06	-0.28
2nd quarter	7.0	-6.92	1.76	0.54	-3.43	4.65	2.38	1.82	0.56	9.75	9.29	0.46
3rd quarter	8.2	2.95	-5.78	0.45	-1.38	-4.85	2.05	0.52	1.53	9.02	8.89	0.13
4th quarter	0.7	1.39	-5.75	-0.75	0.18	-5.17	0.22	-0.15	0.37	4.81	4.86	-0.04
1952												
1st quarter	4.2	0.24	1.51	0.21	0.59	0.71	-0.63	1.23	-1.85	3.11	3.02	0.10
2nd quarter	0.3	4.54	-5.15	0.44	0.37	-5.97	-2.16	-2.18	0.02	3.06	2.46	0.60
3rd quarter	2.6	0.92	3.08	-3.29	-0.21	6.58	-2.31	-1.31	-1.00	0.93	1.67	-0.74
4th quarter	13.8	8.94	4.38	3.20	1.17	0.01	-1.26	0.22	-1.48	1.75	1.07	0.68
1953												
1st quarter	7.7	3.03	1.17	1.95	0.34	-1.11	0.25	-0.18	0.42	3.28	2.67	0.61
2nd quarter	3.1	1.39	0.19	0.26	0.06	-0.13	-0.68	0.17	-0.85	2.18	2.23	-0.04
3rd quarter	-2.4	-0.74	-1.29	0.84	-0.78	-1.34	0.73	0.71	0.03	-1.10	-1.84	0.74
4th quarter	-6.2	-1.78	-4.35	-0.42	-0.16	-3.77	0.25	-0.55	0.80	-0.26	-0.93	0.67
1954												
1st quarter	-2.0	0.66	-0.30	-1.09	0.21	0.58	0.14	-0.76	0.90	-2.45	-3.50	1.05
2nd quarter	0.4	2.99	-0.08	-0.37	1.31	-1.03	0.70	2.16	-1.46	-3.25	-3.37	0.12
3rd quarter	4.5	3.25	3.00	1.04	1.36	0.60	0.38	-0.61	0.99	-2.13	-2.99	0.86
4th quarter	8.2	5.35	2.83	-0.09	1.49	1.43	0.54	0.73	-0.20	-0.54	-0.68	0.15
1955												
1st quarter	12.0	5.84	6.68	0.69	1.86	4.13	-0.38	0.58	-0.96	-0.12	-1.41	1.28
2nd quarter	6.7	4.79	4.11	2.32	0.35	1.44	-1.35	-0.43	-0.91	-0.83	-1.24	0.41
3rd quarter	5.4	3.17	0.93	1.93	-0.55	-0.45	0.78	1.08	-0.31	0.56	0.61	-0.05
4th quarter	2.2	3.07	1.40	1.06	-1.05	1.39	-0.57	0.04	-0.61	-1.74	-1.92	0.19
1956												
1st quarter	-1.9	0.31	-2.16	-0.69	-0.57	-0.90	0.05	0.79	-0.74	-0.03	-0.37	0.33
2nd quarter	3.2	0.75	-0.76	0.63	-0.15	-1.24	1.34	1.28	0.06	1.87	1.46	0.41
3rd quarter	-0.5	0.47	-0.70	0.33	-0.44	-0.59	0.48	0.66	-0.18	-0.73	-0.90	0.16
4th quarter	6.7	3.43	-0.69	-0.09	-0.33	-0.27	1.73	0.93	0.80	2.22	1.88	0.34
1957												
1st quarter	2.4	1.59	-0.89	0.30	-0.30	-0.90	-0.01	1.35	-1.36	1.77	0.94	0.83
2nd quarter	-1.0	0.33	-0.09	-0.10	-0.48	0.49	-0.73	-0.57	-0.16	-0.51	-0.80	0.29
3rd quarter	4.0	2.06	1.46	0.91	-0.25	0.80	-0.26	-0.57	0.32	0.72	0.22	0.49
4th quarter	-4.2	0.07	-5.24	-1.03	-0.03	-4.19	-0.64	-0.57	-0.07	1.65	0.80	0.85
1958												
1st quarter	-10.4	-3.29	-4.21	-2.72	-0.69	-0.80	-2.05	-1.81	-0.24	-0.87	-1.84	0.98
2nd quarter	2.4	2.01	-1.33	-1.61	0.05	0.23	-0.64	0.11	-0.75	2.34	1.80	0.53
3rd quarter	9.6	4.14	4.58	-0.54	1.36	3.76	0.29	0.10	0.20	0.55	-0.26	0.82
4th quarter	9.5	3.13	5.44	1.35	2.10	1.99	-0.97	-0.01	-0.96	1.94	1.24	0.69
1959												
1st quarter	7.9	3.94	3.89	1.11	2.37	0.41	0.76	1.18	-0.42	-0.72	-1.02	0.30
2nd quarter	10.9	4.26	5.69	1.14	0.83	3.73	-0.31	0.63	-0.94	1.32	1.21	0.11
3rd quarter	-0.3	2.72	-4.42	1.14	-0.43	-5.13	0.37	0.59	-0.23	1.03	0.99	0.04
4th quarter	1.4	0.33	2.07	-0.15	-0.63	2.86	-0.04	-0.49	0.45	-0.95	-0.77	-0.18
1960												
1st quarter	9.2	2.47	6.70	1.49	0.65	4.57	1.70	2.30	-0.60	-1.63	-2.24	0.62
2nd quarter	-2.0	3.13	-6.92	0.58	-1.76	-5.74	1.15	1.26	-0.10	0.66	-0.20	0.85
3rd quarter	0.6	-0.99	-0.46	-0.94	-0.60	1.08	0.01	-0.54	0.54	2.07	1.52	0.55
4th quarter	-5.1	0.31	-7.21	-0.18	-0.03	-7.00	1.26	0.43	0.83	0.58	0.16	0.42

... = Not available.

Table 19-3. Contributions to Percent Change in Real Gross Domestic Product—Continued

NIPA Table 1.1.2

Year and quarter	Percent change at seasonally adjusted annual rate, GDP	Personal consumption expenditures	Gross private domestic investment				Exports and imports of goods and services			Government consumption expenditures and gross investment		
			Total	Fixed investment		Change in private inventories	Net exports	Exports	Imports	Total	Federal	State and local
				Nonresidential	Residential							
1961												
1st quarter	2.4	-0.03	1.40	-0.76	0.07	2.08	-0.07	-0.14	0.07	1.12	-0.08	1.20
2nd quarter	7.7	3.89	4.14	0.77	0.07	3.30	-0.48	-0.28	-0.20	0.19	0.45	-0.26
3rd quarter	6.6	1.25	4.84	0.30	1.03	3.51	-1.17	-0.11	-1.06	1.74	1.41	0.32
4th quarter	8.4	5.15	1.11	1.20	0.66	-0.75	0.21	0.62	-0.40	1.95	0.88	1.07
1962												
1st quarter	7.4	2.69	3.66	0.82	0.36	2.48	-0.56	-0.05	-0.51	1.59	1.86	-0.27
2nd quarter	4.4	3.02	-0.56	1.05	0.62	-2.23	1.51	1.88	-0.37	0.47	0.20	0.27
3rd quarter	3.7	2.03	1.10	0.46	-0.02	0.65	-1.38	-1.17	-0.21	1.99	1.52	0.48
4th quarter	1.0	3.53	-2.05	-0.26	-0.03	-1.77	-0.63	-0.42	-0.21	0.13	-0.28	0.41
1963												
1st quarter	5.3	1.74	3.30	-0.06	0.73	2.63	0.88	0.46	0.41	-0.53	-1.25	0.72
2nd quarter	5.1	2.43	0.88	1.13	1.44	-1.70	1.90	2.29	-0.38	-0.12	-0.46	0.35
3rd quarter	7.7	3.45	2.02	1.11	0.39	0.52	-1.53	-1.11	-0.42	3.80	2.76	1.04
4th quarter	3.1	2.10	0.80	1.19	0.63	-1.02	1.05	0.99	0.06	-0.81	-1.35	0.54
1964												
1st quarter	9.3	5.00	2.64	0.93	1.32	0.38	1.30	1.27	0.02	0.33	-0.25	0.58
2nd quarter	4.7	4.42	-0.25	0.95	-1.10	-0.09	-0.02	0.35	-0.37	0.58	-0.31	0.89
3rd quarter	5.6	4.66	1.46	1.29	-0.33	0.50	-0.60	-0.16	-0.44	0.06	-0.36	0.43
4th quarter	1.1	0.71	0.44	0.81	-0.36	0.00	0.17	0.62	-0.45	-0.24	-0.66	0.42
1965												
1st quarter	10.2	5.68	6.36	2.72	0.07	3.56	-1.65	-2.29	0.64	-0.18	-0.56	0.38
2nd quarter	5.5	2.83	-0.09	1.52	0.15	-1.77	1.68	3.59	-1.91	1.10	0.08	1.02
3rd quarter	8.4	4.36	2.34	1.59	0.08	0.67	-1.31	-1.23	-0.07	2.96	1.82	1.14
4th quarter	10.0	7.18	0.32	1.77	-0.41	-1.04	0.62	1.48	-0.86	1.91	1.31	0.60
1966												
1st quarter	10.1	3.74	5.68	1.88	0.42	3.38	-0.82	-0.36	-0.46	1.55	1.05	0.50
2nd quarter	1.4	0.67	-1.22	0.65	-1.47	-0.40	0.45	0.89	-0.45	1.49	1.19	0.31
3rd quarter	2.7	2.80	-0.65	0.51	-0.55	-0.61	-1.82	-0.80	-1.02	2.33	1.86	0.46
4th quarter	3.3	1.02	0.32	-0.12	-1.70	2.14	0.48	0.68	-0.20	1.44	0.38	1.06
1967												
1st quarter	3.6	1.44	-1.83	-0.91	-0.43	-0.49	0.16	0.41	-0.25	3.82	3.30	0.52
2nd quarter	0.0	3.25	-2.69	-0.15	1.58	-4.11	-0.03	-0.20	0.17	-0.51	-0.74	0.23
3rd quarter	3.2	1.27	1.73	-0.21	0.77	1.17	-0.74	-0.51	-0.24	0.97	0.80	0.17
4th quarter	3.1	1.49	1.32	0.84	0.94	-0.46	-0.41	0.58	-0.99	0.65	-0.09	0.74
1968												
1st quarter	8.5	5.97	1.38	1.34	0.11	-0.06	-0.54	0.60	-1.15	1.70	0.93	0.77
2nd quarter	7.0	3.85	2.57	-0.73	0.43	2.87	0.10	0.42	-0.31	0.45	-0.39	0.84
3rd quarter	2.7	4.59	-2.06	0.52	0.30	-2.89	0.01	1.22	-1.21	0.22	-0.40	0.62
4th quarter	1.7	1.09	0.63	1.18	0.21	-0.77	-0.10	-0.27	0.17	0.07	-0.30	0.37
1969												
1st quarter	6.5	2.80	4.16	1.23	0.65	2.28	-0.58	-2.53	1.94	0.10	-0.26	0.36
2nd quarter	1.1	1.54	-0.49	0.45	-0.19	-0.75	0.50	4.08	-3.58	-0.39	-0.75	0.36
3rd quarter	2.5	1.13	1.51	1.14	-0.14	0.52	-0.25	-0.53	0.28	0.12	0.03	0.09
4th quarter	-1.9	1.92	-3.44	-0.25	-1.27	-1.92	0.98	0.74	0.24	-1.34	-1.25	-0.09
1970												
1st quarter	-0.7	1.46	-1.90	-0.23	0.03	-1.70	0.26	0.19	0.08	-0.50	-0.91	0.41
2nd quarter	0.8	1.17	0.20	-0.23	-1.08	1.51	0.57	0.98	-0.41	-1.18	-1.43	0.25
3rd quarter	3.6	2.23	1.00	0.20	0.81	-0.01	-0.03	-0.08	0.05	0.40	-0.64	1.04
4th quarter	-4.2	-0.66	-3.42	-1.61	1.61	-3.43	-0.12	0.21	-0.33	0.00	-0.24	0.24
1971												
1st quarter	11.6	5.09	7.60	0.32	0.96	6.33	0.36	0.09	0.26	-1.42	-1.64	0.22
2nd quarter	2.3	2.34	1.86	0.57	1.80	-0.51	-1.63	-0.05	-1.59	-0.28	-0.60	0.32
3rd quarter	3.2	2.03	0.83	0.18	0.97	-0.32	0.43	0.92	-0.49	-0.08	-0.19	0.12
4th quarter	1.1	4.14	-1.98	0.92	0.79	-3.69	-0.35	-1.93	1.57	-0.67	-1.27	0.60
1972												
1st quarter	7.3	3.34	4.54	1.49	1.44	1.62	-0.89	2.23	-3.12	0.31	0.15	0.16
2nd quarter	9.8	4.83	4.22	0.78	0.45	2.99	0.21	-0.68	0.89	0.55	0.65	-0.10
3rd quarter	3.9	3.77	1.05	0.68	0.05	0.32	0.82	1.30	-0.48	-1.78	-2.16	0.38
4th quarter	6.7	5.83	0.45	2.17	0.80	-2.53	-0.11	0.95	-1.07	0.55	-0.11	0.66
1973												
1st quarter	10.6	4.61	4.47	2.02	0.80	1.65	0.59	1.73	-1.14	0.88	0.67	0.22
2nd quarter	4.7	-0.14	3.36	1.75	-1.19	2.80	1.96	1.20	0.75	-0.47	-0.55	0.08
3rd quarter	-2.1	0.87	-2.72	0.73	-0.95	-2.50	0.78	0.06	0.71	-1.04	-1.52	0.48
4th quarter	3.9	-0.72	2.84	0.34	-1.03	3.53	1.17	1.39	-0.22	0.59	0.02	0.57
1974												
1st quarter	-3.4	-2.09	-4.40	-0.07	-1.48	-2.84	1.38	0.37	1.01	1.69	1.07	0.62
2nd quarter	1.2	1.07	-0.34	-0.11	-0.82	0.59	-0.15	1.56	-1.71	0.58	-0.07	0.65
3rd quarter	-3.8	1.15	-3.85	-0.51	-0.58	-2.76	-1.24	-1.85	0.61	0.12	0.18	-0.06
4th quarter	-1.6	-3.45	0.33	-1.27	-2.33	3.93	1.26	0.90	0.36	0.31	0.29	0.03

Table 19-3. Contributions to Percent Change in Real Gross Domestic Product—Continued

NIPA Table 1.1.2

Year and quarter	Percent change at seasonally adjusted annual rate, GDP	Percentage points at seasonally adjusted annual rates									
		Personal consumption expenditures	Gross private domestic investment				Exports and imports of goods and services			Government consumption expenditures and gross investment		
			Total	Fixed investment		Change in private inventories	Net exports	Exports	Imports	Total	Federal	State and local
				Nonresidential	Residential							
1975												
1st quarter	-4.7	2.15	-11.74	-2.70	-0.93	-8.11	3.84	0.23	3.61	1.08	-0.40	1.48
2nd quarter	3.0	4.21	-2.11	-1.13	0.32	-1.30	1.52	-1.05	2.56	-0.65	-0.28	-0.37
3rd quarter	6.9	3.69	4.53	0.39	1.06	3.08	-2.86	-0.57	-2.29	1.59	0.94	0.65
4th quarter	5.4	2.68	1.64	0.37	0.69	0.58	0.26	1.81	-1.56	0.77	0.11	0.67
1976												
1st quarter	9.3	5.03	6.17	0.73	1.63	3.80	-2.12	-0.23	-1.89	0.24	-0.33	0.56
2nd quarter	3.0	2.23	2.76	0.47	0.50	1.79	-1.04	0.33	-1.37	-0.93	-0.06	-0.86
3rd quarter	1.9	2.63	0.12	0.89	-0.29	-0.47	-0.39	0.94	-1.33	-0.43	-0.09	-0.34
4th quarter	2.9	3.39	0.34	0.83	2.24	-2.73	-0.77	0.34	-1.11	-0.06	0.10	-0.15
1977												
1st quarter	4.9	3.14	3.07	1.74	0.62	0.71	-2.08	-0.51	-1.57	0.78	0.31	0.47
2nd quarter	8.1	1.43	5.23	1.33	2.40	1.50	0.55	0.87	-0.33	0.89	0.60	0.29
3rd quarter	7.4	2.46	3.98	0.99	-0.07	3.06	0.77	0.25	0.53	0.15	0.20	-0.05
4th quarter	0.0	3.69	-1.94	1.56	-0.30	-3.20	-1.53	-1.03	-0.50	-0.27	-0.34	0.07
1978												
1st quarter	1.3	1.35	1.63	0.51	0.10	1.02	-1.83	0.67	-2.50	0.12	0.11	0.01
2nd quarter	16.7	5.68	5.56	4.18	1.14	0.23	3.23	3.34	-0.11	2.27	0.85	1.42
3rd quarter	4.0	1.06	2.45	1.71	0.31	0.43	-0.12	0.35	-0.48	0.61	0.11	0.50
4th quarter	5.4	2.01	1.85	1.62	-0.08	0.31	0.80	1.31	-0.50	0.71	0.29	0.43
1979												
1st quarter	0.8	1.34	-0.03	1.04	-0.54	-0.53	0.14	0.03	0.10	-0.67	0.04	-0.71
2nd quarter	0.4	-0.12	-0.18	-0.21	-0.43	0.46	-0.10	0.09	-0.19	0.78	0.39	0.40
3rd quarter	2.9	2.42	-1.50	1.56	-0.27	-2.79	1.87	1.24	0.63	0.12	-0.05	0.16
4th quarter	1.2	0.68	-1.40	0.10	-0.86	-0.64	1.39	2.22	-0.84	0.51	0.01	0.50
1980												
1st quarter	1.3	-0.45	-0.49	0.55	-1.65	0.61	1.02	0.97	0.05	1.19	1.00	0.19
2nd quarter	-7.8	-5.56	-6.62	-2.68	-3.61	-0.33	4.09	0.75	3.35	0.26	0.87	-0.61
3rd quarter	-0.7	2.72	-5.29	0.38	0.28	-5.95	3.04	-0.07	3.10	-1.14	-0.47	-0.67
4th quarter	7.6	3.44	6.58	1.11	1.66	3.82	-2.30	-0.20	-2.10	-0.08	0.12	-0.20
1981												
1st quarter	8.4	1.15	7.08	0.86	-0.31	6.53	-0.92	0.83	-1.75	1.09	0.74	0.36
2nd quarter	-3.1	0.07	-3.50	1.06	-0.58	-3.99	0.18	0.26	-0.08	0.18	1.04	-0.86
3rd quarter	4.9	1.01	4.46	1.32	-1.28	4.43	-0.36	-0.82	0.46	-0.17	-0.03	-0.14
4th quarter	-4.9	-1.83	-2.89	1.33	-1.55	-2.67	-0.92	0.17	-1.09	0.76	0.40	0.36
1982												
1st quarter	-6.4	1.64	-7.46	-1.28	-0.78	-5.40	-0.52	-1.67	1.15	-0.06	0.08	-0.13
2nd quarter	2.2	0.88	-0.05	-1.98	-0.42	2.35	0.83	0.20	0.63	0.50	0.36	0.14
3rd quarter	-1.5	1.93	-0.68	-1.82	-0.04	1.18	-3.32	-1.62	-1.70	0.57	0.57	0.00
4th quarter	0.4	4.60	-5.61	-1.07	0.92	-5.46	-0.08	-1.56	1.48	1.44	1.13	0.31
1983												
1st quarter	5.0	2.48	2.20	-1.00	2.26	0.94	-0.29	0.51	-0.80	0.63	0.47	0.16
2nd quarter	9.3	5.25	5.88	0.52	1.86	3.50	-2.53	0.10	-2.63	0.73	0.85	-0.11
3rd quarter	8.1	4.71	4.26	2.05	1.70	0.51	-2.31	0.47	-2.79	1.47	1.11	0.36
4th quarter	8.4	4.22	6.83	3.03	0.79	3.01	-1.21	0.63	-1.84	-1.39	-1.36	-0.03
1984												
1st quarter	8.1	2.34	7.29	1.59	0.54	5.17	-2.35	0.66	-3.01	0.82	0.31	0.51
2nd quarter	7.1	3.83	2.34	2.44	0.35	-0.45	-0.91	0.77	-1.68	1.80	1.22	0.58
3rd quarter	3.9	2.06	1.65	1.67	-0.17	0.15	-0.38	0.67	-1.05	0.61	-0.15	0.76
4th quarter	3.3	3.42	-1.28	1.22	0.02	-2.52	-0.58	0.61	-1.19	1.77	1.28	0.49
1985												
1st quarter	3.8	4.30	-2.40	0.61	-0.06	-2.95	0.90	0.01	0.89	0.95	0.42	0.52
2nd quarter	3.5	2.35	1.24	0.73	0.14	0.36	-2.00	-0.12	-1.87	1.86	0.96	0.90
3rd quarter	6.4	4.95	-0.72	-0.76	0.23	-0.18	-0.02	-0.44	0.42	2.19	1.33	0.86
4th quarter	3.1	0.57	2.71	0.84	0.42	1.45	-0.68	0.81	-1.49	0.50	-0.01	0.51
1986												
1st quarter	3.9	2.10	-0.06	-0.68	0.78	-0.16	0.95	0.85	0.10	0.89	-0.21	1.10
2nd quarter	1.6	2.69	-1.50	-1.22	1.05	-1.33	-1.37	0.28	-1.65	1.77	1.22	0.55
3rd quarter	3.9	4.48	-2.08	-0.70	0.31	-1.68	-0.47	0.63	-1.10	1.95	1.51	0.44
4th quarter	2.0	1.65	0.12	0.44	-0.04	-0.28	0.72	1.06	-0.33	-0.46	-0.59	0.13
1987												
1st quarter	2.7	0.10	2.09	-1.26	-0.06	3.41	0.23	0.02	0.21	0.25	0.27	-0.02
2nd quarter	4.5	3.64	0.09	1.03	0.09	-1.02	0.11	1.19	-1.08	0.63	0.60	0.03
3rd quarter	3.7	3.00	0.06	1.40	-0.06	-1.29	0.45	1.31	-0.86	0.17	0.08	0.09
4th quarter	7.2	0.66	5.17	-0.11	0.10	5.18	0.15	1.16	-1.02	1.21	0.62	0.58
1988												
1st quarter	2.0	4.33	-3.88	0.34	-0.42	-3.80	1.98	1.78	0.20	-0.46	-1.01	0.55
2nd quarter	5.2	1.92	1.57	1.11	0.15	0.31	1.48	0.96	0.52	0.21	-0.35	0.56
3rd quarter	2.1	2.20	0.40	0.23	0.01	0.15	-0.35	0.64	-1.00	-0.09	-0.25	0.16
4th quarter	5.4	3.15	0.85	0.47	0.17	0.21	-0.22	1.07	-1.29	1.61	1.10	0.51

Table 19-3. Contributions to Percent Change in Real Gross Domestic Product—Continued

NIPA Table 1.1.2

Year and quarter	Percent change at seasonally adjusted annual rate, GDP	Personal consumption expenditures	Gross private domestic investment				Exports and imports of goods and services			Government consumption expenditures and gross investment		
			Total	Fixed investment		Change in private inventories	Net exports	Exports	Imports	Total	Federal	State and local
				Nonresidential	Residential							
1989												
1st quarter	4.1	0.99	2.48	0.75	-0.12	1.85	1.15	1.02	0.12	-0.49	-0.72	0.23
2nd quarter	2.6	1.25	-0.78	0.62	-0.54	-0.86	0.92	1.57	-0.64	1.25	0.80	0.45
3rd quarter	2.9	2.51	-0.76	1.26	-0.19	-1.84	0.38	0.43	-0.05	0.76	0.35	0.41
4th quarter	1.0	1.20	-0.66	-0.67	-0.36	0.37	0.05	0.60	-0.55	0.43	-0.17	0.60
1990												
1st quarter	4.7	2.19	0.60	0.58	0.17	-0.16	0.64	1.57	-0.93	1.28	0.54	0.74
2nd quarter	1.0	0.85	0.03	-0.77	-0.64	1.43	0.02	0.48	-0.47	0.14	0.05	0.09
3rd quarter	0.0	1.06	-1.42	0.25	-0.92	-0.76	0.39	0.31	0.08	0.00	-0.30	0.30
4th quarter	-3.0	-1.92	-3.70	-0.84	-0.83	-2.03	1.81	0.39	1.42	0.82	0.31	0.51
1991												
1st quarter	-2.0	-1.18	-2.25	-1.14	-0.87	-0.24	1.08	0.18	0.90	0.33	0.27	0.06
2nd quarter	2.6	2.29	-0.22	-0.41	0.31	-0.12	0.26	1.43	-1.16	0.29	0.11	0.18
3rd quarter	1.9	1.14	1.31	-0.40	0.56	1.15	-0.12	0.95	-1.07	-0.38	-0.65	0.27
4th quarter	1.9	-0.24	2.02	-0.23	0.30	1.94	0.43	0.92	-0.49	-0.32	-0.67	0.35
1992												
1st quarter	4.2	4.50	-1.26	-0.19	0.72	-1.79	0.32	0.68	-0.37	0.65	0.02	0.64
2nd quarter	3.9	1.56	3.45	1.50	0.56	1.39	-1.01	0.02	-1.03	-0.08	-0.03	-0.06
3rd quarter	4.0	2.70	0.58	0.78	0.03	-0.24	0.26	0.86	-0.60	0.44	0.40	0.04
4th quarter	4.5	3.14	1.80	1.18	0.51	0.11	-0.47	0.22	-0.70	0.02	0.02	0.00
1993												
1st quarter	0.5	0.92	1.34	0.25	0.07	1.03	-0.93	0.05	-0.98	-0.85	-1.04	0.19
2nd quarter	2.0	2.37	0.48	1.04	0.18	-0.75	-0.72	0.46	-1.18	-0.08	-0.47	0.38
3rd quarter	2.1	2.95	0.01	0.44	0.54	-0.96	-0.67	-0.10	-0.56	-0.22	-0.46	0.24
4th quarter	5.5	2.47	2.97	1.69	0.83	0.45	-0.25	1.29	-1.53	0.29	0.08	0.21
1994												
1st quarter	4.1	3.07	2.47	0.39	0.34	1.74	-0.65	0.34	-0.99	-0.76	-0.90	0.14
2nd quarter	5.3	1.98	3.56	0.81	0.58	2.17	-0.56	1.31	-1.86	0.33	-0.16	0.49
3rd quarter	2.3	1.94	-1.11	0.75	-0.18	-1.68	0.20	1.49	-1.29	1.23	0.71	0.52
4th quarter	4.8	2.71	2.89	1.82	-0.22	1.29	-0.19	0.93	-1.12	-0.64	-0.80	0.16
1995												
1st quarter	1.1	0.39	0.69	1.68	-0.38	-0.61	-0.26	0.72	-0.98	0.28	-0.06	0.34
2nd quarter	0.7	2.21	-1.68	0.29	-0.53	-1.44	-0.11	0.59	-0.70	0.31	-0.05	0.36
3rd quarter	3.3	2.37	-0.58	0.29	0.50	-1.37	1.75	1.92	-0.17	-0.24	-0.27	0.03
4th quarter	3.0	1.87	1.70	0.88	0.38	0.44	0.21	0.68	-0.47	-0.82	-1.06	0.24
1996												
1st quarter	2.9	2.46	0.76	1.09	0.44	-0.77	-0.85	0.56	-1.42	0.49	0.59	-0.10
2nd quarter	6.7	3.02	3.17	1.29	0.73	1.15	-0.71	0.77	-1.48	1.23	0.56	0.67
3rd quarter	3.4	1.74	3.14	1.48	-0.05	1.71	-1.23	0.38	-1.61	-0.25	-0.66	0.40
4th quarter	4.8	2.28	-0.25	1.20	-0.18	-1.27	2.09	2.75	-0.66	0.64	-0.05	0.69
1997												
1st quarter	3.1	2.89	1.40	1.14	0.06	0.21	-1.22	0.82	-2.03	0.06	-0.34	0.40
2nd quarter	6.2	1.27	4.39	1.14	0.22	3.03	-0.18	1.81	-1.99	0.73	0.57	0.16
3rd quarter	5.1	4.42	1.38	2.34	0.08	-1.04	-0.73	1.10	-1.83	0.01	-0.15	0.16
4th quarter	3.0	2.78	1.12	0.37	0.17	0.57	-0.87	-0.04	-0.83	0.01	-0.15	0.16
1998												
1st quarter	4.5	2.98	3.53	1.57	0.35	1.61	-1.65	0.20	-1.85	-0.41	-0.66	0.25
2nd quarter	2.7	4.25	-1.12	1.44	0.47	-3.04	-1.86	-0.48	-1.38	1.40	0.61	0.79
3rd quarter	4.7	3.29	1.57	0.45	0.48	0.64	-0.82	-0.19	-0.63	0.66	-0.19	0.85
4th quarter	6.2	3.71	1.71	1.49	0.44	-0.22	0.13	1.59	-1.46	0.64	0.20	0.44
1999												
1st quarter	3.4	2.68	1.96	0.87	0.16	0.93	-1.67	-0.39	-1.28	0.46	-0.14	0.60
2nd quarter	3.4	4.23	0.05	1.47	0.16	-1.57	-1.35	0.48	-1.83	0.41	0.09	0.32
3rd quarter	4.8	2.90	1.72	1.19	0.11	0.42	-0.75	1.12	-1.87	0.88	0.49	0.39
4th quarter	7.3	3.47	2.65	0.12	0.23	2.30	0.01	1.13	-1.11	1.17	0.58	0.59
2000												
1st quarter	1.0	4.38	-1.30	1.64	0.19	-3.13	-1.53	0.70	-2.23	-0.56	-0.93	0.36
2nd quarter	6.4	1.78	4.65	1.76	-0.16	3.05	-0.98	1.30	-2.27	0.96	0.96	0.01
3rd quarter	-0.5	2.62	-1.84	0.28	-0.38	-1.74	-0.87	1.14	-2.01	-0.37	-0.51	0.15
4th quarter	2.1	2.29	-0.36	0.11	0.02	-0.49	-0.07	-0.31	0.24	0.22	-0.07	0.29
2001												
1st quarter	-0.5	1.07	-2.44	-0.52	0.10	-2.01	-0.04	-0.59	0.56	0.92	0.46	0.46
2nd quarter	1.2	0.67	-1.28	-1.76	0.25	0.23	0.49	-1.45	1.94	1.35	0.52	0.83
3rd quarter	-1.4	1.20	-1.76	-0.83	0.08	-1.02	-0.56	-2.04	1.48	-0.28	0.00	-0.28
4th quarter	1.6	4.71	-3.95	-1.63	-0.18	-2.14	-0.66	-1.11	0.45	1.48	0.51	0.97
2002												
1st quarter	3.4	1.32	2.34	-1.13	0.42	3.05	-1.10	0.43	-1.53	0.85	0.49	0.36
2nd quarter	2.4	1.98	0.05	-1.06	0.51	0.60	-0.46	0.99	-1.45	0.81	0.78	0.03
3rd quarter	2.6	2.02	0.61	-0.12	0.13	0.59	-0.43	0.29	-0.72	0.40	0.19	0.21
4th quarter	0.7	1.74	-0.06	-0.33	0.20	0.07	-1.69	-0.42	-1.27	0.75	0.58	0.17
2003												
1st quarter	1.9	1.84	-0.10	-0.01	0.36	-0.45	0.14	-0.15	0.29	0.05	0.04	0.02
2nd quarter	4.1	2.72	0.54	1.10	0.44	-1.01	-0.50	-0.15	-0.34	1.35	1.40	-0.05
3rd quarter	7.4	3.58	3.16	1.50	1.09	0.57	0.64	1.02	-0.39	0.03	-0.23	0.26
4th quarter	4.2	2.50	2.04	1.07	0.50	0.47	-0.66	1.55	-2.22	0.31	0.33	-0.02

Table 19-4. Chain-Type Quantity Indexes for Gross Domestic Product and Domestic Purchases

(Index numbers, 2000 = 100.)

NIPA Tables 1.1.3, 1.4.3, 2.3.3

Year and quarter	Gross domestic product, total	Personal consumption expenditures		Private fixed investment			Exports and imports of goods and services		Government consumption expenditures and gross investment			Gross domestic purchases
		Total	Excluding food and energy	Total	Nonresidential	Residential	Exports	Imports	Total	Federal	State and local	
1947												
1st quarter	16.0	15.1	...	10.6	8.3	19.6	7.1	3.1	19.5	32.0	12.9	15.0
2nd quarter	16.0	15.3	...	10.3	8.2	18.6	7.1	3.2	19.6	32.1	13.0	15.0
3rd quarter	16.0	15.4	...	10.7	8.0	21.5	6.7	2.8	19.8	32.1	13.3	15.0
4th quarter	16.2	15.4	...	11.6	8.3	25.6	6.0	3.0	19.5	31.0	13.6	15.4
1948												
1st quarter	16.5	15.5	...	12.0	8.8	25.3	5.7	3.4	19.9	32.0	13.5	15.8
2nd quarter	16.8	15.6	...	12.0	8.5	26.8	5.1	3.5	20.8	33.9	13.9	16.2
3rd quarter	16.8	15.7	...	11.9	8.5	26.0	5.3	3.7	21.2	34.7	14.2	16.3
4th quarter	16.9	15.8	...	11.7	8.8	24.1	5.1	3.6	22.1	36.5	14.5	16.3
1949												
1st quarter	16.6	15.8	...	11.0	8.3	22.2	5.7	3.5	22.8	37.3	15.1	16.0
2nd quarter	16.6	16.1	...	10.7	8.0	21.9	5.6	3.4	23.8	38.7	16.0	15.9
3rd quarter	16.8	16.1	...	10.7	7.6	23.7	5.2	3.3	24.0	38.3	16.6	16.1
4th quarter	16.6	16.3	...	11.0	7.5	26.6	4.5	3.4	23.5	36.3	17.0	16.1
1950												
1st quarter	17.3	16.6	...	11.8	7.7	29.7	4.4	3.4	23.1	34.6	17.4	16.8
2nd quarter	17.8	16.9	...	12.8	8.4	32.5	4.5	3.6	23.5	35.4	17.5	17.3
3rd quarter	18.5	17.7	...	13.8	9.1	34.3	4.6	4.5	23.0	34.1	17.5	18.1
4th quarter	18.8	17.2	...	13.5	9.1	32.7	4.9	4.5	24.5	38.2	17.6	18.4
1951												
1st quarter	19.1	17.6	...	13.0	8.9	31.0	5.2	4.5	27.1	45.6	17.4	18.6
2nd quarter	19.4	17.1	...	12.4	9.0	26.8	5.7	4.4	30.9	55.4	17.7	18.8
3rd quarter	19.8	17.3	...	12.2	9.1	25.1	5.8	4.0	34.4	64.9	17.8	19.1
4th quarter	19.8	17.4	...	12.1	8.9	25.3	5.8	3.9	36.2	70.1	17.7	19.1
1952												
1st quarter	20.0	17.5	...	12.2	9.0	26.0	6.1	4.3	37.4	73.3	17.8	19.3
2nd quarter	20.0	17.8	...	12.4	9.1	26.5	5.4	4.3	38.6	76.2	18.2	19.5
3rd quarter	20.2	17.9	...	11.6	8.2	26.2	5.0	4.6	39.0	78.2	17.7	19.7
4th quarter	20.8	18.5	...	12.5	9.0	27.6	5.0	5.0	39.7	79.4	18.1	20.4
1953												
1st quarter	21.2	18.7	...	13.0	9.5	28.0	4.9	4.9	41.1	82.4	18.5	20.8
2nd quarter	21.4	18.9	...	13.1	9.5	28.1	5.0	5.1	42.0	85.0	18.4	21.0
3rd quarter	21.2	18.8	...	13.1	9.7	27.0	5.2	5.1	41.5	82.7	18.9	20.8
4th quarter	20.9	18.7	...	13.0	9.6	26.8	5.0	4.8	41.4	81.6	19.4	20.5
1954												
1st quarter	20.8	18.8	...	12.8	9.3	27.1	4.8	4.6	40.2	77.2	20.1	20.4
2nd quarter	20.8	19.0	...	13.0	9.2	28.9	5.5	5.0	38.8	73.0	20.2	20.4
3rd quarter	21.1	19.2	...	13.5	9.5	30.6	5.3	4.7	37.9	69.4	20.7	20.6
4th quarter	21.5	19.6	...	13.8	9.5	32.5	5.5	4.7	37.6	68.6	20.8	20.9
1955												
1st quarter	22.1	20.1	...	14.3	9.6	35.0	5.7	5.0	37.6	66.9	21.7	21.6
2nd quarter	22.5	20.5	...	15.0	10.2	35.5	5.6	5.3	37.2	65.4	22.0	22.0
3rd quarter	22.8	20.7	...	15.3	10.8	34.7	6.0	5.4	37.4	66.1	22.0	22.2
4th quarter	22.9	21.0	...	15.3	11.1	33.3	6.0	5.6	36.6	63.6	22.1	22.4
1956												
1st quarter	22.8	21.0	...	15.0	10.9	32.4	6.3	5.8	36.6	63.1	22.3	22.3
2nd quarter	22.9	21.1	...	15.1	11.0	32.2	6.7	5.8	37.4	64.8	22.6	22.4
3rd quarter	22.9	21.1	...	15.1	11.1	31.5	6.9	5.8	37.0	63.6	22.7	22.3
4th quarter	23.3	21.4	...	15.0	11.1	31.1	7.2	5.5	38.0	65.9	22.9	22.6
1957												
1st quarter	23.4	21.6	...	15.0	11.2	30.6	7.7	6.0	38.8	67.1	23.5	22.7
2nd quarter	23.4	21.6	...	14.8	11.1	29.9	7.5	6.0	38.5	66.0	23.7	22.7
3rd quarter	23.6	21.8	...	15.0	11.4	29.5	7.3	5.9	38.8	66.3	24.1	22.9
4th quarter	23.4	21.8	...	14.7	11.1	29.4	7.1	5.9	39.5	67.2	24.6	22.7
1958												
1st quarter	22.7	21.5	...	13.8	10.3	28.3	6.4	6.0	39.1	64.8	25.3	22.2
2nd quarter	22.9	21.6	...	13.4	9.8	28.3	6.4	6.3	40.0	66.9	25.7	22.4
3rd quarter	23.4	22.0	...	13.6	9.7	30.4	6.4	6.2	40.3	66.6	26.3	22.9
4th quarter	23.9	22.3	...	14.4	10.1	33.6	6.4	6.5	41.1	68.1	26.8	23.5
1959												
1st quarter	24.4	22.6	18.2	15.3	10.4	37.5	6.8	6.7	40.9	67.0	27.0	23.9
2nd quarter	25.0	23.0	18.6	15.8	10.7	38.8	7.0	7.0	41.5	68.6	27.0	24.5
3rd quarter	25.0	23.3	18.8	16.0	11.0	38.1	7.3	7.1	42.0	70.0	27.1	24.5
4th quarter	25.1	23.3	18.8	15.8	11.0	37.0	7.1	6.9	41.6	69.0	26.9	24.6
1960												
1st quarter	25.6	23.5	19.0	16.3	11.4	38.0	8.0	7.2	40.7	65.9	27.4	25.0
2nd quarter	25.5	23.8	19.3	16.0	11.6	34.9	8.5	7.2	41.1	65.6	28.1	24.8
3rd quarter	25.6	23.7	19.3	15.6	11.3	33.8	8.2	7.0	42.1	67.7	28.5	24.9
4th quarter	25.2	23.7	19.3	15.5	11.2	33.8	8.4	6.7	42.3	67.9	28.8	24.5

. . . = Not available.

Table 19-4. Chain-Type Quantity Indexes for Gross Domestic Product and Domestic Purchases—*Continued*

(Index numbers, 2000 = 100.)

NIPA Tables 1.1.3, 1.4.3, 2.3.3

Year and quarter	Gross domestic product											Gross domestic purchases
	Gross domestic product, total	Personal consumption expenditures		Private fixed investment			Exports and imports of goods and services		Government consumption expenditures and gross investment			
		Total	Excluding food and energy	Total	Nonresidential	Residential	Exports	Imports	Total	Federal	State and local	
1961												
1st quarter	25.4	23.7	19.2	15.3	11.0	33.9	8.4	6.6	42.9	67.8	29.7	24.6
2nd quarter	25.9	24.1	19.6	15.6	11.2	34.0	8.2	6.7	43.0	68.4	29.5	25.1
3rd quarter	26.3	24.2	19.7	15.9	11.3	35.9	8.2	7.2	43.8	70.4	29.8	25.6
4th quarter	26.8	24.7	20.3	16.5	11.7	37.1	8.4	7.3	44.8	71.6	30.6	26.1
1962												
1st quarter	27.3	25.0	20.5	16.8	12.0	37.7	8.4	7.5	45.6	74.3	30.4	26.6
2nd quarter	27.6	25.3	20.8	17.3	12.3	38.9	9.2	7.7	45.9	74.6	30.6	26.8
3rd quarter	27.8	25.5	21.0	17.5	12.5	38.9	8.7	7.8	46.9	76.8	31.0	27.2
4th quarter	27.9	25.8	21.4	17.4	12.4	38.8	8.5	7.9	47.0	76.4	31.3	27.3
1963												
1st quarter	28.3	26.0	21.6	17.6	12.4	40.2	8.7	7.7	46.7	74.5	31.9	27.6
2nd quarter	28.6	26.3	21.9	18.4	12.8	43.1	9.8	7.9	46.6	73.8	32.2	27.8
3rd quarter	29.2	26.6	22.2	18.9	13.2	43.9	9.2	8.1	48.6	77.9	33.1	28.4
4th quarter	29.4	26.8	22.4	19.5	13.6	45.3	9.7	8.1	48.2	75.9	33.5	28.6
1964												
1st quarter	30.1	27.4	23.0	20.2	13.9	48.1	10.3	8.1	48.3	75.5	34.0	29.1
2nd quarter	30.4	27.9	23.4	20.2	14.3	45.6	10.5	8.3	48.7	75.0	34.8	29.5
3rd quarter	30.8	28.4	23.8	20.5	14.8	44.9	10.4	8.5	48.7	74.4	35.2	29.9
4th quarter	30.9	28.5	23.9	20.6	15.1	44.1	10.7	8.7	48.6	73.3	35.6	30.0
1965												
1st quarter	31.7	29.1	24.5	21.6	16.1	44.2	9.5	8.4	48.4	72.4	35.9	30.9
2nd quarter	32.1	29.4	24.7	22.2	16.7	44.6	11.3	9.4	49.1	72.5	36.8	31.2
3rd quarter	32.7	29.9	25.2	22.8	17.3	44.7	10.7	9.4	50.8	75.5	37.9	31.9
4th quarter	33.5	30.8	25.9	23.3	18.0	43.8	11.5	9.9	51.9	77.6	38.4	32.7
1966												
1st quarter	34.4	31.2	26.4	24.2	18.8	44.8	11.2	10.1	52.8	79.3	38.9	33.5
2nd quarter	34.5	31.3	26.4	23.9	19.1	41.2	11.7	10.4	53.7	81.4	39.2	33.6
3rd quarter	34.7	31.7	26.8	23.8	19.4	39.8	11.3	11.0	55.2	84.7	39.6	34.0
4th quarter	35.0	31.8	27.0	23.1	19.3	35.7	11.7	11.1	56.1	85.4	40.7	34.2
1967												
1st quarter	35.3	32.0	27.1	22.6	18.9	34.6	11.9	11.3	58.4	91.3	41.2	34.5
2nd quarter	35.3	32.4	27.5	23.2	18.8	38.5	11.8	11.2	58.1	90.0	41.4	34.5
3rd quarter	35.6	32.6	27.8	23.4	18.7	40.5	11.5	11.3	58.7	91.4	41.5	34.9
4th quarter	35.8	32.8	27.8	24.1	19.1	42.8	11.8	11.9	59.1	91.2	42.3	35.2
1968												
1st quarter	36.6	33.5	28.6	24.7	19.7	43.1	12.2	12.6	60.2	92.8	43.0	35.9
2nd quarter	37.2	34.1	29.0	24.6	19.4	44.2	12.4	12.8	60.4	92.0	43.8	36.5
3rd quarter	37.5	34.7	29.6	24.9	19.6	45.0	13.1	13.6	60.6	91.2	44.5	36.8
4th quarter	37.6	34.8	29.8	25.5	20.2	45.5	13.0	13.5	60.6	90.7	44.9	37.0
1969												
1st quarter	38.2	35.2	30.1	26.3	20.8	47.1	11.4	12.2	60.7	90.2	45.2	37.6
2nd quarter	38.3	35.5	30.3	26.5	21.0	46.6	14.0	14.6	60.4	88.7	45.6	37.7
3rd quarter	38.5	35.6	30.5	26.9	21.6	46.3	13.6	14.4	60.5	88.8	45.7	37.9
4th quarter	38.4	35.9	30.7	26.2	21.5	42.9	14.1	14.3	59.6	86.4	45.6	37.6
1970												
1st quarter	38.3	36.1	30.8	26.1	21.4	43.0	14.2	14.2	59.3	84.7	46.0	37.6
2nd quarter	38.4	36.3	30.9	25.6	21.3	40.1	14.9	14.5	58.5	82.0	46.3	37.6
3rd quarter	38.7	36.6	31.2	26.0	21.4	42.2	14.8	14.5	58.8	80.8	47.3	37.9
4th quarter	38.3	36.5	31.0	26.0	20.6	46.7	15.0	14.7	58.8	80.4	47.6	37.5
1971												
1st quarter	39.4	37.2	31.8	26.6	20.8	49.2	15.0	14.5	57.8	77.3	47.8	38.5
2nd quarter	39.6	37.5	32.2	27.7	21.1	54.1	15.0	15.6	57.6	76.2	48.1	38.9
3rd quarter	39.9	37.8	32.6	28.2	21.1	56.8	15.6	15.9	57.6	75.8	48.2	39.2
4th quarter	40.0	38.5	33.3	29.0	21.6	59.0	14.3	14.9	57.2	73.5	48.8	39.3
1972												
1st quarter	40.7	39.0	33.8	30.3	22.3	63.0	15.8	17.0	57.4	73.8	49.0	40.1
2nd quarter	41.7	39.7	34.4	30.9	22.7	64.2	15.3	16.4	57.7	74.9	48.9	41.0
3rd quarter	42.1	40.3	35.0	31.2	23.0	64.3	16.3	16.8	56.5	70.9	49.3	41.3
4th quarter	42.8	41.3	35.9	32.6	24.2	66.6	17.0	17.5	56.9	70.7	50.0	42.0
1973												
1st quarter	43.9	42.0	36.8	34.0	25.4	68.9	18.2	18.3	57.4	71.8	50.2	43.0
2nd quarter	44.4	42.0	36.9	34.3	26.4	65.4	19.1	17.8	57.1	70.7	50.3	43.3
3rd quarter	44.1	42.1	37.0	34.2	26.9	62.6	19.1	17.3	56.4	67.7	50.8	43.0
4th quarter	44.5	42.0	37.0	33.9	27.1	59.6	20.1	17.5	56.8	67.8	51.4	43.3
1974												
1st quarter	44.2	41.7	37.0	33.1	27.0	55.2	20.3	16.9	58.0	69.9	52.1	42.7
2nd quarter	44.3	41.8	37.1	32.6	27.0	52.8	21.3	17.8	58.4	69.8	52.8	42.8
3rd quarter	43.9	42.0	37.1	32.0	26.7	51.1	20.2	17.4	58.4	70.1	52.7	42.6
4th quarter	43.7	41.4	36.4	30.2	25.9	44.4	20.7	17.3	58.7	70.7	52.8	42.3

Table 19-4. Chain-Type Quantity Indexes for Gross Domestic Product and Domestic Purchases—Continued

(Index numbers, 2000 = 100.)

NIPA Tables 1.1.3, 1.4.3, 2.3.3

Year and quarter	Gross domestic product											Gross domestic purchases
	Gross domestic product, total	Personal consumption expenditures		Private fixed investment			Exports and imports of goods and services		Government consumption expenditures and gross investment			
		Total	Excluding food and energy	Total	Nonresidential	Residential	Exports	Imports	Total	Federal	State and local	
1975												
1st quarter	43.2	41.8	36.8	28.4	24.3	41.6	20.9	15.5	59.4	69.9	54.3	41.4
2nd quarter	43.5	42.4	37.3	28.0	23.7	42.5	20.2	14.3	58.9	69.3	53.9	41.5
3rd quarter	44.2	43.0	38.0	28.7	23.9	45.5	19.9	15.5	60.0	71.0	54.6	42.6
4th quarter	44.8	43.5	38.6	29.2	24.1	47.5	21.0	16.3	60.5	71.2	55.3	43.1
1976												
1st quarter	45.8	44.4	39.3	30.4	24.6	52.3	20.9	17.3	60.6	70.6	55.9	44.3
2nd quarter	46.1	44.8	39.6	30.9	24.9	53.8	21.1	18.1	59.9	70.4	54.9	44.7
3rd quarter	46.4	45.2	40.0	31.2	25.4	52.9	21.7	18.8	59.6	70.2	54.5	45.0
4th quarter	46.7	45.8	40.5	32.8	25.9	59.7	21.9	19.4	59.6	70.4	54.4	45.4
1977												
1st quarter	47.3	46.4	41.0	34.0	26.9	61.5	21.6	20.4	60.1	71.0	54.9	46.2
2nd quarter	48.2	46.6	41.5	35.9	27.7	68.5	22.2	20.5	60.7	72.1	55.2	47.1
3rd quarter	49.1	47.1	42.0	36.4	28.3	68.3	22.3	20.3	60.9	72.6	55.2	47.8
4th quarter	49.1	47.8	42.8	37.1	29.3	67.4	21.6	20.5	60.7	71.8	55.3	48.0
1978												
1st quarter	49.2	48.0	43.0	37.4	29.5	67.8	22.1	21.9	60.8	72.1	55.3	48.3
2nd quarter	51.1	49.1	44.3	40.1	32.0	71.0	24.4	22.0	62.4	73.8	56.9	49.8
3rd quarter	51.7	49.3	44.5	41.2	33.2	72.0	24.7	22.3	62.9	74.1	57.5	50.3
4th quarter	52.3	49.7	44.8	42.1	34.2	71.7	25.7	22.6	63.5	74.7	58.1	50.9
1979												
1st quarter	52.4	49.9	45.0	42.4	35.0	70.1	25.7	22.5	62.9	74.8	57.1	51.0
2nd quarter	52.5	49.9	45.2	42.1	34.9	68.8	25.8	22.6	63.6	75.8	57.6	51.0
3rd quarter	52.9	50.4	45.8	42.9	36.0	67.9	26.7	22.3	63.7	75.6	57.8	51.2
4th quarter	53.0	50.6	45.8	42.5	36.1	65.4	28.4	22.8	64.1	75.6	58.5	51.1
1980												
1st quarter	53.2	50.5	45.7	41.9	36.5	60.4	29.2	22.8	65.1	78.0	58.8	51.2
2nd quarter	52.1	49.3	44.5	38.2	34.6	49.2	29.7	21.1	65.3	80.0	58.0	49.6
3rd quarter	52.0	49.9	45.3	38.6	34.9	50.0	29.7	19.6	64.4	78.9	57.2	49.2
4th quarter	53.0	50.6	46.2	40.1	35.6	54.9	29.5	20.7	64.3	79.2	57.0	50.4
1981												
1st quarter	54.1	50.8	46.5	40.4	36.2	53.9	30.0	21.6	65.2	80.8	57.4	51.6
2nd quarter	53.6	50.8	46.3	40.7	36.9	52.1	30.2	21.6	65.3	83.2	56.3	51.1
3rd quarter	54.3	51.0	46.7	40.7	37.8	48.1	29.6	21.4	65.2	83.1	56.1	51.8
4th quarter	53.6	50.6	46.1	40.6	38.7	43.2	29.7	22.0	65.8	84.0	56.5	51.3
1982												
1st quarter	52.7	50.9	46.5	39.3	37.8	40.7	28.4	21.3	65.7	84.2	56.4	50.5
2nd quarter	53.0	51.1	46.6	37.9	36.4	39.4	28.6	21.0	66.1	84.9	56.6	50.7
3rd quarter	52.8	51.5	47.1	36.9	35.2	39.3	27.3	22.0	66.6	86.2	56.6	50.9
4th quarter	52.9	52.4	48.2	36.8	34.5	42.2	26.1	21.1	67.7	88.8	56.9	51.0
1983												
1st quarter	53.5	53.0	48.8	37.6	33.9	49.3	26.5	21.6	68.2	89.8	57.2	51.6
2nd quarter	54.7	54.0	49.9	39.1	34.3	55.2	26.6	23.2	68.8	91.7	57.0	53.1
3rd quarter	55.8	55.0	50.8	41.4	35.8	60.6	27.0	25.1	70.0	94.3	57.5	54.5
4th quarter	56.9	55.8	51.9	43.8	38.1	63.2	27.5	26.3	68.8	91.0	57.4	55.7
1984												
1st quarter	58.1	56.3	52.6	45.2	39.4	65.0	28.1	28.4	69.5	91.8	58.1	57.1
2nd quarter	59.1	57.1	53.3	47.1	41.3	66.2	28.8	29.6	71.0	94.7	58.8	58.2
3rd quarter	59.6	57.6	53.8	48.1	42.7	65.5	29.4	30.4	71.5	94.3	59.9	58.8
4th quarter	60.1	58.3	54.7	49.0	43.7	65.6	30.0	31.2	73.1	97.4	60.5	59.4
1985												
1st quarter	60.7	59.3	55.7	49.3	44.2	65.4	30.0	30.6	73.9	98.5	61.3	59.8
2nd quarter	61.2	59.8	56.4	49.9	44.9	65.9	29.9	32.1	75.6	100.9	62.5	60.6
3rd quarter	62.2	61.0	57.7	49.5	44.2	66.8	29.5	31.7	77.5	104.3	63.7	61.5
4th quarter	62.6	61.1	57.7	50.5	44.9	68.3	30.4	33.0	78.0	104.2	64.5	62.0
1986												
1st quarter	63.2	61.6	58.3	50.6	44.3	71.3	31.3	33.0	78.8	103.7	66.1	62.5
2nd quarter	63.5	62.3	59.0	50.4	43.2	75.2	31.7	34.4	80.5	107.0	66.9	62.9
3rd quarter	64.1	63.4	60.3	50.1	42.6	76.4	32.4	35.3	82.3	111.0	67.5	63.6
4th quarter	64.4	63.8	60.6	50.5	43.0	76.2	33.6	35.6	81.9	109.3	67.7	63.8
1987												
1st quarter	64.8	63.8	60.7	49.5	41.8	76.0	33.6	35.4	82.1	110.0	67.7	64.1
2nd quarter	65.6	64.7	61.6	50.4	42.8	76.4	35.0	36.3	82.7	111.6	67.8	64.8
3rd quarter	66.1	65.4	62.5	51.4	44.2	76.1	36.5	37.0	82.8	111.7	67.9	65.3
4th quarter	67.3	65.5	62.6	51.4	44.1	76.5	37.8	37.8	83.9	113.4	68.8	66.4
1988												
1st quarter	67.6	66.6	63.6	51.4	44.5	74.9	39.9	37.6	83.4	110.3	69.6	66.4
2nd quarter	68.5	67.1	64.0	52.4	45.6	75.5	41.0	37.2	83.6	109.2	70.5	67.0
3rd quarter	68.9	67.7	64.5	52.6	45.8	75.5	41.8	38.1	83.5	108.4	70.7	67.4
4th quarter	69.8	68.5	65.3	53.1	46.3	76.2	43.1	39.2	85.1	111.6	71.5	68.3

Table 19-4. Chain-Type Quantity Indexes for Gross Domestic Product and Domestic Purchases—Continued

(Index numbers, 2000 = 100.)

NIPA Tables 1.1.3, 1.4.3, 2.3.3

Year and quarter	Gross domestic product, total	Gross domestic product										Gross domestic purchases
		Personal consumption expenditures		Private fixed investment			Exports and imports of goods and services		Government consumption expenditures and gross investment			
		Total	Excluding food and energy	Total	Nonresidential	Residential	Exports	Imports	Total	Federal	State and local	
1989												
1st quarter	70.5	68.7	65.6	53.6	47.1	75.7	44.3	39.1	84.6	109.4	71.9	68.8
2nd quarter	70.9	69.0	66.1	53.7	47.7	73.4	46.3	39.7	85.9	111.8	72.6	69.1
3rd quarter	71.4	69.7	66.8	54.6	49.1	72.6	46.8	39.7	86.7	112.9	73.3	69.5
4th quarter	71.6	70.0	66.9	53.7	48.4	71.1	47.6	40.3	87.2	112.3	74.2	69.7
1990												
1st quarter	72.4	70.6	67.8	54.4	49.0	71.8	49.6	41.2	88.5	114.0	75.4	70.3
2nd quarter	72.6	70.8	67.8	53.2	48.2	69.1	50.2	41.6	88.7	114.2	75.6	70.5
3rd quarter	72.6	71.1	68.0	52.6	48.5	65.1	50.6	41.6	88.7	113.2	76.1	70.5
4th quarter	72.1	70.6	67.6	51.1	47.5	61.5	51.1	40.2	89.6	114.2	76.9	69.6
1991												
1st quarter	71.7	70.3	67.4	49.3	46.3	57.9	51.4	39.4	89.9	115.0	77.0	69.1
2nd quarter	72.2	70.9	67.8	49.3	45.9	59.2	53.3	40.5	90.2	115.4	77.3	69.5
3rd quarter	72.5	71.2	68.2	49.4	45.4	61.7	54.5	41.6	89.8	113.3	77.8	69.9
4th quarter	72.9	71.2	68.3	49.5	45.2	63.0	55.8	42.1	89.5	111.1	78.3	70.1
1992												
1st quarter	73.6	72.3	69.6	50.0	45.0	66.3	56.7	42.5	90.2	111.1	79.4	70.8
2nd quarter	74.3	72.8	70.2	52.0	46.8	68.8	56.8	43.5	90.1	111.0	79.3	71.6
3rd quarter	75.1	73.5	71.0	52.8	47.7	69.0	58.0	44.1	90.6	112.3	79.3	72.3
4th quarter	75.9	74.3	71.7	54.4	49.2	71.3	58.3	44.9	90.6	112.4	79.3	73.2
1993												
1st quarter	76.0	74.6	72.1	54.7	49.5	71.6	58.4	45.9	89.6	108.9	79.7	73.4
2nd quarter	76.4	75.3	72.8	56.0	50.8	72.5	59.1	47.2	89.5	107.4	80.3	73.9
3rd quarter	76.8	76.1	73.5	57.0	51.4	75.0	58.9	47.8	89.3	105.8	80.7	74.4
4th quarter	77.8	76.8	74.3	59.5	53.5	78.7	60.8	49.5	89.6	106.1	81.1	75.5
1994												
1st quarter	78.6	77.6	75.3	60.3	54.0	80.3	61.4	50.6	88.7	102.9	81.3	76.3
2nd quarter	79.6	78.2	75.7	61.7	55.1	83.0	63.4	52.7	89.1	102.4	82.2	77.4
3rd quarter	80.1	78.7	76.4	62.3	56.2	82.1	65.8	54.2	90.5	104.8	83.2	77.8
4th quarter	81.0	79.5	77.4	64.0	58.7	81.1	67.3	55.5	89.8	102.0	83.5	78.8
1995												
1st quarter	81.2	79.6	77.5	65.5	61.0	79.3	68.5	56.7	90.1	101.8	84.1	79.0
2nd quarter	81.4	80.3	78.2	65.2	61.5	76.7	69.4	57.5	90.5	101.6	84.8	79.2
3rd quarter	82.0	81.0	79.0	66.1	61.9	79.1	72.5	57.7	90.2	100.7	84.8	79.5
4th quarter	82.6	81.6	79.7	67.5	63.1	80.9	73.6	58.3	89.2	96.9	85.2	80.0
1996												
1st quarter	83.2	82.3	80.4	69.2	64.7	83.0	74.5	59.9	89.7	98.9	85.0	80.7
2nd quarter	84.6	83.2	81.4	71.5	66.6	86.5	75.7	61.8	91.2	100.8	86.2	82.2
3rd quarter	85.3	83.7	82.2	73.1	68.8	86.3	76.4	63.8	90.9	98.4	87.0	83.1
4th quarter	86.3	84.4	82.9	74.3	70.6	85.4	81.1	64.7	91.7	98.2	88.4	83.7
1997												
1st quarter	87.0	85.3	83.9	75.8	72.4	85.7	82.6	67.4	91.9	97.0	89.2	84.6
2nd quarter	88.3	85.7	84.4	77.4	74.2	86.8	85.9	70.1	92.8	99.1	89.6	85.9
3rd quarter	89.4	87.1	86.0	80.4	78.0	87.2	87.9	72.7	92.8	98.5	90.0	87.1
4th quarter	90.0	88.0	87.0	81.1	78.7	88.1	87.9	73.9	92.8	97.7	90.3	87.9
1998												
1st quarter	91.0	89.0	88.1	83.5	81.3	89.9	88.2	76.6	92.3	95.4	90.7	89.3
2nd quarter	91.6	90.4	89.5	86.0	83.8	92.4	87.3	78.7	94.2	97.8	92.3	90.3
3rd quarter	92.7	91.5	90.7	87.3	84.6	94.9	86.9	79.7	95.0	96.9	94.1	91.5
4th quarter	94.1	92.7	92.2	89.8	87.2	97.2	90.2	82.1	95.9	97.8	94.9	92.8
1999												
1st quarter	94.9	93.6	93.2	91.2	88.8	98.0	89.4	84.2	96.6	97.2	96.2	94.0
2nd quarter	95.7	95.1	94.7	93.4	91.5	98.9	90.4	87.2	97.1	97.7	96.9	95.0
3rd quarter	96.8	96.1	95.8	95.2	93.7	99.5	92.8	90.2	98.3	99.6	97.7	96.3
4th quarter	98.5	97.3	97.0	95.7	93.9	100.7	95.2	92.0	99.9	101.9	98.9	97.9
2000												
1st quarter	98.8	98.8	98.9	98.3	97.1	101.7	96.8	95.6	99.2	98.2	99.7	98.5
2nd quarter	100.3	99.5	99.4	100.6	100.5	100.8	99.6	99.4	100.5	102.1	99.7	100.3
3rd quarter	100.2	100.4	100.5	100.4	101.1	98.7	102.2	102.7	100.0	100.0	100.0	100.4
4th quarter	100.7	101.3	101.2	100.6	101.3	98.8	101.5	102.3	100.3	99.7	100.6	100.9
2001												
1st quarter	100.6	101.7	101.7	100.0	100.2	99.3	100.1	101.3	101.6	101.7	101.6	100.8
2nd quarter	100.9	101.9	102.3	97.7	96.6	100.7	96.7	98.0	103.6	103.9	103.4	100.9
3rd quarter	100.6	102.4	102.8	96.6	94.9	101.2	92.0	95.3	103.2	103.9	102.8	100.7
4th quarter	100.9	104.1	104.7	93.9	91.6	100.2	89.4	94.5	105.3	106.1	104.9	101.3
2002												
1st quarter	101.8	104.6	105.2	92.9	89.3	102.4	90.4	97.3	106.5	108.2	105.6	102.4
2nd quarter	102.4	105.3	105.9	92.1	87.0	105.2	92.8	100.0	107.7	111.5	105.7	103.1
3rd quarter	103.1	106.1	106.8	92.1	86.8	106.0	93.5	101.3	108.2	112.3	106.2	103.8
4th quarter	103.2	106.8	107.3	91.9	86.1	107.1	92.5	103.7	109.3	114.8	106.5	104.4
2003												
1st quarter	103.7	107.5	107.9	92.5	86.1	109.0	92.2	103.2	109.3	114.9	106.6	104.9
2nd quarter	104.8	108.5	109.3	94.9	88.5	111.4	91.8	103.8	111.3	120.8	106.4	106.0
3rd quarter	106.7	109.8	110.6	98.9	91.8	117.2	94.3	104.5	111.3	119.8	107.0	107.7
4th quarter	107.8	110.8	111.4	101.4	94.2	119.9	98.2	108.7	111.7	121.2	107.0	108.9

Table 19-5. Chain-Type Price Indexes for Gross Domestic Product and Domestic Purchases

(Index numbers, 2000 = 100.)

NIPA Tables 1.1.4, 1.6.4, 2.3.4

Year and quarter	Gross domestic product											Gross domestic purchases
	Gross domestic product, total	Personal consumption expenditures		Private fixed investment			Exports and imports of goods and services		Government consumption expenditures and gross investment			
		Total	Excluding food and energy	Total	Nonresidential	Residential	Exports	Imports	Total	Federal	State and local	
1947												
1st quarter	15.1	15.4	...	18.7	22.2	11.9	23.4	16.3	10.8	12.6	8.8	14.8
2nd quarter	15.3	15.5	...	19.4	22.9	12.6	25.1	17.5	10.9	12.5	9.0	15.0
3rd quarter	15.6	15.8	...	19.9	23.6	12.9	26.3	18.4	10.7	12.1	9.2	15.2
4th quarter	15.9	16.2	...	20.3	24.0	13.2	27.0	19.0	10.8	12.1	9.5	15.5
1948												
1st quarter	16.1	16.4	...	20.6	24.1	13.4	27.2	19.5	11.0	12.1	9.8	15.7
2nd quarter	16.3	16.5	...	21.0	24.8	13.6	27.0	19.5	11.1	12.1	10.0	15.9
3rd quarter	16.6	16.8	...	21.7	25.7	13.9	26.7	19.3	11.3	12.3	10.4	16.2
4th quarter	16.6	16.7	...	21.9	26.1	13.9	26.3	19.0	11.4	12.3	10.5	16.2
1949												
1st quarter	16.5	16.6	...	21.9	25.9	14.1	25.8	18.6	11.6	12.8	10.4	16.2
2nd quarter	16.4	16.5	...	21.8	25.8	14.0	25.3	18.4	11.6	12.8	10.3	16.1
3rd quarter	16.3	16.4	...	21.6	25.7	13.7	24.9	18.3	11.4	12.5	10.2	16.0
4th quarter	16.3	16.4	...	21.5	25.6	13.7	24.7	18.4	11.5	12.8	10.2	16.0
1950												
1st quarter	16.2	16.4	...	21.5	25.6	13.7	24.3	18.7	11.5	12.8	10.1	15.9
2nd quarter	16.3	16.5	...	21.9	25.8	14.1	24.3	19.1	11.4	12.6	10.2	16.0
3rd quarter	16.6	16.8	...	22.5	26.4	14.6	24.5	19.8	11.6	12.6	10.5	16.4
4th quarter	16.9	17.1	...	22.9	27.3	14.6	25.0	20.7	11.7	12.6	10.8	16.6
1951												
1st quarter	17.5	17.6	...	23.7	28.2	15.0	26.5	22.4	12.3	13.4	11.1	17.2
2nd quarter	17.6	17.8	...	24.0	28.7	15.2	27.4	23.6	12.2	13.1	11.3	17.3
3rd quarter	17.6	17.8	...	24.2	29.0	15.3	28.3	24.3	12.3	13.1	11.6	17.4
4th quarter	17.8	18.0	...	24.5	29.3	15.4	28.7	24.4	12.4	13.3	11.7	17.6
1952												
1st quarter	17.9	18.1	...	24.6	29.4	15.5	28.0	23.4	12.3	13.1	11.7	17.6
2nd quarter	17.9	18.1	...	24.7	29.5	15.6	27.9	23.0	12.5	13.3	11.8	17.7
3rd quarter	18.1	18.2	...	24.7	29.4	15.8	27.8	22.6	12.6	13.4	12.1	17.8
4th quarter	18.1	18.3	...	24.7	29.4	15.7	27.8	22.2	12.8	13.6	12.1	17.9
1953												
1st quarter	18.2	18.3	...	24.7	29.4	15.7	27.9	22.0	12.7	13.4	12.2	17.9
2nd quarter	18.2	18.4	...	24.8	29.7	15.7	27.9	21.8	12.7	13.5	12.2	17.9
3rd quarter	18.3	18.5	...	25.0	29.9	15.9	27.8	21.7	12.6	13.4	12.2	18.0
4th quarter	18.3	18.5	...	25.0	29.9	15.8	27.7	21.7	12.7	13.5	12.1	18.0
1954												
1st quarter	18.4	18.6	...	25.0	30.0	15.7	27.5	22.0	12.8	13.6	12.1	18.1
2nd quarter	18.4	18.6	...	25.1	30.1	15.8	27.4	22.1	12.9	13.6	12.4	18.2
3rd quarter	18.4	18.6	...	25.1	29.9	15.9	27.4	22.2	13.0	13.8	12.4	18.2
4th quarter	18.5	18.5	...	25.1	30.0	15.9	27.4	22.2	13.1	13.9	12.5	18.2
1955												
1st quarter	18.5	18.6	...	25.1	29.9	16.0	27.5	21.9	13.2	14.1	12.4	18.2
2nd quarter	18.6	18.6	...	25.3	30.0	16.1	27.6	22.0	13.4	14.5	12.5	18.3
3rd quarter	18.8	18.7	...	25.6	30.5	16.3	27.7	22.0	13.6	14.6	12.7	18.5
4th quarter	18.9	18.8	...	26.0	31.2	16.3	27.9	22.1	13.8	14.8	12.8	18.6
1956												
1st quarter	19.1	18.8	...	26.5	32.1	16.4	28.1	22.1	14.0	15.0	13.1	18.8
2nd quarter	19.3	19.0	...	26.8	32.3	16.6	28.4	22.3	14.2	15.2	13.3	18.9
3rd quarter	19.5	19.2	...	27.2	33.2	16.7	28.7	22.4	14.4	15.3	13.5	19.2
4th quarter	19.6	19.3	...	27.4	33.6	16.6	29.1	22.7	14.4	15.4	13.7	19.3
1957												
1st quarter	19.8	19.4	...	27.7	34.2	16.6	29.5	22.7	14.7	15.7	13.8	19.5
2nd quarter	20.0	19.6	...	27.8	34.3	16.6	29.7	22.8	14.9	15.8	14.0	19.6
3rd quarter	20.1	19.7	...	28.0	34.6	16.7	29.8	22.6	15.0	16.0	14.1	19.8
4th quarter	20.2	19.8	...	28.1	34.9	16.6	29.8	22.4	15.0	16.1	14.1	19.9
1958												
1st quarter	20.4	20.1	...	27.9	34.5	16.6	29.5	21.9	15.1	16.3	14.0	20.0
2nd quarter	20.5	20.1	...	28.0	34.7	16.6	29.3	21.7	15.3	16.5	14.1	20.1
3rd quarter	20.6	20.1	...	28.0	34.7	16.6	29.3	21.6	15.4	16.7	14.2	20.2
4th quarter	20.6	20.1	...	28.1	34.8	16.6	29.4	21.6	15.5	16.8	14.3	20.2
1959												
1st quarter	20.7	20.3	20.9	28.1	34.9	16.6	29.2	21.8	15.5	16.6	14.5	20.3
2nd quarter	20.7	20.4	21.0	28.2	35.1	16.6	29.2	21.8	15.4	16.5	14.5	20.3
3rd quarter	20.8	20.5	21.1	28.3	35.2	16.6	29.5	21.9	15.3	16.3	14.5	20.4
4th quarter	20.9	20.6	21.2	28.4	35.3	16.6	29.8	22.1	15.4	16.4	14.5	20.5
1960												
1st quarter	20.9	20.6	21.3	28.4	35.3	16.7	29.8	22.1	15.4	16.4	14.6	20.5
2nd quarter	21.0	20.7	21.3	28.5	35.3	16.8	29.8	22.1	15.5	16.4	14.7	20.6
3rd quarter	21.1	20.8	21.4	28.4	35.3	16.8	29.9	22.2	15.7	16.7	14.8	20.7
4th quarter	21.2	20.9	21.5	28.4	35.2	16.8	29.8	22.1	15.8	16.9	14.8	20.8

... = Not available.

Table 19-5. Chain-Type Price Indexes for Gross Domestic Product and Domestic Purchases—*Continued*

(Index numbers, 2000 = 100.)

NIPA Tables 1.1.4, 1.6.4, 2.3.4

Year and quarter	Gross domestic product, total	Gross domestic product										Gross domestic purchases
		Personal consumption expenditures		Private fixed investment			Exports and imports of goods and services		Government consumption expenditures and gross investment			
		Total	Excluding food and energy	Total	Nonresidential	Residential	Exports	Imports	Total	Federal	State and local	
1961												
1st quarter	21.2	20.9	21.5	28.3	35.1	16.7	30.0	22.2	15.8	16.8	14.9	20.8
2nd quarter	21.2	20.9	21.6	28.3	35.1	16.8	30.4	22.1	15.9	16.9	15.0	20.8
3rd quarter	21.3	21.0	21.7	28.3	35.0	16.8	30.3	22.1	15.9	16.8	15.1	20.9
4th quarter	21.4	21.0	21.7	28.3	35.1	16.8	30.5	22.1	16.0	16.9	15.3	20.9
1962												
1st quarter	21.5	21.1	21.8	28.3	35.1	16.8	30.6	21.8	16.2	17.1	15.5	21.0
2nd quarter	21.5	21.2	21.9	28.4	35.1	16.8	30.3	21.9	16.3	17.1	15.5	21.1
3rd quarter	21.6	21.3	22.0	28.4	35.1	16.8	30.3	21.8	16.3	17.2	15.6	21.2
4th quarter	21.7	21.3	22.0	28.3	35.1	16.8	30.3	21.9	16.5	17.4	15.7	21.2
1963												
1st quarter	21.7	21.4	22.1	28.3	35.1	16.8	30.4	22.1	16.6	17.5	15.8	21.3
2nd quarter	21.8	21.4	22.1	28.3	35.1	16.7	30.3	22.2	16.6	17.5	15.9	21.3
3rd quarter	21.8	21.5	22.2	28.2	35.1	16.5	30.3	22.3	16.6	17.5	15.9	21.4
4th quarter	21.9	21.6	22.3	28.3	35.1	16.6	30.3	22.5	16.9	17.9	16.0	21.5
1964												
1st quarter	22.0	21.7	22.4	28.2	35.1	16.5	30.4	22.7	17.0	18.0	16.1	21.6
2nd quarter	22.1	21.7	22.5	28.4	35.3	16.7	30.4	22.8	17.1	18.1	16.2	21.7
3rd quarter	22.2	21.8	22.5	28.4	35.3	16.8	30.6	22.7	17.2	18.3	16.3	21.8
4th quarter	22.3	21.9	22.6	28.8	35.5	17.2	30.9	22.8	17.3	18.3	16.3	21.9
1965												
1st quarter	22.4	22.0	22.7	28.8	35.5	17.1	31.6	23.0	17.4	18.4	16.5	21.9
2nd quarter	22.5	22.1	22.7	28.8	35.6	17.2	31.5	22.9	17.5	18.5	16.6	22.0
3rd quarter	22.6	22.2	22.8	28.9	35.7	17.1	31.5	23.1	17.6	18.7	16.7	22.1
4th quarter	22.7	22.2	22.9	29.2	35.9	17.6	31.4	23.3	17.9	19.1	16.9	22.3
1966												
1st quarter	22.9	22.4	23.0	29.1	35.8	17.4	32.0	23.4	18.0	19.1	17.1	22.4
2nd quarter	23.1	22.6	23.1	29.6	36.2	18.0	32.2	23.7	18.2	19.1	17.4	22.6
3rd quarter	23.3	22.8	23.3	29.6	36.3	17.9	32.6	23.6	18.5	19.6	17.6	22.8
4th quarter	23.5	22.9	23.5	29.9	36.6	18.3	33.2	23.7	18.6	19.6	17.9	23.0
1967												
1st quarter	23.6	23.0	23.6	30.1	36.8	18.3	33.7	23.7	18.8	19.5	18.2	23.1
2nd quarter	23.8	23.1	23.8	30.2	37.0	18.4	33.7	23.7	19.0	19.8	18.4	23.3
3rd quarter	24.0	23.3	24.0	30.4	37.2	18.5	33.7	23.7	19.2	20.0	18.6	23.5
4th quarter	24.2	23.5	24.2	30.8	37.6	18.9	33.8	23.7	19.5	20.4	18.8	23.7
1968												
1st quarter	24.5	23.8	24.5	31.1	37.8	19.2	34.1	23.8	19.7	20.5	19.1	24.0
2nd quarter	24.8	24.0	24.8	31.4	38.2	19.4	34.8	24.0	20.0	20.8	19.4	24.2
3rd quarter	25.0	24.3	25.1	31.6	38.5	19.4	34.4	24.1	20.2	21.2	19.5	24.5
4th quarter	25.4	24.5	25.4	32.3	39.1	20.1	34.6	24.2	20.6	21.5	19.9	24.8
1969												
1st quarter	25.6	24.8	25.6	32.6	39.4	20.5	35.1	24.3	20.7	21.5	20.2	25.1
2nd quarter	26.0	25.1	25.9	33.0	39.8	20.8	35.2	24.5	21.1	21.8	20.6	25.4
3rd quarter	26.3	25.4	26.2	33.3	40.2	20.9	35.7	24.6	21.6	22.5	21.0	25.8
4th quarter	26.7	25.7	26.5	33.7	40.7	21.2	36.5	25.3	21.9	22.7	21.4	26.1
1970												
1st quarter	27.1	26.0	26.8	33.9	41.1	21.2	36.5	25.5	22.5	23.5	21.8	26.5
2nd quarter	27.4	26.3	27.1	34.7	41.8	22.0	37.2	25.8	22.9	23.7	22.3	26.8
3rd quarter	27.7	26.6	27.4	34.6	42.1	21.4	37.1	26.5	23.3	24.1	22.7	27.1
4th quarter	28.0	26.9	27.8	35.0	42.6	21.6	37.2	26.7	23.6	24.4	23.1	27.4
1971												
1st quarter	28.4	27.2	28.1	35.6	43.2	22.1	38.3	27.4	24.3	25.2	23.6	27.9
2nd quarter	28.8	27.5	28.4	36.1	43.8	22.6	38.4	27.5	24.7	25.7	24.0	28.2
3rd quarter	29.1	27.7	28.7	36.6	44.1	23.0	38.2	27.8	25.1	26.1	24.3	28.5
4th quarter	29.3	27.9	28.9	36.9	44.4	23.4	38.5	28.2	25.4	26.7	24.5	28.8
1972												
1st quarter	29.8	28.2	29.2	37.4	44.9	23.7	39.6	28.7	26.3	28.1	25.0	29.2
2nd quarter	30.0	28.4	29.4	37.6	45.2	23.8	39.9	29.5	26.6	28.3	25.3	29.4
3rd quarter	30.3	28.6	29.6	38.0	45.5	24.2	40.1	29.9	26.9	28.5	25.7	29.7
4th quarter	30.6	28.9	29.8	38.5	45.8	24.9	41.0	30.6	27.4	29.2	26.1	30.1
1973												
1st quarter	31.0	29.2	30.0	38.9	46.2	25.3	42.1	31.5	28.0	29.7	26.7	30.5
2nd quarter	31.5	29.8	30.4	39.6	46.8	25.9	44.0	34.0	28.5	30.1	27.3	31.1
3rd quarter	32.1	30.3	30.7	40.4	47.5	26.8	46.6	35.6	29.0	30.7	27.7	31.6
4th quarter	32.7	31.0	31.1	40.9	48.0	27.2	49.0	38.2	29.5	31.3	28.2	32.2
1974												
1st quarter	33.4	31.9	31.6	41.7	48.8	27.9	52.4	44.3	30.2	31.8	29.0	33.1
2nd quarter	34.1	32.8	32.4	42.9	50.4	28.5	54.2	49.4	31.1	32.5	30.0	34.0
3rd quarter	35.2	33.6	33.3	44.6	52.5	29.4	57.2	52.0	32.1	33.5	31.0	35.0
4th quarter	36.2	34.5	34.1	46.4	54.9	30.2	60.1	53.7	33.2	34.9	31.9	36.1

Table 19-5. Chain-Type Price Indexes for Gross Domestic Product and Domestic Purchases—Continued

(Index numbers, 2000 = 100.)

NIPA Tables 1.1.4, 1.6.4, 2.3.4

Year and quarter	Gross domestic product, total	Gross domestic product										Gross domestic purchases
		Personal consumption expenditures		Private fixed investment			Exports and imports of goods and services		Government consumption expenditures and gross investment			
		Total	Excluding food and energy	Total	Nonresidential	Residential	Exports	Imports	Total	Federal	State and local	
1975												
1st quarter	37.1	35.1	34.7	48.1	57.1	31.0	61.8	54.5	33.9	35.6	32.6	36.8
2nd quarter	37.6	35.6	35.3	49.2	58.6	31.5	61.6	54.6	34.5	36.1	33.3	37.4
3rd quarter	38.3	36.2	35.8	49.8	59.3	31.8	61.5	53.4	35.1	36.8	33.8	38.1
4th quarter	39.0	36.9	36.4	50.5	60.1	32.4	61.8	53.5	35.8	37.9	34.3	38.7
1976												
1st quarter	39.4	37.3	36.9	51.0	60.8	32.6	62.7	54.4	36.3	38.3	34.9	39.2
2nd quarter	39.9	37.6	37.4	51.9	61.6	33.6	63.4	55.2	36.8	38.7	35.4	39.6
3rd quarter	40.4	38.2	38.0	52.6	62.4	34.1	63.8	56.2	37.3	39.3	35.8	40.2
4th quarter	41.1	38.8	38.6	53.5	63.3	34.7	64.9	56.8	38.0	40.5	36.2	40.8
1977												
1st quarter	41.8	39.5	39.2	54.6	64.6	35.5	65.7	58.7	38.8	41.4	36.9	41.6
2nd quarter	42.5	40.1	39.8	55.7	65.6	36.5	66.6	60.4	39.4	41.9	37.6	42.3
3rd quarter	43.0	40.7	40.4	56.9	66.8	37.7	66.3	61.2	39.8	42.1	38.2	43.0
4th quarter	43.8	41.3	41.0	58.1	67.9	38.8	66.6	61.8	40.8	43.4	38.8	43.7
1978												
1st quarter	44.5	42.0	41.7	59.3	68.9	40.0	67.9	62.8	41.3	43.9	39.4	44.4
2nd quarter	45.4	42.9	42.4	60.5	70.1	41.2	69.6	64.4	41.9	44.3	40.1	45.3
3rd quarter	46.1	43.6	43.1	61.7	71.2	42.2	70.8	65.4	42.5	44.9	40.7	46.0
4th quarter	47.1	44.5	43.8	62.9	72.5	43.4	73.1	66.6	43.3	46.1	41.2	46.9
1979												
1st quarter	47.9	45.3	44.4	64.2	74.0	44.2	75.2	69.1	44.1	46.7	42.2	47.8
2nd quarter	49.1	46.5	45.3	65.9	75.7	45.7	78.3	72.7	45.0	47.4	43.2	49.0
3rd quarter	50.1	47.7	46.1	67.5	77.3	47.2	80.1	78.2	46.3	48.4	44.7	50.3
4th quarter	51.1	48.8	47.1	68.9	78.7	48.3	81.6	83.4	47.6	50.4	45.6	51.5
1980												
1st quarter	52.2	50.2	48.2	70.5	80.5	49.6	84.0	90.4	48.8	51.3	46.9	52.9
2nd quarter	53.4	51.5	49.3	72.1	82.4	50.8	85.2	93.6	50.0	52.5	48.2	54.2
3rd quarter	54.6	52.7	50.4	73.7	84.1	51.9	87.6	96.2	51.2	53.3	49.5	55.4
4th quarter	56.1	54.0	51.6	75.3	85.8	53.2	90.5	97.8	53.0	56.1	50.8	56.9
1981												
1st quarter	57.6	55.3	52.7	77.3	88.3	54.4	92.8	100.4	54.4	57.0	52.4	58.4
2nd quarter	58.6	56.3	53.7	79.1	90.5	55.2	93.2	101.0	55.3	57.9	53.4	59.4
3rd quarter	59.7	57.2	54.7	80.4	92.1	55.9	93.3	98.4	56.0	58.5	54.1	60.4
4th quarter	60.7	58.1	55.7	81.9	94.0	56.8	93.6	98.6	57.3	60.5	54.9	61.4
1982												
1st quarter	61.6	58.8	56.5	83.1	95.3	57.6	94.2	98.3	58.2	61.4	55.9	62.2
2nd quarter	62.3	59.4	57.3	84.0	96.3	58.5	94.1	96.6	59.0	62.1	56.7	62.9
3rd quarter	63.2	60.3	58.2	84.5	96.8	59.0	93.4	95.4	59.8	62.6	57.6	63.7
4th quarter	63.9	61.0	59.1	84.6	96.8	59.2	92.9	94.7	60.6	63.7	58.3	64.4
1983												
1st quarter	64.4	61.5	59.9	84.2	96.1	59.5	93.3	92.7	61.0	64.0	58.8	64.8
2nd quarter	64.9	62.1	60.3	83.9	95.5	59.7	93.6	92.7	61.6	64.4	59.4	65.2
3rd quarter	65.5	62.9	61.3	83.7	95.1	60.0	94.1	92.9	62.1	64.9	60.0	65.8
4th quarter	66.0	63.3	61.8	83.9	95.0	60.5	95.0	92.3	62.4	65.0	60.5	66.2
1984												
1st quarter	66.8	64.0	62.4	83.9	94.9	60.9	95.2	92.6	64.1	67.7	61.5	67.1
2nd quarter	67.4	64.6	63.1	84.3	95.2	61.3	95.8	93.1	64.8	68.3	62.1	67.6
3rd quarter	68.0	65.1	63.7	84.6	95.3	61.9	94.8	91.4	65.3	68.8	62.6	68.1
4th quarter	68.4	65.5	64.2	84.8	95.4	62.4	93.8	90.3	65.6	69.0	63.1	68.5
1985												
1st quarter	69.2	66.2	65.0	85.1	95.6	62.7	92.8	88.1	66.5	69.9	63.9	69.1
2nd quarter	69.5	66.7	65.5	85.2	95.7	62.9	92.4	88.5	66.8	69.8	64.5	69.5
3rd quarter	69.9	67.1	66.0	85.5	96.0	63.3	91.4	88.4	67.0	69.7	65.0	69.9
4th quarter	70.3	67.7	66.6	86.1	96.4	64.0	91.3	90.2	67.6	70.4	65.6	70.5
1986												
1st quarter	70.7	68.2	67.3	86.5	96.6	64.8	90.9	90.4	67.7	70.3	65.9	70.9
2nd quarter	71.0	68.2	67.9	87.1	97.3	65.4	90.5	87.6	67.9	70.3	66.2	71.0
3rd quarter	71.5	68.7	68.6	87.9	98.0	66.3	90.2	88.2	68.3	70.4	66.8	71.5
4th quarter	72.0	69.2	69.2	88.5	98.4	67.0	91.0	89.3	68.8	70.5	67.7	72.0
1987												
1st quarter	72.5	70.0	69.8	88.8	98.4	67.7	91.4	91.6	69.5	71.0	68.5	72.7
2nd quarter	72.9	70.6	70.4	88.9	98.3	68.2	92.6	94.0	69.9	71.1	69.1	73.2
3rd quarter	73.5	71.3	71.1	89.0	98.2	68.8	93.0	95.0	70.3	71.3	69.8	73.8
4th quarter	73.9	71.9	71.8	89.8	98.9	69.4	94.5	96.4	70.5	71.4	70.0	74.3
1988												
1st quarter	74.6	72.5	72.6	90.6	99.8	70.1	95.6	97.8	71.2	72.2	70.6	75.0
2nd quarter	75.3	73.3	73.5	91.1	100.3	70.7	97.6	99.5	71.8	72.7	71.2	75.7
3rd quarter	76.2	74.2	74.3	91.6	100.7	71.1	98.8	98.5	72.1	72.8	71.8	76.4
4th quarter	76.8	74.9	75.1	92.4	101.7	71.8	98.6	99.3	72.5	73.0	72.3	77.1

Table 19-5. Chain-Type Price Indexes for Gross Domestic Product and Domestic Purchases—Continued

(Index numbers, 2000 = 100.)

NIPA Tables 1.1.4, 1.6.4, 2.3.4

Year and quarter	Gross domestic product, total	Gross domestic product										Gross domestic purchases
		Personal consumption expenditures		Private fixed investment			Exports and imports of goods and services		Government consumption expenditures and gross investment			
		Total	Excluding food and energy	Total	Nonresidential	Residential	Exports	Imports	Total	Federal	State and local	
1989												
1st quarter	77.6	75.8	75.9	92.9	102.1	72.3	99.6	100.9	73.5	74.3	73.0	77.9
2nd quarter	78.3	76.8	76.6	93.5	102.5	73.2	99.7	102.0	73.9	74.5	73.7	78.8
3rd quarter	78.9	77.3	77.2	93.9	102.9	73.4	99.1	100.2	74.4	75.0	74.1	79.2
4th quarter	79.4	77.9	77.9	94.3	103.4	73.9	98.8	100.7	74.8	74.9	74.9	79.8
1990												
1st quarter	80.4	79.1	78.8	94.9	103.9	74.5	98.9	102.2	75.9	76.0	76.1	80.9
2nd quarter	81.3	79.9	79.9	95.2	104.2	74.8	99.2	100.5	76.7	76.7	76.8	81.6
3rd quarter	82.1	81.0	80.6	95.8	104.9	75.1	100.2	103.4	77.4	77.3	77.7	82.5
4th quarter	82.7	82.0	81.3	96.4	105.7	75.3	101.6	109.2	78.6	78.6	78.8	83.5
1991												
1st quarter	83.7	82.6	82.2	97.1	106.7	75.5	102.0	105.9	79.3	79.7	79.2	84.2
2nd quarter	84.2	83.1	82.9	97.1	106.5	75.8	101.4	103.1	79.4	79.8	79.4	84.5
3rd quarter	84.8	83.7	83.6	97.0	106.2	76.3	100.8	101.8	80.0	80.4	79.9	85.1
4th quarter	85.2	84.3	84.4	96.7	105.9	76.0	101.0	102.9	80.4	81.0	80.2	85.6
1992												
1st quarter	85.8	85.0	85.2	96.5	105.7	75.8	100.9	102.4	81.0	81.9	80.6	86.1
2nd quarter	86.2	85.5	85.8	96.6	105.4	76.5	100.9	103.0	81.6	82.5	81.2	86.6
3rd quarter	86.6	86.1	86.4	96.7	105.3	77.0	101.0	104.6	82.0	83.0	81.5	87.1
4th quarter	87.0	86.7	87.0	96.9	105.2	78.0	100.8	104.2	82.2	82.9	81.9	87.5
1993												
1st quarter	87.7	87.1	87.5	97.4	105.5	78.9	100.8	102.6	83.1	83.9	82.7	88.1
2nd quarter	88.2	87.7	88.2	97.7	105.5	79.7	101.1	103.4	83.6	84.4	83.2	88.6
3rd quarter	88.6	88.0	88.6	98.0	105.5	80.4	100.9	102.5	84.0	85.2	83.4	88.9
4th quarter	89.0	88.4	89.0	98.1	105.5	80.8	100.8	102.2	84.5	85.6	83.8	89.3
1994												
1st quarter	89.6	88.8	89.5	98.6	105.8	81.7	101.3	101.7	85.2	86.2	84.8	89.8
2nd quarter	90.0	89.3	90.1	99.0	106.1	82.2	101.6	103.0	85.8	87.1	85.1	90.3
3rd quarter	90.5	90.1	90.8	99.3	106.2	83.0	102.3	104.7	86.2	87.1	85.7	90.9
4th quarter	91.0	90.5	91.2	99.6	106.0	84.1	102.9	105.2	86.8	87.8	86.3	91.3
1995												
1st quarter	91.6	90.9	91.7	100.0	106.1	85.2	104.0	105.6	87.7	88.8	87.2	91.9
2nd quarter	91.9	91.4	92.2	100.3	106.4	85.6	104.8	107.5	88.1	89.0	87.7	92.3
3rd quarter	92.3	91.8	92.6	100.4	106.4	85.9	104.6	106.7	88.4	89.3	88.0	92.7
4th quarter	92.7	92.2	93.1	100.4	106.2	86.4	104.1	105.8	89.2	90.9	88.3	93.1
1996												
1st quarter	93.3	92.8	93.5	100.1	105.6	86.7	103.9	105.4	90.3	92.2	89.3	93.6
2nd quarter	93.6	93.4	93.9	99.8	104.9	87.1	103.5	105.0	90.0	91.5	89.3	93.9
3rd quarter	94.1	93.7	94.3	100.1	104.9	88.1	102.8	103.8	90.5	91.8	89.9	94.3
4th quarter	94.5	94.4	94.8	100.1	104.7	88.5	101.8	104.0	91.1	92.4	90.4	94.8
1997												
1st quarter	95.0	94.8	95.1	99.9	104.2	89.0	101.5	102.8	91.8	93.3	91.1	95.2
2nd quarter	95.3	95.0	95.6	99.8	103.9	89.4	101.5	100.8	91.9	93.4	91.1	95.3
3rd quarter	95.5	95.2	95.8	99.8	103.6	90.2	101.2	100.2	92.1	93.5	91.4	95.5
4th quarter	95.9	95.5	96.1	99.6	103.1	90.8	100.8	99.5	92.7	94.0	92.1	95.8
1998												
1st quarter	96.1	95.6	96.4	99.1	102.2	91.1	99.8	96.7	93.0	94.3	92.3	95.8
2nd quarter	96.3	95.8	96.7	98.8	101.6	91.7	99.2	95.7	93.2	94.4	92.6	95.9
3rd quarter	96.6	96.1	97.0	98.8	101.1	92.6	98.5	94.5	93.6	94.6	93.2	96.1
4th quarter	96.9	96.4	97.4	98.7	100.7	93.5	98.2	94.5	94.1	94.8	93.7	96.4
1999												
1st quarter	97.3	96.7	97.7	98.9	100.6	94.4	98.0	94.0	94.8	96.1	94.2	96.8
2nd quarter	97.7	97.3	98.2	98.9	100.2	95.4	98.1	95.3	95.6	96.6	95.2	97.3
3rd quarter	98.0	97.9	98.5	98.8	99.7	96.3	98.3	96.6	96.5	97.1	96.1	97.8
4th quarter	98.5	98.4	99.0	98.9	99.6	97.0	98.8	97.9	97.4	97.8	97.2	98.4
2000												
1st quarter	99.3	99.3	99.6	99.5	99.8	98.7	99.5	99.3	99.0	99.5	98.7	99.3
2nd quarter	99.8	99.8	99.9	99.8	99.8	99.6	100.0	99.5	99.4	99.2	99.5	99.7
3rd quarter	100.2	100.2	100.1	100.3	100.2	100.4	100.2	100.5	100.5	100.4	100.5	100.3
4th quarter	100.7	100.7	100.5	100.5	100.2	101.3	100.3	100.7	101.1	100.8	101.3	100.7
2001												
1st quarter	101.5	101.5	101.2	100.4	99.6	102.6	100.3	99.9	101.9	101.3	102.2	101.4
2nd quarter	102.3	102.1	101.7	100.9	99.7	103.9	100.0	98.4	102.4	101.6	102.8	102.0
3rd quarter	102.7	102.3	102.1	101.4	99.8	105.6	99.5	97.1	102.8	102.1	103.1	102.2
4th quarter	103.1	102.4	102.7	101.4	99.6	106.4	98.6	94.6	103.1	102.6	103.3	102.4
2002												
1st quarter	103.5	102.7	103.0	101.1	99.2	106.2	98.3	94.1	104.1	104.4	104.0	102.7
2nd quarter	103.9	103.4	103.5	101.1	99.0	106.7	99.1	96.5	104.9	104.8	105.0	103.3
3rd quarter	104.3	103.9	104.0	101.0	98.6	107.1	99.8	97.3	105.7	105.3	105.8	103.7
4th quarter	104.8	104.3	104.3	101.7	98.8	109.0	99.9	97.4	106.5	106.6	106.5	104.2
2003												
1st quarter	105.5	105.1	104.6	102.2	98.7	110.8	100.9	100.1	108.4	108.8	108.2	105.2
2nd quarter	105.8	105.3	104.9	102.1	98.4	111.3	101.2	99.0	108.3	108.9	108.0	105.3
3rd quarter	106.2	105.7	105.2	102.4	98.4	112.1	101.4	99.6	108.9	109.2	108.7	105.7
4th quarter	106.6	106.0	105.5	103.1	98.7	113.7	102.1	99.8	109.2	109.4	109.0	106.1

Table 19-6. Personal Income and Its Disposition

(Billions of current dollars, except as noted; quarterly data are at seasonally adjusted annual rates.)

NIPA Table 2.1

Year and quarter	Personal income							Less: Personal current taxes	Equals: Disposable personal income	Less: Personal outlays	Equals: Personal saving		Disposable personal income, billions of chained (2000) dollars
	Total	Compensation of employees, received	Proprietors' income with IVA and CCAdj	Rental income of persons with CCAdj	Personal income receipts on assets	Personal current transfer receipts	Less: Contributions for government social insurance				Billions of dollars	Percent of disposable personal income	
1947													
1st quarter	187.6	127.2	36.6	7.0	13.4	9.7	6.3	19.2	168.4	158.1	10.3	6.1	1 096.0
2nd quarter	185.7	128.7	32.4	7.1	13.8	9.6	6.0	19.5	166.2	161.9	4.3	2.6	1 072.8
3rd quarter	193.7	130.0	33.9	7.3	14.2	13.5	5.2	19.7	174.0	165.6	8.4	4.8	1 102.8
4th quarter	197.0	134.3	35.3	7.5	14.2	10.5	4.8	20.8	176.2	169.7	6.5	3.7	1 089.7
1948													
1st quarter	202.3	137.8	36.1	7.7	14.9	10.7	4.8	21.2	181.1	172.7	8.4	4.6	1 107.3
2nd quarter	208.3	139.4	40.4	7.9	14.7	10.4	4.6	18.9	189.3	176.5	12.8	6.8	1 145.3
3rd quarter	214.3	144.6	41.0	7.9	15.2	10.1	4.6	18.2	196.1	179.5	16.6	8.5	1 168.4
4th quarter	214.4	145.8	39.7	8.0	15.6	9.8	4.5	18.4	196.0	180.4	15.6	8.0	1 171.9
1949													
1st quarter	208.3	143.9	35.5	7.9	15.7	10.5	5.2	17.8	190.5	179.2	11.3	5.9	1 147.6
2nd quarter	207.0	142.2	34.9	8.0	15.9	11.0	5.1	17.0	190.0	181.0	9.0	4.7	1 151.4
3rd quarter	206.3	141.0	34.2	8.3	16.0	11.5	4.8	16.3	190.0	180.4	9.6	5.0	1 158.1
4th quarter	207.0	140.5	34.2	8.5	16.5	11.8	4.5	15.8	191.2	183.0	8.2	4.3	1 165.7
1950													
1st quarter	221.6	144.6	35.7	8.8	17.7	20.2	5.3	16.6	205.0	185.7	19.3	9.4	1 252.8
2nd quarter	222.4	150.6	36.3	9.0	18.0	13.8	5.3	17.6	204.8	189.7	15.1	7.4	1 245.4
3rd quarter	231.3	159.0	38.8	9.2	19.0	10.8	5.5	18.9	212.4	203.6	8.8	4.1	1 264.8
4th quarter	240.7	166.8	39.5	9.5	19.6	11.1	5.8	22.5	218.2	201.1	17.1	7.8	1 277.4
1951													
1st quarter	249.6	174.8	42.1	9.7	18.6	11.1	6.6	24.4	225.2	212.4	12.8	5.7	1 276.9
2nd quarter	256.9	180.7	42.5	10.0	19.1	11.4	6.7	26.4	230.6	208.1	22.5	9.8	1 297.5
3rd quarter	260.1	183.0	42.7	10.3	19.2	11.6	6.6	27.8	232.4	210.8	21.6	9.3	1 305.9
4th quarter	265.5	187.0	43.6	10.5	19.5	11.6	6.7	29.6	235.8	214.8	21.1	8.9	1 308.5
1952													
1st quarter	267.5	191.3	41.9	10.8	19.1	11.4	6.9	30.9	236.7	216.2	20.4	8.6	1 308.1
2nd quarter	271.4	192.7	43.1	11.1	19.8	11.5	6.8	31.8	239.6	220.5	19.1	8.0	1 323.9
3rd quarter	278.2	196.6	44.9	11.4	20.0	12.3	6.9	32.3	246.0	223.2	22.8	9.3	1 349.7
4th quarter	284.3	204.1	42.7	11.7	20.5	12.3	7.1	33.1	251.2	231.5	19.7	7.8	1 376.0
1953													
1st quarter	289.0	208.0	43.1	12.0	20.6	12.4	7.1	33.4	255.6	235.3	20.3	7.9	1 395.0
2nd quarter	293.0	211.4	42.4	12.3	21.7	12.3	7.1	33.4	259.6	237.3	22.2	8.6	1 414.5
3rd quarter	293.1	211.6	41.7	12.6	21.9	12.5	7.2	33.2	259.9	238.2	21.8	8.4	1 408.7
4th quarter	292.4	210.1	41.4	12.9	22.1	12.9	7.1	32.9	259.4	237.7	21.7	8.4	1 399.8
1954													
1st quarter	292.4	208.1	42.7	13.2	23.0	13.5	8.1	30.2	262.2	239.7	22.5	8.6	1 407.5
2nd quarter	291.9	207.7	42.0	13.4	22.7	14.1	8.0	30.0	262.0	242.5	19.5	7.4	1 407.4
3rd quarter	294.0	208.3	42.4	13.6	23.4	14.5	8.1	30.0	264.0	245.2	18.8	7.1	1 422.7
4th quarter	299.4	212.6	42.2	13.7	23.9	15.2	8.1	30.5	269.0	249.9	19.1	7.1	1 450.6
1955													
1st quarter	305.3	216.9	43.5	13.8	24.7	15.3	8.9	31.4	273.9	256.3	17.5	6.4	1 471.9
2nd quarter	313.2	223.1	44.5	13.8	25.2	15.6	9.0	32.4	280.7	261.6	19.1	6.8	1 506.9
3rd quarter	320.5	229.1	44.7	13.9	26.1	15.9	9.2	33.4	287.2	266.1	21.1	7.3	1 535.3
4th quarter	325.5	233.6	44.5	14.0	26.7	16.0	9.3	34.2	291.3	270.3	21.0	7.2	1 552.7
1956													
1st quarter	330.9	238.0	44.9	14.1	27.4	16.3	9.9	35.4	295.5	272.1	23.4	7.9	1 568.4
2nd quarter	336.7	242.6	45.4	14.1	27.9	16.6	10.0	36.2	300.4	274.9	25.5	8.5	1 583.9
3rd quarter	341.6	245.7	46.2	14.2	28.3	17.1	10.0	36.9	304.7	278.2	26.5	8.7	1 590.6
4th quarter	349.2	251.6	46.9	14.3	29.2	17.3	10.1	37.9	311.3	283.7	27.7	8.9	1 615.9
1957													
1st quarter	353.3	255.3	47.0	14.4	29.8	18.2	11.4	38.6	314.7	288.3	26.5	8.4	1 618.9
2nd quarter	357.8	257.0	47.8	14.5	30.5	19.4	11.4	39.0	318.9	290.6	28.2	8.9	1 629.5
3rd quarter	362.1	259.7	48.7	14.6	31.0	19.6	11.5	39.2	322.9	295.3	27.7	8.6	1 637.5
4th quarter	361.5	258.1	47.9	14.9	31.1	20.8	11.3	38.8	322.7	297.0	25.8	8.0	1 628.2
1958													
1st quarter	362.0	254.6	50.2	15.2	31.3	22.1	11.3	38.2	323.8	296.6	27.3	8.4	1 613.2
2nd quarter	364.3	254.2	50.3	15.3	31.8	23.9	11.3	37.7	326.6	299.4	27.2	8.3	1 623.7
3rd quarter	372.6	262.2	50.0	15.5	32.1	24.2	11.4	38.9	333.6	304.4	29.2	8.8	1 656.8
4th quarter	377.2	267.2	50.1	15.6	32.2	23.7	11.5	39.4	337.8	308.3	29.5	8.7	1 677.1
1959													
1st quarter	383.8	274.5	50.4	15.6	33.0	24.0	13.7	40.8	343.0	315.9	27.1	7.9	1 688.6
2nd quarter	392.4	281.6	50.7	16.0	34.0	23.9	13.9	42.0	350.5	322.1	28.4	8.1	1 721.0
3rd quarter	394.6	282.3	50.5	16.4	35.1	24.2	13.9	42.7	352.0	327.6	24.4	6.9	1 719.5
4th quarter	400.3	285.5	50.9	16.7	36.3	24.8	13.9	43.7	356.6	329.9	26.7	7.5	1 733.2
1960													
1st quarter	406.7	294.0	50.2	16.9	37.4	24.6	16.4	45.3	361.4	333.6	27.8	7.7	1 753.2
2nd quarter	411.2	296.9	50.9	17.0	37.5	25.3	16.5	46.0	365.2	339.7	25.5	7.0	1 761.8
3rd quarter	413.4	297.6	50.9	17.2	38.1	26.0	16.5	46.5	366.9	339.8	27.0	7.4	1 762.8
4th quarter	414.7	297.1	51.2	17.4	38.5	27.0	16.4	46.4	368.3	342.0	26.3	7.1	1 761.2

Table 19-6. Personal Income and Its Disposition—Continued

(Billions of current dollars, except as noted; quarterly data are at seasonally adjusted annual rates.)

NIPA Table 2.1

Year and quarter	Personal income							Less: Personal current taxes	Equals: Disposable personal income	Less: Personal outlays	Equals: Personal saving		Disposable personal income, billions of chained (2000) dollars
	Total	Compensation of employees, received	Proprietors' income with IVA and CCAdj	Rental income of persons with CCAdj	Personal income receipts on assets	Personal current transfer receipts	Less: Contributions for government social insurance				Billions of dollars	Percent of disposable personal income	
1961													
1st quarter	418.8	298.0	52.4	17.6	38.7	28.8	16.7	46.5	372.3	342.6	29.8	8.0	1 777.6
2nd quarter	424.8	302.2	52.6	17.8	39.5	29.7	16.9	46.9	377.9	347.5	30.4	8.0	1 804.6
3rd quarter	431.8	307.2	53.4	18.0	40.5	29.9	17.1	47.4	384.4	350.5	33.9	8.8	1 829.2
4th quarter	440.6	313.8	54.6	18.2	41.9	29.4	17.3	48.1	392.5	357.9	34.5	8.8	1 865.4
1962													
1st quarter	447.4	320.4	55.4	18.5	42.0	30.0	18.9	49.4	398.0	363.3	34.7	8.7	1 883.4
2nd quarter	454.8	326.4	55.2	18.7	43.6	30.0	19.1	50.9	403.8	369.1	34.7	8.6	1 904.1
3rd quarter	459.4	329.2	55.2	18.9	44.9	30.4	19.2	52.3	407.1	373.2	33.9	8.3	1 914.7
4th quarter	465.2	332.6	55.7	19.1	45.9	31.2	19.3	53.6	411.6	379.7	31.9	7.8	1 930.4
1963													
1st quarter	470.2	337.5	56.0	19.3	46.1	32.6	21.3	54.1	416.1	383.6	32.6	7.8	1 946.0
2nd quarter	475.0	342.4	55.8	19.5	47.1	31.7	21.5	54.3	420.7	387.9	32.7	7.8	1 964.3
3rd quarter	482.0	347.4	56.3	19.6	48.4	32.0	21.8	54.6	427.4	395.3	32.1	7.5	1 986.4
4th quarter	491.3	353.6	57.7	19.6	49.9	32.5	22.0	55.2	436.1	400.3	35.8	8.2	2 019.6
1964													
1st quarter	500.8	360.0	58.1	19.6	51.5	33.6	22.0	53.8	447.1	410.1	37.0	8.3	2 060.6
2nd quarter	510.0	367.4	59.0	19.6	53.1	33.2	22.3	49.7	460.3	418.4	41.9	9.1	2 116.8
3rd quarter	519.4	374.6	59.6	19.7	54.6	33.5	22.5	51.6	467.8	427.7	40.1	8.6	2 144.6
4th quarter	528.1	380.8	60.8	19.6	55.8	33.7	22.7	53.2	474.8	430.5	44.4	9.3	2 169.4
1965													
1st quarter	538.6	387.3	62.2	19.9	57.1	35.0	22.9	57.0	481.7	441.3	40.4	8.4	2 193.3
2nd quarter	547.8	394.1	63.4	20.1	58.8	34.6	23.2	58.4	489.4	448.7	40.7	8.3	2 217.4
3rd quarter	561.7	402.3	64.2	20.3	60.3	38.1	23.6	57.0	504.7	458.1	46.6	9.2	2 278.4
4th quarter	574.8	414.3	65.9	20.3	61.4	36.9	24.0	58.3	516.5	472.2	44.3	8.6	2 324.3
1966													
1st quarter	586.9	426.7	69.4	20.7	62.6	37.8	30.4	61.5	525.3	482.8	42.5	8.1	2 345.9
2nd quarter	596.5	437.8	67.4	20.6	63.6	37.9	30.8	65.6	530.9	488.3	42.6	8.0	2 351.7
3rd quarter	609.6	449.0	67.6	20.9	64.5	39.6	31.9	67.9	541.7	497.6	44.1	8.1	2 381.3
4th quarter	622.8	457.2	68.3	20.9	65.5	43.1	32.2	70.6	552.2	503.6	48.5	8.8	2 408.6
1967													
1st quarter	633.3	463.3	69.1	21.1	67.5	46.1	33.6	71.2	562.2	508.2	53.9	9.6	2 445.0
2nd quarter	640.4	469.0	68.9	21.2	68.7	47.2	34.6	70.9	569.5	517.9	51.6	9.1	2 464.5
3rd quarter	654.1	478.7	71.0	21.2	69.8	48.7	35.2	73.8	580.3	524.9	55.3	9.5	2 488.1
4th quarter	665.4	489.7	70.5	21.1	70.1	50.0	36.0	75.9	589.5	532.6	57.0	9.7	2 506.1
1968													
1st quarter	684.7	504.5	72.2	20.9	72.4	52.4	37.6	78.6	606.2	550.9	55.3	9.1	2 549.8
2nd quarter	704.2	517.6	73.6	20.9	74.7	55.9	38.4	81.7	622.5	565.1	57.4	9.2	2 592.3
3rd quarter	722.0	531.4	75.4	21.0	76.0	57.3	39.1	91.9	630.2	581.9	48.3	7.7	2 597.1
4th quarter	737.2	543.8	76.0	20.8	77.6	58.7	39.7	95.9	641.3	591.2	50.2	7.8	2 613.7
1969													
1st quarter	751.2	555.9	76.2	21.1	80.5	60.4	42.9	102.6	648.6	603.9	44.7	6.9	2 617.5
2nd quarter	769.2	569.8	77.4	21.1	83.0	61.5	43.7	105.7	663.5	616.0	47.5	7.2	2 643.5
3rd quarter	789.5	586.6	78.1	21.3	85.3	62.9	44.6	104.1	685.4	626.7	58.7	8.6	2 696.6
4th quarter	804.0	598.2	77.9	21.2	87.7	64.3	45.3	105.6	698.4	639.2	59.2	8.5	2 716.1
1970													
1st quarter	814.7	606.1	77.6	21.2	89.6	66.1	46.0	104.6	710.1	650.7	59.4	8.4	2 729.4
2nd quarter	836.1	616.3	77.1	20.9	91.9	76.1	46.3	105.5	730.5	660.9	69.6	9.5	2 777.4
3rd quarter	848.2	622.5	79.1	21.5	95.4	76.3	46.7	100.7	747.5	673.2	74.4	10.0	2 814.6
4th quarter	856.1	623.9	79.7	21.8	97.1	80.1	46.5	101.5	754.6	680.2	74.5	9.9	2 804.4
1971													
1st quarter	876.1	641.6	81.8	21.7	99.5	82.0	50.5	98.3	777.8	699.6	78.2	10.1	2 863.6
2nd quarter	898.6	653.5	83.9	22.3	100.3	89.6	51.0	100.7	797.9	714.1	83.7	10.5	2 904.6
3rd quarter	911.3	663.5	85.2	22.7	101.7	89.6	51.3	102.3	809.0	727.1	81.9	10.1	2 916.4
4th quarter	928.0	674.8	88.3	23.1	102.4	91.3	51.9	105.5	822.5	743.9	78.5	9.5	2 946.8
1972													
1st quarter	956.1	702.6	88.5	23.7	105.2	94.3	58.1	119.8	836.4	761.8	74.6	8.9	2 965.0
2nd quarter	972.3	716.2	91.8	20.7	107.6	94.9	58.8	123.4	848.9	780.9	68.0	8.0	2 991.5
3rd quarter	998.6	729.9	96.5	24.6	111.1	96.0	59.5	124.3	874.3	799.8	74.5	8.5	3 053.6
4th quarter	1 043.8	751.9	106.7	24.6	114.6	106.4	60.4	127.1	916.7	825.0	91.6	10.0	3 175.0
1973													
1st quarter	1 064.8	781.6	106.0	24.5	117.2	109.1	73.6	126.4	938.4	849.9	88.5	9.4	3 210.5
2nd quarter	1 094.6	801.1	111.1	24.5	121.1	111.5	74.7	129.2	965.4	866.0	99.4	10.3	3 240.3
3rd quarter	1 122.6	819.9	114.4	23.5	127.6	113.3	76.1	134.1	988.5	884.9	103.6	10.5	3 258.3
4th quarter	1 161.0	842.5	122.4	24.5	132.6	116.5	77.6	140.0	1 021.0	901.6	119.4	11.7	3 297.6
1974													
1st quarter	1 177.8	860.7	115.9	24.7	137.7	121.9	83.1	142.8	1 035.0	918.7	116.3	11.2	3 246.6
2nd quarter	1 203.9	881.9	108.8	24.0	144.0	129.9	84.7	148.9	1 055.0	947.8	107.2	10.2	3 219.9
3rd quarter	1 241.8	904.6	112.9	24.4	149.1	137.1	86.4	154.9	1 086.9	977.4	109.4	10.1	3 231.1
4th quarter	1 267.1	915.7	114.7	24.2	154.7	144.3	86.6	157.6	1 109.5	987.9	121.5	11.0	3 217.3

Table 19-6. Personal Income and Its Disposition—*Continued*

(Billions of current dollars, except as noted; quarterly data are at seasonally adjusted annual rates.)

NIPA Table 2.1

Year and quarter	Personal income							Less: Personal current taxes	Equals: Disposable personal income	Less: Personal outlays	Equals: Personal saving		Disposable personal income, billions of chained (2000) dollars
	Total	Compensation of employees, received	Proprietors' income with IVA and CCAdj	Rental income of persons with CCAdj	Personal income receipts on assets	Personal current transfer receipts	Less: Contributions for government social insurance				Billions of dollars	Percent of disposable personal income	
1975													
1st quarter	1 284.0	919.4	113.2	24.1	159.0	155.9	87.6	158.0	1 126.0	1 015.5	110.5	9.8	3 205.7
2nd quarter	1 314.2	931.7	115.4	23.8	159.9	171.5	88.0	121.1	1 193.2	1 044.5	148.6	12.5	3 354.6
3rd quarter	1 351.9	957.6	122.4	23.7	163.1	174.8	89.8	152.8	1 199.1	1 079.1	120.0	10.0	3 309.1
4th quarter	1 390.1	987.5	126.9	23.2	166.7	177.6	91.8	158.5	1 231.5	1 108.3	123.2	10.0	3 342.0
1976													
1st quarter	1 425.6	1 022.3	127.6	22.9	170.4	181.4	98.9	162.1	1 263.5	1 141.8	121.7	9.6	3 390.9
2nd quarter	1 453.5	1 046.0	129.9	21.9	176.3	179.7	100.4	169.0	1 284.5	1 161.6	122.9	9.6	3 417.5
3rd quarter	1 491.5	1 070.7	133.7	22.1	180.8	186.4	102.2	175.8	1 315.8	1 191.4	124.4	9.5	3 448.0
4th quarter	1 528.5	1 098.0	137.4	22.2	186.2	188.5	103.8	182.4	1 346.1	1 225.9	120.2	8.9	3 473.0
1977													
1st quarter	1 561.0	1 126.9	140.4	22.2	190.2	190.6	109.3	188.4	1 372.5	1 262.7	109.8	8.0	3 479.7
2nd quarter	1 606.6	1 164.3	141.6	20.6	201.0	191.1	112.1	195.3	1 411.3	1 291.8	119.5	8.5	3 517.4
3rd quarter	1 652.4	1 196.8	143.3	20.0	210.5	196.2	114.3	198.2	1 454.3	1 323.9	130.3	9.0	3 570.6
4th quarter	1 712.8	1 233.7	157.5	19.8	219.5	199.0	116.7	208.1	1 504.6	1 363.2	141.4	9.4	3 642.1
1978													
1st quarter	1 750.7	1 269.6	157.8	21.4	224.9	203.1	126.2	211.7	1 538.9	1 394.9	144.0	9.4	3 663.5
2nd quarter	1 811.9	1 318.3	167.3	20.9	230.6	204.9	130.1	222.8	1 589.0	1 454.2	134.8	8.5	3 706.3
3rd quarter	1 866.5	1 355.2	170.4	22.7	237.4	213.6	132.8	236.0	1 630.5	1 486.7	143.8	8.8	3 737.6
4th quarter	1 921.7	1 400.2	171.2	23.3	246.2	216.9	136.0	247.0	1 674.8	1 527.3	147.5	8.8	3 768.3
1979													
1st quarter	1 979.1	1 445.2	178.2	25.0	257.1	222.5	148.8	253.4	1 725.8	1 563.8	162.0	9.4	3 811.7
2nd quarter	2 021.9	1 478.4	178.2	22.1	267.0	227.1	150.9	261.8	1 760.2	1 605.5	154.6	8.8	3 785.2
3rd quarter	2 088.5	1 519.0	181.3	21.8	277.7	242.7	154.2	274.6	1 813.9	1 661.3	152.6	8.4	3 807.2
4th quarter	2 159.2	1 561.2	182.7	26.3	297.2	248.9	157.1	285.0	1 874.2	1 706.8	167.4	8.9	3 841.5
1980													
1st quarter	2 228.2	1 602.7	176.1	29.8	324.0	258.7	163.1	284.2	1 944.0	1 759.2	184.9	9.5	3 869.4
2nd quarter	2 246.8	1 625.1	161.0	25.4	334.6	263.9	163.2	291.6	1 955.2	1 761.2	194.0	9.9	3 800.0
3rd quarter	2 322.8	1 657.4	173.5	26.6	336.0	295.9	166.6	301.6	2 021.2	1 819.7	201.6	10.0	3 839.0
4th quarter	2 433.7	1 722.1	185.9	38.2	360.1	299.3	171.8	318.2	2 115.5	1 890.1	225.4	10.7	3 920.8
1981													
1st quarter	2 492.2	1 774.5	188.5	36.7	378.2	305.9	191.6	330.3	2 161.9	1 950.2	211.6	9.8	3 905.7
2nd quarter	2 544.9	1 808.0	179.6	36.5	405.6	309.3	194.1	342.1	2 202.8	1 984.6	218.3	9.9	3 915.0
3rd quarter	2 645.9	1 846.2	186.3	37.8	445.5	327.9	197.7	356.3	2 289.6	2 027.5	262.2	11.5	4 003.1
4th quarter	2 682.1	1 874.2	177.4	41.0	458.5	330.4	199.4	352.1	2 330.1	2 044.9	285.1	12.2	4 012.8
1982													
1st quarter	2 711.6	1 898.0	170.2	40.1	474.7	335.7	207.2	351.9	2 359.7	2 086.6	273.1	11.6	4 013.3
2nd quarter	2 758.2	1 917.2	175.1	37.6	491.7	344.9	208.4	359.1	2 399.1	2 116.4	282.7	11.8	4 041.9
3rd quarter	2 796.7	1 937.0	176.1	39.6	492.3	361.5	209.8	349.5	2 447.2	2 167.1	280.1	11.4	4 059.3
4th quarter	2 834.7	1 951.1	183.9	38.0	494.7	377.3	210.2	356.0	2 478.7	2 231.5	247.2	10.0	4 066.2
1983													
1st quarter	2 871.5	1 979.2	188.0	38.0	506.4	380.2	220.4	350.3	2 521.2	2 274.0	247.2	9.8	4 100.4
2nd quarter	2 923.3	2 018.5	189.4	38.3	514.4	386.4	223.6	359.0	2 564.3	2 341.0	223.3	8.7	4 132.7
3rd quarter	2 980.0	2 059.9	190.2	35.8	539.3	381.9	227.2	344.9	2 635.1	2 414.5	220.6	8.4	4 191.6
4th quarter	3 068.0	2 114.6	202.4	39.0	558.2	386.5	232.6	355.1	2 712.9	2 469.6	243.3	9.0	4 286.5
1984													
1st quarter	3 166.0	2 184.6	231.6	37.8	569.7	393.4	251.0	360.7	2 805.3	2 517.2	288.2	10.3	4 385.5
2nd quarter	3 255.3	2 235.2	245.9	36.3	596.0	397.8	255.8	370.0	2 885.4	2 578.9	306.5	10.6	4 467.0
3rd quarter	3 338.6	2 281.5	248.7	40.8	627.1	400.5	259.9	383.6	2 955.0	2 620.5	334.5	11.3	4 539.8
4th quarter	3 397.9	2 320.3	247.1	45.8	638.9	408.9	263.1	395.5	3 002.4	2 672.5	330.0	11.0	4 583.9
1985													
1st quarter	3 464.0	2 366.0	263.3	44.1	646.4	419.6	275.4	431.8	3 032.2	2 748.5	283.7	9.4	4 580.0
2nd quarter	3 505.6	2 403.3	261.2	43.3	654.5	422.1	278.8	388.1	3 117.5	2 798.6	318.9	10.2	4 673.4
3rd quarter	3 536.5	2 441.1	261.1	41.0	648.6	427.5	282.8	421.1	3 115.4	2 869.7	245.7	7.9	4 640.4
4th quarter	3 600.6	2 489.2	263.6	39.3	666.6	430.4	288.4	428.5	3 172.2	2 900.4	271.8	8.6	4 688.0
1986													
1st quarter	3 659.1	2 522.7	264.5	38.3	688.9	442.7	297.9	425.8	3 233.4	2 945.6	287.7	8.9	4 744.2
2nd quarter	3 698.0	2 545.3	271.3	36.2	697.5	448.5	300.7	428.9	3 269.1	2 978.6	290.5	8.9	4 793.8
3rd quarter	3 746.2	2 581.4	283.9	31.7	698.7	455.4	305.1	438.9	3 307.2	3 050.8	256.4	7.8	4 813.6
4th quarter	3 786.2	2 631.5	282.9	27.9	697.1	457.3	310.1	455.5	3 330.7	3 091.8	238.9	7.2	4 813.4
1987													
1st quarter	3 847.3	2 678.6	291.7	31.7	699.3	462.5	316.5	450.3	3 397.1	3 124.0	273.0	8.0	4 854.6
2nd quarter	3 900.6	2 721.1	298.5	29.3	704.3	467.6	320.2	511.2	3 389.4	3 191.3	198.1	5.8	4 802.3
3rd quarter	3 973.0	2 767.3	304.7	34.7	722.1	468.7	324.5	488.5	3 484.5	3 258.9	225.6	6.5	4 887.3
4th quarter	4 068.6	2 833.9	313.9	38.1	742.3	471.7	331.2	506.5	3 562.1	3 293.4	268.7	7.5	4 954.1
1988													
1st quarter	4 139.6	2 883.1	333.4	39.1	747.1	489.0	352.1	501.1	3 638.5	3 376.1	262.4	7.2	5 016.9
2nd quarter	4 208.2	2 945.5	339.5	37.2	752.5	492.6	359.1	496.9	3 711.3	3 437.6	273.7	7.4	5 061.3
3rd quarter	4 292.6	2 994.2	350.2	38.4	775.3	498.8	364.4	505.7	3 786.9	3 506.8	280.0	7.4	5 103.3
4th quarter	4 374.5	3 045.9	343.2	47.6	802.1	506.0	370.3	516.3	3 858.2	3 582.7	275.5	7.1	5 149.2

Table 19-6. Personal Income and Its Disposition—Continued

(Billions of current dollars, except as noted; quarterly data are at seasonally adjusted annual rates.)

NIPA Table 2.1

Year and quarter	Personal income							Less: Personal current taxes	Equals: Disposable personal income	Less: Personal outlays	Equals: Personal saving		Disposable personal income, billions of chained (2000) dollars
	Total	Compensation of employees, received	Proprietors' income with IVA and CCAdj	Rental income of persons with CCAdj	Personal income receipts on assets	Personal current transfer receipts	Less: Contributions for government social insurance				Billions of dollars	Percent of disposable personal income	
1989													
1st quarter	4 506.2	3 092.8	367.0	46.1	849.9	530.2	379.8	551.3	3 954.9	3 640.9	314.0	7.9	5 216.3
2nd quarter	4 558.5	3 122.1	360.1	46.5	875.1	537.6	382.8	565.1	3 993.4	3 708.1	285.3	7.1	5 199.1
3rd quarter	4 608.8	3 158.3	359.0	41.5	888.3	548.0	386.4	570.0	4 038.8	3 769.0	269.7	6.7	5 224.9
4th quarter	4 677.8	3 207.7	367.0	38.3	898.6	557.9	391.8	578.2	4 099.5	3 820.1	279.5	6.8	5 259.9
1990													
1st quarter	4 778.8	3 272.8	376.4	44.5	911.4	577.8	404.1	580.6	4 198.2	3 905.6	292.6	7.0	5 307.9
2nd quarter	4 860.8	3 330.5	379.7	47.7	922.3	588.8	408.3	592.7	4 268.1	3 960.9	307.2	7.2	5 338.7
3rd quarter	4 924.5	3 370.2	385.1	54.0	930.9	598.4	414.1	598.8	4 325.7	4 027.8	297.8	6.9	5 343.6
4th quarter	4 950.2	3 379.2	381.1	56.4	931.3	616.1	413.9	598.9	4 351.3	4 051.3	300.0	6.9	5 306.6
1991													
1st quarter	4 965.7	3 394.4	367.9	55.9	932.0	640.0	424.5	578.5	4 387.1	4 066.7	320.4	7.3	5 310.5
2nd quarter	5 025.5	3 426.9	374.2	58.3	934.1	659.8	427.7	583.7	4 441.8	4 124.1	317.7	7.2	5 347.1
3rd quarter	5 071.7	3 461.5	377.2	61.6	935.0	669.1	432.6	588.0	4 483.7	4 170.0	313.7	7.0	5 359.6
4th quarter	5 140.9	3 498.5	389.2	65.3	927.0	696.9	435.9	596.4	4 544.5	4 199.8	344.7	7.6	5 389.4
1992													
1st quarter	5 238.0	3 566.8	409.5	71.6	914.1	724.8	448.7	586.6	4 651.4	4 292.0	359.4	7.7	5 473.9
2nd quarter	5 321.0	3 617.0	425.3	79.8	909.3	743.2	453.7	604.9	4 716.1	4 342.3	373.8	7.9	5 514.6
3rd quarter	5 382.5	3 659.9	432.4	70.8	907.2	769.9	457.8	613.9	4 768.6	4 418.5	350.1	7.3	5 537.4
4th quarter	5 506.5	3 761.0	443.1	89.9	912.7	759.4	459.6	636.9	4 869.6	4 488.7	380.9	7.8	5 619.2
1993													
1st quarter	5 419.5	3 666.6	444.6	90.9	907.7	777.8	468.1	617.9	4 801.6	4 529.2	272.4	5.7	5 512.1
2nd quarter	5 542.3	3 780.5	456.3	95.3	903.8	782.3	475.9	641.2	4 901.1	4 596.9	304.3	6.2	5 590.2
3rd quarter	5 579.6	3 821.2	448.9	94.3	897.5	797.8	480.1	655.3	4 924.3	4 659.8	264.5	5.4	5 597.4
4th quarter	5 692.8	3 911.4	465.5	101.7	898.4	802.4	486.6	672.1	5 020.8	4 725.7	295.1	5.9	5 677.2
1994													
1st quarter	5 668.9	3 873.2	460.9	105.7	905.2	822.6	498.7	670.2	4 998.7	4 795.4	203.3	4.1	5 629.9
2nd quarter	5 813.7	3 973.4	475.1	120.9	931.0	819.6	506.5	695.6	5 118.1	4 859.3	258.8	5.1	5 733.1
3rd quarter	5 891.0	4 009.0	475.9	126.2	967.1	823.3	510.5	693.5	5 197.5	4 941.2	256.3	4.9	5 770.8
4th quarter	5 996.5	4 062.8	481.3	125.9	999.8	843.8	517.1	703.4	5 293.1	5 013.7	279.4	5.3	5 850.9
1995													
1st quarter	6 072.3	4 118.6	483.1	122.6	1 006.7	867.2	525.9	721.4	5 350.9	5 048.1	302.9	5.7	5 886.4
2nd quarter	6 119.2	4 153.2	484.9	122.3	1 012.2	876.8	530.1	742.9	5 376.3	5 123.3	253.0	4.7	5 881.7
3rd quarter	6 174.6	4 197.5	493.9	119.6	1 014.7	884.1	535.2	747.5	5 427.1	5 196.8	230.3	4.2	5 912.1
4th quarter	6 243.0	4 238.7	506.7	124.1	1 032.0	881.6	540.0	764.4	5 478.6	5 260.9	217.6	4.0	5 943.3
1996													
1st quarter	6 371.1	4 291.7	526.0	131.1	1 056.1	910.7	544.4	796.6	5 574.5	5 338.0	236.5	4.2	6 010.0
2nd quarter	6 490.5	4 359.0	547.9	130.7	1 073.2	931.9	552.2	833.9	5 656.6	5 433.6	223.0	3.9	6 059.8
3rd quarter	6 566.0	4 419.1	545.5	132.1	1 100.2	928.0	558.9	838.5	5 727.5	5 492.6	234.9	4.1	6 111.3
4th quarter	6 654.6	4 477.8	553.4	132.0	1 127.4	929.4	565.3	859.4	5 795.3	5 576.0	219.2	3.8	6 142.5
1997													
1st quarter	6 773.1	4 556.4	569.6	130.0	1 146.7	946.2	575.8	895.7	5 877.4	5 663.7	213.7	3.6	6 201.3
2nd quarter	6 847.0	4 617.9	566.8	129.5	1 168.7	946.4	582.2	910.4	5 936.7	5 706.0	230.6	3.9	6 251.9
3rd quarter	6 956.7	4 693.4	579.9	128.2	1 192.4	952.9	590.0	935.9	6 020.8	5 816.1	204.7	3.4	6 323.3
4th quarter	7 083.7	4 790.8	587.9	127.4	1 219.0	959.4	600.7	963.3	6 120.5	5 896.2	224.3	3.7	6 406.6
1998													
1st quarter	7 247.1	4 894.1	606.2	131.0	1 257.6	969.7	611.5	991.2	6 255.9	5 964.2	291.7	4.7	6 543.4
2nd quarter	7 376.0	4 977.6	619.2	135.7	1 287.6	975.8	619.9	1 018.3	6 357.7	6 072.3	285.4	4.5	6 638.6
3rd quarter	7 485.8	5 062.2	632.6	141.6	1 298.8	979.1	628.5	1 037.7	6 448.1	6 167.6	280.5	4.3	6 710.9
4th quarter	7 583.0	5 146.4	653.3	141.6	1 288.8	989.8	636.8	1 061.0	6 522.1	6 272.5	249.6	3.8	6 763.0
1999													
1st quarter	7 658.4	5 242.8	664.3	145.2	1 249.4	1 009.5	652.8	1 071.7	6 586.7	6 346.3	240.4	3.6	6 812.9
2nd quarter	7 728.8	5 297.3	672.0	147.6	1 255.4	1 013.3	656.8	1 090.2	6 638.6	6 489.5	149.1	2.2	6 822.1
3rd quarter	7 823.7	5 371.2	680.6	144.5	1 262.3	1 027.4	662.4	1 115.5	6 708.2	6 593.2	115.0	1.7	6 856.0
4th quarter	7 998.8	5 496.5	696.1	152.1	1 289.7	1 038.1	673.8	1 152.5	6 846.2	6 716.6	129.7	1.9	6 955.6
2000													
1st quarter	8 266.2	5 694.1	709.3	153.8	1 349.9	1 054.6	695.5	1 207.0	7 059.2	6 888.0	171.2	2.4	7 109.7
2nd quarter	8 372.3	5 727.2	726.5	148.5	1 385.6	1 080.8	696.3	1 231.1	7 141.2	6 970.0	171.3	2.4	7 157.5
3rd quarter	8 514.4	5 837.4	735.6	148.2	1 406.2	1 094.8	707.7	1 248.0	7 266.4	7 076.3	190.1	2.6	7 249.3
4th quarter	8 565.8	5 871.9	742.1	150.5	1 406.5	1 106.0	711.2	1 256.6	7 309.3	7 168.1	141.2	1.9	7 259.6
2001													
1st quarter	8 688.7	5 946.2	769.4	155.3	1 397.4	1 149.6	729.2	1 296.6	7 392.1	7 253.5	138.6	1.9	7 283.0
2nd quarter	8 719.9	5 944.6	770.6	161.7	1 388.7	1 185.7	731.5	1 312.3	7 407.6	7 318.8	88.7	1.2	7 252.1
3rd quarter	8 733.1	5 939.3	773.4	176.4	1 373.3	1 202.6	731.9	1 110.3	7 622.8	7 361.2	261.6	3.4	7 452.2
4th quarter	8 754.8	5 938.3	774.2	176.2	1 360.3	1 237.8	731.9	1 230.0	7 524.8	7 484.4	40.5	0.5	7 346.0
2002													
1st quarter	8 803.6	6 010.2	762.2	179.7	1 337.8	1 259.4	745.7	1 065.8	7 737.8	7 528.5	209.3	2.7	7 537.6
2nd quarter	8 897.1	6 068.3	769.0	184.7	1 340.2	1 284.0	749.1	1 052.1	7 845.0	7 635.0	210.0	2.7	7 588.4
3rd quarter	8 895.7	6 086.0	770.4	165.4	1 333.7	1 289.1	748.9	1 046.7	7 849.0	7 722.9	126.1	1.6	7 555.1
4th quarter	8 919.2	6 113.4	776.7	153.8	1 326.7	1 298.1	749.6	1 040.3	7 878.8	7 787.6	91.2	1.2	7 558.0
2003													
1st quarter	9 002.2	6 177.7	794.0	155.5	1 325.9	1 311.4	762.4	1 025.7	7 976.5	7 897.0	79.5	1.0	7 591.2
2nd quarter	9 105.7	6 247.0	825.7	144.1	1 324.7	1 333.1	768.9	1 030.7	8 075.0	7 982.9	92.1	1.1	7 671.1
3rd quarter	9 209.3	6 324.7	852.0	148.8	1 314.4	1 346.2	776.7	941.7	8 267.6	8 107.8	159.8	1.9	7 822.9
4th quarter	9 330.0	6 406.7	864.7	167.1	1 325.8	1 350.7	785.0	1 009.4	8 320.5	8 209.4	111.1	1.3	7 849.6

Table 19-7. Inventories to Sales Ratios
(Seasonally adjusted, ratio of inventories at end of quarter to monthly rate of sales during the quarter, annual data are for fourth quarter.)

NIPA Tables 5.7.5A, 5.7.5B, 5.7.6A, 5.7.6B

Year and quarter	Total private inventories to final sales of domestic business		Nonfarm inventories to			
			Final sales of domestic business		Final sales of goods and structures	
	Current dollars	Chained (2000) dollars	Current dollars	Chained (2000) dollars	Current dollars	Chained (2000) dollars
1947						
1st quarter	5.67	3.73	2.72	2.21	3.43	3.38
2nd quarter	5.59	3.70	2.70	2.21	3.42	3.38
3rd quarter	5.72	3.62	2.64	2.17	3.34	3.33
4th quarter	5.99	3.60	2.69	2.19	3.38	3.34
1948						
1st quarter	5.70	3.62	2.74	2.22	3.45	3.37
2nd quarter	5.67	3.67	2.75	2.24	3.49	3.42
3rd quarter	5.53	3.74	2.82	2.28	3.59	3.49
4th quarter	5.37	3.77	2.83	2.30	3.63	3.51
1949						
1st quarter	5.28	3.76	2.79	2.30	3.61	3.52
2nd quarter	5.00	3.68	2.65	2.24	3.44	3.42
3rd quarter	5.01	3.67	2.64	2.23	3.43	3.40
4th quarter	4.88	3.60	2.60	2.17	3.36	3.30
1950						
1st quarter	4.90	3.56	2.59	2.16	3.36	3.27
2nd quarter	4.89	3.49	2.57	2.14	3.33	3.24
3rd quarter	4.91	3.34	2.58	2.07	3.27	3.10
4th quarter	5.45	3.53	2.87	2.24	3.68	3.39
1951						
1st quarter	5.50	3.55	2.90	2.27	3.73	3.42
2nd quarter	5.52	3.67	3.01	2.39	3.93	3.64
3rd quarter	5.38	3.65	2.94	2.40	3.87	3.64
4th quarter	5.33	3.62	2.89	2.40	3.78	3.61
1952						
1st quarter	5.25	3.66	2.89	2.43	3.81	3.66
2nd quarter	5.08	3.62	2.79	2.38	3.72	3.60
3rd quarter	5.07	3.71	2.85	2.45	3.82	3.71
4th quarter	4.70	3.61	2.76	2.39	3.69	3.59
1953						
1st quarter	4.54	3.56	2.72	2.36	3.65	3.54
2nd quarter	4.47	3.57	2.75	2.38	3.71	3.57
3rd quarter	4.48	3.59	2.79	2.39	3.76	3.59
4th quarter	4.50	3.61	2.76	2.39	3.75	3.59
1954						
1st quarter	4.53	3.59	2.75	2.37	3.72	3.57
2nd quarter	4.47	3.54	2.72	2.32	3.65	3.50
3rd quarter	4.42	3.47	2.69	2.27	3.61	3.43
4th quarter	4.33	3.40	2.64	2.23	3.54	3.35
1955						
1st quarter	4.27	3.34	2.62	2.20	3.51	3.31
2nd quarter	4.17	3.33	2.63	2.21	3.48	3.27
3rd quarter	4.08	3.30	2.64	2.21	3.52	3.29
4th quarter	4.06	3.33	2.71	2.24	3.61	3.36
1956						
1st quarter	4.14	3.36	2.77	2.28	3.69	3.43
2nd quarter	4.18	3.37	2.78	2.30	3.72	3.45
3rd quarter	4.16	3.36	2.80	2.31	3.71	3.47
4th quarter	4.11	3.33	2.79	2.30	3.74	3.48
1957						
1st quarter	4.06	3.33	2.77	2.30	3.71	3.46
2nd quarter	4.09	3.36	2.78	2.33	3.74	3.51
3rd quarter	4.08	3.35	2.78	2.33	3.72	3.50
4th quarter	4.05	3.36	2.74	2.32	3.74	3.52
1958						
1st quarter	4.26	3.44	2.78	2.36	3.78	3.58
2nd quarter	4.20	3.44	2.71	2.33	3.73	3.55
3rd quarter	4.17	3.37	2.67	2.27	3.65	3.47
4th quarter	4.09	3.33	2.65	2.25	3.62	3.42
1959						
1st quarter	4.02	3.25	2.61	2.21	3.54	3.36
2nd quarter	3.98	3.24	2.63	2.23	3.59	3.40
3rd quarter	3.90	3.21	2.61	2.22	3.57	3.38
4th quarter	3.90	3.26	2.67	2.27	3.67	3.48
1960						
1st quarter	3.97	3.27	2.72	2.30	3.70	3.51
2nd quarter	3.90	3.26	2.70	2.30	3.68	3.51
3rd quarter	3.94	3.30	2.73	2.33	3.73	3.55
4th quarter	3.89	3.27	2.67	2.29	3.67	3.51

Table 19-7. Inventories to Sales Ratios—Continued

(Seasonally adjusted, ratio of inventories at end of quarter to monthly rate of sales during the quarter, annual data are for fourth quarter.)

NIPA Tables 5.7.5A, 5.7.5B, 5.7.6A, 5.7.6B

Year and quarter	Total private inventories to final sales of domestic business		Nonfarm inventories to			
			Final sales of domestic business		Final sales of goods and structures	
	Current dollars	Chained (2000) dollars	Current dollars	Chained (2000) dollars	Current dollars	Chained (2000) dollars
1961						
1st quarter	3.87	3.25	2.65	2.27	3.63	3.48
2nd quarter	3.79	3.23	2.61	2.25	3.63	3.48
3rd quarter	3.84	3.25	2.63	2.27	3.63	3.50
4th quarter	3.80	3.20	2.59	2.24	3.58	3.45
1962						
1st quarter	3.81	3.22	2.60	2.27	3.60	3.48
2nd quarter	3.76	3.19	2.57	2.26	3.58	3.48
3rd quarter	3.81	3.21	2.59	2.29	3.61	3.50
4th quarter	3.79	3.21	2.59	2.29	3.60	3.51
1963						
1st quarter	3.78	3.23	2.60	2.30	3.61	3.53
2nd quarter	3.72	3.19	2.57	2.27	3.58	3.50
3rd quarter	3.66	3.17	2.56	2.28	3.56	3.49
4th quarter	3.62	3.15	2.55	2.27	3.56	3.49
1964						
1st quarter	3.54	3.09	2.52	2.24	3.50	3.44
2nd quarter	3.49	3.07	2.52	2.24	3.50	3.45
3rd quarter	3.48	3.05	2.51	2.24	3.49	3.43
4th quarter	3.50	3.07	2.54	2.26	3.54	3.49
1965						
1st quarter	3.52	3.07	2.55	2.28	3.55	3.50
2nd quarter	3.53	3.05	2.54	2.27	3.54	3.49
3rd quarter	3.48	3.04	2.54	2.27	3.53	3.48
4th quarter	3.46	2.99	2.50	2.24	3.47	3.42
1966						
1st quarter	3.49	3.00	2.52	2.26	3.47	3.43
2nd quarter	3.53	3.06	2.56	2.33	3.58	3.56
3rd quarter	3.57	3.09	2.60	2.37	3.63	3.61
4th quarter	3.59	3.16	2.67	2.44	3.74	3.75
1967						
1st quarter	3.58	3.22	2.70	2.50	3.84	3.85
2nd quarter	3.57	3.21	2.68	2.49	3.80	3.83
3rd quarter	3.56	3.24	2.70	2.52	3.83	3.88
4th quarter	3.54	3.25	2.71	2.54	3.86	3.92
1968						
1st quarter	3.51	3.22	2.66	2.51	3.80	3.86
2nd quarter	3.50	3.24	2.65	2.52	3.79	3.90
3rd quarter	3.47	3.22	2.63	2.51	3.75	3.87
4th quarter	3.43	3.23	2.62	2.53	3.76	3.91
1969						
1st quarter	3.46	3.22	2.64	2.53	3.75	3.90
2nd quarter	3.48	3.25	2.64	2.56	3.78	3.95
3rd quarter	3.48	3.28	2.67	2.59	3.82	4.01
4th quarter	3.52	3.30	2.70	2.62	3.89	4.08
1970						
1st quarter	3.52	3.29	2.69	2.61	3.88	4.06
2nd quarter	3.52	3.31	2.70	2.62	3.89	4.10
3rd quarter	3.51	3.29	2.70	2.62	3.91	4.10
4th quarter	3.47	3.29	2.70	2.63	3.92	4.13
1971						
1st quarter	3.51	3.28	2.69	2.63	3.91	4.12
2nd quarter	3.50	3.29	2.68	2.63	3.90	4.12
3rd quarter	3.46	3.29	2.67	2.63	3.88	4.11
4th quarter	3.43	3.24	2.63	2.59	3.83	4.07
1972						
1st quarter	3.39	3.20	2.58	2.57	3.77	4.02
2nd quarter	3.41	3.18	2.57	2.55	3.74	3.98
3rd quarter	3.44	3.17	2.58	2.55	3.76	3.99
4th quarter	3.44	3.09	2.54	2.50	3.66	3.90
1973						
1st quarter	3.52	3.02	2.56	2.47	3.65	3.83
2nd quarter	3.70	3.06	2.62	2.50	3.74	3.88
3rd quarter	3.76	3.08	2.63	2.51	3.77	3.91
4th quarter	3.86	3.13	2.74	2.57	3.91	4.01
1974						
1st quarter	3.91	3.18	2.86	2.63	4.10	4.10
2nd quarter	3.92	3.22	3.00	2.67	4.33	4.18
3rd quarter	4.09	3.25	3.10	2.70	4.49	4.24
4th quarter	4.11	3.37	3.22	2.82	4.73	4.50

Table 19-7. Inventories to Sales Ratios—Continued

(Seasonally adjusted, ratio of inventories at end of quarter to monthly rate of sales during the quarter, annual data are for fourth quarter.)

NIPA Tables 5.7.5A, 5.7.5B, 5.7.6A, 5.7.6B

Year and quarter	Total private inventories to final sales of domestic business		Nonfarm inventories to			
			Final sales of domestic business		Final sales of goods and structures	
	Current dollars	Chained (2000) dollars	Current dollars	Chained (2000) dollars	Current dollars	Chained (2000) dollars
1975						
1st quarter	3.92	3.33	3.10	2.76	4.56	4.41
2nd quarter	3.88	3.26	3.00	2.70	4.44	4.32
3rd quarter	3.82	3.22	2.95	2.66	4.34	4.24
4th quarter	3.69	3.17	2.88	2.62	4.24	4.17
1976						
1st quarter	3.64	3.14	2.86	2.60	4.21	4.13
2nd quarter	3.74	3.17	2.92	2.64	4.31	4.20
3rd quarter	3.69	3.19	2.95	2.66	4.37	4.23
4th quarter	3.62	3.14	2.91	2.63	4.32	4.21
1977						
1st quarter	3.35	3.14	2.92	2.63	4.34	4.20
2nd quarter	3.38	3.11	2.87	2.61	4.26	4.14
3rd quarter	3.44	3.13	2.87	2.62	4.28	4.18
4th quarter	3.55	3.13	2.88	2.62	4.29	4.18
1978						
1st quarter	3.68	3.18	2.94	2.67	4.41	4.28
2nd quarter	3.58	3.06	2.85	2.58	4.21	4.08
3rd quarter	3.60	3.06	2.85	2.58	4.20	4.07
4th quarter	3.63	3.06	2.87	2.58	4.20	4.06
1979						
1st quarter	3.79	3.09	2.94	2.61	4.30	4.10
2nd quarter	3.82	3.13	3.00	2.64	4.42	4.18
3rd quarter	3.81	3.08	3.00	2.60	4.38	4.07
4th quarter	3.82	3.08	3.05	2.60	4.47	4.08
1980						
1st quarter	3.87	3.09	3.14	2.61	4.63	4.10
2nd quarter	3.99	3.20	3.23	2.71	4.84	4.29
3rd quarter	3.94	3.10	3.17	2.64	4.75	4.18
4th quarter	3.86	3.05	3.13	2.60	4.69	4.13
1981						
1st quarter	3.87	3.09	3.16	2.63	4.73	4.15
2nd quarter	3.85	3.10	3.14	2.63	4.74	4.18
3rd quarter	3.81	3.15	3.15	2.67	4.76	4.23
4th quarter	3.78	3.20	3.16	2.71	4.80	4.31
1982						
1st quarter	3.79	3.20	3.13	2.70	4.79	4.31
2nd quarter	3.76	3.20	3.10	2.70	4.76	4.31
3rd quarter	3.72	3.25	3.09	2.73	4.82	4.40
4th quarter	3.58	3.15	2.97	2.64	4.67	4.26
1983						
1st quarter	3.50	3.08	2.87	2.58	4.56	4.18
2nd quarter	3.44	3.02	2.83	2.54	4.49	4.11
3rd quarter	3.36	2.95	2.81	2.51	4.46	4.05
4th quarter	3.35	2.91	2.79	2.49	4.39	3.98
1984						
1st quarter	3.43	2.95	2.85	2.53	4.48	4.04
2nd quarter	3.40	2.96	2.85	2.53	4.49	4.04
3rd quarter	3.39	2.99	2.87	2.57	4.53	4.09
4th quarter	3.36	2.98	2.85	2.56	4.50	4.07
1985						
1st quarter	3.26	2.93	2.77	2.52	4.40	4.02
2nd quarter	3.21	2.93	2.75	2.51	4.38	4.02
3rd quarter	3.12	2.90	2.68	2.48	4.30	3.98
4th quarter	3.15	2.92	2.70	2.50	4.36	4.03
1986						
1st quarter	3.07	2.91	2.64	2.50	4.27	4.01
2nd quarter	3.02	2.91	2.61	2.50	4.25	4.02
3rd quarter	2.95	2.86	2.56	2.46	4.15	3.95
4th quarter	2.91	2.84	2.52	2.44	4.12	3.92
1987						
1st quarter	2.96	2.87	2.57	2.48	4.22	4.02
2nd quarter	2.95	2.83	2.56	2.46	4.20	3.97
3rd quarter	2.93	2.79	2.54	2.42	4.14	3.90
4th quarter	2.98	2.84	2.60	2.47	4.25	3.99
1988						
1st quarter	2.97	2.80	2.57	2.44	4.22	3.94
2nd quarter	2.97	2.77	2.57	2.43	4.20	3.91
3rd quarter	2.98	2.76	2.58	2.44	4.22	3.94
4th quarter	2.96	2.75	2.58	2.43	4.22	3.92

Table 19-7. Inventories to Sales Ratios—*Continued*

(Seasonally adjusted, ratio of inventories at end of quarter to monthly rate of sales during the quarter, annual data are for fourth quarter.)

NIPA Tables 5.7.5A, 5.7.5B, 5.7.6A, 5.7.6B

Year and quarter	Total private inventories to final sales of domestic business		Nonfarm inventories to			
			Final sales of domestic business		Final sales of goods and structures	
	Current dollars	Chained (2000) dollars	Current dollars	Chained (2000) dollars	Current dollars	Chained (2000) dollars
1989						
1st quarter	2.99	2.76	2.60	2.44	4.28	3.94
2nd quarter	2.96	2.77	2.59	2.45	4.25	3.94
3rd quarter	2.90	2.73	2.55	2.43	4.16	3.89
4th quarter	2.92	2.75	2.55	2.44	4.22	3.94
1990						
1st quarter	2.87	2.72	2.51	2.42	4.11	3.88
2nd quarter	2.86	2.75	2.51	2.45	4.16	3.97
3rd quarter	2.89	2.76	2.54	2.46	4.24	4.00
4th quarter	2.90	2.77	2.54	2.46	4.27	4.02
1991						
1st quarter	2.85	2.79	2.49	2.48	4.21	4.05
2nd quarter	2.77	2.76	2.43	2.45	4.12	4.02
3rd quarter	2.74	2.75	2.42	2.45	4.12	4.03
4th quarter	2.75	2.77	2.43	2.46	4.17	4.07
1992						
1st quarter	2.70	2.72	2.36	2.41	4.07	3.98
2nd quarter	2.69	2.71	2.36	2.40	4.08	3.98
3rd quarter	2.66	2.69	2.34	2.39	4.06	3.95
4th quarter	2.63	2.67	2.30	2.36	3.99	3.90
1993						
1st quarter	2.66	2.69	2.33	2.39	4.04	3.96
2nd quarter	2.64	2.68	2.32	2.39	4.02	3.94
3rd quarter	2.60	2.66	2.30	2.38	4.00	3.93
4th quarter	2.57	2.63	2.27	2.35	3.92	3.86
1994						
1st quarter	2.58	2.64	2.26	2.35	3.92	3.87
2nd quarter	2.58	2.66	2.29	2.37	3.96	3.89
3rd quarter	2.58	2.66	2.29	2.36	3.96	3.88
4th quarter	2.60	2.67	2.31	2.38	3.99	3.88
1995						
1st quarter	2.65	2.69	2.36	2.40	4.07	3.91
2nd quarter	2.66	2.69	2.38	2.41	4.13	3.95
3rd quarter	2.62	2.65	2.35	2.39	4.08	3.91
4th quarter	2.61	2.63	2.33	2.38	4.05	3.88
1996						
1st quarter	2.57	2.61	2.30	2.35	3.99	3.84
2nd quarter	2.54	2.58	2.26	2.33	3.93	3.79
3rd quarter	2.55	2.59	2.26	2.33	3.92	3.79
4th quarter	2.49	2.56	2.23	2.30	3.87	3.74
1997						
1st quarter	2.48	2.56	2.21	2.31	3.83	3.73
2nd quarter	2.47	2.59	2.21	2.33	3.84	3.78
3rd quarter	2.44	2.57	2.18	2.32	3.78	3.74
4th quarter	2.44	2.60	2.19	2.34	3.82	3.78
1998						
1st quarter	2.44	2.63	2.20	2.38	3.84	3.84
2nd quarter	2.40	2.62	2.17	2.37	3.79	3.82
3rd quarter	2.37	2.62	2.15	2.37	3.74	3.81
4th quarter	2.33	2.59	2.12	2.35	3.67	3.75
1999						
1st quarter	2.34	2.61	2.12	2.37	3.69	3.80
2nd quarter	2.32	2.59	2.11	2.35	3.67	3.77
3rd quarter	2.33	2.59	2.13	2.36	3.71	3.78
4th quarter	2.35	2.60	2.15	2.37	3.76	3.79
2000						
1st quarter	2.35	2.58	2.15	2.36	3.75	3.76
2nd quarter	2.36	2.60	2.16	2.38	3.79	3.81
3rd quarter	2.37	2.61	2.18	2.40	3.83	3.84
4th quarter	2.39	2.62	2.18	2.40	3.85	3.86
2001						
1st quarter	2.37	2.61	2.16	2.39	3.82	3.84
2nd quarter	2.33	2.61	2.12	2.39	3.76	3.84
3rd quarter	2.29	2.61	2.09	2.39	3.72	3.84
4th quarter	2.20	2.55	2.01	2.33	3.57	3.74
2002						
1st quarter	2.20	2.55	2.01	2.33	3.61	3.77
2nd quarter	2.20	2.55	2.01	2.34	3.65	3.79
3rd quarter	2.21	2.55	2.02	2.34	3.68	3.79
4th quarter	2.22	2.56	2.02	2.35	3.73	3.83
2003						
1st quarter	2.23	2.55	2.03	2.34	3.76	3.80
2nd quarter	2.17	2.51	1.98	2.30	3.66	3.72
3rd quarter	2.15	2.45	1.94	2.24	3.53	3.59
4th quarter	2.15	2.42	1.94	2.22	3.52	3.55

Table 19-8. Federal Government Current Receipts and Expenditures

(National Income and Product Accounts, calendar years, billions of dollars, quarterly data are at seasonally adjusted annual rates.)

NIPA Table 3.2

Year and quarter	Current receipts													
	Total	Tax receipts							Contributions for government social insurance	Income receipts on assets			Current transfer receipts	Current surplus of government enterprises
		Total	Personal current taxes	Taxes on production and imports		Taxes on corporate income				Total	Interest receipts	Rents and royalties		
				Total	Excise taxes	Total	Federal Reserve banks	Other						
1947														
1st quarter	43.4	36.9	18.2	7.8	...	10.9	0.1	10.9	6.2	...	...	...	0.3	...
2nd quarter	42.5	36.4	18.5	7.5	...	10.4	0.1	10.3	5.8	...	...	...	0.3	...
3rd quarter	41.6	36.3	18.7	7.4	...	10.2	0.1	10.1	5.0	...	...	...	0.3	...
4th quarter	43.8	38.9	19.8	7.9	...	11.1	0.1	11.0	4.6	...	...	...	0.3	...
1948														
1st quarter	44.0	39.1	20.1	7.5	...	11.5	0.1	11.4	4.6	...	...	...	0.3	...
2nd quarter	42.5	37.8	17.8	7.9	...	12.1	0.1	12.0	4.3	...	...	...	0.3	...
3rd quarter	41.6	36.9	17.1	7.9	...	11.9	0.2	11.7	4.4	...	...	...	0.3	...
4th quarter	41.4	36.7	17.3	7.9	...	11.5	0.2	11.3	4.3	...	...	...	0.3	...
1949														
1st quarter	39.9	34.6	16.5	7.8	...	10.4	0.2	10.2	5.0	...	...	...	0.3	...
2nd quarter	37.9	32.7	15.6	7.9	...	9.1	0.2	8.9	4.9	...	...	...	0.3	...
3rd quarter	37.4	32.5	14.9	8.1	...	9.5	0.2	9.3	4.6	...	...	...	0.3	...
4th quarter	36.2	31.5	14.5	7.7	...	9.3	0.2	9.2	4.3	...	...	...	0.3	...
1950														
1st quarter	41.4	36.1	15.2	7.9	...	13.0	0.2	12.9	5.1	...	...	...	0.2	...
2nd quarter	45.5	40.2	16.1	8.5	...	15.6	0.2	15.4	5.1	...	...	...	0.2	...
3rd quarter	51.8	46.3	17.4	9.8	...	19.1	0.2	18.9	5.3	...	...	...	0.2	...
4th quarter	56.5	50.7	21.0	8.8	...	20.9	0.2	20.7	5.6	...	...	...	0.2	...
1951														
1st quarter	64.5	57.9	22.8	9.8	...	25.3	0.2	25.0	6.4	...	...	...	0.3	...
2nd quarter	61.6	54.9	24.7	8.8	...	21.4	0.3	21.1	6.5	...	...	...	0.3	...
3rd quarter	60.9	54.3	26.1	8.8	...	19.4	0.3	19.1	6.3	...	...	...	0.3	...
4th quarter	64.6	57.9	27.9	9.3	...	20.7	0.3	20.4	6.4	...	...	...	0.3	...
1952														
1st quarter	64.7	57.8	29.1	9.8	...	19.0	0.3	18.7	6.7	...	...	...	0.3	...
2nd quarter	64.8	58.0	30.0	10.1	...	17.9	0.3	17.6	6.6	...	...	...	0.3	...
3rd quarter	65.3	58.4	30.4	10.1	...	17.8	0.3	17.5	6.6	...	...	...	0.3	...
4th quarter	68.4	61.4	31.2	10.5	...	19.7	0.3	19.3	6.8	...	...	...	0.3	...
1953														
1st quarter	70.1	63.1	31.5	10.8	...	20.8	0.3	20.4	6.8	...	...	...	0.3	...
2nd quarter	70.5	63.3	31.5	11.0	...	20.9	0.3	20.5	6.8	...	...	...	0.3	...
3rd quarter	69.5	62.4	31.2	10.7	...	20.4	0.4	20.0	6.9	...	...	...	0.3	...
4th quarter	64.3	57.3	31.0	10.4	...	15.9	0.3	15.6	6.7	...	...	...	0.3	...
1954														
1st quarter	61.6	53.6	28.1	9.7	...	15.7	0.3	15.4	7.8	...	...	...	0.3	...
2nd quarter	61.7	53.7	27.9	9.6	...	16.2	0.3	15.9	7.7	...	...	...	0.3	...
3rd quarter	62.3	54.3	27.9	9.3	...	17.1	0.3	16.9	7.7	...	...	...	0.3	...
4th quarter	64.4	56.3	28.3	9.5	...	18.4	0.2	18.2	7.8	...	...	...	0.3	...
1955														
1st quarter	68.3	59.5	29.0	10.0	...	20.4	0.2	20.2	8.5	...	...	...	0.3	...
2nd quarter	70.3	61.3	30.1	10.5	...	20.7	0.2	20.4	8.7	...	...	...	0.3	...
3rd quarter	72.0	62.8	31.0	10.6	...	21.2	0.3	20.9	8.9	...	...	...	0.3	...
4th quarter	73.7	64.5	31.8	10.6	...	22.0	0.3	21.7	8.9	...	...	...	0.3	...
1956														
1st quarter	74.2	64.3	32.7	10.6	...	21.0	0.4	20.6	9.5	...	...	...	0.4	...
2nd quarter	75.6	65.6	33.6	10.6	...	21.4	0.4	21.0	9.6	...	...	...	0.4	...
3rd quarter	75.4	65.4	34.2	11.0	...	20.1	0.4	19.7	9.6	...	...	...	0.4	...
4th quarter	78.2	68.1	35.2	11.7	...	21.2	0.4	20.8	9.8	...	...	...	0.4	...
1957														
1st quarter	80.4	69.0	35.7	11.6	...	21.7	0.5	21.3	11.0	...	...	...	0.4	...
2nd quarter	79.9	68.5	36.1	11.6	...	20.8	0.5	20.3	11.0	...	...	...	0.4	...
3rd quarter	79.9	68.4	36.3	11.7	...	20.4	0.6	19.8	11.1	...	...	...	0.4	...
4th quarter	77.1	65.8	35.9	11.3	...	18.6	0.6	18.0	10.9	...	...	...	0.4	...
1958														
1st quarter	73.6	62.2	35.2	11.1	...	16.0	0.6	15.4	10.9	...	...	...	0.4	...
2nd quarter	73.5	62.2	34.7	11.2	...	16.3	0.6	15.8	10.9	...	...	...	0.4	...
3rd quarter	76.7	65.3	35.9	11.1	...	18.4	0.5	17.9	11.0	...	...	...	0.4	...
4th quarter	80.4	68.9	36.2	11.5	...	21.1	0.5	20.7	11.1	...	...	...	0.4	...
1959														
1st quarter	84.9	71.4	37.2	11.9	10.9	22.3	0.7	21.6	13.3	0.0	...	0.0	0.4	-0.1
2nd quarter	88.6	74.9	38.3	12.1	11.0	24.4	0.8	23.6	13.5	0.0	...	0.0	0.4	-0.1
3rd quarter	86.8	73.2	38.7	12.5	11.4	21.9	1.0	20.9	13.4	0.0	...	0.0	0.4	-0.2
4th quarter	87.4	73.7	39.7	12.5	11.4	21.4	1.2	20.2	13.5	0.0	...	0.0	0.4	-0.1
1960														
1st quarter	95.6	78.2	41.1	13.3	12.1	23.6	0.9	22.7	16.0	1.3	1.3	0.0	0.4	-0.2
2nd quarter	94.3	76.8	41.8	13.2	12.1	21.7	0.9	20.8	16.0	1.3	1.2	0.0	0.4	-0.2
3rd quarter	93.7	76.2	42.3	13.1	12.1	20.7	0.9	19.8	16.0	1.5	1.4	0.0	0.4	-0.4
4th quarter	92.2	74.8	42.1	12.9	11.9	19.7	0.8	18.9	15.9	1.4	1.4	0.0	0.4	-0.4

... = Not available.

Table 19-8. Federal Government Current Receipts and Expenditures—Continued

(National Income and Product Accounts, calendar years, billions of dollars, quarterly data are at seasonally adjusted annual rates.)

NIPA Table 3.2

Year and quarter	Current expenditures										Net federal government saving, NIPA (surplus + / deficit -)		
	Total	Consumption expenditures	Government social benefits		Other current transfer payments		Interest payments			Subsidies			
			Total	To persons	Total	Grants-in-aid to state and local governments	Total	To persons and business	To the rest of the world		Total	Social insurance funds	Other
1947													
1st quarter	37.5	21.7	7.7	7.7	3.2	1.4	4.2	...	0.0	0.7	5.9	...	...
2nd quarter	37.3	21.6	7.3	7.3	3.6	1.7	4.1	...	0.0	0.6	5.2	...	...
3rd quarter	39.7	20.6	10.7	10.7	3.8	1.6	4.1	...	0.0	0.5	2.0	...	...
4th quarter	35.8	19.6	7.8	7.8	3.8	1.6	4.1	...	0.0	0.5	7.9	...	...
1948													
1st quarter	36.3	19.6	7.5	7.5	4.6	1.6	4.1	...	0.0	0.5	7.7	...	...
2nd quarter	37.4	21.0	7.2	7.2	4.6	1.7	4.1	...	0.0	0.4	5.1	...	...
3rd quarter	40.2	21.8	7.0	7.0	6.6	1.8	4.1	...	0.0	0.7	1.4	...	...
4th quarter	41.2	22.5	7.0	7.0	6.4	1.9	4.2	...	0.0	1.0	0.2	...	...
1949													
1st quarter	43.3	23.8	7.7	7.7	6.9	1.7	4.3	...	0.0	0.7	-3.4	...	...
2nd quarter	44.4	24.4	8.2	8.2	7.1	1.7	4.3	...	0.0	0.5	-6.5	...	...
3rd quarter	43.9	23.0	8.5	8.5	7.4	2.1	4.3	...	0.0	0.7	-6.5	...	...
4th quarter	42.3	22.2	8.5	8.5	6.6	1.9	4.4	...	0.0	0.7	-6.2	...	...
1950													
1st quarter	49.8	22.1	16.6	16.6	5.8	1.9	4.4	...	0.0	0.9	-8.4	...	...
2nd quarter	42.8	22.1	9.6	9.6	5.7	1.9	4.4	...	0.0	1.0	2.8	...	...
3rd quarter	38.3	20.6	7.2	7.2	5.0	1.9	4.5	...	0.0	0.9	13.5	...	...
4th quarter	42.3	23.6	7.5	7.5	5.4	1.9	4.5	...	0.0	1.3	14.2	...	...
1951													
1st quarter	47.3	28.8	7.5	7.5	5.1	2.0	4.6	...	0.0	1.3	17.2	...	...
2nd quarter	51.6	32.7	7.9	7.9	5.2	2.1	4.6	...	0.0	1.3	10.0	...	...
3rd quarter	55.5	37.4	8.1	8.1	5.1	1.9	4.6	...	0.0	1.1	5.3	...	...
4th quarter	58.7	38.7	8.0	8.0	5.4	2.1	4.7	...	0.0	1.2	6.0	...	...
1952													
1st quarter	57.8	40.8	7.7	7.7	3.8	2.0	4.6	...	0.0	1.0	6.9	...	...
2nd quarter	61.4	43.8	7.6	7.6	4.5	2.1	4.6	...	0.0	0.9	3.4	...	...
3rd quarter	64.2	45.3	8.5	8.5	4.8	2.3	4.6	...	0.1	0.9	1.1	...	...
4th quarter	64.9	46.9	8.5	8.5	3.9	2.3	4.7	...	0.1	0.8	3.5	...	...
1953													
1st quarter	65.8	47.7	8.6	8.6	3.9	1.8	4.7	...	0.1	0.9	4.3	...	...
2nd quarter	67.8	49.2	8.4	8.4	4.8	2.7	4.7	...	0.1	0.6	2.6	...	...
3rd quarter	66.1	47.6	8.6	8.6	4.2	2.3	4.7	...	0.1	0.8	3.5	...	...
4th quarter	67.5	48.8	9.2	9.2	4.2	2.3	4.8	...	0.1	0.4	-3.2	...	...
1954													
1st quarter	65.0	45.9	9.9	9.9	4.1	2.3	4.8	...	0.1	0.3	-3.3	...	...
2nd quarter	63.6	43.6	10.5	10.5	3.7	2.3	4.8	...	0.1	0.9	-1.9	...	...
3rd quarter	63.7	43.1	10.9	10.9	4.3	2.4	4.8	...	0.1	0.6	-1.3	...	...
4th quarter	64.3	43.2	11.4	11.4	4.4	2.3	4.8	...	0.1	0.4	0.0	...	...
1955													
1st quarter	64.7	43.3	11.4	11.4	4.8	2.3	4.7	...	0.1	0.6	3.6	...	...
2nd quarter	63.6	42.8	11.4	11.4	4.4	2.4	4.6	...	0.1	0.8	6.7	...	...
3rd quarter	67.1	45.2	11.6	11.6	4.4	2.5	4.8	...	0.1	0.5	4.9	...	...
4th quarter	65.9	44.4	11.6	11.6	4.3	2.4	4.9	...	0.1	0.7	7.8	...	...
1956													
1st quarter	65.7	43.9	11.9	11.9	4.2	2.4	4.9	...	0.1	0.8	8.5	...	...
2nd quarter	68.8	46.1	12.1	12.1	4.4	2.5	5.1	...	0.1	1.0	6.7	...	...
3rd quarter	67.6	43.9	12.5	12.5	4.5	2.6	5.2	...	0.2	1.4	7.8	...	...
4th quarter	70.9	46.3	12.6	12.6	4.6	2.7	5.7	...	0.2	1.7	7.3	...	...
1957													
1st quarter	74.3	49.1	13.4	13.4	4.6	2.9	5.4	...	0.2	1.7	6.1	...	...
2nd quarter	75.5	49.0	14.5	14.5	4.8	2.8	5.6	...	0.2	1.6	4.3	...	...
3rd quarter	75.5	49.1	14.6	14.6	4.7	2.9	5.7	...	0.2	1.5	4.4	...	...
4th quarter	78.6	50.7	15.7	15.7	4.9	3.1	5.9	...	0.2	1.4	-1.5	...	...
1958													
1st quarter	76.8	49.1	16.8	16.8	4.6	2.9	5.4	...	0.2	1.5	-3.2	-1.3	-1.9
2nd quarter	81.8	51.8	18.6	18.6	5.1	3.3	5.2	...	0.1	1.7	-8.3	-3.6	-4.7
3rd quarter	83.1	50.6	19.0	19.0	5.1	3.2	5.3	...	0.1	1.9	-6.4	-3.5	-3.0
4th quarter	83.9	52.0	18.3	18.3	5.9	4.0	5.6	...	0.2	2.0	-3.5	-2.4	-1.1
1959													
1st quarter	81.7	48.3	18.4	18.4	7.5	3.5	6.4	...	0.2	1.1	3.2	-0.6	3.8
2nd quarter	83.4	50.2	18.3	18.3	8.1	3.9	5.9	...	0.2	0.9	5.2	-0.3	5.5
3rd quarter	83.9	50.7	18.5	18.5	7.2	3.8	6.3	...	0.3	1.1	2.9	-0.7	3.6
4th quarter	85.3	50.7	19.1	19.1	7.8	3.8	6.7	...	0.4	1.1	2.1	-1.2	3.3
1960													
1st quarter	83.9	48.1	19.1	18.9	7.1	3.9	8.6	8.2	0.4	1.0	11.7	1.3	10.3
2nd quarter	86.0	48.6	19.6	19.5	8.0	4.0	8.5	8.2	0.3	1.3	8.2	0.8	7.4
3rd quarter	87.1	50.6	20.3	20.1	6.9	4.0	8.2	7.9	0.3	1.0	6.6	0.2	6.4
4th quarter	90.0	51.7	21.2	21.0	7.7	4.2	8.1	7.8	0.3	1.2	2.2	-0.8	3.0

... = Not available.

Table 19-8. Federal Government Current Receipts and Expenditures—Continued

(National Income and Product Accounts, calendar years, billions of dollars, quarterly data are at seasonally adjusted annual rates.)

NIPA Table 3.2

Year and quarter	Current receipts													
	Total	Tax receipts							Contributions for government social insurance	Income receipts on assets			Current transfer receipts	Current surplus of government enterprises
		Total	Personal current taxes	Taxes on production and imports		Taxes on corporate income				Total	Interest receipts	Rents and royalties		
				Total	Excise taxes	Total	Federal Reserve banks	Other						
1961														
1st quarter	92.2	74.6	42.2	12.9	11.9	19.4	0.7	18.7	16.3	1.4	1.4	0.1	0.5	-0.5
2nd quarter	94.1	76.4	42.5	13.1	12.1	20.7	0.7	20.1	16.4	1.5	1.4	0.1	0.5	-0.6
3rd quarter	96.0	78.0	42.8	13.2	12.1	22.0	0.7	21.3	16.6	1.4	1.4	0.1	0.5	-0.5
4th quarter	99.5	81.0	43.4	13.6	12.5	23.9	0.7	23.2	16.8	1.6	1.5	0.1	0.5	-0.3
1962														
1st quarter	101.0	80.9	44.6	14.0	12.8	22.3	0.8	21.5	18.4	1.6	1.5	0.1	0.5	-0.4
2nd quarter	102.5	82.2	46.0	14.0	12.8	22.1	0.8	21.3	18.6	1.8	1.7	0.1	0.5	-0.5
3rd quarter	104.9	84.5	47.2	14.4	13.2	22.7	0.8	21.9	18.6	1.7	1.6	0.1	0.5	-0.5
4th quarter	106.1	85.7	48.4	14.3	13.1	22.8	0.8	22.0	18.7	1.7	1.6	0.1	0.5	-0.5
1963														
1st quarter	109.1	86.3	48.8	14.4	13.2	22.9	0.8	22.0	20.7	1.7	1.7	0.1	0.6	-0.3
2nd quarter	111.4	88.4	49.0	14.7	13.5	24.5	0.9	23.6	20.9	1.7	1.7	0.1	0.6	-0.3
3rd quarter	112.5	89.3	49.1	14.8	13.6	25.2	0.9	24.3	21.1	1.8	1.7	0.1	0.6	-0.3
4th quarter	114.1	90.5	49.6	15.0	13.7	25.8	0.9	24.8	21.4	1.8	1.7	0.1	0.6	-0.2
1964														
1st quarter	112.7	89.1	48.0	15.0	13.8	25.9	1.5	24.4	21.4	1.9	1.8	0.1	0.6	-0.2
2nd quarter	109.0	85.3	43.7	15.4	14.1	26.0	1.6	24.4	21.6	1.8	1.7	0.1	0.5	-0.2
3rd quarter	111.7	87.6	45.4	15.5	14.2	26.5	1.6	24.9	21.8	2.0	1.9	0.1	0.9	-0.6
4th quarter	113.6	89.1	46.9	15.9	14.5	26.1	1.7	24.5	22.0	1.6	1.5	0.1	1.0	-0.2
1965														
1st quarter	119.5	94.6	50.5	16.4	15.0	27.5	1.2	26.3	22.2	2.0	1.9	0.1	1.0	-0.3
2nd quarter	121.4	96.2	51.9	15.7	14.1	28.4	1.3	27.1	22.4	2.0	1.9	0.1	1.0	-0.2
3rd quarter	119.8	94.3	50.4	14.8	13.1	28.9	1.3	27.6	22.8	2.0	1.9	0.1	1.1	-0.4
4th quarter	123.1	97.6	51.5	15.0	13.3	30.8	1.4	29.4	23.2	1.7	1.6	0.1	1.1	-0.5
1966														
1st quarter	132.5	100.2	54.4	13.9	12.1	31.7	1.5	30.2	29.6	2.0	1.9	0.1	1.1	-0.5
2nd quarter	137.3	104.6	58.0	14.7	12.8	31.7	1.6	30.2	30.0	2.0	1.9	0.1	1.1	-0.6
3rd quarter	139.7	106.1	59.8	14.6	12.7	31.4	1.7	29.7	31.1	2.1	2.0	0.1	1.2	-0.8
4th quarter	142.3	108.2	62.2	14.9	13.0	30.9	1.8	29.0	31.4	2.3	2.1	0.1	1.2	-0.7
1967														
1st quarter	143.2	107.7	62.9	15.0	13.0	29.7	1.9	27.8	32.8	2.3	2.2	0.2	1.0	-0.7
2nd quarter	144.3	107.5	62.6	15.2	13.3	29.4	1.9	27.5	33.7	2.5	2.4	0.2	1.1	-0.6
3rd quarter	147.8	110.3	65.2	15.3	13.5	29.6	1.9	27.8	34.4	2.5	2.4	0.2	1.1	-0.5
4th quarter	152.2	114.0	66.9	15.5	13.5	31.4	2.0	29.4	35.1	2.6	2.4	0.2	1.2	-0.8
1968														
1st quarter	160.9	120.6	68.8	16.2	14.1	35.2	2.3	33.0	36.7	2.9	2.7	0.2	1.1	-0.4
2nd quarter	165.6	124.4	71.4	16.8	14.6	35.9	2.4	33.5	37.5	2.9	2.7	0.2	1.1	-0.3
3rd quarter	176.8	134.8	81.0	17.3	15.0	36.1	2.5	33.5	38.1	3.1	2.9	0.2	1.1	-0.3
4th quarter	181.5	139.3	84.5	17.5	15.1	37.0	2.6	34.4	38.7	2.8	2.6	0.2	1.1	-0.4
1969														
1st quarter	191.0	145.9	90.7	17.4	15.4	37.4	2.8	34.6	41.9	2.6	2.4	0.2	1.1	-0.5
2nd quarter	194.1	148.1	93.3	17.9	15.3	36.5	3.0	33.5	42.7	2.6	2.5	0.2	1.1	-0.5
3rd quarter	191.9	144.8	90.8	18.3	15.8	35.3	3.1	32.2	43.6	2.7	2.5	0.2	1.2	-0.4
4th quarter	193.3	145.4	91.9	18.0	15.6	35.1	3.3	31.8	44.2	2.8	2.6	0.2	1.2	-0.3
1970														
1st quarter	187.2	139.2	90.6	18.0	15.5	30.3	3.4	27.0	44.9	2.9	2.7	0.2	1.2	-1.0
2nd quarter	188.1	140.5	91.4	18.2	15.8	30.5	3.5	27.0	45.2	3.1	2.8	0.2	1.2	-1.8
3rd quarter	184.7	136.5	86.3	18.3	15.8	31.5	3.6	27.9	45.6	3.1	2.8	0.3	1.1	-1.5
4th quarter	183.8	135.9	87.2	18.3	15.7	30.1	3.5	26.6	45.4	3.1	2.9	0.3	1.1	-1.7
1971														
1st quarter	188.5	136.8	83.6	19.5	16.9	33.3	3.4	29.9	49.3	3.2	2.9	0.3	1.1	-2.0
2nd quarter	191.4	138.2	85.1	18.8	16.1	33.9	3.3	30.7	49.9	3.5	3.1	0.3	1.1	-1.3
3rd quarter	191.8	138.7	86.3	19.0	15.8	33.1	3.4	29.8	50.1	3.5	3.1	0.4	1.1	-1.6
4th quarter	195.1	141.1	88.2	19.1	15.1	33.5	3.4	30.1	50.7	3.7	3.3	0.4	1.1	-1.5
1972														
1st quarter	214.1	154.0	100.3	18.3	15.2	35.0	3.2	31.8	56.9	3.5	3.2	0.4	1.2	-1.5
2nd quarter	217.5	156.4	102.4	18.4	15.6	35.2	3.2	32.0	57.5	3.5	3.2	0.4	1.3	-1.2
3rd quarter	220.4	158.4	103.1	18.6	15.7	36.3	3.2	33.1	58.2	3.7	3.3	0.4	1.3	-1.1
4th quarter	228.2	164.7	105.3	19.1	15.9	39.9	3.3	36.6	59.0	3.7	3.3	0.4	1.3	-0.6
1973														
1st quarter	243.5	167.6	104.5	19.7	16.2	43.0	3.7	39.3	72.2	3.8	3.4	0.4	1.4	-1.4
2nd quarter	247.6	170.7	106.9	20.0	16.7	43.5	4.2	39.4	73.3	3.8	3.4	0.4	1.5	-1.8
3rd quarter	250.8	173.4	111.0	19.8	16.7	42.2	4.6	37.6	74.5	3.7	3.3	0.4	1.1	-1.9
4th quarter	259.6	180.9	116.0	20.2	17.0	44.3	4.9	39.4	76.0	3.8	3.3	0.5	1.1	-2.2
1974														
1st quarter	267.2	182.3	119.5	19.9	16.5	42.5	5.1	37.4	81.5	4.0	3.5	0.5	1.3	-2.0
2nd quarter	277.6	190.2	124.8	20.2	16.7	44.8	5.5	39.3	83.1	4.2	3.6	0.5	1.4	-1.2
3rd quarter	288.4	199.8	129.7	20.4	16.5	49.3	5.8	43.5	84.7	4.2	3.7	0.6	1.5	-1.8
4th quarter	284.9	196.6	132.0	20.3	16.5	43.9	5.8	38.1	84.8	4.3	3.8	0.6	1.5	-2.3

Table 19-8. Federal Government Current Receipts and Expenditures—Continued

(National Income and Product Accounts, calendar years, billions of dollars, quarterly data are at seasonally adjusted annual rates.)

NIPA Table 3.2

Year and quarter	Current expenditures											Net federal government saving, NIPA (surplus + / deficit -)		
	Total	Consumption expenditures	Government social benefits		Other current transfer payments		Interest payments			Subsidies				
			Total	To persons	Total	Grants-in-aid to state and local governments	Total	To persons and business	To the rest of the world		Total	Social insurance funds	Other
1961														
1st quarter	89.7	49.8	22.9	22.7	7.5	4.2	7.9	7.6	0.3	1.6	2.5	-2.1	4.6
2nd quarter	93.4	51.2	23.7	23.4	8.7	4.5	7.8	7.6	0.3	2.0	0.8	-2.7	3.5
3rd quarter	93.5	52.2	23.7	23.5	7.5	4.6	7.9	7.6	0.3	2.2	2.5	-2.7	5.2
4th quarter	94.9	53.3	23.1	22.9	8.1	4.7	8.0	7.7	0.3	2.3	4.7	-1.8	6.5
1962														
1st quarter	98.6	56.0	23.6	23.3	8.5	4.9	8.2	7.9	0.3	2.3	2.4	-0.6	3.1
2nd quarter	100.3	56.9	23.4	23.1	9.1	4.9	8.6	8.2	0.3	2.4	2.2	-0.3	2.5
3rd quarter	101.7	58.9	23.7	23.5	8.1	5.2	8.8	8.5	0.3	2.2	3.1	-0.5	3.6
4th quarter	103.7	59.6	24.3	24.1	8.6	5.2	9.0	8.6	0.4	2.2	2.4	-0.8	3.2
1963														
1st quarter	104.9	59.5	25.5	25.3	8.8	5.3	9.0	8.7	0.4	2.0	4.2	-0.2	4.3
2nd quarter	105.0	59.1	24.4	24.2	10.1	5.5	9.2	8.8	0.4	2.2	6.3	1.1	5.2
3rd quarter	106.7	61.8	24.6	24.3	8.6	5.8	9.4	9.0	0.4	2.3	5.9	1.2	4.7
4th quarter	108.9	62.7	25.0	24.8	9.2	6.1	9.6	9.2	0.4	2.4	5.2	1.2	4.0
1964														
1st quarter	110.7	62.7	25.8	25.5	9.6	6.5	9.8	9.4	0.4	2.7	2.0	0.5	1.5
2nd quarter	111.6	62.9	25.2	24.9	10.7	6.5	9.9	9.5	0.4	2.9	-2.6	1.3	-3.9
3rd quarter	110.4	63.4	25.3	25.1	9.0	6.2	10.1	9.7	0.4	2.6	1.3	1.5	-0.2
4th quarter	110.3	62.1	25.4	25.1	9.8	6.6	10.2	9.7	0.5	2.7	3.3	1.7	1.6
1965														
1st quarter	111.9	62.3	26.5	26.2	9.8	6.5	10.3	9.9	0.5	2.9	7.6	0.9	6.7
2nd quarter	114.6	63.1	26.2	25.7	11.8	7.1	10.5	10.1	0.5	3.0	6.8	1.6	5.1
3rd quarter	120.2	66.7	29.5	29.2	10.5	7.5	10.6	10.1	0.5	3.0	-0.4	-1.2	0.8
4th quarter	123.7	70.8	28.2	27.9	10.8	7.6	10.8	10.3	0.5	3.1	-0.6	0.5	-1.1
1966														
1st quarter	127.4	71.3	29.0	28.7	12.6	9.0	11.0	10.5	0.5	3.5	5.0	6.4	-1.4
2nd quarter	133.8	74.5	28.6	28.3	15.3	10.1	11.5	10.9	0.5	3.9	3.5	6.7	-3.2
3rd quarter	138.3	78.6	30.2	29.8	13.6	10.5	11.8	11.2	0.6	4.0	1.4	6.2	-4.8
4th quarter	143.2	79.1	33.1	32.8	14.5	10.7	12.3	11.7	0.6	4.2	-0.9	4.7	-5.6
1967														
1st quarter	152.9	85.2	35.9	35.6	15.3	11.1	12.5	12.0	0.5	4.0	-9.7	3.7	-13.4
2nd quarter	154.7	86.2	36.4	36.1	15.8	11.6	12.4	11.8	0.6	3.8	-10.4	4.3	-14.7
3rd quarter	156.3	87.3	37.5	36.9	15.3	11.6	12.6	12.0	0.6	3.7	-8.5	4.0	-12.5
4th quarter	161.0	89.9	37.9	37.6	16.4	12.7	13.1	12.5	0.7	3.7	-8.8	4.6	-13.4
1968														
1st quarter	166.9	93.7	39.6	39.3	15.6	11.8	13.8	13.1	0.7	4.0	-6.0	4.6	-10.5
2nd quarter	173.0	94.5	42.2	41.8	17.6	13.3	14.5	13.8	0.7	4.2	-7.4	2.9	-10.3
3rd quarter	175.2	95.9	43.2	42.8	17.0	12.6	14.9	14.3	0.7	4.2	1.5	2.6	-1.1
4th quarter	178.9	97.5	43.9	43.5	18.2	13.2	15.1	14.4	0.7	4.2	2.7	2.7	0.0
1969														
1st quarter	176.4	95.4	44.9	44.6	16.6	13.1	15.1	14.3	0.8	4.3	14.6	5.1	9.4
2nd quarter	182.5	97.6	45.7	45.3	19.2	14.0	15.6	14.8	0.8	4.4	11.5	5.5	6.1
3rd quarter	186.2	100.2	46.5	46.1	19.0	15.1	15.9	15.1	0.8	4.6	5.6	6.0	-0.3
4th quarter	190.1	100.3	47.4	47.0	21.0	16.1	16.7	15.9	0.8	4.6	3.2	6.2	-3.0
1970														
1st quarter	189.5	99.8	48.6	48.3	21.5	17.5	17.3	16.4	0.8	4.7	-2.3	6.6	-8.8
2nd quarter	204.0	98.0	57.9	57.5	23.6	18.8	17.5	16.6	1.0	4.8	-15.8	-1.3	-14.5
3rd quarter	204.1	98.4	57.4	56.9	25.0	20.1	18.2	17.0	1.1	4.7	-19.4	0.5	-19.9
4th quarter	206.9	98.3	60.3	59.8	25.5	20.8	18.0	16.9	1.2	4.8	-23.1	-1.7	-21.4
1971														
1st quarter	212.0	101.0	61.5	61.0	27.0	21.6	17.9	16.5	1.3	4.7	-23.6	1.3	-24.9
2nd quarter	221.5	101.9	68.4	67.9	28.8	23.2	17.6	16.0	1.6	4.8	-30.1	-5.1	-25.0
3rd quarter	221.0	102.0	67.7	67.2	28.7	23.5	18.0	15.9	2.1	4.5	-29.1	-4.1	-25.1
4th quarter	225.7	103.0	68.7	68.2	31.3	24.7	18.2	15.9	2.4	4.6	-30.6	-4.2	-26.4
1972														
1st quarter	236.6	108.3	70.7	70.2	33.2	25.7	18.3	15.8	2.5	6.1	-22.6	0.1	-22.7
2nd quarter	245.2	109.4	70.7	70.2	40.3	33.9	18.6	16.0	2.6	6.2	-27.7	0.8	-28.5
3rd quarter	237.0	105.9	70.7	70.3	34.4	26.8	18.8	16.1	2.7	7.1	-16.6	2.0	-18.5
4th quarter	258.9	107.0	81.2	80.6	46.4	40.4	19.4	16.5	2.9	7.0	-30.7	-5.4	-25.3
1973														
1st quarter	258.2	108.5	82.8	82.2	40.1	35.6	21.0	17.6	3.5	5.9	-14.7	6.1	-20.8
2nd quarter	262.3	109.2	84.2	83.6	40.8	34.7	22.4	18.5	3.9	5.6	-14.7	5.7	-20.4
3rd quarter	260.9	107.8	85.7	85.1	39.2	33.9	23.5	19.5	4.0	4.6	-10.1	5.7	-15.8
4th quarter	265.3	109.9	87.9	87.3	38.7	34.9	24.3	20.3	4.0	4.5	-5.7	5.6	-11.3
1974														
1st quarter	275.5	114.0	94.5	94.1	38.9	34.6	24.8	20.8	4.0	3.5	-8.3	9.1	-17.4
2nd quarter	288.4	114.6	101.3	100.7	43.5	35.4	25.6	21.4	4.2	2.8	-10.8	4.1	-14.8
3rd quarter	298.9	119.0	107.1	106.4	41.7	36.8	26.7	22.4	4.3	3.1	-10.5	1.8	-12.3
4th quarter	310.4	124.3	112.6	112.0	43.1	38.2	26.9	22.4	4.5	3.5	-25.4	-2.2	-23.3

Table 19-8. Federal Government Current Receipts and Expenditures—Continued

(National Income and Product Accounts, calendar years, billions of dollars, quarterly data are at seasonally adjusted annual rates.)

NIPA Table 3.2

Year and quarter	Current receipts												Current transfer receipts	Current surplus of government enterprises
	Total	Tax receipts							Contributions for government social insurance	Income receipts on assets				
		Total	Personal current taxes	Taxes on production and imports		Taxes on corporate income				Total	Interest receipts	Rents and royalties		
				Total	Excise taxes	Total	Federal Reserve banks	Other						
1975														
1st quarter	278.3	189.6	132.3	19.9	15.8	37.0	5.5	31.5	85.9	4.5	3.9	0.6	1.5	-3.1
2nd quarter	245.1	156.1	94.6	21.5	16.3	39.6	5.4	34.2	86.2	4.8	4.2	0.6	1.5	-3.4
3rd quarter	288.5	198.0	125.7	23.5	16.6	48.3	5.2	43.2	87.9	5.1	4.5	0.6	1.5	-3.9
4th quarter	296.8	204.4	130.4	24.1	16.8	49.4	5.5	43.9	89.9	5.2	4.5	0.6	1.5	-4.1
1976														
1st quarter	312.1	210.0	132.7	21.0	16.7	55.7	5.8	49.9	96.9	5.7	5.0	0.7	1.5	-2.0
2nd quarter	319.0	215.4	138.4	21.5	17.0	54.8	5.8	49.0	98.3	5.9	5.2	0.7	1.6	-2.2
3rd quarter	326.6	221.2	144.2	21.9	17.1	54.4	5.9	48.5	100.0	6.1	5.4	0.7	1.6	-2.3
4th quarter	332.5	225.9	149.7	21.9	17.3	53.5	6.0	47.5	101.4	5.8	5.1	0.7	1.7	-2.3
1977														
1st quarter	347.0	234.7	154.9	22.2	17.1	56.9	5.9	51.0	106.8	6.5	5.6	0.8	1.7	-2.6
2nd quarter	360.8	245.7	160.6	22.7	17.4	61.7	6.0	55.7	109.4	6.7	5.8	0.9	1.8	-2.7
3rd quarter	367.4	250.2	162.3	23.4	17.6	63.8	5.9	57.9	111.5	6.9	5.9	1.0	2.1	-3.2
4th quarter	378.5	259.1	170.8	23.4	17.9	64.1	6.0	58.1	113.6	6.8	5.8	1.0	2.1	-3.2
1978														
1st quarter	388.7	258.9	173.1	24.2	17.8	60.7	6.3	54.4	123.0	7.6	6.6	1.0	2.3	-3.1
2nd quarter	417.1	282.1	182.7	25.6	18.5	72.8	6.6	66.2	126.8	8.4	7.3	1.1	2.4	-2.5
3rd quarter	434.7	295.7	195.1	25.8	18.5	73.9	7.2	66.7	129.3	8.7	7.6	1.1	2.5	-1.5
4th quarter	453.5	310.7	204.9	26.6	19.1	78.2	7.9	70.3	132.4	9.4	8.2	1.2	2.6	-1.5
1979														
1st quarter	469.1	313.3	211.3	26.2	18.6	74.8	8.2	66.6	145.0	9.9	8.6	1.3	2.7	-1.8
2nd quarter	480.3	322.4	219.7	26.2	18.7	75.4	8.8	66.5	147.0	10.2	8.7	1.4	2.8	-2.1
3rd quarter	492.4	330.9	229.2	25.7	18.4	74.8	9.5	65.3	150.3	10.9	9.4	1.6	2.9	-2.6
4th quarter	503.1	338.3	238.3	25.9	18.6	72.7	10.6	62.1	153.2	11.6	9.9	1.7	3.0	-2.9
1980														
1st quarter	517.2	345.7	237.6	28.0	20.7	78.6	11.6	67.0	159.5	12.1	10.2	2.0	3.1	-3.2
2nd quarter	514.3	341.2	243.6	33.9	27.0	62.1	12.3	49.8	160.3	13.0	10.8	2.2	3.2	-3.4
3rd quarter	533.6	357.3	252.2	36.5	29.3	67.0	11.0	56.0	162.8	14.2	11.8	2.5	3.2	-3.8
4th quarter	563.3	379.5	266.6	37.7	30.4	73.6	11.9	61.7	167.9	15.3	12.5	2.8	4.6	-3.9
1981														
1st quarter	606.6	401.9	277.8	51.0	43.2	71.5	13.0	58.5	187.9	16.6	13.5	3.1	3.9	-3.7
2nd quarter	616.1	406.4	288.4	52.2	43.8	64.3	13.6	50.7	190.3	17.5	14.2	3.4	3.5	-1.7
3rd quarter	631.9	419.0	300.8	49.5	40.7	67.2	14.5	52.7	193.7	18.8	15.2	3.6	3.7	-3.3
4th quarter	623.2	405.0	295.3	48.5	39.1	59.8	15.0	44.8	195.5	20.2	16.4	3.8	3.9	-1.4
1982														
1st quarter	616.5	388.4	294.6	43.9	34.8	48.6	15.1	33.5	203.2	21.6	17.7	3.9	4.9	-1.5
2nd quarter	622.7	393.2	301.1	40.4	31.7	50.4	15.7	34.7	204.3	22.0	18.1	3.9	5.2	-2.0
3rd quarter	611.9	381.7	289.1	40.5	32.2	50.8	15.4	35.4	205.8	22.4	18.5	3.8	5.4	-3.3
4th quarter	615.2	383.7	295.2	40.7	32.4	46.3	14.6	31.7	206.1	22.7	19.0	3.7	5.5	-2.8
1983														
1st quarter	622.1	379.8	289.0	41.5	33.8	48.2	13.9	34.3	216.3	23.2	19.7	3.5	5.5	-2.8
2nd quarter	647.7	401.8	294.7	45.7	36.7	60.2	13.9	46.3	219.6	23.3	19.8	3.4	5.8	-2.8
3rd quarter	641.1	391.5	276.8	45.9	36.2	67.6	14.3	53.3	223.1	24.0	20.6	3.4	6.1	-3.5
4th quarter	658.4	401.2	284.4	46.2	36.1	69.4	14.8	54.6	228.3	24.9	21.4	3.5	6.6	-2.6
1984														
1st quarter	692.5	416.4	287.4	47.4	36.5	80.3	15.4	64.8	246.5	25.5	21.7	3.8	7.1	-3.0
2nd quarter	705.2	423.0	294.1	48.0	35.8	79.5	15.7	63.8	251.2	27.0	23.1	3.9	7.3	-3.1
3rd quarter	711.8	426.1	306.9	47.9	35.7	70.1	16.3	53.8	255.2	26.8	22.9	3.9	7.3	-3.7
4th quarter	726.6	437.4	317.3	47.8	35.5	71.0	16.7	54.3	258.4	27.3	23.5	3.9	7.3	-3.8
1985														
1st quarter	779.8	476.7	352.6	46.8	34.5	75.9	18.2	57.7	270.7	27.7	23.9	3.8	7.9	-3.2
2nd quarter	743.6	429.5	307.1	46.0	34.4	74.5	18.2	56.3	274.1	28.3	24.7	3.6	13.6	-2.0
3rd quarter	781.1	467.3	339.6	47.2	35.1	78.4	17.5	60.8	277.9	30.0	26.6	3.4	8.0	-2.1
4th quarter	788.6	469.1	344.7	45.8	33.1	76.3	17.3	59.0	283.2	30.5	27.4	3.1	7.9	-2.2
1986														
1st quarter	799.2	469.3	341.3	44.8	32.0	81.7	18.7	63.0	292.4	31.5	28.8	2.7	8.0	-2.0
2nd quarter	802.6	470.1	343.9	43.3	29.8	81.4	17.9	63.4	294.9	31.1	28.6	2.5	8.2	-1.7
3rd quarter	816.8	479.2	351.4	44.1	29.8	81.9	17.3	64.6	298.9	32.9	30.6	2.3	7.3	-1.5
4th quarter	842.2	499.9	363.7	43.9	29.7	90.3	17.2	73.1	303.6	30.1	27.8	2.2	9.4	-0.8
1987														
1st quarter	842.3	494.3	357.9	44.4	29.5	90.2	17.2	73.0	309.7	29.3	26.9	2.4	10.0	-1.0
2nd quarter	911.8	560.1	409.7	46.1	30.3	102.3	17.7	84.6	313.2	28.8	26.4	2.4	11.2	-1.5
3rd quarter	906.2	552.6	394.4	46.7	31.3	109.5	18.0	91.5	317.2	27.9	25.5	2.3	10.7	-2.1
4th quarter	926.2	568.9	408.0	47.7	31.8	110.7	18.1	92.7	323.5	25.9	23.6	2.3	11.0	-3.2
1988														
1st quarter	940.0	556.5	401.7	50.0	33.7	102.7	16.7	85.9	344.1	33.9	31.7	2.2	10.1	-4.5
2nd quarter	949.9	561.6	399.6	49.8	33.6	109.5	16.6	92.8	350.8	28.2	26.2	2.0	10.5	-1.3
3rd quarter	961.3	568.1	401.6	50.7	34.2	113.4	17.5	95.9	355.9	27.9	26.0	1.9	11.1	-1.7
4th quarter	981.8	580.5	408.7	50.7	33.9	119.0	18.6	100.4	361.6	29.9	28.0	1.9	11.6	-1.7

Table 19-8. Federal Government Current Receipts and Expenditures—*Continued*

(National Income and Product Accounts, calendar years, billions of dollars, quarterly data are at seasonally adjusted annual rates.)

NIPA Table 3.2

Year and quarter	Current expenditures										Net federal government saving, NIPA (surplus + / deficit -)		
	Total	Consumption expenditures	Government social benefits		Other current transfer payments		Interest payments			Subsidies			
			Total	To persons	Total	Grants-in-aid to state and local governments	Total	To persons and business	To the rest of the world		Total	Social insurance funds	Other
1975													
1st quarter	325.5	125.8	121.2	120.5	47.1	40.7	27.3	22.4	4.9	4.1	-47.2	-9.1	-38.1
2nd quarter	349.3	128.2	134.9	134.2	54.1	45.8	28.1	23.7	4.4	4.1	-104.2	-14.9	-89.3
3rd quarter	350.5	130.2	137.4	136.8	49.3	46.5	29.3	24.8	4.5	4.4	-62.0	-21.1	-40.8
4th quarter	359.6	134.0	138.6	137.8	51.5	47.5	31.0	26.6	4.4	4.8	-62.8	-19.6	-43.2
1976													
1st quarter	364.5	134.2	141.8	141.0	51.3	48.7	32.4	28.0	4.4	5.0	-52.4	-14.9	-37.5
2nd quarter	367.1	136.5	140.1	139.3	52.7	49.5	33.2	28.8	4.4	4.7	-48.1	-12.5	-35.6
3rd quarter	378.3	136.6	145.8	145.0	57.0	50.4	34.1	29.5	4.6	4.9	-51.7	-17.3	-34.3
4th quarter	387.3	141.4	148.1	147.3	57.2	54.4	35.4	30.7	4.7	5.3	-54.8	-17.9	-37.0
1977													
1st quarter	392.3	145.3	150.3	149.4	55.6	52.5	35.6	30.8	4.8	5.6	-45.3	-14.4	-30.9
2nd quarter	400.2	149.5	149.3	148.6	59.4	55.5	36.4	31.3	5.1	5.7	-39.4	-12.0	-27.3
3rd quarter	412.6	151.6	154.9	154.1	62.8	59.1	37.2	31.6	5.6	6.2	-45.2	-14.7	-30.5
4th quarter	425.0	156.5	157.1	156.2	62.2	59.2	39.2	32.6	6.6	10.1	-46.5	-14.2	-32.3
1978													
1st quarter	435.1	158.3	159.1	158.3	67.3	63.5	41.9	34.1	7.8	8.5	-46.3	-5.6	-40.7
2nd quarter	442.6	162.1	158.6	157.7	70.1	66.1	43.8	35.4	8.4	8.1	-25.5	-1.4	-24.1
3rd quarter	454.2	164.0	166.5	165.6	69.3	65.5	46.4	37.8	8.6	8.0	-19.4	-6.3	-13.2
4th quarter	468.1	168.9	169.0	168.0	70.9	67.1	49.2	39.3	9.8	10.1	-14.7	-5.0	-9.7
1979													
1st quarter	475.3	173.2	173.1	172.2	68.4	64.4	52.3	41.2	11.1	8.1	-6.1	4.9	-11.0
2nd quarter	486.5	178.0	176.4	175.4	69.3	65.0	54.4	43.4	11.0	8.5	-6.2	4.5	-10.7
3rd quarter	504.2	177.3	190.8	189.8	72.0	67.6	56.4	45.3	11.1	7.8	-11.9	-4.2	-7.6
4th quarter	524.0	187.5	194.6	193.6	73.7	68.4	59.7	48.4	11.3	8.5	-20.8	-4.5	-16.3
1980													
1st quarter	548.1	195.8	202.5	201.5	75.8	69.3	65.3	52.9	12.3	8.9	-30.9	-2.3	-28.6
2nd quarter	569.1	207.1	207.6	206.6	75.2	70.8	69.7	57.8	11.9	9.3	-54.7	-7.6	-47.0
3rd quarter	602.4	208.1	235.9	234.8	78.7	73.4	70.0	57.8	12.1	9.7	-68.7	-27.7	-41.0
4th quarter	623.5	219.0	236.9	235.7	83.8	75.8	73.9	59.5	14.4	9.9	-60.2	-24.3	-35.9
1981													
1st quarter	645.8	228.1	241.1	239.9	79.5	74.4	87.0	70.8	16.2	10.2	-39.3	-7.3	-32.0
2nd quarter	659.5	237.1	242.2	241.0	79.8	74.5	90.1	72.7	17.4	10.3	-43.4	-6.2	-37.2
3rd quarter	683.0	238.3	260.0	258.7	78.2	71.9	96.0	78.3	17.7	10.7	-51.1	-19.9	-31.2
4th quarter	702.6	249.7	262.2	260.9	75.2	69.2	102.4	84.6	17.9	13.1	-79.4	-22.0	-57.4
1982													
1st quarter	716.8	255.2	265.5	264.6	76.0	68.8	106.5	87.7	18.8	13.5	-100.4	-18.8	-81.6
2nd quarter	728.7	256.5	272.8	271.6	76.1	70.4	110.2	91.9	18.3	13.1	-105.9	-25.5	-80.4
3rd quarter	755.7	265.1	288.2	286.9	75.2	69.0	114.9	94.9	19.9	12.5	-143.8	-38.9	-104.9
4th quarter	792.6	276.6	303.3	301.9	78.3	69.8	115.5	95.4	20.1	18.9	-177.3	-52.0	-125.3
1983													
1st quarter	795.3	280.5	302.9	301.6	75.5	70.6	117.0	98.2	18.9	19.4	-173.2	-41.7	-131.5
2nd quarter	817.2	287.3	308.2	306.9	78.4	72.7	121.0	102.3	18.7	21.0	-169.4	-44.2	-125.3
3rd quarter	826.8	296.3	302.1	300.8	78.8	71.8	127.5	108.5	19.0	21.7	-185.7	-33.5	-152.2
4th quarter	822.2	282.0	304.2	302.9	82.0	71.2	132.8	113.4	19.4	21.0	-163.8	-29.8	-134.0
1984													
1st quarter	846.3	297.2	307.1	305.9	82.0	75.4	139.6	119.8	19.8	20.7	-153.9	-13.0	-140.8
2nd quarter	869.2	310.5	309.2	307.9	84.3	77.4	145.0	124.7	20.3	20.5	-164.0	-9.5	-154.5
3rd quarter	883.5	313.2	309.8	308.6	84.8	75.1	155.2	133.5	21.6	20.4	-171.7	-5.2	-166.5
4th quarter	909.4	319.1	315.8	314.6	92.9	78.8	161.5	138.6	22.9	20.7	-182.8	-7.2	-175.6
1985													
1st quarter	926.8	329.3	324.0	322.7	88.6	79.1	164.3	141.3	23.0	20.7	-147.0	-1.9	-145.1
2nd quarter	940.9	334.5	324.9	323.7	90.9	80.0	169.0	146.1	22.9	20.6	-197.3	1.1	-198.4
3rd quarter	955.5	342.1	328.3	327.1	94.1	81.2	170.1	146.8	23.3	20.9	-174.3	1.7	-176.0
4th quarter	969.9	347.7	329.3	328.0	97.1	83.1	174.2	150.9	23.3	21.6	-181.3	6.1	-187.4
1986													
1st quarter	979.9	347.2	339.2	337.7	93.6	84.8	177.2	152.7	24.5	22.7	-180.7	6.8	-187.5
2nd quarter	1 004.7	357.1	342.9	341.4	102.5	89.0	178.5	154.2	24.2	23.8	-202.1	6.1	-208.2
3rd quarter	1 023.9	365.8	348.6	347.2	106.1	91.8	178.4	153.7	24.8	25.1	-207.1	4.8	-211.9
4th quarter	1 015.6	362.9	350.4	348.3	97.3	84.9	178.5	153.5	25.0	26.5	-173.3	8.0	-181.4
1987													
1st quarter	1 022.8	369.6	354.5	353.0	91.1	82.1	179.7	153.9	25.8	27.9	-180.5	11.2	-191.7
2nd quarter	1 037.8	372.3	358.5	357.1	95.4	85.8	181.5	155.5	26.0	30.1	-126.0	11.5	-137.5
3rd quarter	1 040.5	372.3	358.9	357.4	93.4	83.9	185.2	159.1	26.1	30.9	-134.4	15.7	-150.1
4th quarter	1 065.3	382.8	360.7	359.2	99.0	83.8	191.8	164.9	26.9	30.7	-139.1	22.2	-161.3
1988													
1st quarter	1 082.4	381.5	375.6	374.0	99.4	89.5	195.9	167.0	28.9	29.9	-142.4	31.4	-173.8
2nd quarter	1 080.9	379.9	376.7	375.1	98.6	90.0	196.2	165.3	30.9	29.4	-131.0	38.5	-169.5
3rd quarter	1 089.3	377.0	380.1	378.5	103.3	93.1	200.1	167.2	32.9	28.7	-128.0	42.1	-170.1
4th quarter	1 118.2	391.4	383.9	382.3	109.9	93.8	205.0	170.9	34.1	28.0	-136.4	46.7	-183.2

Table 19-8. Federal Government Current Receipts and Expenditures—*Continued*
(National Income and Product Accounts, calendar years, billions of dollars, quarterly data are at seasonally adjusted annual rates.)

NIPA Table 3.2

Year and quarter	Current receipts													
	Total	Tax receipts							Contributions for government social insurance	Income receipts on assets			Current transfer receipts	Current surplus of government enterprises
		Total	Personal current taxes	Taxes on production and imports		Taxes on corporate income				Total	Interest receipts	Rents and royalties		
				Total	Excise taxes	Total	Federal Reserve banks	Other						
1989														
1st quarter	1 028.2	618.5	437.9	51.3	34.2	126.3	21.2	105.1	371.1	28.4	26.5	1.9	11.8	-1.6
2nd quarter	1 030.8	618.1	446.8	49.7	32.2	119.1	22.1	97.0	374.0	28.2	26.2	2.0	12.0	-1.4
3rd quarter	1 038.5	619.2	455.5	50.5	32.8	110.5	21.5	89.0	377.4	30.3	28.1	2.2	13.1	-1.5
4th quarter	1 052.0	630.9	465.8	49.4	31.8	113.0	21.8	91.1	382.6	27.4	25.1	2.3	12.8	-1.7
1990														
1st quarter	1 057.5	626.9	461.3	50.8	33.1	112.1	22.6	89.6	394.6	27.5	25.1	2.5	12.3	-3.8
2nd quarter	1 075.8	643.0	470.1	51.3	33.5	118.7	23.2	95.5	398.5	26.8	24.3	2.6	12.7	-5.1
3rd quarter	1 093.2	653.9	475.1	51.6	34.2	124.2	24.7	99.5	403.9	27.2	24.6	2.7	13.7	-5.5
4th quarter	1 099.5	647.3	474.3	52.0	35.0	117.5	24.0	93.5	403.4	39.3	36.6	2.7	15.5	-6.0
1991														
1st quarter	1 087.0	627.5	457.3	60.1	43.6	107.4	21.5	85.9	413.5	32.4	29.6	2.8	17.1	-3.5
2nd quarter	1 095.7	632.6	459.2	61.7	45.6	109.0	20.8	88.2	416.3	30.1	27.3	2.8	17.7	-1.0
3rd quarter	1 107.1	638.5	461.9	62.2	45.5	111.8	20.5	91.3	420.8	30.4	27.7	2.8	18.3	-0.9
4th quarter	1 115.3	645.6	467.0	64.6	46.7	111.6	20.3	91.2	423.7	27.5	24.8	2.7	18.6	-0.1
1992														
1st quarter	1 126.8	645.8	459.1	64.0	46.3	120.0	17.8	102.2	436.1	26.5	23.9	2.6	18.4	0.1
2nd quarter	1 143.7	658.8	468.0	63.5	45.5	124.7	17.4	107.3	440.7	25.8	23.2	2.5	18.2	0.2
3rd quarter	1 137.6	649.2	477.2	62.3	43.6	107.1	16.2	90.9	444.5	25.0	22.5	2.5	18.6	0.3
4th quarter	1 180.6	687.8	496.8	65.0	46.1	123.3	15.7	107.5	446.0	25.5	23.0	2.5	22.3	-1.1
1993														
1st quarter	1 174.4	674.6	481.4	62.5	43.9	127.8	16.4	111.4	454.3	26.9	24.3	2.6	21.0	-2.5
2nd quarter	1 218.1	709.6	502.8	65.1	44.9	139.0	16.0	123.1	461.9	26.9	24.2	2.7	20.8	-1.1
3rd quarter	1 226.8	715.5	511.7	65.7	45.2	135.4	15.7	119.7	465.8	26.5	23.8	2.7	20.8	-1.9
4th quarter	1 270.9	753.9	526.1	73.4	53.5	151.6	15.8	135.8	472.2	24.6	21.8	2.7	21.9	-1.6
1994														
1st quarter	1 272.4	741.0	523.3	75.9	55.3	138.9	18.6	120.3	484.1	23.9	21.1	2.8	23.3	0.1
2nd quarter	1 326.8	789.4	553.7	79.0	57.8	153.5	19.5	134.0	491.9	23.4	20.6	2.8	22.0	0.1
3rd quarter	1 331.0	789.4	542.3	80.9	58.9	163.1	20.9	142.1	496.0	23.4	20.7	2.7	22.7	-0.5
4th quarter	1 353.0	807.8	551.4	81.7	59.8	171.4	22.9	148.6	502.7	22.8	20.2	2.6	21.1	-1.4
1995														
1st quarter	1 373.8	817.7	564.6	76.9	56.9	172.6	22.8	149.8	511.9	22.9	20.6	2.3	20.5	0.8
2nd quarter	1 407.3	848.1	590.6	76.1	56.1	177.7	23.8	154.0	516.3	23.8	21.5	2.3	19.5	-0.4
3rd quarter	1 415.2	852.5	586.8	75.8	56.1	185.8	23.6	162.1	521.8	23.1	20.6	2.5	18.9	-1.1
4th quarter	1 429.8	862.0	601.8	74.8	55.1	181.2	23.3	157.8	526.8	25.0	22.2	2.8	17.6	-1.6
1996														
1st quarter	1 470.5	896.1	631.3	73.0	52.9	187.2	19.9	167.3	531.4	26.4	22.9	3.5	18.1	-1.6
2nd quarter	1 519.0	936.4	668.1	71.5	52.2	192.0	20.0	172.0	539.6	26.4	22.6	3.8	18.3	-1.7
3rd quarter	1 529.5	937.5	669.2	72.1	52.4	190.9	20.1	170.8	546.6	27.7	23.5	4.2	18.8	-1.1
4th quarter	1 577.0	959.6	685.2	76.3	58.6	192.4	20.3	172.0	553.5	27.2	22.8	4.4	37.2	-0.5
1997														
1st quarter	1 600.2	990.0	718.0	72.3	53.3	194.9	20.0	174.9	564.5	27.0	22.5	4.5	19.3	-0.6
2nd quarter	1 636.3	1 017.7	733.5	80.1	59.6	199.3	20.5	178.8	571.3	27.0	22.4	4.5	19.6	0.8
3rd quarter	1 672.8	1 046.8	751.8	80.3	60.5	209.6	20.9	188.8	579.4	25.7	21.3	4.5	20.4	0.5
4th quarter	1 703.1	1 067.9	774.0	80.1	60.8	208.2	21.3	186.9	590.2	23.9	19.6	4.4	20.4	0.7
1998														
1st quarter	1 731.4	1 086.0	796.1	79.9	60.5	205.2	26.4	178.9	600.9	22.5	18.3	4.1	21.2	1.0
2nd quarter	1 758.1	1 104.9	816.5	80.5	60.9	202.8	26.6	176.2	609.4	21.8	17.9	3.9	21.4	0.7
3rd quarter	1 792.4	1 131.4	836.3	81.8	62.0	207.7	26.8	181.0	618.2	20.9	17.2	3.7	21.8	0.1
4th quarter	1 813.2	1 145.1	854.5	82.1	62.6	201.3	26.6	174.7	626.7	20.8	17.4	3.5	21.8	-1.4
1999														
1st quarter	1 843.6	1 157.5	864.1	81.7	63.5	206.3	24.0	182.3	643.0	20.8	17.7	3.2	21.9	0.4
2nd quarter	1 869.5	1 179.2	879.7	82.1	64.2	211.4	24.6	186.8	647.1	21.2	17.9	3.4	22.1	-0.2
3rd quarter	1 900.2	1 203.9	899.5	84.2	64.5	213.9	25.3	188.5	652.6	21.5	18.0	3.5	22.5	-0.4
4th quarter	1 951.6	1 242.4	928.7	87.5	66.5	220.2	27.7	192.5	663.9	22.3	18.4	3.8	24.2	-1.2
2000														
1st quarter	2 035.7	1 301.9	975.4	86.7	66.7	233.0	24.7	208.3	685.3	24.5	20.1	4.4	24.8	-0.8
2nd quarter	2 044.9	1 309.4	987.4	88.9	67.0	225.5	25.0	200.6	685.6	25.5	20.7	4.8	25.3	-0.9
3rd quarter	2 066.8	1 322.6	1 011.7	88.1	66.5	215.6	25.6	189.9	696.5	25.0	19.6	5.4	25.8	-3.1
4th quarter	2 068.0	1 320.4	1 021.7	87.5	66.5	203.7	26.1	177.6	699.4	25.9	19.9	6.0	26.7	-4.5
2001														
1st quarter	2 089.2	1 323.0	1 047.3	87.6	65.8	180.7	29.6	151.1	716.4	26.4	19.8	6.6	27.2	-3.8
2nd quarter	2 080.5	1 315.6	1 045.7	86.9	66.3	176.6	28.0	148.7	718.1	25.2	18.6	6.7	27.3	-5.7
3rd quarter	1 895.4	1 132.0	881.0	84.2	64.3	159.7	26.6	133.2	717.9	24.4	17.9	6.5	27.1	-6.1
4th quarter	1 999.6	1 238.1	1 004.1	84.6	64.4	141.6	24.3	117.4	717.6	23.5	17.3	6.2	26.6	-6.2
2002														
1st quarter	1 844.6	1 070.4	846.9	85.1	66.3	131.4	25.4	105.9	731.3	21.3	16.0	5.3	25.4	-3.7
2nd quarter	1 850.5	1 074.1	835.6	87.8	68.0	143.2	25.6	117.6	734.6	20.2	15.1	5.1	24.9	-3.3
3rd quarter	1 847.9	1 066.6	824.4	88.2	67.9	146.9	24.2	122.7	734.3	19.9	15.3	4.7	24.7	2.4
4th quarter	1 846.2	1 064.8	817.7	88.0	67.2	152.2	22.8	129.4	734.9	19.8	15.4	4.4	24.3	2.3
2003														
1st quarter	1 888.6	1 089.7	809.6	90.3	68.6	183.1	24.0	159.1	747.7	19.4	14.7	4.7	25.1	6.6
2nd quarter	1 902.5	1 094.2	811.6	89.6	68.2	183.1	22.8	160.4	754.0	22.8	16.4	6.4	25.4	6.0
3rd quarter	1 816.4	999.3	709.2	88.0	66.7	194.3	21.2	173.1	761.6	24.3	17.0	7.3	25.8	5.5
4th quarter	1 900.6	1 074.9	772.5	89.6	68.1	204.9	20.1	184.8	769.5	25.5	17.9	7.6	25.6	5.0

Table 19-8. Federal Government Current Receipts and Expenditures—Continued

(National Income and Product Accounts, calendar years, billions of dollars, quarterly data are at seasonally adjusted annual rates.)

NIPA Table 3.2

Year and quarter	Current expenditures											Net federal government saving, NIPA (surplus + / deficit -)		
	Total	Consumption expenditures	Government social benefits		Other current transfer payments		Interest payments			Subsidies				
			Total	To persons	Total	Grants-in-aid to state and local governments	Total	To persons and business	To the rest of the world		Total	Social insurance funds	Other
1989														
1st quarter	1 139.6	389.0	404.4	402.8	105.3	94.9	213.5	176.6	36.9	27.4	-111.4	41.8	-153.2
2nd quarter	1 159.4	400.5	408.8	407.2	104.2	95.6	219.1	181.0	38.1	26.8	-128.6	42.6	-171.3
3rd quarter	1 178.0	403.0	414.3	412.6	113.3	101.4	220.9	181.8	39.1	26.5	-139.5	42.9	-182.4
4th quarter	1 192.9	404.5	421.4	419.7	116.5	101.4	223.9	184.6	39.3	26.7	-140.9	45.2	-186.1
1990														
1st quarter	1 226.0	414.9	437.6	435.9	117.7	106.5	229.2	189.2	40.1	26.5	-168.6	43.8	-212.4
2nd quarter	1 247.2	418.1	443.5	441.7	125.7	110.3	233.6	193.1	40.5	26.4	-171.4	43.5	-214.9
3rd quarter	1 258.1	416.4	448.0	446.2	125.9	112.6	241.5	200.6	40.9	26.4	-164.9	45.8	-210.7
4th quarter	1 282.6	429.7	459.5	457.8	121.7	116.3	245.5	203.9	41.6	26.4	-183.1	39.0	-222.2
1991														
1st quarter	1 245.4	443.8	480.9	479.1	46.1	122.8	248.2	206.4	41.8	26.5	-158.4	29.7	-188.1
2nd quarter	1 307.4	442.2	491.2	489.3	96.0	128.1	251.0	210.1	40.9	26.6	-211.7	25.0	-236.6
3rd quarter	1 339.8	438.1	495.0	493.1	129.0	134.9	250.7	209.7	41.1	26.9	-232.7	27.1	-259.7
4th quarter	1 367.4	433.9	509.5	506.5	142.7	140.6	253.9	214.1	39.7	27.5	-252.1	20.9	-273.1
1992														
1st quarter	1 415.3	439.2	539.5	538.0	156.9	143.2	251.7	212.6	39.2	28.0	-288.5	8.8	-297.3
2nd quarter	1 435.4	441.1	551.2	548.5	161.9	146.2	252.6	213.3	39.3	28.6	-291.7	4.5	-296.3
3rd quarter	1 453.7	450.1	555.5	553.5	166.6	152.4	251.8	212.6	39.1	29.8	-316.1	6.5	-322.6
4th quarter	1 473.9	450.3	560.7	559.1	182.5	154.6	248.9	210.2	38.8	31.6	-293.4	6.2	-299.6
1993														
1st quarter	1 475.0	442.7	574.1	572.7	169.9	156.3	253.4	214.6	38.8	34.8	-300.6	3.6	-304.3
2nd quarter	1 486.1	440.0	580.4	578.4	174.8	159.3	253.9	215.2	38.7	36.9	-268.0	5.8	-273.8
3rd quarter	1 500.8	441.2	585.4	583.4	183.0	165.0	254.2	214.3	39.8	37.0	-274.0	4.9	-278.9
4th quarter	1 522.2	443.7	589.5	587.5	201.6	174.1	252.0	211.9	40.1	35.4	-251.3	8.3	-259.5
1994														
1st quarter	1 504.6	437.8	600.4	599.0	183.0	171.2	250.4	209.7	40.7	32.9	-232.2	13.4	-245.5
2nd quarter	1 517.2	438.4	604.3	602.9	185.3	171.6	257.5	215.1	42.3	31.7	-190.3	18.1	-208.4
3rd quarter	1 542.3	446.7	610.0	606.3	190.1	174.9	264.3	219.8	44.6	31.2	-211.3	18.0	-229.3
4th quarter	1 568.6	440.4	615.7	613.9	207.9	181.2	273.2	224.0	49.1	31.4	-215.5	22.4	-237.9
1995														
1st quarter	1 589.0	442.9	631.9	630.7	198.0	185.0	283.1	234.8	48.3	33.0	-215.2	20.7	-235.9
2nd quarter	1 602.6	442.6	640.3	638.2	196.0	184.9	290.2	237.5	52.7	33.5	-195.3	17.9	-213.2
3rd quarter	1 613.9	443.5	646.0	643.9	197.1	185.1	293.4	237.4	56.0	34.0	-198.7	18.6	-217.3
4th quarter	1 608.5	432.8	652.6	650.5	194.0	181.6	294.9	236.6	58.3	34.3	-178.7	18.8	-197.5
1996														
1st quarter	1 652.6	443.6	672.0	669.7	205.8	186.1	296.9	237.2	59.7	34.3	-182.1	8.6	-190.6
2nd quarter	1 662.5	447.6	678.5	676.4	207.0	195.0	294.8	232.0	62.8	34.2	-143.1	11.7	-154.9
3rd quarter	1 662.6	442.2	682.2	680.1	206.0	193.2	298.3	231.2	67.2	33.9	-133.1	16.3	-149.4
4th quarter	1 685.7	451.7	687.4	685.3	214.2	190.3	298.9	227.6	71.4	33.5	-108.7	19.2	-127.8
1997														
1st quarter	1 689.4	453.2	702.8	700.7	202.9	192.4	297.5	223.1	74.4	33.0	-89.2	20.9	-110.1
2nd quarter	1 705.4	461.7	706.0	703.7	206.1	195.5	299.3	221.6	77.7	32.3	-69.1	25.6	-94.7
3rd quarter	1 707.8	457.2	707.7	705.7	209.7	198.4	301.1	220.4	80.7	32.1	-35.0	33.0	-68.0
4th quarter	1 733.1	458.5	708.9	706.7	231.2	208.2	302.0	220.3	81.7	32.4	-30.0	42.8	-72.8
1998														
1st quarter	1 718.4	447.7	716.7	714.4	218.7	207.9	302.3	220.9	81.3	33.1	13.0	46.2	-33.2
2nd quarter	1 729.2	457.9	718.0	715.6	218.2	208.1	301.2	220.1	81.2	33.7	28.9	54.8	-25.8
3rd quarter	1 732.0	451.0	720.5	718.3	225.9	213.0	299.3	220.1	79.2	35.3	60.4	62.1	-1.7
4th quarter	1 760.2	461.8	721.4	719.1	246.6	222.0	292.6	217.1	75.5	37.7	53.0	72.9	-19.9
1999														
1st quarter	1 764.2	467.0	733.4	731.0	238.5	227.0	284.4	210.6	73.8	40.9	79.4	85.5	-6.1
2nd quarter	1 764.8	463.9	736.5	734.2	237.4	223.7	283.3	210.4	72.9	43.6	104.6	89.5	15.1
3rd quarter	1 792.4	477.6	739.3	736.9	250.2	237.6	280.1	205.2	75.0	45.2	107.8	95.3	12.5
4th quarter	1 828.9	491.8	742.9	740.6	265.9	243.2	282.8	206.2	76.5	45.4	122.7	105.9	16.9
2000														
1st quarter	1 823.0	485.7	756.1	753.7	252.1	239.0	285.1	205.6	79.6	43.9	212.7	117.7	95.0
2nd quarter	1 863.5	505.1	771.5	769.3	257.0	242.8	285.7	203.5	82.2	43.8	181.4	105.3	76.1
3rd quarter	1 875.5	501.5	776.8	774.2	271.1	255.0	282.5	198.6	83.9	43.7	191.2	114.1	77.1
4th quarter	1 895.5	505.0	785.1	782.6	282.2	252.6	279.6	193.5	86.2	43.5	172.5	112.2	60.2
2001														
1st quarter	1 932.6	518.4	817.3	814.6	278.1	266.5	274.5	188.6	85.9	44.3	156.6	102.6	54.0
2nd quarter	1 956.9	528.0	831.2	828.5	290.1	278.3	263.7	178.7	85.0	44.0	123.6	95.2	28.4
3rd quarter	1 984.0	532.7	849.4	846.7	286.1	272.8	253.3	173.4	80.0	62.5	-88.6	80.9	-169.5
4th quarter	2 004.3	548.4	867.6	865.0	305.8	286.6	242.8	164.0	78.8	39.7	-4.7	69.3	-74.1
2002														
1st quarter	2 053.1	570.7	897.7	895.1	319.2	291.9	228.5	150.0	78.4	37.0	-208.5	63.9	-272.4
2nd quarter	2 102.1	586.2	924.2	921.5	319.0	304.2	236.5	159.4	77.1	36.1	-251.6	43.6	-295.2
3rd quarter	2 103.1	593.4	927.6	924.8	319.4	305.4	226.2	150.7	75.5	36.6	-255.1	42.2	-297.3
4th quarter	2 148.8	620.3	929.4	926.6	335.4	316.3	224.7	151.3	73.4	39.0	-302.7	40.9	-343.6
2003														
1st quarter	2 170.2	634.3	941.4	938.6	339.4	314.3	213.9	141.9	72.0	42.5	-281.6	48.4	-330.1
2nd quarter	2 266.9	665.7	957.2	954.4	370.3	345.1	217.7	146.7	71.0	54.6	-364.4	41.8	-406.2
3rd quarter	2 249.4	663.0	964.5	961.7	366.6	343.0	210.1	138.2	71.9	45.3	-433.0	44.4	-477.4
4th quarter	2 279.8	671.3	972.5	969.6	378.0	357.2	214.7	141.4	73.3	43.2	-379.2	47.2	-426.4

Table 19-9. State and Local Government Current Receipts and Expenditures

(National Income and Product Accounts, calendar years, billions of dollars, quarterly data are at seasonally adjusted annual rates.)

NIPA Table 3.3

Year and quarter	Current receipts												
	Total	Current tax receipts							Taxes on corporate income	Contributions for government social insurance	Income receipts on assets		
		Total	Personal current taxes		Taxes on production and imports						Total	Interest receipts	Rents and royalties
			Total	Income taxes	Total	Sales taxes	Property taxes	Other					
1947													
1st quarter	14.1	11.5	1.0	...	9.9	...	...	...	0.6	0.2	0.4	...	0.1
2nd quarter	14.7	11.8	1.0	...	10.2	...	...	...	0.6	0.2	0.4	...	0.1
3rd quarter	15.1	12.2	1.0	...	10.6	...	...	...	0.6	0.2	0.4	...	0.1
4th quarter	15.6	12.7	1.0	...	11.1	...	...	...	0.6	0.2	0.4	...	0.1
1948													
1st quarter	16.1	13.2	1.1	...	11.4	...	...	...	0.7	0.2	0.5	...	0.2
2nd quarter	16.6	13.6	1.1	...	11.7	...	...	...	0.7	0.2	0.5	...	0.2
3rd quarter	17.0	13.9	1.1	...	12.1	...	...	...	0.7	0.2	0.5	...	0.2
4th quarter	17.3	14.1	1.1	...	12.3	...	...	...	0.7	0.2	0.5	...	0.2
1949													
1st quarter	17.7	14.6	1.3	...	12.6	...	...	...	0.7	0.2	0.5	...	0.2
2nd quarter	17.9	14.8	1.4	...	12.9	...	...	...	0.6	0.2	0.5	...	0.2
3rd quarter	18.7	15.2	1.4	...	13.2	...	...	...	0.6	0.2	0.5	...	0.2
4th quarter	18.8	15.4	1.4	...	13.4	...	...	...	0.6	0.2	0.5	...	0.2
1950													
1st quarter	19.2	15.8	1.5	...	13.7	...	...	...	0.6	0.2	0.5	...	0.2
2nd quarter	19.7	16.1	1.5	...	14.0	...	...	...	0.7	0.2	0.5	...	0.2
3rd quarter	20.4	16.9	1.5	...	14.6	...	...	...	0.9	0.2	0.5	...	0.2
4th quarter	20.6	17.1	1.5	...	14.6	...	...	...	0.9	0.2	0.6	...	0.2
1951													
1st quarter	21.7	17.9	1.6	...	15.3	...	...	...	1.0	0.2	0.6	...	0.2
2nd quarter	21.6	17.8	1.7	...	15.3	...	...	...	0.9	0.2	0.6	...	0.2
3rd quarter	21.9	18.1	1.7	...	15.6	...	...	...	0.8	0.2	0.6	...	0.2
4th quarter	22.5	18.6	1.7	...	16.0	...	...	...	0.8	0.2	0.6	...	0.2
1952													
1st quarter	22.9	19.0	1.8	...	16.3	...	...	...	0.8	0.3	0.6	...	0.2
2nd quarter	23.4	19.4	1.8	...	16.8	...	...	...	0.8	0.3	0.7	...	0.2
3rd quarter	24.0	19.8	1.8	...	17.2	...	...	...	0.8	0.3	0.7	...	0.2
4th quarter	24.6	20.4	1.8	...	17.7	...	...	...	0.9	0.3	0.7	...	0.2
1953													
1st quarter	24.6	20.7	1.9	...	18.0	...	...	...	0.9	0.3	0.7	...	0.3
2nd quarter	25.8	21.0	1.9	...	18.2	...	...	...	0.9	0.3	0.7	...	0.3
3rd quarter	25.8	21.4	2.0	...	18.6	...	...	...	0.8	0.3	0.7	...	0.3
4th quarter	25.9	21.4	2.0	...	18.8	...	...	...	0.7	0.3	0.7	...	0.3
1954													
1st quarter	26.4	21.7	2.1	...	19.0	...	...	...	0.7	0.3	0.8	...	0.3
2nd quarter	26.6	22.0	2.1	...	19.2	...	...	...	0.7	0.3	0.8	...	0.3
3rd quarter	27.1	22.4	2.1	...	19.5	...	...	...	0.8	0.3	0.8	...	0.3
4th quarter	27.6	22.8	2.1	...	19.9	...	...	...	0.8	0.3	0.8	...	0.3
1955													
1st quarter	28.3	23.6	2.4	...	20.3	...	...	...	0.9	0.3	0.8	...	0.3
2nd quarter	29.0	24.0	2.4	...	20.7	...	...	...	0.9	0.3	0.8	...	0.3
3rd quarter	29.8	24.7	2.4	...	21.3	...	...	...	1.0	0.3	0.9	...	0.3
4th quarter	30.4	25.3	2.4	...	21.9	...	...	...	1.0	0.3	0.9	...	0.3
1956													
1st quarter	31.3	26.1	2.7	...	22.4	...	...	...	1.0	0.4	0.9	...	0.3
2nd quarter	32.0	26.8	2.7	...	23.0	...	...	...	1.1	0.4	1.0	...	0.3
3rd quarter	32.8	27.3	2.7	...	23.6	...	...	...	1.0	0.4	1.0	...	0.3
4th quarter	33.4	27.8	2.7	...	24.1	...	...	...	1.1	0.4	1.0	...	0.3
1957													
1st quarter	34.4	28.5	2.9	...	24.6	...	...	...	1.1	0.4	1.1	...	0.3
2nd quarter	34.7	28.9	2.9	...	25.0	...	...	...	1.0	0.4	1.1	...	0.3
3rd quarter	35.3	29.3	2.9	...	25.4	...	...	...	1.0	0.4	1.1	...	0.3
4th quarter	35.6	29.3	2.9	...	25.5	...	...	...	0.9	0.4	1.1	...	0.3
1958													
1st quarter	35.7	29.7	3.0	1.8	25.8	9.8	13.4	2.7	0.9	0.4	1.1	0.7	0.4
2nd quarter	36.5	30.1	3.0	1.8	26.1	9.8	13.6	2.7	0.9	0.4	1.1	0.8	0.4
3rd quarter	37.2	30.8	3.1	1.8	26.7	10.0	13.9	2.8	1.0	0.4	1.1	0.8	0.4
4th quarter	38.9	31.7	3.1	1.8	27.4	10.3	14.2	3.0	1.2	0.4	1.2	0.8	0.4
1959													
1st quarter	39.1	32.7	3.6	2.0	27.9	10.7	14.4	2.8	1.2	0.4	1.1	0.8	0.3
2nd quarter	40.1	33.2	3.7	2.1	28.2	10.9	14.5	2.9	1.3	0.4	1.1	0.8	0.3
3rd quarter	41.3	34.4	4.0	2.4	29.3	11.4	14.9	2.9	1.1	0.4	1.1	0.9	0.3
4th quarter	42.1	35.1	4.0	2.4	30.0	11.5	15.4	3.0	1.1	0.4	1.2	0.9	0.3
1960													
1st quarter	43.3	36.0	4.2	2.5	30.4	11.8	15.6	3.1	1.4	0.4	1.3	1.1	0.3
2nd quarter	44.2	36.7	4.2	2.5	31.2	12.1	16.0	3.1	1.3	0.4	1.4	1.1	0.3
3rd quarter	44.8	37.3	4.3	2.6	31.8	12.3	16.5	3.1	1.2	0.5	1.3	1.0	0.3
4th quarter	45.5	37.9	4.3	2.6	32.4	12.4	16.9	3.1	1.1	0.5	1.3	1.0	0.3

... = Not available.

Table 19-9. State and Local Government Current Receipts and Expenditures—Continued

(National Income and Product Accounts, calendar years, billions of dollars, quarterly data are at seasonally adjusted annual rates.)

NIPA Table 3.3

Year and quarter	Current receipts—Continued				Current surplus of government enterprises	Current expenditures					Net state and local government saving, NIPA (surplus + / deficit -)		
	Current transfer receipts												
	Total	Federal grants-in-aid	From business (net)	From persons		Total	Consumption expenditures	Government social benefits to persons	Interest payments	Subsidies	Total	Social insurance funds	Other
1947													
1st quarter	1.6	1.4	0.1	0.2	0.4	12.5	10.3	1.6	0.5	...	1.6	...	...
2nd quarter	1.9	1.7	0.1	0.2	0.4	13.1	10.7	1.9	0.5	...	1.6	...	...
3rd quarter	1.9	1.6	0.1	0.2	0.4	14.0	11.1	2.4	0.5	...	1.1	...	...
4th quarter	1.9	1.6	0.1	0.2	0.4	14.3	11.5	2.3	0.5	...	1.3	...	...
1948													
1st quarter	1.9	1.6	0.1	0.2	0.4	15.1	11.8	2.8	0.5	...	1.0	...	...
2nd quarter	2.0	1.7	0.1	0.2	0.3	15.4	12.0	2.8	0.5	...	1.2	...	...
3rd quarter	2.1	1.8	0.1	0.3	0.3	15.8	12.5	2.7	0.5	...	1.2	...	...
4th quarter	2.2	1.9	0.1	0.3	0.3	15.8	13.0	2.4	0.5	...	1.5	...	...
1949													
1st quarter	2.1	1.7	0.1	0.3	0.4	16.2	13.3	2.5	0.5	...	1.5	...	...
2nd quarter	2.0	1.7	0.1	0.3	0.4	16.5	13.4	2.6	0.5	...	1.4	...	...
3rd quarter	2.5	2.1	0.1	0.3	0.4	17.1	13.8	2.7	0.5	...	1.6	...	...
4th quarter	2.3	1.9	0.1	0.3	0.4	17.5	14.1	2.9	0.5	...	1.3	...	...
1950													
1st quarter	2.3	1.9	0.1	0.3	0.4	18.2	14.5	3.2	0.6	...	1.0	...	...
2nd quarter	2.3	1.9	0.1	0.3	0.4	18.9	14.7	3.7	0.6	...	0.7	...	...
3rd quarter	2.3	1.9	0.1	0.3	0.4	18.6	15.0	3.0	0.6	...	1.8	...	...
4th quarter	2.3	1.9	0.1	0.3	0.4	18.8	15.3	2.9	0.6	...	1.8	...	...
1951													
1st quarter	2.5	2.0	0.1	0.3	0.5	19.0	15.6	2.8	0.6	...	2.7	...	...
2nd quarter	2.5	2.1	0.1	0.3	0.5	19.1	15.9	2.6	0.6	...	2.5	...	...
3rd quarter	2.4	1.9	0.1	0.3	0.5	19.5	16.2	2.6	0.6	...	2.4	...	...
4th quarter	2.6	2.1	0.1	0.3	0.5	19.8	16.6	2.6	0.7	...	2.7	...	...
1952													
1st quarter	2.5	2.0	0.1	0.3	0.5	20.0	16.5	2.8	0.7	...	2.9	...	...
2nd quarter	2.5	2.1	0.1	0.3	0.5	21.0	17.3	3.0	0.7	...	2.4	...	...
3rd quarter	2.7	2.3	0.1	0.3	0.5	20.7	17.1	2.9	0.7	...	3.3	...	...
4th quarter	2.7	2.3	0.1	0.3	0.5	21.2	17.5	2.9	0.7	...	3.4	...	...
1953													
1st quarter	2.3	1.8	0.1	0.3	0.5	21.7	18.0	2.9	0.7	...	2.9	...	...
2nd quarter	3.2	2.7	0.1	0.3	0.5	21.8	18.0	3.0	0.8	...	4.0	...	...
3rd quarter	2.8	2.3	0.1	0.4	0.6	22.3	18.4	3.1	0.8	...	3.5	...	...
4th quarter	2.8	2.3	0.2	0.4	0.6	22.3	18.5	2.9	0.8	...	3.6	...	...
1954													
1st quarter	2.9	2.3	0.2	0.4	0.6	22.8	18.9	3.0	0.9	...	3.6	...	...
2nd quarter	2.8	2.3	0.2	0.4	0.7	23.4	19.4	3.0	0.9	...	3.3	...	...
3rd quarter	2.9	2.4	0.2	0.4	0.7	24.1	20.1	3.1	0.9	...	3.0	...	...
4th quarter	2.9	2.3	0.2	0.4	0.7	24.5	20.4	3.1	1.0	...	3.1	...	...
1955													
1st quarter	2.8	2.3	0.2	0.4	0.8	25.3	21.1	3.2	1.0	...	3.0	...	...
2nd quarter	2.9	2.4	0.2	0.4	0.8	25.7	21.3	3.3	1.1	...	3.3	...	...
3rd quarter	3.1	2.5	0.2	0.4	0.9	26.0	21.7	3.3	1.1	...	3.8	...	...
4th quarter	3.0	2.4	0.2	0.4	0.9	26.5	22.1	3.2	1.1	...	3.9	...	...
1956													
1st quarter	3.0	2.4	0.2	0.4	0.9	27.0	22.6	3.3	1.2	...	4.3	...	...
2nd quarter	3.1	2.5	0.2	0.4	0.9	27.6	23.1	3.2	1.2	...	4.5	...	...
3rd quarter	3.3	2.6	0.2	0.4	0.9	28.3	23.8	3.3	1.3	...	4.5	...	...
4th quarter	3.3	2.7	0.2	0.5	0.9	29.0	24.4	3.4	1.3	...	4.3	...	...
1957													
1st quarter	3.6	2.9	0.2	0.5	0.9	29.6	24.8	3.5	1.3	...	4.8	...	...
2nd quarter	3.5	2.8	0.2	0.5	0.9	30.4	25.5	3.5	1.4	...	4.3	...	...
3rd quarter	3.7	2.9	0.2	0.5	0.9	31.3	26.2	3.6	1.4	...	4.1	...	...
4th quarter	3.8	3.1	0.2	0.5	0.9	32.0	26.8	3.7	1.5	...	3.6	...	...
1958													
1st quarter	3.6	2.9	0.2	0.5	0.9	33.0	27.6	4.0	1.5	...	2.7	0.1	2.6
2nd quarter	4.1	3.3	0.2	0.5	0.9	33.9	28.4	4.0	1.5	...	2.6	0.0	2.5
3rd quarter	3.9	3.2	0.2	0.5	0.9	34.6	29.0	4.0	1.6	...	2.6	0.0	2.6
4th quarter	4.7	4.0	0.2	0.5	0.9	35.3	29.5	4.1	1.6	...	3.6	0.0	3.6
1959													
1st quarter	3.9	3.5	0.1	0.3	1.0	36.1	30.0	4.3	1.7	0.0	3.1	0.0	3.0
2nd quarter	4.3	3.9	0.1	0.3	1.1	36.5	30.5	4.3	1.7	0.0	3.6	0.0	3.5
3rd quarter	4.2	3.8	0.1	0.3	1.2	37.1	30.9	4.3	1.8	0.0	4.2	0.0	4.1
4th quarter	4.2	3.8	0.1	0.3	1.2	37.8	31.5	4.4	1.9	0.0	4.3	0.0	4.3
1960													
1st quarter	4.3	3.9	0.2	0.3	1.2	39.0	32.5	4.4	2.1	0.0	4.3	0.0	4.3
2nd quarter	4.4	4.0	0.2	0.3	1.3	40.0	33.4	4.5	2.1	0.0	4.2	0.0	4.2
3rd quarter	4.5	4.0	0.2	0.3	1.3	40.5	33.8	4.6	2.0	0.0	4.3	0.0	4.3
4th quarter	4.7	4.2	0.2	0.3	1.3	41.2	34.5	4.7	2.0	0.0	4.4	0.0	4.3

... = Not available.

Table 19-9. State and Local Government Current Receipts and Expenditures—Continued

(National Income and Product Accounts, calendar years, billions of dollars, quarterly data are at seasonally adjusted annual rates.)

NIPA Table 3.3

Year and quarter	Current receipts												
	Total	Current tax receipts							Taxes on corporate income	Contributions for government social insurance	Income receipts on assets		
		Total	Personal current taxes		Taxes on production and imports						Total	Interest receipts	Rents and royalties
			Total	Income taxes	Total	Sales taxes	Property taxes	Other					
1961													
1st quarter	46.5	38.4	4.3	2.6	32.9	12.6	17.2	3.2	1.2	0.5	1.4	1.0	0.4
2nd quarter	47.6	39.2	4.5	2.7	33.4	12.8	17.5	3.2	1.2	0.5	1.4	1.1	0.4
3rd quarter	48.6	40.1	4.6	2.9	34.1	13.2	17.7	3.2	1.3	0.5	1.4	1.1	0.4
4th quarter	49.6	41.0	4.7	3.0	34.8	13.6	18.0	3.2	1.4	0.5	1.4	1.1	0.4
1962													
1st quarter	50.7	41.8	4.9	3.1	35.5	13.9	18.3	3.2	1.5	0.5	1.5	1.1	0.4
2nd quarter	51.5	42.4	5.0	3.1	36.0	13.9	18.7	3.3	1.5	0.5	1.5	1.1	0.4
3rd quarter	52.5	43.1	5.1	3.2	36.5	14.0	19.2	3.3	1.5	0.6	1.6	1.2	0.4
4th quarter	53.3	43.8	5.2	3.3	37.1	14.2	19.6	3.3	1.5	0.6	1.5	1.1	0.4
1963													
1st quarter	54.1	44.4	5.3	3.3	37.6	14.3	19.9	3.4	1.5	0.6	1.5	1.1	0.4
2nd quarter	55.3	45.2	5.3	3.3	38.3	14.7	20.1	3.5	1.6	0.6	1.6	1.2	0.4
3rd quarter	56.8	46.3	5.5	3.5	39.1	15.3	20.4	3.5	1.7	0.6	1.7	1.3	0.4
4th quarter	57.9	47.1	5.6	3.6	39.8	15.6	20.6	3.5	1.7	0.7	1.7	1.3	0.4
1964													
1st quarter	59.7	48.3	5.8	3.7	40.7	16.1	21.0	3.6	1.8	0.7	1.8	1.4	0.4
2nd quarter	60.7	49.2	6.0	4.0	41.4	16.3	21.4	3.7	1.8	0.7	2.0	1.5	0.4
3rd quarter	61.7	50.5	6.2	4.1	42.4	16.7	21.9	3.7	1.9	0.7	1.9	1.5	0.4
4th quarter	62.9	51.1	6.4	4.2	42.9	16.7	22.4	3.8	1.8	0.7	2.0	1.5	0.4
1965													
1st quarter	64.1	52.2	6.5	4.3	43.8	17.2	22.8	3.8	1.9	0.7	2.1	1.6	0.4
2nd quarter	65.9	53.2	6.5	4.4	44.7	17.8	23.1	3.9	1.9	0.8	2.2	1.8	0.4
3rd quarter	67.3	54.4	6.6	4.4	45.8	18.5	23.3	4.0	2.0	0.8	2.2	1.7	0.4
4th quarter	68.9	55.7	6.8	4.5	46.8	19.2	23.6	4.0	2.1	0.8	2.3	1.8	0.4
1966													
1st quarter	71.8	56.9	7.1	4.8	47.5	19.5	23.9	4.1	2.3	0.8	2.5	2.0	0.5
2nd quarter	74.1	58.0	7.6	5.2	48.2	19.7	24.3	4.2	2.3	0.8	2.6	2.0	0.5
3rd quarter	76.1	59.5	8.0	5.6	49.2	20.2	24.7	4.3	2.2	0.8	2.7	2.2	0.5
4th quarter	77.7	60.6	8.4	6.0	50.1	20.4	25.2	4.5	2.2	0.8	2.7	2.2	0.5
1967													
1st quarter	79.2	61.6	8.3	5.9	50.7	20.4	25.8	4.4	2.6	0.9	2.8	2.2	0.6
2nd quarter	80.7	62.5	8.3	5.9	51.7	20.7	26.6	4.4	2.6	0.9	2.8	2.2	0.6
3rd quarter	83.3	64.8	8.7	6.2	53.5	21.8	27.3	4.5	2.6	0.9	3.1	2.5	0.6
4th quarter	86.8	67.0	9.0	6.5	55.2	22.7	28.1	4.4	2.7	0.9	3.3	2.7	0.6
1968													
1st quarter	89.3	70.2	9.7	7.1	57.2	23.8	28.9	4.5	3.2	0.9	3.4	2.6	0.7
2nd quarter	92.9	72.3	10.3	7.6	58.7	24.6	29.6	4.6	3.3	0.9	3.4	2.7	0.7
3rd quarter	94.6	74.6	10.8	8.1	60.4	25.6	30.3	4.6	3.3	1.0	3.5	2.8	0.7
4th quarter	97.3	76.5	11.4	8.5	61.8	26.2	30.9	4.6	3.4	1.0	3.7	3.0	0.7
1969													
1st quarter	100.1	79.0	11.9	8.9	63.3	27.1	31.6	4.7	3.8	1.0	4.0	3.2	0.8
2nd quarter	103.4	81.1	12.3	9.3	65.1	28.1	32.3	4.7	3.7	1.0	4.2	3.5	0.8
3rd quarter	107.5	83.9	13.4	10.3	67.0	29.1	33.1	4.7	3.5	1.0	4.5	3.7	0.8
4th quarter	110.9	85.9	13.7	10.5	68.8	29.9	34.1	4.8	3.4	1.1	4.7	3.9	0.8
1970													
1st quarter	115.1	88.4	14.0	10.8	70.6	30.6	35.1	4.9	3.8	1.1	4.9	4.1	0.8
2nd quarter	118.6	90.3	14.1	10.9	72.4	31.3	36.2	4.9	3.7	1.1	5.1	4.3	0.8
3rd quarter	122.2	92.5	14.3	11.0	74.3	32.1	37.2	5.0	3.8	1.1	5.2	4.4	0.8
4th quarter	124.5	94.0	14.4	11.0	76.0	32.6	38.2	5.2	3.6	1.1	5.3	4.5	0.8
1971													
1st quarter	128.5	97.1	14.7	11.3	78.3	33.6	39.2	5.5	4.1	1.1	5.4	4.5	0.9
2nd quarter	133.2	100.0	15.6	12.2	80.2	34.5	40.1	5.6	4.2	1.2	5.5	4.6	0.9
3rd quarter	136.7	103.2	16.0	12.5	82.8	36.1	40.9	5.8	4.4	1.2	5.5	4.6	0.9
4th quarter	141.3	106.5	17.3	13.8	84.7	37.3	41.6	5.9	4.5	1.2	5.5	4.6	0.9
1972													
1st quarter	147.2	110.9	19.5	15.9	86.4	38.1	42.2	6.1	5.0	1.3	5.7	4.7	1.0
2nd quarter	159.4	114.5	21.0	17.3	88.5	39.4	42.8	6.3	5.0	1.3	5.8	4.8	1.0
3rd quarter	154.9	116.8	21.2	17.5	90.4	40.3	43.6	6.5	5.2	1.3	6.0	5.0	1.0
4th quarter	172.3	120.1	21.8	18.1	92.5	41.4	44.4	6.7	5.7	1.4	6.3	5.3	1.0
1973													
1st quarter	171.0	123.0	21.9	18.0	95.1	43.0	45.3	6.8	6.0	1.4	6.9	5.8	1.1
2nd quarter	172.4	124.7	22.3	18.4	96.3	43.3	46.1	6.9	6.1	1.5	7.4	6.3	1.1
3rd quarter	175.1	127.6	23.1	19.1	98.7	44.9	46.8	7.0	5.9	1.5	8.0	6.9	1.1
4th quarter	178.9	129.7	24.0	19.9	99.6	45.1	47.3	7.2	6.1	1.6	8.7	7.5	1.1
1974													
1st quarter	180.4	130.6	23.3	19.2	101.0	45.7	47.8	7.5	6.3	1.6	9.4	8.1	1.3
2nd quarter	185.8	134.7	24.1	19.9	104.0	47.8	48.5	7.7	6.6	1.6	10.0	8.7	1.3
3rd quarter	192.0	139.3	25.2	21.0	106.8	49.7	49.3	7.8	7.3	1.7	10.5	9.2	1.3
4th quarter	194.0	139.6	25.6	21.3	107.5	49.4	50.3	7.8	6.5	1.7	10.8	9.5	1.3

Table 19-9. State and Local Government Current Receipts and Expenditures—*Continued*

(National Income and Product Accounts, calendar years, billions of dollars, quarterly data are at seasonally adjusted annual rates.)

NIPA Table 3.3

Year and quarter	Current receipts—Continued					Current expenditures					Net state and local government saving, NIPA (surplus + / deficit -)		
	Current transfer receipts				Current surplus of government enterprises	Total	Consumption expenditures	Government social benefits to persons	Interest payments	Subsidies	Total	Social insurance funds	Other
	Total	Federal grants-in-aid	From business (net)	From persons									
1961													
1st quarter	4.9	4.2	0.2	0.4	1.3	42.4	35.5	4.9	2.0	0.0	4.1	0.0	4.1
2nd quarter	5.2	4.5	0.2	0.4	1.4	43.6	36.5	4.9	2.2	0.0	4.0	0.0	4.0
3rd quarter	5.3	4.6	0.2	0.4	1.3	44.1	36.8	5.0	2.3	0.0	4.5	0.0	4.4
4th quarter	5.4	4.7	0.2	0.5	1.4	45.0	37.5	5.1	2.4	0.0	4.6	0.0	4.6
1962													
1st quarter	5.6	4.9	0.2	0.5	1.3	45.8	38.1	5.2	2.4	0.0	4.9	0.0	4.9
2nd quarter	5.6	4.9	0.2	0.5	1.4	46.5	38.7	5.3	2.4	0.0	5.0	0.0	5.0
3rd quarter	5.9	5.2	0.2	0.5	1.4	47.0	39.2	5.3	2.5	0.0	5.5	0.0	5.5
4th quarter	5.9	5.2	0.2	0.5	1.5	47.8	39.9	5.5	2.4	0.0	5.5	0.0	5.5
1963													
1st quarter	6.0	5.3	0.3	0.5	1.6	48.7	40.7	5.6	2.5	0.0	5.4	0.0	5.3
2nd quarter	6.2	5.5	0.3	0.5	1.6	49.7	41.5	5.7	2.6	0.0	5.5	0.0	5.5
3rd quarter	6.5	5.8	0.3	0.5	1.7	50.8	42.3	5.7	2.7	0.0	6.0	0.0	6.0
4th quarter	6.8	6.1	0.3	0.5	1.6	52.0	43.3	5.8	2.9	0.0	5.9	0.0	5.8
1964													
1st quarter	7.3	6.5	0.3	0.5	1.6	53.2	44.4	6.0	2.9	0.0	6.4	0.0	6.4
2nd quarter	7.3	6.5	0.3	0.5	1.6	54.5	45.3	6.1	3.0	0.0	6.3	0.0	6.2
3rd quarter	7.0	6.2	0.3	0.5	1.7	55.3	46.2	6.2	2.8	0.0	6.5	0.1	6.4
4th quarter	7.4	6.6	0.3	0.5	1.7	56.5	47.2	6.4	2.9	0.0	6.4	0.1	6.3
1965													
1st quarter	7.4	6.5	0.3	0.5	1.7	57.8	48.3	6.5	3.0	0.0	6.2	0.1	6.1
2nd quarter	7.9	7.1	0.3	0.5	1.7	59.3	49.5	6.6	3.2	0.0	6.5	0.1	6.4
3rd quarter	8.3	7.5	0.3	0.5	1.7	60.8	50.9	6.7	3.2	0.0	6.6	0.1	6.5
4th quarter	8.5	7.6	0.3	0.6	1.7	62.1	52.1	6.8	3.2	0.0	6.8	0.1	6.7
1966													
1st quarter	10.0	9.0	0.3	0.6	1.6	64.0	53.7	7.0	3.3	0.0	7.7	0.1	7.6
2nd quarter	11.1	10.1	0.3	0.7	1.6	66.1	55.2	7.5	3.4	0.0	8.0	0.1	7.9
3rd quarter	11.5	10.5	0.3	0.8	1.6	68.2	56.9	7.7	3.5	0.0	8.0	0.1	7.9
4th quarter	11.8	10.7	0.3	0.8	1.6	70.4	58.7	8.2	3.5	0.0	7.3	0.1	7.1
1967													
1st quarter	12.4	11.1	0.5	0.9	1.6	71.7	60.0	8.4	3.3	0.0	7.5	0.1	7.4
2nd quarter	12.9	11.6	0.5	0.9	1.6	73.9	61.5	8.9	3.4	0.0	6.9	0.1	6.7
3rd quarter	13.0	11.6	0.5	0.9	1.5	76.9	63.5	9.5	3.8	0.0	6.4	0.1	6.2
4th quarter	14.2	12.7	0.5	1.0	1.5	79.6	65.3	10.1	4.3	0.0	7.2	0.1	7.1
1968													
1st quarter	13.2	11.8	0.5	1.0	1.6	82.1	67.4	10.6	4.0	0.0	7.2	0.1	7.0
2nd quarter	14.8	13.3	0.5	1.0	1.5	84.7	69.2	11.4	4.1	0.0	8.2	0.1	8.1
3rd quarter	14.1	12.6	0.5	1.0	1.5	87.2	71.3	11.7	4.2	0.0	7.4	0.1	7.3
4th quarter	14.7	13.2	0.5	1.0	1.5	90.1	73.6	12.1	4.3	0.0	7.2	0.2	7.1
1969													
1st quarter	14.7	13.1	0.5	1.0	1.5	92.7	75.9	12.6	4.2	0.0	7.4	0.1	7.3
2nd quarter	15.6	14.0	0.5	1.1	1.5	95.6	78.4	12.8	4.3	0.0	7.8	0.2	7.6
3rd quarter	16.7	15.1	0.5	1.1	1.5	99.0	81.2	13.4	4.4	0.0	8.5	0.2	8.3
4th quarter	17.7	16.1	0.5	1.1	1.5	102.6	83.9	14.0	4.6	0.0	8.2	0.2	8.1
1970													
1st quarter	19.2	17.5	0.6	1.1	1.5	106.9	87.3	14.7	4.9	0.0	8.2	0.2	8.0
2nd quarter	20.6	18.8	0.6	1.2	1.5	110.8	90.0	15.6	5.2	0.0	7.7	0.2	7.5
3rd quarter	21.9	20.1	0.6	1.2	1.5	115.1	93.0	16.6	5.4	0.0	7.1	0.2	7.0
4th quarter	22.6	20.8	0.6	1.3	1.5	119.1	95.8	17.5	5.8	0.0	5.4	0.2	5.2
1971													
1st quarter	23.5	21.6	0.6	1.3	1.4	123.5	99.0	18.3	6.2	0.0	5.0	0.2	4.8
2nd quarter	25.1	23.2	0.6	1.4	1.3	127.1	101.6	19.1	6.4	0.0	6.0	0.2	5.8
3rd quarter	25.5	23.5	0.6	1.4	1.4	130.2	104.2	19.6	6.7	0.0	6.5	0.2	6.2
4th quarter	26.8	24.7	0.6	1.5	1.4	132.9	106.1	20.3	6.9	0.0	8.4	0.2	8.2
1972													
1st quarter	28.0	25.7	0.7	1.6	1.5	138.1	109.1	21.2	7.2	0.0	9.1	0.2	8.8
2nd quarter	36.2	33.9	0.7	1.6	1.6	140.7	111.6	21.6	7.4	0.1	18.7	0.3	18.4
3rd quarter	29.1	26.8	0.7	1.7	1.6	144.8	114.6	22.5	7.6	0.1	10.1	0.3	9.9
4th quarter	42.8	40.4	0.7	1.7	1.6	147.6	117.3	22.5	7.8	0.1	24.6	0.3	24.4
1973													
1st quarter	38.1	35.6	0.9	1.7	1.6	152.1	120.7	23.2	8.1	0.1	18.9	0.3	18.7
2nd quarter	37.2	34.7	0.9	1.7	1.5	156.6	124.2	24.0	8.3	0.1	15.7	0.3	15.4
3rd quarter	36.5	33.9	0.9	1.7	1.4	160.5	127.7	24.2	8.6	0.1	14.6	0.3	14.3
4th quarter	37.6	34.9	0.9	1.8	1.3	165.3	131.4	25.0	8.8	0.1	13.6	0.3	13.3
1974													
1st quarter	37.6	34.6	1.1	1.8	1.2	168.6	136.0	23.4	9.1	0.1	11.8	0.4	11.4
2nd quarter	38.4	35.4	1.1	1.9	1.0	175.2	140.9	24.7	9.4	0.1	10.6	0.4	10.3
3rd quarter	39.9	36.8	1.1	2.0	0.7	182.0	146.3	25.9	9.8	0.1	10.0	0.4	9.6
4th quarter	41.4	38.2	1.1	2.1	0.5	189.1	151.8	27.1	10.1	0.1	4.9	0.4	4.5

Table 19-9. State and Local Government Current Receipts and Expenditures—Continued

(National Income and Product Accounts, calendar years, billions of dollars, quarterly data are at seasonally adjusted annual rates.)

NIPA Table 3.3

Year and quarter	Current receipts												
		Current tax receipts							Taxes on corporate income	Contributions for government social insurance	Income receipts on assets		
	Total	Personal current taxes			Taxes on production and imports								
		Total	Total	Income taxes	Total	Sales taxes	Property taxes	Other			Total	Interest receipts	Rents and royalties
1975													
1st quarter	198.3	140.9	25.7	21.4	109.0	49.5	51.6	7.9	6.1	1.8	11.2	9.9	1.3
2nd quarter	207.6	144.8	26.5	22.1	111.7	50.8	52.8	8.1	6.6	1.8	11.3	9.9	1.3
3rd quarter	213.8	150.3	27.2	22.7	114.9	52.6	54.0	8.3	8.2	1.9	11.2	9.8	1.3
4th quarter	218.6	153.9	28.2	23.6	117.3	53.8	55.2	8.2	8.4	2.0	11.0	9.6	1.3
1976													
1st quarter	225.8	160.0	29.5	24.8	120.9	55.9	56.4	8.5	9.7	2.0	10.5	9.1	1.3
2nd quarter	230.2	163.7	30.6	25.8	123.5	57.2	57.7	8.7	9.6	2.1	10.4	9.0	1.3
3rd quarter	234.9	167.3	31.6	26.7	126.0	58.0	58.9	9.2	9.7	2.2	10.3	9.0	1.3
4th quarter	243.8	171.9	32.6	27.7	129.6	60.0	60.0	9.6	9.6	2.3	10.5	9.1	1.3
1977													
1st quarter	247.9	176.9	33.5	28.6	132.9	61.8	61.5	9.5	10.5	2.5	10.9	9.6	1.3
2nd quarter	256.3	181.6	34.7	29.8	135.5	63.1	62.8	9.6	11.4	2.7	11.4	10.1	1.3
3rd quarter	265.2	186.1	35.9	30.9	138.3	64.7	63.8	9.8	11.8	2.9	11.9	10.6	1.3
4th quarter	270.4	190.3	37.3	32.2	141.1	66.4	64.6	10.0	12.0	3.0	12.5	11.2	1.3
1978													
1st quarter	277.7	192.1	38.6	33.4	143.0	67.3	65.3	10.4	10.5	3.2	13.2	11.8	1.3
2nd quarter	289.5	200.2	40.1	34.7	147.7	70.8	66.1	10.9	12.4	3.3	14.1	12.7	1.3
3rd quarter	287.5	197.6	40.9	35.4	144.2	72.0	61.3	10.9	12.5	3.5	15.1	13.7	1.3
4th quarter	295.5	202.7	42.1	36.5	147.6	74.0	62.3	11.3	13.1	3.6	16.2	14.9	1.3
1979													
1st quarter	298.8	206.3	42.0	36.3	150.6	75.4	63.2	12.0	13.7	3.8	18.2	16.2	1.9
2nd quarter	302.8	208.4	42.1	36.3	152.6	76.3	64.0	12.3	13.8	3.9	19.5	17.5	1.9
3rd quarter	312.8	214.6	45.4	39.6	155.6	77.9	64.8	12.8	13.6	3.9	20.8	18.8	1.9
4th quarter	319.0	218.8	46.6	40.7	159.0	79.6	65.6	13.8	13.2	4.0	22.0	20.0	1.9
1980													
1st quarter	328.0	224.5	46.6	40.4	161.9	81.2	66.5	14.2	16.1	3.6	24.3	21.1	3.1
2nd quarter	329.5	224.1	48.0	41.7	163.3	80.8	67.8	14.7	12.8	2.9	25.6	22.4	3.1
3rd quarter	341.5	231.5	49.4	43.0	168.2	83.5	69.5	15.2	14.0	3.8	26.9	23.7	3.1
4th quarter	353.7	240.0	51.6	45.2	173.3	86.0	71.5	15.8	15.1	4.0	28.3	25.1	3.1
1981													
1st quarter	363.5	249.5	52.5	46.0	180.2	89.6	73.9	16.7	16.8	3.7	29.9	26.5	3.3
2nd quarter	368.1	252.5	53.7	47.0	183.7	89.6	76.2	17.9	15.2	3.8	31.4	27.9	3.3
3rd quarter	374.0	259.5	55.5	48.8	188.3	91.8	78.0	18.5	15.7	3.9	32.7	29.2	3.3
4th quarter	375.3	261.6	56.8	49.9	190.7	92.1	80.2	18.4	14.1	4.0	33.9	30.4	3.3
1982													
1st quarter	380.8	265.4	57.3	50.2	193.9	92.9	82.4	18.5	14.1	4.0	35.2	31.6	3.5
2nd quarter	389.1	270.6	58.1	50.9	198.3	95.5	84.5	18.3	14.3	4.0	36.3	32.6	3.5
3rd quarter	395.0	276.5	60.4	53.1	201.7	97.0	86.3	18.4	14.4	4.1	37.3	33.6	3.5
4th quarter	400.8	280.1	60.8	53.4	206.0	99.3	87.9	18.7	13.3	4.1	38.1	34.5	3.5
1983													
1st quarter	407.6	283.7	61.3	53.7	209.6	101.5	89.3	18.8	12.8	4.0	39.5	35.4	4.0
2nd quarter	423.6	295.9	64.3	56.5	216.0	106.2	90.9	18.9	15.7	4.1	40.7	36.4	4.2
3rd quarter	436.4	307.5	68.1	60.2	222.0	109.9	92.7	19.5	17.4	4.1	42.0	37.5	4.4
4th quarter	446.9	316.4	70.7	62.7	228.0	113.1	94.6	20.3	17.7	4.3	43.5	38.8	4.6
1984													
1st quarter	465.3	328.0	73.3	65.0	234.7	116.8	96.8	21.1	20.1	4.5	44.9	40.0	4.7
2nd quarter	478.1	336.0	75.8	67.4	240.3	119.9	98.8	21.6	19.9	4.7	46.7	41.7	4.9
3rd quarter	481.6	339.0	76.8	68.1	244.7	122.0	100.7	22.0	17.5	4.8	48.6	43.4	5.0
4th quarter	495.6	346.1	78.2	69.3	250.2	125.3	102.5	22.3	17.7	4.8	50.5	45.3	5.1
1985													
1st quarter	506.6	353.9	79.3	70.2	254.7	127.3	104.5	22.9	20.0	4.7	52.9	47.6	5.1
2nd quarter	516.4	360.6	80.9	71.8	260.0	130.6	106.5	23.0	19.6	4.8	54.5	49.1	5.2
3rd quarter	526.1	367.5	81.5	72.2	265.1	132.8	108.5	23.8	20.9	4.9	55.4	49.8	5.4
4th quarter	535.2	372.7	83.7	74.3	268.5	133.8	110.6	24.1	20.5	5.2	56.7	50.9	5.7
1986													
1st quarter	552.7	378.9	84.5	75.0	273.0	136.1	112.6	24.3	21.4	5.5	57.7	51.3	6.2
2nd quarter	554.8	383.6	85.0	75.4	276.6	137.8	114.9	23.8	22.0	5.8	58.3	51.9	6.3
3rd quarter	567.1	392.2	87.5	77.7	282.3	142.0	117.3	23.0	22.4	6.1	58.7	52.3	6.3
4th quarter	572.0	403.5	91.8	81.8	286.8	143.5	119.8	23.5	24.8	6.4	58.9	52.6	6.2
1987													
1st quarter	570.8	405.0	92.4	82.1	291.9	145.1	122.5	24.2	20.7	6.7	58.5	52.4	6.0
2nd quarter	593.2	423.7	101.5	90.9	298.5	148.6	125.1	24.8	23.7	7.0	58.0	52.2	5.6
3rd quarter	594.1	425.5	94.1	83.4	306.0	152.9	127.7	25.4	25.5	7.3	58.0	52.7	5.2
4th quarter	604.1	434.2	98.4	87.5	310.0	154.7	130.3	25.1	25.7	7.7	58.1	53.3	4.6
1988													
1st quarter	616.4	438.9	99.4	88.3	315.5	157.8	132.4	25.3	24.0	8.0	59.0	54.2	4.7
2nd quarter	626.2	446.3	97.2	85.8	323.3	162.3	134.9	26.1	25.8	8.3	59.9	55.2	4.5
3rd quarter	643.4	458.1	104.1	92.5	327.4	163.7	137.7	25.9	26.6	8.5	61.0	56.5	4.3
4th quarter	656.2	467.7	107.6	95.8	332.4	165.8	141.0	25.6	27.8	8.7	62.2	57.8	4.2

Table 19-9. State and Local Government Current Receipts and Expenditures—*Continued*

(National Income and Product Accounts, calendar years, billions of dollars, quarterly data are at seasonally adjusted annual rates.)

NIPA Table 3.3

Year and quarter	Current receipts—Continued					Current expenditures					Net state and local government saving, NIPA (surplus + / deficit -)		
	Current transfer receipts				Current surplus of government enterprises	Total	Consumption expenditures	Government social benefits to persons	Interest payments	Subsidies	Total	Social insurance funds	Other
	Total	Federal grants-in-aid	From business (net)	From persons									
1975													
1st quarter	44.1	40.7	1.2	2.2	0.3	197.7	157.8	29.2	10.5	0.1	0.6	0.4	0.2
2nd quarter	49.4	45.8	1.2	2.3	0.4	205.0	163.5	30.5	10.9	0.2	2.6	0.5	2.1
3rd quarter	50.2	46.5	1.2	2.4	0.3	210.3	167.9	31.0	11.3	0.2	3.6	0.5	3.1
4th quarter	51.3	47.5	1.2	2.6	0.5	215.5	171.1	32.6	11.6	0.2	3.1	0.5	2.6
1976													
1st quarter	52.7	48.7	1.4	2.7	0.5	220.1	174.5	33.4	12.0	0.2	5.7	0.5	5.2
2nd quarter	53.6	49.5	1.4	2.8	0.4	223.7	177.8	33.4	12.4	0.2	6.5	0.6	5.9
3rd quarter	54.7	50.4	1.4	2.9	0.3	228.6	180.9	34.7	12.7	0.2	6.3	0.6	5.7
4th quarter	58.8	54.4	1.4	3.0	0.3	232.8	184.6	35.0	13.0	0.2	11.0	0.7	10.3
1977													
1st quarter	57.2	52.5	1.6	3.2	0.3	238.3	189.2	35.7	13.3	0.2	9.6	0.8	8.8
2nd quarter	60.3	55.5	1.6	3.3	0.3	244.5	193.3	37.5	13.5	0.2	11.8	0.9	10.9
3rd quarter	64.1	59.1	1.6	3.3	0.3	249.5	198.2	37.3	13.8	0.2	15.7	1.1	14.7
4th quarter	64.2	59.2	1.6	3.4	0.4	254.9	202.8	37.7	14.1	0.2	15.5	1.2	14.3
1978													
1st quarter	68.8	63.5	1.9	3.5	0.4	260.9	207.2	39.2	14.3	0.2	16.9	1.3	15.5
2nd quarter	71.6	66.1	1.9	3.6	0.3	266.5	210.7	41.0	14.6	0.2	23.0	1.4	21.6
3rd quarter	71.1	65.5	1.9	3.7	0.2	271.4	215.2	41.3	15.1	0.2	16.1	1.5	14.5
4th quarter	72.8	67.1	1.9	3.8	0.1	276.8	219.6	41.7	15.6	0.3	18.7	1.7	17.1
1979													
1st quarter	70.5	64.4	2.2	4.0	0.0	284.3	225.5	42.4	16.4	0.3	14.5	1.7	12.9
2nd quarter	71.2	65.0	2.2	4.1	-0.2	290.9	229.2	43.5	17.0	0.3	11.9	1.8	10.1
3rd quarter	74.0	67.6	2.2	4.2	-0.4	298.9	236.3	44.5	17.6	0.3	13.9	1.8	12.1
4th quarter	74.9	68.4	2.2	4.3	-0.6	307.4	242.4	46.9	18.0	0.3	11.6	1.8	9.8
1980													
1st quarter	76.2	69.3	2.5	4.4	-0.7	317.3	249.3	49.1	18.4	0.3	10.6	1.4	9.2
2nd quarter	77.9	70.8	2.5	4.6	-0.9	324.0	255.8	49.0	19.0	0.3	5.5	0.7	4.8
3rd quarter	80.7	73.4	2.5	4.8	-1.4	334.0	261.6	52.4	19.6	0.4	7.5	1.5	6.0
4th quarter	83.3	75.8	2.5	5.0	-1.9	342.2	267.0	54.3	20.4	0.4	11.5	1.6	9.9
1981													
1st quarter	82.6	74.4	2.9	5.4	-2.3	351.8	274.4	55.6	21.4	0.4	11.7	1.3	10.4
2nd quarter	83.0	74.5	2.9	5.6	-2.6	360.0	279.9	57.4	22.3	0.4	8.0	1.3	6.7
3rd quarter	80.5	71.9	2.9	5.8	-2.5	366.4	284.9	57.7	23.3	0.4	7.7	1.3	6.4
4th quarter	78.1	69.2	2.9	6.0	-2.2	372.5	290.1	57.7	24.3	0.4	2.8	1.3	1.5
1982													
1st quarter	78.2	68.8	3.2	6.1	-2.0	381.5	296.6	59.0	25.4	0.4	-0.7	1.3	-2.0
2nd quarter	79.9	70.4	3.2	6.3	-1.7	390.6	302.6	61.0	26.5	0.5	-1.4	1.2	-2.7
3rd quarter	78.7	69.0	3.3	6.4	-1.5	397.7	307.4	62.1	27.7	0.5	-2.6	1.2	-3.9
4th quarter	79.7	69.8	3.3	6.6	-1.2	404.8	312.8	62.6	29.0	0.5	-4.0	1.2	-5.2
1983													
1st quarter	81.1	70.6	3.6	6.8	-0.8	415.0	318.4	65.8	30.4	0.5	-7.4	1.2	-8.6
2nd quarter	83.3	72.7	3.6	7.0	-0.4	420.6	322.1	66.3	31.7	0.4	3.0	1.2	1.8
3rd quarter	82.7	71.8	3.6	7.3	0.0	426.6	326.0	67.2	33.0	0.4	9.8	1.2	8.5
4th quarter	82.4	71.2	3.7	7.5	0.2	432.7	329.8	68.3	34.1	0.4	14.2	1.3	12.9
1984													
1st quarter	87.1	75.4	4.0	7.8	0.7	442.8	337.2	69.9	35.2	0.4	22.5	1.4	21.1
2nd quarter	89.6	77.4	4.2	8.0	1.1	451.4	343.9	70.6	36.4	0.4	26.7	1.5	25.3
3rd quarter	87.7	75.1	4.3	8.3	1.6	460.5	351.3	71.3	37.6	0.4	21.1	1.5	19.7
4th quarter	91.6	78.8	4.3	8.5	2.5	470.2	358.2	72.8	38.8	0.4	25.4	1.4	24.0
1985													
1st quarter	92.2	79.1	4.3	8.7	2.9	481.9	367.3	74.9	39.4	0.3	24.7	1.3	23.4
2nd quarter	93.4	80.0	4.4	9.1	3.2	492.4	376.0	76.3	39.8	0.3	24.0	1.2	22.8
3rd quarter	95.0	81.2	4.4	9.4	3.4	504.5	386.9	78.1	39.2	0.3	21.7	1.3	20.4
4th quarter	97.4	83.1	4.5	9.7	3.3	516.2	397.0	79.8	39.2	0.3	19.0	1.5	17.6
1986													
1st quarter	107.6	84.8	12.6	10.2	3.1	526.0	406.9	81.6	37.2	0.3	26.7	1.6	25.0
2nd quarter	104.2	89.0	4.7	10.5	2.9	534.3	413.1	83.6	37.2	0.3	20.5	1.8	18.7
3rd quarter	107.4	91.8	4.8	10.8	2.7	544.3	420.5	85.3	38.3	0.3	22.8	2.0	20.8
4th quarter	100.7	84.9	4.8	11.0	2.5	558.2	430.9	86.9	40.1	0.3	13.8	2.1	11.8
1987													
1st quarter	97.9	82.1	4.8	11.0	2.6	564.8	433.7	88.3	42.6	0.3	6.0	2.1	3.9
2nd quarter	101.7	85.8	4.8	11.1	2.8	573.8	438.7	89.9	44.9	0.3	19.4	2.1	17.3
3rd quarter	100.1	83.9	4.9	11.2	3.1	581.9	442.5	91.6	47.6	0.3	12.2	2.2	9.9
4th quarter	100.2	83.8	5.0	11.4	3.9	592.0	448.9	93.1	49.7	0.3	12.1	2.3	9.8
1988													
1st quarter	106.2	89.5	5.1	11.6	4.2	602.8	459.2	95.3	48.0	0.3	13.6	2.4	11.2
2nd quarter	107.1	90.0	5.2	11.9	4.6	613.0	467.2	97.3	48.1	0.3	13.2	2.5	10.7
3rd quarter	110.7	93.1	5.5	12.1	5.0	622.2	474.0	99.5	48.3	0.4	21.2	2.6	18.6
4th quarter	112.0	93.8	5.7	12.5	5.6	632.6	481.1	101.9	49.3	0.4	23.6	2.6	21.0

Table 19-9. State and Local Government Current Receipts and Expenditures—Continued

(National Income and Product Accounts, calendar years, billions of dollars, quarterly data are at seasonally adjusted annual rates.)

NIPA Table 3.3

Year and quarter	Current receipts												
	Total	Current tax receipts							Taxes on corporate income	Contributions for government social insurance	Income receipts on assets		
		Total	Personal current taxes		Taxes on production and imports						Total	Interest receipts	Rents and royalties
			Total	Income taxes	Total	Sales taxes	Property taxes	Other					
1989													
1st quarter	673.4	480.2	113.4	101.3	340.3	168.7	145.0	26.6	26.6	8.8	64.1	59.7	4.2
2nd quarter	687.0	491.0	118.2	105.8	348.1	172.9	148.4	26.9	24.6	8.9	65.2	60.9	4.1
3rd quarter	694.5	491.0	114.5	102.1	353.8	174.6	151.5	27.7	22.7	9.0	66.3	62.0	4.1
4th quarter	694.3	489.8	112.4	99.8	354.3	173.2	154.5	26.6	23.1	9.3	67.2	63.0	4.0
1990													
1st quarter	721.5	509.9	119.3	106.6	369.1	183.7	156.6	28.7	21.5	9.5	67.5	63.5	3.8
2nd quarter	730.6	514.0	122.6	109.5	368.7	181.2	159.7	27.9	22.7	9.9	68.4	64.4	3.8
3rd quarter	744.3	523.0	123.7	110.8	375.7	185.3	163.1	27.3	23.6	10.2	69.6	64.3	5.0
4th quarter	754.7	529.6	124.6	111.5	382.7	186.9	166.7	29.1	22.2	10.5	68.3	64.0	4.0
1991													
1st quarter	763.0	528.5	121.2	108.0	384.6	184.8	171.2	28.6	22.7	11.0	68.8	64.1	4.3
2nd quarter	778.8	538.2	124.5	111.2	390.3	187.9	174.7	27.7	23.4	11.4	68.3	63.5	4.5
3rd quarter	798.2	549.7	126.1	112.2	399.3	193.1	177.8	28.4	24.2	11.8	67.7	62.7	4.6
4th quarter	816.6	560.8	129.4	115.5	407.1	196.9	180.5	29.7	24.2	12.2	67.1	62.0	4.7
1992													
1st quarter	824.3	564.4	127.5	112.7	412.6	200.6	182.9	29.1	24.4	12.6	66.9	61.1	5.3
2nd quarter	842.7	580.4	136.9	122.3	418.0	201.6	184.4	32.0	25.5	13.0	65.0	60.0	4.6
3rd quarter	851.7	582.6	136.7	121.9	424.0	207.4	185.4	31.3	21.8	13.3	64.1	59.1	4.6
4th quarter	863.9	591.6	140.2	124.6	425.7	207.7	186.0	32.0	25.8	13.6	63.1	58.1	4.6
1993													
1st quarter	862.5	588.6	136.5	121.8	427.6	210.9	184.8	31.8	24.6	13.8	62.0	57.0	4.6
2nd quarter	875.9	598.5	138.3	123.9	433.2	214.7	185.9	32.6	27.0	14.1	61.4	56.3	4.5
3rd quarter	893.2	609.5	143.6	128.7	439.6	217.4	187.8	34.4	26.3	14.2	61.0	55.8	4.5
4th quarter	916.1	622.3	145.9	130.5	446.7	222.5	190.5	33.7	29.7	14.4	60.9	55.8	4.5
1994													
1st quarter	920.9	629.9	146.9	131.4	456.4	225.7	196.0	34.7	26.5	14.6	61.6	56.4	4.5
2nd quarter	931.4	636.9	141.9	125.8	465.5	230.9	198.8	35.8	29.5	14.6	62.4	57.1	4.5
3rd quarter	952.3	652.1	151.2	135.1	469.7	233.1	200.8	35.8	31.2	14.5	63.8	58.5	4.5
4th quarter	966.9	658.0	152.0	136.7	473.4	235.9	201.9	35.6	32.6	14.4	65.0	59.6	4.5
1995													
1st quarter	980.9	665.6	156.8	140.6	478.3	240.4	200.8	37.2	30.5	14.0	66.5	61.1	4.5
2nd quarter	979.1	661.6	152.4	136.1	477.9	239.6	201.6	36.8	31.3	13.7	67.6	62.3	4.5
3rd quarter	997.6	677.2	160.6	144.2	483.7	243.7	203.0	37.0	32.8	13.5	69.1	63.5	4.5
4th quarter	1 003.3	684.1	162.6	146.0	489.4	247.3	204.9	37.2	32.0	13.2	70.4	64.7	4.5
1996													
1st quarter	1 021.7	695.8	165.3	149.0	498.1	252.4	208.1	37.6	32.4	13.0	71.4	65.6	4.6
2nd quarter	1 042.6	705.7	165.9	149.6	506.5	255.7	210.9	40.0	33.3	12.7	72.6	66.7	4.6
3rd quarter	1 049.1	712.4	169.3	152.8	509.9	256.8	213.7	39.4	33.1	12.3	73.9	67.8	4.7
4th quarter	1 059.7	724.5	174.2	157.8	517.0	259.9	216.7	40.5	33.3	11.9	75.1	69.0	4.7
1997													
1st quarter	1 073.4	734.3	177.8	160.7	523.7	262.8	220.0	40.9	32.8	11.3	76.5	70.3	4.8
2nd quarter	1 084.0	741.0	176.9	159.6	530.5	266.8	222.6	41.2	33.5	10.9	77.4	71.1	4.8
3rd quarter	1 106.5	756.0	184.1	166.8	536.6	270.5	224.8	41.3	35.3	10.6	78.3	71.9	4.8
4th quarter	1 125.8	768.5	189.2	171.6	544.3	274.5	226.8	43.0	34.9	10.5	79.1	72.8	4.7
1998													
1st quarter	1 137.5	779.5	195.1	177.2	549.3	277.5	227.7	44.1	35.2	10.6	79.8	73.5	4.6
2nd quarter	1 150.5	791.8	201.8	183.6	555.3	281.4	229.7	44.2	34.7	10.4	80.3	74.1	4.6
3rd quarter	1 165.3	798.6	201.4	183.2	561.6	285.4	232.0	44.2	35.5	10.3	81.2	74.9	4.6
4th quarter	1 199.4	809.7	206.5	188.0	568.9	291.1	234.7	43.1	34.3	10.1	82.4	76.0	4.7
1999													
1st quarter	1 205.1	818.6	207.6	188.8	576.1	292.9	238.3	45.0	34.9	9.8	83.0	76.5	4.8
2nd quarter	1 217.1	831.4	210.4	191.6	585.4	298.8	241.3	45.3	35.6	9.7	84.4	77.7	5.0
3rd quarter	1 249.6	847.3	216.0	196.9	595.4	305.4	244.3	45.7	35.9	9.7	86.0	79.0	5.2
4th quarter	1 275.0	864.3	223.8	204.7	603.7	309.3	247.2	47.1	36.8	9.9	87.7	80.4	5.5
2000													
1st quarter	1 294.4	880.3	231.6	212.2	610.9	313.3	249.9	47.7	37.8	10.3	90.4	82.7	5.9
2nd quarter	1 319.0	898.4	243.7	224.5	618.0	315.7	252.9	49.4	36.7	10.7	91.9	83.9	6.2
3rd quarter	1 330.5	895.4	236.3	216.6	624.1	317.0	256.1	51.1	35.0	11.2	92.8	84.5	6.4
4th quarter	1 333.9	898.8	234.8	215.7	631.2	320.3	259.5	51.5	32.8	11.8	93.7	85.1	6.7
2001													
1st quarter	1 367.2	919.1	249.2	230.1	637.5	322.8	262.6	52.1	32.4	12.7	91.6	83.1	6.6
2nd quarter	1 397.4	937.9	266.6	246.9	639.4	320.5	266.5	52.4	31.9	13.5	89.9	81.4	6.6
3rd quarter	1 354.8	899.9	229.3	209.5	641.4	317.7	271.3	52.4	29.2	14.0	87.7	79.3	6.5
4th quarter	1 372.5	906.2	225.8	205.9	652.9	323.5	276.7	52.7	27.4	14.4	85.9	77.5	6.4
2002													
1st quarter	1 380.9	909.4	218.8	199.0	662.1	324.8	284.1	53.3	28.5	14.4	83.5	75.2	6.2
2nd quarter	1 404.1	919.7	216.5	195.9	672.3	328.6	289.5	54.2	30.9	14.5	81.9	73.7	6.1
3rd quarter	1 423.9	937.3	222.3	201.7	683.0	332.6	294.2	56.1	31.9	14.6	80.9	72.6	6.2
4th quarter	1 438.5	939.7	222.6	201.8	683.8	330.4	298.2	55.3	33.3	14.7	80.1	71.5	6.4
2003													
1st quarter	1 437.7	941.1	216.1	195.0	693.2	335.8	300.5	57.0	31.9	14.7	80.9	71.7	6.7
2nd quarter	1 484.6	955.2	219.0	198.0	703.3	340.8	303.5	59.0	32.9	14.9	80.6	71.2	7.0
3rd quarter	1 511.4	981.9	232.5	210.6	714.0	346.8	306.6	60.7	35.4	15.1	80.6	70.8	7.3
4th quarter	1 545.8	998.8	236.9	214.6	724.3	352.3	309.6	62.4	37.6	15.5	81.7	71.5	7.6

Table 19-9. State and Local Government Current Receipts and Expenditures—Continued

(National Income and Product Accounts, calendar years, billions of dollars, quarterly data are at seasonally adjusted annual rates.)

NIPA Table 3.3

Year and quarter	Current receipts—Continued				Current surplus of government enterprises	Current expenditures					Net state and local government saving, NIPA (surplus + / deficit -)		
	Current transfer receipts					Total	Consumption expenditures	Government social benefits to persons	Interest payments	Subsidies	Total	Social insurance funds	Other
	Total	Federal grants-in-aid	From business (net)	From persons									
1989													
1st quarter	114.0	94.9	6.1	13.0	6.3	646.8	489.8	104.2	52.3	0.4	26.6	2.5	24.1
2nd quarter	115.2	95.6	6.3	13.3	6.6	659.8	498.1	107.3	54.0	0.4	27.2	2.4	24.8
3rd quarter	121.5	101.4	6.5	13.5	6.8	671.7	504.8	111.0	55.6	0.4	22.8	2.3	20.6
4th quarter	121.9	101.4	6.7	13.9	6.2	687.6	515.9	114.8	56.5	0.4	6.7	2.1	4.5
1990													
1st quarter	127.8	106.5	7.2	14.0	6.8	705.7	530.0	118.8	56.5	0.4	15.8	2.0	13.8
2nd quarter	131.7	110.3	6.9	14.5	6.7	720.5	538.5	124.2	57.5	0.4	10.1	2.0	8.2
3rd quarter	134.9	112.6	7.0	15.2	6.6	738.2	549.3	130.3	58.3	0.4	6.1	2.0	4.1
4th quarter	139.6	116.3	7.2	16.0	6.7	757.8	560.8	137.4	59.2	0.4	-3.1	2.0	-5.0
1991													
1st quarter	147.8	122.8	7.8	17.2	6.9	769.9	567.1	141.5	60.9	0.4	-7.0	2.1	-9.1
2nd quarter	153.9	128.1	7.6	18.2	7.0	785.0	570.8	152.2	61.6	0.4	-6.2	2.3	-8.5
3rd quarter	162.0	134.9	7.9	19.2	7.1	798.4	577.4	158.6	62.0	0.4	-0.2	2.4	-2.6
4th quarter	169.2	140.6	8.5	20.1	7.3	819.9	583.2	173.8	62.5	0.4	-3.3	2.6	-5.9
1992													
1st quarter	173.1	143.2	8.9	21.0	7.3	824.6	591.3	170.5	62.4	0.4	-0.3	2.8	-3.0
2nd quarter	176.8	146.2	8.9	21.7	7.5	840.6	599.5	178.6	62.0	0.4	2.1	3.0	-0.9
3rd quarter	183.8	152.4	9.2	22.2	7.9	855.5	607.5	185.8	61.9	0.4	-3.8	3.3	-7.1
4th quarter	187.3	154.6	10.0	22.7	8.2	859.1	612.4	185.0	61.3	0.4	4.8	3.5	1.3
1993													
1st quarter	189.4	156.3	10.1	23.0	8.7	872.5	622.6	188.9	60.6	0.4	-9.9	3.8	-13.7
2nd quarter	193.0	159.3	10.4	23.3	8.9	877.6	627.3	189.7	60.3	0.4	-1.7	4.1	-5.8
3rd quarter	199.3	165.0	10.6	23.7	9.2	893.6	632.8	200.6	59.9	0.4	-0.3	4.3	-4.7
4th quarter	209.2	174.1	11.0	24.1	9.2	900.5	638.5	201.7	59.9	0.4	15.7	4.5	11.1
1994													
1st quarter	207.3	171.2	11.4	24.7	7.5	916.7	651.8	203.6	60.9	0.4	4.2	4.6	-0.4
2nd quarter	208.5	171.6	11.8	25.1	9.0	925.0	659.1	203.9	61.6	0.3	6.4	4.7	1.7
3rd quarter	212.5	174.9	12.1	25.4	9.4	934.5	668.0	203.7	62.5	0.3	17.8	4.7	13.1
4th quarter	219.5	181.2	12.5	25.8	10.0	953.4	674.3	215.7	63.1	0.3	13.5	4.6	8.9
1995													
1st quarter	223.9	185.0	12.9	26.0	11.0	970.8	687.0	220.4	63.1	0.3	10.2	4.4	5.8
2nd quarter	224.5	184.9	13.3	26.3	11.7	978.7	694.0	220.7	63.7	0.3	0.4	4.2	-3.8
3rd quarter	225.5	185.1	13.7	26.6	12.4	984.3	698.7	220.7	64.5	0.3	13.4	3.9	9.4
4th quarter	222.7	181.6	14.1	27.0	13.0	979.0	704.5	208.8	65.4	0.3	24.3	3.7	20.6
1996													
1st quarter	227.8	186.1	14.5	27.2	13.7	998.1	712.9	218.2	66.6	0.3	23.7	3.4	20.2
2nd quarter	237.6	195.0	15.0	27.6	14.0	1 020.7	720.5	232.2	67.7	0.3	21.9	3.0	18.8
3rd quarter	236.5	193.2	15.4	27.9	14.0	1 021.9	728.2	224.8	68.5	0.3	27.2	2.6	24.6
4th quarter	234.4	190.3	15.8	28.3	13.8	1 029.3	737.7	221.7	69.5	0.4	30.4	2.2	28.3
1997													
1st quarter	238.1	192.4	16.3	29.5	13.2	1 043.8	747.0	226.0	70.4	0.4	29.6	1.5	28.1
2nd quarter	242.2	195.5	16.6	30.1	12.6	1 047.7	752.5	223.7	71.1	0.4	36.4	1.2	35.2
3rd quarter	249.6	198.4	20.6	30.6	12.0	1 062.0	761.7	228.0	71.8	0.4	44.4	1.0	43.4
4th quarter	256.5	208.2	17.2	31.0	11.3	1 079.7	774.4	232.4	72.4	0.5	46.1	1.0	45.1
1998													
1st quarter	257.9	207.9	18.8	31.2	9.7	1 088.9	783.1	232.2	73.1	0.5	48.6	1.5	47.1
2nd quarter	257.7	208.1	18.0	31.6	10.2	1 103.7	794.7	235.2	73.4	0.5	46.7	1.7	45.1
3rd quarter	264.8	213.0	19.6	32.1	10.5	1 115.6	807.6	233.9	73.7	0.4	49.7	1.8	47.9
4th quarter	286.6	222.0	31.8	32.8	10.6	1 136.4	820.0	241.7	74.2	0.4	63.0	1.8	61.2
1999													
1st quarter	282.8	227.0	22.4	33.5	10.8	1 156.1	834.3	247.7	73.8	0.4	49.0	1.7	47.3
2nd quarter	280.9	223.7	22.8	34.3	10.7	1 171.8	850.8	246.3	74.2	0.4	45.3	1.7	43.6
3rd quarter	296.1	237.6	23.2	35.3	10.4	1 197.6	867.3	255.1	74.8	0.4	52.0	1.7	50.3
4th quarter	303.3	243.2	23.7	36.4	9.8	1 219.7	883.3	260.3	75.6	0.4	55.3	1.7	53.5
2000													
1st quarter	304.7	239.0	28.0	37.6	8.8	1 238.5	900.6	260.4	77.0	0.5	55.9	1.7	54.2
2nd quarter	310.0	242.8	28.6	38.7	8.0	1 259.5	910.8	269.6	78.5	0.5	59.5	1.9	57.7
3rd quarter	323.8	255.0	29.1	39.8	7.3	1 281.6	923.4	277.4	80.3	0.6	49.0	2.1	46.8
4th quarter	323.0	252.6	29.6	40.8	6.6	1 298.5	936.3	279.2	82.4	0.6	35.4	2.4	33.0
2001													
1st quarter	338.2	266.5	30.1	41.6	5.5	1 334.7	951.7	290.7	84.2	8.0	32.5	2.6	29.9
2nd quarter	351.5	278.3	30.5	42.7	4.6	1 371.6	963.6	308.3	85.3	14.4	25.8	2.7	23.1
3rd quarter	350.0	272.8	33.3	43.9	3.2	1 363.4	976.6	295.9	86.0	4.8	-8.6	2.6	-11.2
4th quarter	363.3	286.6	31.5	45.2	2.8	1 403.1	987.1	326.0	86.6	3.4	-30.6	2.4	-33.0
2002													
1st quarter	370.8	291.9	32.3	46.7	2.8	1 409.8	996.2	324.8	86.9	1.9	-28.8	2.0	-30.8
2nd quarter	384.8	304.2	32.5	48.1	3.2	1 427.7	1 011.5	328.3	87.3	0.7	-23.6	1.7	-25.3
3rd quarter	387.6	305.4	32.9	49.4	3.6	1 445.3	1 023.8	332.0	87.7	1.8	-21.3	1.4	-22.8
4th quarter	400.3	316.3	33.4	50.7	3.7	1 464.8	1 034.6	342.6	87.9	-0.3	-26.3	1.3	-27.6
2003													
1st quarter	397.4	314.3	31.3	51.8	3.6	1 486.6	1 054.8	343.6	87.9	0.3	-49.0	1.1	-50.1
2nd quarter	430.1	345.1	31.9	53.1	3.8	1 490.2	1 051.8	349.7	88.1	0.6	-5.7	1.1	-6.7
3rd quarter	429.9	343.0	32.5	54.4	3.8	1 504.9	1 061.0	355.7	88.9	-0.7	6.5	1.1	5.4
4th quarter	446.1	357.2	33.1	55.8	3.7	1 510.5	1 066.3	352.3	90.7	1.2	35.3	1.2	34.1

Table 19-10. U.S. International Transactions

(Millions of dollars, seasonally adjusted.)

Year and quarter	Exports of goods, services, and income				Imports of goods, services, and income [1]				Unilateral current transfers, net [2]	U.S.-owned assets abroad, net [3]					
											U.S. official reserve assets, net	U.S. government assets other than official reserve assets, net	U.S. private assets, net		
	Total	Goods	Services	Income receipts	Total	Goods	Services	Income payments		Total			Total	Direct investment	Foreign securities
1960															
1st quarter	7 355	4 685	1 543	1 127	-6 050	-3 812	-1 907	-331	-955	-1 066	159	-237	-988	-664	-266
2nd quarter	7 762	4 916	1 715	1 131	-6 078	-3 858	-1 906	-314	-1 154	-1 156	175	-339	-992	-586	-166
3rd quarter	7 650	5 031	1 453	1 166	-5 925	-3 648	-1 970	-307	-889	-956	740	-160	-1 536	-754	-111
4th quarter	7 791	5 018	1 580	1 193	-5 619	-3 440	-1 892	-287	-1 064	-923	1 071	-365	-1 629	-936	-120
1961															
1st quarter	7 827	5 095	1 481	1 251	-5 599	-3 394	-1 912	-293	-989	-1 320	371	-381	-1 310	-774	-135
2nd quarter	7 773	4 806	1 758	1 209	-5 659	-3 438	-1 922	-299	-1 208	-1 029	-320	471	-1 180	-551	-246
3rd quarter	7 757	5 038	1 468	1 251	-6 026	-3 809	-1 900	-317	-887	-1 928	-212	-486	-1 230	-737	-124
4th quarter	8 047	5 169	1 590	1 288	-6 171	-3 896	-1 939	-336	-1 043	-1 260	768	-513	-1 515	-592	-257
1962															
1st quarter	8 015	5 077	1 666	1 272	-6 256	-3 966	-1 971	-319	-1 113	-1 301	427	-406	-1 322	-545	-196
2nd quarter	8 719	5 336	2 004	1 379	-6 402	-4 080	-1 992	-330	-1 272	-1 461	-163	-381	-917	-716	-308
3rd quarter	8 295	5 331	1 567	1 397	-6 455	-4 116	-2 005	-334	-879	-279	881	8	-1 168	-811	-87
4th quarter	8 315	5 037	1 709	1 569	-6 567	-4 098	-2 126	-343	-1 016	-1 134	390	-306	-1 218	-779	-378
1963															
1st quarter	8 428	5 063	1 849	1 516	-6 478	-4 064	-2 057	-357	-1 107	-1 922	32	-482	-1 472	-980	-522
2nd quarter	9 244	5 599	2 150	1 495	-6 674	-4 226	-2 066	-382	-1 371	-2 631	124	-654	-2 101	-874	-536
3rd quarter	8 832	5 671	1 620	1 541	-6 893	-4 372	-2 122	-399	-918	-887	227	-86	-1 028	-721	-100
4th quarter	9 275	5 939	1 731	1 605	-6 926	-4 386	-2 118	-422	-999	-1 831	-5	-440	-1 386	-908	53
1964															
1st quarter	9 885	6 242	1 922	1 721	-6 982	-4 416	-2 140	-426	-993	-2 086	-51	-288	-1 747	-822	20
2nd quarter	9 975	6 199	2 088	1 688	-7 179	-4 598	-2 142	-439	-1 269	-2 018	303	-386	-1 935	-970	-206
3rd quarter	10 009	6 423	1 851	1 735	-7 349	-4 756	-2 153	-440	-935	-2 255	70	-414	-1 911	-1 018	2
4th quarter	10 299	6 637	1 982	1 680	-7 594	-4 930	-2 186	-478	-1 043	-3 200	-151	-592	-2 457	-949	-494
1965															
1st quarter	9 689	5 768	2 047	1 874	-7 395	-4 711	-2 187	-497	-1 037	-1 576	843	-374	-2 045	-1 606	-198
2nd quarter	11 263	6 876	2 448	1 939	-8 208	-5 428	-2 269	-511	-1 478	-1 270	69	-536	-803	-1 250	-147
3rd quarter	10 625	6 643	2 120	1 862	-8 307	-5 516	-2 263	-528	-1 013	-1 454	42	-254	-1 242	-1 030	-209
4th quarter	11 149	7 174	2 212	1 763	-8 802	-5 855	-2 393	-554	-1 058	-1 416	271	-441	-1 246	-1 125	-205
1966															
1st quarter	11 190	7 242	2 124	1 824	-9 068	-6 012	-2 483	-573	-1 140	-1 465	424	-321	-1 568	-1 115	-437
2nd quarter	11 726	7 169	2 705	1 852	-9 390	-6 195	-2 601	-594	-1 547	-1 967	68	-504	-1 531	-1 373	-115
3rd quarter	11 470	7 290	2 301	1 879	-9 912	-6 576	-2 693	-643	-1 073	-1 681	83	-339	-1 425	-1 314	-115
4th quarter	12 068	7 609	2 487	1 972	-10 098	-6 710	-2 717	-671	-1 194	-2 208	-5	-380	-1 823	-1 616	-53
1967															
1st quarter	12 439	7 751	2 731	1 957	-10 248	-6 708	-2 866	-674	-1 315	-1 203	1 027	-643	-1 587	-1 186	-265
2nd quarter	12 275	7 693	2 666	1 916	-10 136	-6 475	-2 986	-675	-1 472	-2 339	-419	-543	-1 377	-964	-261
3rd quarter	12 134	7 530	2 540	2 064	-10 262	-6 526	-3 059	-677	-1 309	-3 155	-375	-551	-2 229	-1 359	-419
4th quarter	12 506	7 692	2 731	2 083	-10 833	-7 157	-2 955	-721	-1 199	-3 060	-180	-685	-2 195	-1 297	-363
1968															
1st quarter	13 016	7 998	2 816	2 202	-11 571	-7 796	-2 997	-778	-1 249	-1 299	912	-706	-1 505	-981	-449
2nd quarter	13 577	8 324	2 936	2 317	-11 885	-8 051	-2 990	-844	-1 363	-2 427	-135	-632	-1 660	-1 172	-283
3rd quarter	14 195	8 745	3 039	2 411	-12 611	-8 612	-3 129	-870	-1 445	-3 447	-572	-568	-2 307	-1 573	-318
4th quarter	14 126	8 559	3 129	2 438	-12 604	-8 532	-3 185	-887	-1 573	-3 803	-1 075	-368	-2 360	-1 568	-519
1969															
1st quarter	12 921	7 468	2 884	2 569	-11 622	-7 444	-3 174	-1 004	-1 177	-2 595	-45	-406	-2 144	-1 556	-366
2nd quarter	15 492	9 536	3 283	2 673	-13 978	-9 527	-3 303	-1 148	-1 645	-3 428	-298	-632	-2 498	-1 663	-498
3rd quarter	15 439	9 400	3 245	2 794	-14 072	-9 380	-3 368	-1 324	-1 319	-3 361	-685	-703	-1 973	-1 548	-546
4th quarter	16 279	10 010	3 394	2 875	-14 329	-9 456	-3 481	-1 392	-1 593	-2 199	-151	-459	-1 589	-1 192	-139
1970															
1st quarter	16 461	10 258	3 235	2 968	-14 458	-9 587	-3 449	-1 422	-1 383	-2 611	481	-399	-2 693	-1 958	-306
2nd quarter	17 419	10 744	3 645	3 030	-14 861	-9 766	-3 690	-1 405	-1 586	-1 725	1 025	-348	-2 402	-2 144	80
3rd quarter	17 267	10 665	3 625	2 977	-15 141	-10 049	-3 715	-1 377	-1 611	-2 146	802	-423	-2 525	-1 718	-517
4th quarter	17 241	10 802	3 666	2 773	-15 443	-10 464	-3 668	-1 311	-1 576	-1 989	1 040	-419	-2 610	-1 771	-333
1971															
1st quarter	17 980	10 920	4 048	3 012	-15 551	-10 600	-3 724	-1 227	-1 746	-2 747	868	-573	-3 042	-2 033	-408
2nd quarter	18 163	10 878	4 087	3 198	-16 764	-11 614	-3 867	-1 283	-1 808	-2 534	839	-567	-2 806	-1 949	-368
3rd quarter	18 676	11 548	3 972	3 156	-17 460	-12 171	-3 861	-1 428	-1 752	-3 390	1 377	-387	-4 380	-2 308	-346
4th quarter	17 564	9 973	4 251	3 340	-16 639	-11 194	-3 948	-1 497	-2 098	-3 084	-18	-355	-2 711	-1 327	9
1972															
1st quarter	19 757	11 833	4 473	3 451	-19 153	-13 501	-4 173	-1 479	-2 297	-3 585	620	-212	-3 993	-2 187	-476
2nd quarter	19 427	11 618	4 233	3 576	-19 105	-13 254	-4 228	-1 623	-2 011	-2 125	-60	-271	-1 794	-1 481	-318
3rd quarter	20 788	12 351	4 634	3 803	-19 767	-14 022	-4 095	-1 650	-2 306	-3 952	96	-518	-3 530	-2 435	203
4th quarter	22 015	13 579	4 503	3 933	-21 212	-15 020	-4 371	-1 821	-1 933	-4 125	50	-566	-3 609	-1 644	-28
1973															
1st quarter	24 681	15 474	4 579	4 628	-23 000	-16 285	-4 613	-2 102	-1 536	-7 886	213	-572	-7 527	-3 785	55
2nd quarter	27 127	17 112	4 828	5 187	-24 301	-17 168	-4 741	-2 392	-1 953	-4 154	11	-423	-3 742	-2 691	-86
3rd quarter	29 329	18 271	5 145	5 913	-24 841	-17 683	-4 640	-2 518	-1 751	-3 189	-23	-608	-2 558	-2 159	-196
4th quarter	31 912	20 553	5 279	6 080	-26 855	-19 363	-4 849	-2 643	-1 674	-7 646	-43	-1 042	-6 561	-2 718	-445
1974															
1st quarter	34 698	22 614	5 189	6 895	-29 643	-21 952	-4 985	-2 706	-3 443	-5 914	-246	1 389	-7 057	900	-600
2nd quarter	37 295	24 500	5 691	7 104	-34 710	-26 346	-5 359	-3 005	-2 475	-10 318	-358	267	-10 227	-1 790	-272
3rd quarter	37 385	24 629	5 633	7 123	-36 004	-27 368	-5 360	-3 276	-1 676	-7 694	-1 002	-354	-6 338	-4 385	-282
4th quarter	39 105	26 563	6 078	6 464	-36 918	-28 145	-5 675	-3 098	-1 656	-10 818	139	-938	-10 019	-3 776	-699

[1] A minus sign indicates imports of goods or services or income payments.
[2] A minus sign indicates net unilateral transfers to foreigners.
[3] A minus sign indicates financial outflows or increases in U.S. official assets.

Table 19-10. U.S. International Transactions—Continued

(Millions of dollars, seasonally adjusted.)

Year and quarter	U.S.-owned assets abroad, net [4] —Continued		Foreign-owned assets in the United States, net [4]								Statistical discrepancy [5]	Balance on	
	U.S. private assets, net—Continued			Foreign official assets in the United States, net	Other foreign assets in the United States, net								
	U.S. claims		Total				U.S. Treasury securities and U.S. currency flows	U.S. securities other than U.S. Treasury securities	U.S. liabilities			Goods and services	Current account
	On unaffiliated foreigners reported by U.S. nonbanking concerns	Reported by U.S. banks, not included elsewhere			Total	Direct investment			To unaffiliated foreigners reported by U.S. nonbanking concerns	Reported by U.S. banks, not included elsewhere			
1960													
1st quarter	38	-96	926	380	546	89	-100	170	-1	388	-210	509	350
2nd quarter	-100	-140	912	435	477	102	-143	118	-50	450	-286	867	530
3rd quarter	-51	-620	381	283	98	93	-99	5	-11	110	-261	866	836
4th quarter	-281	-292	77	377	-300	31	-22	-11	-28	-270	-262	1 266	1 108
1961													
1st quarter	-117	-284	435	438	-3	68	-82	104	73	-166	-354	1 270	1 239
2nd quarter	-164	-219	620	-307	927	86	-38	152	72	655	-497	1 204	906
3rd quarter	-149	-220	934	673	261	58	83	3	14	103	150	797	844
4th quarter	-128	-538	715	-41	756	99	188	66	67	336	-288	924	833
1962													
1st quarter	-186	-395	737	*	737	89	193	145	-14	324	-82	806	646
2nd quarter	-5	112	675	503	172	130	-51	7	-64	150	-259	1 268	1 045
3rd quarter	-181	-89	-277	178	-455	59	-109	-23	16	-398	-405	777	961
4th quarter	17	-78	779	591	188	68	-99	6	-47	260	-377	522	732
1963													
1st quarter	-27	57	1 191	946	245	40	25	14	-36	202	-112	791	843
2nd quarter	-108	-583	1 527	910	617	108	-109	119	69	430	-95	1 457	1 199
3rd quarter	47	-254	205	56	149	105	1	52	11	-20	-339	797	1 021
4th quarter	245	-776	295	75	220	-22	-66	102	-80	286	186	1 166	1 350
1964													
1st quarter	-206	-739	462	393	69	87	32	-42	0	-8	-286	1 608	1 910
2nd quarter	-166	-593	630	227	403	109	-108	14	19	369	-139	1 547	1 527
3rd quarter	-532	-363	769	275	494	56	-65	-30	37	496	-239	1 365	1 725
4th quarter	-204	-810	1 781	763	1 018	70	-5	-27	19	961	-243	1 503	1 662
1965													
1st quarter	286	-527	208	-202	410	184	60	57	3	106	111	917	1 257
2nd quarter	165	429	-330	-194	-136	-21	64	-243	63	1	23	1 627	1 577
3rd quarter	-19	16	587	115	472	147	-149	-227	49	652	-438	984	1 305
4th quarter	-91	175	280	421	-141	104	-106	54	63	-256	-153	1 138	1 289
1966													
1st quarter	-159	143	458	-164	622	143	-102	173	68	340	25	871	982
2nd quarter	-68	25	961	-57	1 018	133	-316	518	78	605	217	1 078	789
3rd quarter	-105	109	909	-342	1 251	-37	66	107	195	920	287	322	485
4th quarter	-110	-44	1 332	-111	1 443	187	-4	108	135	1 017	100	669	776
1967													
1st quarter	-107	-29	401	708	-307	169	-6	133	219	-822	-74	908	876
2nd quarter	-69	-83	1 884	1 100	784	174	-61	329	66	276	-212	898	667
3rd quarter	-40	-411	2 513	548	1 965	127	-36	520	164	1 190	79	485	563
4th quarter	-563	28	2 584	1 098	1 486	228	-32	34	135	1 121	2	311	474
1968													
1st quarter	-231	156	1 374	-533	1 907	367	22	855	207	456	-271	21	196
2nd quarter	-567	362	2 192	-2 007	4 199	133	86	1 122	478	2 380	-94	219	329
3rd quarter	-213	-203	2 809	442	2 367	148	-8	1 124	315	788	499	43	139
4th quarter	-191	-82	3 550	1 321	2 229	160	36	1 312	474	247	304	-29	-51
1969													
1st quarter	-132	-90	3 664	-1 117	4 781	359	-125	1 388	90	3 069	-1 191	-266	122
2nd quarter	-21	-316	3 896	-766	4 662	267	-35	365	181	3 884	-337	-11	-131
3rd quarter	141	-20	3 833	1 256	2 577	261	79	396	345	1 496	-520	-103	48
4th quarter	-114	-144	1 311	-672	1 983	376	13	981	176	437	531	467	357
1970													
1st quarter	-366	-63	2 160	2 830	-670	592	16	304	222	-1 804	-169	457	620
2nd quarter	-73	-265	848	694	154	212	-35	374	534	-931	-95	933	972
3rd quarter	-157	-133	1 940	1 411	529	357	1	720	510	-1 059	-309	526	515
4th quarter	0	-506	1 413	1 975	-562	303	99	792	748	-2 504	354	336	222
1971													
1st quarter	-355	-246	3 092	5 178	-2 086	196	179	559	-62	-2 958	-1 028	644	683
2nd quarter	-131	-358	5 154	5 630	-476	140	1 862	196	-34	-2 640	-2 211	-516	-409
3rd quarter	-337	-1 389	8 726	10 367	-1 641	-293	-795	626	79	-1 258	-4 800	-512	-536
4th quarter	-406	-987	5 997	5 704	293	324	-1 270	908	386	-55	-1 740	-918	-1 173
1972													
1st quarter	-248	-1 082	4 367	2 762	1 605	-136	-3	1 059	-14	699	911	-1 368	-1 693
2nd quarter	-185	190	4 277	1 103	3 174	373	-83	961	250	1 673	-463	-1 631	-1 689
3rd quarter	-241	-1 057	6 382	4 740	1 642	310	-12	718	216	410	-1 145	-1 132	-1 285
4th quarter	-380	-1 557	6 437	1 871	4 566	403	59	1 769	363	1 972	-1 182	-1 309	-1 130
1973													
1st quarter	-809	-2 988	10 743	9 937	806	631	-119	1 718	246	-1 670	-3 002	-845	145
2nd quarter	-202	-763	3 056	-403	3 458	835	-185	489	54	2 265	225	31	873
3rd quarter	-502	299	2 168	-772	2 940	539	-205	1 173	454	979	-1 716	1 093	2 737
4th quarter	-870	-2 528	2 423	-2 736	5 159	795	293	662	281	3 128	1 840	1 620	3 383
1974													
1st quarter	-2 113	-5 244	6 514	-1 138	7 652	1 784	336	712	354	4 466	-2 212	866	1 612
2nd quarter	-588	-7 577	9 962	4 434	5 528	539	60	363	390	4 176	246	-1 514	110
3rd quarter	273	-1 944	9 303	3 062	6 241	1 610	400	227	239	3 765	-1 314	-2 466	-295
4th quarter	-793	-4 751	9 563	4 188	5 375	828	1 001	-925	861	3 610	724	-1 179	531

[4] A minus sign indicates financial outflows or decreases in foreign official assets in the United States.
[5] Sum of credits and debits with the sign reversed.
* = Less than $500,000 (+/-).

Table 19-10. U.S. International Transactions—*Continued*

(Millions of dollars, seasonally adjusted.)

	Exports of goods, services, and income				Imports of goods, services, and income [1]				Unilateral current transfers, net [2]	U.S.-owned assets abroad, net [3]					
													U.S. private assets, net		
Year and quarter	Total	Goods	Services	Income receipts	Total	Goods	Services	Income payments		Total	U.S. official reserve assets, net	U.S. government assets other than official reserve assets, net	Total	Direct investment	Foreign securities
1975															
1st quarter	40 047	27 480	6 454	6 113	-33 797	-24 980	-5 580	-3 237	-2 043	-10 576	-327	-877	-9 372	-4 022	-1 931
2nd quarter	38 675	25 866	6 807	6 002	-31 284	-22 832	-5 309	-3 143	-2 377	-9 591	-28	-875	-8 688	-3 990	-985
3rd quarter	38 347	26 109	5 886	6 352	-33 078	-24 487	-5 379	-3 212	-1 189	-5 099	-333	-745	-4 021	-1 495	-938
4th quarter	40 868	27 633	6 351	6 884	-34 588	-25 886	-5 729	-2 973	-1 467	-14 436	-161	-977	-13 298	-4 736	-2 393
1976															
1st quarter	41 183	27 575	6 556	7 052	-37 464	-28 176	-5 883	-3 405	-1 153	-12 364	-777	-749	-10 838	-3 923	-2 467
2nd quarter	42 309	28 256	6 660	7 393	-39 494	-30 182	-5 980	-3 332	-1 167	-11 701	-1 580	-914	-9 207	-2 017	-1 405
3rd quarter	43 818	29 056	7 311	7 451	-41 737	-32 213	-6 231	-3 293	-2 165	-10 618	-408	-1 428	-8 782	-3 327	-2 751
4th quarter	44 780	29 858	7 444	7 478	-43 416	-33 657	-6 478	-3 281	-1 201	-16 588	207	-1 124	-15 671	-2 682	-2 262
1977															
1st quarter	44 916	29 668	7 494	7 754	-46 360	-36 585	-6 676	-3 099	-1 243	-1 198	-420	-1 062	284	-1 880	-749
2nd quarter	46 796	30 852	7 901	8 043	-48 401	-38 063	-6 940	-3 398	-1 426	-12 182	-24	-885	-11 273	-3 783	-1 784
3rd quarter	47 125	30 752	7 991	8 382	-48 511	-38 005	-6 894	-3 612	-1 371	-6 297	112	-1 001	-5 408	-2 762	-2 177
4th quarter	45 818	29 544	8 098	8 176	-50 495	-39 254	-7 133	-4 108	-1 185	-15 109	-43	-746	-14 320	-3 466	-749
1978															
1st quarter	48 847	30 470	8 704	9 673	-54 471	-42 487	-7 612	-4 372	-1 396	-15 219	187	-1 009	-14 397	-4 771	-1 115
2nd quarter	54 213	35 674	8 772	9 767	-56 513	-43 419	-7 768	-5 326	-1 477	-5 606	248	-1 257	-4 597	-3 250	-1 094
3rd quarter	56 058	36 523	9 203	10 332	-58 300	-44 422	-8 248	-5 630	-1 425	-9 703	115	-1 394	-8 424	-2 753	-510
4th quarter	61 399	39 408	9 673	12 318	-60 587	-45 674	-8 561	-6 352	-1 491	-30 601	182	-999	-29 784	-4 812	-907
1979															
1st quarter	64 530	41 475	9 664	13 391	-63 492	-47 582	-8 649	-7 261	-1 462	-7 841	-2 446	-1 094	-4 301	-5 465	-908
2nd quarter	68 445	43 885	9 713	14 847	-67 584	-50 778	-8 960	-7 846	-1 552	-15 565	322	-970	-14 917	-7 220	-492
3rd quarter	74 411	47 104	9 936	17 371	-71 856	-54 002	-9 329	-8 525	-1 632	-27 156	2 779	-779	-29 156	-7 166	-2 331
4th quarter	80 577	51 975	10 378	18 224	-78 726	-59 645	-9 751	-9 330	-1 949	-14 353	-649	-904	-12 800	-5 370	-995
1980															
1st quarter	85 274	54 237	10 997	20 040	-86 559	-65 815	-10 335	-10 409	-2 174	-12 662	-2 116	-1 441	-9 105	-5 188	-787
2nd quarter	83 441	55 967	11 491	15 983	-82 734	-62 274	-10 106	-10 354	-1 648	-24 724	502	-1 159	-24 067	-2 659	-1 387
3rd quarter	86 148	55 830	12 543	17 775	-79 906	-59 010	-10 292	-10 604	-1 909	-19 666	-1 109	-1 382	-17 175	-4 156	-944
4th quarter	89 578	58 216	12 554	18 808	-84 577	-62 651	-10 760	-11 166	-2 618	-28 761	-4 279	-1 178	-23 304	-7 219	-450
1981															
1st quarter	94 665	60 317	13 684	20 664	-91 024	-67 004	-11 360	-12 660	-2 678	-21 922	-3 436	-1 361	-17 125	-2 044	-473
2nd quarter	96 294	60 141	14 392	21 761	-92 303	-67 181	-11 447	-13 675	-2 763	-24 158	-905	-1 491	-21 762	-5 709	-1 564
3rd quarter	95 013	58 031	14 835	22 147	-89 787	-64 407	-11 236	-14 144	-3 145	-17 945	-4	-1 268	-16 673	-1 124	-697
4th quarter	94 958	58 555	14 446	21 957	-91 082	-66 475	-11 460	-13 147	-3 117	-49 028	262	-976	-48 314	-745	-2 966
1982															
1st quarter	94 006	55 163	16 032	22 811	-90 336	-63 502	-12 749	-14 085	-3 955	-36 335	-1 089	-800	-34 446	-2 695	-628
2nd quarter	96 060	55 344	16 187	24 529	-88 318	-60 580	-13 096	-14 642	-3 953	-42 754	-1 132	-1 727	-39 895	1 074	-471
3rd quarter	90 925	52 089	16 003	22 833	-90 938	-63 696	-12 794	-14 448	-4 027	-23 547	-794	-2 524	-20 229	903	-3 397
4th quarter	85 993	48 561	15 857	21 575	-86 379	-59 864	-13 109	-13 406	-4 611	-25 246	-1 950	-1 080	-22 217	-3 838	-3 488
1983															
1st quarter	86 146	49 198	16 239	20 709	-85 097	-59 757	-12 951	-12 389	-3 566	-28 890	-787	-1 136	-26 967	-862	-1 549
2nd quarter	87 214	49 340	16 093	21 781	-91 096	-64 783	-13 557	-12 756	-3 951	-2 974	16	-1 263	-1 727	-1 842	-2 813
3rd quarter	89 919	50 324	16 308	23 287	-98 481	-70 370	-14 133	-13 978	-4 339	-12 191	529	-1 171	-11 549	-4 861	-1 308
4th quarter	92 831	52 937	15 671	24 223	-102 822	-73 991	-14 337	-14 494	-5 453	-22 318	-953	-1 436	-19 929	-4 962	-1 093
1984															
1st quarter	96 000	52 991	17 353	25 656	-112 576	-79 740	-16 131	-16 705	-4 354	-8 338	-657	-2 033	-5 648	-1 837	758
2nd quarter	100 257	54 626	18 045	27 586	-119 220	-83 798	-16 885	-18 537	-4 476	-25 718	-566	-1 342	-23 811	-1 967	-764
3rd quarter	102 296	55 893	17 936	28 467	-120 533	-83 918	-17 168	-19 447	-5 147	15 298	-799	-1 392	17 489	-3 209	-1 106
4th quarter	101 361	56 416	17 834	27 111	-121 591	-84 962	-17 564	-19 065	-6 359	-21 618	-1 110	-720	-19 789	-9 396	-3 644
1985															
1st quarter	97 794	54 866	18 227	24 701	-116 249	-80 319	-17 707	-18 223	-5 064	-5 491	-233	-760	-4 498	-2 783	-2 474
2nd quarter	97 437	54 154	18 214	25 069	-120 891	-84 565	-18 276	-18 050	-5 235	-2 340	-356	-1 053	-931	-4 374	-2 219
3rd quarter	94 771	52 836	17 961	23 974	-120 285	-83 909	-18 151	-18 225	-5 789	-5 776	-121	-453	-5 202	-4 698	-1 572
4th quarter	97 612	54 059	18 756	24 797	-126 349	-89 295	-18 732	-18 322	-5 911	-31 146	-3 148	-555	-27 444	-7 073	-1 217
1986															
1st quarter	100 332	53 536	21 052	25 744	-129 342	-89 220	-19 855	-20 267	-5 199	-17 406	-115	-266	-17 025	-9 781	-5 930
2nd quarter	102 206	56 828	20 912	24 466	-131 690	-91 743	-19 066	-20 881	-6 208	-24 945	16	-230	-24 731	-7 298	-1 051
3rd quarter	101 288	55 645	21 969	23 674	-132 879	-92 801	-20 448	-19 630	-6 458	-32 615	280	-1 554	-31 341	-4 975	181
4th quarter	103 275	57 335	22 761	23 179	-136 232	-94 661	-20 778	-20 793	-6 269	-36 753	132	29	-36 914	-1 938	2 529
1987															
1st quarter	104 750	56 696	23 602	24 452	-138 887	-96 023	-21 273	-21 591	-5 128	8 177	1 956	-5	6 226	-6 547	-1 749
2nd quarter	111 642	60 202	24 740	26 700	-146 125	-100 648	-22 537	-22 940	-5 502	-26 738	3 419	-168	-29 989	-7 541	-287
3rd quarter	116 688	64 217	24 986	27 485	-151 111	-104 412	-22 833	-23 866	-5 706	-27 791	32	310	-28 133	-8 795	-1 159
4th quarter	123 968	69 093	25 329	29 546	-158 324	-108 682	-24 146	-25 496	-6 926	-32 943	3 742	868	-37 553	-12 150	-2 056
1988															
1st quarter	134 932	75 655	26 598	32 679	-161 810	-109 963	-24 503	-27 344	-6 074	2 892	1 502	-1 597	2 987	-5 037	-4 504
2nd quarter	139 984	79 542	27 567	32 875	-163 265	-110 836	-24 282	-28 147	-5 615	-23 428	39	-854	-22 613	-2 594	1 318
3rd quarter	143 879	80 941	28 453	34 485	-165 901	-110 901	-24 588	-30 412	-5 902	-49 965	-7 380	1 960	-44 545	-7 791	-1 500
4th quarter	149 068	84 092	28 302	36 674	-172 770	-115 489	-25 157	-32 124	-7 685	-36 074	1 925	3 457	-41 456	-7 105	-3 294
1989															
1st quarter	155 853	86 322	30 576	38 955	-178 297	-118 709	-25 140	-34 448	-6 048	-53 703	-4 000	961	-50 664	-12 136	-2 225
2nd quarter	163 435	91 482	31 110	40 843	-182 850	-121 012	-25 241	-36 597	-5 753	-8 202	-12 095	-306	4 199	-7 686	-6 192
3rd quarter	163 560	90 743	32 316	40 501	-178 980	-117 459	-25 792	-35 729	-6 630	-51 678	-5 996	489	-46 171	-8 704	-9 149
4th quarter	165 444	91 369	33 087	40 988	-181 480	-120 485	-26 306	-34 689	-7 739	-61 803	-3 202	87	-58 688	-14 922	-4 504

[1] A minus sign indicates imports of goods or services or income payments.
[2] A minus sign indicates net unilateral transfers to foreigners.
[3] A minus sign indicates financial outflows or increases in U.S. official assets.

Table 19-10. U.S. International Transactions—Continued

(Millions of dollars, seasonally adjusted.)

Year and quarter	U.S.-owned assets abroad, net [4]—Continued		Foreign-owned assets in the United States, net [4]							Statistical discrep-ancy [5]	Balance on	
	U.S. private assets, net—Continued				Other foreign assets in the United States, net							
	U.S. claims		Total	Foreign official assets in the United States, net	Total	Direct invest-ment	U.S. Treasury securities and U.S. currency flows	U.S. securities other than U.S. Treasury securities	U.S. liabilities			Goods and services	Current account
	On unaffiliated foreigners reported by U.S. nonbanking concerns	Reported by U.S. banks, not included elsewhere							To unaffiliated foreigners reported by U.S. nonbanking concerns	Reported by U.S. banks, not included elsewhere			
1975													
1st quarter	353	-3 772	2 788	3 419	-631	278	892	344	359	-2 504	3 581	3 374	4 207
2nd quarter	112	-3 825	4 371	2 244	2 127	870	10	385	55	807	206	4 532	5 014
3rd quarter	-939	-649	2 991	-1 731	4 722	86	2 424	737	-163	1 638	-1 972	2 129	4 080
4th quarter	-883	-5 286	7 021	3 095	3 926	1 369	764	1 038	68	687	2 602	2 369	4 813
1976													
1st quarter	-747	-3 701	7 769	3 699	4 070	1 471	737	1 036	154	672	2 029	72	2 566
2nd quarter	-999	-4 786	8 453	4 039	4 414	1 086	-91	134	-231	3 516	1 600	-1 246	1 648
3rd quarter	616	-3 320	9 120	2 958	6 162	999	3 325	64	-184	1 958	1 582	-2 077	-84
4th quarter	-1 166	-9 561	12 677	6 997	5 680	790	312	51	-317	4 844	3 748	-2 833	163
1977													
1st quarter	-771	3 684	3 062	5 554	-2 492	980	1 181	749	-98	-5 304	823	-6 099	-2 687
2nd quarter	-1 124	-4 582	14 781	7 888	6 893	965	-799	589	-102	6 240	432	-6 250	-3 031
3rd quarter	1 310	-1 779	14 676	8 257	6 419	1 023	1 651	337	768	2 640	-5 622	-6 156	-2 757
4th quarter	-1 355	-8 750	20 703	15 117	5 586	761	401	763	518	3 143	268	-8 745	-5 862
1978													
1st quarter	-2 241	-6 270	18 684	15 448	3 236	1 356	1 381	396	507	-404	3 555	-10 925	-7 020
2nd quarter	315	-98	1 551	-5 113	6 664	2 313	1 493	1 082	304	1 472	7 832	-6 741	-3 777
3rd quarter	-29	-5 132	17 582	4 903	12 679	2 620	-368	296	912	9 219	-4 212	-6 944	-3 667
4th quarter	-1 898	-22 167	29 220	18 440	10 780	1 608	. . .	480	166	5 854	2 060	-5 154	-679
1979													
1st quarter	-3 854	5 926	2 707	-8 697	11 404	1 554	. . .	409	-296	6 773	5 558	-5 092	-424
2nd quarter	716	-7 921	7 663	-9 775	17 438	3 354	743	524	799	12 018	8 593	-6 140	-691
3rd quarter	-1 826	-17 833	25 349	6 036	19 313	3 382	2 402	166	210	13 153	884	-6 291	923
4th quarter	-50	-6 385	5 134	-1 228	6 362	3 588	. . .	252	908	663	9 317	-7 043	-98
1980													
1st quarter	-1 927	-1 203	9 582	-7 413	16 995	3 321	. . .	2 435	340	6 599	6 539	-10 916	-3 459
2nd quarter	144	-20 165	11 373	7 731	3 643	5 756	229	496	1 671	-4 509	14 292	-4 922	-941
3rd quarter	365	-12 440	14 930	7 564	7 366	4 713	222	263	1 252	916	403	-929	4 333
4th quarter	-2 605	-13 030	26 726	7 614	19 112	3 128	2 394	2 263	3 590	7 737	-348	-2 641	2 383
1981													
1st quarter	-2 944	-11 664	9 819	5 502	4 317	3 146	2 486	2 357	121	-3 793	11 140	-4 363	963
2nd quarter	513	-15 002	15 364	-3 159	18 523	5 294	1 641	3 512	13	8 063	7 566	-4 095	1 228
3rd quarter	458	-15 310	17 531	-5 992	23 523	5 505	. . .	704	1 084	16 478	-1 667	-2 777	2 081
4th quarter	-2 404	-42 199	43 519	8 609	34 910	11 251	. . .	332	-301	21 380	4 750	-4 934	759
1982													
1st quarter	2 220	-33 343	27 240	-3 265	30 505	2 154	1 297	1 263	-65	25 856	9 325	-5 056	-285
2nd quarter	-1 095	-39 403	35 260	1 534	33 726	2 945	. . .	2 486	-2 023	26 125	3 653	-2 145	3 789
3rd quarter	3 670	-21 405	18 663	2 694	15 969	2 849	. . .	555	-282	10 756	8 398	-8 398	-4 040
4th quarter	2 028	-16 919	15 424	2 629	12 795	4 685	. . .	1 781	-13	2 896	14 775	-8 555	-4 997
1983													
1st quarter	-4 253	-20 303	16 266	-38	16 304	1 254	. . .	2 873	-2 763	11 227	15 090	-7 271	-2 517
2nd quarter	-590	3 518	16 325	1 612	14 713	3 287	. . .	2 470	-64	4 404	-5 570	-12 907	-7 833
3rd quarter	-1 764	-3 616	20 420	-2 689	23 109	4 059	. . .	1 777	1 311	13 654	4 619	-17 871	-12 901
4th quarter	-4 347	-9 527	35 682	6 960	28 722	1 771	3 452	1 044	1 398	21 057	2 027	-19 720	-15 444
1984													
1st quarter	-3 012	-1 557	23 302	-2 956	26 258	4 858	2 450	1 333	6 092	11 525	5 910	-25 527	-20 930
2nd quarter	-934	-20 146	42 689	-156	42 845	8 625	8 036	362	4 232	21 590	6 411	-28 012	-23 439
3rd quarter	3 987	17 817	7 568	-884	8 452	4 432	6 103	1 447	1 662	-5 192	458	-27 257	-23 384
4th quarter	492	-7 241	44 192	7 136	37 056	6 552	10 512	9 426	4 640	5 926	3 953	-28 276	-26 589
1985													
1st quarter	475	284	18 342	-10 962	29 304	4 913	3 390	9 615	-720	12 106	10 597	-24 933	-23 519
2nd quarter	2 337	3 325	29 334	8 502	20 832	4 376	6 888	7 194	1 724	650	1 619	-30 473	-28 689
3rd quarter	-2 779	3 847	38 263	2 506	35 757	4 839	9 136	11 669	2 801	7 312	-1 265	-31 263	-31 303
4th quarter	-10 375	-8 779	60 179	-1 165	61 344	5 618	6 219	22 484	6 046	20 977	5 528	-35 212	-34 648
1986													
1st quarter	-6 230	4 916	41 489	2 712	38 777	3 431	6 420	18 730	696	9 500	10 042	-34 487	-34 209
2nd quarter	-2 722	-13 660	53 710	15 918	37 792	5 520	4 620	22 752	1 635	3 265	6 851	-33 069	-35 692
3rd quarter	-7 638	-18 909	70 876	15 789	55 087	8 746	-854	17 107	1 947	28 141	-282	-35 635	-38 049
4th quarter	-5 183	-32 322	63 933	1 229	62 704	17 723	-2 277	12 380	-953	35 831	11 975	-35 343	-39 226
1987													
1st quarter	-5 715	20 237	42 247	14 199	28 048	12 883	-2 326	18 372	6 151	-7 032	-11 246	-36 998	-39 265
2nd quarter	712	-22 873	57 331	10 444	46 887	8 593	-731	15 960	5 595	17 470	9 301	-38 243	-39 995
3rd quarter	-1 319	-16 860	83 145	764	82 381	20 763	-1 835	12 676	6 656	44 121	-15 319	-38 042	-40 129
4th quarter	-724	-22 623	65 910	19 980	45 930	16 230	2 649	-4 888	-39	31 978	8 222	-38 406	-41 282
1988													
1st quarter	-3 454	15 982	32 028	24 925	7 103	8 425	6 511	2 423	12 593	-22 849	-2 077	-32 213	-32 952
2nd quarter	-9 954	-11 383	74 531	6 006	68 525	13 717	7 673	9 702	6 742	30 691	-22 325	-28 009	-28 896
3rd quarter	-5 217	-30 037	52 797	-1 974	54 771	13 778	4 743	7 464	6 399	22 387	24 962	-26 095	-27 924
4th quarter	-2 568	-28 489	87 166	10 801	76 365	21 815	7 112	6 764	7 159	33 515	-19 841	-28 252	-31 387
1989													
1st quarter	-9 293	-27 010	66 666	7 700	58 966	18 584	10 961	8 544	6 637	14 240	15 401	-26 951	-28 492
2nd quarter	-5 767	23 844	10 980	-5 114	16 094	15 325	4 789	9 365	12 000	-25 385	22 257	-23 661	-25 168
3rd quarter	-5 924	-22 394	74 068	13 060	61 008	11 519	12 744	10 270	-1 121	27 596	-479	-20 192	-22 050
4th quarter	-6 662	-32 600	73 215	-7 142	80 357	22 846	7 024	10 588	4 570	35 329	12 427	-22 335	-23 775

[4] A minus sign indicates financial outflows or decreases in foreign official assets in the United States.
[5] Sum of credits and debits with the sign reversed.
. . . = Not available.

Table 19-10. U.S. International Transactions—Continued

(Millions of dollars, seasonally adjusted.)

Year and quarter	Exports of goods, services, and income				Imports of goods, services, and income [1]				Unilateral current transfers, net [2]	U.S.-owned assets abroad, net [3]					
										Total	U.S. official reserve assets, net	U.S. government assets other than official reserve assets, net	U.S. private assets, net		
	Total	Goods	Services	Income receipts	Total	Goods	Services	Income payments					Total	Direct investment	Foreign securities
1990															
1st quarter	171 856	95 070	35 016	41 770	-188 962	-124 947	-28 173	-35 842	-6 540	37 828	-3 177	-756	41 761	-10 391	-8 580
2nd quarter	174 266	96 273	35 988	42 005	-186 146	-121 782	-28 764	-35 600	-7 644	-37 204	371	-796	-36 779	-4 651	-11 037
3rd quarter	176 466	97 227	37 402	41 837	-190 664	-124 132	-29 923	-36 609	-7 339	-43 716	1 739	-338	-45 117	-17 898	-1 037
4th quarter	184 389	98 831	39 428	46 130	-193 514	-127 577	-30 795	-35 142	-5 133	-38 142	-1 092	4 205	-41 255	-4 240	-8 111
1991															
1st quarter	181 296	101 258	37 891	42 147	-186 167	-122 326	-29 801	-34 040	15 004	-10 570	-353	549	-10 766	-14 318	-9 960
2nd quarter	180 627	102 674	40 745	37 208	-181 695	-120 103	-29 660	-31 932	3 780	745	1 014	-423	154	-1 230	-12 021
3rd quarter	181 647	104 238	41 860	35 549	-182 800	-122 448	-29 200	-31 152	-2 812	-15 900	3 878	3 256	-23 034	-9 356	-12 550
4th quarter	183 993	105 913	43 766	34 314	-183 906	-126 143	-29 799	-27 964	-5 224	-38 664	1 226	-459	-39 431	-12 987	-11 142
1992															
1st quarter	186 444	108 062	44 164	34 218	-185 439	-127 962	-29 733	-27 744	-6 827	-11 428	-1 057	-259	-10 112	-20 695	-8 668
2nd quarter	186 873	107 941	44 133	34 799	-190 385	-132 484	-29 414	-28 487	-7 887	-16 235	1 464	-302	-17 397	-10 268	-8 196
3rd quarter	188 127	110 847	44 609	32 671	-193 285	-136 048	-30 147	-27 090	-7 441	-13 570	1 952	-392	-15 130	-5 157	-13 059
4th quarter	189 201	112 781	44 343	32 077	-196 399	-140 034	-30 154	-26 211	-10 980	-33 177	1 542	-715	-34 004	-12 145	-19 243
1993															
1st quarter	191 422	112 099	45 984	33 339	-197 831	-142 331	-29 967	-25 533	-7 732	-21 491	-983	487	-20 995	-14 982	-28 208
2nd quarter	193 169	113 257	46 457	33 455	-204 708	-146 800	-30 632	-27 276	-8 455	-45 843	822	-304	-46 361	-23 264	-29 833
3rd quarter	194 153	112 982	46 707	34 464	-205 520	-147 763	-30 893	-26 864	-9 210	-52 975	-544	-194	-52 237	-13 155	-51 940
4th quarter	200 170	118 605	46 766	34 799	-215 744	-152 500	-32 174	-31 070	-11 711	-80 243	-673	-340	-79 230	-32 550	-36 272
1994															
1st quarter	204 240	118 833	48 362	37 045	-220 697	-156 303	-32 780	-31 614	-7 697	-39 740	-59	399	-40 080	-28 554	-19 540
2nd quarter	211 812	122 251	49 978	39 583	-231 447	-163 200	-32 994	-35 253	-8 067	-45 677	3 537	477	-49 691	-14 932	-11 834
3rd quarter	222 795	128 947	50 667	43 181	-244 291	-171 342	-33 596	-39 353	-9 198	-31 948	-165	-323	-31 460	-17 316	-13 368
4th quarter	230 930	132 828	51 391	46 711	-254 574	-177 845	-33 575	-43 154	-11 837	-61 574	2 033	-943	-62 664	-19 367	-18 448
1995															
1st quarter	241 117	138 370	52 173	50 574	-263 078	-183 966	-34 396	-44 716	-8 502	-64 771	-5 318	-553	-58 900	-19 325	-8 596
2nd quarter	248 705	142 520	53 163	53 022	-271 557	-189 910	-35 067	-46 580	-8 154	-118 089	-2 722	-225	-115 142	-15 078	-27 964
3rd quarter	255 495	146 536	56 436	52 523	-272 899	-187 685	-35 574	-49 640	-8 533	-47 311	-1 893	252	-45 670	-21 772	-42 116
4th quarter	259 310	147 778	57 408	54 124	-272 472	-187 813	-36 243	-48 416	-8 913	-122 091	191	-458	-121 824	-42 573	-43 718
1996															
1st quarter	263 221	150 552	57 442	55 227	-279 388	-194 445	-37 059	-47 884	-10 169	-80 431	17	-210	-80 238	-23 759	-43 538
2nd quarter	266 995	152 861	59 350	54 784	-287 281	-200 070	-37 575	-49 636	-8 421	-68 123	-523	-568	-67 032	-15 096	-30 579
3rd quarter	266 854	151 856	58 664	56 334	-293 230	-202 367	-38 805	-52 058	-8 531	-91 580	7 489	105	-99 174	-23 129	-33 178
4th quarter	280 655	156 844	64 029	59 782	-299 457	-206 231	-38 993	-54 233	-11 464	-173 272	-315	-316	-172 641	-29 898	-42 020
1997															
1st quarter	287 298	162 670	62 534	62 094	-313 484	-214 188	-40 519	-58 777	-8 815	-152 729	4 480	-76	-157 133	-29 544	-24 352
2nd quarter	299 738	170 249	64 351	65 138	-318 291	-217 306	-40 950	-60 035	-9 103	-93 152	-236	-298	-92 618	-24 883	-31 275
3rd quarter	303 592	173 155	64 905	65 532	-325 603	-220 853	-42 209	-62 541	-9 503	-119 387	-730	377	-119 034	-21 217	-51 401
4th quarter	300 816	172 292	64 483	64 041	-329 635	-224 123	-42 670	-62 842	-12 988	-120 209	-4 524	65	-115 750	-29 161	-9 824
1998															
1st quarter	302 200	171 060	64 728	66 412	-333 905	-227 353	-43 377	-63 175	-10 869	-72 938	-444	-80	-72 414	-41 844	-17 951
2nd quarter	298 801	165 559	66 228	67 014	-337 651	-228 197	-44 744	-64 710	-11 174	-137 128	-1 945	-483	-134 700	-44 689	-41 461
3rd quarter	293 039	164 054	64 870	64 115	-338 641	-227 430	-45 985	-65 226	-11 956	-57 020	-2 025	188	-55 183	-20 479	9 283
4th quarter	300 761	169 743	67 251	63 767	-345 722	-234 123	-47 157	-64 442	-14 443	-80 745	-2 369	-47	-78 329	-35 634	-74 075
1999															
1st quarter	300 137	164 302	68 829	67 006	-351 303	-238 715	-47 807	-64 781	-10 899	-84 290	4 068	118	-88 476	-68 498	4 196
2nd quarter	307 252	166 144	70 276	70 832	-366 856	-250 093	-49 349	-67 414	-11 316	-180 642	1 159	-392	-181 409	-50 190	-68 182
3rd quarter	319 816	172 989	71 265	75 562	-388 302	-264 363	-50 930	-73 009	-11 092	-125 226	1 951	-686	-126 491	-64 062	-38 290
4th quarter	332 465	180 530	72 109	79 826	-403 270	-276 809	-51 629	-74 832	-13 448	-113 483	1 569	3 710	-118 762	-42 185	-13 960
2000															
1st quarter	341 606	185 253	73 228	83 125	-427 348	-293 664	-54 415	-79 269	-12 129	-214 667	-554	-127	-213 986	-34 934	-31 042
2nd quarter	355 236	191 227	75 384	88 625	-441 169	-301 569	-55 488	-84 112	-12 645	-108 046	2 020	-570	-109 496	-52 029	-36 671
3rd quarter	360 310	198 811	74 780	86 719	-454 026	-312 780	-57 686	-83 560	-13 481	-86 485	-346	114	-86 253	-39 618	-30 863
4th quarter	364 277	196 703	75 593	91 981	-456 650	-316 395	-57 332	-82 923	-17 435	-160 602	-1 410	-358	-158 834	-32 633	-23 332
2001															
1st quarter	350 473	193 976	74 737	81 760	-443 079	-309 396	-56 648	-77 035	-14 083	-211 382	190	77	-211 649	-35 381	-23 855
2nd quarter	334 755	185 030	74 265	75 460	-417 608	-290 214	-58 097	-69 297	-14 690	-84 086	-1 343	-783	-81 960	-26 783	-48 700
3rd quarter	311 400	172 648	71 287	67 465	-401 578	-277 881	-55 330	-68 367	-1 719	37 302	-3 559	77	40 784	-44 327	13 139
4th quarter	296 718	167 058	67 652	62 008	-370 205	-268 409	-53 371	-48 425	-16 087	-108 601	-199	143	-108 545	-35 857	-25 228
2002															
1st quarter	299 663	165 123	71 085	63 455	-392 457	-273 520	-56 447	-62 490	-17 411	-34 144	390	133	-34 667	-30 668	5 325
2nd quarter	312 230	172 034	72 890	67 306	-416 557	-291 395	-56 902	-68 260	-13 562	-133 373	-1 843	42	-131 572	-34 244	-5 886
3rd quarter	317 911	174 371	73 998	69 542	-423 484	-296 778	-58 507	-68 199	-13 427	21 574	-1 416	-27	23 017	-35 834	21 624
4th quarter	312 935	170 305	76 134	66 496	-424 804	-303 035	-61 092	-60 677	-14 980	-52 069	-812	197	-51 454	-34 087	-5 174
2003															
1st quarter	315 676	173 459	74 540	67 677	-437 067	-311 402	-61 983	-63 682	-16 815	-102 665	83	53	-102 801	-40 837	-26 619
2nd quarter	317 367	174 554	73 920	68 893	-434 873	-310 087	-61 767	-63 019	-16 369	-110 962	-170	310	-111 102	-34 049	8 429
3rd quarter	329 508	178 251	77 472	73 785	-444 497	-312 886	-65 087	-66 524	-16 639	-8 138	-611	483	-8 010	-45 206	-28 312
4th quarter	352 336	186 858	81 448	84 030	-461 679	-326 299	-67 501	-67 879	-17 617	-61 647	2 221	-309	-63 559	-53 705	-25 835

[1] A minus sign indicates imports of goods or services or income payments.
[2] A minus sign indicates net unilateral transfers to foreigners.
[3] A minus sign indicates financial outflows or increases in U.S. official assets.

Table 19-10. U.S. International Transactions—Continued

(Millions of dollars, seasonally adjusted.)

Year and quarter	U.S.-owned assets abroad, net [4]—Continued		Foreign-owned assets in the United States, net [4]								Statistical discrepancy [5]	Balance on	
	U.S. private assets, net—Continued			Foreign official assets in the United States, net	Other foreign assets in the United States, net							Goods and services	Current account
	U.S. claims		Total		Total	Direct investment	U.S. Treasury securities and U.S. currency flows	U.S. securities other than U.S. Treasury securities	U.S. liabilities				
	On unaffiliated foreigners reported by U.S. nonbanking concerns	Reported by U.S. banks, not included elsewhere							To unaffiliated foreigners reported by U.S. nonbanking concerns	Reported by U.S. banks, not included elsewhere			
1990													
1st quarter	3 019	57 713	-22 824	-6 421	-16 403	15 774	1 709	1 311	12 904	-48 101	8 661	-23 034	-23 646
2nd quarter	-5 069	-16 022	41 215	6 207	35 008	13 773	6 257	2 114	6 713	6 151	15 356	-18 285	-19 524
3rd quarter	-15 514	-10 668	63 231	13 937	49 294	8 313	6 044	-2 874	16 838	20 973	1 857	-19 426	-21 537
4th quarter	-10 260	-18 644	59 949	20 186	39 763	10 635	2 256	1 041	8 678	17 153	-667	-20 113	-14 258
1991													
1st quarter	-40	13 552	8 347	5 569	2 778	4 076	9 539	5 023	-586	-15 274	-6 969	-12 978	10 133
2nd quarter	7 902	5 503	12 678	-4 913	17 591	13 378	15 661	14 872	-2 549	-23 771	-16 208	-6 344	2 712
3rd quarter	3 341	-4 469	33 236	3 854	29 382	-1 354	3 004	10 310	4 761	12 661	-9 585	-5 550	-3 965
4th quarter	-106	-15 196	56 549	12 879	43 670	7 072	6 022	4 939	-4 741	30 378	-12 923	-6 263	-5 137
1992													
1st quarter	7 562	11 689	31 079	20 988	10 091	2 086	1 986	4 569	5 689	-4 239	-13 692	-5 469	-5 822
2nd quarter	-6 620	7 687	50 304	20 879	29 425	5 916	11 331	10 467	3 954	-2 243	-22 495	-9 824	-11 399
3rd quarter	-3 737	6 823	35 469	-7 524	42 993	2 898	11 008	2 531	4 854	21 702	-9 169	-10 739	-12 599
4th quarter	2 408	-5 024	53 809	6 133	47 676	8 922	26 206	12 476	-924	996	-2 340	-13 064	-18 178
1993													
1st quarter	-6 130	28 325	25 099	10 937	14 162	8 060	16 363	9 694	-215	-19 740	11 291	-14 215	-14 141
2nd quarter	-725	7 461	59 038	17 466	41 572	11 386	5 608	15 205	6 531	2 842	6 949	-17 718	-19 994
3rd quarter	5 896	6 962	85 694	19 073	66 621	11 688	9 658	17 782	288	27 205	-11 910	-18 967	-20 577
4th quarter	1 725	-12 133	112 210	24 277	87 933	20 229	11 652	37 411	3 885	14 756	-4 523	-19 303	-27 285
1994													
1st quarter	-2 215	10 229	90 280	10 568	79 712	5 883	15 412	21 070	5 856	31 491	-26 228	-21 888	-24 154
2nd quarter	-20 966	-1 959	56 842	9 455	47 387	5 767	-798	12 352	4 269	25 797	17 548	-23 965	-27 702
3rd quarter	-960	184	81 934	19 358	62 576	13 709	10 361	13 389	-1 620	26 737	-18 896	-25 324	-30 694
4th quarter	-12 195	-12 654	76 933	202	76 731	20 762	32 699	10 160	-7 203	20 313	20 280	-27 201	-35 481
1995													
1st quarter	-2 631	-28 348	97 915	21 956	75 959	9 924	34 410	12 400	17 764	1 461	-2 506	-27 819	-30 463
2nd quarter	-24 580	-47 520	122 149	37 072	85 077	11 888	30 338	15 851	11 864	15 136	26 992	-29 294	-31 006
3rd quarter	13 729	4 489	116 366	39 302	77 064	16 764	37 194	26 218	13 493	-16 605	-42 481	-20 287	-25 937
4th quarter	-31 804	-3 729	102 132	11 550	90 582	19 200	1 902	22 780	16 516	30 184	42 103	-18 870	-22 075
1996													
1st quarter	-15 210	2 269	85 255	51 771	33 484	28 518	13 646	20 356	4 350	-33 386	21 689	-23 510	-26 336
2nd quarter	-22 000	643	101 405	13 503	87 902	16 184	29 514	24 686	15 259	2 259	-4 418	-25 434	-28 707
3rd quarter	-9 090	-33 777	144 109	23 020	121 089	15 257	44 116	29 719	28 925	3 072	-17 450	-30 652	-34 907
4th quarter	-40 033	-60 690	220 326	38 430	181 896	26 542	77 108	28 511	5 202	44 533	-16 640	-24 351	-30 266
1997													
1st quarter	-38 112	-65 125	173 005	27 763	145 242	28 626	32 537	38 490	25 055	20 534	14 931	-29 503	-35 001
2nd quarter	-9 885	-26 575	140 719	-6 019	146 738	23 150	38 750	45 651	6 461	32 726	-19 638	-23 656	-27 656
3rd quarter	-22 173	-24 243	167 223	23 474	143 749	17 865	42 709	52 544	25 550	5 081	-16 000	-25 002	-31 514
4th quarter	-51 590	-25 175	225 860	-26 182	252 042	35 960	41 221	24 724	59 452	90 685	-63 601	-30 018	-41 807
1998													
1st quarter	-7 822	-4 797	79 170	11 072	68 098	19 759	-5 789	63 237	39 833	-48 942	36 533	-34 942	-42 574
2nd quarter	-20 363	-28 187	155 055	-10 235	165 290	20 391	24 163	56 146	30 722	33 868	32 277	-41 154	-50 024
3rd quarter	-15 658	-28 329	75 963	-46 640	122 603	23 490	2 195	6 628	14 976	75 314	38 818	-44 491	-57 558
4th quarter	5 639	25 741	113 381	25 900	87 481	115 405	24 634	30 304	-62 391	-20 471	26 934	-44 286	-59 404
1999													
1st quarter	-47 211	23 037	109 283	4 381	104 902	28 759	-10 887	49 157	51 307	-13 434	37 260	-53 391	-62 065
2nd quarter	-27 021	-36 016	247 860	-757	248 617	140 759	-8 355	70 205	16 928	29 080	3 871	-63 022	-70 920
3rd quarter	-13 663	-10 476	156 858	12 625	144 233	50 758	8 382	86 202	-8 777	7 668	48 121	-71 039	-79 578
4th quarter	-9 809	-52 808	226 210	27 294	198 916	69 169	-11 230	93 270	16 789	30 918	-24 163	-75 799	-84 253
2000													
1st quarter	-79 800	-68 210	248 698	22 542	226 156	52 094	-17 860	129 306	72 433	-9 817	64 034	-89 598	-97 871
2nd quarter	-25 287	4 491	247 559	6 952	240 607	91 669	-21 894	88 189	28 796	53 847	-40 746	-90 446	-98 578
3rd quarter	-14 121	-1 651	246 185	11 354	234 831	79 979	-12 656	122 138	16 914	28 456	-52 275	-96 875	-107 197
4th quarter	-19 582	-83 287	304 456	1 910	302 546	97 534	-12 258	120 256	52 529	44 485	-33 848	-101 431	-109 808
2001													
1st quarter	-46 769	-105 644	332 155	21 333	310 822	59 145	-15 348	129 474	112 097	25 454	-13 815	-97 331	-106 689
2nd quarter	-7 507	1 030	207 866	-19 965	227 831	59 338	-9 144	108 537	-173	69 273	-25 977	-89 016	-97 543
3rd quarter	1 824	70 140	22 936	15 653	7 283	13 783	205	60 748	-23 171	-44 282	31 956	-89 276	-91 897
4th quarter	43 932	-91 392	219 902	11 038	208 864	34 755	33 692	95 126	-22 643	67 934	-21 470	-87 070	-89 574
2002													
1st quarter	-11 863	2 539	165 989	12 801	153 188	28 407	14 858	73 782	45 704	-9 563	-21 359	-93 759	-110 205
2nd quarter	-23 262	-68 180	229 135	53 312	175 823	2 195	26 020	99 718	20 607	27 283	22 398	-103 373	-117 889
3rd quarter	-4 119	41 346	150 075	17 720	132 355	9 927	56 624	43 931	-242	22 115	-52 288	-106 916	-119 000
4th quarter	-6 181	-6 012	223 047	30 157	192 890	31 882	24 443	68 069	11 921	56 575	-43 782	-117 688	-126 849
2003													
1st quarter	-11 207	-24 138	246 105	48 986	197 119	32 523	13 901	56 723	69 410	24 562	-4 828	-125 386	-138 206
2nd quarter	-22 480	-63 002	218 553	65 245	153 308	-544	54 712	92 407	-2 257	8 990	27 836	-123 380	-133 875
3rd quarter	35 845	29 663	134 202	50 663	83 539	-2 810	49 258	18 090	12 721	6 280	6 385	-122 250	-131 628
4th quarter	-31 090	47 071	230 311	83 679	146 632	10 719	12 201	83 761	4 140	35 811	-41 404	-125 494	-126 960

[4] A minus sign indicates financial outflows or decreases in foreign official assets in the United States.
[5] Sum of credits and debits with the sign reversed.

Table 19-11. Productivity and Related Data

(1992 = 100, seasonally adjusted.)

Year and quarter	Business sector								Nonfarm business sector							
	Output per hour of all persons	Output	Hours of all persons	Compensation per hour	Real compensation per hour	Unit labor costs	Unit nonlabor payments	Implicit price deflator	Output per hour of all persons	Output	Hours of all persons	Compensation per hour	Real compensation per hour	Unit labor costs	Unit nonlabor payments	Implicit price deflator
1947																
1st quarter	32.3	20.2	62.7	6.8	40.7	21.1	18.0	20.0	36.5	19.7	54.0	7.2	43.2	19.9	16.7	18.7
2nd quarter	32.5	20.3	62.6	7.0	41.1	21.5	18.1	20.2	37.4	20.2	54.0	7.4	43.3	19.7	17.7	19.0
3rd quarter	32.3	20.4	63.1	7.0	40.5	21.8	18.9	20.7	36.3	19.7	54.2	7.5	43.3	20.7	18.2	19.8
4th quarter	32.6	20.7	63.6	7.3	40.9	22.4	19.6	21.3	37.8	20.7	54.7	7.7	43.2	20.4	18.6	19.7
1948																
1st quarter	33.4	21.1	63.3	7.4	40.7	22.2	20.3	21.5	37.9	20.9	55.1	7.9	43.4	20.9	18.8	20.1
2nd quarter	34.1	21.6	63.3	7.5	40.5	22.0	21.1	21.7	37.9	20.9	55.0	8.0	43.3	21.2	19.2	20.4
3rd quarter	34.0	21.7	63.9	7.7	41.0	22.7	21.0	22.1	38.0	21.0	55.4	8.2	43.5	21.6	19.5	20.8
4th quarter	34.2	21.7	63.5	7.9	42.3	23.1	20.5	22.1	38.2	21.0	54.9	8.3	44.5	21.7	20.0	21.1
1949																
1st quarter	34.1	21.3	62.6	7.7	41.9	22.7	20.6	21.9	38.6	20.8	54.0	8.3	45.1	21.6	19.8	21.0
2nd quarter	34.2	21.2	62.0	7.6	41.3	22.3	20.6	21.6	39.0	20.7	53.1	8.3	45.0	21.3	19.8	20.8
3rd quarter	35.2	21.5	61.0	7.8	42.3	22.0	20.7	21.5	39.9	21.0	52.5	8.4	45.6	20.9	20.3	20.7
4th quarter	35.3	21.2	60.2	7.8	42.9	22.2	20.2	21.5	39.7	20.7	52.3	8.4	45.7	21.1	19.9	20.6
1950																
1st quarter	36.9	22.3	60.4	8.1	44.5	22.0	20.5	21.4	41.0	21.6	52.7	8.6	47.0	20.9	20.4	20.7
2nd quarter	37.2	23.0	61.8	8.2	44.6	22.0	20.8	21.5	41.5	22.4	54.0	8.7	47.5	21.0	20.4	20.8
3rd quarter	37.9	24.0	63.4	8.3	44.6	22.0	22.0	22.0	42.4	23.6	55.7	8.9	47.6	21.0	21.1	21.0
4th quarter	38.0	24.3	63.8	8.5	44.6	22.4	22.8	22.5	42.5	23.9	56.2	9.1	48.0	21.5	21.3	21.4
1951																
1st quarter	38.0	24.5	64.5	8.8	44.3	23.1	23.7	23.3	42.6	24.3	57.2	9.4	47.2	22.0	22.1	22.1
2nd quarter	38.2	24.8	64.8	9.0	45.1	23.6	23.4	23.6	42.5	24.5	57.7	9.5	47.6	22.5	22.1	22.3
3rd quarter	39.3	25.2	64.0	9.2	45.9	23.4	23.8	23.5	43.5	24.8	57.1	9.7	48.4	22.3	22.7	22.5
4th quarter	39.2	25.2	64.2	9.3	45.6	23.7	24.0	23.8	43.5	24.9	57.1	9.8	48.3	22.6	22.7	22.6
1952																
1st quarter	39.3	25.4	64.6	9.4	45.9	23.8	23.5	23.7	43.7	25.1	57.5	10.0	48.8	22.8	22.4	22.7
2nd quarter	39.6	25.3	63.9	9.6	46.7	24.1	23.0	23.7	43.6	25.0	57.3	10.0	49.1	23.0	22.0	22.6
3rd quarter	39.7	25.5	64.1	9.7	47.0	24.4	23.3	23.9	43.4	25.1	57.7	10.1	49.2	23.3	22.1	22.9
4th quarter	40.3	26.5	65.7	9.9	48.1	24.6	23.0	24.0	44.3	26.2	59.2	10.4	50.4	23.5	22.4	23.1
1953																
1st quarter	40.9	27.0	66.0	10.1	49.0	24.6	22.9	24.0	44.6	26.7	59.8	10.5	51.1	23.6	22.4	23.1
2nd quarter	41.3	27.2	65.9	10.2	49.4	24.7	22.8	24.0	44.7	26.8	59.9	10.7	51.6	23.8	22.3	23.3
3rd quarter	41.3	27.0	65.3	10.3	49.9	25.1	22.4	24.1	44.9	26.7	59.3	10.8	52.0	24.0	22.2	23.3
4th quarter	41.1	26.5	64.3	10.3	49.8	25.1	22.4	24.1	44.8	26.1	58.4	10.9	52.3	24.3	21.8	23.4
1954																
1st quarter	41.1	26.3	63.9	10.4	50.0	25.3	22.3	24.2	44.8	25.8	57.6	11.0	52.6	24.4	21.7	23.4
2nd quarter	41.7	26.3	63.0	10.5	50.8	25.3	22.2	24.1	45.1	25.8	57.2	11.0	52.8	24.3	22.1	23.5
3rd quarter	42.3	26.6	62.7	10.6	51.0	25.0	22.8	24.2	45.9	26.2	56.9	11.1	53.3	24.1	22.4	23.5
4th quarter	42.9	27.1	63.2	10.7	51.9	25.0	22.9	24.2	46.4	26.8	57.7	11.2	54.0	24.0	22.8	23.6
1955																
1st quarter	43.6	28.1	64.4	10.7	51.6	24.5	24.0	24.3	47.4	27.8	58.6	11.3	54.4	23.7	23.5	23.7
2nd quarter	43.9	28.6	65.1	10.8	52.4	24.7	23.8	24.3	47.5	28.2	59.4	11.4	55.0	23.9	23.5	23.8
3rd quarter	43.9	29.0	66.0	10.8	52.4	24.7	24.2	24.5	47.6	28.6	60.0	11.5	55.7	24.2	23.8	24.0
4th quarter	43.6	29.1	66.8	11.0	52.9	25.2	24.1	24.8	47.4	28.8	60.7	11.6	56.2	24.5	23.7	24.2
1956																
1st quarter	43.4	28.9	66.6	11.3	54.3	25.9	23.5	25.0	46.9	28.6	61.1	11.8	57.0	25.2	23.1	24.5
2nd quarter	43.6	29.1	66.8	11.5	55.0	26.3	23.2	25.1	47.1	28.8	61.2	12.1	57.8	25.6	22.9	24.6
3rd quarter	43.6	29.0	66.5	11.6	55.0	26.6	23.6	25.5	47.0	28.7	60.9	12.2	58.1	26.0	23.1	24.9
4th quarter	44.5	29.5	66.4	11.9	55.7	26.7	23.7	25.6	47.5	29.1	61.3	12.4	58.5	26.2	23.2	25.1
1957																
1st quarter	44.7	29.7	66.3	12.1	56.4	27.0	24.1	25.9	48.1	29.5	61.3	12.6	58.9	26.3	23.9	25.4
2nd quarter	44.8	29.5	66.0	12.2	56.5	27.3	24.1	26.1	47.9	29.3	61.2	12.8	59.0	26.6	23.7	25.5
3rd quarter	45.3	29.8	65.9	12.3	56.5	27.2	24.5	26.2	48.6	29.6	60.9	12.9	59.2	26.6	24.0	25.6
4th quarter	45.7	29.5	64.4	12.5	57.2	27.4	24.1	26.2	48.8	29.1	59.7	13.1	59.7	26.9	23.7	25.7
1958																
1st quarter	45.3	28.4	62.7	12.7	57.1	27.9	24.0	26.5	48.0	28.0	58.3	13.1	59.2	27.4	23.2	25.8
2nd quarter	46.0	28.5	62.1	12.7	56.8	27.6	24.6	26.5	48.9	28.1	57.5	13.3	59.3	27.1	23.8	25.9
3rd quarter	46.8	29.3	62.6	12.9	57.9	27.6	25.0	26.6	49.9	29.0	58.1	13.4	60.2	27.0	24.3	26.0
4th quarter	47.3	30.1	63.5	13.0	58.4	27.5	25.5	26.8	50.7	29.9	59.0	13.6	60.8	26.8	25.0	26.1
1959																
1st quarter	47.7	30.8	64.5	13.2	59.0	27.7	25.3	26.8	50.7	30.5	60.2	13.7	61.2	27.0	24.9	26.2
2nd quarter	48.0	31.7	66.1	13.2	59.0	27.5	25.4	26.8	51.4	31.5	61.3	13.8	61.7	26.9	25.1	26.2
3rd quarter	48.3	31.6	65.4	13.4	59.5	27.8	25.2	26.8	51.4	31.4	61.1	13.9	61.8	27.1	24.9	26.3
4th quarter	48.4	31.7	65.4	13.6	59.9	28.1	25.0	26.9	51.3	31.4	61.1	14.1	62.0	27.4	24.8	26.4
1960																
1st quarter	49.7	32.4	65.3	13.9	61.4	28.0	25.3	27.0	52.5	32.3	61.5	14.4	63.2	27.3	25.0	26.5
2nd quarter	48.7	32.1	65.9	13.9	60.8	28.5	24.8	27.1	51.7	31.9	61.6	14.4	63.2	27.9	24.2	26.5
3rd quarter	48.8	32.1	65.8	13.9	60.7	28.4	25.0	27.1	51.9	31.8	61.3	14.5	63.6	28.0	24.4	26.6
4th quarter	48.5	31.5	65.0	14.0	60.9	28.9	24.4	27.2	51.2	31.1	60.7	14.6	63.4	28.5	23.8	26.7

Table 19-11. Productivity and Related Data—Continued

(1992 = 100, seasonally adjusted.)

Year and quarter	Nonfinancial corporations										Manufacturing				
	Output per hour of all employees	Output	Employee hours	Compensation per hour	Real compensation per hour	Unit costs			Unit profits	Implicit price deflator	Output per hour of all persons	Output	Hours of all persons	Compensation per hour	Real compensation per hour	Unit labor costs
						Total	Labor costs	Nonlabor costs							

Year and quarter	Output per hour	Output	Employee hours	Comp per hour	Real comp per hour	Total	Labor costs	Nonlabor costs	Unit profits	Implicit price deflator	Output per hour	Output	Hours	Comp per hour	Real comp per hour	Unit labor costs
1947																
1st quarter	...	...	...	...	...	...	...	...	...	...	...	...	...	...	...	...
2nd quarter	...	...	...	...	...	...	...	...	...	...	...	...	...	...	...	...
3rd quarter	...	...	...	...	...	...	...	...	...	...	...	...	...	...	...	...
4th quarter	...	...	...	...	...	...	...	...	...	...	...	...	...	...	...	...
1948																
1st quarter	...	...	...	...	...	...	...	...	...	...	...	...	...	...	...	...
2nd quarter	...	...	...	...	...	...	...	...	...	...	...	...	...	...	...	...
3rd quarter	...	...	...	...	...	...	...	...	...	...	...	...	...	...	...	...
4th quarter	...	...	...	...	...	...	...	...	...	...	...	...	...	...	...	...
1949																
1st quarter	...	...	...	...	...	...	...	...	...	...	...	...	...	...	...	...
2nd quarter	...	...	...	...	...	...	...	...	...	...	...	...	...	...	...	...
3rd quarter	...	...	...	...	...	...	...	...	...	...	...	...	...	...	...	...
4th quarter	...	...	...	...	...	...	...	...	...	...	...	...	...	...	...	...
1950																
1st quarter	...	...	...	...	...	...	...	...	...	...	...	...	...	...	...	...
2nd quarter	...	...	...	...	...	...	...	...	...	...	...	...	...	...	...	...
3rd quarter	...	...	...	...	...	...	...	...	...	...	...	...	...	...	...	...
4th quarter	...	...	...	...	...	...	...	...	...	...	...	...	...	...	...	...
1951																
1st quarter	...	...	...	...	...	...	...	...	...	...	...	...	...	...	...	...
2nd quarter	...	...	...	...	...	...	...	...	...	...	...	...	...	...	...	...
3rd quarter	...	...	...	...	...	...	...	...	...	...	...	...	...	...	...	...
4th quarter	...	...	...	...	...	...	...	...	...	...	...	...	...	...	...	...
1952																
1st quarter	...	...	...	...	...	...	...	...	...	...	...	...	...	...	...	...
2nd quarter	...	...	...	...	...	...	...	...	...	...	...	...	...	...	...	...
3rd quarter	...	...	...	...	...	...	...	...	...	...	...	...	...	...	...	...
4th quarter	...	...	...	...	...	...	...	...	...	...	...	...	...	...	...	...
1953																
1st quarter	...	...	...	...	...	...	...	...	...	...	...	...	...	...	...	...
2nd quarter	...	...	...	...	...	...	...	...	...	...	...	...	...	...	...	...
3rd quarter	...	...	...	...	...	...	...	...	...	...	...	...	...	...	...	...
4th quarter	...	...	...	...	...	...	...	...	...	...	...	...	...	...	...	...
1954																
1st quarter	...	...	...	...	...	...	...	...	...	...	...	...	...	...	...	...
2nd quarter	...	...	...	...	...	...	...	...	...	...	...	...	...	...	...	...
3rd quarter	...	...	...	...	...	...	...	...	...	...	...	...	...	...	...	...
4th quarter	...	...	...	...	...	...	...	...	...	...	...	...	...	...	...	...
1955																
1st quarter	...	...	...	...	...	...	...	...	...	...	...	...	...	...	...	...
2nd quarter	...	...	...	...	...	...	...	...	...	...	...	...	...	...	...	...
3rd quarter	...	...	...	...	...	...	...	...	...	...	...	...	...	...	...	...
4th quarter	...	...	...	...	...	...	...	...	...	...	...	...	...	...	...	...
1956																
1st quarter	...	...	...	...	...	...	...	...	...	...	...	...	...	...	...	...
2nd quarter	...	...	...	...	...	...	...	...	...	...	...	...	...	...	...	...
3rd quarter	...	...	...	...	...	...	...	...	...	...	...	...	...	...	...	...
4th quarter	...	...	...	...	...	...	...	...	...	...	...	...	...	...	...	...
1957																
1st quarter	...	...	...	...	...	...	...	...	...	...	...	...	...	...	...	...
2nd quarter	...	...	...	...	...	...	...	...	...	...	...	...	...	...	...	...
3rd quarter	...	...	...	...	...	...	...	...	...	...	...	...	...	...	...	...
4th quarter	...	...	...	...	...	...	...	...	...	...	...	...	...	...	...	...
1958																
1st quarter	52.2	25.2	48.2	14.8	66.6	27.0	28.3	23.3	42.2	28.3	...	...	...	...	...	...
2nd quarter	53.0	25.0	47.3	14.9	66.6	26.9	28.1	23.7	43.0	28.4	...	...	...	...	...	...
3rd quarter	54.0	25.8	47.9	15.1	67.6	26.7	28.0	23.2	47.4	28.5	...	...	...	...	...	...
4th quarter	55.1	26.9	48.8	15.2	68.2	26.3	27.7	22.5	53.0	28.7	...	...	...	...	...	...
1959																
1st quarter	55.6	27.8	50.1	15.3	68.5	26.0	27.6	21.8	56.0	28.7	...	...	...	...	...	...
2nd quarter	56.7	29.1	51.4	15.5	69.2	25.7	27.3	21.2	59.2	28.7	...	...	...	...	...	...
3rd quarter	55.9	28.6	51.1	15.6	69.3	26.4	27.9	22.2	52.8	28.8	...	...	...	...	...	...
4th quarter	56.4	28.8	51.2	15.8	69.7	26.6	28.0	22.6	51.8	28.8	...	...	...	...	...	...
1960																
1st quarter	57.3	29.8	52.1	16.1	70.7	26.5	28.0	22.2	54.0	28.9	...	...	...	...	...	...
2nd quarter	56.7	29.5	52.1	16.2	70.8	27.0	28.5	22.8	49.4	29.0	...	...	...	...	...	...
3rd quarter	56.9	29.5	51.8	16.2	70.9	27.1	28.5	23.2	48.5	29.0	...	...	...	...	...	...
4th quarter	57.1	29.2	51.1	16.3	70.9	27.3	28.6	23.8	46.0	28.9	...	...	...	...	...	...

... = Not available.

Table 19-11. Productivity and Related Data—Continued

(1992 = 100, seasonally adjusted.)

Year and quarter	Business sector								Nonfarm business sector							
	Output per hour of all persons	Output	Hours of all persons	Compensation per hour	Real compensation per hour	Unit labor costs	Unit nonlabor payments	Implicit price deflator	Output per hour of all persons	Output	Hours of all persons	Compensation per hour	Real compensation per hour	Unit labor costs	Unit nonlabor payments	Implicit price deflator
1961																
1st quarter	49.0	31.7	64.7	14.1	61.3	28.8	24.6	27.2	51.8	31.3	60.4	14.7	63.9	28.4	24.0	26.8
2nd quarter	50.7	32.4	64.0	14.4	62.7	28.5	25.2	27.3	53.3	32.1	60.2	14.9	64.8	28.0	24.8	26.8
3rd quarter	51.2	33.0	64.4	14.5	62.9	28.4	25.5	27.3	54.0	32.7	60.6	15.0	65.0	27.8	25.2	26.8
4th quarter	51.7	33.6	65.0	14.7	63.5	28.4	25.7	27.4	54.5	33.5	61.4	15.1	65.4	27.8	25.3	26.8
1962																
1st quarter	52.3	34.3	65.7	14.9	63.9	28.4	26.1	27.5	55.5	34.2	61.6	15.4	66.2	27.7	25.7	27.0
2nd quarter	52.5	34.7	66.1	15.0	64.4	28.6	25.9	27.6	55.4	34.5	62.3	15.5	66.4	28.0	25.5	27.1
3rd quarter	53.3	35.0	65.7	15.1	64.7	28.4	26.3	27.6	56.1	34.9	62.2	15.6	66.6	27.8	25.9	27.1
4th quarter	53.7	35.1	65.3	15.3	65.4	28.5	26.1	27.6	56.4	34.9	61.8	15.7	67.1	27.9	25.9	27.1
1963																
1st quarter	54.1	35.6	65.8	15.4	65.5	28.5	26.2	27.7	56.8	35.3	62.2	15.9	67.5	28.0	25.9	27.2
2nd quarter	54.5	36.1	66.2	15.5	65.7	28.4	26.4	27.7	57.3	35.9	62.6	16.0	67.8	27.9	26.1	27.2
3rd quarter	55.6	36.8	66.2	15.7	66.3	28.3	26.9	27.7	58.5	36.7	62.7	16.1	68.0	27.6	26.6	27.2
4th quarter	55.8	37.1	66.5	15.9	66.7	28.5	27.0	27.9	58.5	37.0	63.2	16.3	68.6	27.9	26.5	27.4
1964																
1st quarter	56.5	38.1	67.3	16.0	66.9	28.3	27.4	27.9	59.1	38.1	64.4	16.3	68.3	27.6	27.2	27.4
2nd quarter	56.7	38.5	67.9	16.1	67.3	28.4	27.3	28.0	59.5	38.5	64.7	16.5	68.9	27.7	27.2	27.5
3rd quarter	57.2	39.1	68.3	16.3	68.0	28.5	27.4	28.1	60.0	39.1	65.1	16.7	69.7	27.9	27.3	27.7
4th quarter	56.9	39.1	68.8	16.5	68.3	28.9	27.1	28.2	59.4	39.0	65.7	16.8	69.9	28.3	26.8	27.8
1965																
1st quarter	57.9	40.3	69.6	16.6	68.7	28.7	27.8	28.4	60.2	40.2	66.8	16.9	70.0	28.1	27.6	27.9
2nd quarter	57.9	40.8	70.5	16.7	68.6	28.8	27.9	28.5	60.6	40.8	67.4	17.0	70.0	28.1	27.6	27.9
3rd quarter	59.3	41.7	70.4	16.9	69.2	28.5	28.6	28.5	61.7	41.7	67.6	17.2	70.5	27.9	28.2	28.0
4th quarter	60.2	42.9	71.1	17.1	69.7	28.4	29.1	28.6	62.8	42.9	68.2	17.4	71.2	27.8	28.6	28.1
1966																
1st quarter	61.3	44.0	71.9	17.5	70.7	28.5	29.3	28.8	63.7	44.1	69.2	17.8	71.7	27.9	28.7	28.2
2nd quarter	60.9	44.1	72.4	17.8	71.3	29.2	28.8	29.0	63.3	44.2	69.9	18.0	72.2	28.5	28.5	28.5
3rd quarter	61.0	44.3	72.5	18.1	71.8	29.6	28.8	29.3	63.3	44.5	70.2	18.3	72.6	28.9	28.4	28.7
4th quarter	61.5	44.5	72.4	18.4	72.4	29.9	29.1	29.6	63.8	44.7	70.0	18.5	73.0	29.1	29.0	29.1
1967																
1st quarter	62.1	44.9	72.3	18.5	72.8	29.8	29.4	29.7	64.3	45.0	70.0	18.8	73.8	29.2	29.2	29.2
2nd quarter	62.6	44.8	71.6	18.9	73.7	30.2	29.2	29.8	64.5	44.8	69.5	19.1	74.5	29.6	29.0	29.4
3rd quarter	62.6	45.1	72.1	19.1	73.8	30.5	29.5	30.1	64.7	45.1	69.8	19.4	74.8	29.9	29.2	29.6
4th quarter	62.8	45.4	72.4	19.3	73.9	30.8	29.7	30.4	64.9	45.5	70.1	19.6	75.1	30.2	29.4	29.9
1968																
1st quarter	64.2	46.5	72.5	19.9	75.5	31.1	30.1	30.7	66.4	46.6	70.2	20.2	76.4	30.4	29.9	30.2
2nd quarter	64.8	47.3	73.0	20.3	76.1	31.3	30.6	31.0	67.0	47.5	70.9	20.5	77.0	30.6	30.5	30.6
3rd quarter	64.8	47.6	73.4	20.7	76.5	31.9	30.3	31.3	66.9	47.8	71.4	20.9	77.2	31.2	30.1	30.8
4th quarter	64.7	47.8	73.9	21.1	77.0	32.6	30.4	31.7	66.8	48.0	71.8	21.3	77.8	31.9	30.1	31.2
1969																
1st quarter	65.0	48.7	74.9	21.2	76.4	32.6	31.2	32.1	67.4	48.9	72.5	21.6	77.8	32.0	30.8	31.6
2nd quarter	64.9	48.7	75.1	21.7	77.2	33.5	30.8	32.5	66.8	48.9	73.2	21.9	77.9	32.8	30.5	31.9
3rd quarter	65.0	49.0	75.3	22.2	77.7	34.1	30.7	32.8	66.8	49.1	73.5	22.3	78.2	33.4	30.4	32.3
4th quarter	64.9	48.6	75.0	22.6	78.2	34.9	30.4	33.2	66.5	48.8	73.3	22.7	78.5	34.2	29.9	32.6
1970																
1st quarter	65.1	48.6	74.6	23.1	78.5	35.4	30.4	33.5	66.7	48.7	73.0	23.2	78.7	34.7	30.0	33.0
2nd quarter	66.0	48.7	73.8	23.4	78.4	35.5	31.5	34.0	67.7	48.8	72.1	23.5	78.9	34.8	31.2	33.4
3rd quarter	67.1	49.2	73.3	23.8	79.0	35.5	31.9	34.2	68.8	49.3	71.7	24.0	79.5	34.8	31.6	33.6
4th quarter	66.8	48.5	72.6	24.1	78.9	36.1	32.0	34.6	68.3	48.5	71.1	24.2	79.2	35.5	31.8	34.1
1971																
1st quarter	68.7	50.1	72.9	24.6	79.7	35.8	33.6	35.0	70.3	50.2	71.4	24.7	80.1	35.1	33.3	34.4
2nd quarter	68.8	50.4	73.3	24.9	80.0	36.2	34.1	35.4	70.6	50.5	71.6	25.1	80.6	35.6	33.7	34.9
3rd quarter	69.6	50.9	73.1	25.3	80.6	36.4	34.6	35.7	71.2	51.0	71.6	25.4	81.0	35.8	34.3	35.2
4th quarter	69.0	51.0	73.9	25.5	80.7	37.0	34.2	35.9	70.6	51.1	72.4	25.6	81.0	36.3	33.7	35.4
1972																
1st quarter	69.7	52.2	74.9	26.1	81.8	37.5	34.5	36.4	71.6	52.5	73.3	26.3	82.3	36.7	34.2	35.8
2nd quarter	71.4	53.7	75.3	26.4	82.3	37.1	35.7	36.5	73.0	53.9	73.8	26.6	82.9	36.5	35.1	35.9
3rd quarter	71.6	54.3	75.8	26.8	82.6	37.4	36.0	36.9	73.4	54.5	74.3	27.0	83.4	36.8	35.2	36.2
4th quarter	72.3	55.3	76.5	27.4	83.6	37.8	36.4	37.3	74.0	55.5	75.0	27.5	84.2	37.2	35.0	36.4
1973																
1st quarter	73.7	57.1	77.5	28.2	84.7	38.2	36.8	37.7	75.7	57.6	76.2	28.3	85.1	37.4	35.3	36.6
2nd quarter	73.9	57.9	78.3	28.6	84.3	38.7	37.5	38.2	75.7	58.3	77.0	28.7	84.7	37.9	35.5	37.0
3rd quarter	72.9	57.5	78.8	29.2	84.4	40.0	37.4	39.0	75.1	58.2	77.5	29.3	84.6	39.0	34.9	37.5
4th quarter	73.3	58.1	79.2	29.8	84.0	40.6	38.4	39.8	74.6	58.1	77.8	29.9	84.4	40.1	35.4	38.4
1974																
1st quarter	72.3	57.2	79.2	30.4	83.1	42.0	38.4	40.6	74.5	57.7	77.5	30.6	83.9	41.1	35.9	39.2
2nd quarter	72.5	57.4	79.1	31.3	83.5	43.1	39.2	41.7	74.3	57.8	77.7	31.4	83.9	42.3	37.7	40.6
3rd quarter	71.9	56.6	78.7	32.3	83.7	44.9	39.9	43.0	73.6	57.0	77.4	32.3	83.9	44.0	38.3	41.9
4th quarter	72.5	56.2	77.5	33.0	83.1	45.5	42.4	44.3	74.3	56.6	76.2	33.2	83.5	44.7	40.5	43.1

Table 19-11. Productivity and Related Data—Continued

(1992 = 100, seasonally adjusted.)

Year and quarter	Nonfinancial corporations									Manufacturing					
	Output per hour of all employees	Output	Employee hours	Compensation per hour	Real compensation per hour	Unit costs			Unit profits	Implicit price deflator	Output per hour of all persons	Output	Hours of all persons	Compensation per hour	Real compensation per hour	Unit labor costs
						Total	Labor costs	Nonlabor costs								

Year and quarter	Output per hour	Output	Employee hours	Comp per hour	Real comp per hour	Total	Labor costs	Nonlabor costs	Unit profits	Implicit price deflator	Output per hour	Output	Hours	Comp per hour	Real comp per hour	Unit labor costs
1961																
1st quarter	57.2	28.9	50.6	16.4	71.3	27.5	28.7	24.1	44.8	29.0	...	...	...	...	...	...
2nd quarter	58.7	29.8	50.8	16.6	72.3	27.1	28.4	23.5	49.1	29.0	...	...	...	...	...	...
3rd quarter	59.2	30.4	51.4	16.8	72.6	27.0	28.4	23.3	50.5	29.1	...	...	...	...	...	...
4th quarter	60.0	31.4	52.2	17.0	73.2	26.8	28.2	22.9	53.3	29.2	...	...	...	...	...	...
1962																
1st quarter	60.8	32.0	52.6	17.1	73.8	26.8	28.2	22.8	54.8	29.3	...	...	...	...	...	...
2nd quarter	60.8	32.5	53.4	17.3	74.1	27.0	28.4	23.0	52.7	29.3	...	...	...	...	...	...
3rd quarter	61.4	32.9	53.6	17.4	74.4	27.0	28.3	23.2	53.1	29.3	...	...	...	...	...	...
4th quarter	62.2	33.3	53.6	17.6	74.9	26.9	28.3	23.3	54.3	29.4	...	...	...	...	...	...
1963																
1st quarter	62.5	33.7	53.9	17.7	75.0	26.9	28.3	23.3	54.1	29.3	...	...	...	...	...	...
2nd quarter	63.2	34.5	54.5	17.8	75.3	26.7	28.1	23.0	56.6	29.4	...	...	...	...	...	...
3rd quarter	63.8	34.9	54.7	18.0	75.7	26.7	28.1	23.0	57.2	29.5	...	...	...	...	...	...
4th quarter	64.3	35.3	55.0	18.2	76.4	26.8	28.3	23.0	57.8	29.6	...	...	...	...	...	...
1964																
1st quarter	64.0	36.2	56.5	18.0	75.3	26.7	28.1	22.8	60.0	29.6	...	...	...	...	...	...
2nd quarter	64.3	36.8	57.1	18.2	75.9	26.8	28.2	22.8	59.0	29.7	...	...	...	...	...	...
3rd quarter	64.9	37.5	57.7	18.3	76.5	26.8	28.3	22.9	58.8	29.7	...	...	...	...	...	...
4th quarter	64.6	37.7	58.4	18.4	76.6	27.1	28.6	23.2	57.7	29.9	...	...	...	...	...	...
1965																
1st quarter	65.6	39.0	59.5	18.5	76.6	26.8	28.2	22.9	62.6	30.0	...	...	...	...	...	...
2nd quarter	65.6	39.6	60.4	18.6	76.5	26.9	28.4	22.9	63.2	30.1	...	...	...	...	...	...
3rd quarter	66.1	40.3	61.0	18.8	77.1	26.9	28.4	22.9	63.0	30.2	...	...	...	...	...	...
4th quarter	66.8	41.4	62.0	19.1	77.9	27.0	28.6	22.6	64.0	30.3	...	...	...	...	...	...
1966																
1st quarter	67.2	42.3	63.0	19.3	78.0	27.1	28.7	22.6	64.9	30.5	...	...	...	...	...	...
2nd quarter	67.1	42.8	63.8	19.6	78.7	27.6	29.3	22.9	63.2	30.7	...	...	...	...	...	...
3rd quarter	67.0	43.1	64.3	20.0	79.4	28.0	29.8	23.1	61.1	31.0	...	...	...	...	...	...
4th quarter	67.3	43.5	64.6	20.3	79.9	28.3	30.1	23.4	61.5	31.3	...	...	...	...	...	...
1967																
1st quarter	67.3	43.5	64.6	20.5	80.5	28.6	30.4	23.8	59.5	31.4	...	...	...	...	...	...
2nd quarter	68.1	43.7	64.1	20.8	81.2	28.8	30.5	24.2	58.4	31.5	...	...	...	...	...	...
3rd quarter	68.2	44.1	64.6	21.1	81.4	29.2	30.9	24.5	58.5	31.8	...	...	...	...	...	...
4th quarter	68.8	44.8	65.1	21.3	81.5	29.4	31.0	24.9	59.9	32.1	...	...	...	...	...	...
1968																
1st quarter	69.6	45.6	65.4	21.9	83.0	29.8	31.5	25.3	58.9	32.4	...	...	...	...	...	...
2nd quarter	70.4	46.5	66.1	22.3	83.6	30.0	31.7	25.6	59.9	32.7	...	...	...	...	...	...
3rd quarter	70.8	47.2	66.8	22.7	83.8	30.4	32.0	26.0	58.9	32.9	...	...	...	...	...	...
4th quarter	71.0	47.8	67.3	23.1	84.5	30.9	32.6	26.5	58.9	33.4	...	...	...	...	...	...
1969																
1st quarter	70.7	48.2	68.2	23.3	84.3	31.4	33.0	27.2	57.4	33.8	...	...	...	...	...	...
2nd quarter	70.5	48.6	68.9	23.8	84.5	32.1	33.7	27.8	54.9	34.2	...	...	...	...	...	...
3rd quarter	70.5	48.9	69.4	24.3	85.1	32.8	34.4	28.4	52.4	34.5	...	...	...	...	...	...
4th quarter	70.2	48.7	69.4	24.7	85.5	33.6	35.2	29.2	48.5	35.0	...	...	...	...	...	...
1970																
1st quarter	69.7	48.1	69.0	25.1	85.4	34.5	36.0	30.5	43.4	35.3	...	...	...	...	...	...
2nd quarter	70.6	48.1	68.2	25.5	85.5	34.9	36.2	31.4	45.7	35.8	...	...	...	...	...	...
3rd quarter	71.6	48.5	67.8	26.0	86.2	35.1	36.3	31.9	44.4	35.9	...	...	...	...	...	...
4th quarter	71.4	47.7	66.8	26.3	86.0	35.9	36.8	33.2	41.4	36.3	...	...	...	...	...	...
1971																
1st quarter	73.3	49.2	67.2	26.8	86.9	35.6	36.6	32.8	49.0	36.8	...	...	...	...	...	...
2nd quarter	73.5	49.7	67.6	27.2	87.4	36.0	37.0	33.1	49.5	37.2	...	...	...	...	...	...
3rd quarter	74.0	50.2	67.9	27.5	87.6	36.2	37.2	33.4	49.8	37.4	...	...	...	...	...	...
4th quarter	74.3	51.1	68.8	27.8	87.8	36.3	37.4	33.3	51.0	37.6	...	...	...	...	...	...
1972																
1st quarter	74.5	52.3	70.1	28.2	88.5	36.6	37.9	33.1	52.4	38.0	...	...	...	...	...	...
2nd quarter	75.0	53.4	71.2	28.5	88.9	36.9	38.1	33.6	51.2	38.2	...	...	...	...	...	...
3rd quarter	75.2	54.1	71.9	28.9	89.1	37.0	38.4	33.4	53.5	38.5	...	...	...	...	...	...
4th quarter	76.1	55.6	73.0	29.5	90.2	37.4	38.8	33.5	56.0	39.0	...	...	...	...	...	...
1973																
1st quarter	76.6	56.9	74.2	30.1	90.5	37.8	39.3	33.7	57.0	39.5	...	...	...	...	...	...
2nd quarter	76.1	57.1	75.0	30.6	90.3	38.8	40.3	34.8	53.3	40.1	...	...	...	...	...	...
3rd quarter	75.6	57.0	75.4	31.3	90.5	39.9	41.4	35.8	52.5	41.0	...	...	...	...	...	...
4th quarter	75.4	57.4	76.1	32.0	90.1	40.8	42.4	36.5	53.7	41.9	...	...	...	...	...	...
1974																
1st quarter	74.6	56.7	76.1	32.6	89.1	42.1	43.7	37.9	49.0	42.7	...	...	...	...	...	...
2nd quarter	74.8	56.8	76.0	33.5	89.3	43.3	44.8	39.2	48.5	43.8	...	...	...	...	...	...
3rd quarter	74.1	56.1	75.7	34.5	89.4	45.0	46.5	41.1	46.8	45.2	...	...	...	...	...	...
4th quarter	73.9	54.9	74.3	35.3	88.9	46.7	47.8	43.8	46.6	46.7	...	...	...	...	...	...

... = Not available.

Table 19-11. Productivity and Related Data—Continued

(1992 = 100, seasonally adjusted.)

Year and quarter	Business sector								Nonfarm business sector							
	Output per hour of all persons	Output	Hours of all persons	Compensation per hour	Real compensation per hour	Unit labor costs	Unit nonlabor payments	Implicit price deflator	Output per hour of all persons	Output	Hours of all persons	Compensation per hour	Real compensation per hour	Unit labor costs	Unit nonlabor payments	Implicit price deflator
1975																
1st quarter	73.5	55.2	75.1	34.0	83.8	46.3	44.0	45.4	74.8	55.2	73.8	34.1	84.0	45.6	42.8	44.5
2nd quarter	74.7	55.6	74.5	34.7	84.4	46.4	45.5	46.1	76.0	55.6	73.1	34.8	84.7	45.8	44.3	45.2
3rd quarter	75.4	56.7	75.2	35.2	83.9	46.6	47.5	47.0	76.9	56.7	73.8	35.4	84.5	46.1	45.8	46.0
4th quarter	75.6	57.6	76.3	35.9	84.2	47.6	48.0	47.7	76.9	57.7	75.0	36.1	84.5	46.9	46.2	46.7
1976																
1st quarter	76.6	59.3	77.4	36.8	85.3	48.0	48.3	48.2	78.0	59.5	76.3	36.9	85.4	47.3	47.1	47.2
2nd quarter	77.2	59.8	77.6	37.6	86.2	48.7	48.5	48.6	78.8	60.1	76.3	37.6	86.4	47.8	47.6	47.7
3rd quarter	77.2	60.1	77.9	38.3	86.5	49.6	48.7	49.3	78.9	60.4	76.6	38.5	86.9	48.8	47.8	48.4
4th quarter	77.7	60.7	78.1	39.2	87.3	50.5	49.5	50.1	79.1	60.9	77.0	39.3	87.5	49.7	48.6	49.3
1977																
1st quarter	78.0	61.6	78.9	39.9	87.3	51.1	50.5	50.9	79.5	61.9	77.8	40.0	87.4	50.3	49.5	50.0
2nd quarter	78.2	63.1	80.6	40.5	87.1	51.8	51.2	51.6	79.9	63.4	79.3	40.8	87.6	51.0	50.5	50.8
3rd quarter	79.2	64.4	81.3	41.4	87.8	52.2	52.0	52.1	80.7	64.7	80.2	41.6	88.1	51.5	51.5	51.5
4th quarter	78.3	64.3	82.1	42.1	88.0	53.8	52.4	53.2	79.6	64.4	80.9	42.3	88.4	53.1	51.2	52.4
1978																
1st quarter	78.0	64.4	82.5	43.3	89.1	55.5	51.6	54.0	79.7	64.8	81.3	43.5	89.6	54.7	50.4	53.1
2nd quarter	79.6	67.5	84.9	44.0	88.7	55.3	54.7	55.1	81.2	68.0	83.7	44.3	89.2	54.5	53.2	54.0
3rd quarter	79.7	68.2	85.5	44.9	88.9	56.3	55.6	56.0	81.2	68.6	84.4	45.1	89.4	55.5	54.3	55.1
4th quarter	80.0	69.2	86.5	46.0	89.3	57.5	56.9	57.3	81.7	69.8	85.4	46.2	89.8	56.5	55.6	56.2
1979																
1st quarter	79.5	69.2	87.1	47.3	89.8	59.5	56.3	58.3	81.0	69.6	86.0	47.5	90.2	58.7	54.4	57.1
2nd quarter	79.4	69.3	87.3	48.3	89.4	60.9	58.1	59.8	80.8	69.7	86.3	48.5	89.7	60.0	56.4	58.7
3rd quarter	79.4	69.9	88.0	49.4	89.1	62.3	59.1	61.1	80.7	70.2	87.0	49.6	89.4	61.5	57.4	60.0
4th quarter	79.2	69.9	88.3	50.6	89.0	63.9	59.4	62.2	80.6	70.3	87.2	50.8	89.4	63.1	57.8	61.1
1980																
1st quarter	79.6	70.0	87.9	52.2	89.0	65.5	60.3	63.6	80.9	70.4	87.0	52.3	89.2	64.7	59.3	62.7
2nd quarter	78.7	68.0	86.4	53.5	89.1	68.0	59.9	65.0	80.0	68.4	85.5	53.7	89.4	67.1	60.0	64.5
3rd quarter	78.8	67.9	86.1	54.9	89.3	69.6	61.2	66.4	80.3	68.3	85.1	55.1	89.6	68.6	60.2	65.5
4th quarter	79.6	69.4	87.2	56.3	89.4	70.6	63.9	68.1	81.2	69.9	86.1	56.6	89.9	69.7	62.2	66.9
1981																
1st quarter	81.2	71.1	87.7	57.7	89.3	71.1	67.9	69.9	82.4	71.4	86.6	58.1	89.8	70.5	66.5	69.0
2nd quarter	80.4	70.4	87.5	58.8	89.3	73.1	68.1	71.2	81.3	70.5	86.6	59.1	89.8	72.7	66.6	70.4
3rd quarter	81.5	71.3	87.6	60.1	89.5	73.7	70.5	72.5	82.1	71.1	86.6	60.4	90.0	73.6	69.0	71.9
4th quarter	80.3	70.1	87.3	60.9	89.2	75.9	70.0	73.7	81.0	69.9	86.3	61.3	89.7	75.7	69.0	73.2
1982																
1st quarter	79.8	68.5	85.8	62.5	90.4	78.3	68.4	74.6	80.5	68.3	84.9	62.9	91.0	78.1	67.5	74.2
2nd quarter	80.1	68.9	86.0	63.1	90.4	78.9	69.8	75.5	80.7	68.7	85.2	63.4	90.8	78.6	69.1	75.1
3rd quarter	80.1	68.5	85.5	64.0	90.2	79.9	70.7	76.5	80.8	68.4	84.6	64.4	90.7	79.6	69.8	76.0
4th quarter	80.9	68.5	84.7	64.9	90.4	80.2	72.0	77.1	81.5	68.3	83.8	65.2	90.9	80.0	71.4	76.8
1983																
1st quarter	81.6	69.5	85.1	65.4	90.7	80.1	73.5	77.7	82.6	69.6	84.3	65.9	91.2	79.8	72.8	77.2
2nd quarter	83.1	71.5	86.0	66.0	90.4	79.5	75.8	78.1	84.5	72.0	85.2	66.4	91.0	78.6	75.4	77.4
3rd quarter	83.4	73.2	87.7	66.3	90.0	79.5	77.8	78.9	85.3	74.1	86.9	66.8	90.6	78.2	78.0	78.1
4th quarter	84.1	75.0	89.1	67.2	90.4	79.9	78.5	79.4	85.7	75.9	88.5	67.5	90.8	78.7	78.4	78.6
1984																
1st quarter	84.5	76.8	90.8	68.0	90.3	80.5	79.2	80.0	85.7	77.2	90.2	68.4	90.7	79.8	78.1	79.2
2nd quarter	85.2	78.4	92.0	68.7	90.3	80.6	80.5	80.6	86.2	78.7	91.4	69.0	90.8	80.1	79.4	79.8
3rd quarter	85.6	79.2	92.5	69.6	90.9	81.3	80.7	81.1	86.5	79.4	91.8	70.0	91.4	80.9	79.8	80.5
4th quarter	85.8	79.8	93.0	70.2	90.9	81.8	81.0	81.5	86.6	80.0	92.4	70.5	91.3	81.4	80.0	80.9
1985																
1st quarter	86.1	80.7	93.7	71.1	91.3	82.5	81.8	82.3	86.8	80.8	93.1	71.4	91.7	82.3	81.0	81.8
2nd quarter	86.5	81.5	94.2	71.7	91.3	82.9	82.0	82.6	87.0	81.5	93.7	72.0	91.6	82.7	81.5	82.3
3rd quarter	88.0	82.9	94.3	72.8	92.1	82.8	82.8	82.8	88.1	82.8	94.0	73.0	92.3	82.8	82.7	82.8
4th quarter	88.3	83.6	94.6	74.1	92.9	83.9	82.0	83.2	88.5	83.6	94.4	74.2	93.0	83.8	81.6	83.0
1986																
1st quarter	89.3	84.5	94.6	75.0	93.5	84.1	82.7	83.6	89.6	84.5	94.3	75.2	93.7	83.9	82.6	83.4
2nd quarter	89.8	84.8	94.4	75.7	94.8	84.2	83.1	83.8	90.3	85.0	94.1	75.9	95.0	84.0	83.0	83.6
3rd quarter	90.3	85.7	94.9	76.4	95.2	84.6	83.3	84.1	90.7	85.8	94.6	76.6	95.4	84.5	82.9	83.9
4th quarter	90.0	86.1	95.6	77.7	96.1	86.2	82.2	84.7	90.4	86.2	95.3	77.9	96.3	86.1	81.8	84.5
1987																
1st quarter	89.6	86.6	96.7	77.8	95.2	86.8	82.3	85.1	90.0	86.8	96.5	78.0	95.4	86.7	82.0	84.9
2nd quarter	90.2	87.8	97.2	78.6	95.1	87.0	83.1	85.6	90.6	87.9	97.0	78.7	95.3	86.9	82.8	85.4
3rd quarter	90.4	88.4	97.9	79.4	95.2	87.8	83.6	86.3	90.6	88.6	97.7	79.5	95.4	87.8	83.3	86.1
4th quarter	91.2	90.2	98.9	80.4	95.6	88.2	84.1	86.7	91.5	90.3	98.8	80.5	95.8	88.0	83.7	86.4
1988																
1st quarter	91.4	90.5	98.9	81.7	96.5	89.4	84.1	87.4	91.6	90.6	98.9	81.8	96.6	89.2	83.5	87.1
2nd quarter	91.6	91.9	100.3	82.7	96.7	90.3	84.5	88.1	92.0	92.2	100.3	82.7	96.7	89.9	84.3	87.8
3rd quarter	91.8	92.3	100.5	83.7	96.8	91.2	85.8	89.1	92.2	92.7	100.6	83.7	96.7	90.7	85.4	88.7
4th quarter	92.0	93.6	101.7	84.2	96.4	91.4	87.0	89.8	92.7	94.3	101.7	84.2	96.4	90.8	87.2	89.4

Table 19-11. Productivity and Related Data—Continued

(1992 = 100, seasonally adjusted.)

Year and quarter	Nonfinancial corporations										Manufacturing					
	Output per hour of all employees	Output	Employee hours	Compensation per hour	Real compensation per hour	Unit costs			Unit profits	Implicit price deflator	Output per hour of all persons	Output	Hours of all persons	Compensation per hour	Real compensation per hour	Unit labor costs
						Total	Labor costs	Nonlabor costs								
1975																
1st quarter	75.2	53.8	71.5	36.2	89.3	47.6	48.2	46.1	49.9	47.8	...	...	...	...	...	...
2nd quarter	77.1	54.5	70.7	36.9	89.8	47.5	47.9	46.3	58.5	48.4	...	...	...	...	...	...
3rd quarter	78.3	56.2	71.7	37.6	89.7	47.3	48.0	45.7	69.4	49.3	...	...	...	...	...	...
4th quarter	78.5	57.1	72.7	38.4	89.9	48.0	48.9	45.7	70.3	50.0	...	...	...	...	...	...
1976																
1st quarter	79.5	59.1	74.3	39.1	90.5	48.0	49.1	44.7	74.6	50.3	...	...	...	...	...	...
2nd quarter	79.6	59.5	74.8	39.8	91.5	48.8	50.1	45.5	70.3	50.8	...	...	...	...	...	...
3rd quarter	79.9	60.1	75.3	40.7	92.0	49.6	51.0	45.9	69.3	51.3	...	...	...	...	...	...
4th quarter	79.8	60.3	75.6	41.6	92.7	50.7	52.2	46.8	67.6	52.2	...	...	...	...	...	...
1977																
1st quarter	79.9	61.2	76.6	42.1	92.2	51.3	52.7	47.5	69.2	52.9	...	...	...	...	...	...
2nd quarter	81.6	63.8	78.2	43.0	92.5	51.2	52.7	47.2	76.7	53.5	...	...	...	...	...	...
3rd quarter	83.3	65.8	79.0	44.0	93.2	51.3	52.8	47.2	81.2	53.9	...	...	...	...	...	...
4th quarter	82.2	65.7	79.9	44.9	93.8	53.0	54.6	48.9	77.3	55.2	...	...	...	...	...	...
1978																
1st quarter	82.1	65.8	80.1	46.0	94.7	54.6	56.0	50.7	70.0	56.0	...	...	...	...	...	...
2nd quarter	83.4	68.6	82.3	47.0	94.8	54.8	56.4	50.3	80.5	57.1	...	...	...	...	...	...
3rd quarter	82.7	68.9	83.2	48.0	95.0	55.9	58.0	50.0	79.9	58.0	...	...	...	...	...	...
4th quarter	82.9	70.0	84.3	49.2	95.5	57.1	59.3	51.0	81.3	59.2	...	...	...	...	...	...
1979																
1st quarter	82.6	70.3	85.1	50.3	95.5	58.6	60.9	52.4	76.2	60.2	...	...	...	...	...	...
2nd quarter	82.1	70.2	85.5	51.3	95.0	60.3	62.5	54.3	74.4	61.6	...	...	...	...	...	...
3rd quarter	81.6	70.3	86.2	52.4	94.5	62.0	64.2	56.0	71.5	62.9	...	...	...	...	...	...
4th quarter	81.6	70.6	86.4	53.6	94.4	63.5	65.7	57.6	70.3	64.1	...	...	...	...	...	...
1980																
1st quarter	81.7	70.5	86.2	55.1	94.0	65.5	67.5	60.2	68.8	65.8	...	...	...	...	...	...
2nd quarter	80.6	68.3	84.8	56.5	94.1	68.4	70.1	63.9	59.1	67.6	...	...	...	...	...	...
3rd quarter	81.0	68.2	84.2	57.9	94.1	70.0	71.4	66.1	64.7	69.5	...	...	...	...	...	...
4th quarter	81.9	70.0	85.5	59.4	94.5	71.3	72.6	68.0	73.2	71.5	...	...	...	...	...	...
1981																
1st quarter	82.1	70.7	86.1	60.7	93.9	72.8	73.9	69.9	78.7	73.4	...	...	...	...	...	...
2nd quarter	82.4	71.2	86.5	61.8	93.8	74.4	75.0	72.8	78.9	74.8	...	...	...	...	...	...
3rd quarter	83.6	72.5	86.7	63.1	94.0	75.2	75.4	74.5	87.6	76.3	...	...	...	...	...	...
4th quarter	82.6	71.3	86.3	64.1	93.8	77.5	77.5	77.3	79.4	77.6	...	...	...	...	...	...
1982																
1st quarter	83.0	70.3	84.8	65.5	94.7	79.1	78.9	79.6	73.6	78.6	...	...	...	...	...	...
2nd quarter	83.2	70.4	84.6	66.0	94.5	79.7	79.3	80.7	77.9	79.5	...	...	...	...	...	...
3rd quarter	83.1	69.8	84.0	66.8	94.1	80.7	80.4	81.6	77.8	80.5	...	...	...	...	...	...
4th quarter	83.3	69.2	83.0	67.5	94.1	81.6	81.1	83.2	70.9	80.7	...	...	...	...	...	...
1983																
1st quarter	84.6	70.5	83.4	67.9	94.1	80.9	80.3	82.4	79.3	80.7	...	...	...	...	...	...
2nd quarter	86.0	72.6	84.4	68.6	94.0	80.1	79.8	81.1	89.7	81.0	...	...	...	...	...	...
3rd quarter	86.8	74.6	85.9	69.1	93.7	79.9	79.6	80.9	95.6	81.3	...	...	...	...	...	...
4th quarter	87.2	76.4	87.6	70.1	94.3	80.4	80.4	80.4	97.4	81.9	...	...	...	...	...	...
1984																
1st quarter	87.7	78.4	89.3	70.6	93.7	80.3	80.5	79.7	107.8	82.7	...	...	...	...	...	...
2nd quarter	88.3	80.0	90.6	71.4	93.9	80.7	80.9	80.1	109.2	83.2	...	...	...	...	...	...
3rd quarter	88.7	80.9	91.2	72.5	94.6	81.6	81.7	81.2	105.1	83.7	...	...	...	...	...	...
4th quarter	89.0	81.9	92.0	73.1	94.6	81.9	82.1	81.5	105.1	84.0	...	...	...	...	...	...
1985																
1st quarter	89.3	82.5	92.4	73.9	94.8	82.7	82.7	82.5	102.5	84.4	...	...	...	...	...	...
2nd quarter	89.7	83.3	93.0	74.5	94.8	83.2	83.1	83.4	99.5	84.6	...	...	...	...	...	...
3rd quarter	91.3	84.9	93.0	75.5	95.5	82.6	82.7	82.2	106.1	84.7	...	...	...	...	...	...
4th quarter	91.5	85.3	93.1	76.9	96.3	83.8	84.0	83.2	97.2	85.0	...	...	...	...	...	...
1986																
1st quarter	92.2	85.9	93.2	77.7	96.8	84.5	84.3	84.9	92.4	85.2	...	...	...	...	...	...
2nd quarter	92.1	85.5	92.9	78.3	98.2	85.1	85.1	85.3	89.8	85.5	...	...	...	...	...	...
3rd quarter	92.3	85.9	93.0	79.2	98.7	85.8	85.8	85.7	87.3	85.9	...	...	...	...	...	...
4th quarter	93.1	87.1	93.5	80.3	99.3	86.0	86.2	85.5	87.4	86.2	...	...	...	...	...	...
1987																
1st quarter	93.0	88.1	94.7	80.5	98.5	86.3	86.6	85.6	90.4	86.7	86.4	89.2	103.1	80.0	97.8	92.5
2nd quarter	94.1	89.9	95.6	81.0	98.1	85.8	86.2	84.9	97.6	86.9	88.2	90.7	102.9	80.4	97.3	91.1
3rd quarter	95.0	91.7	96.5	81.8	98.1	85.5	86.0	84.2	104.7	87.3	89.0	92.3	103.6	81.1	97.3	91.1
4th quarter	95.3	92.9	97.4	82.8	98.6	86.3	86.9	84.8	103.0	87.8	89.7	94.6	105.4	81.4	96.8	90.7
1988																
1st quarter	96.4	94.2	97.7	83.7	98.8	86.3	86.8	85.0	108.5	88.3	89.5	95.1	106.2	82.3	97.3	92.0
2nd quarter	96.5	95.4	98.8	84.6	98.9	87.0	87.6	85.4	108.8	89.0	89.9	96.0	106.8	83.0	97.0	92.3
3rd quarter	96.4	95.7	99.4	85.5	98.8	88.1	88.7	86.5	110.0	90.1	90.0	96.5	107.1	83.9	97.0	93.2
4th quarter	96.9	97.5	100.6	85.9	98.4	88.3	88.6	87.2	115.1	90.7	90.7	97.7	107.7	85.1	97.5	93.8

... = Not available.

Table 19-11. Productivity and Related Data—*Continued*

(1992 = 100, seasonally adjusted.)

Year and quarter	Business sector									Nonfarm business sector						
	Output per hour of all persons	Output	Hours of all persons	Compensation per hour	Real compensation per hour	Unit labor costs	Unit nonlabor payments	Implicit price deflator	Output per hour of all persons	Output	Hours of all persons	Compensation per hour	Real compensation per hour	Unit labor costs	Unit nonlabor payments	Implicit price deflator
---	---	---	---	---	---	---	---	---	---	---	---	---	---	---	---	---
1989																
1st quarter	92.2	94.6	102.6	84.4	95.8	91.6	89.4	90.8	92.4	94.8	102.7	84.4	95.8	91.4	88.5	90.3
2nd quarter	92.5	95.2	102.9	84.8	94.7	91.7	91.6	91.7	92.6	95.5	103.1	84.7	94.6	91.4	91.1	91.3
3rd quarter	92.8	95.9	103.3	85.4	94.7	92.0	92.6	92.2	93.0	96.1	103.3	85.3	94.7	91.7	92.3	92.0
4th quarter	92.9	96.0	103.3	86.5	95.1	93.1	92.3	92.8	93.2	96.3	103.4	86.5	95.1	92.8	91.8	92.4
1990																
1st quarter	94.0	97.2	103.4	88.3	95.6	94.0	93.6	93.8	94.1	97.4	103.6	88.1	95.4	93.7	93.1	93.5
2nd quarter	94.6	97.3	102.8	90.3	96.8	95.4	94.0	94.9	94.7	97.6	103.0	90.0	96.5	95.0	93.6	94.5
3rd quarter	95.1	97.1	102.1	91.6	96.7	96.3	94.4	95.6	95.1	97.3	102.3	91.4	96.4	96.1	94.1	95.4
4th quarter	94.3	96.0	101.7	92.3	95.9	97.8	93.8	96.3	94.4	96.1	101.8	92.2	95.8	97.6	93.7	96.2
1991																
1st quarter	94.5	95.2	100.7	93.0	96.2	98.4	95.5	97.3	94.6	95.3	100.7	92.9	96.1	98.2	95.7	97.3
2nd quarter	95.8	95.9	100.1	94.7	97.4	98.8	96.4	97.9	96.0	96.1	100.1	94.6	97.4	98.6	96.5	97.8
3rd quarter	96.4	96.5	100.0	95.7	97.9	99.2	97.5	98.6	96.7	96.6	100.0	95.7	97.8	99.0	97.9	98.6
4th quarter	97.1	97.0	99.9	96.8	98.3	99.6	97.8	99.0	97.3	97.1	99.9	96.7	98.3	99.5	97.9	98.9
1992																
1st quarter	98.9	98.3	99.3	98.7	99.6	99.8	98.7	99.4	98.8	98.3	99.4	98.6	99.5	99.7	98.7	99.4
2nd quarter	99.5	99.4	99.9	99.3	99.6	99.8	99.6	99.7	99.5	99.3	99.8	99.4	99.7	99.9	99.5	99.7
3rd quarter	100.4	100.5	100.0	100.8	100.5	100.4	99.9	100.2	100.4	100.5	100.0	100.8	100.5	100.4	99.7	100.2
4th quarter	101.2	101.9	100.7	101.2	100.2	100.1	101.8	100.7	101.2	102.0	100.7	101.2	100.2	100.0	102.0	100.7
1993																
1st quarter	100.4	101.8	101.5	101.6	100.0	101.2	101.7	101.4	100.4	102.0	101.6	101.4	99.8	101.0	102.3	101.5
2nd quarter	99.9	102.5	102.6	102.0	99.7	102.1	101.6	101.9	99.8	102.7	102.8	101.8	99.5	102.0	101.9	101.9
3rd quarter	100.0	103.1	103.1	102.5	99.7	102.4	102.1	102.3	100.2	103.5	103.3	102.2	99.5	102.0	102.9	102.3
4th quarter	101.0	105.0	104.0	102.8	99.4	101.8	104.4	102.8	100.9	105.2	104.2	102.6	99.2	101.6	104.6	102.7
1994																
1st quarter	101.6	106.3	104.6	104.0	100.3	102.3	104.7	103.2	101.6	106.3	104.6	103.8	100.1	102.2	104.9	103.2
2nd quarter	101.4	107.9	106.5	103.6	99.4	102.2	105.8	103.6	101.5	108.0	106.4	103.6	99.4	102.1	106.2	103.6
3rd quarter	101.1	108.5	107.3	103.6	98.6	102.5	107.2	104.2	101.1	108.5	107.4	103.5	98.5	102.4	107.9	104.4
4th quarter	101.7	110.1	108.2	104.1	98.6	102.3	108.5	104.6	101.9	110.3	108.2	104.1	98.6	102.1	109.3	104.8
1995																
1st quarter	101.3	110.4	109.0	105.0	98.8	103.6	107.7	105.2	101.7	110.7	108.9	104.9	98.8	103.2	108.9	105.3
2nd quarter	101.3	110.5	109.1	105.6	98.7	104.2	107.7	105.5	101.7	110.9	109.0	105.5	98.6	103.8	109.0	105.7
3rd quarter	101.5	111.7	110.1	106.1	98.7	104.6	108.4	106.0	102.0	112.2	110.0	106.1	98.7	104.1	109.3	106.0
4th quarter	102.4	112.8	110.2	107.2	99.2	104.6	109.1	106.3	102.8	113.3	110.2	107.1	99.2	104.2	109.6	106.2
1996																
1st quarter	103.5	113.9	110.0	108.2	99.4	104.5	110.6	106.8	103.7	114.2	110.0	108.2	99.4	104.3	110.8	106.7
2nd quarter	104.6	116.0	110.9	109.3	99.6	104.5	112.0	107.3	104.8	116.3	111.0	109.2	99.5	104.2	111.8	107.0
3rd quarter	105.0	117.2	111.6	110.2	99.8	105.0	111.8	107.5	105.1	117.5	111.8	110.0	99.7	104.6	112.2	107.5
4th quarter	105.2	118.8	112.9	110.7	99.5	105.2	112.8	108.0	105.4	119.2	113.1	110.5	99.4	104.9	113.2	108.0
1997																
1st quarter	104.9	119.9	114.2	111.3	99.5	106.1	113.0	108.7	104.9	120.1	114.4	111.2	99.4	105.9	113.2	108.6
2nd quarter	106.2	122.1	114.9	112.1	100.0	105.5	114.2	108.8	106.2	122.2	115.0	112.0	99.9	105.4	115.1	109.0
3rd quarter	107.3	123.9	115.4	113.4	100.7	105.6	114.9	109.1	107.2	124.0	115.6	113.1	100.5	105.5	115.7	109.3
4th quarter	107.6	124.9	116.1	115.4	101.9	107.2	113.0	109.4	107.5	125.1	116.3	115.1	101.7	107.0	114.0	109.6
1998																
1st quarter	108.5	126.5	116.6	117.6	103.7	108.4	111.4	109.5	108.4	126.8	117.0	117.2	103.4	108.2	112.3	109.7
2nd quarter	108.6	127.4	117.2	119.1	104.8	109.6	109.3	109.5	108.7	127.7	117.5	118.9	104.6	109.4	110.4	109.8
3rd quarter	109.9	129.0	117.5	121.0	105.9	110.1	109.1	109.7	109.8	129.4	117.8	120.7	105.7	110.0	110.2	110.1
4th quarter	110.5	131.5	118.9	121.7	106.2	110.1	109.6	109.9	110.4	131.8	119.4	121.4	105.9	110.0	110.5	110.2
1999																
1st quarter	111.5	132.7	119.0	124.2	107.9	111.3	108.5	110.3	111.3	133.0	119.6	123.6	107.4	111.1	109.5	110.5
2nd quarter	111.8	133.9	119.8	124.6	107.4	111.4	108.9	110.5	111.5	134.3	120.4	124.0	107.0	111.2	110.5	111.0
3rd quarter	112.6	135.7	120.5	125.7	107.6	111.6	109.5	110.8	112.3	136.1	121.2	125.1	107.1	111.4	111.3	111.3
4th quarter	114.4	138.5	121.1	128.0	108.8	112.0	109.8	111.1	114.2	138.9	121.6	127.7	108.5	111.8	111.6	111.7
2000																
1st quarter	114.0	138.6	121.6	132.4	111.5	116.2	105.2	112.1	113.7	138.8	122.1	132.1	111.2	116.2	106.6	112.6
2nd quarter	116.2	141.1	121.5	133.0	111.0	114.4	109.4	112.6	115.8	141.4	122.1	132.5	110.6	114.4	111.0	113.1
3rd quarter	115.9	140.8	121.5	135.6	112.2	117.0	106.2	112.9	115.5	141.1	122.1	135.1	111.8	116.9	107.8	113.5
4th quarter	117.1	141.5	120.8	136.5	112.2	116.6	107.9	113.3	116.6	141.8	121.6	135.9	111.6	116.5	109.4	113.9
2001																
1st quarter	117.0	141.1	120.7	138.8	113.0	118.7	106.4	114.1	116.5	141.4	121.4	138.1	112.5	118.6	107.9	114.6
2nd quarter	118.4	141.4	119.4	139.7	112.8	117.9	109.9	114.9	118.1	141.9	120.2	138.9	112.2	117.6	111.6	115.4
3rd quarter	118.8	140.3	118.1	140.4	113.2	118.2	110.2	115.2	118.5	140.8	118.9	139.6	112.5	117.8	111.9	115.6
4th quarter	120.9	141.0	116.6	141.5	114.2	117.0	113.1	115.6	120.4	141.2	117.3	140.7	113.5	116.8	114.7	116.0
2002																
1st quarter	122.7	142.2	115.9	143.2	115.2	116.7	113.4	115.5	122.4	142.6	116.5	142.6	114.7	116.4	115.1	116.0
2nd quarter	123.2	142.9	116.0	144.4	115.2	117.2	113.6	115.9	122.8	143.2	116.7	143.8	114.7	117.1	115.4	116.5
3rd quarter	124.7	144.3	115.7	145.0	115.0	116.3	115.7	116.1	124.1	144.5	116.4	144.3	114.4	116.2	117.7	116.8
4th quarter	125.0	144.7	115.7	145.5	114.8	116.3	116.8	116.5	124.6	145.0	116.4	144.7	114.3	116.1	118.9	117.2
2003																
1st quarter	126.2	145.5	115.3	147.4	115.3	116.8	117.7	117.1	125.8	145.9	116.0	146.6	114.7	116.6	119.6	117.7
2nd quarter	128.6	147.5	114.7	149.6	116.8	116.4	119.0	117.3	127.8	147.8	115.6	148.7	116.1	116.3	120.4	117.8
3rd quarter	131.2	150.8	114.9	151.7	117.7	115.6	120.8	117.5	130.6	151.1	115.7	150.9	117.1	115.5	122.3	118.0
4th quarter	132.0	152.3	115.4	153.2	118.7	116.0	120.7	117.8	131.7	152.8	116.1	152.5	118.2	115.9	121.9	118.1

Table 19-11. Productivity and Related Data—*Continued*

(1992 = 100, seasonally adjusted.)

Year and quarter	Nonfinancial corporations									Manufacturing				
	Output per hour of all employ-ees	Output	Em-ployee hours	Compen-sation per hour	Real compen-sation per hour	Unit costs			Unit profits	Implicit price deflator	Output per hour of all persons	Output	Hours of all persons	Compen-sation per hour	Real compen-sation per hour	Unit labor costs
						Total	Labor costs	Nonlabor costs								
1989																
1st quarter	95.7	97.2	101.6	86.3	97.8	90.1	90.2	90.1	104.3	91.4	90.9	98.3	108.1	85.4	96.9	94.0
2nd quarter	94.8	96.8	102.1	86.4	96.5	91.4	91.2	92.2	102.1	92.4	90.2	97.5	108.1	85.2	95.2	94.5
3rd quarter	95.0	97.2	102.3	87.0	96.5	92.3	91.6	94.0	100.7	93.0	89.7	96.6	107.8	86.2	95.6	96.1
4th quarter	95.1	97.5	102.6	88.3	97.1	93.4	92.9	94.7	95.4	93.5	90.6	96.6	106.6	87.7	96.5	96.8
1990																
1st quarter	94.4	97.7	103.5	88.8	96.1	94.3	94.1	95.1	97.7	94.6	91.8	97.4	106.1	87.9	95.2	95.8
2nd quarter	95.8	98.6	103.0	90.7	97.3	95.0	94.7	95.6	103.0	95.7	92.5	98.0	106.0	89.6	96.1	96.9
3rd quarter	95.9	98.1	102.3	92.1	97.2	96.6	96.1	97.8	94.7	96.4	93.7	98.2	104.8	90.8	95.9	96.9
4th quarter	96.4	97.8	101.4	92.9	96.5	97.2	96.3	99.7	91.4	96.7	93.7	96.6	103.0	92.1	95.7	98.3
1991																
1st quarter	96.9	97.1	100.2	93.5	96.7	98.0	96.5	102.1	94.1	97.7	93.5	94.5	101.0	93.5	96.7	100.0
2nd quarter	97.9	97.2	99.3	95.2	97.9	98.7	97.3	102.4	93.3	98.2	95.0	95.2	100.2	95.1	97.9	100.2
3rd quarter	98.1	97.5	99.4	96.2	98.3	99.3	98.0	102.6	92.5	98.7	96.4	96.9	100.4	96.2	98.4	99.8
4th quarter	98.4	97.8	99.4	97.1	98.7	99.6	98.7	102.1	91.6	98.9	96.9	97.3	100.4	96.9	98.4	100.0
1992																
1st quarter	99.6	99.0	99.4	98.6	99.6	99.5	99.0	100.7	96.6	99.2	97.8	97.6	99.9	98.3	99.3	100.6
2nd quarter	99.7	99.8	100.1	99.4	99.7	99.7	99.7	99.9	100.6	99.8	99.4	99.7	100.4	99.5	99.8	100.1
3rd quarter	99.9	99.7	99.8	100.9	100.6	100.7	100.9	100.2	95.3	100.2	101.4	100.8	99.4	101.2	100.9	99.7
4th quarter	100.8	101.5	100.7	101.2	100.1	100.1	100.4	99.2	107.3	100.7	101.5	101.8	100.4	101.1	100.0	99.6
1993																
1st quarter	99.6	100.9	101.2	101.1	99.6	101.3	101.5	100.5	104.0	101.5	102.3	103.1	100.8	101.1	99.5	98.8
2nd quarter	100.5	102.6	102.1	101.6	99.3	100.6	101.1	99.2	113.2	101.7	102.2	103.7	101.4	101.7	99.4	99.5
3rd quarter	100.6	103.4	102.7	102.0	99.2	100.9	101.3	99.8	112.5	102.0	102.4	104.0	101.6	102.6	99.8	100.2
4th quarter	101.5	105.1	103.6	102.3	98.9	100.4	100.8	99.2	125.3	102.6	103.8	105.7	101.9	103.7	100.2	99.9
1994																
1st quarter	102.3	106.7	104.4	103.6	99.9	101.4	101.3	101.6	119.8	103.0	104.7	107.0	102.2	105.2	101.4	100.4
2nd quarter	102.5	108.9	106.2	103.4	99.2	100.5	100.8	99.5	131.0	103.2	106.0	109.3	103.1	105.3	101.0	99.3
3rd quarter	102.4	110.1	107.6	103.3	98.3	100.8	100.9	100.5	134.3	103.8	106.2	110.7	104.2	105.7	100.6	99.5
4th quarter	103.1	112.3	108.9	103.9	98.4	100.7	100.8	100.3	139.7	104.2	107.2	113.1	105.4	106.4	100.8	99.2
1995																
1st quarter	102.5	112.6	109.8	104.7	98.6	101.8	102.1	101.2	132.5	104.6	108.5	114.6	105.6	105.6	99.5	97.3
2nd quarter	102.8	113.4	110.3	105.1	98.2	102.1	102.2	101.6	132.4	104.8	109.4	114.4	104.5	107.1	100.1	97.9
3rd quarter	103.6	115.1	111.1	105.5	98.1	101.6	101.8	101.0	141.1	105.1	110.3	114.9	104.2	108.2	100.7	98.1
4th quarter	104.3	116.1	111.3	106.1	98.3	101.6	101.7	101.2	141.3	105.2	111.5	116.0	104.1	109.0	101.0	97.8
1996																
1st quarter	105.7	117.4	111.1	107.2	98.4	101.1	101.4	100.5	148.4	105.4	112.9	115.9	102.7	109.3	100.4	96.8
2nd quarter	106.7	119.6	112.1	108.2	98.6	101.0	101.4	100.0	149.8	105.4	113.2	118.0	104.2	109.6	99.8	96.8
3rd quarter	107.8	121.8	113.0	109.0	98.7	100.7	101.1	99.6	149.3	105.0	114.4	119.7	104.7	110.1	99.8	96.3
4th quarter	108.4	123.7	114.1	109.5	98.5	100.7	101.0	99.6	152.1	105.3	115.0	120.8	105.1	110.4	99.3	96.0
1997																
1st quarter	108.5	125.4	115.5	110.4	98.8	101.3	101.7	100.2	152.7	105.9	115.8	122.6	105.9	110.2	98.5	95.1
2nd quarter	109.3	127.2	116.4	111.0	99.0	101.1	101.6	99.9	152.9	105.7	117.1	123.9	105.8	111.3	99.3	95.1
3rd quarter	110.5	129.6	117.3	111.9	99.4	100.9	101.3	99.8	158.6	106.0	119.0	125.8	105.8	112.4	99.9	94.5
4th quarter	111.1	131.3	118.2	113.6	100.3	101.5	102.3	99.3	153.4	106.1	120.0	128.0	106.7	114.3	100.9	95.2
1998																
1st quarter	111.6	132.6	118.8	116.1	102.4	102.8	104.0	99.4	140.0	106.1	121.7	129.7	106.5	116.6	102.8	95.8
2nd quarter	112.6	134.3	119.3	117.5	103.3	103.0	104.4	99.5	137.0	106.1	122.7	130.2	106.1	118.5	104.2	96.5
3rd quarter	114.1	136.5	119.6	119.2	104.3	103.1	104.4	99.5	140.3	106.4	124.9	130.7	104.7	120.3	105.3	96.3
4th quarter	113.9	137.9	121.1	119.7	104.4	104.0	105.1	101.0	132.9	106.6	125.3	132.3	105.6	120.6	105.2	96.3
1999																
1st quarter	115.9	140.8	121.5	122.6	106.5	104.2	105.8	99.7	134.1	106.8	126.6	132.9	105.0	121.6	105.6	96.0
2nd quarter	116.4	142.4	122.3	122.8	105.9	104.1	105.5	100.3	134.4	106.8	127.4	133.9	105.1	122.3	105.5	96.0
3rd quarter	116.4	143.5	123.3	123.5	105.7	104.9	106.1	101.6	126.9	106.9	127.6	134.7	105.6	123.7	105.9	97.0
4th quarter	117.7	146.0	124.0	125.2	106.4	105.2	106.4	102.2	124.1	106.9	130.7	136.8	104.6	127.0	107.9	97.2
2000																
1st quarter	119.7	149.4	124.7	129.7	109.2	106.8	108.3	102.5	115.3	107.5	132.4	137.9	104.1	133.4	112.3	100.7
2nd quarter	120.4	150.2	124.8	130.4	108.9	107.2	108.3	104.1	116.6	108.0	134.0	139.7	104.2	132.6	110.8	99.0
3rd quarter	121.3	151.5	125.0	132.9	110.0	108.5	109.6	105.4	108.0	108.4	134.0	139.1	103.8	136.1	112.6	101.6
4th quarter	121.6	151.5	124.6	134.4	110.5	109.7	110.6	107.1	97.6	108.6	135.2	137.8	101.9	137.1	112.6	101.4
2001																
1st quarter	122.2	151.3	123.9	135.5	110.4	110.6	111.0	109.6	87.8	108.6	134.9	135.2	100.2	138.4	112.7	102.6
2nd quarter	122.8	150.3	122.4	136.7	110.4	111.6	111.4	112.2	87.3	109.4	135.8	133.3	98.2	137.4	111.0	101.2
3rd quarter	123.0	148.6	120.8	137.9	111.1	112.8	112.1	114.7	79.4	109.8	136.9	131.1	95.8	137.3	110.6	100.3
4th quarter	123.9	147.6	119.1	139.3	112.5	113.4	112.4	116.2	75.8	110.1	140.4	129.7	92.4	139.4	112.5	99.3
2002																
1st quarter	126.3	149.7	118.5	139.9	112.6	111.6	110.8	114.0	89.1	109.6	143.8	130.5	90.7	144.1	115.9	100.2
2nd quarter	127.9	151.4	118.4	141.3	112.7	111.2	110.5	112.9	94.7	109.7	145.7	131.8	90.4	147.0	117.2	100.8
3rd quarter	129.2	152.3	117.9	142.1	112.7	110.7	110.0	112.7	95.7	109.4	147.8	132.4	89.5	148.6	117.8	100.5
4th quarter	130.2	153.1	117.6	142.9	112.8	110.4	109.7	112.3	101.8	109.6	148.8	131.3	88.2	149.9	118.3	100.7
2003																
1st quarter	131.3	153.4	116.8	144.1	112.7	110.7	109.8	113.2	99.2	109.7	151.0	131.3	87.0	155.7	121.8	103.1
2nd quarter	134.1	156.1	116.4	146.3	114.2	109.7	109.1	111.4	111.0	109.8	152.1	130.1	85.6	158.5	123.8	104.2
3rd quarter	137.2	159.4	116.2	148.5	115.3	109.0	108.2	111.1	118.7	109.9	156.0	131.5	84.3	161.6	125.5	103.6
4th quarter	138.9	162.0	116.7	150.0	116.2	108.7	108.0	110.5	123.2	110.0	157.2	133.5	84.9	163.9	127.0	104.2

NOTES AND DEFINITIONS

TABLES 19-1 THROUGH 19-9
SELECTED NATIONAL INCOME AND PRODUCT ACCOUNT DATA

See the Notes and Definitions for Tables 1-1 through 1-10. For *Personal income and its disposition* (Table 19-6), see the Notes and Definitions for Table 4-1. For *Inventories to sales ratios* (Table 19-7), see the Notes and Definitions for Table 5-7. For *Federal and State and local government current receipts and expenditures* (Tables 19-8 and 19-9), see the Notes and Definitions for Tables 6-1 and 6-8.

TABLE 19-10
U.S. INTERNATIONAL TRANSACTIONS

See the Notes and Definitions for Table 7-6.

TABLE 19-11
PRODUCTIVITY AND RELATED DATA

See the Notes and Definitions for Table 9-3.

CHAPTER 20: HISTORICAL DATA FOR SELECTED MONTHLY SERIES

Table 20-1. Industrial Production and Capacity Utilization

(Seasonally adjusted.)

Year and month	Total industry	Manufac- turing (SIC)	Market groups								Capacity utilization (output as percentage of capacity)	
			Consumer goods			Business equipment	Defense and space equipment	Construction supplies	Business supplies	Materials	Total industry	Manufac- turing (SIC)
			Total	Durable	Nondurable							
1947	17.2	16.1	20.7	14.7	23.6	9.3	9.3	24.5	14.0	17.5	...	...
1948	18.0	16.7	21.3	15.3	24.3	9.7	11.0	26.3	14.6	18.3	...	82.5
1949	17.0	15.8	21.2	14.5	24.5	8.4	11.5	24.1	14.4	16.7	...	74.2
1950	19.7	18.3	24.2	19.4	26.5	9.0	13.5	29.0	16.1	20.0	...	82.8
1951	21.3	19.8	24.0	16.8	27.5	11.0	33.1	30.1	17.0	22.1	...	85.8
1952	22.1	20.6	24.5	16.3	28.6	12.5	46.6	29.9	16.9	22.4	...	85.4
1953	24.0	22.5	26.0	19.1	29.4	13.0	55.7	32.1	18.0	24.9	...	89.3
1954	22.7	21.0	25.8	17.7	29.7	11.4	49.1	31.6	18.3	23.0	...	80.1
1955	25.6	23.7	28.8	21.8	32.0	12.4	44.9	36.4	20.5	27.2	...	87.0
1956	26.7	24.6	29.9	21.1	34.1	14.4	43.9	37.4	21.7	27.9	...	86.1
1957	27.1	24.9	30.6	21.1	35.2	14.9	45.9	36.9	22.0	27.8	...	83.6
1958	25.4	23.2	30.3	18.7	36.2	12.6	46.0	35.6	21.8	25.1	...	75.0
1959	28.4	26.1	33.3	22.2	38.7	14.2	48.6	39.9	23.7	28.9	...	81.6
1960	29.0	26.6	34.6	23.4	39.9	14.5	49.9	39.0	24.5	29.3	...	80.1
1961	29.2	26.7	35.3	23.1	41.3	14.1	50.7	39.4	25.3	29.3	...	77.3
1962	31.6	29.1	37.7	26.1	43.2	15.3	58.7	41.7	26.8	31.9	...	81.4
1963	33.5	30.9	39.7	28.3	45.1	16.1	63.3	43.7	28.6	34.0	...	83.5
1964	35.8	33.0	42.0	30.4	47.4	18.0	61.3	46.3	30.6	36.7	...	85.6
1965	39.3	36.5	45.3	35.6	49.4	20.6	67.8	49.2	32.6	41.0	...	89.5
1966	42.8	39.9	47.6	37.8	51.8	23.9	79.7	51.3	35.1	44.6	...	91.1
1967	43.7	40.6	48.7	36.3	54.4	24.4	90.9	52.6	37.0	44.2	87.0	87.2
1947												
January	17.0	15.9	20.5	13.8	23.9	8.9	9.6	23.3	13.9	17.2	...	...
February	17.1	16.0	20.5	14.3	23.5	9.0	9.5	24.0	13.9	17.4	...	...
March	17.2	16.0	20.5	14.6	23.5	9.1	9.3	24.3	13.9	17.9	...	...
April	17.1	16.1	20.5	14.7	23.3	9.2	9.4	24.5	14.1	17.5	...	...
May	17.2	15.9	20.3	14.5	23.1	9.3	9.2	24.8	14.0	17.6	...	...
June	17.2	15.9	20.3	14.7	23.1	9.3	9.2	24.8	13.9	17.4	...	...
July	17.1	15.8	20.4	14.4	23.3	9.2	9.1	24.2	13.9	17.2	...	...
August	17.2	15.9	20.6	14.2	23.6	9.3	9.1	24.6	13.8	17.2	...	...
September	17.3	16.0	20.8	14.7	23.7	9.5	9.1	24.8	13.9	17.4	...	...
October	17.5	16.2	21.1	14.9	24.1	9.5	9.4	24.7	13.9	17.6	...	...
November	17.7	16.5	21.4	15.4	24.3	9.5	9.5	25.2	14.2	18.0	...	...
December	17.8	16.5	21.5	15.6	24.3	9.6	9.7	25.3	14.5	17.8	...	...
1948												
January	17.9	16.6	21.3	15.4	24.2	9.7	9.8	26.4	14.4	17.8	...	84.4
February	17.9	16.6	21.4	15.2	24.4	9.6	10.2	26.1	14.6	17.9	...	84.0
March	17.7	16.6	21.2	15.3	24.1	9.7	10.4	26.2	14.5	17.8	...	83.4
April	17.7	16.5	21.3	15.2	24.4	9.6	10.6	26.1	14.5	17.6	...	82.8
May	18.0	16.7	21.3	14.9	24.4	9.6	10.4	26.3	14.5	18.6	...	83.3
June	18.3	16.9	21.6	15.5	24.6	9.7	10.8	26.0	14.6	18.6	...	83.6
July	18.3	16.9	21.6	15.9	24.3	9.8	11.0	26.7	14.5	18.7	...	83.4
August	18.2	16.8	21.4	15.6	24.1	9.8	11.2	26.6	14.7	18.5	...	82.7
September	18.1	16.7	21.3	15.2	24.2	9.7	11.5	26.2	14.6	18.5	...	81.5
October	18.2	16.8	21.5	15.7	24.3	9.6	11.7	26.8	14.6	18.6	...	81.7
November	18.0	16.6	21.3	15.1	24.3	9.5	12.0	26.0	14.7	18.4	...	80.2
December	17.8	16.5	21.0	14.5	24.2	9.4	12.0	25.8	14.7	18.3	...	79.3
1949												
January	17.6	16.2	20.8	14.1	24.0	9.2	11.8	25.1	14.4	17.9	...	77.9
February	17.5	16.1	20.7	13.9	24.1	9.2	11.8	24.6	14.2	17.8	...	76.9
March	17.1	15.9	20.9	13.8	24.3	9.0	11.7	24.3	14.2	17.1	...	75.9
April	17.0	15.6	20.8	13.9	24.2	8.8	11.5	23.9	14.2	16.9	...	74.2
May	16.8	15.5	20.8	13.8	24.3	8.6	11.7	23.6	14.3	16.4	...	73.2
June	16.8	15.5	21.1	14.1	24.4	8.5	11.8	23.6	14.3	16.2	...	73.1
July	16.7	15.6	21.3	14.6	24.5	8.3	11.7	23.3	14.3	16.1	...	73.1
August	16.9	15.7	21.5	14.8	24.7	8.3	11.5	23.5	14.3	16.4	...	73.6
September	17.1	16.0	21.8	15.3	24.8	8.2	11.3	24.3	14.6	16.7	...	74.8
October	16.4	15.4	21.9	15.6	24.9	7.9	11.0	23.5	14.7	15.0	...	71.7
November	16.9	15.5	21.5	14.7	24.8	7.6	11.7	24.3	14.7	16.3	...	72.0
December	17.2	15.9	21.3	14.5	24.7	7.6	10.8	25.3	14.7	17.1	...	73.6
1950												
January	17.5	16.3	22.2	16.2	25.1	7.8	10.8	25.0	14.9	17.3	...	74.9
February	17.5	16.4	22.2	16.2	25.1	8.0	10.8	26.0	15.3	17.0	...	75.4
March	18.1	16.7	22.7	16.9	25.5	8.1	10.9	26.6	15.3	18.1	...	76.4
April	18.7	17.4	23.3	18.1	25.9	8.3	11.1	28.0	15.6	18.9	...	79.2
May	19.1	17.8	23.8	19.0	26.1	8.7	11.5	28.2	15.7	19.4	...	81.0
June	19.7	18.4	24.5	20.6	26.3	9.0	11.9	29.2	15.9	20.2	...	83.1
July	20.3	19.0	25.2	21.5	26.8	9.3	12.5	30.0	16.3	20.7	...	85.5
August	21.0	19.7	26.0	22.1	27.8	9.9	13.8	30.6	16.7	21.3	...	88.4
September	20.8	19.5	25.4	21.1	27.4	9.6	15.2	30.6	16.5	21.5	...	87.2
October	21.0	19.6	25.2	20.7	27.2	9.8	16.4	30.9	16.8	21.8	...	87.5
November	20.9	19.6	25.1	20.3	27.3	9.9	17.5	31.0	16.8	21.6	...	87.0
December	21.3	19.9	25.5	20.1	28.1	10.1	19.0	31.0	17.1	21.9	...	88.1
1951												
January	21.4	20.0	25.6	19.7	28.4	10.2	21.1	31.3	17.3	21.7	...	88.3
February	21.5	20.1	25.6	19.8	28.4	10.3	24.4	31.0	17.0	21.8	...	88.3
March	21.6	20.2	25.2	19.6	27.9	10.5	27.7	31.1	17.3	22.3	...	88.4
April	21.6	20.2	24.8	18.7	27.7	10.7	30.3	31.0	17.7	22.4	...	88.2
May	21.6	20.1	24.3	17.8	27.5	10.8	31.3	30.7	17.5	22.6	...	87.4
June	21.5	20.0	24.0	16.9	27.4	11.0	33.0	30.5	17.2	22.7	...	86.6
July	21.1	19.6	23.2	15.1	27.2	11.1	34.9	29.8	17.1	22.3	...	84.9
August	20.9	19.4	22.7	14.1	26.9	11.2	36.0	29.6	16.9	21.9	...	83.6
September	21.1	19.5	22.9	14.7	26.9	11.4	37.2	29.6	16.8	22.1	...	83.7
October	21.0	19.4	22.8	14.6	26.9	11.6	38.7	29.3	16.4	21.7	...	83.1
November	21.2	19.6	23.2	14.9	27.2	11.8	41.0	29.1	16.5	21.8	...	83.6
December	21.3	19.8	23.3	15.1	27.4	12.0	41.8	29.2	16.5	21.9	...	83.9

... = Not available.

Table 20-1. Industrial Production and Capacity Utilization—Continued

(Seasonally adjusted.)

| Year and month | Total industry | Manufac-turing (SIC) | Market groups ||||||||| Capacity utilization (output as percentage of capacity) ||
| | | | Consumer goods ||| Business equipment | Defense and space equipment | Construction supplies | Business supplies | Materials | Total industry | Manufac-turing (SIC) |
			Total	Durable	Nondurable							
1952												
January	21.6	19.9	23.5	15.0	27.7	12.3	42.5	29.6	16.6	22.4	...	84.4
February	21.7	20.1	23.7	15.0	28.0	12.4	43.0	29.8	16.6	22.2	...	84.6
March	21.8	20.2	23.8	15.3	28.0	12.5	43.1	29.6	16.6	22.2	...	84.7
April	21.6	20.0	23.8	15.2	28.1	12.5	43.6	29.1	16.5	21.7	...	83.6
May	21.4	19.9	23.8	15.6	27.8	12.6	45.0	28.7	16.4	21.4	...	83.1
June	21.2	19.7	24.4	15.8	28.8	12.6	46.4	28.5	16.8	20.2	...	81.9
July	20.8	19.3	24.0	14.3	28.9	12.0	46.6	28.5	16.9	19.8	...	79.8
August	22.2	20.7	24.5	15.7	28.9	12.2	47.4	30.4	17.0	22.3	...	85.1
September	23.0	21.4	25.1	17.3	28.9	12.5	48.2	30.7	17.3	23.8	...	87.7
October	23.2	21.7	25.5	17.9	29.2	12.7	49.7	31.1	17.5	23.6	...	88.8
November	23.7	22.1	26.0	19.0	29.5	12.8	50.8	31.7	17.7	24.3	...	90.2
December	23.8	22.3	26.0	19.1	29.4	13.0	52.3	31.8	17.6	24.4	...	90.5
1953												
January	23.9	22.4	26.3	19.8	29.4	13.0	53.1	32.3	17.3	24.3	...	90.5
February	24.0	22.6	26.5	20.0	29.6	13.1	54.2	32.8	17.7	24.8	...	91.1
March	24.2	22.8	26.5	20.2	29.4	13.2	55.3	32.9	18.1	25.1	...	91.4
April	24.3	22.9	26.4	20.0	29.6	13.2	56.0	33.0	18.2	25.4	...	91.5
May	24.5	23.0	26.5	20.1	29.7	13.1	57.0	32.3	18.3	25.9	...	91.7
June	24.4	22.8	26.1	19.4	29.6	13.0	57.3	32.1	18.3	25.9	...	90.7
July	24.7	22.9	26.2	19.2	29.5	13.2	57.8	32.5	18.3	26.2	...	91.0
August	24.5	22.9	26.0	19.1	29.4	13.2	57.4	32.4	18.3	25.5	...	90.6
September	24.0	22.4	25.7	18.3	29.2	13.0	57.3	31.8	18.2	24.9	...	88.3
October	23.8	22.2	25.7	18.1	29.3	13.0	56.8	31.9	18.1	24.1	...	87.2
November	23.3	21.6	25.3	17.5	29.1	12.6	53.1	31.3	18.0	23.5	...	84.7
December	22.7	21.1	24.9	16.9	28.8	12.4	53.5	30.6	17.7	22.9	...	82.3
1954												
January	22.5	20.9	25.0	16.6	29.2	12.0	52.5	31.2	17.7	22.7	...	81.3
February	22.6	20.8	25.3	17.0	29.3	11.9	52.1	31.3	17.9	22.6	...	80.8
March	22.5	20.8	25.3	17.0	29.4	11.7	51.4	31.0	17.9	22.4	...	80.2
April	22.3	20.6	25.3	17.2	29.2	11.5	50.5	31.0	18.0	22.4	...	79.4
May	22.5	20.8	25.5	17.5	29.3	11.5	49.7	31.4	17.9	22.7	...	79.8
June	22.5	20.8	25.6	17.7	29.4	11.3	49.0	30.7	18.1	22.9	...	79.9
July	22.6	20.8	25.7	17.5	29.7	11.3	48.8	30.6	17.9	23.0	...	79.4
August	22.5	20.7	25.8	17.6	29.7	11.2	47.8	30.5	18.0	22.9	...	78.8
September	22.6	20.8	26.0	17.7	30.0	11.1	47.3	32.0	18.5	22.7	...	79.2
October	22.8	21.1	26.1	18.0	30.1	11.1	46.8	33.1	18.7	23.2	...	79.7
November	23.2	21.4	26.6	18.5	30.6	11.3	46.6	33.4	19.0	23.7	...	80.9
December	23.5	21.7	27.1	19.2	30.8	11.3	45.9	33.7	19.3	24.1	...	81.8
1955												
January	24.0	22.3	27.7	20.5	31.0	11.4	45.6	34.1	19.4	24.9	...	83.5
February	24.3	22.5	27.8	20.8	31.0	11.6	45.6	34.6	19.6	25.5	...	84.1
March	24.9	23.0	28.3	21.3	31.5	11.7	45.3	35.8	20.2	26.2	...	85.8
April	25.2	23.4	28.5	21.7	31.7	12.1	45.3	36.0	20.1	26.7	...	86.7
May	25.6	23.8	28.9	22.2	31.9	12.3	45.3	36.2	20.4	27.2	...	87.7
June	25.6	23.8	28.7	21.8	31.8	12.4	44.8	36.8	20.6	27.3	...	87.6
July	25.8	23.9	28.8	22.1	31.8	12.4	44.7	36.9	20.5	27.6	...	87.7
August	25.8	23.9	28.9	22.1	31.8	12.5	44.4	36.9	20.4	27.6	...	87.3
September	26.0	24.0	29.0	22.2	32.1	12.6	44.6	37.1	20.8	27.9	...	87.5
October	26.4	24.4	29.6	22.3	32.9	13.2	44.4	37.1	21.0	28.2	...	88.4
November	26.5	24.4	29.6	22.1	33.2	13.2	44.3	37.5	21.3	28.1	...	88.3
December	26.6	24.7	29.8	22.0	33.5	13.5	44.4	37.7	21.2	28.3	...	89.0
1956												
January	26.7	24.6	29.8	21.8	33.6	13.6	43.9	38.3	21.4	28.4	...	88.2
February	26.5	24.5	29.8	21.4	33.7	13.8	43.5	38.2	21.4	27.9	...	87.4
March	26.5	24.5	29.7	21.4	33.7	13.9	42.6	38.1	21.5	27.8	...	87.0
April	26.7	24.8	29.8	21.7	33.7	14.3	42.9	37.9	21.8	28.0	...	87.8
May	26.5	24.5	29.7	21.2	33.8	14.3	43.0	37.4	21.6	27.5	...	86.3
June	26.2	24.3	29.6	20.7	33.9	14.3	43.0	37.0	21.5	27.1	...	85.3
July	25.4	23.3	29.7	20.7	34.0	14.3	43.0	35.1	21.7	24.9	...	81.5
August	26.5	24.4	29.8	20.7	34.3	14.5	43.5	36.9	21.7	27.2	...	84.9
September	27.1	24.8	29.8	20.4	34.3	14.6	43.9	37.8	21.7	28.6	...	86.0
October	27.3	25.0	30.0	20.7	34.5	14.7	45.1	37.6	21.9	29.1	...	86.5
November	27.1	25.0	29.9	20.4	34.4	14.9	45.8	37.2	21.9	28.4	...	85.8
December	27.5	25.3	30.1	21.2	34.4	15.1	46.8	37.9	22.0	29.0	...	86.8
1957												
January	27.4	25.2	30.3	21.3	34.5	15.3	47.0	37.4	22.1	28.4	...	86.2
February	27.6	25.6	30.7	21.7	34.9	15.6	47.2	38.5	22.1	28.6	...	87.0
March	27.6	25.5	30.8	21.6	35.1	15.6	47.2	37.9	22.0	28.5	...	86.4
April	27.2	25.1	30.4	21.0	35.0	15.3	47.3	37.1	22.0	28.1	...	85.0
May	27.1	25.0	30.5	20.9	35.1	15.0	46.6	36.9	22.2	28.0	...	84.2
June	27.2	25.2	30.6	21.2	35.2	15.0	46.8	37.2	22.0	28.1	...	84.6
July	27.4	25.2	30.8	21.0	35.5	15.1	46.3	37.2	22.1	28.3	...	84.3
August	27.4	25.2	30.9	21.6	35.4	15.1	46.4	36.9	22.1	28.3	...	84.2
September	27.1	25.0	30.9	21.5	35.4	14.9	45.4	36.7	22.1	28.0	...	83.2
October	26.7	24.5	30.4	20.7	35.2	14.5	44.4	36.3	21.8	27.5	...	81.4
November	26.1	24.0	30.4	20.7	35.0	14.1	42.9	35.9	21.6	26.5	...	79.4
December	25.6	23.5	30.2	19.7	35.3	13.7	42.5	35.3	21.5	25.7	...	77.5

... = Not available.

Table 20-1. Industrial Production and Capacity Utilization—Continued

(Seasonally adjusted.)

Year and month	Total industry	Manufac- turing (SIC)	Consumer goods			Business equipment	Defense and space equipment	Construction supplies	Business supplies	Materials	Capacity utilization (output as percentage of capacity)	
			Total	Durable	Nondurable						Total industry	Manufac- turing (SIC)
1958												
January	25.1	23.0	29.8	19.0	35.2	13.4	43.0	34.8	21.5	24.9	...	75.7
February	24.6	22.5	29.6	18.3	35.3	12.9	43.4	33.7	21.4	24.1	...	73.8
March	24.3	22.2	29.3	17.7	35.3	12.6	44.2	33.5	21.4	23.5	...	72.7
April	23.9	21.9	29.0	17.0	35.2	12.4	44.9	33.1	21.3	22.9	...	71.3
May	24.1	22.1	29.4	17.6	35.5	12.1	45.4	34.2	21.2	23.2	...	71.9
June	24.8	22.8	30.0	18.1	36.1	12.1	46.7	35.6	21.5	24.2	...	73.9
July	25.1	23.0	30.5	18.4	36.6	12.2	46.8	35.4	21.5	24.8	...	74.3
August	25.6	23.5	30.6	18.7	36.6	12.4	47.2	36.9	21.8	25.6	...	75.7
September	25.9	23.7	30.2	17.4	36.8	12.5	47.5	37.0	22.1	26.2	...	76.2
October	26.2	23.8	30.5	18.3	36.8	12.6	47.5	37.0	22.4	26.6	...	76.4
November	26.9	24.7	32.0	21.4	37.2	12.9	47.9	38.4	22.6	27.4	...	79.1
December	27.0	24.8	32.1	21.5	37.3	13.0	47.9	37.9	22.4	27.4	...	79.0
1959												
January	27.4	25.2	32.5	21.6	37.8	13.2	48.1	38.7	23.0	27.9	...	80.2
February	27.9	25.7	32.7	21.7	38.2	13.4	47.7	39.7	23.2	28.8	...	81.4
March	28.3	26.1	32.7	22.1	38.0	13.5	47.9	40.7	23.4	29.5	...	82.5
April	28.9	26.6	33.3	22.2	38.6	13.9	48.2	41.9	23.4	30.3	...	84.0
May	29.4	27.0	33.4	22.7	38.6	14.4	48.5	42.3	23.4	31.1	...	84.9
June	29.4	27.0	33.3	22.9	38.3	14.7	48.7	42.1	23.7	30.9	...	84.8
July	28.7	26.5	33.7	23.3	38.6	14.7	48.9	40.4	23.9	29.1	...	83.0
August	27.7	25.5	33.7	22.7	39.1	14.6	48.6	37.9	23.9	26.9	...	79.5
September	27.7	25.4	33.6	22.0	39.3	14.5	48.9	37.5	24.0	26.8	...	79.0
October	27.5	25.2	33.5	22.5	38.8	14.4	48.8	37.6	24.0	26.6	...	78.2
November	27.6	25.4	32.7	19.7	39.4	14.1	48.7	38.9	23.9	27.6	...	78.5
December	29.4	27.1	33.8	22.2	39.5	14.4	49.1	41.9	24.2	30.6	...	83.6
1960												
January	30.1	27.9	34.9	24.7	39.7	14.9	49.5	41.6	24.5	31.5	...	85.6
February	29.9	27.6	34.5	24.3	39.3	15.0	49.7	41.2	24.4	31.1	...	84.6
March	29.6	27.3	34.5	23.8	39.6	15.0	50.0	39.9	24.4	30.5	...	83.2
April	29.4	27.1	34.8	23.8	40.0	14.8	49.7	39.9	24.8	29.8	...	82.3
May	29.3	26.9	35.0	24.0	40.2	14.9	50.3	39.5	24.9	29.6	...	81.5
June	29.0	26.6	34.7	23.8	40.0	14.7	49.0	38.8	24.6	29.1	...	80.2
July	28.9	26.6	34.4	22.9	40.0	14.5	50.2	39.2	24.7	29.1	...	79.7
August	28.8	26.4	34.5	23.1	40.0	14.3	50.4	38.2	24.5	29.0	...	79.1
September	28.5	26.2	34.3	22.9	39.9	14.2	50.3	37.9	24.4	28.5	...	77.9
October	28.5	26.1	34.7	23.1	40.3	14.1	49.8	37.9	24.4	28.4	...	77.5
November	28.1	25.6	34.1	22.4	39.9	14.1	50.0	37.5	24.4	27.7	...	75.8
December	27.5	25.2	33.8	21.6	39.9	13.7	49.2	37.0	24.0	26.9	...	74.3
1961												
January	27.6	25.2	33.5	20.8	40.0	13.8	49.7	36.7	24.4	27.2	...	74.1
February	27.5	25.1	33.7	20.7	40.3	13.7	49.4	36.6	24.4	26.9	...	73.5
March	27.7	25.3	33.7	20.7	40.3	13.7	49.3	37.5	24.7	27.2	...	73.9
April	28.3	25.9	34.5	22.2	40.6	13.8	49.4	38.4	24.8	28.0	...	75.4
May	28.7	26.3	34.9	22.9	40.9	13.9	49.4	38.6	24.9	28.9	...	76.4
June	29.1	26.7	35.3	23.7	41.1	14.0	49.4	39.4	25.1	29.3	...	77.3
July	29.5	27.0	35.6	24.1	41.3	14.0	49.7	40.0	25.4	29.7	...	78.1
August	29.7	27.4	35.9	24.1	41.6	14.1	50.0	40.5	25.5	30.3	...	79.0
September	29.7	27.2	35.3	22.8	41.4	14.3	51.1	40.8	25.4	30.3	...	78.2
October	30.3	27.7	36.2	24.0	42.1	14.3	52.2	41.1	25.8	30.9	...	79.6
November	30.7	28.2	36.9	25.1	42.5	14.7	53.5	40.8	26.0	31.3	...	80.8
December	31.0	28.6	37.0	25.6	42.5	14.7	54.4	41.1	26.3	31.7	...	81.6
1962												
January	30.7	28.2	36.7	25.0	42.4	14.7	55.1	39.2	26.3	31.5	...	80.2
February	31.2	28.7	36.9	25.2	42.6	14.9	56.0	41.5	26.5	32.0	...	81.4
March	31.4	28.9	37.2	25.5	42.9	15.1	56.8	42.0	26.4	32.0	...	81.9
April	31.5	29.0	37.5	26.1	42.9	15.2	57.3	41.4	26.4	32.0	...	81.7
May	31.4	28.9	37.7	26.3	43.2	15.2	57.7	41.4	26.9	31.6	...	81.3
June	31.4	28.8	37.5	25.9	43.1	15.3	58.2	41.7	26.8	31.5	...	80.9
July	31.7	29.1	38.1	26.4	43.6	15.5	59.4	41.5	26.8	31.7	...	81.5
August	31.7	29.2	37.7	26.1	43.2	15.6	60.2	42.3	26.9	31.8	...	81.4
September	31.9	29.4	37.9	26.4	43.5	15.6	60.3	42.8	27.2	32.1	...	81.8
October	31.9	29.3	37.8	26.5	43.3	15.7	60.5	42.1	27.2	32.1	...	81.4
November	32.1	29.6	38.1	26.5	43.5	15.7	61.1	42.2	27.3	32.4	...	81.8
December	32.1	29.6	38.2	26.7	43.7	15.6	61.4	42.6	27.2	32.2	...	81.7
1963												
January	32.3	29.8	38.7	27.0	44.3	15.5	64.2	41.5	27.4	32.3	...	81.9
February	32.7	30.0	39.1	27.3	44.8	15.7	63.8	41.6	27.6	32.8	...	82.4
March	32.9	30.2	39.3	27.4	45.0	15.6	63.4	42.1	27.4	33.3	...	82.6
April	33.2	30.6	39.5	27.6	45.2	15.8	63.4	43.5	28.3	33.6	...	83.5
May	33.6	30.9	39.5	28.0	45.0	15.7	63.4	44.5	28.6	34.4	...	84.0
June	33.7	31.0	39.8	28.5	45.1	15.8	63.3	44.3	28.4	34.5	...	83.9
July	33.5	30.9	39.7	28.5	44.9	16.0	62.7	44.2	28.6	34.2	...	83.3
August	33.6	31.0	40.0	28.5	45.4	16.4	62.9	44.3	28.8	33.8	...	83.5
September	33.9	31.2	40.1	29.1	45.2	16.4	63.2	44.0	29.1	34.5	...	83.8
October	34.2	31.5	40.4	29.1	45.6	16.7	63.2	44.6	29.3	34.7	...	84.3
November	34.3	31.6	40.4	29.4	45.6	16.8	62.9	45.2	29.6	34.9	...	84.3
December	34.3	31.6	40.7	29.5	46.0	16.7	63.1	44.5	29.4	34.7	...	84.0

... = Not available.

Table 20-1. Industrial Production and Capacity Utilization—Continued

(Seasonally adjusted.)

Year and month	Total industry	Manufac- turing (SIC)	Market groups								Capacity utilization (output as percentage of capacity)	
			Consumer goods			Business equipment	Defense and space equipment	Construction supplies	Business supplies	Materials	Total industry	Manufac- turing (SIC)
			Total	Durable	Nondurable							
1964												
January	34.6	31.9	41.0	29.5	46.4	17.2	62.5	44.8	29.7	35.0	...	84.5
February	34.8	32.1	41.0	29.7	46.2	17.1	61.9	45.9	29.9	35.5	...	84.7
March	34.8	32.1	40.8	29.5	46.1	17.3	61.8	46.1	30.1	35.5	...	84.4
April	35.4	32.7	41.8	30.2	47.2	17.7	61.6	46.3	30.5	36.0	...	85.6
May	35.6	32.8	42.1	30.4	47.6	17.9	60.6	46.5	30.8	36.3	...	85.6
June	35.7	32.9	42.0	30.7	47.3	18.0	60.2	46.2	30.8	36.5	...	85.4
July	35.9	33.1	42.6	31.2	47.9	18.2	60.1	47.0	30.8	36.6	...	85.9
August	36.2	33.3	42.6	31.5	47.6	18.2	60.4	46.6	30.7	37.3	...	86.1
September	36.3	33.5	42.1	30.7	47.4	18.4	60.8	46.2	30.7	37.9	...	86.2
October	35.8	33.0	41.2	27.5	48.0	18.2	61.2	46.4	30.8	37.2	...	84.6
November	36.9	34.0	42.8	31.3	48.1	18.8	61.8	47.5	31.0	38.3	...	86.8
December	37.3	34.6	43.7	33.1	48.4	19.2	62.3	46.9	31.3	38.8	...	88.0
1965												
January	37.7	35.0	44.3	33.7	49.1	19.1	63.0	47.2	31.6	39.2	...	88.6
February	38.0	35.2	44.4	34.1	49.0	19.5	63.7	48.4	31.7	39.4	...	88.7
March	38.5	35.7	44.8	35.1	49.0	19.7	64.8	48.8	32.0	40.0	...	89.3
April	38.6	35.9	44.7	35.0	48.9	19.9	65.6	48.1	32.0	40.4	...	89.3
May	38.9	36.2	45.0	35.3	49.2	20.2	67.0	48.6	32.4	40.6	...	89.4
June	39.2	36.4	45.1	35.6	49.2	20.5	67.9	48.7	32.5	41.0	...	89.5
July	39.6	36.9	45.1	35.8	49.1	20.8	68.9	50.0	32.5	41.4	...	90.3
August	39.8	37.0	45.1	35.5	49.2	20.8	69.5	49.5	32.8	41.8	...	89.9
September	39.9	37.1	45.7	36.1	49.8	21.2	69.6	49.1	32.8	41.5	...	89.6
October	40.3	37.4	46.0	36.5	50.0	21.5	70.5	49.8	33.2	41.9	...	89.8
November	40.4	37.5	46.2	36.7	50.3	21.9	71.1	50.5	33.4	41.8	...	89.6
December	41.0	38.1	46.5	37.5	50.3	22.4	71.8	51.6	33.9	42.2	...	90.5
1966												
January	41.4	38.5	46.7	37.6	50.5	22.8	73.4	51.5	33.9	42.8	...	90.9
February	41.6	38.7	46.9	37.5	50.8	22.8	74.5	51.1	34.3	43.3	...	90.9
March	42.2	39.2	47.2	37.8	51.2	23.2	75.1	52.1	34.6	44.1	...	91.6
April	42.3	39.5	47.4	38.5	51.1	23.4	76.7	52.1	34.3	44.0	...	91.5
May	42.7	39.7	47.4	37.9	51.4	23.7	78.1	52.3	34.8	44.5	...	91.6
June	42.9	39.9	47.6	37.9	51.7	23.9	79.2	51.6	35.3	44.8	...	91.5
July	43.1	40.1	47.5	37.2	52.0	24.3	80.3	52.1	35.7	44.9	...	91.4
August	43.1	40.2	47.3	36.6	52.1	24.4	81.4	50.5	35.5	45.2	...	91.1
September	43.5	40.5	47.5	36.8	52.2	24.7	82.5	50.5	35.7	45.7	...	91.2
October	43.8	40.9	48.5	38.7	52.6	24.6	83.7	50.6	35.7	45.9	...	91.6
November	43.5	40.5	48.2	37.6	52.9	24.3	85.3	50.6	35.8	45.2	...	90.1
December	43.6	40.7	48.1	37.2	53.0	24.6	86.1	50.5	35.9	45.2	...	90.0
1967												
January	43.8	40.8	48.6	36.2	54.2	24.4	87.6	51.9	36.6	45.0	89.4	89.8
February	43.3	40.3	47.9	35.2	53.8	24.5	88.6	51.4	36.4	44.1	88.0	88.4
March	43.1	40.1	48.1	35.6	53.8	24.4	89.6	51.5	36.4	43.3	87.1	87.5
April	43.5	40.4	48.9	35.8	54.9	24.4	90.4	51.4	36.8	43.7	87.5	87.7
May	43.1	40.1	47.9	35.3	53.7	24.5	91.1	52.2	36.2	43.3	86.4	86.6
June	43.1	40.0	48.1	35.0	54.2	24.4	90.9	52.5	36.4	43.2	86.0	86.1
July	43.0	39.9	48.0	35.4	53.8	23.9	91.4	52.7	36.5	43.2	85.4	85.3
August	43.8	40.6	48.5	35.8	54.3	24.3	91.5	53.3	37.4	44.4	86.6	86.5
September	43.8	40.6	48.6	35.7	54.5	24.2	91.8	53.7	37.6	44.2	86.1	86.1
October	44.1	41.0	49.2	36.4	55.1	24.0	92.5	53.4	37.8	44.7	86.4	86.4
November	44.8	41.7	50.3	38.4	55.6	24.6	92.7	53.8	37.9	45.2	87.3	87.5
December	45.2	42.1	51.1	39.9	55.9	24.9	92.7	53.7	37.9	45.8	87.8	88.0
1968												
January	45.2	42.0	50.4	38.8	55.6	25.0	92.3	54.1	38.0	46.0	87.4	87.4
February	45.4	42.2	50.7	39.4	55.6	25.0	93.4	54.7	38.3	46.0	87.3	87.4
March	45.5	42.3	51.0	39.3	56.2	25.2	91.5	54.8	38.3	46.2	87.3	87.1
April	45.6	42.3	50.9	39.3	56.0	25.1	89.7	55.1	38.7	46.5	87.0	86.8
May	46.1	42.9	51.2	39.8	56.2	25.5	91.0	55.3	39.0	47.2	87.7	87.6
June	46.2	43.0	51.5	40.2	56.4	25.4	91.5	55.3	39.2	47.4	87.6	87.3
July	46.2	42.8	51.4	39.9	56.4	25.2	91.5	55.3	39.2	47.5	87.2	86.7
August	46.3	43.0	52.0	40.4	57.1	25.4	91.7	55.6	39.6	47.1	87.1	86.7
September	46.5	43.1	52.2	40.8	57.2	25.6	91.6	55.2	39.7	47.3	87.0	86.4
October	46.6	43.3	52.5	41.4	57.3	25.9	89.2	55.1	40.0	47.4	86.9	86.6
November	47.2	43.9	53.2	42.3	57.8	25.9	90.1	56.4	40.4	48.1	87.7	87.4
December	47.3	44.0	52.9	42.7	57.1	26.2	89.6	57.5	40.6	48.4	87.6	87.1
1969												
January	47.6	44.2	53.2	42.6	57.6	26.5	89.8	57.9	40.8	48.6	87.8	87.2
February	47.9	44.6	53.6	42.5	58.3	26.5	89.2	58.4	40.7	49.1	88.0	87.6
March	48.3	44.9	54.0	42.8	58.7	26.8	89.5	58.6	42.0	49.4	88.4	87.9
April	48.1	44.7	53.2	41.7	58.1	27.1	88.8	58.1	41.4	49.5	87.8	87.2
May	47.9	44.5	52.8	41.1	57.9	26.9	88.6	57.7	41.8	49.4	87.1	86.5
June	48.4	44.8	53.4	42.5	58.0	27.1	87.4	58.0	42.1	50.1	87.6	86.7
July	48.6	45.1	54.3	42.5	59.4	27.4	87.0	57.5	41.9	50.1	87.8	87.0
August	48.8	45.2	54.2	42.9	59.0	27.3	85.8	57.4	42.0	50.6	87.7	86.8
September	48.8	45.1	53.8	42.5	58.6	27.6	85.3	57.4	41.9	50.7	87.3	86.3
October	48.8	45.2	53.8	42.7	58.5	27.7	84.5	57.6	42.1	50.7	87.1	86.1
November	48.3	44.7	53.4	41.0	58.8	27.0	82.9	57.3	41.8	50.5	85.9	84.9
December	48.2	44.5	53.4	40.8	59.1	26.9	81.9	57.0	42.3	50.2	85.4	84.1

... = Not available.

CHAPTER 20: HISTORICAL DATA FOR SELECTED MONTHLY SERIES

Table 20-1. Industrial Production and Capacity Utilization—Continued

(Seasonally adjusted.)

Year and month	Total industry	Manufac- turing (SIC)	Market groups								Capacity utilization (output as percentage of capacity)	
			Consumer goods			Business equipment	Defense and space equipment	Construction supplies	Business supplies	Materials	Total industry	Manufac- turing (SIC)
			Total	Durable	Nondurable							
1970												
January	47.3	43.5	52.6	38.6	59.0	26.6	80.8	55.2	42.3	49.0	83.5	82.0
February	47.3	43.5	53.1	39.2	59.4	26.7	79.4	55.0	42.0	48.7	83.2	81.8
March	47.2	43.4	53.0	39.5	59.1	26.7	77.7	55.5	42.2	48.6	82.8	81.3
April	47.1	43.3	53.2	39.5	59.5	26.7	75.9	56.0	42.0	48.3	82.4	80.7
May	47.0	43.2	53.5	39.6	59.9	26.7	74.3	56.1	41.9	48.1	82.0	80.3
June	46.9	43.0	53.6	40.3	59.6	26.5	73.0	55.8	41.8	47.9	81.5	79.8
July	47.0	43.2	53.8	40.4	59.8	26.4	71.8	56.5	42.0	48.1	81.4	79.8
August	46.9	42.9	52.9	39.2	59.1	26.4	71.2	56.3	41.6	48.7	81.0	79.0
September	46.6	42.5	52.7	38.1	59.4	25.8	70.5	56.1	41.9	48.4	80.2	78.1
October	45.6	41.6	52.0	35.9	59.8	25.0	69.5	55.6	41.8	47.1	78.4	76.1
November	45.4	41.3	51.7	36.0	59.2	24.8	69.0	54.9	41.8	46.8	77.6	75.4
December	46.4	42.4	53.9	40.2	60.1	25.1	68.2	55.5	41.9	47.9	79.2	77.1
1971												
January	46.8	42.8	54.7	41.8	60.4	24.6	68.7	55.5	42.1	48.6	79.6	77.6
February	46.7	42.8	54.7	42.7	59.8	24.7	67.1	55.9	42.5	48.3	79.2	77.4
March	46.6	42.7	54.8	42.7	60.0	24.5	66.5	55.7	42.1	48.4	78.9	77.0
April	46.9	42.9	55.3	43.0	60.6	24.3	66.6	56.2	42.6	48.7	79.2	77.2
May	47.1	43.2	55.3	43.7	60.3	24.2	67.4	56.5	42.7	49.3	79.4	77.6
June	47.3	43.3	55.7	44.0	60.7	24.3	66.4	57.1	42.5	49.5	79.5	77.5
July	47.2	43.4	56.6	44.9	61.6	24.3	65.9	57.6	43.6	48.3	79.0	77.5
August	46.9	42.9	55.9	44.4	60.8	24.7	65.9	56.6	43.1	48.0	78.4	76.4
September	47.7	43.7	56.5	44.3	61.7	25.3	65.2	58.7	43.8	48.9	79.5	77.7
October	48.0	44.4	57.2	45.2	62.4	25.5	64.8	59.5	44.0	49.1	79.8	78.7
November	48.2	44.5	57.7	45.6	62.8	25.6	64.3	59.7	44.5	49.2	80.0	78.7
December	48.8	45.0	58.1	45.8	63.3	25.8	63.3	60.7	44.7	50.2	80.7	79.3
1972												
January	50.0	46.1	59.0	47.2	63.9	26.6	63.2	62.4	45.5	51.7	82.4	81.1
February	50.5	46.5	59.4	47.5	64.4	27.0	63.5	62.7	46.3	52.3	83.1	81.6
March	50.9	46.9	59.4	47.2	64.6	27.3	64.1	63.3	46.8	52.8	83.5	82.0
April	51.4	47.4	60.1	48.6	64.8	27.8	64.3	63.9	46.8	53.3	84.1	82.7
May	51.4	47.4	59.8	48.1	64.6	27.8	63.7	64.4	47.0	53.4	84.0	82.6
June	51.5	47.6	59.7	48.1	64.6	28.0	63.6	64.7	47.5	53.5	83.9	82.7
July	51.5	47.6	60.2	49.1	64.7	28.0	63.7	65.6	47.4	53.1	83.7	82.5
August	52.1	48.2	60.8	49.3	65.4	28.5	63.4	65.8	48.0	53.9	84.5	83.2
September	52.4	48.5	61.0	49.8	65.5	28.8	63.9	66.2	47.9	54.4	84.9	83.6
October	53.1	49.2	61.9	51.0	66.2	29.3	64.1	67.3	48.7	54.9	85.7	84.5
November	53.7	49.8	62.3	52.1	66.1	29.8	65.9	68.1	48.9	55.8	86.5	85.4
December	54.5	50.6	63.0	53.5	66.4	30.2	66.9	68.2	49.2	56.7	87.5	86.5
1973												
January	54.9	51.0	63.0	53.3	66.4	30.8	68.1	69.2	49.5	57.3	87.9	87.0
February	55.7	51.8	63.7	54.2	67.0	31.5	69.4	70.3	50.0	58.1	88.9	88.1
March	55.8	52.0	63.9	54.3	67.3	31.7	69.0	70.6	50.1	58.0	88.7	88.0
April	55.6	51.8	63.2	53.3	66.8	31.8	68.3	70.2	50.0	58.0	88.1	87.4
May	56.0	52.1	63.6	53.2	67.5	32.3	68.6	70.5	50.3	58.4	88.4	87.7
June	56.0	52.1	63.1	53.1	66.8	32.7	69.1	70.7	50.5	58.5	88.2	87.4
July	56.2	52.3	63.0	53.1	66.7	33.0	70.6	71.2	50.6	58.7	88.2	87.4
August	56.1	52.2	62.4	51.3	66.8	33.1	70.8	71.1	50.7	58.7	87.8	86.9
September	56.5	52.6	63.4	53.0	67.3	33.6	70.7	70.6	50.6	59.0	88.2	87.3
October	56.9	53.0	63.6	52.6	67.7	33.9	71.9	71.1	51.1	59.4	88.5	87.6
November	57.1	53.3	63.7	52.6	68.0	34.1	71.3	71.4	51.0	59.8	88.5	87.9
December	57.0	53.3	62.5	51.4	66.9	34.2	70.7	71.9	50.7	60.1	88.0	87.7
1974												
January	56.7	53.0	61.8	48.9	67.3	34.2	70.7	72.7	50.8	59.6	87.3	86.8
February	56.5	52.8	61.6	48.9	67.0	34.1	71.3	71.1	50.5	59.6	86.7	86.2
March	56.6	52.8	61.8	49.0	67.2	34.5	71.2	71.5	50.7	59.4	86.6	86.0
April	56.5	52.7	61.7	48.8	67.1	34.4	71.4	71.1	50.8	59.4	86.4	85.6
May	56.8	53.0	62.1	48.8	67.9	34.8	71.3	71.3	50.9	59.7	86.6	85.8
June	56.8	53.0	62.4	49.5	67.8	34.8	70.2	70.9	51.3	59.4	86.3	85.6
July	56.7	52.8	62.2	49.0	67.8	34.6	71.1	69.3	50.8	59.6	85.9	85.1
August	56.2	52.4	62.1	49.1	67.7	34.6	73.0	68.6	50.7	58.6	84.9	84.2
September	56.2	52.4	61.6	48.9	67.0	35.1	73.1	68.3	50.4	58.7	84.8	84.0
October	55.9	52.0	61.6	48.3	67.3	35.0	74.1	66.8	50.1	58.4	84.2	83.1
November	54.1	50.5	59.9	46.1	65.9	34.4	73.7	65.0	49.0	55.9	81.3	80.5
December	52.2	48.2	58.0	42.2	65.2	33.0	72.9	61.7	48.0	53.7	78.3	76.7
1975												
January	51.6	47.4	56.8	40.6	64.4	32.4	73.9	61.5	47.3	53.4	77.3	75.3
February	50.5	46.1	56.2	39.6	64.0	31.3	70.4	60.0	46.4	52.1	75.4	73.1
March	49.9	45.5	56.4	40.3	63.9	30.7	70.9	58.1	45.8	51.4	74.5	72.0
April	49.9	45.3	57.5	41.6	64.9	30.3	70.4	57.3	45.9	50.9	74.3	71.6
May	49.8	45.3	57.7	42.5	64.6	30.1	73.9	56.8	45.6	50.7	74.0	71.5
June	50.1	45.7	58.5	42.9	65.6	29.9	74.8	56.7	45.7	51.1	74.4	72.0
July	50.6	46.4	59.9	45.0	66.6	30.0	74.3	57.5	46.2	51.3	75.0	72.9
August	51.0	46.7	60.2	45.6	66.7	29.8	73.6	58.1	46.5	52.0	75.5	73.4
September	51.6	47.5	60.9	46.4	67.4	30.2	75.6	58.8	46.6	52.6	76.2	74.4
October	51.7	47.6	60.9	46.2	67.5	30.1	74.7	59.3	46.7	52.9	76.2	74.4
November	51.9	47.7	61.2	46.3	67.8	30.1	71.8	59.1	46.8	53.1	76.3	74.4
December	52.6	48.4	61.8	47.2	68.2	30.6	74.1	58.8	47.3	54.0	77.2	75.4

Table 20-1. Industrial Production and Capacity Utilization—Continued

(Seasonally adjusted.)

| Year and month | Total industry | Manufac- turing (SIC) | Market groups ||||||||| Capacity utilization (output as percentage of capacity) ||
| | | | Consumer goods ||| Business equipment | Defense and space equipment | Construction supplies | Business supplies | Materials | Total industry | Manufac- turing (SIC) |
			Total	Durable	Nondurable							
1976												
January	53.3	49.0	62.7	48.0	69.2	30.9	74.4	60.5	47.8	54.8	78.1	76.2
February	54.0	49.9	63.0	48.7	69.3	31.1	74.5	61.7	48.1	55.8	78.9	77.3
March	54.0	49.9	62.7	48.6	68.8	31.2	74.2	61.2	48.3	56.0	78.8	77.2
April	54.4	50.3	62.9	48.7	69.1	31.7	73.1	62.1	48.6	56.4	79.2	77.7
May	54.6	50.6	63.5	48.7	70.0	31.9	72.0	62.8	48.8	56.4	79.3	77.9
June	54.6	50.6	63.2	48.5	69.7	32.0	71.1	63.2	48.6	56.6	79.1	77.7
July	54.9	50.9	63.6	48.6	70.2	32.3	69.1	64.3	49.3	56.7	79.4	78.1
August	55.2	51.2	63.8	49.4	70.1	32.8	69.1	63.8	49.4	57.2	79.7	78.3
September	55.3	51.3	63.8	48.9	70.3	32.6	68.7	64.0	50.4	57.2	79.7	78.2
October	55.4	51.3	64.3	49.7	70.7	32.9	68.9	64.0	50.7	57.0	79.6	78.1
November	56.2	52.0	65.4	51.3	71.5	33.9	68.3	64.5	50.9	57.7	80.6	78.9
December	56.9	52.6	66.2	52.7	71.8	34.4	67.3	64.7	51.5	58.5	81.4	79.7
1977												
January	56.6	52.5	66.1	52.6	71.7	34.6	66.5	63.7	51.4	58.0	80.8	79.3
February	57.4	53.4	66.8	53.1	72.6	35.3	66.2	64.9	51.7	58.8	81.7	80.4
March	58.2	54.2	66.9	54.5	71.8	35.8	64.6	66.8	52.3	60.0	82.6	81.5
April	58.7	54.8	67.4	55.0	72.3	36.3	65.1	68.2	52.9	60.5	83.2	82.2
May	59.1	55.2	67.3	55.1	72.2	36.9	64.9	69.4	53.4	61.0	83.6	82.6
June	59.5	55.6	67.8	56.1	72.2	37.6	64.7	69.9	53.9	61.2	83.9	83.0
July	59.7	55.7	68.0	56.2	72.6	38.2	64.5	70.0	54.1	61.2	84.0	82.9
August	59.7	56.0	68.0	56.0	72.7	38.4	63.7	70.5	54.4	61.1	83.8	83.1
September	60.0	56.0	68.0	56.3	72.5	38.7	63.7	69.9	54.4	61.5	83.9	83.0
October	60.1	56.2	68.5	56.2	73.4	38.8	58.3	70.0	54.4	61.7	83.9	83.0
November	60.1	56.2	68.5	56.2	73.4	38.8	57.4	70.3	54.4	61.8	83.7	82.8
December	60.3	56.9	69.1	56.6	74.1	39.5	61.5	70.9	54.9	61.2	83.6	83.6
1978												
January	59.6	56.2	67.6	53.8	73.5	38.8	62.4	70.2	54.8	60.7	82.5	82.3
February	59.7	56.3	68.6	54.9	74.3	39.6	58.9	69.8	54.9	60.5	82.5	82.2
March	60.9	57.3	70.0	56.6	75.4	40.6	64.1	70.9	55.7	61.4	83.8	83.5
April	62.1	58.1	70.5	57.7	75.6	41.3	63.6	72.1	55.8	63.3	85.2	84.5
May	62.4	58.4	70.0	56.9	75.3	41.5	63.9	72.4	56.1	64.0	85.4	84.6
June	62.8	58.8	70.4	57.3	75.8	42.1	64.6	72.9	56.7	64.3	85.8	85.1
July	62.8	58.8	70.2	57.4	75.2	42.4	64.5	73.0	56.7	64.3	85.5	84.8
August	63.0	59.0	70.1	57.0	75.4	42.9	65.1	73.0	56.8	64.5	85.5	84.9
September	63.1	59.3	70.2	56.6	75.7	43.4	65.1	73.3	56.8	64.5	85.5	85.0
October	63.6	59.7	69.9	56.7	75.2	44.2	64.9	73.9	57.1	65.2	85.9	85.3
November	64.0	60.2	70.1	56.9	75.4	45.0	64.5	74.7	57.3	65.7	86.3	85.8
December	64.4	60.7	70.3	57.0	75.6	45.7	65.3	75.7	57.8	66.0	86.6	86.3
1979												
January	64.1	60.3	70.3	57.6	75.3	46.2	65.8	74.7	58.0	65.1	85.9	85.5
February	64.4	60.5	69.7	56.9	74.9	46.9	67.1	74.8	58.4	65.7	86.2	85.6
March	64.6	60.8	70.0	56.7	75.4	47.2	66.6	75.0	58.6	65.9	86.3	85.7
April	64.1	60.1	68.9	54.1	75.1	46.5	65.4	74.1	58.5	65.6	85.3	84.4
May	64.5	60.7	69.3	55.5	75.0	47.6	66.3	74.2	58.6	65.9	85.7	85.1
June	64.5	60.8	69.0	55.0	74.8	47.9	66.9	74.7	58.3	65.9	85.5	85.0
July	64.3	60.8	68.3	54.2	74.3	48.2	68.2	74.9	58.3	65.6	85.1	84.7
August	63.9	60.0	67.8	51.9	74.7	47.5	69.2	73.9	58.6	65.2	84.3	83.4
September	63.9	60.1	68.0	53.7	74.1	48.8	69.7	73.9	57.8	64.8	84.2	83.3
October	64.2	60.2	68.1	53.3	74.3	48.0	71.7	74.3	58.3	65.3	84.4	83.2
November	64.1	60.0	67.9	52.5	74.6	47.9	73.3	74.0	58.5	65.2	84.1	82.8
December	64.2	60.2	68.0	52.3	74.8	48.2	74.8	74.7	58.6	65.1	84.0	82.8
1980												
January	64.5	60.5	67.8	51.3	75.1	48.9	76.1	74.8	58.3	65.7	84.3	83.1
February	64.6	60.5	68.0	51.0	75.5	49.3	79.1	73.9	58.3	65.5	84.2	82.9
March	64.4	60.0	67.7	50.4	75.4	48.9	80.1	72.6	58.1	65.5	83.8	82.1
April	63.1	58.9	66.6	48.2	75.0	48.5	81.0	68.9	57.1	63.9	82.0	80.3
May	61.6	57.1	65.2	45.2	74.5	47.7	81.1	66.4	56.0	62.1	79.9	77.7
June	60.8	56.2	64.9	44.7	74.4	47.1	81.8	65.1	55.4	60.9	78.7	76.3
July	60.4	55.7	65.0	44.5	74.6	47.1	82.8	64.6	55.7	60.1	78.1	75.5
August	60.5	56.1	65.3	44.9	74.8	47.0	82.9	65.4	55.9	60.2	78.1	75.7
September	61.5	57.0	65.8	46.9	74.5	47.7	82.9	67.2	56.7	61.4	79.3	76.8
October	62.2	57.8	66.2	47.7	74.7	48.3	83.8	68.2	56.7	62.2	79.9	77.7
November	63.2	58.9	66.6	48.9	74.6	49.1	85.1	69.5	57.4	63.6	81.1	79.0
December	63.6	59.1	66.5	48.1	74.9	49.2	85.1	69.2	58.1	64.3	81.5	79.0
1981												
January	63.2	58.8	66.5	47.9	75.0	49.5	84.6	68.9	58.2	63.5	80.8	78.5
February	63.0	58.6	66.4	47.9	74.8	49.2	84.4	68.8	57.7	63.3	80.4	78.0
March	63.4	58.8	66.4	48.5	74.5	49.5	84.8	69.1	57.6	63.7	80.6	78.0
April	63.1	59.2	66.6	49.2	74.5	50.0	85.2	69.4	58.0	62.8	80.1	78.3
May	63.5	59.5	67.3	49.9	75.1	50.1	86.1	69.4	58.7	63.2	80.4	78.5
June	63.9	59.3	66.8	49.5	74.6	50.0	86.9	68.3	58.9	64.1	80.7	78.0
July	64.3	59.4	67.3	49.8	75.1	50.1	87.9	68.4	59.3	64.6	81.1	78.0
August	64.2	59.4	67.4	49.4	75.5	50.0	88.8	68.2	58.8	64.5	80.8	77.8
September	63.8	59.1	66.7	48.1	75.2	49.8	90.4	67.5	58.8	64.0	80.0	77.1
October	63.3	58.4	67.0	47.8	75.8	49.5	92.6	65.7	58.4	63.1	79.2	76.1
November	62.6	57.7	66.9	47.1	76.0	48.7	95.1	64.7	58.1	62.0	78.1	75.1
December	61.9	56.7	66.1	45.0	76.1	47.9	97.6	63.2	58.0	61.3	77.1	73.6

Table 20-1. Industrial Production and Capacity Utilization—Continued

(Seasonally adjusted.)

Year and month	Total industry	Manufac-turing (SIC)	Market groups								Capacity utilization (output as percentage of capacity)	
			Consumer goods			Business equipment	Defense and space equipment	Construction supplies	Business supplies	Materials	Total industry	Manufac-turing (SIC)
			Total	Durable	Nondurable							
1982												
January	60.8	55.5	65.3	43.9	75.5	46.4	97.1	61.5	57.4	60.1	75.5	71.9
February	62.0	57.0	67.0	45.5	77.1	47.8	102.6	63.7	58.5	60.9	76.8	73.7
March	61.6	56.6	66.6	45.3	76.7	47.2	104.3	62.1	58.3	60.5	76.1	73.0
April	61.0	56.3	66.6	46.3	76.1	46.9	105.6	62.1	58.1	59.7	75.3	72.4
May	60.6	56.1	66.6	46.2	76.1	46.7	107.0	62.1	57.6	59.0	74.7	72.1
June	60.4	56.1	66.9	46.5	76.5	45.9	107.1	61.5	57.6	58.8	74.3	71.9
July	60.2	56.0	67.1	46.8	76.5	45.7	108.2	61.1	57.6	58.4	73.9	71.6
August	59.7	55.5	66.9	46.1	76.7	44.6	107.5	61.2	57.6	57.8	73.1	70.9
September	59.4	55.2	66.7	45.4	76.7	44.2	108.9	61.3	57.6	57.4	72.6	70.4
October	58.9	54.6	66.8	44.9	77.2	43.2	109.0	60.4	57.4	56.8	71.9	69.5
November	58.6	54.3	66.7	44.9	76.9	42.8	109.1	60.4	57.4	56.5	71.5	69.0
December	58.2	54.0	65.7	44.9	75.5	43.0	108.4	59.7	57.1	56.1	70.9	68.7
1983												
January	59.2	55.4	67.1	46.8	76.5	43.1	107.1	62.0	57.8	57.2	72.1	70.3
February	58.9	55.3	66.4	46.7	75.5	43.0	105.3	61.3	57.9	57.1	71.7	70.1
March	59.4	55.8	66.6	47.3	75.4	43.4	105.8	62.7	58.6	57.6	72.2	70.8
April	60.2	56.5	68.1	48.3	77.2	43.6	105.0	63.4	59.3	58.3	73.1	71.6
May	60.6	57.3	68.4	49.1	77.1	44.1	105.3	64.6	59.5	58.8	73.6	72.5
June	61.0	57.7	68.7	50.0	77.2	44.5	104.9	65.5	59.8	59.2	74.0	73.1
July	61.9	58.5	69.6	51.0	78.0	45.3	106.2	67.0	60.5	60.2	75.1	74.1
August	62.6	58.9	70.2	51.9	78.5	45.7	106.3	67.2	61.3	61.0	75.9	74.5
September	63.5	60.0	71.0	52.9	79.1	47.1	107.7	67.8	62.3	61.8	77.0	75.9
October	64.0	60.7	70.5	53.5	78.0	47.6	109.5	69.1	62.4	62.7	77.5	76.6
November	64.2	60.9	70.5	53.4	78.0	47.9	109.9	68.9	62.7	63.0	77.7	76.8
December	64.6	61.1	70.6	54.7	77.6	48.4	111.2	69.1	63.0	63.4	78.1	76.9
1984												
January	65.9	62.2	72.1	56.0	79.1	49.6	113.9	69.7	64.1	64.6	79.6	78.3
February	66.1	62.8	71.7	56.0	78.5	50.1	116.2	71.0	64.0	65.0	79.7	78.9
March	66.6	63.3	72.2	56.3	79.0	50.7	117.1	71.0	64.9	65.3	80.2	79.3
April	67.0	63.6	72.4	56.1	79.4	51.2	119.7	71.2	64.8	65.7	80.5	79.6
May	67.4	63.8	72.1	55.6	79.4	51.6	120.7	71.4	65.8	66.2	80.9	79.7
June	67.6	64.2	72.0	55.9	79.1	52.3	122.3	72.2	66.0	66.4	81.0	79.9
July	67.8	64.5	72.1	56.5	78.8	53.1	120.6	71.8	66.4	66.6	81.1	80.1
August	67.9	64.6	71.8	56.9	78.2	53.7	124.7	72.0	66.4	66.5	81.1	80.0
September	67.7	64.4	71.6	56.1	78.3	53.9	127.5	72.1	66.2	66.2	80.7	79.6
October	67.6	64.6	72.0	55.6	79.2	54.1	128.3	72.0	66.6	65.6	80.4	79.6
November	67.8	64.8	72.2	56.4	79.0	54.7	127.4	71.6	66.9	65.8	80.5	79.6
December	67.9	65.0	72.6	57.1	79.3	54.9	129.5	72.7	66.4	65.7	80.4	79.7
1985												
January	67.7	64.7	72.1	56.0	79.1	54.6	129.7	71.2	66.5	65.7	80.0	79.1
February	68.1	64.6	72.6	55.9	80.0	54.4	131.0	71.5	67.2	66.0	80.2	78.8
March	68.1	65.1	72.5	56.4	79.6	54.9	133.6	73.0	67.0	65.8	80.1	79.1
April	68.1	65.0	72.2	55.7	79.5	54.5	134.5	73.2	67.4	65.9	79.9	78.8
May	68.2	65.1	72.3	55.8	79.4	54.7	135.2	73.9	67.7	65.9	79.8	78.7
June	68.2	65.2	72.5	55.7	79.9	54.9	137.3	74.0	67.3	65.8	79.6	78.6
July	67.7	64.8	72.3	55.9	79.5	54.4	136.1	73.9	66.9	65.3	79.0	78.0
August	68.1	65.2	72.6	56.2	79.8	54.6	138.6	73.9	67.5	65.5	79.2	78.3
September	68.4	65.3	73.1	56.2	80.5	54.4	139.5	73.9	68.0	65.8	79.3	78.2
October	68.0	65.0	72.9	55.8	80.4	54.3	141.1	73.9	67.4	65.4	78.8	77.8
November	68.2	65.4	73.1	57.2	80.0	54.8	142.8	74.0	67.6	65.4	78.9	78.1
December	68.9	65.6	73.9	57.2	81.2	54.7	143.7	73.9	68.5	66.3	79.5	78.2
1986												
January	69.3	66.4	74.8	58.8	81.7	54.8	144.4	75.5	69.0	66.5	79.9	79.0
February	68.8	66.1	74.2	58.5	81.0	54.3	142.6	74.9	68.4	66.2	79.2	78.5
March	68.3	65.8	73.9	58.4	80.6	54.3	144.1	74.9	68.1	65.4	78.6	78.1
April	68.4	66.1	74.3	58.1	81.3	53.9	144.3	75.3	68.6	65.4	78.5	78.3
May	68.5	66.2	74.6	58.2	81.8	53.8	145.0	75.8	69.2	65.4	78.6	78.4
June	68.3	66.0	74.8	58.8	81.8	53.3	145.5	74.9	69.8	65.0	78.3	78.0
July	68.7	66.4	75.2	59.4	82.0	53.7	147.3	75.5	69.9	65.4	78.6	78.3
August	68.6	66.5	75.2	59.5	82.0	53.7	146.6	76.3	69.8	65.2	78.4	78.4
September	68.7	66.7	75.3	60.0	81.8	53.7	146.1	76.5	70.1	65.3	78.4	78.5
October	69.0	66.9	75.5	60.2	82.1	53.4	146.1	76.3	70.6	65.8	78.6	78.6
November	69.3	67.2	76.1	61.1	82.5	53.5	147.2	77.2	70.6	66.1	78.9	78.8
December	70.0	67.8	76.7	62.2	82.9	54.1	147.1	77.3	71.6	66.7	79.5	79.4
1987												
January	69.6	67.4	75.7	61.4	81.8	54.3	147.5	77.3	71.0	66.4	78.9	78.8
February	70.6	68.5	76.8	62.4	82.9	55.7	148.5	78.5	71.6	67.3	79.9	79.9
March	70.7	68.6	77.1	62.3	83.3	55.3	148.5	78.8	72.0	67.5	79.9	79.9
April	71.2	69.0	77.1	61.9	83.6	55.7	149.0	79.5	72.8	68.1	80.3	80.2
May	71.6	69.5	77.5	62.3	84.0	56.1	148.5	79.9	73.6	68.4	80.7	80.5
June	72.0	69.9	77.9	61.9	84.8	56.7	147.8	80.5	74.1	68.9	81.0	80.8
July	72.5	70.4	78.3	61.6	85.5	57.1	146.9	80.8	74.5	69.4	81.4	81.2
August	73.0	70.7	78.9	62.2	86.1	57.9	148.0	81.1	74.7	69.8	81.8	81.4
September	73.1	71.0	78.5	62.7	85.2	58.5	148.5	81.8	74.8	70.0	81.9	81.7
October	74.1	72.1	79.7	64.6	86.1	59.7	148.1	82.6	75.5	71.0	82.9	82.8
November	74.5	72.5	79.9	64.7	86.3	60.0	149.0	82.9	75.4	71.6	83.2	83.2
December	74.8	72.8	79.8	64.1	86.6	60.6	149.8	82.8	75.6	72.0	83.5	83.5

Table 20-1. Industrial Production and Capacity Utilization—Continued

(Seasonally adjusted.)

Year and month	Total industry	Manufac- turing (SIC)	Market groups								Capacity utilization (output as percentage of capacity)	
			Consumer goods			Business equipment	Defense and space equipment	Construction supplies	Business supplies	Materials	Total industry	Manufac- turing (SIC)
			Total	Durable	Nondurable							
1988												
January	74.8	72.7	80.3	64.0	87.2	60.7	152.7	81.7	76.0	71.7	83.4	83.2
February	75.2	72.9	80.8	64.0	88.1	60.8	150.5	82.3	76.5	72.1	83.8	83.4
March	75.4	73.1	80.8	64.8	87.6	61.2	149.3	82.9	76.4	72.3	83.9	83.6
April	75.7	73.6	81.1	66.1	87.5	61.9	147.6	82.5	76.3	72.7	84.2	84.1
May	75.7	73.6	80.9	66.2	87.1	62.2	147.7	82.7	75.7	72.8	84.1	84.0
June	75.8	73.6	80.9	66.6	86.9	62.5	146.5	81.9	76.0	73.0	84.2	84.0
July	75.9	73.8	81.0	65.0	87.8	62.1	147.6	82.1	76.6	73.3	84.3	84.1
August	76.3	73.9	81.6	65.7	88.4	62.5	146.7	82.0	77.4	73.6	84.7	84.1
September	76.1	74.1	81.1	67.1	87.0	63.1	147.1	81.8	76.7	73.3	84.3	84.3
October	76.5	74.5	81.7	67.6	87.7	63.7	147.9	82.5	77.0	73.5	84.7	84.7
November	76.6	74.7	81.7	68.2	87.3	64.1	147.6	82.6	77.1	73.7	84.8	84.8
December	77.0	75.1	82.1	69.1	87.4	64.1	148.5	83.0	77.4	74.1	85.0	85.1
1989												
January	77.2	75.6	82.1	70.4	86.9	64.8	148.2	84.5	77.4	74.2	85.2	85.6
February	76.8	74.9	82.0	69.6	87.1	64.7	148.3	82.3	77.6	73.6	84.6	84.6
March	77.0	74.8	82.3	68.6	88.0	64.2	147.4	82.4	78.5	74.0	84.7	84.4
April	77.0	74.9	82.2	69.1	87.6	64.8	149.5	81.9	77.8	73.9	84.5	84.2
May	76.5	74.3	81.4	67.7	87.1	63.6	150.4	81.9	77.5	73.7	83.8	83.4
June	76.5	74.4	81.3	66.9	87.3	64.5	150.4	82.2	77.8	73.4	83.7	83.3
July	75.8	73.5	79.6	64.6	85.9	63.8	150.5	81.5	77.1	73.0	82.7	82.2
August	76.5	74.2	80.9	66.8	86.8	64.8	151.0	81.3	77.4	73.4	83.3	82.7
September	76.2	73.9	80.7	67.3	86.2	64.4	150.1	81.7	77.6	73.1	82.8	82.3
October	76.1	73.8	81.0	66.1	87.2	63.7	145.1	81.3	77.5	73.2	82.6	82.0
November	76.3	73.9	81.0	66.2	87.2	64.2	143.0	81.3	77.9	73.4	82.6	81.8
December	76.8	74.0	82.6	67.1	89.1	65.5	146.0	80.6	78.3	73.2	83.0	81.8
1990												
January	76.5	74.0	81.0	63.7	88.3	64.7	146.1	82.5	79.0	73.1	82.4	81.6
February	77.1	75.0	81.8	67.5	87.7	65.6	145.9	83.1	78.9	73.8	83.0	82.5
March	77.4	75.3	82.4	68.7	88.1	66.1	145.1	82.2	79.4	74.0	83.1	82.6
April	77.4	75.2	82.2	67.4	88.4	66.0	144.6	82.0	79.3	74.2	83.0	82.4
May	77.5	75.2	82.0	67.8	88.0	66.6	143.0	81.2	79.8	74.3	82.9	82.2
June	77.7	75.4	82.9	68.8	88.8	66.8	142.5	81.7	79.6	74.3	83.0	82.3
July	77.6	75.3	82.3	67.1	88.7	66.8	142.9	81.0	80.1	74.3	82.7	81.9
August	77.8	75.5	82.4	66.9	88.9	67.0	141.4	80.9	80.0	74.7	82.8	82.0
September	78.0	75.4	83.2	67.4	89.9	66.9	140.4	80.3	80.1	74.6	82.8	81.8
October	77.4	74.9	81.9	65.3	89.0	66.5	141.0	80.1	80.0	74.4	82.1	81.0
November	76.5	74.0	81.1	62.0	89.3	65.0	138.6	79.4	79.6	73.5	81.0	79.9
December	76.0	73.5	80.6	61.0	89.0	64.8	139.6	79.2	79.2	72.7	80.3	79.2
1991												
January	75.7	72.9	81.1	61.4	89.6	64.0	137.9	76.8	78.8	72.4	79.8	78.5
February	75.1	72.5	80.3	59.9	89.1	63.6	136.7	76.0	78.1	72.1	79.1	77.9
March	74.7	71.9	80.3	59.9	89.1	63.8	136.0	75.0	77.1	71.4	78.6	77.2
April	74.9	72.2	80.3	60.9	88.6	63.9	132.3	75.5	77.7	71.7	78.6	77.3
May	75.7	72.7	81.7	62.4	90.1	64.3	129.8	75.9	78.3	72.4	79.3	77.8
June	76.4	73.5	82.9	63.9	91.1	65.2	130.6	76.8	78.9	72.9	80.0	78.5
July	76.4	73.7	82.5	64.9	90.0	65.1	128.9	77.0	78.4	73.4	79.8	78.5
August	76.4	73.8	82.5	64.1	90.3	64.8	130.4	77.5	78.8	73.4	79.8	78.5
September	77.1	74.6	83.6	66.6	90.9	65.6	129.8	77.7	79.2	73.9	80.3	79.2
October	76.9	74.5	83.4	66.4	90.6	65.2	130.1	76.7	78.9	74.0	80.0	78.9
November	76.8	74.3	83.5	66.6	90.6	64.9	129.1	77.5	78.9	73.7	79.8	78.6
December	76.6	74.2	82.5	65.9	89.5	65.2	127.8	77.2	79.0	73.7	79.4	78.4
1992												
January	76.1	73.8	81.6	63.4	89.4	63.9	126.0	77.5	78.8	73.7	78.8	77.8
February	76.8	74.5	82.6	66.0	89.6	65.6	125.7	78.6	79.0	74.0	79.4	78.5
March	77.4	75.2	83.3	67.3	90.1	65.9	125.1	79.0	79.4	74.6	79.9	79.0
April	77.9	75.6	84.1	68.6	90.6	66.6	123.3	79.7	80.0	75.1	80.3	79.3
May	78.2	76.1	84.5	70.7	90.2	67.3	122.7	80.0	80.2	75.3	80.4	79.6
June	78.1	76.2	84.0	69.7	90.0	67.4	122.5	79.9	80.0	75.5	80.3	79.6
July	78.7	76.8	85.0	71.5	90.7	67.9	120.5	80.2	80.6	76.0	80.8	80.1
August	78.5	76.6	85.2	71.0	91.2	67.8	120.6	80.6	80.6	75.3	80.4	79.7
September	78.6	76.6	84.8	70.6	90.7	67.8	120.6	80.4	80.7	75.7	80.3	79.5
October	79.2	77.0	85.9	71.9	91.7	68.1	120.2	80.7	81.2	76.2	80.8	79.8
November	79.6	77.4	86.2	72.7	91.9	68.6	120.2	80.5	81.6	76.6	81.1	80.1
December	79.6	77.3	86.2	73.5	91.5	68.8	120.0	80.8	81.8	76.5	80.9	79.8
1993												
January	79.9	78.0	86.5	74.8	91.4	69.3	119.1	81.2	81.8	76.8	81.1	80.3
February	80.2	78.1	86.8	74.4	91.9	69.1	118.5	81.6	82.3	77.3	81.3	80.3
March	80.3	78.1	86.9	75.1	91.9	69.3	116.9	81.7	83.0	77.2	81.3	80.2
April	80.5	78.5	87.2	75.8	91.9	69.7	117.1	82.1	82.9	77.4	81.3	80.4
May	80.2	78.4	86.5	76.1	90.7	69.9	116.0	83.1	82.6	77.2	80.9	80.2
June	80.4	78.3	86.7	75.7	91.3	69.1	115.0	82.8	82.6	77.6	80.9	79.9
July	80.7	78.6	87.7	76.0	92.5	69.0	115.6	83.6	82.9	77.6	81.1	80.0
August	80.6	78.4	87.6	75.3	92.7	68.6	113.8	83.3	82.8	77.7	80.9	79.6
September	81.0	79.0	87.9	76.9	92.4	69.5	114.4	84.1	83.2	78.0	81.2	80.1
October	81.6	79.5	88.2	79.0	92.0	70.6	114.1	84.9	83.2	78.6	81.6	80.5
November	81.9	79.9	88.4	79.7	91.9	70.8	113.7	85.5	83.2	79.3	81.8	80.7
December	82.4	80.5	88.7	80.4	92.2	71.0	112.7	86.9	83.9	79.9	82.1	81.0

Table 20-1. Industrial Production and Capacity Utilization—Continued

(Seasonally adjusted.)

Year and month	Total industry	Manufacturing (SIC)	Market groups								Capacity utilization (output as percentage of capacity)	
			Consumer goods			Business equipment	Defense and space equipment	Construction supplies	Business supplies	Materials	Total industry	Manufacturing (SIC)
			Total	Durable	Nondurable							
1994												
January	82.9	80.7	89.7	82.0	92.8	71.3	111.3	86.6	84.6	80.1	82.4	81.1
February	82.9	80.9	89.9	82.1	93.1	70.9	109.6	86.0	84.8	80.4	82.3	81.0
March	83.7	81.8	90.4	82.9	93.6	71.6	110.6	87.7	85.3	81.2	82.8	81.8
April	84.1	82.4	90.5	83.8	93.3	72.3	110.6	88.6	85.4	81.7	83.0	82.2
May	84.6	83.0	91.3	84.4	94.1	72.7	109.5	89.1	85.7	82.3	83.3	82.5
June	85.2	83.3	92.0	85.3	94.8	73.2	108.3	89.2	86.4	82.8	83.6	82.5
July	85.3	83.6	91.6	85.5	94.0	74.0	107.4	90.2	86.2	83.2	83.5	82.6
August	85.8	84.3	92.6	87.0	94.8	73.9	106.1	90.2	86.3	83.8	83.7	82.9
September	85.9	84.5	92.0	87.2	94.0	74.2	107.2	90.7	86.6	84.1	83.6	82.8
October	86.6	85.3	92.9	88.0	94.9	75.1	107.8	91.2	87.2	84.7	84.0	83.3
November	87.2	85.9	93.0	87.7	95.1	75.8	109.0	91.6	87.6	85.5	84.2	83.6
December	88.1	87.0	93.7	88.7	95.7	76.6	109.4	92.5	88.3	86.7	84.8	84.3
1995												
January	88.5	87.4	93.8	89.7	95.4	77.3	109.3	92.8	88.6	87.2	84.8	84.3
February	88.5	87.3	94.1	89.5	96.0	77.5	107.7	91.8	88.6	87.2	84.5	83.9
March	88.5	87.4	93.8	89.3	95.7	78.0	107.8	91.4	88.9	87.2	84.2	83.6
April	88.5	87.3	93.6	89.0	95.5	77.9	107.6	90.4	89.0	87.4	83.8	83.1
May	88.7	87.3	93.9	88.1	96.3	78.0	107.1	90.0	89.3	87.5	83.7	82.8
June	89.0	87.7	94.4	88.8	96.7	78.7	107.8	90.3	89.7	87.6	83.6	82.7
July	88.6	87.1	93.9	87.2	96.6	78.4	106.2	89.9	89.7	87.2	82.8	81.8
August	89.8	88.2	95.4	90.2	97.5	80.2	105.9	90.3	90.7	88.2	83.6	82.3
September	90.2	89.0	95.6	91.6	97.2	81.4	105.1	91.9	90.7	88.6	83.6	82.7
October	90.0	88.8	94.8	90.6	96.4	80.9	104.2	91.8	90.7	88.8	83.0	82.1
November	90.3	89.0	95.2	90.8	96.9	81.4	101.7	92.2	91.4	89.0	82.9	81.8
December	90.7	89.4	95.5	91.3	97.2	82.7	101.2	93.3	91.4	89.3	82.9	81.7
1996												
January	90.1	88.7	94.5	88.7	96.8	82.1	100.2	91.5	91.0	88.9	81.9	80.6
February	91.3	89.8	95.8	90.9	97.8	83.9	102.3	92.5	91.9	89.9	82.6	81.1
March	91.1	89.5	95.2	87.9	98.1	83.2	102.5	93.3	91.8	89.9	82.0	80.4
April	91.9	90.5	96.2	92.7	97.7	84.3	102.2	93.8	91.6	90.8	82.3	80.8
May	92.5	91.2	96.3	93.6	97.5	85.1	102.2	94.8	92.5	91.7	82.5	81.0
June	93.4	92.2	97.2	95.6	97.9	86.3	101.6	96.1	92.9	92.5	82.8	81.4
July	93.2	92.5	96.5	95.8	96.8	87.2	101.8	95.8	92.9	92.5	82.3	81.2
August	93.9	93.1	96.4	95.4	96.9	88.5	102.8	97.0	93.9	93.3	82.5	81.4
September	94.5	93.8	97.3	95.5	98.0	89.3	103.3	97.3	94.2	93.7	82.6	81.5
October	94.5	93.8	96.9	94.0	98.1	89.4	102.3	97.4	94.5	94.0	82.3	81.1
November	95.4	94.7	98.0	95.7	99.0	90.9	101.8	98.5	95.5	94.6	82.7	81.5
December	96.0	95.4	98.1	96.9	98.6	92.7	101.5	97.6	96.0	95.2	82.8	81.7
1997												
January	96.3	95.7	97.9	96.4	98.5	93.3	100.0	97.4	96.9	95.8	82.7	81.5
February	97.7	97.3	98.8	98.0	99.1	95.4	100.2	99.1	97.9	97.3	83.5	82.4
March	97.9	97.8	98.9	98.7	99.0	96.4	99.8	99.2	97.5	97.6	83.4	82.5
April	98.4	98.2	98.5	96.6	99.3	97.4	99.6	99.6	98.9	98.4	83.4	82.4
May	98.8	98.7	98.9	97.7	99.3	98.5	99.6	99.7	99.1	98.6	83.3	82.4
June	99.3	99.4	98.9	99.6	98.6	99.9	99.5	99.7	99.4	99.3	83.3	82.5
July	99.9	99.9	99.0	96.9	99.9	100.1	99.6	99.5	100.4	100.3	83.4	82.5
August	100.9	101.1	100.2	101.0	99.9	102.5	100.1	100.2	100.3	101.0	83.8	82.9
September	101.7	101.9	101.2	102.2	100.7	102.2	100.5	100.4	101.3	102.1	84.0	83.1
October	102.5	102.6	102.5	102.4	102.6	102.9	100.1	101.0	102.7	102.5	84.2	83.1
November	103.2	103.5	102.9	105.3	101.9	105.0	99.7	101.6	102.6	103.3	84.3	83.3
December	103.5	103.9	102.3	105.2	101.2	106.3	101.3	102.6	103.0	103.8	84.1	83.1
1998												
January	104.0	104.9	103.0	105.8	101.8	108.1	102.2	103.3	102.8	104.0	84.0	83.3
February	104.3	105.1	102.7	105.6	101.5	108.8	102.7	103.7	103.1	104.5	83.7	83.0
March	104.6	105.3	103.0	106.3	101.6	108.7	102.3	103.5	104.2	104.8	83.5	82.5
April	105.2	106.0	103.9	107.1	102.6	108.6	102.3	104.0	104.8	105.4	83.5	82.6
May	105.7	106.4	104.1	107.3	102.8	109.0	103.6	105.3	105.8	106.0	83.4	82.3
June	105.3	105.8	102.9	101.9	103.2	109.8	103.8	105.0	106.0	105.4	82.6	81.3
July	105.0	105.5	101.9	97.5	103.5	109.9	104.5	105.9	106.7	105.2	81.9	80.7
August	107.1	108.0	105.1	110.1	103.1	113.4	105.3	105.8	107.0	107.0	83.2	82.1
September	106.9	107.7	104.0	109.2	101.9	113.7	104.8	105.7	107.3	107.1	82.6	81.5
October	107.8	108.9	104.9	111.5	102.3	114.8	106.5	106.6	107.5	108.1	82.9	81.9
November	107.5	108.8	104.0	110.6	101.4	114.7	106.2	106.5	107.7	108.0	82.3	81.4
December	107.5	109.0	103.4	110.7	100.5	114.4	105.3	107.2	107.6	108.6	82.0	81.2
1999												
January	108.2	109.4	104.6	111.1	102.1	114.7	105.3	107.3	108.1	109.0	82.2	81.2
February	108.6	110.1	104.9	111.8	102.2	115.4	106.0	107.2	108.1	109.5	82.1	81.3
March	109.0	110.3	104.7	111.2	102.1	115.2	105.6	106.7	109.0	110.6	82.2	81.1
April	109.2	110.6	104.3	112.0	101.4	116.1	104.6	107.1	109.6	111.0	82.1	81.1
May	110.0	111.6	105.6	113.1	102.6	116.9	103.8	107.1	110.0	111.7	82.3	81.5
June	110.1	111.5	104.6	112.6	101.5	116.7	102.6	107.2	110.3	112.6	82.1	81.1
July	110.6	111.9	104.1	112.8	100.8	117.8	101.5	108.4	111.1	113.8	82.3	81.1
August	111.4	112.9	106.1	115.4	102.5	117.7	101.2	107.9	111.1	114.3	82.6	81.5
September	111.1	112.7	105.0	113.6	101.6	117.9	98.5	108.0	111.8	114.4	82.1	81.0
October	112.3	114.0	106.3	116.7	102.4	118.9	98.0	108.9	112.3	115.5	82.7	81.6
November	112.8	114.8	106.3	115.6	102.7	118.7	95.6	109.5	112.8	117.0	82.8	81.9
December	113.7	115.6	107.1	116.0	103.7	119.3	94.1	110.2	113.7	118.1	83.2	82.1

Table 20-1. Industrial Production and Capacity Utilization—Continued

(Seasonally adjusted.)

Year and month	Total industry	Manufac- turing (SIC)	Market groups								Capacity utilization (output as percentage of capacity)	
			Consumer goods			Business equipment	Defense and space equipment	Construction supplies	Business supplies	Materials	Total industry	Manufac- turing (SIC)
			Total	Durable	Nondurable							
2000												
January	113.6	115.6	105.5	118.4	100.6	121.1	93.8	110.6	113.9	118.4	82.8	81.7
February	114.3	116.2	106.8	118.5	102.5	121.5	91.4	110.6	114.4	118.9	83.0	81.8
March	114.8	117.0	106.6	118.1	102.3	123.2	90.9	111.4	115.3	119.5	83.0	82.0
April	115.6	117.8	107.6	119.5	103.2	125.0	89.2	111.3	116.6	120.0	83.3	82.2
May	116.3	118.2	108.2	119.9	103.9	126.4	89.0	110.3	117.3	120.8	83.5	82.2
June	116.4	118.4	108.6	119.9	104.4	126.3	90.1	110.2	116.9	120.8	83.3	82.0
July	115.8	118.1	107.5	116.8	103.9	127.2	91.9	110.8	116.3	120.1	82.7	81.4
August	115.7	117.6	107.8	118.0	103.9	126.2	90.0	109.8	116.3	120.0	82.3	80.8
September	116.2	118.1	108.7	119.1	104.7	127.5	86.4	110.3	116.0	120.3	82.4	80.8
October	115.7	117.6	107.3	116.4	103.8	127.4	91.0	110.0	116.0	120.1	81.8	80.2
November	115.6	117.1	107.5	113.4	105.1	127.0	93.7	109.5	116.3	119.7	81.5	79.6
December	115.3	116.5	108.0	111.8	106.2	126.8	94.1	108.6	116.2	118.7	81.0	79.0
2001												
January	114.2	115.4	106.6	109.2	105.3	126.0	97.8	108.4	115.6	117.4	80.1	78.0
February	113.6	114.8	106.4	109.3	105.0	124.3	97.4	107.6	114.1	116.9	79.5	77.4
March	113.2	114.3	106.1	111.3	103.9	123.4	100.3	107.2	113.3	116.4	79.0	76.9
April	112.8	114.1	106.5	110.7	104.6	122.0	102.0	106.6	112.0	115.9	78.6	76.6
May	112.3	113.5	106.6	111.3	104.5	119.8	102.1	106.3	111.6	115.2	78.1	76.1
June	111.6	112.7	106.3	110.5	104.4	118.1	103.8	105.9	111.2	114.2	77.5	75.4
July	111.1	112.4	106.0	111.8	103.6	117.1	105.1	105.3	110.8	113.7	77.0	75.1
August	110.9	111.8	105.9	110.0	104.0	114.7	104.6	104.2	111.0	114.0	76.7	74.6
September	110.2	111.2	105.4	109.4	103.6	112.8	105.4	103.7	110.0	113.4	76.1	74.1
October	109.9	110.8	105.5	108.3	104.0	111.5	105.0	102.1	110.2	113.3	75.8	73.8
November	109.4	110.5	104.9	110.5	102.6	110.8	104.1	102.2	109.5	112.7	75.3	73.5
December	109.1	110.4	105.4	112.8	102.5	110.1	104.1	102.4	109.4	112.0	75.1	73.4
2002												
January	109.7	111.0	106.3	112.7	103.6	110.0	103.7	101.9	109.2	113.0	75.4	73.7
February	109.9	111.0	106.3	113.7	103.4	109.8	103.3	102.7	109.3	113.4	75.4	73.7
March	110.3	111.4	106.8	113.9	104.0	109.5	103.9	103.9	109.8	113.9	75.6	73.8
April	110.8	111.6	107.0	114.4	104.1	109.4	104.3	103.5	110.7	114.8	75.8	73.9
May	111.0	111.9	106.5	114.9	103.2	109.7	104.5	103.9	111.3	115.3	75.8	74.1
June	111.7	112.6	107.6	116.1	104.4	110.1	105.3	104.0	111.1	116.0	76.2	74.4
July	111.5	112.4	107.5	116.8	103.9	109.0	105.0	102.6	111.6	116.2	76.0	74.3
August	111.5	112.6	107.1	116.8	103.5	109.7	106.1	103.3	111.2	116.1	75.9	74.3
September	111.3	112.5	107.3	117.0	103.6	109.3	107.2	103.4	111.1	115.7	75.7	74.2
October	111.0	111.9	106.7	115.9	103.2	108.8	107.9	103.2	111.7	115.3	75.4	73.7
November	111.2	111.9	106.6	118.8	102.1	109.6	107.1	102.8	111.0	115.9	75.4	73.6
December	110.6	111.3	105.6	116.8	101.5	109.2	109.7	102.1	110.9	115.3	74.9	73.1
2003												
January	111.2	112.0	106.6	119.4	101.9	109.8	110.3	102.7	111.8	115.5	75.2	73.6
February	111.6	112.1	107.0	117.2	103.2	110.6	111.0	101.9	112.6	115.8	75.4	73.5
March	110.8	111.8	106.3	116.4	102.6	110.0	111.0	101.2	111.9	114.7	74.8	73.3
April	110.1	111.1	105.3	115.5	101.4	108.7	110.3	100.6	111.1	114.5	74.2	72.7
May	110.0	111.0	105.5	115.3	101.8	108.6	111.8	100.8	111.0	114.1	74.1	72.6
June	110.0	111.2	105.0	116.2	100.9	109.0	111.8	100.8	110.6	114.4	74.0	72.7
July	110.8	111.8	105.8	118.2	101.3	109.3	112.1	101.5	111.5	115.4	74.5	73.0
August	110.9	111.8	105.7	117.4	101.4	110.0	113.0	101.9	111.2	115.5	74.5	73.0
September	111.5	112.7	106.1	120.8	100.9	111.2	113.7	102.3	111.3	116.4	74.9	73.6
October	111.8	112.9	106.0	119.8	101.1	110.8	113.7	103.1	112.1	116.9	75.0	73.6
November	112.9	114.2	107.1	121.3	102.1	112.7	113.3	104.4	112.8	117.9	75.7	74.4
December	113.1	114.2	107.3	121.2	102.3	113.2	112.4	104.1	113.4	118.2	75.8	74.4

Table 20-2. Summary Consumer and Producer Price Indexes

(Seasonally adjusted.)

Year and month	Consumer Price Index, all urban consumers, 1982–1984 = 100						Producer Price Index, 1982 = 100					
							Finished goods		Intermediate materials, supplies, and components		Crude materials for further processing	
	All items	All items less food and energy	Food	Energy	Transportation	Medical care	Total	Less food and energy	Total	Less food and energy	Total	Crude nonfood less energy
1947												
January	21.5	...	22.8	...	17.9	13.2	...	...	...	...	...	...
February	21.6	...	23.1	...	17.9	13.3	...	...	...	...	...	...
March	22.0	...	23.8	...	18.1	13.3	...	...	...	...	...	...
April	22.0	...	23.5	...	18.3	13.4	26.0	...	23.1	...	30.7	...
May	22.0	...	23.4	...	18.3	13.5	26.1	...	23.0	...	30.4	...
June	22.1	...	23.5	...	18.4	13.5	26.2	...	23.2	...	30.6	...
July	22.2	...	23.8	...	18.5	13.5	26.2	...	23.2	...	31.0	...
August	22.4	...	24.1	...	18.5	13.6	26.3	...	23.3	...	31.6	...
September	22.8	...	24.8	...	18.7	13.7	26.7	...	23.7	...	32.4	...
October	22.9	...	24.9	...	18.8	13.8	26.8	...	24.0	...	33.7	...
November	23.1	...	25.2	...	19.0	13.8	27.1	...	24.3	...	33.9	...
December	23.4	...	25.7	...	19.1	13.9	27.7	...	24.5	...	35.3	...
1948												
January	23.7	...	26.1	...	19.6	14.0	28.1	...	25.0	...	36.2	...
February	23.7	...	25.9	...	19.5	14.0	27.9	...	24.7	...	34.4	...
March	23.5	...	25.3	...	19.6	14.1	28.0	...	24.8	...	33.5	...
April	23.8	...	26.0	...	19.9	14.3	28.1	...	25.1	...	34.2	...
May	24.0	...	26.3	...	19.9	14.3	28.4	...	25.1	...	35.3	...
June	24.2	...	26.5	...	20.0	14.4	28.6	...	25.4	...	36.2	...
July	24.4	...	26.7	...	21.0	14.5	28.8	...	25.4	...	36.1	...
August	24.4	...	26.5	...	21.3	14.6	28.9	...	25.5	...	35.5	...
September	24.4	...	26.3	...	21.4	14.5	28.8	...	25.5	...	34.9	...
October	24.3	...	26.1	...	21.5	14.6	28.7	...	25.5	...	33.8	...
November	24.2	...	25.7	...	21.6	14.7	28.5	...	25.4	...	33.5	...
December	24.0	...	25.5	...	21.6	14.7	28.5	...	25.2	...	33.0	...
1949												
January	24.0	...	25.4	...	21.6	14.7	28.3	...	25.2	...	32.0	...
February	23.9	...	25.3	...	21.8	14.8	28.0	...	24.8	...	30.9	...
March	23.9	...	25.3	...	21.9	14.8	28.0	...	24.7	...	30.8	...
April	23.9	...	25.3	...	22.0	14.8	27.9	...	24.5	...	30.2	...
May	23.9	...	25.2	...	22.2	14.8	27.8	...	24.3	...	30.1	...
June	23.9	...	25.3	...	22.1	14.8	27.7	...	24.1	...	29.7	...
July	23.7	...	24.8	...	22.2	14.8	27.5	...	24.1	...	29.2	...
August	23.7	...	24.8	...	22.3	14.9	27.4	...	23.9	...	29.2	...
September	23.8	...	25.0	...	22.2	14.9	27.4	...	23.9	...	29.5	...
October	23.7	...	24.8	...	22.3	14.9	27.3	...	23.8	...	29.5	...
November	23.7	...	24.8	...	22.3	14.9	27.2	...	23.7	...	29.6	...
December	23.6	...	24.5	...	22.5	14.9	27.2	...	23.8	...	29.6	...
1950												
January	23.5	...	24.3	...	22.4	14.9	27.2	...	23.8	...	29.6	...
February	23.6	...	24.7	...	22.4	15.0	27.2	...	23.9	...	30.5	...
March	23.6	...	24.6	...	22.4	14.9	27.3	...	24.1	...	30.3	...
April	23.6	...	24.6	...	22.4	15.0	27.3	...	24.2	...	30.3	...
May	23.8	...	24.8	...	22.5	15.0	27.5	...	24.6	...	31.6	...
June	23.9	...	25.1	...	22.5	15.0	27.6	...	24.7	...	32.1	...
July	24.1	...	25.6	...	22.7	15.1	28.0	...	25.3	...	33.3	...
August	24.2	...	25.8	...	22.9	15.1	28.6	...	25.6	...	34.0	...
September	24.3	...	25.8	...	22.9	15.2	28.9	...	26.2	...	34.5	...
October	24.5	...	26.0	...	22.9	15.3	29.0	...	26.7	...	34.5	...
November	24.6	...	26.1	...	23.0	15.3	29.4	...	26.9	...	35.4	...
December	25.0	...	26.9	...	23.2	15.4	30.0	...	27.8	...	36.7	...
1951												
January	25.4	...	27.6	...	23.3	15.4	30.5	...	28.5	...	38.2	...
February	25.8	...	28.5	...	23.6	15.5	30.8	...	28.7	...	39.6	...
March	25.9	...	28.4	...	23.8	15.7	30.9	...	28.8	...	39.1	...
April	25.9	...	28.2	...	23.9	15.7	30.9	...	28.8	...	39.1	...
May	26.0	...	28.3	...	24.0	15.8	31.1	...	28.8	...	38.4	...
June	25.9	...	28.0	...	24.1	15.8	31.0	...	28.7	...	38.1	...
July	25.9	...	27.9	...	24.1	15.8	30.8	...	28.4	...	36.8	...
August	25.9	...	27.8	...	24.2	15.9	30.7	...	28.0	...	36.2	...
September	26.0	...	27.9	...	24.4	15.9	30.6	...	28.0	...	35.9	...
October	26.2	...	28.4	...	24.5	16.0	30.8	...	27.9	...	36.7	...
November	26.3	...	28.6	...	24.8	16.1	30.9	...	27.9	...	36.4	...
December	26.5	...	28.9	...	24.9	16.3	30.9	...	27.8	...	36.6	...
1952												
January	26.4	...	28.9	...	25.0	16.3	30.8	...	27.8	...	35.8	...
February	26.4	...	28.6	...	25.2	16.4	30.7	...	27.7	...	35.5	...
March	26.4	...	28.5	...	25.3	16.5	30.9	...	27.6	...	35.0	...
April	26.5	...	28.7	...	25.5	16.5	30.7	...	27.5	...	34.9	...
May	26.5	...	28.7	...	25.6	16.5	30.7	...	27.5	...	34.8	...
June	26.5	...	28.6	...	25.8	16.8	30.7	...	27.6	...	34.6	...
July	26.7	...	28.9	...	26.0	16.9	30.8	...	27.5	...	34.6	...
August	26.7	...	28.9	...	25.9	16.9	30.7	...	27.6	...	34.7	...
September	26.6	...	28.7	...	26.0	16.9	30.6	...	27.6	...	33.8	...
October	26.7	...	28.8	...	26.1	16.9	30.5	...	27.5	...	33.8	...
November	26.7	...	28.8	...	26.2	16.9	30.4	...	27.4	...	33.7	...
December	26.7	...	28.6	...	26.2	17.0	30.2	...	27.3	...	32.9	...

... = Not available.

Table 20-2. Summary Consumer and Producer Price Indexes—Continued

(Seasonally adjusted.)

Year and month	Consumer Price Index, all urban consumers, 1982–1984 = 100						Producer Price Index, 1982 = 100					
							Finished goods		Intermediate materials, supplies, and components		Crude materials for further processing	
	All items	All items less food and energy	Food	Energy	Transportation	Medical care	Total	Less food and energy	Total	Less food and energy	Total	Crude nonfood less energy
1953												
January	26.6	...	28.4	...	26.3	17.0	30.3	...	27.4	...	32.5	...
February	26.6	...	28.3	...	26.2	17.0	30.2	...	27.4	...	32.4	...
March	26.6	...	28.3	...	26.3	17.0	30.3	...	27.5	...	32.4	...
April	26.7	...	28.1	...	26.4	17.1	30.2	...	27.5	...	31.6	...
May	26.7	...	28.2	...	26.4	17.2	30.3	...	27.6	...	31.8	...
June	26.8	...	28.4	...	26.5	17.3	30.4	...	27.7	...	31.4	...
July	26.8	...	28.2	...	26.6	17.3	30.5	...	28.0	...	32.3	...
August	26.8	...	28.3	...	26.7	17.4	30.4	...	27.9	...	31.8	...
September	26.9	...	28.4	...	26.7	17.5	30.4	...	27.9	...	32.0	...
October	27.0	...	28.4	...	26.6	17.5	30.4	...	27.9	...	31.4	...
November	26.8	...	28.1	...	26.3	17.6	30.3	...	27.8	...	31.2	...
December	26.9	...	28.3	...	26.2	17.6	30.4	...	27.8	...	31.7	...
1954												
January	26.9	...	28.5	...	26.5	17.6	30.5	...	27.9	...	32.0	...
February	27.0	...	28.5	...	26.3	17.7	30.4	...	27.9	...	32.0	...
March	26.9	...	28.4	...	26.3	17.7	30.4	...	27.9	...	32.1	...
April	26.9	...	28.4	...	26.4	17.8	30.6	...	27.9	...	32.2	...
May	26.9	...	28.4	...	26.4	17.8	30.6	...	27.9	...	32.1	...
June	26.9	...	28.4	...	26.4	17.8	30.4	...	27.8	...	31.5	...
July	26.9	...	28.4	...	26.0	17.8	30.5	...	27.9	...	31.4	...
August	26.8	...	28.3	...	25.9	17.9	30.4	...	27.9	...	31.3	...
September	26.8	...	28.0	...	25.9	17.9	30.3	...	27.8	...	31.5	...
October	26.7	...	27.9	...	25.4	17.9	30.2	...	27.8	...	31.2	...
November	26.8	...	27.9	...	25.8	18.0	30.3	...	27.9	...	31.4	...
December	26.8	...	27.8	...	25.8	18.0	30.3	...	27.9	...	30.8	...
1955												
January	26.8	...	27.8	...	25.9	18.0	30.4	...	27.9	...	31.1	...
February	26.8	...	28.0	...	25.9	18.1	30.5	...	28.0	...	31.0	...
March	26.8	...	28.0	...	25.9	18.1	30.3	...	28.0	...	30.7	...
April	26.8	...	28.0	...	25.6	18.1	30.4	...	28.1	...	31.0	...
May	26.8	...	27.9	...	25.7	18.2	30.4	...	28.1	...	30.2	...
June	26.7	...	27.7	...	25.8	18.2	30.5	...	28.2	...	30.7	...
July	26.8	...	27.7	...	25.7	18.2	30.4	...	28.4	...	30.4	...
August	26.7	...	27.6	...	25.6	18.3	30.4	...	28.5	...	30.1	...
September	26.8	...	27.8	...	25.7	18.3	30.5	...	28.8	...	30.4	...
October	26.8	...	27.7	...	25.8	18.4	30.6	...	28.9	...	30.4	...
November	26.9	...	27.6	...	26.0	18.5	30.6	...	28.9	...	29.4	...
December	26.9	...	27.6	...	25.8	18.6	30.7	...	29.0	...	29.5	...
1956												
January	26.8	...	27.5	...	25.8	18.6	30.7	...	29.1	...	29.4	...
February	26.9	...	27.5	...	25.8	18.7	30.8	...	29.2	...	29.9	...
March	26.9	...	27.5	...	25.8	18.7	30.9	...	29.4	...	29.8	...
April	26.9	...	27.6	...	25.8	18.8	31.0	...	29.5	...	30.3	...
May	27.0	...	27.8	...	26.0	18.8	31.2	...	29.6	...	30.7	...
June	27.2	...	28.1	...	26.0	18.8	31.4	...	29.6	...	30.5	...
July	27.3	...	28.4	...	26.2	18.9	31.3	...	29.4	...	30.5	...
August	27.3	...	28.2	...	26.3	19.0	31.4	...	29.7	...	31.0	...
September	27.4	...	28.2	...	26.4	19.1	31.6	...	29.8	...	31.0	...
October	27.5	...	28.3	...	27.0	19.1	31.8	...	30.0	...	31.0	...
November	27.5	...	28.4	...	26.9	19.1	31.9	...	30.0	...	31.1	...
December	27.6	...	28.5	...	27.0	19.2	31.9	...	30.1	...	31.7	...
1957												
January	27.7	28.5	28.4	21.3	27.2	19.3	32.1	...	30.3	...	31.3	...
February	27.8	28.6	28.7	21.4	27.4	19.3	32.2	...	30.3	...	31.0	...
March	27.9	28.7	28.6	21.5	27.5	19.4	32.1	...	30.3	...	30.9	...
April	27.9	28.8	28.6	21.6	27.7	19.5	32.3	...	30.2	...	30.8	...
May	28.0	28.8	28.7	21.6	27.6	19.6	32.3	...	30.2	...	30.7	...
June	28.1	28.9	28.9	21.6	27.7	19.7	32.5	...	30.3	...	31.5	...
July	28.2	29.0	29.1	21.5	27.8	19.7	32.6	...	30.3	...	32.0	...
August	28.3	29.0	29.4	21.4	27.8	19.8	32.6	...	30.4	...	32.0	...
September	28.3	29.1	29.2	21.4	27.9	19.8	32.6	...	30.4	...	31.2	...
October	28.3	29.2	29.2	21.4	27.5	19.9	32.7	...	30.3	...	31.0	...
November	28.4	29.3	29.2	21.5	28.3	20.0	32.9	...	30.4	...	31.1	...
December	28.5	29.3	29.2	21.5	28.1	20.1	33.0	...	30.4	...	31.5	...
1958												
January	28.6	29.3	29.8	21.6	28.1	20.2	33.2	...	30.4	...	31.4	...
February	28.7	29.4	29.9	21.3	28.2	20.2	33.2	...	30.3	...	31.9	...
March	28.9	29.5	30.5	21.4	28.3	20.3	33.4	...	30.3	...	32.3	...
April	28.9	29.5	30.6	21.4	28.3	20.4	33.2	...	30.2	...	31.8	...
May	28.9	29.5	30.5	21.5	28.4	20.5	33.2	...	30.3	...	32.4	...
June	28.9	29.6	30.3	21.5	28.4	20.6	33.3	...	30.3	...	32.0	...
July	28.9	29.6	30.2	21.6	28.7	20.7	33.2	...	30.3	...	32.1	...
August	28.9	29.6	30.1	21.7	28.8	20.7	33.2	...	30.4	...	31.9	...
September	28.9	29.7	30.0	21.7	28.9	20.9	33.2	...	30.4	...	31.6	...
October	28.9	29.7	30.0	21.7	28.9	21.0	33.2	...	30.4	...	31.9	...
November	29.0	29.8	30.0	21.4	29.1	21.0	33.2	...	30.5	...	32.1	...
December	29.0	29.9	29.9	21.4	29.2	21.1	33.1	...	30.6	...	31.6	...

... = Not available.

Table 20-2. Summary Consumer and Producer Price Indexes—Continued

(Seasonally adjusted.)

Year and month	Consumer Price Index, all urban consumers, 1982–1984 = 100						Producer Price Index, 1982 = 100					
							Finished goods		Intermediate materials, supplies, and components		Crude materials for further processing	
	All items	All items less food and energy	Food	Energy	Transportation	Medical care	Total	Less food and energy	Total	Less food and energy	Total	Crude nonfood less energy
1959												
January	29.0	29.9	30.0	21.4	29.3	21.1	33.1	...	30.6	...	31.6	...
February	29.0	29.9	29.8	21.6	29.4	21.2	33.2	...	30.7	...	31.4	...
March	29.0	30.0	29.7	21.7	29.6	21.3	33.2	...	30.7	...	31.5	...
April	29.0	30.0	29.5	21.8	29.7	21.3	33.2	...	30.7	...	31.7	...
May	29.0	30.1	29.5	21.8	29.7	21.4	33.3	...	30.9	...	31.5	...
June	29.1	30.2	29.7	21.9	29.8	21.5	33.2	...	30.9	...	31.3	...
July	29.2	30.2	29.6	21.8	29.9	21.5	33.1	...	30.8	...	31.0	...
August	29.2	30.2	29.6	21.9	29.9	21.6	33.0	...	30.8	...	30.7	...
September	29.2	30.3	29.7	21.9	30.0	21.7	33.4	...	30.8	...	30.9	...
October	29.4	30.4	29.7	22.2	30.1	21.7	33.1	...	30.8	...	30.7	...
November	29.4	30.4	29.7	22.2	30.1	21.8	33.0	...	30.9	...	30.5	...
December	29.4	30.5	29.6	22.3	30.1	21.8	33.0	...	30.9	...	30.3	...
1960												
January	29.4	30.5	29.6	22.3	30.0	21.9	33.1	...	30.8	...	30.4	...
February	29.4	30.6	29.5	22.2	30.0	22.0	33.1	...	30.9	...	30.4	...
March	29.4	30.6	29.6	22.3	29.9	22.1	33.4	...	30.9	...	30.7	...
April	29.5	30.6	30.0	22.4	29.9	22.2	33.4	...	30.8	...	30.8	...
May	29.6	30.6	30.0	22.3	29.8	22.2	33.4	...	30.8	...	30.8	...
June	29.6	30.7	30.0	22.4	29.8	22.2	33.4	...	30.9	...	30.4	...
July	29.6	30.6	29.9	22.5	29.8	22.3	33.5	...	30.8	...	30.4	...
August	29.6	30.6	30.0	22.5	29.8	22.3	33.4	...	30.8	...	29.8	...
September	29.6	30.6	30.1	22.6	29.6	22.4	33.4	...	30.8	...	30.0	...
October	29.8	30.8	30.3	22.5	29.6	22.4	33.7	...	30.8	...	30.2	...
November	29.8	30.8	30.5	22.7	29.6	22.5	33.7	...	30.7	...	30.2	...
December	29.8	30.7	30.5	22.6	29.7	22.6	33.6	...	30.7	...	30.3	...
1961												
January	29.8	30.8	30.5	22.7	29.7	22.6	33.6	...	30.6	...	30.4	...
February	29.8	30.8	30.5	22.6	29.8	22.7	33.7	...	30.7	...	30.5	...
March	29.8	30.9	30.5	22.6	29.8	22.7	33.6	...	30.8	...	30.3	...
April	29.8	30.9	30.4	22.2	29.8	22.8	33.4	...	30.7	...	30.2	...
May	29.8	30.9	30.3	22.4	30.0	22.8	33.3	...	30.6	...	29.9	...
June	29.8	31.0	30.2	22.5	30.1	22.9	33.3	...	30.5	...	29.5	...
July	29.9	31.0	30.3	22.5	30.3	22.9	33.3	...	30.5	...	29.7	...
August	29.9	31.1	30.3	22.5	30.4	23.0	33.4	...	30.5	...	30.5	...
September	30.0	31.1	30.3	22.6	30.5	23.1	33.3	...	30.5	...	30.3	...
October	30.0	31.1	30.3	22.4	30.5	23.1	33.3	...	30.4	...	30.3	...
November	30.0	31.2	30.3	22.5	30.4	23.1	33.4	...	30.5	...	30.2	...
December	30.0	31.2	30.3	22.4	30.3	23.2	33.4	...	30.6	...	30.6	...
1962												
January	30.0	31.2	30.4	22.4	30.4	23.2	33.5	...	30.5	...	30.6	...
February	30.1	31.2	30.5	22.6	30.5	23.3	33.6	...	30.6	...	30.5	...
March	30.2	31.3	30.6	22.4	30.5	23.4	33.5	...	30.6	...	30.5	...
April	30.2	31.3	30.7	22.7	30.9	23.4	33.5	...	30.6	...	30.1	...
May	30.2	31.4	30.6	22.7	30.9	23.5	33.4	...	30.6	...	30.1	...
June	30.2	31.4	30.5	22.5	30.9	23.5	33.4	...	30.6	...	29.9	...
July	30.2	31.4	30.4	22.3	30.6	23.6	33.4	...	30.6	...	30.2	...
August	30.3	31.5	30.6	22.4	30.8	23.6	33.5	...	30.6	...	30.5	...
September	30.4	31.5	30.9	22.8	31.0	23.6	33.8	...	30.6	...	31.2	...
October	30.4	31.5	30.8	22.7	30.9	23.7	33.6	...	30.5	...	30.8	...
November	30.4	31.5	30.9	22.7	30.9	23.7	33.6	...	30.5	...	31.0	...
December	30.4	31.6	30.7	22.8	30.9	23.8	33.5	...	30.5	...	30.6	...
1963												
January	30.4	31.5	31.0	22.8	30.6	23.9	33.4	...	30.5	...	30.3	...
February	30.5	31.6	31.1	22.7	30.7	23.9	33.4	...	30.5	...	30.0	...
March	30.5	31.7	31.0	22.7	30.8	23.9	33.3	...	30.5	...	29.6	...
April	30.5	31.7	30.9	22.6	30.8	23.9	33.3	...	30.5	...	29.8	...
May	30.5	31.7	30.9	22.6	30.9	24.0	33.4	...	30.7	...	29.6	...
June	30.6	31.8	31.0	22.5	30.9	24.1	33.5	...	30.7	...	29.9	...
July	30.7	31.8	31.2	22.7	30.9	24.1	33.4	...	30.7	...	30.0	...
August	30.8	31.9	31.2	22.6	31.0	24.2	33.4	...	30.7	...	29.9	...
September	30.7	31.9	31.1	22.5	31.0	24.2	33.4	...	30.7	...	29.8	...
October	30.8	32.0	31.0	22.7	31.2	24.2	33.5	...	30.8	...	29.9	...
November	30.8	32.0	31.2	22.6	31.1	24.3	33.5	...	30.8	...	30.2	...
December	30.9	32.1	31.3	22.6	31.2	24.3	33.4	...	30.8	...	29.4	...
1964												
January	30.9	32.2	31.4	22.8	31.4	24.4	33.5	...	30.8	...	29.8	...
February	30.9	32.2	31.4	22.2	31.3	24.4	33.5	...	30.8	...	29.4	...
March	30.9	32.2	31.4	22.6	31.4	24.4	33.4	...	30.8	...	29.5	...
April	31.0	32.2	31.4	22.5	31.3	24.5	33.5	...	30.8	...	29.5	...
May	31.0	32.2	31.4	22.5	31.3	24.5	33.5	...	30.7	...	29.4	...
June	31.0	32.3	31.4	22.6	31.4	24.6	33.5	...	30.6	...	29.0	...
July	31.0	32.3	31.5	22.5	31.3	24.6	33.5	...	30.7	...	29.2	...
August	31.0	32.3	31.4	22.6	31.4	24.7	33.6	...	30.6	...	29.4	...
September	31.1	32.3	31.6	22.5	31.3	24.7	33.6	...	30.7	...	30.1	...
October	31.1	32.4	31.6	22.5	31.3	24.7	33.6	...	30.8	...	29.8	...
November	31.2	32.5	31.7	22.5	31.4	24.8	33.6	...	30.8	...	29.9	...
December	31.2	32.5	31.7	22.6	31.7	24.8	33.6	...	30.9	...	29.8	...

... = Not available.

Table 20-2. Summary Consumer and Producer Price Indexes—Continued

(Seasonally adjusted.)

Year and month	Consumer Price Index, all urban consumers, 1982–1984 = 100						Producer Price Index, 1982 = 100					
							Finished goods		Intermediate materials, supplies, and components		Crude materials for further processing	
	All items	All items less food and energy	Food	Energy	Transportation	Medical care	Total	Less food and energy	Total	Less food and energy	Total	Crude nonfood less energy
1965												
January	31.3	32.6	31.6	22.8	31.9	24.8	33.6	...	30.9	...	29.5	...
February	31.3	32.6	31.5	22.7	31.8	24.9	33.7	...	30.9	...	29.9	...
March	31.3	32.6	31.7	22.6	31.8	25.0	33.7	...	31.0	...	30.0	...
April	31.4	32.7	31.8	22.9	31.9	25.0	34.0	...	31.1	...	30.4	...
May	31.5	32.7	32.1	23.0	32.0	25.1	34.1	...	31.1	...	30.8	...
June	31.6	32.7	32.6	23.1	31.9	25.1	34.2	...	31.2	...	31.6	...
July	31.6	32.7	32.5	23.0	31.9	25.3	34.1	...	31.2	...	31.2	...
August	31.6	32.7	32.4	23.0	31.9	25.3	34.2	...	31.3	...	31.5	...
September	31.6	32.8	32.3	23.1	31.9	25.3	34.3	...	31.3	...	31.4	...
October	31.6	32.8	32.5	23.0	31.8	25.4	34.4	...	31.3	...	31.8	...
November	31.8	32.9	32.6	23.1	31.9	25.5	34.5	...	31.4	...	32.1	...
December	31.8	33.0	32.8	23.1	32.0	25.5	34.7	...	31.4	...	32.7	...
1966												
January	31.9	33.0	33.0	23.1	31.9	25.6	34.7	...	31.4	...	33.1	...
February	32.1	33.1	33.5	23.2	32.0	25.6	35.0	...	31.6	...	33.7	...
March	32.2	33.1	33.8	23.2	32.1	25.8	35.0	...	31.7	...	33.5	...
April	32.3	33.3	33.8	23.2	32.2	25.9	35.1	...	31.8	...	33.3	...
May	32.4	33.4	33.7	23.2	32.1	26.0	35.1	...	32.0	...	33.0	...
June	32.4	33.5	33.7	23.3	32.2	26.1	34.9	...	32.0	...	33.0	...
July	32.4	33.6	33.5	23.4	32.5	26.3	35.1	...	32.2	...	33.4	...
August	32.6	33.7	34.0	23.3	32.6	26.4	35.4	...	32.3	...	33.5	...
September	32.8	33.8	34.1	23.4	32.6	26.7	35.6	...	32.2	...	33.4	...
October	32.8	34.0	34.2	23.4	32.7	26.9	35.5	...	32.1	...	32.9	...
November	32.9	34.0	34.1	23.5	32.8	27.1	35.5	...	32.2	...	32.3	...
December	32.9	34.1	34.0	23.5	32.6	27.2	35.4	...	32.2	...	32.1	...
1967												
January	32.9	34.2	33.9	23.6	32.6	27.4	35.4	...	32.2	...	32.2	...
February	33.0	34.2	33.8	23.7	32.8	27.5	35.3	...	32.1	...	31.5	...
March	33.0	34.3	33.8	23.6	32.8	27.6	35.3	...	32.1	...	31.1	...
April	33.1	34.4	33.7	23.9	33.0	27.8	35.3	...	32.1	...	30.7	...
May	33.1	34.5	33.7	23.9	33.1	27.9	35.4	...	32.1	...	31.1	...
June	33.3	34.6	34.0	23.8	33.1	28.1	35.7	...	32.2	...	31.4	...
July	33.4	34.7	34.1	23.8	33.3	28.2	35.7	...	32.2	...	31.3	...
August	33.5	34.9	34.3	23.9	33.4	28.3	35.8	...	32.2	...	31.3	...
September	33.6	35.0	34.3	24.0	33.7	28.5	35.8	...	32.3	...	31.2	...
October	33.7	35.1	34.4	23.9	33.6	28.7	35.9	...	32.3	...	31.3	...
November	33.9	35.2	34.5	24.0	33.9	28.8	35.9	...	32.4	...	31.1	...
December	34.0	35.4	34.6	23.9	33.9	29.0	36.0	...	32.6	...	31.5	...
1968												
January	34.1	35.5	34.6	24.0	34.1	29.1	36.1	...	32.6	...	31.4	...
February	34.2	35.7	34.8	24.1	34.2	29.2	36.2	...	32.7	...	31.5	...
March	34.3	35.8	34.9	24.1	34.2	29.4	36.3	...	32.8	...	31.6	...
April	34.4	35.9	35.0	24.0	34.1	29.5	36.5	...	32.8	...	31.7	...
May	34.5	36.0	35.1	24.1	34.1	29.6	36.5	...	32.8	...	31.5	...
June	34.7	36.2	35.2	24.2	34.3	29.7	36.6	...	32.9	...	31.3	...
July	34.9	36.4	35.3	24.2	34.3	29.9	36.7	...	33.0	...	31.6	...
August	35.0	36.5	35.4	24.3	34.4	30.0	36.8	...	33.0	...	31.7	...
September	35.1	36.7	35.6	24.3	34.4	30.2	37.0	...	33.1	...	31.9	...
October	35.3	36.9	35.9	24.3	34.5	30.4	37.0	...	33.2	...	32.1	...
November	35.4	37.1	35.9	24.4	34.7	30.6	37.1	...	33.2	...	32.8	...
December	35.6	37.2	36.0	24.3	34.5	30.8	37.1	...	33.4	...	32.4	...
1969												
January	35.7	37.3	36.1	24.4	34.7	30.9	37.2	...	33.6	...	32.6	...
February	35.8	37.6	36.1	24.4	35.2	31.2	37.2	...	33.7	...	32.3	...
March	36.1	37.8	36.2	24.7	35.8	31.4	37.4	...	33.9	...	32.7	...
April	36.3	38.1	36.4	24.9	35.8	31.6	37.6	...	33.8	...	33.1	...
May	36.4	38.1	36.6	24.8	35.5	31.8	37.8	...	33.9	...	34.0	...
June	36.6	38.3	37.0	25.0	35.6	31.9	38.0	...	34.0	...	34.5	...
July	36.8	38.5	37.3	24.9	35.6	32.1	38.1	...	34.0	...	34.1	...
August	36.9	38.7	37.5	24.9	35.7	32.2	38.2	...	34.2	...	34.4	...
September	37.1	38.9	37.7	25.0	35.6	32.5	38.3	...	34.2	...	34.4	...
October	37.3	39.1	37.8	25.0	35.9	32.3	38.5	...	34.4	...	34.8	...
November	37.5	39.2	38.2	25.0	36.0	32.5	38.8	...	34.6	...	35.2	...
December	37.7	39.4	38.6	25.1	36.2	32.6	38.9	...	34.7	...	35.1	...
1970												
January	37.9	39.6	38.7	25.1	36.6	32.8	39.1	...	35.0	...	35.1	...
February	38.1	39.8	38.9	25.1	36.7	33.0	39.0	...	35.0	...	35.2	...
March	38.3	40.1	38.9	25.0	36.6	33.2	39.1	...	34.9	...	35.6	...
April	38.5	40.4	39.0	25.5	37.1	33.5	39.1	...	35.1	...	35.5	...
May	38.6	40.5	39.2	25.4	37.2	33.7	39.1	...	35.2	...	35.0	...
June	38.8	40.8	39.2	25.3	37.4	33.9	39.2	...	35.3	...	35.0	...
July	38.9	40.9	39.2	25.5	37.6	34.1	39.2	...	35.5	...	35.1	...
August	39.0	41.1	39.2	25.4	37.5	34.3	39.2	...	35.5	...	34.7	...
September	39.2	41.3	39.4	25.6	37.7	34.5	39.6	...	35.6	...	35.5	...
October	39.4	41.5	39.5	25.9	38.1	34.6	39.6	...	35.8	...	35.5	...
November	39.6	41.8	39.5	26.0	38.5	34.8	39.8	...	35.9	...	35.1	...
December	39.8	42.0	39.5	26.2	38.9	35.1	39.8	...	35.9	...	34.5	...

... = Not available.

Table 20-2. Summary Consumer and Producer Price Indexes—Continued

(Seasonally adjusted.)

Year and month	Consumer Price Index, all urban consumers, 1982–1984 = 100						Producer Price Index, 1982 = 100					
							Finished goods		Intermediate materials, supplies, and components		Crude materials for further processing	
	All items	All items less food and energy	Food	Energy	Transportation	Medical care	Total	Less food and energy	Total	Less food and energy	Total	Crude nonfood less energy
1971												
January	39.9	42.1	39.4	26.3	39.2	35.2	39.9	...	36.0	...	34.8	...
February	39.9	42.2	39.5	26.2	39.4	35.4	40.1	...	36.1	...	35.9	...
March	40.0	42.2	39.8	26.2	39.4	35.6	40.2	...	36.3	...	35.4	...
April	40.1	42.4	40.1	26.1	39.4	35.8	40.3	...	36.3	...	36.0	...
May	40.3	42.6	40.3	26.2	39.4	36.0	40.5	...	36.5	...	36.0	...
June	40.5	42.8	40.5	26.3	39.6	36.2	40.6	...	36.7	...	36.2	...
July	40.6	42.9	40.6	26.3	39.6	36.4	40.4	...	36.9	...	35.9	...
August	40.7	43.0	40.6	26.8	39.7	36.5	40.7	...	37.2	...	35.8	...
September	40.8	43.0	40.6	26.9	39.5	36.7	40.7	...	37.2	...	35.7	...
October	40.9	43.1	40.7	27.0	39.5	36.5	40.7	...	37.1	...	36.4	...
November	41.0	43.2	40.9	26.9	39.4	36.6	40.8	...	37.2	...	37.0	...
December	41.1	43.3	41.3	27.0	39.4	36.7	41.1	...	37.4	...	37.2	...
1972												
January	41.2	43.5	41.1	27.0	39.7	36.8	41.0	...	37.5	...	37.8	...
February	41.4	43.6	41.7	26.8	39.6	36.9	41.3	...	37.7	...	38.1	...
March	41.4	43.6	41.6	26.9	39.6	37.0	41.3	...	37.8	...	38.1	...
April	41.5	43.8	41.6	26.9	39.6	37.1	41.3	...	37.9	...	38.7	...
May	41.6	43.9	41.7	27.0	39.7	37.2	41.5	...	38.0	...	39.3	...
June	41.7	44.0	41.9	27.0	39.7	37.3	41.7	...	38.0	...	39.4	...
July	41.8	44.1	42.1	27.1	39.8	37.3	41.8	...	38.1	...	40.0	...
August	41.9	44.3	42.2	27.3	40.0	37.4	42.0	...	38.2	...	40.3	...
September	42.1	44.3	42.5	27.6	40.2	37.4	42.2	...	38.5	...	40.5	...
October	42.2	44.4	42.8	27.7	40.1	37.8	42.0	...	38.7	...	40.9	...
November	42.4	44.4	43.0	27.9	40.3	37.8	42.3	...	39.0	...	42.0	...
December	42.5	44.6	43.2	27.8	40.4	37.9	42.7	...	39.6	...	43.8	...
1973												
January	42.7	44.6	44.0	27.9	40.4	38.0	43.0	...	39.8	...	45.0	...
February	43.0	44.8	44.6	28.2	40.6	38.1	43.5	...	40.4	...	47.1	...
March	43.4	45.0	45.8	28.3	40.7	38.2	44.4	...	41.1	...	49.3	...
April	43.7	45.1	46.5	28.6	41.0	38.3	44.7	...	41.3	...	50.1	...
May	43.9	45.3	47.1	28.8	41.0	38.5	45.0	...	42.2	...	52.5	...
June	44.2	45.4	47.6	29.2	41.2	38.6	45.5	...	43.0	...	55.0	...
July	44.2	45.5	47.7	29.2	41.2	38.6	45.4	...	42.3	...	52.5	...
August	45.0	45.7	50.5	29.4	41.2	38.7	47.0	...	43.5	...	64.1	...
September	45.2	46.0	50.4	29.4	41.1	38.9	46.9	...	43.0	...	60.9	...
October	45.6	46.3	50.7	30.3	41.4	39.6	46.8	...	43.4	...	58.5	...
November	45.9	46.5	51.4	31.5	41.8	39.7	47.2	...	43.8	...	59.0	...
December	46.3	46.7	51.9	32.5	42.2	39.9	47.6	...	44.8	...	59.1	...
1974												
January	46.8	46.9	52.5	34.1	42.8	40.1	48.8	49.7	45.9	47.5	63.3	86.3
February	47.3	47.2	53.6	35.4	43.4	40.3	49.7	50.0	46.8	48.1	64.3	86.5
March	47.8	47.6	54.2	36.9	44.2	40.7	50.2	50.5	48.1	49.5	62.3	88.3
April	48.1	47.9	54.1	37.6	44.7	41.0	50.7	51.1	49.0	50.9	60.6	89.7
May	48.6	48.5	54.5	38.3	45.3	41.4	51.3	52.2	50.6	52.5	58.3	83.8
June	49.0	49.0	54.5	38.6	45.9	42.1	51.3	53.1	51.5	53.7	55.4	82.9
July	49.3	49.5	54.3	38.9	46.4	42.6	52.7	54.0	53.4	55.2	59.8	84.2
August	49.9	50.2	55.1	39.2	46.6	43.2	53.7	55.0	55.8	57.0	62.9	85.5
September	50.6	50.7	56.2	39.3	47.0	43.7	54.3	55.7	55.9	57.6	60.9	82.5
October	51.0	51.2	56.8	39.2	47.3	44.1	55.3	56.7	57.2	58.2	63.2	80.6
November	51.5	51.6	57.5	39.4	47.6	44.4	56.4	57.4	57.8	58.8	64.2	77.6
December	51.9	52.0	58.2	39.6	47.9	44.8	56.4	57.9	57.8	59.1	61.5	71.6
1975												
January	52.3	52.3	58.4	40.0	48.0	45.3	56.7	58.3	58.0	59.6	59.6	69.8
February	52.6	52.8	58.5	40.3	48.3	45.8	56.6	58.7	57.8	59.8	57.9	69.2
March	52.8	53.0	58.4	40.6	48.7	46.3	56.6	59.0	57.4	59.7	57.1	68.2
April	53.0	53.3	58.3	41.0	48.8	46.7	57.1	59.2	57.5	59.7	59.5	67.7
May	53.1	53.5	58.6	41.3	48.9	47.0	57.4	59.3	57.3	59.7	61.2	68.8
June	53.5	53.8	59.2	41.7	49.4	47.4	57.9	59.5	57.3	59.8	61.5	66.5
July	54.0	54.0	60.3	42.5	50.2	47.8	58.4	59.8	57.5	59.9	62.4	66.5
August	54.2	54.2	60.3	42.8	50.6	48.1	58.9	59.9	58.0	60.1	63.0	67.7
September	54.6	54.5	60.7	43.2	51.4	48.5	59.3	60.2	58.2	60.3	64.5	71.2
October	54.9	54.8	61.3	43.5	51.7	48.9	59.8	60.6	58.8	61.0	65.1	71.5
November	55.3	55.2	61.7	43.9	52.4	48.8	60.0	61.0	59.0	61.4	64.4	71.9
December	55.6	55.5	62.1	44.1	52.6	49.3	60.1	61.4	59.2	61.8	64.0	73.1
1976												
January	55.8	55.9	61.9	44.5	53.0	49.7	60.0	61.7	59.4	62.1	63.0	72.4
February	55.9	56.2	61.3	44.4	53.3	50.2	59.9	61.9	59.6	62.3	62.1	73.8
March	56.0	56.5	60.9	44.1	53.8	50.7	60.0	62.2	59.8	62.6	61.5	74.5
April	56.1	56.7	60.9	43.9	54.0	51.0	60.3	62.3	60.0	62.8	63.9	78.1
May	56.4	57.0	61.1	44.1	54.3	51.4	60.4	62.4	60.3	63.2	63.6	80.6
June	56.7	57.2	61.3	44.4	54.8	51.8	60.5	62.8	60.8	63.6	65.2	82.8
July	57.0	57.6	61.6	44.8	55.1	52.3	60.7	63.1	61.1	63.9	64.8	87.3
August	57.3	57.9	61.8	45.2	55.4	52.6	60.9	63.5	61.3	64.3	63.6	84.1
September	57.6	58.2	62.1	45.7	56.0	53.0	61.1	63.9	61.9	64.7	63.4	84.4
October	57.9	58.5	62.4	46.1	56.6	53.2	61.4	64.1	62.0	65.0	63.0	82.2
November	58.1	58.7	62.3	46.8	57.0	53.9	61.9	64.6	62.4	65.3	63.4	81.8
December	58.4	58.9	62.5	47.5	57.3	54.2	62.4	64.9	62.8	65.6	64.5	81.1

... = Not available.

Table 20-2. Summary Consumer and Producer Price Indexes—Continued

(Seasonally adjusted.)

Year and month	Consumer Price Index, all urban consumers, 1982–1984 = 100						Producer Price Index, 1982 = 100					
							Finished goods		Intermediate materials, supplies, and components		Crude materials for further processing	
	All items	All items less food and energy	Food	Energy	Transportation	Medical care	Total	Less food and energy	Total	Less food and energy	Total	Crude nonfood less energy
1977												
January	58.7	59.3	62.7	48.1	57.8	54.6	62.5	65.1	63.0	65.8	64.3	78.7
February	59.3	59.7	63.9	48.1	58.2	54.9	63.2	65.4	63.3	65.9	65.7	79.7
March	59.6	60.0	64.2	48.4	58.7	55.5	63.7	65.7	63.9	66.4	66.6	81.5
April	60.0	60.3	65.0	48.6	59.0	56.0	64.0	65.9	64.4	66.7	68.3	82.1
May	60.2	60.6	65.3	48.9	59.1	56.5	64.4	66.1	64.9	67.1	67.6	82.5
June	60.5	61.0	65.7	48.9	59.1	57.0	64.6	66.5	64.9	67.4	65.5	79.7
July	60.8	61.2	65.9	49.1	59.0	57.3	64.8	66.8	65.1	67.9	64.7	78.8
August	61.1	61.5	66.2	49.5	58.9	57.7	65.2	67.3	65.4	68.2	63.9	79.2
September	61.3	61.8	66.4	49.8	59.1	58.2	65.5	67.8	65.7	68.7	63.7	79.2
October	61.6	62.0	66.6	50.5	59.3	58.4	65.9	68.2	65.8	68.8	64.0	78.5
November	62.0	62.3	67.1	51.3	59.5	58.6	66.4	68.8	66.3	69.1	65.4	78.4
December	62.3	62.7	67.4	51.6	59.8	59.0	66.7	69.0	66.6	69.4	66.4	80.1
1978												
January	62.7	63.1	67.9	51.1	60.1	59.3	67.0	69.2	66.9	69.8	67.3	80.3
February	63.0	63.4	68.6	50.6	60.2	59.9	67.5	69.5	67.4	70.3	68.4	80.6
March	63.4	63.8	69.5	51.0	60.3	60.2	67.8	69.9	67.8	70.6	69.8	80.3
April	63.9	64.3	70.6	51.4	60.4	60.7	68.6	70.6	68.1	71.1	72.1	82.2
May	64.5	64.7	71.6	51.7	60.7	61.1	69.1	71.1	68.7	71.6	72.8	84.6
June	65.0	65.2	72.7	51.9	61.1	61.5	69.7	71.7	69.2	72.2	74.6	87.4
July	65.5	65.6	73.0	52.1	61.6	61.9	70.3	72.3	69.4	72.5	74.2	89.6
August	65.9	66.1	73.3	52.6	62.0	62.4	70.4	72.8	69.9	73.2	73.7	90.4
September	66.5	66.7	73.6	53.2	62.6	62.8	71.1	73.5	70.5	73.7	75.1	92.3
October	67.1	67.2	74.2	54.1	63.3	63.3	71.4	73.4	71.3	74.5	77.0	94.7
November	67.5	67.6	74.7	54.9	63.9	63.8	72.0	74.1	71.9	75.2	77.4	96.3
December	67.9	68.0	75.1	55.9	64.5	64.1	72.8	74.7	72.4	75.6	78.0	96.8
1979												
January	68.5	68.5	76.4	55.8	64.6	64.8	73.7	75.3	73.1	76.3	80.1	96.4
February	69.2	69.2	77.7	55.9	65.2	65.2	74.4	75.9	73.7	77.0	82.1	99.6
March	69.9	69.8	78.4	57.4	66.4	65.7	75.0	76.4	74.6	77.8	83.8	104.2
April	70.6	70.3	79.0	59.5	67.8	66.1	75.8	77.0	75.7	78.9	84.4	105.1
May	71.4	70.8	79.7	62.0	69.1	66.6	76.2	77.4	76.6	79.6	84.7	106.7
June	72.2	71.3	80.0	64.7	70.5	67.1	76.6	78.0	77.5	80.1	85.6	111.6
July	73.0	71.9	80.5	67.3	71.7	67.7	77.4	78.5	78.7	81.1	86.5	109.4
August	73.7	72.7	80.4	69.7	72.7	68.2	78.2	78.8	79.8	81.8	85.5	106.4
September	74.4	73.3	80.9	71.9	73.5	68.7	79.5	79.7	81.1	82.7	87.9	106.5
October	75.2	74.0	81.5	73.5	74.0	69.2	80.4	80.4	82.4	83.9	88.8	108.9
November	76.0	74.8	82.0	74.8	74.7	69.8	81.4	81.0	83.2	84.5	90.0	111.3
December	76.9	75.7	82.8	76.8	75.8	70.6	82.2	81.7	84.0	85.2	91.2	111.3
1980												
January	78.0	76.7	83.3	79.1	78.0	71.4	83.4	83.3	86.0	87.2	90.9	112.6
February	79.0	77.5	83.4	81.9	79.8	72.3	84.6	84.2	87.6	88.2	92.6	115.3
March	80.1	78.6	84.1	84.5	81.8	73.0	85.5	84.7	88.2	88.6	90.8	111.7
April	80.9	79.5	84.7	85.4	82.2	73.6	86.2	85.5	88.5	88.8	88.3	109.9
May	81.7	80.1	85.2	86.4	82.8	74.2	86.6	85.7	89.0	89.1	89.5	107.2
June	82.5	81.0	85.7	86.5	82.7	74.7	87.3	86.6	89.8	89.8	90.1	106.1
July	82.6	80.8	86.6	86.7	83.1	75.2	88.7	87.7	90.5	90.3	94.6	109.6
August	83.2	81.3	88.0	87.2	83.7	75.6	89.7	88.4	91.5	91.1	99.0	112.4
September	83.9	82.1	89.1	87.5	84.6	76.3	90.1	88.8	91.9	91.4	100.4	116.2
October	84.7	83.0	89.8	88.0	85.3	76.9	90.8	89.6	92.8	92.1	102.2	118.2
November	85.6	83.9	90.8	88.8	86.1	77.3	91.4	90.1	93.5	92.6	103.5	119.8
December	86.4	84.9	91.3	90.7	86.8	77.8	91.8	90.4	94.4	93.7	102.7	119.3
1981												
January	87.2	85.4	91.6	92.1	88.5	78.6	92.8	91.4	95.6	94.7	103.4	113.3
February	88.0	85.9	92.1	95.2	90.7	79.2	93.6	92.0	96.1	94.9	104.2	106.2
March	88.6	86.4	92.6	97.4	91.8	79.9	94.7	92.6	97.1	95.6	103.8	108.9
April	89.1	87.0	92.8	97.6	91.7	80.7	95.7	93.5	98.3	96.6	104.2	111.9
May	89.7	87.8	92.8	97.9	92.2	81.4	96.0	94.0	98.7	97.1	103.8	113.7
June	90.5	88.6	93.2	97.3	92.7	82.3	96.5	94.6	99.0	97.7	104.9	115.5
July	91.5	89.8	93.9	97.3	93.5	83.4	96.7	94.8	99.2	98.4	105.0	116.4
August	92.2	90.7	94.4	97.8	93.9	84.3	96.8	95.3	99.7	98.9	104.0	115.5
September	93.1	91.8	94.8	98.6	94.6	85.1	97.2	95.9	99.7	99.3	102.7	112.6
October	93.4	92.1	95.0	99.2	95.5	85.9	97.6	96.5	99.8	99.5	101.2	110.8
November	93.8	92.5	95.1	100.5	96.2	86.8	97.9	97.0	99.9	99.7	99.7	107.5
December	94.1	93.0	95.3	101.5	96.4	87.5	98.3	97.6	100.0	99.8	98.8	106.0
1982												
January	94.4	93.3	95.6	100.6	96.7	88.2	98.9	98.1	100.4	99.9	99.7	101.2
February	94.7	93.8	96.3	98.0	96.2	88.8	98.8	98.1	100.3	100.0	100.0	100.7
March	94.7	93.9	96.2	96.6	95.8	89.6	98.8	98.7	99.9	99.9	99.7	100.0
April	95.0	94.7	96.4	94.2	94.5	90.5	99.0	99.0	99.7	99.8	100.2	101.1
May	95.9	95.4	97.2	95.7	95.1	91.3	99.0	99.4	99.7	100.1	101.9	102.2
June	97.0	96.1	98.1	98.4	97.2	92.2	99.8	99.9	99.8	100.0	101.8	101.0
July	97.5	96.7	98.2	99.3	98.1	93.0	100.2	100.1	100.0	99.8	100.7	101.4
August	97.7	97.1	98.0	99.8	98.2	93.9	100.6	100.6	99.9	99.7	99.8	100.0
September	97.7	97.2	98.2	100.3	98.0	94.7	100.7	100.8	100.0	100.2	99.2	98.9
October	98.1	97.5	98.2	101.7	98.2	95.5	101.0	101.3	99.9	100.2	98.7	97.7
November	98.0	97.3	98.2	102.5	98.2	96.5	101.4	101.6	100.1	100.2	99.2	96.3
December	97.7	97.2	98.2	102.8	97.7	97.2	101.8	102.2	100.1	100.3	98.8	95.9

Table 20-2. Summary Consumer and Producer Price Indexes—Continued

(Seasonally adjusted.)

Year and month	Consumer Price Index, all urban consumers, 1982–1984 = 100						Producer Price Index, 1982 = 100					
							Finished goods		Intermediate materials, supplies, and components		Crude materials for further processing	
	All items	All items less food and energy	Food	Energy	Transportation	Medical care	Total	Less food and energy	Total	Less food and energy	Total	Crude nonfood less energy
1983												
January	97.9	97.6	98.1	99.6	97.6	97.9	101.0	101.8	99.8	100.3	98.8	97.3
February	98.0	98.0	98.2	97.7	96.9	98.8	101.1	102.2	100.0	100.8	100.0	99.8
March	98.1	98.2	98.8	96.8	96.5	99.0	101.0	102.5	99.7	100.8	100.5	102.2
April	98.8	98.6	99.2	98.9	97.8	99.4	101.1	102.4	99.5	100.9	101.2	102.1
May	99.2	98.9	99.5	100.4	98.6	99.9	101.4	102.6	99.8	101.0	100.9	103.4
June	99.4	99.2	99.6	100.6	99.0	100.4	101.6	102.8	100.2	101.3	100.5	104.8
July	99.8	99.8	99.6	100.9	99.6	100.8	101.6	103.1	100.5	101.8	99.5	106.2
August	100.1	100.1	99.7	101.2	100.4	101.4	101.9	103.5	100.9	102.0	102.2	108.4
September	100.4	100.5	100.0	101.0	100.7	101.8	102.2	103.5	101.6	102.3	103.3	109.0
October	100.8	101.0	100.3	100.8	101.1	102.3	102.2	103.6	101.7	102.5	103.2	109.1
November	101.1	101.5	100.3	100.5	101.5	102.8	102.0	103.8	101.8	102.8	102.3	109.9
December	101.4	101.8	100.6	100.0	101.5	103.4	102.3	104.1	101.9	103.1	103.5	111.2
1984												
January	102.1	102.5	102.0	100.2	102.0	104.0	103.0	104.5	102.1	103.4	104.6	111.5
February	102.6	102.8	102.7	101.4	102.2	105.0	103.4	104.7	102.5	103.8	103.8	113.8
March	102.9	103.2	102.9	101.4	102.9	105.2	103.8	105.2	103.0	104.4	105.7	114.8
April	103.3	103.7	102.9	101.7	103.3	105.8	103.9	105.3	103.2	104.5	105.2	115.1
May	103.5	104.1	102.7	101.6	103.7	106.2	103.8	105.3	103.4	104.6	104.5	115.7
June	103.7	104.5	103.1	100.8	103.9	106.7	103.8	105.5	103.6	104.8	103.3	114.1
July	104.1	105.0	103.3	100.5	103.7	107.2	104.0	105.7	103.4	104.9	104.0	112.0
August	104.4	105.4	103.9	100.1	103.8	107.7	103.8	105.9	103.2	105.1	103.3	109.6
September	104.7	105.8	103.8	100.6	104.1	108.1	103.8	106.2	103.1	105.0	102.8	110.5
October	105.1	106.2	104.0	101.1	104.8	108.7	103.6	105.9	103.2	105.1	101.5	108.5
November	105.3	106.4	104.1	100.8	104.9	109.3	104.0	106.2	103.3	105.3	101.9	107.7
December	105.5	106.8	104.5	100.1	104.7	109.8	104.0	106.3	103.2	105.3	101.4	107.3
1985												
January	105.7	107.1	104.7	100.3	105.1	110.2	104.0	106.9	103.1	105.3	99.9	107.4
February	106.3	107.7	105.2	100.3	105.6	110.8	104.1	107.3	102.8	105.3	99.4	107.2
March	106.8	108.1	105.5	101.3	106.3	111.4	104.1	107.6	102.7	105.2	97.6	107.0
April	107.0	108.4	105.4	102.3	106.8	112.0	104.6	107.6	102.9	105.2	96.7	107.4
May	107.2	108.8	105.2	102.2	106.5	112.6	104.9	107.8	103.2	105.3	95.8	105.3
June	107.5	109.1	105.5	102.2	106.5	113.3	104.6	108.2	102.6	105.5	95.2	103.6
July	107.7	109.4	105.5	102.2	106.6	113.9	104.7	108.4	102.3	105.3	94.9	104.3
August	107.9	109.8	105.6	101.2	106.2	114.6	104.5	108.5	102.3	105.3	92.9	103.6
September	108.1	110.0	105.8	101.2	106.2	115.2	103.8	107.9	102.2	105.2	91.8	103.3
October	108.5	110.5	105.8	101.2	106.5	115.8	104.9	108.9	102.3	105.1	94.1	103.7
November	109.0	111.1	106.5	101.8	107.0	116.5	105.5	109.1	102.5	105.1	95.7	103.0
December	109.5	111.4	107.3	102.4	107.5	117.1	106.0	109.1	102.9	105.1	95.5	102.4
1986												
January	109.9	111.9	107.5	102.6	108.0	118.0	105.5	109.3	102.4	105.0	94.2	103.6
February	109.7	112.2	107.3	99.5	107.0	118.8	104.1	109.5	101.2	104.9	90.5	103.5
March	109.1	112.5	107.5	92.6	103.6	119.7	102.8	109.6	99.9	105.0	88.2	103.8
April	108.7	112.9	107.7	87.2	101.0	120.4	102.3	110.1	98.9	104.7	85.6	103.9
May	109.0	113.1	108.2	87.2	101.4	121.2	102.8	110.2	98.7	104.6	86.5	104.1
June	109.4	113.4	108.3	88.8	102.3	121.8	103.1	110.5	98.6	104.7	86.2	104.7
July	109.5	113.8	109.1	85.6	101.1	122.5	102.3	110.7	98.0	104.8	86.4	105.3
August	109.6	114.2	110.1	83.6	100.1	123.2	102.7	110.8	98.0	104.9	86.7	99.7
September	110.0	114.6	110.2	84.4	100.6	124.0	102.9	110.7	98.5	105.1	86.6	100.3
October	110.2	115.0	110.5	82.8	100.5	124.7	103.5	111.8	98.3	105.1	87.4	102.0
November	110.4	115.3	111.1	82.1	100.8	125.5	103.4	112.0	98.3	105.2	87.6	102.8
December	110.8	115.6	111.4	82.5	101.1	126.2	103.6	112.1	98.5	105.3	86.9	104.1
1987												
January	111.4	115.9	111.8	85.4	102.6	126.7	104.1	112.5	99.0	105.6	89.3	105.4
February	111.8	116.2	112.2	87.4	103.5	127.2	104.4	112.3	99.8	105.9	90.2	106.2
March	112.2	116.6	112.4	87.6	103.8	127.8	104.5	112.4	99.9	106.2	90.5	106.5
April	112.7	117.3	112.6	87.6	104.3	128.6	105.1	112.9	100.3	106.5	92.5	107.5
May	113.0	117.7	113.2	87.1	104.4	129.2	105.2	113.0	100.8	107.0	93.8	110.0
June	113.5	117.9	113.9	88.5	105.1	130.0	105.5	113.1	101.4	107.5	94.5	113.2
July	113.8	118.3	113.7	89.2	105.9	130.6	105.7	113.3	101.9	107.9	95.6	115.9
August	114.3	118.7	113.9	90.5	106.6	131.2	105.9	113.6	102.4	108.3	96.5	119.1
September	114.7	119.2	114.3	90.3	106.9	131.9	106.2	113.9	102.6	108.9	96.0	122.8
October	115.0	119.8	114.5	89.6	107.0	132.4	106.0	114.0	103.1	109.6	95.8	126.6
November	115.4	120.1	114.5	90.0	107.3	133.0	106.0	114.2	103.5	110.1	95.1	127.5
December	115.6	120.4	115.1	89.5	107.2	133.5	105.8	114.3	103.8	110.7	94.9	127.9
1988												
January	116.0	120.9	115.6	88.8	107.0	134.4	106.4	115.0	104.1	111.8	94.2	129.4
February	116.2	121.2	115.6	88.7	107.0	135.2	106.3	115.3	104.4	112.2	95.2	131.7
March	116.5	121.7	115.8	88.4	107.0	135.8	106.6	115.6	104.8	112.8	94.1	133.0
April	117.2	122.3	116.4	88.8	107.5	136.7	107.0	115.9	105.5	113.6	95.4	132.1
May	117.5	122.7	116.9	88.5	107.9	137.6	107.2	116.2	106.2	114.3	95.8	130.7
June	118.0	123.2	117.6	88.9	108.3	138.3	107.5	116.6	107.4	114.9	97.0	131.1
July	118.5	123.6	118.8	89.4	108.8	139.1	108.4	117.2	108.3	115.8	96.7	133.2
August	119.0	124.0	119.4	90.1	109.7	139.8	108.8	117.7	108.5	116.3	97.0	134.3
September	119.5	124.7	120.1	89.8	109.9	140.5	109.0	118.1	108.7	116.8	97.0	133.3
October	119.9	125.2	120.3	89.8	110.0	141.4	109.2	118.4	108.6	117.3	96.6	133.6
November	120.3	125.6	120.5	89.8	110.2	142.0	109.6	118.7	108.8	118.0	95.2	136.0
December	120.7	126.0	121.1	89.6	110.4	142.7	110.0	119.2	109.4	118.6	98.1	137.6

Table 20-2. Summary Consumer and Producer Price Indexes—Continued

(Seasonally adjusted.)

Year and month	Consumer Price Index, all urban consumers, 1982–1984 = 100						Producer Price Index, 1982 = 100					
							Finished goods		Intermediate materials, supplies, and components		Crude materials for further processing	
	All items	All items less food and energy	Food	Energy	Transportation	Medical care	Total	Less food and energy	Total	Less food and energy	Total	Crude nonfood less energy
1989												
January	121.2	126.5	121.6	90.3	110.9	143.8	111.1	119.9	110.8	119.5	102.0	140.6
February	121.6	126.9	122.5	90.8	111.7	144.9	111.9	120.5	111.3	119.9	101.7	140.3
March	122.2	127.4	123.2	91.8	112.4	145.8	112.3	120.7	111.9	120.2	102.9	140.6
April	123.1	127.8	123.9	96.6	115.0	146.6	113.1	120.8	112.5	120.5	104.1	140.3
May	123.7	128.3	124.7	97.4	115.8	147.5	114.0	121.6	112.6	120.6	104.5	139.8
June	124.1	128.8	125.1	96.9	115.7	148.6	114.0	122.2	112.5	120.6	103.2	137.9
July	124.5	129.2	125.6	96.7	115.4	149.6	113.8	122.1	112.2	120.3	103.5	135.9
August	124.5	129.5	125.9	94.9	114.5	150.6	113.4	122.7	111.8	120.2	101.2	136.8
September	124.8	129.9	126.3	93.8	113.9	151.8	114.0	123.1	112.1	120.2	102.5	137.5
October	125.4	130.6	126.8	94.4	114.5	152.8	114.6	123.5	112.2	120.3	102.7	137.9
November	125.9	131.1	127.4	93.9	114.4	154.1	114.8	123.9	112.0	120.0	103.5	134.9
December	126.3	131.6	127.8	94.2	114.7	154.9	115.5	124.2	112.2	119.8	105.1	132.8
1990												
January	127.5	132.1	129.7	98.9	117.0	156.0	117.7	124.5	113.7	120.0	106.7	132.7
February	128.0	132.7	130.8	98.2	117.2	157.1	117.6	124.9	112.8	119.9	106.8	131.6
March	128.6	133.5	131.0	97.6	117.3	158.3	117.5	125.3	112.9	120.2	105.1	133.9
April	128.9	134.0	130.8	97.5	117.7	159.6	117.4	125.5	113.1	120.5	102.7	137.0
May	129.1	134.4	131.1	96.7	117.5	160.8	117.5	126.0	113.1	120.6	103.1	138.0
June	129.9	135.1	132.1	97.3	118.0	162.0	117.6	126.4	112.9	120.4	100.6	137.3
July	130.5	135.8	132.8	97.1	118.5	163.4	117.9	126.6	112.8	120.6	101.0	138.0
August	131.6	136.6	133.2	101.6	120.7	164.8	119.2	127.1	114.0	120.8	110.5	140.1
September	132.5	137.1	133.6	106.5	123.2	165.9	120.7	127.7	115.8	121.5	115.8	139.9
October	133.4	137.6	134.1	110.8	125.6	167.3	121.9	128.0	117.4	122.1	125.8	138.4
November	133.7	138.0	134.5	111.2	126.1	168.7	122.6	128.4	117.7	122.3	117.8	135.7
December	134.2	138.6	134.6	111.0	126.9	169.8	122.0	128.6	116.9	122.1	110.8	133.8
1991												
January	134.7	139.5	135.0	108.5	125.5	171.0	122.6	129.5	116.9	122.4	113.3	134.2
February	134.8	140.2	135.1	104.5	123.9	172.1	121.8	129.8	115.9	122.1	104.1	133.7
March	134.8	140.5	135.3	101.9	122.7	173.2	121.3	130.1	114.7	121.7	100.5	131.8
April	135.1	140.9	136.1	101.2	122.5	174.3	121.3	130.4	114.2	121.5	100.2	131.7
May	135.6	141.3	136.6	102.1	123.2	175.2	121.6	130.6	114.1	121.3	100.9	130.4
June	136.0	141.8	137.4	101.1	123.4	176.4	121.4	130.7	113.9	121.3	99.2	126.1
July	136.2	142.3	136.7	100.7	123.3	177.4	121.1	131.0	113.6	121.1	99.4	125.4
August	136.6	142.9	136.2	101.1	124.0	178.8	121.3	131.3	113.8	121.0	99.1	125.8
September	137.0	143.4	136.4	101.5	124.1	179.9	121.5	131.8	114.0	121.0	98.4	125.7
October	137.2	143.7	136.2	101.6	123.9	180.9	121.9	132.3	114.0	121.1	100.8	125.4
November	137.8	144.2	136.7	102.4	124.5	181.9	122.4	132.5	114.1	121.1	100.7	124.4
December	138.2	144.7	137.0	103.1	125.1	183.1	122.3	132.6	114.0	121.1	98.2	123.4
1992												
January	138.3	145.1	136.6	101.5	124.6	184.3	122.0	133.0	113.4	121.0	97.2	123.4
February	138.6	145.4	137.1	101.2	124.5	185.6	122.3	133.1	113.8	121.3	98.6	125.2
March	139.1	145.9	137.6	101.2	125.0	186.8	122.4	133.4	113.9	121.5	97.1	127.7
April	139.4	146.3	137.5	101.4	125.6	187.9	122.5	133.8	114.1	121.7	98.1	128.4
May	139.7	146.8	137.2	102.0	125.9	188.7	122.9	134.3	114.5	121.8	100.3	129.1
June	140.1	147.1	137.6	103.3	126.4	189.6	123.4	134.1	115.1	122.0	101.6	128.8
July	140.5	147.6	137.4	103.7	126.9	190.6	123.3	134.3	115.2	122.1	101.6	129.6
August	140.8	147.9	138.4	103.5	127.0	191.5	123.4	134.3	115.1	122.3	100.7	130.4
September	141.1	148.1	138.9	103.6	127.0	192.4	123.7	134.6	115.3	122.4	102.8	130.4
October	141.7	148.8	138.9	104.3	128.1	193.5	124.2	134.9	115.3	122.4	102.8	128.9
November	142.1	149.2	138.7	105.1	128.7	194.5	124.1	135.1	115.1	122.4	102.5	128.2
December	142.3	149.6	138.8	105.3	128.9	195.3	124.2	135.2	115.1	122.5	101.3	130.5
1993												
January	142.8	150.1	139.1	105.0	129.2	196.4	124.4	135.6	115.4	122.9	101.7	135.0
February	143.1	150.6	139.6	104.3	129.6	197.4	124.7	135.9	115.9	123.5	101.2	136.8
March	143.3	150.8	139.6	104.9	129.4	198.1	125.0	136.1	116.3	123.8	101.7	137.0
April	143.8	151.4	140.0	104.9	129.6	199.1	125.7	136.5	116.6	124.0	103.2	138.4
May	144.2	151.8	141.0	104.3	129.9	200.5	125.7	136.6	116.3	123.7	105.6	140.3
June	144.3	152.1	140.6	103.9	129.9	201.3	125.2	136.4	116.3	123.7	103.8	140.3
July	144.5	152.3	140.6	103.4	130.1	202.2	125.1	136.6	116.3	123.7	101.6	142.1
August	144.8	152.8	141.1	103.4	130.5	202.8	123.9	134.9	116.2	123.9	100.8	140.4
September	145.0	152.9	141.4	103.0	130.4	203.6	124.1	134.9	116.3	124.0	101.2	140.7
October	145.6	153.4	142.0	105.3	132.0	204.5	124.2	135.0	116.4	124.0	103.7	142.6
November	146.0	153.9	142.3	104.4	132.2	205.1	124.4	135.3	116.5	124.3	103.0	144.1
December	146.3	154.3	142.8	103.7	132.1	205.8	124.4	135.7	116.2	124.5	101.7	145.3
1994												
January	146.3	154.5	142.9	102.8	131.7	206.4	124.8	136.3	116.5	124.7	103.8	148.3
February	146.7	154.8	142.7	104.1	132.3	207.2	125.0	136.3	116.9	124.9	102.1	151.0
March	147.1	155.3	142.7	104.3	132.6	207.9	125.1	136.4	117.1	125.1	103.8	151.5
April	147.2	155.5	143.0	103.7	132.8	209.0	125.1	136.6	117.1	125.3	103.8	150.7
May	147.5	155.9	143.3	102.8	132.4	209.7	125.1	137.0	117.2	125.6	102.2	149.7
June	147.9	156.4	143.8	103.1	133.2	210.5	125.2	137.2	117.8	126.3	102.7	151.2
July	148.4	156.7	144.6	104.5	134.4	211.3	125.7	137.3	118.3	126.7	101.7	155.5
August	149.0	157.1	145.1	106.7	136.0	212.2	126.2	137.6	119.1	127.4	101.6	158.8
September	149.3	157.5	145.3	106.1	136.1	213.1	125.9	137.7	119.6	128.4	99.7	160.5
October	149.4	157.8	145.3	105.7	136.2	214.1	125.5	137.4	120.1	129.3	98.6	161.3
November	149.8	158.2	145.6	106.1	136.7	215.0	126.1	137.6	121.0	130.3	99.8	166.6
December	150.1	158.3	146.8	105.9	137.1	215.9	126.6	137.9	121.5	131.0	101.1	169.9

Table 20-2. Summary Consumer and Producer Price Indexes—Continued

(Seasonally adjusted.)

Year and month	Consumer Price Index, all urban consumers, 1982–1984 = 100						Producer Price Index, 1982 = 100					
							Finished goods		Intermediate materials, supplies, and components		Crude materials for further processing	
	All items	All items less food and energy	Food	Energy	Transportation	Medical care	Total	Less food and energy	Total	Less food and energy	Total	Crude nonfood less energy
1995												
January	150.5	159.0	146.7	105.7	137.4	216.6	126.9	138.4	122.8	132.6	102.1	174.5
February	150.9	159.4	147.3	105.8	137.9	217.4	127.2	138.7	123.7	133.7	102.9	176.5
March	151.2	159.9	147.1	105.5	138.4	218.1	127.4	139.0	124.3	134.3	102.3	177.8
April	151.8	160.4	148.1	105.6	139.2	218.6	127.7	139.3	125.0	135.2	103.7	180.2
May	152.1	160.7	148.2	105.8	139.7	219.2	127.8	139.7	125.2	135.5	102.4	179.6
June	152.4	161.1	148.3	106.7	140.6	219.9	127.8	139.8	125.5	135.7	103.0	179.5
July	152.6	161.4	148.5	105.8	139.9	220.6	128.0	140.2	125.6	136.1	101.6	176.4
August	152.9	161.8	148.6	105.6	139.4	221.6	127.9	140.2	125.6	136.1	99.7	173.4
September	153.1	162.2	149.1	104.1	139.1	222.4	128.1	140.2	125.5	136.2	102.0	170.9
October	153.5	162.7	149.5	104.4	139.5	223.0	128.4	141.0	125.4	135.8	101.9	166.6
November	153.7	163.0	149.6	103.4	139.1	223.7	128.7	141.3	125.2	135.5	104.1	163.6
December	153.9	163.1	149.9	104.4	139.1	224.3	129.3	141.5	125.4	135.2	106.5	162.3
1996												
January	154.7	163.7	150.4	106.9	140.4	225.2	129.7	141.5	125.5	134.8	109.8	162.6
February	155.0	164.0	150.8	107.1	140.9	225.7	129.7	141.6	125.0	134.4	111.6	162.1
March	155.5	164.4	151.4	108.3	141.5	226.2	130.5	141.6	125.3	134.1	109.8	158.2
April	156.1	164.6	152.0	111.2	142.9	226.8	130.9	141.6	125.7	133.8	114.2	156.7
May	156.4	165.0	151.9	112.0	143.5	227.4	130.9	142.0	126.2	134.0	114.6	157.6
June	156.7	165.4	152.9	110.3	143.4	228.0	131.3	142.2	125.8	133.9	112.2	154.6
July	157.0	165.7	153.4	110.1	143.0	228.6	131.2	142.2	125.5	133.6	114.6	152.2
August	157.2	166.0	153.9	109.7	143.0	229.1	131.6	142.3	125.6	133.6	115.3	152.5
September	157.7	166.5	154.6	109.8	143.6	229.7	131.7	142.2	126.1	134.0	112.7	153.5
October	158.2	166.8	155.5	110.5	143.9	230.3	132.4	142.3	126.0	133.7	111.9	153.3
November	158.7	167.2	156.1	111.8	144.6	231.0	132.5	142.1	125.8	133.7	115.7	153.0
December	159.1	167.4	156.3	113.9	145.7	231.2	132.9	142.3	126.4	133.9	122.5	153.6
1997												
January	159.4	167.8	155.9	115.2	145.6	231.8	133.0	142.5	126.6	134.1	127.5	156.2
February	159.7	168.1	156.5	115.0	145.2	232.2	132.7	142.4	126.5	134.1	116.6	157.6
March	159.8	168.4	156.6	113.0	145.0	233.0	132.6	142.6	126.1	134.2	107.5	158.7
April	159.9	168.9	156.5	111.0	144.3	233.5	131.8	142.6	125.6	134.1	107.8	155.8
May	159.9	169.2	156.6	108.8	143.3	234.1	131.5	142.4	125.4	134.2	109.1	157.0
June	160.2	169.4	156.9	110.0	143.6	234.4	131.3	142.4	125.4	134.2	106.2	156.9
July	160.4	169.7	157.0	109.1	143.3	234.7	130.9	142.2	125.1	134.2	106.2	155.7
August	160.8	169.8	157.7	110.9	144.1	235.1	131.4	142.3	125.3	134.3	106.8	156.8
September	161.2	170.2	158.0	112.4	144.8	235.5	131.6	142.6	125.5	134.3	108.4	155.8
October	161.5	170.6	158.3	111.8	144.7	236.1	131.9	142.6	125.4	134.3	113.4	156.7
November	161.7	170.8	158.6	111.4	143.9	236.9	131.6	142.4	125.6	134.4	115.8	156.5
December	161.8	171.2	158.7	109.8	143.7	237.8	131.4	142.3	125.4	134.4	108.8	154.2
1998												
January	162.0	171.6	159.5	107.5	143.0	238.1	130.7	142.4	124.6	134.3	102.8	150.4
February	162.0	171.9	159.4	105.1	142.4	238.8	130.6	142.6	124.2	134.2	100.8	150.1
March	162.0	172.2	159.7	103.3	141.5	239.4	130.5	143.3	123.7	134.1	99.5	148.7
April	162.2	172.5	159.7	102.4	140.9	240.3	130.7	143.4	123.6	134.0	100.6	147.3
May	162.6	172.9	160.3	103.2	141.2	241.2	130.5	143.5	123.5	133.9	99.6	146.2
June	162.8	173.2	160.2	103.6	141.4	241.8	130.4	143.5	123.1	133.6	97.1	145.9
July	163.2	173.5	160.6	103.3	141.7	242.5	130.7	143.8	123.0	133.5	97.4	143.4
August	163.4	174.0	161.0	102.1	141.6	243.3	130.4	143.8	122.7	133.4	93.6	139.4
September	163.5	174.2	161.1	101.3	141.2	244.1	130.4	144.0	122.3	133.1	91.4	137.6
October	163.9	174.4	162.0	101.5	141.4	244.8	130.9	144.2	122.2	132.7	93.9	134.0
November	164.1	174.8	162.2	101.1	141.3	245.3	130.8	144.3	122.0	132.5	93.6	131.6
December	164.4	175.4	162.4	100.1	140.9	245.9	131.3	145.8	121.3	132.2	90.2	129.4
1999												
January	164.7	175.6	163.0	99.7	140.8	246.5	131.5	145.2	121.2	132.0	91.0	128.7
February	164.7	175.6	163.3	99.2	140.0	247.3	131.0	145.3	120.8	131.8	89.0	130.5
March	164.8	175.7	163.3	100.4	140.7	247.9	131.3	145.3	121.1	131.9	89.6	129.6
April	165.9	176.3	163.5	105.5	143.6	248.7	131.9	145.3	121.9	132.0	91.3	128.7
May	166.0	176.5	163.8	104.9	143.4	249.3	132.1	145.4	122.2	132.4	96.8	130.5
June	166.0	176.6	163.7	104.5	143.0	250.0	132.2	145.4	122.6	132.8	97.0	131.6
July	166.7	177.1	163.9	106.7	144.6	250.9	132.5	145.4	123.4	133.3	97.3	133.6
August	167.1	177.3	164.2	109.5	145.9	251.7	133.3	145.3	124.1	133.6	102.4	136.3
September	167.8	177.8	164.6	111.8	147.0	252.5	134.2	146.1	124.6	133.9	106.4	138.8
October	168.1	178.1	165.0	112.0	147.6	253.1	134.2	146.5	124.9	134.3	103.8	142.5
November	168.4	178.4	165.3	111.5	147.5	253.9	134.7	146.5	125.4	134.5	109.7	144.4
December	168.8	178.7	165.5	113.8	148.8	254.9	135.0	146.6	125.8	134.7	104.4	147.6
2000												
January	169.3	179.2	165.7	114.7	149.0	255.5	135.1	146.8	126.3	135.1	106.7	149.9
February	169.9	179.4	166.2	118.7	149.9	256.5	136.5	147.3	127.4	135.5	111.2	151.4
March	171.0	180.0	166.5	124.4	153.7	257.7	137.2	147.4	128.4	136.0	113.3	150.8
April	170.9	180.4	166.7	120.8	152.0	258.5	136.9	147.4	128.3	136.5	111.5	149.1
May	171.2	180.7	167.4	119.8	151.9	259.2	137.1	147.8	128.3	136.6	115.1	148.0
June	172.2	181.0	167.4	126.9	155.0	260.3	138.3	147.8	129.4	136.9	124.8	145.7
July	172.7	181.5	168.2	127.4	154.7	261.2	138.3	148.0	129.7	137.1	122.0	143.3
August	172.7	181.9	168.7	124.0	153.3	262.4	138.0	148.2	129.4	136.9	117.6	141.3
September	173.6	182.3	169.0	129.4	155.3	263.3	139.1	148.6	130.3	137.0	125.3	142.6
October	173.9	182.6	169.1	130.0	154.9	264.1	139.4	148.5	130.7	137.1	130.2	141.7
November	174.2	183.1	169.2	129.3	155.0	264.7	140.1	148.8	130.6	136.9	129.0	139.4
December	174.6	183.3	170.0	130.0	155.0	265.6	140.1	148.9	131.0	136.9	141.3	139.3

Table 20-2. Summary Consumer and Producer Price Indexes—Continued

(Seasonally adjusted.)

Year and month	Consumer Price Index, all urban consumers, 1982–1984 = 100						Producer Price Index, 1982 = 100					
							Finished goods		Intermediate materials, supplies, and components		Crude materials for further processing	
	All items	All items less food and energy	Food	Energy	Transportation	Medical care	Total	Less food and energy	Total	Less food and energy	Total	Crude nonfood less energy
2001												
January	175.6	183.9	170.4	134.9	155.4	267.1	141.6	149.6	132.0	137.2	165.6	138.4
February	175.9	184.4	171.2	133.9	155.2	268.4	142.0	149.2	131.8	137.4	141.9	136.6
March	176.0	184.7	171.6	131.4	154.1	269.4	141.4	149.5	131.1	137.4	132.5	135.3
April	176.5	185.1	172.0	133.1	155.1	270.5	142.1	149.8	131.0	137.3	133.2	131.5
May	177.4	185.4	172.5	138.7	157.8	271.3	142.4	150.1	131.1	137.3	130.6	130.8
June	177.8	186.0	173.0	137.6	157.6	272.4	141.9	150.2	131.0	137.0	119.9	129.7
July	177.4	186.5	173.6	129.9	154.1	272.9	140.2	150.5	129.5	136.4	113.1	130.8
August	177.5	186.8	174.0	127.4	153.4	274.3	140.6	150.4	129.2	135.9	112.3	128.5
September	178.1	187.1	174.2	130.9	156.0	275.2	141.3	150.7	129.3	135.9	106.9	128.7
October	177.6	187.4	174.9	122.9	152.9	276.2	139.0	149.8	127.6	135.4	97.4	126.3
November	177.5	188.1	174.9	116.6	150.1	277.3	138.4	150.2	126.8	135.1	102.7	126.2
December	177.2	188.3	174.7	113.2	149.0	278.1	137.7	150.3	125.9	134.8	95.7	125.6
2002												
January	177.6	188.6	175.4	114.3	149.3	279.5	137.7	150.1	125.5	134.7	99.7	125.9
February	177.9	189.0	175.7	112.9	148.5	280.5	138.1	150.2	125.4	134.7	98.7	127.8
March	178.5	189.2	176.0	117.6	150.6	281.6	139.1	150.1	126.3	135.0	103.9	128.6
April	179.4	189.7	176.2	122.2	152.9	282.9	139.1	150.4	127.4	135.3	108.4	131.0
May	179.5	190.0	175.8	121.8	152.7	284.0	138.5	150.3	127.0	135.3	109.3	134.0
June	179.7	190.2	175.8	122.1	152.8	284.6	138.8	150.6	127.3	135.6	105.1	138.2
July	180.1	190.5	176.1	122.9	153.4	286.5	138.6	150.0	127.7	136.0	106.1	140.7
August	180.6	191.1	176.1	123.6	154.0	287.2	138.6	149.9	128.2	136.2	108.1	140.0
September	180.9	191.4	176.6	124.3	154.5	288.0	139.0	150.3	129.0	136.5	110.4	139.8
October	181.2	191.5	176.6	126.6	155.5	289.7	140.0	150.6	129.9	136.7	112.5	139.8
November	181.4	191.8	177.0	126.0	155.1	291.1	139.7	150.4	129.9	136.8	116.7	141.5
December	181.6	192.0	177.2	125.5	154.7	292.0	139.3	149.5	129.7	136.7	119.2	141.4
2003												
January	182.2	192.2	177.1	130.4	156.4	292.4	141.1	150.0	131.1	137.2	127.9	142.7
February	183.2	192.4	178.1	137.5	159.1	293.1	142.8	149.9	133.6	138.2	134.5	147.9
March	184.0	192.5	178.4	144.9	161.4	293.7	144.6	150.8	136.4	138.6	152.3	147.6
April	183.4	192.6	178.4	138.1	158.4	294.3	142.5	150.0	133.2	138.3	128.2	145.8
May	183.3	193.0	178.8	132.9	156.1	295.4	141.9	150.1	132.3	138.4	130.1	145.6
June	183.5	193.1	179.6	133.7	156.3	296.3	142.7	150.1	133.1	138.4	135.7	145.9
July	183.8	193.4	179.8	134.1	156.5	297.4	142.8	150.3	133.3	138.2	131.9	148.6
August	184.5	193.6	180.5	138.3	158.4	298.3	143.5	150.5	134.1	138.4	130.6	151.5
September	185.1	193.7	180.9	142.8	159.9	299.6	143.8	150.5	134.0	138.7	134.1	155.6
October	184.9	194.0	181.8	137.8	157.7	300.3	144.7	151.2	134.4	139.1	137.9	160.3
November	184.6	194.0	182.6	133.7	155.6	301.3	144.5	151.2	134.4	139.3	137.9	167.2
December	184.9	194.1	183.5	134.1	155.3	302.7	144.8	151.0	134.9	139.6	142.6	172.2

CHAPTER 20: HISTORICAL DATA FOR SELECTED MONTHLY SERIES

Table 20-3. Summary Labor Force, Employment, and Unemployment

(Thousands of persons, percent, seasonally adjusted, except as noted.)

Year and month	Noninsti-tutional population [1]	Labor force		Employment, thousands of persons					Employ-ment–population ratio, percent	Unemployment		
		Thousands of persons	Participa-tion rate (percent)	By age and sex			By industry			Thousands of persons		Rate, percent
				Men, 20 years and over	Women, 20 years and over	Both sexes, 16–19 years	Agricultural	Nonagri-cultural		Total	Unem-ployed 15 weeks and over	
1948												
January	102 603	60 095	58.6	39 386	14 556	4 119	8 077	49 984	56.6	2 034	311	3.4
February	102 698	60 524	58.9	39 480	14 621	4 095	7 696	50 500	56.7	2 328	283	3.8
March	102 771	60 070	58.5	39 098	14 481	4 092	7 333	50 338	56.1	2 399	292	4.0
April	102 831	60 677	59.0	39 157	15 001	4 133	7 557	50 734	56.7	2 386	324	3.9
May	102 923	59 972	58.3	39 139	14 712	4 003	7 141	50 713	56.2	2 118	329	3.5
June	102 992	60 957	59.2	39 392	15 213	4 138	7 591	51 152	57.0	2 214	322	3.6
July	103 216	61 181	59.3	39 607	15 348	4 013	7 602	51 366	57.1	2 213	295	3.6
August	103 240	60 806	58.9	39 510	14 994	3 952	7 562	50 894	56.6	2 350	332	3.9
September	103 291	60 815	58.9	39 324	15 207	3 982	7 865	50 648	56.6	2 302	298	3.8
October	103 361	60 646	58.7	39 522	14 956	3 909	7 626	50 761	56.5	2 259	324	3.7
November	103 424	60 702	58.7	39 459	15 054	3 904	7 624	50 793	56.5	2 285	282	3.8
December	103 468	61 169	59.1	39 539	15 137	4 064	7 984	50 756	56.8	2 429	305	4.0
1949												
January	103 529	60 771	58.7	39 233	14 991	3 951	7 790	50 385	56.2	2 596	315	4.3
February	103 559	61 057	59.0	39 117	15 117	3 974	8 022	50 186	56.2	2 849	374	4.7
March	103 665	61 073	58.9	39 015	15 069	3 959	8 008	50 035	56.0	3 030	414	5.0
April	103 739	61 007	58.8	38 993	14 978	3 776	7 911	50 130	55.7	3 260	483	5.3
May	103 845	61 259	59.0	38 701	15 066	3 785	8 067	49 485	55.4	3 707	602	6.1
June	103 930	60 948	58.6	38 632	15 003	3 537	7 802	49 370	55.0	3 776	705	6.2
July	104 042	61 301	58.9	38 405	15 244	3 541	8 021	49 169	55.0	4 111	848	6.7
August	104 121	61 590	59.2	38 610	15 181	3 606	7 604	49 793	55.1	4 193	917	6.8
September	104 219	61 633	59.1	38 744	15 129	3 711	7 297	50 287	55.3	4 049	973	6.6
October	104 338	62 185	59.6	38 394	15 260	3 615	6 814	50 455	54.9	4 916	1 000	7.9
November	104 421	62 005	59.4	38 860	15 422	3 727	7 497	50 512	55.6	3 996	1 056	6.4
December	104 524	61 908	59.2	38 908	15 300	3 637	7 379	50 466	55.3	4 063	961	6.6
1950												
January	104 619	61 661	58.9	38 780	15 255	3 600	7 065	50 570	55.1	4 026	947	6.5
February	104 737	61 687	58.9	38 818	15 339	3 594	7 057	50 694	55.1	3 936	947	6.4
March	104 844	61 604	58.8	38 851	15 366	3 511	7 116	50 612	55.1	3 876	912	6.3
April	104 943	62 158	59.2	39 100	15 831	3 652	7 264	51 319	55.8	3 575	920	5.8
May	105 014	62 083	59.1	39 416	15 628	3 605	7 277	51 372	55.8	3 434	890	5.5
June	105 104	62 419	59.4	39 476	15 953	3 623	7 285	51 767	56.2	3 367	868	5.4
July	105 194	62 121	59.1	39 517	15 793	3 691	7 126	51 875	56.1	3 120	769	5.0
August	105 282	62 596	59.5	39 879	16 124	3 794	7 248	52 549	56.8	2 799	633	4.5
September	105 269	62 349	59.2	39 865	15 902	3 808	6 992	52 583	56.6	2 774	648	4.4
October	105 096	62 428	59.4	39 737	16 175	3 891	7 371	52 432	56.9	2 625	545	4.2
November	104 979	62 286	59.3	39 668	16 195	3 834	7 163	52 534	56.9	2 589	507	4.2
December	104 872	62 068	59.2	39 536	16 149	3 744	6 760	52 669	56.7	2 639	482	4.3
1951												
January	104 844	61 941	59.1	39 595	16 279	3 762	6 828	52 808	56.9	2 305	438	3.7
February	104 604	61 778	59.1	39 695	16 257	3 709	6 738	52 923	57.0	2 117	386	3.4
March	104 629	62 526	59.8	40 013	16 557	3 831	6 858	53 543	57.7	2 125	355	3.4
April	104 541	61 808	59.1	39 804	16 426	3 659	6 722	53 167	57.3	1 919	294	3.1
May	104 491	62 044	59.4	39 752	16 581	3 855	6 752	53 436	57.6	1 856	269	3.0
June	104 488	61 615	59.0	39 538	16 368	3 714	6 529	53 091	57.1	1 995	258	3.2
July	104 504	62 106	59.4	39 483	16 898	3 775	6 601	53 555	57.6	1 950	260	3.1
August	104 536	61 927	59.2	39 508	16 665	3 821	6 790	53 204	57.4	1 933	249	3.1
September	104 588	61 780	59.1	39 416	16 504	3 793	6 558	53 155	57.1	2 067	223	3.3
October	104 690	62 204	59.4	39 555	16 674	3 781	6 636	53 374	57.3	2 194	269	3.5
November	104 740	62 014	59.2	39 504	16 669	3 663	6 699	53 137	57.1	2 178	316	3.5
December	104 810	62 457	59.6	39 691	16 946	3 860	7 065	53 432	57.7	1 960	269	3.1
1952												
January	104 862	62 432	59.5	39 714	17 001	3 745	7 148	53 312	57.7	1 972	282	3.2
February	104 868	62 419	59.5	39 772	16 935	3 755	7 020	53 442	57.7	1 957	248	3.1
March	104 860	61 721	58.9	39 580	16 627	3 701	6 468	53 440	57.1	1 813	234	2.9
April	104 906	61 720	58.8	39 542	16 659	3 708	6 525	53 384	57.1	1 811	242	2.9
May	104 996	62 058	59.1	39 588	16 844	3 763	6 334	53 861	57.3	1 863	219	3.0
June	105 118	62 103	59.1	39 558	16 837	3 824	6 529	53 690	57.3	1 884	210	3.0
July	105 246	61 962	58.9	39 496	16 778	3 697	6 334	53 637	57.0	1 991	194	3.2
August	105 346	61 877	58.7	39 289	16 867	3 634	6 174	53 616	56.8	2 087	211	3.4
September	105 436	62 457	59.2	39 386	17 477	3 658	6 537	53 984	57.4	1 936	249	3.1
October	105 591	61 971	58.7	39 451	17 032	3 649	6 363	53 769	56.9	1 839	230	3.0
November	105 706	62 491	59.1	39 549	17 450	3 749	6 509	54 239	57.5	1 743	216	2.8
December	105 812	62 621	59.2	40 011	17 181	3 762	6 361	54 593	57.6	1 667	238	2.7
1953												
January	106 594	63 439	59.5	40 256	17 482	3 862	6 642	54 958	57.8	1 839	268	2.9
February	106 678	63 520	59.5	40 546	17 321	4 017	6 463	55 421	58.0	1 636	208	2.6
March	106 744	63 657	59.6	40 648	17 397	3 965	6 420	55 590	58.1	1 647	213	2.6
April	106 826	63 167	59.1	40 346	17 242	3 856	6 362	55 082	57.5	1 723	180	2.7
May	106 910	62 615	58.6	40 323	16 983	3 713	5 937	55 082	57.1	1 596	176	2.5
June	106 978	63 063	58.9	40 358	17 301	3 797	6 361	55 095	57.4	1 607	213	2.5
July	107 034	63 057	58.9	40 378	17 341	3 678	6 267	55 130	57.4	1 660	168	2.6
August	107 132	62 816	58.6	40 352	17 108	3 691	6 319	54 832	57.1	1 665	177	2.7
September	107 253	62 727	58.5	40 192	17 063	3 651	6 198	54 708	56.8	1 821	178	2.9
October	107 383	62 867	58.5	40 155	17 236	3 502	6 096	54 797	56.7	1 974	190	3.1
November	107 504	62 949	58.6	40 163	16 974	3 601	6 345	54 393	56.5	2 211	259	3.5
December	107 623	62 795	58.3	39 885	16 599	3 493	5 929	54 048	55.7	2 818	309	4.5

[1] Not seasonally adjusted.

Table 20-3. Summary Labor Force, Employment, and Unemployment—Continued

(Thousands of persons, percent, seasonally adjusted, except as noted.)

Year and month	Noninsti-tutional population [1]	Labor force		Employment, thousands of persons					Employ-ment–population ratio, percent	Unemployment		
				By age and sex			By industry			Thousands of persons		
		Thousands of persons	Participa-tion rate (percent)	Men, 20 years and over	Women, 20 years and over	Both sexes, 16–19 years	Agricultural	Nonagri-cultural		Total	Unem-ployed 15 weeks and over	Rate, percent
1954												
January	107 763	63 101	58.6	39 834	16 574	3 616	6 073	53 951	55.7	3 077	372	4.9
February	107 880	63 994	59.3	39 899	17 162	3 602	6 590	54 073	56.2	3 331	532	5.2
March	107 987	63 793	59.1	39 497	17 022	3 667	6 395	53 791	55.7	3 607	765	5.7
April	108 080	63 934	59.2	39 613	17 015	3 557	6 142	54 043	55.7	3 749	774	5.9
May	108 184	63 675	58.9	39 467	16 975	3 466	6 210	53 698	55.4	3 767	879	5.9
June	108 267	63 343	58.5	39 476	16 894	3 422	6 162	53 630	55.2	3 551	880	5.6
July	108 344	63 302	58.4	39 467	16 777	3 399	6 222	53 421	55.0	3 659	932	5.8
August	108 440	63 707	58.7	39 582	16 868	3 403	6 087	53 766	55.2	3 854	1 002	6.0
September	108 546	64 209	59.2	39 702	17 133	3 447	6 453	53 829	55.5	3 927	1 017	6.1
October	108 668	63 936	58.8	39 618	17 209	3 443	6 242	54 028	55.5	3 666	1 009	5.7
November	108 798	63 759	58.6	39 745	17 213	3 399	5 934	54 423	55.5	3 402	975	5.3
December	108 892	63 312	58.1	39 763	17 121	3 232	5 848	54 268	55.2	3 196	827	5.0
1955												
January	109 059	63 910	58.6	39 937	17 375	3 441	6 113	54 640	55.7	3 157	882	4.9
February	109 078	63 696	58.4	39 964	17 413	3 350	5 854	54 873	55.7	2 969	826	4.7
March	109 254	63 882	58.5	40 111	17 415	3 438	6 242	54 722	55.8	2 918	816	4.6
April	109 377	64 564	59.0	40 120	17 867	3 528	6 363	55 152	56.2	3 049	811	4.7
May	109 544	64 381	58.8	40 410	17 665	3 559	6 327	55 307	56.3	2 747	734	4.3
June	109 680	64 482	58.8	40 444	17 837	3 500	6 243	55 538	56.3	2 701	668	4.2
July	109 792	65 145	59.3	40 751	18 123	3 639	6 438	56 075	56.9	2 632	640	4.0
August	109 882	65 581	59.7	40 747	18 377	3 673	6 575	56 222	57.1	2 784	535	4.2
September	109 977	65 628	59.7	40 920	18 285	3 745	6 819	56 131	57.2	2 678	558	4.1
October	110 085	65 821	59.8	40 858	18 327	3 806	6 728	56 263	57.2	2 830	572	4.3
November	110 177	66 037	59.9	40 936	18 422	3 899	6 655	56 602	57.4	2 780	564	4.2
December	110 296	66 445	60.2	41 063	18 630	3 991	6 653	57 031	57.7	2 761	581	4.2
1956												
January	110 390	66 419	60.2	41 203	18 691	3 859	6 590	57 163	57.8	2 666	561	4.0
February	110 478	66 124	59.9	41 175	18 582	3 761	6 457	57 061	57.5	2 606	545	3.9
March	110 582	66 175	59.8	41 199	18 496	3 716	6 221	57 190	57.3	2 764	521	4.2
April	110 650	66 264	59.9	41 289	18 629	3 696	6 460	57 154	57.5	2 650	476	4.0
May	110 810	66 722	60.2	41 166	18 844	3 851	6 375	57 486	57.6	2 861	506	4.3
June	110 903	66 702	60.1	41 196	18 748	3 876	6 335	57 485	57.5	2 882	516	4.3
July	111 019	66 752	60.1	41 216	18 718	3 866	6 320	57 480	57.5	2 952	523	4.4
August	111 099	66 673	60.0	41 265	18 864	3 843	6 280	57 692	57.6	2 701	543	4.1
September	111 222	66 714	60.0	41 221	19 019	3 839	6 375	57 704	57.6	2 635	577	3.9
October	111 335	66 546	59.8	41 261	18 928	3 786	6 137	57 838	57.5	2 571	530	3.9
November	111 432	66 657	59.8	41 208	18 846	3 742	5 997	57 799	57.3	2 861	575	4.3
December	111 526	66 700	59.8	41 192	18 859	3 859	5 806	58 104	57.3	2 790	567	4.2
1957												
January	111 626	66 428	59.5	41 168	18 740	3 724	5 790	57 842	57.0	2 796	509	4.2
February	111 711	66 879	59.9	41 341	19 115	3 801	6 125	58 132	57.5	2 622	530	3.9
March	111 824	66 913	59.8	41 500	19 066	3 838	5 963	58 441	57.6	2 509	514	3.7
April	111 933	66 647	59.5	41 345	18 937	3 765	5 836	58 211	57.2	2 600	516	3.9
May	112 031	66 695	59.5	41 334	18 897	3 754	5 999	57 986	57.1	2 710	538	4.1
June	112 172	67 052	59.8	41 411	18 973	3 812	6 002	58 194	57.2	2 856	526	4.3
July	112 317	67 336	60.0	41 472	19 262	3 806	6 401	58 139	57.5	2 796	535	4.2
August	112 421	66 706	59.3	41 243	19 020	3 696	5 898	58 061	56.9	2 747	542	4.1
September	112 554	67 064	59.6	41 213	19 116	3 792	5 728	58 393	57.0	2 943	559	4.4
October	112 710	67 066	59.5	41 069	19 160	3 817	5 875	58 171	56.8	3 020	650	4.5
November	112 874	67 123	59.5	40 853	19 082	3 734	5 686	57 983	56.4	3 454	674	5.1
December	113 013	67 398	59.6	40 884	19 285	3 753	6 037	57 885	56.6	3 476	731	5.2
1958												
January	113 138	67 095	59.3	40 617	19 035	3 568	5 831	57 389	55.9	3 875	879	5.8
February	113 234	67 201	59.3	40 336	18 951	3 611	5 654	57 244	55.5	4 303	1 005	6.4
March	113 337	67 223	59.3	40 180	18 968	3 583	5 561	57 170	55.3	4 492	1 128	6.7
April	113 415	67 647	59.6	40 129	18 969	3 533	5 602	57 029	55.2	5 016	1 387	7.4
May	113 534	67 895	59.8	40 253	18 978	3 643	5 647	57 227	55.4	5 021	1 493	7.4
June	113 647	67 674	59.5	40 208	19 008	3 514	5 510	57 220	55.2	4 944	1 677	7.3
July	113 727	67 824	59.6	40 270	19 039	3 436	5 525	57 220	55.2	5 079	1 796	7.5
August	113 835	68 037	59.8	40 343	19 103	3 566	5 673	57 339	55.4	5 025	1 888	7.4
September	113 977	68 002	59.7	40 564	19 033	3 584	5 453	57 728	55.4	4 821	1 795	7.1
October	114 138	68 045	59.6	40 699	19 091	3 685	5 563	57 912	55.6	4 570	1 708	6.7
November	114 283	67 658	59.2	40 684	19 157	3 629	5 571	57 899	55.5	4 188	1 570	6.2
December	114 429	67 740	59.2	40 666	19 170	3 713	5 521	58 028	55.5	4 191	1 490	6.2
1959												
January	114 582	67 936	59.3	40 769	19 292	3 807	5 481	58 387	55.7	4 068	1 396	6.0
February	114 712	67 649	59.0	40 699	19 167	3 818	5 429	58 255	55.5	3 965	1 277	5.9
March	114 849	68 068	59.3	41 079	19 379	3 809	5 677	58 590	56.0	3 801	1 210	5.6
April	114 986	68 339	59.4	41 419	19 498	3 851	5 893	58 875	56.3	3 571	1 039	5.2
May	115 144	68 178	59.2	41 355	19 565	3 779	5 792	58 907	56.2	3 479	965	5.1
June	115 287	68 278	59.2	41 387	19 658	3 804	5 712	59 137	56.3	3 429	963	5.0
July	115 429	68 539	59.4	41 596	19 595	3 820	5 564	59 447	56.3	3 528	889	5.1
August	115 555	68 432	59.2	41 485	19 568	3 791	5 442	59 402	56.1	3 588	889	5.2
September	115 668	68 545	59.3	41 351	19 531	3 888	5 447	59 323	56.0	3 775	895	5.5
October	115 798	68 821	59.4	41 362	19 702	3 847	5 355	59 556	56.1	3 910	883	5.7
November	115 916	68 533	59.1	41 062	19 594	3 874	5 480	59 050	55.7	4 003	982	5.8
December	116 040	68 994	59.5	41 651	19 717	3 973	5 458	59 883	56.3	3 653	920	5.3

[1] Not seasonally adjusted.

Table 20-3. Summary Labor Force, Employment, and Unemployment—Continued

(Thousands of persons, percent, seasonally adjusted, except as noted.)

Year and month	Noninstitutional population [1]	Labor force		Employment, thousands of persons					Employment–population ratio, percent	Unemployment		Rate, percent
				By age and sex			By industry			Thousands of persons		
		Thousands of persons	Participation rate (percent)	Men, 20 years and over	Women, 20 years and over	Both sexes, 16–19 years	Agricultural	Nonagricultural		Total	Unemployed 15 weeks and over	
1960												
January	116 594	68 962	59.1	41 637	19 686	4 024	5 458	59 889	56.0	3 615	915	5.2
February	116 702	68 949	59.1	41 729	19 765	4 126	5 443	60 177	56.2	3 329	841	4.8
March	116 827	68 399	58.5	41 320	19 388	3 965	4 959	59 714	55.4	3 726	959	5.4
April	116 910	69 579	59.5	41 641	20 110	4 208	5 471	60 488	56.4	3 620	896	5.2
May	117 033	69 626	59.5	41 668	20 186	4 203	5 359	60 698	56.4	3 569	797	5.1
June	117 167	69 934	59.7	41 553	20 290	4 325	5 416	60 752	56.5	3 766	854	5.4
July	117 281	69 745	59.5	41 490	20 257	4 162	5 542	60 367	56.2	3 836	921	5.5
August	117 431	69 841	59.5	41 503	20 316	4 076	5 520	60 375	56.1	3 946	927	5.6
September	117 521	70 151	59.7	41 604	20 493	4 170	5 755	60 512	56.4	3 884	982	5.5
October	117 643	69 884	59.4	41 464	20 076	4 092	5 436	60 196	55.8	4 252	1 189	6.1
November	117 829	70 439	59.8	41 543	20 384	4 182	5 513	60 596	56.1	4 330	1 223	6.1
December	118 001	70 395	59.7	41 416	20 332	4 030	5 622	60 156	55.7	4 617	1 142	6.6
1961												
January	118 155	70 447	59.6	41 363	20 325	4 088	5 422	60 354	55.7	4 671	1 328	6.6
February	118 250	70 420	59.6	41 177	20 392	4 019	5 472	60 116	55.5	4 832	1 416	6.9
March	118 358	70 703	59.7	41 273	20 459	4 118	5 406	60 444	55.6	4 853	1 463	6.9
April	118 503	70 267	59.3	41 206	20 145	4 023	5 037	60 337	55.2	4 893	1 598	7.0
May	118 638	70 452	59.4	41 139	20 261	4 049	5 099	60 350	55.2	5 003	1 686	7.1
June	118 767	70 878	59.7	41 349	20 446	4 198	5 220	60 773	55.6	4 885	1 651	6.9
July	118 889	70 536	59.3	41 245	20 252	4 111	5 153	60 455	55.2	4 928	1 830	7.0
August	119 006	70 534	59.3	41 362	20 279	4 211	5 366	60 486	55.3	4 682	1 649	6.6
September	119 107	70 217	59.0	41 400	20 112	4 029	5 021	60 520	55.0	4 676	1 531	6.7
October	119 202	70 492	59.1	41 509	20 338	4 072	5 203	60 716	55.3	4 573	1 481	6.5
November	119 153	70 376	59.1	41 556	20 330	4 195	5 090	60 991	55.5	4 295	1 388	6.1
December	119 214	70 077	58.8	41 534	20 287	4 079	4 992	60 908	55.3	4 177	1 361	6.0
1962												
January	119 300	70 189	58.8	41 547	20 501	4 060	5 094	61 014	55.4	4 081	1 235	5.8
February	119 360	70 409	59.0	41 745	20 693	4 100	5 289	61 249	55.7	3 871	1 244	5.5
March	119 476	70 414	58.9	41 696	20 567	4 230	5 157	61 336	55.7	3 921	1 162	5.6
April	119 702	70 278	58.7	41 647	20 567	4 158	5 009	61 363	55.4	3 906	1 122	5.6
May	119 813	70 551	58.9	41 847	20 558	4 283	4 964	61 724	55.7	3 863	1 134	5.5
June	119 943	70 514	58.8	41 761	20 547	4 362	4 943	61 727	55.6	3 844	1 079	5.5
July	120 128	70 302	58.5	41 671	20 592	4 220	4 840	61 643	55.3	3 819	1 049	5.4
August	120 323	70 981	59.0	41 900	20 841	4 227	4 866	62 102	55.7	4 013	1 081	5.7
September	120 653	71 153	59.0	42 020	20 982	4 190	4 867	62 325	55.7	3 961	1 096	5.6
October	120 856	70 917	58.7	42 086	20 856	4 172	4 816	62 298	55.5	3 803	1 022	5.4
November	121 045	70 871	58.5	41 985	20 794	4 068	4 831	62 016	55.2	4 024	1 051	5.7
December	121 236	70 854	58.4	41 934	20 831	4 182	4 647	62 300	55.2	3 907	1 068	5.5
1963												
January	121 463	71 146	58.6	41 938	20 933	4 201	4 882	62 190	55.2	4 074	1 122	5.7
February	121 633	71 262	58.6	41 876	21 046	4 102	4 652	62 372	55.1	4 238	1 137	5.9
March	121 824	71 423	58.6	42 047	21 162	4 142	4 696	62 655	55.3	4 072	1 087	5.7
April	121 986	71 697	58.8	42 131	21 281	4 230	4 670	62 972	55.5	4 055	1 071	5.7
May	122 162	71 832	58.8	42 145	21 225	4 245	4 729	62 886	55.3	4 217	1 157	5.9
June	122 352	71 626	58.5	42 268	21 185	4 196	4 642	63 007	55.3	3 977	1 067	5.6
July	122 521	71 956	58.7	42 427	21 268	4 210	4 694	63 211	55.4	4 051	1 070	5.6
August	122 667	71 786	58.5	42 400	21 185	4 323	4 604	63 304	55.4	3 878	1 114	5.4
September	122 821	72 131	58.7	42 500	21 317	4 357	4 650	63 524	55.5	3 957	1 069	5.5
October	123 014	72 281	58.8	42 437	21 456	4 401	4 702	63 592	55.5	3 987	1 071	5.5
November	123 192	72 418	58.8	42 415	21 553	4 299	4 694	63 573	55.4	4 151	1 054	5.7
December	123 360	72 188	58.5	42 427	21 481	4 305	4 629	63 584	55.3	3 975	1 007	5.5
1964												
January	123 560	72 356	58.6	42 510	21 462	4 355	4 603	63 724	55.3	4 029	1 057	5.6
February	123 707	72 683	58.8	42 579	21 652	4 520	4 563	64 188	55.6	3 932	1 015	5.4
March	123 857	72 713	58.7	42 600	21 685	4 478	4 366	64 397	55.5	3 950	1 039	5.4
April	124 019	73 274	59.1	42 885	22 110	4 361	4 414	64 942	55.9	3 918	934	5.3
May	124 204	73 395	59.1	43 025	22 103	4 503	4 603	65 028	56.1	3 764	975	5.1
June	124 386	73 032	58.7	42 760	21 995	4 463	4 556	64 662	55.6	3 814	1 047	5.2
July	124 567	73 007	58.6	42 998	21 846	4 555	4 591	64 808	55.7	3 608	1 002	4.9
August	124 731	73 118	58.6	42 963	22 002	4 498	4 573	64 890	55.7	3 655	934	5.0
September	124 920	73 290	58.7	43 009	21 863	4 706	4 619	64 959	55.7	3 712	917	5.1
October	125 108	73 308	58.6	43 023	21 984	4 575	4 550	65 032	55.6	3 726	903	5.1
November	125 291	73 286	58.5	43 171	21 954	4 610	4 496	65 239	55.7	3 551	922	4.8
December	125 468	73 465	58.6	43 109	22 136	4 569	4 322	65 492	55.6	3 651	873	5.0
1965												
January	125 647	73 569	58.6	43 237	22 282	4 478	4 271	65 726	55.7	3 572	793	4.9
February	125 810	73 857	58.7	43 279	22 276	4 572	4 322	65 805	55.7	3 730	919	5.1
March	125 985	73 949	58.7	43 370	22 373	4 696	4 318	66 121	55.9	3 510	796	4.7
April	126 155	74 228	58.8	43 397	22 416	4 820	4 424	66 209	56.0	3 595	796	4.8
May	126 320	74 466	59.0	43 579	22 494	4 961	4 724	66 310	56.2	3 432	736	4.6
June	126 499	74 412	58.8	43 487	22 759	4 779	4 444	66 581	56.1	3 387	786	4.6
July	126 573	74 761	59.1	43 489	22 841	5 130	4 390	67 070	56.5	3 301	683	4.4
August	126 756	74 616	58.9	43 447	22 783	5 132	4 355	67 007	56.3	3 254	733	4.4
September	126 906	74 502	58.7	43 371	22 684	5 231	4 271	67 015	56.2	3 216	732	4.3
October	127 043	74 838	58.9	43 461	22 819	5 415	4 418	67 277	56.4	3 143	672	4.2
November	127 171	74 797	58.8	43 447	22 829	5 448	4 093	67 631	56.4	3 073	645	4.1
December	127 294	75 093	59.0	43 513	22 983	5 566	4 159	67 903	56.6	3 031	659	4.0

[1] Not seasonally adjusted.

Table 20-3. Summary Labor Force, Employment, and Unemployment—Continued

(Thousands of persons, percent, seasonally adjusted, except as noted.)

Year and month	Noninsti-tutional population [1]	Labor force		Employment, thousands of persons					Employ-ment–population ratio, percent	Unemployment		
		Thousands of persons	Participa-tion rate (percent)	By age and sex			By industry			Thousands of persons		Rate, percent
				Men, 20 years and over	Women, 20 years and over	Both sexes, 16–19 years	Agricultural	Nonagri-cultural		Total	Unem-ployed 15 weeks and over	
1966												
January	127 394	75 186	59.0	43 495	23 098	5 605	4 077	68 121	56.7	2 988	623	4.0
February	127 514	74 954	58.8	43 528	23 089	5 517	4 078	68 056	56.6	2 820	594	3.8
March	127 626	75 075	58.8	43 576	23 109	5 503	4 069	68 119	56.6	2 887	583	3.8
April	127 744	75 338	59.0	43 679	23 227	5 604	4 108	68 402	56.8	2 828	575	3.8
May	127 879	75 447	59.0	43 710	23 282	5 505	3 930	68 567	56.7	2 950	534	3.9
June	127 983	75 647	59.1	43 662	23 359	5 754	3 967	68 808	56.9	2 872	475	3.8
July	128 102	75 736	59.1	43 574	23 422	5 864	3 920	68 940	56.9	2 876	427	3.8
August	128 240	76 046	59.3	43 636	23 605	5 905	3 921	69 225	57.0	2 900	464	3.8
September	128 359	76 056	59.3	43 718	23 881	5 659	3 952	69 306	57.1	2 798	488	3.7
October	128 494	76 199	59.3	43 776	23 881	5 744	3 912	69 489	57.1	2 798	494	3.7
November	128 627	76 610	59.6	43 804	24 130	5 906	3 945	69 895	57.4	2 770	464	3.6
December	128 730	76 641	59.5	43 820	24 025	5 884	3 906	69 823	57.3	2 912	488	3.8
1967												
January	128 909	76 639	59.5	44 029	23 872	5 770	3 890	69 781	57.1	2 968	489	3.9
February	129 032	76 521	59.3	43 997	23 919	5 690	3 723	69 883	57.0	2 915	459	3.8
March	129 190	76 328	59.1	43 922	23 832	5 685	3 757	69 682	56.8	2 889	436	3.8
April	129 344	76 777	59.4	44 061	24 161	5 660	3 748	70 134	57.1	2 895	428	3.8
May	129 515	76 773	59.3	44 100	24 172	5 572	3 658	70 186	57.0	2 929	417	3.8
June	129 722	77 270	59.6	44 230	24 303	5 745	3 689	70 589	57.3	2 992	422	3.9
July	129 918	77 464	59.6	44 364	24 416	5 740	3 833	70 687	57.4	2 944	412	3.8
August	130 187	77 712	59.7	44 410	24 600	5 757	3 963	70 804	57.4	2 945	441	3.8
September	130 392	77 812	59.7	44 535	24 683	5 636	3 851	71 003	57.4	2 958	448	3.8
October	130 582	78 194	59.9	44 610	24 802	5 639	4 008	71 043	57.5	3 143	472	4.0
November	130 754	78 191	59.8	44 625	24 914	5 586	3 933	71 192	57.5	3 066	490	3.9
December	130 936	78 491	59.9	44 719	25 104	5 650	4 076	71 397	57.6	3 018	485	3.8
1968												
January	131 112	77 578	59.2	44 606	24 581	5 513	3 908	70 792	57.0	2 878	503	3.7
February	131 277	78 230	59.6	44 659	24 881	5 689	3 959	71 270	57.3	3 001	468	3.8
March	131 412	78 256	59.6	44 663	25 019	5 697	3 904	71 475	57.4	2 877	447	3.7
April	131 553	78 270	59.5	44 753	25 072	5 736	3 875	71 686	57.4	2 709	393	3.5
May	131 712	78 847	59.9	44 841	25 513	5 753	3 814	72 293	57.8	2 740	395	3.5
June	131 872	79 120	60.0	44 914	25 466	5 802	3 806	72 376	57.8	2 938	405	3.7
July	132 053	78 970	59.8	44 935	25 347	5 805	3 820	72 267	57.6	2 883	426	3.7
August	132 251	78 811	59.6	44 897	25 201	5 945	3 736	72 307	57.5	2 768	393	3.5
September	132 446	78 858	59.5	44 893	25 445	5 834	3 758	72 414	57.5	2 686	375	3.4
October	132 617	78 913	59.5	44 884	25 475	5 865	3 741	72 483	57.5	2 689	386	3.4
November	132 903	79 209	59.6	44 996	25 674	5 824	3 758	72 736	57.6	2 715	357	3.4
December	133 120	79 463	59.7	45 262	25 712	5 804	3 746	73 032	57.7	2 685	351	3.4
1969												
January	133 324	79 523	59.6	45 154	25 777	5 874	3 704	73 101	57.6	2 718	339	3.4
February	133 465	80 019	60.0	45 339	26 092	5 896	3 770	73 557	57.9	2 692	358	3.4
March	133 639	80 079	59.9	45 305	26 115	5 947	3 668	73 699	57.9	2 712	353	3.4
April	133 821	80 281	60.0	45 262	26 233	6 028	3 629	73 894	57.9	2 758	386	3.4
May	134 027	80 125	59.8	45 278	26 283	5 851	3 706	73 706	57.8	2 713	387	3.4
June	134 213	80 696	60.1	45 313	26 429	6 138	3 663	74 217	58.0	2 816	368	3.5
July	134 414	80 827	60.1	45 305	26 516	6 138	3 548	74 411	58.0	2 868	377	3.5
August	134 597	81 106	60.3	45 513	26 556	6 181	3 613	74 637	58.1	2 856	373	3.5
September	134 774	81 290	60.3	45 447	26 572	6 231	3 551	74 699	58.1	3 040	391	3.7
October	135 012	81 494	60.4	45 488	26 658	6 299	3 517	74 928	58.1	3 049	374	3.7
November	135 239	81 397	60.2	45 505	26 652	6 384	3 477	75 064	58.1	2 856	392	3.5
December	135 489	81 624	60.2	45 577	26 832	6 331	3 409	75 331	58.1	2 884	413	3.5
1970												
January	135 713	81 981	60.4	45 654	26 908	6 218	3 422	75 358	58.0	3 201	431	3.9
February	135 957	82 151	60.4	45 627	26 828	6 243	3 439	75 259	57.9	3 453	470	4.2
March	136 179	82 498	60.6	45 668	26 933	6 262	3 499	75 364	57.9	3 635	534	4.4
April	136 416	82 727	60.6	45 679	27 114	6 137	3 568	75 362	57.9	3 797	602	4.6
May	136 686	82 483	60.3	45 666	26 739	6 159	3 547	75 017	57.5	3 919	591	4.8
June	136 928	82 484	60.2	45 554	26 904	5 955	3 555	74 858	57.3	4 071	657	4.9
July	137 196	82 901	60.4	45 516	27 083	6 127	3 517	75 209	57.4	4 175	662	5.0
August	137 455	82 880	60.3	45 495	27 011	6 118	3 418	75 206	57.2	4 256	705	5.1
September	137 717	82 954	60.2	45 535	26 784	6 179	3 451	75 047	57.0	4 456	788	5.4
October	137 988	83 276	60.4	45 508	27 058	6 119	3 337	75 348	57.0	4 591	771	5.5
November	138 264	83 548	60.4	45 540	27 020	6 090	3 372	75 278	56.9	4 898	871	5.9
December	138 529	83 670	60.4	45 466	27 038	6 090	3 380	75 214	56.7	5 076	1 102	6.1
1971												
January	138 795	83 850	60.4	45 527	27 173	6 164	3 393	75 471	56.8	4 986	1 113	5.9
February	139 021	83 603	60.1	45 455	27 040	6 205	3 288	75 412	56.6	4 903	1 068	5.9
March	139 285	83 575	60.0	45 520	26 967	6 101	3 356	75 232	56.4	4 987	1 098	6.0
April	139 566	83 946	60.1	45 789	26 984	6 214	3 574	75 413	56.6	4 959	1 149	5.9
May	139 826	84 135	60.2	45 917	27 056	6 166	3 449	75 690	56.6	4 996	1 173	5.9
June	140 090	83 706	59.8	45 879	27 013	5 865	3 334	75 423	56.2	4 949	1 167	5.9
July	140 343	84 340	60.1	46 000	27 054	6 251	3 386	75 919	56.5	5 035	1 251	6.0
August	140 596	84 673	60.2	46 041	27 171	6 327	3 395	76 144	56.6	5 134	1 261	6.1
September	140 869	84 731	60.1	46 090	27 390	6 209	3 367	76 322	56.6	5 042	1 239	6.0
October	141 146	84 872	60.1	46 132	27 538	6 248	3 405	76 513	56.6	4 954	1 268	5.8
November	141 393	85 458	60.4	46 209	27 721	6 367	3 410	76 887	56.8	5 161	1 277	6.0
December	141 666	85 625	60.4	46 280	27 791	6 400	3 371	77 100	56.8	5 154	1 283	6.0

[1] Not seasonally adjusted.

Table 20-3. Summary Labor Force, Employment, and Unemployment—Continued

(Thousands of persons, percent, seasonally adjusted, except as noted.)

Year and month	Noninstitutional population [1]	Labor force		Employment, thousands of persons					Employment–population ratio, percent	Unemployment		
		Thousands of persons	Participation rate (percent)	By age and sex			By industry			Thousands of persons		Rate, percent
				Men, 20 years and over	Women, 20 years and over	Both sexes, 16–19 years	Agricultural	Nonagricultural		Total	Unemployed 15 weeks and over	
1972												
January	142 736	85 978	60.2	46 471	27 956	6 532	3 366	77 593	56.7	5 019	1 257	5.8
February	143 017	86 036	60.2	46 600	28 016	6 492	3 358	77 750	56.7	4 928	1 292	5.7
March	143 263	86 611	60.5	46 821	28 126	6 626	3 438	78 135	56.9	5 038	1 232	5.8
April	143 483	86 614	60.4	46 863	28 114	6 678	3 382	78 273	56.9	4 959	1 203	5.7
May	143 760	86 809	60.4	46 950	28 184	6 753	3 412	78 475	57.0	4 922	1 168	5.7
June	144 033	87 006	60.4	47 147	28 175	6 761	3 402	78 681	57.0	4 923	1 141	5.7
July	144 285	87 143	60.4	47 244	28 225	6 761	3 461	78 769	57.0	4 913	1 154	5.6
August	144 522	87 517	60.6	47 321	28 382	6 875	3 603	78 975	57.1	4 939	1 156	5.6
September	144 761	87 392	60.4	47 394	28 417	6 732	3 568	78 975	57.0	4 849	1 131	5.5
October	144 988	87 491	60.3	47 354	28 438	6 824	3 634	78 982	57.0	4 875	1 123	5.6
November	145 211	87 592	60.3	47 529	28 567	6 894	3 517	79 473	57.2	4 602	1 040	5.3
December	145 446	87 943	60.5	47 747	28 698	6 955	3 596	79 804	57.3	4 543	1 006	5.2
1973												
January	145 720	87 487	60.0	47 701	28 596	6 864	3 456	79 705	57.1	4 326	947	4.9
February	145 943	88 364	60.5	47 884	28 995	7 033	3 415	80 497	57.5	4 452	894	5.0
March	146 230	88 846	60.8	48 117	29 110	7 225	3 469	80 983	57.8	4 394	889	4.9
April	146 459	89 018	60.8	48 098	29 304	7 157	3 407	81 152	57.7	4 459	809	5.0
May	146 719	88 977	60.6	48 068	29 432	7 148	3 376	81 272	57.7	4 329	816	4.9
June	146 981	89 548	60.9	48 244	29 505	7 436	3 509	81 676	58.0	4 363	779	4.9
July	147 233	89 604	60.9	48 452	29 592	7 255	3 540	81 759	57.9	4 305	756	4.8
August	147 471	89 509	60.7	48 353	29 578	7 273	3 425	81 779	57.8	4 305	788	4.8
September	147 731	89 838	60.8	48 408	29 710	7 370	3 342	82 146	57.9	4 350	785	4.8
October	147 980	90 131	60.9	48 631	29 885	7 471	3 424	82 563	58.1	4 144	793	4.6
November	148 219	90 716	61.2	48 764	30 071	7 485	3 593	82 727	58.2	4 396	832	4.8
December	148 479	90 890	61.2	48 902	29 991	7 508	3 658	82 743	58.2	4 489	767	4.9
1974												
January	148 753	91 199	61.3	49 107	29 893	7 555	3 756	82 799	58.2	4 644	799	5.1
February	148 982	91 485	61.4	49 057	30 146	7 551	3 824	82 930	58.2	4 731	829	5.2
March	149 225	91 453	61.3	48 986	30 293	7 540	3 726	83 093	58.2	4 634	849	5.1
April	149 478	91 287	61.1	48 853	30 376	7 440	3 582	83 087	58.0	4 618	889	5.1
May	149 750	91 596	61.2	49 039	30 424	7 428	3 529	83 362	58.0	4 705	880	5.1
June	150 012	91 868	61.2	48 946	30 512	7 483	3 386	83 555	58.0	4 927	926	5.4
July	150 248	92 212	61.4	48 883	30 869	7 397	3 436	83 713	58.0	5 063	924	5.5
August	150 493	92 059	61.2	48 950	30 662	7 425	3 429	83 608	57.8	5 022	960	5.5
September	150 753	92 488	61.4	48 978	30 569	7 504	3 460	83 591	57.7	5 437	1 021	5.9
October	151 009	92 518	61.3	48 959	30 570	7 466	3 431	83 564	57.6	5 523	1 072	6.0
November	151 256	92 766	61.3	48 833	30 424	7 369	3 405	83 221	57.3	6 140	1 128	6.6
December	151 494	92 780	61.2	48 458	30 431	7 255	3 361	82 783	56.9	6 636	1 326	7.2
1975												
January	151 755	93 128	61.4	48 086	30 343	7 198	3 401	82 226	56.4	7 501	1 555	8.1
February	151 990	92 776	61.0	47 927	30 215	7 114	3 361	81 895	56.1	7 520	1 841	8.1
March	152 217	93 165	61.2	47 776	30 334	7 077	3 358	81 829	56.0	7 978	2 074	8.6
April	152 443	93 399	61.3	47 759	30 410	7 020	3 315	81 874	55.9	8 210	2 442	8.8
May	152 704	93 884	61.5	47 835	30 483	7 133	3 560	81 891	56.0	8 433	2 643	9.0
June	152 976	93 575	61.2	47 754	30 618	6 983	3 368	81 987	55.8	8 220	2 843	8.8
July	153 309	94 021	61.3	48 050	30 794	7 050	3 457	82 437	56.0	8 127	2 943	8.6
August	153 580	94 162	61.3	48 239	30 966	7 029	3 429	82 805	56.1	7 928	2 862	8.4
September	153 848	94 202	61.2	48 126	30 979	7 174	3 508	82 771	56.1	7 923	2 906	8.4
October	154 082	94 267	61.2	48 165	31 121	7 084	3 397	82 973	56.1	7 897	2 689	8.4
November	154 338	94 250	61.1	48 203	31 135	7 118	3 331	83 125	56.0	7 794	2 789	8.3
December	154 589	94 409	61.1	48 266	31 268	7 131	3 259	83 406	56.1	7 744	2 868	8.2
1976												
January	154 853	94 934	61.3	48 592	31 595	7 213	3 387	84 013	56.4	7 534	2 713	7.9
February	155 066	94 998	61.3	48 721	31 680	7 271	3 304	84 368	56.5	7 326	2 519	7.7
March	155 306	95 215	61.3	48 836	31 842	7 307	3 296	84 689	56.7	7 230	2 441	7.6
April	155 529	95 746	61.6	49 097	31 951	7 368	3 438	84 978	56.8	7 330	2 210	7.7
May	155 765	95 847	61.5	49 193	32 147	7 454	3 367	85 427	57.0	7 053	2 115	7.4
June	156 027	95 885	61.5	49 010	32 267	7 286	3 310	85 253	56.8	7 322	2 332	7.6
July	156 276	96 583	61.8	49 236	32 334	7 523	3 358	85 735	57.0	7 490	2 316	7.8
August	156 525	96 741	61.8	49 417	32 437	7 369	3 380	85 843	57.0	7 518	2 378	7.8
September	156 779	96 553	61.6	49 485	32 390	7 298	3 278	85 895	56.9	7 380	2 296	7.6
October	156 993	96 704	61.6	49 524	32 412	7 338	3 316	85 958	56.9	7 430	2 292	7.7
November	157 235	97 254	61.9	49 561	32 753	7 320	3 263	86 371	57.0	7 620	2 354	7.8
December	157 438	97 348	61.8	49 599	32 914	7 290	3 251	86 552	57.0	7 545	2 375	7.8
1977												
January	157 688	97 208	61.6	49 738	32 872	7 318	3 185	86 743	57.0	7 280	2 200	7.5
February	157 913	97 785	61.9	49 838	32 997	7 507	3 222	87 120	57.2	7 443	2 174	7.6
March	158 131	98 115	62.0	50 031	33 246	7 531	3 212	87 596	57.4	7 307	2 057	7.4
April	158 371	98 330	62.1	50 185	33 470	7 616	3 313	87 958	57.6	7 059	1 936	7.2
May	158 657	98 665	62.2	50 280	33 851	7 623	3 432	88 322	57.8	6 911	1 928	7.0
June	158 929	99 093	62.4	50 544	33 678	7 737	3 340	88 619	57.9	7 134	1 918	7.2
July	159 185	98 913	62.1	50 597	33 749	7 738	3 247	88 837	57.8	6 829	1 907	6.9
August	159 430	99 366	62.3	50 745	33 809	7 887	3 260	89 181	58.0	6 925	1 836	7.0
September	159 674	99 453	62.3	50 825	34 218	7 659	3 201	89 501	58.1	6 751	1 853	6.8
October	159 915	99 815	62.4	51 046	34 187	7 819	3 272	89 780	58.2	6 763	1 789	6.8
November	160 129	100 576	62.8	51 316	34 536	7 909	3 375	90 386	58.6	6 815	1 804	6.8
December	160 377	100 491	62.7	51 492	34 668	7 945	3 320	90 785	58.7	6 386	1 717	6.4

[1] Not seasonally adjusted.

Table 20-3. Summary Labor Force, Employment, and Unemployment—Continued

(Thousands of persons, percent, seasonally adjusted, except as noted.)

Year and month	Noninstitutional population [1]	Labor force		Employment, thousands of persons					Employment–population ratio, percent	Unemployment		
				By age and sex			By industry			Thousands of persons		
		Thousands of persons	Participation rate (percent)	Men, 20 years and over	Women, 20 years and over	Both sexes, 16–19 years	Agricultural	Nonagricultural		Total	Unemployed 15 weeks and over	Rate, percent
1978												
January	160 617	100 873	62.8	51 542	34 948	7 894	3 434	90 950	58.8	6 489	1 643	6.4
February	160 831	100 837	62.7	51 578	35 118	7 823	3 320	91 199	58.8	6 318	1 584	6.3
March	161 038	101 092	62.8	51 635	35 310	7 810	3 351	91 404	58.8	6 337	1 531	6.3
April	161 263	101 574	63.0	51 912	35 546	7 936	3 349	92 045	59.2	6 180	1 502	6.1
May	161 518	101 896	63.1	52 050	35 597	8 122	3 325	92 444	59.3	6 127	1 420	6.0
June	161 795	102 371	63.3	52 240	35 828	8 275	3 483	92 860	59.5	6 028	1 352	5.9
July	162 034	102 399	63.2	52 190	35 764	8 136	3 441	92 649	59.3	6 309	1 373	6.2
August	162 259	102 511	63.2	52 228	35 856	8 347	3 401	93 030	59.4	6 080	1 242	5.9
September	162 502	102 795	63.3	52 284	36 274	8 112	3 400	93 270	59.5	6 125	1 308	6.0
October	162 783	103 080	63.3	52 448	36 525	8 160	3 409	93 724	59.7	5 947	1 319	5.8
November	163 017	103 562	63.5	52 802	36 559	8 124	3 284	94 201	59.8	6 077	1 242	5.9
December	163 272	103 809	63.6	52 807	36 686	8 088	3 396	94 185	59.8	6 228	1 269	6.0
1979												
January	163 516	104 057	63.6	53 072	36 697	8 179	3 305	94 643	59.9	6 109	1 250	5.9
February	163 726	104 502	63.8	53 233	36 904	8 192	3 373	94 956	60.1	6 173	1 297	5.9
March	164 027	104 589	63.8	53 120	37 159	8 201	3 368	95 112	60.0	6 109	1 365	5.8
April	164 172	104 172	63.5	53 085	36 944	8 074	3 291	94 812	59.8	6 069	1 272	5.8
May	164 459	104 171	63.3	53 178	37 134	8 019	3 272	95 059	59.8	5 840	1 239	5.6
June	164 721	104 638	63.5	53 309	37 221	8 149	3 331	95 348	59.9	5 959	1 171	5.7
July	164 970	105 002	63.6	53 384	37 514	8 108	3 335	95 671	60.0	5 996	1 123	5.7
August	165 198	105 096	63.6	53 336	37 548	7 892	3 374	95 402	59.8	6 320	1 203	6.0
September	165 431	105 530	63.8	53 510	37 798	8 032	3 371	95 969	60.0	6 190	1 172	5.9
October	165 813	105 700	63.7	53 478	37 931	7 995	3 325	96 079	59.9	6 296	1 219	6.0
November	166 051	105 812	63.7	53 435	38 065	8 074	3 436	96 138	60.0	6 238	1 239	5.9
December	166 300	106 258	63.9	53 555	38 259	8 119	3 400	96 533	60.1	6 325	1 277	6.0
1980												
January	166 544	106 562	64.0	53 501	38 367	8 011	3 316	96 563	60.0	6 683	1 353	6.3
February	166 759	106 697	64.0	53 686	38 389	7 920	3 397	96 598	60.0	6 702	1 358	6.3
March	166 984	106 442	63.7	53 353	38 406	7 954	3 418	96 295	59.7	6 729	1 457	6.3
April	167 197	106 591	63.8	53 035	38 427	7 771	3 326	95 907	59.4	7 358	1 694	6.9
May	167 407	106 929	63.9	52 915	38 335	7 695	3 382	95 563	59.1	7 984	1 740	7.5
June	167 643	106 780	63.7	52 712	38 312	7 658	3 296	95 386	58.9	8 098	1 760	7.6
July	167 932	107 159	63.8	52 733	38 374	7 689	3 319	95 477	58.8	8 363	1 995	7.8
August	168 103	107 105	63.7	52 815	38 511	7 498	3 234	95 590	58.8	8 281	2 162	7.7
September	168 297	107 098	63.6	52 866	38 595	7 616	3 443	95 634	58.9	8 021	2 309	7.5
October	168 503	107 405	63.7	53 094	38 620	7 603	3 372	95 945	58.9	8 088	2 306	7.5
November	168 695	107 568	63.8	53 210	38 795	7 540	3 396	96 149	59.0	8 023	2 329	7.5
December	168 883	107 352	63.6	53 333	38 737	7 564	3 492	96 142	59.0	7 718	2 406	7.2
1981												
January	169 104	108 026	63.9	53 392	39 042	7 521	3 429	96 526	59.1	8 071	2 389	7.5
February	169 280	108 242	63.9	53 445	39 280	7 466	3 345	96 846	59.2	8 051	2 344	7.4
March	169 453	108 553	64.1	53 662	39 464	7 445	3 365	97 206	59.4	7 982	2 276	7.4
April	169 641	108 925	64.2	53 886	39 628	7 542	3 529	97 527	59.6	7 869	2 231	7.2
May	169 829	109 222	64.3	53 879	39 759	7 410	3 369	97 679	59.5	8 174	2 221	7.5
June	170 042	108 396	63.7	53 576	39 682	7 040	3 334	96 964	59.0	8 098	2 250	7.5
July	170 246	108 556	63.8	53 814	39 683	7 196	3 296	97 397	59.1	7 863	2 166	7.2
August	170 399	108 725	63.8	53 718	39 723	7 248	3 379	97 310	59.1	8 036	2 241	7.4
September	170 593	108 294	63.5	53 625	39 342	7 097	3 361	96 703	58.7	8 230	2 261	7.6
October	170 809	109 024	63.8	53 482	39 843	7 053	3 412	96 966	58.8	8 646	2 303	7.9
November	170 996	109 236	63.9	53 335	39 908	6 964	3 415	96 792	58.6	9 029	2 345	8.3
December	171 166	108 912	63.6	53 149	39 708	6 788	3 227	96 418	58.2	9 267	2 374	8.5
1982												
January	171 335	109 089	63.7	53 103	39 821	6 768	3 393	96 299	58.2	9 397	2 409	8.6
February	171 489	109 467	63.8	53 172	39 859	6 731	3 375	96 387	58.2	9 705	2 758	8.9
March	171 667	109 567	63.8	53 054	39 936	6 682	3 372	96 300	58.1	9 895	2 965	9.0
April	171 844	109 820	63.9	53 081	39 848	6 647	3 351	96 225	57.9	10 244	3 086	9.3
May	172 026	110 451	64.2	53 234	40 121	6 761	3 434	96 682	58.2	10 335	3 276	9.4
June	172 190	110 081	63.9	52 933	40 219	6 391	3 331	96 212	57.8	10 538	3 451	9.6
July	172 364	110 342	64.0	52 896	40 228	6 369	3 402	96 091	57.7	10 849	3 555	9.8
August	172 511	110 514	64.1	52 797	40 336	6 500	3 408	96 225	57.8	10 881	3 696	9.8
September	172 690	110 721	64.1	52 760	40 275	6 469	3 385	96 119	57.6	11 217	3 889	10.1
October	172 881	110 744	64.1	52 624	40 105	6 486	3 489	95 726	57.4	11 529	4 185	10.4
November	173 058	111 050	64.2	52 537	40 111	6 464	3 510	95 602	57.3	11 938	4 485	10.8
December	173 199	111 083	64.1	52 497	40 164	6 371	3 414	95 618	57.2	12 051	4 662	10.8
1983												
January	173 354	110 695	63.9	52 487	40 268	6 406	3 439	95 722	57.2	11 534	4 668	10.4
February	173 505	110 634	63.8	52 453	40 336	6 300	3 382	95 707	57.1	11 545	4 641	10.4
March	173 656	110 587	63.7	52 615	40 368	6 196	3 360	95 819	57.1	11 408	4 612	10.3
April	173 794	110 828	63.8	52 814	40 542	6 204	3 341	96 219	57.3	11 268	4 370	10.2
May	173 953	110 796	63.7	52 922	40 538	6 182	3 328	96 314	57.3	11 154	4 538	10.1
June	174 125	111 879	64.3	53 515	40 695	6 423	3 462	97 171	57.8	11 246	4 470	10.1
July	174 306	111 756	64.1	53 835	41 041	6 332	3 481	97 727	58.1	10 548	4 329	9.4
August	174 440	112 231	64.3	53 837	41 314	6 457	3 502	98 106	58.2	10 623	4 070	9.5
September	174 602	112 298	64.3	53 983	41 650	6 383	3 347	98 669	58.4	10 282	3 854	9.2
October	174 779	111 926	64.0	54 146	41 597	6 296	3 303	98 736	58.4	9 887	3 648	8.8
November	174 951	112 228	64.1	54 499	41 788	6 442	3 291	99 438	58.7	9 499	3 535	8.5
December	175 121	112 327	64.1	54 662	41 852	6 482	3 332	99 664	58.8	9 331	3 379	8.3

[1] Not seasonally adjusted.

Table 20-3. Summary Labor Force, Employment, and Unemployment—Continued

(Thousands of persons, percent, seasonally adjusted, except as noted.)

Year and month	Noninstitutional population [1]	Labor force		Employment, thousands of persons					Employment–population ratio, percent	Unemployment		
		Thousands of persons	Participation rate (percent)	By age and sex			By industry			Thousands of persons		Rate, percent
				Men, 20 years and over	Women, 20 years and over	Both sexes, 16–19 years	Agricultural	Nonagricultural		Total	Unemployed 15 weeks and over	
1984												
January	175 533	112 209	63.9	54 975	41 812	6 414	3 293	99 908	58.8	9 008	3 254	8.0
February	175 679	112 615	64.1	55 213	42 196	6 415	3 353	100 471	59.1	8 791	2 991	7.8
March	175 824	112 713	64.1	55 281	42 328	6 358	3 233	100 734	59.1	8 746	2 881	7.8
April	175 969	113 098	64.3	55 373	42 512	6 451	3 291	101 045	59.3	8 762	2 858	7.7
May	176 123	113 649	64.5	55 661	43 071	6 461	3 343	101 850	59.7	8 456	2 884	7.4
June	176 284	113 817	64.6	55 996	42 944	6 651	3 383	102 208	59.9	8 226	2 612	7.2
July	176 440	113 972	64.6	55 921	42 979	6 535	3 344	102 091	59.8	8 537	2 638	7.5
August	176 583	113 682	64.4	55 930	42 885	6 348	3 286	101 877	59.6	8 519	2 604	7.5
September	176 763	113 857	64.4	56 095	42 967	6 428	3 393	102 097	59.7	8 367	2 538	7.3
October	176 956	114 019	64.4	56 183	43 052	6 403	3 194	102 444	59.7	8 381	2 526	7.4
November	177 135	114 170	64.5	56 274	43 244	6 454	3 394	102 578	59.8	8 198	2 438	7.2
December	177 306	114 581	64.6	56 313	43 472	6 438	3 385	102 838	59.9	8 358	2 401	7.3
1985												
January	177 384	114 725	64.7	56 184	43 589	6 529	3 317	102 985	59.9	8 423	2 284	7.3
February	177 516	114 876	64.7	56 216	43 787	6 552	3 317	103 238	60.0	8 321	2 389	7.2
March	177 667	115 328	64.9	56 356	44 035	6 598	3 250	103 739	60.2	8 339	2 394	7.2
April	177 799	115 331	64.9	56 374	44 000	6 562	3 306	103 630	60.1	8 395	2 393	7.3
May	177 944	115 234	64.8	56 531	43 905	6 496	3 280	103 652	60.1	8 302	2 292	7.2
June	178 096	114 965	64.6	56 288	43 958	6 259	3 161	103 344	59.8	8 460	2 310	7.4
July	178 263	115 320	64.7	56 435	43 975	6 397	3 143	103 664	59.9	8 513	2 329	7.4
August	178 405	115 291	64.6	56 655	44 103	6 337	3 121	103 974	60.0	8 196	2 258	7.1
September	178 572	115 905	64.9	56 845	44 395	6 417	3 064	104 593	60.3	8 248	2 242	7.1
October	178 770	116 145	65.0	56 969	44 565	6 313	3 051	104 796	60.3	8 298	2 295	7.1
November	178 940	116 135	64.9	56 972	44 617	6 418	3 062	104 945	60.4	8 128	2 207	7.0
December	179 112	116 354	65.0	56 995	44 889	6 332	3 141	105 075	60.4	8 138	2 208	7.0
1986												
January	179 670	116 682	64.9	57 637	44 944	6 306	3 287	105 600	60.6	7 795	2 089	6.7
February	179 821	116 882	65.0	57 269	44 804	6 407	3 083	105 397	60.3	8 402	2 308	7.2
March	179 985	117 220	65.1	57 353	44 960	6 524	3 200	105 637	60.5	8 383	2 261	7.2
April	180 148	117 316	65.1	57 358	45 081	6 513	3 153	105 799	60.5	8 364	2 162	7.1
May	180 311	117 528	65.2	57 287	45 289	6 513	3 150	105 939	60.5	8 439	2 232	7.2
June	180 503	118 084	65.4	57 471	45 621	6 484	3 193	106 383	60.7	8 508	2 320	7.2
July	180 682	118 129	65.4	57 514	45 837	6 459	3 141	106 669	60.8	8 319	2 269	7.0
August	180 828	118 150	65.3	57 597	45 926	6 492	3 082	106 933	60.8	8 135	2 276	6.9
September	180 997	118 395	65.4	57 630	45 972	6 483	3 171	106 914	60.8	8 310	2 318	7.0
October	181 186	118 516	65.4	57 660	46 046	6 567	3 128	107 145	60.9	8 243	2 188	7.0
November	181 363	118 634	65.4	57 941	46 070	6 464	3 220	107 255	60.9	8 159	2 202	6.9
December	181 547	118 611	65.3	58 185	46 132	6 411	3 148	107 580	61.0	7 883	2 161	6.6
1987												
January	181 827	118 845	65.4	58 264	46 219	6 470	3 143	107 810	61.0	7 892	2 168	6.6
February	181 998	119 122	65.5	58 279	46 444	6 534	3 208	108 049	61.1	7 865	2 117	6.6
March	182 179	119 270	65.5	58 362	46 549	6 497	3 214	108 194	61.2	7 862	2 070	6.6
April	182 344	119 336	65.4	58 503	46 746	6 545	3 246	108 548	61.3	7 542	2 091	6.3
May	182 533	120 008	65.7	58 713	47 052	6 669	3 345	109 089	61.6	7 574	2 104	6.3
June	182 703	119 644	65.5	58 581	47 102	6 563	3 216	109 030	61.4	7 398	2 087	6.2
July	182 885	119 902	65.6	58 740	47 229	6 665	3 235	109 399	61.6	7 268	1 921	6.1
August	183 002	120 318	65.7	58 810	47 322	6 925	3 112	109 945	61.8	7 261	1 878	6.0
September	183 161	120 011	65.5	58 964	47 285	6 660	3 189	109 720	61.6	7 102	1 866	5.9
October	183 311	120 509	65.7	59 073	47 533	6 676	3 219	110 063	61.8	7 227	1 794	6.0
November	183 470	120 540	65.7	59 210	47 622	6 673	3 145	110 360	61.9	7 035	1 797	5.8
December	183 620	120 729	65.7	59 217	47 781	6 795	3 213	110 580	62.0	6 936	1 767	5.7
1988												
January	183 822	120 969	65.8	59 346	47 862	6 808	3 247	110 769	62.0	6 953	1 714	5.7
February	183 969	121 156	65.9	59 535	47 919	6 773	3 201	111 026	62.1	6 929	1 738	5.7
March	184 111	120 913	65.7	59 393	48 090	6 554	3 169	110 868	61.9	6 876	1 744	5.7
April	184 232	121 251	65.8	59 832	48 147	6 671	3 224	111 426	62.2	6 601	1 563	5.4
May	184 374	121 071	65.7	59 644	47 946	6 702	3 121	111 171	62.0	6 779	1 647	5.6
June	184 562	121 473	65.8	59 751	48 146	7 030	3 111	111 816	62.3	6 546	1 531	5.4
July	184 729	121 665	65.9	59 888	48 186	6 986	3 060	112 000	62.3	6 605	1 601	5.4
August	184 830	122 125	66.1	59 877	48 467	6 938	3 119	112 163	62.4	6 843	1 639	5.6
September	184 962	121 960	65.9	59 980	48 511	6 865	3 165	112 191	62.4	6 604	1 569	5.4
October	185 114	122 206	66.0	60 023	48 859	6 756	3 231	112 407	62.5	6 568	1 562	5.4
November	185 244	122 637	66.2	60 042	49 254	6 804	3 241	112 859	62.7	6 537	1 468	5.3
December	185 402	122 622	66.1	60 059	49 257	6 788	3 194	112 910	62.6	6 518	1 490	5.3
1989												
January	185 644	123 390	66.5	60 477	49 529	6 702	3 287	113 421	62.9	6 682	1 480	5.4
February	185 777	123 135	66.3	60 588	49 497	6 691	3 234	113 542	62.9	6 359	1 304	5.2
March	185 897	123 227	66.3	60 795	49 503	6 724	3 198	113 824	62.9	6 205	1 353	5.0
April	186 024	123 565	66.4	60 764	49 565	6 768	3 162	113 935	62.9	6 468	1 397	5.2
May	186 181	123 474	66.3	60 795	49 583	6 721	3 125	113 974	62.9	6 375	1 348	5.2
June	186 329	123 995	66.5	61 054	49 542	6 822	3 068	114 350	63.0	6 577	1 300	5.3
July	186 483	123 967	66.5	60 947	49 693	6 832	3 227	114 245	63.0	6 495	1 435	5.2
August	186 598	124 166	66.5	60 915	49 804	6 936	3 284	114 371	63.1	6 511	1 302	5.2
September	186 726	123 944	66.4	60 668	50 015	6 671	3 219	114 135	62.8	6 590	1 360	5.3
October	186 871	124 211	66.5	60 958	49 871	6 752	3 215	114 366	62.9	6 630	1 392	5.3
November	187 017	124 637	66.6	60 958	50 221	6 733	3 132	114 780	63.0	6 725	1 418	5.4
December	187 165	124 497	66.5	61 068	50 116	6 646	3 188	114 642	63.0	6 667	1 375	5.4

[1] Not seasonally adjusted.

Table 20-3. Summary Labor Force, Employment, and Unemployment—*Continued*

(Thousands of persons, percent, seasonally adjusted, except as noted.)

Year and month	Noninsti- tutional population [1]	Labor force		Employment, thousands of persons					Employ- ment– population ratio, percent	Unemployment		
		Thousands of persons	Participa- tion rate (percent)	By age and sex			By industry			Thousands of persons		Rate, percent
				Men, 20 years and over	Women, 20 years and over	Both sexes, 16–19 years	Agricultural	Nonagri- cultural		Total	Unem- ployed 15 weeks and over	
1990												
January	188 413	125 833	66.8	61 742	50 436	6 903	3 210	115 871	63.2	6 752	1 412	5.4
February	188 516	125 710	66.7	61 805	50 438	6 816	3 188	115 871	63.2	6 651	1 350	5.3
March	188 630	125 801	66.7	61 832	50 463	6 908	3 260	115 943	63.2	6 598	1 331	5.2
April	188 778	125 649	66.6	61 579	50 457	6 816	3 231	115 621	63.0	6 797	1 376	5.4
May	188 913	125 893	66.6	61 778	50 646	6 727	3 266	115 885	63.1	6 742	1 415	5.4
June	189 058	125 573	66.4	61 762	50 550	6 671	3 245	115 738	62.9	6 590	1 436	5.2
July	189 188	125 732	66.5	61 683	50 514	6 613	3 192	115 618	62.8	6 922	1 534	5.5
August	189 342	125 990	66.5	61 715	50 635	6 452	3 197	115 605	62.7	7 188	1 607	5.7
September	189 528	125 892	66.4	61 608	50 587	6 329	3 206	115 318	62.5	7 368	1 695	5.9
October	189 710	125 995	66.4	61 606	50 616	6 314	3 270	115 266	62.5	7 459	1 689	5.9
November	189 872	126 070	66.4	61 545	50 541	6 220	3 189	115 117	62.3	7 764	1 831	6.2
December	190 017	126 142	66.4	61 506	50 530	6 205	3 245	114 996	62.2	7 901	1 804	6.3
1991												
January	190 163	125 955	66.2	61 383	50 472	6 085	3 208	114 732	62.0	8 015	1 866	6.4
February	190 271	126 020	66.2	61 117	50 523	6 115	3 270	114 485	61.9	8 265	1 955	6.6
March	190 381	126 238	66.3	61 144	50 422	6 086	3 177	114 475	61.8	8 586	2 137	6.8
April	190 517	126 548	66.4	61 280	50 760	6 069	3 241	114 868	62.0	8 439	2 206	6.7
May	190 650	126 176	66.2	61 052	50 457	5 931	3 275	114 165	61.6	8 736	2 252	6.9
June	190 800	126 331	66.2	61 147	50 585	5 907	3 300	114 339	61.7	8 692	2 533	6.9
July	190 946	126 154	66.1	61 179	50 636	5 753	3 319	114 249	61.6	8 586	2 388	6.8
August	191 116	126 150	66.0	61 122	50 601	5 761	3 313	114 171	61.5	8 666	2 460	6.9
September	191 302	126 650	66.2	61 279	50 864	5 785	3 319	114 609	61.6	8 722	2 497	6.9
October	191 497	126 642	66.1	61 174	50 811	5 815	3 289	114 511	61.5	8 842	2 638	7.0
November	191 657	126 701	66.1	61 201	50 759	5 810	3 296	114 474	61.4	8 931	2 718	7.0
December	191 798	126 664	66.0	61 074	50 728	5 664	3 146	114 320	61.2	9 198	2 892	7.3
1992												
January	191 953	127 261	66.3	61 116	51 095	5 767	3 155	114 823	61.5	9 283	3 060	7.3
February	192 067	127 207	66.2	61 062	51 033	5 658	3 239	114 514	61.3	9 454	3 182	7.4
March	192 204	127 604	66.4	61 363	51 204	5 577	3 236	114 908	61.5	9 460	3 196	7.4
April	192 354	127 841	66.5	61 468	51 323	5 635	3 245	115 181	61.6	9 415	3 130	7.4
May	192 503	128 119	66.6	61 513	51 245	5 617	3 213	115 162	61.5	9 744	3 444	7.6
June	192 663	128 459	66.7	61 537	51 383	5 499	3 297	115 122	61.5	10 040	3 758	7.8
July	192 826	128 563	66.7	61 641	51 458	5 614	3 285	115 428	61.6	9 850	3 614	7.7
August	193 018	128 613	66.6	61 681	51 386	5 759	3 279	115 547	61.6	9 787	3 579	7.6
September	193 229	128 501	66.5	61 663	51 359	5 698	3 274	115 446	61.4	9 781	3 504	7.6
October	193 442	128 026	66.2	61 550	51 373	5 705	3 254	115 374	61.3	9 398	3 505	7.3
November	193 621	128 441	66.3	61 644	51 535	5 697	3 207	115 669	61.4	9 565	3 397	7.4
December	193 784	128 554	66.3	61 721	51 524	5 752	3 259	115 738	61.4	9 557	3 651	7.4
1993												
January	193 962	128 400	66.2	61 895	51 505	5 675	3 222	115 853	61.4	9 325	3 346	7.3
February	194 108	128 458	66.2	61 963	51 573	5 739	3 125	116 150	61.4	9 183	3 190	7.1
March	194 248	128 598	66.2	62 007	51 808	5 727	3 119	116 423	61.5	9 056	3 115	7.0
April	194 398	128 584	66.1	62 032	51 732	5 710	3 074	116 400	61.5	9 110	3 014	7.1
May	194 549	129 264	66.4	62 309	51 996	5 810	3 100	117 015	61.7	9 149	3 101	7.1
June	194 719	129 411	66.5	62 409	52 183	5 698	3 108	117 182	61.8	9 121	3 141	7.0
July	194 882	129 397	66.4	62 497	52 088	5 882	3 126	117 341	61.8	8 930	3 046	6.9
August	195 063	129 619	66.4	62 634	52 294	5 928	3 026	117 830	62.0	8 763	3 026	6.8
September	195 259	129 268	66.2	62 437	52 241	5 876	3 174	117 380	61.7	8 714	3 042	6.7
October	195 444	129 573	66.3	62 614	52 379	5 830	3 084	117 739	61.8	8 750	3 029	6.8
November	195 625	129 711	66.3	62 732	52 531	5 906	3 157	118 012	61.9	8 542	2 986	6.6
December	195 794	129 941	66.4	62 760	52 813	5 891	3 116	118 348	62.0	8 477	2 968	6.5
1994												
January	195 953	130 596	66.6	62 798	53 052	6 116	3 302	118 664	62.2	8 630	3 060	6.6
February	196 090	130 669	66.6	62 708	53 266	6 112	3 339	118 747	62.3	8 583	3 118	6.6
March	196 213	130 400	66.5	62 780	53 099	6 051	3 354	118 576	62.1	8 470	3 055	6.5
April	196 363	130 621	66.5	62 906	53 274	6 110	3 428	118 862	62.3	8 331	2 921	6.4
May	196 510	130 779	66.6	63 116	53 624	6 124	3 409	119 455	62.5	7 915	2 836	6.1
June	196 693	130 561	66.4	63 041	53 393	6 200	3 299	119 335	62.3	7 927	2 735	6.1
July	196 859	130 652	66.4	63 034	53 531	6 141	3 333	119 373	62.3	7 946	2 822	6.1
August	197 043	131 275	66.6	63 294	53 744	6 304	3 451	119 891	62.6	7 933	2 750	6.0
September	197 248	131 421	66.6	63 631	53 991	6 065	3 430	120 257	62.7	7 734	2 746	5.9
October	197 430	131 744	66.7	63 818	54 071	6 223	3 490	120 622	62.9	7 632	2 955	5.8
November	197 607	131 891	66.7	64 080	54 168	6 268	3 574	120 942	63.0	7 375	2 666	5.6
December	197 765	131 951	66.7	64 359	54 054	6 308	3 577	121 144	63.1	7 230	2 488	5.5
1995												
January	197 753	132 038	66.8	64 185	54 087	6 391	3 519	121 144	63.0	7 375	2 396	5.6
February	197 886	132 115	66.8	64 378	54 226	6 324	3 620	121 308	63.1	7 187	2 345	5.4
March	198 007	132 108	66.7	64 321	54 141	6 493	3 634	121 321	63.1	7 153	2 287	5.4
April	198 148	132 590	66.9	64 165	54 366	6 414	3 566	121 379	63.1	7 645	2 473	5.8
May	198 286	131 851	66.5	63 829	54 272	6 320	3 349	121 072	62.7	7 430	2 577	5.6
June	198 453	131 949	66.5	63 992	54 020	6 510	3 461	121 061	62.7	7 427	2 266	5.6
July	198 615	132 343	66.6	63 962	54 476	6 378	3 379	121 437	62.8	7 527	2 311	5.7
August	198 801	132 336	66.6	63 875	54 434	6 543	3 374	121 478	62.8	7 484	2 391	5.7
September	199 005	132 611	66.6	64 179	54 507	6 447	3 285	121 848	62.9	7 478	2 306	5.6
October	199 192	132 716	66.6	64 272	54 692	6 424	3 438	121 950	62.9	7 328	2 272	5.5
November	199 355	132 614	66.5	63 931	54 850	6 407	3 338	121 850	62.8	7 426	2 339	5.6
December	199 508	132 511	66.4	64 041	54 674	6 373	3 352	121 736	62.7	7 423	2 331	5.6

[1] Not seasonally adjusted.

Table 20-3. Summary Labor Force, Employment, and Unemployment—Continued

(Thousands of persons, percent, seasonally adjusted, except as noted.)

Year and month	Noninstitutional population [1]	Labor force		Employment, thousands of persons					Employment–population ratio, percent	Unemployment		
		Thousands of persons	Participation rate (percent)	By age and sex			By industry			Thousands of persons		Rate, percent
				Men, 20 years and over	Women, 20 years and over	Both sexes, 16–19 years	Agricultural	Nonagricultural		Total	Unemployed 15 weeks and over	
1996												
January	199 634	132 616	66.4	64 180	54 580	6 365	3 483	121 642	62.7	7 491	2 371	5.6
February	199 773	132 952	66.6	64 398	54 844	6 397	3 547	122 092	62.9	7 313	2 307	5.5
March	199 921	133 180	66.6	64 506	54 994	6 362	3 489	122 373	63.0	7 318	2 454	5.5
April	200 101	133 409	66.7	64 481	55 067	6 446	3 406	122 588	63.0	7 415	2 455	5.6
May	200 278	133 667	66.7	64 683	55 034	6 527	3 473	122 771	63.0	7 423	2 403	5.6
June	200 459	133 697	66.7	64 940	55 177	6 485	3 424	123 178	63.2	7 095	2 355	5.3
July	200 641	134 284	66.9	65 068	55 362	6 517	3 433	123 514	63.3	7 337	2 297	5.5
August	200 847	134 054	66.7	65 216	55 525	6 431	3 395	123 777	63.3	6 882	2 267	5.1
September	201 061	134 515	66.9	65 169	55 669	6 698	3 448	124 088	63.4	6 979	2 220	5.2
October	201 273	134 921	67.0	65 460	55 750	6 680	3 463	124 427	63.5	7 031	2 268	5.2
November	201 463	135 007	67.0	65 320	55 896	6 555	3 356	124 415	63.4	7 236	2 159	5.4
December	201 636	135 113	67.0	65 435	55 849	6 576	3 445	124 415	63.4	7 253	2 124	5.4
1997												
January	202 285	135 456	67.0	65 679	56 024	6 595	3 449	124 849	63.4	7 158	2 162	5.3
February	202 389	135 400	66.9	65 758	55 955	6 585	3 353	124 945	63.4	7 102	2 140	5.2
March	202 513	135 891	67.1	65 974	56 270	6 647	3 419	125 472	63.6	7 000	2 110	5.2
April	202 674	136 016	67.1	66 092	56 347	6 704	3 462	125 681	63.7	6 873	2 176	5.1
May	202 832	136 119	67.1	66 328	56 446	6 690	3 437	126 027	63.8	6 655	2 121	4.9
June	203 000	136 211	67.1	66 308	56 573	6 531	3 409	126 003	63.7	6 799	2 085	5.0
July	203 166	136 477	67.2	66 422	56 785	6 615	3 422	126 400	63.9	6 655	2 119	4.9
August	203 364	136 618	67.2	66 508	56 852	6 650	3 359	126 651	63.9	6 608	2 004	4.8
September	203 570	136 675	67.1	66 483	56 931	6 605	3 392	126 627	63.9	6 656	2 074	4.9
October	203 767	136 633	67.1	66 511	56 982	6 686	3 312	126 867	63.9	6 454	1 950	4.7
November	203 941	136 961	67.2	66 765	57 039	6 849	3 386	127 267	64.1	6 308	1 817	4.6
December	204 098	137 155	67.2	66 643	57 219	6 817	3 405	127 274	64.0	6 476	1 901	4.7
1998												
January	204 238	137 095	67.1	66 750	56 941	7 035	3 299	127 389	64.0	6 368	1 833	4.6
February	204 400	137 112	67.1	66 856	56 992	6 959	3 284	127 522	64.0	6 306	1 809	4.6
March	204 547	137 236	67.1	66 721	57 080	7 014	3 146	127 650	64.0	6 422	1 772	4.7
April	204 731	137 150	67.0	67 074	57 074	6 985	3 334	127 852	64.1	5 941	1 476	4.3
May	204 899	137 372	67.0	67 164	57 155	7 007	3 360	127 959	64.1	6 047	1 490	4.4
June	205 085	137 455	67.0	67 054	57 156	7 033	3 380	127 874	64.0	6 212	1 613	4.5
July	205 270	137 588	67.0	67 119	57 192	7 018	3 455	127 913	64.0	6 259	1 577	4.5
August	205 479	137 570	67.0	66 985	57 332	7 074	3 509	127 970	63.9	6 179	1 626	4.5
September	205 699	138 286	67.2	67 254	57 520	7 212	3 500	128 399	64.2	6 300	1 688	4.6
October	205 919	138 279	67.2	67 433	57 529	7 036	3 593	128 389	64.1	6 280	1 582	4.5
November	206 104	138 381	67.1	67 591	57 638	7 052	3 375	128 897	64.2	6 100	1 590	4.4
December	206 270	138 634	67.2	67 548	57 840	7 214	3 246	129 320	64.3	6 032	1 559	4.4
1999												
January	206 719	139 003	67.2	67 679	58 256	7 092	3 233	129 802	64.4	5 976	1 490	4.3
February	206 873	138 967	67.2	67 498	58 129	7 229	3 246	129 647	64.2	6 111	1 551	4.4
March	207 036	138 730	67.0	67 660	58 132	7 155	3 238	129 656	64.2	5 783	1 472	4.2
April	207 236	138 959	67.1	67 542	58 260	7 153	3 336	129 615	64.2	6 004	1 480	4.3
May	207 427	139 107	67.1	67 539	58 440	7 331	3 335	129 937	64.3	5 796	1 505	4.2
June	207 632	139 329	67.1	67 700	58 641	7 037	3 386	129 982	64.2	5 951	1 624	4.3
July	207 828	139 439	67.1	67 731	58 490	7 193	3 346	130 146	64.2	6 025	1 513	4.3
August	208 038	139 430	67.0	67 768	58 707	7 117	3 234	130 366	64.2	5 838	1 455	4.2
September	208 265	139 622	67.0	67 882	58 735	7 090	3 173	130 434	64.2	5 915	1 449	4.2
October	208 483	139 771	67.0	67 840	58 921	7 232	3 229	130 758	64.3	5 778	1 438	4.1
November	208 666	140 025	67.1	68 094	59 018	7 198	3 343	130 989	64.4	5 716	1 378	4.1
December	208 832	140 177	67.1	68 217	59 056	7 251	3 260	131 257	64.4	5 653	1 375	4.0
2000												
January	211 410	142 258	67.3	69 424	59 836	7 301	2 611	133 912	64.6	5 698	1 381	4.0
February	211 576	142 452	67.3	69 504	59 886	7 209	2 728	133 901	64.6	5 853	1 307	4.1
March	211 772	142 398	67.2	69 472	59 974	7 222	2 578	134 004	64.5	5 730	1 312	4.0
April	212 018	142 747	67.3	69 505	60 357	7 402	2 505	134 778	64.7	5 483	1 260	3.8
May	212 242	142 369	67.1	69 385	59 950	7 276	2 481	134 118	64.4	5 758	1 326	4.0
June	212 466	142 571	67.1	69 629	60 017	7 277	2 446	134 515	64.4	5 648	1 238	4.0
July	212 677	142 265	66.9	69 551	59 989	6 996	2 401	134 217	64.2	5 749	1 341	4.0
August	212 916	142 562	67.0	69 850	59 726	7 126	2 437	134 309	64.2	5 861	1 386	4.1
September	213 163	142 539	66.9	69 706	60 092	7 110	2 388	134 483	64.2	5 631	1 285	4.0
October	213 405	142 663	66.9	69 776	60 250	7 098	2 316	134 820	64.3	5 540	1 339	3.9
November	213 540	142 959	66.9	69 905	60 282	7 129	2 342	134 942	64.3	5 643	1 319	3.9
December	213 736	143 273	67.0	69 928	60 521	7 182	2 389	135 205	64.4	5 641	1 332	3.9
2001												
January	213 888	143 787	67.2	70 071	60 605	7 114	2 349	135 407	64.4	5 997	1 377	4.2
February	214 110	143 652	67.1	69 935	60 608	7 037	2 359	135 249	64.3	6 072	1 500	4.2
March	214 305	143 873	67.1	69 855	60 893	6 990	2 340	135 320	64.3	6 136	1 521	4.3
April	214 525	143 549	66.9	69 896	60 518	6 861	2 335	134 989	64.0	6 274	1 494	4.4
May	214 732	143 290	66.7	69 849	60 506	6 708	2 357	134 699	63.8	6 227	1 502	4.3
June	214 950	143 323	66.7	69 704	60 336	6 803	2 092	134 725	63.7	6 481	1 521	4.5
July	215 180	143 674	66.8	69 835	60 468	6 788	2 297	134 859	63.7	6 583	1 641	4.6
August	215 420	143 372	66.6	69 636	60 308	6 371	2 314	133 967	63.3	7 057	1 845	4.9
September	215 665	144 020	66.8	69 935	60 282	6 651	2 327	134 565	63.5	7 151	1 944	5.0
October	215 903	144 171	66.8	69 647	60 189	6 611	2 315	134 141	63.2	7 723	2 094	5.4
November	216 117	144 254	66.7	69 440	60 199	6 595	2 228	134 011	63.0	8 020	2 338	5.6
December	216 315	144 369	66.7	69 530	60 137	6 411	2 289	133 770	62.9	8 291	2 465	5.7

[1] Not seasonally adjusted.

Table 20-3. Summary Labor Force, Employment, and Unemployment—*Continued*

(Thousands of persons, percent, seasonally adjusted, except as noted.)

Year and month	Noninsti-tutional population [1]	Labor force		Employment, thousands of persons					Employ-ment–population ratio, percent	Unemployment		
				By age and sex			By industry			Thousands of persons		
		Thousands of persons	Participa-tion rate (percent)	Men, 20 years and over	Women, 20 years and over	Both sexes, 16–19 years	Agricultural	Nonagri-cultural		Total	Unem-ployed 15 weeks and over	Rate, percent
2002												
January	216 506	143 842	66.4	69 323	60 019	6 374	2 360	133 359	62.7	8 126	2 587	5.6
February	216 663	144 546	66.7	69 490	60 456	6 417	2 373	134 046	62.9	8 184	2 623	5.7
March	216 823	144 384	66.6	69 451	60 151	6 503	2 348	133 710	62.8	8 278	2 728	5.7
April	217 006	144 675	66.7	69 555	60 189	6 353	2 375	133 782	62.7	8 578	2 832	5.9
May	217 198	144 902	66.7	69 955	60 224	6 325	2 270	134 236	62.8	8 397	2 948	5.8
June	217 407	144 738	66.6	69 789	60 225	6 339	2 191	134 087	62.7	8 384	2 998	5.8
July	217 630	144 879	66.6	69 854	60 299	6 325	2 341	134 094	62.7	8 400	2 923	5.8
August	217 866	145 146	66.6	70 004	60 572	6 235	2 146	134 639	62.8	8 335	2 872	5.7
September	218 107	145 606	66.8	70 206	60 717	6 414	2 288	135 127	63.0	8 269	2 976	5.7
October	218 340	145 442	66.6	69 978	60 704	6 397	2 421	134 666	62.8	8 363	3 071	5.7
November	218 548	145 109	66.4	69 612	60 754	6 179	2 296	134 269	62.5	8 565	3 105	5.9
December	218 741	145 157	66.4	69 569	60 750	6 141	2 345	134 098	62.4	8 698	3 312	6.0
2003												
January	219 897	145 875	66.3	69 940	61 391	6 117	2 301	135 176	62.5	8 428	3 175	5.8
February	220 114	145 898	66.3	70 174	61 106	6 039	2 205	135 166	62.4	8 581	3 176	5.9
March	220 317	145 818	66.2	70 213	61 219	5 868	2 235	135 054	62.3	8 519	3 168	5.8
April	220 540	146 377	66.4	70 290	61 343	5 945	2 162	135 486	62.4	8 799	3 318	6.0
May	220 768	146 462	66.3	70 182	61 397	5 926	2 194	135 311	62.3	8 957	3 294	6.1
June	221 014	146 917	66.5	70 190	61 610	5 873	2 229	135 348	62.3	9 245	3 510	6.3
July	221 252	146 652	66.3	70 269	61 479	5 856	2 217	135 240	62.2	9 048	3 559	6.2
August	221 507	146 622	66.2	70 324	61 467	5 902	2 327	135 282	62.2	8 929	3 561	6.1
September	221 779	146 610	66.1	70 596	61 191	5 857	2 341	135 401	62.1	8 966	3 511	6.1
October	222 039	146 892	66.2	70 726	61 524	5 846	2 410	135 722	62.2	8 797	3 478	6.0
November	222 279	147 187	66.2	70 964	61 597	5 972	2 418	136 172	62.3	8 653	3 484	5.9
December	222 509	146 878	66.0	71 099	61 521	5 859	2 245	136 180	62.2	8 398	3 403	5.7

[1] Not seasonally adjusted.

Table 20-4. Nonfarm Payroll Employment, Hours, and Earnings

(Wage and salary workers on nonfarm payrolls, seasonally adjusted.)

Year and month	All wage and salary workers, (thousands)					Production or nonsupervisory workers on private payrolls							
		Private				Number (thousands)		Average hours per week		Average hourly earnings, dollars		Average weekly earnings, dollars	
	Total	Total	Goods–producing		Service–providing	Total private	Manufacturing	Total private	Manufacturing	Total private	Manufacturing	Total private	Manufacturing
			Total	Manufacturing									
1946													
January	39 839	34 054	15 031	12 719	24 808	...	10 990	...	40.9	...	0.86	...	35.17
February	39 250	33 472	14 308	11 922	24 942	...	10 292	...	40.4	...	0.85	...	34.34
March	40 192	34 434	15 017	12 545	25 175	...	10 989	...	40.6	...	0.89	...	36.13
April	40 908	35 147	15 439	13 200	25 469	...	11 616	...	40.4	...	0.92	...	37.17
May	41 348	35 616	15 875	13 389	25 473	...	11 758	...	39.8	...	0.93	...	37.01
June	41 732	36 052	16 206	13 598	25 526	...	11 905	...	40.0	...	0.94	...	37.60
July	42 153	36 471	16 461	13 771	25 692	...	12 065	...	40.2	...	0.96	...	38.59
August	42 642	36 961	16 728	13 981	25 914	...	12 241	...	40.6	...	0.98	...	39.79
September	42 908	37 239	16 912	14 135	25 996	...	12 311	...	40.4	...	0.99	...	40.00
October	43 094	37 430	17 002	14 182	26 092	...	12 302	...	40.4	...	1.00	...	40.40
November	43 396	37 757	17 157	14 310	26 239	...	12 421	...	40.3	...	1.02	...	41.11
December	43 379	37 751	17 164	14 301	26 215	...	12 419	...	40.5	...	1.02	...	41.31
1947													
January	43 545	37 926	17 213	14 328	26 332	...	12 445	...	40.5	...	1.03	...	41.72
February	43 563	37 957	17 200	14 278	26 363	...	12 487	...	40.4	...	1.04	...	42.02
March	43 605	38 017	17 196	14 259	26 409	...	12 518	...	40.3	...	1.06	...	42.72
April	43 491	37 933	17 178	14 240	26 313	...	12 531	...	40.5	...	1.06	...	42.93
May	43 637	38 086	17 176	14 189	26 461	...	12 449	...	40.4	...	1.08	...	43.63
June	43 808	38 284	17 253	14 200	26 555	...	12 389	...	40.4	...	1.10	...	44.44
July	43 742	38 218	17 106	14 076	26 636	...	12 265	...	40.4	...	1.10	...	44.44
August	43 958	38 439	17 280	14 200	26 678	...	12 370	...	40.0	...	1.11	...	44.40
September	44 201	38 662	17 398	14 315	26 803	...	12 430	...	40.5	...	1.11	...	44.96
October	44 415	38 849	17 499	14 393	26 916	...	12 464	...	40.5	...	1.13	...	45.77
November	44 486	38 901	17 517	14 414	26 969	...	12 494	...	40.5	...	1.14	...	46.17
December	44 578	38 973	17 563	14 428	27 015	...	12 526	...	40.8	...	1.16	...	47.33
1948													
January	44 686	39 062	17 625	14 438	27 061	...	12 520	...	40.5	...	1.16	...	46.98
February	44 537	38 922	17 447	14 339	27 090	...	12 437	...	40.2	...	1.16	...	46.63
March	44 680	39 057	17 544	14 364	27 136	...	12 489	...	40.4	...	1.16	...	46.86
April	44 369	38 726	17 302	14 183	27 067	...	12 304	...	40.1	...	1.17	...	46.92
May	44 795	39 114	17 508	14 235	27 287	...	12 344	...	40.2	...	1.18	...	47.44
June	45 032	39 296	17 633	14 318	27 399	...	12 402	...	40.3	...	1.19	...	47.96
July	45 160	39 386	17 649	14 359	27 511	...	12 417	...	40.2	...	1.21	...	48.64
August	45 175	39 384	17 655	14 353	27 520	...	12 397	...	40.2	...	1.23	...	49.45
September	45 294	39 489	17 741	14 441	27 553	...	12 450	...	40.1	...	1.24	...	49.72
October	45 250	39 421	17 683	14 390	27 567	...	12 364	...	39.8	...	1.25	...	49.75
November	45 194	39 325	17 599	14 292	27 595	...	12 302	...	39.8	...	1.26	...	50.15
December	45 028	39 140	17 417	14 086	27 611	...	12 127	...	39.6	...	1.26	...	49.90
1949													
January	44 675	38 781	17 170	13 867	27 505	...	11 905	...	39.4	...	1.26	...	49.64
February	44 500	38 607	17 019	13 734	27 481	...	11 792	...	39.4	...	1.26	...	49.64
March	44 238	38 323	16 848	13 581	27 390	...	11 654	...	39.1	...	1.26	...	49.27
April	44 230	38 282	16 685	13 439	27 545	...	11 517	...	38.8	...	1.25	...	48.50
May	43 982	38 020	16 492	13 269	27 490	...	11 352	...	38.9	...	1.25	...	48.63
June	43 739	37 783	16 351	13 178	27 388	...	11 266	...	39.0	...	1.26	...	49.14
July	43 530	37 568	16 222	13 067	27 308	...	11 168	...	39.2	...	1.26	...	49.39
August	43 621	37 636	16 327	13 158	27 294	...	11 251	...	39.2	...	1.25	...	49.00
September	43 784	37 794	16 403	13 225	27 381	...	11 284	...	39.4	...	1.25	...	49.25
October	42 950	36 980	15 739	12 891	27 211	...	10 940	...	39.6	...	1.24	...	49.10
November	43 244	37 294	16 040	12 882	27 204	...	10 964	...	39.1	...	1.24	...	48.48
December	43 516	37 564	16 217	13 062	27 299	...	11 173	...	39.4	...	1.25	...	49.25
1950													
January	43 530	37 596	16 255	13 161	27 275	...	11 258	...	39.6	...	1.27	...	50.29
February	43 298	37 372	16 035	13 169	27 263	...	11 262	...	39.7	...	1.26	...	50.02
March	43 952	37 874	16 482	13 290	27 470	...	11 362	...	39.7	...	1.28	...	50.82
April	44 376	38 282	16 718	13 471	27 658	...	11 528	...	40.3	...	1.29	...	51.99
May	44 717	38 674	17 080	13 780	27 637	...	11 855	...	40.3	...	1.30	...	52.39
June	45 084	39 062	17 288	13 923	27 796	...	11 979	...	40.6	...	1.30	...	52.78
July	45 453	39 363	17 464	14 072	27 989	...	12 107	...	40.9	...	1.31	...	53.58
August	46 187	40 000	17 917	14 461	28 270	...	12 476	...	41.3	...	1.33	...	54.93
September	46 442	40 214	18 040	14 561	28 402	...	12 519	...	40.8	...	1.33	...	54.26
October	46 712	40 463	18 249	14 737	28 463	...	12 659	...	41.1	...	1.36	...	55.90
November	46 778	40 516	18 288	14 762	28 490	...	12 682	...	41.0	...	1.37	...	56.17
December	46 855	40 541	18 283	14 782	28 572	...	12 710	...	40.9	...	1.39	...	56.85
1951													
January	47 289	40 937	18 518	14 950	28 771	...	12 816	...	41.0	...	1.40	...	57.40
February	47 577	41 195	18 666	15 076	28 911	...	12 929	...	40.9	...	1.41	...	57.67
March	47 871	41 461	18 754	15 125	29 117	...	12 936	...	41.0	...	1.42	...	58.22
April	47 856	41 405	18 810	15 166	29 046	...	12 960	...	41.0	...	1.43	...	58.63
May	47 952	41 535	18 829	15 164	29 123	...	12 941	...	41.0	...	1.44	...	59.04
June	48 067	41 568	18 826	15 176	29 241	...	12 934	...	40.9	...	1.45	...	59.31
July	48 061	41 523	18 747	15 110	29 314	...	12 848	...	40.6	...	1.45	...	58.87
August	48 008	41 489	18 709	15 061	29 299	...	12 772	...	40.4	...	1.46	...	58.98
September	47 955	41 403	18 622	14 996	29 333	...	12 659	...	40.4	...	1.46	...	58.98
October	48 009	41 432	18 630	14 973	29 379	...	12 615	...	40.3	...	1.47	...	59.24
November	48 149	41 523	18 617	14 999	29 532	...	12 628	...	40.4	...	1.48	...	59.79
December	48 308	41 620	18 698	15 045	29 610	...	12 667	...	40.7	...	1.49	...	60.64

... = Not available.

Table 20-4. Nonfarm Payroll Employment, Hours, and Earnings—Continued

(Wage and salary workers on nonfarm payrolls, seasonally adjusted.)

Year and month	All wage and salary workers, (thousands)					Production or nonsupervisory workers on private payrolls								
	Total	Private				Number (thousands)		Average hours per week		Average hourly earnings, dollars		Average weekly earnings, dollars		
		Total	Goods–producing		Service–providing	Total private	Manufacturing	Total private	Manufacturing	Total private	Manufacturing	Total private	Manufacturing
			Total	Manufacturing									
1952													
January	48 299	41 710	18 719	15 067	29 580	...	12 675	...	40.8	...	1.49	...	60.79
February	48 522	41 872	18 813	15 105	29 709	...	12 689	...	40.8	...	1.49	...	60.79
March	48 504	41 842	18 775	15 127	29 729	...	12 695	...	40.6	...	1.51	...	61.31
April	48 616	41 954	18 806	15 162	29 810	...	12 713	...	40.3	...	1.51	...	60.85
May	48 645	41 951	18 784	15 143	29 861	...	12 676	...	40.5	...	1.51	...	61.16
June	48 286	41 574	18 419	14 828	29 867	...	12 353	...	40.6	...	1.51	...	61.31
July	48 144	41 407	18 268	14 707	29 876	...	12 233	...	40.2	...	1.50	...	60.30
August	48 922	42 204	18 928	15 279	29 994	...	12 764	...	40.7	...	1.53	...	62.27
September	49 319	42 585	19 206	15 553	30 113	...	13 007	...	41.1	...	1.55	...	63.71
October	49 598	42 782	19 312	15 690	30 286	...	13 122	...	41.2	...	1.56	...	64.27
November	49 816	43 015	19 473	15 843	30 343	...	13 262	...	41.2	...	1.58	...	65.10
December	50 164	43 229	19 610	15 973	30 554	...	13 375	...	41.2	...	1.58	...	65.10
1953													
January	50 145	43 351	19 721	16 067	30 424	...	13 447	...	41.1	...	1.59	...	65.35
February	50 339	43 542	19 841	16 158	30 498	...	13 529	...	41.0	...	1.61	...	66.01
March	50 474	43 690	19 909	16 270	30 565	...	13 620	...	41.2	...	1.61	...	66.33
April	50 432	43 662	19 908	16 293	30 524	...	13 629	...	40.9	...	1.62	...	66.26
May	50 491	43 774	19 930	16 341	30 561	...	13 645	...	41.0	...	1.62	...	66.42
June	50 522	43 788	19 909	16 343	30 613	...	13 636	...	40.9	...	1.63	...	66.67
July	50 536	43 813	19 910	16 353	30 626	...	13 653	...	40.7	...	1.64	...	66.75
August	50 487	43 733	19 834	16 278	30 653	...	13 564	...	40.7	...	1.64	...	66.75
September	50 365	43 616	19 726	16 151	30 639	...	13 419	...	40.1	...	1.65	...	66.17
October	50 242	43 478	19 578	15 981	30 664	...	13 244	...	40.1	...	1.65	...	66.17
November	49 906	43 157	19 315	15 728	30 591	...	12 990	...	40.0	...	1.65	...	66.00
December	49 702	42 959	19 173	15 581	30 529	...	12 847	...	39.7	...	1.65	...	65.51
1954													
January	49 467	42 707	18 963	15 440	30 504	...	12 706	...	39.5	...	1.65	...	65.18
February	49 381	42 598	18 880	15 307	30 501	...	12 593	...	39.7	...	1.65	...	65.51
March	49 158	42 362	18 748	15 197	30 410	...	12 493	...	39.6	...	1.65	...	65.34
April	49 177	42 371	18 602	15 065	30 575	...	12 361	...	39.7	...	1.65	...	65.51
May	48 965	42 136	18 476	14 974	30 489	...	12 282	...	39.7	...	1.67	...	66.30
June	48 896	42 050	18 400	14 910	30 496	...	12 220	...	39.7	...	1.67	...	66.30
July	48 834	41 966	18 280	14 799	30 554	...	12 121	...	39.7	...	1.66	...	65.90
August	48 825	41 933	18 251	14 772	30 574	...	12 089	...	39.8	...	1.66	...	66.07
September	48 881	41 987	18 261	14 805	30 620	...	12 104	...	39.9	...	1.66	...	66.23
October	48 944	42 044	18 321	14 841	30 623	...	12 142	...	39.7	...	1.67	...	66.30
November	49 179	42 215	18 438	14 913	30 741	...	12 206	...	40.1	...	1.68	...	67.37
December	49 331	42 374	18 508	14 967	30 823	...	12 254	...	40.1	...	1.68	...	67.37
1955													
January	49 497	42 544	18 609	15 034	30 888	...	12 309	...	40.4	...	1.69	...	68.28
February	49 644	42 721	18 726	15 138	30 918	...	12 408	...	40.6	...	1.70	...	69.02
March	49 963	43 025	18 910	15 258	31 053	...	12 524	...	40.7	...	1.71	...	69.60
April	50 246	43 287	19 067	15 375	31 179	...	12 626	...	40.8	...	1.71	...	69.77
May	50 512	43 521	19 223	15 493	31 289	...	12 731	...	41.1	...	1.73	...	71.10
June	50 790	43 770	19 351	15 585	31 459	...	12 810	...	40.8	...	1.73	...	70.58
July	50 985	43 936	19 376	15 614	31 609	...	12 818	...	40.7	...	1.75	...	71.23
August	51 112	44 089	19 432	15 679	31 680	...	12 866	...	40.7	...	1.76	...	71.63
September	51 262	44 195	19 427	15 668	31 835	...	12 830	...	40.7	...	1.77	...	72.04
October	51 431	44 313	19 482	15 740	31 949	...	12 896	...	41.0	...	1.77	...	72.57
November	51 592	44 509	19 554	15 813	32 038	...	12 967	...	41.1	...	1.78	...	73.16
December	51 805	44 673	19 608	15 859	32 197	...	13 009	...	40.9	...	1.78	...	72.80
1956													
January	51 975	44 808	19 665	15 882	32 310	...	13 011	...	40.8	...	1.78	...	72.62
February	52 167	44 955	19 731	15 889	32 436	...	12 986	...	40.7	...	1.79	...	72.85
March	52 295	45 043	19 691	15 829	32 604	...	12 905	...	40.6	...	1.80	...	73.08
April	52 375	45 099	19 811	15 909	32 564	...	12 970	...	40.5	...	1.82	...	73.71
May	52 506	45 139	19 825	15 893	32 681	...	12 925	...	40.4	...	1.83	...	73.93
June	52 583	45 216	19 905	15 835	32 678	...	12 836	...	40.3	...	1.83	...	73.75
July	51 954	44 549	19 390	15 468	32 564	...	12 435	...	40.3	...	1.82	...	73.35
August	52 632	45 181	19 922	15 893	32 710	...	12 860	...	40.3	...	1.85	...	74.56
September	52 600	45 119	19 860	15 863	32 740	...	12 822	...	40.5	...	1.87	...	75.74
October	52 781	45 262	19 918	15 937	32 863	...	12 908	...	40.6	...	1.88	...	76.33
November	52 822	45 269	19 886	15 916	32 936	...	12 864	...	40.4	...	1.88	...	75.95
December	52 930	45 346	19 926	15 957	33 004	...	12 882	...	40.6	...	1.91	...	77.55
1957													
January	52 888	45 268	19 833	15 970	33 055	...	12 881	...	40.4	...	1.90	...	76.76
February	53 098	45 452	19 933	15 998	33 165	...	12 885	...	40.5	...	1.91	...	77.36
March	53 156	45 484	19 936	15 994	33 220	...	12 855	...	40.4	...	1.92	...	77.57
April	53 238	45 537	19 887	15 970	33 351	...	12 811	...	40.0	...	1.91	...	76.40
May	53 149	45 436	19 834	15 931	33 315	...	12 762	...	40.0	...	1.92	...	76.80
June	53 066	45 364	19 777	15 873	33 289	...	12 697	...	40.0	...	1.92	...	76.80
July	53 122	45 368	19 735	15 854	33 387	...	12 669	...	40.0	...	1.93	...	77.20
August	53 128	45 371	19 728	15 867	33 400	...	12 673	...	40.0	...	1.94	...	77.60
September	52 932	45 183	19 545	15 710	33 387	...	12 528	...	39.7	...	1.95	...	77.42
October	52 765	44 997	19 421	15 599	33 344	...	12 437	...	39.4	...	1.96	...	77.22
November	52 557	44 788	19 260	15 466	33 297	...	12 301	...	39.2	...	1.96	...	76.83
December	52 385	44 539	19 111	15 332	33 274	...	12 170	...	39.1	...	1.95	...	76.25

... = Not available.

Table 20-4. Nonfarm Payroll Employment, Hours, and Earnings—Continued

(Wage and salary workers on nonfarm payrolls, seasonally adjusted.)

Year and month	All wage and salary workers, (thousands)					Production or nonsupervisory workers on private payrolls								
	Total	Private				Number (thousands)		Average hours per week		Average hourly earnings, dollars		Average weekly earnings, dollars		
		Total	Goods–producing		Service–providing	Total private	Manufac-turing	Total private	Manufac-turing	Total private	Manufac-turing	Total private	Manufac-turing
			Total	Manufac-turing										
1958														
January	52 077	44 256	18 902	15 130	33 175	...	11 969	...	38.9	...	1.95	...	75.86
February	51 576	43 744	18 529	14 908	33 047	...	11 757	...	38.7	...	1.95	...	75.47
March	51 300	43 452	18 335	14 670	32 965	...	11 532	...	38.8	...	1.96	...	76.05
April	51 026	43 158	18 120	14 506	32 906	...	11 373	...	38.9	...	1.96	...	76.24
May	50 913	43 019	18 008	14 414	32 905	...	11 294	...	38.9	...	1.97	...	76.63
June	50 912	42 986	17 984	14 408	32 928	...	11 300	...	39.1	...	1.98	...	77.42
July	51 037	43 065	18 038	14 450	32 999	...	11 349	...	39.3	...	1.98	...	77.81
August	51 233	43 221	18 147	14 524	33 086	...	11 412	...	39.5	...	2.01	...	79.40
September	51 506	43 490	18 331	14 658	33 175	...	11 556	...	39.5	...	2.00	...	79.00
October	51 485	43 454	18 218	14 503	33 267	...	11 394	...	39.6	...	2.00	...	79.20
November	51 943	43 915	18 610	14 827	33 333	...	11 702	...	39.9	...	2.03	...	81.00
December	52 088	43 988	18 592	14 877	33 496	...	11 743	...	39.9	...	2.04	...	81.40
1959														
January	52 481	44 376	18 796	14 998	33 685	...	11 849	...	40.2	...	2.04	...	82.01
February	52 687	44 571	18 890	15 115	33 797	...	11 950	...	40.3	...	2.05	...	82.62
March	53 016	44 884	19 069	15 259	33 947	...	12 078	...	40.4	...	2.07	...	83.63
April	53 320	45 178	19 269	15 385	34 051	...	12 185	...	40.5	...	2.08	...	84.24
May	53 549	45 396	19 378	15 487	34 171	...	12 277	...	40.7	...	2.08	...	84.66
June	53 678	45 535	19 462	15 554	34 216	...	12 330	...	40.6	...	2.09	...	84.85
July	53 803	45 630	19 529	15 623	34 274	...	12 366	...	40.3	...	2.09	...	84.23
August	53 337	45 156	19 049	15 202	34 288	...	11 936	...	40.4	...	2.07	...	83.63
September	53 428	45 189	19 052	15 254	34 376	...	11 984	...	40.4	...	2.08	...	84.03
October	53 359	45 094	18 925	15 158	34 434	...	11 864	...	40.1	...	2.07	...	83.01
November	53 635	45 351	19 108	15 300	34 527	...	11 991	...	39.9	...	2.07	...	82.59
December	54 175	45 807	19 425	15 573	34 750	...	12 254	...	40.3	...	2.11	...	85.03
1960														
January	54 274	45 967	19 491	15 687	34 783	...	12 362	...	40.6	...	2.13	...	86.48
February	54 513	46 187	19 605	15 765	34 908	...	12 434	...	40.3	...	2.14	...	86.24
March	54 458	45 933	19 373	15 707	35 085	...	12 362	...	40.0	...	2.14	...	85.60
April	54 812	46 278	19 446	15 654	35 366	...	12 299	...	40.0	...	2.14	...	85.60
May	54 472	46 040	19 374	15 575	35 098	...	12 218	...	40.1	...	2.14	...	85.81
June	54 347	45 915	19 240	15 466	35 107	...	12 102	...	39.9	...	2.14	...	85.39
July	54 303	45 861	19 170	15 413	35 133	...	12 047	...	39.9	...	2.14	...	85.39
August	54 272	45 800	19 105	15 360	35 167	...	11 986	...	39.7	...	2.15	...	85.36
September	54 228	45 734	19 057	15 330	35 171	...	11 956	...	39.4	...	2.16	...	85.10
October	54 144	45 642	18 952	15 231	35 192	...	11 846	...	39.7	...	2.16	...	85.75
November	53 962	45 446	18 799	15 112	35 163	...	11 726	...	39.3	...	2.15	...	84.50
December	53 743	45 146	18 548	14 947	35 195	...	11 556	...	38.4	...	2.16	...	82.94
1961														
January	53 683	45 119	18 508	14 863	35 175	...	11 473	...	39.3	...	2.16	...	84.89
February	53 556	44 969	18 418	14 801	35 138	...	11 414	...	39.4	...	2.16	...	85.10
March	53 662	45 051	18 438	14 802	35 224	...	11 410	...	39.5	...	2.16	...	85.32
April	53 626	44 997	18 432	14 825	35 194	...	11 444	...	39.5	...	2.18	...	86.11
May	53 783	45 119	18 523	14 932	35 260	...	11 544	...	39.7	...	2.19	...	86.94
June	53 977	45 289	18 618	14 981	35 359	...	11 593	...	40.0	...	2.20	...	88.00
July	54 124	45 400	18 640	15 029	35 484	...	11 639	...	40.0	...	2.21	...	88.40
August	54 299	45 535	18 725	15 093	35 574	...	11 701	...	40.1	...	2.22	...	89.02
September	54 387	45 591	18 730	15 080	35 657	...	11 679	...	39.5	...	2.20	...	86.90
October	54 521	45 716	18 805	15 143	35 716	...	11 731	...	40.3	...	2.23	...	89.87
November	54 743	45 931	18 927	15 259	35 816	...	11 842	...	40.7	...	2.23	...	90.76
December	54 871	46 035	18 981	15 309	35 890	...	11 872	...	40.4	...	2.24	...	90.50
1962														
January	54 891	46 040	18 936	15 322	35 955	...	11 865	...	40.0	...	2.25	...	90.00
February	55 187	46 309	19 109	15 411	36 078	...	11 950	...	40.4	...	2.26	...	91.30
March	55 276	46 375	19 109	15 451	36 167	...	11 970	...	40.6	...	2.26	...	91.76
April	55 601	46 679	19 258	15 524	36 343	...	12 034	...	40.6	...	2.26	...	91.76
May	55 626	46 668	19 253	15 513	36 373	...	12 011	...	40.6	...	2.27	...	92.16
June	55 644	46 644	19 186	15 518	36 458	...	12 006	...	40.5	...	2.26	...	91.53
July	55 746	46 720	19 248	15 522	36 498	...	12 004	...	40.5	...	2.27	...	91.94
August	55 838	46 775	19 251	15 517	36 587	...	11 990	...	40.5	...	2.28	...	92.34
September	55 977	46 888	19 305	15 568	36 672	...	12 033	...	40.5	...	2.28	...	92.34
October	56 041	46 927	19 301	15 569	36 740	...	12 034	...	40.3	...	2.29	...	92.29
November	56 055	46 910	19 260	15 530	36 795	...	11 977	...	40.5	...	2.29	...	92.75
December	56 027	46 901	19 219	15 520	36 808	...	11 961	...	40.3	...	2.29	...	92.29
1963														
January	56 116	46 912	19 257	15 545	36 859	...	11 974	...	40.5	...	2.30	...	93.15
February	56 231	47 000	19 228	15 542	37 003	...	11 965	...	40.5	...	2.31	...	93.56
March	56 322	47 077	19 233	15 564	37 089	...	11 990	...	40.5	...	2.32	...	93.96
April	56 580	47 316	19 343	15 602	37 237	...	12 029	...	40.5	...	2.32	...	93.96
May	56 616	47 328	19 399	15 641	37 217	...	12 066	...	40.5	...	2.33	...	94.37
June	56 658	47 356	19 371	15 624	37 287	...	12 050	...	40.7	...	2.34	...	95.24
July	56 795	47 461	19 423	15 646	37 372	...	12 080	...	40.6	...	2.35	...	95.41
August	56 910	47 542	19 437	15 644	37 473	...	12 060	...	40.6	...	2.34	...	95.00
September	57 078	47 661	19 483	15 674	37 595	...	12 088	...	40.6	...	2.36	...	95.82
October	57 284	47 805	19 517	15 714	37 767	...	12 131	...	40.7	...	2.36	...	96.05
November	57 255	47 771	19 456	15 675	37 799	...	12 072	...	40.7	...	2.37	...	96.46
December	57 360	47 863	19 493	15 712	37 867	...	12 108	...	40.6	...	2.38	...	96.63

... = Not available.

Table 20-4. Nonfarm Payroll Employment, Hours, and Earnings—Continued

(Wage and salary workers on nonfarm payrolls, seasonally adjusted.)

Year and month	All wage and salary workers, (thousands)					Production or nonsupervisory workers on private payrolls							
		Private				Number (thousands)		Average hours per week		Average hourly earnings, dollars		Average weekly earnings, dollars	
	Total	Total	Goods–producing		Service–providing	Total private	Manufac-turing	Total private	Manufac-turing	Total private	Manufac-turing	Total private	Manufac-turing
			Total	Manufac-turing									
1964													
January	57 487	47 925	19 406	15 715	38 081	39 914	12 132	38.2	40.1	2.50	2.38	95.50	95.44
February	57 752	48 171	19 570	15 742	38 182	40 123	12 165	38.5	40.7	2.50	2.38	96.25	96.87
March	57 898	48 287	19 587	15 770	38 311	40 171	12 190	38.5	40.6	2.50	2.38	96.25	96.63
April	57 923	48 279	19 593	15 785	38 330	40 208	12 211	38.6	40.7	2.52	2.40	97.27	97.68
May	58 089	48 419	19 630	15 812	38 459	40 332	12 231	38.6	40.8	2.52	2.40	97.27	97.92
June	58 221	48 552	19 682	15 839	38 539	40 448	12 255	38.6	40.8	2.53	2.41	97.66	98.33
July	58 412	48 735	19 740	15 887	38 672	40 624	12 309	38.5	40.8	2.53	2.41	97.41	98.33
August	58 620	48 888	19 810	15 948	38 810	40 770	12 354	38.5	40.9	2.55	2.42	98.18	98.98
September	58 903	49 117	19 943	16 073	38 960	41 026	12 479	38.5	40.9	2.55	2.44	98.18	99.80
October	58 794	48 949	19 723	15 821	39 071	40 827	12 224	38.5	40.7	2.55	2.40	98.18	97.68
November	59 217	49 338	20 026	16 096	39 191	41 157	12 477	38.6	41.0	2.56	2.42	98.82	99.22
December	59 420	49 523	20 111	16 176	39 309	41 308	12 551	38.7	41.2	2.58	2.44	99.85	100.53
1965													
January	59 583	49 646	20 173	16 245	39 410	41 453	12 603	38.7	41.3	2.58	2.45	99.85	101.19
February	59 800	49 826	20 216	16 291	39 584	41 583	12 644	38.7	41.3	2.59	2.46	100.23	101.60
March	60 003	49 993	20 292	16 353	39 711	41 675	12 701	38.7	41.3	2.60	2.47	100.62	102.01
April	60 258	50 207	20 317	16 418	39 941	41 886	12 752	38.7	41.2	2.60	2.47	100.62	101.76
May	60 492	50 398	20 444	16 477	40 048	42 044	12 792	38.8	41.3	2.62	2.49	101.66	102.84
June	60 690	50 562	20 522	16 554	40 168	42 183	12 854	38.6	41.2	2.62	2.49	101.13	102.59
July	60 963	50 762	20 611	16 669	40 352	42 364	12 962	38.6	41.2	2.63	2.49	101.52	102.59
August	61 228	50 957	20 726	16 732	40 502	42 537	12 994	38.5	41.1	2.64	2.50	101.64	102.75
September	61 490	51 152	20 808	16 802	40 682	42 726	13 046	38.6	41.1	2.65	2.51	102.29	103.16
October	61 718	51 340	20 895	16 864	40 823	42 870	13 100	38.5	41.2	2.66	2.52	102.41	103.82
November	61 997	51 561	21 021	16 962	40 976	43 045	13 175	38.6	41.3	2.67	2.52	103.06	104.08
December	62 321	51 822	21 151	17 051	41 170	43 270	13 243	38.6	41.3	2.68	2.53	103.45	104.49
1966													
January	62 528	51 987	21 214	17 143	41 314	43 401	13 301	38.6	41.5	2.68	2.54	103.45	105.41
February	62 796	52 185	21 315	17 288	41 481	43 552	13 426	38.7	41.7	2.69	2.56	104.10	106.75
March	63 191	52 499	21 515	17 400	41 676	43 801	13 508	38.7	41.6	2.70	2.56	104.49	106.50
April	63 436	52 677	21 568	17 517	41 868	43 959	13 598	38.7	41.8	2.71	2.58	104.88	107.84
May	63 711	52 890	21 675	17 625	42 036	44 138	13 678	38.5	41.5	2.72	2.58	104.72	107.07
June	64 110	53 208	21 846	17 733	42 264	44 390	13 753	38.5	41.4	2.72	2.58	104.72	106.81
July	64 301	53 327	21 872	17 760	42 429	44 484	13 758	38.4	41.2	2.74	2.60	105.22	107.12
August	64 507	53 501	21 972	17 882	42 535	44 596	13 843	38.4	41.4	2.75	2.61	105.60	108.05
September	64 645	53 582	21 948	17 886	42 697	44 659	13 841	38.3	41.2	2.76	2.63	105.71	108.36
October	64 854	53 727	21 991	17 956	42 863	44 789	13 906	38.4	41.3	2.77	2.64	106.37	109.03
November	65 019	53 816	21 988	17 981	43 031	44 834	13 918	38.3	41.2	2.78	2.65	106.47	109.18
December	65 199	53 943	22 008	17 998	43 191	44 916	13 906	38.2	40.9	2.78	2.64	106.20	107.98
1967													
January	65 407	54 092	22 057	18 033	43 350	45 050	13 925	38.3	41.1	2.79	2.65	106.86	108.92
February	65 427	54 074	21 987	17 978	43 440	44 967	13 853	37.9	40.4	2.81	2.67	106.50	107.87
March	65 530	54 133	21 919	17 940	43 611	44 991	13 797	37.9	40.5	2.81	2.67	106.50	108.14
April	65 467	54 032	21 842	17 878	43 625	44 871	13 712	37.8	40.4	2.82	2.68	106.60	108.27
May	65 618	54 144	21 779	17 832	43 839	44 961	13 664	37.8	40.4	2.83	2.69	106.97	108.68
June	65 750	54 216	21 761	17 812	43 989	45 004	13 632	37.8	40.4	2.84	2.69	107.35	108.68
July	65 887	54 343	21 772	17 784	44 115	45 105	13 602	37.8	40.5	2.86	2.71	108.11	109.76
August	66 142	54 552	21 887	17 905	44 255	45 267	13 681	37.8	40.6	2.87	2.73	108.49	110.84
September	66 163	54 540	21 775	17 794	44 388	45 236	13 559	37.8	40.6	2.88	2.73	108.86	110.84
October	66 225	54 583	21 779	17 800	44 446	45 278	13 587	37.8	40.6	2.89	2.74	109.24	111.24
November	66 703	55 008	21 996	17 985	44 707	45 701	13 777	37.9	40.6	2.91	2.75	110.29	111.65
December	66 900	55 165	22 037	18 025	44 863	45 800	13 782	37.7	40.7	2.92	2.77	110.08	112.74
1968													
January	66 805	55 011	21 917	18 040	44 888	45 655	13 798	37.6	40.4	2.94	2.81	110.54	113.52
February	67 214	55 395	22 117	18 056	45 097	45 980	13 793	37.8	40.8	2.95	2.82	111.51	115.06
March	67 296	55 454	22 119	18 067	45 177	46 041	13 803	37.7	40.8	2.97	2.84	111.97	115.87
April	67 555	55 677	22 207	18 131	45 348	46 239	13 858	37.6	40.3	2.98	2.85	112.05	114.86
May	67 652	55 747	22 255	18 190	45 397	46 267	13 900	37.7	40.9	3.00	2.87	113.10	117.38
June	67 904	55 917	22 264	18 228	45 640	46 402	13 921	37.8	40.9	3.01	2.88	113.78	117.79
July	68 126	56 108	22 329	18 265	45 797	46 562	13 953	37.7	40.8	3.03	2.89	114.23	117.91
August	68 328	56 286	22 350	18 254	45 978	46 669	13 903	37.7	40.7	3.03	2.89	114.23	117.62
September	68 487	56 420	22 390	18 252	46 097	46 792	13 914	37.7	40.9	3.06	2.92	115.36	119.43
October	68 720	56 619	22 419	18 293	46 301	46 989	13 974	37.7	41.0	3.07	2.94	115.74	120.54
November	68 985	56 878	22 512	18 346	46 473	47 244	14 028	37.5	40.9	3.09	2.96	115.88	121.06
December	69 245	57 100	22 617	18 410	46 628	47 384	14 044	37.5	40.7	3.11	2.97	116.63	120.88
1969													
January	69 438	57 229	22 644	18 432	46 794	47 528	14 086	37.7	40.8	3.12	2.99	117.62	121.99
February	69 698	57 474	22 755	18 502	46 943	47 697	14 134	37.5	40.4	3.14	3.00	117.75	121.20
March	69 906	57 677	22 813	18 558	47 093	47 852	14 169	37.6	40.8	3.15	3.01	118.44	122.81
April	70 072	57 827	22 815	18 554	47 257	47 959	14 144	37.7	41.0	3.17	3.03	119.51	124.23
May	70 328	58 044	22 899	18 588	47 429	48 122	14 161	37.6	40.7	3.19	3.04	119.94	123.73
June	70 636	58 277	22 981	18 640	47 655	48 330	14 206	37.5	40.7	3.20	3.05	120.00	124.14
July	70 730	58 390	22 990	18 642	47 740	48 434	14 194	37.5	40.6	3.22	3.08	120.75	125.05
August	71 005	58 632	23 111	18 767	47 894	48 616	14 287	37.5	40.6	3.24	3.10	121.50	125.86
September	70 918	58 539	22 988	18 707	47 930	48 524	14 159	37.5	40.6	3.26	3.12	122.25	126.67
October	71 119	58 689	22 976	18 613	48 143	48 669	14 174	37.4	40.5	3.28	3.13	122.67	126.77
November	71 088	58 640	22 840	18 467	48 248	48 589	14 035	37.5	40.5	3.29	3.14	123.38	127.17
December	71 240	58 763	22 884	18 485	48 356	48 638	14 013	37.5	40.6	3.30	3.15	123.75	127.89

CHAPTER 20: HISTORICAL DATA FOR SELECTED MONTHLY SERIES

Table 20-4. Nonfarm Payroll Employment, Hours, and Earnings—Continued

(Wage and salary workers on nonfarm payrolls, seasonally adjusted.)

Year and month	All wage and salary workers, (thousands)					Production or nonsupervisory workers on private payrolls							
	Total	Private			Service-providing	Number (thousands)		Average hours per week		Average hourly earnings, dollars		Average weekly earnings, dollars	
		Total	Goods-producing			Total private	Manufacturing	Total private	Manufacturing	Total private	Manufacturing	Total private	Manufacturing
			Total	Manufacturing									
1970													
January	71 176	58 680	22 726	18 424	48 450	48 564	13 964	37.3	40.4	3.31	3.16	123.46	127.66
February	71 302	58 784	22 747	18 361	48 555	48 600	13 897	37.3	40.2	3.33	3.17	124.21	127.43
March	71 453	58 850	22 738	18 360	48 715	48 690	13 917	37.2	40.1	3.35	3.19	124.62	127.92
April	71 348	58 643	22 552	18 207	48 796	48 479	13 785	37.0	39.8	3.36	3.19	124.32	126.96
May	71 122	58 454	22 336	18 029	48 786	48 287	13 616	37.0	39.8	3.38	3.22	125.06	128.16
June	71 028	58 361	22 241	17 930	48 787	48 226	13 554	36.9	39.8	3.39	3.24	125.09	128.95
July	71 055	58 358	22 195	17 877	48 860	48 242	13 527	37.0	40.0	3.41	3.25	126.17	130.00
August	70 932	58 221	22 105	17 779	48 827	48 089	13 449	37.0	39.8	3.43	3.26	126.91	129.75
September	70 949	58 208	21 988	17 692	48 961	48 101	13 401	36.8	39.6	3.45	3.29	126.96	130.28
October	70 519	57 726	21 477	17 173	49 042	47 619	12 905	36.8	39.5	3.46	3.26	127.33	128.77
November	70 409	57 579	21 345	17 024	49 064	47 466	12 781	36.7	39.5	3.47	3.26	127.35	128.77
December	70 790	57 945	21 673	17 309	49 117	47 778	13 062	36.8	39.5	3.50	3.32	128.80	131.14
1971													
January	70 866	57 988	21 594	17 280	49 272	47 859	13 069	36.8	39.9	3.52	3.36	129.54	134.06
February	70 805	57 928	21 514	17 216	49 291	47 779	13 033	36.7	39.7	3.54	3.39	129.92	134.58
March	70 859	57 951	21 491	17 154	49 368	47 819	12 984	36.7	39.8	3.56	3.39	130.65	134.92
April	71 037	58 092	21 552	17 149	49 485	47 966	12 993	36.8	39.9	3.57	3.41	131.38	136.06
May	71 247	58 277	21 645	17 225	49 602	48 153	13 081	36.7	40.0	3.60	3.43	132.12	137.20
June	71 253	58 245	21 568	17 139	49 685	48 109	13 012	36.8	39.9	3.62	3.45	133.22	137.66
July	71 316	58 305	21 564	17 126	49 752	48 167	13 001	36.7	40.0	3.63	3.46	133.22	138.40
August	71 368	58 327	21 570	17 115	49 798	48 164	12 993	36.7	39.8	3.66	3.48	134.32	138.50
September	71 620	58 552	21 650	17 154	49 970	48 362	13 038	36.7	39.7	3.67	3.48	134.69	138.16
October	71 642	58 527	21 604	17 126	50 038	48 305	13 027	36.8	39.9	3.68	3.50	135.42	139.65
November	71 844	58 696	21 684	17 166	50 160	48 442	13 064	36.9	40.0	3.69	3.49	136.16	139.60
December	72 108	58 918	21 741	17 202	50 367	48 613	13 078	36.9	40.2	3.73	3.55	137.64	142.71
1972													
January	72 445	59 179	21 865	17 283	50 580	49 035	13 173	36.9	40.2	3.80	3.57	140.22	143.51
February	72 652	59 354	21 915	17 361	50 737	49 143	13 235	36.9	40.4	3.82	3.61	140.96	145.84
March	72 945	59 616	22 036	17 447	50 909	49 437	13 316	36.9	40.4	3.84	3.63	141.70	146.65
April	73 163	59 805	22 099	17 508	51 064	49 561	13 373	36.9	40.5	3.86	3.65	142.43	147.83
May	73 467	60 051	22 222	17 602	51 245	49 745	13 451	36.8	40.5	3.87	3.67	142.42	148.64
June	73 760	60 355	22 282	17 641	51 478	49 997	13 475	36.9	40.6	3.88	3.68	143.17	149.41
July	73 709	60 227	22 162	17 556	51 547	49 842	13 387	36.8	40.5	3.90	3.69	143.52	149.45
August	74 137	60 607	22 400	17 741	51 737	50 156	13 562	36.8	40.6	3.92	3.73	144.26	151.44
September	74 268	60 693	22 456	17 774	51 812	50 224	13 572	36.9	40.6	3.94	3.75	145.39	152.25
October	74 672	61 066	22 613	17 893	52 059	50 552	13 681	37.0	40.7	3.97	3.78	146.89	153.85
November	74 965	61 322	22 688	18 005	52 277	50 790	13 783	36.9	40.7	3.98	3.79	146.86	154.25
December	75 270	61 586	22 772	18 158	52 498	51 054	13 902	36.8	40.6	4.01	3.83	147.57	155.50
1973													
January	75 620	61 930	22 955	18 276	52 665	51 349	14 006	36.8	40.4	4.03	3.86	148.30	155.94
February	76 017	62 306	23 160	18 410	52 857	51 686	14 127	36.9	40.9	4.04	3.87	149.08	158.28
March	76 286	62 541	23 262	18 493	53 024	51 901	14 181	37.0	40.9	4.06	3.88	150.22	158.69
April	76 456	62 679	23 316	18 530	53 140	51 982	14 192	36.9	40.8	4.08	3.91	150.55	159.53
May	76 646	62 829	23 382	18 564	53 264	52 082	14 217	36.9	40.7	4.10	3.93	151.29	159.95
June	76 886	63 014	23 485	18 606	53 401	52 234	14 253	36.9	40.7	4.12	3.95	152.03	160.77
July	76 911	63 046	23 522	18 598	53 389	52 238	14 232	36.9	40.7	4.15	3.98	153.14	161.99
August	77 166	63 262	23 559	18 629	53 607	52 393	14 251	36.9	40.6	4.16	4.00	153.50	162.40
September	77 281	63 389	23 548	18 609	53 733	52 410	14 213	36.8	40.7	4.19	4.03	154.19	164.02
October	77 605	63 628	23 641	18 702	53 964	52 655	14 289	36.7	40.6	4.21	4.05	154.51	164.43
November	77 909	63 874	23 719	18 773	54 190	52 847	14 342	36.9	40.6	4.23	4.07	156.09	165.24
December	78 035	63 965	23 779	18 820	54 256	52 954	14 386	36.7	40.6	4.25	4.09	155.98	166.05
1974													
January	78 104	64 014	23 709	18 788	54 395	52 896	14 340	36.6	40.5	4.26	4.10	155.92	166.05
February	78 253	64 118	23 718	18 727	54 535	52 971	14 269	36.6	40.4	4.29	4.13	157.01	166.85
March	78 295	64 143	23 687	18 700	54 608	52 951	14 223	36.6	40.4	4.31	4.15	157.75	167.66
April	78 384	64 193	23 670	18 702	54 714	53 003	14 225	36.4	39.5	4.34	4.16	157.98	164.32
May	78 547	64 326	23 635	18 688	54 912	53 095	14 199	36.5	40.3	4.39	4.25	160.24	171.28
June	78 602	64 363	23 591	18 690	55 011	53 107	14 197	36.5	40.2	4.43	4.30	161.70	172.86
July	78 634	64 346	23 462	18 656	55 172	53 044	14 152	36.5	40.1	4.45	4.33	162.43	173.63
August	78 619	64 291	23 396	18 570	55 223	53 025	14 089	36.5	40.2	4.49	4.38	163.89	176.08
September	78 614	64 192	23 274	18 492	55 340	52 915	14 025	36.4	40.0	4.53	4.42	164.89	176.80
October	78 627	64 143	23 118	18 364	55 509	52 836	13 884	36.3	40.0	4.56	4.48	165.53	179.20
November	78 259	63 727	22 773	18 077	55 486	52 413	13 607	36.1	39.5	4.57	4.49	164.98	177.36
December	77 657	63 098	22 303	17 693	55 354	51 856	13 259	36.1	39.3	4.60	4.52	166.06	177.64
1975													
January	77 297	62 673	21 974	17 344	55 323	51 439	12 933	36.1	39.2	4.61	4.54	166.42	177.97
February	76 919	62 172	21 512	17 004	55 407	50 934	12 622	35.9	38.9	4.63	4.58	166.22	178.16
March	76 649	61 895	21 274	16 853	55 375	50 666	12 483	35.7	38.8	4.66	4.63	166.36	179.64
April	76 463	61 668	21 109	16 759	55 354	50 439	12 407	35.8	39.0	4.66	4.63	166.83	180.57
May	76 623	61 796	21 097	16 746	55 526	50 558	12 406	35.9	39.0	4.68	4.65	168.01	181.35
June	76 519	61 735	21 018	16 690	55 501	50 537	12 371	35.9	39.2	4.72	4.68	169.45	183.46
July	76 768	61 907	20 981	16 678	55 787	50 726	12 374	35.9	39.4	4.73	4.71	169.81	185.57
August	77 154	62 284	21 176	16 824	55 978	51 070	12 538	36.1	39.7	4.77	4.75	172.20	188.58
September	77 232	62 408	21 284	16 904	55 948	51 183	12 617	36.1	39.8	4.79	4.78	172.92	190.24
October	77 535	62 635	21 384	16 984	56 151	51 376	12 687	36.1	39.9	4.81	4.80	173.64	191.52
November	77 679	62 776	21 442	17 025	56 237	51 458	12 700	36.1	39.9	4.85	4.83	175.09	192.72
December	78 017	63 071	21 602	17 140	56 415	51 759	12 811	36.2	40.2	4.87	4.86	176.29	195.37

Table 20-4. Nonfarm Payroll Employment, Hours, and Earnings—Continued

(Wage and salary workers on nonfarm payrolls, seasonally adjusted.)

Year and month	All wage and salary workers, (thousands)					Production or nonsupervisory workers on private payrolls							
	Total	Private			Service–providing	Number (thousands)		Average hours per week		Average hourly earnings, dollars		Average weekly earnings, dollars	
		Total	Goods–producing			Total private	Manufacturing	Total private	Manufacturing	Total private	Manufacturing	Total private	Manufacturing
			Total	Manufacturing									
1976													
January	78 506	63 537	21 799	17 287	56 707	52 182	12 945	36.3	40.3	4.89	4.90	177.51	197.47
February	78 817	63 836	21 893	17 384	56 924	52 430	13 030	36.3	40.4	4.93	4.94	178.96	199.58
March	79 049	64 062	21 980	17 470	57 069	52 615	13 092	36.0	40.2	4.95	4.98	178.20	200.20
April	79 293	64 308	22 050	17 541	57 243	52 810	13 160	36.0	39.6	4.97	4.98	178.92	197.21
May	79 311	64 340	21 988	17 513	57 323	52 802	13 130	36.1	40.3	5.01	5.04	180.86	203.11
June	79 376	64 413	21 982	17 521	57 394	52 830	13 121	36.1	40.2	5.03	5.07	181.58	203.81
July	79 546	64 553	21 988	17 524	57 558	52 973	13 124	36.1	40.3	5.06	5.11	182.67	205.93
August	79 704	64 697	22 038	17 596	57 666	53 072	13 195	36.0	40.2	5.11	5.16	183.96	207.43
September	79 892	64 921	22 142	17 665	57 750	53 268	13 253	36.0	40.2	5.14	5.20	185.04	209.04
October	79 905	64 877	22 037	17 548	57 868	53 165	13 109	35.9	40.0	5.16	5.19	185.24	207.60
November	80 237	65 164	22 207	17 682	58 030	53 362	13 199	35.9	40.1	5.20	5.25	186.68	210.53
December	80 448	65 373	22 261	17 719	58 187	53 543	13 230	35.9	39.9	5.22	5.29	187.40	211.07
1977													
January	80 692	65 636	22 320	17 803	58 372	53 756	13 305	35.6	39.4	5.25	5.35	186.90	210.79
February	80 987	65 931	22 478	17 843	58 509	54 016	13 331	36.0	40.2	5.29	5.36	190.44	215.47
March	81 391	66 341	22 672	17 941	58 719	54 390	13 424	35.9	40.3	5.32	5.40	190.99	217.62
April	81 730	66 655	22 807	18 024	58 923	54 670	13 490	36.0	40.4	5.36	5.45	192.96	220.18
May	82 089	66 957	22 919	18 107	59 170	54 940	13 567	36.0	40.5	5.39	5.49	194.04	222.35
June	82 488	67 281	23 046	18 192	59 442	55 195	13 622	36.0	40.5	5.42	5.54	195.12	224.37
July	82 836	67 537	23 106	18 259	59 730	55 395	13 670	35.9	40.4	5.45	5.58	195.66	225.43
August	83 074	67 746	23 124	18 276	59 950	55 543	13 679	35.9	40.4	5.47	5.61	196.37	226.64
September	83 532	68 129	23 244	18 334	60 288	55 859	13 714	35.9	40.4	5.50	5.65	197.45	228.26
October	83 794	68 331	23 279	18 356	60 515	56 004	13 722	36.0	40.6	5.55	5.69	199.80	231.01
November	84 173	68 658	23 371	18 419	60 802	56 281	13 771	35.9	40.5	5.58	5.72	200.32	231.66
December	84 408	68 870	23 371	18 531	61 037	56 466	13 861	35.8	40.4	5.60	5.75	200.48	232.30
1978													
January	84 595	68 984	23 374	18 593	61 221	56 547	13 917	35.3	39.5	5.65	5.83	199.45	230.29
February	84 948	69 277	23 453	18 639	61 495	56 768	13 950	35.6	39.9	5.68	5.86	202.21	233.81
March	85 461	69 730	23 649	18 699	61 812	57 176	13 992	35.8	40.5	5.72	5.88	204.78	238.14
April	86 163	70 366	24 008	18 772	62 155	57 709	14 037	35.8	40.4	5.78	5.93	206.92	239.57
May	86 509	70 675	24 082	18 828	62 427	57 941	14 096	35.8	40.4	5.81	5.96	208.00	240.78
June	86 951	71 099	24 238	18 919	62 713	58 263	14 129	35.9	40.6	5.86	6.01	210.37	244.01
July	87 205	71 304	24 300	18 951	62 905	58 422	14 152	35.9	40.6	5.89	6.06	211.45	246.04
August	87 481	71 590	24 374	19 006	63 107	58 626	14 187	35.8	40.5	5.92	6.09	211.94	246.65
September	87 618	71 799	24 444	19 068	63 174	58 819	14 241	35.8	40.5	5.96	6.15	213.37	249.08
October	87 954	72 096	24 548	19 142	63 406	59 017	14 291	35.8	40.5	6.02	6.20	215.52	251.10
November	88 391	72 497	24 678	19 257	63 713	59 377	14 388	35.7	40.6	6.05	6.26	215.99	254.16
December	88 674	72 763	24 758	19 334	63 916	59 599	14 459	35.7	40.5	6.09	6.31	217.41	255.56
1979													
January	88 811	72 874	24 740	19 388	64 071	59 659	14 497	35.6	40.4	6.13	6.36	218.23	256.94
February	89 054	73 107	24 784	19 409	64 270	59 840	14 501	35.7	40.5	6.17	6.40	220.27	259.20
March	89 480	73 524	24 998	19 453	64 482	60 216	14 526	35.8	40.6	6.21	6.45	222.32	261.87
April	89 418	73 441	24 958	19 450	64 460	60 067	14 515	35.3	39.3	6.21	6.43	219.21	252.70
May	89 790	73 800	25 071	19 509	64 719	60 368	14 551	35.6	40.2	6.27	6.52	223.21	262.10
June	90 108	74 063	25 161	19 553	64 947	60 583	14 566	35.6	40.2	6.31	6.56	224.64	263.71
July	90 214	74 064	25 163	19 531	65 051	60 558	14 536	35.6	40.2	6.35	6.59	226.06	264.92
August	90 296	74 067	25 059	19 406	65 237	60 516	14 397	35.6	40.1	6.39	6.63	227.48	265.86
September	90 323	74 195	25 088	19 442	65 235	60 629	14 440	35.6	40.1	6.44	6.67	229.26	267.47
October	90 480	74 344	25 038	19 390	65 442	60 746	14 384	35.6	40.2	6.46	6.71	229.98	269.74
November	90 574	74 401	24 947	19 299	65 627	60 778	14 295	35.6	40.1	6.50	6.74	231.40	270.27
December	90 669	74 489	24 970	19 301	65 699	60 860	14 300	35.5	40.1	6.56	6.80	232.88	272.68
1980													
January	90 800	74 599	24 949	19 282	65 851	60 896	14 241	35.4	40.0	6.56	6.82	232.22	272.80
February	90 879	74 653	24 874	19 219	66 005	60 964	14 170	35.4	40.1	6.62	6.88	234.35	275.89
March	90 991	74 695	24 818	19 217	66 173	60 987	14 165	35.3	39.9	6.69	6.95	236.16	277.31
April	90 846	74 263	24 507	18 973	66 339	60 540	13 914	35.2	39.8	6.71	6.97	236.19	277.41
May	90 415	73 961	24 234	18 726	66 181	60 194	13 632	35.1	39.3	6.75	7.02	236.93	275.89
June	90 095	73 654	23 968	18 490	66 127	59 892	13 405	35.0	39.2	6.81	7.10	238.35	278.32
July	89 832	73 414	23 698	18 276	66 134	59 693	13 227	34.9	39.1	6.85	7.16	239.07	279.96
August	90 092	73 682	23 860	18 414	66 232	59 908	13 349	35.1	39.5	6.90	7.24	242.19	285.98
September	90 205	73 875	23 931	18 445	66 274	60 075	13 396	35.1	39.6	6.94	7.30	243.59	289.08
October	90 485	74 099	24 012	18 506	66 473	60 239	13 437	35.2	39.8	7.01	7.38	246.75	293.72
November	90 741	74 350	24 123	18 601	66 618	60 449	13 528	35.3	39.9	7.08	7.47	249.92	298.05
December	90 936	74 563	24 182	18 640	66 754	60 606	13 550	35.3	40.1	7.12	7.52	251.34	301.55
1981													
January	91 031	74 671	24 152	18 639	66 879	60 710	13 545	35.4	40.1	7.18	7.58	254.17	303.96
February	91 098	74 752	24 118	18 613	66 980	60 736	13 518	35.2	39.8	7.22	7.62	254.14	303.28
March	91 202	74 910	24 203	18 647	66 999	60 875	13 550	35.3	40.0	7.28	7.68	256.98	307.20
April	91 276	75 016	24 151	18 711	67 125	60 973	13 594	35.3	40.1	7.32	7.76	258.40	311.18
May	91 286	75 088	24 148	18 766	67 138	60 973	13 633	35.3	40.2	7.36	7.81	259.81	313.96
June	91 482	75 323	24 290	18 789	67 192	61 134	13 632	35.2	40.0	7.41	7.85	260.83	314.00
July	91 594	75 419	24 302	18 785	67 292	61 222	13 629	35.2	39.9	7.45	7.89	262.24	314.81
August	91 558	75 448	24 258	18 748	67 300	61 216	13 573	35.2	40.0	7.52	7.97	264.70	318.80
September	91 471	75 440	24 210	18 712	67 261	61 235	13 565	35.0	39.6	7.56	8.03	264.60	317.99
October	91 371	75 302	24 051	18 566	67 320	61 066	13 399	35.1	39.6	7.58	8.06	266.06	319.18
November	91 162	75 084	23 875	18 409	67 287	60 817	13 235	35.1	39.4	7.63	8.08	267.81	318.35
December	90 884	74 811	23 656	18 223	67 228	60 511	13 033	34.9	39.2	7.63	8.09	266.29	317.13

Table 20-4. Nonfarm Payroll Employment, Hours, and Earnings—Continued

(Wage and salary workers on nonfarm payrolls, seasonally adjusted.)

Year and month	All wage and salary workers, (thousands)					Production or nonsupervisory workers on private payrolls								
	Total	Private			Service-providing	Number (thousands)		Average hours per week		Average hourly earnings, dollars		Average weekly earnings, dollars	
		Total	Goods-producing			Total private	Manufacturing	Total private	Manufacturing	Total private	Manufacturing	Total private	Manufacturing
			Total	Manufacturing									
1982													
January	90 557	74 516	23 362	18 047	67 195	60 206	12 874	34.1	37.3	7.71	8.26	262.91	308.10
February	90 551	74 540	23 361	17 981	67 190	60 277	12 831	35.1	39.6	7.72	8.21	270.97	325.12
March	90 422	74 398	23 214	17 857	67 208	60 140	12 727	34.9	39.1	7.75	8.24	270.58	322.18
April	90 141	74 131	22 996	17 683	67 145	59 867	12 566	34.8	39.1	7.76	8.28	270.05	323.75
May	90 096	74 093	22 884	17 588	67 212	59 840	12 506	34.8	39.1	7.82	8.33	272.14	325.70
June	89 853	73 837	22 643	17 430	67 210	59 589	12 365	34.8	39.2	7.84	8.37	272.83	328.10
July	89 510	73 620	22 434	17 278	67 076	59 411	12 261	34.8	39.2	7.88	8.40	274.22	329.28
August	89 352	73 422	22 268	17 160	67 084	59 203	12 153	34.7	39.0	7.93	8.43	275.17	328.77
September	89 171	73 248	22 146	17 074	67 025	59 069	12 104	34.8	39.0	7.93	8.45	275.96	329.55
October	88 894	72 938	21 879	16 853	67 015	58 750	11 880	34.6	38.9	7.95	8.44	275.07	328.32
November	88 770	72 793	21 736	16 722	67 034	58 613	11 766	34.6	39.0	7.97	8.46	275.76	329.94
December	88 756	72 775	21 688	16 690	67 068	58 585	11 746	34.7	39.0	8.01	8.49	277.95	331.11
1983													
January	88 981	72 958	21 757	16 705	67 224	58 813	11 783	34.8	39.3	8.05	8.52	280.14	334.84
February	88 903	72 899	21 676	16 706	67 227	58 792	11 794	34.5	39.3	8.09	8.59	279.11	337.59
March	89 076	73 071	21 649	16 711	67 427	58 958	11 817	34.7	39.6	8.09	8.59	280.72	340.16
April	89 352	73 362	21 729	16 794	67 623	59 201	11 894	34.8	39.7	8.12	8.61	282.58	341.82
May	89 629	73 624	21 829	16 885	67 800	59 444	11 987	34.9	40.0	8.16	8.64	284.78	345.60
June	90 007	73 987	21 949	16 960	68 058	59 806	12 054	34.9	40.1	8.18	8.66	285.48	347.27
July	90 425	74 414	22 103	17 059	68 322	60 189	12 155	34.9	40.3	8.22	8.71	286.88	351.01
August	90 117	74 101	22 207	17 118	67 910	59 820	12 200	34.9	40.3	8.19	8.71	285.83	351.01
September	91 231	75 189	22 381	17 255	68 850	60 849	12 318	35.0	40.6	8.25	8.76	288.75	355.66
October	91 502	75 516	22 546	17 367	68 956	61 095	12 408	35.2	40.6	8.30	8.80	292.16	357.28
November	91 854	75 857	22 698	17 479	69 156	61 378	12 503	35.1	40.6	8.31	8.84	291.68	358.90
December	92 210	76 202	22 803	17 551	69 407	61 664	12 553	35.1	40.5	8.32	8.87	292.03	359.24
1984													
January	92 657	76 647	22 942	17 630	69 715	61 906	12 617	35.1	40.6	8.37	8.91	293.79	361.75
February	93 136	77 111	23 146	17 728	69 990	62 329	12 703	35.3	41.1	8.36	8.92	295.11	366.61
March	93 411	77 381	23 209	17 806	70 202	62 516	12 768	35.1	40.7	8.40	8.96	294.84	364.67
April	93 774	77 699	23 305	17 872	70 469	62 801	12 814	35.2	40.8	8.44	8.98	297.09	366.38
May	94 082	77 979	23 389	17 916	70 693	63 012	12 840	35.1	40.7	8.43	8.99	295.89	365.89
June	94 461	78 334	23 497	17 967	70 964	63 296	12 871	35.1	40.6	8.47	9.03	297.30	366.62
July	94 773	78 601	23 571	18 013	71 202	63 517	12 901	35.1	40.6	8.51	9.05	298.70	367.43
August	95 014	78 790	23 608	18 034	71 406	63 654	12 906	35.0	40.5	8.51	9.09	297.85	368.15
September	95 325	79 070	23 617	18 019	71 708	63 874	12 880	35.1	40.5	8.55	9.12	300.11	369.36
October	95 611	79 337	23 626	18 024	71 985	64 083	12 868	34.9	40.5	8.54	9.15	298.05	370.58
November	95 960	79 649	23 639	18 016	72 321	64 325	12 846	35.0	40.4	8.56	9.19	299.60	371.28
December	96 087	79 805	23 673	18 023	72 414	64 441	12 848	35.1	40.5	8.60	9.22	301.86	373.41
1985													
January	96 353	80 017	23 672	18 009	72 681	64 657	12 833	34.9	40.3	8.60	9.27	300.14	373.58
February	96 477	80 128	23 621	17 966	72 856	64 758	12 784	34.8	40.1	8.63	9.29	300.32	372.53
March	96 823	80 428	23 661	17 939	73 162	65 007	12 758	34.9	40.4	8.66	9.32	302.23	376.53
April	97 018	80 588	23 644	17 886	73 374	65 115	12 701	34.9	40.4	8.68	9.35	302.93	378.68
May	97 292	80 818	23 632	17 855	73 660	65 307	12 673	34.9	40.4	8.69	9.37	303.28	378.55
June	97 437	80 939	23 592	17 819	73 845	65 382	12 635	34.9	40.5	8.73	9.39	304.68	380.30
July	97 626	81 006	23 549	17 776	74 077	65 432	12 596	34.8	40.4	8.73	9.42	303.80	380.57
August	97 819	81 200	23 546	17 756	74 273	65 615	12 593	34.8	40.6	8.76	9.43	304.85	382.86
September	98 023	81 385	23 528	17 718	74 495	65 750	12 556	34.8	40.6	8.79	9.44	305.89	383.26
October	98 210	81 556	23 529	17 708	74 681	65 917	12 556	34.8	40.7	8.78	9.46	305.54	385.02
November	98 419	81 745	23 520	17 697	74 899	66 069	12 545	34.8	40.7	8.81	9.49	306.59	386.24
December	98 587	81 893	23 518	17 693	75 069	66 197	12 550	34.9	40.9	8.86	9.55	309.21	390.60
1986													
January	98 710	81 995	23 530	17 686	75 180	66 293	12 546	35.0	40.7	8.84	9.53	309.40	387.87
February	98 817	82 058	23 485	17 663	75 332	66 365	12 530	34.8	40.7	8.87	9.56	308.68	389.09
March	98 910	82 155	23 428	17 624	75 482	66 403	12 498	34.8	40.7	8.88	9.58	309.02	389.91
April	99 098	82 333	23 427	17 616	75 671	66 531	12 495	34.7	40.5	8.88	9.56	308.14	387.18
May	99 223	82 433	23 349	17 593	75 874	66 606	12 474	34.8	40.7	8.89	9.59	309.37	390.31
June	99 130	82 351	23 263	17 530	75 867	66 533	12 424	34.7	40.7	8.90	9.58	308.83	389.91
July	99 448	82 669	23 235	17 497	76 213	66 810	12 389	34.6	40.6	8.91	9.60	308.29	389.76
August	99 561	82 761	23 225	17 489	76 336	66 909	12 399	34.7	40.7	8.93	9.61	309.87	391.13
September	99 907	82 997	23 216	17 498	76 691	67 108	12 411	34.6	40.7	8.93	9.60	308.98	390.72
October	100 094	83 125	23 208	17 477	76 886	67 206	12 396	34.6	40.6	8.95	9.62	309.67	390.57
November	100 280	83 275	23 204	17 472	77 076	67 344	12 407	34.7	40.7	8.99	9.64	311.95	392.35
December	100 484	83 463	23 237	17 478	77 247	67 493	12 425	34.6	40.8	9.00	9.66	311.40	394.13
1987													
January	100 655	83 610	23 232	17 465	77 423	67 614	12 405	34.7	40.8	9.01	9.67	312.65	394.54
February	100 887	83 851	23 296	17 499	77 591	67 845	12 438	34.9	41.2	9.04	9.69	315.50	399.23
March	101 136	84 072	23 307	17 507	77 829	67 991	12 446	34.7	41.0	9.06	9.71	314.38	398.11
April	101 474	84 365	23 342	17 525	78 132	68 237	12 465	34.7	40.8	9.07	9.71	314.73	396.17
May	101 701	84 589	23 390	17 542	78 311	68 426	12 481	34.8	41.0	9.10	9.73	316.68	398.93
June	101 872	84 748	23 390	17 537	78 482	68 552	12 482	34.7	40.9	9.10	9.74	315.77	398.37
July	102 218	85 058	23 455	17 593	78 763	68 798	12 521	34.7	41.0	9.11	9.74	316.12	399.34
August	102 388	85 216	23 506	17 630	78 882	68 926	12 560	34.9	40.9	9.17	9.80	320.03	400.82
September	102 617	85 482	23 566	17 691	79 051	69 139	12 614	34.7	40.8	9.18	9.85	318.55	401.88
October	103 109	85 840	23 655	17 729	79 454	69 416	12 637	34.8	41.1	9.21	9.84	320.51	404.42
November	103 340	86 041	23 711	17 775	79 629	69 594	12 678	34.8	41.0	9.26	9.87	322.25	404.67
December	103 634	86 287	23 772	17 809	79 862	69 826	12 707	34.6	41.0	9.27	9.89	320.74	405.49

Table 20-4. Nonfarm Payroll Employment, Hours, and Earnings—Continued

(Wage and salary workers on nonfarm payrolls, seasonally adjusted.)

Year and month	All wage and salary workers, (thousands)					Production or nonsupervisory workers on private payrolls							
	Total	Private			Service–providing	Number (thousands)		Average hours per week		Average hourly earnings, dollars		Average weekly earnings, dollars	
		Total	Goods–producing			Total private	Manufacturing	Total private	Manufacturing	Total private	Manufacturing	Total private	Manufacturing
			Total	Manufacturing									
1988													
January	103 728	86 363	23 668	17 790	80 060	69 833	12 684	34.6	41.1	9.28	9.91	321.09	407.30
February	104 180	86 791	23 769	17 823	80 411	70 228	12 706	34.7	41.1	9.28	9.92	322.02	407.71
March	104 456	87 009	23 824	17 844	80 632	70 371	12 712	34.5	40.9	9.30	9.94	320.85	406.55
April	104 701	87 249	23 880	17 874	80 821	70 578	12 733	34.6	41.0	9.35	9.99	323.51	409.59
May	104 928	87 447	23 896	17 892	81 032	70 693	12 747	34.6	41.0	9.40	10.02	325.24	410.82
June	105 291	87 776	23 951	17 916	81 340	71 000	12 767	34.6	41.1	9.41	10.04	325.59	412.64
July	105 514	88 020	23 966	17 926	81 548	71 210	12 774	34.7	41.1	9.44	10.05	327.57	413.06
August	105 635	88 091	23 926	17 891	81 709	71 273	12 752	34.5	40.9	9.45	10.07	326.03	411.86
September	105 975	88 341	23 942	17 914	82 033	71 456	12 764	34.5	41.0	9.50	10.12	327.75	414.92
October	106 243	88 573	23 987	17 966	82 256	71 649	12 812	34.7	41.1	9.55	10.16	331.39	417.58
November	106 582	88 836	24 030	18 003	82 552	71 872	12 851	34.5	41.1	9.57	10.19	330.17	418.81
December	106 871	89 135	24 054	18 025	82 817	72 144	12 864	34.6	40.9	9.59	10.20	331.81	417.18
1989													
January	107 133	89 359	24 097	18 057	83 036	72 361	12 882	34.7	41.1	9.64	10.23	334.51	420.45
February	107 391	89 579	24 080	18 055	83 311	72 545	12 880	34.5	41.2	9.67	10.26	333.62	422.71
March	107 583	89 761	24 069	18 060	83 514	72 663	12 878	34.5	41.1	9.69	10.29	334.31	422.92
April	107 756	89 916	24 100	18 055	83 656	72 788	12 867	34.6	41.1	9.74	10.28	337.00	422.51
May	107 874	89 998	24 089	18 040	83 785	72 826	12 852	34.4	41.0	9.72	10.30	334.37	422.30
June	107 991	90 079	24 052	18 013	83 939	72 906	12 822	34.4	40.9	9.76	10.33	335.74	422.50
July	108 030	90 125	24 027	17 980	84 003	72 943	12 790	34.5	40.9	9.81	10.36	338.45	423.72
August	108 077	90 088	24 048	17 964	84 029	72 931	12 790	34.5	40.9	9.82	10.39	338.79	424.95
September	108 326	90 299	24 000	17 922	84 326	73 080	12 745	34.4	40.8	9.86	10.41	339.18	424.73
October	108 437	90 404	23 997	17 895	84 440	73 176	12 723	34.6	40.8	9.92	10.43	343.23	425.54
November	108 714	90 657	24 009	17 886	84 705	73 392	12 713	34.4	40.7	9.92	10.44	341.25	424.91
December	108 809	90 734	23 949	17 881	84 860	73 468	12 705	34.3	40.5	9.97	10.49	341.97	424.85
1990													
January	109 144	90 993	23 981	17 796	85 163	73 701	12 739	34.4	40.5	10.00	10.51	344.00	425.66
February	109 397	91 220	24 074	17 896	85 323	73 901	12 848	34.3	40.6	10.06	10.64	345.06	431.98
March	109 618	91 324	24 025	17 870	85 593	73 963	12 823	34.4	40.7	10.10	10.70	347.44	435.49
April	109 652	91 275	23 966	17 845	85 686	73 928	12 806	34.3	40.6	10.12	10.68	347.12	433.61
May	109 801	91 202	23 887	17 796	85 914	73 839	12 755	34.3	40.6	10.14	10.74	347.80	436.04
June	109 820	91 264	23 847	17 774	85 973	73 824	12 736	34.4	40.7	10.19	10.77	350.54	438.34
July	109 773	91 213	23 746	17 704	86 027	73 773	12 675	34.3	40.6	10.21	10.81	350.20	438.89
August	109 569	91 112	23 646	17 647	85 923	73 705	12 622	34.2	40.5	10.23	10.80	349.87	437.40
September	109 485	91 048	23 572	17 610	85 913	73 606	12 601	34.2	40.5	10.27	10.87	351.23	440.24
October	109 321	90 878	23 470	17 574	85 851	73 466	12 576	34.1	40.4	10.29	10.92	350.89	441.17
November	109 175	90 725	23 283	17 428	85 892	73 316	12 439	34.2	40.2	10.31	10.89	352.60	437.78
December	109 118	90 650	23 203	17 395	85 915	73 250	12 413	34.2	40.3	10.33	10.93	353.29	440.48
1991													
January	108 998	90 524	23 060	17 329	85 938	73 103	12 351	34.1	40.2	10.36	10.97	353.28	440.99
February	108 698	90 216	22 903	17 214	85 795	72 815	12 243	34.1	40.1	10.38	10.98	353.96	440.30
March	108 542	90 054	22 780	17 141	85 762	72 666	12 191	34.0	40.0	10.40	11.00	353.60	440.00
April	108 325	89 840	22 687	17 093	85 638	72 496	12 158	34.0	40.1	10.44	11.03	354.96	442.30
May	108 203	89 705	22 617	17 069	85 586	72 395	12 142	34.0	40.1	10.47	11.08	355.98	444.31
June	108 283	89 722	22 569	17 042	85 714	72 417	12 134	34.1	40.5	10.51	11.13	358.39	450.77
July	108 233	89 635	22 508	17 016	85 725	72 383	12 132	34.1	40.5	10.53	11.17	359.07	452.39
August	108 252	89 685	22 493	17 025	85 759	72 435	12 151	34.1	40.6	10.54	11.18	359.41	453.91
September	108 285	89 742	22 467	17 011	85 818	72 453	12 143	34.1	40.6	10.57	11.22	360.44	455.53
October	108 293	89 700	22 416	16 997	85 877	72 421	12 138	34.2	40.6	10.58	11.25	361.84	456.75
November	108 235	89 608	22 315	16 960	85 920	72 350	12 103	34.1	40.6	10.60	11.26	361.46	457.16
December	108 261	89 620	22 274	16 916	85 987	72 394	12 074	34.1	40.7	10.63	11.26	362.48	458.28
1992													
January	108 313	89 625	22 213	16 839	86 100	72 422	12 009	34.1	40.6	10.63	11.24	362.48	456.34
February	108 242	89 553	22 144	16 831	86 098	72 406	12 018	34.1	40.7	10.66	11.30	363.51	459.91
March	108 301	89 586	22 127	16 805	86 174	72 421	12 006	34.1	40.7	10.69	11.33	364.53	461.13
April	108 457	89 718	22 131	16 830	86 326	72 570	12 029	34.3	40.9	10.71	11.36	367.35	464.62
May	108 584	89 831	22 134	16 834	86 450	72 684	12 045	34.2	40.9	10.73	11.39	366.97	465.85
June	108 640	89 878	22 096	16 825	86 544	72 725	12 041	34.1	40.8	10.75	11.41	366.58	465.53
July	108 714	89 897	22 077	16 822	86 637	72 731	12 047	34.2	40.8	10.77	11.43	368.33	466.34
August	108 851	89 968	22 044	16 782	86 807	72 815	12 020	34.2	40.8	10.81	11.47	369.70	467.98
September	108 888	90 059	22 021	16 762	86 867	72 921	12 005	34.3	40.8	10.81	11.46	370.78	467.57
October	109 061	90 233	22 028	16 750	87 033	73 076	12 001	34.2	40.8	10.84	11.47	370.73	467.98
November	109 205	90 364	22 042	16 758	87 163	73 219	12 008	34.2	40.9	10.86	11.49	371.41	469.94
December	109 418	90 540	22 075	16 768	87 343	73 411	12 029	34.2	40.9	10.88	11.51	372.10	470.76
1993													
January	109 725	90 824	22 132	16 790	87 593	73 678	12 056	34.3	41.1	10.92	11.55	374.56	474.71
February	109 962	91 060	22 189	16 806	87 773	73 940	12 075	34.3	41.1	10.93	11.58	374.90	475.94
March	109 916	91 009	22 142	16 795	87 774	73 855	12 074	34.1	40.8	10.98	11.58	374.42	472.46
April	110 223	91 285	22 130	16 771	88 093	74 077	12 055	34.4	41.5	10.98	11.63	377.71	482.65
May	110 496	91 545	22 189	16 766	88 307	74 332	12 056	34.3	41.1	11.01	11.66	377.64	479.23
June	110 660	91 691	22 165	16 742	88 495	74 438	12 038	34.3	41.0	11.02	11.67	377.99	478.47
July	110 960	91 900	22 186	16 742	88 774	74 615	12 041	34.4	41.1	11.04	11.69	379.78	480.46
August	111 119	92 091	22 203	16 741	88 916	74 793	12 049	34.3	41.2	11.07	11.72	379.70	482.86
September	111 359	92 318	22 251	16 768	89 108	74 981	12 081	34.4	41.3	11.09	11.77	381.50	486.10
October	111 638	92 596	22 306	16 778	89 332	75 229	12 093	34.4	41.3	11.11	11.79	382.18	486.93
November	111 901	92 833	22 347	16 800	89 554	75 443	12 116	34.4	41.3	11.14	11.83	383.22	488.58
December	112 203	93 094	22 413	16 815	89 790	75 662	12 142	34.4	41.4	11.17	11.88	384.25	491.83

Table 20-4. Nonfarm Payroll Employment, Hours, and Earnings—Continued

(Wage and salary workers on nonfarm payrolls, seasonally adjusted.)

Year and month	All wage and salary workers, (thousands)					Production or nonsupervisory workers on private payrolls							
		Private				Number (thousands)		Average hours per week		Average hourly earnings, dollars		Average weekly earnings, dollars	
	Total	Total	Goods–producing		Service–providing	Total private	Manufacturing	Total private	Manufacturing	Total private	Manufacturing	Total private	Manufacturing
			Total	Manufacturing									
1994													
January	112 473	93 326	22 463	16 853	90 010	75 875	12 181	34.4	41.4	11.19	11.89	384.94	492.25
February	112 665	93 515	22 451	16 862	90 214	76 075	12 199	34.2	40.9	11.23	11.98	384.07	489.98
March	113 133	93 943	22 549	16 896	90 584	76 436	12 234	34.5	41.7	11.23	11.95	387.44	498.32
April	113 490	94 267	22 640	16 932	90 850	76 734	12 275	34.5	41.7	11.26	11.96	388.47	498.73
May	113 829	94 565	22 704	16 962	91 125	77 013	12 305	34.5	41.8	11.28	11.98	389.16	500.76
June	114 139	94 865	22 765	17 011	91 374	77 265	12 353	34.5	41.8	11.30	12.00	389.85	501.60
July	114 498	95 197	22 808	17 027	91 690	77 566	12 369	34.6	41.8	11.33	12.02	392.02	502.44
August	114 801	95 495	22 877	17 082	91 924	77 802	12 429	34.4	41.7	11.34	12.05	391.23	502.49
September	115 155	95 818	22 947	17 114	92 208	78 069	12 460	34.4	41.6	11.37	12.09	391.13	502.94
October	115 361	96 017	22 974	17 144	92 387	78 253	12 490	34.5	41.8	11.42	12.12	393.99	506.62
November	115 786	96 419	23 051	17 187	92 735	78 600	12 527	34.5	41.8	11.43	12.15	394.34	507.87
December	116 056	96 668	23 096	17 218	92 960	78 839	12 559	34.5	41.8	11.46	12.16	395.37	508.29
1995													
January	116 377	96 980	23 144	17 259	93 233	79 086	12 593	34.5	41.8	11.47	12.19	395.72	509.54
February	116 588	97 181	23 102	17 264	93 486	79 240	12 601	34.4	41.7	11.52	12.25	396.29	510.83
March	116 808	97 381	23 151	17 263	93 657	79 423	12 600	34.4	41.5	11.54	12.25	396.98	508.38
April	116 971	97 537	23 174	17 278	93 797	79 560	12 609	34.3	41.2	11.56	12.25	396.51	504.70
May	116 962	97 544	23 121	17 260	93 841	79 577	12 592	34.2	41.2	11.58	12.28	396.04	505.94
June	117 189	97 744	23 140	17 250	94 049	79 740	12 575	34.3	41.2	11.62	12.31	398.57	507.17
July	117 260	97 823	23 119	17 218	94 141	79 811	12 538	34.3	41.1	11.66	12.38	399.94	508.82
August	117 538	98 109	23 165	17 241	94 373	80 059	12 568	34.3	41.2	11.68	12.39	400.62	510.47
September	117 777	98 347	23 207	17 246	94 570	80 253	12 566	34.3	41.2	11.71	12.41	401.65	511.29
October	117 926	98 462	23 205	17 215	94 721	80 373	12 535	34.3	41.2	11.75	12.44	403.03	512.53
November	118 070	98 607	23 198	17 207	94 872	80 451	12 517	34.3	41.3	11.77	12.45	403.71	514.19
December	118 210	98 744	23 208	17 230	95 002	80 604	12 548	34.2	40.9	11.79	12.49	403.22	510.84
1996													
January	118 192	98 742	23 194	17 206	94 998	80 529	12 520	33.8	39.7	11.84	12.60	400.19	500.22
February	118 627	99 142	23 280	17 229	95 347	80 914	12 531	34.3	41.3	11.86	12.56	406.80	518.73
March	118 882	99 350	23 275	17 192	95 607	81 092	12 489	34.3	41.1	11.88	12.50	407.48	513.75
April	119 047	99 532	23 316	17 204	95 731	81 259	12 505	34.2	41.2	11.94	12.69	408.35	522.83
May	119 376	99 847	23 357	17 221	96 019	81 515	12 514	34.3	41.3	11.96	12.70	410.23	524.51
June	119 647	100 119	23 399	17 226	96 248	81 733	12 526	34.4	41.5	12.02	12.76	413.49	529.54
July	119 875	100 328	23 417	17 222	96 458	81 921	12 516	34.3	41.4	12.04	12.79	412.97	529.51
August	120 078	100 574	23 479	17 255	96 599	82 118	12 543	34.3	41.5	12.08	12.82	414.34	532.03
September	120 296	100 729	23 498	17 253	96 798	82 243	12 544	34.4	41.6	12.12	12.85	416.93	534.56
October	120 534	100 980	23 546	17 268	96 988	82 476	12 558	34.4	41.4	12.14	12.84	417.62	531.58
November	120 826	101 261	23 583	17 276	97 243	82 664	12 561	34.4	41.5	12.19	12.88	419.34	534.52
December	121 003	101 432	23 599	17 285	97 404	82 831	12 569	34.4	41.7	12.23	12.95	420.71	540.02
1997													
January	121 232	101 639	23 619	17 298	97 613	82 973	12 579	34.3	41.4	12.27	12.99	420.86	537.79
February	121 526	101 928	23 686	17 316	97 840	83 252	12 592	34.5	41.6	12.30	13.00	424.35	540.80
March	121 843	102 235	23 738	17 339	98 105	83 478	12 613	34.5	41.8	12.35	13.04	426.08	545.07
April	122 134	102 531	23 767	17 351	98 367	83 727	12 618	34.6	41.8	12.37	13.04	428.00	545.07
May	122 396	102 795	23 809	17 362	98 587	83 943	12 630	34.5	41.7	12.42	13.06	428.49	544.60
June	122 642	102 982	23 834	17 387	98 808	84 080	12 649	34.4	41.6	12.45	13.09	428.28	544.54
July	122 918	103 232	23 860	17 387	99 058	84 320	12 645	34.5	41.6	12.48	13.09	430.56	544.54
August	122 911	103 294	23 951	17 451	98 960	84 264	12 697	34.6	41.6	12.55	13.17	434.23	547.87
September	123 417	103 738	23 997	17 466	99 420	84 659	12 710	34.6	41.7	12.58	13.17	435.27	549.19
October	123 756	104 018	24 053	17 513	99 703	84 869	12 746	34.5	41.8	12.65	13.28	436.43	555.10
November	124 063	104 302	24 111	17 555	99 952	85 053	12 774	34.6	41.8	12.70	13.32	439.42	556.78
December	124 361	104 595	24 183	17 587	100 178	85 288	12 798	34.6	42.0	12.73	13.35	440.46	560.70
1998													
January	124 629	104 859	24 264	17 621	100 365	85 438	12 819	34.6	41.9	12.77	13.34	441.84	558.95
February	124 814	105 028	24 283	17 627	100 531	85 605	12 828	34.6	41.7	12.82	13.39	443.57	558.36
March	124 962	105 170	24 264	17 637	100 698	85 629	12 822	34.5	41.5	12.87	13.43	444.02	557.35
April	125 240	105 424	24 339	17 636	100 901	85 845	12 813	34.5	41.3	12.91	13.41	445.40	553.83
May	125 641	105 766	24 361	17 624	101 280	86 124	12 790	34.5	41.5	12.95	13.45	446.78	558.18
June	125 846	105 967	24 386	17 607	101 460	86 274	12 772	34.4	41.4	12.97	13.43	446.17	556.00
July	125 967	106 037	24 237	17 421	101 730	86 271	12 553	34.5	41.4	12.99	13.34	448.16	552.28
August	126 322	106 363	24 421	17 564	101 901	86 572	12 705	34.5	41.4	13.07	13.46	450.92	557.24
September	126 543	106 558	24 420	17 558	102 123	86 735	12 713	34.4	41.3	13.10	13.53	450.64	558.79
October	126 735	106 734	24 406	17 512	102 329	86 885	12 676	34.5	41.4	13.13	13.52	452.99	559.73
November	127 020	106 976	24 395	17 466	102 625	87 039	12 631	34.5	41.5	13.16	13.54	454.02	561.91
December	127 364	107 285	24 454	17 449	102 910	87 307	12 622	34.5	41.5	13.19	13.56	455.06	562.74
1999													
January	127 477	107 393	24 400	17 426	103 077	87 355	12 604	34.4	41.3	13.25	13.59	455.80	561.27
February	127 873	107 729	24 433	17 394	103 440	87 676	12 574	34.4	41.3	13.28	13.63	456.83	562.92
March	127 997	107 829	24 378	17 368	103 619	87 731	12 562	34.3	41.3	13.32	13.69	456.88	565.40
April	128 379	108 142	24 423	17 342	103 956	87 963	12 539	34.4	41.3	13.37	13.75	459.93	567.88
May	128 593	108 364	24 445	17 333	104 148	88 168	12 535	34.4	41.4	13.42	13.81	461.65	571.73
June	128 850	108 578	24 433	17 294	104 417	88 328	12 504	34.4	41.3	13.45	13.85	462.68	572.01
July	129 145	108 806	24 485	17 319	104 660	88 506	12 530	34.4	41.5	13.50	13.91	464.40	577.27
August	129 338	108 963	24 468	17 288	104 870	88 632	12 502	34.4	41.5	13.54	13.95	465.78	578.93
September	129 525	109 121	24 485	17 281	105 040	88 757	12 496	34.4	41.5	13.60	14.01	467.84	581.42
October	129 947	109 490	24 508	17 275	105 439	89 082	12 484	34.4	41.4	13.62	14.00	468.53	579.60
November	130 242	109 746	24 562	17 283	105 680	89 316	12 488	34.4	41.4	13.64	14.00	469.22	579.60
December	130 536	109 996	24 579	17 277	105 957	89 525	12 490	34.4	41.4	13.68	14.07	470.59	582.50

Table 20-4. Nonfarm Payroll Employment, Hours, and Earnings—Continued

(Wage and salary workers on nonfarm payrolls, seasonally adjusted.)

Year and month	All wage and salary workers, (thousands)					Production or nonsupervisory workers on private payrolls								
	Total	Private				Number (thousands)		Average hours per week		Average hourly earnings, dollars		Average weekly earnings, dollars		
		Total	Goods–producing		Service– providing	Total private	Manufac- turing	Total private	Manufac- turing	Total private	Manufac- turing	Total private	Manufac- turing
			Total	Manufac- turing									

2000													
January	130 730	110 161	24 622	17 281	106 108	89 661	12 487	34.4	41.5	13.74	14.13	472.66	586.40
February	130 876	110 280	24 612	17 283	106 264	89 748	12 480	34.4	41.6	13.78	14.15	474.03	588.64
March	131 369	110 640	24 700	17 298	106 669	90 064	12 489	34.3	41.4	13.83	14.18	474.37	587.05
April	131 677	110 879	24 694	17 304	106 983	90 286	12 480	34.4	41.5	13.89	14.23	477.82	590.55
May	131 908	110 761	24 648	17 280	107 260	90 181	12 468	34.3	41.3	13.92	14.23	477.46	587.70
June	131 883	110 992	24 687	17 305	107 196	90 346	12 473	34.3	41.3	13.97	14.30	479.17	590.59
July	132 043	111 181	24 726	17 331	107 317	90 496	12 480	34.3	41.5	14.02	14.32	480.89	594.28
August	132 015	111 170	24 681	17 289	107 334	90 482	12 434	34.2	41.1	14.05	14.38	480.51	591.02
September	132 104	111 349	24 631	17 229	107 473	90 615	12 383	34.2	41.1	14.11	14.41	482.56	592.25
October	132 134	111 387	24 642	17 213	107 492	90 632	12 356	34.3	41.1	14.17	14.49	486.03	595.54
November	132 317	111 552	24 619	17 201	107 698	90 752	12 335	34.2	41.0	14.21	14.51	485.98	594.91
December	132 441	111 643	24 572	17 175	107 869	90 769	12 302	34.0	40.3	14.26	14.50	484.84	584.35
2001													
January	132 388	111 560	24 511	17 093	107 877	90 716	12 221	34.2	40.7	14.27	14.49	488.03	589.74
February	132 492	111 591	24 467	17 023	108 025	90 700	12 148	34.0	40.5	14.35	14.55	487.90	589.28
March	132 507	111 564	24 405	16 931	108 102	90 670	12 082	34.1	40.5	14.40	14.58	491.04	590.49
April	132 236	111 248	24 258	16 807	107 978	90 447	11 983	34.0	40.6	14.44	14.64	490.96	594.38
May	132 237	111 204	24 134	16 666	108 103	90 390	11 866	34.0	40.4	14.48	14.69	492.32	593.48
June	132 087	110 972	23 981	16 519	108 106	90 164	11 737	34.0	40.4	14.52	14.75	493.68	595.90
July	131 972	110 805	23 855	16 399	108 117	90 079	11 649	34.0	40.6	14.55	14.81	494.70	601.29
August	131 831	110 590	23 681	16 245	108 150	89 927	11 504	33.9	40.3	14.58	14.83	494.26	597.65
September	131 564	110 302	23 543	16 121	108 021	89 663	11 403	33.8	40.1	14.62	14.89	494.16	597.09
October	131 203	109 917	23 379	15 970	107 824	89 329	11 283	33.7	40.0	14.64	14.89	493.37	595.60
November	130 871	109 535	23 202	15 821	107 669	88 987	11 170	33.8	40.0	14.70	14.95	496.86	598.00
December	130 659	109 312	23 085	15 702	107 574	88 842	11 074	33.9	40.2	14.73	15.02	499.35	603.80
2002													
January	130 494	109 123	22 945	15 573	107 549	88 793	10 987	33.8	40.2	14.73	15.05	497.87	605.01
February	130 404	109 006	22 873	15 504	107 531	88 768	10 939	33.8	40.2	14.77	15.11	499.23	607.42
March	130 447	109 010	22 783	15 435	107 664	88 773	10 896	33.8	40.5	14.80	15.15	500.24	613.58
April	130 379	108 933	22 704	15 397	107 675	88 642	10 863	33.9	40.5	14.81	15.17	502.06	614.39
May	130 381	108 872	22 629	15 343	107 752	88 487	10 829	33.8	40.6	14.86	15.23	502.27	618.34
June	130 406	108 881	22 581	15 301	107 825	88 425	10 801	34.0	40.7	14.93	15.27	507.62	621.49
July	130 295	108 807	22 541	15 278	107 754	88 288	10 784	33.8	40.4	14.96	15.29	505.65	617.72
August	130 306	108 722	22 457	15 186	107 849	88 214	10 708	33.9	40.5	15.00	15.33	508.50	620.87
September	130 259	108 680	22 399	15 127	107 860	88 183	10 673	33.9	40.4	15.05	15.37	510.20	620.95
October	130 342	108 750	22 319	15 054	108 023	88 206	10 623	33.8	40.3	15.10	15.46	510.38	623.04
November	130 305	108 712	22 269	14 984	108 036	88 117	10 572	33.8	40.3	15.13	15.48	511.39	623.84
December	130 096	108 501	22 169	14 899	107 927	87 895	10 511	33.8	40.5	15.18	15.54	513.08	629.37
2003													
January	130 190	108 572	22 122	14 838	108 068	87 948	10 465	33.8	40.3	15.18	15.58	513.08	627.87
February	130 031	108 406	22 005	14 770	108 026	87 780	10 406	33.7	40.4	15.27	15.62	514.60	631.05
March	129 921	108 305	21 949	14 717	107 972	87 546	10 346	33.8	40.4	15.27	15.63	516.13	631.45
April	129 901	108 304	21 880	14 623	108 021	87 560	10 263	33.6	40.1	15.25	15.64	512.40	627.16
May	129 873	108 332	21 859	14 574	108 014	87 541	10 233	33.7	40.2	15.31	15.68	515.95	630.34
June	129 859	108 292	21 805	14 514	108 054	87 533	10 181	33.7	40.3	15.34	15.72	516.96	633.52
July	129 814	108 253	21 744	14 452	108 070	87 510	10 136	33.6	40.1	15.40	15.73	517.44	630.77
August	129 789	108 209	21 712	14 404	108 077	87 513	10 104	33.6	40.2	15.41	15.79	517.78	634.76
September	129 856	108 317	21 697	14 375	108 159	87 581	10 077	33.6	40.4	15.41	15.84	517.78	639.94
October	129 944	108 384	21 674	14 351	108 270	87 628	10 058	33.7	40.5	15.43	15.83	519.99	641.12
November	130 027	108 483	21 686	14 344	108 341	87 625	10 048	33.8	40.8	15.46	15.89	522.55	648.31
December	130 035	108 491	21 668	14 324	108 367	87 617	10 044	33.6	40.6	15.45	15.93	519.12	646.76

Table 20-5. Money Stock, Reserves, and Monetary Base

(Averages of daily figures; billions of dollars, seasonally adjusted.)

Year and month	Money stock measures			Reserves, adjusted for change in reserve requirements				
	M1	M2	M3	Total	Nonborrowed	Nonborrowed plus extended credit	Required	Monetary base
1959								
January	138.9	286.6	288.8	11 112	10 560	10 560	10 614	40 425
February	139.4	287.7	289.9	11 129	10 624	10 624	10 675	40 605
March	139.7	289.2	291.4	11 081	10 482	10 482	10 621	40 615
April	139.7	290.1	292.3	11 116	10 424	10 424	10 684	40 694
May	140.7	292.2	294.4	11 058	10 317	10 317	10 637	40 731
June	141.2	294.1	296.3	10 972	10 043	10 043	10 566	40 750
July	141.7	295.2	297.4	11 109	10 148	10 148	10 693	40 896
August	141.9	296.4	298.5	11 168	10 177	10 177	10 720	40 992
September	141.0	296.7	298.8	11 128	10 202	10 202	10 686	41 034
October	140.5	296.5	298.5	11 057	10 150	10 150	10 616	40 903
November	140.4	297.1	299.1	11 052	10 194	10 194	10 609	40 822
December	140.0	297.8	299.7	11 109	10 168	10 168	10 603	40 880
1960								
January	140.0	298.2	300.1	11 081	10 194	10 194	10 567	40 794
February	139.9	298.5	300.4	10 884	10 074	10 074	10 430	40 666
March	139.8	299.4	301.4	10 796	10 155	10 155	10 373	40 616
April	139.6	300.1	302.2	10 767	10 161	10 161	10 341	40 621
May	139.6	300.9	303.0	10 840	10 344	10 344	10 396	40 639
June	139.6	302.3	304.5	10 885	10 451	10 451	10 406	40 689
July	140.2	304.1	306.4	10 994	10 615	10 615	10 493	40 794
August	141.3	306.9	309.3	11 078	10 782	10 782	10 536	40 895
September	141.2	308.4	311.0	11 147	10 932	10 932	10 520	41 040
October	140.9	309.5	312.2	11 216	11 049	11 049	10 554	41 097
November	140.9	310.9	313.6	11 299	11 166	11 166	10 556	41 130
December	140.7	312.4	315.2	11 247	11 172	11 172	10 503	40 977
1961								
January	141.1	314.1	317.1	11 324	11 259	11 259	10 553	40 960
February	141.6	316.5	319.9	11 229	11 096	11 096	10 580	40 945
March	141.9	318.3	321.9	11 108	11 038	11 038	10 563	40 851
April	142.1	319.9	323.8	11 123	11 066	11 066	10 507	40 823
May	142.7	322.2	326.5	11 035	10 940	10 940	10 480	40 791
June	142.9	324.3	328.9	11 087	11 024	11 024	10 497	40 902
July	142.9	325.6	330.5	11 124	11 070	11 070	10 508	40 980
August	143.5	327.6	332.7	11 234	11 169	11 169	10 655	41 227
September	143.8	329.5	334.8	11 289	11 251	11 251	10 709	41 417
October	144.1	331.1	336.5	11 413	11 342	11 342	10 881	41 651
November	144.8	333.4	338.8	11 482	11 384	11 384	10 891	41 782
December	145.2	335.5	340.8	11 499	11 366	11 366	10 915	41 853
1962								
January	145.2	337.5	343.0	11 490	11 403	11 403	10 867	41 864
February	145.7	340.1	346.1	11 301	11 233	11 233	10 799	41 810
March	146.0	343.1	349.4	11 259	11 170	11 170	10 788	41 923
April	146.4	345.5	352.1	11 330	11 258	11 258	10 838	42 096
May	146.8	347.5	354.2	11 384	11 323	11 323	10 867	42 194
June	146.6	349.3	356.3	11 328	11 226	11 226	10 855	42 259
July	146.5	350.8	358.0	11 394	11 302	11 302	10 860	42 398
August	146.6	352.8	360.1	11 355	11 231	11 231	10 826	42 491
September	146.3	354.9	362.5	11 383	11 303	11 303	10 893	42 537
October	146.7	357.2	365.1	11 450	11 387	11 387	10 972	42 700
November	147.3	359.8	368.0	11 492	11 372	11 372	10 936	42 861
December	147.8	362.7	371.3	11 604	11 344	11 344	11 033	42 957
1963								
January	148.3	365.2	374.2	11 567	11 421	11 421	11 062	43 008
February	148.9	367.9	377.2	11 456	11 290	11 290	10 995	43 155
March	149.2	370.7	380.2	11 404	11 255	11 255	10 970	43 289
April	149.7	373.3	383.1	11 449	11 319	11 319	10 992	43 444
May	150.4	376.1	386.2	11 426	11 216	11 216	10 996	43 586
June	150.4	378.4	388.8	11 398	11 139	11 139	10 981	43 780
July	151.3	381.1	391.5	11 530	11 232	11 232	11 075	44 058
August	151.8	383.6	394.5	11 484	11 155	11 155	11 039	44 149
September	152.0	386.0	397.3	11 503	11 184	11 184	11 075	44 339
October	152.6	388.3	400.0	11 457	11 137	11 137	11 060	44 444
November	153.7	391.5	403.8	11 547	11 198	11 198	11 106	44 744
December	153.3	393.2	405.9	11 730	11 397	11 397	11 239	45 003
1964								
January	153.7	395.2	408.5	11 643	11 369	11 369	11 204	45 042
February	154.3	397.6	411.3	11 547	11 261	11 261	11 150	45 112
March	154.5	399.8	413.6	11 563	11 285	11 285	11 177	45 371
April	154.8	401.7	415.8	11 537	11 326	11 326	11 185	45 470
May	155.3	404.2	418.9	11 523	11 263	11 263	11 169	45 651
June	155.6	407.1	422.1	11 595	11 326	11 326	11 220	45 959
July	156.8	410.1	425.5	11 651	11 387	11 387	11 275	46 143
August	157.8	413.4	429.2	11 795	11 480	11 480	11 374	46 410
September	158.7	416.9	433.0	11 863	11 518	11 518	11 432	46 714
October	159.2	419.1	435.9	11 888	11 567	11 567	11 490	46 823
November	160.0	422.1	439.3	11 998	11 598	11 598	11 591	47 106
December	160.3	424.7	442.4	12 011	11 747	11 747	11 605	47 161

Table 20-5. Money Stock, Reserves, and Monetary Base—Continued

(Averages of daily figures; billions of dollars, seasonally adjusted.)

Year and month	Money stock measures			Reserves, adjusted for change in reserve requirements				Monetary base
	M1	M2	M3	Total	Nonborrowed	Nonborrowed plus extended credit	Required	
1965								
January	160.7	427.5	445.8	11 952	11 653	11 653	11 537	47 281
February	160.9	430.4	449.1	11 883	11 479	11 479	11 472	47 500
March	161.5	433.2	452.0	11 884	11 472	11 472	11 518	47 584
April	162.0	435.4	454.5	12 043	11 571	11 571	11 701	47 721
May	161.7	437.1	456.4	11 912	11 417	11 417	11 578	47 799
June	162.2	440.1	459.9	12 005	11 467	11 467	11 643	48 061
July	163.1	442.9	463.3	12 073	11 544	11 544	11 720	48 281
August	163.7	445.8	466.8	12 079	11 531	11 531	11 682	48 453
September	164.9	449.5	471.1	12 071	11 517	11 517	11 662	48 712
October	166.0	452.6	474.9	12 118	11 630	11 630	11 759	49 029
November	166.7	455.7	478.3	12 087	11 655	11 655	11 735	49 234
December	167.8	459.2	482.1	12 316	11 872	11 872	11 892	49 620
1966								
January	169.1	462.0	485.1	12 295	11 875	11 875	11 916	49 850
February	169.6	464.6	487.8	12 193	11 711	11 711	11 846	50 054
March	170.5	467.2	490.8	12 164	11 604	11 604	11 822	50 171
April	171.8	469.3	494.0	12 258	11 621	11 621	11 903	50 439
May	171.3	470.1	495.4	12 263	11 575	11 575	11 922	50 591
June	171.6	471.2	497.1	12 256	11 549	11 549	11 901	50 754
July	170.3	470.9	497.8	12 371	11 629	11 629	11 993	51 019
August	170.8	472.6	499.6	12 165	11 430	11 430	11 798	50 989
September	172.0	475.4	502.3	12 229	11 460	11 460	11 858	51 154
October	171.2	475.7	501.4	12 199	11 465	11 465	11 867	51 200
November	171.4	477.3	502.0	12 205	11 598	11 598	11 820	51 422
December	172.0	480.2	505.4	12 223	11 690	11 690	11 884	51 565
1967								
January	171.9	481.6	509.1	12 334	11 924	11 924	11 931	51 876
February	173.0	485.1	514.5	12 280	11 916	11 916	11 911	52 173
March	174.8	489.7	519.9	12 438	12 237	12 237	12 024	52 494
April	174.2	492.1	522.6	12 488	12 342	12 342	12 138	52 517
May	175.7	497.2	527.7	12 418	12 329	12 329	12 053	52 682
June	177.0	502.0	533.1	12 457	12 351	12 351	12 104	52 867
July	178.1	506.3	537.7	12 722	12 607	12 607	12 304	53 165
August	179.7	510.8	542.5	12 678	12 598	12 598	12 313	53 347
September	180.7	514.7	546.8	12 846	12 758	12 758	12 504	53 670
October	181.6	518.2	550.2	13 088	12 959	12 959	12 752	54 044
November	182.4	521.2	553.9	13 131	12 999	12 999	12 773	54 241
December	183.3	524.8	557.9	13 180	12 952	12 952	12 805	54 579
1968								
January	184.3	527.4	560.4	13 239	12 993	12 993	12 852	54 892
February	184.7	530.4	563.6	13 188	12 815	12 815	12 801	55 171
March	185.5	533.2	567.0	13 186	12 527	12 527	12 849	55 436
April	186.6	535.7	569.2	13 117	12 432	12 432	12 782	55 692
May	188.0	538.9	572.3	13 130	12 389	12 389	12 771	55 872
June	189.4	542.6	575.9	13 251	12 557	12 557	12 923	56 323
July	190.5	545.6	580.6	13 455	12 928	12 928	13 105	56 626
August	191.8	549.4	585.6	13 440	12 875	12 875	13 110	56 976
September	192.7	553.6	590.6	13 435	12 931	12 931	13 074	57 160
October	194.0	557.6	595.8	13 529	13 086	13 086	13 283	57 477
November	196.0	562.4	601.7	13 649	13 104	13 104	13 340	57 887
December	197.4	566.8	607.2	13 767	13 021	13 021	13 341	58 357
1969								
January	198.7	569.3	607.9	13 629	12 893	12 893	13 383	58 597
February	199.3	571.9	609.1	13 714	12 879	12 879	13 460	58 917
March	200.0	574.4	610.8	13 653	12 751	12 751	13 434	58 999
April	200.7	575.7	611.5	13 471	12 468	12 468	13 304	59 062
May	200.8	576.5	611.6	13 844	12 470	12 470	13 589	59 552
June	201.3	578.5	612.1	13 795	12 410	12 410	13 491	59 794
July	201.7	579.5	610.1	13 491	12 239	12 239	13 266	59 713
August	201.7	580.1	607.7	13 784	12 565	12 565	13 547	60 137
September	202.1	582.1	608.5	13 822	12 743	12 743	13 549	60 357
October	202.9	583.4	608.9	13 904	12 754	12 754	13 741	60 633
November	203.6	585.4	613.5	14 172	12 969	12 969	13 943	61 229
December	203.9	587.9	615.9	14 168	13 049	13 049	13 882	61 569
1970								
January	206.2	589.6	616.1	14 087	13 128	13 128	13 914	61 792
February	205.0	586.3	613.3	14 099	13 019	13 019	13 891	61 931
March	205.7	587.3	615.7	14 071	13 173	13 173	13 908	62 205
April	206.7	588.4	619.5	14 209	13 364	13 364	14 057	62 653
May	207.2	591.5	624.3	14 007	13 040	13 040	13 850	62 977
June	207.6	595.2	627.1	14 078	13 197	13 197	13 888	63 189
July	208.0	599.1	635.7	14 159	12 799	12 799	13 993	63 444
August	209.9	604.9	644.8	14 282	13 445	13 445	14 108	63 725
September	211.8	611.2	654.4	14 447	13 847	13 847	14 203	64 087
October	212.9	616.4	662.3	14 480	14 017	14 017	14 274	64 303
November	213.7	621.1	669.3	14 470	14 055	14 055	14 236	64 574
December	214.4	626.5	677.1	14 558	14 225	14 225	14 309	65 013

Table 20-5. Money Stock, Reserves, and Monetary Base—Continued

(Averages of daily figures; billions of dollars, seasonally adjusted.)

Year and month	Money stock measures			Reserves, adjusted for change in reserve requirements				
	M1	M2	M3	Total	Nonborrowed	Nonborrowed plus extended credit	Required	Monetary base
1971								
January	215.5	633.0	685.5	14 604	14 240	14 240	14 371	65 545
February	217.4	641.0	695.8	14 819	14 488	14 488	14 565	66 037
March	218.8	649.9	706.5	14 798	14 479	14 479	14 603	66 378
April	220.0	658.4	713.7	14 759	14 606	14 606	14 591	66 731
May	222.0	666.7	723.3	14 982	14 698	14 698	14 763	67 315
June	223.5	673.0	730.1	15 057	14 564	14 564	14 855	67 678
July	224.9	679.6	738.3	15 125	14 302	14 302	14 941	68 155
August	225.6	685.5	744.0	15 190	14 380	14 380	14 994	68 413
September	226.5	692.5	751.7	15 423	14 928	14 928	15 234	68 751
October	227.2	698.4	760.2	15 211	14 854	14 854	15 049	68 603
November	227.8	704.6	768.3	15 247	14 864	14 864	15 010	68 894
December	228.3	710.3	776.0	15 230	15 104	15 104	15 049	69 108
1972								
January	230.1	717.7	783.8	15 369	15 347	15 347	15 163	69 853
February	232.3	725.7	792.9	15 363	15 331	15 331	15 211	70 368
March	234.3	733.5	800.6	15 480	15 382	15 382	15 291	70 820
April	235.6	738.4	807.9	15 651	15 534	15 534	15 495	71 031
May	235.9	743.4	816.1	15 739	15 628	15 628	15 600	71 525
June	236.6	749.7	824.6	15 909	15 809	15 809	15 706	71 817
July	238.8	759.5	835.5	15 835	15 597	15 597	15 642	72 173
August	240.9	768.7	846.6	16 010	15 623	15 623	15 822	72 623
September	243.2	778.3	856.4	16 000	15 459	15 459	15 788	72 984
October	245.0	786.9	865.8	16 193	15 637	15 637	15 981	73 644
November	246.4	793.9	875.8	16 441	15 833	15 833	16 088	74 370
December	249.2	802.3	885.9	16 645	15 595	15 595	16 361	75 167
1973								
January	251.5	810.3	896.3	16 708	15 548	15 548	16 450	75 925
February	252.2	814.1	906.1	16 714	15 120	15 120	16 516	76 160
March	251.7	815.3	915.0	16 923	15 099	15 099	16 714	76 663
April	252.7	819.7	922.4	16 731	15 020	15 020	16 508	76 962
May	254.9	826.8	932.3	16 672	14 830	14 830	16 533	77 393
June	256.7	833.3	940.7	16 746	14 895	14 903	16 528	77 842
July	257.5	836.5	950.3	16 988	15 035	15 067	16 705	78 531
August	257.7	838.8	959.0	16 796	14 631	14 657	16 624	78 781
September	257.9	839.3	965.8	16 735	14 883	14 909	16 505	79 316
October	259.0	842.6	972.0	16 924	15 448	15 464	16 672	80 173
November	261.0	848.9	977.3	16 978	15 585	15 585	16 753	80 479
December	262.9	855.5	985.0	17 021	15 723	15 723	16 717	81 073
1974								
January	263.8	859.7	993.9	17 222	16 171	16 174	17 060	81 850
February	265.3	864.2	1 002.4	17 125	15 933	15 933	16 941	82 341
March	266.7	870.1	1 010.7	17 131	15 817	15 817	16 997	82 835
April	267.2	872.9	1 020.8	17 298	15 561	15 561	17 116	83 621
May	267.6	874.6	1 029.2	17 423	14 833	15 491	17 263	84 432
June	268.5	877.8	1 037.8	17 367	14 361	15 587	17 169	84 895
July	269.3	881.4	1 043.9	17 486	14 185	15 615	17 323	85 439
August	270.1	884.1	1 048.6	17 391	14 055	15 592	17 203	85 974
September	271.0	887.9	1 052.9	17 385	14 102	15 731	17 204	86 377
October	272.3	893.3	1 058.5	17 349	15 536	16 021	17 228	86 513
November	273.7	898.6	1 063.7	17 453	16 201	16 361	17 248	87 043
December	274.2	902.1	1 069.9	17 550	16 823	16 970	17 292	87 535
1975								
January	273.9	906.3	1 075.5	17 273	16 874	17 010	17 126	87 756
February	275.0	914.1	1 082.7	17 271	17 123	17 176	17 077	88 192
March	276.4	925.0	1 090.0	17 439	17 333	17 370	17 239	88 916
April	276.2	935.1	1 095.8	17 498	17 387	17 398	17 340	89 116
May	279.2	947.9	1 106.0	17 353	17 288	17 291	17 198	89 610
June	282.4	963.0	1 118.7	17 715	17 488	17 504	17 513	90 817
July	283.7	975.1	1 128.7	17 632	17 331	17 351	17 445	91 373
August	284.1	983.1	1 135.1	17 660	17 449	17 461	17 465	91 700
September	285.7	991.5	1 145.8	17 834	17 438	17 452	17 643	92 119
October	285.4	997.8	1 153.8	17 587	17 397	17 408	17 380	92 448
November	286.8	1 006.9	1 163.8	17 849	17 789	17 794	17 566	93 373
December	287.1	1 016.2	1 170.2	17 822	17 692	17 704	17 556	93 887
1976								
January	288.4	1 026.6	1 181.6	17 616	17 537	17 549	17 376	94 281
February	290.8	1 040.3	1 193.5	17 806	17 725	17 734	17 587	95 039
March	292.7	1 050.0	1 204.6	17 875	17 821	17 824	17 651	95 786
April	294.7	1 060.8	1 216.7	17 719	17 675	17 675	17 564	96 479
May	295.9	1 072.1	1 227.6	17 940	17 826	17 826	17 731	97 251
June	296.2	1 077.6	1 236.1	17 946	17 820	17 820	17 732	97 732
July	297.2	1 086.3	1 245.9	17 846	17 714	17 714	17 612	98 234
August	299.0	1 098.7	1 259.2	18 053	17 953	17 953	17 846	98 888
September	299.6	1 110.8	1 268.2	18 009	17 948	17 948	17 808	99 446
October	302.0	1 125.0	1 280.8	18 077	17 983	17 983	17 858	100 066
November	303.6	1 138.2	1 294.5	18 340	18 268	18 268	18 083	100 892
December	306.2	1 152.0	1 310.0	18 388	18 335	18 335	18 115	101 515

Table 20-5. Money Stock, Reserves, and Monetary Base—Continued

(Averages of daily figures; billions of dollars, seasonally adjusted.)

Year and month	Money stock measures			Reserves, adjusted for change in reserve requirements				Monetary base
	M1	M2	M3	Total	Nonborrowed	Nonborrowed plus extended credit	Required	
1977								
January	308.3	1 165.2	1 322.5	18 421	18 353	18 353	18 156	102 237
February	311.5	1 177.6	1 335.5	18 299	18 227	18 227	18 100	102 654
March	313.9	1 188.5	1 348.4	18 405	18 301	18 301	18 190	103 337
April	316.0	1 199.6	1 360.6	18 479	18 406	18 406	18 287	104 076
May	317.2	1 209.0	1 374.0	18 585	18 379	18 379	18 377	104 630
June	318.8	1 217.8	1 387.6	18 471	18 208	18 208	18 324	105 186
July	320.2	1 226.7	1 400.4	18 748	18 425	18 425	18 473	106 394
August	322.3	1 237.0	1 415.1	18 919	17 858	17 858	18 719	107 185
September	324.5	1 246.2	1 428.0	18 873	18 247	18 247	18 664	107 923
October	326.4	1 254.0	1 441.8	18 963	17 658	17 658	18 753	108 750
November	328.6	1 262.4	1 457.1	19 012	18 150	18 150	18 761	109 560
December	330.9	1 270.3	1 470.4	18 990	18 420	18 420	18 800	110 324
1978								
January	334.4	1 279.7	1 486.3	19 290	18 806	18 806	19 023	111 449
February	335.3	1 285.5	1 498.1	19 561	19 155	19 155	19 319	112 450
March	337.0	1 292.2	1 513.0	19 286	18 958	18 958	19 087	112 778
April	339.9	1 300.4	1 528.6	19 408	18 851	18 851	19 260	113 377
May	344.9	1 310.5	1 544.3	19 655	18 443	18 443	19 436	114 418
June	346.9	1 318.5	1 555.4	19 868	18 774	18 774	19 691	115 376
July	347.6	1 324.1	1 567.0	20 118	18 801	18 801	19 921	116 273
August	349.6	1 333.5	1 583.1	19 912	18 772	18 772	19 744	116 904
September	352.2	1 345.0	1 597.1	19 994	18 934	18 934	19 801	118 112
October	353.3	1 352.3	1 611.1	20 109	18 832	18 832	19 947	119 044
November	355.4	1 359.1	1 630.2	19 872	19 169	19 169	19 650	119 733
December	357.3	1 366.0	1 644.6	19 753	18 885	18 885	19 521	120 445
1979								
January	358.6	1 371.6	1 656.8	19 821	18 818	18 818	19 606	121 272
February	359.9	1 377.8	1 669.2	19 396	18 423	18 423	19 187	121 504
March	362.5	1 387.8	1 683.2	19 429	18 439	18 439	19 271	122 065
April	368.0	1 402.1	1 700.9	19 504	18 587	18 587	19 328	122 819
May	369.6	1 410.2	1 711.1	19 553	17 788	17 788	19 412	123 487
June	373.4	1 423.0	1 728.1	19 808	18 390	18 390	19 587	124 635
July	377.2	1 434.8	1 743.3	19 992	18 822	18 822	19 782	125 810
August	378.8	1 446.6	1 761.5	20 008	18 923	18 923	19 786	127 079
September	379.3	1 454.1	1 782.9	20 007	18 667	18 667	19 816	128 309
October	380.8	1 460.4	1 796.7	20 375	18 353	18 353	20 103	129 458
November	380.8	1 465.9	1 798.9	20 398	18 492	18 492	20 153	130 369
December	381.8	1 473.7	1 808.7	20 720	19 248	19 248	20 279	131 143
1980								
January	385.8	1 482.7	1 823.1	20 693	19 452	19 452	20 442	131 998
February	390.1	1 494.6	1 841.8	20 682	19 027	19 027	20 471	132 785
March	388.5	1 499.8	1 850.2	20 703	17 879	17 978	20 517	133 607
April	383.8	1 502.2	1 854.2	20 629	18 174	18 726	20 432	134 740
May	384.8	1 512.4	1 867.1	20 440	19 421	20 164	20 262	134 998
June	389.1	1 529.2	1 884.4	20 575	20 196	20 503	20 372	135 679
July	394.0	1 545.5	1 903.2	20 796	20 401	20 654	20 511	136 637
August	399.2	1 561.5	1 920.8	21 011	20 352	20 594	20 709	137 977
September	404.8	1 574.0	1 935.1	21 232	19 921	20 011	20 977	139 220
October	409.0	1 584.8	1 953.6	21 147	19 837	19 837	20 941	140 150
November	410.7	1 595.7	1 975.2	22 150	20 091	20 091	21 629	141 566
December	408.5	1 599.8	1 995.5	22 015	20 325	20 328	21 501	142 004
1981								
January	411.3	1 606.9	2 020.6	21 673	20 278	20 348	21 298	141 462
February	414.8	1 618.7	2 039.5	21 840	20 536	20 557	21 489	142 270
March	419.0	1 636.6	2 058.1	22 072	21 072	21 086	21 791	143 029
April	427.4	1 659.3	2 086.4	22 187	20 849	20 857	22 018	143 917
May	424.7	1 664.2	2 102.8	22 442	20 219	20 224	22 184	144 587
June	425.2	1 670.3	2 118.4	22 326	20 289	20 295	21 988	145 001
July	427.0	1 681.9	2 137.9	22 329	20 650	20 653	21 989	145 839
August	426.9	1 694.3	2 157.1	22 356	20 936	21 017	22 064	146 467
September	426.9	1 706.0	2 179.2	22 487	21 031	21 332	22 073	146 941
October	428.4	1 721.8	2 204.6	22 296	21 115	21 553	22 018	147 062
November	431.2	1 736.1	2 226.7	22 338	21 675	21 840	21 993	147 749
December	436.7	1 755.4	2 254.6	22 443	21 807	21 956	22 124	149 021
1982								
January	442.7	1 770.4	2 275.8	22 669	21 152	21 349	22 251	149 991
February	441.9	1 774.5	2 284.4	22 551	20 762	20 994	22 248	150 459
March	442.8	1 786.5	2 303.0	22 452	20 898	21 206	22 091	150 660
April	447.2	1 804.0	2 328.5	22 337	20 769	21 014	22 064	151 606
May	446.7	1 815.4	2 343.2	22 402	21 285	21 461	22 043	152 868
June	447.5	1 826.0	2 359.7	22 368	21 164	21 268	22 060	153 861
July	448.1	1 834.3	2 372.2	22 182	21 490	21 541	21 868	154 385
August	451.4	1 849.3	2 396.6	22 348	21 833	21 926	22 036	155 470
September	456.9	1 863.3	2 413.0	22 686	21 752	21 871	22 302	156 629
October	464.5	1 874.7	2 434.9	22 889	22 412	22 553	22 485	157 716
November	471.5	1 888.4	2 447.4	23 354	22 733	22 921	22 952	158 667
December	474.8	1 910.3	2 460.7	23 600	22 966	23 152	23 100	160 127

Table 20-5. Money Stock, Reserves, and Monetary Base—Continued

(Averages of daily figures; billions of dollars, seasonally adjusted.)

Year and month	Money stock measures			Reserves, adjusted for change in reserve requirements				
	M1	M2	M3	Total	Nonborrowed	Nonborrowed plus extended credit	Required	Monetary base
1983								
January	477.2	1 963.3	2 489.0	23 226	22 697	22 854	22 678	161 136
February	484.3	2 000.5	2 517.8	23 901	23 319	23 597	23 466	163 170
March	490.6	2 018.6	2 534.1	24 414	23 621	23 939	23 981	165 052
April	493.2	2 031.9	2 553.9	24 900	23 890	24 295	24 424	166 549
May	500.0	2 046.4	2 569.5	24 860	23 907	24 420	24 411	167 842
June	504.0	2 056.7	2 585.0	25 277	23 641	24 599	24 797	169 393
July	507.8	2 067.8	2 596.0	25 356	23 903	24 480	24 848	170 129
August	510.5	2 076.9	2 609.8	25 376	23 830	24 320	24 929	171 208
September	512.8	2 086.1	2 626.2	25 435	23 994	24 509	24 937	172 411
October	517.2	2 102.2	2 646.1	25 454	24 610	24 866	24 949	173 584
November	518.9	2 115.3	2 673.8	25 396	24 491	24 497	24 867	174 605
December	521.4	2 126.5	2 697.6	25 367	24 593	24 595	24 806	175 467
1984								
January	525.1	2 141.2	2 714.9	25 451	24 736	24 740	24 838	176 896
February	527.5	2 161.4	2 742.5	25 874	25 307	25 312	24 968	177 928
March	531.4	2 178.4	2 772.0	25 821	24 869	24 896	25 153	178 966
April	535.0	2 194.9	2 801.2	25 749	24 516	24 560	25 276	179 959
May	536.7	2 207.5	2 828.4	25 935	22 946	22 983	25 365	180 859
June	540.2	2 218.5	2 850.2	26 138	22 837	24 710	25 379	182 038
July	540.9	2 226.9	2 871.8	26 023	20 099	25 107	25 394	183 052
August	541.0	2 233.6	2 886.0	26 080	18 063	25 106	25 400	183 831
September	543.1	2 247.5	2 904.6	26 125	18 883	25 341	25 475	184 681
October	543.7	2 262.1	2 930.1	26 281	20 264	25 322	25 664	185 272
November	547.6	2 284.8	2 957.8	26 518	21 901	25 738	25 820	186 195
December	551.6	2 309.9	2 990.9	26 896	23 710	26 314	26 061	187 237
1985								
January	556.9	2 336.0	3 017.9	27 064	25 669	26 719	26 321	188 096
February	563.5	2 357.4	3 040.6	27 604	26 315	27 119	26 755	189 666
March	566.4	2 369.4	3 056.5	27 616	26 023	27 082	26 941	190 336
April	570.3	2 378.8	3 062.4	27 899	26 577	27 445	27 163	191 380
May	575.1	2 393.2	3 078.8	28 110	26 846	27 380	27 427	192 784
June	582.3	2 416.3	3 103.6	28 867	27 662	28 328	27 945	194 735
July	589.1	2 433.1	3 112.7	29 162	28 055	28 562	28 322	195 986
August	596.2	2 447.5	3 131.3	29 676	28 604	29 173	28 842	198 027
September	603.5	2 460.1	3 149.9	30 054	28 765	29 421	29 357	199 369
October	607.9	2 471.7	3 167.1	30 502	29 315	29 944	29 758	200 764
November	612.1	2 481.2	3 182.2	30 904	29 164	29 694	29 986	202 151
December	619.8	2 495.7	3 208.3	31 541	30 223	30 722	30 478	203 540
1986								
January	621.4	2 505.6	3 232.7	31 548	30 778	31 275	30 466	204 233
February	625.1	2 516.1	3 250.6	31 675	30 791	31 283	30 661	205 344
March	633.5	2 536.2	3 277.2	32 132	31 372	31 890	31 250	206 960
April	640.8	2 560.9	3 307.6	32 567	31 674	32 308	31 794	208 176
May	651.9	2 588.4	3 330.9	33 313	32 437	33 021	32 435	210 226
June	660.7	2 608.7	3 353.1	33 991	33 188	33 719	33 072	211 820
July	670.4	2 630.5	3 382.0	34 707	33 966	34 344	33 834	213 466
August	678.7	2 650.3	3 407.8	35 249	34 376	34 841	34 508	215 257
September	687.4	2 671.9	3 435.3	35 681	34 672	35 243	34 991	216 859
October	695.0	2 691.9	3 455.5	36 308	35 467	35 964	35 591	218 696
November	705.6	2 705.7	3 467.2	37 288	36 537	36 955	36 387	220 755
December	724.6	2 732.3	3 499.4	38 841	38 015	38 317	37 668	223 432
1987								
January	730.1	2 748.0	3 524.6	39 260	38 681	38 905	38 190	225 362
February	730.7	2 751.7	3 534.2	39 062	38 505	38 788	37 869	226 621
March	733.8	2 757.7	3 542.6	38 914	38 386	38 650	37 993	227 166
April	744.1	2 772.1	3 562.8	39 628	38 635	38 906	38 772	229 096
May	745.8	2 777.2	3 578.1	39 904	38 868	39 156	38 836	230 584
June	743.0	2 778.6	3 593.1	39 546	38 770	39 043	38 313	231 389
July	743.1	2 783.4	3 599.5	39 167	38 494	38 689	38 308	232 071
August	745.1	2 792.4	3 620.2	39 298	38 651	38 783	38 247	233 640
September	747.5	2 803.6	3 642.5	39 204	38 264	38 673	38 420	234 745
October	756.1	2 819.1	3 667.7	39 893	38 950	39 399	38 804	237 168
November	753.5	2 824.2	3 681.7	39 364	38 739	39 133	38 424	238 932
December	750.2	2 831.4	3 686.8	38 918	38 141	38 624	37 899	239 847
1988								
January	756.2	2 852.4	3 709.0	39 480	38 398	38 770	38 228	241 811
February	757.8	2 875.8	3 737.2	39 456	39 059	39 264	38 318	242 830
March	761.8	2 895.7	3 762.2	39 340	37 588	39 066	38 395	243 852
April	768.0	2 915.6	3 788.2	39 698	36 705	39 329	38 814	245 812
May	771.7	2 931.2	3 814.5	40 031	37 453	39 560	38 984	247 494
June	778.4	2 943.4	3 834.2	40 343	37 261	39 814	39 448	249 239
July	781.3	2 953.1	3 850.6	40 579	37 139	39 678	39 688	251 009
August	783.2	2 958.2	3 864.4	40 534	37 293	39 946	39 564	252 130
September	783.7	2 963.1	3 876.1	40 400	37 561	39 620	39 384	253 447
October	783.4	2 971.6	3 890.1	40 458	38 158	39 940	39 405	254 624
November	784.9	2 986.5	3 909.0	40 546	37 684	40 007	39 372	255 769
December	786.6	2 994.4	3 928.9	40 428	38 712	39 956	39 366	256 869

Table 20-5. Money Stock, Reserves, and Monetary Base—Continued

(Averages of daily figures; billions of dollars, seasonally adjusted.)

Year and month	Money stock measures			Reserves, adjusted for change in reserve requirements				Monetary base
	M1	M2	M3	Total	Nonborrowed	Nonborrowed plus extended credit	Required	
1989								
January	785.8	2 997.8	3 937.0	40 409	38 760	39 798	39 265	257 889
February	783.9	2 998.1	3 940.8	40 359	38 872	39 922	39 204	258 286
March	783.1	3 005.8	3 961.6	39 889	38 076	39 411	38 970	259 214
April	779.3	3 012.0	3 970.8	39 580	37 291	38 998	38 767	259 547
May	774.9	3 017.4	3 974.8	39 346	37 626	38 823	38 304	260 307
June	773.4	3 033.4	3 995.0	39 125	37 635	38 551	38 216	261 158
July	777.9	3 058.4	4 018.0	39 477	38 783	38 889	38 494	262 280
August	779.3	3 080.4	4 027.4	39 436	38 761	38 802	38 544	262 873
September	780.8	3 098.6	4 035.0	39 705	39 012	39 034	38 760	263 762
October	786.6	3 120.7	4 047.5	40 170	39 615	39 636	39 130	264 876
November	788.2	3 139.6	4 063.3	40 137	39 788	39 809	39 188	265 748
December	792.8	3 158.4	4 076.9	40 430	40 164	40 184	39 489	267 668
1990								
January	795.1	3 172.7	4 088.8	40 687	40 247	40 272	39 644	269 511
February	797.8	3 185.6	4 095.3	40 732	39 284	39 819	39 732	271 113
March	801.1	3 196.1	4 097.4	40 664	38 540	40 491	39 783	273 058
April	806.3	3 208.8	4 105.7	40 865	39 257	40 641	39 994	275 232
May	804.5	3 206.7	4 107.4	40 773	39 441	40 313	39 819	276 789
June	808.8	3 218.7	4 114.0	40 687	39 806	40 152	39 900	278 960
July	810.2	3 229.9	4 127.5	40 600	39 842	40 122	39 732	281 010
August	815.9	3 247.8	4 143.6	40 900	39 973	40 101	40 025	284 127
September	820.3	3 260.9	4 151.5	41 112	40 487	40 494	40 199	287 265
October	819.7	3 264.9	4 155.0	40 804	39 394	40 412	39 964	289 199
November	822.1	3 269.3	4 150.5	40 925	40 695	40 720	39 998	291 197
December	824.8	3 279.2	4 154.1	41 699	41 374	41 397	40 035	293 262
1991								
January	827.1	3 294.6	4 176.3	42 243	41 709	41 736	40 102	297 714
February	832.5	3 311.6	4 192.5	42 055	41 803	41 837	40 250	300 895
March	838.4	3 328.8	4 199.7	41 818	41 577	41 629	40 633	302 655
April	842.8	3 339.5	4 206.8	41 877	41 646	41 732	40 851	303 031
May	849.0	3 350.6	4 207.1	42 433	42 130	42 218	41 399	304 240
June	857.2	3 360.2	4 208.7	42 734	42 394	42 402	41 741	305 515
July	861.5	3 362.9	4 201.4	43 016	42 409	42 455	42 112	307 243
August	866.7	3 361.5	4 195.4	43 433	42 669	42 969	42 346	309 372
September	870.5	3 362.3	4 189.9	43 587	42 942	43 244	42 657	310 754
October	878.1	3 367.2	4 194.0	44 006	43 746	43 757	42 951	312 743
November	887.3	3 371.6	4 199.0	44 571	44 463	44 464	43 679	314 931
December	896.9	3 379.1	4 207.7	45 451	45 258	45 259	44 461	317 509
1992								
January	910.4	3 388.0	4 213.7	46 325	46 091	46 092	45 333	319 618
February	925.1	3 407.0	4 233.8	47 600	47 522	47 524	46 546	322 587
March	936.5	3 410.7	4 235.2	48 292	48 201	48 203	47 267	324 328
April	944.4	3 408.3	4 225.0	49 061	48 971	48 973	47 934	326 727
May	950.4	3 404.5	4 218.2	49 366	49 212	49 212	48 363	328 812
June	954.2	3 400.1	4 215.9	49 303	49 074	49 074	48 380	330 157
July	963.3	3 401.9	4 217.2	49 799	49 515	49 515	48 824	333 317
August	974.0	3 406.7	4 225.7	50 525	50 275	50 275	49 587	336 992
September	987.8	3 416.9	4 233.1	51 425	51 138	51 138	50 413	340 789
October	1 003.5	3 430.8	4 232.1	52 753	52 610	52 610	51 692	344 612
November	1 016.1	3 434.8	4 228.8	53 685	53 581	53 581	52 643	347 677
December	1 025.0	3 432.8	4 219.7	54 332	54 208	54 209	53 178	350 758
1993								
January	1 030.2	3 426.7	4 201.3	54 901	54 736	54 737	53 639	353 556
February	1 033.4	3 423.1	4 203.9	54 657	54 612	54 612	53 565	355 394
March	1 038.3	3 419.8	4 207.0	54 971	54 879	54 879	53 739	357 853
April	1 047.9	3 420.6	4 209.3	55 367	55 294	55 294	54 263	360 899
May	1 066.1	3 445.4	4 239.7	56 664	56 543	56 543	55 668	364 904
June	1 074.9	3 450.5	4 239.4	57 100	56 919	56 919	56 209	367 907
July	1 084.2	3 450.4	4 235.8	57 760	57 516	57 516	56 693	371 466
August	1 094.2	3 455.0	4 237.0	58 216	57 864	57 864	57 265	374 621
September	1 104.5	3 462.7	4 247.4	58 883	58 455	58 455	57 800	378 335
October	1 112.8	3 465.6	4 253.0	59 563	59 277	59 277	58 485	381 501
November	1 123.8	3 478.9	4 270.8	60 217	60 128	60 128	59 100	384 026
December	1 129.9	3 484.7	4 281.8	60 460	60 378	60 378	59 390	386 465
1994								
January	1 131.8	3 486.0	4 279.0	60 811	60 738	60 738	59 354	390 118
February	1 136.3	3 486.5	4 263.7	60 478	60 407	60 407	59 331	393 272
March	1 140.3	3 492.7	4 275.1	60 296	60 240	60 240	59 315	396 064
April	1 141.2	3 497.7	4 286.4	60 511	60 387	60 387	59 373	398 861
May	1 143.2	3 505.9	4 296.7	59 989	59 789	59 789	59 123	401 453
June	1 145.3	3 494.2	4 294.8	60 076	59 743	59 743	58 962	404 506
July	1 149.7	3 498.9	4 314.7	60 362	59 904	59 904	59 251	407 741
August	1 150.0	3 496.3	4 315.7	60 000	59 531	59 531	58 997	409 693
September	1 151.3	3 496.9	4 324.4	59 825	59 338	59 338	58 780	411 821
October	1 150.0	3 496.5	4 336.1	59 352	58 972	58 972	58 561	413 992
November	1 150.2	3 498.6	4 350.8	59 339	59 090	59 090	58 352	416 698
December	1 150.5	3 497.7	4 364.8	59 369	59 160	59 160	58 209	418 196

Table 20-5. Money Stock, Reserves, and Monetary Base—Continued

(Averages of daily figures; billions of dollars, seasonally adjusted.)

Year and month	Money stock measures			Reserves, adjusted for change in reserve requirements				
	M1	M2	M3	Total	Nonborrowed	Nonborrowed plus extended credit	Required	Monetary base
1995								
January	1 151.0	3 503.2	4 388.5	59 349	59 213	59 217	58 010	420 913
February	1 147.0	3 500.8	4 389.9	58 630	58 571	58 571	57 668	421 679
March	1 146.4	3 501.9	4 410.5	58 220	58 151	58 151	57 405	424 748
April	1 149.8	3 511.8	4 433.2	58 001	57 891	57 891	57 249	427 924
May	1 144.8	3 533.8	4 471.3	57 686	57 537	57 537	56 812	430 620
June	1 143.5	3 559.1	4 509.5	57 432	57 159	57 159	56 449	430 272
July	1 145.0	3 579.1	4 536.6	57 886	57 514	57 514	56 781	430 742
August	1 145.1	3 600.8	4 571.1	57 608	57 326	57 326	56 604	431 417
September	1 140.7	3 611.6	4 590.3	57 363	57 085	57 085	56 394	431 873
October	1 136.2	3 623.6	4 608.2	56 741	56 495	56 495	55 656	432 620
November	1 133.3	3 632.4	4 620.0	56 284	56 079	56 079	55 330	432 993
December	1 127.0	3 641.4	4 630.9	56 430	56 173	56 173	55 140	434 388
1996								
January	1 122.8	3 659.3	4 664.5	55 844	55 806	55 806	54 380	434 699
February	1 118.3	3 674.1	4 693.1	54 616	54 582	54 582	53 760	432 727
March	1 122.1	3 699.2	4 728.7	55 313	55 292	55 292	54 174	435 881
April	1 124.8	3 710.7	4 747.0	55 210	55 120	55 120	54 087	437 012
May	1 116.4	3 721.3	4 783.0	54 083	53 956	53 956	53 177	437 683
June	1 114.8	3 735.0	4 806.3	54 196	53 810	53 810	53 088	440 037
July	1 111.5	3 749.5	4 831.9	53 439	53 071	53 071	52 421	442 570
August	1 100.7	3 758.0	4 851.5	52 221	51 888	51 888	51 263	444 742
September	1 095.0	3 769.0	4 879.3	51 358	50 990	50 990	50 311	446 130
October	1 086.4	3 782.2	4 919.9	50 056	49 768	49 768	49 049	446 824
November	1 081.6	3 796.1	4 939.2	49 761	49 547	49 547	48 709	448 701
December	1 079.3	3 817.0	4 978.8	50 149	49 994	49 994	48 733	451 904
1997								
January	1 080.9	3 831.2	5 006.8	49 653	49 608	49 608	48 429	453 413
February	1 077.6	3 842.3	5 035.7	48 705	48 663	48 663	47 673	454 582
March	1 070.3	3 857.9	5 074.0	47 858	47 701	47 701	46 692	456 322
April	1 062.7	3 874.6	5 114.3	47 370	47 109	47 109	46 361	457 946
May	1 062.9	3 886.2	5 139.9	46 668	46 425	46 425	45 405	459 677
June	1 064.6	3 904.5	5 170.2	46 946	46 579	46 579	45 632	462 167
July	1 065.9	3 923.8	5 228.7	46 780	46 370	46 370	45 563	464 668
August	1 072.8	3 953.3	5 284.6	46 952	46 354	46 354	45 697	466 948
September	1 066.6	3 971.7	5 324.8	46 285	45 848	45 848	44 984	469 343
October	1 066.4	3 990.0	5 369.6	45 972	45 702	45 702	44 557	471 877
November	1 068.8	4 011.8	5 411.0	46 399	46 246	46 246	44 730	475 823
December	1 072.5	4 031.9	5 453.5	46 848	46 523	46 523	45 163	479 826
1998								
January	1 073.7	4 056.1	5 500.8	46 665	46 455	46 455	44 872	482 006
February	1 077.7	4 089.0	5 533.8	45 733	45 675	45 675	44 200	483 334
March	1 076.5	4 115.7	5 603.5	45 863	45 822	45 822	44 512	485 138
April	1 076.7	4 140.8	5 641.8	46 150	46 078	46 078	44 762	487 171
May	1 076.6	4 160.1	5 679.6	45 548	45 395	45 395	44 275	488 928
June	1 075.6	4 184.5	5 718.8	45 454	45 203	45 203	43 838	491 784
July	1 074.9	4 204.2	5 741.7	44 932	44 674	44 674	43 562	494 529
August	1 073.3	4 230.7	5 807.8	45 124	44 853	44 853	43 593	498 135
September	1 078.9	4 272.2	5 874.8	44 859	44 608	44 608	43 164	502 349
October	1 085.2	4 312.8	5 945.5	44 950	44 776	44 776	43 378	506 770
November	1 092.7	4 352.6	6 003.8	44 942	44 859	44 859	43 323	510 374
December	1 096.1	4 384.1	6 044.6	45 254	45 138	45 138	43 741	513 894
1999								
January	1 095.8	4 407.4	6 071.9	44 618	44 412	44 412	43 131	516 450
February	1 096.6	4 434.2	6 119.9	44 251	44 135	44 135	43 055	520 546
March	1 097.4	4 444.4	6 125.7	43 954	43 890	43 890	42 686	524 673
April	1 101.2	4 475.4	6 165.2	43 698	43 532	43 532	42 538	528 463
May	1 100.7	4 494.6	6 193.8	44 066	43 939	43 939	42 845	533 252
June	1 098.8	4 515.0	6 227.9	43 341	43 196	43 196	42 046	536 863
July	1 097.7	4 539.0	6 257.9	42 240	41 931	41 931	41 116	540 564
August	1 097.3	4 560.9	6 290.1	42 123	41 779	41 779	40 963	544 900
September	1 096.6	4 577.3	6 314.9	42 017	41 678	41 678	40 807	550 201
October	1 101.5	4 595.4	6 369.8	41 600	41 319	41 319	40 449	557 447
November	1 109.8	4 619.3	6 456.9	41 846	41 611	41 611	40 516	571 452
December	1 124.0	4 649.0	6 544.7	41 928	41 607	41 607	40 631	593 709
2000								
January	1 120.3	4 677.9	6 595.0	42 272	41 898	41 898	40 252	590 785
February	1 108.6	4 692.1	6 624.2	40 964	40 856	40 856	39 852	572 989
March	1 108.9	4 723.2	6 696.8	40 410	40 231	40 231	39 200	571 426
April	1 111.9	4 775.3	6 761.1	40 620	40 316	40 316	39 463	572 023
May	1 104.8	4 766.6	6 770.1	40 764	40 402	40 402	39 792	573 466
June	1 104.3	4 783.7	6 814.5	40 418	39 938	39 938	39 301	575 614
July	1 103.1	4 798.8	6 865.4	40 254	39 685	39 685	39 111	577 165
August	1 101.4	4 832.8	6 937.5	39 702	39 123	39 123	38 684	577 996
September	1 098.6	4 863.6	6 994.4	39 665	39 187	39 187	38 546	578 617
October	1 098.9	4 881.0	7 017.3	39 416	38 998	38 998	38 267	580 588
November	1 092.3	4 892.4	7 034.8	39 542	39 259	39 259	38 234	582 553
December	1 087.9	4 932.7	7 112.9	38 677	38 467	38 467	37 249	585 104

Table 20-5. Money Stock, Reserves, and Monetary Base—Continued

(Averages of daily figures; billions of dollars, seasonally adjusted.)

Year and month	Money stock measures			Reserves, adjusted for change in reserve requirements				Monetary base
	M1	M2	M3	Total	Nonborrowed	Nonborrowed plus extended credit	Required	
2001								
January	1 095.3	4 988.4	7 223.4	37 847	37 774	37 774	36 463	588 053
February	1 099.4	5 027.4	7 290.0	38 427	38 376	38 376	36 920	589 841
March	1 107.7	5 086.9	7 363.1	38 278	38 220	38 220	36 879	591 977
April	1 110.6	5 151.1	7 498.2	38 354	38 303	38 303	37 077	594 869
May	1 115.5	5 152.4	7 554.8	38 483	38 270	38 270	37 464	598 094
June	1 123.6	5 190.3	7 629.6	39 027	38 798	38 798	37 665	601 500
July	1 135.6	5 221.2	7 669.0	39 568	39 285	39 285	38 160	607 771
August	1 147.3	5 253.4	7 677.6	39 809	39 626	39 626	38 601	615 828
September	1 199.1	5 363.2	7 833.4	58 085	54 700	54 700	39 069	640 082
October	1 162.8	5 355.0	7 875.3	45 476	45 349	45 349	44 150	630 645
November	1 166.5	5 398.1	7 955.9	40 999	40 915	40 915	39 558	630 420
December	1 179.3	5 448.6	8 025.0	41 411	41 344	41 344	39 760	635 936
2002								
January	1 184.6	5 476.0	8 046.1	41 640	41 590	41 590	40 245	641 534
February	1 186.1	5 505.7	8 090.1	41 571	41 541	41 541	40 201	646 160
March	1 190.0	5 517.4	8 110.0	40 883	40 804	40 804	39 462	649 124
April	1 179.9	5 522.7	8 133.6	40 595	40 524	40 524	39 383	652 862
May	1 184.0	5 552.2	8 169.4	39 429	39 317	39 317	38 168	656 818
June	1 188.3	5 573.9	8 180.8	39 288	39 146	39 146	38 049	662 257
July	1 194.2	5 615.8	8 221.6	39 435	39 243	39 243	38 057	668 273
August	1 182.9	5 651.5	8 284.8	39 703	39 370	39 370	38 095	670 801
September	1 190.5	5 677.9	8 321.3	39 036	38 807	38 807	37 550	672 264
October	1 201.8	5 722.7	8 348.3	39 132	38 989	38 989	37 597	674 482
November	1 204.5	5 767.2	8 479.4	39 880	39 609	39 609	38 242	677 713
December	1 217.2	5 794.5	8 552.4	40 442	40 362	40 362	38 433	682 151
2003								
January	1 220.4	5 825.5	8 564.8	40 840	40 813	40 813	39 132	685 645
February	1 235.1	5 867.3	8 601.9	41 095	41 070	41 070	39 129	690 639
March	1 240.6	5 891.1	8 633.4	41 087	41 065	41 065	39 453	693 925
April	1 246.1	5 933.8	8 670.4	40 696	40 666	40 666	39 153	696 642
May	1 257.7	5 985.1	8 725.2	40 884	40 829	40 829	39 263	700 151
June	1 271.0	6 026.1	8 774.6	42 348	42 186	42 186	40 485	702 786
July	1 273.4	6 066.1	8 849.0	43 314	43 183	43 183	41 379	705 363
August	1 281.5	6 106.6	8 888.6	45 252	45 252	45 252	41 814	710 239
September	1 281.4	6 083.9	8 879.6	44 289	44 109	44 109	42 779	712 123
October	1 284.1	6 069.1	8 856.8	43 394	43 287	43 287	41 921	715 834
November	1 283.4	6 065.8	8 844.4	43 034	42 966	42 966	41 545	718 968
December	1 293.4	6 062.5	8 845.6	42 843	42 797	42 797	41 804	720 978

Table 20-6. Interest Rates, Bond Yields, and Stock Price Indexes

(Not seasonally adjusted.)

Year and month	Short-term rates					U.S. Treasury securities		Bond yields			Fixed-rate first mortgages	Stock price indexes		
	Federal funds	Federal reserve discount rate [1]	U.S. Treasury bills, 3-month	U.S. Treasury bills, 6-month	Bank prime rate	1-year	10-year	Domestic corporate (Moody's)		State and local bonds (Bond Buyer)		Dow Jones industrials (30 stocks)	Standard and Poor's composite (500 stocks) [2]	Nasdaq composite
								Aaa	Baa					
1945														
January	...	...	0.38	...	...	...	...	2.69	3.46	...	...	153.95	13.49	...
February	...	...	0.38	...	...	...	...	2.65	3.41	...	...	157.24	13.94	...
March	...	...	0.38	...	...	...	...	2.62	3.38	...	...	157.31	13.93	...
April	...	...	0.38	...	...	...	...	2.61	3.36	...	...	160.34	14.28	...
May	...	...	0.38	...	...	...	...	2.62	3.32	...	...	165.52	14.82	...
June	...	...	0.38	...	...	...	...	2.61	3.29	...	...	167.37	15.09	...
July	...	...	0.38	...	...	...	...	2.60	3.26	...	...	163.92	14.78	...
August	...	...	0.38	...	...	...	...	2.61	3.26	...	...	166.17	14.83	...
September	...	...	0.38	...	...	...	...	2.62	3.24	...	...	177.85	15.84	...
October	...	...	0.38	...	...	...	...	2.62	3.20	...	...	185.06	16.50	...
November	...	...	0.38	...	...	...	...	2.62	3.15	...	...	190.34	17.04	...
December	...	...	0.38	...	...	...	...	2.61	3.10	...	...	192.68	17.33	...
1946														
January	...	...	0.38	...	...	...	...	2.54	3.01	...	...	199.23	18.02	...
February	...	...	0.38	...	...	...	...	2.48	2.95	...	...	198.56	18.07	...
March	...	...	0.38	...	...	...	...	2.47	2.94	...	...	194.23	17.53	...
April	...	...	0.38	...	...	...	...	2.46	2.96	...	...	205.71	18.66	...
May	...	...	0.38	...	...	...	...	2.51	3.02	...	...	206.80	18.70	...
June	...	...	0.38	...	...	...	...	2.49	3.03	...	...	207.33	18.58	...
July	...	...	0.38	...	...	...	...	2.48	3.03	...	...	202.28	18.05	...
August	...	...	0.38	...	...	...	...	2.51	3.03	...	...	199.45	17.70	...
September	...	...	0.38	...	...	...	...	2.58	3.10	...	...	172.74	15.09	...
October	...	...	0.38	...	...	...	...	2.60	3.15	...	...	169.47	14.75	...
November	...	...	0.38	...	...	...	...	2.59	3.17	...	...	168.74	14.69	...
December	...	...	0.38	...	...	...	...	2.61	3.17	...	...	174.29	15.13	...
1947														
January	...	...	0.38	...	...	...	...	2.57	3.13	...	...	176.15	15.21	...
February	...	...	0.38	...	...	...	...	2.55	3.12	...	...	181.43	15.80	...
March	...	...	0.38	...	...	...	...	2.55	3.15	...	...	176.69	15.16	...
April	...	...	0.38	...	...	...	...	2.53	3.16	...	...	171.23	14.60	...
May	...	...	0.38	...	...	...	...	2.53	3.17	...	...	168.63	14.34	...
June	...	...	0.38	...	...	...	...	2.55	3.21	...	...	173.76	14.84	...
July	...	...	0.66	...	...	...	...	2.55	3.18	...	...	183.53	15.77	...
August	...	...	0.75	...	...	...	...	2.56	3.17	...	...	180.08	15.46	...
September	...	...	0.80	...	...	...	...	2.61	3.23	...	...	176.81	15.06	...
October	...	...	0.85	...	...	...	...	2.70	3.35	...	...	181.95	15.45	...
November	...	...	0.92	...	...	...	...	2.77	3.44	...	...	181.52	15.27	...
December	...	...	0.95	...	...	...	...	2.86	3.52	...	...	179.24	15.03	...
1948														
January	...	...	0.97	...	...	...	...	2.86	3.52	...	...	176.30	14.83	...
February	...	...	1.00	...	...	...	...	2.85	3.53	...	...	168.64	14.10	...
March	...	...	1.00	...	...	...	...	2.83	3.53	...	...	169.77	14.30	...
April	...	...	1.00	...	...	...	...	2.78	3.47	...	...	180.05	15.40	...
May	...	...	1.00	...	...	...	...	2.76	3.38	...	...	186.51	16.15	...
June	...	...	1.00	...	...	...	...	2.76	3.34	...	...	191.06	16.82	...
July	...	...	1.00	...	...	...	...	2.81	3.37	...	...	187.07	16.42	...
August	...	...	1.06	...	...	...	...	2.84	3.44	...	...	181.77	15.94	...
September	...	...	1.09	...	...	...	...	2.84	3.45	...	...	180.34	15.76	...
October	...	...	1.12	...	...	...	...	2.84	3.50	...	...	185.16	16.19	...
November	...	...	1.14	...	...	...	...	2.84	3.53	...	...	176.76	15.29	...
December	...	...	1.16	...	...	...	...	2.79	3.53	...	...	176.30	15.19	...
1949														
January	...	...	1.17	...	2.00	...	...	2.71	3.46	...	...	179.63	15.36	...
February	...	...	1.17	...	2.00	...	...	2.71	3.45	...	...	174.54	14.77	...
March	...	...	1.17	...	2.00	...	...	2.70	3.47	...	...	175.87	14.91	...
April	...	...	1.17	...	2.00	...	...	2.70	3.45	...	...	175.63	14.89	...
May	...	...	1.17	...	2.00	...	...	2.71	3.45	...	...	173.93	14.78	...
June	...	...	1.17	...	2.00	...	...	2.71	3.47	...	...	165.60	13.97	...
July	...	...	1.02	...	2.00	...	...	2.67	3.46	...	...	173.34	14.76	...
August	...	...	1.04	...	2.00	...	...	2.62	3.40	...	...	179.25	15.29	...
September	...	...	1.07	...	2.00	...	...	2.60	3.37	...	...	180.92	15.49	...
October	...	...	1.05	...	2.00	...	...	2.61	3.36	...	...	186.57	15.89	...
November	...	...	1.08	...	2.00	...	...	2.60	3.35	...	...	191.49	16.11	...
December	...	...	1.10	...	2.00	...	...	2.58	3.31	...	...	196.78	16.54	...
1950														
January	...	1.50	1.07	...	2.00	...	...	2.57	3.24	...	...	199.75	16.88	...
February	...	1.50	1.12	...	2.00	...	...	2.58	3.24	...	...	203.31	17.21	...
March	...	1.50	1.12	...	2.00	...	...	2.58	3.24	...	...	206.25	17.35	...
April	...	1.50	1.15	...	2.00	...	...	2.60	3.23	...	...	212.76	17.84	...
May	...	1.50	1.16	...	2.00	...	...	2.61	3.25	...	...	219.30	18.44	...
June	...	1.50	1.15	...	2.00	...	...	2.62	3.28	...	...	221.02	18.74	...
July	...	1.50	1.16	...	2.00	...	...	2.65	3.32	...	...	205.31	17.38	...
August	...	1.59	1.20	...	2.00	...	...	2.61	3.23	...	...	216.61	18.43	...
September	...	1.75	1.30	...	2.08	...	...	2.64	3.21	...	...	223.20	19.08	...
October	...	1.75	1.31	...	2.25	...	...	2.67	3.22	...	...	229.24	19.87	...
November	...	1.75	1.36	...	2.25	...	...	2.67	3.22	...	...	229.08	19.83	...
December	...	1.75	1.34	...	2.25	...	...	2.67	3.20	...	...	229.18	19.75	...

[1] Federal Reserve Bank of New York. Through 2002, represents the rate for adjustment credit. Beginning in 2003, represents the rate for primary credit. See Notes and Definitions.
[2] 1941–1943 = 10.
... = Not available.

Table 20-6. Interest Rates, Bond Yields, and Stock Price Indexes—Continued

(Not seasonally adjusted.)

Year and month	Short-term rates					U.S. Treasury securities		Bond yields			Fixed-rate first mortgages	Stock price indexes		
	Federal funds	Federal reserve discount rate [1]	U.S. Treasury bills, 3-month	U.S. Treasury bills, 6-month	Bank prime rate	1-year	10-year	Domestic corporate (Moody's)		State and local bonds (Bond Buyer)		Dow Jones industrials (30 stocks)	Standard and Poor's composite (500 stocks) [2]	Nasdaq composite
								Aaa	Baa					
1951														
January	...	1.75	1.34	...	2.44	...	...	2.66	3.17	...	...	244.41	21.21	...
February	...	1.75	1.36	...	2.50	...	...	2.66	3.16	...	...	253.16	22.00	...
March	...	1.75	1.40	...	2.50	...	...	2.78	3.23	...	...	249.36	21.63	...
April	...	1.75	1.47	...	2.50	...	...	2.87	3.35	...	...	253.02	21.92	...
May	...	1.75	1.55	...	2.50	...	...	2.89	3.40	...	...	254.45	21.93	...
June	...	1.75	1.45	...	2.50	...	...	2.94	3.49	...	...	249.32	21.55	...
July	...	1.75	1.56	...	2.50	...	...	2.94	3.53	...	...	253.61	21.93	...
August	...	1.75	1.62	...	2.50	...	...	2.88	3.50	...	...	264.93	22.89	...
September	...	1.75	1.63	...	2.50	...	...	2.84	3.46	...	...	273.37	23.48	...
October	...	1.75	1.54	...	2.62	...	...	2.89	3.50	...	...	269.85	23.36	...
November	...	1.75	1.56	...	2.75	...	...	2.96	3.56	...	...	259.65	22.71	...
December	...	1.75	1.73	...	2.85	...	...	3.01	3.61	...	...	266.15	23.41	...
1952														
January	...	1.75	1.57	...	3.00	...	...	2.98	3.59	...	...	271.64	24.19	...
February	...	1.75	1.54	...	3.00	...	...	2.93	3.53	...	...	264.72	23.75	...
March	...	1.75	1.59	...	3.00	...	...	2.96	3.51	...	...	264.45	23.81	...
April	...	1.75	1.57	...	3.00	...	...	2.93	3.50	...	...	262.46	23.74	...
May	...	1.75	1.67	...	3.00	...	...	2.93	3.49	...	...	261.63	23.73	...
June	...	1.75	1.70	...	3.00	...	...	2.94	3.50	...	...	268.39	24.38	...
July	...	1.75	1.81	...	3.00	...	...	2.95	3.50	...	...	276.05	25.08	...
August	...	1.75	1.83	...	3.00	...	...	2.94	3.51	...	...	276.70	25.18	...
September	...	1.75	1.71	...	3.00	...	...	2.95	3.52	...	...	272.41	24.78	...
October	...	1.75	1.74	...	3.00	...	...	3.01	3.54	...	...	267.78	24.26	...
November	...	1.75	1.85	...	3.00	...	...	2.98	3.53	...	...	276.38	25.03	...
December	...	1.75	2.09	...	3.00	...	...	2.97	3.51	...	...	285.96	26.04	...
1953														
January	...	1.88	1.96	...	3.00	...	...	3.02	3.51	2.44	...	288.45	26.18	...
February	...	2.00	1.97	...	3.00	...	...	3.07	3.53	2.59	...	283.96	25.86	...
March	...	2.00	2.01	...	3.00	...	...	3.12	3.57	2.65	...	286.79	25.99	...
April	...	2.00	2.19	...	3.03	2.36	2.83	3.23	3.65	2.67	...	275.29	24.71	...
May	...	2.00	2.16	...	3.25	2.48	3.05	3.34	3.78	2.82	...	276.84	24.84	...
June	...	2.00	2.11	...	3.25	2.45	3.11	3.40	3.86	3.03	...	266.89	23.95	...
July	...	2.00	2.04	...	3.25	2.38	2.93	3.28	3.86	2.95	...	270.33	24.29	...
August	...	2.00	2.04	...	3.25	2.28	2.95	3.24	3.85	2.90	...	272.20	24.39	...
September	...	2.00	1.79	...	3.25	2.20	2.87	3.29	3.88	2.87	...	261.90	23.27	...
October	...	2.00	1.38	...	3.25	1.79	2.66	3.16	3.82	2.71	...	270.72	23.97	...
November	...	2.00	1.44	...	3.25	1.67	2.68	3.11	3.75	2.60	...	277.09	24.50	...
December	...	2.00	1.60	...	3.25	1.66	2.59	3.13	3.74	2.59	...	281.15	24.83	...
1954														
January	...	2.00	1.18	...	3.25	1.41	2.48	3.06	3.71	2.50	...	286.64	25.46	...
February	...	1.79	0.97	...	3.25	1.14	2.47	2.95	3.61	2.42	...	292.13	26.02	...
March	...	1.75	1.03	...	3.13	1.13	2.37	2.86	3.51	2.39	...	299.16	26.57	...
April	...	1.63	0.97	...	3.00	0.96	2.29	2.85	3.47	2.47	...	310.93	27.63	...
May	...	1.50	0.76	...	3.00	0.85	2.37	2.88	3.47	2.49	...	322.85	28.73	...
June	...	1.50	0.64	...	3.00	0.82	2.38	2.90	3.49	2.47	...	327.91	28.96	...
July	0.80	1.50	0.72	...	3.00	0.84	2.30	2.89	3.50	2.32	...	341.27	30.13	...
August	1.22	1.50	0.92	...	3.00	0.88	2.36	2.87	3.49	2.26	...	346.06	30.73	...
September	1.06	1.50	1.01	...	3.00	1.03	2.38	2.89	3.47	2.31	...	352.71	31.45	...
October	0.85	1.50	0.98	...	3.00	1.17	2.43	2.87	3.46	2.34	...	358.29	32.18	...
November	0.83	1.50	0.93	...	3.00	1.14	2.48	2.89	3.45	2.32	...	375.71	33.44	...
December	1.28	1.50	1.15	...	3.00	1.21	2.51	2.90	3.45	2.36	...	393.84	34.97	...
1955														
January	1.39	1.50	1.22	...	3.00	1.39	2.61	2.93	3.45	2.40	...	398.43	35.60	...
February	1.29	1.50	1.17	...	3.00	1.57	2.65	2.93	3.47	2.43	...	410.26	36.79	...
March	1.35	1.50	1.28	...	3.00	1.59	2.68	3.02	3.48	2.44	...	408.91	36.50	...
April	1.43	1.63	1.59	...	3.00	1.75	2.75	3.01	3.49	2.41	...	423.00	37.76	...
May	1.43	1.75	1.45	...	3.00	1.90	2.76	3.04	3.50	2.38	...	421.55	37.60	...
June	1.64	1.75	1.41	...	3.00	1.91	2.78	3.05	3.51	2.41	...	440.83	39.78	...
July	1.68	1.75	1.60	...	3.00	2.02	2.90	3.06	3.52	2.54	...	462.17	42.69	...
August	1.96	1.97	1.90	...	3.23	2.37	2.97	3.11	3.56	2.60	...	457.31	42.43	...
September	2.18	2.18	2.07	...	3.25	2.36	2.97	3.13	3.59	2.58	...	476.44	44.34	...
October	2.24	2.25	2.23	...	3.40	2.39	2.88	3.10	3.59	2.51	...	452.65	42.11	...
November	2.35	2.36	2.24	...	3.50	2.48	2.89	3.10	3.58	2.45	...	476.60	44.95	...
December	2.48	2.50	2.54	...	3.50	2.73	2.96	3.15	3.62	2.57	...	484.58	45.37	...
1956														
January	2.45	2.50	2.41	...	3.50	2.58	2.90	3.11	3.60	2.50	...	474.75	44.15	...
February	2.50	2.50	2.32	...	3.50	2.49	2.84	3.08	3.58	2.44	...	475.53	44.43	...
March	2.50	2.50	2.25	...	3.50	2.61	2.96	3.10	3.60	2.57	...	502.67	47.49	...
April	2.62	2.65	2.60	...	3.65	2.92	3.18	3.24	3.68	2.70	...	511.05	48.05	...
May	2.75	2.75	2.61	...	3.75	2.94	3.07	3.28	3.73	2.68	...	495.21	46.54	...
June	2.71	2.75	2.49	...	3.75	2.74	3.00	3.26	3.76	2.54	...	485.33	46.27	...
July	2.75	2.75	2.31	...	3.75	2.76	3.11	3.28	3.80	2.65	...	509.75	48.78	...
August	2.73	2.81	2.60	...	3.84	3.10	3.33	3.43	3.93	2.80	...	511.69	48.49	...
September	2.95	3.00	2.84	...	4.00	3.35	3.38	3.56	4.07	2.93	...	495.03	46.84	...
October	2.96	3.00	2.90	...	4.00	3.28	3.34	3.59	4.17	2.95	...	483.81	46.24	...
November	2.88	3.00	2.99	...	4.00	3.44	3.49	3.69	4.24	3.16	...	479.36	45.76	...
December	2.94	3.00	3.21	...	4.00	3.68	3.59	3.75	4.37	3.22	...	492.02	46.44	...

[1] Federal Reserve Bank of New York. Through 2002, represents the rate for adjustment credit. Beginning in 2003, represents the rate for primary credit. See Notes and Definitions.
[2] 1941–1943 = 10.
... = Not available.

Table 20-6. Interest Rates, Bond Yields, and Stock Price Indexes—Continued

(Not seasonally adjusted.)

Year and month	Short-term rates					U.S. Treasury securities		Bond yields			Fixed-rate first mortgages	Stock price indexes		
	Federal funds	Federal reserve discount rate [1]	U.S. Treasury bills, 3-month	U.S. Treasury bills, 6-month	Bank prime rate	1-year	10-year	Domestic corporate (Moody's)		State and local bonds (Bond Buyer)		Dow Jones industrials (30 stocks)	Standard and Poor's composite (500 stocks) [2]	Nasdaq composite
								Aaa	Baa					
1957														
January	2.84	3.00	3.11	...	4.00	3.37	3.46	3.77	4.49	3.18	...	485.90	45.43	...
February	3.00	3.00	3.10	...	4.00	3.38	3.34	3.67	4.47	3.00	...	466.83	43.47	...
March	2.96	3.00	3.08	...	4.00	3.42	3.41	3.66	4.43	3.09	...	472.77	44.03	...
April	3.00	3.00	3.07	...	4.00	3.49	3.48	3.67	4.44	3.13	...	485.42	45.05	...
May	3.00	3.00	3.06	...	4.00	3.48	3.60	3.74	4.52	3.27	...	500.83	46.78	...
June	3.00	3.00	3.29	...	4.00	3.65	3.80	3.91	4.63	3.41	...	505.29	47.55	...
July	2.99	3.00	3.16	...	4.00	3.81	3.93	3.99	4.73	3.39	...	514.65	48.51	...
August	3.24	3.15	3.37	...	4.42	4.01	3.93	4.10	4.82	3.54	...	487.97	45.84	...
September	3.47	3.50	3.53	...	4.50	4.07	3.92	4.12	4.93	3.53	...	471.80	43.98	...
October	3.50	3.50	3.58	...	4.50	4.01	3.97	4.10	4.99	3.42	...	443.38	41.24	...
November	3.28	3.23	3.31	...	4.50	3.57	3.72	4.08	5.09	3.37	...	436.73	40.35	...
December	2.98	3.00	3.04	...	4.50	3.18	3.21	3.81	5.03	3.04	...	436.96	40.33	...
1958														
January	2.72	2.94	2.44	...	4.34	2.65	3.09	3.60	4.83	2.91	...	445.69	41.12	...
February	1.67	2.75	1.53	...	4.00	1.99	3.05	3.59	4.66	3.02	...	444.16	41.26	...
March	1.20	2.35	1.30	...	4.00	1.84	2.98	3.63	4.68	3.06	...	450.15	42.11	...
April	1.26	2.03	1.13	...	3.83	1.45	2.88	3.60	4.67	2.96	...	446.91	42.34	...
May	0.63	1.75	0.91	...	3.50	1.37	2.92	3.57	4.62	2.92	...	460.04	43.70	...
June	0.93	1.75	0.83	...	3.50	1.23	2.97	3.57	4.55	2.97	...	471.98	44.75	...
July	0.68	1.75	0.91	...	3.50	1.61	3.20	3.67	4.53	3.09	...	488.30	45.98	...
August	1.53	1.75	1.69	...	3.50	2.50	3.54	3.85	4.67	3.35	...	507.55	47.70	...
September	1.76	1.91	2.44	...	3.83	3.05	3.76	4.09	4.87	3.54	...	521.81	48.96	...
October	1.80	2.00	2.63	...	4.00	3.19	3.80	4.11	4.92	3.45	...	539.85	50.95	...
November	2.27	2.40	2.67	...	4.00	3.10	3.74	4.09	4.87	3.32	...	557.11	52.50	...
December	2.42	2.50	2.77	3.01	4.00	3.29	3.86	4.08	4.85	3.33	...	566.44	53.49	...
1959														
January	2.48	2.50	2.82	3.09	4.00	3.36	4.02	4.12	4.87	3.42	...	592.30	55.62	...
February	2.43	2.50	2.70	3.13	4.00	3.54	3.96	4.14	4.89	3.36	...	590.72	54.77	...
March	2.80	2.92	2.80	3.13	4.00	3.61	3.99	4.13	4.85	3.30	...	609.13	56.15	...
April	2.96	3.00	2.95	3.27	4.00	3.72	4.12	4.23	4.86	3.39	...	617.00	57.10	...
May	2.90	3.05	2.84	3.33	4.23	3.96	4.31	4.37	4.96	3.57	...	630.80	57.96	...
June	3.39	3.50	3.21	3.52	4.50	4.07	4.34	4.46	5.04	3.71	...	631.52	57.46	...
July	3.47	3.50	3.20	3.82	4.50	4.39	4.40	4.47	5.08	3.71	...	662.81	59.74	...
August	3.50	3.50	3.38	3.87	4.50	4.42	4.43	4.43	5.09	3.58	...	660.58	59.40	...
September	3.76	3.83	4.04	4.70	5.00	5.00	4.68	4.52	5.18	3.78	...	635.49	57.05	...
October	3.98	4.00	4.05	4.53	5.00	4.80	4.53	4.57	5.28	3.62	...	637.35	57.00	...
November	4.00	4.00	4.15	4.54	5.00	4.81	4.53	4.56	5.26	3.55	...	646.43	57.23	...
December	3.99	4.00	4.49	4.85	5.00	5.14	4.69	4.58	5.28	3.70	...	671.36	59.06	...
1960														
January	3.99	4.00	4.35	4.74	5.00	5.03	4.72	4.61	5.34	3.72	...	655.39	58.03	...
February	3.97	4.00	3.96	4.30	5.00	4.66	4.49	4.56	5.34	3.60	...	624.89	55.78	...
March	3.84	4.00	3.31	3.61	5.00	4.02	4.25	4.49	5.25	3.57	...	614.70	55.02	...
April	3.92	4.00	3.23	3.55	5.00	4.04	4.28	4.45	5.20	3.56	...	619.98	55.73	...
May	3.85	4.00	3.29	3.58	5.00	4.21	4.35	4.46	5.28	3.60	...	615.63	55.22	...
June	3.32	3.65	2.46	2.74	5.00	3.36	4.15	4.45	5.26	3.55	...	644.39	57.26	...
July	3.23	3.50	2.30	2.71	5.00	3.20	3.90	4.41	5.22	3.50	...	625.83	55.84	...
August	2.98	3.18	2.30	2.59	4.85	2.95	3.80	4.28	5.08	3.33	...	624.47	56.51	...
September	2.60	3.00	2.48	2.83	4.50	3.07	3.80	4.25	5.01	3.42	...	598.10	54.81	...
October	2.47	3.00	2.30	2.73	4.50	3.04	3.89	4.30	5.11	3.53	...	582.47	53.73	...
November	2.44	3.00	2.37	2.66	4.50	3.08	3.93	4.31	5.08	3.40	...	601.14	55.47	...
December	1.98	3.00	2.25	2.50	4.50	2.86	3.84	4.35	5.10	3.40	...	609.54	56.80	...
1961														
January	1.45	3.00	2.24	2.47	4.50	2.81	3.84	4.32	5.10	3.39	...	632.20	59.72	...
February	2.54	3.00	2.42	2.60	4.50	2.93	3.78	4.27	5.07	3.31	...	650.02	62.17	...
March	2.02	3.00	2.39	2.54	4.50	2.88	3.74	4.22	5.02	3.45	...	670.57	64.12	...
April	1.49	3.00	2.29	2.47	4.50	2.88	3.78	4.25	5.01	3.48	...	684.90	65.83	...
May	1.98	3.00	2.29	2.45	4.50	2.87	3.71	4.27	5.01	3.43	...	693.03	66.50	...
June	1.73	3.00	2.33	2.54	4.50	3.06	3.88	4.33	5.03	3.52	...	691.46	65.62	...
July	1.17	3.00	2.24	2.45	4.50	2.92	3.92	4.41	5.09	3.51	...	690.67	65.44	...
August	2.00	3.00	2.39	2.66	4.50	3.06	4.04	4.45	5.11	3.52	...	718.64	67.79	...
September	1.88	3.00	2.28	2.68	4.50	3.06	3.98	4.45	5.12	3.53	...	711.02	67.26	...
October	2.26	3.00	2.30	2.66	4.50	3.05	3.92	4.42	5.13	3.42	...	703.01	68.00	...
November	2.61	3.00	2.48	2.70	4.50	3.07	3.94	4.39	5.11	3.41	...	724.74	71.08	...
December	2.33	3.00	2.60	2.88	4.50	3.18	4.06	4.42	5.10	3.47	...	728.44	71.74	...
1962														
January	2.15	3.00	2.72	2.94	4.50	3.28	4.08	4.42	5.08	3.34	...	705.15	69.07	...
February	2.37	3.00	2.73	2.93	4.50	3.28	4.04	4.42	5.07	3.21	...	711.95	70.22	...
March	2.85	3.00	2.72	2.87	4.50	3.06	3.93	4.39	5.04	3.14	...	714.20	70.29	...
April	2.78	3.00	2.73	2.83	4.50	2.99	3.84	4.33	5.02	3.06	...	690.29	68.05	...
May	2.36	3.00	2.69	2.78	4.50	3.03	3.87	4.28	5.00	3.11	...	643.71	62.99	...
June	2.68	3.00	2.73	2.80	4.50	3.03	3.91	4.28	5.02	3.25	...	572.65	55.63	...
July	2.71	3.00	2.92	3.08	4.50	3.29	4.01	4.34	5.05	3.27	...	581.79	56.97	...
August	2.93	3.00	2.82	2.99	4.50	3.20	3.98	4.35	5.06	3.23	...	602.50	58.52	...
September	2.90	3.00	2.78	2.93	4.50	3.06	3.98	4.32	5.03	3.11	...	597.02	58.00	...
October	2.90	3.00	2.74	2.84	4.50	2.98	3.93	4.28	4.99	3.02	...	580.67	56.17	...
November	2.94	3.00	2.83	2.89	4.50	3.00	3.92	4.25	4.96	3.04	...	628.83	60.04	...
December	2.93	3.00	2.87	2.91	4.50	3.01	3.86	4.24	4.92	3.07	...	648.38	62.64	...

[1] Federal Reserve Bank of New York. Through 2002, represents the rate for adjustment credit. Beginning in 2003, represents the rate for primary credit. See Notes and Definitions.
[2] 1941–1943 = 10.
... = Not available.

Table 20-6. Interest Rates, Bond Yields, and Stock Price Indexes—Continued

(Not seasonally adjusted.)

Year and month	Short-term rates					U.S. Treasury securities		Bond yields			Fixed-rate first mortgages	Stock price indexes		
	Federal funds	Federal reserve discount rate [1]	U.S. Treasury bills, 3-month	U.S. Treasury bills, 6-month	Bank prime rate	1-year	10-year	Domestic corporate (Moody's)		State and local bonds (Bond Buyer)		Dow Jones industrials (30 stocks)	Standard and Poor's composite (500 stocks) [2]	Nasdaq composite
								Aaa	Baa					
1963														
January	2.92	3.00	2.91	2.96	4.50	3.04	3.83	4.21	4.91	3.10	...	672.10	65.06	...
February	3.00	3.00	2.92	2.98	4.50	3.01	3.92	4.19	4.89	3.15	...	679.74	65.92	...
March	2.98	3.00	2.89	2.95	4.50	3.03	3.93	4.19	4.88	3.05	...	674.63	65.67	...
April	2.90	3.00	2.90	2.98	4.50	3.11	3.97	4.21	4.87	3.10	...	707.12	68.76	...
May	3.00	3.00	2.93	3.01	4.50	3.12	3.93	4.22	4.85	3.11	...	720.84	70.14	...
June	2.99	3.00	2.99	3.08	4.50	3.20	3.99	4.23	4.84	3.21	...	719.15	70.11	...
July	3.02	3.24	3.18	3.31	4.50	3.48	4.02	4.26	4.84	3.22	...	700.75	69.07	...
August	3.49	3.50	3.32	3.44	4.50	3.53	4.00	4.29	4.83	3.13	...	714.16	70.98	...
September	3.48	3.50	3.38	3.50	4.50	3.57	4.08	4.31	4.84	3.20	...	738.53	72.85	...
October	3.50	3.50	3.45	3.58	4.50	3.64	4.11	4.32	4.83	3.20	...	747.53	73.03	...
November	3.48	3.50	3.52	3.65	4.50	3.74	4.12	4.33	4.84	3.30	...	743.24	72.62	...
December	3.38	3.50	3.52	3.66	4.50	3.81	4.13	4.35	4.85	3.27	...	759.96	74.17	...
1964														
January	3.48	3.50	3.52	3.64	4.50	3.79	4.17	4.39	4.83	3.22	...	777.07	76.45	...
February	3.48	3.50	3.53	3.67	4.50	3.78	4.15	4.36	4.83	3.14	...	793.02	77.39	...
March	3.43	3.50	3.54	3.72	4.50	3.91	4.22	4.38	4.83	3.28	...	812.19	78.80	...
April	3.47	3.50	3.47	3.66	4.50	3.91	4.23	4.40	4.85	3.28	...	820.96	79.94	...
May	3.50	3.50	3.48	3.60	4.50	3.84	4.20	4.41	4.85	3.20	...	823.13	80.72	...
June	3.50	3.50	3.48	3.56	4.50	3.83	4.17	4.41	4.85	3.20	...	817.65	80.24	...
July	3.42	3.50	3.46	3.56	4.50	3.72	4.19	4.40	4.83	3.18	...	844.25	83.22	...
August	3.50	3.50	3.50	3.61	4.50	3.74	4.19	4.41	4.82	3.19	...	835.31	82.00	...
September	3.45	3.50	3.53	3.68	4.50	3.84	4.20	4.42	4.82	3.23	...	863.55	83.41	...
October	3.36	3.50	3.57	3.72	4.50	3.86	4.19	4.42	4.81	3.25	...	875.27	84.85	...
November	3.52	3.62	3.64	3.81	4.50	3.91	4.15	4.43	4.81	3.18	...	880.03	85.44	...
December	3.85	4.00	3.84	3.95	4.50	4.02	4.18	4.44	4.81	3.13	...	866.73	83.96	...
1965														
January	3.90	4.00	3.81	3.94	4.50	3.94	4.19	4.43	4.80	3.06	...	889.91	86.12	...
February	3.98	4.00	3.93	4.00	4.50	4.03	4.21	4.41	4.78	3.09	...	894.42	86.75	...
March	4.04	4.00	3.93	4.00	4.50	4.06	4.21	4.42	4.78	3.17	...	896.45	86.83	...
April	4.09	4.00	3.93	3.99	4.50	4.04	4.20	4.43	4.80	3.15	...	907.72	87.97	...
May	4.10	4.00	3.89	3.95	4.50	4.03	4.21	4.44	4.81	3.17	...	927.50	89.28	...
June	4.04	4.00	3.80	3.86	4.50	3.99	4.21	4.46	4.85	3.24	...	878.07	85.04	...
July	4.09	4.00	3.84	3.90	4.50	3.98	4.20	4.48	4.88	3.27	...	873.44	84.91	...
August	4.12	4.00	3.84	3.95	4.50	4.07	4.25	4.49	4.88	3.24	...	887.71	86.49	...
September	4.01	4.00	3.92	4.07	4.50	4.20	4.29	4.52	4.91	3.35	...	922.20	89.38	...
October	4.08	4.00	4.03	4.19	4.50	4.30	4.35	4.56	4.93	3.40	...	944.78	91.39	...
November	4.10	4.00	4.09	4.24	4.50	4.37	4.45	4.60	4.95	3.45	...	953.31	92.15	...
December	4.32	4.42	4.38	4.55	4.92	4.72	4.62	4.68	5.02	3.54	...	955.20	91.73	...
1966														
January	4.42	4.50	4.59	4.71	5.00	4.88	4.61	4.74	5.06	3.52	...	985.93	93.32	...
February	4.60	4.50	4.65	4.82	5.00	4.94	4.83	4.78	5.12	3.64	...	977.15	92.69	...
March	4.65	4.50	4.59	4.78	5.35	4.97	4.87	4.92	5.32	3.72	...	926.43	88.88	...
April	4.67	4.50	4.62	4.74	5.50	4.75	4.75	4.96	5.41	3.56	...	943.46	91.60	...
May	4.90	4.50	4.64	4.81	5.50	4.93	4.78	4.98	5.48	3.65	...	890.71	86.78	...
June	5.17	4.50	4.50	4.65	5.52	4.97	4.81	5.07	5.58	3.77	...	888.83	86.06	...
July	5.30	4.50	4.80	4.93	5.75	5.17	5.02	5.16	5.68	3.95	...	875.89	85.84	...
August	5.53	4.50	4.96	5.27	5.88	5.54	5.22	5.31	5.83	4.12	...	817.55	80.65	...
September	5.40	4.50	5.37	5.79	6.00	5.82	5.18	5.49	6.09	4.12	...	791.66	77.81	...
October	5.53	4.50	5.35	5.62	6.00	5.58	5.01	5.41	6.10	3.93	...	778.11	77.13	...
November	5.76	4.50	5.32	5.54	6.00	5.54	5.16	5.35	6.13	3.86	...	806.56	80.99	...
December	5.40	4.50	4.96	5.07	6.00	5.20	4.84	5.39	6.18	3.86	...	800.88	81.33	...
1967														
January	4.94	4.50	4.72	4.74	5.96	4.75	4.58	5.20	5.97	3.54	...	830.55	84.45	...
February	5.00	4.50	4.56	4.59	5.75	4.71	4.63	5.03	5.82	3.52	...	851.12	87.36	...
March	4.53	4.50	4.26	4.22	5.71	4.35	4.54	5.13	5.85	3.55	...	858.12	89.42	...
April	4.05	4.10	3.84	3.89	5.50	4.11	4.59	5.11	5.83	3.60	...	868.66	90.96	...
May	3.94	4.00	3.60	3.80	5.50	4.15	4.85	5.24	5.96	3.89	...	883.74	92.59	...
June	3.98	4.00	3.54	3.89	5.50	4.48	5.02	5.44	6.15	3.96	...	872.66	91.43	...
July	3.79	4.00	4.21	4.72	5.50	5.01	5.16	5.58	6.26	4.02	...	888.51	93.01	...
August	3.90	4.00	4.27	4.83	5.50	5.13	5.28	5.62	6.33	3.99	...	912.48	94.49	...
September	3.99	4.00	4.42	4.96	5.50	5.24	5.30	5.65	6.40	4.12	...	923.46	95.81	...
October	3.88	4.00	4.56	5.07	5.50	5.37	5.48	5.82	6.52	4.29	...	907.55	95.66	...
November	4.13	4.18	4.73	5.25	5.68	5.61	5.75	6.07	6.72	4.34	...	865.44	92.66	...
December	4.51	4.50	4.97	5.49	6.00	5.71	5.70	6.19	6.93	4.43	...	887.20	95.30	...
1968														
January	4.60	4.50	5.00	5.24	6.00	5.43	5.53	6.17	6.84	4.29	...	884.78	95.04	...
February	4.71	4.50	4.98	5.17	6.00	5.41	5.56	6.10	6.80	4.31	...	847.20	90.75	...
March	5.05	4.66	5.17	5.33	6.00	5.58	5.74	6.11	6.85	4.54	...	834.76	89.09	...
April	5.76	5.20	5.38	5.49	6.20	5.71	5.64	6.21	6.97	4.34	...	893.38	95.67	...
May	6.11	5.50	5.66	5.83	6.50	6.14	5.87	6.27	7.03	4.54	...	905.23	97.87	...
June	6.07	5.50	5.52	5.64	6.50	5.98	5.72	6.28	7.07	4.49	...	906.82	100.53	...
July	6.02	5.50	5.31	5.41	6.50	5.65	5.50	6.24	6.98	4.33	...	905.33	100.30	...
August	6.03	5.48	5.09	5.23	6.50	5.43	5.42	6.02	6.82	4.21	...	883.73	98.11	...
September	5.78	5.25	5.19	5.25	6.45	5.45	5.46	5.97	6.79	4.38	...	922.82	101.34	...
October	5.91	5.25	5.35	5.41	6.25	5.57	5.58	6.09	6.84	4.49	...	955.48	103.76	...
November	5.82	5.25	5.45	5.60	6.25	5.75	5.70	6.19	7.01	4.60	...	964.13	105.40	...
December	6.02	5.36	5.96	6.06	6.60	6.19	6.03	6.45	7.23	4.82	...	968.39	106.48	...

[1] Federal Reserve Bank of New York. Through 2002, represents the rate for adjustment credit. Beginning in 2003, represents the rate for primary credit. See Notes and Definitions.
[2] 1941–1943 = 10.
... = Not available.

Table 20-6. Interest Rates, Bond Yields, and Stock Price Indexes—Continued

(Not seasonally adjusted.)

Year and month	Short-term rates					U.S. Treasury securities		Bond yields			Fixed-rate first mortgages	Stock price indexes		
	Federal funds	Federal reserve discount rate [1]	U.S. Treasury bills, 3-month	U.S. Treasury bills, 6-month	Bank prime rate	1-year	10-year	Domestic corporate (Moody's)		State and local bonds (Bond Buyer)		Dow Jones industrials (30 stocks)	Standard and Poor's composite (500 stocks) [2]	Nasdaq composite
								Aaa	Baa					
1969														
January	6.30	5.50	6.14	6.28	6.95	6.34	6.04	6.59	7.32	4.85	...	935.00	102.04	...
February	6.61	5.50	6.12	6.30	7.00	6.41	6.19	6.66	7.30	4.98	...	931.31	101.46	...
March	6.79	5.50	6.02	6.16	7.24	6.34	6.30	6.85	7.51	5.26	...	916.52	99.30	...
April	7.41	5.95	6.11	6.13	7.50	6.26	6.17	6.89	7.54	5.19	...	927.38	101.26	...
May	8.67	6.00	6.04	6.15	7.50	6.42	6.32	6.79	7.52	5.33	...	954.88	104.62	...
June	8.90	6.00	6.44	6.75	8.23	7.04	6.57	6.98	7.70	5.75	...	896.62	99.14	...
July	8.61	6.00	7.00	7.24	8.50	7.60	6.72	7.08	7.84	5.75	...	844.02	94.71	...
August	9.19	6.00	6.98	7.19	8.50	7.54	6.69	6.97	7.86	6.00	...	825.46	94.18	...
September	9.15	6.00	7.09	7.32	8.50	7.82	7.16	7.14	8.05	6.26	...	826.72	94.51	...
October	9.00	6.00	7.00	7.29	8.50	7.64	7.10	7.33	8.22	6.09	...	832.52	95.52	...
November	8.85	6.00	7.24	7.62	8.50	7.89	7.14	7.35	8.25	6.30	...	841.10	96.21	...
December	8.97	6.00	7.82	7.90	8.50	8.17	7.65	7.72	8.65	6.82	...	789.23	91.11	...
1970														
January	8.98	6.00	7.87	7.78	8.50	8.10	7.79	7.91	8.86	6.63	...	782.93	90.31	...
February	8.98	6.00	7.13	7.22	8.50	7.59	7.24	7.93	8.78	6.22	...	756.22	87.16	...
March	7.76	6.00	6.63	6.58	8.39	6.97	7.07	7.84	8.63	6.05	...	777.63	88.65	...
April	8.10	6.00	6.51	6.60	8.00	7.06	7.39	7.83	8.70	6.65	...	771.65	85.95	...
May	7.94	6.00	6.84	7.02	8.00	7.75	7.91	8.11	8.98	7.00	...	691.97	76.06	...
June	7.60	6.00	6.68	6.86	8.00	7.55	7.84	8.48	9.25	6.93	...	699.30	75.59	...
July	7.21	6.00	6.45	6.51	8.00	7.10	7.46	8.44	9.40	6.42	...	712.81	75.72	...
August	6.61	6.00	6.41	6.55	8.00	6.98	7.53	8.13	9.44	6.17	...	731.98	77.92	...
September	6.29	6.00	6.12	6.46	7.83	6.73	7.39	8.09	9.39	6.31	...	759.39	82.58	...
October	6.20	6.00	5.91	6.21	7.50	6.43	7.33	8.03	9.33	6.37	...	763.74	84.37	...
November	5.60	5.85	5.28	5.42	7.28	5.51	6.84	8.05	9.38	5.71	...	769.28	84.28	...
December	4.90	5.52	4.87	4.89	6.92	5.00	6.39	7.64	9.12	5.47	...	821.51	90.05	...
1971														
January	4.14	5.23	4.44	4.47	6.29	4.57	6.24	7.36	8.74	5.35	...	849.04	93.49	...
February	3.72	4.91	3.70	3.78	5.88	3.89	6.11	7.08	8.39	5.23	...	879.69	97.11	...
March	3.71	4.75	3.38	3.50	5.44	3.69	5.70	7.21	8.46	5.17	...	901.29	99.60	...
April	4.15	4.75	3.86	4.03	5.28	4.30	5.83	7.25	8.45	5.37	7.31	932.54	103.04	...
May	4.63	4.75	4.14	4.36	5.46	5.04	6.39	7.53	8.62	5.90	7.43	925.51	101.64	...
June	4.91	4.75	4.75	4.97	5.50	5.64	6.52	7.64	8.75	5.95	7.53	900.45	99.72	...
July	5.31	4.88	5.40	5.63	5.91	6.04	6.73	7.64	8.76	6.06	7.60	887.81	99.00	...
August	5.56	5.00	4.94	5.22	6.00	5.80	6.58	7.59	8.76	5.82	7.70	875.41	97.24	...
September	5.55	5.00	4.69	4.97	6.00	5.41	6.14	7.44	8.59	5.37	7.69	901.22	99.40	...
October	5.20	5.00	4.46	4.60	5.90	4.91	5.93	7.39	8.48	5.06	7.63	872.15	97.29	...
November	4.91	4.90	4.22	4.38	5.53	4.67	5.81	7.26	8.38	5.20	7.55	822.11	92.78	...
December	4.14	4.63	4.01	4.23	5.49	4.60	5.93	7.25	8.38	5.21	7.48	869.92	99.17	...
1972														
January	3.50	4.50	3.38	3.66	5.18	4.28	5.95	7.19	8.23	5.12	7.44	904.65	103.30	...
February	3.29	4.50	3.20	3.63	4.75	4.27	6.08	7.27	8.23	5.28	7.33	914.37	105.24	...
March	3.83	4.50	3.73	4.12	4.75	4.67	6.07	7.24	8.24	5.31	7.30	939.23	107.69	...
April	4.17	4.50	3.71	4.23	4.97	4.96	6.19	7.30	8.24	5.43	7.29	958.17	108.81	...
May	4.27	4.50	3.69	4.12	5.00	4.64	6.13	7.30	8.23	5.30	7.37	948.22	107.65	...
June	4.46	4.50	3.91	4.35	5.04	4.93	6.11	7.23	8.20	5.33	7.37	943.44	108.01	...
July	4.55	4.50	3.98	4.50	5.25	4.96	6.11	7.21	8.23	5.41	7.40	925.94	107.21	...
August	4.80	4.50	4.02	4.55	5.27	4.98	6.21	7.19	8.19	5.30	7.40	958.36	111.01	...
September	4.87	4.50	4.66	5.13	5.50	5.52	6.55	7.22	8.09	5.36	7.42	950.60	109.39	...
October	5.04	4.50	4.74	5.13	5.73	5.52	6.48	7.21	8.06	5.18	7.42	944.10	109.56	...
November	5.06	4.50	4.78	5.09	5.75	5.27	6.28	7.12	7.99	5.02	7.43	1 001.20	115.05	...
December	5.33	4.50	5.07	5.30	5.79	5.52	6.36	7.08	7.93	5.05	7.44	1 020.32	117.50	...
1973														
January	5.94	4.77	5.41	5.62	6.00	5.89	6.46	7.15	7.90	5.05	7.44	1 026.82	118.42	...
February	6.58	5.05	5.60	5.83	6.02	6.19	6.64	7.22	7.97	5.13	7.44	974.05	114.16	...
March	7.09	5.50	6.09	6.51	6.30	6.85	6.71	7.29	8.03	5.29	7.46	957.36	112.42	...
April	7.12	5.50	6.26	6.52	6.61	6.85	6.67	7.26	8.09	5.15	7.54	944.12	110.27	...
May	7.84	5.90	6.36	6.62	7.01	6.89	6.85	7.29	8.06	5.15	7.65	922.41	107.22	...
June	8.49	6.33	7.19	7.23	7.49	7.31	6.90	7.37	8.13	5.17	7.73	893.90	104.75	...
July	10.40	6.98	8.01	8.12	8.30	8.39	7.13	7.45	8.24	5.40	8.05	903.61	105.83	...
August	10.50	7.29	8.67	8.65	9.23	8.82	7.40	7.68	8.53	5.48	8.50	883.73	103.80	...
September	10.78	7.50	8.29	8.45	9.86	8.31	7.09	7.63	8.63	5.10	8.82	909.99	105.61	...
October	10.01	7.50	7.22	7.32	9.94	7.40	6.79	7.60	8.41	5.05	8.77	967.63	109.84	...
November	10.03	7.50	7.83	7.96	9.75	7.57	6.73	7.67	8.42	5.18	8.58	878.99	102.03	...
December	9.95	7.50	7.45	7.56	9.75	7.27	6.74	7.68	8.48	5.12	8.54	824.08	94.78	...
1974														
January	9.65	7.50	7.77	7.65	9.73	7.42	6.99	7.83	8.48	5.22	8.54	857.25	96.11	...
February	8.97	7.50	7.12	6.96	9.21	6.88	6.96	7.85	8.53	5.20	8.46	831.33	93.45	...
March	9.35	7.50	7.96	7.83	8.85	7.76	7.21	8.01	8.62	5.40	8.41	874.01	97.44	...
April	10.51	7.60	8.33	8.32	10.02	8.62	7.51	8.25	8.87	5.73	8.58	847.79	92.46	...
May	11.31	8.00	8.23	8.40	11.25	8.78	7.58	8.37	9.05	6.02	8.97	830.26	89.67	...
June	11.93	8.00	7.90	8.12	11.54	8.67	7.54	8.47	9.27	6.13	9.09	831.45	89.79	...
July	12.92	8.00	7.55	7.94	11.97	8.80	7.81	8.72	9.48	6.68	9.28	783.01	82.82	...
August	12.01	8.00	8.96	9.11	12.00	9.36	8.04	9.00	9.77	6.71	9.59	729.30	76.03	...
September	11.34	8.00	8.06	8.53	12.00	8.87	8.04	9.24	10.18	6.76	9.96	651.29	68.12	...
October	10.06	8.00	7.46	7.74	11.68	8.05	7.90	9.27	10.48	6.57	9.98	638.62	69.44	...
November	9.45	8.00	7.47	7.52	10.83	7.66	7.68	8.89	10.60	6.61	9.79	642.11	71.74	...
December	8.53	7.81	7.15	7.11	10.50	7.31	7.43	8.89	10.63	7.05	9.62	596.50	67.07	...

[1] Federal Reserve Bank of New York. Through 2002, represents the rate for adjustment credit. Beginning in 2003, represents the rate for primary credit. See Notes and Definitions.
[2] 1941–1943 = 10.
... = Not available.

Table 20-6. Interest Rates, Bond Yields, and Stock Price Indexes—Continued

(Not seasonally adjusted.)

Year and month	Short-term rates					U.S. Treasury securities		Bond yields			Fixed-rate first mortgages	Stock price indexes		
	Federal funds	Federal reserve discount rate [1]	U.S. Treasury bills, 3-month	U.S. Treasury bills, 6-month	Bank prime rate	1-year	10-year	Domestic corporate (Moody's)		State and local bonds (Bond Buyer)		Dow Jones industrials (30 stocks)	Standard and Poor's composite (500 stocks) [2]	Nasdaq composite
								Aaa	Baa					
1975														
January	7.13	7.40	6.26	6.36	10.05	6.83	7.50	8.83	10.81	6.82	9.43	659.09	72.56	...
February	6.24	6.82	5.50	5.62	8.96	5.98	7.39	8.62	10.65	6.39	9.11	724.89	80.10	...
March	5.54	6.40	5.49	5.62	7.93	6.11	7.73	8.67	10.48	6.73	8.90	765.06	83.78	...
April	5.49	6.25	5.61	6.00	7.50	6.90	8.23	8.95	10.58	6.95	8.82	790.94	84.72	...
May	5.22	6.12	5.23	5.59	7.40	6.39	8.06	8.90	10.69	6.97	8.91	836.55	90.10	...
June	5.55	6.00	5.34	5.61	7.07	6.29	7.86	8.77	10.62	6.94	8.89	845.70	92.40	...
July	6.10	6.00	6.13	6.50	7.15	7.11	8.06	8.84	10.55	7.07	8.89	856.29	92.49	...
August	6.14	6.00	6.44	6.94	7.66	7.70	8.40	8.95	10.59	7.17	8.94	815.52	85.71	...
September	6.24	6.00	6.42	6.92	7.88	7.75	8.43	8.95	10.61	7.44	9.13	818.29	84.67	...
October	5.82	6.00	5.96	6.25	7.96	6.95	8.14	8.86	10.62	7.39	9.22	831.27	88.57	...
November	5.22	6.00	5.48	5.80	7.53	6.49	8.05	8.78	10.56	7.43	9.15	845.52	90.07	...
December	5.20	6.00	5.44	5.85	7.26	6.60	8.00	8.79	10.56	7.31	9.10	840.80	88.70	...
1976														
January	4.87	5.79	4.87	5.14	7.00	5.81	7.74	8.60	10.41	7.07	9.02	929.34	96.86	...
February	4.77	5.50	4.88	5.20	6.75	5.91	7.79	8.55	10.24	6.94	8.81	971.72	100.64	...
March	4.84	5.50	5.00	5.44	6.75	6.21	7.73	8.52	10.12	6.91	8.76	988.55	101.08	...
April	4.82	5.50	4.86	5.18	6.75	5.92	7.56	8.40	9.94	6.60	8.73	992.52	101.93	...
May	5.29	5.50	5.20	5.62	6.75	6.40	7.90	8.58	9.86	6.87	8.77	988.82	101.16	...
June	5.48	5.50	5.41	5.77	7.20	6.52	7.86	8.62	9.89	6.87	8.85	985.60	101.77	...
July	5.31	5.50	5.23	5.53	7.25	6.20	7.83	8.56	9.82	6.79	8.93	993.20	104.20	...
August	5.29	5.50	5.14	5.40	7.01	6.00	7.77	8.45	9.64	6.61	9.00	981.63	103.29	...
September	5.25	5.50	5.08	5.30	7.00	5.84	7.59	8.38	9.40	6.51	8.98	994.38	105.45	...
October	5.02	5.50	4.92	5.06	6.77	5.50	7.41	8.32	9.29	6.30	8.93	951.96	101.89	...
November	4.95	5.43	4.75	4.88	6.50	5.29	7.29	8.25	9.23	6.29	8.81	944.58	101.19	...
December	4.65	5.25	4.35	4.51	6.35	4.89	6.87	7.98	9.12	5.94	8.79	976.87	104.66	...
1977														
January	4.61	5.25	4.62	4.83	6.25	5.29	7.21	7.96	9.08	5.87	8.72	970.63	103.81	...
February	4.68	5.25	4.67	4.90	6.25	5.47	7.39	8.04	9.12	5.88	8.67	941.75	100.96	...
March	4.69	5.25	4.60	4.88	6.25	5.50	7.46	8.10	9.12	5.89	8.69	946.10	100.57	...
April	4.73	5.25	4.54	4.80	6.25	5.44	7.37	8.04	9.07	5.72	8.75	929.12	99.05	...
May	5.35	5.25	4.96	5.20	6.41	5.84	7.46	8.05	9.01	5.75	8.82	926.30	98.76	...
June	5.39	5.25	5.02	5.21	6.75	5.80	7.28	7.95	8.91	5.62	8.86	916.57	99.29	...
July	5.42	5.25	5.19	5.40	6.75	5.94	7.33	7.94	8.87	5.63	8.94	908.21	100.18	...
August	5.90	5.27	5.49	5.83	6.83	6.37	7.40	7.98	8.82	5.62	8.94	872.27	97.75	...
September	6.14	5.75	5.81	6.04	7.13	6.53	7.34	7.92	8.80	5.51	8.90	853.37	96.23	...
October	6.47	5.80	6.16	6.43	7.52	6.97	7.52	8.04	8.89	5.64	8.92	823.96	93.74	...
November	6.51	6.00	6.10	6.41	7.75	6.95	7.58	8.08	8.95	5.49	8.92	828.52	94.28	...
December	6.56	6.00	6.07	6.40	7.75	6.96	7.69	8.19	8.99	5.57	8.96	818.80	93.82	...
1978														
January	6.70	6.37	6.44	6.70	7.93	7.28	7.96	8.41	9.17	5.71	9.02	781.08	90.25	...
February	6.78	6.50	6.45	6.74	8.00	7.34	8.03	8.47	9.20	5.62	9.16	763.58	88.98	...
March	6.79	6.50	6.29	6.63	8.00	7.31	8.04	8.47	9.22	5.61	9.20	756.37	88.82	...
April	6.89	6.50	6.29	6.73	8.00	7.45	8.15	8.56	9.32	5.79	9.36	794.66	92.71	...
May	7.36	6.84	6.41	7.02	8.27	7.82	8.35	8.69	9.49	6.03	9.58	838.56	97.41	...
June	7.60	7.00	6.73	7.23	8.63	8.09	8.46	8.76	9.60	6.22	9.71	840.25	97.66	...
July	7.81	7.23	7.01	7.44	9.00	8.39	8.64	8.88	9.60	6.28	9.74	831.72	97.19	...
August	8.04	7.43	7.08	7.37	9.01	8.31	8.41	8.69	9.48	6.12	9.79	887.93	103.92	...
September	8.45	7.83	7.85	7.99	9.41	8.64	8.42	8.69	9.42	6.09	9.76	878.64	103.86	...
October	8.96	8.26	7.99	8.55	9.94	9.14	8.64	8.89	9.59	6.13	9.86	857.70	100.58	...
November	9.76	9.50	8.64	9.24	10.94	10.01	8.81	9.03	9.83	6.19	10.11	804.30	94.71	...
December	10.03	9.50	9.08	9.36	11.55	10.30	9.01	9.16	9.94	6.50	10.35	807.96	96.11	...
1979														
January	10.07	9.50	9.35	9.47	11.75	10.41	9.10	9.25	10.13	6.46	10.39	837.39	99.71	...
February	10.06	9.50	9.32	9.41	11.75	10.24	9.10	9.26	10.08	6.31	10.41	825.18	98.23	...
March	10.09	9.50	9.48	9.47	11.75	10.25	9.12	9.37	10.26	6.33	10.43	847.85	100.11	...
April	10.01	9.50	9.46	9.49	11.75	10.12	9.18	9.38	10.33	6.28	10.50	864.97	102.07	...
May	10.24	9.50	9.61	9.54	11.75	10.12	9.25	9.50	10.47	6.25	10.69	837.41	99.73	...
June	10.29	9.50	9.06	9.06	11.65	9.57	8.91	9.29	10.38	6.12	11.04	838.65	101.73	...
July	10.47	9.69	9.24	9.24	11.54	9.64	8.95	9.20	10.29	6.13	11.09	836.96	102.71	...
August	10.94	10.24	9.52	9.49	11.91	9.98	9.03	9.23	10.35	6.20	11.09	873.55	107.36	...
September	11.43	10.70	10.26	10.20	12.90	10.84	9.33	9.44	10.54	6.52	11.30	878.51	108.60	...
October	13.77	11.77	11.70	11.66	14.39	12.44	10.30	10.13	11.40	7.08	11.64	840.52	104.47	...
November	13.18	12.00	11.79	11.82	15.55	12.39	10.65	10.76	11.99	7.30	12.83	815.79	103.66	...
December	13.78	12.00	12.04	11.84	15.30	11.98	10.39	10.74	12.06	7.22	12.90	836.14	107.78	...
1980														
January	13.82	12.00	12.00	11.84	15.25	12.06	10.80	11.09	12.42	7.35	12.88	860.75	110.87	...
February	14.13	12.52	12.86	12.86	15.63	13.92	12.41	12.38	13.57	8.16	13.04	878.22	115.34	...
March	17.19	13.00	15.20	15.03	18.31	15.82	12.75	12.96	14.45	9.16	15.28	803.57	104.69	...
April	17.61	13.00	13.20	12.88	19.77	13.30	11.47	12.04	14.19	8.63	16.33	786.35	102.97	...
May	10.98	12.94	8.58	8.65	16.57	9.39	10.18	10.99	13.17	7.59	14.26	828.20	107.69	...
June	9.47	11.40	7.07	7.30	12.63	8.16	9.78	10.58	12.71	7.63	12.71	869.86	114.55	...
July	9.03	10.87	8.06	8.06	11.48	8.65	10.25	11.07	12.65	8.13	12.19	909.79	119.83	...
August	9.61	10.00	9.13	9.41	11.12	10.24	11.10	11.64	13.15	8.67	12.56	947.33	123.50	...
September	10.87	10.17	10.27	10.57	12.23	11.52	11.51	12.02	13.70	8.94	13.20	946.68	126.51	...
October	12.81	11.00	11.62	11.63	13.79	12.49	11.75	12.31	14.23	9.11	13.79	949.17	130.22	...
November	15.85	11.47	13.73	13.50	16.06	14.15	12.68	12.97	14.64	9.56	14.21	971.09	135.65	...
December	18.90	12.87	15.49	14.64	20.35	14.88	12.84	13.21	15.14	10.20	14.79	945.97	133.48	...

[1] Federal Reserve Bank of New York. Through 2002, represents the rate for adjustment credit. Beginning in 2003, represents the rate for primary credit. See Notes and Definitions.
[2] 1941–1943 = 10.
... = Not available.

Table 20-6. Interest Rates, Bond Yields, and Stock Price Indexes—Continued

(Not seasonally adjusted.)

Year and month	Short-term rates					U.S. Treasury securities		Bond yields			Fixed-rate first mortgages	Stock price indexes		
	Federal funds	Federal reserve discount rate [1]	U.S. Treasury bills, 3-month	U.S. Treasury bills, 6-month	Bank prime rate	1-year	10-year	Domestic corporate (Moody's)		State and local bonds (Bond Buyer)		Dow Jones industrials (30 stocks)	Standard and Poor's composite (500 stocks) [2]	Nasdaq composite
								Aaa	Baa					
1981														
January	19.08	13.00	15.02	14.08	20.16	14.08	12.57	12.81	15.03	9.66	14.90	962.14	132.97	...
February	15.93	13.00	14.79	14.05	19.43	14.57	13.19	13.35	15.37	10.09	15.13	945.51	128.40	...
March	14.70	13.00	13.36	12.81	18.05	13.71	13.12	13.33	15.34	10.16	15.40	987.18	133.19	...
April	15.72	13.00	13.69	13.45	17.15	14.32	13.68	13.88	15.56	10.62	15.58	1 004.86	134.43	...
May	18.52	13.87	16.30	15.29	19.61	16.20	14.10	14.32	15.95	10.77	16.40	979.53	131.73	...
June	19.10	14.00	14.73	14.09	20.03	14.86	13.47	13.75	15.80	10.67	16.70	996.27	132.28	...
July	19.04	14.00	14.95	14.74	20.39	15.72	14.28	14.38	16.17	11.14	16.83	947.95	129.13	...
August	17.82	14.00	15.51	15.52	20.50	16.72	14.94	14.89	16.34	12.26	17.29	926.26	129.63	...
September	15.87	14.00	14.70	14.92	20.08	16.52	15.32	15.49	16.92	12.92	18.16	853.39	118.27	...
October	15.08	14.00	13.54	13.82	18.45	15.38	15.15	15.40	17.11	12.83	18.45	853.26	119.80	...
November	13.31	13.03	10.86	11.30	16.84	12.41	13.39	14.22	16.39	11.89	17.83	860.43	122.92	...
December	12.37	12.10	10.85	11.52	15.75	12.85	13.72	14.23	16.55	12.91	16.92	878.29	123.79	...
1982														
January	13.22	12.00	12.28	12.83	15.75	14.32	14.59	15.18	17.10	13.28	17.40	853.42	117.28	...
February	14.78	12.00	13.48	13.61	16.56	14.73	14.43	15.27	17.18	12.97	17.60	833.16	114.50	...
March	14.68	12.00	12.68	12.77	16.50	13.95	13.86	14.58	16.82	12.82	17.16	812.34	110.84	...
April	14.94	12.00	12.70	12.80	16.50	13.98	13.87	14.46	16.78	12.58	16.89	844.93	116.31	...
May	14.45	12.00	12.09	12.16	16.50	13.34	13.62	14.26	16.64	11.95	16.68	846.74	116.35	...
June	14.15	12.00	12.47	12.70	16.50	14.07	14.30	14.81	16.92	12.44	16.70	804.37	109.70	...
July	12.59	11.81	11.35	11.88	16.26	13.24	13.95	14.61	16.80	12.28	16.82	818.41	109.38	...
August	10.12	10.68	8.68	9.88	14.39	11.43	13.06	13.71	16.32	11.23	16.27	832.11	109.65	...
September	10.31	10.00	7.92	9.37	13.50	10.85	12.34	12.94	15.63	10.66	15.43	917.27	122.43	...
October	9.71	9.68	7.71	8.29	12.52	9.32	10.91	12.12	14.73	9.68	14.61	988.73	132.66	...
November	9.20	9.35	8.07	8.34	11.85	9.16	10.55	11.68	14.30	10.06	13.83	1 027.76	138.10	...
December	8.95	8.73	7.94	8.16	11.50	8.91	10.54	11.83	14.14	9.96	13.62	1 033.10	139.37	...
1983														
January	8.68	8.50	7.86	7.93	11.16	8.62	10.46	11.79	13.94	9.50	13.25	1 064.31	144.27	...
February	8.51	8.50	8.11	8.23	10.98	8.92	10.72	12.01	13.95	9.58	13.04	1 087.40	146.80	...
March	8.77	8.50	8.35	8.37	10.50	9.04	10.51	11.73	13.61	9.20	12.80	1 129.58	151.88	...
April	8.80	8.50	8.21	8.30	10.50	8.98	10.40	11.51	13.29	9.04	12.78	1 168.43	157.71	...
May	8.63	8.50	8.19	8.22	10.50	8.90	10.38	11.46	13.09	9.11	12.63	1 212.86	164.10	...
June	8.98	8.50	8.79	8.89	10.50	9.66	10.85	11.74	13.37	9.52	12.87	1 221.47	166.39	...
July	9.37	8.50	9.08	9.26	10.50	10.20	11.38	12.15	13.39	9.53	13.42	1 213.94	166.96	...
August	9.56	8.50	9.34	9.51	10.89	10.53	11.85	12.51	13.64	9.72	13.81	1 189.22	162.42	...
September	9.45	8.50	9.00	9.15	11.00	10.16	11.65	12.37	13.55	9.58	13.73	1 237.04	167.16	...
October	9.48	8.50	8.64	8.83	11.00	9.81	11.54	12.25	13.46	9.66	13.54	1 252.20	167.65	...
November	9.34	8.50	8.76	8.93	11.00	9.94	11.69	12.41	13.61	9.74	13.44	1 250.00	165.23	...
December	9.47	8.50	9.00	9.17	11.00	10.11	11.83	12.57	13.75	9.89	13.42	1 257.65	164.36	...
1984														
January	9.56	8.50	8.90	9.01	11.00	9.90	11.67	12.20	13.65	9.63	13.37	1 258.89	166.39	...
February	9.59	8.50	9.09	9.18	11.00	10.04	11.84	12.08	13.59	9.64	13.23	1 164.45	157.25	...
March	9.91	8.50	9.52	9.66	11.21	10.59	12.32	12.57	13.99	9.94	13.39	1 161.98	157.44	...
April	10.29	8.87	9.69	9.84	11.93	10.90	12.63	12.81	14.31	9.96	13.65	1 152.72	157.60	...
May	10.32	9.00	9.83	10.31	12.39	11.66	13.41	13.28	14.74	10.49	13.94	1 143.42	156.55	...
June	11.06	9.00	9.87	10.51	12.60	12.08	13.56	13.55	15.05	10.67	14.42	1 121.14	153.12	...
July	11.23	9.00	10.12	10.52	13.00	12.03	13.36	13.44	15.15	10.42	14.67	1 113.29	151.08	...
August	11.64	9.00	10.47	10.61	13.00	11.82	12.72	12.87	14.63	9.99	14.47	1 212.82	164.42	...
September	11.30	9.00	10.37	10.47	12.97	11.58	12.52	12.66	14.35	10.10	14.35	1 213.52	166.11	...
October	9.99	9.00	9.74	9.87	12.58	10.90	12.16	12.63	13.94	10.25	14.13	1 199.30	164.82	...
November	9.43	8.83	8.61	8.81	11.77	9.82	11.57	12.29	13.48	10.17	13.64	1 211.31	166.27	247.00
December	8.38	8.37	8.06	8.28	11.06	9.33	11.50	12.13	13.40	9.95	13.18	1 188.96	164.48	242.53
1985														
January	8.35	8.00	7.76	8.00	10.61	9.02	11.38	12.08	13.26	9.51	13.08	1 238.16	171.61	260.85
February	8.50	8.00	8.27	8.39	10.50	9.29	11.51	12.13	13.23	9.65	12.92	1 283.23	180.88	285.52
March	8.58	8.00	8.52	8.90	10.50	9.86	11.86	12.56	13.69	9.77	13.17	1 268.84	179.42	280.43
April	8.27	8.00	7.95	8.23	10.50	9.14	11.43	12.23	13.51	9.42	13.20	1 266.38	180.62	280.90
May	7.97	7.81	7.48	7.65	10.31	8.46	10.85	11.72	13.15	9.01	12.91	1 279.41	184.90	287.51
June	7.53	7.50	6.95	7.09	9.78	7.80	10.16	10.94	12.40	8.69	12.22	1 314.00	188.89	290.45
July	7.88	7.50	7.08	7.20	9.50	7.86	10.31	10.97	12.43	8.81	12.03	1 343.17	192.54	302.04
August	7.90	7.50	7.14	7.32	9.50	8.05	10.33	11.05	12.50	9.08	12.19	1 326.19	188.31	298.25
September	7.92	7.50	7.10	7.27	9.50	8.07	10.37	11.07	12.48	9.27	12.19	1 317.95	184.06	287.94
October	7.99	7.50	7.16	7.33	9.50	8.01	10.24	11.02	12.36	9.08	12.14	1 351.58	186.18	285.37
November	8.05	7.50	7.24	7.30	9.50	7.88	9.78	10.55	11.99	8.54	11.78	1 432.89	197.45	304.36
December	8.27	7.50	7.10	7.14	9.50	7.67	9.26	10.16	11.58	8.42	11.26	1 517.02	207.26	320.24
1986														
January	8.14	7.50	7.07	7.16	9.50	7.73	9.19	10.05	11.44	8.08	10.88	1 534.85	208.19	328.54
February	7.86	7.50	7.06	7.11	9.50	7.61	8.70	9.67	11.11	7.44	10.71	1 652.74	219.37	348.79
March	7.48	7.10	6.56	6.57	9.10	7.03	7.78	9.00	10.50	7.08	10.08	1 757.36	232.33	368.28
April	6.99	6.83	6.06	6.08	8.83	6.44	7.30	8.79	10.19	7.19	9.94	1 807.06	237.98	382.54
May	6.85	6.50	6.15	6.19	8.50	6.65	7.71	9.09	10.29	7.54	10.14	1 801.81	238.46	388.49
June	6.92	6.50	6.21	6.27	8.50	6.73	7.80	9.13	10.34	7.87	10.68	1 867.71	245.30	398.60
July	6.56	6.16	5.83	5.86	8.16	6.27	7.30	8.88	10.16	7.51	10.51	1 809.92	240.18	385.90
August	6.17	5.82	5.53	5.55	7.90	5.93	7.17	8.72	10.18	7.21	10.20	1 843.45	245.00	375.62
September	5.89	5.50	5.21	5.35	7.50	5.77	7.45	8.89	10.20	7.11	10.01	1 813.48	238.27	358.26
October	5.85	5.50	5.18	5.26	7.50	5.72	7.43	8.86	10.24	7.08	9.97	1 817.06	237.36	355.05
November	6.04	5.50	5.35	5.41	7.50	5.80	7.25	8.68	10.07	6.84	9.70	1 883.65	245.09	358.08
December	6.91	5.50	5.53	5.55	7.50	5.87	7.11	8.49	9.97	6.87	9.31	1 924.09	248.61	354.90

[1] Federal Reserve Bank of New York. Through 2002, represents the rate for adjustment credit. Beginning in 2003, represents the rate for primary credit. See Notes and Definitions.
[2] 1941–1943 = 10.
... = Not available.

Table 20-6. Interest Rates, Bond Yields, and Stock Price Indexes—Continued

(Not seasonally adjusted.)

Year and month	Short-term rates					U.S. Treasury securities		Bond yields		State and local bonds (Bond Buyer)	Fixed-rate first mortgages	Stock price indexes		
	Federal funds	Federal reserve discount rate [1]	U.S. Treasury bills, 3-month	U.S. Treasury bills, 6-month	Bank prime rate	1-year	10-year	Domestic corporate (Moody's)				Dow Jones industrials (30 stocks)	Standard and Poor's composite (500 stocks) [2]	Nasdaq composite
								Aaa	Baa					
1987														
January	6.43	5.50	5.43	5.44	7.50	5.78	7.08	8.36	9.72	6.66	9.20	2 065.13	264.51	384.24
February	6.10	5.50	5.59	5.59	7.50	5.96	7.25	8.38	9.65	6.61	9.08	2 202.34	280.93	411.71
March	6.13	5.50	5.59	5.60	7.50	6.03	7.25	8.36	9.61	6.65	9.04	2 292.61	292.47	432.19
April	6.37	5.50	5.64	5.90	7.75	6.50	8.02	8.85	10.04	7.55	9.83	2 302.66	289.32	422.75
May	6.85	5.50	5.66	6.05	8.14	7.00	8.61	9.33	10.51	8.00	10.60	2 291.12	289.12	416.64
June	6.73	5.50	5.67	5.99	8.25	6.80	8.40	9.32	10.52	7.79	10.54	2 384.02	301.38	423.70
July	6.58	5.50	5.69	5.76	8.25	6.68	8.45	9.42	10.61	7.72	10.28	2 481.73	310.09	429.01
August	6.73	5.50	6.04	6.15	8.25	7.03	8.76	9.67	10.80	7.82	10.33	2 655.02	329.36	448.45
September	7.22	5.95	6.40	6.64	8.70	7.67	9.42	10.18	11.31	8.26	10.89	2 570.81	318.66	442.82
October	7.29	6.00	6.13	6.69	9.07	7.59	9.52	10.52	11.62	8.70	11.26	2 224.58	280.16	385.05
November	6.69	6.00	5.69	6.19	8.78	6.96	8.86	10.01	11.23	7.95	10.65	1 931.88	245.01	318.76
December	6.77	6.00	5.77	6.36	8.75	7.17	8.99	10.11	11.29	7.96	10.65	1 910.07	240.96	314.55
1988														
January	6.83	6.00	5.81	6.25	8.75	6.99	8.67	9.88	11.07	7.69	10.43	1 947.35	250.48	339.29
February	6.58	6.00	5.66	5.93	8.51	6.64	8.21	9.40	10.62	7.49	9.89	1 980.65	258.13	353.58
March	6.58	6.00	5.70	5.91	8.50	6.71	8.37	9.39	10.57	7.74	9.93	2 044.32	265.74	375.55
April	6.87	6.00	5.91	6.21	8.50	7.01	8.72	9.67	10.90	7.81	10.20	2 036.14	262.61	377.23
May	7.09	6.00	6.26	6.56	8.84	7.40	9.09	9.90	11.04	7.91	10.46	1 988.91	256.12	371.88
June	7.51	6.00	6.46	6.71	9.00	7.49	8.92	9.86	11.00	7.78	10.46	2 104.95	270.68	385.99
July	7.75	6.00	6.73	6.99	9.29	7.75	9.06	9.96	11.11	7.76	10.43	2 104.23	269.05	391.43
August	8.01	6.37	7.06	7.39	9.84	8.17	9.26	10.11	11.21	7.79	10.60	2 051.28	263.73	379.60
September	8.19	6.50	7.24	7.43	10.00	8.09	8.98	9.82	10.90	7.66	10.48	2 080.07	267.97	382.17
October	8.30	6.50	7.35	7.50	10.00	8.11	8.80	9.51	10.41	7.46	10.30	2 144.33	277.40	385.02
November	8.35	6.50	7.76	7.86	10.05	8.48	8.96	9.45	10.48	7.46	10.27	2 099.04	271.02	372.90
December	8.76	6.50	8.07	8.22	10.50	8.99	9.11	9.57	10.65	7.61	10.61	2 148.59	276.51	375.80
1989														
January	9.12	6.50	8.27	8.36	10.50	9.05	9.09	9.62	10.65	7.35	10.73	2 234.68	285.41	389.33
February	9.36	6.59	8.53	8.55	10.93	9.25	9.17	9.64	10.61	7.44	10.65	2 304.31	294.01	404.09
March	9.85	7.00	8.82	8.85	11.50	9.57	9.36	9.80	10.67	7.59	11.03	2 283.10	292.71	404.00
April	9.84	7.00	8.65	8.65	11.50	9.36	9.18	9.79	10.61	7.49	11.05	2 348.92	302.25	417.14
May	9.81	7.00	8.43	8.41	11.50	8.98	8.86	9.57	10.46	7.25	10.77	2 439.57	313.93	435.99
June	9.53	7.00	8.15	7.93	11.07	8.44	8.28	9.10	10.03	7.02	10.20	2 494.89	323.73	447.63
July	9.24	7.00	7.88	7.61	10.98	7.89	8.02	8.93	9.87	6.96	9.88	2 554.04	331.93	446.70
August	8.99	7.00	7.90	7.74	10.50	8.18	8.11	8.96	9.88	7.06	9.99	2 691.12	346.61	461.83
September	9.02	7.00	7.75	7.74	10.50	8.22	8.19	9.01	9.91	7.26	10.13	2 693.41	347.33	469.28
October	8.84	7.00	7.64	7.62	10.50	7.99	8.01	8.92	9.81	7.22	9.95	2 692.01	347.40	469.69
November	8.55	7.00	7.69	7.49	10.50	7.77	7.87	8.89	9.81	7.14	9.77	2 642.50	340.22	454.69
December	8.45	7.00	7.63	7.42	10.50	7.72	7.84	8.86	9.82	6.98	9.74	2 728.47	348.57	449.02
1990														
January	8.23	7.00	7.64	7.55	10.11	7.92	8.21	8.99	9.94	7.10	9.90	2 679.24	339.97	439.35
February	8.24	7.00	7.74	7.70	10.00	8.11	8.47	9.22	10.14	7.22	10.20	2 614.19	330.45	424.53
March	8.28	7.00	7.90	7.85	10.00	8.35	8.59	9.37	10.21	7.29	10.27	2 700.13	338.47	436.10
April	8.26	7.00	7.77	7.84	10.00	8.40	8.79	9.46	10.30	7.39	10.37	2 708.27	338.18	429.00
May	8.18	7.00	7.74	7.76	10.00	8.32	8.76	9.47	10.41	7.35	10.48	2 793.82	350.25	442.60
June	8.29	7.00	7.73	7.63	10.00	8.10	8.48	9.26	10.22	7.24	10.16	2 894.84	360.39	462.31
July	8.15	7.00	7.62	7.52	10.00	7.94	8.47	9.24	10.20	7.19	10.04	2 934.23	360.03	455.83
August	8.13	7.00	7.45	7.38	10.00	7.78	8.75	9.41	10.41	7.32	10.10	2 681.89	330.75	396.33
September	8.20	7.00	7.36	7.32	10.00	7.76	8.89	9.56	10.64	7.43	10.18	2 550.69	315.41	368.57
October	8.11	7.00	7.17	7.16	10.00	7.55	8.72	9.53	10.74	7.49	10.18	2 460.54	307.12	338.02
November	7.81	7.00	7.06	7.03	10.00	7.31	8.39	9.30	10.62	7.18	10.01	2 518.58	315.29	347.72
December	7.31	6.79	6.74	6.70	10.00	7.05	8.08	9.05	10.43	7.09	9.67	2 610.92	328.75	370.21
1991														
January	6.91	6.50	6.22	6.28	9.52	6.64	8.09	9.04	10.45	7.08	9.64	2 587.60	325.49	376.67
February	6.25	6.00	5.94	5.93	9.05	6.27	7.85	8.83	10.07	6.91	9.37	2 863.05	362.26	442.59
March	6.12	6.00	5.91	5.92	9.00	6.40	8.11	8.93	10.09	7.10	9.50	2 920.12	372.28	469.10
April	5.91	5.98	5.65	5.71	9.00	6.24	8.04	8.86	9.94	7.02	9.49	2 925.55	379.68	496.32
May	5.78	5.50	5.46	5.61	8.50	6.13	8.07	8.86	9.86	6.95	9.47	2 928.43	377.99	490.93
June	5.90	5.50	5.57	5.75	8.50	6.36	8.28	9.01	9.96	7.13	9.62	2 968.14	378.29	490.38
July	5.82	5.50	5.58	5.70	8.50	6.31	8.27	9.00	9.89	7.05	9.58	2 978.19	380.23	489.37
August	5.66	5.50	5.33	5.39	8.50	5.78	7.90	8.75	9.65	6.90	9.24	3 006.09	389.40	513.25
September	5.45	5.20	5.22	5.25	8.20	5.57	7.65	8.61	9.51	6.80	9.01	3 010.36	387.20	520.56
October	5.21	5.00	4.99	5.04	8.00	5.33	7.53	8.55	9.49	6.68	8.86	3 019.74	386.88	528.92
November	4.81	4.58	4.56	4.61	7.58	4.89	7.42	8.48	9.45	6.73	8.71	2 986.13	385.92	536.58
December	4.43	4.11	4.07	4.10	7.21	4.38	7.09	8.31	9.26	6.69	8.50	2 958.66	388.51	544.10
1992														
January	4.03	3.50	3.80	3.87	6.50	4.15	7.03	8.20	9.13	6.54	8.43	3 227.06	416.08	615.73
February	4.06	3.50	3.84	3.93	6.50	4.29	7.34	8.29	9.23	6.74	8.76	3 257.27	412.56	632.05
March	3.98	3.50	4.04	4.18	6.50	4.63	7.54	8.35	9.25	6.76	8.94	3 247.42	407.36	619.60
April	3.73	3.50	3.75	3.87	6.50	4.30	7.48	8.33	9.21	6.67	8.85	3 294.10	407.41	582.79
May	3.82	3.50	3.63	3.75	6.50	4.19	7.39	8.28	9.13	6.57	8.67	3 376.79	414.81	581.47
June	3.76	3.50	3.66	3.77	6.50	4.17	7.26	8.22	9.05	6.49	8.51	3 337.79	408.27	566.66
July	3.25	3.02	3.21	3.28	6.02	3.60	6.84	8.07	8.84	6.13	8.13	3 329.41	415.05	568.72
August	3.30	3.00	3.13	3.21	6.00	3.47	6.59	7.95	8.65	6.16	7.98	3 307.46	417.93	569.00
September	3.22	3.00	2.91	2.96	6.00	3.18	6.42	7.92	8.62	6.25	7.92	3 293.93	418.48	580.68
October	3.10	3.00	2.86	3.04	6.00	3.30	6.59	7.99	8.84	6.41	8.09	3 198.70	412.50	585.01
November	3.09	3.00	3.13	3.34	6.00	3.68	6.87	8.10	8.96	6.36	8.31	3 238.49	422.84	630.86
December	2.92	3.00	3.22	3.36	6.00	3.71	6.77	7.98	8.81	6.22	8.22	3 303.15	435.64	661.28

[1] Federal Reserve Bank of New York. Through 2002, represents the rate for adjustment credit. Beginning in 2003, represents the rate for primary credit. See Notes and Definitions.
[2] 1941–1943 = 10.

CHAPTER 20: HISTORICAL DATA FOR SELECTED MONTHLY SERIES 469

Table 20-6. Interest Rates, Bond Yields, and Stock Price Indexes—Continued

(Not seasonally adjusted.)

Year and month	Short-term rates					U.S. Treasury securities		Bond yields			Fixed-rate first mortgages	Stock price indexes		
	Federal funds	Federal reserve discount rate [1]	U.S. Treasury bills, 3-month	U.S. Treasury bills, 6-month	Bank prime rate	1-year	10-year	Domestic corporate (Moody's)		State and local bonds (Bond Buyer)		Dow Jones industrials (30 stocks)	Standard and Poor's composite (500 stocks) [2]	Nasdaq composite
								Aaa	Baa					
1993														
January	3.02	3.00	3.00	3.14	6.00	3.50	6.60	7.91	8.67	6.16	8.02	3 277.73	435.23	691.13
February	3.03	3.00	2.93	3.07	6.00	3.39	6.26	7.71	8.39	5.87	7.68	3 367.26	441.70	681.71
March	3.07	3.00	2.95	3.05	6.00	3.33	5.98	7.58	8.15	5.64	7.50	3 440.73	450.16	684.49
April	2.96	3.00	2.87	2.97	6.00	3.24	5.97	7.46	8.14	5.76	7.47	3 423.62	443.08	665.33
May	3.00	3.00	2.96	3.07	6.00	3.36	6.04	7.43	8.21	5.73	7.47	3 478.18	445.25	686.45
June	3.04	3.00	3.07	3.20	6.00	3.54	5.96	7.33	8.07	5.63	7.42	3 513.81	448.06	695.38
July	3.06	3.00	3.04	3.16	6.00	3.47	5.81	7.17	7.93	5.57	7.21	3 529.44	447.29	703.40
August	3.03	3.00	3.02	3.14	6.00	3.44	5.68	6.85	7.60	5.45	7.11	3 597.03	454.13	725.15
September	3.09	3.00	2.95	3.06	6.00	3.36	5.36	6.66	7.34	5.29	6.92	3 592.29	459.24	745.94
October	2.99	3.00	3.02	3.12	6.00	3.39	5.33	6.67	7.31	5.25	6.83	3 625.81	463.90	771.31
November	3.02	3.00	3.10	3.26	6.00	3.58	5.72	6.93	7.66	5.47	7.16	3 674.71	462.89	764.04
December	2.96	3.00	3.06	3.23	6.00	3.61	5.77	6.93	7.69	5.35	7.17	3 744.10	465.95	762.94
1994														
January	3.05	3.00	2.98	3.15	6.00	3.54	5.75	6.92	7.65	5.31	7.06	3 868.37	472.99	787.77
February	3.25	3.00	3.25	3.43	6.00	3.87	5.97	7.08	7.76	5.40	7.15	3 905.62	471.58	787.81
March	3.34	3.00	3.50	3.78	6.06	4.32	6.48	7.48	8.13	5.91	7.68	3 816.99	463.81	785.93
April	3.56	3.00	3.68	4.09	6.45	4.82	6.97	7.88	8.52	6.23	8.32	3 661.49	447.23	732.30
May	4.01	3.24	4.14	4.60	6.99	5.31	7.18	7.99	8.62	6.19	8.60	3 708.00	450.90	727.76
June	4.25	3.50	4.14	4.55	7.25	5.27	7.10	7.97	8.65	6.11	8.40	3 737.58	454.83	723.21
July	4.26	3.50	4.33	4.75	7.25	5.48	7.30	8.11	8.80	6.23	8.61	3 718.31	451.40	713.49
August	4.47	3.76	4.48	4.88	7.51	5.56	7.24	8.07	8.74	6.21	8.51	3 797.48	464.24	738.87
September	4.73	4.00	4.62	5.04	7.75	5.76	7.46	8.34	8.98	6.28	8.64	3 880.60	466.96	763.94
October	4.76	4.00	4.95	5.39	7.75	6.11	7.74	8.57	9.20	6.52	8.93	3 868.10	463.81	762.46
November	5.29	4.40	5.29	5.72	8.15	6.54	7.96	8.68	9.32	6.97	9.17	3 792.44	461.01	760.42
December	5.45	4.75	5.60	6.21	8.50	7.14	7.81	8.46	9.10	6.80	9.20	3 770.30	455.19	734.96
1995														
January	5.53	4.75	5.71	6.21	8.50	7.05	7.78	8.46	9.08	6.53	9.15	3 872.46	465.25	758.01
February	5.92	5.25	5.77	6.03	9.00	6.70	7.47	8.26	8.85	6.22	8.83	3 953.73	481.92	784.24
March	5.98	5.25	5.73	5.89	9.00	6.43	7.20	8.12	8.70	6.10	8.46	4 062.78	493.15	807.16
April	6.05	5.25	5.65	5.77	9.00	6.27	7.06	8.03	8.60	6.02	8.32	4 230.67	507.91	825.34
May	6.01	5.25	5.67	5.67	9.00	6.00	6.63	7.65	8.20	5.95	7.96	4 391.58	523.81	859.77
June	6.00	5.25	5.47	5.42	9.00	5.64	6.17	7.30	7.90	5.84	7.57	4 510.77	539.35	906.04
July	5.85	5.25	5.42	5.37	8.80	5.59	6.28	7.41	8.04	5.92	7.61	4 684.78	557.37	979.36
August	5.74	5.25	5.40	5.41	8.75	5.75	6.49	7.57	8.19	6.06	7.86	4 639.27	559.11	1 009.59
September	5.80	5.25	5.28	5.30	8.75	5.62	6.20	7.32	7.93	5.91	7.64	4 746.76	578.77	1 051.00
October	5.76	5.25	5.28	5.32	8.75	5.59	6.04	7.12	7.75	5.80	7.48	4 760.48	582.92	1 022.15
November	5.80	5.25	5.36	5.27	8.75	5.43	5.93	7.02	7.68	5.64	7.38	4 935.82	595.53	1 046.64
December	5.60	5.25	5.14	5.13	8.65	5.31	5.71	6.82	7.49	5.45	7.20	5 136.11	614.57	1 047.04
1996														
January	5.56	5.24	5.00	4.92	8.50	5.09	5.65	6.81	7.47	5.43	7.03	5 179.38	614.42	1 024.95
February	5.22	5.00	4.83	4.77	8.25	4.94	5.81	6.99	7.63	5.43	7.08	5 518.74	649.54	1 094.02
March	5.31	5.00	4.96	4.96	8.25	5.34	6.27	7.35	8.03	5.79	7.62	5 612.25	647.07	1 092.65
April	5.22	5.00	4.95	5.06	8.25	5.54	6.51	7.50	8.19	5.94	7.93	5 579.86	647.17	1 135.63
May	5.24	5.00	5.02	5.12	8.25	5.64	6.74	7.62	8.30	5.98	8.07	5 616.71	661.23	1 220.54
June	5.27	5.00	5.09	5.25	8.25	5.81	6.91	7.71	8.40	6.02	8.32	5 671.52	668.50	1 205.08
July	5.40	5.00	5.15	5.30	8.25	5.85	6.87	7.65	8.35	5.92	8.25	5 496.27	644.07	1 105.61
August	5.22	5.00	5.05	5.13	8.25	5.67	6.64	7.46	8.18	5.76	8.00	5 685.51	662.68	1 134.25
September	5.30	5.00	5.09	5.24	8.25	5.83	6.83	7.66	8.35	5.87	8.23	5 804.01	674.88	1 186.44
October	5.24	5.00	4.99	5.11	8.25	5.55	6.53	7.39	8.07	5.72	7.92	5 996.22	701.45	1 234.04
November	5.31	5.00	5.03	5.07	8.25	5.42	6.20	7.10	7.79	5.59	7.62	6 318.36	735.67	1 259.83
December	5.29	5.00	4.91	5.04	8.25	5.47	6.30	7.20	7.89	5.64	7.60	6 435.87	743.25	1 292.15
1997														
January	5.25	5.00	5.03	5.10	8.25	5.61	6.58	7.42	8.09	5.72	7.82	6 707.05	766.22	1 345.41
February	5.19	5.00	5.01	5.06	8.25	5.53	6.42	7.31	7.94	5.63	7.65	6 917.46	798.39	1 349.17
March	5.39	5.00	5.14	5.26	8.30	5.80	6.69	7.55	8.18	5.76	7.90	6 901.14	792.16	1 282.86
April	5.51	5.00	5.16	5.37	8.50	5.99	6.89	7.73	8.34	5.88	8.14	6 657.51	763.93	1 225.00
May	5.50	5.00	5.05	5.30	8.50	5.87	6.71	7.58	8.20	5.70	7.94	7 242.33	833.09	1 352.56
June	5.56	5.00	4.93	5.13	8.50	5.69	6.49	7.41	8.02	5.53	7.69	7 599.61	876.29	1 422.45
July	5.52	5.00	5.05	5.12	8.50	5.54	6.22	7.14	7.75	5.35	7.50	7 990.65	925.29	1 531.14
August	5.54	5.00	5.14	5.19	8.50	5.56	6.30	7.22	7.82	5.41	7.48	7 948.42	927.74	1 596.74
September	5.54	5.00	4.95	5.09	8.50	5.52	6.21	7.15	7.70	5.39	7.43	7 866.59	937.02	1 660.15
October	5.50	5.00	4.97	5.09	8.50	5.46	6.03	7.00	7.57	5.38	7.29	7 875.82	951.16	1 682.17
November	5.52	5.00	5.14	5.17	8.50	5.46	5.88	6.87	7.42	5.33	7.21	7 677.35	938.92	1 600.97
December	5.50	5.00	5.16	5.24	8.50	5.53	5.81	6.76	7.32	5.19	7.10	7 909.82	962.37	1 567.00
1998														
January	5.56	5.00	5.04	5.03	8.50	5.24	5.54	6.61	7.19	5.06	6.99	7 808.36	963.36	1 570.23
February	5.51	5.00	5.09	5.07	8.50	5.31	5.57	6.67	7.25	5.10	7.04	8 323.62	1 023.74	1 714.87
March	5.49	5.00	5.03	5.04	8.50	5.39	5.65	6.72	7.32	5.21	7.13	8 709.48	1 076.83	1 781.27
April	5.45	5.00	4.95	5.06	8.50	5.38	5.64	6.69	7.33	5.23	7.14	9 037.43	1 112.20	1 852.30
May	5.49	5.00	5.00	5.14	8.50	5.44	5.65	6.69	7.30	5.20	7.14	9 080.09	1 108.42	1 836.39
June	5.56	5.00	4.98	5.12	8.50	5.41	5.50	6.53	7.13	5.12	7.00	8 872.96	1 108.39	1 795.74
July	5.54	5.00	4.96	5.03	8.50	5.36	5.46	6.55	7.15	5.14	6.95	9 097.15	1 156.58	1 941.58
August	5.55	5.00	4.90	4.95	8.50	5.21	5.34	6.52	7.14	5.10	6.92	8 478.54	1 074.63	1 784.75
September	5.51	5.00	4.61	4.63	8.49	4.71	4.81	6.40	7.09	4.99	6.72	7 909.80	1 020.64	1 663.43
October	5.07	4.86	3.96	4.05	8.12	4.12	4.53	6.37	7.18	4.93	6.71	8 164.47	1 032.47	1 615.69
November	4.83	4.63	4.41	4.42	7.89	4.53	4.83	6.41	7.34	5.03	6.87	9 005.78	1 144.43	1 888.72
December	4.68	4.50	4.39	4.40	7.75	4.52	4.65	6.22	7.23	4.98	6.72	9 018.68	1 190.05	2 071.03

[1]Federal Reserve Bank of New York. Through 2002, represents the rate for adjustment credit. Beginning in 2003, represents the rate for primary credit. See Notes and Definitions.
[2]1941–1943 = 10.

Table 20-6. Interest Rates, Bond Yields, and Stock Price Indexes—Continued

(Not seasonally adjusted.)

Year and month	Short-term rates					U.S. Treasury securities		Bond yields			Fixed-rate first mortgages	Stock price indexes		
	Federal funds	Federal reserve discount rate [1]	U.S. Treasury bills, 3-month	U.S. Treasury bills, 6-month	Bank prime rate	1-year	10-year	Domestic corporate (Moody's) Aaa	Domestic corporate (Moody's) Baa	State and local bonds (Bond Buyer)		Dow Jones industrials (30 stocks)	Standard and Poor's composite (500 stocks) [2]	Nasdaq composite
1999														
January	4.63	4.50	4.34	4.33	7.75	4.51	4.72	6.24	7.29	5.01	6.79	9 345.86	1 248.77	2 357.80
February	4.76	4.50	4.44	4.44	7.75	4.70	5.00	6.40	7.39	5.03	6.81	9 322.94	1 246.58	2 356.99
March	4.81	4.50	4.44	4.47	7.75	4.78	5.23	6.62	7.53	5.10	7.04	9 753.64	1 281.66	2 391.14
April	4.74	4.50	4.29	4.37	7.75	4.69	5.18	6.64	7.48	5.08	6.92	10 443.50	1 334.76	2 537.89
May	4.74	4.50	4.50	4.56	7.75	4.85	5.54	6.93	7.72	5.18	7.15	10 853.88	1 332.07	2 512.60
June	4.76	4.50	4.57	4.82	7.75	5.10	5.90	7.23	8.02	5.37	7.55	10 704.03	1 322.55	2 520.96
July	4.99	4.50	4.55	4.58	8.00	5.03	5.79	7.19	7.95	5.36	7.63	11 052.22	1 380.99	2 741.26
August	5.07	4.56	4.72	4.87	8.06	5.20	5.94	7.40	8.15	5.58	7.94	10 935.48	1 327.49	2 642.45
September	5.22	4.75	4.68	4.88	8.25	5.25	5.92	7.39	8.20	5.69	7.82	10 714.03	1 318.17	2 807.95
October	5.20	4.75	4.86	4.98	8.25	5.43	6.11	7.55	8.38	5.92	7.85	10 396.89	1 300.01	2 815.28
November	5.42	4.86	5.07	5.20	8.37	5.55	6.03	7.36	8.15	5.86	7.74	10 809.80	1 391.00	3 230.55
December	5.30	5.00	5.20	5.44	8.50	5.84	6.28	7.55	8.19	5.95	7.91	11 246.37	1 428.68	3 739.88
2000														
January	5.45	5.00	5.32	5.50	8.50	6.12	6.66	7.78	8.33	6.08	8.21	11 281.27	1 425.59	4 013.49
February	5.73	5.24	5.55	5.72	8.73	6.22	6.52	7.68	8.29	6.00	8.33	10 541.93	1 388.87	4 410.87
March	5.85	5.34	5.69	5.85	8.83	6.22	6.26	7.68	8.37	5.83	8.24	10 483.38	1 442.21	4 802.99
April	6.02	5.50	5.66	5.81	9.00	6.15	5.99	7.64	8.40	5.75	8.15	10 944.32	1 461.36	3 863.64
May	6.27	5.71	5.79	6.10	9.24	6.33	6.44	7.99	8.90	6.00	8.52	10 580.28	1 418.48	3 528.42
June	6.53	6.00	5.69	5.97	9.50	6.17	6.10	7.67	8.48	5.80	8.29	10 582.93	1 461.96	3 865.48
July	6.54	6.00	5.96	6.00	9.50	6.08	6.05	7.65	8.35	5.63	8.15	10 662.98	1 473.00	4 017.69
August	6.50	6.00	6.09	6.07	9.50	6.18	5.83	7.55	8.26	5.51	8.03	11 014.51	1 485.46	3 909.60
September	6.52	6.00	6.00	5.98	9.50	6.13	5.80	7.62	8.35	5.56	7.91	10 967.88	1 468.05	3 875.82
October	6.51	6.00	6.11	6.04	9.50	6.01	5.74	7.55	8.34	5.59	7.80	10 440.96	1 390.14	3 333.82
November	6.51	6.00	6.17	6.06	9.50	6.09	5.72	7.45	8.28	5.54	7.75	10 666.08	1 375.04	3 055.42
December	6.40	6.00	5.77	5.68	9.50	5.60	5.24	7.21	8.02	5.22	7.38	10 652.52	1 330.93	2 657.81
2001														
January	5.98	5.52	5.15	4.95	9.05	4.81	5.16	7.15	7.93	5.10	7.03	10 682.76	1 335.63	2 656.86
February	5.49	5.00	4.88	4.71	8.50	4.68	5.10	7.10	7.87	5.18	7.05	10 774.58	1 305.75	2 449.57
March	5.31	4.81	4.42	4.28	8.32	4.30	4.89	6.98	7.84	5.13	6.95	10 081.33	1 185.85	1 986.66
April	4.80	4.28	3.87	3.85	7.80	3.98	5.14	7.20	8.07	5.27	7.08	10 234.52	1 189.84	1 933.93
May	4.21	3.73	3.62	3.62	7.24	3.78	5.39	7.29	8.07	5.29	7.15	11 004.95	1 270.37	2 181.13
June	3.97	3.47	3.49	3.45	6.98	3.58	5.28	7.18	7.97	5.20	7.16	10 767.19	1 238.71	2 112.05
July	3.77	3.25	3.51	3.45	6.75	3.62	5.24	7.13	7.97	5.20	7.13	10 444.50	1 204.45	2 033.98
August	3.65	3.16	3.36	3.29	6.67	3.47	4.97	7.02	7.85	5.03	6.95	10 314.70	1 178.50	1 929.71
September	3.07	2.77	2.64	2.63	6.28	2.82	4.73	7.17	8.03	5.09	6.82	9 042.57	1 044.64	1 573.31
October	2.49	2.02	2.16	2.12	5.53	2.33	4.57	7.03	7.91	5.05	6.62	9 220.75	1 076.59	1 656.43
November	2.09	1.58	1.87	1.88	5.10	2.18	4.65	6.97	7.81	5.04	6.66	9 721.83	1 129.68	1 870.06
December	1.82	1.33	1.69	1.78	4.84	2.22	5.09	6.77	8.05	5.25	7.07	9 979.89	1 144.93	1 977.71
2002														
January	1.73	1.25	1.65	1.73	4.75	2.16	5.04	6.55	7.87	5.16	7.00	9 923.80	1 140.21	1 976.77
February	1.74	1.25	1.73	1.82	4.75	2.23	4.91	6.51	7.89	5.11	6.89	9 891.05	1 100.67	1 799.72
March	1.73	1.25	1.79	2.01	4.75	2.57	5.28	6.81	8.11	5.29	7.01	10 500.95	1 153.79	1 863.05
April	1.75	1.25	1.72	1.93	4.75	2.48	5.21	6.76	8.03	5.22	6.99	10 165.18	1 112.03	1 758.80
May	1.75	1.25	1.73	1.86	4.75	2.35	5.16	6.75	8.09	5.19	6.81	10 080.48	1 079.27	1 660.31
June	1.75	1.25	1.70	1.79	4.75	2.20	4.93	6.63	7.95	5.09	6.65	9 492.44	1 014.05	1 505.49
July	1.73	1.25	1.68	1.70	4.75	1.96	4.65	6.53	7.90	5.02	6.49	8 616.52	903.59	1 346.09
August	1.74	1.25	1.62	1.60	4.75	1.76	4.26	6.37	7.58	4.95	6.29	8 685.48	912.55	1 327.36
September	1.75	1.25	1.63	1.60	4.75	1.72	3.87	6.15	7.40	4.74	6.09	8 160.78	867.81	1 251.07
October	1.75	1.25	1.58	1.56	4.75	1.65	3.94	6.32	7.73	4.88	6.11	8 048.12	854.63	1 241.91
November	1.34	0.83	1.23	1.27	4.35	1.49	4.05	6.31	7.62	4.95	6.07	8 625.72	909.93	1 409.15
December	1.24	0.75	1.19	1.24	4.25	1.45	4.03	6.21	7.45	4.85	6.05	8 526.66	899.18	1 387.15
2003														
January	1.24	...	1.17	1.20	4.25	1.36	4.05	6.17	7.35	4.90	5.92	8 474.59	895.84	1 389.56
February	1.26	[1]2.25	1.17	1.18	4.25	1.30	3.90	5.95	7.06	4.81	5.84	7 916.18	837.62	1 313.26
March	1.25	[1]2.25	1.13	1.13	4.25	1.24	3.81	5.89	6.95	4.76	5.75	7 977.73	846.62	1 348.50
April	1.26	[1]2.25	1.13	1.14	4.25	1.27	3.96	5.74	6.85	4.74	5.81	8 332.09	890.03	1 409.83
May	1.26	[1]2.25	1.07	1.08	4.25	1.18	3.57	5.22	6.38	4.41	5.48	8 623.41	935.96	1 524.18
June	1.22	[1]2.20	0.92	0.92	4.22	1.01	3.33	4.97	6.19	4.33	5.23	9 098.07	988.00	1 631.75
July	1.01	[1]2.00	0.90	0.95	4.00	1.12	3.98	5.49	6.62	4.74	5.63	9 154.39	992.54	1 716.85
August	1.03	[1]2.00	0.95	1.03	4.00	1.31	4.45	5.88	7.01	5.10	6.26	9 284.78	989.53	1 724.82
September	1.01	[1]2.00	0.94	1.01	4.00	1.24	4.27	5.72	6.79	4.92	6.15	9 492.54	1 019.44	1 856.22
October	1.01	[1]2.00	0.92	1.00	4.00	1.25	4.29	5.70	6.73	4.89	5.95	9 682.46	1 038.73	1 907.89
November	1.00	[1]2.00	0.93	1.02	4.00	1.34	4.30	5.65	6.66	4.73	5.93	9 762.20	1 049.90	1 939.25
December	0.98	[1]2.00	0.90	0.99	4.00	1.31	4.27	5.62	6.60	4.65	5.88	10 124.66	1 080.64	1 956.98

[1]Federal Reserve Bank of New York. Through 2002, represents the rate for adjustment credit. Beginning in 2003, represents the rate for primary credit. See Notes and Definitions.
[2]1941–1943 = 10.
... = Not available.

Table 20-7. Composite Indexes of Economic Activity and Selected Index Components

Year and month	Cyclical composite indexes, 1996 = 100				Selected components of leading index			Selected component of coincident index	Selected component of lagging index
	Leading	Coincident	Lagging	Ratio, coincident to lagging	Vendor performance (slower deliveries, diffusion index, percent)	Interest rate spread, 10-year Treasury bond less federal funds [1]	Index of consumer expectations [1,2]	Personal income less transfer payments (billions of 1996 dollars)	Consumer installment credit outstanding (percent of personal income)
1959									
January	58.5	36.1	78.9	45.8	61.8	1.54	95.2	1 758.3	12.9
February	59.2	36.4	79.2	46.0	67.3	1.53	95.8	1 769.1	12.9
March	59.8	36.7	79.2	46.3	66.3	1.19	96.4	1 785.3	12.9
April	59.7	37.1	79.5	46.7	64.8	1.16	96.9	1 797.4	13.0
May	59.9	37.4	79.9	46.8	63.0	1.41	97.5	1 812.3	13.0
June	59.8	37.5	80.1	46.8	63.7	0.95	97.2	1 819.2	13.1
July	59.7	37.3	80.6	46.3	59.1	0.93	96.9	1 816.3	13.3
August	59.3	36.8	81.6	45.1	57.4	0.93	96.7	1 806.8	13.5
September	59.4	36.8	82.0	44.9	57.5	0.92	96.4	1 806.7	13.6
October	58.9	36.8	82.6	44.6	58.5	0.55	96.1	1 809.9	13.7
November	58.4	37.0	82.4	44.9	54.6	0.53	95.8	1 822.4	13.7
December	59.5	37.7	82.2	45.9	53.7	0.70	98.7	1 842.4	13.9
1960									
January	59.2	38.0	81.7	46.5	46.2	0.73	101.7	1 852.5	13.8
February	58.7	38.0	82.0	46.3	31.7	0.52	104.6	1 853.2	13.9
March	58.0	37.9	82.5	45.9	28.8	0.41	102.6	1 854.0	14.0
April	58.2	38.1	82.5	46.2	28.9	0.36	100.6	1 859.4	14.1
May	58.2	37.9	83.2	45.6	32.3	0.50	98.6	1 863.6	14.1
June	58.3	37.7	83.7	45.0	34.8	0.83	98.2	1 862.1	14.2
July	58.3	37.7	83.9	44.9	35.8	0.67	97.9	1 863.1	14.2
August	58.5	37.7	83.7	45.0	38.0	0.82	97.5	1 859.8	14.3
September	58.4	37.6	83.4	45.1	37.3	1.20	96.1	1 860.4	14.3
October	58.3	37.6	83.3	45.1	36.2	1.42	94.8	1 865.8	14.3
November	58.2	37.4	83.3	44.9	37.6	1.49	93.4	1 854.1	14.4
December	58.2	37.1	83.6	44.4	40.4	1.86	93.9	1 841.8	14.5
1961									
January	58.6	37.1	83.7	44.3	39.2	2.39	94.4	1 858.9	14.6
February	58.6	37.0	83.5	44.3	41.1	1.24	94.9	1 859.4	14.4
March	59.5	37.2	82.9	44.9	42.1	1.72	96.0	1 868.6	14.4
April	59.9	37.3	82.5	45.2	47.5	2.29	97.0	1 874.5	14.3
May	60.3	37.6	82.0	45.9	47.9	1.73	98.1	1 884.9	14.2
June	60.9	37.9	81.5	46.5	49.3	2.15	98.2	1 901.1	14.1
July	60.9	38.0	81.0	46.9	49.4	2.75	98.4	1 905.6	14.0
August	61.5	38.2	81.0	47.2	50.6	2.04	98.5	1 913.5	14.1
September	61.2	38.3	81.2	47.2	50.7	2.10	97.9	1 918.3	14.1
October	61.7	38.6	81.2	47.5	52.4	1.66	97.4	1 938.2	14.0
November	62.3	38.9	81.0	48.0	51.1	1.33	96.8	1 957.5	14.0
December	62.6	39.1	81.4	48.0	55.8	1.73	99.0	1 967.8	14.0
1962									
January	62.5	39.0	81.8	47.7	57.1	1.93	101.2	1 963.7	14.0
February	63.0	39.2	81.6	48.0	56.2	1.67	103.4	1 974.0	14.0
March	62.9	39.4	82.0	48.0	57.0	1.08	101.1	1 987.8	14.0
April	62.8	39.6	82.1	48.2	47.4	1.06	98.8	1 998.9	14.1
May	62.5	39.6	82.4	48.1	45.2	1.51	96.5	2 001.9	14.2
June	62.1	39.6	82.7	47.9	43.3	1.23	95.5	2 007.6	14.3
July	62.4	39.8	82.8	48.1	45.1	1.30	94.4	2 015.4	14.3
August	62.5	39.8	83.0	48.0	43.7	1.05	93.4	2 017.1	14.4
September	62.7	40.0	83.0	48.2	45.1	1.08	95.3	2 019.9	14.4
October	62.8	40.0	83.0	48.2	46.7	1.03	97.3	2 024.0	14.5
November	63.5	40.2	83.1	48.4	48.7	0.98	99.2	2 035.9	14.5
December	63.5	40.1	83.3	48.1	50.1	0.93	99.4	2 046.1	14.6
1963									
January	63.9	40.2	83.3	48.3	50.4	0.91	99.7	2 040.0	14.6
February	64.3	40.4	83.3	48.5	51.0	0.92	99.9	2 045.0	14.8
March	64.7	40.6	83.3	48.7	54.9	0.95	98.0	2 053.7	14.9
April	65.1	40.8	83.4	48.9	58.2	1.07	96.0	2 060.4	15.0
May	65.3	40.9	83.5	49.0	56.4	0.93	94.1	2 068.0	15.0
June	65.4	41.0	83.7	49.0	56.3	1.00	95.1	2 080.9	15.0
July	65.3	41.1	83.7	49.1	43.6	1.00	96.0	2 081.4	15.2
August	65.4	41.1	84.3	48.8	48.5	0.51	97.0	2 089.4	15.3
September	65.9	41.3	84.3	49.0	49.7	0.60	97.0	2 103.4	15.3
October	66.1	41.6	84.4	49.3	47.4	0.61	97.0	2 116.8	15.4
November	66.2	41.6	85.1	48.9	48.7	0.64	97.0	2 120.5	15.4
December	66.4	41.7	85.1	49.0	47.6	0.75	97.8	2 136.3	15.5
1964									
January	66.7	41.9	84.9	49.4	55.3	0.69	98.6	2 137.9	15.6
February	67.0	42.1	85.0	49.5	51.9	0.67	99.4	2 156.5	15.6
March	67.2	42.2	85.2	49.5	60.3	0.79	98.7	2 166.4	15.7
April	67.5	42.4	85.6	49.5	57.7	0.76	97.9	2 180.2	15.8
May	67.9	42.7	85.2	50.1	61.4	0.70	97.2	2 194.6	15.8
June	68.0	42.8	85.3	50.2	57.6	0.67	97.8	2 203.9	15.9
July	68.4	43.0	85.2	50.5	61.8	0.77	98.5	2 212.7	16.0
August	68.7	43.1	85.8	50.2	66.2	0.69	99.1	2 230.2	16.0
September	69.2	43.4	86.0	50.5	71.9	0.75	99.8	2 239.2	16.1
October	69.0	43.2	86.3	50.1	71.2	0.83	100.4	2 241.2	16.2
November	69.3	43.6	86.0	50.7	70.3	0.63	101.1	2 256.0	16.1
December	69.5	44.0	86.0	51.2	67.8	0.33	101.7	2 277.8	16.1

[1] Not seasonally adjusted.
[2] Copyright, University of Michigan, Survey Research Center, first quarter 1966 = 100.

Table 20-7. Composite Indexes of Economic Activity and Selected Index Components—Continued

Year and month	Cyclical composite indexes, 1996 = 100				Selected components of leading index			Selected component of coincident index	Selected component of lagging index
	Leading	Coincident	Lagging	Ratio, coincident to lagging	Vendor performance (slower deliveries, diffusion index, percent)	Interest rate spread, 10-year Treasury bond less federal funds [1]	Index of consumer expectations [1,2]	Personal income less transfer payments (billions of 1996 dollars)	Consumer installment credit outstanding (percent of personal income)
1965									
January	70.0	44.2	86.6	51.0	68.5	0.29	102.4	2 281.5	16.2
February	70.0	44.4	87.0	51.0	68.1	0.23	103.0	2 293.2	16.4
March	70.4	44.7	87.1	51.3	65.9	0.17	103.2	2 304.1	16.4
April	70.5	44.9	87.6	51.3	69.4	0.11	103.4	2 313.6	16.6
May	70.7	45.0	88.0	51.1	68.9	0.11	103.7	2 327.4	16.6
June	70.8	45.2	88.0	51.4	69.3	0.17	103.9	2 333.8	16.7
July	70.9	45.5	88.1	51.6	65.1	0.11	104.1	2 349.2	16.7
August	71.0	45.7	88.2	51.8	65.4	0.13	104.3	2 361.2	16.7
September	71.2	45.8	88.4	51.8	61.2	0.28	105.3	2 379.7	16.4
October	71.8	46.2	88.6	52.1	59.1	0.27	106.3	2 404.5	16.7
November	72.4	46.5	88.8	52.4	65.1	0.35	107.3	2 421.8	16.6
December	72.8	46.8	89.0	52.6	73.5	0.30	104.9	2 434.3	16.6
1966									
January	72.8	47.0	89.2	52.7	74.9	0.19	102.4	2 440.4	16.7
February	72.9	47.2	89.7	52.6	80.1	0.23	100.0	2 450.8	16.7
March	73.5	47.6	89.8	53.0	86.4	0.22	98.7	2 462.2	16.7
April	73.3	47.7	90.3	52.8	79.3	0.08	97.3	2 463.2	16.7
May	72.7	47.8	90.8	52.6	74.6	-0.12	96.0	2 471.8	16.7
June	72.3	48.2	91.3	52.8	71.6	-0.36	94.2	2 487.0	16.6
July	72.0	48.3	91.8	52.6	73.1	-0.28	92.5	2 499.2	16.6
August	71.7	48.4	91.9	52.7	74.3	-0.31	90.7	2 505.8	16.5
September	71.5	48.6	91.9	52.9	72.4	-0.22	90.5	2 511.4	16.4
October	71.2	48.8	91.6	53.3	68.7	-0.52	90.4	2 523.2	16.3
November	71.0	48.8	92.3	52.9	62.6	-0.60	90.2	2 532.4	16.3
December	70.9	48.9	92.2	53.0	57.9	-0.56	92.3	2 528.7	16.3
1967									
January	71.2	49.1	92.3	53.2	48.2	-0.36	94.3	2 551.6	16.2
February	70.9	49.0	92.5	53.0	49.9	-0.37	96.4	2 549.9	16.2
March	71.1	49.1	92.6	53.0	38.0	0.01	95.7	2 560.3	16.1
April	71.3	49.2	92.6	53.1	36.9	0.54	95.0	2 560.7	16.2
May	71.8	49.2	92.4	53.2	34.4	0.91	94.3	2 565.2	16.1
June	72.4	49.3	92.9	53.1	36.5	1.04	94.7	2 575.2	16.1
July	72.7	49.4	92.8	53.2	40.9	1.37	95.1	2 587.8	16.0
August	73.6	49.7	92.4	53.8	44.8	1.38	95.5	2 598.3	16.0
September	73.5	49.8	92.4	53.9	46.5	1.31	94.0	2 600.8	16.0
October	73.7	49.8	92.5	53.8	51.1	1.60	92.6	2 596.8	16.0
November	74.0	50.3	92.2	54.6	51.4	1.62	91.1	2 612.3	16.0
December	74.4	50.7	92.2	55.0	49.9	1.19	92.2	2 638.3	15.9
1968									
January	74.3	50.6	92.1	54.9	50.6	0.93	93.2	2 640.8	15.8
February	74.7	50.8	92.5	54.9	53.9	0.85	94.3	2 662.3	15.8
March	75.0	51.0	92.7	55.0	54.0	0.69	92.8	2 674.9	15.7
April	74.4	51.1	92.9	55.0	49.0	-0.12	91.4	2 684.5	15.7
May	74.4	51.4	93.3	55.1	49.4	-0.24	89.9	2 699.9	15.7
June	74.7	51.6	93.4	55.2	49.9	-0.35	89.8	2 712.1	15.7
July	75.1	51.8	93.3	55.5	55.9	-0.52	89.7	2 729.0	15.7
August	74.6	51.8	93.7	55.3	47.8	-0.61	89.6	2 737.6	15.6
September	75.4	52.0	93.5	55.6	48.4	-0.32	90.3	2 749.7	15.6
October	76.1	52.2	93.7	55.7	53.3	-0.33	90.9	2 753.9	15.7
November	76.3	52.5	93.8	56.0	61.0	-0.12	91.6	2 765.2	15.8
December	76.3	52.7	94.1	56.0	58.3	0.01	93.7	2 775.0	15.8
1969									
January	76.5	52.8	94.5	55.9	63.6	-0.26	95.9	2 775.9	15.9
February	76.6	53.0	94.6	56.0	60.1	-0.42	98.0	2 786.6	15.9
March	76.4	53.2	95.0	56.0	60.5	-0.49	95.7	2 799.2	15.9
April	76.7	53.3	95.3	55.9	63.9	-1.24	93.4	2 808.9	15.9
May	76.0	53.4	95.8	55.7	64.9	-2.35	91.1	2 819.1	15.9
June	75.7	53.7	96.0	55.9	67.0	-2.33	89.6	2 828.6	15.9
July	75.3	53.8	96.0	56.0	65.7	-1.89	88.1	2 844.5	15.8
August	75.3	54.1	96.3	56.2	70.3	-2.50	86.6	2 862.8	15.8
September	75.5	54.1	96.2	56.2	68.9	-1.99	84.3	2 868.5	15.8
October	75.0	54.3	96.2	56.4	66.8	-1.90	81.9	2 875.1	15.8
November	74.6	54.1	96.2	56.2	64.1	-1.71	79.6	2 876.0	15.8
December	74.2	54.1	96.5	56.1	66.8	-1.32	78.3	2 878.5	15.7
1970									
January	73.5	53.9	97.0	55.6	57.9	-1.19	77.1	2 873.7	15.8
February	72.8	53.9	96.9	55.6	57.7	-1.74	75.8	2 875.4	15.7
March	72.5	53.9	97.0	55.6	49.3	-0.69	74.3	2 882.7	15.7
April	71.8	53.9	96.7	55.7	48.7	-0.71	72.7	2 889.8	15.3
May	72.3	53.8	96.3	55.9	67.2	-0.03	71.2	2 892.2	15.4
June	72.5	53.8	96.4	55.8	66.1	0.24	72.7	2 885.6	15.5
July	72.5	53.9	95.8	56.3	49.8	0.25	74.2	2 900.6	15.4
August	72.8	53.8	96.0	56.0	46.1	0.92	75.7	2 908.6	15.4
September	72.8	53.8	95.5	56.3	46.5	1.10	74.2	2 908.6	15.3
October	72.5	53.3	95.6	55.8	39.0	1.13	72.8	2 884.1	15.4
November	72.5	53.1	95.3	55.7	37.8	1.24	71.3	2 880.9	15.3
December	73.8	53.6	94.4	56.8	37.5	1.49	72.8	2 886.8	15.3

[1] Not seasonally adjusted.
[2] Copyright, University of Michigan, Survey Research Center, first quarter 1966 = 100.

Table 20-7. Composite Indexes of Economic Activity and Selected Index Components—*Continued*

Year and month	Cyclical composite indexes, 1996 = 100				Selected components of leading index			Selected component of coincident index	Selected component of lagging index
	Leading	Coincident	Lagging	Ratio, coincident to lagging	Vendor performance (slower deliveries, diffusion index, percent)	Interest rate spread, 10-year Treasury bond less federal funds [1]	Index of consumer expectations [1,2]	Personal income less transfer payments (billions of 1996 dollars)	Consumer installment credit outstanding (percent of personal income)
1971									
January	74.5	53.9	94.1	57.3	39.8	2.10	74.4	2 919.5	15.4
February	75.2	53.9	93.9	57.4	44.2	2.39	75.9	2 919.6	15.4
March	75.6	54.0	93.6	57.7	45.0	1.99	75.9	2 930.9	15.4
April	76.0	54.2	93.2	58.2	48.9	1.68	75.9	2 938.0	15.4
May	76.3	54.4	93.0	58.5	49.4	1.76	75.9	2 948.4	15.4
June	76.5	54.5	92.5	58.9	47.9	1.61	76.7	2 947.8	15.2
July	76.5	54.4	92.9	58.6	47.4	1.42	77.6	2 949.6	15.5
August	76.6	54.5	93.3	58.4	49.7	1.02	78.4	2 966.9	15.5
September	77.0	54.8	93.2	58.8	48.9	0.59	78.0	2 968.9	15.6
October	77.1	54.9	92.9	59.1	50.9	0.73	77.6	2 979.2	15.7
November	77.5	55.2	92.8	59.5	50.9	0.90	77.2	2 993.9	15.7
December	78.7	55.5	92.6	59.9	53.3	1.79	81.8	3 018.8	15.7
1972									
January	79.3	56.0	91.3	61.3	55.2	2.45	86.3	3 038.7	15.6
February	79.9	56.2	91.1	61.7	52.6	2.79	90.9	3 054.1	15.6
March	80.2	56.5	91.4	61.8	57.1	2.24	88.0	3 070.7	15.6
April	80.2	56.8	91.7	61.9	55.0	2.02	85.1	3 093.4	15.7
May	80.3	57.1	91.9	62.1	56.1	1.86	82.2	3 105.9	15.8
June	80.5	57.1	92.2	61.9	57.7	1.65	85.2	3 074.4	16.1
July	81.0	57.2	92.4	61.9	61.7	1.56	88.3	3 124.4	15.9
August	82.0	57.8	92.0	62.8	62.9	1.41	91.3	3 157.7	15.9
September	82.7	58.1	91.8	63.3	65.5	1.68	90.1	3 172.6	15.9
October	83.0	58.6	91.9	63.8	73.0	1.44	89.0	3 221.9	15.7
November	83.5	59.1	91.8	64.4	74.5	1.22	87.8	3 248.0	15.7
December	83.9	59.5	91.7	64.9	80.7	1.03	83.0	3 268.8	15.8
1973									
January	84.1	59.8	92.4	64.7	83.7	0.52	78.1	3 255.3	16.1
February	84.1	60.1	93.0	64.6	85.2	0.06	73.3	3 275.6	16.1
March	83.6	60.2	93.5	64.4	87.5	-0.38	71.3	3 277.7	16.2
April	83.0	60.3	94.2	64.0	86.7	-0.45	69.3	3 281.5	16.2
May	82.8	60.5	94.5	64.0	86.6	-0.99	67.3	3 302.7	16.3
June	82.6	60.6	95.3	63.6	85.6	-1.59	65.9	3 314.5	16.3
July	82.1	60.8	95.6	63.6	85.2	-3.27	64.4	3 327.7	16.4
August	81.6	60.7	96.4	63.0	86.7	-3.10	63.0	3 315.7	16.4
September	81.5	60.9	96.5	63.1	90.1	-3.69	64.4	3 337.4	16.4
October	81.5	61.4	96.2	63.8	88.7	-3.22	65.7	3 369.4	16.3
November	81.4	61.8	96.5	64.0	96.8	-3.30	67.1	3 379.7	16.3
December	80.2	61.7	96.9	63.7	92.8	-3.21	61.2	3 371.8	16.3
1974									
January	80.0	61.5	97.3	63.2	91.8	-2.66	55.3	3 335.4	16.3
February	79.4	61.4	97.2	63.2	88.8	-2.01	49.4	3 313.2	16.3
March	79.7	61.4	97.3	63.1	88.9	-2.14	54.2	3 289.0	16.3
April	78.9	61.3	97.8	62.7	82.1	-3.00	59.1	3 270.3	16.4
May	78.7	61.5	98.4	62.5	74.5	-3.73	63.9	3 279.6	16.3
June	78.0	61.5	98.8	62.2	73.1	-4.39	61.8	3 284.4	16.2
July	77.4	61.5	99.2	62.0	69.2	-5.11	59.7	3 297.0	16.1
August	76.4	61.3	99.8	61.4	66.3	-3.97	57.6	3 280.8	16.1
September	75.1	61.2	100.2	61.1	51.8	-3.30	55.5	3 274.5	16.0
October	74.5	61.0	100.4	60.8	45.3	-2.16	53.3	3 279.9	15.8
November	73.4	60.4	100.4	60.2	34.0	-1.77	51.2	3 251.6	15.8
December	72.2	59.6	100.7	59.2	23.2	-1.10	50.8	3 236.3	15.6
1975									
January	71.9	59.3	99.9	59.4	19.5	0.37	50.4	3 224.6	15.6
February	71.9	58.8	99.0	59.4	15.9	1.15	50.0	3 205.3	15.5
March	72.5	58.4	98.4	59.3	17.3	2.19	56.6	3 203.6	15.5
April	74.1	58.4	97.3	60.0	21.7	2.74	63.2	3 199.0	15.3
May	75.0	58.5	96.3	60.7	22.7	2.84	69.8	3 215.1	15.2
June	75.5	58.6	94.1	62.3	24.9	2.31	70.1	3 220.8	14.6
July	76.6	58.8	93.9	62.6	28.7	1.96	70.4	3 222.8	14.8
August	76.9	59.2	93.4	63.4	35.1	2.26	70.7	3 253.0	14.6
September	77.3	59.4	93.2	63.7	43.8	2.19	70.4	3 265.8	14.6
October	77.8	59.6	93.1	64.0	44.8	2.32	70.2	3 282.2	14.5
November	78.1	59.7	92.9	64.3	46.8	2.83	69.9	3 291.5	14.5
December	78.3	60.1	92.7	64.8	41.2	2.80	73.7	3 293.1	14.6
1976									
January	79.7	60.7	92.7	65.5	54.0	2.87	77.4	3 316.7	14.5
February	80.7	61.0	92.5	65.9	56.1	3.02	81.2	3 340.0	14.5
March	80.8	61.2	92.3	66.3	56.7	2.89	80.6	3 358.5	14.5
April	80.8	61.5	92.1	66.8	57.3	2.74	80.1	3 379.8	14.6
May	81.1	61.6	91.9	67.0	58.3	2.61	79.5	3 392.7	14.5
June	81.2	61.7	91.7	67.3	58.6	2.38	81.5	3 392.5	14.6
July	81.7	61.9	91.6	67.6	54.0	2.52	83.5	3 408.5	14.6
August	81.9	62.1	91.6	67.8	55.2	2.48	85.5	3 421.8	14.5
September	82.2	62.2	91.7	67.8	52.6	2.34	85.6	3 428.5	14.6
October	82.0	62.2	92.0	67.6	49.0	2.39	85.8	3 433.3	14.6
November	82.5	62.7	91.9	68.2	47.2	2.34	85.9	3 463.9	14.6
December	83.2	63.1	91.7	68.8	53.3	2.22	85.3	3 472.3	14.6

[1] Not seasonally adjusted.
[2] Copyright, University of Michigan, Survey Research Center, first quarter 1966 = 100.

Table 20-7. Composite Indexes of Economic Activity and Selected Index Components—Continued

Year and month	Cyclical composite indexes, 1996 = 100				Selected components of leading index			Selected component of coincident index	Selected component of lagging index
	Leading	Coincident	Lagging	Ratio, coincident to lagging	Vendor performance (slower deliveries, diffusion index, percent)	Interest rate spread, 10-year Treasury bond less federal funds [1]	Index of consumer expectations [1,2]	Personal income less transfer payments (billions of 1996 dollars)	Consumer installment credit outstanding (percent of personal income)
1977									
January	83.0	63.1	91.8	68.7	55.3	2.60	84.8	3 460.2	14.6
February	83.5	63.5	91.8	69.2	65.1	2.71	84.2	3 470.9	14.6
March	84.1	63.9	91.7	69.7	49.6	2.77	84.0	3 489.6	14.7
April	84.1	64.2	92.0	69.8	54.6	2.64	83.8	3 508.0	14.8
May	84.2	64.5	92.0	70.1	55.4	2.11	83.6	3 531.0	14.9
June	84.5	64.9	92.5	70.2	53.3	1.89	82.9	3 542.8	15.0
July	84.5	65.1	92.5	70.4	58.3	1.91	82.2	3 556.0	15.0
August	84.4	65.3	92.8	70.4	53.5	1.50	81.5	3 568.8	15.0
September	84.5	65.6	93.0	70.5	56.7	1.20	79.6	3 599.7	15.1
October	84.4	66.0	93.1	70.9	53.6	1.05	77.8	3 648.4	15.1
November	84.5	66.3	93.4	71.0	56.3	1.07	75.9	3 665.4	15.1
December	84.6	66.5	93.1	71.4	57.1	1.13	75.8	3 676.4	15.1
1978									
January	83.7	66.2	93.9	70.5	55.6	1.26	75.7	3 662.2	15.2
February	84.1	66.6	94.0	70.9	63.4	1.25	77.2	3 680.7	15.2
March	84.3	67.2	94.2	71.3	58.9	1.25	69.5	3 706.8	15.3
April	85.0	68.0	94.1	72.3	57.1	1.26	71.1	3 738.3	15.3
May	85.0	68.2	94.4	72.2	57.4	0.99	73.0	3 741.0	15.4
June	85.1	68.6	95.0	72.2	61.1	0.86	68.1	3 762.9	15.6
July	84.8	68.7	95.3	72.1	59.4	0.83	72.0	3 773.9	15.6
August	85.0	69.0	95.4	72.3	60.6	0.37	67.0	3 787.5	15.7
September	85.2	69.1	95.9	72.1	60.0	-0.03	69.8	3 802.9	15.7
October	85.4	69.5	96.0	72.4	64.7	-0.32	71.7	3 818.8	15.7
November	84.5	69.8	96.8	72.1	64.5	-0.95	62.8	3 831.5	15.8
December	83.9	70.1	96.9	72.3	63.5	-1.02	53.8	3 854.8	15.8
1979									
January	83.9	70.1	97.2	72.1	66.4	-0.97	58.4	3 861.1	15.8
February	84.0	70.3	97.5	72.1	64.0	-0.96	62.2	3 881.0	15.9
March	84.4	70.8	97.0	73.0	66.7	-0.97	53.7	3 895.8	15.9
April	83.2	70.3	98.2	71.6	75.6	-0.83	53.3	3 856.0	16.0
May	83.7	70.7	98.1	72.1	63.7	-0.99	54.9	3 856.0	16.1
June	83.4	70.7	98.9	71.5	61.4	-1.38	51.4	3 865.4	16.1
July	82.5	70.8	99.2	71.4	57.4	-1.52	44.2	3 869.4	16.0
August	82.7	70.8	99.6	71.1	52.9	-1.91	49.3	3 875.4	16.1
September	82.8	70.7	100.3	70.5	50.7	-2.10	53.6	3 876.1	16.1
October	81.8	70.9	100.7	70.4	46.9	-3.47	49.5	3 897.0	16.1
November	81.4	71.0	101.1	70.2	46.8	-2.53	52.0	3 917.2	16.0
December	81.0	71.1	101.1	70.3	42.2	-3.39	51.5	3 931.3	16.0
1980									
January	81.4	71.3	101.3	70.4	42.1	-3.02	54.1	3 933.7	15.8
February	81.7	71.2	101.5	70.1	46.0	-1.72	54.9	3 920.1	15.9
March	79.1	71.0	102.8	69.1	39.1	-4.44	44.3	3 905.9	15.7
April	77.4	70.4	103.6	68.0	36.9	-6.14	44.4	3 869.0	15.7
May	77.4	69.7	102.9	67.7	29.8	-0.80	45.3	3 845.1	15.5
June	79.0	69.5	101.8	68.3	32.4	0.31	53.0	3 846.8	15.3
July	80.2	69.3	99.8	69.4	36.3	1.22	53.4	3 832.4	15.1
August	81.3	69.6	98.6	70.6	40.1	1.49	59.6	3 848.6	15.0
September	82.2	70.1	97.5	71.9	41.2	0.64	67.2	3 868.0	14.8
October	82.6	70.7	96.9	73.0	46.5	-1.06	68.9	3 933.4	14.5
November	82.5	71.1	97.0	73.3	46.8	-3.17	76.2	3 957.4	14.4
December	81.4	71.3	97.8	72.9	50.1	-6.06	59.7	3 977.0	14.3
1981									
January	81.2	71.2	98.3	72.4	49.7	-6.51	67.2	3 954.2	14.3
February	81.1	71.2	98.3	72.4	48.5	-2.74	61.4	3 943.0	14.3
March	81.9	71.2	98.2	72.5	48.7	-1.58	61.4	3 952.7	14.2
April	82.6	71.2	98.0	72.7	51.2	-2.04	68.1	3 954.8	14.2
May	82.1	71.3	99.1	71.9	50.2	-4.42	72.9	3 968.5	14.2
June	81.2	71.5	99.3	72.0	47.9	-5.63	70.5	3 996.2	14.1
July	80.9	71.8	99.3	72.3	44.9	-4.76	66.4	4 037.8	13.9
August	81.3	71.8	99.5	72.2	49.6	-2.88	70.1	4 059.9	13.8
September	80.7	71.7	100.2	71.6	45.9	-0.55	68.3	4 060.5	13.9
October	79.9	71.4	99.8	71.5	37.7	0.07	61.5	4 056.2	13.9
November	79.7	71.1	99.6	71.4	40.5	0.08	55.6	4 051.4	13.8
December	79.9	70.8	99.2	71.4	41.2	1.35	56.8	4 042.3	13.8
1982									
January	79.4	70.3	99.3	70.8	40.1	1.37	62.9	4 031.0	13.9
February	79.9	70.7	98.4	71.8	40.8	-0.35	58.7	4 042.8	13.9
March	79.4	70.6	97.8	72.2	36.4	-0.82	53.1	4 047.9	13.8
April	80.0	70.5	97.9	72.0	38.2	-1.07	61.1	4 066.3	13.8
May	80.2	70.5	97.6	72.2	42.1	-0.83	62.0	4 074.3	13.8
June	80.0	70.2	97.6	71.9	45.2	0.15	60.1	4 055.2	13.8
July	80.5	69.9	97.2	71.9	45.8	1.36	57.6	4 043.1	13.7
August	80.3	69.7	97.0	71.9	45.3	2.94	60.9	4 040.8	13.7
September	81.2	69.5	96.6	71.9	45.9	2.03	66.9	4 032.7	13.7
October	81.6	69.2	95.9	72.2	46.5	1.20	70.4	4 023.7	13.7
November	82.1	69.2	95.0	72.8	46.9	1.35	71.0	4 026.0	13.6
December	82.9	69.1	94.0	73.5	48.6	1.59	67.9	4 041.2	13.7

[1] Not seasonally adjusted.
[2] Copyright, University of Michigan, Survey Research Center, first quarter 1966 = 100.

Table 20-7. Composite Indexes of Economic Activity and Selected Index Components—Continued

Year and month	Cyclical composite indexes, 1996 = 100				Selected components of leading index			Selected component of coincident index	Selected component of lagging index
	Leading	Coincident	Lagging	Ratio, coincident to lagging	Vendor performance (slower deliveries, diffusion index, percent)	Interest rate spread, 10-year Treasury bond less federal funds [1]	Index of consumer expectations [1,2]	Personal income less transfer payments (billions of 1996 dollars)	Consumer installment credit outstanding (percent of personal income)
1983									
January	84.3	69.5	93.3	74.5	46.7	1.78	65.2	4 044.5	13.7
February	85.1	69.4	93.2	74.5	49.9	2.21	71.2	4 044.9	13.7
March	86.1	69.8	92.8	75.2	50.8	1.74	80.9	4 063.6	13.7
April	86.8	70.0	92.7	75.5	52.7	1.60	86.9	4 064.5	13.7
May	87.8	70.4	92.2	76.4	51.9	1.75	93.4	4 094.1	13.7
June	88.5	70.9	92.3	76.8	56.8	1.87	89.2	4 104.2	13.8
July	88.9	71.3	92.4	77.2	58.9	2.01	91.1	4 127.0	13.8
August	88.7	71.2	92.8	76.7	60.2	2.29	88.2	4 115.0	13.9
September	89.1	72.1	92.7	77.8	60.7	2.20	85.8	4 153.1	13.9
October	89.8	72.6	92.6	78.4	62.8	2.06	86.1	4 204.9	13.9
November	90.0	73.0	93.1	78.4	67.5	2.35	87.9	4 231.1	14.0
December	90.1	73.5	93.3	78.8	62.1	2.36	91.0	4 272.4	14.1
1984									
January	90.9	74.1	93.2	79.5	64.4	2.11	97.0	4 312.1	14.1
February	91.1	74.4	94.1	79.1	61.5	2.25	93.2	4 330.6	14.3
March	91.0	74.7	94.6	79.0	65.5	2.41	97.7	4 358.3	14.3
April	90.8	75.1	95.1	79.0	64.6	2.34	91.4	4 395.9	14.3
May	91.2	75.4	95.6	78.9	62.5	3.09	90.6	4 416.4	14.5
June	90.6	75.9	96.1	79.0	56.2	2.50	89.8	4 458.2	14.7
July	90.6	76.1	96.7	78.7	59.1	2.13	91.9	4 491.7	14.7
August	89.9	76.3	97.3	78.4	55.2	1.08	93.7	4 506.2	14.8
September	89.8	76.5	97.6	78.4	52.8	1.22	96.4	4 542.0	14.8
October	89.8	76.6	97.9	78.2	49.3	2.17	91.6	4 536.4	15.0
November	90.2	77.0	97.7	78.8	48.1	2.14	91.5	4 565.0	15.0
December	90.8	77.1	97.7	78.9	48.8	3.12	87.9	4 587.5	15.1
1985									
January	91.2	77.2	97.9	78.9	50.4	3.03	90.3	4 588.8	15.2
February	91.2	77.4	98.0	79.0	48.6	3.01	86.5	4 593.1	15.4
March	91.4	77.6	98.2	79.0	46.7	3.28	87.3	4 611.9	15.5
April	91.2	77.7	98.2	79.1	46.1	3.16	87.0	4 613.1	15.7
May	91.5	78.0	98.6	79.1	48.0	2.88	84.2	4 617.9	15.9
June	91.8	77.9	98.6	79.0	47.1	2.63	91.1	4 634.3	15.9
July	91.8	77.9	98.9	78.8	45.7	2.43	87.4	4 621.3	16.1
August	92.0	78.3	98.9	79.2	46.6	2.43	86.3	4 631.1	16.2
September	92.3	78.4	98.7	79.4	49.5	2.45	84.2	4 638.7	16.4
October	92.1	78.5	99.5	78.9	50.0	2.25	80.8	4 673.6	16.4
November	92.0	78.7	99.4	79.2	48.5	1.73	84.5	4 670.1	16.6
December	92.5	79.0	99.6	79.3	49.3	0.99	88.1	4 710.0	16.5
1986									
January	92.6	79.1	99.4	79.6	50.1	1.05	85.3	4 688.2	16.7
February	92.7	79.1	99.6	79.4	49.8	0.84	87.8	4 713.1	16.7
March	92.7	79.3	99.9	79.4	50.5	0.30	86.9	4 755.7	16.7
April	93.2	79.5	99.3	80.1	50.7	0.31	88.5	4 759.0	16.8
May	93.4	79.5	99.4	80.0	50.2	0.86	87.5	4 766.3	16.9
June	93.9	79.5	99.3	80.1	49.9	0.88	90.3	4 768.8	17.0
July	93.8	79.8	99.3	80.4	49.9	0.74	88.5	4 777.4	17.0
August	93.9	79.9	99.2	80.5	50.8	1.00	85.9	4 794.1	17.1
September	94.1	80.3	98.6	81.4	49.6	1.56	81.3	4 795.9	17.2
October	94.5	80.3	99.3	80.9	51.3	1.58	87.1	4 795.7	17.4
November	94.4	80.5	99.1	81.2	52.0	1.21	81.6	4 816.6	17.3
December	95.0	80.9	98.7	82.0	52.8	0.20	78.3	4 818.9	17.2
1987									
January	94.9	80.6	99.4	81.1	51.5	0.65	80.9	4 821.5	17.1
February	95.6	81.3	98.6	82.5	51.2	1.15	81.6	4 836.6	17.0
March	95.8	81.4	98.5	82.6	51.9	1.12	83.3	4 851.3	16.8
April	95.8	81.6	98.6	82.8	52.8	1.65	84.7	4 846.9	16.9
May	95.9	81.9	98.8	82.9	54.0	1.76	80.6	4 869.5	16.9
June	96.2	82.1	98.9	83.0	56.8	1.67	80.8	4 874.3	16.9
July	96.6	82.4	98.7	83.5	58.9	1.87	83.3	4 890.9	16.9
August	96.6	82.7	98.8	83.7	60.3	2.03	85.8	4 923.7	16.9
September	96.8	82.9	99.0	83.7	61.5	2.20	84.2	4 928.7	16.9
October	96.7	83.4	99.2	84.1	62.2	2.23	80.4	4 966.5	16.9
November	96.1	83.6	99.2	84.3	64.9	2.17	72.7	4 991.9	16.9
December	96.0	84.1	99.0	84.9	62.7	2.22	76.7	5 047.2	16.7
1988									
January	95.8	84.0	99.4	84.5	62.0	1.84	80.9	5 014.2	16.8
February	96.5	84.4	99.2	85.1	61.2	1.63	81.9	5 037.7	16.8
March	96.7	84.8	99.4	85.3	57.3	1.79	85.2	5 046.9	16.8
April	96.6	84.9	99.7	85.2	58.6	1.85	82.4	5 055.3	16.9
May	96.6	85.1	99.8	85.3	56.9	2.00	87.3	5 063.3	16.9
June	97.3	85.4	100.1	85.3	65.6	1.41	85.7	5 080.5	16.8
July	96.6	85.6	99.9	85.7	58.4	1.31	82.3	5 107.6	16.8
August	96.7	85.7	100.1	85.6	57.4	1.25	88.8	5 111.0	16.8
September	96.5	85.9	99.9	86.0	55.2	0.79	89.5	5 117.6	16.8
October	96.6	86.2	100.2	86.0	54.8	0.50	87.0	5 145.2	16.7
November	96.5	86.4	100.3	86.1	52.1	0.61	86.3	5 149.6	16.7
December	96.7	86.9	100.1	86.8	53.0	0.35	85.5	5 191.5	16.6

[1] Not seasonally adjusted.
[2] Copyright, University of Michigan, Survey Research Center, first quarter 1966 = 100.

Table 20-7. Composite Indexes of Economic Activity and Selected Index Components—Continued

Year and month	Cyclical composite indexes, 1996 = 100				Selected components of leading index			Selected component of coincident index	Selected component of lagging index
	Leading	Coincident	Lagging	Ratio, coincident to lagging	Vendor performance (slower deliveries, diffusion index, percent)	Interest rate spread, 10-year Treasury bond less federal funds [1]	Index of consumer expectations [1,2]	Personal income less transfer payments (billions of 1996 dollars)	Consumer installment credit outstanding (percent of personal income)
1989									
January	96.7	87.2	100.4	86.9	53.9	-0.03	89.9	5 235.9	16.7
February	96.3	87.2	101.1	86.3	54.0	-0.19	88.8	5 240.4	16.7
March	95.5	87.3	101.6	85.9	52.5	-0.49	87.6	5 254.2	16.8
April	95.8	87.4	101.2	86.4	52.2	-0.66	83.2	5 244.3	16.8
May	95.2	87.2	102.0	85.5	49.1	-0.95	80.1	5 222.0	16.9
June	95.0	87.3	102.3	85.3	46.5	-1.25	82.0	5 237.4	16.9
July	95.1	87.2	102.4	85.2	46.1	-1.22	85.5	5 250.6	16.9
August	95.3	87.6	102.0	85.9	44.0	-0.88	80.3	5 255.8	16.9
September	95.5	87.5	101.8	86.0	43.9	-0.83	88.6	5 252.5	16.9
October	95.3	87.5	102.2	85.6	43.3	-0.83	87.2	5 265.3	16.9
November	95.6	87.8	102.0	86.1	42.5	-0.68	84.3	5 290.9	16.9
December	95.9	88.1	102.0	86.4	43.5	-0.61	85.5	5 300.6	16.9
1990									
January	96.2	88.0	101.5	86.7	48.2	-0.02	83.4	5 295.4	16.8
February	95.6	88.5	101.4	87.3	44.4	0.23	81.3	5 318.0	16.7
March	96.1	88.7	101.5	87.4	47.2	0.31	81.3	5 320.3	16.6
April	95.7	88.7	101.4	87.5	47.2	0.53	83.9	5 349.3	16.5
May	95.6	88.8	101.4	87.6	48.2	0.58	79.3	5 336.2	16.5
June	95.7	88.9	101.4	87.7	49.8	0.19	76.6	5 344.9	16.4
July	95.5	88.9	101.6	87.5	46.4	0.32	77.3	5 366.0	16.4
August	94.9	88.8	101.4	87.6	50.1	0.62	62.9	5 335.8	16.5
September	94.3	88.6	101.5	87.3	48.9	0.69	58.8	5 330.9	16.4
October	93.6	88.2	101.5	86.9	48.1	0.61	50.9	5 284.8	16.5
November	93.1	87.9	101.6	86.5	48.6	0.58	52.8	5 282.1	16.5
December	93.2	87.7	101.4	86.5	47.2	0.77	53.7	5 289.9	16.3
1991									
January	92.9	87.3	101.5	86.0	44.4	1.18	55.2	5 235.6	16.3
February	93.5	87.2	100.9	86.4	44.7	1.60	62.0	5 233.8	16.3
March	94.1	87.0	100.8	86.3	43.9	1.99	84.5	5 238.9	16.3
April	94.5	87.2	100.0	87.2	45.0	2.13	74.7	5 248.5	16.2
May	94.8	87.3	99.5	87.7	46.0	2.29	71.5	5 243.7	16.1
June	95.2	87.5	98.9	88.5	47.1	2.38	75.9	5 273.9	15.9
July	96.0	87.6	98.5	88.9	49.6	2.45	74.4	5 257.9	15.9
August	95.5	87.6	98.1	89.3	48.3	2.24	75.3	5 259.0	15.8
September	95.5	87.8	97.7	89.9	48.8	2.20	76.4	5 270.4	15.7
October	95.5	87.7	97.4	90.0	50.2	2.32	70.5	5 251.2	15.6
November	95.4	87.7	97.2	90.2	50.1	2.61	61.9	5 266.2	15.6
December	95.0	87.6	97.0	90.3	49.4	2.66	61.5	5 292.4	15.4
1992									
January	95.5	87.7	96.2	91.2	48.7	3.00	59.1	5 285.1	15.4
February	95.9	88.0	95.7	92.0	49.3	3.28	61.8	5 321.2	15.2
March	96.6	88.1	95.4	92.3	50.3	3.56	70.3	5 326.0	15.2
April	96.6	88.4	95.1	93.0	47.4	3.75	70.5	5 336.4	15.1
May	96.7	88.5	94.9	93.3	50.0	3.57	71.2	5 356.9	15.0
June	96.6	88.6	94.4	93.9	50.8	3.50	70.7	5 364.2	14.9
July	96.5	88.9	94.0	94.6	52.5	3.59	67.6	5 360.5	14.9
August	96.4	88.6	94.3	94.0	50.3	3.29	69.5	5 336.7	14.8
September	96.5	88.9	94.1	94.5	51.2	3.20	67.4	5 370.3	14.8
October	96.7	89.2	93.8	95.1	48.6	3.49	67.5	5 396.3	14.7
November	97.3	89.5	94.1	95.1	51.3	3.78	78.2	5 414.8	14.7
December	98.1	90.4	93.2	97.0	51.5	3.85	89.5	5 620.5	14.3
1993									
January	97.7	89.6	94.1	95.2	52.3	3.58	83.4	5 337.8	14.9
February	97.7	89.8	94.2	95.3	51.7	3.23	80.6	5 336.0	15.0
March	97.0	89.6	94.4	94.9	52.7	2.91	75.8	5 311.2	15.0
April	97.4	90.2	94.2	95.8	52.8	3.01	76.4	5 420.6	14.8
May	97.1	90.4	94.2	96.0	51.5	3.04	68.5	5 437.6	14.8
June	97.3	90.5	94.2	96.1	50.4	2.92	70.4	5 428.7	14.8
July	97.0	90.6	94.4	96.0	51.0	2.75	64.7	5 424.6	14.9
August	97.3	90.8	94.4	96.2	51.8	2.65	65.8	5 442.5	14.9
September	97.4	91.1	94.4	96.5	51.3	2.27	66.8	5 438.2	15.0
October	97.6	91.4	94.2	97.0	50.7	2.34	72.5	5 450.9	15.1
November	97.9	91.7	94.1	97.4	50.9	2.70	70.3	5 467.1	15.2
December	98.6	92.6	93.8	98.7	51.5	2.81	78.8	5 669.9	14.9
1994									
January	98.6	91.9	94.6	97.1	54.4	2.70	86.4	5 408.9	15.5
February	98.3	92.3	94.3	97.9	57.0	2.72	83.5	5 470.3	15.5
March	99.0	92.9	94.3	98.5	55.4	3.14	85.1	5 494.5	15.6
April	99.1	93.3	94.3	98.9	57.2	3.41	82.6	5 569.8	15.6
May	99.2	93.7	94.6	99.0	60.2	3.17	84.2	5 608.2	15.7
June	99.1	94.0	95.0	98.9	60.3	2.85	82.7	5 603.4	15.8
July	98.8	94.2	95.1	99.1	58.1	3.04	78.5	5 611.5	15.9
August	99.1	94.7	95.2	99.5	61.6	2.77	80.8	5 619.8	16.1
September	99.1	94.9	95.6	99.3	62.5	2.73	83.5	5 647.8	16.2
October	99.4	95.3	95.8	99.5	64.9	2.98	85.1	5 692.7	16.2
November	99.3	95.7	96.4	99.3	64.7	2.67	84.8	5 687.8	16.4
December	99.3	96.1	96.7	99.4	64.8	2.36	88.8	5 705.5	16.6

[1] Not seasonally adjusted.
[2] Copyright, University of Michigan, Survey Research Center, first quarter 1966 = 100.

Table 20-7. Composite Indexes of Economic Activity and Selected Index Components—Continued

Year and month	Cyclical composite indexes, 1996 = 100				Selected components of leading index			Selected component of coincident index	Selected component of lagging index
	Leading	Coincident	Lagging	Ratio, coincident to lagging	Vendor performance (slower deliveries, diffusion index, percent)	Interest rate spread, 10-year Treasury bond less federal funds [1]	Index of consumer expectations [1,2]	Personal income less transfer payments (billions of 1996 dollars)	Consumer installment credit outstanding (percent of personal income)
1995									
January	99.1	96.4	97.2	99.2	62.7	2.25	88.4	5 721.4	16.7
February	98.5	96.5	97.8	98.7	60.7	1.55	85.9	5 725.0	16.8
March	98.0	96.6	98.1	98.5	56.9	1.22	79.8	5 730.6	17.0
April	97.8	96.6	98.7	97.9	56.3	1.01	83.8	5 735.1	17.1
May	97.6	96.7	99.0	97.7	53.3	0.62	80.1	5 725.7	17.3
June	97.7	97.0	99.5	97.5	51.8	0.17	84.1	5 744.1	17.4
July	98.0	96.8	99.7	97.1	51.3	0.43	87.4	5 752.9	17.5
August	98.4	97.4	99.6	97.8	49.1	0.75	86.1	5 756.1	17.7
September	98.5	97.6	99.7	97.9	50.0	0.40	78.8	5 779.9	17.9
October	98.3	97.7	99.9	97.8	48.4	0.28	80.8	5 790.1	17.9
November	98.2	98.0	99.9	98.1	45.3	0.13	79.7	5 820.9	18.2
December	98.6	98.3	99.9	98.4	47.5	0.11	83.7	5 836.8	18.2
1996									
January	97.7	98.1	100.0	98.1	47.8	0.09	78.7	5 843.3	18.2
February	98.7	98.7	99.9	98.8	49.5	0.59	77.8	5 897.6	18.2
March	99.2	98.9	99.8	99.1	49.6	0.96	86.2	5 918.9	18.3
April	99.6	99.2	99.8	99.4	49.4	1.29	83.0	5 923.7	18.3
May	100.0	99.6	99.8	99.8	49.9	1.50	79.2	5 948.3	18.4
June	100.5	100.0	99.8	100.2	52.8	1.64	84.0	5 991.6	18.4
July	100.5	100.1	100.2	99.9	50.8	1.47	86.5	5 988.0	18.6
August	100.5	100.5	100.0	100.5	51.9	1.42	87.3	6 017.4	18.6
September	100.7	100.8	100.1	100.7	50.0	1.53	90.1	6 040.9	18.6
October	100.7	101.0	100.1	100.9	50.9	1.29	89.9	6 045.0	18.6
November	100.9	101.4	100.1	101.3	51.2	0.89	93.9	6 066.5	18.6
December	100.9	101.6	100.3	101.3	52.0	1.01	91.8	6 092.2	18.6
1997									
January	101.2	101.5	100.4	101.1	49.7	1.33	91.3	6 119.1	18.6
February	102.1	102.1	100.2	101.9	52.1	1.23	94.9	6 147.6	18.6
March	102.1	102.4	100.2	102.2	53.1	1.30	93.6	6 176.6	18.6
April	102.2	102.7	100.3	102.4	53.4	1.38	92.5	6 185.6	18.7
May	102.6	102.9	100.5	102.4	55.0	1.21	96.6	6 216.0	18.7
June	102.8	103.4	100.5	102.9	54.6	0.93	98.9	6 239.7	18.6
July	103.5	103.8	100.2	103.6	54.7	0.70	102.6	6 271.8	18.6
August	103.4	104.0	100.4	103.6	55.2	0.76	100.3	6 312.5	18.6
September	103.8	104.6	100.6	104.0	54.8	0.67	100.7	6 331.5	18.6
October	104.1	104.9	100.9	104.0	54.9	0.53	102.8	6 364.5	18.6
November	104.3	105.5	101.1	104.4	55.2	0.36	102.3	6 415.9	18.5
December	104.1	105.8	101.1	104.6	53.9	0.31	96.1	6 451.4	18.4
1998									
January	104.2	106.2	101.2	104.9	53.0	-0.02	102.2	6 516.5	18.2
February	104.9	106.7	101.4	105.2	52.8	0.06	104.2	6 568.2	18.2
March	105.0	107.0	101.9	105.0	53.0	0.16	101.9	6 612.2	18.3
April	105.2	107.4	101.8	105.5	52.4	0.19	104.3	6 644.0	18.5
May	105.2	107.8	101.9	105.8	51.5	0.16	101.7	6 681.3	18.5
June	104.8	107.9	102.4	105.4	50.9	-0.06	99.3	6 722.8	18.5
July	105.1	107.9	102.5	105.3	50.2	-0.08	100.0	6 741.1	18.5
August	105.4	108.6	102.6	105.8	50.3	-0.21	98.3	6 774.3	18.5
September	105.2	108.9	102.7	106.0	50.8	-0.70	93.9	6 799.2	18.5
October	105.4	109.3	102.6	106.5	49.8	-0.54	87.5	6 811.5	18.6
November	106.4	109.5	102.5	106.8	50.4	0.00	94.3	6 843.8	18.5
December	106.6	109.8	102.4	107.2	48.5	-0.03	91.9	6 853.8	18.6
1999									
January	107.1	110.0	103.0	106.8	51.0	0.09	95.7	6 856.6	18.6
February	107.7	110.5	103.0	107.3	50.8	0.24	103.6	6 883.1	18.7
March	107.8	110.6	103.3	107.1	52.3	0.42	99.0	6 890.3	18.8
April	107.5	110.8	103.5	107.1	49.5	0.44	97.4	6 880.2	18.8
May	108.1	111.2	103.4	107.5	52.1	0.80	97.6	6 900.6	18.9
June	108.6	111.4	103.1	108.1	52.6	1.14	99.8	6 920.6	18.9
July	108.8	111.7	103.6	107.8	54.0	0.80	99.2	6 929.4	19.0
August	108.8	112.1	103.8	108.0	51.4	0.87	98.4	6 959.1	19.0
September	108.8	112.1	104.2	107.6	55.8	0.70	101.5	6 947.3	19.1
October	109.0	112.7	104.1	108.3	56.2	0.91	97.1	7 014.9	19.0
November	109.4	113.3	104.4	108.5	56.8	0.61	101.0	7 070.4	18.9
December	110.0	113.8	104.8	108.6	56.7	0.98	101.1	7 128.0	18.8
2000									
January	110.3	114.3	105.0	108.9	55.0	1.21	108.6	7 231.2	18.7
February	109.6	114.4	105.7	108.2	54.4	0.79	107.8	7 265.6	18.6
March	109.8	114.9	105.5	108.9	54.3	0.41	101.7	7 291.1	18.7
April	110.1	115.3	105.8	109.0	55.4	-0.03	103.7	7 297.3	18.8
May	109.6	115.4	105.9	109.0	55.4	0.17	104.8	7 297.6	18.8
June	109.6	115.6	106.5	108.5	54.5	-0.43	100.8	7 328.5	19.0
July	109.4	115.7	106.3	108.8	53.9	-0.49	104.5	7 387.8	19.0
August	109.2	115.8	106.8	108.4	53.5	-0.67	104.0	7 410.1	19.2
September	109.3	116.0	107.0	108.4	49.6	-0.72	103.4	7 407.9	19.3
October	109.0	115.9	107.6	107.7	51.1	-0.77	100.7	7 419.8	19.5
November	108.6	115.9	108.1	107.2	50.2	-0.79	101.6	7 412.5	19.6
December	108.1	115.9	107.9	107.4	52.8	-1.16	90.7	7 394.7	19.7

[1] Not seasonally adjusted.
[2] Copyright, University of Michigan, Survey Research Center, first quarter 1966 = 100.

Table 20-7. Composite Indexes of Economic Activity and Selected Index Components—Continued

Year and month	Cyclical composite indexes, 1996 = 100				Selected components of leading index			Selected component of coincident index	Selected component of lagging index
	Leading	Coincident	Lagging	Ratio, coincident to lagging	Vendor performance (slower deliveries, diffusion index, percent)	Interest rate spread, 10-year Treasury bond less federal funds [1]	Index of consumer expectations [1,2]	Personal income less transfer payments (billions of 1996 dollars)	Consumer installment credit outstanding (percent of personal income)
2001									
January	108.2	115.7	106.6	108.5	49.5	-0.82	86.4	7 424.0	19.7
February	108.1	115.8	106.3	108.9	50.1	-0.39	80.8	7 428.6	19.8
March	107.8	115.6	106.1	109.0	48.1	-0.42	83.9	7 436.0	19.9
April	107.9	115.2	106.0	108.7	47.5	0.34	82.2	7 393.8	20.0
May	108.5	115.1	105.6	109.0	46.0	1.18	85.4	7 371.1	20.1
June	108.6	114.7	105.0	109.2	47.5	1.31	86.9	7 362.9	20.1
July	108.9	114.7	104.9	109.3	47.0	1.47	88.4	7 366.8	20.2
August	108.7	114.7	104.5	109.8	46.8	1.32	85.2	7 364.7	20.3
September	108.0	114.1	104.6	109.1	47.3	1.66	73.5	7 353.9	20.4
October	108.1	114.4	103.9	110.1	49.1	2.08	75.5	7 330.0	20.5
November	109.0	114.1	103.5	110.2	48.5	2.56	76.6	7 332.5	20.8
December	110.3	114.0	103.4	110.3	48.8	3.27	82.3	7 352.1	20.9
2002									
January	110.8	114.1	103.3	110.5	50.8	3.31	91.3	7 337.3	20.9
February	111.0	114.1	103.0	110.8	51.1	3.17	87.2	7 350.3	20.9
March	111.1	114.0	103.0	110.7	52.6	3.55	92.7	7 358.6	21.0
April	110.8	114.2	102.5	111.4	53.6	3.46	89.1	7 353.1	21.0
May	111.4	114.3	102.2	111.8	53.9	3.41	92.7	7 363.8	21.0
June	111.1	114.5	102.0	112.3	54.9	3.18	87.9	7 374.6	21.1
July	111.0	114.4	101.9	112.3	54.8	2.92	81.0	7 339.2	21.2
August	110.8	114.4	101.9	112.3	53.7	2.52	80.6	7 319.4	21.3
September	110.3	114.3	101.6	112.5	56.5	2.12	79.9	7 306.1	21.3
October	110.3	114.3	101.5	112.6	53.1	2.19	73.1	7 317.5	21.3
November	111.0	114.4	101.2	113.0	51.8	2.71	78.5	7 312.9	21.3
December	111.1	114.2	101.1	113.0	52.4	2.79	80.8	7 300.7	21.3
2003									
January	111.0	114.4	101.1	113.2	52.0	2.81	72.8	7 313.9	21.5
February	110.6	114.2	101.2	112.8	52.4	2.64	69.9	7 318.8	21.4
March	110.4	114.2	101.0	113.1	53.4	2.56	69.6	7 324.1	21.3
April	110.5	114.1	100.7	113.3	50.1	2.70	79.3	7 345.1	21.4
May	111.6	114.3	100.5	113.7	51.4	2.31	91.4	7 392.9	21.4
June	112.0	114.4	99.8	114.6	50.6	2.11	86.4	7 412.5	21.3
July	112.8	114.7	99.6	115.2	51.4	2.97	83.7	7 430.0	21.3
August	113.2	114.7	99.6	115.2	53.3	3.42	82.5	7 437.9	21.3
September	113.3	114.9	99.0	116.1	53.1	3.26	80.8	7 451.6	21.4
October	113.9	115.2	99.0	116.4	54.1	3.28	83.0	7 488.2	21.4
November	114.2	115.6	98.4	117.5	56.0	3.30	88.1	7 542.8	21.2
December	114.5	115.8	98.0	118.2	58.6	3.29	89.8	7 550.6	21.2

[1] Not seasonally adjusted.
[2] Copyright, University of Michigan, Survey Research Center, first quarter 1966 = 100.

CHAPTER 20: SELECTED HISTORICAL DATA FOR MONTHLY SERIES

NOTES AND DEFINITIONS

TABLE 20-1
INDUSTRIAL PRODUCTION AND CAPACITY UTILIZATION

See the Notes and Definitions for Tables 2-1 through 2-3.

TABLE 20-2
SUMMARY CONSUMER AND PRODUCER PRICE INDEXES

See the Notes and Definitions for Tables 8-1 through 8-4.

TABLE 20-3
SUMMARY LABOR FORCE, EMPLOYMENT, AND UNEMPLOYMENT

See the Notes and Definitions for Tables 10-1 through 10-3.

TABLES 20-4
NONFARM PAYROLL EMPLOYMENT, HOURS, AND EARNINGS

See the Notes and Definitions for Tables 10-5 through 10-10.

TABLE 20-5
MONEY STOCK, RESERVES, AND MONETARY BASE

See the Notes and Definitions for Tables 12-1 through 12-3.

TABLE 20-6
INTEREST RATES, BOND YIELDS, AND STOCK PRICE INDEXES

See the Notes and Definitions for Tables 12-9 and 12-10.

TABLE 20-7
COMPOSITE INDEXES OF ECONOMIC ACTIVITY AND SELECTED INDEX COMPONENTS

See the Notes and Definitions for Table 1-8.

PART D

REGIONAL AND STATE DATA

CHAPTER 21: REGIONAL AND STATE DATA

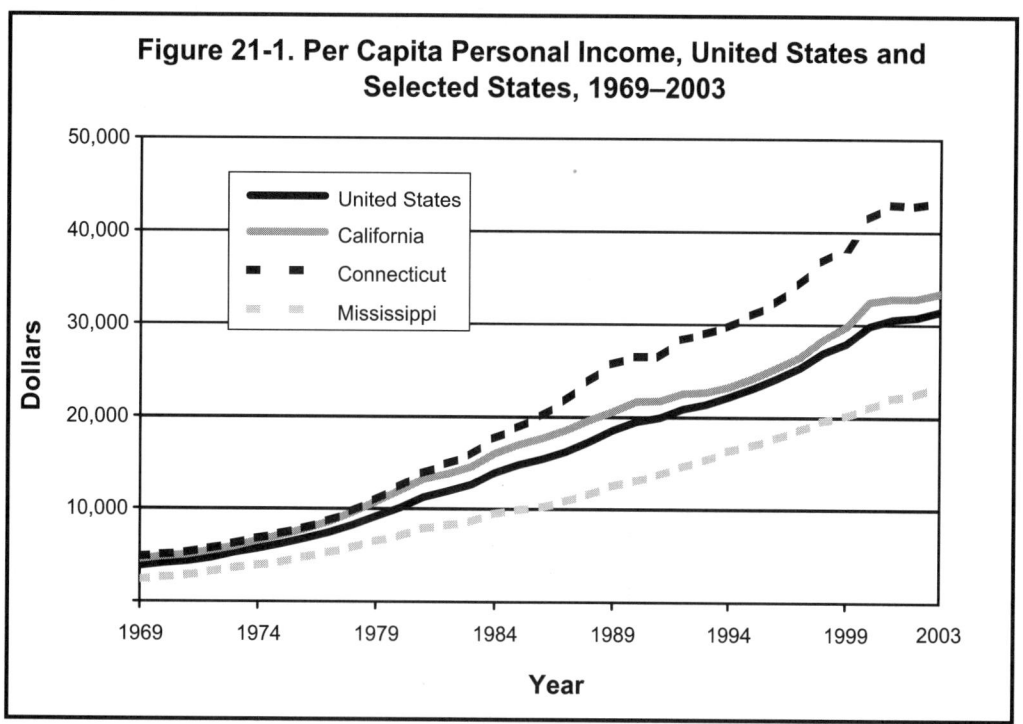

Figure 21-1. Per Capita Personal Income, United States and Selected States, 1969–2003

- Per capita personal income (total personal income divided by the size of the population) provides one measure of the affluence of states and regions and how they have changed over time. To provide examples, Figure 21-1 above shows the time path since 1969 for the U.S. total; for the largest state in terms of both population and total income (California); for the state with the highest per capita income in 2003 (Connecticut); and for the state with the lowest (Mississippi). (The District of Columbia, which is shown in the tables in order to complete the coverage of the United States, has even higher per capita income than Connecticut, but is not really comparable with the states in many respects since it consists entirely of a central city area.) (Table 21-2)
- These data are not adjusted to remove the effects of inflation or the effects of different costs of living in different states or regions. In addition, they are averages ("means") and, because of the skewed distribution of income, do not necessarily approximate the income of the typical, or "median," person in the state. Median income data for recent years are shown in Table 3-12 of this volume. (See "Expanded Historical Statistics…" at the beginning of this volume for a discussion of means and medians. The District of Columbia provides an extreme example of the difference. Despite its high per capita income, the District's *median* income is low and its poverty rate is high.) However, per capita income data can be useful for assessing and comparing the economic and fiscal capacities of the states.

Table 21-1. Gross Domestic Product by Region and State

(Billions of dollars; index numbers, 1996 = 100.)

Year	United States	New England							Mideast						
		Total	Connect-icut	Maine	Massa-chusetts	New Hamp-shire	Rhode Island	Vermont	Total	Delaware	District of Columbia	Maryland	New Jersey	New York	Pennsyl-vania
VALUE															
1977	1 985.7	103.7	29.5	7.6	49.7	6.4	7.3	3.4	402.1	6.0	15.2	35.5	66.8	178.0	100.6
1978	2 249.0	116.5	33.0	8.4	55.6	7.5	8.0	4.0	446.5	6.6	16.6	39.4	74.2	197.4	112.3
1979	2 503.9	129.5	36.7	9.3	61.6	8.5	8.9	4.5	490.1	7.2	18.1	43.4	82.7	215.4	123.2
1980	2 731.6	143.0	40.6	10.2	68.2	9.4	9.7	4.9	530.0	7.8	19.6	47.3	90.5	234.3	130.6
1981	3 069.8	159.1	45.1	11.2	76.0	10.6	10.8	5.5	585.0	8.7	21.4	52.8	100.6	259.4	142.0
1982	3 217.6	171.4	49.0	12.1	81.7	11.4	11.4	5.8	621.3	9.3	22.6	56.0	107.3	280.3	145.7
1983	3 446.6	189.3	53.9	13.1	90.9	12.7	12.3	6.3	674.5	10.4	24.3	61.9	119.1	303.4	155.3
1984	3 866.3	215.7	61.2	14.9	104.0	14.9	13.8	7.0	752.6	11.7	26.4	69.8	134.6	339.2	171.0
1985	4 151.4	237.5	66.6	16.1	115.1	16.8	15.2	7.7	812.9	13.0	28.4	77.0	147.0	366.7	180.8
1986	4 355.9	259.9	72.8	17.5	126.1	18.7	16.5	8.3	872.5	14.1	30.0	84.2	159.7	393.6	190.9
1987	4 683.2	289.1	81.4	19.4	139.6	21.5	17.9	9.3	949.2	15.8	32.4	92.5	176.2	425.6	206.7
1988	5 092.2	317.2	89.7	21.7	152.3	23.3	19.7	10.5	1 040.3	17.1	35.6	102.7	197.6	462.5	224.7
1989	5 411.4	333.8	95.0	23.1	159.2	24.1	21.0	11.3	1 093.1	19.2	38.2	109.6	208.4	479.6	238.2
1990	5 706.7	339.7	98.9	23.5	160.0	23.9	21.6	11.8	1 144.8	20.3	40.4	115.0	217.0	502.2	249.9
1991	5 895.4	344.0	100.4	23.6	161.5	24.9	21.8	11.8	1 171.6	22.2	42.2	117.6	224.3	504.7	260.6
1992	6 209.1	357.1	103.8	24.4	167.3	26.4	22.7	12.6	1 234.4	23.1	44.5	120.7	235.5	535.3	275.3
1993	6 513.0	373.3	107.9	25.4	175.7	27.5	23.6	13.2	1 282.9	23.8	46.6	126.4	246.7	551.2	288.2
1994	6 930.8	394.4	112.4	26.5	188.0	29.4	24.4	13.7	1 341.3	25.1	47.5	134.0	258.1	575.6	301.1
1995	7 309.5	416.2	118.6	28.0	197.5	32.4	25.7	14.0	1 403.3	27.6	48.4	139.5	271.4	597.6	318.8
1996	7 715.9	439.6	124.2	28.9	210.1	35.1	26.7	14.7	1 471.8	29.0	48.5	145.1	285.7	633.8	329.7
1997	8 225.0	471.3	135.0	30.4	223.6	37.5	29.4	15.5	1 547.5	31.3	50.5	154.6	300.0	663.4	347.3
1998	8 750.2	503.9	142.7	32.2	241.4	40.5	30.8	16.3	1 649.5	32.7	52.1	164.1	316.9	718.7	365.0
1999	9 251.5	533.3	149.0	34.1	257.8	43.4	31.9	17.2	1 720.2	34.7	55.4	173.8	332.2	743.9	380.2
2000	9 891.2	582.9	161.9	36.3	283.1	47.4	36.1	18.1	1 837.6	37.2	60.0	185.0	357.5	798.4	399.5
2001	10 137.2	594.7	166.2	37.4	287.8	47.2	36.9	19.1	1 900.2	40.5	64.5	195.0	365.4	826.5	408.4
QUANTITY INDEX															
1977	58.6	54.4	56.0	61.4	54.1	39.2	64.5	49.9	64.8	51.4	88.3	59.2	54.0	67.4	69.3
1978	61.8	57.2	58.8	63.2	56.8	43.2	66.3	55.0	67.2	53.3	90.8	61.5	56.3	69.9	72.0
1979	63.7	59.3	61.1	64.8	58.9	45.8	68.4	57.4	68.8	53.8	91.9	63.1	58.5	71.3	73.4
1980	63.6	60.3	62.2	65.9	59.9	47.1	68.3	59.1	68.4	52.8	91.1	63.2	58.7	71.1	71.9
1981	65.2	61.7	63.2	66.6	61.4	48.7	69.7	60.9	69.2	53.7	89.4	64.6	59.9	72.3	72.0
1982	64.1	62.0	63.9	67.4	61.5	49.3	69.0	60.3	68.6	54.1	86.8	63.8	59.7	72.8	69.1
1983	66.0	65.3	67.0	70.2	65.3	52.5	71.1	62.8	70.9	58.3	88.0	67.0	63.6	74.6	70.8
1984	71.0	71.3	72.6	75.7	71.6	59.3	76.3	66.4	75.6	62.6	90.2	72.0	68.7	79.5	74.8
1985	73.9	75.6	76.1	79.2	76.4	64.9	80.7	70.6	78.3	67.2	91.6	76.4	72.2	81.9	76.4
1986	75.4	79.8	80.3	83.0	80.6	69.6	84.6	73.8	80.8	69.6	92.7	80.3	75.6	84.4	77.8
1987	78.7	86.0	87.1	88.6	86.5	77.8	88.4	79.8	85.1	75.3	95.9	85.0	80.8	88.5	81.9
1988	82.8	91.4	92.9	95.5	91.5	81.8	94.4	86.9	89.9	78.1	100.3	91.0	87.1	92.9	85.7
1989	84.7	92.6	94.5	97.8	92.2	81.6	97.1	91.0	91.1	84.2	103.2	93.6	88.6	93.0	87.5
1990	85.9	90.6	94.5	96.1	89.1	77.8	95.8	91.4	91.8	86.1	104.9	94.5	88.7	93.6	88.4
1991	85.7	88.4	92.3	93.4	86.6	78.5	92.6	88.5	90.2	88.9	103.0	92.7	88.4	90.3	88.9
1992	87.8	89.0	92.5	93.5	87.0	80.9	93.3	92.2	92.1	88.4	104.4	92.3	90.3	92.6	91.2
1993	89.7	90.4	93.2	94.3	88.8	82.1	94.6	94.1	93.1	89.6	105.6	93.8	91.9	92.8	92.9
1994	93.4	93.3	94.6	96.0	92.9	85.9	95.2	96.3	95.0	91.9	104.4	96.7	93.8	94.8	94.7
1995	96.3	96.1	97.3	97.7	95.4	93.0	98.2	96.4	97.0	97.4	102.5	98.0	96.2	96.1	98.0
1996	100.0	100.0	100.0	100.0	100.0	100.0	100.0	100.0	100.0	100.0	100.0	100.0	100.0	100.0	100.0
1997	104.9	105.4	106.8	103.6	104.6	105.9	107.9	104.4	103.1	103.9	101.6	104.4	102.9	102.7	103.4
1998	110.2	111.2	111.3	107.6	111.4	114.0	110.8	108.6	108.0	105.5	102.3	108.7	106.7	109.7	106.8
1999	115.1	116.4	114.9	112.1	117.7	121.3	112.8	113.3	111.7	110.2	105.7	113.1	110.6	113.2	110.0
2000	120.5	125.0	122.4	116.7	127.0	131.4	125.1	118.6	117.0	115.1	111.5	117.7	116.5	119.4	113.5
2001	121.0	125.0	123.2	117.6	126.5	129.1	125.5	123.1	118.3	123.3	115.6	120.8	116.5	120.9	113.6

Note: These data have not been updated by BEA since the previous edition of *Business Statistics*, and therefore are not strictly consistent with the National Income and Product Account data shown elsewhere in this volume.

Table 21-1. Gross Domestic Product by Region and State—Continued

(Billions of dollars; index numbers, 1996 = 100.)

Year	Great Lakes						Plains							
	Total	Illinois	Indiana	Michigan	Ohio	Wisconsin	Total	Iowa	Kansas	Minnesota	Missouri	Nebraska	North Dakota	South Dakota
VALUE														
1977	389.8	115.4	47.4	88.1	98.1	40.9	148.6	26.3	20.3	36.3	41.8	13.5	5.3	5.1
1978	434.9	128.7	53.3	98.1	109.1	45.7	168.8	30.1	22.6	41.1	47.1	15.5	6.5	6.0
1979	472.0	140.3	57.7	104.2	119.2	50.6	188.3	32.8	26.2	46.4	51.8	17.1	7.3	6.7
1980	484.8	146.5	58.4	102.9	123.7	53.4	197.7	34.0	28.0	49.7	53.7	17.9	7.6	6.8
1981	529.7	160.0	63.8	113.3	134.9	57.7	220.7	37.7	31.6	54.6	58.8	20.4	9.9	7.6
1982	536.1	163.6	63.5	113.2	136.3	59.5	225.9	36.6	33.0	56.4	61.6	20.6	10.0	7.7
1983	574.0	172.1	67.9	125.0	145.9	63.0	237.7	36.7	34.8	60.6	66.4	21.2	10.0	8.1
1984	646.2	192.7	77.4	141.0	165.0	70.1	269.2	41.0	38.1	69.9	76.0	24.1	10.8	9.3
1985	688.3	205.7	81.1	151.3	175.9	74.2	282.8	42.4	40.5	74.4	79.5	25.4	10.8	9.8
1986	726.7	217.9	85.7	161.1	184.0	78.1	293.2	43.1	41.3	77.9	85.0	25.8	9.8	10.2
1987	767.5	231.8	92.0	167.6	193.7	82.4	311.4	45.2	44.0	84.0	90.4	26.8	10.2	10.8
1988	825.0	250.3	99.2	178.2	207.4	90.0	332.4	48.8	46.3	90.1	97.1	29.0	9.7	11.3
1989	871.7	263.5	106.7	186.9	219.3	95.4	353.8	52.7	48.3	96.2	102.7	31.2	10.6	12.1
1990	908.0	275.8	110.8	190.8	230.0	100.4	370.5	55.8	51.5	100.4	104.8	33.5	11.5	13.0
1991	934.9	285.7	114.2	194.2	235.9	104.9	386.8	57.7	53.6	103.9	110.4	35.5	11.6	14.1
1992	996.2	303.2	123.6	206.7	250.4	112.3	410.8	61.1	56.3	111.9	116.0	37.6	12.7	15.1
1993	1 052.0	317.2	131.5	222.9	260.9	119.5	424.0	62.8	58.4	115.4	119.7	38.7	12.9	16.3
1994	1 138.9	342.3	141.7	246.8	280.8	127.2	459.5	69.2	62.2	125.0	130.0	42.0	13.9	17.2
1995	1 191.4	359.5	148.4	254.2	295.7	133.7	484.0	71.7	64.1	131.8	139.5	44.1	14.5	18.3
1996	1 243.6	375.9	155.1	265.1	306.3	141.0	516.2	77.0	68.2	141.5	146.5	47.8	15.9	19.4
1997	1 317.4	400.3	163.0	279.5	326.5	148.2	547.8	81.7	73.0	152.3	155.8	49.3	15.9	19.8
1998	1 396.8	423.2	176.1	293.2	346.6	157.7	575.1	83.1	76.6	163.0	163.4	51.3	17.1	20.6
1999	1 456.6	440.9	181.3	312.1	357.4	164.9	598.4	85.5	80.2	171.5	168.9	53.5	17.1	21.7
2000	1 523.4	466.3	189.8	323.7	370.6	173.0	635.0	89.7	84.5	186.1	177.1	55.6	18.6	23.5
2001	1 537.0	475.5	189.9	320.5	373.7	177.4	647.9	90.9	87.2	188.0	181.5	57.0	19.0	24.3
QUANTITY INDEX														
1977	68.6	67.5	65.2	75.3	69.6	61.2	62.5	68.8	67.2	55.4	64.3	59.5	71.0	57.3
1978	71.4	70.2	68.1	78.2	72.1	64.0	65.7	72.9	68.8	58.3	67.5	63.0	79.6	61.1
1979	72.1	71.3	68.6	77.4	73.3	66.1	68.0	74.2	73.2	61.0	69.2	64.8	81.6	63.8
1980	68.5	68.7	64.7	70.4	70.3	65.0	66.4	72.5	71.9	60.6	66.5	63.7	77.8	60.8
1981	68.9	69.3	65.3	70.5	70.8	64.9	68.5	74.8	73.9	62.2	66.9	67.3	89.6	64.2
1982	65.4	66.4	61.1	65.7	66.9	63.3	66.5	69.6	72.9	60.9	65.9	65.2	86.3	62.4
1983	67.5	67.2	62.8	70.0	69.4	64.5	67.1	66.8	73.5	62.9	68.0	63.8	84.5	61.8
1984	73.0	72.1	68.8	76.2	75.6	68.9	72.8	71.8	77.4	69.8	74.4	69.4	87.9	67.7
1985	75.6	74.4	70.5	79.6	78.4	71.3	74.9	73.4	80.6	72.6	75.4	72.2	87.7	70.3
1986	76.9	76.1	71.9	81.1	79.0	72.4	75.3	72.4	80.5	73.2	77.6	71.3	81.5	71.5
1987	79.2	78.8	75.3	82.3	81.3	74.4	77.7	73.9	83.7	76.8	80.2	71.8	82.0	72.1
1988	82.5	82.3	78.5	85.1	84.1	78.7	80.2	77.2	85.3	79.5	83.3	75.1	76.3	72.7
1989	84.0	83.7	81.4	86.1	85.7	80.3	82.3	80.3	85.9	81.9	85.0	77.7	80.3	74.7
1990	84.5	84.5	81.9	84.9	86.8	81.7	83.2	82.4	87.8	82.4	83.8	80.9	83.1	78.0
1991	84.0	84.5	81.6	82.9	85.9	82.7	84.2	83.0	88.8	82.6	85.0	83.7	82.7	82.2
1992	87.0	87.4	86.2	85.4	88.7	86.4	87.1	85.9	90.8	86.7	86.8	86.5	88.4	85.7
1993	89.5	89.0	89.3	89.5	90.1	89.9	87.6	86.2	91.5	87.0	87.1	86.6	87.0	90.0
1994	94.6	94.0	94.1	96.5	94.7	93.4	92.7	93.0	95.4	92.0	92.2	92.1	92.3	93.4
1995	97.0	96.8	96.7	97.4	97.7	95.8	95.6	95.0	96.3	94.5	96.9	94.7	94.5	96.8
1996	100.0	100.0	100.0	100.0	100.0	100.0	100.0	100.0	100.0	100.0	100.0	100.0	100.0	100.0
1997	104.6	104.9	103.8	104.1	105.1	104.2	105.0	105.9	105.8	106.3	104.7	102.4	99.8	101.6
1998	109.4	109.4	110.7	107.7	110.2	109.5	108.8	107.0	109.8	112.3	107.9	105.3	106.5	104.9
1999	113.0	113.0	113.1	113.0	112.6	113.6	112.2	109.6	113.7	117.0	110.1	108.9	106.1	110.8
2000	116.5	117.5	117.1	115.6	115.1	117.7	117.2	113.6	117.3	124.9	113.7	112.0	112.2	118.4
2001	115.3	117.5	114.9	112.2	114.0	118.6	117.2	113.0	118.4	123.9	114.2	112.1	112.0	119.6

Note: These data have not been updated by BEA since the previous edition of *Business Statistics*, and therefore are not strictly consistent with the National Income and Product Account data shown elsewhere in this volume.

Table 21-1. Gross Domestic Product by Region and State—Continued

(Billions of dollars; index numbers, 1996 = 100.)

Year	Southeast												
	Total	Alabama	Arkansas	Florida	Georgia	Kentucky	Louisiana	Mississippi	North Carolina	South Carolina	Tennessee	Virginia	West Virginia
VALUE													
1977	389.5	26.5	14.9	66.4	41.2	28.5	39.4	16.0	44.1	20.3	33.6	44.1	14.7
1978	444.9	30.4	17.3	77.5	46.8	32.0	45.3	17.9	50.4	23.3	38.3	49.5	16.3
1979	497.6	33.6	19.0	88.8	52.2	35.3	52.1	20.2	55.3	26.0	42.4	54.9	17.8
1980	549.5	36.1	20.1	101.4	56.9	36.7	64.0	21.5	59.8	28.2	45.4	60.5	19.1
1981	622.9	40.1	22.6	116.0	64.3	40.6	77.7	24.2	66.7	31.6	50.5	68.0	20.5
1982	654.5	41.4	23.2	125.6	69.1	41.6	79.1	24.9	69.7	32.9	52.3	73.4	21.2
1983	708.7	45.1	25.0	139.8	77.4	43.3	77.8	26.2	78.4	36.4	57.3	81.3	20.8
1984	799.8	49.8	28.3	158.8	89.5	49.0	83.8	29.2	89.8	42.0	64.7	92.2	22.8
1985	859.5	53.6	29.1	173.5	99.3	51.7	85.1	30.7	98.2	44.7	69.3	100.7	23.5
1986	907.7	56.1	30.4	188.1	108.9	53.5	76.2	31.4	106.3	48.4	74.2	110.3	23.9
1987	981.1	60.8	32.3	207.3	117.9	56.8	77.0	33.8	114.7	53.3	81.5	121.1	24.5
1988	1 066.6	65.8	34.6	227.2	127.7	61.2	83.7	36.0	126.2	58.2	87.8	131.8	26.4
1989	1 133.7	68.3	36.8	244.6	135.0	65.1	86.6	37.7	135.9	62.3	92.4	141.8	27.3
1990	1 190.3	71.6	38.4	258.3	141.4	67.9	94.9	39.2	141.1	66.1	95.0	148.2	28.3
1991	1 245.5	76.0	41.3	269.8	148.7	70.8	95.9	41.3	147.5	68.8	102.0	154.0	29.3
1992	1 320.7	81.1	44.6	285.5	160.8	76.7	91.2	44.2	160.0	71.9	111.8	161.8	30.9
1993	1 400.3	84.5	47.2	305.0	172.2	80.9	95.6	47.4	168.8	76.0	119.8	170.8	32.2
1994	1 504.1	89.7	50.9	325.6	187.6	86.9	104.1	51.4	182.2	81.5	129.7	179.7	34.8
1995	1 599.4	95.5	53.8	344.8	203.5	91.5	112.2	54.6	194.6	86.9	136.8	189.0	36.3
1996	1 684.3	99.3	56.8	366.3	219.5	95.5	116.9	56.6	204.3	89.9	142.1	200.0	37.2
1997	1 791.6	104.2	59.1	389.5	235.7	101.5	123.5	58.7	221.6	95.4	151.7	212.1	38.3
1998	1 905.3	109.7	61.3	415.6	254.9	107.6	122.6	61.7	241.2	101.4	162.2	228.0	39.0
1999	2 030.0	115.1	65.0	442.6	276.5	112.4	133.9	64.2	260.6	106.8	170.8	241.5	40.5
2000	2 145.9	119.3	66.8	471.6	295.5	117.2	145.0	66.2	272.9	112.2	177.4	260.8	40.9
2001	2 205.6	121.5	67.9	491.5	299.9	120.3	148.7	67.1	275.6	115.2	182.5	273.1	42.4
QUANTITY INDEX													
1977	52.8	59.5	56.7	43.0	42.2	62.5	78.8	61.0	49.5	48.9	52.2	53.4	78.7
1978	56.1	63.5	60.8	46.8	44.8	65.3	83.1	63.0	52.8	52.4	55.8	56.1	80.5
1979	58.0	65.0	61.6	49.9	46.9	67.0	83.0	65.3	54.3	54.8	57.5	57.9	81.3
1980	58.7	64.7	60.5	52.6	47.3	65.1	86.0	64.0	54.6	55.1	56.9	58.9	81.0
1981	60.6	65.6	62.6	55.0	49.1	66.8	89.8	66.2	56.2	57.0	58.2	60.5	79.7
1982	59.8	63.8	60.7	55.8	49.8	64.3	86.5	64.2	54.9	55.8	57.0	60.7	77.4
1983	62.1	66.8	62.9	59.0	53.1	64.2	84.9	65.5	57.9	59.3	60.1	63.4	74.2
1984	67.2	70.7	68.3	63.8	58.6	70.1	89.9	70.7	63.5	65.4	65.0	68.2	78.7
1985	70.0	73.9	69.0	67.0	62.8	72.4	90.4	72.5	67.4	67.5	67.4	71.5	79.4
1986	72.0	75.0	70.2	69.9	66.4	72.3	86.8	72.5	69.9	70.7	69.7	75.3	79.7
1987	75.5	79.0	72.6	74.2	69.6	75.1	86.3	76.7	72.9	75.4	74.2	79.8	80.4
1988	79.3	82.5	75.2	78.6	72.7	78.4	91.4	78.8	77.2	79.5	77.2	83.7	84.0
1989	81.2	82.6	77.1	81.6	74.2	80.4	89.9	79.4	79.7	82.2	78.3	86.8	84.3
1990	82.0	83.8	77.7	82.9	75.1	81.1	92.4	79.4	79.6	84.6	77.8	87.3	85.3
1991	82.8	86.1	81.3	83.5	76.1	81.5	92.1	81.2	79.6	85.1	80.5	86.7	86.0
1992	85.3	89.5	85.7	85.8	80.0	85.7	86.2	84.8	83.3	86.8	85.9	88.0	88.8
1993	88.2	90.9	88.3	88.9	83.4	88.5	88.0	88.2	86.2	89.5	89.5	90.6	90.8
1994	92.9	94.2	93.2	92.6	89.0	93.8	94.6	93.7	92.3	94.1	94.6	93.8	96.0
1995	96.5	97.3	96.3	95.7	94.0	97.1	99.7	98.0	96.7	97.7	97.6	96.3	98.3
1996	100.0	100.0	100.0	100.0	100.0	100.0	100.0	100.0	100.0	100.0	100.0	100.0	100.0
1997	104.6	103.4	103.2	104.3	105.6	104.9	103.3	102.2	106.7	104.9	105.1	104.0	101.2
1998	109.4	107.1	105.6	109.4	112.0	109.2	103.4	105.9	113.6	109.5	110.4	109.2	101.5
1999	114.3	111.2	111.3	114.7	119.1	111.6	110.8	109.2	118.9	113.9	114.5	112.3	105.1
2000	117.9	113.1	112.8	119.7	125.2	114.7	107.6	110.1	122.2	118.1	117.3	118.5	103.9
2001	118.4	112.8	112.2	121.9	124.8	115.2	107.2	108.8	120.5	118.5	118.6	120.8	104.8

Note: These data have not been updated by BEA since the previous edition of *Business Statistics*, and therefore are not strictly consistent with the National Income and Product Account data shown elsewhere in this volume.

Table 21-1. Gross Domestic Product by Region and State—Continued

(Billions of dollars; index numbers, 1996 = 100.)

Year	Southwest					Rocky Mountain					
	Total	Arizona	New Mexico	Oklahoma	Texas	Total	Colorado	Idaho	Montana	Utah	Wyoming
VALUE											
1977	185.1	19.2	10.4	23.9	131.6	54.8	25.2	7.0	6.4	10.4	5.7
1978	213.0	22.8	11.9	27.1	151.1	64.3	29.4	8.3	7.5	12.1	6.9
1979	246.9	27.2	13.6	31.6	174.5	73.6	34.0	9.2	8.2	13.9	8.3
1980	291.6	30.3	16.2	37.7	207.4	83.5	38.4	9.8	9.0	15.5	10.8
1981	348.7	33.4	19.1	45.5	250.6	95.7	44.1	10.5	10.3	17.6	13.3
1982	369.5	34.3	19.9	49.5	265.8	100.1	47.7	10.5	10.3	18.6	13.1
1983	377.7	38.3	20.6	48.0	270.9	104.8	50.5	11.6	10.6	19.9	12.2
1984	415.5	44.5	22.3	51.9	296.8	114.9	56.0	12.5	11.2	22.3	12.9
1985	442.0	49.3	23.5	53.4	315.8	120.4	59.0	13.0	11.2	24.1	13.0
1986	425.8	54.6	22.5	49.0	299.6	119.9	59.9	13.1	11.2	24.5	11.2
1987	435.7	59.1	23.2	48.9	304.7	125.1	63.4	13.8	11.6	25.2	11.1
1988	475.0	63.4	24.0	52.8	334.8	132.6	66.7	15.0	11.9	27.2	11.7
1989	503.2	66.0	25.5	54.7	357.0	140.3	70.0	16.7	12.8	28.7	12.0
1990	541.9	68.9	27.2	57.8	388.1	150.6	74.7	17.7	13.4	31.4	13.4
1991	565.7	71.9	30.9	59.7	403.3	159.4	79.4	18.7	14.1	33.7	13.6
1992	598.6	79.0	32.9	62.0	424.7	170.5	85.8	20.4	15.1	35.7	13.6
1993	640.3	85.5	37.1	65.0	452.6	185.0	93.6	22.8	16.2	38.4	14.1
1994	687.2	95.7	41.8	67.0	482.7	200.0	101.5	24.9	17.0	42.2	14.4
1995	730.6	104.6	42.2	70.0	513.9	214.9	109.0	27.2	17.5	46.3	14.9
1996	785.0	112.9	44.1	74.9	553.2	230.7	117.1	28.1	18.1	51.5	15.9
1997	858.1	122.3	47.8	79.4	608.6	249.2	129.6	29.4	18.9	55.1	16.2
1998	905.0	132.9	48.5	82.2	641.4	266.4	139.9	31.0	20.0	59.1	16.4
1999	958.0	144.6	49.2	85.4	678.8	287.1	152.3	34.6	20.6	62.6	17.0
2000	1 035.3	153.5	52.6	90.9	738.3	315.3	169.3	36.8	21.7	68.4	19.1
2001	1 073.8	160.7	55.4	93.9	763.9	324.1	173.8	36.9	22.6	70.4	20.4
QUANTITY INDEX											
1977	54.2	38.8	53.1	71.9	55.0	53.2	50.0	52.1	77.6	45.6	72.0
1978	57.4	42.7	56.1	75.2	58.1	57.6	54.1	56.6	83.3	49.1	78.8
1979	59.8	46.9	56.7	78.7	60.0	60.3	57.7	57.7	83.5	51.5	81.9
1980	62.0	48.1	58.4	82.4	62.3	62.2	59.6	58.0	83.6	52.6	89.7
1981	65.2	49.1	59.5	87.3	65.9	64.6	62.2	58.1	87.0	54.7	94.0
1982	65.3	47.1	58.5	89.8	66.1	63.8	63.3	55.5	83.2	54.2	88.2
1983	65.3	50.1	59.3	85.6	66.0	64.3	64.0	58.0	82.7	55.8	83.3
1984	69.8	55.8	62.6	90.3	70.4	67.9	67.9	60.1	84.4	60.2	87.8
1985	72.6	59.7	64.8	91.5	73.3	69.3	69.1	61.6	82.4	63.3	88.8
1986	70.7	63.7	63.4	85.6	70.7	68.2	68.3	60.2	81.7	62.9	83.6
1987	70.7	66.4	63.4	83.6	70.4	69.1	70.0	61.5	81.9	62.9	81.8
1988	74.9	69.0	64.1	88.1	75.2	71.1	71.5	64.5	80.9	65.8	86.4
1989	76.2	69.4	65.4	87.6	76.9	72.6	72.4	69.0	84.2	66.9	85.4
1990	78.2	70.0	66.7	88.3	79.5	75.0	74.3	71.1	85.5	70.5	90.1
1991	79.7	70.6	74.1	89.0	80.8	77.2	76.4	73.0	87.7	73.3	91.7
1992	82.6	75.6	77.3	90.4	83.4	80.6	80.3	77.5	91.7	75.7	91.2
1993	86.2	79.6	85.7	92.4	86.8	85.2	85.2	84.2	95.4	79.4	94.4
1994	91.1	87.1	95.6	93.6	91.2	90.2	90.4	90.1	97.8	85.3	96.1
1995	95.2	93.4	96.8	95.9	95.4	95.0	95.0	97.5	98.8	91.2	98.3
1996	100.0	100.0	100.0	100.0	100.0	100.0	100.0	100.0	100.0	100.0	100.0
1997	107.6	107.0	108.0	104.4	108.1	106.3	108.7	104.3	103.0	104.8	100.7
1998	113.7	115.8	112.3	107.9	114.2	112.5	115.8	110.4	107.5	110.7	103.7
1999	119.1	125.2	114.0	110.9	119.4	119.9	124.3	123.4	110.1	115.8	106.1
2000	124.2	131.8	118.7	113.7	124.5	128.7	135.1	132.0	113.2	123.4	110.4
2001	126.5	136.1	124.5	114.8	126.3	129.6	136.0	131.1	114.6	124.1	115.0

Note: These data have not been updated by BEA since the previous edition of Business Statistics, and therefore are not strictly consistent with the National Income and Product Account data shown elsewhere in this volume.

Table 21-1. Gross Domestic Product by Region and State—Continued

(Billions of dollars; index numbers, 1996 = 100.)

Year	Far West						
	Total	Alaska	California	Hawaii	Nevada	Oregon	Washington
VALUE							
1977	312.1	7.5	229.5	9.4	7.5	22.3	36.0
1978	360.2	9.1	263.6	10.5	9.1	25.9	42.0
1979	405.9	10.8	295.1	12.0	10.6	29.1	48.2
1980	451.4	15.0	328.2	13.4	12.1	30.7	52.0
1981	508.0	21.5	368.5	14.5	13.6	32.1	57.7
1982	538.8	23.1	393.2	15.5	14.2	31.9	60.8
1983	579.8	22.3	426.0	16.9	15.3	33.9	65.4
1984	652.5	23.6	484.5	18.6	16.9	37.9	71.1
1985	708.2	25.9	529.4	20.0	18.4	40.0	74.5
1986	750.2	18.6	567.4	21.5	20.0	42.1	80.5
1987	824.1	22.0	624.6	23.4	22.2	45.0	86.9
1988	903.2	21.4	685.1	26.0	25.4	49.7	95.6
1989	981.8	22.9	743.5	28.8	28.5	53.5	104.7
1990	1 060.8	24.8	798.9	32.3	31.6	57.8	115.5
1991	1 087.5	22.0	814.7	34.0	33.7	60.6	122.5
1992	1 120.7	22.4	831.6	35.5	36.5	64.1	130.6
1993	1 155.2	23.0	847.9	36.3	39.9	69.8	138.2
1994	1 205.3	23.1	879.0	36.8	45.0	75.1	146.3
1995	1 269.7	24.8	925.9	37.2	49.4	81.1	151.3
1996	1 344.7	25.8	973.4	37.5	54.6	91.7	161.8
1997	1 442.4	26.6	1 045.3	38.5	59.2	97.5	175.2
1998	1 548.1	24.7	1 125.3	39.4	63.8	102.9	192.0
1999	1 667.9	25.6	1 213.4	40.7	69.5	110.4	208.5
2000	1 815.7	28.1	1 330.0	42.5	75.5	121.4	218.1
2001	1 853.8	28.6	1 359.3	43.7	79.2	120.1	223.0
QUANTITY INDEX							
1977	53.4	64.6	53.9	62.7	33.7	54.5	52.5
1978	57.2	70.5	57.7	65.5	37.9	58.1	56.8
1979	59.7	74.0	59.9	69.2	40.7	60.5	60.4
1980	61.1	84.9	61.4	71.0	41.9	59.9	60.5
1981	62.8	97.9	63.3	69.6	43.5	57.9	62.0
1982	62.4	100.5	63.1	69.6	42.7	54.4	61.3
1983	64.4	97.6	65.5	72.1	43.7	54.9	62.4
1984	69.3	102.2	71.3	74.3	46.1	58.7	64.7
1985	72.8	113.2	75.3	76.2	48.1	60.2	65.4
1986	74.9	92.7	78.0	78.6	50.3	61.1	68.1
1987	79.6	108.4	83.2	82.5	53.2	63.1	71.1
1988	84.4	107.0	88.2	88.1	58.3	67.2	75.4
1989	88.4	108.7	92.4	94.2	63.1	69.4	79.5
1990	91.8	107.8	95.3	101.7	68.0	72.5	84.4
1991	90.8	97.3	93.8	102.7	69.9	73.7	86.3
1992	91.1	97.5	93.1	104.3	73.8	75.7	89.3
1993	91.3	98.7	92.3	103.5	78.8	79.6	91.6
1994	93.1	98.0	93.6	102.2	86.2	83.6	94.5
1995	96.0	102.3	96.8	101.2	91.7	88.7	95.2
1996	100.0	100.0	100.0	100.0	100.0	100.0	100.0
1997	105.6	101.1	105.7	100.5	105.4	105.9	106.5
1998	112.1	96.7	112.6	100.4	110.9	112.5	114.6
1999	119.5	97.2	120.2	101.5	118.0	121.5	122.6
2000	127.7	95.9	129.3	103.7	125.0	136.1	125.4
2001	127.9	95.0	129.4	103.6	127.4	136.1	125.2

Note: These data have not been updated by BEA since the previous edition of *Business Statistics*, and therefore are not strictly consistent with the National Income and Product Account data shown elsewhere in this volume.

Table 21-2. Personal Income and Employment by Region and State

(Millions of dollars, except as noted.)

Year	Personal income, total	Derivation of personal income								Per capita (dollars)		Population (thousands)	Total employment (thousands)
		Earnings by place of work			Less: Contributions for government social insurance	Plus: Adjustment for residence	Equals: Net earnings by place of residence	Plus: Dividends, interest, and rent	Plus: Personal current transfer receipts	Personal income	Disposable personal income		
		Nonfarm	Farm	Total									
UNITED STATES													
1969	772 235	631 338	17 243	648 581	43 792	-163	604 626	105 287	62 322	3 836	3 321	201 298	91 057
1970	832 429	671 582	17 463	689 045	46 012	-175	642 858	114 838	74 733	4 085	3 582	203 799	91 282
1971	897 952	719 396	17 970	737 366	50 859	-198	686 309	123 395	88 248	4 342	3 853	206 818	91 586
1972	987 137	793 438	21 733	815 171	58 897	-229	756 045	132 962	98 130	4 717	4 129	209 275	94 317
1973	1 105 605	884 639	34 658	919 297	75 183	-244	843 870	148 887	112 848	5 231	4 607	211 349	98 433
1974	1 217 556	968 564	29 813	998 377	84 873	-264	913 240	170 677	133 639	5 707	5 002	213 334	100 118
1975	1 329 892	1 034 062	28 873	1 062 935	88 975	-313	973 647	185 821	170 424	6 172	5 489	215 457	98 907
1976	1 469 467	1 160 623	24 993	1 185 616	100 987	-339	1 084 290	200 695	184 482	6 754	5 965	217 554	101 597
1977	1 627 310	1 295 462	24 254	1 319 716	112 699	-377	1 206 640	225 919	194 751	7 405	6 509	219 761	105 049
1978	1 831 117	1 467 160	28 073	1 495 233	130 827	-410	1 363 996	256 812	210 309	8 245	7 215	222 098	109 689
1979	2 053 827	1 641 985	29 875	1 671 860	152 274	-398	1 519 188	298 510	236 129	9 146	7 952	224 569	113 289
1980	2 298 255	1 795 158	20 392	1 815 550	165 669	-454	1 649 427	368 611	280 217	10 114	8 802	227 225	114 231
1981	2 580 600	1 969 935	27 169	1 997 104	195 066	-443	1 801 595	459 858	319 147	11 246	9 746	229 466	115 304
1982	2 764 886	2 066 560	24 558	2 091 118	208 173	-520	1 882 425	527 092	355 369	11 935	10 410	231 664	114 557
1983	2 949 883	2 206 755	17 235	2 223 990	225 148	-508	1 998 334	567 273	384 276	12 618	11 114	233 792	116 057
1984	3 275 805	2 452 535	31 814	2 484 349	256 554	-579	2 227 216	647 861	400 728	13 891	12 294	235 825	121 091
1985	3 511 344	2 639 477	31 950	2 671 427	280 384	-603	2 390 440	695 617	425 287	14 758	13 008	237 924	124 510
1986	3 708 199	2 798 353	33 079	2 831 432	302 395	-575	2 528 462	728 615	451 122	15 442	13 626	240 133	126 970
1987	3 934 655	2 997 457	39 409	3 036 866	322 010	-608	2 714 248	752 842	467 565	16 240	14 226	242 289	130 400
1988	4 237 460	3 253 621	39 109	3 292 730	360 256	-651	2 931 823	809 089	496 548	17 331	15 271	244 499	134 507
1989	4 571 133	3 446 466	45 677	3 492 143	383 938	-664	3 107 541	920 199	543 393	18 520	16 231	246 819	137 200
1990	4 861 936	3 655 379	46 760	3 702 139	408 654	-737	3 292 748	973 575	595 613	19 477	17 108	249 623	139 381
1991	5 032 196	3 762 522	41 579	3 804 101	428 560	-788	3 374 753	991 122	666 321	19 892	17 578	252 981	138 606
1992	5 349 384	4 017 224	49 550	4 066 774	453 745	-797	3 612 232	987 898	749 254	20 854	18 478	256 514	139 162
1993	5 548 121	4 191 800	47 244	4 239 044	476 585	-798	3 761 661	996 465	789 995	21 346	18 862	259 919	141 779
1994	5 833 906	4 395 182	49 932	4 445 114	507 172	-860	3 937 082	1 069 567	827 257	22 172	19 550	263 126	145 224
1995	6 144 741	4 622 731	39 675	4 662 406	531 848	-893	4 129 665	1 137 710	877 366	23 076	20 286	266 278	148 983
1996	6 512 485	4 868 019	54 906	4 922 925	554 248	-914	4 367 763	1 219 791	924 931	24 175	21 089	269 394	152 150
1997	6 907 332	5 180 807	52 982	5 233 789	586 178	-969	4 646 642	1 309 556	951 134	25 334	21 941	272 647	155 608
1998	7 415 709	5 591 837	49 748	5 641 585	623 147	-1 022	5 017 416	1 419 686	978 607	26 883	23 163	275 854	159 628
1999	7 796 137	5 975 196	49 774	6 024 970	660 395	-1 030	5 363 545	1 410 543	1 022 049	27 939	23 974	279 040	162 955
2000	8 422 074	6 460 197	44 482	6 504 679	701 650	-1 060	5 801 969	1 536 284	1 083 821	29 847	25 472	282 178	166 759
2001	8 718 165	6 664 435	44 726	6 709 161	729 953	-1 093	5 978 115	1 546 319	1 193 731	30 580	26 244	285 094	166 960
2002	8 868 261	6 795 584	33 800	6 829 384	746 784	-1 162	6 081 438	1 504 300	1 282 523	30 795	27 149	287 974	166 500
2003	9 148 680	7 063 339	47 294	7 110 633	771 483	-1 194	6 337 956	1 475 401	1 335 323	31 459	28 019	290 810	166 990
NEW ENGLAND													
1969	49 110	38 952	292	39 244	2 634	850	37 460	7 541	4 110	4 185	3 580	11 735	5 516
1970	52 799	41 507	304	41 811	2 769	856	39 898	8 000	4 902	4 445	3 868	11 878	5 518
1971	56 146	43 683	281	43 964	3 008	884	41 840	8 432	5 874	4 680	4 130	11 996	5 454
1972	60 795	47 663	285	47 948	3 449	941	45 440	8 949	6 406	5 029	4 372	12 088	5 573
1973	66 585	52 617	395	53 013	4 355	997	49 655	9 734	7 195	5 481	4 795	12 148	5 783
1974	72 433	56 312	427	56 739	4 823	1 084	52 999	10 905	8 530	5 958	5 204	12 157	5 843
1975	77 693	58 564	310	58 874	4 913	1 171	55 131	11 426	11 135	6 381	5 657	12 176	5 685
1976	84 949	64 843	426	65 269	5 515	1 300	61 053	12 228	11 667	6 959	6 121	12 207	5 811
1977	93 075	71 649	382	72 030	6 127	1 453	67 356	13 611	12 109	7 593	6 663	12 257	6 007
1978	103 505	80 717	393	81 110	7 097	1 636	75 649	15 052	12 804	8 413	7 334	12 303	6 280
1979	115 950	90 631	376	91 006	8 287	1 868	84 587	17 099	14 264	9 392	8 123	12 345	6 515
1980	131 495	100 572	365	100 936	9 186	2 184	93 935	21 156	16 404	10 629	9 164	12 372	6 641
1981	147 313	110 056	468	110 524	10 801	2 360	102 084	26 458	18 771	11 846	10 151	12 436	6 692
1982	160 475	117 752	511	118 263	11 790	2 538	109 011	30 943	20 521	12 871	11 095	12 468	6 694
1983	173 474	128 988	477	129 465	13 042	2 671	119 094	32 462	21 918	13 829	12 050	12 544	6 828
1984	194 956	145 754	564	146 318	15 170	2 851	134 000	37 985	22 971	15 422	13 505	12 642	7 198
1985	210 807	159 769	554	160 324	16 763	3 009	146 570	40 070	24 166	16 546	14 396	12 741	7 447
1986	227 430	173 818	572	174 390	18 460	3 186	159 116	42 941	25 374	17 722	15 338	12 833	7 687
1987	247 610	191 880	637	192 517	20 144	3 353	175 726	45 790	26 095	19 119	16 431	12 951	7 828
1988	272 305	212 023	653	212 677	22 610	3 553	193 620	50 631	28 054	20 811	18 091	13 085	8 082
1989	291 087	221 728	601	222 329	23 600	3 478	202 207	57 540	31 340	22 083	19 157	13 182	8 072
1990	300 474	226 118	683	226 801	24 139	3 468	206 130	59 311	35 033	22 712	19 749	13 230	7 918
1991	304 280	225 468	629	226 097	24 576	3 464	204 986	58 851	40 443	22 969	20 068	13 248	7 585
1992	320 794	238 304	790	239 094	25 752	4 699	218 041	58 892	43 861	24 172	21 092	13 271	7 624
1993	330 058	247 633	733	248 366	26 959	4 136	225 544	59 163	45 351	24 752	21 510	13 334	7 748
1994	344 112	258 270	681	258 951	28 549	3 937	234 339	62 048	47 724	25 687	22 279	13 396	7 843
1995	361 504	270 708	604	271 313	30 077	4 736	245 972	64 974	50 558	26 832	23 136	13 473	7 938
1996	382 164	285 093	694	285 787	31 483	5 568	259 872	70 219	52 073	28 194	24 026	13 555	8 069
1997	404 990	304 268	598	304 867	33 623	5 185	276 428	74 302	54 260	29 687	25 007	13 642	8 228
1998	435 052	327 646	622	328 268	35 767	6 648	299 149	80 797	55 106	31 677	26 452	13 734	8 402
1999	458 597	351 831	674	352 505	38 053	6 557	321 009	80 582	56 796	33 126	27 510	13 838	8 562
2000	503 961	388 102	674	388 776	41 223	6 869	354 422	89 556	59 982	36 121	29 522	13 952	8 776
2001	524 389	402 167	592	402 759	42 662	6 300	366 397	92 825	65 167	37 328	30 815	14 048	8 834
2002	528 913	405 168	492	405 660	43 123	5 737	368 274	90 235	70 403	37 420	32 118	14 134	8 774
2003	540 069	417 251	562	417 813	44 010	5 709	379 513	88 236	72 320	38 018	33 013	14 205	8 742

Table 21-2. Personal Income and Employment by Region and State—Continued

(Millions of dollars, except as noted.)

Year	Personal income, total	Derivation of personal income								Per capita (dollars)		Population (thousands)	Total employment (thousands)
		Earnings by place of work			Less: Contributions for government social insurance	Plus: Adjustment for residence	Equals: Net earnings by place of residence	Plus: Dividends, interest, and rent	Plus: Personal current transfer receipts	Personal income	Disposable personal income		
		Nonfarm	Farm	Total									

CONNECTICUT

1969	14 502	11 126	66	11 193	752	728	11 169	2 385	947	4 834	4 081	3 000	1 417
1970	15 432	11 725	71	11 796	783	722	11 735	2 552	1 146	5 078	4 405	3 039	1 414
1971	16 222	12 144	69	12 213	840	746	12 119	2 679	1 423	5 299	4 669	3 061	1 388
1972	17 478	13 231	68	13 299	968	785	13 115	2 857	1 505	5 694	4 943	3 070	1 416
1973	19 119	14 722	80	14 802	1 234	808	14 376	3 114	1 629	6 230	5 448	3 069	1 480
1974	20 906	15 985	83	16 068	1 395	841	15 514	3 474	1 918	6 797	5 942	3 076	1 511
1975	22 386	16 629	75	16 704	1 423	916	16 197	3 643	2 546	7 257	6 437	3 085	1 468
1976	24 327	18 206	82	18 289	1 577	1 011	17 723	3 895	2 708	7 883	6 908	3 086	1 493
1977	26 849	20 256	83	20 339	1 778	1 121	19 682	4 336	2 832	8 693	7 620	3 089	1 546
1978	29 896	22 830	80	22 910	2 062	1 273	22 121	4 855	2 920	9 660	8 383	3 095	1 616
1979	33 675	25 755	79	25 833	2 421	1 449	24 861	5 564	3 250	10 863	9 353	3 100	1 675
1980	38 470	28 754	83	28 837	2 682	1 695	27 850	6 884	3 737	12 357	10 587	3 113	1 709
1981	43 267	31 541	82	31 622	3 157	1 878	30 343	8 611	4 313	13 828	11 797	3 129	1 732
1982	46 731	33 642	108	33 750	3 431	2 035	32 354	9 582	4 796	14 887	12 683	3 139	1 731
1983	49 978	36 347	105	36 452	3 735	2 156	34 873	9 925	5 180	15 804	13 807	3 162	1 749
1984	55 880	40 799	129	40 928	4 304	2 309	38 932	11 532	5 416	17 572	15 437	3 180	1 831
1985	59 962	44 509	127	44 636	4 740	2 448	42 343	11 875	5 743	18 731	16 308	3 201	1 890
1986	64 552	48 289	140	48 429	5 210	2 609	45 827	12 650	6 075	20 024	17 335	3 224	1 948
1987	70 599	53 653	142	53 795	5 699	2 736	50 832	13 487	6 279	21 741	18 642	3 247	1 997
1988	77 821	59 457	156	59 613	6 394	2 923	56 142	14 902	6 777	23 784	20 660	3 272	2 053
1989	84 330	62 593	139	62 732	6 705	2 815	58 842	17 888	7 600	25 684	22 327	3 283	2 047
1990	87 251	64 508	182	64 689	6 927	2 780	60 542	18 214	8 495	26 504	23 121	3 292	2 018
1991	87 567	64 814	162	64 975	7 123	2 745	60 597	17 496	9 474	26 512	23 128	3 303	1 937
1992	93 615	68 000	187	68 187	7 344	3 958	64 801	17 646	11 168	28 362	24 471	3 301	1 917
1993	95 882	70 520	211	70 731	7 609	3 375	66 497	17 760	11 625	28 975	24 859	3 309	1 938
1994	98 467	72 709	187	72 896	7 970	3 139	68 065	18 343	12 059	29 693	25 468	3 316	1 920
1995	103 199	75 954	173	76 128	8 349	3 901	71 680	18 686	12 834	31 045	26 418	3 324	1 958
1996	108 189	79 217	162	79 379	8 695	4 689	75 373	19 607	13 210	32 424	27 105	3 337	1 989
1997	115 134	85 414	157	85 571	9 240	4 219	80 549	20 963	13 622	34 375	28 349	3 349	2 015
1998	123 918	91 518	182	91 699	9 733	5 609	87 575	22 535	13 807	36 822	30 068	3 365	2 043
1999	129 807	97 457	201	97 658	10 205	5 450	92 903	22 759	14 145	38 332	31 148	3 386	2 076
2000	141 570	106 464	191	106 655	10 785	5 678	101 549	25 164	14 858	41 495	33 388	3 412	2 114
2001	147 323	111 496	182	111 678	11 110	5 060	105 628	25 932	15 763	42 919	34 608	3 433	2 123
2002	147 856	112 661	150	112 811	11 529	4 501	105 783	25 119	16 955	42 751	35 846	3 459	2 118
2003	150 801	116 041	186	116 227	11 742	4 440	108 925	24 543	17 333	43 292	36 774	3 483	2 107

MAINE

1969	3 106	2 505	74	2 578	181	-23	2 375	419	312	3 131	2 782	992	443
1970	3 400	2 705	77	2 782	193	-18	2 571	459	370	3 411	3 068	997	446
1971	3 647	2 872	66	2 937	211	-17	2 709	500	438	3 591	3 278	1 016	443
1972	3 993	3 159	64	3 223	241	-20	2 962	541	490	3 859	3 502	1 035	453
1973	4 509	3 497	147	3 644	301	-11	3 332	593	583	4 309	3 875	1 046	470
1974	5 034	3 799	195	3 993	337	-6	3 650	681	703	4 749	4 278	1 060	478
1975	5 397	4 063	81	4 143	357	-19	3 767	732	899	5 029	4 578	1 073	475
1976	6 215	4 722	163	4 885	422	-23	4 440	800	975	5 702	5 170	1 090	498
1977	6 766	5 177	128	5 305	461	-25	4 819	908	1 038	6 121	5 556	1 105	513
1978	7 483	5 820	89	5 909	531	-23	5 355	1 013	1 115	6 708	6 053	1 115	532
1979	8 349	6 478	74	6 552	607	-17	5 929	1 160	1 260	7 422	6 658	1 125	546
1980	9 406	7 140	48	7 189	670	-14	6 504	1 431	1 471	8 347	7 464	1 127	555
1981	10 415	7 663	117	7 780	773	-50	6 956	1 782	1 677	9 193	8 153	1 133	554
1982	11 282	8 134	103	8 238	835	-49	7 354	2 089	1 839	9 925	8 739	1 137	556
1983	12 108	8 841	71	8 913	912	-40	7 961	2 157	1 989	10 577	9 432	1 145	568
1984	13 506	9 831	117	9 948	1 045	-30	8 873	2 534	2 099	11 687	10 481	1 156	591
1985	14 602	10 729	102	10 831	1 133	-9	9 689	2 693	2 221	12 556	11 209	1 163	610
1986	15 789	11 659	92	11 751	1 246	29	10 535	2 951	2 304	13 494	11 976	1 170	635
1987	17 231	12 834	135	12 969	1 362	48	11 655	3 219	2 357	14 546	12 789	1 185	658
1988	18 912	14 270	117	14 387	1 549	61	12 900	3 513	2 500	15 710	13 851	1 204	692
1989	20 499	15 283	124	15 406	1 657	60	13 810	3 997	2 693	16 803	14 827	1 220	708
1990	21 402	15 741	166	15 907	1 704	58	14 261	4 135	3 006	17 376	15 387	1 232	707
1991	21 681	15 603	121	15 724	1 721	75	14 078	4 144	3 459	17 526	15 627	1 237	683
1992	22 606	16 216	176	16 392	1 818	119	14 692	4 099	3 815	18 253	16 343	1 239	686
1993	23 156	16 678	157	16 835	1 925	179	15 088	4 049	4 018	18 639	16 688	1 242	697
1994	24 092	17 239	148	17 387	2 033	240	15 593	4 298	4 201	19 387	17 292	1 243	708
1995	25 044	17 679	123	17 802	2 110	310	16 002	4 613	4 429	20 140	17 965	1 243	710
1996	26 484	18 406	151	18 558	2 171	364	16 750	4 991	4 743	21 203	18 801	1 249	720
1997	27 830	19 332	106	19 438	2 290	436	17 584	5 279	4 967	22 179	19 509	1 255	733
1998	29 710	20 612	138	20 750	2 417	511	18 844	5 744	5 122	23 596	20 576	1 259	753
1999	31 016	21 939	154	22 092	2 555	580	20 118	5 619	5 279	24 484	21 343	1 267	770
2000	33 173	23 226	146	23 371	2 666	701	21 406	6 179	5 588	25 972	22 491	1 277	792
2001	35 102	24 713	117	24 829	2 812	726	22 743	6 342	6 017	27 324	23 744	1 285	796
2002	36 295	25 664	91	25 755	2 849	708	23 614	6 217	6 464	28 030	24 932	1 295	799
2003	37 781	26 798	80	26 878	2 926	726	24 678	6 100	7 004	28 935	25 963	1 306	805

Table 21-2. Personal Income and Employment by Region and State—Continued

(Millions of dollars, except as noted.)

Year	Personal income, total	Derivation of personal income							Per capita (dollars)		Population (thousands)	Total employment (thousands)
		Earnings by place of work			Less: Contributions for government social insurance	Plus: Adjustment for residence	Equals: Net earnings by place of residence	Plus: Dividends, interest, and rent	Plus: Personal current transfer receipts	Personal income	Disposable personal income		
		Nonfarm	Farm	Total									

MASSACHUSETTS

1969	23 734	19 262	66	19 328	1 259	-126	17 943	3 635	2 156	4 201	3 572	5 650	2 679
1970	25 568	20 590	69	20 659	1 323	-108	19 228	3 791	2 550	4 483	3 872	5 704	2 679
1971	27 271	21 783	63	21 846	1 443	-111	20 292	3 960	3 019	4 752	4 161	5 739	2 644
1972	29 436	23 667	62	23 729	1 647	-110	21 972	4 151	3 313	5 109	4 398	5 762	2 697
1973	32 081	26 017	70	26 088	2 069	-134	23 885	4 481	3 716	5 547	4 811	5 784	2 787
1974	34 754	27 700	69	27 769	2 269	-150	25 350	5 001	4 404	6 016	5 205	5 777	2 811
1975	37 217	28 668	68	28 737	2 290	-155	26 292	5 195	5 731	6 459	5 678	5 762	2 728
1976	40 233	31 440	76	31 516	2 550	-182	28 784	5 513	5 936	6 998	6 107	5 749	2 756
1977	43 770	34 557	79	34 636	2 811	-224	31 600	6 073	6 098	7 620	6 619	5 744	2 833
1978	48 413	38 736	103	38 839	3 242	-287	35 310	6 635	6 468	8 430	7 297	5 743	2 959
1979	53 926	43 372	90	43 461	3 788	-361	39 312	7 453	7 161	9 385	8 050	5 746	3 079
1980	60 920	48 178	105	48 283	4 217	-483	43 583	9 165	8 172	10 602	9 053	5 746	3 142
1981	68 062	52 825	116	52 940	4 985	-599	47 357	11 417	9 289	11 798	9 987	5 769	3 155
1982	74 684	56 835	131	56 966	5 488	-729	50 749	13 894	10 041	12 941	11 082	5 771	3 157
1983	81 246	62 745	164	62 909	6 135	-906	55 867	14 737	10 642	14 009	12 057	5 799	3 230
1984	91 835	71 536	182	71 719	7 218	-1 180	63 321	17 321	11 194	15 723	13 603	5 841	3 422
1985	99 445	78 467	160	78 627	7 995	-1 366	69 266	18 465	11 714	16 910	14 544	5 881	3 533
1986	107 119	85 208	175	85 383	8 777	-1 502	75 104	19 692	12 323	18 148	15 531	5 903	3 629
1987	116 181	93 682	153	93 835	9 558	-1 683	82 595	20 913	12 673	19 575	16 660	5 935	3 661
1988	127 622	103 283	173	103 456	10 690	-1 917	90 848	23 126	13 647	21 341	18 412	5 980	3 770
1989	134 399	107 024	152	107 175	11 056	-2 040	94 080	24 930	15 390	22 342	19 178	6 015	3 743
1990	138 782	108 597	151	108 748	11 227	-2 089	95 432	26 109	17 241	23 043	19 795	6 023	3 647
1991	141 024	108 226	171	108 396	11 401	-2 295	94 700	26 555	19 770	23 432	20 272	6 018	3 480
1992	147 930	114 834	171	115 005	11 992	-2 401	100 613	26 696	20 622	24 538	21 281	6 029	3 510
1993	152 578	119 513	166	119 679	12 610	-2 613	104 456	26 951	21 171	25 176	21 745	6 061	3 576
1994	160 322	125 587	151	125 738	13 431	-2 824	109 483	28 393	22 445	26 303	22 639	6 095	3 645
1995	168 623	132 142	148	132 289	14 231	-2 891	115 167	29 801	23 655	27 457	23 458	6 141	3 680
1996	178 797	140 371	169	140 540	15 029	-3 153	122 358	32 042	24 397	28 933	24 439	6 180	3 744
1997	189 885	149 449	169	149 619	16 164	-3 428	130 027	34 439	25 419	30 498	25 500	6 226	3 833
1998	203 987	161 510	107	161 617	17 279	-3 656	140 683	37 686	25 618	32 524	26 916	6 272	3 917
1999	216 221	175 021	106	175 127	18 592	-4 247	152 288	37 540	26 393	34 227	28 126	6 317	3 989
2000	240 209	195 723	116	195 839	20 551	-5 116	170 173	42 108	27 928	37 756	30 311	6 362	4 097
2001	249 238	200 596	97	200 693	21 150	-5 094	174 449	44 174	30 615	38 944	31 803	6 400	4 124
2002	249 889	199 402	97	199 499	20 949	-4 886	173 664	42 920	33 306	38 913	33 268	6 422	4 065
2003	253 528	203 659	111	203 769	21 222	-4 838	177 710	41 937	33 881	39 408	34 088	6 433	4 024

NEW HAMPSHIRE

1969	2 705	1 992	21	2 012	129	232	2 116	386	203	3 736	3 295	724	334
1970	2 883	2 113	16	2 130	135	220	2 215	427	241	3 886	3 409	742	334
1971	3 123	2 270	14	2 284	150	230	2 364	467	292	4 098	3 662	762	336
1972	3 454	2 525	16	2 541	176	252	2 617	515	322	4 419	3 888	782	350
1973	3 905	2 882	21	2 902	229	284	2 957	568	380	4 870	4 340	802	374
1974	4 304	3 119	13	3 132	257	329	3 204	644	455	5 267	4 673	817	381
1975	4 655	3 266	17	3 283	266	359	3 375	694	586	5 608	5 049	830	370
1976	5 298	3 787	19	3 806	310	411	3 906	768	624	6 255	5 588	847	394
1977	5 992	4 304	18	4 322	353	480	4 449	883	660	6 873	6 109	872	418
1978	6 918	5 032	19	5 051	420	572	5 203	993	723	7 739	6 817	894	446
1979	7 933	5 762	21	5 784	503	681	5 962	1 144	827	8 700	7 653	912	469
1980	9 104	6 397	14	6 410	560	849	6 699	1 435	969	9 850	8 698	924	483
1981	10 323	7 062	23	7 084	669	959	7 375	1 812	1 135	11 021	9 703	937	494
1982	11 382	7 629	19	7 648	741	1 050	7 957	2 180	1 246	12 010	10 698	948	500
1983	12 517	8 563	17	8 580	841	1 174	8 913	2 274	1 331	13 064	11 631	958	520
1984	14 211	9 694	21	9 715	977	1 390	10 129	2 674	1 408	14 547	12 997	977	556
1985	15 763	10 930	24	10 954	1 125	1 513	11 342	2 947	1 474	15 815	14 018	997	589
1986	17 407	12 256	24	12 280	1 285	1 598	12 594	3 267	1 546	16 981	14 957	1 025	622
1987	19 252	13 814	43	13 856	1 430	1 723	14 150	3 524	1 579	18 261	16 067	1 054	639
1988	21 178	15 254	45	15 299	1 621	1 876	15 554	3 910	1 714	19 563	17 335	1 083	665
1989	22 615	15 864	34	15 898	1 700	1 968	16 166	4 531	1 918	20 475	18 157	1 105	665
1990	22 817	15 773	43	15 817	1 720	2 004	16 101	4 568	2 149	20 512	18 292	1 112	648
1991	23 518	15 619	44	15 663	1 740	2 190	16 113	4 543	2 863	21 189	19 031	1 110	621
1992	24 594	16 706	51	16 758	1 845	2 247	17 159	4 384	3 051	22 002	19 777	1 118	633
1993	25 273	17 449	43	17 492	1 924	2 370	17 938	4 383	2 953	22 376	20 016	1 129	647
1994	26 972	18 492	41	18 532	2 082	2 468	18 919	4 696	3 358	23 607	21 141	1 143	670
1995	28 647	19 637	36	19 673	2 228	2 456	19 901	5 131	3 615	24 748	22 094	1 158	685
1996	31 045	20 859	42	20 901	2 352	2 624	21 173	6 302	3 570	26 427	23 434	1 175	701
1997	32 420	22 536	39	22 575	2 536	2 829	22 869	5 830	3 721	27 257	23 770	1 189	722
1998	35 149	24 694	42	24 736	2 753	2 946	24 928	6 363	3 858	29 147	25 403	1 206	745
1999	37 125	26 424	45	26 469	2 929	3 410	26 949	6 244	3 932	30 380	26 278	1 222	763
2000	41 429	29 364	42	29 405	3 210	4 043	30 239	6 986	4 204	33 398	28 568	1 240	785
2001	42 707	30 309	38	30 347	3 355	4 036	31 028	7 113	4 566	33 922	29 275	1 259	795
2002	43 468	31 068	29	31 096	3 416	3 876	31 556	6 930	4 982	34 109	30 344	1 274	793
2003	44 686	32 451	39	32 490	3 540	3 893	32 842	6 785	5 059	34 703	31 197	1 288	799

Table 21-2. Personal Income and Employment by Region and State—Continued

(Millions of dollars, except as noted.)

| Year | Personal income, total | Derivation of personal income ||||||||| Per capita (dollars) || Population (thousands) | Total employment (thousands) |
| | | Earnings by place of work ||| Less: Contributions for government social insurance | Plus: Adjustment for residence | Equals: Net earnings by place of residence | Plus: Dividends, interest, and rent | Plus: Personal current transfer receipts | Personal income | Disposable personal income | | |
		Nonfarm	Farm	Total									

RHODE ISLAND

1969	3 591	2 901	8	2 909	230	65	2 744	500	347	3 853	3 392	932	440
1970	3 902	3 117	9	3 126	245	66	2 948	531	423	4 104	3 653	951	440
1971	4 137	3 278	8	3 286	267	61	3 081	560	497	4 292	3 824	964	436
1972	4 510	3 614	8	3 621	306	56	3 371	593	546	4 619	4 066	976	447
1973	4 853	3 873	6	3 880	381	71	3 569	659	625	4 962	4 372	978	452
1974	5 142	3 973	9	3 982	410	88	3 660	749	734	5 393	4 744	954	439
1975	5 543	4 113	9	4 121	415	82	3 788	783	972	5 857	5 257	946	424
1976	6 090	4 631	9	4 641	472	89	4 257	840	993	6 408	5 699	950	442
1977	6 670	5 096	8	5 104	520	103	4 687	943	1 040	6 983	6 224	955	459
1978	7 317	5 661	9	5 670	597	102	5 176	1 031	1 111	7 644	6 714	957	475
1979	8 141	6 305	7	6 312	684	110	5 738	1 168	1 235	8 510	7 401	957	484
1980	9 181	6 882	8	6 890	746	124	6 268	1 484	1 428	9 677	8 476	949	486
1981	10 263	7 431	9	7 440	851	155	6 744	1 885	1 634	10 769	9 441	953	486
1982	11 036	7 803	27	7 831	902	209	7 137	2 105	1 794	11 566	10 196	954	477
1983	11 890	8 425	37	8 462	988	265	7 739	2 238	1 913	12 432	10 998	956	482
1984	13 183	9 384	32	9 416	1 135	334	8 615	2 603	1 965	13 705	12 183	962	507
1985	14 161	10 162	42	10 204	1 220	394	9 378	2 696	2 087	14 615	12 968	969	522
1986	15 174	10 991	43	11 034	1 336	419	10 118	2 886	2 171	15 526	13 697	977	541
1987	16 310	11 910	41	11 951	1 435	488	11 004	3 071	2 236	16 482	14 393	990	550
1988	17 980	13 160	42	13 202	1 603	563	12 162	3 427	2 391	18 045	15 865	996	564
1989	19 559	13 860	32	13 892	1 669	625	12 848	4 098	2 612	19 546	17 184	1 001	565
1990	20 126	14 136	31	14 167	1 716	665	13 117	4 123	2 887	20 006	17 639	1 006	555
1991	20 262	13 810	32	13 842	1 722	693	12 814	3 940	3 509	20 049	17 741	1 011	528
1992	21 129	14 666	30	14 696	1 835	712	13 573	3 902	3 654	20 867	18 541	1 013	534
1993	21 913	15 207	30	15 237	1 924	754	14 067	3 880	3 966	21 586	19 141	1 015	538
1994	22 450	15 657	26	15 683	2 011	828	14 500	4 007	3 943	22 097	19 553	1 016	538
1995	23 620	16 395	25	16 420	2 080	860	15 200	4 253	4 167	23 225	20 544	1 017	541
1996	24 609	16 919	24	16 943	2 113	929	15 759	4 623	4 227	24 106	21 213	1 021	544
1997	25 983	17 758	16	17 774	2 218	990	16 547	4 940	4 497	25 341	22 080	1 025	550
1998	27 501	18 856	16	18 872	2 348	1 074	17 598	5 315	4 587	26 670	23 111	1 031	558
1999	28 568	19 810	16	19 826	2 459	1 177	18 544	5 232	4 792	27 459	23 757	1 040	570
2000	30 697	21 255	16	21 271	2 619	1 344	19 996	5 713	4 988	29 216	25 060	1 051	584
2001	32 229	22 356	15	22 371	2 748	1 340	20 964	5 706	5 559	30 434	26 157	1 059	587
2002	33 156	23 271	14	23 285	2 850	1 300	21 735	5 568	5 853	31 035	27 295	1 068	589
2003	34 369	24 627	17	24 644	2 996	1 243	22 891	5 440	6 038	31 937	28 325	1 076	596

VERMONT

1969	1 473	1 167	57	1 224	83	-27	1 113	215	144	3 370	2 921	437	203
1970	1 614	1 256	61	1 318	89	-27	1 202	241	172	3 617	3 154	446	205
1971	1 745	1 337	60	1 397	98	-24	1 276	265	205	3 841	3 444	454	206
1972	1 924	1 467	67	1 534	111	-21	1 402	291	230	4 153	3 657	463	211
1973	2 118	1 626	71	1 697	141	-20	1 536	320	262	4 521	4 028	469	220
1974	2 293	1 736	58	1 794	155	-17	1 622	356	315	4 847	4 319	473	222
1975	2 494	1 826	60	1 886	162	-11	1 712	380	401	5 197	4 654	480	220
1976	2 786	2 056	77	2 133	184	-6	1 943	411	431	5 742	5 172	485	228
1977	3 028	2 259	65	2 325	203	-2	2 119	467	441	6 152	5 494	492	236
1978	3 478	2 637	94	2 731	244	-2	2 485	526	467	6 980	6 227	498	252
1979	3 924	2 960	104	3 064	284	5	2 785	609	530	7 760	6 878	506	261
1980	4 414	3 220	107	3 327	310	14	3 031	756	627	8 613	7 607	513	266
1981	4 983	3 535	122	3 657	366	18	3 309	950	724	9 664	8 505	516	271
1982	5 359	3 708	122	3 831	393	24	3 461	1 093	805	10 324	9 175	519	272
1983	5 735	4 067	82	4 150	431	22	3 740	1 131	864	10 959	9 764	523	279
1984	6 341	4 510	82	4 592	490	28	4 130	1 321	889	12 040	10 759	527	290
1985	6 873	4 972	100	5 071	549	30	4 552	1 394	928	12 968	11 528	530	302
1986	7 388	5 414	98	5 512	607	33	4 939	1 494	956	13 834	12 238	534	313
1987	8 037	5 987	123	6 110	661	41	5 490	1 576	971	14 875	13 053	540	323
1988	8 792	6 599	120	6 720	752	47	6 014	1 753	1 025	15 992	14 109	550	337
1989	9 685	7 105	121	7 226	814	50	6 461	2 097	1 126	17 365	15 268	558	344
1990	10 096	7 362	111	7 473	845	49	6 677	2 163	1 256	17 876	15 759	565	344
1991	10 227	7 396	100	7 497	869	56	6 684	2 173	1 369	17 985	15 951	569	337
1992	10 919	7 881	175	8 056	918	64	7 202	2 165	1 552	19 065	16 964	573	344
1993	11 257	8 265	127	8 392	967	72	7 498	2 140	1 619	19 485	17 310	578	352
1994	11 809	8 586	128	8 714	1 022	86	7 778	2 311	1 719	20 226	17 998	584	361
1995	12 370	8 901	100	9 001	1 079	100	8 022	2 490	1 858	21 002	18 697	589	365
1996	13 040	9 321	146	9 467	1 123	115	8 460	2 655	1 925	21 964	19 418	594	370
1997	13 738	9 779	111	9 890	1 175	138	8 853	2 850	2 035	23 002	20 160	597	375
1998	14 788	10 457	137	10 594	1 238	164	9 521	3 153	2 115	24 629	21 515	600	386
1999	15 650	11 180	153	11 333	1 313	187	10 207	3 188	2 255	25 881	22 577	605	394
2000	16 883	12 070	163	12 234	1 392	219	11 060	3 407	2 416	27 680	24 010	610	404
2001	17 790	12 696	143	12 840	1 487	231	11 585	3 558	2 647	29 024	25 298	613	409
2002	18 247	13 103	111	13 214	1 531	239	11 922	3 481	2 844	29 603	26 340	616	409
2003	18 904	13 674	130	13 805	1 583	245	12 467	3 431	3 006	30 534	27 486	619	411

Table 21-2. Personal Income and Employment by Region and State—Continued

(Millions of dollars, except as noted.)

Year	Personal income, total	Derivation of personal income								Per capita (dollars)		Population (thousands)	Total employment (thousands)
		Earnings by place of work			Less: Contributions for government social insurance	Plus: Adjustment for residence	Equals: Net earnings by place of residence	Plus: Dividends, interest, and rent	Plus: Personal current transfer receipts	Personal income	Disposable personal income		
		Nonfarm	Farm	Total									
MIDEAST													
1969	181 847	152 341	1 093	153 435	11 063	-1 763	140 609	25 972	15 266	4 318	3 681	42 111	19 435
1970	196 035	162 686	1 051	163 737	11 648	-1 676	150 413	27 506	18 116	4 611	3 985	42 517	19 469
1971	209 754	172 600	959	173 559	12 763	-1 757	159 039	28 964	21 751	4 893	4 285	42 870	19 304
1972	226 753	187 174	952	188 126	14 524	-1 928	171 674	30 644	24 435	5 274	4 553	42 992	19 526
1973	246 067	204 210	1 373	205 582	18 181	-2 067	185 334	33 415	27 318	5 744	4 988	42 837	19 973
1974	267 975	219 769	1 272	221 041	20 147	-2 304	198 590	37 559	31 826	6 274	5 427	42 709	19 960
1975	289 442	231 378	1 180	232 557	20 828	-2 632	209 098	39 856	40 487	6 774	5 949	42 728	19 485
1976	313 595	251 815	1 263	253 078	22 884	-2 988	227 206	42 683	43 707	7 350	6 424	42 667	19 568
1977	341 719	275 240	1 081	276 321	24 856	-3 397	248 068	47 609	46 041	8 032	6 982	42 547	19 855
1978	375 225	304 666	1 290	305 957	28 197	-3 929	273 831	52 546	48 848	8 845	7 660	42 412	20 412
1979	413 568	335 719	1 499	337 218	32 242	-4 599	300 377	59 582	53 610	9 764	8 395	42 358	20 900
1980	461 074	366 473	1 115	367 589	35 077	-5 472	327 039	72 378	61 657	10 907	9 373	42 272	20 962
1981	513 728	400 069	1 477	401 546	40 900	-6 096	354 550	89 636	69 543	12 137	10 351	42 329	21 061
1982	555 698	423 565	1 441	425 007	43 908	-6 361	374 738	103 732	77 228	13 112	11 214	42 382	20 945
1983	592 905	451 999	1 072	453 071	47 823	-6 483	398 764	110 628	83 513	13 936	12 083	42 544	21 140
1984	655 004	499 159	1 879	501 037	54 352	-6 832	439 853	128 241	86 910	15 345	13 339	42 687	21 891
1985	700 965	537 095	1 993	539 089	59 534	-7 145	472 409	137 210	91 346	16 380	14 176	42 794	22 485
1986	745 867	576 142	2 176	578 318	64 727	-7 570	506 021	143 331	96 515	17 349	15 010	42 991	22 996
1987	797 403	624 822	2 275	627 096	69 438	-8 069	549 589	148 639	99 174	18 463	15 832	43 190	23 505
1988	868 226	685 292	2 183	687 475	78 001	-8 776	600 698	162 243	105 285	19 989	17 295	43 435	24 124
1989	935 223	723 215	2 551	725 765	82 280	-9 049	634 436	186 854	113 933	21 457	18 486	43 585	24 412
1990	989 039	762 655	2 443	765 098	86 817	-9 850	668 431	195 844	124 764	22 601	19 569	43 762	24 476
1991	1 016 388	773 800	2 066	775 866	89 611	-10 425	675 831	199 744	140 813	23 063	20 110	44 071	23 904
1992	1 069 395	820 468	2 600	823 069	94 257	-12 216	716 596	195 997	156 802	24 090	21 021	44 392	23 796
1993	1 095 679	845 769	2 537	848 306	97 857	-12 146	738 302	192 182	165 194	24 502	21 308	44 717	23 915
1994	1 133 109	872 295	2 302	874 598	102 909	-11 974	759 714	202 048	171 348	25 197	21 864	44 970	24 084
1995	1 189 144	911 867	1 783	913 650	106 722	-13 142	793 786	213 982	181 376	26 317	22 793	45 186	24 376
1996	1 252 041	955 150	2 727	957 877	109 947	-13 630	834 300	226 610	191 130	27 588	23 716	45 384	24 602
1997	1 319 270	1 009 108	1 877	1 010 985	114 752	-14 012	882 222	243 551	193 498	28 944	24 665	45 580	24 971
1998	1 404 640	1 081 158	2 370	1 083 528	121 047	-15 313	947 168	259 099	198 373	30 654	25 973	45 822	25 416
1999	1 467 261	1 145 465	2 430	1 147 895	127 305	-16 820	1 003 770	257 372	206 119	31 824	26 804	46 106	25 900
2000	1 580 733	1 231 448	2 699	1 234 147	135 130	-15 670	1 083 347	279 930	217 456	34 079	28 578	46 384	26 540
2001	1 625 769	1 266 507	2 574	1 269 081	141 248	-15 151	1 112 682	275 967	237 120	34 866	29 166	46 629	26 641
2002	1 649 049	1 286 225	1 675	1 287 900	144 287	-15 963	1 127 650	268 250	253 148	35 188	30 346	46 864	26 591
2003	1 694 203	1 330 005	2 526	1 332 531	148 330	-16 402	1 167 799	262 868	263 536	35 983	31 375	47 084	26 645
DELAWARE													
1969	2 382	1 992	55	2 047	139	-43	1 865	378	139	4 411	3 642	540	271
1970	2 530	2 132	35	2 167	147	-48	1 971	394	165	4 597	3 822	550	275
1971	2 765	2 349	38	2 387	168	-60	2 159	411	194	4 891	4 107	565	280
1972	3 040	2 606	49	2 655	196	-68	2 391	434	215	5 298	4 436	574	293
1973	3 392	2 928	96	3 023	253	-97	2 674	471	248	5 858	4 899	579	305
1974	3 695	3 171	82	3 253	282	-108	2 863	528	303	6 336	5 322	583	302
1975	3 969	3 340	91	3 432	293	-110	3 029	532	408	6 742	5 746	589	292
1976	4 355	3 693	84	3 776	325	-121	3 331	586	438	7 347	6 177	593	296
1977	4 696	3 989	56	4 045	352	-133	3 560	659	477	7 895	6 647	595	296
1978	5 155	4 431	60	4 492	402	-162	3 928	728	499	8 617	7 258	598	304
1979	5 677	4 876	54	4 929	460	-184	4 285	819	572	9 480	7 917	599	312
1980	6 394	5 412	12	5 424	512	-230	4 682	1 018	694	10 748	8 970	595	312
1981	7 051	5 814	42	5 856	592	-249	5 015	1 255	781	11 831	9 799	596	314
1982	7 593	6 231	65	6 296	648	-270	5 378	1 386	829	12 673	10 645	599	317
1983	8 172	6 723	78	6 801	704	-316	5 781	1 507	884	13 498	11 500	605	326
1984	9 046	7 399	96	7 495	780	-356	6 359	1 739	948	14 792	12 692	612	341
1985	9 884	8 096	104	8 200	865	-397	6 938	1 950	997	15 987	13 735	618	359
1986	10 484	8 526	143	8 669	926	-398	7 345	2 061	1 078	16 706	14 318	628	372
1987	11 293	9 338	114	9 452	1 007	-454	7 992	2 178	1 124	17 730	15 263	637	389
1988	12 308	10 204	181	10 386	1 144	-498	8 744	2 326	1 238	19 006	16 443	648	405
1989	13 655	11 136	192	11 327	1 255	-607	9 465	2 848	1 342	20 743	17 911	658	417
1990	14 343	11 826	139	11 966	1 333	-678	9 954	2 948	1 442	21 422	18 474	670	423
1991	15 089	12 312	130	12 442	1 406	-688	10 348	3 110	1 631	22 090	19 224	683	417
1992	15 754	13 178	114	13 292	1 448	-996	10 848	3 091	1 815	22 670	19 768	695	416
1993	16 224	13 504	109	13 613	1 510	-944	11 159	3 123	1 942	22 967	19 973	706	423
1994	16 884	14 216	120	14 337	1 611	-1 106	11 619	3 202	2 063	23 530	20 343	718	427
1995	17 811	14 687	87	14 774	1 701	-930	12 143	3 402	2 265	24 407	21 105	730	445
1996	19 063	15 455	120	15 575	1 790	-952	12 833	3 724	2 506	25 727	22 071	741	456
1997	19 895	16 449	95	16 544	1 895	-1 228	13 421	3 926	2 548	26 475	22 427	751	468
1998	21 565	17 776	140	17 916	1 983	-1 410	14 523	4 356	2 687	28 252	23 933	763	485
1999	22 416	19 089	139	19 228	2 131	-1 690	15 407	4 200	2 809	28 925	24 518	775	497
2000	24 277	20 358	122	20 480	2 233	-1 733	16 514	4 705	3 058	30 871	26 279	786	508
2001	25 423	21 616	182	21 798	2 369	-1 855	17 574	4 512	3 337	31 955	27 118	796	505
2002	26 183	22 410	59	22 469	2 433	-1 885	18 151	4 425	3 606	32 487	28 382	806	502
2003	27 240	23 453	122	23 576	2 525	-2 012	19 038	4 363	3 839	33 321	29 420	817	504

Table 21-2. Personal Income and Employment by Region and State—Continued

(Millions of dollars, except as noted.)

Year	Personal income, total	Derivation of personal income								Per capita (dollars)		Population (thousands)	Total employment (thousands)
		Earnings by place of work			Less: Contributions for government social insurance	Plus: Adjustment for residence	Equals: Net earnings by place of residence	Plus: Dividends, interest, and rent	Plus: Personal current transfer receipts	Personal income	Disposable personal income		
		Nonfarm	Farm	Total									

DISTRICT OF COLUMBIA

1969	3 423	6 168	0	6 168	252	-3 208	2 708	481	234	4 492	3 842	762	678
1970	3 755	6 720	0	6 720	274	-3 512	2 934	519	302	4 973	4 276	755	674
1971	4 129	7 309	0	7 309	299	-3 828	3 182	572	375	5 500	4 791	751	669
1972	4 482	7 918	0	7 918	343	-4 161	3 414	622	447	6 027	5 218	744	671
1973	4 748	8 441	0	8 441	414	-4 449	3 578	658	512	6 472	5 588	734	664
1974	5 228	9 285	0	9 285	472	-4 910	3 904	729	595	7 254	6 290	721	676
1975	5 709	10 269	0	10 269	521	-5 523	4 225	744	741	8 038	7 007	710	680
1976	6 080	11 186	0	11 186	573	-6 095	4 518	794	768	8 732	7 494	696	677
1977	6 577	12 269	0	12 269	609	-6 741	4 919	871	787	9 647	8 371	682	683
1978	6 949	13 370	0	13 370	668	-7 527	5 175	965	810	10 371	8 904	670	696
1979	7 366	14 631	0	14 631	770	-8 486	5 375	1 088	903	11 236	9 512	656	709
1980	7 845	16 125	0	16 125	859	-9 728	5 538	1 283	1 025	12 291	10 450	638	707
1981	8 610	17 541	0	17 541	1 002	-10 675	5 864	1 614	1 133	13 519	11 349	637	696
1982	9 352	18 647	0	18 647	1 074	-11 326	6 247	1 838	1 267	14 747	12 452	634	681
1983	9 796	19 582	0	19 582	1 292	-11 702	6 588	1 883	1 325	15 490	13 204	632	676
1984	10 829	21 323	0	21 323	1 463	-12 630	7 231	2 185	1 414	17 098	14 596	633	699
1985	11 516	22 794	0	22 794	1 678	-13 423	7 693	2 408	1 415	18 148	15 475	635	713
1986	12 135	24 283	0	24 283	1 845	-14 271	8 166	2 500	1 469	19 013	16 245	638	733
1987	12 829	26 112	0	26 112	2 015	-15 322	8 775	2 540	1 514	20 141	17 067	637	746
1988	14 042	28 785	0	28 785	2 312	-16 846	9 626	2 789	1 626	22 273	19 061	630	769
1989	15 063	30 522	0	30 522	2 550	-17 953	10 019	3 418	1 626	24 133	20 667	624	777
1990	16 025	32 860	0	32 860	2 813	-19 150	10 897	3 393	1 734	26 473	22 858	605	788
1991	16 564	34 558	0	34 558	2 987	-20 356	11 215	3 371	1 978	27 567	24 027	601	774
1992	17 279	36 614	0	36 614	3 172	-21 744	11 698	3 395	2 186	28 916	25 315	598	768
1993	17 857	38 062	0	38 062	3 319	-22 634	12 110	3 354	2 394	29 996	26 358	595	767
1994	18 169	38 961	0	38 961	3 470	-23 190	12 301	3 432	2 437	30 835	26 876	589	747
1995	18 151	39 471	0	39 471	3 530	-23 538	12 403	3 374	2 373	31 266	27 245	581	740
1996	18 766	39 820	0	39 820	3 567	-23 410	12 843	3 343	2 580	32 786	28 275	572	721
1997	19 580	41 000	0	41 000	3 676	-24 077	13 247	3 757	2 575	34 488	29 380	568	717
1998	20 562	42 956	0	42 956	3 907	-25 176	13 873	3 980	2 709	36 379	30 608	565	721
1999	21 115	46 459	0	46 459	4 268	-27 665	14 527	3 862	2 726	37 030	30 716	570	735
2000	23 102	48 999	0	48 999	4 493	-28 346	16 160	4 124	2 818	40 428	33 385	571	757
2001	25 618	52 259	0	52 259	4 918	-28 793	18 548	4 106	2 964	44 731	37 610	573	760
2002	26 125	55 243	0	55 243	5 306	-31 126	18 810	4 019	3 296	45 902	39 607	569	773
2003	26 651	57 569	0	57 569	5 583	-32 688	19 298	3 970	3 383	47 305	41 143	563	777

MARYLAND

1969	16 230	11 866	131	11 997	750	2 154	13 401	1 885	944	4 196	3 482	3 868	1 679
1970	17 951	12 944	120	13 064	815	2 512	14 761	2 064	1 126	4 558	3 857	3 938	1 702
1971	19 640	14 079	93	14 172	916	2 764	16 020	2 248	1 373	4 883	4 190	4 023	1 729
1972	21 555	15 481	127	15 608	1 059	3 000	17 549	2 433	1 574	5 282	4 457	4 081	1 781
1973	23 861	17 260	208	17 468	1 353	3 203	19 318	2 727	1 816	5 807	4 929	4 109	1 846
1974	26 329	18 949	163	19 112	1 531	3 478	21 058	3 166	2 105	6 370	5 369	4 133	1 868
1975	28 656	20 109	202	20 311	1 622	3 864	22 553	3 456	2 647	6 893	5 918	4 157	1 846
1976	31 444	22 281	173	22 454	1 806	4 179	24 827	3 767	2 850	7 537	6 473	4 172	1 866
1977	34 306	24 337	128	24 465	1 972	4 586	27 079	4 190	3 037	8 179	6 965	4 195	1 919
1978	38 027	27 080	182	27 262	2 258	4 953	29 957	4 720	3 350	9 029	7 673	4 212	2 003
1979	42 135	29 946	158	30 104	2 607	5 388	32 885	5 449	3 801	9 977	8 430	4 223	2 061
1980	47 296	32 846	56	32 902	2 861	5 961	36 002	6 767	4 526	11 187	9 511	4 228	2 075
1981	52 794	36 134	127	36 261	3 377	6 434	39 318	8 289	5 187	12 388	10 415	4 262	2 102
1982	57 330	38 006	142	38 149	3 613	7 008	41 544	10 013	5 774	13 386	11 336	4 283	2 090
1983	61 841	41 516	88	41 604	4 071	7 382	44 916	10 630	6 296	14 337	12 313	4 313	2 158
1984	68 984	46 396	263	46 659	4 672	8 079	50 065	12 282	6 636	15 803	13 558	4 365	2 253
1985	75 325	50 925	275	51 201	5 285	8 729	54 645	13 665	7 015	17 069	14 721	4 413	2 356
1986	81 069	55 292	285	55 577	5 863	9 361	59 075	14 510	7 484	18 068	15 593	4 487	2 443
1987	87 696	60 547	298	60 845	6 352	10 136	64 629	15 295	7 771	19 208	16 379	4 566	2 572
1988	95 867	66 462	364	66 826	7 276	11 230	70 780	16 800	8 288	20 582	17 765	4 658	2 668
1989	103 528	70 968	362	71 330	7 861	12 077	75 546	18 953	9 029	21 900	18 724	4 727	2 726
1990	109 686	75 228	351	75 579	8 417	12 546	79 708	20 088	9 890	22 852	19 591	4 800	2 760
1991	113 436	76 595	305	76 901	8 725	13 216	81 392	20 961	11 083	23 304	20 135	4 868	2 683
1992	118 847	79 974	353	80 327	9 032	14 068	85 363	21 012	12 472	24 139	20 951	4 923	2 656
1993	122 906	83 059	329	83 388	9 386	14 474	88 476	21 446	12 984	24 720	21 406	4 972	2 679
1994	128 523	86 718	311	87 029	9 944	14 942	92 026	22 861	13 636	25 587	22 085	5 023	2 726
1995	133 814	90 440	219	90 659	10 331	14 992	95 320	24 048	14 446	26 393	22 676	5 070	2 788
1996	140 035	93 880	398	94 279	10 678	15 347	98 947	25 566	15 522	27 393	23 396	5 112	2 827
1997	147 843	100 100	274	100 374	11 326	15 310	104 358	27 583	15 901	28 666	24 091	5 157	2 891
1998	157 784	106 978	331	107 309	12 034	16 649	111 924	29 550	16 310	30 317	25 610	5 204	2 947
1999	167 075	114 411	349	114 760	12 769	17 611	119 603	30 200	17 272	31 796	26 813	5 255	3 018
2000	181 957	124 081	354	124 435	13 613	19 892	130 715	32 998	18 245	34 257	28 800	5 312	3 092
2001	191 257	131 843	295	132 138	14 619	20 313	137 832	33 529	19 896	35 527	29 967	5 383	3 127
2002	198 544	138 112	154	138 266	15 328	21 149	144 087	33 052	21 405	36 427	31 463	5 451	3 155
2003	206 166	144 264	296	144 559	15 956	22 245	150 848	32 535	22 783	37 424	32 659	5 509	3 183

Table 21-2. Personal Income and Employment by Region and State—Continued

(Millions of dollars, except as noted.)

Year	Personal income, total	Derivation of personal income								Per capita (dollars)		Population (thousands)	Total employment (thousands)
		Earnings by place of work			Less: Contributions for government social insurance	Plus: Adjustment for residence	Equals: Net earnings by place of residence	Plus: Dividends, interest, and rent	Plus: Personal current transfer receipts	Personal income	Disposable personal income		
		Nonfarm	Farm	Total									

NEW JERSEY

Year	Personal income, total	Nonfarm	Farm	Total	Contrib.	Adjust.	Net earnings	Div/Int/Rent	Transfer	Per cap income	Disp income	Population	Employment
1969	32 013	24 081	104	24 186	1 827	3 117	25 476	4 325	2 212	4 512	3 913	7 095	3 061
1970	34 663	26 049	99	26 149	1 957	3 071	27 263	4 712	2 689	4 821	4 225	7 190	3 125
1971	37 285	27 829	93	27 922	2 168	3 155	28 908	5 100	3 276	5 120	4 549	7 282	3 119
1972	40 492	30 383	88	30 472	2 482	3 354	31 343	5 485	3 664	5 519	4 835	7 337	3 184
1973	44 253	33 599	126	33 725	3 128	3 511	34 109	6 012	4 132	6 033	5 331	7 335	3 288
1974	48 161	36 184	137	36 320	3 458	3 701	36 564	6 748	4 848	6 566	5 779	7 335	3 301
1975	51 810	37 723	96	37 819	3 541	3 983	38 261	7 211	6 338	7 057	6 299	7 341	3 191
1976	56 579	41 568	101	41 669	3 930	4 326	42 065	7 673	6 842	7 704	6 809	7 344	3 248
1977	62 009	45 747	111	45 858	4 313	4 720	46 265	8 526	7 218	8 446	7 383	7 342	3 325
1978	68 857	51 302	126	51 428	4 985	5 301	51 744	9 431	7 681	9 360	8 160	7 356	3 464
1979	76 525	56 860	126	56 985	5 744	6 057	57 298	10 684	8 544	10 379	8 956	7 373	3 555
1980	86 355	62 436	114	62 549	6 325	7 159	63 384	13 209	9 763	11 707	10 084	7 376	3 608
1981	96 485	68 287	148	68 436	7 378	7 797	68 854	16 668	10 963	13 025	11 188	7 407	3 643
1982	104 313	73 032	165	73 198	8 007	8 339	73 529	18 766	12 018	14 038	12 070	7 431	3 651
1983	112 659	79 741	191	79 932	8 979	8 573	79 526	20 155	12 978	15 086	13 118	7 468	3 753
1984	124 744	88 809	199	89 008	10 422	8 976	87 562	23 648	13 533	16 598	14 501	7 515	3 933
1985	133 915	96 368	226	96 594	11 391	9 355	94 558	25 171	14 186	17 701	15 321	7 566	4 049
1986	143 017	104 150	228	104 378	12 485	9 953	101 846	26 320	14 852	18 763	16 212	7 622	4 146
1987	154 440	114 160	260	114 420	13 605	10 505	111 321	27 770	15 350	20 134	17 237	7 671	4 248
1988	169 577	126 764	260	127 024	15 329	10 836	122 531	30 701	16 345	21 988	19 041	7 712	4 349
1989	181 461	133 204	254	133 458	15 980	10 339	127 816	36 138	17 506	23 487	20 354	7 726	4 386
1990	190 753	139 588	234	139 821	16 641	10 556	133 736	37 702	19 315	24 572	21 381	7 763	4 344
1991	194 174	140 848	220	141 068	17 191	10 647	134 524	37 633	22 016	24 847	21 700	7 815	4 204
1992	207 904	150 184	237	150 421	18 256	12 656	144 821	37 478	25 604	26 382	23 084	7 881	4 201
1993	213 222	156 037	268	156 305	18 953	13 077	150 429	36 017	26 776	26 824	23 357	7 949	4 228
1994	220 859	162 295	286	162 581	20 037	13 144	155 688	38 032	27 139	27 558	23 897	8 014	4 264
1995	233 937	170 507	284	170 790	20 840	14 226	164 176	40 712	29 049	28 941	25 158	8 083	4 330
1996	248 320	179 807	303	180 110	21 722	15 672	174 060	43 856	30 404	30 470	26 299	8 150	4 386
1997	263 420	189 111	248	189 359	22 502	18 451	185 309	47 048	31 063	32 051	27 411	8 219	4 446
1998	282 721	203 154	261	203 415	23 902	20 798	200 311	50 775	31 636	34 115	28 914	8 287	4 524
1999	294 385	213 763	234	213 997	25 071	22 436	211 362	50 143	32 881	35 215	29 600	8 360	4 595
2000	323 554	233 138	304	233 441	26 854	25 657	232 244	56 234	35 076	38 372	32 015	8 432	4 755
2001	332 700	238 138	269	238 407	27 975	27 433	237 865	56 158	38 677	39 122	32 796	8 504	4 784
2002	337 853	244 742	257	244 999	28 590	24 814	241 222	54 655	41 975	39 399	34 038	8 575	4 791
2003	345 557	252 919	266	253 185	29 036	25 092	249 241	53 405	42 912	40 002	34 967	8 638	4 807

NEW YORK

Year	Personal income, total	Nonfarm	Farm	Total	Contrib.	Adjust.	Net earnings	Div/Int/Rent	Transfer	Per cap income	Disp income	Population	Employment
1969	83 071	70 374	435	70 810	5 283	-3 370	62 156	13 177	7 738	4 588	3 866	18 105	8 496
1970	89 047	74 870	415	75 285	5 525	-3 320	66 440	13 696	8 912	4 874	4 182	18 272	8 468
1971	94 929	79 090	405	79 495	6 021	-3 426	70 047	14 132	10 750	5 169	4 499	18 365	8 348
1972	101 465	84 851	347	85 199	6 786	-3 682	74 731	14 735	11 999	5 529	4 758	18 352	8 350
1973	108 510	91 179	465	91 644	8 402	-3 900	79 342	15 873	13 295	5 964	5 159	18 195	8 468
1974	117 015	96 764	435	97 199	9 177	-4 124	83 898	17 692	15 425	6 475	5 582	18 073	8 395
1975	125 715	101 226	372	101 598	9 443	-4 471	87 683	18 518	19 514	6 972	6 100	18 032	8 175
1976	134 312	108 634	395	109 029	10 240	-4 915	93 875	19 655	20 782	7 472	6 514	17 975	8 128
1977	145 284	117 785	325	118 110	11 004	-5 468	101 638	21 900	21 746	8 138	7 069	17 852	8 202
1978	158 202	129 462	425	129 887	12 359	-6 121	111 407	24 010	22 785	8 928	7 721	17 720	8 381
1979	173 257	142 323	530	142 853	14 064	-6 979	121 810	27 111	24 336	9 825	8 437	17 634	8 591
1980	193 492	156 467	521	156 988	15 326	-8 203	133 459	32 079	27 955	11 015	9 424	17 567	8 622
1981	216 592	172 221	535	172 756	17 978	-8 899	145 788	39 247	31 556	12 329	10 454	17 568	8 700
1982	235 868	185 233	512	185 745	19 580	-9 865	156 300	45 045	34 523	13 409	11 352	17 590	8 710
1983	252 521	197 967	363	198 331	21 209	-10 334	166 787	48 380	37 353	14 277	12 282	17 687	8 771
1984	281 237	219 483	484	219 967	23 922	-11 005	185 040	56 657	39 540	15 848	13 687	17 746	9 058
1985	300 295	236 364	552	236 916	26 226	-11 661	198 999	59 537	41 739	16 877	14 473	17 792	9 293
1986	320 223	254 715	645	255 360	28 610	-12 570	214 180	61 820	44 223	17 956	15 381	17 833	9 494
1987	341 560	275 384	727	276 111	30 469	-13 388	232 255	63 931	45 375	19 115	16 212	17 869	9 552
1988	372 671	301 956	642	302 598	34 131	-14 143	254 284	70 236	48 252	20 777	17 818	17 941	9 768
1989	400 769	316 180	764	316 944	35 868	-13 782	267 294	80 513	52 962	22 286	18 986	17 983	9 841
1990	423 897	332 467	745	333 212	37 849	-14 083	281 280	84 547	58 069	23 523	20 183	18 021	9 817
1991	434 304	334 699	617	335 316	38 691	-14 151	282 475	86 538	65 291	23 965	20 750	18 123	9 567
1992	453 737	354 874	728	355 602	40 470	-17 429	297 702	83 690	72 344	24 867	21 525	18 247	9 494
1993	462 008	362 389	792	363 181	41 543	-17 363	304 275	80 922	76 811	25 143	21 650	18 375	9 516
1994	475 979	370 458	665	371 123	43 347	-17 370	310 406	85 003	80 570	25 785	22 197	18 459	9 551
1995	501 667	389 360	545	389 905	44 952	-19 760	325 193	90 770	85 704	27 082	23 268	18 524	9 601
1996	528 363	411 259	777	412 036	46 314	-22 529	343 193	95 589	89 580	28 424	24 212	18 588	9 686
1997	557 024	436 661	474	437 135	48 332	-25 017	363 785	103 491	89 748	29 857	25 245	18 657	9 819
1998	591 847	469 379	716	470 096	51 014	-28 639	390 443	108 539	92 864	31 555	26 461	18 756	10 015
1999	619 659	498 632	827	499 459	53 642	-30 402	415 415	108 354	95 889	32 816	27 296	18 883	10 220
2000	663 005	537 852	770	538 623	57 239	-34 495	446 888	115 784	100 334	34 900	28 883	18 997	10 455
2001	678 874	550 275	881	551 156	59 511	-35 642	456 003	112 830	110 041	35 590	29 133	19 075	10 488
2002	680 182	545 959	654	546 613	59 851	-32 361	454 401	109 146	116 634	35 548	30 191	19 134	10 407
2003	696 531	561 240	802	562 043	61 464	-32 550	468 029	106 934	121 567	36 296	31 188	19 190	10 412

Table 21-2. Personal Income and Employment by Region and State—*Continued*

(Millions of dollars, except as noted.)

| Year | Personal income, total | Derivation of personal income ||||||||| Per capita (dollars) || Population (thousands) | Total employment (thousands) |
| | | Earnings by place of work ||| Less: Contributions for government social insurance | Plus: Adjustment for residence | Equals: Net earnings by place of residence | Plus: Dividends, interest, and rent | Plus: Personal current transfer receipts | Personal income | Disposable personal income | | |
		Nonfarm	Farm	Total									
PENNSYLVANIA													
1969	44 729	37 860	367	38 227	2 810	-413	35 003	5 726	4 000	3 810	3 311	11 741	5 250
1970	48 088	39 971	382	40 353	2 930	-379	37 044	6 121	4 923	4 071	3 566	11 812	5 226
1971	51 007	41 943	331	42 274	3 190	-362	38 722	6 501	5 783	4 292	3 802	11 884	5 159
1972	55 719	45 934	341	46 275	3 658	-372	42 246	6 935	6 537	4 680	4 060	11 905	5 247
1973	61 303	50 803	479	51 282	4 632	-336	46 314	7 675	7 315	5 158	4 504	11 885	5 402
1974	67 547	55 417	455	55 872	5 228	-341	50 302	8 695	8 550	5 693	4 947	11 864	5 419
1975	73 581	58 711	417	59 128	5 407	-374	53 347	9 395	10 840	6 184	5 460	11 898	5 302
1976	80 825	64 453	510	64 963	6 010	-362	58 591	10 207	12 027	6 799	5 984	11 887	5 353
1977	88 847	71 112	462	71 574	6 607	-361	64 606	11 463	12 778	7 478	6 545	11 882	5 429
1978	98 035	79 020	497	79 518	7 526	-372	71 620	12 692	13 723	8 263	7 205	11 865	5 564
1979	108 608	87 084	631	87 715	8 596	-395	78 724	14 431	15 452	9 147	7 935	11 874	5 672
1980	119 692	93 188	412	93 600	9 194	-431	83 975	18 022	17 695	10 085	8 769	11 868	5 638
1981	132 196	100 071	625	100 697	10 573	-413	89 710	22 563	19 923	11 148	9 628	11 859	5 605
1982	141 241	102 416	557	102 972	10 986	-246	91 740	26 684	22 817	11 924	10 389	11 845	5 495
1983	147 915	106 470	352	106 822	11 570	-86	95 166	28 072	24 677	12 495	11 020	11 838	5 455
1984	160 164	115 749	837	116 585	13 094	104	103 596	31 729	24 839	13 556	11 964	11 815	5 606
1985	170 050	122 548	836	123 384	14 059	251	109 576	34 479	25 995	14 447	12 738	11 771	5 714
1986	178 939	129 176	875	130 051	14 998	356	115 408	36 121	27 409	15 187	13 418	11 783	5 808
1987	189 585	139 281	876	140 157	15 991	453	124 619	36 926	28 040	16 052	14 096	11 811	5 998
1988	203 661	151 121	737	151 857	17 810	685	134 733	39 391	29 537	17 193	15 134	11 846	6 165
1989	220 748	161 204	980	162 184	18 766	878	144 296	44 984	31 467	18 603	16 334	11 866	6 265
1990	234 334	170 686	973	171 659	19 763	959	152 855	47 166	34 314	19 687	17 344	11 903	6 342
1991	242 822	174 787	794	175 581	20 611	908	155 877	48 130	38 814	20 265	17 949	11 982	6 259
1992	255 874	185 645	1 169	186 813	21 879	1 229	166 163	47 330	42 381	21 235	18 796	12 049	6 262
1993	263 462	192 717	1 039	193 756	23 147	1 243	171 853	47 321	44 289	21 738	19 236	12 120	6 302
1994	272 695	199 647	919	200 566	24 499	1 607	177 675	49 517	45 504	22 414	19 776	12 166	6 369
1995	283 764	207 402	648	208 051	25 368	1 868	184 551	51 675	47 539	23 262	20 443	12 198	6 471
1996	297 494	214 929	1 128	216 057	25 875	2 242	192 423	54 532	50 538	24 344	21 258	12 220	6 525
1997	311 509	225 787	786	226 573	27 021	2 549	202 101	57 746	51 662	25 475	22 096	12 228	6 631
1998	330 161	240 915	921	241 836	28 206	2 465	216 095	61 899	52 167	26 961	23 301	12 246	6 724
1999	342 611	253 111	881	253 992	29 424	2 889	227 456	60 613	54 542	27 937	24 101	12 264	6 836
2000	364 838	267 020	1 148	268 169	30 697	3 355	240 827	66 085	57 926	29 697	25 575	12 285	6 973
2001	371 897	272 376	947	273 323	31 856	3 393	244 860	64 831	62 206	30 240	26 094	12 298	6 977
2002	380 162	279 761	550	280 311	32 779	3 446	250 978	62 952	66 232	30 835	27 227	12 329	6 963
2003	392 058	290 560	1 039	291 599	33 765	3 511	261 344	61 660	69 053	31 706	28 266	12 365	6 962
GREAT LAKES													
1969	161 216	134 765	2 823	137 588	9 310	287	128 564	21 319	11 332	4 040	3 475	39 904	17 785
1970	169 065	139 828	2 468	142 296	9 504	262	133 055	22 464	13 547	4 193	3 647	40 320	17 630
1971	181 621	149 081	2 856	151 936	10 425	334	141 845	23 673	16 103	4 471	3 941	40 622	17 549
1972	198 554	163 794	3 114	166 907	12 096	383	155 195	25 387	17 973	4 864	4 227	40 824	17 933
1973	222 988	183 726	5 158	188 884	15 629	435	173 689	28 362	20 937	5 446	4 759	40 947	18 710
1974	242 749	197 733	4 588	202 321	17 400	535	185 457	32 361	24 931	5 915	5 153	41 037	18 911
1975	261 436	205 408	5 752	211 160	17 671	628	194 118	35 288	32 030	6 360	5 614	41 105	18 399
1976	289 361	232 056	4 759	236 815	20 243	776	217 348	37 821	34 192	7 026	6 144	41 187	18 891
1977	321 800	260 950	4 757	265 707	22 759	959	243 908	42 176	35 716	7 782	6 770	41 353	19 508
1978	357 361	292 752	4 425	297 177	26 310	1 185	272 053	46 904	38 404	8 609	7 452	41 510	20 196
1979	394 863	321 395	5 134	326 529	29 955	1 405	297 979	53 456	43 428	9 489	8 182	41 611	20 520
1980	428 890	334 970	3 223	338 193	30 983	1 681	308 891	65 489	54 510	10 287	8 933	41 694	20 024
1981	468 448	357 480	3 605	361 085	35 487	1 440	327 038	80 802	60 608	11 248	9 729	41 648	19 862
1982	489 802	361 458	2 869	364 327	36 419	1 338	329 246	92 540	68 016	11 805	10 344	41 492	19 315
1983	514 149	380 781	-168	380 614	38 830	1 319	343 102	98 364	72 682	12 429	10 929	41 366	19 335
1984	568 589	421 539	4 319	425 858	44 244	1 423	383 037	111 096	74 456	13 736	12 136	41 393	20 120
1985	603 916	450 343	4 886	455 229	48 176	1 462	408 515	117 214	78 187	14 581	12 835	41 418	20 605
1986	634 420	475 878	4 409	480 287	51 707	1 531	430 111	122 456	81 853	15 304	13 487	41 455	21 050
1987	665 925	504 152	4 956	509 108	54 365	1 600	456 343	125 466	84 116	16 012	14 013	41 590	21 651
1988	711 001	546 216	3 304	549 520	60 533	1 724	490 711	132 499	87 791	17 042	14 974	41 721	22 219
1989	762 846	576 310	6 917	583 227	64 389	1 763	520 600	148 027	94 218	18 218	15 925	41 873	22 717
1990	804 166	605 942	5 825	611 767	68 063	1 966	545 671	155 614	102 881	19 105	16 725	42 091	23 093
1991	828 639	624 201	3 411	627 612	71 309	2 014	558 316	157 550	112 773	19 499	17 154	42 496	23 003
1992	884 713	669 058	5 717	674 776	75 713	2 245	601 308	159 796	123 609	20 621	18 213	42 903	23 126
1993	918 620	700 714	5 058	705 771	80 221	2 335	627 886	161 006	129 728	21 228	18 651	43 275	23 512
1994	975 700	745 488	5 695	751 183	86 536	2 549	667 196	174 775	133 729	22 384	19 607	43 590	24 215
1995	1 021 606	781 585	3 253	784 838	91 002	2 683	696 520	184 396	140 689	23 259	20 302	43 924	24 876
1996	1 073 297	812 452	6 713	819 165	93 998	2 994	728 161	197 605	147 531	24 261	21 032	44 239	25 274
1997	1 132 660	856 122	6 766	862 889	98 451	3 340	767 777	212 193	152 690	25 457	21 951	44 494	25 674
1998	1 207 487	916 993	5 562	922 556	103 148	3 466	822 873	229 877	154 737	26 996	23 179	44 728	26 131
1999	1 255 454	969 950	4 158	974 108	108 420	3 884	869 572	224 886	160 996	27 918	23 964	44 969	26 548
2000	1 333 971	1 024 233	4 264	1 028 498	111 902	4 245	920 840	242 503	170 627	29 497	25 334	45 223	26 986
2001	1 360 054	1 041 257	4 242	1 045 498	114 660	4 500	935 338	237 665	187 050	29 931	25 841	45 440	26 695
2002	1 381 209	1 061 827	2 391	1 064 218	116 022	4 522	952 718	230 080	198 411	30 266	26 715	45 635	26 441
2003	1 423 692	1 101 654	4 780	1 106 434	118 913	4 814	992 336	225 230	206 126	31 060	27 712	45 837	26 371

Table 21-2. Personal Income and Employment by Region and State—Continued

(Millions of dollars, except as noted.)

| Year | Personal income, total | Derivation of personal income ||||||| Per capita (dollars) || Population (thousands) | Total employment (thousands) |
| | | Earnings by place of work ||| Less: Contributions for government social insurance | Plus: Adjustment for residence | Equals: Net earnings by place of residence | Plus: Dividends, interest, and rent | Plus: Personal current transfer receipts | Personal income | Disposable personal income | | |
		Nonfarm	Farm	Total									
ILLINOIS													
1969	47 931	39 958	897	40 854	2 717	93	38 230	6 465	3 236	4 342	3 715	11 039	5 179
1970	50 835	42 176	706	42 882	2 811	18	40 089	6 909	3 837	4 570	3 930	11 125	5 144
1971	54 555	44 885	870	45 755	3 075	-23	42 657	7 307	4 592	4 868	4 253	11 206	5 105
1972	59 248	48 794	980	49 774	3 518	-42	46 214	7 865	5 169	5 263	4 538	11 258	5 156
1973	66 374	54 070	1 822	55 892	4 491	-59	51 342	8 884	6 149	5 895	5 119	11 260	5 351
1974	72 753	59 101	1 649	60 750	5 079	-71	55 600	10 143	7 010	6 453	5 580	11 274	5 442
1975	79 270	62 185	2 439	64 625	5 196	-96	59 332	10 952	8 986	7 011	6 150	11 306	5 342
1976	86 597	69 306	1 693	70 999	5 882	-76	65 040	11 641	9 916	7 623	6 623	11 360	5 458
1977	95 420	76 897	1 695	78 592	6 516	-10	72 066	12 982	10 372	8 366	7 250	11 406	5 587
1978	105 497	85 870	1 482	87 352	7 467	78	79 963	14 494	11 039	9 226	7 972	11 434	5 748
1979	115 966	93 950	1 809	95 759	8 483	163	87 439	16 503	12 024	10 152	8 709	11 423	5 811
1980	125 838	99 447	350	99 797	8 955	262	91 104	20 148	14 585	11 005	9 464	11 435	5 688
1981	139 569	106 465	1 497	107 962	10 275	198	97 885	24 927	16 758	12 196	10 471	11 443	5 684
1982	147 604	109 368	899	110 267	10 717	126	99 676	29 528	18 401	12 921	11 284	11 423	5 583
1983	153 546	114 125	-498	113 627	11 259	90	102 458	31 385	19 703	13 459	11 829	11 409	5 542
1984	169 736	126 062	1 202	127 264	12 809	-15	114 440	35 223	20 073	14 873	13 150	11 412	5 746
1985	178 529	133 155	1 697	134 852	13 762	-83	121 007	36 571	20 951	15 661	13 801	11 400	5 814
1986	187 025	141 045	1 404	142 449	14 767	-142	127 540	37 776	21 710	16 424	14 487	11 387	5 927
1987	197 603	151 176	1 415	152 591	15 637	-230	136 723	38 717	22 163	17 347	15 145	11 391	6 072
1988	212 011	164 930	838	165 768	17 418	-361	147 989	41 099	22 923	18 613	16 346	11 390	6 232
1989	225 574	173 261	2 143	175 404	18 470	-376	156 558	44 657	24 358	19 770	17 247	11 410	6 342
1990	238 499	183 093	1 722	184 815	19 637	-281	164 897	47 026	26 576	20 824	18 168	11 453	6 440
1991	245 434	188 369	928	189 298	20 599	-294	168 405	48 337	28 693	21 215	18 634	11 569	6 416
1992	263 702	201 612	1 882	203 494	21 736	-337	181 421	49 557	32 724	22 550	19 905	11 694	6 397
1993	271 174	209 580	1 641	211 222	22 937	-497	187 788	49 132	34 254	22 962	20 164	11 810	6 487
1994	285 537	219 921	2 095	222 015	24 452	-515	197 048	53 003	35 486	23 969	20 964	11 913	6 658
1995	301 688	232 445	556	233 001	25 762	-778	206 461	57 378	37 849	25 123	21 920	12 008	6 822
1996	320 081	243 715	2 345	246 061	26 827	-831	218 403	61 828	39 850	26 449	22 924	12 102	6 925
1997	337 897	258 356	2 167	260 523	28 338	-874	231 312	65 874	40 712	27 729	23 849	12 186	7 029
1998	360 095	276 720	1 487	278 207	30 089	-853	247 265	71 525	41 305	29 343	25 103	12 272	7 185
1999	373 385	293 094	935	294 029	31 536	-1 049	261 445	69 859	42 081	30 212	25 763	12 359	7 282
2000	400 373	311 686	1 338	313 024	33 038	-1 343	278 642	76 913	44 818	32 187	27 414	12 439	7 416
2001	407 965	317 019	1 359	318 378	33 981	-1 509	282 888	76 782	48 294	32 592	27 926	12 517	7 370
2002	412 262	321 202	723	321 926	34 412	-1 448	286 066	74 233	51 964	32 754	28 817	12 586	7 282
2003	420 156	328 419	1 348	329 767	35 085	-1 292	293 391	72 664	54 101	33 205	29 532	12 654	7 244
INDIANA													
1969	18 956	16 014	541	16 555	1 097	25	15 483	2 194	1 279	3 686	3 186	5 143	2 327
1970	19 678	16 472	371	16 843	1 116	58	15 785	2 393	1 500	3 782	3 309	5 204	2 291
1971	21 408	17 530	588	18 118	1 229	118	17 008	2 609	1 790	4 078	3 607	5 250	2 290
1972	23 453	19 484	496	19 980	1 442	151	18 689	2 794	1 970	4 428	3 876	5 296	2 367
1973	27 049	21 954	1 218	23 172	1 865	195	21 502	3 211	2 335	5 076	4 487	5 329	2 483
1974	28 975	23 614	721	24 335	2 091	256	22 500	3 718	2 757	5 416	4 713	5 350	2 493
1975	31 211	24 291	1 085	25 376	2 122	301	23 555	4 144	3 512	5 833	5 170	5 351	2 405
1976	34 912	27 780	1 065	28 846	2 440	351	26 756	4 491	3 665	6 500	5 704	5 372	2 489
1977	38 717	31 429	712	32 141	2 757	413	29 798	5 070	3 849	7 163	6 263	5 405	2 578
1978	43 272	35 403	716	36 119	3 196	467	33 390	5 646	4 236	7 945	6 916	5 446	2 671
1979	47 781	38 926	655	39 581	3 636	544	36 489	6 425	4 867	8 727	7 565	5 475	2 713
1980	51 469	40 144	361	40 505	3 725	667	37 447	7 937	6 085	9 374	8 188	5 491	2 632
1981	56 488	43 131	291	43 422	4 306	716	39 832	9 856	6 800	10 307	8 961	5 480	2 611
1982	58 448	43 147	297	43 445	4 399	781	39 827	11 044	7 577	10 689	9 376	5 468	2 530
1983	61 123	45 482	-265	45 218	4 660	830	41 388	11 576	8 159	11 214	9 902	5 450	2 550
1984	68 027	50 091	738	50 829	5 257	993	46 565	12 904	8 558	12 463	11 055	5 458	2 653
1985	71 838	53 092	668	53 760	5 685	1 080	49 155	13 675	9 008	13 159	11 631	5 459	2 709
1986	75 378	55 967	564	56 532	6 093	1 177	51 615	14 251	9 512	13 820	12 243	5 454	2 769
1987	79 846	60 020	753	60 773	6 466	1 249	55 556	14 592	9 698	14 589	12 872	5 473	2 865
1988	84 969	64 859	274	65 132	7 244	1 375	59 263	15 428	10 277	15 472	13 654	5 492	2 953
1989	92 341	68 990	946	69 937	7 759	1 442	63 619	17 555	11 167	16 717	14 678	5 524	3 030
1990	97 213	72 440	838	73 278	8 221	1 513	66 570	18 516	12 127	17 491	15 368	5 558	3 090
1991	100 361	75 515	212	75 728	8 700	1 536	68 563	18 421	13 377	17 869	15 752	5 616	3 091
1992	108 029	80 908	771	81 679	9 257	1 752	74 173	18 631	15 224	19 037	16 844	5 675	3 139
1993	113 428	85 485	849	86 334	9 860	1 940	78 415	18 951	16 062	19 764	17 431	5 739	3 216
1994	120 278	90 848	766	91 614	10 664	2 091	83 042	20 481	16 756	20 761	18 225	5 794	3 306
1995	125 269	94 943	330	95 273	11 170	2 342	86 445	21 817	17 006	21 408	18 757	5 851	3 400
1996	132 103	98 763	1 144	99 907	11 546	2 486	90 847	23 246	18 010	22 368	19 528	5 906	3 439
1997	138 794	103 913	1 185	105 098	12 122	2 648	95 625	24 734	18 435	23 306	20 247	5 955	3 496
1998	149 336	112 167	763	112 931	12 830	2 679	102 779	27 448	19 109	24 894	21 572	5 999	3 567
1999	154 842	118 361	300	118 660	13 446	3 032	108 246	26 616	19 980	25 615	22 206	6 045	3 626
2000	165 285	124 719	553	125 272	13 888	3 374	114 757	28 997	21 531	27 134	23 649	6 092	3 673
2001	168 431	125 816	672	126 488	14 115	3 474	115 847	28 904	23 680	27 492	24 015	6 126	3 611
2002	171 841	129 644	126	129 770	14 532	3 368	118 606	28 117	25 119	27 910	24 842	6 157	3 583
2003	178 415	135 807	787	136 594	15 026	3 431	124 999	27 590	25 827	28 797	25 882	6 196	3 590

Table 21-2. Personal Income and Employment by Region and State—Continued

(Millions of dollars, except as noted.)

Year	Personal income, total	Derivation of personal income								Per capita (dollars)		Population (thousands)	Total employment (thousands)
		Earnings by place of work			Less: Contributions for government social insurance	Plus: Adjustment for residence	Equals: Net earnings by place of residence	Plus: Dividends, interest, and rent	Plus: Personal current transfer receipts	Personal income	Disposable personal income		
		Nonfarm	Farm	Total									
MICHIGAN													
1969	36 523	30 769	345	31 115	2 203	107	29 019	4 945	2 559	4 159	3 571	8 781	3 640
1970	37 346	31 039	334	31 374	2 193	112	29 293	4 837	3 216	4 198	3 654	8 897	3 558
1971	40 372	33 744	305	34 049	2 446	104	31 706	4 827	3 839	4 500	3 951	8 972	3 571
1972	44 824	37 704	420	38 124	2 901	112	35 336	5 170	4 318	4 967	4 285	9 025	3 687
1973	50 345	42 829	555	43 384	3 794	138	39 728	5 691	4 925	5 550	4 824	9 072	3 858
1974	53 956	44 629	640	45 270	4 077	140	41 333	6 471	6 153	5 923	5 174	9 109	3 854
1975	57 435	45 633	570	46 204	4 087	154	42 271	7 088	8 076	6 306	5 595	9 108	3 695
1976	64 660	52 806	471	53 277	4 789	197	48 685	7 665	8 311	7 092	6 200	9 117	3 844
1977	72 818	60 448	552	61 000	5 485	223	55 737	8 547	8 534	7 952	6 888	9 157	4 016
1978	80 986	68 222	500	68 722	6 394	270	62 598	9 312	9 076	8 801	7 551	9 202	4 188
1979	89 110	74 493	534	75 027	7 197	310	68 140	10 504	10 467	9 635	8 269	9 249	4 234
1980	95 460	75 328	525	75 853	7 181	355	69 026	12 625	13 809	10 314	8 983	9 256	4 039
1981	102 206	79 421	505	79 927	8 188	384	72 123	15 456	14 627	11 098	9 634	9 209	3 992
1982	105 189	78 622	402	79 025	8 242	393	71 176	17 682	16 331	11 540	10 147	9 115	3 837
1983	111 468	83 679	214	83 893	8 948	427	75 372	18 812	17 284	12 320	10 797	9 048	3 881
1984	123 531	93 384	540	93 924	10 351	491	84 064	21 990	17 477	13 651	11 999	9 049	4 059
1985	134 083	102 618	653	103 271	11 659	512	92 124	23 920	18 039	14 773	12 895	9 076	4 257
1986	142 459	109 552	482	110 035	12 629	495	97 900	25 643	18 915	15 607	13 642	9 128	4 373
1987	147 486	113 544	660	114 204	12 973	512	101 743	26 291	19 452	16 053	13 984	9 187	4 511
1988	156 961	122 341	580	122 921	14 386	523	109 058	27 631	20 272	17 028	14 901	9 218	4 612
1989	168 637	129 411	967	130 378	15 261	517	115 634	31 067	21 937	18 225	15 878	9 253	4 742
1990	176 189	134 549	757	135 305	15 869	457	119 893	32 537	23 758	18 922	16 571	9 311	4 825
1991	181 655	137 697	645	138 343	16 406	472	122 409	32 558	26 688	19 324	17 028	9 400	4 754
1992	192 788	148 021	740	148 760	17 435	599	131 924	32 883	27 981	20 338	18 040	9 479	4 783
1993	201 574	155 626	742	156 368	18 536	663	138 494	33 204	29 876	21 129	18 567	9 540	4 843
1994	217 812	169 356	566	169 922	20 325	763	150 360	37 309	30 143	22 694	19 888	9 598	5 016
1995	227 466	177 753	711	178 464	21 386	734	157 812	38 018	31 635	23 508	20 487	9 676	5 175
1996	237 193	183 594	629	184 222	21 903	758	163 077	40 784	33 333	24 306	21 040	9 759	5 282
1997	248 821	191 430	655	192 086	22 969	849	169 966	43 479	35 376	25 367	21 857	9 809	5 363
1998	265 098	205 821	633	206 454	24 035	892	183 312	46 690	35 096	26 919	23 077	9 848	5 416
1999	278 062	218 175	838	219 013	25 441	995	194 567	45 859	37 635	28 095	24 099	9 897	5 519
2000	294 227	230 621	560	231 181	26 411	1 005	205 775	49 515	38 938	29 553	25 436	9 956	5 629
2001	299 284	233 483	417	233 900	26 349	1 077	208 628	47 328	43 328	29 913	25 967	10 005	5 539
2002	302 019	236 590	468	237 058	26 775	1 121	211 405	45 834	44 780	30 072	26 678	10 043	5 480
2003	314 460	248 570	599	249 169	27 470	1 138	222 837	44 749	46 874	31 196	27 985	10 080	5 449
OHIO													
1969	41 407	35 347	409	35 757	2 360	-187	33 210	5 298	2 899	3 920	3 394	10 563	4 695
1970	43 597	36 742	426	37 167	2 409	-178	34 580	5 623	3 394	4 086	3 589	10 669	4 683
1971	46 381	38 669	407	39 076	2 605	-128	36 343	6 026	4 012	4 321	3 856	10 735	4 627
1972	50 350	42 095	497	42 592	2 987	-125	39 479	6 435	4 436	4 685	4 116	10 747	4 710
1973	56 071	47 155	658	47 813	3 865	-153	43 795	7 113	5 163	5 208	4 581	10 767	4 902
1974	61 593	50 967	784	51 752	4 312	-129	47 311	8 081	6 200	5 721	5 020	10 766	4 964
1975	65 710	52 665	802	53 468	4 338	-75	49 055	8 726	7 929	6 101	5 402	10 770	4 809
1976	72 585	58 965	777	59 742	4 944	-85	54 713	9 389	8 483	6 750	5 946	10 753	4 889
1977	80 707	66 238	664	66 902	5 557	-98	61 246	10 549	8 912	7 493	6 561	10 771	5 034
1978	89 417	73 903	613	74 515	6 407	-116	67 993	11 843	9 581	8 283	7 233	10 795	5 207
1979	99 084	81 302	745	82 047	7 332	-138	74 578	13 566	10 940	9 176	7 960	10 799	5 298
1980	108 500	85 191	559	85 750	7 615	-153	77 983	16 735	13 783	10 046	8 770	10 801	5 215
1981	118 192	91 268	155	91 423	8 706	-463	82 254	20 621	15 316	10 956	9 510	10 788	5 151
1982	123 709	92 078	260	92 338	8 892	-585	82 861	23 070	17 778	11 500	10 105	10 757	4 983
1983	131 008	97 188	-77	97 111	9 600	-706	86 805	25 186	19 017	12 201	10 737	10 738	4 978
1984	144 833	107 686	857	108 543	10 920	-841	96 782	28 427	19 624	13 488	11 941	10 738	5 183
1985	153 758	114 774	855	115 630	11 858	-930	102 842	29 995	20 921	14 323	12 641	10 735	5 316
1986	160 469	120 111	669	120 780	12 681	-964	107 135	31 178	22 157	14 955	13 220	10 730	5 430
1987	167 984	126 814	722	127 536	13 449	-1 001	113 086	31 871	23 026	15 612	13 688	10 760	5 582
1988	179 628	137 023	772	137 795	14 928	-1 053	121 815	33 627	24 186	16 634	14 648	10 799	5 720
1989	192 358	144 303	1 149	145 453	15 919	-1 092	128 441	38 088	25 828	17 763	15 559	10 829	5 843
1990	203 630	151 641	1 166	152 807	16 872	-1 079	134 856	40 065	28 709	18 743	16 446	10 864	5 905
1991	209 066	155 532	663	156 195	17 692	-1 082	137 421	40 360	31 285	19 100	16 824	10 946	5 882
1992	221 277	165 885	1 121	167 006	18 756	-1 284	146 967	40 372	33 938	20 062	17 709	11 029	5 893
1993	229 065	173 029	912	173 941	19 815	-1 346	152 780	41 056	35 230	20 634	18 149	11 101	5 998
1994	242 146	183 511	1 127	184 638	21 316	-1 485	161 837	43 717	36 592	21 712	19 067	11 152	6 175
1995	252 003	190 711	892	191 603	22 425	-1 408	167 769	45 671	38 563	22 495	19 675	11 203	6 341
1996	262 201	196 924	1 231	198 156	23 039	-1 367	173 749	48 328	40 124	23 322	20 217	11 243	6 437
1997	278 049	207 342	1 734	209 076	23 706	-1 451	183 918	52 712	41 419	24 656	21 308	11 277	6 541
1998	294 292	220 595	1 258	221 853	24 264	-1 567	196 022	56 190	42 079	26 017	22 405	11 312	6 660
1999	304 464	232 218	752	232 970	25 366	-1 597	206 007	55 044	43 413	26 859	23 164	11 335	6 747
2000	320 538	243 185	936	244 121	25 426	-1 526	217 168	57 209	46 161	28 208	24 264	11 363	6 836
2001	325 719	247 062	806	247 868	26 695	-1 404	219 770	55 612	50 337	28 607	24 687	11 386	6 758
2002	331 968	252 239	215	252 454	26 339	-1 420	224 695	53 709	53 564	29 098	25 578	11 409	6 688
2003	342 533	261 498	877	262 376	26 882	-1 419	234 070	52 575	55 887	29 953	26 649	11 436	6 669

Table 21-2. Personal Income and Employment by Region and State—Continued

(Millions of dollars, except as noted.)

Year	Personal income, total	Derivation of personal income								Per capita (dollars)		Population (thousands)	Total employment (thousands)
		Earnings by place of work			Less: Contributions for government social insurance	Plus: Adjustment for residence	Equals: Net earnings by place of residence	Plus: Dividends, interest, and rent	Plus: Personal current transfer receipts	Personal income	Disposable personal income		
		Nonfarm	Farm	Total									
WISCONSIN													
1969	16 398	12 676	630	13 307	934	249	12 622	2 418	1 359	3 746	3 212	4 378	1 944
1970	17 609	13 399	631	14 030	974	253	13 308	2 702	1 599	3 979	3 460	4 426	1 954
1971	18 906	14 252	686	14 938	1 070	264	14 132	2 904	1 870	4 239	3 737	4 460	1 957
1972	20 679	15 717	721	16 437	1 248	287	15 477	3 123	2 080	4 597	4 007	4 498	2 014
1973	23 149	17 717	907	18 624	1 615	313	17 322	3 462	2 365	5 123	4 476	4 518	2 116
1974	25 472	19 421	793	20 215	1 841	339	18 713	3 948	2 811	5 613	4 878	4 538	2 159
1975	27 810	20 632	855	21 488	1 928	345	19 905	4 378	3 527	6 086	5 345	4 570	2 148
1976	30 606	23 199	752	23 951	2 188	390	22 154	4 634	3 818	6 676	5 829	4 585	2 211
1977	34 137	25 939	1 133	27 072	2 444	432	25 061	5 027	4 049	7 400	6 437	4 613	2 293
1978	38 190	29 355	1 114	30 468	2 847	487	28 108	5 609	4 472	8 245	7 113	4 632	2 382
1979	42 922	32 724	1 391	34 115	3 307	526	31 334	6 457	5 131	9 199	7 958	4 666	2 465
1980	47 623	34 859	1 429	36 288	3 507	550	33 330	8 044	6 249	10 107	8 786	4 712	2 449
1981	51 994	37 195	1 157	38 352	4 011	604	34 945	9 943	7 107	11 001	9 506	4 726	2 424
1982	54 851	38 243	1 011	39 254	4 170	623	35 707	11 216	7 928	11 599	10 118	4 729	2 382
1983	57 004	40 307	457	40 764	4 363	677	37 079	11 405	8 520	12 073	10 632	4 721	2 385
1984	62 462	44 316	982	45 298	4 908	794	41 185	12 553	8 724	13 190	11 645	4 736	2 478
1985	65 709	46 704	1 012	47 716	5 212	883	43 387	13 053	9 269	13 840	12 219	4 748	2 509
1986	69 089	49 203	1 289	50 491	5 536	966	45 920	13 608	9 560	14 528	12 822	4 756	2 551
1987	73 006	52 599	1 405	54 004	5 840	1 071	49 235	13 994	9 777	15 280	13 406	4 778	2 621
1988	77 433	57 064	840	57 904	6 557	1 240	52 587	14 715	10 132	16 057	14 102	4 822	2 702
1989	83 936	60 344	1 712	62 056	6 980	1 272	56 348	16 660	10 927	17 283	15 140	4 857	2 759
1990	88 635	64 219	1 342	65 561	7 464	1 356	59 453	17 470	11 711	18 072	15 801	4 905	2 834
1991	92 124	67 086	963	68 049	7 912	1 381	61 518	17 875	12 731	18 557	16 260	4 964	2 860
1992	98 917	72 633	1 204	73 837	8 530	1 515	66 822	18 353	13 742	19 683	17 253	5 025	2 913
1993	103 379	76 993	914	77 907	9 073	1 575	70 409	18 663	14 306	20 331	17 768	5 085	2 969
1994	109 927	81 854	1 141	82 995	9 780	1 695	74 910	20 265	14 752	21 413	18 666	5 134	3 060
1995	115 180	85 733	764	86 497	10 258	1 793	78 032	21 513	15 636	22 215	19 310	5 185	3 140
1996	121 718	89 456	1 363	90 819	10 682	1 947	82 085	23 420	16 214	23 273	20 091	5 230	3 191
1997	129 099	95 081	1 024	96 106	11 316	2 167	86 957	25 394	16 748	24 514	21 034	5 266	3 245
1998	138 667	101 690	1 421	103 111	11 930	2 314	93 495	28 024	17 148	26 175	22 382	5 298	3 303
1999	144 702	108 102	1 333	109 435	12 631	2 502	99 306	27 509	17 887	27 135	23 236	5 333	3 374
2000	153 548	114 023	877	114 900	13 138	2 736	104 498	29 870	19 179	28 573	24 500	5 374	3 431
2001	158 654	117 876	988	118 864	13 519	2 861	108 206	29 039	21 410	29 352	25 277	5 405	3 418
2002	163 118	122 152	859	123 011	13 964	2 901	111 947	28 187	22 984	29 987	26 424	5 440	3 408
2003	168 128	127 359	1 169	128 528	14 445	2 956	117 039	27 651	23 437	30 723	27 295	5 472	3 420
PLAINS													
1969	58 083	44 468	4 157	48 626	3 164	-414	45 048	8 096	4 940	3 585	3 134	16 202	7 506
1970	62 780	47 467	4 378	51 845	3 342	-358	48 145	8 844	5 791	3 840	3 394	16 350	7 516
1971	67 510	50 815	4 554	55 369	3 697	-355	51 317	9 541	6 651	4 098	3 665	16 475	7 544
1972	74 631	55 480	6 091	61 571	4 228	-361	56 982	10 399	7 250	4 506	3 979	16 563	7 731
1973	87 442	61 770	11 224	72 994	5 405	-399	67 190	11 804	8 448	5 259	4 681	16 628	8 065
1974	92 655	68 191	7 590	75 782	6 194	-432	69 156	13 651	9 848	5 558	4 866	16 672	8 219
1975	101 551	73 769	7 410	81 179	6 600	-423	74 155	15 275	12 120	6 065	5 380	16 743	8 181
1976	109 353	83 446	4 328	87 774	7 518	-521	79 735	16 453	13 165	6 485	5 716	16 864	8 438
1977	121 183	92 400	5 110	97 510	8 276	-659	88 574	18 694	13 914	7 150	6 291	16 950	8 657
1978	137 405	104 056	7 733	111 789	9 619	-819	101 350	20 900	15 155	8 069	7 080	17 028	8 958
1979	151 909	116 763	6 495	123 259	11 228	-989	111 041	23 892	16 975	8 885	7 731	17 097	9 247
1980	164 453	126 038	1 769	127 807	12 066	-1 146	114 596	29 583	20 275	9 557	8 314	17 208	9 250
1981	186 200	135 956	5 340	141 296	13 919	-1 338	126 039	37 048	23 113	10 785	9 363	17 264	9 212
1982	198 366	140 880	3 935	144 815	14 702	-1 344	128 769	43 844	25 753	11 472	9 977	17 292	9 082
1983	208 000	149 764	1 509	151 273	15 683	-1 434	134 156	46 139	27 705	12 006	10 597	17 325	9 196
1984	232 330	165 627	6 435	172 062	17 725	-1 604	152 733	50 727	28 870	13 366	11 911	17 382	9 512
1985	245 609	175 442	7 372	182 814	19 127	-1 714	161 973	53 060	30 576	14 114	12 556	17 402	9 664
1986	256 417	183 830	7 972	191 802	20 442	-1 829	169 531	54 841	32 046	14 743	13 149	17 393	9 754
1987	269 790	195 341	9 709	205 050	21 670	-1 940	181 440	55 378	32 971	15 480	13 717	17 428	10 009
1988	282 070	208 831	7 312	216 144	24 068	-2 103	189 972	57 506	34 591	16 088	14 260	17 533	10 221
1989	302 898	221 060	9 071	230 131	25 672	-2 186	202 274	63 155	37 469	17 215	15 193	17 595	10 427
1990	320 841	233 098	10 157	243 255	27 311	-2 429	213 515	66 828	40 499	18 129	15 987	17 698	10 617
1991	333 016	242 685	7 919	250 604	28 836	-2 481	219 286	69 176	44 554	18 663	16 544	17 843	10 667
1992	355 443	260 395	10 305	270 700	30 671	-2 726	237 302	69 859	48 282	19 718	17 507	18 026	10 778
1993	364 761	272 319	6 124	278 443	32 318	-2 813	243 312	70 294	51 155	20 031	17 720	18 210	11 004
1994	389 452	288 145	10 081	298 225	34 685	-3 032	260 509	75 507	53 436	21 188	18 730	18 381	11 301
1995	406 860	303 842	5 682	309 524	36 499	-3 171	269 854	80 406	56 600	21 934	19 298	18 550	11 611
1996	437 288	320 004	13 336	333 340	38 271	-3 394	291 675	86 163	59 450	23 378	20 468	18 705	11 836
1997	460 385	339 516	10 525	350 041	40 508	-3 805	305 728	93 219	61 438	24 422	21 257	18 851	12 054
1998	492 324	365 434	9 778	375 212	43 015	-4 066	328 132	100 976	63 216	25 928	22 520	18 988	12 316
1999	511 507	387 838	7 398	395 236	45 317	-4 402	345 517	99 915	66 075	26 737	23 251	19 131	12 510
2000	545 882	412 558	7 075	419 634	47 513	-4 695	367 426	107 850	70 606	28 327	24 565	19 271	12 696
2001	563 202	425 890	6 752	432 642	49 309	-4 816	378 517	107 112	77 573	29 080	25 292	19 368	12 687
2002	574 808	438 710	4 302	443 011	50 721	-4 866	387 424	103 848	83 536	29 532	26 212	19 464	12 653
2003	594 716	455 874	8 410	464 284	52 511	-5 063	406 709	101 921	86 086	30 391	27 243	19 569	12 670

Table 21-2. Personal Income and Employment by Region and State—Continued

(Millions of dollars, except as noted.)

| Year | Personal income, total | Derivation of personal income ||||||| Per capita (dollars) || Population (thousands) | Total employment (thousands) |
| | | Earnings by place of work ||| Less: Contributions for government social insurance | Plus: Adjustment for residence | Equals: Net earnings by place of residence | Plus: Dividends, interest, and rent | Plus: Personal current transfer receipts | Personal income | Disposable personal income | | |
		Nonfarm	Farm	Total									
IOWA													
1969	10 256	7 109	1 222	8 331	544	82	7 869	1 532	856	3 656	3 225	2 805	1 289
1970	10 931	7 541	1 197	8 738	568	89	8 259	1 680	992	3 865	3 436	2 829	1 295
1971	11 450	8 046	997	9 043	627	88	8 504	1 819	1 127	4 015	3 609	2 852	1 297
1972	12 835	8 774	1 464	10 237	720	94	9 611	2 008	1 216	4 487	3 968	2 861	1 316
1973	15 472	9 873	2 712	12 586	931	88	11 742	2 326	1 404	5 402	4 817	2 864	1 374
1974	16 035	11 078	1 694	12 772	1 094	84	11 762	2 647	1 626	5 591	4 853	2 868	1 407
1975	17 919	12 052	1 945	13 997	1 169	100	12 928	2 974	2 017	6 219	5 488	2 881	1 407
1976	19 111	13 718	1 204	14 922	1 324	92	13 689	3 207	2 215	6 582	5 758	2 904	1 455
1977	21 145	15 318	1 204	16 522	1 461	65	15 126	3 677	2 341	7 255	6 352	2 914	1 488
1978	24 433	16 950	2 412	19 362	1 675	61	17 748	4 104	2 581	8 370	7 352	2 919	1 514
1979	26 220	18 993	1 540	20 533	1 960	71	18 644	4 683	2 892	8 989	7 816	2 917	1 557
1980	27 930	20 155	683	20 838	2 067	92	18 863	5 661	3 405	9 585	8 320	2 914	1 541
1981	31 569	21 304	1 611	22 915	2 325	118	20 708	6 986	3 876	10 856	9 429	2 908	1 513
1982	32 477	21 296	797	22 093	2 354	192	19 931	8 126	4 419	11 245	9 870	2 888	1 476
1983	33 153	22 192	-7	22 185	2 430	206	19 961	8 456	4 737	11 550	10 226	2 871	1 479
1984	36 836	23 961	1 434	25 395	2 688	239	22 945	9 038	4 853	12 886	11 579	2 859	1 506
1985	38 171	24 690	1 729	26 419	2 815	278	23 882	9 139	5 151	13 490	12 122	2 830	1 503
1986	39 389	25 379	2 106	27 485	2 947	270	24 808	9 237	5 344	14 108	12 706	2 792	1 501
1987	41 242	27 165	2 442	29 606	3 158	266	26 714	9 068	5 460	14 905	13 297	2 767	1 523
1988	42 415	29 167	1 627	30 794	3 529	307	27 572	9 142	5 700	15 321	13 634	2 768	1 567
1989	45 981	30 999	2 366	33 365	3 774	315	29 906	9 985	6 091	16 596	14 707	2 771	1 611
1990	48 358	32 713	2 250	34 963	4 010	323	31 276	10 473	6 609	17 389	15 369	2 781	1 646
1991	49 808	34 164	1 730	35 894	4 221	373	32 047	10 663	7 098	17 804	15 785	2 798	1 665
1992	53 082	36 360	2 558	38 918	4 467	399	34 850	10 565	7 667	18 834	16 768	2 818	1 680
1993	53 098	38 164	846	39 010	4 718	380	34 672	10 408	8 018	18 716	16 590	2 837	1 702
1994	57 873	40 512	2 762	43 273	5 082	386	38 577	10 982	8 314	20 301	18 042	2 851	1 735
1995	60 012	42 462	1 817	44 279	5 345	446	39 380	11 848	8 785	20 929	18 559	2 867	1 796
1996	64 862	44 253	3 653	47 907	5 541	498	42 863	12 750	9 248	22 521	19 962	2 880	1 826
1997	68 297	46 672	3 610	50 283	5 838	578	45 023	13 731	9 543	23 623	20 794	2 891	1 852
1998	71 704	50 255	2 391	52 646	6 175	663	47 134	14 800	9 770	24 701	21 725	2 903	1 894
1999	73 285	53 167	1 402	54 569	6 422	737	48 885	14 310	10 090	25 118	22 076	2 918	1 914
2000	77 763	55 681	1 656	57 336	6 609	832	51 560	15 416	10 787	26 554	23 389	2 929	1 934
2001	79 692	56 992	1 716	58 708	6 819	813	52 702	15 355	11 635	27 178	24 001	2 932	1 916
2002	81 925	58 697	1 651	60 348	7 027	851	54 173	14 903	12 849	27 905	25 113	2 936	1 908
2003	83 604	61 279	1 438	62 716	7 332	856	56 240	14 598	12 766	28 398	25 725	2 944	1 910
KANSAS													
1969	7 937	5 721	457	6 178	423	441	6 196	1 052	689	3 550	3 111	2 236	1 029
1970	8 583	6 035	599	6 633	444	439	6 629	1 151	803	3 818	3 372	2 248	1 017
1971	9 320	6 510	700	7 210	494	430	7 146	1 258	916	4 149	3 718	2 246	1 022
1972	10 411	7 208	956	8 163	575	453	8 041	1 386	984	4 616	4 096	2 256	1 048
1973	11 936	8 099	1 378	9 477	737	468	9 208	1 577	1 151	5 271	4 669	2 264	1 090
1974	12 943	9 079	1 049	10 127	856	483	9 754	1 865	1 323	5 707	4 997	2 268	1 122
1975	14 136	10 059	797	10 856	938	497	10 415	2 108	1 613	6 204	5 501	2 279	1 133
1976	15 432	11 388	575	11 963	1 070	514	11 407	2 245	1 780	6 713	5 947	2 299	1 169
1977	16 876	12 551	489	13 040	1 176	559	12 423	2 527	1 926	7 281	6 407	2 318	1 208
1978	18 712	14 255	273	14 528	1 375	604	13 757	2 854	2 102	8 021	7 033	2 333	1 252
1979	21 422	16 102	695	16 796	1 617	652	15 832	3 272	2 318	9 126	7 924	2 347	1 298
1980	23 578	17 658	97	17 755	1 760	729	16 724	4 098	2 756	9 953	8 629	2 369	1 312
1981	26 764	19 350	333	19 683	2 059	755	18 378	5 210	3 176	11 223	9 638	2 385	1 326
1982	28 988	20 045	570	20 615	2 184	778	19 209	6 215	3 564	12 072	10 413	2 401	1 310
1983	30 221	21 125	373	21 498	2 289	754	19 963	6 457	3 800	12 511	11 018	2 416	1 327
1984	33 274	23 302	740	24 042	2 569	799	22 272	7 085	3 918	13 726	12 216	2 424	1 370
1985	35 078	24 466	802	25 268	2 735	844	23 376	7 570	4 131	14 451	12 810	2 427	1 375
1986	36 501	25 581	930	26 510	2 901	826	24 436	7 731	4 334	15 005	13 399	2 433	1 375
1987	38 146	26 820	1 168	27 988	3 017	901	25 872	7 818	4 456	15 599	13 818	2 445	1 428
1988	40 070	28 412	1 136	29 549	3 319	911	27 140	8 254	4 675	16 275	14 422	2 462	1 440
1989	42 157	30 030	818	30 847	3 504	960	28 303	8 725	5 128	17 048	14 988	2 473	1 463
1990	44 876	31 495	1 372	32 867	3 708	975	30 134	9 174	5 568	18 085	15 971	2 481	1 483
1991	46 541	32 815	1 017	33 832	3 928	953	30 857	9 652	6 032	18 626	16 517	2 499	1 498
1992	49 867	35 362	1 395	36 757	4 178	967	33 546	9 637	6 685	19 692	17 554	2 532	1 511
1993	51 729	36 977	1 338	38 315	4 384	1 062	34 992	9 670	7 067	20 234	17 973	2 557	1 534
1994	54 164	38 811	1 397	40 208	4 671	932	36 469	10 383	7 312	20 990	18 609	2 581	1 561
1995	56 073	40 611	786	41 396	4 843	1 099	37 653	10 758	7 662	21 558	18 995	2 601	1 609
1996	59 729	42 595	1 484	44 079	5 057	1 159	40 180	11 579	7 970	22 845	20 036	2 615	1 642
1997	63 356	45 464	1 405	46 869	5 387	1 066	42 548	12 456	8 352	24 041	20 923	2 635	1 686
1998	67 800	49 032	1 290	50 322	5 757	1 096	45 661	13 654	8 485	25 483	22 171	2 661	1 734
1999	70 158	51 703	1 364	53 066	6 013	996	48 050	13 305	8 804	26 195	22 775	2 678	1 752
2000	74 570	55 091	705	55 796	6 259	1 103	50 640	14 437	9 492	27 694	24 048	2 693	1 771
2001	77 399	57 463	786	58 249	6 499	980	52 730	14 210	10 459	28 662	25 003	2 700	1 781
2002	78 290	58 882	227	59 109	6 648	940	53 401	13 704	11 184	28 870	25 731	2 712	1 770
2003	80 466	60 706	811	61 517	6 815	974	55 676	13 431	11 359	29 545	26 602	2 724	1 759

CHAPTER 21: REGIONAL AND STATE DATA

Table 21-2. Personal Income and Employment by Region and State—Continued

(Millions of dollars, except as noted.)

Year	Personal income, total	Derivation of personal income								Per capita (dollars)		Population (thousands)	Total employment (thousands)
		Earnings by place of work			Less: Contributions for government social insurance	Plus: Adjustment for residence	Equals: Net earnings by place of residence	Plus: Dividends, interest, and rent	Plus: Personal current transfer receipts	Personal income	Disposable personal income		
		Nonfarm	Farm	Total									

MINNESOTA

1969	14 157	11 177	709	11 886	782	-33	11 071	1 925	1 161	3 767	3 270	3 758	1 691
1970	15 411	11 948	863	12 811	826	-29	11 956	2 081	1 373	4 039	3 554	3 815	1 699
1971	16 417	12 736	786	13 522	911	-28	12 582	2 242	1 593	4 262	3 789	3 852	1 706
1972	17 845	13 821	946	14 767	1 038	-30	13 699	2 384	1 762	4 615	4 040	3 867	1 780
1973	21 033	15 462	2 165	17 628	1 336	-38	16 254	2 713	2 065	5 414	4 804	3 885	1 878
1974	22 671	17 045	1 626	18 671	1 528	-34	17 110	3 139	2 423	5 815	5 059	3 898	1 921
1975	24 432	18 413	1 247	19 660	1 615	-34	18 011	3 497	2 924	6 223	5 454	3 926	1 920
1976	26 580	20 697	767	21 464	1 847	-43	19 574	3 797	3 210	6 718	5 854	3 957	1 977
1977	29 978	22 914	1 485	24 398	2 045	-55	22 298	4 305	3 375	7 533	6 552	3 980	2 034
1978	33 703	26 160	1 605	27 765	2 412	-70	25 283	4 795	3 624	8 416	7 284	4 005	2 123
1979	37 603	29 778	1 221	30 998	2 858	-88	28 052	5 498	4 052	9 312	7 983	4 038	2 222
1980	41 898	32 485	934	33 418	3 111	-92	30 215	6 826	4 857	10 256	8 838	4 085	2 254
1981	46 460	35 134	1 018	36 152	3 609	-131	32 411	8 474	5 575	11 299	9 705	4 112	2 241
1982	49 807	36 680	804	37 484	3 842	-154	33 488	10 050	6 268	12 056	10 420	4 131	2 201
1983	52 586	39 255	107	39 362	4 165	-183	35 014	10 814	6 758	12 698	11 023	4 141	2 228
1984	59 664	44 180	1 421	45 601	4 800	-238	40 563	12 009	7 092	14 350	12 587	4 158	2 335
1985	63 458	47 404	1 322	48 726	5 238	-286	43 202	12 721	7 535	15 166	13 306	4 184	2 399
1986	67 102	50 169	1 622	51 791	5 657	-327	45 807	13 423	7 873	15 957	14 047	4 205	2 432
1987	71 516	53 912	2 125	56 036	6 067	-378	49 591	13 802	8 123	16 886	14 738	4 235	2 526
1988	75 230	58 303	1 237	59 540	6 819	-458	52 263	14 392	8 575	17 511	15 311	4 296	2 598
1989	82 088	62 152	2 022	64 174	7 304	-442	56 428	16 338	9 322	18 923	16 520	4 338	2 653
1990	87 318	66 158	1 916	68 073	7 823	-469	59 781	17 517	10 020	19 891	17 304	4 390	2 712
1991	90 050	68 981	1 159	70 140	8 310	-477	61 354	17 909	10 787	20 278	17 739	4 441	2 736
1992	96 401	74 824	1 396	76 220	8 954	-513	66 753	17 938	11 710	21 443	18 707	4 496	2 781
1993	98 571	77 927	177	78 104	9 436	-519	68 149	18 065	12 357	21 636	18 790	4 556	2 835
1994	105 971	82 409	1 287	83 696	10 146	-568	72 983	19 968	13 021	22 985	19 964	4 610	2 923
1995	112 209	87 062	503	87 565	10 708	-614	76 244	22 161	13 804	24 078	20 814	4 660	3 015
1996	121 195	92 732	1 886	94 618	11 367	-684	82 567	24 182	14 447	25 716	21 986	4 713	3 077
1997	128 388	98 786	1 152	99 938	12 044	-777	87 117	26 524	14 747	26 953	22 994	4 763	3 129
1998	139 553	107 639	1 556	109 195	12 946	-837	95 412	28 941	15 200	28 993	24 649	4 813	3 202
1999	146 722	115 346	1 071	116 418	13 821	-946	101 650	29 205	15 867	30 106	25 784	4 873	3 275
2000	157 964	124 400	1 016	125 416	14 734	-1 040	109 642	31 339	16 983	32 018	27 187	4 934	3 344
2001	162 751	128 693	735	129 427	15 351	-1 130	112 946	30 824	18 981	32 647	27 863	4 985	3 363
2002	166 718	132 419	686	133 105	15 741	-1 122	116 242	29 927	20 550	33 179	28 893	5 025	3 357
2003	172 217	137 754	1 063	138 817	16 372	-1 139	121 306	29 397	21 514	34 039	29 965	5 059	3 364

MISSOURI

1969	16 551	14 162	442	14 604	954	-758	12 892	2 232	1 427	3 567	3 085	4 640	2 216
1970	18 037	15 085	516	15 600	1 004	-702	13 895	2 451	1 691	3 850	3 376	4 685	2 203
1971	19 431	16 087	563	16 649	1 108	-683	14 858	2 623	1 950	4 114	3 643	4 723	2 200
1972	21 140	17 456	704	18 161	1 261	-703	16 197	2 833	2 111	4 448	3 889	4 753	2 242
1973	23 542	19 089	1 206	20 295	1 584	-737	17 975	3 119	2 449	4 931	4 358	4 775	2 325
1974	25 235	20 650	627	21 277	1 766	-763	18 748	3 596	2 890	5 273	4 624	4 785	2 341
1975	27 602	21 920	687	22 607	1 841	-773	19 993	3 955	3 654	5 756	5 120	4 795	2 291
1976	30 433	24 747	460	25 208	2 095	-850	22 263	4 277	3 893	6 309	5 570	4 824	2 365
1977	33 839	27 557	706	28 263	2 330	-990	24 943	4 832	4 064	6 984	6 167	4 845	2 424
1978	37 743	30 825	905	31 730	2 695	-1 143	27 892	5 431	4 420	7 748	6 792	4 871	2 513
1979	42 199	34 195	1 164	35 359	3 087	-1 307	30 965	6 234	5 000	8 631	7 529	4 889	2 580
1980	45 893	36 617	225	36 843	3 284	-1 524	32 034	7 778	6 082	9 324	8 143	4 922	2 554
1981	51 359	39 478	759	40 237	3 795	-1 663	34 779	9 743	6 836	10 413	9 054	4 932	2 549
1982	54 839	41 306	338	41 644	4 051	-1 730	35 863	11 522	7 454	11 125	9 625	4 929	2 525
1983	58 534	44 455	-110	44 345	4 387	-1 758	38 199	12 327	8 008	11 840	10 468	4 944	2 571
1984	65 162	49 343	410	49 754	4 995	-1 886	42 873	13 930	8 359	13 097	11 642	4 975	2 679
1985	69 812	52 925	785	53 710	5 477	-2 003	46 230	14 765	8 817	13 962	12 364	5 000	2 753
1986	73 310	55 978	571	56 549	5 908	-2 052	48 589	15 438	9 282	14 595	12 937	5 023	2 816
1987	77 057	59 356	728	60 084	6 219	-2 177	51 687	15 811	9 559	15 239	13 466	5 057	2 854
1988	81 340	63 171	648	63 819	6 842	-2 265	54 712	16 541	10 087	16 006	14 179	5 082	2 905
1989	86 570	66 431	893	67 324	7 283	-2 395	57 646	17 997	10 927	16 988	14 975	5 096	2 960
1990	90 407	69 167	682	69 849	7 670	-2 626	59 553	19 014	11 839	17 627	15 536	5 129	2 993
1991	94 900	71 308	561	71 869	8 001	-2 639	61 229	19 883	13 789	18 353	16 312	5 171	2 962
1992	100 945	76 098	804	76 903	8 440	-2 814	65 648	20 548	14 749	19 349	17 240	5 217	2 977
1993	104 699	79 308	493	79 801	8 857	-2 922	68 022	20 881	15 796	19 862	17 654	5 271	3 061
1994	111 005	84 013	680	84 693	9 506	-2 917	72 270	22 179	16 556	20 848	18 466	5 324	3 134
1995	115 948	88 669	232	88 901	10 081	-3 143	75 678	22 666	17 604	21 559	19 013	5 378	3 218
1996	122 469	92 921	1 040	93 961	10 514	-3 277	80 170	23 802	18 497	22 548	19 777	5 432	3 277
1997	129 992	98 557	1 096	99 654	11 141	-3 484	85 029	25 766	19 197	23 716	20 701	5 481	3 349
1998	137 619	105 196	614	105 810	11 671	-3 691	90 448	27 453	19 718	24 923	21 683	5 522	3 405
1999	142 925	111 165	247	111 411	12 281	-3 767	95 363	26 837	20 725	25 697	22 345	5 562	3 450
2000	152 722	117 772	657	118 429	12 842	-4 056	101 530	29 030	22 162	27 243	23 677	5 606	3 497
2001	157 235	120 372	630	121 002	13 284	-3 920	103 798	28 997	24 440	27 897	24 261	5 636	3 480
2002	160 962	124 044	183	124 226	13 643	-3 931	106 652	28 122	26 187	28 391	25 240	5 670	3 469
2003	165 967	128 305	829	129 134	14 010	-4 063	111 062	27 604	27 301	29 094	26 121	5 704	3 474

Table 21-2. Personal Income and Employment by Region and State—Continued

(Millions of dollars, except as noted.)

Year	Personal income, total	Derivation of personal income								Per capita (dollars)		Population (thousands)	Total employment (thousands)
		Earnings by place of work			Less: Contributions for government social insurance	Plus: Adjustment for residence	Equals: Net earnings by place of residence	Plus: Dividends, interest, and rent	Plus: Personal current transfer receipts	Personal income	Disposable personal income		
		Nonfarm	Farm	Total									
NEBRASKA													
1969	5 261	3 800	596	4 397	269	-100	4 028	804	430	3 570	3 140	1 474	704
1970	5 642	4 121	534	4 655	289	-107	4 259	885	498	3 792	3 363	1 488	715
1971	6 197	4 438	681	5 120	320	-110	4 689	946	562	4 120	3 719	1 504	728
1972	6 874	4 879	800	5 679	364	-119	5 196	1 059	619	4 527	4 014	1 518	748
1973	8 042	5 466	1 219	6 685	467	-123	6 095	1 207	741	5 261	4 678	1 529	775
1974	8 379	6 078	759	6 837	541	-133	6 164	1 369	847	5 449	4 785	1 538	793
1975	9 523	6 579	1 099	7 677	579	-140	6 959	1 528	1 036	6 178	5 535	1 541	790
1976	9 970	7 478	579	8 056	661	-147	7 248	1 620	1 103	6 437	5 743	1 549	811
1977	10 817	8 151	522	8 673	723	-146	7 805	1 838	1 174	6 959	6 128	1 554	831
1978	12 534	9 128	1 074	10 202	832	-169	9 201	2 030	1 303	8 030	7 111	1 561	855
1979	13 527	10 202	740	10 943	970	-198	9 775	2 300	1 451	8 647	7 555	1 564	877
1980	14 403	11 053	98	11 151	1 051	-215	9 885	2 824	1 693	9 160	8 015	1 572	879
1981	16 722	11 887	822	12 708	1 209	-255	11 244	3 526	1 952	10 593	9 351	1 579	874
1982	17 984	12 352	760	13 111	1 287	-262	11 562	4 272	2 151	11 370	9 889	1 582	864
1983	18 630	12 989	540	13 528	1 355	-276	11 897	4 405	2 327	11 759	10 498	1 584	870
1984	20 826	14 329	1 150	15 479	1 525	-328	13 627	4 758	2 441	13 109	11 846	1 589	889
1985	21 978	15 089	1 442	16 531	1 651	-353	14 527	4 859	2 593	13 869	12 527	1 585	902
1986	22 565	15 614	1 406	17 020	1 756	-351	14 913	4 942	2 710	14 333	12 942	1 574	902
1987	23 549	16 436	1 630	18 066	1 859	-347	15 860	4 916	2 772	15 032	13 521	1 567	930
1988	25 095	17 477	2 026	19 503	2 069	-380	17 054	5 148	2 893	15 969	14 355	1 571	953
1989	26 497	18 526	1 834	20 360	2 209	-389	17 761	5 633	3 102	16 825	15 022	1 575	971
1990	28 444	19 736	2 182	21 918	2 372	-382	19 164	5 915	3 365	17 983	16 031	1 582	994
1991	29 563	20 678	1 979	22 658	2 508	-420	19 730	6 226	3 608	18 524	16 566	1 596	998
1992	31 184	21 948	2 087	24 034	2 630	-458	20 947	6 313	3 924	19 349	17 329	1 612	1 005
1993	32 105	23 084	1 735	24 818	2 769	-472	21 577	6 341	4 187	19 750	17 656	1 626	1 027
1994	34 012	24 518	1 787	26 306	2 961	-479	22 865	6 779	4 367	20 751	18 515	1 639	1 068
1995	36 006	26 296	1 311	27 607	3 101	-524	23 982	7 377	4 647	21 730	19 290	1 657	1 077
1996	39 382	27 887	2 555	30 442	3 264	-579	26 599	7 822	4 961	23 530	20 879	1 674	1 103
1997	40 576	29 465	1 823	31 288	3 462	-653	27 173	8 272	5 131	24 061	21 132	1 686	1 118
1998	43 314	31 387	1 723	33 110	3 686	-684	28 741	9 096	5 477	25 542	22 392	1 696	1 144
1999	45 116	33 311	1 472	34 783	3 874	-762	30 146	9 148	5 822	26 465	23 175	1 705	1 166
2000	47 329	35 157	963	36 120	4 031	-825	31 263	9 991	6 075	27 627	24 091	1 713	1 183
2001	49 300	36 479	1 342	37 821	4 198	-861	32 762	9 871	6 667	28 679	25 119	1 719	1 182
2002	49 872	37 659	859	38 517	4 368	-899	33 250	9 581	7 041	28 869	25 790	1 728	1 178
2003	52 755	39 347	2 160	41 507	4 536	-935	36 036	9 413	7 306	30 331	27 404	1 739	1 184
NORTH DAKOTA													
1969	1 910	1 227	379	1 605	103	-52	1 450	277	183	3 076	2 759	621	274
1970	1 999	1 367	300	1 667	115	-55	1 497	291	212	3 230	2 920	619	281
1971	2 314	1 500	428	1 928	130	-58	1 741	325	248	3 693	3 397	627	284
1972	2 769	1 681	661	2 342	148	-62	2 132	361	276	4 388	4 027	631	288
1973	3 914	1 901	1 521	3 422	190	-65	3 167	437	310	6 189	5 686	632	300
1974	3 878	2 155	1 153	3 308	225	-78	3 005	517	356	6 114	5 444	634	308
1975	4 063	2 443	934	3 377	257	-84	3 037	606	420	6 363	5 695	638	314
1976	3 990	2 796	470	3 266	295	-99	2 872	654	464	6 183	5 531	645	326
1977	4 160	3 038	266	3 304	304	-106	2 894	760	506	6 409	5 764	649	331
1978	5 258	3 471	855	4 326	355	-118	3 852	853	553	8 082	7 246	651	345
1979	5 392	3 890	491	4 382	414	-136	3 831	948	613	8 269	7 390	652	354
1980	5 174	4 232	-396	3 837	448	-153	3 235	1 216	723	7 907	6 932	654	356
1981	6 819	4 733	361	5 094	530	-176	4 388	1 601	830	10 340	9 098	660	360
1982	7 383	5 006	298	5 304	574	-179	4 551	1 902	930	11 036	9 929	669	361
1983	7 734	5 256	358	5 614	615	-182	4 817	1 882	1 035	11 430	10 361	677	366
1984	8 410	5 555	599	6 154	654	-188	5 312	1 988	1 110	12 358	11 252	680	368
1985	8 710	5 682	688	6 370	680	-188	5 502	2 029	1 179	12 866	11 731	677	365
1986	8 796	5 704	682	6 386	702	-184	5 500	2 011	1 285	13 137	12 032	670	359
1987	9 057	5 927	780	6 707	732	-186	5 789	1 924	1 344	13 699	12 489	661	365
1988	8 343	6 144	-70	6 074	798	-192	5 083	1 912	1 348	12 731	11 485	655	369
1989	9 338	6 373	426	6 798	846	-198	5 754	2 116	1 468	14 447	13 075	646	373
1990	10 166	6 714	751	7 465	908	-194	6 363	2 231	1 573	15 943	14 457	638	376
1991	10 351	7 091	594	7 685	978	-203	6 504	2 245	1 602	16 282	14 746	636	385
1992	11 277	7 550	1 021	8 570	1 044	-222	7 304	2 214	1 759	17 669	16 085	638	390
1993	11 351	8 033	602	8 635	1 131	-242	7 262	2 236	1 853	17 703	16 006	641	400
1994	12 255	8 481	994	9 475	1 207	-258	8 011	2 368	1 876	19 006	17 244	645	414
1995	12 221	8 888	404	9 292	1 255	-283	7 754	2 490	1 977	18 865	17 008	648	421
1996	13 702	9 354	1 272	10 627	1 312	-319	8 995	2 631	2 075	21 068	19 084	650	429
1997	13 440	9 791	336	10 127	1 357	-344	8 425	2 861	2 154	20 686	18 560	650	433
1998	14 810	10 390	950	11 340	1 414	-371	9 555	3 065	2 190	22 872	20 620	648	440
1999	14 934	10 837	658	11 495	1 446	-402	9 647	2 994	2 293	23 180	20 863	644	443
2000	16 097	11 360	962	12 322	1 503	-428	10 391	3 244	2 462	25 109	22 598	641	447
2001	16 470	12 063	567	12 631	1 564	-467	10 600	3 338	2 531	25 884	23 209	636	449
2002	16 780	12 639	383	13 023	1 636	-492	10 895	3 221	2 664	26 471	24 124	634	451
2003	18 078	13 429	1 037	14 466	1 723	-532	12 210	3 150	2 717	28 521	26 248	634	456

Table 21-2. Personal Income and Employment by Region and State—Continued

(Millions of dollars, except as noted.)

| Year | Personal income, total | Derivation of personal income ||||||||| Per capita (dollars) || Population (thousands) | Total employment (thousands) |
| | | Earnings by place of work ||| Less: Contributions for government social insurance | Plus: Adjustment for residence | Equals: Net earnings by place of residence | Plus: Dividends, interest, and rent | Plus: Personal current transfer receipts | Personal income | Disposable personal income | | |
		Nonfarm	Farm	Total									
SOUTH DAKOTA													
1969	2 010	1 272	353	1 625	90	6	1 541	275	194	3 009	2 739	668	303
1970	2 177	1 371	369	1 740	96	6	1 650	305	222	3 265	3 005	667	305
1971	2 381	1 498	400	1 897	107	6	1 797	329	255	3 546	3 304	671	306
1972	2 757	1 662	560	2 221	121	7	2 107	368	282	4 070	3 795	677	309
1973	3 502	1 879	1 022	2 901	159	7	2 749	426	327	5 158	4 776	679	323
1974	3 515	2 107	681	2 789	184	8	2 613	520	382	5 169	4 717	680	326
1975	3 877	2 303	701	3 004	201	10	2 814	607	456	5 689	5 271	681	326
1976	3 837	2 622	273	2 895	225	12	2 682	654	501	5 586	5 108	687	336
1977	4 368	2 871	439	3 310	238	13	3 085	755	528	6 339	5 875	689	342
1978	5 023	3 267	609	3 877	275	15	3 617	832	574	7 287	6 708	689	355
1979	5 545	3 603	644	4 247	323	16	3 941	956	648	8 048	7 387	689	360
1980	5 577	3 839	128	3 966	344	18	3 640	1 180	758	8 073	7 317	691	354
1981	6 507	4 070	437	4 507	391	14	4 130	1 508	869	9 437	8 582	690	349
1982	6 887	4 196	368	4 564	411	12	4 165	1 756	966	9 972	9 022	691	345
1983	7 142	4 492	249	4 741	442	5	4 304	1 798	1 040	10 306	9 486	693	354
1984	8 159	4 956	680	5 636	493	-2	5 141	1 918	1 099	11 701	10 887	697	364
1985	8 401	5 186	604	5 791	532	-5	5 254	1 978	1 169	12 029	11 172	698	367
1986	8 755	5 406	656	6 062	572	-11	5 478	2 060	1 217	12 578	11 691	696	368
1987	9 223	5 725	837	6 563	617	-19	5 926	2 040	1 257	13 251	12 251	696	383
1988	9 577	6 156	708	6 865	691	-26	6 148	2 116	1 313	13 717	12 669	698	390
1989	10 267	6 550	713	7 263	750	-36	6 476	2 360	1 431	14 737	13 548	697	398
1990	11 273	7 115	1 005	8 120	821	-56	7 243	2 505	1 525	16 172	14 822	697	412
1991	11 803	7 647	879	8 526	891	-69	7 567	2 599	1 638	16 774	15 396	704	423
1992	12 687	8 253	1 045	9 298	958	-85	8 255	2 645	1 787	17 799	16 328	713	434
1993	13 207	8 827	935	9 761	1 025	-99	8 638	2 693	1 877	18 289	16 682	722	445
1994	14 172	9 401	1 173	10 574	1 113	-128	9 333	2 849	1 989	19 392	17 775	731	467
1995	14 390	9 854	629	10 482	1 167	-152	9 163	3 106	2 121	19 501	17 777	738	475
1996	15 948	10 262	1 446	11 708	1 216	-192	10 300	3 396	2 252	21 488	19 661	742	482
1997	16 335	10 781	1 102	11 883	1 278	-191	10 413	3 609	2 313	21 949	19 849	744	488
1998	17 523	11 534	1 255	12 789	1 366	-243	11 180	3 967	2 376	23 488	21 251	746	497
1999	18 367	12 309	1 185	13 494	1 459	-258	11 777	4 116	2 474	24 475	22 019	750	509
2000	19 438	13 099	1 116	14 215	1 535	-280	12 400	4 393	2 645	25 722	23 164	756	519
2001	20 355	13 827	976	14 803	1 594	-230	12 979	4 517	2 859	26 847	24 228	758	517
2002	20 261	14 370	313	14 682	1 658	-213	12 811	4 389	3 061	26 644	24 403	760	519
2003	21 629	15 054	1 072	16 126	1 723	-224	14 179	4 326	3 124	28 299	26 188	764	522
SOUTHEAST													
1969	133 396	107 868	4 024	111 892	7 217	1 134	105 808	16 202	11 386	3 071	2 698	43 440	19 085
1970	146 106	116 499	4 011	120 510	7 781	1 014	113 743	18 589	13 773	3 323	2 949	43 974	19 254
1971	161 148	127 812	4 227	132 039	8 838	988	124 189	20 686	16 273	3 580	3 202	45 013	19 635
1972	181 308	144 522	4 922	149 444	10 454	1 049	140 039	22 857	18 412	3 940	3 482	46 019	20 523
1973	207 012	164 064	7 235	171 299	13 505	1 118	158 913	26 278	21 821	4 405	3 915	46 992	21 636
1974	231 338	181 835	6 604	188 439	15 476	1 237	174 199	30 756	26 383	4 824	4 270	47 955	22 069
1975	253 040	193 691	5 947	199 638	16 283	1 478	184 832	33 964	34 244	5 187	4 675	48 788	21 642
1976	282 944	219 142	6 323	225 465	18 670	1 667	208 462	37 160	37 323	5 714	5 112	49 514	22 351
1977	314 834	246 134	5 721	251 855	20 907	1 900	232 848	42 236	39 748	6 258	5 581	50 312	23 208
1978	358 185	281 063	6 871	287 935	24 367	2 207	265 774	48 856	43 555	7 008	6 217	51 113	24 309
1979	404 319	315 506	6 775	322 281	28 409	2 574	296 446	57 632	50 241	7 779	6 860	51 977	25 020
1980	457 351	349 106	4 103	353 209	31 472	3 121	324 858	72 622	59 871	8 649	7 623	52 881	25 378
1981	518 648	385 765	6 570	392 335	37 325	3 556	358 566	91 563	68 520	9 671	8 495	53 627	25 676
1982	556 499	405 718	6 722	412 439	40 014	3 774	376 199	104 262	76 038	10 258	9 056	54 249	25 579
1983	600 314	437 897	4 862	442 759	43 707	3 836	402 888	114 568	82 858	10 943	9 740	54 856	26 113
1984	671 395	490 730	8 332	499 062	49 941	4 023	453 144	130 915	87 337	12 094	10 838	55 515	27 396
1985	723 822	530 457	7 382	537 838	54 907	4 222	487 154	143 419	93 250	12 880	11 476	56 199	28 243
1986	769 051	565 084	6 887	571 971	59 646	4 445	516 769	152 882	99 400	13 525	12 057	56 861	28 986
1987	821 022	608 702	8 255	616 958	63 886	4 748	557 820	159 675	103 527	14 270	12 660	57 536	29 714
1988	887 860	658 337	10 858	669 195	71 716	5 205	602 684	174 165	111 012	15 276	13 616	58 120	30 732
1989	964 369	698 612	11 314	709 926	77 054	5 561	638 432	202 339	123 598	16 419	14 573	58 733	31 473
1990	1 027 597	742 219	10 581	752 800	82 334	6 324	676 790	215 541	135 266	17 266	15 364	59 516	32 068
1991	1 074 251	768 714	12 167	780 881	86 845	6 868	700 903	220 417	152 931	17 756	15 887	60 501	31 940
1992	1 148 896	827 937	13 040	840 977	92 810	7 344	755 511	217 769	175 616	18 679	16 736	61 508	32 402
1993	1 206 516	874 804	12 636	887 440	98 854	7 742	796 328	225 313	184 875	19 295	17 248	62 531	33 414
1994	1 278 747	924 517	13 835	938 352	106 194	7 667	839 825	243 165	195 757	20 114	17 930	63 574	34 368
1995	1 354 691	977 844	12 425	990 270	112 353	8 006	885 923	258 650	210 118	20 970	18 645	64 602	35 493
1996	1 437 179	1 031 269	14 127	1 045 396	117 639	7 546	935 303	278 888	222 988	21 904	19 354	65 611	36 336
1997	1 523 242	1 093 453	14 329	1 107 781	124 948	8 337	991 170	300 536	231 535	22 853	20 070	66 655	37 295
1998	1 633 535	1 178 179	12 881	1 191 060	133 230	8 240	1 066 071	328 652	238 811	24 155	21 113	67 627	38 306
1999	1 716 450	1 258 627	13 444	1 272 072	141 274	9 685	1 140 483	326 126	249 841	25 032	21 854	68 569	39 177
2000	1 840 460	1 347 513	12 238	1 359 751	148 752	8 106	1 219 106	354 362	266 993	26 485	23 091	69 490	39 981
2001	1 924 739	1 401 196	13 191	1 414 387	156 010	7 949	1 266 325	363 240	295 174	27 381	23 968	70 295	40 010
2002	1 975 666	1 447 537	7 040	1 454 576	161 231	9 289	1 302 635	354 287	318 744	27 769	24 822	71 146	40 011
2003	2 047 938	1 514 833	11 162	1 525 995	167 906	9 609	1 367 698	348 924	331 316	28 436	25 647	72 019	40 285

Table 21-2. Personal Income and Employment by Region and State—Continued

(Millions of dollars, except as noted.)

Year	Personal income, total	Derivation of personal income								Per capita (dollars)		Population (thousands)	Total employment (thousands)
		Earnings by place of work			Less: Contributions for government social insurance	Plus: Adjustment for residence	Equals: Net earnings by place of residence	Plus: Dividends, interest, and rent	Plus: Personal current transfer receipts	Personal income	Disposable personal income		
		Nonfarm	Farm	Total									

ALABAMA

1969	9 384	7 734	277	8 011	551	137	7 597	895	891	2 728	2 412	3 440	1 411
1970	10 202	8 284	247	8 531	590	136	8 076	1 029	1 097	2 957	2 657	3 450	1 413
1971	11 199	9 013	276	9 289	655	144	8 778	1 136	1 284	3 202	2 889	3 497	1 423
1972	12 466	10 050	345	10 395	765	171	9 801	1 234	1 431	3 521	3 152	3 540	1 471
1973	14 103	11 284	532	11 816	983	188	11 021	1 401	1 681	3 939	3 527	3 581	1 526
1974	15 715	12 656	335	12 991	1 136	198	12 053	1 651	2 010	4 332	3 874	3 628	1 552
1975	17 537	13 669	410	14 079	1 221	204	13 061	1 876	2 600	4 765	4 307	3 681	1 543
1976	19 851	15 672	475	16 148	1 421	218	14 944	2 068	2 839	5 312	4 773	3 737	1 594
1977	21 914	17 571	380	17 951	1 595	247	16 603	2 317	2 995	5 793	5 199	3 783	1 651
1978	24 773	19 942	504	20 447	1 840	270	18 877	2 634	3 262	6 461	5 782	3 834	1 714
1979	27 615	22 041	516	22 557	2 102	297	20 753	3 061	3 801	7 137	6 355	3 869	1 739
1980	30 564	23 944	205	24 149	2 281	328	22 196	3 908	4 460	7 836	6 966	3 900	1 736
1981	34 004	25 812	485	26 297	2 648	427	24 076	4 920	5 008	8 678	7 698	3 919	1 724
1982	35 988	26 702	407	27 110	2 787	448	24 771	5 681	5 536	9 168	8 216	3 925	1 692
1983	38 491	28 731	289	29 020	3 053	441	26 409	6 087	5 996	9 784	8 766	3 934	1 722
1984	42 692	31 793	476	32 270	3 428	493	29 335	7 020	6 337	10 803	9 731	3 952	1 787
1985	45 944	34 347	462	34 809	3 740	503	31 572	7 678	6 694	11 566	10 352	3 973	1 831
1986	48 553	36 390	453	36 843	3 937	525	33 432	8 158	6 963	12 164	10 889	3 992	1 868
1987	51 502	38 824	537	39 361	4 163	533	35 731	8 652	7 119	12 826	11 419	4 015	1 923
1988	55 120	41 549	800	42 349	4 651	529	38 228	9 467	7 426	13 698	12 287	4 024	1 982
1989	59 911	43 962	934	44 896	4 972	548	40 472	11 047	8 391	14 865	13 266	4 030	2 019
1990	63 679	46 896	820	47 716	5 317	525	42 924	11 528	9 227	15 723	14 047	4 050	2 061
1991	67 250	49 183	1 097	50 280	5 674	555	45 161	11 899	10 191	16 406	14 714	4 099	2 073
1992	71 977	52 870	990	53 860	6 061	610	48 408	11 974	11 595	17 327	15 578	4 154	2 110
1993	74 863	55 245	1 001	56 246	6 437	659	50 468	12 097	12 298	17 764	15 941	4 214	2 172
1994	79 265	58 052	1 055	59 107	6 899	751	52 958	13 285	13 021	18 606	16 637	4 260	2 193
1995	83 534	60 851	798	61 649	7 276	827	55 200	14 302	14 033	19 441	17 344	4 297	2 256
1996	86 972	63 130	918	64 048	7 512	837	57 374	14 810	14 788	20 081	17 842	4 331	2 290
1997	91 419	65 943	998	66 940	7 863	938	60 015	15 979	15 425	20 930	18 528	4 368	2 335
1998	97 012	69 795	1 095	70 890	8 212	1 049	63 728	17 454	15 830	22 025	19 500	4 405	2 385
1999	100 662	73 138	1 307	74 445	8 569	1 116	66 992	17 154	16 517	22 722	20 095	4 430	2 405
2000	105 807	76 023	955	76 977	8 783	1 238	69 433	18 725	17 648	23 768	21 050	4 452	2 416
2001	110 612	79 173	1 237	80 410	9 144	1 261	72 527	18 955	19 130	24 765	22 042	4 466	2 391
2002	113 647	82 089	809	82 898	9 514	1 268	74 652	18 468	20 527	25 374	22 925	4 479	2 379
2003	118 260	85 952	1 140	87 092	9 895	1 306	78 503	18 159	21 598	26 276	23 937	4 501	2 385

ARKANSAS

1969	4 978	3 744	342	4 086	279	30	3 837	557	584	2 602	2 320	1 913	800
1970	5 458	3 997	411	4 408	297	20	4 131	643	683	2 828	2 535	1 930	805
1971	6 072	4 470	404	4 874	341	19	4 552	719	801	3 079	2 795	1 972	831
1972	6 854	5 090	477	5 567	406	18	5 178	783	893	3 396	3 070	2 018	867
1973	8 167	5 770	909	6 679	526	14	6 166	918	1 083	3 967	3 575	2 058	902
1974	9 156	6 492	827	7 319	610	7	6 716	1 125	1 315	4 359	3 899	2 100	927
1975	10 066	6 943	789	7 733	640	6	7 099	1 298	1 669	4 664	4 250	2 158	905
1976	11 175	8 051	636	8 687	746	-4	7 938	1 415	1 823	5 153	4 636	2 169	941
1977	12 481	9 058	721	9 778	849	-8	8 921	1 625	1 935	5 655	5 104	2 207	981
1978	14 489	10 332	1 171	11 503	990	-14	10 499	1 863	2 127	6 466	5 834	2 241	1 022
1979	15 924	11 480	988	12 469	1 137	-15	11 317	2 168	2 439	7 018	6 284	2 269	1 033
1980	17 221	12 474	363	12 837	1 227	-3	11 607	2 726	2 888	7 524	6 704	2 289	1 035
1981	19 545	13 435	845	14 280	1 430	-22	12 828	3 446	3 270	8 523	7 605	2 293	1 030
1982	20 511	13 892	638	14 530	1 506	-18	13 006	3 949	3 556	8 940	7 927	2 294	1 014
1983	21 884	15 108	412	15 520	1 642	-48	13 830	4 205	3 849	9 491	8 520	2 306	1 043
1984	24 523	16 870	876	17 746	1 873	-68	15 806	4 682	4 035	10 571	9 564	2 320	1 084
1985	26 203	17 956	858	18 815	2 010	-72	16 733	5 197	4 273	11 260	10 163	2 327	1 104
1986	27 307	18 898	798	19 696	2 153	-94	17 449	5 356	4 502	11 710	10 593	2 332	1 116
1987	28 308	19 854	931	20 785	2 262	-112	18 411	5 264	4 634	12 085	10 882	2 342	1 143
1988	30 223	21 094	1 343	22 436	2 517	-146	19 774	5 587	4 862	12 901	11 639	2 343	1 177
1989	32 334	22 306	1 229	23 535	2 686	-146	20 703	6 261	5 371	13 781	12 395	2 346	1 197
1990	34 076	23 763	1 013	24 776	2 875	-210	21 692	6 572	5 813	14 460	12 987	2 357	1 211
1991	36 043	25 233	1 102	26 334	3 074	-236	23 024	6 611	6 408	15 124	13 625	2 383	1 238
1992	39 162	27 465	1 393	28 859	3 347	-259	25 252	6 771	7 139	16 209	14 621	2 416	1 263
1993	40 822	28 886	1 315	30 201	3 564	-289	26 348	6 946	7 528	16 619	14 977	2 456	1 309
1994	43 272	30 657	1 452	32 108	3 859	-312	27 937	7 420	7 915	17 350	15 563	2 494	1 337
1995	45 829	32 388	1 496	33 883	4 070	-282	29 531	7 802	8 497	18 076	16 170	2 535	1 391
1996	48 679	33 700	1 910	35 610	4 223	-273	31 114	8 536	9 028	18 926	16 920	2 572	1 414
1997	50 955	35 253	1 887	37 140	4 427	-272	32 441	9 102	9 411	19 590	17 424	2 601	1 435
1998	53 810	37 573	1 615	39 188	4 659	-275	34 254	9 853	9 703	20 489	18 146	2 626	1 462
1999	56 052	39 646	1 813	41 459	4 884	-301	36 274	9 738	10 040	21 137	18 749	2 652	1 482
2000	58 726	41 852	1 218	43 070	5 065	-346	37 659	10 411	10 656	21 926	19 377	2 678	1 504
2001	62 233	43 921	1 451	45 372	5 296	-348	39 728	10 701	11 805	23 118	20 539	2 692	1 498
2002	63 505	45 595	700	46 295	5 501	-378	40 415	10 369	12 720	23 466	21 167	2 706	1 497
2003	66 224	47 403	1 540	48 943	5 721	-375	42 847	10 190	13 187	24 296	22 103	2 726	1 497

Table 21-2. Personal Income and Employment by Region and State—Continued

(Millions of dollars, except as noted.)

Year	Personal income, total	Derivation of personal income								Per capita (dollars)		Population (thousands)	Total employment (thousands)
		Earnings by place of work			Less: Contributions for government social insurance	Plus: Adjustment for residence	Equals: Net earnings by place of residence	Plus: Dividends, interest, and rent	Plus: Personal current transfer receipts	Personal income	Disposable personal income		
		Nonfarm	Farm	Total									

FLORIDA

1969	24 265	17 587	636	18 224	1 132	-22	17 070	5 002	2 194	3 654	3 215	6 641	2 857
1970	27 412	19 648	546	20 194	1 272	-20	18 903	5 865	2 645	4 004	3 566	6 845	2 966
1971	30 744	21 806	640	22 446	1 472	-14	20 960	6 598	3 187	4 292	3 846	7 163	3 082
1972	35 396	25 330	739	26 068	1 796	-11	24 261	7 382	3 753	4 707	4 148	7 520	3 338
1973	41 436	29 862	837	30 699	2 420	-10	28 269	8 608	4 559	5 227	4 634	7 927	3 666
1974	46 570	32 988	908	33 897	2 780	-1	31 116	9 957	5 496	5 599	4 981	8 317	3 766
1975	50 491	34 395	1 000	35 395	2 859	-9	32 527	10 783	7 181	5 911	5 362	8 542	3 676
1976	55 378	37 742	1 037	38 779	3 168	10	35 621	11 798	7 959	6 369	5 738	8 695	3 730
1977	62 064	42 319	1 035	43 354	3 570	22	39 806	13 548	8 710	6 982	6 273	8 889	3 929
1978	71 641	49 021	1 236	50 256	4 245	25	46 037	15 921	9 683	7 845	7 000	9 132	4 235
1979	82 755	56 229	1 312	57 541	5 105	22	52 458	19 076	11 221	8 738	7 743	9 471	4 457
1980	97 741	64 498	1 671	66 169	5 915	16	60 270	24 129	13 341	9 933	8 764	9 840	4 695
1981	113 537	73 001	1 405	74 406	7 194	111	67 323	30 619	15 595	11 139	9 811	10 193	4 881
1982	122 669	77 823	1 784	79 608	7 902	134	71 839	33 177	17 653	11 715	10 236	10 471	4 970
1983	136 037	85 908	2 474	88 382	8 777	160	79 765	36 964	19 309	12 655	11 331	10 750	5 185
1984	152 157	97 483	1 835	99 318	10 141	210	89 387	42 201	20 568	13 782	12 455	11 040	5 529
1985	166 837	107 129	1 841	108 970	11 349	255	97 876	46 765	22 196	14 698	13 130	11 351	5 809
1986	180 125	116 036	1 977	118 013	12 556	312	105 768	50 446	23 910	15 438	13 740	11 668	6 055
1987	194 991	127 575	2 145	129 719	13 658	373	116 434	53 207	25 351	16 253	14 440	11 997	6 140
1988	213 834	140 308	2 705	143 013	15 504	450	127 959	58 106	27 768	17 376	15 504	12 306	6 443
1989	238 049	149 588	2 484	152 072	16 800	531	135 803	70 930	31 317	18 836	16 792	12 638	6 654
1990	254 984	160 352	2 079	162 431	17 966	637	145 102	75 602	34 280	19 564	17 525	13 033	6 800
1991	264 449	165 073	2 458	167 531	18 866	683	149 348	76 318	38 783	19 780	17 842	13 370	6 775
1992	278 700	176 786	2 461	179 247	20 071	748	159 925	71 444	47 331	20 417	18 411	13 651	6 820
1993	293 167	188 108	2 534	190 641	21 391	803	170 054	75 621	47 492	21 050	18 942	13 927	7 061
1994	308 508	197 779	2 163	199 942	22 925	865	177 882	80 344	50 282	21 666	19 450	14 239	7 294
1995	329 885	210 690	2 183	212 873	24 318	933	189 489	86 064	54 333	22 691	20 321	14 538	7 554
1996	351 355	224 299	1 931	226 229	25 622	1 005	201 612	92 335	57 407	23 655	20 962	14 853	7 804
1997	372 094	236 991	2 117	239 108	27 216	1 101	212 993	99 454	59 647	24 502	21 513	15 186	8 068
1998	402 454	257 448	2 512	259 960	29 239	1 224	231 945	109 355	61 154	25 987	22 728	15 487	8 368
1999	423 834	277 556	2 928	280 484	31 118	1 351	250 717	109 423	63 693	26 894	23 509	15 759	8 656
2000	457 539	301 755	1 750	303 505	33 266	1 514	271 753	117 914	67 872	28 511	24 812	16 048	8 933
2001	478 656	313 240	1 997	315 237	35 506	1 574	281 305	122 987	74 364	29 266	25 611	16 355	9 109
2002	492 218	326 009	1 892	327 901	37 054	1 537	292 383	119 584	80 251	29 489	26 397	16 692	9 191
2003	510 090	343 136	1 580	344 716	38 800	1 575	307 491	118 186	84 413	29 972	27 089	17 019	9 334

GEORGIA

1969	14 317	12 274	416	12 690	786	-76	11 828	1 427	1 063	3 146	2 743	4 551	2 119
1970	15 556	13 140	394	13 535	836	-69	12 629	1 628	1 299	3 378	2 989	4 605	2 121
1971	17 197	14 398	453	14 851	951	-65	13 835	1 817	1 545	3 651	3 266	4 710	2 167
1972	19 340	16 305	467	16 772	1 127	-57	15 588	2 012	1 740	4 023	3 549	4 807	2 253
1973	21 988	18 369	783	19 153	1 444	-55	17 653	2 325	2 009	4 481	3 984	4 907	2 356
1974	24 235	20 004	666	20 670	1 626	-55	18 989	2 736	2 510	4 852	4 312	4 995	2 374
1975	26 088	20 923	633	21 555	1 679	-45	19 832	2 931	3 326	5 157	4 673	5 059	2 313
1976	29 155	23 887	625	24 513	1 945	-77	22 492	3 117	3 547	5 688	5 107	5 126	2 400
1977	32 319	27 068	360	27 428	2 188	-97	25 143	3 496	3 680	6 201	5 535	5 212	2 503
1978	36 742	30 792	562	31 354	2 550	-79	28 724	4 015	4 002	6 951	6 163	5 286	2 622
1979	41 292	34 539	592	35 130	2 972	-97	32 062	4 670	4 560	7 659	6 711	5 391	2 705
1980	46 192	38 226	34	38 260	3 309	-114	34 837	5 901	5 454	8 420	7 409	5 486	2 747
1981	52 395	42 185	517	42 702	3 929	-28	38 745	7 431	6 218	9 409	8 246	5 568	2 785
1982	56 834	45 089	679	45 767	4 283	-69	41 416	8 627	6 792	10 059	8 872	5 650	2 802
1983	62 289	49 717	471	50 188	4 794	-112	45 282	9 631	7 376	10 874	9 574	5 728	2 886
1984	71 237	56 949	950	57 899	5 610	-176	52 113	11 242	7 882	12 209	10 814	5 835	3 081
1985	78 332	63 162	781	63 943	6 359	-193	57 390	12 490	8 451	13 137	11 561	5 963	3 224
1986	85 000	69 039	822	69 860	7 115	-238	62 507	13 491	9 001	13 970	12 305	6 085	3 354
1987	91 395	74 555	891	75 446	7 642	-238	67 566	14 383	9 446	14 721	12 894	6 208	3 455
1988	99 402	80 830	1 151	81 981	8 534	-232	73 215	15 990	10 198	15 738	13 860	6 316	3 568
1989	107 069	85 130	1 349	86 479	9 075	-192	77 211	18 537	11 321	16 701	14 648	6 411	3 633
1990	114 643	90 735	1 257	91 991	9 719	-113	82 159	19 906	12 577	17 603	15 464	6 513	3 689
1991	120 222	93 943	1 552	95 495	10 196	-129	85 170	20 604	14 449	18 070	15 985	6 653	3 645
1992	130 041	102 108	1 638	103 746	10 930	-179	92 637	21 206	16 198	19 075	16 909	6 817	3 722
1993	137 607	108 791	1 480	110 271	11 683	-166	98 422	21 819	17 366	19 719	17 402	6 978	3 891
1994	148 234	116 226	1 947	118 173	12 644	-214	105 315	24 283	18 637	20 711	18 252	7 157	4 046
1995	158 858	125 131	1 784	126 914	13 582	-297	113 036	25 942	19 880	21 677	19 043	7 328	4 215
1996	172 113	134 974	1 881	136 855	14 509	-350	121 996	28 738	21 378	22 945	20 029	7 501	4 362
1997	182 868	144 033	1 861	145 894	15 538	-434	129 922	31 166	21 779	23 795	20 630	7 685	4 477
1998	198 782	157 534	1 823	159 357	16 845	-552	141 960	34 433	22 389	25 279	21 792	7 864	4 640
1999	212 081	171 018	1 994	173 012	18 195	-582	154 235	34 086	23 761	26 359	22 695	8 046	4 778
2000	230 356	185 385	1 650	187 035	19 367	-728	166 940	37 570	25 845	27 989	24 054	8 230	4 892
2001	241 128	192 090	1 967	194 057	20 176	-777	173 104	39 325	28 699	28 724	24 817	8 395	4 905
2002	246 781	195 700	1 378	197 078	20 531	-817	175 730	38 612	32 439	28 884	25 559	8 544	4 881
2003	254 104	203 067	2 246	205 313	21 060	-818	183 436	38 050	32 618	29 259	26 146	8 685	4 893

Table 21-2. Personal Income and Employment by Region and State—Continued

(Millions of dollars, except as noted.)

Year	Personal income, total	Derivation of personal income								Per capita (dollars)		Population (thousands)	Total employment (thousands)
		Earnings by place of work			Less: Contributions for government social insurance	Plus: Adjustment for residence	Equals: Net earnings by place of residence	Plus: Dividends, interest, and rent	Plus: Personal current transfer receipts	Personal income	Disposable personal income		
		Nonfarm	Farm	Total									

KENTUCKY

1969	9 444	7 416	423	7 839	511	174	7 502	998	944	2 953	2 585	3 198	1 332
1970	10 229	7 993	388	8 381	549	164	7 996	1 129	1 104	3 166	2 801	3 231	1 336
1971	11 132	8 708	403	9 110	616	107	8 601	1 233	1 298	3 375	3 014	3 298	1 360
1972	12 329	9 651	501	10 152	716	101	9 538	1 351	1 441	3 696	3 256	3 336	1 392
1973	13 901	10 965	573	11 538	922	59	10 675	1 508	1 719	4 123	3 676	3 372	1 461
1974	15 670	12 264	657	12 921	1 063	26	11 883	1 736	2 051	4 586	4 010	3 417	1 496
1975	17 119	13 218	475	13 693	1 124	11	12 580	1 956	2 583	4 935	4 413	3 469	1 465
1976	19 247	15 045	550	15 595	1 293	-23	14 279	2 146	2 822	5 452	4 857	3 530	1 523
1977	21 702	17 051	675	17 727	1 454	1	16 273	2 471	2 959	6 071	5 363	3 575	1 579
1978	24 378	19 341	595	19 936	1 690	12	18 259	2 949	3 171	6 750	5 945	3 611	1 645
1979	27 686	21 634	667	22 301	1 950	4	20 355	3 634	3 697	7 598	6 696	3 644	1 668
1980	29 965	22 940	549	23 488	2 064	28	21 453	4 059	4 453	8 178	7 238	3 664	1 646
1981	33 296	24 726	928	25 654	2 396	-8	23 250	5 022	5 025	9 072	7 981	3 670	1 639
1982	35 477	25 629	895	26 524	2 528	-18	23 979	6 013	5 485	9 631	8 498	3 683	1 621
1983	36 630	26 730	224	26 954	2 655	12	24 311	6 379	5 941	9 915	8 796	3 694	1 629
1984	41 139	29 648	1 109	30 757	3 001	-65	27 691	7 230	6 218	11 132	9 978	3 695	1 683
1985	42 974	31 166	865	32 031	3 219	-76	28 736	7 731	6 506	11 631	10 379	3 695	1 706
1986	44 492	32 459	636	33 095	3 420	-48	29 626	8 055	6 811	12 065	10 775	3 688	1 742
1987	47 171	34 929	722	35 651	3 652	-78	31 920	8 207	7 044	12 807	11 388	3 683	1 775
1988	49 914	37 047	770	37 817	4 064	-91	33 663	8 782	7 469	13 564	12 072	3 680	1 827
1989	53 733	39 213	1 125	40 338	4 355	-138	35 845	9 698	8 190	14 612	12 920	3 677	1 877
1990	57 026	41 431	1 045	42 475	4 677	-101	37 697	10 361	8 968	15 437	13 621	3 694	1 918
1991	60 160	43 101	1 068	44 168	4 961	-142	39 065	10 831	10 264	16 162	14 347	3 722	1 915
1992	64 671	47 009	1 306	48 315	5 389	-413	42 513	10 982	11 176	17 175	15 251	3 765	1 962
1993	66 791	49 229	1 104	50 333	5 737	-424	44 172	11 012	11 606	17 520	15 527	3 812	2 006
1994	70 148	51 763	1 139	52 901	6 169	-538	46 194	11 785	12 169	18 225	16 110	3 849	2 047
1995	73 389	54 066	714	54 780	6 482	-573	47 725	12 581	13 084	18 879	16 625	3 887	2 123
1996	77 819	56 573	1 131	57 704	6 740	-641	50 323	13 607	13 889	19 854	17 443	3 920	2 155
1997	82 436	59 950	1 163	61 112	7 129	-657	53 326	14 482	14 627	20 855	18 218	3 953	2 203
1998	87 851	64 022	1 042	65 064	7 498	-595	56 970	15 845	15 035	22 043	19 218	3 985	2 244
1999	91 462	68 223	796	69 019	7 993	-686	60 340	15 528	15 593	22 763	19 834	4 018	2 291
2000	98 845	72 430	1 442	73 872	8 182	-719	64 972	17 137	16 736	24 414	21 346	4 049	2 332
2001	101 419	74 486	963	75 448	8 485	-998	65 964	17 305	18 150	24 935	21 786	4 067	2 303
2002	104 055	77 310	344	77 654	8 835	-1 071	67 749	16 848	19 459	25 442	22 609	4 090	2 285
2003	108 515	81 885	651	82 536	9 171	-1 371	71 995	16 593	19 927	26 352	23 603	4 118	2 302

LOUISIANA

1969	10 453	8 655	239	8 894	568	3	8 328	1 164	961	2 888	2 569	3 619	1 440
1970	11 281	9 160	280	9 441	591	3	8 852	1 275	1 154	3 090	2 788	3 650	1 429
1971	12 299	9 931	318	10 249	657	-9	9 583	1 398	1 318	3 314	2 994	3 711	1 445
1972	13 462	10 934	345	11 280	756	-22	10 502	1 511	1 450	3 578	3 210	3 762	1 488
1973	15 076	12 125	576	12 701	960	-38	11 703	1 688	1 685	3 979	3 582	3 789	1 550
1974	17 188	13 722	609	14 331	1 117	-55	13 159	2 055	1 974	4 499	4 013	3 821	1 598
1975	19 297	15 506	416	15 921	1 242	-84	14 595	2 262	2 439	4 964	4 478	3 887	1 641
1976	21 951	17 920	452	18 372	1 453	-114	16 805	2 456	2 689	5 555	4 962	3 952	1 702
1977	24 561	20 222	452	20 674	1 625	-141	18 907	2 760	2 893	6 116	5 448	4 016	1 756
1978	28 160	23 540	369	23 909	1 929	-188	21 791	3 219	3 150	6 913	6 113	4 073	1 848
1979	32 076	26 737	498	27 235	2 273	-234	24 727	3 764	3 585	7 749	6 801	4 139	1 899
1980	37 067	30 700	169	30 869	2 595	-339	27 934	4 857	4 276	8 777	7 680	4 223	1 968
1981	42 887	35 149	261	35 411	3 182	-365	31 864	6 247	4 775	10 013	8 692	4 283	2 036
1982	45 962	36 735	260	36 995	3 383	-343	33 268	7 185	5 509	10 560	9 307	4 353	2 029
1983	47 894	37 172	228	37 400	3 376	-324	33 701	7 922	6 271	10 897	9 716	4 395	1 990
1984	51 348	39 558	318	39 875	3 661	-317	35 897	8 921	6 530	11 669	10 466	4 400	2 032
1985	53 398	40 512	226	40 738	3 773	-286	36 679	9 685	7 034	12 113	10 853	4 408	2 020
1986	52 905	39 217	230	39 447	3 665	-231	35 551	9 633	7 720	12 005	10 887	4 407	1 939
1987	53 052	39 221	393	39 614	3 621	-196	35 797	9 438	7 818	12 212	11 052	4 344	1 915
1988	55 908	41 436	627	42 062	3 989	-176	37 898	9 817	8 193	13 036	11 845	4 289	1 947
1989	59 437	43 499	461	43 961	4 215	-142	39 604	10 879	8 955	13 976	12 620	4 253	1 966
1990	64 052	47 034	381	47 414	4 569	-119	42 726	11 456	9 870	15 173	13 689	4 222	2 019
1991	67 628	49 404	448	49 852	4 912	-137	44 803	11 583	11 242	15 900	14 381	4 253	2 044
1992	72 000	52 211	554	52 765	5 126	-137	47 503	11 497	13 000	16 771	15 233	4 293	2 052
1993	75 161	54 150	566	54 717	5 360	-139	49 218	11 725	14 218	17 413	15 788	4 316	2 100
1994	80 043	57 071	659	57 729	5 785	-165	51 779	12 536	15 727	18 411	16 667	4 347	2 140
1995	83 535	59 857	675	60 532	6 073	-193	54 265	13 530	15 741	19 077	17 228	4 379	2 209
1996	87 036	62 305	870	63 175	6 355	-217	56 603	14 435	15 999	19 786	17 690	4 399	2 254
1997	91 432	65 945	715	66 660	6 742	-233	59 685	15 415	16 331	20 681	18 373	4 421	2 305
1998	96 677	70 309	453	70 762	7 137	-255	63 370	16 684	16 622	21 772	19 385	4 440	2 355
1999	98 200	71 733	616	72 349	7 217	-249	64 884	16 193	17 123	22 014	19 650	4 461	2 374
2000	103 151	74 913	502	75 415	7 380	-260	67 775	17 700	17 676	23 080	20 576	4 469	2 404
2001	110 407	79 904	498	80 402	7 845	-138	72 418	17 568	20 420	24 722	22 068	4 466	2 408
2002	113 277	82 563	243	82 806	8 093	-133	74 581	17 009	21 688	25 307	22 946	4 476	2 407
2003	117 074	86 400	598	86 997	8 347	-155	78 495	16 714	21 865	26 038	23 796	4 496	2 428

Table 21-2. Personal Income and Employment by Region and State—Continued

(Millions of dollars, except as noted.)

| Year | Personal income, total | Derivation of personal income ||||||||| Per capita (dollars) || Population (thousands) | Total employment (thousands) |
| | | Earnings by place of work ||| Less: Contributions for government social insurance | Plus: Adjustment for residence | Equals: Net earnings by place of residence | Plus: Dividends, interest, and rent | Plus: Personal current transfer receipts | Personal income | Disposable personal income | | |
		Nonfarm	Farm	Total									

MISSISSIPPI

Year	Personal income	Nonfarm	Farm	Total	Contrib.	Adj.	Net earnings	Div/Int/Rent	Transfer	Per cap income	Disp income	Population	Employment
1969	5 303	4 160	346	4 506	291	35	4 249	503	552	2 389	2 172	2 220	909
1970	5 813	4 432	391	4 823	311	36	4 549	575	689	2 617	2 369	2 221	917
1971	6 450	4 860	433	5 293	351	58	4 999	637	814	2 847	2 619	2 266	939
1972	7 352	5 594	490	6 084	422	73	5 735	699	918	3 187	2 889	2 307	979
1973	8 439	6 321	688	7 010	539	93	6 564	810	1 065	3 591	3 276	2 350	1 019
1974	9 308	7 013	510	7 523	616	123	7 029	966	1 313	3 913	3 534	2 379	1 031
1975	10 086	7 510	372	7 882	654	150	7 378	1 077	1 631	4 203	3 859	2 400	1 001
1976	11 529	8 587	572	9 159	757	182	8 584	1 167	1 779	4 744	4 321	2 430	1 039
1977	12 870	9 678	606	10 284	851	223	9 655	1 312	1 903	5 232	4 779	2 460	1 071
1978	14 345	10 993	449	11 442	984	279	10 737	1 513	2 095	5 766	5 206	2 488	1 102
1979	16 263	12 205	699	12 904	1 131	337	12 110	1 762	2 392	6 485	5 835	2 508	1 117
1980	17 695	13 168	178	13 346	1 216	425	12 555	2 275	2 865	7 007	6 305	2 525	1 114
1981	19 928	14 416	327	14 743	1 429	455	13 770	2 909	3 250	7 849	7 011	2 539	1 110
1982	21 064	14 802	421	15 223	1 505	473	14 191	3 298	3 575	8 238	7 494	2 557	1 083
1983	22 021	15 557	99	15 656	1 597	530	14 589	3 494	3 939	8 576	7 768	2 568	1 091
1984	24 278	16 979	473	17 452	1 777	594	16 270	3 935	4 074	9 417	8 581	2 578	1 121
1985	25 602	17 983	433	18 416	1 917	624	17 123	4 211	4 268	9 892	9 010	2 588	1 129
1986	26 440	18 749	198	18 946	2 045	609	17 511	4 409	4 520	10 194	9 323	2 594	1 136
1987	27 962	19 641	584	20 224	2 135	647	18 736	4 516	4 710	10 802	9 845	2 589	1 147
1988	29 832	20 962	731	21 693	2 387	688	19 994	4 819	5 019	11 561	10 576	2 580	1 176
1989	32 164	22 257	562	22 819	2 564	731	20 986	5 682	5 496	12 495	11 374	2 574	1 196
1990	33 754	23 567	433	24 001	2 712	754	22 042	5 754	5 958	13 089	11 910	2 579	1 210
1991	35 607	24 634	538	25 172	2 885	813	23 100	5 871	6 635	13 702	12 525	2 599	1 218
1992	38 199	26 425	641	27 066	3 073	832	24 824	5 926	7 449	14 559	13 319	2 624	1 241
1993	40 596	28 534	547	29 081	3 335	852	26 598	6 057	7 940	15 290	13 941	2 655	1 294
1994	43 805	30 802	818	31 620	3 668	854	28 805	6 598	8 402	16 291	14 801	2 689	1 343
1995	45 973	32 211	681	32 892	3 850	943	29 985	6 900	9 088	16 885	15 314	2 723	1 374
1996	48 646	33 488	1 067	34 555	3 977	986	31 565	7 416	9 665	17 702	16 004	2 748	1 398
1997	51 514	35 315	1 174	36 490	4 175	1 124	33 439	8 016	10 058	18 550	16 733	2 777	1 424
1998	54 820	37 875	958	38 833	4 421	1 204	35 616	8 889	10 315	19 545	17 593	2 805	1 462
1999	56 719	39 635	955	40 590	4 614	1 310	37 286	8 748	10 685	20 053	18 038	2 828	1 488
2000	59 837	41 267	724	41 991	4 707	1 506	38 790	9 547	11 500	21 007	18 937	2 848	1 493
2001	62 892	42 314	939	43 253	4 820	1 657	40 090	9 921	12 881	22 008	19 892	2 858	1 469
2002	64 328	43 838	283	44 121	5 030	1 680	40 771	9 698	13 859	22 440	20 543	2 867	1 471
2003	67 258	45 803	926	46 730	5 201	1 758	43 286	9 550	14 422	23 343	21 545	2 881	1 472

NORTH CAROLINA

Year	Personal income	Nonfarm	Farm	Total	Contrib.	Adj.	Net earnings	Div/Int/Rent	Transfer	Per cap income	Disp income	Population	Employment
1969	15 272	12 885	667	13 553	899	16	12 670	1 495	1 107	3 036	2 655	5 031	2 458
1970	16 661	13 881	666	14 546	971	13	13 589	1 734	1 337	3 267	2 879	5 099	2 469
1971	18 181	15 184	622	15 805	1 101	10	14 714	1 898	1 568	3 496	3 108	5 201	2 490
1972	20 569	17 280	743	18 023	1 308	4	16 720	2 094	1 756	3 884	3 409	5 296	2 602
1973	23 407	19 492	1 155	20 647	1 677	2	18 972	2 398	2 038	4 349	3 844	5 382	2 720
1974	25 830	21 304	1 101	22 405	1 900	8	20 513	2 784	2 532	4 730	4 155	5 461	2 743
1975	27 932	22 239	1 058	23 297	1 977	14	21 334	3 077	3 521	5 046	4 541	5 535	2 647
1976	31 206	25 131	1 141	26 272	2 271	15	24 016	3 409	3 781	5 579	4 966	5 593	2 754
1977	34 239	28 005	849	28 854	2 512	22	26 364	3 884	3 992	6 040	5 352	5 668	2 851
1978	38 715	31 757	1 133	32 890	2 922	21	29 989	4 424	4 303	6 744	5 950	5 740	2 948
1979	42 946	35 519	746	36 264	3 390	18	32 892	5 133	4 921	7 403	6 474	5 802	3 051
1980	48 344	38 941	639	39 580	3 727	23	35 875	6 599	5 870	8 195	7 172	5 899	3 060
1981	54 553	42 821	1 040	43 860	4 393	-20	39 448	8 334	6 772	9 158	8 000	5 957	3 082
1982	58 508	44 892	1 058	45 950	4 648	-30	41 272	9 694	7 542	9 720	8 615	6 019	3 051
1983	63 973	49 669	628	50 296	5 177	-49	45 070	10 770	8 132	10 527	9 304	6 077	3 138
1984	72 997	56 515	1 283	57 798	5 974	-83	51 741	12 659	8 596	11 842	10 517	6 164	3 306
1985	79 417	61 714	1 152	62 866	6 593	-147	56 126	14 075	9 217	12 699	11 245	6 254	3 410
1986	85 223	66 483	1 136	67 619	7 231	-210	60 179	15 243	9 802	13 481	11 928	6 322	3 512
1987	91 611	72 355	1 137	73 492	7 803	-292	65 397	16 016	10 198	14 306	12 552	6 404	3 631
1988	99 786	78 675	1 477	80 152	8 776	-351	71 025	17 733	11 028	15 398	13 589	6 481	3 774
1989	108 309	83 928	1 712	85 640	9 430	-403	75 807	20 186	12 316	16 497	14 460	6 565	3 864
1990	114 926	88 090	2 122	90 212	10 017	-447	79 748	21 605	13 573	17 246	15 196	6 664	3 928
1991	119 927	90 607	2 382	92 989	10 504	-430	82 055	22 291	15 581	17 677	15 648	6 784	3 889
1992	129 957	99 375	2 308	101 682	11 395	-451	89 836	22 782	17 339	18 842	16 720	6 897	3 989
1993	137 865	105 214	2 587	107 800	12 178	-467	95 155	23 608	19 101	19 575	17 325	7 043	4 113
1994	146 620	111 617	2 804	114 421	13 105	-520	100 797	25 958	19 865	20 400	17 982	7 187	4 227
1995	156 407	118 415	2 701	121 115	13 922	-592	106 601	27 715	22 091	21 295	18 716	7 345	4 380
1996	167 416	124 934	3 001	127 935	14 596	-648	112 691	30 754	23 972	22 320	19 548	7 501	4 487
1997	180 163	134 089	3 024	137 114	15 663	-716	120 735	34 165	25 263	23 530	20 508	7 657	4 631
1998	193 223	144 640	2 365	147 005	16 692	-704	129 609	37 408	26 206	24 743	21 400	7 809	4 746
1999	203 187	155 058	2 158	157 216	17 797	-771	138 648	36 606	27 933	25 560	22 136	7 949	4 850
2000	218 668	166 192	2 579	168 771	18 748	-885	149 137	39 633	29 898	27 071	23 398	8 078	4 925
2001	225 742	170 519	2 796	173 315	19 563	-779	152 973	39 483	33 285	27 545	23 888	8 195	4 883
2002	230 696	175 409	1 224	176 633	19 984	-766	155 882	39 002	35 811	27 775	24 601	8 306	4 870
2003	237 931	182 610	1 443	184 053	21 065	-761	162 227	38 404	37 300	28 301	25 306	8 407	4 872

Table 21-2. Personal Income and Employment by Region and State—Continued

(Millions of dollars, except as noted.)

Year	Personal income, total	Derivation of personal income								Per capita (dollars)		Population (thousands)	Total employment (thousands)
		Earnings by place of work			Less: Contributions for government social insurance	Plus: Adjustment for residence	Equals: Net earnings by place of residence	Plus: Dividends, interest, and rent	Plus: Personal current transfer receipts	Personal income	Disposable personal income		
		Nonfarm	Farm	Total									
SOUTH CAROLINA													
1969	7 229	6 159	186	6 345	416	115	6 044	648	536	2 813	2 495	2 570	1 170
1970	7 928	6 657	187	6 844	448	116	6 511	748	669	3 051	2 738	2 598	1 196
1971	8 690	7 253	202	7 456	509	128	7 075	837	778	3 265	2 935	2 662	1 215
1972	9 766	8 206	212	8 417	599	145	7 963	927	876	3 592	3 168	2 718	1 262
1973	11 148	9 348	300	9 648	773	159	9 035	1 070	1 043	4 017	3 562	2 775	1 328
1974	12 652	10 492	339	10 830	897	174	10 107	1 228	1 318	4 450	3 939	2 843	1 365
1975	13 721	10 992	274	11 266	927	185	10 524	1 384	1 814	4 731	4 297	2 900	1 326
1976	15 460	12 649	232	12 880	1 088	220	12 013	1 528	1 919	5 256	4 713	2 941	1 376
1977	16 945	13 977	185	14 162	1 198	243	13 207	1 733	2 005	5 669	5 066	2 989	1 411
1978	19 167	15 871	243	16 114	1 389	261	14 985	1 978	2 204	6 303	5 616	3 041	1 467
1979	21 577	17 805	256	18 062	1 607	285	16 740	2 294	2 544	6 990	6 160	3 087	1 510
1980	24 270	19 666	33	19 699	1 777	320	18 242	2 939	3 088	7 743	6 846	3 135	1 527
1981	27 402	21 686	168	21 854	2 095	350	20 110	3 721	3 571	8 619	7 584	3 179	1 541
1982	29 155	22 456	192	22 649	2 199	383	20 832	4 401	3 922	9 089	8 081	3 208	1 518
1983	31 715	24 588	49	24 637	2 470	396	22 564	4 967	4 184	9 806	8 717	3 234	1 552
1984	35 810	27 767	266	28 033	2 850	443	25 627	5 769	4 414	10 945	9 789	3 272	1 631
1985	38 534	29 706	194	29 899	3 096	500	27 303	6 447	4 783	11 666	10 407	3 303	1 664
1986	40 900	31 674	88	31 762	3 393	564	28 934	6 922	5 045	12 235	10 915	3 343	1 706
1987	43 838	34 116	248	34 364	3 631	608	31 341	7 310	5 188	12 968	11 518	3 381	1 748
1988	47 510	37 151	347	37 498	4 110	628	34 016	7 959	5 535	13 924	12 439	3 412	1 820
1989	51 381	39 690	363	40 053	4 463	581	36 171	8 569	6 640	14 864	13 172	3 457	1 871
1990	55 647	42 754	295	43 049	4 817	505	38 737	9 845	7 064	15 894	14 095	3 501	1 926
1991	57 987	43 771	394	44 164	5 035	492	39 621	10 219	8 148	16 241	14 522	3 570	1 898
1992	61 377	46 294	376	46 671	5 305	502	41 867	10 391	9 119	16 953	15 186	3 620	1 910
1993	64 220	48 564	338	48 902	5 641	506	43 767	10 666	9 788	17 531	15 681	3 663	1 944
1994	68 050	50 654	484	51 138	5 982	611	45 767	11 730	10 553	18 365	16 384	3 705	1 992
1995	71 688	53 328	381	53 709	6 326	731	48 115	12 272	11 301	19 124	16 980	3 749	2 051
1996	76 144	55 854	463	56 318	6 540	851	50 628	13 319	12 197	20 058	17 724	3 796	2 094
1997	81 004	59 171	474	59 645	6 942	1 000	53 702	14 486	12 816	20 987	18 473	3 860	2 154
1998	86 854	63 512	341	63 853	7 403	1 074	57 524	15 912	13 418	22 161	19 440	3 919	2 209
1999	91 716	67 945	418	68 363	7 786	1 169	61 747	15 705	14 264	23 075	20 238	3 975	2 257
2000	98 270	71 951	489	72 441	8 132	1 398	65 707	17 289	15 274	24 426	21 503	4 023	2 291
2001	101 681	73 711	585	74 296	8 415	1 374	67 255	17 443	16 983	25 046	22 123	4 060	2 265
2002	104 540	76 276	161	76 437	8 732	1 379	69 084	17 084	18 372	25 474	22 910	4 104	2 257
2003	108 398	79 603	527	80 130	9 039	1 394	72 486	16 787	19 125	26 138	23 720	4 147	2 271
TENNESSEE													
1969	11 487	9 905	252	10 157	659	-155	9 342	1 168	977	2 948	2 607	3 897	1 789
1970	12 480	10 539	265	10 804	695	-155	9 954	1 330	1 197	3 170	2 827	3 937	1 785
1971	13 776	11 592	262	11 854	789	-165	10 900	1 481	1 396	3 435	3 087	4 010	1 817
1972	15 518	13 153	321	13 475	937	-192	12 346	1 634	1 538	3 796	3 407	4 088	1 924
1973	17 714	14 916	488	15 403	1 211	-181	14 011	1 886	1 816	4 280	3 842	4 138	2 025
1974	19 663	16 476	312	16 788	1 383	-191	15 214	2 230	2 220	4 680	4 202	4 202	2 055
1975	21 405	17 344	244	17 588	1 430	-190	15 968	2 503	2 933	5 024	4 557	4 261	1 983
1976	24 104	19 654	366	20 021	1 639	-184	18 197	2 714	3 193	5 568	5 030	4 329	2 052
1977	26 795	22 168	294	22 463	1 846	-241	20 376	3 066	3 354	6 087	5 503	4 402	2 135
1978	30 593	25 576	312	25 888	2 151	-308	23 429	3 500	3 664	6 857	6 164	4 462	2 228
1979	34 236	28 396	333	28 730	2 480	-358	25 891	4 079	4 266	7 552	6 777	4 533	2 282
1980	37 994	30 627	188	30 815	2 675	-425	27 714	5 143	5 136	8 259	7 406	4 600	2 264
1981	42 404	33 394	352	33 746	3 142	-460	30 144	6 435	5 825	9 163	8 216	4 628	2 263
1982	45 249	34 683	297	34 979	3 338	-417	31 224	7 632	6 393	9 739	8 780	4 646	2 224
1983	48 130	37 357	-38	37 318	3 650	-430	33 238	8 022	6 869	10 329	9 331	4 660	2 247
1984	53 966	41 775	402	42 178	4 188	-430	37 559	9 213	7 194	11 515	10 468	4 687	2 354
1985	57 984	45 092	326	45 419	4 588	-447	40 384	9 952	7 648	12 297	11 140	4 715	2 411
1986	61 771	48 341	232	48 574	5 017	-487	43 069	10 493	8 209	13 035	11 819	4 739	2 490
1987	66 412	52 507	297	52 804	5 430	-520	46 855	10 907	8 650	13 885	12 531	4 783	2 593
1988	71 640	56 628	382	57 011	6 057	-534	50 420	11 925	9 294	14 856	13 464	4 822	2 680
1989	76 859	59 936	430	60 366	6 500	-560	53 306	13 327	10 225	15 833	14 298	4 854	2 753
1990	81 700	63 314	423	63 737	6 916	-595	56 226	14 157	11 317	16 692	15 122	4 894	2 796
1991	85 914	66 124	490	66 613	7 353	-592	58 668	14 403	12 842	17 298	15 728	4 967	2 795
1992	93 807	72 514	653	73 167	7 953	-432	64 782	14 590	14 435	18 577	16 893	5 050	2 855
1993	99 074	77 377	577	77 954	8 566	-562	68 825	14 785	15 463	19 284	17 504	5 138	2 960
1994	105 846	83 132	626	83 758	9 339	-666	73 752	15 881	16 212	20 233	18 318	5 231	3 079
1995	112 793	88 380	437	88 818	9 959	-757	78 102	17 027	17 665	21 174	19 132	5 327	3 164
1996	118 374	92 275	374	92 649	10 314	-732	81 602	18 221	18 551	21 854	19 628	5 417	3 214
1997	124 699	97 431	485	97 916	10 941	-935	86 039	19 343	19 317	22 676	20 290	5 499	3 288
1998	133 620	104 721	235	104 955	11 589	-1 088	92 278	21 026	20 316	23 989	21 452	5 570	3 373
1999	140 395	111 391	103	111 494	12 204	-1 285	98 006	21 138	21 252	24 898	22 293	5 639	3 435
2000	148 833	116 833	383	117 216	12 650	-1 456	103 110	22 659	23 065	26 099	23 410	5 703	3 496
2001	154 439	120 900	312	121 212	13 061	-1 507	106 644	22 642	25 153	26 879	24 164	5 746	3 458
2002	159 833	126 331	-88	126 243	13 633	-1 439	111 171	21 791	26 871	27 606	25 271	5 790	3 451
2003	166 867	132 626	155	132 782	14 227	-1 401	117 153	21 291	28 423	28 565	26 389	5 842	3 475

Table 21-2. Personal Income and Employment by Region and State—Continued

(Millions of dollars, except as noted.)

Year	Personal income, total	Derivation of personal income								Per capita (dollars)		Population (thousands)	Total employment (thousands)
		Earnings by place of work			Less: Contributions for government social insurance	Plus: Adjustment for residence	Equals: Net earnings by place of residence	Plus: Dividends, interest, and rent	Plus: Personal current transfer receipts	Personal income	Disposable personal income		
		Nonfarm	Farm	Total									
VIRGINIA													
1969	16 396	13 209	210	13 419	800	956	13 575	1 842	978	3 554	3 046	4 614	2 148
1970	17 658	14 220	210	14 430	871	851	14 411	2 068	1 179	3 789	3 265	4 660	2 158
1971	19 443	15 651	191	15 842	1 000	877	15 719	2 312	1 413	4 091	3 561	4 753	2 196
1972	21 655	17 464	251	17 715	1 167	933	17 480	2 553	1 621	4 485	3 849	4 828	2 263
1973	24 393	19 683	351	20 034	1 484	1 005	19 555	2 902	1 937	4 971	4 300	4 907	2 384
1974	27 300	21 863	312	22 175	1 701	1 134	21 608	3 391	2 301	5 484	4 710	4 978	2 451
1975	30 141	23 555	262	23 816	1 821	1 394	23 389	3 804	2 947	5 961	5 245	5 056	2 425
1976	33 619	26 394	233	26 627	2 071	1 617	26 173	4 227	3 219	6 550	5 730	5 133	2 501
1977	37 455	29 520	165	29 685	2 302	1 857	29 240	4 763	3 452	7 195	6 259	5 206	2 585
1978	42 386	33 282	286	33 568	2 621	2 191	33 137	5 432	3 816	8 021	6 936	5 284	2 697
1979	47 656	37 211	151	37 362	3 050	2 588	36 900	6 376	4 380	8 950	7 730	5 325	2 769
1980	54 457	41 357	64	41 421	3 388	3 164	41 198	8 052	5 208	10 144	8 770	5 368	2 802
1981	61 447	45 860	265	46 125	4 022	3 394	45 497	9 937	6 013	11 287	9 696	5 444	2 820
1982	66 758	49 328	119	49 447	4 381	3 464	48 530	11 657	6 572	12 154	10 521	5 493	2 832
1983	72 551	53 913	42	53 955	4 947	3 450	52 459	12 984	7 108	13 038	11 411	5 565	2 905
1984	81 186	60 988	321	61 309	5 702	3 561	59 168	14 498	7 520	14 385	12 677	5 644	3 054
1985	87 821	66 828	223	67 051	6 436	3 680	64 295	15 489	8 037	15 366	13 459	5 715	3 198
1986	94 892	72 660	270	72 930	7 211	3 835	69 555	16 820	8 517	16 328	14 311	5 812	3 335
1987	102 769	79 524	366	79 890	7 910	4 048	76 029	17 893	8 847	17 324	15 066	5 932	3 501
1988	111 768	86 420	520	86 939	8 962	4 431	82 408	19 911	9 449	18 514	16 190	6 037	3 582
1989	120 816	92 214	634	92 848	9 725	4 664	87 787	22 688	10 342	19 740	17 185	6 120	3 681
1990	127 129	96 150	670	96 819	10 329	5 419	91 909	23 997	11 223	20 449	17 872	6 217	3 726
1991	131 913	98 849	604	99 453	10 804	5 950	94 600	24 995	12 318	20 934	18 384	6 301	3 666
1992	139 901	104 962	658	105 619	11 403	6 420	100 636	25 388	13 876	21 811	19 200	6 414	3 684
1993	146 273	109 985	524	110 509	11 991	6 862	105 381	26 218	14 674	22 470	19 726	6 510	3 758
1994	153 654	115 007	629	115 636	12 705	6 853	109 783	28 374	15 497	23 305	20 389	6 593	3 842
1995	160 470	120 085	553	120 637	13 240	7 072	114 469	29 315	16 686	24 056	21 007	6 671	3 931
1996	169 001	126 723	570	127 292	13 902	6 519	119 910	31 117	17 974	25 034	21 761	6 751	4 012
1997	179 654	135 507	428	135 935	14 876	7 060	128 119	33 037	18 498	26 307	22 746	6 829	4 111
1998	191 711	145 903	436	146 339	15 969	6 758	137 128	35 425	19 158	27 780	23 662	6 901	4 185
1999	204 586	157 576	360	157 936	17 243	8 158	148 851	35 604	20 132	29 226	24 664	7 000	4 282
2000	220 845	171 986	521	172 507	18 568	6 275	160 214	39 100	21 531	31 084	26 212	7 105	4 407
2001	233 639	182 659	454	183 113	19 652	5 980	169 441	40 205	23 993	32 483	27 528	7 193	4 438
2002	239 480	187 508	163	187 671	20 326	7 341	174 686	39 319	25 475	32 860	28 690	7 288	4 440
2003	248 554	196 621	391	197 012	21 303	7 714	183 423	38 611	26 520	33 651	29 604	7 386	4 475
WEST VIRGINIA													
1969	4 868	4 138	30	4 169	324	-79	3 766	503	599	2 788	2 443	1 746	652
1970	5 428	4 548	25	4 573	350	-82	4 141	566	722	3 108	2 752	1 747	660
1971	5 965	4 945	25	4 970	395	-100	4 474	620	870	3 369	2 999	1 770	670
1972	6 601	5 465	30	5 495	455	-114	4 926	678	997	3 673	3 256	1 797	684
1973	7 240	5 929	44	5 973	567	-117	5 288	765	1 186	4 010	3 579	1 805	700
1974	8 051	6 562	28	6 590	647	-131	5 812	897	1 343	4 438	3 916	1 814	711
1975	9 157	7 399	14	7 412	709	-158	6 545	1 012	1 600	4 975	4 407	1 841	717
1976	10 268	8 408	3	8 412	817	-195	7 400	1 115	1 753	5 469	4 821	1 877	739
1977	11 488	9 497	-2	9 495	915	-226	8 354	1 263	1 871	6 028	5 324	1 906	758
1978	12 796	10 617	12	10 629	1 056	-263	9 309	1 407	2 080	6 663	5 903	1 920	781
1979	14 293	11 710	17	11 727	1 211	-273	10 242	1 616	2 435	7 371	6 488	1 939	791
1980	15 841	12 567	8	12 575	1 297	-301	10 978	2 034	2 829	8 118	7 129	1 951	784
1981	17 249	13 280	-23	13 257	1 467	-280	11 511	2 542	3 196	8 827	7 765	1 954	764
1982	18 325	13 687	-29	13 659	1 552	-234	11 872	2 948	3 505	9 399	8 318	1 950	743
1983	18 700	13 448	-16	13 432	1 569	-191	11 672	3 143	3 885	9 614	8 555	1 945	724
1984	20 063	14 404	22	14 426	1 735	-139	12 551	3 544	3 968	10 408	9 303	1 928	735
1985	20 777	14 860	20	14 880	1 826	-118	12 936	3 698	4 143	10 896	9 729	1 907	735
1986	21 444	15 139	46	15 185	1 905	-91	13 189	3 856	4 400	11 392	10 221	1 882	735
1987	22 010	15 602	6	15 608	1 977	-26	13 605	3 883	4 523	11 849	10 624	1 858	742
1988	22 922	16 238	4	16 242	2 166	8	14 084	4 066	4 772	12 524	11 283	1 830	755
1989	24 305	16 886	31	16 917	2 268	87	14 736	4 535	5 034	13 454	12 034	1 807	762
1990	25 980	18 133	44	18 177	2 420	70	15 827	4 759	5 394	14 493	12 965	1 793	783
1991	27 152	18 794	34	18 828	2 580	41	16 289	4 793	6 071	15 095	13 554	1 799	784
1992	29 105	19 919	62	19 981	2 756	103	17 328	4 819	6 959	16 112	14 543	1 806	794
1993	30 077	20 721	64	20 785	2 971	106	17 919	4 758	7 400	16 548	14 936	1 818	806
1994	31 301	21 758	60	21 819	3 113	149	18 854	4 971	7 477	17 194	15 464	1 820	827
1995	32 328	22 444	23	22 467	3 255	194	19 406	5 202	7 721	17 727	15 924	1 824	844
1996	33 622	23 016	11	23 026	3 350	208	19 885	5 599	8 139	18 445	16 540	1 823	853
1997	35 005	23 825	3	23 827	3 435	360	20 753	6 705	8 363	19 243	17 200	1 819	864
1998	36 722	24 847	7	24 853	3 566	401	21 689	6 367	8 666	20 226	18 068	1 816	878
1999	37 557	25 707	-4	25 704	3 654	455	22 504	6 204	8 849	20 729	18 509	1 812	879
2000	39 582	26 926	26	26 951	3 905	568	23 615	6 676	9 292	21 901	19 536	1 807	887
2001	41 893	28 279	-7	28 272	4 047	651	24 876	6 705	10 312	23 253	20 768	1 802	883
2002	43 305	28 909	-69	28 840	3 998	688	25 531	6 503	11 272	23 993	21 724	1 805	882
2003	44 665	29 727	-34	29 693	4 078	744	26 359	6 387	11 919	24 672	22 521	1 810	882

Table 21-2. Personal Income and Employment by Region and State—Continued

(Millions of dollars, except as noted.)

| Year | Personal income, total | Derivation of personal income ||||||| Per capita (dollars) || Population (thousands) | Total employment (thousands) |
| | | Earnings by place of work ||| Less: Contributions for government social insurance | Plus: Adjustment for residence | Equals: Net earnings by place of residence | Plus: Dividends, interest, and rent | Plus: Personal current transfer receipts | Personal income | Disposable personal income | | |
		Nonfarm	Farm	Total									
SOUTHWEST													
1969	54 214	44 504	1 499	46 003	2 889	-71	43 044	6 920	4 250	3 320	2 912	16 328	7 219
1970	59 884	48 244	1 824	50 069	3 105	-84	46 880	7 968	5 037	3 603	3 197	16 621	7 311
1971	65 468	52 674	1 670	54 344	3 502	-88	50 754	8 830	5 883	3 834	3 443	17 077	7 457
1972	72 894	58 803	2 002	60 805	4 087	-106	56 612	9 690	6 592	4 165	3 698	17 503	7 807
1973	83 245	66 442	3 284	69 726	5 309	-119	64 298	11 110	7 836	4 639	4 139	17 943	8 215
1974	94 055	75 785	2 119	77 904	6 216	-80	71 608	13 094	9 354	5 124	4 528	18 354	8 511
1975	106 022	84 534	2 094	86 628	6 833	-47	79 748	14 446	11 827	5 643	5 060	18 789	8 633
1976	119 729	96 956	2 068	99 024	7 905	24	91 143	15 644	12 942	6 213	5 537	19 270	9 001
1977	134 097	110 113	1 847	111 959	9 030	-222	102 707	17 649	13 741	6 803	6 017	19 710	9 467
1978	154 990	128 346	1 666	130 011	10 769	-359	118 884	20 872	15 235	7 680	6 778	20 180	10 043
1979	179 873	148 041	2 960	151 001	12 999	-351	137 651	24 817	17 406	8 658	7 569	20 777	10 539
1980	207 566	169 583	1 510	171 092	14 993	-456	155 643	31 513	20 410	9 688	8 443	21 426	10 944
1981	243 542	196 004	2 820	198 824	18 612	-188	180 023	40 197	23 321	11 077	9 553	21 985	11 485
1982	266 878	211 431	2 338	213 769	20 507	-250	193 012	47 492	26 373	11 710	10 171	22 791	11 717
1983	282 870	221 074	2 388	223 462	21 383	-180	201 899	51 515	29 455	12 086	10 706	23 405	11 747
1984	313 020	244 032	2 649	246 681	24 036	-180	222 465	59 312	31 243	13 165	11 737	23 776	12 310
1985	337 065	261 602	2 557	264 159	26 108	-147	237 904	65 691	33 470	13 948	12 430	24 166	12 686
1986	344 430	265 084	2 559	267 643	26 812	-32	240 799	67 158	36 473	14 010	12 609	24 585	12 551
1987	354 107	271 650	3 504	275 153	27 210	59	248 002	67 579	38 526	14 309	12 814	24 748	12 860
1988	375 506	289 186	4 149	293 336	29 947	156	263 545	71 110	40 851	15 105	13 591	24 860	13 137
1989	402 842	306 386	4 078	310 464	31 925	238	278 777	78 949	45 116	16 060	14 378	25 083	13 331
1990	433 473	329 983	4 921	334 904	34 487	336	300 752	82 704	50 017	17 058	15 253	25 411	13 646
1991	454 182	346 721	4 471	351 193	37 087	293	314 399	84 341	55 442	17 524	15 752	25 917	13 850
1992	487 472	372 640	5 286	377 926	39 441	332	338 816	84 232	64 424	18 401	16 609	26 491	13 978
1993	514 272	396 136	6 178	402 314	41 994	380	360 700	84 645	68 927	18 966	17 091	27 116	14 427
1994	546 291	419 859	5 256	425 116	45 155	401	380 362	92 027	73 902	19 670	17 702	27 772	14 943
1995	580 621	446 364	4 263	450 627	47 850	381	403 158	98 193	79 269	20 430	18 351	28 420	15 498
1996	622 613	479 691	3 922	483 613	51 087	383	432 909	105 301	84 403	21 455	19 136	29 020	15 990
1997	674 420	523 385	5 083	528 468	55 200	372	473 640	112 833	87 948	22 765	20 174	29 625	16 588
1998	732 215	572 873	4 924	577 797	59 764	378	518 411	122 915	90 889	24 214	21 371	30 240	17 179
1999	776 129	614 351	7 023	621 375	63 353	467	558 488	122 930	94 711	25 177	22 236	30 827	17 543
2000	850 326	676 366	4 669	681 035	67 860	527	613 701	135 901	100 723	27 089	23 839	31 391	18 052
2001	892 506	710 497	5 171	715 668	71 698	377	644 348	136 313	111 846	27 948	24 709	31 935	18 210
2002	903 255	715 542	5 606	721 148	73 174	379	648 353	132 643	122 259	27 776	25 070	32 520	18 214
2003	934 521	744 279	6 223	750 502	76 001	421	674 923	130 314	129 284	28 246	25 742	33 085	18 278
ARIZONA													
1969	6 039	4 715	203	4 918	322	-26	4 570	977	492	3 477	3 053	1 737	711
1970	6 884	5 320	180	5 499	362	-29	5 108	1 183	593	3 835	3 385	1 795	747
1971	7 855	6 070	201	6 270	430	-28	5 812	1 333	711	4 143	3 701	1 896	786
1972	9 010	7 060	205	7 265	525	-32	6 708	1 485	817	4 485	3 965	2 009	850
1973	10 450	8 237	239	8 476	695	-31	7 750	1 715	984	4 917	4 396	2 125	925
1974	11 814	9 076	384	9 460	791	-41	8 628	1 996	1 189	5 311	4 721	2 224	955
1975	12 679	9 474	217	9 691	816	-47	8 828	2 190	1 661	5 545	5 045	2 286	935
1976	14 254	10 665	329	10 994	916	-47	10 031	2 399	1 825	6 071	5 487	2 348	976
1977	16 080	12 261	266	12 527	1 061	-56	11 409	2 746	1 924	6 625	5 945	2 427	1 048
1978	18 974	14 559	317	14 876	1 292	-69	13 515	3 289	2 171	7 536	6 705	2 518	1 149
1979	22 475	17 302	398	17 700	1 606	-71	16 023	3 981	2 471	8 518	7 530	2 639	1 241
1980	26 073	19 463	476	19 939	1 810	-80	18 049	5 055	2 969	9 524	8 458	2 738	1 285
1981	29 889	21 780	414	22 194	2 178	-14	20 003	6 396	3 490	10 636	9 365	2 810	1 317
1982	31 598	22 582	397	22 979	2 300	-6	20 672	7 032	3 893	10 934	9 668	2 890	1 320
1983	34 656	24 757	327	25 083	2 581	4	22 506	7 886	4 263	11 673	10 413	2 969	1 383
1984	39 524	28 362	527	28 890	3 019	8	25 878	9 075	4 571	12 886	11 526	3 067	1 511
1985	43 833	31 695	492	32 187	3 436	21	28 772	10 101	4 961	13 769	12 250	3 184	1 632
1986	47 730	34 645	472	35 117	3 825	41	31 332	10 956	5 442	14 427	12 851	3 308	1 712
1987	51 506	37 301	636	37 937	4 093	68	33 912	11 648	5 946	14 985	13 324	3 437	1 777
1988	55 246	40 178	763	40 942	4 571	110	36 480	12 244	6 522	15 627	13 971	3 535	1 847
1989	59 413	41 787	690	42 477	4 863	168	37 781	14 075	7 557	16 403	14 598	3 622	1 880
1990	62 649	44 065	653	44 718	5 151	228	39 795	14 485	8 369	17 005	15 131	3 684	1 910
1991	65 390	46 059	729	46 787	5 487	224	41 524	14 561	9 304	17 260	15 379	3 789	1 918
1992	69 609	49 518	673	50 190	5 855	250	44 586	14 323	10 700	17 777	15 906	3 916	1 940
1993	74 370	53 127	796	53 923	6 325	268	47 866	14 923	11 580	18 293	16 325	4 065	2 026
1994	81 555	58 376	585	58 961	7 003	281	52 239	16 941	12 375	19 212	17 103	4 245	2 158
1995	88 333	63 463	833	64 296	7 298	302	57 300	17 890	13 143	19 929	17 717	4 432	2 275
1996	95 514	69 410	752	70 162	8 213	331	62 279	19 267	13 968	20 823	18 306	4 587	2 406
1997	103 557	75 371	745	76 116	8 833	365	67 648	21 308	14 601	21 861	19 157	4 737	2 515
1998	113 370	83 272	871	84 143	9 576	410	74 977	23 290	15 103	23 216	20 250	4 883	2 631
1999	120 857	90 179	926	91 105	10 295	469	81 279	23 414	16 165	24 057	20 966	5 024	2 722
2000	132 558	99 949	684	100 633	11 159	522	89 997	25 454	17 107	25 661	22 327	5 166	2 819
2001	138 741	104 268	820	105 087	11 729	564	93 923	25 360	19 458	26 189	22 922	5 298	2 856
2002	143 680	107 731	1 056	108 786	12 109	549	97 227	24 883	21 570	26 406	23 654	5 441	2 873
2003	150 295	113 819	854	114 672	12 685	567	102 554	24 491	23 249	26 931	24 324	5 581	2 923

Table 21-2. Personal Income and Employment by Region and State—Continued

(Millions of dollars, except as noted.)

Year	Personal income, total	Derivation of personal income								Per capita (dollars)		Population (thousands)	Total employment (thousands)
		Earnings by place of work			Less: Contributions for government social insurance	Plus: Adjustment for residence	Equals: Net earnings by place of residence	Plus: Dividends, interest, and rent	Plus: Personal current transfer receipts	Personal income	Disposable personal income		
		Nonfarm	Farm	Total									

NEW MEXICO

1969	2 942	2 399	107	2 506	152	-22	2 332	350	261	2 910	2 588	1 011	395
1970	3 262	2 592	131	2 723	163	-22	2 538	399	325	3 188	2 849	1 023	399
1971	3 601	2 856	129	2 986	188	-22	2 775	448	378	3 419	3 106	1 053	416
1972	4 043	3 225	136	3 362	221	-20	3 121	500	422	3 752	3 380	1 078	440
1973	4 551	3 610	179	3 789	283	-17	3 489	562	500	4 122	3 716	1 104	461
1974	5 143	4 078	147	4 225	328	-15	3 881	662	601	4 553	4 086	1 130	478
1975	5 876	4 596	176	4 772	367	-13	4 393	745	738	5 054	4 618	1 163	491
1976	6 601	5 263	123	5 386	421	-12	4 953	823	825	5 523	5 003	1 195	512
1977	7 429	5 981	134	6 116	481	-11	5 623	937	869	6 064	5 486	1 225	539
1978	8 515	6 872	167	7 039	565	-11	6 463	1 098	954	6 802	6 091	1 252	568
1979	9 666	7 746	206	7 952	667	-9	7 275	1 290	1 101	7 549	6 751	1 281	593
1980	10 929	8 561	179	8 740	740	-3	7 996	1 623	1 310	8 346	7 483	1 309	598
1981	12 415	9 637	128	9 765	893	-15	8 857	2 062	1 497	9 316	8 255	1 333	613
1982	13 559	10 281	115	10 396	972	-17	9 407	2 506	1 647	9 942	8 789	1 364	621
1983	14 594	10 921	126	11 046	1 035	-13	9 998	2 797	1 800	10 467	9 476	1 394	633
1984	16 030	12 030	145	12 176	1 165	-6	11 005	3 102	1 923	11 315	10 286	1 417	658
1985	17 376	12 929	207	13 136	1 272	1	11 865	3 450	2 060	12 080	10 958	1 438	678
1986	17 993	13 270	193	13 463	1 333	9	12 139	3 637	2 217	12 301	11 212	1 463	684
1987	18 769	13 784	240	14 024	1 376	24	12 671	3 753	2 345	12 695	11 443	1 479	703
1988	19 816	14 537	320	14 857	1 514	35	13 378	3 926	2 512	13 296	11 995	1 490	739
1989	21 173	15 319	381	15 700	1 614	43	14 129	4 246	2 797	14 078	12 637	1 504	754
1990	22 708	16 407	416	16 822	1 737	51	15 136	4 525	3 046	14 924	13 413	1 522	767
1991	24 302	17 549	402	17 951	1 887	64	16 128	4 783	3 391	15 625	14 088	1 555	790
1992	25 963	18 776	484	19 260	2 006	81	17 335	4 848	3 781	16 273	14 687	1 595	803
1993	27 753	20 215	533	20 748	2 167	99	18 680	4 977	4 096	16 959	15 254	1 636	831
1994	29 662	21 511	463	21 974	2 357	117	19 734	5 506	4 421	17 631	15 831	1 682	863
1995	31 701	22 924	397	23 321	2 524	130	20 926	5 925	4 849	18 426	16 566	1 720	905
1996	33 345	23 626	413	24 039	2 597	150	21 592	6 472	5 282	19 029	17 034	1 752	915
1997	34 961	24 728	559	25 287	2 722	173	22 739	6 804	5 418	19 698	17 529	1 775	929
1998	37 046	26 134	614	26 748	2 852	196	24 091	7 261	5 694	20 656	18 382	1 793	945
1999	38 046	26 974	726	27 700	2 967	224	24 957	7 061	6 028	21 042	18 681	1 808	951
2000	40 318	28 692	504	29 196	3 115	250	26 332	7 545	6 441	22 134	19 577	1 822	973
2001	44 083	31 240	702	31 942	3 339	251	28 854	8 032	7 198	24 101	21 504	1 829	978
2002	45 801	32 739	535	33 275	3 521	262	30 016	7 898	7 887	24 730	22 358	1 852	989
2003	47 807	34 445	638	35 082	3 700	267	31 649	7 771	8 387	25 502	23 234	1 875	1 005

OKLAHOMA

1969	8 111	6 305	272	6 576	402	63	6 237	1 018	855	3 200	2 818	2 535	1 107
1970	8 919	6 802	355	7 157	431	65	6 791	1 147	981	3 475	3 098	2 566	1 120
1971	9 729	7 391	332	7 723	484	64	7 303	1 295	1 130	3 716	3 356	2 618	1 132
1972	10 675	8 155	413	8 568	558	73	8 084	1 351	1 240	4 017	3 574	2 657	1 183
1973	12 172	9 095	729	9 825	720	83	9 188	1 578	1 406	4 518	4 058	2 694	1 221
1974	13 600	10 387	446	10 832	846	107	10 094	1 842	1 663	4 977	4 400	2 732	1 256
1975	15 237	11 530	399	11 928	928	142	11 142	2 043	2 052	5 497	4 936	2 772	1 269
1976	16 879	12 960	333	13 293	1 054	177	12 416	2 217	2 245	5 978	5 339	2 823	1 305
1977	18 853	14 807	178	14 985	1 198	153	13 940	2 525	2 388	6 578	5 841	2 866	1 359
1978	21 405	17 011	167	17 178	1 417	149	15 911	2 923	2 571	7 348	6 456	2 913	1 428
1979	24 956	19 487	628	20 115	1 687	164	18 592	3 413	2 952	8 403	7 364	2 970	1 483
1980	28 906	22 648	257	22 905	1 964	171	21 113	4 383	3 410	9 506	8 279	3 041	1 551
1981	33 952	26 334	324	26 657	2 443	196	24 411	5 667	3 874	10 966	9 414	3 096	1 630
1982	37 938	28 875	483	29 358	2 741	201	26 817	6 753	4 368	11 833	10 086	3 206	1 678
1983	38 747	28 987	208	29 196	2 738	239	26 697	7 257	4 794	11 776	10 372	3 290	1 642
1984	41 833	31 099	368	31 467	2 968	288	28 787	8 072	4 974	12 732	11 328	3 286	1 672
1985	43 614	32 036	375	32 411	3 108	330	29 632	8 668	5 314	13 332	11 874	3 271	1 656
1986	43 291	31 358	638	31 996	3 118	378	29 256	8 388	5 647	13 309	12 100	3 253	1 595
1987	43 171	31 321	558	31 880	3 135	425	29 169	8 126	5 875	13 448	12 062	3 210	1 607
1988	45 023	32 621	760	33 381	3 457	473	30 397	8 414	6 212	14 216	12 753	3 167	1 617
1989	48 111	34 557	792	35 349	3 696	497	32 151	9 342	6 618	15 272	13 632	3 150	1 632
1990	50 971	36 644	847	37 490	3 966	560	34 084	9 765	7 121	16 187	14 280	3 149	1 664
1991	52 565	38 020	610	38 630	4 241	590	34 978	9 845	7 742	16 554	14 749	3 175	1 678
1992	55 958	40 450	815	41 266	4 469	610	37 406	9 876	8 676	17 376	15 553	3 221	1 690
1993	57 937	42 261	865	43 125	4 721	645	39 049	9 774	9 115	17 814	15 947	3 252	1 726
1994	60 283	43 590	821	44 412	4 979	701	40 133	10 474	9 676	18 374	16 410	3 281	1 759
1995	62 395	45 122	275	45 397	5 194	739	40 942	11 142	10 311	18 861	16 826	3 308	1 810
1996	65 944	47 523	373	47 896	5 379	767	43 284	11 886	10 773	19 743	17 523	3 340	1 861
1997	69 720	50 339	680	51 018	5 605	840	46 253	12 369	11 098	20 671	18 213	3 373	1 908
1998	74 118	53 674	572	54 246	5 882	874	49 238	13 431	11 448	21 766	19 161	3 405	1 957
1999	77 565	56 264	872	57 136	6 050	925	52 011	13 537	12 017	22 567	19 887	3 437	1 975
2000	84 310	60 883	715	61 598	6 355	1 008	56 251	15 290	12 770	24 410	21 519	3 454	2 015
2001	90 198	65 696	634	66 330	6 796	1 007	60 541	15 527	14 130	26 015	23 007	3 467	2 024
2002	90 077	65 318	746	66 064	7 034	1 027	60 057	14 887	15 134	25 812	23 168	3 490	2 005
2003	93 290	67 937	1 170	69 107	7 287	1 054	62 874	14 631	15 785	26 567	24 042	3 512	1 980

Table 21-2. Personal Income and Employment by Region and State—Continued

(Millions of dollars, except as noted.)

Year	Personal income, total	Earnings by place of work			Less: Contributions for government social insurance	Plus: Adjustment for residence	Equals: Net earnings by place of residence	Plus: Dividends, interest, and rent	Plus: Personal current transfer receipts	Per capita (dollars)		Population (thousands)	Total employment (thousands)
		Nonfarm	Farm	Total						Personal income	Disposable personal income		

TEXAS

1969	37 122	31 086	917	32 003	2 013	-86	29 905	4 575	2 642	3 361	2 941	11 045	5 005
1970	40 820	33 530	1 159	34 689	2 150	-97	32 443	5 240	3 137	3 633	3 221	11 237	5 045
1971	44 282	36 357	1 008	37 365	2 400	-102	34 864	5 754	3 664	3 847	3 451	11 510	5 123
1972	49 166	40 363	1 248	41 611	2 784	-128	38 699	6 354	4 114	4 181	3 709	11 759	5 334
1973	56 072	45 501	2 136	47 636	3 610	-155	43 871	7 254	4 947	4 665	4 150	12 019	5 608
1974	63 498	52 244	1 143	53 387	4 251	-132	49 004	8 593	5 901	5 176	4 562	12 268	5 822
1975	72 230	58 934	1 302	60 236	4 722	-130	55 384	9 469	7 377	5 747	5 131	12 568	5 938
1976	81 994	68 068	1 282	69 351	5 514	-94	63 743	10 205	8 047	6 355	5 638	12 903	6 207
1977	91 735	77 063	1 269	78 332	6 290	-308	71 734	11 442	8 560	6 954	6 118	13 192	6 521
1978	106 096	89 904	1 015	90 918	7 495	-428	82 995	13 562	9 539	7 860	6 925	13 498	6 898
1979	122 776	103 506	1 727	105 234	9 039	-434	95 760	16 133	10 883	8 841	7 696	13 887	7 222
1980	141 659	118 911	598	119 509	10 479	-544	108 486	20 452	12 721	9 880	8 563	14 338	7 511
1981	167 287	138 253	1 954	140 207	13 099	-356	126 753	26 073	14 460	11 344	9 736	14 746	7 925
1982	183 782	149 693	1 344	151 037	14 494	-427	136 116	31 201	16 466	11 987	10 406	15 331	8 098
1983	194 872	156 409	1 728	158 137	15 029	-410	142 699	33 576	18 598	12 372	10 940	15 752	8 088
1984	215 633	172 540	1 609	174 149	16 884	-471	156 795	39 062	19 777	13 471	11 989	16 007	8 469
1985	232 242	184 943	1 482	186 424	18 291	-499	167 635	43 472	21 135	14 272	12 708	16 273	8 721
1986	235 416	185 811	1 256	187 067	18 535	-459	168 072	44 177	23 167	14 215	12 784	16 561	8 560
1987	240 661	189 243	2 070	191 313	18 606	-457	172 250	44 052	24 360	14 479	12 975	16 622	8 773
1988	255 422	201 850	2 306	204 156	20 405	-461	183 290	46 527	25 605	15 325	13 812	16 667	8 934
1989	274 145	214 722	2 215	216 937	21 751	-471	194 715	51 286	28 144	16 312	14 626	16 807	9 064
1990	297 146	232 867	3 006	235 873	23 633	-504	211 737	53 929	31 480	17 421	15 623	17 057	9 304
1991	311 926	245 094	2 731	247 824	25 471	-585	221 768	55 152	35 005	17 929	16 165	17 398	9 465
1992	335 941	263 896	3 314	267 209	27 111	-609	239 489	55 185	41 267	18 916	17 128	17 760	9 545
1993	354 213	280 534	3 984	284 518	28 782	-633	255 104	54 972	44 137	19 503	17 633	18 162	9 844
1994	374 791	296 382	3 387	299 769	30 815	-698	268 256	59 105	47 430	20 189	18 236	18 564	10 163
1995	398 192	314 855	2 758	317 613	32 834	-790	283 990	63 236	50 966	21 003	18 928	18 959	10 507
1996	427 810	339 131	2 385	341 516	34 898	-865	305 753	67 676	54 380	22 120	19 802	19 340	10 808
1997	466 182	372 947	3 099	376 046	38 041	-1 006	337 000	72 351	56 831	23 616	20 991	19 740	11 236
1998	507 681	409 793	2 867	412 660	41 453	-1 102	370 104	78 933	58 644	25 186	22 282	20 158	11 646
1999	539 661	440 935	4 499	445 434	44 041	-1 151	400 241	78 918	60 502	26 250	23 251	20 558	11 895
2000	593 139	486 842	2 765	489 607	47 231	-1 254	441 122	87 612	64 405	28 313	24 964	20 949	12 245
2001	619 483	509 293	3 015	512 308	49 833	-1 445	461 030	87 394	71 060	29 028	25 705	21 341	12 353
2002	623 697	509 754	3 270	513 024	50 510	-1 460	461 054	84 975	77 669	28 693	25 961	21 737	12 347
2003	643 129	528 079	3 562	531 640	52 328	-1 466	477 846	83 420	81 863	29 076	26 582	22 119	12 369

ROCKY MOUNTAIN

1969	16 945	13 223	881	14 104	884	15	13 235	2 364	1 345	3 428	3 003	4 943	2 216
1970	18 959	14 580	995	15 575	965	16	14 626	2 732	1 601	3 763	3 337	5 038	2 271
1971	21 075	16 293	959	17 252	1 105	19	16 166	3 038	1 871	4 058	3 621	5 194	2 343
1972	23 910	18 534	1 260	19 794	1 323	22	18 493	3 327	2 090	4 454	3 945	5 368	2 482
1973	27 460	21 163	1 742	22 905	1 732	22	21 195	3 823	2 442	4 968	4 399	5 527	2 646
1974	31 054	23 917	1 825	25 741	2 006	25	23 760	4 457	2 838	5 497	4 842	5 650	2 740
1975	34 301	26 568	1 373	27 942	2 181	37	25 797	4 974	3 529	5 933	5 293	5 782	2 778
1976	38 235	30 309	1 016	31 325	2 515	42	28 852	5 503	3 879	6 463	5 731	5 916	2 912
1977	42 875	34 583	675	35 258	2 873	44	32 429	6 301	4 146	7 053	6 225	6 079	3 060
1978	49 768	40 290	941	41 231	3 414	54	37 872	7 330	4 536	7 949	7 005	6 257	3 257
1979	56 617	46 043	731	46 773	4 095	54	42 733	8 734	5 150	8 793	7 695	6 439	3 406
1980	64 677	51 329	946	52 275	4 581	78	47 772	10 865	6 040	9 811	8 603	6 592	3 482
1981	73 822	57 702	1 039	58 740	5 544	49	53 245	13 518	7 059	10 949	9 552	6 743	3 571
1982	79 932	61 325	814	62 138	6 011	51	56 179	15 721	8 032	11 578	10 131	6 904	3 608
1983	85 115	64 682	1 132	65 814	6 402	53	59 465	16 820	8 830	12 099	10 771	7 035	3 654
1984	92 828	70 926	1 028	71 953	7 181	72	64 845	18 766	9 217	13 058	11 680	7 109	3 817
1985	97 850	74 902	831	75 733	7 736	90	68 087	19 988	9 775	13 651	12 184	7 168	3 882
1986	100 722	76 478	1 226	77 704	8 060	112	69 756	20 475	10 491	13 989	12 528	7 200	3 876
1987	104 000	78 751	1 569	80 320	8 246	137	72 212	20 659	11 129	14 433	12 871	7 206	3 908
1988	109 048	83 306	1 618	84 924	9 098	174	76 000	21 332	11 717	15 140	13 505	7 203	4 047
1989	118 433	88 587	2 194	90 781	9 785	209	81 205	24 296	12 932	16 372	14 524	7 234	4 142
1990	127 012	95 147	2 682	97 829	10 634	245	87 439	25 594	13 979	17 387	15 368	7 305	4 260
1991	134 339	101 315	2 427	103 742	11 630	275	92 386	26 574	15 379	17 967	15 926	7 477	4 364
1992	144 661	110 240	2 489	112 730	12 591	306	100 445	27 139	17 077	18 796	16 640	7 696	4 464
1993	156 042	119 490	3 211	122 701	13 759	338	109 281	28 341	18 420	19 656	17 367	7 939	4 657
1994	166 759	128 150	2 035	130 184	14 930	389	115 643	31 818	19 299	20 408	17 969	8 171	4 919
1995	179 084	136 956	1 965	138 920	15 894	453	123 479	34 611	20 994	21 371	18 790	8 380	5 080
1996	192 538	146 540	2 182	148 723	16 746	525	132 502	37 720	22 316	22 478	19 636	8 565	5 284
1997	206 054	157 536	2 191	159 727	17 842	595	142 480	40 740	22 835	23 560	20 448	8 746	5 475
1998	223 844	171 306	2 411	173 716	18 724	689	155 681	44 601	23 562	25 100	21 698	8 918	5 663
1999	239 693	186 425	2 798	189 223	20 083	791	169 932	44 939	24 822	26 356	22 713	9 094	5 815
2000	264 024	206 838	1 994	208 831	21 824	857	187 864	49 481	26 680	28 491	24 437	9 267	6 013
2001	279 475	218 533	2 546	221 079	22 884	918	199 114	51 087	29 274	29 639	25 686	9 429	6 054
2002	283 224	222 136	1 865	224 001	23 133	917	201 784	49 727	31 714	29 588	26 254	9 572	6 043
2003	291 133	229 436	2 396	231 831	23 680	958	209 110	48 909	33 114	30 053	26 944	9 687	6 061

Table 21-2. Personal Income and Employment by Region and State—Continued

(Millions of dollars, except as noted.)

Year	Personal income, total	Derivation of personal income								Per capita (dollars)		Population (thousands)	Total employment (thousands)
		Earnings by place of work			Less: Contributions for government social insurance	Plus: Adjustment for residence	Equals: Net earnings by place of residence	Plus: Dividends, interest, and rent	Plus: Personal current transfer receipts	Personal income	Disposable personal income		
		Nonfarm	Farm	Total									

COLORADO

1969	7 967	6 340	249	6 589	388	2	6 204	1 158	605	3 678	3 191	2 166	1 001
1970	9 003	7 073	287	7 361	427	2	6 935	1 337	730	4 048	3 558	2 224	1 032
1971	10 164	8 031	300	8 331	499	3	7 835	1 478	850	4 412	3 902	2 304	1 072
1972	11 509	9 226	331	9 557	606	4	8 956	1 611	943	4 786	4 174	2 405	1 149
1973	13 217	10 612	438	11 051	797	3	10 256	1 853	1 108	5 296	4 640	2 496	1 243
1974	14 861	11 793	533	12 326	905	4	11 426	2 152	1 284	5 848	5 101	2 541	1 276
1975	16 379	12 907	462	13 369	966	8	12 411	2 357	1 611	6 333	5 602	2 586	1 285
1976	18 137	14 577	334	14 911	1 104	9	13 816	2 562	1 759	6 890	6 066	2 632	1 340
1977	20 343	16 562	263	16 825	1 260	12	15 578	2 900	1 865	7 546	6 598	2 696	1 411
1978	23 488	19 364	205	19 569	1 505	20	18 085	3 373	2 031	8 490	7 400	2 767	1 505
1979	27 101	22 430	213	22 643	1 837	20	20 827	3 992	2 282	9 512	8 242	2 849	1 594
1980	31 259	25 394	285	25 679	2 101	28	23 606	5 007	2 646	10 746	9 320	2 909	1 654
1981	36 126	29 007	302	29 309	2 592	6	26 723	6 295	3 108	12 131	10 462	2 978	1 722
1982	39 663	31 705	181	31 886	2 901	3	28 988	7 153	3 523	12 955	11 156	3 062	1 765
1983	42 631	33 698	356	34 055	3 128	0	30 926	7 807	3 898	13 604	12 016	3 134	1 794
1984	46 846	37 094	421	37 516	3 537	8	33 986	8 752	4 108	14 778	13 111	3 170	1 892
1985	49 537	39 247	391	39 639	3 833	17	35 823	9 414	4 300	15 438	13 661	3 209	1 926
1986	51 108	40 374	393	40 768	4 039	23	36 751	9 742	4 614	15 786	14 010	3 237	1 925
1987	53 063	41 724	475	42 199	4 136	35	38 098	9 992	4 974	16 275	14 392	3 260	1 915
1988	55 884	44 002	576	44 578	4 510	50	40 119	10 531	5 234	17 130	15 185	3 262	1 981
1989	60 652	46 648	615	47 263	4 834	66	42 495	12 314	5 844	18 515	16 307	3 276	2 017
1990	64 748	49 807	912	50 719	5 235	91	45 576	12 915	6 256	19 575	17 201	3 308	2 054
1991	68 283	52 974	630	53 604	5 731	103	47 976	13 357	6 950	20 160	17 740	3 387	2 101
1992	73 794	57 765	669	58 434	6 212	117	52 339	13 665	7 791	21 109	18 569	3 496	2 149
1993	79 697	62 827	812	63 639	6 819	130	56 949	14 405	8 344	22 054	19 345	3 614	2 249
1994	85 671	67 176	566	67 742	7 376	147	60 513	16 341	8 817	23 004	20 120	3 724	2 362
1995	92 704	72 272	535	72 807	7 887	169	65 088	17 858	9 758	24 226	21 175	3 827	2 441
1996	100 233	78 009	671	78 680	8 425	187	70 442	19 492	10 299	25 570	22 174	3 920	2 537
1997	107 873	84 641	685	85 326	9 109	207	76 424	21 010	10 439	26 846	23 068	4 018	2 647
1998	118 493	93 252	787	94 039	9 537	233	84 736	23 100	10 657	28 784	24 565	4 117	2 751
1999	128 860	103 383	934	104 318	10 435	262	94 145	23 323	11 392	30 492	25 948	4 226	2 840
2000	144 394	117 038	567	117 605	11 567	290	106 328	25 955	12 111	33 371	28 236	4 327	2 950
2001	152 713	123 450	764	124 213	12 146	334	112 401	27 015	13 296	34 482	29 577	4 429	2 967
2002	153 593	123 919	533	124 452	12 044	339	112 747	26 300	14 546	34 124	29 982	4 501	2 937
2003	157 043	127 208	730	127 937	12 223	358	116 072	25 835	15 135	34 510	30 694	4 551	2 923

IDAHO

1969	2 290	1 675	250	1 925	127	12	1 810	286	194	3 239	2 887	707	315
1970	2 525	1 828	264	2 092	137	14	1 969	328	229	3 520	3 165	717	324
1971	2 755	2 001	247	2 248	154	15	2 108	378	269	3 730	3 354	739	332
1972	3 144	2 279	317	2 596	183	16	2 429	409	306	4 119	3 727	763	347
1973	3 658	2 588	450	3 038	240	18	2 816	491	351	4 677	4 200	782	365
1974	4 316	2 963	625	3 588	282	22	3 328	567	421	5 341	4 758	808	381
1975	4 626	3 367	383	3 750	316	28	3 462	640	524	5 560	4 999	832	393
1976	5 218	3 917	339	4 256	370	35	3 922	705	591	6 088	5 466	857	419
1977	5 715	4 417	236	4 653	418	35	4 271	818	627	6 469	5 793	883	435
1978	6 595	5 124	304	5 427	487	42	4 982	944	669	7 240	6 465	911	460
1979	7 264	5 665	227	5 892	567	48	5 372	1 110	781	7 789	6 942	933	470
1980	8 198	6 040	402	6 442	605	61	5 899	1 365	934	8 648	7 719	948	466
1981	9 032	6 497	423	6 920	702	53	6 271	1 690	1 071	9 387	8 297	962	463
1982	9 368	6 479	391	6 869	718	62	6 214	1 925	1 229	9 621	8 590	974	453
1983	10 143	7 008	581	7 589	782	64	6 871	1 972	1 300	10 330	9 293	982	464
1984	10 973	7 715	496	8 211	874	77	7 414	2 212	1 346	11 074	10 002	991	474
1985	11 572	8 162	454	8 617	933	84	7 767	2 362	1 442	11 641	10 490	994	476
1986	11 833	8 305	475	8 780	961	100	7 919	2 392	1 521	11 949	10 827	990	476
1987	12 366	8 689	592	9 282	995	109	8 396	2 404	1 566	12 554	11 348	985	490
1988	13 300	9 437	670	10 106	1 127	124	9 104	2 515	1 682	13 493	12 172	986	512
1989	14 647	10 188	876	11 065	1 235	139	9 969	2 855	1 824	14 729	13 143	994	529
1990	15 918	11 099	990	12 089	1 358	152	10 884	3 067	1 968	15 724	13 988	1 012	552
1991	16 692	11 780	816	12 596	1 482	174	11 289	3 210	2 194	16 030	14 280	1 041	570
1992	18 318	13 082	858	13 940	1 613	191	12 518	3 340	2 460	17 093	15 135	1 072	590
1993	20 073	14 337	1 080	15 416	1 767	210	13 860	3 568	2 644	18 103	16 066	1 109	616
1994	21 422	15 629	761	16 390	1 951	238	14 676	3 957	2 789	18 707	16 593	1 145	651
1995	22 871	16 455	836	17 291	2 074	281	15 498	4 350	3 023	19 426	17 206	1 177	672
1996	24 360	17 184	947	18 131	2 134	326	16 323	4 718	3 319	20 248	17 898	1 203	694
1997	25 367	17 966	779	18 745	2 223	369	16 891	5 068	3 408	20 648	18 173	1 229	713
1998	27 287	19 127	959	20 086	2 337	437	18 185	5 544	3 557	21 789	19 192	1 252	740
1999	29 068	20 676	1 046	21 722	2 480	504	19 746	5 546	3 776	22 786	19 988	1 276	759
2000	31 290	22 587	867	23 453	2 676	524	21 302	5 909	4 079	24 076	20 960	1 300	788
2001	33 090	23 442	1 049	24 492	2 726	532	22 297	6 225	4 568	25 044	21 934	1 321	796
2002	33 963	24 151	1 002	25 153	2 803	536	22 885	6 125	4 953	25 287	22 813	1 343	801
2003	34 954	25 079	977	26 057	2 886	550	23 721	6 032	5 201	25 583	23 239	1 366	809

Table 21-2. Personal Income and Employment by Region and State—Continued

(Millions of dollars, except as noted.)

Year	Personal income, total	Derivation of personal income								Per capita (dollars)		Population (thousands)	Total employment (thousands)
		Earnings by place of work			Less: Contributions for government social insurance	Plus: Adjustment for residence	Equals: Net earnings by place of residence	Plus: Dividends, interest, and rent	Plus: Personal current transfer receipts	Personal income	Disposable personal income		
		Nonfarm	Farm	Total									

MONTANA

Year	Personal income	Nonfarm	Farm	Total	Contrib.	Adj.	Net earn.	Div.	Transfer	PC Pers.	PC Disp.	Pop.	Emp.
1969	2 276	1 613	239	1 853	127	-1	1 724	342	209	3 279	2 872	694	298
1970	2 518	1 736	289	2 025	137	-1	1 886	390	241	3 611	3 215	697	301
1971	2 684	1 897	249	2 145	152	-1	1 992	411	280	3 774	3 404	711	307
1972	3 116	2 133	398	2 531	179	0	2 352	454	310	4 332	3 863	719	319
1973	3 628	2 389	573	2 961	229	0	2 733	535	360	4 987	4 432	727	333
1974	3 947	2 700	462	3 162	264	1	2 899	626	423	5 354	4 743	737	344
1975	4 347	3 012	396	3 409	285	3	3 126	707	514	5 802	5 190	749	344
1976	4 696	3 447	222	3 669	326	3	3 346	781	569	6 191	5 495	759	359
1977	5 104	3 886	68	3 954	371	4	3 588	903	613	6 617	5 835	771	372
1978	5 998	4 430	299	4 729	435	3	4 297	1 027	674	7 650	6 791	784	390
1979	6 466	4 887	115	5 003	500	6	4 509	1 197	759	8 193	7 171	789	397
1980	7 144	5 204	118	5 322	537	14	4 799	1 453	892	9 058	7 955	789	394
1981	8 124	5 659	223	5 881	626	25	5 281	1 811	1 032	10 214	9 007	795	396
1982	8 566	5 811	168	5 979	656	18	5 341	2 069	1 155	10 654	9 502	804	392
1983	9 009	6 143	123	6 265	701	9	5 573	2 170	1 266	11 067	9 912	814	400
1984	9 609	6 570	42	6 611	760	6	5 857	2 401	1 351	11 706	10 528	821	410
1985	9 793	6 745	-86	6 659	792	3	5 871	2 494	1 429	11 909	10 718	822	409
1986	10 148	6 704	233	6 938	810	-2	6 126	2 496	1 525	12 470	11 331	814	404
1987	10 448	6 895	314	7 209	833	-3	6 373	2 477	1 598	12 978	11 700	805	408
1988	10 640	7 260	106	7 366	931	0	6 435	2 519	1 686	13 296	11 917	800	419
1989	11 707	7 646	413	8 059	997	-2	7 059	2 801	1 847	14 641	13 043	800	427
1990	12 361	8 097	386	8 483	1 077	-4	7 402	2 935	2 024	15 448	13 795	800	436
1991	13 213	8 693	544	9 237	1 182	-11	8 043	3 045	2 125	16 318	14 656	810	447
1992	13 928	9 376	467	9 843	1 291	-2	8 550	3 087	2 291	16 867	15 115	826	459
1993	15 012	10 094	769	10 863	1 432	1	9 432	3 112	2 467	17 770	15 939	845	473
1994	15 384	10 634	366	11 001	1 518	6	9 489	3 343	2 552	17 861	15 939	861	497
1995	16 084	10 964	322	11 286	1 534	9	9 761	3 604	2 719	18 349	16 402	877	507
1996	16 880	11 402	295	11 697	1 538	12	10 171	3 835	2 874	19 047	16 983	886	523
1997	17 688	11 814	329	12 143	1 555	14	10 602	4 174	2 912	19 877	17 660	890	529
1998	18 857	12 596	337	12 932	1 598	18	11 353	4 489	3 015	21 130	18 738	892	540
1999	19 373	13 176	391	13 567	1 651	22	11 938	4 443	2 991	21 585	19 087	898	548
2000	20 716	14 077	244	14 321	1 733	26	12 614	4 763	3 339	22 932	20 236	903	559
2001	22 281	15 288	311	15 599	1 848	32	13 783	4 894	3 604	24 594	21 808	906	566
2002	22 526	15 907	26	15 933	1 957	31	14 007	4 744	3 775	24 744	22 261	910	574
2003	23 651	16 870	226	17 095	2 052	33	15 076	4 682	3 894	25 775	23 356	918	583

UTAH

Year	Personal income	Nonfarm	Farm	Total	Contrib.	Adj.	Net earn.	Div.	Transfer	PC Pers.	PC Disp.	Pop.	Emp.
1969	3 238	2 694	73	2 766	176	2	2 593	397	248	3 093	2 734	1 047	444
1970	3 611	2 960	77	3 036	191	2	2 847	465	298	3 389	3 032	1 066	455
1971	4 023	3 280	76	3 356	218	3	3 141	530	353	3 655	3 296	1 101	467
1972	4 516	3 682	87	3 769	260	5	3 515	599	402	3 980	3 569	1 135	494
1973	5 052	4 137	129	4 266	339	8	3 936	645	472	4 323	3 873	1 169	523
1974	5 688	4 687	95	4 782	396	11	4 398	752	538	4 745	4 244	1 199	545
1975	6 392	5 211	66	5 277	433	14	4 859	860	673	5 180	4 693	1 234	553
1976	7 328	6 013	73	6 086	502	17	5 601	997	730	5 760	5 157	1 272	580
1977	8 356	6 910	63	6 972	575	22	6 419	1 151	786	6 348	5 671	1 316	613
1978	9 623	7 971	70	8 041	678	27	7 390	1 357	876	7 054	6 291	1 364	651
1979	11 035	9 048	81	9 129	810	36	8 354	1 683	998	7 792	6 923	1 416	679
1980	12 519	10 013	58	10 071	897	52	9 226	2 118	1 175	8 501	7 584	1 473	689
1981	14 206	11 235	41	11 276	1 082	54	10 247	2 582	1 377	9 374	8 325	1 515	699
1982	15 541	11 929	45	11 974	1 170	54	10 857	3 100	1 583	9 973	8 852	1 558	709
1983	16 803	12 704	36	12 739	1 268	43	11 514	3 564	1 726	10 535	9 469	1 595	721
1984	18 546	14 162	55	14 216	1 449	38	12 805	3 961	1 779	11 431	10 325	1 622	764
1985	19 794	15 128	55	15 183	1 579	40	13 644	4 217	1 932	12 048	10 849	1 643	793
1986	20 663	15 740	85	15 825	1 666	35	14 193	4 380	2 090	12 426	11 176	1 663	805
1987	21 361	16 368	129	16 497	1 729	25	14 792	4 328	2 241	12 729	11 392	1 678	835
1988	22 287	17 390	208	17 598	1 931	24	15 691	4 263	2 333	13 192	11 803	1 689	870
1989	23 891	18 574	202	18 777	2 095	22	16 703	4 613	2 575	14 005	12 546	1 706	903
1990	25 817	20 227	246	20 473	2 293	17	18 197	4 795	2 825	14 913	13 197	1 731	944
1991	27 573	21 772	228	22 000	2 518	11	19 493	4 973	3 106	15 492	13 786	1 780	967
1992	29 601	23 606	278	23 883	2 726	6	21 164	5 013	3 424	16 115	14 331	1 837	985
1993	31 810	25 462	303	25 765	2 956	7	22 817	5 244	3 750	16 756	14 857	1 898	1 032
1994	34 437	27 633	222	27 855	3 253	7	24 609	5 966	3 862	17 566	15 481	1 960	1 109
1995	37 218	30 017	170	30 187	3 545	1	26 643	6 434	4 141	18 478	16 210	2 014	1 158
1996	40 386	32 475	182	32 657	3 777	1	28 881	7 115	4 390	19 529	17 085	2 068	1 225
1997	43 667	35 231	206	35 436	4 050	1	31 387	7 681	4 599	20 600	17 977	2 120	1 277
1998	47 019	38 008	240	38 248	4 301	-5	33 943	8 258	4 818	21 708	18 937	2 166	1 317
1999	49 343	40 340	256	40 596	4 519	-1	36 076	8 188	5 078	22 393	19 488	2 203	1 349
2000	53 561	43 559	201	43 760	4 797	4	38 967	9 148	5 447	23 878	20 802	2 243	1 388
2001	56 332	45 985	275	46 260	5 032	16	41 244	9 129	5 959	24 711	21 655	2 280	1 393
2002	57 732	47 322	199	47 521	5 146	10	42 384	8 896	6 452	24 898	22 320	2 319	1 392
2003	59 327	48 835	265	49 100	5 286	21	43 835	8 722	6 770	25 230	22 802	2 351	1 403

CHAPTER 21: REGIONAL AND STATE DATA

Table 21-2. Personal Income and Employment by Region and State—Continued

(Millions of dollars, except as noted.)

Year	Personal income, total	Derivation of personal income								Per capita (dollars)		Population (thousands)	Total employment (thousands)
		Earnings by place of work			Less: Contributions for government social insurance	Plus: Adjustment for residence	Equals: Net earnings by place of residence	Plus: Dividends, interest, and rent	Plus: Personal current transfer receipts	Personal income	Disposable personal income		
		Nonfarm	Farm	Total									

WYOMING

1969	1 173	902	69	971	66	*	905	180	89	3 567	3 148	329	158
1970	1 303	983	78	1 060	72	0	989	212	103	3 904	3 466	334	159
1971	1 449	1 084	87	1 172	81	-1	1 090	240	119	4 261	3 811	340	165
1972	1 626	1 215	125	1 340	96	-3	1 242	255	129	4 689	4 240	347	172
1973	1 905	1 436	152	1 588	128	-7	1 453	299	152	5 390	4 806	353	182
1974	2 242	1 774	109	1 883	159	-14	1 711	360	172	6 151	5 388	365	194
1975	2 557	2 071	66	2 137	182	-16	1 939	411	208	6 722	5 986	380	203
1976	2 857	2 356	47	2 403	213	-23	2 167	458	232	7 224	6 383	395	214
1977	3 357	2 809	44	2 853	249	-30	2 574	529	254	8 157	7 210	412	231
1978	4 033	3 402	63	3 465	309	-39	3 118	630	286	9 361	8 254	431	250
1979	4 752	4 012	95	4 107	381	-56	3 670	752	331	10 517	9 137	452	267
1980	5 556	4 677	84	4 761	442	-77	4 243	922	392	11 718	10 216	474	280
1981	6 335	5 304	51	5 354	542	-88	4 724	1 140	471	12 883	11 159	492	290
1982	6 794	5 400	29	5 429	566	-85	4 779	1 474	541	13 417	11 831	506	288
1983	6 528	5 129	37	5 166	523	-62	4 581	1 306	640	12 791	11 409	510	275
1984	6 854	5 385	14	5 399	561	-56	4 782	1 440	633	13 576	12 208	505	277
1985	7 154	5 619	17	5 636	600	-55	4 982	1 501	672	14 317	12 871	500	278
1986	6 971	5 355	39	5 394	584	-43	4 767	1 464	740	14 064	12 754	496	265
1987	6 762	5 076	58	5 134	553	-28	4 553	1 458	751	14 177	12 801	477	260
1988	6 938	5 218	59	5 276	601	-23	4 652	1 504	782	14 918	13 463	465	265
1989	7 536	5 530	88	5 618	622	-16	4 979	1 714	842	16 440	14 729	458	267
1990	8 167	5 916	148	6 064	671	-12	5 381	1 881	906	18 002	16 149	454	272
1991	8 579	6 096	209	6 305	717	-2	5 586	1 988	1 005	18 680	16 816	459	279
1992	9 020	6 412	218	6 630	748	-7	5 874	2 034	1 112	19 346	17 430	466	282
1993	9 450	6 771	247	7 018	785	-10	6 224	2 012	1 215	19 976	17 925	473	286
1994	9 845	7 077	119	7 197	832	-9	6 356	2 211	1 278	20 498	18 364	480	299
1995	10 207	7 248	102	7 350	854	-7	6 489	2 366	1 352	21 039	18 848	485	302
1996	10 678	7 472	87	7 558	872	-2	6 685	2 559	1 434	21 875	19 159	488	306
1997	11 459	7 884	193	8 076	905	3	7 175	2 806	1 478	23 412	20 413	489	309
1998	12 189	8 323	88	8 411	952	6	7 465	3 209	1 515	24 836	21 613	491	315
1999	13 050	8 849	170	9 020	998	5	8 027	3 439	1 584	26 536	23 044	492	319
2000	14 063	9 576	115	9 692	1 051	13	8 653	3 706	1 704	28 463	24 500	494	328
2001	15 060	10 368	147	10 516	1 131	4	9 389	3 825	1 846	30 502	26 546	494	333
2002	15 410	10 836	106	10 942	1 183	1	9 761	3 661	1 988	30 892	27 466	499	338
2003	16 157	11 444	198	11 642	1 233	-4	10 405	3 638	2 114	32 235	28 991	501	342

FAR WEST

1969	117 424	95 215	2 474	97 689	6 630	-201	90 858	16 873	9 693	4 409	3 844	26 635	12 295
1970	126 801	100 771	2 433	103 204	6 899	-205	96 099	18 736	11 966	4 679	4 150	27 101	12 313
1971	135 230	106 438	2 464	108 902	7 521	-222	101 159	20 230	13 842	4 905	4 400	27 570	12 301
1972	148 290	117 467	3 108	120 575	8 736	-228	111 611	21 709	14 970	5 312	4 687	27 918	12 742
1973	164 806	130 648	4 247	134 895	11 068	-231	123 596	24 360	16 850	5 818	5 173	28 328	13 405
1974	185 296	145 021	5 388	150 410	12 611	-328	137 471	27 894	19 931	6 434	5 701	28 801	13 865
1975	206 409	160 150	4 808	164 958	13 666	-524	150 768	30 591	25 051	7 034	6 308	29 346	14 104
1976	231 301	182 055	4 812	186 867	15 736	-640	170 491	33 204	27 606	7 728	6 872	29 929	14 625
1977	257 728	204 392	4 682	209 074	17 871	-454	190 750	37 643	29 335	8 435	7 456	30 553	15 287
1978	294 707	235 270	4 753	240 023	21 055	-385	218 583	44 352	31 772	9 420	8 274	31 285	16 235
1979	336 728	267 888	5 905	273 793	25 059	-360	248 374	53 298	35 056	10 534	9 196	31 965	17 141
1980	382 747	297 087	7 361	304 449	27 313	-444	276 692	65 005	41 051	11 676	10 198	32 780	17 549
1981	428 897	326 903	5 851	332 754	32 478	-226	300 050	80 635	48 212	12 828	11 219	33 434	17 744
1982	457 237	344 431	5 928	350 359	34 820	-268	315 271	88 558	53 408	13 414	11 834	34 086	17 618
1983	493 057	371 570	5 962	377 532	38 277	-290	338 966	96 777	57 314	14 202	12 585	34 719	18 044
1984	547 683	414 770	6 608	421 378	43 906	-332	377 140	110 819	59 724	15 506	13 759	35 321	18 847
1985	591 310	449 866	6 376	456 241	48 033	-379	407 829	118 965	64 516	16 408	14 491	36 037	19 498
1986	629 862	482 039	7 279	489 318	52 540	-418	436 360	124 532	68 970	17 109	15 112	36 815	20 070
1987	674 798	522 159	8 505	530 664	57 052	-496	473 116	129 655	72 026	17 927	15 676	37 641	20 926
1988	731 443	570 428	9 031	579 459	64 283	-583	514 592	139 604	77 247	18 978	16 721	38 542	21 944
1989	793 435	610 569	8 951	619 521	69 234	-677	549 609	159 037	84 789	20 070	17 510	39 534	22 626
1990	859 336	660 218	9 468	669 686	74 869	-796	594 021	172 139	93 175	21 160	18 510	40 610	23 304
1991	887 101	679 618	8 488	688 106	78 666	-795	608 645	174 471	103 985	21 413	18 881	41 428	23 293
1992	938 010	718 181	9 322	727 503	82 509	-781	644 213	174 213	119 583	22 214	19 711	42 226	22 994
1993	962 172	734 935	10 767	745 702	84 623	-771	660 308	176 520	126 345	22 482	19 937	42 798	23 102
1994	999 736	758 458	10 047	768 505	88 214	-797	679 494	188 179	132 063	23 104	20 458	43 271	23 551
1995	1 051 231	793 565	9 699	803 264	91 451	-840	710 973	202 498	137 761	24 031	21 186	43 745	24 111
1996	1 115 366	837 819	11 205	849 024	95 077	-906	753 041	217 285	145 040	25 169	21 950	44 314	24 760
1997	1 186 310	897 418	11 612	909 031	100 854	-980	807 197	232 181	146 931	26 331	22 751	45 054	25 324
1998	1 286 611	978 248	11 199	989 447	108 453	-1 065	879 930	252 769	153 913	28 093	24 115	45 798	26 214
1999	1 371 257	1 060 709	11 848	1 072 557	116 590	-1 192	954 775	253 792	162 690	29 486	24 949	46 506	26 901
2000	1 502 717	1 173 138	10 869	1 184 007	127 447	-1 298	1 055 262	276 701	170 754	31 837	26 519	47 200	27 715
2001	1 548 032	1 198 390	9 658	1 208 048	131 482	-1 171	1 075 394	282 110	190 528	32 284	27 302	47 951	27 828
2002	1 572 137	1 218 439	10 430	1 228 869	135 093	-1 176	1 092 599	275 231	204 307	32 323	28 379	48 639	27 773
2003	1 622 409	1 270 007	11 236	1 281 243	140 133	-1 240	1 139 870	268 999	213 540	32 894	29 173	49 323	27 939

* = Less than $50,000, but the estimates for this item are included in the total.

Table 21-2. Personal Income and Employment by Region and State—Continued

(Millions of dollars, except as noted.)

Year	Personal income, total	Derivation of personal income								Per capita (dollars)		Population (thousands)	Total employment (thousands)
		Earnings by place of work			Less: Contributions for government social insurance	Plus: Adjustment for residence	Equals: Net earnings by place of residence	Plus: Dividends, interest, and rent	Plus: Personal current transfer receipts	Personal income	Disposable personal income		
		Nonfarm	Farm	Total									

ALASKA

1969	1 412	1 377	1	1 378	94	-26	1 258	100	54	4 769	4 071	296	144
1970	1 602	1 564	2	1 566	105	-47	1 414	116	72	5 263	4 573	304	149
1971	1 772	1 729	2	1 730	118	-61	1 551	130	91	5 600	4 901	316	153
1972	1 945	1 904	2	1 905	134	-76	1 695	146	103	5 956	5 141	326	158
1973	2 274	2 113	2	2 115	165	-94	1 856	171	247	6 823	5 978	333	167
1974	2 809	2 839	2	2 841	241	-210	2 391	210	209	8 148	6 964	345	189
1975	3 963	4 479	4	4 482	407	-614	3 462	264	237	10 683	9 055	371	227
1976	4 767	5 631	4	5 635	526	-885	4 224	309	233	12 125	10 279	393	243
1977	4 929	5 213	5	5 218	463	-454	4 301	350	278	12 405	10 554	397	237
1978	5 028	5 078	5	5 083	434	-326	4 324	406	299	12 501	10 819	402	237
1979	5 334	5 318	3	5 321	467	-289	4 565	477	293	13 219	11 291	404	241
1980	6 025	5 962	3	5 965	527	-329	5 109	573	343	14 866	12 947	405	244
1981	6 934	6 965	2	6 967	666	-473	5 827	701	406	16 569	14 127	418	253
1982	8 335	8 057	3	8 060	775	-565	6 720	891	724	18 538	16 050	450	278
1983	9 365	8 985	2	8 987	851	-623	7 513	1 061	791	19 174	16 869	488	298
1984	10 019	9 678	2	9 680	947	-639	8 094	1 243	682	19 503	17 375	514	310
1985	10 821	10 137	2	10 139	969	-632	8 539	1 396	886	20 321	18 184	532	318
1986	10 780	9 835	7	9 841	918	-571	8 353	1 431	996	19 807	17 938	544	311
1987	10 440	9 294	9	9 303	859	-533	7 911	1 490	1 038	19 357	17 373	539	312
1988	10 789	9 583	11	9 594	930	-556	8 108	1 564	1 117	19 907	17 972	542	318
1989	11 834	10 444	5	10 449	1 027	-618	8 804	1 793	1 237	21 628	19 231	547	330
1990	12 617	11 042	8	11 050	1 097	-654	9 299	1 950	1 369	22 804	20 147	553	341
1991	13 207	11 579	8	11 588	1 164	-700	9 724	2 020	1 463	23 161	20 666	570	349
1992	14 004	12 222	8	12 230	1 228	-734	10 268	2 109	1 627	23 786	21 320	589	353
1993	14 709	12 689	11	12 699	1 305	-753	10 641	2 253	1 814	24 538	22 023	599	361
1994	15 113	12 874	12	12 886	1 357	-771	10 759	2 499	1 855	25 050	22 402	603	366
1995	15 415	12 990	13	13 003	1 366	-778	10 859	2 624	1 932	25 504	22 822	604	367
1996	15 704	13 041	14	13 055	1 365	-793	10 897	2 728	2 079	25 805	23 003	609	371
1997	16 402	13 389	16	13 405	1 400	-783	11 222	2 928	2 252	26 759	23 765	613	377
1998	17 085	13 884	17	13 900	1 448	-834	11 619	3 015	2 451	27 560	24 401	620	383
1999	17 557	14 132	20	14 152	1 464	-832	11 856	2 970	2 730	28 100	24 932	625	384
2000	18 741	14 859	15	14 874	1 527	-887	12 461	3 191	3 090	29 863	26 422	628	395
2001	20 162	16 217	16	16 234	1 631	-937	13 665	3 248	3 250	31 868	28 314	633	402
2002	20 899	17 045	16	17 061	1 717	-993	14 350	3 202	3 347	32 580	29 413	641	410
2003	21 576	17 985	14	18 000	1 790	-1 040	15 169	3 140	3 267	33 254	30 272	649	418

CALIFORNIA

1969	89 273	71 819	1 701	73 521	4 830	-132	68 559	13 099	7 616	4 529	3 958	19 711	9 033
1970	96 313	75 965	1 705	77 670	5 020	-116	72 534	14 479	9 300	4 810	4 275	20 023	9 057
1971	102 428	80 044	1 704	81 749	5 452	-126	76 170	15 564	10 694	5 034	4 526	20 346	9 036
1972	112 265	88 387	2 170	90 557	6 337	-129	84 090	16 654	11 520	5 454	4 815	20 585	9 369
1973	124 037	97 808	2 928	100 737	7 979	-116	92 642	18 638	12 757	5 944	5 298	20 868	9 844
1974	138 721	107 848	3 645	111 493	9 020	-131	102 342	21 263	15 116	6 552	5 819	21 173	10 163
1975	153 525	117 689	3 272	120 961	9 606	-21	111 333	23 200	18 992	7 129	6 411	21 537	10 287
1976	171 635	132 990	3 478	136 468	10 984	82	125 566	25 082	20 987	7 825	6 972	21 935	10 633
1977	191 542	149 938	3 545	153 483	12 566	-70	140 847	28 417	22 278	8 570	7 589	22 350	11 119
1978	218 788	172 547	3 490	176 037	14 800	-80	161 157	33 545	24 086	9 580	8 429	22 839	11 803
1979	250 061	196 345	4 575	200 920	17 658	-57	183 205	40 390	26 465	10 753	9 406	23 255	12 462
1980	284 455	218 407	5 591	223 999	19 245	-90	204 664	49 064	30 727	11 951	10 443	23 801	12 777
1981	319 962	241 392	4 357	245 749	23 075	248	222 921	60 883	36 159	13 175	11 537	24 286	12 969
1982	341 593	255 578	4 604	260 182	24 980	253	235 455	66 508	39 630	13 763	12 136	24 820	12 899
1983	369 132	277 336	4 235	281 571	27 658	261	254 174	72 635	42 324	14 556	12 871	25 360	13 219
1984	413 355	312 504	4 913	317 417	32 083	235	285 569	83 619	44 168	15 994	14 147	25 844	13 852
1985	448 335	340 854	4 952	345 807	35 345	182	310 644	89 931	47 760	16 956	14 918	26 441	14 359
1986	478 832	366 896	5 389	372 285	38 927	123	333 481	94 051	51 300	17 668	15 548	27 102	14 787
1987	515 252	399 627	6 612	406 238	42 578	40	363 700	98 032	53 520	18 549	16 142	27 777	15 394
1988	557 867	435 774	6 967	442 741	47 865	-3	394 873	105 733	57 261	19 599	17 202	28 464	16 133
1989	601 456	463 473	6 809	470 282	51 198	-20	419 064	119 685	62 706	20 585	17 899	29 218	16 550
1990	648 263	497 550	7 230	504 780	55 042	-79	449 660	129 702	68 901	21 638	18 871	29 960	16 965
1991	662 728	507 383	6 210	513 593	57 255	-69	456 269	129 807	76 651	21 750	19 154	30 471	16 870
1992	696 670	531 743	6 799	538 541	59 325	-71	479 146	128 895	88 629	22 492	19 957	30 975	16 510
1993	707 906	538 682	7 800	546 482	60 172	-3	486 306	128 042	93 558	22 635	20 067	31 275	16 484
1994	730 529	552 103	7 583	559 686	62 187	12	497 510	135 370	97 650	23 203	20 544	31 484	16 659
1995	765 806	576 839	7 281	584 120	64 041	-3	520 075	145 317	100 414	24 161	21 263	31 697	17 059
1996	810 448	607 170	8 183	615 354	66 134	-13	549 206	155 712	105 530	25 312	22 011	32 019	17 466
1997	860 545	650 342	8 753	659 095	70 388	-110	588 597	166 048	105 900	26 490	22 793	32 486	17 787
1998	936 009	711 197	8 260	719 456	75 771	-120	643 565	181 283	111 160	28 374	24 258	32 988	18 504
1999	999 228	772 928	9 163	782 091	82 306	-183	699 602	182 484	117 142	29 828	25 087	33 499	19 024
2000	1 103 842	866 034	8 089	874 122	91 271	-351	782 500	199 052	122 290	32 466	26 718	34 000	19 626
2001	1 134 884	882 514	7 135	889 649	94 991	-361	794 297	204 062	136 525	32 864	27 493	34 533	19 712
2002	1 149 144	893 945	7 852	901 797	97 591	-313	803 893	198 841	146 410	32 831	28 651	35 002	19 666
2003	1 185 302	930 481	8 433	938 914	100 992	-281	837 642	194 091	153 570	33 403	29 458	35 484	19 737

NOTES AND DEFINITIONS

TABLE 21-1
GROSS DOMESTIC PRODUCT BY STATE AND REGION

SOURCE: U.S. DEPARTMENT OF COMMERCE, BUREAU OF ECONOMIC ANALYSIS (BEA)

The data for gross product (value added) by state and region, as of the deadline for this year's *Business Statistics*, had not been revised and updated to reflect the 2003 comprehensive revision of the National Income and Product Accounts (NIPAs). (See the Notes and Definitions to Chapter 1 for a description of the comprehensive revision.) In the absence of new data, *Business Statistics* reproduces the current-dollar values and quantity indexes from last year's edition, updated June 2003. The Notes and Definitions that follow are consistent with the June 2003 data.

Gross state product (GSP) is the sum of the value added, previously known as gross products originating (GPOs), in all industries in the state. In concept, each industry's gross product originating in the state is equal to its gross output (sales or receipts and other operating income, commodity taxes, and inventory change) in that state minus its intermediate inputs (consumption of goods and services purchased from other U.S. industries or imported) in that state, and the sum of all states would therefore equal U.S. gross domestic product (GDP). For explanation of GDP, see the Notes and Definitions to Tables 1-1 through 1-12. GSP and GPO are calculated only on an annual basis.

Definitions and notes on the data

The value of an industry's GPO is equal to the market value of its gross output (which consists of sales or receipts and other operating income, commodity taxes, and inventory change) minus the value of its intermediate inputs (which consist of energy, raw materials, semifinished goods, and services that are purchased from domestic industries or from foreign sources). In concept, this is equal to the sum of labor and property-type incomes earned in that industry in the production of GDP plus commodity (indirect business) taxes. Property-type income is the sum of corporate profits, proprietors' income, rental income of persons, net interest, capital consumption allowances, business transfer payments, and the current surplus of government enterprises less subsidies.

In practice, gross state product, like national GDP by industry, is measured using the incomes data rather than data on gross output and intermediate inputs, which are not available on a sufficiently detailed and timely basis.

Therefore, the *value* of *gross domestic product by state* is defined as the sum of labor and property-type incomes originating in each of 63 industries in that state plus indirect business taxes. Because of insufficient information, the statistical discrepancy is not allocated to individual industries or states.

The *quantity indexes* of gross state product are aggregates of the real output of each industry in the state, net of intermediate inputs, based on chained constant-dollar estimates, and expressed as index numbers, 1996 = 100. They are derived by applying national implicit deflators calculated for each industry group to the current-dollar GSP estimates for that industry group and applying the chain-type index formula used in the national accounts to aggregate the industry groups to the state total.

To the extent that a state's output is produced and sold in national markets at relatively uniform prices, or sold locally at national prices, GSP captures the differences across states that reflect the relative differences in the mix of goods and services that the states produce. However, real GSP does not capture geographic differences in the prices of goods and services produced and sold locally.

Data availability and references

The latest available (as of press time) values for GSP by state and industry are published in "Gross State Product by Industry, 1999–2001," *Survey of Current Business*, June 2003. This article contains a description of the methodology and references to other relevant materials. Further detail and historical values back to 1977 can be found on the BEA Web site <http://www.bea.gov>.

TABLE 21-2
PERSONAL INCOME AND EMPLOYMENT BY STATE AND REGION

SOURCE: U.S. DEPARTMENT OF COMMERCE, BUREAU OF ECONOMIC ANALYSIS (BEA)

This table contains annual time-series data on personal income and employment for the United States, each state, the District of Columbia, and eight geographic regions. Comprehensively revised data for 1969 through 2002 were released in April 2004 and are consistent in definitions, methodology, and data with the 2003 comprehensive revision of the NIPAs (see Chapters 1 and 4). In September 2004, the data for 2001 through 2003 were revised or newly estimated consistent with the midyear revision of the NIPAs.

The sum for the United States of state personal incomes that is shown in the table here is somewhat smaller than U.S. personal income as shown in the NIPAs in Chapters 1 and 4, because of slightly different definitions. The national total of the state estimates consists of only the income earned by persons who live in the United States and of foreign residents who work in the United States.

The measure of personal income in the NIPAs is broader. It includes the earnings of federal civilian and military personnel stationed abroad and of U.S. residents on foreign assignment for less than a year, and it includes the investment income that is received by federal retirement plans of federal workers stationed abroad. Earnings of foreign residents are included only if they live and work in the United States for a year or more. There are also statistical differences reflecting differences in the timing of the availability of source data.

Definitions

A state's *personal income* is the personal income (as defined below) of persons resident in that state, not persons working in that state. Its derivation from source data on earnings by place of work is shown in the succeeding columns of Table 21-2, and explained below.

Earnings by place of work include wage and salary disbursements, all supplements to wages and salaries (including employer contributions for government social insurance and all other benefits), and farm and nonfarm proprietors' income paid to persons working in the state.

Contributions for government social insurance, which is subtracted from total earnings, includes both the employer and the employee contributions. As it was before the 2003 revision, personal income is net of all contributions for government social insurance, though not of other taxes on wages or other income.

Adjustment for residence. Earnings by place of work are adjusted to a place-of-residence basis by BEA to account for interstate and international commuting. The difference between earnings by place of residence and earnings by place of work is shown in the "Adjustment for residence" column. This adjustment is a net figure: income received by state (or area) residents from employment outside the state, minus income paid to persons residing outside the state but working in the state. There is a negative adjustment for the United States as a whole, reflecting net payments to foreign residents working in the United States.

The effect of interstate commuting can be seen in its most extreme form by comparing the District of Columbia, with its adjustment for residence of negative $33 billion representing net payments to persons living outside D.C. in 2003, to Maryland, which received an adjustment for residence of a positive $22 billion net from employment sources outside the state in that year.

Dividends, interest, and rent are as defined in U.S. personal income, including the capital consumption adjustment for rental income of persons.

Total employment is the total number of jobs, full-time plus part-time; each job that any person holds is counted at full weight. The employment estimates are on a place-of-work basis. Both wage and salary employment and self-employment are included. The main source for the wage and salary employment estimates is Bureau of Labor Statistics estimates from unemployment insurance data (the ES-202 data), which also provides benchmarks for the payroll employment measures (see Table 10-5 and the Notes and Definitions thereto). Self-employment is estimated mainly from individual and partnership federal income tax returns.

This concept of employment differs from that in the Current Population Survey (CPS), which is derived from a monthly count of persons employed; any individual appears only once in the CPS in a given month no matter how many different jobs he or she might hold. (See the Notes and Definitions to Tables 10-1 through 10-3.) In addition, a self-employed individual who files more than one Schedule C income-tax filing will be counted more than once in the state figures. Finally, the state figures include members of the armed forces, who are not covered in the CPS. Because of these differences and other possible reporting inconsistencies, the BEA estimates are different from, and usually larger than, state employment estimates from the CPS.

The employment estimates correspond closely in coverage to the earnings estimates. However, the earnings estimates include the income of limited partnerships and of tax-exempt cooperatives, for which there are no corresponding employment estimates.

Per capita income is total income divided by the state's population. It is therefore an average or "mean," subject to the qualifications discussed in "Expanded Historical Statistics…" at the beginning of this volume, under the heading "Whose Standard of Living?" For recent data on median household income by state, which give a better idea of the income of a typical resident of the state, see Table 3-12 in Chapter 3.

The states are divided into regions by BEA as follows:

- **New England:** Connecticut, Maine, Massachusetts, New Hampshire, Rhode Island, Vermont
- **Mideast:** Delaware, District of Columbia, Maryland, New Jersey, New York, Pennsylvania
- **Great Lakes:** Illinois, Indiana, Michigan, Ohio, Wisconsin
- **Plains:** Iowa, Kansas, Minnesota, Missouri, Nebraska, North Dakota, South Dakota
- **Southeast:** Alabama, Arkansas, Florida, Georgia, Kentucky, Louisiana, Mississippi, North Carolina, South Carolina, Tennessee, Virginia, West Virginia
- **Southwest:** Arizona, New Mexico, Oklahoma, Texas
- **Rocky Mountain:** Colorado, Idaho, Montana, Utah, Wyoming
- **Far West:** Alaska, California, Hawaii, Nevada, Oregon, Washington

These BEA regional groupings differ from the region and division definitions used by the U.S. Bureau of the Census.

Data availability and references

The comprehensive revision of state personal income for the years 1969–2002 and preliminary estimates for 2003 is presented in "Comprehensive Revision of State Personal Income," *Survey of Current Business*, May 2004. Revised and updated data for 2001 through the second quarter of 2004 were presented in a press release dated September 28, 2004, and are to be described in the October 2004 issue of the *Survey of Current Business*. These articles and all current and historical data are on the BEA Internet site at <http://www.bea.gov>.

INDEX

INDEX

A
ACCESSORIES
  Definitions, 86
ACCOUNTING
  Receipts of taxable firms, 339
ACKNOWLEDGEMENTS
  Editorial staff, xiii
AFRICA
  Growth rates in real GDP, 274
AGE
  Income distribution and poverty
    poor people 16 years and over by work experience, 62
    poverty status of persons by age, 60
  Poverty
    status of persons by age, 60
    total rates for children and seniors, 54
AGGREGATE HOURS
  Definitions, 240
  Indexes of aggregate weekly hours, 311
AGGREGATE INCOME
  Shares of aggregate income received by families, 53
  Shares of aggregate income received by household, 52
AGRICULTURE
  Definitions, 204
  Prices
    farmers' prices received and paid, 198
ALABAMA
  Median income and poverty rates by state, 67
ALASKA
  Median income and poverty rates by state, 67
ALTERNATIVE DEFINITIONS OF INCOME
  Income distribution and poverty
    median income and poverty rates based on, 64
    poverty rate, 65
AMUSEMENT AND RECREATION
  Receipts of taxable firms, 339
  Revenue of tax-exempt firms, 339
APPAREL INDEX
  Definitions, 200
ARIZONA
  Median income and poverty rates by state, 67
ARKANSAS
  Median income and poverty rates by state, 67
ASIA
  Growth rates in real GDP, 274
ASIAN NEWLY INDUSTRIALIZED COUNTRIES (NICS)
  Definitions, 180
  Growth rates in real GDP, 274
ASSETS
  Commercial banks, 251
  Credit market assets held by sector, 268
  Household assets, 257
  Money stock measures, 248
  Saving and investment; business sales and inventories
    chain-type quantity indexes for net stock of fixed assets, 98
    current-cost net stock of fixed assets, 97

AUGMENTED UNEMPLOYMENT RATE
  Definitions, 236
AUTOMOTIVE REPAIR
  Receipts of taxable firms, 339
AVERAGE HOURLY EARNINGS
  Generally, 232, 309
AVERAGE WEEKLY EARNINGS
  Generally, 233, 310
AVERAGE WEEKLY HOURS
  Generally, 229, 308
  Indexes of aggregate weekly hours, 231
  Production or nonsupervisory workers by NAICS industry, 308
  Selected industries, 230

B
BALANCE ON CURRENT ACCOUNT
  Definitions, 175
BALANCE ON GOODS
  Definitions, 175
BALANCE ON INCOME
  Definitions, 175
BALANCE ON SERVICES
  Definitions, 175
BALANCE ON UNILATERAL TRANSFERS
  Definitions, 175
BANKS AND BANKING
  Aggregate reserves of depository institutions and monetary base, 250
  Commercial bank credit and selected liabilities, 251
  Consumer credit, 261
  Credit market debt outstanding, 253
  Money stock measures, 248
  Selected components of the money stock, 249
BENCHMARK ADJUSTMENTS
  Definitions, 239
BENEFITS
  Definitions, 215
BONDS
  Common stock prices and yields, 264
  Definitions, 271
  Historical data, 461
  Notes on the data, 271
  Selected interest rates and bond yields, 262
BORROWING
  Federal government, 117
  National saving, investment, and borrowing, 1946–2003, 87
  Net lending or borrowing, 106
  State and local government, 124
BRITISH THERMAL UNIT
  Defined, 246
BUILDING MATERIALS
  Inventories, 337
  Sales, 334
BUILDING PERMITS
  Construction and housing, 319
  Definitions, 32

525

Housing starts, 319
New construction put in place, 317
BUSINESS CURRENT TRANSFER PAYMENTS, NET
Definitions, 28
BUSINESS SALES AND INVENTORIES
see **SAVING AND INVESTMENT; BUSINESS SALES AND INVENTORIES**
BUSINESS SERVICES
Receipts of taxable firms, 339

C

CALIFORNIA
Median income and poverty rates by state, 67
CAMPS
Revenue of tax-exempt firms, 339
CANADA
Growth rates in real GDP, 274
Real GDP per capita, 275
CAPACITY UTILIZATION
Data availability, 47
Definitions, 47
Generally, 35, 413
Historical data, 413
Indexes by market groups, 36
Indexes by NAICS industry groups, 40
Industrial production and capacity utilization, 35, 413
NAICS industry groups, 43
Notes on the data, 46
References, 47
Revisions, 47
CAPITAL ACCOUNT TRANSACTIONS
Definitions, 106
CAPITAL CONSUMPTION
Definitions, 142
CAPITAL EXPENDITURES
Saving and investment; business sales and inventories
1996–2002, 103
companies with employees, by NAICS industry sector, 1998–2002, 104
CENTRAL AND EASTERN EUROPE
Growth rates in real GDP, 274
CHAINED-DOLLAR ESTIMATES
Definitions, 26
CHAIN-TYPE PRICE INDEXES
Foreign trade and finance, 150
Gross domestic product and domestic purchases, 9, 370
Inflation indicators, 1946–2003, 183
CHAIN-TYPE QUANTITY INDEXES
Federal government
consumption expenditures and gross investment, 118, 119
government output, 138
Foreign trade and finance, 149, 152
Government
consumption expenditures and gross investment, 118, 119, 125
government output, 138

Gross domestic product and domestic purchases, 8, 366
Personal consumption expenditures by major type of product, 79
Saving and investment; business sales and inventories
net stock of fixed assets, 98
private fixed investment by type, 95
State and local government
consumption expenditures and gross investment, 125
CHANGE IN PRIVATE INVENTORIES
Defined, 25
Gross domestic product, 4
Real gross domestic product, 5
CHECKABLE DEPOSITS
Definitions, 265
CHILDREN
Poverty rates for children, 54
CIGARETTES
Definitions, 86
CITIES
Income distribution and poverty
poverty status of persons inside and outside metropolitan areas, 61
CIVILIAN LABOR FORCE
Defined, 235
CIVILIAN NONINSTITUTIONAL POPULATION
Defined, 235
CIVILIAN POPULATION AND LABOR FORCE
Employment, hours, and earnings
general data, 220
insured unemployment, 224
unemployment rates, 222
International comparisons, 279
CLOTHING
Definitions, 86
Inventories, 337
Sales, 334
COAL
Energy supply and consumption, 244
COLORADO
Median income and poverty rates by state, 67
COMMERCIAL BANKS
Credit and selected liabilities, 251
Credit market debt outstanding, 253
Data availability, 267
Definitions, 266
Notes on the data, 266
COMMODITY GROUPS
Producer price indexes, 196
COMMONWEALTH OF INDEPENDENT STATES
Growth rates in real GDP, 274
COMPENSATION
Defined, 27
Employment cost indexes
total compensation, 208
wages and salaries, 209
Gross domestic income
defined, 23

INDEX

type of income, 17
Wages and salaries
see **WAGES AND SALARIES**

COMPOSITE INDEXES
Gross domestic product
economic activity and selected index components, 12
Historical data, 471

CONNECTICUT
Median income and poverty rates by state, 67

CONSTRUCTION AND HOUSING
Building permits, 319
Definitions, 342
Home sales and prices, 319
Housing starts, 319
New construction put in place, 317

CONSUMER CREDIT
Data availability, 271
Defined, 270
Generally, 261

CONSUMER INCOME AND SPENDING
Chain-type quantity indexes: expenditures by major type of product, 79
Data availability, 85
Definitions, 83
Disposition of personal income, 74
Personal consumption expenditures: current and constant dollars, 76
Personal consumption expenditures by major type of product, 77
Personal consumption expenditures by type of expenditure, 81
Personal income and its disposition, 74
Personal saving rate, 1946–2003, 73
References, 85
Revisions, 85
State and regional data
annual data, 489

CONSUMER PRICE INDEXES
All items, 1946–2003, 190
Data availability, 201
Definitions, 199
General data, 184
Historical data, 423
Inflation indicators, 1946–2003, 183
International comparisons, 278
References, 201
Summary consumer and producer price indexes, 423
Supplemental indexes, 201

CONSUMPTION OF FIXED CAPITAL
Definitions, 29, 106

CORPORATIONS
Gross value added of domestic corporate business, 21
Gross value added of nonfinancial domestic corporate business, 22
Profits
defined, 28
inventory valuation adjustment (NAICS basis), 214
inventory valuation adjustment (SIC basis), 212

COSTS
Employment costs, productivity, and profits, 207

CREDIT MARKET
Credit market assets held by sector, 268
Data availability, 268
Debt outstanding, 253
Definitions, 267
Notes on the data, 267
Sectors owing debt, 267

CREDITS
Definitions, 174

CRUDE OIL
Energy supply and consumption, 244

CURRENCY
Definitions, 265

CURRENT COST
Definitions, 177

CURRENT-DOLLAR
Real gross domestic product, 7

CURRENT PAYMENTS TO THE REST OF THE WORLD
Definitions, 173

CURRENT RECEIPTS FROM THE REST OF THE WORLD
Definitions, 173

CURRENT SURPLUS OF GOVERNMENT ENTERPRISES
Definitions, 141

CURRENT TAXES AND TRANSFER PAYMENTS (NET)
Definitions, 174

CURRENT TRANSFER RECEIPTS
Definitions, 141

CYCLICAL INDICATORS
National income and product and cyclical indicators, 3

D

DEBITS
Definitions, 174

DEBT
Aggregate reserves of depository institutions and monetary base, 250
Commercial bank credit and selected liabilities, 251
Consumer credit, 261
Credit market debt outstanding, 253
Federal government
debt by fiscal year, 136
Gross domestic product
debt as a percent of GDP, 1945–2003, 256
Household financial obligations, 257
Money stock measures, 248
Mortgage debt outstanding, 260
Ratio of household debt service to personal income, 1980–2003, 259

DEBT HELD BY FEDERAL RESERVE SYSTEM
Definitions, 145

DEBT HELD BY PRIVATE INVESTORS
Definitions, 145

DEBT HELD BY SOCIAL SECURITY FUNDS
  Definitions, 145
DEFENSE SPENDING
  Chain-type quantity indexes for expenditures and
      investment, 116, 119
  Defense and nondefense consumption expenditures
      by type, 115
  Government spending as a percent of GDP, 1945–2003,
      132
  National defense consumption expenditures and
      gross investment, 116
DEFINITIONS
  Accessories, 86
  Aggregate hours, 240
  Agriculture, 204
  Alternative definitions of income, 70
  Apparel index, 200
  Asian Newly Industrialized Countries, 180
  Augmented unemployment rate, 236
  Average poverty thresholds, 69
  Balance on current account, 175
  Balance on goods, 175
  Balance on income, 175
  Balance on services, 175
  Balance on unilateral transfers, 175
  Benchmark adjustments, 239
  Benefits, 215
  Bond yields, 271
  Break in series: travel and passenger fares, 179
  British thermal unit, 246
  Budget, 140
  Building permits, 32
  Business current transfer payments, net, 28
  Capacity utilization, 47
  Capital account, 175
  Capital account transactions, 106
  Capital consumption, 142
  Chained-dollar estimates, 26
  Change in private inventories, 25
  Checkable deposits, 265
  Civilian employment, 235
  Civilian labor force, 235
  Civilian noninstitutional population, 235
  Civilian workers, 216
  Clothing, 86
  Commercial banks, 266
  Compensation, 27
  Compensation of employees, received, 83
  Compensation per hour, 215
  Construction and housing, 342
  Consumer credit, 270
  Consumer income and spending, 83
  Consumer price indexes, 199
  Consumption of fixed capital, 29, 106
  Contributions for government social insurance, 84
  Contributions for social insurance, 141
  Corporate profits, 28
  Credit market, 267
  Credits, 174

  Currency, 265
  Current cost, 177
  Current payments to the rest of the world, 173
  Current receipts from the rest of the world, 173
  Current surplus of government enterprises, 141
  Current taxes and transfer payments (net), 174
  Current tax receipts, 141
  Current transfer receipts, 141
  Debits, 174
  Debt held by Federal Reserve System, 145
  Debt held by other U.S. government accounts, 145
  Debt held by private investors, 145
  Debt held by Social Security funds, 145
  Delinquency rates, 269
  Demand deposits, 265
  Direct defense expenditures, 180
  Direct investment, 177
  Disposable personal income, 84
  Dividends, 29
  Durable goods, 85
  Earnings, 69, 241
  Economic affairs, 143
  Education, 86, 143
  Education and communication, 200
  Employer contributions, 27
  Employment, hours, and earnings, 235
  Employment costs, productivity, and profits, 215
  Employment to population ratio, 235
  Energy, 246
  Euro Area, 180
  Eurodollars, 265
  European Union, 180
  Exchange rates, 283
  Exports and imports of goods and services, 173
  Extended credit, 266
  Families, 68
  Family assistance, 84
  Farmers, 204
  Federal budget, 140
  Federal government debt held by the public, 144
  Federal grants-in-aid, 142
  Final sales, 26
  Financial account, 175
  Financial obligations, 269
  Food, 86
  Food and beverage index, 200
  Foreign official assets, 176
  Foreign trade and finance, 173
  Foreign travel, 86
  GDP price indexes, 26
  General public service, 143
  Gini coefficient, 69
  Goods, 178
  Government, 141
  Government consumption expenditures, 25, 142
  Government net saving, 106
  Government social benefits, 84, 142
  Gross domestic income, 23
  Gross domestic product, 23, 301

INDEX

Gross domestic purchases, 26
Gross government investment, 25, 106, 142
Gross investment, 143
Gross national income, 23, 107
Gross national product, 23
Gross nonresidential fixed investment, 107
Gross output, 142
Gross private domestic investment, 106
Gross private fixed investment, 107
Gross public debt—total, 144
Gross saving, 106
Household assets, 269
Household operation, 86
Households, 68
Housing, 86
Housing and community services, 143
Housing index, 200
Housing starts, 344
Imputation, 24
Income, 69
Income distribution and poverty
   generally, 68
   income and poverty rates based on alternative definitions of income, 64
Income receipts and payments, 174
Income receipts on assets, 141
Income security, 143
Index of coincident economic indicators, 32
Index of consumer expectations, 32
Index of lagging economic indicators, 32
Index of leading economic indicators, 31
Industrial production index, 46
Industry groups, 46
Initial claims, 32
Interest, 141
Interest payments, 142
Interest rates, 271
Interest rate spread, 32
Interest receipts, 141
Intermediate goods and services purchased, 142
International comparisons, 282
International transactions, 174
Inventories to sales ratios, 107
Inventory valuation adjustment, 29
Jewelry, 86
Key sector statistics, 342
Labor force participation rate, 235
Large time deposits, 265
Liabilities, 269
License fees, 179
Local government, 141
Long-term unemployed, 235
Manufacturers' new orders, 32
Manufacturing, 345
Market groups, 46
Market value, 177
Mean income, 69
Median and average weeks unemployed, 235
Median income, 68

Medical care, 86
Medical care index, 200
Merchants, 348
Money supply, 32
Mortgages, 270
NAICS
   employment, hours, and earnings, 313
   industry definitions: with rough derivation from SIC, 289
National income, 24
Net exports of goods and services, 25
Net interest, 27
Net lending or borrowing, 106, 140, 173
Net national product, 24
Net operating surplus, 27
Net saving, 142
Net worth, 269
Nondurable goods, 85
Nonresidential equipment and software, 25, 107
Nonresidential fixed investment, 25
Nonresidential structures, 107
Notes and definitions, xvi
On-budget and off-budget, 144
Organization of Petroleum Exporting Countries, 180
Outlays, 144
Outlays by function, 144
Output, 142
Output per hour of all persons, 216
Overtime hours, 240
Passenger fares, 179
Personal business, 86
Personal care, 86
Personal consumption expenditures, 24, 85
Personal current taxes, 84, 141
Personal current transfer receipts, 84
Personal dividend income, 84
Personal income, 83
Personal income receipts on assets, 84
Personal interest income, 84
Personal outlays, 84
Personal saving, 84, 106
Petroleum and petroleum products, 342
Poverty, 69
Poverty population, 69
Poverty thresholds, 69
Preface to the book, xv
Prices, 200
Private capital consumption adjustment, 29
Private capital consumption allowances, 29
Private fixed investment, 25
Private remittances and other transfers, 175
Private transportation index, 200
Producer price indexes, 202
Product and income by industry, 301
Production, 46
Production or nonsupervisory workers, 239
Productivity, 216
Profits after tax, 29
Proprietors' income with inventory valuation, 28, 83

Public order and safety, 143
Quintiles, 69
Racial classifications, 68
Real gross private investment, 107
Real or chained dollar estimates, 26
Receipts, 144
Recreation, 86, 200
Regional data, 519
Religious activities, 86
Rental income of persons, 28, 83
Rents, 141
Repayments on U.S. credits, 176
Repurchase agreements, 265
Required reserves, 266
Research, 86
Residential private fixed investment, 25, 107
Retail trade, 347
Royalties, 141, 179
Saving and investment; business sales and inventories, 106
Savings deposits, 265
Seasonal adjustment, 239
Selected annual data, 356
Services, 85, 178
Small time deposits, 265
Software, 25
Sources of financing, 144
State and regional data, 519
State government, 141
Stock prices, 32
Stocks and bonds, 271
Subsidies, 27, 142
Supplements to wages and salaries, 27
Taxes on corporate income, 29, 141
Taxes on production and imports, 27, 141
Tobacco, 86
Total compensation, 215
Total consumption expenditures, 143
Total reserves, 266
Total surplus, 144
Transportation, 86
Travel, 179
U.S. bank claims, 177
U.S. government grants, 175
U.S. nonbank claims, 177
U.S. official reserve assets, 177
Undistributed offsetting receipts, 144
Undistributed profits, 29, 106
Unemployed persons, 235
Unemployment rate, 236
Unrelated individuals, 68
Value added, 142
Vendor performance, 32
Wage and salary accruals, 27
Wage and salary disbursements, 83
Welfare activities, 86
Wholesale trade, 348
Work experience, 69

DELAWARE
  Median income and poverty rates by state, 67
DELINQUENCY RATES
  Definitions, 269
  Household assets, financial obligations, and delinquency rates, 257
DEMAND DEPOSITS
  Definitions, 265
DEPARTMENT STORES
  Inventories, 337
  Sales, 334
DEPOSITORY INSTITUTIONS
  Aggregate reserves, 250
DIRECT INVESTMENT
  Definitions, 177
DISTRICT OF COLUMBIA
  Median income and poverty rates by state, 67
DIVIDENDS
  Defined, 29
DOLLAR
  Value of the U.S. dollar, 1973–2003, 281
DURABLE GOODS
  Definitions, 85
  New orders for durable goods, 315
  Unfilled orders, 330

E
EARNINGS
  Wages and salaries
    see **WAGES AND SALARIES**
E-COMMERCE
  Service industries, 341
ECONOMIC AFFAIRS
  Definitions, 143
ECONOMIC GROWTH AND CHANGE
  Historical data, 471
EDITORIAL STAFF
  Acknowledgements, xiii
EDUCATION
  Definitions, 86, 143, 200
ELECTRONICS AND APPLIANCES
  Inventories, 337
  Sales, 334
EMPLOYMENT, HOURS, AND EARNINGS
  Average hourly earnings, 232, 309
  Average weekly earnings, 233, 310
  Average weekly hours, 229, 308
  Civilian employment and unemployment, 221, 222
  Civilian population and labor force, 220
  Civilian unemployment rates, 222
  Data availability, 237
  Definitions, 235
  Establishment
    defined, 238
  Federal government, 137, 139
  Generally, 219
  Government, 137, 139
  Historical data, 433, 443

Indexes of aggregate weekly hours, 231
Insured unemployment, 224
Labor force participation rate, 1948–2003, 219
NAICS
    average hourly earnings of production or nonsupervisory workers, 309
    average weekly earnings of production or nonsupervisory workers, 310
    average weekly hours of production, 308
    definitions, 313
    indexes of aggregate weekly hours, 311
    indexes of aggregate weekly payrolls, 312
    nonfarm employment by NAICS sector and industry, 304
    production or nonsupervisory workers on private payrolls, 307
Net new nonfarm payroll jobs by NAICS industry group, 1990–2003, 303
Nonfarm payroll employment, 226, 443
Nonsupervisory workers on private nonfarm payrolls, 228
Notes on data, 236
Production workers on private nonfarm payrolls, 228
References, 237
State and local government, 137, 139
State and regional data
    annual data, 489
Total nonfarm payroll employment, 1946–2003, 225
Unemployment rates
    data, 1948–2003, 219
    general data, 221, 222

EMPLOYMENT COST INDEXES
Data availability, 216
Measuring changes, 215
Notes on the data, 216
References, 216
Total compensation, 208
Wages and salaries, 209

EMPLOYMENT COSTS, PRODUCTIVITY, AND PROFITS
Change in labor productivity, nonfarm business, 1948–2003, 207
Definitions, 215
Employment Cost Index, 215
Generally, 207
Productivity
    related data, 210

ENERGY
Consumption and prices, 1949–2003, 243
Consumption per dollar of real gross domestic product, 245
Definitions, 246
Generally, 243
Notes on the data, 246
References, 246
Supply and consumption, 244

ENGINEERING
Receipts of taxable firms, 339

EURO AREA
Definitions, 180
Growth rates in real GDP, 274

EURODOLLARS
Definitions, 265

EUROPEAN UNION
Definitions, 180
Growth rates in real GDP, 274

EXCHANGE RATES
Definitions, 283
International comparisons, 280
Value of the U.S. dollar, 1973–2003, 281

EXPENDITURES
Consumer income and spending
        see **CONSUMER INCOME AND SPENDING**
Receipts and expenditures
        see **RECEIPTS AND EXPENDITURES**

EXPERIMENTAL POVERTY MEASURES
Generally, 71

EXPORT PRICE INDEXES
Data availability, 181
U.S. foreign trade and finance, 172

EXPORTS
U.S. foreign trade and finance
        see **FOREIGN TRADE AND FINANCE**

EXTENDED CREDIT
Definitions, 266

F

FAMILIES
Income distribution and poverty
    definitions, 68
    median family income, 49, 51
    poverty status by type of family, 56
    poverty thresholds by family size, 55
    shares of aggregate income received, 53
Poverty
    average poverty thresholds by family size, 55
    status by type of family, 56

FARMERS
Definitions, 204
Prices
    prices received and paid by farmers, 198

FEDERAL GOVERNMENT
Borrowing, 117
Chain-type quantity indexes
    consumption expenditures and gross investment, 118, 119
    government output, 138
Current receipts and expenditures, 112, 382
Current tax receipts, 141
Defense and nondefense consumption expenditures by type, 115

Defense spending as a percent of GDP, 1945–2003, 132
Definitions, 141
Employment, 137, 139
Historical data
  current receipts and expenditures, 112, 382
Investment
  net investment, 117
Lending, 117
National defense
  consumption expenditures and gross investment, 116, 119
Net investment, 117
Outlays
  receipts and outlays by fiscal year, 133
Output, 117
Receipts and expenditures
  consumption expenditures and gross investment, 114
  current receipts and expenditures, 112, 382
  data availability, 143
  debt by fiscal year, 136
  defense and nondefense consumption expenditures by type, 115
  national defense consumption expenditures and gross investment, 116
  receipts and outlays by fiscal year, 133
  references, 143
Saving and dis-saving, 1946–2003, 111
Transactions in the national income and product accounts, 148

FEDERAL GOVERNMENT DEBT HELD BY THE PUBLIC
Definitions, 144

FEDERAL GRANTS-IN-AID
Definitions, 142

FEDERAL RESERVE
Debt held by Federal Reserve System defined, 145

FINAL SALES
Definitions, 26
Gross domestic product, 10

FINANCIAL MARKETS
Common stock prices and yields, 264
Credit market debt outstanding, 253
Data availability, 176
Federal funds rate, 1962–2003, 247
Money stock measures, 248
Mortgage debt outstanding, 260
Selected components of the money stock, 249
Selected interest rates and bond yields, 262
Treasury securities rate, 1962–2003, 247

FISCAL YEAR
Federal government
  debt by fiscal year, 136

FIXED ASSETS
Saving and investment; business sales and inventories
  chain-type quantity indexes for net stock, 98
  current-cost net stock, 97

FIXED INVESTMENT
Gross domestic product, 4

Real gross domestic product, 5

FLORIDA
Median income and poverty rates by state, 67

FOOD AND BEVERAGE INDEX
Definitions, 200

FOOD AND FOOD PRODUCTS
Definitions, 86
Inventories, 337
Sales, 334

FOOD SERVICES SALES
Inventories, 337
Retail and food services sales, 334

FOREIGN OFFICIAL ASSETS
Definitions, 176

FOREIGN TRADE AND FINANCE
Balance, receipts, and payments on current account, 1946–2003, 147
Balance on current account and financial inflows and outflows, 1960–2003, 153
Chain-type price indexes for exports and imports, 150
Chain-type quantity indexes for exports and imports, 149, 152
Data availability, 176
Definitions, 173
Export and import price indexes, 172
Exports and imports of selected NIPA types of product, 151, 152
Goods
  U.S. exports and imports of goods and services, 162
  U.S. exports and imports of goods by principal end-use category, 165
  U.S. exports of goods by end-use and advanced technology categories 163
  U.S. exports of goods by selected regions and countries, 166
  U.S. imports of goods by end-use and advanced technology categories, 164
  U.S. imports of goods by selected regions and countries, 168
Gross domestic product, 4
Historical data
  U.S. international transactions, 154, 398
International investment position of the U.S. at year-end, 160
Notes on the data, 175
Real gross domestic product, 5
Receipts, payments, and balance on current account, 1946–2003, 147
References, 176
Trade balances on goods and services, 1960–2003, 161
Transactions in the national income and product accounts, 148
U.S. export and import price indexes, 172
U.S. exports and imports of goods and services, 162
U.S. exports and imports of goods by principal end-use category, 165
U.S. exports of goods by end-use and advanced technology categories, 163

U.S. exports of goods by selected regions and
    countries, 166
U.S. exports of services, 162, 170
U.S. imports of goods by end-use and advanced
    technology categories, 164
U.S. imports of goods by selected regions and
    countries, 168
U.S. imports of services, 162, 171
U.S. international transactions, 154, 398

FOREIGN TRAVEL
Definitions, 86

FRANCE
Growth rates in real GDP, 274
Real GDP per capita, 275

FURNITURE AND HOME FURNISHINGS
Inventories, 337
Sales, 334

G

GASOLINE
Inventories, 337
Sales, 334

GENERAL MERCHANDISE
Inventories, 337
Sales, 334

GENERAL PUBLIC SERVICE
Definitions, 143

GEORGIA
Median income and poverty rates by state, 67

GEOTHERMAL ENERGY
Energy supply and consumption, 244

GERMANY
Growth rates in real GDP, 274
Real GDP per capita, 275

GINI COEFFICIENT
Definitions, 69

GOODS
Chain-type quantity indexes for exports and imports
    of goods, 149
Definitions, 85, 178
Foreign trade and finance
    U.S. exports and imports of goods and services, 162
    U.S. exports and imports of goods by principal
        end-use category, 165
    U.S. exports of goods by end-use and advanced
        technology categories, 163
    U.S. exports of goods by selected regions and
        countries, 166
    U.S. imports of goods by end-use and advanced
        technology categories, 164
    U.S. imports of goods by selected regions and
        countries, 168
Foreign trade balances on goods, 1960–2003, 161

GOVERNMENT
Chain-type quantity indexes
    consumption expenditures and gross investment,
        118, 119, 125
    government output, 138
Consumption expenditures, 114, 123
Current tax receipts, 141
Definitions, 141
Employment, 137, 139
Federal government
    current receipts and expenditures, 112
    debt by fiscal year, 136
    employment, 137, 139
Gross domestic product
    defense spending as a percent of GDP, 1945–2003, 132
Gross investment, 114
National defense consumption expenditures and
    gross investment, 116, 119
State and local government
    chain-type quantity indexes for expenditures
        and investment, 125
    consumption expenditures and gross investment,
        123, 130, 131
    current receipts and expenditures, 121, 126, 128
    output, lending and borrowing, and net investment,
        124

GOVERNMENT CONSUMPTION EXPENDITURES
Definitions, 25, 142
Gross domestic product, 4
Real gross domestic product, 5

GOVERNMENT NET SAVING
Definitions, 106

GOVERNMENT SOCIAL BENEFITS
Definitions, 84, 142

GROSS DOMESTIC INCOME
Definitions, 23
Income
    relationship of GDP and personal income, 14
Type of income, 17

GROSS DOMESTIC PRODUCT
Chain-type price indexes, 9, 370
Chain-type quantity indexes, 8, 366
Composite indexes
    economic activity and selected index components, 12
Contributions to percent change in real gross
    domestic product, 6
Current-dollar and real GDP, 1946–2003, 7
Debt as a percent of GDP, 1945–2003, 256
Definitions, 23, 301
Difference between GNP and GDP, 16
Domestic income of corporate business, 21, 22
Energy
    consumption per dollar of real GDP, 245
Final sales, 10
Generally, 4
Government
    defense spending as a percent of GDP, 1945–2003, 132
Gross and net national product, 14
Historical data
    chain-type quantity indexes, 366
    quarterly series, 357
    real GDP, 1939–1947, 353
    real gross domestic product, 361, 362

state and regional data, 484
Industry profiles
 data availability, 302
 definitions, 301
 GDP by NAICS industry group, 299, 300
 GDP by SIC industry group, 298
 notes on the data, 301
 references, 302
International comparisons
 definitions, 282
 growth rates in real GDP, 274
 real GDP per capita, 275
 real GDP per capita, United States and Japan, 1960–2003, 273, 275
 real GDP per employed person, 276
National income and product and cyclical indicators, 3
National income by type of income, 19
Output per capita, 3
Per capita product and income and population, 11
Percent changes in current-dollar and real GDP, 7
Price indexes defined, 26
Product and income by industry
 value added by NAICS industry group, 299, 300
 value added by SIC industry group, 298
Real gross domestic product, 5, 6, 362
Regional data, 484
State data, 484
GROSS DOMESTIC PURCHASES
Defined, 26
Gross domestic product, 4
Real gross domestic product, 5
GROSS GOVERNMENT INVESTMENT
Definitions, 25, 106, 142
GROSS INVESTMENT
Definitions, 143
GROSS NATIONAL INCOME
Definitions, 23, 107
GROSS NATIONAL PRODUCT
Defined, 23
Difference between GNP and GDP, 16
GROSS NONRESIDENTIAL FIXED INVESTMENT
Definitions, 107
GROSS OUTPUT
Definitions, 142
GROSS PRIVATE DOMESTIC INVESTMENT
Definitions, 25, 106
GROSS PRIVATE FIXED INVESTMENT
Data, 90
Definitions, 107
Saving and investment; business sales and inventories, 76
GROSS PUBLIC DEBT—TOTAL
Definitions, 144
GROSS SAVING AND INVESTMENT
Definitions, 106

H
HAWAII
Median income and poverty rates by state, 67

HEALTH AND PERSONAL CARE
Receipts of taxable firms, 339
Revenue of tax-exempt firms, 339
Sales, 334
HIGH-TECH
Capacity utilization: total manufacturing and high tech, 35, 413
HISPANIC ORIGIN
Income distribution and poverty
 definitions, 68
 poverty status by Hispanic origin, 56
HISTORICAL DATA
Bond yields, 461
Capacity utilization, 413
Chain-type price indexes, 9, 370
Chain-type quantity indexes, 366
Composite indexes, 471
Consumer price indexes, 423
Economic growth and change, 471
Employment, hours, and earnings, 433, 443
Federal government
 current receipts and expenditures, 112, 382
Foreign trade and finance
 U.S. international transactions, 154, 398
Gross domestic product
 chain-type price indexes, 9, 370
 chain-type quantity indexes, 366
 contributions to percent change in real GDP, 5, 6, 362
 quarterly series, 357
 real GDP, 1939–1947, 353
 real gross domestic product, 361, 362
 state and regional data, 484
History of this publication, xvi
Income, 74, 374
Interest rates, 461
Inventories to sales ratios, 378
Labor force, 433
Monetary base, 453
Money stock, 453
Nonfarm payroll employment, hours, and earnings, 226, 443
Personal income and its disposition, 74, 374
Producer price indexes, 423
Production, 413
Productivity and related data, 404
Real GDP, 361, 362
Regional and state data
 per capita personal income, 1969–2003, 483
Reserves, 453
Selected aggregate economic data, 1939–1947, 354
State and local government
 receipts and expenditures, 126, 128, 390
Stock price indexes, 461
Summary consumer and producer price indexes, 423
Summary labor force, employment, and unemployment, 433
U.S. international transactions, 154, 398
Unemployment rates, 433
War and the economy, xxxiii

HOTELS
  Receipts of taxable firms, 339
HOURS OF WORK
  Average hourly earnings, 232, 309
  Average weekly hours, 229, 308
  Civilian population and labor force, 220
  Indexes of aggregate weekly hours, 231
  Nonfarm payroll employment, hours, and earnings, 226, 443
  Private nonfarm payrolls, 229
  Selected industries, 230
HOUSEHOLD DEBT
  Ratio of household debt service to personal income, 1980–2003, 259
HOUSEHOLD INCOME
  Median household income, 49, 50, 63
  Shares of aggregate income received, 52
HOUSEHOLD OPERATION
  Definitions, 86
HOUSING
  Definitions, 86
  Housing starts and building permits, 319
  New construction put in place, 317
HOUSING AND COMMUNITY SERVICES
  Definitions, 143
HOUSING INDEX
  Definitions, 200
HOUSING STARTS
  Building permits, 319
  Construction and housing, 319
  Definitions, 344
  Home sales and prices, 319
HYDROELECTRIC POWER
  Energy supply and consumption, 244

I
IDAHO
  Median income and poverty rates by state, 67
ILLINOIS
  Median income and poverty rates by state, 67
IMPORT PRICE INDEXES
  Data availability, 181
  U.S. foreign trade and finance, 172
IMPORTS
  Gross domestic product, 4
  Oil and gas, 316
  Petroleum and petroleum products, 316
  Real gross domestic product, 5
  U.S. foreign trade and finance
    see **FOREIGN TRADE AND FINANCE**
IMPUTATION
  Defined, 24
INCOME
  Alternative definitions of income, 64, 65
  Consumer income and spending
    see **CONSUMER INCOME AND SPENDING**
  Definitions
    alternative definitions of income, 70
  Factor income by type, 1948 and 2000, 13
  Foreign transactions in the national income and product accounts, 148
  Gross domestic income
    defined, 23
    relationship of GDP and personal income, 14
    type of income, 17
  Historical data, 74, 374
  Median household income, 49, 50, 63
  National income and product and cyclical indicators
    see **NATIONAL INCOME AND PRODUCT AND CYCLICAL INDICATORS**
  Per capita personal income, 1969–2003, 483
  Per capita product and income and population, 11
  Personal income and employment, 489
  Personal income and its disposition, 74, 374
  Ratio of household debt service to personal income, 1980–2003, 259
  Selected services: estimated revenue for employer firms, xxv
  Shares of aggregate income received, 52
  Type of income, 19
  Value added, 13
INCOME DISTRIBUTION AND POVERTY
  Age
    poor people 16 years and over by work experience, 62
    poverty status of persons by age, 60
    total rates for children and seniors, 54
  Alternative definitions of income
    median income and poverty rates based on, 64
    poverty rate, 65
  Alternative measures and state data, 63
  Average poverty thresholds
    defined, 69
  Cities
    poverty status of persons inside and outside metropolitan areas, 61
  Data availability, 71
  Definitions
    generally, 68
    income and poverty rates based on alternative definitions of income, 64
  Earnings
    defined, 69
  Experimental measures of before-tax and after-tax income, 66
  Experimental poverty measures, 71
  Families
    defined, 68
    median family income, 49, 51
    poverty status by type of family, 56
    poverty thresholds by family size, 55
    shares of aggregate income received, 53
  Gini coefficient
    defined, 69

Hispanic origin
  defined, 68
  poverty status by Hispanic origin, 56
Household income
  median and mean household income, 49, 50, 63
  shares of aggregate income received, 52
Households
  defined, 68
Income
  defined, 69
Mean income
  defined, 69
Median household income, 49, 50, 63
Median income
  defined, 68
  income and poverty rates by state, 67
  poverty rates based on alternative definitions of income, 64
Metropolitan areas
  poverty status of persons inside and outside metropolitan areas, 61
Notes on the data, 71
Poverty population
  defined, 69
Race
  defined, 68
  poverty status by race, 56
Sex
  median earnings by sex, 51
  poverty status of persons by sex, 60
Unrelated individuals
  defined, 68
Work experience
  poor people 16 years and over by work experience, 62
Work experience
  defined, 69

INCOME RECEIPTS AND PAYMENTS
Definitions, 174

INCOME SECURITY
Definitions, 143

INDEX OF COINCIDENT ECONOMIC INDICATORS
Definitions, 32

INDEX OF CONSUMER EXPECTATIONS
Definitions, 32

INDEX OF LAGGING ECONOMIC INDICATORS
Definitions, 32

INDEX OF LEADING ECONOMIC INDICATORS
Definitions, 31

INDIANA
Median income and poverty rates by state, 67

INDUSTRIAL PRODUCTION AND CAPACITY UTILIZATION
Capacity utilization
    see CAPACITY UTILIZATION
Historical data, 35, 413
Production
    see PRODUCTION

INDUSTRIAL PRODUCTION INDEXES
Capacity utilization by NAICS industry groups, 43
Definitions, 46
Industry groups, 40
International comparisons, 277
Market groups, 36

INDUSTRY GROUPS
Defined, 46

INDUSTRY PROFILES
Gross domestic product
  data availability, 302
  definitions, 301
  GDP by NAICS industry group, 299, 300
  GDP by SIC industry group, 298
  notes on the data, 301
  references, 302
NAICS industry definitions: with rough derivation from SIC, 289
Structure of U.S. industry, 287

INFLATION INDICATORS
Prices, 1946–2003, 183

INFLOWS
Balance on current account and financial inflows, 1960–2003, 153

INITIAL CLAIMS
Definitions, 32

INSURANCE
Unemployed insured, 224

INTEREST PAYMENTS
Definitions, 142

INTEREST RATES
Definitions, 271
Historical data, 461
Notes on the data, 271
Personal interest income, 84
Selected interest rates and bond yields, 262

INTEREST RATE SPREAD
Definitions, 32

INTEREST RECEIPTS
Definitions, 141

INTERMEDIATE GOODS AND SERVICES PURCHASED
Definitions, 142

INTERNATIONAL COMPARISONS
Civilian labor forces, 279
Consumer price indexes, 278
Data availability, 284
Definitions, 282
Exchange rates, 280
Generally, 273
Gross domestic product
  definitions, 282
  growth rates in real GDP, 274
  real GDP per capita, 275
  real GDP per capita, United States and Japan, 1960–2003, 273, 275
  real GDP per employed person, 276
Industrial production indexes, 277

References, 284
Unemployment rates, 279
Value of the U.S. dollar, 1973–2003, 281
INTERNATIONAL TRANSACTIONS
Balance on current account and financial inflows and outflows, 1960–2003, 153
Definitions, 174
Investment position of the U.S. at year-end, 160
Trade balances on goods and services, 1960–2003, 161
U.S. international transactions, 154, 398
INVENTORIES
Building materials, 337
Clothing and accessories, 337
Contributions to percent change in real gross domestic product, 6
Corporations
  inventory valuation adjustment (NAICS basis), 214
  inventory valuation adjustment (SIC basis), 212
Department stores, 337
Electronic and electrical equipment, 337
Food and food products, 337
Food services sales, 337
Furniture and home furnishings, 337
Gasoline, 337
General merchandise, 337
Gross domestic product, 4
Manufacturing
  manufacturers' inventories, 325
  manufacturing and trade sales and inventories, 101
  real manufacturing and trade sales and inventories, 102
Motor vehicle sales, 332, 337
Petroleum and petroleum products, 337
Real gross domestic product, 5
Retail inventories, 337
Saving and investment; business sales and inventories generally, 88
  inventories to sales ratios, 99
  manufacturing and trade sales and inventories, 101
  real manufacturing and trade sales and inventories, 102
Wholesale trade, 338
INVENTORIES TO SALES RATIOS
Definitions, 107
Historical data, 378
Private nonfarm inventory/sales ratios, 1947–2003, 100
INVESTMENT
Federal government
  chain-type quantity indexes for expenditures and investment, 118, 119
  consumption expenditures and gross investment, 114
  defense and nondefense consumption expenditures by type, 115
  international investment position of the U.S. at year-end, 160
  national defense consumption expenditures and gross investment, 116
  net investment, 117
Gross government investment, 106
Gross nonresidential fixed investment defined, 107
Gross private domestic investment, 106
Gross private fixed investment by type, 90
Gross private fixed investment defined, 107
National saving, investment, and borrowing, 1946–2003, 87
Real gross private fixed investment by type, 93
Real gross private fixed investment defined, 107
Residential private fixed investment, 107
Saving and investment; business sales and inventories *see* **SAVING AND INVESTMENT; BUSINESS SALES AND INVENTORIES**
State and local government
  chain-type quantity indexes, 125
  consumption expenditures and gross investment, 123, 130, 131
  net investment, 124
IOWA
Median income and poverty rates by state, 67
ITALY
Growth rates in real GDP, 274
Real GDP per capita, 275

J
JAPAN
Growth rates in real GDP, 274
Real GDP per capita, United States and Japan, 1960–2003, 273, 275
JEWELRY
Definitions, 86

K
KANSAS
Median income and poverty rates by state, 67
KENTUCKY
Median income and poverty rates by state, 67
KEY SECTOR STATISTICS
Definitions, 342
Home sales and prices, 319
Housing starts and building permits, 319
Manufacturers' inventories, 325
Manufacturers' new orders, 328
Manufacturers' shipments, 320
Manufacturers' unfilled orders, 330
Merchant wholesalers, 338
Motor vehicle sales and inventories, 332, 337
New construction put in place, 317
New orders for durable goods, 315
Petroleum and petroleum products, 316
Receipts of taxable firms, 339
Retail and food services sales, 334
Retail inventories, 337
Revenue by NAICS industry, 1998–2002, 340, 341
Revenue of tax-exempt firms, 339

L

LABOR FORCE
  Historical data, 433
LABOR FORCE PARTICIPATION RATE
  Definitions, 235
LARGE TIME DEPOSITS
  Definitions, 265
LEGAL SERVICES
  Receipts of taxable firms, 339
  Revenue of tax-exempt firms, 339
LENDING
  Federal government, 117
  State and local government, 124
LIABILITIES
  Bank credit and selected liabilities, 251
  Definitions, 269
  Household assets, liabilities, net worth, and financial obligations, 257
  Mortgage debt outstanding, 260
LIBRARIES
  Revenue of tax-exempt firms, 339
LICENSE FEES
  Definitions, 179
LOCAL GOVERNMENT
  see **STATE AND LOCAL GOVERNMENT**
LONG-TERM UNEMPLOYED
  Definitions, 235
LOUISIANA
  Median income and poverty rates by state, 67

M

MAINE
  Median income and poverty rates by state, 67
MALTA
  Growth rates in real GDP, 274
MANAGEMENT
  Receipts of taxable firms, 339
  Revenue of tax-exempt firms, 339
MANUFACTURING
  Average weekly hours of production, 308
  Capacity utilization: total manufacturing and high-tech, 35, 413
  Definitions, 345
  Employment, hours, and earnings, 220
  Generally, 303
  Inventories
    manufacturers' inventories, 325
    manufacturing and trade sales and inventories, 101
    merchant wholesalers, 338
    real manufacturing and trade sales and inventories, 102
  Key sector statistics
    new orders for durable goods, 1959–2002, 285
  New orders
    defined, 32
    manufacturers' new orders, 328
  Sales
    merchant wholesalers, 338
  Shipments
    manufacturers' shipments, 320
  Unfilled orders
    manufacturers' unfilled orders, 330
MANUFACTURING AND TRADE INVENTORIES
  Saving and investment; business sales and inventories, 101
MANUFACTURING AND TRADE SALES
  Saving and investment; business sales and inventories, 101
MARKET GROUPS
  Defined, 46
  Industrial production indexes by market groups, 36
MARKET VALUE
  Definitions, 177
MARYLAND
  Median income and poverty rates by state, 67
MASSACHUSETTS
  Median income and poverty rates by state, 67
MEAN INCOME
  Definitions, 69
MEDIAN INCOME AND EARNINGS
  Income distribution and poverty
    see **INCOME DISTRIBUTION AND POVERTY**
MEDICAL CARE
  Consumer prices, 1946–2003, 190
  Definitions, 86
MEDICAL CARE INDEX
  Definitions, 200
MEMBERSHIP ORGANIZATIONS
  Revenue of tax-exempt firms, 339
MERCHANTS
  Definitions, 348
  Inventories, 338
  Sales, 338
METROPOLITAN AREAS
  Income distribution and poverty
    poverty status of persons inside and outside metropolitan areas, 61
MICHIGAN
  Median income and poverty rates by state, 67
MIDDLE EAST
  Growth rates in real GDP, 274
MINNESOTA
  Median income and poverty rates by state, 67
MINORITIES
  Hispanic origin
    see **HISPANIC ORIGIN**
  Race
    see **RACE**
MISSISSIPPI
  Median income and poverty rates by state, 67
MISSOURI
  Median income and poverty rates by state, 67

MONETARY BASE
  Historical data, 453
MONEY AND FINANCIAL MARKETS
  Aggregated reserves of depository institutions and monetary base, 250
  Bond yields, 262
  Commercial bank credit and selected liabilities, 251
  Common stock prices and yields, 264
  Consumer credit, 261
  Credit market debt outstanding, 253
  Data availability, 265
  Definitions, 265
  Delinquency rates, 257
  Federal funds rate, 1962–2003, 247
  Generally, 247
  Interest rates, 262
  Money stock measures, 248
  Mortgage debt outstanding, 260
  Notes on the data, 265
  Selected components of the money stock, 249
  Selected interest rates and bond yields, 262
  Treasury securities rate, 1962–2003, 247
MONEY STOCK
  Historical data, 453
MONEY STOCK MEASURES
  General data, 248
MONEY SUPPLY
  Definitions, 32
MONGOLIA
  Growth rates in real GDP, 274
MONTANA
  Median income and poverty rates by state, 67
MORTGAGES
  Debt outstanding, 260
  Definitions, 270
MOTELS
  Receipts of taxable firms, 339
MOTION PICTURES
  Receipts of taxable firms, 339
MOTOR VEHICLES
  Inventories, 332, 337
  Sales, 334
MUSEUMS
  Receipts of taxable firms, 339
  Revenue of tax-exempt firms, 339

N
NAICS
  Capital expenditures by major industry sectors, 1998–2002, 104
  Definitions
    employment, hours, and earnings, 313
    industry definitions: with rough derivation from SIC, 289
  Employment, hours, and earnings
    average hourly earnings of production or nonsupervisory workers, 309
    average weekly earnings of production or nonsupervisory workers, 310
    average weekly hours of production, 308
    definitions, 313
    indexes of aggregate weekly hours, 311
    indexes of aggregate weekly payrolls, 312
    net new nonfarm payroll by NAICS industry group, 1990–2003, 303
    nonfarm employment by NAICS sector and industry, 304
    production or nonsupervisory workers on private payrolls, 307
  Industry groups, 40, 43
  Introduction to NAICS, 287
  Key sector statistics, 315
  Manufacturing
    inventories, 325
    new orders, 328
    shipments, 320
    unfilled orders, 330
  Output change by NAICS industry group, 297
  Revenue by NAICS industry, 1998–2002, 340, 341
  Service industries
    revenue, 1998–2002, by NAICS industry, 340, 341
NATIONAL DEFENSE
  Federal government
    consumption expenditures and gross investment, 116, 119
NATIONAL INCOME AND PRODUCT AND CYCLICAL INDICATORS
  Chain-type price indexes for gross domestic product, 9, 370
  Chain-type quantity indexes for gross domestic product, 8, 366
  Composite indexes of economic activity and selected index components, 12
  Corporations
    gross value added of domestic corporate business, 21
    gross value added of nonfinancial domestic corporate business, 22
  Data availability, 30, 33
  Definitions
    generally, 23
  Factor income by type, 1948 and 2000, 13
  Final sales, 10
  Generally, 3
  Gross and net national product and national income, 14
  Gross domestic product, 4
  Income and value added, 13
  Index of coincident economic indicators, 32
  Index of lagging economic indicators, 32
  Index of leading economic indicators, 31
  Nonfinancial corporate business, 22
  Output per capita, 3
  Per capita product and income and population, 11
  Real gross domestic product, 5
  References, 30, 33

Type of income, 19
NATURAL GAS
　Energy supply and consumption, 244
NEBRASKA
　Median income and poverty rates by state, 67
NET EXPORTS OF GOODS AND SERVICES
　Definitions, 25
NET INTEREST
　Definitions, 27
NET INVESTMENT
　Federal government, 117
　State and local government, 124
NET LENDING OR BORROWING
　Definitions, 106, 140, 173
NET NATIONAL PRODUCT
　Definitions, 24
　Gross and net national product and national income, 14
NET OPERATING SURPLUS
　Definitions, 27
NET SAVING
　Definitions, 142
NET WORTH
　Definitions, 269
NEVADA
　Median income and poverty rates by state, 67
NEW HAMPSHIRE
　Median income and poverty rates by state, 67
NEW JERSEY
　Median income and poverty rates by state, 67
NEW MEXICO
　Median income and poverty rates by state, 67
NEW ORDERS
　Manufacturers' new orders, 328
NEW YORK
　Median income and poverty rates by state, 67
NONDURABLE GOODS
　Definitions, 85
NONRESIDENTIAL EQUIPMENT AND SOFTWARE
　Definitions, 25, 107
NONRESIDENTIAL FIXED INVESTMENT
　Definitions, 25
NONRESIDENTIAL STRUCTURES
　Definitions, 107
NORTH CAROLINA
　Median income and poverty rates by state, 67
NORTH DAKOTA
　Median income and poverty rates by state, 67
NUCLEAR POWER
　Energy supply and consumption, 244

O
OHIO
　Median income and poverty rates by state, 67
OIL AND GAS
　Domestic production, 316
　Energy supply and consumption, 244
　Imports, 316
　Stocks, 316

OKLAHOMA
　Median income and poverty rates by state, 67
ON-BUDGET AND OFF-BUDGET
　Definitions, 144
ORDERS
　Manufacturers' new orders, 328
　Unfilled orders, 330
OREGON
　Median income and poverty rates by state, 67
ORGANIZATION OF PETROLEUM EXPORTING COUNTRIES (OPEC)
　Definitions, 180
OUTFLOWS
　Balance on current account and financial outflows, 1960–2003, 153
OUTLAYS
　Definitions, 144
　Federal government
　　receipts and outlays by fiscal year, 133
OUTLAYS BY FUNCTION
　Definitions, 144
OUTPUT
　Change by NAICS industry group, 297
　Definitions, 142
　Federal government, 117
　Producer price indexes for the net output of selected NAICS groups, 197
　State and local government, 124
OUTPUT PER CAPITA
　National income and product and cyclical indicators, 3
OVERTIME HOURS
　Definitions, 240

P
PASSENGER FARES
　Definitions, 179
PENNSYLVANIA
　Median income and poverty rates by state, 67
PERSONAL BUSINESS
　Definitions, 86
PERSONAL CARE
　Definitions, 86
PERSONAL CONSUMPTION EXPENDITURES
　Current dollars, constant dollars, and price indexes, 76
　Defined, 24, 85
　Gross domestic product, 4
　Price indexes for personal consumption expenditures, xxiii
　Real gross domestic product, 5
　Type of expenditure, 81, 82
　Type of product, 77, 79
PERSONAL INCOME
　Definitions, 83
　Historical data, 74, 374
　Ratio of household debt service to personal income, 1980–2003, 259
　State and regional data, 489
PERSONAL INCOME RECEIPTS ON ASSETS
　Definitions, 84

PERSONAL SAVING
   Definitions, 106
   Households and non-profit institutions serving households, xxii
   Saving rate, 1946–2003, 73

PERSONAL SERVICES
   Receipts of taxable firms, 339

PETROLEUM AND PETROLEUM PRODUCTS
   Definitions, 342
   Domestic production, 316
   Energy supply and consumption, 244
   Imports, 316
   Inventories, 337
   Sales, 334
   Stocks, 316

POVERTY
   Age
      status of persons by age, 60
      total rates for children and seniors, 54
   Alternative definitions of income, 65
   Data availability, 71
   Definitions, 69
   Experimental measures of before-tax and after-tax income, 66
   Families
      average poverty thresholds by family size, 55
      status by type of family, 56
   Hispanic origin
      status by Hispanic origin, 56
   Income distribution and poverty
      see **INCOME DISTRIBUTION AND POVERTY**
   Median income and earnings
      income and poverty rates by state, 67
      poverty rates for persons based on alternative definitions of income, 64
   Metropolitan areas
      status of persons inside and outside of, 61
   Notes on the data, 71
   Poor people 16 years and over by work experience, 62
   Race
      status by race, 56
   Sex
      status of persons by sex, 60
   Total rates for children and seniors, 54

POVERTY POPULATION
   Definitions, 69

POVERTY THRESHOLDS
   Definitions, 69

PREFACE
   History of the book, xvi
   Notes and definitions, xvi
   Plan of the book, xv

PRICES
   Consumer price indexes, 184
   Consumer prices: all items, 1946–2003, 190
   Data availability, 203
   Definitions, 200
   Energy consumption and prices, 1949–2003, 243
   Farmers
      prices received and paid by farmers, 198
   Home sales and prices, 319
   Indexes for personal consumption expenditures, xxiii
   Inflation indicators, 1946–2003, 183
   Notes on data, 202
   Producer price indexes and purchasing power of the dollar, 191
   Producer price indexes by major commodity groups, 196
   Producer price indexes for net output of NAICS industry groups, 197
   Purchasing power of the dollar, 191
   References, 203
   U.S. export and import price indexes, 172

PRIVATE CAPITAL CONSUMPTION ADJUSTMENT
   Definitions, 29

PRIVATE CAPITAL CONSUMPTION ALLOWANCES
   Definitions, 29

PRIVATE INVESTMENT
   Chain-type price indexes for gross domestic product, 9, 370
   Chain-type quantity indexes for gross domestic product, 8, 366
   Definitions, 25
   Gross nonresidential fixed investment, 107
   Gross private domestic investment, 106
   Gross private fixed investment, 107
   Private fixed investment by type, 1948 and 2000, 92
   Real gross private fixed investment, 107
   Residential private fixed investment, 107

PRIVATE REMITTANCES AND OTHER TRANSFERS
   Definitions, 175

PRIVATE TRANSPORTATION INDEX
   Definitions, 200

PRODUCER PRICE INDEXES
   Commodity groups, 196
   Data availability, 201
   Definitions, 202
   Historical data, 423
   Net output of selected NAICS industry groups, 197
   Notes on data, 202
   Purchasing power of the dollar, 191
   References, 201
   Summary consumer and producer price indexes, 423
   Supplemental indexes, 201

PRODUCER PRICES
   see **PRICES**

PRODUCT AND INCOME BY INDUSTRY
   Data availability, 302
   Definitions, 301
   Gross domestic product
      value added by NAICS industry group, 299, 300
      value added by SIC industry group, 298
   Notes on the data, 301

Output change by NAICS industry group, 297
References, 302
PRODUCT INDICATORS
National income and product and cyclical indicators, 3
PRODUCTION
Data availability, 47
Definitions, 46
Figures for productivity and related data, 84
Generally, 35, 413
Historical data, 413
Indexes by market groups, 36
Indexes by NAICS industry groups, 40
Industrial production and capacity utilization, 35, 413
NAICS industry groups, 43
Notes on the data, 46
References, 47
Revisions, 47
PRODUCTIVITY
Data availability, 217
Definitions, 216
Employment costs, productivity, and profits
generally, 207
related data, 210
Historical data, 404
Notes on the data, 217
References, 218
Revisions, 217
PROFITS
Corporations
definitions, 28
inventory valuation adjustment (NAICS basis), 214
inventory valuation adjustment (SIC basis), 212
Employment costs, productivity, and profits
generally, 207
PROFITS AFTER TAX
Definitions, 29
PUBLIC ORDER AND SAFETY
Definitions, 143
PURCHASING POWER OF THE DOLLAR
Generally, 191

Q
QUINTILES
Definitions, 69

R
RACE
Income distribution and poverty
definitions, 68
poverty status by race, 56
REAL ESTATE
Receipts of taxable firms, 339
REAL GROSS DOMESTIC PRODUCT
Contributions to percent change in real gross
domestic product, 5, 6, 362
Current-dollar and real GDP, 1946–2003, 7
Energy consumption per dollar of real gross
domestic product, 245
Generally, 5

Growth rates in real GDP, 274
Historical data, 361, 362
International comparisons: real GDP per capita, 275
International comparisons: real GDP per employed
person, 276
**REAL GROSS PRIVATE FIXED INVESTMENT
BY TYPE**
Data, 93
REAL GROSS PRIVATE INVESTMENT
Definitions, 107
REAL OR CHAINED-DOLLAR ESTIMATES
Definitions, 26
RECEIPTS AND EXPENDITURES
Capital expenditures, 1996–2002, 103
Capital expenditures for companies by NAICS
industry sector, 1998–2002, 104
Definitions, 144
Federal government
consumption expenditures and gross investment, 114
current receipts and expenditures, 112, 382
data availability, 143
debt by fiscal year, 136
defense and nondefense consumption expenditures
by type, 115
national defense consumption expenditures and
gross investment, 116
receipts and outlays by fiscal year, 133
references, 143
Foreign trade and finance
receipts, payments, and balance on current
account, 1946–2003, 147
Personal consumption expenditures
see **PERSONAL CONSUMPTION
EXPENDITURES**
Price indexes for personal consumption
expenditures, xxiii
Selected services: estimated revenue for employer
firms, xxv
Service industries
receipts of taxable firms, 339
State and local government
chain-type quantity indexes, 125
consumption expenditures and gross investment,
123, 130, 131
current receipts and expenditures, 121, 126, 128
historical data, 126, 128, 390
receipts and expenditures, 1946–2003, 120
RECREATION
Definitions, 86, 200
Revenue of tax-exempt firms, 339
REGIONAL DATA
Data availability and references, 519
Definitions, 519
Gross domestic product, 484
Per capita personal income, 1969–2003, 483
Personal income and employment
annual data, 489
RELIGIOUS ACTIVITIES
Definitions, 86

RENTAL INCOME OF PERSONS
   Definitions, 28, 83
RENTS
   Definitions, 141
REPAYMENTS ON U.S. CREDITS
   Definitions, 176
REPURCHASE AGREEMENTS
   Definitions, 265
REQUIRED RESERVES
   Definitions, 266
RESEARCH
   Definitions, 86
   Receipts of taxable firms, 339
   Revenue of tax-exempt firms, 339
RESERVES
   Historical data, 453
RESIDENTIAL PRIVATE FIXED INVESTMENT
   Definitions, 25, 107
RESTAURANTS
   Food services sales, 334
RETAIL TRADE
   Definitions, 347
   Inventories, 337
   Quarterly U.S. retail sales: total and e-commerce, xxiv
   Sales, 334
RHODE ISLAND
   Median income and poverty rates by state, 67
ROYALTIES
   Definitions, 141, 179
RUSSIA
   Growth rates in real GDP, 274

S
SALARIES
            see **WAGES AND SALARIES**
SALES
   Building materials, 334
   Clothing, 334
   Department stores, 334
   Electronics and appliances, 334
   Final sales, 10
   Furniture and home furnishings, 334
   Gasoline, 334
   General merchandise, 334
   Health and personal care, 334
   Inventories to sales ratios, 378
   Merchant wholesalers, 338
   Motor vehicles, 334
   Petroleum products, 334
   Private nonfarm inventory/sales ratios, 1947–2003, 100
   Quarterly U.S. retail sales: total and e-commerce, xxiv
   Retail and food services sales, 334
   Saving and investment; business sales and inventories
      inventories to sales ratios, 99
      manufacturing and trade sales and inventories, 101
      real manufacturing and trade sales, 102
   Wholesale trade, 338
SAVING AND INVESTMENT; BUSINESS SALES AND INVENTORIES
   Assets
      chain-type quantity indexes for net stock of fixed assets, 98
      current-cost net stock of fixed assets, 97
   Capital account transactions, 106
   Capital expenditures
      1996–2002, 103
      companies with employees, by NAICS industry sector, 1998–2002, 104
   Chain-type quantity indexes
      net stock of fixed assets, 98
      private fixed investment by type, 95
   Consumption of fixed capital, 106
   Data availability, 108
   Definitions, 106, 107
   Expenditures
      capital expenditures, 1996–2002, 103
      companies with employees by major NAICS industry sector, 1998–2002, 104
   Fixed assets
      chain-type quantity indexes for net stock of fixed assets, 98
      current-cost net stock, 97
   Generally, 88
   Government net saving, 106
   Gross government investment, 106
   Gross national income, 107
   Gross nonresidential fixed investment, 107
   Gross private domestic investment, 106
   Gross private fixed investment by type, 90
   Gross private fixed investment defined, 107
   Gross saving, 106
   Inventories to sales ratios, 99
   Manufacturing and trade sales and inventories, 101
   National saving, investment, and borrowing, 1946–2003, 87
   Net lending or borrowing, 106
   Nonresidential equipment and software, 107
   Nonresidential structures, 107
   Personal saving, 106
   Personal saving rate, 1946–2003, 73
   Private fixed investment by type, 1948 and 2000, 92
   Private nonfarm inventory/sales ratios, 1947–2003, 100
   Real gross private fixed investment by type, 93
   Real gross private investment, 107
   Real manufacturing and trade sales and inventories, 102
   References, 108
   Residential private fixed investment, 107
   Sales
      inventories to sales ratios, 99
      manufacturing and trade sales and inventories, 101
      real manufacturing and trade sales, 102
   Saving and investment generally, 88

Undistributed profits, 106
SAVINGS
Federal government saving and dis-saving, 1946–2003, 111
Households and non-profit institutions serving households, xxii
National saving, investment, and borrowing, 1946–2003, 87
Personal saving rate, 1946–2003, 73
SAVINGS DEPOSITS
Definitions, 265
SEASONAL ADJUSTMENT
Definitions, 239
SELECTED ANNUAL DATA
Aggregate economic data, 1939–1947, 354
Definitions, 356
Real GDP, 1939–1947, 353
SENIORS
Poverty rates for seniors, 54
SERVICE INDUSTRIES
E-commerce, 341
NAICS
revenue, 1998–2002, by NAICS industry, 340, 341
Receipts and expenditures
receipts of taxable firms, 339
Revenue of selected industries, 1998–2002, 340, 341
Revenues of tax-exempt firms, 339
SERVICES
Chain-type quantity indexes for exports and imports of services, 149
Definitions, 178
Foreign trade balances on services, 1960–2003, 161
U.S. exports of services, 162, 170
U.S. imports of services, 162, 171
SEX
Income distribution and poverty
median earnings by sex, 51
poverty status of persons by sex, 60
SHIPMENTS
Manufacturers' shipments, 320
SMALL TIME DEPOSITS
Definitions, 265
SOCIAL SECURITY
Debt held by Social Security funds defined, 145
SOCIAL SERVICES
Receipts of taxable firms, 339
Revenue of tax-exempt firms, 339
SOFTWARE
Definitions, 25
SOURCES OF FINANCING
Definitions, 144
SOUTH CAROLINA
Median income and poverty rates by state, 67
SOUTH DAKOTA
Median income and poverty rates by state, 67

SPENDING
Consumer income and spending
disposition of personal income, 74
personal consumption expenditures by major type of product, 77
personal consumption expenditures by type of expenditure, 81
personal income and its disposition, 74
STATE AND LOCAL GOVERNMENT
Borrowing, 124
Chain-type quantity indexes
consumption expenditures and gross investment, 125
Current receipts and expenditures, 1946–2003, 120
Definitions, 141
Employment, 137, 139
Historical data
receipts and expenditures, 126, 128, 390
Investment
consumption expenditures and gross investment, 123, 130, 131
Lending, 124
Net investment, 124
Output, 124
Receipts and expenditures
chain-type quantity indexes, 125
consumption expenditures and gross investment, 123, 130, 131
current receipts and expenditures, 121, 126, 128
historical data, 126, 128, 390
receipts and expenditures, 1946–2003, 120
STATE DATA
Data availability and references, 519
Definitions, 519
Gross domestic product, 484
Income and poverty
median income and poverty rates by state, 67
Per capita personal income, 1969–2003, 483
Personal income and employment
annual data, 489
STOCK PRICE INDEXES
Historical data, 461
STOCK PRICES
Definitions, 32
STOCKS AND BONDS
Common stock prices and yields, 264
Definitions, 271
Notes on the data, 271
Personal dividend income, 84
Selected interest rates and bond yields, 262
SUBSIDIES
Definitions, 27, 142

T
TENNESSEE
Median income and poverty rates by state, 67

TEXAS
  Median income and poverty rates by state, 67
TOBACCO
  Definitions, 86
TOTAL CONSUMPTION EXPENDITURES
  Definitions, 143
TOTAL RESERVES
  Definitions, 266
TOTAL SURPLUS
  Definitions, 144
TRADE
  Foreign trade and finance
        see **FOREIGN TRADE AND FINANCE**
TRADE BALANCES
  Foreign trade balances on goods and services, 1960–2003, 161
TRANSPORTATION
  Definitions, 86
  Receipts of taxable firms, 339
TRAVEL
  Definitions, 179
TURKEY
  Growth rates in real GDP, 274

U
U.S. FOREIGN TRADE AND FINANCE
        see **FOREIGN TRADE AND FINANCE**
UNDISTRIBUTED OFFSETTING RECEIPTS
  Definitions, 144
UNDISTRIBUTED PROFITS
  Definitions, 106
UNEMPLOYMENT RATES
  Civilian unemployment
    data, 1948–2003, 219
    general data, 221, 222
  Definitions, 236
  Historical data, 433
  Insured unemployment, 224
  International comparisons, 279
  Rates of unemployment, 221, 222
UNFILLED ORDERS
  Manufacturing
    manufacturers' unfilled orders, 330
UNITED KINGDOM
  Growth rates in real GDP, 274
  Real GDP per capita, 275
UNITED STATES
  International transactions, 154, 398
  Median income and poverty rates by state, 67
  Real GDP per capita, United States and Japan, 1960–2003, 273, 275
UTAH
  Median income and poverty rates by state, 67

V
VALUE ADDED
  Definitions, 142
VENDOR PERFORMANCE
  Definitions, 32
VERMONT
  Median income and poverty rates by state, 67
VIRGINIA
  Median income and poverty rates by state, 67
VOCATIONAL SCHOOLS
  Receipts of taxable firms, 339
  Revenue of tax-exempt firms, 339

W
WAGES AND SALARIES
  Average hourly earnings, 232, 309
  Average weekly earnings, 233, 310
  Average weekly hours, 229, 308
  Civilian population and labor force, 220
  Data availability, 216
  Defined, 27
  Disbursements defined, 83
  Employment cost indexes
    total compensation, 208
    wages and salaries, 209
  Gross domestic income
    defined, 23
    type of income, 17
  Indexes of aggregate weekly hours, 231
  Indexes of aggregate weekly payrolls, 312
  National income by type of income, 19
  Nonfarm payroll employment, 226, 443
  Per capita personal income, 1969–2003, 483
  Per capita product and income and population, 11
WAR AND THE ECONOMY
  Historical data, xxxiii
WASHINGTON
  Median income and poverty rates by state, 67
WELFARE ACTIVITIES
  Definitions, 86
WEST VIRGINIA
  Median income and poverty rates by state, 67
WHOLESALE TRADE
  Definitions, 348
  Inventories, 338
  Sales, 338
WISCONSIN
  Median income and poverty rates by state, 67
WORK EXPERIENCE
  Definitions, 69
  Income distribution and poverty
    poor people 16 years and over by work experience, 62
WYOMING
  Median income and poverty rates by state, 67